P9-DDX-817

HANDBOOK OF RESEARCH

ON TEACHING

THE ENGLISH LANGUAGE ARTS

HANDBOOK

OF RESEARCH ON

TEACHING THE

ENGLISH LANGUAGE ARTS

Sponsored by the International Reading Association

and the National Council of Teachers of English

EDITED BY

JAMES FLOOD
JULIE M. JENSEN
DIANE LAPP
JAMES R. SQUIRE

DISCARDED
JENKS LRC
GORDON COLLEGE

JENKS L.R.C.
GORDON COLLEGE
255 GRAPEVINE RD.
WENHAM. MA 01984-1895

MACMILLAN PUBLISHING COMPANY
NEW YORK
Collier Macmillan Canada
TORONTO
Maxwell Macmillan International
NEW YORK   OXFORD   SINGAPORE   SYDNEY

LB
1576
.H234
1991

Copyright © 1991 by
International Reading Association and National Council of Teachers of English

All rights reserved. No part of this book may be reproduced or
transmitted in any form or by any means, electronic or mechanical,
including photocopying, recording, or by any information storage and
retrieval system, without permission in writing from the Publisher.

Macmillan Publishing Company
866 Third Avenue, New York, N.Y. 10022

Collier Macmillan Canada, Inc.
1200 Eglinton Avenue East, Suite 200
Don Mills, Ontario M3C 3N1

Library of Congress Catalog Card Number: 90-38726

Printed in the United States of America

printing number
1 2 3 4 5 6 7 8 9 10

Library of Congress Cataloging-in-Publication Data

Handbook of research on teaching the English language arts / edited by
    James Flood . . . [et al.].
        p.   cm.
    "Sponsored by the International Reading Association and the
National Council of Teachers of English."
    Includes index.
    ISBN 0-02-922382-2
    1. Language arts.   I. Flood, James.   II. International Reading
Association.   III. National Council of Teachers of English.
LB1576.H234   1991
428′.007′073—dc20   90-38726
                                                     CIP

Figures in Chapter 31C from *Teaching Reading Vocabulary,* 2d ed., by Dale
D. Johnson and P. David Pearson, copyright © 1984 by Holt, Rinehart and
Winston, Inc., reprinted by permission of the publisher.

CONTENTS

v

Part
IV
ENVIRONMENTS FOR ENGLISH LANGUAGE ARTS TEACHING 423

Part V

RESEARCH ON TEACHING SPECIFIC ASPECTS OF THE ENGLISH LANGUAGE ARTS CURRICULUM 557

PREFACE

Research in the teaching of the English language arts seldom has been summarized and interpreted as a unified field of study. The profession has seen reviews of research on reading, many studies of research on writing and on response to literature, or on such specialized skills as spelling or listening, or even punctuation and handwriting. Given intensive past examinations of separate language arts components, compiling a handbook on the teaching of all English language arts proved particularly challenging. Indeed, the very separation of professional associations in the English language arts has seemed to reflect the isolation of English teaching components so often seen in the classroom, and has made joint sponsorship of the National Council of Teachers of English and the International Reading Association of critical importance.

To understand how teaching the English language arts became what it is today, theoretical and historical perspective is needed. Hence, the initial chapters of this *Handbook* present diverse perspectives on historical and comtemporary influences on the ways the English Language Arts are taught and learned.

But different bodies of research also influence decision-making—experimental, ethnographic, literary, and so on. Chapters in the second section show in different ways some of these approaches to defining sound teaching of the subject, and chapters in the third section discuss what we know about the characteristics of learners at various levels that seem to have relevance for the teaching and learning of language.

The fourth section deals with the environments for teaching the English language arts, the nature of the classroom, the fashion in which teachers are educated, the ways in which they might be encouraged to grow to engage in their own research. Research on instructional materials that are needed for effective teaching of the English Language Arts also are discussed in this section.

Then, finally, a large section focuses on the content of the English language arts, the skills and strategies basic to learning the subject, and our present and future directions for teaching the English Language Arts.

For each of the five sections, the editors have invited prominent scholars and professional leaders, not simply to compile and summarize findings, but to assess the significance of research, evaluate new developments, find relationships to scholarship in related fields, examine current conflicts, controversies, and issues, and identify tomorrow's priorities for English language arts teaching.

No attempt has been made to maintain a unified perspective beyond that implied in the organization of this *Handbook*. Rather, the general editors encouraged the strength and richness that emerges as each author or team of authors develops a unique point of view.

The editors are grateful to each of the authors for their willingness to serve the sponsoring organizations. We also thank the many critic readers listed herein. They offered incisive and lively comments, which assisted the authors in preparing final copy. We thank Lloyd Chilton, Executive Editor of Macmillan Publishing Company, for his insight and leadership in making this project a reality. We also thank Marilyn James of York Production Services for her tireless and competent efforts in completing this volume. Finally, this *Handbook* is a statement on the unification of the language arts and on cooperation among organizations devoted to the language arts. It would have been impossible without the endorsement and guidance of the elected leadership, editorial boards, and staff liaisons representing the National Council of Teachers of English and the International Reading Association.

Informed teaching of the English language arts is central to the success of our schools and to the future of our society. We hope that this *Handbook* will remind readers of ways to make their teaching better informed.

James Flood
Julie M. Jensen
Diane Lapp
James R. Squire

ABOUT THE CONTRIBUTORS

Virginia G. Allen is Associate Professor, Language, Literature and Reading, Ohio State University at Marion, Ohio.

Arthur N. Applebee is Professor of Education, State University of New York at Albany, and Director of the Center for the Learning and Teaching of Literature.

Kathryn H. Au is Educational Psychologist with the Kamehameha Schools, Honolulu, Hawaii.

Mary A. Barr is Director of the California Literature Project for the California State Department of Education.

James F. Baumann is Professor of Curriculum and Instruction, University of Georgia.

Michael D. Beck is President of BETA, Inc. of Pleasantville, New York.

June Canwell Birnbaum is Visiting Assistant Professor of English Education at Rutgers University.

David Bloome is Associate Professor, School of Education, University of Massachusetts at Amherst.

Rita S. Brause is Professor of Education at Fordham University, New York.

James. H. Britton is Emeritus Professor of Education, University of London.

Bertram Bruce is Principal Scientist at Bolt, Beranek and Newman, Cambridge, Mass., and Associate Director of the Center for the Study of Reading.

Frederick R. Burton is a Principal with Dublin City Schools, Columbus, Ohio.

Robert C. Calfee is Professor of Education and Psychology, Stanford University.

Courtney B. Cazden is Professor of Education, Harvard University Graduate School of Education.

Jeanne S. Chall is Professor, Harvard University Graduate School of Education, and Director, Harvard Reading Laboratory.

Marilyn J. Chambliss, a graduate student at Stanford University, received her Ph.D. from that institution in December, 1989.

Merron Chorny is Emeritus Professor of Education at the University of Calgary.

Marie M. Clay is Professor of Education at the University of Auckland, New Zealand.

Carole Cox is Associate Professor at the Graduate School of Education, California State University, Long Beach.

Bernice E. Cullinan is Professor of Education at New York University.

Mary E. Curtis is Director of Research, Boystown, Omaha NE

Thomas G. Devine is Professor of Education, University of Lowell, Lowell, Mass.

John Dixon is an educational consultant residing in London, England.

Janice A. Dole is Assistant Professor, Department of Educational Studies, University of Utah.

Dolores Durkin is Professor of Education, University of Illinois, Urbana-Champaign, and senior staff member, Center for the Study of Reading.

Anne Haas Dyson is Associate Professor, School of Education, University of California at Berkeley.

Margaret M. Early is Professor and Chair, Instruction and Curriculum, College of Education, University of Florida.

Janet Emig is University Professor of English Education at Rutgers University, and 1988–89 president of the National Council of Teachers of English.

Marcia Farr is Associate Professor of English and Linguistics at the University of Illinois, Chicago.

Roger Farr is Director, Center for Reading and Language Studies, Indiana University.

Edmund J. Farrell is Professor of English Education, University of Texas, Austin.

Joan T. Feeley is Professor, Curriculum and Instruction, The William Paterson College of New Jersey.

Sheila M. Fitzgerald is Professor of Education, Michigan State University.

James Flood is Professor of Reading and Language Arts at San Diego State University.

Sara Warshauer Freedman is Professor of Education and Director of the Center for the Study of Writing, University of California, Berkeley.

Lee Galda is Associate Professor, Department of Language Education, University of Georgia.

Allan A. Glatthorn is Professor of Education, East Carolina University.

Yetta M. Goodman is Professor of Education, University of Arizona.

Donald H. Graves is Professor of Education, University of New Hampshire.

Judith L. Green is Professor of Education, The Ohio State University.

Alfred H. Grommon is Emeritus Professor of Education and English, Stanford University.

Jane Hansen is Professor of Education, University of New Hampshire.

Mary Kay Healy is Research and Training Director, Puente Project, University of California, Berkeley.

Patricia A. Herman is Senior Curriculum Researcher, Kamehameha Schools, Honolulu, Hawaii.

Elfrieda H. Hiebert is Associate Professor of Education, University of Colorado.

George Hillocks, Jr. is Professor, Departments of Education and English Language and Literature, The University of Chicago.

Richard E. Hodges is Professor of Education, University of Puget Sound.

Roselmina Indrisano is Professor and Chairman, Department of Developmental Studies and Counseling, Boston University.

Angela M. Jaggar is Professor of Education, New York University.

Julie M. Jensen is Professor of Education, University of Texas at Austin.

Edward J. Kameenui is Chair, Special Education Area, Teacher Education Division, University of Oregon.

James L. Kinneavy is Professor of English, University of Texas at Austin.

Susan Shurberg Klein is Senior Research Associate with the U.S. Department of Education.

Diane Lapp is Professor of Reading and Language Development at San Diego State University.

V. Cindy Mall is a Visiting Practitioner at the Center for the Study of Reading, University of Illinois.

Miriam G. Martinez is Assistant Professor, Southwest Texas State University.

Robert J. Marzano is Senior Program Director of the Mid-Continent Regional Educational Laboratory.

Jana M. Mason is Professor of Education, University of Illinois at Urbana-Champaign, and senior staff member, Center for the Study of Reading.

John S. Mayher is Professor of English Education. New York University.

Paula Menyuk is Professor of Education, Boston University.

James Moffett is an educational consultant in Madera, California.

Dianne L. Monson is Professor of Education, University of Minnesota.

Lesley Mandel Morrow is Professor of Education, Rutgers University.

Miles A. Myers, formerly President of the California Federation of Teachers, became Executive Director of the National Council of Teachers of English in 1990.

Thomas Newkirk is Associate Professor of English and Director of the Freshman English Institute, University of New Hampshire.

James W. Ney is Professor of English, Arizona State University.

Roy C. O'Donnell is Professor, Department of Language Education, University of Georgia.

Jean Osborn is Associate Director, Center for the Study of Reading, University of Illinois.

Jeanne R. Paratore is Associate Professor of Education, Boston University, and Director of the Center for Assessment and Design of Learning.

John J. Pikulski is Professor of Education, University of Delaware.

Gay Su Pinnell is Associate Professor of Education, The Ohio State University, where she is also Director of the Reading Recovery Project.

Robert E. Probst is Professor of English Education, Georgia State University.

Alan C. Purves is Professor of Education, Director of the Center for Literacy, and Associate Director of the Center for the Learning and Teaching of Literature. State University of New York at Albany.

Louise M. Rosenblatt is Professor Emerita of English Education. New York University.

Nancy L. Roser is Professor of Education, University of Texas at Austin.

Leo P. Ruth is Supervisor of Student Teachers at the University of California, Berkeley.

Diane Lemonnier Schallert is Associate Professor of Educational Psychology, University of Texas at Austin.

Sam Leaton Sebesta is Professor of Education, University of Washington.

John S. Simmons is Professor, English Education and Reading, Florida State University.

Carl B. Smith is Professor of Education, Indiana University.

Michael Smith is Assistant Professor, Department of Education, University of Chicago.

James R. Squire is a retired Senior Vice President of Silver Burdett & Ginn, for whom he continues to serve as Executive Consultant.

Sandra Stotsky is Research Associate and Director of the Writing Workshop for the Harvard Graduate School of Education.

Dorothy S. Strickland is New Jersey State Professor of Reading, Rutgers University.

Elizabeth Sulzby is Professor of Education, University of Michigan.

Denny Taylor is a senior research fellow with the Institute of Urban and Minority Education, Teachers College, Columbia University.

Robert J. Tierney is Professor of Education at The Ohio State University.

Frederick B. Tuttle, Jr., Ph.D. is Assistant Superintendent, Curriculum and Administration, Needham Public Schools.

Eileen Tway is Professor of Education, Miami University, Oxford, Ohio.

Richard L. Venezky is Unidel Professor of Educational Studies, University of Delaware.

Betty Jane Wagner is Professor, Reading and Language Department, Foster G. McGaw Graduate School, National-Louis University, Evanston, Ill.

Merlin C. Wittrock is Professor and Head, Division of Educational Psychology, Graduate School of Education, U.C.L.A.

Walt Wolfram is Professor of Communication Sciences, University of the District of Columbia, and Director of Research, Center for Applied Linguistics.

Amy Zaharlick is Associate Professor at The Ohio State University.

READERS AND CONTRIBUTORS

The general editors and authors express particular appreciation to the following individuals who served as readers for diverse chapters of this manuscript and offered many valuable suggestions:

Ira Aaron, University of Georgia
Richard Abrahamson, University of Houston
JoBeth Allen, University of Georgia
Donna E. Alvermann, University of Georgia
Patricia L. Anders, University of Arizona
Mary C. Austin, University of Hawaii
Richard Beach, University of Minnesota
Isabel L. Beck, University of Pittsburgh
Glenda L. Bissex, Northeastern University
Rexford Brown, Education Commission for the States
Dwight Burton, Florida State University
John B. Carroll, University of North Carolina at Chapel Hill
Donna Christian, Center for Applied Linguistics
Carolyn Colvin, San Diego State University
Kathleen A. Copeland, University of Illinois at Urbana-Champaign
William Corcoran, James Cook University, Australia
William V. Costanzo, Westchester Community College, New York
Patricia M. Cunningham, Wake Forest University
Arthur Daigon, University of Connecticut
Thomas G. Devine, University of Lowell
Deborah R. Dillon, Purdue University
Priscilla A. Drum, University of California at Santa Barbara
Edward R. Fagan, Pennsylvania State University
Nancy Farnan, San Diego State University
Sharon Ryan Flood, San Diego State University
Irene West Gaskins, Benchmark School, PA
Celia Geneshi, Ohio State University
Anne Ruggles Gere, University of Michigan
Ernest T. Goetz, Texas A&M University
Kenneth S. Goodman, University of Arizona
Michael Graves, University of Minnesota
Robert A. Gundlach, Northwestern University
Martha Rapp Haggard, Sonoma State University
Janet Hickman, Ohio State University
Elfrieda Hiebert, University of Colorado
James V. Hoffman, University of Texas at Austin
Robert F. Hogan, National Council of Teachers of English

Sarah Hudelson, Arizona State University
Susan Hynds, Syracuse University
Dale D. Johnson, Boston, Massachusetts
Michael L. Kamil, Ohio State University
Lannie S. Kanevsky, McGill University
Barbara Kiefer, University of Oregon
Martha King, The Ohio State University
Walter Kintsch, University of Colorado
Judith A. Langer, State University of New York, Albany
Walter D. Loban, University of California, Berkeley
Leslie Mandel Morrow, Rutgers University
John C. Maxwell, National Council of Teachers of English
John S. Mayher, New York University
Walter H. MacGinitie, Friday Harbor, WA
H. Thomas McCracken, Youngstown University
John D. McNeil, University of California at Los Angeles
Gregory Morris, Pittsburgh Public Schools, PA
Joseph O. Milner, Wake Forest University
Lorri Neilsen, Mt. St. Vincent University, Nova Scotia
David G. O'Brien, Purdue University
Donna Ogle, National College of Education
Miles C. Olson, University of Colorado at Boulder
P. David Pearson, University of Illinois at Urbana-Champaign
A. D. Pellegrini, University of Georgia
Chris Pratt, University of Western Australia
Gordon M. Pradl, New York University
Robert Probst, Georgia State University
Raymond Rodrigues, Colorado State University
H. Alan Robinson, Hofstra University
Mary W. Salus, Boston, MA
Jay Samuels, University of Minnesota
Judith A. Schickedanz, Boston University
Jerrie Cobb Scott, Central State University, Wilberforce, OH
Michael Spooner, National Council of Teachers of English
Robert E. Shafer, Arizona State University
Timothy Shanahan, University of Illinois at Chicago
Jennifer Stevenson, Hilites for Children
Judith Solsken, University of Massachusetts, Amherst

Erwin Steinberg, Carnegie Mellon University
Patricia Stock, Syracuse University
Brian V. Street, University of Sussex
Sandra Stotsky, Harvard Graduate School of Education
Charles Suhor, National Council of Teachers of English
Lynne Thrope, Josten's Learning Corporation, San Diego
Gail E. Tompkins, California State University, Fresno
Lynn Quitman Troyka, City University of New York

Gladys V. Veidemanis, North High School, Oshkosh, WI
Ken Watson, Sydney, Australia
Rose-Marie Weber, State University of New York at Albany
Jerri Willet, Amherst, MA
Sandra Wilde, Michigan State University
Karen D. Wood, University of North Carolina at Charlotte
Brooke Workman, West High School, Iowa City

HANDBOOK OF RESEARCH

ON TEACHING

THE ENGLISH LANGUAGE ARTS

Part

·I·

THEORETICAL BASES FOR ENGLISH LANGUAGE ARTS TEACHING

THE HISTORY OF THE PROFESSION

James R. Squire

Although its antecedents date back 2,500 years, teaching the English Language Arts in today's schools has been shaped largely by the forces of the last century. Teachers in classical Greece emphasized rhetoric. The medieval trivium of grammar, rhetoric, and logic formed the core of an education provided for future churchmen or noblemen. Not until the rise of the common school did teaching reading, writing, and spelling in the mother tongue occupy the major attention of schoolmasters (Smith, 1985; Venezky, 1984). The literature that was studied in academies and the early grammar schools was usually written in Greek or Latin. Indeed, major universities, like Oxford, did not offer a degree in English until 1896. Psalters, ABC's, and Hornbooks, used for beginning lessons in the mother tongue in colonial America, were based on sixteenth- and seventeenth-century British models and taught the rudiments of language through religious and moralistic content (Smith, 1985; Squire, 1988; Venezky, 1984). Primers containing fragments from the Bible or from established literary works used to teach reading in a one-classroom school were well established by 1790, when Noah Webster's spelling books appeared. Developed as a way of seeking standardization of variant English spellings, the Webster spellers became the most widely used texts for teaching reading as well as spelling (Robinson, 1977; Smith, 1985). Spelling and reading thus became associated in teaching English for the next half century (Goodman, Freeman, Murphy, & Shannon, 1988). Webster's intent was to standardize spelling, but the result in terms of instruction was to link beginning reading with pronunciation and with words (Chall and Squire, in press).

For three quarters of a century from the first edition in 1836, the graded McGuffey readers became so widely used that an estimated two million copies were published. This primer series controlled vocabulary and provided graded levels of difficulty to satisfy the requirements of the multigrade level classrooms of the time; they thus established the pattern for subsequent elementary school textbook series. Graded spellers to accompany each reader were soon published, thus linking reading and spelling, and establishing the concept of grade level standards in the two subjects. The early moralistic content in elementary school readers yielded to informational content (to make the books seem more relevant to children) and then to the literary, often presented in fragments and snippets, and the tradition that textbook content defined curriculum content was implanted in American education (Robinson, 1977; Smith, 1985; Venezky, 1984).

By the early years of this century, a substantial number of educational publishers had arisen, each offering schools diverse yet similar basal reading and spelling programs based on the mold that had emerged (Chall & Squire, in press). Twentieth-century authors were to add workbooks and ancillary material and expand terse teachers' manuals into expensive teacher editions with reproduced pages, questions and answers, and teaching support materials, which limited the preparation and planning needed by the teacher. A pattern of instruction that relied on basal readers was well established by 1930 (Mavrogenes, 1985). By 1980, it would be followed by more than 90 percent of American classrooms (Institutional Tracking Service, 1980). Spelling programs were developed independently of the readers from early in this century and normally were selected and used independently by schools. Reading and spelling thus formed the core of elementary school education in the language arts; writing and grammatical study came later.

Curiously, textbooks dealing with writing in the elementary school did not appear until early in this century, and then focused on penmanship, manuscript form, and elements of grammar and usage (Burrows, 1955). Indeed, not until the mid-1960s was composition stressed below the high school levels, and only during the 1980s has writing been seen to share a priority with reading in the primary school (Chall, Conard, & Harris, 1977; Graves, 1978). As the recent emphasis on the total writing process has grown, proponents have increasingly urged that the teaching of spelling, grammar, usage, and other skills be embedded within the overall process, although evidence that teachers are moving in this direction remains scant (Applebee, Langer, & Mullis, 1986a,b,c).

As school enrollments expanded during the early years of this century, children were separated into age/grade level classrooms, each with its own teacher (Smith, 1985). Earlier stress on oral reading in elementary school instruction (with some emphasis on phonics and alphabetic method) yielded to silent reading, the result partially of research in pedagogy, partially of the publication of silent reading tests, and partially, perhaps, from the emphasis on "economy of time" and practicality during the first quarter of the century (adults do their reading silently—why should they be taught orally?) (Judd & Buswell, 1922; Smith, 1985). The result: less emphasis on word analysis and decoding methods; more on whole words, meaning, and fluency (Chall & Squire, 1988). Further, with spelling instruction so carefully limited to pronunciation and oral usage, the close tie between readers and spellers was broken and independent spellers began to appear. Until the late 1960s, elementary school classrooms and the readers and spellers used in them followed this general approach.

ORIGINS OF SECONDARY SCHOOL ENGLISH

Until the first quarter of the twentieth century, content in secondary school English classrooms focused largely on the study of major literary works, primarily those mandated for college entrance (Mason, 1960b; Piché, 1967; Rosewall, 1965). President Charles Eliot of Harvard University, for example, recommended a celebrated five-foot shelf of books that he felt all Americans should know. Until World War I, and for a time thereafter, few students other than the college-bound completed high school. Hence, college requirements predominated in determining the high school English curriculum. The National Conference on Entrance Examinations for Colleges formed in 1894 and the Committee of Ten in 1892 were influential in identifying the literary works to be read and in recommending universal completion of an English curriculum designed to develop understanding, expression, and familiarity with good literature (Applebee, 1974). The result, early in the century, was an increase in literary studies, particularly studies of major English writers, and a decrease in independent courses of rhetoric, grammar, and analysis. English as a subject combining literature with the teaching of all essential skills thus became established (Applebee, 1974), although separate high school courses in literature and composition, sometimes even in grammar, are found as late as 1968 (Smith, 1932, 1939; Squire & Applebee, 1968). The teaching of reading for all children, however, was largely ignored as a subject for secondary school, although remedial or corrective reading was a matter of continuing concern. Children were to be taught to read in the grammar school; they then read to learn in the secondary. Those reading skills that were addressed inevitably related to literary analysis. Required works read by all were largely traditional, as George Norwell, then state supervisor for New York, demonstrated in 1950 when he reported the reactions of New York students to 5,000 selections that regularly appeared in junior and senior high school anthologies. (Olson, 1969)

In 1911, the National Council of Teachers of English (NCTE) was organized, largely to protect high school departments against slavish adherence to college requirements (Hosic, 1921; Hook, 1979). For the next 75 years, its book lists for high school, junior high, and elementary schools sought to advance wide reading by children and young people (Applebee, 1974; Fay,

1968; Hook, 1979; Mason, 1960a). Some freedom of choice by teachers and schools was thus encouraged, and growth in non-academic curricula and the requirements for acculturating millions of new Americans led to some relaxation in the procrustean yardstick of college requirements. Still, the rise of freshman composition courses and entrance examinations in writing, coupled with the continued emphasis of the College Entrance Examination Board (CEEB) on Scholastic Aptitude Tests (SAT), so influential in determining entrance requirements, meant that the requirements of college preparation were never far from crucial professional consideration, even as nonacademic English programs emerged to satify other needs (Applebee, 1974; Hays, 1936; see also the Commission on English's review of the impact of tests in 1931). From interpretations of college requirements have come the theme-a-week, ultimately ossified into "the five-paragraph essay," with its stress on expository writing, which has held unity, coherence, and emphasis to be the greatest value in writing. To understand the uniqueness of this stress in American English teaching, see reports from the recent international assessment of writing (Purves & Takala, 1982).

Instruction in English grammar was particularly strong in junior high schools, where the need for teaching a Latin-based schoolroom grammar was created by the heavy Latin enrollments in grade nine. Learning Latin by grammatical methods, students encountered difficulties if they did not command the grammar of their native tongue. Speech education, or the teaching of speaking and listening, was much talked about in professional conferences (as it is today), but rarely applied in the classroom, perhaps because specialists in oral language left the National Council of Teachers of English to form their own association in 1922 (Veith, 1952). A curriculum in speech education for all young people beyond the primary level has been little more than a desired goal. Indeed, as late as 1968, a national study reported that as few as 15 percent of pupils graduating from high school had had any formal instruction in speech (Squire & Applebee, 1968). Jewett's review of 238 courses of study also confirms the emphasis on traditional literature, English grammar, and some composition (1958).

Reading remains a major focus of the elementary school language arts curriculum, requiring as much as half of all instructional time in language arts and around 40 percent of all textbook expenditures (Squire, 1988). Grammar dominated the junior high school until the 1960s, and literature the high school (85 percent of the instructional time) (Squire & Applebee, 1968). This has been the prevailing pattern until recent reform movements. (See Applebee, 1974; Applebee, 1978; Squire & Applebee, 1968.)

MAJOR CURRICULUM REFORMS

If the revolt against college domination of the curriculum early in this century represented one significant thrust that influenced subsequent decisions in English teaching, other forces also impacted teaching decisions. For example, the Clapp report (1926) was part of an Economy of Time Movement, which emphasized minimum essentials and·emerged shortly after

World War I. It directed attention to language competencies needed in various occupations (Applebee, 1974). These were the first of many attempts to emphasize the functional aspects of English teaching and efficiency in teaching, much as did the Effective Schooling studies of the 1970s and 1980s (Applebee, 1974). Both movements raised questions about the practicality of the content to be emphasized and the ways in which time tended to be wasted in schools. And both occurred as schools sought to adjust curriculum and instruction to strong waves of immigrant children.

From the Hosic report on reorganization of high school English in 1917 to Dora V. Smith's evaluation of schools in 1933, professional leaders tried to define priorities. Smith, for example, reported more children conjugating English verbs in six tenses than engaged in all other English activities combined (1941). These early attempts to define functional aspects of the subject led to Stormazand and O'Shea's efforts to define the essentials of language as distinct from niceties (1924), to O'Rourke's attempt to define minimum essentials (1934), and, ultimately, to Robert C. Pooley's (1946) efforts to classify instruction in English grammar and usage into elements to be emphasized, elements to be taught, if possible, and elements to receive no instruction. The recommendations were carried to the schools through the *English Journal,* a professional periodical owned by W. Wilbur Hatfield, then executive secretary of NCTE, which became the official journal of the Council. But its stress on high school concerns led C.C. Certain in 1927 to found *Elementary English* (now *Language Arts*) to give voice to problems of teaching the language arts in the elementary school. Certain's journal became the official organ for NCTE's elementary section two years later (Petty, 1983), and changes in lower level curriculum are more easily traced from that time. The inclusion of pedagogical considerations of reading as well as of the other language arts within the same journal lead Council leaders ultimately to promote consideration of integrated language arts within the classroom (Hook, 1979; Smith, 1952). Still, the continued domination of Council meetings by secondary school concerns led Certain, Harry A. Greene, and Emmett Betts to found the National Conference for Research in English (NCRE) in 1933 to provide for gatherings of those concerned with educational research, particularly research in reading and the other language arts (Petty, 1983). Indeed, for the next three decades, NCRE normally met with the American Educational Research Association (AERA), perhaps one of the reasons why research findings did not loom large in discussions of English teaching during the early years. NCRE tried to publicize findings regularly in *Elementary English,* but the journal reached few secondary school teachers, and not all of those in English Education.

THE EXPERIENCE CURRICULUM

The teaching of the English language arts during the 1930s and 1940s was only partially touched by experimentation then underway in progressive education in American schooling. But the significant lesson—that young people taught by content-free educational methods stressing higher thought processes did as well or better in higher education as students graduated from more rigid content-bound programs—had little impact on national decision making, largely because the findings were not released until the early 1940s when Americans were more occupied with World War II than with improving education (Aikin, 1942). NCTE's leaders did embrace the functional emphasis in Progressive Education (PEA) and the concern with the individual student (Simmons, Shadiow, and Shafer, 1990), but did not retreat from an interest in subject matter. More influential than the PEA—perhaps the most influential title in English teaching during the century—was the 1935 publication, *An Experience Curriculum in English,* by the NCTE Commission on the Curriculum, edited by W. Wilbur Hatfield, then secretary-treasurer of the Council and editor of the *English Journal.* The report stressed the importance of experiences *in* literature and language and experiences *through* literature and language. Although isolated instruction in reading, grammar, literature, and writing would continue for the next 50 years, professional leaders from the late 1930s began to talk about the project method, about integrating the language arts in "meaningful" classroom activities, about "functional teaching" of English, and about correlating English studies with those in other subjects. Almost two decades later, another commission, this time headed by Dora V. Smith, popularized concern for integrated language arts (i.e., reading, writing, speaking, listening) (Smith, 1952) and published four volumes to illuminate how this integrated language arts philosophy could influence curriculum in schools and in teacher education (Broening, 1956; Grommon, 1963; Mackintosh, 1954). The term "language arts" rose to professional popularity among elementary school teachers at this time, since it suggested the integration of skills and experiences; English, the term still used in the high school, suggested subject matter, and often, subject matter taught in isolation. Today's concern with "whole language" and integration of reading and writing dates back to such curriculum efforts.

SKILL IN READING

The stress on language activities and experiences and on children's literature in the elementary school, which marked much of the profession, if not the teaching, during the 1940s through the 1960s, made reading specialists increasingly dissatisfied with the quality of instruction. Too little attention was being directed to basic skills. The rise of standardized tests and the development of age-grade norms in reading provided evidence that many children were not developing needed competence in basic reading skills (a development increasingly apparent with the children from lower socioeconomic groups with their characteristic problems in learning language). Early NCTE meetings frequently saw as many debates on "skills" versus experience-oriented instruction as do our conventions today. Paul Witty, a highly regarded advocate of an experience curriculum, was seen as one who wanted to teach "the whole child," while Stella Center, an early leader in teaching the skills of reading, was concerned more with "the hole in the child" (Hook, 1979).

Dissatisfied with the state of skill instruction in the early 1950s, and unable to find an adequate voice for their views within NCTE and its journals, a group of national reading specialists and a group of remedial reading teachers formed separate associations shortly after World War II—the National Association of Remedial Teachers in 1946 and the International Council for the Improvement of Reading Instruction in 1947. The bulletin of the latter association became *The Reading Teacher* in 1951, and the two groups merged to form the International Reading Association (IRA) in 1955 (Jerrolds, 1977). Many reading specialists who had been active in NCTE elementary section left the organization. Initially concerned with the curriculum in reading skills and remedial reading, with NCTE remaining the major center for those interested in children's literature, oral language, and writing, IRA has grown over the past 35 years to be a broadly based association with an extensive publishing program dealing with all aspects of the English language arts. Further, from the very beginning, its affiliated associations included Canadian chapters, and it has focused on international concerns both in its journals and in a biennial World Congress on reading. *The Reading Teacher,* its journal for elementary school, and the *Journal of Reading* for secondary school teachers, have consistently provided guidelines for reading instruction. Over the past 25 years, these journals have been particularly influential in suggesting methods and strategies for teaching reading even more than in the other language arts.

The teaching of reading has continued to be influenced by commercial instructional materials, with Komolski reporting by the mid-1970s that more than 90 percent of all classroom teaching decisions were influenced by the textbooks (EPIE Institute, 1977). The widespread use of basal reading programs from the early years of the century, and particularly the development beginning in 1930 of modern graded basals by leaders like William S. Gray, Arthur Gates, and David H. Russell, provided detailed manuals of teaching strategies (some say too detailed), which were followed extensively, sometimes even blindly and sluggishly, by classroom teachers. By 1980, virtually all K–6 classrooms were using such manuals (ITS, 1980) and were often organizing much of the language arts instruction around the basal programs. However, recent criticism of the uses of basal reading approaches, concentrating on their overemphasis on skill drills and underemphasis on literary and language processing experience, suggests that today's elementary school classrooms are changing (Anderson, Hiebert, Scott, & Wilkinson, 1985; Goodman et al., 1988).

COMPOSITION AND RHETORIC

Although the teaching of rhetoric and writing historically has been a significant dimension of English, the emergence of concern with contemporary rhetorics and with the relationship of instruction in grammar and usage to writing (or the lack of such relationship) dates mostly from the founding of the Conference on College Composition and Communication (CCCC) in 1949 within NCTE, and to the influence of its annual meeting and its quarterly journal. Initially focused on college freshman composition and on preparation for it, the CCCC served as a national center within the profession for those concerned with the teaching of writing throughout the K–college curriculum. CCCC

leaders were responsible for publication of *The State of Knowledge about Composition* in 1963, a review of research which forcefully rejected grammar-based approaches in improving children's writing (Braddock, Lloyd-Jones, & Schoer, 1963). The CCCC conference and its journal provided a way of communicating to schools information about the newer grammars and rhetorics that were advanced in the 1960s and 1970s. Members of the organization lobbied vigorously for stronger preparation of high school and elementary school teachers in writing (Committee on National Interest, 1961, 1964). As recently as 25 years ago, half of the nation's high school teachers of English had not studied composition beyond freshman composition, and almost no elementary school teacher had formally studied language development or the teaching of writing. That such conditions largely have changed today is due in no small measure to the efforts of CCCC leaders.

TEACHER EDUCATION

During the early part of this century, many elementary school teachers had been educated in the two-year normal schools and lacked extensive course work in the subject matter of English or its teaching. Donald Durrell noted, for example, that in 1930, when he began teaching at Boston University, not a single course on teaching reading was offered in the nation's colleges (Squire, 1988). Emphasis on preparation of language arts teachers and stronger certification standards in the subject began earnestly after World War II when NCTE and, later IRA provided concrete recommendations to state certification authorities for strengthening preparation for teaching subject matter. (See Austin, Morrison, & Kenny, 1961; Committee on National Interest, 1964; English Teacher Preparation Study, Grommon, 1968.)

The strengthening of certification standards for teaching in elementary school and the rising interest in research in reading and the other language arts led during the 1930s and 1940s to the rise of major university centers for preparing teachers, administrators, and faculty for teacher training. During this period, many universities developed laboratory schools or demonstration centers, making it possible for would-be teachers and administrators to study and sometimes participate in the proper teaching of English language arts. A few of the university centers developed such powerful philosophies that they influenced an entire generation of teacher educators and classroom teachers. At the University of Chicago, for instance, William S. Gray, supported by Ralph Tyler, Helen Robinson, Hilda Taba, Guy Buswell, and others, created in reading education a distinct point of view, not only through their graduate programs, but through such publications as an annual summary of research in reading (Gray, 1933–1960), and through an influential and unique 25-year series of summer reading conferences at the University of Chicago.

Perhaps the strongest influence on teaching the other language arts was the program Dora V. Smith administered at the University of Minnesota, which stressed the importance of children's literature and meaningful language arts teaching. The experiments in progressive education at Ohio State University, and, particularly, its laboratory school, led by Paul Witty, Lou LaBrant, and Edgar Dale, were probably the most significant influences on introducing free reading. Teachers College, Columbia University, given its base in New York and its distinguished faculty in curriculum and instruction, became both a national center for training teachers and educational leaders in reading, with Arthur Gates and, later, Roma Gans and Ruth Strang, and a center for the English communication arts, where Lennox Gray and Francis Shoemaker, during the 1940s and 1950s, perpetuated a communication arts model based on the philosophy of Suzanne Langer (1942), furthered by the multimedia theories of Marshall McLuhan (1964). These centers were important not only for stimulating bodies of research and theory published at the time, but for training teacher educators, school administrators, and young research professors who sallied forth to schools of education and teacher training institutions across the land during expansion of higher education in the 1950s. Thus was the influence of William S. Gray or Arthur Gates spread throughout the nation, as were the unique points of view of Dora V. Smith of Lennox Gray on the teaching of English. Many teachers were educated during the 1960s and 1970s by professional leaders whose attitudes had been shaped at these university centers. Their importance to the history of teaching and learning the English language arts was profound, but today few such centers continue.

With a decline in interest in teacher education during the 1960s and 1970s, centers for research in English and reading became less common. Individual leaders, not institutional centers, became more common. Laboratory schools were closed. Teacher training moved into the public school classroom so as to become more "realistic," and beginning teachers were often denied an opportunity to see theory in practice. Thus, the kind of advanced study of theory, research, and practice in teaching reading, writing, literature, and oral language with teams of high level educators has been lost during the recent decades, and the views associated with any particular center for study have been less influential.

Today's federally supported centers, such as the Center for the Study of Reading at the University of Illinois at Urbana-Champaign, may be opening a new era to today's graduate students. Cognitive psychologists concerned with comprehension and the thinking process have been gathered at Illinois, and their work has dominated professional discussions about reading. The attitudes of large numbers of tomorrow's educational leaders may be influenced by the philosophies which emerged at the Illinois center, as others will be influenced by the programs at the Center for the Study of Writing (University of California at Berkeley) and the Center for the Learning and Teaching of Literature (State University of New York at Albany). Such institutions may again assert the kind of leadership once associated with the earlier institutional centers. Indeed, some of the more influential of recent publications have come from such centers. (See Anderson et al., 1985; Applebee, Langer, & Mullis, 1985; 1986a,b,c; 1988.)

Further, as this report is written, a renewed concern about the quality of the nation's teachers and the ability of American schools to attract outstanding young teachers has led to calls for the reform of teacher education, the most significant of which appears to be the Holmes Report (Olson, 1987), and the Carnegie Commission on Teacher Education (*A Nation Prepared*, 1986). It seems likely that the reform effort, which stresses sound academic preparation as well as pedagogy, will exert a critical influence on education for several years.

ACADEMIC REFORM

Despite the work of the early centers in improving aspects of the English language arts, a report on the state of the profession in 1960, read into the Congressional Record as part of the deliberations leading to an extension of the National Defense Education Act of 1958 to include English, called for teacher institutes, curriculum development, and research to strengthen the teaching of the "bed rock" subject in the schools. Squire and others reported at that time that half of the nation's teachers of English were ill-prepared in the subject (Committee on National Interest, 1961).

The late 1950s and early 1960s were marked by a school reform movement in which Nobel Laureates and professors in academic subjects worked with teachers to provide new instructional materials in an attempt to strengthen academic achievement, most notably in school mathematics, sciences, and foreign languages. NCTE joined with the Modern Language Association (MLA) and other college English associations to identify "The Basic Issues in the Teaching of English" that needed to be resolved and which required federal support (Modern Language Association, 1959, Squire, 1963.). Reform efforts in English focused largely on funding research and curriculum development projects (Project English), and on support for three years of summer training institutes for teachers (see Shugrue, 1968). Stronger preparation in English was stressed in nationally-oriented projects (Shugrue & Everett, 1968.)

A "Spiral Curriculum" model, advanced by Jerome Bruner (1960), stressed that children could be introduced early to mature concepts, then repeatedly and systematically reexposed to the ideas as they matured (Bruner, 1960). This model of learning appealed to professors who wished to strengthen the teaching of subject matter and led to a strengthening of instructional components in composition and language in the elementary school and to some attempts to strengthen literary content. Conant's (1959) widely emulated report on high schools stressed the need for four years of English and for a strong writing program. Extensive federally sponsored research, which has continued since that day, supported such influential studies as Loban's 13-year study of language development, Strickland's analysis of the importance of informing language arts teaching by concepts from language and linguistic research (Strickland, 1962); Hanna's linguistically based analysis of the regularity of English orthography in spelling (Hanna, Hanna, Hodges, & Rudolph, 1966); and the First Grade Reading Studies (Bond & Dykstra, 1967), where a series of comparisons of classroom teaching pointed to a need for many approaches to beginning reading even while emphasizing the value of early phonics instruction.

At this time, also, Chall (1967) reviewed research in beginning reading and added her powerful call for "code-oriented," not "meaning-oriented" beginning reading instruction. Although her findings seemed initially controversial to those addicted to meaning emphasis in beginning reading instruction, they had a profound influence on subsequent materials and methods. The summer institutes for teachers of the English language arts were based on a tripod model of curriculum (language, literature, composition) with separate courses in each subject taught by academic professors following a pattern developed and pioneered in 1961 by the CEEB's Commission on English (Gerber, 1973). The institute thus provided a way of educating members of academic college departments about schools and teachers and about recent scholarly developments in the disciplines (Commission on English, 1965). From this effort came a stress on basic skills and basic content in the elementary school, ultimately to include writing, spelling, some grammar, and attention to the study of literature in depth and to rhetoric in the high school (Shugrue, 1968). The long-range effects of Project English thus can be seem more in powerful research studies and in the education of teacher leaders than in curriculum development, although the units, courses, and books developed at such diverse English curriculum centers as Hunter College, Florida State University, University of Nebraska, and University of Oregon did for a time dominate professional discussion (Simmons, Shadiow, and Shafer, 1990).

LITERATURE

Historically, the curriculum in literature has consisted of great works from traditional western literature deemed suitable for reading by boys and girls. Many of the works were moralistic, much as was the content of early basal readers. *Silas Marner* and *A Tale of Two Cities* were seen as excellent ways of inculcating Victorian values, then under seige, as were many standard selections, e.g., "Abou Ben Adam," "Say Naught the Struggle Not Availeth," and "The Chambered Nautilus." Like university scholars early in the century, teachers emphasized literary history or the backgrounds of literature (the togas of Rome, the theatres of Shakespeare, the lives of the Romantic poets). When Smith conducted her field studies of secondary English school teaching in the late 1930s, she found the teaching of literature dominated by the selections existing within the large anthology (Smith, 1941), the single resource, largely developed as an economic measure during The Great Depression to make worthwhile literature available to students in the classroom. Such anthologies, like the basal reading programs in the elementary school, tended to provide a relatively uniform national curriculum in literature for grades 7–12, the more so since two anthology programs, Scott Foresman's *Literature and Life,* first published in 1922–24, and Harcourt Brace Jovanovich's *Adventures* series, first published in 1932, have dominated secondary school English classrooms for the past 50 years (Applebee, 1974; Searles, 1942).

School libraries often could not be supported at that time and inexpensive paperback editions of works did not appear widely until after World War II. The college entrance requirements of earlier years remained the most important determinant of content (Applebee, 1974), much as the elementary school reader provided the literary curriculum for the lower level. Yet, anthologies and readers were useful, also, in providing for a prescreening of selections so that only those judged appropriate for the young might be included in course offerings, and schools and teachers could avoid the censorship issues that surfaced strongly in the McCarthy era and have continued ever since (Association of American Publishers, American Library Association, Association for Supervision and Curriculum Development, 1981; Committee on Right to Read, 1962; Jenkinson, 1979; Moffett, 1988). Thus, many of today's readers and anthologies contain works adapted to be more acceptable to schools (Goodman et al., 1988). Further, instructional purpose increasingly required books tailored to special groups of learners. Vocabulary control and graded readability criteria led to more and more selections being written or rewritten specifically for school programs.

Literary scholarship changed in the nation's universities late in the 1930s and 1940s when Brooks and Warren (1938) and Wellek and Warren (1949) forced attention to works themselves and to internal interrelationships of language and metaphor within the selections. This emphasis on text—the insights of "The New Criticism"—found support for teaching in the CEEB Institute of the early 1960s, which, at about the time that literary ventures at universities were turning away from exclusive concern with text, succeeded in directing the attention of school teachers and examiners to a study of texts in depth. The Advance Placement program in literature, also sponsored by CEEB, furthered such emphasis by the kind of test questions asked on its examinations (Commission on English, 1965). Thus, the study of major works in depth came to secondary school teaching. (See, particularly, the recommendations of Lynch and Evans, 1983.) Among the more influential literary scholars was Shakespearean student Northrup Frye, whose *Anatomy of Criticism* (1957) defined the importance of metaphor in learning literature, and whose *Educated Imagination* (1964) provided guidance to teachers in schools seeking to expand literary education. Of unique importance also during this period of academic reform was the John Hay Fellow Program, which provided a selected number of outstanding teachers with advanced work in literature at outstanding graduate schools. Directed by historian, Charles Keller, the John Hay program developed an informed alumni association which provided opportunities for teachers from diverse school districts to discuss teaching in the school. The interdisciplinary humanities course, introduced in many high schools during the Sixties, probably owes its origin to the work of these teachers (Applebee, 1974).

Largely unnoticed during the period was work on the reader's response to literature initiated by Richards (1929) and Rosenblatt (1938). Influential primarily on researchers rather than on classroom teachers (Purves & Beach, 1971; Squire, 1964), concern with the response of the reader did not emerge widely in schools until a professional reaction to the formalism of the academic reform movement occurred during the late 1960s (Squire and Applebee, 1968). Subsequent publication of another seminal work from Rosenblatt (1978) and release of major new research works (Cooper, 1982; Purves and Beach, 1972), led teachers to think again about the reader in relation to the literary text. Recently, the state of California has recommended major attention to children's response to literature, not merely to literature per se (1987).

URBAN SCHOOL REFORM

The academic reform of the late 1950s and early 1960s was short-lived, even though it formed the impetus for redirecting an entire generation of English teachers. Rising concern with educating children from lower socioeconomic groups in reading and language led to the massive "Great Society" programs of the Lyndon Johnson administration and to various federal programs, which sought to equalize opportunity for all (Corbin & Crosby, 1965; Jewett, 1964). Because language deprivation is an almost universal characteristic of children reared in poverty, many federal and state initiatives of this period emphasized headstart programs in reading and language, multimedia approaches, expanded library services, special tutoring, and similar initiatives in urban schools.

Also important for the classroom teacher was an increased awareness of special problems in teaching bilingual children both within the general classroom and in special classes (Allen, 1966). TESOL, The Association for Teachers of English to Speakers of Other Languages, was formed in 1966 in a series of conferences sponsored by NCTE, IRA, Modern Language Association (MLA), and the Speech Association of America (Hook, 1979). The continued increase of new Americans entering classrooms during the 1970s and 1980s, particularly Americans speaking Hispanic and Asian languages, has mandated a new commitment to multiculturalism. One of the ways that professional associations responded to the new needs was through formation of special interest subgroups. Witness, for example, the organization of spring conferences by the same organization; the extensive preconvention and postconvention programs of such organizations as IRA and NCTE; as well as formation of special "job-alike" associations such as the Conference on English Education (CEE), the Conference for Secondary School English Department Chairpersons, and the NCTE assemblies for literature and research (Hook, 1979, p. 263). English teaching had become so complex it required specialization. Each special interest group required its own programs and publications. Leaders of NCTE increasingly chose to view the association as a national forum for all groups and individuals interested in English, rather than an organization with a unified viewpoint. The conferences, assemblies, and expanded activities were seen as a way of responding to diverse educational interests, and moving conferences around the nation, a way of serving a diversity of teachers (Hook, 1979, p. 205).

But the Coleman Report in 1966 suggested that schooling had little influence on the learning of such children, and the debate over its findings stimulated extensive attempts to define exactly how the classroom teacher does influence learning. Thus, Edmonds (1979), Rosenshine and Stevens (1984), and Berliner and Rosenshine (1977), among others, led teams into schools that were achieving instructional goals in reading and (sometimes) writing and reported on the characteristics of effective schooling. Initially, most such studies were in urban schools, but later studies extended the findings to schools of all kinds. Instructional leadership, direct instruction, time-on-task, and stress on academic achievement were found to be characteristic of quality instruction in these studies (Denham & Lieberman, 1980), and teachers everywhere struggled to apply these ideas to their teaching. A decade earlier, Squire and Applebee had conducted a similar survey of successful high school English programs in the United States and England (1968, 1969), and their results, like the more widely publicized studies of effective teaching in the elementary school, provided similar teaching models.

Also influential in the urban school reform efforts were anecdotal descriptions of teaching in the slums and of responding to individual children. Among the more influential were titles by Kozol (1968), Herndon (1971), and Kauffman (1965). Most of the writings of these so-called "Romantic Critics" emphasized the teaching of the language arts.

TESTING AND ACCOUNTABILITY

Both in their assessment of successful teaching and in their recommendations for school improvement, educational leaders seeking to improve instruction in reading and instruction in language and writing were influenced by the increase in academic testing which began to pervade the schools in the 1960s and 1970s. Criterion-referenced assessment measures focused on specific skills were developed for elementary school reading; national, statewide, and district-wide accountability of pupil competence assessment in reading (Valencia & Pearson, 1987) became commonplace in 48 of the states by the early 1980s. Process assessment of growth in reading as well as product assessment emerged as matters of educational concern. Samplings of student writings were assessed in two thirds of the states (Applebee, Langer, & Mullis, 1986b).

The National Assessment of Educational Progress (NAEP), first from a base with The Education Commission of the States and later with Educational Testing Service, published national "report cards" every 5 or 6 years on how schools were doing in reading, writing, and other subjects. The data initially indicated a perceptible improvement in scores as the teaching effectiveness movement took hold, but continued to show low scores by minority children and children of low socio-economic status. Only in the 1986 reading assessment did the improvement halt (Applebee, Langer, & Mullis, 1988).

Given the emphasis on skill development in reading and writing as part of "back to the basics," and the single level of purpose of most instruments used in assessments, small wonder that our classrooms tended more and more to emphasize skill development and drill and practice. Public criticism of schooling drove administrators to rely on test score improvement in responding to critics, and the tests themselves drove teachers to overemphasize specific skills. "Mastery Learning" as a teaching model seemed to fit the demand (Bloom, 1982). So extensive did skill drill become in American schools that the Commission on Reading of the National Academy on Education (NAE) reported in 1985 that 80 percent of the time devoted to reading at the primary level was spent on skill drills (Anderson et al., 1985). Durkin (1983) and Applebee (1978) also reported a low level of teaching based on their classroom observations.

But if the academic formalism of the early 1960s led, on the one hand, to a counter-effort in which students engaged in drills and testing, it also stimulated an interest in productive language (Applebee, 1978; Durkin, 1983). To counter an overemphasis on "basics," many teachers sought interactive programs. (See Moffett, 1968). Alternative schools, or "storefront schools," stressing "open education," emphasized expression during the late 1960s and early 1970s. For a time, natural language activities were introduced into elementary classrooms and free electives replaced the standardized high school English curriculum. During this interval, some secondary schools reported offering as many as 272 different courses, many of short duration (Hillocks, 1972; Squire & Applebee, 1968). Teachers, encouraged to offer courses reflecting their own interests, tried to interest the young with such relevant English courses as "The Cookery of the Midwest," "Broadway Musical Comedy," "The History Plays of Shakespeare," or "Women I," "Women II," and "Women III."

The excesses of the new freedom defeated itself. In schooling, as in life, one cannot sustain freedom without discipline. The extreme liberalism of many experiments seemed to strengthen the belief that children did need skills and were not acquiring them. Doubt had been planted, of course, concerning the value of teaching subject matter unrelated to children's needs. In 1966, the Anglo-American Seminar at Dartmouth College provided opportunity for 60 international professors, teacher-educators, and teachers to review the teaching of the English language arts for three intensive weeks. The seminar occurred at a moment of watershed in the history of English teaching. Americans were just completing a series of curriculum projects known as Project English, which, for the most part, attempted to apply academic reforms in literature, grammar, and composition to the classroom. The British were struggling between twin philosophies—a basic literary outlook associated with literary critic F. R. Leavis and the Cambridge school (Frank Whitehead, Dennis Thomson, Dennis Harding, David Holbrook), and the views of leaders from the London Institute of Education, who emphasized the power of writing in transforming learning (James Britton, Harold Rosen, Nancy Martin). In the long run, the London group became ascendent in England and their influence can be seen in publications of the next decade as well as in reports from the New Hampshire conference. (See Her Majesty's Stationery Office, 1975; Squire & Applebee, 1969.)

The recommendations from the Dartmouth Seminar called for a growth model of learning stressing creativity, expressive writing, and response to literature (Dixon, 1967; Muller, 1967). Given the climate of the time, the recommendations were slow to reach fulfillment, but some of the views found fruit in the interactive model of teaching proposed by James Moffett and his fellows (1968, 1976) and in the emphasis on responding to literature associated with Alan Purves (1973). Literature teaching, however, was never again to dominate professional life as it did earlier in our history; composition and composing increasingly attracted attention. Those who sought more naturalistic teaching, based on the experience of pupils, were encouraged by an independent series of studies by James Britton (1970, 1975) and Louise Rosenblatt (1978).

WRITING AS PROCESS

The Dartmouth Seminar had stressed the creativity inherent in writing and how writing could contribute to an individual's growth. Meanwhile, rhetoric again began to loom large in college scholarly inquiries and "new rhetorics" began to attract attention, among them the work by Francis Christensen (Applebee, 1974; Moffett, 1968), and the publications by James Britton and colleagues (Britton, 1970, 1975). Emig's seminal study of the composing process appeared at about the same time, focusing the profession's attention on how children learn to write, not on what they write (Emig, 1971). Moffett and Britton, almost as effective as international analysts as they were as researchers or philosophers, continued to stress the importance of writing in learning. Donald Murray (1986) and Mina Shaughnessy (1977) helped a generation of teachers clarify their thinking about the process of composing, and Donald Graves (1978) popularized such concepts with elementary teachers.

In 1974, James Gray initiated a writing project at the University of California at Berkeley that stressed the reeducation of teachers in composition. Gray's 6-week and 8-week institutes concentrated on teachers writing for other teachers, and, thus, teaching one another. Extended a year or two later to a series of statewide California institutes, and, ultimately, to 152 other institutes or writing projects in 46 states and 6 foreign countries, plus the Department of Defense Schools around the world, the Writing Project network now reaches some 60,000 elementary and secondary school teachers annually (Gray, 1987).

At the least, writing projects have provided an instrument to communicate concern about, and experiences with, teaching writing and new research in composing. Follow-up programs, a quarterly newsletter, and a national alumni association, formed within the National Council of Teachers of English, help to maintain the excitement of being a writing teacher. Similar projects at the University of Iowa, at Bread Loaf in Vermont (and in England), in New Jersey, and elsewhere, have also been influential, particularly in the Midwestern and New England regions. The impact on the profession in focusing attention on writing as central to English teaching and then to the teaching of all subjects has been incalculable.

COMPREHENSION OF READING

If the teaching of reading in the 1960s and 1970s concentrated on specific skills, teaching in the 1980s has stressed the teaching of comprehension. Cognitive psychologists studying human learning in the mid-1960s found themselves focusing on language learning, since it is through language that a person develops concepts. Researchers in psycholinguistics, such as Kenneth Goodman and Frank Smith, directed attention to the interrelationships of oral and written language (Smith, 1971). Such work contributed strongly to insights into the processes of writing, but, even more, to research on the processes of comprehension. The 1976 creation by the federal government of a Center for the Study of Reading at the University of Illinois provided a focus for much of the work of the cognitive psychologists (so much so that initially some reading people feared that the Center was not being controlled by "specialists in reading"). Through a series of reports, conferences, and publications at the Center and related to the Center's work has come new insights into comprehension which have informed today's teaching: the importance of prior knowledge, text structure, and writing and speaking in relation to text (Flood, 1984; Pearson, 1984). This vision sees reading less as a collection of specific skills to be mastered than as an integrated sequence of processes closely associated with writing. Further, study of the processes of comprehension led to awareness of metacognition, the reader's awareness of what he is learning and his ability to assess his own progress (Baker & Brown, in press). The impact on today's teaching can be gleaned in part by noting the heavy stress placed on comprehension in today's textbooks as contrasted with yesterday's, and by the concern expressed by professional leaders over the failure of some teachers to apply the findings of research in comprehension (Durkin, 1983; Mason & Osborn, 1983). Although most assessment instruments still focus on specific skills, leaders in reading are now calling for tests focusing on comprehension, and some experimental changes are underway (Squire, 1987.) The impact on how the profession views the teaching of reading has been manifest. Just contrast today's IRA convention programs with the programs of the 1950s, or review the new history of reading comprehension just published by IRA (Robinson, Faraone, Hittleman, and Unruh, 1990.)

Much of the research on comprehension has stressed the interrelationship of the language arts—the importance of early experiences with literature to beginning reading, say, or the value of writing after reading as a way of encouraging students to process the ideas they acquired. The result has been heightened interest in interrelating the language arts, most particularly seen in the Whole Language movement in primary classrooms with its rejection of traditional basal instruction (Goodman et al., 1988). The little research available suggests that integrated whole language approaches may be more effective in the initial stages of teaching reading, but not subsequently as skill development is stressed (Stahl & Miller, 1988). Almost certainly the current movement will result in more balanced stress on literature, writing, and oral language, and less emphasis on separate instruction in language skills, spelling, or grammar.

ORAL LANGUAGE

Far less research has been devoted to the teaching of speaking and listening than to the other language arts. In the early years of this century, Departments of English celebrated "Better Speech Days" as a way of emphasizing clarity in communication, but this interest largely waned after specialists in oral language left NCTE in 1922 to form their own organization, the Speech Association of America, now the Speech Communication Association (Applebee, 1974; Hook, 1979). For many years

research in oral language was mostly initiated by university speech departments and seldom filtered down to teachers of English Language Arts since the latter were educated in Departments of English and Education.

Speaking and listening were emphasized as two of the four language arts by the Commission on the English Curriculum in 1952 (Smith, 1952), and in 1948, The Conference on College Composition and Communication brought together college faculty members interested in oral as well as written communication (Hook, 1979), but oral language seldom has received the stress in schools or in research accorded writing, reading, and literature. As late as 1968, Squire and Applebee reported almost all high school teachers of English professing to assume responsibility for speech education, but only 15 percent of the graduating seniors were found to have completed course work in oral English.

Indeed, until the most recent decades, much of the research in oral language which affected classroom teaching was conducted by structural linguists and their followers, who believed deeply that oral language was *the* language, and that writing and reading were secondary. "There is no language apart from the speaker active in expression," wrote Charles C. Fries, and his grammar studies along with those of Marckwardt, Allen, McDavid, and others focused on oral language—oral pattern practice, variations in spoken dialects, and audiolingual approaches (Marckwardt, 1963). Such pedagogy proved to be particularly influential in teaching English as a second language. For teaching native-language speakers, one of the more influential pedagogical reports reflecting these views was Robert C. Pooley's *Teaching English Usage,* which stressed oral practice in establishing appropriate expression (1946).

The rise of transformational grammar with its emphasis on self-generation of expression, the Dartmouth Seminar with its stress on individual creation through language (Wilkinson, 1970), and particularly recent concern with the integration of the language arts and the reawakening of interest in the emergence of literacy, have given new emphasis to oral language, particularly in relation to the other language arts (see Pinnell and Jaggar, this text). Loban's monumental 12-year study of the development of competence in oral language not only provided a base study on children's competence in oral language, but pointed up many critical interrelationships (Loban, 1976). In recent years cooperative learning, reciprocal teaching and response-oriented teaching of literature have renewed interest in oral processing of ideas and in the ways in which oral language processing can contribute to improved comprehension and written communication (Cazden, 1988). In addition, the discovery of Heath and others that at-risk children frequently lack opportunity in school or out of school to exchange ideas orally with others seems to be leading to a new emphasis in our classrooms (Heath, 1983).

TEACHING CONDITIONS

Concern with teaching during past decades has also meant concern with teaching conditions. Crucial, perhaps, to the teaching of the English language arts has been the repeated concern with class size, teacher-pupil ratios, library and classroom book supply, censorship, certification of teachers (see the discussion above on teacher education), and the quality of teachers. The American Federation of Teachers and the National Education Association have been instrumental in seeking improved salaries; but NCTE, IRA, and the American Association of School Librarians (AASL) have addressed such critical subject issues as the size of classes and the instructional materials needed.

Class size has concerned English teachers for more than 50 years. Certainly, if teachers are to read children's writing regularly and hold conferences with individual children, the number of pupil contacts must be manageable. (Committee on National Interest, 1961). Research has seldom shown that smaller classes result in more effective instruction (Braddock, 1963; U.S. Department of Education, 1988), but the effort to demonstrate the importance of a low teacher-pupil ratio continues. Many instructional leaders feel that overly heavy teaching loads contribute to "teacher burnout." Most recognize the importance of teacher-student ratios that permit conferencing. Given that annotation of a single student theme to improve thinking requires at least 10 minutes per theme (Dusel, 1956), secondary school teachers with 150–200 students early found it impossible to assign and annotate papers on a regular basis. Leaders seeking to increase the amount of writing in our classrooms have generally supported smaller classes. Certainly, those who believe in interaction recognized the need for class sizes that stimulate the exchange of ideas. The NCTE repeatedly has resolved in annual convention that no more than four classes of 25 students each be established as a standard teaching load (Hook, 1979).

Censorship has been a continuing concern of teachers of literature. Communities have objected even to traditional titles, based at different times on political issues, profanity, morality, ethnic-stereotypes, and so on (Jenkinson, 1979). Working especially closely with ALA's Freedom of Information Office, the National Council of Teachers of English throughout its history has insisted that the suitability of any work for student reading must be judged in relation to the student's level of development and in relation to critical appraisals of the worth of the selection (see Applebee, 1974, p. 221.). During the 1960s, the Council, under the leadership of Edward Gordon, developed an extended form for parents to request reconsideration of a book—a widely used instrument that did much to decrease casual protests.

In 1961, Squire and others reported that more than 10 million children were attending elementary schools without central libraries, resulting in a widespread effort to create a better collection of books during the next two decades (Committee on National Interest, 1961). Today, the concern is less with the libraries and textbooks themselves (most schools have improved schoolwide collections) than with their use and with the supply of books for children from lower socioeconomic groups (Anderson et al., 1985; Chall, 1967). The importance of providing time for conferencing and adequate staff development, the need for effective supervision, and the importance of reducing interruption to academic instruction are other recent concerns about the conditions of teaching (Committee on National Interest, 1964). A related effort sought to ensure an adequate supply of up-to-date textbooks for all children (AAP and NEA, 1972; Denham & Lieberman, 1980). Perhaps most important has been the increased awareness during recent years for improving the morale of teachers and for attracting better qualified teachers to the classroom (Anderson et al., 1985; Goodlad, 1985). "Teacher empowerment" has been the "buzzword" of the late 1980s, apparent in professional as well as union associations, so much so that at times the term seems to suggest a new sentimentalism. Still, the renewed focus on teaching is overdue. (Myers, 1985) And the work of the Holmes Commission and the Carnegie Commission on Teacher Education seeks to assure schools of better teachers (A Nation Prepared, 1987; Olson, 1977). An improvement in salaries and strengthened recruitment efforts have also characterized the recent efforts to achieve excellence in the schools.

THE INTERNATIONALIZATION OF ENGLISH TEACHING

The early years of the century saw the teaching of English in America, Canada, England, and other English-speaking countries develop almost independently, albeit derived from many British models. But cross-national communication began in earnest after World War II and most of today's teaching is strongly influenced by ideas initiated in other countries. From its inception, the IRA has been international with vigorous professional Canadian leadership and has sponsored a biennial series of international conferences from Singapore to Dublin. TESOL brought together teachers concerned with ESL and EFL teaching through the world (Hook, 1979). The formation of the British National Association of Teachers of English (NATE) in 1965, and the Canadian Council of Teachers of English (CCTE) in 1968, provided associations to further cross-national dialogue. (See, for example, Squire, 1966.) The Anglo-American Dartmouth Seminar in 1966 saw the organization of an international steering committee that planned subsequent international conferences such as those held at York University in 1970, Melbourne in 1976, and Ottawa in 1978. An International Federation of English Associations has been formed to maintain communication from country to country and to plan international conferences on a multiyear cycle. International exchanges of beginning teachers have been sponsored by such institutions as the University of Connecticut, Florida State University, and Rutgers; and the National Writing Project at Berkeley has held workshops in three other countries. Further, the International Assessment of Educational Progress, operating out of Stockholm, has provided comparative studies of the teaching of reading, literature, and writing (Purves, 1974, 1982; Thorndike, 1974). These efforts have informed teachers of new ideas for teaching the English language arts from every country, and have made available internationally the resources of gifted teachers like Marie Clay in language development, Eva Malmquist in reading, Dorothy Heathcote in drama, James Britton in writing, and Louise Rosenblatt in literature.

THE EXCELLENCE REFORM MOVEMENT

Alarmed at falling test scores, reports of educational deprivation, and vocal public criticism of American schools, the United States Department of Education in 1983 issued *A Nation at Risk,* a painfully written call for educational reform, lest the nation condemn itself to "drowning in a sea of mediocrity" (National Commission on Excellence, 1983). Supported by 28 major studies of the quality of teaching, the most influential of which were by Goodlad (1985) and Sizer (1986), and an estimated 480 separate task forces and committees appointed by states, professional societies, and large school districts, the "Excellence Reform Movement," as it has been tagged, sought to improve the teaching of basic skills in reading and writing as well as in mathematics and to strengthen the academic content of the school. The Secretary of Education publicly introduced the report with support from the President of the United States, and called for an end to "the dumbing down" of textbooks (Bell, 1989). The Holmes Group and a Carnegie Task Force called for reform of teacher education (*A Nation Prepared,* 1987; Olson, 1987). The National Academy of Education published a monograph on improving reading instruction and reading in content areas (Anderson et al., 1985). Report after report pointed to the significance of writing in improving comprehension and thinking (Graves, 1978). Especially significant has been concern with improving basic literacy for children at risk (Chall, 1985; Venezky, Kaestle, & Sum, 1987). Much of the previous decade's work in writing and thinking and writing across the curriculum led to increased calls for writing in every subject as a way of improving learning (Corbett, 1987; Squire, 1987). Trying to direct attention to outstanding teachers and teaching, the NCTE initiated a Centers of Excellence program to direct attention to classrooms and schools regularly achieving excellence. So focused had been the claims for attention to reading and writing in English classrooms that it appeared for a time that literature might suffer. Articulate advocates of strong programs in literature, however, particularly those seeking programs in traditional literature, began to emphasize the importance of cultural literacy and of familiarizing children and young people with the best that has been known and thought in the world (California State Department of Education, 1987; Hirsch, 1987; Ravitch & Finn, 1987; Squire, 1987). A National Assessment on Cultural Literacy revealed some American children less familiar with Bible stories, legends and myths, and traditional literature than many would wish (Applebee, Langer & Mullis, 1988). Even as this is written, schools are responding to such changes and strong efforts to restore a literature emphasis to the classroom appear likely. (See, for example, Westbury & Purves, 1988.)

PROCESS VERSUS CONTENT

Conflict between the content of English education and the processes of language learning has sparked professional debate in recent years and seems likely to continue. Do we teach the skills of reading or the process of comprehension? Is rhetoric our subject or the processes of composing? Should we teach literature or focus on response to literature? William Bennett, Secretary of Education in 1987 and 1988, stressed the importance of content in literature as well as in reading and composition (Bennett, 1979), yet a coalition of English Associations (NCTE, NLA, College English Association, CCCC, CEE, and others) meeting for 3 weeks during the summer of 1987, asserted the importance of process in learning language and responding to literature, and the value of looking at instruction in relation to the growing capacities of readers and writers and not in relation to inert content alone. Their report, released in early 1989, seems likely to stimulate a new debate in professional discussion (Lloyd-Jones & Lunsford, 1989).

VIEWING ENGLISH TEACHING FROM BOOKS

One way of ascertaining current and developing views of the profession of the teaching of the English language arts is to look at widely read books that have defined the role of the teacher at different times. During the past half century, the conception of what a teacher of English is and does appears to have progressed from early, oversentimentalized portraits of Mr. Chips (Hilton, 1934), or Miss Dove (Patton, 1954), to the pixilated Miss Gurney in the popular 1950s television series, "Mr. Peepers," or to Bel Kaufmann's giddy *Up the Down Staircase* (1965), to the repressed sexuality of Blanche Dubois (Williams, 1980). Is it the centrality of our subject in education that leads to so much satirization of English teaching? Two of the most profoundly influential portraits of teaching English have come from Jacques Barzun (1944) and Sylvia Ashton-Warner (1963), both emphasizing the humanity at the core of English instruction. Ruth Strickland's widely influential portrait of the elements in a language arts classroom set the standard for a géneration of teachers (1969). Lou LaBrant's *We Teach English* (1951) provided a similar assertion of value for secondary teachers. And Neil Postman and Samuel Weingartner perhaps best reflected the values of the romantic critics in *Teaching As Subversive Activity* (1969). Important personal credos with respect to teaching English have appeared by Moffett (1968), Macrorie (1970), G. B. Harrison (1962), and others. These views have shaped what thousands of teachers think and feel about the teaching of the English language arts, and, perhaps more accurately than any school survey or research, reflect how many feel about the profession today.

THE PROFESSION FACES THE FUTURE

Teachers of the English Language Arts today face new responsibilities as they look at their changing classrooms. The aging white population coupled with increasing minorities in our schools point to critical new priorities. The very young children currently in our society seem to represent a new kind of pluralism. The traditional "ideal" family now embraces only 6 percent of our households, and two thirds of the world's immigration is still to the United States (Hodgkinson, 1988). Further, the problems of poverty loom large. If we have faced continued problems in teaching basic English skills to the children of poverty (Chall, 1985; Venezky et al., 1987), the fact that 40 percent of today's children are poor—13 million—necessitates continued attention to literacy (Hodgkinson, 1988). The recent emphasis on strengthening academic requirements may only exacerbate the problems of schooling. Shortly after the year 2000, we will become a nation in which one out of three children is nonwhite. English will remain our national language, but teaching it will be a continued challenge, particularly when tomorrow's language arts classrooms will become steadily more Asian, more Hispanic, more African American, and less white.

The growing economic and cultural influence of these nonwhite American cultures should support sound efforts in our schools. But our inability thus far to recruit large numbers of nonwhite teachers, particularly teachers from new American cultural groups, may not bode well for the future. Nor may our persistent concern with a narrow definition of "cultural literacy." At a time when the cultural antecedents of America are changing, our school curriculum in English must also be prepared to change. Fortunately, the historical resiliency of teachers of the English language arts and their professional leaders should help to face the challenge.

References

Aikin, W.M. (1942). *The story of the eight year study.* New York: Harper and Bros.

Allen, H.B. (1966). *TENES: A survey of the teaching of English to non-English speakers.* Urbana, IL: NCTE.

Anderson, R.A., Hiebert, E., Scott, J., & Wilkinson, I. (1985). *Becoming a nation of readers.* Champaign, IL: National Academy of Education, National Institute of Education, Center for the Study of Reading.

Applebee, A. (1974). *Tradition and reform in the teaching of English: A history.* Urbana, IL: National Council of Teachers of English.

Applebee, A. (1978). *Writing in the secondary school.* Urbana, IL: National Council of Teachers of English

Applebee, A., Langer, J., & Mullis, I. (1985). *The reading report card.* Princeton, NJ: Educational Testing Service.

Applebee, A., Langer, J., & Mullis, I. (1986a). *Learning to be literate in America.* Princeton, NJ: Educational Testing Service,

Applebee, A., Langer, J., & Mullis, I. (1986b). *The writing report card.* Princeton, NJ: Educational Testing Service

Applebee, A., Langer, J., & Mullis, I. (1986c). *Writing trends across the decades.* Princeton, NJ: Educational Testing Service

Applebee, A., Langer, J., & Mullis, I. (1988). *Who can read.* Princeton, NJ: Educational Testing Service

Ashton-Warner, S. (1963). *Teacher.* New York: Simon & Schuster.

Association of American Publishers, American Library Association, & the Association for Supervision and Curriculum Development. (1981). *Limiting what students should read.* Washington, D.C.: Association of American Publishers.

Association of American Publishers, & National Education Association. (1972). *Selecting instructional materials for purchase.* Washington, D.C.: National Education Association.

Austin, M., Morrison, C., & Kenny, H.J. (1961). *The torchlighters.* Cambridge, MA: Harvard University Press.

Baker, L., & Brown, A. (in press). Metacognitive skill and reading. In P.D., R. Barr M. Kamil and D. Pearson (Eds.), *Handbook of research in reading,* Vol II. New York: Longman.

Barzun, J. (1944). *Teacher in America.* Boston: Little Brown & Co.

Bell, T. (1989). *The Thirteenth Man, A Reagan Cabinet Memoir.* New York: The Free Press.

Bennett, W. (1979). *To reclaim a legacy: A report on the humanities in higher education.* Washington, D.C.: National Endowment for the Humanities.

Berliner, D.C. & Rosenshine, B. (1977). The acquisition of knowledge in the classroom. In R.C. Anderson, R.J. Spiro & W.E. Montague (Eds.), *Schooling and the acquisition of knowledge.* Hillsdale, NJ: Erlbaum.

Bloom, B. (1982). *Human characteristic and school learning.* New York: McGraw Hill.

Bond, G., & Dykstra, R. (1967). The cooperative research programs in first grade reading instruction. *Reading Research Quarterly, 2* (Winter), 5–41.

Braddock, R., Lloyd-Jones, R., & Schoer, L. (1963). *Research in written composition.* Urbana, IL: National Council of Teachers of English.

Britton, J. (1970). *Language and learning.* Portsmouth, NH: Heinemann/Boynton.

Britton, J., Martin, N., McLeod, A., & Rosen, H. (1975). *The development of writing abilities.* London: Macmillan.

Broening, A. (1956). *The English language arts in the secondary school.* New York: Appleton Century Crofts.

Brooks, C., & Warren, R.P. (1938). *Understanding poetry.* New York: D. Appleton Century.

Bruner, J. (1960). *The process of education.* Cambridge, MA: Harvard University Press.

Burrows, A.T. (1955). Composition: Prospect and retrospect. In H.A. Robinson (Ed.), *Reading and writing instruction in the United States: Historical trends.* Urbana, IL: ERIC and International Reading Association.

California State Department of Education. (1987). *Handbook for planning an effective literature program.* Sacramento, CA: Author.

Carnegie Commission on Teacher Education. (1986). A nation prepared: Teachers for the 21st century. *Chronicle of higher education, 32*(May 21), 43–51.

Cazden, C. (1988). *Classroom discourse: The Language of Teaching and Learning.* Portsmouth, N.H.: Heineman.

Chall, J.S. (1967). *The great debate.* New York: McGraw-Hill. Also, revised 1984.

Chall, J.S. (1985). *Growth in reading ability.* New York: McGraw-Hill.

Chall, J.S., Conard, S., & Harris, S. (1977). *An analysis of textbooks in relation to falling SAT scores.* New York: College Entrance Examination Board.

Chall, J.S. & Squire, J.R. (in press). Publishing and textbooks. In P.D. Pearson et al. (Eds.), *Handbook of research in reading* (2nd ed.). New York: Longman.

Clapp, J.M. (1926). *The place of English in American life.* Chicago, IL: National Council of Teachers of English.

Coleman, J. (1966). *Equality of educational opportunity.* Washington, D.C.: U.S. Government Printing Office.

Commission on English. (1931). *Examining the examination in English.* Cambridge, MA: Harvard University Press.

Commission on English. (1965). *Freedom and discipline in English.* New York: College Entrance Examination Board.

Committee on the National Interest. (1961). *The national interest and the teaching of English: A report on the status of the profession.* Urbana, IL: National Council of Teachers of English.

Committee on the National Interest. (1964). *The national interest and the continuing education of teachers: A report on the status of the profession of English.* Urbana, IL: National Council of Teachers of English.

Committee on the Right to Read of National Council of Teachers of English. (1962). *The students' right to read.* Urbana, IL: National Council of Teachers of English.

Conant, James B. (1959). *The American high school today.* New York: McGraw-Hill.

Cooper, Charles. (1982). *Researching response to literature and the teaching of literature: Points of departure.* Norwood, NJ: Ablex.

Corbett, E.P.J. (1987). Teaching composition: Where we've been and where we're going. *College Composition and Communication, 38,* 444–452.

Corbin, R., & Crosby, M. (1965). *Language programs for the disadvantaged.* Urbana, IL: National Council of Teachers of English.

Denham, C., & Lieberman, A. (1980). *Time to learn.* Washington, D.C.: National Institute of Education and U.S. Department of Education.

Dixon, J. (1975). *Growth through English* (3rd ed.). London: Oxford University.

Durkin, D. (1983). *Is there a match between what elementary teachers do and what basal manuals recommend* (Technical Report No. 44). Urbana, IL: Center for the Study of Reading, University of Illinois.

Dusel, W. (1956). *Determining an efficient load in English.* San Leandro, CA: Central California Council of Teachers of English.

Edmonds, R. (1979). Effective schools for the urban poor. *Educational Leadership. 37,* 15–34.

Emig, J. (1971). *The composing processes of twelfth grades.* Urbana, IL: National Council of Teachers of English.

EPIE Institute. (1977). *Report on a national study of the nature and quality of instructional materials most used by teachers.* (EPIE Report No. 78). New York: Educational Products Information Exchange.

Fay, R.S. (1968) *The reform movement in English teaching, 1910–1917.* Doctoral dissertation, Harvard University. (University Microfilms No. 68-12,068)

Flood J. (Ed.). (1984). *Promoting reading comprehension: Cognition, language, and structure of prose.* Newark, DE: International Reading Association.

Frye, Northrop. (1957). *The anatomy of criticism.* Princeton, NJ: Princeton University Press.

Frye, Northrop. (1964). *The educated imagination.* Bloomington, IN: Indiana University Press.

Gerber, J.C. (1963). The 1962 summer institutes of the Commission on English. *PMLA, 78,* 9–25.

Goodlad, J. (1985). *A place called school.* New York: McGraw-Hill.

Goodman, K.S., Freeman, S., Murphy, S., & Shannon, P. (1988). *Basal reader report card.* Des Moines, IA: Richard Owen.

Graves, D.F. (1978). *Balance the basics and let them write.* New York: Ford Foundation.

Gray, J. (1987). *The Bay Area writing project, model of university-school collaboration.* Berkeley: University of California.

Gray, W.S. (1933). SUmmary of reading investigations. *Journal of Educational Research, 21* (February), 401–24. (Published annually in this journal until 1960 and thereafter by International Reading Association).

Grommon, A.H. (1963). *The education of teachers of English for American schools and colleges.* New York: Appleton Century Crofts.

Grommon, A.H. (1968). A history of the preparation of teachers of English. *The English Journal, 57*(4), 484–527.

Hanna, P., Hanna, J.S., Hodges, R.E., & Rudolph, Jr., E.H. (1966). *Phonemegrapheme correspondencies as cues to spelling improvement.* Washington, D.C.: U.S. Department of Health, Education and Welfare.

Harrison, G.B. (1962). *The profession of English.* New York: Harcourt, Brace, and World.

Hatfield, W.W. (Ed.). (1935). *An experience curriculum in English.* New York: D. Appleton-Century.

Hays, Edna. (1936). College entrance requirements in English: Their effects on the high schools. Contributions to *Education, No. 675.* New York: Teachers College, Columbia University.

Heath, S.B. (1983). *Ways with words.* Cambridge: Cambridge University Press.

Her Majesty's Stationery Office. (1975). *A language for life: Report of the committee of inquiry under chairmanship of Sir Alan Bullock.* London: Author.

Herndon, J. (1971). *The way it's spozed to be.* New York: Simon & Schuster.

Hillocks, G. (1972). *Alternatives in English: A critical appraisal of elective programs.* Urbana, IL: National Council of Teachers of English.

Hillocks, G. (1986). *Research on written composition and new directions for teaching.* Urbana, IL: National Council of Teachers of English and National Conference on Research in English.

Hilton, J. (1934). *Goodbye Mr. Chips.* Boston: Little Brown & Co.

Hirsch, E.D. (1987). *Cultural literacy.* Boston: Houghton Mifflin Co.

Hodgkinson, H.L. (1988). Using demographic data for long range planning, *Phi Delta Kappan* 70:166–70 (Oct. 1988).

Hook, J.N. (1979). *A long way together.* Urbana, IL: National Council of Teachers of English.

Hosic, J.F. (1917). *Reorganization of English in the secondary schools.* (Bulletin No. 2., Government Printing Office). Washington, D.C.: Government Printing Office.

Hosic, J.F. (1921). The National Council of Teachers of English. *English Journal, 10*(1), 1–10.

Institutional Tracking Service (1980). *Reading/Language Arts.* White Plains, NY: Author.

Jenkinson, E.B. (1979). *Censors in the classroom: The mind benders.* Carbondale, IL: Southern Illinois University Press.

Jerrolds, R.W. (1977). *Reading reflections: The history of the International Reading Association.* Newark, DE: International Reading Association.

Jewett, Arno. (1958). *English language arts in American high schools* (Bulletin No. 13). Washington, D.C.: U.S. Office of Education.

Jewett, Arno. (1964). *Improving the English skills of culturally different youth.* Washington, D.C.: U.S. Department of Health, Education and Welfare.

Judd, C.H., & Buswell, G.T. (1922). *Silent reading.* Chicago, IL: University of Chicago.

Kaufmann, Bel. (1965). *Up the down staircase.* Englewood Cliffs, NJ: Prentice Hall.

Kozol, J. (1968). *Death at an early age.* Boston: Houghton Mifflin.

LaBrant, Lou L. (1951). *We teach English.* New York: Harcourt brace.

LaBrant, Lou L. (1961). The uses of communication media. In M. Willis (Ed.), *The guinea pigs grow up.* Columbus, OH: Ohio University Press.

Langer, Suzanne. (1942). *Philosophy in a new key.* Cambridge, MA: Harvard University Press.

Lloyd-Jones, R., & Lunsford, A. (1989). *The English coalition conference: Democracy through language.* Urbana, IL: National Council of Teachers of English and Modern Language Association.

Loban, W.D. (1976). *Language development: Kindergarten through grade twelve* (Research Report No. 18). Urbana, IL: National Council of Teachers of English.

Lynch, J., & Evans, B. (1983). *High school English textbooks: A critical examination.* Boston: Little Brown & Co.

Mackintosh, H.K. (1954). *Language arts for today's children.* New York: Appleton Century Crofts.

Macrorie, K. (1970). *Uptaught.* New York: Hayden.

Marckwardt, A.H. (1963). Research in the teaching of English language and linguistics (a summary). In R.W. Rogers (Ed.), *Proceedings of the Allerton Park Conference on Research in the Teaching of English.* Unpublished U.S.O.E. Project #G-1006.

Mason, J. (1960a). *The National Council of Teachers of English—1911–1926.* Doctoral dissertation, George Peabody College of Education. (University Microfilms No. 62-5681).

Mason, J. (1960b). The teaching of literature in American high schools, 1885–1900. In R.C. Pooley (Ed.), *Perspective in English.* New York: Appleton Century.

Mason, J. & Osborn, J. (1983). When do children begin reading to learn. *A survey of practices in grades two to five* (Technical Report No. 261). Urbana, IL: Center for the Study of Reading, University of Illinois.

Mavrogenes, N.A. (1985). William Scott Gray: Leader of teachers and shaper of American reading instruction (Doctoral dissertation, University of Chicago).

McLuhan, M. (1964). *Understanding media: The extensions of man.* New York: McGraw-Hill.

Modern Language Association, National Council of Teachers of English, College English Association, & American Studies Association. (1959). The basic issues in the teaching of English. *PMLA, 74,* 1–12.

Moffett, J. (1968). *Teaching in a universe of discourse.* Boston, MA: Houghton Mifflin.

Moffett, J. (1988). *Storm in the mountains: A case study of censorship, conflict, and consciousness.* Carbondale, IL: Southern Illinois University Press.

Moffett, J., & Wagner, B.J. (1976). *A student centered language arts curriculum, grades K–12* (2nd ed.). Boston: Houghton Mifflin Co.

Muller, H. (1967). *The uses of English.* New York: Holt, Rinehart & Winston.

Murray, D. (1986). *Writing to learn.* New York: Holt, Rinehart & Winston.

Myers, M. (1985). The need for a new professionalism. In M. Chorny (Ed.), *Teacher as learner* (pp. 107–120). Calgary, Alberta: Language in Curriculum Project, University of Calgary.

National Commission on Excellence. (1983). *A Nation at risk: The Imperative for Educational Reform.* Washington, D.C.: U.S. Department of Education.

Norvell, G. (1950). *The reading interests of young people.* Boston: D.C. Heath.

Olson, J.W. (1969). The nature of literature anthologies in the teaching of high school English, 1917–1957 (Doctoral dissertation, University of Wisconsin). *University Microfilms No. 69-22-454.*

Olson, L. (1987). An overview of the Holmes Group. *Phi Delta Kappan, 68,* 619–21.

O'Rourke, L.J. (1934). *Rebuilding the English curriculum to involve greater mastery of essentials.* Washington, D.C.: The Psychological Institute.

Patton, F. (1954). *Good morning, Miss Dove.* New York: Dodd Mead.

Pearson, P.D., Barr, R., Kamil, M., & Mosenthal, P. (Eds.). (1984). *Handbook of research on reading.* New York: Longman.

Petty, W.J. (1983). *A history of the national conference on research in English.* Urbana, IL: National Council of Teachers of English.

Piche, G.L. (1967). Revision and reform in secondary school English curriculum 1870–1900 (Doctoral dissertation, University of Minnesota).

Pooley, R.C. (1946). *Teaching English usage.* New York: Appleton Century.

Postman, N., & Weingartner, S. (1969). *Teaching as a subversive activity.* New York: Delacorte.

Purves, A.C. (1974). *Literature education in ten countries.* New York: John Wiley & Co.

Purves, A., & Beach, R. (1972). *Literature and the reader.* Urbana, IL: National Council of Teachers of English.

Purves, A.C. et al. (Eds.). (1973). *Responding—A literature program for grades 7–12.* Boston, MA: Ginn and Company.

Purves, A.C. & Takala, S. (1982). An international perspective on the evaluation of written composition. In A.C. Purves and S. Takala (Eds.), *Evaluation in education: An international review series* (pp. 207–290). New York: Pergamon Press.

Ravitch, Diane, & Finn, Chester E. (1987). *What do our seventeen-year olds know?* A Report on the First National Assessment of History and Literature. New York: Harper & Row.

Richards, I.A. (1929). *Practical Criticism.* New York: Harcourt Brace.

Robinson, H.A., Faraone, V., Hittleman, D., Unruh, E. (1990). *Reading Comprehension Instruction 1783–1987.* Neward, Del.: International Reading Association.

Robinson, H.A. (Ed.). (1977). *Reading and writing instruction in the United States: Historical trends.* Urbana, IL: ERIC and International Reading Association.

Rosenblatt, L. (1938). Literature as Exploration. New York: Progressive Education Association. (Now in 4th edition, Modern Language Association, 1982.)

Rosenblatt, L. (1978). *The reader, the text, and the poem.* Carbondale, IL: Southern Illinois University.

Rosenshine, B. & Stevens, R. (1984). Classroom instruction in reading. In P.D. Pearson (Ed.), *Handbook of research on reading.* New York: Longman.

Rosewall, P.T. (1965). *A historical survey of recommendations and proposals for the literature curricula of American secondary schools since 1892.* Lincoln: University of Nebraska.

Searles, J.F. (1942). Some trends in the teaching of literature since 1900 in American high schools (Doctoral dissertation, University of Wisconsin).

Shaughnessy, M. (1977). *Errors and expectations: A guide for teachers of writing.* New York: Oxford Publishing Co.

Shugrue, M.F. (1968). *English in a decade of change.* New York: Pegasus.

Shugrue, M. & Everett, E. (1968). English teacher preparation study. *English Journal, 57*(4), 475–83.

Simmons, John S., Shadiow, Linda, & Shafer, Robert E. (1990). History of the teaching of English in the United States. In Robert E. Shafer, James Britton, & Ken Watson (Eds.), *Teaching and learning English worldwide.* Clevedon, Avon, England: Multilingual Matters, Ltd.

Sizer, T. (1986). *Horace's compromise.* Boston: Houghton Mifflin Co.

Smith, D.V. (1939). *Evaluating instruction in secondary school English.* New York: Appleton Century Crofts.

Smith, D.V. (1941). *Evaluating instruction in secondary school English.* Chicago: National Council of Teachers of English.

Smith, D.V. (1932). *Instruction in English* (Bureau of Education, Bulletin No. 17). Washington, D.C.: U.S. Government Printing Office.

Smith, D.V. (Ed.). (1952). *The English language arts.* New York: Appleton Century Crofts.

Smith, F. (1971). *Psycholinguistics and reading.* New York: Holt, Rinehart and Winston.

Smith, Nila B. (1985, 1934). *American reading instruction.* Newark DE: International Reading Association.

Squire, J.R. (1963). College English departments and professional efforts to improve English teaching. *PMLA, 78*(4), 36–38.

Squire, J.R. (1964). *The response of adolescents to four short stories.* Urbana, IL: National Council of Teachers of English.

Squire, J.R. (1966). *A common purpose.* Urbana, IL: National Council of Teachers of English.

Squire, J.R. (1967). English at the crossroads: The national interest report plus eighteen. *The English Journal, 52*(6), 381–97.

Squire, J.R. (Ed.). (1987). The state of assessment in reading. *The Reading Teacher, 40,* (themed issue).

Squire, J.R. (1988). Studies of textbooks: Are we asking the right questions. In P. Jackson (Ed.), *Contributing to educational change.* Berkeley, CA: McCutchan Publishing Co.

Squire, J.R. &, Applebee, A. (1968). *High school English instruction today: The national study of high school English.* New York: Appleton Century Crofts.

Squire, J.R. & Applebee, A. (1969). *Teaching English in the United Kingdom.* Urbana, IL: National Council of Teachers of English.

Stahl, D. (1965). *A history of the English curriculum in American high schools.* Chicago, IL: Lyceum Press.

Stahl, S.A. & Miller, P.D. (1988). The language experience approach for beginning reading. Unpublished research report, Western Illinois University, Macomb, IL.

Stormzand, M.J., & O'Shea, M.V. (1924). *How much English grammar?* Baltimore: Warwick and York.

Strickland, R. (1962). *The language development of children, its relationship to the language of reading textbooks, and the quality of reading of selected school children.* Bloomington, IN: School of Education, Indiana University.

Strickland, R. (1969). *Language arts in the elementary school* (3rd ed.). Boston: D.C. Heath.

Thorndike, R. (1974). *Reading education in ten countries.* New York: John Wiley.

U.S. Department of Education. (1988). *Class size and public policy: Politics and panaceas.* Washington, D.C.: U.S. Department of Education.

Valencia, S. & Pearson, P.D. (1987). Time for a change. *The Reading Teacher, 40,*726–33.

Veith, D.P. (1952). A historical analysis of the relations between English and speech since 1910 (Doctoral dissertation, Teachers College, Columbia University).

Venezky, R.L. (1984). History of reading research. In P.D. Pearson (Ed.), *Handbook of research on reading* (pp. 3–35). New York: Longman.

Venezky, R.L., Kaestle, C.F., & Sum, A.M. (1987). *The subtle danger.* Princeton, NJ: Educational Testing Service.

Wellek, R., & Warren, R. (1949). *Theory of literature.* New York: Harcourt Brace.

Westbury, A. & Purves, A. (1988). Cultural literacy and the idea of general education. *National Society for the Study of Education Eighty-Seventh Yearbook, Part II.* Chicago: University of Chicago Press.

Wilkinson, A. (1970). The concept of oracy. *English Journal 59,* 70–77.

Williams, T. (1980). *A streetcar named desire.* New York: New Directions.

HISTORICAL CONSIDERATIONS: AN INTERNATIONAL PERSPECTIVE

John Dixon

History as Living Present

I went to a one-room school through eighth grade. We had countywide examinations, the purpose of which I am not quite sure [about]. What I do recall is that it was a real feather in a teacher's cap to have his or her eighth-grade pupils score at or near the top of that list. At any rate, the other eighth-grade students and I spent every afternoon of the last two months of the school year in the entryway asking each other questions from every standardized achievement test that the teachers could get their hands on. I have no doubt that every other entry to every other one-room school was similarly occupied by eighth graders hot in pursuit of the knowledge embedded in standardized tests.

Robert Dykstra (1987)

History invites us both to record what happened and to ask why. It suggests we study small-scale institutions, like classrooms, and ask how what goes in them is related to what goes on in bigger institutions, like school boards, subject associations, state legislatures, national offices of education—and, wider still, in the society at large, or internationally.

Why did Robert Dykstra's teachers take county tests so seriously? What alternatives had they access to? What power had they, individually or as a group, to propose an alternative? How common was their experience? What, if anything, has happened since in that county to change the tests, the alternatives, or who has power to decide? What conflicts, if any, have there been over different models of education? History invites you to ask such questions.

Once you begin to ask them, and only then, historical research becomes usable, fascinating, and never-ending. This brief article must start, then, by prompting you to look at what's going on in your classroom, in your school and board, and to ask questions; to realize that you, like Robert Dykstra, are a part of history and therefore need to ask how you were formed as

a student, and equally, perhaps, how you are being formed as a teacher now.

FORMATIVE EXPERIENCES OF THE OLDER GENERATION

Teachers roughly aged 60 to 65 (and I am one of them) went to school in the 1930s and early 1940s: in the Depression years, for the most part. The times were hard, with little cash for education. They reached their teens during a world war; some of the oldest fought in it. Education faced specific, narrow demands. Many went to college immediately after the War, however, and with luck caught the feeling that humanity was capable after all of building a better world.

Looking into a sample of their schools in the 1930s, Dora V. Smith saw "methods conditioned by desks nailed to the floor"; it is a powerful image. "Question and answer procedures with the teacher in command, and recitation around the class of sentences written out at home the night before represent by far

18

the most common activities of the average high school class in New York State" (1941). "Regimentation of pupils was the rule; individualization, the exception." For a handful to be sent out into the entry to ask each other questions, then, would still have been a radical innovation.

Literature was the major element in English courses for the secondary schools (Applebee, 1974). In half the junior high schools, this meant the study of a literary anthology textbook, which successive presidents of the National Council of Teachers of English (NCTE) worked hard to write and disseminate, in order to encourage wider reading. Unfortunately, in many cases that one anthology was all the school could afford in the 1930s. It easily became the dominating book, and its assignments the inevitable goal of reading. In New York, 60 percent of teachers in Dora Smith's 1941 sample testified that what determined their classroom practices was the textbook available, not the official course of study.

Senior high school kept to the study of classic works; half the schools in a national sample had no other method of organizing the course, just the list of texts (Smith, 1933). Following the recent "unit" method, schools would give up on average 4 weeks to the study of *Julius Caesar, Macbeth,* or *As You Like It,* for instance; some allowed as much as 9 weeks for the one text. Of the 30 most frequently used texts, not one was contemporary.

What was the force behind this curriculum? It was the early traditions of college entrance exams. Apart from the omission of the "Bunker Hill Oration," 25 to 40 years had passed "with little change in the requirements except to add a few more titles in kind plus the nineteenth century novel" and possibly an 11th grade program in American literature. In 1931, the College Entrance Examination Board found that the best two predictors of college achievement were the new Scholastic Achievement Test, on the one hand, and the high school record, on the other. Read candidly, this result might have suggested radical change in their own examinations. But, though their "restricted text exam" finally was set aside 10 years later, they still hung on, like colleagues elsewhere in the English-speaking world, to their right to "test the candidate's ability to paraphrase or to make a precis, or to interpret the subtler qualities of a poem read at sight," by whatever methods their examiners were accustomed to.

Also in 1931, the Board concluded that English teachers in the lower levels "cannot afford to ignore the value of these [standardized] tests in classroom work" and recommended "recurrent" practice throughout the year. (So young Dykstras were actually getting off lightly.)

For Dora Smith, "no impression remains more vivid after conference with hundreds of teachers throughout the country than the fear [sic] under which they labor because of the requirements (real or imaginary) of the institutions higher up" (1933). A characteristic result was "deadly and uninteresting routine" (1941).

A Model of External Domination

Teachers and students were dominated, then, by higher institutions, by textbooks or set texts, and by tests or exams. How could this model be so widespread? After all, since its foundation in 1911 NCTE had given the various "clubs" and "associations" of English teachers both a national voice and a forum for discussion. In the 1930s alone, the pages of "English Journal" had been open to many new ideas, including:

a. The Committee for Film or "Photoplay Appreciation" (beginning 1932);
b. The early work of the Radio Committee (beginning 1936);
c. An invited series, for instance, on Hemingway, Dos Passos, and contemporary Left-Wing literature in 1933. (Applebee, 1974; Hook, 1979).

In a major report in 1936, NCTE recommended, among other things, the abandonment of formal grammar teaching, except as an elective for seniors, and a curriculum based on "selected experiences," each unit forming an "organic whole." (Hatfield 1935).

A minority of classrooms were affected by these and other "progressive" ideas, as we shall see, but the majority were not. To realize why takes an act of historical imagination. First, let's imagine the social constraints: whole regions thrown into the poverty line or starvation; more than one in three unemployed and job opportunities shrivelling; savage cutting of salaries and funds for education—the days "of crisis and chaos" with which the 1930s began (DeBoer, 1932). Thus, within that ambience, the inexorable clinging on to recognizable results: success with college entry tests.

Consider then the teachers and their preparation, solidly based on college Anglo-Saxon and Middle English, for a start; on an academic tradition modelled on the study of the ancient classics. Admittedly, a sizable minority had the initiative to set up flourishing extracurricular programs in drama, journalism and debate; there was still no feedback, however, about their work in class. After all, what recognition would such activities get in standardized tests for college entrance, "an examination system that takes cognizance chiefly of facts and skills" (Smith, 1941).

Teachers who persisted had "to meet, study and assimilate several new psychologies, at least one new sociology, and a score of isms. We have had to grapple with such concepts as 'the child centred school," the activity program, the socialized recitation, the project method, correlation, two- and three-track plans, and the unit plan . . . all movements . . . [that] have added immeasurably to the science and art of teaching" (Pooley, 1939). Against "local insistence upon more formal elements of instruction", and without adequate institutions to prepare themselves for revolutionary changes in class, most teachers, not surprisingly, felt a growing chasm between practice and theory, which they were powerless to deal with (Applebee, 1974).

Historical circumstances like these have almost inevitable outcomes. Without special support, teachers (like students) learn to accept the targets set them from above, and getting through the textbook assignments becomes yet another imposed task, for teachers as well as students. Thus, authority comes to rest in tests and exams, and status depends on who comes out on top. It is a model of external domination—but then, for over a decade, almost everyone felt inescapably fettered and chained by economic and social forces. You had to learn to endure.

If you had support and unusual enterprise, you joined the groups who resisted: who escaped the "serfdom" of college entrance by exam, who struggled to democratize school and classroom, who looked for "experiences" relevant to adolescents, who took modern, American literature and media seriously. But with so much to learn at once, only exceptional teachers and students could swim against the tide, and then with difficulty.

Alternative Models in the 1930s

When Dora V. Smith spotted the desks nailed to the floor, she clearly had other possibilities in mind, desks (or chairs) that could be moved, grouped and arranged according to the classroom activity. Her critical observer role (like ours today) depended on a knowledge of alternatives that had been important in her own formation.

Indeed, from the 1910s there had been a concerted movement across the English-speaking world to escape from the limited horizons—and achievements—of a test-dominated model. Here, for example, is a liberal inspector in the United Kingdom Board of Education describing the kind of elementary school practices that he and his colleagues were hoping to promote in 1914:

The good modern school will have a generous course in English. The children will not only be taught to read aloud, but will have plenty of practice, in *reading for enjoyment and for information*. . . [The] children will read *six or seven [books] or even more* in each year, and those supplied to the older children will include standard books in travel and fiction. . . Children will be taught to consult books for reference and in their later years will *look up and prepare the subject matter of their essays themselves*. Composition, a starved subject under the old conditions, . . will be practised throughout the school, *orally or in written form* or both, and the children will take as naturally to *recording their ideas* with the pen as to uttering them in speech. . . [In] all the best schools, much will be made of English poetry, no longer in the shape of a formal recitation lesson, but by the children reading and learning numerous poems *often chosen by themselves* (from personal archives, my emphases).

The stress is on real books (not practice readers); on recording their own ideas (not reproducing the teacher's or the text's), using speech (as well as writing); on choosing poems individually, and on preparing subject matter by themselves (not being told by teacher). Clearly, behind this model there is a whole new philosophy. (See also the chapter by Goodman on alternative modes of testing, this text.)

In the 1910s and immediately after World War I, there were international exchanges and practical contributions to a model along these lines. At that time the Child Study movement with Froebel, Montessori, and others gradually had set up a wide interest in children's development, in their questions and responses, the stories and poems they became involved in, their ways of thinking, and the choices they were capable of making. New ideas on adolescence (Hall 1904) spreading through the United States from the 1900s, raised questions about the ways

high school subjects like English might be affecting a vital phase in students' lives. New aspirations for active participation in democracy (Dewey, 1918) promoted a move to individual rather than class work, and to extensions of student choice and autonomy. All this was submerged in the classrooms of the Depression years, surviving only as a minority aspiration.

INTERLUDE: COLLEGE AND SCHOOLS IN THE FIFTIES

Most of us 60- to 65-year-olds went through college in the 1940s just before another revolution, the "new criticism." By the early 1950s, according to Welleck (1953), it predominated among younger staff members in the United States and would come to dominate graduate training, sweeping aside the historical, philological, and genre courses that had originally won English studies a place in the university. So some of our current 60- to 65-year-olds may have felt themselves no sooner graduated than obsolete.

About the same period, academic critics opened up on the progressive movement: "Crisis in Education" (1949), "And Madly Teach" (1949), "Quackery in the Public Schools" (1953), "Educational Wastelands" (1953). The call from college was for "minds made free by discipline" (Applebee 1974). Finally, as the Cold War intensified and political witch-hunts began, progressivism was linked with "communism."

In line with a new focus on the academically gifted, the Advanced Placement Program was established, including from 1955 a series of exams. In English, these immediately established textual analysis and "new" criticism as major new goals (for underprepared teachers).

In 1957, however, the growing excitement in the United States about courses for "Students of Superior Ability" turned into a wave of shock: the Soviet Union had launched the first rocket into space, the Sputnik. "Only massive upgrading of the scholastic standards of our schools will guarantee the future prosperity and freedom of the Republic" wrote Admiral Rickover (1958). How would a new generation respond?

FORMATIVE EXPERIENCES OF TEACHERS NOW 30 TO 35

This generation went to school in the 1960s and early 1970s, during a world-wide economic boom. In their early years money, was thrown—recklessly at times—into new education projects to try to secure "massive upgrading" of standards. Yet while they were still in elementary school, the nation fell into turmoil, positively through the Civil Rights movement, negatively through the war in Vietnam. Volunteer, be conscripted, or protest? This group faced inexorable choices, the men especially. For some of the women, on the other hand, there were new horizons, through the resurgence of the Women's Rights Movement. But before this age group were all through college in the 1970s, the advanced capitalist economies felt the first jolt in what was to become a long-term crisis of overproduction.

Surveying the best of their high schools in the mid-1960s, Jim Squire and Roger Applebee found "little reason for rejoicing" (1968). Each school had been selected because of outstanding English students (generally NCTE award winners) but, significantly, that gave little indication of the strength of the English department. For this reason, the mainstream practices and norms that were observed probably stand for what was then going on in many average to above average schools across the country.

Half the class time was spent in literary studies. "Macbeth" and "Julius Caesar" were studied in half the college preparatory classes; "Hamlet," "Silas Marner," "The Scarlet Letter," "A Tale of two Cities," and "The Return of the Native," in 40 percent. In these classes, then, authors were still dead, and formed a rather odd canon. But with two-, three- and five-track systems of instruction there was wide variation in the texts on offer. (Was it because of the *teachers'* formative experiences that, after Shakespeare, *The Grapes of Wrath* was the next "most significant text" listed by students?)

How about the teaching? Research observers attended, more often than not, talks by the teacher (or a student) on the age in which the work was written, the writer, the literary genre (in abstraction from the given text), or simply isolated facts. Analytical reading (dealing with a play line by line, for example) were rare: when it happened, the observers noted, it often lead to a more emotional response with greater sophistication.

Associated with these talks, there were oral questions from the teacher that were often self-defeating, curtailing discussion and interest, and were frequently answered by the teachers themselves. Students were expected to accept the thematic interpretation, to answer an assigned series of questions, and possibly to follow a mimeographed study guide.

As well as factual quizzes on the text, there were writing assignments. Much of the writing was superficial. Some questions invited imaginative construction beyond the text ("William Dane confesses. . ."—a "questionable" approach, according to the observers, who were happier to report the national impact of advanced placement tests. The latter ensured that, in honors classes at least, the analytical study of a particular poem or passage was attempted.

After a decade of pressure for advanced academic courses, targeted on the "gifted" (i.e., the students most able to teach themselves and each other), how can these classroom practices be explained? Perhaps the answer lay in the model of reform itself. A test-led change in classroom practices still leaves teachers passive and dominated by external demands. Outstanding individuals escape, it's true, but the majority feel no energies released in *them* for changing habitual ways of working with students. And without workshop discussion and practice, there was no vehicle for such changes at the time. This helps to explain the important finding that "outstanding" teaching had not spread throughout a department; it could only do so if teachers were accustomed to taking joint initiatives and organizing work together.

The results of a test-led curriculum were inevitably most clearly observable in writing instruction. Little or no thought was being given as to how a student's writing ability could be improved. Thus "for most teachers [in the sample], correcting papers is synonymous with teaching writing." Actually one third of papers collected were not corrected, and in a further third corrections were limited to gross errors in spelling and usage. Only 17 percent of the teachers said that their comments were designed to teach writing and thinking.

What teachers had learned from testing was a negative point of view, a search for student error. But this was reinforced by the composition-grammar texts they used: these had twice as many pages on grammar, usage, and mechanics as on units beyond the sentence. Many teachers had rejected the books available, according to the observers, but not, it seems, the stance.

The remaining 30 percent or so of the time in class was spent on "confused" language programs, on developmental reading programs, or (occasionally) on speech. Confusion over language was only to be expected: Lynch and Evans (1963) had found that most textbooks taught the same content at every grade level. As to reading development, while department chairs agreed that the fundamental purpose was to help students become active and critical readers, the only vehicle widely used was the packaged system, a prescribed set of texts and assignments.

By contrast, when this age-group entered college in the early 1970s, they found the profession split. Radical questions were being asked: "The subject of English in this country has been used to inculcate a white, Anglo-Saxon, Protestant ethic. . . My own feeling is that the game is just about played out" (Fisher, 1969).

College responded in the early 1970s by adopting a mixed program. On the one hand, they added new electives: women's studies, African American literature, ethnic literatures, film studies, psychoanalysis and literature, the literature of adolescence, science fiction. On the other hand, they preserved the standard period studies, either as a requirement or an advised course for the English major (Ohmann, 1976). Presumably, it was this evasion of theoretical issues that opened the floodgates in the 1980s.

These, then, were some of the formative experiences of the generation now aged 30 to 35. Naturally, there was variation (for better, and for worse); but the pattern above is easily recognizable to a teacher in the 1950s and early 1960s, whether in the Australasia, Canada or the United Kingdom. In those countries, the focus on academic students and exam targets was probably more insistent, if anything, and the practices that resulted were in many ways comparable.

In retrospect, one might say that there was a price to be paid for the 1950s' aggressive rejection of "progressive" aspirations, of their quest for individual choice, for student (and teacher) autonomy, for independent projects, and for active learning. The staleness of many high school programs was perhaps a significant factor in shaping the outbreak of radical, even anarchic, college protest that spread across the United States in the later 1960s, and linked up with other, world-wide movements.

COMPONENTS OF THE CURRENT SCENE

So far I have taken two generations now teaching in school, and briefly sketched some mainstream traditions that may have shaped their current practices. In retrospect, U.S. observers of the 1930s and the 1960s clearly pointed to a model of dominated teaching, whether by tests, textbooks, or canonical texts. Indeed, over the same period, it would not be difficult to present evidence showing the same model at work throughout the English-speaking world. Not surprisingly, then, there are currently teachers, departments and even whole regions still working to that model (generally under the new banner of an "objectives-driven" curriculum, "objectively measured").

Equally, during the past two decades, some readers will have experienced, however briefly, a sharply opposed model of teaching, in terms of:

a. The purposes of teacher-student (and student-student) dialogue (Barnes, 1976);
b. The initiatives allowed for in student writing, and the roles of teacher and fellow students in response to what's written (Britton, 1967; Emig, 1971; Graves, 1983);
c. The multicultural choices and purposes underlying what is read, listened to, or viewed, and the active roles taken by students in such "readings" and the discussions that follow (Meek, Wardlow, & Barton, 1977, Thompson, 1987);
d. The place of speech (oracy), role play and drama within such work (Heathcote, 1976) [All references could be multiplied.]

Taken singly, these changes have their parallels and forerunners in exceptional classrooms of the earlier period, especially in elementary schools. What is significantly different today is the kind of theoretical frame available to integrate the planning, practices, and evaluation of English "lessons." Even in the last 10 years, new ways have been discovered of making explicit—and thus differentiating among—students' achievements in using speech and writing for personal and social ends. (And in consequence, there has been a devastating critique of traditional assumptions behind "measuring" instruments.)

Even more important, however, has been the breakthrough in forms of teacher education. Extended "workshops," summer schools, writing (and reading) project networks have developed forms in which teacher-students make active contributions, experiencing for themselves the break from dominated classrooms. Already some teachers have become partners in research, and empowered teachers in turn empower their students (Boomer, 1982).

In most countries, these changes affect a minority. It is easier and cheaper for central administrators in the advanced economies to apply tests, make international comparisons, and, in a period of economic depression, to call on teachers nationally for better "output." So, in societies with greater wealth than ever before, an historical struggle continues. Will education, perhaps the central example today of social enterprise, win through to a new plateau in the "western democracies"? This history is still in the making, and, whether active or passive, we are part of it right now.

Can we learn from history, from historical research? Turning round to your current classroom, your department, your school, board, and state or national offices, do you still see teachers and students hemmed in and dominated by external forces? What precise forms are those forces taking today? And within your experience, how are they being resisted, or even, in some places, transformed? Where can you get support and encouragement for taking teaching and learning another step on the road to democracy? Either we learn from history, or we suffer it.

References

Historical Background

Applebee, A.N. (1974). *Tradition and Reform in the Teaching of English*. Urbana, Ill.: National Council of Teachers of English.

Bell, B.I. (1949). *Crisis in Education*. New York: H. Renergy.

Bestor, A. (1955). *Educational Wastelands*. Urbana, IL: Univ. of Illinois Press.

DeBoer, J.J. (1932). The Materials of the English Curriculum. In *English Journal* 21:(Jan. 1932) 68–69 [See Applebee.]

Dewey, J. (1916). *Democracy and Education*. New York: Macmillan.

Dyskra, R. (1987). Introduction. In J.R. Squire (Ed.), *The Dynamics of Language Learning*. Urbana, Ill.: ERIC Clearinghouse.

Fisher, J. (1969). Movement in English. (ADE Bulletin 22) New York: Modern Language Associates.

Hatfield, W.W. (1935). An Experience Curriculum in English. New York: D. Appleton Century.

Lynch, J.J., & Evans, B. 91963). *High School English Text-books: A Critical Examination*. Boston: Little, Brown & Co.

Lynd, A. (1953). *Quackery in the Public Schools*. New York: Grosset & Dunlap.

Ohmann, R. (1976). *English in America*. New York: Oxford University Press.

Pooley, R.C. (1939). Varied Patterns of Approach in the Teaching of Literature. *English Journal*, May 1939. [See Applebee.]

Rickover, H.G. (1959). *Education and Freedom*. New York: Dutton.

Smith, D. (1933). *Instruction in English*. Washington, D.C.: Government Printing Office.

Smith, D. (1941). *Evaluating Instruction in Secondary School English*. Chicago: National Council of Teachers of English.

Squire, J.R. & Applebee, R.K. (1968). *High School English Instruction Today*. New York: Appleton-Century-Crofts.

Wellek, R. (1953). Literary Scholarship. In Merle Curti, Ed., American Scholarship in the Twentieth Century. Cambridge: Harvard U. Press, 1983.

Pioneers of Current Developments

Barnes, D. (1976). *From Communication to Curriculum*. London: Penguin.

Boomer, G. (1982). *Negotiating the Curriculum*. Sydney: Ashton Scholastic.

Britton, J.N. (1967). (Ed.). *Talking and Writing*. London: Methuen.

Emig, J. (1971). *The Composing Process of Twelfth Graders*. Urbana, IL: National Council of Teachers of English.

Graves, D. (1983). *Writing: Teachers and Children at Work*. Portsmouth, N.H.: Heinemann.

Heathcote, D. (1980). *Exploring the Theatre and Education*. London: Heineman, 1980.

Meek, M., Wardlow, A., & Barton G. (1977). (Eds.). *The Cool Web: The Pattern of Children's Reading*. London: Bodley Head.

Wagner, B.J. (1976). *Dorothy Heathcote: Drama as a Learning Medium*. Washington, D.C.: National Education Association.

Thompson, J. (1987). *Understanding Teenagers' Reading*. New York: Nichols Publishing Co.

· 3 ·

INFLUENCES OF RELATED DISCIPLINES

3A. LINGUISTICS AND TEACHING THE LANGUAGE ARTS

Paula Menyuk

The study of linguistics has long influenced teaching the English Language Arts in this country. Linguistic theory has changed over this time. One of the more dramatic changes occurred some 30 years ago. This was the advent of transformational or, more accurately, generative grammar (Chomsky, 1965). Previoius language theories were influenced by behaviorists' theories of learning. Language was described as a set of learned habits and was acquired by learning these habits through stimulus, response, and reward conditions. Generative theories hold that language knowledge is represented in the mind as a system of rules, and that language is acquired by an active learner. Only those influences arising from this latter theory, in its various forms, will be discussed here, since current linguistic influences on teaching the language arts all stem from this dramatic change.

The aspects of current linguistic theory most germane to the teaching of the language arts are theoretical positions now held about the nature of language knowledge and its acquisition, about the process of language acquisition and application of linguistic knowledge in learning, and about how differing socio-cultural experiences can affect what the child knows when entering school. These aspects are studied by linguists, psycholinguists and sociolinguists. These, then, will be the topics covered in this chapter. The implications of theory in each of these areas for practice will be touched upon.

LANGUAGE KNOWLEDGE AND ACQUISITION

All linguistic theories, both current and past, have described language as an arbitrary symbolic system composed of units at different levels, which are embedded into each other. When speaking, sounds are combined to produce words, words are combined to produce utterances, and utterances are combined to produce discourse. In comprehending language these units are used to get at the meanings of words, utterances, and discourse. Language is used to represent categories and relations that people find important to talk about. Since language is such an arbitrary and symbolic system, questions arise about what

language knowledge is and about what causes acquisition of this knowledge.

Nature of Language Knowledge

Theories of the nature of language knowledge are really theories about the nature of human minds. Thus, when it was held that language knowledge consisted of habits that were learned to respond appropriately in certain situations because the environment rewarded such behaviors, then humans could be conceived of as having the ability to learn habits and associate these with certain situations. Man could imitate, memorize, and generalize behaviors that are similar to those observed in other species. Current theories suggest that humans have the unique, species-specific ability to test various hypotheses about the structure of language, to develop rules of a particular language and remember them, and to use these rules to generate appropriate language (Premack, 1985).

The distinction between these two positions that often has been pointed to is that the first seems to depict the human as a passive learner, whereas the second conceives of the human as an active learner. The fact that a person is considered an active learner in current linguistic and psycholinguistic theories suggests that efforts to teach language to human learners should actively engage them in the learning process. Such active engagement consists of providing opportunities to test hypotheses about language, rather than simply requiring that learners memorize bits of language for use in certain situations. Activities such as asking children to judge the goodness of sentences that do and do not violate linguistic rules, to complete sentences that require a dependent and logical clause ("because," "although," and "if-then" clauses), and to combine sentences are a few activities that require such hypothesis testing.

There is no disagreement among current linguistic theorists that language knowledge is generative rather than memorized. The child's language acquisition is described as the acquisition of a set of language rules. Because of the biological structure of humans, the human infant is designed to process or test

TABLE 3A–1. Examples of Language Knowledge and Use at Various Ages

Ages	Knowledge	Use
1 year	Word or jargon phrase Shoe or Wuzzat shoe	Command, request, state Shoe!, Shoe?, Shoe.
3 years	Embedded sentences I see the boy who's there.	Polite requests Can I have a cookie?
5 years	Complement sentences I know that he'll come.	Bargaining If you give me a ... I'll
10 years	Figurative language He's as fast as a tiger.	Riddles What has four wheels ...

hypotheses and remember language input in particular ways. As children develop, these hypotheses about how language is structured are modified by particular language input. In other words, the set of rules available to children changes as the child develops and recognizes what are and are not permissible structures in their particular language.

The evidence of developmental change is clear in the types of utterances and discourse understood and produced at various ages. A 3-year-old child is markedly different in language knowledge from the child aged 1, the 5-year-old is remarkably different from the 3-year-old, the 10-year-old from the 5-year-old, and so on until some adult level of knowledge is achieved. Not only does a child's structural knowledge change in time, but, also, knowledge of how to use structures (Menyuk, 1988). This latter knowledge has been termed pragmatic knowledge. Because there are systematic changes in knowledge that have been described in numerous books on language development, materials for teaching language can be designed to fit the varying developmental levels of children within a classroom. Children will vary in terms of the sophistication of their linguistic knowledge and also in the ways in which they can use this knowledge. Table 3A–1 presents some examples of structural and pragmatic knowledge at the ages cited above.

Causes for Language Development

Some questions have been raised about what causes developmental changes in knowledge of structure and use. Some hold that children have the innate ability to acquire knowledge of the structure of a language because of the constraints on the structures in all languages (Wexler & Cullicover, 1980). Others hold that acquisition of such knowledge is based on certain cognitive abilities. Categorization abilities explain the acquisition of vocabulary (Clark, 1983). Information processing abilities, for example, the ability to determine and remember the distributional characteristics of language, are said to explain acquisition of structural aspects of language (Maratsos, 1983). If this *is* the way word meaning and syntax is acquired, then such theorizing should have implications for teaching. Teachers should, perhaps, wait for certain cognitive developments before teaching about certain aspects of language. Teachers should think about the information processing complexity in the language tasks they give. These are not needless concerns. However, these positions, similar to Piaget's position, hold that al-

though interaction with the environment is crucial, the child's acquisition of language knowledge is a closed process independent of the influence of teaching. Other positions are more open, in that they attempt to describe the possible influences of teaching.

Another theory describes the child's acquisition of at least pragmatic knowledge as a product of "motherese" or of how mothers interact with their infants. Mothers support their infant's communication interaction by providing frames for them to interact within (like peek-a-boo games) and by encouraging them to take a turn (Bruner, 1985). Bruner described this as "scaffolding" and within the child's "zone of proximal development" (Vygotsky, 1978), and as such, can extend the child's knowledge of, at least, how to communicatively interact (pragmatic knowledge). Such interaction can provide children with the opportunity to test their hypotheses about language, and, indirectly, lead to learning structural knowledge. Similarly, communicative interaction in the classroom, during which students and teachers take turns, can provide the older child with the opportunity to test hypotheses about language.

Others suggest that there are direct effects of caregivers' input on children's knowledge acquisition because such input is simplified and clarified by the use of contextual information (Snow, 1986). Still others hold that communicative interaction is crucial for the acquisition of structural knowledge, because it is only through *discourse* that such structural knowledge can be acquired. For example, it is only through discourse by and with others that the child determines the use of anaphora (Hickman, 1985) or which chunks of the language one can negate or question (Foley & Van Valin, 1984). In this latter view, what the child learns are the relations between forms and functions, rather than simply a set of abstract linguistic rules. Regardless of theoretical differences, all these theorists point to the importance of communicative interaction in the language development.

The role of teaching is to provide support *and* the data from which a child can draw conclusions about the structure and use of the language. Such input can also extend the child's knowledge by having a more expert language-user interact with the child within that child's zone of proximal development. For example, it has been observed that mothers shift from requesting actions on objects (Roll the ball!) to requesting information (Do you want the ball?) from their infants during the second year of life. They apparently do so as soon as their infants give some indication that they understand a number of lexical items. Such requests are then within the infant's zone of proximal development. However, this shift also presents a greater challenge to the language learner because it requires knowledge of language apart from the ordinary context (what one ordinarily does with a ball). The child is required to attend to the language itself to achieve an appropriate response, and, in this way, learns more about language.

Both closed and open system theories of language acquisition have importance for teaching the language arts. The former stress the importance of keeping in mind the developmental changes that occur in the child's linguistic competence due to innate and cognitive factors. The latter stress the importance of communicative *interaction* as a vehicle for language growth.

(See chapters by Cazden, Dyson, Flood and Lapp, this Handbook.)

THE ACQUISITION PROCESS

The process by which language is acquired has been described as one of developing strategies for mapping meaning onto a fast fading signal. In hearing individuals, this signal is acoustic. The process also has been described as one that changes in the degree to which there is reliance on the context for interpretation of that signal. As acquisition begins, the infant is highly dependent on the surface structure (the acoustics) of the signal to derive meaning. At later stages, higher order knowledge (or rules) allows the child to chunk and interpret the signal with minimal use of the acoustic signal itself. At this stage, the child is imposing meaning on the signal. At the beginning stages of development, the infant is highly dependent on context for interpreting the meaning of a word or phrase. At later developmental stages, the child achieves a decontextualized knowledge of the signal's meaning.

The process of achieving decontextualized knowledge of language is gradual. For example, in first learning the meaning of a word, a child relies heavily on having present the item or action that is denoted by the word. Mothers initially talk about the "here and now." Later, the child understands the meaning of the word in all linguistic and situational context. Relying heavily on situational context at first and later linguistic context alone applies to the learning of all aspects of language. It takes the child a long time to achieve such knowledge for the complex aspects of language such as passive and relative sentences. Early on, children rely on real-world knowledge to understand passive sentences such as "The baby was fed by the mother" and relative sentences such as "The boy who read the book ran away." Later in development, they understand these structures in contexts where real-world knowledge does not help comprehension. This is the case in reversible passives ("The boy was chased by the girl.") and relatives ("The boy who kissed the girl ran away."). Not until the middle childhood years does such knowledge become operational (Karmiloff-Smith, 1979). Being able to metaprocess language *(to bring to conscious awareness what one knows about language)* is a product of this decontextualization process. Many of the activities that the child engages in in school, such as following directions and learning to read, require meta-processing. Therefore, teachers need to keep in mind the limits of the young child's decontextualized knowledge of language (see, also, Sulzby, this Handbook).

Various psycholinguistic models of language processing have been presented that might account for the developmental processes described above (Carroll, 1986). One model, a parallel processing model, seems to best explain developmental changes (for example, Marslen-Wilson & Tyler, 1980). Such a model describes the language processer as accessing all aspects of the language (phonological, lexical, and syntactic) as soon as some meaningful chunk has occurred. At the process' beginning stages, the phonology and meaning of a single word are probably accessed and some predictions made about what may follow depending on context and real-world knowledge. How-ever, as more data are collected, the word might be incorporated into a meaningful phrase, and as still more data are collected, the chunk becomes the clause and complete sentence. The young child's chunks would be smaller and more limited (limited in the sense of lexical and syntax knowledge) than those of the older child, and, therefore, processing would be slower and also more limited. Nevertheless, even the young child attempts to access all levels of language while trying to map meaning onto the signal. In fact, the child needs all levels of language present to process effectively. Isolating aspects of language from each other places a burden on the young child's limited processing ability.

This model of the process of language acquisition has both developmental and process implications. The developmental implications are that there are limits in the amount and type of language that can be processed at various ages, and there are limits on the *conditions* under which language can be processed. The processing implications are that the conditions that provide the most favorable opportunities for language interpretation are those that provide materials that are within the child's competence limits, and do so under conditions where both the context of the situation and the context of the language allow the child to access units from all levels of the language. At later stages of development such props to understanding need not be present.

APPLICATION OF LINGUISTIC KNOWLEDGE

Teachers of the language arts are concerned with how oral language knowledge is applied in the acquisition of written language knowledge. Psycholinguistic theories clearly have impacted reading and writing theories. Current theories hold that the process of reading requires bringing to conscious knowledge what one knows about various language levels. This, in turn, requires that the child have thorough knowledge of the units (sounds, words, and structures) that are being read, so they can be easily brought to conscious awareness. The parallel processing model for language acquisition described above has been applied to the reading process with one addition. In the reading process the child must *initially* translate the written signal into an oral language signal so meaning can be mapped onto the written signal. Just as in oral language processing, when this translation takes place, all levels of language knowledge are accessed and used to predict what might follow in the sequence (Perfetti & McCutchen, 1987). Once the child becomes familar with this translation process with a set of words and structures, this process takes place automatically with that particular set of words and structures. As the material to be read becomes more complex phonologically, lexically, and syntactically, this process of first conscious awareness and then automaticity is repeated. It is repeated throughout life as the reader approaches text that is unfamiliar in structure and topic (Menyuk, 1983).

Earlier, I described the developmental process of decontextualization of oral language knowledge. Because reading requires bringing language units to conscious awareness, such decontextualized knowledge is required in that process. This suggests that practice in achieving awareness of linguistic units of varying size and complexity can be a bridge to reading. Kindergarten teachers engage children in such awareness tasks on the phonological level (rhyming and segmentation), but such practice can be carried out with language units at all levels and throughout the school years. The domain in which such practice can occur should change as the children achieve more and more complex knowledge of oral language units (Menyuk, 1988). This practice can be carried out not only in the oral language mode, but also in reading and writing. Written language provides even greater opportunity to think and talk about language units, because these units do not disappear when they're in writing.

The relation between reading and writing has been described as analogous to the relation between listening and speaking. This implies that writing development is highly dependent on reading. To some extent that is true. However, writing is more highly dependent on oral language knowledge, in its beginning stages, than it is on reading (Perera, 1986). That is, beginning writing once past the problems of handwriting and spelling (the mechanics stage), appears to be talking in written form. Children, initially, write what they say. Thus, in the early stages, writing accesses speech in its phonological, lexical, syntactic and discourse forms. In the more mature stages of writing, speech and writing forms become more and more dissimilar. The forms used in writing become similar to those found in reading and, therefore, probably dependent on frequent reading of varied literary forms.

To interpret and remember what we have read, and to write so that others can interpret and remember what we have written, requires knowledge that goes beyond that of linguistic knowledge. Cognitive strategies of gist extraction, inferencing, organization, use of schema (word knowledge), and planning are some of the cognitive strategies that must be used in effective reading and writing (Rumelhart, 1981; Flower & Hayes, 1980). It also should be obvious that to map meaning onto written text and to generate meaning always requires accessing the various aspects of language. In order to map meaning accurately onto written text and to generate comprehensible text, this access process must be constantly monitored. Thus, throughout the development of reading and writing, linguistic knowledge is constantly called upon. In the emphasis on cognitive strategies in reading and writing, this fact may be ignored, but the language arts teacher must constantly be aware of it. In fact, the problem for the language arts teacher is to teach both aspects of these written language processes so that students can determine the relations between them. Stages in the development of reading and writing, to which a number of researchers have pointed, are presented in Table 3A–2. The writer selected accomplishments of each stage that make clear the dependency of these processes on language experience and knowledge.

SOCIOLINGUISTICS AND TEACHING THE LANGUAGE ARTS

Different children coming to school bring with them different levels of knowledge about language structure and use. That

TABLE 3A–2. Stages in the Development of Reading and Writing

Reading	Writing
Emergence of literacy	Handwriting and spelling
Print awareness	Writing equals saying
Decoding	Writing and saying differentiated
Reading for literal meaning	Writing and saying integrated
Inferencing while reading	Writing in different genres

is, some children are more linguistically mature than others when they enter school. In addition, children bring with them different sociolinguistic experiences. In particular, they bring different notions about the purpose of language use, different rules of conversational interaction, and different rules of discourse organization. When the children come from sociolinguistic backgrounds that are similar to that of the teachers', then these differences create few problems in communications in the school. When children come from sociolinguistic backgrounds that are markedly different from that of their teachers, then difficulties can arise. Some of these problems can be avoided if teachers, particularly language arts teachers, are aware of the nature of the distinctions that exist both in language knowledge and language use. The latter differences will be discussed first.

Differences in expectations about classroom communication on the part of teachers and students can be very disruptive of the learning that is supposed to be going on. Several studies of such communication indicate discrepancies between teacher and child expectations in common classroom communications, due to sociolinguistic differences. For example, in "Show and Tell," the teacher expects the child to follow the expected format of telling. This format is one of sequential narration of a story with a setting, episodes, and conclusion, a story grammar format (Mandler, 1983). Children from minority sociolinguistic backgrounds use a different format, one similar to that used in cultures in which oral stories are used to relate the history and culture of the people. This format includes lengthy departures from the sequence, and then return to it. Presumably, children using this kind of format in Show and Tell have been considered "disordered" by their teacher (Michaels, 1981).

The most common situation in mainstream classrooms is that of teacher as lecturer and guide. Classroom communication is usually one-way: the teacher giving directions and asking questions and the students answering. Such interaction is contrary to the expectations of children from minority sociolinguistic groups, who expect more of a shared situation in the classroom (Menyuk, 1988).

There are other roles that teachers can and do take. One role is that of guide and learner (Heath, 1985). The term that is used to describe this situation is "reciprocal teaching" (Brown, Palinscar, & Armbruster, 1987; Cole & Hall, 1982). In this situation, teachers shift from being experts to being guides, then coaches, and, finally, learners along with the children.

All of the above findings point to differences in discourse

styles that can affect classroom interactions and, therefore, the teaching of language arts to minority children. In addition to differences in discourse styles, children from different sociolinguistic groups can come to school with varying degrees of knowledge of the English language and varying degrees of decontextualized knowledge of language. In sum, these children may have a different set of structural rules, as well as a different set of pragmatic rules. These differences can affect how ready these children are to engage in learning the English language arts.

The patterns of language input discussed in a previous section that are said to be necessary for language development do not occur in all sociocultural environments (Ochs & Schieffelin, 1984). Despite these differences in input, all children throughout the world acquire language. However, much of the sociolinguistic research with children from minority sociocultural backgrounds indicates that differences in patterns of caregivers-child communicative interaction may be the source of differences in degree of decontextualized knowledge of language that a child has on entering school (Heath, 1983). As pointed out previously, such decontextualized knowledge, which leads to the ability to metaprocess language, is necessary for many school tasks. The ability to metaprocess language is particularly crucial in learning to read and write. Differences in metaprocessing abilities can be overcome. At least one study indicates that, if children from a minority sociocultural background are given enough experience in metaprocessing, they can learn to read as successfully as children from the majority culture (Piestrup, 1973).

Children who come to school with limited knowledge of English pose a different kind of problem to the teacher of English language arts. If decontextualized knowledge of the language is needed in reading, writing, and other school tasks, it is clear that children with little English will have difficulty in these tasks. This is especially so if they also have little or no decontextualized knowledge of their own language. The educational implications for these children are a matter of great argument, and the research carried out thus far leaves more questions than answers (Willig, 1982). Sociolinguistic research, however, has indicated that bilingualism per se can give the child a cognitive advantage in decontextualized knowledge of language (Hakuta, Ferdman, & Diaz, 1987). Therefore, educational programs that foster bilingualism in children may put them at a cognitive advantage in learning to read, write and use language creatively.

IMPLICATIONS FOR TEACHING

Throughout this chapter, I have referred to what I believe are the important contributions of linguistic, psycholinguistic, and sociolinguistic research to the teaching of the English language arts. They will be summarized here. First, such research has provided information about the patterns of language development and language use in both majority and minority group children. Such information can be used in the selection of developmentally appropriate materials and contexts for teaching. Second, the research has shown the conditions under which language is learned and grows. Communication interaction between the child and more mature users of the language is vital for such growth. Linguistic meta-abilities are best learned when children are asked to actively think and talk about language. Third, this research also has shown that metaprocessing abilities are crucial to learning to read and write. Finally, such research has shown that there are important differences in different sociocultural groups that should affect how they are taught. There are differences in styles of communication interaction, the important context for language learning. There are also differences in experiences with decontextualized use of language. These latter differences can adversely affect learning of reading and writing, but adverse effects can be overcome with appropriate attitudes and teaching.

References

Brown, A., Palinscar, A., and Armbruster, B. (1987). Inducing comprehension fostering abilities in interactive learning situations. In H. Mandl, N. Stein & T. Trabasso (Eds.), *Learning and comprehension of texts* (pp. 273–304). Hillsdale, N.J.: Erlbaum.

Bruner, J. (1985). Vygotsky: A historical and conceptual perspective. In J. V. Wertsch (Ed.), *Culture communication and cognition* (pp. 21–34). Cambridge: Cambridge University Press.

Carroll, D. (1986). *Psychology of language*. Monterey, CA.: Brooks/Cole.

Chomsky, N. (1965). *Aspects of the theory of syntax*. Cambridge, MA.: M.I.T. Press.

Clark, E. (1983). Meanings and concepts. In J. Flavell & E. Markman (Eds.), *Handbook of child psychology, Vol. III* (pp. 787–840). New York: John Wiley & Sons.

Cole, M. & Hall, W. (1982). A model system for the study of learning disabilities. *Quarterly Newsletter of the Laboratory of Comparative Human Cognition, University of California SanDiego, 4*, 39–66.

Flower, L. & Hayes, J. (1980). The dynamics of composing: Making plans and juggling constraints. In L. W. Gregg & E. R. Steinberg (Eds.), *Cognitive processes in writing* (pp. 31–50), Hillsdale, NJ.: Erlbaum.

Foley, W. & Van Valin, R. (1984). *Functional syntax and universal grammar*. Cambridge: Cambridge University Press.

Hakuta, K., Ferdman, B. M., & Diaz, R. M. (1987). Bilingualism and cognitive development: Three perspectives. In S. Rosenberg (Ed.), *Advances in applied psycholinguistics, Vol. II* (pp. 284–319). Cambridge: Cambridge University Press.

Heath, S. B. (1983). *Ways with words*. Cambridge: Cambridge University Press.

Heath, S. B. (1985). The cross-cultural study of language acquisition. *Papers on research in Child Language Development Vol. 24*. Stanford, CA.: Stanford University.

Hickman, M. (1985). The implications of discourse skills in Vygotsky's developmental theory. In J. Wertsch (Ed.), *Culture, communication and cognition* (pp. 236–257). Cambridge: Cambridge University Press.

Karmiloff-Smith, A. (1979). Language development after five. In P. Fletcher & M. Garman (Eds.), *Language acquisition: Studies in first language development* (pp. 307–324). Cambridge: Cambridge University Press.

Mandler, J. M. (1983). Representation. In J. Flavell & E. Markman (Eds.), *Handbook of child psychology, Vol. III* (pp. 420–494). New York: John Wiley & Sons.

Maratsos, M. (1983). Some current issues in the study of the acquisition of grammar. In J. Flavell & E. Markman (Eds.), *Handbook of child psychology, Vol. III* (pp. 707–786). New York: John Wiley & Sons.

Marslen-Wilson, W. & Tyler, L. (1980). The temporal structure of spoken language understanding. *Cognition, 8,* 1–71.

Menyuk, P. (1983). Language development and reading. In T. Gallagher & C. Prutting (Eds.), *Pragmatic issues: Assessment and intervention* (pp. 151–170). San Diego, CA.: College Hill Press.

Menyuk, P. (1988). *Language development: Knowledge and use.* Glenview, IL.: Scott Foresman/Little Brown College Division.

Michaels, S. (1981). Sharing time: Children's narrative styles and differential access to literacy. *Language in Society, 10,* 49–76.

Ochs, E. & Schieffelin, B. (1984). Language acquisition and socialization: three stories and their implications. In R. Levine (Ed.), *Culture theory: Essays on mind, self, and emotion* (pp. 276–320). Cambridge: Cambridge University Press.

Perera, K. (1986). Language acquisition and writing. In P. Fletcher & M. Garman (Eds.), *Language acquisition: Studies in first language development* (2nd ed.) (pp. 494–518). Cambridge: Cambridge University Press.

Perfetti, C. & McCutchen, D. (1987). Schooled language competence: linguistic abilities in reading and writing. In S. Rosenberg (Ed.), *Advances in applied psycholinguistics, Vol. 2* (pp. 105–141). Cambridge: Cambridge University Press.

Piestrup, A. (1973). Black dialect interference and accomodation of reading instruction in first grade. *Monographs of the Language Behavior Research Laboratory, No. 4.* U. of California, Berkeley.

Premack, D. (1985). "Gavagai!" or the future history of the animal language controversy. *Cognition, 19,* 207–296.

Rumelhart, D. E. (1981). Schemata: The building blocks of cognition. In J. T. Guthrie (Ed.), *Comprehension and teaching: Research reviews* (pp. 3–26). Newark, DE.: International Reading Association.

Snow, C. E. (1986). Conversations with children. In P. Fletcher & M. Garman (Eds.), *Language acquisition: Studies in first language development, second edition* (pp. 69–89). Cambridge: Cambridge University Press.

Vygotsky, L. (1978). *Mind in society.* Cambridge, MA.: Harvard University Press.

Wexler, K. & Cullicover, P. W. (1980). *Formal principles of language acquisition.* Cambridge, MA.: M.I.T. Press.

Willig, A. (1982). The effectiveness of bilingual education: Review of report. *NABE Journal, 6,* 1–19.

3B. THE CONTRIBUTION OF PSYCHOLOGY TO TEACHING THE LANGUAGE ARTS

Diane Lemonnier Schallert

How does the mind work? How do individuals respond to their environment and make meaning of their life experience? What are the particular processes they go through as they deal with language? What factors, manipulable or not, can influence the individual's experience? These are essentially a psychologist's questions. Though very similar to questions posed in a number of other disciplines, the psychologist, or researcher engaged in a psychological study, addresses them by a particular methodological approach. Scholarship that is psychological in nature may begin with the same kind of logical analysis, informed intuition, or well-chosen and well-described example as may linguistic or philosophical treatises. With no claim that it is somehow superior to approaches common to other disciplines, what makes a work psychological in its methodology is the manner in which conclusions are grounded in data, in objectively verifiable, generalizable, or at the very least, consensually supported findings.

What has been psychology's contribution to our understanding of the teaching of the language arts? As one of my graduate students pointed out, this is perhaps similar to the question of what has been the role of religion in society, to some so all-encompassing as to require a book-length treatise and to others irrelevant. Knowing full well that I am oversimplifying, I will address the question by describing the empirical and theoretical literature in three areas, with the first a much longer section that lays the groundwork for a number of concepts in the other sections:

1. How people learn,
2. How they process language, and
3. How they are influenced by the social, emotional, motivational context in which they find themselves.

I have chosen these areas by considering first what is involved in any teaching situation (my answer: teachers and learners, with all their affective and cognitive baggage, working together in a highly influential social context to achieve some goal that involves at least in part the learning of something new). I then considered what teaching the language arts in particular might require (my answer: a particular attention to language, including a focus on reading and writing). My next concern was with what teachers and educational researchers would most likely find interesting and/or informative (my answer: probably more interested in information about learners and how they work than in how teachers teach, although always there is likely to be a great deal of interest in any information about particularly effective techniques for fostering learning). Finally, I considered what was actually there in the psychological literature that related to these first three concerns, perhaps derived from relatively artificial experimental settings or of a rather esoteric theoretical nature but, as much as possible, re-presenting the most compelling explanations I could find. With each recycling of these concerns, my goal has been to capture those aspects of psychological work that would give a faithful representation of its nature and show its relevance to an understanding of teaching the language arts. With the hope that I have been at least partly successful, I turn first to a discussion of what psychologists might say about how people learn.

HOW PEOPLE LEARN

Learning as a construct has had a peculiar history in psychology. For decades, learning theories dominated the lively, sometimes contentious, discourse of psychologists. Even so, there was rather general agreement on the underlying framework that explained learning. That framework, called behavior theory, with its emphasis on the relationship between environmental events and outwardly observable responses, has certainly waned in importance in psychology. Its influence today is only vestigial in certain prejudices about methodology that psychologists, even the most cognitive among us, are prone to have. With the decline of a behavior theory perspective and the rise of a cognitive approach, interest in learning per se, that is, in changes in people's behavioral and cognitive repertoire, withered. Cognitive psychologists studied memory and theories of information processing and knowledge representation, not learning. It is only in the last 10 years or so that cognitive psychologists have turned their direct attention to learning (Shuell, 1986).

Although relatively new, a cognitive conception of learning already has obvious characteristics. The following are those that are particularly relevant to the teaching of the language arts:

- The learner as an active constructor of meaning.
- The role of prior knowledge in comprehension and knowledge acquisition.
- The interactive and parallel nature of information processing and, in particular, the constraints on the system that result from limits on working memory capacity.
- Problem solving and metacognitive processes.

The "Active" Learner. In cognitive conceptions of learning, individuals are not passive repositories of associations stamped in by the environment as behaviorists proposed. Rather, learners are seen as active, constructive, interacting minds, always putting their personal touch on what gets learned. Studies by Bransford and his colleagues (c.f., Bransford & Johnson, 1972, 1973; Bransford & Franks, 1971) among many (c.f., Brewer, 1977; Loftus & Palmer, 1974; Schallert, 1976) have become classic demonstrations of how individuals transform what they hear or read to reflect the interpretation they have given to materials presented to them. Bartlett's (1932) description of how people remember something meaningful from what they have heard has made the phrase "effort after meaning" a part of our unmarked vocabulary.

What exactly do cognitive psychologists mean when they describe the learner as active? In the next subsection, we will discuss the role of prior knowledge in learning, surely the major way in which a learner contributes directly to what is learned. Generally, what is meant by "active" is that the learner's genetic makeup and previously acquired repertoire play as much a role in learning as the actual learning situation and to-be-learned information. In addition, active refers to an attribute of how the learner deals with the information, not simply laying down traces as presented but selecting, combining, and transforming that information to create mental products that are not in one-to-one correspondence with what was presented. Thus, Rothkopf's (1970) concept of mathemagenic activities and Wittrock's (1974) generative learning are part of our accepted description of effective learning.

Prior Knowledge. If one theme from a cognitive psychology perspective has had an impact in the last 20 years in explaining how people learn, it would have to be that of the role of prior knowledge in comprehension and knowledge acquisition. At its most general, the claim is that what one already knows influences the quantity and quality of what one can learn. Because the claim is hardly disputable in its general form, it may seem easy to dismiss. In what I present here, I have explored what it means by considering the many controversies it has generated in order to show that, in fact, how prior knowledge influences learning is still an interesting issue.

One of the earliest controversies arose when David Ausubel (1960; see also Ausubel, Novak, & Hanesian, 1978) proposed that meaningful learning occurs when two conditions are met: the learner must adopt a meaningful learning set, that is, an intention to relate the new information to existing cognitive structures; and the material to be learned must be potentially meaningful, that is, it must have the possibility of being related to the learner's own existing cognitive structures (Ausubel, 1961). Thus, from Ausubel's perspective, learning occurs when one's current organization of knowledge is changed, either because a subsuming concept has been elaborated with the new information, or because existing concepts are now connected by a new subsuming concept.

The controversy surrounding Ausubel's notions were not so much about his general description of learning, although his ideas, proposed just at the beginning of the cognitive revolution, met a less-than-friendly response, but about his pedagogical notion of the "advance organizer." By advance organizer, Ausubel did not mean something that is presented in advance that tells the learner the organization of the to-be-learned information. Outlines, previews, headings, objectives, as helpful as they may be to learning, are not advance organizers. An advance organizer is something that allows the learner to remember what he or she already knows that will somehow subsume the new information.

In Ausubel's view, knowledge grows by changing the organization of existing knowledge and, thus, new information will be learned only if it is properly anchored into the existing orga-

nized knowledge. When Ausubel described the advance organizer, he said it needed to be written at a higher level of abstraction and generality. This was an unfortunate choice of words, because it led to hundreds, perhaps thousands of experiments testing the effectiveness of what were called advance organizers using impossibly vague, abstract prose. Rather than having the effect Ausubel hoped they would have of reminding learners of what they already knew, these supposed advance organizers were themselves simply not understood. Currently, there is a much better understanding, largely due to the excellent work of Mayer (1979), of Ausubel's advance organizers and of the conditions necessary for their effectiveness, although it is very easy to find misuses of the term.

A second controversy relates to the more recent construct of "schema," a theoretical label for cognitive structures or concepts proposed by cognitive scientists as a basic unit of knowledge. Much has been written about schemata, both at the theoretical and empirical level (c.f., Anderson, 1977, 1984; Black, 1985; Rumelhart & Ortony, 1977; Schank & Abelson, 1977; Schallert, 1982, 1987; Spiro, Vispoel, Schmitz, Samarapungavan, & Boerger, 1987; Tierney & Cunningham, 1984; Voss & Bisanz, 1985). Suffice it to say here that the construct was developed to answer the need for describing knowledge of the world, and not simply knowledge of the language, in explaining how people (and computers) understand linguistic input. From the beginning, schemata were meant to help us unpack the role of prior knowledge in comprehension and knowledge acquisition. With the mechanism of "instantiation," we had a way of describing how, moment by moment, a person's existing conception interacts with the input to result in comprehension. We also had a different perspective in explaining why someone might fail to learn or understand: not because of low intelligence or a deficiency in the ability to engage the basic comprehension processes, but because of missing or unactivated background knowledge presupposed by the new input (Bransford, 1979, 1984).

Problems arose when, in the name of schema theory or with allusion to the role of prior knowledge in the reading process, less-than-ideal recommendations were made and implemented in the development of reading and instruction materials. One cannot expect children to be very successful with stories that require too many leaps to knowledge that has only recently been acquired. A graduate student who is also teaching second grade in a predominantly urban, African American school recounted that the basal materials in her class had a story about two children discussing their fears as they faced a cello and piano recital. The manual suggested teachers explain what recitals and the instruments are, "teach the prior knowledge required." Perceptively, she felt that this would not work, at least not with her kids. The background knowledge would be so new and itself so tenuously supported by what the children already knew that it would not be of much help when it came to understanding the story.

A related problem was demonstrated by Omanson, Beck, Voss, and McKeown (1984). It is not just any prior knowledge that will help young readers have a successful interaction with text. The commercial program they analyzed had a tendency to lead teachers and students into explorations of concepts that were often only tangentially related to a story to be read. Their revised materials, which emphasized reminding students of what they know about central, critical aspects of the story, were much more successful with the students. For their part, Omanson and colleagues are themselves subject to the criticism of implying that there is one, correct, best interpretation of a story, something that would run not only against prevailing views of literary theory about the validity and value of individual reader responses, but that might be seen as violating a basic aspect of schema notions of comprehension, the individualized nature of the process. Thus, as is not unusual in applying any notion from psychology to instruction, the ramifications of a schema view are not simple.

A third controversy surrounding discussions of prior knowledge relates to its role in knowledge acquisition rather than simply comprehension. In the early 1980s when I reviewed the literature related to schema theory (Schallert, 1982), I came to the conclusion that there was little direct empirical or theoretical work dealing with how schemata are acquired in the first place and how they change. We had come a good way in explaining comprehension, but we had made little progress in explaining knowledge acquisition. Learning had been ignored. Since then, progress has been made along several lines, three of which I will mention. As you will see, there are once again debates generated at every turn.

One line of progress has been the work on learning from informative text, an area that is often slighted in language arts instruction and was also slighted by researchers interested in the psychology of reading until recently. When students encounter text that is meant to teach them something new, they often face not only unfamiliar rhetorical forms and intents, but also a stepped-up barrage of new words expressing new concepts. Effective vocabulary instruction, therefore, would seem crucial (Beck, Perfetti, & McKeown, 1982). However, as Nagy, Herman, and Anderson (1985) pointed out, it is unlikely that children learn much of their vocabulary through direct instruction. The numbers simply argue against it. Rather, children must be learning new vocabulary more indirectly, from the language they hear and, primarily, from the language they read. In his seminal analysis of reading acquisition, Stanovich (1986) described the situation as one ripe for *Matthew* effects, those with better vocabularies can read and understand more advanced prose which will, in turn, expose them to more new vocabulary items and ideas.

Students reading informative prose face not only new words and new ideas, but also ideas that conflict with what they currently know. In such a situation, prior knowledge is no longer consonant with what is to be learned. Alvermann, Smith, and Readence (1985) found, in fact, that when the information to be learned conflicts with what students believe, it is better not to have students call to mind what they already know. They seem better able to learn the new information if their own contradictory position is allowed to remain dormant. However, one wonders about the kind of learning these students are evidencing. As Spiro (1980) demonstrated, it is very easy for subjects to compartmentalize information so that they hold incompatible ideas. In a study by Eaton, Anderson, and Smith (1984), it was found that, unless teachers directly helped their students to

think about their current beliefs and to prepare themselves to change these beliefs, compartmentalization again occurred. As part of their analysis, Eaton, Anderson, and Smith demonstrated how the teachers' commercial materials, including the teacher's guide, did not help teachers address the misconceptions of students and, in fact, worked against this. Thus these studies demonstrate once again how complex the relationship of prior knowledge to learning is.

A second line of work related to explaining how knowledge can be changed is the work on elaborations. Bransford and his colleagues have shown in a number of studies (Bransford, 1984; Bransford, Stein, Shelton, & Owings, 1981) how important it is in learning something new that its significance and the reasons why certain distinctions are being made be shared with the learners. In his most recent work, Bransford (1988; Bransford, Sherwood, & Hasselbring, in press) has cogently argued for multiple access to ideas using different forms of media and a rich learning context so that children will experience what it means truly to understand and learn. Where is the controversy in these ideas? Here, there is not the hot debate I see in some of the other aspects that relate to how prior knowledge works. There is, however, a widely cited finding by Reder and Anderson (1980) to the effect that learners will perform better when presented with an unelaborated summary than when the same information is enriched with examples and explanations. The resolution comes from a consideration of how knowledge is tested, of what it is that the learner must do with what has been learned. If learning is measured soon after exposure and requires little more than a direct recall of the main facts, it seems better to have been exposed simply to those facts. If, instead, learning is for the long term and is meant to provide a rich basis for application and transfer, then the elaborations recommended by Bransford and others are best.

A third line of work is represented by several direct theoretical and empirical descriptions of how knowledge changes. These run the gamut in terms of fitting well with the earlier agenda of explaining the comprehension process. For example, Rumelhart and Norman (1978) described three qualitatively different kinds of schema change: accretion, tuning, and restructuring. Focusing on restructuring in particular, Vosniadou and Brewer (1987) made a distinction between weak and radical restructuring and proposed different instructional approaches for each. Both works are very compatible with schema theory, with Anderson's (1977) early attempt at explaining how accommodative and assimilative processes might account for knowledge change. J. Anderson's (1983) ACT theory, on the other hand, is not nearly as compatible with schema notions nor does it as centrally deal with the role of prior knowledge in learning something new.

Finally, Spiro (Spiro et al., 1987) has presented a theory of knowledge acquisition that he claims is "beyond" schema theory. He begins by pointing to the distinction between domains of knowledge that are well-structured and those that are ill-structured. His chief complaint with schema notions is that they imply a learner who is not flexible, who approaches new input with precompiled knowledge structures that cannot deal with the rich variability naturally encountered in the world. By extension, he goes on to say, such views of the learner encourage teaching that oversimplifies new concepts so that transfer in ill-structured domains is almost necessarily precluded. Instead, he proposes that knowledge must be assembled from fragments to fit each new situation, such knowledge having been derived from a different instructional approach. Cognitive flexibility requires an approach that depends on case-based presentations that treat "a content domain as a landscape that is explored by 'criss-crossing' it in many directions" (p. 178). The controversy here is not so much with the substance of his ideas but with his view of schema theory. I would argue that rather than representing an abrupt break with schema notions, Spiro's theory represents exactly how it needed to evolve.

Thus, to summarize this long section on prior knowledge, we have considered three areas where controversy has arisen in discussions of the seemingly obvious assertion that prior knowledge influences learning:

• The frequent misinterpretation of Ausubel's advance organizer.

• The misapplication of schema notions in instructional settings.

• The long delay over direct considerations of how exactly knowledge changes.

This last topic was itself addressed in terms of three lines of recent work:

• How people learn from informative prose in terms of acquiring the vocabulary needed and dealing with situations where they hold strongly held contradictory beliefs.

• The complex role of elaborations in learning.

• Theories that specifically describe knowledge change and not simply knowledge use.

The Nature of Information Processing and Limited Capacity Constraints. One of the earliest interests of cognitive psychologists was in describing humans as information processing systems. This is an area that continues to trouble and challenge psychologists. For example, very recent models of information processing are presenting a rather different view of the system, one that involves the related constructs of distributed memory, connectionist models, neural nets, and unmediated representations of knowledge (cf., McClelland, 1988). It remains to be seen how these newer ideas will be incorporated into generally accepted notions about information processing. For the present, "current wisdom" is the conception of the system as comprised of interactive, parallel processes that inform each other in an orchestration aimed at accomplishing a task (c.f., Lesgold & Perfetti, 1981).

Such a view entails a particular characteristic that is highly relevant in learning and the acquisition of expertise. In engaging in the more or less conscious processes involved in performing a task, the learner is constrained by having limited resources available in terms of cognitive capacity. Eventually, the learner experiences overload and must give up attending to what one of the tasks or subprocesses requires. However, a learner is usually not prevented forever from attempting the

particular configuration of subtasks that led to overload. With experience and practice, some of the tasks or components of the task that were requiring major chunks of cognitive capacity can become so well learned that they can be accomplished automatically or with little attention devoted to them. This is one of the more predictable shifts that occurs when one moves from novice to expert status in a domain. Thus, expert drivers, expert readers, expert writers are similar in that many components of the task have become routine so that more resources can be devoted to the more complex aspects of the task. It is a bitter irony for novices that exactly when they need the most available resources to deal with the difficult part of a task, they do not have the resources available; too much precious attention and effort is being devoted to the simpler aspects of the task.

There is an important lesson for educators to learn from such a conception of the information processing system. When students are introduced to new domains of knowledge, to new academic tasks, teachers should allow for an initial period during which the ultimate goals of the task may not be addressable simply because simpler aspects are still not routine. We may want students to appreciate and write about Shakespeare's complex views of the human condition. However, students who are just learning how to formulate an essay or worse yet, who are still having difficulty reading, will likely fall short of expectations. One solution, which is only too frequently implemented, is to give students who cannot meet expectations simpler, and often, less valued tasks. From the perspective of the information processing model described here, practice with simpler tasks may help learners achieve automaticity for simpler tasks. However, another possibility is to encourage more practice, perhaps under conditions where there is more room for less-than-perfect performance, with the complex task itself.

The "Higher" Processes of Problem Solving and Metacognition. In addition to describing the process of learning proper, a cognitive view of learning is concerned with the broader issue of thinking as represented by problem solving and metacognition. Problem solving is a set of processes that are invoked when one wants to achieve a particular goal but does not know quite how to get there from the current state. It is an area that has received much attention and generated exciting findings and rich descriptions of human cognition (c.f., Mayer, 1983; Newell & Simon, 1972). For example, Johnson-Laird and Wason (1977) found that people made many fewer errors on tasks requiring conditional reasoning when the statements to be judged referred to potentially real situations rather than to abstract systems. In fact, amount of domain knowledge seems to be a critical dimension that differentiates successful from unsuccessful problem solvers in a particular area (Chase & Simon, 1973; Larkin, McDermott, Simon, & Simon, 1980). In addition, Larkin and colleagues found that experts in a domain use different strategies in reaching a solution than do novices.

In the current literature, problem solving is presented as a general process of human cognition. Although much of the research on problem solving has involved the domain areas of logic, mathematics, physics, and computer science, the field is not restricted to these areas. In fact, characterizing the comprehension process as problem solving is not unusual (e.g. Mayer,

1983) and the description easily fits, especially when comprehension is in any way effortful. Similarly, current writing models owe much to findings about and descriptions of problem solving. Thus, in terms of applications to the language arts, problem solving literature offers insight into any language use situations where "thinking out" might be required, including situations where analysis, critical judgment, and logical reasoning arise.

A related area, which also characterizes a cognitive conception of learning, is the field of metacognition, the ability of a learner to reflect on his or her cognitive state and to monitor and engage appropriate strategies to accomplish goals. One interpretation of what it means to engage metacognition initially led to an attempt to catalogue all the different strategies learners can engage in and to try to relate success to particular strategies. This effort has not been very successful. There were too many instances where poor performers or younger learners were engaging in either the same strategies or in more strategies than successful and older learners. Success does not seem assured simply because a particular strategy has been engaged.

Currently, it is more accepted to talk not of metacognitive strategies but of strategic cognition (Garner, 1987; Paris, 1988; Paris, Lipson, & Wixson, 1983). A global description of strategic cognition is that the learner will be cognizant of pursuing a particular goal, will engage whatever strategic operations are needed to achieve the goal, will monitor continually whether the goal is being approached, and will change the goal when that seems appropriate. In terms of instructional implications, such a view of the learner would lead away from a curriculum that would present strategies as separate skills and toward a curriculum that would stress the importance of knowing what goal one is trying to accomplish and how to manage the complex task of reaching the goal.

Section Summary. What has been the impact on the professional field of language arts of the cognitive characterization of learning? In many ways, we have a situation where the foundational science, psychology, "discovered" what the practitioners had known all along. Language arts educators did not need the evidence from the typically short, contrived, artificially presented texts of the cognitive psychologists (but see the many clever passages invented by Bransford and colleagues in Bransford & Johnson, 1973, and by many others) to realize that students will naturally and continually interpret the language they read and hear in ways that reflect how they are thinking about the text. This the language arts educators already knew. What psychology contributed by its own shift in focus was a change in how educators thought of students' contribution, an appreciation for what the learner is doing, for the active processes that can be engaged by tasks appropriately designed, for the reasons why differences in performance might be encountered.

HOW PEOPLE PROCESS LANGUAGE

Perhaps fueled by the Chomsky-Skinner debates of the late 1950s, cognitive psychologists' fascination with language, with how people understand and use it, has endured. In fact, implicit in many models of human information processing and comprehension is the focus on how language is processed and comprehended, and much of the research base for cognitive views of learning described in the previous section applies to cognitive views of how language is used. From such a perspective, language comprehension is (a) an active process by which (b) an individual's intentions to reach a particular goal (c) strategically guide the selection and use of particular aspects of prior knowledge (d) to construct a reasonable accounting of the current linguistic input, (e) constrained by the limits of what can be attended to in current consciousness. In current models, language production is similarly described.

One could argue that a cognitive psychology view of how language is used is often not particularly sensitive to the nature of language as such. When the information to be processed or learned comes in linguistic form, no particular distinction related to its linguistic nature is proposed. From the perspective of teaching the language arts, this may be unfortunate as language may make distinctive demands that entail important differences in how it is processed. There are, of course, large exceptions (witness the field of psycholinguistics) from which I will elaborate on two concepts in the first section below. I will then discuss briefly psychological views of reading and of writing.

Key Psycholinguistic Constructs. When cognitive psychologists attempt to understand the linguistic aspects of psycholinguistic events, they naturally turn to linguists for help. In current explanations of language use, few linguists have had as much influence as Grice and Halliday who have contributed to the two psychological notions of coherence and the given-new contract. Both of these constructs are particularly relevant to language arts.

The given-new contract, most clearly developed by Clark and Haviland (1977), begins with Halliday's (1967) analysis of the language into "given" and "new" information, a distinction signalled in the syntax and intonation of any utterance that identifies what aspect a listener or reader is expected to have already established in current working memory (the "given") and what aspect is being introduced for the first time (the "new"). Clark and Haviland then drew on Grice's (1975) communicative contrast to propose the following description of how people process language. The speaker (or writer) attempts to construct utterances so that what is signalled as "given" information indeed matches with what he or she believes the listener (or reader) already knows and so that "new" information is in fact new. The listener (or reader) agrees to view utterances in the same way.

Thus, in interpreting utterances, the listener (or reader) identifies what is given and what is new, searches memory for something to match the given, and establishes what is found in the memory search as the antecedent for the given information. The new information then is interpreted in light of the context provided by all that has been constructed as the antecedent for the given. Interesting difficulties arise whenever the memory search does not yield a direct match with the given and a bridging inference must be made in order to establish the basis for connecting together the ideas expressed in the language. Clark and Haviland (1977) found that texts requiring bridging inferences were more difficult to understand.

The construct of coherence refers to the nature of language to allow a comprehender to perceive a continuity in the ideas being expressed (Beaugrande & Dressler, 1981). Related once again to the linguistic analyses of both Grice and of Halliday, coherence becomes a psychological constraint that impinges on language users by leading them to expect that utterances will clearly delineate conceptual continuity. Coherence is related to the given-new contract mentioned above. Sanford and Garrod (1981), for example, demonstrated that, over and above the kind of syntactic analysis necessary to establish Clark and Haviland's given-new analysis, a semantic analysis takes place that connects the ideas being expressed into a coherent whole.

The potential power of coherence and the related given-new contract as constructs is not to be underestimated by language arts educators. Approaching texts with the expectation that they should express ideas that hang together and that the language should reveal as clearly as possible this underlying coherence can help students experience a productive transaction both as authors and as readers.

The Psychology of Reading. I have already discussed many constructs that describe the psychological process of reading comprehension. The role of prior knowledge in comprehension, capacity constraints on the processing system, the strategic nature of comprehension, and the nature of textual communication that would lead a reader to expect coherence are some examples. There are, of course, many other constructs and empirical findings that have made a significant difference in our views of the comprehension process. However, seen in the face of space constraints, I must mention the model of discourse comprehension presented by van Dijk and Kintsch (1983). By representing the reading process as a strategic coordination at many levels, van Dijk and Kintsch emphasized the goal-directed nature of language activities. In their model, the complex interplay of many sources of influence, from the word level all the way to the discourse-social-cultural level, are represented as they bear on the construction of a particular proposition from a text being processed. What is unusual about the model is the connection that is made between very global knowledge factors, very dynamic processing factors, and the minute particulars of responding to linguistic input. Unlike many cognitive psychologists interested in comprehension, van Dijk and Kintsch take the nature of language very seriously in their model.

For language arts educators, reading comprehension is perhaps the most interesting aspect of reading. However, it is but one component of the broad ability to read on which much psychological work has been done. Currently, there seems to be consensus on the role of facile word recognition in the whole act of reading, represented most cogently by Stanovich (1986). In his interactive-compensatory model, Stanovich argued that in order for comprehension of text to occur, the reader must be in a situation to devote most of his or her cognitive capacity to constructing the meaning of the message. Decoding and word recognition, subcomponents of the process, must be executed so as not to interfere with the amount of

capacity necessary to figure out the meaning of the message. Any difficulty encountered in figuring out individual words may divert precious cognitive energy from meaning making.

Stanovich argued that a major task of learning to read is to make word recognition and decoding automatic, something that will most easily result from much experience with reading. In his analysis of factors that result in individual differences in reading acquisition, Stanovich pointed to the many instructional, motivational, and experiential factors that increase the advantage of successful readers over unsuccessful readers, so that those who most need the exposure to print, who must need the best instructional environment, are the ones least likely to get it. His analysis of reading and reading acquisition in terms of "rich-get-richer" effects, not just at the level of processes involved in reading but also at the level of contextual and societal effects on literacy, provides a powerful explanatory tool for language arts educators.

The Psychology of Writing. When it comes to the area of writing, the contribution of psychology is in a somewhat disputed state. Beginning in the late 1970s, a number of theorists and researchers, most notably Flower and Hayes (1981, 1984; Flower, Hayes, Carey, Schriver, & Stratman, 1986) and Scardamalia and Bereiter (1986), explored the usefulness of representing writing as a problem-solving cognitive task. Their efforts led to a fruitful portrayal of the writing process as a recursive coordination of a number of subprocesses including planning, language generation, and revising, all influenced by the constraints of audience and goal concerns and by prior knowledge. In this view, writers are represented as attempting to solve the problem of how best to meet their goals with written language.

For all that was right about the description of writing that such a view afforded, it has recently met a flurry of criticism so that the cognitive approach is often maligned when contrasted with a newer emphasis on the social nature of writing (Faigley, 1986; Nystrand, 1986, 1989). Dissatisfaction with the cognitive approach to describing the writing process arose, I believe, because of three factors. The first has to do with an unfortunate collocation between cognitive models of the writing process and instructional process approaches to teaching writing, simply because both use the term "process" in their descriptions. As the field of writing instruction has come to be dissatisfied with the most common interpretation of process approaches to instruction, that dissatisfaction has spilled over to efforts to describe the writing process. Note that this first possibility is most likely not part of the reason why the serious thinker/researcher is rejecting the cognitive perspective on writing. However, I have frequently enough encountered the confusion among graduate students in rhetoric and language arts education to believe that it supports, by popular influence, the move away from the cognitive model.

A more serious concern with "cognitive" models of writing comes from the emphasis these generally place on the thinking, or cognitive, aspect of writing at the expense of modelling the particular difficulties that arise when thoughts must be translated into words. Writing, after all, is a language activity. As McCutchen (1984) persuasively argued, writing cannot be represented simply as a problem-solving activity where the writer's only important problem is to plan out what to say. Simply because of the nature of language, the writer is often led along unpredicted paths and much of the hair-pulling that a writer experiences has to do with encountering difficulties in coming up with the actual words to express meaning. Thus, one complaint that has been raised about cognitive models of the writing process is that they have not been sensitive enough to the special problems caused by the linguistic nature of writing. In fairness to the researchers most closely associated with a cognitive approach to writing, recent work in that tradition (c.f., Flower, et al., 1986; Kaufer, Hayes, & Flower, 1986) has addressed exactly this issue quite well.

However, the most serious concerns with a cognitive approach to writing surely have been generated because of its characterization of the writing process as a fundamentally solitary, individual process. In some ways, it is exactly in this aspect that a cognitive process model is so psychological in nature. Current representations of writing as a social-interactive activity emphasize, by contrast, the social moves and roles that constitute any language activity (Nystrand, 1989). Research in this newer tradition is much more likely to involve writers in tasks that represent real writing to real audiences rather than the contrived, researcher-designed task to write for a generic or fictitious audience typical of research from a cognitive perspective. And, although there is obvious room for a rapprochement between the two approaches by studies that would focus on the psychological process of how individuals represent to themselves, and are influenced by, the social context in which writing occurs (Flower, 1989), at this time, the debate seems to be only heating up.

LEARNING IN A SOCIAL/MOTIVATIONAL/ EMOTIONAL CONTEXT

The newer work in writing, in which models that seem to be solely cognitive are criticized and replaced by more social models, represents in a microcosm some of the same broad changes that are taking place in cognitive models of learning. Current psychological work is likely to show a much greater sensitivity than was true 10 years ago to broader contextual factors that might influence the learning process. Although the change in focus may seem painfully slow to educational researchers and especially to practitioners, psychologists are more and more turning their attention to describing the learning process as it is influenced by, on the one hand, the instructional setting and on the other hand, the emotional and motivational proclivities of the learner.

How People Teach. In terms of psychological studies of teaching, there have been several lines of work that have contributed to an understanding of what is involved in teaching. A full appreciation of these approaches would well begin with a review of the latest edition of the *Handbook of Research on Teaching* edited by Wittrock (1986) and the special issue of the *American Psychologist,* edited by Glaser and Takanishi (1986), devoted to "Psychological Science and Education." A sketch of this work would have to include the productive approach that flourished

in the late 1970s and early 1980s using a process-product paradigm. In this approach, teachers and classrooms were observed so as to identify factors that seemed to make a difference in student achievement. More recently, psychological studies of teaching have been concerned with characterizing teachers' thought processes and decision making (Clark & Peterson, 1986). One finding from this literature is that, for example, teachers are responding not just in terms of what they believe will influence students' ability to learn and understand content, but also in terms of a host of contextual factors such as what has recently happened in the classroom or what particular students will find manageable. In this section, I would like to highlight two additional key concepts reflecting how a psychological analysis may enhance our understanding of teaching.

One of these is Doyle's (1983) construct of *academic work,* the representation of classroom life in terms of tasks that teachers set up and that students attempt to accomplish. A natural unit of classroom time, from this view, is the activity, something that has temporal and physical unity and provides a program of action on a focal content. An activity, or academic task, is defined by four parameters:

a. The products that must be produced,
b. The processes that it engenders,
c. Available resources, and
d. The significance of the task in terms of grading and other evaluation.

Doyle (1983, 1989) reported that different academic tasks had different consequences for how classrooms worked, both in terms of management and learning opportunities for the students. One important contribution of such a characterization of the classroom is the opportunity it affords for capturing in one snapshot content, process, and context, what Doyle (1989) called "curriculum in action." Characterizing teaching and learning in terms of academic tasks allows for a consideration of such often separated concerns as relate to discipline content (curriculum), student learning and motivation, management, and process descriptions of exactly what is taking place in the classroom.

A second approach currently having much impact on conceptualization of teaching owes much to the psychological tradition established by the Russian psychologist, Lev Vygotsky (1978). Palincsar and Brown (1984), for example, used Vygotsky's construct of expert scaffolding and zone of proximal development to develop an intervention program involving reciprocal teaching of comprehension strategies. The hallmark of a Vygotskian approach to teaching and learning is the focus on how a learner, who may not be able to accomplish a task on her own, may be much more adept when a more expert individual provides help. The learner's state in terms of development or knowledge acquisition is called the zone of proximal development, and the type of help that the more expert is providing is referred to as scaffolding. Scaffolding occurs whenever someone in the role of teacher provides as much help to the learner as is required in order to accomplish a particular task. In the early stages of acquisition, this may require that the teacher perform nearly all aspects of the task. As the learner becomes more accomplished in the task, the teacher gradually withdraws the direct and indirect help and lets the learner take over. Palincsar and Brown (1984) were successful in using such notions to guide the development of a powerful intervention that helped academically delayed seventh graders learn how to read grade-level informative texts with good comprehension.

Thus, some of the most exciting psychological work on teaching takes a perspective that includes much more attention to context, social factors, and group influence than might have been expected even 10 years ago. I would claim this newer work maintains its identification as psychological study by virtue of its focus always on individuals and how each individual, teacher or learner, constructs an inner reality and public program of action in response to the social world. For language arts educators, such work highlights the importance of structuring classroom work that will encourage students to approach a task in a most beneficial way. The concept of scaffolding, in particular, supports instructional programs where students find themselves doing much more than might have been expected simply because the right kind of help was provided.

Goal-Oriented and Emotional Nature of Human Functioning. A final area of psychological work that can help elucidate how people learn and teach is represented by concerns with how motivational and emotional factors influence learning and understanding. Earlier conceptions of motivation and emotion generally took either of two approaches: a behavior theory focus on environment-response connections with the individual portrayed as a passive responder to external contingencies, or a dynamic personality perspective with motivation and emotion depicted as the result of global internal states. Recent developments in views of motivation emphasize a third possibility altogether, a social-cognitive approach where motivation and emotion are mediated by the individual's cognitive interpretations of situations. Such a view provides for a much easier integration with models of learning, teaching, and comprehension discussed above and for more successful recommendations for intervention.

One of the best examples of this newer generation of models is offered by the work of Dweck (1986; Dweck & Leggett, 1988) on adaptive and maladaptive motivational patterns. In this view, a learner who takes a certain view on ability will then approach a task with a particular goal which will lead to particular behavior patterns in the face of success and failure. People who believe their ability for a particular task is fixed will likely approach the task with a performance goal, a goal to demonstrate their abilities in the best light possible. In the face of success, all will be well. With the first signs of failure, however, the learners will give up trying to accomplish the task. On the other hand, learners who believe that ability for a task is something that increases with practice will seek challenge and approach tasks with the goal of increasing competence. Such learners will show high task involvement and persistence even when the task proves to be quite difficult.

Dweck and her colleagues (see Dweck, 1986, and Dweck & Leggett, 1988, for a review) found that such patterns of motivational attribution were predictive of the amount of effort students of all ages were willing to devote to tasks. They also found

that maladaptive attributional patterns could be changed with interventions aimed specifically at the views (schemata, if you will) the learners had of their ability. Similarly, Ames and Archer (1988) found that the classroom environment influenced students to adopt more or less adaptive approaches to their learning. When in classrooms that they perceived as encouraging competence or mastery goals, students exhibited motivational processes that were in line with the more adaptive pattern identified by Dweck. When in classrooms that they perceived as emphasizing absolute performance levels, students assumed a performance-oriented, low challenge seeking, low persistence pattern of motivation. Thus, learning was found to be intimately influenced by the students' conception of their ability and of the classroom context their teachers offered.

Finally, the intersection of emotional-motivational factors and cognitive processes has been represented in a model of human intentionality by Young and Schallert (1988, 1989). Here, individuals are represented as initiating different cognitive operations in the service of complex, interleaved plans. What should be particularly interesting to an educator about this model is the portrayal of individuals as continually goal-directed, setting up internal criteria by which they will know whether the goal is being reached. These criteria, which are in fact often revised as a particular task unfolds, act as a sort of magnet to guide successive approximations to the goal. Dweck's performance and learning goals can easily be fit into the intentionality model. Young and Schallert also characterized different stances toward a task that an individual can take. For example, a student may approach a task with a sincere and open attitude, one that will allow for a facile incorporation of the information or ability into her current knowledge. Or, a student may not agree with or like or understand the information being presented and yet, because of the situation's exigency, must pretend to know it. Unfortunately, many learning environments throw young people into situations where they adopt a stance to pseudo-incorporate the information or skill. They learn, in a manner of speaking, well enough for the performance assessments set up by the system, but they do not fully integrate what has been presented with their prior knowledge.

Why researchers and educators interested in the teaching of the language arts should be interested in psychological studies of how the larger context in which learning occurs influences its course perhaps needs little explicating. I will only point to what I see are distinctive dimensions of the teaching of the language arts. When students are learning about their language, when they are engaged in writing at the request of their teachers, when they are exploring their response to literature, they place themselves in uniquely vulnerable positions. Classroom systems and teacher responses, unless carefully designed and humanely thoughtful, can easily crush their personal investments and future motivation to engage fully in these learning situations.

CLOSING

In summary, psychology can legitimately be portrayed, I believe, as a foundational science for education. Given the focus of this volume on the teaching of the language arts, those aspects of psychological work that inform more directly how language is used, how comprehension and production occur, and then, what teaching involves and motivational affective variables that impinge on the learning process, were presented. There are many ways in which psychological studies provide a rigorous basis for understanding what is going on in the teaching and learning of the language arts.

And yet, there are many ways in which the discipline of psychology and that of the language arts educator diverge in terms of goals, approach to the learner, and views of inquiry. Psychologists can seem foreign to educators, especially to those that take as their content discipline some field in the humanities. The scientific approach of the psychologist with its tendency to objectify the individual and the mind, can easily offend the artist in the language arts educator. In the face of this potential for divergence, it is important to remember the many ways in which world views of the two disciplines agree. Psychologists and language arts educators are fascinated with language, with the particulars of how a message and its expression are related and can influence comprehension. Both are more likely to be interested in how individuals work rather than groups.

Finally, if we take literary studies as a central aspect of the language arts, the psychologist easily fits in. Authors and readers often explore the minds and hearts of characters in ways that reflect the same need to understand the human condition as psychologists have. In fact, it is not unusual for psychological constructs to be presented in literary works before these are explored by the psychologist. There is much room for a mutually satisfying and beneficial relationship here.

References

Alvermann, D., Smith, L. C., & Readance, J. E. (1985). Prior knowledge activation and the comprehension of compatible and incompatible text. *Reading Research Quarterly, 20,* 420–436.

Ames, C., & Archer, J. (1988). Achievement goals in the classroom: Students' learning strategies and motivation processes. *Journal of Educational Psychology, 80,* 260–267.

Anderson, J. R. (1983). *The architecture of cognition.* Cambridge, MA: Harvard University Press.

Anderson, R. C. (1977). The notion of schemata and the educational enterprise. In R. C. Anderson, R. J. Spiro, & W. E. Montague (Eds.), *Schooling and the acquisition of knowledge,* pp. 415–431. Hillsdale, NJ: Erlbaum.

Anderson, R. C. (1984). Role of the reader's schema in comprehension, learning and memory. In R. C. Anderson, J. Osborn, & R. J. Tierney (Eds.), *Learning to read in American schools: Basal readers and content texts,* pp. 243–257. Hillsdale, NJ: Erlbaum.

Ausubel, D. P. (1960). The use of advance organizers in the learning and retention of meaningful verbal material. *Journal of Educational Psychology, 51,* 267–272.

Ausubel, D. P. (1961). In defense of verbal learning. *Educational Theory, 11,* 15–25.

Ausubel, D. P., Novak, J. D., & Hanesian, H. (1978). *Educational psychology: A cognitive view, (2nd Ed.).* New York: Holt, Rinehart and Winston.

Bartlett, F. C. (1932). *Remembering: A study in experimental and social psychology.* London: Cambridge University Press.

Beaugrande, R. de, & Dressler, W. U. (1981). *Introduction to text linguistics.* London: Longman.

Beck, I. L., Perfetti, C. A., & McKeown, M. G. (1982). Effects of long-term vocabulary instruction on lexical access and reading comprehension. *Journal of Educational Psychology, 74,* 506–521.

Black, J. B. (1985). An exposition on understanding expository text. In B. K. Britton & J. B. Black (Eds.), *Understanding expository text,* pp. 249–267. Hillsdale, NJ: Erlbaum.

Bransford, J. D. (1979). *Human cognition: Learning, understanding, and remembering.* Belmont, CA: Wadsworth.

Bransford, J. D. (1984). Schema activation and schema acquisition: Comments on Richard C. Anderson's remarks. In R. C. Anderson, J. Osborn, & R. J. Tierney (Eds.), *Learning to read in American schools: Basal readers and content texts,* pp. 259–272. Hillsdale, N.J.: Erlbaum.

Bransford, J. D. (1988). Invited address presented at the annual meeting of the National Reading Conference, Tucson, Arizona.

Bransford, J. D., & Franks, J. J. (1971). The abstraction of linguistic ideas. *Cognitive Psychology, 2,* 331–350.

Bransford, J. D., & Johnson, M. K. (1972). Contextual prerequisites for understanding: Some investigations of comprehension and recall. *Journal of Verbal Learning and Verbal Behavior, 11,* 717–726.

Bransford, J. D., & Johnson, M. K. (1973). Considerations of some problems of comprehension. In W. G. Chase (Ed.), *Visual information processing,* pp. 383–438. New York: Academic Press.

Bransford, J. D., Sherwood, R., & Hasselbring, T. (in press). Effects of the video revolution on development: Some initial thoughts. In G. Foreman & P. Puffall (Eds.), *Constructivism in the computer age.*

Bransford, J. D., Stein, B. S., Shelton, T. S. & Owings, R. A. (1981). Cognition and adaptation: The importance of learning to learn. In J. Harvey (Ed.), *Cognition, social behavior, and the environment.* Hillsdale, NJ: Erlbaum.

Brewer, W. F. (1977). Memory for the pragmatic implications of sentences. *Memory & Cognition, 5,* 673–678.

Chase, W. G., & Simon, H. A. (1973). Perception in chess. *Cognitive Psychology, 4,* 55–81.

Clark, C. M., & Peterson, P. L. (1986). Teachers' thought processes. In M. C. Wittrock (Ed.), *Handbook of research on teaching, (3rd Ed.),* pp. 255–296. New York: Macmillan.

Clark, H. H., & Haviland, S. E. (1977). Comprehension and the Given-New contract. In R. O. Freedle (Ed.), *Discourse production and comprehension.* Norwood, NJ: Ablex.

Doyle, W. (1983). Academic work. *Review of Educational Research, 53,* 159–199.

Doyle, W. (1989). Classroom knowledge as a foundation for learning. Paper presented at a conference on Foundational Studies in Teacher Education: A Re-Examination, University of Illinois, Urbana-Champaign.

Dweck, C. S. (1986). Motivational processes affecting learning. *American Psychologist, 41,* 1040–1048.

Dweck, C. S., & Leggett, E. (1988). A social-cognitive approach to motivation and personality. *Psychological Review, 95,* 256–273.

Eaton, J., Anderson, C. W., & Smith, E. L. (1984). Students misconceptions interfere with science learning: Case studies of fifth-grade students. *Elementary School Journal, 84,* 367–379.

Faigley, L. (1986). Competing theories of process. *College English, 48,* 527–542.

Flower, L. (1989). Cognition, context, and theory building. *College Composition and Communication, 40,* 282–311.

Flower, L. S., & Hayes, J. R. (1981). A cognitive process theory of writing. *College Composition and Communication, 32,* 365–387.

Flower, L. S., & Hayes, J. R. (1984). Images, plans, and prose: The representation of meaning in writing. *Written Communication, 1,* 120–160.

Flower, L. S., Hayes, J. R., Carey, L., Schriver, K., & Stratman, J. (1986). Detection, diagnosis, and the strategies of revision. *College Composition and Communication, 37,* 16–53.

Garner, R. (1987). *Metacognition and reading comprehension.* Norwood, NJ: Ablex.

Glaser, R., & Takanishi, R. (1986). Special issue: Psychological science and education. *American Psychologist, 41,* 1025–1168.

Grice, H. P. (1975). Logic and conversation. In P. Cole & J. L. Morgan (Eds.), *Syntax and semantics, Vol. 3: Speech acts,* pp. 41–58. New York: Academic Press.

Halliday, M. A. K. (1967). Notes of transitivity and theme in English, Part 1. *Journal of Linguistics, 3,* 37–81.

Johnson-Laird, P. N., & Wason, P. C. (1977). A theoretical analysis of insight into a reasoning task. In P. N. Johnson-Laird & P. C. Wason (Eds.), *Thinking: Readings in congitive science.* Cambridge, England: Cambridge University Press.

Kaufer, D., Hayes, J. R., & Flower, L. S. (1986). Composing written sentences. *Research in the Teaching of English, 20,* 121–140.

Larkin, J. H., McDermott, J., Simon, D. P., & Simon, H. A. (1980). Expert and novice performance in solving physics problems. *Science, 208,* 1335–1342.

Lesgold, A. M. & Perfetti, C. A. (1981). *Interactive processes in reading.* Hillsdale, NJ: Erlbaum.

Loftus, E. F., & Palmer, J. C. (1974). Reconstruction of automobile destruction: An example of the interaction between language and memory. *Journal of Verbal Learning and Verbal Behavior, 13,* 585–589.

Mayer, R. E. (1979). Can advance organizers influence meaningful learning? *Review of Educational Research, 49,* 371–383.

Mayer, R. E. (1983). *Thinking, problem solving, cognition.* New York: W. H. Freeman and Company.

McClelland, J. L. (1988). Connectionist models and psychological evidence. *Journal of Memory and Language, 27,* 107–123.

McCutchen, D. (1984). Writing as a linguistic problem. *Educational Psychologist, 19,* 226–238.

Nagy, W. E., Herman, P. A., & Anderson, R. C. (1985). Learning words from context. *Reading Research Quarterly, 20,* 233–253.

Newell, A., & Simon, H. A. (1972). *Human problem solving.* Englewood-Cliffs, NJ: Prentice-Hall.

Nystrand, M. (1986). *The structure of written communication: Studies in reciprocity between writers and readers.* Orlando, FL: Academic Press.

Nystrand, M. (1989). A social-interactive model of writing. *Written Communication, 6,* 66–85.

Omanson, R. C., Beck, I., Voss, J., & McKeown, M. (1984). The effects of reading lessons on comprehension: A processing description. *Cognition and instruction, 1,* 45–67.

Palincsar, A. S., & Brown, A. L. (1984). Reciprocal teaching of comprehension-fostering and comprehension-monitoring activities. *Cognition and Instruction, 1,* 117–175.

Paris, S. G. (1988). Models and metaphors of learning strategies. In C. E. Weinstein, E. T. Goetz, & P. A. Alexander (Eds.), *Learning and study strategies: Issues in assessment, instruction, and evaluation,* pp. 299–321. San Diego: Academic Press.

Paris, S. G., Lipson, M. Y., & Wixson, K. K. (1983). Becoming a strategic reader. *Contemporary Educational Psychology, 8,* 293–316.

Reder, L. M., & Anderson, J. R. (1980). A comparison of texts and their summaries: Memorial consequences. *Journal of Verbal Learning and Verbal Behavior, 19,* 121–134.

Rumelhart, D. E. & Norman, D. A. (1978). Accretion, tuning, & restructuring: Three modes of learning. In J. W. Cotton & R. L. Klatzky (Eds.), *Semantic factors in cognition,* pp. 37–53. Hillsdale, NJ: Erlbaum.

Rumelhart, D. E., & Ortony, A. (1977). The representation of knowledge in memory. In R. C. Anderson, R. J. Spiro, & W. E. Montague (Eds.), *Schooling and the acquisition of knowledge,* pp. 99–135. Hillsdale, NJ: Erlbaum.

Sanford, A. J., & Garrod, S. C. (1981). *Understanding written language: Explorations of comprehension beyond the sentence.* Chichester, England: John Wiley & Sons.

Scardamalia, M., & Bereiter, C. (1986). Written composition. In M. C. Wittrock (Ed.), *Handbook of research on teaching. (3rd Ed.),* pp. 778–803. New York: Macmillan.

Schallert, D. L. (1976). Improving memory for prose: The relationship between depth of processing and context. *Journal of Verbal Learning and Verbal Behavior, 15,* 621–632.

Schallert, D. L. (1982). The significance of knowledge: A synthesis of research related to schema theory. In W. Otto & S. White (Eds.), *Reading, expository material,* pp. 13–48. New York: Academic Press.

Schallert, D. L. (1987). Thought and language, content and structure in language communication. In J. R. Squire (Ed.), *The dynamics of language learning,* pp. 65–79. Urbana, Ill.: ERIC Clearinghouse.

Schank, R. C. & Abelson, R. P. (1977). *Scripts, plans, goals, and understanding: An inquiry into human knowledge structures.* Hillsdale, NJ: Erlbaum.

Shuell, T. J. (1986). Cognitive conceptions of learning. *Review of Educational Research, 56,* 411–436.

Spiro, R. J. (1980). Accommodative reconstruction in prose recall. *Journal of Verbal Learning and Verbal Behavior, 19,* 84–95.

Spiro, R. J., Vispoel, W. L., Schmitz, J. G., Samarapungavan, A., & Boerger, A. E. (1987). Knowledge acquisition for application: Cognitive flexibility and transfer in complex content domains. In B. C. Britton & S. Glynn (Eds.), *Executive control processes,* (pp. 177–199). Hillsdale, NJ: Erlbaum.

Stanovich, K. E. (1986). Matthew effects in reading: Some consequences of individual differences in the acquisition of literacy. *Reading Research Quarterly, 21,* 360–407.

Tierney, R. J., & Cunningham, J. W. (1984). Research on teaching reading comprehension. In P. D. Pearson (Ed.), *Handbook of reading research,* pp. 609–655. New York: Longman.

van Dijk, T. A., & Kintsch, W. (1983). *Strategies of discourse comprehension.* New York: Academic Press.

Vosniadou, S., & Brewer, W. F. (1987). Theories of knowledge restructuring in development. *Review of Educational Research, 57,* 51–67.

Voss, J. F., & Bisanz, G. L. (1985). Knowledge and the processing of narrative and expository texts. In B. K. Britton & J. B. Black (Eds.), *Understanding expository text,* pp. 173–198. Hillsdale, NJ: Erlbaum.

Vygotsky, L. (1978). Mind in society: The development of higher psychological processes. (M. Cole, V. John-Steiner, S. Scribner, & E. Souberman, Eds. and Trans.) Cambridge, MA: Harvard University Press.

Wittrock, M. C. (1974). Learning as a generative process. *Educational Psychologist, 11,* 87–95.

Wittrock, M. C., (Ed.) (1986). *Handbook of research on teaching. (3rd Ed.).* New York: Macmillan.

Young, E. L., & Schallert, D. L. (1988). The influence of personal intentions and external constraints on college students' writing. Paper presented at the meeting of the Southwest Educational Research Association, San Antonio.

Young, E. L., & Schallert, D. L. (1989). The intentional nature of a writer's response to social constraints. Paper presented at the American Educational Research Association, San Francisco.

3C. CHILD DEVELOPMENT
Marie M. Clay

Theories in developmental psychology and theories about teaching the English language arts are furthest apart when developmental psychology has nothing to say about teaching, when it attends focally to the evidence that the child constructs his own knowledge, and when it fails to address the roles assigned by society to teachers. Conversely, when teaching is seen as the delivery into children of content and skill by didactic instruction, or the use of teacher-proof curricula that calls for no developmental wisdom, or nothing more than publishers' programs, these positions ignore the highly relevant insights about children's learning that exist in developmental psychology. The work of both disciplines is closely allied when researchers document in precise ways the effects on children of real-world interactions and when they search for theoretical explanations of how and why children's responses change over time. The two disciplines have shared interests in recent studies of parent-child interaction, tutoring by novice tutors, adults talking with children especially in schools (Cazden, 1988), all of which show how the apprentice learner gradually assumes a self-monitored role.

The child study movement of the early 1900s emerged from the innovation and international interchange of the 1930s as developmental psychology (Senn, 1975). Like the parent discipline of psychology, it placed high value on empirical evidence gained under controlled conditions and theories grounded in data. The methodological and theoretical uniqueness and challenge of a developmental orientation (Baltes, 1983) are reflected in its goals, namely

1. To describe change over time in behaviors, abilities, and processes,
2. To explain what occurs, and
3. To optimize opportunities for enhanced development.

Optimization may call for interventions that establish external or internal resources to allow for optimal development, or programs that modify problematic behavior. A diversity of philosophical, theoretical, and methodological orientations are found at the cutting edge of current debates (Lerner, 1983), but there is a major focus today on internal, cognitive, strategic, and affective variables as prior and causative. Learning contexts influence behaviors and cognitive processes in important ways, and the problem of how to study the process of learning during interactions is a challenge to researchers.

Interpreted broadly, formal education fits comfortably into this goal of optimization: its central enterprise can be seen as a myriad of interventions in children's lives during formative years of change. Educational researchers also record cumulative change over time as children learn, with their empirical evidence ranging from that gained under controlled conditions (evaluation or assessment) to telling accounts in individual biographies. In such descriptive research, learning is conceptualized broadly as something that occurs in or out of school, with or without instruction. Such research recognizes that some changes in children occur under the control of historical and societal factors, others are determined by the child's selection of what to attend to, many are brought about in interaction with significant others, and some result from what is delivered more formally in classroom programs.

There is no clear distinction between the two disciplines when educational researchers pursue questions to the level of explanatory theory tested against competing alternatives, or when developmental psychologists test theories in interventions in the real world of schools. More commonly, developmental psychologists focus more on research designs and questions that will yield explanations and educational researchers attend to effective optimization as a goal. There is a search for both a better explanation and a more effective program.

Since 1970, the need of societies to solve problems by changing the next generation of school children produced different research pressures in psychology and education, complicating the transfer of information between them. Education received calls for accountability and for higher standards while hearing arguments to narrow its focus, which seemed blind to what was known about child development, while developmental psychology broadened its scope from highly controlled experimental studies to consider the ecologies within which children learned (Bronfenbrenner, 1979). In part this led to a more culturally aware and activist stance, and involvements in interventions with underprivileged children (Weikart, Rogers, Adcock, & McClelland, 1971).

In this paper, brief comment on research interests shared by the two disciplines in oral language, writing, and reading is followed by a more general analysis of congruence and communicative distance between them.

THE ACQUISITION OF LANGUAGE

Oral Language

Language acquisition has been richly generative of challenges to educators. It is clearly cumulative, its foundation is laid before entry to school, and most of it is completed in interaction with significant others but without direct instruction (Lindfors, 1987). Preschoolers use it to code cognitive stores of information and acquire processes for accessing that information. They derive order and structure for language from massively different and diverse samples, test and refine their values for production, and are barely conscious of any of these processes. The learning is often initiated by the child, although adults and older children may pace the learning and provide appropriate information that the child is able to use. It does not proceed by accurate performance with the use of correct grammar. This is important, because how would the brain construct self-monitoring and self-correction processes if it never made an imperfect response? By being partially correct, the child progresses to more control over complexity in the use of language. Accuracy is the outcome, not the process, of learning.

In the 1960s as psychologists came to terms with the linguists' conceptual approaches to syntax, attention to detailed protocols of individual progress placed the spotlight on the importance of interrelationships between parts of the utterance and the organization of language on several levels. When linguists began to explore the links between structure and meaning, developmental psychologists found themselves in familiar territory with knowledge about cognition and how we understand language. As interest turned to the pragmatics of language use, it was easy for educators to recognize the influence of familiar contextual variables—settings, home influences, cultural factors, discourse factors, dialect differences. By 1975, oral language was seen in rich perspective, with important implications for teaching, for the valuing of cultures, and for bilingual education. Since then, the interactions of language, culture, and education have received attention as ethnomethodological approaches have been tested and refined (Heath, 1983), cultural factors explored (Au & Kawakami, 1984), and classroom discourse analyzed (Cazden, 1988).

Perhaps because children seem to have well-formed response systems for comprehending and producing language prior to entering school, the continuing development of oral language during schooling is not often seen by teachers to be important. In fact individual differences in oral language achievement vary greatly. While teachers see oral language as central to writing and reading acquisition, they often do not recognize the need to foster its further development. Multicultural or bilingual challenges in most English-speaking countries have led to a new awareness of oral language issues, which may direct more attention to the ways in which the language of the child at home undergoes further development during schooling.

Writing

Three slim volumes appeared by 1978 with detailed observations of young children writing (Clay, 1975; Graves, 1978; Read, 1975). Graves placed prime emphasis on the observation of the writing processes used by children who were encouraged to be writers. Read discovered children who analyzed the sounds they could hear in their own pronunciation of sentences and invented a writing system for themselves. Clay collected weekly writing samples from an age cohort of children in five schools throughout their first year of school. An area that had been confined by beliefs about motor incoordination, having to be correct, needing to read before you could write, and getting images of spellings into the brain, began to expand with new vigor. Today even preschool children are seen as writers. Attention focussed on

a. How to look at children's writing,
b. How to look for processes of change, and
c. How to evaluate change.

Writing acquisition had surprising similarities to oral language. Children made responses that were systematic rather than random, and they occurred across children, even across countries

and languages (Ferreiro & Teberosky, 1982; Goodman, in press) as if children were operating on rules they had discovered for themselves. Children were hard to shift from such positions pointing to cognitive involvements. Questions were needed to elicit the rules or assumptions that children were using. Researchers could almost see cognitive processes in operation as they recorded children in classrooms composing messages, and monitoring their oral production against their written composition at sound, sound cluster, word, or phrase level within the text as a whole, using recursive strategies of reviewing and revising (Graves, 1983; King & Rentel, 1979).

Reading

By analogy reading acquisition might have been viewed constructively, i.e., something that the child put together, except that reading instruction has a long history of polarized theoretical positions. In lay minds, there are two superficial descriptions of beginning reading instruction, one at the letter level (phonics) and one at the word level (sight vocabulary). A wealth of writing on communication, information, and linguistic theory (Miller, 1951) showed how language transmits information on several levels. Research directed the attention of teachers to variables that found no place in the stripped-down versions of decoding and sight vocabulary theories—research on children's syntactic errors in reading, the role of context and meaning, the links within stretches of texts called cohesive variables (Chapman, 1983), and memory experiments that showed how children related prior experience to new text. These research results were consistent with textual approaches to reading and writing.

Strategic reading is seen by many educators as something that older readers learn: rereading to comprehend (Garner, Wagoner, & Smith, 1983), skimming ahead for organizational structure, using context to process unfamiliar words (Potter, 1982), summarizing text to ensure understanding and remembering (Palincsar & Brown, 1984), and comprehension monitoring (Wagoner, 1983). That earlier forms of each of these strategies occur in the young reader (Baker, 1984; Clay, 1979) if instruction allows for it, is inconsistent with the advocacy of "decoding first and comprehension later." Unlike oral language and writing research, there have been few continuous longitudinal studies of reading processes in formation, with a result that young speakers and writers are seen as building their competencies and young readers receive them from their teachers and/or texts. The weight of research on early reading is on how cognition and teaching interact at the level of phonological awareness, to the neglect of other levels of language knowledge which might be powering the progress. Recent attention to the interactions of reading with writing may take us out of this strange situation (Langer, 1986). [See chapter by Tierney on longitudinal studies.]

THE CONTRIBUTION OF DEVELOPMENTAL THEORY

In the first half of this century psychoanalytic theory with its focus on the study of the individual child provided a strong developmental emphasis for the education of young children in British education from the time of Susan Isaacs (1935) to the Plowden Report (1967). In the United States, the strong influences on education from psychology were from associationist or behavioral theories, which could be applied to children being instructed in groups; at that time developmental psychology studied children's development before they went to school and in their out-of-school lives. In contrast to Britain and the United States, the Soviet Union's developmental psychology was directed, even in the 1930s, to pedagogical issues (although it only reached Western countries in translation to the 1960s) and work from that period is central to important research on children's learning today (Vygotsky, 1962, Wertsch, 1958).

For 50 years Piaget's theory of cognitive development evolved, expanded, and provided an approximation to a theory that might account for all development and learning, an "inclusive model" (Cairns & Valsiner, 1984). Children not only carried out cognitive operations, but used processing strategies, coded experiences, and compiled records of experiences stored as memory schemas. Piaget's description of assimilatory and accommodation processes presents teachers with the option of going with the child or against the child in one to one teaching, but provides only very general guidance for the design of day-to-day cumulative instruction of groups for children in classrooms (Goodman, in press). Critical evaluation of the contribution of Piagetian theory to teaching has led to the concept of the competent preschooler (Donaldson, 1979) and to theories that challenge the role of conflict in cognitive change (Bryant, 1982, 1984).

Current analysis of Vygotsky's theory is focused not on his concept of inner speech, only partially on his social theory, and mostly on his concept of the zone of proximal development. His challenge to current teaching practice is that he sanctions shared activity between tutor and learner so that the learner can complete more difficult tasks with help that he would not complete on his own. He is supported in the beginning but gradually takes over the entire task. The help of the expert becomes unnecessary as learners become able to assume control. Education does not have to be an activity on which the child must always work solo on unseen material. While these ideas can be easily fitted to concepts of teaching they do not reflect the depth of the theory which claims that the shared and supported activity allows the child to construct some inner generating system, which will initiate and manage learning of this kind independently on future occasions.

Many abilities are now regarded in developmental psychology as "alterable variables" and potential targets for education. Researchers study the procedures children use to get to solutions, like cognitive strategies and self-monitoring (Flavell, 1982), and provide explanations of how we understand speech and texts arguing that 'scripts' have causal effects on achievement (Schank & Abelson, 1977). Even intelligence is seen as a matter of dynamic processes, rather than fixed static states (Sternberg, 1984; Pintrich, Cross, Kozma, & McGeachie, 1986).

How do developmental theories influence teachers' assumptions about children? The explanations provided, particularly in language and cognitive areas, have created for teachers a vocabulary and knowledge structures that allow them to think beyond what the child does to what may be occurring in children's heads. It is the purpose of scientific study to go beyond the detailed variability of individual differences and the surface plausibility of what is observed, to less obvious phenomena and more general statements of relationships. This is a position to be treated very seriously. Education needs to know why developmental psychology works in the ways it does.

However, the need to test particular developmental theories on certain age groups has led to an uneven spread of information with most attention going to the preschool years (ages 4 to 6), followed by the early elementary years (ages 6 to 9), and the intermediate years (ages 9 to 12) (McCandless & Geis, 1975), and with adolescence a poorly researched age group. Recent research on infants and toddlers has overcome an earlier neglect, and lifespan developmental psychology is theoretically strong but empirically young. Such coverage serves early childhood education well but not schooling in later years.

Theories of child development influence teachers' assumptions about why children behave the way they do, rather than their decisions about how and what to teach. There are particular risks when the theories applied belong to another age, arose from a different knowledge base, and may be distorted by the time-warp. For example Wertsch (1985) had to use Soviet authorities who wrote long after Vygotsky's death to explicate Vygotsky's work; Gesell's attempt to characterize the mismatch between some children's learning needs and instruction demands is used today to exclude children from instruction and so from opportunities to learn. Bloom's (1971) theory of how the scores of average achievers can be lifted two standard deviations by teaching in certain ways can be applied as a concept of mastery learning that looks like pouring content into empty vessels more demandingly.

THE CONTRIBUTION OF METHODOLOGY

In the area of methodology, the two professional areas can negotiate concurrent rather than derivative exchanges. A question in education may be explored by the newest methodology and the best available analytic logic in developmental psychology at the point of beginning the investigation. "Join our team and when we get there you will know as much as we do and avoid the lag in the transfer of information," could be a useful idea.

Critical for more effective interchange between the two disciplines is a need to appreciate the logical linkages between theoretical issues, research designs, statistical analyses, and interpretations (Baltes, Reese, & Nesselroade, 1977; Bryant & Bradley, 1985; Pintrich et al., 1986). Theory testing and experimental controls in psychology are necessary to answer some kinds of questions for which observational and participant observation methodologies are not alternatives, because they address important but different questions.

Experimental or longitudinal studies that compare age groups can only produce descriptions or change in children consistent with discreet stages. Gradual change in process or knowledge, which teachers find a better match to what they see in classrooms, is more likely to emerge from intensive longitudinal studies of change over short intervals.

Where developmental psychology has paid detailed attention to what happens in the course of development, with manipulative and precise measurement of change in children's responses, it provides good models for education, and for teachers to monitor whether good outcomes are occurring. Ideas of where, when, and how to begin teaching, of the changes that may be expected over time, of the track that most children take, of the variability to be expected, and of different developmental paths to the same outcomes could emerge from developmental research designed for this purpose.

Piaget's clinical method, used to study children's cognitions in depth, had an important impact on the acceptability of talking to children about their understanding. (Ferreiro & Teberosky, 1982; Karmiloff-Smith, 1979). Roger Brown (1973) and his eminent students began a search for description of language acquisition with in-depth data from the language of three children. The new emphases required careful recording of daily change, small scale manipulations, and analyses of particular features, trying to model the inner structure to account for the outer behaviors. Studies in the Soviet Union of sensory features used a similar kind of detailed observation, asking what was behind the behavior change.

Longitudinal research is highly relevant to the understanding of change over time needed in education; it is essential for the study of prediction, for understanding the origins of individual differences, and for the evaluation of outcomes of educational programs (Sontag, 1971). It is a method too rarely used, and almost never applied to a total cohort of children across the whole normal curve, varying in age as they do in real classrooms and under the normal school conditions within which children are taught. Yet descriptive data of learning processes in classrooms is very useful in education (Nicholson, 1984). If teachers became researchers of change over time in the day-to-day, small-scale sense (Pinnell & Haussler, in press) this could enrich assessment and evaluation of children's progress.

Detailed description of process changes in successful learners may well provide teachers with appropriate guides for what the poor learners need to be taught to do in what education regards as 'basic' subjects (Clay, 1985).

DIFFERENT PRIORITIES

While there are many points of congruence between the two disciplines, there are many reasons for communicative distance to arise between research on teaching the English language arts and research in developmental psychology. A recognition of some of these reasons may improve the potential for dialogue between two important areas of research endeavour.

Questions and Answers

While developmental psychology must take time to pose its questions and systematically test its explanations in a scientific way, education must act on today's best available knowledge for current programs and tomorrow's plan for changes. Teachers need answers to build into practice: psychologists want ques-

tions that lead to breakthroughs in understanding. Researchers in both disciplines will be problem solving in similar areas but with different goals. What counts as relevant is different and is liable to lead one group to ignore what the other group is finding out.

Selecting the Subjects

Teachers must deal with all children; they present the kind of diversity that developmental psychology seeks to control in its research designs. Teachers face the average majority, extreme subgroups, and particular individuals with learning challenges all at the same time. In order to obtain a clear test of an hypothesis, developmental psychologists select appropriate samples of children. Their findings may be clear but will usually apply only to some of the children in a mixed classroom who have to be taught today, and only extremely rarely to all of them. This problem can lead to impatience on the part of educators with psychological research and an unwillingness to consider its findings.

'The Whole Learner' versus 'Particular Processes'

The teacher's job is to work with all aspects of the child's functioning impinging on a single task. Teachers know that it is the individual child who interacts in some holistic way with the specific task at a particular time. Developmental psychology tries, in its advocacy, to remember the whole organism, and research has been directed to the links between perception and reading, cognition and language, culture and learning, classroom discourse and child learning, and contexts and outcomes. However, it is the nature of the developmental psychologist's work to search for explanations in specialized areas, to tease out the specific, eschew the complex, explicate processes, avoid global theory, and oppose unwarranted generalization, thus tending to exclude holistic theories.

COMMON RESEARCH PROBLEMS

Achievement Outcomes Do Not Define Curricula Inputs

Research findings of what children typically do at selected ages describe in step-wise form sequences of achievements, which are the outcomes of learning. Those error-free end-results, which are the outcome of many false starts, half-correct processes, and much self-correction en route to a recognizable product or achievement, have sometimes been built into curricula by educators in their perfected form. The appropriate research questions relate to how this "now perfect performance" was acquired, and records of the changes that took place en route to perfect performance will provide a better guide for the curricula of learning than study of the perfect outcomes of instruction.

Education is not about putting in the outcomes; it is about knowing what inputs, in what contexts, give rise to the desired achievement outcomes. In current debates about phonological segmentation in reading, metacognitive awareness in oral language, or the importance of correctness in writing, the distinction is not made between where you begin and where you end, but between inputs that give rise to outcomes.

For example, if the child learner constructs knowledge from learning interactions, then finding that competent readers score well on tests of phonological awareness do not imply that one should teach phonics, but, rather, that one should study change over time in younger children and document the sequences of interactions by which they reach that final tested state. Perhaps, like language acquisition, there are many inputs of different kinds which can contribute to the desired outcome. The fact that most children learn to read in very different instructional programs suggests that this may be the case. Developmental psychology is rich in understandings of this problem in a slightly different form. It accepts that change over time must be studied on individuals who change over time. Language acquisition research has illustrated how individuals learn from different language samples on different time scales, taking different paths to similar goals of talking fluently. What they need to learn cannot be interpolated from the average scores of separate samples of 3-, 4-, 5-, 6- and 7-year-olds. In the school years, it has been common for designers of educational interventions to try to achieve change in individuals on the basis of evidence derived from cross-sectional norms. Differences between individuals do not describe what is required to achieve change within or by individuals, and interventionists in both disciplines have often failed to recognize this (Montada & Filipp, 1976). A normative description of change is a gross approximation and does not provide a satisfactory basis for designing an instructional sequence.

Interactions Are Hard to Study

Riegel (1979), impressed by the dialectical world view of developmental psychology, chided the discipline for describing either the responses of the adult (parent or teacher) or the child during learning interactions and not doing the harder task of studying the interactions themselves. Two design and analysis problems are that interactions occur in sequences, and that any one response affects the subsequent responses of either or both parties. (That is, of course, one description of instruction.) Research designs in behavioral psychology, language acquisition research, the studies of Bruner (Bruner & Sherwood, 1976; Bruner & Garton, 1978), classroom discourse, and ethnomethodological research could be the source of innovative methodologies for interaction research. An emphasis on the sensitive observation of children shifts easily to the observation of interactions, and a new guide to the observation of interactions (Bakeman & Gottam, 1986) will be helpful.

SOME FINAL THOUGHTS

A Beginning Has Been Made

Vygotsky's theories (1962; Wertsch, 1985) of the support system provided by others for the learner at the growing edge of their competence (Bruner, 1986) come almost as a confirmation of recent developments (Au & Kawami, 1984; Clay, 1985; Palincsar & Brown, 1984) and adults have been shown to work in this way tutoring preschool children (Wood, Bruner, & Ross, 1976). "Teachers scaffold budding reading skills through prompts and examples and then foster individual control of reading by gradually removing social supports" (Pintrich et al., 1986). There is more than a scaffold involved, however, because the learning in the language and cognitive areas leaves the learner not only with the production of performance but with the inner structures and functions capable of generating these (Karmiloff-Smith, 1986).

Updating the Knowledge Base

A somewhat disturbing claim in recent years has been that we can predict very little about the way an individual will change from infancy to adulthood (Lipsitt, 1982), or about the way selected behaviours will be achieved from one historical era to another (Baltes et al., 1977; Elder, 1974; Lerner, 1983). Group predictions often do not hold up for individuals, and they do not hold up even for groups if the social contexts in which we learn are undergoing change. These claims are disturbing, because education operates on assumptions about accumulating expertise and continual change in expected directions during childhood (Kagan, 1983), and the degree and direction of expected change are derived from the average majority. Awareness of such claims implies that knowledge about children gained from research should be checked at quite short intervals, since today's research populations may be responding differently than the original research populations. Replication studies should be funded, as neither discipline would want its outdated information to limit the learning opportunites of today's children. This becomes more important today, because an hypothesis currently receiving some attention from developmental psychologists is that schooling may influence cognitive development in important ways.

References

Au, K. & Kawakami, A. (1984). Vygotskian perspectives on discussion processes in small group reading lessons. In P. Peterson, L. Wilkinson & M. Hallinan (Eds.). *The social context of instruction: Group organization and group processes* (pp.). New York: Academic Press.

Bakeman, R. & Gottman, J. M. (1986). *Observing interaction: An introduction to sequential analysis.* Cambridge: Cambridge University Press.

Baker, L. (1984). Children's effective use of multiple standards for evaluating their comprehension. *Journal of Educational Psychology, 76,* 588–597.

Baltes, P. B. (1983). Lifespan developmental psychology: Observations on history and theory revisited. In R. M. Lerner (Ed.). *Developmental* psychology: Historical and philosophical perspectives Hillsdale, N.J.: Lawrence Erlbaum, pp. 79–111.

Baltes, P. B., Reese, H. W., & Nesselroade, J. R. (1977). *Lifespan developmental psychology: Introduction to research methods.* Monterey, CA: Brooks/Cole.

Bloom, B. (1971). Mastery learning. In J. H. Block, (Ed.). *Mastery learning: Theory and practice* New York: Holt, Rinehart & Winston.

Bronfenbrenner, U. (1979). *The ecology of human development.* Cambridge: Harvard University Press.

Brown, A. & Palincsar, A. S. (1982). Inducing strategic learning from text by means of informed self-control training. In S. J. Samuels (Ed.). *Issues in reading diagnosis (Special Issue), Topics in Learning and Learning Disabilities, 2,* 1–17.

Brown, R. (1973). *A first language: The early stages.* Cambridge: Harvard University Press.

Bruner, J. S. & Sherwood, V. (1976). Early rule structure: The case of peek-a-boo. In Bruner, J. S., Jolly, A., and Sylva, K. *Play: Its role in development and evolution.* Harmondworth: Penguin.

Bruner, J. S. & Garton, A. (Eds.). (1978). *Human growth and development.* Oxford: Clarendon Press.

Bruner, J. S. (1986). *Actual minds: Possible worlds.* Cambridge, Mass.: Harvard University Press.

Bryant, P. E. (1982). The role of conflict and agreement between intellectual strategies in children's ideas about measurement. *British Journal of Psychology, 73,* 243–252.

Bryant, P. E. (1984). Piaget, teachers and psychologists. *Oxford Review of Education, 10,* (3), 251–259.

Bryant, P. & Bradley, L. (1985). *Children's reading problems.* Oxford: Blackwells.

Cairns, R. B. & Valsiner, J. (1984). Child psychology. In M. R. Rozenweig & L. W. Porter, (Eds.). *Annual Review of Psychology, 35,* 553–578.

Cazden, C. B. (1988). *Classroom discourse: The language of teaching and learning.* Portsmouth, N.H.: Heinemann Educ. Books.

Chapman, L. J. (1983). *Reading development and cohesion.* London: Heinemann Educational Books.

Clay, M. M. (1975). *What did I write?* Auckland: Heinemann Publishers.

Clay, M. M. (1979). *Reading: The patterning of complex behaviour.* Auckland: Heinemann Publishers.

Clay, M. M. (1985). *The early detection of reading difficulties.* Auckland: Heinemann Publishers.

Donaldson, M. (1979). *Children's minds.* New York: W. W. Norton.

Elder, G. H. (1974). *Children of the great depression.* Chicago: University of Chicago Press.

Ferreiro, E. & Teberosky, A. (1982). *Literacy before schooling.* Portsmouth, N.J.: Heinemann Educational Books.

Flavell, J. J. (1982). On cognitive development. *Child Development, 53,* 1–10.

Garner, R., Wagoner, S. & Smith, T. (1983). Externalizing question-answer strategies of good and poor comprehenders. *Reading Research Quarterly, 16,* 439–447.

Goodman, Y. (In press) *Literacy development: Psychogenesis and pedagogical implications.* Newark, Delaware: International Reading Association.

Graves, D. H. (1978). *Balance the basics: Let them write.* New York: Ford Foundation.

Graves, D. (1983). *Teachers and children at work.* Portsmouth, N. H.: Heinemann Educational Books.

Heath, S. B. (1983). *Ways with words.* Cambridge: Cambridge University Press.

Isaacs, S. (1935). *Children we teach.* London: University of London Press.

Kagan, J. (1983). Developmental categories and the premise of connectivity. In R. M. Lerner, (Ed.). *Developmental psychology* (see below).

Karmiloff-Smith, A. (1979). *A functional approach to child language.* Cambridge: Cambridge University Press.

Karmiloff-Smith, A. (1986). From meta-processes to conscious access: Evidence from children's metalinguistic and repair data. *Cognition, 23,* 95–147.

King, M. & Rentel, V. (1979). Towards a theory of early writing development. *Research in the Teaching of English, 13,* (3), 243–253.

Langer, J. A. (1986). *Children reading and writing: Structures and strategies.* Norwood, N.J.: Ablex.

Lerner, R. M. (1983). (Ed.). *Developmental psychology: Historical and philosophical perspectives.* Hillsdale, N.J.: Lawrence Erlbaum.

Lindfors, J. W. (1987). *Children's language and learning.* (2nd ed.). Englewood Cliffs, N.J.: Prentice-Hall.

Lipsitt, L. P. (1982). Infancy and life-span development. In T. M. Field, A. Huston, H. C. Quay, L. Troll, & G. E. Finlay (Eds.). *Review of Human Development* New York: Wiley.

McCandless, B. R., & Geis, M. F. (1975). Current trends in developmental psychology: In H. W. Reese (Ed.). *Advances in child development and behaviour, 10,* 1–8, New York: Academic Press.

Miller, G. (1951). *Language and communication.* New York: McGraw-Hill.

Montada, L. & Fillip, S. H. (1976). Implications of life-span developmental psychology for childhood education. In H. W. Reese (Ed.). *Advances in child development and behaviour, 11,* 253–266. New York: Academic Press.

Nicholson, T. (1984). Experts and novices: A study of reading in the high school classroom. *Reading Research Quarterly, XIX,* (4), 436–451.

Palincsar, A. S. & Brown, A. L. (1984). Reciprocal teaching of comprehension monitoring activities. *Cognition and Instruction, 2,* 117–175.

Pinnell, G. S., & Haussler, M. (In press). *Negotiating meaning through language: Impact of research on schools and teaching.* Newark, Delaware: NCTE and International Reading Association.

Pintrich, P. R., Cross, D. R., Kozma, R. B. & McGeachie, W. J. (1986). Instructional psychology. In M. R. Rozenweig & L. W. Porter, *Annual Review of Psychology,* Palo Alto: Annual Reviews, 611–654.

Plowden, B. (1967). *Children and their primary schools.* London: Her Majesty's Stationery Office.

Potter, F. (1982). The use of linguistic context: Do good and poor readers use different strategies? *British Journal of Educational Psychology, 52,* 16–23.

Read, C. (1975). *Children's categorizations of speech sounds in English.* (Research Report 17). Urbana, Ill.: National Council of Teachers of English.

Riegel, K. F. (1979). *Foundations of dialectical psychology: Some historical and ethical considerations.* New York: Academic Press.

Schank, R. C. & Abelson, R. P. (1977). *Scripts, plans, goals and understanding.* Hillsdale, N.J.: Erlbaum.

Senn, M. J. E. (1975). Insights on the child development movement in the United States. *Monograph of the Society for Research in Child development, 40* (3).

Sontag, L. W. (1971). The history of longitudinal research: Implications for the future. *Child Development, 42,* 987–1002.

Sternberg, R. J. (Ed.). (1984). *Mechanisms of cognitive development.* New York: W. H. Freeman.

Vygotsky, L. S. (1962). *Thought and language.* Cambridge, Mass.: MIT Press.

Wagoner, S. (1983). Comprehension monitoring: What it is and what we have to know about it. *Reading Research Quarterly, 18:* 328–346.

Weikart, D. P., Rogers, L., Adcock, C., and McClelland, D. (1971). *The cognitively-oriented curriculum.* Urbana, Ill.: University of Illinois.

Wertsch, J. V. (1985). *Vygotsky and the social formation of mind.* Cambridge, Mass.: Harvard University Press.

Wood, D., Bruner, J. S., & Ross, G. (1976). The role of tutoring in problem-solving. *Journal of Child Psychology and Child Psychiatry, 17,* 89–100.

3D. ANTHROPOLOGY AND RESEARCH ON TEACHING THE ENGLISH LANGUAGE ARTS

David Bloome

The primary contributions of anthropologically based research on teaching the English language arts lie in the attention that it focuses on minority student* education and on the redefinition of basic concepts such as education, language, teaching, and schooling; it is this attention to the education of minority students and the redefinition of basic concepts that makes them inseparable. Although commonly used in educational literature the term "minority" is problematic. Minority is often used to refer to non-dominant groups or oppressed groups rather than to a simple numerical relationship. By calling particular ethnic groups minorities instead of by labels that more accurately describe relationships among ethnic groups and classes, obfuscates important issues. In addition, some ethnic groups that are labelled minorities are the majority in some geographical areas and overall may constitute the majority in North America if not specifically in the United States. In this chapter, I use the term minority to refer to non-dominant ethnic and linguistic groups.

The research interest in minority students derives from a concern for educational equality (e.g., Drake, 1978; Jacob & Jordan, 1987) and from the inherent cross-cultural nature of anthropological research. Historically, anthropologists have studied people of cultures different from the mainstream culture of the anthropologist, and traditionally this has meant studying people who were geographically far away. More recently, there have been calls for studies about people within our own society (e.g., Cole, 1982; Jones, 1982; Nader, 1982; Spradley & Rynkiewich, 1975). Regardless of whether a study is conducted near or far, the intent is to develop insight and understanding through comparison. It is through attention to similarities and differences, continuity and change, conformity and conflict, that anthropologically based research makes visible the cultural basis of mainstream society, minority groups, and the contact between them.

With regard to teaching the English language arts, part of the hidden cultural agenda is taking for granted definitions of education, language, learning, teaching, and schooling. Such definitions greatly influence how we act and how we interpret what happens around us, and, like many other fundamental concepts, it is resistant to change and illumination except at a superficial level. Such basic concepts are extensions of the everyday cultural worlds in which we live, and thus seem to be common sense. Anthropologically based research has the power to show that common sense is a cultural system and not necessarily common sense to all (Geertz, 1983). However, to date, the contribution of anthropologically based research on teaching the English language arts is more promise than reality, more shadow than substance. The taken-for-granted, common-sense definitions of education, language, learning, teaching, and schooling have been challenged in a relatively small number of anthropologically based studies. Even more limited are the

attempts to apply such redefinitions in a substantive manner in schools and classrooms.

In this chapter, I focus on directions for redefinition of education, language, teaching, and schooling suggested by recent anthropologically based research on teaching the English language arts. In so doing, I highlight issues concerned with minority students, since as stated earlier, the redefinition of basic concepts and attention to minority students are inseparable. I begin by first discussing the concept of culture in anthropological research since that frames the redefinitions of education, language, teaching, and schooling. Then, I discuss issues in the choice of English, both as the language of schooling and as a topic of study. Thereafter, I discuss how recent anthropologically based research redefines education, language (including literacy and literature), teaching, and schooling. (See Emihovich, in press; and Erickson, 1982a, 1982b, for discussion of anthropologically based redefinitions of learning in education.)

Two notes are important before continuing. First, for the purposes of this chapter I have made a distinction between ethnographic research in education and anthropologically based research. At present, what passes for ethnographic research in education may or may not be based on theoretical constructs from cultural anthropology; it may only have the trappings of anthropological methods. (See Zaharkick & Green, this volume, for a discussion of ethnographic research methods; also, see McDermott & Hood, 1982.) Further, ethnographic research in Great Britain, among other places, tends to be grounded more in sociology than anthropology (see Hammersley & Atkinson, 1983). Second, it should be noted that given the limited length of the chapter, it is impossible to review or even cite all related studies.

DEFINING CULTURE

Anthropological perspectives vary in their definitions of culture. Tylor (1871) defined culture as "that complex whole which includes knowledge, belief, art, morals, law, custom, and any other capabilities and habits acquired by man as a member of society" (in Peacock, 1986, p. 3). Cultural anthropologists have built on Tylor's definition by attending less to surface features of culture as definition and more to the underlying processes, structures, and dynamics as definition. In brief, among the perspectives taken are: *functionalism* (e.g., Malinowski, 1922), where attention is focused on how a cultural system functions to meet the needs of people; *structuralism* (e.g., Levi-Strauss, 1963), where attention is focused on how underlying themes (usually thought of as binary oppositions such as freedom versus conformity) structure cultural phenomena; *psychological anthropology* (e.g., Harrington, 1978; Wallace, 1961;

*I want to thank Anne Gere, Diane Lapp, Earl Seidman, Judith Solsken, Patricia Stock, Denny Taylor, Jerri Willett, and an anonymous reviewer, for critical and editorial comments on early drafts of this chapter. Whatever problems remain are solely my responsibility.

Whiting & Whiting, 1975), where attention is focused on the relationship of the individual and the culture; *cognitive anthropology* (e.g., Frake, 1969, 1980; Goodenough, 1970, 1981; Quinn & Holland, 1987; Tyler, 1969), where attention is focused on shared cultural models and the standards people hold for perceiving, believing, evaluating, communicating, and acting; *symbolic interactionist* (e.g., Geertz, 1973), where attention is focused on the meaning and significance of what people do; and, *linguistic anthropology* (e.g., Gumperz & Hymes, 1972; Hymes, 1974), where attention is focused on the relationship of language and culture. Different perspectives are not necessarily taken as mutually exclusive; for example, much recent work in the ethnography of communication builds on symbolic interactionist definitions of culture. (Chilcott, 1987, and Peacock, 1986, provide discussion of various anthropological definitions of culture.)

One can point out commonality in the various approaches to culture. Culture is learned and shared. It is taken for granted. It is studied holistically. But these commonalities, while important, do not provide a consensual definition of culture nor reveal much about what an anthropological perspective is. It is not so much commonalities in definitions of culture that define an anthropological view, but more so the arguments and questions one is likely to have in studying the way people live. A few of these arguments and questions are:

What are the particularities of a cultural group? How do their local cultural conditions (practices and understandings) change and yet remain the same over time, place, and situation? What is it that changes and what remains the same? And, where are the particularities and interpretive practices of a cultural group located?

How shall and can we understand the sense that people make of their world? of what they do?

What does it mean that culture is shared? And, if shared what is it that is shared?

How are the local conditions, doings, and understandings of a cultural group connected to other forces (e.g., historical, economic, and geographical)?

What are the varieties of cultural doings and understandings in which people engage? And what constitutes a difference in cultural doings and understandings?

How can the varieties of local cultural conditions be taken as commentaries on each other? (This question is paraphrased from Geertz, 1983, p. 233).

How do the particularities of what people (as a cultural group) do inform a broader view of human behavior?

A major and continuing argument is between mentalist and materialist definitions of culture; that is, whether culture is in the head or in the doing. Is culture a knowledge that is, to a greater or lesser degree, shared by a group or does culture transcend individuals and exist in the interactions and histories that individuals have with each other? In support of in-the-head definitions is the work of cognitive anthropologists and others who have shown how cultural knowledge varies across cultures, is shared by members of a culture, and how cultural knowledge frames how people interpret behavior and act on the world (e.g., Quinn & Holland, 1987). However, as Keesing

(1987), who cautiously supports more recent in-the-head definitions of culture, points out:

[A] cognitive view of culture, while potentially allowing us to interpret the distribution and variability of knowledge and the situational co-construction of shared worlds, renders it difficult to capture the publicness and collectiveness of culture as symbol systems (Geertz, 1972). As Varenne (1984:291) has perceptively written in critically assessing "individualist" theories of culture, the collective tradition of a people is in an important sense external and transcendent in relation to any individual; such a cultural tradition ["] is *always already there*. It is in this sense that ideology, or culture, is an external social fact that is part of the environment of individuals. To the extent that it is part of the environment, it is something to which individuals will adapt and against which they may react. . . ["] (p. 372) [original emphasis]

In *The Interpretation of Cultures* (1973), Geertz gives an extended discussion of an alternative to conceptions of culture as in the head.

Culture, this acted document, is public, like a burlesqued wink or a mock sheep raid. Though ideational, it does not exist in someone's head; though unphysical, it is not an occult entity. . . . Once human behavior is seen as (most of the time; there *are* true twitches) symbolic action—action, which like phonation in speech, pigment in painting, line in writing, or sonance in music, signifies—the question as to whether culture is patterned conduct or a frame of mind, or even the two somehow mixed together, loses sense. The thing to ask about a burlesqued wink or a mock sheep raid is not what their ontological status is. It is the same as that of rocks on one hand and dreams on the other—they are things of this world. The thing to ask is what their import is: what it is, ridicule or challenge, irony or anger, snobbery or pride, that, in their occurrence and through their agency, is getting said. (p. 10)

It may be difficult for those raised in Western cultures, with its emphasis on individualism and with the recent hegemony of psychological explanations of behavior (especially in education, see McDermott & Hood, 1982), to conceive of human phenomena being located outside of the individual without defining that phenomena as mystical or ethereal. Nonetheless, it is in understanding definitions of culture as more than in-the-head phenomena that the potential exists for anthropological research on teaching the English language arts to provide an alternative to psychological and humanistic perspectives already extant.

ENGLISH ITSELF

English is the dominant language of instruction in many countries, including countries where English is not the dominant native language. English is both the language of schooling and a topic for extended study (grammar and literature). In areas where English is not the native language, teaching in English may be justified by educators noting that many scientific and technical books are written in English, or because English was (is) the language of much colonial education, and, despite national independence, in many cases English retains its hierarchical status.

In the United States, English is so much so the language of

education that when another language is used, that other language is viewed as only part of a transitional phase to English, and even still the use of another language may be controversial. Further, the dominance of English extends to the common-sense notion that the United States is a monolingual country (which is far from accurate, see Burger, 1973; Fergussen & Heath, 1981; Heath, 1981).

The official language of education is not any English but a specific English often referred to as Standard English.* Those who do not speak Standard English in school are often viewed as disadvantaged, less academically capable, or, more generously, needing to learn to code-switch into Standard English in order to be successful in the mainstream society. Whether there is or is not a Standard English, whether there is a single Standard English dialect or several varieties, whether middle-class whites do or do not actually speak Standard English, whether students who do not speak Standard English are or are not disadvantaged, less academically capable or need to learn to code-switch, and whether the differences between Standard English and other varieties of English are significant enough to make any real difference, these are less issues from an anthropological perspective than the meanings people give to Standard English and that they give meaning to the use of Standard English at all. As Saville-Troike (1982, p. 243) points out, "The choice of language for education is a major consideration in multilingual contexts, and reflects the power structure in the country, attitudes toward group identities, and educational philosophy and priorities." Yet, educators, researchers, and others, take for granted Standard English as the language for education and as a topic of study. Educational opportunities associated with using students' native languages and dialects (e.g., Elsasser & Irvine, 1985) or with multiple languages and dialects (e.g., Burger, 1973; Fishman, 1982) are rarely even conceived.

Perhaps as important as choosing English as the language of education, is the way that choice is enacted. African American and Hispanic students are often made to feel less academically capable and that their home, community, and culture are less valuable because they do not speak Standard English. By not speaking Standard English, some African American minority students may be at risk of being referred to special education or of being placed in less academically challenging situations (e.g., Collins, 1987; Labov, 1982; Smitherman, 1981). Trueba (1989) describes how the push for English language dominance in schools can lead to what he calls cultural trauma for some non-native English-speaking students, resulting in some cases in severe psychological disorders.

EDUCATION REDEFINED

Anthropologists often define education as cultural transmission (e.g., Gearing, 1973; Spindler, 1963), passing a culture from one generation to the next. Building on education as cultural transmission, Spindler & Spindler (1987, p. 3) define education as a "*calculated intervention* in the learning process." A major contribution of anthropologically based research has been to remind researchers and educators that calculated interventions do not only occur in school and that education within schools is connected to the broader society.

Studies of education in non-Western and less well-known societies provide important perspectives for understanding variation and possibility in education. While societies with or without formal schooling may explicitly teach and may teach abstract knowledge, Mead (1970) points out that a contrast can be made between conceptions of education as seeking to learn versus seeking to teach. The difference is not an issue of motivation, but rather of cultural organization and transmission. Firth (1936) describes the difference in his study of the Tikopia.

The cardinal points of education in a native society such as Tikopia are its continuity in both a temporal and a social sense, its position as an activity of kinsfolk, its practicality—not in the sense of being directed to economic ends, but as arising from actual situations in daily life—and its nondisciplinary character. A certain subordination to authority is required and is sometimes impressed by forcible and dramatic methods, but these are sporadic and the individual is a fairly free agent to come and go as he likes, to refuse to heed what is being taught him. All this is in direct contrast to a system of education for native children wherever it is carried out under European tutelage. Such consists usually of periodic instruction while segregation, intermitted by intervals of relaxation and rejoining of the normal village life, and imparted not by kinsfolk of the children but by strangers, often from another area, even when non-Europeans. This instruction is given not in connection with practical situations of life as they occur, but in accord with general principles, the utility of which is only vaguely perceived by the pupils. Moreover, it is disciplinary, the pupils are under some degree of direct restraint and may even suffer punishment for neglect of appointed tasks. (p. 134)

Study of education among the Tikopia and other non-European groups (following Firth's use of European) and cross-cultural comparison across European educational systems (e.g., Spindler & Spindler, 1987) and across contemporary Western and non-Western education systems (e.g., Duranti & Ochs, 1986; Elsmon & Hallett, 1989; Kalab, 1976; Leacock, 1976; Nwa-Chil, 1976; Wagner, Messick, & Spratt, 1986) reveal basic cultural meanings, assumptions, and agendas in both the group being studied and in our own educational systems (e.g., see Goody, 1968, 1987, on literacy, culture, and society in traditional and Western societies). By equating education with schooling, we assume limited possibility in role relationships, organization, the structure of knowledge, and the assignment of meaning to behavior. Further, we downgrade the importance of nonschool locations for learning (with the exception of settings that mimic schooling or prepare for schooling) despite anthropological studies showing the importance of such settings (e.g., Bloome, 1989; Heath, 1983; Taylor, 1983).

Socialization and Enculturation

Socialization refers to how and what a person learns (or needs to learn) in order to assume a role within society. Enculturation refers to the beliefs, values, and feelings as other as-

---

*The term Standard English is problematic because it suggests a standard by which other varieties of English and other languages are measured and compared. While such measurements and comparisons may occur, there is nothing inherent in Standard English that makes it a standard."

pects that accompany becoming a member of a cultural group. Given the holistic and broad ranging inquiry of anthropological study, socialization and enculturation are often used interchangeably. (In this chapter, socialization is used to refer to both socialization and enculturation.)

How socialization occurs continues to be an important research topic. Recent theoretical discussions tend to view socialization as a constructed, interactive process rather than deterministic (Mehan, 1980). Parents, teachers, and others seek to help children become members of their society (although not necessarily compliant members), and they take actions to do so based on their historical experiences, their understanding of how children learn, and the educational and school experiences of their cultural group. Children are not passive, they want to act on their world and understand it in ways compatible with how others see it (at least sufficiently compatible in order to get things done). Children, based on what parents, teachers, and others do, and on the results of their own actions, construct models of how the world (the world of their society) operates, of how they fit into the world, and of what is expected of them, what they can expect of themselves, and how they might be able to meet those expectations. Children are participants in constructing meaning and the outcomes of events in which they participate. Although research attention has primarily focused on children, socialization is a lifespan process. Throughout one's life, members of a cultural group act to conform and inform each other's public behavior (Schleffelin & Ochs, 1986a).

There are many levels at which socialization occurs. At a somewhat obvious level, for example, are issues of dress. But there are deeper levels, less accessible to conscious reflection and attention. For example, in Western culture, including the United States, individualism is an important ideology shaping many of our beliefs, feelings, activities, and understandings across a wide range of endeavors. Individualism is evident, among other places, in the dominant Western religions (e.g., individual salvation), governments (e.g., one person one vote), sports (e.g., the superstar), economies (e.g., free market), and education (e.g., individual instruction and achievement). Individualism is taken for granted, learned not as an explicit focus of a curriculum or an educational agenda but rather because it is deeply and broadly embedded in the organization and structure of events and institutions in which people and children participate on a daily basis.

With regard to teaching the English language arts, questions need to be asked about how people are socialized as students of the English language arts, what underlying hidden cultural ideologies are embedded in the teaching practices in the English language arts, and where socialization to classroom practice is located (e.g., in child rearing practices, in schooling, in peer play). For example, how does what happens in English language arts classes influence what students think language is? how it is used? how language is interpreted? where the authority for use and interpretation of language lies? what a narrative is and how it is constructed? How does what happens in English language arts classes define students as individuals? as a group? as members of a speech community? and which speech communities? as members or nonmembers of nonschool groups such as their native community? How does what happens in English language arts classes define and give interpretation to

those who are not there (e.g., students in other tracks and schools, students in other countries studying in other languages and literatures, people both older and younger)? How does what happens in English language arts classes structure the interpretation of relationships among students from various different communities? How does what happens in English language arts classes contribute to the socialization agendas of schooling and nonschool education, broadly considered? How does what happens in an English language arts class contribute to a system of meanings and actions that extends beyond the classroom? The questions above are but a small sample of the questions that need to be asked.

Also of recent concern to anthropologically based research is differentiation in how socialization occurs and its consequences within and across groups. Part of the recent agenda has been to understand that differentiation, especially with regard to gender issues (e.g., Pittman & Eisenhart, 1988), and racial and ethnic issues (e.g., Cazden & Hymes, 1972; Cook-Gumperz, Gumperz & Simons, 1981; Gilmore, 1987; Hart, 1982; Hymes, 1981; Wilcox, 1982). Differentiation in socialization has been linked to broader social and economic forces. For example, Ogbu (1974, 1979) has suggested that job ceilings, which limit what employment opportunities minority students will be able to get, affect the education of minority students.

Cultural Reproduction

Differentiation in socialization is part of the way in which cultural reproduction occurs. The structure and organization of a society is reproduced by differentiating opportunities for learning and by differentiating language experiences. As Hymes (1980) states about language socialization:

Depending on gender, family, community, and religion, children are raised in terms of one configuration of the use and meaning of language rather than another. The particular configuration will affect the opportunities and access they have for other uses and meanings of language. Depending on social, economic, political factors, they will come to be able to use and experience language in some ways and not in others. Often, the result will be less than justice or vision would require. (p. vi)

There is considerable debate about whether social and cultural differences in language socialization inherently affect educational opportunities both in and outside of school or whether such differences are inappropriately used as justifications for denying access to minority students. Bernstein (1981), among others, has suggested that the hierarchial class structure of society tends to produce language codes which respectively, restrict and enable working-class and middle-class children's use of language for academic learning. However, studies primarily in the United States and by American scholars outside the United States have shown the sophistication of language use in non-middle class and non-Western groups (e.g., Labov, 1972; Schieffelin & Ochs, 1986b; Wells, 1986) and how subtle, inappropriate gatekeeping processes deny access to minority language users (e.g., Cook-Gumperz, Gumperz & Simons, 1981; Gumperz, 1982a, 1982b).

It is important to note that cultural differences are not the same thing as differentiation. Differentiation is part of the calculated intervention in learning. It is differentiation (whether through schooling practices, familial practices, or the structure of society), not cultural differences, that raise questions of equality and justice.

Differentiation can involve the explicit curriculum or how a curriculum is implemented. For example, two classes with the same grammar curriculum may still have different experiences in learning grammar. In one classroom, the teacher may focus on correct grammatical performance, while in another classroom students explore relationships between grammar and meaning. However, differentiation can occur even when students are given the same experiences. Given differences in the social and cultural context, the same activity in a working class school and a bourgeois school will not have the same meaning. Even within the same school and same classroom, similar activities will have different meanings dependent on the social and cultural context in which they are done.

Over time, differentiation may lead to distinct communities. For example, Borko and Eisenhart (1989) show how reading groups within the same classroom could be considered different communities, with different ways of interacting with each other, with the teacher, and with print (similar findings are reported by Eder, 1982, 1986). Movement from one group to another was not only a matter of demonstrating appropriate ability with print but more so congruence with the culture of the other reading group.

From an anthropological perspective, there are at least two key issues in the study of cultural reproduction: (a) What is being reproduced and how? and (b) What is changing and how? In addition, there may be reproduction at one level but not at another. For example, reader-response approaches to literature (e.g., Rosenblatt, 1978) require a change in the form and structure of instruction in many classrooms. Students' responses to text are viewed as integral rather than right or wrong so teacher questioning and teacher evaluation are transformed. However, at a deeper level, such changes maintain culturally based definitions of reading and writing activity as individual activity with individual accountability.

It is also important to explore how change may be stability. That is, given an ever-changing world, one can ask how things might change in cultural form and structure in order for the culture to remain substantively the same. For example, changes in definitions of writing as process instead of product affected how writing was taught and evaluated. Writing could not be evaluated as formerly done on the basis of grammar, spelling, and form. Indeed, there were questions about whether writing, as process, could be evaluated at all. Various types of holistic writing assessments were created. In holistic assessment, especially that done in large-scale assessment, evaluators may read for content, importance, and communicability, but the function of writing for evaluation remains constant. The writing is still primarily done for individual assessment; content, importance, and communicability are redefined as assessment. In effect, the change in assessment maintains individual accountability, individual comparison, and definitions of writing instruction as progressive individual skill accumulation. The change in evaluation maintained the former social relationships of students, teachers, and evaluators with regard to authority for what determines what counts as good writing and how it should be done.

LANGUAGE, LITERACY, AND LITERATURE REDEFINED

Among the questions of concern to many English educators are: Should grammar be taught? Should phonics or comprehension be emphasized? Should form or process in writing be emphasized? What works of literature should be taught? These questions are primarily questions of instructional efficiency and assume underlying definitions of language, literacy, and literature. Language is a communicative and referential system, literacy is a written representation of language, and literature is a body of written works. Acquiring language, literacy, and literature is, respectively, the development of a linguistic competence, decontextualized modes of language use (reflecting decontextualized modes of thinking), and knowledge of a common (canonized) set of literary works understood according to common (standard) literary dimensions (e.g., plot, theme, character, genre).

From an anthropological perspective, language, literacy, and literature are cultural processes. They are cultural processes because their nature reflects the broader culture in which they are embedded and because they do cultural work (e.g., socialization, assign meaning to behavior and experience). Rather than asking about linguistic competence, questions are asked about communicative competence, what constitutes appropriate language use in various situations by various language users for various purposes. Rather than asking about decontextualized modes of language, questions are asked about the meaning of the use of written language, how that use is distributed, for what purposes written language is used, what modes of thinking are associated with written language in what situations, and how language is contextualized (rather than whether it is or is not). Rather than asking about the cannon of literary works and literary dimensions, questions are asked about the nature, use and meaning of narrative: What is the variation in how narratives are structured and defined? In what situations are what kinds of narratives used? What is the meaning of their use? How are different narratives related? Who gets to tell what narratives? How? What roles do narratives play in the cultural life of the community?

Anthropologically based definitions of language, literacy, and literature provide alternatives to questions of instructional efficiency. To ask about instructional efficiency requires assumption of *an* ideal that can be attained or approached. From an anthropological perspective, ideals are cultural constructions, not givens.

Language as Communicative Competence

According to Cazden (1972), the first presentation of Hymes' paper "On Communicative Competence" was in June 1966, at Yeshiva University. In that paper, Hymes laid out three assumptions underlying a definition of language as communicative competence.

1. Each social relationship entails the selection and/or creation of communicative means considered specific and appropriate to it by its participants.
2. The organization of communicative means in terms of social relationships confers a structure that is not disclosed in the analysis of the means separately.
3. The communicative means available in a relationship conditions its nature and outcome. (Hymes, 1971, p. 60)

Hymes ties communicative competence directly to issues of equality in education, particularly for minority children. Rather than describing their language as deficient, their language (and that of other children) would be described as a consequence of the setting, function, means of language behavior, and of social and power relationships across settings. In terms of communicative competence, characterizations of minority children's language in classrooms as inadequate, lazy, underdeveloped, nonverbal, incoherent, or even lacking language are taken as indicators of the power, social, and cultural relationships between classroom settings and the settings in which minority children first learn and use language.

From the perspective of communicative competence, questions are asked about how children learn to use language appropriately in the classroom to interact with teachers and peers and to engage in academic tasks (e.g., Bloome, 1987; DeStefano, Pepinsky, & Sanders, 1982; Erickson, 1982a; Green & Wallat, 1981; Mehan, 1979; Michaels, 1981; Wallat & Green, 1979). Questions are also asked about the language made available in classrooms, and how that language is differentiated across schools, classrooms, and groups (e.g., Borko & Eisenhart, 1989; Collins, 1986; Eder, 1982, 1986). Questions are asked about what differences emerge between minority students and standards for language use in classrooms, what meaning and social identities are assigned to those differences, and how those differences are treated (e.g., Heath, 1982a, 1983). Questions are asked about the relationship of language in and out of classrooms (e.g., Gilmore, 1986; Heath, 1983; Michaels & Collins, 1984; Miller, Nemoianu, & DeJong, 1986; Miller, 1986; Taylor, 1983; Zinsser, 1986). Questions are also asked about how the social and cultural structure of schooling influences what and how language is used and how the language used in school reproduces (or reconstructs) the social and cultural organization of society (e.g., Cook-Gumperz, 1986; Cook-Gumperz & Gumperz, 1982).

The questions above erase the boundaries between language as a topic of study (e.g., grammar instruction) and language as a means of social engagement, socialization, and cultural transmission. From the perspective of communicative competence, it is a whole. Both in school and out, students interact with others through language, and they use language to define situations, themselves, boundaries between situations and settings, and the social, power, cultural and cross-cultural relationships among settings. Structuring teacher-student interaction to promote appropriate classroom language (e.g., responding with a complete sentence, speaking one at a time,

raising hands to get turns, speaking in Standard English) and formalizing language study as grammar instruction are both part of an enactment of a consistent cultural agenda of socialization to language and through language.

Literacy as Cultural Practice

Anthropologically based research has also been concerned with the role of schooling in defining literacy. For example, Scribner and Cole (1981) argue that the cognitive consequences often associated with becoming literate (e.g., Goody, 1968, 1987) are much more so a consequence of schooling. Written language practices and learning outside of and distinct from classroom education do not tend to have the same cognitive consequences. For anthropologists, the questions raised by Scribner and Cole (1981), Goody (1968, 1987), among others, are part of a broader set of questions about the role of literacy in socialization and cultural reproduction (Cook-Gumperz, 1986).

Literacy is often treated as a social and cultural identity, especially if one is not literate (Smith, 1987a). For example, Scollon and Scollon (1979, 1981, 1984) show that how one interprets written language reflects broader cultural themes. It is not a matter of the use of culturally based knowledge for interpretation, but rather, what is considered to be culturally appropriate norms for how to use a text to construct meaning. Scollon and Scollon suggest that Western cultures restrict interpretation to the text and standardized interpretations, whereas other cultures may vary in the degree to which they do so. Reder and Green (1983) make a similar point. In their study of an Alaskan fishing village, they describe how literacy, as a set of differing social practices across various community domains, identifies insiders and outsiders. The nature of the literacy practices and consequently who gets defined as an insider or an outsider are historically based, but evolve and change, simultaneously changing people's identities as insiders or outsiders. Literacy, then, can be viewed as a specific set of culturally based discourse practices.

With regard to social configuration, literacy has primarily been defined as the interaction between a solitary text and a solitary reader or writer. As Shuman (1983) states:

Notions of standardized and literary texts imply a model of solitary readers and writers. The model, as conceived by reader-response theorists and some educational literacy scholars, insists upon the individuality both of authors and of an "ideal reader." The study of reading and writing in everyday life requires an alternative model which moves beyond studies of the distances between reader and writer as imposed by printed texts and gives attention to conventions for interpreting written texts created in collaborative reading and writing interaction. (p. 69)

In addition to viewing literacy as involving an individual reader or writer alone with a text, literacy is often equated with (1) conscious learning (often through schooling), (2) modality-specific processes of production, (3) detachment of writer from his or her audience, (4) conscious planning and systematic organization, and (5) permanency of text and accurate reproduction of knowledge, (6) elevation of text through depersonalization and decontextualization, and (7) lexical elaboration and syntactico-semantic complexity (Akinnaso, 1982). These features are not peculiar to written language (Tannen, 1982), for example, in so-called nonliterate (nontechnologically advanced) societies ritual communication is different from everyday talk in much the same way that written language differs from ordinary conversation in literate societies (Akinnaso, 1982).

Given the diverse cultural practices of literacy, often obfuscated by narrow academic and school definitions, Szwed (1981) outlines an agenda for the anthropological study of literacy by avoiding too close a definition of literacy, separating literacy from instruction, and by embracing the diverse ways literacy is practiced (also see Basso, 1974, on the ethnography of writing).

> I propose that we step back from the question of instruction, back to an even more basic "basic," the *social meaning* of literacy: that is, the roles these abilities play in social life; the varieties of reading and writing available for choice; the contexts for their performance; and the manner in which they are interpreted and tested, not by experts, but by ordinary people in ordinary activities. (p. 14) [original emphasis]

Similar issues with definition of a literacy curriculum are raised by Florio and Clark's (1982) study of writing in an elementary classroom. They show that the writing curriculum of the classroom was embedded in the various functions performed by writing. Writing to participate in community, writing to know oneself, writing to occupy free time, and writing to demonstrate academic competence constituted an informal writing curriculum. Beyond that one classroom, the implication is that the social functions writing performs constitute the actual writing curriculum (as opposed to what's stated in formal curricular documents). Varenne and McDermott (1986) push further the issue of the cultural context of literacy curriculum, instruction and evaluation.

> Simply to ask "why Sheila can read" does not force us to wonder what difference it makes that *she* can read (while Joe cannot), or how it became enough of a cultural focus that someone officially decided that she *can* read (while Joe can *not*).... To focus on Sheila (or Joe) obscures the social forces that organize her reading into an institutional concern and a symbolically recognizable fact. (p. 190)

By defining literacy as social and cultural practices with social and cultural consequences, anthropologically based research raises questions about the validity of definitions of literacy as a psychological process, about definitions of literacy curriculum as skill acquisition, and about the agenda of schooling as promotion of universal literacy. Shuman (1986) summarizes the issue well: "The idea of literacy begins with texts, but in turning to the question of contexts, literacy undermines itself, and the privileged status of writing becomes a question of who is entitled to grant the privilege" (p. 200).

Literature as Storytelling

One of the decisions English faculty usually make, whether at a college, high school, or elementary school, is what litera-

ture to include as part of the curriculum. In elementary schools, questions may be asked about the quality of the literature versus its usefulness in promoting reading achievement. (While the choice between quality literature and literature which promotes reading achievement is an artificial choice, the rewriting of children's literature in basal readers and the use of stories chosen primarily for their adherence to readability formulas, use of rebus symbols and initial teaching alphabets or limited vocabulary, and so on, may suggest to some educators that instructional needs and quality literature are mutually exclusive choices). At secondary and college levels, questions may be asked about classics and the traditional cannon versus contemporary and relevant literature. The questions being asked and the supporting arguments given can be viewed as a debate over what counts as the literary cultural capital of the society and what value or priority is given to the literary domain compared with other domains (e.g., skill development).

However, beyond the choice of stories and books are questions about the location of literature and who gets to decide what is and what is not literature. In what has become a classic article, Bohannon (1971) describes her attempt to tell *Hamlet* to the Tiv in West Africa. She was unable to tell them the story as she wanted because their understanding of stories, what could and could not be in a story, how a story would be organized, and the relationship of story to the real world, differed greatly from Bohannon's. They continually interrupted her and, at the end of her telling concluded, "[Y]ou must tell us some more stories of your country. We, who are elders, will instruct you in their true meaning, so that when you return to your own land your elders will see that you have not been sitting in the bush, but among those who know things and who have taught you wisdom" (p. 25). Since Bohannon (1971) lacked authority among the Tiv to decide what is and what is not literature and what the nature of literature should be, at that time and place, she had to yield to their definition of literature.

From an anthropological perspective, the issue is not merely what books or stories are chosen as literature, but who gets to do the choosing, as well as how, when and under what circumstances and what meanings are assigned to those choices. (There are, of course, many educators also concerned about who gets to choose, and they arrive at that concern in many different ways; e.g., a concern with democratic rights in the classroom, a concern for motivating students by allowing them to choose.)

Underlying definitions of literature is the organization of story as narrative and of narrative performance. Children, through their interaction with parents, teachers, peers, and others, learn culturally specific ways of organizing, understanding, and performing narratives (e.g., Bauman, 1982; Cook-Gumperz & Green, 1984; Heath & Branscombe, 1986). When diverse cultural groups, each with their own definition of literature, come into contact in educational settings, there is potential for conflict. The definitions held by less powerful groups are liable to be viewed as alien or not valid and given token or no visibility. That is, less powerful groups may not be entitled to tell their stories, to have their stories be part of the literature or told in their way. As a result, the historical and everyday experiences of such groups and the experience of their ways of storytelling are not validated through inclusion in a school literature. What's at stake with regard to entitlement is not only the story, but who is entitled to be a storyteller, a listener, and a repeater of the story (Shuman, 1986). Part of the agenda of anthropologically based research on literature is description of the nature of entitlement within and across groups, and what happens to entitlement when there is contact among diverse cultural groups.

TEACHING/SCHOOLING

Teaching in schools consists of more than managing classrooms, providing academic tasks, and evaluating students. These activities, and others, must be done in a way that looks like school. That is, educators, parents, children, and others, have implicit cultural models for what school looks like and when teaching does not look like school, questions may be raised about whether the activities can be called education. In brief, teaching in large part must be about doing school.

By "The School" we mean a cultural system of political consequences, that is, a set of historically derived, comparatively arbitrary, interactionally constraining, discourse conventions used to deal with experience. These conventions can take the forms of traditional sayings, typical conversations, more or less ritualized performances, legitimately constructed consequences, and so on. (Varenne & McDermott, 1986, p. 190)

Among the discourse conventions that characterize teaching and schooling are teacher initiation, student response, and teacher evaluation patterns (hereafter I-R-E sequences) of classroom interaction (e.g., Mehan, 1979). I-R-E sequences may have multiple functions from providing feedback to students to managing errant behavior. I-R-E sequences provide the teacher with authority for determining what knowledge is right and important to know and what forms of discourse need to be used to express having knowledge. Most importantly, I-R-E sequences identify the setting as doing school.

The asking of known information questions, such as occurs in I-R-E sequences, is not compatible with the ways of using language children learn in some cultures (e.g., Boggs, 1972; Dumont, 1972; Heath, 1982b; Phillips, 1972, 1983; Smith, 1987b). To ask a question to which one already knows the answer makes no sense to many children because they are unfamiliar with the meaning, sense, routine, function, or public display of doing so. For other children, the asking of known information questions is compatible with the ways of using language that they have learned at home. The result is that some children find doing school an extention of the ways of using language at home while other children find doing school alien and at best a cross-cultural adventure.

Cultural differences in how language is used at home and in teaching includes how participation in events is structured. Erickson and Mohatt (1982), Phillips (1972, 1983), Shultz, Florio and Erickson (1982), among others, have shown that the participation structures of classroom events may, at times, confuse or distance some minority children because of subtle but powerful differences with the participation structures of analogous events in home settings. Au (1980) has suggested that when participation structures in classroom events are similar to the participation structures of events in home settings, then children's participation will increase.

In my work, I have identified a series of discourse practices or strategies called procedural display, which are also associated with doing school (Bloome, 1987; Bloome, Puro & Theodorou, in press). Procedural display can be defined as the display by teachers and students to each other of a set of interactional procedures that count as getting through the lesson. Displaying getting through the lesson is not the same thing as engagement in the substantive academic content or intent of the lesson.

Among other aspects of the cultural context of doing school are the construction of us and them distinctions between teachers and parents (Anderson-Levitt, 1987) and the evaluation of individual children as successes and failures (e.g., McDermott, 1977, Taylor, 1988). These aspects of doing school are not inherent in schooling but rather are culturally and socially determined ways of organizing and assigning meaning and identity.

The importance of phenomena like I-R-E sequences, crosscultural differences in participation structures, procedural display, creation of us and them distinctions, and evaluation of individual children as successes and failures, are that they, among other discourse conventions associated with doing school, constitute a context that gives meaning to the practices and events involved in teaching the English language arts.

ENDING COMMENTS

The general mission of anthropology in part can be said to be to help overcome the limitations of the categories and understandings of human life that are part of a single civilization's partial view. (Hymes, 1980, p. 92)

Although there have been calls for anthropologically based research on teaching the English language arts (e.g., Freeman, Samuelson, & Sanders, 1986; Kanter, Kirby, & Goetz, 1981), with the exception of a relatively small number of studies, anthropologically based research on teaching the English language arts remains more promise than practice, more shadow than substance. Anthropologically based research calls for redefinition of the fundamental concepts that define teaching the English language arts. The definitions held of education, language, learning, literacy, literature, teaching, and schooling, among others, are questioned and reformulated.

In this chapter, I have discussed some broad directions for anthropological redefinition of education, language, literacy, literature, teaching, and schooling. A great deal more discussion is needed of how basic concepts in the teaching of the English language arts get redefined from various anthropological perspectives. I have also discussed how the definitions we hold affect the education of minority students. The promise and substance of anthropologically based research on teaching the English language arts lie, in large part, in the possibilities and vision it yields for social equality in and through educational settings.

References

Akinnaso, F. N. (1982). The literate writes and the nonliterate chants: Written language and ritual communication in sociolinguistic perspective. In W. Frawley (Ed.), *Linguistics and literacy* (pp. 7–36). New York: Plenum Press.

Anderson-Levitt, K. (1987). *School and home as 'us' and 'them' in urban France.* Paper presented at annual meeting of the American Anthropological Association, Chicago.

Au, K. (1980). Participation structures in a reading lesson with Hawaiian children: Analysis of a culturally appropriate instructional event. *Anthropology and Education Quarterly, 9*(2), 91–115.

Basso, K. H. (1974). The ethnography of writing. In R. Bauman & J. Sherzer (Eds.) *Explorations in the ethnography of speaking* (pp. 425–432) New York: Cambridge University Press.

Bauman, R. (1982). Ethnography of children's folklore. In P. Gilmore & A. Glatthorn (Eds.) *Children in and out of school* (pp. 172–186). Washington, D.C.: Center for Applied Linguistics.

Bernstein, B. (1981). Codes, modalities, and the process of cultural reproduction: A model. *Language in Society, 10*(3), 327–364.

Bloome, D. (1987). Reading and writing as a social process in a middle school classroom. In D. Bloome (Ed.), *Literacy and schooling* (pp. 123–149). Norwood, NJ: Ablex.

Bloome, D. (1989). Locating reading and writing. In C. Emihovich (Ed.), *Locating learning across the curriculum: Ethnographic perspectives.* Norwood, NJ: Ablex.

Bloome, D., Puro, P., & Theodorou, E. (1989). Procedural display and classroom lessons. *Curriculum Inquiry, 19* (3), pp. 265–292.

Boggs, S. T. (1972). The meaning of questions and narratives to Hawaiian children. In C. Cazden, V. John, & D. Hymes (Eds.), *Functions of language in the classroom* (pp. 299–330). New York: Teachers College Press.

Bohannon, L. (1971). Shakespeare in the bush. In J. P. Spradley & D. W. McCurdy (Eds.), *Conformity and conflict: Readings in cultural anthropology* (pp. 13–23). Boston: Little, Brown.

Borko, H. & Eisenhart, M. (1989). Reading ability groups as literacy communities. In D. Bloome (Ed.), *Classroom and literacy.* Norwood, NJ: Ablex.

Burger, H. (1973). Cultural pluralism and the schools. In C. S. Brembeck & W. H. Hill (Eds.), *Cultural challenges to education: The influence of cultural factors in school learning* (pp. 5–18). Lexington, MA: Lexington Books.

Cazden, C. (1972). Preface. In C. Cazden, V. John, & D. Hymes (Eds.), *Functions of language in the classroom* (pp. vii–ix). New York: Teachers College Press.

Cazden, C., John, V., & Hymes, D. (Eds.). (1972). *Functions of language in the classroom.* New York: Teachers College Press.

Chilcott, J. H. (1987). Where are you coming from and where are you going? The reporting of ethnographic research. *American Educational Research Journal, 24*(2), 199–218.

Cole, J. B. (1982). Toward a new anthropology: Introduction. In J. B. Cole (Ed.), *Anthropology for the eighties: Introductory readings* (pp. 449–455). New York: The Free Press.

Collins, J. (1986). Differential instruction in reading groups. In J. Cook-Gumperz (Ed.), *The social construction of literacy* (pp. 117–137). NY: Cambridge University Press.

Collins, J. (1987). Using cohesion analysis to understand access to knowledge. In D. Bloome (Ed.), *Literacy and schooling* (pp. 70–97). Norwood, NJ: Ablex.

Cook-Gumperz, J. (1986). Introduction: the social construction of literacy. In J. Cook-Gumperz (Ed.), *The social construction of literacy* (pp. 1–15). NY: Cambridge University Press.

Cook-Gumperz, J., & Green, J. (1984). A sense of story: Influences on children's storytelling ability. In D. Tannen (Ed.), *Coherence in spoken and written discourse* (pp. 201–218). Norwood, NJ: Ablex.

Cook-Gumperz, J., & Gumperz, J., & Simons, H. (1981). *School-home ethnography project.* Final report to the U.S. Dept. of Education. Washington, D.C.: U.S. Dept. of Education.

DeStefano, J., Pepinsky, H., & Sanders, T. (1982). Discourse rules for literacy learning in a classroom. In L. Wilkinson (Ed.), *Communicating in the classroom* (pp. 101–130). New York: Academic Press.

Drake, S. C. (1978). Reflections on anthropology and the Black experience. *Anthropology and Education Quarterly, 9*(2), 85–109.

Dumont, Jr., R. V. (1972). Learning English and how to be silent: Studies in Sioux and Cherokee classrooms. In C. Cazden, V. John, & D. Hymes (Eds.), *Functions of language in the classroom* (pp. 344–369). New York: Teachers College Press.

Duranti, A., & Ochs, E. (1986). Literacy instruction in a Samoan village. In B. Schieffelin & P. Gilmore (Eds.), *The acquisition of literacy: Ethnographic perspectives* (pp. 213–232). Norwood, NJ: Ablex.

Eder, D. (1982). Differences in communicative styles across ability groups. In L. Wilkinson (Ed.), *Communicating in the classroom* (pp. 245–264). New York: Academic Press.

Eder, D. (1986). Organizational constraints on reading group mobility. In J. Cook-Gumperz (Ed.), *The social construction of literacy* (pp. 138–155). Cambridge, England: Cambridge University Press.

Eismon, T., & Hallett, M. (1989). The acquisition of literacy in religious and secular schools. In D. Bloome (Ed.), *Classrooms and literacy* (pp. 264–287). Norwood, NJ: Ablex.

Elsasser, N., & Irvine, P. (1985). English and Creole: The dialectics of choice in a college writing program. *Harvard Educational Review, 55*(4), 399–415.

Emihovich, C. (Ed.). (1989). *Locating learning across the curriculum: Ethnographic perspectives.* Norwood, NJ: Ablex.

Erickson, F. (1982a). Classroom discourse as improvisation: Relationships between academic task structure and social participation structure in lessons. In L. Wilkinson (Ed.), *Communicating in the classroom* (pp. 153–182). New York: Academic Press.

Erickson, F. (1982b). Taught cognitive learning in its immediate environments: A neglected topic in the anthropology of education. *Anthropology and Education Quarterly, 13*(2), 148–180.

Erickson, F., & Mohatt, G. (1982). Cultural organization of participation structures in two classrooms of Indian students. In G. Spindler (Ed.), *Doing the ethnography of schooling: Educational anthropology in action.* New York: Holt, Rinehart, & Winston, pp. 132–174.

Fergussen, C. A., & Heath, S. B. (Eds.). (1981). *Language in the USA.* Cambridge, England: Cambridge University Press.

Firth, R. (1936). *We, the Tikopia: A sociological study of kinship in primitive Polynesia.* Boston: Beacon Press.

Fishman, J. (1982). Whorfism of the third kind: Ethnolinguistic diversity as a worldwide societal asset. *Language in Society, 11*(1), 1–14.

Florio, S., & Clark, C. (1982). The functions of writing in an elementary classroom. *Research in the Teaching of English, 16*(2), 115–130.

Frake, C. O. (1969). The ethnographic study of cognitive systems. In S. Tyler (Ed.), *Cognitive anthropology* (pp. 28–40). New York: Holt, Rinehart and Winston.

Freeman, E. B., Samuelson, J., & Sanders, T. (1986). Writing instruction: New insights from ethnographic research. *Journal of Research and Development in Education 19*(2), 10–15.

Gearing, F. O. (1984; 1973). Toward a general theory of cultural transmission. *Anthropology and Education Quarterly, 15*(1), 29–37.

Geertz, C. (1972). Deep play: Notes on the Balinese cockfight. *Daedalus,* 101:1–37. (Reprinted in C. Geertz (1973). *The interpretation of cultures.* New York: Basic Books).

Geertz, C. (1973). *The interpretation of cultures.* New York: Basic Books.

Geertz, C. (1983). *Local knowledge: Further essays in interpretive anthropology.* New York: Basic Books.

Gilmore, P. (1986). Sub-rosa literacy: Peers, play, and ownership in literacy acquisition. In B. Schieffelin & P. Gilmore (Eds.), *The acquisition of literacy: Ethnographic perspectives* (pp. 155–170). Norwood, NJ: Ablex.

Gilmore, P. (1987). Sulking, stepping and tracking: The effects of attitude assessment on access to literacy. In D. Bloome (Ed.), *Literacy and schooling* (pp. 98–120). Norwood, NJ: Ablex.

Goodenough, W. H. (1970). *Description and comparison in cultural anthropology.* New York: Cambridge University Press.

Goodenough, W. H. (1981). *Culture, language, and society.* Menlo Park, CA: Benjamin/Cummings.

Goody, J. (Ed.) (1968). *Literacy in traditional societies.* Cambridge, England: Cambridge University Press.

Goody, J. (1987). *The interface between the written and the oral.* Cambridge, England: Cambridge University Press.

Green, J., & Wallat, C. (1981). Mapping instructional conversations—a sociolinguistic ethnography. In J. Green & C. Wallat (Eds.), *Ethnography and language in educational settings* Norwood, NJ: Ablex. pp. 161–205.

Gumperz, J. J. (1982a). *Discourse strategies.* London: Cambridge University Press.

Gumperz, J. J. (Eds.). (1982b). *Language and social identity.* London: Cambridge University Press.

Gumperz, J. J., & Hymes, D. (Eds.) (1972). *Directions in sociolinguistics: The ethnography of communication.* New York: Holt, Rinehart & Winston.

Hammersley, M., & Atkinson, P. (1983). *Ethnography: Principles in practice.* London: Tavistock.

Harrington, C. (1978). Psychological anthropology and education: a delineation of a field of injury. In *Anthropology and education* (pp. 74–356). (No place of publishing given): National Academy of Education.

Hart, S. (1982). Analyzing the social organization for reading in one elementary school. In G. Spindler (Ed.), *Doing the ethnography of schooling: Educational anthropology in action.* New York: Holt, Rinehart & Winston, pp. 410–439.

Heath, S. B., & Branscombe, A. (1986). The book as narrative prop in langue acquisition. In B. B. Schieffelin & P. Gilmore (Eds.), *The acquisition of literacy: Ethnographic perspectives* (pp. 16–34). Norwood, NJ: Ablex.

Heath, S. (1981). English in our language heritage. In C. Ferguson & S. Heath (Eds.), *Language in the USA* (pp. 6–20). New York: Cambridge University Press.

Heath, S. (1982a). Questioning at home and at school: A comparative study. In G. Spindler (Ed.), *Doing the ethnography of schooling: Educational anthropology in action.* New York: Holt, Rinehart & Winston, pp. 102–131.

Heath, S. (1982b). What no bedtime story means: Narrative skills at home and school. *Language in Society, 11,* 49–76.

Heath, S. (1983). *Ways with words: Language, life, and work in communities and classrooms.* New York: Cambridge University Press.

Hymes, D. (1971). On linguistic theory, communicative competence, and the education of disadvantaged children. In M. L. Wax, S. Diamond, & F. O. Gearing (Eds.), *Anthropological perspectives on education* (pp. 51–66). New York: Basic Books.

Hymes, D. (1974). *Foundations in sociolinguistics: An ethnographic approach.* Philadelphia: University of Pennsylvania Press.

Hymes, D. (1980). *Language in education: Ethnolinguistic essays.* Washington, D.C.: Center for Applied Linguistics.

Hymes, D. (Project Director). (1981). *Ethnographic monitoring of children acquisition of reading/language arts skills in and out of the classroom.* Final report submitted to the National Institute of Education, Washington, D.C.

Jacob, E., & Jordan, C. (Eds.) (1987). *Explaining the school performance of minority students.* A theme issue of *Anthropology and Education Quarterly, 18*(4).

Jones, D. J. (1982). Towards a native anthropology. In J. B. Cole (Ed.), *Anthropology for the eighties: Introductory readings* (pp. 471–482). New York: The Free Press.

Kalab, M. (1976). Monastic education, social mobility, and village structure in Cambodia. In C. J. Calhoun & F. A. J. Ianni (Eds.), *The anthropological study of education* (pp. 61–74). The Hague: Mouton.

Kanter, K. J., Kirby, D. R., & Goetz, J. P. (1981). Research in context: Ethnographic studies in English education. *Research in the Teaching of English, 15*(4), 293–309.

Keesing, R. M. (1987). Models, "folk" and "cultural": Paradigms regained? In D. Holland & N. Quinn (Eds.), *Cultural models in language and thought* (pp. 369–393). New York: Cambridge University Press.

Labov, W. (1972). *Language in the inner city: Studies in the Black English vernacular.* Philadelphia: University of Pennsylvania Press.

Labov, W. (1982). Objectivity and commitment in linguistic science: The case of the Black English trial in Ann Arbor. *Language in society, 11*(2), 165–202.

Leacock, E. B. (1976). Education in Africa: Myths of "modernization." In C. J. Calhoun & F. A. J. Ianni (Eds.), *The anthropological study of education* (pp. 240–250). The Hague: Mouton.

Levi-Strauss, C. (1963). *Structural anthropology.* New York: Basic Books.

Malinowski, B. (1922). *Argonauts of the western Pacific.* London: Routledge.

McDermott, R. P. (1977). Social relations as contexts for learning in school. *Harvard Educational Review, 47*(2), 198–213.

McDermott, R. P., & Hood, L. (1982). Institutionalized psychology and the ethnography of schooling. In P. Gilmore & A. Glatthorn (Eds.), *Children in and out of school* (pp. 232–249). Washington, D.C.: Center for Applied Linguistics.

Mead, M. (1970). Our education emphases in primitive perspective. In J. Middleton (Ed.), *From child to adult* (pp. 1–13). Garden City, NY: The Natural History Press.

Mehan, H. (1979). *Learning lessons: Social organization in the classroom.* Cambridge, MA: Harvard University Press.

Mehan, H. (1980). The competent student. *Anthropology and Education Quarterly, 11*(3), 131–152.

Michaels, S. (1981). "Sharing time": Children's narrative styles and differential access to literacy. *Language in Society, 10*(3), 423–443.

Michaels, S., & Collins, J. (1984). Oral discourse styles: Classroom interaction and the acquisition of literacy. In D. Tannen (Ed.), *Coherence in spoken and written discourse* (pp. 219–244). Norwood, NJ: Ablex.

Miller, P. (1986). Teasing as language socialization and verbal play in a white working-class community. In B. Schieffelin & E. Ochs (Eds.), *Language socialization across cultures* (pp. 199–212). Cambridge, England: Cambridge University Press.

Miller, P., Nemoianu, A., & DeJong, J. (1986). Early reading at home: Its practice and meanings in a working class community. In B. Schieffelin & P. Gilmore (Eds.), *The acquisition of literacy: Ethnographic perspectives* (pp. 3–15). Norwood, NJ: Ablex.

Nader, L. (1982). Up the anthropologist—perspectives from studying up. In J. B. Cole (Ed.), *Anthropology for the eighties: Introductory readings* (pp. 456–470). New York: The Free Press.

Nwa-Chil, C. C. (1976). Resistance to early Western education in eastern Nigeria. In C. J. Calhoun & F. A. J. Ianni (Eds.), *The anthropological study of education* (pp. 43–60). The Hague: Mouton.

Ogbu, J. (1974). *The next generation.* New York: Academic Press.

Ogbu, J. (1979). *Minority education and caste.* New York: Academic Press.

Peacock, J. L. (1986). *The anthropological lens: Harsh light, soft focus.* New York: Cambridge University Press.

Phillips, S. U. (1972). Participant structures and communicative competence: Warm Springs children in community and classroom. In C. Cazden, V. John, & D. Hymes (Eds.), *Functions of language in the classroom* (pp. 370–394). New York: Teachers College Press.

Phillips, S. U. (1983). *The invisible culture: Communication in classroom and community on the Warm Springs Indian Reservation.* New York: Longman.

Pittman, M. A., & Eisenhart, M. (Eds.), (1988). *Women, culture and education.* A special issue of *Anthropology and Education Quarterly, 19*(2), 67–196.

Quinn, N., & Holland, D. (1987). Culture and cognition. In D. Holland & N. Quinn (Eds.), *Cultural models in language and thought* (pp. 3–40). New York: Cambridge University Press.

Reder, S., & Green, K. R. (1983). Contrasting patterns of literacy in an Alaska fishing village. *International Journal of the Sociology of Language, 42,* 9–39.

Rosenblatt, L. M. (1978). *The reader, the text, the poem: The transactional theory of the literary work.* Carbondale, IL: Southern Illinois University Press.

Saville-Troike, M. (1982). *The ethnography of communication: An introduction.* New York: Basil Blackwell.

Schieffelin, B., & Ochs, E. (1986a). Language socialization. *Annual Review of Anthropology, 15,* 163–191.

Schieffelin, B., & Ochs, E. (1986b). *Language socialization across cultures.* Cambridge, England: Cambridge University Press.

Scollon, R., & Scollon, S. (1979). *Literacy as interethnic communication: An Athabaskan case.* Austin, TX: Southwest Educational Development Laboratory.

Scollon, R., & Scollon, S. (1981). *Narrative, literacy, and face in interethnic communication.* Norwood, NJ: Ablex.

Scollon, R., & Scollon, S. (1984). Cooking it up and boiling it down: Abstracts in Athabaskan children's story retellings. In D. Tannen (Ed.), *Coherence in spoken and written discourse* (pp. 173–200). Norwood, NJ: Ablex.

Scribner, S., & Cole, M. (1981). *The psychology of literacy.* Cambridge, MA: Harvard University Press.

Shultz, J., Florio, S., & Erickson, F. (1982). Where's the floor? Aspects of the cultural organization of social relationships in communication at home and in school. In P. Gilmore & A. Glatthorn (Eds.), *Children in and out of school* (pp. 88–123). Washington, D.C.: Center for Applied Linguistics.

Shuman, A. (1983). Collaborative literacy in an urban multiethnic neighborhood. *International Journal of the Sociology of Language, 42,* 69–81.

Shuman, A. (1986). *Storytelling rights: The uses of oral and written texts by urban adolescents.* New York: Cambridge University Press.

Smith, D. (1987a). Illiteracy as a social fault. In D. Bloome (Ed.), *Literacy and schooling.* (pp. 55–64). Norwood, NJ: Ablex.

Smith, D. (1987b). Reading and writing in the real world: Explorations into the culture of literacy. In R. Parker & F. Davis (Eds.), *Developing literacy: Young children's use of language.* Newark, DE: International Reading Association, pp. 173–189.

Smitherman, G. (1981). "What go round come round": King in perspective. *Harvard Educational Review, 51*(1), 40–56.

Spindler, G. (Ed.) (1963). *Education and culture.* New York: Holt, Rinehart & Winston.

Spindler, G., & Spindler, L. (1987). Issues and applications in ethnographic methods. In G. Spindler & L. Spindler (Eds.), *Interpretive ethnography of education: At home and abroad* (pp. 1–7). Hillsdale, NJ: Lawrence Erlbaum Associates.

Spradley, J. P., & Rynkiewich, M. A. (Eds.). (1975). *The Nacirema: Readings on American culture.* Boston: Little, Brown.

Szwed, J. (1981). The ethnography of literacy. In M. F. Whiteman (Ed.), *Variation in writing: Functional and linguistic-cultural differences.* Hillsdale, NJ: Erlbaum, pp. 13–24.

Tannen, D. (1982). The oral/literate com=continuum in discourse. In D. Tannen (Ed.), *Spoken and written language: Exploring orality and literacy.* Norwood, NJ: Ablex, pp. 1–16.

Taylor, D. (1983). *Family literacy.* Exeter, NH: Heinemann Educational Books.

Taylor, D. (1988). Ethnographic educational evaluation for children, families and schools. *Theory Into Practice, 27*(1), 67–76.

Trueba, H. (1989). English literacy acquisition: From cultural trauma to learning disabilities in minority students. *Linguistics and Education, 1*(2), pp. 125–152.

Tyler, S. (Ed.). (1969). *Cognitive anthropology.* New York: Holt, Rinehart and Winston, Inc.

Varenne, H. (1984). Collective representation in American anthropological conversations about culture. *Current Anthropology, 25*(3), 281–299.

Varenne, H., & McDermott, R. P. (1986). "Why" Sheila can read: Structure and indeterminancy in the reproduction of familial literacy. In B. B. Schieffelin & P. Gilmore (Eds.), *The acquisition of literacy: Ethnographic perspectives* (pp. 188–212). Norwood, NJ: Ablex.

Messick, B. M., & Spratt, J. (1986). Studying literacy in Morocco. In B. Schieffelin & P. Gilmore (Eds.), *The acquisition of literacy: Ethnographic perspectives* (pp. 233–260). Norwood, NJ: Ablex.

Wallace, A. (1961). *Culture and personality.* New York: Randon House.

Wallat, C., & Green, J. 91979). Social rules and communicative contexts in kindergarten. *Theory Into Practice, 18*(4), 275–284.

Wells, G. (1986). *The meaning makers: Children learning language and using language to learn.* Portsmouth, NH: Heinemann Educational Books.

Whiting, B. B., & Whiting, J. M. (1975). *Children of six cultures: A psychocultural analysis.* Cambridge, MA: Harvard University Press.

Wilcox, K. (1982). Differential socialization in the classroom: Implications for equal opportunity. In G. Spindler (Ed.), *Doing the ethnography of schooling.* NY: Harcourt-Brace-Jovanovitch, pp. 456–488.

Zaharlick, A. & Green, J. (This volume).

Zinsser, C. (1986). For the Bible tells me so: Teaching children in a Fundamentalist church. In B. B. Schieffelin & P. Gilmore (Eds.), *The acquisition of literacy: Ethnographic perspectives* (pp. 55–74). Norwood, NJ: Ablex.

3E. LITERARY THEORY
Louise M. Rosenblatt

Assumptions concerning literature underlie at least tacitly any teaching of literature and any research on the teaching of literature. What texts fall under the heading of literary? What are appropriate ways of interpreting literary texts? Consciously or unconsciously, teachers are guided by answers to such questions, answers often assimilated automatically from their own education or from the established practices in their field. Basic to literature teaching are not only assumptions about the learning process but also assumptions about the nature of the reading process, the relationship between the reader and the text. Ultimately, the underlying theoretical implications involve such matters as assumptions about the nature of language and its relation to how human beings know their world, or "reality"— the problem philosophers term "epistemology" or the theory of knowledge.

Such problems, now grouped under the heading of literary theory, or sometimes critical theory, have occupied thinkers since Plato and Aristotle, especially at times of cultural and intellectual change. In the United States since the late 1960s and early 1970s, literary theory has been increasingly discussed in professional journals and publications, and it has emerged as a distinct field of academic specialization. Proponents of various alternative theories are competing for representation in graduate and undergraduate university departments. Since such theories ultimately have implications for teaching and research, this chapter will sketch the major outlines of recent developments in this highly controversial field. In such short compass, only very reductive accounts are posssible, concentrating on competing theories that are the subject of concern in the universities.

Works by authors' names appearing in this text are in References but fuller bibliographies may be found in surveys that are beginning to appear (e.g., Eagleton, 1983; Graff, 1987; Leitch, 1988; Wellek, 1986).

DOMINANT THEORIES BEFORE 1950

In the colleges, only the Greek and Latin literatures were at first deemed proper for study, and they were approached primarily as objects of grammatical and rhetorical, or philological analysis. When, for various reasons, the shift was made to English texts, there was no problem following the model of the philological study of literature in the German universities. Philology was the main concern of Francis Child when in 1896 he was appointed the first professor of English literature at Harvard. Moreover, his reading list included works in what today would be considered fields other than literary, such as history or philosophy. When later in the century courses were introduced that focused more on works now defined as imaginative, concern for scholarship dictated, in addition to textual analysis, largely a biographical and historical approach.

The Romantic movement had produced a body of theory that, on the one hand, supported this view of the literary work as primarily a reflection of the writer's biography and times. On the other hand, the Romantic view of the organic nature of art, with its emphasis on the poem as a poem, derived from Kant and the German philosophers mainly through the writings of Coleridge, did not fit easily into the scientific or scholarly academic scheme. An influential theoretical strand in both the universities and schools was Matthew Arnold's (1880) neoclassical emphasis on the potentialities of literature as the transmitter of ethical and spiritual ideals, and of the critic as concerned with propagating "the best that is known and thought in the world."

As the study of English and American literature became an accepted part of the college and university curriculum in the early decades of the twentieth century, these, not always consistent, approaches contributed to shaping the program. Linguistic and textual analysis, the study of Anglo-Saxon, the history of literary periods and movements, the concern for objective scholarship, and the concentration on works deemed good or great characterized the usual English program. The graduate school emphasized especially scholarly research and historical accuracy. The undergraduate program sought to promote knowledge of the canon, viewed largely in terms of great writers and literary periods.

Certain assumptions concerning the study of literature can be discerned as having prevailed over the whole educational spectrum until recent decades. No matter whether the work was viewed largely as a linguistic document, as a reflection of its world (i.e., of reality), or as an organic expression of a creative mind, the general assumption was that competent readers could interpret the text and agree on the author's intended meaning, on "what the text meant." A pedagogical result of these theoretical assumptions was the college classroom lecture in which the instructor expounded and analyzed the work and its background. Classroom recitations and written examinations were designed to establish whether the student had acquired this knowledge.

From the earliest days, the dominance of factually oriented literary study and research in the universities led some to complain that the values of literature as an art were being neglected, and to defend the acceptability of criticism as an academic subject. An indication of the continuing struggle is that a historian of the "profession of literature" (Graff, 1987) uses the title "Scholars versus Critics" for chapters covering the years from 1915 to 1965.

Literature in the Schools

Long before literature in English was introduced into the college curriculum, literary texts were being used in schools in teaching reading and were being justified as a means of inculcating moral and social attitudes. Histories of the teaching of English in the schools (e.g., Applebee, 1974), histories of American education (e.g., Cremin, 1961), and accounts of the academic profession (Berlin, 1984, 1987; Graff, 1987) show that the treatment of literature over the K–12 spectrum has not necessarily reflected developments in the universities. In the early twentieth century, when emphasis shifted from college preparation to a more democratic concern for the general student, professional educators turned away from the academic model offered by the colleges. Emphasis on the personal and social needs and interests of the individual student, and on education as a process of growth emerged in the 1920s and reached its height as the progressive education movement in the 1930s and the early 1940s. Except for a few colleges (e.g., Sarah Lawrence and Bennington), progressive ideas influenced teaching methods and curriculum mainly in the schools. However, pressures from the growing demands of mass education led to the distortions of progressive ideas that in the 1950s produced the movement for education for "life adjustment." Not until the 1960s do we find a convergence of attitudes among school and college theorists (Applebee, 1974, pp. 107–245). The present chapter is concerned primarily with developments after the mid-century, with the emergence and prevalence of New Criticism formalism, and the current reaction against it.

THE NEW CRITICISM

In the late 1930s, a group calling themselves the New Critics emerged, and by the mid-century they had gained academic preeminence in the universities. The prevalent concern with the history of literature and with literature as a reflection of biographical and social factors, the New Critics claimed, led to neglect of literature as an art. They reacted also against the Romantic emphasis on the personality of the author and the critic. The New Critics urged an impersonal "intrinsic" analysis of "the poem itself," as an autonomous entity, instead of study of "extrinsic" biographical or historical materials. Their attacks on "the intentional fallacy" diminished the importance of the author, and attacks on "the affective fallacy" decried the concern with the reader's response. (Wellek & Warren, 1949; Wimsatt and Beardsley, 1954)

A Formalist Process of Analysis

The New Critics called for an objective approach to the work. The poem was presented as an autonomous entity embodying its meaning and existing in its own right as a unified system whose workings could be objectively studied and analyzed. Thus the central concern was no longer the message of the text, its ethical or intellectual import, and its relation to author and social context. Interest turned rather to analysis of the text as a formal structure. Though this approach was in various ways new, it developed to an extreme one component of the traditional approach, the emphasis on formal analysis of the text.

In *Understanding Poetry,* an anthology for the college introductory course, Cleanth Brooks and Robert Penn Warren (1938) set forth a technique of "close reading" that exemplified the New Criticism. Explication of the text demanded categorization of genre, analysis of such matters of technique as the structure of the work (the relation of its parts to the whole), verse forms, patterns of imagery and metaphor, and definitions of the technical means by which effects such as irony were produced. Belief in the "affective fallacy" (Wimsatt and Beardsley, 1954) discouraged interest in the potential personal significance of texts for the student reader.

In the following decades, other anthologies by these and other authors and theoretical writings supporting this approach enjoyed increasing success. In 1949, Wellek and Warren's *Theory of Literature* provided theoretical support for the formalist position. Various competing critical positions—e.g., the Chicago neo-Aristotelians, such as Crane, (1952) or the myth or "archetypal" critics, such as Northrop Frye (1957)—also enjoyed high prestige. By the mid-century, however, the New Criticism was dominant in the universities.

In the 1950s and 1960s, formalist approaches to literature were increasingly imposed on the earlier traditional historical patterns of program organization in the colleges. Introductory courses (and anthologies) were usually organized by genres, with some advanced courses for English majors concentrating on periods. Graduate studies reflected a similar division between formalist critical concerns and historical or linguistic research. This pattern still predominates in the late 1980s, as college catalogues and the sales of college "introduction to literature" texts demonstrate.

"READER RESPONSE" THEORIES

Reaction against the New Criticism

In the late 1960s, the unrest in the universities generated by the Vietnam War and the feeling that formalist criticism was propagating an endless flow of sterile explications of literary works opened the way for the propounding of alternative views on the literary work and critical method. In the 1970s and 1980s, a multiplicity of journals, books, and conference reports on controversial problems of literary criticism and interpretation produced a wide range of theoretical positions. By 1980, literary theory had emerged as a distinct field of academic specialization, increasingly seeking representation in university departments of English, first in graduate schools and in scattered instances in undergraduate courses.

The "Reader Response" Spectrum

The New Critics viewed the text as an entity embodying a determinate message or meaning. Rejection of this assumption was a major point of agreement among the various competing literary theories in the late 1980s. No matter by what philosophic paths they had arrived at their differing positions, and no matter how different the implications derived, they saw the reader as actively involved in the process of making meaning. Hence their being loosely grouped under the label of "reader response criticism" when anthologies on current literary theory (Suleiman, 1980; Tompkins, 1980) were published. By that time, theoretical groupings had differentiated themselves under a variety of labels. Given the need for brevity, the following discussion will characterize them mainly in terms of the emphases in their treatment of the reader-text relationship, since this has the clearest pedagogical implications.

Reader-Oriented Theories

The reader emerges as paramount in psychoanalytically oriented theories. For Holland, (1975a, 1975b) applying "ego psychology" developed by followers of Freud (e.g., Erikson, 1963), the reader's personality, manifested in his "identity theme" or "defense mechanism," dominates the interaction with an ultimately passive text. The reader's characteristic modes of adaptation and defense—expectations, desires, fantasies—shape the reader's interpretation. Although theoretically the constraints of the text are recognized, attention is focused mainly on the reader's response as a means of discovering the reader's identity theme. Although more eclectic psychologically, Bleich (1975, 1978) also makes the reader's response the central object of analysis and the source of self-understanding. Bleich's titles, *Readings and Feelings* and *Subjective Criticism,* underline his reaction against the impersonality of classrooms dominated by traditional or New Criticism approaches. He stresses various ways of eliciting students' primary emotional responses and distrusts the distancing effect of the intellectual aspects of interpretation. Instead of the orthodox concern with objectivity of interpretation, he maintains the emphasis on the reader as against the text by postulating a process of negotiation for a consensus among readers in the classroom. More recently, he has tended toward a greater emphasis on the social aspect.

Text-Oriented Theories

From the early 1970s to the early 1980s, the structuralists were considered the bringers of a new theoretical emphasis. After about 1975, they were displaced as a center of attention by the poststructuralists, more frequently termed "deconstructionists." Both are rooted in the French tradition stemming from the linguist, Saussure (1966). His stress on the arbitrary relationship between the sign and the signified, the word and its object, gave rise to a dyadic view of language as a closed system. This focused on the underlying codes, rules, and conventions, which he termed *langue,* that could be abstracted and analyzed apart from actual speech, termed *parole.* The anthropologist Levi-Strauss (1966) applied to analysis of cultures a process of analysis similar to the formal structural analysis that linguists applied to language.

The influence of the structuralist movement on literary theory became apparent in the early 1970s in the United States in the writings, e.g., of Chatman, (1978); Culler, (1975); Riffaterre, (1978); and Scholes (1974). Jakobson, (1960) with roots in Russian formalism, was a powerful ally. Rejecting historical and interpretive approaches, they brought to the literary text the type of formal analysis linguists applied to language. Just as the linguists were interested in abstract syntactic patterns of language, so the structuralist critics were interested, not in explication of

meaning as conceived by individual readers, but in revealing the underlying conventions and codes to be found in the text.

To this view of language the poststructuralists (Hartman, (1975); Derrida, (1976, 1978); de Man, (1979); Fish, (1980); Miller, (1982); and Scholes (1985) brought an extreme philosophical relativism, derived largely from Heidigger and Nietzsche (see Passmore, 1972, 1985). They rejected the rationalist tradition of Western culture and the idea of the connection between experience and knowledge. Traditionally, the assumption has been that the sign or word referred to a thing, that language mirrored reality. Questioning the referential and mimetic aspects of language, some poststructuralists carried the idea of the indeterminancy of language—the idea that there is no single, unvarying meaning of a text—to the point of such phrasings as "the unreadability" of the text. They developed a deconstructionist technique of reading, especially exemplified in the writings of Derrida, (1976, 1978) based on the assumption that every text contained its own contradiction and could be shown to self-deconstruct. Moreover the poststructuralist philosophic views led to a Nietzschean denial of the importance of the individual. Language and cultural codes dominate, or "write," both author and reader. Thus, despite being originally grouped with the reader-response critics, both the structuralists and the poststructuralists carried to an even greater extreme the New Critics' formalist preoccupation with the text.

Stanley Fish, (1980) probably the most widely read reader-response theorist in the 1980s, started from a scholarly New Critical position and moved through various stages from simple discovery of the reader's activity to poststructuralism. Recognizing the universality of the interpretive act, he ends up attributing authority for the interpretive process to neither the reader nor the author but to the "interpretive communities" to which they belong and which are responsible for their activities and the texts those activities produce. This leads to a sociological interest in the politics of the literary profession. Fish sees no practical implications for teaching flowing from his theory, and in practice he seems to continue scholarly concentration on the text.

In the late 1970s, increasing criticism of the poststructuralists' and deconstructionists' antihumanism declared that it cut off the literary work from the world, banished the author, devalued the personal ethical and emotional responses of the reader, and ruled out traditional historical and biographical critical approaches (Abrams, (1977); Graff, (1987); Searle, (1977); Wellek (1986); Todorov, 1987; Booth (1988). Deconstructionists countered often with complex theoretical arguments.

Reader-Plus-Text-Oriented Theories

Theorists who present the reading process as the relationship between the reader and the text still may differ in their interpretation of these terms and in their emphasis on one or the other. Grouped under the label of "reception theory," the German theorists, Iser (1978) and Jauss, (1982), stem from phenomenological philosophy (see Passmore, 1972, 1985). Iser, who has been more widely read in the United States, presents a complex temporal model of the reading process in terms of an interaction. The text is seen as setting particular requirements for an "implied reader," but also having gaps that the reader must fill. Different readers will therefore "concretize" the text differently. Each will seek to create a consistent structure and at the same time accommodate the shifting perspectives presented by the text. In analyses of the interaction between reader and text, the text receives most attention because it is ultimately determinate.

Jauss (1980), less well-known in the United States, starts with the reader-text assumption, but is concerned mainly with developing a new type of literary history based on investigation of "the horizon of expectations" that explains the audience reception of literary works.

The transactional theory (Rosenblatt, 1938, 1978, 1983), draws on the American philosophy of Pragmatism (Dewey (1929); James, (1890); Peirce, 1932, 1933). Instead of an "interaction" between reader and text that is seen as separate, completely defined entitles acting on one another, "transaction," following Dewey & Bentley (1949), designates a reciprocal or circular relationship in which each conditions the other. Thus the "self" of the reader and the text are conceived as more flexible, taking on their character during the transaction, which is an event conditioned also by its particular context. The importance of the cultural or social context is stressed, but transactional theory sees the convention or code, as, e.g., in language, as always individually internalized. Each reader draws on a personal reservoir of linguistic and life experiences. The new meaning, the literary work, whether poetic or nonpoetic, is constituted during the actual transaction between reader and text.

Whether the reading event will produce a literary or nonliterary work depends, according to Rosenblatt, on the reader's stance toward the contents of consciousness during the transaction with the text. The same text can be read either "efferently" (e.g., to analyze its syntax or as a historical document) or "aesthetically." In an efferent reading of a text, the attention is focused on abstracting out, analyzing, and structuring what is to be retained after the reading, as, e.g., information, logical argument, or instructions for action. In an aesthetic reading, attention is focused on what is being lived through, the ideas and feelings being evoked and organized during the transaction. This experience constitutes the literary work that is the object of response and interpretation.

When the reader response movement developed in the 1970s and 1980s, Rosenblatt's *Literature as Exploration* (1938, 1983) was recognized as the first statement of the reader response approach (Tompkins, 1980, p.xxvi), and has gone through four editions. A theory of literature presented as the basis for a theory of teaching, it was favorably received by both university and school groups. Although after the mid-century the New Criticism dominated in the colleges, the book continued to be influential in the schools (Applebee, 1974, pp. 123–25, 131. See also the chapter by Probst, this Handbook.)

Feminist, African American, Ethnic, Marxist, and Other Critics

Various critical groups concerned primarily with particular causes or ideologies are usually grouped under the general reader response rubric, e.g., feminist critics (Fetterly, 1977; Gilbert and Gubar, 1979; Showalter, 1985), African American or ethnic critics (Christian, 1985; Gates, 1984), or Marxist and cultural critics (Eagleton, 1983; Jameson, 1972; Lentricchia, 1980; Mailloux, 1982; Said, 1983). Some of these groups tend to draw on the general reader response approach, although others find deconstructionism especially congenial.

The cultural critics adopt a political, social-historical approach drawing largely on Foucault's (1980) theories about power and sometimes colored by a Marxist anticapitalist ideology. Like the deconstructionists, they seek behind the manifest meanings of the text, the hidden assumptions; these, they claim, support the ideology of the status quo and must be resisted. Those deconstructionists who stress the importance of the institutional context in the teaching of literature tend to view the theoretical controversies under such rubrics as "the politics of literature." The theoretical groups discussed in this section typically seek to impose their ideologies on the selection of works read and the point of view from which the students respond, interpret, and evaluate.

Theoretical Controversies in the Universities

At the end of the 1980s, although the newer approaches are filtering in, formalist methods continue to dominate in the large majority of college and graduate literature classes. The usual pattern is inculcation of a formalist method of textual analysis: close reading of the text, study of genres, and analysis of linguistic techniques, with some mix of history, literary history, and biography. The teacher's task is seen as being expounder of theme and form, presumably as reflective of the intentions of the author. Neither the student reader's response nor the implications of the work for "real life" are much considered.

Yet the situation of literature and the humanities in the university is confused and unstable. All levels of the educational establishment are under attack from a wide range of points of view. Some critics of the university are calling for a return to the emphasis on literature as a transmitter of traditional values; others are concerned with teaching a common body of information about frequently mentioned literary and other works; others are seeking to change the canon to reflect the antiestablishment views of diverse minority groups. Literary theorists belonging to the various categories sketched in this article are not only challenging the dominant traditional approach, but are also competing against one another in efforts to introduce a new literature curriculum. In a few large universities, there are strong representations of exponents of reader response, deconstructionism, and cultural criticism.

PEDAGOGICAL IMPLICATIONS

A history of the teaching of English (Applebee, 1974) reports in all periods dissatisfaction at the lack of success in achieving the humanistic goals of literature teaching that schools profess and the failure to understand that these aims are in conflict with the continuing emphasis on specific knowledge or content. Literature is treated as a body of knowledge rather than as a series of experiences. Methods of teaching appropriate to the transmission of knowledge of the content or techniques of literary works are not primarily adapted to producing readers capable of evoking literary works for themselves, or of deriving the pleasures and insights claimed for literary study. If students are to learn to experience literature—to read aesthetically—the need evidently is for different methods and a different educational climate from the traditional teacher-dominated explication of literary texts.

When the competing theoretical positions are looked at from the point of view of implications for educational method and pedagogical procedures, the division falls elsewhere than between the old formalism and historicism on the one hand and the new so-called reader response approaches on the other. Educationally, the division falls between on the one hand, the text-oriented traditional, New Critical, structuralist, and poststructuralist theories and on the other hand, the reader-oriented and reader-plus-text-oriented theories.

Text-oriented theories tend most readily to continue traditional approaches to the teaching of literature. New formulations of literary conventions can be taught, and radical deconstructive methods of analysis of content can be imparted without changing anything in the traditional teacher-dominated and text-centered classroom. Similarly, the canon can be changed or new items introduced into the reading lists without affecting instructional methods. Accounts of the theoretical developments in the past half-century have tended to designate the various trends in terms of critical methods of interpretation without making explicit their implications involving the educational environment, instructional methods, and the relations between teachers and students. Even those among the recent theoreticians who, departing from earlier denigration of educational concerns, admit that their theories stem from classroom discussions, do not concern themselves with their pedagogical implications, and, in some instances, reveal that they disregard them and continue traditional practices.

Reader-oriented and reader-plus-text-oriented theories, in their agreement that readers must draw on past experiences in order to evoke the literary work, tend directly and indirectly to challenge traditional methods of literature teaching. Readers are encouraged to pay attention to their own literary experiences as the basis for self-understanding or for comparison with others' evocations. This implies a new, collaborative relationship between teacher and student. Emphasis on the reader need not exclude application of various approaches, literary and social, to the process of critical interpretation and evaluation.

Ethics of Indoctrination

Agreement that the teaching of literature has social and political implications has not produced widespread discussion of educational ethics, especially the problem of covert versus overt indoctrination. Attention has been focused rather on the politics of gaining control of the academic institution.

Some support the teacher's explicit affirmation of a social or political point of view. Some of the neo-Marxist theorists, for example, call for a revision of the curriculum in those terms. Others support explicit affirmation of the democratic values of the importance of individual human beings and their right to freedom of thought and expression. Given such explicit basic values, they contend, the student can participate through literary experiences in a diversity of worlds and systems of value, can become acquainted with diverse interpretive frames of reference, and can be helped to critically develop a personal hierarchy of values that recognizes the rights of others.

References

Abrams, M. H. (1979). How to do things with texts. *Partisan Review, 46,* 566–588.

Abrams, M. H. (1977). The limits of pluralism: deconstructive angel. *Critical inquiry 3,* 425–38.

Abrams, M. H. (1953). *The mirror and the lamp: romantic theory and the critical tradition.* New York: Oxford University Press.

Arnold, M. (1880). *Essays in criticism.* New York: Macmillan.

Applebee, A. N. (1974). *Tradition and reform in the teaching of English: a history.* Urbana, IL: National Council of Teachers of English.

Berlin, J. A. (1984). Writing instruction in nineteenth-century American colleges. Carbondale: Southern Illinois University Press.

Berlin, J. A. (1987). *Writing instruction in American colleges 1900–1985.* Carbondale: Southern Illinois University Press.

Bleich, D. (1975). *Reading and feelings: an introduction to subjective criticism.* Urbana, IL: National Council of Teachers of English.

Bleich, D. (1978). *Subjective criticism.* Baltimore: Johns Hopkins University Press.

Booth, W. C. (1988). *The company we keep.* Berkeley: University of California Press.

Brooks, C., and R. P. Warren, (Eds.). (1938). *Understanding poetry.* New York: Henry Holt.

Chatman, S. (1978). *Story and discourse.* Ithaca: Cornell University Press.

Christian, B. (1985). *Black feminist criticism: perspectives on black women writers.* New York: Pergamon.

Crane, R. S. (Ed). (1952). *Critics and criticism: ancient and modern.* Chicago: University of Chicago Press.

Cremin, L. A. (1961). *The transformation of the school: Progressivism in American education.* New York: Vintage Books.

Culler, J. (1975). *Structuralist poetics: structuralism, linguistics, and the study of literature.* Ithaca: Cornell University Press.

de Man, P. (1979). *Allegories of reading.* New Haven: Yale University Press.

Derrida, J. (1976). *Of grammatology.* (G. C. Spivak, Trans.). Baltimore: Johns Hopkins Press.

Derrida, J. (1978). *Writing and difference.* (Alan Bass, Trans.). Chicago: University of Chicago Press.

Dewey, J. (1929). *The Quest for certainty.* New York: Minton Balch.

Dewey, J. & Bentley, A. F. (1949). *Knowing and the known.* Boston: Beacon Press.

Eagleton, T. (1983). *Literary theory: an introduction.* Minneapolis: University of Minnesota Press.

Erikson, E. H. (1963). *Childhood and society.* New York: W. W. Norton.

Fetterly, J. (1977). *The resisting reader: a feminist approach to American fiction.* Bloomington: Indiana University Press.

Fish, S. (1980). *Is there a text in this class? The authority of interpretive communities.* Cambridge: Harvard University Press.

Foucault, M. (1980). *Power/knowledge: selected interviews and other writings.* C. Gordon (Ed.). New York: Random House.

Frye, N. (1957). *The anatomy of criticism.* Princeton: Princeton University Press.

Gates, H. L. (1984). *Black literature and literary theory.* New York: Methuen.

Gilbert, S., & Gubar, S. (1979). *The madwoman in the attic: the woman writer and the nineteenth-century literary imagination.* New Haven: Yale University Press.

Graff, G. (1987). *Professing literature.* Chicago: University of Chicago Press.

Hartman, G. (1975). *The fate of reading.* Chicago: University of Chicago Press.

Holland, N. (1975a). *5 readers reading.* New Haven: Yale University Press.

Holland, N. (1975b). *Poems in persons: an introduction to the psychoanalysis of literature.* New York, Norton.

Iser, W. (1978). *The act of reading: A theory of aesthetic response.* Baltimore: Johns Hopkins University Press.

Iser, W. (1974). *The implied reader.* Baltimore: Johns Hopkins University Press.

Jakobson, R. (1960). Linguistics and poetics. In T. A. Sebeok (Ed.), *Style in language,* pp. 350–377. Cambridge, MA: MIT Press.

James, W. (1890). *The principles of psychology.* New York: Henry Holt.

Jameson, F. (1972). *The prison-house of language.* Princeton: Princeton University Press.

Jauss, H. R. (1982). *Towards an aesthetic of reception.* (T. Bahti, Trans.). Minneapolis: University of Minnesota Press.

Leitch, V. B. (1988). *American literary criticism from the thirties to the eighties.* New York: Columbia University Press.

Lentricchia, F. (1980). *After the new criticism.* Chicago: University of Chicago Press.

Levi-Strauss, C. (1966). *The savage mind.* Chicago: University of Chicago Press.

Mailloux, S. (1982). *Interpretive conventions: the reader in the study of American fiction.* Ithaca: Cornell University Press.

Miller, J. H. (1982). *Fiction and repetition.* Cambridge, Mass.: Harvard University Press.

Passmore, J. (1972). *A hundred years of philosophy.* London: Penguin Books.

Passmore, J. (1985). *Recent philosophers.* La Salle, IL: Open Court Publishing.

Peirce, C. S. (1932, 1933). In P. Weiss & C. Hartshorne (Eds.). *Collected papers.* Cambridge, MA: Harvard University Press.

Riffaterre, M. (1978). *Semiotics of poetry.* Bloomington: Indiana University Press.

Rorty, R. (1979). *Philosophy and the mirror of nature.* Princeton: Princeton University Press.

Rosenblatt, L. M. (1938). *Literature as exploration.* New York: Appleton-Century.

Rosenblatt, L. M. (1983). *Literature as exploration.* 4th edition. New York: Modern Language Association.

Rosenblatt, L. M. (1978). *The reader, the text, the poem: the transactional theory of the literary work.* Carbondale, IL: Southern Illinois University Press.

Said, E. W. (1983). *The world, the text, and the critic.* Cambridge: Harvard University Press.

Saussure, F. de (1966). *Course in general linguistics* (W. Baskin, Trans.). New York: McGraw-Hill.

Scholes, R. (1974). *Structuralism in literature.* New Haven: Yale University Press.

Scholes, R. (1985). *Textual power: literary theory and the teaching of English.* New Haven: Yale University Press.

Searle, J. (1977). Reiterating the differences: a reply to Derrida. *Glyph 1* (pp. 198–208). Baltimore: Johns Hopkins University Press.

Showalter, E. (Ed.). (1985). *The new feminist criticism: essays on women, literature, and theory.* New York: Pantheon.

Suleiman, S. R., & Crosman, I. (Eds.). (1980). *The reader in the text.* Princeton: Princeton University Press.

Todorov, T. (1987). *Literature and its theorists.* (C. Porter, Trans.) Ithaca: Cornell University Press.

Tompkins, J. (Ed.). (1980). *Reader-response criticism.* Baltimore: Johns Hopkins Press.

Wellek, R. (1986). *American criticism, 1900–1950, Vol. 6 of A history of modern criticism.* New Haven: Yale University Press.

Wellek, R., & Warren, A. (1949). *Theory of literature.* New York: Harcourt Brace.

Wimsatt, W. K., & Beardsley, M. (1954). The affective fallacy. In W. K. Wimsatt (Ed.), *The verbal icon: studies in the meaning of poetry.* Lexington: University of Kentucky Press.

· 4 ·

INSTRUCTIONAL MODELS FOR ENGLISH
LANGUAGE ARTS, K–12

Edmund J. Farrell

Curriculum models imply instructional models. In his introduction to *Three Language-Arts Curriculum Models,* Mandel (1980) discriminates among a competencies model, which he equates with the mastery learning of language skills; a heritage model, in which the values and traditions of the culture are transmitted; and a process or student-centered model, in which emphasis is upon the language processes that lead to the individual growth of each student. (For an earlier discussion of these models, see Dixon, 1967, pp. 1–13.) About the relation of instruction to this curricular triad, Mandel comments, "whatever the pedagogical choice might be, all pedagogical paradigms, if understood correctly, are devoted to process, competencies, and heritage" (p. 4). He discriminates as follows among the three:

Whereas a competencies model can fairly clearly state behavior expected to occur . . . a process approach focuses more on watchfulness, the observation of what is developing at a given moment of instruction and then the harnessing of its energy . . . In the heritage model, the underlying assumption is that the way to acquire skills and knowledge is to submit to something larger than oneself, that is to the culture. By culture I mean traditions, history, the time-honored values of civilized thought and feeling . . . and the skills that make it possible to share in one's culture and to pass it on. (p. 8)

After asserting that it is reasonable to assume that particular models will be best suited for specific kinds of learning, Mandel concludes his introduction by calling "for a true and strict eclecticism: selection from what appears to be the *best* in various doctrines, methods, or styles" (p. 12).

COMPLEXITIES OF THE CURRICULUM

Because of the complexity of the curriculum (or curricula) of the English language arts, any single instructional model, particularly a monolithic one, will perforce distort what takes place in the classroom. First, the enormous content and the myriad skills traditionally associated with the subject are not stable (e.g., literature accretes, and knowledge about how students attain literacy steadily alters as a consequence of scholarship); second, like other areas of the curriculum, the English language arts are subject to cultural influences and trends (on this point, see Applebee, 1974; Glatthorn, 1980; Squire, 1977); third, the curriculum involves the performance of tens of thousands of teachers and millions of students, each of whom brings to the classroom peculiarities in aptitudes, interests, and prior life experiences. In short, the curriculum and the instructional modes it implies are dynamic and resist verbal encapsulation.

This is not to deny the value of words like "mastery teaching," "heritage," or "student-centered" in suggesting curricular emphases at a given time. But curricula might be described in other ways. For example, Goodlad (1977) hypothesized that five curricula exist simultaneously in the schools: the *ideal curriculum,* what scholars propose be taught; the *formal curriculum,* what has been mandated by a controlling agency, such as the state or local district; the *perceived curriculum,* what teachers believe they are teaching; the *operational curriculum,* what observers actually see being taught; and the *experiential curriculum,* what students believe they are learning.

Certainly one who examines research in English language arts can find discrepancies among the curricula Goodlad hypothesizes. In the 1960s professional publications like *Media and Methods* and the *English Journal* repeatedly ran articles on the need to incorporate instruction on mass media within the English language arts. But in analyzing data from 32,580 minutes of observation in 1,609 English classes in 116 exemplary schools, Squire and Applebee (1968) found only 1.3 percent of classroom time given to mass media. When teachers in the same study were asked on individual questionnaires to rank their own practices, the large majority reported giving discussion first priority; however, observers noted only 20 percent of class time being devoted to discussion, in comparison to 21 percent of time being given to lecture and 22 percent to recitation. Despite emphasis by scholars on the importance of both process and practice in writing (see, e.g., Britton, 1978; Emig, 1971; Graves, 1983; Moffett, 1981a; Tate, 1987), Applebee (1981) found in an observational study of writing in the content areas of two midwestern high schools that only 10 percent of observed time in English classes was devoted to writing of at least paragraph length and that the amount of time devoted to prewriting activities averaged just over 3 minutes. Summaries of research on written composition (Braddock, Lloyd-Jones, & Schoer, 1963; Hillocks, 1986) report little relationship between instruction in formal grammar and students' proficiency in writing; yet in analyzing observational data from his national study of 38 elementary and secondary schools, Goodlad (1984) concluded that in English language arts

the dominant emphasis throughout was on teaching basic language skills and mastering mechanics—capitalization, punctuation, paragraphs, ... parts of speech, etc. These were repeated in successive grades of the elementary years, were reviewed in the junior high years, and reappeared in the low track classes of the senior high schools. (p. 205)

Some Cautionary Words

In reading what follows on mastery, heritage, and process models for instruction in English language arts, the reader is asked, then, to bear the following in mind:

1. The three descriptors may be inadequate to capture the full dynamics of what falls under the rubric of English language arts or of teachers' classroom behaviors. Other descriptors might be equally useful but equally inadequate.
2. The descriptors are convenient for presenting the work of scholars. However, there has been a continuing historical lag between scholars' theories, findings, and recommendations and teachers' instructional practices.
3. Argument rather than research most often provides credence for the worth of a curriculum model and the instructional model it implies. To date, American education has lacked both the money and the sophistication in research needed for long-range longitudinal evaluation of the efficacy of a given curricular/instructional model, one used in a variety of school settings, K–12. What research exists is short-range and usually limited to a handful of classes. In the absence of valid and reliable longitudinal research, one encounters much faddism in American education, with the persuasive rhetoric of one group or another being ascendant for brief periods.
4. Programs of teacher education appear to devote little time to the examination of models, to the argumentation and research that undergird them, and to the implications of each for the health of a democratic society. Once in the classroom, individuals have little time to consciously reflect on their pedagogical practices. The consequence is that K–12 teachers of English often appear atheoretical to classroom observers, unconsciously eclectic, unaware of the models—

whether competency, heritage, or process—to which given behaviors provide tacit support.
5. Highly innovative instructional practices, ones requiring schooling to be conceptually restructured, are difficult to implement on a broad scale.

Causes for this difficulty are complex. Widely implemented instructional models must be accommodated to the prevailing institutional model of education. Schools as presently structured derive their models from early twentieth-century industry. It is a model with industrial metaphors ("school plant planning," the "products of the school," "teacher load") and with concerns—"efficiency," "accountability"—derived principally from an historic alliance with business. (For documentation and perspectives on this alliance, see Callahan, 1962; McNeil, 1988a; Spring, 1972). It is a model that, in the secondary schools, segments knowledge into discrete subjects and appears to move students along, conveyor-belt fashion, from one station to another where they are analogically "processed" by teachers. It is a model that easily perpetuates a static instructional model, one in which teachers see their central role as that of purveying knowledge to an ostensibly passive audience:

We observed [from 1,016 classroom visits in 38 schools] that, on the average, about 75% of class time was spent on instruction and that nearly 70% of this was "talk"—usually teacher to students. Teachers out-talked the entire class of students by a ratio of about three to one. Clearly, the bulk of this teacher talk was instructing in the sense of telling. (Goodlad, 1984, p. 229)

Because of the complex contextual constraints on education posed by the institutional model, well-publicized efforts in recent decades to reform education by altering the distribution of time and the pattern of instruction, have been largely unsuccessful. One rarely reads these days about modular scheduling, team teaching, or Individually Prescribed Instruction (IPI), innovations highly publicized in the professional literature of the 1960s and 1970s (Bush & Allen, 1964; Talmage, 1975, Trump, 1959).

Recent school-based reform projects, some as outgrowths of observational studies in the schools, call for restructuring the roles and responsibilities of teachers and, in some cases, redesigning the curriculum. At least five networks of affiliated schools support these grassroot endeavors: Mortimer Adler's Paideaia Group, Theodore Sizer's Coalition of Essential Schools, John Goodlad's National Network for Educational Renewal, the National Education Association's Mastery in Learning Project, and the American Federation of Teachers' Research-in-to-Practice Practitioners Network. How influential any or all of these networks become waits to be seen. Their greatest strength seemingly lies in their ability to accommodate greater than usual pedagogical and curricular diversity at local levels. Nevertheless, as was true for earlier reform movements, their greatest challenge appears to be that of overcoming inertia inherent in the prevailing and pervasive industrial model for schooling. On this point, McNeil (1988a) comments, "Designing structures that make skills hospitable to our best, most learned, and skilled

TABLE 4–1. A Brief Overview of Instructional Models for English Language Arts, K–12

Proponent	Areas of Skills/Content	Instructional Level	Comment
		Mastery	
Bloom, B.	Reading	Elementary	Focuses on skills; reduces student (LFM) variability; relies heavily on tests
Hunter	All areas	Elem/Sec	Focus on teacher's instructional strategies, not content; gives little attention to creativity
Keller (PSI)	Reading	Sec/Col	Focuses on skills; provides for independent progress and more student variability than LFM; stresses achievement testing
Reid (ECRI)	Lang. arts	Elementary	Is highly structured and atomistic; makes heavy demands of teachers; gives little attention to creativity
		Heritage	
Bennett	Literature (composition, speech)	Secondary	Is prescriptive; lacks detail; gives no attention to skills or students' interests
Bloom, A.	Literature/classics	Sec/Col	Is highly prescriptive; lacks detail; focuses on narrow canon of works
Hirsch	Literature	K–12	Emphasizes content, not teaching method; is implicitly but moderately prescriptive
Ravitch/ Finn	Literature	Elem/Sec	Is moderately prescriptive; gives little attention to skills or students' interests and abilities
		Process	
Britton	All areas, espec. comp.	Elem/Sec/Col espec. K–9	Provides less detail than Moffett; is integrated, student-centered, creative
Kinneavy	Composition	Col/Sec	Emphasizes communication triangle and centrality of writer's aim
Moffett	All areas	K–13 (mostly elem)	Is student-centered, developmental, interdisciplinary; encourages creativity
Rosenblatt	Literature (creative writing)	All levels (less elem)	Focuses on student in relationship to text; provides for diversity but uses text to verify response

teachers and our most eager students is even more complicated today than transferring schools into factories was in the early days of this century" (p. 339).

THE MASTERY MODEL

Mastery teaching, most closely associated with the competencies model for English language arts (Mandel, 1980), derives its present theoretical basis from Carroll (1963), and its popularity from Bloom (1968, 1971, 1974, 1976, 1981), who claims that as high as 95 percent of all students can master content and skills if they are given the instructional time they need. Motivational features are that all students can expect success from their efforts, that students assume considerable responsibility for evaluating their own progress, and that errors are accepted as a natural part of the learning process. So far as it applies to English programs, mastery learning has been used mainly for

teaching reading and writing skills, particularly (but not exclusively) in the elementary grades.

Major Characteristics

The model requires that instructional objectives be clearly formulated and that course content be broken into small discrete units for learning. The units are organized hierarchically to permit mastery at increasing levels of complexity. The teacher normally introduces a new unit to the whole class in accordance with his or her customary teaching style (style of presentation is not prescribed in mastery learning programs). Following the unit introduction, the teacher provides students with instructional materials for applying the new concepts.

To determine each student's level of understanding (formative evaluation), the teacher develops brief, ungraded, student-scored diagnostic-progress tests. Results from the tests keep both teacher and student apprised of the student's progress toward mastery of instructional objectives. A summative test determines grades, which are noncompetitive in that any student mastering the unit within the designated instructional time is given an *A*. Until a student demonstrates mastery on the summative test, he or she is given an *I* (incomplete). (Students who master the unit quickly are given "enrichments," which permit them to pursue more intensely or broadly the material covered on formative tests.) Based upon performance on the test, a student is given additional instructional material. These "correctives," which differ from the teacher's group instruction, may include supplementary print or audiovisual materials, academic games, small-group study sessions, affective exercises, and peer tutoring. This cycle of diagnostic test—corrective instruction continues until students have achieved mastery.

Variant Models

Personalized Systems of Instruction. A principal variant of Bloom's Learning for Mastery Model (LFM) is Keller's (1968) Personalized System of Instruction (PSI), which finds its theoretical basis in B. F. Skinner's operant conditioning. Students utilizing PSI proceed through hierarchical written curriculum materials at their own pace, assisted by a teacher or possibly an aide. After completing the unit material, the student is given a unit mastery test. Success on the test permits advancement to the next unit; otherwise, the student is provided unit correctives to restudy the unmastered material. Until the student demonstrates mastery on one form of the unit test, the cycle repeats.

Stallings and Stipek (1986), who present an overview and summary of research on mastery learning, point out that in LFM classrooms students are expected to work on their own time to master material so that the class can proceed in concert to the next unit of study. The consequence theoretically is that this method, which has been used principally in elementary classrooms, should reduce variability in achievement levels among students. In contrast, the PSI method, which has been used largely in high schools and colleges, could result in increased variability in mastery because the progress of fast learners is not delayed by that of slow learners, as sometimes occurs when whole-class instruction is used.

The Exemplary Center for Reading Instruction. Conceptually related to Bloom's LFM is the Exemplary Center for Reading Instruction (ECRI), a program that has been taught to teachers at sites throughout the nation. Founded in 1966 in Salt Lake City, Utah, and directed by Ethna Reid, ECRI "is a total language arts instructional program. It provides instruction simultaneously in reading, oral language, spelling, comprehension, and other activities in a highly structured, systematic pattern that ensures mastery" (Reid, 1986, p. 511). Designed to be a supplement to current basal instruction, ECRI "can be best described as a highly structured, teacher-directed, mastery learning approach" (p. 513). The program, which occupies 80 to 120 minutes of the school day, is divided into three major components of instruction—skills time (20 to 30 minutes), practice time (40 to 60 minutes), and backup skills time (20 to 30 minutes).

Skills time is used for introducing new skills, for example, vocabulary words, sentence patterns, and strategies for comprehension. A three-step process is employed for instruction: demonstration, prompt, and practice. ECRI teachers typically use eight methods for introducing new words. Comprehension is divided into four levels (literal, interpretive, critical, and creative), which are broken down into 90 discrete skills. Teachers are expected to have students employ daily the expressive skills of speaking and writing as well as the receptive skills of reading and listening. During practice time, students usually work independently as the teacher confers with individuals, administers mastery tests, or holds small-group conferences. Once summative evaluations are successfully completed during practice time, students move on to the next skill level. Backup skills time is devoted to instruction in penmanship, proofing through dictation, and spelling.

Research Findings

Stallings and Stipek (1986) report that most of the studies in this country of LFM's effectiveness have been conducted in elementary schools and have been short term, with intervention lasting from 2 to 4 weeks. Further, the studies have focused principally upon mathematics and science, not language arts. (For an example of how mastery learning might be used to teach the concept of noun, see Glatthorn, 1977, pp. 211–212.) Reid (1986) cites studies indicating that ECRI has led to substantial gains in reading achievement for elementary school students and for secondary students experiencing reading difficulties.

In general, evidence suggests mastery learning programs have been reasonably successful in increasing the percentage of students who master the basic curriculum in the subjects investigated (Block & Burns, 1976). Nevertheless, criticism has been advanced that the programs are overly structured, even mechanistic; that they fail to develop proficiency in speaking or listening skills; that they lead to decreased motivation in highly competitive (usually high ability) students; that they imply too narrow a view of education, giving too little attention to creativity; that they make unrealistic demands on teachers (Stallings & Stipek, 1986, pp. 745–746), and that they are inappropriate for learning certain processes, for example, writing, "because it would be difficult to ascertain at what point the student has 'mastered' the ability to write" (Guam Department of Education, 1987, *Teaching for mastery,* draft copy. Agana, Guam, 3).

The Madeline Hunter Instructional Skills Program

Used in elementary and secondary schools throughout the United States is the instructional skill model developed by Madeline Hunter of the School of Education, University of California, Los Angeles. While not a mastery learning program per se, it does share some similarities with such programs: it assumes that nearly all students can learn the basic school curriculum, it derives its authority from research in human learning and human behavior, and it is highly structured. Further, Hunter

(1985) has said that Mastery Teaching is among the several names by which her program is known. Unlike other mastery programs, however, it appears to focus more on teachers' instructional strategies than on students' progress through a sequence of formative and summative tests. Consequently, though the Hunter model is presented here under the general rubric of *The Mastery Model,* it seems equally appropriate to curricula placed under *The Heritage Model.*

Hunter (1984) presents three "templates" by which she believes the quality of teaching can be described, interpreted, and evaluated. The first template is an analysis of the teacher's decisions about content, learners' behavior, and the teacher's own instructional behavior. The second template is lesson design. For this Hunter provides a seven-step model, with brief commentary on each step: 1. anticipatory set; 2. objective and purpose; 3. input; 4. modeling; 5. checking for understanding; 6. guided practice; 7. independent practice. (Hunter acknowledges that some educators have used the design to measure "correctness" in teaching, a use she says she never intended. Further, she acknowledges a teacher's professional right to decide which steps to omit in a given lesson.) The third template is the Teaching Appraisal for Instructional Improvement Instrument (TA III), developed "to document changes in teachers' decisions and behaviors and to validate the positive influence of those changes on students' learning gains in terms of academic achievement, positive self-concept, reduced problems of discipline and vandalism as well as increased teacher satisfaction" (1984, p. 177). In using TA III, the observer answers and documents a number of questions having to do with the appropriateness and effectiveness of the instruction. Hunter recommends that the observer create during observation a "script tape," an anecdotal record of what transpires during instruction.

Script tapes provide categories of information which can be made available to teachers in instructional conferences. Formative conferences can be used to help teachers identify and label productive behaviors; develop useful, alternative behaviors; analyze their own teaching; and identify errors that need improvement. In addition, such conferences can help excellent teachers continue their growth. Evaluative conferences, which are summative, should occur only after a number of formative conference interactions (1984, pp. 179–183).

In response to Hunter (1984), Costa (1984) questioned the scientific soundness of Hunter's program, suggesting that modern science acknowledges an indeterminancy not found in Hunter's assertion that research-based theory has now been translated into practice. After observing that such "instructional strategists" as Taba, Lozanov, Adler, Glasser, Bruner, and Montessori "might conceive the acts of teaching, learning, and supervising quite differently" from Hunter (p. 196), Costa comments. The concept of science portrayed throughout [her] chapter is one of reducing teaching, learning, curriculum, and supervision to their lowest common denominators" (p. 198).

Hunter (1985) rebuts what she considers to be myths about her instructional model, among them, that it is rigid and stifles creativity; that it was created to evaluate teachers; that it applies only to elementary teaching; and that it consists of a limited set of learning principles. With regard to the "myth" that the model does not apply to the arts, to discovery learning, or to cooperative learning, Hunter writes:

Any style of teaching or learning may be used, but the teacher remains responsible for learning outcomes. The more skilled the teacher is in using the model, the more independent and successful learners can become and the greater the variety of teaching and learning styles that can be used. (p. 59)

Although Hunter (1985) refers to a number of research studies that she believes have corroborated the propositions of her model, Stallings and Stipek (1986) report that "there has been little experimental research on its implementation by teachers or on its effects upon students" (p. 742).

Weakness in the Model

One problem that mastery programs appear to share is their reliance upon achievement tests to validate their worth. Paper and pencil tests intended to measure the acquisition of skills overlook many areas critical to English language arts, among them, effectiveness of oral communication, appreciation of literature, development of values, understanding and appreciation of media. Further, most achievement tests fail to measure style and expression in writing done in various modes for various audiences. (For a discussion of the limitations of tests as they affect English teaching, see Task Force on Measurement and Evaluation of English, 1975.) In short, mastery programs, by and large, present a limited view of what most English educators believe important to the field. In focusing primarily on instructional strategies rather than on students' performance on sequential tests, Hunter appears to escape criticism about the narrowness of curricular goals.

THE HERITAGE MODEL

Evidenced early in American education was concern for transmitting the values and traditions of the culture. As Applebee (1974) points out:

The New England Primer, Webster's *Grammatical Institute,* and the McGuffey readers ... provided a common background of culture and allusion, a common heritage for a nation too young to have any other. *The Primer* spread a common catechism, Webster's *Institute* advanced a common system of spelling and promoted a chauvinistic nationalism, McGuffey's readers created a literary heritage, even if one based on fragments and precis. (p. 5)

Applebee reports that Webster purposefully designed his *Blue-Backed Speller,* published in 1783, "to foster the unity and common culture which he sensed that the nation lacked" (p. 3).

Since Webster's time, any number of individuals, committees, and commissions have sensed that the nation has lacked a common culture and have criticized the schools—elementary through college—for not providing it (Applebee, 1974, *passim*). With respect to English teaching, most often falling under attack have been literature programs for failing to contain works of sufficient merit to satisfy those doing the criticizing. Either explicit or implicit in this criticism is usually the belief that there exists a corpus of literature that has enduring worth because of its content, style, and ethical value, and that within this corpus are works accessible to virtually all students. These works constitute the student's literary and, in part, cultural heritage. (For works reflecting this position, see for example, Adler, 1940; Lynch & Evans, 1963; Ravitch & Finn, 1987; Stone, 1961; Van Doren, 1943.)

In preference to specifying particular works to be taught at a given grade or level, proponents of the heritage model often recommend that teachers, knowledgeable about the youngsters they face, should themselves make choices from within the corpus. Rather than relying solely on individual choice, however, the Commission on English of the College Entrance Examination Board (1965) suggested that in the secondary school, the curriculum in literature be determined by departmental consensus and that it consist mainly of American and English literature. Recognizing that the corpus is ever expanding, the Commission made a concession to modernity:

Along with major and minor classics [the literature curriculum] will certainly include a selection of more recent books. These may or may not become part of the classic heritage, but they are important because literature does not possess absolutely fixed values and because the classic heritage must be understood as an evolving tradition, open at one end. (pp. 47–48)

Recent Proponents of the Heritage Model

The National Commission on Excellence in Education (1983) recommended that the teaching of English in high school should, among other things, "equip graduates to ... know our literary heritage and how it enhances imagination and ethical understanding, and how it relates to the customs, ideas, and values of today's life and culture" (p. 25). In 1987 a number of publications appeared that amplified in one way or another the Commission's recommendation (Bennett, 1987; A. Bloom, 1987; Cheney, 1987; Hirsch, 1987; Ravitch & Finn, 1987).

Alan Bloom

Bloom's *The Closing of the American Mind: How Higher Education Has Failed Democracy* (1987) is a critique of the modern university and of the students who inhabit it. An unexpected best seller, the book is divided into three parts, the first dealing with contemporary students, the second with political philosophy, and the third with the present state of university education. In the text, Bloom traces the history of Western civilization through the contributions of a number of philosophers, chief among them Socrates, Machiavelli, Hobbes, Locke, Rousseau, Nietzche, and Heidegger. From Socrates, who believed the use of reason to be the highest fulfillment of our natures, to Heidegger, who endorsed National Socialism in the name of philosophy, Bloom finds a progressive decline in the importance given to the role of intellect in society. This decline accounts for what he believes to be a cultural crisis in America. He finds a new kind of student now occupying the university, one who is un-

read and antiintellectual, the product of public-school teachers who fell under the sway of the "moral relativism" of the 1960s. He argues for the reading of "the greatest texts" from childhood on, believes that failure to read "good books" strengthens "our most fatal tendency—the belief that here and now is all there is" and finds feminism to be "the latest enemy of the vitality of classic texts" (pp. 64–65). The struggles against elitism and racism in the 1960s and 1970s he believes had little effect on students' relation to books.

Radicals had at an earlier stage of egalitarianism already dealt with the monarchic, aristocratic and antidemocratic character of most literary classics by no longer paying attention to their manifest political content.... And as for racism, it just did not play a role in the classical literature ... and no great work of literature is ordinarily considered racist (p. 65)

The popularity of Bloom's book suggests that its theses struck a responsive cord within many book reviewers and readers. But it also provoked controversy. Barber (1988) and Rorty (1988), for example, faulted the book for being antidemocratic, and Menand (1987) found it to be anti-young people. In a generally favorable review, Scholes (1988) concluded that *The Closing of the American Mind...* "is a smart, thoughtful, and occasionally hateful book" (p. 326).

E.D. Hirsch, Jr

Of more direct pertinence to a chapter on instructional models for English is Hirsch's *Cultural Literacy: What Every American Needs to Know* (1987), another surprising best seller. Citing the work of various psycholinguists and reading specialists, Hirsch argues that cultural literacy depends on the sufficiency of shared relevant background information (schemata) that readers within a nation can bring to bear on texts. Hirsch finds the information necessary for cultural literacy to be national in character, differing from one nation to another; rarely detailed or precise; and marked more by stability than change.

Cultural literacy lies *above* the everyday levels of knowledge that everyone processes and *below* the expert level known only to specialists. It is that middle ground of cultural knowledge possessed by the "common reader." It includes information that we have traditionally expected our children to receive in school, but which they no longer do. (p. 19)

The failure of the schools to transmit the information necessary for cultural literacy is attributed to shifts in educational policy occurring between the issuance of the *Report of the Committee of Ten on Secondary School Studies* (National Education Association, 1883) and the publication of the *Cardinal Principles of Secondary Education* (Kingsley, 1918). While the earlier report "assumed that all students would take the same humanistic subjects and recommended giving a new emphasis to natural sciences," the later one rejected focus on subject matter, stressing instead "the seven fundamental aims of education in a democracy: 1. Health. 2. Command of fundamental processes. 3. Worthy home membership. 4. Vocation. 5. Citizenship. 6. Worthy use of leisure. 7. Ethical character" (pp. 117–118).

Dewey's Influence. Hirsch (1987) credits the shift in policy to the influence of John Dewey, whose educational philosophy amalgamated European romanticism, which stressed the uniqueness and natural development of the child, and American pragmatism, which stressed utility and direct application of knowledge. The full flowering of this shift, according to Hirsch, has led to the following: an emphasis upon generic skills without reference to content; the creation of academic "tracks" and of elective courses, together which have fragmented the curriculum horizontally and vertically and prevented students from acquiring knowledge in common (on this point, see Powell, Farrar, & Cohen, 1985); the decline of scores on the verbal Scholastic Aptitude Test and on national assessments of reading; and, in toto, to the debasement of cultural literacy in America.

Hirsch (1987) asserts that disadvantaged children have been most adversely affected by the school's failure to impart information critical to their attainment of cultural literacy and, with it, access to the economic benefits of the dominant culture. To those who claim the literate culture in our land: it excludes nobody; it cuts across generations and social groups and classes..." (p. 21). (For rebuttals of this point, see Coser, 1987; and Gray, 1988.)

A Two-Part Curriculum. To reverse the decline he perceives in cultural literacy, Hirsch (1987) recommends a two-part curriculum modeled after that proposed by Graham (1984). One part, the extensive curriculum, would have the following as its content:

traditional literate knowledge, the information, attitudes, and assumptions that literate Americans share—cultural literacy.... [T]his curriculum should be taught not just as a series of terms, or list of words, but as a vivid system of shared associations ... [T]his extensive network of associations constitutes the part of the curriculum that has to be known by every child and must be common to all the schools of the nation. (Hirsch, 1987, pp. 127–128)

The intensive curriculum, which could accommodate diversity in temperaments and aims of students, teachers, and schools, would encourage "a fully developed understanding of a subject, making one's knowledge of it integrated and coherent" (p. 128).

To acquire from the extensive curriculum the network of associations or schemata necessary for cultural literacy, students would not have to study identical materials. For example, not all high school graduates would have to read *Romeo and Juliet,* but all would have to know something about it. There would be no national core curriculum or list of great books to be read. Content for the extensive curriculum would come in good part from a total revision of language-arts texts, which Hirsch (1987) finds too concerned at present with readability formulas and skills, too devoid of traditional lore and factual material. He desires textbooks that, as in earlier decades, "consciously aimed to impart cultural literacy" (p. 112).

The List. In an attempt to identify and publish the contents of cultural literacy, Hirsch (1987) and two colleagues from the University of Virginia, one a historian and the other a physicist, compiled a list of about 5,000 items that appears in an appendix

to *Cultural Literacy* ... and that was later augmented, with items defined, for *The Dictionary of Cultural Literacy* (Hirsch, Kett, & Trefil, 1988). Included are authors' names, book titles, cities, historical events, proverbs, political personages, and scientific concepts intended to reflect a high-school level of literacy. When the first list was submitted to 100 outside consultants, otherwise unidentified, the authors found "a strong consensus about the significant elements in our core literate vocabulary," a consensus that "extended to educated Americans of different ages, sexes, races, and ethnic origins" (Hirsch, 1987, p. 136).

The popularity of Hirsch's *Cultural Legacy* ... like that of Bloom's *The Closing of the American Mind,* suggests that it contained an argument of fundamental appeal to tens of thousands of Americans, among them such prominent educators as William Bennett, U.S. Secretary of Education; Albert Shanker, President, American Federation of Teachers; Bill Honig, Superintendent of Public Instruction in California; and Richard Anderson, Director, Center for the Study of Reading, University of Illinois. As might be expected, the book also prompted some tepid or adverse reviews (see, e.g., Coser, 1987; Gray, 1988; Scholes, 1988; Squire, 1988; Tschudi, 1988; and Warnock, 1987). Called into question most often were Hirsch's assumptions that students in earlier generations always learned the material to which they were exposed; that learning factual information about literature is equivalent to having lived through experiences with literature; that literate culture is not class-biased; and that once the contents of cultural literacy are identified, the method of teaching them is not highly significant. Also questioned strongly was the adequacy of a list of items to serve as a gauge of literacy, as well as Hirsch's statement that "only a few hundred pages of information stand between the literate and illiterate, between dependence and autonomy" (Hirsch, 1987, p. 143). In a positive review, Scott (1988) argued that Hirsch's model of reading, though not one strongly supported by the profession of English, had widespread public support. He held that "the profession's negative response to Hirsch's book is not only intellectually shortsighted ... but also politically inept" (p. 338).

At this point, only time can determine what lasting influence, if any, Hirsch's work will have on American public education in general and, in particular, on the content and teaching of the English language arts.

Lynne Cheney, Diane Ravitch, and Chester Finn, Jr.

American Memory, by Cheney (1987) and *What Do Our 17-Year-Olds Know,* by Ravitch and Finn (1987) both report on a national assessment of 11th graders' knowledge of history and literature. The assessment, funded by the National Endowment for the Humanities (chaired by Cheney), was administered early in 1986 by the National Assessment of Educational Progress (NAEP). A national sample of approximately 8,000 students responded to 141 multiple-choice questions in history and 121 in literature. The sample, was reportedly representative "of students within a large number of sub-groups of the population, including gender, race, and number attending public and nonpublic schools...." (Ravitch & Finn, p. 3). No student answered all questions. Matrix sampling was employed, wherein each student takes only a portion of a large text, and results are averaged for groups. The literature assessment was composed principally of questions

that could be answered correctly on the basics of rather superficial knowledge about major writers and works of Western literature. Yet on the average question, just 51.8 percent of the students supply correct answers, a lower average score than the 54.5 percent giving the right answer to the average history question.... (p. 85)

Cheney (1987), whose pamphlet treated the data in general terms, reported that most students were unfamiliar with such writers as Dante, Chaucer, Dostoevsky, Austin, Whitman, Hawthorne, Melville, and Cather. (She, as well as Ravitch and Finn, seemed unaware that 11th graders would probably not encounter figures like Chaucer and Austin in the school curriculum until 12th grade when English literature is normally taught. Only students taking a course in world literature would likely be familiar with Dante and Dostoevsky, while Cather would probably not be taught until late in the 11th grade, when modern American literature is traditionally introduced. This comment is offered as clarification, not as an excuse of students' generally poor performance.)

Cheney (1987) found "language arts" (p. 10), basal readers (p. 15), teacher-education programs (p. 23), education specialists (p. 26), and literature textbooks (p. 28) in good part responsible for students' deficient knowledge of literature. The term "language arts" suggests process rather than content; basal readers follow readability scales and contain little substantive literature; time spent in education courses could be better spent in content courses; education specialists stress skills and process rather than substance; more meritorious works should appear in literature anthologies.

Echoing some of the complaints made by A. Bloom (1987), Ravitch and Finn (1987) contended that students' poor performance on the assessment reflected the dissolution of what once had been an established literature curriculum:

Since the mid-1960s, the professional consensus that supported the established literature curriculum has dissolved as a result of criticism from many quarters—from blacks, because black writers were ignored; from feminists, because women writers were neglected; from those who believed that students would prefer literature that was contemporary and relevant to their own lives; and from those who on principle opposed the very idea of a canon, regardless of its content or its capaciousness. Today, there is assuredly no canon, and no one could venture a confident guess as to what is read by American students at any point in their schooling (p. 10).

Ravitch and Finn (1987) asserted that rather than substantially revising the curriculum to correct its limitations—reconstructing it through a mix of classic and contemporary works and authors—... scholars and educators judged the very idea of the traditional curriculum to be irrelevant...." However, maintained the authors, the real problem "lay not in the idea of a coherent literature curriculum, but in the failure of those who could not or would not make the effort to show how traditional and modern literature together can ... help us better

understand ourselves and our society" (p. 10). The traditional curriculum having lost its authority, the only remaining source of authority for language arts was reading specialists' research, "which yields technical rather than literary standards for what students ought to read" (p. 11).

One may be somewhat puzzled by the authors' assertion that the traditional high school canon of literature collapsed after the mid-1960s. On pp. 186–187 they present charts comparing books that students in 1986 had reported reading in public school to books that students over two decades earlier had reported being assigned (Anderson, 1964). The charts appear to reflect considerable stability in the curriculum. For example, 33 percent of students reported reading *Tale of Two Cities* in school in 1963, as compared to 21 percent in 1986; 27 percent in 1963 had read *The Adventures of Huckleberry Finn,* as compared to 45 percent in 1986; 33 percent had read *The Red Badge of Courage* in 1963, while 30 percent had read it in 1986; 32 percent in 1963 had read *The Scarlet Letter,* as compared to 39 percent in 1986. The charts do, however, list only novels. With the exception of novels and certain Shakespearean plays—*Romeo and Juliet, Julius Caesar, Macbeth, Hamlet*—one might find in the curriculum of the past quarter century considerable instability for drama, poetry, short stories, and essays.

Advancing the same arguments as Hirsch (1987), who served on the literature committee for the assessment and whose work they cite, Ravitch and Finn (1987) attributed students' weak performance to the education profession's belief "that *what* children learn is unimportant compared to *how* they learn; ... that skills can be learned without content ..." (p. 17). They repeated Hirsch's (1987) belief that students who lack sufficient background knowledge are culturally handicapped, incapable of carrying on complex transactions in conversation or reading (pp. 18–19).

After conceding that data in their book cannot verify that contemporary youth know less about the past than did their predecessors, Ravitch and Finn (1987) made a number of recommendations, among them the following: that more time be devoted to teaching literature, from the earliest grades through high school; that publishers of readers for schools include among their selections a generous proportion of important literary works and a balanced mix of classic and contemporary poems; that textbook publishers solicit the advice of English teachers and literature scholars in selecting contents for reading textbooks and literature anthologies; that all students, not just the gifted or college bound, be provided "a hefty dose of good literature"; and that all those concerned with the quality of literature in the schools "should strive to define the essential ingredients of a coherent literature curriculum, from the earliest grades through high school ..." (pp. 216–220).

One could advance against the assessment of 17-year-olds' knowledge of literature the same criticism advanced against the list of items included in Hirsch's *Cultural Literacy* (1987), namely, that nodding acquaintance with names of authors, characters, and works is not comparable to lived-through experiences with literature. Recognizing the validity of this potential charge, Ravitch and Finn (1987) lamented from time to time about the limitations of the multiple-choice format (see, for example, comments on pp. 21 and 246). The authors, perforce, left to future assessments and teachers "to probe whether students have drawn meaning for their own lives from what they have read . . ." (pp. 22–23).

As with Hirsch's work, one must await the influence, if any, that findings from the First National Assessment of Literature and History have upon the content of literature programs, K–12. Ravitch and Finn, as with Hirsch, leave open the question of instructional mode or modes. Nevertheless, the heavy emphasis upon factual recall found in both books would seem to lead inexorably to even heavier teacher domination and prescriptiveness than Squire and Applebee (1968), Goodlad (1984), and Powell, Farrar and Cohen (1985) have already found in English programs.

William J. Bennett

At the end of 1987, then Secretary of Education William J. Bennett released a proposed core curriculum for high schools. Titled *James Madison High School: A Curriculum for American Students,* the document called for students to complete a total of 36 semester units of required work to be eligible for graduation, including eight semesters of English. The proposed program followed broadly the recommendations of the National Commission on Excellence in Education (1983).

The proposed titles for the mandatory courses in English revealed a heavy emphasis to be given literature: Introduction to Literature (9th grade); American Literature (10th grade); British Literature (11th grade); Introduction to World Literature (12th grade). Although Bennett recommended for each year that writing assignments be regularly made and that students be given experience in "classroom speaking," he specified most clearly what literary works and authors he believed might be included.

For the 9th grade he suggested that the syllabus be "confined to recognized masterworks of Western literature" and might include "a few books of Homer's *Odyssey,* parts of the the Bible, sonnets and plays of Shakespeare, *Huckleberry Finn,* and a Dickens novel." The syllabus for the 10th grade would "spotlight the distinctive American achievement in literature." Authors mentioned for possible inclusion were Franklin, Irving, Hawthorne, Poe, Whitman, Twain, Melville, Dickinson, Faulkner, Wharton, Hemingway, O'Neill, Fitzgerald, Frost, Ralph Ellison, and Robert Penn Warren. For the 11th grade a "good" syllabus might include Chaucer, Shakespeare, Donne, Milton, Swift, Blake, Wordsworth, Keats, Austen, the Brontes, Dickens, George Eliot, Hardy, Conrad, T. S. Eliot, and Shaw. A sound syllabus for the 12th grade would feature numerous works in translation by such authors as Sophocles, Virgil, Dante, Cervantes, Moliere, Balzac, Chekhov, Dostoevsky, Zola, Mann, and Ibsen. In addition, selections from Japan, China, the Near East, Africa, or Latin America might be introduced, depending on the teacher's knowledge and interest (p. 13).

Rothman (1988) reported that when Bennett's curricular outline was released, educators generally responded favorably to its academic rigor "but questioned whether such a program would be useful to the many students unwilling or unable to master it" (p. 1). Once again, as with the recommendations of Hirsch, Ravitch, and Finn, only time will determine how widely Bennett's proposals are adopted and with what success.

Unsettled Issues

Although desire for the schools to transmit a literary heritage through "good" or "great" works of literature has been recurrent in American education, specification of particular works for particular grades becomes ever more problematic for levels beyond the local: the corpus of potential literature grows steadily with time, and the clientele of public education is far more diverse than it was early in the nation's history. In recognition of these facts, neither the Commission on English (1965) nor members of the Anglo-American Conference at Dartmouth (Muller, 1967) would specify particular works to be taught all students, relying instead on the judgments of teachers in local schools.

Is Hirsch (1987) correct in believing that cultural literacy, as it pertains to English programs, depends in part upon students having intensive experiences with a limited number of highly reputable works of literature? If so (and the point is certainly moot), what corpus of works from which to draw, what instructional conditions, and what instructional behaviors can best help students acquire valuable schemata, schemata that will lead to their reading increasingly complex works on their own? Do these conditions and behaviors need to vary in accordance with students' ages, interests, aptitudes, and experiential backgrounds? If so, in what specific ways?

In like vein, if Bennett (1987) is correct in saying that the curriculum he has proposed can "work" for all students, under what conditions can it work, and by what criteria is it to be judged successful? How, specifically, do teachers in "successful" schools carry out instruction in literature? What measures are used to assess the levels of students' engagement, comprehension, and appreciation of the works they read? What long-range commitments to literature do students evince? How are writing programs and "classroom speaking" effectively joined to the literature curriculum? What are the measures of successful incorporation?

In short, in keeping with many prior proposals to reform the literature curriculum, recent recommendations appear marked more by persuasive rhetoric than by evidence.

THE PROCESS MODEL

More student-centered than either the mastery or heritage models, the process model for instruction asks that the teacher establish the most favorable conditions wherein students can make meaning for themselves. Rather than requiring that students master a set body of content or skills before progressing further, or that as part of their heritage, they become familiar with specific authors and works, the process model places a premium on diversity, on the varied ways by which individuals, each unique, construct knowledge from experience.

The process-oriented teacher may well have a class or a group of students read a work in common, but the teacher will honor the different ways in which the work is experienced and evaluated. (At issue at present is the extent to which a literary heritage can be transmitted via a process approach, i.e., must reading works of acknowledged literary merit lead to teacher-dominated classrooms and to uniformity of response? Can process approaches provide for scope as well as depth?) If skills are taught, they will be taught not in isolation but in relationship to significant language activities in which students are occupied. Emphasis is not on right answers but on the making of meaning. Probst (1984) condemns extensive testing because it distorts students' conception of knowledge, implying to them that knowledge is a commodity that either teachers or books can provide. He comments:

Knowledge is not such a simple matter. It cannot be bought and sold—it must be made. It is the product of the mind's interaction with the world. At such, it can change and grow. If knowledge is out there to be found, there is no possibility for progress—we can only know what is already known. (p. 216)

Some Major Theorists

What follows is a description of the theories that four individuals—Louise Rosenblatt, James Moffett, James Britton, and James Kinneavy—have advanced with respect to teaching the English language arts. Although Rosenblatt's work has long been read and discussed in college methods courses on the teaching of English, and although it is relevant to the teaching of literature at any level, it appears to date to be most influential upon literature programs in the secondary schools. While Moffett treats the entire English curriculum, K–12, his model has been most easily and readily accommodated in elementary schools. Like Moffett, Britton deals with the whole spectrum of the English language arts, though not from as complete a conceptual model and not in the detail that Moffett provides. In the recent past, Britton's research on composition has most strongly affected the English curriculum, particularly in elementary and middle schools. Finally Kinneavy's theory of discourse has been most influential upon writing programs in colleges and, to a lesser extent, secondary schools. In short, some of the theories to be described are more inclusive of the English curriculum than are others. Some may appear to be more process or student-centered than do others. Each has implications for instructional practice. [All four theorists have contributed chapters to this handbook.]

Louise Rosenblatt

The past quarter century has witnessed a flow of books concerned in some respect with how readers respond to texts (see, for example, Barthes, 1975; Bleich, 1975, 1978, 1985; Cooper, 1985; Corcoran & Evans, 1987; Culler, 1983; Fish, 1980; Holland, 1975a, b, 1985; Iser, 1978; Probst, 1984; Purves, 1972, 1985; Purves & Beach, 1972; Purves & Rippere, 1968; Slatoff, 1970; Suleiman & Crosman, 1980; Tompkins, 1980a). The field represented by those books, that of reader-response criticism, is not conceptually unified. Still it has found a common ground in the United States in its opposition to the major tenet of New Criticism, that there exists an objective text apart from its effects upon readers. As Tompkins (1980b) notes, "[R]eader-response critics argue against locating meaning in the text, against seeing the text as a fixed object, and in favor of a criticism that recognizes the reader's role in making meaning" (p. 223).

Since its initial publication in 1938, Rosenblatt's *Literature as Exploration* not only has had a considerable influence on the teaching of literature in the schools but has furnished the theoretical basis for research in the teaching and study of literature (Purves, 1976, pp. iii–iv). Hailed as a work that "stands preiminent in its field" (Squire, 1968, p. vi) and as "a classic" likened in its importance to Milton's *Areopagitica* and Shelley's *Defense of Poetry* (Purves, 1976, p. iv), *Literature as Exploration* is now regarded as the first book in this country to advance a reader-response theory. The brief discussion that follows cannot do justice to the richness and lucidity of the text, though it will attempt to highlight some of its more salient points. (Future page references to the work will be made to the fourth edition, 1983.)

Denying the existence of either generic text or generic reader, Rosenblatt asserts that the literary work results from a complex transaction between reader and text, a transaction that accords with contemporary schema theory:

The literary work exists in the live circuit set up between reader and text: the reader infuses intellectual and emotional meanings into the pattern of verbal symbols, and those symbols channel his thoughts and feelings. Out of this complex process emerges a more or less organized imaginative experience. (p. 25)

Though each transaction is unique, differing even for the same reader from one reading to the next, human beings share enough in common to be able to communicate with each other about how they have experienced a given work. To assure the vitality of that experience, Rosenblatt suggests that students be allowed to express freely their reactions to a selection in both writing and class discussions. As a consequence of the open exchange of response, students will return to the text to clarify their individual responses. Through free expressions and clarification, they may discover that more than one interpretation is possible and that some interpretations are more defensible than others. Throughout, the text remains a constraint against total relativism or subjectivity.

Rosenblatt views literatre as having social and esthetic elements, substance and form, that are inextricably interrelated, though theoretically distinguishable. Emphasis upon only one value—social or esthetic—diminishes the work of art. "The crux of the matter is that the text embodies verbal stimuli toward a special kind of intense and ordered experience—sensuous, intellectual, emotional—out of which social insights may arise" (1983, pp. 31–32). Although students can gain pleasure from knowledge about literary form and artistry, particularly through their engaging in imaginative writing themselves," . . . all the student's knowledge about literary history, about authors, and periods and types, will be so much useless baggage if he has not been led primarily to seek in literature a vital personal experience" (p. 59). Preoccupation with what can be taught and tested diverts teachers from the primary aim of literature study, to enhance students' ability to read and enjoy literature (p. 64).

Rosenblatt stresses that in making literature available to students, teachers must remain sensitive to the emotional concerns of young people, to their levels of maturity, and to the social forces at work upon them, all of which color their responses. Arguing that the essence of literature is the rejection of stereotyped reactions, she views the teacher's role as that of helping readers "develop flexibility of mind, a freedom from rigid emotional habits" that will enable them "to enter into the esthetic experiences the artist has made possible" (1983, p. 104).

In their attempts to clarify their personal response, to be sure they have taken into account all that the work has to offer, students will become more aware of such matters as diction, rhythm, structure, point of view, and genre. Further, to better understand themselves and the literature, they may seek additional information about the author and the work, information that should be assimilated into their primary responses.

Pursuit of additional information may lead them to study the social, economic, intellectual, and philosophical conditions surrounding the author's life, a study which, in turn, may lead them to a consideration of the work's reception in its own day as compared to its present-day reception. The value of this comparison will come from "seeing that the reader's own reactions, like the work of art, are the organic expression not only of a particular individual but also of a particular cultural setting" (Rosenblatt, 1983, p. 118). Out of such insight may come still deeper concerns with human relations, with the text's implicit system of values, with questions of good and evil, and of a human's relationship to the world. To be a catalyst for students' investigations, and to help them avoid stereotypic and prejudicial thinking, teachers need to be at least conversant with the processes and basic concepts of the social sciences. Characteristic to these is the scientific method, which fosters inquiry and an attitude of tentativeness. Rosenblatt finds the method to be complimentary, not antithetical, to the artistic spirit and the exploration of literature.

In revealing their own attitudes toward experience, their own values, teachers must avoid inculcating dogmatism and guard against promoting noncommital relativism. The task of education is to provide students with the knowledge, mental habits, and motivation that will enable them to solve their own problems independently, to formulate with increasing maturity their own systems of values and philosophy. Literature can abet that task, according to Rosenblatt (1983), for it helps acculturate individuals, frees them from provincialism, makes them aware of alternative forms of thought and behavior, assists them in resolving personal problems and in making sound choices, and redirects their potentially antisocial behavior. It can help individuals develop the kind of imagination critical to the well-being of a democracy.

To liberate imaginations, teachers need to provide students a broad range of literature, including works, both present and past, that reflect cultures quite different from the students' own. Teachers should not, however, force young people to confront "classics" in which archaic language or ways of life confound their understanding. Such works can await students' greater maturity: "To force such works upon the young prematurely defeats the long-term goal of educating people to a personal love of literature sufficiently deep to cause them to seek it out for themselves at the appropriate time" (Rosenblatt, 1983, p. 218). The test is whether the child or adolescent is intellectually and emotionally ready for what the book has to offer.

Rosenblatt (1983) asserts that the same habits of mind developed for making sound judgments about literature will serve students in developing sound insights into ordinary human experience: "[T]hrough discussion and reflection on his response to literature, the student may learn to order his emotions and to rationally face people and situations he is emotionally involved in" (pp. 238–239). She believes that literature can root in specific lived-through human situations the generalizations and abstractions of the social sciences. Teachers in both areas share a responsibility to the student's development as a whole person. "It is not half so important that the student should acquire history, sociology, and literature as it is that he should see exemplified in each of these fields certain unifying concepts concerning human nature and society" (p. 271). Understanding builds upon understanding in an ever-widening spiral: "The development of literary appreciation will depend upon a reciprocal process: An enlargement of the student's understanding of human life leads to increased esthetic sensitivity, and increased esthetic sensitivity makes possible more fruitful human insights from literature" (p. 273).

Strengths and Limitations. In *The Reader, the Text, the Poem,* Rosenblatt (1978) elaborates her transactional theory of the literary work, treats such topics as interpretation and evaluation, and discriminates between aesthetic reading, in which the reader is primarily concerned with what he or she is experiencing during the actual reading event, and efferent reading, in which the reader's attention is fixed on the uses to be made of what is read. The book, which centers on the reader's contribution in the two-way transactional relationship with the text, has implications for instruction but does not directly deal with classroom situations. Even in her earlier work, Rosenblatt (1938) offers less an instructional model for English language arts than a set of attitudes, an approach or stance, that she believes teachers should adopt toward the teaching of literature. The teacher of literature that she implies in her work—flexible, undogmatic, compassionate, well-versed in literature, and familiar with the methods and major findings of the social sciences—seems more the ideal teacher of English than the one most often observed (Goodlad, 1984; Powell et al., 1985; Squire & Applebee, 1968). Roemer (1987) raises questions about whether most teachers, including those supportive of reading-response theory, can conduct classrooms without communicating "a set of dominant values and manners which the students transgress at their own peril" (p. 912).

The problem of teachers exerting pedagogical authority may be less severe in the elementary than in the secondary school. Although she draws most of her illustrations of teaching from the high school or college years, Rosenblatt (1983) reports that elementary teachers were quick to see the implications of her work. She notes that "perhaps they were less hampered by the baggage of literary history and literary terminology" (p. ix).

Ironically, though reader-response criticism appears to be increasingly influential in colleges and universities (e.g., Roemer, 1987; Suleiman & Crosman 1980; Tompkins, 1980a), the "baggage" to which Rosenblatt referred has recently become more predominate in high-school anthologies of literature, in which one finds handbooks of literary forms and techniques; units tightly organized by chronology, genre, or both; and frequent questions on aspects of form (see, for example, *McDougal, Littel Literature,* rev. ed., 1987; *Adventures in Literature,* Heritage ed. rev., Harcourt Brace Jovanovich, 1985; or *America Reads,* Classic ed., Scott, Foresman, 1989).

Needed Research. Rosenblatt (1985) has called for research to test her belief that most questions posed in classrooms, literature anthologies, and research projects promote efferent rather than aesthetic reading. While Purves and Beach (1972) report that studies of response to literature tend to support Rosenblatt's transactional theory of criticism, Hansson (1985) has said that we know virtually nothing as yet about "what goes on in the reading processes where the latent meanings, qualities, and structures of works of literature are realized in the minds of readers" (p. 226). Among studies Hansson believes needed are ones to determine at what age level and in what contexts students are ready to study a particular work. With respect to classroom practice, Fillion and Brause (1987) assert that "we know very little from research about how literature teaching is manifested in classrooms and how such teaching influences learning (literary or otherwise) or about the role of literary texts in language education" (p. 215). In short, the extent to which Rosenblatt's transactional theory is influencing present classroom instruction is unknown. One might reasonably surmise that current textbooks and testing programs are undermining what widespread influence it might exert.

James Moffett

Through books for teachers (Moffett, 1968a, b; Moffett, 1981 a, b; Moffett & Wagner, 1983), student texts (Moffett, 1973; Moffett, Baker, & Cooper, 1987; Moffett, Bolchazy, & Friedberg, 1987a; Moffett & Tashlike, 1987b; Moffett, Wixon, P., Wixon, V., Blau, & Phreaner, 1987c), and readers (Moffett, 1985a; Moffett & McElheny, 1966), James Moffett offers one of the most fully developed models for teaching the English langauge arts, K–12 (Kuykendall, 1972; Myers, 1986; Pope & Kutiper, 1988; Stanek, 1972; Stanford & Stanford, 1980). Maintaining that English, like foreign language and mathematics, is a symbol system rather than an empirical subject like history or physics, Moffett (1968a) believes that students need to learn how to operate the system in oral and written form. English he construes "as all discourse in our native language—any verbalizing of any phenomena, whether thought, spoken, or written; whether literary or non-literary" (Moffett, 1968a, p. 9); consequently, he would include as part of language arts materials not only literature but "many reading selections, periodicals, games, and visuals that draw subject matter from history and the behavioral and physical sciences..." (Moffett & Wagner, 1983, p. 41).

The theory underlying many of Moffett's contributions is to be found in *Teaching the Universe of Discourse* (1968a). Influenced by the work in general semantics of Alfred Korzybski and

TABLE 4–2. Moffett's Spectrum of Discourse

Interior Dialogue (ecogentric speech)			P
Vocal Dialogue (socialized speech)	*Recording, the drama of what is happening.*	PLAYS	O
Correspondence Personal Journal Autobiography Memoir	*Reporting, the narrative of what happened.*	FICTION	E T
Biography Chronicle History	*Generalizing, the exposition of what happens.*	ESSAY	R
Science Metaphysics	*Theorizing, the argumentation of what will, may happen.*		Y

S. I. Hayakawa and the developmental theories of Jean Piaget and, to a lesser degree, Lem Vygotsky, Moffett proposes a sequential curriculum for teaching the language arts, one corresponding to a student's intellectual and emotional growth and based on a hierarchy of abstraction:

The hypothesis is that speaking, writing, and reading in forms of discourse that are successively more abstract makes it possible for the learner to understand better what is entailed at each stage of the hierarchy, to relate one stage to another, and thus to become aware of how he and others create information and ideas. The goal is not so much to attain the higher levels as it is to practice abstracting all along the way. No greater value is ascribed to one level than to another. (1968a, p. 25)

Moffett describes modes of discourse as occurring in the form of two progressions, the first involving an increasing distance between speaker and audience *(I-you),* or the rhetorical relation; the second involving an increasing distance between speaker and subject *(I-it),* or the referential relation. The first progression is from reflection, to conversation, to correspondence, to publication (p. 33). The second progression is from drama, to narrative, to exposition, to logical argumentation (p. 35). Both progressions are then combined into a hierarchy of levels of abstraction called *The Spectrum of Discourse* (p. 47): Moffett concedes that this linear model fails to capture the simultaneous play between speaker-listener and speaker-subject, or to indicate that "something of every level is found at every other level" (p. 48). Moreover, the model fails to reflect the great variability in students' rate of linguistic and intellectual growth (p. 54).

Student Variability. To accommodate student variability, Moffett and Wagner (1983) propose a student-centered language-arts curriculum which would promote the "three things that are hardest for the schools to bring about ... individualization, interaction, and integration" (p. 46). The curriculum would foster individualization by allowing students to select and sequence their own activities and materials; interaction, by arranging for students to teach each other; integration, by interweaving subjects so that students could synthesize knowledge structures in their own minds (p. 25). The student-centered classroom would ideally permit students "access at any time to any activity, book, person, medium, materials, and methods" (p. 29). It would mix students of different abilites and even ages, have in it a minimum of three or four grades "worth of things to do and things to do them with," and might require the use of aides and persons from the community as well as a differentiated teaching staff (p. 30). Ability tracking would not be used, and student self-evaluation based upon feedback from a number of sources would be preferable to letter grades.

Materials for each classroom would include "reading matter, recordings of some reading selections, language games, activity directions on cards and posters, photos and films, media equipment, and raw materials for making things" (p. 63). Using the media equipment and raw materials, students would regularly augment the other classroom supplies by creating for themselves what they felt was needed. Activity cards, which would replace teacher presented lessons and conventional textbooks, would be central to individualizing the classroom, enabling students at any time to choose from a wide spectrum of activities and freeing the teacher to work with individuals or small groups. Because materials and activities for the whole of elementary and secondary school would be broken into four stages, each representing a share of student growth and each spanning several years, students would have available the same materials for several years running (p. 61).

Objectives. Moffett and Wagner (1983) divide all discourse objectives for the English language arts into nine kinds, corresponding roughly to a developmental sequence of growth and reflecting the hierarchy of levels of abstraction presented under *The Spectrum of Discourse* (Moffett, 1968a, p. 47). Students could practice each kind by speaking, listening, reading, and writing, and they would be expected to be able to send and receive each kind effectively in oral or written form:

1. Word play (riddles, puns, tongue twisters, much poetry)
2. Labels and captions (language joined with pictures of objects, graphs, maps, and so on)
3. Invented dialogue (discussion and transcripts)
4. Actual dialogue (discussion and transcripts)
5. Invented stories (fiction, fables, tales, much poetry, and so on)
6. True stories (autobiography, memoir, biography, reportage, journals, and so on)
7. Directions (for how to do and how to make)
8. Information (generalized fact)
9. Ideas (generalized thought) (p. 22)

Even younger children could practice all nine kinds concurrently, "either by speaking some kinds before they can write them, or reading them before they can speak them, or by sending and receiving very short or very long continuities" (p. 556). Since the discourse areas are conceived as being multimedia, they might involve the use of nonprint media as well as words.

In contrast to discourse objectives, literacy objectives bridge oral and written language, irrespective of type of discourse:

1. The student will be able to sound out with normal intonation any text that he can understand if read to him.
2. The student will be able to transcribe whatever he can say or understand orally. (p. 23)

The discourse and literacy objectives would assure that reading in the elementary schools is treated as a subject integral to the language arts, and that composition in the secondary schools bears a relationship to literature (pp. 19–20).

Implications for Instruction. The implied teachers for the curriculum that Moffett advocates would have to be creative, self-assured, and highly tolerant of diversity. Like the teachers of literature implied in Rosenblatt's work, they would need to be broadly educated, familiar with concepts, methods, and resources in the social and physical sciences as well as in the humanities. However, unlike Rosenblatt's implied teachers, they would not give print literature a privileged place in the curriculum: it would compete with content from other subjects for students' attention. Moreover, students would be as much encouraged to write literature as to read it. Rather than being concerned principally with students' mastery of discrete skills or their familiarity with a cultural or literary heritage, teachers would be primarily interested in helping students gain control over language through using it in increasingly sophisticated ways. "Through reading, writing, and discussing whole, authentic discourses—and using no textbooks—students can learn better everything that we consider of value in language and literature than they can by the current substantive and particle approach" (Moffett, 1968a, p. 7).

Teachers would be creators and managers of resources, making themselves available as needed for coaching, conferencing, and participating in small-group discussions. Student choice would be central to learning, with instruction individualized in providing each student maximum access to human and material resources. Because students would be going in diverse and sometimes unpredictable directions, teachers would not be able to rely on set lesson plans or sequences of instruction (Moffett & Wagner, 1983, pp. 28, 54–55). The classroom would be active and at times filled with noise as students engaged in such oral language activities as dramatic improvisations, rehearsed readings of texts, brainstorming, panels and topic discussions.

Moffett and Wagner (1983) find that open education, or its counterpart in England, the "integrated day," most resembles the mode of classroom operation they advocate (p. 53). The mode, similar to that supported by Dixon (1967), is one they believe can be viewed as reactionary rather than radical:

Individual programs, different working parties doing different things at the same time, kids teaching kids, nongraded heterogeneity—these all went on in the one-room schoolhouse. Such "innovations" would in fact be a return to an earlier American tradition. . . . (Moffett & Wagner, p. 49)

The authors acknowledge that the "thoroughgoing humanistic individualization" at which both their curriculum and open education aim has not been widely implemented in the United

States, an acknowledgment supported by observational studies of secondary classrooms (Applebee, 1981; Boyer, 1983; Goodlad, 1984; Powell et al., 1985; Sizer, 1984; Squire & Applebee, 1968).

The reasons for only marginal implementation of a more humanistic and open educational system are many, including those Moffett and Wagner (1983) earlier provide: the trend of institutions is toward standardization, isolation; and compartmentalization, not toward individualization, interaction, and integration (p. 46). Even if this were not so, Moffett's curriculum for the English language arts would likely encounter resistance, particularly at the secondary level. Among other things, it requires that secondary English teachers no longer conceive of themselves as content specialists in language and literature; that they no longer try to control the substance and pace of students' learning; that they live comfortably with numerous activities occurring simultaneously in the classroom. Further, unlike mastery or heritage models that individual secondary teachers might adopt, Moffett's process model, essentially interdisciplinary, requires the commitment of administration and staff to a total restructuring of the curriculum. Nevertheless, because the model is so thoroughly conceptualized and persuasively presented, it will continue to gain adherents among those who find individual learners' productive and receptive uses of language, not decontextualized skills or inherited content, to be central to the English language arts.

Implications for Research. Warnock (1984) states that researchers have been far more interested than teachers in Moffett's scheme by which individuals learn to differentiate the universe of discourse through apprehending progressively more abstract relations to audience and subject. But Warnock fails to define "researcher" or to support his assertion. Certainly Moffett has had an influence on thinking and research methodology of Britton (1972, 1978); further, Kinneavy (1980a) has found much in common between his own theory of discourse and that of Moffett. Nevertheless, the curriculum and instructional responsibilities that Moffett builds upon his theory of discourse seem not to have attracted researchers, perhaps because they do not lend themselves to the types of controls familiar to empirical research. Further, the "success" of the curriculum and instructional model he presents is contingent on the kind of future society that Americans wish. One may surmise that a student who had experienced Moffett's curriculum for 13 years would differ appreciably as a mature citizen from one who had been involved for 13 years in mastery learning. But proof would be hard to establish.

On a more modest but nevertheless complex scale, Dillon (1987) and Fillion and Brause (1987) have called for greater research efforts into the theoretical stance in language instruction that has been dominant in the professional literature since the Dartmouth Seminar in 1966, a stance whose pedagogical aspects are explicitly expressed in Britton (1972), Dixon (1967), and Moffett (1968a, b).

Awareness of the deep, overriding importance of purpose and meaning for language use and development (both oral and written) has been with us at least since the Dartmouth Seminar, but has not yet characterized our research efforts.

. . . I think our research should deal explicitly with these deep-structure headings of purpose and meaning, rather than allow them to remain implicit and tacit, for they are always present. (Dillon, 1987, pp. 186–187)

James Britton

Britton's ideas are presented most completely in two works, *Language and Learning* (1972) and *The Development of Writing Abilities (11–18),* (Britton, Burgess, Martin, McLeod, & Rosen, 1975), each of which will be discussed in some detail.

Influenced by the work of Cassirer, Sapir, Langer, Bruner, Malinowski, Vygotsky, Luria, Moffett, George Kelly, D. W. Harding, and Roger Brown, Britton (1972) presents as central to his book the theory that we build "a representation of the world as we experience it, and from this representation, this cumulative record of our own past, we generate expectations which, as moment by moment the future becomes the present, enable us to interpret the present" (p. 12).

Language learning begins with listening (p. 37), while talk is the means by which we habitually bring our representations of experience up to date, not necessarily as we encounter actualities, but through recollecting them and interpreting them (p. 19). The capability of language to classify and order objects and events at different levels of generality permits higher forms of thought process, including reasoning (p. 28). However, in our world representation or "verbally organized world schema," we organize more than words. Into it are woven interiorized sensory images, pre-verbal patterns of feeling, and post-verbal patterns of ideas and beliefs (p. 29).

Drawing on the work of Harding (1937, 1963), Britton (1972) distinguishes between two distinctive roles we adopt with respect to language—participant or spectator.

As participants, we use language to interact with people and things and make the wheels of the world . . . go round. As spectators, we use language to contemplate what has happened to us or to other people, or what might conceivably happen; . . . we improvise upon our world representation . . . to enrich it, to embroider it, to fill its gaps and extend its frontiers, or to iron out its inconsistencies. (p. 8)

The participant role is characterized by the need to decide and act, to get things done. As participants, we use language to inform, instruct, persuade, plan, argue, and explain. Free from the demands of the world, as spectators we use language to create make-believe play; to day dream; to relate and to listen to experiences, gossip and tales; to read or write fiction, drama, and poetry (p. 122). (For further discussion of these roles, see Applebee, 1985; Britton, 1977, 1978, 1984; Britton et al., 1975; and Harris, 1988.)

Early Schooling. Britton (1972) views the early years of schooling as an opportunity for students to continue and refine their use of language in the role of spectators through a unified body of activity, a body that would include stories and poems

TABLE 4–3. Britton's Function Categories

Participant role		Spectator role
TRANSACTIONAL	EXPRESSIVE	POETIC

both read and written, dramatic play, and talk that would accompany and mediate these events. Mingled with them would be activities in the participant role, activities which in the course of time would develop into a second unity (pp. 128, 152).

According to Britton (1972), the process of composing in writing should be wedded to that of reading, and both should be related to students' spoken language (p. 159). Elementary teachers should not use graded readers, which isolate a "sight vocabulary" from the child's speech vocabulary. The latter should be fully employed in beginning reading through having the child either dictate or write selections (p. 162). Talk is the most likely means by which students first investigate, explore, and organize new fields of interest. "talk . . . prepares the environment into which what is taken from reading may be accommodated: and from that amalgam the writing proceeds" (p. 166).

Both speech and writing may function in expressive, transactional, or poetic ways. Expressive speech or writing is language close to the self of the speaker or writer and relies heavily upon context for its interpretation, on the listener's or reader's knowledge of the speaker's or writer's situation (p. 168). Change from expressive to transactional speech or writing occurs when participant demands require that language be used for some transaction, "to get something done in the world" (p. 169). (For an objection to Britton's use of the word "transactional," see Rosenblatt, 1985). The move from expressive to poetic function occurs when language in the spectator role is used to present "an object to be contemplated in itself and for itself" (Britton, 1972, p. 175). In moving toward the transactional function, expressive language becomes more public and explicit; in moving toward the poetic function, it becomes more public and implicit, relying upon the formal arrangement of sounds, words, images, ideas, events, and feelings to give resonance to items (p. 177). Britton et al. (1975) present these language functions and roles schematically as shown in Table 4–3.

From the earliest stages, children should have available a wide range of reading material relevant to their interests and capable of challenging their powers to make sense of what they read (164). The relationship between child and teacher in the primary school should first be one "of simple reciprocity . . . an acceptance of each by the other, as persons" (p. 182). Once this relationship is secured, then the teacher can establish a professional relationship with individual children (p. 188).

Later Schooling. Because young children have few practical responsibilities, their expressive speech tends to "undergo organization in the direction—ultimately—of art, of poem, story, or play" (Britton, 1972, p. 216). As children grow into adolescence, they exchange a world of objects, including non-human creatures, for a world of persons and ideas (pp. 219, 230). In

helping effect that exchange, teachers in the secondary schools should continue to encourage expressive talk and writing, media through which students discover and explore their thoughs and feelings. Classroom talk is critical not only to adolescents' pursuit of ideas but to their establishing relationships with others:

Perhaps the most important general implication for teaching . . . is to note that anyone who succeeded in outlawing talk in the classroom would have outlawed life in the adolescent: the web of human relations must be spun in school as well as out. (p. 223)

A major task for adolescents is that of integrating their personalities, of reconciling their perceptions of themselves with the impressions they make upon others, of becoming aware of the relationship between what they believe and how they behave. Their preoccupation with forging separate identities for themselves is reflected in their behavior and in their talk, writing, and reading. "In the participant role they will discuss, argue, confess, explore, theorize: in the spectator role, they are likely to intensify their improvisations upon 'the world as I have known it'" through day-dreaming, dramatic improvisations, and reading and writing poetry and fiction (Britton, 1972, p. 225).

The main stream of writing in the English class will be in the spectator role, providing adolescents opportunities to use writing as a means of exploring and imposing order upon their experiences (Britton, 1972, p. 249). With younger adolescents in particular, the teacher must be a sympathetic reader, one who invites students to share experiences (p. 253). More sophisticated adolescent writers may move from writing for the teacher as a familiar and sympathetic audience to writing for an unknown audience. Although most writing in the English class will range from expressive to poetic in the spectator role, older adolescents, in particular, should have opportunities to produce transactional writing at a fairly high theoretical level. The development of transactional writing, speaking, and reading is the responsibility of teachers of all subjects, however, not just those in English (pp. 262–264).

Like their counterparts in the elementary schools, secondary teachers should make available to students a wide range of reading, realizing that those who elect the second-rate may be ascending the first rung of a ladder that will lead them to increasingly complex and artistic works (Britton, p. 268).

Not only books, but films, television, and stage plays should be sources for adolescents' experiences (Britton, 1972, p. 264). With respect to books, students should have access to works ranging from "light" to classic (p. 267). The reading of ephemeral literature may start some students on the path toward works that will make increasingly more complex demands of them and provide them with greater satisfaction (p. 268).

The Development of Writing Abilities (11–18). This report, completed by Britton et al. in 1975, has been said to be "undoubtedly the most influential study in writing across the curriculum in the last fifteen years" (Kinneavy, 1987, p. 361). From 1967 to 1971, the researchers collected 2,122 "scripts" or pieces of writing by 500 students divided among the first, third, fifth, and seventh years of secondary schools in England, with students' ages ranging roughly from 11 to 18. Produced principally for classes in history, geography, religious education, science, and English, the scripts were classified according to the major function categories described by Britton (1972) and earlier suggested by Jakobson (1960)—transactional, expressive, and poetic. The transactional function was further divided into "informative" and "conative," with subdivisions for each, those for informative being expanded from Moffett's (1968a) abstractive scale, the movement from a close to a distant relationship between writer and topic. Level of abstraction was found to be a highly significant index of development from ages 11 to 18, but comparatively few students reached the theorizing stage. Functions were determined by whether the writer's language signaled that the reader was to act in the role of participant or that of spectator. The participant role was allied with the transactional function, the spectator with the poetic, while either or both roles might be evoked by the expressive function. Stull (1984) declared that the use of these function categories in the study represented "a breakthrough in discourse theory" (p. 132).

Besides categorizing each script according to its function, the researchers categorized each according to its intended audience: self, teacher, wider audience (known), or unknown audience. The category "teacher" was subdivided into "child or adolescent to trusted adult"; "pupil to teacher, general (teacher-learner dialogue)"; "pupil to teacher, particular relationship . . . based upon a shared interest and expertise. . ."; and "pupil to examiner, . . . as a demonstration of material mastered . . . with the expectation of assessment rather than response" (Britton et al., 1975, provide a fold out table of function and audience categories, with definitions, following the Index, p. 226).

Analysis of Data. A major hypothesis regarding the development of writing ability in school that was expressive language, that is, language that reflects the user's immediate concerns and mood, would be the matrix from which differentiated forms of mature writing—transactional, poetic, as well as expressive—would be developed:

> . . . that what children write in the early stages should be a form of written-down expressive speech, and what they read should also be, generally speaking, expressive. As their writing and reading progress side by side, they will move from this starting point into the three broadly differentiated kinds of writing . . . and, in favourable circumstances, their mode of doing so will be by a kind of shuttling between their speech resources . . . and the written forms they meet. . . . Britton et al, 1975, pp. 82–83).

However, since very little of the writing examined was expressive (from 6 percent in the first year to 4 percent in the seventh year) the hypothesis was neither proved nor disproved. About the paucity of expressive writing—what there was of it was found almost exclusively in English (11 percent) and religious education (11 percent)—the authors comment.

> Our disappointment arises from our belief that expressive writing, whether in participant or spectator role, may be at any stage the kind

of writing best adapted to exploration and discovery. . . . Moreover, it represents . . . the move into writing most likely to preserve a vital link with the spoken mode in which up to this point all a child's linguistic resources have been gathered and stored. (Britton et al., 1975, p. 197)

Distribution by function categories revealed that, overall, 63.4 percent of the scripts were transactional, rising from 54 percent in the first year to 84 percent by the seventh year; 5.5 percent wre expressive, and 17.6 percent were poetic, which peaked in the fifth year (24 percent) and dwindled by the seventh year (7 percent). ("Additional" (8 percent) and "miscellaneous" (4.9 percent) categories account for missing percentages.) As with expressive writing, poetic writing was found almost exclusively in English (39 percent) and religious education (12 percent), with history responsible for 2 percent (Britton et al., 1975, pp. 164, 165, 168).

With respect to intended audience, the researchers found that 39 percent of the scripts overall were to teacher, general (teacher-learner dialogue), with the percentage steadily declining from year one (51 percent) to year seven (19 percent). In contrast, the percentage of scripts to the teacher as examiner rose steadily from year one (40 percent) to year seven (61 percent), for an overall average of 49 percent (Britton et al., 1975, pp. 130–131). In English, the percentage of scripts to teacher, general, declined from 83 percent in year one to 34 percent in year seven, while those to the teacher as examiner rose from 6 percent in year one to 41 percent in year seven (p. 135). Examination of the interrelation of audience and function revealed that 67 percent of transactional writing, which formed the largest proportion of writing in the sample, was for an examining audience. "By contrast there was hardly any evidence of association between expressive writing and an examining audience; and only 5 percent of poetic writing was judged to be of this kind" (p. 188).

The authors indicate that the use in England of public or external examinations may have accounted in good part for the high percentage of scripts written to the teacher as examiner, not to the actual teacher in the classroom, however, but to a spectral one hovering in the background, "a shadowy figure of an 'external examiner' whom teachers and pupils have conspired together to conjure up" (Britton et al., 1975, p. 195). Nonetheless, Britton and his colleagues emerged from the study continuing to believe that students need more opportunities and stronger incentive to choose their own audiences so as "to be able, when the occasion arises, to write as someone with something to say to the world in general" (p. 192).

A Brief Evaluation. Unquestionably Britton's emphasis on the importance of expressive language has influenced the uses of informal discussion, "brain-storming" techniques, free writing and journal writing in American schools. Further, his belief that students need to write for audiences other than the teacher, particularly the teacher as examiner, has encouraged the practice of peer editing and the stipulation in writing assignments of varied audiences. Britton can also be credited, at least in part, for insistence that students be given opportunity to take "ownership" of their writing by determining for themselves matters of content, audience, and purpose (Atwell, 1987; Calkins, 1986;

Graves, 1981, 1983). D'Angelo (1987) cites several articles and books that argue for greater use of expressive writing in the college curriculum. Particularly noteworthy is a book edited by Fulwiler and Young (1982), dealing with the importance of Britton's major function categories to writing and learning across the collegiate curriculum.

Warnock (1979) contends that the classificatory scheme developed by Britton and his colleagues represents a taxonomy (a description), not a theory (an explanation), and is therefore unprovable. He also questions the assumption "that there is such a thing as a taxonomy of discourse that is good for all occasions and purposes" (p. 8). Knoblauch (1980) maintains that both Britton and Kinneavy, by establishing static schemes, ignore the complexity of an author's purpose and audience as these function in actual composing (p. 154). Rosenblatt (1985) has raised issue not only with Britton's use of the word *transactional* but with Britton's (1984) suggestion that his "spectator" and "participant" categories are interchangeable with her "aesthetic" and "efferent" categories. Finally, Harris (1988) has taken exception to Britton's restriction of the spectator role to the writing of "verbal objects," that is to the writing of literature and "artlike" scripts, such as those composed by schoolchildren (Britton, 1984). Harris argues that concern for unity and form is as pertinent to a verbal transaction as to a verbal object, and that one can take on the role of spectator in non-poetic as well as poetic discourse: "... the act of stepping back, of theorizing, of gaining a critical distance from events and ideas seems a vital part of how one learns *any* discipline, of how one enters into any form of talk or writing" (p. 45).

Instructional Implications. While the instructional model suggested by Britton's work (Britton, 1972, 1977, 1978, 1984; Britton et al., 1975) is not as detailed as that developed by Moffett, it shares with the latter a primary emphasis on students' psycholinguistic development rather than on their mastery of skills or familiarity with works of literature that ostensibly help constitute their cultural heritage.

Like Rosenblatt, Britton sees literature being accorded a prominent place in English studies, but, like Moffett, he places greater emphasis on students' own creation of "verbal objects" than does Rosenblatt. Though he has not spelled out as fully as has Moffett a curriculum for English language arts, Britton, like Moffett, wants teachers to engage students in a full spectrum of language activities—reading, writing, listening, and speaking. Moreover, he wants language in the classroom to be used for real purposes, not for "dummy runs": "... [children] must practise language in the sense in which a doctor 'practises' medicine..., and not in the sense in which a juggler 'practises' a new trick before he performs it" (Britton, 1972, p. 130). Finally, like Moffett, Britton believes that secondary education must be restructured if it is to enable adolescents to develop to their full potential intellectually, aesthetically, socially, and morally:

What is required today ... is an urgent look at our secondary education having in mind the need of the adolescent to become himself.... to make important choices: ... to be trusted. There is much that wants altering both in the way institutions are organized and controlled and in the way teaching and learning are related in the classroom. (p. 272)

TABLE 4–4. Kinneavy's Communication Triangle

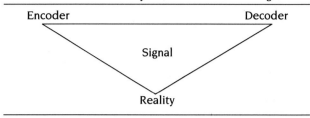

James Kinneavy

Fundamental to Kinneavy's theoretical ideas on discourse (Kinneavy 1969, 173, 1980a, b; Kinneavy, Cope, & Campbell, 1976a, b; Kinneavy, McCleary, & Nakadate, 1985) is his belief that any act of communication involves an encoder (the speaker or writer), a decoder (the audience or reader), reality (subject matter or the outer world), and a signal (language, or the text itself). Kinneavy represents the relationship of these four components via a communication triangle (Table 4–4), the use of which he traces back to Aristotle (1980b, p. 19).

Although all four components exist on any occasion of communication, one component will be dominant. Associated, therefore, with each of these components is a discourse aim, which Kinneavy views as being all important: "The aim of discourse determines everything else in the process of discourse" (Kinneavy, 1980b, p. 48). If focus is upon the encoder (the speaker-writer), the aim is expressive; upon the decoder (audience), persuasive; upon reality (subject matter), referential; upon the signal (language, text), literary. These aims result in four kinds of discourse—expressive, persuasive, referential (which is subdivided into exploratory, scientific, and informative), and literary. "Each of these uses of language has its own processes of thought ... its own logic or logics ... its own organizational patterns and stylistic peculiarities" (p. 40). Kinneavy denotes most of *A Theory of Discourse* (1980b), his major work, to a discussion of these distinguishing characteristics.

In developing ideas for a particular aim and kind of discourse, a speaker or writer will predominantly use one of four modes of discourse: description, narration, classification, or evaluation. Not an application of the communication triangle, modes "are grounded in certain philosophic concepts of the nature of reality..." and answer the question of what a text is about (p. 36). Just as there can be only one dominant aim in any discourse, there can be only one dominant mode, though elements of other modes may appear.

Expressive discourse includes conversations, journals, diaries, gripe sessions, prayers, manifestos, contracts, constitutions, religious credos, and declarations of independence. Exploratory referential discourse includes dialogues, seminars, questionnaires, and interviews; informative referential discourse takes in weather reports, news stories, telephone directories, textbooks, articles, essays, and summaries; and scientific referential discourse includes descriptive analyses, literary criticism, taxonomic categories, and history. Examples of persuasive discourse are editorials, political speeches, religious sermons, and advertising. Literary discourse embodies short stories, novels, drama, poetry, movies, songs, jokes, puns, and TV shows (Kinneavy, 1980b, pp. 39, 61).

Kinneavy (1980b) finds no inherent qualitative differences with respect to the uses of language:

In the communications framework, no use of language is considered superior to any other. Information is a good use of language, so is science, and so is persuasion. Simple expression is as good in itself as science. Each achieves a different *and* valid purpose. To achieve a specific purpose, a specific aim of language must be used. Persuasion is bad science, but good rhetoric; and science may be good reference discourse but bad literature. (p. 66)

Evaluation. To date, Kinneavy's theory of discourse has had strongest influence upon the college teaching of composition. While D'Angelo (1987) cites a number of college textbooks based on Kinneavy's ideas, none to date appears to have been written for elementary or secondary schools. However, the departments of education in both Texas (Texas Education Agency, 1988) and Wisconsin (Last, Benson, Chandler, & Bethke, 1986) have incorporated Kinneavy's theoretical framework in their language arts curriculum guides, K–12. Greenhalgh (1983) discusses how Kinneavy's aims might be combined with Britton's audience categories in a writing program for elementary schools, while Polnac (1983) describes the influence of Kinneavy's aims and modes upon a community college writing program. Summer writing programs held under the aegis of the National Writing Project have also helped disseminate Kinneavy's theory among public school teachers, as have his consultancies with schools and with state departments of éducation in New York, Colorado, and New Mexico.

The theory has received a mixed reception from scholars and teachers. Hunter (1986) finds fault with Kinneavy's reliance on the communication triangle, since "a theory of speaking ought not be the foundation for a theory of writing" (p. 286). He argues that reading-writing differs from speaking-listening as a kind of thinking. Further, he claims that Kinneavy's theory is not neutral, that it grants least significance to the persuasive aim and too much significance to the referential aim. O'Banion (1982) finds Kinneavy's "categories . . . static and his approach . . . too closely tied to literary criticism to be helpful in composition" (p. 196). He nevertheless concludes that *A Theory of Discourse* "certainly has helped move English studies toward 'some initial order' " and that it "must be required reading for anyone wishing to do better" (p. 200). Larson (1987) finds "unconvincing" Kinneavy's suggestion of a correspondence between discourse aim and organizational plan (p. 58). Odell, Cooper, and Courts (1978) question Kinneavy's analysis of written products, not of the choices writers actually make, to determine the aims or "purposes" of discourse (p. 6). Odell (1979) calls for research to determine the extent to which students view composing as a process of making choices and the degree to which they justify choices by referring to their basic purposes in writing (pp. 40–41). Fulkerson (1984) believes *A Theory of Discourse* to be more useful for rhetorical critics than for teachers, that it presents a wide range of rhetorical issues worth probing in depth. "Instead of a finished taxonomy upon which we build curricula and syllabuses, Kinneavy has provided a complex set of hypotheses to be tested, used, and modified through rhetorical criticism" (p. 54).

Crusius (1984) offers strong support for Kinneavy's theory of discourse, arguing that "we should adopt [it] as the paradigm for our field, thinking with his concepts, developing his categories, extending his system in principled ways, until it either becomes adequate and complete or reveals innate shortcomings that call for a new . . . set of ideas" (p. 1). In a later article, Crusius (1985) suggests that Kinneavy's theory can benefit from internal development in the ends or aims of discourse and the relationship of the modes to heuristic or topical systems. Harris (1979) argues for applying Kinneavy's theory to courses in technical writing, while Hagaman (1980, 1982) finds Kinneavy's ideas useful in teaching students to revise compositions. Ruskiewiez (1983), disagreeing with O'Banion's (1982) critique that found Kinneavy's threory too static to account for writing processes, attempts "to show how Kinneavy's system has been and continues to be a practical framework for process-oriented courses in rhetorical composition" (p. 38).

If Kinneavy's *A Theory of Discourse* does not dwell explicitly on the precise mechanisms of what we have come to understand as writing process, neither does it ignore the essential cognitive motions of process—the generation, arrangement, formulation and evaluation of ideas. Perhaps the best evidence of Kinneavy's thoroughness is the ease with which a process-structured course can be imposed upon his framework and the conceptual richness that results from such a juncture. (p. 41)

Comparison. When Kinneavy (1980a) compared his model for teaching composition to those of Moffett (1968a), Britton et al. (1975), and D'Angelo (1975), he concluded that the "four . . . contemporary rhetorics are compatible with each other and can be incorporated into a meta-system which profits from the strengths of each component system but yet respects each component system" (p. 51). Lending support to the inclusion of Kinnevy's discourse model under a process model of instruction are three further conclusions that Kinneavy drew from his comparative study, the first acknowledging a deficiency in his own model:

The psychological developmental sequences for the presentation of these various types of discourse and audiences are critical for a workable educational program. The research of Britton and Moffett is a healthy beginning . . . and needs to be supplemented. . . . Without such a supplement, Kinneavy's and D'Angelo's systems are Brunerian systems without level adjustments.

These four authors favor the holistic teaching of composition over the isolated teaching of parts of the theme (such as grammar, paragraph, etc.).

The teaching of composition ought to be related to the situational and cultural contexts of the student whenever possible. (pp. 51–52)

After summarizing Kinneavy's comparative study, Burnham (1984) opined that the synthesis Kinneavy derived "seems plausible and ready for testing" (p. 203).

Summary Comments

As Purves and Beach (1972) note, curriculum is "the architecture of instruction" (p. 152). A curriculum concerned primarily with students' mastery of particular language, skills implies an instructional model different from one implied by a curriculum emphasizing students' cognitive and affective growth through their participation in a wide and increasingly complex variety of language activities. A teacher's encouragement of expressive speech, dramatic improvisation, and emotional engagement in literature would likely seem alien to the first curriculum, natural to the second. In similar vein, a curriculum stressing the transmission through literature of a cultural heritage would invite instructional behaviours different from those invited by a curriculum emphasizing either process or mastery. While it is true that a given curriculum may attempt to incorporate elements of all three models—mastery, process, and heritage—it is also true, as Mandel (1980a) notes,

… that most teachers tend to gather their intellectual and emotional resources together in one kind of teaching more than another, that schools and districts usually favor one kind of curriculum emphasis over another, and that students profit from learning in an environment which, while richly heterogeneous, is conscious of its dominant curricular style, goals, and values. (p. 10).

A central issue at present has to do with the degree to which teachers of the English language arts have "ownership" of the curriculum and of subsequent instructional strategies. One of the many reports emanating from the English Coalition Conference, held in July 1987, speaks of the classroom dominance of the lecture-and-recitation mode of teaching:

In recent years many states, regions, and local school boards have used this model to dictate curriculum and either directly or indirectly dictate the instructional models that will be used to reach curricular goals. This model dictates not only expected student outcomes, usually in terms of isolated learner behaviors, but often teacher behaviors which presumably will help learners master language objectives.

[T]his model … is no longer suitable…. If the schools are to prepare students for the demands of a world … dominated by new techno-logies and the information explosion, then teachers and students must be freed from a model of teaching and learning that denies that language learning is an interactive process. (*English for the 90's and Beyond, Final report: Strand A-2. Secondary.* Duplicated report, p. 5. English Coalition Conference. Aspen Institute for Humanistic Studies. Queenstown, MD.)

Whether the coalition will be more successful than the Anglo-American Seminar (Dixon, 1967, Muller, 1967) in establishing a learner-centered curriculum awaits time's passage. To encourage the development of such a curriculum, Moffett (1985b) has called for a "new covenant between school and home," one which would enlist laity as voluntary aides in the classroom liberation of students' thought and behavior. With the assistance of aides, students would learn to use speaking, reading, and writing as modes of inquiry into matters important to themselves. Further, according to Moffett, involvement of lay persons would result in their sharing with teachers accountability for the results of instruction and in their becoming "disenchanted with our current testing practices" (p. 55).

A word needs to be said about current systems of teacher appraisal, which, along with written curricula, favor some instructional behaviors over others. To date, the English profession appears not to have exerted much influence on the systems, which tend to be subject generic rather than subject specific. In 1987 teachers in Texas were evaluated on forms calling for the exhibition of 55 discrete teachers behaviors within a single class hour (Texas Education Agency, 1986–87). The appraisal systems, which control teachers' ascension on career ladders, exert tremendous influence over pedagogy. (McNeil, 1988b) If the profession as a whole is to follow the lead of the English coalition in endorsing a student-centered curriculum, then it must be sure that instructional appraisal of teachers of English language arts is concordant with that endorsement.

References

Adler, M. (1940). *How to read a book: The art of getting a liberal education.* New York: Simon & Schuster.

Anderson, S. (1964). *Between the Grimms and "The Group": Literature in American High schools.* Princeton, NJ: Educational Testing Service.

Applebee, A. N. (1974). *Tradition and reform in the teaching of English: A history.* Urbana, IL: National Council of Teachers of English.

Applebee, A. N. (1981). *Writing in the secondary school: English and the content areas.* (Research report No. 21). Urbana, IL: National Council of Teachers of English. ED 197347.

Applebee, A. N. (1985). Studies in the spectator role: An approach to response to literature. In C. R. Cooper (Ed.), *Researching response to literature and the teaching of literature: Points of departure* (pp. 87–103). Norwood, NJ: Ablex.

Atwell, N. (1987). *In the middle: Writing, reading, and learning with adolescents.* Upper Montclair, NJ: Boynton/Cook.

Barber, B. (1988). The philosopher despot: Allan Bloom's elitist agenda. *Harper's, 276* (1652), pp. 61–65.

Barthes, R. (1975). *The pleasure of the text.* (R. Miller, Trans.). New York: Hill & Wang.

Bennett, W. J. (1987). *James Madison high school: A curriculum for American students.* Washington, DC: U.S. Department of Education.

Bleich, D. (1975). *Readings and feelings.* Urbana, IL: National Council of Teachers of English.

Bleich, D. (1978). *Subjective criticism.* Baltimore: Johns Hopkins University Press.

Bleich, D. (1985). The identity of pedagogy and research in the study of response to literature. In C. R. Cooper (Ed.), *Researching response to literature and the teaching of literature: Points of departure* (pp. 253–272). Norwood, NJ: Ablex.

Block, J., & Burns, R. (1976). Mastery learning. *Review of Research in Education, 4,* 3–49.

Bloom, A. (1987). *The closing of the American mind.* New York: Simon & Schuster.

Bloom, B. (1968). Learning for mastery. *Evaluation Comment, 1* (2). University of California at Los Angeles: Center for the Study of Evaluation of Instructional Programs.

Bloom, B. (1971). Mastery learning and its implications for curriculum development. In E. W. Eisner (Ed.), *Confronting curriculum reform* (pp. 17–49). Boston: Little, Brown.

Bloom, B. (1974). An introduction to mastery learning theory. In J. H.

Block (Ed.), *Schools, society, and mastery learning* (pp. 4–14). New York: Holt, Rinehart & Winston.

Bloom, B. (1976). *Human characteristics and school learning: A theory of school learning.* New York: McGraw Hill.

Bloom, B. (1981). *All our children learning.* New York: McGraw Hill.

Boyer, E. L. (1983). *High school: A report on secondary education in America.* New York: Harper & Row.

Braddock, R., Lloyd-Jones, R., & Schoer, L. (1963). *Research in written composition.* Urbana, IL: National Council of Teachers of English.

Britton, J. (1972). *Language and learning.* Harmondsworth, Middlesex, England: Penguin Books Inc. (First published by Allen Lane, The Penguin Press, 1970).

Britton, J. (1977). Language and the nature of learning: An individual perspective. In J. R. Squire (Ed.), *The teaching of English: The seventy-sixth yearbook of the national society for the study of education. Part I* (pp. 1–38). Chicago: University of Chicago Press.

Britton, J. (1978). The composing processes and the functions of writing. In C. Cooper & L. Odell (Eds.), *Research on composing* (pp. 13–28). Urbana, IL: National Council of Teachers of English.

Britton, J. (1984). Viewpoints: The distinction between participant and spectator role language in research and practice. *Research in the Teaching of English, 18* (3), 320–331.

Britton, J., Burgess, T., Martin, N., McLeod, A. & Rosen, H. (1975). *The development of writing abilities (11–18).* London: Macmillan Education, Ltd.

Burnham, C. C. (1984). Research methods in composition. In M. G. Moran and R. F. Lunsford (Eds.), *Research in composition and rhetoric: A bibliographic sourcebook* (pp. 191–210). Westport, CT: Greenwood Press.

Bush, R. N., & Allen, D. W. (1964). *A new design for high school education: Assuming a flexible schedule.* New York: McGraw Hill.

Calkins, L. M. (1986). *The art of teaching writing.* Portsmouth, NH: Heineman.

Callahan, Raymond E. (1962). *Education and the cult of efficiency.* Chicago: University of Chicago Press.

Carroll, J. (1963). A model for school learning. *Teachers College Record, 64,* 723–733.

Cheney, L. V. (1987). *American memory: A report on the humanities in the nation's public schools.* Washington, DC: U.S. Government Printing Office.

Commission on English. (1965). *Freedom and Discipline in English.* Princeton, NJ: College Entrance Examination Board.

Cooper, Charles R. (Ed.). (1985). Introduction. *Researching response to literature and the teaching of literature: Points of departure* (pp. ix–xix). Norwood, NJ: Ablex.

Corcoran, B., & Evans, E. (Eds.). (1987). *Readers, texts, teachers.* Upper Montclair, NJ: Boynton/Cook.

Coser, L. A. (1987). Remedial acculturation. *Science, 236,* 973.

Costa, A. L. (1984). A reaction to Hunter's knowing, teaching, and supervising. In P. L. Hosford (Ed.), *Using what we know about teaching* (pp. 196–203). Alexandria, VA: Association of Supervision and Curriculum Development.

Crusius, T. (1984). A brief plea for a paradigm and for Kinneavy as paradigm. *Freshman English News, 12* (1), 1–3.

Crusius, T. (1985). Thinking (and rethinking) Kinneavy. *Rhetoric Review, 3* (2), 120–130.

Culler, J. (1983). *On deconstruction: Theory and criticism after structuralism.* Ithaca, NY: Cornell University Press.

D'Angelo F. (1975). *A conceptual theory of rhetoric.* Cambridge, MA: Winthrop Publishing Co.

D'Angelo, F. (1987). Aims, modes, and forms of discourse. In G. Tate (Ed.), *Teaching composition: 12 bibliographic essays* (rev. ed. pp. 131–154). Forth Worth: Texas Christian University Press.

Dillion, D. (1987). Commentary. In J. R. Squire (Ed.), *The dynamics of language learning: Research in reading and English* (pp. 184–88).

Urbana, IL: ERIC Clearinghouse on Reading and Communication Skills and the National Conference on Research in English.

Dixon, J. (1967). *Growth through English: A report based on the Dartmouth seminar.* Reading, England: National Association for the Teaching of English.

Emig, J. (1971). *The composing process of twelfth graders.* Urbana, IL: National Council of Teachers of English.

Fillion, B., & Brause, R. S. (1987). Research into classroom practices: What have we learned and where are we going? In J. R. Squire (Ed.), *The dynamics of language learning: Research in reading and English* (pp. 201–225). Urbana, IL: ERIC Clearinghouse on Reading and Communication Skills and the National Conference on Research in English.

Fish, S. (1980). *Is there a text in this class? The authority of interpretive communities.* Cambridge, MA: Harvard University Press.

Fulkerson, P. P. (1984). Kinneavy on referential and persuasive discourse: A critique. *College Composition and Communication, 35* (1), 43–56.

Fulwiler, T. E. & Young, A. (1982). *Language connections: Writing and reading across the curriculum.* Urbana, IL: National Council of Teachers of English.

Glatthorn, A. A. (1977). Creating learning environments. In J. R. Squire, (Ed.), *The teaching of English: The seventy-sixth yearbook of the national society for the study of education, Part I* (pp. 197–230). Chicago: University of Chicago Press.

Glatthorn, A. A. (1980). *A guide for developing an English curriculum for the eighties.* Urbana, IL: National Council of Teachers of English.

Goodlad, J. (1977). What goes on in our schools. *Educational Researcher 6,* 3–6.

Goodlad, J. (1984). *A place called school: Prospects for the future.* New York: McGraw Hill.

Graham, P. A. (1984). Schools: Cacophony about practice, silence about purpose. *Daedalus, 113* (Fall), 29–57.

Graves, D. H. (1981). Break the welfare cycle: Let writers choose their topics. In D. H. Graves (Ed.), *A case study observing the development of primary children's composing, spelling, and motor behaviors during the writing process* (Final Report, 388–394. NIE Grant No. G-78-0174). Durham, NH: University of New Hampshire.

Graves, D. H. (1983). *Writing: Teachers and children at work.* Exeter, NH: Heinemann.

Gray, D. (1988). What *does* every American need to know? *Phi Delta Kappan, 69* (5), 386–88.

Greenhalgh, C. (1983). When children begin: Considering aim and audience in the elementary writing program. *English in Texas, 14* (1), 14–23.

Guam Department of Education. (1987). *Teaching for Mastery.* Draft copy. Agana, Guam.

Hagaman, J. (1980). Using discourse analysis scales to encourage thoughtful revision in a Kinneavy-framed advanced composition course. *Journal of Advanced Composition, 1,* 79–85.

Hagaman, J. (1982). A comparative analysis of revisions made by advanced composition students in expressive, persuasive, and information discourse. *Journal of Advanced Composition, 3,* 126–135.

Hansson, G. (1985). Verbal scales in research on response to literature. In C. R. Cooper (Ed.), *Researching response to literature and the teaching of literature: Points of departure* (pp. 212–232). Norwood, NJ: Ablex.

Harding, D. W. (1937). The role of the onlooker. *Scrutiny, 6* (3), 247–258.

Harding, D. W. (1963). *Experience into words.* New York & London: Cambridge University Press.

Harris, E. (1979). Applications of Kinneavy's theory of discourse to technical writing. *College English, 40,* 625–632.

Harris, J. (1988). The spectator as theorist: Britton and the functions of writing. *English Education, 20* (1), 41–50.

Hillocks, G., Jr., (1986). *Research on written composition: New directions for teaching.* Urbana, IL: ERIC Clearinghouse on Reading and Communication Skills.

Hirsch, E. D., Jr., (1987). *Cultural literacy: What every American needs to know.* Boston: Houghton Mifflin.

Hirsch, E. D., Jr., kett, J., & Trefil, J. (1988). *The dictionary of cultural literacy.* Boston: Houghton Mifflin.

Holland, N. N. (1968; rpt. 1975a). *The dynamics of literary response.* New York: Norton.

Holland, N. N. (1975b). *5 readers reading.* New Haven: Yale University Press.

Holland, N. N. (1985). Readers reading reading. In C. R. Cooper (Ed.), *Researching response to literature and the teaching of literature: Points of departure* (pp. 3–21). Norwood, NJ: Ablex.

Hunter, M. (1984). Knowing, teaching, and supervising. In P. L. Hosford (Ed.), *Using what we know about teaching* (pp. 169–192). Alexandria, VA: Association for Supervision and Curriculum Development.

Hunter, M. (1985). What's wrong with Madeline Hunter? *Educational Leadership, 42,* 57–60.

Hunter, P. (1986). "that we have divided/In three our kingdom": The communication triangle and a theory of discourse. *College English, 48* (3), 279–287.

Iser, W. (1978). *The act of reading: A theory of aesthetic response.* Baltimore: Johns Hopkins University Press.

Jakobson, R. (1960). Closing statement: Linguisticss and poetics. In T. A. Sebeok (Ed.), *Style in language* (pp. 350–377). Cambridge, MA: MIT Press.

Keller, F. (1968). Goodbye, teacher ... *Journal of Applied Behavior Analysis, 1,* 79–89.

Kingsley, C. D. (Ed.). (1918). *Cardinal principles of secondary education: A report on the commission on the reorganization of secondary education, appointed by the National Education Association* (Bulletin, 1918, No. 35). Washington, DC: U.S. Government Printing Office.

Kinneavy, J. L. (1969). The basic aims of discourse. *College Composition and Communication, 20* (4), 297–304.

Kinneavy, J. L. (1973). Theories of composition and actual writing. *Kansas English, 59* (4), 3–17.

Kinneavy, J. L. (1980a). A pluralistic synthesis of four contemporary models for teaching composition. In A. Freeman & I. Pringle (Eds.), *Reinventing the rhetorical tradition* (pp. 37–52). Conway, AR: L & S Books.

Kinneavy, J. L. (1980b). *A theory of discourse.* New York: W. W. Norton. (Originally published in 1971. Englewood Cliffs, NJ: Prentice Hall)

Kinneavy, J. L. (1987). Writing across the curriculum. In G. Tate (Ed.), *Teaching composition: 12 bibliographic essays* (rev. ed., pp. 353–377). Forth Worth: Texas Christian University Press.

Kinneavy, J. L., Cope, J., & Campbell, J. (1976a). *Aims and audiences in writing.* Dubuque, IA: Kendall/Hunt Publishing Co.

Kinneavy, J. L., Cope, J., & Campbell, J. (1976b). *Writing basic modes of organization.* Dubuque, IA: Kendall/Hunt Publishing Co.

Kinneavy, J. L., McCleary, W. J., & Nakadate, N. (1985). *Writing in the liberal arts tradition.* New York: Harper & Row.

Knoblauch, C. H. (1980). Intentionality in the writing process: A case study. *College Composition and Communication, 31* (2), 153–159.

Kuykendall, C. (1972). Sequence without structure. *English Journal, 61* (5), 715–22.

Larson, R. L. (1987). Structure and form in non-narrative prose. In G. Tate (Ed.), *Teaching Composition: 12 bibliographical essays* (rev. ed., pp. 39–82). Fort Worth: Texas Christian University Press.

Last, E., Benson, J., Chandler, A., & Bethke, E. (1986). *A guide to curriculum planning in English language arts.* Madison, WI: Wisconsin Department of Public Instruction.

Lynch, J., & Evans, B. (1963). *High school English textbooks: A critical examination.* Boston: Little, Brown.

Mandel, B. J. (Ed.). (1980). *Three language-arts curriculum models: Prekindergarten through college.* Urbana, IL: National Council of Teachers of English.

McNeil, L. (1988a). Contradictions of control, part I: Administrators and teachers. *Phi Delta Kappan, 69* (5), 333–339.

McNeil, L. (1988b). Contradictions of control, part 3: Contradictions of reform. *Phi Delta Kappan, 69* (7), 478–485.

Menand, L. (1987). Mr. Bloom's planet. *New Republic, 196* (21), 38–41.

Moffett, J. (1968a). *Teaching the universe of discourse.* Boston: Houghton Mifflin.

Moffett, J. (1968b). *A student-centered language-arts curriculum, grades K–13: A handbook for teachers.* Boston: Houghton Mifflin.

Moffett, J. (Ed.). (1973). *Interaction: A student-centered arts and reading program.* Boston: Houghton Mifflin.

Moffett, J. (1981a). *Active voice, A writing program across the curriculum.* Upper Montclair, NJ: Boynton/Cook.

Moffett, J. (1981b). *Coming on center: Englsih education in evoluation.* Upper Montclair, NJ: Boynton/Cook.

Moffett, J. (Ed.). (1985a). *Points of departure: An anthology of nonfiction.* New York: New American Library.

Moffett, J. (1985b). Hidden impediments to improving English reading. *Phi Delta Kappan, 67* (1), 50–56.

Moffett, J., Baker, M., & Cooper, C. (1987d). *Active voices IV: A writer's reader (College).* Upper Montclair, NJ: Boynton/Cook.

Moffett, J., Bolchazy, M., & Friedberg, B. (1987a). *Active voices I: A writer's reader (Grades 4–6).* Upper Montclair, NJ: Boynton/Cook.

Moffett, J., & McElheny, K. R. (Eds.). (1966). *Points of view: An anthology of short stories.* New York: New American Library.

Moffett, J., & Tashlik, P. (1987b). *Active voices II: A writer's reader (Grades 7–9).* Upper Montclair, NJ: Boynton/Cook.

Moffett, J., & Wagner, B. J. (1983). *Student-centered language arts and reading, K–13: A handbook for teachers* (3rd ed.). Boston: Houghton Mifflin.

Moffett, J., Wixon, P., Wixon, V., Blau, S., & Phreaner, J. (1987c). *Active voices III: A writer's reader (Grades 10–12).* Upper Montclair, NJ: Boynton/Cook.

Muller, H. (1967). *The uses of English.* New York: Holt, Rinehart & Winston.

Myers, M. (1986). The teaching of writing in the secondary schools. In A. Petrosky & D. Bartholomae (Eds.), *The teaching of writing: Eighty-fifth yearbook of the national society for the study of education, Part II* (pp. 148–169). Chicago: University of Chicago Press.

National Commission on Excellence in Education (1983). *A nation at risk: The imperative for educational reform.* Washington, DC: U.S. Government Printing Office.

National Education Association (1883). *Report of the committee of ten on secondary school studies.* Washington, DC: U.S. Government Printing Office.

O'Banion, J. D. (1982). *A theory of discourse:* A retrospective. *College Composition and Communication, 33* (2), 196–201.

Odell, L. (1979). Teachers of composition and needed research in discourse theory. *College Composition and Communication, 30* (1), 39–45.

Odell, L., Cooper, C. R., & Courts, C. (1978). Discourse theory: Implications for research in composing. In C. Cooper & L. Odell (Eds.), *Research on composing: Points of departure* (pp. 1–12). Urbana, IL: National Council of Teachers of English.

Polnac, L. (1983). When theory meets practice: using Kinneavy's aims in a community college program. *English in Texas, 14* (1), 32–37.

Pope, C., & Kutiper, K. (1988). James Moffett: Prophet and practitioner. *English Journal, 76* (7) 86–88.

Powell, A. G., Farrar, E., & Cohen, D. K. (1985). *The shopping mall high school.* Boston: Houghton Mifflin.

Probst, R. E. (1984). *Adolescent literature: Response and analysis.* Columbus, OH: Charles E. Merrill.

Purves, A. (Ed.). (1972). *How porcupines make love: Notes on a response-centered curriculum.* Lexington, MA: Xerox College Publishing.

Purves, A. (1976). Foreward. In L. M. Rosenblatt, *Literature as exploration.* (4th ed., pp. iii–iv). New York: Modern Language Association.

Purves, A. (1985). That sunny dome: Those caves of ice. In C. R. Cooper (Ed.), *Researching response to literature and the teaching of literature: Points of departure* (pp. 54–69). Norwood, NJ: Ablex.

Purves, A., & Beach, R. (1972). *Literature and the reader: Research in response to literature, reading interests, and the teaching of literature.* Urbana, IL: National Council of Teachers of English.

Purves, A., & Rippere, V. (1968). *Elements of writing about a literary work: A study of response to literature.* Urbana, IL: National Council of Teachers of English.

Ravitch, D., & Finn, C. E., Jr. (1987). *What do our 17-year-olds know? A report on the first national assessment of history and literature.* New York: Harper & Row.

Reid, E. R. (1986). Practicing effective instruction: The exemplary center for reading instruction approach. *Exceptional Children, 52* (6) 510–519.

Roemer, M. G. (1987). Which reader's response? *College English, 49* (8), 911–921.

Rorty, R. (1988). That old-time philosophy. *New Republic, 198* (14), 28–33.

Rosenblatt, L. M. (1938). *Literature as exploration.* New York: Appleton-Century. (New York: Noble & Noble, 1968 [rev. ed.]; London: Heinemann, 1970 [3rd ed.]; New York: Noble & Noble, 1976 [rev. ed.cb; New York: Modern Language Association, 1983 [4th ed.]).

Rosenblatt, L. M. (1978). *The reader, the text, the poem: The transactional theory of the literary work.* Carbondale: Southern Illinois University Press.

Rosenblatt, L. M. (1985). The transactional theory of the literary work: Implications for research. In C. R. Cooper (Ed.), *Researching response to literature and the teaching of literature: Points of departure* (pp. 33–53). Norwood, NJ: Ablex.

Rothman, R. (1988). Bennett offers high school's 'ideal' content. *Education Week, 7* (15 & 16), pp. 1, 26.

Ruskiewiez, J. J. (1983). Where process meets product: Applying Kinneavy's A Theory of Discourse. *English in Texas, 14* (1), 38–44.

Scholes, R. (1988). Three views of education: Nostalgia, history, and voodoo. *College English, 50* (3), 323–332.

Scott, P. (1988). A few words more about E. D. Hirsch and Cultural Literacy. *College English, 50* (3), 333–338.

Sizer, T. R. (1984). *Horace's compromise: The dilemma of the American high school.* Boston: Houghton Mifflin.

Slatoff, W. J. (1970). *With respect to readers: Dimensions of literary response.* Ithaca, NY: Cornell University Press.

Spring, J. H. (1972). *Education and the rise of the corporate state.* Boston: Beacon Press.

Squire, J. R. (1968). Foreword. In L. M. Rosenblatt, *Literature as exploration.* (rev. ed., pp. v–vi). New York: Noble and Noble.

Squire, J. R. (Ed.). (1977). *The Teaching of English: The seventy-sixth yearbook of the national society for the study of education. Part I.* Chicago: University of Chicago Press.

Squire, J. R. (1988). Basic skills are not enough. *Educational Leadership, 45* (4), 76–77.

Squire, J. R., & Applebee, R. K. (1968). *High school English instruction today.* New York: Appleton-Century-Crofts.

Stallings, J., & Stipek, D. (1986). Research on early childhood and elementary school teaching programs. In M. C. Wittrock (Ed.), *Handbook of research on teaching* (3rd. ed., pp. 727–753). New York: Macmillan.

Stanek, L. W. (1972). Hesse and Moffett team teach the theory of discourse. *English Journal, 61* (6), 985–993.

Stanford, B., & Stanford, G. (1980). Process curriculum for high school students. In B. J. Mandel (Eds.), *Three language-arts curriculum models* (pp. 138–154). Urbana, IL: National Council of Teachers of English.

Stone, G. W., Jr. (Ed.). (1961). *Issues, problems, and approaches in the teaching of English.* New York: Holt, Rinehart, & Winston.

Stull, W. L. (1984). Literature, literary theory, and the teaching of composition. In M. Moran & R. Lunsford (Eds.), *Research in composition and rhetoric* (pp. 125–53). Westport, CT: Greenwood Press.

Suleiman, S. R., & Crosman, I. (Eds.). (1980). *The reader in the text: Essays on audience and interpretation.* Princeton, NJ: Princeton University Press.

Talmage, H. (Ed.). (1975). *Systems of individualized education.* Berkeley, CA: McCutchan.

Task Force on Measurement and Evaluation of English. (1975). *Common sense and testing in English.* Urbana, IL: National Council of Teachers of English.

Tate, G. (Ed.) (1987). *Teaching composition: 12 bibliographical essays.* Fort Worth: Texas Christian University Press.

Texas Education Agency. (1986–87). *Teacher appraisal system: Teacher orientation manual.* Austin, TX: Texas Education Agency.

Texas Education Agency (1988). *English language arts framework, kindergarten through grade twelve.* Austin, TX: Texas Education Agency.

Tompkins, J. P. (Ed.). (1980a). *Reader-response criticism: From formalism to post-structuralism.* Baltimore: Johns Hopkins University Press.

Tompkins, J. P. (1980b). The reader in history: The changing shape of literary response. In J. P. Tompkins (Ed.), *Reader-response criticism: From formalism to post-structuralism* (pp. 201–232). Baltimore, MD: Johns Hopkins University Press.

Trump, J. L. (1959). *Images of the future: A new approach to secondary schools.* Washington, DC: National Association of Secondary School Principals.

Tschudi, S. (1988). Slogans indeed: A reply to Hirsch. *Educational Leadership, 45* (4), 72–74.

Van Doren, M. (1943). *Liberal education.* New York: Henry Holt.

Warnock, J. (1979). Brittonism. *Rhetoric Society Quarterly, 9* (Winter), 7–15.

Warnock, J. (1984). The writing process. In M. G. Moran & R. F. Lunsford (Eds.), *Research in composition and rhetoric: A bibliographic sourcebook* (pp. 3–26). Westport, CT: Greenwood Press.

Warnock, J. (1987). Review: Cultural literacy: What every American needs to know. *College Composition and Communications, 38* (4), 486–490.

WHO DECIDES? POLICYMAKERS IN ENGLISH LANGUAGE ARTS EDUCATION

Leo Ruth

Since the initiation of the public school system ... national leaders have periodically issued statements of a "literacy crisis" and have launched reform programs designed to eliminate illiteracy.
(Harvey Graff, 1987)

The morning begins in Mary Hart's seventh-grade English classroom with companionable milling around. In clusters, some children share gossipy stories about events in the neighborhood; some reenact favorite moments from television; some browse in the classroom library. It is a friendly gathering where everyone fits. The bell rings. Thirty-six children tumble into chairs at tables that crowd the room. Ms. Hart invites Lee to read the school announcements. Afterwards, Ms. Hart nods at Maria, Tyrone, and Rick, who slowly pull themselves out of their seats and quietly make their way to the door. Rick, the last one to exit, kicks the door closed with a downward thrust of his heel on the way out.

These three are members of the "pullout" class. They represent a cohort whose numbers are legion in the nation. They are participating in the school practice universal at all grade levels of sending children needing remedial reading or ESL instruction out of their "regular" classroom to another room to spend some part of the hour with a specialist teacher. This phenomenon of the pullout class is a common institutional reform inspired by the latest manifestation of the "literacy crisis" referred to in the epigraph that begins this chapter.

This scenario of the pullout class poses the basic policy question: Who decides? Who determines the policy underlying the practice of delivering remedial instruction through a pull-

out program? What policies underlie determination of the students eligible for special instruction? Who decides what assessment instruments should be used to select students for special classes? How do the curriculum, methods, and materials of instruction differ in pullout classes and regular classes? What knowledge has been called upon to support this national pullout policy? Does the practice relate to administrative convenience in complying with federal or state funding regulations? What is the relation of sources and levels of financial support to the establishment of this policy? What is the position of formally organized professional groups in English, reading, and ESL concerning this practice? And, most important of all, is this pullout policy really the best way to serve the literacy needs of students? The answers to these questions come later in this chapter when the impact of federal policy on local programs is considered.

This chapter inquires into the roots of policymaking in the English language arts. Policymaking is essentially a political process of negotiating arrangements to attain power and influence over the conduct of curriculum in the English language arts. For many people "politics" connotes dubious practices. Thus, it is not surprising that until the turbulent late 1960s and early 1970s, many members of the English profession innocently declared themselves to be "above politics." Even many of the leaders in English believed themselves to be "apolitical." Yet the

I am grateful to my official reader, John Maxwell, to my university colleagues, Kenneth Lane and Jon Wagner, and to my editor, James Squire, who took time from their own valuable work to read several earlier versions of this chapter. Their ongoing interest and wise suggestions proved to be vital to the development of the chapter. I alone, however, am responsible for this interpretation of policy in the English language arts. Deborah Dashow Ruth helped make the language of the manuscript more coherent and more artful.

history of any organized profession is necessarily a history of political arrangements. For, if "politics is the pursuit of what is desired" (Fuller, 1989, p. 139), as Michael Oakeshott argues, then the English profession has engaged in politics the moment it drafted its first statement of intention to "create a *representative* body, which could reflect and render effective the will of the various local associations and of individual teachers" (cited in Applebee, 1974, p. 52).

The National Council of Teachers of English was founded in 1911 in a protest against the prevailing political arrangement that supported college domination of the high school English curriculum (Applebee, 1974). Throughout its history, the various leaders of the NCTE, on behalf of its members, have periodically articulated important values, goals, and processes for teaching the English language arts that the profession desired to pursue. These policy statements were prepared with the intention of guiding the thinking of other professionals, legislators, jurists, bureaucrats, and citizens. Although a historian or a political scientist would construe these activities as political in nature, the English profession itself, until very recently, was less likely to interpret its work from a political perspective. Thus, it was not until the time of the volatile, consciousness-raising movements of the 1960s and 1970s, that "politics" surfaced in the organizational rhetoric. The NCTE Board of Directors took official notice in 1975 of its political function by establishing the standing committee called SLATE (Support for the Learning and Teaching of English). This committee on social and political concerns "seeks to influence public attitudes and policy decisions affecting the teaching of the English language arts . . . [to] publicize policies adopted by the NCTE membership . . . [and to] help create an environment for free and responsible teaching and learning," according to the SLATE membership leaflet (n.d.).

The present composition of the English language arts as a school subject has evolved through the political struggles of various professional and social interests seeking to use the school to express particular purposes and values. For example, the roots of elementary reading instruction derive from the religious concerns of colonial times. New England Puritans who felt obliged to teach their children how to read the *Bible* made reading a priority subject for home instruction. But because reading also was important for knowing society's laws, it very early became a subject of concern within the arena of government. The Massachusetts Bay Colony passed a law in 1642 that empowered the selectmen (the board of town officers) to remove from their parents any children who had not been taught "to read and understand the principles of religion and the capital laws of this country" (quoted in modern spelling in Cremin, 1970, p. 124, cited by Monaghan & Saul, 1987, p. 86).

Today varying conceptions of functional and cultural literacy often compete with one another for ascendance. Federal, state, and local government units, as well as special interest groups, all vie with one another to formulate policy for the English language arts. Sometimes the three levels of government work together; sometimes they work independently; sometimes they are adversaries. All three levels are interrelated by a complex web of laws and regulations and ingrained traditions of custom and prior practice. At each of these levels of government, many

special interest groups and individuals also compete for influence.

The tangled paths of policy influences are so difficult to follow that they can easily lead the analyst into confusion and frustration. However, complex, contrary tendencies should be expected. The historian Sheldon Rothblatt (1988) points out that "modern culture exists on diversity, flexibility, and individual initiative" and that "we should not therefore expect much agreement about an ideal type called an 'educated person' " (p. 20). Nor, adds Rothblatt, should we think that in the past there once was common agreement about the norms of cultural literacy. Gerald Graff and M. Warner (1989) also challenge the "myth of the lost cultural consensus" popularized by former Secretary of Education William J. Bennett and in best-selling books like those by E. D. Hirsch, Jr. (1987), and Allan Bloom (1987). Thus, the maintenance of a commonly agreed upon vision of the English language arts as a field of study grows more difficult as the field evolves, as social conditions change, and as government intervention increases. The primary purpose of this chapter is to describe how the members of these varied spheres of interest seek to exercise power and influence over the English language arts through political processes of policymaking.

A SEARCH FOR TENDENCIES AND TRENDS IN POLICYMAKING

Tendencies Toward Differentiation and Integration in Organizations

Sociologists have observed in social processes that generally appear in the life of organizations, the tendency to move in cycles of differentiation and integration. This process is evident in the organizational development of the English language arts field. As the profession of English teaching grew in complexity and size, a division of labor occurred, with numerous specializations, distinctions, and factions appearing. As the teaching of English has matured as a profession, it has tended to divide into specialized professional bodies, sometimes as subgroups within a parent organization, but often as independent organizations. For example, separate, but sometimes overlapping, constituencies have been organized in professional associations to speak for English, reading, speech, drama, journalism, modern languages (including English), teaching English as a second language, and so forth. Each of these organizations functions to define and maintain power over the boundaries of its curriculum area and over the qualifications of its practitioners. Thus, establishing a new curriculum domain provides a new political arena where its members determine what policy issues matter and how to interact with the larger body politic. This chapter, however, will be limited to the policymaking activities of the NCTE and the International Reading Association (IRA).

As an organization grows larger, there tends to be an increase in differentiation as perceived interests of members diverge. The result of this process in the NCTE is reflected in the table of contents of its *1989 Directory*. The contents (NCTE, 1989) show that the Council is structured by educational level into three "sections:" elementary, secondary, and college. Other permanent divisions in the Council are six "commissions" relating to the following subject concerns: composition, curriculum, language, literature, media, and reading. Three more permanent NCTE substructures, defined by the special interests of professional role, are called "conferences": the Conference for Secondary English Department Chairpersons; the Conference on College Composition and Communication; and the Conference on English Education. Eleven other permanent substructures called "assemblies" relate to various areas of the English language arts curriculum and profession. Six "standing committees" deal with certain enduring issues of the profession, while current, relatively short-term concerns are addressed by 43 "committees." Collectively, these 72 agencies provide within a single organizational structure a range of social arenas where English language arts curriculum issues and questions are identified and professional policies are negotiated.

Paradoxically, even as any large organization responds to the differences in backgrounds, interests, roles, and functions of its members, it must also seek to unite them internally for their greater good. Outside of its own membership, it must also seek alliance or coalition with other professional organizations or governmental entities sharing a core of policy interests. Differentiation and partition of function often lead to conflict, lack of coordination, and loss of control. The response to differentiation is an attempt to overcome differences by providing mechanisms for communication, collaboration, even reintegration. The history of NCTE then is partly a history of collaborative efforts with other organizations, with governmental bodies, and with emerging special interest groups such as the "whole language" movement among elementary language arts teachers. Throughout this chapter there are examples of this process of differentiation and integration and how it has had an influence on public policy decisions affecting the English language arts.

Inclinations Toward Development of Rival Positions

Another major tendency related to the first is harder to characterize, but nonetheless evident. There are policymaking groups, both inside and outside of the profession, that represent to one another rival or contrary positions in their conceptions of what content and arrangements are most desirable for the field of English language arts. The very use of the orientative metaphors, "inside" and "outside," suggests the existence of divergent conceptions. In curriculum theory, this divergence could mean "skills" vs. "whole language" approaches, or "subject-centered" vs. "student-centered" approaches, and so forth. In organizational theory, this divergence could mean "open" classroom vs. "structured" classroom, or "preformulated objectives" vs. "expressive outcomes," and so forth. As two opposite strains of belief develop in a conceptual area, the tensions that arise may be dispelled in several ways: 1) an agreement may be reached to divide the conceptual territory, resulting in a form of complementarity in content as viewed from the perspective of the whole curriculum; 2) the strains may be played out in competition for power and resources; or 3) one strain may be

ignored for a time, remaining latent until conditions change to favor it. Rival positions may develop within virtually any domain of the English language arts; reading provides a notable example. The sociologist Kai Erikson (1976) theorizes, in another context, that a line of conceptual divergence, which he calls an *"axis of variation"* (p. 82), is part of the natural order of things in any culture. He suggests that polarities function to draw attention to the meaningful contrasts in the culture. The tendency toward development of rival positions within the English language arts is evident at many points in this chapter.

Public Policy Trends: Federal, State, and Local

Outside the profession of the English language arts there are policymakers within the three levels of governance who are determining both broad and specific public policies impinging upon the English language arts. These policymakers include secretaries of education at the national level, state governors and legislators, state school boards and state superintendents of instruction, local school boards, local administrators, community pressure groups, jurists, test-makers, textbook publishers, unions, private foundations, and university academics. These policymakers collaborate or compete to attain the political arrangements they desire, "making deals" to shape the dominant trends in public educational policy. During the last 25 years, these policies have constrained the discretionary powers of teachers and other "grass roots" policymakers in the school. Eight conspicuous major public policy trends are currently affecting the welfare of professionals in the English language arts. The trends include:

1. Decline in local control of school policy;
2. Nationalization of state educational policies leading to uniformity of policies between states;
3. Decline of public confidence in professional expertise and in educational research;
4. Growth of reliance upon standardized tests for accountability;
5. Increase in legal challenges of educational policies by concerned citizens;
6. Growth of bureaucratic, rule-based management systems with a consequent narrowing of the realm of professional choice;
7. Growth of reform-motivated reports about the relationship between schooling and society, the economy, and employment—most prepared with minimal involvement of teachers and professional educators;
8. Recent countermovement to emancipate and professionalize teachers, placing them at the center of policymaking, action, and inquiry.

The two major tendencies of social forces in professional organizations and the eight public policy trends identified here integrate this account of the power and politics in the English language arts across three levels of governance. A definition of key terms will follow the discussion of the search for sources in the study of policy in the English language arts. Then we will present a sample of typical policy activities at each level of government and in the courts. Next comes a brief examination of the part special interest groups play in policy formation: publishers, teacher unions, professional associations, university academics, and others. The chapter concludes with an examination of the role of the "grass roots" policymaker, the teacher, and the presentation of a set of recommendations.

THE SEARCH FOR STUDIES OF POLICY IN ENGLISH LANGUAGE ARTS

Studies of the nature and development of public policy in the English language arts have so far been seriously neglected in the scholarship of the field. Even though there is an intense public focus on what English language arts teachers do, few policy analysts have examined the curriculum choices in English language arts as policy decisions and consequential political acts. Yet, definitions of literacy in English do determine what knowledge in English will be transmitted, what types of instruction will receive public funds. The definitions of literacy held by professionals and by members of the public play a large part in determining what culture will be conveyed.

The act of choosing a story or a method of teaching writing constitutes a policy decision about what knowledge and culture and what processes of thinking will be emphasized to students. The act of selecting a particular item of nonstandard English usage for children to learn, to eliminate, or replace with a valued standard form inevitably involves incorporating prior values and interests into instruction. Likewise, the act of choosing a particular literary work and the strategies for teaching it is an act that has potential for shaping and organizing the social and cultural consciousness of the children so instructed. Thus, the act of designing an English language arts program—tacitly, if not consciously—engages curriculum decision-makers at every level of occurrence in social, philosophical, and political decisions about what counts as valuable knowledge.

Different intellectual traditions and social values underlie the debates between scholars, legislators, and citizens about what forms of literacy to develop in English classrooms. Thus, divergent and sometimes incompatible and unstated assumptions shape emerging policies affecting allocation of academic learning time, specification of teacher competencies, content and frequency of achievement testing, and standards and expectations for English language arts courses.

There is then a larger sociopolitical-historical context in which the content, procedures, and organization of an English language arts program are designed to function. But who decides what knowledge will be transmitted in English language arts classrooms? Where does this knowledge come from? Who creates it? In whose interest is it selected, organized, evaluated and presented? Who decides what the processes of instruction are to be in English language arts classrooms?

The interrelated issues of policy, power, and politics in constructing the English language arts curricula have received scant attention in either the theoretical or research literature of English education. With few exceptions, scholars in the English language arts do not analyze the complex interplay of individu-

als, social groups, and governmental structures in shaping the policy decisions that form the political economy of the English language arts.

Policy analysis is not yet a coherent field of study in the English language arts; nevertheless, several writers in English education have contributed works with valuable insights into various power structures in the profession. Venezky's (1986) "modern" history of reading instruction does call attention to the neglect of the historical study of the development of reading as a curriculum area, and it attempts to lay "a foundation for an integrated history of American reading instruction through an analysis of the major findings and central controversies of this field" (p. 130), but Venezky does not attempt to analyze the sociopolitical-historical forces underlying the development of the field. Similarly there has been little systematic historical exploration of the issues, forces, and motivations shaping the development of English as a curriculum area beyond Applebee's (1974) general history, which seeks to "trace the broad movements in the theory and practice of the teaching of English from its origin to the present day" (p. ix). Clifford's (1987) report moves closer to the present, providing a brief historical account of alternating pressures for separation and integration of the teaching of reading and writing in the schools. J. N. Hook (1979), a former executive secretary of the National Council of Teachers of English (NCTE), presents his personal history of the first 67 years of the NCTE, giving a valuable inside view of the processes and results of policymaking by the leaders of the profession.

In the area of reading, Monaghan and Saul (1987) offer one of the few available policy studies in the field with their report on the impact of social and political forces in evolving definitions of reading and writing as school subjects. Fraatz (1987), a political scientist, has investigated the "politics of reading" to determine what political dimensions are evident in the "opportunities for success" provided in elementary reading programs by the "grass roots policymakers"—teacher, principals, reading specialists, district administrators, and parents. Goodman, Shannon, Freeman, and Murphy (1988) have prepared an extensive report on politics and policies of publishing and adopting basal readers. Moffett (1988b) has contributed a case study of censorship of a language arts and reading series, an in-depth analysis of the ways policy decisions are made at a "grass roots" level by parents, ministers, school board members, school officials, teachers, jurists, and officers of government.

North (1987) examines the professional and academic forces at work in defining and constructing the field of composition into a high status academic subject. Berlin (1987) has studied the ideological and social origins of the major rhetorics operative in American colleges in the twentieth century. Ohmann (1987) has scanned, from a Marxist perspective, English composition, criticism, literature, literacy and the basics, and English teaching to identify alignments of interest and power that dominate the culture of the English profession. Shor's (1986) depiction of the "culture wars" underlying the processes of educational policymaking from 1969 to 1984 provides insight into what happened in the English language arts during this period. Shor traces the course of three great "culture wars" for school reform: the war for "careerism" from 1971 to 1975; the war on "illiteracy" from 1975 to 1982; the war for "excellence" and against "mediocrity" from 1982 to 1984. What happened in the arena of academic politics to influence the origins and directions of literary studies in America from 1874 to 1937 is developed in Graff and Warner's (1989) anthology of original documents written by the founders of literary studies.

In the absence of a research tradition in policy analysis within English language arts scholarship, this chapter draws upon the general literature of policy analysis and curriculum studies to define the relationships of power, influence, and politics and to provide information about their interrelation and operation at the three levels of governance (Beyer & Apple, 1988; Eisner, 1985; Popkewitz, 1987a, 1987b; Spring, 1985, 1988; Tanner, 1988; Wirt & Kirst, 1982).

POLICY, POWER, AND POLITICS DEFINED

Before moving on to discuss the nature and impact of public policy upon English education specifically, it is necessary to define several terms that recur throughout this chapter. Educational policy is made by anyone who has the power to prescribe a particular course of action for others to follow. *Power* means having the authority to make demands and set constraints on any of the people occupying various roles in an educational system. In this chapter, power generally refers to the ability of a policymaker to affect, influence, or control what happens in English language arts education. Although the term *influence* (as a word) is related to power, it embraces a different set of working relationships between the actors in a decision-making event. The difference between an exercise of power and an exercise of influence is largely strategic, hinging on the appeal to authority that the policymaker adopts to get people to follow rules and plans that they themselves did not devise. The policymaker may seek compliance with his view by asserting his legal or institutional authority or by appealing to the intellectual authority of reason, logic, evidence, or to the authority of ethics and human conscience.

The main sources of power and influence can be found in the control of resources (money, information), in the authority of a role in an institution (jurist, legislator, board member, superintendent, principal, teacher), and in the authority of knowledge (expertise, wisdom). These sources of power and influence give their possessors the capacity to initiate demands and impose constraints. *Demands* include statutory obligations, institutional requirements, and standards of performance placed on individuals or units within educational structures. *Constraints* start with space, materials, and money; but they also include schedules, curricula, classroom organization—anything that formally or informally sets boundaries to behavior in the educational setting of a language arts classroom in an elementary or secondary school. Between the demands and the constraints of educational policy lies the realm of choice. Policymakers at all levels of educational systems find it tempting to add to demands and constraints and to set limits to choice, believing thereby to achieve accountability, predictability, and quality control.

The nature of the authority for policymaking at national,

state, and local levels with examples of its impact upon English language arts is explored in the sections below.

POWER AND CONTROL AT THE FEDERAL LEVEL

The National Interest and the Teaching of English

The federal government does not have the power to control local public schools directly. But it does have the power to control the spending of federal money. If a school system is reluctant to adopt certain programs, materials, or curricula, the federal government can "persuade" that school to adopt these changes by granting it money. It can also "jawbone" state and local decision-makers and provide incontrovertible data to promote federal values as perceived by the officials in office in both the legislative and executive branches of government.

The development of *categorical aid* became a powerful tool of federal influence and control. For example, initially, the 1958 National Defense Education Act (NDEA) contained financial aid for the improvement of mathematics, science, and foreign languages; thus these subjects became linked with national policy objectives. But the NDEA had failed to link English to the "national interest." The situation called for a dramatic lobbying effort on the part of the English profession, and it came in a report on *The National Interest and the Teaching of English* (1961) produced by the NCTE Committee on National Interest chaired by the newly appointed Executive Secretary of the Council, James Squire. This policy report made what Applebee (1974) has called "a direct and shrewd presentation of the importance of English to the national welfare, coupled with a startling documentation of instructional inadequacies" (p. 199). Although the NDEA was not broadened in 1961 to include English, the Council's efforts did succeed in attracting funds from the United States Office of Education to initiate Project English (Hook, 1979).

Project English established at major universities curriculum study centers which developed and tested a number of curricular patterns drawing on help from classroom teachers. Project English also sponsored some fifty or more basic research projects, including a series of cooperative studies of beginning reading instruction that came to be known as the First Grade Studies. The Project established also a small number of demonstration centers, and it sponsored a series of semi-annual conferences on such issues as teaching English to "culturally different" youth. According to Squire (1987), one of these conferences on research in the teaching of English (Carnegie Institute of Technology, 1962), developed recommendations which "defined for years the priorities used by the Cooperative Research Branch of the U.S. Department of Health, Education, and Welfare in allocating research funds" (p. 387).

In 1964, the NCTE's Committee on National Interest issued a second report on *The National Interest and the Continuing Education of Teachers of English*. This volume described in great detail the inadequacy of the preparation of many secondary teachers of English and most elementary school teachers. Finally, in response to the Project English activity and to the National Interest reports, the National Defense Education Act was broadened in 1964 to include English, reading, and the teaching of English to second language speakers. Hook sums up NCTE's role in national policy formation: "It is certain that NCTE had firmly assumed a leadership role and, through its publications, conferences, and supplying of personnel, had demonstrated to Congress, USOE, and other groups some of the kinds of changes that were needed to teach more effectively a subject basic to almost all other learning" (p. 198).

This National Interest episode illustrates the power of moral and political suasion that an active national professional association can marshall to influence the policy makers at the federal level. It illustrates how a national association when it is in a sense "accredited" with the authority to make "official" statements can function to define issues, provide ideas, and prompt the officials who have the actual power to determine policy. This episode in the history of curriculum policy in the English language arts suggests that such policy is made in a variety of arenas and at a variety of levels.

The Office of Education as a Policymaker

Until the establishment of Title VI of the 1964 Civil Rights Act, the United States Office of Education (elevated to cabinet status as the Department of Education in 1980) had traditionally defined its role as a servant of the state and local educational systems. Given the doctrine of local control and the opposition of federal control, the Office of Education disbursed money usually with a minimum of requirements and regulation. However Title VI established the precedent for using federal funds as a means of controlling state and local educational policy, completely reversing the traditional relationship. Title VI required the witholding of federal funds from institutions practicing racial, religious, or ethnic discrimination. In 1972, Title IX of the Higher Education Act extended federal protection of civil rights to include means of ending sex discrimination and further expanded the activities of the Office of Education into writing guidelines to end discrimination in schools.

According to Joel Spring (1985), the pattern that emerged in the 1970's found the American school system functioning under three levels of control: federal, state, and local. State governments imposed regulations and requirements upon local districts, which in turn administered these regulations and requirements in terms of local needs. Additionally, the federal government intervened in state and local educational policies by providing the money and planning for innovative programs under provisions of the Elementary and Secondary Education Act (ESEA) and, later, under ESEA amendments such as the Bilingual Education Ethnic Heritage legislation.

At the end of the Carter administration, the U.S. Office of Education became a separate Department of Education, with cabinet status for its secretary. President Reagan came to office in 1980 favoring termination of the Department of Education. He cut its budget and staff, rendering its continued existence precarious. Reagan wanted to reduce federal control over local school systems by giving greater administrative control to state and local governments. His administration sought to achieve this objective by revoking existing rules and regulations and by reducing the level of enforcement. Within a year of President Reagan's election, the Department of Education had revoked 30 sets of rules governing 19 programs. Joel Spring (1985) sees in these events an important political lesson

in the real power of the presidential office to control and shape educational policies. Congress can pass legislation, and the courts can make decisions regarding education, but how that legislation is carried out and how the court decisions are applied depend on the actions of the executive branch of the federal government. (p. 197)

The President and the Secretary of Education as Policymakers

The power of the presidential office to shape educational policies through controls implemented by federal education agencies is especially evident in the recent history of the fate of educational research under several recent administrations. The long and complex story of shifting federal priorities with increasing trends toward politicization of research agendas is detailed in an important collection of articles (Justiz and Bjork, 1988) published for the American Council on Education. These articles trace the development of a succession of federal agencies charged with initiating, funding, and overseeing research conducted in the nation's institutions of higher education.

In the early 1970s policy makers began to argue that past educational policy and programs had failed because research had not been conducted before implementation. Thus during the administration of President Richard Nixon in the early seventies came the establishment of the National Institute of Education (NIE), created as a vehicle to make wise use of available government funds for educational research. By designating priority areas, the NIE established a new research agenda in reading and writing for the educational community. To overcome problems of fragmented educational research, the USOE had earlier established (circa 1966) a total of fourteen centers and twenty laboratories to mount large-scale research on major educational concerns. But once established, the regional laboratories and the R & D centers found survival precarious as successive administrations struggled to gain control of these institutions against congressional resistance. Thus, by 1988 there remained only 6 labs and 10 R & D centers to sponsor the bulk of federally funded educational research. Among the R & D centers were separate centers for the study of reading, writing, and literature. Clark and Astuto (1988) report that the current level of support for the unsolicited grants programs has shrunk to the $1.0 million level of 1956, when the Cooperative Research Program was first funded.

Clark and Astuto's (1988) portrayal of the changing federal role in educational research casts the administration in a larger role than it once held in determining what is to be emphasized in research. They predict that the big winners in federal support will be national data collection (a statistical census type of function), outcomes-reporting through a reconstructed National Assessment of Educational Progress, and dissemination through "what works" types of reports. Clark and Astuto see the big losers under current federal policies as basic and applied research and evaluation and school improvement programs.

The following excerpt from an article in NCTE *Council-Grams*[1] (1989, January) seems to bear out some of the Clark and Astuto predictions, while it also further illustrates the nature of presidential power and influence for affecting the course of education:

Issues papers released during the campaign have shown that Bush sees education as the reponsibility of the states. An article signed by him in the October [1988] *Phi Delta Kappan* spells out a six-point "strategy for excellence in education," in which the federal government plays the role of "catalyst," providing incentives and encouraging "local experimentation with new ideas," a formula Bush says "has worked so well in business."

Bush declares his intention to focus on results and reward success.... Proposed "National Merit Schools" primarily serving disadvantaged students could get federal awards based on their size and averaging $100,000, to be used as they choose—"for lab equipment, library books, computers, or rewards for teachers and principals."

[Bush] favors state-administered competency testing for promotion and graduation, as well as state-by-state comparisons of educational performance through the National Assessment of Educational Progress.

Bush cites his wife Barbara's efforts on behalf of literacy and says he wants Chapter 1 [in the Education Consolidation Improvement Act] resources better targeted for the disadvantaged. (p. 1)

The Chief agent in executing the presidential agenda for education is the Secretary of the Department of Education. Terrel H. Bell and William J. Bennett, both serving as secretaries under the same president, present a study in contrasts as educational policy makers.

Terrel Bell. "We could have changed the course of history in American education if the President had stayed with the issue through the implementation phase of the school reform movement" (quoted in Miller, 1987, p. 1), concluded Terrel Bell upon reviewing his years as Secretary of Education under President Reagan. Bell, in contrast to the flamboyant style of his successor William Bennett, rather quietly appointed the National Commission on Excellence in Education on August 26, 1981, naming as chairman, David Gardner, then President of the University of Utah. Given the Reagan administration's agenda for dismantling the Department of Education, its curtailment of federal spending, and its advocacy of controversial policies, such as tuition tax credits and school prayer, many of the members of the Commission were dubious about its prospects, according to Lynn Olson (1988) who has studied recently released early drafts of *A Nation at Risk,* staff memoranda, letters and other Commission papers hitherto unavailable.

When it came out in April 1983, the Commission's report, *A Nation at Risk: The Imperative for Educational Reform* jolted the nation with its grim message about a "rising tide of mediocrity" in our educational system. This report has had a major impact upon education even though six years later many of its recommendations had not yet been realized. Its recommendations focused on five areas:

1. Stronger content in high school as reflected in Five New Basics which included 4 years of English;
2. More rigorous and measurable standards and higher expectations for academic performance and student conduct;
3. More time, more effectively used for learning the New Basics;
4. Better prepared, better rewarded and more highly respected teachers;
5. Public commitment to providing leadership and funding necessary to achieve these reforms.

The report set off reverberations through the states, and many of its recommendations were echoed in a flurry of further reform reports. Coming out the year before the presidential election, the report afforded a useful vehicle to Reagan for projecting an image of himself as a friend of education. Guthrie and Koppich (1988) describe the scene:

For the first time in any significant way since the days of Theodore Roosevelt, the nation experienced effective use of the Presidential 'bully pulpit'. President Reagan was quick to recognize the significance of *A Nation at Risk* and the intense public concern it had awakened. He made repeated statements regarding the importance of renewed educational rigor to the nation's future. He admonished state and local officials, as well as parents and educators, to make the changes necessary to restore America's schools to their past levels of prominence. He was careful to specify, however, that the financial burden of reform, if there was any, should be borne by states and localities. (p. 29)

William J. Bennett. When Terrel Bell resigned, President Reagan appointed William J. Bennett Secretary of Education in 1985. Some observers marveled that William Bennett as head of an agency once marked for extinction could rise so rapidly to become one of the Reagan cabinet's most visible members. Using his Secretarial Office as a "bully pulpit," Bennett devoted a good deal of his time to speech making and capturing headlines by making controversial policy and political statements.

During his administration, Bennett issued three major reports on curricular reform: *First Lessons: A Report on Elementary Education in America* (Fall, 1986); *James Madison High School: A Curriculum for American Students* (Fall, 1987), and *James Madison Elementary School: A Curriculum for American Students* (Fall, 1988). These reports offer guidelines for local districts, but they are not a "statement of federal policy," according to Bennett (cited in Rothman, 1988, p. 26). According to Rothman's (1988) summary of *First Lessons,* Bennett identified reading as the elementary school's most important responsibility. He urged the use of phonics rather than the "look-say" method and called for more challenging and entertaining books to make children desire to read. Rothman reports that *First Lessons* was criticized on several grounds, including the failure to address the problems of "at-risk" children and the unrealistic conclusion that improvements could be made without much cost.

The *Madison High School* report proposed a rigorous core curriculum which would require students to spend three-

---

[1]This periodical, sent to leaders of the NCTE and its affiliate councils, digests information from the nation's educational presses about current national and state policy issues considered relevant to the English profession.

fourths of their time in required academic course work, including four years of English. The proposed English curriculum would be required of all students. Reading lists for each grade would be comprised of "recognized masterworks of Western literature." Rothman (1988) reported that the Secretary argued that all students—not just those with high ability or motivation—should be exposed to such a curriculum. He claimed that low-achieving students would respond if schools raised expectations for them.

On the eve of departing his post as Secretary of Education, Bennett released one more report on what should be done to correct the shortcomings of American education. On August 30, 1988, he introduced *James Madison Elementary School.* As described in a *Council-Grams* (1988) report, Bennett

outlined what he termed "a sound elementary school core curriculum." [According to his plan] "Kindergartners through third-graders would study phonics, reading, grammar, writing and elementary composition. In fourth through sixth grade, children would be introduced to critical reading, book reports, spelling and vocabulary. Seventh-grade instruction would stress more composition, and by eighth grade, students would be analyzing literature." (*ED [Education Daily]:* 8/31) (p. 3)

In propounding these national curricula for elementary and secondary schools, Bennett made deep incursions into the curriculum development territory once held to be the sacred domain of local school boards. It is difficult to assess at this point how Bennett's recommendations may fare among a plethora of competing proposals. Not only has hortatory intervention in curriculum increased at the national level, it also has increased substantially at the state level.

POWER AND CONTROL AT THE STATE LEVEL

The Tenth Amendment to the Constitution of the United States specifies that "the powers not delegated to the United States by the Constitution, nor prohibited by it to the States, are reserved to the States respectively, or to the people." Since the Constitution makes no reference to education, this function is reserved to the states. The provision of state constitutions coupled with this Amendment have been taken to mean that the burden of policy making for schools falls on state governments. Although the state held the constitutional authority to oversee public education, it did not exercise its full powers until recent decades, leaving it to the boards at local levels to create the basic policies governing schools. After 1965 the shift of power from the local authority to the state was dramatic and swift. As Wirt and Kirst have put it, "local control as a value and operational fact has declined to the vanishing point" (Wirt & Kirst, 1982, p. 196). Today the state is increasingly inclined to oversee all state educational business. The initiators of policy at the state level include the governor, the legislature, and the chief state school officer.

The Governor as Policymaker

Governors are important policy leaders in defining issues. Recently, policy analysts have noted a growing uniformity in

educational policies across the states. Some analysts see this uniformity arising from the fact that the governors and state legislators share a common pool of resources to draw upon for guidance in determining the policy stances they will take. Joel Spring (1988, pp. 80–81), for example, attributes this nationalization of state policies to the work of three organizations: the National Governors' Association, the Council of Chief State School Officers, and the Education Commission of the States. He illustrates how uniformity in policy between states occurs through the strengthening of ties between governors in the activities of an agency such as the Education Commission of the State (ECS) in its development of task force reports such as *Action for Excellence.* According to the copyright page of one of its publications (Green, 1987), ECS was founded in 1965 as a "non-profit, nationwide interstate compact. The primary purpose of the commission is to help governors, state legislators, state education officials and others to develop policies to improve the quality of education at all levels." In 1986, the National Governors' Association issued its own school reform report, *Time for Results.* The NCTE *Council-Grams* (1988) provides an update of this report which illustrates how the governors' policy concerns about proliferation of testing could shift the emphasis upon teaching basic skills in English language arts to more productive matters, if the governors' concerns are ever acted upon. According to *Council-Grams,* the National Governors' Association update on *Time for Results* said

that the "virtual explosion in state testing efforts" since 1983 (the *Nation at Risk* year) may be a start, but it is no answer to meeting students' needs for education.

"We need to know what our students know, what they should know, and what kinds of programs will help them learn what they need to know," said NGA chairman John Ashcroft, governor of Missouri. Tests of basic skills that are "easy to measure" must give way to serious efforts by the states to determining their education needs and "test what's important"—students' ability to communicate complex ideas, respond to novel situations, and learn new skills. (*ED [Education Daily]:* 8/8/88) (p. 5)

The governors now seem to be leaning toward seeking more sophisticated indicators of performance than the simplistic standardized tests mandated by so many of their state legislatures as accountability measures and control mechanisms.

The State Legislature as Policymaker

By the beginning of the 1980s educational issues had climbed to the top of the list of priorities in the state legislatures across the land. The states responded swiftly and intensively to *A Nation at Risk* (1983) and other reports on the decline of education. Between 1982 and 1984, over 200 state commissions were formed to review the status of education and make recommendations for its improvement. Many state legislatures immediately enacted omnibus education bills. California's reform vehicle Senate Bill 813 contained more than 80 provisions. There proved to be a remarkable similarity from state to state in the rhetoric of the educational excellence movement and its realization through the provisions of state level educational reform legislation. Guthrie and Koppich (1988) attribute this phenomenon to "the widespread and uniform network of ideas that have been fostered by *A Nation at Risk*" (p. 29).

Wirt and Kirst (1982) also document the dramatic increase, beginning in the mid-1960s, in state legislated control of education. The main areas of control are evident in state administration of federal grants, state role in education finance, state requirements for accountability, state programs for children with special needs, and state efforts to stimulate experimentation. Wirt and Kirst (1982) have selected the area of the "accountability mandate" to exemplify the nature of the growth of state control. They report that between 1966 and 1976, 35 states passed laws mandating various forms of accountability dealing with teacher evaluation, assessment of curricula to meet state standards, setting of objectives for local education authorities, minimum competency standards for high school graduation. Wirt and Kirst (1982) mention that some four thousand reports about these activities were published in this period.

Accountability by testing. "Power is exercised through the ability to assign categories that provide identity to those to whom the categories are to be applied. The techniques of sorting, classifying, and evaluating of people enable the exercise of sovereignty" (Popkewitz, 1987a, p. ix). Tests are a chief means of exercising this form of sovereignty. Tests are now used to sort, classify, and evaluate students for placement, promotion, graduation, or college admission; teachers and administrators for certification, accountability, reward, or dismissal; school systems for accountability, reward, censure, or allocation of resources. The widespread replacement of human judgment by tests in the decision-making processes in education results from the fact that "Policymakers have mandated that the [test] results be used *automatically* to make such decisions" (Madaus, 1988, p. 87). Such has not always been the case.

George Madaus (1988) has described the evolution of the use of test results to inform policy. He says that from the 1920s to the 1960s standardized tests had little or nothing to do with state or federal policy. But in the 1950s and 1960s the large expenditures for curriculum development and compensatory programs led federal and state policymakers to request student test data to appraise the effectiveness of these programs. So test scores began to be used as a primary indication of educational attainment. More recently the various educational reform reports have used National Assessment of Educational Progress (NAEP) and Scholastic Aptitude Test (SAT) data both to portray the mediocre state of American education and to lobby for programs to address the weaknesses. According to Madas, the data from standardized tests have become an important source of the negative descriptions of the status of American education.

Where standardized tests once served primarily as indicators of achievement, they now have become our primary instrument of accountability. From the 1960s onward state legislatures have used such tests as a mechanism of power to leverage reforms. This growing use of tests in the policy sphere was revealed by a fifty-state survey of reform measures conducted by *Education Week* in 1985: Thirty-seven states already had some type of assessment program and six additional states were considering such a program (Madaus, 1988).

Now that the evolution to test-based accountability is virtually complete, various scholars are observing the occurrence of unintended policy consequences. Koretz (1988) questions these "unintended costs:"

we must face the fact that test-based accountability has not always worked as advertised . . . there are disturbing signs that it has substantial unintended costs. In making measurement-driven educational policy a cornerstone of the reform movement, we have made a more powerful change in the educational system than many people anticipated. (p. 48)

Madaus (1988), too, has noted the costs of measurement-driven policy, declaring that "It is testing, not the 'official' stated curriculum, that is increasingly determining what is taught, how it is taught, what is learned, and how it is learned" (p. 83).

In principal the official standardized tests are supposed to provide neutral, "objective" assessments of student accomplishment in locally determined curricula in the English language arts. In effect, however, these externally mandated tests are covertly prescriptive, implying the curriculum that should be known to the examinees. Thus, in practice as success and failure in school language arts come to be measured almost entirely by these tests, it is not surprising to find that both students and teachers consider preparation for these tests to have priority over other school goals in language arts that are unrelated to the tests. Consequently, the several dominant widely used achievement tests actually constitute a "hidden" national language arts curriculum—affecting selection of content, student work strategies, and the nature of the teacher-student interaction. The local course of study in the English language arts yields to the pressure of the district or state mandated test policy, focusing on what is needed to pass the test, with a consequent loss of attention to the broad social or personal goals the English language arts might serve in the local community. Teachers are sometimes quite explicit in letting students know that the real objective of the course is to pass the exam rather than to master the subject under study.

Quoting a high school English department chairman, Madaus (1988) offers a telling example of the corrupting effects of accountability testing in the area of English language arts on the Georgia Regents' Testing Program, a program designed to assess minimum competencies in reading and writing on the part of college preparatory students. The department chair speaks:

Because we are devoting our best efforts to getting the largest number of students past the essay exam . . ., we are teaching to the exam, with an entire course, English III, given over to developing one type of essay writing, the writing of a five-paragraph argumentative essay written under a time limit on a topic about which the author may or may not have knowledge, ideas, or personal opinions. (p. 96)

The Georgia Regents' Test provides an example of what Madaus (1988) calls a "high stakes test." Such a test transfers control over the curriculum to the testing agency. Madaus thinks that this shift of power from the local education authority to the state department of education is well understood by policymakers who are mandating graduation and promotion tests, but he believes that the implications of this shift "have not received sufficient attention and discussion" by members of the profession (p. 98).

The State Superintendent of Instruction as Policymaker

Traditionally, the states have allowed curriculum content specifications to be developed at the local level. The state education office has sometimes specified course titles and issued advisory curriculum frameworks. For example, in California, until a recent policy of "curriculum alignment" was adopted, the major curriculum instruments were only loosely related, having been developed within different administrative units of the state department. The state achievement tests developed in one unit were not always closely aligned with the curriculum frameworks and the textbook specifications generated in other units. But the criticism of local district standards in reform documents such as *A Nation at Risk* (1983) spurred the efforts of state departments of education to adopt new more stringent methods of influencing local academic efforts. How a state superintendent of instruction is accomplishing this policy shift can be observed by following the efforts of California's current State Superintendent of Public Instruction Bill Honig to reshape the K–12 curriculum in the English language arts.

Honig came into office with a plan for reform that he hoped to foster in California. Honig's vision of a "traditional education" in the English language arts is embodied in *Raising Expectations: Model Graduation Requirements* (1983), a policy document for the profession and in *Last Chance for Our Children* (1985), a popular treatment of his ideas aimed at educators and the general citizenry, where he declares that "significantly, a traditional education has high expectations of all parties concerned—students, teachers, parents, and administrators—and holds them accountable" (p. 42).

The reform efforts in the English language arts started by Honig in 1983 came to fruition in the *English Language Arts Framework for Grades K–12* (1987). The *Framework* endorsed among other things:

- A literature-based English language arts program for all students, giving attention to a range of thinking processes through focus on ethical, aesthetic, and cultural values;
- The integration of listening, speaking, reading, and writing and the teaching of language skills in meaningful contexts;
- A school environment where teachers of all subjects encourage students to read widely, to write frequently, and to listen and speak effectively;
- Teacher preparation programs in the English language arts which insure that teachers are prepared to implement an effective program of instruction;
- Assessment of the full range of goals of the langauge arts program with alternative methods other than the common objective tests.

Once the *English Language Arts Framework* (1987) was in place, the adoption of instructional materials compatible with the *Framework* became the next step. That adoption process was completed in June 1988. Rather than offer a Californian's view of the policy implications of this adoption, we present here a commentary on its significance from the perspective of an NCTE *Council-Gram* (1989) reporter who draws upon an account in the *New York Times*:

The [California] board of education in that influential state has adopted a policy of switching from basal readers to literature-based textbooks to help its three-million-plus elementary students learn to read. Further, it has cut its purchases of workbooks and flash cards used for drill by about one-fourth. "Such material was seen as taking time away from direct reading and writing," David S. Wilson reported in the *New York Times* October 19 [1988].

The decision to rely on anthologies and novels in original form rather than [on] what were portrayed as less imaginative 'dumbed-down' texts is expected to influence other states and the plans of book publishers," Wilson added, noting that 10 percent of the country's textbook purchases are made by California. [The state board] is also requiring publishers to label any stories that have been adapted or abridged. And the board has "encouraged teachers to give students more time to read in class." (p. 6)

The English Language Arts Assessment Task Force is now working to further advance the "alignment" of curriculum framework, texts, and tests. Honig and his Task Force recognize this phase of the operation as an essential step. The preface to a "Preview Edition" of the report states

The influence of assessment on the curriculum that teachers offer students is recognized as a significant barrier to the full implementation of the *English-Language Arts framework*. Unless assessment measures and practices are revised to focus on a literature-based, student-constructed expression of meaning, classroom practices are likely to remain rooted in a formalistic, specific skills-based approach. . . . We suggest that assessment measures instituted for accountability purposes and targeted on a formalistic superstructure of subskills have drawn teachers and their students away from meaningful classroom learning activities. (Mentor, 1988, p. 1)

This new goal of state control of "alignment" of frameworks, texts, tests, school accreditation, and teacher training being developed in California provides a method that can significantly affect local policy and classroom content, overcoming local inclinations to ignore or thwart state policy. Kirst (1989) indicates that "curricular alignment" is a method being adopted in other states.

POWER AND CONTROL AT THE LOCAL DISTRICT LEVEL

Americans in most communities exercise control over their schools through some type of appointed or elected board of education whose members are supposed to represent the population at large. These boards of education formulate educational policy, which is then administered by a central office headed by the local district superintendent. The line of administrative power reaches into each elementary or secondary school through the building principal who has responsibility for administering school policy at that level.

In addition to the increases in state and federal involvement in policy issues relating to school curricula, as noted above, there has also been an increase in regulation of local district practices as a result of judicial decisions. Such increases in policy activity at the federal and state levels have meant a decline of power at the local level. Wirt and Kirst (1982) have described the 1970s as a time when local control became much more limited as "the political web surrounding the school district tightened and included many more participants" (p. v). One result of the burgeoning development of new power groups during the last 25 years is that

the local superintendent has lost his once pre-eminent position in setting the district agenda and controlling decision outcomes. The superintendent and school board have become a reactive force, trying to juggle diverse and changing coalitions across different issues. (pp. 20–21)

Because the social composition and political world of local districts vary, the complex issues of power and control also vary from community to community. It is possible here to sample only a few of the kinds of forces that regulate or influence development of language arts policy at the local level.

Impact of Federal Policy on Local Program Structure

Why does nearly every school in the nation have some form of "pullout" remedial class? Richard Allington's (1986) study of the impact of federal policy constraints on local compensatory reading programs offers an answer. He suggests that such a program structure results from overly conservative interpretations of federal program regulations. Local authorities recognize that the federal funding is being provided to *supplement* not *supplant* the funds from local sources. Thus, an accounting problem arises in keeping track of programs and their funding sources. Allington (1986) claims:

The pullout structure produces a more easily followed "audit trail". . . . Simply put, a pullout program enables local and state education personnel to verify compliance with the "supplement not supplant" regulation with ease. The pullout program structure clearly was not motivated by pedagogical concerns, adquate empirical evidence, or learning theory, but rather by the perceptions, or misperceptions, of federal program requirements by local and state education personnel. . . . While several alternatives to pullout structures obviously comply with the regulations, movement away from that traditional program design is not evident. (p. 267)

Allington (1986) argues that this separation of students has unintended negative consequences that result in a fragmentation of school experience for these Title I students. He cites Kaestle and Smith (1982) as showing that these students are often required to "deal simultaneously with reading and mathematics instruction from two different textbooks, taught in two different styles . . ." (pp. 263–264).

The near universal "pullout" class seems to offer a classic example of a trend toward bureaucratization and dehumanization of school program structures through the application of federal and/or state regulations at local levels. Linda Darling-

Hammond (1988) has concluded that "as education becomes rule-based, it is bureaucratized and thus inevitably further dehumanized . . ." (p. 20). Ironically, educators at local levels are finding themselves in regulatory straitjackets even as they attempt to comply with the reforms recommended by state authorities. According to an *Education Week* report abstracted in the NCTE *Council-Grams* (1989), the National Governors' Association had promised 16 outstanding school districts a reduction in regulations if they would implement the NGA reform agenda proposed in *Time for Results* (1986). But two years later, local school leaders claimed that instead of reductions, federal and state regulations had actually increased to the extent that

they have resorted to "educational banditry" to unsnarl the red tape. . . . They now think nothing short of a blanket exemption will give their schools the flexibility they need to try new ideas. (*ED [Education Week]*: 11/23/88) (p. 6)

Impact of Pressure Groups on Local District Textbook Selection

Parent groups, taxpayer associations, and other special interest constituencies have become ever more strident in their efforts to influence and shape the educational policies adopted by local school boards. Materials and procedures within the area of the English language arts increasingly have become a favorite target of powerful pressure groups. Ardent speakers arise in various local board meetings to champion a favored teaching method—"phonics" versus "look-say"—or to warn against "invidious" instructional approaches—journal writing and discussions of values—or to challenge "humanistic" textbook selections. The dynamics of the complex U. S. political system as it involves the interaction of special interest groups, school officials, local politicians, and even the courts are especially well-revealed in the case of textbook selection, which is still a local matter even though there may be state constraints on the range of choices.

In most states, a local textbook selection committee composed of educators (teachers and administrators) from a county or a district administrative unit traditionally has selected the textbooks and library books used in the elementary schools. At the secondary level the textbook selection may be made within subject departments at the school site. Generally, these choices become major concerns of the community and the school board only when a local individual or group protests the content.

What happened when a storm of protest did arise over local textbook choices is recounted in James Moffett's (1988b) *Storm in the Mountains*. Moffett provides a fully documented history of the efforts of certain local citizens to protest the adoption of language arts and reading textbooks in 1974 in Kanawha County, West Virginia. Here began what George Hillocks, Jr. has called "the most prolonged, intense, and violent textbook protest this country has ever witnessed" (cited in Moffett, 1988b, p. 26). Moffett's dramatic account of this firestorm of protest led by fundamentalist groups offers more than the usual censorship case study. His detailed analysis of the underlying psychology and motives of the protestors enriches his insightful history of how a local censorship case came to have broad national policy effects.

The Kanawha County protestors lost in the courts, but they won a larger victory, according to Moffett (1988b):

The fact that nothing like it has occurred since gives a good indication of how effective it was: no publisher has dared to offer to schools any textbooks of a comparable range of subjects and ideas and points of view to those the protestors vilified and crippled in the market. Theoretically returned to Kanawha County schools, they may as well not have been. In many other ways the bitter controversy closed up its own school system as much as it did textbook editorial offices. (p. 26)

Defeats in the courts have not discouraged would-be censors of school material. According to a *Council-Grams* (1988) summary of censorship activities, People for the American Way, a civil liberties group, in its annual report, *Attacks on Freedom to Learn* (1988), cites 157 attempts at censorship, about a third of them successful. A second report on censorship from the American Library Association and the American Association of School Administrators has estimated that the number of challenges to library books and school materials has increased by 168 percent within the last 5 years. Despite decisions such as the following, by the U.S. Supreme Court, efforts at censorship seem to be increasing:

We hold that local school boards may not remove books from school library shelves simply because they dislike the ideas contained in those books and seek by their removal to prescribe what shall be orthodox in politics, nationalism, religion, or other matters of opinion. (U.S. Supreme Court, *Board of Island Union Free School District v. Steven A. Pico,* 1982) (cited in Spring, 1985, p. 256)

Impact of Court Decisions on Local Book Selection

Most English teachers probably do not consider themselves to be in jeopardy of losing their positions when they select literary works for use in class or as outside reading. Yet certain school boards have dismissed teachers for making "improper" choices of literature, such as Vonnegut's "Welcome to the Monkey House" or Salinger's *Catcher in the Rye* or stories that contain "dirty" words. Algeo and Zirkel (1987) have reviewed seven cases involving lawsuits in which the courts were asked to review a teacher's termination or non-renewal as a violation of legal rights to academic freedom in the selection of literary works. Their review of decisions in state and federal courts reveals a split in the courts over the extent of the English teacher's academic freedom in choosing literature to teach. During the 1980s English language arts teachers (as well as social studies and science teachers) found increasing numbers of legal challenges to their freedom of choice in book selection on the grounds that their adoptions were infringing upon the constitutional rights of some children to free exercise of religion. The two cases presented below illustrate how the First Amendment is invoked by fundamentalist religious groups to protest the teaching of "secular humanism," and how such actions influence educational policymaking.

Mozert v. Hawkins County Board of Education (1986 & 1987). Bob and Alice Mozert and their children brought action in 1986 against the Hawkins County Public Schools in the U.S. District Court of Eastern Tennessee, seeking injunctive relief and money damages for alleged violation of the children's First Amendment right to free exercise of religion. Briefly, the story behind this action is as follows: A small group of parents of fundamentalist Christian faith objected on religious grounds to the school-adopted basal readers, the 1983 edition of the Holt, Rinehart & Winston reading series placed in grades 1 through 8. The parents asked the school to provide an alternative reading program because, according to them, the Holt reading series allegedly contained sacrilegious and un-American doctrine. Jenkinson (1987) reports that these parents saw a portrayal of secular humanism in *Goldilocks,* and they found advocacy of a particular religion or antireligious sentiment in the play version of *Diary of Anne Frank* and in the poem "The Blind Men and the Elephant." Wynn and Wynn (1988) further note that these parents found dangerous portrayals of magic and supernatural acts in *Cinderella* and *King Arthur,* and they saw a favorable depiction of witchcraft in the *Wizard of Oz.* When the school system refused to provide the alternative reading curriculum and suspended students for refusing to use the adopted reading textbooks, eleven families withdrew their children from the schools and instituted a law suit.

The *Federal Reporter* (1987) traces the course of the litigation. In legal round one, the U.S. District Court for the Eastern District of Tennessee limited the plaintiffs' allegations and granted the School District's motion to dismiss. The plaintiffs appealed. The Court of Appeals reversed and remanded the case to District Court. In the second legal round, District Court Judge Thomas Gray Hull, finding in favor of the plaintiffs, summarized their complaint as follows:

The plaintiffs believe that, after reading the entire Holt series, a child might adopt the views of a humanist, a pacifist, an anti-Christian, a vegetarian, or an advocate of a "one-world government." Plaintiffs sincerely believe that the repetitive affirmations of these philosophical viewpoints is [sic] repulsive to the Christian faith—so repulsive that they must not allow their children to be exposed to the Holt series. This is their religious belief. (quoted in Flygare, 1987, p. 474)

In his December 14, 1986, decision, Judge Hull found that the constitutional rights of the plaintiffs had been violated. He did not require the school system to provide alternative textbooks, but he did order the school officials to allow students whose religious beliefs were offended by the Holt series to "opt out" of reading instruction. An appeal was brought before the U.S. Court of Appeals (Sixth Circuit), where Chief Judge Lively (August 24, 1987) held that the requirement that public school students study a basic reader series chosen by school authorities did not create an unconstitutional burden under the free exercise clause. The lower court decision was reversed and remanded with directions to dismiss the complaint.

Smith v. Board of School Commissioners of Mobile County (1987). An even more serious challenge to the school's authority to select textbooks came in March 1987 when U.S. District Court Judge Brevard Hand made a much more sweeping decision than the one in the *Mozert* case. In the case of *Smith v. Board of School Commissioners of Mobile County* Judge Hand ruled that 44 state-adopted textbooks in social studies and home economics promoted a religion of secular humanism in violation of the First Amendment, and he ordered the books removed from the schools. However, an appeal was taken to the U.S. Court of Appeals (Eleventh Circuit), where on August 26, 1987, Circuit Judge Johnson held that the use of the textbooks did not advance secular humanism or inhibit theistic religion in violation of the Establishment Clause, even assuming secular humanism was a religion. The lower court decision was reversed and remanded with directions. If the *Smith* decision had stood, it would have had a much more profound significance than *Mozert* because it required the elimination of curriculum materials for *all* students, not just the excusing of the offended individuals from using them.

Evangelical Christians are not the only parental groups to challenge the use of particular literary selections on religious grounds. The plaintiff in one of the earliest of such cases, *Rosenberg v. Board of Education of the City of New York,* sought judicial review of the use of *Oliver Twist* and *The Merchant of Venice* in schools, arguing that both works promoted prejudice against Jews. The state court held that there was "no proof that the books had been approved with anti-racial, anti-religious, or other malevolent intent" and refused to interfere with the discretion of the school board (Algeo & Zirkel, 1987, p. 180).

Residual Effects of Protests and Litigation on Local Book Selection. Many educators are concerned about the impact of legal cases such as these and others which threaten to proscribe the range of texts which can be introduced into classrooms. Jenkinson (1987) observes that even though relatively few cases reach the courts, dozens of protests over textbooks occur throughout the United States each month at the local level. Thus, the specter of protests leading to lengthy and costly litigation through the courts may very well threaten to weaken the determination of publishers, school officials, and teachers to defend their textbook decisions. Self-censorship or overly conservative selection policies then loom as an unfortunate consequence of fear of potential court action. Donelson (1987) quotes an American Civil Liberties Union document, *Censorship in the South: A Report of Four States, 1980–85* that suggests

[S]elf censorship may be widespread. A Louisiana librarian wrote, "My main observation is that teachers, librarians, media personnel, and supervisors practice self-censorship— let's do it for them before they do it to us." (p. 210)

The process whereby self-imposed censorship and a more conservative text selection policy can enter state and local deliberation in choosing texts can be seen in the response of one state level administrator to the *Mozert* decision. In his review of that case, Charles L. Glenn (1987), director of equal educational opportunity for the Massachusetts Department of Education calls for "flexibility of approach and parental choice." Mr. Glenn argues:

Why fight with parents over whether their children will read a particular story, if there is another one they find more acceptable that will achieve the same result? I have read the *Wizard of Oz* aloud to my children several times, but I can't see that we have any business making a free public education dependent on accepting that particular book. (p. 455)

Taking local school systems to court can lead to policy decisions with broad-ranging consequences for the freedom of editorial choice of authors in developing textbook content and for the freedom of professionals in selecting textbooks at all levels of authority. Even though the decisions in the *Mozert* and the *Smith* cases were overturned at the appellate level in 1987, it is likely that memory of such litigation will trigger procedures to avoid controversy for years to come. It may become increasingly difficult for publishers and schools to sponsor the degree of intellectual freedom that the distinguished historian, Lawrence A. Cremin (Olson, 1988), has insisted must be preserved. Interviewed by Lynn Olson of *Education Week,* Cremin carefully challenged the popular view that the public school should be totally reflective of the local sentiments and that local citizens should have full control of it. He declared that this arrangement works only to a certain degree:

A free society owes it to its children to have the schools at a certain point begin to make the children aware of points of view, to make the children aware of knowledge, to make the children aware of phenomena and experience that they will not get in their families or in their neighborhoods. (p. 5)

It does seem obvious that in a mobile society many children will end up living elsewhere and be unprepared for the divergent views they may encounter in new environments unless schools have prepared them to be open-minded, active, thoughtful learners in a democratic society.

POWER AND CONTROL OVER LANGUAGE POLICY BY THE COURTS

The Supreme Court and other federal courts have never questioned the principle that education is a function of the states. Thus for many years the federal courts did not review educational practices unless they violated provisions of the United States Constitution. The decades of the 1960s and 1970s, however, initiated a period of court-mandated reform as the federal judiciary expanded the scope of its review of educational practices. Examining trends in educational policy, Yudorf, Kirp, Van Geel, & Levin (1982) have concluded that during the past 35 years "decisions once made by school administrators and local boards of education have increasingly become the province of the courts" (p. xxiii). Yudorf et al. (1982) noted two trends in these developments: "As the reach of law expands, distinctions between law and politics begin to blur. . . . What has diminished is dependency on professional expertise" (p. 813). For example, the courts now address questions once left to professionals: What language shall we teach in our classrooms? How much attention must we pay to the home language of the child?

The Lau Decision and Bilingual Programs

The courts have ruled that "the primary task of the schools is to teach standard English, and that other languages and 'black English' are to be used as means to achieve that goal" (Spring, 1985, p. 260). In the case of *Lau, et al. v. Nichols, et al., 1974*, the Supreme Court ruled that the lack of special instruction to help non English-speaking students learn standard English violated Title VI of the 1964 Civil Rights Code:

It seems obvious that the Chinese-speaking minority receives fewer benefits than the English-speaking majority from the respondents' school system which denies them a meaningful opportunity to participate in the educational program—all earmarks of the discrimination banned by the regulations. (cited in Spring, 1985, p. 260)

The Supreme Court did not specify bilingual education as the only solution to the problem found by the Court, but the original regulations issued by the U.S. Department of Education did focus on the provision of bilingual programs. What began as a pedagogical problem became a volatile social policy issue with many political overtones, prompting bitter controversy and further litigation.

The Ann Arbor Decision on Black English

Although the Supreme Court did not specify a remedy for the situation covered by the *Lau* decision, the U.S. District Court of Michigan did provide a remedy in a case involving children from nonstandard English backgrounds. After reviewing the evidence, the court argued that there is a possible relationship between poor reading ability and the school's failure to take into account the home language of black children. Therefore, in the case of *Martin Luther King Junior Elementary School Children et al. v. Ann Arbor School District* on July 12, 1979, Judge Charles W. Joiner directed the school system to develop within 30 days a plan to identify children speaking black English and to "use that knowledge in teaching such students how to read standard English" (cited in Spring, 1985, p. 260).

Many regarded this ruling, which came to be known as the Ann Arbor Decision, as establishing an important precedent in the education of black students who are dialect speakers (Farr, 1980). But what has happened since the Ann Arbor decision? Has it been effective? Nicholas Bountress (1987), who had earlier written two articles describing the significance of the Ann Arbor Decision, conducted a computer search of the literature ten year later to answer these questions. He turned up no new information, only "repetitive discussions of the case itself." Bountress reports that "while the plan had been implemented, no information was gathered and disseminated that indicated whether or not teacher attitudes had been altered or pupil performance had been improved" (p. 19).

Thus, a unique opportunity for gathering information that might improve the educational progress of dialect-speaking children was lost, according to Bountress (1987), who concluded:

Judge Joiner's ruling did provide public recognition of black English and demonstrated that the nation's legal system can intervene when the

schools allow dialectal interference to disrupt the progress of minority children. However, two crucial lessons remain. The courts cannot legislate teacher sensitivity nor can they develop more effective educational programs. (p. 19)

The Ann Arbor experience suggests that judicial decisions are not self-activating. It remains for the educational profession itself, as the ultimate policymakers, to act to sustain the life and force of the judicial intent behind this or any other court mandate.

POWER AND INFLUENCE OF SPECIAL INTEREST GROUPS

Outside of the court system and the other federal, state, and local educational governance structures already discussed in this chapter, there are myriad special interest groups seeking to wield influence over the English language arts curriculum to make it serve the interests and ideologies of their constituencies. Previous sections have shown how religious special interest groups have organized to attempt to influence critical decisions about the English curriculum. But besides the various religious bodies there are a great many other special interest groups seeking to influence what is taught in school: corporations, business organizations, publishers, private foundations, accrediting agencies, universities, parent-teacher associations, advocates for students with special needs, teachers' organizations, professional associations, organized community pressure groups, and nonaffiliated individuals. Representatives of these various constituencies lobby the lawmakers and bureaucrats at all levels of governance to fight for their moment in the curriculum. Sometimes the special interest groups enter the political arena of educational policymaking as allies, sometimes as combatants. Because a chapter has its limits only a small sample of the universe of special interest groups can be considered here: textbook publishers, teacher unions, professional associations, and universities.

Power and Influence of Publishers

Textbooks control access to knowledge. The widespread use of the textbook, thus, gives publishers enormous power to package the knowledge delivered in the English language arts curriculum as well as in other subject areas. The pervasive use of textbooks has been well documented (Eisner, 1985; Anderson, Hieber, Scott & Wilkinson, 1985; Apple, 1986; Goldstein, 1978; Spring , 1988; Tanner, 1988). For example, Daniel Tanner (1988) reports that the textbook is " 'the predominant resource,' accounting for up to 80 percent of the subject matter in the course of study" (Tanner, 1988, p. 122). Citing other sources, Michael Apple (1986) concurs:

Whether we like it or not, the curriculum in most American schools is not defined by courses of study or suggested programs, but by one particular artifact, the standardized, grade-level-specific text in mathematics, reading, social studies, science (when it is even taught), and so on. The impact of this on the social relations of the classroom is also immense. It is estimated, for example, that 75 percent of the time elementary and secondary students are in classrooms and 90 percent of their time on homework is spent with text materials. (p. 85)

Apple (1986) suggests that textbook content is selected, structured, and "managed" in classrooms in ways that constrain socialization and interaction.

The textbook in the United States today is now increasingly "systems managed." It is more and more rationalized and geared to testing programs and competency measures, especially at the elementary level; but with the growth of statewide high school competency tests, this rationalization and standardization are growing rapidly there as well. . . . Though the textbook can be partly liberatory [sic] since it can provide needed knowledge where that information is missing, the text often becomes one aspect of the systems control I discussed earlier. Little is left to the teacher's discretion as the state becomes even more intrusive into the kinds of knowledge that must be taught, the end products and goals of that teaching, and ways it must be carried on. (p. 82)

Publishers of textbooks and tests make significant policy decisions for all students when they select and format the knowledge that they present to the world. Yet amazingly little critical attention has been devoted to textbooks. Tanner (1988), for example, expresses surprise, as does Apple (1986), about "how little research has been conducted on how textbooks influence teaching and learning . . . considering the great disputations attaching to the content and uses of the textbook" (p. 140). Apple suggests that we need to have a "long-term *and* theoretically and politically grounded ethnographic investigation that follows a curriculum artifact such as a textbook from its writing to its selling (and then its use)" (p. 104). Although Goodman et al's (1988) *Report Card on Basal Readers* does not achieve the breadth of Apple's proposed model study, it does offer our most comprehensive investigation yet of designing, marketing, and using one kind of text, basal readers. Another important source of recent studies of textbook knowledge, authority, language, form, and production is de Castell, Luke and Luke's (1989) cross disciplinary collection of critical readings.

Publishers are susceptible to the same policy directives and political issues that move other sectors of the educational world. For example, in the early 1980s, California required the rewriting of textbooks in science and mathematics because the existing textbooks failed to present the content and to develop the desired conceptual understandings presented in frameworks recently developed in the state. Later in the decade, the developers of the "California Reading Initiative" pressured publishers for more "literature-based" elementary school reading texts. For example, a 10-page memorandum from the California State Department of Education (Oct. 5, 1987), distributed to publishers, explicitly spelled out the implications of California's "meaning-centered," "student-centered," "integrated language arts program." The impressive speed with which publishers have responded to California's textbook criticisms and recommendations is understandable when we take into account the purchasing power represented by California's 12 percent share of the entire nation's textbook market. Tanner (1988) quotes California State Superintendent Honig as remarking that "publishers are willing to make changes based on quality criteria, if

we ask them, and educators across the country have applauded our efforts" (p. 137). This interaction between a state agency and publishers demonstrates how the individuals shaping one state's policies may influence the shape of textbooks (and curricula) across the nation.

Although Tanner (1988) lauds the professionals in California for basing their current decisions on the best of available professional knowledge, Tanner reminds us that California is also the state where professional educators once collaborated with special interest groups to demolish for narrow political reasons *Building America,* a series used in social studies classes in the 1940s. Tanner challenges educators to shoulder their responsibility as professionals to withstand "ill-conceived and narrowly directed" policy initiatives: "The mark of a profession is that decisions are based upon the best available evidence, not on political opportunism or expediency" (p. 138).

Power and Influence of Teacher Unions

Many English language arts teachers are members of one of the two major teacher unions, the American Federation of Teachers (AFT) or the National Education Association (NEA). From time to time, the AFT and the NEA have had a profound impact on policies affecting the conditions of employment for English language arts teachers as a part of their general mission to improve the lot of all teachers. The major goals of these organizations have traditionally been linked to the protection and improvement of teachers' salaries and welfare and to the aim of increasing teacher participation in decision-making processes through collective bargaining. Both the AFT and the NEA have sought to develop alternative structures to the corporate model that places teachers at the very bottom of a power hierarchy.

In the early 1980s the AFT, under the leadership of Albert Shanker, shifted from the more narrow focus on teachers' salaries and welfare issues to concentrate on larger issues of educational reform such as developing tougher entrance exams for the field, professionalizing the teaching force, raising curriculum standards, strengthening classroom discipline, creating coalitions with business, and so forth. Shanker hoped to encourage and to convey to the public the willingness of the union and its teachers to lead the way to various needed reforms. Policy shifts along similar lines were to come later within the NEA.

Power and Influence of Professional Associations

Powerful and effective lobbies have been organized around the curriculum functions of the school. Because the basic subjects such as English and mathematics never had to fight for a place in the curriculum, they were less likely to be mandated by state law (Kirst, 1984). The newer subject areas such as physical education, vocational education, and driver training organized into powerful professional associations which became very influential at the state level (e.g., Four years of physical education are mandated for most high school students). Michael Kirst (1984), a member of the California State Board of Education (1975–1981), found academic subject groups weakly organized at the state level in contrast to other areas:

During the more than seven years I spent on the state board of education, the math or English teachers never requested an opportunity to speak or never lobbied. But the vocational education and physical education teachers pushed for some specific policy every year. A consequence of this lobbying is the large percentage of the curriculum held by vocational education, as much as 24 percent in some schools. The teachers in traditional academic areas like math and social studies relied on college entrance requirements to assure their place in the curriculum. When colleges lowered their academic requirements in the 1970s, these academic subjects lost some of their priority. (pp. 54–55)

The Influence of English Associations. Kirst, apparently, is unaware of the concerted effort made in the early 1970s by members of the English professional associations in California to defeat the state-legislated and federally supported accountability scheme then known as PPBS (Planning, Programming, Budgeting Systems), a Pentagon model of cost-benefit analysis adapted to educational decision making and curriculum planning. There is at least this one instance where the appearance of activists in English before legislative committees and the State Board won the day: PPBS was never adopted in California. It is true that the California Association of Teachers of English (CATE) like other English councils in the nation, has not made a practice of systematically mounting official lobbying campaigns. However, CATE has achieved notable policy effects through the informal efforts of its legislative representative for the past decade, Kenneth Lane, who also writes for *California English* a monthly column, "Legislative Report," which serves to raise the political consciousness of the CATE membership.

The major professional effort to influence public policy in English studies at the national level comes through the leadership of the NCTE. Historically the National Council has taken an active role in policymaking, beginning with James Hosic's report on the reorganization of English in the secondary schools in 1917. One later example of the NCTE's lobbying role in attaining federal funding for the support of research and training in English language arts in the 1960s has been presented above in the discussion of the National Interest statements and Project English.

The direct efforts of the NCTE Council leaders to influence national legislation and national policy intensified in the decade of the sixties when the focus of American education moved from state and local districts to Washington, D. C. James Squire, then Executive Secretary of NCTE, described the scene during those years in his *Eight Year Report 1960–1967:*

Beginning almost "hat in hand" outside each USOE office, the Executive Secretary and Council leaders (with support and encouragement of loyal members within) built solid and substantial relationships within the Office of Education, the United States Information Agency, and other government groups. Our mission has been to improve the teaching of English, and Council members have responded magnificently. Despite continued national disputes over federal-local control, the Council has clearly stood for strengthened English instruction: extension of NDEA to include English, TESOL [Teaching English to Speakers of Other Languages], reading, programs for the disadvantaged; improved school and college libraries; expansion of the research and development programs to provide support for English; expansion of state and local supervisory and consultant services in English and subject matter fields; support for the National Endowment for the Arts and Humanities; inclusion of support for literature in the USOE curriculum and research projects; improvement of quality in the NDEA English institute programs; protection of the profession's interest in the revision of copyright laws. On such issues our purposes have been clear, and we have managed to speak with a relatively unified voice. On other national educational issues—the national assessment, for instance, or the public-private school controversy—the issues related to English teaching are less evident, Council membership is divided, and NCTE performs its most effective service merely by trying to keep members informed. (pp. 16–17)

Squire (1967) foresaw the consequences of the shift of federal funding to the states and the political burdens it would place upon many state English councils ill-prepared to advance policy proposals at the state level. He said:

We seem to be facing a relentless effort to channel federal funds and federal projects through individual state departments of education. Yet in far too few of our states are the leaders of English—elementary, secondary, and college—ready to speak in a united voice. How the Council meets this responsibility will depend in large measure on the effectiveness of our affiliated state associations. (p. 18)

Squire's assessment of the professional condition in English at state levels finds some confirmation in Kirst's (1974, 1981) recognition of the absence of official representatives from state English associations in California's political forums.

Nevertheless, professional associations in the English language arts at the national level—notably, the NCTE and the IRA—have continued into the 1980s to influence the shaping of curriculum policies, determination of research agendas, and appropriation of funds. This influence has been attained largely through the ongoing dialogue that NCTE and IRA national and state councils maintain about the content of English, reading, and other language arts through journals and other publications, conferences, commissions, special task forces, and targeted lobbying efforts both in Washington, D.C., and in some state capitals.

How this dialogue has been sustained by NCTE, can be seen by examining its policy documents issued over a period of 70 years for the purpose of shaping the thinking of the profession and the public. The titles suggest the range of policy concerns: the Hosic Report written in collabortion with the NEA and the U.S. Bureau of Education, *Reorganization of English in Secondary Schools* (1917); Hatfield's *An Experience Curriculum in English* (1935); Smith's *Basic Aims of English Instruction* (1942); Smith, Broening, and Perrin's five volumes on the English curriculum (1952–1965) developed under the auspices of NCTE's Commission on the English Curriculum; *The Basic Issues in the Teaching of English* (1958) formulated in collaboration with the Modern Language Association (MLA), American Studies Association (ASA), and the College English Association (CEA); Squire's *The National Interest and the Teaching of English* (1961); *The Student's Right to Read* (1960); Corbin and Crosby's *Language Programs for the Disadvantaged* (1965); Dixon's *Growth Through English* (1967), a report of the Anglo-American Seminar on the Teaching of English (Dartmouth Conference) as co-sponsor with the MLA and the National Association of Teachers of English, England (NATE); the CCCC's policy statement on "Students' Right to Their Own Language" (adopted 1972, published 1974); Mellon's *The National Assessment and the Teaching of English* (1975); Purves' *Common Sense and Testing in English* (1975); Hillock's *The English Curriculum Under Fire: What Are the Real Basics?* (1982); and others. In an effort to counter the "basic skills," "minimum competency" movement, the NCTE joined with a set of representatives from a number of educational associations in 1979 to develop a general statement on "The Essentials of Education." In 1982 the NCTE followed with its own statement on "The Essentials of English."

The tendencies toward differentiation and integration that have characterized NCTE's history took a turn toward integration in the first gathering of the Coalition of English Associations which, in 1984, met at NCTE headquarters to develop a statement, "Some Plain Truths about Teaching English," to speak to the neglect of English studies in the reform reports of that time. By 1987, the foundations had been laid for the Coalition to draft the most recent policy statement about the teaching of English language arts, which evolved from a three week "summit meeting," July 6–24, 1987 attended by some 60 representatives of all levels of schooling from eight major language arts professional associations: NCTE, MLA, CCCC, CEA, the Association of Departments of English (ADE), the College Language Association (CLA), the Conference on English Education (CEE), and the Conference for Secondary School English Department Chairpersons (CSSEDC). The formal conference report, *The English Coalition Conference: Democracy through Language* (Lloyd-Jones & Lunsford, 1989), calls for a restructuring of the way the English language arts are taught at all levels of instruction. A synopsis of the report in *Language Arts* (March, 1989) noted the following recommendations:

The report (arranged in three "strands" [plus additional resolutions and appendices]) says that for elementary school, the aim of language arts teaching should be to help youngsters learn to learn—to become readers and writers who use language to reflect on and make sense of their world and to become active members of society. The curriculum for this goal is recursive, deepening and expanding in secondary school, where fluency in language arts is sought. At the college level, wide reading and varied writing assignments leading toward "exemplary command of English" are among the aims.

In place of the usual "tripod" of English studies—language, literature, and composition, with the teacher as dispenser of knowledge—the Coalition offers a model in which the teacher coaches students, often in groups, through integrated language activities of reading, writing, reflecting, interpreting, speaking, and listening. . . .

The Coalition calls for a shift of emphasis in teacher education from *how to teach* to *how to learn,* integration of coursework, collabortion between college English and education departments and the schools, and recognition that teaching is not only a science but an art.

To support better learning of English, the Coalition says, administrators need to know classrooms from the inside, treat teachers as professional colleagues, and share decision making for curriculum and budget. Administrators and policymakers need to reduce teacher-student ratios at all levels and reorganize the school or college day into longer periods than the standard 50 minutes to permit sustained writing and discussion. (pp. 347–348)

As Wayne Booth (1989) says in the Foreword to the Coalition report, "our colleagues in English . . . travel under many different names: language arts, communications studies, media studies, linguistics, composition, rhetoric, and so on" (p. viii). Thus, the Coalition conference provided an important forum for uniting constituencies within the field of English who "were not, for the most part, accustomed to talking with one another," (Lloyd-Jones & Lunsford, 1989, p. xviii) to deliberate about the common goals of teaching the English language arts that apply to all levels from elementary classes to doctoral programs.

The Influence of Reading Associations. The process of differentiation and integration in English studies moved toward differentiation in the late 1940s, sorting out the professional groups in reading who were dissatisfied with a perceived lack of attention by the NCTE to the area of reading. This divergence of interests led to formation of the International Reading Association (IRA), chartered in 1953, which arose from the merger of the International Council for the Improvement of Reading Instruction (ICIRI) formed in 1948 and the National Association of Remedial Teachers (NART) formed in 1947. The unification that formed IRA was completed on December 31, 1955, when ICIRI and NART closed their books (Jerrolds, 1979).

Monaghan and Saul (1987) have traced the forces that helped the IRA to grow rapidly in its membership. They point out that the existence of the field's theoretical base—as defined through the work of its early scholars, William S. Gray, Arthur Gates, David Russell, and others—provided a core of knowledge useful to the founding of a professional organization. In contrast, no comparable, coherent theoretical knowledge base was yet available for writing during this period. Composition, as an academic field for the development of theory and research, was not to take substantive form until the mid-1970s.

The growth of reading as a profession was abetted unintentionally by the publication of Rudolf Flesch's *Why Johnny Can't Read* (1955), according to Monaghan and Saul (1987). Even though the leaders of the reading profession denounced the book, it nevertheless created a public furor and helped to give reading instruction its high visibility. The polarized debate that was set off provides an example of the tendency toward development of rival positions described earlier in this chapter. This arousal of varied sources of public concern influenced policy decisions for funding and for the establishment and certification of experts in reading. The enlarged axis of concern led to growth of the ranks and the influence of IRA. During this period, the position of "reading specialist" began to emerge as a new field of expertise. By 1956 there were reading specialists in both schools and colleges, and by 1960 seven states had sanctioned the certification of reading specialists as a specific profession (Monaghan & Saul, 1987). The growth of the professionalization of reading instruction was also helped by the massive infusion of resources directed to it by President Johnson's Great Society policies. The Elementary and Secondary Education Act (ESEA) of 1965 provided more than a billion dollars to help disadvantaged children. Because no school subject was considered more important than reading, a substantial portion of the funding of ESEA was earmarked for remedial programs in reading under the Title I provision of the Act.

In contrast to the more direct role of NCTE in generating policy statements for English, the history of the IRA indicates that a number of IRA leaders sought to avoid taking policy stands because they "believed that it was best to avoid dissension" (Jerrolds, 1979, p. 145). One must conclude from Jerrolds' history that it was the rare IRA president who entered into any sort of "controversy." Thus, President Donald L. Cleland's support for the "Right to Read" project in 1969 was an exception to the typical IRA leadership stance of nonalignment on policy issues. IRA established its first legislative committee in 1972.

IRA's first resolution committee was established in 1962 in response to Arthur I. Gates' urging of the leadership to respond to then current criticisms of the teaching of reading. Jerrolds (1979) reports on this first committee's restrictions on the content of resolutions:

[It] saw as its purpose the task of aiding the IRA in speaking out to educators and laypersons, nationally and internationally, with regard to critical issues in the teaching of reading. They decided to make a distinction between controversial issues and wholesale assaults on the reading program. The committee felt that controversial issues reflected honest differences of opinion; they were debatable and would not be the subject of resolutions by the IRA. (p. 101)

According to Jerrolds (1979), the resolutions committee decided to answer only the "gross exaggerations" and "assaults" that could do "damage to the field of reading" (p. 101). It also agreed that resolutions would not attack persons or organizations and would be stated in general terms. But when the committee did consider a resolution recommending "that producers of reading materials and devices make their publicity and advertising conform to professional standards of ethics and avoid exaggerated or unwarranted claims" (p. 101), this forthright position seemed to go too far for Gates, who served as advisor to the committee. He wrote:

I feel until the line of action and general intention of the International Reading Association in such matters are clear the committee should be cautious. (quoted in Jerrolds, 1979, p. 101)

The organization heeded Gates' advice: During the next two administrations the "resolutions" committee was called the "timely issues" committee; thereafter, it once again became a "resolutions" committee, but it continued to move very cautiously until the end of the 1970s. Since 1979, when the IRA Board adopted a position on "minimum competencies" opposing the use of a single assessment as a basis to determine promotion or graduation, the IRA has adopted and circulated 24 Board Position statements and Resolutions. These policy statements range across such matters as Misuse of Grade Equivalents (1981), Courts Should Not Make Reading Policy (1981), Continuation of the U.S. Department of Education (1982), Multiliteracy Statement (1985), Selection of Instructional Materials (1986), Ethnic Minorities in Teaching Materials (1988), Reading Assess-

ment (1988), Textbook and Reading Program Censorship (1988), and so forth.

Even though the adoption of 13 resolutions in 1988 indicates a considerable acceleration in the IRA's willingness to take stands on policy issues, its primary goals remain focused on improving the quality of reading instruction through the study of the reading process and teaching techniques, and the dissemination of reading research through conferences, journals, and other publications. In keeping with this goal the IRA currently has over 150 publications in print on reading and related topics. The Director of IRA's Division of Research and Development, A. A. Farstrup (personal communication, April 14, 1989) offers his view of IRA's role as a forum for clarification of ideas rather than as an initiator of policy:

There are many widely varying points of view and philosophies represented within the Association. I view the Association as a forum for the competition and clarification of these ideas and philosophies rather than as an institution whose job it is to advocate specific points of view unless there is a strong consensus across the entire membership with regard to particular issues. Certainly when the question revolves around matters of basic literacy and the importance of literacy we can all agree on the correct stance to adopt. When the issues revolve around contrasting, underlying philosophies of education—for example whether we should insist on highly structured teacher directed lessons or whether we should follow an approach where the teacher is not as directive—then the Association's role as an open forum becomes very important.

The major policy statements about reading have come from outside the IRA. Other agencies have moved to fill the policy vacuum left by IRA's historic policy of nonalignment with the various positions on reading instruction. For example, in 1969, when James E. Allen, Jr., United States Commissioner of Education, sought information that would guide his proposed Right-to-Read program, he turned to the Committee on Reading, a special task force of the National Academy of Education. Six years later, the Committee issued its report, *Toward a Literate Society* (Carroll & Chall, 1975), with a number of policy recommendations for "a national strategy for attacking the reading problem," which included recommendations for legislative and administrative actions at federal, state, and local levels.

The next major policy document to appear was the *Yearbook* of the National Society for the Study of Education, *Becoming Readers in a Complex Society,* under the joint editorship of Alan Purves (Purves & Niles, 1984), a past president of the NCTE and Olive Niles, a past president of the IRA. Threaded through the work are a number of policy positions advanced from the individual perspectives of the contributors rather than as official representations of viewpoints of their respective professional associations. The most recent major policy document on reading, *Becoming a Nation of Readers* (Anderson et al, 1985), was again produced by the Commission on Reading of the National Academy of Education, this time with the sponsorship of the National Institute of Education (NIE) and with research support from the Center for the Study of Reading (CSR), which also prepared the manuscript.

Though the IRA may not have sponsored the major policy documents on reading, it has not been without influence on the curriculum in reading. Most of the leading reading experts are members, and they are writing the nation's reading curricula under contract to the publishers of basal readers (Goodman et al, 1988).

POWER AND INFLUENCE OF UNIVERSITIES

Influence in Defining the Subject

Authority to Define College Entrance Requirements. Universities have played an expanding policy role in exercising power and influence over schools and their English language arts programs, both directly and indirectly. One form of direct influence is seen in the setting of academic entrance requirements. At the turn of the century, colleges and universities attempted to control the curriculum of the newly evolving high schools. Charles W. Eliot, president of Harvard, with his Committee of Ten, issued recommendations in 1893 that set the pattern for modern academic subjects in the high school. During the first two decades of the twentieth century, the university directly influenced the forming of the English curriculum of schools by setting course requirements for admission to the university. The university's continued influence in this direction is seen today at the national level in such documents as the College Board's policy statement, *Academic Preparation for College: What Students Need to Know and Be Able to Do* (1983), which identifies reading, writing, speaking, and listening as among the "basic academic competencies" which "can be defined in measurable terms" (p. 7). The university's influence at the state level can be seen in policy documents such as the *Statement on Competencies in English and Mathematics Expected of Entering Freshmen* (1982) jointly developed by the Academic Senates of the California Community Colleges, the California State University, and the University of California. Through policy statements such as these, the university defines the sanctioned version of academic English in the lower schools.

Authority to Credential Language Arts Teachers. A second important influence comes through the university's role in training and recommending candidates for state teaching credentials. Even though there are certain political constraints on the university teacher preparation curriculum imposed by state departments of education, certifying agencies, and examinations (National Teacher Examination), the university still maintains control of the content of its own courses. English language arts teachers typically are required to take four to six years of college or university work, including certain required courses in English departments and schools or departments of education, before certification, the specific patterns varying with state requirements. It is instructive to note that in *The English Coalition Conference: Democracy Through Language* report, it is the "College Strand" that carries the definition of the "restructured" English major and notes its implications for teacher preparation in English education. However, given the nature of participation and collaboration from all levels of schooling in this conference, it seems likely that the Coalition's enlarged vision of English education received intellectual direction from all teaching levels.

Authority over Definition of Research Models. At the graduate level, the university establishes scientific models of research for the study of schooling and curriculum. It defines the rules of data collection, analysis, and reporting—imitating dominant natural science models. It defines Truth as residing in these procedures, which so often neglect to take into account the social context where this discourse is formed. The university fosters a certain style of scientific discourse which has had only limited applicability to research in the English language arts. However, in recent years there has been a shift in the social sciences away from research methods based on natural science models to models using techniques developed by ethnographers and literary critics. A recent working party in English education has concluded:

Research studies which emphasize the complex interaction of many contextual variables come closer to capturing the real world of English classrooms than do those which isolate and manipulate a single variable. The logistics of carrying out such naturalistic/ethnographic studies are such, however, that the findings seem more difficult to generalize than the traditional experimental paradigm has assumed.... While a great deal of research has been done in the last two decades on student learning and theoretical descriptions of such areas as composition studies, language development, and reader response to literature, this research has not been successfully integrated into a comprehensive theory, nor have its implications for classroom practice been sufficiently studied. (Angelotti, et al, 1988, pp. 234–235)

Authority over Construction of a Field of School Knowledge. The relation of university scholarship to the professionalization of knowledge has been discussed by various commentators (Clifford, 1987; Monaghan & Saul, 1987; Popkewitz, 1987a, 1987b). For example, Popkewitz (1987b) generalized about the power of scholarly expertise in structuring school knowledge: "What is defined as school knowledge reflects interests that have the power to structure definitions and communication patterns available in a society" (p. 347). Monaghan and Saul (1987), using historical examples, show just how this power of professional educators in universities to structure definitions of reading and writing, combined with social and political forces, have contributed to the disparity in the attention given to these two subjects in schools. Applebee (1974) also has commented on the influence of scholarship in defining the content of secondary English:

Virtually every development in scholarship in English studies has been seen as offering the inevitably proper definition of the content of the secondary school class. Grammar and rhetoric in the eighteenth century, philology in the nineteenth, sociology during the thirties, semantics in the forties, and the New Criticism in the sixties have been taken up and transplanted by enthusiastic teachers; and each has ben supplanted in its turn by equally enthusiastic proponents of a newer critical perspective. (p. 246)

To Applebee's list could be added the recent adoption in schools of still newer definitions of school content in the English language arts emanating from developments in reader response theory and theories of composing processes.

Authority over Construction of Composition as an Academic Discipline. Exactly how a field of knowledge is chartered in the university is the subject of Stephen North's *The Making of Knowledge in Composition* (1987). North (1987) attempts to show in detail the social process of constructing the field of "knowledge" that has come to be called "composition," both in the worlds of practitioners and scholars. It is a study of how composition "knowledge" is made mostly at the university in various "methodological communities": These are occupied by "groups of inquirers more or less united by their allegiance to one such [methodological community], to an agreed-upon set of rules for gathering, testing, validating, accumulating and distributing what they regard as knowledge" (p. 1). North (1987) plots out the story of how a discipline such as composition is "colonized" (to borrow Ivor Goodson's (1988) term) in the academic world—how its knowledge base is established through the various modes of inquiry of competing research colonies and how these colonies gain their adherents and resource allocations. North offers a very detailed account of the complex, often problematic processes in the world of classroom practitioners and the world of university level "knowledge-making" communities engaged in constructing the practice and field of "composition" in the universities and in the schools.

Authority of Expert Knowledge. Obviously, an important influence on the formation of policy in English language arts comes through the university's role as a provider of expert knowledge for policy makers such as legislators, judges, state and local bureaucrats and for policy implementors such as administrators and teachers. Thus scholars and researchers, individually as valued consultants or collectively through research centers, have had a profound impact on the English language arts. Federally-funded research centers such as the Center for the Study of Reading (University of Illinois, Urbana), for example, have influenced our conception of reading processes among other things. The more recently funded Center for the Study of Writing (University of California, Berkeley) and the Center for the Learning and Teaching of Literature (State University of New York at Albany) promise to be influential in the future as their research agendas produce needed scholarship in the areas of writing and literature. Academics also have been particularly influential in implementing federal and state legislation as a network of personnel has moved back and forth among universities, professional associations, and government agencies.

Scholars such as Louise Rosenblatt in literature; James Britton in language; John Dixon in English curriculum; Donald Graves in children's writing; Jean Chall, William S. Gray, and Kenneth Goodman in reading have affected teaching practice and the design of English language arts curricula through their writings, professional addresses, and consultancies. These scholars, affiliated with colleges and universities, and the occasional independent scholar such as James Moffett and his student-centered holistic language arts curriculum, plus others too numerous to identify here, have all contributed to the dynamic of the creation and distribution of knowledge that has given form and direction to the English language arts.

Authority to Collaborate on Projects with Teachers. With the aid of funds from federal, state, and foundation sources some academics have been directly involved in collegial working relationships with teachers to improve instruction in the English language arts. One type of school-university partnership is exemplified in the work of James Gray and his development of the National Writing Project (NWP). In the mid-1970s, James Gray, a supervisor of teacher education in the School of Education at the University of California, Berkeley established the Bay Area Writing Project (BAWP) which later expanded into NWP. From the start, this model always recognized the central role of the teacher in changing the teaching of writing in the English language arts curriculum. The NWP inservice model, which was one of the earliest partnership models whereby a higher education institution collaborates on an equal footing with local districts in training teachers to teach other teachers how to teach writing better, has literally swept the nation and is now in position at more than 150 sites across the country.

Though the NWP espouses "no single curriculum or methodology" (Gray, 1988, pp. 1–2) it does advance a platform of conceptions, theories, and beliefs which constitute a tacit set of policies for guiding instruction in composition. For example, its model for designing an inservice program in teaching writing is founded upon the following beliefs: knowledge comes from practice as well as research; the most valuable expertise comes from the teacher; thus, teachers are the best teachers of other teachers and the university expert functioning in a "top-down" model of staff development no longer offers a viable approach to inservice education; teachers of writing come to understand the process of writing through actual writing; effective staff development occurs as teachers meet and confer at home sites on a regular basis, and so forth. With teachers at its center, the NWP model does have an implicit theory of what is true, what is desirable, and what is teachable and learnable in writing as it promotes images of good teaching. Moffett (1988a) has called this model, "the most positive development in English education during the '70's—indeed during the whole period since World War II" (p. 68).

The Bay Area Writing Project and subsequently the National Writing Project centers surely represent one of the earliest efforts in the nation to break with the dominant, academic top-down transmission model of reform. These centers honor the wisdom of practice, recognize teachers as professionals, and encourage them to lead the way to reforms in the teaching of the English language arts. Thus Gray and other leaders of the prototype writing projects intuitively recognized the teacher as the prime mover in curriculum change. For it is the teacher who, as a "grass roots" policymaker, transforms the curriculum that is written into the curriculum that is realized in practice.

THE ULTIMATE POLICYMAKERS: TEACHERS IN ENGLISH LANGUAGE ARTS

The making of laws and regulations does not end the policy-making process. Laws and regulations are not self-executing.

Janet White (1988) has observed that "The primary teacher, when in sole charge of a class, has the power to reshape the whole curriculum" (p. 9). Clark (1988) contends that "Teachers are policymakers, although they are not recognized as such in most of the literature on educational policymaking" (p. 177). Teachers make curriculum decisions moment by moment which directly affect students:

It makes little difference what the secretary of education says works, what the governor includes in his program, or what the school board adopts for the district administration to implement, *if* none of these actions affects what happens between the teacher and the student. (Clark, 1988, p. 17)

Recent classroom research has called into question the rationalistic bases of many prior reform models (Garman & Hazi, 1988; Goodlad, 1987; Sizer, 1986; Stedman, 1987; Wise, 1979, 1988). Wise (1988) explains why the intrusive, legislated, rationalistic models of planning and supervision do not work:

Because students are not standardized in their needs, stages of development, home environments, preconceptions, or learning styles, a given stimulus does not produce a predictable response. A teacher must make decisions based on knowledge of the student, of the subject matter, and of pedagogy to create the right conditions of learning. Appropriate instructional decisions must be made at the point of service delivery. (p. 332)

Policies which attempt to tighten control of what happens in classrooms by standardizing instructional planning, supervision, and evaluation fail because these well-intentioned rationalistic models erode teacher professionalism and autonomy, emphasize narrow, measurable goals and lead to a decline in the quality of education for all students, according to Wise (1979).

Larry Cuban (1986) observed that in spite of a century of reform efforts, the durable core of teaching practice has not changed. He suggests that because most such "well-intentioned and highly motivated" reformers have been nonteachers, they were simply unable to take into account the "survival needs" of teachers in a demanding teaching environment. Cuban says:

Until state policymakers and national cheerleaders for change understand clearly the consequences for teachers of the reforms they propose, those reforms are likely to prove counterproductive for students and for the teaching profession. And the would-be reformers will continue to thrash about blindly, seeking clear-cut solutions to irreconcilable dilemmas arising from the structural conditions within which teachers labor. (p. 11)

A belated recognition of the teacher's power to shape curriculum has finally led some reformers to look to the teacher at the local school site to discover how reforms might be brought to life. According to John Goodlad (1987), there is a growing body of evidence that the familiar top-down, linear approach to change with its "pathological emphasis on accountability" will not work. He sees an emerging alternative to this authoritarian approach:

One-way directives are replaced by multiple interactions; leadership by authority is replaced by leadership by knowledge; following rules and regulations is replaced by providing more room for decision making; mandated behavior is replaced by inquiring behavior; accountability is replaced by high expectations, responsibility, and a level of trust that includes freedom to make mistakes. . . . Educational improvement calls for increasing the authority and decision-making space of the large numbers of individuals who constitute the base of the pyramid. . . . empowering principals and teachers—those closest to the processes of students' learning. (p. 4)

In other words, no policy is ever self-executing. It requires a teacher to make the actual classroom decision that activates any policy received from any level of authority. The following letter to the "Questions and Answers" column of the *Reading Teacher* provides a "real world" example of "grassroots policymaking" in reading classrooms:

Q. I'm a 2nd grade teacher and this is my first year of teaching. I love teaching reading and I love the school. The principal meets with new teachers every 2 weeks to help us with any problems, and I think he knows more about really teaching reading than the university professors I had.

There's only one thing that really bothers me. My principal is very much against teaching reading skills. He insists that kids learn by reading and that kids who read and write get better in reading. He frequently says that the word superiority effect proves that kids recognize words as wholes and not by using phonic skills.

This is the direct opposite of what I learned as an undergraduate. We learned phonic terms, designed phonics lessons, and in our reading methods course we had to teach a phonics lesson. I was told that there was a ton of research to show that phonics works.

I asked another 2nd grade teacher whether she teaches phonics and she said she did, but that she just doesn't make a big deal about it, and that the principal doesn't make a big deal about it either since the kids she teaches do well in reading.

Is my principal right and were my university professors wrong? (Pikulski, 1987, p. 831)

The two second-grade teachers and their principal in this elementary school are active policymakers. The principal has made a policy choice by introducing a new reading pedagogy. This new approach threatens the familiar knowledge and practices of the two teachers, creating the dilemma of requiring them to decide between rival methods of teaching reading. The more experienced of the two understands very well her "realm of choice" between the demands and the constraints placed upon her, and she acts accordingly. The newer teacher chooses to consult her professional association for help in rescuing her from this pedagogical quandary. Who decides policy? Each one does, the principal and the two teachers, in his or her own time and place in school. Yet, the three may not consider themselves "grassroots policymakers" as they make their instructional decisions day-by-day. This simple example suggests that even though a reform policy may begin anywhere—in Secretary Bennett's Madison Elementary School scheme, in a professor's university course or in a principal's inservice program for new teachers—the legislated "reform" can finally come to life only in the classroom where a teacher interacts with students.

In concluding his address to the Third International Conference for the Teaching of English held in Sydney, Australia in 1980, James Britton (1982) proposed a toast to the 1980s as the "decade of the teacher."

ARRANGEMENTS OF POWER AND POLICYMAKING

1. Organizational Structures: Who decides?
   a. Decision-making authorities: Who are they? What powers do they have?
   b. Rule-making authorities: Who decides what regulations are imposed, what goals are set, what work norms are enforced?

2. Resource Allocation: Who gets what?
   a. Finance: Who controls the distribution of money?
   b. Information: Who gets what data? Who controls the channels of information?
   c. Human and material resources: Who controls the deployment of people and allocation of materials?

3. Strategy Initiatives: How is control or influence attained and used?
   a. Rewards and sanctions: Who distributes rewards or imposes sanctions?
   b. Social contact: Who initiates or prohibits meetings of people: 1) inside the administrative unit; or 2) between the people in separate units?
   c. Bargaining and negotiation: Who is authorized to attempt to persuade others to follow a particular course of action?
   d. Autonomy and professional authority: Who determines the boundaries of professional authority and responsibility?

FIGURE 5–1. Arrangements of power and policymaking.

As we have developed our view of learning as interactive, and that of curriculum as negotiable; as we have recognised the dramatic effect of intentions upon performance, by teachers as well as by students; as it has become clear that teaching consists of moment-by-moment interactive behavior, behavior that can only spring from inner conviction—I think we are, perhaps for the first time, ready to admit that what the teacher can't do in the classroom can't be achieved by any other means. (Britton, 1982, p. 11)

Here in the United States at the beginning of the 1990s, we may finally be entering the age of the teacher. According to Milbrey McLaughlin (1987), current thinking in the world of policy analysis holds that "policy-directed change ultimately is a problem of the smallest unit" (p. 171). And as Gene Maeroff argues in his book, *The Empowerment of Teachers: Overcoming the Crisis of Confidence* (1988), "if elementary and secondary education in America improves, it will be, more than anything else, because of the part teachers play" (p. 1). In the end, the question is what part should the teacher in English language arts play in policymaking?

CONCLUSION: WHO DECIDES?

The Power of Professional English Language Arts Teachers

There is a new vision of the professional (Carnegie, 1986; Maeroff, 1988; Tucker & Mandel, 1986) that could entrust English language arts teachers with greater power in policymaking. For example, in Rochester, New York (Urbanski, 1987) and in Cerritos, California (Sickler, 1988) new management structures have been developed both at the school and the district levels; new decision-making structures are beginning to invest teachers with authority to determine curriculum, select teaching materials, create relevant forms of student assessment, and participate in the selection and evaluation of peers. Such new forms of shared governance are giving teachers a sense of au-

thority and recognizing them as experts, conferring on them status as "real" professionals. As respected professionals they are being empowered to organize the school day and the school's resources in ways that best suit the educational needs of their students.

New power arrangements, more than ever before, are bringing teachers into the center of the political arena to join the company of all the other decision-makers whose institutional or societal position confers on them the authority to influence or to shape the policies affecting the English language arts. Along with the acquisition of more authority, all teachers will need to master the discourse of policymaking which deals essentially with the interrelation of power structures, allocation of resources, and strategies for deciding policy. English language arts teachers will find themselves grappling with a set of basic policy questions that interest political scientists and policy analysts: Who decides? Who gets what? How is control attained? These questions apply across all policy contexts from the kindergarten classroom to the congressional committee. The outline below poses key questions in relation to three areas of concern: organizational *structures* that give authority to policy makers, the *resources* that policy makers draw upon, and the *strategies* that policy makers use to make effective their decisions.

Arrangements of Power and Policymaking

1. Organizational Structures: Who decides?
   a. Decision-making authorities: Who are they? What powers do they have?
   b. Rule-making authorities: Who decides what regulations are imposed, what goals are set, what work norms are enforced?
2. Resource Allocation: Who gets what?
   a. Finanace: Who controls the distribution of money?
   b. Information: Who gets what data? Who controls the channels of information?

c. Human and material resources: Who controls the deployment of people and allocation of materials?

3. Strategy Initiatives: How is control or influence attained and used?

a. Rewards and sanctions: Who distributes rewards or imposes sanctions?

b. Social contact: Who initiates or prohibits meetings of people: 1) inside the administrative unit; or 2) between the people in separate units?

c. Bargaining and negotiation: Who is authorized to attempt to persuade others to follow a particular course of action?

d. Autonomy and professional authority: Who determines the boundaries of professional authority and responsibility?

As this chapter has shown, policy is not simply made by one unit and executed by another. Rather, policy is the overall result of many forces with divergent interests impinging on each other in the context of various levels of governance, all the way from classrooms to courtrooms.

RECOMMENDATIONS

It is unfortunate that no strong theory and no coherent field of policy studies in the English language arts have yet been developed. As social conditions change, as governmental interventions increase, and as teacher participation in policymaking advances, such studies are more sorely needed than ever. But the entire field of policy studies in education is no more than 20 years old, and those who have pioneered this field have not directed their attention to the English language arts. Little attention to the study of policymaking has come from within the profession, possibly because many members of the English profession have tended to resist involving themselves with politics and policymaking, preferring to direct their attention to what they consider loftier matters. Hence, the field of English language arts is rarely studied either by members within its own profession, or by scholars outside of it. However, a recent study group on research in English education has recognized the knowledge gap in policy studies and the importance of investigating such issues: "We have little research from an English Education perspective on how the socio-political climate constrains teachers from testing to censorship, from curricular con-

trol to professional autonomy (Angelotti et al, 1988, pp. 234–235).

It would seem that the more profound a profession's understanding of policymaking activity, the less likely will that profession be at the mercy of plausible but mistaken policy applications from without. The more thoroughly a profession understands its own history, the less likely that profession will be to embrace the illusions that await the ill-informed. If a profession is to advance to higher ground, it must understand where it has stood before. As a case in point, Gerald Graff (Graff & Warner, 1989), who has studied the institutional history of literary studies, assesses the "cultural literacy" controversy from the breadth of his historical perspective, concluding that

because [the] defenders of the past [such as Education Secretary William Bennett, Allan Bloom, and E. D. Hirsch] know little about the actual past [of humanities education], they are unaware that the diagnoses they offer were already clichés a hundred years ago, and that the cures they have recommended have been repeatedly tried and have always led to futility. (pp. 1–2)

In the absence of any tradition of policy studies in the English language arts, the policy initiative is thus left open to anyone who dares seize it. Who should decide the key policy question in the English language arts—what knowledge is most worth communicating through the English language arts? The ongoing dialogue about this policy issue in relation to the concreteness of real classrooms could inject new vitality into the profession. Gerald Graff (1989), for example, in considering a redefinition of literary studies, wonders whether it is possible to imagine one "whose goal would be not to establish a tradition or a consensus so much as to clarify differences and conflicts" (p. 13). Whoever makes such policy decisions shapes the education of our future citizens, especially the cultural literacy they may attain.

The initial question still remains: Who decides what is good policy for the English language arts? If the answer is the English profession, then the professional community has no choice but to recognize its need to consider matters of strategy, politics, and public relations, leading to the exercise of power. Kirst (1984) puts the matter bluntly: "When a constituency is so well organized that it becomes a lobby, it has power" (p. 55). Most importantly, if the profession is to exercise its power wisely and effectively at all levels of goverance, it must make room for the establishment of policy study as a legitimate field of inquiry within English education.

References

Academic Senates of the California Community Colleges, the California State University, & the University of California. (1982). *Statement of competencies in English and mathematics expected of entering freshmen.* Sacramento, CA: California Roundtable for Educational Opportunity (the California State Department of Education, distributor).

Algeo, A. M., & Zirkel, P. A. (1987). Court cases on teaching literature in the secondary schools. *Educational Horizons, 65,* 179–182.

Allington, R. L. (1986). Policy constraints and effective compensatory reading instruction: A review. In J. V. Hoffman (Ed.), *Effective teach-*

ing of reading: Research and practice (pp. 261–291). Newark, DE: International Reading Association.

Anderson, R. C., Hieber, E. H., Scott, J. A., & Wilkinson, I. A. G. (1985). *Becoming a nation of readers: The report of the commission on reading.* Champaign, IL: Center for the Study of Reading, University of Illinois.

Angelotti, M., Brause, R., Mayher, J., Pradl, G., & Appleby, B. (1988). On the nature and future of English education: What the grayhairs' gathering was really about. *English Education, 20,* pp. 230–244.

Apple, M. W. (1986). *Teachers & texts: A political economy of class and gender relations in education.* New York: Routledge & Kegan Paul.

Applebee, A. N. (1974). *Tradition and reform in the teaching of English: A history.* Urbana, IL: National Council of Teachers of English.

Berlin, J. A. (1987). *Rhetoric and reality: Writing instruction in American colleges, 1900–1985.* Carbondale, IL: Southern Illinois University Press.

Berlin, J. A. (1988). Rhetoric and ideology in the writing class. *College English, 50,* 477–494.

Beyer, L. E., & Apple, M. W. (Eds.). (1988). *The curriculum: Problems, politics, and possibilities.* Albany, NY: State University of New York Press.

Bloom, A. (1987). *The closing of the American mind: How higher education has failed democracy and impoverished the souls of today's students.* New York: Simon & Schuster.

Bountress, N. G. (1987). Educational implications of the Ann Arbor decision. *Educational Horizons, 66,* 18–19.

Britton, J. (1982). Opening address: English teaching retrospect and prospect. In R. D. Eagleson (Ed.), *English in the eighties* (pp. 1–12). Adelaide, Australia: Australian Association for the Teaching of English (Heinemann & Boynton/Cook).

California State Department of Education. (1983). *Raising expectations: Model graduation requirements.* Sacramento, CA: California State Deparment of Education.

California State Department of Education. (1987). *English-language arts framework for California public schools, kindergarten through grade twelve.* Sacramento, CA: California State Department of Education.

California State Department of Education. (1987, October 5). Improvement of English-language arts instruction in California: Implications for the adoption of instructional materials for grades K–8 (memorandum to publishers). Sacramento, CA: California State Department of Education.

Carnegie Task Force on Teaching as a Profession. (1986). *A nation prepared: Teachers for the 21st century.* New York: Carnegie Forum on Education and the Economy.

Carroll, J. B., & Chall, J. S. (Eds.) (1975). *Toward a literate society: The report of the committee on reading of the national academy of education.* New York: McGraw Hill.

Clark, D. L., & Astuto, T. A. (1988). Changes in federal education research policy. In M. J. Justiz & L. G. Bjork (Eds.), *Higher education research and public policy* (pp. 65–89). New York: American Council on Education & Macmillan.

Clark, R. W. (1988). Who decides? The basic policy issue. In L. N. Tanner (Ed.), *Critical issues in curriculum: The Eighty-seventh Yearbook of the National Society for the Study of Education: Part I* (pp. 175–205). Chicago: University of Chicago Press.

Clifford, G. J. (1987). *A sisyphean task: Historical perspectives on the relationship between writing and reading instruction* (Technical Report No. 7). Berkeley, CA: University of California, Center for the Study of Writing.

College Entrance Examination Board. (1983). *Academic preparation for college: What students need to know and be able to do.* New York: The College Board.

Cuban, L. (1986). Persistent instruction: Another look at constancy in the classroom. *Phi Delta Kappan, 68,* 7–11.

Darling-Hammond, L. (1988, April 20). In Commentary: Thinking about education: On the "cult of efficiency" in schools. *Education Week,* p. 20.

De Castell, S., Luke, A., & Luke, C. (Eds.). (1989). *Language, authority, and criticism: Readings on the school textbook.* London: The Falmer Press.

Donelson, K. (1987). Six statements/questions from the censors. *Phi Delta Kappan, 69,* 208–214.

Eisner, E. (1985). *The educational imagination: On the design and evaluation of school programs* (2nd ed.). New York: Macmillan.

Erikson, K. T. (1976). *Everything in its path: Destruction of community in the Buffalo Creek flood.* New York: Simon and Schuster.

Farr, M. (Ed.). (1980). *Reactions to Ann Arbor: Vernacular black English and education.* Washington, DC: Center for Applied Linguistics.

Flygare, T. J. (1987). Some thoughts about the Tennessee textbook case. *Phi Delta Kappan, 68,* 474–475.

Fraatz, J. M. B. (1987). *The politics of reading: Power, opportunity, and prospects for change in America's public schools.* New York: Teachers College Press.

Fuller, T. (Ed.). (1989). *The voice of liberal learning: Michael Oakeshott on education.* New Haven, CT: Yale University Press.

Garman, N. B., & Hazi, H. M. (1988). Teachers ask: Is there life after Madeline Hunter? *Phi Delta Kappa, 69,* 669–672.

Glenn, C. L. (1987). Textbook controversies: A "Disaster for public schools"? *Phi Delta Kappan, 68,* 451–4.

Goldstein, P. (1978). *Changing the American schoolbook: Law, politics, technology.* Lexington, MA: Lexington Books (D.C. Heath).

Goodlad, J. I. (1987). Structure, process, and agenda. In J. I. Goodlad (Ed.), *The ecology of school renewal: The Eighty-sixth Yearbook of the National Society for the Study of Education: Part I* (pp. 1–20). Chicago: University of Chicago Press.

Goodman, K. S., Shannon, P., Freeman, Y. S., & Murphy, S. (1988) *Report card on basal readers.* Katonah, NY: Richard C. Owen.

Goodson, I. F. (1988). *The making of curriculum: Collected essays.* London: The Falmer Press.

Graff, G., & Warner, M. (Eds.) (1989). *The origins of literary studies in America.* New York: Routledge.

Graff, H. J. (1987). *The legacies of literacy: Continuities and contradictions in Western culture and society.* Bloomington, IN: Indiana University Press.

Gray, J. R. (1988). *National writing project: Model and program design.* Berkeley, CA: University of California, National Writing Project.

Green, J. (1987). *The next wave: A synopsis of recent education reform reports* (Advance Copy, Report No. TR-87-1). Denver, CO: Education Commission of the States.

Guthrie, J. T. (Ed.). (1984). *Responding to "A Nation at Risk": Appraisal and policy guidelines.* Newark, DE: International Reading Association.

Guthrie, J. W., & Koppich J. (1988). Exploring the political economy of national education reform. In W. L. Boyd & C. T. Kerchner (Eds.), *The politics of excellence and choice in education: The 1987 Yearbook of the Politics of Education Association* (pp. 25–47). New York: The Falmer Press.

Hirsch, Jr., E. D. (1987). *Cultural literacy: What every American needs to know.* Boston: Houghton Mifflin.

Honig, B. (1985). *Last chance for our children: How you can help save our schools.* Reading, MA: Addison Wesley.

Hook, J. N. (1979). *A long way together: A personal view of NCTE's first sixty-seven years.* Urbana, IL: National Council of Teachers of English.

International Reading Association. (1988). IRA facts (leaflet). Newark, DE: International Reading Association.

Jenkinson, E. B. (1987). The significance of the decision in "Scopes II." *Phi Delta Kappan, 68,* 445–450.

Jerrolds, B. W. (1979). *Reading reflections: The history of the International Reading Association.* Newark, DE: International Reading Association.

Justiz, M. J., & Bjork, L. G. (Eds.). (1988). *Higher education research and public policy.* New York: American Council on Education (Macmillan)

Kirst, M. W. (1984). *Who controls our schools? American values in conflict.* New York: W. H. Freeman.

Kirst, M. W. (1989). Who should control the schools? Reassessing current policies. In T. J. Sergiovanni & J. H. Moore (Eds.), *Schooling for tomorrow: Directing reforms to issues that count* (pp. 62–89). Boston: Allyn and Bacon.

Koretz, D. (1988) Arriving in Lake Woebegon: Are standardized tests exaggerating achievement and distorting instruction? *American Education, 12,* 8–15, 46–52.

Lloyd-Jones, R., & Lunsford, A. A. (Eds.). (1989). *The English coalition: Democracy through language.* Urbana, IL: National Council of Teachers of English.

Madaus, G. F. (1988). The influence of testing on the curriculum. In L. N. Tanner (Ed.), *Critical issues in curriculum: The Eighty-seventh Yearbook of the National Society for the Study of Education* (pp. 83–121). Chicago: University of Chicago Press.

Maeroff, G. I. (1988). *The empowerment of teachers: Overcoming the crisis of confidence.* New York: Teachers College Press.

McLaughlin, M. W. (1987). Learning from experience: Lessons from policy implementation. *Educational Evaluation and Policy Analysis, 9,* 171–178.

Mentor, S. (1988). *As curriculum improves so must assessment: Framework friendly strategies to leverage improvement: Report of the English language arts assessment task force* (Preview Edition, Asilomar, March 9–11). Sacramento, CA: California State Department of Education.

Miller, J. A. (1987, October 28). Bell recounts tenure as chief of ED in book. *Education Week,* p. 1.

Moffett, J. (1988a). *Coming on center: Essays in English education* (2nd Ed.). Portsmouth, NH: Boynton/Cook, Heinemann.

Moffett, J. (1988b). *Storm in the mountains: A case study of censorship, conflict, and consciousness.* Carbondale, IL: Southern Illinois Press.

Monaghan, E. J., & Saul, E. W. (1987). The reader, the scribe, the thinker: A critical look at the history of American reading and writing instruction. In T. S. Popkewitz (Ed.), *The formation of school subjects: The struggle for creating an American institution* (pp. 85–122). London: The Falmer Press.

Mozert v. Hawkins County Bd. of Educ., 827 F.2d 1058, (6th Cir. (Tenn.), Aug. 24, 1987).

National Council of Teachers of English Committee on the National Interest, (1961). *The national interest and the teaching of English.* Urbana, IL: National Council of Teachers of English.

National Council of Teachers of English. (1989). *1989 directory.* Urbana, IL: National Council of Teachers of English.

NCTE to you: Information, news, announcements. (1989). *Language Arts, 66,* 347–348.

North, S. M. (1987). *The making of knowledge in composition: Portrait of an emerging field.* Upper Montclair, NJ: Boynton/Cook.

Ohmann, R. (1987). *Politics of letters.* Middletown, CT: Wesleyan University Press.

Olson, L. (1988, March 16). History: "A lamp to light the present" [Interview with Lawrence A. Cremin] *Education Week,* pp. 5, 20.

Olson, L. (1988, April 27). Inside "A Nation at Risk": A view from the cutting room floor. *Education Week,* pp. 1, 22–23.

Pikulski, J. J. (1987) Questions and answers. *The Reading Teacher, 40,* 831–832.

Popkewitz, T. S. (1987a). *Critical studies in teacher education: Its folklore, theory, and practice.* London: The Falmer Press.

Popkewitz, T. S. (1987b). Knowledge and interest in curriculum studies. In T. S. Popkewitz (Ed.), *The formation of school subjects: The struggle for creating an American institution.* London: The Falmer Press.

Purves, A. N., & Niles, O. (Eds.). (1984). *Becoming readers in a complex society: The Eighty-third Yearbook of the National Society for the Study of Education: Part I.* Chicago: University of Chicago Press.

Rothblatt, S. (1988). General education on the American campus: A historical introduction in brief. In I. Westbury & A. C. Purves (Eds.), *Cultural literacy and the idea of general education: The Eighty-*seventh Yearbook of the National Society for the Study of Education: Part II* (pp. 9–29). Chicago: University of Chicago Press.

Rothman, R. (1988, January 13). Bennett offers high school's "ideal" content. *Education Week,* 1, 26–27.

Shor, I. (1986). *The culture wars: School and society in the conservative restoration, 1969–1984.* Boston: Routledge & Kegan Paul.

Sickler, J. L. (1988) Teachers in charge: Empowering the professionals. *Phi Delta Kappan, 70,* 354–375.

Sizer, T. R. (1986). Rebuilding: First steps by the coalition of essential schools. *Phi Delta Kappan, 68,* 38–42.

Smith v. Board of School Commissioners of Mobile County, 827 F.2d 684 (11th Cir. (Ala.) Aug. 26, 1987).

Spring, J. (1985). *American education: An introduction to social and political aspects* (3rd ed.). New York: Longman.

Spring, J. (1988). *Conflict of interests: The politics of American education.* New York: Longman.

Squire, J. R. (1967, November). *The eight year report of the executive secretary.* Champaign, IL (Urbana): National Council of Teachers of English.

Squire, J. R. (1987). Retrospect and prospect. In J. R. Squire (Ed.), *The dynamics of language learning: Research in reading and English* (pp. 387–393). Urbana, IL: ERIC Clearinghouse on Reading and Communication Skills.

Staff. (1988, November). Bennett's elementary school: ambitious plan raises questions. NCTE *Council-Grams,* p. 3.

Staff. (1988, November). Books old and new raise censors' ire. NCTE *Council-Grams,* p. 6.

Staff. (1988, November). Governors push for better measures of school success. NCTE *Council-Grams,* p. 5.

Staff. (1988, November). Teachers reveal limits of their decision making. NCTE *Council-Grams,* p. 5.

Staff. (1989, January). In the states: California switches to literature-based reading texts. NCTE *Council-Grams,* p. 6.

Staff. (1989, January). Looking ahead: George Bush's federal agenda for education. NCTE *Council-Grams,* p. 1.

Staff. (1989, January). Regulatory straitjacket still binds, participants in reform plan say. NCTE *Council-Grams,* p. 6.

Stedman, L. C. (1987). It's time we changed the effective schools formula. *Phi Delta Kappan, 69,* 215–224.

Tanner, D. (1988). The textbook controversies. In L. N. Tanner (Ed.), *Critical issues in curriculum: The Eighty-seventh Yearbook of the National Society for the Study of Education: Part I* (pp. 122–142). Chicago: University of Chicago Press.

Tucker, M., & Mandel, D. (1986). The Carnegie report—A call for redesigning the schools. *Phi Delta Kappan, 68,* 24–27.

Urbanski, A. (1987, October 28). Restructuring the teaching profession. *Education Week,* p. 1, 25, 32.

Venezky, R. L. (1986). Steps toward a modern history of American reading instruction. In E. Z. Rothkopf (Ed.), *Review of Research in Education 13.* Washington, DC: American Educational Research Association.

White, J. (1988). *Changing practice: A collaborative study between SCDC national writing project and the NFER department of language: Part one: (September 1986–February 1988).* Slough, England: National Foundation for Education and Research.

Wirt, F. M., & Kirst, M. W. (1982). *Schools in conflict: The politics of education.* Berkeley, CA: McCutchan Publishing.

Wise, A. E. (1979). *Legislated learning: The bureaucratization of the American classroom.* Berkeley, CA: University of California Press.

Wise, A. E. (1988). Legislated learning revisited. *Phi Delta Kappan, 69,* 328–333.

Wynn, R., & Wynn, J. L. (1988). *American education* (2nd ed.). New York: Harper & Row.

Yudorf, M. G., Kirp, D. L., van Geel, T., & Levin, B. (1982). *Kirp and Yudorf's educational policy and the law: Cases and materials* (2nd ed.). Berkeley, CA: McCutchan Publishing.

·6·

CURRENT ISSUES AND FUTURE DIRECTIONS

James Britton
Merron Chorny

The accumulation of new discoveries changes the relationships that unify knowledge within a field and requires revised or novel integrating frameworks for the effective understanding and application of what is known. Thus, Bell (1977) indicated the need for an overarching framework to organize anew the burgeoning discoveries in science, and Ulam (1976) saw the need for a new, more flexible theory that would unify the rapidly expanding concerns of mathematics. In such theories and frameworks lies the prospect of developing new modes of consciousness as well as new perspectives for furthering and applying knowledge; restoring the integrity of knowledge maintains the integrity of self and of society.

For several decades now there has been a similar concern for a unifying conception of subject English, but earlier attempts have failed to embrace the variety of concerns legitimately represented in English lessons—have failed, in fact, to achieve a unification that would affect both classroom practices and educational research.

The problem remained, and no doubt these earlier efforts served to maintain the concern for a solution and indicate its direction. The outcome has been the progressive emergence of a body of shared, related ideas that is evolving into a new perspective within the profession of English teaching.

In spite of periodic endeavors to modify the nature and function of English programs in schools, in light of new knowledge and changing times, the ideas that informed teaching and learning in earlier decades of public education can be perceived as having remained dominant. To summarize our view of the traditional perspective in English we present assumptions underlying it, in relation to ideas that inform the emerging perspective in the language arts: The focus of the traditional perspective is on elements of language usage, rather than upon processes by which language mastery is acquired; on the development of language skills in isolation, rather than on contexts of which they are constituent parts; on the skills of reading, often without complementary reference to the skills of writing, rather than on the process of mastering the written language, with its effect on cognitive growth; on literature and knowledge about works of literature, rather than on the experience of response to such works; on learning in school, without recognition of the knowledge and language that students bring to school; all these in association with a sense that teachers are to be the sole arbiters and dispensers of knowledge in the classroom.

Broad generalization can overstate: Attempts to characterize even small jurisdictions cannot do justice to reality; schools and teachers differ widely. Nevertheless, evidence over the past decade, in the major English-speaking countries, indicates a trend by central authorities to reorganize public education consistent with reconfirmation of the traditional perspective and assumptions noted above. Our purpose here is not simply to polarize the two perspectives, nor to dismiss the traditional assumptions as inappropriate; some will continue to have relevance. Rather, the intent is to propose that in themselves, they are too narrow and inadequate for our time. For the English language arts specifically, they limit classroom expression of the potential inherent in new knowledge and understanding about the nature of language, learning, and teaching and thus circumscribe the complementary contributions that schools could make to enable youth to develop as learners and as persons entering a world in which change is a constant.

TOWARD A NEW PERSPECTIVE

The Dartmouth International Seminar of 1966 set the stage for a new perspective regarding the concerns of the English lesson and shed new light on the role of research in English education. For a traditional view of English as focusing on product, Dartmouth added a sense of process; for a view of language learning as a means to literacy narrowly conceived, it proposed a recognition of the role of language in all learning. Finally, a sense of the learner as a passive receiver gave way to a recognition of learning as an activity to be pursued.

Here lay the promise of a unifying theory: In the act of using language to explore their own experiences and develop their own ideas, students would be encouraged within the class community to acquire self-knowledge and world-knowledge in the course of learning to use and understand language.

The Dartmouth Seminar was a month-long learning experience involving teachers from all school levels as well as scholars in related disciplines representing three countries and their systems of education. A wide variety of experience, commitment, and viewpoint contributed to an agenda that produced reflective discussion, challenge, and, at times, confrontation. It was a crucible of intense critical examination that achieved finally a surprising degree of consensus.

In the half decade that followed, a number of publications explored, extended, and refined the central concepts of this consensus. *Growth Through English* (Dixon, 1967) presented a synthesis of key ideas from the Seminar and indicated how they might be implemented. *Teaching the Universe of Discourse* (Moffett, 1968) confirmed the recognition of children as natural learners of language and learners through language, and presented a view of the developmental processes involved. *Language, the Learner and the School* (Barnes, Britton & Rosen, 1969) drew attention to the role of language in interactive learning and to the need for studies of classroom language. *Language and Learning* (Britton, 1970) proposed learning as the main characteristic of humankind and language as its principal means. In relation to English education, it reintegrated language and the learner and offered a unifying framework for language development and use. *The Composing Processes of Twelfth Graders* (Emig, 1971) pointed to the need to re-examine existing assumptions about teaching writing and their practical effects. *The Development of Writing Abilities (11–18)* (Britton, Burgess, Martin, McLeod, Rosen, 1975), a longitudinal study of students' writing, extended insights about function and audience categories in school writing. In a series of pamphlets in the early 1970s (collected in *Writing Across the Curriculum,* 1983), Nancy Martin worked with teachers to explore children's uses of talk and writing in the classroom and indicated afresh the importance of teachers' participation in classroom research. *The Dynamics of Language Learning* (Squire, 1987), reporting proceedings of the Mid-Decade Seminar (1985) of the National Conference on Research in Education, re-assessed and coordinated research in areas of the language arts and examined the research implications for language development, teaching and learning in relation to classroom practice. These publications and others created links between new perspectives and classroom practices, and they indicated directions for research based on holistic views of language development.

The Dartmouth Seminar also had other effects: It created an organizational context for continuing dialogue within the international community of English education. Largely through the efforts of James Squire, a liaison body was set up to facilitate cooperation and exchange among professional English associations. Now named the International Federation for the Teaching of English (IFTE), the body includes the English associations of Australia, Barbados, Canada, England and Wales, New Zealand, and the United States. Under its auspices, Dartmouth has been followed by conferences in York, England, in 1971; Syndney, Australia, in 1980 (Eagleson, 1982); Detroit in 1984 (Tchudi,

1985); and Ottawa in 1986 (attended by members from nearly twenty countries). In 1979, the Canadian Council of Teachers of English (CCTE) sponsored an international conference in Ottawa that has been celebrated as the most important discussion of writing in a generation (Freedman & Pringle, 1980; Pringle and Freedman, 1981).

These conferences have embodied the spirit and the critical procedures of the Dartmouth Seminar. In Ottawa, for example, a context was provided in which teachers and scholars, internationally, could share their views of English and engage in critical reexamination and exchange: and this with the express purpose of evaluating, extending and refining the assumptions that inform English education.

The evolution of the new perspective in English and its translation into programs and practice continues. A recent highlight in this process has been the three-week English Coalition Conference, sponsored by eight national language associations, including the National Council of Teachers of English, in the United States, and held at the Aspen Institute's Wye Plantation in Maryland during the summer of 1987. Sixty teachers of English, representing the sponsoring bodies as well as all levels of schooling discussed current issues, examined theoretical bases for informed change and formulated resolutions for programs and practice to provide for a "fresh view of the field." A report on the meeting, *The English Coalition Conference: Democracy Through Language* (Lloyd-Jones & Lunsford, 1989) highlights proposed emphases that include recognition of the student as active learner, interactive classroom learning, correlation of students' school and out-of-school knowledge and learning, an integrated approach in language arts and English programs, interrelation of skills study with content within contexts of students' language use, and a learning centered-approach to English studies. A related publication, *Stories to Grow on: Demonstrations of Language Learning in K–8 Classrooms* (Jensen, J., 1989) focuses on one aspect of the conference. Other publications on the conference are expected.

Thus, for two decades now, within circles and networks in the countries concerned, teachers and researchers have collaborated in developing the new perspectives that contribute to a unifying theory for subject English. Communal activity has been the key; yet each group works within its own terms and its own context, selecting from the pool of promising ideas to create their own rationales by integrating the new into their known experience and understanding of language, learning, and teaching.

Implicit in this perspective is a recognition that our knowledge is still evolving and that tacit learning processes that are imperfectly understood still play important roles. In pursuit of fuller understanding, appeal has been made to a range of other disciplines. In this context, Sapir, Vygotsky, Kelly and Polanyi are key figures; they are complemented by work, among others, of Rosenblatt, Langer, Moffett, Emig, Britton, Nancy Martin, Douglas Barnes, John Dixon, and extended by Applebee, Graves, Murray, Ken and Yetta Goodman, Frank Smith, Michael Halliday, Garth Boomer. What they share is their acknowledgment of tacit learning processes, their emphasis on the human potential for learning (rather than its limitations), and the importance of a learning environment.

The new perspective in English is still evolving. We do not offer it here as an established theory or as a package to be applied to cure the presumed ills of English teaching. Its potential for practice lies in personal choices from its ideas, implemented in individual ways within local contexts.

The Report of the Bullock Committee, set up in 1972 by the British government to examine "reading and the uses of language in schools," incorporates among its recommendations many of the ideas that inform the new perspective, and develops their relevance for practice. An excerpt from the report, *A Language for Life* (1975) conveys the sense of interrelationships proposed by the committee for unifying language in classroom practice:

4.9 It is a confusion of everyday thought that we tend to regard "knowledge" as something that exists independently of someone who knows. "What is known" must in fact be brought to life afresh within every "knower" by his own efforts. To bring knowledge into being is a formulating process, and language as its ordinary means, whether in speaking or in writing or the inner monologue of thought. Once it is understood that talking and writing are means to learning, those more obvious truths that we learn also from other people by listening and reading will take on a fuller meaning and fall into a proper persepctive. Nothing has done more to confuse current educational debate than the simplistic notion that "being told" is the polar opposite of "finding out for oneself." In order to accept what is offered when we are told something, we have to have somewhere to put it; and having somewhere to put it means that the framework of past knowledge and epxerience into which it must fit is adequate as a means of interpreting and apprehending it. Something approximating to "finding out for ourselves" needs therefore to take place if we are to be successfully told. The development of this individual context for a new piece of information, the forging of the links that give it meaning, is a task that we customarily tackle by talking to other people.

4.10 In the Committee's view there are certain important inferences to be drawn from a study of the relationship between language and learning:

(i) all genuine learning involves discovery, and it's as ridiculous to suppose that teaching begins and ends with "instruction" as it is to suppose that "learning by discovery" means leaving children to their own resources;

(ii) language has a heuristic function; that is to say, a child can learn by walking and writing as certainly as he can by listening and reading;

(iii) to exploit the process of discovery through language in all its uses is the surest means of enabling a child to master his mother tongue. (p. 50)

Although this statement refers to student learning, it has relevance also in its content and its approach to teacher learning as well.

In such mental process as polarizing, classifying, categorizing, structuring, and sequencing, we possess highly refined means for the acquisition of knowledge. However, having established these constructs, we may also tend to regard them as constant and absolute. Indeed, we have tended to polarize constructs of education into teaching-learning, knowledge-knower, subject-child, objective-subjective, knowing-feeling, form-content. Similarly, having established structures of knowledge, we may tend to equate them with structures for teaching and learning. It is doubtful that we could sustain comfortably now, as we did a couple of decades ago, that the way we hold knowledge

of English, in terms of its perceived structure and assumed sequence of development, can be used directly as a model for teaching, or be assumed, further to be the framework for learning.

For the understanding and application of knowledge, a further stage of operation is involved. This is the input for teacher learning that is projected by the Bullock citation. It transcends polarities, establishes new relationships, emphasizes informing personal contexts, and intimates new shapes of consciousness in thinking. To refine their work, teachers, like their students, can make choices from new ideas, indwell in them, convert them into practice, and test and refine them. Teacher learning, in this context, is a continual reforming of one's theory. Such a view of evolving transformation of teaching dispels the notion of change, proposed by some, who would impose complete new frameworks of English upon schools. Inherent in such proposals is an insistence that teachers surrender personal construct systems that they already hold about English, an impossible expectation and chaotic in its effect if it were within the realm of possibility.

The basic strategies of knowing may be a factor also in the perceived fragmentation of English in school programs. As English curricula set out skills, processes, modes, and goals, listed as discrete items to be covered within a year of study, yet without a related informing and unifying context, they project a fragmented view of the subject. Through the structure, they also imply a teaching method. As a result, classroom instruction may be focused on the items, which can then be dealt with separately and sequentially by the use of assigned drills and exercises. Such categorizations also need to be transcended by new structures, recombinations and relationships, by a view of language that is encompassing, coherent, and vital. This is the tacit promise of the evolving perspective. In its terms, teachers structure learning situations within which students talk, write, read, and listen under the guidance of the teacher/expert. The teacher is alert to the students' use of specified curriculum skills and processes, mentally ticking the curriculum items off, as it were, and assessing the proficiency of their expression in the course of the ongoing work.

Inherent in any consideration of the implications of theory and research for classroom practice is the issue of change. Before we continue with out own reflections on change, we want to state our belief that change in English teaching, based on the evolving perspective of theory and research, has been proceeding for more than a decade, not universally, but in scattered areas, and without public fanfare. New knowledge about language and the learner as well as about the role of language in learning is being taken on, applied and tested. Theory and research relating to reading, writing, literature, and talk is being assessed and transformed into practice in schools. Collaborative learning is more evident in classrooms. The shared and reported experiences in the international English community, discussed earlier, are one area of confirmation. The confirmation is extended by articles in professional English journals as well as by presentations at regional, national, and international English conferences in which teachers report about their transformed practice.

Further confirmation comes from personal knowledge of

the work of many teachers we have been privileged to observe, including instances of a language-based program of work in social studies, mathematics, science, and art. Though such confirmations may not constitute hard evidence, they indicate a trend that cannot, in today's circumstances, be ignored.

What is remarkable and significant in this development is that it has often proceeded in contexts of constraint and adversity. Talk with teachers who have successfully transformed their practice in a large and respected educational jurisdiction in Canada elicited concerns such as these:

a. Narrow concept of leadership in schools,
b. Limitations of teachers' authority to make professional decisions,
c. Growth of methods of control that progressively infect lower levels of the school hierarchy,
d. Decision makers' apparent lack of context for understanding what teachers are trying to do,
e. Constraining effect of external tests and examinations,
f. Increasing course and class loads that affect the quality of teachers' work.

These teachers are confident, informed, and successful; they know not only how to survive but also how to prevail. Their concern is for the future of English and of their students.

When the focus is directed sharply upon a single situation, the factors affecting change appear in dramatic perspective. A teacher who is already a master at transforming practice is developing, with a colleague, a new language program within a new school assignment. Neither teacher has any free periods; they cannot plan together in class time. Though the school teacher-pupil ratio is 16, neither of them has a class load less than 30. An administrator, when the students wrote about their own experiences, commented that the writing was "too personal." Yet at the end of the year, when the two teachers arranged a parents' evening, 250 parents attended to view and discuss the program; no one complained about the personal nature of the work and many congratulated the teachers on their success.

This simple account reflects some of the complexity involved in change. In the course of their work, the teachers had to maintain professional and collegial relations, sustain a sense of school unity and common purpose, transcend interpersonal difficulties, and make sensitive decisions. They demonstrate not only strong professional ability, but also social and political skills of a high order. It is seldom recognized that English programs may constitute a profound social process, not only for the development of literacy, but for the refining of thought and values as well.

Shirley Brice Heath (1983), in her concluding comments on her study of schools, children, language, and learning in a multicultural community, writes:

But structural and institutional changes in the schools and patterns of control from external sources, such as the federal and state governments, have forced many of the teachers described here to choose either to leave the classroom or revert to transmitting only mainstream language and culture patterns. (p. 368)

And Lorraine Cockle (1988), reflecting on the effect of her graduate research in relation to her teaching experience comments:

Realistically speaking, teachers are not entirely free to work with children in ways that conscience, intention and research might suggest would be most conducive to personally meaningful learning. Education, too, is a hierarchy of levels and aside from the marginal control that is exerted upon the classroom encounter by the demands of curriculum and skill objectives (and the objective accountability for both), society, itself, may impose all kinds of restrictions upon what may or may not go on in a classroom. Real questions, real thoughts cannot be precertified for safety, and thinking which might question the authority of any external source, whether it be religion or science, is likely to be seen as threatening or subversive by one group or another. (Chorny, 1988, p. 201)

Even within such constraining contexts, many teachers are taking the responsibility and the risk of evolving their own informing rationales and of refining their practice in English. In the process they are not only demonstrating their own commitment to self-sustaining learning, but also are creating situations in which their students can explore and discover through language development of their own continuing learning habits.

OBSTACLES TO PROGRESS

As an extension of the concern about constraints, we want to focus briefly on three issues that tend to inhibit the evolution of teacher practice: accountability, external testing, and major external proposals for change in English. Within levels of government and the upper levels of education hierarchy is an understandable continuing sense of responsibility about the quality of education. The first must be responsive to the public; the second, to the first. While the intention is reasonable, some of the forms of its expression create conflicts and tensions between what teachers believe and do as contrasted to what they perceive the public appears to want them to do. Some of the forms of expression of the intended responsibility suggest, however, the evolution of a sub-culture of education, a cult of control, as it were, that in instances seems committed to the realization of Orwell's *1984*, as though determined to bring it forth, even if through Caesarian section after misdiagnosis. It may have reached its most abysmal form in the idea of "teacher-proof materials," an odious term for an invidious intent. It is ironic that in countries committed to a free enterprise philosophy, that some would want to deny schools the opportunity to be enterprising or free.

Within the concern for accountability, external tests and examinations have been the principal instruments for determining achievement in English in schools. Again, the argument regarding external tests may be less about their intent than with the forms of assessment, though ultimately the two cannot be separated. Despite assurances to the contrary, the tests, in most of their forms, focus essentially on surface structures, out of context, and give little attention to the processes of language. The external tests affect teachers and English teaching in at least three ways: First, as an official and authoritative act emphasizing discrete "skills and abilities," they convey in their implicit expectations a limited view of English to teachers who may be prepared to change instruction. Further, for teachers who have transformed practice in relation to new knowledge, such tests demean and devalue their efforts. As one teacher put it, "All the students in my classes passed the examination with good marks; however, the examination did not test what the students had learned, knew, and could do in reading and writing." Finally, tests not only inhibit innovations in practice, but through this inhibition adversely affect teachers' attitudes toward teaching and students.

This decade has seen the rise of an international concern about education. In large part, this concern grows out of the expected needs for a highly trained work force that a technologically transformed society is assumed to require by the end of the century. Because communication is seen to be a major factor in the new work force, the emphasis within this concern is being placed on proficiency in the mother tongue.

In the United States, England, and Canada, this concern is being expressed in major re-examinations of school organization and of English programs. Inherent in these reexaminations is a tension about future directions, between the forming ideas and rationale for English evolved over the last two decades and some of the current proposals for reform, which reflect those of the "search for excellence" of a generation ago.

Despite such constraints, change in English, based in current theory and research, is proceeding. However, the tension between evolving practice and external proposals for change remains. At issue is the continuing development of English programs relevant to society's needs at this time and the autonomy and authority of teachers and schools.

Implicit in an undertaking to make the findings of research and theory in English more accessible to teachers is the issue of continuing learning and of change, a process about which our knowledge is still limited. The transformation of an idea into practice may be one of the most difficult and complex tasks in education. Its roots are in the impact of new ideas that change a teacher's theoretical perspective, the ways of thinking about English and English teaching; the new perspective transforms personal practice. The implementation of the ideas lies less in new curricula and jurisdictional schemes and more in the personal use of the ideas as alternatives for solving educational problems, though a facilitating curriculum may increase the likelihood of problem solving. However, most proposals for reform in education whether instituted by governments or by jurisdictions, rarely take personal change into account.

Essentially, the prevailing point of view relating to change in education is prescriptive, in that new directions are externally set; deterministic, in that prejudgments of future needs are externally formulated; and categorical, in that particular items of skills and abilities, assumed basic to future needs, are externally specified. Within this point of view, the means proposed are antithetical to the realization of the reforms sought.

In the first instance, the prescriptive approach imposes change upon individuals, teachers, who have not been part of the planning process, and, invariably, neither makes provision for an in-service process to involve teachers in the proposal nor demands of the initiators a subsequent evaluation and account-

ing of its consequences. Second, past experience warns us about the elusive nature of the future to prediction, as well as about the transitory qualities of predictions for change. Finally, if we could predict accurately, the hope of preparing youth for the future would rest more in the processes of language and learning and less in the predetermined ends of constituent skills and prespecified information. This is not to deny anticipation, planning, and action. However, these need to be considered from a different perspective; its focus would be on individuals within a social context.

Although social institutions propose change in society-encompassing terms, within the structure of society individuals are the sources of action and reaction. Collectively and interactively, they create the nature and direction of change: Change in educational practice must include individual teachers as an integral part of the process. Inherent in the process needs to be a trust that teachers can evolve their informing rationales in relation to new knowledge out of their interactions with students and colleagues, with the support of interested university teachers. Further, they need more freedom than they have now to transform, test, and evolve their practice. Teachers, like students, need scope to pursue individual intentions for their own learning and opportunity to explore and to discover new knowledge in theory and in practice, to relate it to what they already know, to invest the new with relevance. Essentially, each teacher negotiates the curriculum into practice in personal ways to meet both the expectations of society and the needs of students.

Ultimately, theories of teaching are defined largely by theories of learning. Our teaching is built upon what we have chosen to believe about the role of language in children's learning, but we must adapt to meet a range of demands that constitute the teaching situation and the system in which we practise. While claiming that the potential for change in English teaching rests mainly on individual teachers, we need to recognize also that their efforts must be supported by collaborative networks of some sort. If we are ever to narrow the gap between the emergence of new ideas and their implementation, we have to conceive of the potential for change as an essential ingredient in the educational enterprise as a whole.

To this end, collaboration by workers at all levels and in all branches is called upon. Our concerns here suggest that the stage of initial teacher education would make a suitable starting point. If the emerging perspective in English education is to be presented to them, it will have to be clearly incorporated in our own dealings with the students: not simply to present a visible model, but to initiate learning experiences for them that carry conviction. It is not too early, we believe, to engage students in observational research projects, collecting and analyzing linguistic data in classroom situations. Experience of the way in which knowledge is transformed into practice should provide an inner sense of the role of learning in the act of teaching.

Other agencies will necessarily be involved. In any school or jurisdiction there are related issues of maintaining continued professional relationship, securing approval and support, coping with political expediencies. Accounts of successful innovative programs along these lines will be of value.

The potential of such sharing of experience is evident in Goodhall's (1988) account of his involvement, as principal, in trying to transform practice in two elementary schools. His statement traces the evolution of change both within himself and in the collaborative activity of the whole staff, from the origins of their informing ideas to their application in the classrooms and the outcomes in terms of children's language and learning, illustrating work across the grades. Parents' comments on the work extend the account, which records both successes and difficulties, frustrations and failures. Goodhall concludes:

Perhaps when we stop operating schools as though they were psychological clinics and behaviour modification laboratories, when we treat children as intelligent beings rather than bearers of deficit systems and patients in need of treatment, more schools will be more amenable and productive places for learning. It is not, or so it seemed to us, endless funding and specialization, but knowledge of intellectual development and original work on everyone's part in schools that will make the difference, and of course, willing, informed and capable teachers, who will take risks to learn and to try—above all, such teachers. (Chorny, 1988, p. 93)

A concept of teacher as researcher is increasingly tending to break down the customary distinction. Examples abound both of individual teachers seeking answers to their own questions and networks of teachers collaborating in inquiries, sometimes with the assistance of university-based research colleagues. Thus, the locus of change begins to move from external agencies to operations internal to the school system.

It becomes increasingly apparent that schools need to revitalize their relations with parents and the public, who all too often feel excluded from policy in education and starved of information. The home as partner to the school in a child's education is a valuable concept that must be protected. It may act as a support for innovative successful teaching when it is under threat from remote or less involved quarters. Schools that find means of strengthening the liaison deserve encouragement and emulation.

The world of work constitutes another potential ally and potential problem. There are clearly common interests, and the more these are recognized and understood, the more successful will schooling become. Although English in the classroom will demand a broader spectrum of outcomes than many employers would recognize, ignorance of the other's needs and aspirations for the learner can only be a brake on progress. There are signs today that in-house training for beginning workers and apprentices may be on the increase, owing to a better understanding between employers and educators of their respective responsibilities. New knowledge does not directly solve problems; rather, it creates problems to solve. New ideas modify our personal perspectives and have implications for changes in practice. Eisner (1984), Jensen and Squire (1987) propose that in addition to the scientific language of educational research, we need accounts of changing ideas and changing practices in more personal terms, expressive of the life of a classroom. For these we shall look to teachers.

We were encouraged to find in a recent comprehensive survey of research into the teaching and learning of writing the following concluding paragraph:

As educators—whether our dominant function is as teacher, researcher, administrator, or some other role—we are united in our concerns for students, our commitment to teaching, and our desire that our work contribute to the education of future generations. (Freedman, Hass Dyson, Flower & Chafe, 1987, p. 39)

It is in the spirit of this declaration that we shall consider here the theoretical and philosophical bases underlying current educational issues and indicating the direction of future research in the field.

A VIEW OF EDUCATIONAL RESEARCH

It is our view that experimental research in education should not primarily be concerned to prove something, but rather to explore, to make discoveries that initiate new lines of thought. Researching some areas may well be cumulative, adding established fact to established fact to the end that our knowledge of some physical or even biological phenomenon becomes ever more complete. In the social sciences a different logistic prevails on account of the impossibility of controlling all significant variables; and in education we have yet another case, since any understanding derived from research findings can be no more than a partial contribution to the practice of teaching. What we look for fromm the educational research of the future is, therefore, not a direct outcome in classroom practice but a contribution to *thinking*: what Michael Polanyi (1962, p. 294) would no doubt call a *fiduciary* relationship, an effect upon the beliefs by which we set and adjust the course of our lives, including our professional lives.

George Kelly has relevant (and amusing) things to say in describing what he calls "humanistic methodology in psychological research." He is concerned with the way an experimenter sees his own role:

If he is one who imagines himself accumulating nuggets of ultimate truth he will place his primary research emphasis on the unassailability of his fragmentary findings. If he supports something at the .05 level of confidence, he is encouraged; if he pushes it to the .01 level, he is gratified; if it turns out at the .001 level, he is ecstatic; and if it reaches the .0001 level, he wonders how one writes an application for the Nobel Prize. The research objective of such a man is to nail something down, once and for all. . . . But if the experimenter sees himself exploring only one of many alternative constructions of man, with the best ones yet to be devised, he will be on a continual lookout for fresh perspectives emerging out of his research experience. (Kelly, 1969, p. 139)

It seems to us that the challenge educational research has to meet is that of enriching the knowledge relevant to school an classroom practices that is available to educators. The curriculum theorist, Joseph Schwab, long ago warned us of the complexities involved in such a task, a warning that has largely fallen on deaf ears, we believe. The kind of theoretical understanding that scholarly research contributes will not, he claims, affect educational processes unless it draws upon studies of educational practice—"the discipline concerned with choice and action"—and, in addition, applies fruits of a concern he calls *eclectic*—"the arts by which unsystematic, uneasy, but usable focus on a body of problems is effected among diverse theories, each relevant to the problems in a different way" (Schwab, 1969, p. 1).

Such a view clearly supports the need to loosen the constrictions that a physical sciences model of research has for long tended to impose upon the practice of educational research. As Steve North has recently pointed out, among researchers of different methodologies it is still the experimentalists who reckon to be—and are often accounted—the final arbiters of the value of what is discovered by any method (North, 1987, p. 151).

Certainly, educational research in recent years has seen a decline in positivistic approaches accompanied by an increasing concern with contexts. There will of course remain a need for statistical surveys that supply information by which to plan courses of action, as for example the distribution of special services, to meet the needs of the average student in particular populations. And no doubt tried and reliable methods along these lines will continue to attract some of the less able students at the doctoral level. (Methodology to hand rather than a genuine recognition of a problem may all too often provide the starting point for such students' enquiries. On the other hand, students tackling their first research project have often asked original and valuable questions and explored new ground in looking for answers; we would certainly see this as a continuing strength in future research.)

Schwab's notion of *the eclectic,* referred to above, must raise the whole question as to the nature of education as an area of study. Clearly, scholarly study of the theory of English as a timetable subject borrows a great deal from other recognized disciplines—notably psychology, linguistics, and sociology. But answers to its problems are rarely satisfied from any one such source: What is usually required is a fresh synthesis of elements from a variety of sources. Such a synthesis has been earlier referred to as constituting a pre-disciplinary theory (Britton, 1977, p. 2). It is pre-disciplinary in the sense that in abstracting from the particularities of the data under study, it stops short of the level of abstraction demanded by a discipline, by psychology, say, or linguistics or sociology. Each of these disciplines will carry the abstraction process to a point where its governing theory will distinguish it from the theories of neighboring disciplines. But the educational theorist cannot afford to omit the insights gained from sociology, for example, or from linguistics, as he applied psychological theory to educational practices and is similarly placed in applying theories borrowed from the other disciplines. His theorizing, in other words, must articulate fully with the concrete data below it, the data under study, and abandon the idea of articulating with the governing theory of any one of the disciplines he is applying.

However complicated that may sound, it must be recognized as a form of the process by which an English teacher must construct a *rationale* for his own teaching, a cognitive structure constantly submitted to the results of classroom experiment. As we have said earlier, the links we covet for scholarly research in education are with *thinking* rather than directly with action.

We hope that such a view of educational research may encourage educationists to undertake inquiry that integrates a range of language uses. American research to date has tended to focus on, for example, teaching and learning in freshman composition courses. The most comprehensive account of research into writing processes, that by Steve North, seems to set English literature over against rhetoric as alternative aspects of subject English. The uses of language—speaking, listening, writing, reading, dramatic improvisation—mark out a field which is essential context for any interpretation of English on the curriculum. It is worth recording that one of the first enquiries taken up by the newly formed Centre for Studies in Writing was a study of the relation between writing and reading. Nevertheless, U.S. research finds its basic organizational pattern in establishing separate centers for research into reading, writing, literary studies, whereas the activity that surrounds and supports them, talking, does not make an appearance.

If future research in the field of English education is to pursue a policy of exploration rather than authentication or proof, it must move in the direction of interpretation and analysis in terms of "soft" or "subjective" categories, those categories that, in Karl Popper's view are open to falsification by "a critical attitude of reasonableness" rather than by hard empirical evidence (Popper, 1976, p. 115).

No doubt, educational research in recent years has seen a decline in the use of "hard" categories, and positivistic experimental designs as the influence of sociological and anthropological approaches have gained ground, and as the necessity has been recognized of taking historical, social, and institutional contexts into account.

Perhaps the most helpful recommendation we could make regarding the philosophical grounds of future research is that it should employ a conception of knowledge and belief in line with modern thinking, what Polanyi, for example, has called a "post-critical philosophy" (Polanyi, 1962, pp. 266–68) or George Kelly calls "constructive alternativism" and sees as descended from phenomenological roots (Kelly, 1963, pp. 40–43). Today, we must add Bruner's recent publication, *Actual Minds, Possible Worlds* (Bruner, 1986), to the catalog and take particular note of the kinds of information he derives, not from argument or exposition, but from narrative.

Polanyi has suggested that one's ability to apply explicit knowledge in solving a problem situation calls upon "tacit powers." In describing the nature of these tacit powers and their relationship to explicit knowledge—say, a verbal statement of principle—Polanyi develops arguments that make it possible for us to claim here that we can have confidence in the outcomes of "teaching by hunch" and qualitative findings in research with no reservations that do not also apply to our confidence in the findings of scientific enquiry. Where there is conflict between scientific and public opinion, Polanyi, a scientist, supports, as might be expected, the claims of science: But he does so on grounds very different from those widely held by both scientists and public.

Consider, for example his conception of a scientist's approach to a research problem:

Each scientist starts then by sensing a point of deepending coherence, and continues by feeling his way towards such coherence. His questing imagination, guided by intuition, forges ahead until he has achieved success or admitted failure. The clues supporting his surmises are largely unspecifiable; his feeling of their potentialities hardly definable. Scientific research is one continued act of tacit integration—like making out an obscure sight, or being engaged in painting a picture, or in writing a poem. (Polanyi, 1969, p. 82)

Such ideas are, assuredly, less startling to us than they might have been some 30 years ago. Thomas Kuhn (1970) has familiarized us with the contrast that exists between the strictly codified practices of "normal science" and the "constellations of beliefs, values, techniques" that constitute in his terms a "paradigm," the framework of assumptions within which the controlled enquiries of normal science are carried out. As long ago as 1958, George Kelly introduced a psychological paper with this uncompromising statement: "This paper throughout, deals with half-truths only. Nothing that it contains is, or is intended to be, wholly true" (Kelly, 1969, p. 66). Recognizing that the individual view of the observer must inevitably color his perceptions, and that a similar effect operates upon his subsequent interpretation and analysis of what he observes, and again upon his most abstract, theoretical conclusions, Kelly accepts this "approximateness" as a principle and sees scientific discovery as a program of successive approximations. In this sense, any theory he proposes stands as one way of explaining, recognizes the existence of alternative ways, and embraces the principle of its own eventual displacement.

We need hardly point out the dangers attached to the view we are putting forward. Generalizing from our experience, developing theoretical explanations to account for phenomena, then attempting to sharpen that process by drawing upon the theories generated by psychologists, linguists, sociologists, yet stopping short of the independent frames of reference of those disciplines, could lead to a fatal eclecticism. Categories that have been divorced from the systems they comprise may be seen as rough equivalents and so become distorted to the point where anything means everything, and so, finally nothing at all. Yet the remedy is as evident as the disease: It lies in allowing full rein to the control exercised by the phenomenon. While our intuitively guided construing of the phenomenon throughout all our interactions with it remains the effective arbiter of our reflecting and theorizing, we protect ourselves from irresponsibilities, whether of eclecticism or similar kinds of distortion.

In *Actual Minds, Possible Worlds,* Bruner pursues the idea that forms of discourse reflect two complementary action patterns, those of *cause* and *effect* and those of *intentions* and *outcomes.* The ideal forms of discourse, "a well-formed argument" and "a good story" (the latter, of course representing "intentions and outcomes") introduce his general thesis in these words:

There are two modes of cognitive functioning, two modes of thought, each providing distinctive ways of ordering experience, of constructing reality. The two (though complementary) are irreducible to one another. Efforts to reduce one mode to the other or to ignore one at the expense of the other inevitably fail to capture the rich diversity of thought. . . . A good story and a well formed argument are different natural kinds. Both can be used as means for convincing another. Yet what

they convince of is fundamentally different: Arguments convince one of their truth, stories of their lifelikeness. The one verifies by eventual appeal to procedures for establishing formal and empirical proof. The other establishes not truth but verisimilitude. (Bruner, 1986, p. 11)

Ethnographic research, it is claimed, sets out to put words to a way of life. Shirley Brice Heath introduces her book *Ways with Words* by calling it a record of "the natural flow of community and classroom life over nearly a decade"—life in three neighboring South Carolina communities—and later adds:

The reader should see *Ways with Words* as an unfinished story, in which the characters are real people whose lives go beyond the decade covered by the book, and for whom we cannot, within these pages, either resolve the plot or complete the story. Through these pages, however, the reader should move very close to a living understanding of the ways of behaving, feeling, believing, and valuing of the children, their community members, and their townspeople teachers. (Brice Heath, 1983, pp. 8 & 13)

As means to such ends, we shall surely rely at least as much upon the writer's ability to produce "a good story" as we do upon her ability at "well-formed argument." Without taking on here the vexed question of how a novel with a message relates, as discourse, to a piece of political propaganda, we must surely recognize that narrative as contrasted with argument (Bruner's second world and, by earlier analysis, our spectator role utterance) has the means to communicate aspects of experience that are incommunicable in ordinary discursive language. As Susanne Langer has put it, "What discursive symbolism—language in its literal use—does for our awareness of things about us and our relation to them, the arts to for our awareness of subjective reality, feeling and emotion; they give form to inward experiences and thus make them conceivable" (Langer, 1962, p. 82).

The means by which literary discourse succeeds where non-literary language fails are still highly problematic: Here is an area for scholarly analysis and research, and surely that area belongs above all in the field of studies relating to subject English.

Within a context of commitment to professional growth by teachers, new perspectives of English continue to evolve. Further, studies of classroom language and the role of language in learning extend the scope of our knowledge. Major publications report reexamination and refinement of the evidence that enriches our conception of English teaching: Arnold, 1983; Britton, 1984; Chorny, 1988; Farmer, 1986; Lightfoot & Martin, 1988; Medway, 1980; Meek & Miller, 1984; Squire, 1987; Tchudi, 1986.

Strong confirmation of the notion of teachers as learners derives from published researches over recent years: Much of it has been produced at the masters and doctoral levels.

Evidence is provided of the importance of talk as an instrument of children's learning (McIvor, 1978; Mowat, 1979; Searle, 1973). Students in their groups create social contexts in which they raise issues, exchange ideas, seek solutions, learn to handle differences, develop shared meanings and points of view, and make discoveries.

Central to this learning process is the use of expressive language, talk and writing. Rooted in the social transactions of past generations, it is the means by which people define themselves, establish relationships, share and develop ideas. Expressive language may be intimately related to inner speech, mediating between thought and its expression. It has been regarded as a route to mastery of both transactional and poetic modes, the languages of discourse and reflection (Paquette, 1981).

Through talk in class discussion, in small groups, in individual conferences with students, teachers are able to serve as the "wise adult," to extend a learner's potential within "the zone of proximal development" (Vygotsky, 1978, p. 86). It is through this process (sometimes referred to as scaffolding) that a teacher's intentions and a student's may interrelate.

However, the notion is open to misunderstanding: Tensions are likely to exist between a teacher's sense of responsibilities and a student's purposes (Searle, 1984, pp. 480–482). The solution lies in conceiving such exchanges as successive approximations that, by enhancing the student's learning, also serve the goals of English. By such means teachers and students, as also students working in groups, develop shared intentions (Sadownik, 1982).

The role of narrative in learning is being rediscovered. Spectator role discourse, and other forms of narrative, in their focus on the concrete, on personal experience, serve to bridge the gap that students often perceive as divorcing their own language from the language demanded in school. Personal narrative probably frees the writer to focus on process because the narrated material is familiar. For teachers, there is the bonus of getting to know their students as individuals.

Paquette, on the basis of his two-year experience teaching a group of students who had previously been placed in remedial courses in English, concludes:

For me, the most telling discovery was that none of the boys construed their respective teachers as genuine readers with whom they were making contact through writing. . . . What they [the teachers] seemed to be unaware of was the potential value of their personal participation as genuine readers of the boys' ideas, thoughts, and feelings—the importance of a writer having a sense of there being somebody at the other end of the process, a reader willing to try to enter the mind and world of the writer and to divine what he was striving to say. (Chorny, 1988, p. 461)

Reading studies that reflect recent work in language have extended our concept of the work of English lessons. Iveson (1988) has examined children's early experiences of literacy in a context of classroom talk, writing, and reading in relation to home experiences. Bechervaise (1988) traces the development of reading in ten families in Australia, through three generations, in relation to levels of family support, economic circumstances, and school experiences.

Novel approaches to the study of literature have included accounts of the role of personal constructs in reading (Washburn, 1978), of the influence of personal constructs on the individual intention pursued in response (Sadownik, 1982), and of the interaction of reading, talk, and writing in the forming of response (Montgomery, 1980).

Studies that relate in-school with out-of-school learning have focused on the use of language and reveal that students bring to school abilities to learn and to think that are evidenced in school learning (Mowat, 1979; Paquette, 1981; Searle, 1981). In a study of teacher intervention based on a thematic unit dealing

with the status of women in society, Scott (1986) discovered a range of external influences on school learning and set about to explore these within class activities in English lessons.

By setting boundaries upon the operations of language and learning on the basis of present understandings, we may be excluding supportive processes we cannot yet explain. Writing half a century ago, Vygotsky warned of the error of separating intellect and affect in our concept of mentality. Representing thought as self-generating results precludes the development of "a dynamic system of meaning in which the affective and intellectual unite" (Vygotsky, 1962, p. 8). His conclusion:

Thought itself is engendered by motivation, i.e. by our desires and needs, our interests and emotions. Behind every thought, there is an affective-volitional tendency, which holds the answer to the last "why" in the analysis of thinking. (p. 150)

Kelly's theory of personal constructs integrates cognition, action, and inherent feeling (1963). Polanyi recognizes the interaction between knowing and feeling in his view of personal knowledge. We emphatically share their views and would warn against imposing a disjunction between thought and feeling, between cognitive and affective modes of representation. We must overcome the lingering sense that feeling is mental operation at a lower level; we need to find new ways of exploring its role in the processes of learning.

We have stressed the practical nature of the outcomes aimed at in educational research. This being the case, let us say in conclusion that any informed scrutiny of English teaching practices today would suggest that the kind of research most urgently and immediately needed would be inquiries into the conditions that favor change in school and classroom procedures, and, above all, into the conditions that result in resistance to change. There is no shortage, we believe, of models of improved practice derived from research, but they seem to exist for the most part in a context of deep-seated institutional reluctance to apply them. A degree of conservatism in the profession, and inertia in the system and indifference or hostility on the part of the public—these offer themselves as rough and ready judgments on the state of affairs but afford no detailed evidence by which the situation might be improved. Here, we suggest, is a field of activity for practicing teachers at all levels of the educational system—an intimate working knowledge and an experienced sensibility—of classroom practices would be a prime qualification for such projects, a notion of "action research" its governing methodology. Especial insights might result from classroom cooperation between the teacher *in situ* and a professional researcher as observer.

It would be important, in any such undertaking, to study the relationship in any teaching situation between the strictly educative function of the institution and whatever child-minding or social control functions were deemed legitimate.

Teachers who succeeded in pursuing such enquiries would, *sui generis,* be exceptional teachers, and findings from their projects would need to be supported by studies over a broader range of teaching situations. In particular, we should like to know what are the classroom concomitants of various conceptions of the teaching/learning community? Where learning is seen as exploration, discovery, and the students' questions are more important than their answers, does the quality of the learning improve? How productive, in fact, is it when children learn from each other as well as from teacher and text-book, and is anything lost when they generate a classroom regime of cooperation rather than competition? How important are the social bonds between one classroom population and another within the school?

Such questions are, clearly, the beginnings of a list that

might be vastly extended. School/community relationships will foster or restrict or prohibit change in teaching strategies in ways that have been little studied: Influences, both within the community and beyond it that promote or inhibit teacher professionalism must materially affect the potential for change in the classroom.

Western societies in general seem to have entered a phase in their history in which inquiries of this kind are matters of urgency.

References

Arnold, R. (1983). *Timely voices: English teaching in the 1980's*. Melbourne: Oxford University Press.

Barnes, D., Britton, J., & Rosen, H. (1969). *Language, the learner and the school*. Harmondsworth, Eng.: Penguin Books.

Bell, D. (1977). Teletex & technology. *Encounter, 48*, 9–29.

Bechervaise, N. E. (1988). *The reader and the family: Cross-generational studies of readers and their reading*. Unpublished doctoral dissertation, Monash University, Melbourne, Australia.

Britton, J. (1970). *Languae and learning*. London: Allen Lane The Penguin Press.

Britton, J. (1977). Language and the nature of learning: an individual perspective. In J. Squire (Ed.), *The teaching of English, 76th Yearbook of the National Society for the Study of Education*. Chicago: Chicago University Press.

Britton, J. (1984). *English teaching: An international exchange*. London: Heinemann Educational Books, on behalf of the International Federation for the Teaching of English.

Britton, J., Burgess, T., Martin, N., McLeod, A., & Rosen, H. (1975). *The development of writing Abilities* (11–18). London: Macmillan Education.

Bruner, J. (1986). *Actual minds, possible worlds*. Cambridge, MA: Harvard University Press.

Bullock, A. (1975). *A language for life*. London: Her Majesty's Stationery Office.

Chorny, M. (Ed.). (1985). *Teacher as learner*. Calgary: University of Calgary, Language in the Classroom Project.

Chorny, M. (Ed.). (1988). *Teacher as researcher*. Calgary: University of Calgary, Language in the Classroom Project.

Cockle, L. (1988). When is art? Art, language and the spectator role. In M. Chorny (Ed.), *Teacher as researcher* (pp. 175–205). Calgary: University of Calgary, Language in the Classroom Project.

Dixon, J. (1967). *Growth through English*. Oxford University Press.

Eagleson, R. D. (Ed.). (1982). English in the eighties. Melbourne: Australian Association for the Teaching of English.

Eisner, E. W. (1984). Can educational research inform educational practice? *Phi Delta Kappan, 67*, 447–452.

Emig, J. (1971). *The composing processes of twelfth graders*. Urbana, IL: National Council of Teachers of English.

Farmer, M. (Ed.). (1986). *Consensus and dissent: Teaching English past, present and future*. Urbana, IL: National Council of Teachers of English.

Freedman, A., & Pringle, I. (Eds.). (1980). *Re-inventing the rhetorical tradition*. Ottawa, CAN: Canadian Council of Teachers of English.

Freedman, S. W., Haas Dyson, A., Flower, L., & Chafe, V. (1987). *Research in writing: past, present, and future*. Berkeley, CA: Center for the Study of Writing, University of California and Carnegie Mellon University.

Goodhall, P. E. (1988). Some dimensions of classroom language. In M. Chorny (Ed.), *Teacher as researcher*. Calgary: University of Calgary, Language in the Classroom Project.

Heath, S. B. (1983). *Ways with words*. New York: Cambridge University Press.

Iveson, M. L. (1988). *Teaching and learning literacy: A descriptive study of the reading and writing experiences of grade one children*. Unpublished doctoral dissertation, University of Calgary, Calgary, Alberta.

Jensen, J. M. (1987). Commentary. In J. R. Squire (Ed.), *The dynamics of language and learning*. Urbana, Ill: ERIC Clearinghouse on Reading and Communication Skills and the National Conference on Research in English.

Jensen, J. M. (Ed.). (1989). *Stories to grow on: Demonstrations of language learning in K–8 classrooms*. Exeter, NH: Heinemann Educational.

Kelly, G. A. (1963). *A theory of personality*. New York: W. W. Norton.

Kelly, G. A. (1969). The strategy of psychological research. In B. Maher (Ed.), *Psychology and personality* (pp. 114–132). New York: John Wiley.

Kuhn, T. S. (1970). *The structure of scientific revolutions*. Chicago: University of Chicago Press.

Langer, S. (1962). *Philosophical Sketches*. Baltimore: Johns Hopkins Press.

Lightfoot, M., & Martin, N. (Eds.). (1988). *The word for teaching is learning: Essays for James Britton*. London: Heinemann Educational Books and Portsmouth, NH: Boynton/Cook in association with the National Assocation for the Teaching of English.

Lloyd-Jones, R., & Lunsford, A. A. (Eds.). (1989). *The English coalition conference:* Democracy through language. Urbana, IL: National Council of Teachers of English.

Martin, N. (Ed.). (1983). *Writing across the curriculum*. Upper Montclair, NJ: Boynton/Cook.

McIvor, A. K. (1978). *The language of English 23 students*. Unpublished master's thesis, University of Calgary, Calgary, Alberta.

Medway, P. (1980). *Finding a language*. London: Writers and Readers Publishing Cooperative in association with Chameleon.

Meek, M., & Miller, J. (1984). *Changing English: Essays for Harold Rosen*. London: Heinemann Educational Books for the Institute of Education, University of London.

Moffett, J. (1968). *Teaching the universe of discourse*. Boston: Houghton-Mifflin.

Mohr, M. M. & Maclean, M. S. (1987). *Working together*. Urbana, IL: National Council of Teachers of English.

Montgomery, D. (1980). *Reading, talking and writing to learn*. Unpublished master's thesis, University of Calgary, Calgary, Alberta.

Mowat, W. (1979). *The roots of real concepts*. Unpublished master's thesis, University of Calgary, Calgary, Alberta.

North, Stephen (1987). *The making of knowledge in composition*. Upper Montclair, NJ: Boynton/Cook.

Paquette, J. (1981). *A study of the influence of sense of audience on the writing processes of eight adolescent boys*. Unpublished doctoral dissertation, University of London, Institute of Education.

Paquette, J. (1988). The audience in the writer. In M. Chorny (Ed.), *Teacher as researcher* (pp. 433–461). Calgary: University of Calgary, Language in the Classroom Project.

Polanyi, M. (1962). *Personal knowledge.* Chicago: Chicago University Press.

Polanyi, M. (1969). *Knowing and being.* Chicago: Chicago University Press.

Polanyi, M., & Prosch, H. (1975). *Meaning.* Chicago: Chicago University Press.

Popper, Karl (1976). *Unended quest.* London: Fontana.

Pringle, I., & Freedman, A. (Eds.). (1981). *Teaching writing learning.* Ottawa, CAN.: Canadian Council of Teachers of English.

Sadownik, A. (1982). *Constructs and intention in response.* Unpublished master's thesis. University of Calgary, Calgary, Alberta.

Sapir, E. (1961). *Culture, language and society.* Berkeley: University of California Press.

Schwab, J. (1969). The practical: a language for curriculum. *The school review, 78,* 1–23.

Scott, H. C. (1986). *An examination of the effect of teacher intervention on adolescent learning.* Unpublished master's thesis, University of Calgary, Calgary, Alberta.

Searle, D. (1973). The classroom language activity of five selected high school students. Unpublished master's thesis, University of Calgary, Calgary, Alberta.

Searle, D. (1981). *Two contexts for adolescent language: Classroom learning and the discussion of extra-school experience.* Unpublished doctoral dissertation, University of London, Institute of Education.

Searle, D. (1984). Scaffolding: who's building whose building? *Language arts, 61,* 480–83.

Squire, J. R. (Ed.). (1987). *The dynamics of language learning: Research in reading and English.* Urbana, IL: ERIC Clearinghouse on reading and communication skills and the National Conference on Research in English.

Tchudi, S. (Ed.). (1985). *Language, schooling, and society.* Upper Montclair, NJ: Boynton/Cook.

Tchudi, S. (Ed.). (1986). *English teachers at work: Ideas and strategies from five countries.* Upper Montclair, NJ: Boynton/Cook.

Ulam, S. (1976). *Adventures of a mathematician.* New York: Scribner.

Vygotsky, L. S. (1962). *Thought and language.* Cambridge, MA: Massachusetts Institute of Technology.

Vygotsky, L. S. (1978). *Mind in society.* Cambridge, MA: Harvard University Press.

Washburn, W. (1978). *Response to a literary work of art.* Unpublished doctoral dissertation, University of Calgary, Calgary, Alberta.

METHODS OF RESEARCH ON ENGLISH LANGUAGE ARTS TEACHING

7

UNDERSTANDING RESEARCH ON TEACHING
THE ENGLISH LANGUAGE ARTS:
AN INTRODUCTION FOR TEACHERS

Sandra Stotsky
with Cindy Mall

In everyday life, we often do research to find practical solutions for immediate problems; we look for something that "works," even if we don't really know why it works. The immediate purpose of academic research in education, however, is to seek empirical evidence for explanatory generalizations, or theories, about the relationships among teaching practices, learning processes, and educational outcomes. The larger purpose of academic research is the development of theoretical knowledge.

Theoretical knowledge consists of systematically formulated and organized generalizations that explain the nature or behavior of a particular phenomenon. In the English language arts, these explanatory generalizations, or theories, constitute our knowledge about what happens as language teachers and language learners interact, what their interactions mean to them, why they take place, and what effects they have on the quality of language learning. The purpose of these theories is not only to explain what we can observe but also to predict what will or might happen. In essence, a theory is an educated "guess" about cause and effect for a particular phenomenon. A theoretical model derived from a theory tries to organize all the seemingly relevant elements of the phenomenon in a way that may account for its occurrence, and the model serves as a guide in formulating hypotheses for empirical studies of the phenomenon.

The purpose of much of the research in the English language arts is to determine how valid a particular thoery is in explaining a particular phenomenon. The more validity a theory has, the more support it has, the more researchers can use it to guide further research, and the more teachers can rely on it as a general guide for pedagogical practice. Nevertheless, no matter how much explanatory strength a theory has, for exam-

ple, no matter how much empirical evidence has been obtained to support the theory, theories in the English language arts, as in other areas, are always tentative. Problems constantly arise or new facts are discovered, that do not seem to be explained by existing theories. Moreover, our ability to understand any educational phenomenon is always limited by the complexity of human behavior. Every theory is simply the best explanation we have at the moment for a particular educational question or concern. Thus, academic research on teaching the English language arts is a continuous, never-ending process of systematic inquiry for enhancing the explanatory power of theoretical discourse on language teaching and learning.

This chapter is intended to give K–12 teachers an introduction to understanding the basic categories and functions of research in teaching the English language arts. It was designed with the assumption that most teachers do not have extensive backgrounds in understanding educational research. It was also designed to highlight, as much as possible, studies that tell us something about teaching or the teacher's role in the learning process in order to compensate for the fact that there have been relatively few studies in the past two decades devoted to the teacher's role in stimulating student learning in the English language arts (Peters, 1987). Although much of the research in the English language arts is addressed chiefly to other researchers or doctoral students (e.g., the research on planning processes in composing), or is of primary concern to public policymakers or educational administrators (e.g., large program evaluations), the illustrative research in this chapter was selected, as much as possible, for its potential appeal to classroom teachers or curriculum developers.

The chapter begins with a brief overview of what research

is and what it is not. It then describes the two basic modes of academic inquiry—conceptual work and empirical research—with a discussion of empirical research in the English language arts divided into two categories: qualitative and quantitative methods. It concludes by suggesting how teachers might recognize these major categories of research in classroom-oriented studies and how they might go about determining the theoretical value of a study's findings. However, the chapter also suggests why the usefulness of a particular study to a particular practitioner may not necessarily depend on the theoretical value of its findings. Thus, the overall purpose of this chapter is to help teachers become more intelligent consumers of, as well as participants in, educational research.

WHAT IS RESEARCH?

Academic research on teaching the English language arts is a planned, methodical exploration of some aspect of language teaching and learning. Regardless of the nature of the question or problem the researcher is investigating, researchers plan what they are going to do and proceed by systematically gathering data of some kind to address the question or problem. Data are facts. Sometimes they may be easily established and verified by others (e.g., the works of literature that secondary school teachers recommend for whole class instruction, as in Stotsky and Anderson, in-press). Or they may have a subjective quality and their status as facts depends on what researchers report they have observed (e.g., how teachers respond to student writing, as in Freedman, 1987). Or they may be quantities resulting from criteria or instruments that assess the quality of language teaching and learning. But researchers do more than provide their readers with data to inspect (e.g., a list of the readings certain teachers assign their classes; a detailed description of how particular teachers respond to student writing; or the distribution of achievement scores). They also interpret the meaning of these data. Researchers then suggest how their findings contribute to the development of theoretical knowledge about the process of language teaching and language learning and the effects of this process on the students' development as a speaker, listener, reader, and writer of the English language.

In the English language arts, as in other subject areas, one must distinguish a research study from instructional materials that operationalize the pedagogical implications of research findings. For example, a workbook on the editing process by Epes and Kirkpatrick (1987) provides exercises designed to help adult basic writers discover whether they are most prone to overlooking either missing words, missing endings, or reversed letters. The exercises are based on many years of teaching, joint research (e.g., Epes and Kirkpatrick, 1979), and Epes' (1985) in-depth case study of 26 unskilled adult students, all of which suggested that unskilled adult writers show different patterns of errors in their writing. While the material in Epes and Kirkpatrick's workbook is clearly derived from their research findings, it is not the research itself. A bibliography (as in Epes and Kirkpatrick's workbook) or an introductory section should suggest the body of research on which an instructional text is based.

It is also important to distinguish academic research from field-testing instructional material. Before mass distribution of newly created instructional material, field-testers for publishing companies attempt to determine the material's usability in selected classrooms representative of the intended market. Their goal is to find out if the material needs to be revised (and made more useful), not if the the theoretical knowledge that the material was designed to reflect should be revised. Field-testing is also done by teachers. As Calkins (1985) points out, many of the studies conducted by teacher-researchers in their own classrooms are also examples of field-testing. Teachers often try out their own or others' ideas in their own classrooms. But, Calkins suggests, "Will this work in my classroom?" is not an academic research question.

Finally, one must distinguish academic research from personal narratives describing a successful teacher's philosophy, approach, and experiences in the classroom, such as Eliot Wigginton's (1985) account of the *Foxfire* project, or Nancie Atwell's (1987) book on teaching writing and reading in a middle school. Books or articles of this nature can stimulate other practitioners' thinking, provide them with much useful pedagogical advice, and offer rich insights for researchers to use in creating or revising theory. But in themselves, they do not constitute academic research, a form of inquiry characterized by, among other things, the professional detachment of the inquirer, the systematic collection and write-up of data to address an explicit problem or question, and the use of a codified methodology (Chilcott, 1987).

Good research provides teachers with concepts to think with and ideas to think about. It also raises questions to stimulate their thinking about what they see or do in the classroom. But its purpose is not to propose a specific solution to a particular teacher's classroom problems, to advocate a particular pedagogical practice, or to provide instructional materials for teachers or students. Rather, its purpose is to enhance a teacher's ability to make intelligent instructional decisions. It is from this general perspective that teachers should examine academic research.

THE BASIC MODES OF ACADEMIC INQUIRY IN TEACHING THE ENGLISH LANGUAGE ARTS

In order to understand the nature of empirical research on teaching the English language arts, it is useful to distinguish first the two basic modes of academic inquiry. In its categorization of doctoral dissertations for determining awards each year (e.g., *Educational Researcher,* 1988, p. 30), the American Educational Research Association (AERA) suggests two broad categories of academic inquiry concerned with the improvement of the educational process: conceptual and empirical work.

Conceptual Inquiry

Conceptual work is theoretical or philosophical in nature and is usually referred to as scholarship rather than research. It focuses on an examination of the assumptions and conditions that shape teaching and learning and on the formulation of broad principles for models of teaching and learning. It may draw insights from the results of existing empirical research, but it is not concerned with gathering new data from systematic observations to provide evidence for support of its propositions. The work of John Dewey (1938) is a prime example of conceptual inquiry in the field of education. He saw a need for active learning within a coherent intellectual framework, and he stressed the development of a curriculum that moved progressively in the direction of a "more objective intellectual scheme of organization" from roots in the student's experience. But Dewey did not actually gather data from classroom observations to show that experience-based activities could lead to better and more meaningful learning than formal text-based discussion. We accept or reject his ideas according to how sensible, insightful, and well-reasoned we judge them to be.

The work of James Moffett (1968) is a notable example in the field of composition teaching. He proposed principles for developing a series of composition assignments that he believed could, over time, enhance growth in abstract thinking. Although he showed examples of student writing to illustrate the use of his principles in actual writing assignments, he, too, did not gather data from classrooms to show that the use of the principles he articulated did, in fact, improve student thinking.

Empirical Research

In contrast to purely conceptual work, empirical research focuses on the collection, analysis, and interpretation of data that can be sensed or experienced in some way, either to answer research questions, to test hypotheses derived from theories, and/or to develop hypotheses or theories. Examples of different forms of empirical research, according to the AERA, are experimental research, survey research, participant observational research, audiovisual recording analysis, in-depth interviewing, and empirical historiography.

Although North (1987) distinguishes four "communities" of empirical researchers in the field of composition (experimentalists; clinicians, or case study researchers; formalists, or model-builders; and ethnographers), most educational researchers have in recent years grouped various methods for empirically investigating questions of interest in English language arts into two basic categories of methods. This chapter uses the terms "qualitative" and "quantitative" to designate these two groups of methods because they seem to be the most commonly used terms in recent articles, including those in *Educational Researcher,* an official journal of the AERA. However, the terms qualitative, holistic, phenomenological, hypothesis-generating, participant-observational, ethnographic, longitudinal, humanistic, naturalistic, field-based, interpretivistic, or hermeneutical are often used interchangeably, even though some researchers do not see them all as interchangeable; unfortunately, no clear definitions can be found that distinguish among all these various terms. Similarly, the terms positivistic, scientific, hypothesis-testing, or quantitative are also often used interchangeably.

However distinct these two groups of methods may be in theory and in practice, a question we will return to later, all methods can contribute to the development of theoretical knowledge in teaching the English language arts.

In the next section, we look at the general features of these two broad categories of methods. Other chapters deal separately with various types of studies using these methods (see, for example, the chapters on case studies or ethnographic studies), and readers should consult these chapters for further illustrations and more detailed explanations of these specific types.

Qualitative Methods

Researchers use qualitative methods to investigate how language teaching and language learning take place in the complexity of their natural settings. They may explore the process of language teaching and language learning as these occur in the classroom, the home, or the community. Qualitative methods, by definition, feature qualitative data—the researcher's description of what participants do or say about themselves and their activities in an educational setting. Studies featuring qualitative methods tend to focus on small numbers of participants and a thorough understanding of small, complete units of social interaction; hence, "thick" descriptions, or masses of details, are a salient characteristic of these studies. Researchers then analyze and interpret these details and often formulate categories for classifying their data. If their studies are not theory-based, they may propose tentative generalizations based on their data, and these tentative generalizations may be referred to as "grounded theory" because the theory has been derived from the data.

For example, Florio and Clark (1982) observed an elementary classroom to find answers to the following questions: "What opportunities for writing do students find in school? How is writing used by students to meet those opportunities? How do students come to differentiate among the functions of writing and the forms appropriate to them? What role does the teacher play in this process? What other contextual forces are operant (p. 116)?" After lengthy observations and an analysis of what they saw and heard, they concluded that, among other things, they could identify four different purposes for student writing in this classroom: students wrote to participate in community, to know themselves and others, to demonstrate academic competence, and to occupy free time. By providing categories for understanding how the teacher and her students used and talked about writing in this classroom, this study contributes to the formulation of a theory about the social meaning of written literacy in the classroom.

Studies featuring qualitative methods tend to be exploratory in nature. Sometimes qualitative researchers do not decide in advance all the aspects of the phenomenon under investigation they will explore; they hope to discover possibly important aspects that may not have been noted yet. On the other hand, sometimes they explore the possible significance of features that have been noted but which have not yet been considered relevant to an understanding of a particular phenomenon. For example, Wong (1988) examined teacher/student talk in writing conferences at an engineering school over a 3-month period. The descriptive research she had reviewed found that teachers tend to initiate talk in writing conferences, despite a view by eminent teachers of writing that the writing conference should be more like a "natural conversation," with both parties initiating talk. Wong hypothesized that a writing conference might be less dominated by the teacher if students had more technical knowledge than their tutors with respect to the content of their writing. She discovered from this small case study involving two tutors and four tutees that this variable seemed to have some influence on the teacher/student conference; students writing technical papers did engage in more give-and-take dialogues than did the students in the research Wong had reviewed. Thus, her study contributes to a better understanding of why conferences do not seem to be natural conversations and helps in the elaboration of a "complete theory of conferencing for guiding instruction" (p. 459).

Researchers using qualitative methods not only make their own interpretation about what they see and hear, they frequently explore what the language learning and teaching activities mean to the participants as well (although researchers using quantitative methods may also examine this). They try to discover the participants' point of view, thoughts, and feelings and why they think, feel, or behave as they do. For example, Hudson (1986) asked 20 children in several elementary grades to tell her whether the pieces of writing they had done at home and at school over the course of several months were self-sponsored or school-sponsored. By obtaining the children's perceptions of their own writing, she found that many children often did not distinguish assignments given by the teacher from those they wrote on their own, seeing many school assignments as self-sponsored if they had a personal interest in them. Hudson did not determine whether or not their teachers had kindled their interest in the school assignments they perceived as self-sponsored, but she was able to conclude that the traditional dichotomy between self-sponsored and school-sponsored writing may be misleading, and that students' personal investment in their writing may not depend on their having chosen the topic themselves. Hudson also found a much wider variety of purposes for writing in the classroom than Florio and Clark (largely because she asked the children for their perception of their purposes and categorized what she found in a different way), suggesting the importance of multiple descriptive studies of an observed phenomenon.

Quantitative Methods

Studies featuring quantitative methods are apt to be concerned with the discovery of broad principles of language teaching and learning that will hold across many students, classrooms, or schools. These studies are usually characterized by a testable theory, concrete data obtained by a reproducible methodology, and a methodology that allows confirmation or disconfirmation of the theory (Becker, 1987). In order to make valid generalizations across many students, classrooms, or schools, quantitative researchers may use representative populations or randomly chosen subjects in experimental and control groups, or carefully constructed comparison groups. Drawing on the results of other relevant research to shape and justify their specific focus of interest, they decide in advance on all the variables to be examined, specify the relationships among them that are to be investigated, and measure them (statistically) in prescribed ways (Howe, 1988). A study using a quantitative method usually proceeds by systematically manipulating its specific variables to test the predictions made by the theory informing the study. Quantitative methods, by definition, feature quantified data (facts) expressed as quantities so that objective measurements are possible.

Hillocks' (1986) integrative review of research in written composition provides an examination of many well-done studies using quantitative methods. As part of a meta-analysis, a statistical treatment of the quantified findings of experimental studies with similar purposes and variables that makes the results of each individual study interpretable in relation to the others, Hillocks showed that studies exploring the effects of similar writing strategies or modes of writing instruction produced similar amounts of gain in students, despite differences in the individual studies with respect to such contextual variables as population and grade level. (For example, students in sentence-combining studies showed about the same amount of improvement in their writing, despite differences among these studies in the classroom setting.) This indicated that the findings of well-designed experimental studies in composition may be generalized across varied instructional contexts; for example, sentence-combining activities may have a beneficial effect on writing in any classroom.

Not all studies using quantitative methods focus directly on cause and effect relationships. Many such studies are correlational rather than experimental. They seek to discover whether one entity is related to another, and if so, how or to what extent. Researchers may then try to infer cause and effect, but must do so carefully. For example, a study by Anderson, Wilson, and Fielding (1986) found a relationship between outside-of-school book reading and reading achievement in fifth-grade students. In itself, this study cannot establish a causal relationship between outside-of-school book reading and reading achievement. But it still can suggest that teachers and parents might assign a "higher priority" to outside-of-school book reading, and it does provide a rationale for a rigorous study comparing an experimental curriculum stressing outside-of-school reading with one not doing so.

It is important to note that not all quantitative research is oriented to the validation of theory; in fact, a great deal of it in and outside of academic settings does not directly concern theory at all. Some of it is conducted to assess instructional programs. Descriptive data are frequently gathered and quantified to provide a vast variety of factual information, such as faculty or student profiles. Other kinds of studies without a theoretical orientation also use quantitative methods; studies on word frequencies, or studies detailing the objective characteristics of oral or written texts, such as parts of speech, types of words, or misspelled words, are among the best examples. Often these collections of data are used in other research or for creating instructional materials, such as vocabulary or spelling text-books.

ARE QUANTITATIVE AND QUALITATIVE METHODS INCOMPATIBLE?

Howe (1988) argues that no incompatibility between quantitative and qualitative methods exists in theory or in practice. In an examination of qualitative and quantitative methods with respect to the design of a study, the analysis of data, and the interpretation of results, Howe suggests that differences exist primarily in the assumptions researchers are willing to make and in how much attention they pay to "closely experienced" data—data based on their own observations and their own understanding of their interactions with participants in the research setting. There are, in fact, many commonalities among the methods used for empirical research.

To begin with, both categories of methods can be used to enhance theoretical knowledge. On one hand, empirical studies can be pre-theoretical, and their findings can help to create theory. As Jacob (1988) notes in an examination of six academic "traditions" that emphasize descriptive studies, all these traditions see descriptive studies preceding the testing of specific theories and hypotheses. On the other hand, empirical studies can be based on theory, and their findings can help to strengthen, revise, or disconfirm it. Case study research, as Calkins (1985) points out, as well as experimental research, is often, if not usually, theory-based, and can contribute to the confirmation, revision, or disconfirmation of theory (e.g., the case studies by Wong, 1988, and Epes, 1985).

Second, as Jacob notes, all researchers are interested in minimizing or controlling bias despite differences in how they obtain their data or in the kind of data they collect. Jacob notes that even qualitative researchers want to report their data as objectively as possible, even when they report on subjective aspects of behavior as participant-observers-researchers who not only observe their subjects but interact with them and, possibly, influence them.

Third, all researchers collect, analyze, and interpret data. No facts of any kind ever interpret themselves. Moreover, all researchers present their data to the reader in some form. A researcher's argument is always based on evidence available to the reader, with a careful exploration of alternative explanations of the data (Howe, 1988).

Finally, studies using either quantitative and qualitative methods to investigate teaching in the English language arts can take place in the classroom or in other natural settings. Both kinds of methods can also be used in laboratory settings.

It may be the case that studies using qualitative methods have not, in general, focused on an assessment of the quality of teaching and learning activities. They have perhaps more often sought to describe the process of language teaching and learning in its natural settings and to understand the meaning of what happened in the classroom from both the researcher's and the participants' perspectives. It may also be the case that studies using quantitative methods have not, in general, focused

on all the details of various contexts for language teaching and learning. They have perhaps more often sought to discover the precise role of individual elements in the process of language teaching and learning in order to determine their influence on the quality of language learning. Nevertheless, Kantor, Kirby, and Goetz (1981) note: "Quantitative strategies can be associated with investigation of processes, grounded theory, and close examination of contexts, while qualitative approaches can serve the study of outcomes, hypothesis testing, and generalizable conclusions" (p. 295). Thus, each group of methods does not necessarily cluster around a completely different set of interests, and methods from both groups can be, and have been, combined for purposes often associated with one or the other group.

Jacob (1988), too, concludes that "researchers are presented with a range of research options, not just an all-or-nothing approach between qualitative research and positivistic research" (p. 23). And, indeed, more and more studies on the English language arts today use both qualitative and quantitative methods. Researchers may creatively combine the case-study method of investigation with some of the advantages of a quantified study as Epes (1985) did in a model case study; using 26 carefully selected subjects in comparison groups, Epes was able to test hypotheses and tentatively establish causal relationships. Researchers can also codify and quantify classroom observations and use comparison groups based on seemingly important differences to explore possible causal factors. For example, Wendler, Samuels, & Moore (1989) conducted observations of three groups of elementary school teachers (teachers who had received an award for excellence in teaching, teachers with a master's degree, and a group of teachers with significantly fewer years of teaching experience and reading courses) to determine the amount of time they spent on comprehension instruction using basal readers and to see if there were differences among them in the use of the best comprehension instruction practices suggested by research. Finding that all three groups spent very little time on pre-reading activities and direct comprehension instruction, the researchers were able to conclude that graduate-level course work in reading may not be influencing comprehension instruction in the way it should and suggested we need to find out why.

Witte (1987) also believes that the field of composition research is "large enough . . . to make good use of both qualitative and quantitative methodologies and to embrace both the logic of discovery and the logic of validation" (p. 207). Moreover, he feels that it must do both if the field of research is "to meet its obligations to itself *and* to the larger social context which sustains it" (p. 207).

In sum, both qualitative and quantitative methods are useful, are used together, and should be used together in empirical research on the English language arts. Moreover, both qualitative and quantitative methods can be used in both pre-theoretical and theoretically motivated research; that is, both groups of methods serve both functions of empirical research—studies using qualitative methods may be theory-based, and studies using quantitative methods may be pre-thoretical. This suggests that what teachers should first note when reading research on teaching the English language arts is not what methodology the study uses, or whether the data are qualitative or quantitative in nature, but rather how the study contributes to the development of theoretical knowledge and how well scientific reasoning is demonstrated in its design and in the analysis, presentation, and interpretation of its findings. As Stotsky (1989) concludes in a review of several recent books on teaching the English language arts, the value of theoretical knowledge and scientific thinking may well be what is at stake in the controversy about which empirical methods are more or less useful for research on teaching the English language arts.

DETERMINING THE THEORETICAL VALUE OF A STUDY'S FINDINGS

As we have suggested above, perhaps the most important question for teachers to ask when reading a classroom-oriented study on teaching the English language arts is how it contributes to the development of theoretical knowledge. To answer that question, they need to ascertain whether the study is pre-theoretical or based on theory. Pre-theoretical studies help us to create theories, while theory-based studies help us to validate theories and build a knowledge base. Teachers need to ask: Is a study exploratory and pre-theoretical, one in which the researcher seeks to describe what is happening in a particular educational setting and to generate questions or explanations for further research? Do its findings contribute to the construction of theory, to the formulation of a tentative generalization that might explain its findings? Or does a study begin with a formulated theory and seek to gather evidence that validates the theory? Do its findings contribute to the strengthening of a theory, to the revision or confirmation of a formulated theory that predicted the findings?

Teachers may determine the theoretical value of a study's findings by distinguishing theory-based studies from pre-theoretical studies. Any empirical study can give teachers insights and useful ideas for the classroom, as we shall point out below. But studies whose findings clearly validate an articulated theory about a particular phenomenon should probably carry more weight than pre-theoretical studies about that phenomenon, all other things being equal. This is particularly the case when the theory-based studies have resulted in converging evidence, or similar findings, using a variety of methodologies, teachers, and students. And theories that account for all available evidence or that have been validated by a great deal of empirical evidence from a variety of sources and types of studies deserve more consideration than theories with little or no empirical evidence to validate them. Thus, when administrators or curriculum makers wish to develop recommendations for formal policy in English language arts, or when researchers wish to propose directions for future research, or when teachers consider making basic changes in classroom practices, they should pay especial attention to research whose findings provide strong empirical evidence to validate a comprehensive theory. The larger the body of research whose findings support the theory, the greater its explanatory power, and the more fruitful a practical translation of its pedagogical implications should be.

Although it is beyond the scope of this chapter to enumerate and explain in detail the questions educators might use to determine whether a study in the English language arts is pre-theoretical or theoretically-motivated, the following questions may be somewhat useful.

1. What exactly seems to be the purpose of the study? Does it seek to describe language teaching and learning in one specific context and to generate generalizations after data have been collected (as in Florio and Clark's study)? Or does it seek to validate a proposed principle of language teaching and learning (as in Wong's study)? The first kind of study is pre-theoretical; the second, theory-based.
2. Does the study begin with a series of questions or a statement of the researcher's focus of interest (as in Florio and Clark's study)? If so, it *may* be pre-theoretical; however, researchers sometimes phrase their hypotheses in the form of questions so that the presence of questions does not necessarily indicate a pre-theoretical study. If a study begins with specific hypotheses (as in Epes' study), then it is theoretically motivated.
3. Is the study informed by an explicit theoretical framework? If so, the study is theoretically motivated. If not, the study *may* be pre-theoretical. (Sometimes a theoretically motivated study is poorly written up and the reader can find little, if any, mention of its particular theoretical framework.)

Needless to say, a researcher's methodology should flow from his or her purpose for a study. If the methodology of a study is not guided by what the researcher seeks to do, then the study is conceptually flawed. And if the researcher's methodology is based on his or her values or beliefs, rather than on the purpose for the study, then rational discussion is not possible.

It is often not easy to determine exactly how a study contributes to the development of theoretical knowledge, for example, whether it seeks to create or confirm theory. Teacher discussion groups can be especially helpful. As teachers talk to each other about their understanding of the same study, the meaning of research concepts can be illuminated and the researcher's goals and reasoning process clarified. Comparing individual interpretations of a research report in teacher discussion groups may be the most fruitful way for teachers of the English language arts to learn how to interpret research.

HOW ACADEMIC AND CLASSROOM INQUIRY AND PRACTICE ARE RELATED

For policy-making purposes or basic changes in pedagogical practices, educators should pay close attention to studies whose findings strengthen theoretical knowledge about teaching the English language arts. However, the usefulness of a particular study to a classroom teacher is not necessarily determined by the study's orientation to theory and the theoretical value of its findings. According to Chilcott (1987) and Calkins (1985), most school ethnographic studies lack a theoretical basis. Their findings, therefore, do not contribute to the strengthening of an

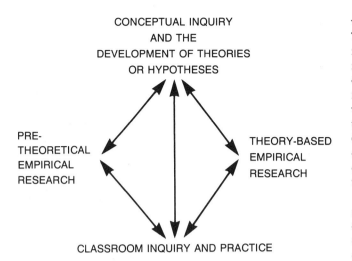

CONCEPTUAL INQUIRY
AND THE
DEVELOPMENT OF THEORIES
OR HYPOTHESES

PRE-
THEORETICAL
EMPIRICAL
RESEARCH

THEORY-BASED
EMPIRICAL
RESEARCH

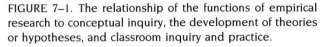

CLASSROOM INQUIRY AND PRACTICE

FIGURE 7–1. The relationship of the functions of empirical research to conceptual inquiry, the development of theories or hypotheses, and classroom inquiry and practice.

articulated theory; at best they contribute only to the formulation of a tentative generalization. Nevertheless, classroom descriptions can give (and have given) teachers stimulating and useful ideas. For example, elementary grade teachers can learn about a remarkable classroom project and the kinds of civic writing even young children can do from the description of the model imaginary community called "Betterburg" that second-grade students planned, organized, and managed in their classroom for the school year under the direction of their teacher (Florio and Frank, 1982).

The findings of experimental research support articulated generalizations about students or classrooms across specific contexts; they do not tell us about specific students or specific contexts. Nevertheless, they can be directly useful to individual practitioners. For example, the results of the studies on reciprocal teaching and guided cooperative learning by Palincsar and Brown (1983) and Brown and Palincsar (1986) suggest the value of a variety of group learning procedures for improving reading comprehension. Teachers can easily adapt these procedures for their own classrooms, and probably many have done so.

Even the fruits of conceptual inquiry can serve teachers directly as a source of inspiration and guidance. For example, Dewey's ideas on the value of experiential learning within an articulated and organized intellectual framework served as the primary academic source for the writing curriculum Wiggenton designed around the publication of the journal *Foxfire*. Wiggenton drew on relatively little, if any, empirical research to guide his thinking about classroom and community-based learning activities for his Appalachian Mountain students. Moffett's ideas have also directly influenced many teachers, such as Dellinger (1982), who developed a series of assignments and activities for teaching composition to her high school students that reflects almost wholly the use of the principles Moffett proposed.

Figure 7–1 shows the reciprocal nature of the relationship between the basic modes of academic inquiry and classroom inquiry and practice. At the base of the figure is the classroom

where the teaching of the English language arts takes place. Teachers often do practical problem-solving in their own classrooms without reference to academic inquiry, and the practical research they do can be very useful to other teachers. But their questions can serve as a stimulus for pre-theoretical empirical research, purely conceptual inquiry, and theoretically motivated empirical research, as the three arrows suggest. In return, the insights and findings of all modes of academic inquiry (whether or not this inquiry is based on the classroom teacher's questions) can stimulate teachers' thinking by expanding the contexts and the constructs they use for viewing their work in their own classroom.

Figure 7–1 also shows how the two functions of empirical research are related to conceptual inquiry and the development of theory. As the figure suggests, pre-theoretical research can contribute to conceptual inquiry and the formulation of hypotheses or theoretical generalizations (grounded theory). Reciprocally, theoretical thinking can lead to further exploratory, pre-theoretical research. Hence, the bi-directional arrow. As the figure also shows, empirical research also proceeds from hypotheses or formulated theories and seeks evidence to validate them. The findings of this research may support or disconfirm these hypotheses or theories and provide a rationale for further theory-based empirical research (or even further exploratory pre-theoretical research). Hence, the bi-directional arrow here as well. It is important to note that theoretical generalizations can be formulated without prior pre-theoretical research and do not necessarily result in empirical research.

In theory and in practice, therefore, as Figure 7–1 suggests, all modes and functions of academic inquiry can be useful to teachers. In turn, all modes and functions of academic inquiry can and should be responsive to teachers' questions and concerns. For teachers are not simply pragmatic or eclectic in all they choose to do in the classroom. For the most part, they are highly principled with respect to the goals of formal education. Their ideas about how they think students learn to become informed, self-sufficient, and responsible citizens through their English language arts programs are as worthy of consideration as are the ideas of academic researchers.

JUDGING THE USEFULNESS OF RESEARCH FINDINGS FOR CLASSROOM PRACTICE

Although we have discussed how teachers might determine the theoretical value of a study's findings, we have not suggested how they might judge their usefulness for their classroom. Whether or not a study is pre-theoretical or theoretically motivated, the following questions may be helpful.

First, how applicable are the study's concepts to the teacher's classroom? The educational level of the study may make a considerable difference. Concepts useful at the elementary school level may have little meaning for adult learners, while those useful for adult learners may be inappropriate for young children. On the other hand, teachers may still wish to consider the adaptability of any concept for different educational levels.

Second, are the location of the teacher's school (rural, urban, or suburban), class size, and the students' level of ability in English similar to the school's setting, class size, and student ability in the study? Clearly, teachers should be cautious about applying the findings from any one study if their classroom differs substantially from the classroom in the study.

Third, are only small numbers of students involved in the study? If so, teachers should exercise caution unless a study's findings are consistent with those from a large body of research. If the study is unique, and its findings have not been replicated in any way, then the pedagogical implications of its findings should be considered with extreme tentativeness. One study should be seen as only a possible piece of a puzzle, with firm knowledge accumulating only slowly over time as evidence comes in from a variety of sources and types of studies.

Fourth, is other research negatively portrayed? A study should be able to stand on its own merits. If the researchers appears biased, both the conceptualization of the study and the interpretation of the data may be affected.

Fifth, are the teachers in the study criticized or demeaned in some way? Are they portrayed as resistant to new ideas? Does the researcher appear to believe that his or her ideas are the "correct" ones? Such a stance is patronizing to teachers, even if the researcher is also a teacher. But more importantly, negative attitudes towards teachers may also signal a bias in the interpretation of a study's findings. For example, most, if not all, studies of the differences between school talk and home talk have viewed these differences as sources of conflict that prevent students from learning in school. These studies then imply that teachers need to adjust their curricula accordingly. The possibility that differences between home and school talk have no necessary bearing on school learning, or that differences between the two may even stimulate school learning, has not been explored and might well be. While no professional practice is above examination and criticism, it is useful for teachers to note whether the researcher explored alternative explanations for negatively interpreted findings, and whether evidence was provided to show that what the researcher found actually influences student achievement.

Finally, are teachers urged to adopt specific practices on the basis of one study? As our discussion of empirical research implied, the findings of any one study are apt to be too context-specific or too general for blanket recommendations and for unqualified or automatic application to any one classroom. Even if a body of similar research findings supports strong generalizations about the effects of a particular classroom practice, no generalization necessarily applies to all classrooms in exactly the same way. Ultimately, what is best for particular students can best be determined by the teacher's professional judgment in light of what the best evidence suggests.

CONCLUDING REMARKS

Serious educational research in the English language arts is only about 100 years old. Today, educators have the opportunity to gain insights and information from studies using a broad array of methodologies. Moreover, given the complexities of any research with human beings, teachers can legitimately expect researchers to use all methods of research and to gather both qualitative and quantitative data for investigating questions in teaching the English language arts. To deserve serious consideration, any specific conclusions about the teaching of the English language arts should be supported by a variety of pre-theoretical and theoretically motivated studies.

Teachers have many complex questions for researchers to address such questions as: What are ways to assess growth in reading and writing ability? How can parents assist their children's development as readers and writers? Do the results of a literature-based approach to reading instruction differ from the results of other approaches? Why are more boys than girls remedial readers and writers, and what can the schools do about it? What are the effects on reading and writing achievement in English if a young non-English-speaking child's native language is used for beginning reading and writing instruction? Such questions require a variety of research methodologies as well as many different studies using similar methodologies, if teachers are to have confidence in the conclusions of these studies.

However, it is worth keeping in mind that findings from different studies on the same topic may just as easily be inconsistent or contradict each other as converge (Mathison, 1988). And they may just as easily support or contradict teachers' intuitions or experiences. Mixed findings do not invalidate academic research, nor do findings that contradict teachers' intuitions invalidate their judgment. To the contrary, mixed findings provide new and useful information, and they suggest how complex the problem is. The best wisdom suggests that we should not expect one or two studies, no matter how well done, to provide answers to complex questions of classroom practice in teaching the English language arts. In the final analysis, how teachers read and interpret research on teaching the English language arts depends on the respect researchers and teachers have for each other, the respect researchers have for other researchers, and the respect researchers have for the moral and intellectual goals that most teachers have for their students.

References

Anderson, R., Wilson, P., & Fielding, L. (1986). Growth in reading and how children spend their time outside of school (Tech. Report No. 389). Urbana-Champaign, IL: University of Illinois, Center for the Study of Reading.

Atwell, N. (1987). *In the Middle: Writing, reading, and learning with adolescents.* Portsmouth, NH: Boynton/Cook, Heineman.

Becker, H. (1987). The importance of a methodology that maximizes falsifiability: Its applicability to research about Logo. *Educational Researcher, 16*(5), 11–16.

Brown, A., & Palinscar, A. (1986). *Guided, cooperative learning and individual knowledge acquisition* (Technical Report No. 372). Urbana-Champaign, IL: University of Illinois, Center for the Study of Reading.

Calkins, L. (1985). Forming research communities among naturalistic researchers. In B. McClelland & T. Donovan (Eds.), *Perspectives on research and scholarship in composition*. New York: Modern Language Association.

Chilcott, J. (1987). Where are you coming from and where are you going? The reporting of ethnographic research. *American Educational Research Journal, 24*(2), 199–218.

Dellinger, D. (1982). Out of the heart: How to design writing assignments for high school courses. The National Writing Project, Berkeley, CA: University of California.

Dewey, J. (1938). *Experience and education*. New York: Macmillan Publishing.

Educational Researcher. (1988, January–February). p. 30.

Epes, M. (1985). Tracing errors to their sources: A study of the encoding processes of adult basic writers. *Journal of Basic Writing, 4* 4–33.

Epes, M., & Kirkpatrick, C. (1978). *Investigating error in the writing of nontraditional college students*. (ERIC Document Reproduction Service No. ED 168 018.)

Epes, M., & Kirkpatrick, C. (1987). *Editing your Writing*. New York: Prentice Hall.

Florio, S., & Clark, C. (1982). The functions of writing in an elementary classroom. *Research in the Teaching of English, 16*(2), 115–130.

Florio, S., & Frank, J. (1982). Literacy and community in the classroom: A case study of Betterburg. In B. Beyer & R. Gilstrap (Eds.), *Integrating Writing and Social Studies, K–6* (pp. 31–42). Boulder, CO: Social Science Education Consortium.

Freedman, S. (1987). *Response to student writing* (NCTE Research Report No. 23). Urbana, IL: National Council of Teachers of English.

Hillocks, G. (1986). *Research on written composition: New directions for teaching*. Urbana, IL: NCRE and ERIC Clearinghouse on Reading and Communication Skills.

Howe, K. (1988). Against the quantitative-qualitative incompatibility thesis or dogmas die hard. *Educational Researcher, 17*(8), 10–16.

Hudson, S. (1986). Context and children's writing. *Research in the Teaching of English, 20*(3), 294–316.

Jacob, E. (1988). Clarifying qualitative research: A focus on traditions. *Educational Researcher, 17* (1) 16–24.

Kantor, K., Kirby, D., & Goetz, J. (1981). Research in context: Ethno-graphic studies in English education. *Research in the Teaching of English, 15,* 293–310.

Mathison, S. (1988). Why triangulate? *Educational Researcher, 17*(2), 13–17.

Moffett, J. (1968). *Teaching the universe of discourse*. Boston: Houghton Mifflin.

North, S. (1987). *The making of knowledge in composition: Portrait of an emerging field*. Montclair, NJ: Boynton/Cook.

Palincsar, A., & Brown, A. (1983). *Reciprocal teaching of comprehension-monitoring activities* (Tech. Report No. 269). Urbana-Champaign, IL: University of Illinois, Center for the Study of Reading.

Peters, W. (Chair). (1987). *Effective English teaching: Concept, research, and practice*. CEE Commission on Research in Teacher Effectiveness. Urbana, IL: National Council of Teachers of English.

Stotsky, S. (1989). How to restore the professional status of English teachers: Three useful but troubling perspectives [Essay review of *Consensus and dissent: Teaching English past, present, and future,* NCTE Yearbook, M. N. Farmer, 1986; *Effective English teaching: concept, research, practice,* W. H. Peters (Chair), and the CEE Commission on Research in Teacher Effectiveness, 1987; and *Working together: A guide for teacher-researchers,* M. M. Mohr & M. S. MacLean, 1987.] *College English, 51*(7), 750–758.

Stotsky, S., & Anderson, P. (in press). *Works of literature recommended for whole-class instruction by New England Area teachers of English*. Report of research for the New England Association of Teachers of English.

Wendler, D., Samuels, S. & Moore, V. (1989). Comprehension instruction of award-winning teachers, teachers with master's degrees, and other teachers. *Reading Research Quarterly, 24*(4), 382–398.

Wigginton, E. (1985). *Sometime a shining moment: The Foxfire experience*. New York: Doubleday.

Witte, S. (1987). [Review of *Research on Written Composition: New Directions for Teaching*]. G. Hillocks, Jr., *College Composition and Communication, 38* (2), 202–207.

Wong, I. (1988). Teacher-student talk in technical writing conferences. *Written Communication, 5*(9), 444–460.

8

THEORY, RESEARCH, AND PRACTICE IN TEACHING ENGLISH LANGUAGE ARTS

Roy C. O'Donnell

In an ideal world, educational theory might be formulated and tested through competently designed and carefully executed research and then disseminated to teachers who would apply it in their classrooms. In the real world, however, such a logical progression can seldom be discerned. In fact, the relationships among educational theory, research, and practice are sometimes so obscure as to be impossible to trace. Consequently, the assertion has often been made that there is little or no relationship between theory and practice.

THE GAP BETWEEN RESEARCH AND PRACTICE

In "Research in the Teaching of English: The Troubled Dream," Dwight Burton (1973) alludes to the fact that despite the positive connotations the word "research" has in our culture, "in the humanistic-oriented English teaching profession there has been an abiding uneasiness with quantitative methods and perhaps with the empirical approach generally" (p. 160). He acknowledges that research seems to have had little to do with either curriculum structure or teaching methods in English, but says "we have the feeling that answers are just around the corner if we but design the right studies" (p. 160).

As evidence of disappointments and frustrations with the fruits of research, Burton cites the "state of knowledge" reports published by the National Council of Teachers of English (Braddock, Lloyd-Jones, & Schoer, 1963; Petty, Herold & Stoll, 1968; Purves & Beach, 1972), which emphasize that research has *not* accomplished more than it has. He says "most reviewers of research shake their heads sadly over the quality of much of what they review, and listings of common faults that make research inconclusive or invalid are strikingly similar over the past twenty-five years" (p. 161). As a possible explanation for the disappointment, he says we may have "expected too much of an effort that is relatively young and we may have underestimated the difficulty of probing, for our particular reasons, the

mysteries of human behavior, its development and change" (p. 161).

In addition to problems stemming from the "fragmentary, isolated, unrelated nature" of much of the research concerned with the teaching of English, Burton sees dissemination of findings as a basic problem. Most doctoral research does not get beyond the supervisory committee, and many of the small grant projects end in undisseminated reports to the sponsoring agency. He sees cause for hope of improvement, however, through the expanded publications program of NCTE and then-recent establishment of the NCTE/ERIC Clearinghouse on Reading and Communication Skills. This development, in addition to the increased commitment of the profession generally to research and the "virtual explosion" of research activity during the 1960s, was viewed with optimism.

That dissemination of research findings has been a basic problem is strongly supported by Edward R. Fagan's (1972) study of English teachers' understanding of research. Fagan surveyed a national sample randomly drawn from National Council of Teachers of English membership lists in each of four categories: elementary, secondary, college, and English education. Of the four groups sampled, English educators were most cognizant of, and willing to apply, research findings to their teaching. College English teachers reported awareness of bibliographical and historical studies but desultory application of the findings to their teaching; those who taught composition were sometimes influenced to alter their teaching by findings of studies reported in *College Composition and Communication*. Fagan found that the majority of elementary and secondary teachers in his sample were almost totally unaware of research; consequently, research findings could have no direct influence on their teaching.

This lack of awareness of research is documented by Theodore W. Hipple and Thomas R. Giblin (1971) in their study of the professional reading of English teachers. On the basis of data from 386 teachers who responded to a questionnaire sent to 580 randomly selected teachers of English in Florida, the authors concluded that: "The practicing secondary school English teacher in Florida is not likely to be engaged in much professional reading related either to education in general or to teaching English in particular. Furthermore, his university preparation has not been remarkably rich with professional reading experiences" (p. 153). Less than half (41.6 percent) of these teachers held membership in the National Council of Teachers of English, and slightly more than half (55.2 percent) held membership in the Florida Council of Teachers of English. Only 41 percent of these teachers subscribed to *English Journal* (*Research in the Teaching of English* was not included in the survey). Of the books that contained then current information relevant to the teaching of English, *Freedom and Discipline in English* (Commission on English, 1965) was unknown to 58 percent of the teachers, and only 6 percent claimed to have read it; Dixon's (1967) *Growth Through English* was unknown to 75.5 percent, and only 2.8 percent claimed to have read it; Evans and Walker's (1966) *New Trends in the Teaching of English* was unknown to 55.7 percent, and only 4.9 percent claimed to have read it; Rosenblatt's (1938) *Literature as Exploration* was unknown to 69.7 percent, and only 2.3 percent claimed to have read it.

Given the probability that Florida English teachers on the whole are among the more sophisticated in the nation, these figures leave a rather dismal impression indeed. This dismal impression is reinforced by a more recent survey of Michigan teachers reported by Clinton S. Burhans, Jr. (1985). He surveyed a random sampling of 141 teachers in south-central Michigan with an instrument consisting of 55 names of theorists, researchers, and authorities in cognitive and developmental psychology, learning theory, linguistics, language acquisiton, reading, writing, and literary experience and response, with instructions or circle the names recognized, identify their field or specialty, and give the title or subject of the book or article read. He found that respondents on the average recognized only three names, identified fewer than two, and had read or were familiar with the works of less than one. Commenting on his results, Burhans says they:

suggest that teachers in general and English teachers in particular do little professional reading, at least not in reading, writing, literary response, and related fields. The conclusion seems inescapable: Where these basic activities are involved, most teachers, including English teachers, are teaching from obsolete information and knowledge by unsupported and often discredited methods. (p. 95).

THE INDIRECT IMPACT OF THEORY AND RESEARCH

In a paper presented at the Third International Conference on the Teaching of English, Garth Boomer (1982) attempts to assess the impact of research on classroom practice during the 15 years beginning in 1966. On the basis of approximately 150 interviews with experienced secondary English teachers seeking promotion to the position of "faculty head" in Australian schools, Boomer makes the following generalizations:

- It is rare for a teacher to be able to engage in detailed debate about the significance of advances in our understanding of language learning.

- Teachers may have heard of Britton, Barnes, Moffett and Halliday, but few have read them (apart from the odd quotations). Fewer still have the ability to discuss in detail the implications of the work of these people for English reading.

- While many have been exposed to language theory in their preservice education, it seems that most have not retained what they did in such a way that it can inform and shape their classroom practice. Attempts to revive memories usually result in vague references.

- When challenged to become engaged in consideration of theories and research, most teachers will unashamedly, some aggressively, say that they are essentially practitioners and question the usefulness of the theorists.

- Teachers are able to talk reasonably fluently on topics and slogans which have currency (Language Across the Curriculum; "Remedial" Reading; Streaming; Course Books; "Back to Basics"). Their talk is informed by praxis and discussion with colleagues rather than by reading or attendance at courses.

- Central curriculum guides are not well known in most schools. They may have been read superficially but they do not provide a continuing reference point.

- There are outstanding examples of teachers with a well-articulated personal theory of English teaching, but, by and large, teachers are operating, effectively or not, on implicit notions. (pp. 140–141)

Included in the significant influences on the English teacher, in addition to theories and research, are political ideology, economic change, societal myths, professional habits, past study, textbooks, colleagues, administrators, parents, students, and so forth. Boomer sees "the umbrella of western/national/state politics and 'ruling' ideology along with economic (therefore technological and social) structure" as the chief determiner of the "force field" within which English teaching is contained. In harmony with this "macro" umbrella, he sees an equally significant "micro control" coming from the individual's "political/ethical profile." He says, "Many of the values and beliefs embedded in the macro structure are implicit and tend to be reproduced unobtrusively from era to era, decade to decade, as part of the 'hidden curriculum' of culture" (p. 134).

A subset of what Boomer calls "these all-embracing habits" includes the influence of colleagues and students, along with textbooks and examinations. He sees these influences as "second order" forces. New theories and research are ranked at a "third order" level, along with the influence of the teacher's professional training, curriculum guides, conferences, community groups, and school administrators. Boomer recognizes that there is room for debate about the relative significance of these factors, and he acknowledges that his assessment is largely subjective. But he says that he can call upon some aspects of his own research and the research of others to support the relatively low status which he ascribes to research. He does not, however, offer this as an argument for the discontinuation of research. He says, "My conception of research is that it is a crucial component in the various conversations of teachers, and of society, aspects of which conversations will eventually become part of the established mythos and thereby exert considerable influence indirectly on the course of education" (p. 136).

Although he ranks research and theory as a "third order" influence, he does not thereby discount the significance of that influence. It is his view that "liberated" teachers must have developed an "articulated set of principles and theories to justify, explain and inform what they do" (p. 141). While this set of principles may be articulated by teachers examining their own practice and reflecting upon it, these teachers would benefit from the challenge of engaging with the minds of theorists and philosophers who bring new perspectives. Since researchers are part of the "ecological system," what they do changes the balance of the system in some way. What Boomer does not find is evidence of many *direct* relationships between researchers and teacher. Textbooks which attempt to take account of emerging theories are cited as one example of relatively direct influence on practice, but in general, "there seems to be a more subtle and probably more powerful dissemination process at work" (p. 141).

Boomer attempts to explain this process by comparing researchers and theorists with story tellers whose "yarns eventually become part of the mythos of a culture" (p. 141). In his view, during the period under consideration,

English teachers in varying degrees and sometimes in partisan factions have come under the spell of certain powerful weavers of tales. It is not the details of the research, the ins and outs of the plot, which remain with teachers; it is the ruling metaphors or frames of mind, the ideas, which have somehow caught their imagination and inspired them to be better teachers than they are. The story tellers are, of course, not just theorists and researchers. Politicians, principals, religious leaders, playwrights, and teachers themselves can claim the conch shell if their story is generative or compelling enough. (p. 141)

"What catches fire," he says, "depends on the present state of the 'eco' system of ideas and practice." Furthermore, it depends on "the ethical/political profile, the established frame of mind of those who listen to the story." It is Boomer's belief that, "Theory does not catch on because it is true but rather because it vibrates positively and sympathetically with the growing intuitions and beliefs of the teacher." Consequently, "Research which threatens the deep-seated personal constructs of a teacher will be rejected or not heard" (p. 141). This belief is the basis for Boomer's hypothesis that the most influential figures in research and theory in English teaching are the "metaphor makers." His list of top metaphor makers includes Noam Chomsky, Lev Vygotsky, Susanne Langer, George Mead, Michael Halliday, Jerome Bruner, and Basil Bernstein. He says, "These people tell stories in their own right but most have come to influence English teachers through superb intermediaries, story tellers . . ." (p. 142).

Boomer is ultimately quite optimistic about the impact of research. Although he qualifies his comments by allowing that he may be deluding himself, he identifies four areas in which, as a result of research activity, "English teaching will never be the same again" (p. 142). The four areas are discussed under these headings: Language Learning, Fiction and Culture, Function and Form, and Class and Control.

Boomer associates the notion of language as a resource for personal growth, popularized by John Dixon (1967) in *Growth Through English,* with George Kelly's conception of the way the human mind works. Kelly's conception of "the human being as born scientist hypothesizing about the world and acting on these hypotheses" (p. 142) inspired much of the work of James Britton. Vygotsky's work has helped to show the links between language and thinking, and Bruner and the cognitive psychologists have helped to clarify the role of various media of symbolic representation in human learning. He refers to Frank Smith, Kenneth Goodman, James Britton, James Moffett, John Dixon, and Douglas Barnes as the "popular storytellers," whose "stories" have been realized in changing pedagogy in English classrooms. "Directly or indirectly through the work of people such as Britton and Barnes," he says, "enlightened English teachers are providing more time and opportunity for student talk and interim formulation of thought in writing" (p. 143).

Although less sure about the origins of metaphors in the area of Fiction and Culture and their effects on classroom practice, Boomer asserts that there is an emerging new picture of literature as a "fundamental human activity." He credits Susanne Langer and others with the enlargement of our conception of literature: "Whenever human beings begin to construct an image of life, a fiction, then they are using the 'literary' function of language" (p. 143). Harold Rosen and others have encouraged the extension of the range of literature used in classrooms. "At its best," Boomer says, "this influence on English teaching has led to less precious teaching of literature, more vigorous making of literature and more intensive meaning of literature to unearth cultural and political meaning as well as plot" (p. 144).

Michael Halliday's conception of human beings learning language in social interaction within the context of culture has encouraged teachers to take more seriously both the form and function of language. This conception emphasizes the meaning of language, and its influence can be seen in classrooms where children are becoming their own researchers into the language of the community and the classroom. "Study of the language, in this way," Boomer says, "inevitably leads children to consider the appropriateness of language to situation, the falsity of the notions of correctness, and the effect of relative status of participants on language exchange" (p. 144).

Regardless of the merit of Basil Bernstein's early work on restricted and elaborated codes in language, Boomer thinks Bernstein has been an influential metaphor maker. He has led English teachers to look closely at the way language is used as a means of control: "He has forced us to consider the 'middle classness' of schools and the effect which this has on the language and learning of those who have learnt alternative values and styles of meaning exchange" (p. 144). His work has helped discredit the view of the underachieving child as a deficient language user.

In an article published in *Research in the Teaching of English,* James Squire (1976) challenges the "myth" that research has had little or no impact on the nature and quality of education. In spite of the fact that there are no examples of research providing overnight solutions to educational problems, he says "it can be clearly demonstrated that on the long, hard, never-ending trail to improvement of education, research does play an important role" (p. 63). The evidence for the significant impact of research in education can be found, not in direct and dramatic one-to-one relationships between research findings and subsequent changes in practice, but in "the slower, long-range effects that shape and influence the direction of change in curriculum and instruction" (p. 63).

As an example of the long-range effects of research on practice, Squire cites the field of elementary reading. The basal reader approach to the teaching of reading, which dominated the field until newer research identified its deficiencies and suggested other approaches, can be traced to studies done by Arthur Gates in the early 1920s. Gates found that the "teach, practice, and test" sequence could be organized in instructional materials that were more effective than the "helter-skelter" approaches current at that time. "Refined and improved by William W. Grey and David Russell, among others, incorporating findings by Thorndike and his colleagues on vocabulary control," Squire says,

this 'basal' approach became the most wide-spread approach to the teaching of reading for three or four decades during a period when college and school resources for teacher education were sorely limited and a large majority of elementary-school teachers lacked the professional certification required today. (p. 64)

Another example cited by Squire is illustrative of the potential influence of a body of independent studies undertaken over a long period of time. Collectively, the numerous studies of reading interests of young people have influenced curriculum choices made by teachers, librarians, and textbook publishers. Although no single study in this category may seem impressive, "taken together they tend to yield similar findings with respect to differences in taste and reader response associated with age, sex, social and cultural differences" (p. 64). Consequently, these studies have had an obvious impact on the literature taught in schools.

These examples of the long-range effects of research and the collective impact of related studies are supportive of Squire's belief that:

the most apparent influence results over the long run from the continued impact of a large number of related studies that seem to point in the same direction, studies that tend to change the attitudes of educational leaders and ultimately teachers, studies that ultimately become translated into practical, manageable ideas, techniques, or materials that seem to assist the teacher in the classroom or result in classroom experiences which support the teacher's role. (p. 64)

THEORY AND PRACTICE IN THE TEACHING OF LITERATURE

The history of literature in the schools, as traced by Arthur Applebee (1974) in his *Tradition and Reform in the Teaching of English,* shows that changes in theory have been followed by changes in practice. Taught variously for its moral, ethical, and

cultural content and its disciplinary and esthetic values, literature had by the turn of the century gained a prominent place in the English curriculum. After the revolt against college domination of the high school program, there was a rejection of the analytic approach to literary studies, with instructional approaches "moving instead toward an emphasis on the work as a whole, and of the ideas or values embodied in it" (p. 55). Commenting on the 1917 *Reorganization of English in Secondary Schools,* Applebee says, "The main points discussed in the report paralleled those that had prominence in the professional literature. The justifications for literary studies fall into three categories—cultural, vocational, social and ethical" (p. 66). Excellence of style was to be subordinated to social value of content and power to arouse interest. The course was to be structured around expressional and interpretive experiences of social value to students. The report provided two reading lists for each grade level, one of books for class work and one for individual reading. The distribution of works was planned to correspond to the emotional and intellectual stages of the students. The 12th-grade course, organized chronologically, included both American and British literature.

During the decades between the first and second World Wars, the search for a new and coherent framework for teaching English led to elaboration of the metaphors of "experience" and "exploration" as the heart of the educational process. The emphasis on experience led to the treatment of literature as a vicarious experience of events. Acceptance of the idea of vicarious experience involved judgments of the moral content of literary works and led to problems for progressive teachers who wished to include works of contemporary authors in their courses. These problems called attention to the need for new techniques of literary criticism. Applebee cites the reformulation provided by Llewellyn Jones in which the emphasis on experience was continued without a direct relationship with values; experience was dependent on form rather than content. In Applebee's words:

This analysis provided teachers with the ideal solution of the problem of twentieth century literature. Its emphasis on experience continued the easy link with the methodological and philosophical proposals of Kilpatrick and Dewey. At the same time, by substituting intellectual order for moral value it justified the approaches of the new authors. The process of assimilation was not easy, especially for teachers in whom the previous approaches were thoroughly ingrained, but the direction was at least clear. Increasingly during the twenties and throughout the thirties, discussions of literature were phrased in terms of the experience which the work under study would provide. (p. 112)

Rather than becoming a developed critical approach, however, experience was "the underlying goal toward which the various approaches were oriented." Applebee mentions Sterling A. Leonard's use of literary types to structure a high school course that would group together "experiences presenting similar sorts of difficulties in reading and interpretation," as well as Mabel Irene Rich's 1921 anthology organized by types. Teachers who valued understanding of the social and cultural milieu in which literary works originated supported historical studies, and those "whose concern were more directly pedagogical turned to the instructional unit as the major way to insure that students would achieve a proper 'experience' " (p. 112).

Although the movement toward literature as experience remained a movement away from the formal study of literature, support for the movement was not unanimous, and advocates of other emphases continued to speak out. Applebee cites the 1919 convention address of NCTE president Joseph M. Thomas in which he acknowledged the criticism that had been directed to earlier forms of literary study but went on to argue that their shortcomings were no reason to abandon the great tradition of literature. There were calls for discipline, concentration, and "intellectual courage," which were really arguments for a return to mental discipline and attention to great books.

The experience approach was given added impetus, however, by the NCTE Curriculum Commission's *An Experience Curriculum in English* (1935), which was intended as a pattern for schools to use in developing their own curricula. Units lasting from 5 to 15 days, themselves organized into "experience strands" were taken as the basic element around which to structure the curriculum. In the literature component emphasis was placed on pupils' experiences, using informal discussion to broaden horizons and refine perception. Potentially harmful experiences were to be excluded. In his critique, Applebee says,

In spite of the rhetoric, the units do not in any significant way lead to—and were not meant to lead to—important experiences through literature. What they do attempt is to provide the functional skills that were considered prerequisite to the actual experience of literature. The experiences that are offered, on the kindest judgment, are better than the earliest philological approaches; but they are artificial and lifeless in their own way. (pp. 120–121)

For evidence of the extent to which classroom procedures were influenced by new theoretical concerns, Applebee cites Dora V. Smith's (1933) monograph prepared as part of the National Survey of Secondary Education and her 1939 *English Journal* article, "Implications of the New York Regents' Inquiry for the Teaching of English." In the National Survey, she found a mix of traditional and progressive approaches to instruction. She found evidence of provision for individual differences of learners and widespread use of the unit method of instruction, which she believed was beneficial in helping teachers concentrate on the literary work as a whole. While philological analysis of texts had given way to broader discussions, a great deal of time continued to be devoted to the study of single texts. Although she noted a trend toward wider individual reading in some states, she found little evidence that this was the dominant practice. The main alternative she found to organization by lists of classics was the study of types or genres, which at least some teachers were able to handle "without undue stress on form and technique."

In the New York study, Smith found that the movement toward wide or extensive reading had been curtailed by the economic depression, but she saw evidence of a "wholesome emphasis" on literary selections themselves rather than emphasis on facts about authors and literary periods. In general, newer instructional approaches, such as the project method and small group work, were not widely used and attention to individual needs was limited. Although New York had adopted a liberal statewide course of study, a majority of teachers reported that textbooks, rather than the course of study, determined what went on in classrooms.

A more intensive survey conducted some 30 years later by Squire and Applebee (1968) showed that an average of 52 percent of class time in the schools observed was devoted to the study of literature. As in the Smith study, classes were devoted largely to lectures and recitation. Single anthologies were still widely used, but often supplemented by paperbacks. More than half of the teachers rated close textual study as being of great importance, but evidence of its widespread use was not obvious. Selections chosen for study were more "literary" than during the life adjustment era, but the threat of censorship restricted the use of some major twentieth century-works.

In addition to her observation of classroom procedures, Smith (1933) looked at the qualifications of English teachers, and her findings emphasize the importance of teacher education programs, as well as the availability of good textbooks in the implementation of an effective instructional program in English. Smith's concern that the teacher preparation gave too little attention to the literary interests of high school students had earlier led her to organize a course in literature for adolescents as part of the teacher–training program at the University of Minnesota. When adolescent needs emerged as a focal point of the curriculum during the 1940's, the instructional uses of literatue addressing interests peculiar to adolescents received widespread attention. Dwight Burton, one of Smith's students and later editor of *English Journal,* became a leader in the movement to legitimize such literature in school programs in the 1950s. Such books as *The Yearling, The Diary of Anne Frank,* and *The Catcher in the Rye* began to receive serious attention from teachers (Applebee, 1974, p. 156).

What the experience metaphor had failed to accomplish for teaching literature in the schools was perhaps more nearly achieved by means of the exploration metaphor. In *Literature as Exploration,* Louise M. Rosenblatt (1938) recognized the central importance of experience through literature, but she did not accept the premise of the Curriculum Commission that the teacher's attention should focus primarily on experiences *with* literature. She concluded that none of the current ways of using literature were likely to lead to a personal response on the part of a reader, and it was the intimate personal response of the student rather than the content of the literary work that should be the concern of the teacher. Ability to respond maturely to progressively more complex writings was, in her view, more important than ability to distinguish among various literary forms. Rosenblatt's instructional approach was student-centered, emphasizing group discussion and exchange of ideas. She recognized the need for individuals to learn "the various superstructures of ideas, emotions, modes of behavior, moral values" of their particular society and the potential of literature to illustrate the various ways of life open to an individual reader. What she proposed was not just a continuation of the tradition of prescriptive character building by providing models of human behavior to imitate. In Applebee's words:

The new view of the teaching of literature would help the student to experience many models, good and bad, and to learn to deal critically and intellectually with the emotional reactions they would necessarily arouse. It was truly to be, in terms of her title, an *exploration* of the reader's own nature, during which he would gradually "become aware of potentialities for thought and feeling within himself, acquire clearer perspective, develop aims and a sense of direction." Viewed in this way, literature had a "very real, and even central" role in the "social and cultural life of a democracy"; it was to engender the cultural patterns and modes of behavior that would control that society's future. (pp. 124–125)

Although the immediate impact of Rosenblatt's *Literature as Exploration* on classroom practice may have been less than revolutionary, the long-range influence has been considerable. The third edition of the book was issued in 1968, and the reader's response to literature, which she emphasized, has been the topic of numerous studies (e.g., Squire, 1964; Wilson, 1966; Purves and Rippere, 1968; Cooper, 1969; and Galda, 1982). Buttressed by the work of Norman Holland (1968), David Bleich (1975), Wolfgang Iser (1978), and Stanley Fish (1980), the role of individual response in the teaching of literature has come to be widely recognized by English educators. Illustrative of efforts to heighten English teachers' awareness of the importance of the individual reader's response is a recent *English Journal* article by Robert E. Probst (1986). In answer to the question, "Can young adult literature work with modern critical theory?" he says:

Teachers persuaded by the visions of literature and reading proposed by such theorists as Rosenblatt and Iser might begin by searching for books likely to create the tensions that will lead to active, involved reading, books that, by presenting students with differences in perceptions and values, will provoke them into committed reading. (pp. 35–36)

Probst goes on to explain how Normal Klein's (1972) *Mom, the Wolf Man and Me* can be presented to students in a way to encourage individual response and discussion. "However teachers manage to initiate the talk," he says, "the purpose is not to reach consensus, to agree upon an interpretation or an assessment of the work." "Rather," he goes on to say, "the purpose is for individuals to work out their own readings, to create out of the text literary works that are appropriate and satisfying for the readers" (p. 37). At the end of the article is a selected bibliography to guide teachers in their further reading on literary theory and related topics.

A recent NCTE publication, *Literature in the Classroom: Readers, Texts, and Contexts,* edited by Ben F. Nelms (1988), has as one of its objectives to "Relate the teaching of literature to current modes of literary criticism and to reader-response theory." The chapters on interpretive approaches to literature include references to Fish (1980), Bleich (1975), Iser (1980), Rosenblatt (1978), Barthes (1971), Scholes (1985), and Fetterly (1978), and the fact that 10 of the 23 authors are classroom teachers might suggest that newer critical approaches are being widely used in the schools. (See, also, the chapters in this handbook by Rosenblatt and Probst.)

If the survey reported by Ellis (1987) is representative, however, the reality may be otherwise. He observed 93 classes, grades 9–12, in five Georgia schools. Using a grid to record the results of direct classroom observation, he found that two thirds (ranging from just over half to more than four fifths) of instruc-

tional time in literature classes was focused on basic factual information. Inferential/interpretive matters occupied less than one fourth of class time, and application of literature content to contemporary experience took less than one tenth of class time. While no claim is made for total representation, the sample was selected to include diversity of student ability, demographic features, and geographic dispersal throughout the state. Similar surveys in other states might yield different results, but one suspects that the application of teaching methods growing out of newer critical approaches to literature have yet to be widely adopted by classroom teachers.

THEORY AND PRACTICE IN THE TEACHING OF LANGUAGE

In the area of language teaching, the application of research findings has been uneven. On the one hand, negative results of studies of the practical value of grammar study have been widely rejected or ignored. On the other hand, studies of the value of sentence combining exercises derived from transformational-generative grammar have led to their acceptance in many schools.

As early as 1906, Franklin S. Hoyt reported a low statistical correlation between knowledge of grammar and skills in reading and writing and consequently questioned the place of grammar in the elementary school curriculum. His study was replicated by Louis W. Rapeer (1913) with similar results. The NCTE Curriculum Commission (1935), in *An Experience Curriculum in English,* recommended that since "there is no scientific evidence of the value of grammar which warrants its appearance as a prominent or even distinct feature of the course of study" (p. 228), formal grammar should be restricted to an elective course at the high school level. This elective course would be "designed to present systematic and logical grammar to those high-school seniors who presumably will enjoy it and profit by it." It was not to be "practical" or "functional," nor "prescriptive" grammar, but rather "grammar as a body of classified knowledge about language" (p. 289). Nearly three decades later in their comprehensive review of research in written composition, Braddock, Lloyd-Jones, and Schoer (1963) stated in "strong and unqualified terms" that "the teaching of formal grammar has a negligible or, because it usually displaces some instruction and practice in actual composition, even a harmful effect on the improvement of writing" (p. 38).

Despite the weight of research evidence, however, many educators have refused to give up their emphasis on grammar, and numerous studies have been carried out in the attempt to find evidence to prove its value. With the development of the newer linguistics-based grammars, these efforts received additional impetus. White (1965) compared the effects of teaching structural linguistics, the effects of teaching traditional school grammar, and the effects of teaching no grammar to 7th-graders. The structural linguistics group scored higher than the others on the STEP Writing and Essay Tests and on teacher assigned themes, but the only significant difference was on the STEP Writing Test, which does not involve an acutal writing sample. The effects of generative versus traditional grammar were studied by Harter (1978), working with 7th-graders, Davenport

(1971) with 9th-graders, and Fry (1972) with junior high school students. None of these researchers found significant differences in writing quality of the students in the comparison groups.

One of the more recent, and more carefully executed, studies of the role of grammar in the secondary school English curriculum was done by Elley, Barham, Lamb, and Wyllie (1976) in New Zealand. They examined the effects of three courses of study: one emphasizing the transformational grammar (TG) strand developed in the Oregon Curriculum (Kitzhaber, 1970), one with extra reading and writing in lieu of grammar in the Reading-Writing (RW) course of the Oregon Curriculum, and one based on Smart's (1969) *Let's Learn English in the 70's,* with an emphasis on traditional school grammar. Their main purpose was "to determine the direct effects of a study of transformational grammar on the language growth of secondary school pupils." Their results showed that the effects were negligible.

Similarly, those pupils who studied a course containing elements of traditional grammar showed no measurable benefits. The RW group, who studied no formal grammar for three years, demonstrated competence in writing and related language skills fully equal to that shown by the two grammar groups. After two years, no differences were detected in writing performance or language competence; after three years, small differences appeared in some minor conventions of·usage favoring the TG group, but these were more than offset by the less positive attitudes which they showed towards their English studies. No differences were found in the School Certificate English results of the three groups, nor in a follow-up exercise twelve months later. (pp. 17–18)

The authors go on to say: "It is difficult to escape the conclusion that English grammar, whether traditional or transformational, has virtually no influence on the language growth of typical secondary school students" (p. 18). Even so, grammar continues to have a prominent place in English textbooks, many teachers continue to devote a great deal of time to attempts to teach it, and school critics continue to blame teachers who question the value of grammar.

Research studies on sentence combining and construction completed since the mid-1960s are reviewed in Hillock's (1986) *Research on Written Composition.* He identifies Hunt's (1965) study of grammatical structures at three grade levels as a major impetus for a pedagogy designed to help students increase the length of their syntactic structures. Hunt found a steady increase in number of words per terminable syntactic unit (T-unit) from grade 4 to grade 8 to grade 12 and suggested the possibility of a curriculum designed to deliberately hasten syntactic growth. Drawing on the theory of transformational grammar, he showed how many of the longer units could be accounted for as combinations of simpler structures. Exercises combining simple structures could possibly enhance the process of syntactic growth. In Mellon's (1969) study, sentence combining exercises were used to help students understand the structures taught in transformational grammar. Mellon predicted that knowledge of concepts of transformational grammar reinforced by concrete application to sentence combining problems would result in more complex or "mature" syntactic structures in student writing. Using Hunt's T-unit as a measure of complexity, he found evidence to support his hypothesis.

The pedagogical use of sentence combining exercises was further encouraged by the results of O'Hare's (1973) study. Hypothesizing that gains similar to those achieved by Mellon could be obtained without using the terminology of transformational grammar, O'Hare devised a series of sentence combining problems for an experiment with seventh grade students. He reported that his seventh-graders at the end of the experiment wrote well beyond the syntactic maturity level of those in a control group and in some respects at a level similar to that of the 12th-graders in Hunt's study. Furthermore, he claimed that the experimental students wrote compositions of superior quality.

Other studies that have reported significant gains in quality of student writing, along with increases in T-unit and clause length, are those by Combs (1976), Pedersen (1978), Stewart (1978), and Daiker, Kerek, and Morenberg (1978). These studies represent a range of grade levels, including the freshman year of college. Other studies have found evidence that disadvantaged or remedial students especially benefit from work with sentence combining exercises (Hunt & O'Donnell, 1970; Perron, 1975; Schuster, 1977). Kerek, Daiker, and Morenberg (1980) make an additional claim for the instructional value of these exercises:

Sentence combining instruction helps build confidence because it is positive in approach, it emphasizes the learning of new skills rather than the avoidance of old errors, and it subordinates every other course consideration to students' writing. After a semester of sentence combining, students usually feel better about their writing. (p. 1151)

Other studies cited by Hillocks include those of Schuster (1976), whose experimental groups exhibited fewer errors in mechanics and usage in their posttest essays than in their pretest essays, and Obenchain (1979), who also found a reduction in errors. Countering these studies are those of Maimon and Nodine (1978), who reported that sentence combining practice produced more errors on a rewriting passage, and Hake and Williams (1979), who reported a higher "flaw count" with increased length of T-units. They also reported that students whose pretest and posttest compositions were judged incompetent increased the length of their T-units, while those whose posttest compositions showed significant improvement decreased their mean T-unit length.

Although these findings undoubtedly provide a basis for questions about the efficacy of instruction in sentence combining, it should be recognized that syntactic complexity in and of itself is not meritorious and that errors made by writers seeking a higher level of proficiency may be signs of growth rather than regression. Researchers and critics alike have sometimes seemed to overlook the fact that complexity is only one aspect of syntactic maturity and that syntactic maturity is only one facet of linguistic maturity (See O'Donnell, 1973, for elaboration of this point).

Commenting on the mixed results of the various studies, Hillocks says "It would appear that increased mean T-unit or clause length for an individual is *not* necessarily an indication of increased quality for that individual, despite findings that show increased syntactic maturity for groups to be a concomitant of increased quality" (pp. 148–149). Given the complexity of the interaction of syntactic and semantic factors with various rhetorical considerations, that conclusion should not be surprising. An observation recorded before many of the sentence combining experiments were conducted still seems pertinent:

What is needed is a program of instruction that would on the one hand increase the student's repertoire of syntactic structures, and on the other hand sharpen his awareness of syntactic options. . . . Ability to use syntax appropriately and effectively has to be developed in situations requiring the effective and appropriate use of language. Therefore, it is more the province of rhetoric than grammar. The point to be noted is that knowledge of how to construct a variety of sentences can be an asset to the student who is striving for effective expression. (O'Donnell, 1972, p. 349)

While it may be true that some advocates of sentence combining have overstated their case, it is also true, as Charles Cooper (1975) observed, that "no other single teaching approach has ever consistently been shown to have a beneficial effect on syntactic maturity and writing quality" (p. 72).

Unlike the earlier studies on the effects of teaching traditional grammar, these studies on sentence combining have had an impact on the contents of English textbooks. Examples include such diverse texts as *Building English Skills,* published by McDougal and Littel (1985), and Wariner's (1986) *English Grammar and Composition,* published by Harcourt Brace Jovanovich. Since the textbook is one of the most influential determinants of what is taught in school, it seems reasonable to conclude that research on the effects of sentence-combining exercises is one of the most obvious examples of research that has influenced classroom practice.

THEORY AND PRACTICE IN THE TEACHING OF COMPOSITION

The impact of theory and research on the teaching of written composition is explored by Arthur N. Applebee (1986) in the 85th yearbook of the National Society for the Study of Education. He describes the traditional approach to writing instruction in American schools as "prescriptive and product-centered":

At the sentence level, instruction has emphasized correct usage and mechanics; at the text level, it has emphasized the traditional modes of discourse (narration, description, exposition, persuasion, and sometimes poetry). In this approach, instruction usually consists of analyzing classic examples of good form, learning the rules that govern those classic examples, and practicing following the rules (either in exercises of limited scope or by imitating the classic models). In turn, success in writing has been measured by the ability to incorporate those rules into one's own writing. (p. 95)

During the past two decades there have been efforts to shift from the traditional approach to "process approaches" in writing instruction. These approaches, in general, are characterized by instructional activities designed to help students think through and organize their ideas before they write and "to rethink and revise their initial drafts." In more detail, Applebee says:

Instructional activities typically associated with process approaches include brainstorming, journal writing, focus on the students' ideas and experiences, small-group activities, teacher/student conferences, the provision of audiences other than the teacher, emphasis on multiple drafts, postponement of attention to editing skills until the final draft, and elimination or deferment of grading. For convenience in instruction, process activities are often partitioned into stages such as prewriting, drafting, revising, and editing, usually with the caveat that the processes are recursive rather than linear, complex rather than simple. (pp. 95–96)

Although he offers little empirical evidence to support his view, Applebee sees the current emphasis on process-oriented approaches as a clear instance of research driving practice. He credits Janet Emig's (1971) examination of the writing processes of 8 high school seniors as the seminal work from which similar studies "emphasizing the essentially heuristic, problem-solving nature of writing about new material" have sprung. General findings of these studies include the following:

1. Writing involves a number of recursively operating subprocesses (for example, planning, monitoring, drafting, revising, editing) rather than a linear sequence.
2. Expert and novice writers differ in their use of those subprocesses.
3. The processes vary depending upon the nature of the task. (p. 96)

More recent process-oriented studies cited by Applebee have suggested that the processes also vary depending on the instructional context (Dyson, 1984), personal history (Florio, 1979), and the writer's knowledge of the topic (Langer, 1984). He says, "The journal literature for the past decade has been dominated by suggestions on how such approaches can be best implemented, and influential programs such as the National Writing Project have helped make the works of such scholars as Emig [1971], Britton [1970], and Moffett [1968] more widely known" (p. 97).

The use of electronic word processors as a means of achieving instruction goals in written composition has been investigated in several research studies. The work of Bradley (1982), Daiute (1982), Whithey (1983), and others is reviewed by Fagan and Detterbeck (1988). They view word processing as a natural vehicle for teaching writing as a process, and identify several benefits resulting from the use of word processors in writing instruction. Among these are ease in editing, pride in accomplishment, immediate reinforcement of student interaction, and active involvement in learning.

In view of the growing acceptance of process-oriented writing instruction and the accumulation of research and practical knowledge about writing processes, Applebee addresses the success of process approaches against three criteria: "(a) How widely have they been adopted? (b) When adopted, how successfully are they implemented? and (c) When implemented, do they lead to noticeable improvement in students' writing?" (p. 97).

Although process approaches are dominant in professional literature, there is apparently the usual gap between educational theory and practice. In Applebee's (1981) study of the status of writing instruction in secondary schools, he found no evidence of a widespread movement toward process-oriented assignments. The typical pattern of instruction followed by teachers was to give an assignment, have the students complete it, and comment extensively on the finished product. Prewriting activities were limited and few papers went beyond the first draft. Peer response groups, editing sessions, deferment of grading, etc., were found in the minority of classrooms. The findings of the National Assessment of Educational Progress (1980) were similar: less than 10 percent of the 17-year-olds in this study were engaged in the full range of process-oriented activities. In his examination of elementary school instruction, Graves (1978) also found little evidence of process-oriented writing instruction; in fact, there were few writing activities of any sort.

In answering the question of how successfully process approaches are implemented when transferred from laboratory to classroom, Applebee reports findings of a series of studies done by him and Judith Langer (Applebee & Langer, 1982). Planned as a way to develop a series of models of effective instruction, as well as a way to provide evidence of the effectiveness of process-oriented writing instruction, the studies actually resulted instead in the identification of "some serious problems in current conceptualizations of writing processes" (Applebee, 1986, p. 102). There is an evident conflict between the institutional forces shaping instruction and the values in process-oriented instruction in writing. Applebee says:

Process instruction takes time, which must come at the expense of other activities; process instruction stresses the student's role as author with something of value to say, reducing the teacher's role as transmitter of information; and process instruction focuses on the skills needed in the context of particular activities, rather than as part of a separate curriculum organized around the logic of the subject matter. (p. 104)

In answering the question, "Does process-oriented instruction improve students' writing?" Applebee cites George Hillocks' (1984) meta-analysis of experimental studies published between 1963 and 1982. The four broad approaches described by Hillocks are:

a. Traditional, product-oriented, teacher-centered instruction,
b. Individualized instruction,
c. Natural process instruction, and
d. The environmental mode of instruction.

The "natural process" is further described as student-centered, activity-based, and process-oriented, and the "environmental mode" as a structured approach often involving inquiry-based learning and group problem solving.

Disputing Hillocks' interpretation of the data as evidence that process-oriented instruction is less effective than the alternatives, Applebee believes the data provide support for the effectiveness of process-oriented instruction. The difference lies in their contrasting classifications of the "environmental mode," which Applebee sees as a version of process-oriented instruction. He thinks "environmental" instruction might better be labeled "structured process" in contrast to "natural process." Thus, in Applebee's opinion, Hillocks' meta-analysis reinforces the view that process-oriented approaches to instruction offer many advantages over traditional, product-oriented modes of instruction.

Although Applebee finds that process-oriented approaches have not been as widely adopted nor as successfully implemented as one might wish, he thinks the evidence of their effectiveness is convincing. It is his contention that "writing processes in general, and the nature of process-oriented instruction in particular, have been underconceptualized." He says, "In the first flush of enthusiasm, process-oriented instruction was embraced simplistically and naively; in the next wave of reform, we must carry it toward a more sophisticated maturity" (p. 97). Although there have been significant developments in theory and research in writing (e.g., Kinneavy, 1971; Graves, 1975) and in dissemination of information about the teaching of writing (Gray & Myers, 1978), more research, as well as better implementation of theory in classroom practice, is needed. (Much of this recent research is reflected in the articles in this handbook written by Kinneavy, Hausen and Graves, and Dyson and Freedman.)

CONCLUSION

Theory and research in literature, language, and composition have definitely had a positive impact on the teaching of English, but in order to achieve maximum impact on classroom practice, theory has to become a part of the "lore" of the times; it must work its way into the "ecological system." The path followed in doing that is seldom direct. Given the reading interests and habits of teachers, it is not realistic to expect that a newly formulated theory will be tested by research and immediately implemented as a result of publication in a research journal. The more likely progression is through the professional literature read by students in preservice and in-service training programs, reinforced by new concepts incorporated in the textbooks used daily in the classrooms. Thus, it is likely that there will always be a gap between theory and practice. Even so, Squire's (1976) assertion that research "has made a difference, does make a difference, and will make a difference" still rings true.

References

Applebee, A. N. (1974). *Tradition and reform in the teaching of English: A history.* Urbana, IL: National Council of Teachers of English.

Applebee, A. N. (1981). *Writing in the secondary school: English and the content areas* (Report No. 21). Urbana, IL: National Council of Teachers of English.

Applebee, A. N. (1986). Problems in process approaches: Toward a Reconceptualization of process instruction. In A. R. Petrosky & D. Bartholemae (Eds.), *The Teaching of Writing,* Eighty-fifth Yearbook of the National Society for the Study of Education, Part II, (pp. 95–113). Chicago: NSSE.

Applebee, A. & Langer, J. (1982). Moving toward excellence: Writing and learning in the secondary school curriculum. (Proposed to the National Institute of Education.) Stanford, CA: Stanford University.

Barthes, R. 91971). The structuralist activity. In H. Adams (Ed.), *Critical Theory Since Plato*. New York: Harcourt Brace Jovanovich.

Bleich, D. (1975). *Readings and feelings*. Urbana, IL: National Council of Teachers of English.

Boomer, G. (1982). The English teacher, research and change (1966–1980). In R. D. Eagleson (Ed.), *English in the Eighties*. Adelaide, Australia: Australian Association for the Teaching of English.

Braddock, R., Lloyd-Jones, R., & Schoer, L. (1963). *Research in Written Composition*. Champaign, IL: National Council of Teachers of English.

Bradley, V. (1982). Improving students' writing with microcomputers. *Language Arts, 59,* 732–743.

Britton, J. N. (1970). *Language and Learning*. Harmondsworth, England: Allen Lane, Penguin Press.

Building English Skills (1985). Evanston, IL: McDougal, Littel & Co.

Burhans, C. S., Jr. (1985). *English teachers and professional reading. English Education, 17*(2), 91–95.

Burton, D. L. (1973). Research in the teaching of English: The Troubled dream. *Research in the Teaching of English, 7*(2), 160–189.

Combs, E. E. (1976). Further effects of sentence-combining practice on writing ability. *Research in the Teaching of English, 10,* 137–149.

Commission on English. (1965). *Freedom and discipline in English*. New York: College Entrance Examination Board.

Cooper, C. R. (1969). *Preferred modes of literary response: The characteristics of high school juniors in relation to the consistency of their reactions to three dissimilar short stories*. Unpublished doctoral dissertation, University of California at Berkeley.

Cooper, C. R. (1975). Research roundup: Oral and written composition. *English Journal, 64,* 72–74.

Curriculum Commission. (1935). *An experience curriculum in English* (English Monograph No. 4, National Council of Teachers of English). New York: D. Appleton-Century Company.

Daiker, D., Kerek, A., & Morenberg, M. (1978). Sentence combining and syntactic maturity in Freshman English. *College Composition and Composition, 29,* 36–41.

Daiute, C. (1982). Writing, creativity and change. *Childhood Education, 59,* 227–231.

Davenport, H. D. (1971). The effects of instruction in generative grammar on the writing ability of students in the ninth grade (Doctoral dissertation). *Dissertation Abstracts International, 31,* 4594-A.

Dixon, J. (1967). *Growth through English*. Reading, England: National Association for the Teaching of English.

Dyson, A. H. (1984). Learning to write/Learning to do school: Emerging writers' interpretations of school literacy tasks. *Research in the Teaching of English, 18,* 233–64.

Elley, W. B., Barham, I. H., Lamb, H., & Wyllie, M. (1976). The role of grammar in a secondary school English curriculum. *Research in the Teaching of English, 10*(1), 5–21.

Ellis, W. G. (1987). What are you teaching? Literature. *English Journal, 76*(3), 108–112.

Emig, J. (1971). *The composing processes of twelfth graders* (Report No. 13). Urbana, IL: National Council of Teachers of English.

Evans, W. H., Walker, J. L. (1966). *New trends in the teaching of English in secondary schools*. Chicago: Rand McNally and Co.

Fagan, E. R. (1972). *Analysis of English Teachers' understanding of research reports in the language arts*. (Report to NCTE Research Foundation). Urbana, IL: National Council of Teachers of English.

Fagan, E. R., & Detterbeck, P. H. (1988). Status report: Micros for word processing. *The English Record, 38*(3), 11–14.

Fetterly, J. (1978). *The resisting reader: A feminist approach to American fiction*. Bloomington: Indiana University Press.

Fish, S. (1980). *Is there a text in this class? The authority of interpretive communities*. Cambridge: Harvard University Press.

Florio, S. (1979). The problem of dead letters: Social perspectives on the teaching of writing. *Elementary School Journal, 80,* 1–7.

Fry, D. J. (1972). The effects of transformational grammar upon the writing performance of students of low socio-economic backgrounds (Doctoral dissertation). *Dissertation Abstracts International, 32,* 4835-A.

Galda, L. (1982). Assuming the spectator stance: An examination of the responses of three young readers. *Research in the Teaching of English, 16,* 1–20.

Graves, D. H. (1975). An examination of the writing processes of seven year old children. *Research in the Teaching of English, 9,* 227–241.

Graves, D. H. (1978). Research update: We won't let them write. *Language Arts, 55,* 635–640.

Gray, J., & Myers, M. (1978). The Bay Area Writing Project. *Phi Delta Kappan, 59,* 410–413.

Hake, R. L., & Williams, J. M. (1979). Sentence expanding: Not can, or how, but when. In D. Daiker, A. Kerek, & M. Morenberg (Eds.), *Sentence combining and the teaching of writing*. Conway, AR: University of Akron and University of Central Arkansas.

Harter, M. T. (1978). A study of the effects of transformational grammar on the writing skills of seventh graders (Doctoral dissertation). *Dissertation Abstracts International, 39,* 2794-A.

Hillocks, G. (1984). What works in teaching composition: A meta-analysis of experimental treatment studies. *American Journal of Education, 93,* 133–170.

Hillocks, G. (1986). *Research on written composition: New directions for teaching*. Urbana, IL: National Council of Teachers of English.

Hipple, T., & Giblin, R. (1971). The professional reading of English teachers in Florida. *Research in the Teaching of English, 5*(2), 153–164.

Holland, N. (1968). *The dynamics of literary response*. New York: Oxford University Press.

Hoyt, F. S. (1906). Grammar in the elementary curriculum. *Teachers College Reocrd, 8,* 467–500.

Hunt, K. W. (1965). *Grammatical structures written three grade levles* (NCTE Research Report No. 3). Champaign, IL: National Council of Teachers of English.

Hunt, K. W., & O'Donnell, R. C. (1970). *An elementary school curriculum to develop better writing skills*. Tallahassee, FL: The Florida State University. (ERIC Document Reproduction Service No. ED 050 108).

Iser, W. (1978). *The act of reading: A theory of aesthetic response*. Baltimore: Johns Hopkins University Press.

Iser, W. (1980). The reading process: A phenomenological approach. In J. Tompkins (Ed.), *Reader-response criticism*. Baltimore: Johns Hopkins University Press.

Kerek, A., Daiker, D. A., & Morenberg, M. (1980). Sentence combining and college composition. *Perceptual and Motor Skills, 51,* 1059–1157.

Kinneavy, J. L. (1971). *A theory of discourse: The aims of discourse*. New York: Norton.

Kitzhaber, A. R. (Ed.). (1970). *The Oregon curriculum: A sequential program in English*. New York: Holt Rinehart & Winston.

Klein, N. (1972). *Mom, the Wolf man, and me*. New York: Pantheon.

Langer, J. A. (1984). The effects of available information on responses to school writing tasks. *Research in the Teaching of English, 18,* 27–44.

Maimon, E. P., & Nodine, B. F. (1978). Measuring syntactic growth: Errors and expectations in sentence-combining practice with college freshmen. *Research in the Teaching of English, 12,* 233–244.

Mellon, J. C. (1969). *Transformational sentence combining: A method for enhancing the development of syntactic fluency in English composition* (NCTE Research Report No. 10). Champaign, IL: National Council of Teachers of English.

Moffett, J. (1968). *Teaching the universe of discourse*. Boston: Houghton Mifflin.

National Assessment of Educational Progress (1980). *Writing achievement, 1969–79, I–III*. Denver, CO: Education Commission of the States.

Nelms, B. F. (Ed.). (1988). *Literature in the classroom: Readers, texts, and contexts*. Urbana, IL: National Council of Teachers of English.

Obenchain, A. (1979). Developing paragraph power through sentence combining. In D. Daiker, A. Kerek, & M. Morenberg (Eds.), *Sentence combining and the teaching of writing* (pp. 3–33). Conway, AR: University of Akron and University of Central Arkansas.

O'Donnell, R. C. (1972). Is grammar really dead? *The Educational Forum, 36*(3), 343–350.

O'Donnell, R. C. (1973). Some aspects of language development in school age children. *The High School Journal, LVI,* 312–317.

O'Hare, F. (1973). *Sentence combining: Improving student writing without formal grammar instruction* (NCTE Research Report No. 15). Urbana, IL: National Council of Teachers of English.

Pedersen, E. L. (1978). Improving syntactic and semantic fluency in writing of language arts students through extended practice in sentence-combining. *Dissertation Abstracts International, 38,* 5892-A.

Perron, J. D. (1975). An exploratory approach to extending the syntactic development of fourth-grade students through the use of sentence-combining methods. *Dissertation Abstracts International, 35,* 4316-A.

Petty, W., Herold, P., & Stoll, E. (1968). *The state of knowledge about the teaching of vocabulary*. Champaign, IL: National Council of Teachers of English.

Probst, R. E. (1986). Mom, Wolfgang and me: Adolescent literature, critical theory, and the English classroom. *English Journal, 75*(6), 33–39.

Purves, A. C., & Beach, R. (1972). *Literature and the reader: Research in response to literature, reading interests, and the teaching of literature*. Urbana, IL: National Council of Teachers of English.

Purves, A. C., & Rippere, V. (1968). *Elements of writing about a literary work: A study of response to literature*. (NCTE Research Report No. 9). Urbana, IL: National Council of Teachers of English.

Rapeer, L. W. (1913). The problem of formal grammar in elementary education. *Journal of Educational Psychology, IV,* 125–137.

Rosenblatt, L. M. (1938). *Literature as Exploration*. New York: Appleton-Century Co.

Rosenblatt, L. M. (1968). *Literature as Exploration* (3rd ed.). New York: Noble and Noble.

Rosenblatt, L. M. (1978). *The reader, the text, the poem*. Carbondale: Southern Illinois University Press.

Scholes, R. (1985). *Textual power: Literary theory and the teaching of English*. New Haven: Yale University Press.

Schuster, E. H. (1977). *Forward to basics through sentence-combining*. Paper presented at the Annual Meeting of the Pennsylvania Council of Teachers of English. (ERIC Document Reproduction Service No. ED 133 774).

Schuster, E. H. (1977). *Using sentence combining to teach writing to inner-city students*. Paper presented at the Annual Meeting of the National Council of Teachers of English. (ERIC Document Reproduction Service No. ED 150 614).

Smart, P. R. (1969). *Let's learn English in the 70's*. Wellington, New Zealand: A. H. & A. W. Reed.

Smith, D. V. (1933). *Instruction in English*. National Survey of Secondary Education (Monograph No. 20). Washington, D.C.: Government Printing Office.

Smith, D. V. (1939). Implications of the New York Regents' Inquiry for the teaching of English. *English Journal, 28*(3), 177.

Squire, J. R. (1964). *The responses of adolescents while reading four short stories* (NCTE Research Report No. 2). Urbana, IL: National Council of Teachers of English.

Squire, J. R. (1976). Research can make a difference. *Research in the Teaching of English, 10*(1), 63–65.

Squire, J. R., & Applebee, R. K. (1968). *High school English instruction today: The national study of high school English programs*. New York: Appleton-Century-Crofts.

Stewart, M. F. (1978). Freshman sentence combining: A Canadian project. *Research in the Teaching of English, 12,* 257–68.

Warriner, J. E. (1986). *Warriner's English Grammar and Composition*. New York: Harcourt Brace Jovanovich.

White, R. H. (1965). The effect of structural linguistics on improving English composition compared to that of prescriptive grammar or the absence of grammar instruction (Doctoral dissertation). *Dissertation Abstracts International, 25,* 5032.

Whithey, M. (1983). The computer & writing, *English Journal,* 24–31.

Wilson, J. R. (1966). *Responses of college freshmen to three novels* (NCTE Research Report No. 7). Urbana, IL: National Council of Teachers of English.

· 9 ·

MAJOR RESEARCH PROGRAMS*

Margaret Early

The purpose of this chapter is to review major research programs from 1960 through 1988 that have influenced the teaching of English language arts either directly (though such influence is not always verified by hard data) or potentially as findings are made known through journals, teacher education courses, professional conferences, curriculum guides, and textbooks. We define as "major programs" research efforts involving numbers of experienced researchers and their assistants working together over extended periods of time in centers or other units based in universities, professional organizations, or private companies and supported by federal, state, or private funding. Research emanating from such programs is long-term, cumulative, and well publicized.

Because our concern is with the impact of research on teaching, we shall look, too, at institutional efforts to disseminate research, such as the Regional Laboratories, selecting those with special emphasis on language arts. Since major research programs have produced many important studies and stimulated many more that are integral to the reviews in other chapters of this handbook, we include in this chapter only studies that have historical significance, illustrate the work of a particular center, or appear to have significant actual or potential impact on teaching.

Because major research programs related to teaching the English language arts must be viewed within the context of larger educational research movements, this chapter inevitably trespasses on matters that are not strictly "English" and not strictly "research." We cannot avoid considering

a. The influence of federal support;
b. The interaction of research with policy-making and curriculum development;
c. The changing philosophies of research and the consequent changes in research methods;
d. The blurring of demarcations between research and theory and application.

In an attempt to present major research programs chronologically, we begin with the influence of federal support, as exemplified in Project English, and try to retain a chronological perspective throughout the chapter. However, the time line snaps intermittently, and the reader is signaled to "see below" or referred to another chapter. For example, the Curriculum Study Centers were being funded by Project English in the same time period that the research and development centers and the regional laboratories were getting started, but this chapter begins with the former and ends with the latter because regional laboratories and R&D Centers are still in operation. In considering that still influential movement in the last section of this chapter, we shall deal also with the other four themes noted at the beginning of this paragraph.

PROJECT ENGLISH

To begin arbitrarily in 1960 is not to suggest that major research programs focused on the teaching of English were unheard of before that date. But the 1960s marked a new beginning. The National Defense Education Act of 1958 was aimed at strengthening instruction in mathematics, science, and foreign languages. The omission of English led the National Council of Teachers of English to lobby vigorously for its inclusion, using among other tactics the publication of 1961 of *The National Interest and the Teaching of English* (Committee on the National Interest, 1961) a compilation of statistics which showed shocking deficiencies in the preparation of English teachers and revealed their lack of confidence in teaching writing and reading. (In the early 1960s, 70 percent of secondary English teachers did not "feel well prepared" to teach writing; 87 percent expressed similar doubts about teaching reading.) It was not until October, 1964, that Congress extended NDEA to include English and reading, but more immediate repercussions from the publication of such statistics included the establishment of Project English by the Cooperative Research Branch of the U.S. Office of Education, the sponsorship of summer institutes for English teachers by the Commission on English of the College Entrance Examination Board (with Educational Testing Service

The author acknowledges the assistance of John Zbikowski (University of Wisconsin, White Water) in the preparation of this chapter.

and federal funds), a research-planning conference funded by the Carnegie Corporation and directed by Louise Rosenblatt, and a review of research on teaching composition sponsored by the NCTE Research Committee and aided by federal funds (Braddock, Lloyd-Jones & Schoer, 1963).

Project English, designed to "sponsor an increasing amount of research and experimentation in the area of English instruction," resulted in 20 curriculum study centers, 6 demonstration centers, some 50 basic research studies, and a series of conferences including one on research needed in teaching English (Steinberg, 1963). At the cost of a few million dollars, Project English, with its emphasis on writing and reading, initiated a surge of research productivity that is with us still. Although we cannot link multiple effects to a single catalyst, we can find in Project English several ideas that propel current research. For example, the curriculum centers brought together teachers in elementary and secondary schools, teacher educators, educatonal psychologists, and scholars in literature and linguistics to identify content, write curricula, and try them out in real classrooms.

The Nebraska Center illustrates a typical collaboration. It was codirected by a professor of literature (Paul Olson) and a high school teacher (Frank Rice), and it produced an integrated K–12 curriculum in literature, language, and composition, which implemented the concept of the unifying force of archetypal patterns across all literature as articulated by a literary critic (Northrop Frye). Classroom teachers were involved from the beginning, though probably to react more often than to initiate. Nebraska's degree of collaboration was perhaps typical; teachers were participants but university professors—subject specialists more than education specialists—dominated the study centers.

The center at Northwestern University illustrates another, to-be-expected characteristic of the study centers: a tendency to translate theory into curricular materials directly, in the absence of supportive research. Ten years before case studies of writers' processes became popular in journal articles and conference papers, the group at Northwestern was producing curriculum materials aimed at developing students' understanding of the writing process and the interaction of style, audience, and situation. Like other centers that took writing as their focus, the scholar-teachers at Northwestern (led by Wallace Douglas) rejected the accepted practice of teaching writing as a body of skills to be applied to teacher-imposed assignments and instead studied composition as a discipline in its own right.

The University of Oregon, the third center to be established, presents another example of the modus operandi of all the study centers. What was to be studied first was content, what was to be delivered were packages of content labeled by grade level and sometimes by "types" of students. Not surprisingly, the shape of the package was the curriculum guide and the textbook, since these were what teachers turned to in deciding what would happen in their classrooms. Making content the first aim of the study centers did not mean that Project English was oblivious to questions of how that content was to be delivered, but funds ran out before the centers could study secondary aims of how students learned from the new materials and how teachers interacted with learners and content. In any case, other agents than the centers would take over the delivery of their products, insuring that the impact was felt in many classrooms even if it was not systematically measured.

Two agents of delivery were ready in the mid-1960s. The NDEA Institutes in reading and English, established in 1964 under an expansion of the National Defense Education Act, reached thousands of teachers at more than 300 institutes in the summers of 1965, 1966, and 1967. As conduits of the voluminous materials produced by the study centers, these institutes permitted staff members and participants to consider in detail not only the content of the units but methods of teaching them. Shugrue (1968) stated flatly: "Unquestionably, the NDEA institutes have been the single most influential mode of promoting curriculum change in the last five years." Although unverified (and probably unverifiable) by research, this opinion reflects the optimism and energy that federal support unleashed in the 1960s.

The second delivery agent was the publishing industry. Materials from the Carnegie-Mellon Center, the University of Orgeon, and Hunter College became literature anthologies. The Nebraska Curriculum was published in 1966 and 1967 by the University of Nebraska Press. Either wholly and directly, as in these examples, or partially and by indirection, much of the Study Center materials found their way into commercial publications. Some remained as "fugitive" or private publications. Dissemination was widespread, but the effects on teaching and learning remain subject to speculation.

Two study centers deserve mention because they focused on teachers rather than school curricula. The Illinois State-Wide Curriculum Study Center in the Preparation of Secondary School English Teachers (ISCPET) was a coalition of 20 colleges and universities that undertook research on the preparation of English teachers, examined their own curricula for teachers, and issued, among other publications, a statement of qualifications for teachers. The English Teacher Preparation Study (ETPS) was a nationwide effort sponsored by the Modern Language Association, NCTE, and the National Association of State Directors of Teacher Preparation and Certification; its purpose was to assist state certification officers to evaluate programs and individuals' preparation and to help college and university personnel improve offerings for preservice teachers. Guidelines for the preparation of both elementary and secondary teachers were the chief product.

As their name implies, demonstration centers were more directly concerned with methods of teaching than were study centers, though here again the relationship to research was tenuous whether one considers the source of the pedagogy being demonstrated or the effects of the centers on teachers' practices. The center at Syracuse University, a collaboration between the Jamesville-DeWitt School District and the university's Reading and Language Arts Center, produced 10 films and a guide for using them as the core for inservice courses on teaching reading in secondary schools. Here the intent was clearly to demonstrate how to teach reading through content such as history and science as well as English, a theory that had been expounded for at least two previous decades and that had a research base of sorts even in the early 1960s. The effects of the film-based course did not go untested, even though the funding for the project was consumed by the production of the films. Results of these evaluations and of related research appeared in a series of monographs published by the Reading and Language Arts Center.

The center at Euclid Central Junior High School outside of Cleveland was directed by George Hillocks, then chair of the English department, in cooperation with Western Reserve University. Visitors were invited to observe teachers using a new curriculum they had developed for average, honors, and remedial students in grades 7–9. The observers could discuss units and obtain copies of them for use in their own classrooms. Federal funding for this center ended in 1965, and Hillocks moved on to university-based teacher education and research. The center continued to operate, and in 1966 sponsored a conference for 300 teachers from 23 states supported solely by local funds. (Shugrue, 1968).

Though undocumented, the effects of Project English are undeniable. From the perspective of 25 years later, it is easy to cite the limitations of the centers and individual research projects, some of which will be mentioned in this and subsequent chapters. But it is more important to recognize the impact of those few million dollars expended on "increasing the amount of research and experimentation in the area of English instruction." (Dershimer, 1976). If the centers stopped short of basic and applied research, they nevertheless provided the makings of future studies: theories of instruction, especially those related to writing; new approaches to the study of language including explorations of structural linguistics and transformational grammar that led to lessons in sentence combining; new assessments of the literary canon then in place and a rethinking of the order and range of literature; and, most important, the researchers themselves. Many of the centers proved to be training grounds for future researchers, supplying them with ideas to be pondered, materials to be tested, methodologies to be tried, and funds to support their graduate studies. Out of the curriculum study centers and the funded research projects emerged at least two generations of researchers.

Their influence can be seen in two professional organizations, which were closely connected to the Cooperative Research Program: the National Council of Teachers of English and the International Reading Association. In the half decade of Project English, NCTE's Research Committee came to life, launching a series of research monographs many of which are now often labeled "classic" or "seminal," for example, Loban's two monographs on language development (1964, 1976), Squire's *Responses of Adolescents While Reading Four Short Stories* (1964), Emig's *Composing Processes of Twelfth Graders* (1971), Mellon's (1969) and O'Hare's (1973) monographs on sentence combining. These titles illustrate the profession's earlier concern with learning process; the 22nd and 23rd reports in the series, *How Writing Shapes Thinking* (Langer & Applebee, 1987) and *Response to Student Writing* (Freedman, 1988), indicate the later concern with teaching.

Not satisfied to stimulate and disseminate research by means of the Research Committee alone, the Council established the Trustees of the Research fund to sponsor small studies especially by classroom teachers. In 1967, it added a quarterly jour-

nal, *Research in the Teaching of English*. Similarly, the other professional organization, IRA, composed chiefly of elementary classroom teachers and teacher educators, gave research a prominent place on its agenda. The *Reading Research Quarterly* began publication in 1965, and a director of research was added to the headquarters staff in 1971.

Project English did more than serve a public relations function. It helped to make research in teaching English and reading as popular with professors of English and English educators as it had been in the first half of the century with educational psychologists. Among the studies it funded were many that addressed significant problems and a few that continue to influence current investigations, as will be seen in other chapters in this volume.

Before turning to a few of these studies, we should note that the centers reflected the then-prevailing view that improvement of student learning would result from improved curricula, with minimum attention to teaching strategies, and that improvement could be measured by standardized tests, writing samples, and attitude inventories. Twenty years later, the importance of content is being stressed again. This time, however, we have a sufficient research on teaching effectiveness to insure that attention to *what* does not stifle concern for *how* that content is taught.

In Project English centers, as in individual studies supported through the Cooperative Research Program, not enough attention was directed to teachers and classrooms as sources of researchable questions, although there was a tentative move in that direction as teachers working with the centers were invited to engage in "action research." Today, as teachers' roles are being redefined as part of a movement to restructure schools, there is perhaps a stronger chance that the teacher-as-researcher idea will take hold. (See Part II, Chapter 14.)

A contemporaneous evaluation of the centers by Carlsen and Crow (1967) faults them for "lack of concern for how the learner learns," for attending almost exclusively to the content of English without "testing and probing of new beliefs," and for failing to carry on basic research on unsolved problems. Carlsen and Crow cite as an exception to this failure the center at Florida State University directed by Dwight Burton, which made systematic comparisons among the curricula it was producing and trying out in the schools and noted failures as well as successes. These critics wonder if Project English will have as little lasting effect as the Eight Year Study of the Progressive Education Association has had.

Commenting on the centers seven years later, Applebee (1974) is more sanguine. He notes the short time (3 to 5 years) for which the projects were funded and commends them for producing the "first sets of academically oriented material for the high school course, [and for] involving university professors of the liberal arts once again in the process of curriculum development in English. (p. 203)" He takes special note of two centers that departed from the academic model in an effort to serve disadvantaged students, the one at Hunter College in New York City led by Marjorie Smiley, the other at the University of Michigan led by Daniel Fader. Both programs recognized the need to capture students' interests first and foremost, to get them to read whatever they would, and to postpone concern for academic content ordered logically and sequentially until student involvement was assured. Applebee is cautious about Fader's claims for the success of the Michigan program, but acknowledges that this center (as well as Florida State's) attempted to study its effectiveness.

Individual Studies Coming Out of Project English

Project English supported 50 or more individual research studies between 1961 and 1967. While many of these had implications for teaching the language arts, few focused on teachers. Typical studies investigated language itself for cues to improvement of instruction (e.g., Paul Hanna's (1966) study of the consistency of phoneme-graphme relationships in the spelling of 10,000 English words); or analyzed students' use of grammatical structures in writing (e.g., Hunt, O'Donnell, Griffin & Norris, 1967); or attempted to identify elements within reading performance which accounted for reading achievement (e.g., Holmes & Singer's studies of the substrata factor theory, 1961). Such studies were impelled by new linguistic theories, particularly transformational grammar, and new data from linguists' studies of spoken English, and were constricted by traditions of empirical research, which had dominated educational psychology since the turn of the century. The way to find out how students acquire language skills was to define large groups by certain traits—age, sex, socioeconomic studies, race, region, parents, grade placement, type of school, and so forth—and compare them using standard measures, holding variables constant. Longitudinal studies would be desirable, but unlikely, with short-range funding; so developmental studies usually meant comparing different learners at various stages.

A further restriction on the nature and scope of Project English and Cooperative Research studies was imposed by the enabling legislation which had specified research on reading and writing, with the intention of improving instruction in "basic skills." Many of the curriculum and demonstration centers skirted this restriction by insisting on the integration of literature, language, and composition, many featuring thematic units based in literature. But most individual research projects confined themselves strictly to reading or writing and examined language and linguistics only as they related to these two skills. One that broke out of that pattern was the National Study of High School English Programs (Squire & Applebee, 1968) undertaken by NCTE and the University of Illinois.

Looking in English Classrooms

Clearly focused on teaching and the instructional context, the National Study was based on observations of English classes in 158 high schools, selected as "consistently educating outstanding students in English," and located in 45 states. The observations made in 1963 to 1964 were supplemented by interviews with teachers, administrators, and students and by questionnaires from 1331 teachers and 13,291 students in these schools. In its focus on teachers, the study sought data on their preparation, continuing education, and involvement in professional organizations, their attitudes toward teaching, and perceptions of general and specific goals, classroom management, and the selection of instructional materials. Instructional context was interpreted largely as teaching conditions, that is, numbers of students, classes, and hours spent teaching, preparing, correcting papers, conferring with students, handling school routines. Although teachers were queried on such issues as goals, student motivation, close reading, values of textbooks and workbooks, grading compositions, assigning term papers, teaching grammar and usage, and other dimensions of language, there was no attempt to analyze teachers' beliefs and to relate them to practice.

In these assumed-excellent English programs, it was not surprising to find that 72 percent of the teachers had been English majors, that more than half had master's degrees, that nearly half had sabbatical privileges, and a fifth could receive stipends for summer study. The quality of teachers' preparation was judged high, an especially important issue at a time when many underqualified teachers were being hired to meet the needs of an expanding school population. In these select schools, teachers' morale was also high though conditions were far from ideal. Complaints about the paper load were related less to having too many students or too many classes than to nonteaching requirements.

Classroom observations and questionnaires yielded information on teaching practices. More than half of class time (52 percent) was devoted to literature instruction, 16 percent to composition, 13.5 percent to language, and about 18 percent to everything else (speech, reading, media, etc.). Based on 32,580 minutes of class time, the observers reported the following methods of instruction: recitation (22 percent), discussion (195. percent), lecture (21 percent), student presentation (14 percent), silent study (10 percent), "Socratic questioning" (2 percent) and group work (2 percent). Some differences between grade levels were reported: recitation dropped from 29 percent to 21 percent and discussion rose from 15 percent to 21 percent between 10th– grade and 12th. In these schools with strong English programs for the college bound, observers found few accommodations being made for the interests and abilities of terminal students. In his introduction to the published report, Floyd Rinker concluded, "The chief concern in the teaching of writing continues to be correctness rather than content, logic, organization, and style. The neglect of language study is common." (Squire and Applebee, 1968, 1969)

One of the values of this current-practices study of the 1960s is that it offers a standard of comparison for subsequent studies. One of those, *Teaching English in the United Kingdom* by Squire and Applebee (1969), was undertaken three years later and was also supported by the Cooperative Research Program. The content emphasis in British classrooms showed literature taking 39 percent of class time compared with 52 percent in American high schools. Speech at 14 percent and drama and miscellaneous at nearly 17 percent accounted for emphases that scarcely registered in the American study. Composition at 13.3 percent was slightly less than the equivalent American figure. Teaching practices observed in British classrooms were accorded very similar time allotments as in the American study, except that the British spent somewhat less time in recitation and lectures and more time in student presentation and drama.

"Socratic questioning" was in both countries equally minuscule, and group work was found only slightly more often (3.5 percent) in the United Kingdom.

Another study, this one limited to writing, also supported in large part by federal funds and sponsored by NCTE, invites interesting comparisons in methods of research as well as findings. More than 15 years after the data collection of the first study, Applebee (1981) selected different foci and a radically different design for what is still essentially a study of current practices. First, instead of the broad coverage (158 schools) of the earlier study, which limited observations in two days in each school, the later study placed the limitation on the number of schools (2) and expanded the observations to 309 lessons observed over 25 weeks, though for any given teacher the number of observations might have been as few as one or as many as 11, and was on average between 3 and 4. Second, Applebee added the dimension of writing in content areas in addition to English and chose 9th and 11th grades only. Because even extended observations in two high schools yield case studies rather than studies of current practices, he relied on a national questionnaire to add breadth. From the observational phase completed in the 1979 to 1980 school year, data comparable to that collected in 1964 to 1965 can be extracted. For instance, in grade 11 in one-of-the-two schools (the city high school), teacher-led discussion took 28 percent of the time; teacher presentation, 5 percent; student presentation, 2 percent; group work, 11 percent; individual work, 33 percent.

The relatively low incidence of observed writing in this study corresponds to the 1968 finding that only a small proportion of English instruction was devoted to writing. Of course, the two studies are comparable in only very limited respects. Reflecting a trend in language-arts research in the late 1970s, Applebee identified a number of specific variables to look at in addition to the time allocated to writing instruction (what the earlier study reported). For example, he looked at purposes and audiences for writing and, more significantly, he included five school subjects in addition to English.

THE FIRST GRADE STUDIES

In spite of limitations in design and execution, the First Grade Studies yielded excellent returns on the investment of funds by the Cooperative Research Program. Their importance resides in two dimensions: what was learned about organizing and managing a truly cooperative research effort; the impact of the findings on future studies and on teacher education. More than 20 years after a summary of the studies was published in the *Reading Research Quarterly* (Bond & Dykstra, 1967) these two dimensions are worth revisiting.

The idea for the First Grade Studied emerged in 1959 from a group of reading educators convened by the National Conference on Research in English and sponsored by the Carnegie Foundation. Two days of sometimes heated discussion of the merits of one approach or another to the teaching of beginning reading led to a consensus that the various methods should be compared in a study that would apply the same measures as children entered and left first grade.

In the next few years, effrots funding sources were identified. At just about the same time, the Cooperative Research Program, having been directed by Congress to focus on reading and writing, was looking to support a major study on a basic question: what are the most effective ways of teaching beginning reading? Proposals were solicited and the 27 projects selected came from state and local education agencies as well as from universities. while each one compared different instructional approaches or different kinds of first grade populations, each was committed to using the same data-gathering instruments. Researchers set up the Coordinating Center at the University of Minnesota and the 27 project directors convened for the first time in June, 1964, to prepare to collect data the following school year. The instructional approaches that were to be studied included basal reading series, basals supplemented by phonics, the initial teaching alphabet, linguistic readers, language experience, phonics/linguistics, and basals supplemented by trade books. Except for the standard instruments used in all of the studies, they were not subject to the same research procedures. There was considerable variation from one study to another in the kinds of additional information collected, variable control, and the amount and kind of classroom observations.

Basically, the studies sought answers to three questions:

1. To what extent are various pupil, teacher, class, school, and community characteristics related to pupil achievement in first grade reading and spelling?
2. Which of many approaches to initial reading instruction produces superior reading and spelling by the end of first grade?
3. Is any program uniquely effective or ineffective for pupils with high- or low-readiness for reading?

The sophistication of the first question was greatly diminished by the limited means employed to define and describe "characteristics." Anything more sophisticated than statistics obtainable from test scores, questionnaires, and school records was beyond the budget and beyond the generally-accepted research methods of the 1960s. The second and third questions betray a simplified view of reading instruction cherished by the public even today but not subscribed to by most reading educators either then or now. If the unlikelihood of any one approach emerging as a "winner" was as clear to many of the researchers before they undertook the studies as it was afterwards, then what reason could there have been for such a major effort? One, of course, might have been to satisfy public demand and in so doing to prove the fallacy of the "one best method" point of view. More important, the First Grade Studies sought facts to penetrate the emotional turbulence that, then as now, surrounds any discussion of how to teach beginning reading. Unfortunately, seeking answers to the questions by applying standard measures focused attention on outcomes and concealed differences in effects that may have been observable in the classes using different approaches.

The study of teachers, if not teaching, implied in the first question was limited to demographic data and "teaching effectiveness as rated by supervisors." An attempt to measure teachers' attitudes toward reading by a standard scale was abandoned. Some studies included interview with teachers and classroom observations, but the data collected could not be compared across 27 projects. Questions asked about characteristics of teachers, pupils, classes, schools, and communities were answered by naive data collection and analysis.

Nevertheless, the First Grade Studies yielded findings that were significant to the future of research even if they failed to answer the questions raised about methods and materials. The major finding was that differences were greater among classes using the same methods than they were across methods. No approach was better than the others in producing superior reading and spelling by the end of first grade; none proved "uniquely effective or ineffective for pupils with high or low readiness for reading." Thus the First Grade Studies contributed to the mounting conviction among researchers that measuring outcomes should give way to studying processes, both how students learn and how teachers teach, and the circumstances in which learning and teaching take place. In the next two decades, research emphases would shift in just that sequence—learning, teaching, context—and only very recently would include the interactions among the three. (See, for example, the study of first grade reading by Anderson, Evertson & Brophy, 1979.)

Some of the research of the 1960s and 1970s that studied learners was interpreted as contradictory to the prime conclusion drawn from the First Grade Studies, namely, that researchers make a difference. From studies that showed the powerful effects on learning, particularly on literacy, of poverty, home language, community and school environments, and cultural attitudes toward education (e.g., Jencks, 1972), it was assumed that teachers might have negligible impact on learning outcomes. Contesting that assumption led to the next major research focus, teacher effectiveness.

THE BEGINNING TEACHER EVALUATION STUDY

In the beginning, the research that investigated relationships between teachers' behaviors, beliefs about content, and attitudes toward learners and matters of instruction tended not to be subject-specific. In the same period that generalists in elementary education were becoming involved in teacher effectiveness studies, researchers in the language arts pursued questions of process in learning rather than teaching. (Important psycholinguistic studies were being undertaken at this time not only in universities but in Research and Development Centers, a movement that followed Project English and will be discussed later in this chapter.) But educational psychologists and elementary curriculum specialists who pursued questions of teacher effectiveness had to examine the teaching of something, and that something often turned out to be reading. Such was the case in a major effort growing out of a need for "empirically grounded information about teaching" expressed by the California Commission for Teacher Preparation and Licensing. Called the Beginning Teacher Evaluation Study, this long-term project was supported by the National Institute of Education (NIE), Educational Testing Service (ETS), and the Far West Lab-

oratory for Educational Research and Development. Its second phase, a field study of 41 2nd-grade and 54 5th-grade teachers in eight California school districts, was conducted by ETS.

The comprehensive data-gathering of Phase II of BTES suggests how abortive were the First Grade Studies in attempting to relate teacher (and classroom) characteristics to pupil outcomes. More limited geographically than the First Grade Studies, BTES tested approximately 2,700 pupils in 43 schools in the fall and spring of 1973–74, allotted 400 days of observation to 95 teachers, and videotaped each one. Teachers, principals, and pupils responded to an array of assessment procedures including interviews to document teachers' performances and backgrounds, aptitudes, cognitive styles, attitudes, and expectations. The aim of Phase II was to "gather sufficient data to develop hypotheses about teaching and learning," and these hypotheses were to be tested in successive phases. The report on Phase II (McDonald & Elias, 1975–76) filled five volumes, figured in numerous policy decisions affecting teacher evaluation, and led to subsequent studies of teaching functions such as presentation, monitoring, and feedback.

Some of the hypotheses generated by Phase II of the BTES had immediate and widespread impact on the teaching of reading—on the advice offered by reading educators, on the policies promulgated by state and local boards of education, and on the studies undertaken by reading researchers as well as by teacher educators. A sampling of the findings will have to suffice to suggest the impact. In general, pupils who read better at the end of the year were the same ones who read better at the beginning of the year. In short, what pupils brought with them to 2nd grade and to 5th grade accounted for about 80 percent of end-of-the-year achievement in reading. But about 15 percent of the variation among children could be attributed to factors relating to teacher behavior, and what teachers did influenced learning rate among good readers as well as poor.

A critical finding was that a classroom management pattern that worked well at 2nd grade did not necessarily work well at 5th grade. The use of a variety of materials was not so important in grade 5 as it was in grade 2. In 5th grade, the study suggests, teacher-pupil interaction must be more sustained around fewer materials. Teachers arranged reading instruction for individuals, small groups, and the class as a whole. No one of these arrangements used exclusively was as effective as a pattern which included all three. The critical feature seemed to be the degree to which management patterns maintained a reasonably high level of pupil involvement. Pupils learn when their minds are engaged. In this study what determined this engagement in learning was the amount of direct instruction to pupils by teachers. Appropriate materials were not enough. Direct instruction seemed to be the key in improving reading achievement scores in grades 2 and 5.

Direct instruction, time on task or academic learning time, teacher monitoring and feedback, quality of questions and explanations—all these concepts emerged from teacher-effectiveness studies just as opinion-makers were clamoring for accountability and "back to the basics." The channels from research to practice were amazingly open, the result perhaps of improved dissemination through R & D Centers and Regional Educational Laboratories and of media interest in education news. Implementation of findings from studies offering limited generalizability often outran the cautious interpretations made by conscientious researchers. To be sure, "implementation" was more prompt at the policy-making levels than in the classrooms. Nevertheless, the resulting increase in student assessments and measures of teacher performance have altered classroom practices, causing some educators to blame research for a decline in student-centered and process-oriented language-arts classes which they see as having peaked in the late 1960s, early 1970s (Moffett, 1985).

A MAJOR RESEARCH PROGRAM IN TEACHING WRITING

One of the more influential long-term investigative efforts related to language-arts instruction is the series of studies that began with Donald Graves (1981) and his colleagues at the University of New Hampshire and have been extended in other sites, notably in New York City by Lucy Calkins (1983) working out of Teachers College, Columbia, and in Boothbay Harbor, Maine, where teacher Nancie Atwell has chronicled the growth of her middle school students in reading and writing (1987). Their studies and others spinning off from the original studies at Atkinson Academy (New Hampshire) will be amply referred to in later chapters. (See, for example, the chapter by Hansen and Graves.) They are included here to illustrate several trends related to programmatic research. For one thing, the studies have been funded by federal and foundational grants. For another, they are examples of cooperative research, though they are linked less formally than other studies we have cited. Spanning more than a decade, they illustrate the transition from product- to process-centered research in language arts. This transition from product to process in studying learning was accompanied by changes in methodology from empirically based analyses to descriptive, anecdotal, and example-filled documentation, more like reportage than research and, consequently, more readable. And they exemplify the profession's mounting concern for the role that teachers play in the learning process.

Two aspects of Graves' work signal important developments in the nature of research on language arts. One is the emphasis on collaboration, the blurring of distinctions between teachers and researchers, a trend eagerly promoted in the mid 1980s. (See chapter by Burton, this Handbook.) This emphasis, in turn, is reflected in the way the research is reported: classroom narratives that chronicle both children's development as writers and teachers' efforts to help them. The effect of this style of reporting is to make the distinction between research and practice difficult to discern. This body of research is simultaneously research on learning and on teaching, combining findings, implications, and applications in single reports. Given the persuasive use of recognizable classroom incidents to illustrate every point, it is not surprising that Graves' (1981), Calkins' (1983), and Atwell's (1987) work (to select just three examples) is received enthusiastically by language-arts specialists who spread the word to teachers.

Through their early studies, Graves and his colleagues came to view writing in terms of natural development. As a corollary of this, the form of instruction that they recommend is an indirect one, a "waiting, responsive type of teaching," according to Graves. Effective teaching in this view involves such behaviors as arranging the classroom to establish an atmosphere conducive to writing, grouping students for conferences, publishing their writing, and asking facilitating questions. Above all, it advocates letting children set their own agenda—choosing topics, writing, drawing, inventing spelling, finding their own structures.

The response to the New Hampshire studies has not been uniformly enthusiastic. For example, Hillocks (1986, p. 13–18) criticizes the reports on the grounds that, although their points are illustrated with anecdotes, the authors provide no means to confirm that the anecdotes are typical of what they observed. (Sixteen children were observed over a two-year period, 8 from the beginning of grade 1 to the end of grade 2, from the beginning of grade 3 to the end of grade 4.) While acknowledging the importance of the studies, Hillocks points out that they make inferences about cause-effect relationships without considering alternative explanations and without controlling for instructional variables.

Response to studies like these, including many from British researchers whose influence can be traced in Graves' and others' studies of the composing process, depends on how broad a definition one gives to research. Among educators in language arts, the consensus appears to be toward a latitudinarian view as can be seen in the following accounts of two other developments related to writing instruction.

THE IOWA WRITING PROJECTS

The present-day Iowa Writing Project is rooted in a history of writing instruction in that state that goes back at least four decades to the University of Iowa Programs in writing and rhetoric, the CEEB summer institutes, and the NDEA institutes which succeeded them. In the 1950s and 1960s, faculty from the university's English department played key roles in the organizations most active in turning policy-makers' attention to the need for improving English instruction, especially the teaching of composition. John Gerber, at the time chair of the Iowa English department, was president of NCTE in 1955. He had taken a lead in forming the Conference on College Composition and Communication and was actively involved in planning the CEEB summer institutes, which would provide the tripod model—language, literature, and composition—as a focus for the NDEA institutes. Richard Braddock and Richard Lloyd-Jones, collaborating with their researcher colleague Lowell Schoer, had produced for NCTE a summary of 504 studies of writing, *Research in Written Composition* (Braddock, Lloyd-Jones, & Schoer, 1963), which is regarded by some as a "charter of modern Composition" (North, 1987, p. 17). It is not surprising that this team, joined by Carl Klaus in 1962 as associate director with Braddock, should have placed special emphasis on writing in the NDEA institutes they organized for Iowa English teachers over the next several summers.

While the institutes offered courses in literature and linguistics as well as composition, it was writing that offered the most challenge and the greatest opportunity for innovation. Realizing that most teachers had had no practice in writing since their freshman year in college, Klaus and his colleagues designed a course that gave them a fresh and sustained writing experience. In addition to taking the tripod courses, NDEA institute participants were expected to develop a curriculum project they could put into action when they returned to their schools, but teachers often returned to situations not conducive to curricular change. Recognizing this, Klaus and his colleagues developed a special institute in 1967, one whose focus was exclusively on composition and whose clientele were not teachers but supervisors and principals.

In a second development of the original institutes, Klaus developed one for college teachers of composition. Funded by the National Endowment for the Humanities inn 1977, the program ran for two successive years and involved two groups of freshman writing directors. They spent six months studying cognitive psychology, philosophy of language, educational theory, course design, composition, and linguistics, and then designed a new freshman program for their institution and a writing-across-the-curriculum scheme to go with it.

The NEH institutes were followed by several years of follow-up to counteract what Klaus sees as the potential victimizing of the teacher, which can result, he says, "if you send teachers back to classrooms all energized but with no support group to help them." (personal communication, March 1988). To be considered for admission, participants had to have written assurances from their department chairs and academic deans that they would be given the opportunity to try out model courses they developed in the institute. The department chairs and deans also were required to attend part of the institutes to familiarize them with the concepts and methods presented.

An example of practitioner-oriented research followed, as Klaus and others evaluated successful college writing programs and published their findings in *Courses for Change in Writing* (1984). Running from 1977 to 1984, this program was the largest federally-funded project for the improvement of the teaching of writing at the college level.

At about the same time that the Iowans were developing the projects just described, a group in San Francisco's Bay Area were working on similar ideas. Later, when the Bay Area Writing Project (on its way to becoming the National Writing Project) reached out to Iowa, James S. Davis of the Grant Wood Area Education Agency, together with colleagues from other AEA's, consulted Klaus and Lloyd-Jones about a University of Iowa affiliation with the BAWP. After due consideration, the group decided not to affiliate, because while they admired the BAWP as "an immensely impressive project, it was not necessarily just right for a geographic, social, and cultural setting such as existed in Iowa." (J. S. Davis, personal communication, Feburary 1988). Remaining independent of NWP, the Iowa Writing Project, now in its 11th year, has more than 30 institutes; over 3,000 teachers have been through the program, a significant number for a rural state. When a majority of teachers in a school have participated in this inservice program, changes can be made in the writing curriculum, according to Lloyd-Jones, "regardless of what the principal proposes." (personal communication, February 1988).

A collaboration of four Area Education Agencies, the Iowa Department of Education, and the University of Iowa, the IWP began with Title IV-C funds but has continued to flourish after this funding ended. With funding, however, more formal research could be undertaken than is possible now. Davis regrets this limitation but says that as project director he keeps copious records and consciously fosters dissertation-level research such as a current examination of participants' histories as writers and as teachers of writing. (personal communication, Feburary 1988)

THE NATIONAL WRITING PROJECT

The National Writing Project (NWP) has emerged, in the opinion of many educators, as a premier model for the development and diffusion of effective strategies for teaching writing. Through its emphasis on recruiting teacher expertise from the classroom, on teachers teaching teachers, on networking, follow-up, and the involvement of school administrators, NWP seems to have found an effective solution to the problem of limited adoption of findings, a problem that has beset most educational research and development projects. Nor must we limit NWP's merits to dissemination.

By stretching our definition of research to embrace "the making of knowledge," it can be argued that NWP has produced "research" or "knowledge" specifically of how teachers learn to teach writing. James Gray, the NWP Director who developed in the early 1970s the Bay Area Writing Project from which the national projects emerged, has been quoted by Gomez (1985) as referring to "teacher expertise, that special kind of knowledge which comes out of practice, that is more important than research." Whether or not we accept practitioners' lore (North, 1987) as research on teaching, we must recognize NWP's influence on our changing concepts of research; that is, the emergence of the teacher and the classroom as sources of research ideas, not simply as subjects of others' investigations or as vehicles for verifying or demonstrating results of others' research.

The writing projects have also produced conventional research data. NWP has spawned a variety of evaluation efforts and some more broad-based research as well (Scriven, 1980). These have included studies of the impact of writing project models on student writing (Pritchard, 1987) and on student attitudes towards writing, as in the study of the New Jersey Writing Project by Emig (1982, p. 2030) reported in a dissertation by King (1980).

The writing projects have actively fostered teachers' participation in research. Rather than presenting participants with a set of prescriptions derived from research, the projects encourage them to conduct their own investigations, sometimes in co-operation with university educators. The most notable recent example is Perl and Wilson's (1986) ethnographic study of five Long Island teachers. Similarly related to NWP is Freedman's national survey of 560 NWP teachers and 715 of their students inquiring into response practices. This survey is supplemented by an ethnographic study of two NWP 9th-grade teachers (Freedman, 1988).

A final argument for including NWP in this review is that is has given rise to an R & D Center for the Study of Writing—to be treated in the last section of this chapter.

Beginning with the Bay Area Writing Project in 1974, the projects had multiplied by 1988 into a network of 166 sites located in all but 4 of the 50 states and in 6 foreign countries. Although with this growth have come modifications of the original plan, the essential idea is that expert writing teachers from elementary, middle and secondary schools should come together in summer institutes of 4 to 6 weeks' duration to improve their own writing and to further develop their strategies for teaching writing. As a consequence of this intensive experience in writing and teaching writing, participants return to their school districts as teacher-consultants ready to conduct inservice sessions in their own and other districts. Participants are nominated by, and if selected by the summer institute staff will be funded by their administrators, who are committed to sponsoring their inservice roles. When these conditions are met, NWP practitioners are in a good position to effect change. The spread of the projects has greatly expanded the chances that teachers almost everywhere can come into contact with ideas promulgated in the summer institutes. The success of NWP with teachers has been widely accepted even in the absence of much hard data. Its consequent, expected success with students has yet to be seen. It is by no means reflected in the only substantial evidence yet available—the performance of thousands of students on writing tasks set by the National Assessment of Educational Progress. (See below.)

What accounts for NWP's reputation as an extraordinarily effective inservice effort? Most observers credit these features:

1. The respect accorded to teachers as the real experts, the possessors of classroom lore;
2. The absence of top-down, authority-to-practitioner communication;
3. The rituals of the institute sessions that promote self-esteem, camaraderie, and mutual support;
4. The mystique with which writing itself is infused, as self-therapy, as craft and as art, and as higher-order thinking.

Its long-term impact on students will depend on the durability of these features as they are translated into grassroots inservice and thence to classrooms in all kinds of schools. Of crucial importance is maintaining the high quality of participants by keeping the summer institues selectively invitational. This system is costly and therefore in danger of being watered down by projects serving less-than-affluent areas. (BAWP itself continues to be highly selective, choosing 20 teachers each summer from more than a hundred nominees.) To the extent that school administrators are not financially, as well as morally, committed to the NWP scheme, the chances of affecting students' writing diminish.

RESEARCH CENTERS AND EDUCATIONAL LABORATORIES

The most far-reaching and long-lasting phase of the Cooperative Research Act of 1954 resulted from the 1965 amendment (Title IV of the Elementary and Secondary Education Act) in the creation of Research and Development Centers to conduct basic and applied research on educational problems. By 1969, there were 12 centers located at major universities across the country. Two of them had been authorized as feasibility sites prior to 1965, and one of these is still operating, funded through 1990. None of the 1969 centers was charged exclusively with studying the English language arts, but several were so broadly conceived (e.g., learning, teaching, teacher education, cognitive learning, educational differences, early childhood education) that studies of language acquisition in its several dimensions were inevitably included in their research agenda. Each center received $500,000 annually in a 5-year reimbursement contract. By fiscal 1969, over $11 million had been allocated to the centers. By the time the National Institute for Education was created in 1972, the centers and regional laboratories accounted for most of its budget. (Chase & Walter, 1982)

Between 1969 and 1985, new centers were added and some of the original were phased out. In the most recent round of funding in 1985, 19 university-based R&D Centers were authorized through fiscal 1990. Three of these are related exclusively to language arts and will be described in the last section of this chapter. First, however, we shall briefly describe the total research and development design that embraced the centers, the Regional Educational Laboratories, a dissemination network (ERIC), and a plan for evaluation (NAEP) as it was conceived in the early 1960s and as it took shape over the next 25 years.

Because R&D facilities were a new idea in education in the 1960s, they drew inspiration at first from other fields; agriculture, rural sociology, medicine, and engineering are cited by Chase and Walter. Following leads from research and development in these fields, Guba and Clark (1965) proposed for the R & D Centers a linear model that began with basic research, moved to field testing, then to demonstration for practitioners' reaction, followed by diffusion and adoption. Thus research results included projects and procedures as well as findings. For example, from the Wisconsin Center for R & D in Cognitive Learning came an objectives-based management system, Individually Guided Instruction (IGE), which produced a spin-off, the Wisconsin Design for Reading Skill Development which, for a time, had a marked influence on elementary school reading programs.

Such successful transfer from research to practice was an exception however. So in time, the linear model was modified to allow greater interaction among researchers, disseminators (largely college-based educators), and school personnel. But new concepts of educational research and new ways of conducting research developed gradually, and in the meantime, and in the original scheme of things, the top-down, producer-to-consumer model for the functioning of the R & D centers had to be buttressed by additional agencies. So the Regional Educational Laboratories were created with the primary function of implementing research and theory through developing materials, demonstrating their use, and providing schools with technical assistance. The laboratories would conduct some research, but largely this was of the sort that evaluates newly installed practices and materials. To increase the speed of dissemination of information coming from the R & D centers and the RELs, as well as from independent researchers and theorists, the ERIC network came into being. The Educational Resources Information Clearinghouse for English began operation in 1968, expanded in 1972 to become the Reading and Communications Skills Clearinghouse (ERIC/RCS) including speech, theater, and journalism, and was housed for 20 years at NCTE headquarters. It is now located at Indiana University. Still another element was added as a guide to the direction of research and development: a national assessment of educational progress (NAEP) would be conducted annually. First conceived in 1963, the first assessment would be made in 1969. (See below.) Finally, to oversee the operations of this network (excluding NAEP), the National Institute for Education (NIE) was established in 1972 as a discrete unit within the Office of Education. In 1986, NIE was abolished and a new Office of Educational Research and Improvement (OERI) was established to oversee the operations of the R & D Centers only. The OERI years have seen increased concentration on publishing findings, but, once again, controversy has developed over the relationship between the centers and the administratively separate laboratories.

Current R & D Centers

Besides the centers on reading, writing, and literature, others among the 19 centers operating today are concerned at least secondarily with teaching the language arts. One that has produced considerable research related to teaching reading and writing is the Institute for Research on Teaching at Michigan State University. For more than 12 years, this center has focused on the roles of teachers rather than on students, looking not simply at teachers' behaviors but at their planning, thinking, and decision-making. From the beginning (1976), IRT has developed research studies in collaboration with teachers. In studies affecting reading, IRT researchers have examined such issues as how beginning teachers learn to use basal texts and teachers' manuals (Ball & Feiman-Nemser, 1986), and how experienced teachers monitor students' comprehension (Duffy, Roehler, Book, Meloth, Vavrus, Putnam & Wesselman, 1986) and modify their instructional strategies (Duffy, Roehler & Putnam, 1987; Anthony & Raphael, 1987). One example among several from this center involving writing instruction is the series of ethnographically oriented studies in elementary classrooms conducted by Florio and others (1984) showing inconsistency in scheduling and monitoring students' writing. Related to inferences from these studies about writing practices is the finding from another IRT study (Schmidt & Buchmann, 1983) that elementary teachers spend more time teaching reading than any other subject. Studies that demonstrate the interrelatedness of research on teaching, writing, and reading are illustrated by one by Raphael, Englert, and Kirschner (1986) examining the impact of text structure and social context on comprehension and production of expository text and students' metacognitive knowledge about writing. See Porter and Brophy (1987).

In the April, 1988, directory of projects funded by OERI, this Michigan State center is listed as operating the Center for the Learning and Teaching of Elementary Subjects. Its mission focuses on problem-solving and higher-order thinking, specifi-

cally addressing issues of content; how teachers frame and focus their teaching to best utilize their resources; in what ways good teaching is subject-matter specific. Literature is identified as one of six elementary education areas to be studied.

Also located at Michigan State is the National Center for Research on Teacher Education, established in 1986 explore "teacher education as one of many influences on teachers." The Center's researchers are engaged in studying 11 preservice and inservice programs for educating teachers, asking how particular kinds of learning situations influence teachers of writing (and mathematics) in elementary and secondary schools. The Center's statement of purpose underscores a significant change of direction in the 20-year history of the educational R & D movement; it declares conceptual development to be as important as gathering empirical data in helping to inform teacher education policy and practice.

Already by 1981 the mission of the centers had veered away from development and dissemination of products, although some product development still takes place. For example, the Center for Research on Elementary and Middle Schools at Johns Hopkins recently developed the Cooperative Integrated Reading and Composition (CIRC) program, a system for managing small-group instruction in reading and writing. CREMS personnel testing the CIRC program have reported that it results in improved standardized test scores in reading, vocabulary, language expression, and spelling. Related, too, to teaching language arts are periodic surveys by CREMS of the uses of microcomputers in primary and middle level classrooms. A recent survey shows language arts to be one of two subjects in elementary schools for which computers are used most.

One of the original R & D centers, the Wisconsin Center for Educational Research has become an umbrella organization, which includes (since 1984) the National Center on Effective Secondary Schools, which is exploring ways to improve achievement for all students, especially the disadvantaged. among its constituent projects is one on higher-order thinking skills in the school curriculum being conducted by Fred Newmann, its director. Here also Martin Nystrand and colleagues recently have completed a major review of tests of reading and writing, which could have far-reaching implications for the way instruction is evaluated. They have also been engaged in a study measuring the processes, discourse, and content of instruction in a sample of 8th and 9th grade English and social studies classes, examining the use of learning logs and relating close analysis of discourse to the differential treatment of students, especially disadvantaged and low-achieving students. At the elementary level, work continues at the WCER on studies of children's linguistic and cognitive development; for example, recent studies have investigated prosody and structure in children's syntactic processing and in the use of phonetic cues in spelling and reading (Nystrand, personal communication, February 1988).

The Center for the Study of Evaluation at the University of California at Los Angeles is related to the teaching the language arts through its affiliation with the International Association for the Evaluation of Educational Achievement (IEA), which is engaged in a 17-country study of written composition. Recently, CSE reported findings that seemed to indicate that the writing skills of American students are considerably better than the most recent NAEP results suggested. (See below.)

The ERIC Clearinghouse on Languages and Linguistics is located at the Center for Applied Linguistics, which was founded in 1959, and is *not* one of the centers created by the federal movement under discussion here. However, its contributions to the whole field of English teaching over the last 40 years cannot be overlooked. The work of scholars at the CAL has given direction to the discussion of such issues as "whole language" instruction and the teaching of standard English to speakers of minority dialects or other languages (Shuy, 1981).

The Regional Laboratories

Originally, the Regional Educational Laboratories were expected to identify one or two high-priority problems in their respective regions and to concentrate research and development efforts on these problems. Over the years, the activities of the RELs have been various, but they continue to include the development and pilot testing of innovative curricula, assisting state educational agencies and local school systems in planning and evaluation, and providing technical assistance in solving various educational problems. Of the first 20 RELs, only 6 remain today:

Appalachia Educational Laboratory (Charleston, WV)
Far West Laboratory for Educational Research and Development (San Francisco)
Mid-Continent Regional Educational Laboratory (Aurora, CO)
Northwest Regional Educational Laboratory (Portland, OR)
Research for Better Schools (Philadelphia)
Southwest Educational Development Laboratory (Austin)

The 3 newest RELs were created in 1984, to make a total of 9 currently:

North Central Regional Educational Laboratory (Elmhurst, IL)
Regional Laboratory for Educational Improvement of the Northeast and Islands (Andover, MA)
Southeastern Educational Improvement Laboratory (Research Triangle Park, NC)

Some of the early efforts of the RELs related to instruction in reading or language arts reflect diverse interpretations of their mission. Two labs in New York and Pennsylvania took an "engineering" approach to research. Working with the learning R & D Center in Pittsburgh, Research for Better Schools (RBS) and the now-defunct ERIE devoted much effort to implementing Pittsburgh's Individually Programmed Instruction System. Others were involved somewhat more directly in basic research. For example, the Far West Laboratory was instrumental in conducting the Beginning Teacher Evaluation Study. In general, wherever innovations were attempted, evaluations took place, and the result was increased concern for monitoring educational processes and outcomes generally.

Initially, only two RELs were devoted principally to language arts and communication, one in Atlanta and the other in Albu-

querque, and both now no longer operating. Others interested in such fields as urban education (The Center for Urban Education was a REL despite its title) and computer-assisted instruction (SWRL) took on problems related to reading and language arts. Laboratories with broad goals made reading and writing instruction part of a larger agenda. The Southwest Educational Development Laboratory's work in bilingual education proved useful to later researchers in reading instruction.

More recently, several RELs have addressed issues of concern to language-arts teachers and researchers. The Appalachia Educational Laboratory (with others) sponsored the group that produced the *Research within Reach* series, including the most recent monograph, subtitled *Secondary School Reading* (Alvermann, Moore & Conley, 1987). The North Central Regional Educational Lab, through its higher-order thinking skills program, is working with school districts to implement ideas developed by program associate Beau Fly Jones focused on reading comprehension. NCREL's rural education program assists local agencies in planning efforts to improve early literacy.

The role of some RELs in curriculum development has diminished recently in favor of technical assistance and service. Research for Better Schools is a case in point. But along with its emphasis on helping schools develop policies and conduct evaluations, RBS also conducts a program aimed at improving cognitive skills. At the Northwest Regional Educational Laboratory, Richard Stiggins has been concerned with classroom applications of writing assessment as part of the lab's Center for Classroom Assessment. NWREL has produced a handbook on writing evaluation for teachers, which draws on experience in holistic, analytic, and primary trait scoring. The Southeast Educational Improvement Laboratory is an important sponsor of the activities of the National Writing Project affiliates in its region.

National Assessment of Educational Progress (NAEP)

As noted above, NAEP was conceived in 1963 and authorized in 1965 along with the interdisciplinary R & D centers to serve as the evaluative strand in the design. To defuse political resistance to the idea of a national assessment, the exploratory committee set up the USOE recommended handing the project to the Education Commission of the States, which administered the assessments until 1983, when the Educational Testing Service took over. Seed money for the project in the amount of $500,000 came from the Ford Foundation's Fund for the Advancement of Education, and in 1968 Congress appropriated a million dollars. Since 1969, more than a million 9-, 13- and 17-year-olds, and, periodically, young adults have been tested by NAEP in 10 different subject areas, including reading, writing, and literature.

Of the four components of the national educational network we have been describing in this section, NAEP probably has the strongest impact on teaching the language arts. Legislators, taxpayers, educators, and school boards heed test results, and NAEP has been effective in publicizing its results through the media and through its own publication, *The Nation's Report Card,* a series of readable, well-designed pamphlets. Originally conceived as a sampling by age-level ("a stratified, multistage probability sample") permitting generalizations to be applied to the school population nationally, NAEP began in 1983 to assess students by grade as well as by age. Moreover, because questions used in the assessments are now made available to state and local agencies, NAEP directly contributes to the control that state-mandated testing can impose on teaching practices. Whether this control is beneficial or harmful depends, or course, on the quality of the questions, how they are administered, the uses to which achievement results are put, and the information provided by the assessment to aid interpretation of results. In recent assessments, NAEP has attempted to explore the contexts of learning through surveys of students, teachers, and administrators, asking questions about teaching strategies, resources, out-of-school experiences, attitudes, and demographics. For instance, in surveying writing achievement in the school years 1973 to 1974, 1978 to 1979, and 1983 to 1984, NAEP has used increasingly sophisticated assessment techniques. The 1983 to 1984 assessment looked at process-oriented writing activities as it queried students about such matters as planning, revising and editing, the type of teacher feedback, the amount of sharing with others, and their attitudes, purposes, and values vis-a-vis writing.

Such background information helps consumers deal with findings like these:

1. Only 25 percent of 11th-graders reached adequate performance on analytic writing;
2. Fewer than one third of all students on any persuasive writing task wrote responses judged adequate or better;
3. Less than 9 percent of 4th-graders wrote stories judged adequate or better.

Findings such as these lead NAEP Director Archie LaPointe in introducing the report (Applebee, Langer, Mullis, 1986) to conclude: "Performance in writing in our schools is, quite simply, *bad*." (p. 3) From there to the major conclusion that "students at all grade levels are deficient in higher-order thinking skills" is an easy step (p. 11).

Similar though less drastic conclusions were reached by the same team after studying findings from the 1986 assessment of reading achievement. This was the fifth reading assessment since 1971, made after a two-year interval instead of the usual four, and for that reason as well as possible distortions in achievement scores, it is not included in NAEP's usual trend reporting over what would have been a 15-year period. Instead, the pamphlet *Who Reads Best?* (Applebee, Langer, & Mullis, 1988) reports on factors related to reading achievement, and in doing so reveals findings on instruction and academic climate that are additional evidence of the shift in research interest from learning to teaching.

For example, a section on "The Effective Teacher" outlines the kinds of before-and-after reading activities teachers conduct in order to improve students' ability to comprehend. Between grades 7 and 11, there is an increase in the use of previewing and a decrease in reading aloud and highlighting difficult words. Over 45 percent of 7th- and 11th-grade students reported that they never had the opportunity to exchange ideas in group discussion.

Another finding indicative of the teaching focus suggests that teachers use a broader range of strategies with better readers than with poorer readers.

As with the writing assessment, this one also shows students at all three levels having particular difficulty elaborating upon or defending their interpretations of written texts.

Assessed less frequently than reading and writing, literature has figured in only one full-scale assessment (1974) and one in 1986 limited to 11th-graders. The latter was funded by the National Endowment for the Humanities at a time when critics of education were charging that emphasis on the skills of reading and writing was resulting in the neglect of content. Developed by NAEP's learning area committee for literature, the test was administered to a sample of 8,000 high school juniors along with a comparable measure of their knowledge of facts of American history. Responses to multiple-choice items revealed considerable gaps in 11th-graders' acquaintance with authors and works that they might be expected to know. An analysis of the outcomes by Chester Finn and Diane Ravitch, *What Do Our 17-Year-Olds Know?* (1987) captured media attention and fueled the debate as to whether or not American students should have a common curriculum in literature.

Whereas the 1986 assessment tested students' recognition of certain authors and works, the 1974 assessment measured not only this factor but also comprehension of imaginative language, how four age groups responded to literature (i.e., became engaged in, interpreted, and evaluated works), and how they felt about reading literature. The majority of respondents professed a willingness to read at least one type of literature (usually the novel) outside of school assignments, but the most widely quoted finding from this assessment was that the majority of students had difficulty explaining why they made certain inferences about a work—still another failure, many educators concluded, in the application of higher-order thinking.

The actual and potential influence of NAEP on teaching is described by Ralph Tyler in his introduction to a 1975 summary of results. As quoted by Johnson (1975), he points to the use of assessment data to "document educational inequities and secure money for their remediation"; to serve as "starting points for the creation of personal or local teaching objectives;" and to suggest to educators "implications for curriculum, textbook, and classroom" (Johnson, 1975, xii)

A major research effort in themselves, the assessments also stimulate research on teaching by invoking hypotheses and by providing baseline data and instrumentation.

R & D CENTERS FOR THE LANGUAGE ARTS

Of the 19 R & D Centers currently operating, three are devoted exclusively to one aspect of language arts: reading, writing, or literature. The newest of these, located at the State University of New York at Albany and directed by Arthur Applebee, is studying the learning and teaching of literature in grades K–12. Barely underway at this writing, it promises to "provide an intellectual focus for literature research and practice." One emphasis will be on the content and organization of literature instruction in "unusual programs" in the United States and abroad. A second emphasis is on interactions between classroom approaches and what readers learn to do. A third strand will be assessment.

Reading Research and Education Center (RREC)

Originally established as the Center for the Study of Reading in 1976, this center, housed at the University of Illinois and now directed by Richard C. Anderson grew out of a conference sponsored by NIE in 1974. One of the conclusions reached at this conference, according to information provided by the Center, was that research in reading, to that time, had been "fragmented and noncumulative", that there was a need for coordinating federal and private efforts in building on sound research, and that researchers doing important theoretical studies should be attracted to applied studies as well. From the beginning, this Center has been concerned with the practical consequences of research it has undertaken and has made vigorous efforts to disseminate research-based knowledge not only to practitioners and other researchers but to the public at large. In 10 years, the Center staff produced more than 400 technical reports. Between 1981 and 1986, Center research appeared in 288 articles in professional and popular journals. In 1985 alone, research produced by the Center was cited 159 times in the *Reading Research Quarterly* (Synopsis, 1986).

Probably the most widely read, praised, and contested publication prepared at the Center is *Becoming a Nation of Readers* (Anderson, Hiehert, Scott & Wilkinson, 1985), which in layman's language interprets findings from selected research, much of it emanating from the Center but including some earlier studies of reading and substantial amounts of recent related work in areas such as teacher effectiveness. The book concludes with 17 unequivocal recommendations of which the following is most pertinent to the subject of this *Handbook:* "Teachers should devote more time to comprehension instruction. Teacher-led instruction in reading strategies and other aspects of comprehension promotes reading achievement, but there is very little direct comprehension instruction in most American classrooms" (p. 118).

In its first 10 years, the Center's research has been wide ranging, concerned, for example, with emerging literacy, schema theory, how phonics skills relate to beginning reading, metacognition, automaticity, scaffolding, reciprocal teaching, conceptual mapping, testing, motivation, sustained reading, use of students' and teachers' time in reading instruction, questioning strategies, and learning academic content through reading. Directly related to research on teaching and illustrative, too, of the Center's mission to engage in applied studies and affect practice are its efforts to study how textbooks are written, purchased, and used and, consequently, to improve instructional texts. Studies sponsored by the Center have popularized the notion of "considerate texts" and have led researchers and teachers to concentrate on how to help students comprehend many that are inconsiderate. The Center, together with the Association of American Publishers, has organized three confer-

ences for senior editors and executives of educational publishing houses, and has a project underway to improve textbook adoption practices.

As the recently-renewed and renamed Center moves into its next five years funded by OERI, it has identified four foci, all of which reflect new trends in research that it has helped to bring about. One of these emphasizes instruction and extends to improving teacher education. Studies either proposed or undertaken represent a greater acknowledgment of both the context of instruction and the teacher's role than was characteristic of much previous research in reading. For example, one study promises to develop "a model approach to an integrated classroom language arts environment, paying special attention to accommodating teachers' beliefs and practices." Another series of studies will focus on classroom transactions to provide insight into the influence of various environmental factors on teachers' and students' behavior (Synopsis, 1986).

Center for the Study of Writing (CSW)

Supported for five years with a $4 million grant from OERI, this Center, established in 1985 at the University of California, Berkeley with Sarah Freedman as director, has a major branch at Carnegie Mellon University with Linda Flower and John Hayes as co-directors (Freedman, Dyson, Flower & Chafe, 1987). CSW is specifically geared toward redefining the relationship between research and practice in teaching writing. Thus, it is not mere coincidence that an important component is the National Writing Project network, which has been instrumental in fostering inquiry among teachers and in making research findings useful to them. One of the Center's ambitious aims is to develop a social-cognitive theory of writing, answering a need for greater theoretical coherence and co-ordination of effort, which has been as lacking in writing research as it was in reading when an R & D Center in that discipline was called for in 1974.

One of three program areas targeted by CSW is writing and instruction; another area investigates interactions between writing and reading, speaking, and access to computers; the third area deals with the social contexts of writing and writers' thinking processes. The Center has sponsored several projects so far within these areas all focusing on some transition in the learner's experience—from home to school, for example, from school to the workplace, from high school to college.

These studies include Anne Haas Dyson's examination of the transition from home to school. In this two-year study, Dyson has looked at relationships among speech, drawing, and writing, the role of peer interaction in the acquisition of literacy, and how individual differences affect the boundaries between talking and drawing and writing. (See chapter 35 by Dyson and Freedman, this handbook.) As Carnegie Mellon, Flower and her colleagues have been studying the thinking strategies of college freshman and "expert" writers (e.g., Nelson & Hayes, 1988). One insight reported by Flower is that learning to analyze text features may have little or no impact on what students do when they write their own texts (Freedman et al., 1987).

One of the more ambitious studies underway is a comparison of peer response and effective instruction in the United States and Great Britain. Other studies include analysis of the writing of prize-winning college students, a comparison of the literacy demands of entry-level jobs and instruction at community colleges, and an examination of the effects of various forms of writing evaluation on school curriculums. (Information in this and the preceding paragraph was derived from a brochure published at Carnegie Mellon University, *Accent on Research,* 1987, which is no longer available and so not referenced.)

In keeping with its commitment to produce a theoretical groundwork for research in writing, the Center has sponsored discussions of linguistic and psychological issues. Chafe and Danielwicz's 1988 analysis of properties of spoken and written language and Flower's explorations of cognition in reading and writing are examples. The Center's first technical reports also have included reviews of research and historical overviews of particular issues such as that by DiPardo and Freedman (1988) on groups in the writing classroom.

A FEW OBSERVATIONS

Several impressions emerge from this selective review of major research programs and research-related activities in teaching English over the last 30 years. Most striking is the rapid growth of a field that had been sketchily defined in the first half of this century. The National Conference on Research in English had been in existence since 1932, but its small membership and limited research efforts did little in its first 30 years to help define the field. Reading remained a field apart, its research dominated in the early years of this century by educational psychologists more concerned with learning than with teaching. While lip service has been paid to the relatedness of language arts at least since the 1920s, it was not until the late 1960s, with the development of psycholinguistics, that reading research began to merge with broader examinations of literacy and the effects of literacy on academic studies. (Affiliations between the R & D centers for reading and for writing are but one sign of that merger.)

A more inclusive definition of research in English has been accompanied by an expanding body of research and growing number of researchers. This growth may have been an inevitable effect of the burgeoning of school populations and public interest in education in the 1960s, but it was nourished by federal and foundational dollars. With relatively modest but sustained Congressional support in the 1960s and 1970s, educational researchers were able to design and redesign a total national effort to produce significant research, to disseminate findings and implement them, and to assess outcomes. However imperfect the plan has proved in 25 years of trial and error, its overall effects have been salutary. In general, the most serious complaint about federal support for educational research is that it has lost momentum in the 1980s. Yet even within this overall decline, resources for the study of literacy have been maintained. As new studies multiply and quality improves, we remember that what we have learned about teaching English in recent years and what we will learn from ambitious R & D projects now being mounted we owe in no small part to those edu-

cators in the 1960s who lobbied for a place for English in the Cooperative Research Program.

Growth has resulted also from collaboration. At first, *collaboration* referred chiefly to interdisciplinary action—literary scholars working with teacher educators, psychologists with linguists, specialists in reading with experts in speech and composition, for example. Today collaborative research is more likely to mean involving classroom teachers as researchers. If a single trend stands out in the recent history of educational research, it is the increasing value assigned to the role of the teacher in research, not only as the subject of investigation or as a source of problems and data to be analyzed by others, but as a key participant in defining classroom variables and identifying appropriate directions for change.

When teachers are considered to be professionals whose beliefs and thought processes are critically important, gaps between research and implementation are lessened. Insights into contextual factors are heightened. Such has been the experience at the Institute for Research on Teaching where since 1976 classroom teachers have been hired half time to conduct research along with Michigan State professors (Porter, 1987). As has been noted in this review, the writing projects have also been a significant force in promoting collaborative research.

This trend toward collaboration goes along with the greater emphasis on "critical" and "interpretive" approaches to research that Soltis (1984) cites, and it is evident also in the process-outcome studies of teacher effectiveness that have multiplied in the last 15 years.

Collaborative research is an effect, too, of the modifications in R & D technologies that have taken place over three decades. The "engineering" approach to professional knowledge that Guba and others articulated in the early 1960s has been criticized not only by observers like Schon (1983) but by researchers within and outside the R & D establishment. Guba himself has become one of the foremost critics of the positivistic approach to educational research and evaluation. Instead of thinking of educational innovations as something researchers develop in laboratory settings to be installed by administrators in classrooms, educators are coming to realize that it is teachers who not only must implement changes but must recognize the need for change. No longer is research-based knowledge thought of as something to be transmitted through a chain of command from university personnel to regional research coordinators to statewide agencies and down to building administrators who then pass the innovation along through training programs to teachers who act as technicians. If such a reversal in thinking has not yet become widespread, it has at least been planted and nourished by major research programs in English in recent years.

Cooperative research has a different shade of meaning from *collaborative.* Best exemplified in this review by the First Grade Studies, its aim is to strengthen research by focusing the efforts of many researchers on a few significant issues. Thus inconsequential studies might be avoided and conflicting results minimized or reasonably accounted for. Thus, too, policy-makers and practitioners might be deterred from over-interpreting tentative results and rushing to implement minor studies and major enthusiasms. Perhaps one of the disappointments of this review is that the spread of cooperative research has been sluggish and more accidental than planned. Lack of adequate federal funding has left the cooperative research effort to the professional organizations and private foundations.

Synthesis, a primary goal of the Cooperative Research Program, has moved forward as a result of individual effort (e.g., Chall, 1967, Hillocks, 1986) and the requirements of Office of Education directives. Dissemination of synthesized results through ERIC and more effectively through the publications of the RELs and R & D centers has made it possible for researchers as well as educators to build on a defined knowledge base. (See chapter 16 by Smith & Klein, this handbook.)

Overall the impression left by this review is an optimistic one. The substantial benefits accruing to the teaching of English from expenditures on research in the recent past should persuade legislators as well as private foundations of the value of increased investments in the future.

References

Alvermann, D. E., Moore, D. W., & Conley, M. W. (1987). *Research within reach: Secondary school reading.* Newark, DE: International Reading Association.

Anderson, L. M., Evertson, C. M., & Brophy, J. E. (1979). An experimental study of effective teaching in first-grade reading groups. *The Elementary School Journal, 79,* 193–223.

Anderson, R. C., Hiebert, E. H., Scott, J. A., & Wilkinson, I. A. G. (1985). *Becoming a nation of readers: The report of the commission on reading.* Washington: The National Institute of Education.

Anthony, H. E., & Raphael, T. E. (1987). *Using questioning strategies to promote students' active comprehension of content area material.* Occasional Paper No. 109. East Lansing, MI: Michigan State University, Institute for Research on Teaching.

Applebee, A. N. (1974). *Tradition and reform in the teaching of English.* Urbana, IL: National Council of Teachers of English.

Applebee, A. N. (1981). *Writing in the secondary schools: English and the content areas.* Research Report No. 21. Urbana, IL: National Council of Teachers of English.

Applebee, A. N., Langer, J. A., & Mullis, I. V. S. (1986, November). *The writing report card: Writing achievement in American schools.* Princeton, NJ: Educational Testing Service.

Applebee, A. N., Langer, J. A., & Mullis, I. (1988). *Who reads best?: Factors related to reading achievement in grades 3, 7, and 11.* Report No. 17-R-01 from NAEP. Princeton, NJ: Educational Testing Service.

Atwell, N. (1987). *In the middle: Writing, reading, and learning with adolescents.* Montclair, NJ: Boynton/Cook.

Ball, D. L., & Feiman-Nemser, S. (1986). *Using textbooks and teachers' guides: What beginning teachers learn and what they need to know.* Research Series No. 174. East Lansing, MI: Michigan State University, Institute for Research on Teaching.

Bond, G. L., & Dykstra, R. (1967). The co-operative research program in first-grade reading instruction. (entire issue) *Reading Research Quarterly, 2*(4).

Braddock, R., Lloyd-Jones, R., & Schoer, L. (1963). *Research in written composition.* Champaign: National Council of Teachers of English.

Calkins, L. M. (1983). *Lessons from a child: On the teaching and learning of writing.* Exeter, NH: Heinemann.

Carlsen, G. R., & Crow, J. (1967). Project English curriculum centers, *English Journal,* (56), 986–93.

Chafe, W., & Danielewicz, J. (1988). Properties of spoken and written language. In R. Horowitz & J. Samuels (Eds.). *Comprehending written language.* New York: Academic Press.

Chall, J. S. (1983). *Learning to read: The great debate.* (2nd ed.). First ed published 1967, New York: McGraw-Hill.

Chase, F. S. & Walter, J. E. (1982). Research laboratories and centers. In *Encyclopedia of Educational Research* (5th ed.). Mitzel, H. E. (Ed.). New York: The Free Press (Macmillan). 1618–1627.

Committee on the National Interest. (1961). *The national interest and the teaching of English.* Urbana, IL: National Council of Teachers of English.

Dershimer, R. A. (1976). *The federal government and educational research and development.* Lexington, MA: D. C. Heath.

DiPardo, A. & Freedman, S. W. (1988). Peer response groups in the writing classroom: Theoretic foundations and new directions. *Review of Educational Research, 58,* 119–149.

Duffy, G. G., Roehler, L. R., Book, C., Meloth, M., Vavrus, L., Putnam, J., & Wesselman, R. (1986). The relationship between explicit verbal explanations during reading skill instruction and student awareness and achievement: A study of reading teacher effects. *Reading Research Quarterly, 21,* 237–252.

Duffy, G. G., Roehler, L. R., & Putnam, J. (1987). Putting the teacher in control: Basal reading textbooks and instructional decision making. *Elementary School Journal, 87,* 357–366.

Emig, J. (1971). *The composing processes of twelfth graders.* Research Report No. 13. Champaign, IL: National Council of Teachers of English.

Emig, J. (1982). Writing, composition, and rhetoric. *Encyclopedia of educational research* (5th ed.). Mitzel, H. E., (ed.). New York: The Free Press (Macmillan). 2021–2036.

Finn, C. E., & Ravitch, D. (1987). *What do our 17-year-olds know?* New York: Harper and Row.

Florio, S., & Clark, C., with Elmore, J., Martin, J., Maxwell, R. & Metheny, W. (1984). The environment of instruction: The forms and function of writing in a teacher-developed curriculum. In G. Duffy, L. Roehler, & J. Mason (Eds.), *Comprehension instruction: Perspectives and suggestions* (pp. 104–115). New York: Longman.

Freedman, S. W. (1987). *Response to student writing.* Research Report No. 23. Urbana, IL: National Council of Teachers of English.

Freedman, S. W., & DiPardo, A. (1988). Peer response groups in the writing classroom: Theoretic foundations and new directions. *Review of Educational Research 58*(2), 119–149.

Freedman, S. W., Dyson, A. H., Flower, L., & Chafe, W. (1987). *Research in writing: Past, present, and future.* Technical Report No. 1. Berkeley, CA: University of California Center for the Study of Writing.

Gomez, M. L. (1985). *The Wisconsin writing project: An exemplar of current efforts at planned school change through staff development.* (Doctoral dissertation, University of Wisconsin). *Dissertation Abstracts International. 47/01.* 152A.

Graves, D. H. (1981). *A case study observing the development of primary children's composing, spelling, and motor behaviors during the writing process.* Final Report. NIE Grant No. G-78-0174. See also Graves, D. H. (1983). *Writing: Teachers and children at work.* Exeter, NH: Heinemann.

Guba, E. G., & Clark, D. L. (1965). An examination of potential change roles in Education. Paper presented at the *Symposium on Innovation and Planning School Curricula* held by the NEA Committee for study of instruction, Airiel House, VA. (October) Cited in Chase, F. S., & Walter, J. E. (1982).

Hanna, Paul R., with Hanna, Jean S., Hodges, Richard E., & Rudorf, Edwin H., Jr. (1966). *Phoneme-grapheme correspondences as cues to spelling improvement.* Washington, DC: Government Printing Office.

Hillocks, G. (1986). *Research on written composition: New directions for teaching.* Urbana, IL: ERIC Clearinghouse on Reading and Communication and the National Conference on Research in English. (NCTE Stock No. 40750) (13–18).

Holmes, J. A. & Singer, H. (1961). *The substrata-factor theory: Substrata-factor differences underlying reading ability in known groups.* U.S. Office of Education, Final Report No. 538, SAE 8176. (See summary in *Theoretical Models and Processes of Reading* (3rd ed.). Singer, H. & Ruddel, R. (Eds.). (1985) Newark, DE: International REading Association.

Hunt, K. W. (1965). *Grammatical structures written at three grade levels.* Champaign, IL: National Council of Teachers of English.

Jencks, C., *et al.* (1972). *Inequality: A reassessment of the effect of family and schooling in America.* New York: Basic Books.

Johnson, S. S. (1975). *Update on education: A digest of the National Assessment of Educational Progress.* Denver, CO: Education Commission of the States.

King, B. (1980). *Two modes of analyzing teacher and student attitudes towards writing: The Emig Attitude Scale and the King Construct Scale.* (Doctoral dissertation, Rutgers University). *Dissertation Abstracts International,* Vol. 40.

Klaus, C. H., & Jones, N. (Eds.). (1984). *Courses for change in writing: A selection from the NEH/Iowa Institute.* Upper Montclair, NJ: Boynton/Cook. (Published in cooperation with the Institute on Writing of the University of Iowa.

Langer, J., & Applebee, A. (1987). *How writing shapes thinking.* Research Report No. 22. Urbana, IL: National Council of Teachers of English.

Loban, W. (1964). *The language of elementary school children.* Research Report No. 1. Champaign, IL: National Council of Teachers of English.

Loban, W. (1976). *Language development: Kindergarten through grade 12.* Research Report No. 18. Urbana, IL: National Council of Teachers of English.

McDonald, F. J. & Elias, P. J. (1975–76). *The effects of teaching performances on pupil learning.* (Beginning teacher evaluation study, Phase II, Final Report; 5 vols.) Princeton, NJ: Educational Testing Service.

Mellon, J. C. (1969). *Transformational sentence combining.* Research Report No. 10. Champaign, IL: National Council of Teachers of English.

Moffett, James (1985). Hidden impediments to improving English teaching. *Phi Delta Kappan, 67*(1), 50–56.

Nelson, J., & Hayes, J. R. (1988). *How the writing context shapes college students strategies for writing from sources.* Technical Report No. 16. Berkeley, CA: University of California, Center for the Study of Writing.

North, S. M. (1987). *The making of knowledge in composition: Portrait of an emerging field.* Upper Montclair, NJ: Boynton/Cook.

O'Donnell, R. C., Griffin, W. J., & Norris, R. C. (1967). *Syntax of kindergarten and school children: A transformational analysis.* Research Report No. 8. Champaign, IL: National Council of Teachers of English.

O'Hare, F. (1973). *Sentence-combining: Improving student writing without formal grammar instruction.* Research Report No. 15. Urbana, IL: National Council of Teachers of English.

Perl, S., & Wilson, N. (1986). *Through teachers' eyes: Portraits of writing teachers at work.* Portsmouth, NH: Heinemann.

Porter, A. C. (1987). Teacher collaboration: New partnerships to attack old problems. *Phi Delta Kappan,* 147–152.

Porter, A., & Brophy, J. (1987). *Good teaching: Insights from the work of the Institute for Research on Teaching.* Occasional Paper No. 114. East Lansing, MI: Michigan State University, Institute for Research on Teaching.

Pritchard, R. J. (1987). Effects on student writing of teacher training in the national Writing Project model. *Written Communication 4,*(1), 51–67.

Raphael, T. E. Englert, C. S., & Kirschner, B. W. (1986). *The impact of text structure instruction and social context on students' comprehension and production of expository text.* Research Series No. 177. East Lansing, MI: Michigan State University, Institute for Research on Teaching.

Schon, D. A. (1983). *The reflective practitioner: How professionals think in action.* New York: Basic Books.

Schmidt, W., & Buchmann, M. (1983). Six teachers' beliefs and attitudes and their curricular time allocations. *Elementary School Journal, 84,* 162–172.

Scriven, M. (1980). *Executive summary of the Bay Area Writing Project evaluation.* Berkeley, CA: University of California BAWP.

Shugrue, M. F. (1968). *English decade of change.* New York: Pegasus.

Shuy, Roger (1981). Holistic view of language. *Research in the Teaching of English. 15,* 101–111.

Soltis, J. F. (1984). On the nature of educational research. *Educational Researcher. 13*(10) 5–10.

Squire, J. R. (1964). *The responses of adolescents while reading four short stories.* Research Report No. 2. Champaign, IL: National Council of Teachers of English.

Squire, J. R., & Applebee, R. K. (1968). *High school English instruction today: The national study of high school English programs.* New York: Appleton-Century-Crofts.

Squire, J., & Applebee, R. K. (1969). *Teaching English in the United Kingdom.* Urbana, IL: National Council of Teachers of English

Steinberg, E. R. (Ed.). (1963). *Needed research in the teaching of English: Proceedings of a Project English research conference.* May 5–7, 1962. Washington: U.S. Government Printing Office.

Synopsis (1986). A summary prepared by staff of the Reading Research and Education Center. Urbana, IL: University of Illinois.

· 10 ·

THE DESIGN OF EMPIRICAL RESEARCH

Robert C. Calfee
Marilyn J. Chambliss

Empirical research is a systematic approach for answering certain types of questions. Through empirical studies, social science researchers seek to discover factors that influence human thought and behavior and to understand when and why these influences occur. This tradition plays a significant role in creating and validating social and psychological theories about how people think and act. In language arts, for instance, data-based research has led to models of the processes by which readers comprehend (e.g., Pearson, 1984) and writers compose (e.g., Bereiter & Scardamalia, 1987).

Empirical research also searches for answers to practical questions. A high school English teacher seeks to improve her students' understanding of formal arguments. A middle school teacher aims to encourage his students toward more analytic comprehension. A remedial reading teacher wants to improve vocabulary instruction so that students score higher on standardized tests. While these questions can be informed by scholarship and conceptual analysis, the primary goals are pragmatic.

Empirical research is *disciplined* (Cronbach & Suppes, 1969). It is distinguished "by the ways observations are collected, evidence is marshalled, arguments are drawn, and opportunities are afforded for replication, verification, and refutation" (Shulman, 1988, p. 4). Empirical research is often equated with quantitative methods, replete with statistics and experimentation, and opposed to qualitative methods, to ethnography, and to naturalistic inquiry. We think this contrast is misleading for several reasons. First, it leads a researcher to concentrate on methodology rather than conceptualization. Second, it implies a choice between "hard-headed" and "soft-hearted" approaches. Third, it overlooks the fact that virtually all significant educational problems call for a mix of methods, and all require rigorous conceptualization and creative design. Shulman (1988) advises novice researchers, "Become *skilled and experienced* in at least two methodologies..., become *aware* of the rich variety of methods of disciplined inquiry..., [and] do not limit your education to methodology alone" (p. 16). Our notion of empirical research design encompasses the

breadth of systematic approaches for collecting evidence to support trustworthy understandings.

We take our audience to be varied: researchers, college teachers of research methods, and high school teachers who rely on research as a guide to practice, among others. Based on our estimate of who is most likely to use the *Handbook*, we focus on a graduate student who is planning a dissertation. This individual is probably a practitioner who has returned for advanced work, who is interested in an investigation with the potential for practical benefits. The chapter is also intended for those who want to read research reports with an informed and critical eye, to enhance their professional knowledge and as a guide for improving instruction. We assume that the reader is already familiar with basic concepts of social science and educational research.

The chapter has four sections. The first examines the task of framing a research question. The next three sections provide additional detail on principles of research design, the process of constructing a design, and the task of interpretation. To demonstrate practical application of the concepts, we introduce a vignette early in the chapter that we will follow through the four sections. We include relatively few references, but provide an annotated selection of research texts at the end of the chapter.

Research Strategy: Question to Answer

Evidence supporting a trustworthy understanding of a problem seldom comes by happenstance: *design* is essential. But design presupposes a topic, a task, a theme. In this section, we present an overview of three elements that are essential for a design to take shape: framing the research question, selecting the context of the study, and thinking forward to the task of interpretation. The serial nature of print forces us to present these in sequence, but they are actually interactive and recursive.

159

Framing an answerable question. The initial phase in empirical research is the formulation of a workable scientific question, one that is answerable by objective evidence. For instance, suppose that you are the high school teacher mentioned at the beginning of the chapter. You want to help your 9th-graders recognize well reasoned and coherent arguments. Assume that you are familiar with Toulmin's (1958) concept of argument (evidence, a claim, and a warrant for joining the two), and that this structure has become critical in your thinking. You also plan to explore the concept of comprehension as reconstruction (Wittrock, Marks, & Doctorow, 1975; Spivey, 1987). You think that students have genuine mastery of the argument structure when they can compose as well as comprehend.

As you reflect on the issues, you weigh several options, including the three listed below:

- What is the essence of a good argument?
- What do my students already know about the concept of argument?
- How might I teach my students to comprehend, critique, and compose various types of arguments?

The first question cannot be answered empirically; the answer depends on value judgments. Objective evidence cannot be brought to bear on this issue, but you can employ other approaches. You might inquire, for instance, "How can I best present the concept of argument as a curriculum goal?" For this question, Toulmin's scholarship might be quite helpful.

The second and third questions, in contrast, are starting points for empirical study. For instance, students' responses to the question, "What makes this a strong argument?" can reveal their thinking processes. Observing the results of different instructional approaches on student performance can provide evidence about the third question.

Setting the study context. This phase entails choices: the researcher must decide what evidence is relevant to the question, how to gather it, and how to analyze and interpret the data. It helps to know the territory: what you already know about research on comprehension of argument texts, about comprehension and composition in general, about effective instructional practices, and so on. Part of the task is to review the literature; this can be daunting when you have a "full platter" as in the present instance. By selecting a few "best-evidence" papers as starting points and working backwards from there (Calfee, 1985, Ch. 2; Slavin, 1986), you can shape the job into manageable proportions. You should also bring your professional knowledge and experience into the mix.

You must decide how and where you will collect data. The *how* of data collection encompasses both passive and active facets; the researcher observes and intervenes, describes and experiments. Imagine a young boy examining an ant hill. One moment he is the naturalist, observing the hectic activity in the insect community. Suddenly compelled to intervene, he pokes a stick into the hole and then covers the hill with sand.

To observe or to intervene? Most texts on research methodology separate these two approaches, one section on naturalistic approaches and a second on experiments. As noted at the outset, *experimental, quantitative,* and *statistical* are often bound together in a package labelled *empirical,* and contrasted with *naturalistic, qualitative,* and *descriptive* (presumably nonempirical) techniques. Fortunately, the joining of quantitative and qualitative methods is becoming more commonplace (Ragin, 1987). Both approaches are clearly empirical, in the sense that they both rely on objective evidence. In addition, the various facets are separable; you can design a naturalistic investigation that relies on quantitative methods, or an experimental study that employs qualitative assessments.

The *where* of data collection is also frequently represented as a contrast between real classroom situations and laboratory environments, the latter presumably unreal. Like the previous contrast, this one is misleading. On the one hand, the laboratory presumably allows control over extraneous fluctuations in conditions, whereas the classroom is a "wild and crazy" place. On the other hand, the practical value of laboratory findings is questioned, whereas classroom-based research is assumed to be directly applicable. Neither stereotype stands close scrutiny. The key is to identify the contextual factors that influence performance, to design the conditions of data collection so that these factors are adequately controlled, and to ensure that the plan incorporates linkages to the domain of generalizability.

Let us look briefly at how these concepts might apply to the vignette. Start with the *where*. Suppose you discover that two teachers in your school employ different approaches to argument instruction, one fairly traditional, the other more innovative. The traditional teacher relies on lecture and discussion to cover standard pro-con forms of argument, with assigned readings and an essay assignment. The second teacher leads students through several forms of argument, emphasizing the role of warrants in linking evidence to a claim. She integrates comprehension and composition in each lesson.

You have the makings of a natural experiment. The plan seems simple enough; your task as researcher will be to visit and describe. On reflection, you realize that the reality is more complex. For instance, your questions may influence both teachers and students. These effects are not necessarily "bad," but they illustrate how research almost always entails some intervention.

You then begin to think about a planned experiment, with classes assigned to contrastive treatments, one traditional and the other more innovative. This approach resembles the studies covered in Chapter 9 on *Major Research Programs.* This plan also seems simple enough at first. You construct materials for the two instructional treatments and select tests to assess performance at the beginning and end of the study.

Your advisor raises several questions. The two treatments differ in several ways—the goals, reading materials, teaching approach, and student activities, to name a few. If the results favor the innovative approach, how can you identify the critical elements? How can you be sure that the treatments are implemented as you intend? What if the tests do not mesh with critical elements of the instruction? You realize that, even in a planned experiment, you may have to play the naturalist's role.

Making sense of the evidence. Assume that the study is complete—you are satisfied with the design, and the data are in the bag. You have completed the analyses. The job is almost finished—or is it?

Data do not answer questions; people do. In order for the evidence to have meaning, you must develop an argument that addresses several issues. How far can you trust the evidence; how far can you generalize the findings; how convincingly can you persuade others of your interpretation? The basic point is simple: you should reflect on what you will say in response to various outcomes—*before you collect the data*. You can organize this task around two options: a) the findings confirm your expectations, or b) they surprise you. The reason for this exercise is equally simple: it helps you refine your research design.

Suppose the results turn out as you predicted. Students in the novel treatment for analyzing and composing arguments do better on final exam and express greater enthusiasm for the course than those in the traditional approach. What does this result mean? Your answer is straightforward; the innovative approach is superior, supporting your notions about what students need to learn and how they can best learn it.

The researcher's task is seldom so simple. You should expect challenges. How else can the results be interpreted? This question is both practically and theoretically important. The intent is to establish the validity of the findings, to ensure that the interpretation holds up to close scrutiny. Addressing this challenge is seldom easy. The researcher is usually close to the problem and invested in the expected conclusion. Imagining other possibilities does not come readily. One remedy is to ask colleagues for alternatives. You will be surprised at the creative ideas that emerge from this exercise. For instance, the novelty of your favored approach may stimulate both teachers and students; what will happen when the method becomes humdrum? The technique worked for this class, but will students apply the ideas in other classes and situations? The approach takes extra work; if another teacher decides to try it with modifications, what are the critical features?

On the other hand, suppose the results do not come out as expected? You may have difficulty imagining this outcome. Given all your planning, thinking, and work, how could this happen! The most frequent disappointment occurs when an innovative treatment produces little or no effect, when the null hypothesis (no difference) cannot be rejected. This result can come about for either or both of two reasons. First, the treatment may actually not be effective—hard to accept, but possible. Second, student performance may vary so widely that random fluctuations swamp the effect. It's like a slot machine, which costs you on each play; you do not notice the loss because sometimes you win and sometimes you lose. A well-conceived research design allows you to identify sources of variability in performance, so that you can tell whether you are winning or losing.

Planning an empirical investigation is not a sequential activity. The process begins with a question. You wrestle with the details, and suddenly the shape of the question changes. You think about how to interpret various outcomes, and the design takes a different form. Each phase has distinctive features, but the process is recursive and interactive. When you read a research report, it may resemble bowling; the investigator sets

- **FACTOR:** A variation in treatment conditions, in subject characteristics, or in instrumentation, that is identified by the researcher to achieve control over the performance outcomes in a study; also referred to as an *independent variable*.

- **LEVEL OF A FACTOR:** A particular choice or selection from the possible variations in a factor.

- **MEASURE:** Result of observation or measurement of performance under specified conditions; also referred to as a *dependent variable*.

- **TREATMENT FACTOR:** Variation in environmental conditions under direct control of the researcher. *Amount of time allowed for revising a draft* is a treatment factor; *5, 10,* and *30 minutes* are levels.

- **PERSON FACTOR:** Pre-existing characteristic of a person or group, identified by the researcher in designing a plan for selecting a sample for investigation. *Undergraduate major* is a person factor; *English, Engineering,* and *Political Science* are levels.

- **OUTCOME FACTOR:** Facet used in designing a measurement package (e.g., test, observation, interview, or questionnaire). *Writing topic* is an instrument factor; *contemporary writing styles, earthquake preparation,* and *world conflicts* are levels.

- **NUISANCE FACTOR:** A variation included in the design of an investigation to ensure adequate control, not necessarily because of conceptual or practical importance. *Class period* is a nuisance factor; *early and late morning and afternoon* are levels.

FIGURE 10–1. Technical vocabulary for research design terminology.

the pins, throws the ball, and counts how many pins fall. Reality is different. "Some of the most excellent inquiry is free-ranging and speculative in its initial stages, trying what might seem to be bizarre combinations of ideas and procedures, restlessly casting about . . ." (Cronbach & Suppes, 1969, p. 16).

Principles of Design

This section of the chapter develops the foundational concepts of research design. Any field of study evolves in stages or paradigms. At the beginning is the careful examination of intuitive experiences and ideas. Later comes the evolution of theory. Along the way, investigators must rely on informed guesses. Educational research is in this middle stage today, and hence our emphasis in this chapter on disciplined planfulness.

We first explain the three fundamental barriers that design techniques help surmount: validity, confounding, and control. Then we discuss four fundamental principles: the overall concept of design, the elements of design, connection of the elements, and integration around a theme. We will employ a technical vocabulary that has evolved over the past several decades; the critical terms are shown in Figure 10–1. This table should be helpful as you proceed through the chapter.

Three Fundamental Barriers. In conducting a research study, the researcher must keep in mind three critical issues—validity, confounding, and control—that can undermine the value of the outcomes. Design methods help you safeguard against these threats.

The validity of a research study, as for a test, refers to the trustworthiness of various interpretations of the evidence; does the finding mean what you think it means (Messick, 1988)? Validity can be compromised in several ways, but most of the shortcomings arise when you fail to think through the path that leads from the initial question to the final interpretation. The concept of test validity is a useful metaphor. Suppose a student's test score indicates she reads two grade levels below expectation. Should you assign the student to a remedial program? The answer depends not only on the test score, but on the interpretation. The validity of the test for this decision can be questioned in several ways: Is the test suitable for this purpose? Were the testing conditions appropriate? What other evidence is available? What are the costs and benefits of the decision for the student?

Similar questions can be posed for a research study. The principles are the same; the validity of the findings depends not only on the data but on the interpretation. Is the plan of the study adequate? To what extent does the context allow generalization to other situations? How does the finding mesh with other studies? What are the cost-benefit implications of various decisions springing from the study? The more you know about the answers to these questions, the more secure will be the validity. One purpose of research design is to increase the chances that outcomes are valid. As Cronbach (1988) puts it, "Validators should do what the detached scientist would do; [the key ingredient is] a vigorous, questing intellect. . . ." (p. 14)

The second barrier, confounding, occurs when two variables are intertwined. The effect of the primary factor cannot be separated from the confounded factor, and the findings are completely compromised. Consider how confounding might arise in your study if you select two teachers to employ two different instructional approaches. Suppose you find a striking difference in student outcomes. The finding can result from the teacher, the program, or some combination of the two. Given these possibilities, the evidence cannot be interpreted with any confidence. This difficulty is virtually impossible to repair after the fact.

Confounding is the major shortcoming of designs that contrast an innovative approach and a traditional method, the classical experimental-control technique. A quarter-century ago, Cronbach (1963) pointed out the many limitations of this design, which still appears in the empirical literature. Our advice to you, if you propose such a study, is to give the matter further thought. Any comparison of two groups probably means confounded variables, and hence is subject to multiple interpretations. A more complex design can pull the confounded variables apart.

Inadequate control is the third concern, and it occurs when unintended fluctuations obscure answers to the research question. Eliminating unwanted fluctuations is essential because of the critical importance of variability in educational research. On the one hand, explainable variability is the payoff. You predict that performance under the novel treatment will differ from the traditional approach, presumably because of the treatment. On the other hand, unexplainable variability is a threat; large differences in student performance within the two conditions may obscure the treatment effect. The goal, then, is to plan a design and arrange conditions so that systematic variability is maximized and unexplained variability is minimized—this, in a nutshell, is the essence of the concept of control.

Control encompasses the various methods employed to strengthen validity. Chief among these methods is design, but other issues are also important. We will discuss design in the next section, and focus here on ancillary issues.

For instance, if your findings are to be generalized to other situations, the evidence should presumably be based on a random sample from some population of interest, or at least you should know how nonrandom the data are. Social science research typically relies on "handy" random samples. You have access to teachers and students in a particular school, not exactly a chance selection, but typical of schools in the area. Some teachers will cooperate with you; others will not. Or you may search for a "purposive" sample, a situation selected because it meets conditions important for your hypotheses. These constraints and decisions may limit the generalizability of your findings. The important point for control is to be aware of these constraints, and to document events for yourself and your audience.

A second non-design control issue is the maintenance of uniformity during data collection. A well-constructed design provides control over certain variables, but other conditions are likely to be free-floating. For instance, suppose your study spans a five-week period. You should consult the calendar—what upcoming events may influence instruction or assessment? If the critical posttest is scheduled on the day before a big football game, students may not give full attention to the task.

What is happening in the lives of students and teachers during the study? If several students know that they are moving in two months, their engagement in the program may be lessened. If a teacher is in the midst of a divorce or fighting with the Internal Revenue Service, this may not be the best time for a new program—nor, for that matter, to handle a traditional approach. These scenarios exemplify the difficulty of establishing uniformity. You should make every effort to keep conditions constant. You also should be sensitive to discrepancies, and document them.

The concept of design. Thus far we have outlined the steps in conceiving a design from question to answer. We have specified three barriers that empirical design can surmount. Until now we have begged a crucial question: What does a good research design look like? In this section we present our concept of empirical design.

A well-planned design is the key to isolating treatment effects from background noise. It is the best hedge against lack of validity, confoundings, and inadequate control. Textbooks on research design often stress the procedures and mechanics of the task, including statistical methods. We start instead with underlying principles of design, which apply equally to descriptive and experimental investigations, to quantitative and to qualitative approaches.

Many human endeavors rely on the concept of design, sometimes through recognition and appreciation of naturally occurring patterns, more often through creation and construction. As Simon (1981) notes, design is the feature that distinguishes between the natural and the artificial, between happenstance and the artifices of humankind. All designs have three essential ingredients (Calfee & Chambliss, 1987). First is a set of distinctive elements, what Simon calls "nearly decomposable components." Second are the linkages that bind individual elements together. Third is the theme that gives overall shape and meaning to the enterprise.

A well-crafted written argument illustrates the concept. The theme comes from the claim, which sets the author's overall purpose. The shaping of a coherent theme is where art joins technology. The elements are the sources of evidence, the concrete statements that support the claim. Toulmin (1958) proposes a model whereby *warrants* (principles about how the world works) link the evidence to the claim. In a complex argument where linkages between the claim and the evidence are not readily apparent, warrants are made explicit by statements that explain how the evidence offered supports the claim.

For instance, consider the claim that "World political systems have converged on a single model combining socialistic economics and democratic politics." The claim may appear simple on the surface, but is actually quite complex. The daily newspapers are a rich source of evidence. Warrants link world events to the claim by explaining how each event is, indeed, an instance where socialistic economics and democratic politics have combined. A well-designed composition presenting this argument would clearly state the claim, only offer as evidence the facts, examples, and so on that are warranted (linked to the claim by warrants), and include explicit warrant statements linking the argument parts. The three characteristics of good design would be present.

Now let us consider the application of design principles for planning the research study. The elements include the factors that influence performance: the treatment or environmental variations, differences between individuals, and various methods for assessing performance. The elements are linked by one of two relationships, "crossing" or "nesting," described below. The theme encompasses the overarching objectives of the research. A design with these three characteristics will generate a data structure to inform your research questions in a trustworthy and generalizable fashion.

Factorial elements. A factor is a variable that the researcher defines and controls in order to evaluate its influence on performance (see Figure 10–1). Some factors can be directly controlled; others depend on careful observation of natural variations. In your study, for instance, your initial reflections turn up serveral candidates as factors for inclusion in the design: argument type, instructional method, prior student experience with arguments, age and sex of students, teacher experience with the genre, and choice of a written or oral test.

As suggested earlier, your best strategy at the outset is to cast a wide net—brainstorm, think divergently. The idea is not to create a shopping list of every conceivable variable, but to identify a range of factors that may substantially influence performance or inform your understanding of the phenomenon.

Novice researchers tend to begin with one or two factors of central interest, relying on "randomness" to handle other effects. This strategy leaves too much to chance. Keep in mind

the following principle: *if you ignore factors that influence performance, variability from these sources does not disappear; instead, it confuses the picture.* In a well-controlled study, the researcher pins down important sources of variability, to ensure that systematic effects stand out clearly against background noise.

For practical purposes, we distinguish three primary types of factors: treatment factors; person or individual-difference factors; and outcome factors (Figure 10–1). A fourth category, nuisance or control factors, is also useful in preparing a design.

A *treatment factor* is an environmental facet directly controllable by the researcher. Argument type and instructional method might serve as treatment factors in your study. You introduce students to two types of arguments depicted in Figure 10–2: a simple version where all the evidence supports a single claim, and a complex form where different facets of a claim are supported by different pieces of evidence. You arrange two types of instruction: one where students receive model arguments to stody, and one where students are explicitly taught the argument structure.

A "person factor" is an intrinsic characteristic of an individual or group. Age, sex, ability, and prior experience are examples. These factors should be taken into account when selecting teachers, students, and classes. If you know that some students have been taught about arguments while others are unfamiliar with the concept, then you should include experience as a design factor.

In addition to controlling a factor of importance in its own right, you can also assess the interaction between experience and other factors. An interaction occurs when the effect of one variable depends on conditions associated with another factor. For instance, experienced students may not benefit from the special treatment, but novices may be helped a lot. This particular effect is an example of aptitude-treatment interaction, where students respond to variation in a treatment factor differentially depending on person characteristics (Cronbach & Snow, 1981).

"Outcome factors" direct the choice of measures in an investigation. Like treatment factors, they can often be directly manipulated by the researcher, although this opportunity is often overlooked. The tendency is to select an off-the-shelf instrument without thinking about its relation to the research questions. Suppose your school administers a standardized comprehension test. Should you employ this test to assess the relative effectiveness of the two programs? Probably not. Most tests use rather vague expositions, not the argument genre; they tap the students' ability to recognize, not to reflect or to compose. You might use the test as an index of general student ability, but in designing the assessment system you should construct measures that directly assess students' ability to handle argument structures, that demonstrate their ability to craft a persuasive text, and that reveal attitudes and confidence about these tasks.

In addition to deciding on the factors to include in a design, you also need to choose the levels for each factor. Sometimes the decision is straightforward; if sex is a factor, then male and female are obvious choices. For a factor like undergraduate major, the range of options is greater, and the selection requires more thoughtfulness. If revision time is a treatment variable, the number of options is virtually infinite, and you have to esti-

Simple Claim with One Warrant

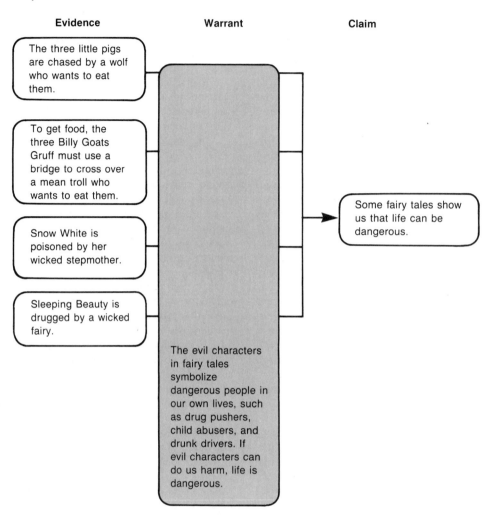

mate the relation between this factor and performance. For instance, does performance increase steadily with time? Or might it increase for a while and then tail off? Or perhaps, beyond a certain point, might further time actually lead to a poorer outcome? And for each question, what are candidate values?

What are the instructional options in your study? We suggested earlier that you might ask students to read model arguments, or you could teach the argument structure directly. On reflection, what about a level (a condition) that combines the two? Now the factor has three levels (Figure 10–3). But how are instruction and reading to be combined into this third level? Students could first study the models in small groups with minimal guidance, and then end the session with a guided discussion. Or you could incorporate the models as examples for guided discovery during class discussion. A third approach is to lecture the students about argument structures and then assign the models as exercises. Which plan should you employ in the design? The answer depends on your resources, and on your judgment about what you can learn from each plan.

Linkages. Two factors can be joined in either of two ways: *crossed* (every level of the first factor is combined with every level of the second factor), or *nested* (the levels of the second factor differ at each level of the first factor). The contrast, shown in (Figure 10–4), parallels the contrast between a matrix and a hierarchy. In a matrix, every level on the first dimension is combined with every level of the second dimension. In a hierarchy, while the lower levels have a common thread, they do not connect to other points at the same level. When a set of factors is crossed, you can assess the main effects of each factor as well as the interactions among them. When factors are nested, only the main effects can be evaluated.

These two methods for connecting factors have two advantages. First, like Lego blocks or Tinker toys, they combine in virtually infinite ways to join any number of factors. While the previous definitions express relations between a pair of factors, any number of factors may be joined by combinations of crossing and nesting.

Second, the methods ensure that any factorial design is free

Complex Claim with Many Warrants

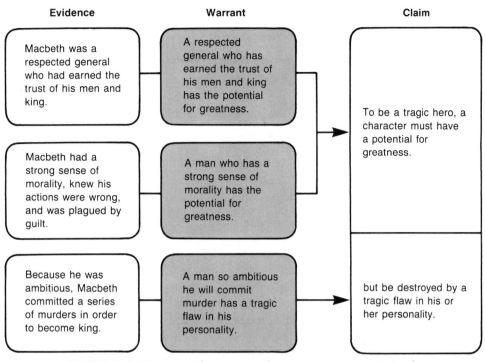

FIGURE 10–2. Diagrams of two types of argument structure: A simple claim with one warrant and a complex claim with many warrants.

from confounding, that the effects of any two factors are independent of one another. This assurance has two caveats. First, each combination must be assigned an equal (or proportionate) number of observations. Second, the strategy does not guarantee that any given factor is not confounded with other factors not in the design.

The alternative to a factorial design is to simply cast a broad net for available data. Unintentional confounding can result because of natural covariation. Suppose that some cells or combinations are underrepresented or altogether missing, which is not unusual in survey studies. For instance, you distribute a questionnaire, and then discover that the respondents fall into two configurations: English majors with high verbal and low math SATs, and engineering majors with low verbal and high math SATs. If you find differences in responses, these can reflect the effects of undergraduate major, verbal aptitude, math aptitude, or any combination of the three factors. You can often predict such patterns in advance; by preparing a design in advance, you can select a sample that allows you to separate the various facets.

How does the researcher decide whether to cross or nest a particular pair of factors in planning a design? The linkage can depend on the situation. Consider the design in (Figure 10–5), for instance. Factor STRUCTURE represents the argument structure. In Many-One-One, all evidence goes directly through a single warrant to a single claim. In Many-Many-One, each evidence source has its own warrant, all converging on a single claim. Finally, in Many-Many-Many, multiple sources of evidence and warrants support different parts of a complex claim. The other two factors are simpler. In Factor PRESENCE, the warrant is either stated or implicit. The third factor, EXAMPLES, covers the researcher's choice of specific texts and topics to replicate the various treatment conditions.

In (Figure 10–5), the researcher has chosen to cross STRUCTURE and PRESENCE. The reasoning is that the combinations make sense, and that the interaction between the two factors deserves attention. EXAMPLES is nested within STRUCTURE but crossed with PRESENCE; two different passages are selected for each structure, and then used with or without the warrant statement. The researcher reasons that the same passage is unlikely to fit all three structures, but that a passage can serve equally well for the two levels of the PRESENCE factor.

Notice that in (Figure 10–5) different students are assigned to each of the twelve combinations. STUDENTS can be viewed as a factor nested within the three treatment factors. An important consideration in planning a design is the decision about how to assign individuals or groups to various treatment combinations. The issue often appears in research texts as the choice of a between-subject or within-subject plan, but it is better described as a crossing versus nesting of persons with other design factors.

The decision to nest students within conditions as in (Figure 10–5) might arise from the following rationale. Suppose you have a couple of cooperative colleagues who will make their classes available to you for a preliminary study. You will have only an hour with each class, but your procedures allow you to

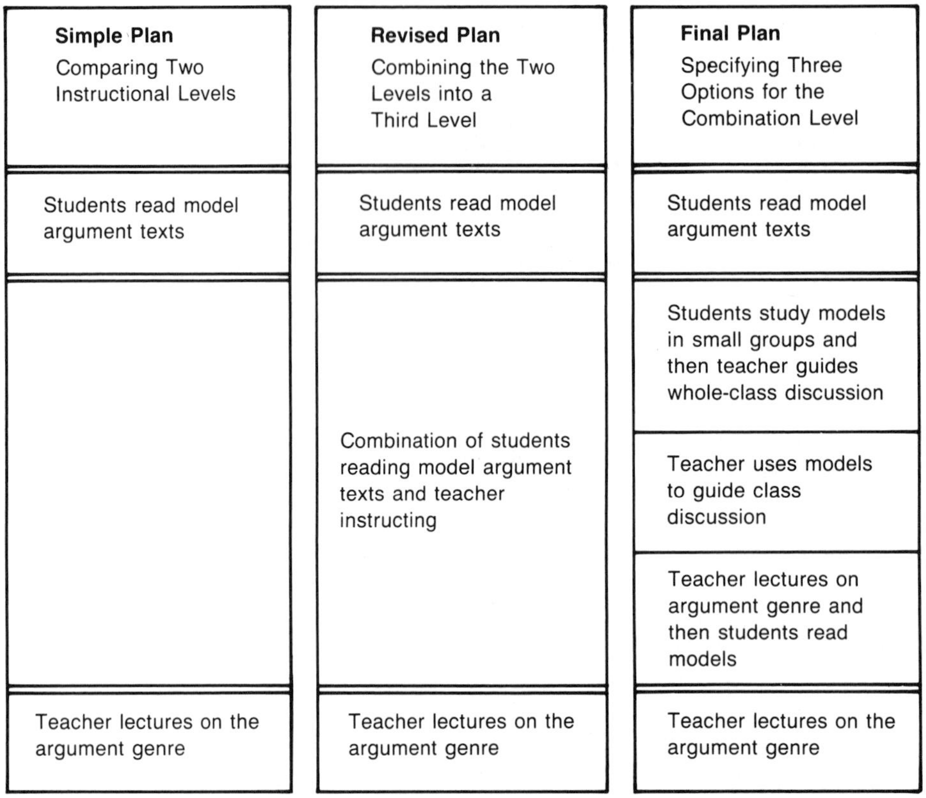

Simple Plan Comparing Two Instructional Levels	Revised Plan Combining the Two Levels into a Third Level	Final Plan Specifying Three Options for the Combination Level
Students read model argument texts	Students read model argument texts	Students read model argument texts
		Students study models in small groups and then teacher guides whole-class discussion
	Combination of students reading model argument texts and teacher instructing	Teacher uses models to guide class discussion
		Teacher lectures on argument genre and then students read models
Teacher lectures on the argument genre	Teacher lectures on the argument genre	Teacher lectures on the argument genre

FIGURE 10–3. Choosing levels for an instructional factor from a simple plan with two levels to a final plan with options for five levels.

assign the various treatment combinations at random to students within each class. With about 30 students per class, you can assign 5 students to each combination; this example does not control for any person factors.

In contrast, suppose you have access to an advanced placement class with 20 students, that your study fits well with the instructional program, and that the students are interested in the investigation. Practically speaking, you have virtually unlimited time with each student. A design suitable for these conditions is shown in (Figure 10–6), with 10 students assigned in the warrant-stated level and ten to the warrant-implicit level. Students in each group study all combinations of structures and examples. The student factor is thus crossed with structure and examples and nested within the stated-implicit factor. The reason for this nesting is that high-achieving students might recognize variations in the PRESENCE factor, and realize the need to fill in the warrants when these are missing.

The decision to nest or cross persons with other factors reflects both practical and theoretical considerations. Practically speaking, the researcher sometimes has little or no choice. For instance, individual-difference factors like sex or personality dictate that individuals be nested within the levels of a factor. A person is either male or female, impulsive or reflective. Treatment factors can generally be crossed with person factors, and sometimes it makes sense to do so. If a treatment combination

takes only a minute or two to administer and the student is available for an hour, the researcher should probably administer as many conditions as possible. This decision means crossing the student with several factors.

Crossed and nested person designs provide qualitatively different information. If each student is tested under a single condition as in (Figure 10–5), the researcher cannot assess how individuals react to different combinations. When each individual is tested under several conditions, then contrasts in performance are measurable. To be sure, the researcher must then attend to performance changes due to the testing itself. People improve with practice; they also become fatigued with time. Several techniques (e.g., counterbalancing through Latin Square designs) provide control over these influences, but the key issue is the researcher's sensitivity to such "nuisance" factors.

Theme. The final ingredient in a design is the conceptual framework that guides selection of the factors and decisions about how to combine them. While we have placed this topic at the end of our list, it is of paramount importance. The thematic foundation of a research study requires knowledge of the territory, experience in dealing with the issues, and a large dollop of intuition and art. On the other hand, the task can also be guided by systematic strategy, for which Simon (1981) gives

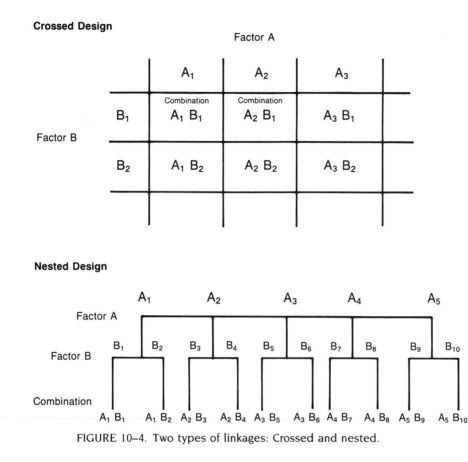

FIGURE 10–4. Two types of linkages: Crossed and nested.

counsel. Although some systems appear complex on the surface, Simon argues all are fashioned around a relatively small set of separable components, each with a distinctive internal structure, each linked in simple ways to one another (Calfee, 1981). We applied this notion earlier to the composing of an argument and the planning of a study. It also applies to the conceptualizing of a research problem.

The key is to look for the joints that divide a complex system into a small number of simpler entities. Carving a turkey is a metaphor. A turkey can pose quite a challenge to the novice carving the Thanksgiving bird. The trick is to find the joints, so the carver can divide a big job into relatively small ones. Think about messes, lumps, chunks. If you carve a problem into a lot of little pieces, you will be overwhelmed. If you try to handle the problem as a whole, you will be confused by the apparent complexity. Human beings can effectively handle a few items at a time; the key is to keep it simple—more to the point, make it simple.

How do you know when you have hit a joint in a conceptual domain? We suggest that when the technical language and relations in one chunk differ from those in another chunk, you have found a starting point. Locating the chunks, then, is the key to analysis of a complex question; it also lays the foundation for synthesis, for relating the chunks to one another.

Let us apply this reasoning to the vignette. Your initial thinking about argument was fuzzy and complex. On the one hand, you saw the issues as one-dimensional: the best method

seemed obvious. On the other hand, you were soon burdened by technical details. We advise you now to look for a few joints, which allow you to divide the big problem into manageable chunks that organize the details. You have already moved in this direction by focusing on two thematic areas: forms of argument and styles of integrated instruction. Both areas have a distinctive technical base; each can be considered as an entity in its own right.

You can apply the divide-and-conquer principle to each of the two domains. For instance, how can you handle the complexities of instruction: pedagogical method, materials, and management? The answer is implicit in the question. Divide the instructional chunk into a handful of distinctive subchunks, and decide which are critical to the research question. To be sure, the chunks will need to be related to one another, but the capacity to assess interactions is inherent in the technology of factorial design.

Creating the design

In this section of the chapter we discuss how the concepts and procedures described above apply to your construction of a specific research plan. This is the time when you move from divergent to convergent thinking, from strategy to tactics.

You have identified two thematic issues: clarity in assessing argument genre curricular goals for your students, and instruc-

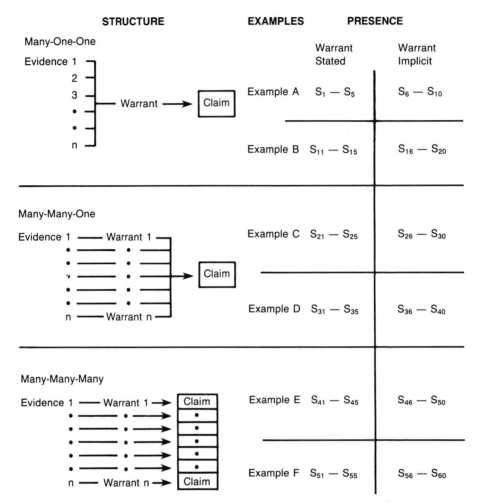

FIGURE 10–5. Linking STRUCTURE, PRESENCE, EXAMPLES, and SUBJECTS into a design.

tional support to help students learn both to comprehend the point of a writer's argument and to support a point in their own writing. You have raised researchable questions for each issue. What processes do 9th-graders use as they work their way through a written argument? How do they use their knowledge about arguments (if any) when they write? Both are assessment questions. Your instructional question is: What combination of didactics, examples, and discussion will improve student skills?

How do you formalize a plan of action? You have several options, but certain principles can guide your decisions. First, the thematic chunks—argument text structures and instructional approaches—need to be expanded into operational factors. Second, you should consider two or three bite-sized investigations rather than putting all of your eggs into a single basket. Third, keep the ultimate goal in mind, and be careful not to drown in details. The factors selected for the design should support the thematic foundations of the study, while ensuring that the design controls significant sources of extraneous variability. The sections that follow offer some practical advice about the process of preparing a plan.

Big picture and first steps. The first task is to remember where you are going, and to keep moving in that direction. You have shaped the elements of a plan; an image of the research problem is taking shape in your mind's eye. How should you proceed next? One approach is to plan a full-scale experiment. Another is to develop a series of ministudies. A third is to initiate a naturalistic investigation of observation, interview and assessment. Our recommendation is that you work at the extremes of this continuum, collecting preliminary data while also refining the big picture.

Developing a conceptual framework requires abstract thinking, but it can also be aided in practical ways. For instance, a graphic layout can help you document the evolution of your research plan. Figure 10–7 shows a midstream road map that might fit your project. The matrix arranges the two thematic elements as column headings; the rows show the factorial categories central to any research plan. Imagine the sketch as a structure for laying out ideas; the entries in the figure are illustrative. Creating the plan is a dynamic enterprise; use "Post-Its," or record your thoughts on a word-processor. Ask colleagues

Factor PRESENCE: Warrant Stated

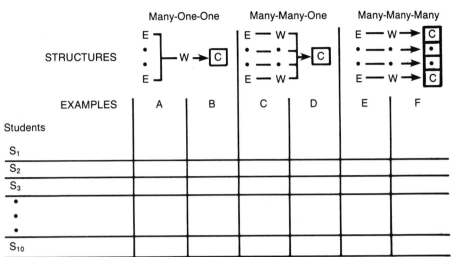

FACTOR PRESENCE: Warrant Implicit

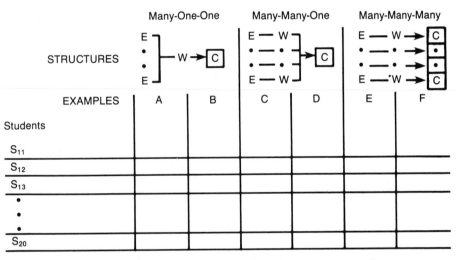

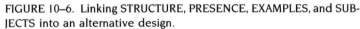

FIGURE 10–6. Linking STRUCTURE, PRESENCE, EXAMPLES, and SUB-JECTS into an alternative design.

for comment and criticism. Be flexible; the one constancy is change.

Our second recommendation is that, as your plans take shape, you spend time in classrooms with teachers and students, looking and listening, trying out your ideas and procedures and materials in realistic settings. This suggestion does not assume you have an empty head; to the contrary, what you see and hear will be guided by the conceptual framework spread around your walls. But before the design is cast in stone, check the context. Approach this task with explicit questions in mind. What are the major sources of evidence? What variations are especially critical? Where are you least certain and most confused? What questions should you pose to informants? What answers do you expect, and how can you follow up for clarification?

These early forays into the field make great demands on research methodology. You are still framing the research question. You are still developing the instruments. The decisions you base on pilot information are critical, and will determine the shape of the real study. Yet in making these decisions you must rely on relatively unreliable evidence.

We might do well in social science research to adopt a more organic and decision-oriented approach, a more deliberative and interactive process: "Given what I have learned thus far, what is the most sensible direction for my next move?" Custom (and the reliance on the set-piece proposal) often lead the novice researcher (as well as others) to persist with an original course of action even when it is clear that things are not going as planned. Research is a problem-solving activity, and depends on flexibility and feedback for success.

	Assessment	Instruction
Treatments	Text differences	Task differences for teachers & students Comprehension & composition
Subjects	Different levels of expertise	Different levels of expertise
Outcomes	Performance measures	Performance measures Transfer measures Satisfaction measures

FIGURE 10–7. An overall design for assessing and instructing comprehension and composition of arguments.

Evolution of a strategy. Following classroom visits and reflection on the issues, you begin to formulate your research plan. Studying the charts around your walls, you may feel overwhelmed. Too many factors, too many combinatins, too much data to assemble and interpret. Simon's suggestion to search for parsimony is now the remedy.

Our experience suggests that the initial stage of an instructional study (after the "walking around" phase) is often most effectively directed toward the development of an assessment system to uncover psychological processes—cognition, behavior, and motivation. The assessment stage answers your assessment research questions and gives you valuable information for designing instruction. Much more is involved than the development of a test. The second stage explores the impact of instructional interventions, not to demonstrate the efficacy of a particular approach, but to gain an understanding of the relation between instruction and learning. The two sections below explore how to pursue a strategy crafted along these lines.

The assessment study. Figure 10–8 depicts a plan for the assessment phase. The plan incorporates three tasks: identify text type; search for argument parts; integrate the parts into a mental representation of the complete argument. Your knowledge of comprehension research (e.g. Kintsch & Yarborough, 1982; Meyer, Brandt, & Bluth, 1980; Meyer & Freedle, 1984) suggests to you that these tasks are basic to effective comprehension. Some factors, like text characteristics, have specific variations for each component. For instance, the contrast between infor-

mational and argumentative patterns will show whether students recognize the argument pattern.

The general treatment factors apply to all three components. For example, individual differences in reading achievement are likely to influence student performance in all three tasks, and must be included to control extraneous variability and evaluate interactions.

The instructional study. Figure 10–9 lays out a plan for instructional factors. This design has two components, the first designed to aid students to comprehend the argument schema, and the second to assist them in composing an argument text. As in Figure 10–8, the plan is designed as a matrix crossing the two components with the three general factorial categories. Factors for the comprehension component depend on outcomes from the assessment study, which reveal areas where students have difficulty. Factors for the composition component come from the writing model proposed by Hayes and Flower (1980): planning, translating, and reviewing.

A few words about the structure of the design. Because teaching presumably has lasting effects, different students are assigned to each instructional combination; in this instance, students must be nested in a factor, because an individual student cannot learn one instructional strategy, erase it, and then learn another. In making these and other decisions, basic design principles provide the base for moving from initial conceptualization to final plan.

Interpretation

We now make another pass at the question raised earlier: With the data in hand, how does a researcher interpret and generalize the findings? The critical issue is validity—the trustworthiness of the interpretations. This task of establishing validity comprises two subtasks: internal validity and external validity (Campbell & Stanley, 1966; Cook & Campbell, 1979; Porter, 1988). Internal validity addresses the question, "To what degree can I trust the evidence that I have within my grasp?" External validity asks, "To what degree can I extend the findings to other situations?"

Answers to these questions depend partly on factors controlled by the design and partly on factors that are free-floating (Figure 10–10). The first test of internal validity, *conceptual clarity,* depends on the design factors. Now that the data are in, how clearly can you tell what happened? To what degree do the factors appear as compelling representatives of the constructs (the underlying concepts) that you chose to represent the research question? To what degree can you make sense of patterns in the data? Complex interactions may be appealing when you first think about a problem, but they can also render interpretation difficult. To what extent did the treatments work as intended? Secrest, West, Phillips, Redner, and Yeaton, (1979) refine this point: "The essence of construct validity is that one has a good understanding of the conceptual meaning of the treatment. . . . It refers to our interpretation of the treatments, not the treatments themselves" (p. 17).

The second test of internal validity, situational stability, is the

Comprehension Processes			
Identify Text Type	**Look for Argument Parts**	**Integrate Parts**	**General Factors**
Specific Factors			
Treatment Factors Text Structure Argument or informational	Claim Presence Claim present or absent Evidence Presence Support or superfluour information	Argument Structure Simple claim/individual warrants or simple claim/one warrant or complex claim/individual warrants Warrant Presence Warrant explicit or implicit	Examples Order
Person Factors Text Knowledge Know text schemata or not	Argument Knowledge Know how to find argument parts or not	Argument Structure Knowledge Know argument structures or not	Vocabulary skills Prior experience
Outcome Factors Identify Text Type Argument or informational	Identify Argument Parts List the point and support or not	Summarzie the Argument Write a summary of the argument or not	

FIGURE 10–8. A design for assessing the comprehension of arguments.

degree to which the evidence allows you to project the basic findings with confidence to other contexts, without modification of the original design. What about the influence of factors that you decided to ignore; either directly or through interactions, how may they influence the outcome? If the sample of participants is too small or too homogeneous, then you may not be able to extend the findings. If the instruments are too specialized, you may again be hesitant to recommend your results to others.

The next two categories go beyond the details of your original design to extension of the underlying principles. Researchers seldom limit their interpretive scope to a particular study. You are interested not just in the program that you have developed, whatever shape it may take in the final design, but in the concepts that undergird this program. Researchers aspire to broadly generalizable statements, and here the issue of validity takes a different shape.

Figure 10–10 has two entries under this heading. First is conceptual match. In going beyond the original conditions, while staying close to the original conception, how safe are you in projecting your results? The key here is again the clarity of the original conceptualization, and the degree to which the conditions can be implemented in a similar manner in a different context.

Your argument program shows considerable promise on its test flight. The program employs a process approach, with techniques for prewriting, for creating a draft, and for revision, each incorporating a student planning guide and an evaluation form. Teachers receive intensive staff development in the concepts and the procedures. A colleague plans to implement the program in a different setting, but must modify it to fit local conditions. What are the boundaries? Surely the program is not limited to specific wording or format. If staff development has to be reduced from a week to two days, what to keep and what to jettison?

Next comes the situational match, which is related to what Cronbach (Cronbach, Gleser, Nanda, & Rajaratnam, 1972) calls generalizability. Suppose a user wants to change the program and apply it to a different situation—what are the chances that the results apply under these circumstances? Your program has been tested under one set of conditions, with certain factors under control. The students are from middle-class backgrounds, the classes are relatively small, the teachers are experienced professionals, and resources are available for staff devel-

	Process to be Taught		General Factors
	Comprehend Argument	Compose Argument	
	Specific Factors		
Treatment Factors	Instructional Content Identify text type or find claim and evidence or integrate to match text or a combination	Instructional Content Planning or translating or reviewing or a combination	Teacher Tasks Direct instruction or providing argument models or a combination Student Tasks Individual practice or small group practice or whole class practice or a combination
Person Factors	Argument Knowledge Know argument type or not Reading Skills Level of decoding skill Level of vocabulary skill	Writing Skills Level of spelling skill Level of sentence mechanics skills Level of paragraph development skills	Prior experience
Outcome Factors	State Author's Point in Argument Text Accurately or not State Speaker's Point in Class Discussion Accurately or not State Speaker's Point in Political Speech Accurately or not	Write an Argument Competently or not Prepare a Debate Competently or not	Fill Out Motivation Questionnaire High or low interest Teacher Observation of Students Comprehending and Constructing Arguments Students competent or not

FIGURE 10–9. A design for instructing students to comprehend and compose arguments.

opment and collegial interactions. Can the findings be applied in situations where these conditions do not hold? If the treatment is powerful, then the variation in local contexts should not matter. An investigation should ideally provide linkages that inform judgments about the transferability of the findings.

Answers to these questions require human judgment. Informed judgment is enhanced when you understand the conceptual issues. Interpretation is generally a matter of pattern detection, a task in which the human mind excels.

Final Thoughts

Research is problem-solving—with real problems. Empirical data are part of the process, though not always the most significant element. Educational and social science research are particularly demanding because the theoretical foundations are weak—and because researchers tend to overlook the theoreti-

cal tools that are available (Suppes, 1974). But "the times are a-changing," and rapidly. The cognitive revolution, the practical emphasis on educating rather than training, and the challenge of helping every individual realize his or her full potential—the road ahead is exciting and demanding.

Educational and social science research is still in the "sleepwalking" phase (Koestler, 1968). Even the best of our theories are heuristic more than formal, and we must often rely on experience and intuition. Success rests most frequently from doing several things right rather than the one best answer (Slaving, 1986; Tyack, 1974). Cronbach (1975) paints a dim prospect for generalizable research in education, portraying a hall of mirrors with infinitely complex and intricate interactions.

The problems are clearly daunting, but we are optimistic. Whether as producer or consumer of empirical research, you should consider the "divide and conquer" strategy. A series of modest but well-designed studies is likely to be more informative than a single humongous effort. Critical experiments are rare in

	Conditions Within Immediate Domain of Study (design remains constant)	Conditions Beyond Domain of Study (design changes; underlying concepts remain constant)
Factors Within the Design	CONCEPTUAL CLARITY (Affected by the design factors) • Clarity of concepts • Size & simplicity of effects • Inadvertent confounding	CONCEPTUAL MATCH (Affected by the replicability of underlying concepts) • Repeatability of plan • Interactions • Faithfulness to plan
Factors Outside the Design	SITUATIONAL STABILITY (Affected by the effect of factors in the situation) • Extraneous factors, direct & interactive • Reliability of measures • Size of sample; number of observations	SITUATIONAL MATCH (Affected by the degree of similarity between situations) • Presence of new conditions & contexts • Reliance on new tests • Different people & groups

FIGURE 10–10. Factors both within a design and within a situation that affect the trustworthiness of interpretations.

our business; any single investigation may provide one or two insights—often from a mistake that suggests what not to do.

While we do not recommend a fixed algorithm for planning empirical research, the strategy exemplified in the vignette often works quite well. First, learn something about the territory through an assessment study. Conduct a survey or check out a test. Your goal is not to prove the validity of an instrument, but to determine whether you have an effective method for exploring the territory. Then experiment; try out a series of instructional treatments, perhaps one or two chunks at a time. Innovations are difficult to implement, and you are more likely to succeed by proceeding in phases. It is important to assess the actual implementation, and to examine in detail the full range of potential effects (positive and negative). You may not be able to complete an in-depth evaluation for every participant, but you can always select a few individuals for careful study, for contrast with the thinner data from the entire group.

Our main message throughout is the essential importance of *design*—basic building blocks, linkages, and an overarching theme. These components assume different shapes in different stages of an investigation, but if you build on them consistently, they give coherence and unity to the effort. You are likely to learn something from the experience, and to gain satisfaction from the enterprise.

References

Bereiter, C., & Scardamalia, M. (1987). *The psychology of written composition.* Hillsdale, NJ: Lawrence Erlbaum Associates, Publishers.

Calfee, R. C. (1981). Cognitive psychology and educational practice. In D. Berliner (Ed.), *Review of educational research* (pp. 3–73). Washington DC: American Educational Research Association.

Calfee, R. C. (1985). *Experimental methods in psychology.* New York: Hold, Rinehart, and Winston.

Calfee, R. C., & Chambliss, M. J. (1987). The structural design features of large texts. *Educational Psychologist, 22,* 357–378.

Campbell, D. T., & Stanley, J. C. (1966). *Experimental and quasi-experimental designs for research.* Chicago: Rand McNally.

Cook, T. D., & Campbell, D. T. (1979). *Quasi-experimentation: Design and analysis issues for field settings.* Chicago: Rand McNally.

Cronbach, L. J. (1963). Evaluation for course improvement. *Teachers College Record, 64,* 97–121. Also in R. W. Heath (Ed.), *New curricula.* New York: Harper and Row, 1964.

Cronbach, L. J. (1975). Beyond the two disciplines of scientific psychology. *American Psychologist, 30,* 116–127.

Cronbach, L. J. (1988). Five perspectives on the validity argument. In H. Wainer and H. I. Braun (Eds.), *Test validity.* Hillsdale, NJ: Erlbaum Associates.

Cronbach, L. J., Glesser, G. C., Nanda, H., & Rajaratnam, N. (1972). *The dependability of behavioral measurements: Theory of generalizability for scores and profiles.* New York: Wiley.

Cronbach, L. J., & Snow, R. E. (1981). *Aptitudes and instructional methods/A handbook for research on interactions.* New York: Irvington Publishers, Inc.

Cronbach, L. J., & Suppes, P. (Eds.). (1969). *Research for tomorrow's schools: Disciplined inquiry for education.* New York: Macmillan Publishing Co.

Hayes, J. R., & Flower, L. S. (1980). Identifying the organization of writing processes. In L. W. Gregg, & E. R. Steinberg (Eds.), *Cognitive processes in writing* (pp. 3–30). Hillsdale, NJ: Lawrence Erlbaum Associates.

Kintsch, W., & Yarborough, J. C. (1982). Role of rhetorical structure in text comprehension. *Journal of Educational Psychology, 74,* 828–834.

Koestler, A. (1968). *The sleepwalkers.* New York: Macmillan.

Messick, S. (1988). The once and future issues of validity: Assessing the meaning and consequences of measurement. In H. Wainer and H. I. Braun (Eds.), *Test validity.* Hillsdale, NJ: Erlbaum Associates.

Meyer, B. J. F., Brandt, D. H., & Bluth, G. J. (1980). Use of top-level structure in text: Key for reading comprehension on ninth-grade students. *Reading Research Quarterly, 16,* 72–103.

Meyer, B. J. F., & Freedle, R. O. (1984). Effects of discourse type on recall. *American Educational Research Journal, 21,* 121–143.

Pearson, P. D. (Ed.) (1984). *Handbook of reading research.* New York: Longman.

Porter, A. C. (1988). Comparative experiments in educational research. In R. Jaeger (Ed.), *Complementary methods for research in education* (pp. 391–411). Washington, DC: American Educational Research Association.

Ragin, C. C. (1987). *The comparative method.* Berkeley, CA: University of California Press.

Secrest, L., West, S. G., Phillips, M. E., Redner, R., & Yeaton, W. (1979). Introduction. In L. Secrest (Ed.), *Evaluation studies review annual,* Vol. *4* (pp. 15–35). Beverly Hills, CA: Sage Publications.

Shulman, L. S. (1988). Disciplines of inquiry in education: An overview. In R. Jaeger (Ed.), *Complementary methods for research in education* (pp. 3–58). Washington, DC: American Educational Research Association.

Simon, H. A. (1981). *The sciences of the artificial* (2nd ed.). Cambridge, MA: MIT Press.

Slavin, R. (1986). Best evidence synthesis: An alternative to meta-analytic and traditional reviews. *Educational Researcher, 15* (9), 5–11.

Slavin, R. E. (1984). Component building: A strategy for research based instructional improvement. *Elementary School Journal, 84,* 255–269.

Spivey, N. N. (1987). Constructing constructivism: Reading research in the U.S. *Poetics, 16,* 169–92.

Suppes, P. (1974). The place of theory in educational research. *Educational Researcher, 3,* 3–10.

Toulmin, S. E. (1958). *The uses of argument.* Cambridge: The University Press.

Tyack, D. B. (1974). *The one best system; A history of American urban education.* Cambridge, MA: Harvard University Press.

Wittrock, M. C., Marks, C., & Doctorow, M. (1975). Reading as a generative process. *Journal of Educational Psychology, 67,* 484–489.

A BRIEF ANNOTATED BIBLIOGRAPHY OF TEXTBOOK REFERENCES ON EMPIRICAL METHODOLOGY

Literally hundreds of methodology textbooks have been published during the past decade covering various domains of social science and educational research. Our intention here is not a compendium, but a "consumer's guide" along with some examples. Most of the references are relatively recent, but a few older pieces are also included because of their significance.

What are the major dimensions for comparison? How should this large collection be clustered? Practically speaking, what features of a methods textbook should a novice researcher attend to? If we had more time and energy, we might have turned these into serious research questions! As it is, we will rely on intuition and experience. One major contrast, however, is the difference between cookbook and conceptual approaches. Both have their place, to be sure, and we are not making value judgments in identifying this dimension. An explanatory treatment necessarily means that the author can cover fewer details; a "how to" focus assumes that the user understands the issues. We will note that most of the textbooks claiming a conceptual emphasis in our sample did not meet this challenge; virtually all fell back into the routines of the scientific method as applied to social science research.

A second important distinction is between an emphasis on field-based research (evaluation methods) and those that take a disciplinary orientation (often psychological, but in recent years other perspectives are appearing—sociological and anthropological, for instance). The field-based methods have their origins in the landmark work of Campbell and his collaborators (Campbell & Stanley, 1966 [a reprint of a 1963 chapter]; Cook & Campbell, 1979). The aim is generally practical and immediate. Disciplinary perspectives more often aim to yield generalizable theoretical findings.

Size is a third consideration. The more comprehensive works are daunting in their magnitude. The slim introductions generally provide little guidance beyond the undergraduate level—research as a course requirement. We assume the *Handbook* audience to be at the graduate level, and hence needing a deeper treatment. The midrange textbooks are probably most valuable—if you can find the configuration that meets your particular needs. These texts do the best job of combining how and why, but always within a limited range of methodologies.

Finally, the books vary widely in their coverage of specific areas important in the research enterprise. Moreover, the same label takes quite different shape from one text to another. Almost all include sections on design and validity, for instance, but the interpretation of these concepts is by no means the same for all authors. Some texts can almost be described as statistics books with some contextual background about research methods, while other texts do not cover statistics at all. Most recent texts attempt to cover both quantitative and qualitative techniques, but usually weighted in one direction or the other, often reflecting the disciplinary orientation. The pragmatics of such tasks as reviewing the literature and composing a research report are included in some texts but not others.

We would extend Shulman's advice—gain some familiarity with a range of methodology texts. Begin by locating the section of the library that contains this material. Check the copyright (including the first edition; a text may be out of date conceptually, even though it was published last year). Skim the table of contents. How is the presentation organized? Do you see familiar terminology? Does the balance in the presentation mesh with your needs? Go to a few sections dealing with topics familiar to you. Is the presentation readable, or are you overwhelmed by jargon? Does the author provide workable examples?

In short, treat the domain of methodology textbooks as a market place. Shop carefully and wisely, and take advantage of what works for you. Here now is a brief sample from contemporary offerings:

Babie, E. (1986). *The practice of social research.* Belmont, CA: Wadsworth Publishing Company.

A comprehensive text based on a sociological perspective. On first glance, it is well designed around a few significant topics: inquiry, design, observation, analysis, and contextual issues. The working out of the details falls short of the initial promise, but the thoughtful reader can fill in the missing pieces.

Cook, T. D., & Campbell, D. T. (1979). *Quasi-experimentation/Design and analysis issues for field settings.* Chicago: Rand McNally College Publishing Company.

This text extends a line of research methodology for field experiments that goes back to the early 1960s. The emphasis is on techniques for improving the validity of studies that aim to evaluate innovative treatments. It is an advanced treatment that assumes considerable prior knowledge.

Eichelberger, R. T. (1989). *Disciplined inquiry/Understanding and doing educational research.* New York: Longman.

A standard introduction to educational research methods, distinguished by the attention to philosophy of science issues.

Jaeger, R. M. (Ed.). (1988). *Complementary methods for research in education.* Washington, DC: American Educational Research Association.; Morgan, G. (Ed.). (1983). *Beyond method/Strategies for social research.* Beverly Hills, CA: Sage Publications.; Brewer, M. B., & Collins, B. E. (Eds.). (1981). *Scientific inquiry and the social sciences.* San Francisco: Jossey/Bass Publishers.

These three volumes illustrate an approach to methodology based on joining forces in an edited collection. All in all, the result is generally uneven. Some individual contributions are significant, but we would recommend that the novice researcher rely on more coherent presentations.

Krathwohl, D. R. (1985). *Social and behavioral science research/A new framework for conceptualizing, implementing, and evaluating research studies.* San Francisco: Jossey-Bass Publishers.

Another extension of the "Campbell-Stanley" approach to the design of field-based studies. This work is advanced, and follows through on the promise to take a conceptual approach. It provdes few practical guides for action, however.

Mitchell, M., & Jolley, J. (1988). *Research design explained.* New York: Holt, Rinehart and Winston, Inc.

Typical of many introductions to research methodology that promise a conceptual approach and user-friendly writing. This text takes a psychological perspective, and the basic plan is solid. But the writing is "busy" and "jargony," and the substance is lacking in many instances. For instance, internal validity is equated with the establishment of cause-effect relations.

Williamson, J. B., Karp, D. A., Dalphin, J. R., & Gray, P. S. (1982). *The research craft/An introduction to social research methods.* Boston: Little, Brown and Company.

A relatively-advanced text, which begins from a sociological perspective, but has considerable breadth (e.g., a section on historical methods). The basic stance is quantitative more than qualitative, as in the coverage of survey methods.

Borg, W. R., & Gall, M. D. (1989). *Educational research/An Introduction.* New York: Longman.

Virtually a handbook, this enormous text covers essentially every topic in the territory. The writing lays out the techniques in a straightforward manner, with less attention to the rationale behind the various methods. Qualitative methods receive less attention than quantitative approaches.

McMillan, J. H., & Schumacher, S. (1989). *Research in education/A conceptual approach.* Glenview, IL: Scott, Foresman and Company.

A broad treatment of educational research paradigms, covering a wide array of designs and methods, both quantitative and qualitative. Although it promises a conceptual approach, it comes across as a cookbook. In many respects it is a miniature version of Borg and Gall.

Slavin, R. E. (1986). *Research methods in education/A practical guide.* Englewood Cliffs, NJ: Prentice-Hall, Inc.

Typical of a variety of relatively low-level introductions to research methods, including basic designs, statistical techniques, computer packages, and practical matters like gaining access to schools.

Tuckman, B. W. (1988). *Conducting educational research.* New York: Harcourt Brace Jovanovich, Inc.

A condensed version of Borg and Gall. Practically oriented.

Kirk, R. E. (1982). *Experimental design/Procedures for the behavioral sciences.* Belmont, CA: Wadsworth, Inc.

A standard approach to factorial design methods and associated statistical techniques. The approach is primarily "how to," with an emphasis on quantitative terminology. This text includes a compendium of different designs and is more comprehensive than most.

Fetterman, D. M. (1989). *Ethnography/Step by step.*

A qualitative version of Tuckman, but briefer and more focused.

Marshall, C., & Rossman, G. B. (1989). *Designing qualitative research.* Newbury Park, CA: Sage Publications.

This text on qualitative methods builds around the notion of the *argument* that supports an investigation. This theme has also appeared in recent discussions of validity, and emphasizes the logic of proving a point as the key to scientific inquiry.

Miles, M. B., & Huberman, A. M. (1984). *Qualitative data analysis/A sourcebook of new methods.* Newbury Park, CA: Sage Publications.

Probably the current classic on qualitative methods. Smaller than Borg and Gall, but equivalent in its scope and impact.

·11·

STUDIES OF READING AND WRITING GROWTH: LONGITUDINAL RESEARCH ON LITERACY DEVELOPMENT

Robert J. Tierney

How does literacy develop? This question is one of the major concerns of educators and, you would expect, one of the major pursuits of literacy research. Understanding how literacy develops is a prerequisite to responding to readers and writers and to planning their educational experiences. Therefore, how do we pursue answers to this question? Here the answer seems rather obvious—initiate studies which examine how students change across time. Ideally, this would involve longitudinal studies of the same individuals at different times rather than different individuals at different times. The present paper represents an attempt to examine longitudinal studies of reading and writing growth with two major questions: how do readers and writers develop; and what are some of the methodological considerations involved in longitudinal studies.

In preparation for this paper, a great deal of time was spent gathering information about longitudinal research: scanning the research for examples of longitudinal research on particular topics of relevance to the language arts; and reviewing discussions of research methodologies for tenets by which longitudinal studies might be conducted and reviewed. Unfortunately, the task was more formidable than expected. At the time, neither a substantial review of longitudinal research dealing with methodological issues nor a thorough review of those longitudinal studies pertaining to reading and writing development existed. Most discussions of research in the social sciences included a mere mention of longitudinal research; and with a few exceptions, reviews of reading and writing research only incidentally mentioned the extent to which longitudinal studies have been pursued. Perhaps this should have come as no surprise. For longitudinal studies are expensive to pursue and are apt to be viewed as unrewarding if a rapid turnaround in research is an investigator's goal. This may account for the enor-

mous number of cross-sectional studies comparing students at different ages rather than studies of the same students at these different ages.

These limitations aside, the current review examines several longitudinal studies of readers and writers. Since a limited number of longitudinal studies have been conducted (or, if they have been conducted, do not exist in the mainstream research outlets) and most of these relate to a few research areas (mostly early reading and writing development) a review of longitudinal studies is more illustrative than explanatory. It is illustrative in terms of:

1. The implications which emerge from such studies, especially the development principles which can be drawn about language learning;
2. The theoretical frameworks which guide their implementation and interpretation; and
3. The methodological considerations which emerge for consideration.

Longitudinal Studies of Reading and Writing in the Early Years

Over the past 30 years, studies of children's initial encounters with print and beginning school experiences represent the majority of longitudinal studies conducted to date. Especially in recent years, there have appeared several case studies of young children and observational studies of several children, which have examined reading and writing development across time. The antecedents of such studies seem to be rather a mixed set. Some of them have their roots in developmental psychology, which dominated the field from 1910 to 1930. For example, in the early part of this century a number of maturational psychologists detailed the early development of young children. For instance, based upon his observations of several children at various ages and the same children at different times, Gesell (1925, 1928, 1940) detailed what he termed a reading gradient—a scale which represented the book handling and related behaviors which were typical of children at different ages. Other studies have their roots in clincial studies based upon case histories of students with difficulty learning to read. In this regard, the work of Vernon (1957) in England, Schonell (1956) in Australia and Monroe (1932) in the United States may be most notable. Still others have their roots in case studies focused on reader's response to storybooks (White, 1954). Finally, many have roots in a reaction to or movement away from correlational studies, which compared skills considered to be related to later reading achievement with each other (e.g., Dykstra, 1966; Barrett, 1965).

A study that has received a great deal of attention is Durkin's (1966) longitudinal studies of early readers in which she examined the impact of home experiences upon later reading achievement in hopes of answering several questions: How many children learn to read before they start school? Do they have any traits that distinguish them from other children? What are their family backgrounds? What do their families report about how they learned to read? Do they stay ahead as they move through the grades? Durkin found 49 children out of 5,103 in Oakland, California and 180 children out of 4,465 in New York who could read a list of primary level words at the beginning of first grade. The early readers were retested at least once a year for several years, and the results on these tests were related to various factors in the preschool situation as well as measures such as IQ, sex, data from personality tests, teacher ratings, and interviews with parents. In addition, the progress of the early readers was compared with that of equally-bright students who were not early readers. Furthermore, a number of these early readers were selected for case studies. Several of Durkin's findings challenged popular beliefs about early reading experiences. Her studies in "no way corroborate the pessimistic predictions about the future achievement of early readers" (p. 133). After six years of schooling, early readers maintained their advantage. Her findings also challenged the belief that IQ and socioeconomic factors of other traits were effective predictors of success. Neither IQ nor selected personality traits nor other measures suggested a particular advantage for any of these factors. Instead, what proved to be salient were factors related to how parents and siblings encouraged, nurtured, and responded to the reading interests of these children. Durkin stressed that what appeared to be important was "the presence of parents who spend time with their children; who read to them; who answer their questions and their requests for help; and who demonstrate in their own lives that reading is a rich source for relaxation, information and contentment." (p. 136). She also stressed that a great deal of early readers' interest in print and learning to read was tied to their interest in learning to "print and spell," and their curiosity about what words "say."

In addition to being partially replicated (Tobin & Pikulski,

1988), several lines of research have addressed some of the same issues raised by Durkin. In particular, a number of studies have examined through parents' diaries, parent-child and teacher-child interactions, and other data young children's storybook reading experiences—its features and relationship to literacy development. Dorothy White's *Books Before Five,* originally published in 1954, represents one of the earliest, best known diary accounts of story reading. White's diary describes a three-year period (2–5 years old) of her daughter's story reading experience. White's diary chronicles her daughter's response to a caring parent who shares various books with her daughter and notes sensitively the nature of her responses including acquisition of written language, but especially meaning making. As Somerset points out in the foreword, there are two sets of issues explored implicitly throughout and explicitly on occasion in the diary:

… we find on the intellectual side the following lines clearly marked: a gradual understanding of the meaning of drawings and pictorial symbols, growth in comprehending the meaning of words, the growth of memory, the emergence of the distinction between 'real' and 'pretendy', 'true' and untrue'. On the aesthetic side, too, we find a great deal of interesting material: the joy in sounds and words, in rhymes and rhythms, and a dawning perception of literary form not only in verse but even in prose stories. And, of course, many phases of a child's emotional life—its joys, its fears, its likes and dislikes, its interests—are to be found illustrated in these pages. On all such matters the textbooks of psychology have much to tell us in a generalized manner, but here we can see them happening in the life of one child. (p. xvi)

Over the past 15 years other parents have told the story of their children's development as readers and writers in conjunction with story reading. In 1979, Butler described her reflections of her grandchild, Cushla, and the role of story reading on her ongoing cognitive and social development. In 1980, Bissex described the literacy development of her son Paul in conjunction with his early reading and writing development. In 1983, Crago and Crago reported the preschool discoveries of their daughter Anna as she encountered pictures and stories. In 1989, Wolf offered a case study of her daughter, Lindsey, from 3 years 2 months to 4 years 6 months of age.

Apart from diary studies, a number longitudinal studies of parent-child interaction together with studies involving repeated readings of storybooks have led to a gradual refinement in our understanding of the nature and role of story reading and especially its significance to ongoing literacy development. For example, a study by Ninio and Bruner (1978) with children 8–18 months suggests a rich but rather routinized dialogue between parent and child occurs during story reading. As Ninio and Bruner stated, the interactions around books had a "structured interactional sequence that had the texture of dialogue" (p. 6) with the parent's dialogue centering upon labelling and the child smiling, pointing, vocalizing and acquiring the turn-taking rules underlying such dialogues. Investigations by Snow (1983) and Snow and Goldfield (1982, 1982) indicate that this type of routine interactions with parents affords children the security whereby they can link ideas from these experiences. Snow's studies and, more recently, studies by Teale (1986), Teale and Sulzby (1986 a & b), Sulzby (1985 a & b), and Sulzby

& Teale (1985) suggest that routine does not mean mindless repetition. In repeated readings of a storybook children move from elaboration and labeling to a concern with motive and causal issues. Teale (1984) has noted that they shift their focus from character identification to what the characters are doing. Furthermore, the nature of their social interactions between child and parent shift as the child assumes more responsibility for the reading. Describing the changes in the language and social interaction that took place over 14-months as a mother and child read a counting book, Teale and Sulzby (in press) found important shifts in responsibility as the child gained more and more control over the task. In fact, after eight months of the mother initiating the reading, the child spontaneously read the material.

In an effort to detail children's use of text cues, some studies have focused upon how children respond to and use print as a source for making meaning across repeated story readings. For example, Cochran-Smith (1984) described in some detail the behaviors of children enrolled in a nursery school over a period of 18 months. According to Cochran-Smith, the students demonstrated that they "were coming to know . . . a great deal about print." (p. 252). The 3- to 5-year-olds knew reading and writing were integral and meaningful parts of the everyday world and were effective ways to accomplish many of their own purposes and needs. Furthermore, they knew how to organize and use print, relate print to oral language, relate their own knowledge to decontexualized print of storybooks, achieve and apply understandings, and integrate the use of reading and writing into their lives.

Other work has studied in more detail the shifts that occur in such behaviors (i.e., student's use of cues) across time. For example, Sulzby (1985), reported a longitudinal study in which the "emergent reading" attempts of 24 children at the beginning and end of their kindergarten year were compared and examined against similar data acquired from repeated readings with story books by 2-, 3-, and 4-year-olds. By using a classification scheme to characterize the reading behaviors of children, Sulzby (1985a) was able to demonstrate the extensive repertoire of strategies students have acquired as a result of story book reading and the types of changes which occur across time but seem relatively stable across books. Tables 11–1 and 11–2 include comparisons made of the kindergarteners at the beginning and end of the year, as well as a comparison with 2-, 3-, and 4-year-olds. Sulzby contends, as several of these researchers who have pursued longitudinal studies have stressed, literacy is not learned by rote procedures but occurs in conjunction with negotiations between the child, parent, text, and other features of context.

Adopting a slightly different orientation, Pappas and Brown (1987) explored in detail the extent to which 27 kindergarteners were developing an understanding of the register of shared reading including the linguistic awareness necessary to understand stories. As they stated,

. . . learning to read is fundamentally an extension of the functional potential of language. During the preschool years young children learn a lot about the lexicogrammatical realizations of the language system so that they are able to control a variety of different oral language registers to express their meanings. They learn to adjust their linguistic choices

TABLE 11–1. Classification Scheme for Emergent Reading of Favorite Storybooks in the Kindergarten Year

Reading Attempt Type	Major Categories (and Sub-categories)	
	Beginning of Year	End of Year
A. Attempts Governed by Print	5	10
Reading independently	(1)	(3)
Reading with strategies imbalanced	(1)	(2)
Reading aspectually	(1)	(5)
Refusing to read based on print awareness	(2)	(0)
B. Attempts Governed by Pictures, Stories Formed		
1. Written language-like	6	7
Reading verbatim-like story	(1)	(0)
Reading similar to original story	(3)	(2)
Reading and story-telling mixed	(2)	(5)
2. Oral language-like	5	5
Monologic story-telling	(2)	(3)
Dialogic story-telling	(3)	(2)
C. Attempts Governed by Picture, Stories Not Formed	4	0
Following the action	(2)	(0)
Labelling and commenting	(2)	(0)
D. Refusals (low-level) and/or Dependent Reading	4	2

Note. N = 24

to meet the features of particular social contexts—the setting, the participants, and the specific task at hand. To become literate, however, the young child has to come to terms with certain important characteristics of written language—its sustained organization, its characteristic rhythms and structures, and the disembedded quality of written language. Thus, an essential aspect of the extension of the functional potential of language involves young children's coming to understand that the registers of written language are different from those of speech. (p. 160–161)

Rather than focus upon children's role-like word-by-word response to the repeated reading of a story, Pappas and Brown (1987) focused on the children's approximations of the author's wordings and extrapolations from the story. Across repeated readings Pappas and Brown found that children made extensive use of extrapolations and approximations and their use seemed integral to their realizations of the potentials of written language (including their constructing an understanding of the social conflicts and plans of characters pertaining to the story). What is noteworthy is the socio-semiotic perspective adopted by Pappas and Brown. Their analyses brings to the fore the social nature of literacy and literacy learning, as well as the extent to which meaning-making is inherently constructive. As they concluded,

While young children's reading-like behavior in previous research might have been explained in terms of rote meory, the results reported in this study indicate that this is not the cause. The ontogenesis of the registers of written language appears to be just as much a constructive process as we have seen in other areas of children's cognitive/linguistic development. (Pappas & Brown, 1987, p. 175)

TABLE 11–2. Percentage of Children Reading at Increasing Levels of
Sophistication by Age

Categories Reading Attempts	Age				
	Two's[a] (n = 8)	Three's[a] (n = 12)	Four's[a] (n = 12)	Five's November[b] (n = 24)	Five's May[b] (n = 24)
Governed by print	0%[c]	17	25	21	42
Written Language-Like Stories	13	17	33	25	30
Oral Language-Like Stories	25	17	17	21	21
Stories Not Formed	13	17	8	17	0
Refusals (Low-level) and/or Dependent Reading	50	33	17	17	8

[a]Date from Study II; counted here is only the first storybook attempt by each child on entry into a longitudinal study (Sulzby, 1983-b)

[b]Data from Study I; reading attempts are the beginning and end of kindergarten by the same subjects. (Sulzby 1983b)

[c]Percentages may not sum to 100 due to rounding.

Along similar lines, Yaden, Smolkin, and Conlon (1989) have been interested in the hypothesis that "story reading may provide an opportunity for children not only to explore many aspects of the book itself, but also to acquire new ways of communicating, and to sharpen, refine, and compare their own view of the world with the perspectives they encounter in books" p. 207. To this end, they have reported studies in which the questions and inquiries of preschoolers (3 to 5 years) regarding print and pictures have been described. On a weekly basis for periods of one and two years, they collected, transcribed, and analyzed the questions and inquiries of nine children. Children's questions were classified as pertaining to graphic forms, word meaning, story text, pictures and book conventions. Their findings suggested that over one or two years, even the least inquisitive child would ask over 1,000 questions, and these represented a full range of question types. While most students asked questions about pictures, some students moved toward asking questions about the story text. At no time did students ask many questions about the conventions of books. While the researchers tended to decline from suggesting trends or developmental patterns (due to the variations which were found across students, the story selections themselves, and the interactional style of parents, and other variables), the researchers concluded that storybook reading offered children a foundation from which they might begin to master reading. As they stated,

Perhaps it is safest to say that story books provide a variety of information about the way print communicates meaning and represents the sounds of oral language, just as environmental print may influence children's acquisition of print knowledge. In another way, exposing children to as many sources of written information in the environment as possible before school cannot help but give them the kind of foundation needed for successful mastery of this most complicated human invention. (Yaden, Smolkin, & Conlon, 1989, p. 211)

Given the wealth of these data, it seems unfortunate that these data were not considered in a more open-ended fashion that showed what the child's inquisitiveness contributed. Studies of literacy acquisition have not been restricted to children's responses to story reading. Apart from a number of cross-sec-

tional studies of different children at different ages (e.g., Goodman, 1986; Harste, Burke & Woodward, 1984; Hiebert, 1978), a few longitudinal studies were done that focused upon the link between what is commonly referred to as "print awareness" and reading ability. The key tenet underlying such pursuits is the notion that children acquire an understanding of literacy as a result of their interactions with every-day print. As Goodman (1986) argued, environmental print encounters are at the root of the child developing a model for the features of written language. As she stated: "the development of print awareness in environmental contexts is the root of literacy most common to all learners and the most well developed in the preschool years" and serves to facilitate the child's development of "a model . . . which includes rules about the features of written language in situational contexts" (p. 7). Unfortunately, very few longitudinal studies have examined this claim either directly or in detail. One example is a study by Kontos (1988) who examined the relationship between print awareness and reading achievement from the beginning of preschool to the end of first grade for 47 subjects. Print awareness measures included a battery of tests directed at various aspects of print and book awareness along with a researcher-constructed measure of the children's knowledge of the communicative functions of print. Other measures included a test of knowledge of sound symbol correspondence, writing measure and a prereading phonics inventory. Across six time periods from spring of the preschool year to fall of 1st-grade the intercorrelations between these variables and their relationship to performance on the Metropolitan Reading Test and California Test of Basic Skill (involving a composite score based upon several tests including tests of component skills) were determined. Despite the fact that some of her reading measures were similar to the measures of reading subskills used as predictors, print awareness, especially as measured by Clay's battery of tests, did emerge as a significant predictor. Kontos argued that the role of print awareness seemed to be intertwined with the role of other literary knowledge and skills.

Research on writing development has been another major area for study. In the past 15 years this area of research has received a great deal of attention as researchers began asking questions about the child's conceptions of written language rather than concentrating on how well the letters and words are formed and conventions adopted. In this regard, the work of Ferreiro and Teberosky (1982) has been most seminal. Based upon their analyses of children's writing at various ages, they described hypotheses governing children's writing. Central to their work was the thesis that children operate according to certain assumptions (e.g., writing is a way of representing speech and objects, a principle of minimal quantity in terms of number of letters, a principle of individual variation of letters within words, the syllabic principle), which they construct and upgrade to account for new encounters.

To date, a number of researchers have offered a longitudinal perspective on the understandings children acquire as they write. Read (1971) and Chomsky (1979) have described in some detail the assumptions which tend to undergird a child's invented spellings. Harste, Burke and Woodward (1984 a & b) and DeFord (1987) have offered several examples of how young children's writing develops across time. Bissex's (1980) and Baghban's (1984) case studies of their children are devoted primarily to tracing their early writing development. Graves (1982) and Calkins (1982) have offered rich descriptions of writing development across time as students begin writing and conferencing with others. The longitudinal studies of Sulzby and her colleagues (1983a, 1985a; Sulzby, Barnhart, & Hieshima, in press; Sulzby and Teale, 1985) in general support the findings of the aforementioned studies. While highlighting the active and constructive nature of meaning-making by the child, they argue that children's writing might be informed more by adult conventions than other researchers would support.

Taken together, the longitudinal research on early reading and writing to date has confirmed some beliefs at the same time as it has added definition and stimulated a number of issues. The view of the child as an active meaning maker constructing his or her own hypotheses in the context of daily negotiations with print and others is substantiated repeatedly. Left unanswered is how such constructions are achieved. Some key factors seem to have been identified, but their interrelationship and the mechanisms students use to contruct these hypotheses seem relatively undefined. What seems most promising are those studies that have adopted a more expansive, differentiated view of literacy which is situation-based—namely, studies that have been willing to address the complex configurations of variables which constitute literacy events.

A number of recent studies seem to be on the verge of moving us toward a more expansive view of the child's reading and writing development. For example, in conjunction with an eight-month study exploring the nature of literacy learning among 3- and 4-year-olds enrolled in a daycare situation, Rowe (1987) pursued detailed analyses in hopes of understanding the saliency of interactions with others and prior experiences in literacy learning. Her analyses prompted her to hypothesize that the links and negotiations children have with others' and their own past experience was central to their ongoing literacy learning. As she stated,

... as children formed new communicative goals, they flexibly combined various aspects of their existing knowledge, or linked their existing knowledge to available demonstrations, to construct situation-based hypotheses which were their communicative goals (p. 110).

In accordance with this view, Rowe (1987) suggested literacy events in the classrooms

... provided opportunities for children to *observe* another at work, to *talk* with that person in order to expand and develop their ideas, to *observe* again, and often to *incorporate new ideas* into their own texts. Sometimes children used the demonstrations of others as starting points for developing their own ideas ... At other times, children chose to use available demonstrations conservatively; that is, they chose to stick as close to the demonstration as possible until they felt they understood it fully. In either case, the construction of intertextual ties appeared to be supported by interaction in which (a) the activities of other authors were familiar and understandable, (b) the participants worked collaboratively to reach shared meanings through conversations, and (c) conversation and demonstration were linked to form interaction demonstrations. It was by observing the demonstrations of others, by exchaning meanings in conversation, and by authoring their own texts that children formed shared meanings about literacy. (p. 106)

Rowe's work has a number of parallels with the work by Dyson (1983, 1985, 1986, 1988) who has explored the role of the tensions which occur as various texts (oral, written, drawings) transact. As she stated,

children's major developmental challenge is not simply to create a unified text world but to move among multiple worlds, carrying out multiple roles and coordinating multiple space/time structures. That is, to grow as writers of imaginary worlds and, by inference, other sorts of text worlds as well, children must differentiate, and work to resolve the tensions among, the varied symbolic and social worlds within which they write—worlds with different dimensions of time and space. And it is our own differentiation of these competing worlds that will allow us as adults to understand the seemingly unstable worlds, the shifts of time frames and points of view, that children create. (1988, p. 356)

It is noteworthy that the studies of both Rowe and Dyson extrapolated their principles of literacy learning based upon detailed analyses of both individuals and groups across different literacy situations. These leanings concur with the implications drawn in conjunction with a longitudinal study by Galda, Pellegrini, and Cox (1989) in which a determination of the relationship among play and literacy development. Galda, et al. (1989) suggested that when literacy was defined in more global terms using general measures, including those extrapolated from past studies of literacy development, the interrelationship among play, literacy interaction, and other factors are apt to be diminished and obscured.

The past decade has been a period of enormous growth in our understanding of early literacy learning. The sheer number of studies, including longitudinal studies, focusing upon early literacy development is larger than any other 10-year period. Despite the inroads that have been made, studies of early literacy development appear to retreat to interpretations of findings reflecting one side or other of a debate about the goals of literacy. The debate involves whether children should be viewed as learning a set of stable literacy conventions based upon adult norms or whether literacy learning should be viewed as more inventive. Whereas there appears to be little disagreement among researchers that children actively construct their own set of rules for literacy during the early years, substantial disagreements appear to exist in some of the assumptions pertaining to the goals or standards by which such rules, hypotheses, or principles are governed. In particular, whereas some researchers verge on the view that literacy learning involves acquiring adult conventions; other researchers contend that literacy should not be viewed as emerging. In accordance with this latter position, literacy is viewed as involving respect for what and how literacy is negotiated in different situations rather than how literacy measures up to adult conventions. What seems to distinguish this view is that literacy can be viewed as open to refinement or closed with static conventions. Accordingly, literacy involves refinement, invention and development in conjunction with pursuing the power to negotiate meanings in different contexts rather than being tied to eventually acquiring a standard set of conventions for so doing. Perhaps it might be useful to pursue a view of literacy that somewhat merges the two positions. An amalgamation of such views might suggest that literacy has many of the features of "jazz" music—a mixture of improvisations, inventions, allusions, variations, and standard themes inspired by the combination of players and context.

Longitudinal Studies of Literacy Acquisition During the Beginning School Years

Several longitudinal studies of reading and writing development describe the stages students pass through as they learn to read and write in school. Clay (1966, 1982), for example, pursued a longitudinal study of children during their first year of school in New Zealand. To this end, she collected weekly records of reading (including running records of their oral reading of books that they were assigned to read) for a sample of 100 children from six schools, and administered a battery of 17 tests (tests of language skills, auditory and visual perception, a reading readiness battery) within two weeks of school entry, midyear, and when the child was 6 years old. In hopes of attaining a comparative perspective on the data, Clay examined the data across three ability groups (high, middle, and low). Her conclusions served two purposes: a description of the strategies of successful readers and a developmental description of the stages they pass through. Good readers, she observed, manipulate a "network of language, spatial, and visual perception cues and sort these implicitly but efficiently, searching for dissonant relations and best-fit solutions. Redundancy in cue sources allows for confirming checks and acts as a stimulus to error correction" (p. 28). In terms of stages, she claimed that children move from a reliance upon information from their oral language experience and knowledge of situation to the use of an expanded set of cues which include visual dimensions, word knowledge and associations of letter and sound. As she stated, cues from these sources for a long time are "piece meal, unreliable and unstable" but become efficient as the use of these cuing systems simultaneously become more differentiated. In accordance with these conclusions and other findings, she argued for maintaining a difficulty level of approximately 95 percent

accuracy so that students will be challenged to apply a range of cues rather than rely upon a limited repertoire or for which success is dependent upon a restricted use of cues, say an overreliance upon auditory cues.

Whereas Clay's approach and findings suggest the need for a rather open-ended view of reading development, a number of studies have tended to adopt and be restrained by a priori models of reading development and a focus upon decoding. Perhaps the most elaborate longitudinal study to date was an investigation launched by the Center for the Study of Reading at the University of Illinois in 1985. To date, an interim report (Meyer, Wardrop & Hastings, 1989) detailing preliminary analyses of data from the first cohort of children through kindergarten, first grade, and second grade has been released. The primary focus of the Illinois study is on how children develop the ability to comprehend. As Meyer, et al. (1989) stated,

How do children develop the ability to comprehend over time? In the process of ferreting out answers to this question, several more focused research questions have emerged. What kinds of home experiences contribute to the development of reading comprehension ability? What is the nature of these activities? What sort of things do children do independently that contribute to the development of reading comprehension ability? How much reading instruction is there in the lower elementary grades? What are the characteristics of this instruction? How do activities in the home and the school jointly influence the development of children's reading comprehension ability. (p. 12)

To answer these questions, the research team at Illinois adopted a tentative model of comprehension development, which they have been testing. Their model assumes that various home and school factors together with student aptitude and student-initiated activity combine to influence reading comprehension development. In all, the model includes eight general constructs (home background characteristics, student's ability at the time they entered school, the characteristics of the instructional materials, teacher's management and instructional style, home support for literacy development, and independent reading), which were measured in different ways at different times in accordance with some important a priori decisions. For example, they decided to exclude any measure of independent reading prior to the 3rd grade, and decided to characterize teaching style in terms of micro-level analyses of decoding activities and silent reading activities rather than other features such as shared reading, reading-writing experiences, conferencing and story talk. Using this top-down approach, the Illinois team has done extensive observations of classrooms as well as extensive use of questionnaires and published tests. Perhaps due to the size of their sample, none of their measures of basic abilities are what might be termed open-ended—for example, their measures of reading comprehension include cloze procedures, multiple-choice items, and so on, but do not include any type of free recall or miscue analysis. Their measures of decoding do not include a measure which addresses the students' use of decoding strategies in context. The first cohort includes 240 students from the three districts selected for study. The schools from which they were drawn represent a suburban school with diverse ethnic mix and two small Midwestern towns. While the reading programs in each school differ somewhat, they appear

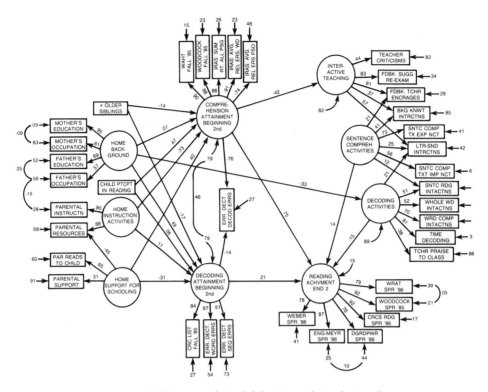

FIGURE 11–1. Final Structural Model for Second Grade Reading.

to be traditional given their alignment with a basal approach and their orientation to the teaching of skills.

Using analysis procedures that seek to create a path model with a certain "goodness of fit" (in conjunction with factor analysis techniques to accommodate the use of multiple measures), the research team has generated a model of the interrelationship between variables, which maximizes the variance accounted for at each grade level. Figure 11–1 represents the model generated for the 2nd grade. Tables 11–3 and 11–4 provide intercorrelational matrices of the data. As the researchers point out: the "model they are presenting is not the only possible model for these interrelationships, but it is the one obtained when we applied the criteria and diagnostic/revision procedures described" (Meyer, et al. 1989, p. 41). Their findings, to date, seem to support and extend some of the findings of other research. Home factors emerged as closely related to end-of-year achievement and, at grade 2 interacted with teacher behavior. Not surprising, the entry-level achievement of students predicted success at the end of each grade level and, beginning in the 1st grade, interacted with teaching practices to affect achievement—in other words, as they stated "What teachers do appears to be influenced by the skills the pupils bring with them" (Meyer, et al. 1989, p. 49). Also, the relationship between decoding attainment, reading comprehension and activities that focus upon letters or texts became complex by the end of the 2nd grade. As Meyer, et al. (1989) pointed out, the decoding and comprehension appear to be more distinct variables by the end of the 2nd grade. That is, decoding activities tended to be less clearly related to reading comprehension and sometimes

appear to be negatively correlated. Examine, if you will, the intercorrelations between decoding and those reading comprehension indices shaded on Tables 11–3 and 11–4 versus the correlation of reading comprehension with the amount of student participation in reading and more sentence level activities. At grade 1 a similar trend is apparent. Decoding has a limited and sometimes negative relationship to comprehension. In general, these data point to an issue—the nature of the relationship between decoding and reading development—which has been an important facet of a number of longitudinal studies in reading.

A number of studies have attempted to sort out the precise nature of the interrelationships between component skills and reading, as well as how the development of these skills interface with different instructional experiences. Taken together, these studies, to which I will now turn, seem to suggest that phonics appears to bear a relationship with reading that changes across time and does not appear to be causal. By the end of the 2nd grade, the relationship between phonics and reading for meaning is slight. Furthermore, there appears to be no advantage, and some disadvantages, for emphasizing phonics over reading for meaning. Students who are encouraged to read for meaning have comparable phonic segmentation and superior reading for meaning abilities to students who have received a strict phonics emphasis.

To assess the viability of a model of literacy acquisition that posits decoding as crucial, Juell, Griffith, and Gough (1986) studied changes in the pattern of relationship of scores on various tests across 80 students during grades 1 and 2 who were enrolled either in classrooms using a basal approach or in classrooms receiving synthetic phonics daily on top of the basal reading material.

We begin with the simple view of reading . . . that reading is composed of a. decoding and b. listening comprehension. This is not to suggest that either of the components, decoding and listening comprehension, is simple in itself but to argue that these two skills are the critical components of reading. That is, we suppose that reading crucially involves decoding, the ability to translate print into linguistic form. But we do not suppose that decoding alone is sufficient for reading. Having derived the linguistic form represented in print, the reader must then comprehend that form. To do this, we suppose that the reader employs the same mechanisms, the same knowledge of morphology, syntax, semantics and pragmatics that are used in the comprehension of spoken language in order to understand decoded print. We recognize that written text has certain distinctive characteristics from speech with differential impact upon the comprehension process . . . But we are inclined to agree with those researchers who emphasize the commonality of the demands of written and spoken language upon the comprehender. Thus, we believe that given perfection in decoding, the quality of reading will depend entirely on the quality of the reader's comprehension; if the listening comprehension is poor, then his reading comprehension will be poor, no matter how good his decoding. (p. 244)

Figure 11–2, while not explicating the various nuances, details the general model that guided the selection of tests and data analysis. In terms of data collection, a battery of tests were given either at the beginning of grade 1 or periodically during grades 1 and 2. Some of the measures represented a standard fare of published tests; others seem somewhat limited. For example, ciphering knowledge was based upon the students' ability to pronounce nonsense words; exposure to print was assessed in terms of the number of words the students had confronted in their basals. What was apparent in their analyses was some specificity of effects. In particular, phonemic awareness tends to be most clearly related to those tasks which, in a restrictive sense, seem tied to phonemic awareness, such as spelling-sound knowledge. Furthermore, its relationship to reading comprehension, perhaps due to a ceiling effect, became quite diminished by the end of the 2nd grade. The results of their analyses for the second grade are included on Figure 11–2.

Whereas those studies that have tended to focus upon phonemic awareness to the exclusion of other variables suggest a strong relationship between phonemic segmentation and reading achievement, those studies that have looked at some of the other variables suggest a more tempered and sometimes different viewpoint. Take, if you will, some of those studies that have attempted to sort out the relationship between decoding and reading in the context of different instructional approaches. For example, Calfee and Piontkowski (1981) pursued a longitudinal study of the acquisition of decoding skills of 50 1st-graders in 10 classrooms. The design, which included four categories of data-diagnostic decoding tests, oral reading, and comprehension measures, standardized achievement test, and classroom observations, allowed for an investigation of the patterns of reading acquisition of "component skills" during regular classroom instruction and to examine the relationship of these patterns to the instructional program. In terms of the relationship

between component skills and reading acquisition, there appeared to be some transfer from decoding to oral reading and comprehension, but not vice versa. In other words, those students who were comprehending successfully may or may not have the same level of decoding skills. In terms of the effects of instruction, the results were somewhat predictable. Student performance on the various tests suggested that students learn what they are taught. In particular, target students in the reading-for-meaning programs tended to perform better on reading passages than in response to isolated words; target students in the programs emphasizing phonics performed better on decoding tasks rather than reading passages. The findings from this study underline the impact of differences in instructional emphases and illustrate the power of longitudinal studies to inform our understanding of development. As Calfee and Piontkowski (1981) argued in the closing statement of their study:

Understanding how readers become "good" or "poor" readers is not impossible, but it requires longitudinal, multivariate data with appropriate information about teaching styles and programs. Such research will not only clarify our knowledge of the acqusition of reading; it is also likely to yield the practical tools for assessment and instruction. (p. 372)

In recent years, a number of studies have adopted the multivariate viewpoint advocated by Calfee and Piontkowski and the possibility that the pattern of relationships between variables will vary with differences in instruction. Recently, Perfetti, Beck, Bell, and Hughes (1987) reported the results of a longitudinal study of the relationship between phonemic knowledge and reading for 1st graders (N = 82) in different instructional programs (basal with readiness, basal without readiness, and a direct code teaching method). Various measures were included throughout the year to assess phonemic knowledge, word reading, and curriculum progress. At four points throughout the year phonemic blending and analysis were tested while other tests were less frequent. In general, the results suggest that those students who were given opportunities to read progressed more and were as able to perform adequately on decoding tasks; students who received an emphasis upon decoding progressed less and their decoding abilities did not necessarily transfer to reading. Based upon partial time-lag correlations, the authors argued that reading gains had a reciprocal relationship with an ability to phonemically analyze (deletion task, e.g., remove the "k" sound from cat), but reading contributed to the ability to delete, which in turn contributed to reading rather than the ability to delete making a contribution by itself. As they stated:

What is clear is that learning to read can begin in a variety of ways, most of which may require only minimal explicit knowledge of speech segments. Thus, the rudimentary ability to manipulate isolated segments may be necessary for significant progress in reading. However, it is reading itself, we suggest, that enables the child to be able to analyze words and to manipulate their speech segments. It is not that the reader performs such manipulations on the orthography. Rather, learning some orthographic principles through reading enables the discoveries, including the alphabetic principle, can happen without direct instruction as well as with it. Although the direct teaching of the code may

TABLE 11-3. Correlations of First Grade Measures of Student Ability, Classroom Process Variables, and Home Support for Literacy Development

	Child Ptcpt in Reading	Parental Resources	Parental Support	Parental Instruction	Amount Homework	WRAT Fall '84	Woodcock Fall '84	Chicago Fall '84	WRAT Spring '85	IRAS Avg. Ret Ers WD	IRAS Avg. Ret Rate W	IRAS Avg. Ret Ers PSG	IRAS Avg. Ret Rate P	IRAS Sum Ret all PSG	Woodcock Spring '85	Err Dect Decode Errs	Err Dect Word Errs	Err Dect Seq. Errs	Ltr-snd Intrctns
Child Ptcpt in Reading	1.000																		
Parental Resources	0.285	1.000																	
Parental Support	0.440	0.194	1.000																
Parental Instruction	0.036	0.294	0.116	1.000															
Amount Homework	0.019	-0.012	0.011	0.220	1.000														
WRAT Fall '84	0.320	0.175	0.141	-0.140	-0.183	1.000													
Woodcock Fall '84	0.211	0.073	0.059	-0.108	-0.162	0.827	1.000												
Chicago Fall '84	0.257	0.109	0.130	-0.143	-0.096	0.762	0.646	1.000											
WRAT Spring '85	0.306	0.139	0.061	-0.277	-0.279	0.675	0.541	0.650	1.000										
IRAS: Avg. Ret. Ers, WD	-0.330	-0.161	-0.137	0.292	0.238	-0.587	-0.430	-0.624	-0.812	1.000									
IRAS: Avg. Ret. Rate, W	-0.332	-0.247	-0.137	0.098	0.145	-0.564	-0.407	-0.566	-0.625	0.619	1.000								
IRAS: Avg. Ret. Ers, PSG	-0.412	-0.197	-0.153	0.138	-0.258	-0.533	-0.367	-0.556	-0.785	0.793	0.595	1.000							
IRAS: Avg. Ret. Rate, P	-0.385	-0.253	-0.210	0.047	0.159	-0.605	-0.471	-0.575	-0.673	0.667	0.724	0.721	1.000						
IRAS: Sum Rt, all PSG	0.327	0.122	0.063	-0.227	-0.211	0.581	0.446	0.665	0.785	-0.749	-0.584	-0.687	-0.562	1.000					
Woodcock Spring '85	0.315	0.198	0.103	-0.189	-0.232	0.684	0.587	0.694	0.848	-0.772	-0.667	-0.718	-0.668	0.772	1.000				
Err Dect: Decode Errs	-0.335	-0.160	-0.123	0.248	0.245	-0.607	-0.435	-0.635	-0.802	0.822	0.659	0.815	0.774	-0.747	-0.760	1.000			
Err Dect: Word Errs	0.212	0.146	0.185	0.036	-0.097	0.236	0.173	0.255	0.368	-0.362	-0.266	-0.512	-0.489	0.325	0.346	-0.471	1.000		
Err Dect: Seq. Errs	0.170	0.134	0.147	0.057	-0.185	0.222	0.164	0.250	0.304	-0.299	-0.185	-0.343	-0.289	0.330	0.308	-0.299	0.429	1.000	
Ltr-Snd Intrctns	-0.010	-0.088	-0.035	-0.056	0.072	-0.142	-0.109	-0.084	-0.054	0.057	0.056	0.072	0.043	0.015	-0.055	0.047	-0.090	-0.028	1.000
Whole Wd Intrctns	0.027	-0.140	0.020	-0.035	0.230	-0.094	-0.081	-0.036	-0.106	0.057	0.045	0.089	0.001	-0.047	-0.122	0.031	-0.079	-0.022	0.595
Sntc Rdg Intrctns	-0.038	-0.127	-0.038	-0.094	0.118	-0.082	-0.007	0.018	0.007	-0.049	-0.075	0.029	-0.074	0.035	0.004	-0.033	-0.091	-0.054	0.654
Bkg Knwl Intrctns	0.044	-0.019	0.038	-0.020	0.056	0.103	0.109	0.103	0.121	-0.173	-0.204	-0.075	-0.181	0.103	0.155	-0.097	-0.064	0.010	0.320
Sntc Comp Tx Exp Nct	-0.146	-0.117	-0.076	0.033	-0.004	-0.234	-0.118	-0.207	-0.128	0.142	0.176	0.200	0.163	-0.098	-0.173	0.190	-0.096	0.077	0.680
Sntc Comp Tx Impl Nct	-0.026	-0.076	0.020	0.039	0.081	-0.069	-0.045	-0.084	-0.090	0.046	0.047	0.038	0.016	-0.034	-0.101	0.063	0.000	0.016	0.427
Time Dcd no Text	0.132	0.013	0.056	-0.041	0.351	0.177	0.127	0.241	0.104	-0.135	-0.190	-0.141	-0.199	0.111	0.109	-0.158	0.046	-0.099	0.148
Time Ded with Text	0.018	-0.073	-0.029	-0.068	-0.029	-0.137	-0.147	-0.098	0.027	-0.045	-0.100	-0.014	-0.092	0.000	-0.009	-0.065	-0.060	-0.060	0.463
Time Rdg in Text	0.074	-0.066	0.066	-0.105	0.161	0.118	0.070	0.221	0.137	-0.238	-0.187	-0.141	-0.233	0.136	0.094	-0.187	-0.086	0.025	0.310
Fdbk: Rept Question	-0.099	-0.112	-0.043	-0.069	-0.059	-0.193	-0.145	-0.197	-0.115	0.117	0.176	0.190	0.143	-0.121	-0.200	0.128	-0.071	0.085	0.207
Fdbk: Tchr Leads	-0.021	-0.031	-0.028	-0.140	-0.125	-0.134	-0.120	-0.066	-0.024	-0.015	0.019	0.025	0.046	0.006	-0.045	0.007	-0.009	-0.035	0.273
Frequency Scatwork	0.063	0.041	0.042	0.053	-0.248	0.034	-0.071	-0.072	0.080	-0.054	0.007	-0.121	-0.071	0.029	0.032	-0.096	0.220	0.185	-0.053
Tchr Crit to Class	0.054	0.105	0.028	0.019	0.215	-0.015	-0.037	-0.068	-0.062	0.071	-0.069	0.035	-0.058	-0.038	-0.016	-0.052	0.050	-0.150	0.245
No. Adults in Home	-0.135	-0.108	-0.134	-0.012	-0.096	-0.124	-0.009	-0.062	-0.095	0.057	0.151	0.134	0.195	-0.088	-0.064	0.118	-0.084	-0.118	-0.036
Mother's Education	0.010	0.200	0.114	0.050	-0.255	0.248	0.176	0.205	0.146	-0.170	-0.216	-0.154	-0.224	0.141	0.173	-0.253	0.197	0.151	-0.176
Father's Education	0.120	0.165	0.126	0.033	-0.236	0.319	0.211	0.294	0.238	-0.221	-0.237	-0.252	-0.275	0.194	0.244	-0.299	0.135	0.080	-0.245
Mother's Occupat'n	-0.025	0.113	0.030	0.009	-0.169	0.140	0.095	0.088	0.112	-0.093	-0.131	-0.104	-0.127	0.069	0.119	-0.173	0.142	0.008	-0.074
Father's Occupat'n	0.034	0.108	0.087	-0.109	-0.249	0.234	0.158	0.231	0.185	-0.180	-0.207	-0.172	-0.242	0.169	0.220	-0.215	0.124	0.089	-0.171

TABLE 11–3. Correlations of First Grade Measures of Student Ability, Classroom Process Variables, and Home Support for Literacy Development

	Whole Wd Intrctng	Sntc Rdg Intrctng	Bkg Knwl Intrctng	Sntc Comp Tx Exp Nct	Sntc Comp Tx Impl Nct	Time Ded No Text	Time Ded with Text	Time Rdg in Text	Fdbk: Rept Question	Fdbk: Tchr Leads	Frequency Seatwork	Tchr Crit to Class	No. Adults in Home	Mother's Education	Father's Education	Mother's Occupat'n	Father's Occupat'n
Whole Wd Intrctns	1.000																
Sntc Rdg Intrctns	0.636	1.000															
Bkg Knwl Intrctns	0.302	0.515	1.000														
Sntc Comp Tx Exp Nct	0.436	0.534	0.274	1.000													
Sntc Comp Tx Impl Nct	0.447	0.390	0.291	0.473	1.000												
Time Ded No Text	0.356	0.406	0.334	−0.166	0.087	1.000											
Time Ded with Text	0.248	0.434	0.289	0.440	0.243	−0.184	1.000										
Time Rdg in Text	0.599	0.628	0.607	0.171	0.390	0.619	0.158	1.000									
Fdbk: Rept Question	0.244	0.138	0.185	0.480	0.077	−0.339	0.202	0.068	1.000								
Fdbk: Tchr Leads	0.330	0.247	0.003	0.179	0.163	−0.054	0.196	0.111	0.011	1.000							
Frequency Seatwork	0.002	−0.319	−0.318	0.041	0.126	−0.675	0.031	−0.333	0.270	0.095	1.000						
Tchr Crit to Class	0.087	0.183	0.035	0.019	−0.112	0.233	0.261	−0.194	−0.154	0.009	−0.289	1.000					
No. Adults in Home	−0.034	0.035	0.016	0.062	0.023	−0.097	0.058	−0.030	0.020	−0.010	0.018	−0.055	1.000				
Mother's Education	−0.144	−0.132	−0.023	−0.138	0.035	−0.118	−0.174	−0.078	−0.119	−0.014	0.234	−0.005	−0.030	1.000			
Father's Education	−0.187	−0.209	−0.078	−0.211	−0.078	−0.111	−0.171	−0.109	−0.171	−0.083	0.189	−0.069	−0.017	0.640	1.000		
Mother's Occupat'n	−0.127	−0.094	−0.056	−0.080	−0.063	−0.078	−0.155	0.070	−0.042	−0.016	0.135	0.004	−0.077	0.508	0.344	1.000	
Father's Occupat'n	−0.165	−0.096	−0.043	−0.161	−0.012	−0.024	−0.122	−0.066	−0.196	−0.009	0.028	0.029	0.021	0.531	0.664	0.390	1.000

TABLE 11–4. Correlations of Second Grade Measures of Student Ability, Classroom Process Variables, and Home Support for Literacy Development

	WRAT Fall '85	Woodcock Fall '85	IRAS: Avg Ret Ers, WD	IRAS: Avg Ret Ers, PSG	IRAS: Sum Rt all PSG	Err Dect Word Errs	Err Dect Decode Errs	Err Dect Sntc Errs	Circ List Fall '85	Wrat Spr '86	Woodcock Spr '86	Crcs Rdg Spr '86	Dg Rd Pwr Spr '86	Eng-Meyer Spr '86	Weber Spr '86	Mother's Education	Father's Education	Mother's Occupat'n	Father's Occupat'n
WRAT Fall '85	1.000																		
Woodcock Fall '85	0.825	1.000																	
IRAS: Avg Ret Ers, WD	-0.855	-0.774	1.000																
IRAS: Avg Ret Ers, PSG	-0.696	-0.588	0.710	1.000															
IRAS: Sum Rt all PSG	0.769	0.804	-0.795	-0.623	1.000														
Err Dect Word Errs	0.398	0.289	-0.335	-0.369	0.277	1.000													
Err Dect Decode Errs	-0.781	-0.683	0.828	0.774	-0.706	-0.477	1.000												
Err Dect Sntc Errs	0.376	0.353	-0.308	-0.303	0.353	0.339	-0.392	1.000											
Circ List Fall '85	0.435	0.439	-0.412	-0.376	0.396	0.590	-0.488	0.416	1.000										
Wrat Spr '86	0.811	0.711	-0.696	-0.592	0.642	0.304	-0.616	0.277	0.351	1.000									
Woodcock Spr '86	0.729	0.756	-0.697	-0.598	0.687	0.370	-0.676	0.368	0.497	0.759	1.000								
Crcs Rdg Spr '86	0.725	0.701	-0.738	-0.616	0.709	0.403	-0.717	0.370	0.554	0.712	0.803	1.000							
Dg Rd Pwr Spr '86	0.534	0.634	-0.519	-0.426	0.557	0.291	-0.479	0.372	0.467	0.555	0.706	0.676	1.000						
Eng-Meyer Spr '86	0.623	0.657	-0.630	-0.542	0.643	0.355	-0.620	0.330	0.544	0.640	0.787	0.795	0.744	1.000					
Weber Spr '86	0.589	0.543	-0.614	-0.528	0.513	0.391	-0.620	0.312	0.442	0.587	0.696	0.714	0.535	0.687	1.000				
Mother's Education	0.136	0.213	-0.182	-0.145	0.188	0.180	-0.201	0.208	0.340	0.168	0.272	0.258	0.358	0.280	0.197	1.000			
Father's Education	0.210	0.268	-0.228	-0.245	0.263	0.271	-0.256	0.220	0.299	0.214	0.308	0.272	0.343	0.289	0.257	0.674	1.000		
Mother's Occupat'n	0.065	0.074	-0.098	-0.071	0.050	0.141	-0.096	0.091	0.150	0.120	0.209	0.161	0.231	0.177	0.132	0.497	0.356	1.000	
Father's Occupat'n	0.172	0.220	-0.197	-0.202	0.220	0.117	-0.177	0.157	0.230	0.205	0.226	0.196	0.255	0.232	0.187	0.546	0.656	0.403	1.000
# Older Siblings	-0.094	-0.121	0.165	0.075	-0.113	-0.010	0.103	-0.142	-0.192	-0.025	-0.124	-0.099	-0.107	-0.089	-0.031	-0.041	-0.028	0.055	0.073
Par Reads to Child	-0.059	-0.035	0.058	0.062	-0.022	-0.062	0.059	-0.006	-0.027	0.008	-0.008	-0.010	-0.035	-0.050	-0.017	0.245	0.201	0.268	0.148
Child Prcpt in Reading	0.147	0.131	-0.140	-0.133	0.126	0.024	-0.131	0.110	0.054	0.148	0.183	0.208	0.191	0.175	0.151	-0.010	0.040	-0.158	-0.149
Parental Resources	-0.007	0.075	0.031	-0.025	-0.023	-0.008	0.011	0.054	0.046	-0.057	0.066	0.027	0.036	0.005	-0.053	-0.090	-0.020	-0.205	-0.157
Parental Support	0.068	0.036	-0.111	-0.019	0.101	0.010	-0.062	0.100	0.125	0.059	0.114	0.087	0.037	0.031	0.095	0.179	0.191	0.075	0.057
Parental Instructn	-0.147	-0.154	0.169	0.080	-0.229	-0.016	0.180	-0.033	-0.078	-0.160	-0.138	-0.180	-0.170	-0.189	-0.182	-0.005	0.007	-0.062	-0.196
Ltr-Snd Intrctns	-0.120	-0.186	0.176	0.129	-0.180	0.022	0.129	-0.065	-0.112	-0.094	-0.125	-0.140	-0.177	-0.166	-0.092	-0.147	-0.158	-0.158	-0.096
Whole Wd Intrctns	-0.068	-0.165	0.093	0.084	-0.115	0.045	0.054	-0.031	-0.096	-0.148	-0.175	-0.177	-0.268	-0.226	-0.175	-0.234	-0.151	-0.079	-0.070
Sntc Rdg Intrctns	0.120	0.077	-0.086	-0.120	0.041	0.102	-0.150	0.009	0.112	0.129	0.096	0.125	0.024	0.067	0.205	-0.147	-0.065	-0.174	-0.089
Bkg Knwl Intrctns	-0.161	-0.199	0.158	0.067	-0.201	0.046	0.078	0.029	-0.064	-0.116	-0.101	-0.106	-0.107	-0.099	-0.058	-0.083	-0.148	-0.029	-0.129
Wrd Comp Intrctns	0.155	0.076	-0.165	-0.104	0.139	0.059	-0.165	0.096	0.041	0.074	0.010	0.050	-0.049	-0.007	0.035	-0.235	-0.136	-0.134	-0.165
Sntc Comp Tx Exp Nct	-0.001	0.014	-0.048	-0.101	0.030	0.041	-0.096	-0.036	0.012	0.034	0.106	0.091	0.061	0.103	0.151	-0.039	-0.033	-0.170	-0.161
Sntc Comp Tx Imp Nct	0.007	-0.009	0.015	-0.036	0.008	0.091	-0.016	0.090	0.090	0.015	0.041	0.023	0.001	0.046	0.015	-0.069	-0.073	-0.147	-0.114
Time Decoding	0.111	0.021	-0.073	-0.022	0.033	0.048	-0.069	0.044	0.000	0.036	-0.046	0.032	-0.210	-0.111	-0.002	-0.286	-0.185	-0.261	-0.122
Fdbk: Tchr Enc'rages	-0.233	-0.286	0.243	0.212	-0.280	-0.004	0.202	-0.102	-0.195	-0.180	-0.241	-0.248	-0.215	-0.224	-0.146	-0.127	-0.215	-0.059	-0.082
Fdbk: Sugg Re-exam	-0.249	-0.306	0.305	0.209	-0.300	-0.011	0.261	-0.062	-0.140	-0.189	-0.258	-0.310	-0.254	-0.307	-0.227	-0.195	-0.194	-0.022	-0.032
Tchr Praise to Class	0.156	0.167	-0.153	-0.043	0.158	0.054	-0.120	0.072	0.116	0.137	0.106	0.147	0.146	0.126	-0.014	0.254	0.205	0.178	0.219
Teacher Criticism	0.154	0.144	0.159	0.167	-0.113	-0.092	0.154	-0.069	-0.221	-0.124	-0.128	-0.175	-0.060	-0.110	-0.135	-0.079	-0.055	0.033	0.004

TABLE 11–4. Correlations of Second Grade Measures of Student Ability, Classroom Process Variables, and Home Support for Literacy Development

	# Older Siblings	Par Reads to Child	Child Prcpt in Reading	Parental Resources	Parental Support	Parental Instructn	Ltr-Snd Intrctns	Whole Wd Intrctns	Sntc Rdg Intrctns	Bkg Knwl Intrctns	Wrd Comp Intrctns	Sntc Comp Tx Exp Nct	Sntc Comp Tx Imp Nct	Time Decoding	Fdbk: Tchr Enc'rages	Fdbk: Sugg Re-exam	Tchr Praise to Class	Teacher Criticisms
# Older Siblings	1.000																	
Par Reads to Child	0.021	1.000																
Child Prcpt in Reading	−0.060	0.054	1.000															
Parental Resources	−0.090	0.114	0.451	1.000														
Parental Support	−0.002	0.201	0.092	0.195	1.000													
Parental Instructn	−0.102	0.404	0.359	0.431	0.203	1.000												
Ltr-Snd Intrctns	0.059	−0.105	−0.034	0.002	0.040	0.079	1.000											
Whole Wd Intrctns	0.083	−0.200	−0.049	−0.006	−0.085	−0.023	0.321	1.000										
Sntc Rdg Intrctns	−0.047	−0.071	0.034	0.072	0.078	−0.030	0.316	0.021	1.000									
Bkg Knwl Intrctns	0.123	−0.074	−0.028	−0.042	−0.147	0.039	0.394	0.238	0.066	1.000								
Wrd Comp Intrctns	−0.023	−0.165	0.027	0.035	0.093	−0.086	0.331	0.367	0.407	0.128	1.000							
Sntc Comp Tx Exp Nct	−0.017	−0.060	0.012	−0.014	0.001	0.024	0.303	0.084	0.242	0.356	0.163	1.000						
Sntc Comp Tx Imp Nct	0.060	−0.146	0.007	0.047	0.022	−0.064	0.253	0.380	0.202	0.357	0.354	0.448	1.000					
Time Decoding	−0.033	−0.151	−0.073	−0.027	0.062	−0.064	0.517	0.576	0.417	0.145	0.621	0.179	0.239	1.000				
Fdbk: Tchr Enc'rages	0.062	−0.049	−0.103	−0.039	−0.067	0.048	0.609	0.235	0.269	0.430	0.229	0.221	0.223	0.285	1.000			
Fdbk: Sugg Re-exam	0.095	−0.067	−0.070	0.051	0.035	0.133	0.559	0.290	0.260	0.358	0.226	0.020	0.204	0.311	0.659	1.000		
Tchr Praise to Class	−0.063	0.176	−0.021	−0.031	−0.026	0.067	−0.395	−0.101	−0.270	−0.212	−0.301	−0.211	−0.033	−0.269	−0.116	−0.152	1.000	
Teacher Criticisms	0.032	−0.031	−0.073	−0.126	−0.087	0.009	0.461	0.115	−0.007	0.166	0.233	0.018	−0.155	0.124	0.348	0.243	−0.382	1.000

ACQUISITION OF LITERACY

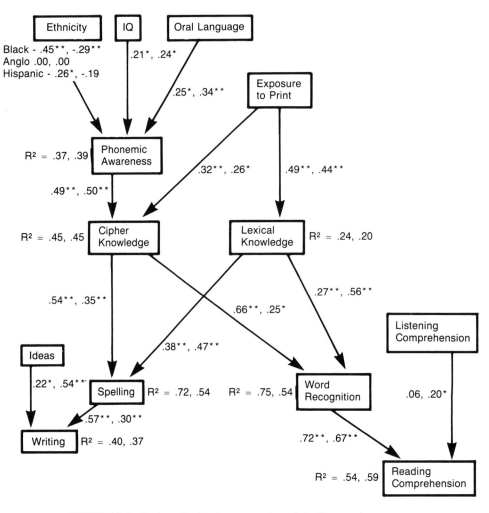

FIGURE 11–2. Path analysis of proposed model of literacy acquisition. (Path coefficients for the straight arrows are standardized regression coefficients. The first listed number represents first grade, and the second number represents second grade. *$p < .05$. **$p < .01$.)

have some consequences for analytic phonemic knowledge, they are fairly subtle. Children taught by direct code instruction do not seem to learn any more (or less) about deletion than do other children. However, their improvement in decoding may depend less on phonemic analytic abilities than does the improvement of children not taught coding directly. (p. 317–318)

Likewise, in a 15-month longitudinal study that began with children aged 3 years, Maclean, Bryant, and Bradley (1987) found a strong and specific relationship between knowledge of nursery rhymes and the development of phonological skills, particularly the detection of rhyme and alliteration, which remained significant when differences in IQ and social background were controlled.

Studies by Mason (1980) and by Maclean, et al. (1987) make a similar argument based upon their pursuit of the origins of

phonological awareness. Mason (1980; Mason & McCormick, 1979; 1981) has reported a number of studies in which she has examined the reading development of students enrolled in informal preschool and nursery school situations. Based upon parent questionnaires describing the children's interests in words, letters, and learning to read and tests directed at letter and word recognition and word learning, Mason (1980) has argued that the progress that students appear to make in knowledge of reading and skill in recognizing and reading words can best be described as involving three levels. As she stated:

The changes made in knowledge of reading and skill in recognizing letters and words, spelling and writing were best described in terms of three levels of development. The first level is denoted by children's ability to read at least one printed word, usually their name or a few signs and labels. They can also recite the alphabet, recognize a few letters, and may print letters. At the second level, they read a few short and very common words from books, print, and spell short words and begin to try reading new words by looking at the first consonant. At the third level, they notice and begin to use the more complex letter-sound congruences and letter-pattern configurations. Thus, first level children recognize words by context, second-level children begin to use letter and word-sound cues, and third-level children rely on a sounding-out strategy to identify words. Mason defines third-level children as readers; first and second-level children as prereaders. (pp. 515–516)

Vellutino and Scanlon (1987) reached similar findings regarding the interrelationship between phonic segmentation and reading ability. Vellutino and Scanlon (1987) compared the relationship of oral reading scores (acquired at the end of 1st and 2nd grade) and IQ, various phonemic segmentation measures, vocabulary and syntactic abilities. Word recognition, phonemic segmentation (especially consonant substitution) abilities, and use of contextual cues proved to be better predictors of oral reading performance than vocabulary measures and syntactic skills at the end of grades 1 and 2.

In a slightly different vein, Stanovich, Cunningham and West (1981) have suggested that the interrelationship between automaticity of word recognition various across time. Stanovich, et al. (1981) adopted a longitudinal approach in hopes of assessing changes in automaticity of letter and word recognition across skilled and less skilled readers in the 1st grade; and developing an understanding of its development and role in reading improvement. An automated process was defined as "one that can take place while attention is directed elsewhere." Across two experiments various measures of response times were obtained at different times of the year (late September, mid-February, April for experiment one; December, April for experiment two) for two groups of first graders (n = 24 for both experiment one and two). The data from experiment one suggested that for both skilled and less skilled readers there was little difference in their automaticity between February and late April indicating "a flattening out by the end of 1st grade" (p. 64). In experiment two, Stanovich et al.'s data confirmed the possibility that the chief difference between skilled and less skilled readers by the end of 1st grade was speed of recognition rather than automaticity. As they point out, the results are consistent with Ehri and Wilce (1979), who argued that success in reading should be assessed in regard to three criteria: accuracy, automaticity, and speed. And from their results, they argue, one could conceptualize these as stages beginning with accuracy.

The sheer number of longitudinal studies of beginning reading that have focused upon the acquisition of decoding skills suggest certain preoccupations. First, research has tended to be preoccupied with decoding to the exclusion of other literacy understandings. There are a host of facets of being literate which have barely been touched upon. They include: child's aesthetic development, view of interpretative authority, genre, cognitive processes such as self-questioning, on-line thinking, the student's use of multiple sources of information, criteria for self-selection, self-assessment. A second preoccupation of these studies has been the tendency to isolate reading from the other language arts. For example, to date, there exists a dearth of longitudinal studies that examine the interface between early writing development and reading development despite the belief

orginally espoused by Chomsky (1979) that children will learn to read by writing. As she stated:

Children who have been writing for months are in a very favorable position when they undertake learning to read. They have at their command considerable phonetic information about English, practice in phonemic segmentation, and experience with alphabetic representation. These are some of the technical skills that they need to get started. They have, in addition, an expectation of going ahead on their own. They are prepared to make sense, and their purpose is to derive a message from the print, not just to pronounce the words. (pp. 51–52)

Certainly, several descriptive studies suggest that there is a strong interface between reading and writing during these years, but careful study using longitudinal procedures are lacking.

A related problem is that very few longitudinal studies of writing exist and those that do tend not to examine writing and reading together. In fact, studies of writing development during the beginning school years have been dominated by cross-sectional comparisons of students varying in age or ability rather than studies that have looked at the same children at different ages. Perhaps the only exceptions to that are the studies by Loban reported in the next section and the work by Rentel and King (1983) and Hilgers (1986) which represent rather disparate concerns and approaches.

In Hilger's study (1987), four children were studied repeatedly as they evaluated pieces of writing in hopes of gleaning developmental trends in the standards students used to evaluate their texts and how they applied these criteria. In general, the students' aesthetic response (i.e., whether or not they liked a piece) was the most prevalent criteria used by all four students across this period. While Hilgers suggested there was no clear developmental trends, students, with age, tended to increase in the number of criteria that they employed as well as the time that they spent evaluating essays. In terms of how and when students employed criteria, the trends were not straightforward. Some students applied criteria during planning, others during revision, or both. Furthermore, students tended to use certain skills in their own writing prior to employing that same skill as a basis for evaluating essays. Often, opportunities to discuss certain skills seemed tied to their use.

In the Rentel and King study (1983), written narrative texts were elicited from 36 children stratified by sex, socioeconomic class, dialect, and school at intervals of four monhts over the children's first four years of schooling. A subsample of the texts of 16 of these children was then used as the basis for an examination of coherence in the students' narratives. Specific to their study, the data revealed that students developed what the researchers deemed to be a coherent text at a very young age and that differences in the coherence of these text was tied to their use of identity and similarity relationships for purposes of tying together events. Of relevance to the potential of longitudinal studies to inform developmental appreciations, their comments regarding these findings are noteworthy. As Rentel and King stated:

Children marshal their linguistic resources and bend them to the task of writing almost in defiance of the law of adult expectations. From second grade onward, the sample of children's texts we investigated thwarted our expectations about levels of coherence we could expect within them. Our expectation was that cohesive harmony scores would improve gradually over a period of several years. They did not. Cohesive harmony scores increased significantly from the point at which children could navigate the rudiments of a fictional narrative—for most, at the beginning of second grade. We expected roughly parallel emergence of identity and similarity relations in children's texts. Identity and similarity relations followed a course separate from each other in the sense that identity relations took precedence in children's earliest texts, while similarity relations came to dominate their fourth-grade texts. We expected that reiteration would be an important chain-forming relation in children's first stories, but would gradually diminish as a chain-forming strategy. It did not; instead, reiteration was a basic chain-forming strategy from the outset of writing and grew in its importance as a chain-forming resource over the entire four years of development we studied.

Our initial expectations of coherence in children's texts probably were not unlike those of most adults. Nor is it likely that our views differed significantly from those held by teachers. Adult expectations are in part probably the product of generalizing from the problems that children seem most concerned about at the outset of learning to write: spelling, orientations, editing, and topic. (p. 31)

Taken together, the longitudinal studies of literacy development during the beginning school years are quite sobering. One should be sobered by the problems associated with these sets of longitudinal studies—especially the shortcomings arising due to problems with scope. Since longitudinal studies have the potential to include an enormous number of variables, most researchers have chosen to restrict themselves by adopting a priori models of literacy development that limit the number of variables. Without discounting the worth of these separate studies, as a set they suggest a predilection with phonics to the exclusion of other variables. Reconsider the studies of literacy development during the years prior to formal schooling. Unlike studies dealing with early literacy development, the studies addressing the school years have adopted a rather narrow view of literacy and a restricted and rather static view of its sociosemiotic character or situation-based variation.

A related problem pertaining to measurement—most of the longitudinal studies of literacy during the early school years have developed or selected tests with certain assumptions. The question arises: Are these assumptions considered tenable? Are these assumptions predisposed to a certain view of literacy development? Rather than being open-ended without preset notions, the goals of most of the aforementioned research has been largely to prove a model rather than develop one. Furthermore, such recurring tendencies make syntheses across studies difficult lest recurring results may be more a sign of repeated error than reemerging truth.

Take, if you will, the findings pertaining to phonics. It is appearing to conclude that while one or two studies may point to the important role played by phonics in early literacy development, the studies as a set suggest that over time phonics offers little advantage and some disadvantages. In particular, by the end of 2nd grade, students receiving a reading-for-meaning emphasis appeared to be better comprehenders yet did not appear to lack phonic segmentation abilities. As stated earlier, phonics appears to bear a relationship with reading which changes across time and which does not appear to be causal. But can

such synthesis be assumed? Are such studies comparable or collapsible? Would different sets of measures of different kinds of analyses or different points of view yield different results, sets of results, and syntheses?

Longitudinal Studies Directed at the Study of Reading and Writing in Later Years

The number of longitudinal research studies quickly diminishes as the focus of such studies becomes the student moving through the elementary school, high school, or college. As the focus of the child's learning moves away from beginning reading and writing, so extrapolations about development have tended to depend almost solely upon comparisons of sophisticated and less sophisticated learners, experts and novices, good and poor, knowledgeable and less knowledgeable, or younger and older students. Such dichotomous comparisons have offered researchers worthwhile descriptions of what students might aspire to, but they have offered only highly speculative insights into how students might advance their own learning toward the aspirations which are set. Indeed, an interesting ramification of this void are educational practices that naively pursue the eradication of those behaviors associated with novice-like performance or that assume that expert-like behavior can be explicitly taught by carefully mimicking such behavior. What seems missing are those understandings and appreciations of student behaviors that emerge when researchers follow development of the same individual across time and when researchers ask themselves to identify the students' views of literacy.

There do seem to be a some exceptions to this trend. First, there are a number of case studies of readers and writers. For example, Bissex (1980) extended the case study of her son through his elementary schooling experience. Numerous case studies have been pursued of professional writers by biographers. Johnson (1985) pursued a case study of an adult who had minimal reading abilities. Holland (1975) offered case studies of a college student's reading. Petrosky (1976) and Cooper (1985) have pursued case studies of readers' responses to stories. These tend to be more descriptive than biographical so that a longitudinal perspective is less forthcoming.

In recent years there appears to have been an increase in what might be termed program evaluations and the use of longitudinal methodology to follow up on the lasting impact of a program. Central to such pursuits is an examination of trends across time. For example, researchers will trace the progress of students who were returned to the regular classroom after being involved in programs such as Reading Recovery—a program for "at risk" students. At the heart of these program evaluations is a concern for enduring effects including whether or not the program has worked. In addition, any other advantages or disadvantages can be noted. There are two reasons why such studies were excluded from the present view. First, the number of such studies would require a review beyond the scope of this paper. Second, with very few exceptions, program evaluations focus almost solely on a program's effectiveness and not upon the nature of change across time.

Essentially only a few studies exist that adopt what might be viewed as longitudinal methodology and longitudinal perspective. Studies by Wells (1986) and Loban (1967) are among the most notable. Beginning with children at the age of 15 months and continuing with a subsample of these children until the end of elementary school, Wells reported his attempt to address the question: Why were some children, usually lower in socio-economic status, failing to become literate and failing at school? Wells chronicles their language development by referring to data acquired by interviews, tape-recorded conversations, and assessments by the teacher. A number of recurring themes are developed by Wells. One theme he develops throughout the book is the notion that children need to be equal partners in conversation if they are to succeed. He argues that the types of partnership that parents have with children are lacking from schools. As Wells stated, ". . . schools are not providing an environment that fosters language development. For NO child was the language experience of the classroom richer than that of the home—not even for those believed to be 'linguistically deprived' " p. 87. He argues that a child's contributions should be taken seriously, that they should be viewed as and encouraged to be active meaning makers. A second theme is tied to what Wells describes as the most striking finding from the whole longitudinal study—their finding that achievement of children varied little from the time they entered elementary school to the time they ended (p. 147) Students who were assessed as high at age 5 were high at age 10. Moreover, the explanation for differences entering school seemed governed by the values developed for literacy. Wells argues that it is not the mechanics of literacy that were important, but the purposes for reading and writing that the child had acquired. In turn, a third major theme developed by Wells was that the single most important activity that parents can pursue is reading or telling stories. Storying, he argued, is "sustained meaning-building organization of written language." p. 151. In accordance with this view, he reiterates a concern for the gulf between schools and home, which he uses as a basis for drawing the implication with which he effectively closes his story of these children:

We are the meaningmakers—every one of us; children, parents, and teachers. To try to make sense, to construct stories, and to share them with others in speech and in writing is an essential part of being human. For those of us who are more knowledgeable and more mature—parents and teachers—the responsibility is clear; to interact with those in our care in such a way as to foster and enrich their meaning-making. (p. 222)

While Wells' longitudinal study has no exact counterpart in other countries, a longitudinal study conducted by Loban in the 1950s and 1960s has numerous parallels. In the 1950s and 1960s Loban (1967) pursued a 13-year longitudinal study of over 200 students during the entire course of their schooling (kindergarten through grade 12). The study was concerned with the use and control of language, the rates of growth and interrelationships of language abilities. As Loban stated:

From the outset, the basic purpose of the research has been to accumulate a mass of longitudinal data on each aspect of linguistic behavior, gathering the information in situations identical for each subject and using a cross-section of children from a typical American city so that findings could be generalized to any large urban area. (p. 1)

In particular, Loban delineates patterns of growth in language and details how proficiency was acquired. Taped oral interviews and a wide range of tests and inventories including lists of books read were used to measure reading achievement, listening ability, written language abilities, as well as ability and fluency in oral language (on an annual basis). Loban, similar to Wells, found that later success followed from earlier achievements. Just as Wells argued that later success was dependent upon the quality of home experience, so Loban argued that a strong oral language base, especially the ability to use language flexibly, seemed to be tied to a student's success as a reader and writer. As Wells also found, there appeared to be marked differences in the oral language of students in families of lower socioeconomic status. Like Wells, Loban lamented what appeared to be the gulf between home and school, which appeared to detract from facilitating ongoing language learning.

Finally, a study by Fitzgerald, Spiegel and Webb (1985) represents a worthwhile attempt to examine one of the numerous findings arising from the cross-sectional research on reader's understanding—in particular, they focus upon the nature of the readers' understanding of stories. To this end, at the beginning of both the 4th and 6th grades, they had 30 subjects respond to two stories that were presented in scrambled form. Knowledge of structural features was determined mainly by structural complexity in story productions and the degree to which scrambled stories were restructured into canonical versions. Knowledge of story content was examined in the story productions by determining the amount and nature of conflict, conflict resolution and by analyses of actions occurring in the stories. Their data yielded no important differences in terms of changes in the students knowledge of the content of stories (knowledge of conflict, response, and resolution did not seem to change from a rather restricted range—especially use of internal conflict), but did suggest that students had increased in their knowledge and use of complex story structures. They made greater use of embedded episodes, used the various story categories more often and appeared to use thier knowledge of story structure to aid in recall.

Concluding Remarks

In the introduction of this paper I argued that longitudinal studies were crucial to the advancement of our understanding of how literacy develops. To date, research on reading and writing has been dominated by extrapolations about development based upon a comparison of literacy learners at different ages, ability levels, and so on. I have stressed that such comparisons may be problematic if your goal is to understand how a literacy learner advances from one age to another or from one ability to another and so on. A number of the longitudinal researchers cited here attest to the fact that when they studied the same literacy learners across time their hunches about development were often challenged and subsequently revised. Some were taken aback with the speed with which literacy developed, the repertoire of literacy learning abilities children had and used at very young ages, the flattening out of certain literacy learnings, the extent to which the relationship between certain variables changed across time, and the extent to which some variables remained closely related to the child's literacy learning across time.

Repeatedly, researchers seem to be sensitive to the child's active construction of meaning-making systems and ongoing negotiation of meanings. Across the various studies the picture of meaning making that emerges is one in which the child is not becoming a meaning maker; the child is already a meaning maker. Furthermore, meanings seemed to be negotiated by the child using a variety of cues and systems simultaneously and the child's increasing facility with these cues and systems comes from being involved with meaning making experiences that challenge the child in the context of making meaning to use these cues, skills and systems.

Despite the fact that longitudinal research seems essential to answer questions regarding how literacy develops, such pursuits are neither straightforward nor problem-free. Indeed, longitudinal research seems plagued by many of the same problems of any research pursuit. Studies are limited by the researchers' view of literacy, selected biases, and awareness (or lack of awareness) of previous research. Such can shape the questions that are asked, the variables included for study, the methods used to assess these variables, and the procedures for analysis and interpretation. Across the various studies, relatively widespread use was made of instruments that lacked precision or offered a somewhat distorted glimpse of the variable being assessed. In some cases the method used to assess a predictor variable given one name seemed to closely match that used to assess a criterion variable given another name. Obviously, some of the problems seem unavoidable—particularly, problems devising methods of measuring or describing facets of literacy at an early age or facets which seem amorphous.

Longitudinal research is riddled with problems related to the interpretation of findings. In a number of studies, researchers had a tendency to move from statements about relationships between variables to statements of causality. In a number of cases, a license to make causal inferences seemed to arise whenever multiple regression procedures and the use of path models were enlisted to afford a "best fit." Researchers should be reminded that, regardless of the sophistication of the statistical analyses, these data remain correlational. The limitations surrounding the use of path analysis procedures is not restricted to just ascribing causality. The use of path analysis models often precludes the consideration of alternative constellations of variables or ways of configuring relationships that are less straightforward. Researchers using path analysis should acknowledge the extent to which their approach adopts an a priori model, which is then validated, rather than a more open-ended approach to modelling a configuration of variables.

Wells (1986), in the introduction to "The Meaning Makers", stated:

... there can be no true stories. The evidence is never so complete or so ambiguous as to rule out alternative interpretations. The important criteria in judging the worth of a story are: does it fit the facts as I have observed them and does it provide a helpful basis for future action? p xiii

It should be stressed that longitudinal research is not excluded from the various problems associated with generating reasonable interpretations. Just as in any study, there are constraints on the generalizability of findings to other sites, subjects, times, and so on. There may be a danger in longitudinal studies of assuming that comparisons across age levels and abilities will avail themselves. Certainly longitudinal studies do not involve making inferences based upon a comparison of the responses of different individuals, but despite the fact that the individuals might be the same, the context, including time, is not.

References

Baghban, M. J. M. (1984). *Our daughter learns to read and write: A case study from birth to three*. Newark, DE: International Reading Association.

Barnhart, J. E., & Sulzby, E. (1986, April). How Johnny can write: Children's uses of emergent writing systems. Paper presented at the annual meeting of the American Educational Research Association, San Francisco.

Barrett, T. (1965). The relationship between measures of prereading, visual discrimination and first grade reading achievement: A review of the literature. *Reading Research Quarterly, 1,* 51–76.

Bissex, G. (1980). *Gyns at wrk: A child learns to read and write*. Cambridge: Harvard University Press.

Bloome, D. (1985). Bedtime story reading as a social process. In J. A. Niles and R. V. Lalik (Eds.), *Issues in literacy: A research perspective* (pp. 287–294). 34th Yearbook of the National Reading Conference. Rochester, NY: National Reading Conference.

Butler, Dorothy (1979). *Cushla and her books*. London: Hodder and Stoughton.

Calfee, R., & Piontkowski, D. (1981). The reading diary: Acquisition of decoding. *Reading Research Quarterly, 16,* 346–373.

Calkins, L. (1983). *Lessons from a child*. Portsmouth: Heineman.

Chomsky, C. (1979). Approaching reading through invented spelling. In L. B. Resnick & P. A. Weaver (Eds.) *Theory and Practice of Early Reading*, Vol. 2, Hillsdale, NJ: Erlbaum.

Clark, M. M. (1976). *Young fluent readers*. London: Heinemann.

Clay, M. M. (1982). *Observing young children: Selected papers*. Exeter, NH: Heinemann Educational Books.

Cochran-Smith, M. (1984). *The making of a reader*. Norwood, NJ: Ablex.

Cooper, C. (1985). Researching response to literature and the teaching of literature: points of departure. Norwood: Ablex.

Crago, M. & Crago, H. (1983). *Prelude to literacy: a preschool child's encounter with picture and story*. Carbondale: Southern Illinois University Press.

Doake, D. (1981). *Book experience and emergent reading behavior*. Unpublished doctoral dissertation, University of Alberta.

Durkin, D. (1966). *Children who read early*. New York: Teachers College Press.

Dykstra, R. (1966). Auditory discrimination abilities and beginning reading achievement. *Reading Research Quarterly, 1,* 5–34.

Dyson, A. H. (1982). The emergence of visible language: Interrelationships between drawing and early writing. *Visible Language, 16,* 360–381.

Dyson, A. H. (1983). The role of oral language in early writing. *Research in the Teaching of English, 17,* 1–30.

Dyson, A. H. (1985). Individual differences in emerging writing. In M. Farr (Ed.), *Advances in writing research, Vol. 1: Children's early writing development* (pp. 59–126). Norwood, NJ: Ablex.

Dyson, A. H. (1986). Children's early interpretations of writing: Expanding research perspectives. In D. B. Yaden and S. Templeton (Eds.), *Metalinguistic awareness and beginning literacy* (pp. 201–218). Portsmouth, NH: Heinemann.

Dyson, A. H. (1988). Negotiations among multiple worlds: The space/time dimensions of young children's composing. *Research in the Teaching of English, 22,* (4), 355–390.

Ehri, L. C., & Wilce, L. S. (1979). Does word training increase or decrease interference in a Stroop task? *Journal of Experimental Child Psychology, 27,* 352–364.

Ferreiro, E., & Teberosky, A. (1982). *Literacy before schooling.* Exeter, NH: Heinemann.

Fitzgerald, J., Spiegel, D. L., & Webb, T. B. (1985). Development of children's knowledge of story structure and content. *Journal of Educational Research, 79,* 2, 101–108.

Galda, L. et al. (1989). A short-term longitudinal study of preschooler's emergent literacy. *Research in the Teaching of English, 23,* (3), 292–309.

Gesell, A. L. (1925). *The mental growth of the preschool child.* New York: Macmillan.

Gesell, A. L. (1928). *Infancy and human growth.* New York: Macmillan.

Gesell, A. L. (1940). *The first five years of life.* New York: Harper A& Bros.

Goodman, K. S., & Goodman, Y. M. (1979). Learning to read is natural. In L. B. Resnick & P. Weaver (Eds.), *Theory and practice of early reading* (pp. 137–154). Hillsdale, NJ: Erlbaum.

Goodman, Y. M. (1986). Children coming to know literacy. In W. H. Teale & E. Sulzby (Eds.), *Emergent literacy: Writing and reading* (pp. 1–14). Norwood, NJ: Ablex.

Goodman, Y. M., & Altwerger, B. (1981). *Print awareness in preschool children: A study of the development of literacy in preschool children* (Occasional Paper No. 4). Program in Language and Literacy, Arizona Center for Research and Development. Tucson: University of Arizona.

Graves, D. (1982). Patterns of child control of the writing process. In R. D. Walshe (Ed.), *Donald Graves in Australia.* Exeter, NH: Heinemann.

Green, J. L., & Harker, J. O. (1982). Reading to children: A communicative process. In J. A. Langer & M. T. Smith-Burke (Eds.), *Reader meets author/Bridging the gap: A psycholinguistic and sociolinguistic perspective* (pp. 196–221). Newark, DE: International Reading Association.

Harste, J. C., Woodward, V. A., & Burke, C. L. (1984a). Examining our assumptions: A transactional view of literacy and learning. *Research in the Teaching of English, 18,* 84–108.

Harste, J. C., Woodward, V. A., & Burke, C. L. (1984b). *Language stories and literacy lessons.* Portsmouth, NH: Heinemann.

Hiebert, E. H. (1978). Preschool children's understandings of written language. *Child Development, 49,* 1, 231–234.

Hiebert, E. H. (1981). Preschool children's understanding of written language. *Reading Research Quarterly* 16, 230–260.

Hilgers, L. L. (1986). How children change as critical evaluators of writing: Four three-year case studies. *Research in the Teaching of English, 20,* (1), 36–55.

Holland, N. (1975). *5 readers reading.* New Haven & London: Yale.

Johnson, P. (1985). Understanding reading disability: a case study approach. *Harvard Educational Review, 55,* 153–157.

Juell, C., Griffith, P. L., & Gough, P. B. (1986). Acquisition of literacy: A longitudinal study of children in first and second grade. *Journal of Educational Psychology, 78* (4), 243–255.

Kontos, S. (1988). Development and interrelationships of reading knowledge and skills during kindergarten and first grade. *Reading Research and Instruction, 27* (2), 13–28.

Kontos, S., & Mackley, H. (1985, April). *Development and interrelationships of reading knowledge and skills during kindergarten and first grade.* Paper presented at the annual meeting of the American Educational Research Association, Chicago, IL.

Laberge, D., & Samuels, S. J. (1974). Toward a theory of automatic information processing in reading. *Cognitive Psychology, 6,* 293–323.

Loban, W. (1964). Language ability: Grades seven, eight, and nine. University of California-Berkeley. USOE Cooperative Research Project. (ERIC Document Reproduction Service No. ED 001275)

Loban, W. (1967). Language ability: Grades ten, eleven and twelve. University of California-Berkeley. USOE Cooperative Research Project No. 2387 Contract No. EI-4-10–31, (ERIC Document Reproduction Service No. ED 0014477)

Loban, W. (1976). The development of language abilities, K–12. Urbana: National Council for Teachers of English.

Maclean, M., Bryant, P. & Bradley, L. (1987). Rhymes, nursery rhymes and reading in early childhood. *Merrill-Palmer Quarterly, 33* (3), 255–282.

Martinez, J., & Teale, W. H. (1987). The ins and outs of a kindergarten writing program. *The Reading Teacher, 40,* 444–451.

Mason, G., & Blanton, W. (1971). Story content for beginning reading instruction. *Elementary English, 48,* 793–796.

Mason, J. (1977). *Reading readiness: A definition and skills hierarchy from preschoolers' developing conceptions of print* (Tech. Rep. No. 59). Urbana: University of Illinois, Center for the Study of Reading.

Mason, J. (1980). When *do* children begin to read: An exploration of four-year-old children's letter and word reading competencies. *Reading Research Quarterly, 15,* 203–227.

Mason, J. (1977b). Suggested relationships between the acquisition of beginning reading skills and cognitive development. *Journal of Educational Research, 70,* 195–199.

Mason, J., & McCormick, C. (1979). *Testing the development of reading and linguistic awareness* (Tech. Rep. No. 126). Urbana: University of Illinois, Center for the Study of Reading.

Mason, J., & McCormick, C. (1981). *An investigation of prereading instruction: A developmental perspective* (Tech. Rep. No. 224). Urbana: University of Illinois, Center for the Study of Reading.

Mason, J., McCormick, C., & Bhavnagri, N. (1986). How are you going to help me learn? Lesson negotiations between a teacher and preschool children. In D. B. Yaden & S. Templeton (Eds.), *Metalinguistic awareness and beginning literacy* (pp. 159–172). Portsmouth, NH: Heinemann.

McCormick, C. E., & Mason, J. M. (1986). Intervention procedures for increasing preschool children's interest in knowledge about reading. In W. H. Teale & E. Sulzby (Eds.), *Emergent literacy: Writing and reading* (pp. 90–115). Norwood, NJ: Ablex.

Meyer, L. A., Wardrop, J. A., & Hastings, C. N. (1989). *Interim report of trends from a longitudinal study of the development of reading comprehension ability.* Champaign, IL: Center for the Study of Reading.

Monroe, M. (1932). *Children who cannot read.* Chicago: University of Chicago Press.

Ninio, A. (1980). Picture-book reading in mother-infant dyads, belonging to two subgroups in Israel. *Child Development, 51,* 587–590.

Ninio, A., & Bruner, J. S. (1979). The achievement and antecedents of labelling. *Journal of Child Language, 5,* 5–15.

Pappas, C. C., & Brown, E. (1987). Learning to read by reading: Learning how to extend the functional potential of language. *Research in the Teaching of English, 21,* (2), 160–184.

Perfetti, C. A., Beck, I., Bell, L. C., & Hughes, C. H. (1987). Phonemic knowledge and learning to read are reciprocal: A longitudinal study of first graders. *Merrill-Palmer Quarterly, 33* (3), 283–319.

Petrosky, A. R. (1976). The effects of reality perceptions and fantasy on response to literature: Two case studies: *Research in the Teaching of English, 10,* 239–256.

Read, C. (1971). Pre-school children's knowledge of English phonology. *Harvard Educational Review, 41,* 1–34.

Rentel, V. & King, M. (1983). *A longitudinal study of coherence in children's written narratives* (Report NIE-6-81-0063).

Rowe, D. W. (1987). Literacy learning as an intertextual process. In J. E. Readence & R. Scott Baldwin (Eds.), *Research in literacy: Merging perspectives.* Rochester, NY: National Reading Conference.

Schonell, F. J. (1956). *Diagnostic and attainment testing.* London: Oliver and Boyd.

Scollon, R., & Scollon, S. B. K. (1981). *Narrative, literacy, and face in interethnic communication.* Norwood, NJ: Ablex.

Snow, C. E. (1983). Literacy and language: Relationships during the preschool years. *Harvard Educational Review, 53,* 1165–189.

Snow, C. E., 7 Goldfield, B. A. (1982). Building stories: The emergence of information structures from conversation. In D. Tannen (Ed.), *Analyzing discourse: Text and talk* (pp. 127–141). Georgetown University Round Table on Languages and Linguistics. Washington, DC: Georgetown University Press.

Snow, C. E., & Goldfield, B. A. (1983). Turn the page, please: Situation-specific language acquisition. *Journal of Child Language, 10,* 535–549.

Somerset, H. C. D. (1954). Forward to *Books before five.* by D. White.

Stanovich, K. E., Cunningham, A. E., & West, R. F. (1981). A longitudinal study of the development of automatic recognition skills in first graders. *Journal of Reading Behavior, XIII* (1), 57–74.

Sulzby, E. (1985a). Children's emergent reading of favorite storybooks: A developmental study. *Reading Research Quarterly, 20,* 458–481.

Sulzby, E. (1985b). Kindergarteners as writers and readers. In M. Farr (Ed.), *Advances in writing research, Vol. 1: Children's early writing development* (pp. 127–199). Norwood, NJ: Ablex.

Sulzby, E. (1986a). Young children's concepts for oral and written text. In K. Durkin (Ed.), *Language development during the school years* (pp. 95–116). London: Croom Helm.

Sulzby, E. (1986b). Writing and reading: Signs of oral and written language organization in the young child. In W. H. Teale & E. Sulzby (Eds.), *Emergent literacy: Writing and reading* (pp. 50–89). Norwood, NJ: Ablex.

Sulzby, E., & Teale, W. H. (1985). Writing development in early childhood. *Educational Horizons, 64,* 8–12.

Sulzby, E., Barnhart, J., & Hieshima, J. (in press). Forms of writing and re-reading from writing: A preliminary report. In J. Mason (Ed.), *Reading/writing connections.* Boston: Allyn and Bacon.

Teale, W. H. (1984, November). *Learning to comprehend written language.* Paper presented at the annual convention of the National Council for Teachers of English, Detroit, MI. (ERIC Document Reproduction Service No. ED 255-871)

Teale, W. H. (1986). Home background and young children's literacy development. In W. H. Teale & E. Sulzby (Eds.), *Emergent literacy: Writing and reading* (pp. 173–206). Norwood, NJ: Ablex.

Teale, W. H., & Sulzby, E. (1986a). Emergent literacy as a perspective for examining how young children become writers and readers. In W. H. Teale & E. Sulzby (Eds.), *Emergent literacy: Writing and reading* (pp. vii–xxv). Norwood, NJ: Ablex.

Teale, W. H., & Sulzby, E. (Eds.) (1986b). *Emergent literacy: Writing and reading.* Norwood, NJ: Ablex.

Teale, W. H., & Sulzby, E. (in press). Literacy acquisition in early childhood: The roles of access and meditation in storybook reading. In D. A. Wagner (Ed.), *The future of literacy in a changing world.* New York, NY: Pergamon Press.

Tobin, A. W. & Pikulski, J. J. (1988). A longitudinal study of the reading of achievement of early and non-early readers through sixth grade. In J. E. Readence & R. Scott Baldwin (Eds.), *Dialogues in literacy research.* Chicago, IL: National Reading Conference.

Torrey, J. W. (1969). Learning to read without a teacher. A case study. *Elementary English, 46,* 550–556, 658.

Vellutino, F. R., & Scanlon, D. M. (1987). Phonological coding, phonological awareness and reading ability: Evidence from a longitudinal and experimental study. *Merrill-Palmer Quarterly, 33,* 321–363.

Vernon, M. (1957). *Backwardness in reading: A study of its origins.* Cambridge: Cambridge University Press.

Vygotsky, L. S. (1978). *Mind in society.* Cambridge, MA: Harvard University Press.

Vygotsky, L. S. (1981). The genesis of higher mental functions. In J. V. Wertsch (Ed.), *The concept of activity in Soviet psychology* (pp. 144–188). White Plains, NY: M. E. Sharpe.

Wells, C. G., & Raban, B. (1978). *Children learning to read* (Final Report to the Social Science Research Council). University of Bristol, Bristol, England.

Wells, G. (1986). *The meaning makers: Children learning language and using language to learn.* Portsmouth: Heinemann.

White, D. (1954). *Books before five.* Auckland: New Zealand Council for Educational Research.

Wolf, S. A. (1989). Thinking in play: a young child's response to literature. Paper presented at National Reading Conference, Austin, Texas.

Yaden, Jr., D. B., Smolkin, L. B., & Conlon, A. (1989). Preschoolers questions about pictures print, convention, and story text. *Reading Research Quarterly, 24,* 2, 188–214.

·12·

CASE STUDY

June Birnbaum
Janet Emig

Within the past 20 years, case study as a mode of inquiry has come to represent a major strand in English language-arts research. A scan of the literature reveals hundreds of inquiries in which researchers recount how children acquire and develop language, as well as hundreds of others that characterize their histories and processes as speakers, listeners, writers, and readers. Still other studies have examined individual issues, texts, concepts, programs, and curricula.

History

The neurologist Oliver Sacks, in the preface to his *The Man Who Mistook His Wife for a Hat* (1985), traces case study back to Hippocrates, the first physician, and credits Hippocrates with creating the concept of case study through his presentations of diseases as having a course "from their first intimations to their climax or crisis, and thus to their fatal or happy resolution." Sacks suggests, in fact, that the origin of case study can be found, even earlier, in "that universal and prehistorical tradition by which patients have always told their stories to doctors."

In his historical overview, Sacks regards the late nineteenth century as the high point in the writing of "richly human clinical tales" with the case studies of neurologist Hughlings Jackson (1931) and of the psychoanalyst Sigmund Freud (1956) as exemplars. Within the twentieth century A. R. Luria is, in his opinion, the greatest writer of case study. Luria's case studies of such brain-damaged veterans of World War I as *S* (1972) and *Z* (1960) are famous instances.

Within this century, Wilder Penfield and Perot (1963), Sherrington (1940), and Bruno Bettelheim (1950) have also produced case studies of importance within the fields of neurology and psychiatry, as has Sacks himself (1989). In light of this history, it is not surprising that Steven North in his recent taxonomy of our field (1987) places case study inquirers in a category he terms "clinicians."

Definition. Case study is defined here, following Yin (1981a, 1981b), as an empirical study that investigates a contemporary phenomenon within its real-life context when the boundaries between phenomenon and context are not clearly evident and when multiple sources of evidence are used. In addition, to qualify as a case study, the data must be in some way representative of the phenomenon under scrutiny. As Shulman (1986) cautions, mere/exclusive description of an individual or event does not qualify.

Lincoln and Guba (1985) set forth other crucial characteristics and advantages of case study as a mode of inquiry:

1. Contrasting naturalistic with positivistic inquiries, they note that case study inquirers tend to reconstruct the respondents' constructions (*emic* inquiry) while positivistic inquirers "tend toward a construction that they bring to the inquiry *a priori*" (etic).
2. Case studies build on the reader's tacit knowledge, thus providing "a measure of vicarious experience since case study presents a holistic and lifelike description, like those readers normally encounter in their experience of the world.
3. Case studies are effective in demonstrating the interplay between inquirer and respondent.
4. They provide the reader opportunities to probe for internal consistency.
5. The case study provides what Geertz (1988) defines as "thick description," so necessary for judgments of transferability.
6. They provide a grounded assessment of context.

An additional value of case study is that it can frequently serve as one of three angles in triangulated investigation, thus helping to provide validity.

Case Study. Prior to Strang, Robinson, and Emig, case study, as our review will reveal, was not regarded as a legitimate mode of inquiry in English language-arts research. A major reason for its lack of status was the domination in the post-World War-II period by behaviorist psychology with its tenet that only large-scale experimental studies conducted under ostensibly controlled and context-stripped conditions provided validity and generalizability of findings (Mishler, 1979).

At first, perhaps consequently, individual case researchers worked in isolation, at times idiosyncratically, without models. Some current surveyors of the field seem unaware in their critiques of early work of this pervading domination by behaviorism, and early difficulty in getting case studies published in the reputable journals of any of the social sciences. Now, however, not only is case study honored; but the case for case study is being made with greater and greater sophistication (Guba, 1978; Yin 1984; Lincoln & Guba, 1985; Shulman, 1986; Wilson & Godmundsdottir, 1987). These examinations seem closely allied with a powerful questioning of the rationale for the prior domination of the positivistic paradigm over educational research (Carini, 1975; Engle, 1975; Patton, 1975; Bronfenbrenner, 1977; Guba, 1978; Mishler, 1979; Firestone, 1987); and more specifically over English language-arts research (Emig, 1969, 1981; Bissex, 1987; Dyson, 1988, 1989; McCarthy, 1987).

Language Acquisition and Development

Studies of children's language acquisition and development have classically proceeded as case study. Perhaps in part because of the difficulty in finding large numbers of subjects, investigators have studied a few children—frequently their own—as the most available source of data (Piaget, 1930; Weir, 1970). With the exception of Piaget, case studies of bilingualism occurred earlier than those focusing upon monolinguistic acquisition and development—Chao (1951), English and Chinese, for example. Other bilingual studies include Bowermann's of Finnish (1973), Rydin's of Swedish (1971); and Tolbert's of Mexican/Spanish (1971). Monolingual studies, many using transformational-generative syntactic analysis, began with Bellugi (1964); Cazden (1972); and Brown (1973).

The goal of these investigations has been to make apt intra- and inter-linguistic characterizations of how normal children first develop and use language. For the most part longitudinal, many exhibit the characteristics delineated by Lincoln and Guba (1987) as those marking successful case study reporting:

1. Repeated purposeful probing;
2. Ongoing sampling design;
3. Hypothesis-generation that is fluid, refined, and grounded; and
4. Non-exploitive sharing of findings with subjects, or least, when the subjects are very young, with the subjects' families.

Studies of exceptional language development range from those examining the highly gifted to those examining the retarded, the isolated, and the abused. Primary accounts of brilliant writers can take the form of autobiography (Welty, 1984; Sartre, 1964); or occur as exemplars often supporting a general thesis, as with Gardner's examination in *Frames of Mind: A Theory of Multiple Intelligences* (1983) of the extraordinary linguistic abilities of the poets T. S. Eliot and Stephen Spender. Classic among studies of the retarded is Luria and Yudovich's examination of Russian twins (1971); of the isolated, Itard's study of the wild boy of Aveyon (1962); and of the abused, Curtiss's study of Genie (1977).

Listening. Perhaps because of the formidable methodological challenges involved, there have been, to our knowledge, no discrete case studies of listening and attending behaviors and processes involving subjects with normal hearing. A very few involving partially- or totally-deaf subjects have, however, been made (Prinz & Nelson, 1985). Sacks (1989) provides a case study of the status of "sign" as a symbolic modality within the deaf community (see below).

Invented Spelling. Since invented, spelling can be regarded developmentally as a common precursor of abilities to write, so this brief account logically precedes a discussion of the use of case study in the domain of writing. Beginning with Read (1971) a number of parent/scholars conducted studies of how their children "invented" the orthographic systems of American English. Noteworthy here is Bissex's study of her son, Paul making "thick" documentation by collecting and analyzing all texts he produced between the ages of 4 and 9, from signs on his bedroom door, to original newspaper and school writing (1984).

Writing. Emig (1969) was the first researcher to make a case study of the composing processes of successful English-speaking student writers; Brown had looked at how a prototypical French school boy learned to write (1965). Using protocol analysis, she examined the processes of eight 12th-graders as they wrote in what she called the reflexive and extensive modes. Through interviews she also collected the writing histories of the subjects. She set her findings against the dicta in the most widely used composition and rhetoric handbooks and developed a tentative profile of the composing processes of 17-year-olds. Her case study of Lynn became the prototye for now over 1,000 case studies of non-professional writers from the ages of 4 and 5 (Dyson, 1988) to 79 (Harrienger, 1988). Others who looked at successful student writers include Calkins (1983), Stallard (1974), Mishel (1974), Matsuhashi (1981), Sterling and Freedman (1987), and Berkenkotter, Huckin and Ackerman (1988).

Pianko (1977) and Perl (1979) examined the composing processes of less skilled writers—specifically, college freshmen—as did Sommers (1980), who focussed upon their revising practices. Holbrook (1968) had conducted very sophisticated case studies of 13 D-stream, or supposedly limited ability, 16-year-olds in a Cambridgeshire, England, comprehensive school, studies that were accompanied by a psychiatrist's analysis of emotional growth represented by selected student texts. Newkirk (1984) conducted an equally sophisticated study of composing as a process of psychic reintegration with Ann, a college freshman. Contributing importantly and eloquently to this set is the intellectual autobiography of Mike Rose (1989), against a powerful analysis of like students whom he teaches in the Writing Center at UCLA.

In recent studies, the press of context upon the processes and outcomes of writing has been examined with greater and greater thoroughness (Hull, 1989). Representative here is Kamler (1980), who scrutinized the complex interaction among Jill, 7-year-old writer; her teacher; a single piece of writing; and the climate for writing within Jill's 2nd grade classroom. Mano

(1985) studied the rich interplay among her subject, 16-year-old Simon; his mother, a college instructor of writing; and the investigator herself. That study is also noteworthy in its use of contemporary rhetorical theory—specifically, Kenneth Burke's conception of the representative anecdote, as defined in his *Grammar of Human Motives* (1945).

As inquiries into linguistic and specifically writing processes developed, more and more methodological procedures were devised, many with concomitant, not unexpected uses of technology. Perhaps Weir, who audiotaped the presleep soliloquies of her son, Anthony, was among the first her. Pianko (1977) may have been the first to videotape her subjects as they composed. The most dramatic use of technology may have been Glassner's procedure of having his subjects undergo EEG's as they composed, with the record of their brain waves subsequently analyzed by a computer program that divided these into right-and-left-brain activities (1981). More and more sophisticated observational and codificational schemes have been developed as well (Perl, 1979; Matsuhashi, 1981; Flower and Hayes, 1981).

Gender differences across the processes of writing have been observed and analyzed from the outset, the first being Graves (1975), who noted differences in the ratio of drawing to writing between girls and boys, as well as differences between the size of the conceptual domains the two genders addressed, with boys far more frequently writing about the larger world.

The writing across the curriculum movement, in which teachers of subjects other than English involve students in writing to learn, began in the late 1960s with the work of the London Schools' Council under the direction of James Britton and Harold Rosen. The illustrative documents published by the team used mini-case studies to exemplify how writing could help teach the concepts of science (Medway 1973) and social studies (Martin, 1980). In the United States Goodkin (1982) made case studies of instructors of nursing, business, and chemistry within a community college to show the uses of writing in teaching such subjects. McCarthy (1987) analyzed the differing, even conflicting, demands made upon a college freshman by examining writing requirements in his composition, literature, and biology classes.

One of the most perceptive and thorough efforts to deploy case study in examining the writing of children is represented by the work of Dyson (1983, 1987, 1988). She states the thesis she is exploring as follows:

children's major developmental challenge is not simply to create a unified text but to move among multiple worlds, carrying out multiple roles and coordinating multiple space/time structures (Dyson, 1988, p. 2).

Noteworthy also in these studies is the highly self-conscious and explicit setting-forth of supporting theory.

Teachers of Writing. Recently, researchers have begun to add to portraits of student writers, characterizations through case study of teachers presenting writing to students. Many informal self-characterizations of teachers teaching can be found in the documents of such writing projects and programs as the Bread Loaf School of English and the National Writing Project. More

systematic and dense is the Perl and Wilson study *Through Teachers' Eyes* (1986), in which they present portraits of six teachers, grades 1, 4, and 5, 8, 11, 12, using a wide repertoire of data: observational logs, periodic summaries, teachers' journal, students' writing, students' journals, dialog from conferences, peer-writing group conversation, classroom discussions, and even after-school exchanges.

Reading. In 1910, Huey wrote, "We have surely come to the place where we need to know just what the child normally does when he reads, in order to plan a natural and economic method of learning to read" (p. 9). Yet in the next half century, few heeded what was a clear call for case study. As recently as 1984, only two entries for case study appeared in the index to *The Handbook of Research in Reading*. In Johnston's (1985) survey of the methods used, he cited one by Morgan in 1896 on congenital word blindness and Olson's 1938 recommendation of case study as the most scientific method available. Yet Johnston concluded nearly 50 years later that case studies remained underrepresented in the literature.

Robinson (1975) and Venezky (1984) provide some reasons for reading researchers' reluctance to engage in case study. With the advent of standardized tests around 1920, researchers moved away from the more difficult and time-consuming task of studying natural reading behavior and toward tightly controlled experimental and correlational studies based in laboratories. Often these experimental psychologists valued the elegance of their design over the relevance of their findings for reading classrooms. Others viewed case studies as "soft science" and too untidy to report in the prescribed format of many of the reading journals.

Kamil (1984) acknowledged the prevailing distrust of naturalistic inquiry into reading but forecast the growth of descriptive and ethnographic studies and a tendency to use case studies in conjunction with experimental research as complementary modes of investigation. Indeed, two recent studies have included postexperimental interviews to augment the investigators' interpretations of their quantitative data (Lehr, 1988; Sandowski, Goetz and Kangiser, 1988).

Since the early 1970s, however, the number of case studies in reading has grown dramatically, matching the increased use of naturalistic inquiry in all areas of language development. The majority have appeared as full texts, e.g., Bissex, 1980; Baghban, 1984; chapters in texts, e.g., Snow and Ninio, 1986; or as dissertations, e.g., Bartoli, 1986; Walker-Brown, 1987. Of those found in journals, more have been published in NCTE-sponsored publications than in IRA journals. These case studies tend to address one or more of the following areas:

Instructional programs and practices;
Factors associated with successful reading achievement;
Observations of readers' response to literature.

In spite of the relative paucity of case studies prior to the 1970s, each of these areas had been addressed in at least one case study earlier in the century. Each was undertaken by investigators with closer ties to the classroom than to the laboratory and each of the researchers was or has emerged as a major figure in the field: W. S. Gray, H. Robinson, D. Durkin and J. Squire. We will describe these studies briefly and then review recent exemplars that have extended the four areas of inquiry.

Instructional Programs and Practice

In 1933, W. S. Gray published his monograph concerning the outcomes of a multi-year program to improve reading instruction in five Chicago schools. Data included participant-observers' diaries and field notes from conferences and interviews with school personnel and students concerning organization and instruction, yearly reading scores, and students' reading diaries. Ongoing analysis of the data led to refinement in the improvement program. The cyclical nature of collecting data, analyzing them, revising questions and/or hypotheses and collecting new data—the hallmark of case study—was, as Venezsky (1984) commented, unique at that time.

Reading Achievement. In 1946, H. M. Robinson published *Why Pupils Fail in Reading,* a study of 30 subjects, ages 6 to 15, of normal intelligence but with low reading scores. A team of medical, psychological, and reading specialists and social workers studied the readers and their families. Additional data came from scores on standardized reading tests, filmed eye movements, and oral reading samples. The multiple evaluations of each subject, followed by reexamination of results to modify treatment, exemplifies the triangulation of data that is another hallmark of case study.

Two decades later, in 1966, D. Durkin published *Children Who Read Early: Two Longitudinal Studies,* based on her California investigations of 1st grade early-readers and her New York study of 1st grade readers and on-readers. As Durkin notes, her experiences in the California study, begun in 1958, led her to modify the design of her second study while retaining her original research questions. Her second study of 158 subjects included 30 nonreaders as well as readers for intensive study through parent interview, questionnaires, teacher rating, personality tests as well as intelligence and reading tests. In addition to presenting data for the entire group, Durkin included brief case studies of several subjects.

Apart from her results from this study, Durkin contributed much to the evolution of case study research and to studies of early literacy. First, she recognized the impact of the observer's presence on natural behavior. Second, she acknowledged changes in attitude toward early reading that occurred between 1958 and 1961. Her use of the results of her first study to refine the design and instrumentation of her second study while retaining her original questions is typical of case study (Mishler, 1979, Guba, 1978, Lincoln and Guba, 1985). Finally, she provided the foundation for subsequent case studies of early readers such as Torrey (1969) and Clark (1976).

Response to Literature. The third area of inquiry readers' response to literature led researchers to widen their focus of inquiry to include readers' psychological and emotional responses especially to literature. Although earlier studies, such as I. A. Richards (1942), had examined students' reactions to

poems upon completion, J. Squire's was the first to attempt to examine their reactions while reading (1964). Squire studied the responses of 52 9th and 10th graders to four stories by stopping each reader at five points in the story to explore his or her response while reading as well as upon completion.

To complement his findings from the large group, Squire selected 13 for case studies. In addition to the quantitative and response data obtained for all subjects, information concerning these 13 was obtained from interviews from school personnel and observations of each subject in his or her classroom. Although Squire did not present his case studies in his monograph, his frequent reference to them as confirmatory evidence illustrates their value.

Recent Case Studies. In the last two decades, the number of case studies in reading has grown remarkably. This increase seems to reflect a general dissatisfaction with experimental research expressed by a National Institute of Education-sponsored committee on teaching, testing and learning in 1979: ". . . we need ways of describing that are more informative and insightful than percentiles or stanines. . . . As we have indicated, descriptive materials are important starting points for much scientific work and for teaching " (Tyler & White, p. 363). Yet a decade later, reviewers of research in reading still expressed dissatisfaction with the paucity of applicable findings and recommend more naturalistic inquiries. (Fillion & Brause, 1987; Smith-Burke, 1987).

After we eliminated purely ethnographic studies such as Wolf and Perry (1988), survey studies such as Applebee (1977) or Brown (1977) and single episode observation of subjects such as Haas and Flower (1988), our review of the literature yielded nearly 50 case studies in reading published during the last two decades. Although the number represents a quantum leap from the prior 40 years, it remains a small, but important, proportion of the total studies in reading.

These case studies represent extensions of lines of inquiry pursued in their predecessors as well as new explorations in types of design and areas of study. Features of design in this generation have included changes in the relation of the investigator to the subject(s). In addition to the traditional researcher, parents studied their own children, e.g., Bissex 1980; Baghban 1984; Yaden 1988; teacher studied their own students, e.g., Meek, Armstrong, Austerfield, Graham and Plackett 1983; Atwell 1987; and an observer-and-teacher-team studied the teacher's student, a welfare mother, and the latter's field notes as she learned how to read stories to her young son (Heath & Thomas 1984). A second change in design regarded the age range of subjects. While the first generation of studies included subjects from ages 5 to 15, the second included subjects from infancy, e.g., Baghban, 1984; to adulthood, e.g., Feathers and White (1987). The many studies investigating precursors to literacy are extensions of Durkin's (1966) retrospective research into early literacy. These studies also extend Torrey's methodology, because they include observations of parents', teachers', and students' literacy-related behaviors at home and or at school, e.g., Amarel, Bussis, and Chittenden, 1977; Jacob, 1984; Martinez and Teale, 1988; Taylor, 1983. Amarel et al. commented that their research filled an "odd gap in reading . . . in natural settings." (p. 2). The third change in design concerned site and instrumentation. Researchers moved beyond classrooms to follow their subjects into their homes and playgrounds, e.g., Taylor, 1983; Jacobs, 1984; and added videotapes to their data-gathering procedures, e.g., Birnbaum, 1982; Washburn, 1979.

As suggested above, the areas of study no longer fell neatly into the categories dividing the first generation of case studies. Instead many sutdies overlap two or more as investigators recognized the connections among the four language processes and the need to broaden their scope of inquiry to obtain data from as many sources as possible. For example, Wells (1986) drew six case studies from his observations of 32 children as they advanced from 15 months to 10 years and another 128 from 3½ or 5½ years to 10. His data included observations of progress in oral language acquisition, parent-child communication, students' reading and writing development profiles across the period, general academic histories and exit interviews that included story-telling ability and self-projections about their future. Thus Well's conclusions about his six subjects were contextualized by his broader ethnographic research as well as his analysis of these children's histories.

Birnbaum's (1982) study of the reading and writing behaviors of 4th and 7th graders offers another example of not only the merging of categories but the need in case study to adjust the initial design to address emerging data. The initial purpose of the year-long study had been to investigate the reading and writing processes, products, and histories of good readers and writers. The design included at least 40 hours of in-class observation of each subject in language-arts activities, multiple videotaped episodes of silent reading and writing behaviors, two audiotaped reading and writing episodes, interviews with parents, teacher and the students, as well as a review of academic records at the end of data collection. Early data analysis revealed differences in student levels of proficiency; therefore the focus of the study shifted from a search for shared characteristics for all subjects to a search for differential patterns. As both Wells and Birnbaum illustrate, the broader the scope of inquiry, the less likely that the study can be neatly pigeon-holed. Yet most of the reading case studies still can be sorted into one of the categories on the basis of their major emphasis.

Investigation of instructional programs divide into those that focused on curriculum and methodology and those that examined student response to instruction.

Investigators of reading instruction have studied the amount and types of comprehension activities found in reading classes (Durkin, 1978–79), in basal materials (Durkin, 1984), and the effects of in-service training on teacher' classroom behaviors (Ryskamp, 1986). Other observers have compared the match or mismatch of instruction in Chapter I students' regular and remedial reading classes (Allington, Stuetzal, Shake & Lamarche, 1986) and the impact of innovative or nontraditional methods of teaching reading on low-achieving readers (Atwell, 1987; Feathers & White, 1987; Luce, 1985; Meek, Armstrong, Austerfield, Graham & Plackett, 1983). Other investigators of student behaviors have observed the impact of placement in either a meaning-based or a skill-based program on beginning readers' perception of reading (Bondy, 1984; Rasinski & DeFord, 1988), the types and amounts of reading required in vari-

ous content area courses (Dolan, Harrison & Gardner, 1979; Cole, 1979), the amount and range of school-sponsored and self-sponsored writing done by 8th graders, and amount of writing done by students in reading classes that were purported to include a writing component (Howard, 1987), and the effect of instructors' representation of the purpose and audience for a research assignment upon college student's cognitive strategies as they carried out the assignment (Nelson & Hayes, 1988).

The distinguishing feature of all these case studies is that they probed beyond scores, printed curricular goals, and scope and sequence charts to observaton of instruction and materials and their effects upon students. As more case studies in this area appear, we may move closer to knowing not only what reading programs accomplish but why.

Recent case studies of factors associated with low reading achievement have focused, as had Robinson (1946), on individuals and used their academic and nonacademic experiences as explanatory tools. Recognition of the need for representative portraits of disabled readers led Harris (1970) to collect 16 such studies and publish them in a casebook. He noted in his preface that journals seldom published case studies even though they provided rich data concerning reading disability. The following year Tiela and Becker (1971) published an annotated bibliography of case studies in this area that were conducted between 1950 and 1970.

In the last decade, several researchers have included descriptions of subjects with low reading achievement within studies of larger populations (Birnbaum, 1982; Harste, Woodward & Burke, 1984; McDermott, 1985; Wells, 1986) or of programs (Meek et al., 1983). Two recent case studies have reflected the field's growing interest in looking beyond the characteristics associated with low achievement in reading to observe the interaction of subjects and their academic and nonacademic environments as they move toward the label of "reading disabled" (Bartoli, 1986; Walker-Brown, 1987). A case study of three adult disabled readers using a combination of retrospective, introspective, and think-aloud techniques yielded a picture of the complex cognitive, emotional, and social causes and effects of reading disability as borderline illiterates trv to cope with life (Johnston, 1985).

Case studies of successful readers, which began with Durkin's research (1966), reflect not only a continuing interest in characteristics of early readers but also a recent interest in older readers, as well as a desire to investigate the precursors of early literacy. Case studies of early readers have included more direct observations of both parent and child over longer periods of time and have widened to include not only samples of the child's reading but his or her writing, drawing, and problem solving (Clark, 1976) and the role of literacy in the families and homes of early readers (Taylor, 1983). In an appraisal of her own study from the vantage point of nearly a decade, Clark (1984) reflected researchers' growing interest in the connections among language processes influenced by the work of Bissex (1980), Harste, et al. (1984), and Taylor (1983). In retrospect, she wished that she had attended more closely to the children's writing rather than confining her interest to letter formation and spelling, and had studied children more closely as "hypothesis testers and rule makers."

During the last decade, an important outgrowth of the early-reader studies has been the many investigations of emergent literacy from infancy to the onset of conventional reading and writing behaviors. Many of them have been based on an ethnographic or case study design, and, in some instances employ both, e.g., Heath, (1983). Teale (1986) divides them into four categories: uses of environmental print, acquisition of concepts about print, story book reading, and preschool instructional programs. Teale and Sulzby (1986) as well as Wolf and Perry (1988) provide reviews of this literature. One strategy has been to obtain oral histories of proficient readers (Williams, 1986) or of the impact of childhood and adolescent reading experiences upon proficient college readers and writers (Birnbaum, 1986). Another has been to observe and question skilled readers while they read (Briggs, 1984; Henrichs, 1986).

The use of case studies to explore the nature of readers' response to literature has also profliferated since Squire first investigated adolescents' interpretations of short stories. The increased interest parallels the shift in theories of literary criticism, mirroring developments in cognitive psychology and linguistics, and the recognition of the active role of the reader in constructing the meaning of the text, e.g. Bleich (1975), Fish, (1980), Iser (1978), Rosenblatt (1938, 1978). As Rosenblatt's dates indicate, she recognized the active nature of the transaction between the reader and the text decades before other response theorists.

Although many studies during the last two decades have reported investigations of response to literature, most have not been case studies as defined in this chapter, e.g., Applebee (1977), Beach and Wendler (1987), Brown (1977), Hickman (1980), Purves and Beach (1972), Studier (1981). The case studies can be divided into age related categories.

Pre-school studies have included observations of children's changing response to repeated readings of favorite stories (Baghban, 1984; Snow & Ninio, 1987; Yaden, 1988). Case studies of primary, elementary, and middle school students' response to literature have ranged from repeated observations of kindergarten students' browsing patterns in the library (Martinez & Teale, 1988); analysis of a 2nd grader's corpus of writing for stylistic devices that seemed influenced by her reading of literature (Temple, Burris, Nathan & Temple, 1988) to a study of a mainstreamed 8th grader's explorations of literature in a class where personal response was encouraged after years of being in skills-oriented classes where correct completion of dittos was valued. (Atwell, 1988) and a comparative study of teachers of literature-based reading classes, who believed in whole language, with those who still believed in a subskills philosophy while trying to use a literature-centered approach (Zarrillo, 1989).

At the pre-secondary level, two studies merit attention, because each represents the two lines of inquiry suggested by Purves and Beach (1972). These are the cognitive and affective states of the reader and the context for reading a text as influences upon reader response. Galda (1982) exemplifies the first avenue of investigation and Atwell (1987) represents the second.

Galda examined the responses of three 5th graders to two novels during individual and group discussions of each novel. Using transcripts from the discussions, Galda found that all three subjects tended to evaluate characters and their actions. Further analysis, based on the findings of Applebee (1977) and Petrosky (1976), revealed subtle differences in the overall responses of each of the subjects. These ranged from one subject's typical piece-meal, subjective interpretation of each text, which precluded virtual experiencing of the text, to another's ability to enter the story world and interpret it as a whole.

Acting as teacher-researcher, Atwell (1987) published a study of her 8th grade students' year-long progress in a reading-writing workshop where connections between the two processes were fostered. Against this background, Atwell presented case studies of five students and their changes in attitudes and behaviors as they explored literature and their own writing.

At the secondary and postsecondary levels, case studies have focussed on either readers' cognitive and affective states or on the context, i.e., stimulus, setting, purpose, as influences upon reader response—two areas recommend for research by Purves and Beach (1972). Holland (1975), Petrosky (1976), and Washburn (1979) exemplify the first approach, and Marshall (1987) and McCarthy (1987) exemplify the second.

Holland used psychoanalytic measures to search for adult readers' personal identity themes and then compared their interpretations of literary texts, obtained in repeated interviews, with their psychological profiles. He concluded that readers' internal states markedly influenced their perception and interpretation of texts. Petrosky, like Holland, used psychoanalytic measures to profile 9th grade readers but added Piaget's theory of stage development as an additional framework for his study of four readers' response to fiction and poems. His analysis of their twice-weekly interviews during a three-month period revealed that readers' level of cognitive development as well as their emotional state combined to influence their interpretation of texts. Washburn furthered this line of research by using a Kelly Repertory Grid to elicit the personal construct system of four high school seniors. He videotaped them as they read four short stories and verbalized their responses, then videotaped their reactions and explanations of their earlier videotaped behaviors.

In a recent case study Marshall (1987) investigated the external environment's effect on reader response, the other element cited by Purves and Beach (1972). After several months of observing a high school teacher and her literature classes, Marshall developed case studies of six students based on repeated observations, interviews, and a collection of their writing about the literature. He found that "good" students, as identified by the teacher, had learned to read the teacher and rather cynically gave her what she wanted while "poor" students resented her exclusive emphasis on formal analysis of texts. In a followup study of these students, Marshall found that long-term retention of literary texts was equal whether the students engaged in personal response writing or formal papers about the literature. McCarthy's case study of a college student's progress in three courses, which was cited in the review of case studies in writing, revealed another example of the influence of context upon response to literature. Although her subject successfully wrote in response to demands made in his English 101 and biology courses, he could not fathom how the poetry instructor wanted him to respond to the literature. Thus as Marshall's and McCarthy's studies indicate, some literature classes may encourage students to learn to read and respond to the teacher rather than the text.

Thus far, reflecting both the assumptions and the emphases of most literature in the field, we have treated case study as an examination or characterization of persons. Yet Yin notes (1984), in the definition of case study which we espouse (p. 1) that case study investigates phenomena; and in both an actual and a logical sense, persons represent but a subset of phenomena. Within education, other subsets of legitimate phenomena to examine include concepts, issues, curricula, and programs, all of which have also received treatment through case study.

For example, significant issues in the field of English language arts have been examined through case study. One of the most telling and eloquent of these is James Moffett's *Storm in the Mountains* (1988), with its descriptive subtitle 'A Case Study of Censorship, Conflict and Consciousness'. In his analysis of the vast religious and political complexities of the highly publicized 1974 conflict in Kanawha County, West Virginia, over adoption of a cluster of language-arts textbooks, including several he authored, Moffett interweaves historical and media accounts with interviews he holds with many of the parties in the dispute—school board members, politicians, parents, children—interviews that he presents in the form of a dramatic script. He also employs as organizing theme his interpretation of the rhetorical term *agnosis,* thus orchestrating classical and contemporary modes of analysis.

In March, 1986, the deaf students at Gallaudet University in Washington, D.C., the sole liberal arts university for the deaf in the world, staged a 7-day uprising when their Board of Trustees selected a hearing president for the school and forced the board to replace her with a deaf president.

Through case study Sacks (1988, 1989) analyzed this compelling instance of curricular reform (although to characterize the events at Gallaudet merely as an instance of curricular reform would be as inaccurate as to characterize the 1974 events in Kanawha County as an instance of a moment that intertwined issues of theory, research, curriculum, politics, and culture, with consideration of the legitimacy of a communicative modality sign. Sacks served as eyewitness to the events leading within that week to the selection of a deaf president, interplaying, as Moffett did for censorship, a rich historical account of Sign with descriptions of the chief participants in the conflict and of their interplay.

The case study of Gallaudet differs from that of Kanawha in major ways, making it worthy of this separate citation. Moffett's account was retrospective, with his return 8 years later to the

county to analyze what had transpired. Sacks was present for all the events, serving as an on-site observer, not as an instigator-observer. Also, the issue at Gallaudet was more powerfully one of opposing theories that found their support in research rather than in theology, although in both cases the participants proceeded from deeply held personal beliefs and practices.

Trends and Future Directions

Five trends are currently noteworthy within case study inquiry in the English language arts. First, many recent studies are characterized by greater immediacy, with ongoing, recurrent on-site and in-process observations a steady feature. Second, researchers are providing denser and richer contextualizations for the phenomena and subjects under scrutiny. Third, if indeed a clear demarcation ever separated the domains of case study and ethnography, such a boundary now grows increasingly blurred, even to the point, in some cases, of disappearing entirely. Fourth, case study finds itself as a mode more and more contextualized within multilayered, multidimensional inquiries for which it represents but one source of data and of combined qualitative-quantitive knowing. Fifth, substantive studies that feature, in Dyson's happy term *symbol-weaving,* as between drawing and writing, or of speaking and signing, are growing more common, appropriate in an era more and more concerned with developmental and with neuroscientific insights.

We agree with Geertz (1988) that case studies represent, in his recent metaphor, "theaters of language", quite as significantly matters of rhetorical stances, decisions, and style as of methods of data collection and analysis. The rhetorical dimensions of case study, how those case studies are literally written, require more explicit acknowledgment and attention, perhaps using as model Geertz's own analysis, of the writings of four anthropologists: Levi-Strauss, Malinowski, Benedict, and Evans-Pritchard.

Conclusion

Since case study documents dense and specific human history, the mode may flourish especially under those psychological and political arrangements that honor uniqueness—under, that is, mature democracies and political systems. The status of case study in a culture may well prove then an index not only of investigative but also of societal sophistication.

References

Allington, R., Stuetzal, H., Shake, M., & Lamarche, S. (1986). What is remedial reading? A descriptive study. *Reading research and instruction, 26*(1), 15–30.

Amarel, M., Bussis, A., & Chittenden, E. (1977). *An approach to the study of beginning reading: longitudinal case studies.* Paper presented at the National Reading Conference, New Orleans, La.

Applebee, A. (1977). A sense of story. *Theory into Practice, 16,* 342–347.

Atwell, N. (1987). *In the middle: Writing, reading, and learning with adolescents.* Portsmouth, N.H.: Heinemann.

Atwell, N. (1988). A special writer at work. In T. Newkirk & N. Atwell, (Eds.), *Understanding writing: ways of observing, learning and teaching K–8.* (2nd ed.). Portsmouth, N.H.: Heinemann.

Baghban, M. S. M. (1984). *Our daughter learns to read and write: A case study from birth to three.* Newark, Del.: International Reading Association.

Bartoli, J. S. (1986). Exploring the process of reading/learning disability labeling: An ecological systems approach. *Dissertation Abstract Index, 47* (5), Nov., 1672-A.

Bondy, E. (1985). *Children's definitions of reading: Products of an interactive process.* Paper presented at the annual meeting of the American Educational Research Association. Chicago.

Beach, R. & Wendler, L. (1987). Developmental differences in response to a story. *Research and education, 21,* Oct., 286–297.

Berkenkotter, C., Huckin, T. N. & Ackerman, J. (1988). Conventions, conversations and the write: Case study of a student in a rhetoric, Ph.D. program. *Research in the Teaching of English, 22,* Feb., 9–44.

Bettelheim, B. (1950). *Love is not enough: The treatment of emotionally disturbed children.* Glencoe, Il.: Free Press.

Birnbaum, J. C. (1982). The reading and composing behavior of selected 4th- and 7th-grade students. *Research in the teaching of English, 16,* 241–260.

Bissex, G. L. (1980). *GNYS at Wek: A child learns to write and read.* Cambridge: Harvard University Press.

Bissex, G. L. (1987). The child as teacher. In H. Goelman, A. Oberg, & F. Smith, (Eds.), *Awakening to Literacy.* Portsmouth, N.H.: Heinemann.

Bleich, D. (1975). *Readings and feelings: an introduction to subjective criticism.* Urbana, Il.: National Council of Teachers of English.

Bowermann, M. (1973). *Early syntactic development: A cross-linguistic study with special reference to Finnish.* Cambridge, Eng.: Cambridge University Press.

Briggs, S. L. (1984). Professional reading in English as a second language: six case studies of graduate students at an American university. *Dissertation Abstract Index, 45,* 9–10, 2817-A.

Brown, G. H. (1977). Development of story in children's reading and writing. *Theory into Practice, 16,* 357–362.

Brown, R. B. (1973). *A first language: the early stages.* London: George Allen & Unwin, Ltd.

Brown, R. W. (1965). How the French boy learns to write. Champaign, Ill: National Council of Teachers of English.

Burke, K. (1945). *Grammar of human motives.* Berkeley, Ca.: University of California Press.

Calkins, L. (1983). *Lessons from a child: on the teaching and learning of writing.* Exeter, N.H.: Heinemann.

Carini, P. (1975). *Observation and description: An alternate methodology for the investigation of human phenomena.* North Dakota Study Group on Evaluation Monographs. Grand Forks, ND.: University of North Dakota Press.

Cazden, Courtney, B. (1972). *Language in early childhood education.* Washington, D.C.: National Association for the Education of Young Children.

Chao, Y. R. (1951). The Cantian idiolect: An analysis of the Chinese spoken by a 28-months-old child. In W. J. Fishel. (Ed.). *Semitic and oriental studies.* University of California Publications in Semitic Philology, XI. Berkeley and Los Angeles: University of California Press.

Clark, M. M. (1976). *Young fluent readers: What can they teach us?* London: Heinemann.

Clark, M. M. (1984). Literacy at home and at school: Insights from a study of young fluent readers. In H. Goelman, A. Oberg, and F. Smith, (Eds.), *Awakening to literacy.* Portsmouth, N.H.: Heinemann.

Cole, J. (1979). Topic work with first-year secondary pupils. In E. Lunzer and K. Gardner (Eds.), *The effective use of reading.* London: Heinemann.

Curtiss, S. (1977). *Genie: A psycholinguistic study of a modern-day "wild child".* New York: Academic Press.

Dolan, T., Harrison, C., & Gardner, K. (1979). The incidence and context of reading in the classroom. In E. Lunzer and K. Gardner. (Eds.), *The effective use of reading.* London: Heinemann.

Durkin, D. (1966). *Children who read early: Two longitudinal studies.* New York: Teachers College Press.

Durkin, D. (1978–79). What classroom observations reveal about reading comprehension instruction. *Reading Research Quarterly, 14,* 481–533.

Durkin, D. (1984). Do basal readers teach reading comprehension? In R. C. Anderson, J. Osborn, R. J. Tierney, (Eds.), *Learning to read in American schools: Basal reader and content texts.* Hillside, N.J.: Erlbaum.

Dyson, A. H. (1983). The role of oral language in early writing processes. *Research in the Teaching of English, 17,* 1–30.

Dyson, A. H. (1987). Individual differences in beginning composing: An orchestrated vision of learning to compose. *Written communication, 4,* 411–442.

Dyson, A. H. (1988). *Drawing, talking and writing: Rethinking writing development. Occasional Paper No. 3.* Center for the Study of Writing. Berkeley, Ca.: University of California.

Dyson, A. (1989). The multiple world of child writers: A study of friends learning to write. New York: Teachers College Press.

Dyson, A. (1988). *Negotiating among multiple worlds: The space/time dimensions of young children's composing.* Technical Report #15, May, 1988. Berkeley, CA: Center for the Study of Writing.

Emig, J. A. (1969). *Components of the composing process among 12th-grade writers.* Unpublished doctoral dissertation, Harvard University.

Engle, B. S. (1975). *A handbook on documentation.* Grand Forks, ND.: University of North Dakota Press.

Feathers, K. M. & White, J. H. (1987). Learning to learn: case studies of the process. *Reading research and instruction, 26*(4), 264–74.

Fillion, B., & Brause, R. S. (1987). Research in classroom practices: What have we learned and where are we going? In J. R. Squire, (Ed.), *The dynamics of language learning: Research in reading and English,* Urbana, Il: National Council on Research in English and ERIC.

Firestone, W. A. (1987). Meaning in method: the rhetoric of qualitative and quantitative research. *Educational Researcher, 16*(7), 16–21.

Fish, S. (1980). *Is there a text in this class?* Cambridge, Ma.: Harvard University Press.

Flower, L. & Hayes, J. R. (1981). A cognitive process theory of writing. *College Composition and Communication, 32,* 365–387.

Flower, L. & Hayes, J. R. (1981). The cognition of discovery: Defining a rhetorical problem. *College Composition and Communication, 31,* 27–43.

Freud, S. (1956). The relation of the poet to day-dreaming and Leonardo da Vinci and a memory of his childhood. *Collected Papers,* (J. Riviere, Trans.) New York: Basic Books.

Galda, L. (1982). Assuming the spectator stance: An examination of the responses of three young readers. *Research in the Teaching of English, 16,* 1–20.

Gardner, H. (1983). *Frames of mind: A theory of multiple intelligences.* New York: Basic Books.

Geertz, C. (1988). *Works and Lives: The Anthropologist as Author.* Stanford, Ca.: Stanford University Press.

Glassner, B. (1981). Lateral specialization of the modes of composing. Unpublished doctoral dissertation, Rutgers University.

Goodkin, V. (1982). *The Intellectual consequences of writing: Writing as a tool for learning.* Doctoral thesis. Rutgers University.

Graves, D. H. (1975). An examination of the writing process of seven year old children. *Research in the Teaching of English, 9,* 227–241.

Gray, W. S. (1933). *Improving instruction in reading.* (Supplemental Educational Monographs, No. 40). Chicago: University of Chicago Press.

Guba, E. G. (1978). *Toward a methodology of naturalistic inquiry in educational evaluation.* C S E Monograph series in evaluation, 8. Los Angeles, Ca.: Center for the School of Evaluation, U.C.L.A. Gradute School of Education.

Haas, C. & Flower, L. (1988). Rhetorical reading strategies and the construction of meaning. *College Composition and Communication 39*(2), 167–183.

Harrienger, M. (1988). *Discursivity, subjectivity and empowerment: el-*

derly ill women. Doctoral dissertation in progress, Purdue University.

Harris, A. J., (Ed.). (1970). *Casebook on reading disability.* New York: David M. McKay.

Harste, J. C., Woodward, V. A. & Burke, C. L. (1984). *Language stories and literacy lessons.* Portsmouth, N.H.: Heinemann.

Heath, S. B. (1983). *Ways with words: Language, life and work in communities and classrooms.* Cambridge: Cambridge University Press.

Heath, S. B. & Thomas, C. (1984). The achievement of pre-school literacy for mother and child. In H. Goelman, A. Oberg, & F. Smith, (Eds.), *Awakening to literacy.* Portsmouth, N.H.: Heinemann.

Henrichs, M. (1985). Character of highly proficient freshmen college readers. *Dissertation Abstract Index, 48,* 1160-A.

Hickman, J. (1980). Children's response to literature: What happens in the classroom. *Language Arts, 57,* 524–529.

Holbrook, D. (1968). *English for the rejected: Training literacy in the lower streams of the secondary school.* Cambridge, Eng.: Cambridge University Press.

Holland, N. (1975). *Five readers reading.* New Haven, Ct.: Yale University Press.

Howard, K. C. (1987). *Writing in the reading classroom: Teachers' methods, materials, and beliefs.* Unpublished doctoral dissertation, University of Georgia.

Huey, E. B. (1910). *The psychology and pedagogy of reading.* New York: Macmillan.

Hull, G. A. (1989). Research on writing: Building a cognitive and social understanding of composing. In L. B. Resnick & L. E. Klopfer: *Toward the Thinking of Curriculum: Current Cognitive Research 1989.* ASCD Yearbook: CSL: University of Pittsburg.

Iser, W. (1978). *The act of reading: a theory of aesthetic response.* Baltimore: The Johns Hopkins University Press.

Itard, J. M. G. (1962). *Wild Boys of Aveyon.* Englewood Cliffs, N.J.: Prentice Hall.

Jackson, H. In Taylor, J. (1931, 1958). *Selected writings of Huglings Jackson.*

Jacob, E. (1984). Learning literacy through play: Puerto Rican kindergarten children. In H. Geolman, A. Oberg, & F. Smith, (Eds.), *Awakening to literacy.* Portsmouth, N.H.: Heinemann.

Johnston, P. H. (1985). Understanding reading disability: a case study approach. *Harvard Educational Review, 55*(2), May, 153–77.

Kamil, M. L. (1984). Current traditions of reading research. In P. D. Pearson, R. Barr, M. L. Kamil & P. Mosenthal, (Eds.), *Handbook of reading research.* New York: Longman.

Kamler, B. (1980). One child, one teacher, one classroom: the story of one piece of writing. *Language Arts, 57,* 680–93.

Lehr, S. (1988). The child's developing sense of theme as a response to literature. *Reading Research Quarterly 23*(3), 337–357.

Lincoln, Y. & Guba, E. G. (1985). *Naturalistic inquiry.* Beverly Hills, Ca.: Sage.

Loban, W. (1976). *Language development kindergarten through grade twelve.* Urbana, Ill: National Council of Teachers of English.

Luce, C. H. (1985). Terry makes sense: an ethnographic account of a high school peer tutoring event. *Dissertation Abstracts Index* 3 Sept. 847–848-A.

Luria, A. R. (1960). *The mind of a mnemonist: A little book about a vast memory.* (L. Solotaroff, Trans.) NY: Basic Books.

Luria, A. R. (1972). *The man with a scattered world: The history of a brainwound.* (L. Solotaroff, Trans) NY: Basic Books.

Luria, A. R. & la Yudovich, F. (1971). In J. Simon (Ed.), *Speech and the development of mental processes in the child.* Harmonsworth, Middlesex, Eng.: Penguin Books.

Mano, S. (1985). *Simon's writing develops: A case study of a successful adolescent writer.* Doctoral dissertation. University of Southern California.

Marshall, J. D. (1987). The effects of writing on student's understanding of literary texts. *Research in the Teaching of English, 21,* 30–63.

Martin, N. (1980). *The Martin report: case study from government high schools in Western Australia.* Education Dept. Western Australia.

Martinez, M. & Teale, W. H. (1988). Reading in a kindergarten classroom library. *Reading Teacher, 41,* 568–572.

Matsuhashi, A. (1981). Pausing and Planning: The tempo of written discourse production. *Research in the Teaching of English 15,* 113–34.

McCarthy, L. (1987). A stranger in a strange land: a college student writing across the curriculum. *Research in the Teaching of English, 21* (3), October: 233–265.

McDermott, R. P. (1974). Achieving school failure: An anthropological approach to illiteracy and social stratification. In G. Spindler, (Ed.), *Education and cultural process: Toward an anthropology of education.* New York: Holt, Rinehart and Winston.

McDermott, R. P. (1985). Achieving school failure: An anthropological approach to illiteracy and social stratification. In Singer, H. and Ruddell, R. B. (Eds.) *Theoretical Models and Processes of Reading,* 3rd Edition. Newark, Del.: International Reading Association.

Medway, P. (1973). *From talking to Writing.* Project: Writing Across the Curriculum). London: London School Council.

Meek, M., Armstrong, S., Austerfield, V., Graham, J. & Plackett, E. (1983). *Achieving literary: longitudinal studies of adolescents learning to read.* London: Routledge and Kegan Paul.

Mishel, T. (1974). A case study of a twelfth grade writer. *Research in the Teaching of English, 8,* 303–14.

Mishler, E. G. (1979). Meaning in context: Is there any other kind? *Harvard Educational Review, 49,* 1–19.

Moffett, J. (1988). Storm in the mountains: A case study of censorship, conflict and consciousness. Carbondale, Il.: Southern Illinois University Press.

Nelson, J. & Hayes, J. R. (1988). *How the writing context shapes students' strategies for writing from sources.* Technical Report, No. 16. Pittsburgh: Pa.: Center for the Study of Writing.

Newkirk, T. (1984). Anatomy of a breakthrough: Case study of a freshman writer. In Beach, R. and Bridwell, C. (Eds.) *New Directions in Composition Research.* New York: Guilford Press.

Newkirk, T. (1989). *More than stories: the range of children's writing.* Portsmouth, N.H.: Heinemann.

North, S. M. (1987). *The making of knowledge in composition: Portrait of an emerging field.* Montclair, N.J.: Boynton/Cook.

Patton, M. Q. (1975). *Alternative evaluation research paradigm.* Grand Forks, N.D.: University of North Dakota Press.

Penfield, W. & Perot, P. (1963). The brain's record of visual and auditory experience: A final summary and discussion. *Brain, 86,* 595–696.

Perl, S. (1979). The composing processes of unskilled college writers. *Research in the Teaching of English, 13,* 317–33.

Perl, S. & Wilson, N. (1986). *Through teachers' eyes: portraits of writing teachers at work.* Portsmouth, N.H.: Heinemann.

Petrosky, A. R. (1976). The effects of reality perception and fantasy on response to literature: Two case studies. *Research in the Teaching of English, 10,* 239–257.

Piaget, J. (1930). *The language and thought of the child.* (M. Gabain, Trans.). New York: Meridan, 1955.

Pianko, S. (1977). *The composing art of college freshman writers: A description.* Unpublished doctoral dissertation, Rutgers, the State University.

Prinz, & Nelson, K. (1985). *Making sense; the acquisition of shared meaning.*

Purves, A. & Beach, R. (1972). *Literature and the reader: research in response to literature, reading interests and the teaching of literature.* Urbana, Il.: National Council of Teachers of English.

Rasinski, T. V. & Deford, D. E. (1988). First graders' conceptions of literacy: a matter of schooling. *Theory Into Practice, xxvii,* 53–61.

Read, C. (1971). Pre-school children's knowledge of English phonology. *Harvard Educational Review, 23,* 17–38.

Richards, I. A. (1942). *How to read a page.* New York: Norton.

Robinson, H. M. (1946). *Why pupils fail in reading.* Chicago: The University of Chicago Press.

Robinson, H. M. (1975). Insights from research: children's behaviors while reading. In W. P. Page (Ed.), *Help for the Reading Teacher.* Urbana, Il: National Council of Teachers of English.

Rose, M. (1989). *Lives on the boundary.* New York: The Free Press.

Rosenblatt, L. (1938/1983). *The reader, the text, the poem: the transactional theory of the literary work.* Carbondale: Southern Illinois University Press.

Rosenblatt, L. (1978). *Literature as exploration.* (4th ed.). New York: Modern Language Association.

Rydin, I. (1971). A Swedish child in the beginning of syntactic development and some cross-linguistic comparisons. Unpublished paper. On file with Roger Brown, Harvard University, Cambridge, Ma.

Ryskamp, C. V. (1986). Making sense of sense: An observational case study of comprehension in third grade classrooms. *Dissertation Abstract Index, 47* (7) Jan. 2526-A.

Sacks, O. (1985). *The man who mistook his wife for a hat.* New York: Simon and Schuster.

Sacks, O. (1989). *Seeing Voices.* Berkeley, Ca.: University of California Press.

Sandowski, M., Goetz, E. T., & Kangiser, S. (1988). Imagination in story response: relationships between imagery, affect, and structural importance. *Reading and Research Quarterly, 23,* (3).

Sartre, J. (1964). *The words.* (B. Frechtman, Trans.) NY: George Braziller.

Sherrington, C. S. (1940). *Man on his nature.* Cambridge, Eng.: Cambridge University Press.

Shulman, L. (1986). Those who understand: Knowledge growth in teaching. *Educational Researcher, 15*(2), 4–14.

Smith-Burke, M. T. (1987). Classroom practices and classroom interaction during reading instruction: What's going on? In J. Squire, (Ed.), *The dynamics of language learning: Research in reading and English.* Urbana, Il: National Council on Research in English and ERIC.

Snow, C. E. & Ninio, A. (1986). The contracts of literacy: What children learn from learning to read books. In W. H. Teale, & E. Sulzby, (Eds.), *Emerging literacy: Writing and reading.* Norwood, N.J.: Ablex.

Sommers, N. (1980). Revision strategies of student writers and experienced writers, *College Composition and Communication, 31,* 378–388.

Squire, J. R. (1964). *The reading of adolescents while reading four short stories.* National Council of Teachers of English research report. No. 2. Champaign, Ill.: National Council of Teachers of English.

Stallard, C. K. (1974). An analysis of the writing behavior of good student writers. *Research in the Teaching of English, 8,* 206–18.

Sterling, M. & Freedman, S. W. (1987). A good girl writes like a good girl: written response to student writing. *Written Communication, 4*(Oct.), 343–369.

Studier, C. (1981). Children's response to literature. *Language Arts, 58,* 425–429.

Taylor, D. (1983). *Family literacy: young children learning to read and write.* Exeter, N.H.: Heinemann.

Teale, W. H. (1984). Reading to young children: Its significance for literacy development. In H. Goelman, A. Oberg, & F. Smith, (Eds.), *Awakening to Literacy.* Portsmouth, N.H.: Heinemann.

Teale, W. H. & Sulzby, E. (1986). Introduction: emergent literacy as a perspective for examining how young children become writers and readers. In Teale, W. H. and E. Sulzby (Eds.) *Emergent Literacy: Writing and Reading.* Norwood, N.J.: Ablex.

Temple, C., Burris, N., Nathan, R., Temple F. (1988). *The beginnings of writing.* Second edition. Boston: Allyn and Bacon, Inc.

Tiela, T. M. & Becker, G. L. (1971). Case studies in reading: an annotated bibliography. Newark, Del.: International Reading Association.

Tolbert, K. (1971). Pepe Joy: Learning to talk in Mexico. Unpublished paper. On file with Roger Brown, Harvard University, Cambridge, Ma.

Torrey, J. W. (1969). Learning to read without a teacher: A case study. *Elementary English, 46,* 550–556.

Tyler, R. & White, S. (Eds.) (1979). *Teaching, testing and learning.* Washington, D.C.: National Council of Teachers of Education.

Venezky, R. L. (1984). The hsitory of reading research. In P. D. Pearson, R. Barr, M. L. Kamil & P. Mosenthal, (Eds.), *Handbook of reading research.* New York: Longman.

Walker-Brown, P. A. (1987). Toward a dynamic assessment model for understanding literacy learning difficulties of adolescents: Case studies in a Mennonite high school. *Dissertation Abstracts Index, 48,* (3) Sept. 619-A.

Washburn, W. V. (1979). *Responding to a literary work of art.* Unpublished doctoral dissertation, The University of Calgary.

Weir, R. (1970). *Language in the crib.* The Hague: Mouton.

Wells, G. (1986). *The meaning makers: Children learning language and using language to learn.* Portsmouth, N.H.: Heinemann.

Welty, E. (1984). *One writer's beginnings.* Cambridge, Ma.: Harvard University Press.

Williams, G. L. (1986). Literacy acquisition in retrospect: a composite view of academicians and professionals. *Dissertation Abstract Index, 47*(7) Jan. 2527-A.

Wilson, S. N. & Gudmundsdottir, S. (1987). What is this a case of? Exploring some conceptual issues in case study. *Education and urban society, 20*(1), Nov. 42–54.

Wolf, D. P. & Perry, M. D. (1988). Becoming literate: beyond scribes and clerks. *Theory in practice, 27*(1), Winter, 44–52.

Yaden, D. (1988). Understanding stories through repeated read-abouts: How many does it take? *Reading Teacher, 41,* 556–560.

Yin, R. K. (1981a). The case study as a serious research strategy. *Knowledge: creation, diffusion, utilization, 3* (September) 97–114.

Yin, R. K. (1981b). The case study crisis: some answers. *Administrative Science Quarterly, 26*(March), 58–65.

Yin, R. K. (1984). *Case study research: Design and methods.* Beverly Hills: Sage.

Zarrillo, J. (1989). Teachers' interpretations of literature-based reading. *The Reading Teacher, 43* (October) 22–28.

·13·

ETHNOGRAPHIC RESEARCH

Amy Zaharlick
Judith L Green

The most common questions asked about ethnography are: Just what is ethnography? Isn't ethnography the same as participant observation? Don't you just go into the field, look at what is happening, write down everything you see, and then write up your observations for others? If I go into a classroom setting for a year, is that enough to call my study ethnographic? Can I just go into one classroom or look at one student and do ethnography? Isn't ethnography totally subjective? Can I use ethnography if I want to know which program is best? I want to go out and do an ethnographic study; can you tell me what I need to do? You can't generalize across studies, can you? Your descriptions are really vignettes or anecdotes; they're not "real" data, are they? What book can I read to help me analyze ethnographic data? Just what is ethnography good for?

Questions like these have been asked repeatedly of ethnographers by those who want to find new ways to explore educational issues, processes, or phenomena that are part of daily life in classrooms and other educational settings (e.g., home, community, churches). However, the ways in which these questions are posed suggest that those making the questions equate ethnography with method in the same way someone would ask about doing analysis of variance or multiple regression analysis. Just as a statistician would ask about the question being explored before discussing the appropriateness of particular statistical tests, so would the ethnographer, since question and method are inextricably interrelated in ethnographic research. In addition, the ethnographer is concerned about the theory or theories underlying the study since ethnography is an approach to the study of everyday life that is driven by cultural theory (Wilcox, 1982). Therefore, the issue is not do I "do" ethnography or some other approach, but whether or not ethnography is the appropriate approach to use given the questions to be explored and the theory guiding the research.

In this chapter we will develop a framework that can be used to guide decisions about the use of ethnography as an approach to the study of educational issues and processes related to English language arts. This framework will reflect new directions in ethnography grounded in contemporary views of ethnographic research in anthropology, sociology, and education. To develop this framework, three questions will be explored:

1. What makes ethnography a unique approach, or what is meant by the statement that "ethnography is a theoretically driven approach?"
2. What is involved in doing ethnography?
3. What are appropriate ways of presenting ethnographic findings to different audiences?

In answering these questions, we will make visible the theoretical assumptions underlying the approach, the tenets of the community of scholars engaging in this type of research, and the types of questions that can be addressed. Throughout the discussion, we will highlight how this approach can be used by those concerned with research on English language arts.

DEFINING ETHNOGRAPHY

Ethnography is more than a set of field methods, data collection techniques (tools), analysis procedures, or narrative description. It is a theoretically driven, systematic approach to the study of everyday life of a social group which includes a planning phase, discovery phase, and a presentation of findings phase (e.g., Agar, 1980; 1986; Goetz & LeCompte, 1984; Hammersley & Atkinson, 1983; Heath, 1982a; Hymes, 1982; Spradley, 1979; 1980).

Underlying ethnography is a series of orienting principles: ethnography is a culturally driven approach; ethnography involves a comparative perspective; ethnographic fieldwork involves an interactive-reactive approach; and ethnography is the basis for ethnology. These principles distinguish ethnography from other forms of inquiry in the social and behavioral sciences. While each of these principles is presented as a discrete element of a larger process in the sections that follow, they are interrelated.

The brief definition of ethnography provided above provides a starting point for the discussion that follows. A more comprehensive definition of ethnography will be developed as the chapter unfolds and various aspects of the process of "doing" ethnography (the process) and "writing" an ethnography (the product) are considered.

Ethnography Is a Culturally Driven Approach

Ethnography is guided by a concern for exploring the human condition to illuminate the nature of "social being." The goal of the ethnographer is to explore, describe, and compare the cultures of different groups in order to obtain a general understanding of similarities and differences among peoples and cultural processes (e.g., literacy, communication, socialization, educating children). Thus, ethnographers identify and explore the cultural patterns of everyday life and the consequences for participants of being members of particular cultural groups (e.g., religious, social, ethnic, educational, and/or bluebirds reading group). Ethnography, therefore, is a deliberate inquiry process guided by a particular point of view (i.e., cultural theory).

Cultural Theories: Orienting Perspectives

To illustrate how cultural theory orients an ethnographer in the study of a social group, we will explore the ways in which a theory influences how the ethnography will be undertaken (e.g., the data collected, the types of tools used, the questions explored, and the types of findings possible). The purpose of this discussion is to demonstrate how the theory selected by the ethnographer influences what is learned about a particular culture or social group. In a later section of this paper, we discuss in greater depth how two particular theoretical perspectives (i.e., cognitive anthropology and ethnography of communication) have been used productively to explore language and literacy processes in everyday educational settings.

As will become evident, each theoretical perspective serves to orient the researcher to certain aspects of life and to neglect others. That is, the theory of culture serves to frame a general attitude about how the cultural phenomena or cultural group are to be studied and explained.

Just as a photographer must aim and focus a camera in order to capture a scene, so too must an ethnographer focus on what the theory suggests is important in order to describe, and possibly explain, some particular aspects of culture or even define what constitutes a holistic description of the culture. Thus, a theory can be thought of as a lens through which the ethnographer views the everyday life of participants in a social group and the occurrence and interpretation of social events. The value of the lens is the degree to which it permits the ethnographer to see and record the particular aspects of interest.

Two examples of how different theoretical perspectives can be used to study literacy in a social group will be presented to illustrate the influence of theory on the "doing" of ethnography:

cultural ecology and ethnography of communication. For the purpose of this discussion, single theories have been selected. In actual studies, ethnographers may use complementary theories to explore the complexity of everyday life.

A Cultural Ecological Perspective. An ethnographer who is concerned with the literacy resources of a particular group of people (e.g., American Indians; Blacks in Stockton, California; Hispanics in New Mexico) would need to select a cultural theory that supports an exploration of literate behavior, actions, or resources in the community or group at large. One possible theory that could be used is *cultural ecology.* This theory would lead the ethnographer to ask questions about: who is or is not literate within a community or social group; how literacy resources are distributed within the community; who has access to such resources; how resources are associated with power; how literacy resources function to reproduce the social order (e.g., workers vs. elites); and how the beliefs and values (the ideology) of a group support a particular type of social order.

The ethnographer who seeks to understand literacy from this perspective will describe the allocation of resources (e.g., budgets, uses of funds, distribution patterns of books in schools) and will explore the relationship of such resources to social categories (e.g., ethnicity, class, gender). The categories to be explored are researcher defined categories (etic categories) derived from the theory or past research and are not categories that reflect the meanings of those involved in the culture (emic categories).

The ethnographer who adopts this theoretical orientation would use interviews, participant observations, document analysis, and historical analysis. The interviews would focus on politicians, bureaucrats, leaders, literacy program directors and personnel, and producers of materials. Participant observation would focus on decision making and distribution within an organization, government funding programs, school system resource distribution, newspaper subscriptions by subgroup within the culture, and policies of textbook companies and adoption committees. The ethnographer would also examine policy documents and the history of material resource distribution within the culture.

Another way to think about this approach is that the ethnographer asks who makes the decisions about literacy, with what outcomes, with what ensuing rights and responsibilities, under what conditions, for what purpose, when and where. These questions permit the ethnographer to explore the political climate and structure of a social group in order to understand why some members of the group have access to certain types of literacy and others do not (see Ogbu, 1974; 1978; 1982 for an example of this perspective).

Ethnography of Communication. Cultural ecology can be contrasted with an ethnography of communication perspective. Those seeking to understand literacy from this perspective might also focus on a particular social group (e.g., black students in schools, American Indians, Southeast Asian refugees, or Hispanics). The ethnographer of communication would focus on the actions and interactions of members of the social group both within group and in cross-cultural situations to determine how literacy functions for members of the social group. However, the ethnographer would be concerned with how participants become members of a social group, what the rights and obligations of membership are, how the interactions between and among members of the social group influence what counts as literacy, how literacy functions to support and/or constrain participation in the culture, and ultimately, how literacy influences everyday interactions in the social world (e.g., Cook-Gumperz, 1986; Gumperz, 1986; Gumperz & Hymes, 1972; Hymes, 1982; Saville-Troike, 1982). While resources would be of interest, the focus would be on the use of literacy and the knowledge members of the social group need to acquire to participate in all types of literacy events and to engage in literate behavior (both oral and written) (Heath, 1982b; 1983).

The ethnographer of communication does not begin with a predefined view of literacy but identifies what counts as literacy to members of the social group. This definition is obtained by exploring the meanings members have for different literacy events and behaviors, the norms and expectations for literate behavior, and the ways literacy functions in daily life (Bloome, 1981; 1987; Bloome & Green, 1982; Cochran-Smith, 1984; Fishman, 1988; Taylor, 1983; Taylor & Dorsey-Gaines, 1988). Thus, the ethnographer of communication focuses on locating literacy from participants' views.

This theoretical perspective would guide the ethnographer to explore who does what in relation to literacy with whom, under what conditions, for what purpose, with what outcomes, when and where. While these are similar questions to those posed for the cultural ecological theory, they differ in focus. Ethnographers of communication focus on detailed analysis of the talk and actions between and among individuals in particular social contexts. They depend heavily on participant observation and the use of videotapes and/or audiotapes to record the everyday interactions and action of participants in the everyday events of social life.

In addition to taped recordings, ethnographers of communication would record the unfolding events in fieldnotes and would note when, where, and with whom a literacy event took place. They would be concerned with identifying the conventions that support and/or constrain participation in literacy events in order to understand how the discourse patterns of the members influence access within the culture and across cultural contexts (e.g., in crosscultural settings such as schools, doctors' offices, counsellors offices, job interviews, and mother-child events).

Ethnographers of communication would also use photographs and documents. However, they would explore the documents to identify the literacy demands required of participants to produce and use such documents. While these ethnographers, like the cultural ecologist, might be concerned with access to literacy, their focus would be different as would the general approach to the study of literacy in community and the tools they would use.

As illustrated above, the goals of the ethnographer influence the theory selected and nature of the research process. The ethnographer uses culture as the orienting concept and its theoretical underpinnings to approach the study of the everyday life of a social group. In this way, the ethnographer establishes a "boundary" for the research that frames question formulation, research design, methods and techniques used to collect and analyze data, and the presentation of the findings.

Ethnography Involves a Comparative Perspective

The influence of a cultural perspective can be seen in the comparative nature of this approach. Ethnographers are constantly comparing what they are observing and identifying in one situation with other similar situations within and across groups in order to identify and explain the cultural beliefs and practices of the group under study. Ethnography, therefore, is concerned with the descriptive study of a group's customary ways of life. These include ways of:

- accomplishing the everyday events of daily life;
- interpreting actions and interactions;
- establishing, checking, interpreting, modifying, suspending, and reestablishing the norms and expectations for daily life adhered to by members of the group;
- the nature, range and role of artifacts (i.e., materials, items of culture such as books, written materials, visual documents, buildings);
- establishing and limiting the range of possible action;
- constructing the roles and relationships that exist within the group;
- defining the rights and obligations that membership in the group places on members;
- developing the cultural knowledge required for appropriate participation;
- and exploring how particular cultural practices function within the social group (e.g., literacy, formal schooling, child care, ability grouping).

In other words, ethnographers seek understandings of the customary actions, beliefs, knowledge, and attitudes of a social group as reflected in the ways of engaging in everyday life. In this way, ethnography is an approach that takes a holistic and comparative perspective to understanding the human condition within the group being studied and then to compare this group with other groups.

Ethnography Involves a Holistic Perspective

In an ethnographic study, an ethnographer will use a holistic perspective to describe the broad context and patterns of life to understand how the parts (pieces of culture) relate to the "whole" culture. However, while ethnographers are concerned with the "whole," they may elect to take a more "focused" look at particular aspects or elements of everyday life either within a more comprehensive ethnography or as a topic-oriented approach to ethnography (Hymes, 1982)—e.g., the ways in which contacts among members are initiated; the range of literacy options available; the ways in which literacy is used to define group membership; the ways in which younger members of the culture acquire knowledge of the cultural patterns and expectations of daily life; the types and functions of speech events, and so forth. (See Green, 1983, for a description of topic-oriented studies of teaching-learning as linguistic processes.) The difference between a topic-oriented and a comprehensive ethnography is in the scope of the studies and the types of questions being examined. The comprehensive level permits broad-level explorations of cultural patterns while the topic-oriented permits a close examination of particular aspects of culture.

The problem for those seeking to understand the nature of the part-whole relationship is one of understanding what is meant by the term "whole." Some ethnographers argue that "whole" refers to the community level (e.g., Lutz, 1981; Ogbu, 1974), while others argue that "whole" does not equate with size but with the identification of a "bounded" social unit. Erickson (1977), for example, argues that ethnographic work is "holistic,"

not because of the size of the social unit, but because the units of analysis are considered analytically as wholes, whether that whole be a community, a school system . . . or the beginning of one lesson in a single classroom (p. 59).

Holistic, in this instance, does not mean that a single event can be analyzed and then reported as an ethnography but rather that the analysis must consider how the individual parts relate to the broader whole (e.g., beginnings of other lessons, other aspects of lessons, other aspects of classroom life, beginnings of other types of speech events outside of the classroom). Thus, an individual event may be analyzed in depth to explore and identify the cultural demands or elements of the event (e.g., the ways in which it is accomplished, the social and academic demands for participation, the roles and relationships among members, and the communicative requirements for participation). However, the exploration will not stop with the analysis of the individual event. Rather, the information obtained from this analysis will be used as the basis for the exploration of other aspects of the culture or phenomenon. In this way, a "piece of culture" can be examined indepth to identify larger cultural issues and elements.

The notion of holistic has methodological implications for the study of everyday life in cultural contexts (e.g., school, home, church, playground). Observations made of individual "wholes" are compared to other similar wholes and to larger wholes within the group under study. For example, an ethnographer might elect to study reading within the social unit called classroom. Once this decision has been made, the ethnographer would then need to observe the period of classroom life called "reading" by the participants.

To explore the nature of "reading" in the everyday lifeworld, or culture, of the classroom, the ethnographer would need to examine the beginning and ending boundaries of this event as defined by the actions of the participants in the local setting. Once the boundaries of the event are established, the ethnographer would then explore what occurs within the events of reading through a complete cycle of occurrence. A cycle of reading in a classroom could be a series of completed lessons, a unit of instruction, a week, or a grading period. The length or boundaries of a cycle depend on how this aspect of culture is defined by the participants and not on predetermined criteria set by the ethnographer. Thus, while reading as an activity in the daily life of the classroom might occur throughout the year, it is also composed of cycles of instruction or occurrence within the larger whole. These cycles can be explored in their own right and then the findings compared across instances of occurrence to obtain a more "comprehensive" understanding of "what counts as reading" in the local context for the local participants.

In addition, once a unit of observation is determined *within* the local setting, the ethnographer might wish to take a more focused look at how the local event(s) are accomplished within "reading" in the classroom (e.g., compare high group with low group). The focus will depend on the question being explored. The ethnographer might then select a "representative" lesson (one for high group and one for low group) and analyze the social and academic demands and structure of the lesson. Another course of action that the ethnographer might take would be to explore when and how other instances of reading that occur outside of the "official" reading event are defined and accomplished.

This approach to the study of reading from a cultural perspective differs from those of other perspectives in which the definition of reading is assumed prior to entry into the context of the study or is assumed to be stable across all instances of occurrence. While the ethnographer may elect to focus on reading and may derive information from the literature about the nature of reading in classroom contexts, the ethnographer will not begin with a preset definition of "reading." Rather, the ethnographer will examine whether the participants in the social group have an event called "reading," and will explore how it is accomplished, what counts as reading, when and where it occurs, who can participate, what functions and purposes it serves, and what the outcomes are of participating in the event called reading and engaging in the processes of reading. In instances where the cultural group does not have a "formal" event called reading, the ethnographer will make principled decisions about how to locate instances of reading in the group under study (c.f., Anderson, Teale, & Estrada, 1980; Heath, 1983). (For examples of ethnographic studies of reading in classroom contexts see Anderson, Teale, & Estrada, 1980; Bloome, 1981; 1983; 1987; Cochran-Smith, 1984; Collins, 1983; 1986; Cook-Gumperz; 1986; Griffin, 1977; Heap, 1980; 1988; Heath, 1982b; McDermott, 1976; Moll, 1986; Moll & Diaz, 1985; Taylor, 1983; Taylor & Dorsey-Gaines, 1988.)

In these cases, the ethnographer would move between a more comprehensive look at the culture (classroom) and a focused look at individual elements of the culture, or from a more focused look to a more comprehensive examination of a cultural phenomenon (reading). In this way the ethnographer can explore how information obtained from "focused" explorations of specific aspects of culture reflect larger aspects of the culture (e.g., the values, attitudes, knowledge, beliefs, ways of evaluating, expectations for participation, types of cultural knowledge) (e.g., Geertz, 1973; Goodenough, 1981; Gumperz, 1986; Spradley, 1980). Thus, ethnography is concerned with the relationship of the parts to the whole. (For examples of such comparisons see Bloome, 1981; 1987; Bloome & Green, 1982; Cazden, John & Hymes, 1972; Collins, 1983; Cook-Gumperz, 1986; Cook-

Gumperz, Gumperz, & Simons, 1981; Erickson & Mohatt, 1982; Fishman, 1988; Florio & Shultz, 1979; Gilmore & Glatthorn, 1982; Green & Wallat, 1981; Gumperz, 1982; 1986; Heath, 1983; Hymes, 1981; Lemke, 1990; Michaels, 1986; Moll & Diaz, 1985; Philips, 1972; 1983; Reder & Green, 1983; Scollon & Scollon, 1981; 1984; Scribner & Cole, 1981; Shuman, 1986; Spindler, 1982; Taylor, 1983; Taylor & Dorsey-Gaines, 1988; Wolcott, 1967.)

Ethnographic Fieldwork Involves an Interactive-Reactive Approach

While ethnography involves three phases—prefieldwork or planning, fieldwork or discovery, and presentation of findings—these phases are not discrete; rather, they often co-occur and continue throughout a study. That is, ethnography is not the linear process that is generally associated with most forms of educational research in which all decisions about a study are made prior to beginning data collection and all analyses are undertaken once all of the data are collected. Rather, ethnography is a dynamic, interactive-reactive approach to research.

The interactive-reactive nature of ethnography stems, in part, from the comparative nature of the research process and the need to explore the part-whole relationship. In addition, an ethnographer will also bring differing views, methods, theories, and data together to obtain an understanding of the meanings held by participants as reflected in their actions and perceptions. By bringing these views together, that is, by triangulating perspectives, the ethnographer is able to explore and refine the questions that were of interest at the onset of the study and generate questions that could not be anticipated before entry into the "field." Thus, ethnographers must continually adapt their questions and plans to the local conditions of the setting as their studies progress (e.g., Denzin, 1978; Spradley, 1980).

Another way to view the ethnographic research design and process is to view it as responsive not simply reactive. That is, while the ethnographer enters with a plan for study, local conditions and interpretations influence what can and will be seen, the ways in which the initial question is refined and new questions identified, and how the information can and will be obtained (e.g., Goetz & LeCompte, 1984; Hammersley & Atkinson, 1983; Spindler, 1982). Each modification in design is a response to local conditions, to factors previously not known, or to new understandings. Decisions to modify the design are deliberate decisions guided by a variety of factors including the need for new data, the emergence of key issues not previously considered; the identification of directions or issues not appropriate to the group or topic under study; comparisons of data, perspectives, and theories (triangulation); and problems of gaining access to the needed information, persons, or events (e.g., Hammersley & Atkinson, 1983; Heath, 1982; Spradley, 1980).

Ethnography Is the Basis for Ethnology

The comparative nature of this approach suggests still another way in which ethnography differs from other forms of educational and social science research. The concern for under-

standing the human condition does not end with a concern for the individual group being studied. Rather, ethnographers are concerned with understanding commonalities and variability in the human condition both within and across groups. Therefore, the interrelationship between ethnography (the descriptive study of the everyday life of a social group) and ethnology must be understood. Ethnology is the comparative science concerned with how and why cultures differ and are similar. By comparing human behavior and cultural phenomena under various conditions, in all places throughout time, the ethnographer develops the understanding necessary to explain the situated nature of human behavior and cultural phenomena.

Ethnologists seek to understand how and why people today and in other times are similar and different in their customary ways of thinking and acting. Ethnology, then, is concerned with the different dimensions (domains) of culture (e.g., communication, educational systems, folk art, music, religion, literacy, politics, economics, marriage customs, kinship) and with the ways in which cultural patterns within these domains vary across groups and across time. Ethnologists are also concerned with the dynamics of culture—that is, how various cultures develop and change as well as with the relationship of beliefs and practices within a cultural group.

Thus, ethnography and ethnology are intimately connected. In fact, an ethnographer is best thought of as one type of ethnologist. The ethnographer collects and analyzes data from particular social groups (cultures), or on a particular phenomenon to provide a graphic description of those groups and phenomena that will serve as a basis for doing ethnology or cross-cultural/group comparisons. The ethnologist, or cross-cultural researcher, is interested in discovering why certain cultural characteristics or patterns can be found in some social groups but not in others. Why, for example, do some groups have a belief in a high god or supreme being, a written language system, particular types of materials (e.g., books, films, games), particular ways of using language, or particular ways of schooling or educating their children.

The bases for exploring and testing possible answers to these questions are the ethnographic data from many cultures and/or social groups. The ethnologist uses these data to try to arrive at general explanations of cultural/group variation; that is, to identify what is generic across cultures/groups; and what is situation specific. Even in the case of generic elements of culture, the ethnologist seeks to understand how the generic occurs within a specific social group (Hammersley & Atkinson, 1983). Thus, ethnography and ethnology presume one another and together they contribute spirally to building knowledge.

The Comparative Perspective: An Application to English Language Arts

To understand how ethnology and ethnography are related to educational issues, especially those concerned with the English language arts, we must return to our discussion of what is meant by culture and how the comparative perspective provides a basis for theory development. As discussed previously, there are different theories of culture; however, on a general level, ethnographers would agree that culture is what is learned and held in common by members of a group. Culture, therefore, is not "out there" to be found and is not simply transmitted from one person to the next. It is not an object. One is neither "cultured" nor "not cultured." All members of a social group are cultural beings in that they share and have learned the customary patterns for engaging in everyday life.

To illustrate how a cultural orientation to the study of English language arts in everyday school settings (e.g., classrooms) might be developed, we will draw on work in cognitive anthropology and ethnography of communication. The general definition of culture that will guide this discussion and the selection of the illustration is based on the work of cognitive anthropologists Goodenough (1981) and Spradley (1979; 1980). Culture, according to these theorists, can be defined as the standards for the patterned ways of perceiving, believing, acting, and evaluating (c.f., Goodenough 1981). Culture also involves "local" meanings and knowledge (c.f., Geertz, 1983).

This way of defining culture focuses on the meanings that members of social groups have for their customary actions, objects, places, interactions, events, institutions, processes, and so forth. (For other definitions of culture, see Kroeber & Kluckhohn, 1963, and for contributions of a cultural perspective to English language arts see Bloome, this volume.) This view of culture also permits discussion of culture on a local level as well as a societal level or cross-national level. Groups of people who engage in interaction with each other over time develop a set of norms and expectations, have rights and obligations placed on them for participating in the group, and develop roles and relationships among members of the group. In other words, a group develops patterned ways of engaging in life together, of seeing and interpreting the patterned ways of life, of holding members accountable to the norms and expectations of such life, and of making sense out of the world around them.

This view of culture permits us to speak of the culture of a reading group, a classroom, a school, a Camp Fire group, an ethnic group, a church, a community, or a nation. It also assumes that a person belongs to different cultural groups at the same time. For example, a student is simultaneously part of the "peer culture" (Bloome & Theodorou, 1988; Kantor, 1988), the culture of the fourth grade class, the bluebirds reading group, and other groups beyond the classroom walls (e.g., home, community, ethnic group, religious group). The ethnographer, therefore, must consider both the observed patterns of culture of the specific group under study (e.g., classroom, reading group within the classroom) and the patterns of norms and expectations for engaging in daily life individuals bring to the local situation.

For example, Gumperz and Cook-Gumperz and their colleagues (Collins, 1983; Collins & Michaels, 1986; Cook-Gumperz, 1979; 1986; Cook-Gumperz, Gumperz, & Simons, 1981; Michaels, 1981; 1984; 1986; Michaels & Cazden, 1986; Michaels & Collins, 1984; Michaels & Cook-Gumperz, 1979) found that specific ways of participating and demonstrating socially and academically appropriate knowledge were associated with particular speech events (e.g., reading group, circle time). Michaels (1981) found that in the "circle time event" in kindergarten and first grade there were expected ways of "telling a story." Stu-

dents were to stand up, share one event, and then sit down. The narrative form they were to use had a beginning, a middle, and an end.

Some students in the classrooms studied did not tell stories in this way but used another form that Michaels called "topic associating." The narrative form of these stories was more like chains of loosely related actions or events with the topic left on the tacit level. This way of telling stories was related to the patterned ways of telling stories in the students' home community (See Au, 1980; Boggs, 1972; Scollon & Scollon, 1984, for discussion of narrative styles among those of Hawaiian and Athabaskan ancestry respectively; and Door-Bremme, 1982; Florio & Shultz, 1979; Shultz, Florio, & Erickson, 1982; Kantor, Elgas, & Fernie, 1989; Green, Kantor & Rogers, in press; and Wallat & Green, 1979; 1982, for other examples of patterns of circle time.)

Thus, some of the students' stories did not match the expected norms of the circle time group, or rather, the norms of the teacher who held an asymmetrical role within the group. However, the students' actions were consistent with storytelling in the students' home and ethnic group. A problem arose for these students when the teacher did not accept the ways in which they told their stories. In one instance, the teacher told a student that she had already shared one thing part way through her story. The student sat down. When interviewed later by the ethnographer, the student commented that she was always being interrupted by the teacher and did not get a chance to finish sharing.

This example demonstrates the complexity of group membership and the crosscultural nature of this everyday activity for students. The conflict in cultural patterns and ways of interpreting events can be seen in the following:

1. The teacher had developed a set of norms for participating in circle time;
2. She assumed that all of the students shared or had learned these norms;
3. The actions of one subgroup of students indicated that they did not share the norms or had not learned how to participate in the group in the way the teacher expected;
4. The teacher's actions did not help the students learn how to "do" group in circle time; rather, her actions set up a tacit problem for the subgroup of students; and
5. These students knew something was wrong but did not understand the nature of the problem and, therefore, did not participate in the expected way.

This conflict or clash in cultural patterns became problematic in that the teacher based her assessment of students' abilities on student performance in circle time.

The work by Michaels (1986) and Collins and Michaels (1986) indicates that the teacher may have underestimated student narrative ability. This work suggests that performance in classroom settings is often due to students' perceptions of the task and to prior experiences, not to actual ability. (See Green, Kantor, & Rogers, in press; and Moll, 1986; Moll and Diaz 1985; for an elaboration of this argument. See Rogers, 1987, 1988 for a discussion of student perceptions of classroom requirements for task performance vs. personal interpretations of texts.)

Without knowledge of cultural patterns of the various social groups in which the students participated, the ethnographer (Michaels) would not have known how to interpret the actions of the students. Because Michaels was able to explore both the home and school actions of the students and because she had knowledge of how storytelling occurred in other cultures, she was able to ask the students and teacher questions that led to her interpretation. In addition, members of the research team were able to plan a series of tasks that provided a basis for additional data on narrative ability (Collins & Michaels, 1986; Cook-Gumperz, Gumperz, & Simons, 1981; Michaels, 1986). These tasks including collecting narratives between parents and students in the home, planning sessions in a science lab for communication between students, showing a film to elicit storytelling, and having students sequence story cards and tell the story indicated on the cards (Cook-Gumperz, Gumperz, & Simons, 1981; Green, 1983). The narratives produced in these differing situations provided information that was then compared with actual classroom performance to determine factors that led to the interpretation of cross-cultural communication problems.

The storytelling example above shows the relationship between the ethnography of life in the classroom and the comparative study both within the research project and across contexts. The ethnogrpahy provided a description of what was ordinary in the social context of the circle time event in the classroom, about the teacher's expectations for appropriate performance, and about individuals' failure to perform in expected ways. The comparative aspects of the study, the other tasks and the review of previous literature, led to the development of a hypothesis about factors that support and constrain the students' performances.

In a later study, Michaels (1984) gave student narratives from her ethnographic study to adults representing two different ethnic groups; one set of adults matched the students' background and the other matched the teacher's. Those adults who matched the teacher's background did not rate the students' narratives as "well-formed" stories. Many of those whose background were more like the students' indicated that the stories were well-formed and were similar to "down home" stories; that is, stories that matched their sense of storytelling in community but not at school.

Thus, by engaging in systematic description within a particular geographic unit (a classroom), by focusing on a recurrent event within this unit (circle time), by considering what was ordinary and predictable and what was unpredictable or problematic (narrative performance), and by comparing narrative performance across events and settings, the ethnographic research team (Cook-Gumperz, Gumperz, Michaels & Collins) was able to identify factors that influenced or contributed to student performance. What this example highlights, then, is that ethnography is always comparative, that to understand what one sees in one event may often require knowledge of performance in other events, that events and people within them have a history that is visible in the face-to-face actions of the event if one knows how to *see* and what questions to ask, and that a cultural perspective provides a conceptual basis for understanding what is occurring and what might be explored. In addition, this example illustrates how an ethnographic study can be used as a basis for further exploration within a cultural perspective; that is, this example demonstrates ways in which hypothesis generation and testing can occur within and across studies.

DOING ETHNOGRAPHY

In the first half of this chapter, ethnography was defined as an interactive-reactive, context responsive approach to the study of everyday life of a social group driven by cultural theory. In this section, we will discuss how the concepts and issues raised in the first section influence the design, implementation, analysis, and presentation of ethnographic findings. The discussion will be presented in three parts. The first part focuses on what is involved in planning and initiating an ethnographic study: the prefieldwork phase. The second part focuses on what is involved in the fieldwork phase of the ethnographic process. The third part focuses on the presentation of ethnographically derived information and findings.

The first two phases reflect the "context of discovery;" that is, the context in which ethnographic data are identified, collected, and interpreted/analyzed. The latter phase reflects the "context of presentation"; that is, the decisions about audience, ways of writing an ethnography, and ways of linking or comparing the study with other related research. This way of presenting the discussion reflects the dual nature of the term ethnography, as a process and as a product; that is, ethnographers talk about "doing ethnography" and about "writing an ethnography" (Agar, 1980; Berreman, 1968).

The distinction between the context of discovery and the context of presentation (Heap, 1989) is needed since this way of formulating the research process further distinguishes ethnographic research from empirical research in which the context of discovery is followed by the context of justification. (For a discussion of the context of discovery-justification relationship see Kaplan, 1964). While these phases and contexts will be treated as discrete in the discussion, in actuality they are interrelated and overlapping. Thus, like the study of culture, the research process involves consideration of the part-whole relationship.

Given the question-driven nature and cultural orientation of ethnographic research, we have elected to ground the discussion of design and methodology in a specific topic for study: What is the nature of English language arts? Our goal is to highlight the decisions that need to be made in order to design, implement, and report an adequate ethnographic study. It is not our intention to describe an actual study. The issues raised will be used to identify the general categories within which decisions must be made. These categories form a general decision-making framework that can be used to highlight decisions that need to be considered in future studies. The problem facing persons using these categories, however, is one of deciding which are appropriate for their studies, since the design of ethnographic research must be "fine-tuned" to the questions, group, topic and issues under study. Therefore, the framework is illustrative not definitive, and descriptive not prescriptive. It is a point of departure, not a "recipe" for research. Thus, the overall purpose of this section is to highlight the logic of design, implementation, and presentation associated with ethnographic research.

Although we will explore all three of the phases of ethnographic research (prefieldwork, fieldwork, and presentation of findings), we will focus on the decisions involved in the prefieldwork phase since this phase influences the design and contour of the ethnographic study. As will be demonstrated below, the decisions on ethnographer makes before entering the field establishes boundaries for the study and influences the types of information that can and will be obtained from the study. Books on ethnographic methods and techniques for the fieldwork portion of a study abound, yet information about the prefieldwork phase and its relationship to the other phases is limited. Thus, rather than simply restating what has been written about extensively elsewhere, we have elected to focus on issues of theory-method relationship and issues of design. Throughout the discussion, however, we will provide references to work about "doing" ethnography in the field. Finally, we will describe the directions being developed for presentation of ethnographic findings. As will become evident, this phase of the ethnographic process is undergoing reexamination, and new directions are being developed.

The Context of Discovery: Prefieldwork

The prefieldwork phase of any ethnographic study begins with an initial question that can be answered about the culture under study. The question, however, is not a decontextualized question, but rather, stems from the goals of the researcher. For example, the question of what is English language arts may appear specific on the surface. However, unless we know why the question is asked, we do not know the purpose of the study: Is the researcher concerned with how English language arts is defined and enacted in a foreign country? In the United States? Or in a bilingual education setting? Thus, the question of what is English language arts must be placed in the research context. No ethnographic question can be context independent.

The Research Context. The question of what is English language arts is being posed in this instance to provide basic information about what students in the K–12 school sector have an opportunity to learn as a result of formal schooling in the United States. By embedding the question in the statement of the problem, we have begun to delimit the boundaries of the ethnography. The selection of this more focused question, then, locates the study in a particular PLACE (formal school settings in the United States), establishes a TIME frame (the current situation for English education), and identifies a particular GROUP (students in K–12). In addition, the selection of English language arts establishes this study as a TOPIC-ORIENTED as opposed to a comprehensive or community-oriented ethnography. That is, the focus of the study is on a particular aspect of the culture of schooling, English language arts, and not on the totality of schooling or community life.

Although certain boundaries have been established for the question, these boundaries are still too general for an ethnographic study. Topic-oriented ethnography requires observation of the "piece of culture" of a social group through a complete cycle of occurrence. The first problem facing us is one of defining the social group.

While we can talk about the nation as the most macrolevel group to which all people in the United States belong, this level of group membership is not productive for this study nor feasible since the nation has no national curriculum in English language arts. Rather, we know that states are the official macrolevel units for curriculum oversight. However, in most states, the state sets general content area guidelines for districts: it is at the district level, therefore, that most decisions about content, specific knowledge, and materials are decided. Thus, the most appropriate level at which to begin delimiting this study appears to be the district level. Hence, our study could begin with systematic observation of what "counts" as English language arts at the district level and explore how this phenomenon is reflected in the daily actions, interactions, and products (e.g., materials, memos, guides, policies, programs, professional development activities) of the personnel at the various levels of the district (e.g., school board, superintendent's staff, curriculum supervisors, inservice leaders, building administrators, classroom teachers). (See Barr & Dreeben, 1983 for an example of how information can be traced across levels of the school district to the classroom level.)

However, arguments have been made in the curriculum field that documents such as a course of study are not the curriculum (e.g., McCutcheon, 1982; Weade, 1987). Rather, the curriculum is what students have an opportunity to learn in the ordinary events of life in classrooms (Berman, 1986; Chandler & Green, 1988; King, 1986; Tanner & Tanner, 1990; Weade, 1987; Weade & Evertson, 1988). Thus, the way in which the issue of curriculum as well as other aspects of schooling are conceptualized and the theoretical orientations used in the conceptualization further influence the way in which the study will be designed and where and how it will be implemented. For our study, we view the classroom as the appropriate level to begin the exploration of the English language arts, since we agree with the argument that it is at this level that the curriculum is constructed and reconstructed in the daily interactions among teacher, students, and material resources (Chandler & Green, 1988; Weade, 1987).

Although some may argue that classroom-level studies cannot provide an understanding of English language arts at a national level, we argue that we must first understand how it is constructed across individual classrooms. Studies of individual classrooms can then be compared in an ethnological study and a more general picture of English language arts can be developed. In addition, analysis of individual classrooms highlights elements that need to be examined and can provide the data for the development of a survey instrument that will provide national-level data. However, the response to the question as we have posed it and conceptualized the phenomenon must begin with an understanding of particular classrooms in particular school districts.

In addition, the selection of the classroom level as a place to begin does not mean that we will ignore the other levels of interaction with the English language arts in which the classroom is embedded (e.g., the school, district, state). Rather, it means that we will begin by exploring indepth what occurs in particular classrooms and then explore the relationship of other levels of context as indicated in the analysis of face-to-face interactions (e.g., text selection decisions, material provisions, grouping policies, content decision procedures, documents provided to the teacher). In this way we will explore English language arts from a situated perspective and then move to a comparison across situations (e.g., classrooms) as well as to an exploration of the local situation (the classroom) in the larger community contexts.

Developing Conceptual Frameworks for an Ethnographic Study. Another way to view the example just presented is to see it as showing how initial decisions involved in the design of ethnography are influenced by the conceptual framework (mental grid) being used for the study. Such frameworks are needed since ethnographers do not enter the field as "blank slates." Rather, ethnographers need to learn as much as possible about the cultural group or phenomenon to be studied. This knowledge forms a mental grid for the study. For example, in the study by Gumperz and Cook-Gumperz and their colleagues described previously (Cook-Gumperz, Gumperz, & Simons described in Evertson & Green, 1986 and Green, 1983), the mental grid included knowledge and assumptions about cultural behavior and phenomena derived from previous research on discourse processes, conversational analysis, ethnography of communication, classroom organization, teaching-learning processes, adult-child interactions, child language, cross-cultural communication, evaluation of performance, socialization, reading acquisition and development, metalinguistic awareness, sociolinguistics, and cognitive development. In other words, the conceptual framework is based on a review of relevant literature in which information about the setting, group, and processes are identified prior to entry into the field.

The mental grid or framework suggests ways of conceptualizing the phenomena of interest as well as factors that the researchers may need to consider for the specific group under study. The framework provides a place to begin the design of the research. What distinguishes ethnographic research (and some other forms of qualitative research) from other types of educational and social science research is the way in which the mental grid or conceptual framework is used. This framework is not used rigidly or to limit what is to be observed or to be explored; rather, the framework forms a basis for making initial decisions about the question to be asked, the group to be studied, the types of information that are potentially available, the types of data that may be collected, and the approaches to analysis of the data that are appropriate.

Once the researcher enters the field, this information "goes on hold"; that is, the ethnographer enters the field knowledgeable yet open-minded. The ethnographer does not use the predetermined descriptions or theories to control and delimit the study. Instead, these theories are used to help identify the initial types of data to be collected. During the study, often the researcher will have to "rework" the descriptions of phenomena or the information obtained from previous work. Given the goal of understanding the cultural knowledge and ways of life of a social group, such revisions of previously identified information are logical and necessary. These revisions or reworkings of concepts, phenomena, and processes enable us to develop new understandings about the situated nature of phenomena of daily life within and across social groups. These new understandings help to refine, extend, and modify theory and provide the basis for comparative research across groups (i.e., ethnology).

As suggested above, the research context includes the purpose or goal of the research and a conceptual framework (mental grid) that is based on a review of the literature. This context influences question formulation and research design including: the selection of the site, the group being studied, the time frame for the study, and the initial focus. Thus, while cultural theory guides the overall research, other conceptual and theoretical work is also included in the perspective and the knowledge of culture the researcher takes into the field (Birdwhistell, 1977).

To explore the question of what is English Language Arts, then, requires more than a set of techniques. It requires information about the ways in which the English language arts have been examined and conceptualized in the past. In addition, English language arts is not the sole focus of schools or English educators. Therefore, knowledge is needed about how schools work, how curriculum is defined, how language functions, the nature of life in classrooms, how language is learned in classroom contexts, how language influences learning in other content areas, how language at home and community influence student performance and perceptions within classroom events, among other topics.

The discussion above identifies the first category of questions that must be considered: THE RESEARCH CONTEXT. Table 13–1 provides representative questions to be addressed.

Each of these questions in the Research Context category has consequences for the design of the study, but they do not complete the prefieldwork or design phase of the study. Rather, they may be viewed as a general framework within which to design the overall study. In the remainder of this section, we will identify the additional issues and questions that must be considered in the prefieldwork phase. To facilitate the discussion we will identify additional categories and related questions and issues that need to be included in a formal research proposal.

The Research Proposal. Once the research context and the conceptual framework have been established, the formal proposal for research can be developed. This proposal includes statements about what will be studied and why (e.g., literacy, community life, religious rituals, socialization to schooling), who will be studied, where the study will take place, what the design will be, what methods (techniques/tools) will be used, what analysis procedures are proposed, and how the findings will be reported. Also included will be a statement of the significance of the study and how it will contribute to knowledge and/or theory development or understandings of practice.

The categories within the proposal and representative questions associated with each are described in Table 13–2. As indi-

TABLE 13–1. The Research Context Representative
Questions

Sub-category	Questions
Question formulation	What group or topic will be studied? Why?
	What is the purpose/goal of the study?
Conceptual framework	What information or literature exists from studies in similar cultural settings?
	What information exists about the processes or phenomena that will be observed (e.g., language, discourse, literacy, language arts, classroom processes, schooling, curriculum, etc.?
	How do you conceptualize the phenomena to be examined?
	What theoretical perspective(s) will you use to guide your research?
Decision points for design	Who will you study?
	Where will you begin your study?
	What boundaries will be needed for your study (e.g., time, group, place, topic, etc.)?

cated in Table 13–2, there are six categories of information that are generally included in an ethnographic proposal: statement of the purpose and rationale; population parameters; access process; role(s) of the ethnographer; tools and techniques to be used for data collection; and data collection and analysis procedures. For each category identified, questions or topics that need to be addressed are presented. Finally, where appropriate, key sources of information are provided. These sources provide indepth discussions of the issues raised. Discussion of each of these points is not possible within the scope of this paper. The information in this table, then, can be thought of as a framework to guide development of a proposal and further exploration of the issues involved.

These components of the proposal are similar to the components of any research proposal. However, what makes these components different from those in other research proposals are the elements found in each category and the types of questions that must be considered in planning and designing a culturally sensitive and culturally driven research project.

Access. All researchers who wish to work in naturally occurring settings must gain access, but the nature and the types of access differ with the style of research. Access in ethnographic studies involves more than permission to engage in a classroom study. Here, it involves negotiated initial entry and often negotiation of access to additional persons, institutions, or settings as the study unfolds given the interactive-reactive, context-responsive nature of ethnographic research. The members of the social group (e.g., classroom) become formal and informal collaborators in the research. That is, the researcher needs the support

and cooperation of those members of the social group (the classroom) who hold "cultural knowledge" about the meaning of the events, actions, objects and behaviors the ethnographer observes as well as the beliefs, values, and attitudes of members of the group. The specific types of research-collaborator relationships will depend on the purpose of the study and the information needed to understand the roles and relationships, norms and expectations, rights and obligations, and consequences of membership in the social group.

Access, then, in an ethnographic study is never totally obtained. Rather, the ethnographer initially gains access to the setting, but must negotiate and renegotiate access to particular sub-groups (e.g., students, high group readers, teachers in the school, parents, and administrators, among others.) Each time the researcher adds a component or elects a new focus within the study, the researcher will need to gain access anew. (See Corsaro, 1985, for description of the social history of his ethnography.) This process, however, is not as formal, in most instances, as were the original access procedures. The degree of formality needed will depend on the nature of the modification to the study. For example, if the researcher needs information from the students' files but has not received permission to access them, the researcher may need to get formal permission from the parents, school district, teacher, students, and/or the human subjects review committee of the researcher's home institution.

The following example, will demonstrate the complexity of this issue and the sensitivity involved in gaining access. Chandler (1989) in a description of the entry process for a comparative study of curriculum as it is constructed by participants in three reading classrooms was faced with a series of audiences at different levels: teacher, students, building administration, district and university. Figure 13–1 provides a graphic representation of the layers of entry Chandler faced.

Chandler began with the teacher, who also wanted to engage in research in her own classroom. Chandler and the teacher decided that Chandler would undertake an ethnographic study of life in three of the teachers' reading classes (taught back-to-back,) and the teacher would use the data for her own study. Thus, these researchers would collaborate at the level of the data collection but not be coinvestigators on each other's project.

As indicated in Table 13–1, Chandler and the teacher needed to negotiate time commitment, access to documents, methods to be used, rights and obligations of researcher, and ethical issues. Each of these areas contained matters requiring further negotiation. One example will be used to illustrate the complex nature of this process. Consider the area of time commitment. The teacher and researcher had to consider when interviews would occur, how the research would be undertaken (e.g., collaborative research), and how presentations at meetings would be handled. In other words, they had to establish a social contract for their relationships within and across aspects of research from entry to presentations. Thus, time commitment involved more than simply deciding on when the researcher would visit the classroom. It involved the negotiation of complex interpersonal dimensions.

Establishing the agreement with the teacher did not end the

process of entry. Once, this agreement had been reached, the next step involved getting permission from others in the district since the classroom was part of a larger social system. At this point a problem arose in identifying who needed to provide permission. What became evident was that the teacher did not hold all of the cultural knowledge to complete this task and needed to find her own informant who knew who to contact and what was required.

The teacher learned through her explorations that she had the right to engage in research in her classrooms under a professional development provision of her contract. She identified persons at the school and district levels who were involved in the permission process. As indicated in Figure 13–1, each level had different concerns. The administration of the school was concerned with four areas: a) the time commitment, not of the individual teacher but of others in the school; b) the role of teacher and researcher in the project and in the school; c) access to documents; and d) ethics of the researcher. This latter factor involved issues of district permission, research reciprocity, and confidentiality.

Once school-level access had been obtained, the teacher and researcher needed to obtain district permission. Once again, two concerns were raised, permission and ethics. Ethics was defined at this level as confidentiality and reciprocity. At the district level this involved obtaining "fee waivers" from the university that teachers could use to take classes. Thus, the district was concerned with reciprocity for permitting the research as well as confidentiality.

The need for reciprocity required another level of access—access to the university. The university has a negotiated agreement with districts that provides "fee waivers" for each quarter of university research conducted in the district. In order to receive these fee waivers, the university had to approve the research study.

These areas of access demonstrate the complex interrelationships among levels of the social system in which the classroom was embedded. These levels of access, however, were not the only levels. Once all permissions had been obtained, the teacher and researcher still had to obtain access from the students. Once again, this involved several concerns: access to student documents and records, time commitment of students, ethics, and researcher roles. The latter involved considering what types of participant observation would be used, how and when interviews would be conducted, and what roles within the classroom context the researcher would take.

The concerns listed above suggest that access is an ongoing and complex process and that what one is accessing is a social system not a setting. As Chandler states:

... entry is not a linear process, as it is never fully gained and is a continually renegotiated process the researcher may need to revisit and then revisit again ... the complexity that comes from these multiple layers needs to be understood. By understanding this complexity and the part-whole relationships that exist in school settings, entry, as seen through the multiple layers embedded in the context of a larger whole, becomes a constructed process that is never fully gained. (p. 6)

Access, then, is more than entry into a physical setting. Access also involves issues of roles and relationships among multi-ple groups of people (teacher, administrators, students, researcher, district personnel, university personnel). Each role and relationship entails certain rights and obligations for the researcher. Each of the levels and the issues of concern of those at each level can support and/or constrain the research. Access, therefore, is a socially constructed process that must be established, monitored, maintained, and reestablished over the course of the context of discovery as well as the context of presentation. In other words, access does not end when the researcher exits the physical setting.

Role. Access is also closely related to the role(s) that the reseacher assumes during the project. The goal of the researcher using a cognitive anthropological approach to the study of everyday life in classrooms is to obtain the emic, or the insider's, perspective and beliefs about life in classrooms. Thus, the researcher may want to assume a role or engage in participant observation that involves total immersion into the setting at specific times. For example, in the Cook-Gumperz, Gumperz, & Simons (1981) study, Michaels became an "aide" to the classroom teacher. This role permitted her to ask questions about what to do in the classroom, how life in the classroom was conducted, why materials were being used in particular ways, how students were grouped, and so forth. In this way, Michaels was able to explore the theory of pedagogy in action and to ask questions on a "real need-to-know" basis.

In this study, Michaels was also able to take an etic, or outsider's, perspective and record (in fieldnotes and on videotape) the descriptions that formed the basis of explorations of discourse strategies and narrative knowledge needed to understand how student linguistic performance was related to access to learning. At still other times, Michaels was able to involve students in natural experiments to obtain further information about student linguistic and communicative competence (Michaels, 1986; Collins & Michaels, 1986).

This example demonstrates the range of roles an ethnographer may take. What is not generally discussed in descriptions of role taking in ethnographic research is the fact that the role the ethnographer assumes may influence access to some groups and certain types of knowledge. What this caution suggests is that each decision within the study influences other decisions and may influence what the ethnographer "sees" and can access.

The category of role distinguishes ethnographic research (and some forms of qualitative research) from most other types of research. Role in an ethnographic study is often dynamic and shifting, while role in more experimental or clinical studies is generally unidimensional. Thus, the ethnographer must consider what types of role are available or feasible.

Selection of Tools and Techniques. As indicated in Table 13–2, the ethnographer plans the types of data collection that will be used in the fieldwork phase. To select tools and techniques that will be used at the outset of the study, the ethnographer must consider who will be studied, under what conditions, for what purpose, in what ways, when, where, and with what expected outcomes. Thus, the ethnographer attempts to

TABLE 13–2. The Research Proposal: Categories and Questions

Category	Questions/Topics	Sources
Present Purpose and Rationale for the Study	This category reflects the information and decisions made in the research context. (See Table 1.)	
Describe Population Parameters	This category includes a description of the group to be studied and the site of the study. (See Table 1.)	
Describe Ways You Gained Access	What types of involvement and/or contact have you had with the group that will be studied?	Shaffir, Stebbins, Turowetz, 1980.
	What type of social contract have you established with the group to insure anonymity, access to needed settings and information (e.g., homes, schools, public agencies, people, special ceremonies or service groups)?	Erickson & Wilson, 1982.
	How will you address the ethical and human subjects issues (e.g., protection of participants, community)?	American Anthropological Association, 1971; Society for Applied Anthropology, 1974.
	What types of formal permissions will be needed and how will they be obtained?	
	Who will be your contact person (if appropriate)?	
	Will you have a co-investigator who is a member of the group or will you need to establish a local consultant, key informant or advisory group from the local social group?	Bloome, 1981; Taylor & Dorsey-Gaines, 1988.
Describe the role(s) you plan to assume in the ethnography.	In what ways will you participate in the settings? Which of the following roles will you assume and why? a. participant observer b. observer participant c. interviewer d. insider or member of the group (e.g., teacher, specialist)	Shaffir, Stebbins, & Turowetz, 1980.
	With which group in the setting will you be aligned or identified (e.g., students, teachers, administrators, visitors, parents or other)?	
	How will the role(s) you adopt influence access to certain groups and information?	
	How will your role change over time?	
	How will gender issues that might influence access to information and particular settings be considered?	Denzin, 1989.
Describe the tools and techniques that you plan to use to collect the data	Which of the following field methods (tools and techniques) do you plan to use in the study and how will they be used?	Bernard, 1988; Ellen, 1984; Edgerton & Langness, 1974; Hammersley & Atkinson, 1983.
	a. field notes (descriptive, personal, theoretical, methodological)	Corsaro, 1981; 1985.
	b. recording devices (e.g., audiotapes, videotapes, still photographs)	Erickson & Wilson, 1982.
	c. interviews (formal, informal, structured, open-ended)	Spradley, 1979. Crane & Angrosino, 1984.
	d. surveys	
	e. questionnnaires	
	f. artifacts (e.g., materials and objects found in the setting)	
	g. types of observations (general, topic-focused, focused on an individual)	Spradley, 1980; McCall & Simmons, 1969.
	h. natural experiments to explore specific observed phenomena in more "controlled" ways	Green, 1983.
	i. diaries (e.g., participant, research)	

TABLE 13–2. The Research Proposal: Categories and Questions (*Continued*)

Category	Questions/Topics	Sources
Describe the schedule for data collection and analysis that you plan to use at the outset of the study.	How will the data collection techniques be sequenced?	Spindler, 1982; Spradley, 1980.
	What time line do you use for each type of data you plan to collect?	
	How will you index the data so that you can organize and retrieve information and begin analyses? Will you need:	Green, 1983; Werner & Schoepfle, 1987.
	a. a system for cross referencing data (fieldnotes, videotapes, artifacts, interviews, diaries, experiments, photographs)?	
	b. a system for transcribing fieldnotes and video/audiotapes?	Cochran-Smith, 1984; Ochs, 1979.
	c. a way of recording events observed and the participants, topics, organizational structure, participation structure (constituent phases or major sub-parts of the event), roles and relationships of participants, content summary to permit data retrieval for comparative analysis within and across events in the study.	Erickson, cited in Green, 1983.
	d. a time-date code added to your videotapes?	
	Will you use a computer data management system (e.g., Ethnograph Notebook 2)?	Werner & Schoepfle, 1987.
	Do you have a plan for data analysis?	
	Will you do a "pilot" or protoanalysis to explore:	Heap, 1986.
	a. the theory-method-analysis relationship?	Cochran-Smith, 1984.
	b. whether the data you collect will provide you with the information needed to answer your questions?	
	c. whether the scope and design of the study as initially planned is manageable and feasible?	
	d. the types of data, length of time, placement of equipment, types of interviews possible, literature that might be appropriate, the appropriate analysis strategies/techniques (e.g., domain analysis, linguistic/discourse analysis, statistical analysis, content analysis)?	

anticipate the types of data that will be collected and proposes an initial schedule of collection (Spindler, 1982).

The tools and techniques that the ethnographer uses include: participant observation, interviews, observational records (e.g., fieldnotes, audio/videotape records, photographs), maps, documents and/or artifact collections, and diaries. Just which tools will be used and when they will be used depend on the questions, the nature of the access negotiated at the outset of the study, and the roles the researcher will assume during the study. (For a description of each of the tools and techniques see the sources provided in Table 13–2.) As in the case of access and roles, the tools used will vary within the study as new issues are identified that could be determined in the prefieldwork phase. However, the ethnographer does enter the fieldwork phase with a plan of action.

Data Collection Procedures. The collection and analysis procedures that are specified during the prefieldwork phase of the study are those that appear logical given the information, questions, and knowledge available prior to the actual fieldwork phase. As we have discussed above, the ethnographer enters

the field with as much prior knowledge as possible and with a conceptual framework. This information permits the ethnographer to develop a proposed or initial schedule for data collection and analysis. However, like other aspects of this research approach discussed above, the schedule is subject to revision and modification as a result of issues, problems, and new insights or directions that are identified during fieldwork.

For example, if the question under study is how do students learn to go to school, then past research would indicate that audio and video recordings as well as participant observation and fieldnotes would be needed from the beginning moments of teacher-student contact (Brooks, 1985; Dorr-Bremme, 1982; Florio, 1978; Kantor, 1988; Kantor, Elgas, & Fernie, 1989; Wallat, Green, Conlin, & Haramis, 1981). However, if the questions focus on how students gain access to instruction in language arts, the ethnographer might want to enter the context and observe how time is spent on what, with whom, under what conditions, for what purpose, where, with what outcomes before beginning videotape or audiotape recording. By observing general patterns of life in the classroom and developing a map of the structure of that life, the ethnographer can use recordings more

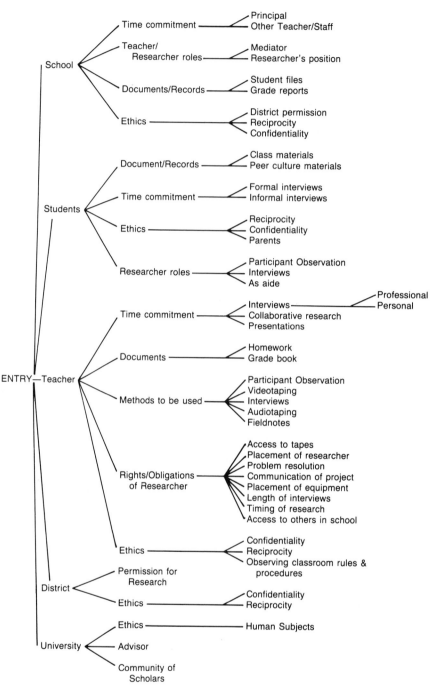

FIGURE 13–1.

selectively. That is, the ethnographer may begin with a comprehensive exploration of life in the classroom and then move to a more focused exploration (e.g., Cochran-Smith, 1984; Cook-Gumperz, Gumperz, & Simons, 1981; Corsaro, 1985; Spradley, 1980). Still others will stay at a comprehensive or macro level throughout most of the study (e.g., Fishman, 1988; Heath, 1983; Taylor, 1983; Taylor & Gaines, 1988). Just how a research schedule will be developed depends on the questions under study,

the negotiated access, the level of observation required, and the conditions within the setting.

Data Analysis: Initial Explorations. The issue of data analysis is related to both the questions under study and the site at which the study is undertaken. To illustrate this point, we will draw a distinction between community-oriented studies and school-oriented studies. The difference between these two types of studies is related to the nature of the two steps of communities: community in the everyday sense of the term and a school community. A community is an ongoing entity that is always entered midstream. In other words, a community does not have a beginning point of existence that the ethnographer can observe, or an ending point. Rather, the ethnographer has a beginning point of entry and an ending point within the ongoing life of a community.

In contrast, a classroom or even a school community is reconfigured each school year. That is, by law and policy decision, schools exist for a given period of time each year. Each year, teachers, students, and in some instances, administrators meet anew. That is, a school may lose and gain some teachers and students. When the members of the group shift, the school culture does not remain the same, but rather, each year the culture must be reconstructed and established for that particular group of teachers, students, administrators, support staff and parents. The same is true of classrooms. Each year a teacher receives a new group of students with whom she or he will live and work for a specified period of time (e.g., a year, a grading period, a quarter, or three out-of-four-quarters). An ethnographer can enter the beginning point of a school year and in a particular classroom. Therefore, the ethnographer can observe the ways in which the culture of the school for that year and that classroom are established, maintained, and completed. At the end of the year or term, members of the particular classroom and often of the school may leave the classroom or school community and be assigned to new classrooms or schools.

Thus, due to the nature of the culture of schools in the United States, classroom ethnographies have a different time-bounded nature than community-oriented ethnographies. These differences lead to different approaches to the design, collection and analysis of data. In community ethnographies, the ethnographer begins data collection and analysis immediately upon entry (Taylor & Dorsey-Gaines, 1988). If the data being collected are not adequate or appropriate to answer the questions of interest, then the ethnographer can modify collection and add new directions or techniques. The community will continue its own lifeworld while the ethnographer adjusts the research design. Although unique events occur that the ethnographer may miss, the general aspects of life will recur and will be available to the ethnographer at another time.

A classroom, however, is a unique type of community. It occurs only once in a given time period. To observe a classroom through a complete cycle of occurrence, the ethnographer must enter with the members and leave with them. Even though other classrooms will exist and a subgroup of students may remain together, the next classroom will be a different community with its own rights and obligations, norms and expectations, and roles and relationships. Thus the classroom community is a unique event. The time-bounded nature of classrooms places special demands on an ethnographer, who does not have time to make many mistakes or who fails to understand the way the classroom is being established. The establishment of the classroom culture usually occurs only once. (Reorganizations of classes after the school year begins is an exception to this rule.)

The uniqueness of the classroom as a time-bounded cultural group means that the ethnographer must begin the study with information about camera placement, observation strategies, data collection schedules, and negotiation of roles more defined than in a community-oriented study. The beginning of school happens only once, and norms are established during those beginning moments for the group that will become a community for the coming school year (e.g., Brooks, 1985; Green & Harker, 1982; Kantor, Elgas, & Fernie, 1989; Wallat & Green, 1979, 1982). Thus, the ethnographer cannot wait to collect information that occurs only at the "beginning of culture formation."

To insure that data collected is appropriate and sufficient to answer the questions of interest, a protoanalysis, (Heap, 1986) or a pilot study is suggested. (See Cochran-Smith, 1984 for an example of how a pilot period can be used to frame an ethnographic study of life in a particular classroom.) The ethnographic pilot phase is not a separate study but rather a systematic attempt to determine what theoretical orientations and conceptualizations of phenomena are appropriate and useful, what data need to be collected, what collection strategies and tools are the most appropriate, what roles and relationships are appropriate for the researcher in the particular situation, and what analysis procedures will yield the desired information. This latter aspect of a pilot phase is important given the nonrecurrence of particular aspects of classroom life (e.g., beginning of school, beginning of a particular unit of instruction, the formation of new reading or other instructional groups).

The pilot phase of a classroom ethnography can help frame the primary collection phase of a particular cycle of occurrence (a school year). However, while a pilot phase will allow the ethnographer to "shake down" theoretical perspectives and data collection and analysis procedures, the ethnographer must remain open and flexible in the study of the new cultural group (the next year's class). Pilots, therefore, will need to occur in a time period that precedes the one that is of main interest (the new school year) (c.f., Cochran-Smith, 1984). This will help the ethnographer avoid the "if only I had known that I needed that information" syndrome in this setting that does not permit repair or revisitation of certain phenomena.

The previous discussion of the ethnographic prefieldwork identifies key elements and decision-making areas for an ethnographic study. As indicated above, this phase is crucial to the success of a systematic ethnographic research study because the decisions made in this phase set the framework for the other phases—fieldwork and presentation of findings. In the remaining sections of this chapter we will briefly discuss these remaining phases of ethnographic research.

The Context of Discovery: Fieldwork

Ethnographic fieldwork has been characterized as an interactive-reactive cycle of inquiry in which the researcher enters the field with an ethnographic question about the culture of the group or topic of interest (Spradley, 1980). The ethnographer then begins to collect and index data using a variety of ethnographic tools or techniques. Analysis of data begins immediately. The ethnographer refines the initial question as the unfolding patterns of everyday life become visible through observations and initial data analysis.

The ethnographer also begins formal and informal interviews to learn whether the initial patterns and impressions being developed (the etic perspective) reflect those of the members of the culture (the emic perspective). This type of data collection-verification process is called triangulation. The ethnographer uses the member's perspective in a contrastive way. If the member's perspective and the ethnographer's match, then the ethnographer feels reasonably sure that a "piece of cultural knowledge" has been identified and this information can be used to guide a stranger's understanding of the culture.

If the perspectives do not match, the ethnographer will seek additional information and then reexamine the data collected to uncover whether there are different perspectives or whether the analysis was inaccurate or incomplete. A lack of match does not automatically invalidate the ethnographer's interpretation or observations, since some aspects of culture are available to members only at a tacit level. In addition, no single member of a culture "holds" all cultural knowledge. Rather, cultural knowledge is a "group" phenomenon. The ethnographer must extract this knowledge from different members of the group (e.g., women, men, children; teachers, students, administrators, parents, support personnel; or high-reading group members, low-reading group members, middle-reading group members, teacher). Members of a culture hold differential knowledge related to their roles and relationships with others in the cultural group.

The ethnographer's task is to develop a "cultural grammar" of the life in the particular culture under study. As Mead (1972) has pointed out, the description obtained is only one description not "the" description. The purpose of the ethnography is to develop a description that captures "daily life" for members of the culture and that can be used by a "stranger" (the ethnographer and others) to guide participation in the culture under study. That is, the ethnographer and other strangers (Agar, 1980) should be able to use the ethnography to participate in the social group in culturally appropriate ways without breaking the cultural norms or ignoring the rights and obligations for participation in daily life. In addition, the ethnography should enable the stranger (or members of the social group) to understand the consequences of adhering to or breaking cultural patterns. Thus, the ethnography will enable a stranger to anticipate the types of events, actions, attitudes, evaluations, and interactional expectations that will occur within and across time in the setting.

For example, Erickson & Mohatt (1982) explored the ways in which native (American Indian) and non-native teachers taught Indian students. What they discovered was that there was a difference in the ways in which the native and non-native teachers interacted with students especially at the beginning of lessons. The native teacher simply began the lesson and students "tuned in" as she got their attention. The non-native teacher would not begin the lesson until he had all of the students looking at him. This particular style did not match the interactional expectations of Indian students or the larger Indian community. This information was shared with school staff and the Indian group and provided a basis for understanding why the native teacher had less "trouble" with the students and was more successful. Thus, Erickson & Mohatt provided information that was unavailable to members of the social group (Indian community) that was then used to develop the group's understanding of an ordinary aspect of daily life and its consequences for a subgroup (the students and their teachers).

Observing Patterns of Culture. As indicated above, the fieldwork phase of an ethnography is used to obtain understandings of cultural knowledge in systematic ways. One way to accomplish this goal has been used by cognitive anthropologists. These ethnographers often begin by asking a series of questions: who can do what, where, when, in what ways, for what purpose, under what conditions, with what expected outcomes. These questions are based on the assumption that actions of participants in a social group are goal-directed and governed by socially constructed norms and expectations. Thus the ethnographer begins an exploration of culture by observing features of the various social situations (Spradley, 1980) that form the basis for identification of a pattern and eventually themes. Spradley (1980) identifies the following features of culture:

1. Space: the physical place or places
2. Actor: the people involved
3. Activity: a set of related acts people do
4. Act: single actions that people do
5. Object: the physical things that are present
6. Event: a set of related activities that people carry out
7. Time: the sequencing that takes place over time
8. Goal: the things people are trying to accomplish
9. Feeling: the emotions or reactions felt and expressed (p. 78)

These features of a social situation provide a point of entry and a framework for the observations of the patterns of everyday life. A pattern is a statement of the relationship among features within and across contexts. Patterns can be identified by asking questions such as:

• Can you describe in detail all the places (objects, acts, activities, events, time periods, actors, goals, and feelings)?
• Where are objects (persons, events, activities) located?
• What are all the ways activities incorporate objects (people, acts, activities)?
• What are all the ways space (objects, acts, events, time) is used by actors? (pp. 82–83)

In addition, patterns can be identified by asking who does what, with whom, under what conditions, for what purpose, with what outcomes, when, and where.

These questions are illustrative not definitive. In any ethnography, the ethnographer may emphasize certain features over others. The key is to collect as much information as possible to begin to understand and uncover the complex relationships among pesons and the relationship of persons to objects and places in the environment; that is, the pattern of daily life. Spradley (1980) provides one way to explore the relationship among the features of culture and to identify specific types of cultural patterns:

1. Strict inclusion: X is a kind of Y
   kinds of actors, activities, events, objects, relationships, goals, time, etc.
2. Spatial: X is a part of Y
   parts of activities, places, events, objects (e.g., books, articles, written texts)
3. Rationale: X is a reason for doing Y
   reasons for actions, carrying out activities, staging events, feelings, using objects, arranging space, seeking goals
4. Location for action: X is a place for doing Y
   places for activities, where people act, where events are held, for objects, and for seeking goals
5. Function: X is used for Y
   uses for objects, events, acts, activities, places
6. Means-end: X is a way to do Y
   ways to organize space, to act, to stage events, to become actors, to acquire information (e.g., to read, write, speak, interpret information)
7. Sequence: X is a step in Y
   steps for achieving goals, in an act, in an event, in an activity, in becoming an actor
8. Attribution: X is an attribute of Y (characteristic)
   characteristics of objects, places, time, actors, activities, events.
9. Cause-effect: X is a result of Y (p. 93)
   results of activities, acts, events, feelings

Although these questions and the categories of relationships appear to focus on a community-oriented ethnography, they can also be used to guide fieldwork for topic-oriented ethnographies. For example, if the goal of the ethnographer is to understand what English language arts is in a particular classroom or school, then the ethnographer would tailor the questions to this goal and ask questions such as: What is a language-arts event? What types of events "count" as language arts in this setting? Where does the event take place? Who are the actors in the event? What types of objects are used in the event (e.g., texts, pencils, paper, films, pictures, oral histories)? How do actors in the events perceive the event and feel about the event? What are the consequences for participation or lack of participation in the event for different members of the social group? and so forth.

Using ethnographic tools to record the events and activities of everyday life, at the beginning of the study, the ethnographer will want to take a comprehensive look at the unfolding life of the social group (e.g., the classroom) so that all of the events of language arts can be identified. The ethnographer will enter the study with a working definition of what constitutes a language arts event but will ultimately refine this definition as he or she comes to understand what "counts" as a language-arts event for that group. Once the ethnographer has obtained an understanding and description of the general pattern of daily life, she or he may elect to take a more focused look at a particular subaspect of such life (e.g., language arts participation of students who are non-English speakers or are low-group readers). Once the focused look has been completed, the ethnographer will re-embed this information into the general description to further explore how the part is influenced by or related to the "whole." (See Gumperz, 1986 for a description of inter-active sociolinguistics, which involves individual speech event analysis against the fabric of an ethnography.) Thus, comes the notion that ethnography is an interactive-reactive, context responsive approach to the study of the everyday life of a cultural group.

Exiting the Field. For the ethnographer, knowing when enough data has been collected is often problematic. In community-oriented ethnographies, the ethnographer may need to exit the field when the contractual period has ended, when the ethnographer believes that sufficient data has been collected to answer the questions of interest, or when the ethnographer "runs out of money" or must return to the university. In school-oriented ethnographies, the naturally occurring breaks in the school cycle may influence when the ethnographer leaves the field. There is no one way to determine when enough data have been collected without engaging in initial analysis during the collection/fieldwork phase. Ethnographers cannot wait until they exit the field to begin data analysis given the context-dependent nature of this approach.

Ethnographers may exit the field at specific points and then reenter at later points to collect additional information, to triangulate perspectives, or to verify the patterns uncovered during analysis. At such times, the ethnographer will need to negotiate reentry and begin once again the interactive-reactive cycle described above. Thus, each decision within the process of ethnography, from initiating a study through exiting the field, must be principled decisions.

The Context of Presentation

The context of presentation begins with having to make a decision—"Why write or speak about this ethnography?" The answer to this question will shape the ethnography (Heap p.c.). The ethnographer, therefore, must decide on an audience and then determine what this audience needs and expects in order to accept the findings as evidence of cultural patterns and descriptions of life in everyday contexts. An ethnography, therefore, is not a single entity, but rather, like the ethnographic process itself, is tailored to the context of use. This aspect of ethnography has led to recent reexamination of what it means to write an ethnography (Clifford & Marcus, 1986; Van Maanen, 1988).

For example, Van Maanen (1988) suggests that there are three principal ways of writing ethnography: realistic, fieldwork confessional, and impressionistic. He also identifies some emerging ways: critical, formal, literary, and jointly told. Table 13–3 presents a summary description of each of these styles of writing ethnography.

These different styles indicate that in writing the ethnographic report, the ethographer transforms "what is known or learned" into a new category, "what is communicated." The transformation of knowledge into communication implies the shifting of material. Although events happen one after another or are written down one after another, this arrangement is rarely the way the ethnographer wishes to convey events or information about phenomena. This means that the ethnogra-

TABLE 13–3. Styles of Writing Ethnography

Style	Description
Realistic	Single author typically narrates this style in a dispassionate, third-person voice; includes the comings and goings of members of the culture, theoretical coverage of certain features of the culture, and hesitant account of why the work was undertaken; result is an author-proclaimed description and explanation for certain specific, bounded, and observed cultural practices.
Fieldwork Confessional	Highly personalized style; attempt to explicitly demystify fieldwork or participant-observation by showing how the technique is practiced in the field; includes stories of infiltration, fieldwork rapport, minimelodramas of hardships, and accounts of what fieldwork did to the fieldworker.
Impressionistic	Presents the doing of fieldwork rather than the doer or the done; tries to startle the audience with striking stories; first-person account; uses words, metaphors, phrasings, imagery, and expansive recall of fieldwork experience to produce a tightly focused, vibrant, exact, but necessarily imaginative rendering of fieldwork; not about what usually happens but about what rarely happens.
Critical	Studies strategically situated to shed light on larger social, political, symbolic, or economic issues; often have a Marxist edge and a concern for representing social structure as seen through the eyes of disadvantaged groups.
Formal	Attempt to build, test, generalize and exhibit theory; analytic goals include the derivation of generalizations through inductive and inferential logic; representations of persons, places, activities, belief systems, and activities, when not the specific target of study, are limited and used only to provide a context for the textualized data under review.
Literary	Author explicitly borrows fiction-writing techniques to tell the story; find stylistic contrasts, use of dialogue and monologue, strong story lines organized around themes of general social interest, dense characterization, dramatic plots, flashbacks and flashforwards, and alternative points of view.
Jointly Told	Jointly authored texts (fieldworker and native) to reveal the discursive and shared character of all cultural descriptions.

Source: Van Maanen, J. (1988). *Tales of the field: On writing ethnography*. Chicago: University of Chicago Press.

pher must decide on the manner and sequence of the written or spoken presentation.

The manner and sequences of presentation differ according to the audience (e.g., members of the social group; policy makers; funding agency; other ethnographers; and practitioners such as teachers, doctors, lawyers, or the general public) and theoretical orientation or style of the ethnographer (e.g., critical, formal, literary, collaborative, realistic, impressionistic, or fieldwork confessional). In addition, the ethnography is also influenced by the type of ethnographic study (e.g., whole community-oriented, school-oriented, topic-oriented).

Another way to consider these issues is that the context of discovery and the cultural dimensions of everyday life do not occur in neat or ordered ways. As suggested above, the context of discovery is often circular and recursive. A reader will not be interested in the ebbs and flows of every "piece of culture" or the "nitty gritty" aspects of doing ethnography. Rather, the reader will expect a formal text of some type that will inform the reader about culture and the consequences of membership in particular social groups. Thus, the task of the ethnographer is to reconstruct the findings about culture in a coherent and orderly fashion.

What is evident in this discussion is that there is no simple, linear relationship between the context of discovery and the context of presentation. Like the decisions made within the context of discovery, the decisions about what information to present, how, and to whom must be principled decisions. These decisions are critical since it is not possible to present all of the descriptions obtained, the findings identified, or the knowledge uncovered. Thus, an ethnography is a selective account that has a goal and a point of view.

A CLOSING AND AN OPENING

In this chapter, we have explored the nature of ethnography as a culturally driven, systematic inquiry process that seeks to explore what is learned from participating in the everyday life of a social group. What was argued is that ethnography is and can be a productive way of exploring what is learned about English language arts in educational settings (e.g., community, home, school, classroom).

The chapter identifies a series of factors involved in using ethnography. These factors can be captured in the following themes:

1. Ethnography is a theoretically driven approach to the study of the everyday life of a social group.
2. Ethnography is driven by cultural theory and involves exploring how the parts observed within a social group are interrelated (part-whole relationship).
3. The particular cultural theory that a researcher elects to use will focus attention on certain aspects and domains of culture and ignore others. It will also entail exploration of different phenomena and different levels of analysis using a variety of fieldwork tools in different ways.
4. The ethnographic process has three phases: the context of discovery includes the prefieldwork and fieldwork phases and the context of presentation includes the postfieldwork or writing phase. Each of these contexts has unique elements, but the contexts often overlap. That is, ethnography is not a linear process but rather an interactive-reactive, context responsive process.
5. Ethnography is not something external to a social setting.

The ethnographer must gain access to the social setting. Access involves negotiations of roles and relationships for the researcher, and rights and obligations of the researcher in the social settings as well as access to information.

6. Ethnography also involves a comparative perspective, both within a study and across studies. Thus, ethnography is one type of ethnology.

The purpose of this chapter was not to explore each aspect of ethnography (e.g., fieldwork) but to identify and describe the key issues. In so doing, we laid a foundation for exploring what is involved at different points in an ethnographic study. In addition, we presented illustrative examples of how ethnography has and can be used to study particular phenomena (e.g., English language arts, life in classrooms).

Throughout the chapter, we have identified a wide variety of sources for the reader. This strategy was used intentionally to provide a guide for further study. This chapter, then, like an ethnographic project, will continue after the person exits the field. What we hope will happen next is that as researchers build on the work in this chapter, they will engage in a critical dialogue about the nature of ethnography in educational settings and will begin to explore what is involved in moving educational ethnography into the arena of ethnology in order to better understand the dynamics of life in schools and the nature of educational processes.

References

Agar, M. H. (1980). *The professional stranger: An informal introduction to ethnography.* New York: Academic Press.

Agar, M. H. (1986). *Speaking of ethnography.* Sage university paper series on qualitative research methods (Vol. 2). Beverly Hills, California: Sage.

American Anthropological Association. (1971). *Principles of professional responsibility.* Washington, D.C.: American Anthropological Association.

Anderson, A. B., Teale, W. B., & Estrada, E. (1980). Low income children's preschool literacy experiences: Some naturalistic observations. *The Quarterly Newsletter of the Laboratory of Human Cognition, 2–3,* 59–65.

Au, K. (1980). Participation structures in a reading lesson with Hawaiian children: Analysis of a culturally appropriate instructional event. *Anthropology and Education Quarterly 11,* 2, 91–115.

Barr, R. & Dreeban, R. (1983). *How schools work.* Chicago: University of Chicago Press.

Berman, L. M. (1986). Perception, paradox, and passion: Curriculum for community. *Theory into Practice 25,* 1, 41–45.

Bernard, H. R. (1988). *Research methods in cultural anthropology.* Newbury Park, California: Sage Publications, Inc.

Berreman, G. D. (1968). Ethnography: Method and product. In J. A. Clifton, (Ed.), *Introduction to cultural anthropology: Essays in the scope and methods of the science of man* (pp. 337–373). Boston, Massachusetts: Houghton-Mifflin.

Birdwhistell, R. (1977). Some discussion of ethnography, theory, and method. In J. Brockman (Ed.), *About Bateson* (pp. 101–141). New York: E. P. Dutton.

Bloome, D. (1981). *An ethnographic approach to the study of reading among black junior high school students.* Unpublished doctoral dissertation, Kent State University.

Bloome, D. (1983). Classroom reading instruction: A socio-communicative analysis of time-on-task. *Thirty-second Yearbook of the National Reading Conference.* Rochester: National Reading Conference.

Bloome, D. (1987). Reading and writing as a social process in a middle school classroom. In D. Bloome (Ed.), *Literacy and schooling* (pp. 123–149). Norwood, New Jersey: Ablex Publishing Company.

Bloome, D. & Green, J. (1982). The social contexts of reading: A multidisciplinary perspective. In B. A. Hutson (Ed.), *Advances in Reading/Language Research,* Volume I, 309–338. Greenwich, Connecticut: JAI Press.

Bloome, D. & Theodorou, E. (1988). Analyzing teacher-student and student-student discourse. In J. L. Green and J. O. Harker (Eds.), *Multiple perspective analyses of classroom discourse* (pp. 217–248). Norwood, New Jersey: Ablex Publishing Corporation.

Boggs, S. T. (1972). The meaning of questions and narrations to Hawaiian children. In C. B. Cazden, V. P. John, and D. Hymes (Eds.), *Functions of language in the classroom* (pp. 299–327). New York: Teachers College Press.

Brooks, D. M. (1985). The teacher's communicative competence: The first day of school. *Theory Into Practice, 24,* 1, 63–70.

Cazden, C. B., John, V. P. & Hymes, D. (Eds.) (1972). *Functions of language in the classroom.* New York: Teachers College Press.

Chandler, S. (1989). Issues of gaining entry. Paper presented at The Tenth Annual University of Pennsylvania Ethnography in Education Research Forum, February 24–25, 1989.

Chandler, S. & Green, J. L. (1988). Puzzlements: When is instruction? When is curriculum? Paper presented at the Bergamo Conference, Dayton, Ohio.

Clifford, J. & Marcus, G. E. (Eds.) (1986). *Writing culture.* Berkeley: University of California Press.

Cochran-Smith, M. (1984). *The making of a reader.* Norwood, New Jersey: Ablex Publishing Corporation.

Collins, J. (1983). Linguistic perspectives on minority education: Discourse analysis and early literacy. Unpublished doctoral dissertation, University of California, Berkeley.

Collins, J. (1986). Differential instruction in reading groups. In J. Cook-Gumperz (Ed.), *The social construction of literacy* (pp. 117–137). New York: Cambridge University Press.

Collins, J. & Michaels, S. (1986). Speaking and writing: Discourse strategies and the acquisition of literacy. In J. Cook-Gumperz (Ed.), *The social construction in literacy* (pp. 207–222). New York: Cambridge University Press.

Cook-Gumperz, J. (1979). Communicating with young children in the home. *Theory into Practice 18,* 4, 207–212.

Cook-Gumperz, J. (Ed.) (1986). *The social construction of literacy.* New York: Cambridge University Press.

Cook-Gumperz, J., Gumperz, J. & Simons, H. D. (1981). *School-home ethnography project* (Final Report, NIE G-78-0082). Washington, D.C.: National Institute of Education.

Corsaro, W. (1981). Entering the child's world: Research strategies for field entry and data collection. In J. L. Green and C. Wallat (Eds.), *Ethnography and language in educational settings* (pp. 117–146). Norwood, New Jersey: Ablex Publishing Corporation.

Corsaro, W. (1985). *Friendship and peer culture in the early years.* Norwood, New Jersey: Ablex Publishing Corporation.

Crane, J. G. & Angrosino, M. V. (1984). *Field projects in anthropology: A student handbook* (2nd ed.). Prospect Heights, New Jersey: Waveland Press, Inc.

Denzin, N. K. (1978). *The research act: A theoretical introduction to sociological methods* (2nd ed). New York: McGraw-Hill.

Denzin, N. K. (1989). *The research act: A theoretical introduction to sociological methods* (3rd ed.). Englewood Cliffs, New Jersey: Prentice-Hall.

Dorr-Bremme, D. (1982). *Behaving and making sense: Creating social organization in the classroom.* Unpublished doctoral dissertation, Harvard University.

Edgerton, R. B. & Langness, L. L. (1974). *Methods and styles in the study of culture.* San Francisco: Chandler and Sharp.

Ellen, R. F. (ed.) (1984). *Ethnographic research: A guide to general conduct.* Orlando, Florida: Academic Press.

Erickson, F. (1977). Some approaches to inquiry in school-community ethnography. *Anthropology and Education Quarterly 8, 2,* 58–69.

Erickson, F. & Mohatt, G. (1982). Cultural organization of participation procedures in two classrooms of Indian students. In G. Spindler (Ed.), *Doing the ethnography of schooling: Educational anthropology in action* (pp. 132–174). New York: Holt, Rinehart and Winston.

Erickson, F. & Wilson, J. (1982). *Sights and sounds of life in schools: A reference guide to film and video tape for research and education.* (Research series 125). East Lansing: Michigan State University, Institute for Research on Teaching.

Evertson, C. & Green, J. L. (1986). Observation as inquriy and method. In M. C. Wittrock (Ed.), *Handbook of research on teaching* (3rd ed., pp. 161–213). New York: Macmillan.

Fishman, A. R. (1988). *Amish literacy.* New Hampshire: Heinneman.

Florio, S. (1978). *Learning how to go to school: An ethnography of interaction in a kindergarten/first grade classroom.* Unpublished doctoral dissertation, Harvard University, Graduate School of Education.

Florio, S. & Shultz, J. (1979). Social competence at home and at school. *Theory into Practice 18,* 234–243.

Geertz, C. (1973). *The interpretation of cultures.* New York: Basic Books.

Geertz, C. (1983). *Local knowledge: Further essays in interpretive anthropology.* New York: Basic Books.

Gilmore, P. & Glatthorn, A. A. (Eds.) (1982). *Children in and out of school: Ethnography and education.* Washington, D.C.: Center for Applied Linguistics.

Goetz, J. P. & LeCompte, M. D. (1984). *Ethnography and qualitative design in educational research.* Orlando, Florida: Academic Press.

Goodenough, W. H. (1981). *Culture, language, and society.* Menlo Park: California: Cummings.

Green, J. L. (1983). Research on teaching as a linguistic process: A state of the art. In E. Gordon (Ed.), *Review of Research in Education,* 10 (pp. 152–252). Washington, D.C.: American Educational Research Association.

Green, J. L. & Harker J. O. (1982). Gaining access to learning: Conversational, social, and cognitive demands of group participation. In L. Wilkinson (Ed.), *Communicating in the classroom* (pp. 183–221). New York: Academic Press.

Green, J. L., Kantor, R. M. & Rogers, T. (In Press). Exploring the complexity of language and learning in the life of the classroom. In B. Jones and L. Idol (Eds.), *Dimensions of thinking, cognitive instruction, and implications for reform.* In the series *Dimensions of thinking: A framework for curriculum and instruction,* Volume II. Earlbaum.

Green, J. L. & Wallat, C. (Eds.) (1981). *Ethnography and language in educational settings.* Norwood, New Jersey: Ablex Publishing Corporation.

Griffin, P. (1977). How and when does reading occur in the classroom. *Theory Into Practice, 16,* 5, 376–383.

Gumperz, J. (1982). *Discourse strategies.* New York: Cambridge University Press.

Gumperz, J. (1986). Interactive sociolinguistics in the study of schooling. In J. Cook-Gumperz (Ed.), *The social construction of literacy* (pp. 45–68). London, Cambridge University Press.

Gumperz, J. J. & Hymes, D. (Eds.) (1972). *Directions in sociolinguistics: The ethnography of communication:* New York: Basil Blackwell Inc.

Hammersley, M. & Atkinson, P. (1983). *Ethnography: Principles in practice.* New York: Tavistock Publications.

Heap, J. L. (1980). What counts as reading? Limits to certainty in assessment. *Curriculum Inquiry, 10,* 3, 265–292.

Heap, J. L. (1986). Maxims. Speech given at International Reading Association Meetings, Atlanta, Georgia.

Heap, J. L. (1988). A situated perspective on literacy events. Occasional paper, Project on the Socio-cultural Organization of Collaborative Writing. Toronto: Ontario Institute for Studies in Education.

Heap, J. L. (1989). The context of presentation. Occasional paper, Project on Moral and Civil Dimensions of Access to Writing Literacy. Toronto: Ontario Institute for Studies in Education.

Heath, S. B. (1982a). Ethnography in education: Defining the essentials. In P. Gilmore and A. A. Glatthorn (Eds.), *Children in and out of school: Ethnography and education* (pp. 33–55). Washington, D.C.: Center for Applied Linguistics.

Heath, S. B. (1982b). Questioning at home and at school. A comparative study. In G. Spindler (Ed.), *Doing the ethnography of schooling: Educational anthropology in Action* (pp. 102–131). New York: Holt, Rinehart and Winston.

Heath, S. B. (1983). *Ways with words: Language, life, and work in communities and classrooms.* New York: Cambridge University Press.

Hymes, D. H. (1981). *Ethnographic monitoring of children's acquisition of reading/language arts skills in and out of the classroom.* Final Report to the National Institute of Education. Washington, D.C.: U.S. Department of Education.

Hymes, D. H. (1982). What is ethnography? In P. Gilmore and A. A. Glatthorn (Eds.), *Children in and out of school: Ethnography and education* (pp. 21–32). Washington, D.C.: Center for Applied Linguistics.

Kantor, R. (1988). Creating school meaning in preschool curriculum. *Theory Into Practice, 27,* 25–35.

Kantor, R., Elgas, P., & Fernie, D. (1989). First the look and then the sound: Creating conversations at preschool circletime. *Early Childhood Research Quarterly 4,* 4, 433–449.

Kaplan, A. (1964). *The conduct of inquiry.* San Francisco: Chandler Publishing Company.

King, N. R. (1986). Recontextualizing the curriculum. *Theory into Practice 25,* 1, 36–40.

Kroeber, A. L. & Kluckhohn, C. (1963). *Culture: A critical review of concepts and definitions.* New York: Vintage Books, Random House.

Lemke, J. (1990). *Talking science.* Norwood, New Jersey: Ablex Publishing Corporation.

Lutz, F. W. (1981). Ethnography—The holistic approach to understanding schooling. In J. L. Green and C. Wallat (Eds.), *Ethnography and language in educational settings* (pp. 51–63). Norwood, New Jersey: Ablex Publishing Corporation.

McCall, G. J. & Simmons, J. L. (Eds.) (1969). *Issues in participant observation: A text and a reader.* Reading, Massachusetts: Addison-Wesley.

McCutcheon, G. (1982). What in the world is curriculum theory? *Theory into Practice 21,* 1, 18–22.

McDermott, R. P. (1976). *Kids make sense: An ethnographic account of the interactional management of success and failure in one first grade classroom.* Unpublished doctoral dissertation, Stanford University.

Mead, M. (1972). *Blackberry winter: My early years.* New York: William Marrow.

Michaels, S. (1981). "Sharing time": Children's narrative styles and differential access to literacy. *Language and Society 10,* 3, 423–442.

Michaels, S. (1984). Listening and responding: Hearing the logic in children's classroom narratives. *Theory into Practice 28,* 218–225.

Michaels, S. (1986). Narrative presentations: An oral preparation for literacy with first graders. In J. Cook-Gumperz (Ed.), *The social construction of literacy* (pp. 94–116). New York: Cambridge University Press.

Michaels, S. & Cazden, C. (1986). Teacher-child collaboration as oral preparation for literacy. In B. Schieffelin and P. Gilmore (Eds.), *The acquisition of literacy: Ethnographic perspectives* (pp. 132–154). Norwood, New Jersey: Ablex Publishing Corporation.

Michaels, S. & Collins, J. (1984). Oral discourse styles: Classroom interaction and the acquisition of literacy. In D. Tannen (Ed.), *Coherence in spoken and written discourse* (pp. 219–244). Norwood, New Jersey: Ablex Publishing Company.

Michaels, S. & Cook-Gumperz, J. (1979). A study of sharing time with first grade students: Discourse narratives in the classroom. In C. Chiarello, C. Chiarello, J. Kingston, E. E. Sweetser, J. Collins, H. Kawasaki, J. Manley-Buser, D. W. Marschak, C. O'Connor, D. Shaul, M. Tobey, H. Thompson, K. Turner (Eds.), *Proceedings of the Fifth Annual Meeting of the Berkeley Linguistics Society* (pp. 87–103). Berkeley, California: Berkeley Linguistics Society.

Moll, L. C. (1986). Wrting as communication: Creating strategic learning environments for students. *Theory Into Practice* 25, 2, 102–108

Moll, L. C. & Diaz, S. (1985). Ethnographic pedagogy: Promoting effective bilingual instruction: In E. Garcia & R. V. Padilla (Eds.), *Advances in bilingual education research* (pp. 127–149). Tucson: University of Arizona Press.

Ochs, E. (1979). Transcription as theory. In E. Ochs & B. Schieffelin (Eds.), *Developmental pragmatics* (pp. 43–72). New York: Academic Press.

Ogbu, J. U. (1974). *The next generation: An ethnography of education in an urban neighborhood.* New York: Academic Press.

Ogbu, J. U. (1978). *Minority education and caste: The American system in cross-cultural perspective.* New York: Academic Press.

Ogbu, J. U. (1982). Cultural discontinuities and schooling. *Anthropology and Education Quarterly* 13, 4, 290–307.

Philips, S. U. (1972). Participant structures and communicative competence: Warm Springs children in community and classroom. In C. B. Cazden, V. P. John, and D. Hymes (Eds.), *Functions of language in the classroom* (pp. 370–394). New York: Teachers College Press.

Philips, S. U. (1983). *The invisible culture: Communication in classroom and community on the Warm Springs Indian Reservation.* New York: Longman.

Reder, S. & Green, K. R. (1983). Contrasting patterns of literacy in an Alaska fishing village. *International Journal of the Sociology of Language 42,* 9–39.

Rogers, T. (1987). Exploring a socio-cognitive perspective on the interpretive processes of junior high school students. *English Quarterly, 20* (3), 218–230.

Rogers, T. (1988). *Students as literary critics: The interpretive theories, processes and experiences of ninth grade students.* Unpublished doctor dissertation, University of Illinois at Urbana-Champaign.

Saville-Troike, M. (1982). *The ethnography of communication.* Oxford: Blackwell.

Scollon, R. & Scollon, S. (1981). *Narrative, literacy, and face in interethnic communication.* Norwood, New Jersey: Ablex Publishing Company.

Scollon, R. & Scollon, S. (1984). Cooking it up and boiling it down: Abstracts in Athabaskan children's story retellings. In D. Tannen (Ed.), *Coherence in spoken and written discourse* (pp. 173–200). Norwood, New Jersey: Ablex Publishing Corporation.

Scribner, S. & Cole, M. (1981). *The psychology of literacy.* Cambridge, Massachusetts: Harvard University Press.

Shaffir, W. B., Stebbins, R. A., & Turowetz, A. (Eds.) (1980). *Fieldwork experience: Qualitative approaches to social research.* New York: St. Martin's Press.

Shultz, J., Florio, S., & Erickson, F. (1982). Where's the floor? Aspects of the cultural organization of social relationships in communication at home and in school. In P. Gilmore and A. Glatthorn (Eds.), *Children in and out of school* (pp. 88–123). Washington, D.C.: Center for Applied Linguistics.

Shuman, A. (1986). *Storytelling rights: The uses of oral and written texts by urban adolescents.* New York: Cambridge University Press.

Society for Applied Anthropology. (1974). Statement on professional and ethical responsibilities. *Human Organization 33* (3), opposite p. 219.

Spindler, G. D. (1982). *Doing the ethnography of schooling: Educational anthropology in action.* New York: Holt, Rinehart and Winston.

Spradley, J. P. (1979). *The ethnographic interview.* New York: Holt, Rinehart and Winston.

Spradley, J. P. (1980). *Participant observation.* New York: Holt, Rinehart and Winston.

Tanner, D. & Tanner, L. (1990). *The History of school curriculum.* New York: Macmillan.

Taylor, D. (1983). *Family literacy.* Exeter, New Hampshire: Heinemann Educational Books.

Taylor, D. & Dorsey-Gaines, C. (1988). *Growing up literate: Learning from inner-city families.* Portsmouth, New Hampshire: Heinemann.

Van Maanen, J. (1988). *Tales of the field: On writing ethnography.* Chicago: University of Chicago Press.

Wallat, C. & Green, J. L. (1979). Social rules and communicative contexts in kindergarten. *Theory into Practice 18* (4), 275–284.

Wallat, C. & Green, J. L. (1982). Construction of social norms. In K. Borman (Ed.), *Socialization of children in a changing society* (pp. 97–122). Hillsdale, New Jersey: Lawrence Erlbaum Associates.

Wallat, C., Green, J. L., Conlin, S. M., & Haramis, M. (1981). Issues related to action research in the classroom—The teacher and researcher as a team. In J. L. Green and C. Wallat (Eds.), *Ethnography and language in educational settings* (pp. 87–113). Norwood, New Jersey: Ablex Publishing Corporation.

Weade, R. (1987). Curriculum 'n' Instruction: The construction of meaning. *Theory into Practice 26* (1), 15–25.

Weade, R. & Evertson, C. (1988). The construction of lessons in affective and less affective classrooms. *Teaching and Teacher Education 4* (3), 189–213.

Werner, O. & Schoepfle, G. M. (1987). *Systematic fieldwork: Ethnographic analysis and data management.* Newbury Park: Sage Publications.

Wilcox, K. (1982). Ethnography as a methodology and its application to the study of schooling: A review. In G. Spindler (Ed.), *Doing the ethnography of schooling* (pp. 456–488). New York: Holt, Rinehart and Winston.

Wolcott, H. (1967). *A Kwakiutl village and school.* New York: Holt, Rinehart and Winston.

TEACHER-RESEARCHER PROJECTS: AN ELEMENTARY SCHOOL TEACHER'S PERSPECTIVE

Fredrick R. Burton

It is no secret that positivistic research, which traditionally emphasizes quantitative measures and experimental designs, has not only been ignored by public school teachers, but has alienated them as well. Such research designs attempt to break down the teaching-learning environment by isolating and controlling its variables. If successful, such experimental procedures yield a design that is "pure" and "findings" that are reported in journals edited by and written for other researchers. However, these studies have failed to make visible the rich complexity of classroom life as children and adults experience it. For many teachers, these studies have findings, but no meaning. And after-all, meanings, not findings are what ultimately make a difference in education.

Fortunately, there are many who are attempting to reconceptualize what constitutes good research in education. The focus of the teacher-researcher movement is one such example. It is an effort to get teachers "off the bench and into the game."

Background of the Teacher-Researcher Movement

The idea that teachers should be active producers of research knowledge is not new (Corey, 1953, 1954; Shumsky, 1958; Wann, 1952). Recently, with the interest in collaborative action research surfacing, the idea of teacher participation in research is once again being discussed, debated, and clarified. Yet, putting the idea into practice is still relatively rare in education, although there are notable exceptions, particularly in Great Britain and the United States.

Historically, conceptual work on the teacher-researcher focused on the procedures that teachers should use to conduct experiments in their own classrooms. Although Corey (1954) believed that the intent of the teacher-researcher differed from traditional experimental research, the ends being the improvement of practice rather than the discovery of educational laws, he saw no difference in their procedures that he called the "scientific method." These procedures usually involved a linear progression through the following stages:

1. Identification of a problem
2. Generation of hypothetical solutions
3. Experimental testing of solutions
4. Critically examining the results and choosing the best solutions
5. Retesting.

This emphasis on a set of methodological procedures continued to be emphasized later by others (Longstreet, 1982; Stenhouse, 1975).

Much of the research and theoretical literature regarding teacher-researchers comes from England (May, 1982). May, who has worked for the Center for Action Research in Education at the University of East Anglia, distinguishes between the teacher as research student and the teacher as researcher. The teacher as research student perspective holds that teachers should strive to fit what they do into a traditional experimental framework in much the same way Corey (1953) did with the teachers he worked with in the United States.

In contrast to this view, May (1982) describes the teacher as researcher perspective as a more desirable approach:

It seems at once clear that the language which the naturalistic paradigm demands of the teacher is that of the everyday practice of teaching. True, the techniques by which data is collected in the process of such research are not part of the everyday practice of most teachers. Nevertheless, they are techniques which may readily be understood and could be used by teachers inclined towards researching the experiences within their classrooms without their having to adopt any narrowly prescriptive theoretical perspectives. (p. 28)

However, an overemphasis on method does nothing to distinguish teacher-researcher projects from its positivistic predecessors. In the past, being a teacher-researcher merely meant that with some training and encouragement classroom teachers could also do the same sort of tradtional experimental studies that university professors had been doing for decades. In order to truly understand the nature of teacher-researcher studies as an alternative to the traditional research paradigm, it is important to look beyond method and begin to: 1) question the nature of research itself, and 2) consider the psychological processes rather than the methodological procedures of doing teacher-researcher studies.

Defining Teacher-Researcher Studies

Simply stated, teacher-researcher studies are attempts to illuminate pedagogical acts by re-searching experience. The aim of the teacher-researcher is not to create educational laws (as is sometimes done in the physical sciences) in order to predict and explain teaching and learning. Instead, the teacher-researcher attempts to make visible the experience of teachers and children acting in the world. This is accomplished through a process called theorizing.

Theorizing, if defined as the articulation and critical examination of directly experienced phenomena leading to increased understanding (Vallance, 1982), is at the very center of doing research as a classroom teacher. In his own attempt to develop a theory of the teacher-researcher, Van Manen (1984) states that "research and theorizing themselves are pedagogic forms of life and therefore inseparable from it" (p. 21). Thus, teaching, theorizing, and research are all intimately bound together. Teacher-researchers believe that they can best serve the large educational community as well as their classrooms by immersing themselves in problemmatic situations. Rather than embrace the naive empiricism that characterizes a consumer orientation toward curriculum, teacher-researchers not only observe, but actually live through educational experiences. Jackson (1968) succinctly puts forth this idea that experiencers themselves must become theorizers who speak as researchers in the academic community:

… the growth in our understanding of what goes on in these environments need not be limited to the information contained in the field notes of professional teacher-watchers. In addition to participant observers it might be wise to foster the growth of observant participators in our schools—teachers, administrators, and perhaps even students, who have the capacity to step back from their own experiences, view them analytically, and talk about them articulately. (pp. 175–176)

Although linking the idea of the teacher-researcher to the process of theorizing as defined by curriculum theorists such as Vallance is intriguing, there is still a need to be more exact about what teacher-researchers actually do. Drawing on phenomenology, psycholinguistics, Deweyan philosophy, and my own experience as a teacher-researcher, I have characterized what teacher-researchers do as they conduct classroom inquiry

(Burton, 1985; 1986). This characterization involves action, reflection, and their reciprocal nature.

Action and Reflection: Teacher-Researcher Processes

The nature of action can be distinguished from being a rote or technical undertaking. (A technical approach to action suggests a type of behavior that is ritualistic, a sort of habitual response.) However, this concept of action can be dismissed when considering the idea of intentionality. Phenomenologists (e.g. Stewart & Mickunas, 1974) rightly argue that to be conscious is to be conscious of some thing. Action, then, is purposeful. Teacher-researcher inquiry is research that is full of purpose, yet there is a necessary degree of uncertainty.

Action also entails observation; however, it is a type of observation that is what Carini (1979) describes as "impressionistic observation." One day I asked Alan, a sandy-haired, freckled 9-year-old boy in my classroom to try doing some writing. After a week, he had produced virtually no text. My impression of Alan for the week was that writing was not a way he preferred to express his knowledge (whereas he was quite "fluent" in art and drama).

Action is a necessary condition for doing teacher-researcher inquiry, but it is not a sufficient condition. Teacher-researchers must go beyond their actions and their impressions in a manner that Schutz (1967) best describes:

When, by my act of reflection, I turn my attention to my living experience, I am no longer taking up my position within the stream of pure duration, I am no longer simply living within that flow. The experiences are apprehended, distinguished, brought into relief, marked out from one another; the experiences which were constituted as phases within the flow of duration now become objects of attention as constituted experiences. (p. 51)

In order to understand the multiple layers of meaning and the fullness of actions and impressions in my classroom, I must reflect in a systematic, disciplined manner. As I returned to my reflective journal and discussed my observations and reflections with colleagues, I discovered that my earlier impression of Alan was misdirected. Furthermore, it was only through the processes of acting and reflecting over time that I later began to view Alan as a "methodical" rather than as a "reluctant" writer.

Because my actions provide substance for my reflections, and because these reflections inform my future encounters with children, there is a reciprocal relationship between the two processes of action and reflection. To be a teacher-researcher, then, is to be a teacher and a learner. Freire (1985) states:

I consider it an important quality or virtue to understand the impossible separation of teaching and learning. Teachers should be conscious every day that they are coming to school to learn and not just to teach. This way we are not just teachers but teacher learners. It is really impossible to teach without learning as well as learning without teaching. We cannot separate one from the other; we create a violence when we try. Over a period of time we no longer perceive it as violence when we continually separate teaching from learning. Then we conclude that the teacher teaches and the student learns. That unfortunately is when students are convinced that they come to school to be taught and that being taught often means transference of knowledge. (pp. 16–17)

The reciprocity of action and reflection is the essence of being a teacher-researcher or in Friere's words a "teacher-learner." Action is the content of reflection; reflection is the driving force behind action for it strengthens and gives intentions sustenance and elevates them from their status as mere impressions. Reflection is not merely an act of looking backward to what is known, nor is it an exercise in short-term memory. Instead, it is grounded in the impressions gathered and sifted out while acting in the classroom. These impressions are then systematically reflected upon in order to produce fresh, new meanings (which then of course point to new actions).

Tools For Teacher-Researchers

While the tools that teacher-researchers use to conduct their studies may involve quantitative measures, it is more likely that data gathering will involve ways that evoke the qualitative dimensions of classroom life. Tools such as field-notes, collecting artifacts, audio and video tape recordings, short- and long-term lesson plans, outside observations by colleagues, and record keeping by students, have long been used by anthropologists and others using a naturalistic research paradigm. Field-notes, usually the most commonly used form of data gathering, often take the form of teacher journals maintained over time. While there are some very fine examples of articles based on teacher journals (Armstrong, 1980; Bohstedt, 1979), I will offer some examples and explanations of field-notes taken from my own experiences as a teacher-researcher.

My field-notes are usually divided into two levels: general narrative notes and what Carini (1979) calls "reflective observations." General narrative field-notes are mostly descriptive of the larger classroom context that frames the more specific acts of the children. These notes include information about the nature of long-term (usually 8 to 10 weeks in duration) integrated class studies (e.g., "Folktale Study", "Middle Ages Study") as well as direct and indirect teaching events such as a planned booksharing event, which would sometimes lead to an unplanned discussion of literary structure. These notes also contain methodological notes to myself as well as what I call "thought ramblings," for example, notes concerning how I am feeling about the year or specific times such as my annual frustration with the disruptive nature of having to administer a week of standardized tests to my class. Below are some examples of general narrative fieldnotes:

1/5 Decided on theme for next week: "The Human Body". There is a twist. Earlier, we studied note-taking and organization. So an information-oriented unit seems logical. However, I'd like the kids to utilize creative reporting methods. I want them to use unique formats and am using existing informational books as models and examples. Some books and their corresponding formats are:

Book	Format
Paddle-to-the-Sea	journey
Unbuilding and Castle	narrative
Wild Mouse	journal
Animal Fact/Animal Fable	Q & A
All Upon a Sidewalk	journey
If You Lived With the Sioux ...	Q & A
Ashanti-to-Zulu	ABC
Charlie Needs a New Cloak	fiction

I'd like to see kids impart information through narrative. Doing so, they would be dealing with informative and poetic functions at the same time. They must attend to information and to the story structure itself. Will go to Grandview library tonight.

2/6 In order to get the ball rolling on the human body drafts, I gave/made extra time for working on them today. We didn't have read aloud although I did read Tim's published book, "World War II". His reaction was like most of the authors/kids—impressed, embarrassed, but proud that I was taking the time to read his book to an audience and that I was taking it seriously.

While kids worked on the human body study drafts, I conferenced with 4–6 kids. There was a buzz of talk, but most of it seemed related to their work. About 20–25 minutes into the writing time, I gathered them into the meeting area primarily for the purpose of building momentum. As kids shared, they reinforced, on a collective level, that we do have a *class* study—i.e. that each individual is contributing knowledge to the group and - through feedback - the group is contributing to individual kids.

2/23 *Notes to Myself*
Immediate tasks:
1. revise literary links chart
2. begin thematic analysis
3. portrayal
   a. a chronolgical portrayal of single kid
   b. thematic portrayal
*either way, my purpose is to tell stories that
—reveal and exemplify my categories, themes, motifs
—tell story of larger context
4. read
   a. introspective & retrospective analysis
   b. Carini
   c. Spradley

In contrast, reflective observations are focused on specific writing and literary events as well as children and their various projects. This form of data collection has embedded within it an analysis component, as Carini (1979) states:

Through description of the person's projects in the world—that is, through the mediums that the person is drawn to and uses and the motifs that recur in his representations, the observer brings to bear the convergent viewpoints offered by the world setting and by time. To do this, the mediums and motifs need to be reflected upon to determine the range of meanings they hold and can preserve. Within this range, it is then possible to describe the particular person's relationship to both medium and motif. (p. 63)

Many of my field notes contain reflective observations on children. However, insight can often come through reflecting on children's projects such as their art work or their written compositions as well. Below are some examples of both types:

9/26 Alan never seems to be with the group and often plays alone. He has received a lot of attention from me lately; unfortunately, most of his attention has revolved around negative behaviors—e.g. wandering out of the meeting area or simply not starting to work during writing time . . .

9/28 In an individual writing conference with me, Alan discusses an idea in which he plans to write a modern version of the "Cinderella" story. He appears to be shaping/creating his story as he talks—perhaps through his talk. At one point in the conference, he describes what is going to happen. As he does so, he orally edits and revises and says that certain parts of his description may not actually come out in his writing. I am glad he wants to share this with me—anything to improve our relationship . . .

12/14 Alan started an untitled story about 1 and 1/2 months ago, around Halloween. The setting of this story is "trick-or-treat" night. He has created an eerie mood much like (in his words) William Sleator's *Into the Dream,* a book I had read aloud to the class earlier . . .

2/23 Jane and Kinthia
J and K set about doing a 3-d map of the setting of *The Green Book.* They started it about 4 weeks ago, right after we finished reading the book. I simply suggested that someone might like to do a project with the book. After brainstorming with the class, J and K decided that the map idea was good. They worked on it steadily over the weeks. Occasionally, the rhythm of their work would be interrupted by a disagreement (see earlier notes) or "acts of God"—e.g. J went to Florida for a week. And now it sits here in the school gym to be viewed tonight during the school "Achievement Fair". It will be interesting to see the comments of the outside "judge".

Although the project is clearly theirs, it certainly has my stamp on it too. After all, I was the one that slowed them down when they were glueing and taping down pine needles to the cardboard. It didn't look very aesthetic.

I was also the one who asked them and encouraged them to revisit the book. They have shown care for the details. Boulder Valley, the mountains, the lake, huts, and the gardens of the original book are all part of their map.

As I observe their project, one other thing seems apparent—i.e. the writing to go with it seems so hurried. they crammed it in on the day that the project was due. Nonetheless, it was done and I'm not sure that it would have been much different if they would have had more time. As it stands, the writing is primarily descriptive. Captions are done to show, tell, reveal bits about the book. The joy seemed to be in the crafting of the model, not the writing.

3/12 Amy—Analysis of her story, "The Glass Eye"
Background: Since about the last week in January we have been studying "The Human Body". The last 6–7 weeks have consisted of the following general activities in roughly this sequence: 1) choosing a topic; 2) gathering and reading resource books; 3) going through a notetaking process; 4) making sketches; 5) more artwork and models with more care; 6) listening to informational books read aloud and used as models; 7) writing drafts of reports using a variety of formats; 8) sharing products along he way; 9) speakers and dissections interwoven; 10) display; and 11) bookmaking and illustrations.

Background on Amy: Amy is a thin, tall girl with dishwater blond stringy hair. She giggles a lot. I get the impression through our conversations that she has a lot of responsibility at home and also that she has a close family. She walks her younger sister, Catlin, home everyday.

Reflection on the writing itself: Amy's piece appears to reflect her experience—literary and life. The obvious literary connection is her reference to Beverly Cleary's book, *Dear Mr. Henshaw,* a book we had read aloud and just finished. According to X. J. Kennedy's textbook on literature, this is a literary allusion—i.e. a direct reference to a person, place, or thing in fiction. Kennedey argues that such allusions "enrich" story.

Although she hasn't shared it yet, my guess is that the class will notice the allusion.

Her opening, which I think has been influenced by Peter and Sherry, strikes me as particularly effective. Those first 3 lines draw you in as a reader. Looking across her other pieces (e.g. "The Search for the White Stallion's Parents" and "My Sister and the China Horse"), she has not used this direct entry into story through dialogue in the past. Instead, she used an opening similar to that found in many folktales. This willing to experiment marks a point of growth for her. Other points of interest: passage of time; her description of the hospital based on her experience; the dream as a harbinger; her character names—e.g. Dr. Rock; Nurse Able; Nancy Chinn

The importance of reflecting on childrens' projects to obtain higher-order knowledge is sometimes underestimated. However, Dewey (in Archambault, 1974) believed that "thought confers upon physical events and objects a very different status and value from those which they possess to a being that does not reflect" (p.214). Thus, to reflect critically upon an object, in the above examples of childrens' writing, is to endow it with meaning and significance.

Why Do Teacher-Researcher Studies?

Although understanding the process of doing teacher-researcher studies is often neglected in the current literature, this understanding does not point to why it is important to conduct such studies in the first place. The fact that teacher-researcher studies are rarely conducted is not in itself a rationale for doing so. Perhaps the most powerful reason for conducting observer-as-participant studies in education is their potential for generating insider knowledge useful to educators in a manner that does not disrupt the classroom, but instead potentially enriches the quality of education that children receive.

While much of the rationale for doing teacher-researcher studies has come from curriculum theorists, language researchers and theorists are also beginning to call for this type of research. Britton (1983) argues the importance of teacher-researcher studies in the language arts. He develops three dimensions of doing such research, the most basic one characterized as a process of discovery that takes place during the teaching day:

As human beings, we meet every new situation armed with expectations derived from past experiences or, more accurately, derived from our interpretations of past experience.
We face the new, therefore not only with knowledge drawn from the past but also with developed tendencies to interpret in certain ways. It is in submitting these to the test of fresh experience—that is, in having our expectations and modes of interpreting either confirmed or disconfirmed or modified that learning, the discovery, takes place. (p. 90)

Finally, another reason for fostering teacher-researcher inquiry is that these studies may be an important step in defining a paradigm of research that is truly educational rather than being haphazardly adapted from other disciplines. According to Stenhouse (1981), this would be research "in" rather than "on" educational settings. Although research "on" educational settings is undoubtedly necessary (e.g., historical, philosophical, psychological, and sociological studies), research "in" classrooms seeks to understand and to portray the educational intentions of the participants.

Conclusion

Teachers who "re-search" their own experiences and those of children as well find that their teaching provides substance for their research and that the act of research enriches and illuminates their teaching. Doing research, then, is not something extra that teachers might do. Rather, research is something teachers *must* do if they are to become tactful observers and participants in the classroom culture that they are continually helping to create anew with children every day of the school year.

NOTABLE EXAMPLES OF TEACHER-RESEARCH PROJECTS

Below are some notable examples of teacher-researcher projects that were initiated and conducted by teachers themselves or in collaboration with colleagues both inside and outside the United States. Some are books comprised entirely of teacher-researcher projects.

Armstrong, M. (1980). *Closely Observed Children.* London: Writers and readers.

Enright, L. (1981). The diary of a primary classroom. In J. Dixon (Ed.), *A teacher's guide to action research.* London: Grant McIntyre.

Hansen, J., Newkirk, T., & Graves, D. (1985) *Breaking ground: Teachers relate reading and writing in the elementary school.* London: Heinemann Educational Books.

Jensen, J. (1988). *Stories to grow on.* London: Heinemann Educational Books.

Milz, V. (1980). First graders can write: Focus on communication. *Theory Into Practice, 14,* pp.179–185.

Mohr, M. (1987). *Working together: A guide for teacher researchers.* Urbana, Illinois: NCTE Publications.

Paley, V. *Wally's Stories.* Cambridge, MA: Harvard University Press, 1981.

Rowland, S. (1978). Notes from Sherard: Split-pins galore. *Outlook, 29,* 28–34.

References

Archambault, R. D., Ed. (1974). *John Dewey on Education.* Chicago: University of Chicago Press, Phoenix Edition.

Armstrong, M. (1980). *Closely observed children: The diary of a primary classroom.* London: Writers and Readers.

Bohstedt, J. (1979). Old tales for young tellers. *Outlook, 33,* 31–45.

Britton, J. (1983). A quiet form of research. *English Journal, 72,* 89–92.

Burton, F. (1985). *The Reading-writing connection: A one year teacher-as-researcher study of third-fourth grade writers and their literary experiences.* Unpublished doctoral dissertation, The Ohio State University.

Burton, F. (1986). Research concurrents: A teacher's conception of the action research process. *Language Arts, 63,* 718–723.

Carini, P. (1979). *The art of seeing and the visibility of the person.* Grand Forks, ND: University of North Dakota Press.

Corey, S. M. (1953). *Action research to improve school practices.* New York: Teachers College Press.

Corey, S. M. (1954) Action research in education. *Journal of Educational Research, 47,* 375–380.

Dewey, J. (1974) Why reflective thinking must be an educational aim. In R. D. Archambault (Ed.), *John dewey on education.* Chicago: University of Chicago Press.

Freire, P. (1985). Reading the world and reading the world: an interview with Paulo Freire. *Language Arts, 62,* 15–21.

Jackson, P. (1968). *Life in classrooms.* New York: Holt, Rinehart, and Winston.

Longstreet, W. (1982). Action research: a paradigm. *Educational Forum, 46,* 135–158.

May, N. (1982). The teacher-as-researcher movement in Britain. In W. and A. Schubert (Eds.), *Conceptions of curriculum knowledge: Focus on students and teachers.* Published by Special Interest Group on the Creation and Utilization of Curriculum Knowledge.

Schutz, A. (1967). *The phenomenology of the social world.* (G. Walsh & F. Lehnert, Trans.). Evanston, IL: Northwestern University Press.

Shumsky, A. (1958). *The action research way of learning: an approach to in-service education.* New York: Teachers College Bureau of Publications.

Stenhouse, L. (1975). *Introduction to curriculum research and development.* London: Heinemann Education Books.

Stenhouse, L. (1981). What counts are research? *British Journal of Educational Studies, 29,* 103–114.

Stewart, D. & Mickunas, A. (1974). *Exploring phenomenology.* Chicago: American Library Association.

Vallance, E. (1982). The practical uses of curriculum theory. *Theory Into Practice, 21,* 4–10.

Van Manen, M. (1984, April). *Action research as theory of the unique: from pedagogic thoughtfulness to pedagogic tactfulness.* Paper presented at the annual meeting of the American Educational Research Association, New Orleans.

Wann, D. (1952). Teachers as researchers. *Educational Leadership, 9,* 489–495.

·15·

CLASSROOM-BASED STUDIES

Dolores Durkin

Commonly, undergraduate programs in education get students who are prospective teachers into classrooms as soon as possible on the assumption that contacts with reality area a source of important information. Observations that are not preceded by adequate preparation, however, lead the most perceptive of the undergraduates to conclude, "I see, but I do not understand."

Because seeing is not always complemented with understanding in classroom-based studies, this chapter explores some ways to achieve understanding. Why changing classroom practices with the intention of improving them is anything but easy is the last topic covered. Only a few studies are cited to serve as illustrations of the various types covered here.

DESCRIPTIVE STUDIES

It would be difficult to dispute the contention that the best way to learn how language arts is taught is through classroom observation. The first group of classroom studies, describing writing in secondary schools, was selected because the chief investigator, Arthur Applebee, did not stop at one study, which is all too common; nor did he rely only on classroom observations to collect data.

The second group of descriptive studies is commonly referred to as the "school effectiveness" research. Even though these widely-known, highly influential studies have been reviewed extensively, they are dealt with here because, unlike Applebee, those conducting the studies were as interested in measuring the outcomes of classroom practices as they were in the practices themselves. When compared, the two groups of studies also serve well in showing that the words "effective" and "improvement" have anything but uniform definitions.

Writing in Secondary Schools

The studies directed by Applebee (1981) started with observations in two high schools. One was a comprehensive city

school; the other, a university-sponsored laboratory school. The observations, which began in October, 1979, and ended in April, 1980, added up to 13,293 minutes. Findings led Applebee to conclude, "Across subjects and grades, the typical writing assignments is a page or less . . . completed within a day (either in class or taken home to finish), and serving an examining function" (p. 99).

Other informative comments are in another report of the same study (Applebee, Lehr, & Auten, 1981) and include the following:

Prewriting: "In a typical assignment, just over three minutes elapsed from the time the teachers began to discuss or pass out the assignment until students began writing" (p. 80).
Writing: "If prewriting activities were limited, those designed to help students while they were writing were almost nonexistent. . . . This may be because many assignments functioned as tests of subjects rather than explorations of new material" (p. 80).
Editing: "Errors in mechanics were the most frequent focus of (teachers') responses" (p. 81).

Applebee and his colleagues continued to study writing in secondary schools with additional classroom observations as well as case studies (1986). Applebee says of this work, "The results from the various substudies converged to provide a remarkably consistent portrait of students' experiences in learning to write" (p. 98). Even when studies were conducted in school where the best instruction was likely to be found, the elements of process writing (e.g., prewriting discussions, peer response groups, editing sessions, and the presence of an audience) were mostly used in mechanistic ways, making them "just another series of practice exercises" (p. 103).

The secondary teachers continued to assign topics and purposes for writing, and to act not as collaborators but as evaluators also led Applebee to predict that process-oriented writing will never become a reality in classrooms if neither the role of the teacher nor the reasons for writing change.

As will be seen in the next section, Applebee's conception of improvement is at odds with the underlying school effectiveness research.

School Effectiveness Studies

Two events accounted for, or at least encouraged, the large number of studies grouped under the heading school effectiveness research. One was a charge that became common in the 1960s: Schools with large minority populations are minimally successful in helping students achieve academically. As is customary, academic achievement was described in relation to test scores, in particular, to reading scores. The other impetus was the well-known Coleman et al. report (1966), which claimed that schools are unable to overcome deficits related to out-of-school factors, and thus make little difference in the lives of a substantial number of students.

Fostered by the leadership of Ronald Edmonds (1979), a number of studies were undertaken to identify features of "schools that work" with poor minority students. Features that received considerable attention included: (1) a strong leader who is knowledgeable about reading and actively involved in the reading program, which is clearly articulated and systematically implemented; and (2) a faculty that has high expectations for students and gives special attention to reading and mathematics. Like the critics, the researchers equated success with high test scores.

Soon, others undertook similar studies that broadened the focus to include more than minority children and concentrated on classrooms. A well-publicized finding in this large collection of studies is that high scores on achievement tests are associated with such factors as:

1. Amount of direct instruction provided;
2. Amount of time students are "engaged" with academic activities; and
3. A teacher's effectivenss in managing a classroom and monitoring students' work. (Brophy & Good, 1986)

Even though the school effectiveness studies had obvious flaws, the widespread attention they received and the influence they wielded are to be expected, given the fact researchers showed that schools *can* make a difference, at least insofar as test scores are concerned. It is also possible that the frequency with which this sizable number of studies reported similar data assigned the findings more credence than they merited. Whatever the explanation, criticism soon mounted.

At first, the critics called attention to obvious flaws:

1. Correlational data do not explain what causes what;
2. Tests used to assess effectiveness are questionable, not only because of what they evaluate, but also because of what they do not examine;
3. Group scores mask individual differences, which means that schools might not have been effective with sizable numbers of students;
4. Assigning importance to something like "time on task" is meaningless unless the nature of the tasks is known;

5. Failure to distinguish between data that originated in classroom observations and data that came from less reliable sources, such as questionnaires, makes it impossible to know whether a close match exists between what actually took place in the classrooms and what was assumed to have taken place.

Later, it was only natural to wonder about the stability of the effectiveness over time.

Still later, more questions were raised including those in an article by Good and Weinstein (1986). One of their concerns will be discussed because it moves beyond descriptions of what is observed in classrooms to thoughts about explanations.

The concern involves the assumption that variables such as amount of direct instruction and tested outcomes have a linear relationship. If they do, the greater the amount of such instruction, the higher the scores.

Contrary to that view, Good and Weinstein suggest that nonlinear relationships may be much more common than is typically recognized. They propose that one nonlinear pattern is likely to be an "inverted *U*." With this pattern, "optimal student performance is associated with a certain level of a classroom process (or teacher behavior), so that teachers who exhibit too little or too much of this process have less positive effects on students than do teachers who use the right amount" (p. 1094). The authors continue, "Many school-effect variables probably have nonlinear relationships, but the paucity of observational data (in the school effectivenss research) makes it impossible to assess the claim.... Unfortunately, too many advocates of change based on the school effectiveness literature assume linear relationships—if a little is good, more is certain to be better" (p. 1094).

DESCRIPTIVE AND EXPLANATORY RESEARCH

Support for "the more the better" is apparent in a classroom-observation study of kindergartens where the objective was learning how children are prepared to read or how to teach reading itself (Durkin, 1987). Because a second goal was to identify what was or was not done with reading in the 42 classes observed, this study illustrates classroom-observation research that attempts to explain as well as describe what is seen. What cannot be overlooked as the study is reviewed is that it is impossible for any researcher to know with certainty whether what appears to be explanations tell the whole story or, even, whether the story reflects facts, perceptions, or excuses.

Before the study of kindergartens is reviewed, attention should be focused on what are sometimes called "constraints" (Duffy & Roehler, 1986), because it was the identification of constraints under which the kindergarten teachers worked that shed light on why they did what they were observed to be doing.

Constraints

Constraints are factors or forces that affect what teachers do or do not do in classrooms. At first glance, constraint may appear to have only negative consequences. For that reason, it must be kept in mind that in addition to preventing teachers from doing what is desirable, constraints also function in keeping them from doing what is undesirable. Used here, then, constraints may have positive or negative consequences.

Constraints can be divided into external forces (outside the classroom) and internal (inside the classroom) forces. External constraints include expectations that originate with administrators, teachers, and parents, and the means used by a school system to evaluate student progress and teacher effectiveness. In recent years, external constraints that originate in state- and federally-mandated programs and tests are too visible to overlook.

Internal constraints that derive from teachers themselves include their knowledge both of what can be taught and what needs to be taught to a particular group of students; their overall teaching ability, along with a willingness to work and plan; their willingness and ability to change when that is likely to result in doing something better; and their ability in class management. How teachers themselves define "effective teacher" is of considerable influence, too.

Internal constraints also have to do with students, which explains why it is not uncommon, nor undesirable, for teachers to change some of their behaviors from year to year. Examples of internal constraints that originate in students include their age, ability, motivation, interests, and past experiences in school. Class size is yet another internal constraint.

When reading instruction is the concern, basal reader series often fall into both categories of constraints (Shannon, 1987). More specifically, when teachers are asked why they use basal programs to decide both what to teach and how to teach it, a common explanation is that such use is mandated by a school or district. On the other hand, when administrators are questioned about faculty dependence on basal materials, they often describe it as the teachers' own choice.

Such discrepancies need to be kept in mind when the kindergarten study referred to earlier is summarized in the following section in a framework that highlights constraints.

Kindergarten Study: Illustrative Constraints

That external and internal constraints affect how classroom time is spent is clearly illustrated with findings from the observation study of 42 kindergarten classes. The same study also demonstrates that understanding the reasons that lie behind what goes on in classrooms typically requires information sources other than observations.

Given the purpose of the study, the most apparent and influential constraint was comercial materials designed to initiate phonics instruction. Their pervasive influence on reading instruction was supported by the fact that what was taught and how it was taught in all 42 classes adhered closely to the materials, in this case, to reading readiness workbooks in basal reader series. This meant the phonics instruction was decontextualized. That is, learning sounds was not related to figuring out the identity of unfamiliar written words but to the names of pictures and objects.

Also observed was the kindergarten teachers' reliance on whole class instruction to teach phonics. The fact that directing instruction to large numbers of 5-year-olds created a restless, inattentive audience, combined with the equally clear fact that the children varied in ability, hardly helped to explain the reliance on whole class teaching.

As it turned out, explanations for much of what was seen came from interviews held with the teachers after they had been observed. A few reported sources of influence are listed below in the context of constraints:

External Constraints

1. The need to mark reading readiness items on the kindergarten report card, which corresponded closely to the content covered in the readiness workbooks.
2. Expectations of first-grade teachers that all the sounds the readiness workbooks presented would be taught so that the first preprimer in the basal series could be used at the beginning of first grade.

Internal Constraints

1. The kindergarten teachers' lack of experience in teaching reading.
2. The belief that kindergarten children are not ready to learn to read. (Because the phonics instruction in the workbooks did so little with words, it was considered to be readiness, not reading instruction.)
3. Absence of a teacher's aide made whole class instruction necessary.

It is likely the interviews would never have yielded the information they did had the kindergarten teachers not been observed earlier. In fact, it has been demonstrated that teachers' own accounts of what they do in their classrooms are not a reliable source of information (Rosenshine, 1978). On the other hand, what the observers in the kindergarten study saw would not have been understood had the interviews been omitted. All of this supports the contention that combinations of different sources of data are usually required when the goal of a study is to learn not only what occurs in classrooms but also why it occurs. Understanding what accounts for what is seen is essential, should it be concluded that what is observed needs to be changed.

INCREASED KNOWLEDGE: AN IMPETUS FOR CHANGE

Anyone who keeps up with the literature knows that a sizable number of classroom-based studies have been, and are being, done for the purpose of changing and presumably improving classroom practices. This is noticeably true for practices dealing with reading comprehension. That topic, therefore, will serve to underscore with three examples how increased knowledge has moved researchers toward efforts to reform classroom practices in numbers that are unprecedented.

The three examples pertain to

1. What is done during the reading period, presumably, to add to students' abilities to comprehend;
2. What is done when content subjects are taught, presumably, to help students learn content; and
3. What is done with poor readers, presumably to remedy deficiencies.

The underlying theme of the following three sections is that the large number of intervention studies being reported indicates not that classroom practices have deteriorated but that researchers have gotten smarter. In addition, in recent years, articles about writing, especially about that of younger children have been as common as reports about comprehension. Thus far, however, case studies of individuals or small groups have been the primary methods used for learning what is done with writing as well as for reforming it. The fact that the director and one of the codirectors of The Center for the Study of Writing have both underscored the need to broaden the focus of writing research (Hays, 1986; Freedman, 1986) suggests that classroom studies should be forthcoming.

Reading Comprehension

Even though the popularity of classroom-based research is relatively new (Fillion & Brause, 1987), the relatively few studies undertaken earlier to learn what is done to teach reading (e.g., Durkin, 1974, 1975) revealed practices that duplicated our own experiences in acquiring reading ability: Once elementary school students are able to read, teachers tend to spend much of the reading period assigning students selections to read, assessing comprehension afterwards with numerous questions, and assigning and checking large numbers of practice exercises originating in workbooks and ditto sheets. Even though some educators lamented this use of time, the criticism was too little and too quiet to stir up much attention.

All that changed starting in the late 1970s when researchers studying comprehension began to stress the importance not only of teaching students how to comprehend but also of preparing them for reading by activating, or adding to, relevant knowledge and by establishing purposes for the reading that, in turn, allow for comprehension monitoring. With these reports, data about what is done in classrooms (Durkin, 1978, 1979) that were similar to what was reported earlier now won widespread attention. In turn, large numbers of classroom-based intervention studies were begun and continue to be reported (Pearson & Dole, 1987).

Content Subject Instruction

Our own experiences as students are enough to verify that instruction in such areas as social studies has traditionally concentrated on covering content, and that a common means for achieving the goal was a round-robin reading of the text followed by, or interspersed with, assessment questions. Again, little attention went to these practices until researchers began in the 1970s to report data about the nature of expository text structure, including the existence of inconsiderate text; about the influence on comprehension of knowing about text structure; and about such aids to comprehending as semantic webbing and semantic feature analysis. The availability of these reports explains why classroom-observation studies of content-subject instruction (e.g, Durkin, 1978, 1979; Pearson & Gallagher, 1983) won attention in the 1980s, even though they describe what existed for some time. In this case, subsequent reform efforts with classroom-based research have concentrated on a great variety of ways to help students learn how to learn from expository text.

Procedures Used with the Lowest Reading Groups

Again, anyone familiar with classrooms knows that the work done with the poorest readers commonly includes the use of overly difficult material read aloud in round-robin reading fashion. Because of the difficulty, classroom observers hear many interruptions during the reading caused by words that cannot be read or are read incorrectly.

More specific information from classroom-observation studies, especially those done by Richard Allington (1977, 1980, 1983), indicates that more instructional time is spent on individual words than on the meaning of connected text, and that literal comprehension questions are sometimes the only kind used. Allington (1983) also found that students in higher-level reading groups read about three times as many words per day as do the poorer readers, even when each group receives approximately equal instructional time.

Placed in juxtaposition with what are now thought to be the cognitive processes underlying reading, the following summary account of work done with poor readers (Shannon, 1985) clarifies once more why calls for reform and intervention studies are common:

... students in low groups are often placed in difficult materials in which they misread at least one in every ten words. This difficulty inhibits low group students' use of context, forces them to read word by words, and makes them rely on phonic characteristics of unknown words. Their frequent mistakes trigger student and teacher interruptions, and the unfortunate cycle begins anew. (p. 608)

CLASSROOM-BASED INTERVENTION STUDIES

The purpose of this final section is not to review intervention studies prompted by newer conceptions of the comprehension process; that would require far more pages than were allotted to the whole of the chapter. Instead, the more circumscribed goal is to identify a few characteristic flaws in recent intervention studies, some of which are rooted in the fact that every classroom is a highly complex social community.

Typical Intervention Studies

Were the description "intervention study" confined to research in which the goal is to alter certain practices not just for a brief amount of time but until other practices thought to be more effective are identified, the number of such studies would be reduced substantially. This is so because the pattern of researcher behavior is to introduce a new presumably better, way of doing something, to evaluate the outcomes, to compare the outcomes with those of the "customary" way of working, and to report the findings. Whether negative results are reported as consistently as positive outcomes is impossible to know.

Efforts to do a little better have teachers rather than researchers implement the experimental procedure. The teachers may also use the new way of working for a longer amount of time than is common. Even when these improvements are made, classroom observations are not always used to learn whether the teachers are carrying out the new procedures correctly and consistently. This is a serious omission because, as researchers such as Duffy and Roehler (1986) have learned, teachers sometimes use an experimental procedure only at the time they are observed. Whenever classroom observations are a part of a research design, another but related problem is the common requirement to let teachers know ahead of time when they will be observed.

Noticeable by their absence in practically all the current intervention studies are attempts by researchers to learn whether teachers continue to use what is demonstrated to be effective, once the official study ends. Such an omission bypasses an opportunity to learn what is involved in bringing about altered behavior that lasts longer than the duration of a study.

Problems in Achieving Long-Term Change

My own experience as a reformer suggest that much more is required to change teachers' behavior than is either acknowledged or implied in reports of intervention studies. Part of the complexity of realizing change was referred to in the earlier discussion of constraints. A brief review of other impediments to reform brings the chapter to a close. A number of researchers have written about the complex nature of changing teacher behavior, for instance, Barr (1986) and Duffy (1982). An effort was made, therefore, not to repeat any of the excellent points stated elsewhere.

To begin, the fact that humans do not change unless they want to change cannot be dismissed from the mind of any serious informer. Basic to successful efforts to achieve long-term improvement, therefore, are teachers who are convinced that something other than what they customarily do might be better. Such conviction can be considered authentic only when the person is aware of the requirements of a proposed change.

Reformers also need to recognize that having teachers try alternative procedures or materials for purposes of a study is essentially different from their continuing to use them. This is true for many reasons including the fact that, in the first instance, the researcher is available to serve as the scapegoat should outcomes not be positive. At a time when the outcomes of schooling are carefully, sometimes publicly, scrutinized, taking risks when no scapegoat is available is hardly appealing.

Not appealing to teachers, either is the increased amount of work that may be required to continue using a new teaching method. It is particularly unappealing when the reward system in a school is such that extra effort is not among the variables considered when decisions are made about salary increments.

Extra work is likely to be viewed differently when the whole of a faculty is involved in a reform movement. In such cases, industry seems natural—that is, is part of what is expected of everyone. Knowing that improvements made at one grade level will not be disregarded at subsequent levels is important, too, and is yet another reason to have faculty-wide participation.

And this leads to the last point that will be made. Only when researchers are committed to long-term efforts to work with a faculty is there any chance of achieving long-lasting change and, presumably, long-lasting improvement. Ideally, too, a member of the school administration will be actively involved, because it is his or her interest and commitment that keeps the momentum going; that can assure regularly scheduled faculty meetings to discuss what is being undertaken; and that can permit classroom observations done for the purpose of learning whether recommended changes have been internalized in ways that allow for consistent implementation. Smith-Burke (1987) alludes to the complexity of successful reform efforts when she states, "It takes long-term inservice training and a great deal of support to help teachers begin to revise their teaching . . ." (p. 239).

References

Allington, R. L. (1977). If they don't read, how they ever gonna get good? *Journal of Reading, 21,* 57–61.

Allington, R. L. (1980). Teacher interruption behaviors during primary-grade oral reading. *Journal of Educational Psychology, 72,* 371–377.

Allington, R. L. (1983). The reading instruction provided readers of differing reading abilities. *Elementary School Journal, 83,* 548–559.

Applebee, A. N. (1981). Writing in the secondary school (NCTE Research Report No. 21). Urbana, IL: National Council of Teachers of English.

Applebee, A. N. (1986). Problems in process approaches: Toward a reconceptualization of process instruction. In A. R. Petrosky & D. Bartholomae (Eds.), *The teaching of writing,* Eighty-fifty Yearbook of the National Society of Education, Part II. Chicago, IL: University of Chicago Press.

Applebee, A. N., Lehr, F., & Auten, A. (1981, Sept.) Learning to write in the secondary school: How and where. *English Journal, 70* September, 78–82.

Barr, R. (1986). Studying classroom reading instruction. *Reading Research Quarterly 21*(3), 231–236.

Brophy, J., & Good, T. L. (1986). Teacher behavior and student achievement. In M. C. Wittrock (Ed.), *Handbook of research on teaching,* (3rd ed.), New York: Macmillan, 328–375.

Coleman, J. S., Campbell, E. Q., Hobson, C. J., McPartland, J. M., Weinfield, F. D., & York, R. L. (1966). *Equality of educational opportunity.* Washington, D.C.: U.S. Government Printing Office.

Duffy, G., & Roehler, L. (1986). Constraints on teacher change. *Journal of Teacher Education, 37,* 55–58.

Durkin, D. (1974, 1975). A six year study of children who learned to read in school at the age of four. *Reading Research Quarterly, 10*(1), 9–61.

Durkin, D. (1978, 1979). What classroom obsrevations reveal about reading comprehension instruction. *Reading Research Quarterly, 14*(4), 481–533.

Durkin, D. (1987). A classroom-observation study of reading instruction in kindergarten. *Early Childhood Research Quarterly, 2*(3), 275–300.

Edmonds, R. (1979). Some schools work and more can. *Social Policy, 9,* 28–32.

Fillion, B., & Brause, R. S. (1987). Research into classroom practices: What have we learned and where are we going? In J. R. Squire (Ed.), *The dynamics of language learning.* Urbana, IL: ERIC Clearinghouse on Reading and Communication Skills, 201–225.

Good, T. L., & Weinstein, R. S. (1986). Schools make a difference: Evidence, criticisms, and new directions. *American Psychologist, 41*(10), 1090–1097.

Pearson, P. D., & Dole, J. A. (1987). Explicit comprehension instruction: A review of research and a new conceptualization of instruction. *Elementary School Journal, 88,* 151–165.

Pearson, P. D., & Gallagher, M. C. (1983). The instruction of reading comprehension (Technical Report No. 297). Urbana: University of Illinois, Center for the Study of Reading.

Rosenshine, B. V. (1978). Review of teaching styles and pupil progress. *American Educational Research Journal, 15,* 163–169.

Shannon, P. (1987). Commercial reading materials, a technological ideology, and the deskilling of teachers. *Elementary School Journal, 87,* 307–329.

Shannon, P. (1985). Reading instruction and social class. *Language Arts, 62,* 604–613.

Smith-Burke, M. T. (1987). Classroom practices and classroom interaction during reading instruction: What's going on? In J. R. Squire (Ed.), *The dynamics of language learning.* Urbana, IL: ERIC Clearinghouse on Reading and Communication Skills, 226–265.

· 16 ·

SYNTHESIS RESEARCH IN LANGUAGE ARTS INSTRUCTION

Carl B. Smith
Susan S. Klein*

When William S. Gray was cataloging reading research more than 50 years ago, do you think he could have foreseen the explosion of research in language arts since the end of World War II? Gray's annual summaries of research became a major contribution to the profession, and the annual summary of research in reading has been carried forward over the past 20 years by Sam Weintraub and his associates. Today, it is almost inconceivable that a language-arts dissertation or major study would not make use of current annual summaries in reading, English, and instruction.

Summaries and syntheses of research hold treasures for many people besides those who are writing their dissertations. Teachers and administrators who wrestle with daily decisions about curriculum and instruction can find guidance in documents that examine research across numerous studies on the same issue. This chapter defines synthesis research and offers criteria for judging the value of a synthesis paper. It also gives examples of language-arts synthesis documents in categories that may be useful to teachers.

Knowledge synthesis is here defined as a cluster of activities often called literature review, research review, interpretive analysis, integrative review, research integration, meta-analysis, state of the art summarizing, evaluation synthesis, or best evidence synthesis. It involves pulling together related extant knowledge from research, evaluation, and practice on specified topics or issues.

WHERE TO START

English language-arts education has so many individual pieces of research that it is difficult for individuals to know where to start when they examine research questions. Under the broad headings of reading, writing, and teaching language arts, each one could generate 10,000 studies, assuming a person had access to all the major research data bases, such as ERIC, Psychological Abstracts, Education Index, and so on. Modern computerized search techniques make it possible to refine a library search and thus limit the available studies to the specific interests of the researcher. One can then locate documents that pertain to a question about "the value of prewriting activities on composition performance in the junior high school," and similar narrowly defined topics. But even then, the list of available studies may far exceed the time or the energy that the researcher can devote to analyzing all material. That's where synthesis research enters the picture.

As the number of studies on a particular topic multiply, it becomes increasingly valuable to have and to use resources that summarize or synthesize that research. There, for example, the annual summary of research in English and the annual summary of research in reading become invaluable. For the same reason handbooks, such as this one, and the *Handbook on Reading Research,* offer educators summarized and synthesized views of the broad literature. Besides the pertinent studies that answer an individual's research question directly, it is helpful to have the same question seen in a broader perspective through the summaries prepared by individuals and by organizations such as federally funded educational labs and the ERIC/ Reading and Communication Skills Clearinghouse.

Cyclical trends in education remind educators of the value of reviewing past research as well as present studies. Doctoral dissertations, for instance, could serve the profession well through their literature reviews by offering syntheses of the top-

*The ideas in this chapter from Dr. Klein are based on "Research and Practice: Implications for Knowledge Synthesis in Education" (Klein, 1989) and do not necessarily reflect the views of her employer, the U.S. Department of Education.

ics under consideration and by placing these topics in historical perspective. An historical view of a particular issue might reveal the manner in which old questions keep arising and how research has changed our perception or knowledge of a particular issue. The use of children's literature in the curriculum, for example, and the integration of the language arts were major concerns in the early 1960s and became issues again in the 1980s. A synthesis of that research over those 25 years can give insight into the similarities and the differences of those two issues in two separated decades. Merely reading a half-dozen studies of recent vintage would deprive the researcher of an important perspective and might limit the value of his or her conclusions.

In an article on how to use research evidence from many studies, Light and Pillemer (1984) suggest two major strategies for synthesis research and conflict resolution: "One strategy is to read through the various findings and reach a series of impressionistic conclusions. A second approach is to apply precise analytic procedures to the collection of studies." Among the specific benefits of synthesizing data, they found that it increases the power of the data. It is well known that the larger the sample size, the more likely an effect will be detected as statistically significant. By pooling the information from a number of smaller studies into a single analysis, it is possible to improve the power of statistical tests. As an example, Light and Pillemer discussed two studies that measured the number of books in a child's home and correlated that information with the child's achievement test scores. In the first study, which included homes having mostly fewer than 200 books, there was no noticeable effect on school performance. But when they added a second study asking the same question, they found a significant effect as the number of books in the home rose into the 200 to 400 range. Then there was a significant increase in the achievement scores (p. 181). As the number of books in a home pushed beyond 200, there was a corresponding increase in school grades. But those effects were noticeable only when the data from the two studies were meshed together.

Another value of synthesis research is that it helps us to view conflict in a constructive way. Suppose that two studies reveal conflicting outcomes. Synthesis research gives us an opportunity to look for explanations about divergent findings. Were the treatments different in some significant way? Were data collected in a similar fashion? Were the populations different? Thus, conflict acts as a a warning to the reviewer, indicating that a more detailed analysis needs to be conducted. Pillemer and Light suggest that an investigator may find a resolution to conflict in other content areas where similar studies have been conducted.

PURPOSES OF KNOWLEDGE SYNTHESIS

The general purposes of knowledge synthesis are:

1. To increase the knowledge base by identifying new insights, needs, and research agenda that are related to specific topics;

2. To improve access to evidence in a given area by distilling and reducing large amounts of information efficiently and effectively;

3. To help readers make informed decisions or choices by increasing their understanding of the syntheses topic; and

4. To provide a comprehensive, well-organized content base to facilitate interpretation activities such as the development of textbooks, training tools, guidelines, information digests, oral presentations, and videotapes

In the 1975 *Catalog of NIE Education Projects,* Spencer Ward categorized 72 of the 660 catalog entries as knowledge synthesis products. Most of these knowledge synthesis products were developed by the ERIC Clearinghouses and Research and Development (R&D) Centers and Laboratories (Ward, 1976, p. 12). A recent search of the Office of Educational Research and Improvement/National Institute of Education (OERI/NIE) project information database from 1979 to 1988, indicates a wide variety of knowledge synthesis projects ranging from an inexpensive commissioned paper to an elaborate meta-analysis.

An examination of the ERIC *Resources in Education* (RIE) database as of 1988, indicates that 2,030 U.S. Department of Education sponsored documents were classified as Information Analysis Products and/or identified as knowledge synthesis, information analysis, literature review, meta-analysis, integrative analysis, integrative review, evaluation synthesis, or state of the art reviews. (Because all types of ERIC Clearinghouse produced documents are coded as ERIC Information Analysis Products, this total for knowledge synthesis documents is inflated.) This federal contribution represents 12 percent of all such knowledge synthesis documents in the ERIC RIE database. Putting this in a larger perspective, it is interesting to note that 6 percent of all documents in both the RIE (16,805) and *Current Index to Journals in Education* (CIJE) (20,891) ERIC database fit this broad knowledge synthesis definition.

In 1977, Ward addressed the problem of the uneven quality of synthesis papers by organizing a conference to plan follow-up research. Information on much of the subsequent R&D is described in *Knowledge Structure and Use: Implications for Synthesis and Interpretation* (Ward and Reed, 1983). In addition to developing useful synthesis products in a wide variety of areas ranging from mathematics to school desegregation, the NIE dissemination group developed models that use a consensus building process for synthesis work. The "Research Within Reach" series supported by this group demonstrated how a consensus process can be used to identify and respond to teachers' questions. The viability of this approach is indicated by *Research Within Reach: Secondary School Reading* (Alvermann, Moore, & Conley, 1988). The dissemination group's most recent R&D on knowledge synthesis was a project by Harris Cooper covering 1982 to 1985. Cooper surveyed knowledge synthesis producers (including authors of ERIC Information Analysis products). Survey questions addressed reviewers' content expertise, knowledge synthesis goals and procedures (Cooper, 1983, 1986a, 1986b, in press). Some of this work is also reflected in *The Integrative Research Review* (Cooper, 1984), which describes how general research methods may be used to guide knowledge synthesis work.

While researchers supported by the NIE Dissemination group used meta-analyses and other synthesis approaches for their substantive work, some researchers refined these methods or developed new synthesis approaches. For example, through his work at the Johns Hopkins R & D Centers, Robert Slavin (1986, 1987) developed a knowledge synthesis procedure called "best evidence synthesis." Numerous other researchers, such as Gregg Jackson, Robert Rich, Herbert Walberg, Richard Light, and their colleagues produced many synthesis products and wrote thoughtfully on the synthesis process (Light & Pillemer, 1984; Jackson, 1980; 1984; Rich, 1983; Walberg & Haertel, 1980).

WHAT HAS BEEN LEARNED ABOUT IMPROVING KNOWLEDGE SYNTHESIS?

The profession is starting to learn about the characteristics and potential indicators of quality knowledge synthesis because the federal government has funded a great deal of knowledge synthesis; and individuals are conducting some research on knowledge synthesis practices and examining R&D on knowledge synthesis.

The discussion of these characteristics and indicators will be grouped into four criteria clusters that are based on similar clusters developed by Klein (1976) for the review and selection of knowledge interpretation products such as instructional or training materials. Additional quality indicators were based on results from Klein's 1987 survey of ERIC Clearinghouse knowledge synthesis practices and criteria, a review of research on knowledge synthesis in education and related areas, and discussion with managers of knowledge synthesis work.

Intrinsic Qualities
The intrinsic quality of a knowledge synthesis document may be judged by experts. Often it is necessary to use different reviewers for these different criteria. For example, it may be advisable to have one or more experts in the content area covered, experts in the knowledge synthesis methodologies used, experts in writing, and educational equity experts for the social fairness criteria.
1. *Nature of Knowledge Synthesis Content.*
   Is the coverage sufficiently comprehensive and inclusive or at least representative?
   Is the evidence sufficiently central or pivotal to the topic? (Cooper, 1986b, p. 17)
   Is the topic not too small or too large for this comprehensive coverage? (Katz, 1986)
   Is the evidence (information) based on extant research, development, evaluation, and/or practice?
   Is the evidence sufficiently current and timely and of cutting edge interest?
   Are significant variables, assumptions, interactions, and analytic questions clearly defined and addressed?
   Are the evidence, analyses, syntheses, and conclusions accu-

rate and appropriately qualified and interpreted (i.e., with context, size and validity limitations) so that the reader will not reach wrong conclusions?
   Are the evidence and analyses free of bias with respect to particular views? However, it may be appropriate for the author(s) to take either a neutral or espousal position when stating conclusions and implications (Cooper, 1986b).
2. *Technical Quality.*
   Were appropriate knowledge synthesis methodological procedures for acquiring, evaluating, analyzing, combining, and describing exact evidence used—whether it was quantitative, qualitative or both?
   There are now many well developed procedures for various types of synthesis for quantitative and qualitative evidence. These are described in many guides on meta-analyses, a book on meta-ethnography (Noblit & Hare, 1988), articles on evaluation synthesis (Chelimsky & Morra, 1984; Slavin, 1986; 1987) and books on research review (Cooper, 1984; Light & Pillemer, 1984).
   Were these appropriate knowledge synthesis methodological procedures for acquiring, evaluating, analyzing, combining and explaining the evidence described in the body of the knowledge synthesis or in an easily accessible appendix?
   Were the context and assumptions for the analytic framework and relevant variables presented so that the syntheses of the evidence is meaningful?
   Was it clear whether the synthesis was intended to serve as an honest broker or advocate and whether it was intended to present evidence for alternatives or "best" solutions?
   Cooper (1985) pointed out that two of the seven AREA research review award winners from 1978 to 84 were espousal rather than neutral in their presentations.
   Is the information balanced in that it resolves, rather than obscures, inconsistencies in the evidence being synthesized? (See Cooper, 1986b, p. 7; Roberts, 1983, p. 479.)
3. *Social Fairness.*
   Does it adhere to standards for the elimination of social group bias?
   Does it report relevant information regarding sex, race, ethnicity, age, and socioeconomic status in evidence covered, and in the conclusions?
4. *Communications Quality.*
   Is the knowledge synthesis well written? Developed logically? Appropriately focused, clear, and organized for the intended readers? Internally congruent and consistent?
   Does it adhere to document design guidelines for clear writing such as those discussed by Landesman and Reed (1983)?
   Is the level of detail (parsimony) and terminology appropriate for key audiences?
   "As reviewers move from addressing specialized researchers to addressing the general public, they em-

ploy less jargon and detail while often paying greater attention to the implications of the work being covered." (Cooper, 1985, p. 7)

Does it adhere to professional writing standards such as appropriate use of the American Psychological Association style manual, use of requested type size, format, length, permissions relating to copyrighted material, and so on, needed by the publisher?

Is it dry and mechanical, or interesting and stimulating?

Are creative formats such as discussing the evidence in terms of alternatives, or in terms of user questions and answers used when appropriate?

Desirability, Utility, Effectiveness

These criteria can be judged by potential and actual users of the knowledge synthesis.

1. *Desirability.*

Is there a need or demand for a current knowledge synthesis on a given topic or would the work be redundant with existing syntheses?

Is there a sufficiently large evidence base that would involve many institutions and states?

Is the knowledge synthesis likely to address its intended purposes such as increasing knowledge in an area?

Do those who are sponsoring the knowledge synthesis work, or doing it, feel that the topic is educationally significant?

2. *Utility/Practicality.*

Is the product appropriate for its intended users such as specialized scholars, general scholars, practitioners, policy makers or general public? (Dervin, 1983)

Is the knowledge synthesis presented in a physically appealing way so that recipients will want to read it?

Is the knowledge synthesis product user friendly? For example, is it appropriately selfcontained so that its use does not depend heavily on other resources?

Is the size of the topic manageable in terms of user comprehension? (Katz, 1986).

Is the knowledge synthesis formatted and developed in such a way that it will be accessible to potential users (i.e., a chapter in a handbook or encyclopedia article, or published as an easily available monograph, book, or review journal article?)

Is the knowledge synthesis appropriately marketed or better yet, distributed for a sufficiently low cost or for free? (It may be possible to judge user satisfaction to some extent based on sales, but purchases may be limited because of a "thin market" audience or because the document is not part of an established "product line.")

Is the knowledge synthesis appropriately linked to one or more knowledge interpretation efforts to increase its visibility and potential utility?

Does the knowledge synthesis contain a sufficient amount of appropriate interpretations?

> Research suggests that the utility of the knowledge synthesis is generally increased by clear interpretations (Cooper, 1986b), but such interpretations may

simplify the information so that scholarly detail is omitted.

3. *Effectiveness.*

Can the users comprehend the knowledge synthesis and remember what they have read?

Is there any evidence that the readers learned from the knowledge synthesis as indicated by cognitive or behavioral tests?

Is there any evidence that the readers confirmed or changed their attitudes about a topic based on the knowledge synthesis?

To what extent was knowledge synthesis information used in knowledge interpretations or for direct decision making?

To what extent was knowledge synthesis information used to supplement the working knowledge of the reader? (Kennedy, 1983)

To what extent has the knowledge synthesis been cited in other work?

Knowledge Synthesis Development Options

Aside from adhering to the logical technical synthesis procedures suggested in the intrinsic quality criteria, little is known about what constitutes an effective knowledge synthesis process. Thus, the following are provided as exploratory questions rather than quality indicators.

1. *Who Should Do the Knowledge Synthesis?*

Experts in the content area? Multidisciplinary experts? Experts in synthesis methodology? Experts in writing for specific audiences? Potential knowledge synthesis users? A combination of any of these?

2. *Should Multiple Individuals or Groups be Involved in the Synthesis Process?*

Does the use of multiple participants increase the credibility of the work? (Ward, 1983, p. 553).

If so, should the synthesis process be structured for consensus development and iterative reviews, collaborative work, or adversarial work? (Klein, Gold, Stalford, 1986; Stalford, 1987)

Glaser (1980, p. 79) suggested the value of developing a state of the art consensus document by iterative reviews and revisions of the drafts by multiple contributors.

Vian and Johansen (1983, p. 494) suggested ways that computer conferencing may be used for collaborative synthesis work.

Should the synthesis process be structured to obtain guidance from specific audiences such as potential knowledge synthesis users?

3. *What Systematic Knowledge Synthesis Processes are Best?*

Chelimsky and Morra (1984, p. 78) note that one of the characteristics of evaluation synthesis is "that designing backward from the information needed is both feasible and likely to ensure the relevance, timeliness, and use of the work performed." This approach differs from some research syntheses where the topic is determined based on the availability of the data.

CONCLUSIONS

The questions and criteria provided above can help individuals evaluate a particular document. Since purpose, breadth of coverage, and the nature of the analysis all contribute to the value of a synthesis paper, those criteria should be applied as appropriate.

When an important decision about instruction or curriculum development needs to be made about language arts, the decision-makers want information. Knowledge synthesis documents offer that kind of summary information. Whether the issue concerns children with specific reading disabilities, process writing strategies, the effect of using children's fiction in a reading program, or the impact of sociocultural influences, there are synthesis studies available. Appended to this chapter are samples of synthesis documents arranged in several frequently used categories. They include only a small fraction of the synthesis papers available in the ERIC database and are presented here merely to indicate the variety that might be useful to language arts educators. (A more complete list of language-arts synthesis references is available as a published bibliography from ERIC/RCS, Indiana University, Bloomington, IN 47405.)

References

Alvermann, D., Moore, D., & Conley, M. (Eds.). (1988). *Research within reach: Secondary school reading.* Newark, DE: International Reading Association. (ED 282 187).

Chelimsky, E. & Morra, L. G. (1984). Evaluation synthesis for the legislative user (chap. 5). In W. H. Yeaton, & P. M. Wortman (Eds.), *Issues in Data Synthesis.* In New Directions for Program Evaluation, Evaluation Research Society (pp. 75–89). Washington, D.C.: Jossey-Bass.

Cooper, H. (1984). *The integrative research review: A systematic approach,* Applied Social Research Methods Series, (Vol. 2). Newbury Park, CA: Sage Publications.

Cooper, H. (1986a). Literature-searching strategies of integrative research reviewers. A first survey. *Knowledge Creation, Diffusion, Utilization* (pp. 372–383).

Cooper, H. (1986b). Moving beyond meta-analysis. Paper presented at a conference Workshop on the Future of Meta-analysis sponsored by the National Committee on Statistics, Oct. 19–21, Hedgeville, WV.

Cooper, H. (1983). Six reviews of research on desegregation and black achievement: What they tell about knowledge synthesis. Paper presented at the American Educational Research Association Annual Meeting, Montreal, Canada.

Cooper, H. (1985). A taxonomy of literature reviews. Paper presented at the annual meeting of the American Educational Research Association, Chicago.

Dervin, B. (1983). Information as a user construct: The relevance of perceived information needs to synthesis and interpretation. In S. A. Ward, & L. J. Reed (Eds.), *Knowledge Structure and Use: Implications for Synthesis and Interpretation* (pp. 153–184). Philadelphia: Temple University Press.

Glaser, E. M. (1980). Using behavioral science strategies for defining the state-of-the-art. *The Journal of Applied Behavioral Science, 16,* 79–92.

Jackson, G. B., (1980). Methods for Integrative Reviews. *Reviews of Educational Research, 50*(3), 438–460.

Katz, L. G. (1986). Issues in the dissemination of child development knowledge. *Professionalism, Child Development, and Dissemination: Three Papers,* ERIC Clearinghouse on Elementary and Early Childhood Education.

Kennedy, M. M. (1983). Working knowledge. *Knowledge, Creation, Diffusion, Utilization, 5*(2), 193–211.

Klein, S. S. (1976). Toward consensus on minimum criteria for educational products. *Criteria for Reviewing Educational Products* (1978). Educational Products Information Exchange Institute and the ERIC Clearinghouse on Information Resources, Syracuse, NY. (ED147318)

Klein, S. S., Gold, N. & Stalford, C. (1986). The convening process: A new technique for applying knowledge to practice. *Educational Evaluation and Policy Analysis, 8*(2), 189–204.

Klein, S. S. (1989). Research and Practice: Implications for Knowledge Synthesis in Education. Knowledge: Creation, Diffusion, Utilization. Vol. 11 No. 1 Sept. p. 58–78. Sage Publications, Inc.

Landesman, J., & Reed, L. (1983). How to write a synthesis document for educational practitioners. In S. A. Ward & L. J. Reed (Eds.), *Knowledge Structure and Use: Implications for Synthesis and Interpretation* (pp. 576–642). Philadelphia: Temple University Press.

Light, R. J., & Pillemer, D. B. (1984). *Summing up: The science of reviewing research.* Cambridge, MA: Harvard University Press.

National Institute of Education. (1975). *Catalog of NIE Education Products* (Vols. 1 & 2). U.S. Department of Health, Education and Welfare, Washington, DC.

Noblit, G. W., & R. D. Hare. (1988). Meta-ethnography: synthesizing qualitative studies. Qualitative Research Methods Series. Newbury Park, CA: Sage Publications.

Rich (1983). Knowledge Synthesis and Problem Solving. In S. A. Ward & L. J. Reed (Eds.), *Knowledge Structure and Use: Implications for Synthesis and Interpretation* (pp. 285–312). Phildelphia: Temple University Press.

Roberts, J. (1983). Quick turnaround synthesis/interpretation for practitioners. In S. A. Ward & L. J. Reed (Eds.), Knowledge Structure and Use: Implications for synthesis and interpretation (pp. 423–486). Philadelphia: Temple University Press.

Slavin, R. E. (1986). Best-evidence synthesis: An alternative to meta-analytic and traditional reviews, *Educational Researcher, 15* (9), November, 5–11.

Slavin, R. E. (1987). Best-evidence synthesis: Why less is more. *Educational Researcher,* 16(4), 15.

Stalford, C. B. (1987). Congruence in theory and practice: The convening process and the consensus development program. *Knowledge: Creation, Diffusion, Utilization, 9*(1), 4–18.

Strike, K., & Posner, G. (1983). Epistemological problems in organizing social science knowledge for application. In S. A. Ward, & L. J. Reed (Eds.), *Knowledge Structure and Use: Implications for Synthesis and Interpretation.* (pp. 45–84). Philadelphia: Temple University Press.

Strike, K. & Posner, G. (1983). Types of synthesis and their criteria. In S. A. Ward & L. J. Reed (Eds.), *Knowledge Structure and Use: Implications for Synthesis and Interpretation.* (pp. 343–362). Philadelphia: Temple University Press.

Vian, K. & Johansen, R. (1983). Knowledge synthesis and computer-based communications systems: Chaging behaviors and concepts. In S. A. Ward & L. J. Reed (Eds.), *Knowledge Structure and Use: Implications for Synthesis and Interpretation.* (pp. 489–514). Philadelphia: Temple University Press.

Walberg, H. J. & Haertel, E. H. (Eds.). (1980). Research Integration: The state-of-the-art [Entire issue] Evaluation in Education, 4(1).

Ward, S. (1976). Summary of results of survey of current NIE synthesis activities. Memorandum to Harold Hodgkinson, Emerson Elliott and NIE Association Directors. March 1. National Institute of Education, Washington, D.C.

Ward, S. A. & Reed, L. J. (Eds.). (1983). *Knowledge Structure and Use: Implications for Synthesis and Interpretation.* Philadelphia: Temple University Press.

APPENDIX: REPRESENTATIVE SYNTHESIS DOCUMENTS

Reading

AN: EJ349079
AU: Dehart, Florence E.; Pauls, Leo W.
TI: Computerized Searches on Articles Reporting Reading Research: A Closer Look.
PY: 1987
JN: Reading Horizons; v27 n3 p209–17 Apr 1987
AV: UMI
DE: Databases; Language Usage; Online Searching; Psycholinguistics; Reading Instruction; Reading Research
ID: Computerized Search Services
AB: Compares the terminology used in three different computerized search services—CIJE, LLBA/Online, and PsycINFO—and shows how the choice of terminology used by them impedes retrieval. Suggests compensatory measures. (FL)

AN: ED276970
AU: Manning-Dowd, Alice
TI: The Effectiveness of SSR: A Review of the Research.
PY: [1985]
NT: 8 p.
PR: EDRS Price—MF01/PC01 Plus Postage
DE: Elementary Education; Research Needs
DE: Reading Attitudes; Reading Comprehension; Reading Instruction; Reading Research; Sustained Silent Reading; Teaching Methods
AB: In the past two decades, sustained silent reading (SSR) has gained attention as a component in many schools' reading programs. Some advocates of SSR differ slightly in their recommendations of specific rules, but most agree on the following guidelines: (1) no interruptions; (2) everyone reads, including the teacher; (3) students choose their own reading material; (4) no required reports; (5) a wide variety of reading materials should be available in the classroom; and (6) the time period should be increased gradually. Research conducted to determine the effects of SSR has produced mixed results, but most researchers seem to agree that SSR has a positive effect on reading comprehension and on students' attitudes about reading at all grade levels. However, research is less conclusive on the effect of SSR on students' reading achievement. of the studies considered, six found SSR to have a significant positive effect on reading scores, whereas five showed no significant improvement. Since SSR appears to positively influence attitudes toward reading, it also appears that its benefits are long range. More research is necessary to determine conclusively the relationship between SSR as a method of reading practice and students' reading achievement. A two-page bibliography concludes the document. (JD)

AN: ED272840
AU: Robinson, Karlen
TI: Visual and Auditory Modalities and Reading Recall: A Review of the Research.
PY: [1985]

NT: 13 p.
PR: EDRS Price—MF01/PC01 Plus Postage.
DE: Comprehension; Learning Processes; Learning Strategies; Memory; Responses; Sensory Integration
DE: Auditory Stimuli; Cognitive Processes; Reading Ability; Reading Research; Recall Psychology; Visual Stimuli
AB: Of particular interest to those exploring student's learning modalities is the relationship between the visual and auditory systems and reading recall. Among the findings of studies that have investigated this relationship are the following: (1) reading competency is dependent as much on auditory processing as on visual processing; (2) when visual and auditory signals are presented simultaneously, subjects generally respond to the visual input and are often unaware that an auditory signal has occurred; (3) auditory stimuli are processed more rapidly than visual stimuli; (4) when preschool children's evaluation and integration of visual and auditory information was compared with that of adults both groups were found to have available continuous and independent sources of information; (5) memory training increases a child's ability to retain stimuli; (6) under audio/video mismatch conditions, memory for audio information is reduced more than memory for video information; however, comprehension and recognition of audio information is similar in the audio only and audio/video match conditions; (7) children recall logical sequences better than illogical ones; and (8) children of all ages show a correspondence between strategy use and metamemory as assessed by verbalization of relationships among pictures during specific questioning; however, when a more typical general question format is used to assess metamemory, strategy use precedes verbalized knowledge of strategy use. In general, most studies show that visual stimuli tend to dominate other modalities in both perceptual and memory tasks. A three-page list of references concludes the document. (HOD)

AN: EJ325185
AU: Sippola, Arne E.
TI: What to Teach for Reading Readiness—A Research Review and Materials Inventory.
PY: 1985
JN: Reading Teacher; v39 n2 p162–67 Nov 1985
AV: UMI
DE: Child Development; Learning Processes; Primary Education
DE: Learning Readiness; Reading Instruction; Reading Materials; Reading Readiness; Reading Readiness Tests; Reading Research
AB: Reviews literature on different aspects of reading readiness, then presents a reading readiness material analysis inventory constructed according to the findings of the review. Explains how the instrument can be used by educators to compare readiness program materials. (FL)

AN: ED223971
AU: Spangler, Katy
TI: Readability: A Review and Analysis of the Research.

PY: 1980
NT: 51 p.
PR: EDRS Price—MF01/PC03 Plus Postage.
DE: Comparative Analysis; Literature Reviews, Research Design; Research Methodology; Test Reviews
DE: Cloze Procedure; Readability Formulas, Reading Research; Test Interpretation; Test Validity
AB: This paper reviews seven research studies on the subject of readability. The first study reviewed is itself an extensive review of 30 readability formulas described by George A. Klare. Of these, five formulas considered to be interesting, unusual, or classic on the basis of high validity, simplicity or complexity, common or uncommon variables, and other unusual features were chosen for analysis. The five formulas include those by I. I. Lorge (1939), G. D. Spache (1953, 1974), W. B. Elley (1969), J. R. Bormuth (1966, 1969), and Harris-Jacobson (1975). In addition, the initial research on cloze procedure by W. L. Taylor (1953) is reviewed to give balance to the overview of readability research. Each review consists of an analysis of the research backing the formulas, specifically the theoretical framework, the research design, the results, the author's evaluation, and a summary including comments on the usefulness and the face validity of the formulas. After the reviews, a synthesis of the studies attempts to answer the following questions: (1) What is readability and how is it calculated? (2) How good is the research on readability—what are its strengths and limitations? (3) How do readability measures compare? and (4) What are some practical implications for use of these formulas? (HOD)

AN: EJ297934
AU: Wiesendanger, Katherine D.; Birlem, Ellen D.
TI: The Effectiveness of SSR: An Overview of the Research.
PY: 1984
JN: Reading Horizons; v24 n3 p197–201 Spr 1984
AV: UMI
DE: Program Effectiveness; Research Problems
DE: Reading Improvement; Reading Instruction; Reading Research; Research Utilization; Sustained Silent Reading
AB: Reviews research concerning sustained silent reading and lists factors that are important in determining whether such a reading program is successful. (FL)

Writing

AN: ED240586
AU: Cronnell, Bruce; And Others
TI: Cooperative Instructional Application of Writing Research. Final Report. Volume Three.
CS: Southwest Regional Laboratory for Educational Research and Development, Los Alamitos, Calif.
PY: 1982
NT: 642 p.; For related documents, see CS 208 143–144
PR: EDRS Price—MF03/PC26 Plus Postage.
DE: Annotated Bibliographies; Basic Skills; Elementary Education; Multiple-Choice Tests; Surveys; Test Items; Test Results; Writing Skills

DE: Achievement Tests; Educational Assessment; Language Arts; Minimum Competency Testing; Writing Evaluation; Writing Research
ID: Theory-Practice Relationship
AB: The last of three volumes studying the relationship between writing research and instruction, this four-part report focuses on writing assessment. The first section details specifications for an instrument assessing student writing samples and the following composition skills: word processing, sentence processing, paragraph development, organizational skill, use of dictionary and reference sources, spelling, and writing mechanics. It also reports on the administration of such an assessment instrument to students from grades 1 to 6 in the Los Angeles Unified School District. The second section discusses specifications for competency based assessment of the following language arts skills: (1) listening, (2) grammar usage, (3) sentence structure, (4) capitalization and punctuation, (5) language expression, (6) spelling, (7) literature, and (8) study skills, media literacy, and nonverbal communication. The third section briefly describes the reading, mathematics, and language proficiency surveys and review exercises administered to entering high school students in the Sacramento City Unified School District, and the final section presents an annotated bibliography of assessment reports. (MM)

AN: ED254848
AU: Davis, David J.
TI: Writing across the Curriculum: A Research Review.
PY: [1984]
NT: 29 p.
PR: EDRS Price—MF01/PC02 Plus Postage.
DE: Higher Education; Learning Theories; Literature Reviews; Writing Processes; Writing Skills
DE: Content Area Writing; Interdisciplinary Approach; Student Attitudes; Teacher Attitudes; Teaching Methods; Writing Research
ID: Writing across the Curriculum
ID: Writing Programs
AB: A review of dozens of journal articles and books on the subject of writing across the curriculum reveals the following basic assumptions that seem to characterize most college writing across the curriculum programs: (1) writing is a complex and developmental process; (2) writing should be used to promote learning; (3) the teaching of writing is the responsibility of the entire academic community and of every teacher; (4) the teaching of writing should be integrated across departmental lines; (5) writing serves several functions in the educational context; (6) the universe of discourse is broad; and (7) the teaching of writing should occur during the entire four undergraduate years. Studies also support the assumption that writing increases student learning. It is clear, however, that there is little common agreement on how best to go about fostering writing skills among disciplines operating with quite diverse rhetorical conventions. In addition, few individual faculties seem to have developed a systematic approach giving overall direction to their own practices toward student writing. The apparent broad inter-

est in student writing is accompanied by fragmentation of attitudes, expectations, and practices in that direction. These studies suggest that English departments would serve themselves and the total campus well by seeking ways to cooperate with their colleagues in other disciplines to accomplish what is obviously a widely shared goal—the development of skilled writers. A 33-item reference list is included. (HOD)

AN: ED225147
AU: Faigley, Lester; Skinner, Anna
TI: Writers' Processes and Writers' Knowledge: A Review of Research. Technical Report No. 6.
CS: Texas Univ., Austin.
PY: 1982
NT: 71 p.; Prepared through the Writing Program Assessment Project. Figures may not reproduce.
PR: EDRS Price—MF01/PC03 Plus Postage.
DE: Cognitive Processes; Educational Theories; Elementary Secondary Education; Higher Education; Literature Reviews
DE: Prewriting; Revision Written Composition; Writing Composition; Writing Instruction; Writing Processes; Writing Research
ID: Theory-Practice Relationship
AB: After a short introductory chapter to this literature review on composing processes, the second chapter examines research that covers the timing and content of planning, planning subprocesses, employing planning strategies, and instruction in planning. Studies in the third chapter are divided into two sections, oral and written discourse production and instruction in producing texts. The sections in the fourth chapter deal with research concerning classification systems for revision changes, revising strategies, why writers revise, and instruction on revision. The final chapter deals with studies that outline the kinds of knowledge a writer possesses about language, the conventions of writing, and a particular writing situation. This chapter argues that examining a writer's knowledge is essential to understanding changes in composing and suggests directions for future research. The studies cited in the document are then listed. (JL)

AN: ED280063
AU: Funderburk, Carol
TI: A Review of Research in Children's Writing.
PY: [1986]
NT: 13 p.
PR: EDRS Price—MF01/PC01 Plus Postage.
DE: Cognitive Development; Cognitive Processes; Developmental Stages; Educational Theories; Language Acquisition; Language Arts; Literature Reviews; Prewriting; Research Proposals; Surveys; Teaching Methods; Theory-Practice Relationship
DE: Piagetian Theory; Primary Education; Reading-Writing Relationship; Writing Processes; Writing Research
ID: Invented Spelling; Piaget, Jean
AB: Recent research into the composing processes of children owes much to Piaget's postulate that cognitive development is linear—that children progress through stages of develop-

ment whereby tasks are mastered at certain levels of cognitive understanding. The stages of children's writing processes (prewriting, composing, revising), as well as language development, drawing, and reading have been examined by Donald Graves, L. M. Calkins, and Glenda Bissex, among others. In one study, C. Temple, R. Nathan, and N. Burris concluded that children make the same discoveries in the same order. Susan Sowers detailed her observation of a first-grade class, in which she used the techniques of invented spelling, writing conferences, and writing about assigned topics to compile children's writing for publishing. Issues currently being examined include the use of drawing as a prewriting exercise, and the relationships between scribbling, drawing, and talking. The issues of invented spelling and writing before reading have profound implications for new directions in elementary education. A growing amount of research indicates that reading is a highly abstract task and should follow rather than precede writing instruction. Frances Kane's work advocates the progression of thinking, drawing, writing, and reading. The link between Piaget's stages of cognitive development and its writing counterparts is a promising area of research. (NKA)

AN: ED229766
AU: Mosenthal, Peter, Ed.; And Others
TI: Research on Writing: Principles and Methods.
PY: 1983
AV: Longman Inc., 1560 Broadway, New York, NY 10036 ($25.00 cloth).
NT: 324 p.
PR: Document Not Available from EDRS.
DE: Elementary-Secondary Education; Higher Education; observation; Research Needs; Research Problems; Student-Teacher Relationship; Writing Processes; Writing Readiness
DE: Experiments; Holistic Approach; Research Design; Research Methodology; Writing Instruction; Writing Research
AB: Designed to alleviate the confusion caused by the existence of a multiplicity of approaches to writing research, the four parts of this book present explicit discussions of research principles and methods used by researchers actively working within a variety of disciplines. The two chapters in Part 1 describe very broad views of the entire research endeavor. The four chapters in Part 2 show how classical experimental projects are used to examine the processes used by readers in evaluating student composition, the development of writing abilities in children, the writing development of children who are just beginning to write, and the control of writing processes. The three chapters in Part 3 describe the use of observational approaches to study the composing processes of adult writers, the on-the-job writing of workers, and the role of the teacher in the student's writing process. Chapters in Part 4 examine two other approaches, recounting the long tradition of interest in writing disabilities and reviewing approaches to text analysis. (JL)

AN: ED236674
AU: Moss, Kay
TI: The Developmental Aspects of the Writing Processes of

Young Children: A Review of Related Research. Instructional Research Laboratory Technical Series #R83003.

CS: Texas A and M Univ., College Station. Instructional Research Lab.

PY: [1982]

NT: 24 p.

PR: EDRS Price—MF01/PC01 Plus Postage.

DE: Elementary Education; Literature Reviews; Teacher Role; Verbal Development; Writing Readiness

DE: Developmental Stages; Language Acquisition; Writing Instruction; Writing Processes; Writing Research

AB: To determine the designs, procedures, and findings of studies related to an investigation of the developmental aspects of the writing processes of children, a literature search was made of documents indexed in "Current Index to Journals in Education" (CIJE) and "Resources in Education" (RIE). A search was also made of the literature in Psychological Abstracts, Comprehensive Dissertation Index, and the Language and Language Behaviors Index. From the analysis it would seem that most of the literature regarding the writing processes of young children has been concerned specifically with developmental aspects. Research conclusions suggest that teachers should question children to help them expand their ideas about writing and options for writing those ideas. Teachers should also encourage other children to set standards for their writing and encourage other children to provide feedback. In particular, the research findings of Donald Graves suggest that children should be encouraged by their teachers to focus on the message rather than on its form and to realize that words are only temporary. His findings also show that informal classroom settings promote writing and that unassigned writing seems to stimulate boys' writing and results in longer compositions. (HOD)

Integration of Language Arts

AN: ED260409

AU: Froese, Victor; Phillips-Riggs, Linda

TI: Dictation, Independent Writing, and Story Retelling in the Primary Grades [and] Research in Reading and Writing Should be Progressive: A Response to Froese.

PY: 1984

NT: 37 p.; Papers presented at the Colloquium on Research in Reading and Language Arts in Canada (Lethbridge, Alberta, Canada, June 7–9, 1984).

PR: EDRS Price—MF01/PC02 Plus Postage.

DE: Communication Research; Communication Skills; Expressive Language; Language Processing; Language Skills; Research Needs; Research Problems; Speech Communication

DE: Dictation; Integrated Activities; Language Arts; Story Telling; Writing Research; Writing Skills

AB: In addressing selected aspects of the language arts from the context of an integrative language paradigm, this paper focuses on the results of three studies recently completed in Manitoba, which help to shed some light on three modes of expression—dictation, independent writing, and retelling—in the primary grades. The first part of the paper discusses the background and need for the studies—their purposes, methods and procedures, findings, and conclusions and implications. The second part of the paper is a response by Linda Phillips-Riggs, which outlines the main points of Froese's paper and discusses the weaknesses of his paper and of the three studies cited. Some research ideas are presented, followed by a conclusion. (EL)

Summaries of Research

AN: EJ332975

AU: Marshall, James D.; Durst, Russel K.

TI: Annotated Bibliography of Research in the Teaching of English.

PY: 1986

JN: Research in the Teaching of English; v20 n2 p198–215 May 1986

AV: UMI

DE: Language Acquisition; Reading-Writing Relationship; Rhetoric; Writing Evaluation; Writing Processes

DE: Educational Research; English Teacher Education; Language Processing; Literature; Writing Instruction; Writing Research

ID: Writing Contexts

ID: Text Analysis

AB: Describes recent research studies in the areas of writing (contexts, status surveys, instruction, processes, text analysis, assessment rhetoric), language (processing, development, interrelationships, language and schooling), literature, and teacher education. (HOD)

Children with Disabilities

AN: EJ358541

AU: Barnett, Janette

TI: Research on Language and Communications in Children Who have Severe Handicaps: A Review and Some Implications for Intervention.

PY: 1987

JN: Educational Psychology; v7 n2 p117–28 1987

DE: Language Handicaps

DE: Communication Research; Interpersonal Communication; Nonverbal Communication; Psycholinguistics; Severe Disabilities; Speech Communication

AB: Presents a critical discussion of some contemporary literature on the language development and communication problems of persons with severe handicaps. States that for meaning to be transmitted from one person to another, a social-interactive context is required. Draws implictions for care givers and therapists. (Author/JDH)

AN: EJ344038

AU: Battacchi, Marco W.; Manfredi, Marta-Montanini

TI: Recent Research Trends in Italy: Cognitive & Communicative Development of Deaf Children.

PY: 1986

JN: Sign Language Studies; n52 p210–18 Fall 1986

DE: Foreign Countries; Language Acquisition; Special Education; Total Communication

DE: Cognitive Development; Communication Research; Communicative Competence Languages; Deafness; Exceptional Child Research

ID: Italy

AB: A review of recent research trends in Italy regarding cognitive and communicative development of deaf children indictes that deaf children's potential for communicative and cognitive growth is enormous. This potential may be realized if provision is made for an educational environment based on a multiple code, gestural communication, spoken language, reading, and writing. (CB)

AN: ED223988

AU: Coots, James H.; Snow, David P.

TI: Understanding Poor Reading Comprehension: Current Approaches in Theory and Research.

CS: Southwest Regional Laboratory for Educational Research and Development, Los Alamitos, Calif.

PY: 1980

NT: 28 p.

PR: EDRS Price—MF01/PC02 Plus Postage.

DE: Academic Aptitude; Learning Theories; Reading Rate; Reading Skills

DE: Decoding Reading; Reading Ability; Reading Comprehension; Reading Difficulties; Reading Processes; Reading Research

AB: Two views of the sources of poor reading comprehension are currently distinguishable in the research literature: a decoding sufficiency view and a comprehension skills view. The decoding sufficiency view argues that decoding is the only skill that must be acquired for general language comprehension. The broader, comprehension skills hypothesis argues that a deficiency in any of several basic component skills could thwart reading comprehension mastery. R. M. Golinkoff's major review of studies comparing good and poor comprehenders posited three components of comprehension: decoding, lexical access, and text organization. Research on decoding has yielded some hypotheses relating decoding speed to comprehension, but problems of study design cast some doubt on these conclusions. Research on lexical access ability indicates that poor comprehenders do not typically lack this ability; however, if cognitive overload during reading is more frequent among poor comprehenders, it is likely that lexical access functioning will deteriorate. Most clearly, text organization research has consistently shown that poor comprehenders are word-by-word readers while good comprehenders employ higher level strategies. (JL)

AN: EJ352216

AU: Goodacre, Elizabeth

TI: Reading Research in Great Britain—1985.

PY: 1987

JN: Reading; v21 n1 p16–29 Apr 1987

DE: Elementary Secondary Education; Foreign Countries; Learning Disabilities; Reading Difficulties; Reading Interests; Reading Materials; Reading Tests; Skill Development; Teaching Methods

DE: Educational Technology; Reading Instruction; Reading Research; Reading Skills

ID: Great Britain

AB: Reviews research in the areas of reading standards and tests, reading development, dyslexia and specific reading retardation, and reading materials and interests. (FL)

Sociocultural Influences

AN: EJ337085

AU: Plant, Richard M.

TI: Reading Research: Its Influence on Classroom Practice.

PY: 1986

JN: Educational Research; v28 n2 p126–31 Jun 1986

DE: Elementary Education; Teacher Responsibility; Teacher Role

DE: Classroom Techniques; Delivery Systems; Reading Research; Research Methodology; Teacher Attitudes

ID: Great Britain

AB: An attempt is made to assess the influence of recent reading research on current classroom practice. It is argued that its overall effect is minimized by a combination of researcher/practitioner disagreement on what constitutes reading, the overreliance by researchers on a particular methodology, and the inadequacy of much of the machinery for dissemination. (Author/CT)

AN: EJ331092

AU: Subervi-Velez, Federico A.

TI: The Mass Media and Ethnic Assimilation and Pluralism: A Review and Research Proposal with Special Focus on Hispanics.

PY: 1986

JN: Communication Research: An International Quarterly; v13 n1 p71–96 Jan 1986

AV: UMI

DE: Ethnic Groups; Research Methodology

DE: Acculturation; Communication Research; Cultural Pluralism; Hispanic Americans; Literature Reviews; Mass Media

AB: Provides an integrated assessment of literature about communication research on Hispanic and other ethnic groups within the context of assimilation and pluralism. (PD)

Teacher Effectiveness

AN: ED233389

AU: Farr, Marcia

TI: Writing Growth in Young Children: What We Are Learning from Research. The Talking and Writing Series, K–12: Successful Classroom Practices.

CS: Dingle Associates, Inc., Washington, D.C.

PY: 1983

NT: 22 p.

PR: EDRS Price—MF01/PC01 Plus Postage.

DE: Basic Skills; Child Development; Child Language; Elementary Education; Language Experience Approach; Language Skills; Language Usage; Models; Oral Language; Writing Instruction

DE: Classroom Research; Developmental Stages; Language Acquisition; Writing Processes; Writing Research; Writing Skills

ID: Theory-Practice Relationship

AB: Prepared as part of a series applying recent research in oral and written communication instruction to classroom practice, this booklet describes several classroom-based studies that have examined children's writing development and synthesizes what they have shown about the process. The first section of the booklet analyzes the term "writing development"; presents a model of literacy acquisition and use devised by J. C. Harste, C. L. Burke, and V. Woodard; and discusses the work of D. H. Graves and his associates in this area. The second section discusses children's transition from oral to written language and reviews the research conducted by M. L. King and V. M. Rentel. The third section examines how written language growth is related to teaching and discusses King's, Rentel's, and Graves' findings on instructional approaches and S. Sowers's work with the concept of scaffolding. (FL)

AN: ED265576

AU: Phelps, Lynn A.; Smilowitz, Michael

TI: Using Research as a Guide for Teaching Interpersonal Communication Competencies.

PY: 1985

NT: 18 p.; Paper presented at the Annual Meeting of the Speech Communication Association (71st, Denver, CO, November 7–10, 1985).

PR: EDRS Price—MF01/PC01 Plus Postage.

DE: Higher Education; Speech Communication; Speech Curriculum; Speech Improvement; Speech Instruction; Speech Skills

DE: Communication Research; Interpersonal Communication; Interpersonal Competence

AB: Twenty years of research in interpersonal communication have provided teachers with a basis for identifying the competencies that should be taught in introductory interpersonal communication courses, including empathy, social composure, and conflict management. However, other issues such as "performance vs. knowledge," the affective dimension, and the situational nature of competency are still being researched and debated. Five suggestions for instructors who teach basic interpersonal communication courses are (1) review various conceptualizations of interpersonal competence and select factors deemed crucial for students to process (2) select a basic textbook that treats those factors, (3) encourage students to critically examine their own behaviors, (4) use exercises that provide the opportunity to observe others who process useful skills and that provide opportunities to practice in a nonthreatening environment, and (5) allow students to make their own choices. (DF)

AN: EJ313480

AU: Rupley, William H.; Wise, Beth S.

TI: Methodological and Data Analysis Limitations in Teacher Effectiveness Research: Threats to the External Validity of Significant Findings.

PY: 1984

JN: Journal of Reading Education; v10 n1 p8–18 Fall 1984

NT: The Organization of Teacher Education in Reading, 1917 15th Av., Greeley, CO 80631; $6.00, includes membership.

DE: Classroom Research

DE: Data Collection; Reading Research; Research Methodology; Research Problems; Teacher Effectiveness; Validity

AB: Notes that major changes have occurred in the factors investigated and the data collection procedures employed in teacher effectiveness research and that the generalizability of significant findings continues to be limited by methodological and experimental design problems. (FL)

AN: ED275152

AU: Zamel, Vivian

TI: In Search of the Key: Research and Practice in Composition.

PY: 1983

NT: 14 p.; In: Handscombe, Jean, Ed.; And Others. On TESOL '83. The Question of Control. Selected Papers from the Annual Convention of Teachers of English to Speakers of Other Languages (17th, Toronto, Canada, March 15–20, 1983); see FL 015 035.

PR: EDRS Price—MF01/PC01 Plus Postage.

DE: Classroom Techniques; Diaries; Error Patterns; Higher Education; Research Needs; Second Language Instruction; Writing Composition

DE: English-Second Language; Writing Exercises; Writing Instruction; Writing Processes; Writing Research

AB: It is important that teachers help students to realize that writing is not simply a product, or a means to an end, but an exploratory, cyclical process. Research has shown that skilled writers conceptualize the effect of their writing as a whole, as a generative process, whereas unskilled writers are distracted by surface-level features and are less aware of the exploratory nature of writing. In light of these findings, methods are proposed for teachers to involve students in the composing process and thereby better prepare them to become independent writers. Some of these activities include: allowing students to be creative and purposeful in their writing; initiating free-writing activities that develop skills for exploring and discovering fresh ideas; and observing students' writing processes closely and noting areas of difficulty. (TR)

Literature Curriculum

AN: EJ345213

AU: Sawyer, Wayne

TI: Literature and Literacy: A Review of Research.

PY: 1987

JN: Language Arts; v64 n1 p33–39 Jan 1987

AV: UMI

NT: Theme Issue: Literature and Literacy.

DE: Beginning Reading; Childrens Literature; Reading Improvement; Reading Strategies

DE: Learning Processes; Learning Theories; Literacy; Literature; Reading Research; Theory-Practice Relationship

AB: Reviews the major theoretical statements regarding the contribution of literature to reading development, nothing that they fall into two interwoven strands: the notion of learning to read through literature, and learning to read literature. Evaluates the empirical evidence supporting the claim that literature plays an important role in learning to read. (JD)

AN: ED235506

AU: Sword, Jeane

TI: The What and How of Book Selection: Research Findings.

PY: 1982

NT: 18 p.; Paper presented at the Annual Meeting of the National Council of Teachers of English Spring Conference (1st, Minneapolis, MN, April 15–17, 1982).

PR: EDRS Price—MF01/PC01 Plus Postage.

DE: Elementary Education; Evaluation Criteria; Fiction; Holistic Evaluation; Intermediate Grades; Kindergarten; Oral REading; Reading Aloud to Others; Resource Materials; Surveys

DE: Childrens Literature; Reading Materials; Reading Material Selection; Reading Research; Teacher Attitudes

AB: A review of the literature on read-aloud programs reveals two studies that extensively examine program content and practices and teacher procedures. The first study, conducted in 1969, compiled responses from 582 intermediate teachers of grades four, five, and six throughout the United States. The second study, conducted in 1979, surveyed 29 kindergarten teachers in a large northern Minnesota city. Findings from the studies showed that in both kindergarten and intermediate grades the largest category of books teachers read orally to children is fiction. In the intermediate grades study, the quality of teacher selected books was determined by checking the list of titles against two standard bibliographies: "Children's Catalog," and "The Elementary School Library Collections." The kindergarten study used a set of criteria for evaluating the quality of plot, characterization, and style of picture story books. In consideration of personal teachre evaluation of a given book, two facts stood out: 85 percent to 100 percent of the teachers relied on their own knowledge in book selection; but in regard to quality of literature chosen, only one-fourth to two-fifths of the books selected for the read-aloud programs were categorized as top quality. The most frequently used book selection aids were "The Instructor," for intermediate teachers, and the "Bibliography of Books for Children" for kindergarten teachers. (HOD)

·17·

CONTEMPORARY METHODOLOGICAL ISSUES AND FUTURE DIRECTIONS IN RESEARCH ON THE TEACHING OF ENGLISH

M. C. Wittrock

Educational research has contributed substantially to our knowledge about teaching of English, which includes teaching reading, writing, composition, and literature. The chapters in this section of the *Handbook* make that point clear through their portrayal of the recent history and development of the research contributions to the study of English teaching.

This section also serves as a prologue to the future of teaching English research and as a provocative source of suggestions about future directions in research, directions that include close ties between researchers and teachers, and between research and practice. These directions also focus upon understanding how teachers' and students' cognitive and affective processes, their thoughts and feelings, lead to learning and achievement in teaching English.

The focus upon understanding how teachers and students use their strategies, background knowledge, and emotions to construct meaning from teaching leads to fundamental changes in the design and conduct of research studies, and to fundamental changes in teaching English, including reading, writing, composition, and literature. We become less interested in standardized testing, norming, ranking, and comparison of students, teachers, classes, schools, and states, because these comparisons do not help us much to understand how teaching functions, how students learn, and how we might improve our teaching and their learning. We also become less interested in simplistic input-output models of teaching (e.g., time correlates positively with achievement), not because they are false, but because they do not lead to an understanding of how and why teaching leads learners to construct meanings and interpretations that enhance their achievement.

We become more interested in learning about the interests, background knowledge, schema, learning strategies, and meta-cognitive processes of our students. Tests that will provide teachers with these types of information have diagnostic value for designing teaching through understanding student thoughts and emotions. We become more interested in models of teaching that go beyond the products of learning to include the critical role of the teachers' and the learners' constructive or generative processes in building meaning as they read and write, as they interpret literature, and as they teach and learn.

EARLY CONTRIBUTIONS TO EDUCATIONAL RESEARCH

Since the early empirical educational research studies in America in the first half of the nineteenth century, teaching English and language continues to be a most important area to study. In 1845, after Horace Mann questioned the effectiveness of teaching in the Boston Schools, a subcommittee of the Boston School Committee decided to examine the children from ages 7 to 14 years in the Boston Writing and Grammar Schools (Travers, 1983, pp. 86–87). To measure achievement in writing, which included handwriting, arithmetic, and sometimes algebra, and orthography (spelling), reading, geography, grammar, and history, the subcommittee developed and used printed achievement tests. The scores on these tests were used to rank the Boston Schools and to compare them with one another.

In this survey, measurement and evaluation of student achievement in grammar, writing, and other basic subjects taught in grammar schools began to be used on a large scale basis to provide empirical data about student achievement. At the same time these data were used to evaluate the effectiveness of the Boston Schools.

In New York, Joseph Mayer Rice, a zealous educational reformer, tried unsuccessfully for several years to convince teachers to accept his ideas, which were not supported with data. Rice singled out one school in New York City, generally considered excellent over 25 years, as an example of needed reform. That school's program was designed to "immobilize," "automatize," and "dehumanize" each student, who was required to stare straight ahead, presumably at the teacher, from whom came all knowledge. Speed and efficiency were highly valued in school lessons, which were dominated by drill and practice (Travers, 1983, p. 100).

Even though Rice published these comments widely, including articles in *Forum,* a well-read journal, they received very little attention among the public or among professional educators. Two years later, Rice decided that his comments were probably being treated as the opinion of one person, not as objective or scientific findings. In 1895, Rice decided to collect data about teaching and learning, especially about time to learn and its relation to student achievement. He chose spelling as the subject he would study. After some preliminary research, Rice developed a spelling test, consisting of spelling words embedded in sentences, which he gave to about 13,000 children across the country. He found that differences in achievement across schools serving upper socioeconomic and lower socioeconomic levels were small, but differences across age levesl were large. He also found that time on task had almost no positive correlation with learning: 10 to 15 minutes of teaching spelling each day produced about the same achievement as did 40 to 50 minutes of daily spelling teaching.

Rice's empirical research on spelling, and later on arithmetic, lead to a series of influential articles on teaching, for which he is still remembered today. His research data also changed his own earlier conceptions of student freedom in schools to emphasize the importance of the teacher in the classroom. Rice's decision to collect data on teaching spelling shows the impact that research can have upon the public and upon the profession. Those research data from students were more convincing than were his earlier comments about teaching practices, which were discredited as personal opinion, even when they presented jarring accounts of rigid and immobilizing teaching procedures in the public schools.

The central role of English and language teaching and testing in educational research appears again in the seminal work of Edward L. Thorndike. Although he is better known for his research on human learning and transfer, Thorndike led in introducing in America statistics that were being developed in Great Britain. In 1904, he published a book entitled *An Introduction to the Theory of Mental and Social Measurements.* His knowledge of research methods and his ability to gather empirical data to evaluate theories of learning and transfer led to some important changes in teaching language.

Thorndike's identical elements theory of transfer of learning stated that transfer occurred when elements present in an initial learning situation occurred again in a lter situation. His theory contrasted sharply with the formal discipline theory of transfer accepted by many teachers of foreign language. Formal discipline theory stated that the mind consisted of faculties, such as memory, reason, and will, which are strengthened by the exercise provided by the most difficult subjects then taught, such as Latin, Greek, and mathematics.

With his identical elements theory to challenge formal discipline theory, and with his knowledge of statistics and research methods to challenge the beliefs of teachers, Thorndike (1924) conducted an empirical study on the effects upon reasoning of different subjects taken in high school. Mathematics, Greek, and Latin produced no greater reasoning ability then did physical education or drama. However, he found that students in the more difficult courses did have higher reasoning abilities than did other students at the beginning of the study, a factor which he adjusted statistically.

As a result of Thorndike's research on transfer, Latin was largely discredited as a way to increase intelligence and reasoning, and as a way to teach English, or other school subjects. These results decimated the justification for teaching Latin. Without the benefit of Thorndike's expertise in statistics and research methods, the teachers of Latin and English who disagreed with Thorndike were left with the formidable task of mounting equally defensible support for their theories and beliefs. The support was not forthcoming. The study of Latin in high schools declined sharply in the next twenty years, in part because of Thorndike's research.

Thorndike's contributions to the teaching of vocabulary and reading (and to arithmetic) are known and are still influential. Reading consisted of recognizing and comprehending words, he maintained. The comprehensibility of vocabulary was related to its frequency of use in daily life. Thorndike gathered data about the frequencies of words children encounter in reading books, especially classic stories, textbooks, newspapers, and poetry. In 1921, he published the *Teachers Word Book,* which later was expanded (Thorndike & Lorge, 1944).

Thorndike's theories of vocabulary in comprehension still influence the teaching of reading of English and foreign languages and still influence our conceptions of sentence and text difficulty, for example, as they occur in readability formulas.

These examples of early contributions show some ways that educational research has contributed to our knowledge about teaching English. They show some of the power of data and research methods to influence teachers and the public, as did Rice's findings about spelling and Thorndike's findings about teaching Latin. They also show how some of the close ties became established between achievement testing and educational research. They imply how difficult it may be to move to more appropriate research methods for understanding teacher and student thoughts and affective processes not measured by conventional achievement or intelligence tests but nevertheless that are critical to understanding and improving teaching English.

RECENT DEVELOPMENTS

In the early development of empirical educational research, achievement testing and the ranking and evaluation of learners, teachers, schools, and districts were commonly employed research methods. The Boston School Committee used them to study the effectiveness of the Boston Writing and Grammar

Schools. Joseph M. Rice employed them to study spelling and to gain public support for this ideas about educational reform. E. L. Thorndike used them to discredit the formal discipline theory of transfer of learning and to change the teaching of foreign language in America.

From these beginnings grew more elaborate and sophisticated empirical methods for conducting educational research. In the twentieth century, educational researchers borrowed and adapted research methods from other fields of study. For example, from agriculture came our fundamental elements of experimental design, including experimental groups, control groups, and random assignment of participants. Our basic statistical procedures for analyzing experiments, analysis of variance and analysis of covariance, also came from research on agriculture. These design and statistical techniques were both products of one Englishman, Ronald Fisher.

From biology we obtained correlation techniques (Pearson), path analysis (Sewall Wright), discriminant analysis, and multivariate analysis of variance. From neurology and medicine came the case study. From psychology came a broad array of techniques, including factor analysis, canonical correlation, reliability, validity, Q-sorts, scaling methods, and social interaction analysis. From sociology we derived survey methods, sampling techniques, and latent-structure analysis.

The chapters of this section of the *Handbook* summarize well the progression of recent events in the research on the teaching of English. In these chapters we see how educational researchers used these and other research methods to study and to try to improve the teaching of English.

Before we turn to these concepts, we need to consider a parallel progression of events that involves models of teaching and learning. The research methods I mentioned were employed to study and to test conceptions about English teaching and learning. To understand the changes that occurred in the teaching of English, we need to see the close relations between these conceptions of learning and teaching and the methods of research appropriate for studying them.

The models of learning and teaching English that were dominant in Joseph Rice's times emphasized student verbatim learning and repetition of the teacher's words (Travers, 1983). In those days, there was little concern for student thoughts. E. L. Thorndike, through his model of instrumental learning, stated that learning was the acquisition of specific behaviors by being rewarded for performing them at the right times and in the right places, which strengthened connections between the situation and the behaviors or responses. Later, B. F. Skinner added to Thorndike's model the concept of reinforcement, which replaced Thorndike's notion of reward as the process of maintaining or increasing behavior, and the concept of behavioral objectives, as a way of knowing when to reinforce behavior. This highly influential conception of learning developed by Thorndike and Skinner again stressed student behaviors, that is, things that can be measured on commonly used tests. The model did not emphasize student and teacher thoughts and feelings, cognitions and affective processes, interpretations, comprehension, images, emotions, learning strategies, motives, metacognitions, or relations between literature and experience. These cognitive and affective processes were not considered

appropriate for scientific study because they were difficult or impossible to measure objectively.

However, Thorndike's and Skinner's highly influential models led to a focus upon teaching measurable and testable specific behaviors, such as facts, vocabulary, and verbatim information. That narrow focus obtained scientific rigor in research on the teaching of English, but at the expense of ignoring, or at least minimizing, its essence, the comprehension and understanding that comes from reading, writing, and speaking.

Because Thorndike's and Skinner's models of learning omitted the constructive or generative nature of language learning, they had great difficulty in explaining basic linguistic events among children and adults. These models could not adequately explain how infants create novel sentences, how the implicit rules of language are learned and applied to construct or to understand an infinite set of rule-governed sentences or utterances. For these reasons, cognitive models of learning arose and supplanted these earlier models. These earlier models, however, still impact the teaching of English through their focus on learning measurable behaviors defined and identified by precise objectives, and taught by reinforcers presented frequently, discriminately, and contingently.

In the late 1950s and increasingly in the 1960s, cognitive models of learning and knowledge acquisition arose and supplanted the model developed by Thorndike and Skinner. Largely through the pioneering works of Noam Chomsky in linguistics and David Ausubel and others in educational psychology, human learning was conceived as a process of construction of meaning by the learners using their background of experience and their strategies of learning. Student and teacher thoughts and emotions became the center of interest within these cognitive models. In the teaching of English, these models led to fundamental changes. Comprehension and student interpretations of sentences, stories, text, and plays came to the foreground. Reading became far more than converting graphemes into phonemes. It became a process of constructing meanings and interpretations of text using one's knowledge and experience.

In this section of the *Handbook* we see the combined influences of the developments in the conceptions of learning and teaching and in the advances in research methods needed to study these emerging concepts.

John Dixon reports how standardized achievement tests that were used for predicting college achievement influenced the curriculum and the instruction in literature in junior and senior high school. In the 1930s and 1940s, the high school teachers followed the college curriculum, using classics in senior high school and anthologies in junior high school. The methods of instruction emphasized recitation and regimentation.

Later, during the 1950s and 1960s, methods of teaching English in the high schools changed, but there was still an emphasis on learning isolated facts about authors. Teacher-made tests were still centered on facts, rather than on interpretations. Teaching of writing still focused on correcting mistakes in students' grammar and syntax.

In the 1970s, the curriculum and the teaching methods changed further. The introduction of women's studies, ethnic literature, and science fiction in the college curriculum paralleled the introduction of greater student choice in reading, increased student and teacher autonomy in the classroom, independent student projects, and active learning. These college curricular and procedural changes also influenced high school teaching practices.

Dixon calls the model that dominated teaching during the 1970s an "objective-driven" one that emphasized "objective measurement." Teaching English in the high school was still driven by the requirements of the standardized tests, which were used to construct objectives for the teachers to attain. Nonetheless, change was beginning to occur in the high school English classrooms. Student initiated writing, student interpretations of literature, and active, thoughtful learning began to find a place in the English classroom. These changes paralleled the changes in the study of learning and instruction. Dixon's chapter records well the progression in changes in thinking about teaching English and its impacts upon teaching practices in high schools.

Dolores Durkin reports an interesting progression in research on classroom studies. The earlier work she presents tried to explain student achievement test scores by correlating them with school and home factors. High achievement test scores, which meant success in those days, correlated with the amount of direct instruction, with the amount of engaged time (in contrast to Rice's finding), and with the teachers' management skills. These data implied that schools could make a difference, in spite of the findings from other studies that indicated achievement in school was largely determined by home and societal factors over which the schools had little control.

These studies of school effectiveness used a simple "input-output" model or "process-product" model that correlates stimulus or environmental variables with output or behavioral variables. These studies reflect the model of learning developed to study measurable behavior, and the research methods appropriate for it. Not many teaching interventions were tried, and not much explanatory research existed either.

Durkin reports that in the 1970s researchers began to change their interests. They conducted more intervention studies than they had previously. The interventions focused on teaching and monitoring comprehension. They conducted observational research on how students learn from expository text, and on how students use their background knowledge to construct meaning for text. They began to observe how teachers try to teach comprehension. They found that teachers often did not teach comprehension, but did assign readings, assess or evaluate comprehension, and check workbook exercises.

These findings also evidence the progression in conceptions of learning and in research methods I described earlier in this chapter. The input-output correlational models and their statistical methods were gradually supplanted by 1) observations about students' and teachers thought processes and ways of learning and teaching comprehension, and 2) intervention studies designed to teach comprehension. Those changes in research methods evidenced the move to the study of cognitive processes and their role in learning English. The move brought with it observational and experimental research methods designed to investigate the student and teacher mental activities that lead to comprehension.

Janet Emig and June Birnbaum show how the case study can be used to study language processes in their real-life contexts. Squire (1964) used it to study 9th- and 10th-grade student responses to literature while they were reading. He had them stop five times during the reading of four stories to give their responses and interpretations.

This type of research method provides insightful descriptions that achievement tests, percentile ranks, means, and standard deviations cannot provide. Yet, this type of research method, the case study, was not often used in research in English teaching during the first 60 years of this century. The models of learning and the accepted canons of research methods left little place or use for case studies. The shift in interest to students' cognitive and emotional thought processes began to change these perceptions. As a result, we have seen an increase in the numbers of case studies that are recently being conducted, as Emig and Birnbaum have noted. The case study method deserves attention for its utility in understanding the cognitive processes of learning and teaching English. (For additional reading of a case study, I suggest the excellent little book, *The Mind of a Mnemonist*, by A. R. Luria, 1968. In this book, Luria reports his 30-year case study of S, who had phenomenal abilities and strategies for remembering information.)

Roy O'Donnell, in his chapter on "Theory, Research, and Practice" and Margaret Early, in her chapter on "Major Research Programs," address the difficult problems of relating research to practice. O'Donnell shows the research value of studying teachers' thoughts and beliefs about teaching. He states that many English teachers feel uneasy with quantitative and empirical methods. Many English teachers do little reading of professional, research-based articles. Many of these teachers question the usefulness of theories of English teaching or learning. However, he reports that research and theories of English teaching do influence English teachers, albeit not as much as do political, ideological, or economic factors, which influence them the most, and colleagues, students, textbooks, and administrators, which influence their teaching the second most frequently. O'Donnell also emphasizes that there is no doubt that research influences English teaching, as we have repeatedly seen in other chapters in this section. The question is "how" does research influence practice.

The major research programs discussed by Margaret Early, such as Project English, the National Writing Project, and the federally-funded National Research and Development Centers and Regional Laboratories, were all designed, in part, to facilitate the relation between research and practice. As a founder and first director of one of these R & D centers (the Center for the Study of Evaluation at UCLA), I experienced first hand some of the findings reported accurately by O'Donnell and Early. The early model of research leading to development, which was to lead to change in practice, did not produce the intended effects. Neither did the simplistic notion that well-written research articles, prepared especially for English teachers, would lead to major improvements in practice.

Instead, as I experienced it, and as O'Donnell reported it, teachers tend more to be influenced by the overarching models of teaching and by the metaphors of teaching that cumulate from long lines of converging research findings. In addition, when these world views and models mesh with the teachers' understandings of their classroom activities, and illuminate and enrich these understandings, than teaching practices change and lasting improvements occur.

Those discoveries help me to understand why research findings about the lack of value of teaching grammar did not reduce its teaching in schools; but research findings about the value of sentence combining and construction that were designed to increase the length and complexity of students' syntactic structures did lead to changes in teaching. Early reports one implication of these findings about ways to enhance the applications of research. She finds that researchers should invest less time in measuring outcomes and invest more time in studying teachers' and students' processes of teaching and learning English. I would include in that advice more time in studying teachers' background knowledge and beliefs, much as we now study readers' background knowledge and experience. Teachers bring preconceptions and models to their interpretations of research findings. These long-standing conceptual structures are robust. They are stable and useful to their creators. To modify them in a constructive way requires a compelling and convincing model or theory: one that carefully conducted, cumulative research can provide.

FUTURE DIRECTIONS

The prologue I have presented in this chapter implies a clear direction for the future. The direction is from assessing student behaviors on achievement tests and intelligence tests and from correlating those behaviors directly with characteristics of the classroom, the school, the home, and the society (Wittrock and Baker, in press.) The direction is toward researching and understanding the cognitive and affective language processes of learners and teachers that mediate achievement in language learning and language teaching (Wittrock, 1974, 1978, 1981, 1983, 1987). The move is from input-output models to cognitive approaches that give ideas about how students and teachers think and feel, about how they use their background knowledge and strategies to generate or construct meaning and interpretations from literature and expository text (Wittrock, 1974, 1990).

The move is toward research that uses case studies and observational methods to study the background knowledge and strategies of learners and teachers (Erickson, 1986). The direction is toward measuring and recording the thought processes of learners as they read and write using process tracing and verbal protocols (Ericsson & Simon, 1980). Process tracing involves methods such as 1) think alouds, 2) retrospective interviews, and 3) stimulated recalls. Verbal protocols are written records of learners' responses during learning that can be used to infer their mental operations.

Another direction is toward measuring the number and quality of ideas, sentences, pictures, and the like, constructed by learners in an experiment or other intervention study, such as one Linden and I (1981) conducted on reading comprehension. In that study, we gathered data from school children to evidence their different thought processes, for example, the sentences and the images that the treatments asked them to generate. Those data enabled us to measure how well the treatments were actually inducing the intended cognitions, and how extensively the induced cognitions were correlated to retention and comprehension. These relations among treatments, thought processes, and comprehension can be analyzed statistically with conditional probability analyses or path analyses and other multivariate regression techniques.

In addition to measuring the learners' and teachers' preconceptions and their thought processes during learning and teaching of English, we need to employ appropriate measures and teach knowledge acquisition, including comprehension (Pearson & Johnson, 1978; McNeil, 1987), semantic maps (Heimlich & Pittelman, 1986), and hierarchical cognitive structures (Naveh-Benjamin, McKeachie, Lin, & Tucker, 1986).

Another move is toward multivariate analyses that are appropriate for relating contexts, preconceptions, and beliefs to 1) thought processes during learning, and 2) to comprehension, retention, and affective responses. Some of these multivariate statistical procedures are already available. See Muthén (1989) and Linn (1986) for discussions of them, including structural equation analyses, metanalyses, and path analyses.

SUMMARY

In sum, the study of learning and teaching English involves devising methods to research the mental processes of language. These invisible cognitive and affective language processes were avoided by researchers early in this century. With the recent shift to the study of cognition, we have seen parallel innovations in research methods. The combination of a shift to research on cognition and a concomitant development of innovative research methods to study it brings fundamental language processes into the foreground of the scientific study of English teaching. The combination also promises to unite the researchers of teaching and the teachers of English in the study of English teaching.

References

Erickson, F. (1986). Qualitative methods in research on teaching. In M. C. Wittrock (Ed.), *Handbook of research on teaching* (3rd ed.). (pp. 119–161). New York: Macmillan.

Ericsson, K. A., & Simon, H. A. (1980). Verbal reports as data. *Psychological Review, 87,* 215–251.

Heimlich, J. E., & Pittelman, S. D. (1986). *Semantic mapping: Classroom applications.* Newark, DE: International Reading Association.

Linden, M., & Wittrock, M. C. (1981). The teaching of reading comprehension according to the model of generative learning. *Reading Research Quarterly, 17*(1), 44–57.

Linn, R. (1986). Quantitative methods in research on teaching. In M. C. Wittrock (Ed.), *Handbook of research on teaching* (3rd ed.) (pp. 92–118). New York: Macmillan.

Luria, A. S. (1968). *The mind of a mnemonist.* New York: Basic Books.

Muthén, B. (1989). Teaching students of educational psychology new sophisticated statistical techniques. In M. C. Wittrock & F. Farley (Eds.), *The future of educational psychology*. Hillsdale, NJ: Lawrence Erlbaum.

Naveh-Benjamin, M., McKeachie, W. J., Lin, Y., & Tucker, D. G. (1986). Inferring students' cognitive structures and their development using the "ordered tree" technique. *Journal of Educational Psychology, 78,* 130–140.

NcNeil, J. D. (1987). *Reading comprehension: New directions for classroom practice* (2nd ed.) Glenview, IL: Scott Foresman.

Newall, A., & Simon, H. A. (1972). *Elements of a theory of human problem solving*. Englewood Cliffs, NJ: Prentice Hall.

Pearson, P. D., & Johnson, D. D. (1978). *Teaching reading comprehension*. New York: Holt, Rinehart, and Winston.

Squire, J. R. (1964). *The responses of adolescents while reading four short stories* (NCTE Research Report No. 2). Urbana, IL: National Council of Teachers of English.

Travers, R. M. W. (1983). *How research has changed American schools*. Kalamazoo, MI: Mythos Press.

Thorndike, E. L. (1904). *An introduction to the theory of mental and social measurements*. New York: Science Press.

Thorndike, E. L. (1924). Mental discipline in high school studies. *Journal of Educational Psychology, 15,* 1–22.

Thorndike, E. L., & Lorge, I. (1944). *The teacher's word book of 30,000 words*. New York: Teachers College, Columbia University.

Wittrock, M. C. (1974). Learning as a generative process. *Educational Psychologist, 11,* 87–95.

Wittrock, M. C. (1978). The cognitive movement in instruction. *Educational Psychologist, 13,* 15–30.

Wittrock, M. C. (1981). Reading comprehension. In F. J. Pirozzolo & M. C. Wittrock (Eds.), *Neuropsychological and cognitive processes of reading*. New York: Academic Press.

Wittrock, M. C. (1983). Writing and the teaching of reading. *Language Arts, 60,* 600–606.

Wittrock, M. C. (1987). Process-oriented measures of comprehension. *The Reading Teacher, 734–737.*

Wittrock, M. C. (1990). Generative processes of comprehension. *Educational Psychologist, 24,* 345–376.

Wittrock, M. C., & Baker, E. L. (in press). *Cognition and testing*. Englewood Cliffs, NJ: Prentice-Hall.

RESEARCH ON LANGUAGE LEARNERS

·18·

OUR STUDENTS

Rita S. Brause
John S. Mayher

We need to understand who our students are by exploring the intimate relationship between their social experiences and their dreams. This knowledge informs our understanding of our students as they function within schools. We will consider the social contexts in which our students live and their unique qualities as learners as these influence their participation and achievement in English language classrooms.

THE SOCIAL/CULTURAL CONTEXTS IN WHICH OUR STUDENTS LIVE

Most of American society is comprised of people who moved here from other lands. Coming from diverse backgrounds, we were united in our hopes for freedom of opportunity in America. Once here, we sought to become part of American society. Our schooling experiences were intended to unify us as a society (Cremin, 1988), providing us with formal instruction within a uniquely American institution. The government funds public schools with the expectation that schooling will enable students to become responsible, productive citizens within American society.

But American society is changing daily. There are increasing rates of immigration, divorce, unemployment, poverty, crime, homelessness, teenage parenting and abuse of drugs, alcohol and children. There is concern for nuclear annihilation, depletion of our resources, and environmental pollution. Competition prevails to the exclusion of cooperation; there is a lack of social responsibility. The rich are "obscenely richer and the poor are poorer" (Tobin, 1988, p. 44). Our students live within this complex society and are affected by it whether they live in cities or suburbs, in apartments or on farms.

Schools are prominent institutions in that society. We experience school as students, continuing this connection with schooling as adults by watching TV sit-coms and movies set in schools. The popularity of these events suggests the key role of schools in our lives. American public education was established

to perpetuate the democratic principles on which our country was founded: freedom and liberty for all, the pursuit of happiness, the constant quest for a "better" life. Embedded in these dreams is a concept of freedom, of equality for all.

Three major issues concerning the social contexts in which our students live will be addressed in this section: American Culture; What the Census Tells Us; and School Practices.

American Culture

There are two competing conceptions of American Culture: one advocates cultural homogeneity adopting one common culture by replacing traditions established in other countries; the second advocates cultural pluralism wherein multiple cultures respectfully coexist. The first is labelled the *Melting Pot* metaphor; the second is sometimes called the *American Casserole or Stew*. While these metaphors have been criticized as simplistic (Lieberson & Waters, 1988), they provide us with useful constructs to understand how popular conceptions of the nature of American society influence our students' goals.

The American Melting Pot. Schools that hold the *melting pot* perspective of equality of opportunity socialize students by transmitting a common, predetermined body of knowledge about the culture as well as about academic content (Cremin, 1988). Recent school reform proposals consistent with this metaphor focus on all students completing a uniform "basic" curriculum, and meeting predetermined standards.

Curriculum practices compatible with the melting pot metaphor seek to reduce differences in student background by imposing common experiences with the same books and workbooks. This has resulted in a *de facto* national curriculum controlled by published texts and tests despite the apparent student differences across school districts and schools. The tests, particularly, are designed to distinguish those who have achieved mastery of an arbitrary set of facts and skills from those who have not. Those who do not score successfully on tests get additional repetition or remedial opportunities to catch up. Success in traditional schools is equated with scores on standardized tests and graduation with age cohorts. Students who adopt the values of the mainstream culture succeed on these standardized tests.

Rodriguez (1982) powerfully relates his experiences of living the melting pot metaphor. He rejected his family's traditions and language for the longterm goal of "becoming American." He spoke only English, ate American dishes, and celebrated American holidays. He believed that to make it in American society, he had to be "melted" to conform with the "mainstream" His family made sure he had access to those traditions, and he was successful in joining the so called mainstream. But the cost was high. As an adult, he realizes he has *A Hunger of Memory* for the culture he lost, yet he still believes that his route was the correct one to choose.

Schools are subsets of our society, which combine practices which are evident in the larger society with unique rules which make schools distinct. While schools cannot be responsible for the rest of society, educators in schools are accountable for the procedures implemented in those settings. It is clear that schools generally reward students who give evidence of holding the values of our society's middle class. These include abiding by bureaucratic and other traditions, seeking to increase wealth, and competing for recognition particularly through verbal facility or athletic prowess. These values are implicit in schools that venerate tradition without thinking about consequences; encourage competition for grades instead of valuing the learning essential for living; and reward students who are good citizens by following the school rules. Students who either do not realize that there are different values inherent in school than at home, or those who consciously decide not to buy into these values, find themselves in a difficult position. When rules are clear and acceptable to some and either unclear or unacceptable to others, then there is an unfair advantage given to those in the first group. Schools in fact perpetuate the status quo, in the main. Yet schools theoretically seek to provide equal opportunity for all, contradicting the status quo.

The ultimate outcome of such a conflict is that the students who know the rules succeed—and those who do not, do not. Not coincidentally, perhaps, those who know the rules come from homes that are more "mainstream" than the others, thereby the schooling experience serves to credential the "in" group—and keeps the out group at bay—with the appearance of objective criteria. According to McLaren (1989), we blame the students who fail for their failure "rather than looking for ways in which the class and educational systems militate against the success of those who are economically powerless and who are discriminated against by gender and race" (p. 219).

Hirsch (1987) and Ravitch and Finn (1987) implicitly advocate the melting pot metaphor, suggesting there is one body of literary and general cultural knowledge essential for all Americans. When Hirsch's list is used to design curriculum and assessment policies, it institutionalizes the melting pot metaphor. Equality of opportunity is available only to those who choose to follow established or so called majority practices, foregoing their own individual interests, and their "Roots" in Haley's (1976) term. The freedom implicit in this metaphor is the freedom to be successful by joining the mainstream, established traditions and practices of the elected, powerful governing elite.

The American Casserole. In contrast, others have hailed diversity as the hallmark of a democracy. Apple (1986), Aronowitz and Giroux (1988), Gardner (1983) and McNeil (1986) suggest that critical literacy, or divergent thinking, is at the heart of a democratic education. The casserole metaphor values diversity: differences in knowledge; differences in experiences; differences in values and beliefs. These result in a diversity of perspectives shared among all learners. Programs fostering these values are individually negotiated in individual classrooms drawing on the unique experiences of the students and teachers in each setting (Boomer, 1982). Learning cannot be prepackaged nor easily measured by standardized tests; alternative assessment strategies are needed. Equality is realized by all students being equally nurtured and challenged to grow.

As noted in the discussion of the melting pot metaphor, it is by no means accidental that schools have adopted a restricted set of values, skills and knowledge as they have. The choices made in setting up schools that feature tracking and a standard curriculum reflecting distinctions between those who have the skills and those who do not, have been made by the people who control the schools. Since they are based on choices, then it is possible for other choices to be made that would value plurality rather than uniformity and seek to enhance the strengths each child brings to school rather than labelling many as deficient (Giroux, 1983).

A school which values cultural pluralism or the American casserole metaphor recognizes the unique contributions of individuals, sponsors activities that encourage students to learn-how-to-learn, acquire knowledge, and develop a social conscience (Holmes Group, 1988, p. 2). Recent proposals that are consistent with this view focus on holistic, integrated learning and personal growth of individual students. The individual learner's background knowledge and interests enable individuals to contribute differently to the larger society, the heart of cultural pluralism.

The casserole or American stew is consistent with Hodgkinson's (1988) call for a "pluralistic society," one that simultaneously respects the individual heritage of its members while uniting to work towards a common dream and goal. Bilingual programs that encourage the development of both languages are consistent with the casserole metaphor (Mayher, 1975, for example). This model celebrates each individual's knowledge and helps to enhance knowledge of the world, strategies for understanding the world, and concepts of social responsibility for participation in that world. The equality of opportunity embedded in this model is the professional support provided to each student to guarantee equivalent accomplishments at the end of the program. And the freedom implicit in this metaphor is the freedom to be proud of one's heritage while learning, respecting and valuing other cultures and backgrounds.

WHAT THE CENSUS TELLS US

Our students experience American society in diverse ways. Three interdependent aspects of our society influence the equality of opportunity experienced by our students: demographic phenomena, families, and schooling. But before trying to use and interpret these data, we must examine their accuracy. The US Census Bureau collects demographic data every 10 years with interim updates. Although cumulatively overwhelming, these statistics provide a limited, biased picture of our students.

The way we, as educators, describe our students both reflects our expectations as we work with them and our implicit social constructs. If we categorize students by the color of clothes they wear, the cost of those clothes, or the length of time worked to pay for those clothes, students would be placed in different groupings. Although we find it convenient to talk about our students by labelling them, we need to acknowledge the effect of such labels, particularly as these influence the quality of each program offered.

Demographic data are collected to quantify the services needed by distinct populations, such as the aged or the newborn. These data are used to plan educational facilities, to provide adequate educational resources, and to monitor program effectiveness as related to educational achievement. They tell us who live where, but they frequently fall short of catching the shifts that happen as suburbs become more and more urban or as exurbs lose their farms to new housing tracts. The ways in which the people are counted then, influence the quantity of services provided and the evaluation of the impact of educational programs on the population. We will first consider the issue of categories used in these reports as these reflect our society's biases and the biases found in our schools.

Limits of Demographic Data

Biases are revealed in the radically different facilities provided for rich and poor and white and African American. The number of English language programs offered to different students reveal different expectations—for one, power, for the other, dependence. These differences are subtly revealed in the presentation or obfuscation of data. To acquire information presented herein, which is essential for sensitivity to the diversity and magnitude of our current population, required extensive digging. In several cases, numerous data sources need to tapped to extrapolate the information. For example, the economic range in American family incomes, seemingly an easy number to access, was obtained using 3 different sources. The fact that we had difficulty obtaining these data caused us to be suspicious about the categories and their presentation, particularly when these data influence the planning and evaluation of English language-arts programs nationwide.

The labelling of individuals based on ethnicity or race (in contrast to other characteristics such as eye color) reflects an implicit bias in our society. Additionally, any basis for determining ethnicity is highly controversial, being neither objective nor scientific. The 1980 US Census report (US Bureau of Census, 1983) used categories of Black, White and Hispanic noting that "Hispanics can be either Black or White". And the groupings change: in 1987 they named the groups differently: White, Black and Others (US Bureau of the Census, 1987). There is no scientific, objective basis for these categories.

Such categorical distinctions are subject to sociopolitical manipulation as well. The objectivity of the categorical systems suggested by demographers is called in question when data concerning ethnicity and school achievement, for example, are combined in one table. By doing so, a relationship is implied, which is simultaneously an inappropriate and misleading use of statistics. Further, such tables provide encouragement for the perpetuation of biases and stereotypes in assessing the potential for achievement of those students categorized by ethnic labels.

Demographic categories reveal nothing about individuals. Within group variation among students is ignored. Members of the "same" group may vary widely in such factors as goals, experiences, feelings, sense of security, and academic proficiencies. Dividing people into such groups frequently magnifies the differences between such groups, rather than revealing commonalities across groups.

"Minority" is a term used in describing the population. The term, however, is not directly related to raw numbers, as evidenced by the fact that women who comprise more than 50 percent of the population are often characterized as a minority. Further, lumping diverse groups together as "minorities" denies each group its own identity. Using the term sometimes reflects the so called majority's denigration of another group as a "minority" implying lesser importance.

There have been predictions/warnings that soon there would be a "Minority Majority," an oxymoron. The language games reveal that the majority numbers have not translated into majority power. It is the powerful majority that is disempowering others with the use of these labels. The figures reported are confusing as well. Due in part to the large population, subsamples are used. Each report uses a different data base, and comparisons across reports are inappropriate. Some report data in percentages, some round out numbers. Some data are self-reports, others are tabulators' observations. Definitions of terms such as "drop out" are defined in conflicting ways across studies.

The Educational Misuse of Demography

Standardized tests are used as a basis for assessing student learning. These instruments are inherently flawed in their design, and have been found to discriminate against "minority" students. They are designed using a theory which is pervasive, but unsubstantiated: namely that any group of people will distribute themselves along a normal curve with most falling in the middle, and few at the two extremes. Following the normal curve hypothesis, half of those tested are designated below average. Although these data are purported to be useful only as group data, they are reported with individual student names, and comparisons are constantly presented between students. Thus, students scoring below average are considered educational failures. The scores are also subject to manipulation. Both Koretz (1988) and *Education Week*, (10/26/88) raise doubts about the value of these tests, since districts select tests that their students will score well on. Further, real national comparisons are impossible according to *Education Week*, when "no more than three states use the same national tests" (p. 11).

Yet the press still reports, and many educators discuss, test scores as though they were based on solid criteria. So we are warned that students' SAT scores have declined significantly, bottoming out at 425 on the verbal portion in 1983 (*OERI, 1987a*); and that only 52 percent of high school students identified *Raisin in the Sun* as a play about an African American family planning to move into a white suburb (Ravitch and Finn, 1987). These declines make us *A Nation at Risk,* according to the National Commission on Excellence (1983). Although our students are not doing well in school on the barometers used to assess growth as we look at such data, we must always be aware of these limitations on categories and procedures used to generate them.

What does the Census Tell Us about Inequities across Race and Gender? In 1986, the total US population reached a record of 241.5 million. There were 39.6 million students enrolled in 1984 (OERI, 1984, p.16) with significant increases noted for the Asian-Pacific Island population (+ 44 percent, according to Hodgkinson, 1988) and the Hispanic population (+ 34 percent according to the New York Times, 9/7/88, p. A20). We are becoming a more multiracial society than we ever have been (Orfield & Monfort, 1988).

The fact that the census reports data by ethnicity reveals an implicit assumption that student achievement is influenced by the ethnic group with which they are associated. Thus, students from one group, for example, "Asian-Pacific Island" population, may be expected, as a group, to be significantly different from another group, say "Hispanics" from this reporting.

From the melting pot perspective, those differences are intended to diminish with time. It seems, however, that people are given one label and live with that one for life. It is unclear at which point in a multi-generational perspective, a person whose ancestors immigrated to this country will be considered "American." In fact, only American Indians are native to this land. Yet some are always reminded of their heritage (Italian Americans, for example) while others are not (African Americans, for example). There is an inherent bias in such differential treatments.

Most recently, there has been a move to use the term African American to denote the origins of "Black" people, analogous to the label of Asian American. Although this consistency is long overdue, the purposes of labelling are still suspect, particularly as these ethnic differences correspond to school achievement and school resources. There are two related, but different perspectives to consider in light of these data:

1. Labels and heritage are used to explain causality of differences, assuming hereditary factors; and
2. The uniqueness of each individual is concealed by the labels.

There is an implicit effort to make American society homogeneous, despite environmental and personal differences which distinguish individuals in our society. The homogeneity sought reflects the biases/prejudices/values of those in power who seek to mold society in their image. Those who are diferent are ostracized and denigrated. Since the power elite are mainly white, of Western European heritage, and relatively rich, that model becomes the standard against which others are mea-

sured. School goals and, particularly, English-language educators need to address this tension in values present in our society by carefully organizing students and their curriculum to consider the ramifications of such biases.

In the largest school districts, the so called "minority" population has been steadily increasing. In 1950, 1 in 10 students represented a designated "minority"; in 1980, the "minority" count was 7 of 10 (Bencivenga, 1983). Recently, California reported that more than half of its school children represented "minority" groups. Even more striking are the figures from urban districts. Central city school districts enroll only 3 percent of the white student population. Such schools "have become almost irrelevant to the nation's white population" (Fiske, 1988, p.16).

The African Americans, Hispanics, and Asian Americans who collectively have replaced whites in central city schools are to a large extent segregated from each other (Fiske, 1988). Nationwide, urban "children go to schools that are almost totally segregated by race and class.... It may well be that the[se] children ... in ... underclass schools are even more comprehensively isolated from mainstream middle-class society than were the Black children of the South" (Fiske, 1987, p.24). A recent report by a New York State Task Force on the Education of Children and Youth at Risk concludes that "racism clearly underlines much of the problem" with the schools today (Kolbert, 1988, p.1).

Nor is the picture much brighter in the suburbs. In many cases, residential shifts and school consolidation have brought "minority" children to many suburban schools, creating tensions that have been "solved" by internal school segregation via tracking (Oakes, 1985). And even where so called "minority" students are not present in large numbers, Powell, Farrar, and Cohen (1985) and Sedlack, Wheeler, Pullin, and Cusick (1986) point a grim picture of alienation, boredom and cynicism. The "Shopping Mall High Schools" of the suburbs don't seem to have found the answer any more than their urban counterparts as to how to make the school experience meaningful for their students.

The long range educational implications of these reports are revealed in the percentages of high school graduates from various groups who have succeeded in school to the extent of enrolling in college. College enrollments have increased, but not equally across ethnic groups. (NYT, 8/30/88, p. A17). The absolute numbers of students in all groups have increased from 1976 to 1986, but the percentage of white high school graduates going to college has gone up from 32.9 percent to 34.5 percent, while the percentage of African American graduates enrolling has declined from 33.4 percent to 28.6 percent and that of Hispanic graduates from 35.8 percent to 29.4 percent during this decade (*Chronicle of Higher Ed. Almanac,* 1988, p. 81).

These differences reflect such contrasts as ethnicity and wealth. When we look at the census categories distinguishing these graduates, we note dramatic differences. "Three out of four Blacks and four out of five Latinos fail to complete high school within four years" (Kolbert, 1988, p. 32).

Despite apparent correlations between ethnicity and school achievement or completion rates, when income data are considered, a very different picture emerges. African American and Hispanic middle-class children "perform like white middle class children . . . [G]iven the opportunity, youth from every ethnic background can realize their potential" (Hodgkinson, 1988, p. 13). Genuine equality of opportunity would result in poor children achieving similarly to their more affluent peers.

Males continue to attend school longer and have slightly higher graduation rates than females. In 1980, 65.8 percent of females graduated from high school and completed a median of 12.4 years whereas 67.3 percent of males achieved a median of 12.6 years of schooling (US Bureau of Census, 1983). But unlike the data on ethnic minorities, these gender figures are improving. "As recently as 1960, American colleges and universities were predominantly male preserves. Only 1 in 3 of all students were female. Today half of all college students are women" (Conf. Bd. & US Bureau of Census, 1986, p.20). Successful high school completion and college enrollments by gender are now generally more equal than any other characteristic used to report demographic data.

How Do Families Influence Schooling?

Our students do not live in isolation. They are usually members of a family. These family structures exert a powerful influence on our students' education goals and their ability to participate in life at school. The size of the gap between the language and values of the school and those at home predicts the level of success the student is likely to achieve in school. Since the family experience has been such an important predictor of school success, it is essential that educators reconceptualize schooling so that all students, regardless of family background, will have not only access to a high quality education, but be nurtured to succeed in such a setting. This perspective conflicts with those that blame school failure on the students' background rather than taking responsibility for the schools' effects during the 15,000 hours our students are in school. English-language educators need to be knowledgeable about our students' families as a basis for designing successful programs that bridge the gap between experience and expectation, fulfilling our democratic responsibility for equality in educational experience for all.

Part of the reason for the increasingly poor fit between schools and students has been a dramatic shift in the nature of the American family. The traditional American family structure of a "breadwinner father, homemaker mother and two school-aged children ... now account[s] for only 7 percent of US households, [it is changing] to a single parent, most often female, with no major job skills (Hodgkinson, 1988, p. 11). Approximately 25 percent of children now live in single-parent homes and most of these are poor (Ellwood, 1988). In those homes where there are two parents, most often both are working outside the home in both cities and suburbs.

One of the important implications of this shift is the extent to which school personnel, from administrators to the individual teacher in a class, have shifted their mental model of who stands behind each child in their class or school. Insofar as we are still thinking of families in Norman Rockwell terms, we may not be able to see our students and their lives with any degree of accuracy. Proposals for increasing homework, for example,

assume parental supervision and support. Where that is not forthcoming, a "more homework policy" may actually have the ironic effect of further widening the achievement gap it is intended to narrow.

Other implications for the future can be derived from such data as the increased frequency with which teenagers are giving birth. These children having children most likely come from low-income households and usually have to drop out of school to care for their babies. This perpetuates a vicious cycle in our society. "Early childbearing is highly correlated with lower educational attainment" for both the mother and the child (Wetzel, 1987, p. iv). "Education is associated with parenting skills and child development; the children of teen parents also suffer. They tend to score lower than the children of older parents on standardized intelligence tests and they perform less well in school" (Kenney, 1987, p. 729). Our students live in families which have varying economic resources, expectations for schooling, and language traditions. These, in turn, are influenced by the economy at large.

How Does Economic Background Influence Schooling?

The financial resources available to our students are likely to influence both the breadth and depth of their previous experiences and the time available for continuing to enhance their education (by adults or by themselves). There is a widening gap between the rich and the poor—with the rich getting proverbially richer and the poor getting children. The consequences of such a phenomenon are revealed by the increasing numbers of our students who live in homes (or are homeless) with incomes at or below the poverty level. Since money is needed for basic survival (food, clothing, and shelter), that becomes a higher priority than education, which is considered a luxury in that content.

Our language-education programs need to be sensitive to our students' economic concerns, particularly focusing on ways to become independent of social service systems. The conflicting values implicit in the individual affluence of people who adopt competitive, independent, entrepreneurial perspectives, in contrast to the unionization of employees who receive the legislated minimum wage needs to be considered within the framework of a democratic society. Literary works need to be studied from a perspective that enlightens the relationship between the individual's power in society and the economic conditions that prevail. The English curriculum needs to be responsive to these issues, reflecting on the impact of society's rules and schools' contribution to the differences across the population, intent on devising alternative practices that might alleviate the poverty our students experience.

Aldrich (1988) notes that fewer than 1 percent of the population owns 20 percent of the wealth in our nation. This disproportionate share of economic resources results in a large percentage of people having very limited funds. Income reports are difficult to obtain, and when they are available, quartile rankings disguise the extent of the disparities Aldrich reports. Even so, it is clear that "minorities" are not prospering. In a recent report, grouped by ethnicity 51.6 percent of the Hispanic population, 40.8 percent of the African American population and only 17 percent of the white population fit into the lowest SES quartile. In contrast only 11.8 percent of the Hispanic population, and 13.1 percent of the African American population, but 32.5 percent of the white population are listed in the highest quartile (OERI, 1987c). In a different report, we are told the incomes of "13.5 percent of the nation (32.5 million Americans) [fall] below the poverty line, with less than 4 percent of the nation's total disposable income" (Glazer, 1988). Although we do not know the actual figures, the trends are dramatic, and reflect the differential economic support available to our students by ethnic background. White students are more likely to have richer resources available to help them understand the world. They are less likely to be concerned with economic hardships and therefore are free to focus on other matters, *i.e.* education.

Economically-advantaged students are increasingly working after school. In the main, they do so not to contribute to their family income, but to provide consumer items for their own lifestyle, whether it be designer outfits or gas for their car. While such work may provide valuable experience and a useful taste of employment requirements, it nevertheless distracts from attention to school work and has severely restricted the time available for school-related extracurricular activities.

The dilema that educators face is one of making school and school-related activities sufficiently meaningful and rewarding to compete with the lure of the mall and McDonald's. In schools that have become themselves increasingly like shopping malls (Powell, et al., 1985), there is little countervailing pressure against the consumer ethos. For students who have watched as many hours of TV commercials as contemporary students have (Postman, 1987), the power of purchasing solutions to all of life's problems must be directly and energetically addressed by educators if schools are to regain a place of central importance in teenagers' lives. Schools dominated by boring and trivial requirements can hardly compete.

The implications of the impact of these social class phenomena on educational success are still considered controversial. Nevertheless, Jencks, et al. (1980) and Bowles and Gintis(1976) have made a compelling case for the conclusion that income levels of parents are the single most important factor in predicting school success. And when low incomes correlate highly with minority status, poor minority students are coming to school with two strikes against them.

Poverty is related to unemployment, and the real unemployment rate is very high. The average civilian unemployment rate for 1980–87 was reported to be 7.8 percent (Tobin, 1988). The federal government's current (1988) unemployment rate of 5.8 percent nationwide excludes people who are not actively searching for a job, and those out of work in excess of 6 months. When these people are included, the numbers are frightening. For example, 45 percent of people in New York City over the age of 16 [who are not students] were neither employed nor looking for work (Lueck, 1988). Some of these may be homemakers and mothers or others who are in effect working in unpaid, caring positions in their families, but the larger percentage are people who have given up looking for employment. Additionally, the percentages conceal the fact that increasing

numbers of people are unemployed, keeping pace with the increasing numbers of people of age to join the workforce.

According to the *1980 Census,* of the 11.5 million 16 to 19 year-olds enrolled in schools, 4 million are employed. Approximately 33 percent of the white students are employed, contrasted with 13 percent of the African American population. Opportunities for employment are associated with ethnic factors. Those who need the income more are less likely to get the jobs.

One of the consequences of poverty and unemployment is that many students are involved in the drug world in two ways—as users and suppliers. OERI (1987b) documented the pervasiveness of drugs and alcohol noting that in 1985 17.3 percent of seniors used cocaine, 60.6 percent used illicit drugs, and 92.3 percent consumed alcohol. These figures are sobering as we note the devastating effects of these substances on students' brains and lives. As suppliers, they wear beepers to class, responding to buy signals, leaving the school building and their education behind. Money accumulates quickly, easily and in large denominations. Students feel successful in contrast to their painful experiences in classrooms where they are anonymous, denigrated for their limited academic achievement, isolated from their peers, denied opportunities to participate in decisions affecting their education, and denied access to knowledge essential for becoming self-reliant.

What Do Parents and Students Expect from Schooling?

Schools are alien places for many of our students. Schools expect different levels of success—some students are deemed "college material" while others are asked what they will do when they "leave school," implying that these students are not expected to graduate. These different treatments are apparent in distinguishing between students of diverse ethnic backgrounds. Students come to accept differential treatment—with some seeing useful models, achieving increasing independence, and getting much encouragement, while others receive isolated drills, are denigrated for their errors, and handicapped from accepting increasing responsibility. These significant differences in treatment and expectation result in significantly different outcomes. For a select few, school is a very positive experience, resulting in an enhanced self-esteem and access to strategies for lifelong learning. For most it is a negative experience. Some never recover their self-esteem or their inquisitiveness and desire to increase their knowledge with which they entered school. These differences perpetuate the status quo, in that a select few people in our society are rich and respected.

Traditionally, "each generation of Americans achieves a higher level of education than the one before" (Conf. Bd. & US Bureau of Census, 1986, p. 16). Enrollment in school for longer periods of time may be noted in comparing statistics from 1940 when 24.5 percent of Americans were high school graduates and the median length of schooling was 8.6 years to those in 1980 when 66.5 percent of the population graduated from high school, with the median schooling increasing to 12.5 years (US Bureau of the Census, 1983). With high school graduation, an accomplishment of the majority of the population, the importance of all groups obtaining their diplomas is self-evident. In

1986, 72 percent of 17-year-olds graduated from high school, in contrast to 56 percent in 1950 (Conf. Bd. & US Bureau of Census, 1986, p. 34–6).

Although overall students are staying in school a longer time and numerically more are achieving high school diplomas, there are dramatic exceptions. "More than half the 300,000 students in the city's high schools failed to qualify for diplomas within four years," (Daley, 1988, p. B4). These figures are troubling for two reasons. We know most of urban students represent large numbers of so called "minorities" and their dropping out reveals the gap between them and the schools. Additionally, the role of education in providing access to the good life is especially important for the "minorities" and the poor who inhabit most urban areas. "The likelihood of dropping out is inversely related to family income and varies directly with parental educational attainment and occupational status" (Wetzel, 1987, p. 17).

When we look at children in different social and economic classes, major differences become apparent. There are many different ways in which our students' school success is influenced by the nature of the support they receive at home. Grant and Sleeter (1988) found students' home backgrounds limited "the school's aspirations for its clients. What the home background did limit was the help parents could give. They told their children to 'get a good education,' 'to do what the teacher says,' most did not know that they should have been telling their children which courses to take, and demanding that teachers do more teaching" (p. 21). Their uninformed view of how schools work deprived their children of important opportunities.

Students and parents believe that schools are organized to help all succeed. They believe that school is the great equalizer where all must attend and all will have similar opportunities to succeed. It is with these implicit beliefs in mind that parents entrust their children to the schools and that students go to school daily. Yet the schools persistently fail to achieve these ends. Students who succeed despite the abundance of negative school experiences, prove they are *Invulnerable* in Anthony and Cohler's terms (1987) and they are persisters in Tinto's (1987) terms, important qualities of Americans.

The Languages of Home

Another success factor of concern to language educators is the nature of our students' linguistic environments. There are three interdependent dimensions of this issue that are of particular concern: English Dominance, Linguistic Differences and Background for Literacy.

English Dominance. "In 1985, language minority students (from homes where English is not the first language) made up 43 percent of the kindergarten enrollments in the [NYC] public schools" (Reyes, 1987). Urban schools are more likely to enroll students with limited exposure to English, placing a considerable responsibility on the schools for helping students develop English proficiency. English-language proficiency is no longer exclusively an urban concern, and recent immigrants are spreading to both suburbs and rural areas.

Students who succeed in school are more likely to be English dominant. Only 8 percent of high school seniors rated themselves as non-English-dominant. Students whose homes and school experiences encourage learning English promote the likelihood that these students will graduate. Schools which provide programs that both value the students' home language, while supporting their acquisition of English proficiency facilitate the possibility that students will succeed in school. We have found such classrooms to be exciting places for students and teachers, accomplishing the dual objective of facilitating the growth of English proficiency while respecting the students' mother tongue (Mayher, 1975). Since English is the dominant language of the nation, it is important for schools to provide programs which support students' learning in ways which are most consistent with current knowledge of factors which influence learning, (Bruner, 1986; Kelly, 1955; Salmon, 1985; and Vygotsky, 1978).

Linguistic Differences. The different ways parents talk with their children have dramatic consequences for their participation in English language-arts classrooms. One area where this is particularly dramatic is in the use of "directives". Delpit (1988) provides helpful contrasts as in (1) and (2) below:

(1) "Boy, get your rusty behind in that bathtub."
(2) "Isn't it time for your bath?"

Both of these statements are intended by the parents who utter them to expedite their child's taking a bath. But (1) is more typical of the working class home, while (2) is more frequently heard in middle-class homes. A child in a working-class home who heard (2) would believe he had real options, which the child in the middle-class home would know are illusory. However, when children from working-class homes enter school and hear such questions, they misconstrue the implicit meanings of language prevailing in the classroom. This may result in their being considered a discipline problem, or being placed in a special class for behavior disordered children.

Samples (3) and (4) capture critical characteristics of school language.

(3) We're going to take a test.
(4) T: Who knows what day it is today?
    S: Friday
    T: Very good.

The teacher who says (3) is not taking the test. The collaboration implicit in this statement is deceptive. Rather, the teacher will administer the test, and the students will take the test. Students who ask if the teacher is also going to take the test may be considered insolent, and disciplined for the transgression.

When asking (4) the teacher is seeking students who know the answer to so indicate by facing her, raising their hands, and making eye contact (Brause, Mayher and Bruno, 1985). Students who call out answers are usually either ignored or ostracized. Implicit in this teacher-student interchange is that the teacher knows the answer, and it is the students who have to come up with what's in the teacher's mind. The students need to figure out if the teacher wants them to say the day of the week and/or the date. The teacher is usually not posing a real question—as revealed by the evaluation (Very good). In a real conversation, the teacher would say "thank you," thereby expressing gratitude for the information. Successful students learn to use and interpret language in school that is consistent with the school norms.

There is no necessary superiority or inferiority inherent in such linguistic differences, but schools have fairly rigid value systems that students must adopt to succeed. Rather than assuming that difference always means deficiency, English language educators need to help students have the option of succeeding in mainstream society. The differences between language styles of home and school are significant for many students, and rather than tracking such students away from success, we must find ways to bridge the gaps.

Another linguistic difference that distinguishes homes (both working class and middle class) from schools is the way language is used to discuss issues. Parents in both working-class and middle-class homes talk with their children as they initiate them into the practices and traditions of the community (Heath, 1983; Wells, 1986). They learn how to read books, prepare meals, repair motors and play ball. When parents engage their children in these activities, they intersperse language as they proceed, sharing ideas and information. These utterances are contextually relevant and purposefully focused on the accomplishment of the activity (with asides on different, but personally important issues, as time permits). It is equally likely that children or adults choose the focus of the talk.

At home there is time and opportunity for implicit negotiation of topics. Parents engage in pleasant, informative conversations with the opportunity for increased understanding, a bonus, as in (5).

(5) **Parent**: We'll be going to the country on Saturday so you will see your friend Geoffrey again.
   Child: How many days before Saturday?
  Parent: Well today is Thursday, then comes Friday and then Saturday. Do you think you and Geoffrey might go to the river and look for your friends, the ducks?

The most rewarding conversations are ones in which each person tries to understand the other's perspectives, avoiding assumptions, and sharing beliefs freely. All are encouraged to participate collaboratively in the discussion, with no one monopolizing the discussion, and specific opportunities designated for those who haven't gotten a turn to present their views. The focus is on being together, to help each other accomplish something together. Rushing is inconsistent with real conversations that are responsive, engaging, and exciting for all participants. And personal remembrances or connections with experiences in other settings are encouraged. The style is colloquial with technical labels applied retrospectively, and contextually.

Children benefit from these types of conversations enhancing their understanding while becoming increasingly fluent language users. Children who are proficient in conversing with their parents, however, are not necessarily proficient in participating in classroom discussions. There are different ways to talk at home and at school, and these do seem to break along economic lines. When the school is a traditional, teacher-centered experience (Brause and Mayher, 1985) and the home is collaborative, these differences can have an effect on schooling. The conversation in classrooms is very different from family dialogues (as in (5)). Middle-class parents more deliberately prepare their children to participate in school-type "conversations" as in (6).

(6) Parent: Show Grandma how nicely you say the days of the week.

These parents school their children in classroom-type dialogue, in which participants are required to display knowledge about abstract, impersonal information, as the names of the planets in the universe, and the plots of stories. Even though at home, the children know the information the parents know, and the children have no personal reason for recalling these arbitrary facts at that particular time, such dialogues as (6) are treated as a game. And those who participate in them become good game players. They get experience at school-talk in preparation for school. In such homes, children are encouraged to "play school" and to learn through doing so that the teacher controls who talks, what is said, what is acceptable, what knowledge students are expected to display, and how they are to display it.

Traditional teacher-centered schools demand this kind of understanding. Hull (1985), for example, reported on children being asked to read the teacher's mind as in (7).

(7) I'm thinking about being alone—another word beginning with s (p. 165).

Unlike home conversations, school-talk is really monologic in quality, since the teacher controls all. Students fill in the blanks in the monologue, as in workbook exercises, and tests (Mayher and Brause, 1986). Teachers question students seeking only one acceptable answer. Student questions are considered digressions, or attempts to subvert the teacher's control. Students are restricted to regurgitating facts presented in textbooks and teacher statements. They are restricted in their observations, experiences and focus. They are restricted in the ways in which they can try to make sense of the information being presented. The teacher selects topics for discussion from the curriculum, often resulting in neither the teacher nor the student being personally interested in the topic. There is a constant concern for time—[we need to hurry]—and few students actually get turns-at-talk, with most eavesdropping on the answers of other students whose responses allow the teacher to move the lesson along. The participants frequently remark that they are bored in these settings, they are uninvolved, and forget the facts that they learn exclusively for regurgitation on tests. For students to get opportunities to talk and be successful in traditional classrooms, they must know the rules. But these rules are never explicitly stated, so students who do not know the game frequently violate the teacher's expectations and get penalized for doing so.

Students' homes prepare them differently for school. School

experiences are fairly predictable, with the overwhelmingly traditional organization of classrooms, consistent for the past 90 years at least, identified by Cuban (1984), particularly in their valuing of one linguistic dialect over others. If schools are to fulfill the casserole metaphor, and foster a pluralistic society, multiple dialects and languages must be respected, encouraged, and developed, while simultaneously providing access to the variety of mainstream, public English. We need to consider the efficacy of the traditional school practices both in light of current research and theory into language and learning and in light of our students' experiences as successful learners outside of school.

Background for Literacy. Children's drawings frequently include words, labels, or comments (Harste, Woodword, & Burke, 1984). From these initial writing efforts, children use their drawings to help them create narratives, alternating between elaborating on the text and the drawing (Graves, 1983). When these drawings and stories are posted on refrigerators at home, and shared enthusiastically with friends, children are subtly rewarded and encouraged to enter the literacy club, as when they look at books, and tell stories corresponding to the illustrations (Smith, 1988).

On the other hand, homes that are short on paper or space to display children's drawings and stories, provide less support for these activities, which are closely connected to reading and writing (Taylor & Dorsey-Gaines, 1988). Children who are deprived of these opportunities for exploring with literacy at home, live and work in the same classrooms where children are encouraged. This creates a major gap between the experiences of the two groups—and their readiness for more demanding literacy activities. Parents who understand the literacy environment of schools are more likely to specifically select preschool programs that are literacy-oriented, in that they provide the child with opportunities to see others writing and reading, and to engage in those activities with their children (Cochran-Smith, 1983). Such values, implicit in parental choice of program, carry over into the children's learning prior to school and at school. When school activities and goals are respected and valued by parents, children adopt the same values. According to Applebee, Langer, and Mullis, (1988), Chomsky (1972) and Wells (1986), homes that value education prepare children for schooling in a variety of ways such as by having more books and other reading materials.

Wells (1986) conducted an extensive longitudinal study of the language in children's homes. He found that all of the children were equivalent in their language ability when they entered school. A major difference was in their experiences being read-to. Those who were read-to knew much more about literate language and therefore were able to participate in those types of activities more readily than children without these experiences, and they continued to grow more rapidly as readers and writers through the first six years of school.

Anderson, Wilson, and Fielding (1988) studied the out-of-school reading of children in 2nd and 5th grades. They found "staggering differences" between children in the amount of reading . . . and that a small difference in the quantity of reading can greatly influence achievement. Time spent reading books was the best predictor of a child's growth as a reader from the second to the fifth grade" (p. 297). However, there are important differences in the achievement by ethnicity. White students' scores exceed those of African American and Hispanic students. Since schooling does not seem to overcome the early differences across these groups, we must reexamine the normal practices of literacy education.

When evaluating the writing of students in grades 3, 7, and 11, an increasing percentage of student writing is evaluated as "satisfactory" or "elaborated," and fewer are receiving the designation of "minimal" or "inadequate" (Applebee, et al., 1988, Table 2.4) However, 36 percent of students in grade 11 are evaluated with the two lowest designations. Considering the length of time these students have attended school, it seems essential to revise teaching practices that do not help students achieve the goals we have set. Rather, differences are perpetuated and magnified, consistent with other schooling practices.

Schooling Practices

In looking at schooling practices we are making two apparently contradictory arguments:

1. Schools are all the same.
2. Schools are different.

Schools are similar in many respects. They have a curriculum. They administer tests. They are housed in isolated buildings. They are organized by age and neighborhood. They have a predictable range of resources: textbooks, televisions, teachers, blackboards, bookcases. They have similar equipment—chairs and desks. They are staffed with one teacher per classroom. The teacher does the talking and the students do the listening. Schools in one place look like schools in all other places—so much so that Cuban (1984) remarked on the similarity between schools, across the nation and across grades, as well as comparing those in 1890 to those in 1980. These similarities among schools do not reveal the quality of the educational transactions within them.

These are the source of the differences among schools. The *people* distinguish one school from another. The life in these buildings embodied in the students, teachers, and administrators, can vary widely in background, expectations and their commitment to equal education for all. These factors strongly influence the nature of the transactions that occur in the schools as noted by one of us (Brause, 1987) returning to one school after 25 years.

In most classrooms, whole class lessons prevail with students answering teacher questions (Goodlad, 1983). During these events, there is a tacit agreement among the participants not to embarrass each other (Powell, et al., 1985). Operationalizing that agreement involves students and teachers not asking questions to which the intended respondent does not have the answer. Implicit in such treaties is the belief that there are a finite number of correct answers—and that there is an objective, but predetermined body of knowledge which all should know. Smith (1986) describes such pratices as an *Insult to Intel-*

ligence, but they are central to the normal game of schooling. Students who play the game well, succeed in school; those who do not, do not.

Applebee et al. (1988) note that students in 11th grade read to answer predetermined, externally imposed questions, clearly an outcome of their schooling experiences. All the reasons language educators introduce children to books suggested by Applebee, et al. (talk with friends, learn something new, imagine myself in the story and to relax) decrease in importance as students go through the grades. The one item that almost doubles in student choice is "to answer questions about it." These students who have made it to the 11th grade know that reading in school serves one essential purpose—to prove that they have read by responding to the teacher's questions. These successful students are testwise and schoolwise. Those who are more adept at psyching out the situation and ascertaining the responses that will be more highly valued by the raters, are rewarded with higher scores. There is increasing evidence to support the view that this testwiseness is prevalent in so-called mainstream environments (Heath, 1983). Those in other settings view the task through different lenses and fail to meet the expectations of the test maker who establishes the reward system. In such a context, it is no surprise that students from different backgrounds perform differently on standardized achievement measures.

In some schools teachers are concerned about their students becoming self-respecting learners who use a variety of strategies for acquiring information collaboratively. They have high expectations for themselves and their students. They know their students as individuals, and they are committed to being instrumental in their students' learning while continuing to learn themselves about their students as learners and about the content of their instruction. They search out experiences and materials that are personally meaningful to students, engaging them in the process of learning, helping students individually and collectively to become critically literate. They have confidence in the students' innate abilities to learn and their own ability to help students learn. Programs established in Hawaii's Kamehameha schools (Au, 1980), and Michigan's Perry Preschool Project (Schweinhart, Weikart, & Larner, 1986), for example, provide persuasive evidence of the efficacy of such programs, particularly helping students considered "at risk" to succeed in school. We know the teacher's expectations can have dramatic impact on students' self-concept and learning (Peters, 1971; Rosenthal and Jacobson, 1968).

Programs offered in schools vary. Preschool programs are distinguished by their focus on daycare and autonomous play (Klass, 1986) or socialization and other school-like activities (Cochran-Smith, 1983). Schools establish different tracks for student placement, grouping students with similar scores on standardized tests in the same room. This grouping results in segregation. Some students are relegated to special services, a euphemism for low-expectation groups, and others are guided to advanced placement courses. Erickson and Shultz (1982) document the guidance counselor's role in perpetuating ethnic bias. Gartner and Lipsky (1987) note the disproportionately high representation of "minority" students enrolled in special education courses. They also indicate a paucity of evidence of student success in these programs.

TABLE 18–1. Enrollments in Honors and Remedial English Programs

Honors Program		Remedial Program
4.7%	White students	4.2%
2.2%	Black students	4.5%
2.1%	Hispanic students	4.5%
8.3%	Asian & Pacific Island students	1.6%
2%	American Indian students	5.2%

Source: OERI, 1987a.

Tracking has been studied by Oakes (1985) and Powell, et al. (1985) revealing so called "minority" students are more highly represented in programs that are considered less rigorous. The enrollments in 11th-grade Remedial and Honors English programs are instructive in this regard (Table 18–1).

There are important consequences to student placement. Some programs lead to college admission, others do not. Students who are enrolled in remedial courses, and less rigorous programs, are denied access to higher education. More importantly, students whose education is viewed as one of remedying their deficient background, rather than an expansion of their experiences, are singularly denigrated by their schooling experiences. "All the national commissions are telling the schools to pick winners, but we need the schools to *create* the winners.... We need to make sure that every kid succeeds in school" (Hodgkinson, 1988, p. 14).

Tracking separates, and perpetuates differences in students' home backgrounds. The racial segregation embedded in these practices causes us to question all tracking. The effect of these practices handicaps students from kindergarten through grade 12.

Weikart and colleagues (Beruetta-Clement, Schweinhart, Barnett, Epstein, & Weikart, 1984; Schweinhart, et al., 1986) show the differential effect of children's participation in preschool programs and their achievement in later school grades. Those who participated in the "transactional" model of learning at the Perry Preschool Project at age 3 were followed to the age of 19, with the results indicating lasting benefits of the preschool program in contrast to those who attended no preschool program. Students stayed in school longer, were more likely to go to college, received higher scores on standardized tests, had fewer teenage births, and fewer arrests. A subsequent study (Schweinhart, et al., 1986) comparing students in the Perry program with 2 other programs [the Distar program and a traditional nursery program] found significant differences in the students' sense of responsibility, self-esteem and similar indicators of success for the students who participated in the transactional, Perry preschool program. School programs differ in their impact on children.

In more traditional schools, students are viewed as empty vessels in need of filling throughout schooling—with the teacher controlling all movement in the room, all topics for discussion, and the assessment of learning. These teachers frequently have low expectations for students achieving in their class or graduating from high school; they have little faith in the students as individuals and do not trust them to be able to work

TABLE 18–2. Characteristics of Students who Succeed and Fail

School Succeeders	School Failures
White	"Minority"
Suburban	Urban
Middle class family	Working class or poor family
English proficient	English is a second language
Trend to small family	Large family and/or single parent
Parent(s) employed	Parent(s) unemployed
Stable community	Transient community
Expect to succeed	Expect to fail
Regular attendance	Frequent absence
Spacious school building	Overcrowded school
Optimistic teachers	Dispirited teachers
Sociable with peers	Socially isolated
Teacher knows student names	Students are anonymous
"Academic" classes	"Skills" classes
Graduate from high school	Dropout prior to high school graduation

independently, always perceiving the need to move the students in a lock-step process to facilitate monitoring. To accommodate this view, they break the curriculum into arbitrary, atomistic and trivial facts, which they present to the students as truths, in abstraction, and assess their ability to regurgitate information (Gold, 1988; Hull, 1985). These teachers believe they know all they need to know to teach their students, never questioning the efficacy of established practices, or the validity of beliefs or strategies.

Inequality in Our Students' Lives

When we look at students' experiences in schools, there seems to be a problem with operationalizing the concept of equality of opportunity. We note characteristics that tend to distinguish these two groups: those who are succeeding using the schools' value system and those who are failing in that system (Table 18–2).

School and the real world are one. Historically, public schools have perpetuated society's biases—helping students similar to the power group to succeed while encouraging others who are different from the power group (particularly in physical characteristics) to drop out.

INTERPRETING THE DATA

Given the undoubted reality that schools are not helping all children get an equal opportunity to participate in the American Dream of access to higher education and economic opportunity, what assessments have been made of this situation and what alternatives have been suggested to help deal with these problems? The analyses vary, but most of them end up blaming the children, their parents, or some other aspect of their social milieu. Further, as Rose (1988) has recently pointed out, the evaluations themselves frequently exhibit what he calls "cognitive reductionism," which involves finding a single, and simplistic cause for such problems, which then limits efforts to provide

alternative educational environments to help such students catch up.

Some of the evaluations blame the schools. This is the tack taken by The National Commission on Excellence (1983) and by William Bennett and his allies such as Ravitch and Finn (1987) and even Hirsch (1987). In this case, the critique is essentially that schools have failed to have sufficient content in the curriculum, sufficiently high standards for students, and sufficiently professional (i.e. subject-content knowledgeable) teachers. They urge a return to a period when American education worked, although they are vague about when that was, because in that golden age everyone knew more and worked harder. They blame the progressive movement and, particularly, its renewal in the late 1960s for our current problems even though, for example, the NAEP data and studies like those of Goodlad (1983) suggest that the real culprit was the emphasis on atomistic skills of decoding and encoding, of the back-to-basics movement which marked the 1970s conservative response to the 60's.

Most significant of all, however, both the identification of problems and the suggestion for reform embodied in much of the current focus on renewing American education take for granted that so called "minority" children will never be able to fully participate in the pursuit of educational excellence. Test data and the demographic realities of the lack of success by "minorities": in completing high school and/or higher education are taken at face value to show that since they aren't doing well, it means they can't do well. This version of the self-fulfilling prophecy provides a built-in excuse for school failure, and thereby lets the schools off the hook of responsibility by, in effect, saying, we are not to blame for the low achievements of some students; they simply do not have the potential to succeed.

Are Schools "Fair"?

The belief in schools can only be sustained if one can assume that the schools and the tests they employ to assess and track students are fundamentally accurate and fair. As noted earlier, this belief is a basic keystone of the American faith in education, a conviction that schools are the great equalizer, the one institution in American society that is both dedicated to and effective at treating every child equally and giving all an equal chance at academic success. While there is no question that schools should, and we believe they could, function that way, we have already cited considerable evidence to show that they just do not do so for all children.

Who's Responsible?

Rather than continuing to blame the victim—to put the onus of responsibility for failure exclusively on the shoulders of the children (and/or their parents), perhaps it is time to try a new tack. This would recognize that the demographic realities we have described do present new challenges to schools, particularly that of viewing all students, especially children of color, of non-English-speaking backgrounds, or of poor and/or single parent families as likely to succeed. Such an approach would require a significant reconceptualization of the tasks facing schools and of the kinds of education programs required to serve effectively the students who are actually enrolled. It would require school people to recognize that the "drop out" problem is not the result of the inadequate potential of the drop outs, but a powerful statement of the failure of schools to help students achieve academic success.

Such a reconceptualization would demand that schools live up to the educational cliche of starting where the students really are. But it would also demand the abandonment of the more or less overt assumption that students who come to school with backgrounds and motivations different from those of the teacher are thereby permanently and inevitably condemned to low standards of achievement and are more than likely to drop out before completing school. It would also require a renewed commitment not only to equality of opportunity, but to equality of results. This latter is a much more controversial goal since the presumption of the inequality of talent and ability is so pervasive, but unless schools commit themselves to such a goal, the current practices of segregation and tracking will continue to make a mockery of equality of opportunity.

FROM A PROBLEM TO AN OPPORTUNITY

A commitment to equality of results for schooling must be based on the overwhelming commonalities of our species specific human potential for learning. This requires a focus, not on the relatively minor differences that distinguish us from each other, but on the common potential of our genetic endowment as human beings. The fact that children are more alike when they enter kindergarten than they ever are again in school—a conclusion that can be drawn from virtually every study of school achievement—is the most powerful evidence we have that schools are part of the problem, not part of the solution to inequality of achievement.

Those of us in language education know, for example, that, by the time they get to school, all but a minute fraction of the student population have acquired a spoken language system of infinite potential, of normally flexible creativity, and with enormous riches of conceptual understanding. But children whose spoken language system is not English, or whose variety of English is not similar to the regional standard, and/or whose parents have not read to them extensively before they get to school, find themselves immediately behind the literacy eight ball. The statistics further show that virtually all of the remedial programs attempted so far have exacerbated, rather than helped close the literacy gap. Providing an educational environment that will genuinely solve these problems will not be easy, but the preschool and followup data (Au, 1980; Bereutta-Clement, et al., 1984; Cochran-Smith, 1983 and Schweinhart, et al., 1986) show it can be done.

But it won't be done by schools which continue to assume that difference means deficiency. In a genuinely pluralistic society—a real casserole—differences can be celebrated and built on as sources of strength. They can be used to provide a space for the transition to mainstream educational attainment as effective transitional bilingual programs do now. They can be a source of individual pride and group self-esteem, rather than a continued source of racist and cultural stereotyping. And they can be a source of creating and renewing our commitment to the kind of pluralistic culture that emphasizes our common humanity at its base, as well as our common Americanism as a nation of immigrants who hold common aspirations for ourselves, our children, and our casserole culture.

From Vision to Reality

Transforming schools is never an easy task as Cuban (1984) has shown. Nevertheless, schools do change. Current pressures for accountability and the use of standardized tests to achieve it have changed schools dramatically in the last decade. Our interpretation of the demographic data, however, shows that these changes have been overwhelmingly counterproductive for the most needy of our students. The limited and limiting tests have emphasized and exaggerated the differences among our students. This has had the effect of emphasizing what they cannot do, rather than what they can do. Further, it has labeled them as potential or actual failures and greased the skids toward their early departure from school.

In order to break this vicious cycle, we must take a new look at who our students are and what they can do. We must emphasize their competencies and achievements constantly striving to expand each student's repertoire, and build on these as the potential foundation for even higher levels of success. We have to believe that excellence is possible for all children, and we have to find approaches to teaching and learning which will narrow the gap between the ideal and the real. If it is *conceivable* that all students can achieve higher levels of critical literacy—to be able to use language as readers, writers, speakers and listeners with power and imagination and critical acumen—then it should be *achievable* given the power of the oral systems all of them bring with them to school. But it would not be achieved as long as we treat differences as symptoms of negative limits on the potential for achievement, when we continue to assume that children who come to school without the groundwork for literacy under their belts will never be able to catch up, and hold to the belief that our current tests measure unchangeable limits of potential.

An Uncommon Sense Education for All

The kinds of schools we need for the students we really have—of all colors, of all cultural and linguistic heritages, of both sexes—are what one of us has called uncommon sense schools (Mayher,1990)—schools that believe in the common human potential of all learners and that build curricula and learning environments that meet the needs of real students by building on their strengths rather than cataloging their deficiencies. Such schools seek excellence for all, not as a pipe dream, but as a commitment to enhancing the common human potential of all students.

The realities they confront of ethnic, racial, and gender stereotyping can be changed by eliminating tracking and developing effective strategies for students of mixed proficiencies, by recognizing and developing effective assessment measures that evaluate children's best work, and by making students partners in the learning process through negotiating the curriculum. When students collaborate with teachers in establishing and implementing the curriculum, there is real dialog in which the interests of students are paramount in identifying the enterprises in which students will engage, and the teacher finds ways to use these experiences to expand students' concepts about the world and strategies for learning. In such a partnership, teams of students design and accept responsibility for accomplishing tasks and collaborating with peers and the teacher in the process of simultaneously accomplishing a project and become increasingly educated. See Boomer (1982) for additional details concerning this concept.

In such schools, everyone not only can learn to use language powerfully in all four modes, but can do so in a framework that helps them learn how to learn, using language and all of the other symbol systems they need to do so. Until we try such approaches we really don't have any idea what the potential for excellence of all students really is. But whatever the possibilities for change in uncommon sense directions, we cannot continue to let the growing number of so called minority children in our schools serve as the perennial reason to excuse our failures. Their numbers will continue to grow. Our challenge is to use this opportunity to rebuild our schools so that they actually help all children have equal access to the American Dream—to make the American ideal that education should serve to provide equality of access to the good life a reality for our students, not an illusion.

References

Aldrich, N.W. Jr. (1988) *Old money.* NY: Alfred Knopf.

Anderson, R.C., Wilson, P.T., & Fielding, L.G. (1988). Growth in reading and how children spend their time outside of school. *Reading research quarterly, 23*(3), 285–303.

Anthony, E.J., & Cohler, B.J. (Eds.), (1987). *The invulnerable child.* NY: Guilford.

Apple, M.W. (1986). *Teachers and texts: A political economy of class and gender relations in education.* NY: Routledge and Kegan Paul.

Applebee, A.N., Langer, J.A. & Mullis, I.V.S. (1988). *Who reads best? Factors related to reading achievement in grades 3, 7 and 11.* Princeton, NJ: ETS.

Aronowitz, S. & Giroux, H.A. (1988). Schooling, culture, and literacy in the age of broken dreams: A review of Bloom and Hirsch. *Harvard educational review, 58*(2), 172–194.

Au, K.H. (1980). Participation structures in a reading lesson with Hawaiian children: Analysis of a culturally appropriate instructional event. *Anthropology and education quarterly, 11,* 91–115.

Bencivenga, J. (1983, March 11). Huge minority enrollment challenges public education. *Christian science monitor,* pp. 7.

Beruette-Clement, J., Schweinhart, L., Barnett, W., Epstein, A. & Weikart, D. (1984). *Changed lives: The effects of the Perry preschool program on youths through age 19.* (Monographs of the High/Scope Educational Research Foundation, 8), Ypsilanti, MI: High/Scope Press.

Boomer, G. (Ed.), (1982). *Negotiating the curriculum: A teacher-student partnership.* Sydney, Australia: Ashton Scholastic.

Bowles, S. & Gintis, H. (1976). *Schooling in capitalist America.* London: Routledge and Kegan Paul.

Brause, R.S. (1987). School days: Then and now. *Anthropology and education quarterly, 18*(1), 53–5.

Brause, R.S. & Mayher, J.S. (1985). Learning through teaching: Language at home and at school. *Language arts, 62*(8), 870–5.

Brause, R.S., & Mayher, J.S. & Bruno, J. (1985). *An investigation into bilingual students' classroom communicative competence.* Rosslyn, VA: National Clearinghouse for Bilingual Education.

Bruner, J. (1986). *Actual minds, possible worlds.* Cambridge: Harvard University Press.

Chomsky, C. (1972). Stages in language development and reading exposure. *Harvard educational review, 42*(1), 1–33.

Chronicle of higher education almanac. (1988, September 1).

Cochran-Smith, M. (1983). *The making of a reader.* Norwood, NJ: Ablex.

Conference Board & US Bureau of the Census. (1986). *How we live:*

Then and now (a joint study). Washington, DC: US Government Printing Office.

Cremin, L. (1988). *American education: The metropolitan experience 1876–1980.* NY: Harper & Row.

Cuban, L. (1984). *How teachers taught: Constancy and change in American classrooms 1890–1980.* NY: Longman.

Daley, S. (1988, June 21). Hispanic dropout rate is highest in study of New York City schools. *The New York Times.* pp. A1, B4.

Delpit, L.D. (1988). The silenced dialogue: Power and pedagogy in educating other people's children. *Harvard educational review, 58*(3), 280–298.

Education Week (1988, October 26). Study of southern students' test scores raises doubts on worth of nationally normed exams, p. 11.

Ellwood, D.T. (1988). *Poor support: Poverty in the American family.* NY:Basic Books.

Erickson, F. & Shultz, J. (1982). *The counselor as gatekeeper: Social interaction in interviews.* NY: Academic Press.

Fiske, E.B. (1987, July 26). Hispanic pupils' plight cited in study. *New York Times,* p. 24.

Fiske, E.B. (1988, June 23). School integration patterns change. *New York Times,* p. 16.

Gardner, H. (1983). *Frames of mind: The theory of multiple intelligences.* NY: Basic Books.

Gartner, A. & Lipsky, D.K.(1987). Beyond special education: Toward a quality system for all students. *Harvard educational review, 57*(4), 367–95.

Giroux, H, (1983). *Theory and resistance in education.* South Hadley, MA: Bergin & Garvey Publ.

Glazer, N. (1988). *The limits of social policy.* Cambridge: Harvard U.P.

Gold, D.L. (1988, November 2). Some reforms counterproductive for young, group says. *Education Week,* p. 5.

Goodlad, J. (1983). *A place called school.* NY: McGraw-Hill.

Grant, C.A. & Sleeter, C.E. (1988). Race, class, and gender and abandoned dreams. *Teachers college record, 90*(1), 19–40.

Graves, D.H. (1983). *Writing: Teachers and children at work.* Portsmouth, NH: Heinemann.

Haley, A. (1976). *Roots.* Garden City, NY: Doubleday.

Harste, J.C., Woodward, V.A., & Burke, C.L. (1984). *Languages stories and literacy lessons.* Portsmouth, NH: Heinemann.

Heath, S.B. (1983). *Ways with words: Language, life and work in communities and classrooms.* NY: Cambridge UP.

Hirsch, E.D. Jr. (1987). *Cultural literacy: What every American needs to know.* Boston: Houghton Mifflin.

Hodgkinson, H. (1988). The right schools for the right kids. *Educational leadership, 45*(5), 10–14.

Holmes Group Forum, (1988). *111*(1) p. 2–3.

Hull, R. (1985). *The language gap: How classroom dialogue fails.* NY:Methuen.

Jencks, C., Bartlett, S., Corcoran, M., Crouse, J., Eaglesfield, D., Jackson, G., McLelland, K., Mueser, P., Olneck, M., Schwartz, J., Ward, S. & Williams, J. (1980). *Who gets ahead?* NY: Basic Books.

Kelly, G. (1955). *A theory of personality.* NY: Norton.

Kenney, A.M. (1987). Teen pregnancy: An issue for schools. *Phi delta kappan, 68*(10), 728–736.

Klass, C.S. (1986). *The autonomous child.* Philadelphia: Falmer Press.

Kolbert, E. (1988, October 22). A NY report says racism creates two tiers of schools. *New York Times,* pp. 1, 32.

Koretz, D. (1988). Arriving in Lake Wobegon: Are standardized tests exaggerating achievement and distorting instruction? *American education, 12*(2), 8–15.

Lieberson, S. & Waters, M.C. (1988). *From many strands: Ethnic and racial groups in contemporary America.* NY: Russell Sage Foundation.

Lueck, T.J. (1988, August 3). 45 percent of New Yorkers are outside labor force. *New York Times,* pp. A1, B4.

Mayher, J.S. (1990). *Uncommon Sense: Theoretical practice in language education.* Portsmouth, NH:Boynton/Cook.

Mayher, J.S. (1975). *An evaluation of the elementary grades bilingual project.* Unpublished manuscript for the NYC Board of Education and US office of Education.

Mayher, J.S. & Brause, R.S. (1986). Teachers can make a difference. Presentation at the NCTE Spring Conference, Houston.

McNeil, L. (1986). *Contradictions of control: School structure and school knowledge.* NY: Routledge and Kegan Paul.

McLaren, P. (1989). *Life in schools.* Boston: Longman.

National Commission on Excellence in Education. (1983). *A nation at risk: The imperative of educational reform.* Washington, DC: US Government Printing Office.

New York Times (1988, August 30). US reports significant rise in education of workforce, p. A17.

New York Times (1988, September 7). US Hispanic population is up 34% since 1980, p. A20.

Oakes, J. (1985). *Keeping track: How schools structure inequality.* New Haven:Yale UP.

Office of Educational Research and Improvement (OERI). (1984). *The conditions of education: A statistical report, 1984 edition.* (NCES 84-401) Washington, DC: US Government Printing Office.

OERI. (1987a). *The conditions of education: A statistical report, 1987 edition.* (CS 87-365) Washington, DC: US Government Printing Office.

OERI. (1987b). *Elementary and ssecondary education indicators in brief.* (IS 87-106) Washington, DC: US Government Printing Office.

OERI. (1987c). *Transition from h.s. to postsecondary education: Analytical studies.* (CS 87-309c) Washington, DC: US Government Printing Office.

Orfield, G. & Monfort, C. (1988). *Racial change and desegregation in large school districts: Trends through the 1986–1987 school year.* Alexandria, VA: National School Boards Association.

Peters, W. (1971). *A class divided.* Garden City, NY: Doubleday.

Postman, N. (1987). *Amusing ourselves to death.*

Powell, A.G., Farrar, E., & Cohen, D.K. (1985). *The shopping mall high school: Winners and losers in the educational marketplace.* Boston: Houghton Mifflin.

Ravitch, D. & Finn, C.E. Jr. (1987). *What do our 17-year-olds know? A report on the first national assessment of history and literature.* NY: Harper & Row.

Reyes, L.O. (compiler) (1987). *Demographies of Puerto Rican/Latino students in NY and the US.* Unpublished manuscript: Aspira of NY Inc.

Rodriguez, R. (1982). *A hunger of memory.* Boston: Godine.

Rose, M. (1988). Narrowing the mind and page: Remedial writers and cognitive reductionism. *College composition and communication, 39*(3), 267–302.

Rosenthal, R. & Jacobson, L. (1968). *Pygmalion in the classroom: Teacher expectation and pupils' intellectual development* NY: Holt, Rinehart & Winston.

Salmon, P. (1985). *Living in time: A new look at personal development.* London: Dent.

Schweinhart, L.J., Weikart, D.P., & Larner, M.B. (1986). A report on the high/scope preschool curriculum comparison study: Consequences of three preschool curriculum models through age 15. *Early childhood research quarterly, 1*(1), 15–45.

Sedlack, M.W., Wheeler, C.W, Pullin, D.C. & Cusick, P.A. (1986). *Selling students short: Classroom bargins and academic reform in the American high school.* New York: Teachers College Press.

Smith, F. (1986). *Insult to intelligence: The bureaucratic invasion of our classrooms.* NY: Arbor House.

Smith, F. (1988). *Joining the literacy club: Further essays into education.* Portsmouth, NH: Heinemann.

Taylor, D. & Dorsey-Gaines, C. (1988). *Growing up literate: Learning from inner-city families.* Portsmouth, NH: Heinemann.

Tinto, V. (1987). *Leaving college: Rethinking the causes and cures of student attrition.* Chicago: U. of Chicago Press.

Tobin, J. (1988, October 23). The rise and fall of the American economy (review of the *The great u-turn* by B. Harrison & B. Bluestone) *New York Times Book Review,* 43–4.

US Bureau of the Census (1983). *Characteristics of the population: General social and economic characteristics: US summary.* (PC 80-1-c1). Washington, DC: US Government Printing Office.

US Bureau of the Census (1987). *Estimates of the population of the US, by age, sex and race: 1980 to 1986.* (Series p-25, No. 1000) Washington, DC: US Government Printing Office.

Vygotsky, L.S. (1969) *Mind in society.* In M. Cole, V. John-Steiner, S. Scribner, & E. Souberman, (Eds.), Cambridge: Harvard UP., pp. 19-119.

Wells, G. (1986). *The meaning makers: Children learning language and using language to learn.* Portsmouth, NH:Heinemann.

Wetzel, J.R. (1987). *American youth: A statistical snapshot.* NY: The Wm. T. Grant Foundation.

·19·

THE LEARNER DEVELOPS

19A. THE DEVELOPMENT OF THE YOUNG CHILD AND THE EMERGENCE OF LITERACY

Elizabeth Sulzby

If we look at the history of education in the United States during this century, we will notice a dearth of information about the reading and writing of young children from birth through kindergarten age for most of that period, even though a few hearty researchers and practitioners (e.g., Hildreth, 1932; Huey, 1908; Iredell, 1989; see also Mathews, 1966, and Teale & Sulzby, 1986) were pointing to the need to study reading and writing in the pre-1st-grade years. Beginning faintly in the mid-1960s, increasing slightly during the 1970s, and burgeoning in the 1980s and early 1990s, research in emergent literacy has itself emerged into a solid area of investigation that differs in approach as well as in age range.

Sulzby (1989, in press) defines *emergent literacy* the "the reading and writing behaviors of young children that precede and develop into conventional literacy." Emergent literacy research treats reading and writing as being interrelated phenomena, with related developmental paths, and treats the young child's literacy development as the relevant object of study (Goodman, 1980, 1984; Mason & Allen, 1986; Teale & Sulzby, 1986). Now as we enter the 1990s it is commonplace to hear the words *emergent literacy* in schools or professional meetings or to read them in professional journals or reviews. But, while labels change, Dickinson (1989) and others warn us that instructional practices may move only slowly.

Definitions of term are in flux, both in literacy research and early childhood research, in general. In this chapter, the term *young child* will be used somewhat loosely to denote the child from birth through the end of kindergarten. This is certainly not the end of early childhood, but it is still the boundary, in general, between instruction based upon a model of development that posits the concepts of the young child as being different from conventional concepts. As can be seen below, the assumption that all children hold conventional, adult concepts for linguistic units and for literacy practices in 1st grade is also questionable, but this review ends somewhat arbitrarily at the end of kindergarten and focuses most heavily upon the prekindergarten-aged child. The terms *preschool* and *preschooler* have ambigious meaning. If we refer to children's age, children not yet in kindergarten could be called *preschoolers* and might not enrolled in any kind of school; other preschoolers will be enrolled in institutes called *preschools* that have instructional programs. In the review that follows, terms referring to age and to type of school or child care institutes will be distinguished.

The actual focus of this chapter is upon a developmental period for children, rather than merely upon their chronological age or institutional affiliation with day cares, preschools, or public schools. It discusses young children prior to their entry into conventional literacy. This period was earlier referred to as "prereading" or "reading readiness" (with children's writing being ignored, for the most part). The shift in terminology signals a shift in conceptions both of young children and of literacy.

The age range is typically from infancy through about age 7, although a few children begin to read and write conventionally as early as 4 or 5, and some do not reach that level of understanding until age 8 or 9. The onset of formal schooling is as variable as is the age range. There are formal lessons in many home settings and there are a variety of attitudes and practices toward instruction in child care, preschool, kindergarten and 1st grade settings—ranging from child-centered programs in which almost all choice is left to the child, through interactive settings in which teachers respond to children's interests and activities, through teacher-centered settings with direct, highly-sequenced instruction.

Teale and Sulzby (1986) provided an extensive history of the shifts in perspective toward the literacy development of young children in the US during the twentieth century. They point out that the immediately preceding view toward early literacy—"reading readiness"—represented a step forward from a view of young children's literacy as dependent upon maturation or neural ripening. Findings from early research in children's maturation were interpreted as providing evidence that a lock-step approach to introducing all children to reading instruction simultaneously with 1st-grade entry was untenable. Morphett and Washburne (1931) seemed to provide evidence for the need of differentiating instruction according to the mental age of the individual child. While this study was quite flawed and immediately refuted, it was quite influential. Researchers (Betts, 1946; Gates, 1937; Gates & Bond, 1936; Gates, Bond & Russell, 1939) found, instead, that instruction would begin earlier if methods were changed. This group ushered in the era of reading readiness as the product of experience, and for the next 40 years or so, reading readiness was the model that ruled research in early literacy. The research paradigm was the search for behaviors of the young child that predicted subsequent achievement in instruction in reading.

Models of reading (and writing) have, of course, changed dramatically during this century. A simple way of expressing the different between the models of reading from the reading readiness perspective and that of emergent literacy is the boundary into conventional reading. From a reading readiness perspective, reading meant an accurate reproduction of the printed words on a page of conventionally spelled words. To put it even more simply, a child was reading when he or she could say and interpret the words in simple texts like basal pre-primers and primers. Prior to that, the child was a prereader and the period was the prereading of readiness period during which the child should be learning the necessary precursors to real reading. Research was the search for what these precursors were, but they were viewed as being different in kind from reading and writing. For example, precursors studied have varied from knowing letter names and sounds to such competencies as maze tracing or balancing on a walking beam (Betts, 1946).

From an emergent literacy perspective, reading begins long before that time and emergent behaviors such as protoreading (Pappas, 1986) or emergent reading (Teale, 1984) are treated as an integral part of reading development. Recently, some researchers (e.g., Sulzby, 1989, in press) have been suggesting that more attention should be paid to the shift from emergent into conventional patterns of reading and writing. The precursors of conventional reading and writing are different under the emergent literacy perspective. They are emergent behaviors and concepts of reading and writing themselves. Examples are children "reading" from books by looking at the pictures or scribbling letters to grandparents.

While emergent literacy is relatively new as an area of research, it has had a vigorous beginning. There have been a number of quite detailed reviews of emergent literacy in recent years (Mason, 1986; Mason & Allen, 1986; Sulzby & Teale, in press; Teale, 1987; Teale & Sulzby, 1986) and a number of books containing collections of emergent literacy research studies (Allen & Mason, 1989; Morrow & Smith, 1989; Strickland & Morrow, 1989; Teale & Sulzby, 1986; Yaden & Templeton, 1986). This review will not attempt to go into detail about many of the older studies that have been discussed elsewhere. Instead, this chapter presents a synopsis of what has been learned about children's emergent reading and writing and some of the challenges for future research. The section that follows frames the current research in emergent literacy with its immediate predecessors.

The Legacy of Earlier Research

Many lines of research and theorizing about young children have contributed to today's research in emergent literacy. A ma-

jor contribution was made by the research in child language acquisition during the 1960s as an aftermath of the so-called Chomskyan Revolution in linguistics. That research revealed that many of the previous explanations of children's language were too simplistic; young children were now seen a being active in their language acquisition, generating hypotheses about how language operates, and testing these hypotheses in linguistic interaction with their parents and other speakers. Children's errors were interpreted as revealing their conceptual understandings of language, picking up on suggestions made earlier by Piaget (1959). Researchers (e.g., Clark 1978) began to study such phenomena as overgeneralization or overextension and the developmental paths of children's semantic and syntactic behavior, as revealed in their production of language and responses to elicitations based upon hypothesized developmental paths. Researchers of early literacy began to turn to language acquisition research and to theories of language as a resource in reconceiving their own studies. In the sections that follow, three other parts of the legacy of earlier studies is reviewed: the studies of early or precocious readers, of metalinguistic awareness, and of environmental print.

Precocious Reader Studies. This line of research developed relatively early and was not initially informed by the shift in conceptions of child language acquisition or child development in general. Yet its contribution began to provide a missing link in earlier approaches to beginning reading (see Teale, 1978). As early as the mid-1960s, Durkin (1966) was conducting research that focused upon children who come to school already reading. In a sense, Durkin was one of the first to operationalize a definition of conventional reading in a manner which would illuminate children's previous development. Her definition, however, was quite traditional but it was in line with the theory and measurement instruments of the day. Teachers and parents had been reporting that some children came to school already reading. In order to select a sample of such children to study, Durkin used as her criteria the ability to read correctly from a list of common words and the ability to score at a level on a standardized reading test sufficiently high for it to be unlikely that the child was not actually reading conventionally.

Using similar techniques, Durkin (1966), Clark (1976), and Tobin (1981) then used traditional methods to study these precocious or early readers. They interviewed parents about the children's experiences prior to school entry. Durkin (1966) and Clark (1976) found that early readers were quite variable in most characteristics, including I. Q. There was quite a bit of consistency in parents' reports of key experiences: parents read to these children; these were curious children who elicited adult attention and help; and parents enjoyed the company of these children.

The early-reader studies were important for at least three reasons:

1. They focused attention on what children knew prior to formal schooling, as did the metalinguistic awareness and environmental print studies;
2. They begin to lay the groundwork for distinguishing the ini-

tial onset of conventional literacy, a topic that is just beginning to be investigated currently; and

3. They provided the basis for hypotheses about key factors of early experiences that seemed relevant to later reading achievement.

While these studies were only retrospective, they provided a grounding for hypotheses to be investigated in current studies of family literacy which are prospective in nature.

Metalinguistic Awareness Studies. Early research in children's metalinguistic awareness (Papandropoulou & Sinclair, 1974; Sinclair, Jarvella, & Levelt, 1978) began to provide specific evidence that young children's concepts for terms such as *word, letter, sentence,* or *sound* during the preschool and early elementary school years are quite different from mature adult concepts. Reading and writing researchers (e.g., Downing, 1979; Downing & Oliver, 1973–1974; Meltzer & Herse, 1969; Reid, 1966) furthered this research, extending it to slow that when children were commonly introduced to formal instruction (which assumed that children's and adults' concepts are isomorphic), usually in 1st grade, children typically still do not understand metalinguistic terms. This line of research continues to the present day and is represented most strongly in the research of Ferreiro (1985, 1986; Ferreiro & Teberosky, 1982), discussed below.

Environmental Print Studies. At about the same time that researchers in metalinguistic awareness were showing that children knew less than most had presumed and knew it differently, other researchers were showing that quite young children are, in fact, learning about written language from their environment. The studies of *environmental print* (Goodman, 1980; Hiebert, 1978, 1981; McGee, Lomax, & Head, 1988) have been quite important in this regard. Hiebert tested 3- and 4-year-old children with familiar written words. These children showed meaningful responses to the words, declining as contextual support was stripped. Goodman and Altweger (1981) showed that children as young as 3, from varying ethnic and socioeconomic backgrounds, showed indications of being aware of print in their environment. Harste, Woodward, & Burke (1984) showed that children in this age range gave semantically appropriate responses to complex parts of common household and restaurant product containers and wrappers. These studies (see also Mason, 1980) showed that children were picking up much information about the functions and features of printed material from their environment. Researchers such as Hiebert (1980, 1981, 1986) urged that these findings be interpreted to mean that children should be involved with print in their environment, in meaningful interactions, during the preschool years. What these earlier studies did not yet do, however, was to investigate the social environment and how adults and children interact with environmental print.

From these lines of early research, a number of implications were being drawn that affected emergent literacy research during the late 1970s and 1980s. First, since children of every socioeconomic level and I.Q. level might become early readers and since parents' memories for early experience showed some

consistency, it seemed important to begin studying children's development in process, through observational studies, rather than through predictive or retrospective designs. Second, children's concepts about literacy were seen as being qualitatively different from conventional concepts; tracing the development of those concepts became a new task for research. Third, children were viewed as constructing their concepts from experiences with the environment; it remained the task for research to define and explore the nature of that environment in detail. It should be pointed out also that these lines of research, particularly the last two, can be viewed as part of emergent literacy research and many of those researchers would today use that term to describe their viewpoints.

In the sections that follow, children's emergent reading and writing development will be examined, starting with a look at studies of home literacy.

Literacy Development in Homes

Since children are now viewed as entering school with much knowledge about literacy, it was inferred that they gained this knowledge from the home and their parents. Interviews with parents (Clark, 1976; Durkin, 1966; McCormick & Mason, 1986; Tobin, 1981; see also Tobin & Pikulski, 1988) provided evidence of a variety of experiences in the home that were fruitful for research. Furthermore, since children differ in their literary knowledge, it was further speculated that differences in home literacy environments should help explain individual and cultural differences. Conducting studies of home literacy in which researchers actually enter the home, however, is extremely difficult and labor-intensive; it is also quite intrusive, not matter how congenial the researchers might be. Hence there are relatively few studies to review, although they are longitudinal in nature and provide a rich body of knowledge. Some of these studies were focused upon particular kinds of literacy, such as storybook reading, rather than upon the broad question of what the home provides in literacy events and support for development. Because of these difficulties of conducting research in the home, a number of relevant studies have been conducted by bringing parent-child dyads into a laboratory setting and attempting to recreate literacy events similar to those seen in the natural home setting.

Ethnographic techniques seem to be the primary methodological tool for studies that were actually based in the home setting. While researchers attempt to spend as much time in the home as possible, they also solicit the participation of parents as informants. While any given study includes only a few families, across studies the numbers are beginning to be quite impressive. Heath (1983) studied working-class African American and white and "mainstream" families in the Piedmont Carolinas. Taylor (1983) and Taylor and Dorsey-Gaines (1988) studied six middle-income suburban white families and six low-income urban African American families. Teale and colleagues (Anderson, Teale, & Estrada, 1980; Anderson & Stokes, 1984; Teale, 1986) studied the six low-income families each from three ethnic groups, Anglo, Hispanic, and African American in the San Diego area. Sulzby and Teale (1987) studied eight families, divided equally between low- and middle-income Anglo and Hispanic families, in the San Antonio area.

Only the latter study was focused upon a particular part of literacy (storybook reading). Commonalities across the other studies included, first, the reports that all children, regardless of ethnicity and socioeconomic background, were included in some kinds of "literacy events," events in which literacy played an integral part. Second, literacy events were functional in nature and only rarely focused upon literacy for the sake of learning literacy. Third, each family had some kind of recurring literacy events; literacy events could be classified by type or domain, even though the domains and distributions differed across families.

In addition to varying across families, these domains differed in regard to how closely they appeared to match school-like domains. Researchers in the San Diego study (Teale, 1986) reported nine domains which they described as follows: Daily Living Activities, Entertainment, School-Related Activities, Work, Religion, Interpersonal Communication, Participating in Information Networks, Storybook Time, and Literacy for the Sake of Teaching/Learning Literacy. The social nature of these events from the researchers' reports is obvious and often entails relatively constrained reference to the actual printed text and much use of talk about the social world in which the text plays a part. In many of these events, children are often present but not physically involved with the text; at other times, such as storybook time or school-related events, children are the focus of the involvement with texts.

Heath (1983) reported that children would often be present in events such as newspaper reading or form completion by adults in which the text itself was secondary to both the social interaction and oral discussion about how the text should be interpreted or negotiated. In situations like this, it would be reasoned that children would learn how to use texts functionally to get things done. In contrast, some researchers have reported times in which a text is not even present, yet participants use written language structures or registers. Heath (1986) reported that when families are enclosed in cars making trips together, their language becomes more decontextualized as members try to relate or refer to nonpresent events. Scollon and Scollon (1981) showed how their 2-year-old used written language structures and intonation in dictating stories into a taperecorder.

Document of differences across domains are not clearcut but are suggestive. Health (1983) documented differences in parental storybook reading styles and how they expected their children to participate in storybook reading. These differences were tied to social class, ethnicity, and age of the child. Working-class African American families in her study did not read storybooks with their young children, although they took part in other literacy events with them. Working-class white families read to their children but began to limit the child's participation from active verbal responding to quiet listening or responding to low-level, literal retelling elicitations when children reached about age 3. Prior to that age, children were encouraged to respond actively and allowed to make imaginatie ties to other aspects of their social world. At age 3 and after, children of mainstream families were also expected to listen to longer stretches of a storybook than they did when they were younger, but their imaginative verbal interactions were still encouraged.

One of the most important findings from studies of family literacy is the variability within socioeconomic and ethnic groups (see Miller, Nemoianu, & DeJong, 1986). First, no group has been found to have a "deprived literacy background," if by that we meant that the children have no literacy. All families studied thus far take part in literacy events, and children are included in these events. This finding matches the finding in elicitation studies that children of all social backgrounds readily show some levels of emergent reading and writing behaviors. Second, these studies have shed light on findings masked by group comparisons that show socioeconomic status (SES) and ethnic group differences. There is great variability within any given group. Just simple participation in a given group does not automatically mean that a child has a particular kind of literacy development. Again, this finding is relevant to the reports of elicitation studies that there are no major differences in the patterns of emergent literacy development.

It has been one of the contributions of emergent literacy research to devise methods so children will demonstrate their emergent literacy. Child language development and cognitive development research has been plagued by criticisms of the artificiality of tasks used and the threat that such task demands underestimate children's knowledge. Many of the tasks and settings used in the research below has grown from observations of the home literacy studies. While our definitions of natural are vague (see Teale, 1984), they seem to involve the criterion that the child seems to do the task without the need for adult pressure, becomes engrossed in the task, and seems to perform with patterns similar to those observed without research intervention. Not all of these studies involve researcher elicitation or structuring, however; naturalistic research occurs in these studies as well.

Reading to Children and Children Reading Emergently

Storybook reading appears to be a fairly widespread social routine among families of differing backgrounds, across many literate cultures (Bus & van IJzendoorn, 1988; Heath, 1983; Ninio, 1980; Snow & Ninio, 1986; Snow, 1983; Snow & Goldfield, 1983; Snow & Ninio, 1986) uses the notion of a routine to mean a recurring event that has its own event structure. Young children appear to be very dependent upon and comforted by routines in daily living, but routines appear to serve an additional function. They have expected social roles for participants and expected subroutines. Storybooks themselves can be conceived to be social products in which cultural values and concepts about the nature of young children are embedded. Snow and Ninio (1986) claimed that, in the process of reading to their children across ages and times, both Israeli and U.S. parents negotiate social contracts with their children that move children in successive stages from oral interaction about the physical nature of the text (it's for reading and not for eating), closer and closer to responding to the oral reading of the actual words of the text. Sulzby and Teale (1987; Teale & Sulzby, 1987) reported that low- and middle-income Anglo and Hispanic parents in the

San Antonio area gradually moved from an oral interactive storybook reading style to a "let's listen to the story" style in which the words of the text were read verbatim. They further reported, however, that each of the eight focal children in their study began to voluntarily reenact the texts independently.

There have been a number of studies (Doake, 1985; Pappas, 1987; Teale, Martinez, & Glass, 1989) of children beginning to reenact or read emergently from familiar storybooks. Sulzby (1985a, 1988, Sulzby & Teale, 1987) has devised a simple elicitation of asking children to "Read me your book," after books have been read repeatedly to them. Sulzby (1988) reported that children from ages 2 through 5 in a day care setting almost all responded by reading when asked to after their teachers had read books to them repeatedly. The remainder responded in some appropriate fashion, including reading interactively with an adult. When presented with a favorite book from home after 11 months of day care storybook reading, however, all the children gave an independent "emergent reading" of the book (except for one child who brought in an obviously new book). Sulzby and Teale (1987) found that low-income incipiently bilingual (Spanish-English) preschoolers also read emergently in both languages at ages 4 and 5. They suggest, in comparing these data with their home literacy study, that children gradually internalize a form of reading that has been socially-created from the interaction between the parent and child. Additionally, this social-creation appears to be shaped at least in part by a set of cultural expectations about what the "bedtime story" (Heath, 1983) is or should be.

Storybook reading has become a research arena for the examination of social/cultural differences and interventions. Following suggestions from Heath's (1982a, 1982b, 1983; Heath with Thomas, 1984) research, Edwards (1989) found that African American Head Start mothers in Louisiana with very low literacy skills themselves have needed to be taught how to read to their children. Whitehurst, et al. (1988) were able to train mothers of 21- to 35-month-old toddlers to vary their bookreading linguistic interchanges and found subsequent significant increases in the children's expressive language usage. Pellegrini and his colleagues (Pellegrini, Brody, & Sigel, 1985; Pellegrini, Perlmutter, Galda, & Brody, in press) have found that most parents of even language-delayed children or low-income African American children make some accommodation for the abilities of their children during reading interactions. They found that African American Head Start mothers in Georgia (with higher literacy levels than Edwards' sample) used a more interactive style with expository texts than with narratives. They showed sensitivity also to the level of their children's familiarity with the text. Bus and IJzendoorn (1988), studying emotional development in relation to emergent literacy, found different patterns of interaction depending upon the text type. In studying parent-child dyads in The Netherlands, they found that children who were judged to be securely attached to their mothers responded more actively than children judged to be insecurely attached and also required less control strategies by the parents.

These studies of storybook reading were typically conducted within a Vygotskiian (Vygotsky, 1978, 1981) framework. It was assumed that children internalize patterns from social interaction and that a facilitative framework in which parents raise ex-

pectations only in relation to children's increasing abilities would be beneficial. Indeed, most of the findings appear to be consistent with this outlook.

A question that remains to be answered in sufficient detail is how emergent storybook reading eventuates in conventional reading. The finding that reading to children is associated with higher subsequent achievement scores has been replicated many times with different methodologies (see Teale, 1984; Wells, 1985). Sulzby (1985a, 1988) has classified children's emergent storybook reading behavior into an 11-point classification scheme with developmental properties. The final point on that scale is reading conventionally from print and the subcategories just preceding conventional reading indicate that children are beginning to coordinate knowledge about letter-sound relationships, about word stability, and about comprehension of written language just prior to the time they begin to read conventionally, moving strategically across these bodies of knowledge. We need much more research into the topic of the transition into conventional literacy, both as it is seen in reading and in writing, the next topic for review.

Writing as an Emergent Phenomenon

As with storybook reading, research in emergent writing has been heavily influenced by studies of home literacy. Read's (1970, 1975) influential study of invented spelling was based upon hypotheses that arose from retrospective reports and naturalistically gathered writing samples from parents of preschoolers. Clay (1975) also used voluntary compositions by young children. Teale (1986), Taylor (1983) and Taylor and Dorsey-Gaines (1988) observed children writing at home with their parents. Taylor reported that parents treated scribbling and other forms of writing as writing and called it writing.

Rowe (1987, 1988) and Dyson (1982a, 1982b, 1983, 1984, 1985, 1987, 1988) used naturalistic techniques to "hang out" where children in preschools, kindergartens, and 1st grades write. Rowe used a technique of writing in front of children while they write and observing their social interaction. Dyson observed how children negotiate or change a teacher's assigned task as they also negotiate their various social worlds with peers in the classroom.

Sulzby (1983) and Harste, Woodward, & Burke (1984) elicited story compositions by young children, by encouraging and accepting any form of writing produced by the child. They used techniques derived from observations of home literacy studies, particularly the technique of asking children to write without any apology or acceptance of the idea that children cannot write. Sulzby (1983, 1988) reported the use of the prompt, "It doesn't have to be like grown-up writing, just write it your own way," as an effective means of eliciting children's emergent writing.

Other researchers (Ferreiro, 1978, 1985; Ferreiro & Gomez Palacio, 1985; Ferreiro & Teberosky, 1982; Tolchinsky-Landsman & Levin, 1985, 1987) have asked children to write dictated words or sentences composed by adults. While the initial elicitation for the child to write words, phrases, or sentences from lists is similar to that used by researchers of invented spelling

(Gentry, 1980; Henderson & Beers, 1980; Morris, 1980, 1981), the follow-up interviews and analyses are quite different. The Piagetian-based researchers typically conduct clinical interviews in order to infer children's concepts about what writing is, how it gets done, and how it can be read from. They tend to interpret children's responses along lines of epistemological distinctions about children's underlying concepts of representation (see below); the invented spelling researchers tend to be more concerned with the exact orthographic patterns that children are acquiring and their sequence. Recent research in invented spelling (e.g., Chi, 1988; Ferroli & Shanahan, 1987; Richgels, 1986a, 1986b; Richgels, McGeee, Hernandez, & Williams, 1988) has begun use tasks in which invented spelling has been elicited in sentential contexts and across compositional tasks, rather than simply from lists of isolated words.

Children have been observed to write in emergent forms from infancy onward. Researchers of home literacy (Taylor, 1983; also see Teale, 1986) have noted that parents use the simple terms "write" and "read" when describing their toddlers' and preschoolers' emergent literacy behaviors, rather independently of how close to conventional the forms are. Parents occasionally may refer to the child's writing as scribbling, but often they just use the unhedged term "writing" to refer to emergent forms and functions. In homes where adults encourage children's interaction with print, children are typically included in "literacy events" in which writing is used functionally. However, children themselves often write spontaneously, just as they spontaneously do independent emergent storybook readings.

From naturalistic observations of this spontaneous writing behavior, as well as from more manipulative studies, we can begin to build a picture of when children begin to write and the forms that such writing takes. Sulzby (1989; Sulzby & Teale, 1985) has offered one sequence for when mainstream children from the USA typically begin to write with different writing forms such as scribbling, drawing, nonphonetic letterstrings, invented spelling, and conventional orthography. This sequence is generally comparable to some of the reports from Harste, Woodward, & Burke (1984; Harste & Woodward, 1989; also see Bissex, 1980, for the latter end of this development). Both sets of researchers refer primarily to the forms of writing used in connected discourse.

Tolchinsky-Landsmann and Levin (1985, 1987), drawing from the work of Ferreiro (1978; Ferreiro & Teberosky, 1982), offer a somewhat different sequence; the Spanish-speaking children are depicted as showing writing forms at a somewhat older age than Sulzby reports, but only efforts in which a quantitative match between written units and the requested terms were treated as analyzable. In other words, the researchers looked for matches between spoken and written words (thus holistic relationships between intended text and forms of writing such as continuous scribble or drawing would not be analyzed). This age difference runs counter to expectations because the Ferreiro methods tend to use requests for or observe children writing isolated words or phrases and sentences suggested by an adult. Children in U.S. English-speaking samples tend to use more "advanced" writing forms with smaller linguistic units, such as words or phrases, and less advanced-

appearing forms for their own compositions of connected discourse. Bearing these differences in mind, let us examine the two sequences.

Tolchinsky-Landsmann and Levin (1987) suggest that the aspect of linearity is typically shown by Ferreiro's Spanish-speaking children between the ages of 3 and 4. The child will have neither sufficient marks to represent syllabic or phonemic element nor a stereotypical estimate of how long a "word" should be; instead, the child may use one or two elements per sentence, representing only the nouns or may use a long string with no indication of a systematic relationship between marks and speech stimulus. Four- to 5-year-olds, however, begin to try to use hypotheses about length of word and referential characteristics and come into conflicts that eventually lead, about a year later, to beginning explorations of phonetically-based writing. In applying Ferreiro's analytic scheme, Tolchinsky-Landsmann and Levin (1987. p 135) noted that forms such as drawing and "long series of characters, often ligated, that could not be counted precisely" were treated as unanalyzable.

Using children's free attempts to compose stories, letters, or notes, Sulzby (1989) suggests that nonletter forms such as early scribbling or drawing frequently function as writing for the young child. Undifferentiated scribble begins at about age 12 to 18 months. This becomes differentiated into drawing and writinglike scribble between ages 2 and 3, for most U.S. mainstream children. Drawing may be used by the child either as drawing itself or as writing; children continue an ambivalence about whether drawing can or cannot be writing from this age well into kindergarten and sometimes 1st grade. Children typically begin to write with letters during the third, but sometimes as late as the fourth year. Most of this writing is comprised of nonphonetic letterstrings, but the child may also produce some conventional-appearing items (particularly the child's name) but not hold a conventional concept for them. Also, with any given writing form, children can use a range of compositional and reading systems (Sulzby, 1989). While it can appear earlier or later for a few children, invented spelling typically makes its appearance during kindergarten or 1st grade. Nurss (1988) has made for a useful compilation of various reports of age of acquisition of writing forms from 1936 to the present time and then used these in examining writing by Norwegian kindergarten (ages 3 to 6) children. The Norwegian children followed a similar sequence from those proposed by Sulzby and Ferreiro, but more in line with the time of acquisition suggested by Ferreiro. Unfortunately, the task used was to ask children to draw and then write; drawing was excluded from being considered a writing form.

It has become clear that it is insufficient simply to look at the forms of writing that children use. Clay (1975), Ferreiro (1982, 1986) and Sulzby (1983, 1989) warn that researchers and practitioners alike must examine children's underlying conceptions. Clay (1975) looked beyond the forms to underlying principles such as linearity and recurrence and resisted treating the appearance of forms of writing as alone being indicative of development. When Galda, Pellegrini, and Cox (1989) treated a logical analysis of the forms of writing as a developmental scheme and then correlated preschoolers' use of these forms with emergent reading, they found a low correlation and concluded an independent line of development for reading and writing. Unfortunately, such a conclusion cannot be drawn from such a design. However, the question of the relationships between emergent reading and writing is an important and complex one, perhaps changing over time as suggested by the theory of Stanovich (1986) and by Shanahan's (1984) research with school-aged children. Much more research is needed before strong conclusions can be drawn about the relationships between reading and writing during the emergent period.

Ferreiro (1978, 1985, 1986; Ferreiro & Gomez Palacio, 1982; Ferreiro & Teberosky, 1982) has also investigated children's interpretations of how different pieces of writing can be read and has asked children to produce writing. She also interviewed the children about the relationship between the forms of their writing, their rereading, and the symbolic relationships involved, using clinical interviews Ferreiro's work does not furnish an inventory of writing forms, as such.

Sulzby (1983, 1985b; Sulzby, Barnhart, & Hieshima, 1989) also claims that looking at the appearance of forms of writing alone is misleading. In a study of kindergarten children, Sulzby (1981) had analyzed children's rereading from dictated and handwritten stories and devised a seven-point categorizations of emergent writing. That categorization system glossed over the forms of writing and focused almost entirely upon rereading. It furnished useful rankings of children and correlations with other measures, but she has cautioned (Sulzby, 1988; Sulzby, Barnhart, & Hieshima, 1989) that it lacked the precision needed to understand the relationship between writing and rereading.

Sulzby (1989) designed a study of five classrooms in which children were invited to write "your own way" after a discussion and modeling of ways in which kindergarteners often write. Over kindergarten and 1st grade, Teachers and researchers did not overtly push children to shift writing forms. Scribble, drawing, nonphonetic letter strings, invented spelling, and conventional orthography were the major writing forms used by children throughout the study, although other forms such as rebus, abbreviation, or idiosyncratic forms showed up on rare occasions, usually in 1st grade.

Children only gradually began to produce conventionally-readable writing (writing in full invented spelling and/or conventional orthography). Children did not immediately read conventionally themselves from this readable writing that had been phonetically encoded (Kamberelis & Sulzby, 1988). Throughout kindergarten and 1st grade children continued to move back and forth across forms as writing, even as they approached the ability to write conventionally. Change was found, not so much in the forms of writing, but in the language that surrounded the writing—compositional and rereading. By the end of 1st grade, however, all the children were writing conventionally. Similar patterns of development have been reported by Allen, et al. (1989; Allen & Carr, 1989). Vukelich and Edwards (1988) found similar patterns when they collected weekly writing samples from children in a university-run kindergarten.

In summary, it can be seen that emergent reading and writing are robust behaviors with young children; children show

them freely in conducive settings. Additionally, while the patterns are not simply, researchers are making good progress in describing the paths of development for certain parts of reading and writing. However, the picture is far from being complete.

In the studies of home literacy, storybook reading, and writing, the role of talking was often observed and analyzed by the researchers. The section that follows recounts recent shifts in concepts about how oral and written language are related and the roles they may play in emergent literacy.

Oral Language and Written Language

During the 1970's we saw an explosion of research in child language acquisition, which almost universally meant oral language acquisition. Instead of being viewed at faulty imitators of adult language, children were viewed as being active in the construction of language, creating hypotheses about how language operates, and testing these hypotheses in communicative contexts—texts which were primarily face-to-face and dependent upon oral speech. Oral language was viewed as being relatively easy to acquire and somewhat consistent across cultures. While views of oral language acquisition have changed and become more complex—adults are viewed as being more active in the process which is viewed as being interactive; the speed and ease of acquisition without teaching has been questioned; and cross-cultural differences are viewed as greater and more important—the basic idea that oral language is actively constructed by the children in interaction with the environment has been maintained. Children's concepts about oral language are different from those of adults and change predictably as children grow older.

Similarly, written language has come to be viewed as a developmental phenomenon and children have come to be viewed as active constructors of concepts about written language. Coinciding in time with this view has been a resurgence in interest in oral and written language relationships by linguists, literacy critics, historians, psychologists, and anthropologists (Chafe, 1982; Good, 1977, 1982; Heath, 1982a; Ong, 1982; Rubin, 1978; Shatz, 1984; Tannen, 1982, 1984). A number of researchers (e.g., Harste, Woodward, & Burke, 1984; King & Rentel, 1981; Martlew, 1988; Scollon & Scollon, 1981; Sulzby, 1981) posited that we need to think about the child as acquiring both oral language and written language from within a given cultural background. They conducted studies that focused on signs that the children is learning about both oral and written language during the preschool years. These early studies led to a number of conclusions.

First, speech and oral language are not synonymous; children's speech can contains signs that they are acquiring knowledge about the ability to use written language patterns or registers long before they are reading and writing conventionally. Children's ability to speak with oral and written language registers has been used as an important way to investigate emergent literacy. Purcell-Gates (1988) found that children who have been read to extensively before schooling used features of a written language register when they were asked to create a story to fit a wordless picturebook. Sulzby (1985a, 1988) found that when children "read" from favorite storybooks, some children use language that sounds conversational, others use a storytelling structure and intonation, and others use written language patterns. Pappas' (1986, 1988; Pappas & Brown, 1987, 1988; ; see also Purcell-Gates, 1988, in press) research on *protoreading* (using a term adapted from Halliday, 1975) concluded that children often use a written language register in response to both narrative and expository texts.

Second, written language is not synonymous with print. Writers have to learn not only the conventions of encoding in print but also what it is that gets written and how it is expressed. King and Rentel's (1981) research with conventional writers showed that children in grades 1–4 still use patterns more appropriate to an oral, face-to-face context when they write.

The notions of *contextualization, decontextualization,* and *recontextualization* have been important in emergent literacy research. The reader is viewed as having needs for a text to provide sufficient context for it to be able to be read when the author is not present (Olson, 1977). It is relatively well-established that young children often use features more appropriate to an oral, interactive context when writing; one measure of growth in writing is the ability to provide sufficient contextual cues within the text itself (Cox, Shanahan, & Sulzby, 1990). Conversely, children often use a written language register when composing with unreadable forms of writing (Sulzby, Barnhart, & Hieshima, 1989). In a somewhat different vein, researchers in metalinguistic awareness (Papapdropoulou & Sinclair, 1978) and emergent literacy (Ferreiro, 1986; Ferreiro & Teberosky, 1982; Tolchinsky-Landsmann & Levin, 1987; see also Barnhart, 1986) have shown that children do not necessarily expect that everything they say or that someone else says needs to be represented graphically: the 3-year-old may think that only nouns are "parts" of a spoken sentence or need to be written.

The research summarized above and much of the other research in this chapter provides some evidence that the young child is acquiring both oral and written language prior to conventional reading and writing. It seems likely that sorting out oral and written language relationships across different tasks, texts, and situations may be important learning for young children. Research in this area has begun to provide evidence for children's development in all of the "language arts"—listening and speaking as well as reading and writing. As can be seen below, literacy itself can be broadened to encompass other forms of symbolizing in addition to traditional reading and writing.

Other Forms of Symbolizing

In the research reviewed above, we dealt with the child's emerging concepts for storybooks as defined both by the conventional printed text, as defined through parent-child interaction, and as defined by the child's reenactment of books. We dealt with writing as the child's use of forms in order to compose a message and dealt with drawing as a form of writing. Here, we discuss a brief bit of research and much speculation about how writing and other forms operate as symbol systems for the young child. Children appear to learn about the symbols used in writing and how to read them in a complex of symbols; part of their task is learning to sort out the symbol systems. Additionally, however, communicating in writing and reading from texts appears also to involve interpreting alternative forms. Highly proficient reading and writing, which we assume should be an attainable outcome as children grow older, involves varying degrees of interpreting various symbol systems of which alphabetic writing is only part, although a crucial part.

We know, for example, that children often confuse the metalinguistic labels and their referents (word and sound, letter and number, drawing and writing). On the surface, these problems often appear to be simply an issue of getting a term properly connected (e.g., Mickish, 1974; Papandropoulou & Sinclair, 1974; Pontecorvo, Orsolini, Zucchermaglio, & Rossi, 1987). However, the issues appear to be far more complex. There are at least three possibilities whenever a child makes a confusion, any one of and any combination of which might be in operation. The first possibility, that of confusing label and referent, may indeed be the case, but does not account for the persistence of the naming/referring problem that we see over the early childhood years. Second, the child may be seeing a connection between the forms of symbolizing that we no longer consciously think about. Third, the environment may be offering examples that lead the child to see relationships that we are no longer unaware of.

Let us consider drawing and writing, for example. At around age 2, many children begin to distinguish between scribble that they use as drawing and scribble that they use as writing. They may request an adult to "write Grandma" or "draw Grandma" and protest if the adult misinterprets their request, even if they reversed the labels. If confusion about labels were the only issue, simple feedback should correct this problem.

A number of children appear to be ambivalent about whether drawing can be a form of writing well into kindergarten age. They seem to use drawing appropriately when asked to draw, yet they may also use drawing when asked to write. Additionally, they "read" back from the drawing, sometimes even agreeing to "point while you are reading." Only gradually do children reach a point of articulating the differences in a stable fashion (Sulzby, 1983). At this point, children typically show a clear distinction between written text and drawing used as illustration. At this point in development, children begin to use *rebus,* rather than using rebus as a lower point in development to aid the understanding of letter-sound based symbolism. Another theoretical speculation (Sulzby, 1989) is that some children begin to deal with the "text" or "composition" as being both the entirety of the orthographically-encoded passage and any also surrounding illustrations, similarly to the way in which many publishing authors do. Thus drawing for the child becomes reorganized in a different manner into writing and representation systems in general.

We must, however, consider how children experience drawing in acts of reading and writing. Illustrations are a key, if not primary, part of texts for young children (Smolkin, Conlon, & Yaden, 1988). Illustrations so dominate many labelling and concept books that the child may have difficulty noticing the print on the page. Additionally, children's illustrators often mix media by inserting dialogue balloons, labels, or expletives into the drawings (Sulzby, 1988). This, from children's books it is not often immediately evident which form of symbol is being read from. Again, if we invite children to "write a story" or "write a book" we may be inviting the mixing of the media. An issue for research is keeping the task definitions straight in our own designs and being alert for child redefinitions.

As seen in the work from Project Zero (Gardner & Wolfe, 1983, Gardner, Wolfe, & Smith, 1975; Wolfe & Gardner, 1981), children's use of drawing has its own developmental track as does writing. We need additional research that examines drawing used for drawing purposes and writing used for writing purposes, as well as the substitution of one for the other, both overtly at the graphic level and covertly through the means with which children compose and talk about their creations.

Ferreiro (1986; Ferreiro & Teberosky, 1982; see also Pontecorvo, 1984) has addressed some attention to numbers as a form of symbolization, contrasting them with letters. Numbers have a different relationship to pronunciation and to referential meaning than do letters. Numbers may name a set, serve as a counting unit, or indicate ordinal value; thus they are ambiguous within their canonical symbol system (Fuson, 1988). They have no assigned sound value and the Arabic numerals, for example, are pronounced in different ways in different languages (Ferreiro & Teberosky, 1982). Letters name only themselves. Yet letters also indicate sounds as they occur in words. Letters "name themselves" and stand for sounds. If a child does not yet understand these complexities, the two forms may appear to be highly similar. They are formed within the same units

of physical space, through the same media, and in acts of accounting or inventorying.

Another tool for writing as well as reading is the computer, which is a machine with multifaceted potential, depending both upon the hardware configuration and software used with it (Papert, 1980). It appears that young children can use the computer as an emergent literacy tool (Murphy & Appel, 1984; Sulzby, Olson, & Johnston, 1989) and as a tool for writing collaboration in the early conventional period (Dickinson, 1986; Heap, 1989). Emergent writers move across representation systems, depending upon what the software will allow, in many unpredicted manners. Exploring children's emergent writing with different kinds of computer capabilities is an area of research that is just in its infancy but offers important avenues to study children's development (Sulzby, Olson, & Johnston, 1989). For example, children explore notation systems for music without the computer (Bamberger, 1986), but computer programs now allow the child to pick out a tune on an on-screen piano keyboard and see the notation for staves, notes, and timing created on the screen immediately. We have little idea of the effects of such representational possibilities on children's growing sense of what it means to be literate and how they can create, using such evolving tools.

We should not forget, in all of this speculation, that the child is working out relationships that may not have immediate resolution or may be resolved differently as children grow older or gain experience than we currently might think possible (see Stanovich, 1986). Harste, Woodward, and Burke (1984) have alerted researchers to the importance of considering a broad range of semiotic functions when studying children's literacy development.

References

Allen, J. B., & Carr, E. (1989). Collaborative learning among kindergarten writers: James learns how to learn at school. In J. B. Allen & J. M. Mason (Eds.), *Risk makers, risk takers, risk breakers: Reducing the risks for young literacy learners* (pp. 30–47). Portsmouth, NH: Heinemann.

Allen, J. B., Clark, W., Cook, M., Crane, P., Fallon, I., Hoffman, L., Jennings, K. S., & Sours, M. A. (1989). Reading and writing development in whole language kindergartens. In J. Mason (Ed.), *Reading and writing connections* (pp. 121–146). Needham Heights, MA: Allyn & Bacon.

Allen, J. B., & Mason, J. M. (Eds.), (1989). *Risk makers, risk takers, risk breakers: Reducing the risks for young literacy learners.* Portsmouth, NH: Heinemann.

Anderson, A. B., & Stokes, S. J. (1984). Social and institutional influences on the development and practice of literacy. In H. Goelman, A. Oberg, & F. Smith (Eds.), *Awakening to literacy* (pp. 24–37). Exeter, NH: Heinemann.

Anderson, A. B., Teale, W. H., & Estrada, E. (1980). Low-income children's preschool literacy experiences: Some naturalistic observations. *The Quarterly Newsletter of the Laboratory of Comparative Human Cognition, 2,* 59–65.

Bamberger, J. (1986). Cognitive issues in the development of musically gifted children. In R. J. Sternberg & J. Davidson, *Conceptions of giftedness.* New York: NY: Cambridge University Press.

Barnhart, J. E. (1986). *Written language concepts and cognitive development in kindergarten children.* Unpublished doctoral dissertation, Northwestern University, Evanston, IL.

Betts, E. A. (1946). *Foundations of reading instruction.* New York: American Book.

Bissex, G. (1980). *GNYS at work: A child learns to write and read.* Cambridge, MA: Harvard University Press.

Bus, A. G., & van IJzendoorn, M. H. (1988). Mother-child interactions, attachment and emergent literacy: A cross-sectional study. *Child Development, 59,* 1262–1272.

Chafe, W. A. (1982). Integration and involvement in speaking, writing, and oral literature. In D. Tannen (Ed.), *Spoken and written language: Exploring orality and literacy* (pp. 35–54). Norwood, NJ: Ablex.

Chi, M. M-Y. (1988). Invented spelling/writing in Chinese-speaking children: The developmental patterns. *National Reading Conference Yearbook, 37,* 385–296.

Clark, E. V. (1978). Awareness of language: Some evidence from what children say and do. In A. Sinclair, R. J. Jarvella, & W. M. Levelt (Eds.), *The child's conception of language.* New York: Springer-Verlag.

Clark, M. M. (1976). *Young fluent readers: What can they teach us?* London, ENG: Heinemann.

Clay, M. M. (1975). *What did I write?* Auckland, NZ: Heinemann.

Cox, B. E., Shanahan, T., & Sulzby, E. (1990). Good and poor elementary readers' use of cohesion in writing. *Reading Research Quarterly, 25,* 47–65.

Dickinson, D. K. (1986). Cooperation, collaboration and a computer: Integrating a computer into a first-second grade writing program. *Research in the Teaching of English, 20*(4), 357–378.

Dickinson, D. (1989). Effects of a shared reading program on one Head Start language and literacy environment. In J. B. Allen & J. M. Mason (Eds.), *Risk makers, risk takers, risk breakers* (pp. 125–153). Portsmouth, NH: Heinemann.

Doake, D. (1985). Reading-like behavior: Its role in learning to read. In A. Jagger & M. T. Smith-Burke (Eds.), *Observing the language learner* (pp. 82–98). Newark, DE: International Reading Association.

Downing, J. (1979). *Reading and reasoning.* New York: Springer-Verlag.

Downing, J., & Oliver, P. (1973-1974). The child's conception of a word. *Reading Research Quarterly, 9,* 568–582.

Durkin, D. (1966). *Children who read early.* New York: NY: Teachers College Press.

Dyson, A. H. (1982a). Reading, writing and language: Young children solving the written language puzzle. *Language Arts, 59,* 829–839.

Dyson, A. H. (1982b). The emergence of visible language: Interrelationships between drawing and early writing. *Visible Language, 16,* 360–381.

Dyson, A. H. (1983). The role of oral language in early writing. *Research in the Teaching of English, 17,* 1–30.

Dyson, A. H. (1984). Learning to write/learning to do school: Emergent writers' interpretations of school literacy tasks. *Research in the Teaching of English, 18,* 233–264.

Dyson, A. H. (1985). Individual differences in emergent writing. In M. Farr (Ed.), *Advances in writing research, Vol. 1: Children's early writing development* (pp. 59–126). Norwood, NJ: Ablex.

Dyson, A. H. (1987). Individual differences in beginning composing: An orchestral vision of learning to compose. *Written Communication, 4,* 411–422.

Dyson, A. H. (1988). Negotiating among multiple worlds: The space/time dimensions of young children's composing. *Research in the Teaching of English, 22*(4), 355–390.

Edwards, P. A. (1989). Supporting lower SES mothers' attempts to provide scaffolding for bookreading. In J. B. Allen & J. Mason (Eds.), *Reading the risks for young learners: Literacy practices and policies.* Portsmouth, NH: Heinemann.

Ferreiro, E. (1978). What is written in a written sentence? A developmental answer. *Journal of Education, 160,* 25–39.

Ferreiro, E. (1985). Literacy development: A psychogenetic perspective. In D. Olson, N. Torrance, & A. Hildyard (Eds.), *Literacy, language, and learning* (pp. 217–228). Cambridge, ENG: Cambridge University Press.

Ferreiro, E. (1986). The interplay between information and assimilation in beginning literacy. In W. H. Teale & E. Sulzby (Eds.), *Emergent literacy: Writing and reading* (pp. 15–49). Norwood, NJ: Ablex.

Ferreiro, E., & Gómez Palacio, M. (1982). *Análisis de las pertubaciones en el proceso aprendizaje de la lectoescritura* [Analysis of variations in the process of literacy development]. (5 vols.) Mexico City: Office of the Director General of Special Education.

Ferreiro, E., & Teberosky, A. (1982). *Literacy before schooling.* Exeter, NH: Heinemann.

Ferroli, L., & Shanahan, T. (1987). Kindergarten spelling: Explaining its relationship to first-grade reading. *National Reading Conference Yearbook, 36,* 93–99.

Fuson, K. (1988). *Children's counting and concepts of number.* New York: Springer-Verlag.

Galda, L., Pellegrini, A. D., Cox, S. (1989). A short-term longitudinal study of preschoolers' emergent literacy. *Research in the Teaching of English, 23,* 292–309.

Gardner, H., & Wolf, D. (1983). Waves and streams of symbolization: Notes on the development of symbolic capacities in young children. In D. Rogers & J. Sloboda (Eds.), *The acquisition of symbolic skills* (pp. 1–37). New York, NY: Plenum.

Gardner, H., Wolfe, D., & Smith, A. (1975). Artistic symbols in early childhood. *NYU Education Quarterly, 6,* 13–21.

Gates, A. I. (1937). The necessary mental age for beginning reading. *Elementary School Journal, 37,* 497–508.

Gates, A. I., & Bond, G. L. 91936). Reading readiness: A study of factors determining success and failure in beginning reading. *Teachers College Record, 37,* 679–85.

Gates, A. I., Bond, G. L., & Russell, D. H. (1939). *Methods of determining reading readiness.* New York: Bureau of Publications, Teachers College, Columbia University.

Gentry, J. R. (1980). Early spelling strategies. *Elementary School Journal, 79,* 88–92.

Goodman, Y. (1980). The roots of literacy. In M. P. Douglass (Ed.), *Claremont reading conference 44th yearbook.* Claremont, CA: Claremont Graduate School.

Goodman, Y. (1984). The development of initial literacy. In H. Goelman, A. Oberg, & F. Smith (Eds.), *Awakening to literacy* (pp. 102–109). Exeter, NH: Heinemann.

Goodman, Y. & Altweger, B. (1981). *Print awareness in preschool children: A study of the development of literacy in preschool children.* (Occasional Paper No. 4). Tucson, AZ: University of Arizona, Program in Language and Literacy, Arizona Center for Research and Development, College of Education.

Goody, J. (1977). *The domestication of the savage mind.* Cambridge, ENG: Cambridge University Press.

Goody, J. (1982). Alternative paths to knowledge in oral and literature cultures. In D. Tannen (Ed.), *Spoken and written language: Exploring orality and literacy* (pp. 201–215). Norwood, NJ: Ablex.

Halliday, M. A. K. (1975). *Learning how to mean: Explorations in the development of language.* NY: Elsevier North Holland.

Harste, J. C., & Woodward, V. A. (1989). Fostering needed change in early literacy programs. In D. S. Strickland & L. M. Morrow (Eds.), *Emerging literacy: Young children learn to read and write* (pp. 147–159). Newark, DE: International Reading Association.

Harste, J. C., Woodward, V. A., & Burke, C. L. (1984). *Language stories and literacy lessons.* Portsmouth, NH: Heinemann.

Heap, J. L. (1989). Sociality and cognition in collaborative computer writing. In D. Bloome (Ed.), *Classrooms and literacy* (pp. 135–157). Norwood, NJ: Ablex.

Heath, S. B. (1982a). Protean shapes in literacy events: Ever-shifting oral and literate traditions. In D. Tannen (Ed.), *Spoken and written language: Exploring orality and literacy* (pp. 91–117). Norwood, NJ: Ablex.

Heath, S. B. (1982b). What no bedtime story means: Narrative skills at home and school. *Language in Society, 11,* 49–76.

Heath, S. B. (1983). *Ways with words: Language, life and work in communities and classrooms.* Cambridge, MA: Harvard University Press.

Heath, S. B. (1986). Separating "things of the imagination" from life: Learning to read and write. In W. H. Teale & E. Sulzby (Eds.), *Emergent literacy: Writing and reading* (pp. 156–172). Norwood, NJ: Ablex.

Heath, S. B. with Thomas, C. (1984). The achievement of preschool literacy for mother and child. In H. Goelman, A. Oberg, & F. Smith (Eds.), *Awakening to literacy* (pp. 51–72). Exeter, NH: Heinemann.

Henderson, E. H. & Beers, J. W. (Eds.). (1980). *Developmental and cognitive aspects of learning to spell.* Newark, DE: International Reading Association.

Hiebert, E. H. (1978). Preschool children's understanding of written language. *Child Development, 49,* 1231–1238.

Hiebert, E. H. (1980). The relationship of logical reasoning ability, oral language comprehension, and home experiences to preschool children's print awareness. *Journal of Reading Behavior, 12*(4), 313–324.

Hiebert, E. H. (1981). Developmental patterns and interrelationships of preschool children's print awareness. *Reading Research Quarterly, 16*(2), 236–260.

Hiebert, E. H. (1986). Issues related to home influences on young children's print-related development. In D. Yaden & S. Templeton (Eds.), *Metalinguistic awareness and beginning literacy: Conceptualizing what it means to read and write* (pp. 145–158). Portsmouth, NH: Heinemann.

Hildreth, G. (1932). Developmental sequences in name writing. *Child Development, 3,* 1–14.

Huey, E. B. (1908). *The psychology and pedagogy of reading.* New York: Macmillan.

Iredell, H. (1989). Eleanor learns to read. *Education, 19,* 233–248.

Kamberelis, G., & Sulzby, E. (1988). Transitional knowledge in emergent literacy. *National Reading Conference Yearbook, 37,* 95–106.

King, M., & Rentel, V. (1981). *How children learn to write: A longitudinal study.* (Final report to the National Institute of Education, RF Project 761861/712383 and 765512/711748). Columbus, OH: Ohio State University Research Foundation.

Martlew, M. (1988). Children's oral and written language. In A. D. Pellegrini (Ed.), *Psychological bases for early education* (pp. 77–122). Chichester, ENG: John Wiley & Sons.

Mathews, M. M. (1966). *Teaching to read: Historically considered.* Chicago: University of Chicago Press.

Mason, J. M. (1980). When do children begin to read: An exploration of four year old children's letter and word reading competencies. *Reading Research Quarterly, 15,* 203–227.

Mason, J. M. (1986). Prereading: A developmental perspective. In P. D. Pearson (Ed.), *Handbook of research in reading, Vol. 1* (pp. 505–543). New York: Longman.

Mason, J. M., & Allen, J. B. (1986). A review of emergent literacy with implications for research and practice in reading. *Review of Research in Education, 13,* 3–47.

McCormick, C. E., & Mason, J. M. (1986). Intervention procedures for increasing preschool children's interest in and knowledge about reading. In W. H. Teale, & E. Sulzby (Eds.), *Emergent literacy: Writing and reading* (pp. 90–115). Norwood, NJ: Ablex.

McGee, L., Lomax, R., & Head, M. (1988). Young children's written language knowledge: What environmental and functional print reading reveals. *Journal of Reading Behavior, 20,* 99–118.

Meltzer, N. H., & Herse, R. (1969). The boundaries of written words as seen by first graders. *Journal of Reading Behavior, 1,* 3–14.

Mickish, V. (1974). Children's perception of written word boundaries. *Journal of Reading Behavior, 6,* 19–22.

Miller, P., Nemoianu, A., & DeJong, J. (1986). Early reading at home: Its practice and meanings in a working class community. In B. Schieffelin & P. Gilmore (Eds.), *The acquisition of literacy: Ethnographic perspectives* (pp. 3–15). Norwood, NJ: Ablex.

Morphett, M. V., & Washburne, C. (1931). When should children begin to read? *Elementary School Journal, 31,* 496–508.

Morris, D. (1980). Beginning readers' concept of word. In E. H. Henderson, & J. W. Beers (Eds.), *Developmental and cognitive aspects of learning to spell* (pp. 97–111). Newark, DE: International Reading Association.

Morris, D. (1981). Concept of word: A developmental phenomenon in the beginning reading and writing program. *Language Arts, 58,* 659–668.

Morrow, L. M., & Smith, J. (Eds.). (1989). *The role of assessment and measurement in early literacy research.* Englewood Cliffs, NJ: Prentice-Hall.

Murphy, R. T., & Appel, L. R. (1984). *Evaluation of the Writing to Read Instructional System, 1982-1984: Second year report.* Princeton, NJ: Educational Testing Service.

Ninio, A. (1980). Picture-book reading in mother-infant dyads belonging to two subgroups in Israel. *Child Development, 51,* 587–590.

Nurss, J. R. (1988). Development of written communication in Norwegian kindergarten children. *Scandinavian Journal of Educational Research, 32,* 33–48.

Olson, D. R. (1977). From utterance to text: The bias of language in speech and writing. *Harvard Educational Review, 47*(3), 257–281.

Ong, W. J. (1982). *Orality and literacy: The technologizing of the words.* New York: Methuen.

Papandropoulou, I., & Sinclair, H. (1974). What is a word? Experimental study of children's ideas on grammar. *Human Development, 17,* 241–258.

Papandropoulou, I., & Sinclair, H. (1974). What is a word? Experimental study of children's ideas on grammar. *Human Development, 17,* 241–258.

Papert, S. (1980). *Mindstorms: Children, computers, and powerful ideas.* New York, NY: Basic Books.

Pappas, C. C. (1986). *Learning to read by reading: Exploring text indices for understanding the process.* (Final report to the Research Committee for the Research Foundation of the National Council of Teachers of English No. R85:21). Lexington, KY: University of Kentucky.

Pappas, C. C. (1987). Exploring the textual properties of "protoreading." In R. Steele & T. Threadgold (Eds.), *Language topics: Essays in honour of Michael Halliday* (Vol. 1, pp. 137–162). Amsterdam, NET: John Benjamins.

Pappas, C. C. (1988, December). *Exploring the ontogenesis of the registers of written language: Young children tackling the "book language" of information books.* Paper presented at the 38th annual meeting of the National Reading Conference, Tucson, AZ.

Pappas, C. C., & Brown, E. (1987). Learning to read by reading: Learning how to extend the functional potential of language. *Research in the Teaching of English, 21,* 160–184.

Pappas, C. C., & Brown, E. (1988). The development of children's sense of the written story language register: An analysis of the texture of "pretend reading." *Linguistics and Education, 1,* 45–79.

Pellegrini, A. D., Brody, G. H., & Sigel, I. E. (1985). Parents' book-reading habits with their children. *Journal of Educational Psychology, 77*(3), 332–340.

Pellegrini, A. D., Perlmutter, J. C., Galda, L., & Brody, G. H. (in press). Joint book reading between Black Head Start children and their mothers. *Child Development.*

Piaget, J. (1959). *The language and thought of the child.* (3rd ed.). London, ENG: Routledge & Kegan Paul.

Pontecorvo, C. (1984). Figure, parole, numeri: Un problema di simbolizzazione. *Età evolutiva, 18,* 5–33.

Pontecorvo, C., Orsolini, M., Zucchermaglio, C., & Rossi, F. (1987, December). *Metalinguistic skills in children: What develops?* Paper presented at the National Reading Conference, St. Petersburg, FL.

Purcell-Gates, V. (1988). Lexical and syntactic knowledge of written narrative held by well-to-read kindergarteners and second graders. *Research in the Teaching of English, 22* (2), 128–160.

Read, C. (1970). *Children's perceptions of the sound of English.* Unpublished doctoral dissertation, Harvard University, Cambridge, MA.

Read, C. (1975). *Children's categorization of speech sounds in English.* (NCTE Res. Rep. No. 17). Urbana, IL: National Council of Teachers of English.

Reid, J. (1966). Learning to think about reading. *Educational Research, 9,* 56–62.

Richgels, D. J. (1986a). An investigation of preschool and kindergarten children's spelling and reading abilities. *Journal of Research and Development in Education, 19,* 41–47.

Richgels, D. J. (1986b). Beginning first graders' "invented spelling" ability and their performance in functional classroom writing activities. *Early Childhood Research Quarterly, 1*, 85–97.

Richgels, D. J., McGee, L. M., Hernandez, S., & Williams, N. (1988). Kindergarteners' attention to graphic detail in functional print: Letter name knowledge and invented spelling ability. *National Reading Conference Yearbook, 37*, 77–84.

Rowe, D. W. (1987). Literacy learning as an intertextual process. *National Reading Conference Yearbook, 36*, 101–112.

Rowe, D. W. (1988, April). *The impact of author/audience interaction on preschoolers' literacy learning*. Paper presented at the annual meeting of the American Educational Research Association, New Orleans, LA.

Rubin, A. D. (1978). A theoretical taxonomy of the differences between oral and written language (Tech. Rep. No. 35). Urbana/Champaign, IL: University of Illinois, Center for the Study of Reading.

Scollon, R., & Scollon, S. B. K. (1981). *Narrative, literacy, and face in interethnic communication*. Norwood, NJ: Ablex.

Shanahan, T. (1984). The nature of reading-writing relations: An exploratory multivariate analysis. *Journal of Educational Psychology, 76*, 357–363.

Shatz, M. (1984). A song without music and other stories: How cognitive process constraints influence children's oral and written narratives. In D. Schiffrin (Ed.), *Meaning, form, and use in context: Linguistic applications*. Washington, DC: Georgetown University Press.

Sinclair, A., Jarvella, R. J., & Levelt, W. J. M. (Eds.) (1978). *The child's conception of language*. New York: Springer-Verlag.

Smolkin, L. B., Conlon, A., & Yaden, D. B. (1988). Print salient illustrations in children's picture books: The emergence of written language awareness. *National Reading Conference Yearbook, 37*, 59–68.

Snow, C. E. (1983). Literacy and language: Relationships during the preschool years. *Harvard Educational Review 53*(2), 165–189.

Snow, C. E., & Goldfield, B. A. (1982). Building stories: The emergence of information structures from conversation. In D. Tannen (Ed.), *Analyzing discourse: Text and talk* (pp. 127–141). Washington, DC: Georgetown University Press.

Snow, C. E., & Goldfield, B. A. (1983). Turn the page, please: Situation-specific language acquisition. *Journal of Child Language, 10*, 535–549.

Snow, C. E., & Ninio, A. (1986). The contracts of literacy: What children learn from learning to read books. In W. H. Teale & E. Sulzby (Eds.), *Emergent literacy: Writing and reading* (pp. 116–138). Norwood, NJ: Ablex.

Stanovich, K. (1986). Matthew effects in reading: Some consequences of individual differences in the acquisition of literacy. *Reading Research Quarterly, 21*, 360–407.

Strickland, D. S., & Morrow, L. M. (Eds.). (1989). *Emerging literacy: Young children learn to read and write*. Newark, DE: International REading Association.

Sulzby, E. (1981, August). *Kindergarteners begin to read their own compositions: Beginning readers' developing knowledges about written language project*. Final report to the Research Foundation of the National Council of Teachers of English. Evanston, IL: Northwestern University.

Sulzby, E. (1983, September). *Beginning readers' developing knowledges about written language*. (Final report to the National Institute of Education NIE-G-80-0176). Evanston, IL: Northwestern University.

Sulzby, E. (1985a). Children's emergent reading of favorite storybooks: A developmental study. *Reading Research Quarterly, 20*, 458–481.

Sulzby, E. (1985b). Kindergarteners as writers and readers. In M. Farr (Ed.), *Advances in writing research, Vol. 1: Children's early writing development* (pp. 127–199). Norwood, NJ: Ablex.

Sulzby, E. (1988). A study of children's early reading development. In A. D. Pellegrini (Ed.), *Psychological bases for early education* (pp. 39–75). Chichester, ENG: Wiley.

Sulzby, E. (1989). Assessment of writing and of children's language while writing. In L. Morrow & J. Smith (Eds.), *The role of assessment and measurement in early literacy instruction* (pp. 83–109). Englewood Cliffs, NJ: Prentice-Hall.

Sulzby, E. (in press). Roles of oral and written language in children approaching conventional literacy. In C. Pontecorvo (Ed.), *L a costruzione del primi testi scritti nel bambino*. Roma: La Nuova Italia.

Sulzby, E., Barnhart, J., & Hieshima, J. (1989). *Forms of writing and rereading from writing: A preliminary report*. In J. Mason (Ed.), *Reading and writing connections* (pp. 31–63). Needham Heights, MA: Allyn & Bacon. Also (1989) Tech Rep. No. 20, Center for the Study of Writing, University of California, Berkeley, CA.

Sulzby, E., Olson, K. A., & Johnston, J. (1989). *The computer and young children: An emergent literacy perspective*. Working paper No. 1, Computers in Early Literacy (CIEL) Research Project. Institute for Social Research, The University of Michigan, Ann Arbor, MI.

Sulzby, E., & Teale, W. H. (1985). Writing development in early childhood. *Educational Horizons, 64*, 8–12.

Sulzby, E. & Teale, W. H. (1987, November). *Young children's storybook reading: Longitudinal study of parent-child interaction and children's independent functioning*. (Final report to The Spencer Foundation). Ann Arbor, MI: The University of Michigan.

Sulzby, E., & Teale, W. H. (in press). Emergent literacy. In P. D. Pearson, R. Barr, M. L. Kamil, & P. Mosenthal (Eds.), *Handbook of reading research, Vol. 2*. New York: Longman.

Tannen, D. (1982). The oral/literate continuum in discourse. In D. Tannen (Ed.), *Spoken and written language: Exploring orality and literacy* (pp. 1–16). Norwood, NJ: Ablex.

Tannen, D. (1984). Spoken and written narrative in English and Greek. In D. Tannen (Ed.), *Coherence in spoken and written discourse* (pp. 21–44). Norwodd, NJ: Ablex.

Taylor, D. (1983). *Family literacy*. Exeter, NH: Heinemann.

Taylor, D., & Dorsey-Gaines, C. (1988). *Growing up literate: Learning from inner-city families*. Portsmouth, NH: Heinemann.

Teale, W. H. (1978). Positive environments for learning to read: What studies of early readers tell us. *Language Arts, 55*, 922–932.

Teale, W. H. (1984). Reading to young children: Its significance in the process of literacy development. In H. Goelman, A. Oberg, & F. Smith (Eds.), *Awakening to literacy* (pp. 110–121). Exeter, NH: Heinemann.

Teale, W. H. (1986). Home background and young children's literacy development. In W. H. Teale & E. Sulzby (Eds.), *Emergent literacy: Writing and reading* (pp. 173–206). Norwood, NJ: Ablex.

Teale, W. H. (1987). Emergent literacy: Reading and writing development in early childhood. *National Reading Conference Yearbook, 36*, 45–74.

Teale, W. H., Martinez, M. G., & Glass, W. L. (1989). Describing classroom storybook reading. In D. Bloome (Ed.), *Classrooms and literacy* (pp. 158–188). Norwood, NJ: Ablex.

Teale, W. H., & Sulzby, E. (Eds.). (1986). *Emergent literacy: Writing and reading*. Norwood, NJ: Ablex.

Teale, W. H., & Sulzby, E. (1987). Literacy acquisition in early childhood: The roles of access and meditation in storybook reading. In D. A. Wagner (Ed.), *The future of literacy in a changing world* (pp. 111–130). New York, NY: Pergamon Press.

Tobin, A. W. (1981). *A multiple discriminant cross-validation of the factors associated with the development of precocious reading achievement*. Unpublished doctoral dissertation, University of Delaware, Newark, DE.

Tobin, A. W., & Pikulski, J. J. (1988). A longitudinal study of the reading achievement of early and nonearly readers through sixth grade. *National Reading Conference Yearbook, 37*, 49–58.

Tolchinsky-Landsmann, L., & Levin, I. (1985). Writing in preschoolers: An age related analysis. *Applied Psycholinguistics, 6,* 319–339.

Tolchinsky Landsmann, L., & Levin, I. (1987). Writing in four- to six-year-olds: Representation of semantic and phonetic similarities and differences. *Journal of Child Language, 14,* 127–144.

Vukelich, C., & Edwards, N. (1988). The role of context and as-written orthography in kindergarteners' word recognition. *National Reading Conference Yearbook, 37,* 85–93.

Vygotsky, L. S. (1978). *Mind in society: The development of higher psychological processes.* Cambridge, MA: Harvard University Press.

Vygotsky, L. S. (1981). The genesis of higher mental functions. In J. V. Wertsch (Ed.), *The concept of activity in Soviety psychology* (pp. 144–188). White Plains, NY: M. E. Sharpe.

Wells, C. G. (1985). Pre-school literacy related activities and success in school. In D. Olson, N. Torrance, & A. Hildyard (Eds.), *Literacy, language and learning: The nature and consequence of literacy* (pp. 229–255). Cambridge, ENG: Cambridge University Press.

Whitehurst, G. J., Falco, F. L., Lonigan, C. J., Fischel, J. E., DeBaryshe, B. D., Valdez-Menchaca, M. C., & Caulfield, M. (1988). Accelerating language development through picture book reading. *Developmental Psychology, 24,* 552–559.

Wolfe, D., & Gardner, H. (1981). On the structure of early symbolization. In R. L. Schiefelsbusch (Ed.), *Early language: Acquisition and intervention* (pp. 287–327). Baltimore, MD: University Park Press.

Yaden, D. B., Smolkin, L. B., & Conlon, A. (1989). Preschoolers' questions about pictures, print conventions, and story text during reading aloud at home. *Reading Research Quarterly, 24,* 188–214.

Yaden, D. B., & Templeton, S. (Eds.). (1986). *Metalinguistic awareness and beginning literacy.* Portsmouth, NH: Heineman.

19B. DEVELOPMENT IN THE ELEMENTARY SCHOOL YEARS

Dorothy S. Strickland
Joan T. Feeley

We can never escape our fundamental beliefs and understandings. What we believe or think we know about our world affects everything we do. As teachers, we accumulate a set of beliefs about how children learn and develop. These understandings begin with our experiences as family members and participants in society. They are expanded and refined through the courses we take as preservice and inservice teachers, through our interactions with other professionals, and through our everyday dealings with children in the classroom. The belief systems we develop play a large part in determing the decisions we make about what to teach, how it will be taught, and how we view the effectiveness of our instruction. They are a powerful influence on determing what new methods and approaches we take into our classrooms, and they guide the way we implement them.

Our belief systems are extremely powerful. Yet, despite their power, they are often taken for granted. Methods and materials, and not understandings about children's learning, consume most teachers' time and energy. It is rare to hear teachers ask, "What theories of language and literacy development underly these new materials or this new approach?" or "How can I implement this new program so that it is consistent with what I know about how children learn?"

We believe that teachers' knowledge about language learning is a major source of empowerment. It enables them to take control over methods and materials and to make informed curricular decisions. It was with these thoughts in mind, that we set out to write this chapter on language development during the elementary school years. It is our belief that a better understanding of children as language learners will lead to improved classroom instructional practices.

THE LEARNER DEVELOPS: AN OVERVIEW

Elementary school-age children have been described as "being everywhere." They are on the playground, at the local store, at the pizza shop, traveling on the school bus, in the movies, and many other places. They are the most visible of all age groups. Yet, adults appear to pay less attention to this age group than they do to children during infancy, early childhood, and adolescence (Collins, 1984). One reason for this might be because school and friends take up much of children's time during the elementary years. Another might be that the physical and psychological changes that children undergo during the middle childhood period do not attract adult attention since they are not as obvious as the changes that occur at other stages of development (Shonkoff, 1984).

Many changes do occur during this developmental period, however. In addition to the shift to more formalized instruction, children are challenged to expand their world to include new acquaintances and experiences outside their immediate neighborhoods. They are introduced to new social rules and expectations, and they are likely to be exposed to people from diverse cultural and linguistic backgrounds. All of these factors require children to make important changes in their ability to think about their world and to relate their own life experiences to the life experiences of others. These changes are of great significance to each child and to those interested in the language-arts education of children.

In this chapter, our major focus is on children's oral and written language and their literary development. In order to provide a wholistic framework for our discussion, we begin with an outline of children's physical, cognitive, and social-emotional development during the elementary school years.

Physical development during the elementary years is generally slower than that during early childhood, but it is steady and sustained. Coordination becomes increasingly developed and control is attained on motor tasks of increasing complexity and difficulty. In relating children's motor development to appropriate toys, Bee (1985) suggests that children 7 and 8 years old can usually ride a bicycle easily, skip rope, and play most games that require hitting, kicking, or throwing a ball. Previous practice with small-muscle coordination makes the elementary school-age child much more skillful with model building, arts and crafts, and even sewing.

Cognitive development during the middle childhood years has been characterized by Piaget (1970) as the period of concrete operations. This refers to children's ability to operate on the basis of rules when they examine and interact with phenomena. Reversibility and conservation are two key mental operations that children grasp during this period. Reversibility refers to the child's understanding that a basic property of any action is that it can be undone or reversed—either physically or mentally—and return to the original position. Thus, the clay can once again be formed into a ball and the milk can be poured back into a taller, thinner glass.

Classification and seriation are important cognitive operations that flourish during this period. According to Ziegler and Finn-Stevenson (1987):

During the middle childhood years, children begin to have an understanding that there is a hierarchical relationship between subordinate and superordinate classes—German Shepherds, Collies, and Great Danes belong to subordinate class of dogs and a superordinate class of animals. (p. 490)

The ability to arrange objects in an orderly series demonstrates systematic, planful thinking on the part of the school-age child. (p. 491)

One way in which this planful behavior is demonstrated is the way that 6-year-olds begin to assign roles to individuals during dramatic play. Another is the increased interest in games with rules and creation of rules in play activities as children move through the grades.

Social and emotional development during the elementary years is generally characterized by excitement and joy. Children experience a growing sense of personal awareness as they interact with peers and adults outside the family. They become increasingly aware of how other people will react to their actions and ideas. Selman (1976) suggests that during these years, children evidence ability to infer accurately other people's thoughts and feelings, and they realize that since other people can do the same, their own thoughts and feelings are the object of other people's thinking.

Having the ability to take the perspective of others, the child becomes better able to communicate, since effective communication depends on the assessment of what other people already know and what they need to know. The ability to understand how people think and feel also enhances empathy, the ability to understand and vicariously feel what another person is feeling. (Zigler & Finn-Stevenson, 1987, pp. 530-531)

Other important changes that occur during the elementary years involve the child's moral development and behavior. As children grow, they develop greater understanding of rules and appropriate behavior, and they increase in their ability to reason about moral issues. Self-concept, whether negative or positive, is greatly influenced during this period by children's relationships with parents, peers, and teachers.

The aspects of children's physical, cognitive, and social-emotional development, which we have highlighted above, should be kept in mind as the research on children's language and literacy is discussed. It is the interdependence of all aspects of the child's life and learning that help provide us with a profile of what these children are like and how we can best support them as they learn to read, write, and enjoy literature.

ORAL LANGUAGE DEVELOPMENT

By the time children enter kindergarten, they know a great deal about language. They have a vocabulary of several thousand words, and they have internalized the phonology and linguistic structures of their language (Berko, 1958; Brown, 1973; Klima & Bellugi-Klima, 1966; *McNeil*, 1970; Menyuk, 1969; Templin, 1987). They know that language is functional, and they use it to share ideas and facilitate their own purposes. Children continue to grow in language competence throughout the elementary-school years. Their increasing language ability reflects a growing understanding of the physical and social world around them. As the range of their experiences increases, new concepts are formed and expressed through language. Their growing cognitive abilities also affect language development.

One of the most comprehensive studies of language development in school-age children was done by Walter Loban (1963). Loban followed children from kindergarten through grade 12. He started with 338 kindergartners, 30 of whom were rated exceptionally high in language development and 24 rated exceptionally low. Tracking these children over several years revealed that all of them increased the number of words spoken each year and increased their effectiveness in speaking. The

high language-ability group maintained its superiority, increased complexity of sentence structure, and added vocabulary until it was about double that of the low language-ability group. Although recent change in the way we view nonstandard dialects may alter the way we construe these findings, the differences remain impressive. The high-ability group children used a greater number of less common words and were more fluent in language use than the low group or the remaining randomly-chosen subjects. In addition, the high group continuously used a greater variety of sentence structures and were distinguished by greater effectiveness in their use of language.

Several instructional implications may be drawn from Loban's work. Once considered less fluent or linguistically disadvantaged, children in a regular school situation seem to be increasingly less able in other language areas when compared with the more capable children. The difference could be the result of teaching practices, since the children who speak well and fluently are the ones who get the most opportunities to talk, while those less ready with words and assurance are sometimes ignored. Loban recommended less teacher reliance on workbook drill and more emphasis on encouraging speech to express ideas, attitudes, and values of concern to the learners. Rather than drill in usage, he suggested that teachers work with the individual to achieve coherence and organization in talking.

We believe these findings have implications relevant to teacher atitudes about children's language. Teachers who feel that the language of a particular student or group of students is deficient may indeed give those students fewer opportunities to speak in the belief that they are incapable of communicating well. Such teachers may be intolerant of language differences or they may act out of genuine concern for putting children in situations where they may not be as successful as others. In either case, they deny children the opportunity to demonstrate and build on what they do know about language in an atmosphere that is risk free and encouraging.

Another extensive study of elementary school children (Chomsky, 1969, 1972) involved their understanding of certain sentence structures. Chomsky found several sentence structures that school-age children consistently misinterpreted prior to a certain stage of development. Five of these proved to be acquired in a sequence, revealing developmental stages. Although the order of acquisition was constant, children varied greatly in their rate of acquisition.

First of these misinterpretations concerned the word *see*. A doll, whose eyes closed when lying down, was laid on a table. The children were asked, "Is the doll hard to see or easy to see?" Later, the doll was placed out of sight and the children were asked the same question. Children under 5 1/2 years old said the doll was hard to see in both instances. Beyond that age some children began to interpret the question correctly. By age 9 all children did.

The words *asked* and *promised* presented a second problem as used in the following sentences: (1) John asked Bill to leave. (2) John promised Bill to leave. Although all the children understood the meaning of *promised* in other types of sentences, children younger than 51/2 years old interpreted *promised* the same as *asked*. By age 9 all interpreted it correctly.

A third problem also involved the word *ask*. When children were told, "Ask Bruce what to feed the dog," the most frequent responses were, "What do you want to feed the dog?" or "What are you going to feed the dog?" Only one third of the group gave the correct response, "What should I feed the dog?"

A fourth problem involved referents of words in certain syntactic structures. When told, "Mother scolded Gloria for answering the phone and I would have done the same," many children thought "the same" meant "I would have answered the phone" rather than " I would have scolded Gloria."

When *although* was substituted for *and* in the sentence above, only 4 children of 36, the most advanced, made the correct distinction. When the less familiar concept of *although* was added to the uncertainty of the referent for same, difficulties increased.

Chomsky's study reminds us that children's language development is ongoing throughout the school-age years. The need to probe and explore their understandings and interpretations of language is a necessary part of classroom practice.

Numerous other researchers have examined the continued evolution of language during this period (Bormouth, Carr, Manning, & Pearson, 1970; Carroll, 1970; and Strickland, 1962). Their research has confirmed the fact that semantic and syntactic acquisition of language continues at least until age 9 or 10. This research is of vital importance to classroom teachers, as it relates to the cognitive and linguistic demands of the typical elementary classroom. It suggests:

1. That teachers need to be aware of the conditions under-which the remarkable accomplishments of children's first language learning occurs and
2. that teachers need to provide experiences that are open ended and flexible enough to accommodate a range of language backgrounds and competencies.

Strickland and Taylor (1989) observed that home language learning conditions are characterized by an atmosphere of success and child centeredness. They suggest that the home learning enviroment is a generally positive one, where adults use language with children rather than at them. They also contend that at home, children acquire spoken language in a meaningful context. Language learning and concept development are related to meaningful activities, objects, and situations in the child's environment. In addition, in language learning situations at home, the child is presented with the whole system to be learned. It is neither sequenced by some external force nor is it put into a skills array or management system. Finally, they remind us that none of these features, so characteristic of first language learning at home, requires standard forms. What *is* required is adult-child interaction where the focus is on whole language used in a meaningful context. We believe that these understandings, based on observations of children in natural settings outside of school, can serve as basic principles upon which to build the language curriculum in school.

Language experiences that accommodate a range of linguistic backgrounds and competencies help support children's ongoing language development. The value of open ended, multi-level language activities was demonstrated by Strickland (1973), who participated in a study to examine the possibility of expanding the speech of lower socioeconomic area African American kindergarten children to include some standard dialect forms. Children in an experimental group listened daily to selected children's literature and took part in oral language activities such as creative dramatics, choral speaking, puppetry, and role playing. They participated in the imitation and repetition of language patterns used in the literature. All activities involved the children in active dialogue. The control group experienced the same daily oral reading of children's literature, but their follow-up activities did not include oral language participation by the children.

The procedures with the experimental group proved a successful way to expand the language repertoire of these linguistically different 5-year-olds without attempting to expunge or discredit their home language. Children began to include more standard dialect in their normal speech, an expansion of language rather than a substitution. An extension of the study to primary grades (Cullinan, Jaggar, & Strickland, 1974) yielded similar results. Kindergarteners made the most dramatic gains, however, as demonstrated by their ability to repeat standard English sentences, an indication of growth in language proficiency. We believe that the dramatic effects of these kinds of activities on the language development of children, who are generally thought to be at a linguistic disadvantage in the schools, offers direction for working with *all* children to increase their communicative competence.

While other researchers studied children's developing ability to understand and use various grammatical structures, Halliday (1975) analyzed children's speech in terms of the functions to which children put it. Halliday suggests a system of development that begins with the words "I want _____," representing the instrumental use of language. In the order they evolve, the seven functions, and examples of each use of speech, are as follows:

Instrumental	I want
Regulatory	Do as I tell you
Interactional	Me and you
Personal	Here I come
Heuristic	Tell me why
Imaginative	Let's pretend
Informative	I've got something to tell you

Informative use of language is generally the last to develop in children. The child uses it least and is least able to understand its use by others. Teachers of young children are generally aware of the danger of the overuse of telling as a means of transmiting information. They know the importance of involving children in firsthand experiences that require experimentation, demonstration, and manipulation of real objects. We believe that this kind of direct involvement is equally important throughout the elementary grades. In the process of developing a concept through first-hand experience, children begin to acquire the appropriate representational speech to describe and refer to that experience. They develop conceptual frameworks that help them internalize the ideas so that they are better able to think and talk about what they know and extend their ideas to new situations. Teachers who rely too heavily on merely telling children the information they want them to acquire risk promoting mindless regurgitation of that information without depth of understanding or ability to extend it to new learnings.

While most of the research on children's language development has focused on speech, the development of listening is also of critical importance. Listening is the primary source of language. It is the foundation upon which all the other communication processes develop. The very young child is channelled to speech, reading, and writing through listening. Studies of physical disabilities (Brown, as cited in Lundsteen, 1976), such as hearing disorders and brain damage, have pointed to the interdependence among the various language processes with listening at the base. As language is expanded and developed, listening remains the primary mode for acquiring linguistic knowledge and skill. Because evidence of listening is indirect, researchers have been unable to learn a great deal about its development. Thus, no developmental stages of listening have been determined.

Some attention has been given to the amount of time children spend listening in school. Wilt (1950) found that out of a five-hour school day, elementary school children spent 2 1/2 hours listening to others—primarily the teacher. Lundsteen (1971) reports that children may hear at least 20 times as many oral contributions from classmates as they themselves give. The need to nurture children's listening development is well established in the literature. Children need planned, consistent help in learning to think about, react, and respond to what they hear.

Bromley (1988) gives two reasons for teaching children how to listen: children and adults spend enormous amounts of time each day listening; and the ability to be an effective listener is of major importance not only for learning in the classroom but also for survival in the everyday world where listening to news reports, political, and consumer messages is a daily occurrence. In addition, the ability to listen for appreciation and enjoyment makes life fuller and more satisfying. Reviews by Devine (1978), Duker (1969), and Pearson and Fielding (1982) cite numerous studies indicating that students who receive systematic instruction in listening improve in their abilities to process the information received and understand and remember it better.

Language and Thought

Language and thought are so interconnected that it is impossible to discuss one without the other. Meaningful communication would be unattainable in the absence of thought. The construction of meaning, whether it be through listening, speaking, reading, or writing, is rooted in thought. Piaget (1955) and Vygotsky (1962) are two researchers who have greatly influenced our knowledge of the development of thinking in children. Piaget stressed the idea that young children learn by acting upon their environment. They learn as they manipulate, explore, experiment, invent, and discover. He suggested that by imposing adult language upon children's cognitive structures, we may actually impede their development rather than promote it. Piaget conceded that adults do act as language models for children; however, he believed that adult language could not expand the thinking of the child beyond the limits of the child's own cognitive development.

Recent researchers have turned to Vygotsky in order to better understand the role of the adult in children's language development. According to Vygotsky, the social context in which children learn to speak is extremely important. Vygotsky emphasized the interaction between the child and the language of the environment. Thus the role of the adult becomes crucial in language development. He believed that the dialogue between children and their parents or teachers played a major role in the creation of thought.

Research examining the dynamics of family storybook reading (Taylor & Strickland, 1986) confirm Vygotsky's notions about the critical role of parents in the development of children's language and thought. Audio recordings of 20 families of varied backgrounds and family structures were collected as they engaged in shared book experiences. Parents were interviewed as they listened to the tapes and reflected on their experiences. Although each family established its own unique routines and style of book sharing, certain aspects of the experience seemed to prevail. The talk between parent and child was critical to furthering children's understandings of the content of the book as well as their understandings about stories and concepts about print. For example, regardless of socioeconomic status, ethnic or educational background, parents instinctively relate new concepts to something the child already knows. They expand on vocabulary by using synonyms or brief explanations where needed. They augment the text in places where a problem is anticipated, and they listen and respond to their child's questions and comments about storyline, characters, pictures, words, and letters. It is no wonder that children fortunate enough to have had such experiences are likely to acquire literacy with ease (Clark, 1976; Durkin, 1966; Torrey, 1969).

The theories of both Piaget and Vygotsky have implications for the classroom. Teachers should avoid confusing children by presenting with them with abstract ideas in adult language before they have the background of concrete experiences to act as a framework for understanding. The importance of adult-child dialogue, however, cannot be overestimated. Interactive language between child and adult is a significant part of every stage of the child's language development. Teachers need to be aware of their important role in the language and cognitive development of children.

In summary, although children have acquired most of the basic structures of English by the time they enter school, their language development continues throughout the elementary school years. During the elementary years, children not only expand their use of syntactic structures, they acquire new ones. Children improve in effectiveness and control of language by building and expanding on already learned patterns. Children who are proficient in oral language tend to be higher achievers on measures of vocabulary and other espects of language and literacy development.

Teachers need to be aware what is known about children's language development, including what has been learned about the conditions under which children are successful language learners outside of school. This information can help provide the basic for planning school experiences. The language curriculum should provide a wide variety of experiences that accommodate a range of language backgrounds and competencies. Following is a discussion of studies about language in the classroom. Suggestions are offered for improving the language learning that takes place there.

Oral Language in the Classroom

Studies of classroom discourse reveal a great deal about whether or not oral language is being fostered at school. Cazden (1988), Dillon and Searle (1981), and Mehan (1979) indicate that the basic interactional pattern in classrooms is characterized by teacher initiation, student response, and teacher evaluation. Mehan's investigation of a combined 1st, 2nd, and 3rd grade class further revealed that 81.1 percent of the instructional sequences were teacher-initiated while only 17.9 percent were student-initiated.

Nearly three decades ago, Flanders' (1962) research on classroom interaction indicated that in a 5-hour day, most teachers talked nearly 2 hours and 20 minutes. Dividing the remaining 67 minutes among 30 children, Flanders suggested that each child was permitted only 2 minutes of talking time throughout the day. Flanders developed the Rule of Two Thirds: two thirds of classroom time is devoted to talk, two thirds of the talk is teacher talk, and two thirds of what the teacher says is merely giving factual information or directions for assignments.

Researchers agree that if schools are to foster children's language development, children need opportunities to use their language resources and to build on them. Yet, studies suggest that the restrictive environment of the school is not conductive to language development. According to Dillon and Searle (1981), the classroom language code of students they studied was restricted while the home language was elaborated. The restricted or limited code seen in the classroom failed to make use of the children's full range of language and learning abilities. Several researchers have offered suggestions for change.

Pinnell (1985) suggests that teachers use the system developed by Halliday or one developed by others such as Smith (1977), Tough (1977), or Wood (1977) in order to observe how children use language. Whatever the system, Pinnell asserts that sensitive observation can help a teacher determine children's competence in using language that relates to real life situations. "Observing and recording children's language behavior is a viable way to look at what they can do, thus giving an effective starting point for instruction" (p. 60).

Michaels and Foster (1985) reported on the use of student-run sharing time in an ethnically mixed 1st and 2nd grade classroom. Students successfully altered their style of communication according to whether they were speaking in a narrative or reportorial mode. Because these sessions were student controlled, pupils were in a better positioin to demonstrate their discourse skills and improve them.

Conferences with peers and teachers during the writing process is another important way to extend language development (Graves, 1983). During writing conferences, students exchange ideas with others in order to improve writing in progress or simply respond to a completed work. During the exchange, students must talk and listen to the talk of others as they explain,

clarify, and extend their ideas. Opportunities to engage in literature response groups is another way to expand children's language use. These share sessions are generally student directed and involve a student's presentation of a book he or she has read, followed by student reactions.

Strickland in collaboration with a group of teacher-researchers (Strickland, Dillon, Funkhouser, Glick, & Rogers, 1989), examined the nature and quality of the classroom dialogue during liturature response groups. Children in grades 1, 2, 4 and 6 were involved. Specifically, the following questions were asked: What was the content of the talk during literature response groups? What functions of language were in use by the students? What evidence of students' reading comprehension was demonstrated? Data were collected by the classroom teachers through observations using field notes and audio and video tape recordings. The findings supported the teachers' intuitive sense and informal observation that literature response groups provide an excellent resource for student learning through talk and support for literacy development.

The content of the discussion included talk about the storyline or topic of the books; the authors and their works; literary elements such as characterization, setting, plot, theme, and genre; the writer's craft and use of literary devices; and students' own personal understandings, including the relationship of the reading to their personal lives.

Growing competence in the following linguistic tasks were evident at all grade levels in the study:

1. Sensitivity to the need to organize information when giving explanations so that they can be better understood by others,
2. Adjustment of the style of speech to suit audience and purpose,
3. sensitivity to the discrepancy between the speaker's information and experiential background and that of the audience,
4. Awareness of differences in point of view, and
5. Analysis of information in relation to the points or problems under discussion.

Through their talk, students also demonstrated application of various aspects of reading comprehension, including ability to: recall important facts and details, arrange facts in sequential order, distinguish between fact and fantasy, identify cause and effect relationships, predict outcomes, compare and contrast ideas and information, and monitor their own comprehension. One of the most significant outcomes of this research was the opportunity it gave teachers to examine systematically the language learning environment in their classrooms and to make adjustments based on their observations and reflections regarding children's language behavior and growth.

Two other methods that effectively promote learning in and through oral language are reciprocal teaching and cooperative learning. These strategies are useful across the curriculum, and they may be used by both young and old students. In reciprocal teaching (Palinscar & Brown, 1985) students are involved in summarizing, question-generating, clarifying, and predicting as they read texts or observe phenomena. As with literature response groups, both teacher and students share responsibility for the conduct of the discussion. While the discussion is cognitively focused on a particular content, the talk is complex and multidimensional and avoids the restrictive question-answer pattern of recitation.

Cooperative learning strategies offer another valuable means of promoting students' communication skills as they use language for learning. When children engage in cooperative learning tasks, they must work together to complete a particular objective. The functions of language required as they work are multifaceted. They must make their ideas clear to others and extend themselves a bit to appreciate another's perspective on a problem. Johnson (1984) suggest that this kind of guided classroom interaction has both social, value-shaping outcomes and cognitive meaning-making benefits.

Instructional scaffolding and inquiry teaching are strategies that may be infused into the many opportunities for class discussion throughout the day. Lehr (1985) describes instructional scaffolding as a widely applicable technique in which the teacher initially provides a relatively high degree of verbal structure—a "scaffold" that assures a firm grounding for student discourse—then gradually withdraws ther structure as students become increasingly capable of building conceptual edifices on their own.

Inquiry teaching, a strategy frequently used in social studies and science, is an interactive method that has been expanded and refined in recent years. Hillocks (1986) reports that inquiry methods—teacher and student question/discussion-generating techniques—underlie numerous studies in which students show writing improvement. The trend toward encouraging students to generate questions for each other and to share responsibility for determining topics and the course of group discussion are major breakthroughs in promoting competence and confidence in oral language. Collins (1986) describes how teachers use inquiry strategies during class discussion. Teachers help guide the course of the talk by helping students become aware of misconceptions, highlighting what is known and not known, and setting future directions for class activities.

Other opportunities for students to expand their oral language in school include dramatics; storytelling and retelling; activities involving brainstorming, planning, and problem solving; and hands-on activities associated with content areas such as mathematics, social studies, and science. Activities of this type allow students to expand their oral language abilities by applying and refining what they already know. Equally important, they offer teachers excellent opportunities to make informed curricular decisions as they bring what they know about children's language development together with their observations of children's language in use.

WRITTEN LANGUAGE DEVELOPMENT

Shanahan (1984) describes reading and writing as related processes, Tierney and Pearson (1984) see them as similar composing processes, and Harste, Woodward, and Burke (1984) characterize them as processes of context-driven meaning-making and communication. Langer (1986) agrees with but goes beyond these explanations. Even for young children, she sees reading and writing as being both purposeful and cognitive ac-

tivities that are used to help one conceptualize personal experience and world knowledge. Calling reading and writing the "interplay of mind and text" that brings about new learning, Langer says that they must be considered as they change over time. However one tries to explain the connection between reading and writing, it is evident that the two processes depend on one's exposure to and uses of written language. This section will report what the research says about how children in the elementary school years develop as readers and writers and what it all means for classroom teachers.

Primary Years (K–2)

When Don Graves (1983) asked children just beginning school if they could read and write only 15 percent answered that they could read while 85 percent said they could write. Accordingly, we will begin with writing because of young children's perception of themselves as writers and the tremendous body of research on this area produced during the past fifteen years (e.g. Baghban, 1984; Bissex, 1980; Calkins, 1983, 1986; Clay, 1975; De Ford & Hartse, 1982; Dyson, 1983; Ferriero & Teberosky, 1983; Graves, 1981; Hansen, 1987; Hartse, Woodward, & Burke, 1984; King & Rentel, 1979).

Writing. If this review were being written a decade ago, writing in kindergarten and grade 1, except for the literal meaning of forming letters, would not have received much attention. Children were not expected to write/compose until the latter half of grade 1, and the major focus was put on learning to read. Writing was thought to begin through group and individual dictation that the teacher would write and the children would copy (Burrows, 1986). But, according to the vast amount of literature cited above, school beginners know much more about producing written language than we had expected.

Most kindergartens begin to write by drawing and scribbling (Sulzby, 1985a; Temple, Nathan, Burris, & Temple, 1988). They will write such things as messages, grocery lists, stories and notes, and "pretend read" them to you. As soon as they can write a few letters (e.g., those in their name), they begin to add these and other letter-like marks to their drawings/scribbles, showing that they know writing is not completely arbitrary but that it involves certain kinds of special marks (Clay, 1975). Temple et al. (1988) call this the prephonemic stage. Gentry (1981) notes that the scribbling stage parallels the babbling stage in oral language development.

When their informal exposure to written language through environmental print is augmented by more direct experiences with print such as group reading of a "big book" (Holdaway, 1979) and group composing of text via the language experience approach (Hall, 1981; Stauffer, 1980), children begin to internalize the alphabetic principle. They may use one or two letters, usually consonants, to stand for whole words. Temple et al. (1988) call this the early phonemic stage and give the following example: RCRBKDN = Our car broke down. With the accompanying illustration, the message is perfectly understandable. Forester (1980) compares this writing with the holophrases children begin to utter around the age of two.

With daily meaningful reading/writing experiences, children move into the letter-name stage in which vowels begin to appear along with prominent consonants (Chomsky, 1979; Read, 1986; Temple et al., 1988). By now they know the names of the letters but not necessarily which letters represent which sounds; active learners, they invent spellings according to their own phonemic rules, for example, "chran" for "train," "yet/ yent" for "went," and "pan" for "pen." Soon standard spellings are mixed with invented spellings, and children are said to be in a transitional stage. Throughout the elementary school years, spelling tends to become more standard, but invented spellings can be found at all levels.

Taking a more global perspective of beginning spellers, Harste et al. (1984) suggest that children may be using three strategies: spelling the way it sounds ("jress" = "dress"); spelling the way it looks ("fro" = "for"); spelling the way it means ("wasapanataem" = the conceptual unit, "once upon a time"). They caution against attention to spelling in the early years, since spelling is the biggest constraint that fives and sixes see in writing. Some children realizing that there is a "right way" to write may temporarily refuse to "spell it like it sounds" or even to write much at all (Bissex, 1980). The public nature of writing also makes it risky business.

However, children do not move through these suggested phases evenly. Some may skip and appear to go from drawing directly to invented spelling. In her year-long study of 183 children in whole language kindergartens, Allen (1989) has found that growth patterns were very individual, with children often adding to their repertoire of writing behaviors without abandoning their old behaviors. For example, although prephonemic writing was the highest category observed during the first quarter and remained high through the second and third quarters, children were attempting more and more phonemic writing as the year unfolded. By the fourth quarter, 72 percent of the children were using some invented spelling. The numbers of children operating in three or more categories moved from 38 percent in the first quarter to 73 percent in the fourth.

Another very important finding of the Allen study was that growth was not limited by the level of literacy sophistication that the children brought with them to kindergarten. While children who came in with advanced skills continued their growth, those who entered with very little observable knowledge of reading and writing also made great gains. Instruction that continued exploration and invention of language made the difference.

Children will develop this control over written language if they are encouraged to write frequently in a workshop atmosphere in which they draw/write about real events in their own lives and read their work to peers in all-group share time (Graves, 1983; Hansen, 1987; Hansen & Graves, 1983).

Graves (1983) says that when fives and sixes first start writing, they think their writing is good, and their self-centeredness protects them from their audiences. It is only toward the end of 1st grade that they begin to realize that others may not agree with them. By grade 2, children become much more concerned about their product and audience acceptance. They want their work to look like the basals and trade books they can now read. Share time can become risky business.

Besides being risky business, writing is noisy business.

Dyson (1983) found that kindergartners talk to themselves as they draw and write, with oral language investing the graphics with meaning. Allen and Carr (in press) learned that they talk to each other to generate topics and develop them, to match print to pictures and letters to sounds, and to learn how "to do school."

Calkins (1986) believes that talk helps young children to hold onto their thoughts while pencils and markers are selected to get them down on paper. She says that both talking and drawing are necessary adjuncts to writing in kindergarten and grade 1. By grade 2, drawing becomes less necessary, but talking with others, as rehearsal for writing and for feedback on drafts, become even more important. Seven-year-olds find emotional support in peer review. It appears that writing can be very social business, too.

Young children demonstrate their egocentricity in their writings. Manning, Manning, and Hughes (1987) found that personal content dominated the journals of 1st-graders who wrote about themselves and their feelings and their families and pets. Demonstrating the effect of leaving home for wider vistas, they also wrote information pieces about school, holidays, and seasons.

Calkins (1986) says that 1st-graders' early "published" pieces can be characterized as "all-about" or attribute books in which they tell everything they know about the topic. Toward the end of the year, many move toward writing narratives, that is, stories in which events are chronologically ordered. The main revision strategy for this age is adding on more information as it occurs to them. As 2nd-graders move away from "all-about" books, they begin to write "bed-to-bed" stories which are chronologically written but include everything that is remembered, with all events being given equal weight. Calkins characterizes this time as a period of great growth in writing.

Writers in the primary years are active, noisy, risk-takers, internalizing the rules of written language as they use it to construct meaning in social situations.

Reading. Smith (1985) describes reading as an active, constructive process in which one applies different kinds of knowledge (knowledge of the world, the language system, and the content) to make meaning from written language. While only 15 percent of school beginners *believe* they can read (Graves, 1983), almost all have some control over this process, but the range is wide. While most can read varying amounts of environmental print, such as stop signs, McDonald's, A&P, and food labels, some who have been read to frequently can "pretend-read" familiar picture books, and a few can read notes, signs, and picture books that they have not encountered before (Hartse et al., 1984; Taylor, 1983).

Over the past decade, the term "reading readiness" has given way to the new concept of "emergent literacy." Lapp and Flood (1978) define reading readiness as the necessary level of preparation children should attain before beginning formal reading instruction. Alphabet and word recognition, vocabulary knowledge, and visual discrimination are cited as possible predictors of reading readiness. In traditional readiness programs, prescribed skills in these areas are directly taught to get children "ready" to read.

On the other hand, emergent literacy looks at both reading and writing (literacy) as they are in the process of emerging in the everyday lives of children from their earliest years (Teale & Sulzby, 1986). Morrow (1989) says that the concept assumes that children acquire knowledge about oral and written language before coming to school. In their review of emergent literacy, Mason and Allen (1986) describe the social and linguistic contexts (community and parental priorities) and the special demands of written language that can affect how children develop as readers and writers. Children who have had many meaningful experiencs with print such as being read to often and experimenting with writing, and more ready for school reading programs than those who have not had such exposures.

Children lacking these experiences, come to school in a state of "cognitive confusion" about the functions of print and the terms we use in formal reading instruction (Downing, 1970). Adults take it for granted that children know what they mean when they talk about a "word," a "letter," a "sound," but simple experiments with preschoolers proved otherwise (Feeley, 1984). In early seminal research, Downing and Oliver (1973–1974) found that many beginners lack concepts about these terms and other prints conventions. Clay (1979, 1985) has developed a simple test for assessing this metalinguistic knowledge. Called Concepts About Print (CAP), the test consists of a story book, with text on one side and pictures on the other, which is read to the child who is asked to help the tester. It explores concepts such as whether the child knows that print, not pictures, tells the story, what letters and words are, what some punctuation marks mean. Clay (1989) describes how educators from many parts of the world have adapted and used this instrument. Goodman & Altwerger (1981) recommend informal bookhandling tasks to assess this kind of knowledge.

Children come to school able to understand and respond to thousands of spoken words (Anderson & Freebody, 1981), but their ability to recognize words in print relates again to their preschool activities with written language. Most will be able to recognize their names and can quickly learn to read the names of their classmates, signs and labels in their classroom, and a basic vocabulary of common words from language experience and shared book activities (Johnson & Pearson, 1984; Mason & Au, 1986). Writing, too, adds to children's stock of sight words. When they compared the vocabulary produced by children in a writing-focused 1st grade with the vocabulary they would have encountered in a basal reading series, Gunderson and Shapiro (1988) found that the young writers produced 18 times the number of words found in the basals! (Studies like this need to be conducted on a regular basis to see what changes may occur as teachers begin to integrate literature and writing activities into their basal programs and use the most current editions of basals that are more likely to contain a wide variety of selections from the best of children's literature.)

Chall (1983) has proposed a six-stage model of reading acquisition which no longer seems to fit with the current concept of emergent literacy. Her stages are: prereading (birth to 6), decoding (6 to 7), fluency (7 to 8), reading to learn (any age), multiple viewpoints (high school), and reconstruction (college and beyond). We now know that young children bring a wide range of literacy skills to their early school experiences (Teale

& Sulzby, 1986) and that readers at all levels reconstruct text according to their background knowledge (Anderson & Pearson, 1984; Smith, 1985).

Bussis, Chittenden, Amarel, and Klausner (1985), who documented the development of reading ability in 26 children from K–2, posit that, from the outset, reading is the act of orchestrating diverse knowledge bases to construct meaning from text. They found that all their subjects began school with some knowledge of letter-sound correspondences, a small "sight word" vocabulary, a belief that reading had to make sense, and their own preferred learning styles. How they grew into able readers makes fascinating reading. Although exposed to an array of diverse reading programs (phonics, language experience, various basals), all had teachers who read to them everyday, provided a large selection of trade books with time to read, and encouraged written composition frequently.

Admitting that it might be dangerous to try to talk about stages in learning to read because the process is so idiosyncratic, Weaver (1988) has suggested phases that children may go through, similar to those noted in spelling development. In the schema emphasis phase stage, which is compared with the prephonemic stage in spelling, children exhibit reading-like behavior, turning pages and "reading" from prior knowledge of story and picture clues. In the semantic/syntactic emphasis phase, which is like the phonemic or invented spelling stage in writing, they continue to use schematic knowledge and picture clues but begin to read some words in context. Miscues at this stage are likely to fit the context semantically and syntactically but may not reflect the actual words on the page, for example "bird" for "canary."

Bussis et al. (1985) noted "quasi-reading" among their kindergartens and cited the work of Neisser (1967) to try to explain this phonemenon. Young readers probably have not "memorized" the 200 or so words in a story that they "pretend-read," but rather, they remenber the phrase structures, chunking the meaning units and rehearsing them as adults do to remember telephone numbers. They wrote, "What Janny and other quasi-readers committed to memory were not individual words but the phrase structures of a story. The individual words flowed from the structures" (p. 87).

When Sulzby (1985b) studied the emergent storybook reading attempts of preschoolers and children at the beginning and end of kindergarten, she found a developmental progression across age levels. When asked to read or "pretend-read" a story, they went from "reading" no real stories to stories which they used oral language-like structures at first and finally written language-like structures. Bussis et al. (1985) also report that their quasi readers read in a "book voice."

According to Weaver (1988), in the grapho-phonemic emphasis phase children tend to read exactly what is on the page, with "sounding out" strategies producing "cainery" for "canary" even when they know it stands for a type of bird. This over-reliance on the grapho-phonemic cueing system may be a reflection of children's attempts to master this cue system in addition to the others; this phase corresponds to the transitional stage in writing when invented forms appear along with standard spellings.

Describing this early reading stage which occured anywhere from the end of kindergarten to grade 2, Bussis et al. (1985)

found that half of their subjects (Cluster B) revealed learning styles that caused them to value accuracy and linearity (getting the words right in order of appearance) over momentum (fluency). These readers would skip words and would frequently stop to sound out (even though blending sounds proved difficult for all the children). On the other hand, the other half (Cluster A) exhibited a penchant for momentum, forging ahead with word approximations or substitutions to produce a text which sounded like language.

Further supporting a development trend, in her storybook reading study, Sulzby (1985b) noted that independent reading seemed to begin when children started to attend more closely to the print on the page. Also Allen (1989) found the relationships between reading measures (letter/sound/word recognition and simple text reading) and the use of letters in spelling were very strong by the end of kindergarten.

Bussis et al. (1985) believe that, within their holistic (Cluster A) or linear (Cluster B) learning styles, children gradually orchestrate what they know about books, grammatical structures, literary styles, information encoded in writing, and the conventions of print to negotiate text. The one common characteristic of all their subjects that was observed around this time was mobility. During the time of physical development when they have begun to play active, organized games and have gained control over small muscle coordination through drawing, model building, and arts and crafts, children need to be able to move around in their interactions with written language. Although Bussis et al. (1985) found relationships between more sophisticated uses of invented spelling and reading skill, they found no relationship between reading and the mechanical aspects of writing. Often children whose handwriting was classified as "poor" or "messy" were very able readers.

Weaver (1988) says that when children are able to use all language cue systems (semantic, syntactic, and grapho-phonemic) to sample and predict text, they are in the simultaneous use phase and are likely to be using mostly conventional spelling when they write.

In looking at what primary children like to read, we again note egocentricity. They like to listen to/read stories about children their own age and about families and animals. They also enjoy fairy tales, folk literature, humor, and modern fantasy (Feeley, 1981). Studying kindergarten children's use of a classroom library, Martinez and Teale (1988) found that familiar books with predictable texts, reflecting the above genres, were most likely to be selected. Bussis et al. (1985) also found that young children read informational materials that meet their specialized interests or school assignment needs. During the course of their longitudinal study, every child elected to read some nonfiction texts on such far-ranging topics as care of animals, space exploration, and making puppets.

Written Language in the Classroom: The Primary Years

Given the profile of the primary school child as an active, social, mobile, inductive thinker who goes from whole to part in learning the uses and conventions of written language, we suggest the following implications, based on those offered by Hartse et al. (1984), Mason and Au (1986), and Schwartz (1988):

1. There should be a rich print enviroment: a class library filled with appropriate literature; language experience stories on charts; songs, poems, chants, and notices in bold manuscript around the room; and prominent reading and writing centers (Feeley, 1982).
2. Children should be given many opportunities to test out their hypotheses about print in a risk-free atmosphere. In the primary years, Smith, Goodman, and Meredith (1976) say that children are between the stages Piaget calls "intuitive" (4 to 7) and concrete operations (7 to 11) and need interactive experiences with written language. Tunmer, Herriman, and Nesdale (1988) found that children's ability to acquire metalinguistic skills depends on their operativity or level of concrete operational thought. "Big books" that are read together several times before children read them to themselves and each other are one example of an activity that encourages hypothesis testing (Holdaway, 1979). Language experience activities (Hall, 1981; Stauffer, 1980) and uninterrupted reading and writing time (Hansen, 1987) are others.
3. Ellermeyer (1988) says that literacy programs for young children should focus on broadening each child's experiential background; as the conceptual base grows, so will the vocabulary for reading and writing. Reading and writing should not be isolated from each other or from other curricular areas. They are tools for getting things done and should be presented in realistic contexts.
4. Choice should be an integral part of the language program: chldren should be able to write about topics they know and read books of their own choosing.
5. Meaning should be at the center of all language activities: skills should be taught within the context of real reading and writing situations rather than in isolated workbook and worksheet activities.
6. Teachers should read to children daily and write with them, modeling the dynamic processes of reading and writing.

Middle Elementary Years

About the age of 8 or 9, most children can integrate the three cue systems (semantic, syntactic, and grapho-phonemic) as they gain more and more control over written language. The middle elementary years mark the period in which reading and writing become increasingly more important in the everyday lives of children.

Writing. Our views about the teaching and learning of writing in the middle grades have undergone some changes in recent years. In their classic longitudinal study of writing in the elementary school first reported in 1939, Burrows, Jackson, and Saunders (1984) theorized that children produced mainly two kinds of writing (practical and personal) and to help them develop as writers, we should handle each differently. Practical or utilitarian writing of such things as reports, letters, and records should be more directly guided by teachers with mechanics directly taught through group compositions and editing conferences. On the other hand, personal writing of stories and poems develops when children are exposed to good literature and encouraged to write by themselves. For example, after hearing stories about the antics of five bears, the 9- and 10-year-olds in their study began to write their own original bear stories, with one boy producing more than 25! While practical writing is "corrected" before a final copy is written, personal writing, which is done for enjoyment, is usually just read to the teacher or group.

Burrows et al. (1984) found that the 5th- and 6th-graders in their study grew in both composing techniques and mechanics through their approach. While they observed a gradual increase in the ability to handle mechanics in personal writing, they also found that the spontaneity and freedom enjoyed in imaginative, personal writing carried over to the reporting of information in practical writing situations.

The new view of teaching writing as a process (Calkins, 1986; Graves, 1983: Hansen, 1987) suggests continuing in the middle grades the workshop approach begun in the primary years. As children engage in writing personal narrative and specialty reports, and move toward genre writing, with feedback from teachers and peers, they will gain further control over written language.

Perhaps because of their new-found control over the mechanics of written language, 3rd-graders in writing process classrooms seem to be preoccupied with correctness and conventions (Calkins, 1986). Selecting giant topics and writing events in a chain-like manner, they like to demonstrate their new knowledge. For instance, once a convention like dialog or exclamation is learned, it tends to appear in great abundance.

Reflecting typical Piagetian concrete operational thinking, 8-year-olds do not consider things in their mind's eye but write everything out completely. They may draft three leads or ending to select from and revise by copying a draft over with a few changes. Bereiter and Scardamalia (1982) say young children lack a central executive function to enable them to reflect on their writing, to shuttle back and forth between talking, listening, writing, and reading. They like to write short pieces that are technically correct but often lack "voice."

Studying children in grades 3 to 7 who were trying to write suspense stories, Bereiter and Scardamalia (1984) found that they were only moderately successful, even when revising after instruction and exposure to a model. They hypothesize that children may not be able to do the high level of planning that this type of narrative requires.

To promote planning and more reflective revisions, Graves (1983) suggests encouraging peer and teacher conferences about works in progress. The listener provides the needed executive structure to help writers "resee" their drafts. Scardamalia and Bereiter (1983) conducted a series of studies in which executive support was offered as children wrote. These "simulation by intervention" studies encouraged revision mainly at a local level; according to these researchers, children may need formal operational thought for reprocessing or revising texts in more global ways.

However, Calkins (1983; 1986) says that children begin to be able to reread to revise in grades 4 to 6, especially if they are in workshop situations in which they read their pieces to others for reaction and response. Soon they will be able to hold their own internal conferences; she quotes Vygotsky who said that what children can do today in cooperation with others, they can do alone tomorrow. Shifting from the concrete approach taken by younger children who write everything out, middle-graders write out only portions of alternative leads, endings, and titles, and "just think about" others as they move toward more representational thought. Writing becomes a means of thinking and rethinking.

By the age of 10, children can view their writing through the eyes of a reader. As they do more writing in their minds, they can begin to experiment, going back and forth from writing to reading. As they gain control over time and content, their writings become more multidimensional: they can shift between narrative and description and narrative and dialogue in one piece.

Although younger children want their writing to be correct, reflecting exactly what happened in real life, older children begin to weave together truth and fiction, learning to shape language to please an audience. Instead of telling everything from the beginning, they will start with the event to be highlighted. Writers in the middle elementary grades can take on the voice of a third person as they write genre and expository pieces as well as personal narrative. As they grow in competence and confidence, they find new ways to integrate writing into their lives (Calkins, 1986).

Reading. Because of wide difference in abilities and experiences and the idiosyncratic nature of literacy development itself, describing readers in the middle grades is a difficult task. Third-graders exhibit a growing independence in reading. Relying heavily on cues in the text, they can figure things out for themselves. They see print as literal truth and think that what the book says is right. Although they can read orally with meaning and expression, they like to read to themselves both for pleasure and information. By this time, most have internalized several print grammars, both narrative and simple expository, to help them make sense of written language appropriate to their experiential background (Cochrane, Cochrane, Scalena, & Buchanan, 1984).

Although narrative is the mainstay of the learning to read materials found in the primary grades, 8-year-olds have a clear, consistent knowledge of exposition (Langer, 1986). They can talk about the differences between stories and reports and know that they are used in different ways. Langer (1986), who studied 8- to 14-year-olds, found that the younger children were less likely to set goals as they read and showed little concern with author or audience. However, the older children in her study were more able to temper their interpretations in light of the author's intentions.

As they move through the elementary school, children's ability to comprehend written language is limited only by their prior knowledge in general and their knowledge of text structures and topics specifically (Mason & Au, 1986). Schema theory posits that reading is the interaction between a reader and a text (Anderson & Pearson, 1984). Readers are actively constructing text, based on what they already know (schemata) and what the author has written. Serving many purposes, schemata help the reader make inferences, summarize, remember, add new knowledge, and make decisions about what is important (McNeil, 1970).

Lipson (1983) had middle-grade children who were either Catholic or Jewish in religious affiliation read passages about receiving first communion and making a bar mitzvah. Each group recalled more from and read faster their culturally familiar passage. Marr and Gromley (1982) reported that 4th-graders had significantly better recall on passages about familiar rather than unfamiliar topics.

Smith (1985) says that reading comprehension is raising questions about a text and getting answers. Middle-grade children are active readers who can ask questions as they read rather than just read to answer questions raised by others (Palincsar & Brown, 1984; Singer, 1978; Stauffer, 1975; Wong, 1985).

Besides being active readers, children in the middle grades are strategic readers. Meyers and Paris (1978) found that they are aware of a variety of reading strategies and know how to use them, acquiring metacognitive capabilities as they go through the grades. Babbs and Moe (1983) define metacognition as the ability to monitor one's own thinking. Garner (1987) proposes that teachers actively promote metacognition by modeling comprehension strategies, having children practice them in a variety of situations and content areas, and encouraging students to teach each other about the reading process.

Vocabulary is another adjunct to comprehension (Davis, 1944). Although children build their meaning vocabulary from direct experiences, they add thousands of words each year from their reading of trade books and content area texts. Nagy and Anderson (1984) found that books read in the elementary grades contain approximately 90,000 different words. While children learn some words through direct instruction, they pick up many more within the context of their in-school and out-of-school reading.

Middle-graders are exposed to written language in a variety of forms. Besides their school texts, trade books and own writing, they read magazines, comics, newspapers, baseball and bubblegum cards, hobby books, directions, TV listings, video games, directories, scout manuals, computer manuals, and a host of other print materials that may be a part of their environments.

As for choice in trade books, from 4th grade on, strong sex differences emerge. Girls seek fiction more than do boys, especially stories with mystery-adventure, social empathy, and fantasy themes. Boys, while expressing interest in some fictional works like mysteries and science fiction, show more preference for nonfiction categories like sports, history, biography, and science (Feeley, 1981; Graham, 1986; Wolfson, Manning & Manning, 1984).

In the much publicized ChildRead survey, Burgess (1985) found that children in grades 4 to 7 selected books on the basis of appearance, author, and recommendations of peers and adults, especially parents and librarians. (Unfortunately, teachers were not viewed as resources for recreational reading.) While most showed a preference for one kind of reading, supporting the interests research cited above, all children read a variety of materials. A new area of general interest was the nonfiction category, "technology," which Burgess attributes to the current focus on computers. interestingly, some are using nonfiction collections heavily for recreational reading. All children claimed to have at least one favorite book that they have reread as many as four or five times.

Towards the end of the elementary school years, as they move from concrete thinking toward formal operational thought, able readers can easily make inferences from print, discuss several aspects of a piece, and challenge its validity. They can process materials further and further removed from their own experiences, with reading providing a major source for continued schema development and refinement (Cochrane, et al. 1984).

Written Language in the Classroom: The Middle Grades

For the 8- to 14-year-olds that she studied, Langer (1986) found the dominant concern was with the meanings they were developing while reading and writing. She wrote:

Though children's behavior was always dominated by the content of the text-worlds being created, the differing purposes underlying reading and writing led to different problems and emphases in the reasoning operations.... Reading, with the author's text to channel the reader's ideas, led to more focusing on specific content, and to validating of the text world that was being developed. Writing, on the other hand, forces the writer to take more overt control of the process, and this led to a greater focus on the strategies that could be used to create their meanings. In each case, the children relied upon operations that helped them to make sense—either of their own or someone else's ideas. (p. 139)

Accordingly, for reading and writing programs in the middle elementary school, the focus should always be on meaning-making, and the following recommendations are offered:

1. Reading and writing should be taught through a process approach (Calkins, 1986; Graves, 1983; Hansen, 1987). The conference aspect, in which listeners provide the external executive function needed by children still in the concrete operational thinking stage, works well for both reading and writing. While teaching writing as process has been rapidly gaining acceptance over the past decade, a new thrust toward teaching reading as process is just emerging. While Hornsby, Sukarna, and Parry (1988) suggest a conference approach, Hancock and Hill (1988) and Routman (1988) offer models for literature-based reading programs, and Five (1988) describes her own transition from a structured basal reader program to a reading process approach. In order to teach reading through books and to encourage recreational reading, teachers must immerse themselves in appropriate children's literature. The ChildRead survey (Burgess, 1985) found that middle-graders welcomed and appreciated book talks by their teachers.

2. Before reading and writing, children should be encouraged to engage in schema activation activities so that they can make use of what they know about topics to aid in meaning-making. Langer (1984) used a Pre Reading Plan (PReP) to assess children's text-specific background knowledge before they read. She found that the measure was a reliable and significant predictor of comprehension; also, the activity significantly raised background knowledge and thus improved comprehension.

McNeil (1987) suggests that webbing, semantic mapping, structured overviews, and other background-generating techniques such as the Directed Reading-Thinking Activity (Stauffer, 1975) and Au's Experience-Text-Relationship (Mason & Au, 1986) should be taught and modeled.

3. There should be increasing attention to expanding children's knowledge about text structures. Langer (1986) found that even 8-year-olds understood exposition, but they tended to use mainly description/collections, dominated by the title, when they wrote reports. She suggests starting with the known approach and moving to other rhetorical structures; for example, after a child wrote a report on English horseback riding and another on western riding, she could be encouraged to compare the two in a new piece.

Armbruster, Anderson, and Ostertag (1987) taught 5-graders to recognize and summarize a conventional text structure, problem/solution. As measured by responses to a main-idea essay question and written summaries, the student's ability to abstract the macrostructure of a problem/solution text was significantly improved.

4. Vocabulary should be expanded through constructing networks of ideas; it is best developed in meaningful contexts (McNeil, 1984). While Mezynski's literature review (1983) concluded that vocabulary training had little effect on reading comprehension, Gipe (1978-79) found an interactive context method superior to other methods, including the time-honored dictionary approach, for developing vocabulary and comprehension among 3rd- and 5th-graders.

5. Children in the middle grades can begin to be reflective about their reading and writing. They can learn to step back and monitor their attempts at meaning-making. Stevens, Madden, Slavin, and Farnish (1987), who taught 3rd- and 4th-graders comprehension and metacomprehension activities in a cooperative learning approach to reading and writing instruction, found significant effects on several measures of literacy achievement.

Paris, Cross, and Lipson (1984) successfully taught 3rd- and 5th-graders to monitor their reading through a program called Informed Strategies for Learning (ISL). The students learned to plan, evaluate, and regulate their own comprehension, becoming significantly more aware of reading strategies and improving their performance on comprehension measures.

6. Writing across the curriculum holds much promise as a way to enhance learning in the content areas. Langer (1986) found that children were more able to talk about what strategies they used and how their knowledge changed after writing than after reading. She says that writing seems to be useful in helping children focus on developing an understanding of subject matter and recommends writing to learn in the content areas. Five and Rosem (1985) provide an excellent example of reading and writing to learn in their description of an American history unit in grade 5.

LITERARY DEVELOPMENT

Researchers studying children's concept of story have noted certain developmental trends. As in the learning of any concept, young children formulate a general sense or idea of what stories are all about, focusing on beginnings, endings, and obvious attempts. For example, McNeil (1987, p. 25) reports a kindergarten child's retelling of "The Lion and the Mouse" as follows: "A lion got trapped in a net and mighty mouse came and saved him." These early notions of story are gradually modified and refined as children continue to encounter new stories in a variety of situations.

Perhaps the first evidence of the developing sense of story in children is their use of language to create a special or private world. This is thought to be the forerunner to the child's use of language to create a world of make-believe, involving dramatic play and leading dramatic play and leading to the gradual acquisition of the specific conventions that constitute a sense of story. As children mature, their stories increase in length and complexity. The characters, settings, and actions become further removed from the here and now of the immediate environment. Children gradually gain greater control over the events in their stories, moving from a loose collection of related events to tightly-structured narratives which link a set of events to each other and to a common theme (Applebee, 1978). A 5th-grader produced a much more detailed retelling of the "The Lion and the Mouse" than did the kindergartner quoted above, including all attempts and reactions and even the theme or moral, ". . . sometimes little can help big" (McNeil, 1987, p. 29). According to McConaughy (1980), this older child is approaching an adult concept of story because of the attention to cause and effect and inferencing beyond the text.

Whaley (1981) found that when reading stories, older children were better at predicting events than younger children. She concluded that the expansion of a story sense in older students enabled them to predict more of the story structures. Mandler (1978) found that children seem to organize their recall according to an ideal story structure. They tap into their existing concept of story as they attempt to remember new stories. Younger children tend to emphasize the outcomes of specific action sequences rather than the specific events and their causes. As children mature, their story retellings appear to move away from a simple, ideal concept of story toward a more complex adult model.

Analyses of children's written stories reveals the same developmental patterns. Sutton-Smith (1981) reports that young children organize their stories around basic pairs of actions such as chase and escape and that they tend to repeat these actions in their written stories. For example, three first-graders who had made doughnuts with their class that morning were composing a follow-up written piece (Long & Bulgarella, 1985). Instead of recording how doughnuts were made, they decided to write about a man who made doughnuts that came alive, "... kinda like Raggedy Ann and Andy" (p. 167). To avoid being eaten up, the doughnuts run away. Because one child in the group wanted a happy ending, both the doughnuts and the man go to a "cellabrashun" where they had "... wine and cake ... and they both had a good time" (p. 171).

As children mature in written expression, multiple pairs of actions with supporting elements become apparent, suggesting a movement toward the elaboration of event structures. For instance, two 4th-grade boys we observed in a local elementary school had developed a super hero named "Machine Gun Joe," a tough army sergeant who saved Americans around the world, from Olympic athletes in Korea to kidnapped ambassadors in Italy. Each episode was connected by a staccato reprise: "It was a mean job, but somebody had to do it!"

Langer (1986) found that story forms used by 8-year-olds were similar in basic structure to those used by the 14-year-olds, even though the older children's stories had more detail. She hypothesized that although children enter school with a firm knowledge of story structure, limited opportunities to use more complex and varied story forms as they go through the grades may account for lack of growth in this genre. While elementary school teachers generally encourage the writing of narratives, upper grade and high school curricula focus mainly on expository writing.

In summary, the research focusing on the development of story in children suggests that virtually all children are exposed to story to some degree; that they begin to develop a concept of story at an early age; and that as they mature their concept of story expands.

Linking Literary Development to Reading and Writing

Researchers studying the development of story in children have linked their findings to children's development of reading and writing. The role of prior knowledge and experience in reading and writing suggests that learners who have had many experiences with stories and who have developed a strong schema for stories make use of that framework as they read and write. Listeners and readers are said to use their knowledge of story structure to guide them in anticipating the events in a story. They make predictions based about what will occur next in a story, a process believed to be essential to reading comprehension. Prior knowledge of what a story is helps facilitate recall of a text (Mandler & Johnson, 1977; Stein, 1979). Story schema actually acts as a guide or road map for retrieving story information. It may help a student to decide when a portion of a story is complete or incomplete and serve to assist in filling in or inferring information that may have been forgotten.

The learner's preexisting concept of story is equally as important in producing stories as it is in comprehending them. Several researchers who have analyzed children's written stories found story narratives to be the most prevalent structure (Applebee, 1978; Britton et al., 1975; Sutton-Smith, 1981). Story schema may be activated during the first stage of the writing process when ideas are being conceived (Britton et al., 1975). The author draws upon the story elements of setting, character, and plot during the writing of the story and these may serve as a framework for revision as well.

Literary Development in the Classroom

Researchers and curriculum specialists have sought to apply what has been learned about the relationship between children's knowledge of story and the development of literacy. These efforts have produced a variety of strategies for using story structure. Although there is some disagreement as to whether the direct teaching of story structure is either necessary or helpful, there is universal agreement about the need to expose students to an abundance of stories in a variety of ways and to expand that exposure to include activities that strengthen their concept of story (Strickland, 1984). Actually, explicit knowledge about story grammar may be most important for teachers as they plan literature experiences for their students.

Vacca, Vacca, and Gove (1987) do not advocate the direct teaching of the technical terms of story elements. Rather, they say that children will develop story schema informally through varied experiences with well structured stories. For example, since Moldofsky (1983) noted that most fiction found in the elementary grades develops around a problem, it is important for children to recognize the central part played by this element. An appropriate strategy is to have children relate problems in their own lives to those in stories they read and write.

The popular practice of reading familiar stories over and over again for young children appears to promote their sense of story structure. Morrow (1988) found that the responses of children who were exposed to repeated readings of three selected stories over a 10-week period focused significantly more on story structure than did those of a group who were read different stories or a control group who were not exposed to storybook reading.

It is important to select books with predictable plots for young readers and to introduce stories with complicated plots or unexpected twists only after children have the cognitive base and literary experiences to deal with them. Stein and Trabasso (1982) found that readers and listeners tend to retell story events in time order even when an author has altered the order or special effects such as in mysteries and suspense stories. Brewer and Lichtenstein (1981) explain that different schemata may be operating. "Event schemas" represent readers' or listeners' knowledge about cause/effect and time relationships in a story, whereas "story schemas" represent their knowledge about constructing narratives. Younger children will have more difficulty reading stories that are not temporally ordered. Older children who have had more experience with stories of various genres and who are beginning to move toward more formal operational thought can deal with event and story schemas simultaneously.

Whole group and small group discussions about books allow children to share and reflect upon their interpretations of literary experiences. Sloan (1984) offers teachers a series of questions for use in helping students strengthen their understanding of stories in relationship to various aspects of story structure. Galda (1982) used creative dramatics to help young children develop their reading comprehension and sense of story. According to Galda, when players discuss things such as roles, props, and story settings, they become more aware of aspects of the story which they individually might not have noticed (p. 53). Storytelling and retelling, as suggested in the oral language section of this chapter, are excellent means of deepening children's understandings of how narratives work, both for reading and writing. Cambourne (1984) developed a retelling strategy that makes use of children's story schema as they make and confirm their own predictions and retellings and compare them with the predictions and retellings of others.

Strickland and Feeley (1985) offer a model for improving story reading and writing that draws upon a variety of modes of language. In this model, students focus on a particular genre of literature over an extended time. They listen to selections read aloud by the teacher and respond to literature through activities such as discussion, dramatics, and art. Book talks and displays related to the genre help to stimulate children's desire to read similar works on their own. As interest in the genre increases, children discuss its features and are encouraged to include the type of story under study in their writing repertoires. Immersing students in the study of a a particular genre helps them to internalize the structure and strengthens their sensitivity and appreciation of literary form as readers and writers.

FINAL THOUGHTS

Children bring their growing mastery over oral language and a wonderful sense of industry to their elementary school experience. Once in school, they begin to internalize in a formal way the rules of written language as they experiment with reading and writing in realistic social settings. With further exposure to the literature of the school-age years, they flesh out their emerging concept of story and learn to control expository as well as narrative text. Schematic knowledge grows in leaps and bounds as reading and writing extend what is learned through direct and vicarious experiences.

As for thinking processes, language learners in elementary school go from nonconservers who have difficulty dealing with print simultaneously as letters, sounds, and meanings to strategic readers who can understand a passage at several levels and reflective writers who can plan, draft, and reprocess text to achieve specific goals. Also, metacognition develops as children are encouraged to reflect on the reading, writing, listening, and speaking they and others do. The sense of industry and experimentation that characterizes middle childhood produces great growth in language, thinking, and knowledge during the elementary school years.

References

Allen, J. (1989). Reading and writing development. In J. Mason (Ed.), *Reading and writing connections*. Needham Heights, MA: Allyn and Bacon.

Allen, J., & Carr, E. (in press). Collaborative learning among kindergarten writers: James learns how to learn at school. In J. Allen & J. Mason (Eds.), *Risk makers, risk takers, risk breakers: Reducing the risks for young literacy learners*. Portsmouth, NH: Heinemann.

Anderson, R. C., & Freebody, P. (1981). Vocabulary knowledge. In J. T. Guthrie (Ed.), *Comprehension and teaching: Research reviews* (pp. 77–117). Newark, DE: International Reading Association.

Anderson, R. C., & Pearson, P. D. (1984). A schema-theoretic view of basic processes in reading. In P. D. Pearson (Ed.), *Handbook of reading research* (pp. 255–291). New York: Longman.

Applebee, A. N. (1978). *The child's concept of story*. Chicago: The University of Chicago Press.

Armbruster, B. B., Anderson, T. H., & Ostertag, J. (1987). Does text structure/summarization instruction facilitate learning from expository text? *Reading Research Quarterly, 22*, 331–346.

Babbs, P. J., & Moe, A. J. (1983). Metacognition: A key for independent learning from text. *The Reading Teacher, 32*, 422–426.

Baghban, M. (1984). *Our daughter learns to read and write: A case study from birth to three*. Newark, DE: International Reading Association.

Bee, H. (1985). *The developing child*. New York: Harper and Row.

Bereiter, C., & Scardamalia, M. (1982). From conversation to composition: The role of instruction in a developmental process. In R. Glaser (Ed.), *Advances in instructional psychology* (Vol. 2, pp. 1–64). Hillsdale, NJ: Erlbaum.

Bereiter, C., & Scardamalia, M. (1984). Learning about writing from reading. *Written Communication, 1*, 163–188.

Berko, J. (1958). The child's learning of English morphology. *Word, 14*, 150–77.

Bissex, G. L. (1980). *GYNS at WRK: A child learns to read and write*. Cambridge, MA: Harvard University Press.

Bormouth, J. R., Carr, J., Manning, J., & Pearson, D. (1970). Children's comprehension of between—and within—sentence syntactic structures. *Journal of Educational Psychology, 61*, 349–357.

Brewer, W. R., & Lichtenstein, E. H. (1981). Event schemas, story schemas, and story grammars. In A. D. Buddely & J. D. Lang (Eds.), *Attention and performance* IX (pp. 160–189). Hillsdale, NJ: Earlbaum.

Britton, J., Burgess, T., Martin, N., McLeod, A., & Rosen, H. (1975). *The development of writing abilities*. London: MacMillan Education Ltd.

Bromley, K. (1988) . *Language arts: Exploring connections*. Boston: Allyn and Bacon.

Brown, R. (1973). *A first language: The early stages*. Cambridge: Harvard University Press.

Burgess, S.A. (1985). Reading but not literate: The ChildRead survey. *School Library Journal, 31*, 27–30.

Burrows, A. (1968). *What research says to the teacher: Teaching composition*. Washington: National Education Association.

Burrows, A., Jackson, D. C., & Saunders, D. O. (1984). *They all want to write*, 4th ed. New York: Library Professional Publications.

Bussis, A.M., Chittenden, E. A., Amarel, M., & Klausner, E. (1985). *Inquiry into meaning: An investigation of learning to read*. Hillsdale, NJ: Earlbaum.

Calkins, L. M. (1983). *Lessons from a child*. Portsmouth, NH: Heinemann.

Calkins, L. M. (1986). *The art of teaching writing*. Portsmouth, NH: Heinemann.

Cambourne, B. (1984). *Retelling as a pedagogical strategy: Summary thoughts*. Paper presented at Miscue Update Conference, Detroit, MI.

Carroll, J. (1970). *Comprehension by 3rd, 6th and 7th graders of words having multiple grammatical functions. Final report*. Princeton, NJ: Educational Testing Service.

Cazden, C. (1988). *Classroom discourse*. Portsmouth, NH: Heinemann.

Chall, J. (1983). *Stages of reading development.* New York: McGraw-Hill.

Chomsky, C. (1969). *The acquisition of syntax in children from 5 to 10 (Research Monography No. 57).* Cambridge, MA: MIT Press.

Chomsky, C. (1972). Stages in language development and reading exposure. *Harvard Educational Review, 42* 1–33.

Chomsky, C. (1979). Approaching reading through invented spelling. In L. B. Resnick & P. A. Weaver (Eds.), *Theory and practice of early reading* (pp. 43–65). Hillsdale, NJ: Erlbaum.

Clark, M. M. (1976). *Young fluent readers.* London: Heinemann.

Clay, M. (1975). *What did I write?* Portsmouth, NH: Heinemann.

Clay, M. (1979). *Concepts about print tests.* Portsmouth, NH: Heinemann.

Clay, M. (1985). *The early detection of reading difficulties.* Portsmouth, NH: Heineman.

Clay, M. (1989). Concepts about print in English and other languages. *The Reading Teacher, 42,* 268–276.

Cochrane, O., Cochrane, D., Scalena, S., & Buchanan, E. (1984), *Reading, writing, and caring.* New York: Richard C. Owens.

Collins, W. A. (1984). Conclusion: The status of basic research on middle childhood. In W. A. Collins (Ed.), *Development during middle childhood: The years from six to twelve* (pp.94–109). Washington, DC: National Academy Press.

Collins, A. (1986). *A sample dialogue based on a theory of inquiry reading.* Technical Report No. 367. Urbana, IL: Center for the Study of Reading.

Cullinan, B., Jagger, A., & Strickland, D. (1974). Language expansion for black children in the primary grades: A research report. *Young children, 29,* 98–112.

Davis, F. B. (1944). Fundemantal factors of comprehension in reading. *Psychometrika, 9,* 185–197.

DeFord, D., & Hartse, J. (1982). Child language research and curriculum. *Language Arts, 59,* 590–600.

Devine, T. (1978). Listening: What do we know after 50 years of research and theorizing? *Journal of Reading, 21,* 296–303.

Dillon, D., & Searle, D. (1981). The role of language in one first grade classroom. *Research in the Teaching of English, 15,* 311–328.

Downing, J. (1970). Children's concepts of language in learning to read. *Educational Research, 12,* 106–112.

Downing, J., & Oliver, P. (1973-1974). The child's conception of a word. *Reading Research Quarterly, 9,* 468–482.

Duker, S. (1969). Listening. In R. L. Ebel (Ed.), *Encyopedia of educational research* (pp. 747–752). London: Collier-Macmillan.

Durkin, D. (1966). *Children who read early.* New York: Teachers College Press.

Dyson, A. H. (1983). The role of oral language in early writing processes. *Research in the Teaching of English, 17* (1), 1–30.

Ellermeyer, D. (1988). Kindergarten reading program to grow on. *The Reading Teacher, 41,* 402–405.

Feeley, J. T. (1981). What do our children like to read? *NJEA Review, 54*(8), 26–27.

Feeley, J. T. (1982). A print environment for beginning readers. *Reading, 16,* 23–50.

Feeley, J. T. (1984). Print and reading: What do preschoolers know? *Day Care and Early Education, 11,* 26–28.

Ferreiro, E., & Teberosky, A. (1983). *Writing before schooling.* Portsmouth, NH: Heinemann.

Five, C. L. (1988). From workbook to workshop: Increasing children's involvement in the reading process. *The New Advocate, 1,* 103–113.

Flanders, N. A. (1962). Using interaction analysis in the inservice training of teachers. *Journal of Experimental Education, 30,* 313–16.

Forester, A. D. (1980). Learning to spell by spelling. *Theory into Practice, 19,* 186–193.

Galda, L. (1982). Playing about a story: Its impact on comprehension. *The Reading Teacher, 36,* 52–55.

Garner, R. (1987). *Metacognition and reading comprehension.* Norwood, NJ: Ablex.

Gentry, J. R. (1981). Learning to spell developmentally. *The Reading Teacher, 34,* 378–381.

Gipe, J. P. (1978–1979). Investigating techniques for teaching word meanings. *Reading Research Quarterly, 14,* 624–644.

Goodman, Y. M., & Altwerger, B. (1981). *Print awareness in preschool children: A working paper.* Tuscon, AZ: Program in Languages and Literacy, University of Arizona.

Graham, S. (1986). Assessing reading preferences: A new approach. *New England Reading Association Journal, 21* (1), 8–11.

Graves, D. H. (1981). *A case study observing the development of primary children's composing, spelling, and motor behaviors during writing process.* Durham, NH: University of New Hampshire. (ERIC Document Reproduction Service No. ED 218–653).

Graves, D. H. (1983). *Writing: Teachers and children at work.* Portsmouth, NH: Heineman.

Gunderson, L., & Shapiro, J. (1988). Whole language instruction: Writing in 1st grade. *The Reading Teacher, 41,* 430–437.

Hall, M. A. (1981). *Teaching reading as a language experience.* Columbus, OH: Merrill.

Halliday, M. A. K. (1975). *Explorations in the functions of language.* London: Edward Arnold.

Hancock, J., & Hill, S. (1988). *Literature-based reading programs that work.* Portsmouth, NH: Heinemann.

Hansen, J. (1987). *When writers read.* Portsmouth, NH: Heinemann.

Hansen, J., & Graves, D. L. (1983). The author's chair. *Language Arts, 60,* 176–183.

Harste, J. C., Woodward, V. A., & Burke, C. L. (1984). *Language stories and literacy lessons.* Portsmouth, NH: Heinemann.

Hillocks, G. (1986). *Research on written composition: New directions for teaching.* Urbana, IL: ERIC Clearinghouse on Reading and Communication Skills and the National Conference on Research in English.

Holdaway, D. (1979). *Foundations of literacy.* Portsmouth, NH: Heinemann.

Hornsby, D., Sukarna, D., & Parry, J. (1988). *Read on: A conference approach to reading.* Portsmouth, NH: Heinemann.

Johnson, D. D., & Pearson, P. D. (1984). *Teaching reading vocabulary.* New York: Holt, Rinehart, and Winston.

King, M. L., & Rentel, V. (1979). Towards a theory of early writing development. *Research in Teaching English, 13,* 243–253.

Klima, E. S., & Belugi-Klima, U. (1966). Syntactic regularities in the speech of children. In J. Lyons & R. Wales (Eds.), *Psycholinguistic Papers* (pp. 145–156). Edinburgh: Edingburgh University Press.

Lapp, D. & Flood, J. (1978). *Teaching reading to every child.* New York: Macmillan.

Langer, J. A. (1984). Examining background knowledge and text comprehension. *Reading Research Quarterly, 19,* 468–481.

Langer, J. A. (1986). *Children reading and writing.* Norwood, NJ: Ablex Publishing.

Lehr, F. (1985). Instructional scaffolding. *Language Arts, 62,* 667–672.

Lipson, M. Y. (1983). The influence of religious affiliation on children's memory for text information. *Reading Research Quarterly, 18,* 448–457.

Loban, W. (1963). *Language development: Kindergarten through grade 12.* Urbana, IL: National Council of Teachers of English.

Long, R., & Bulgarella, L. K. (1985). Social interaction and the writing process. *Language Arts, 62,* 166–172.

Lundsteen, S. (1971). *Listening: Its impact on reading and the other language arts.* Urbana, IL: National Council of Teachers of English.

Lundsteen, S. (1976). *Children learn to communicate.* Englewood Cliffs, NJ: Prentice-Hall.

Mandler, J. (1978). A code in the node: The use of story schema in retrieval. *Discourse Processes, 1,* 1–13.

Mandler, J. M., & Johnson, N. S. (1977). Remembrance of things parsed: Story structure and recall. *Cognitive Psychology, 9* (1), 111–151.

Manning, M., Manning, G., & Hughes, J. (1987). Journals in first grade: What children write. *The Reading Teacher, 41,* 311–315.

Marr, M., & Gromley, K. (1982). Children's recall of familiar and unfamiliar text. *Reading Research Quarterly, 18,* 89–104.

Martinez, M., & Teale, W. (1988). Reading in a kindergarten classroom library. *The Reading Teacher, 41,* 568–573.

Mason, J. M., & Allen, J. (1986). A review of emergent literacy with implications for research and practice in reading. In E. Rothkopf (Ed.), *Review of research in education* (pp. 3–47). Washington, DC: American Educational Research Association.

Mason, J. M., & Au, K. H. (1986). *Reading instruction for today.* Glenview, IL: Scott Foresman.

McConaughy, S. H. (1980). Using story structure in the classroom. *Language Arts, 57,* 157–165.

McNeil, J. (1970). *The acquisition of language: The study of development psycholinguistics.* New York: Harper & Row.

McNeil, J. D. (1987). *Reading comprehension: New directions for classroom practice* (3rd ed.). Glenview, IL: Scott Foresman.

Mehan, H. (1979). *Learning lessons.* Cambridge, MA: Harvard University Press.

Menyuk, P. (1969). Syntactic structures in the language of children. *Child Development, 34,* 407–22.

Meyers, M., & Paris, S. G. (1978). Children's metacognitive knowledge about reading. *Journal of Educational Psychology, 70,* 680–690.

Mezynski, K. (1983). Issues concerning the acquisition of knowledge: Effect of vocabulary training on reading comprehension. *Review of Educational Research, 53,* 253–279.

Michaels, S., & Foster, M. (1985). Peer-peer learning: Evidence from a student-run sharing time. In Jaggar, A. & Smith-Burke, M. (Eds.), *Observing the Language Learner* (pp. 143–158). Newark, DE: International Reading Association.

Moldofsky, P. B. (1983). Teaching children to determine the central story problem: A practical application of schema theory. *The Reading Teacher, 36,* 749–745.

Morrow, L. M. (1988). Young children's responses to one-to-one story readings in school settings. *Reading Research Quarterly, 23,* 89–107.

Morrow, L. M. (1989). New perspectives in early literacy. *The Reading Instruction Journal, 32,* 8–15.

Nagy, W. E., & Anderson, R. C. (1984). How many words are there in printed school English? *Reading Research Quarterly, 19,* 304–330.

Neisser, U. (1967). *Cognitive psychology.* New York: Appleton-Century-Crofts.

Palinscar, A. M., & Brown, A. (1984). Reciprocal teaching of comprehension. *Cognition and Instruction, 1,* 117–175.

Palinscar, A. M., & Brown, A. L. (1985). Reciprocal teaching: Activities to promote "reading with your mind." In T. L. Harris & E. J. Cooper (Eds.), *Reading, thinking, and concept development,* (pp. 147–159). New York: The College Board.

Paris, S. G., Cross, D. R., & Lipson, M. Y. (1984). Informed strategies for learning: A program to improve children's reading awareness and comprehension. *Journal of Educational Psychology, 76,* 239–242.

Pearson, P. D., & Fielding, L. (1982). Research update: Listening comprehension. *Language Arts, 59,* 617–629.

Piaget, J. (1955). *The language and thought of the child.* New York: Meridian Books.

Piaget, J. (1970). Piaget's theory. In P. H. Mussen (Ed.), *Carmichael's manual of child psychology* (pp. 116–129). New York: Wiley.

Pinnell, G. S. (1985). Ways to look at the functions of children's language. In A. Jaggar & M. T. Smith-Burke (Eds.), *Observing the language learner* (pp. 57–72). Newark, DE: International Reading Association; Urbana, IL: National Council of Teachers of English.

Read, C. (1986). *Children's creative spelling.* Boston, MA: Routledge & Kegan.

Routman, R. (1988). *Transitions: From literature to literacy.* Portsmouth, NH: Heinemann.

Scardamalia, M., & Bereiter, C. (1983). The development of evaluative, diagnostic, and remedial capabilities in children's composing. In M. Martlew (Ed.), *The psychology of written language: Developmental and educational perspectives* (pp. 67–95). London: John Wiley.

Schwartz, J. I. (1988). *Encouraging early literacy: An integrated approach to reading and writing in N–3.* Portsmouth, NH: Heinemann.

Selman, R. L. (1976). Social cognitive understanding: A guide to educational and clinical practice. In T. Lickona (Ed.), *Moral development and behavior* (pp. 299–316). New York: Holt, Rinehart and Winston.

Shanahan, T. (1984). The nature of the reading-writing relation: An exploratory multivariate analysis. *Journal of Educational Psychology, 76* 466–477.

Shonkoff, J. P. (1984). The biological substrate and physical health in middle childhood. In W. A. Collins (Ed.), *Development during middle childhood: The years from six to twelve* (pp. 213–254). Washington: National Academy Press.

Singer, H. (1978). Active comprehension. *The Reading Teacher, 31,* 901–908.

Sloan, G. (1984). *The child as critic.* New York: Teachers College Press.

Smith, E. B., Goodman, K. S., & Meredith, R. (1976). *Language and thinking in school.* New York: Holt, Rinehart, Winston.

Smith, F. (1977). The uses of language. *Language Arts, 54,* 638–644.

Smith, F. (1985). *Reading without nonsense.* New York: Teachers College Press.

Stauffer, R. G. (1975). *Directing the reading-thinking process.* New York: Harper and Row.

Stauffer, R. (1980). *The language experience approach to teaching reading.* New York: Harper and Row.

Stein, N. (1979). How children understand stories: A developmental analysis. In L. G. (Ed.), *Current topics in early childhood education* (Vol. 11, pp. 261–290). Norwood, NJ: Ablex Pulishing Corporation.

Stein, N. L., & Tabasso, T. (1982). What's in a story? Critical issues in comprehension and instruction. In R. Glaser (Ed.), *Advances in instructional psychology* (Vol. 2, pp. 213–254). Hillsdale, NJ: Erlbaum.

Stevens, R. J., Madden, N. A., Slavin, R. E., & Farnish, A. M. (1987). Cooperative integrated reading and composition. *Reading Research Quarterly, 22,* 433–454.

Strickland, D. (1973). A program for the linguistically different black children. *Research in the Teaching of English, 7,* 79–86.

Strickland, D. (1984). Building children's knowledge of stories. In J. Osborn, P. Wilson, & R. Anderson (Eds), *Reading education: Foundations for a literate America.* Lexington, MA: Lexington Press.

Strickland, D., with Dillon, R., Funkhouser, L. Glick, M. & Rogers, C. (1989). Research currents: Classroom dialogue during literature response groups. *Language Arts, 66,* 192–200.

Strickland, D. S., & Feeley, J. T. (1985). Using children's concept of story to improve reading and writing. In T. Harris & E. Cooper (Eds.), *Reading, thinking, and concept development* (pp. 163–175). New York: College Board.

Strickland, D. & Taylor, D. (1989). Family storybook reading: Implications for children, families, and curriculum. In D. Strickland & L. Morrow (Eds.), *Emerging literacy: Young children learn to read and write.* Newark, DE: International Reading Association.

Strickland, R. (1962). The language of elementary school children: Its relationship to the language of reading textbooks and the quality of reading of selected children. *Bulletin of the School of Education, 38*(4). Bloomington, IN: Indiana University.

Sulzby, E. (1985a). Kindergartens as writers and readers. In M. Farr (Ed.), *Advances in writing research: Vol. I. Children's early writing development* (pp. 127–199). Norwood, NJ: Ablex.

Sulzby, E. (1985b). Children's emergent reading of favorite storybooks: A development study. *Reading Research Quarterly, 20,* 458–481.

Sutton-Smith, B. (1981). *The folkstories of children.* Philadelphia: University of Pennsylvania Press.

Taylor, D. (1983). *Family literacy: Young children learning to read and write.* Portsmouth, NH: Heinemann.

Taylor, D., & Strickland, D. (1986). *Family storybook reading.* Portsmouth, NH: Heinemann.

Teale, W., & Sulzby, E. (Eds.). (1986). *Emergent literacy: Writing and reading.* Norwood, NJ: Ablex.

Temple, C. A., Nathan, R. G., Burris, N. A., & Temple, F. (1988). *The beginnings of writing.* Boston, MA: Allyn and Bacon.

Templin, M. (1987). *Certain language skills in children: Their development and interrelationships.* Minneapolis: University of Minnesota Press.

Tierney, R. J., & Pearson, P. D. (1984). Toward a composing model of reading. In J. Jensen (Ed.), *Composing and comprehending* (pp. 33–46). Urbana, IL: National Conference on Research in English.

Torrey, J. W. (1969). Learning to read without a teacher: A case study. *Elementary English, 46,* 550–556.

Tough, J. (1977). *Talking and learning: A guide to fostering communication skills in nursery and infant schools.* London: Schools Council Publications.

Tunmer, W. E., Herriman, M. L., & Nesdale, A. R. (1988). Metalinguistic abilities and beginning reading. *Reading Research Quarterly, 23,* 134–158.

Vacca, J. L., Vacca, R. T., & Gove, M. (1987). *Reading and learning to read.* Boston, MA: Little, Brown and Company.

Vygotsky, L. S. (1962). *Thought and language.* Cambridge, MA: MIT Press.

Weaver, C. (1988). *Reading process and practice.* Portsmouth, NH: Heinemann.

Whaley, J. F. (1981). Story grammar and reading instruction. *The Reading Teacher, 34,* 762–771.

Wilt, M. (1950, April). Study of teacher awareness of listening as a factor in elementary education. *Journal of Educational Research, 43,* 626–636.

Wolfson, B. J., Manning, G., & Manning, M (1984). Revisiting what children say their reading interests are. *Reading World, 24*(2), 4–10.

Wood, B. S. (Ed.). (1977). *Development of functional communication competencies: PreK-grade 6.* Urbana, IL: ERIC Clearinghouse on Reading and Communication Skills.

Wong, B. Y. (1985). Self-questioning instructional research. *Review of Educational Research, 55,* 227–268.

Zigler, E. F., & Finn-Stevenson, M. (1987). *Children: Development and social issues.* Lexington, MA: D. C. Heath and Company.

19C. THE TRANSITION YEARS: MIDDLE SCHOOL

John J. Pikulski

This chapter focuses upon the developmental characteristics of what, for this *Handbook,* have been termed the "transition years," the period when language learners are attending middle schools. Unfortunately there is a lack of consistency in how educators and psychologists define both terms "transition years" and "middle schools."

In the developmental psychology literature there has been a discernible shift in labeling these years. Preadolescence was the preferred term through most of the 1970s, followed by a shift to the use of the term early adolescence. Joan Lipsitz's seminal book *Growing Up Forgotten* (1977) brought not only widespread visibility to the period of early adolescence, but also popularized that term. This shift in terminology was solidified with the establishment of a journal that focused exclusively upon the developmental aspects of this age group, *The Journal of Early Adolescence.* Although there is not universal agreement on the ages encompassed by the term early adolescence (Thornburg, 1974; Lipsitz, 1977), the ages of 10 to 14 are a reasonable frame of reference and will be the focus of this chapter.

Redl's 1943 article "Preadolescents—What makes them tick?" marks the beginnings of systematic concern with and study of early adolescents. However, little systematic attention was devoted to theory or research on early adolescents until recently. Through the decade of the 1970s less than a total of 50 articles or books had been written focusing on the uniqueness of these ages (Thornburg, 1983). However, the decade of the 1980s witnessed and explosion of publication about early adolescents. Twenty years ago there was only one journal that dealt with developmental research related to this age youngster, *Adolescence.* There are now at least seven additional journals including *Journal of Early Adolescence, Journal of Adolescent Research, Journal of Adolescence, Youth and Society, Journal of Adolescent Health Care, Journal of Youth and Adolescence, Journal of Child and Adolescent Psychiatry* (Adams, 1987). Readers interested in remaining current about the psychosocial, cognitive, and language development of early adolescents can consult these journals.

The definition of "middle school" is also shifting. The pattern of eight grades for elementary school and four years for high school became very popular after the Civil War, and maintained its popularity through the first decade or two of the twentieth century until the seventh- to ninth-grade junior high school was introduced. Junior high schools then grew in numbers, reaching a peak in the 1960s; thereafter they declined in popularity, to be replaced in many areas by the concept of the middle school. (McEwin, 1983; Alexander & George, 1981) While there were probably less than 100 middle schools in 1960, there were approximately 5,000 in existence by 1980 (Alexander & George, 1981).

Kindred, Wolotkiewicz, Mickelson, Coplein & Dyson (1976) suggest that the middle school organization and concept grew out of dissatisfaction with the degree to which junior schools were serving as a transition between elementary and high schools. There was widespread criticism that junior high schools had, in many cases, developed departmentalization, rigid scheduling, interscholastic athletics, and so on, to the point where they became miniaturized high schools and failed to address the psychological and social characteristics of the early adolescent (Moss, 1969). The middle school movement was begun to address these criticisms. Kindred et al. (1976), after reviewing several surveys of school organization, conclude that the most common organizational patterns for the middle school are either a three-grade pattern (grades six through eight) or a four-year plan (grades five through eight). This operational definition of a middle school agrees with the definition of early adolescence cited earlier because children in grades five through eight are, roughly, between the ages of 10 to 14.

In a handbook devoted to language-arts research, it would seem most appropriate to focus on the development of oral language, writing, reading, and spelling; however, early adolescence is a period of time whem humans develop physically, and perhaps cognitively and psychosocially, at a faster rate than any other time since the first years of life. Therefore, in addition to reviewing some of the research and theory that has accumulated about language development of early adolescents, brief reviews will be presented of the physical, cognitive, and psychosocial development of this age group in order to acquaint readers with major works and theories of development, to offer a few illustrations of recent research, and to serve as an introduction to the reader who decides to seek further information about these areas, which are inextricably related to the language and literacy development of early adolescents.

Following the reviews of the physical, cognitive, and psychosocial development of early adolescents, the remainder of this chapter addresses areas of oral language development, reading, writing, and spelling.

PHYSICAL DEVELOPMENT

The physical changes that are part of early adolescence are perhaps the most obvious changes that are occuring. Brooks-Gunn (1987), Mereidith (1974), and Richards and Peterson (1987) provide comprehensive and detailed synopses of the physical changes occurring anywhere from 8 years of age, prior to early adolescence, through what is referred to as the puberal crisis, which usually occurs by age 14.

Educators would have little professional interest in these physical changes were it not for the well established relationship that these physical changes have on the self-concept and behavior of the early adolescent, which certainly can influence classroom behavior and learning, including language development. Boxer, Tohin-Richards, & Petersen (1983) use the term "biopsychosocial development" to designate the complex interplay among the biological, social, and psychological domains of development. The rate of bodily change that takes place in the years immediately preceding puberty are faster and more dramatic than at any other period of life other than infancy, strikingly dramatic when compared to the slower anatomical changes that occur during the rest of a lifetime.

One major and obvious biological change of early adolescence is the adolescent "growth spurt" that occurs. There is great variability in the timing of that growth from one child to the next, and there are also well established differences between boys and girls.

There is research evidence that suggests the timing of pubertal changes on various psychosocial adjustments have differential effects on boys and girls. Girls' growth spurt is, on the average, two years earlier than that of boys. For girls the age period of 10 to 14 years represents the completion of most of the major growth changes; however, the range of differences is significant since normal girls can mature physically as early as 7.2 years and as late as 13.5. For boys the range is narrower, but nonetheless substantial, from 9.5 to 14 (Chumlea, 1982; Tanner, 1971).

The classic work of Jones (1958) indicated that early maturation carries a distinct advantage for boys, but a disadvantage for girls. Jones and Mussen (1958) found that early maturing boys were given more leadership roles, were more popular, excelled in athletic ability, were perceived as more attractive by adults and peers, and enjoyed considerably enhanced heterosexual status. Early maturing girls were listless, submissive, lacking in poise, and indifferent in social situations. Such girls were felt to rarely achieve a high degree of popularity, prestige, or leadership. Late maturing girls, on the other hand were described as being more outgoing, confident, assured, and possessing leadership ability. (See also Mussen & Jones, 1957; and Duncan, Ritter, Dornbusch, Gross, & Carlsmith, 1985.) Simmons et al. (1983) found that early maturing girls had lower academic performance and more school behavior problems.

Duncan et al. (1985) maintain that the feelings attached to early and late maturation are the results of the social values attached to thinness and muscularity. The body changes that accompany pubertal changes in girls, increased body fat, are not viewed positively, while the increased height, weight, and muscularity of boys is seen as desirable (Tobin Richards et al.,1983). Duncan et al. (1985) express concern that naturally occurring body changes for girls conflict with social values and contribute to very negative consequences such as anorexia nervosa, and that these attitudes are so deeply ingrained that they are insensitive to intervention programs.

Richards and Peterson (1987) more generally suggest that a well documented trend for earlier physical growth and sexual maturity than in the past, referred to as the "secular trend," has influenced the interests, attitudes, and social sophistication of today's adolescents and created pressures on them at an earlier age, pressures that they may be psychosocially prepared to accept.

Summary

Although physical changes are among the most obvious effects of early adolescents, these changes have complex effects on psychosocial adjustment. Early bodily changes in adolescents has been associated with positive psychological effects in boys, but negative effects in girls. Because adolescents are maturing earlier than in past generations they may be facing greater pressures, and these psychosocial influences in turn can be expected to effect school adjustment and learning in all areas, including language and literacy.

PSYCHOSOCIAL DEVELOPMENT IN EARLY ADOLESCENCE

Discussions of the psychosocial development of adolescents have generally been, and continue to be, dominated by a Freudian orientation. Anna Freud (1969) was one of the most important popularizers of the position that adolescence is necessarily a time of psychological "storm and stress." She maintained that with puberty came adult sexual drives which result in a deterioration in the balance of psychological forces achieved in childhood (Lerner and Spanier, 1980; Gallatin, 1980; Hopkins, 1983).

Erickson (1968) modified Freud's theories to include less emphasis on sexual forces and more emphasis on social forces. His theory builds around the resolution of what are termed "normative crises." For example, the earliest developmental stage involves developing "trust from mistrust"; from the age of 6 to puberty, the crisis involves moving from a sense of "feelings of inferiority to feelings of industriousness." Adolescence growth includes acquiring a sense of indentity from a sense of role confusion. Hamachek (1980) makes the important point that a child's younger years of development have been contributing continuously to a growing sense of self and that adolescence is not a time when self-concept is "created," but that it is a time when it expands and undergoes substantial maturation, tending to continue in the direction it started if the basic experiences and significant others remain essentially the same. The social learning theorist Bandura (1964, 1969) also suggests that adolescence may not require the massive adjustments and changes the Freudian theorists have suggested. He notes that many adolescents have adopted the values of their parents by this period and that friction with parents may actually be reduced. Although early adolescence is a time when children move away from close ties with parents to stronger peer group relationships, even this is not necessarily a source of friction because many adolescents tend to form friendships with those who share similar values.

Thus, there is some evidence to suggest that the development of a concept of self, so frequently seen as a central part of adolescence, may, in fact, be better conceptualized as a continuation of earlier development, though at an accelerated pace. Likewise, the conceptualization of adolescence as a time of storm and stress may certainly occur, but not in all adolescents. Hopkins (1983) reviews research that documents the turning of adolescent interest away from parents to the peers. There is often a dramatic shift in social orientation from family to peers from 4th to 10th grade; around seventh and eighth grade the peer groups often become *more* influential than parents. However, the greater influence of peers does not extend equally to all areas of psychosocial functioning. Sebald and White (1980) suggest that the more important the situation and the decision, the more likely that adolescents will comply with parental rather than peer values when the two conflict. It is on more trivial matters, such as dress, where peer compliance is much stronger, though in the important area of drug use, peers may be more influential (Brook, Lukoff & Whiteman, 1980).

Effects of Television in Psychosocial Development

Because television viewing is frequently a concern among professionals interested in language development and school achievement in general, a small sampling of the available research is reviewed here.

Wroblewski and Huston (1987) indicate that early adolescents watch more television than any other age group except the elderly. While some surveys done before the 1980s suggested that early and late adolescents actually showed reduced interest in television, this situation seems to have changed with the introduction of MTV and related music video channels that are part of cable television (Singer & Singer, 1987).

Singer and Singer (1987) show that correlates of heavy television include: increased restlessness, increased aggressive behavior, increased fearfulness and suspicion about the world, less imaginativeness and playfulness, and variety of cognitive limitations. Children exposed to large amounts of television tend to see the world as a domain of rapidly passing, fragmented experiences with heavy doses of violence, sexual teasing, and hypermobility.

Signorielli (1987) provides evidence that heavy television viewers are more likely to hold negative attitudes and to have more negative self-concepts. Early adolescents tend to be depicted as good or cute, but they serve the role of enhancing the status of adults and are often also depicted on television as being victimized, and in ill health, and later in adolescence are seen smoking, drinking, and engaged in drug abuse. She concludes, "The overall image is thus one that conveys a sense of unimportance and devaluation of children and childhood" p. 267.

One form of television programming that has been of particular concern because of its impact on early adolescents is a stress on music videos and rock music. Greenfield et al. (1987) indicate that some of the anxieties that have been expressed may not have a foundation in fact. They found that young children, fourth graders, simply did not understand the general message of lyrics with sexual messages. A second finding was that a music video reduces the emotional response of a young audience, and also seems to reduce, perhaps because of the distractive nature of many of the videos, the viewers' understanding of the lyrics. Thus, video presentations of rock music are not highly likely to have the effects their critics feared.

Singer and Singer (1987) offer practical suggestions and guidelines for parents' use in regulating and guiding the television viewing of adolescents, as well as useful lists of resources and addresses of agencies that are concerned with the influence of television on children and the regulation of television.

Sexual Identity and Its Effects on Achievement

The Spring 1987 (volume 7, no. 1) publication *Journal of Early Adolescence* is a themed issue that presents a recent, excellent set of articles addressing the issue of sex differences in academic achievement among early adolescents. Studies are reported from England, Scotland, Canada, South Africa, and the United states. Space does not permit the review of individual studies of the relationship of early adolescent sex and achievement in academic areas. However, recent research (Lewis & Hoover, 1983; Martain & Hoover, 1987; Viser, 1987; Williams & Kerr, 1987) strongly suggests that the relationship of sex to academic achievement is far from a simple, straightforward or even stable relationship. As with so many relationships in the social sciences, this relationship appears to depend on how and where academic achievement is measured. There are at least a few studies that suggest a strong need to reconsider the stability of generalizations that are drawn including the belief that as children enter early adolescence girls perform better than boys in language related areas and that boys have a better achievement record in mathematics and science. The sex of the early adolescent appears to interact in very complex ways with a variety of social, educational, and psychological characteristics. The differences in the results of studies from country to country and trends over time strongly suggest that any sex differences found are the results of the social, educational, and psychological characteristics and not biological, constitutional sex characteristics.

When sex differences have been found in achievement, it appears that developmental considerations are of great importance and that early adolescence is probably a crucial period of development of the attitudes, self-concept factors and aspirations affecting academic achievement.

Given the very strong likelihood that social psychological factors most likely play the most important role in shaping those patterns, parents and teachers must avoid limiting student achievement because of prejudices about the importance to or potential of an academic area to a child of a particular sex (Sabers, Cushing & Sabers, 1987).

Summary

Thus, although Freudian psychology has very much popularized the preadolescent period as a time of "storm and stress," reflecting a disturbed psychosocial balance resulting from sexual urges, more recent psychological formulations have placed greater emphases on social factors and have looked at the stress as varying from early adolescent to early adolescent and as more of a reflection of general life-span development than specifically linked to a particular aspect of early adolescence. There is good evidence that most early adolescents turn from parents as the point of reference to peers, but there is at least some suggestion that in major life decisions parents may still be the more important influence. Television does seem to influence the psychosocial development of early adolescence, but again, recent research suggests that the influence may not be as strong as was initially thought, and that family and ongoing social relationships can seriously mitigate the influence of television. Although some developmental trends with regard to academic achievement appear to reflect sex identity, even the results in this area seem less firm than had previously been suggested by the research literature.

In general, the newer research and developments in the psychosocial development of early adolescents suggest that social forces may be more influential, relative to hormonal forces, and that individual differences among early adolescents are more prominent than is popularly believed. In some respects the research reviewed in this section may be most beneficial to teachers and other educaters concerned about the language/literacy development of early adolescents in suggesting the need to guard against the potential stereotypical biases that are frequently held about early adolescents.

COGNITIVE/INTELLECTUAL DEVELOPMENT

Interest in the development of early adolescents' reasoning goes back at least to the time of Plato and Aristotle, both of whom attached special significance to the growth in thinking that needed to occur during this transition period between childhood and adulthood (Sisson, Hersen & Van Hasselt, 1987).

Discussions of cognitive development in early adolescence are almost always dominated by a Piagetian framework. For example, in the recent *Handbook of Adolescent Psychology* (Van Hasselt & Hersen 1987), three separate chapters present summaries of Piaget's developmental theory of cognitive development. Given the widespread acceptance and attention given to Piaget's formulations, they will be summarized briefly. (For a fuller discussion see Kaufman and Flaitz, 1987.)

Early adolescence marks the transition from the concrete operations period, typically seen as lasting from about ages 7 to 10 or 11, to the period of formal operations, which begins around age 11. During the stage of concrete operations, children can engage in active mental manipulation, but only for ideas and objects for which they have had direct, concrete experience. Formal operations is marked by the ability to think in abstract terms rather than in terms of concrete, observable events or objects.

Piaget divides the period of formal operations into two stages: one lasting from approximately age 11 to 14 years of age, termed the transitional period; the other lasting, from 14 or 15 to maturity. McKinney and Vogel (1987) and Elkind (1978) indicate there are a number of key overlapping operations that appear during formal operations; some examples follow.

First, the person can use logic and reason to generate possibilities beyond what had been experienced in reality, while the non-formal operational thinker can merely extend the experiences from reality. For example, given the problem: "All three-legged snakes are purple; I am hiding a three legged snake; guess its color," Young children, bound by their experiences, cannot solve the problem. On the other hand, a child at the formal operations level can accept the false premises of the problem and arrive at the logical solution. Formal operations brings this ability to engage in hypothetical reasoning (Hopkins, 1983).

A second feature of formal opertions thought is the ability to use a second symbol system or a set of symbols for another set of symbols, as for example, the use of algebraic expressions to symbolize numbers. This ability also allows a child to recognize that a single work can take on double meanings, and children now become able to deal with metaphor, double entendre, and cartoons in an abstract way.

A third newly acquired feature of early adolescent thinking is the capacity to construct ideal and contrary-to-fact situations. An important feature of formal operational thought is the ability to deal with what is possible along with what is actual. It is this capacity that allows the adolescent to think about the future in a way not thought about before. This capacity also creates some conflict and problems for the developing adolescent because when he or she compares that which is, to that which might be, and often finds the former very lacking, the early adolescent is often disillusioned by family, church, and other social institutions.

During the formal operations period, abstract thought becomes possible and grows to the extent to which it is used. However, early adolescents are in the very beginning of this stage, so that there is not a consistent and refined use of abstract thought. Formal operations is the very last stage of cognitive development in Piaget's formulations so that the approaches to thinking and learning that are developing during this period of time are the ones that will be used through maturity. (See Flavell, 1963, 1985; Ginsburg & Opper, 1979; Inhelder & Piaget, 1958, for further discussions of Piaget's theory.)

There have been attempts to apply more specifically the results of achieving the stage of formal operations on academic performance. McMahon (1974), for example, discussed the implications of Piaget's and Elkind's work as it applied to science, social studies, and mathematics. The general implication of McMahon's suggestions is that with early adolescence and the appearance of formal operational thought, more abstract forms of teaching and learning are made possible. While McMahon does not specifically address the relationship between Piaget's theory and development in language and literacy areas, many of the suggestions that he offers about teaching and learning have implications for these areas as well. In addition there are several places in the second half of this chapter where research findings in areas of language arts seem to reflect what might have been predicted from a Piagetian framework.

Elkind (1967, 1974, 1978) has tended to focus his discussions of the effects of attaining formal operations during the early adolescence period on the general psychosocial behavior, rather on the more narrow intellectual development or academic/learning performance. He maintains that the maturing cognitive structure allows the early adolescent to experience social and psychological phenomena that were not a part of the childhood experience. Elkind (1967) notes, for example, that the development of prejudices or cliques do not appear before early adolescence, and that their appearance is a reflection of the new cognitive structures that are developing. The new cognitive structures do not cause the experiences or the reactions of the early adolescents, but they allow for them to take place.

Elkind has also presented (1967) a highly regarded, frequently cited discussion of the role of egocentrism in early adolescence. In the earlier period of concrete operations, children have difficulty differentiating between actual perceptual phenomena and their own mental products based on those phenomena; however, formal operations thought not only allows the early adolescent to conceptualize his or her own thought, but to conceptualize the thoughts of others as well, an important consideration of language, including reading and writing. However, the egocentrism of early adolescence is inconsistency in being able to distinguish between one's own thoughts and the thoughts of others. For example, this can lead adolescents to believe that others are as concerned with their appearance and behavior as they themselves are. This in turn leads Elkind to posit two constructs steamming form early adolescent egocentrism that are used to explain a great deal of early adolescent behavior. One of the constructs is an "imaginary audience." The early adolescent is continuously constructing and reacting to an imaginary audience that is always scrutinizing and judging his or her behavior because, as a result of a failure to distinguish between the conceptualizing of their own thought and the thought of others, early adolescents feel that others are as vitally interested in them as they are in themselves.

The second interesting construct Elkind posits is that of a "personal fable." Elkind describes it this way: "Perhaps because he believes he is of importance to so many people, the imaginary audience, he comes to regard himself, and particularly his feelings, as something special and unique. Only he can suffer with such agonized intensity or experience such exquisite rapture" (p. 1031). Elkind points to manifestations of the personal fable of early adolescents in the characters of Twain's Tom Sawyer, Goethe's Young Werther and Salinger's Holden Caufield. (See Enright et al (1979) and Hudson and Gray (1986) for research related to these constructs.)

Summary

Recent discussions of the cognitive/intellectual development of early adolescents has been dominated by Piagetian psychological constructs. According to this theory early adolescent are moving from the period of concrete operations to the period of formal operations, a period in which more abstract reasoning is possible. Thus, early adolescents would seem able to take on more sophisticated, advanced tasks in reading and writing. They should be able to appreciate subtleties in literature and be capable of more critical responses than ever before.

There has also been a great deal of theorizing about how the developing cognitive structures of the adolescent affect emotional and social responses, including a form of egocentrism in which early adolescents assume that others are as preoccupied with their behavior and appearance as they are.

LANGUAGE ARTS

While there are many areas of the language arts and literacy that could be explored in a review such as this, this chapter will concentrate on only four areas: oral language development, reading, writing, and spelling.

Language Development

There is a remarkable spate of recent information about general language development among early adolescents. As Obler

(1988) points out: "The primary focus of developmentalists' work on language acquisition has been children aged 1 to 6." Even in a chapter entitled "Language Beyond Childhood" (Obler, 1988) there is more information presented about children between the ages of 6 to 10 than there is about early adolescents. Phillips (1985) referring to research on the oral language development of children beyond the age of 9 concludes that "almost none exists" (p. 60). Similarly, Reed (1986) indicated that "there is no cohesive, integrated body of knowledge regarding normal language development during adolescence" (p. 229). Even Chomsky's seminal study (1969), which is so frequently cited to show that syntactic development extends beyond the preschool years, focuses its attention on children between the ages of 5 and 10.

Obler notes that there are linguistic developments which take place during adolescence and even adulthood, but goes on to point out that these are not treated within a developmental framework. Obler offers the rationale for the different treatment in later childhood and early adolescence and beyond that early language development represents the development of a core language that all children are expected to learn and generally, in fact, do learn, while the special language skills that are learned in adolescence and adulthood are "relatively optional." As examples of the kinds of language development that occur in these later periods, Obler cites developing the language and vocabulary of one's profession or occupation, foreign language acquisition, typing, effective speaking, and learning the appropriate registers of language that are needed in various settings.

However, a recent publication, an edited work by Marilyn Nippold (1988), makes an outstanding professional contribution by summarizing the research on the language development of children between the ages of 9 and 19, an age range is somewhat broader than that presented in this chapter. It seems the best available source for educators interested in an in-depth discussion of adolescent language development.

Nippold's recent (1988) edited volume leads to the conclusion that there are rather systematic, but comparatively subtle, changes and advancements in language development during adolescence. After acknowledging that the developmental language changes at earlier ages are much more perceptible and measurable, she concludes:

the linguistic changes that occur during later childhood and adolescence are much more subtle, a phenomenon which undoubtedly has reinforced the view that "not much happens in the language department beyond the preschool years." However, the research suggests that language development during the 9-through-19 range unfolds in a slow and protracted manner, and that changes become obvious only when sophisticated linguistic phenomena are analyzed and non-adjacent age groups (e.g. 9-year olds and 12-year olds) are compared. Documenting language growth in older children and adolescents requires that written forms of communication be scrutinized in addition to spoken forms. (p. 3)

Nippold (1988) presents an excellent review of the somewhat limited research on the development of lexical knowledge during the early adolescent period. Based largely on the work of Miller and Gildea (1987), Nippold maintains that at about fourth grade and through the period of early adolescence, written text becomes the major source of word meanings. This contention is much in line with developmental theories of reading (see section on reading later in this chapter) that suggest around fourth grade students begin to deal with reading materials containing unfamiliar information and vocabulary. To that point reading materials, though containing printed words that children may have difficulty identifying, are nonetheless words to which they attach meaning when they hear them. Nippold (1988) also hypothesizes that children's abilities to independently infer word meanings from contextual clues becomes an important factor in vocabulary development beyond third grade. Unfortunately, there appear to be no clear developmental studies of such abilities among early adolescents, though there are a few studies (Jenkins, Mattlock & Slocum, 1989; Herman and Weaver, 1988) that suggest children in the middle school grades can improve their ability to acquire word meaning from context, thus clearly implying room for improvement in this area. Unfortunately, it is not clear as to whether such improvements typically take place without instructional intervention.

Nippold (1988) reviews the remaining information about lexical development within two broad concepts—word classes and word definitions.

The research in the area of word classes is further divided into research on verbs, adverbs, and connectives. In each area she concludes that there are subtle but steady developments through early adolescence and beyond, generally through adulthood. As an example of the kind of development that occurs with verbs, Nippold (1988) summarizes the developmental research of Astington & Olson (1987) on accurate understanding of "literate" verbs. Literate verbs are words like know, assert, hypothesize, and contradict that are used to convey varying states of knowing. These can be subdivided into a metacognitive set of words (remember, infer, assume) and a metalinguistic set (assert, predict, and affirm). Relatively good evidence is presented to show that children do grow in their interpretation of these verbs through early adolescence and that sophistication in comprehending subtles among these verbs continues through college levels.

Though Nippold (1988) cites only one study on the acquisition of subtle differences in meaning of adverbs, there is some beginning evidence of such development. There is a greater number of studies to support growing sophistication in the understanding of connectives, which are conjunctions and relative pronouns that convey relationships between words, phrases or clauses. There is within this section of Nippold's chapter, sufficient detail to provide teachers of early adolescents with words and instructional activities that might be beneficial for improving students understanding of this class of words.

The bulk of the research on early adolescents' abilities to deal with word definitions suggests that there are qualitative development differences in the definitions which children give through early adolescence. As they get older, children, tend to give fewer descriptive definitions (e.g., an orange is round or is orange); they also tend to decrease the number of functional definitions (e.g., an orange is something you eat) and increase the number of categorical or superordinate definitions they give (e.g., an orange is a fruit).

Though treated in separate chapters entitled "Verbal Reasoning," "Figurative Language," and "Linguistic Ambiguity," Nippold (1988) deals with the more abstract qualities of words and word combinations. These chapters should be consulted by the interested reader since space limitations prevent such discussions in this chapter.

Thus, while there are not dramatic changes in lexical knowledge during early adolescence, there is a base of research findings that provide good evidence showing there are subtle and consistent developments that occur. (See also the chapters by Baumann and Kameeni and by Mason, Herman and Au, this handbook.)

Scott (1988) presents a comprehensive review of available information on the syntactic development among adolescents. She, however, focuses most of that review on syntactic development as it occurs in written forms, concluding that there is very little evidence of growing syntactic maturity during adolescence. However, she also makes the point that this is probably a limitation of the extant research which has not developed the appropriate methodologies to measure growth in this area.

Given the shift of attention of the early adolescent from parents to peer groups, one might expect to find information about the development of registers of language for communication within early adolescent peer groups. Both Cooper and Anderson-Inman (1988) and Stephens (1988) provide some beginning information on this topic, but each of these chapters presents very limited information. Stephens, for example reviews evidence that early adolescents generally gain in their ability to adjust the style of their speech to their audience, adjusting their speech for peers, adults, and younger children. Cooper and Anderson-Inman review some theories about the importance of language changes among early adolescents as a way of helping them to establish a greater sense of identity by separating themselves from the language of earlier childhood. They also review some evidence to suggest that adolescents become more guarded in the use of language which "openly makes fun" of others and that they develop greater abilities in communicating with peers of the opposite sex.

Given the onset of puberty, one might also expect to find that peer language diifferences based on sex identity might be found among early adolescents. Warren-Leubecker and Bohannon (1988) review some interesting research in the area that they term "genderlect." Indeed, linguistic differences between males and females is a fairly commonly explored topic. For example, children through early adolescents grow in their ability to distinguish sentences that are deemed stereotypically male or female utterances. Edelsky (1977) studied fourth-, third- and sixth-grade children and found that as the children grew older, their stereotypes became increasingly like those of adults.

Cooper and Anderson-Inman (1988) present an excellent, well-integrated summary of gender differences in language usage among adolescents concluding, among other things, that girls tend to use more prestige forms of language while boys tend to use more nonstandard forms, that boys tend to be more dominating than girls by making more interruptions and exerting more topic control, and that adolescent males and females tend to use language for different purposes when verbally interacting with same sexed peer groups. With respect to the latter point, girls try to use words mainly to create and maintain close relationships, to criticize others in acceptable ways, and to interpret accurately the speech of other girls. Boys tend to use language to assert their positions of dominance, to attract and maintain an audience, and to assert themselves while others are speaking. The Cooper and Anderson-Inmaan (1988) chapter should be consulted for the details of the research on adolescent gender differences in language use.

Summary

Although certainly there was research conducted on the oral language development of early adolescents and whereas chapters such as that by Obler (1988) summarized some useful information, until very recently (Nippold, 1988) there appears to have been no depository for information on this topic. There is now a growing body of information to suggest that while there are no highly noticeable, dramatic developments in oral language abilities during early adolescence, there are systematic, subtle changes. Vocabulary continues to grow, though at a slower rate, the types of definitions that early adolescents offer undergo qualitative changes, various word classes are interpreted more precisely, slang and other characteristics of adolescents begin to appear, and gender differences become more apparent.

Reading. Whereas the available information on language development of early adolescents appears very limited and does not point to the need for, or perhaps the potential for, substantial "developmental growth," there is a vast amount written about the reading of early adolescents, and there appears to be clear agreement among researchers that there are substantial opportunities for even average and above average early adolescents to improve their reading abilities. In dramatic contrast to the limited information available on the language development of early adolescents, whole texts have been written about reading and the middle school child (e.g., Duffy, 1975; Early, 1984; Smith and Barrett, 1974). Although the bulk of the materials appear to be descriptive in nature, it is possible to locate a huge volume of research as well. The most recently available *Summary of Investigation Related to Reading* (Weintraub, 1988), for example, reviews and provides annotations for 24 studies done during the course of one year that showed improved reading among students in grades four through eight as a result of some instructional intervention. Most of the studies demonstrated improved comprehension or vocabulary development; only one of the studies concerned itself with improving word recognition skills through the use of root words and affixes.

Smith and Barrett (1974) also take the position that early adolescents still need instruction in reading and challenge the assumption that "most children do not need some form of reading skills instruction beyond the elementary grades" p. 11. They point to needs in vocabulary development, word attack skills, and comprehension. There is a substantial amount of research to suggest that general reading skills of early adolescents can be improved. Chall in her work *Stages of Reading Development* (1983) presents a stage theory that describes the development

of reading skills from essentially birth through maturity. Children in the middle school would fall into what Chall labels "Stage 3." To provide context for this stage, which is the focus of this chapter, the three preceding stages will be very briefly described.

Chall begins her descriptions with Stage 0, which she labels as the "Prereading Stage," that transcends approximately the ages of birth though entrance into first grade. This stage involves the greatest amount of linguistic and cognitive change and growth, the foundations for later literacy skills. It is the stage during which children learn about the functions of language, where they not only rapidly develop important language skills, but also begin to develop control over language and a metalinguistic awareness of how that language operates.

Stage 1 is the "Initial Reading or Decoding Stage," and developmentally it lasts through grades one or two. The major task to master during this stage of development is "learning the arbitrary set of letters and associating these with the corresponding parts of spoken words" p. 16.

Stage 2, "Confirmation, Fluency and Ungluing from Print," is what others might label the child's achievement of decoding skills' automaticity. At this stage separate skills are merged into more effective strategies, and decoding becomes a less deliberate, conscious, attention draining activity. Chall maintains that at this stage children read to confirm what they already know rather then reading to learn new information.

Thus, the stages of development that precede Stage 3 are ones where important psychological, linguistic, and cognitive foundations are laid down for more mature reading, and during which children develop efficient mechanisms for dealing with the decoding aspects of reading.

Stage 3, "Reading for Learning the New: A First Step," begins before the middle school grades, around third or fourth grade; however, Chall's formulation suggests that this stage continues throughout the middle school years, in fact, up to the high school years. Indeed, this stage is so broadly conceived that she divides it into Stages 3A and 3B. Both of these substages, however, reflect the shift from dependence on limited decoding skills and the need to develop decoding skills, to the growing importance on prior knowledge, language development, and cognitive development as critical aspects of reading development. As Chall puts it: "During Stages 1 and 2 what is learned concerns more the relating of print to speech while Stage 3 involves more then relating of print to ideas. Very little new information about the world is learned from reading before Stage 3; more is learned from listening and watching."

In Stage 3A the reader is at the very beginning of acquiring new information from text. The level of sophistication, however, is not very high. Most of the expository materials that students read in grades four through six are introduction to subject areas and supposedly require only limited background knowledge.

Chall's description of Stage 3 seems to reflect some of the limitations that would be expected of a third- or fourth-grade child who is, according to Piagetian theory, still at the stage of concrete operational thought. As children move into early adolescence and the stage of formal operations, fewer of these limitations should be expected.

Stage 3B is marked by a growing ability to read more complex materials and to react critically to different viewpoints. Stage 3B, indeed, seems more descriptive of what could be expected of a learner in the stage of formal operational thought. In Stage 4 students are expected to more fully deal with more than one point of view.

Early (1984) also presents a general overview of the middle school reader, though not within the kind of developmental framework used by Chall. Early's formulations are more descriptive. Given the widespread influence of her work on reading at the middle school level, her basic descriptions seem worth noting. In addition, these formulations will be used as the basis for organizing some of the research that exists on the development of reading skills among early adolescent.

Early suggests the following major characteristics of middle grade readers.

First, she concludes that oral reading will be fairly accurate and fluent among early adolescents. She, like Chall, suggests that the basics of decoding have been mastered. Limitations in oral reading or word identification are very likely to be due to limitations in word meaning rather than in "skills for decoding per se." This conclusion is not to suggest that there are not some early adolescents who have problems with reading or decoding. Some of the research related to range of individual differences in reading among middle grade students will be reviewed later in this section of the chapter.

There is surprisingly little data on the achievement of fluency on the part of developing readers. In fact even data on rate of reading that might be seen as one manifestation of fluency is difficult to find. Harris and Sipay (1984) do present a table that indicates at grade four children read at the rate of 170 word per minute (wpm), and that this improves to 195 wpm at grade five, and 230 wpm at grade six. Thereafter, improvement seems less significant (seventh = 246 wpm; eighth = 267 wpm, ninth = 260 wpm). The minor drop in rate from eighth to ninth grade is not a typographical error, but illustrates the apparent variability from level to level. Harris and Sipay (1984) themselves acknowledge the limitations of rate measures such as the above, which they apparently calculated from composite data from several standardized tests. They review research that clearly shows which rate of reading will vary dramatically with level of text challenge and purpose. As just one indication of how wide reading rate can vary, in a study of very proficient, talented early adolescent readers (Tobin and Pikulski, 1988), a silent reading rate of only 116.2 wpm was obtained for sixth graders; this is very significantly lower than the rate of 230 wpm reported for "average" sixth graders by Harris and Sipay. However, those in the Tobin and Pikulski study were reading challenging material under testing conditions where they knew they would be asked to recall as much of the content as possible. In short there is some evidence to support the conclusion that fluency and rate improves and continues to improve though early adolescence, but absolute measures of that fluency have not been made.

Second, Early (1984) concludes that basic reading comprehension skills have been mastered by the time students reach middle school. Readers at this level deal well with literal aspects of comprehension and can connect details that are rather obviously related. She also points out: "They tend to be literal minded and may, therefore, be confused by metaphors and symbols, and to miss historical and literary allusions because they haven't read widely. They can think critically about text which refers to concrete experiences; they have trouble dealing with abstractions" (p. 83). These are very interesting conclusions, and while Early does not cite evidence for them, they are surprisingly congruent with the expectations that might be drawn from the perspective of Piagetian explanations of cognitive development among early adolescents. Some evidence for the conclusions drawn by Early is provided by the results of the National Assessment of Educational Progress (NAEP) data Educational Testing Service (1985) that will be reviewed at the end of this section of the chapter.

Another aspect of Early's conclusion is that once basic reading skills have been mastered, the need to apply these skills to content area texts should be considered. Dupuis (1984) edited a volume that attempted to summarize the research available on reading in the areas of English, social studies, science, foreign languages, mathematics, music, physical education, and health. While the length of this chapter prevents a review of the important considerations of applying reading to subject area texts, because it is an issue of vital concern to teachers of early adolescents, those interested should consult the available research.

Third, Early (1984) cites as the chief characteristic of middle school readers, the fact that they don't read much. She maintains that their reading is limited because of restricted background that they bring to the reading of many texts, and their background remains restricted because they fail to use reading as a tool for extending, adding to that background.

Although it is difficult to quantify what is meant by early adolescents "not reading much," there is evidence from a fairly recent NAEP Educational Testing Service (1985) report to suggest that early adolescents read less than they did at earlier ages. While 54 percent of the nine-year-olds in that survey reported that they read on a daily basis, the percentage drops to 35 percent by age 13. That survey also reported that while 81 percent of the nine-year-olds reported that they enjoyed reading very much, the percentage drops to about 50 for 13-year-olds. The 1988 NAEP report (Applebee, Langer & Mullis, 1988) also gives self-report information on the reading habits of 13-year-olds. It accents the finding from earlier reports that show there is a decrease in reading at seventh grade. For example, while 66 percent of the third-grade readers reported reading a novel or part of a novel at least on a monthly basis, the percentage drops to 45 for seventh graders. There is, on the other hand, a significant increase in the percentage of seventh graders (67 percent) who read parts of the newspaper on at least a weekly basis, up from 34 percent of the third graders. This section of the NAEP report also makes it apparent that children with poor reading abilities tend to read less. For example, while some 14 percent of the students in the upper quartile of reading achievement reported never finishing parts of a story or novel, almost 24 percent of the students scoring in the lowest quartile reported never reading such materials.

Thus, there is fairly substantial evidence that as children move into early adolescence, they engage in less reading. Unfortunately the reasons are not clear as to why this occurs. Early

(1984), as noted above, attributes the decrease, at least in part, to limitations in background of experience; however, it also seems likely that the fast occurring physical changes and the psychosocial preoccupations that are part of early adolescence, and perhaps increased interest in television viewing, as noted earlier in this chapter, play as an important role, if not more so than experiental limitations.

Smith and Barrett (1974) allude to what may be another very important characteristic of early adolescent readers, their willingness to engage in reading if it will satisfy their personal needs. In spite of Early's conclusion that early adolescents do not read extensively, there is no evidence to show that they cannot be motivated to read. Given the wide range of individual differences and the rapid changes they are undergoing, it would appear that teachers need to present a wide array of books and topics in order to appeal to any one early adolescent's interests.

Finally, a characteristic alluded to but not specifically listed by Early deserves special mention, that is, the wide range of reading abilities, experiences, and interests that exist among early adolescents. Smith and Barrett (1974) make the point that instruction has the effect of widening individual difference so that "in a typical sixth grade population, for example, it would be unusual to find the general level of reading achievement ranging from what we would expect of third graders to what we would expect of eighth or ninth graders." However, this estimate does not consider the certain existence of severe reading problems among at least some early adolescents so that even an estimate of a six-year range of achievement among this age group of students is an underestimation of the full variability. Harris and Sipay (1985), based on data from standardized test scores, conclude that the scores of students at the beginning of fifth grade can range from as low as 2.3 to as high as 12.5, a span of 10 years. Similarly, Rubin (1975) reports of comprehension scores for fifth graders as ranging from 1.8 to 9.5 +. However, the score of 1.8 is the lowest possible tabled score representing the lowest level of the test, and the 9.5 + is obviously an open-ended score. These sources of information about individual differences in reading suggest that the range is likely to be even greater at the upper ages of early adolescence. If there is one conclusion that is firmly established regarding the reading of early adolescents, it is that there is an enormous range of abilities.

Some more specific empirical information about the reading development of early adolescents is obtainable from the *National Assessment of Educational Progress Examinations* (NAEP), which are administered in reading approximately every five years. These results are reviewed here both for their general interest and because they fit into the developmental framework suggested by Chall and the conclusions drawn by Early. The results reported in 1985 offer some information about the trends in the development of reading skills for students aged 13, who would fall into the age range of early adolescence, as well for students aged 9 and 17. Data from comparable NAEP examinations are available since 1971. In terms of trends of achievement, the overall picture for 13-year-olds is mildly encouraging. They showed statistically significant improvement during the 1970s, though their achievement remained steady between the 1980 and 1985 assessment.

The NAEP study reported the 1985 results according to five levels of reading attainment. It may be somewhat informative to look at the percentage of 13-year-old students who were able to meet the criteria for these various levels of proficiency.

The lowest level of proficiency, labeled "rudimentary," was defined as the level of proficiency needed to follow simple directions or to read a few simple sentences and to then answer factual questions. "Performance at this level suggests the ability to carry out simple, discrete reading tasks" p. 15. Obviously, this level of proficiency also requires the mastery of basic decoding skills. In the 1984 assessment, 99.8 percent of the 13-year-olds were able to meet the criteria for mastering rudimentary skills, up very slightly from the first testing that was done in 1970. These results are in line with Chall's expectation that students at this age would be beyond the decoding stage of learning to read and offer confirmation for Early's conclusion that basic word identification skills have been mastered.

The second level of proficiency, termed "basic," requires application of comprehension strategies to simple stories and relatively noncomplex expository passages. "Proficiency at this level suggests the ability to understand specific and sequentially related information" (p. 15). Ninety four point five percent of the 13-year-olds achieved this level of proficiency in 1985, up from 92.3 percent in 1970, a statistically significant increase.

The third level, "intermediate" level skills, also showed improvement for 13-year-olds, (60.0 percent, up from 57.0 percent) but this change was not statistically significant. Intermediate level reading requires application of comprehension strategies to relatively lengthy stories and informational passages. "Proficiency at this level suggests the ability to search for specific information, interrelate ideas, and make generalizations" (p. 17).

Thirteen-year-olds did not fare very well in dealing with the two highest levels of complexity. "Adept" level items required students to understand, summarize, and explain a broad range of passages including stories, poems, and information and graphic forms. "Performance at this level suggests the ability to find, understand, summarize and explain relatively complicated information" p. 15. Only about 11 percent of the 13-year-olds could succeed at this level of proficiency, up insignificantly from about 9 percent in 1970. Finally, 13-year-olds showed no discernable improvement in achieving the "advanced" level of proficiency; less than 1 percent passed at any assessment point. Items at this level entailed restructuring and synthesizing ideas presented in passages using specialized content, difficult vocabulary, sophisticated syntax, and specialized genres. "Performance at this level suggests the ability to synthesize and learn from specialized materials" (p. 15).

Unfortunately the results of the 1987 NAEP reading assessment were not reported using the same scale as in previous assessments and because of that NAEP officials termed a "precipitous" drop in achievement for the 17- and 9-year olds, drops that were termed "anomalous" and "unbelievable" (Applebee, Langer & Mullis, 1988). Therefore, the results of the 1987 evaluation are presented in a somewhat more descriptive form. As one example, there was an attempt made in the 1987 assessment to evaluate student's ability to read and to respond in writing to that reading. Students read two stories and one social studies expository piece and were then to make comparisons, draw, and defend conclusions, or make comparisons between what they had read and their own experiences. In general, the results were dissapointing for all groups, 3rd, 7th and 11th graders. For the seventh graders, more than a third failed to read a simple story and draw a reasonable conclusion, even at a minimally satisfactory level. On the expository material, more than 36 percent drew one comparison between information in the short article and their own experiences, and more than 60 percent made unsatisfactory comparisons. Only slightly more than 3 percent made minimal comparisons and virtually none made satisfactory or elaborated comparisons. The authors of the report conclude: "These findings are disturbing, but not surprising. They parallel the findings of earlier NAEP reading and writing assessments, which indicated that students in American schools can read with surface understanding, but have difficulty when asked to think more deeply about what they have read, to defend or elaborate upon their ideas, and to communicate them in writing" (Applebee, Langer, Mullis, 1988, p. 25).

Summary

Thus, although the above review represents but a very small portion of the information that exists about the development of reading abilities of middle school students, a number of conclusions seem warranted. Middle grade children who have not encountered difficulty in learning to read have mastered basic word identification, decoding, and basic comprehension skills. They are moving into the stage of being able to learn more significant amounts of information from their reading since attention can be focused on comprehending more difficult and new ideas rather than on figuring out the pronunciation of words. On the other hand, early adolescents appear to encounter much difficulty in responding to the more demanding, critical, and creative aspects of reading comprehension. There is also a disturbing downturn in the reading habits of early adolescents. Finally, there is a very wide range of reading abilities among readers at this age and grade, ranging from essentially nonreaders through readers who are so talented that their abilities are not fully tapped through standard measures of reading.

Writing

Although the volume of research dealing with writing, both composition and spelling, is growing rapidly and substantially (see Braddock, Lloyd-Jones, & Schoer, 1963; Freedman, Dyson, Flower, & Chafe, 1987; Hillocks, 1986, for comprehensive reviews), writing has certainly not received the widespread research attention accorded reading. For example, Graves (1984) in an article entitled "A New Look at Writing Research begins by noting, "First, the bad news. Only 156 studies of writing in the elementary grades, or average of six annually, have been done in the United States in the last 25 years. Writing research was in such low esteem from 1955 to 1972 that 84% of all studies were done by dissertation alone" p. 92. Elsewhere he notes that almost 70 per cent of all of the research on writing was

concerned with what the teacher was doing in the classroom, and that only 12 per cent of the studies concerned themselves with what children did when they wrote. Graves does optimistically note that there is a fast growing interest in research on writing.

This chapter is not a comprehensive review of the research that is related to the develoment of writing in early adolescents, but the reviews cited at the beginning section of this chapter make it clear that far more research on composition and spelling exists than could possibly be included here; therefore, spelling will be dealt with in a separate section. In addition, the area of composition will be addressed in three major sections. The results of the trends in the development of writing abilities, as reflected in the National Assessment of Educational Progress reports of writing, will be summarized to provide some perspective. The remaining studies of composition will be addressed under two major headings, one on the development of syntactic complexity research as reflected in written composition, and the other on which audience is dealt with by the early adolescent writer. (For additional views, see chapter by Dyson and Freedman, this handbook.)

TRENDS IN WRITING ACHIEVEMENT FOR EARLY ADOLESCENTS

The National Assessments of Educational Progress (NAEP) have been conducted in the area of writing in 1974, 1979, and 1984. This section of the chapter will begin by briefly reviewing the results of those tests as a way of providing some perspective for the more specific research that exists. Applebee, Langer and Mullis (1988) provide the basis for this summary and for the conclusions drawn about trends in writing achievement.

The national assessments of writing evaluated students, aged 9, 13, and 17, in their abilities to deal with three types of writing: informative, persuasive, and imaginative. Students were given assigned tasks in each of these three areas and asked to write in response to the task. Writings were then rated as to whether they were at the "not rated," "unsatisfactory," "minimal," "adequate," or "elaborative" level of proficiency. In order to illustrate the nature of the assessments, this chapter will give fairly full explanations of the results of the informative writing and more limited explanations for persuasive and imaginative writing.

Informative writing was defined as writing for presenting information and sharing ideas. It can include a wide range of writings from a young child's description of a new toy to a full research report in science. Through this type of writing students think about ideas, refine them, and formulate them clearly. One of the informative writing tasks presented to children in the NAEP to asked them to described for a friend a reproduction of a surrealistic painting by Dali.

To accomplish the above tasks students needed to "select, organize, and present the details of the painting and to convey them in terms of the whole painting "Applebee, Langer, and Mullis, (1988), p. 10. Writings that were "not rated" included papers that were blank, undecipherable, off task, or contained a statement to the effect that the students did not know how to do the task.

Writings that were rated as "unsatisfactory" were ones that provided minimal information, misinformation, or details that were disorganized.

Writings that were rated "minimal" provided some details, but the details were not organized so that the reader could visualize how the parts of the picture might fit together.

Writings that were rated "adeqate" were ones where the writer described and interrelated most of the details of the picture.

Writings that were rated "elaborated" were ones where the writers provided a full description within an organized framework that provided a context for the reader.

For early adolescents there was a significant improvement in performance on the informative writing task in 1984 as compared with 1979, the two assessment points at which comparison data are available. When the 1979 and 1984 results were compared, there was a 1 percent decrease in the percentage of papers that were not ratable (from 1 percent to 0), a 7 percent decrease in the percent rated as unsatisfactory (from 25 percent to 18 percent), a 2 percent increase in those rated as minimal (from 61 percent to 63 percent), a 3 percent increase in the percent rated adeqate (from 14 percent to 17 percent) and a 2 percent increase in those rated as elaborated (from 0 to 2 percent). Although the improvement of the 13-year-olds over the 5 year periods is encouraging, the overall level of performance remains disappointingly low, with less than 20 percent of the 13-year-olds having their writings rated as "adequate" or "elaborated." The vast majority of the writings were rated as "minimal" or less.

In looking at the results of the informative writing, there are clear developmental trends toward improved writing performance as children become older. Of the 9-year-olds, only about 3 percent of the writings were rated as adequate or better in 1984; as noted, slightly less than 20 percent of the 13-year-olds were so rated; and that percentage increases to just over 38 percent for 17-year-olds.

By and large the trends are similar for 13-year-olds for the other two types of writing that were assessed. For persuasive writing, in 1979 only 6 percent of the writings of 13-year-olds were rated as adequate or better, while in 1984 the percentage had increased to almost 10 percent. Finally, for imaginative writing, data exist that permit comparisons for all three NAEP writing evaluations. Here the data suggest caution in interpreting a long-range trend of improvement in the writings of 13-year-olds because the data indicate that from 1974 there was a drop in writing achievement for this age group followed by a recovery in 1984. For example, in 1974 about 16 percent of the 13-year-olds' imaginative writings were rated as adequate or better, but the percentage drops to less than 12 percent in 1979, and then improves to almost 17 percent in 1984; thus, achievement over the decade shows no significant improvement. Indeed, when Applebee et al. review the full data available they conclude: "The writing performance of 13-year-olds between 1974 and 1979 showed increases on some tasks but decreases on others, with more declines than improvements. However, the

nearly uniform improvement between 1979 and 1984 on all tasks assessed by NAEP indicates a recovery from previous declines at age 13. Writing performance in the early 1980's seems to have recovered to 1974 levels for this age group" (p. 48).

The data available from NAEP do not directly address the question of what might have caused the achievement trends that were found for 13-year-olds; however, there are some suggestions as to what might account for the positive trends between 1979 and 1984. Thirteen-year-olds in 1984 reported that they spent more time in planning and revising activities and that they were more likely to receive comments, as opposed to just a grade, from teachers. For example, in 1979 only 24 percent of the students indicated that their papers were returned with written suggestions for improving the writing, but the percentage was up to 33 percent in 1984. In 1979 38 percent of the students indicated that they usually wrote a paper more than once before turning it in, while that percentage rose to 46 percent in 1984. The percentage of students who reported that they were usually encouraged to jot down ideas or make notes about a topic before writing about it increased from 41 percent in 1979 to 47 percent in 1984.

One might also look to the possiblilty that the improvement of 13-year-olds from 1979 to 1984 might due to an increased amount of writing; however, the survey data do not support this conclusion. For example, in 1979 55 percent of the 13-year-olds reported that they spent a third or more of their time in English class on writing activities; this increased insignificantly to 56 percent in 1984. Similarly, in 1979 the average number of papers 13-year-olds reported writing was three, and the figure was almost identical for 1984.

Although the results of the NAEP in the area of writing are not dismal, they are certainly not positive. Early adolescents remain very limited in their ability to deal with the three types of writing tasks called for in the NAEP; it is particularly disappointing to see the small percentages of students whose writings are rated as adequate or elaborated. In a more detailed analysis of the 1984 NAEP writing results Applebee, Langer, and Mullis (1988) note that students do well in responding at a minimal or surface level to writing tasks, but they reach the very important conclusion that "When the tasks became more complex, requiring more extended reasoning in order to plan and carry out the writing, only small percentages of students at any grade were able to perform adequately" (p. 17).

Syntactic Development of Writing

Studies of the syntax of early adolescent children tend to be fairly extensive and very quickly reach a level of complexity that is impossible to deal with in a summary chapter of this sort; therefore, only a sampling of such studies will be offered. One of the factors leading to the complexity is that they almost always deal with ages that are more extensive than those being considered in this chapter.

A pioneering study of syntactic development was that of LaBrant (1933) who studied the written compositions of 1007 individuals in grades 4 through 12. For purposes of this chapter, one of the subgroups was a group of 482 pupils in grades four to nine. Given that La Brant analyzed 161,518 words, it is not surprising that the report of her results is just short of 500 pages. La Brant used both dependent and independent clauses as the unit of analysis for her study; however, her unit of analysis has been criticized (Hunt, 1965; O'Donnell, Griffin & Norris, 1967) because she counted compounded verbs as separate clauses so that the sentence "I am studying books and working hard" was counted as two separate clauses. One might also question the generalization of results because the compositions that were analyzed for grades four to nine were elicited by a faculty member from the University of Kansas who implied that serious consideration was being given to changing the school year to a year-round session, and that the children's written opinions were being solicited in writing with a 20-minute time limit. Interestingly La Brant reports that "The sincerity and subsequent absorption of the writers in the content is indicated by threats to quit school or to join the navy to show in various ways marked defiance to any move to lengthen the school year. In only one case does the pupil generalize throughout the paper" (p. 16).

La Brant's major finding showed there was a clear tendency for the proportion of subordinate clauses to increase between grades four and nine, and that this was a reflection of increasing language sophistication, which she found to be related to both chronological and mental age. She attempted to place the clauses into categories such as clauses of time, place, and so on, but she found no systematic changes in use of the categories, though she reports that the content becomes more "exact and specific." For example, she found that with increasing maturity, time clauses change from the more general "when" clauses to "after," "until," and "while." She also reported that the length of clauses remained comparatively constant between ages 8 and 16, based on her definition of a clause.

A major contribution to the information available about early adolescents' writing ability comes from the classic 1965 study by Kellogg Hunt. The study is best known for its introduction of the T-unit (the minimal terminable unit), which is essentially an independent clause with any other words or sentence parts that accompany it, including subordinate clauses.

Hunt used the T-unit to study syntactic differences at three grade levels: 4th, 8th, and 12th, thus, ages were just before, near the end of and beyond the early adolescent level. Hunt did find significant differences in the mean length of T-units (p. 1) between all grade levels. Thus, syntactic complexity in written compositions continues to develop during the period of adolescence; indeed it appears to continue to develop beyond the upper limits of adolescence.

In his 1965 study, he also found differences between grade levels for average clause length, the ratio of clauses per T-unit, and average sentence length. These refections of complexity and elaboration also appear to be developing during early adolescence. It is important to note that Hunt looked at development over fairly long periods of time, four years. Had adjacent age levels been studied, it seems unlikely that signigicant differences would have been found.

Early adolescents also appear to increase the number of noun clauses and adjectives they use in their writing as compared with fourth graders. However, this function does not reach maturity during early adolescence, because there is another significant increase in the use of such clauses from 8th to 12th grade (Hunt, 1965).

In general, Hunt's work showed that during the period of preadolescence, children use increasingly more complex syntax, moving away from strings of main clauses toward more use of subordinate clauses that modify the main clauses. Studies by O'Donnell, Griffin, and Norris, 1967, and Dixon, 1970, have confirmed and extended Hunt's findings by adding to the specificity of the types of changes that contribute to the increased complexity.

Both units work, and the work of O'Donnell, Griffin, and Norris suggest that although sex differences favoring girls exist prior to preadolescence on the dimension of syntactic complexity, the differences become insignificant during this period of development.

Though Hunt's findings were built on a very limited population of students (only nine girls and nine boys at each of three grade levels), there has been sufficient replication of the finding that syntactic complexity as reflected in T-units continues over the period of preadolescence (Hillocks, 1986). However, interestingly research has found little correlation between mean number of words in T-units and rated quality of composition.

Loban (1976) studied the oral and written language development of children from 1st through 12th grade in seminal, longitudinal studies, one of the few longitudinal research efforts to look at writing development. However, the major focus of Loban's work was on the early development of the children, and although he reported increasing syntactic forms through all grade levels studied, there is little that conflicts with or goes beyond Hunt's findings.

More recently Dixon (1970) analyzed portions of narratives written by fourth, eighth, and twelfth graders as well as college seniors. He too examined words per T-unit, intra T-unit coordinators, and several other linguistic and syntactic variables, and he concluded that the length of T-units was the linguistic variable most associated with grade level, and hence, the most accurate reflection of syntactic and linguistic maturity.

Syntactical developmemt studies of the writing of early adolescents that received early, extensive study seem consistent in suggesting that the complexity of written forms continues to develop through the early adolescent and that the T-unit remains a reasonable measure of syntactic maturity. Hillock (1986) in his extensive review cites no recent studies of the syntactic development of the written compositions of early adolecents, though he does point out several attempts in the 1970s to develop single, more refined measures of syntactic complexity but also dismisses them as not very informative or helpful. More recent work in writing appears to have moved to other approaches such as the analysis of writing (see Freedman et al, 1987).

One dimension of writing that has received some research attention is Sense of Audience, which examines if writers are able to adjust their writing to fit the needs, interests, and other characteristics of various types of audiences. The pioneering work in this area, dealing with oral language, was done by Piaget (1926, 1955) with young children in the preoperational stage of cognitive development. Piaget's young children, trapped in egocentric thought, were not able offer very clear directions or explanations to others. During the 1960s and 1970s there was substantial research published about children' abilities to adapt oral messages to various types of audiences (see Kroll, 1985, for summary). However, there has been only a trickling of studies that have addressed preadolescents' abilities to adapt their writings to various audiences. Unfortunately, even those studies that do exist do not lead to consistent results.

Smith and Swan (1978) asked groups of sixth graders, college freshmen, and upperclassmen to rewrite an expository piece that had been presented to them in simple kernel sentences; they were then asked to revise it on two occasions. The first time they were asked to rewrite it to make it more comprehensible for someone their own age; on another occasion they were asked to rewrite the original piece to make it more comprehensible for someone who had just learned to read. It was found that although the college students were able to rewrite the material so that it was syntactically less complex for the child just beginning to read, the sixth-grade students were not able to do so. The researchers concluded that sixth-grade students had not yet developed the ability to adjust syntactic complexity for the audience they were addressing.

Using different topics and procedures than those used in the study summarized above, Crowhurst and Piche' (1979) also found that sixth graders failed to adjust the level of syntactic complexity of their writing depending on the audience for which they were writing, either a classmate or an adult. No significant differences were found on measures of T-units and number of words per clause. On the other hand, 10th-grade students who were also included in the study were able to adjust their writing for the two types of audiences; significant differences were found on the measures of syntactic complexity for the two pieces of writing, the one for the friend and the other for an adult. The results of their study also suggests that early adolescents do not have good skills in adjusting their writing for different audiences, but there is the suggestion that this ability may be developing during this period because it is found among 10th graders.

Bracewell, Scardamalia, and Bereiter (1978), working with students in grades 4, 8, and 12, asked subjects to describe shapes to someone younger than themselves, someone the same age, and to an adult so that the person receiving the descriptions could draw the shapes. Some simplification of directions was found at all age levels, but clear differences did not appear to exist until grade 12.

Kroll (1985) attempted to more carefully pinpoint the ages at which skill development of addressing various audiences appears by sampling the writings of students at grades 5,7,9, and 11. Subjects were first shown a 6-minute nonverbal cartoon and then were given a 310 word version of the cartoon; the written version deliberately used rather complex syntactic forms and lexical items. Students sere asked to rewrite the story so that it would be more understandable to third-grade students. The results indicated that there was a significant reduction in the

lexical complexity as reflected in a measure of the mean number of words per syllable for targeted vocabulary items and in syntactic complexity as reflected in mean number of clauses per T-unit at all grade levels.

Scardamalia, Bereiter, and McDonald (1978) taught students in grades 4,6,9, and 11 the rules for playing a relatively complex board game and then asked these students to write a description that would teach others to play the game. Their written descriptions were scored both for clarity of ideas and for number of ideas included. The researchers found a progressive, significant increase in the clarity ratings, but found that the number of ideas included increased significantly between grades 4 and 6 and then remained fairly steady for grades 6 to 9, and increased significantly again between grades 9 and 11.

The results of the limited amount of research summarized in this section permit few clear conclusions. The writing activities that subjects were asked to perform were widely different from study to study. However, there does appear to be a foundation of results that suggest even students in grades 5 and 6 can make some adjustments for audience, but that the results may depend on the dimensions used to evaluate whether the writer has made some adjustments. On the other hand, early adolescent writers seem to have substantial difficulty in revising materials in order to make them suitable for a particular audience. Even after a very comprehensive review in this area, Hillocks (1986) concludes that there are not nearly enough studies on this topic and that there are many questions that remain to be answered.

Britton, Burgess, Martin, McLeod, and Rosen (1975), in what is among the most well-known studies of writing, looked at preadolescents and adolescents and the topic of audience in a somewhat different way. There were interested in the audiences that students were most likely to address within the context of a school setting, rather than the issue of whether students are able to adjust their writing to various types of audiences. Britton et al. analyzed some 2,122 pieces of writing from a sample of 500 boys and girls ages 11 to 18 from 85 classes in 65 schools scattered throughout England. The goal was to collect six pieces of writing from each child, with two of the pieces collected in English classes and the remaining four to include one piece each from history, geography, religious education, and science.

Britton et al. (1975) used a very complex system of analysis and complex definitions for 13 different types of school audiences. The complexity of that system does not permit a full discussion of the results. However, the results suggested that there were only minor changes as children move from the beginning to the end of the preadolescent period. Major differences were found in only two categories. There was a reduction in the percentage of items that were classified as "teacher-learner dialogue" (from 51 percent to 45 percent). Writing, which falls into this category, is defined as "writing for a specifically educational adult, but as part of an ongoing interaction; and in expectation of response rather than formal evaluation." However, this trend continues so that as students reach the end of their high school careers, this category drops to only 19 percent of their writing.

As students produce fewer pieces of writing in the category

of teacher-learner dialogue, there is a concomitant increase in the percentage of pieces classified in the category pupil to examiner (from 40 percent to 45 percent). This category is defined as "writing for a specifically educational adult, as a demonstration of material mastered or as evidence of ability to take up a certain kind of style; it is a culminating point rather than a stage in a process of interaction with the expectation of assessment rather than response." The trend continues beyond the period of adolescence so that by the end of high school the percent of writings that fall into this category reaches 61.

Though the Britton study has received widespread attention, the results of the study of students writing for various audiences have limited implications given the fact that it is over a decade old, used procedures that were not clearly defined and controlled, and resulted in limited information. The major conclusion to be drawn is that preadolescent students in England in the early 1970s addressed the teacher in about 90 percent of their writings, and that there was some tendency for teachers to become increasingly evaluative as students moved through this period of time.

Spelling. Much of the research and descriptive work in the area of spelling development appears to center on younger children; for example, the ERIC/RCS REVIEW by Lehr (1986) is devoted largely to development at preschool and first-grade levels; however, there have been a few attempts to more comprehensively describe spelling development through the grades, and a sufficient body of research findings to suggest the spelling development is far from being complete by the middle grades (Anderson, 1985; Frith, 1980; Gould, 1976).

For the most part, the research and writings cited above take a developmental approach in trying to understand spelling in the middle grades. The position favored by these writers is that children's spelling development and the errors in spelling that they make are not haphazard, but reflective of systematic development that is a function of both age and experience. One of the most recent and most comprehensive discussions of spelling as a developmental process is that of Henderson and Templeton (1986). They posit the existence of five stages of spelling development, and suggest approximate times at which these stages might be reached. The general expectation is that children in grades 4 through 6 would be involved with Stage 4 level of development and that students beyond those levels would be involved with Stage 5.

As with the description of Chall's stages of development, this chapter will very quickly summarize the earlier stages of development and then describe, in slightly more detail, the stages at which middle school children would be expected to function.

Basic to the entire developmental framework of the Henderson-Templeton formulation are three fundamental "ordering" principles in the English spelling system:

1. English spelling is alphabetic. There is a more or less systematic relationships between letters and sounds within words.
2. There are within-word patterns that govern spelling. Though there are many deviations and many spellings that are unpredictable (e.g., representation of vowel sounds), there are patterns (e.g, the sequence of consonants as in a word com-

posed of a consonant, a vowel, and a consonant, as the word "cat") that help to predict the correct spelling.
3. Meaning of words is often reflected by spelling, and therefore, word meanings can be an important clue to spelling, and spelling can be a valuable clue for word meaning.

The stages of development described by Henderson and Templeton revolve around these three central concepts. Stage 1 is referred to as a "preliterate period." Although written productions of children at this stage may reflect some understandings of form and print, there is still no understanding of even the first "ordering" principle, which is a relationship between letters and sounds.

Stage 2 is the period during which there is movement into matching letters and sounds alphabetically. At this stage of development children begin to become familiar with conventional spelling forms so that they start to progress beyond attempting to represent oral words in a simple, linear fashion; they are beginning to understand that there are patterns to spelling.

At Stage 3, children move further away from the surface of speech sounds and begin to show an awareness for within-word patterns. Also at Stage 3, children begin to reflect awareness of the third ordering principle of spelling, meaning. For example, they recognize that past tense is conveyed by the inflectional ending spelled *ed* regardless of whether that ending has the sound *t* as in clapped, *d* as in wanted, or *d* as in saved.

Children enter into Stage 4 typically between the fourth and sixth grades. By Stage 3 children have good understanding of within-word patterns for single syllable words, but have difficulty with polysyllable words and are unfamiliar with the conventions that govern "syllable juncture." For example, they are unaware of the conventions that help with deciding whether syllables are doubled at the point of junture or not. From the discussion presented by Henderson and Templeton, it appears that much of the spelling difficulty and subsequent growth in Stage 4 centers around within-word patterns that affect multisyllable words.

Stage 5, typically reached in the middle to late part of the middle school years has, in this formulation, a clear focus on building an understanding of the relationship of spelling and meaning. A child who knows the meaning of the word *condemn* will be aided in inferring or recognizing the meaning of the word *condemnation* by the presence of the letter *n* in both of the words in spite of the fact that the letter *n* is silent in *condemn.* Likewise, thinking about the word *condemnation* in which the sound for the letter *n* is heard will serve to remind a student that the word *condemn* contains a silent letter. There appears to be substantial linguistic evidence and strong professional opinion, but little empirical evidence to support this stage of development (Chomsky & Hall, 1968; DiStefano & Hagerty, 1985; Anderson, 1986).

Henderson and Templeton (1986) present only a modicum of research to support their theory; however, there appears, at the same time, that there is virtually no data to challenge the basic formulations of the theory. Although Groff (1986) challenges some implications of a developmental approach for instructional practice, he does not challenge the tenants of the developmental description. Groff maintains the need for direct instruction in bringing about spelling ability in children; however, there is nothing in the Henderson-Templeton model leading to the conclusion that spelling instruction is not necessary. In fact, the 1984 Henderson and Templeton article contains many suggestions on how spelling instruction should focus on the developmental trends that children show. That article even suggests validity for the use of spelling lists. The authors, however, stress the equal importance of knowledgeable teachers dealing with the spelling responses of individual students as they write connected, meaningful productions.

Marsh, Friedman, Welch and Desberg (1980) present an alternative developmental spelling skills theory. Marsh et al. posited only three major stages of development. The first stage is when substitution strategies are used as a major approach to reading and are sometimes used in spelling as well. A substitution strategy largely involves using context/language clues to produce a word in reading, even if that word has no orthographic relationship to the word in the text. Such a strategy, analogous to Stage 1 in the Henderson and Templeton formulation, is obviously unproductive for spelling. The second shift is to the use of sequential decoding strategies to apply, first knowledge of letter sound associations to the spelling of words, and later combining such information with knowledge of conditional rules (e.g., that a single vowel between two consonants has a short vowel sound). This stage is very similar to combined Stages 2 and 3 as proposed by Henderson and Templeton.

Interestingly, from the point of view of this chapter, it is around the age of 10, fifth grade, that Marsh et al. (1980) posit a movement into the third major stage of development, the use of analogy strategies. Through a series of ingenious research studies, Marsh et al. document that at about fifth grade, children no longer rely solely on decoding strategies for spelling but begin to search for an analogue word that they already know in order to spell a word that they do not know. It is well established in the research literature that adults rely upon such a strategy. Such a strategy becomes necessary as decoding strategies become less reliable as more and more multi-syllabic words are encountered whose spellings are meaning, rather than phonemically based. Another important point make by Marsh et al. is that children are probably not able to use the analogy strategy effectively before fifth grade because they had not, until that point, built up a sufficient number of visual word forms in mental storage to use as analogues. Unfortunately, space prohibits discussion of other developmental formulations for explaining the establishment of spelling skills. For example, Ehri (1980) and Bryant and Bradley (1980) suggest somewhat different explanations than those reviewed above, but the two chosen for review here are more comprehensive in scope, and the remaining two do show substantial overlap with those reviewed here.

In this section, two fairly comprehensive formulations explaining the development of spelling skills were briefly reviewed. Although the emphases of the two formulations are different, particularly as they relate to typical children in the middle grades, there are many similarities. Both clearly suggest that middle grade students must go beyond using phonological strategies and even knowledge of conditions rules based on orthographic patterns for spelling. Henderson and Templeton stress the importance of the meaning connection among lexically related words as clues to spelling, while Marsh et al. stress analogy to orthographically similar words. Using both of these strategies does not seem at all incompatible. There is little research, however, to address the effectiveness of such approaches to improving the spelling abilities of middle grade students. (See also discussion by Hodges, chapter 36.)

CONCLUSIONS

The period of early adolescence, the period of time when a child is likely to be attending a middle school, is a very dynamic period marked by some rapid changes. Perhaps most obvious are the marked physical changes that are characteristic of this period. This is truly a time of transition as the child recognizes that the physical changes that are occurring are moving him or her toward adulthood. Thus, the physical changes bring about psychosocial changes, as for example, as the early adolescent moves increasingly to view his or her peeer group as the more important point of reference, at least for more day-to-day activities and decisions. One of the most striking points made by this review, however, particularly in the area of psychosocial development, is the challenge to some commonly held notions about early adolescence, for example, that it is necessarily a time of "stress and storm," or that it is necessarily a time when students develop differential abilities based on sex identity. Much appears to depend upon social factors such as the nature of the relationship that has existed between the early adolescent and his or her parents.

The early adoloescent is also undergoing substantial cognitive changes, which may, in fact, be influencing psychosocial and academic functioning. According to Piagetian developmental psychology, the early adolescent is moving into the period of formal operations and is becoming more and more capable of abstract thought and in working with symbol systems. It appears to be a time when there is a need for teachers to provide guidance, but also a time for teachers to set intellectual challenges before the early adolescent, who is probably able to respond at a higher, more critical level than ever before.

The research on the development of literacy skills is remarkably in line with what might be predicted from the research and theory on cognitive development. In reading, the middle school student is typically beyond needing to attend to word identification or decoding demands and can now focus on more critical and abstract aspects of reading, although the data that exist are very discouraging as to the extent to which students at this level actually do meet the higher level demands of reading. There is also incontrovertible evidence that shows among early adolescents there is an enormous range of reading abilities. Some early adolescents are still unable to deal with the most fundamental, decoding aspects of reading, while others are able to make very advanced, mature response to reading. In the area of writing and composition, it appears that overall achievement for early adolescents has been stable over the last decade, with some periods of inconsistency. As with students at other grade levels, it appears that early adolescents do reasonably well with simple writing tasks, but evidence considerable difficulty with tasks requiring higher order thinking. Early adolescene is a period when the syntactic development of composed materials shows increasing complexity; the research is less clear with respect to students' ability to adjust the nature of their writing to address different types of audiences. In short, writing skills are developing somewhat during this period of time; however, there is substantial room for improving these skills among early adolescents. Even the area of spelling, which is often seen as a more mechanical skill, shows change during the periods of early adolescence, where straightforward phonemic or orthographic responses are no longer sufficient

for dealing with longer, more complex word forms. At this stage of development, more abstract analogies need to be drawn and meanings become a clue to spelling.

The decade of the 1980s has witnessed an enormous upsurge in interest from the area of developmental psychology in the study of the early adolescent. Although there has been some parallel interest shown by those concerned about literacy development, it does not appear to be focused on this age group. Given the dynamic nature of the development of the early adolescent, it appears to be a period of time that deserves much attention by those concerned about teaching and developing language/literacy skills.

References

Adams, G. R. (1987). Reflections. *The Journal of Early Adolescence, 7,* v–vii.

Alexander, W. M., & George, P. S. (1981). *The exemplary middle school.* New York: Holt, Rinehart and Winston.

Anderson, K. F. (1986). The development of spelling ability and linguistic strategies. *The Reading Teacher, 39,* 140–147.

Applebee, A. N., Langer, J. A., & Mullis, I. V. (1988). *Who reads best? Factors related to reading achievement in grades 3, 7, and 11.* Princeton, NJ: Educational testing Service.

Bandura, A. (1964). The stormy decade: Fact or Fiction? *Psychology in the Schools, 1,* 224–231.

Bandura, A. (1969). *Principles of behavior.* New York: Holt, Rinehart and Winston.

Barritt, L. S., & Kroll, B. M. (1978). Some implications of cognitive-develop[mental psychology of r research in composing. In C. R. Cooper & L. Odell (Eds.), *Research on composing: Points of departure.* Urbana, IL: National Council of Teachers of English.

Braddock, R., Lloyd-Jones, R., & Schoer, L. (1963). *Research in written composition.* Urbana, IL: National Council of Teachers of English.

Britton, J., Burgess, T., Martin, N., McLeod, A., & Rosen, H. (1975). *The development of writing abilities* (pp. 11–18). London: Macmillan Press.

Brook, J. F., Lukoff, I. F., & Whiteman, M. (1980). Initiation into adolescent marijuana use. *Journal of Genetic Psychology, 137,* 133–142.

Brooks-Gunn, J. (1987). Pubertal processes: Their relevance for developmental research. In V. B. VanHasselt & M. Hersen (Eds.), *Handbook of adolescent psychology.* New York: Pergamon Press.

Bryant, P. E., & Bradley, L. (1980). Why children sometimes write words which they do not read. In U. Frith (Ed.), *Cognitive processes in spelling.* New York: Academic Press.

Chall, J. S. (1983). *Learning to read: The great debate.* New York: McGraw-Hill.

Chall, J. S. (1983). *Stages of Reading Development.* New York: McGraw-Hill.

Chomsky, N., & Hall, M. (1968). *The sound patterns of English.* New York: Harper and Row.

Chomsky, C. (1969). The acquisition of syntax in children from five to ten. Cambridge, MA: MIT Press.

Chumlea, W. C. (1982). Physical growth in adolescence. In B. B. Wolman (Ed.), *Handbook of Developmental Psychology.* Englewood Cliffs, NJ: Prentice-Hall.

Cooper, D. C., & Anderson-Inman, L. (1988). Language and Socialization. In M. A. DiStefano, P. P., & Hagerty, P. J. Teaching spelling at the elementary level: A realistic perspective. *The Reading Teacher, 38,* 373–377.

Crowhurst, M., & Piche', G. L. (1979). Audience and mode of discourse effects on syntactic complexity at two grade levels. *Research in the Teaching of English, 13,* 101–109.

Duffy, G. G. (Ed.). (1975). *Reading in the middle school.* Newark, DE: International Reading Association.

Dixon, E. (1970). *Indexes of syntactic maturity* The University of Chicago. (ERIC Document Reproduction Service No. ED 091748).

Dupuis, M. M. (Ed.). (1984). *Reading in the content areas: Research for teachers.* Newark, DE: International Reading Association.

Early, M. (1984). *Reading to learn in grades 5 to 12.* New York: Harcort Brace Jovanovich.

Edelsky, C. (1977). Acquisition of an aspect of communicative competence: Learning what it means to talk like a lady. In S. Ervin-Tripp & C. Mitchell-Kernan (Eds.), *Child discourse.* New York: Academic Press.

Ehri, L. C. (1980). The development of orthographic images. In U. Frith (Ed.), *Cognitive processes in spelling.* New York: Academic Press.

Elkind, D. (1967). Egocentrism in adolescence. *Childhood development, 38,* 4, 1025–1034.

Elkind, D. (1974). Cognitive structure and experience in children and adolescents. In H. D. Thornburg (Ed.), *Preadolescent Development.* Tucson, AZ: University of Arizona Press.

Elkind, D. (1978). *The child's reality: Three developmental themes.* Hillsdale, NJ: Lawrence Erlbaum.

Erickson, E. H. (1968). *Identity: Youth and crisis.* New York: Norton.

Flavell, J. H. (1963, 1985). *The developmental psychology of Jean Piaget.* New York: Van Nostrand.

Freud, A. (1969). Adolescence as a developmental disturbance. In G. Caplan & S. Lebovici (Eds.), *Adolescence.* New York: Basic Books.

Frith, U. (1980). Unexpected spelling problems. In U. Firth (Ed.), *Cognitive processes in learning to spell.* London: Academic Press.

Gallatin, J. (1980). Theories of Adolescence. In J. F. Adams (Ed.), *Understanding Adolescence.* Boston: Allyn and Bacon.

Ginsburg, M., & Opper, S. (1979). *Piaget's theory of intellectual development* (2nd ed.). Englewood Cliffs, NJ: Prentice Hall.

Gould, S. M. (1976). Spelling isn't reading backwards. *Journal of Reading, 20,* 220–225.

Graves, D. (1984). A new look at writing research. In D. Graves (Ed.), *A researcher learns to write: Selected articles and monographs.* Exeter, NH: Heinemann Books.

Groff, P. (1986). The implications of developmental spelling research: A dissenting view. *Elementary School Journal, 86,* 317–323.

Hamachek, D. E. (1980). Psychology and the development of the adolescent self. In D. F. Adams (Ed.), *Understanding Adolescence.* Boston: Allyn and Bacon.

Harris, A, J., & Sipay, E. R. (1985). *How to increase reading ability: A guide to developmental and remedial methods.* New York: Longman.

Hillocks, G. S. (1986) *Research on written composition: New directions for teaching.* Urbana, IL.: ERIC Clearninghouse on Reading and Communication Skills and the National Conference on Research in English.

Henderson, E. H., & Templeton, S. (1986). A developmental perspective of formal spelling instruction through alphabet, pattern, and meaning. *The Elementary School Journal, 86,* 305–316.

Hopkins, J. R. (1983). *Adolescence: The transition years.* New York: Academic Press.

Hudson, L., & Gray, W. M. (1986). Formal operations, the imaginary audience and the personal fable. *Adolescence, 21,* 751–765.

Hunt, K. W. (1965). *Grammatical structures written at three grade levels* (NCTE Report No. 3). Urbana, IL: National Council of Teachers of English.

Inhelder, B., & Piaget, J. (1958). *The growth of logical thinking from childhood to adolescence.* New York: Basic Books.

Jones, M. C., & Mussen, P. H. (1958). Self conceptions, motivations and interpersonal attitudes of early- and late-maturing girls. *Child Development, 29,* 491–501.

Kaufman, S. A., & Flaitz, J. (1987). Intellectual growth. In V. B. VanHasselt & M. Hersen (Eds.), *Handbook of adolescent psychology.* New York: Pergamon Press.

Kroll, B. M. (1985). Rewritten a complex story for a young reader: The development of audience-adapted writing skills. *Research in the Teaching of English, 19,* 120–139.

Lehr, F. (1986). Invented spelling and language development. *The Reading Teacher, 39,* 452–454.

Lerner, R. M., & Spanier, G. B. (1980). *Adolescent development: A life span perspective.* New York: McGraw Hill.

Lewis, J. C., & Hoover, H. D. (1987). Differential prediction of academic achievement in elementary and junior high school by sex. *Journal of Early Adolescence, 7,* 107–116.

Lipsitz, J. (1977). *Growing up forgotten.* Lexington, MA: D. C. Heath.

Marsh, G., Friedman, M., Desberg, P., & Welsh, V. (1980). In U. Frith (Ed.), *Cognitive processes in learning to spell.* London: Academic Press.

Martin, D. J., & Hoover, H. D. (1987). Sex differences in educational achievement: A longitudinal study. *Journal of Early Adolescence, 7,* 65–84.

McKinney, J. P., & Vogel, J. (1987). Developmental theories. In V. B. VanHasselt & M. Hersen (Eds.), *Handbook of adolescent psychology.* New York: Pergamon Press.

McMahon, M. P. (1974). Intellectual capabilities of the preadolescent. In H. D. Thornburg (Ed.), *Preadolescent development.* Tucson, AZ: University of Arizona Press.

Meredith, H. V. (1974). A synopsis of pubertal; changes in youth. In H. D. Thornburg (Ed.), *Preadolescent development.* Tucson, AZ: University of Arizona Press.

Miller, G. A. & Gildea, P. M. (1987). How children learn words, *Scientific American, 257,* 94–99.

Moss, T. C. (1969). *Middle school.* Boston: Houghton Mifflin.

Nippold, M. A. (1988). The literate lexicon. In M. A. Nippold (Ed.), *Later language development.* Boston: Little, Brown and Company.

Nippold, M. A. (Ed.) (1988) *Later language development.* Boston: Little, Brown and Company.

Obler, L. K. (1988). Language beyond childhood. In J. B. Gleason (Ed.), *The development of language* (2nd Ed.). Columbus, OH: Merrill.

Phillips, T. (1985). Beyond lip-service: Discourse development beyond the age of nine. In G. Wells & J. Nicholls (Eds.), *Language and learning: An interactive perspective* (pp. 59–82). Philadelphia: The Falmer Press.

Piaget, J. (1955). *The language and thought of the child* (M. Gabain, Trans,). New York: New American Library. (Original work published 1926)

Redl, F. (1943). Preadolescents—What makes them tick? *Child Study, 19,* 44–48.

Reed, V. A. (1986). Language-disordered adolescents. In V. A. Reed (Ed.), *An introduction to children with language disorders (pp. 228-249).* New York: MacMillan.

Richards, M., & Peterson, A. C. (1987). Biological theoretical models of adolescent development. In V. B. VanHasselt & M. Hersen (Eds.), *Handbook of adolescent psychology.* New York: Pergamon Press.

Sabers, D. Cushing, K., & Sabers, D. (1987). Sex differences in reading and mathematics for middle school children. *Journal of Early Adolescence, 7,* 117–128.

Sebald, H., & White, B. (1980). Teenagers' divided reference groups: Uneven alignment with parents and peers. *Adolescence, 15,* 979–984.

Signorielli, N. (1987). Children and adolescents on television: A consistent pattern of devaluation. *Journal of Early Adolescence, 7,* 255–278.

Singer, D. G., & Singer, J. L. (1987). Practical suggestions for controlling television. *Journal of Early Adolescence, 7,* 365–369.

Sisson, L. A., Hersen, M., & Van Hasselt, V. B. (1987). Historical perspectives. In V. B. Van Hasselt & M. Hersen (Eds.), *Handbook of adolescent psychology.* New York: Pergamon Press.

Smith, R. J., & Barrett, T. C. (1974). *Teaching reading in the middle grades.* Reading, MA: Addison Wesley.

Smith, W. L., & Swan, M. B. (1978). Adjusting syntactic structures to varied levels of audience. *Journal of Experimental Education, 46,* 29–34.

Tanner, J. M. (1971). *Growth in adolescence.* Oxford: Blackwell Scientific Publications.

Thornburg, H. D. (Ed.). (1974). *Preadolescent Development.* Tucson, AZ: University of Arizona Press.

Thornburg, H. D. (1983). Is early adolescence really a stage of development? *Theory into Practice, 22,* 79–83.

Tobin, A. W., & Pikulski, J. J. (1988). A longitudinal study of the reading achievement of early and non-early readers through sixth grade. In J. E. Readence & R. S. Baldwin (Eds.), *Dialogues in literacy research: Thirty-seventh yearbook of the National Reading Conference.* Chicago, IL: National Reading Conference.

Van Hasselt, V. B., & Hersen, M. (Eds.). (1987). *Handbook of adolescent psychology.* New York: Pergamon Press.

Viser, D. (1987). The relationship of parental attitudes and expectations to children's mathematics achievement and behavior. *Journal of Early Adolescence, 7,* 1–12.

Warren-Leubecker, A. and Bohannon, J. N. (1988). Pragmatics: Language in social contexts. In J. B. Gleason (Ed.), *The development of language* (2nd Ed.). Columbus, OH: Merrill

Weintraub, S. (1988). On reviewing instructional research. In S. Weintraub (Ed.), *Annual summary of investigations related to reading July, 1986 to June 30, 1987* (pp. v–vi). Newark, DE: International Reading Association.

Williams, J. D., & Kerr, P. D. (1987). Changes in sex differences in Scottish examination results since 1976. *Journal of Early Adolescence, 7,* 85–106.

Wrobelski, R., & Huston, A. C. (1987). Televised occupational stereotypes and their effects on early adolescents: Are they changing? *Journal of Early Adolescence, 7,* 283–298.

19D. THE JUNIOR HIGH SCHOOL YEARS

John S. Simmons

As the twenty-first century approaches, the presence of the junior high school per se has diminished significantly throughout the United States. In most cases, it has been replaced by the middle school, generally moving the student population from a grade 7, 8, 9 framework to a 6, 7, 8 configuration. The reasons for this shift have been both demographic-political and philosophical. Throughout the country, the wholesale integration of public schools, beginning roughly in the mid-1960s, has caused some school buildings to be dangerously overcrowded, while others have been vacated. In general, it has proven easier for large numbers of school districts to add the ninth grade population to their senior high school buildings and accommodate grades 6, 7, and 8 in facilities originally contructed as junior highs. The integration of minority children in the elementary schools, coupled with the accretion of kindergarten as a mandatory school year during the past half century, has also led these districts to move their sixth-grade populations into the middle school in order to ease widespread overcrowding.

Much of the above adjustment has come about because of practical necessity. The philosophical rationale is considerably more complex and, in many cases, an equivocal mask for the political motivation that was at the core of the change. A number of published school supporters advance the belief that the curriculum be student rather than content centered. It is their conviction that courses of study be designed around principles of (early) adolescent growth and development rather than around learning hierarchies related to the traditional areas of subject matter study. They cite the early adolescent's lack of intellectual, cultural, and social maturity as significant factors in transforming the curriculum into one whose primary emphasis is on the development of the "whole student," in the students' physical, emotional, and social maturation, rather than providing a curriculum that presents an externally imposed set of academic goals. (Atwell, 1987; Lipsitz, 1984) Very recently, however, there are signs that the trend may be reversing somewhat. The Houston public school system, for example, is currently moving the sixth grade back into the K–6 structure. Only time will tell whether this represents a trend.

Many secondary teacher educators, educational sociologists, and classroom teachers would argue that the reorganization of the junior high school into a 6, 7, 8 alignment has, in fact, done little to alter the actual curricular offerings of those schools. They would argue that the inclusion of grade 6 and the lopping off of grade 9 has simply transformed the traditional English, social studies, science, math bill-of-fare into one that sixth graders encounter a year earlier than their scholastic predecessors. They contend further that the same extracurricular activities offered in junior high programs, especially interscholastic athletics, remain substantially present in the middle schools. Thus, they conclude, the movement from junior high to middle school, in the curricular sense, is largely cosmetic.

Having thus noted this current state of early adolescent confusion, the writer will proceed in a description of the "old" junior high school alignment as it reflects the current English language-arts course of study, alluding here and there to ways that middle school theory has made inroads into that course of study, as well as describing ways that the political mood of the country has had its effect on what the early adolescent now receives in the way of E.L.A. instruction.

The incorporation of reading instruction into junior high English language-arts curricula may well be as good a place to begin this review as any. For a long time, it had been known that not much instruction in reading was going on beyond the elementary grade levels. In the 1940s, when the junior high school became a fact of life, many reading authorities voiced great concern about the fact that, in moving from a 1–8 to a 6–3–3 configuration, most schools were in effect doing away with two years of developmental and corrective reading instruction. (Bond & Wagner, 1966) The reasoning they offered for this contention was that the grades 1–8 schools were staffed with elementary school teachers who were trained to teach reading. The junior highs were staffed with secondary-school-trained teachers whose focus had been on academic English rather than on teaching the skills of communication.

That little reading instruction was being incorporated into junior high English language-arts curricula has been well corroborated over the past 40 years. Margaret Early's classic study on reading in the New York (state) junior high schools can serve as an excellent example of this curricular oversight. She found that fewer than one fourth of the junior high schools in that state were providing reading programs led by a trained reading teacher, and that the ninth grade reading test scores of those schools that had employed a reading teacher were no better than those of students in schools where no such teacher had been hired (1957).

Concern with the lack of organized reading instruction in the junior high years was exacerbated by the school integration movement that began with the 1954 landmark Supreme Court decision, Brown v. Kansas. As the heretofore segregated school systems of first the deep South, and later the cities of the Northeast and industrial Midwest, began opening their doors to African American students, it became quickly evident that these newly integrated youngsters were weak in many academic abilities and that low reading ability was indicative of their limitations. During this period of school population upheaval, African American students were entering previously all-white schools with appallingly low reading test scores often clustered around grades 1–3. (Shugrue, 1968) In the desire of the Kennedy-Johnson administrations to solve problems, such federally sponsored programs as Title (now Chapter) I, Title III, and the NDEA summer reading institutes were created to train teachers of reading at all levels; to provide basic skills instruction to students at all levels; and to fund the purchase of reading instructional materials at all levels. A lot of money went into these efforts, but because of the hasty, precipitous nature of the overall effort, a disappointingly large number of school systems received little or no real assistance with their problem. Prominent among these disappointed schools were junior highs. In fact, few secondary teachers were trained in any of the federally sponsored programs, few effective remedial components were added, and a relatively miniscule amount of truly helpful instructional materials was added to those in use at the junior high level (Martin, 1967). Overlooked by most of the "all-school reading instruction training programs" was the need for the inclusion of all-content area teachers in such staff development, as cited by Loren Grissom in an early but significant study of secondary school reading instruction programs (1961).

With the passing of the Great Society and the onset of the behaviorist spirit of the Nixon administration, reading, as a national educational concern, soon took center stage. The watchword of that era was *accountability,* and the behavioral psychologists who now occupied the seats of power in the United States Office of Education wanted to see results, a code word for test scores. Reading was an area that they felt to be highly testable, and since literacy was a vital factor in academic success, the teaching of reading gained in stature in the junior high curricula of the 1970s. One of the few educational programs actually funded during the Nixon-Ford years was the Right To Read Program. Through it, a great many state and local in-service workshops were held for teachers, although the great majority of attendees were from elementary ranks, teachers whose undergraduate training had been inadequate.

The Right To Read Program, however, affected junior high curricula to a significant degree. Its main impact was causing many English language-arts courses of study to be taken over by reading. In other words, in some schools, English became reading at the junior high level. Highly systematized, workbook-oriented courses of study supplanted those that had previously included literature study, some linguistics, oral activity, and written composition. This narrow reading approach was flourishing in the junior high schools at the very time when the psycholinguistic work of Frank Smith and Kenneth Goodman was beginning to gain nationwide scholarly esteem. (Smith & Goodman, 1976; Smith, 1986) One major thrust of this scholarship was to debunk the rigid, prescriptive, memorization-focused reading instruction being foisted on junior high school students and their teachers, many of whom were totally untrained in reading. Because their approach was significantly different from the traditional basal reader program, their highly logical linguistically based approaches were used in few schoolwide reading curricula.

Narrow, prescriptive reading instruction in the junior high schools were given considerable impetus with the advent of statewide testing in the latter part of the 1970s. Influenced by the National Assessment of Educational Progress (N.A.E.P.) testing efforts of the previous decade (Mellon, 1975), it was first introduced to Florida in the 1976 Accountability Act of the state legislature. (Turlington & Williams, 1975) In the fall of 1977, it was put into operation through tests in reading, "writing," (in the sense of multiple-choice items on mechanics and spelling), and mathematics at grades 3, 5, 8, and 11, with a Functional Literacy Test provided in grade 11 as well. This set of "basic skills" tests provided the model for systems that quickly went into operation across the nation. In a frighteningly large number of school districts, the testing mechanism became the great motivator for curricular change; teaching for the test was the obvious modus operandi for junior high school English teachers well into the 1980s.

The results of the Florida Functional Literacy Test did provide one useful set of data that thoughtful English teachers have heeded in secondary schools throughout the Sunshine State and far beyond. The data revealed that students in secondary schools were significantly deficient in the following four areas of reading:

1. To infer an idea from a selection
2. To infer a cause or effect of an action
3. To distinguish between fact and opinon
4. To identify an unstated opinion (*Guide to Statewide Assessment,* 1987)

These reading activities all can be placed under the rubric of critical reading. At this writing, 12 years of testing in Florida have consistently reflected the same weaknesses. Thus, junior high English courses of study have become motivated to include critical reading activity, and this movement has given rise to a discernible increase in literature study at grades 7, 8, and 9—literature being perceived as a most appropriate vehicle for critical reading instruction.

Probably the most significant document of the 1980s, as a stimulus for change in junior high reading instruction, was the 1983 publication of the results of the Gardner Commission study, titled A Nation at Risk. This now celebrated tract led many junior high English programs to abandon basic skills reading workbooks, to opt for more literature study, and to accelerate the increase in critical reading instruction. The academic English models, exemplified by many of the Project English Curriculum Study Centers of the 1960s, were now coming back into vogue. This academically oriented reading renaissance has been given further impetus by the publication of *Cultural Literacy* by Professor E. D. Hirsch (University of Virginia) in 1983 and its revelations concerning the considerable ignorance of their cultural history evidenced by the sample of America's young people tested by Professor Hirsch. As the 1990s approach, there is evidence that another series of statewide tests is on the way, this time focusing on cultural rather than functional literacy. Such a testing program is bound to have a salutary effect on reading instruction in junior high English classes.

LITERATURE

The study of literature in the junior high schools in the United States has seen some significant changes take place—and some serious controversies arise—over the half century. As the junior high curricula have evolved, the centrality of content area study was strengthened; i.e., the subject matter traditionally offered at the senior high school level was extended down into the junior high grades. This was easy to accomplish in most content areas; e.g. history, geography, mathematics, earth sciences, grammar. All of these areas of study were introduced in earlier grades (usually by fourth grade), and their introduction was almost invariably conducted in a tone of high seriousness. To the students who would wrestle with them they were posed as hard subjects, ones that one must approach with concentration and a spirit of solemnity. The one subject that didn't fit this mold was literature.

As customarily introduced in the early grades, literature was seen to be an enjoyable change of pace from the grind of arithmetic, spelling, reading drills, and so on, as was singing (music) and drawing (art). While the two latter areas had usually been relegated to electives roles by the junior high years, literature remained as part of English, one of the Big Four (or in some places where foreign languages were introduced early, the Big Five). Thus, as part of the required junior high academic regimen, the perception of literature as a curricular entity had to undergo a transition in the minds of students as well as uprooted elementary teachers. Once an enjoyable change-of-pace activity, literature now became serious business, to be approached as would a series of math problems or a scientific hypothesis. To add to this drastic change in tone, most teachers urged their students to retain their enjoyment and appreciation of works that they must now look at only with steely eyes. Too many teachers were insensitive to the intellectual schizophrenia that their expectations were causing in their still relatively immature students (Simmons, 1989).

Literature remains the only usually required curricular commodity for which the perspective must change from reading/enjoying to studying. And, to those who sensed this need, the junior high years provided the framework in which the transition had to take place. If students were to be adequately prepared for the rigors of British, American, and World Literature that would be served up to them in the senior high school English course of study, they had to begin viewing literary works as vehicles for serious reflections and oral/written reactions during grades 7, 8, and 9. How to accomplish this goal was an issue that came to the surface in curricular debate soon after junior high schools became the way of the world about 50 years ago. As this review is written, the battle continues to rage in many places, and with renewed vigor.

The earlier thinking on how to effect the philosophical transition among early adolescents described above was through a steady diet of classics and book report assignments. Supporters of the classics approach were pretty sure that they knew what those classics were. They developed long lists of such works as they believed to purvey significant cultural messages, lists heavily weighted with novels, narrative and lyric poems, and essays by writers of earlier times. (Not too much drama, if any.) An emphasis could be found on works by Victorian British authors and genteel American poets (Longfellow, Holmes, Lowell, Whittier). These landmark literary selections could provide for the introduction to serious study because they contained, in symbolic fashion, some of the great precepts of the Protestant Ethic.

The problem was that these selections made for terribly dull reading; they were bloated and stylistically convoluted. To cope with this burdensome reading, responsible students slogged stoically through the text while others found *Classic Comics, Masterplots, Cliff Notes,* book jacket summaries, and other opportunistic dodges. When response was demanded, book reports, assigned regularly and almost invariably written outside of class, became the usual means of analytic, interpretive response. Seldom were these report tasks placed in any meaning-

ful or imaginative context. ("For your third assignment, write a 250–500 word report on …") The products were seldom placed within the framework of the writing process, and the use of the speaking voice approach to develop them was unheard of. In the latter approach, instruction is given in the presence of three basic components: the identity of speaker, audience, and treatment of content in any composed statement. These components are commonly referred to as *voice, tone,* and *attitude* by most rhetoricians. Composition authority Bruce Lockerbie suggests that these elements be clearly identifiable in all writing assignments presented to young people (1963). The sharing of responses, both intellectual and emotional, did not happen very often in the junior high classroom. The procedure of read, write, get your grade, and read some more became a common sequence of events as students ploughed through their initiation into the world of serious literary study.

But back to the literature itself. During the decades of the 1940s, 1950s, and 1960s, a relatively new genre began to emerge in book stores, on school library shelves, and eventually in some junior high classrooms: that of the young adult novel. The content of the classics had been consistently criticized as having little or nothing to do with the real world of contemporary American adolescent experience by such developmental psychologists as Robert Havighurst (1948) and such pioneer English educators as Dora V. Smith (1950) and Lou La Brant (1951). The Young Adult (YA) novel, emerging from the Horatio Alger/*Little Women, Little Men* traditions of an earlier phase of the twentieth century (Zane Grey, Grace Livingston Luce Hill, Louisa May Alcott, Edgar Rice Burroughs, Helen Doyle Boylston, et al.) was being written about adolescent experience with which junior high students could emphathize. Such authors as Marjorie Kinnan Rawlings, Fred Gipson, Paul Annixter, John R. Tunis, and Esther Forbes began producing works whose subject matter related closely to the world of young readers. The rise in popularity of cheap paperback editions of all manner of reading material coincided nicely with the emergence.

By the late 1950s, Young Adult fiction had been established as a genre worthy of scholarly investigation. Dunning's 1958 study of popular YA novels provided a structural and thematic analysis of widely read contemporary works. Dwight Burton's text *Literature Study in the High Schools* (1960) included an extended review of the nature of such fiction. Dorothy Petitt concluded an impressive study in 1960 on the well-written novel for adolescents; she linked scholarly treatises on long fiction to the widely read YA novels of that day. Courses in YA fiction began to appear in English Education programs throughout the nation; and the *English Journal,* under Burton's editorship, added a regular feature column titled "Junior Book Roundup."

Although this literary addition has proven a godsend to junior high English teachers who would assist their students through the transition described earlier, it has not been without its critics. One of the deliberate characteristics of this genre has been that it is easy to read. Dunning found that the YA novel of the late 1950s was about 60 percent as long as its "adult" counterpart (about 150–200 pages), which persists today. He also found such stylistic conventions as one, third person narrator; a plot relatively free of flashbacks, interior monologue, subplots, and stream-of-consciousness; an easily identifiable protagonist and confict, and others. To some critics of softness in modern education, those characteristics condemned YA fiction; pejorative labels such as unsophisticated, simplistic, trivial, and episodic were applied. To these critics, the YA novels lacked the richness of the classics and therefore were unworthy of consideration for use in classrooms. One of the first such attackers was the Council for Basic Education, a group that denounced YA literature as one more example of the disastrous Deweyan Revolution they claimed to be going on in the schools. (Lynch & Evans, 1963) Another critic, Frank Jennings, chose the *English Journal* for publication in 1954 of a now-famous denunciation of all YA novels. About ten years later, the recently formed Commission on English or the College Entrance Examination Board, in a major text titled *Freedom and Discipline in English,* raised serious questions about the legitimacy of what they labeled as "junior books" in the fostering of bona fide literary study in secondary schools (1965). Such opposition to the in-class use of YA novels has persisted into the present day, as will be noted later in this discussion.

Despite this ongoing opposition to its use in the junior high classroom, the genre gained in popularity and literary status during the decade of the 1960s. Late in that decade, however, it took a turn thematically that was to cause teachers who used it for all-class study no end of difficulty. Dunning had labelled the YA novel as "consistently wholesome and insistently didactic." Petitt had found it to be largely free of taboos. More recent YA novelists, however, have chosen to deal with subject matter that some parents and other citizens find objectionable, a trend which probably began in 1967–68 with the publication of S. E. Hinton's *The Outsiders,* Robert Lipsyte's *The Contender,* and Paul Zindel's *The Pigman.* Those books deal, to one degree or another, with gang violence, racial hatred, teenage alcohol and drug use, explicit sex, and negative adult stereotypes. In the decade of the 1970s, there followed an avalanche of well written YA novels based on contemporary social problems that most English Educators applauded as providing literary realism but which a growing segment of increasingly vocal fundamentalist-conservative adults deemed unfit for classroom or library. Muller's 1973 doctoral study, essentially a replication of Petitt's analysis of well written YA novels, took note of this change in theme and tone. This new direction is also discussed in Burton's third edition of *Literature Study in the High Schools* (1975), and more recently in Donelson and Nilsen's first and second editions of *Literature for Today's Young Adults* (1980, 1985). Recent attacks on contemporary YA writers such as Robert Cormier, Judy Blume, Norma Mazer Fox, and Robin Brancato have been made by Jerry Falwell's Moral Majority, Phyllis Schlafly's Eagle Forum, Pat Robertson, Tim La Haye, and other fundamentalist zealots. In the 1980s, the American Library Association and People for the American Way have reported a dramatic increase in school censorship cases. As the report is written, the YA novel continues to face strident criticism coast to coast.

A totally different problem facing junior high teachers of literature has been the continuing paucity of worthwhile literary materials other than the novels just described. Many must fall back on standard anthologies that, as a result of textbook publishers' weak-kneed reaction to reactionary pressures, have become increasingly bland and trivialized. There is no great fund of Young Adult short fiction to be found, and almost no quality drama within the intellectual and emotional range of early adolescents. In 1966, Dunning, Lueders and Smith produced an anthology of largely modern poetry, *Reflections on a Gift of Watermelon Pickle and Other Modern Verse,* which became immediately popular with a large number of English teachers. These same authors followed it up in 1969 with a somewhat more abstruse and less popular collection titled *Some Haystacks Don't Even Have Any Needles.* Both anthologies are still in print, and in use, today. They were not, sad to say, followed by a series of useful poetry volumes.

During the Project English days of the 1960s, several curriculum study centers produced literature instructional units that focused on mythology (classical and other), American folk lore, legends, and, to a lesser degree, Biblical narrative. The 1970s saw a movement away from such materials toward (as previously noted) selections representing the contemporary, the controversial, and the realistic in thematic concentration. Now, in the era of "quality" emphasis, following the publication of *A Nation at Risk* and *Cultural Literacy,* there is evidence of a resurgence of interest in the publication and teaching of such culturally stimulating materials. (See, for example, the 1989. edition of the *Adventures* series published by Harcourt, Brace, Jovanovich.)

For junior high students at the lower end of the academic spectrum, there continues to be a dearth of worthwhile materials. Scholastic Magazines has made a valiant effort with its monthly publication of *Voice* magazine, but much of the literature provided therein is trendy and superficial. Globe Books has recently published a series of literary anthologies that largely consists of simplistic selections, many of which have been rewritten or, in the argot of publishers, "dumbed down" (Potter & McCummery, 1987). There are various and sundry collections around today, but the problem of finding worthwhile textual materials that can be effectively used by junior high teachers to assist in guiding their student through the transition described earlier remains a formidable one.

In the area of teaching strategies, the last few years have seen a significant increase in interest in reader response, a movement that has had an impact across the entire curricular spectrum. The great revival of interest in Louise Rosenblatt's *Literature as Exploration,* (1968) first published in 1938, symbolizes the rapidly growing appeal of reader response activity in the classroom. Rosenblatt's more recent text, *The Reader, the Text and the Poem* (1978), has given even more impetus to the movement, and Robert Probst's *Adolescent Literature* (1984) continues to provide sound pedagogical advice to teachers who wish to involve their students in literary response transactions. Such strategies have inspired teachers at the junior high level to lead their students into far more vital and diverse interactions with literary works than did their predecessors in earlier decades. As a further comprehensive and ongoing teacher resource, the National Council of Teachers of English has, since 1978, published the periodical *ALAN Review* (Assembly on Literature for Adolescents, National), a journal that continues to offer philosophical overviews, instructional frameworks, YA novel analyses, author interviews, and a wealth of other pertinent contributions. Its contents are most frequently directed toward junior high school teachers of English, and its potential benefits for them are manifold.

Thus the literature landscape for junior high school at the beginning of the 90s is a kind of crazy quilt of trial and error, movement and reaction. While the censorship issue will continue its ominous influence on what teachers can and will introduce, the quality of YA novels, the return of usable background material in mythology, and so forth, the continuing search for appropriate transitional literary selections, and the reader response impact are all causes for cautious optimism. Given a few breaks, a brighter day may be in the offing.

WRITING

It is in written composition that the teaching of English in junior high schools has made its greatest strides. In the early (1940s) days of this scholastic unit, "real" composition instruction was almost totally absent. Drills and skills centered around isolated elements of language structure were the rule of the day. Literature instruction, as described earlier in this discussion, was both restricted and stultified, but there was, at least something going on. Extended encounters with spelling lists, often culminated by oral contests, were found to be in widespread use. And, in some "progressively" oriented districts, a loosely organized core curriculum in English featured a potpourri of sophomoric language activities, group projects, reviews of current events, life management skills, considerations of community activities, and so on, all in the name of language development. Largely invisible in all of this was any semblance of effective, systematic, research-based instruction in writing.

As the decade of the 1950s progressed, another fact of life contributed to the exclusion of writing instruction in junior highs: that of dramatically rising school populations. By the second half of that decade, the "war babies" began to enter the seventh grade across the country. By the early 1960s, they were filling the junior high schools beyond their reasonable capacities—and this with school integration (described earlier) just over the next hill. As has been the custom throughout this century, English was a required subject at all three levels. Thus, the English classes were always the largest ones in grades 7, 8, and 9. It was not uncommon to find English teachers burdened with five classes of 40 (or more) students each, for a load of 200 + per day. Just counting their noses required great effort, let alone have them write anything during the class period. Thus the penchant for workbook activities, oral spelling workouts, and objective testing instruments became a means of survival for these beleaguered teachers, whose classes were frequently also being used for distributing administrative dicta, guidance department events, community promotions, ad nauseam. Junior high English teachers had to guard their overall teaching time for the subject itself, and the spectre of mounds of compositions waiting for them on Friday afternoons led the great majority to reiterate the refrain from Herman Melville's famous short novel, *Bartleby, the Scrivener:* "I would prefer not."

The two activities that most of these teachers offered as their writing programs consisted mainly of assigning book reports, and the provision of lengthly sessions with a text on grammar, usage, and mechanics (capitalization, punctuation, and spelling). The book report penchant has already been described. To many teachers, it represented a nice blending of instruction in literature and composition, though, in fact, the mere assignment of the task provided neither. By assigning an annual series of book reports, grading, then returning them, teachers were really testing what they hadn't taught, although most, in refusing to admit this fact, felt vindicated by their willingness to wade through the huge paper load that resulted from each assignment.

The "grammar matter" is and has been a far more enigmatic one in the teaching of secondary school English. Consideration of it in relation to instruction in writing will be brief, in that the issues of grammar teaching must be revisited as part of the discussion of language study in junior high schools. For starters, English Educators have had to cope with the belief among classroom teachers that intensive grammar study increases students' capacity to compose in writing as long as someone has been keeping score. The fact that a plethora of research evidence dating at least as far back in English education as the year 1903 (Rice) seems to have had absolutely no effect on the belief among a very large cadre of junior high English teachers that this transfer does not and never has taken place. To review even a representative sample of this twentieth century research making the case against any positive impact of grammar study on writing improvement does not seem to be a worthy use of time and space in this chapter. Suffice it to say, at least for the moment, that this lack of transfer represent most consistent finding in all the research compiled in the teaching of secondary English over the past 85 years. Still, teachers deny, often indignantly, its validity. And this rejection of empirical data exists today. Hartwell's 1985 review of recent research on the transfer issues includes a summary of recent instances in which it (the data) has been ignored and even vilified by classroom teachers and college English authorities alike. As this chapter is being written, the phoenix continues to rise from the ashes.

During the 1960s, a grammatical system that some educators believed might someday compete with or even replace traditional, Latinate grammar made its presence felt. A transformational generative grammar (T-G) introduced by Noam Chomsky in his 1957 text *Syntactic Structures* began to find its way into English education research designs and school textbooks in the early years of the very next decade. In 1964, Donald Bateman and Frank Zidonis first published the results of an experimental study done with 10th-grade English students at Ohio State University; in this study, a group that had been given instruction in T-G grammar wrote slightly better post-test themes than did a group which had received no T-G grammar instruction (1966). Two years later, John Mellon reported similar results with a group of 10th graders he had treated with T-G grammar instruction at Harvard University. (Mellon rather casually added that he had included some sentence games with the instruction given to his experimental group—a fact that will be considered shortly.)

As this research was going on, Paul Roberts, a well known linguist at that time, published first *English Sentences* (1961) and then English Syntax (1964). Both of these books were aimed at school audiences and purported to present T-G grammar to young people in a comprehensible manner. Soon after completing these publications, he was commissioned by Harcourt, Brace, Jovanovich, Inc. to begin work on a language-based textbook series for students grades 3–12. Roberts' tragic accidental death in 1967 saw the premature end of this undertaking. Books for grades 11 and 12 were never completed, and the series, although enjoying an enormous nationwide initial sale, was never revised and quickly went out of use.

The great hope raised through all this research and development was that a grammar had finally been found which actually could improve student writing. Most junior high teachers, when asked first to learn the complex, formulaic system, were in general agreement that it would not fulfill this goal. By the middle of the 1970s, most attempts at teaching T-G grammar in any school system had been pretty well abandoned. A by-product of this renowned endeavor, however, has made a lasting impact on writing instruction at all curricular levels. It has been mentioned that Mellon included some sentence games in his study. This did not escape the attention of Frank O'Hare, a doctoral student at Florida State University in 1967. In 1971, O'Hare completed an experimental study with 7th graders in which the sentences games, now called Sentence Combining (S-C), were proven to affect both the syntactic maturity and overall quality of writing of these students.

The dramatic research results from O'Hare's study gave impetus to the widespread publication of S-C school texts as well as further research by Combs (1975), Stotsky (1975), Straw (1975), Sullivan (1977) and many others attempting to link S-C techniques with various aspects of language development, primarily writing, and largely with students at elementary, middle, and junior high levels. Concurrently, the practice of S-C activity became quickly popular among junior high teachers everywhere. It continues to occupy substantial class time today and is seen by not a few English Educators as an antidote, if not a replacement for, the grammar-as-writing instructional approach that had so dominated junior high English curricula virtually from their beginnings. While much research completed subsequent to the O'Hare study has not corroborated his finding that S-C did have a positive effect on overall quality of writing, it has demonstrated consistently that the technique does cause substantial improvement in the syntactic maturity of early adolescents.

Although some may argue otherwise, this writer believes that the "Great Writing Era" in which English teachers, and indeed teachers in other subject matter areas now find themselves began with the publication of a cover story titled "Why Johnny Can't Write" appearing in the December 8, 1975, issue of *Newsweek* magazine. Using data from the 1972 NAEP results and a series of annual Scholastic Aptitude Test (SAT) scores, the article delivered a scathing attack on U.S. teachers at all levels for their alleged unwillingness to teach, assign, and evaluate writing, as well as a denunciation of the approaches used by those teachers who made some effort to do so. Stimulated by the expressed concern of large numbers of citizens, states and school districts throughout the country began to focus on writing instruction as a high curricular priority.

The timing of this new effort was fortuitous. Five years before the publication of the *Newsweek* article, a number of U.S. English scholars, educators, and supervisors had attended the second Anglo-American seminar on the teaching of English in York, England. While, on the whole, this seminar received far less publicity than the first one (held at Dartmouth College in Hanover, New Hampshire in August, 1966), a highly instructive curricular concept was provided the Americans by British educators present. One of the titles used to describe it was Writing Across the Curriculum. This effort featured frequent, intensive writing activity to be implemented at all grade levels and in all subject matter areas. Writing, then, became the province—and responsibility—of all teachers. No longer did junior or senior high school teachers have to assume that it was their responsibility to introduce the teaching of written composition to their students; it would already have been done, and in a fairly extensive manner during the earlier grades. Moreover, in this approach, it was no longer left solely to English teachers to shoulder the burden of writing instruction; their counterparts in all subject matter areas became engaged in the teaching, assigning, and evaluation of writing within the courses of study for their students as well. In the ensuing months and years, Writing Across the Curriculum was raised as an innovative curricular possibility at state and national education conferences and was described in a variety of professional publications. Now, in the aftermath of the *Newsweek* bombshell, some curricular leaders saw their chance to try it.

At the same time, sentence combining was being used widely in junior high classrooms, replacing some of the grammar study, as previously noted. And, in the summer of 1975, a group of teachers from several grade levels and several subject matter areas, all from schools in the greater San Francisco area, were invited to attend a summer workshop in the processes and teaching of writing. This workshop took place at the University of California, Berkeley. It was directed by James Gray, a member of the University of California, Berkeley English department and came to be known as the Bay Area Writing Project. A number of junior high school teachers, in English and other subject matter areas, attended.

When compared to the massive federal funding that underwrote the National Defense Education Act (NDEA) institutes of the 1960s, the Bay Area Writing Project (BAWP), which quickly burgeoned into the National Writing Project (NWP), was run on a shoestring. Existing on small grants from participating school districts and in-kind contributions from the University, it met modest expenses and paid the teacher-enrollees the handsome stipend of $500 (no travel or per diem). The initial success of BAWP inspired consortia of school districts in other parts of the country to buy in, and soon the National Writing Project headquarters, under Gray's direction, was founded at Berkeley, gaining further funding support from the California State Department of Education and the National Endowment for the Humanities.

In 1990, as the NWP heads into its 15th year of summer institutes, some 169 of these (usually) four-week sessions will be held. Because no large sums of federal or private philanthropic funds have ever been added to the movement (projects exist almost exclusively on local contributions), the NWP continues to represent a phenomenally popular, successful venture in staff development. Its operation is based on four fundamental assumptions that date back to the original BAWP undertaking:

1. Curriculum change cannot be accomplished by transient consultants who briefly appear, never to be seen again, or by change agents who insist that everyone see the problem in the same way.
2. A substantial body of knowledge exists concerning the teaching of writing, much of which is fairly new.
3. Curriculum change cannot be accomplished with a packet of teacher-proof materials.
4. Field-based research can make a significant contribution to the improvement of instruction. (Gray & Myers, 1978)

When seen in current NWP institute guidelines, these assumptions take the following shape:

1. To teach writing effectively, teachers must write themselves in a variety of modes and with frequency.
2. Teachers can teach each other. There is a wealth of effective, practical pedagogy to be shared.
3. All writers need audiences. Thus much of what is written in the institute is shared, responded to, revised.
4. Teachers who participate in the summer program then become in-service educators. This is a commitment each of them must make at the outset.

On a nationwide basis, the majority of participants have come from the elementary, middle, and junior high grade levels, thus promoting the belief of many writing authorities that instruction in written composition must begin early in the curriculum and continue as a developmental process all the way through grade 12. In this continuum, the junior high teachers, in all subject matter areas, play the vital role of assisting their students in adapting their writing techniques to the academic demands of the several courses of study they will encounter.

A concept that has grown in status and teacher appeal and has become one of the main areas of study and application in NWP institutes is the writing process. The fundamental belief that the process of writing needs to be taught deliberately, systematically, and extensively in the classroom has deeply affected writing instruction at all levels during the decade of the 1980s. Whether its stages are identified as prewriting, drafting, sharing, revising, and editing (one common model) or by another set of labels, is not terribly important. The fact is this new concentration on how a piece of writing evolves has made significant changes in what goes on in English classes, junior high and other, when composition is the focal point. First and foremost, actual writing has become the time-consuming aspect of class periods. In their 1968 study of secondary English programs, Squire and Applebee noted that English teachers were spending roughly 17 percent of their time in writing instruction. As those teachers have begun to devote more attention to the writing process, that figure has increased dramatically.

Second, the product of student writing has become less of a vital factor in evaluating student ability. In another era, when the book report, and other assigned pieces were written en-

tirely outside the classroom, teachers had to rely on those products to determine what progress their students were making as writers. As the notion grew that written work should be viewed consistently as a series of drafts, the teacher could see students' writing in various stages of development. Third, the interaction that can provide personal, face-to-face, non-threatening feedback to the writer has become an integral part of the writing process. Whether called cross-teaching (Moffett, 1968) or peer evaluation or other such labels, the sharing of and responses to drafts have provided ways for the junior high teachers to observe closely the individualized nature of writing styles as they grow and develop. Finally, the integration of revising into class activity has removed much of the onus from that phase of the process. Junior high students of yore, when faced with the demand (or plea) that they revise, often reacted with attitudes running the gamut from indifference to overt hostility. The linking of revising to drafting and sharing has probably done as much to change early adolescents' attitudes about writing as any other single factor.

The inclusion of the writing process as a major element in secondary (and elementary and college) English language-arts instruction has helped to unify what had for a long time been a chaotic aspect of curricular implementation. More than any other factor, it has stood to represent the attempt of U.S. teachers, teacher educators, and curriculum supervisors to make Writing Across the Curriculum a reality on this side of the Atlantic. Some excellent publications have emerged to assist teachers in realizing this inclusion, among them the California State Department of Education's *Practical Ideas for Teaching Writing* (1986) and the New York State Department of Education's *Composition in the Language Arts Curriculum, K–12* (1986). Significantly, both of those publications have evolved largely from the ideas of classroom teachers rather than from professional textbook writers.

Hand in hand with the implementation of innovative writing instructional practices into the junior high ELA curriculum has been the addition of a series of workable, consistent, and positive approaches to evaluating student writing. For too many years, the use of cryptic, largely negative, and often picayune red pencil markings constituted evaluation of what early adolescents had written in school. Most of these young people lacked the perspective and self-confidence to understand these comments and, more importantly, to incorporate them into subsequent writing tasks. Their problems in interpreting the markings were exacerbated by the fact that few teachers had the inclination or took the time to follow up the return of those papers with individual conferences of even the most perfunctory variety. Some of the valuable insights into meaningful evaluation practices articulated over 20 years ago by the Education Testing Services writing consultant Paul Diederich went largely unnoticed and/or unheeded by the great majority of junior high teachers (1974). More recently, the works of Charles Cooper and his partner Lee Odell (1977), Ken Macrorie (1984), Donald Murray (1982), and Minah Shaughnessy, (1977), to name a few researchers/scholars, have added a wealth of clear, practical data to the literature concerning effective judging of student writing. Much of this material can be directly related to junior high students who are at so difficult a stage of self-consciousness. Much time in the NWP summer institues has been devoted to introducing and sharing these findings and ideas with teachers across the 50 states.

As the influence of the above named evaluation researchers has grown, such practices as peer evaluation (already mentioned), conferring, primary trait scoring, holistic scoring, progressive rating of revisions, and other such techniques have augmented traditional, analytic methods used by teachers to reflect to students the status, the strengths, and limitations of their writing at a given point. Through these more recent techniques, many of which are conducted during class time, students and teachers can communicate more honestly, intimately, and progressively on what progress has been made and what still needs to be made.

LANGUAGE

In a quantitative sense, teaching language and linguistics has been the most significant aspect of junior high school English during the past half century. The majority of junior high teachers have demonstrated a deep commitment to teaching Latinate grammar, formal usage, and the mechanics of written expression (capitalization, punctuation, and spelling) for as long as the junior high school has been an operative unit in the school system.

This adherence has proved to be a durable one. For most of the 1930s and 1940s, English teachers of grades 7, 8, and 9 were highly partial to Tressler's *English in Action* (1925) series, a strict adherent to traditional grammar and usage principles and processes. Then, in 1946, Harcourt, Brace, and World published John E. Warriner's series *English Grammar and Composition.* It was this set of textbooks that established the strongest cause-and-effect links between grammar/usage knowledge and composition proficiency. As such, it quickly became the favorite text series of teachers in junior high schools (and later, middle schools) throughout the United States. The tremendous popularity of these books has endured through every "movement" and "reform" in the secondary English curriculum. As this essay is written, the 1987 edition of the series has maintained its record of sales in schools nationwide. To the original six-book series (grades 7–12) has been added an "Introduction to–" text for use in the 6th grade, thus acknowledging the widespread movement to middle school organizational patterns. The title of the series has also been changed to *English Composition and Grammar,* a reflection of the recent increase in emphasis on writing instruction in U.S. public schools. This enduring popularity has made Warriner's the best-selling textbook series in the history of American education.

The fierce adherence of U.S. junior high teachers (and to a slightly lesser degree, senior high teachers) to traditional grammar teaching in general and the Warriner's series in particular remains somewhat of a phenomenon. As was stated earlier, it has withstood the accumulation of data generated by 85 years of research pointing unequivocally to the lack of transfer between grammar knowledge and language development of young people—this despite the fact that these data have been emphasized by linguistic scholars and English educators for a very long time. It has prevailed despite the work of Otto Jespersen (1956), Charles E. Fries (1940), and other historical linguists whose scholarship provides a thorough review of the inconsistencies and inadequacies of the Latinate grammatical system. The usage component has continued to embrace a doctrine of correctness in the face of all the research evidence produced by S. A. Leonard (1935), Albert Marckwardt and Fred G. Walcott (1938), and Robert Pooley (1974), (to name only the most prominent researchers), all of whom have concluded that a relativistic position toward the teaching of English usage is the only tenable one (Finegan, 1980).

It has also survived the challenges of "new" grammars—structural/descriptive of the 1940s and 1950s, and transformational/generative of the 1960s and 1970s. Although these modern grammatical systems have become the source of intense scholarly concern among university-based linguists, they have never made a lasting impression on the secondary school English curriculum, especially on its junior high component.

Why this near-fanatical loyalty has persisted is truly hard to state with any degree of assurance. Some psycholinguists feel that grammar study has left the position of mere knowledge among secondary school English teachers and entered the realm of values. The theory goes that in the minds of the teachers it is as fundamentally important to teach grammar as it is to teach patriotism, sound health habits, and the Protestant work ethic. Whatever the nature of the influence, it is undeniably a visceral issue for an amazingly large number of teachers. When you attack their grammar program, you attack them; and when this happens, reasoned argument ceases to function in any persuasive sense.

Thus, despite the introduction of any competing linguistic systems, it is traditional grammar and prescriptive, "right-wrong" usage that continues to hold sway today in junior high English curricula. For a brief moment, in the now fabled 1960s, some other text materials found their way into print and even into use here and there. These texts, for the most part, presented linguistics in cultural, sociological, and psychological frameworks (Postman, Morine & Morine, 1963; Allen, 1966; *Language of Man,* 1968; Summerfield, 1968; Glatthorn, 1971). They described the language learning process and how various aspects of linguistics—dialectology, relativistic usage, syntactic variety, semantics, and history—related to that process. Probably because of such political and social factors as school integration, Anglo-American professional dialogues, federally sponsored teacher institutes and curriculum study centers, student activism, and the quest for relevance, broader perspectives on language study did have some impact on junior high English curricula. Urban rioting, the Vietnam protest movement, the collapse of the Great Society domestic programs, and the rise of accountability in school systems (the latter culminating in the Great Testing Movement of the 1970s) all provided for an early departure for the linguistic adventurism of the previous decade.

Some linguistic needs of early adolescents, however, forced junior high school English teachers to reconsider and, in some cases, to reorganize their approaches to the study of language. The main preoccupation with linguistics during the first half of this century was clearly with its written form. Most work in grammar, usage, and mechanics came in the form of textbook and workbook activity. Oral work seldom had to do with those aspects of linguistics. With the coming of full-scale integration in the 1960s and 1970s, however, some changes had to be made. Large numbers of African American students entering previously all-white school systems spoke and wrote in a dialect with which their teachers were largely unfamiliar. In order to foster real communication in the classroom, oral aspects of the language took priority. The syntax of many African American students was widely divergent from the models offered in Warriner's. Their morphological constructs provided problems with possessives, verb forms, and adjective-adverb formulations. Their pronunciation of a great many words was deemed to be nonstandard, and their usage choices failed to reflect a sense of correct or formal English. Thus, in many classes, the teaching of major linguistic elements shifted from written to oral emphasis. Moreover, as the population of the Sun Belt began to expand rapidly, primarily during the past 25 years, junior high teachers throughout such growth states as Florida, Texas, New Mexico, Arizona, and (Southern) California frequently found their classes predominated by Hispanic students to whom English had to be taught as a second language. To discuss this development thoughtfully is not within the area of this writer's expertise. It is an area, however, that has been the focus of national attention, and radical changes in linguistic instructional strategies have been made in large numbers of junior high classes, with more to come. Ironically, this shift in demographics has forced considerable innovation in language teaching on many junior high English teachers in recent years.

School integration and the presence of large numbers of students who spoke other languages did have one broad-based effect on the English language-arts curriculum. It forced teachers, curriculum specialists, and teacher educators to face more directly the issue of what to do about standard English as a priority. Simply stated, the question was, "Should we force everyone to learn one style of English, or should we attempt to relate that style to the several linguistic styles of a clearly heterogeneous school population?" This concern has become especially pointed in junior high years because (1) early adolescents are moving through such a variety of physical, motivational, and temperamental changes, and (2) it is in these years that many students encounter their first professionally trained teachers of *English*. A variety of influences (political, social, scholarly, ethnic) has made this issue a highly volatile one in a great many school systems. An excellent case in point on the national level was provided by the great controversy caused by the 1974 adoption by the National Council of Teachers of English of a resolution titled "The Students' Right to Their Own Language." It read:

We affirm the students' right to their own patterns and varieties of language—the dialects of their nurture or whatever dialects in which they find their own identity and style. Language scholars long ago denied that the myth of a standard American dialect has any validity. The claim that any one dialect is unacceptable amounts to an attempt of one social group to exert its dominance over another. Such a claim leads to false advice for speakers and writers, and immoral advice for humans. A nation proud of its diverse heritage and its cultural and racial variety will preserve its heritage of dialects. We affirm strongly that teachers must

have the experiences and training that will enable them to respect diversity and uphold the right of students to their own language.

This resolution had first been debated in 1972 by the NCTE subgroup, the Conference on College Composition and Communication (CCCC). It was then the subject of bitter debate, first by the resolutions committee of the CCCC, and then by the corresponding committee of the parent organization. Although supported by a majority of Council members who happened to be present and voting at that lively New Orleans session, it did not necessarily represent the philosophy of the full Council membership, let alone the thousands of nonmember English teachers then on the job nationwide.

Whatever lofty ideals were represented by the resolution, and regardless of the intense commitment of its advocates, the real impact of the resolution was greatly diminished by the political events of the 1970s. Throughout that entire decade, the growing war cry among state and local educational leaders continued to be, "Back to the Basics." This cry gained in influence by the implementation of the Great Testing Movement described earlier in this chapter. In English curricula, this turning back was marked primarily by a return to Latinate grammar, formal rule-based usage, and prescribed mechanics. Since the junior high English curriculum featured a heavy emphasis on language study, and less concern with literature and composition, the return to these "old" linguistic preoccupations was most evident. The movement turned to the reinstituttion (where any changes had in fact occurred) to the grammar text, workbook, spelling list motif of yore. In 1977 (the year statewide testing began), a new edition of Warriner's broke all sales records. The Roberts' English series was permanently consigned to the dust bin, and memorization took over for language-in-action as the modus operandi in junior high English classes.

As the junior high curriculum entered the 1980s, a small fissure in the traditional language wall could be noted. A meeting in Sydney, Australia, held in August of 1980, produced the text *English in the 80's* (Eagleson, 1982), a much more liberalized view of language study than had been adopted during the Back to the Basics days. The meeting was convened by a new organization, the International Federation on the Teaching of English (IFTE), a congregation of English teachers from the English-speaking world. In contrast with their U.S. colleagues, the representatives from such countries as Great Britain, Scotland, Ireland, Canada, Australia, and New Zealand (to name the big ones) advocated a far more pluralistic, deductive, student-centered curricular approach that they more frequently labelled as "Whole Language." (Halliday, 1978; Wilkinson, Barnsley, Hannah, & Swan, 1980; Downes, 1984; Doughty, Pearce, & Thornton, 1971). The scheme concentrated on the language of the students, rather than that of the textbook, as a point of departure. The teacher's job, in Whole Language, was to provide the environment for students to present their language (both oral and written); to solicit language products from those students; and then to provide for classroom analyses of elements of those products, both their content and form. It was in the inspection of the formal elements that the familiar components of grammar, usage, and mechanics, as well as semantic, phonological, dialectal, and dictional ones, would be dealt with. The concept gained enthusiastic acceptance from many U.S. participants, and the mid-1980s has seen a resurgence of professional interest in studying language from other than a textbook perspective.

The IFTE group, still small but vocal, met at Michigan State University in East Lansing in 1984 and at Carlton University in Ottawa in 1986. The former meeting produced a collection of essays, *Language, Schooling, and Society* (1985), which has received a good deal of attention from U.S. English educators. As this chapter is written, there is some evidence that Whole Language teaching is being adopted in some elementary schools, fewer middle schools and junior highs, and virtually no senior high systems. As many would-be reforms testify, the anvil of tradition is very hard to overcome. The writing movement described earlier, plus some elements of literature instruction emphasizing reader response techniques, have facilitated somewhat the integration of Whole Language activities into the junior high English teachers' courses. In particular, the National Writing Project participants' growing influence on curricula has opened the door to student-centered language activities; moreover, this influence has raised skeptical considerations of the value of heavily traditional grammar study in the junior high. In the immediate future, the NWP influence possibly will increase, and the testing impetus will diminish, thus creating new opportunities for language experience activities in junior high ELA classrooms.

CONCLUSION

The current status of language study is, to a significant degree, symbolic of the struggles occurring within the junior high curriculum in English language arts today. The refusal of tradition-bound English teachers to accept such innovative possibilities as Whole Language study can be seen reflected in approaches to reading, literature, and writing. There is a deeper division, however, among spokespersons for effective English instruction in junior highs today. This division concerns the basic goals to be pursued at this level of the curriculum. The quality movement of the mid-1980s touched off by the Gardner and Carnegie Commission reports has rallied a large number of educators to the cause of academic English study. These advocates would have the schools provide a prescriptive, heavily cognitive set of offerings. These include literature featuring challenging works; formally arranged composition tasks; and traditional, rule-bound linguistic study, abounding in technical and abstract conceptual material. That these proponents are having their way can be evidenced by the amount of quality oriented legislation passed in an imposing number of states during the past five years.

Standing in opposition to this philosophy are those student-centered educators who see the junior high school years as a period of transition in the intellectual, emotional, and social lives of young people. To them, the English language-arts curriculum should be experience-centered, and classroom activities should focus on correlative experience as offered in literary selections, personally oriented writing tasks, and Whole Language activities. Theirs would be a basically inductive rather than a prescriptive approach to immersing early adolescents in the understanding, use, and appreciation of American English. Although these English Educators are outnumbered at the moment, their arguments—articulate, even eloquent—continue to be published. As the final decade of the twentieth century approaches, the debate is still in progress. The issues may sometimes be recursive, but seldom are they trivial. What is really at stake is the linguistic ability of young people.

References

The adventures in literature program. (1989). Orlando, FL: Harcourt, Brace, Jovanovich.

Allen, H. B. (1966). *New dimensions in English.* Wichita, KS: McCormick-Mathers.

Atwell, N. (1987). *In the middle: Writing, reading and learning with adolescents.* Upper Montclair, NJ: Boynton Cook.

Bateman, D., & Zidonis, F. (1966). *The effect of a study of transformational grammar on the writing of ninth and tenth graders* (Report No. 6). Urbana, IL: National Council of Teachers of English.

Bond, G. L., & Wagner, E. B. (1966). *Teaching the child to read.* New York: Macmillan.

Burton, D. L. (1960). *Literature study in the high schools.* New York: Holt, Rinehart & Winston.

Chomsky, N. (1957). *Syntactic structures.* The Hague, Holland: Mouton & Co.

Combs, W. E. (1975). *Some further effects of sentence combining exercises in the secondary language arts curriculum.* Unpublished doctoral dissertation, University of Minnesota, Minneapolis.

Composition in the English language arts curriculum, K–12. (1986). Albany, NY: New York State Department of Education.

Cooper, C. R., & Odell, L. (1977). *Evaluating writing: Describing, measuring, judging.* Urbana, IL: National Council of Teachers of English.

Diederich, P. (1974). *Measuring growth in English.* Urbana, IL: National Council of Teachers of English.

Donelson, K. L., and Nilsen, A. P. (1985). *Literature for today's young adults* (2nd ed.). Glenview, IL: Scott, Foresman.

Doughty, P., Pearce, J., & Thornton, G. (1971). *Language in use.* London, England: Edward Arnold.

Downes, W. (1984). *Language and society.* London, England: Fontana.

Dunning, S. A. (1959). *A definition of the role of the junior novel based on analyses of thirty novels.* Unpublished doctoral dissertation, Florida State University, Tallahassee.

Dunning, S., Lueders, E., & Smith, H. (1969). *Some haystacks don't even have any needle and other modern poems.* Chicago: Scott, Foresman.

Dunning, S., Lueders, E., & Smith, H. (1966). *Reflections on a gift of watermelon pickle and other modern verse.* Chicago: Scott, Foresman.

Eagleson, R. D. (Ed.) (1982). *English in the eighties.* Sydney, Australia: Association for the Teaching of English.

Early, M. J. (1957, October). About successful reading programs. *English Journal, 56* (7), 395–396.

Finegan, E. T. (1980). *Attitudes toward English usage: The war of words.* New York: Teachers College Press.

Freedom and discipline in English. (1965). New York: College Entrance Examination Board.

Fries, C. C. (1940). *American English grammar.* New York: Appleton-Century-Crofts.

Glatthorn, A. (1971). *Dynamics of language.* Boston: D. C. Heath.

Gray, J., & Myers, M. (1978, February). The bay area writing project. *Phi Delta Kappan,* 410–414.

Grissom, L. V. (1961, October). Characteristics of successful reading improvement programs. *English Journal,* 461–464.

A guide to statewide assessment results. (1987, Spring). Tallahassee, FL: Florida Department of State.

Halliday, M. A. K. (1978). *Language as a social semiotic.* London, England: Edward Arnold.

Hartwell, P. (1985, February). Grammar, grammars, and the teaching of grammar. *College English, 47* (2), 102–127.

Havighurst, R. (1948). *Developmental tasks and education,* Chicago: University of Chicago Press.

Hinton, S. E. (1967). *The outsiders.* New York: Bantam.

Hirsch, E. D., Jr. (1983). *Cultural literacy.* Boston: Houghton, Mifflin.

Jennings, F. G. (1954, December). Literature for adolescents, pap or protein. *English Journal, 65,* 526–531.

Jespersen, O. (1956). *Growth and structure of the English language.* Garden City, NY: Doubleday.

La Brant, L. (1951). *We teach English.* New York: Harcourt, Brace.

The language of man. (1968). Chicago: MacDougal-Littell.

Leonard, S. A. (1935). *Curent English usage.* (Monograph No. 1), Chicago: Inland.

Lipsitz, J. (1984). *Successful schools for young adolescents.* New Brunswick, ME: Transaction Books.

Lipsitz, R. (1967). *The contender.* New York: Bantam.

Lockerbie, B. (1963, November). The speaking voice approach. *English Journal,* 596–600.

Lynch, J. J., & Evans, B. (1963). *High school English textbooks: A critical examination.* Boston: Atlantic-Little, Brown.

Macrorie, K. (1984). *Writing to be read* (3rd ed.). Upper Montclair, NJ: Boynton Cook.

Marckwardt, A. H. & Walcott, F. G. (1938). *Facts about current English usage.* New York: Appleton-Century-Crofts.

Martin, W. R. (1967). *Effects of inclusion of title III materials in secondary school reading programs in the upper midwest.* Unpublished doctoral dissertation, University of Minnesota, Minneapolis.

Mellon, J. C. (1975). *National assessment and the teaching of English.* Urbana, IL: National Council of Teachers of English.

Mellon, J. C. (1967). *Transformational sentence combining.* (Report No. 10). Urbana, IL: National Council of Teachers of English.

Moffett, J. (1968). *Teaching the universe of discourse.* Boston: Houghton Mifflin.

Muller, A. P. (1973). *The currently popular adolescent novel as transitional literature.* Unpublished doctoral dissertation, Florida State University, Tallahassee.

Murray, D. (1982). *Learning by teaching: Selected articles on writing and teaching.* Upper Montclair, NJ: Boynton Cook.

A Nation at Risk. (1983). Washington, D.C.: U.S. Department of Education.

O'Hare, F. (1973). *Sentence combining: improving student writing without formal grammar instruction* (Report No. 15). Urbana, IL: National Council of Teachers of English.

Petitt, D. J. (1960). *A study of the qualities of literary excellence which characterize selected fiction for younger adolescents.* Unpublished doctoral dissertation, University of Minnesota, Minneapolis.

Pooley, R. C. (1974). *The teaching of English usage.* Urbana, IL: National Council of Teachers of English.

Postman, N., Morine, J., & Morine, L. (1963). *Postman language series.* New York: Holt, Rinehart & Winston.

Potter, R. R., & McCummery, R. D. (1987). *The collector's anthology.* New York: Globe Books.

Practical ideas for teaching writing as a process. (1986). Sacramento, CA: California Department of Education.

Probst, R. E. (1984). *Adolescent literature: Response and analysis.* Columbus, OH: Merrill.

Rice, J. M. (1905). Educational research: The results of a test in language and English. *Forum, 35,* 204–295.

Roberts, P. (1961). *English sentences.* New York: Harcourt, Brace, Jovanovich.

Roberts, P. (1964). *English syntax.* New York: Harcourt, Brace, Jovanovich.

Rosenblatt, L. (1968). *Literature as exploration* (rev. ed.). New York: Noble.

Rosenblatt, L. (1978). *The reader, the text, and the poems: Transactional theory of the literary work.* Carbondale, IL: Southern Illinois University Press.

Shaughnessy, M. P. (1977). *Errors and expectations.* New York: Oxford University Press.

Shugrue, M. F. (1968). *English in a decade of change* (pp. 19–22). New York: Pegasus.

Simmons, J. S. (1989, Spring). Crossing the straits. *Books for the junior high years. Focus: Teaching English language arts.* Athens, OH: Southeastern Ohio Council of Teachers of English.

Smith, D. V. (1950). Guiding individual reading. *Reading in the high school and college* (Yearbook No. 47, Part 2), Chicago: University of Chicago Press.

Smith, F., & Goodman, K. (1976). *Psycholinguistics and reading.* New York: Holt, Rinehart & Winston.

Smith, F. (1986). *Understanding reading* (3rd ed.). Hillsdale, NJ: Lawrence Elbaum Association.

Squire, J., & Applebee, R. (1968). *High school English instruction today.* New York: Appleton-Century-Crofts.

Stotsky, S. L. (1975). Sentence combining as a curricular activity: Its effect on language development and reading comprehension. *Research in the teaching of English, 9,* 30–71.

Straw, S. (1975). *The effect of sentence combining and sentence reduction on measures of syntactic fluency, reading, comprehension and listening comprehension in fourth grade students.* Unpublished doctoral dissertation, University of Minnesota, Minneapolis.

Sullivan, M. A. (1977). *The effects of sentence combining exercises on syntactic maturity, quality of writing, and attitudes of students in grade eleven.* Unpublished doctoral dissertation, State University of New York at Buffalo.

Summerfield, G. (1968). *Voices.* Chicago: Rand McNally.

Tchudi, S. (Ed.). (1985). *Language, schooling, and society.* Upper Montclair, NJ: Boynton Cook.

Tressler, A. (1925). *English in action.* Boston: D.C. Heath.

Turlington, R. D. & Wiliams, E. (1975). *Education policy for the state of Florida.* Tallahassee, FL: FLorida Department of Education.

Warriner, J. (1946). *English grammar and composition.* New York: Harcourt, Brace.

Warriner, J. (1988). *English composition and grammar* (Benchmark ed.). Orlando, FL: Harcourt, Brace, Jovanovich.

Why Johnny can't write. (1975, December 8). *Newsweek,* 58–63.

Wilkinson, A., Barnsley, G., Hannah, P., & Swan, M. (1980). *Assessing language development.* London, England: Oxford University Press.

Zindel, P. (1968). *The pigman.* New York: Bantam.

19E. THE HIGH SCHOOL YEARS
Thomas Newkirk

This chapter focuses on development, and for that reason it begins with a problem of definition—development *toward what*. It is perhaps possible to view development as a purely neurophysiological event, the unfolding of innate intellectual abilities that occurs along a predetermined path. But recent studies of language development have rejected this biological view in favor of one that gives more importance to culture (e.g., Harste, Woodward & Burke, 1984; Heath, 1983) and views development as an interaction between biological potential and cultural patterns. This dialectical view of development is grounded in the work of Lev Vygotsky (1978) who viewed the learner as gradually appropriating thought patterns that are first manifest in interactions with others. According to Vygotsky, all thought is social or (interpersonal) before it is internalized (or intrapersonal). Put another way, his major work *Mind in Society* might just as well be entitled *Society in Mind*.

This view of development forecloses any possibility of reducing language development to universal stages or patterns, appealing as that possibility might be. In order to understand the high school learner, it is therefore necessary to consider the institution where that learner spends 180 days a year, and to understand the often conflicting demands placed on that institution. This chapter's thesis is that studies of intellectual development, measured through language performance, indicate a "low ceiling" for most high school students and that this impeded development is related to the diffuse structure and mission of the high school.

The charter for the modern comprehensive high school was written by James Conant in *The American High School Today* (1959). There he asked the fundamentally important question:

Can a school at one and the same time provide a good general education for all the pupils as future citizens of a democracy, provide elective programs for the majority to develop useful skills, and educate adequately those with a talent for handling advanced academic subjects—particularly foreign languages and mathematics? (p. 15)

Conant describes this challenge more expansively in *The Comprehensive High School* (1967):

The comprehensive high school is a particularly American phenomenon because it offers, under one administration and under one roof (or series of roofs), secondary education for almost all high school age children of one town or neighborhood. It is responsible for educating the boy who will become an atomic scientist and the girl who will marry at eighteen; the prospective captain of a ship and the future captain of industry. It is responsible for educating the bright and the not bright children with different vocational and professional ambitions and various motivations. It is responsible, in sum, for providing good and appropriate education, both academic and vocational, for all young children within a democratic environment which the American people believe serves the principles they cherish. (p. 3)

If anything, this chapter has expanded in recent years: high schools have become the front line for combating social problems such as alcoholism, AIDS, and drug addiction. They are expected to provide special support for students with learning difficulties as well as those with emotional and physical handicaps. School administrators are evaluated on their ability to raise academic standards, invariably measured in standardized test scores, and at the same time to retain potential dropouts, often weaker students who will pull those scores down. Parents want their adolescents to receive individual attention from teachers, yet will often resist the elimination of options or electives that fragment the school day and make this attention impossible. Schools claim that critical thinking is a primary goal, yet the high school schedule works against the individual attention implicit in that goal; typically, teachers are expected to meet up to 175 students per day in periods as short as 40 minutes, though often shorter because of interruptions. As Goodlad observes in *A Place Called School*, "We want it all" (1984, p. 33).

Often the calls for higher standards or for a greater emphasis on writing as a mode of thinking ignore the complexity of the high schools' mandate. Some of the calls for reform (e.g., *A Nation at Risk*, 1983) suggest that these intellectual goals are paramount, if unrealized, in high schools and that by exhortation or by relatively straightforward measures like lengthening the school day or requiring more courses for graduation, schools can be recalled to their true mission. Powell, Farrar, and Cohen (1985) provide a more provocative reason for the apparent neglect of critical-thinking high schools. They compare the high school to a shopping mall:

Both types of institutions are profoundly consumer-oriented. Both try to hold customers by offering something for everyone. Individual stores or departments, and salespeople or teachers, try their best to attract customers by advertisements of various sorts, yet in the end the customer has the final word. (p. 3)

In this mall one of the "specialty shops" is the honors program where critical thinking and in-depth engagement has a "clientele." But for the general student, the unspecial student, the pattern is one of accommodation, or what Powell, Farrar, and Cohen call "treaties"; the unspecial student may willingly work at essentially uninteresting worksheets if that means he or she can get a good grade without having to go beyond full-in-the-blank work. One teacher described the treaty process this way:

We have all compromised on our values. Inside the classroom, students will work for me or I see to it that they don't stay there. But I don't give them nearly as much homework as I would like because I have been beaten down; too many simply will not do it. (Boyer, 1983, p. 144)

The shopping mall school can best be viewed as an adaptable and enduring democratic institution; it is doing "what comes naturally in a popular democracy; paying attention to their constituents (p. 239)." One of the greatest virtues of the shopping mall school is its adaptability, its ability to deal with the contrary visions of education that were explicit in Conant's charter. As a result we have:

... institutions that are remarkably flexible, ambitious, and tolerant, capable of making room for many different sorts of students and teachers and many different wishes for education. They are institutions nicely suited to cope with America's fickle and political educational sensibilities. All are important strengths, but they have had crippling effects. They have stunted the high schools' capacity to take all students seriously. They have blocked teachers' capacity to cultivate those qualities long valued in educated men and women—the ability to read well and critically, to write plainly and persuasively, and to reason clearly. (Powell, Farrar, & Cohen, p. 309)

It is the general student who suffers most. James Squire and Roger Applebee in their 1968 survey of high school English instruction noted that the better students were expected to do close reading of texts, whereas weaker students were asked to learn historical facts. "The honors student thinks, while his less gifted peers regurgitate"(1968, p. 174).

Recent surveys of high school instruction assessment of student performance reinforce the observations made above. In this view I begin by examining status studies that provide a picture of instructional practices and student achievement. The review then shifts to sections on language development, response to literature, and the teaching of writing. These divisions are, of course, convenient fictions; they do not indicate support for the tripod model of the English curriculum with three clear components (literature, composition, and language). Ultimately any discussion of how English is taught cannot, finally, be divorced from an examination of the high school itself. The structure of the high school—the bell schedule, the size of the classes, the politics of curriculum development—all contribute directly to the development of the high school learner.

STATUS STUDIES

The most extensive of recent surveys has been Goodlad's examination of 38 schools, a project involving 20 trained data collectors that gathered data from 8,624 parents, 1,350 teachers, and 17,163 student. The researchers made detailed observations in over 1,000 classrooms, making it the largest observational study ever conducted in this country. His conclusions make for painful reading. In these classes students "made scarcely any decisions about their learning" (p. 229). Over 75 percent of class time was spent on instruction and nearly 70 percent of this was usually teacher to student. Only 5 percent of instruction was designed to elicit any student response and *not even 1 percent required some kind of open response involving reasoning or perhaps an opinion from the student* (p. 229). Boyer in his Carnegie Foundation study of high schools found the same pattern:

Most discussion in classrooms when it occurs, calls for simple recall (What were the provisions of the Treaty of 1763?) or the application of an idea (Use the periodic table to find an atomic number). Occasionally students are asked to develop explanations (If we release ammonia in one corner of the room why is it possible to smell it in the opposite corner?) But serious intellectual discussion is rare. (p. 146)

Written work resembles this oral recitiation method. Goodlad found that English language-arts classes emphasized a "kind of repetitive reinforcement of basic skills of language usage throughout the twelve grades—a heavy emphasis on mechanics in the topics covered by teachers, textbooks stressing these topics, and workbooks, worksheets, and quizzes emphasizing short answers and the recall of specific information (p. 207)."

Goodlad's conclusions are supported by a smaller survey conducted by Fillion (1979) and (Applebee (1981). Fillion examined three Canadian schools and found the most common student form of writing was copying. Applebee's study involved 259 observations of ninth-and-tenth-grade classes at two schools. He found that 44 percent of class time was spent on some form of writing, broadly defined, but most of this writing was very brief (short answer or fill-in-the-blank) or note-taking. Writing a paragraph or longer occurred about 3 percent of the time. Even some of the writing that seemed to call for analytic thought actually called for a summary of class notes. Applebee gives these examples:

Western Europe on the eve of the Reformation was a civilization going through great changes. In a well-written essay describe the political, economic, social, and cultural changes Europe was going through at the time of the Reformation.

Select some phase of twentieth century American literature and discuss it in a theme of 300–500 words. Turn in polished draft only (p. 74).

Applebee concludes that these assignments "become reasonable tasks only when they are interpreted by students as requests to summarize material previously presented in lessons or texts" (p. 74). Surveys conducted by the National Assessment of Educational Progress indicate that when students are expected to write at length, 82 percent of their writing is in the form of essays or reports; formal academic writing, then, is stressed almost to the exclusion or personal or creative writing (Applebee, Langer, & Mullis, 1987a), a result similar to that found by British researchers in the 1970s (Britton, Burgess, Martin, McLeod, Rosen, 1975).

Another barrier to analytic thinking may be the textbooks themselves. Analysis, if it is to occur, must begin with a response, such as outrage, delight, disagreement, approval, puzzlement, and the potential for response is enhanced if the text has a strong point of view. Fitzgerald (1979) in her survey of U.S. history texts notes a significant change in textbooks that occurred in the 1890s. Up until that time, textbooks would often openly reveal the opinions of the author, but in the 1890s history texts began to assume the tone of objectivity and impersonality. From the 1890s on, Fitzgerald concludes, "what textbooks said about American history would appear to children to be the truth" (p. 52). Fitzgerald particulary deplores the evasiveness of contemporary books; frequently "problems" (e.g., "the race problem") seem to arise through a kind of historical spontaneous generation; they occur without human agency. They happen. Fitzgerald criticizes many of these books as irresponsible history, but this evasiveness, this lack of any point of view that students can identify, also reduces the range of options a reader might assume. These books, mainly committee documents, seem to demand not response, but acceptance. They suggest what Friere (1970) has called a "banking" concept of education where information is passed on, for example, deposited, in students, rather than a curriculum that fosters critical consciousness.

The results of the various National Assessment of Educational Progress (NAEP) suggest students have learned what they have been taught; they are generally strong on factual recall of information, and on the mechanics of writing, but they seem to lack the ability to critically explore their ideas or responses (Applebee, Langer, & Mullis, 1987b). These results indicate that the recent focus on achieving rudimentary or minimal competence, going back to the basics, is misdirected. The vast majority of students achieve competence on this minimal level. The problems lie with the more complex tasks, hardly a surprising conclusion in the light of the surveys of teaching methods already cited.

One of the major innovations of NAEP was a redefinition of reading competence. Traditionally reading comprehension has been tested through multiple-choice questions that were either literal, inferential, or interpretive. NAEP developed a more exacting definition:

In school and in society, we expect a reader to be able to analyze, evaluate, and extend the ideas that are being presented, just as we expect a writer to elaborate upon and defend judgments that are expressed. We expect people to know how to get information and how to use it and shape it to suit their needs. (Applebee, Langer, & Mullis, 1987b, p. 9)

This definition necessitates a form of assessment that links reading and writing (or speaking) because it is through writing and speaking that we elaborate and shape understandings.

The 1979-1980 assessment of 39,000 student was the first to link reading and writing. The authors state:

When reading is divorced from the process of discussing the meaning of a work (as it often is in teaching and testing) comprehension can be misunderstood to be a sudden "click" of meaning measurable only through short answer and multiple choice questions that require little struggle for full understanding. (*Reading, Writing, and Thinking*, 1981, p. ix)

The 1979-1980 assessment used a four-stage model of response that began with

1. Initial comprehension leading to
2. Preliminary interpretations followed by
3. Reexamination of the text in light of these interpretations, leading to
4. Extended and documented interpretation.

In the 1979-1980 assessment, students seemed able to handle the first two steps of this process but were unable to move to steps three and four. The students also seemed able to handle inferential multiple-choice questions, but they had far more difficulty on open-ended questions. When asked to write, students were often unable to do more than summarize. The authors concluded that students seemed to lack experience with reading/writing tasks that involve critical thinking or problem-solving. (It should be noted that students had only 9 minutes to complete the reading/writing task on the 1979-80 assessment. This time limitation may have precluded some of the more elaborated responses the authors were hoping for.)

This theme is echoed in two recent NAEP publications, *The Writing Report Card* (Applebee, Langer, & Mullis, 1986b) and *The Reading Report Card* (Applebee, Langer, & Mullis, 1986a) that report on the 1984 writing and reading assessment. Both assessment reports contain some good news: reading scores and writing scores are up from the previous assessment, and students report that they are doing more writing than they had been reported 5 years earlier. But again the percentage of students who can go beyond minimally adequate written responses or intermediate comprehension was found to be disturbingly low. For example, on the persuasive writing task only 23 percent of the 11th graders wrote better than a minimal response and only 2 percent were classified as "elaborated." Though the reading results were more positive, with 44 percent of 17-year-olds reading at the "adept" or "advanced" level, the authors conclude that:

. . . by and large 17-year-olds do not have consistent control of the reading skills or strategies needed to comprehend material such as primary source historical documents, scientific documents, or financial and technical documents—those often needed to achieve excellence in academic, business, or government environments. (1986b, p. 28)

Compelling as the evidence from the NAEP assessments appears, some of the conclusions may be overstated. For example, in *The Writing Report Card* the authors state that "students at all grade levels are deficient in higher older thinking skills" (p. 11). Clearly, their performance on these tasks may have been deficient, but it is not clear whether this difficulty represents a generalized deficit in "higher order thinking" ability or whether it is an inability on the part of student to apply their intelligence to these tasks and to demonstrate it in these writing tasks. For example, in one of the persuasive writing tasks, students are presented with this hypothetical situation: their school is going to split sessions and they have to write a letter to the principal indicating if they want a morning or an afternoon session and why. The samples of student work included in *Writing: Trends Across the Decade* (Applebee, Langer, & Mullis, 1974-1984) suggest the differences between pieces that were evaluated high and low may not be clear indications of "higher order thinking." Students who wanted the morning sessions so they could play with their friends in the afternoon (certainly an honest position) were evaluated lower than students who claimed they had piano lessons or had to work for money. It is at least possible that many of the minimal responses indicate a lack of familiarity with this kind of letter and not a deficit in thinking ability.

Whatever their limitations, these surveys of instruction and performance are painfully consistent. There is a consistent and repetitive attention to basic facts and skills and a corresponding lack of attention to intellectual development: the ability to think rationally, the ability to use, evaluate, and interrelate knowledge. "Coverage" becomes the goal of teaching, or perhaps the rationale for not spending on more in-depth learning. Perhaps the most striking observation made in these studies is the *absence* of any sense of crisis; students, for the most part are content (if not happy) in their classes. Seventy-two percent of high school students, for example, claim to like English and 94 percent of them rate English as important. Slightly over half find the workload in their English classes to be "just right" (Goodlad, pp. 116–117). As Ted Sizer notes, "No one seems upset" (1984, p. 21).

RESEARCH ON LANGUAGE DEVELOPMENT

This section examines research studies that contribute to an understanding of language development. The critical issue in this research is whether instruction should focus on the sentence level, or whether growth in syntactic competence is the result the writer's attempts to deal with more global rhetorical issues. Polanyi's (1958) distinction between focal and subsidiary awareness can clarify this issue. In his famous example, Polanyi claims that when we pound a nail we are attending to the head of the hammer hitting the nail; we are *focally* aware of the impact, the straightness of the nail and its progress into the board. We are aware in a *subsidiary* way of our grip on the handle and the movements we make in hitting the nail. Should we shift our focal attention to the grip or to the mechanics of moving the hammer, we would be unable to pound the nail. Rhetoricians would argue that writers develop not by shifting their focal awareness to the level of sentence structure, but by using language in a variety of situations, for a variety of purposes and audiences.

Perhaps the most regularly researched question in the area of composition concerns the effect of formal grammar instruction on writing Braddock, Lloyd Jones, and Schoer (1963) in their survey of research concluded that this one issue had been resolved: formal grammar instruction had been shown to be an ineffective way of teaching writing and, because such instruction often took away time from actual writing practice, it probably had a negative effect on writing development. Although some have questioned this sweeping dismissal (e.g., Kolnn, 1981), clearly there is no reason to believe that formal, traditional grammar instruction should occupy the prominent position it holds in many English curricula. Hartwell (1985) has recently suggested that while experimentation may not be able to resolve the issue, grammar instruction can be abandoned on theoretical grounds. He argues that any claim for the effectiveness of grammar instruction rests on premises that, when made explicit, can be immediately recognized as implausible.

Ten years before the Braddock, Lloyd Jones, and Schoer survey, Walter Loban had begun his 13-year longitudinal study of oral and written language development. In 1953 Loban selected 338 kindergarten pupils and twice each year for the next 13 years collected oral samples and (beginning in 4th grade) written samples of discourse in order to a) determine changes in syntactic development over this 12-year period and b) to determine which features of this development contribute to what teachers considered proficiency. Loban found that in both oral and written language, the key index of growth, and the key dif-

ference between stronger and weaker language users, was elaboration or modification within the main clause. Older (and better) language users tended to use longer communication units because they used greater elaboration of subject and predicate, used more embedding, and used more dependent clauses of all kinds.

Hunt (1965), whose research paralleled Loban's, helped to consolidate Loban's conclusions by introducing the concept of a T-unit that he used to designate the main clause and all modification or elaboration of that clause. A major index of language growth became words/T-unit. Since young children tend to connect short main clauses with "and," they tend to use relatively few words/T-unit. But as they mature they begin to use a range of appositives, prepositional phrases, and dependent clauses that increase the number of words/T-unit. Other researchers used Hunt's unit of measurement (e.g., O'Donnell, Griffin, & Norris, 1967) to conclusively show that the words/T-unit ratio went up in both oral and written discourse as writers matured.

The T-unit became an important unit of measurement in sentence-combining research in the late 1960s and 1970s. This research shifted from the normative question (How do writers develop?) to one of experimental intervention (How can we speed up this development?). Mellon (1969) in a large and carefully designed study tried to determine the effects of cued sentence-combining practice where students are given the sentence components and "cues" for combining. Interestingly, at the time of his study, Mellon did not view sentence-combining as a way of teaching writing, but as a form of linguistic play that could increase student's awareness of various language forms. His position seems somewhat different in the epilogue of his study, written two years later, which emphasizes the linguistic growth that sentence combining can enhance.

Other researchers did not share Mellon's ambivalence. O'Hare (1973) simplified the sentence-combining practice and in a much smaller study reported extraordinary differences between control and experimental groups. O'Hare also found that the writing quality of work done by the experimental groups was ranked higher than that of the control groups. Subsequent researchers were unable to reproduce the magnitude of difference found by O'Hare, but they generally found fairly strong evidence of differences in syntactic fluency (later called "syntactic maturity") with less conclusive results on improvement in writing quality (Combs, 1976; Stewart, 1978). The most thorough study, conducted with College freshmen at Miami University (Morenberg, Daiker, & Kerek, 1979), showed superior results on both syntactic maturity and writing quality for the sentence-combining group.

The Miami study was the last major one on sentence-combining. In part, the point had been proven, sentence-combining could accelerate writing development. But a follow-up of the Miami study showed that students in the control groups caught up with the experimental groups (1980), raising questions about the permanence of the gains. If the method only temporarily accelerates development that would occur through reading, writing, and speaking experiences, is it really such an advance? Finally, rhetorically-based models of development seemed to offer more productive explanations of development.

Moffett's *Teaching the Universe of Discourse* (1968) remains the most innovative and profound attempt to base the English curriculum on principles of development. Too often, Moffett claims, curricula are set up around divisions in the subject matter (e.g., American Lit—10th grade; British Lit—11th grade) rather than on an understanding of ways learners develop. Moffett writes:

… The sequence of psychological development should be the backbone of curriculum continuity, and the logical formulations of the subject should serve only as an aid in describing this natural growth. Meshing learner and learned, in the case of a native language, is a matter of translating inner reality into the public realm of the subject. (1968, pp. 14–15)

Drawing on the work of Piaget, Moffett suggests that abstraction or de-centering is a central principle in growth; as the learner develops, he or she is more capable of moving beyond an immediate experience and audience. The learner, for example, may begin by recounting an experience, but the more mature learner can abstract from it, can generalize or theorize, can treat the experience as an instance of a more general concept. The child can also begin to frame discourse to meet the demands of increasingly unfamiliar audiences that demand greater explicitness. Syntactic development, then, is a by-product of the learners attempt to deal with increasingly more demanding rhetorical and intellectual tasks.

The other major attempt to ground a model of language development on principles of intellectual development was that of James Britton and his colleagues who collaborated on *The Development of Writing Abilities* (1975, pp. 11–18), perhaps the most influential piece of research in the past 20 years. Like Moffett, the Britton team viewed the young language learner as working within an intimate context where the language is largely "expressive"—highly contextualized where the speaker or writer assumes that the listener or reader shares common background knowledge and interests. As the language learner matures, he or she can move beyond this expressive matrix in one of two directions: toward the transactional (informing and persuading) where the speaker/writer must provide contextual information, anticipate the audience's position, and answer possible objections. Or the speaker/writer moves toward the poetic that Britton et al. define broadly to include jokes, anecdotes, stories as well as poetry, plays, and novels. What all poetic discourse has in common is its attention to form, the way we shape inchoate experience into a structure that allows us to take what Britton calls a spectator role.

Britton and his colleagues validated their discourse model by applying it to over 2,000 pieces, written by British secondary students in all subject areas. This categorization clearly revealed ways that students were stifled by the demands placed upon them. Virtually all the writing students did was transactional, and the potential of writing in the spectator mode was largely unrealized; the only exception was in English, but once students beagn to prepare for exams (around the fifth year), that writing, too, became almost exclusively transactional. Similarly, students rarely wrote expressive discourse; the only examples of expressive discourse were in English and religious educa-

tion, and this category accounted for only 5.5 percent of the sample. Finally, teachers generally took on the role of "examiner," particularly in non-English subjects; by the time students reached their seventh year, the teacher acted as "examiner" 61 percent of the time. Writing, by this point, was essentially a means of testing the student.

Britton viewed the student as occupying an impossible rhetorical position, writing on a given topic to someone who knew more about the topic, not for any purpose of communication, but simply to demonstrate if certain material had been mastered. Even more limiting, the student was cut off from the resources of speech (or as the British would prefer "talk") or expressive language that, according to his model, is the "matrix," the starting point, for more formalized expression. The alternative, implicit in *The Development of Writing Abilities,* became explicit of subsequent work by the Language Across the Curriculum team under the direction of Nancy Martin (Martin, D'Arcy, Newton, & Parker, 1976). This team began to publish a series of pamphlets illustrating ways that informal, speech-like writing (writing that assumed the teacher was engaged in a dialogue, not acting as examiner) could be used in a variety of subject areas. This work had a major influence on the Writing Across the Curriculum movement in the United States (e.g., Fulwiler, 1988).

While these discourse-based models of development represented a clear advance over more atomistic word counts, they too are open to the criticism. Typically, models of discourse development claim that some kinds of discourse are more advanced than others. Moffett, for example, claims that written argument is more advanced than written narrative. In Bloom's (1959) widely used taxonomy of the cognitive domain, evaluation occupies a higher plane than summarizing or analyzing. And the NAEP reports regularly equate "higher order thinking" with analysis. There is a tendency, then, in many of these models to claim a natural progression from "lower" level cognitive processes, those that are empathetic, affective, situated, narrative, and strongly dependent on memory, to "higher" levels that are distanced, "autonomous," "dependent on abstraction, analysis, and reflection."

A major problem with these hierarchies is their hidden ideological bias. Although Moffett argues for a natural progression, from a Vygotskian point of view any progression is an interaction of biological potential with cultural patterns and the values implicit in those patterns. No model of development is natural or neutral. Most developmental models reflect a preference for the theoretical over the practical, for the abstract over the particular, for objectivity over subjectivity. Those capabilities at the top of the hierarchies are typically ones valued in the educational institutions where the hierarchies are developed. The university, which values analytic reasoning above storytelling, is likely to place it at a higher level. A novelist would draw the map a different way.

There is nothing inappropriate in constructing these hierarchies. The problem comes when a particular order is perceived as natural, as the neutral mapping of a domain, as an objective reading of nature. Feminists like Gilligan (1982) have made this objection to Kohlberg's (1981) model of moral development; she has argued that women's moral decision-making is more contextual, less tied to abstract principles of good and bad (Kohlberg's highest level). Kohlberg's model, she argues, is not neutral, but reflects a male bias. Similarly, Belenky, Clinchy, Goldberger, and Tarule (1985) argue that models of academic achievement may discriminate against women because their personal, empathetic, connected styles of engagement are viewed as less rigorous, less developed, than the more distanced, argumentative styles of men. No developmental scheme is innocent of ideology.

THE DEVELOPMENT OF LITERARY RESPONSE

Virtually all studies of literary response trace back to one source, I. A. Richards' *Practical Criticism* (1929). Richards presented a group of Cambridge students with 13 poems (with the names of the poets removed) and asked them to analyze the poems. Most of *Practical Criticism* is taken up with a discussion of the inadequacies of the responses that include: stock responses, irrelevant personal associations, inappropriate critical predispositions, sentimentality, and the inhibition of emotional response. Richards viewed these protocols as signs of the breakdown of literary education.

Researchers in this country who drew from Richards' study took a less pathological approach towards reader response. One of the most painstaking projects was James Squire's (1964) study of 52 ninth and tenth graders who were reading four short stories. Each student was asked to comment aloud at six carefully chosen spots in each story, and these oral commentaries were then classified into six categories: literary judgment, interpretational responses, narrational reactions (retellings), associational responses, self-involvement responses, and prescriptive judgements. In addition to some of the same difficulties found by Richards, Squire found that students were often limited by a search for certainty and a "happiness binding," a resistance to conclusions that were not upbeat. Purves and Rippere (1968) developed a more systematic and comprehensive taxonomy of responses grouped around four major categories: involvement engagement, perception, interpretation, and evaluation. This category system proved capable of reliable coding of responses and was used in a number of subsequent studies (summarized by Applebee, 1977).

Virtually all of the literary response studies were short-term studies (usually dissertations) that examined a single age group and therefore provided little information about the development of literary response. Unfortunately, the profession lacks longitudinal data of the type that Loban has provided on the development of syntax. Research on the development of literary responses has focused on asking students of differing ages to repond to texts and, on the basis of these responses, to suggest a developmental model. Svennson (1985) has made a useful distinction between "cognitive-developmental" and "cultural-developmental" studies of literary response.

Svennson cites Applebee's (1978) study as cognitive-developmental. According to Applebee, the individual's capacity to respond is tightly linked to Piagetian stages of development. The capacity to analyze literature, for example, is dependent upon the emergence of the formal operations' stage that occurs between ages 12 and 15. Up until that time the child's response is one of "exacting literalism." With the emergence of formal operations, the adolescent can begin to examine characters' motives, the structure of a work, and the reasons for personal reactions of pleasure or distaste.

Applebee's linking of "formal operations" with the capacity for analysis is common among language educators who attempt to "apply Piaget" (see also Lindemann, 1982). Yet, models like this one are open to challenge. Even if one accepts Piaget's stage theory of development (see Boden, 1980 for a skeptical review), it does not follow that all analysis is dependent upon the emergence of formal operations. Although the analysis students may *change* as they begin to perform formal operations, much younger children can, for example discuss why character did what he did or they can articulate reasons why they like or dislike a piece of literature (Calkins, 1983; Hemming, 1985). It is a serious misreading of Piaget to equate the capacity to analyze with "formal operations." The central question should be not *when* students begin analyzing but *how* their ability to analyze changes as they mature.

Svennson, drawing on the work of Fish (1980), argues for the superiority of cultural-developmental models that view development in literary response as a form of socialization. Students in high school enter an "interpretive community" with its own particular strategies for reading. In other words, changes in reading behavior are not viewed as the inevitable outcome of neurophysiological development but as the acquisition of accepted ways of reading. In her own study, Svennson found that older students tended to read symbolic meaning into poems whereas younger students stayed closer to the literal meaning. She also found that the older students were more able to justify or explain their symbolic strategies. In many cases the older students could apply conventional symbolic motifs (light = good; darkness = evil) where younger students did not apply them.

The developmental work of Beach and Wendler (1987) parallels that of Svennson. It examines the responses of students at four levels (8th, 11th, college freshmen and juniors) to two short stories. The authors note three shifts across this age span:

While younger students conceived of characters' actions as autonomous physical behaviors, older students viewed characters' actions as embedded within socially or psychologically defined contexts.
While younger students understood characters' perceptions in terms of immediate feelings, older students conceived of them in terms of characters' social psychological beliefs.
While younger students conceived of characters' goals in terms of characters' immediate or short-term needs, older students saw characters' goals in terms of long-term plans or strategies.

In general, older students viewed characters in a wider context whereas younger readers reacted more to the immediate action rather than its wider implications. Unlike Svennson, Beach and Wendler attribute this change to the capacity of older students to operate at the level of "formal operations." Yet, the work of Nancie Atwell (1987) with dialogue journals at least raises the possibility that the eighth graders are capable of the more theoretical responses given by older students; the performance of younger students in the Beach and Wendler study may reflect the instruction they receive (e.g., a focus on summarizing books and literal questions) rather than any inherent developmental limitations.

In fact, the cognitive-developmental models of response may foster a type of fatalism. If a student's difficulty with analysis is due to the lack of formal operational thinking, and if this stage of thinking occurs on a biological timetable, a teacher naturally may attribute the difficulty to the student's lack of development and not to inadequate instruction. These models, by suggesting biological ceilings for students at particiular ages, may actually have the effect of lowering expectations. By contrast, the cultural developmental model, although not ignoring the biological component of development, assigns a far greater role to culture to the ways talk, reading and writing function in the students' environment. While biology cannot be changed, culture can.

The high point in work literary response may have been the Winter 1976 issue of *Research in the Teaching of English,* which was entirely devoted to response to literature. But there was a significant decrease in empirical work on reader response in the late 1970s. In part, attention seemed to shift from empirical studies to more speculative work in literary theory. It is also possible that the elements of response approach, so dominant in this wave of research, may have failed to elucidate or explain the complex ways that texts and readers transact. This failure may have been due to the breadth of the elements; simply classifying responses as "evaluative" or "interpretive" misses the more central question of the *nature* of the evaluation or interpretation going on. Finally, there was a clear shift of interest away from literary response and toward the study of the writing process, a shift initiated by Janet Emig's *The Composing Processes of Twelfth Graders* (1971).

THE WRITING PROCESS

Shifting attention to the writing process in the 1970s represents both a scholarly and a political redirection. On the one hand, it was comprised of a set of investigations into the nature of the composing process; but it was also an attack on traditional instruction. And fittingly, both of these elements were present in the research study that is widely acknowledged as the starting point for this movement, Janet Emig's monograph, *The Composing Process of Twelfth Graders* (1971).

For her case studies, Emig collected background information on the subjects, carefully observed their writing behavior, elicited oral composing protocols, and interviewed the subjects about their processes; in effect, she employed the means of data-gathering that would be refined and used by subsequent researchers of the writing process. Most of her report is taken up with one of her subjects, Lynn, a good student who, despite her verbal facility, seems to consistently avoid risks in her writing, particularly when it comes to revealing feelings.

Emig goes well beyond her data in her conclusions where she blames Lynn's schools, and by extension school writing instruction in general, for inhibiting student development:

This inquiry strongly suggests that, for a number of reasons, school-sponsored writing experienced by older secondary students is a limited, and limiting experience. The teaching of composition at this level is essentially unimodal, with only extensive [what Britton called "transactional"] writing given sanction in many schools. Almost by definition, this mode is other-directed—in fact it is other-centered. The concern is with sending a message, a communication out into the world for the edification, the enlightenment, and ultimately the evaluation of another. Too often the other is a teacher, interested chiefly in a product he can criticize rather than in a process he can help initiate through empathy and support. (p. 97)

This statement might serve as the political manifesto of the writing process movement, whatever its merits as a research conclusion.

Research on writing processes drew on Emig's research methods. Flower and Hayes (1980, 1981) refined oral composing as a method for uncovering the cognitive dimensions of the writing process, and particularly the differences between skilled and novice writers. Sommers (1980) and Bridwell (1980) focused on revision processes and demonstrated that students rarely made major changes in their writing after a first draft. Matsuhashi (1981) refined Emig's mode of observation, and using a double camera she was able to monitor pauses in composing; she found students had different pause patterns when they shifted from narrative to expository writing, indicating that the cognitive processes for composing in these models might be different. Perl (1979) combined oral composing protocols and observations of writing behavior to illustrate how basic writers seemed to fixate on surface features.

Emig's political attack may have been even more influential than her research innovations. At the time of her study, composition was almost subsumed under literature; Squire and Applebee (1968) found that two thirds of composition topics were tied to literature. Moreover, students were asked to write about literature in a distanced way; the structure for papers was typically thesis-support and the tone impersonal (the first-person often prohibited). What Louise Rosenblatt (1978) called the "transaction" of reading, the narrative moment-by-moment activity of interpretation, seemed incompatible with the rigid requirements of the formal argumentative essays students were asked to write. One guide for students even stated, "When your professor reads a paper, he is less interested in the actual process by which you arrived at the thesis than by the *result* of the process, the thesis itself, supported by a clear, lively, organized argument" (1974).

One solution to this undue restriction on writing possibilities was to allow students freedom in choosing topics. Elbow (1973) and Macrorie (1968) demonstrated ways that freewriting could help writers discover ideas, insights, and topics; the activity of nonstop writing could act as a heuristic to allow these submerged possibilities to take shape. Murray (1968) similarly claimed that if students are to be treated as writers, they should be allowed to choose topics they know and care about. In this way they could write from a position of authority rather than write to an authority.

Other means of responding were also proposed. Elbow (1973), Moffett (1968), and Macrorie (1968) proposed student writing groups, where response would come from peers rather than the teacher acting as evaluator. Garrison (1974), Carnicelli (1980), and Murray (1968) demonstrated ways in which one-on-one writing conferences could also remove the teacher from the limiting role of evaluator and could help provide the empathy and support Emig claimed was lacking in traditional instruction.

Like most challenges to the staus quo, this one at times was taken to extremes. Brannon and Knoblauch (1982) invoked the metaphor of "ownership" to describe the students' relationship to their own texts; it follows that the expectations of teachers, schools, or communities could be viewed as infringements on the expressive rights of students. If students are given almost complete freedom in choosing what they want to write, they might stay close to the narrative forms that are most familiar to them and avoid forms of analytic writing that are less familiar. Unless one takes the extreme position, arguing that discourse forms are somehow innate in the learners mind, like the basic grammar of the language, it not clear how students will learn new forms in a classroom where they receive no structured assistance in their writing.

Equally troublesome was the polarizing of process and product, as if teachers and researchers had to choose between the two. The focus on process was primarily intended to redirect attention to teaching writing. Christensen commented, at about the time of Emig's study, that students were not "taught" to write, they were "expected" to write (1967, p. 3). And, as Murray repeatedly reminded his readers, written products do not reveal the process of their production—"you can't infer the pig from the sausage" (1980, p. 3). Yet, successful employment of writing processes is, to a considerable extent, dependent upon an awareness of the type of product or text to be produced. Correlational studies consistently show that writing ability is strongly related to reading ability and to the availability of reading material in the home (Applebee, Langer, & Mullis, 1987a); students inevitably draw on the knowledge of language conventions and discourse structures they gain through reading when they write. By polarizing process and product, these reformers may have obscured their dynamic interdependence and unwisely minimized the ways that reading exemplary texts provides goals and cultural landmarks, which writers use to guide their processes.

The sharpest critique of some writing process approaches came in George Hillocks' (1986) encyclopedic review of over 2000 studies in composition. The centerpiece of Hillocks' critique is a meta-analysis of experimental studies that he compares four broadly defined approaches to composition teaching: the presentational, the individual, the natural process, and the environmental. The presentational mode includes methods that emphasize teacher lecture or teacher-led discussions, use of models, specific objectives, and teacher feedback only when papers are returned. The natural process mode includes general objectives (e.g., fluency, voice), free-writing, extensive peer interaction, generally positive feedback, and opportunities for revision. The environmental mode shares some elements with the natural process mode; it avoids teacher lecture and it engages the student in a process of planning, drafting, and revision. It also encourages group interaction. It differs from natural process in that the goals are more specific (e.g., to increase the use of details and specific language), and the student is

guided through a structured process designed around the more specific goals. The final mode, the individualized mode includes one-on-one instruction including tutorial and programmed learning approaches.

In his meta-analysis, Hillocks grouped 29 treatments (4 presentational, 9 natural process, 9 environmental, 6 individualized), and for each mode he compared the average difference in improvement between the experimental and control groups. He concluded that the environmental approach was statistically superior and demonstrably more effective than the other three modes. Hillocks speculates that the natural process approaches are less effective because of the generalized nature of the tasks students are asked to perform, a particular example being free-writing. According to Hillocks, free-writing can be performed successfully by using "low-level strategies," a "what-next strategy" that does not call for the student to engage in a systematic process of exploration or to attempt new and more difficult forms.

Hillocks' conclusions can be criticized on a number of counts. His category natural process is almost a caricature of the positions taken by the educators he criticizes—Emig, Calkins, Elbow, Graves, Murray; they would argue that the conference approach, for example, can be a rigorous form of inquiry, and has been since the time of Socrates. The set of studies used by Hillocks is quite small (26), and in the presentational category only two studies are used, neither of which has ever been published in a research journal (of the 26 studies only 6 have appeared in research journals). Finally, there is an ex post facto quality to this meta-analysis; the studies, for the most part, were not designed to test Hillocks' categories.

Applebee (1986) maintains that Hillocks' results can be seen as affirming many of the major innovations of the writing process movement:

Hillocks' argument involves a semantic sleight of hand . . . that can produce a serious misinterpretation of what his data mean. The "environmental" mode that Hillocks champions is itself a version of process-oriented instruction and draws on a panoply of techniques he seems to be attacking. (p. 105)

Applebee credits Hillocks' study with shifting the emphasis away from global generalized processes to processes that are specifically linked with various writing tasks, an approach he calls structured process.

Applebee notes that process approaches, particularly those that adhere to what Bizzell calls a "pedagogy of personal style" (1986), are mismatched with traditional subject-centered notions of instruction in secondary schools. English teachers, for example, continue to view themselves primarily as literature teachers; over 70 percent of student surveyed in th 1986 literature assessment reported that over half of their class time was spent on literature (Applebee, Langer, & Mullis, 1987a). A process pedagogy stressing free choice of topics will naturally be viewed by these teachers as taking time and effort away from their primary mission. Applebee concludes that, "put simply, process-oriented approaches may be, by definition, impossible to implement successfully, given traditional notions of instruction" (1986, p. 108).

Attempts to relate process techniques with the more traditional aims of English classes—the analysis of literary texts—may be met with less resistance. Researchers like Marshall (1987) and Durst (1984) claim that the traditional, thesis-driven critical analysis paper, may actually preclude the kind of analysis it is intended to foster. Marshall quotes one student:

In a limited essay, it's already written. I mean there's an opening paragraph where you tell what it's about. This is always very technical. Automatic. The first sentence is always "In blank's novel" and there's the title. It's all by formula, it's just to what degree. And then you have the example for one character and then an example for another and then you compare the two people and then you conclude. And that's it. It's totally set. (pp. 38–39)

Statements like this one lend support to Bartholomae's indictment of this form of school writing:

When, for example, we ask students to write about texts, the tyranny of the thesis often invalidates the very act of analysis we hope to invoke. Hence in assignment after assignment, we find students asked to reduce a novel, a poem, or their own experience into a single sentence, and then to use the act of writing in order to defend or "support" that single sentence. Writing is used to close a subject down rather than open it up, to put an end to discourse, rather than to open up a project. (1983, p. 311)

Zeigler (1985) has similarly argued that the *closed* thesis driven essay dominates academic writing at the expense of more *open* forms, suggesting to students that "the ability to support an assertion is more important than the ability to examine an issue (p. 458)." The school essay has come to bear little resemblance to the essay as it was originally defined by Montaigne, an "essai" or attempt, a trial to see what one knows and thinks about a subject. Contemporary essayists, Montaigne's heirs, also view that form as fluid, and exploration and not a logical proof. Edward Hoagland (1976) writes:

A personal essay is like a human voice talking, its order, the mind's natural flow, instead of a systemized outline of ideas. Though more wayward or informal than an article or treatise, somewhere it contains a point which is its real center, even if the point couldn't be uttered in fewer words than the essayist has used. Essays don't usually boil down to a summary, as articles do.... (in Smart, 1985, p. 223)

Much of the current work on reader response and the ways writing can be used to respond to texts (e.g., Atwell, 1985, 1987: Bartholomae and Petrosky, 1986; Bleich 1975; Lindberg, 1986; Nelms, 1988; Newkirk, 1984: Petrosky, 1982; Probst, 1988) are attempts to reclaim the essay, to provide space for the "human voice talking."

SCHOOL REFORM

This chapter began with the claim that student's language development is not a natural biological unfolding but rather reflects and gains direction from the culture of the school; as Vygotsky claimed 50 years ago, reversing Piagetian logic, instruction preceeds development. Studies of high school instruction and student achievement in U.S. schools provide a clear illustration of Vygotsky's contention. Instruction emphasizes the acquisition of factual information and repetitive exercises dealing with the mechanics of language, to the neglect of objectives dealing with critical thinking and intellectual development. Similarly, students seem to attain a basic competence on reading and writing, but they have difficulty in the extension and elaboration of their ideas. They have learned what they have been taught.

It is unlikely that this problem identified in virtually all of the high school reports can be remedied through exhortation or accountability schemes, tougher graduation requirements, or career ladders, all of which would leave the basic structure of the high school and the working conditions of teachers unchanged. The first article to appear in the *English Journal,* which began publication in 1912, identified the workload of the high school teacher as the major obstacle to effective writing instruction. Entitled, "Can Good Composition Teaching Be Done Under Present Conditions?" it began:

No.

This is a small and apparently unprotected word, occupying a somewhat exposed position; but it is upborne by indesputable truth. (Hopkins, 1912, p. 1)

Hopkins' essay recounts the attempts to assign the responsibility for teaching writing to English teachers without any reduction in teacher-pupil ratio. Writing, Hopkins contends, can only be learned through writing; in the terminology of the day it was a "laboratory subject." Yet, the demands of responding to student writing were causing teachers to "resign, break down, perhaps become permanent invalids, having sacrificed ambition, health, and in not a few instances even life, in the struggle to do all the work of them" (p. 1).

A 1977 survey of teaching conditions in English suggest that the teacher-student ratio has actually worsened in the time since Hopkins wrote. The typical load is five classes per day, and in randomly selected schools 28.7 percent of classes had 26 to 30 students, and 30.2 percent had more than 31 students (Applebee, 1978). It is hardly surprising that instruction is largely presentational, that it focuses on information and mechanical skills that can be efficiently tested. Given this teaching load, it is also understandable why teachers rely on formulaic essay writing, considering the heavy burden of response that a 150 student load places on them.

Reformers like Sizer argue that high schools could be organized in different ways; that this pattern of requiring a teacher to meet a large number of students for a short time each day is an accommodation schools make to the "shopping mall" concept. The fragmented day is a necessary compromise if students are to have an array of options to choose from. Sizer's recommendation is to renegotiate the compromises schools make: school academic departments, rather than imitating the divisions of the university, could be consolidated into four areas: inquiry and expression, mathematics and science, literature and arts, and philosophy and history. In exchange for teaching more broadly defined subjects, teachers would teach fewer students and therefore be able to break out of the presentational mode and provide more individualized attention.

The Horace in the title of Sizer's book *Horace's Compromise* (1984) is an English teacher and his day is filled with compromises, shortcuts necessitated by demands of high school teaching. If he gives even 5 minutes of his time *per week* to the written work of each student, he is committed to 10 hours of outside work, in addition to class preparation, committe work, and time spent as drama advisor. Sizer writes, "Most jobs in the real world would have a gap between what would be nice and what is possible. The tragedy for many high school teachers is that the gap is chasm, not to be crossed by reasonable and judicious adjustments" (p. 20). It is of course possible to suggest that through heroic measures teachers can cross this chasm, but few professions can rely on heroism.

The crisis in language development is not simply one of ineffectual teaching methods that can, without great disruption, be replaced by more efficient ones. Teachers like Horace need no convincing, on a theoretical level, of the value of in-dividual attention to writing or reading. What they lack is the same thing teachers in Hopkins' time lacked, working conditions that make this individualized attention possible. And, according to Sizer a key factor in making the necessary changes is the empowerment of teachers. Sizer finishes his day at Horace's home, and he listens to him talk bitterly about all of the "top-down" solutions to the current high school crisis. Sizer concludes:

The empowerment of Horace could make a difference. Underneath his defensiveness, he knows that. For some reason, we start morbidly comparing the U.S. Army's top-down activities in Vietnam to the Viet Cong peasant army. Could Horace be a peasant soldier. We slide off the analogy: it isn't right. But he persists in this direction. If I had my way . . . he goes on. It all rings right, because Horace knows how he could find a way to improve each student's self-esteem, how standards could be raised, how sloppy routines could be shaped up. I leave dinner, knowing that Horace is the key. (p. 201)

References

Applebee, A. N. (1978). *The child's concept of story: Ages two to seventeen.* Chicago: University of Chicago Press.

Applebee, A. N. (1977). "ERIC/RCS report: The elements of response to a literary work: What have we learned." *Research in the Teaching of English, 11,* 255–271.

Applebee, A. N. (1974). *Tradition and reform in the teaching of English: A history.* Urbana, IL: National Council of Teachers of English.

Applebee, A. N. (1978). *A survey of teaching conditions in English, 1977.* Urbana, IL: ERIC/National Council of Teachers of English.

Applebee, A. N. (1986). "Problems in process approaches: Toward a reconceptualization of process instruction." In A. Petrosky, D. Bartholomae (Eds.), *The teaching of writing: Eighty-fifth yearbook of the national society for the study of education, part II.* Chicago: National Society for the Study of Education.

Applebee, A. N. (1981). *Writing in the secondary school: English and the content areas* (Research Report 21). Urbana, IL: National Council of Teachers of English.

Applebee, A. N., Langer, J. A and Mullis I. V. S (nd.). *Writing trends across the decade, 1974–1984.* Princeton, NJ: Educational Testing Service.

Applebee, A. N., Langer, J. A. Mullis I. V. S. (1986a). *The reading report card: Progress toward excellence in our schools.* Princeton, NJ: Educational Testing Service.

Applebee, A. N., Langer, J. A. Mullis I. V. S. (1986b). *The writing report card: Writing achievement in american schools.* Princeton, NJ: Educational Testing Service.

Applebee, A. N., Langer, J. A. Mullis. I. V. S. (1987a). *Literature and U.S. history: The instructional experience and factual knowledge of high school juniors.* Princeton, NJ: Educational Testing Service.

Applebee, A. N., Langer, J. A. Mullis I. V. S. (1987b). *Learning to be literate in America: Reading, writing, and reasoning.* Princeton, NJ: Educational Testing Service.

Atwell, N. (1987). *In the middle: Writing, reading and learning with adolescents.* Portsmouth, NH: Heinemann/Boynton Cook.

Atwell, N. (1985). Reading and writing from the inside out. In J. Hansen, T. Newkirk, D. Graves (Eds.), *Breaking ground: Teachers relate reading and writing in the elementary school.* Portsmouth NH: Heinemann.

Bartholomae, D. (1983). Writing assignments: Where writing begins. In P. Stock (Ed.), *Fforum: Essays on theory and practice in the teaching of writing.* Portsmouth, NH: Heinemann/Boynton Cook.

Bartholomae, D., A. Petrosky. (1986). *Facts, artifacts, and counterfacts: Theory and method for a reading and writing course.* Portsmouth, N. H.: Boynton Cook/Heinemann.

Beach, R., L. Wendler. (1987). Development differences in response to a story. *Research in the Teaching of English 21* 286–297.

Belenky, M. F., B. M. Clinchy, N. R. Goldberger, J. M. Tarule. (1986). *Women's ways of knowing : The development of self, voice, and mind.* New York: Basic Books.

Bizzell, P. (1986). Composing processes: An overview. In A. Petrosky, D. Bartholomae (Eds.), *The teaching of writing: Eighty-fifth yearbook of the national society for the study of education. part II.* Chicago: National Society for the Study of Education.

Bleich, D. (1975). *Readings and feelings: An introduction to subjective criticism.* Urbana, IL: National Council of Teachers of English.

Bloom, B. (Ed.) (1959). *Taxonomy of educational objectives: The classification of goals by a committee of college and university examiners.* New York: Longman, Green.

Boden, M. (1980). *Jean Piaget.* New York: Viking.

Boyer, E. (1983). *High school: A report on secondary education in America.* New York: Harper and Row.

Braddock, R., R. L. Jones, L. Schoer. (1963) *Research in written composition.* Urbana, IL: National Council of Teachers of English.

Brannon, L., Knoblauch, C. H. (1982). On students' rights to their own texts: A model of teacher response. *College Composition and Communication 33,* 157–166.

Bridwell, L. (1980). Revising strategies in twelfth grade students' transactional writing." *Research in the Teaching of English 14,* 197–222.

Britton, J., Burgess, T, Martin, N., McLeod, A., Rosen, H. (1975). *The development of writing abilities. 11–18.* London: Mcmillan Education.

Calkins, L. (1983). *Lessons from a child* Portsmouth: Heinemann.

Carnicelli, T. (1980). The writing conference: A one-to-one conversation. In T. Donovan, B. McClelland (Eds.), *Eight approaches to teaching composition.* Urbana, IL: National Council of Teachers of English.

Christensen, F. (1967). *Notes toward a new rhetoric.* New York: Harper and Row.

Combs, W. (1976). Further effects of sentence-combining on writing ability. *Research in the Teaching of Englislh 10,* 137–149.

Conant, J. B. (1959). *The American high school today.* New York: McGraw Hill.

Conant, J.B. (1967). *The comprehensive high school*. New York: McGraw Hill.

Durst, R. (1984). The development of analytic writing. In A. Applebee, *Contexts for Learning to Write: Studies of Secondary School Instruction*. Norwood. NJ: ABLEX.

Elbow, P. (1973). *Writing without teachers*. New York: Oxford University Press.

Emig, J. (1971). *The composing process of twelfth graders*. (Research Report 13). Urbana, IL: National Council of Teachers of English.

Fillion, B. (1986). Language across the curriculum: Examining the place of language in our schools." In T. Newkirk (Ed.) *To compose: Teaching writing in high school and college*. Portsmouth, NH.: Heinemann.

Fish, S. (1980). *Is there a text in this class?: The authority of interpretive communities*. Cambridge, Massachusetts: Harvard University Press.

Fitzgerald, F. (1979). *America Revised*. New York: Vintage Books.

Flower, L., Hayes, J. R. (1981). A cognitive process theory of writing. *College Composition and Communication 32*, 365–387.

Flower, L., Hayes, J. R. (1980). The dynamics of composing: Making plans and juggling constraints. "In Gregg, L. W., Steinberg, E. R, (Eds.), *Cognitive Processes in Writing*. Hillsdale, NJ: Lawrence Earlbaum.

Friere, P. (1970). *Pedagogy of the oppressed. New York: Herder and Herder*.

Fulwiler, T. (1988). The journal book. Portsmouth, NH.: Boynton Cook/Heinemann.

Garrison, R. (1974). One-to-one: Tutorial instruction in freshman English. *New Directions for Community Colleges 2* (1) 55–84.

Gilligan, C. (1982) *In a different voice: Psychological theory and women's development*. Cambridge, MA: Harvard University Press.

Goodlad, J. (1984). *A place called school: Prospects for the future*. New York: McGraw Hill.

Harste, J., Woodward, V., Burke, C. (1984). *Language stories and literacy lessons*. Portsmouth, NH.: Heinemann.

Hartwell, Patrick. (1985). Grammar, grammars, and the teaching of grammar. *College English, 47*, 105–127.

Heath, S. B. (1983). *Ways with words: Language, life, and work in communities and classrooms*. Cambridge, England: Cambridge University Press.

Hemming, H. (1985). Reading: A monitor for writing. In J. Hansen, T. Newkirk, and D. Graves (Eds.), *Breaking ground: Teachers relate reading and writing in the elementary school*. Portsmouth, NH.: Heinemann.

Hillocks, G. (1986). *Research on written composition: New directions for teaching*. Urbana, IL: National Conference on Research in English.

Hopkins, E. M. (1912). Can good composition teaching be done under present conditions. *English Journal, 1*, 1–7.

Hunt, K. (1977). Early blooming and late blooming syntactic structures. In C. Cooper and L. Odell (Eds.), *Evaluating writing: Describing, measuring, judging*. Urbana, IL: National Council of Teachers of English.

Hunt, K. (1965). *Grammatical structures written at three grade levels* (Research Report 3). Urbana, IL: National Council of Teachers of English.

Kohlberg, L. (1981) *The philosophy of moral development*. New York: Harper and Row.

Kolnn, M. (1981). Closing the books on alchemy. *College Composition and Communication, 32*, 139–151.

Lindberg, G. (1986). Coming to words: Writing as process and the reading of literature. In T. Newkirk, (Eds.), *Only connect: Uniting reading and writing*. Portsmouth, NH: Boynton Cook.

Lindemann, E. (1982) *A rhetoric for writers*. New York: Oxford University Press.

Loban, W. (1976). *Language development: Kindergarten through grade twelve*. (Research Report 18). Urbana, IL: National Council of Teachers of English.

Macrorie, K. (1968). *Writing to be read*. Rochelle Park, NJ: Hayden.

Marshall, J. (1987). The effects of writing on students' understanding of literary texts. *Research in the Teaching of English, 21*, 30–63.

Martin, N., D'Arcy, P., Newton, B., Parker, R. (1976). *Writing and learning across the curriculum, 11–16*. Portsmouth, N.H.: Boynton Cook, 1976.

Matsuhashi, A. (1981). Pausing and planning: The tempo of written discourse production. *Research in the Teaching of English, 15*, 113–134.

Mellon, J. (1969). *Transformational sentence combining*. (Research Report 10). Urbana, IL: National Council of Teachers of English.

Moffett, J. (1968). *Teaching the universe of discourse*. Boston:Houghton Mifflin.

Morenberg, M., Daiker, D., Kerek, A. (1978). Sentence combining at the college level: An experimental study. *Research in the Teaching of English, 12*, 245–256.

Morenberg, M., Daiker, D., Kerek, A. (1980). Sentence-Combining over a three-year period: A case study." Paper, annual meeting of the CCC. ED 186 921.

Murray, D. (1968). *A writer teaches writing*. Boston: Houghton Mifflin.

Murray, D. (1980). Writing as process: How writing finds it's own meaning. In T. Donovan and B. McClelland (Eds.). *Eight approaches to teaching composition*. Urbana, IL: National Council of Teachers of English.

A Nation At Risk (1983). (Report by the National Commission on Excellence.) Wasington, D.C.: Government Printing Office.

Nelms, B. F., (Ed.). (1988). *Literature in the classroom: Readers, texts, and contexts*. Urbana, IL: National Council of Teachers of English.

Newkirk, T. (1984). Looking for trouble: A way to unmask our readings. *College English, 46*, 756–766.

O'Donnell, R., Griffin, W., Norris, R. (1967) *Syntax of kindergarten and elementary school children: A transformational nalysis*. (Research Report 8). Urbana, IL: National Council of Teachers of English.

O'Hare, F. (1973) *Sentence combining: Improving student writing without formal grammar instruction*. (Research Report 15). Urbana, IL.: National Council of Teachers of English.

Odell, L., Cooper, C. (1976). Describing responses to works of fiction. *Research in the Teaching of English, 10*, 203–225.

Perl, (1979). The composing process of unskilled college writers. *Research in the Teaching of English, 13*, 317–336.

Petrosky, A. (1982). From story to essay: Reading and writing." *College Composition and Communication, 33*, 19–36.

Polanyi, M. (1958). *Personal knowledge: Toward a post-critical philosophy*. Chicago: University of Chicago Press.

Powell, A., Farrar, E., Cohen, D. (1985). *The shopping mall high school*. Boston: Houghton Mifflin.

Probst, R. (1988). *Response and analysis: Teaching literature in junior and senior high*. Portsmouth, NH: Boynton Cook/Heinemann.

Purves, A. & V. Rippere. (1968). *Elements of writing about a literary work: A study of response to literature*. (Research Report 9). Urbana, IL: National Council of Teachers of English.

Reading, Writing, and Thinking: Results From the 1979–1980 Assessment of Reading and Literature. Denver: National Assessment of Educational Progress.

Richards, I. A. (1929) *Practical Criticism*. New York: Harcourt, Brace, and World.

Rosenblatt, L. (1978). *The reader, the text, and the poem: The transactional theory of the literacy work*. Carbondale, IL: Southern Illinois University Press.

Sizer, T. (1984). *Horace's compromise: The dilemma of the American high school*. Boston: Houghton Mifflin.

Smart, W. (1985). *Eight modern essayists* (Fourth Edition). New York: St. Martins.

Sommers, N. (1980). Revision Strategies of Student Writers and Experienced Writers. *College Composition and Communication, 31,* 378–388.

Stewart, M. (1978). Freshman Sentence Combining: A Canadian Project. *Research in the Teaching of English, 12,* 257–268.

Squire, J. (1964). *The responses of adolescents while reading four short stories.* (Research Report 2). Urbana, IL: National Council of Teachers.

Squire, J., Applebee, R. (1968). *High school English instruction today.* New York: Appleton Crofts.

Style Sheet. (1974). Los Angeles, CA.: Department of English, UCLA.

Svensson, C. (1985). *The construction of poetic meaning: A cultural-developmental study of symbolic and non-symbolic strategies in the interpretation of contemporary poetry.* Malmo, Sweden: Liber Forlag.

Vygotsky, L. (1978). *Mind in society.* Cambridge, MA: Harvard University Press.

Zeigler, W. "The exploratory essay: Enfranchising the spirit of inquiry in college composition." *College English, 47,* 454–466.

19F. CATCHING UP AND FILLING IN: LITERACY LEARNING AFTER HIGH SCHOOL

Richard L. Venezky

The earliest studies ever recorded on reading, performed in France at the end of the eighteenth century, assessed the ability of adults to read different type fonts. From that time until the present, adults have been the primary subjects of psychological studies of reading, yet the improvement of literacy abilities beyond childhood, and especially beyond high school, has an impoverished empirical base, anchored primarily in research on reading in children. Darkenwald (1986), for example, in surveying 236 journal articles published between 1975 and 1980 on adult literacy education, found fewer than 12 that qualified as research. Although we know with great certainty the average number of milliseconds a skilled adult will fixate during silent reading and the distance in letter spaces from the fovea where single letters can no longer be recognized, we have almost no data on how decoding ability develops for those who acquire it after their teens, or even on how different instructional approaches influence reading strategies for this same population. On one hand, assumptions made for children are often extended without question to adults; on the other, lessons acquired in the investigation of child learning are ignored in the study of adults.

The review of adult literacy learning that follows has two specific goals. One is to point out major gaps in the empirical base for adult literacy learning, but to do so in a manner that might lead to improved research. At present many issues center more on personal opinions than they do on empirical results; problems are seldom pursued to satisfactory closure; and no well-defined cutting edge for research exists. The healthy competition among researchers that is evidenced in low temperature fusion, genetics, and superconductivity, for example, has no counterparts in the field of adult literacy. Critical response to experiments is almost nonexistent, thus allowing some poorly designed and poorly executed studies to be touted as gospel, and some excellent ones to remain in cluttered obscurity.

My second goal is to raise for discussion the possibility that the K–12 language-arts curriculum is a major contributor to the problems of the postsecondary literacy learner. By focusing so narrowing on "good" literature as a basis for literacy learning, the schools are denying to many, and especially those who drop out early, the essential skills they need for coping with everyday literacy demands.

Although the interest of this chapter is in literacy in the broadest terms, that is, the utilization of reading, writing, numeracy, and document processing for social ends, studies on adult literacy are, with a few exceptions (e.g., Mikulecky, 1980), studies of adult reading. Therefore, reading will be the focus here although "literacy" will occasionally be used, mostly as a reminder even to the writer that the empirical base required for principled literacy instruction includes more than a knowledge of how reading is acquired. Because adult reading interests and basic processing habits has been reviewed extensively elsewhere (e.g., Gibson & Levin, 1975; Gray & Munroe, 1929;

Buswell, 1937; Murphy, 1975; Pearson, 1984; Sharon, 1973, 1974), little mention will be made of these topics. Instead, attention is focused on those areas of research that illuminate the needs of the low reading ability adult. Many other important topics are not covered due to space limitations, including bilingualism and the social context of literacy learning.

By research is meant true empirical studies, with reasonable and appropriate experimental designs. However, the finding from 30 years ago that the definitions of research for adult education were "exceedingly liberal" remains true today (Brunner, Wilder, Kirschner, & Newberry, 1959, cited in Weber, 1975, p.156). For gauging what has changed in research and practice on adult literacy between the 1950s and how, the reader is encouraged to consult the overview of adult education research by Brunner et al. (1959), and Weber's (1975) insightful review. French (1987) presents an extensive, up-to-date overview and bibliography on the entire field of adult literacy, including literacy research, while Cook (1977) reviews the twentieth-century history of adult literacy education. A brief review of both research and practice can be found in Sticht (1988).

THE THEORETICAL BASE FOR ADULT LITERACY LEARNING

Three issues from the literature are discussed here as illustrations of both the promise and the problems with research on adult literacy learning: stages of development, processing modality, and processing mode. All relate to theories of reading and reading development, but none has been extensively studied or debated. At the and of this section several important research issues that have received limited attention in adult literacy research are presented.

Stages of Reading Development

The earliest approximation to a stage model for reading development was published by Mann (1839), in which mechanical and mental parts for reading were defined. Mann did not present these parts as a developmental sequence, but that could be inferred from his presentation. In this century several stage models for reading development have been proposed, based upon observations of children's reading habits. The two most elaborate of these are Gray (1937) and Chall (1983), both of which posit five levels or stages for reading development. The validity and utility of either of these models for adult learners, however, remains to be demonstrated. Although children tend to follow similar paths from total unawareness of letters and words to fully mature reading, adults who are in need of literacy instruction are a far more diverse group, both in reading ability and in background knowledge. Some low literate adults, either

343

for reasons of health or opportunity, have had limited exposure to reading instruction, while others have passed through eight or more years of instruction, acquiring, in some cases, faulty strategies for coping with the demands of print.

Malicky & Norman (1982), for example, analyzed the reading strategies of 16 adults who were full-time students in an adult basic education program. The subjects ranged in age from 18 to 35 years, and in reading levels from readiness to sixth grade, based upon a reading inventory. From an analysis of oral reading errors obtained at different times during the course, different patterns of processing changes were detected. For example, for one group of readers who upon entry overrelied on graphemic cues, a shift was made towards a more balanced reliance upon both graphemic and grammatical cues. This group, however, made no gains in reading ability. Another group that did make gains in reading ability showed slightly less ability than the no-gain group to use semantic cues.

In a related study, Leibert (1983) compared the oral reading errors of adult basic education students to elementary level students with comparable reading levels. For children, rate of reading as well as accuracy of recall declined with passage difficulty, while for the adults only rate of reading declined over the same set of passages. Given the vastly different knowledge and experience bases that adults and children bring to a reading task, plus the superior experience that most adults have had with language communication, differences in processing strategies should be expected, even for those who produce similar scores on reading tests. Even the approaches to taking tests may differ. Adults, according to Karlsen (1970), take fewer risks than children and therefore tend to omit items on a test they are not sure of rather than guessing at them. Sticht (1982) has also found from a series of comparisons of adult and children in reading and reading related tasks that processing strategies often differ for those who appear to be at the same reading level.

A different form of developmental model for reading is implied by a reading maturity scaling developed by Gray and Rogers (1956). From studies of adult reading interests, attitudes, and abilities, a scaling procedure was devised and built around

1. Interest in reading;
2. Purposes for reading;
3. Recognition and construction of meaning;
4. Reaction to and use of ideas apprehended; and
5. Kinds of material read.

Within each category three or four topics were defined, with a five-point scale for evaluating subjects on each of these. Thus, interest in reading was evaluated for (a) enthusiasm for reading, (b) amount of time spent reading, (c) breadth of interest, and (d) depth of interest (Sticht, 1982, p. 76). What is important about this scheme is that it defines the mature adult reader in terms not only of latent skill, as measured on a reading test, but also in terms of interests, breadth and depth of actual reading practices, willingness to relate ideas read to other information, concepts, and kinds of materials read. The school's responsibility in literacy training is not only to engender the skills required for competent reading, but also to encourage the full application of this ability for personal and social ends. Studies done

over the last 60 years indicate that many adults have little interest in reading beyond the more shallow components of newspapers and magazines, and that book reading for all but the highly educated is minimal at best (Gray & Munroe, 1929; Gray, 1956; Gray & Rogers, 1956; Kirsch & Jungeblut, 1986; Sharon, 1973, 1974.)

In reviewing studies and opinions on stages of reading, it is difficult to ignore the paucity of empirical data to support any stage-by-stage model for adult learners. Nevertheless, if stages that characterize literacy development in adults can be verified, then attention could shift to the instructional implications of each stage and especially to the instructional strategies that most effectively assist progression from stage to stage.

Processing Modality and Reading Capacity

The relationship of listening comprehension to reading comprehension is a theme that threads its way through the last 50 years or so of reading research. It has been argued that because reading is language based and language is acquired first by most people through listening, a comparison of listening to reading ability might reveal capacity to learn to read (e.g., Goldstein, 1940). Several dissertations have been done on the topic, a few standardized tests developed, and at least two monographs published (Goldstein, 1940; Sticht, Beck, Hauke, Kleiman, & James, 1974). One hypothesis drawn from this work is that listening (i.e., auding) ability represents an upper bound on reading ability, particularly after eighth grade, and that mature reading can be defined as that quality of reading where comprehension is at least equivalent to listening comprehension. The problems with this notion are first that we know less about the development of listening comprehension than we do about reading comprehension, and second, that the relationship of listening comprehension to reading comprehension is more complex than most recent studies admit, depending upon, among other variables, the difficulty level of the text and the intelligence of the reader/listener. Goldstein (1940), whose work in this area remains as the most thorough, found from studies of adults (ages 18 to 65) that

1. Superiority of listening over reading decreases with increasing difficulty of the text. For easy texts, listening is superior to reading regardless of intelligence;
2. Difference between listening and reading ability increases with decreasing intelligence; and
3. Passages that are equivalent for reading may not be equivalent for listening.

The use of a listening/reading ratio as an indicator of learning capacity engenders a number of risks, based upon the findings of Goldstein (1940) and others. Persons who measure low in listening comprehension may do so for a variety of reasons, none of which are well understood. Then, persons with low listening ability might be helped best by extensive reading training, especially because beyond the initial levels of learning, self-instruction becomes more practicable with reading training than listening training. The claim that listening ability for adults represents an upper bound for reading ability has no empirical support. The differences between the two might provide useful diagnostic information, particularly about the mechanics of reading, but even this awaits more careful analysis.

Processing Modes

From studies done early in this century that appeared to show that eye movements varied according to text content (e.g., Judd & Buswell, 1922), suggestions were made for remedial reading programs built around different types of reading for different subject areas. McCaul (1944), for example, proposed that literature be used to increase reading speed, social studies for improving organization ability, and science for precision and accuracy. Dixon (1951), in criticizing the studies done up to that time, pointed out that Judd and Buswell (1922) based their results on only four college students, made no tests for significance of differences, and did not equate passages for conceptual load, vocabulary, or any other internal variable. (Judd & Buswell, 1922, report fixations per line for reading fiction, geography, rhetoric, easy verse, French grammar, blank verse, and algebra.) Studies by Terry(1922), Tinker(1928), Stone(1941), and others were found to suffer from similar problems.

Dixon (1951) replicated these studies, using reading speed and various eye movement variables as dependent measures, but equated passages for objective difficulty, using the Flesch and Lorge readability formulas. Passages were selected from the fields of education, history, and physics, and the subjects were university professors and graduate students from these same areas. Subjects read a single practice passage in each area and then the test passage, answering five general yes-no questions after each reading. The results showed no intrinsic subject matter differences. Each group of subjects read fastest from its own field, and no group was significantly better than any other. As would be expected from modern data, individual variation within fields was as wide if not wider than differences across fields.

While Dixon (1951) has rejected the idea of subject-based differences in reading habits, at least as assayed by reading speed and eye movements, this study is limited to a single type of reading task, albeit, the one most commonly encountered in schooling (i.e., read the passage for general meaning and answer questions on it afterwards). Other investigators have pursued the notion of reading differences by attending to task differences in reading (and occasionally writing).

Other Agendas

Missing from the adult studies are attempts to relate reading strategies to reading instruction. Barr (1972), for example, found a strong influence of instruction on the types of oral reading errors made by children in first grade. There is every reason to assume that similar influence occurs with adult learners. Also missing is a serious consideration of the role of automaticity in fluent reading behavior. In executing complex skills, the ability to do lower order skills rapidly and without overt attention

has been shown to be critical for successful performance (Anderson, 1985). For reading this appears to be especially true (LaBerge & Samuels, 1974; Perfetti, 1985). Word recognition, whether acquired through intensive phonics or through any other means, needs to be done rapidly if processing attention is to be available for higher level comprehension. Where adult literacy educators now debate whether or not to teach phonics, they should be debating how to build up rapid word recognition.

The role of vocabulary in literacy acquisition is yet another area where little research has been done and few questions have been asked. Exactly how important vocabulary is to reading performance, we are not sure, but its importance is not doubted seriously. Through the school years reading vocabulary increases on the average at the rate of approximately 5,000 words per year, assuming a conservative definition of the term word(Miller & Gildea, 1987). For the poorer readers, for the dropouts, and for those especially from limited English environments, English vocabulary acquisition is significantly below this figure. Among those adults most in need of literacy training, vocabulary learning is problematic, due in part to the low level of literacy use in the environments in which many of them exist (Taylor, Wade, Jackson, Blum, & Goold, 1980). Improved vocabulary training may be as important for adult literacy as any of the abilities currently driving literacy instruction.

A final issue to consider (but clearly not the only one not covered here so far) is that of situated versus decontextualized knowledge. Opinion among adult educators appears to favor strongly the placing of literacy training within the contexts that adults are most familiar with and which most clearly distinguish the adult world from that of the child (French, 1987). Yet there should be reservations about the extent to which effective literacy learning can be divorced from a classroom, intellectual setting. Scribner and Cole(1981), for example, found among the Vai that the cognitive consequences of literacy learning from a natural setting were inferior to those from a schooling environment. Other researchers have found that years of completion of formal schooling is a better predictor of Wechsler Adult Intelligence scores than age (Birren & Morrison, 1961), although this may reflect subject selectivity as much as schooling consequences. At a minimum, the current debate over situated learning should be observed closely by adult reading researchers, and perhaps used as a guide for reseearch planning.

ADULT READING TASKS

Most researchers agree that school and adult reading requirements diffier, but exactly how to characterize this difference is not settled. Caylor & Sticht (1973), Diehl & Mikulecky (1980), and others have made a distinction between reading-to-learn and reading-to-do. The former, which applies to reading tasks in which new information is obtained for non-immediate purposes, characterizes most in-school reading requirements, while the latter is typical of reading tasks faced by adults, particularly job related reading tasks. Mikulecky (1982) analyzed the reading tasks of 48 high school juniors, 51 adult technical school students, and 150 workers drawn from a cross section of occupations, using interviews and a variety of reading assessment procedures. High school students differed significantly from middle-level workers in reading demands encountered, in literacy competencies, and in reading strategies employed. The workers, for example, had significantly higher percentage of reading-to-do tasks (generally with learning occurring in the process), and used problem solving techniques, note taking, and underlining more often. The students, on the other hand, employed rereading as their primary strategy for getting meaning from a text. Blue-collar workers rated accurate reading as more important than technical school students did, while professionals had a significantly broader scope of reading materials than all the other groups and tended to strive more to relate what they read to what they already knew.

Although the reading-to-learn vs. reading-to-do contrast captures a portion of the difference between school-based reading and job reading, it does not give a complete characterization of these differences. First, schooling by definition has a high reading-to-learn component. Without it, much of our mass educational system would be ineffective. But some reading-to-learn can and does require reading-to-do. Instructions, such as for laboratory experiments and for assignments in general fit this class, and many math word problems do also. But even within the pure reading-to-learn, class, reading strategies may differ according to purpose for reading (Bond & Bond, 1941). How a student reads a history passage, for example, might depend upon whether the goal is passing a short-answer test, answering an essay test, developing a poster representation of the content, or finding a topic for a report.

Elementatry school reading differs dramatically from adult reading both in types of materials used for reading instruction and in reading tasks. Within the context of the basal reader, the central goals of reading are defined around the characteristics of narrative fiction: getting the main point of the story, understanding the authors purpose, following the plot, and building character representations. Nonfiction is underrepresented relative to its importance in the school curriculum and is often taught as if it were a flawed form of fiction (Venezky, 1982). Fiction tends to have a total text focus, a high aesthetic component, subtlety by intention, and an emphasis more on general than particular understanding. Most expository writing, in contrast, is information focused, low on aesthetic aspirations, direct, and requiring attention to details. In elementary school reading classes the primary reading task remains constant and is seldom made overt: read and understand the entire passage, with emphasis at the higher grades on plot, character, and the author's intentions. For adult reading (other than fiction), tasks vary considerably, but usually have a problem solving flavor: find how much sugar we need to make four quarts of blackberry jam; determine which foods I can eat on my diet; find what time the movie starts. These differences apply not only to the tasks involved but also to the strategies that readers need to be successful in the tasks (Gutherie & Kirsch, 1987).

Every day reading tasks can be characterized by three phases: locate information, operate on what is found, and respond. All three phases can vary in difficulty, although the first two tend to have the greatest range of complexity. How difficult any one will be depends first on the task and then on the text.

Finding from *Lincoln's Gettysburg Address,* for example, who brought forth a new nation is a significantly easier task than deciding how in the *Address* Lincoln resolves the paradox in the *Declaration of Independence* of equality being both a natural right and a right that could be altered by popular consent. Assessing text difficulty by readability measures ignores the role of reading task in directing reading strategy. Readability measures have some (limited) utility for elementary school reading so long as reading is based primarily upon narrative fiction and the reading task is to read and digest it all. When realistic reading tasks are required, readability indexes fail.

Although almost 98 percent of the young adults assessed in the recent NAEP Adult Literacy Survey could do the most basic tasks, very few could do the more difficult tasks, all of which were drawn from ordinary literacy needs (Kirsch & Jungeblut, 1986). Even though a higher proportion of young adults achieved at the higher levels than in-school 17-year-olds, an alarming number of young adults, including a disproportionate percentage of minorities, performed at what were labeled the basic and the rudimentary levels. For example, 97 percent of the respondents filled in a phone number correctly on a phone message form, but only 68 percent wrote a correct message, stating the two items of information given orally. Over 90 percent found the correct main idea of a poem that had repeated clues to its theme, but only about 38 percent could do this same task correctly with a poem that had almost no redundancy. Many respondents had difficulties composing messages or letters that reported information. In addition to the phone message difficulties, only about 31 percent wrote a satisfactory letter to a credit department, giving appropriate information about an error in a monthly credit card bill.

In all of these tasks the processing demands rather than the document form were the primary determinant of task difficulty. Furthermore, the traditional division of comprehension tasks into literal and inferential categories did not predict task difficulty. Some literal tasks, for example, were more difficult than some inferential tasks. In some cases the vocabulary differences between the task specification and the matching text information created the difficulty; in other cases it was the presence of redundant information; and in others, it was the number of features or items of information that had to be attended for successful completion of the task. Furthermore, the factors that created difficulties in these tasks were similar to the factors that determine difficulty of math word problems (Carpenter, Corbitt, Kepner, Lindquist, & Reys, 1980).

Problem solving is poorly taught in American schools, if by problem solving we mean the types of tasks reflected in the NAEP science and math assessments. In a recent comparison of American 13-year-olds with 13-year-olds from another industrialized countries, the American students ranked last in mathematics and in the bottom one third in science. In general, the more complex the task, the poorer the American performance relative to the others (Lapointe, Mead, & Phillips, 1989). If a large component of adult literacy needs require problem-solving skills, then American schools are failing to provide a major portion of what adults need. The root of this problem is centered in two time-honored school practices. The first is to base reading instruction primarily upon narrative fiction; the second is to isolate reading practice from the content areas. Learning to read legal arguments, editorials, repair manuals, and the like is at least as important for success in school and later life as learning to read and enjoy "good" fiction, yet the latter is favoured disproportionately over the former for reading instruction.

CONCLUSIONS

Research on adult literacy learning, if it is to inform adult instruction, must become more focused on serious problems, become more sensitive to the major issues emerging from cognitive studies within and without reading, and must be subjected to the same intensive peer review that sustains and drives research in other fields. Whether there are five or six stages to adult literacy development is a far less important issue than whether or not self-sustained literacy learning can take place before automaticity in word recognition is achieved. And to argue over the relative merits of phonics and whole-world instruction is not only to trivialize reading research, but also to divert attention from true issues.

For building adult instruction, the time has come to realize that most adult reading is characterized better by a problem-solving view than it is by a traditional reading comprehension view. And although the evidence for assessing literacy needs in adults is not as extensive as we would like it to be, a pattern can be discerned wherein the best readers are able to transfer their school-based skills to adult reading tasks, the average ones do so with difficulty, and the poorer ones hardly at all. Elementary and high school reading instruction has, for at least the past century, been constructed around "good literature," leaving most students to acquire information processing skills on their own. What is needed is an expanded view of literacy instruction, wherein locating and operating on information can share stage center with reading and enjoying fiction. The schools in general are not doing an adequate job in teaching problem solving, and adult literacy failures are a special case of this. So long as reading instruction and reading assessment are mired in grade level equivalents, readability indexes, and other over simplifications of a narrative fiction orientation, literacy in America will continue to slide. Nevertheless, enough good research on adult literacy learning exists to foster the hope that with sufficient funding and a more focused research orientation, major contributions could be made towards the improvement of adult literacy learning.

References

Anderson, J. R. (1985). *Cognitive psychology and its implications.* New York: W. H. Freeman.

Barr, R. (1972). The influence of instructional conditions on word recognition errors. *Reading Research Quarterly, 7,* 509–579.

Birren, J. E., & Morrison, D. F. (1961). Analysis of the WAIS subtests in relation to age and education. *Journal of Gerontology, 16,* 363–369.

Bond, G. L. & Bond, E. (1941). *Development of reading in high school.* New York: Macmillan.

Brunner, E. de S., Wilder, D. S., Kirschner, C., & Newberry, J. S. (1959). *An overview of adult education research.* Chicago: Adult Education Association of the U.S.A.

Buswell, G. T. (1937). How adults read. *Supplementary Educational Monographs, 45.* Chicago: University of Chicago Press.

Carpenter, T. P., Corbitt, M. K., Kepner, H. S., Jr., Lindquist, M. M., & Reys, R. E. (1980). National assessment: A perspective of students' mastery of basic mathmatics skills. In M. M. Lindquist (Ed.), *Selected issues in mathematics education.* Berkeley, CA: McCutchan Publishing.

Caylor, J. S., & Sticht, T. G. (1973). *Development of a simple readability index for job reading material.* Alexandria, VA.: Human Resources Research Organization.

Chall, J. S. (1983). *Stages of reading development.* New York: McGraw-Hill.

Cook, W. D. (1977). *Adult literacy education in the United States.* Newark, DE: International Reading Association.

Darkenwald, G. G. (1986). *Adult literacy education: A review of the research and priorities for future inquiry.* New York: Literacy Assistance Center.

Diehl, W. A., & Mikulecky, L. (1980). The nature of reading at work. *Journal of Reading, 23,* 221–227.

Dixon, W. R. (1951). Studies of the eye movements in reading of university professors and graduate students. In W. C. Morse, F. A. Ballantine, & W. R. Dixon (Eds.), *Studies in the psychology of reading.*

Monographs in Education, 4. Ann Arbor, MI: University of Michigan Press.

French, J. (1987). *Adult literacy: A source book and guide.* New York: Garland.

Gibson, E., & Levin, H. (1975). *The psychology of reading.* Cambridge, MA: MIT Press.

Goldstein, H. (1940). *Reading and listening comprehension at various controlled rates.* (Contributions to Education, No. 821). New York: Bureau of Publications, Teachers College, Columbia University.

Gray, W. S. (1937). The nature and organization of basic instruction in reading. In W. S. Gray (Ed.), *Thirty-sixth Yearbook of the National Society for the Study of Education, Part I.* Bloomington, IL: Public School Publishing.

Gray, W. S. (1956). How well do adults read?. In N. B. Henry (Ed.), *Fifty-fifth Yearbook of the National Society for the Study of Education.* Chicago: National Society for the Study of Education.

Gray, W. S., & Munroe, R. (1929). *The reading interests and habits of adults: A preliminary report.* New York: Macmillan.

Gray, W. S., & Rogers, B. (1956). *Maturity in reading: Its nature and appraisal.* Chicago: University of Chicago Press.

Gutherie, J., & Kirsch, I. (1987). Distinctions between reading comprehension and locating information in a text. *Journal of Educational Psychology, 79,* 220–228.

Judd, C. H., and Buswell, G. T. (1922). Silent reading: A study of the various types. *Supplementary Educational Monographs, 23.* Chicago: University of Chicago Press.

Karlsen, B. (1970). Educational achievement testing with adults—some research findings. In W. S. Griffith & A. P. Hayes (Eds.), *Adult basic education: The state of the art.* Washington, DC: Government Printing Office.

Kirsch, I. S., & Jungeblut, A. (1986). *Literacy: Profiles of America's young adults.* (Report No. 16-PL-02). Princeton, NJ: National Assessment of Educational Progress.

LaBerge, D., & Samuels, S. J. (1974). Toward a theory of automatic information processing in reading. *Cognitive Psychology, 6,* 293–323.

LaPointe, A. E., Mead, N. A., & Phillips, G. W. (1989). *A world of difference: An international assessment of mathematics and science.* Princeton, NJ: Educational Testing Service.

Leibert, R.E. (1983). Reading profiles of ABE students and children on an informal reading inventory. *Reading Psychology: An International Quarterly, 4,* 141–150.

Malicky, G., & Norman, C. A. (1982). Reading strategies of adult literates. *Journal of Reading, 25,* 731–735.

Mann, H. (1839). Mechanical, mental stages in reading. *American Annals of Education,* 289–299.

McCaul, R. L. (1944). The effect of attitude upon reading interpretation. *Journal of Educational Research, 37,* 451–458.

Mikulecky, L. (1980). Functional writing in the workplace. In L. Gentry (Ed.), *Research and instruction in practical writing.* Los Alamitos, CA: Southwest Regional Laboratory for Educational Research and Development.

Mikulecky, L. (1982). Job literacy: The realtionship between school preparation and workplace actuality. *Reading Research Quarterly, 17,* 400–420.

Miller, G. A., & Gildea, P. M. (1987). How children learn words. *Scientific American, 257*(3), 94–99.

Murphy, R. T. (1975). *Adult functional reading study.* Princeton, NJ: Educational Testing Service.

Pearson, P. D. (Ed.) (1984). *Handbook of reading research.* New York: Longman.

Perfetti, C. (1985). *Reading ability.* New York: Oxford University Press.

Scribner, S., & Cole, M. (1981). *Psychology of literacy.* Cambridge, MA: Harvard University Press.

Sharon, A. T. (1973, 1974). What do asults read?. *Reading Research Quarterly, 9,* 148–169.

Sticht, T. G. (1982). *Basic skills in defense.* Alexandria, Va.: Human Resources Research Organization.

Sticht, T. G. (1988). Adult literacy education. In E. Rothkopf (Ed.), *Review of Research in Education, Vol. 15.* Washington, DC: American Educational Research Association.

Sticht, T. G., Beck, L. J., Hauke, R. N., Kleiman, G. M., & James, J. H. (1974). *Auding and reading: A developmental model.* Alexandria, VA: Human Resources Research Organization.

Stone, L. G. (1941). Reading reactions for various types of subject matter. *Journal of Experimental Education, 10,* 64–77.

Taylor, N., Wade, P., Jackson, S., Blum, I., & Goold, L. (1980). A study of low-literate adults: Personal, environmental and program considerations. *The Urban Review, 12*(2), 69–77.

Terry, P. W. (1922). How numerals are read. *Supplementary Educational Monographs, 18.* Chicago: University of Chicago Press.

Tinker, M. A. (1928). A photographic study of eye-movements in reading formulas. *Genetic Psychology Monographs, 3,* 68–182.

Venezky, R. L. (1982). The origins of the present-day chasm between adult literacy needs and school literacy instruction. *Visible Language, 16,* 113–126.

Weber, R. M. (1975). Adult illiteracy in the United States. In J. B. Carroll & J. S. Chall (Eds.), *Toward a literate society.* New York: McGraw-Hill.

RESPONDING TO INDIVIDUAL DIFFERENCES

AMONG LANGUAGE LEARNERS

20A. CHILDREN AT RISK

Jeanne S. Chall
Mary E. Curtis

Our concern in this chapter is with those children who have a high probability of encountering school difficulties because of a reading or related language problem.

We have chosen reading as our major focus for several reasons. First, from the earliest scientific studies of education, success in learning to read has been linked to school achievement. Among school subjects, problems in reading constitute the majority of referrals for learning difficulties. Thus, most students at risk for academic achievement are at risk in reading. Second, it is becoming increasingly apparent that poor reading is a common factor underlying high school dropout, delinquency, teenage pregnancy and unemployment (e.g., see Davidson & Koppenhaver, 1988). In other words, difficulty in reading and related language skills places children at risk not only for success in school, but for personal, social, and civic well being as well. Finally, among the language arts, reading has been by far the one most often studied in children at risk. Analysis of what is known about the reading abilities of these children may yield some insights about the less investigated areas of oral language and writing.

Although important differences exist among the millions of children in this country who are "at risk", all have two characteristics in common: their performance in school lags behind that expected for their age (i.e., their achievement is below national norms), and their school performance lags behind their potential for achievement (i.e., they have the intellectual capacity to do better). In this chapter we present some of the theories and research related to why these children are at risk, focusing on their problems with reading and related language tasks, and the instructional approaches that have been found to be effective in working with them. Because other chapters in this volume address bilingual/ESL children and those who speak nonstandard English dialects, we concern ourselves with those from families of low socioeconomic status, and those with reading or related language disabilities.

Low-Income Children

Almost every study that relates socioeconomic status (SES) to achievement in school finds that middle-class children are more advanced, age for age, than low SES children (Coleman, Hobson, McPartland, Mood, Weenfeld, & York, 1966; Morris, 1959; NAEP, 1985). This is so not only in this country, but in other countries as well (Thorndike, 1973).

In the United States, the relationship between SES and reading and writing achievement is most clearly demonstrated by the results of the National Assessment of Educational Progress (NAEP). On each of its five assessments of reading, from 1971 to 1986, NAEP's results have shown a large gap between the achievement of disadvantaged urban children and their more advantaged age peers. Moreover, the longer that students are in school, the greater this gap becomes, such that by age 17, low SES children read below the level achieved by advantaged 13-year-olds (NAEP, 1985). With regard to writing, a similar performance gap is found between advantaged and disadvantaged students (NAEP, 1981). Thus, NAEP's results seem to confirm conclusions drawn earlier by Coleman and his associates (1966) that differences in family background are the strongest predictor of verbal achievement, and that differences in verbal achievement increase with age.

Why is it that so many children from low-income families are are at risk for reading and writing achievement, and why does their performance lag farther and farther behind as they proceed through school?

Because a large proportion of low SES children are members of minority groups, considerable debate has taken place about whether it is their minority group membership that places them at risk. Increasingly, however, there is consensus that their socioeconomic status is the significant factor in their academic difficulties (Wilson, 1987).

During the 1970s, a popular view was that dialect differences, particularly among low SES African American children, were responsible for difficulties in acquiring literacy. As a consequence, efforts were made to teach these children to read from special dialect readers (rather than traditional reading textbooks), or from stories dictated by the children and written down in dialect by the teacher (Baratz & Shuy, 1969). Such approaches were short lived, however, in part because dialect readers were not acceptable to parents, but also because a considerable number of studies found that dialect had little effect on reading comprehension (e.g., see Simons, 1979).

Another view, one of more current interest, stems from differences that have been identified in the ways that various social and ethnic groups use oral and written language. Low-income children come from a variety of ethnic groups, groups whose expectations and uses of language can differ from those practiced in schools. As a result, low reading and writing achievement of low income children has been attributed to a mismatch between the more mainstreamed style of language use in school instruction and the various styles of language use in this group of learners.

Heath (1983a, 1983b, 1986) is among those who have espoused this view, based on her study of the language and culture of three communities—a white working class community, an African American working class community, and a mainstream, school-oriented community—and the ways in which the school achievement of children from the three communities differed. Heath found that children in the white working class community experienced success in the primary grades, but by the fourth grade, they had begun to experience declines. The children in the African American working class community began to fail in grade 1, and by grade 3, their failures were well established (although a few were successful in later grades). Among the mainstream children, most were academically successful, graduating from high school and planning to go on to higher education.

From her observational work, Heath concluded that the differences in academic achievement of these three groups were related to differences in language in the three communities, differences such as the ways in which questions and narrative structures were used. This has lead Heath to suggest that teachers of low SES children modify their instruction so that the children are surrounded with many different kinds of talk that will lead them to academic success. For example, Heath (1983a) described a first-grade teacher of a class of 19 African students who were, according to readiness test results, "potential failures" (p. 284). Heath noted that the teacher used activities such as: teaching the shapes of letters as structured symbols that appeared in the children's communities; teaching the sounds of letters; teaching sound-symbol correspondences (i.e., phonics); teaching the configurations of certain function words; teaching sight words; reading (along with choral reading and rereading) from hardcover readers (projected on the overhead); asking children to predict what would happen next in a story, and to make up other endings to stories.

At the end of the year, all but one child (who went to a class for emotionally handicapped children) were reading on or above grade level. In other words, low SES first graders whose language was judged at the beginning of first grade to be different from that required in school were able, with proper instruc-

tion, to succeed in learning to read. Heath has stressed the importance of the kinds of oral language underlying these activities; however, it should be noted that most of the above activities have long been recognized as effective techniques for teaching reading to children at all social levels (e.g., see Harris & Sipay, 1985).

The Kamehameha Early Education Project is also cited as an example of the success of using linguistically and culturally appropriate styles of instruction. In the Kamehameha project, targeted at low-achieving, native Hawaiian children, improvement in reading skills was found after introduction of more oral participation and opportunities for children to help each other—practices that matched, it was proposed, an Hawaiian-Polynesian style of learning (Au & Mason, 1981). What is interesting, however, is that the increased amount of oral reading and encouragement of collaboration among children were procedures commonly used to teach reading to *all* children about 70 years ago, before emphasis on silent reading for meaning was introduced in the early grades (e.g., see Chall, 1967). Furthermore, such practices are ones that have been used successfully in teaching students with reading difficulty (Chall & Curtis, 1990; Palincsar & Brown, 1984; Roswell & Natchez, 1989). Thus, it may be that future research will reveal that the success of the Kamehameha Project stems more from the kinds of instructional techniques it uses than from its cultural "matching". It may even be that techniques like these prove to be helpful in promoting success in learning to read for all low-achieving children, regardless of their culture.

Still another view why low SES children are at risk is that the kind of oral language environment that stimulates literacy development is found less often in their homes than in those of middle-class children (e.g., see Snow, 1983). In particular, practices such as paraphrasing, expanding on children's utterances, and adult-child book sharing—practices that provide links between oral language development and literacy skills—are less prevalent in low income homes (Rice, 1989). Hence, according to this view, it is not low SES per se that places a child at risk as much as a need for certain kinds of linguistic and educational stimulation (e.g., see Bloom, 1976).

Early intervention programs such as Head Start, Sesame Street and The Electric Company were, in fact, designed to provide these kinds of stimulation, and evidence suggests their success in doing so (e.g., see Chall, 1983a; Woodhead, 1988). However, initial gains in the language and literacy achievement of low SES children have not been maintained as the children grow older (e.g., see Caldwell, 1987; Chall, Jacobs & Baldwin, 1990; Lazer, Darlington, Murray, & Snipper, 1982), suggesting that a good start, in and of itself, is not enough.

An explanation why early intervention effects dissipate with age, and why the gap between lower-and middle-class children widens as they grow older, can be found when acquisition of language and literacy are viewed as developmental processes, ones that go through various stages.

Menyuk (1988) has described the following sequence in language development: from ages 1 to 3 the average child acquires from 2000 to 3000 lexical items (words); from ages 3 to 5, they can rhyme words. reconstruct segmented words familiar to them, and they have command of basic morphological rules;

from 5 to 8, children learn more complex phonological aspects of language—segmenting words into sounds, blending separate sounds into words—and they learn more elaborate syntactic structures; from age 8 on up they develop further in various aspects of language such as pragmatics, semantics, and phonology.

Beyond these more general developmental changes in language, the nature of reading and writing also change with their development, from global, meaning-oriented tasks, to ones requiring mastery and fluency with print, to use of reading and writing for the purposes of learning new information and perspectives (Bereiter, 1980; Chall, 1979, 1983a). As the tasks of reading and writing change, so too do the demands for cognition, language, and skills for dealing with print.

For children from low-income families, the stages of literacy development may be much the same as for their more advantaged peers; print skills are more essential for success in the early grades, language and cognition more essential later on. However, if growth in some aspect of low-income children's language or literacy development becomes delayed by conditions at home or experiences in school, these delays can affect their later development (Stanovich, 1986).

A study of children from low-income families in grades 2 to 7 provides support for this explanation (Chall & Jacobs, 1983; Chall, Jacobs, & Baldwin, 1990; Chall & Snow, 1982). When children were tested at the end of the second grade, they scored, as a group at grade level on all reading and vocabulary tests. A year later, at the end of third grade, they were still at, or very close to, grade level. By the end of fourth grade, however, average scores for the children on three of the tests—word meaning, word recognition, and spelling—had slipped below grade level. By grade 7, most of children were substantially below grade level.

The writing development of these children followed the same pattern as their reading, stronger development in grades 2 and 3, with decelerated gains from grades 4 to 7. Overall, the students were strong in ideas but weak in organization, structure, and form. Interestingly, similar trends were reported by Shaughnessy (1977) in the writing of at-risk college students, difficulty with syntax and structural forms rather than with ideas.

A longitudinal study of low income children in grades 1 through 4 reported recently by Juel (1988) helps us to understand further trends in these children's literacy development. Juel found that children who entered grade 1 with little awareness about the relationships among words, letters, and sounds were children who experienced problems in learning to read. And, when children experienced reading failure in grade 1, the probability was quite high that they were still having problems in grade 4.

In contrast to the reading results, Juel found that poor writers in grade 1 were not always poor writers by grade 4. However, early poor readers tended to become poor writers, and poor readers experienced less growth in their ability to tell a story than did good readers.

Hence, findings from studies of low-income children's language and literacy development support the view that language is related to literacy differently at different points of develop-

ment. When children first learn to read, at ages 5 or 6, most native speakers have sufficient lexical and syntactic development to cope with reading material they are expected to read. Those children who experience difficulty usually have difficulty with the phonological aspects of language (i.e., phonological awareness), that is, hearing rhymes, hearing the separate sounds in words, blending them to form words, and relating them to print. Research also suggests that when given good instruction in print and phonemic skills, low-income children can progress as expected in the primary grades because their reading and writing tasks deal with words that are already in their oral language vocabularies.

When reading and writing tasks become more complex (requiring fluency as well as knowledge of less familiar words and language patterns), cognitive and linguistic demands become greater. The materials to be read are no longer familiar, and knowledge of word meanings and problem-solving skills have a stronger role to play in reading. And, if instruction does not meet their needs in these areas, low SES children who were successful initially may begin to falter.

Before going into the kinds of instructional approaches that research has shown to be effective for children at risk, however, let us first discuss another group of these children: those who experience difficulties in school because of reading and related language disabilities.

Children with Learning Disabilities

These children at risk have been referred to by a variety of labels—poor readers, disabled readers, or as having specific or developmental language disabilities. More recently, the term dyslexia has had wider use, although in federal law 94-142, the term learning disability is still used.

Estimates based on research over several decades are that from 10 to 15 percent of the population fall within this category, that is, their reading and writing achievement is significantly below their intellectual capacities. Why this is so has been the subject of psychological, medical, and educational research for more than 100 years.

During the 1940s and 1950s, psychiatrists interested in reading disability proposed various theories of the unconscious as the cause of reading failure. One impetus for such theories came from Robinson's (1946) landmark study of reading disability in which she concluded that the most frequent characteristics of her population were social and emotional difficulties. Recognition of social and emotional disturbances in reading disabled children led many to assume that individual or family therapy was needed before a child could benefit from remediation in reading. As Roswell and Natchez (1989) point out, however, this assumption may be incorrect:

A diagnostician might discover that a student with learning difficulty has personality disturbances and needs psychotherapy. If this choice alone is instituted and the student still does not learn within a reasonable length of time, he or she will fall further and further behind. Even worse, whatever emotional problems were present will be exacerbated through daily academic failure. This does not discredit the psychodynamic stance. It simply states that when other factors continue undetected or ignored, the individual can try, even try *hard,* only to flounder, fumble, and finally despair. (p. 52)

During the 1960s and 1970s, neurological theories of reading disability, which place the major cause on differences in the development and organization of the brain, became increasingly popular. Although first proposed in the United States by Orton (1937), the neurological view became more prevalent as scientific knowledge and technology advanced. Neurological factors such as premature birth, perceptual-motor development, and difficulty with sequencing and blending of sounds were identified as significant reading failure in young children (deHirsch, Jansky, & Langford, 1966; Jansky & deHirsch, 1972). Brain study following the accidental death of a young man who had suffered from severe reading disability since childhood revealed abnormalities in those areas known to deal with language (Galuburda & Kemper, 1979). And several types of reading disability were associated with different language difficulties (e.g., See Doehring, Trites, Patel, & Fiedorowicz, 1981).

Legal mandates were another important impetus for the neurological approach. State and federal laws enacted on behalf of children with reading and learning disabilities specifically excluded those whose difficulties were primarily the result of "sensory, motor, intellectual, or emotional handicap, or lack of opportunity to learn" (Lerner, 1976, p. 427). Thus, only those with learning disabilities that could be attributed to neurological origins could be eligible for assistance in state and federally funded programs.

Although the instructional implications of a neurological view of reading disability have not been straightforward (e.g., see Chall & Peterson, 1986), Orton's recommendation for a highly structured direct phonics procedure to help severely disabled students with difficulties in dealing with printed symbols is one that is still followed in some remedial programs. In addition, treatment of deficits associated with reading and writing difficulties (e.g., gross and fine motor coordination, memory, attention, auditory discrimination and perception, and so on) is an approach that has been used. Deficit training is based on the assumption that reading and writing difficulties are only symptoms, symptoms that will go away as deficits in more basic psychological processing improve. Deficit training has become less prevalent, however, due to research that questions its effectiveness (e.g., see Arter & Jenkins, 1979; Chall, 1978), although specific focus continues on the oral language development of those preschool children who lag significantly behind their peers (Rice, 1989).

In contrast to single factor explanations of reading and related language disabilities, such as the social-emotional or neuropsychological, the treatment followed today in most schools and university clinics is based on a multifactor view (e.g., see Chall & Curtis, 1987). Prevalent since the 1920s, beginning with the work of Gray (1922) and Gates (1922), a multifactor view assumes that any of several factors can "cause" difficulties in learning to read or write: inadequate methods of teaching, insufficient time spent on reading and writing, family circumstances, differences in brain organization, and so on. Beyond the underlying causes, however, a multifactor approach assumes that the academic difficulties of children with a reading or related language disability can be treated directly, through individual testing and use of methods and materials based on the strengths and weaknesses in the relevant language and literacy skills that are uncovered (see also Brown & Campione, 1986).

In terms of reading, this means a diagnostic and remedial focus on components such as accuracy and fluency in word identification; breadth and depth of knowledge of word meanings; success in literal and inferential understanding of what has been read; application of strategies for monitoring and improving understanding (e.g., see Roswell & Natchez, 1989).

With regard to writing, a multifactor approach focuses on knowledge and skills affecting the writing process, such as the ability to organize ideas, use strategies for writing, produce text fluently, as well as on aspects of the written product such as syntax and spelling (e.g., see Lynch & Jones, 1989; Shaughnessy, 1977).

Up to this point, we have described some of the theories and research related to why two different groups of children—those from low-income families and those with reading and related language and learning disabilities—are at risk for academic success because of their reading and writing difficulties. In the sections that follow, we would like to give a brief overview of some features of instruction that research has shown to be effective with both of these groups.

Early Intervention

Prevention of reading failure even before formal instruction begins goes back at least 60 years. The early studies, called studies of reading readiness, were influenced by child development research that found there was an optimal time for learning various tasks.

The first readiness study in reading (Morphett & Washburne, 1931) found that mental age was the best predictor of beginning reading success, and recommended a mental age of 6 and 1/2 as the optimal time for beginning reading instruction. Gates (1937), on the other hand, found that the minimal mental age for beginning reading varied with the instructional program, the teacher, and the learning environment. With easy methods and materials and well organized teaching, even a mental age of 5 was sufficient for learning to read.

Gates notwithstanding, from the 1930s to the early 1960s, schools tended to delay formal teaching for those children who were presumed to lack readiness, even though there seemed to be no controlled studies that supported such an approach. Research in the 1960s and 1970s, however, suggested that early intervention is more effective than delay. Studies of children taught to read early (Durkin, 1974–1975), along with studies on the effectiveness of Head Start (Zigler & Valentine, 1979) and the improved reading scores on the National Assessment of the 1980 cohort of 9-year-olds, who had an earlier, more systematic start in reading instruction than the 1970 cohort (NAEP, 1985), all pointed to the value of early intervention.

Most recently, work in the area of "emergent literacy" has reminded us that very young children know much about language and literacy, particularly when those children come from linguistically rich environments (e.g., see Teale & Sulzby, 1986). However, research on emergent literacy has had little to say about children who may lack readiness skills, and the kinds of intervention that may be necessary with them. Other studies do suggest, on the other hand, that if one waits for readiness skills to emerge, and does not intervene, the child at risk will not make it (e.g., see Juel, 1988). Moreover, the nature of the intervention may make a difference (see Slavin, Karweit, & Madden, 1989; Slavin & Madden, 1989). In particular, programs that provide children at risk with good oral language skills do not seem to have as much effect over time as those that provide systematic early instruction in reading. Based on their work in this area, Slavin and his associates have concluded that:

Well-structured preschool and kindergarten programs can prepare students to learn to read in 1st grade, but perhaps the most important single element of prevention is to use programs in 1st grade to ensure students who do not make adequate progress in reading will receive immediate and intensive assistance. (Slavin & Madden, 1989)

Slavin and his associates have further noted that instructional strategies found to be successful with low achievers are often similar to ones found to be effective for all children.

Direct and Explicit Instruction

Research that makes comparisons among the effectiveness of specific kinds of approaches to teaching language arts has been limited. Overall, however, studies of instructional practices (Slavin et al., 1989) and teacher influences on student achievement (Brophy, 1986) suggest that the following features are important for children at risk: well-defined instructional objectives through which teachers help students to relate new information and skills to what they already know and can already do; and opportunities to apply new knowledge and skills, and to evaluate the effectiveness of those applications.

Results from the study by Chall and her associates of children from low-income families lend further support to these conclusions. For students in the intermediate grades who made at least the expected year's growth from one school year to the next, classroom observations and teacher interviews revealed the following: reading instruction was provided on or above the child's reading level (not below); direct instruction was given in comprehension of texts in reading, social studies, science, health, and other content areas; meaning vocabulary was stressed during content-area instruction as well as during reading and language arts; diverse materials were provided on a wide range of reading levels, some of which challenged even the best readers; frequent field trips and other activities were conducted that exposed students to new experiences and new vocabulary and helped to build up background knowledge for reading about the unfamiliar; homework was assigned in reading that included workbooks in the earlier grades, and reading of trade books and content-area materials in the later grades; and the children's parents were in direct personal contact with their teachers (see Chall & Snow, 1982; Chall, Jacobs & Baldwin, 1990.)

In other words, the factors that were related to greater gains and to higher levels of achievement among these low-income students were similar to the factors identified as contributing to success for all children: a good, strong start in the primary grades, followed in the intermediate and upper elementary grades by structured and challenging instruction in reading, writing, and vocabulary, opportunities for reading stimulating trade books that varied widely, and many opportunities to practice literacy skills. Thus, even when stimulation for language and literacy development was not prevalent in their homes, instruction in school was able to meet these children's needs. When neither school nor home provided this stimulation, however, the children were unable to progress at expected levels.

Intervention studies show that direct and explicit instruction in identifying words (e.g., see Chall, 1967, 1983b) in unknown word meanings and background knowledge (e.g., see Snider, 1989), and in strategies such as summarizing and generating questions (e.g., see Palincsar & Brown, 1984) all can improve the reading achievement of children at risk. Furthermore, when instruction in comprehension strategies involves learning to construct a dialogue around a text, oral language skills of children at risk may be affected as well. For instance, reciprocal teaching as a listening activity was tested by Palincsar and Brown (1989) with first and second graders who were identified as at risk for academic difficulty. After 30 days of instruction given by the classroom teacher, the first-grade students achieved criterion performance on similar listening tasks, and were observed to "spontaneously engage their teachers in similar discussion during small-group reading time" (p. 36).

With respect to writing, direct instruction in spelling and handwriting has lead to improvements for learning disabled students (see review by Lynch & Jones, 1989). Interventions that are more process-oriented, such as teaching strategies for planning and revising, have also proven to be promising (Lynch & Jones, 1989). This latter result is consistent with Hillock's (1986, 1987) more general finding that writing instruction that is explicit and direct is more effective than that which is more "natural" and indirect.

Matching Instruction to Students' Needs

The issue of whether methods of teaching reading can be matched to learning styles for more effective learning is a perennial one. Currently, concerns are being raised again over whether children from different cultures learn best by different methods, and whether visual methods (sight, whole words) work better for children who are visual learners, while phonics methods work better for auditory learners. Because little previous research has demonstrated success in matching methods to learning styles (Cronbach & Snow, 1977), future research in this area will need to show that attention to some kind of style per se is the factor that is important for success in the learning of children at risk.

What research has revealed as important for children at risk is instruction that is matched to their academic needs. As Slavin and Madden (1989) have summarized:

Virtually all of the programs found to be instructionally effective for students at risk assess student progress frequently and use the results to modify groupings or instructional content to meet students' individual needs. (pg. 11)

In other words, when students are not accurate or fluent in dealing with print, then these skills need to be addressed in order for their reading and writing to improve. When students are proficient with print, then instruction in word meanings, background knowledge, text structures, strategies for comprehending or composing, may each be necessary for improvement. Only through assessment of students' strengths and needs in language and literacy, viewed within the context of their point in literacy development, can appropriate instructional decisions be made.

Technology and At-Risk Children

Bransford and Hesselbring (1987) have discussed available research on three areas in which effective use of technology can potentially enhance the learning of at-risk students. The first is through the use of the microcomputer to develop fluency in reading, described by Bransford and Hesselbring as the rapid and almost effortless recognition of familiar text. Without fluency, they note, students' attention becomes overloaded because "there is too much complexity to manage" (p. 18). Fluency allows students to direct their attention to higher level processing.

The second area of research is concerned with the use of the microcomputer and video technology to create "semantically rich contexts" for learning, problem solving and discovery that can facilitate comprehension. Bransford and Hesselbring suggest that video technology can be used as a "source of analogy for understanding other stories" (p. 28), and to help children understand the importance of literacy. They note further that the goal should not be to replace reading with video activities, but to build on reading through the use of those activities.

The third area currently being investigated by Bransford and others is the use of videodiscs in combination with textbooks. Bransford and Hesselbring suggest that making students "producers of information in academically-focused tasks" (p. 32) will result in increased learning.

Concluding Remarks

The search for the causes, the cures, and preventative measures of failure in language and literacy has been a long one. And the lessons learned so far, if implemented, can help children at risk to achieve well.

What we need to remember is that the vast majority of children who lag behind in reading and writing can be helped, whether they are behind because of a less academically stimulating home or school environment, or because of a learning disability that may or may not be neurologically based. The research on both groups of children points to the benefits of instruction that is designed to raise their level of reading and writing development. For those not at risk, a facilitative but non-interventionist view of literacy may be effective. But, for children at risk, a more formal, "direct" kind of instruction, aimed at building on their strengths while addressing their needs, has been shown to be the most beneficial.

References

Arter, J. A., & Jenkins, J. R. (1979). Differential diagnosis-prescriptive teaching: A critical appraisal. *Review of Educational Research, 49,* 517–555.

Au, K. H., & Mason, J. M. (1981). School organizational factors in learning to read: The balance of rights hypothesis. *Reading Research Quarterly, 17,* 115–151.

Baratz, J. C., & Shuy, R. (1969). (Eds.). *Teaching black children to read.* Washington, DC: Center for Applied Linguistics.

Bereiter, C. (1980). *Development in writing.* In L. W. Gregg & E. R. Steinberg (Eds.), Cognitive processes in writing (pp. 73–93). Hillsdale, NJ: Erlbaum.

Bloom, B. S. (1976). *Human characteristics and school learning.* New York: McGraw-Hill.

Bransford, J., & Hesselbring, T. (1987). *Technology can help children who are at risk of school failure.* Proceedings of the Conference on Technology and Students at Risk of School Failure, St. Charles, IL, June 28-30, 1987 (Eric Document Reproduction Service No. ED 295 590)

Brophy, J. (1986). Teacher influences on student achievement. *American Psychologist, 41,* 1069–1077.

Brown, A. L., & Campione, J. C. (1986). Psychological theory and the study of learning disabilities. *American Psychologist, 41,* 1059–1068.

Caldwell, B. (1987). Staying ahead: The challenge of third-grade slump. *Principal, 66,* 10–14.

Chall, J. S. (1967). *Learning to read: The great debate.* New York: McGraw-Hill.

Chall, J. S. (1978). A decade of research on reading and learning disabilities. In S. J. Samuels (Ed.), *What research has to say about reading instruction* (pp. 31–42). Newark, DE: IRA.

Chall, J. S. (1979). The great debate: Ten years later, with a modest proposal for reading stages. In L. B. Resnick & P. A. Weaver (Eds.), *Theory and practice of early reading* (Vol. 1, pp. 29–55). Hillsdale, NJ: Erlbaum.

Chall, J. S. (1983a). *Stages of reading development.* New York: McGraw-Hill.

Chall, J. S. (1983b). *Learning to read: The great debate* (2nd ed.) New York: McGraw-Hill.

Chall, J. S., & Curtis, M. E. (1987). What clinical diagnosis tells us about children's reading. *The Reading Teacher, 40,* 784–788.

Chall, J. S., & Curtis, M. E. (in press). Teaching the disabled or below average reader. In A. E. Farstrup & S. J. Samuels (Eds.), *What research has to say about reading instruction.* Newark, DE: IRA.

Chall, J. S., & Jacobs, V. J. (1983). Writing and reading in the elementary grades: Developmental trends among low SES children. *Language Arts, 60,* 617–626.

Chall, J. S., Jacobs, V. A., & Baldwin, L. E. (1990). *The reading crisis: Why poor children fall behind.* Cambridge, MA: Harvard University Press.

Chall, J. S., & Peterson, R. W. (1986). The influence of neuroscience on educational practice. In S. L. Friedman, K. A. Klivington, & R. W.

Peterson (Eds.), *The brain, cognition, and education* (pp. 287–318). New York: Academic Press.

Chall, J. S., & Snow, C. (1982). *Families and literacy*. Washington, DC: National Institute of Education.

Coleman, J. S., Campbell, E. Q., Hobson, C. J., McPartland, J., Mood, A. M., Weenfeld, F. D., & York, R. L. (1966). *Equality of educational opportunity*. Washington, DC: U.S. Government Printing Office.

Cronbach, L. J., & Snow, R. E. (1977). *Aptitudes and instructional methods: A handbook for research on interactions*. New York: Halstead Press.

Davidson, J., & Koppenhaver, D. (1988). *Adolescent literacy: What works and why*. New York: Garland.

de Hirsch, K., Jansky, J. J., & Langford, W. S. (1966). *Predicting reading failure*. New York: Harper & Row.

Doehring, D. G., Trites, R. L., Patel, P. G., & Fiedorowicz, C. A. M. (1981). *Reading disabilities: The interaction of reading, language, and neuropsychological deficits*. New York: Academic Press.

Durkin, D. (1974–1975). A six year study of children who learned to read in school at the age of four. *Reading Research Quarterly, 10,* 9–61.

Galuburda, A. M., & Kemper, L. (1979). Cytoarchitectonic abnormalities in developmental dyslexia: A case study. *Annals of Neurology, 6,* 94–100.

Gates, A. I. (1922). *Psychology of reading and spelling with special reference to disability* (Contributions to Education No. 129). New York: Bureau of Publications, Columbia University, Teachers College.

Gates, A. I. (1937). The necessary mental age for beginning reading. *Elementary School Journal, 37,* 497–508.

Gray, W. S. (1922). *Remedial cases in reading: Their diagnosis and treatment* (Supplementary Educational Monograph No. 22). Chicago: University of Chicago Press.

Harris, A. J., & Sipay, E. R. (1985). *How to increase reading ability* (8th ed.) New York: Longman.

Heath, S. B. (1983a). *Ways with words: Language, life, and work in communities and classrooms*. Cambridge: Cambridge University Press.

Heath, S. B. (1983b). Research currents: A lot of talk about nothing. *Language Arts, 60,* 999–1007.

Heath, S. B. (1986). Taking a cross-cultural look at narratives. *Topics in Language Disorders, 7,* 220–227.

Hillocks, G. (1986). *Research on written composition*. Urbana, IL: NCRE and ERIC.

Hillocks, G. (1987). Synthesis of research on teaching writing. *Educational Leadership, 44,* 71–83.

Jansky, J., & deHirsch, K. (1972). *Preventing reading failure*. New York: Harper & Row.

Juel, C. (1988). Learning to read and write: A longitudinal study of 54 children from first through fourth grades. *Journal of Educational Psychology, 80,* 437–447.

Lazar, I., Darlington, R. B., Murray, H. W., & Snipper, A. S. (1982). Lasting effects of early education: A report from the Consortium for Longitudinal Studies. *Monograph of Society for Research in Child Development, 47.*

Lerner, J. W. (1976). *Children with learning disabilities* (2nd ed.). Boston: Houghton Mifflin.

Lynch, E. M., & Jones, S. D. (1989). Process and product: A review of the research on LD children's writing skills. *Learning Disability Quarterly, 12,* 74–86.

Menyuk, P. (1988). *Language development*. Glenview, IL: Scott Foresman & Company.

Morphett, M. J., & Washburne, C. (1931). When should children begin to read? *Elementary School Journal, 31,* 496–503.

Morris, J. (1959). *Reading in the primary school: An investigation into standards of reading and their association with primary school characteristics* (National Foundation for Educational Research in England and Scotland), London: Newnes Educational Publishing Company.

National Assessment of Educational Progress (1981). *Reading, thinking, and writing*. Denver, CO: NAEP.

National Assessment of Educational Progress (1985). *The reading report card: Progress toward excellence in our schools*. Princeton, NJ: ETS.

Orton, S. T. (1937). *Reading, writing, and speech problems in children*. London: Chapman and Hall.

Palincsar, A. S., & Brown, A. L. (1984). Reciprocal teaching of comprehension-fostering and monitoring activities. *Cognition and Instruction, 1,* 177–195.

Palincsar, A. S., & Brown, A. L. (1989). Instruction for self-regulated reading. In L. B. Resnick & L. E. Klopfer (Eds.), *Toward the thinking curriculum: Current cognitive research* (pp. 19–39). Alexandria, VA: ASCD.

Rice, M. L. (1989). Children's language acquisition. *American Psychologist, 44,* 149–156.

Robinson, H. M. (1946). *Why pupils fail in reading*. Chicago: University of Chicago Press.

Roswell, F., & Natchez, G. (1989). *Reading disability: A human approach to learning* (4th ed.). New York: Basic Books.

Shaughnessy, M. (1977). *Errors and expectations*. New York: Oxford.

Simons, H. D. (1979). Black dialect, reading interference, and classroom interaction. In L. B. Resnick & P. A. Weaver (Eds.), *Theory and practice of early reading* (Vol. 3, pp. 111–129). Hillsdale, NJ: Erlbaum.

Slavin, R. E., Karweit, N. L., & Madden, N. A. (1989). *Effective programs for students at risk*. Needham Heights, MA: Allyn & Bacon.

Slavin, R. E., & Madden, N. A. (1989). What works for students at risk: A research synthesis. *Educational Leadership, 64,* 4–13.

Snider, V. E. (1989). Reading comprehension performance of adolescents with learning disabilities. *Learning Disability Quarterly, 12,* 87–96.

Snow, C. E. (1983). Literacy and language: Relationships during the preschool years. *Harvard Educational Review, 53,* 165–189.

Stanovich, K. E. (1986). Matthew effects in reading: Some consequences of individual differences in the acquisition of reading. *Reading Research Quarterly, 21,* 360–407.

Teale, W., & Sulzby, E. (Eds.) (1986). *Emergent literacy*. Norwood, NJ: Ablex.

Thorndike, R. L. (1973). *Reading comprehension education in fifteen countries: An empirical study*. New York: Wiley.

Wilson, W. J. (1987). *The truly disadvantaged: The inner city, the underclass, and public policy*. Chicago: University of Chicago Press.

Woodhead, M. (1988). When psychology informs public policy: The case of early childhood intervention. *American Psychologist, 43,* 443–454.

Zigler, E. F., & Valentine, J. (Eds.). (1979). *Project Head Start: A Legacy of the War on Poverty*. New York: Free Press.

20B. TEACHING BILINGUAL AND ESL CHILDREN
Virginia G. Allen

Recent statistics present a rather startling portrait of the American school population. According to the 1980 United States census, there were at least 2.7 million children aged 5 to 14 years who were living in homes in which languages other than English were usually spoken (Waggoner, 1984). This is a rapidly growing group. The United States is now undergoing a wave of immigration comparable in numbers to the great flood of immigrants who arrived in this country from 1900 to 1920. The new immigrants are a young group. Although the mean age of the population in the United States is 30 and getting older, the average ages of some of the recently arrived immigrant groups are sharply lower (McCarty & Carrera, 1988).

These figures demonstrate the dramatic and growing impact of immigration patterns upon American schools. Some cities, such as Los Angeles and New York, have high concentrations of immigrants. Schools in such areas are hard pressed to provide rapidly the numbers of qualified teachers and programs to support and educate this large and diverse group of students. In other areas of the country, refugee resettlement programs have meant that many school systems are enrolling a very small number of immigrant children. These school systems find difficulty in developing strong programs for just a few children.

That schools have problems in dealing with these ethnic and linguistic minority students is documented by the high dropout rates. About 45 percent of Hispanic students do not complete high school. Forty percent of this group leave school before the 10th grade (Cortes, 1986). School systems, however, have a legal obligation to provide instructional programs designed to meet the needs of language-different children (Teitelbaum and Hiller, 1977). The keystone of this mandate is the decision made by the United States Supreme Court in the case of *Lau v. Nichols*. In 1970 a class action suit was filed on behalf of the Chinese-speaking students against the San Francisco Unified School District. In 1974 the Supreme Court ruled that offering students instruction in a language they did not yet understand was not providing them with equal access to the education system. The ruling stated that:

... there is no equality of treatment merely by providing students with the same facilities, textbooks, teachers and curriculum; for students who do not understand English are effectively foreclosed from any meaningful education. (U.S. Supreme Court, 414 U.S. 563)

Children whose home language is not English are often lumped together as LEPs, that is, children of Limited English Proficiency. Such a label, although it may seem convenient, tends to support the mistaken belief that these children are a group with similar needs and they can be treated in similar ways. However, the single dimension of likeness, the need to acquire the English language as a second language, is a slim one. On the other hand, the differences among these children are many and have great educational significance.

Although the English language is an important part of what these children need to learn, it is not the whole or even the central purpose of their schooling experience. Like all children they need to acquire the strategies and the skills that will make them lifelong learners. Therefore, this chapter will review the research in second-language acquisition as this knowledge applies to the schooling of children who are taking on English as a new language.

The first part of this chapter will focus on an examination of the processes of children's second-language acquisition. We will discuss research on the following: theories of second-language acquisition, strategies of second-language learners, the role of L1 in L2 acquisition, and the acquisition of literacy in a second language. The second part of this chapter will explore how knowledge of second-language acquisition can help teachers make instructional decisions for ESL learners. The following topics will be examined: cultural considerations, program models, and the development of supportive classrooms for ESL children.

SECOND-LANGUAGE ACQUISITION

The linguistic task facing second-language learners is a complex one. It cannot be defined simply as learning the forms, structures, and vocabulary of the new language. It also means learning how to use that language for a wide variety of purposes and in a wide variety of settings. For children, it means learning how to use that language in the school setting in order to achieve academic success. In other words, these children need both to learn a language and to use that language for learning. It is vital, then, that teachers who are working with children learning English as their second language develop some understanding about the processes of second-language acquisition.

How do people take on another language? Babies raised in bilingual settings have demonstrated that, not only do they acquire their first language with ease, but that they can simultaneously learn a second language. Without being formally taught, these children are able to sort out the linguistic input they receive from the world around them, develop separate grammars and lexicons, and produce native speech in two languages (Hakuta, 1986). Other persons, who have learned a foreign language in the classroom, find the task much more formidable.

Many theorists are dealing with second-language acquisition. Researchers are examining the psycholinguistic processes of language development as well as the social contexts in which that development occurs (Lindfors, 1987; McLaughlin, 1984; Stern, 1983). There is strong support for the creative, constructive nature of second-language learning, a view that sees children not as passive receptors of language, but as active interactors with that language. Children organize and categorize the language that surrounds them, constructing and reconstructing the rules of that language. Like first-language learners, they hypothesize, test, and revise those rules based on the continuing feedback they receive (Dulay & Burt 1974). One of the theorists in second-language acquisition who has been especially influential in linking theory and practice is Stephen Krashen. Krashen (1981) makes a distinction between language acquisition and language learning. Acquisition, he suggests, is taking on a language naturally, the way a child does. It takes place in informal settings and is a subconscious process. It occurs because there is a real need to use language. Language learning, on the other hand, happens when one is taught a language. It takes place in formal settings. Krashen claims that language learning, that is, conscious knowledge of the rules of the language, only serves as a monitor. It permits the speaker to listen to his speech and match it with his knowledge of the rules of the language, and then make corrections. In other words, the learner can edit his linguistic output.

Another component of Krashen's theory of language acquisition is the Input Hypothesis. Language is acquired when the learner receives comprehensible input. The language may be understandable because of a strong and supportive context or because the learner and the speaker share knowledge or experience. For language growth to occur it is important that the learner receive input that is not only comprehensible but just slightly beyond his or her current level of competence.

In addition, there are attitudinal factors that have a strong relationship to how a language is acquired. Dulay and Burt (1977) proposed the Affective Filter Hypothesis. They posited that high anxiety situations raise a filter between the language input the learner is receiving and the language processing centers of the brain. Low anxiety settings, on the other hand, will lower the filter allowing the input to be processed. Krashen (1982) suggests that an insistence on producing language before the student feels ready to do so will create a high affective filter and thus impede language acquisition.

Strategies of Second-Language Learners

The strategies that children use as they interact with speakers of the new language play a significant role in language acquisition. Wong Fillmore (1976) studied five Mexican children, aged 5 to 7 years, who were acquiring English in a bilingual school. Each of these Mexican children was paired with an English-speaking friend. Among the data collected were videotapes of weekly sessions during which each pair of children played together in an informal setting. She found that children used formulaic expressions as useful chunks of language that allowed them to communicate before they were able to manipulate structures in the new language. Expressions such as "Gimme," "What's that?" and "My turn" let children get into the ongoing activities and to become participants. Wong Fillmore was able to identify several strategies that the children used as they worked their way into English.

1. They assumed that what people were saying was directly related to the ongoing situation.
2. They learned a few stock expressions, or formulaic speech, and started to talk.
3. They looked for patterns that recurred in the language.
4. They made the most of the language they had.
5. They spend their major effort on getting across meaning and saved the refinements for later.

She found great variations, both in the approaches these children used in learning English and in the amount of English they acquired by the end of her year-long study. She concluded that the children who made the most progress in English were those who were strongly interested in socializing with their English-speaking peers. It seemed that because these children were so outgoing they were able to elicit more English language input. However, later studies have demonstrated that one cannot assume that the more non-English speaking children socialize with English speakers, the greater will be their English language development.

Saville-Troike (1984) analyzed the English language development of an ESL class composed of young newcomers to the United States. Seven different languages were spoken by the children who made up this group. She found that these children were able to communicate with minimal use of English by using language formulas, gestures, and mime in order to socialize and accomplish their purposes. Significantly, she noted that children's ability to share meaning with peers did not necessarily help them communicate effectively within the classroom setting. The five students who were the highest achievers academically made minimal use of English for social purposes. Three of the five used their native language to socialize. The other two rarely socialized with children in any language. Clearly, there is a wide range of differences in the way children learn a second language.

In another study, Wong Fillmore (1983) examined individual differences in order to find out how children's language-learning style characteristics and their social style characteristics affected their success in language learning. This project involved observing the English language development of 60 non-English speaking Cantonese and Spanish speakers from kindergarten through grade 2. By the end of year two, the researchers were able to identify two groups of students: "the good language learners" and "the poor language learners." Although within the group of good language learners there were, as expected, many children who were sociable, outgoing, and talkative, there were also children who were shy and introverted. At least half of the poor language learners were also labeled as quiet and withdrawn. The difference in success seemed to lie in the engagement of the children with classroom activities. Good language learners, though quiet, observed, listened and attended. Poor language learners were disengaged.

Another significant difference was found in whether the second-language learner chose to interact more frequently with adults or with children. The Chinese children were concerned about meeting the expectations of the adult, and they interacted frequently with the teacher. The Hispanic children were more interested in interacting with peers. In classrooms where the teacher is the main source of English, the adult-oriented child will receive more English input. In classrooms in which many of the second-language children share a native language and when those children are peer-oriented, the amount of English language input will be diminished. The makeup and the organization of a classroom shape the language that the child receives.

Wong Fillmore also found that the amount of time a child requires to become a proficient user of the second language has been greatly underestimated. She concluded that most children require from 4 to 6 years to be competent users of English. For some children it may take as long as 5 to 8 years.

The Role of First Language in Second-Language Acquisition

The role that the knowledge of a first language has on the acquistion of a second has raised a number of questions. The contrastive analysis hypothesis, which grew from the work of Charles Fries (1945), posits that when the structures of the first language and those of the second language differ, the second-language speaker's errors are marked by an interference of first language patterns. Where the first and second language are similar, in structure or vocabulary, for example, transfer from L1 to L2 can be made. A knowledge of contrastive analysis permits the second-language teacher to identify areas of conflict and to structure lessons so the learner can avoid mistakes that might be caused by interference. It also permits one to discover those aspects of the two languages that are similar and thus simplify the teaching/learning task. Later researchers have viewed second-language learners' errors in a broader context. Selinker (1972) uses the term "interlanguage" to label the intermediate system the learner develops that lies between the native language and the target language. This view of the language learner's task suggests that part of the second-language learning process is hypothesizing about how the new language works, testing out those hypotheses and, in all likelihood, making errors in the process of so doing. Errors, then can serve as windows on the language acquisition process and many of them should be seen as growth points.

Language Proficiency and Competence

One view of proficiency is defined in terms of the linguistic aspects of the language learning task. Linguistic proficiency would be demonstrated by a control of the sound system, structures, and vocabulary of the language, by being able to create, organize and understand language. But the ability of the native speaker to use language goes beyond skill in handling the forms of the language. Hymes (1974) recognized these abilities and coined the term "communicative competence," which he defined as an understanding of how to use language with different persons, in different settings, and for different purposes. Communicative competence clearly requires knowledge of linguistic forms and structures, but goes beyond it. When we talk with others our conversations follow understood rules. For example, although a adult may say to a child, "Stop playing around and eat your dinner," a child may not make that remark to an adult. There is a way to talk in classrooms and a way to talk on the playground. There are appropriate ways to interrupt, to make a request, to end a conversation. Second-language learners need not only know how to form grammatical sentences, but how to use the language they know in appropriate ways. Canale and Swain (1980) suggest that second-language learners also develop another aspect of communicative competence that first-language learners do not need, that is the ability to compensate, to get around problems caused by language limitations.

For school-age children who are acquiring a second language, there is yet another dimension of language competence that is demanded of them. They need to be able to communicate within the context of the classroom. Cummins (1979, 1980, 1981, 1986) has pointed out that there is a difference between context embedded language and context reduced language. For example, the language that occurs among the children in the playhouse corner may be complex and imaginative, but it is richly supported by the context. The language a teacher uses to discuss the long and short sound of vowels is more abstract and is context reduced. Therefore, children who are competent users of a language in one setting, may appear less competent in another setting. In addition, schools require literacy.

Acquiring Literacy in a Second Language

Just as language acquisition means more that acquiring the forms and structures of a second language, literacy means more than decoding and encoding the written forms of a language. Heath (1984) says that to be literate in today's schools means that one must be able to talk and write about language, to explain and sequence implicit knowledge and rules of planning, and to speak and write for multiple functions in appropriate forms. If second-language learners are to succeed in schools, it will happen, not because they are able to sound out words, but because they are literature in the largest sense of that term.

Reading does not begin in the classroom. Children who are learning English in American schools are surrounded by English print within and outside the classroom. Goodman, Goodman and Flores (1979) report that preschool children who were speakers of Navaho, Spanish, and Arabic were responding to the print in their environment. Hudelson (1984) found that older children were able to read some environmental print even though they had been in the United States for only a few months. Just as children seize on chunks of formulaic speech, so too do children draw on the meaningful chunks of print that surround them.

Writing in the Second Language. Studies of young writers show that children hypothesize, test, and revise their knowledge of writing forms in ways that are similar to their discovery of oral language systems, and that these explorations may begin before they start to read (Bissex, 1980; Read, 1975). Edelsky (1986) conducted an extensive study of the writing development of a group of primary children enrolled in a bilingual school. She analyzed the children's written products to see how their writing developed over time and to discover in what ways their writing in Spanish was related to their writing in English. She did not find that first language writing interfered with writing in the second language. Rather, the children used their Spanish to help them fill in when necessary. Knowledge of Spanish print helped them to go beyond what they had done before. However, in classroom observations, Edelsky found that both the Spanish and English print environments were meager. Just as children need a rich input of language if they are to become speakers of English, so too do they need a rich input of print of all kinds if they are to become readers and writers.

Hudelson's (1984) examination of the writing of young Hispanic children led her to suggest that ESL learners should be encouraged to explore writing in English before they have complete control of the new language. The children's written pieces will be a reflection of their stage of language development. Second-language learners frequently draw upon their understanding of first-language print as they approach the task of writing in the second language. Hispanic students will use their knowledge of Spanish orthography in spelling English words (Edelsky, 1982, 1986; Hudelson, 1984; Zutell & Allen, 1988). More experiences with print and books will support children's moves to control the conventions of written language.

Reading in the Second Language. In planning reading programs for second-language learners, one major issue is whether to teach children to read in their native language, or to require that they begin to read in English. Because literacy and oral language are closely linked, it would seem helpful to let children begin to read the language they already know (Goodman, Goodman & Flores, 1979; Hudelson 1981, 1987). This allows children to draw upon their knowledge of the sounds, structures, and meaning of their language as they move into print. For some second-language learners, opportunities to use their native language may be limited because of the teacher's lack of knowledge of the child's language or because of an unavailability of materials in the native language.

Formerly, many held the view that children learning a second language should not be permitted to read and write until they demonstrated control of the oral language. Researchers have shown that second-language learners can begin to read and write English long before they have mastered the forms of that language. Indeed, reading and writing experiences support language acquisition (Hudelson, 1984; Rigg, 1981; and Urzua, 1987).

Goodman and Goodman (1978) studied children from four different nationality groups (Arabic, Navaho, Samoan, and Spanish) as they read in English. It was found that factors other that first language determined how well the children were able to read in English. All of the children, despite limitations in English, were able to read and retell stories. Background knowledge was a significant factor in how well they read and recalled. The more these children knew about the content, the easier it was for them to read and understand the text.

The culturally different student, however, may not share the background of knowledge that many text writers expect. P. Johnson (1981) studied the effects of language complexity and cultural background on the reading comprehension of text. The results showed that the cultural origin of he story had more effect on comprehension than did the level of syntactic and semantic complexity. Steffensen, Joag-dev and Anderson (1979) had adults from the United States and from India read letters about an Indian and an American wedding. The researchers concluded that background knowledge had a profound influence on how well a text would be understood and remembered.

Rigg (1986) analyzed the reading miscues of four Southeast Asian children as they read from materials that were being used in the children's schools. She found that the difficulty level of the text was related to the background knowledge of the child and to shifts in text structure. The story that was most easily read by the children was a narrative that followed a familiar folktale format. A second story, about the winter olympics, was more difficult. It shifted from a journalistic style to a narrative style and then back again. The third story shifted back and forth between narrative and expository text. This text created real problems for the readers. Rigg suggests that material for young ESL readers have a recognizable and unshifting structure. She makes a strong plea for authentic texts rather than materials designed to meet a readability formula that requires short words and short sentences.

A study on the effectiveness of a reading program based on the use of a large number of carefully selected children's story books was carried out by Elley and Mangubhai (1983). They conducted a "book flood" in the fourth and fifth grade classes of eight rural Fijian schools. The classes were randomly assigned to one of three groups. In one group, teachers read aloud to the children each day; books were discussed and extended through a variety of activities. In another group children were read aloud to each day and given a daily sustained silent reading period. In the control group, the children were taught reading through a graded reading program. At the end of eight months, the pupils in the book flood groups progressed in reading and listening at twice the normal rate. After 20 months, the pupils' gains had increased and spread to related language skills.

The value of well-selected, authentic texts as a literacy program core for second-language learners cannot be underestimated. Well-written books supply an input of rich, cohesive language that supports children's acquisition of vocabulary and syntax in a way that talk alone cannot (Allen, in press).

MAKING INSTRUCTIONAL DECISIONS FOR ESL CHILDREN

The classroom provides a context for language acquisition that is different in many aspects from the home context in which the first language was acquired. In school settings, the things that are talked about and the ways that talk occurs can differ sharply from the discourse patterns of the home (Heath, 1983; Wells, 1981). While language in the home is used for real purposes, the language in the classroom is often contrived. In the home the language is adjusted to meet the needs of young children. In many classrooms most of the language input comes from the teacher, who often is talking not to one child, but to a group of children. The dimensions of the language acquisition task change because literacy receives much greater emphasis. Of great significance is the fact that when the child enters school, the purposes and underlying rules for language change. In the home children frequently initiate language in order to meet their needs. In the classroom it is more likely that children respond to language in order to meet the demands of an adult. Language acquisition strategies that worked well in the informal setting of the home may not work as well in the formal setting of the school.

Children in the classroom are expected to do more than learn English. They need to move ahead cognitively as well as linguistically. They are expected to acquire the skills and knowledges set forth in curriculum guides and in courses of study.

While children learning a first language are given a great deal of time to take on a wide variety of functions of language, for children learning a second language, there is frequently pressure to move very quickly into more academic and abstract language uses.

In examining the ways schools work to meet the needs of children who are learning English as a second language, it is vital to keep in mind that such programs need to help children become competent users of English, but more importantly, become successful learners. Cummins (1979) suggests that children who have well-developed skills in their first language, will be more able to develop those skills in their second language. When children have learned how to learn, they can transfer those skills to their new language.

Cultural Considerations

The cultural background of the child must be considered in planning educational experiences. The way children learn at home may not match the way they are expected to learn in school. Philips (1972) identified ways in that Native American children on the Warm Springs Reservation learned rather complex skills at home. They took on segments of the task in cooperation with the adult. Later, the child in privacy would try out and self-test this new skill. Speech played a very minimal part of both the learning process and the demonstration of skill acquisition. In the school setting, where children were expected to acquire most of their new knowledge through language, these capable children appeared less than competent.

There are differences in the way children from different culture groups interact in the classroom. Wong Fillmore (1986) reports finding differences in English language development depending on children's cultural background. Opportunities for Hispanic children to interact with English-speaking peers were an important factor in helping them acquire both speaking and comprehension skills. For the Chinese children, on the other hand, interactions with the teacher were more beneficial. The Hispanic children did well when the teacher's instructions were clear and the lessons well organized, but they became inattentive when the teacher was unclear. The Chinese students, on the other hand, became even more attentive in situations in which understanding was difficult.

Heath (1986) points out the importance of considering the genres of discourse used by different cultural groups. A genre refers to the type of organizing units into which smaller units may fit. Every culture has these recurring organizational patterns—ways of telling a story or a joke, ways of recounting an experience or giving directions. Heath states that these genres act as plans or maps for discourse. She believes that children's success in school is largely dependent upon the extent to which they are able to use the specific genres that are most valued in school settings. For example, two genres that are central to school learning are label quests and meaning quests. A label quest is simply asking for a name. Naming activities are very common with young children in the American culture. Parents commonly play the "what's this?" game with their children. In classrooms being able to provide correct labels continues to be

of great importance. Meaning quests are probes for explanation. Parents from the very beginning model this genre. "You're cranky because you're tired, aren't you?" or by restating children's comments, "You mean that. . . ." In schoolrooms teacher talk and textbook questions follow similar patterns.

Heath studied how genres were used in the homes of both Chinese-American and Mexican-American families. She found that both groups used a range of genres, but that these genres were used differently by each culture group. The importance of the child's ability to command a wide variety of genres may help to explain why some studies have shown that children who come from homes where the native language is used almost exclusively, tend to perform better than children who come from homes in which families try to use English rather than the mother tongue (Dolson, 1985). Parents who are communicating in their own language with ease and fluency are able to demonstrate a full range of genres. The children will be able to use their home language to name, explain, plan, narrate, and summarize. When children don't have access to these kinds of demonstrations in the home, they will need to grow in their understandings of how one uses a variety of genres.

Teachers' understandings of how different culture groups learn, interact, and use language can assist them to organize instruction in ways to support the culturally different learner. A lack of knowledge in this area can set up barriers to children's learning.

Types of School Programs

The school programs designed to assist children who are in the process of acquiring English as their second language have often been organized by focusing on the language in which instruction is delivered. Bilingual approaches involve the use of two languages for the instruction of language minority children. Transitional bilingual programs are ones in which children's first language is used as a medium of instruction until they become fluent enough to receive all their instruction in English. ESL is a part of such programs. It is expected that the amount of instruction offered in the child's native language will decrease as the child's ability to use English increases. Almost all bilingual programs in the United States would be identified as transitional programs. Another model, the maintenance bilingual program, offers instruction in two languages throughout the child's schooling experience. The goal is to develop the child's fluency and literacy in two languages (Fishman, 1979; Trueba, 1979).

The need for bilingual education has been strongly debated. Folk wisdom might seem to suggest that time spent using the first language is time taken away from learning the new language. Therefore, some make the assumption that bilingual instruction will retard children's English language development. Proponents of bilingual education point out that the use of the child's first language allows education to begin immediately without waiting for the child to develop fluency in English. It takes time to acquire a second language. Until children are fully competent in English, their first language can serve as a support to learning (Cummins, 1980). Because reading and writing are closely linked with oral language development, pedagogically it makes sense to help children move into literacy by building on the firm base of their first language (Edelsky, 1986; Hudelson, 1987).

A number of researchers have reviewed studies on the effectiveness of bilingual programs and have come to conflicting conclusions (Baker & DeKanter, 1981; Danoff, 1978; Hakuta & Gould, 1987; Troike, 1978). After doing a meta-analysis of selected studies on the efficacy of bilingual education, Willig (1985) concluded that the evidence supported bilingual programs. However, she also pointed out that the research on bilingual education was frequently inadequate in design. Hakuta and Gould (1987) reviewed the research and found that studies in both psychology and linguistics support the use of the native language in instructional programs. They point out that there is a deficiency of research on bilingual education in the area of program evaluation. They state that, "Evaluation research provokes political heat because programmatic labels often represent different partisan interests (e.g., U.S. English groups arguing against bilingual programs, or Hispanic groups opposing efforts to reduce the use of the native language)" (p. 43).

For a full discussion of the issues and research in bilingual education, see Wong Fillmore and Valdez (1986), "Teaching Bilingual Learners," in *Handbook of Research on Teaching,* third edition.

Although bilingual education is at one end of the instructional continuum, at the other end are instructional models that offer instruction in English only: submersion, immersion, and ESL (English as a Second Language). Submersion cannot truly be considered a program, for in this model the child is simply placed into the monlingual classroom and allowed to sink or swim. In immersion programs, the second language learner is enrolled in the monolingual classroom, but the teacher understands the child's native language and therefore is able to shape instruction with the child's needs in mind. In English as a Second Language (ESL) programs, the child is in the regular classroom setting for most of the day, but is pulled out of the classroom to receive special instruction in English as a second language.

Developing Supportive Classrooms for Second-Language Learners

Although many school districts provide support systems such as ESL instruction and tutoring programs, these alone cannot offer sufficient assistance to children who are acquiring English as a second language. The ESL teacher works with these students for only a small portion of the day. The children will spend the largest part of the day in the regular classroom. Even in school systems that have bilingual programs, the bilingual student will be moved into the regular classroom, usually within two years. However, few mainstream teachers have been prepared to instruct linguistically and culturally different children. Penfield (1987) surveyed regular classroom teachers and found that although many of them felt that the ESL student should be integrated into the regular classroom, they also believed that such placements created problems. Few of the teach-

ers in this survey considered themselves competent to integrate the acquisition of English with the learning of curricular content.

Teachers can, however, create a classroom environment that will allow linguistically and culturally different children both to acquire English and to move ahead cognitively. In order for this to happen, teachers will need to examine the amount and types of linguistic input that children receive and the ways language is used in their classrooms. Using knowledge about second-language acquisition, teachers can provide opportunities that will allow students to grow into their new language.

Providing Language Input. Language-different children in mainstream classrooms are surrounded by English. However, if that language is to serve as input for English-language development, it must be comprehensible. Wong Fillmore (1982) studied the instructional language of teachers as a source of linguistic input for second-language learners. She observed and analyzed instruction in four bilingual kindergartens for one school year. At the end of that year the data showed that in two classrooms nearly all of the children who began the year with no English had learned some English. In the other two classrooms, the observers agreed that only 60 percent of the non-English speakers had learned any English, while the rest were judged to have made no progress. The researchers concluded that when teacher talk was a valuable source of language input to second-language learners, it was because teachers shaped their language to meet these learners' needs. They simplified their language, used gestures, and linked talk to a strong context. While the child's native language was used occasionally to explain concepts that were difficult to make clear in English, direct translation was not used, nor were the two languages mixed. These teachers were making their language comprehensible by keeping the learner's special needs in mind, involving the children in talk, and judiciously using the native language when necessary.

Using Language in the Classroom. One cannot look at linguistic input without also examining the interaction patterns in the classroom. The teacher is one source of language input. Peers provide an equally rich lode of language, but only if classrooms are organized in ways that encourage children to work together on tasks that involve purposeful talk. Both the composition and the organization of the classroom have an effect on the amount of English that second-language learners acquire (Wong Fillmore, 1982). When classes are composed almost entirely of children with limited English, the teacher becomes the central source of language input. If the non-English speaking children share a language, they will tend to use their home language when working together. If they do not share a language and use English to communicate, the English vocabulary will be diminished and the forms of the language simplified and often faulty. When classrooms have fairly equal mixtures of native and nonnative speakers, student interactions can become a major part of the language input that second-language learners receive.

D. Johnson (1983) experimented with the use of peer tutoring with Spanish-speaking elementary children. The peer tutoring sessions were designed to provide a structured setting for natural language practice between a limited English speaker and a native English speaker. She found that the peer tutoring techniques increased the children's vocabulary comprehension. Johnson concluded that young fluent English speakers are a valuable source of L2 input. She suggests that those designing ESL programs for children include ways that bring about opportunities for real and purposeful language interaction. August (1987) also found peer tutoring to be effective in helping Mexican-American children to acquire English. However, she found that it did not help English-speaking children to learn Spanish. As do Edelsky and Hudelson (1980), she posits that the status of the language has a marked effect on its acquisition.

Frequently, L2 learners are limited in the opportunities to use language for a variety of purposes. D. Johnson (1988) set up experiences that let young ESL students take on the teacher's role. Children were taught how to do an activity and then paired with another child in order to teach that activity. Each pair was a cross-language one. This experience created a need for children to use language to explain, describe, and to respond to questions. Johnson concluded that a major part of the ESL instructor's task is to set up the social conditions that will bring about the meaningful and purposeful use of English.

Allen (1986) compared the ways young second-language learners used language as they responded to literature and as they worked together on a science project. The literary theme supported narration and discussion. It helped draw out large cohesive chunks of language as children retold stories, created their own written or oral narratives, or discussed books. The science exploration provided opportunities for children to describe precisely, to record and share observations. It developed vocabulary in very concrete and precise ways. Hester (1984) describes a model developed for the SLIPP (Second Language in the Primary School) Project, a project for linguistically and culturally different children in Great Britain. The focus was on helping children acquire English by giving them firsthand experiences, and by creating opportunities for them to work collaboratively in ways that encouraged the use of language. The teachers in this project found that thematic work allowed them to organize activities in ways that created real purposes for a wide variety of language functions and that used peer interaction as a support for language acquisition. The theme provided a strong contextual support that helped children gain access to meaning. Creating opportunities to talk is not sufficient. Teachers need to consider the linguistic dimensions of the learning tasks.

Supportive classrooms are important for all learners, but if children are to acquire both English as a second language and content knowledge, they are essential. Enright and McCloskey (1985) describe such a classroom as one that is organized so children can collaborate on purposeful activities stemming from their own interests. It is a classroom in which learning is viewed as holistic.

This perspective of language learning has been described by many (Altwerger, Edelsky and Flores, 1987; Goodman & Goodman, 1978; Harste, Newman, 1985; Woodward and Burke, 1984). Providing classrooms that present language and literacy as integrated processes seems a powerful way of supporting second-language learners as they take on their new language (Edelsky, 1986; Hudelson, 1984).

Conclusion

It takes time to become a proficient user of a second language. While some children rather quickly take on a new language, for many others the time frame is much longer. There is strong evidence that most children require from 4 to 6 years to reach the level of proficiency needed to participate fully in the academic setting (Cummins 1981; Wong Fillmore, 1986). Support for these students, although it may change in both focus and amount, needs to continue until the child is able to achieve academic success.

The research discussed in this chapter strongly suggests that teachers who are working with second-language learners need to provide classrooms where these children will be able to:

Acquire the language naturally, using the language for real purposes.

Receive linguistic input that is made comprehensible by a strong and supportive context.

Experiment with, hypothesize about, and try out language in low anxiety settings.

Work with English-speaking peers on meaningful tasks that create opportunities and real reasons to talk, write and read together.

Use language for a broad variety of functions, both social and academic.

Clearly, much of what has been described as supporting the language development of English as a second language, learners will also support the growth of children whose native language is not English.

Finally, it is important that these children who are taking on English as their second language be viewed not as an educational problem, but as a rich and valued resource. They bring much to our schools and to the society. They need time and the sensitive and knowlegeable support of educators if they are to be prepared to take their place in the world outside the classroom.

References

Allen, V. (in press). Literature as a support to language acquisition. In P. Rigg and V. Allen (Eds.), *When they don't all speak English*. Urbana, IL: National Council of Teachers of English.

Allen, V. (1986). Developing contexts to support second language acquisition. *Language Arts, 63,* 61–66.

Altwerger, B., Edelsky, C., & Flores, B. (1987). Whole language: What's new? *The Reading Teacher, 41,* 144–154.

August, D. L. (1987). Effects of peer tutoring on the second language acquisition of Mexican American children in elementary school. *TESOL Quarterly, 21,* 717–736.

Baker, K. A. & De Kantor, A. A. (1981, September). *Effectiveness of bilingual education: A review of the literature*. Washington, DC: U.S. Department of Education, Office of Planning, Budget, and Evaluation.

Bissex, G. L. (1980). *GYNS AT WRK: A child learns to write and read.* Cambridge, MA: Harvard University Press.

Canale, M. & Swain, M. (1980). Theoretical bases of communicative approaches to second language teaching and testing. *Applied Linguistics, 1,* 1–47.

Cortes, C. E. (1986). The education of language minority students: A contextual interaction model. In California State Department of Education. *Beyond language: Social and cultural factors in schooling language minority students* (pp. 299–343). Los Angeles, CA: California State University, Evaluation, Dissemination and Assessment Center.

Cummins, J. (1979). Linguistic interdependence and the educational development of bilingual children. *Review of Educational Research, 49,* 222–251.

Cummins, J. (1980). The cross-lingual dimensions of language proficiency: Implications for bilingual education and the optimal age issue. *TESOL Quarterly, 14,* 175–187.

Cummins, J. (1981). Four misconceptions about language proficiency in bilingual education. *NABE Journal, 5,* 31–45.

Cummins, J. (1986). Impowering minority students: A framework for intervention. *Harvard Educational Review, 56,* 18–36.

Danoff, M. N. (1978). *Evaluation of the impact of ESEA Title VII Spanish/ English Bilingual Education Program: Overview of study and findings.* Palo Alto, CA: American Institute for Research.

Dolson, D. P. (1985). The effects of Spanish home language use on the scholastic performance of Hispanic pupils. *Journal of Multilingual Multicultural Development, 6,* 135–155.

Dulay, H., & Burt, M. (1974). New perspective on the creative construction process in child second language acquisition. *Language Learning, 24,* 253–378.

Dulay, H. & Burt, M. (1977). Remarks on creativity in language acquisition. In M. Burt, H. Dulay, and M. Finnochiaro (Eds.), *Viewpoints on English as a second language* (pp. 95–126). New York: Newbury House.

Edelsky, C. (1982). Writing in a bilingual program: The relationship of L1 and L2 texts. *TESOL Quarterly, 16,* 211–228.

Edelsky, C. (1986). *Writing in a bilingual program: Habla una vez.* Norwood, NJ: Ablex.

Edelsky, C., & Hudelson, S. (1980). *Language acquisition and a marked language. NABE Journal, 5,* 1–16.

Elley, W. B., & Mangubhai, F. (1983). The impact of reading on second language learning. *Reading Research Quarterly, 19,* 53–67.

Enright, D. S., & McCloskey, M. L. (1985). Yes, talking!: Organizing the classroom to promote second language acquisition. *TESOL Quarterly, 19,* 431–454.

Fishman, J. A. (1979). Bilingual education: What and why? In H. T. Trueba and C. Barnett-Mizrahi (Eds.), *Bilingual multicultural education and the professional: From theory to practice* (pp. 11–19). Rawley, MA: Newbury House.

Fries, C. C. (1945). *Teaching and learning English.* Ann Arbor, MI: University of Michigan Press.

Goodman, K., & Goodman, Y. (1978). Reading of American children whose language is a stable rural dialect of English or a language other than English (NIE-C-00-3-0087). Washington, DC: U.S. Department of Health, Education and Welfare.

Goodman, K., Goodman, Y., & Flores, B. (1979). *Reading in the bilingual classroom: Literacy and biliteracy.* Rosslyn, VA: National Clearinghouse for Bilingual Education.

Hakuta, K. (1986). *Mirror of language: The debate on bilingualism.* New York: Basic Books.

Hakuta, K., & Gould, L. J. (1987). Synthesis of research on bilingual education. *Educational Leadership, 44,* 33–45.

Harste, J., Woodward, V., & Burke, C. (1984). *Language stories & literacy lessons,* Portsmouth, NH: Heinemann.

Heath, S. B. (1983). *Ways with words.* Cambridge: Cambridge University Press.

Heath, S. B. (1984). Literacy or literate skills? Consideration for ESL/EFL learners. In P. Larson, E. L. Judd, & D. S. Messerschmitt (Eds.), *On TESOL '84: A brave new world for TESOL* (pp. 15–28). Washington, DC: Teachers of English to Speakers of Other Languages.

Heath, S. B. (1986). Sociocultural contexts of language development. In *Beyond language: Social and cultural factors in schooling language minority students* (pp. 143–186). Los Angeles, CA: California State University, Evaluation, Dissemination and Assessment Center.

Hester, H. (1984). Peer interaction in learning English as a second language. *Theory into Practice, 23,* 208–217.

Hudelson, S. (1981). *Learning to read in different languages.* Washington, DC: Center for Applied linguistics.

Hudelson, S. (1984). Kan yu ret an rayt en Ingles: Children become literate in English as a second language. *TESOL Quarterly, 18,* 221–238.

Hudelson, S. (1987). The role of native language literacy in the education of language minority children. *Language Arts, 64,* 827–841.

Hymes, D. (1974). *Foundations of sociolinguistics: An ethnographic approach.* Philadelphia: University of Pennsylvania Press.

Johnson, D. M. (1983). Natural language learning by design: A classroom experiment in social interaction and second language acquisition. *TESOL Quarterly, 17,* 55–88.

Johnson, D. M. (1988). ESL children as teachers: A social view of second language use. *Language Arts, 65,* 154–163.

Johnson, P. (1981). Effects on reading comprehension of language complexity and cultural background of a text. *TESOL Quarterly, 15,* 159–181.

Krashen, S. (1981). *Second language acquisition and second language learning.* Oxford, England: Pergamon.

Krashen, S. (1982). *Principals and practice in second language acquisition.* Oxford, England: Pergamon.

Lindfors, J. (1987). *Children's language and learning,* 2nd ed. Englewood Cliffs, NJ: Prentice-Hall.

McCarty, J. & Carrera, J. W. (1988). *New voices: Immigrant students in U.S. public schools.* Boston, MA: The National Coalition of Advocates for Students.

McLaughlin, B. (1984). *Second language acquisition in childhood.* (Vol 1, Preschool children Second Edition). Hillsdale, NJ: Erlbaum Associates.

Newman, J. (1985). *Whole language: Theory in use.* Portsmouth, NH: Heinemann.

Penfield, J. (1987). ESL: The regular classroom teacher's perspective. *TESOL Quarterly, 21,* 21–40.

Philips, S. (1972). Participant structures and communicative competence: Warm Springs children in community and classroom. In C. Cazden, V. John, & D. Hymes (Eds.), *Functions of language in the classroom* (pp. 370–394). New York: Teachers College Press.

Read, C. (1975). *Children's categorizations of speech sounds in English.* (Research Rep. No. 17). Urbana, IL: National Council of Teachers of English.

Rigg, P. (1981). Beginning to read in English the LEA way. In C. W. Twyfor, W. Diehl, & R. Feathers (Eds.), *English as a second language: Moving from theory* (pp. 81–90). *Monographs in Teaching and Learning 4.* Bloomington, IN: Indiana University.

Rigg, P. (1986). Reading in ESL: Learning from kids. In P. Rigg & D. S. Enright (Eds.), *Children with ESL: Integrating perspectives* (pp. 55–92). Washington, DC: Teachers of English to Speakers of Other Languages.

Saville-Troike, M. (1984). What *really* matters in second language learning for academic achievement. *TESOL Quarterly, 18,* 199–220.

Selinker, L. (1972). Interlanguage. International Review *of Applied Linguistics, 10,* 209–231.

Steffensen, M., Joag-dev, C., & Anderson, R. (1979). A cross-cultural perspective on reading comprehension. *Reading Research Quarterly, 15,* 10–29.

Stern, H. H. (1983). *Fundamental concepts of language teaching.* Oxford, England: Oxford University Press.

Teitelbaum, H., & Hiller, J. J. (1977). Bilingual education: The legal mandate. *Harvard Educational Review, 47,* 138–170.

Troike, R. C. (1978). *Research Evidence for the effectiveness of bilingual education.* Rosslyn, VA: National Clearinghous for Bilingual Education.

Trueba, H. T. (1979). Bilingual-education models: Types and designs. In H. T. Trueba & C. Barnett-Misrahi (Eds.), *Bilingual multicultural education and the professional: From theory to practice* (pp. 54–73). Rawley, MA: Newbury House.

Urzua, C. (1987). "You stopped too soon": Second language children composing and revising. *TESOL Quarterly, 21,* 279–304.

U.S. Supreme Court. (1974). Lau Nichols, 414 U.S. 563.

Waggoner, D. 91984). The need for bilingual education: Estimates from the 1980 census. *NABE Journal, 8,* 1–14.

Wells, G. (1981). *Learning through interaction.* Cambridge, England: Cambridge University Press.

Willig, A. C. (1985). A meta-analysis of selected studies on the effectiveness of bilingual education. *Review of Educational Research, 55,* 269–318.

Wong Fillmore, L. (1976). The second time around: Cognitive and social strategies in second language acquisition. Unpublished doctoral dissertation, Stanford, CA.

Wong Fillmore, L. (1982). Instructional language as linguistic input: Second language learning in classrooms. In L. C. Wilkinson (Ed.), *Communicating in the classroom* (pp. 283–296). New York: Academic Press.

Wong Fillmore, L. (1986). Research currents: Equity or excellence. *Language Arts 63,* 474–481.

Wong Fillmore, L., & Valadez, C. (1986). Teaching bilingual learners. In M. C. Wittrock (Ed.) *Handbook of research on teaching* (pp. 648–685). New York: Macmillan.

Zutell, J., & Allen, V. (1988). The English spelling strategies of Spanish-speaking bilingual children. *TESOL Quarterly, 22,* 333–339.

20C. DIALECTS, CULTURE, AND TEACHING THE ENGLISH LANGUAGE ARTS

Marcia Farr

Within the last 20 years, there has been increasing recognition of the multicultural nature of many Western English-speaking societies. The fact of multiculturalism, of course, has existed for much longer than 20 years in these societies, but this fact seems to have become particularly salient, especially in educational arenas, since the substantial civil rights gains in the United States in the last several decades. The recognition of multiculturalism comes none too soon, as nonwhite minority populations increase and European-origin white populations decrease, at least in the United States. A recent strategic planning report at the University of Illinois at Chicago, in fact, predicted that, if immigration and birth rates remain at current levels, "Within one hundred years, non-Hispanic whites of European origin will no longer constitute a majority of the American population" (Sima, 1987). Clearly, it is high time that majority attitudes be realigned with the realities of this changing population. This chapter will address the significance of such multiculturalism for the classroom, focusing on the teaching of the English language arts (i.e., reading, writing, and speaking "standard" English). In particular, this chapter will review research on culturally "nonmainstream" populations, focusing on those in the United States, and discuss how this research can inform effective language arts teaching.

Before synthesizing what research has documented regarding the cultural and linguistic characteristics of nonmainstream groups, a few definitions are in order. The terms "mainstream" and "nonmainstream" are used here following Heath (1983):

Mainstreamers exist in societies around the world that rely on formal education systems to prepare children for participation in settings involving literacy. Cross-national descriptions characterize these groups as literate, school-oriented, aspiring to upward mobility through success in formal institutions, and looking beyond the primary networks of family and community for behavioral models and value orientations. (Chapter 7, note 2, pp. 391–2)

Thus, nonmainstream refers to those groups who do not fit the characteristics described above for typically middle-class mainstreamers.

Closely related to the notion of nonmainstream is the term "dialect." Originally referring to "a regional speech pattern (Alsatian, Cajun, and so on) within a nation in which another pattern dominates officially (as determined by the government, the schools, and so on)" (Ducrot & Todorov, 1983), this term has been extended to include social speech patterns as well (Wolfram & Fasold, 1974). A dialect, then, is either a regional variety of a language (e.g., Southern English in the U.S.) or a social variety of a language (e.g., African American vernacular English in the United States). Both kinds of varieties, of course, coexist with usually one "official" or "national" language of a country (in English-speaking countries, some form of "standard" English). It is important to point out that standard, national languages often start out as regional dialects themselves, becoming

the national standard because of the social, economic, and political power of the region in which they are used.

"Culture" is an equally important term to define for the purposes of this chapter, but it is a difficult one. Numerous definitions have been offered by anthropologists through the years (Geertz, 1973, chap. 1), but recently a cognitive definition has been favored by many. Spradley, for example, in his widely-used methodological text, *Participant Observation* (1980), refers to three fundamental aspects of human experience with which ethnographers, or those who study culture, must deal: what people do, what people know, and the things people make and use (1980, p. 5). Of these three aspects, Spradley puts primary emphasis on what people know, or on cultural knowledge. He thus essentially defines "culture as *the acquired knowledge people use to interpret experience and generate behavior*" (1980, p. 6; italics in original). In other words, culture can be viewed as a (cognitive) system of knowledge that both gives rise to behavior and is used to interpret experience.

CULTURAL AND LINGUISTIC DIFFERENCES

As should be clear from the definitions of dialect and culture above, all normal human beings, having been enculturated into one group or another, possess both linguistic and cultural competence; that is, their minds possess the knowledge both to speak the language of their group and to behave in ways appropriate to that group. This is as true for mainstream as for nonmainstream people, of course. Because schools in Western societies are part of mainstream culture, the linguistic and cultural competence expected within them closely resembles the language and culture of mainstream people. Heath (1983), for example, has shown how members of the mainstream culture she studied used "expository talk" that was similar to school-taught expository prose on the job (in her study as mill executives and teachers) and at home as parents. Children from nonmainstream groups, in contrast, enter school with a set of linguistic and cultural resources that in some respects differ from, and even conflict with, rather than resemble, those of the school culture. As has been repeatedly argued, such children do not possess linguistic or cultural deficits (although that is a widespread conventional belief among many mainstreamers); rather, some of their cognitive and linguistic skills are simply different from those of their mainstream counterparts.

A substantial body of sociolinguistic research has documented some of the linguistic characteristics of nonmainstream American English dialects, including African American vernacular English (Fasold, 1972; Labov, 1972a; Kochman, 1972; Wolfram, 1969); Puerto Rican English (Wolfram, 1974; Zentella, 1981); Appalachian English (Wolfram & Christian, 1976); varieties of American Indian English (Wolfram, Christian, Potter, &

Leap, 1979); Vietnamese English (Wolfram & Hatfield, 1984; and others (Amastae & Elias-Olivares, 1982; Ferguson & Heath, 1981; Labov, 1980) The primary finding of all this work is that nonmainstream varieties of English, in fact of any language, are as complex and as regularly patterned as are mainstream varieties. That is, speakers of these nonstandard dialects often have different linguistic rules in their grammars; again, contrary to conventional ''wisdom'' among mainstreamers, they do not have linguistic deficits.

Other sociolinguistic research has focused on culturally-embedded aspects of language use, rather than on the grammatical characteristics of nonstandard dialects. Much of this work has been carried out within the conceptual framework developed by Hymes (1972, 1974) for what he termed ''the ethnography of communication.'' These studies have taken place both within classrooms (Cazden, John, & Hymes, 1972; Cherry Wilkinson, 1982; Cook-Gumperz, 1986; Gilmore & Glatthorn, 1982; Green & Wallat, 1981) and within home and community contexts (Bauman & Sherzer, 1974; Gumperz 1982a, 1982b; Heath, 1983; Kochman, 1981; Scollon & Scollon, 1979, 1981; Tannen, 1982, 1984). This work has found that ways of using language can vary extensively from one cultural group to another and that such differences can cause miscommunication between speakers from different groups. School classrooms are a particularly significant arena for such cross-cultural communication, and the learning of literacy, in particular, is often a context in which communicative systems not only differ, but conflict. That is, when learning to read and to write, many students from mainstream groups are faced with a conflict between their own cultural and linguistic systems (and their own sense of identity) and those of the standard written language. The difficulties inherent in resolving such conflicts provide one explanation for low literacy levels among these populations.

A few other studies have focused on the writing of nonmainstream students (Charrow, 1981; Cronnell, 1981; Farr Whiteman, 1981; Reed, 1981; Valadez, 1981) or on literacy in homes and other nonschool community settings (Fishman, 1988; Heath, 1983; Moll & Diaz, 1987; Scribner & Cole, 1981; Shieffelin & Cochran-Smith, 1984; Street, 1984; Taylor & Dorsey-Gaines, 1988; Teale, 1986).

The research on language variation and writing has identified particular linguistic features characteristic of the ''home language'' of various nonmainstream groups that occur in the writing of children, adolescents, and adults from these groups. For example, when a BVE speaker writes the sentence *Mickey have so many friend,* it illustrates two home language features: *have* rather than *has* and *friend* rather than *friends* (Farr Whiteman, 1981). Work in this area has identified similar characteristics in the writing of African American vernacular English speakers, Latino and Indian bilinguals, and deaf users of American sign language.

Most of the work on the relation of home language to literacy learning explicitly advocates what Baugh (1981) terms ''ethnosensitivity,'' rather than ethnocentricity, on the part of those teaching such students. In this view, an emphasis is placed on understanding and building on the cultural values and linguistic patterns of nonmainstream students.

The work of literacy in community settings has found that literacy is not a single entity that occurs in different context, but a social practice that varies according to the particular use to which it is put in each context. Likewise, the cognitive demands of writing and reading, and the cognitive effects of learning to do so, also vary according to particular uses. Thus, as uses of language and literacy may differ between school and nonschool contexts, so apparently do the cognitive styles that underlie these uses.

For a more detailed review of sociolinguistic research and its relevance to the teaching and learning of writing, see Farr (1986). This review synthesizes research on nonmainstream cultural groups and provides specific examples, drawn from the research, of particular conflicts between mainstream and nonmainstream communicative systems. Examples are provided for conflicts at the phonological, syntactic, semantic, pragmatic, and discourse levels of language, as well as at the broader cultural level of language use.

POLITICAL ISSUES

Recognition of the differences between the linguistic and cultural resources of nonmainstream students and those that are needed for success in mainstream schools leads to decisions that are essentially political in nature. Such decisions constitute a language policy regarding *what* language arts should be taught to a multicultural student population. As Fasold and Shuy pointed out years ago, there are essentially three positions that can be assumed in this situation: eradication, biloquialism, and appreciation of dialect differences (Fasold & Shuy, 1970, p. xi).

Eradication, the traditional policy ''long nourished in the English profession'' (Fasold & Shuy, 1970, p. x), assumes the undesirability of speech patterns associated with nonmainstream groups and attempts to rid students of these features, replacing them with more desirable ''standard'' ones. This, in fact, describes the status quo in most schools, and, without a concerted effort to develop a different language policy, this position will probably prevail. Whether it succeeds or not, and for many, in the United States at least, so far it has not, is a separate question.

Biloquialism calls for the learning of new, standard patterns without eliminating the old nonstandard ones. Often called bidialectalism or biculturalism (as parallels to bilingualism), this position attempts to provide mainstream linguistic and cultural resources to nonmainstream speakers, while avoiding negative attitudes toward nonmainstream cultures and dialects. The goal of this kind of instruction is to enable students to switch from one linguistic style to another, guided by a sense of appropriateness to the context in which the language is used. Since all speakers, mainstream and nonmainstream alike, shift among more or less formal styles, depending on context, to some degree, this position should be a relatively natural one. It also has the advantage of appearing to be the most reasonable position, presenting a compromise between the two more extreme positions of eradication and appreciation of dialect differences.

Appreciation of dialect differences is the logical opposite of eradicationism. This position holds that, since research has clearly shown nonmainstream dialects to be the linguistic equals of mainstream or standard language, it is wrong to insist on replacing such dialects with the national standard. Moreover, as many have argued (see, for example, Sledd, 1972, 1988), the time and effort spent on eradication, with remarkably unsuccessful results, would be better spent on enlightening mainstreamers about the naturalness of variation in language and eliminating their prejudices against nonmainstream groups.

Although these three positions were described two decades ago, the situation remains almost the same today. There is as yet no widespread consensus on which to base a new language policy. Two decades ago, however, the discussion revolved primarily around oral language, with some attention to reading (Baratz & Shuy, 1969; Fasold & Shuy, 1970; Feigenbaum, 1970; Shuy, 1980). As writing has gained in prominence as an educational and research issue, however, the situation has shifted somewhat. Researchers recently have begun to address the concerns of reading and writing together, joining the emerging field of literacy studies (Langer, 1988).

Some studies of literacy have emphasized its importance in modernization and all the processes (e.g., urbanization, industrialization) that go along with it (Goody, 1977, 1986, 1987; Goody & Watt, 1963; Ong, 1982). This view holds that literacy brings with it cognitive changes that are necessary for coping in modern industrial society. A number of researchers have critiqued this view as being ethnocentrically biased in favor of Western culture and have provided counter evidence, from anthropological studies, of supposedly literate cognitive processes in nonliterate cultures (Finnegan, 1988; Street, 1984). Moreover, Levine (1986) has questioned the necessity of standard English literacy for many kinds of employment, while acknowledging the continued use by employers of literacy tests to select workers, apparently for other reasons. Other kinds of employment do involve literacy (for a review, see Gundlach, Farr, & Cook-Gumperz, in press), although the kinds of writing and reading vary widely.

The debate among literacy researchers continues. Recently, Heath (1986), in discussing modern literacy, has suggested two factors that are either precursors or consequences of it: an attitude toward language that sees it as an object in itself, an object that can be broken into parts and analyzed; and institutional reinforcements for literacy, which provide contexts in which people talk about written texts. She then calls for studies of Goody's "middle groups," populations that are neither entirely oral nor literate according to mainstream norms, but use literacy in a variety of nonacademic ways both at home and at work. Such studies, Heath claims, will yield important information about aspects of modern literacy that as yet have been unstudied. Her call is reminiscent of the biloquialism discussed above in its emphasis on accepting local, nonmainstream standards as part of the definition of literacy, rather than simply defining literacy as standard and mainstream.

Once again, then, the most reasonable position seems to be that of biloquialism, the teaching of mainstream patterns as an expansion of students' linguistic repertoires, not as a replacement for indigenous dialects or local ways of using language and literacy. Although this position seems to avoid the injustice of eradicationism, as well as the not-very-practical idealism, some would say, of leaving indigenous dialects unchanged, one

must question whether it is as attainable as it appears to be. It is certainly true that both bilingualism and bidialectalism exist in societies around the world, indicating that, in themselves, these phenomena are natural and attainable. It then must be asked why that has not happened in, for example, the United States, to a greater extent that it has. The work of two researchers in particular, Fred Erickson and John Ogbu, has suggested some explanations for this.

Ogbu (1987) argues that some minorities in modern urban industrial societies form "a collective oppositional identity" for support and survival that makes "intercultural learning or crossing cultural/language boundaries . . . problematic" (Ogbu, 1987, p. 164). In other words, a vernacular dialect is one set of symbols supporting an identity opposed to the forces that denigrate the vernacular culture. To learn mainstream language and cultural patterns, then, is tantamount to denying one's identity and joining forces with those who are rejecting one's group.

Erickson (1984) offers explanations drawn from the micropolitical processes in communicative interactions between individuals. In discussing the miscommunication, in the classroom and elsewhere, that can result from cultural differences in language form and use, he cites studies (Giles & Powlesland, 1975; Labov, 1972b; Piestrup, 1973; Erickson & Shultz, 1982) that show such differences seem to increase in contexts where there is conflict (for example, if such differences lead to negative perceptions of a student by a teacher). When there is no conflict (for example, when instruction is congruent with the culture of the students), such differences can be "sidestepped." The implication here is that these micropolitical processes, reflecting more macro ones from the larger society, may be partially responsible for so many students not learning, or not choosing to use, standard English.

Clearly, the problem of teaching standard English and literacy is more complicated than was thought, by many, two decades ago. Biloquialism still seems to be the most reasonable position, but if it is to be a truly effective policy for language and literacy learning, it will have to be supported by a reality that makes oppositional identity formation unnecessary. Such a reality, of course, will require social change beyond the scope of language-arts teaching Language-arts teaching, however, can contribute to broader, more long-term social change if efforts are made within teacher education programs to negate the use of cultural and linguistic differences as resources for conflict. Instead, as will be discussed in the next section, such differences can be viewed as positive resources that can be used to make instruction more effective with nonmainstream students.

EDUCATIONAL ISSUES

Ethnographic studies of local uses of language and literacy have been used to improve instruction in two ways: by modifying instruction to be congruent with what research has shown to be local ways of using language, and by involving students themselves in doing, and writing up the results of, ethnographic research in their own communities. Heath (1983) provides a model for both uses. Her ethnographic research on language acquisition in one African American and one white southern, rural, working class community was used in the local school to modify instruction to students from these communities. Moreover, in a science classroom, students were involved in ethnographic research in their communities on such topics as ways of growing foodstuffs; they then compared these local ways with scientific approaches in an effort to determine "whether or not science could explain why the local folk methods either worked or did not work" (Heath, 1983, p. 317).

Researchers in Hawaii and in San Diego, California, also have applied the results of ethnographic research to instruction. Au (1980) and Au and Jordan (1981) report on the successful results obtained by modifying reading instruction to be more congruent with the Hawaiian "talk story," a local speech event identified and described by ethnographers (Watson, 1975; Watson-Gegeo & Boggs, 1977). Diaz, Moll, and Mehan (1986) and Moll and Diaz (1987) report on another use of ethnographic research results in the classroom. In this project, the use of "social content: the substance of ... discourse, parents' educational values, life history, and conditions of ... sample families" (Diaz, Moll, & Mehan, 1986, p. 223) to reorganize instruction increased student participation in lessons and, consequently, improved student performance.

Other studies have provided an understanding of the principles underlying effective language-arts instruction. Before summarizing two such studies that have focused on teaching students from nonmainstream groups, it is important to emphasize that it is not so much the pedagogical technique itself that promotes learning, as it is the principles underlying successful techniques. Even the most successful and innovative technique can be misapplied, or can be inappropriate for a particular classrooms, teacher, or cultural group. An acutal incident (reported in Zemelman & Daniels, 1988) may be helpful as an example here.

Recently, a sixth-grade student in a highly regarded middle school in a suburb of Chicago was observed going over her well written essay, erasing more sophisticated words and replacing them with simpler ones. Then she crossed out the simpler words, and drew arrows from them toward the more sophisticated ones written in the margins of the paper. When asked what she was doing, she replied, "I'm doing the writing process. We have to do it this way; it's what the teacher wants." The point of this story, of course, is that, although an emphasis on writing process is in general a welcome improvement to the traditional focus only on written products, replacing one rigid system with another doesn't really improve instruction at all. In short, the principles (e.g., the teacher turning over much of the responsibility for writing to the student) underlying the studies of writing process instruction (see, for example, Graves, 1983; Calkins, 1983; Perl & Wilson, 1986; Zemelman & Daniels, 1988) are equally as important as the focus on process itself.

For nonmainstream students, misapplications of instructional improvements such as the one described above add insult to injury. Most of the schools, in the United States at least, these students attend are already burdened with problems that have little to do with instruction itself. Consequently, any instructional changes made in such schools not only should reflect the underlying principles of successful techniques, but also should be congruent with the realities of such schools. Three essential principles will be discussed below; for a more detailed synthesis of such research, see Farr and Daniels (1986), which presents 15 principles of effective writing instruction for nonmainstream (and other) students. See also Langer and Applebee (1986), which describes five components for effective literacy instruction for all students.

The most important principle of effective instruction for nonmainstream students is that of ethnosensitivity (Baugh, 1981). It is crucial that teachers understand that their own views of the world, or ways of using language in that world, are not necessarily shared by others. A deep understanding of cultural and linguistic differences, either through living in another culture or through pre-service or in-service coursework, can help reduce the ethnocentrism that is widespread in Western societies. Teachers, like most other members of these societies, are generally unaware of the extent to which they believe that their own cultural and linguistic patterns are natural or logical, nor do they generally realize how they tend to interpret others' behavior according to their own cultural norms. For example, indirectness in language or other behavior can signify respect or politeness in one culture and dishonesty in another. If a teacher and a student are from different cultures, or subcultures, the very same behavior can be interpreted quite differently by each of them. Because communication between teacher and student is crucial to effective teaching and learning, it should be clear why ethnosensitivity is so important.

A second principle involves structuring activities that comprise functional and interactive communication and allow students to feel "ownership" of their own writing. That is, writing intended as actual communication is much more effective in engaging students in literacy learning. Staton, Shuy, Kreeft Payton, and Reed (1988) provide an example of this. Staton et al. studied the use of dialogue journals in a sixth-grade classroom in a multicultural section of Los Angeles (the students in this particular classroom, for example, spoke 13 different languages). Their teacher, who had been using dialogue journals for 17 years, asked her students to write in English daily entries in the journal, to which she wrote short responses. Even those students who had minimal literacy skills in English were asked to write, as best they could, at least three sentences per day. The teacher did not evaluate this writing, but, instead, responded to it as a natural form of communication between two people who were writing and reading rather than talking.

Analysis of the journals over the course of a year showed substantial growth in writing, including an increase in quantity, elaboration of student-initiated topics, fluency, and control of English syntax (Kreeft & Shuy, 1985; Staton, Shuy, Kreeft Payton, and Reed, 1988). Moreover, these students experienced, some for the first time, writing and reading for a purpose of their own. They eagerly read the teacher's responses to their own entries and wrote copiously, some even ending the year with several filled notebooks comprising their year-long dialogue journal.

Heath & Branscombe (1985) also showed that structuring activities which comprise functional and interactive communication help students learn how to write and read in mainstream ways. In this study, ninth-grade, remedial track English students (primarily nonmainstream African Americans and a few nonmainstream whites in a southern city) being taught by Branscombe wrote and read long letters to and from Heath and her family, whom the students did not know; they also corresponded with Branscombe's regular track eleventh-grade students.

As in the journals of the Staton study, the letters emphasized "real" communication, i.e., an interaction between writers and readers about thoughts, ideas, and other information. Branscombe's students, over the course of the year, became comfortable operating as writers and readers and learned much about school literacy in the process. They learned, for example, that (mainstream) expository writing requires "linguistic devices and background information in explicated form if the addressee is to understand the (writer)" (Heath & Branscombe, 1985, p. 26).

A third principle is also illustrated by both the Staton et al. and the Heath and Branscombe studies: the need for abundant experience with written texts. Such texts are replete with the linguistic responses of Western literacy such as standard grammar, explicit connectives (e.g., *therefore, consequently, although*), Latinate vocabulary, a clear sequencing of "points," allusions to other written texts, and so on. The more experience students have with such texts, the more easily they will acquire the particular linguistic devices and cultural orientation that they contain. This means that extensive reading and writing of extended discourse is necessary, not the reading and writing of multiple choice or fill-in-the-blank forms. Unfortunately, it is the latter that now prevails in most U.S. schools, and particularly in schools serving nonmainstream populations (Goodlad, 1984).

In the Staton study, students daily read the teacher-written reponses to their dialogue journal entries. These responses, although not correcting student entries, modeled standard literate prose, for example, often the teacher would use a word, spelled correctly, that the student had misspelled). Moreover, the teacher's responses provided a framework (here termed "scaffolding" according to Bruner's extension of Vygotskyan theory) for the students to use in learning new reasoning processes. As students wrote back to the teacher, they too began to model standard literacy and mainstream reasoning processes. In the Heath and Branscombe study, the students read, and attempted to write, the kind of expository prose to or from an unknown audience that school literacy so often requires.

It is important to stress that in both of these studies, the emphasis in the activities was on the actual communication in reading and writing, not on the linguistic forms of mainstream literacy. That is, these activities did not involve rote drills and 1exercises in which students practiced literate forms. In contrast, the students, while actually writing and reading with another real writer/reader, were abundantly exposed to such literate forms. These students had multiple and redundant opportunities to become familiar with literate language resources in dialogue with the teacher and others, and through the journals, letters, and books, but resources were less emphasized than the interaction itself.

CONCLUSION

At the beginning of this chapter, it was noted that nonmainstream cultural groups, taken together, are increasingly no longer the minority in the United States. Within 100 years, in fact, such groups will outnumber non-Hispanic European-origin whites. The primary argument of this chapter has been that this reality must be addressed within our educational system, or that system will be doomed to repeat its current failures with nonmainstream populations. Apart from more widespread social change, especially in mainstream attitudes and values, a number of improvements in the current educational system can be made. These include:

1. Improving literacy instruction for all students, mainstream and nonmainstream alike, in ways that are consonant with the principles underlying successful techniques that have been documented by research;
2. Requiring all current and future teachers to take coursework that presents the results of sociolinguistic research on nonmainstream groups in order to develop ethnosensitivity and to explode the myths of ethnocentrism; and
3. Using ethnographic research to identify community uses of language and literacy and to modify instruction so that it connects such community practices with practices in the classroom.

References

Amastae, J., & Elias-Olivares, L. (Eds.). (1982). *Spanish in the United States: Sociolinguistic aspects*. Cambridge, England: Cambridge University Press.

Au, K. (1980). Participation structures in a reading lesson with Hawaiian children. *Anthroplogy and Education Quarterly, 11,* 91–115.

Au, K., & Jordon, C. (1981). Teaching reading to Hawaiian children: Finding a culturally appropriate solution. In H. Trueba, G. Guthrie, & K. Au (Eds.), *Culture and the bilingual classroom*. Rowley, MA: Newbury House.

Baratz, J., & Shuy, R. (Eds.). (1969). *Teaching black children to read*. Washington, DC: Center for Applied Linguistics.

Baugh, J. (1981). Design and implementation of writing instruction for speakers of non-standard English: Perspectives for a national neighborhood literacy program. In B. Cronnell (Ed.), *The writing needs of linguistically different students*. Los Alamitos, CA: SWRL Research and Development.

Bauman, R., & Sherzer, J. (Eds.). (1974). *Explorations in the ethnography of speaking*. Cambridge, England: Cambridge University Press.

Calkins, L. (1983). *Lessons from a child: On the teaching and learning of writing*. Exeter, NH: Heinemann.

Cazden, C., John, V., & Hymes, D. (1972). *Functions of language in the classroom*. New York: Teachers College Press.

Charrow, V. (1981). The written English of deaf adolescents. In M. Farr Whiteman (Ed.), *Variation in writing: Functional and linguistic-cultural differences*. Hillsdale, NJ: Erlbaum.

Cherry Wilkinson, L. (Ed.). (1982). *Communicating in the classroom*. New York: Academic Press.

Cook-Gumperz, J. (Ed.). (1986). *The social construction of literacy*. Cambridge, England: Cambridge University Press.

Cronnell, B. (Ed.). (1981). *The writing needs of linguistically different students*. Los Alamitos, CA: SWRL Research and Development.

Diaz, S., Moll, L., & Mehan, H. (1986). Sociocultural resources in instruction: A context-specific approach. In *Beyond language: Social and cultural factors in schooling language minority students*. Los Angeles: Evaluation, Dissemination and Assessment Center, California State University.

Ducrot, O., & Todorov, T. (1983). *Encyclopedic dictionary of the sciences of language*. Baltimore: Johns Hopkins University Press.

Erickson, F. (1984). School literacy, reasoning, and civility: An anthropologist's perspective. *Review of Educational Research, 54,* 525–46. Washington, D.C.: American Educational Research Association.

Erickson, F., & Shulz, J. (1982). *The counselor as gatekeeper: Social interaction in interviews*. New York: Academic Press.

Farr Whiteman, M. (1981). Dialect influence in writing. In M. Farr Whiteman (Ed.), *Variation in writing: Functional and linguistic-cultural differences*. Hillsdale, NJ: Erlbaum.

Farr, M. (1986). Language, culture, and writing: Sociolinguistic foundations of research on writing. In E. Rothkopf (Ed.), *Review of Research in Education 13*. Washington, DC: American Educational Research Association.

Farr, M., & Daniels, H. (1986). *Language diversity and writing instruction*. Urbana, IL: NCTE.

Fasold, R. (1972). *Tense marking in Black English*. Washington, DC: Center for Applied Linguistics.

Fasold, R., & Shuy, R. (1970). Preface to *Teaching standard English in the inner city*. Washington, DC: Center for Applied Linguistics.

Feigenbaum, I. (1970). *English now*. New York: New Century.

Ferguson, C., & Heath, S. B. (Eds.). (1981). *Language in the U.S.A.* Cambridge, England: Cambridge University Press.

Finnegan, R. (1988). *Literacy and orality: Studies in the technology of communication*. Oxford and New York: Oxford University Press.

Fishman, A. (1988). *Amish literacy: What and how it means*. Portsmouth, NH: Heinemann.

Geertz, C. (1973). *The interpretation of cultures*. New York: Basic Books.

Giles, H., & Powesland, P. F. (1975). *Speech style and social evaluation*. London: Academic Press.

Gilmore, P., & Glatthorn, A. (Eds.). (1982). *Children in and out of school: Ethnography and education*. Washington, DC: Center for Applied Linguistics.

Goodlad, J. (1984). *A place called school*. New York: McGraw-Hill.

Goody, J., & Watt, I. (1963). The consequences of literacy. *Comparative Studies in History and Society, 5,* 304–45.

Goody, J. (1977). *The domestication of the savage mind*. Cambridge, England: Cambridge University Press.

Goody, J. (1986). *The logic of writing and the organization of society*. Cambridge, England: Cambridge University Press.

Goody, J. (1987). *The interface between the written and the oral*. Cambridge, England: Cambridge University Press.

Graves, D. (1983). *Writing: Children and teachers at work*. Exeter, NH: Heinemann.

Green, J., & Wallat, C. (Eds.). (1981). *Ethnography and language in educational settings*. Norwood, NJ: Ablex.

Gumperz, J. J. (1982a). *Discourse strategies*. Cambridge, England: Cambridge University Press.

Gumperz, J. J. (Ed.). (1982b). *Language and social identity*. Cambridge, England: Cambridge University Press.

Gundlach, R., Farr, M., & Cook-Gumperz, J. (in press). Writing and reading in the community. In A. Dyson (Ed.), *Writing and reading: Collaboration in the classroom?* Urbana, IL: NCTE.

Heath, S. B. (1983). *Ways with words: Language, life and work in communities and classrooms*. Cambridge, England: Cambridge University Press.

Heath, S. B. (1986). Critical factors in literacy development. In S. de Castell, A. Luke, & K. Egan (Eds.), *Literacy, society, & schooling: A reader*. Cambridge, England: Cambridge University Press.

Heath, S. B., & Branscombe, A. (1985). "Intelligent writing" in an audience community: Teachers, students, and researcher. In S. Freedman (Ed.), *The acquisition of written language: Response and revision*. Norwood, NJ: Ablex.

Hymes, D. (1972). Models of the interaction of language and social life. In J. Gumperz & D. Hymes (Eds.), *Directions in sociolinguistics: The ethnography of communication*. New York: Holt, Rinehart & Winston.

Hymes, D. (1974). *Foundations in sociolinguistics*. Philadelphia: University of Pennsylvania Press.

Kochman, T. (Ed.). (1972). *Rappin' and stylin' out: Communication in urban black America*. Urbana, IL: University of Illinois Press.

Kochman, T. (1981). *Black and white styles in conflict*. Chicago: University of Chicago Press.

Kreeft, J. P., & Shuy, R. W. (1985). *Dialogue writing: Analysis of student-teacher interactive writing in the learning of English as a second language*. (Final Rep. to the National Institute of Education, NIE-G-83-0030). Washington, DC: Center for Applied Linguistics.

Labov, W. (1972a). *Language in the inner city: Studies in the Black English Vernacular*. Philadelphia: University of Pennsylvania Press.

Labov, W. (1972b). *Sociolinguistic patterns*. Philadelphia: University of Pennsylvania Press.

Labov, W. (Ed.). (1980). *Locating language in time and space*. New York: Academic Press.

Langer, J. (1988). The state of research on literacy. *Educational Researcher, 17,* (3), 42–6.

Langer, J., & Applebee, A. (1986). Reading and writing instruction: Toward a theory of teaching and learning. In E. Rothkopf (Ed.), *Review of Research in Education, 13*. Washington, DC: American Educational Research Association.

Levine, K. (1986). *The social context of literacy*. London: Routledge & Kegan Paul.

Moll, L., & Diaz, R. (1987). Teaching writing as communication: The use of ethnographic findings in classroom practice. In D. Bloome (Ed.), *Literacy, language and schooling*. Norwood, NJ: Ablex.

Ogbu, J. (1987). Opportunity Structure, Cultural Boundaries, and Literacy. In J. Langer (Ed.), *Language, literacy, & culture*. Norwood, NJ: Ablex.

Ong, W. J. (1982). *Orality and literacy: The technologizing of the word*. New York: Methuen.

Perl, S., & Wilson, N. (1986). *Through teachers' eyes: Portraits of writing teachers at work*. Portsmouth, NH: Heinemann.

Piestrup, A. (1973). *Black dialect interference and accomodation of reading instruction in first grade*. (Monograph No. 4). Berkeley: Language-Behavior Research Laboratory.

Reed, C. (1981). Teaching teachers about teaching writing to students from varied linguistic social and cultural groups. In M. Farr Whiteman (Ed.), *Variation in writing: Functional and linguistic-cultural differences*. Hillsdale, NJ: Erlbaum.

Schieffelin, B. B., and Cochran-Smith, M. (1984). Learning to read culturally: Literacy before schooling. In H. Goelman, A. Oberg, and F. Smith (Eds.), *Awakening to literacy*. Exeter, NH: Heinemann.

Scollon, R., & Scollon, S. B. K. (1979). *Linguistic convergence: An ethnography of speaking at Fort Chipewyan*. New York: Academic Press.

Scollon, R., & Scollon, S. B. K. (1981). *Narrative, literacy, & face in interethnic communication*. Norwood, NJ: Ablex.

Scribner, S., & Cole, M. (1981). *The psychology of literacy*. Cambridge, MA: Harvard University Press.

Shuman, A. (1986). *Storytelling rights*. Cambridge, England: Cambridge University Press.

Shuy, R. (1980). Vernacular Black English: Setting the issues in time. In Farr Whiteman, M. (Ed.), *Reactions to Ann Arbor: Vernacular Black English and education*. Washington, DC: Center for Applied Linguistics.

Sima, C. (1987). *Strategic planning brief vol. 1 no. 5. The Hispanic community of the future: Implications for UIC student enrollment*. Chicago: University of Illinois at Chicago.

Sledd, J. (1972). Doublespeak: Dialectology in the service of big brother. *College English, 33*, 439–56.

Sledd, J. (1988). Product in process: From ambiguities of Standard English to issues that divide us. *College English, 50*, (2), 168–76.

Spradley, J. (1980). *Participant observation*. New York: Holt, Rinehart & Winston.

Staton, J., Shuy, R., Kreeft Payton, J., & Reed, L. (1988). *Dialogue journal communication: Classroom, linguistic, social, and cognitive views*. Norwood, NJ: Ablex.

Street, B. (1984). *Literacy in theory and practice*. Cambridge, England: Cambridge University Press.

Tannen, D. (Ed.). (1982). *Spoken and written language: Exploring orality and literacy*. Norwood, NJ: Ablex.

Tannen, D. (Ed.). (1984). *Coherence in spoken and written discourse*. Norwood, NJ: Ablex.

Taylor, D., & Dorsey-Gaines, C. (1988). *Growing up literate: Learning from inner-city families*. Portsmouth, NH: Heinemann.

Teale, W. (1986). Home background and young children's literacy development. In W. Teale and E. Sulzby (Eds.), *Emergent literacy: Writing and reading*. Norwood, NJ: Ablex.

Valadez, C. (1981). Identity, power and writing skills: The case of the Hispanic bilingual student. In M. Farr Whiteman (Ed.), *Variation in writing: Functional and linguistic-cultural differences*. Hillsdale, NJ: Erlbaum.

Watson, K. (1975). Transferable communicative routines: Strategies and group identity in two speech evetns, *Language in Society, 4*, 53–72.

Watson-Gegeo, K. & Boggs, S. (1977). From verbal play to talk-story: The role of routines in speech events among Hawaiian children. In S. Ervin-Tripp & C. Mitchell-Kernan (Eds.), *Child discourse*. New York: Academic Press.

Wolfram, W. (1969). *A sociolinguistic description of Detroit Negro speech*. Washington, DC: Center for Applied Linguistics.

Wolfram, W. (1974). *Sociolinguistic aspects of assimilation: Puerto Rican English in New York City*. Washington, DC: Center for Applied Linguistics.

Wolfram, W., & Christian, D. (1976). *Appalachian speech*. Washington, DC: Center for Applied Linguistics.

Wolfram, W., Christian, D., Potter, L., & Leap, W. (1979). *Variability in the English of two Indian communities and its effects on reading and writing*. (Final rep. to the National Institute of Education, NIE-G-77-0006). Washington, DC: Center for Applied Linguistics.

Wolfram, W., & Fasold, R. (1974). *The study of social dialects in American English*. Englewood Cliffs, NJ: Prentice-Hall.

Wolfram, W., & Hatfield, D. (1984). *Tense marking in second language learning: Patterns of spoken and written English in a Vietnamese community*. Washington, DC: Center for Applied Linguistics.

Zemelman, S. & Daniels, H. (1988). *A community of writers: Teaching writing in the junior and senior high school*. Portsmouth, NH: Heinemann.

Zentella, A. C. (1981). 'Hablamos los dos. We speak both': Growing up bilingual in El Barrio. Unpublished doctoral dissertation, University of Pennsylvania.

20D. TEACHING THE GIFTED
Frederick B. Tuttle, Jr.

A common misconception about gifted students is that they are automatically destined for high achievement because of their abilities and, consequently, do not require additional attention. In an analysis of gifted education in the United States, Ericson (1986) found that although most are aware of the "gifted," they do not place a priority on gifted education. Indeed, even this interest and awareness seems to be cyclical, depending on media coverage and the need for educated workers. Too often the very traits and abilities that characterize students as "gifted" also often place them at a disadvantage in many classes. As William West (1980) has stated, "A truism regarding teaching is that good teaching magnifies individual differences" (p. 10). With this magnification of individual differences, the need to address the particular traits of gifted students becomes even more apparent. Consequently, teachers should become attuned to the characteristics and needs of gifted students so they can modify curricula and programs appropriately to address these particular individual differences.

CHARACTERISTICS AND NEEDS

Although many educators have provided general definitions of gifted and talented students, most schools rely on the U.S. Office of Education definition that states gifted students are those:

possessing demonstrated or potential abilities that give evidence of high performance capability in areas such as intellectual, creative, artistic, leadership capability, or specific academic fields, and who require services or activities not ordinarily provided by the school in order to fully develop such capabilities. (Public Law 97-35, 1981, sec. 582)

General definitions such as this, however, are seldom appropriate for specific programs for they do not highlight the unique characteristics of the gifted population upon which the differentiation of instruction should be based. The analysis of processing strategies of students, however, does provide insight into some of the differences and similarities between gifted and other individuals in their approaches to learning. In his theory of intellectual giftedness, Sternberg (1986) describes mental processes as a triad. "Metaprocesses, performance processes, and knowledge-acquisition processes. Metaprocesses are used to plan, monitor, and evaluate one's problem solving; performance processes are used to carry out the instructions of the metaprocesses; knowledge-acquisition processes are used to figure out how to solve the problems in the first place" (p. 145). Although academically talented students may perform well on conventional tests (e.g., group achievement tests) because of their strong metaprocessing abilities, they do not always function exceptionally well in the world outside academia. The ability to apply one's intelligence to the everyday world—to synthesize ideas, skills, and realities—marks the intellectually gifted individual. This ability, however, is not readily acknowledged or even recognized in most school environments.

Using Sternberg's theory as a base, Shore (1987) explains giftedness as "... not a single cognitive style, but flexibility or adaptability of styles, ... an essential ingredient of successful university or other high level thinking" (p. 38). His hypothesis is "that the interaction between level of metacognition and the availability and flexibility of cognitive styles is an important characteristic of giftedness.... The highest levels are attained when alternate strategies are available and metacognitive processes govern not only performance with individual strategies, but the switching process as well" (p. 38). The knowledge-acquisition process described by Sternberg and the adaptability of cognitive process described by Shore are apparently supported by other studies. Schofield and Ashman (1987) compared three groups (gifted, high average, and low average) of fifth and sixth graders relative to a simultaneous/successive model of cognitive processing. They found that the gifted group was superior to the others in both simultaneous processing and high level planning. Differences between gifted and other students for processing information were also described by Hafenstein (1987). She found that the intellectually gifted students used "simultaneous" processing techniques while others used "sequential" processing strategies.

Dweck and Bempechat (1983) raise other concerns about the concepts of intelligence and the consequent effect on teaching and learning. If teachers and students believe that intelligence is an "entity," a "rather stable global trait" (as is often portrayed through standardized tests), they "tend to subscribe to the idea that they possess a specific, fixed amount of intelligence, that this intelligence is displayed through performance, and that the outcomes or judgments indicate whether they are or are not intelligent" (p. 243). On the other hand, if they believe that intelligence is "incremental," subject to change through learning and experience, they envision intelligence as "an ever-expanding repertoire of skills and knowledge, one that is increased through one's own instrumental behavior" (p. 244). Teachers who hold the "entity" theory often perceive students "who perform the tasks quickly and easily" (p. 252) as the most intelligent, while teachers who believe in the "incremental" theory "would likely provide for all children challenging, long-term tasks that require planning and persistence in search of resolution" (p. 252).

Some studies have focused on processes more closely associated with English language-arts classes. Kempton (1986) employed think aloud techniques in his examination of ways high and low creatively gifted high school students approach creative problem solving. After analyzing their verbalization of strategies as well as solutions to problem solving, Kempton found the highly creative students had more responses that he categorized as "strategies," "facilitative," and "solution," while the low creative students had more "rereading," "inhibitive," and "silence" responses. In addition, he also found that the productivity of the high creative students increased over time, while that of the low creative students decreased. In her analysis of reading processing strategies, Fehrenback (1987) used think aloud techniques to compare processes used by 30 gifted and 30 average students in grades 8, 10, and 12. She found that gifted students related information read to personal and content area knowledge, analyzed and evaluated information, and predicted outcomes to a greater degree than the average students. The average students, on the other hand, showed a greater concern with word pronunciation than the gifted. These studies highlight an important characteristic of gifted students: the ability to comprehend and synthesize relationships among a variety of sources. Although this ability is seldom addressed on academic tests, it is of paramount importance to teachers of English and language arts as it distinguishes the verbally gifted from the good student.

In his analysis of the content of the English class, Charles Suhor (1988) stresses the importance of "process." Reading, for example, is not merely a decoding of symbols of an accumulation of information about literature but rather "reading is a meaning-making process in which the background knowledge and personal experience of the reader interact with the text" (p. 34). An important concept throughout the English language-arts curriculum is connection-making, which requires the ability to draw relationships among a wide range of ideas, experiences, and feelings. "Not only are students linked with the minds and emotions of authors, they are also put in touch with their own ideas and feelings, because the processing of personal experiences through language gives clearer form to their impressions of the world" (p. 45). Because gifted students tend to employ a variety of cognitive processes simultaneously, while other students tend to operate in a more sequential manner, instruction for gifted students should encourage drawing of relationships at an earlier stage than would be appropriate for other students.

In English language-arts classes, many of the attributes associated with the verbally talented such as being perceptive, critical, sensitive, and, especially, able to see relationships should be highly valued in act as well as in theory. Yet, many of these characteristics sometimes pose difficulties for students in school situations, often masking their actual abilities. For example, when a student sees relationships among diverse ideas unforeseen by the teacher, the teacher may consider the response in class to be incorrect or inappropriate. In addition, gifted students; answers on group standardized tests are sometimes wrong because these individuals recognized several of the possible responses as equally correct. Sternberg (1986) suggests that individuals with high knowledge-acquisition processes (synthetic intellectual giftedness) are at risk as students since they "may come to percieve themselves as not particularly intelligent because of their lesser test scores and the lesser reinforcement they received in school" (p. 145). They are also at risk in later life because they "may view themselves as 'putting one over' on the world rather than as capable people in their own right" (p. 145).

Table 20D–1 depicts several characteristics associated with giftedness that pose potential difficulties in school settings.

Although individuals may, indeed, be verbally talented, they may not always demonstrate their abilities easily. This is especially true of the underachieving gifted particularly when identification depends on performance, usually demonstrated by

TABLE 21D–1. Characteristics Associated with Giftedness

Characteristic	Sample Potential Difficulty
Characteristic	Continually raises questions that sometime interfere with the teacher's lesson; needs access to a variety of materials
Persistence	Focuses on areas of personal interest, sometimes at the expense of work in other areas often required by the teacher; is viewed as stubborn
Critical Thinking	Is reluctant to submit work that is not perfect; may not even begin a project because of feeling that it may not reach own excessively high standards; criticizes peers and teachers, causing negative reactions and feelings
Abstract Thinking	Neglects details once generalizations are mastered; jumps to conclusions about specifics; impatient with teacher's focus on specific steps or details in a procedure; becomes frustrated by others' inability to understand general concepts quickly; designs own procedures that may be in conflict with those taught by the teacher
High Verbal Ability	Dominates class and informal discussions; is sarcastic of others; argues for the sake of argument, detracting from the progress of the lesson; uses humor not always understood or accepted by others.

Adapted from Tuttle, Becker, and Sousa, *Characteristics*, 1988, p. 30

high motivation and achievement. Motivation, for example, is a major component of Renzulli's (1978) popular definition of gifted, the other two being above average ability and creativity. Underachieving students seldom demonstrate either high achievement or motivation. Indeed, Witmore (1980) defines underachieving gifted as those who demonstrate a marked discrepancy between their superior abilities and performance. As a result not only are teachers frustrated because these students do not live up to their potential, but underachieving gifted students often demonstrate negative behaviors and feelings. Some of these include school phobia, poor attendance and participation, very low self-esteem, unhealthy self-concepts resulting in difficulties coping emotionally, lack of self-confidence, and inferiority feelings (p. 88).

After reviewing several popular definitions of gifted, including Renzulli's, Gagné (1985) presents a model that incorporates both high achievement and high, but unrealized, potential. In his model "motivation serves as a catalyst in the actualization of exceptional gifts into exceptional talents" (p. 111) rather than as an essential characteristic of the gifted. In drawing a distinction between gifted and talented, Gagné states that "one can be gifted without necessarily being talented (as with the case of underachievers), but not vice versa" (p. 103).

To include all appropriate gifted students in a program, identification methods should be sufficiently broad to encompass gifted students whose potential abilities are unrecognized. Moreover, the identification measures and procedures should be directly related to both the characteristics and needs of the gifted students under consideration and the demands of the program. As Roach and Bell (1986) state, "All students must have the opportunity to be chosen. The purpose of identification is to find those exceptional students who indicate a need so great that they require special services not ordinarily provided by schools" (p. 395).

To create and maintain an effective program, educators should continually examine the relationships among the goals of the program, the characteristics of the learners, and the actual teaching practices. Therefore, the identification procedures described below should be viewed in relation to the particular learning characteristics required by the program.

IDENTIFICATION

Tests. The use of standardized tests to locate gifted students is common and controversial. Because of the apparent objectivity and the ease of administration, most school systems include these tests as part of their screening procedures. On the other hand, many educators are wary of extensive use of standardized tests because of potential cultural or socioeconomic bias (Richert, 1987), the limitations of student response, arbitrary "cutoff" scores, low ceilings, and questions aimed at lower cognitive skills such as recall and comprehension. With reference to testing in English language arts, Suhor (1988) states, "Testing students' knowledge of content is important, but evaluation of student progress in English can never be reduced soley to content testing. Students 'know' English when they 'do' English well—stating significant ideas clearly in discussions, writing (and revising) with power and grace, reading with insight and enjoyment" (p. 52). Many educators have found that group standardized tests "frequently fail to locate those individuals who have gifts in other areas (e.g., intellectual and creative abilities) and even many who are actually academically talented" (Tuttle, 1987, p. 7).

Other educators, however, have found standardized tests valuable in locating gifted students, especially from large populations. After studying the effects of using the Scholastic Aptitude Test to locate gifted seventh graders for the Midwest Talent Search Project, VanTassel-Baska (1986) concluded, "While no one test could possibly find all talented individuals, the use of the SAT through the talent search mechanism has found large numbers of students not otherwise uncovered in an efficient and effective manner. It remains the challenge to find other measures as successful" (p. 189). The Johns Hopkins Program for Verbally Gifted Youth uses high test scores on standardized tests to select seventh graders for their program. First, students must score "above the 97th percentile on the verbal, numerical, or total score of an in-grade achievement tests such as the Iowa Test of Basic Skills. . . . Students who score 430 or higher on the verbal portion of the SAT (Scholastic Aptitude Test) at grade seven (430 is the mean score for high school seniors) are considered verbaly precocious" (Fox, 1982, p. 14). In a study of gifted youths, Scruggs and Mastropieri (1985) used students who in grades 7 and 8 scored at least 370 on the verbal section of the SAT.

To help mitigate the potential problems of these standardized tests, several educators advocate the use of culture fair and/or creativity tests. Instruments such as the Raven Progressive Matrices (culture fair) and the Torrence Tests of Creative Thinking (creativity) often use nonverbal or open-ended stimuli to assess reasoning abilities of students. These instruments provide students, especially many minority students, an opportunity to demonstrate abilities sometimes overlooked by the traditional standardized tests. Although tests may provide some information for program developers, they are less useful for the classroom teacher unless they closely reflect the actual curriculum. The less formal inventories and ratings constructed on the basis of learning characteristics appropriate for that program may be more useful for the teacher.

Inventories and Ratings. Although teacher nomination is the most commonly used method of locating students for gifted programs, several researchers and educators have found it to be unreliable without special training. (Buchanan, 1987; Gear, 1976; Jacobs, 1971; Pegnato & Birch, 1959) Gear (1978) found that with appropriate in-service training, however, teachers become more accurate in identifying the gifted students. Students, on the other hand, are sometimes better predictors of gifted ability among their peers than teachers (Buchanan, 1987). This may be espcially true if the desired traits include leadership or intellectual abilities among underachieving or minority students. Although sometimes considered self-serving and unreliable, many parent inventories and nominations have been more effective in identifying giftedness than teacher nominations, especially in young children (Jacobs, 1971). Since children often exhibit their gifted traits more readily outside the restrictions of the classroom, it is not surprising that peers and parents have more accurate insight into these characteristics than many teachers. If the inventories are constructed in relation to specific aspects of the program, such as creative writing or critical thinking, teachers may glean valuable information from students and parents. For example, if the inventory asks students to list three others who "have the most ideas and solutions to problems" or "whom would you go to for help on a composition" the teacher might locate some talent that would be overlooked by test scores.

Student Products. According to Fox (1982) a major attribute of "verbal giftedness, creative writing aptitude, is more difficult to identify and categorize (than other attributes of verbally talented). Since creative writing is not a standard curriculum offering and since it cannot be assessed by customary standardized achievement or aptitude measures, it is often excluded from the category of specific academic aptitude" (p. 12). Although creativity tests and teacher checklists are sometimes used to asses student abilities in writing, most educators in English language arts agree that actual writing samples are necessary to assess writing ability. From this research in creativity Wallach (1976) supports the use of student products for identification of talent, suggesting that for students who score in the upper ranges of tests, student products should be used to project future accomplishment. In their examination of the gifted reader, Catron and Wingenbach (1986) emphasize performance over

IQ, achievement, or creativity. They indicate that a "gifted reader is quick to integrate prior knowledge and experience with text information, is comfortable and productive in the application of higher level thinking skills (analysis, synthesis, and evaluation) to the written text, and is capable of communicating the outcome of this individualized processing of print" (p. 134). This echoes the processes described previously. As Sternberg states, we "would do well to remember a fundamental principle of psychological measurement: The best predictor of a given set of behaviors is that very set of behaviors exhibited in the past. . . . (We) should not write her off because of low scores on tests that are irrelevant to these abilities" (pp. 146–147).

Recommended Procedures. Procedures for identifying students for gifted programs should include multiple criteria using a variety of instruments selected to highlight learning characteristics of the population for which the particular program is designed. Many schools use a two-stage process with the first being a general screening and the second a case study, incorporating student products and, possibly, observation of process. The screening might include several instruments such as group tests with relatively low cutoff scores (e.g., 85th percentile), teacher nominations with trained teachers, peer and parent inventories. Because the numbers of students would not be so large, the second stage could include more individual assessments such as interviews, individual testing, and especially, examination of individual student products and performance. The approach selected should take into account both the characteristics and needs of the population and the requirements of the gifted program.

PROGRAMS AND PRACTICES

Programs for gifted students range from totally separate schools and classes to differentiated activities within the regular classroom. For totally separate programs, students are homogeneously grouped for all of their instruction. For semiseparated designs, students are homogeneously grouped only for specific gifted activities. In integrated programs the classroom teacher is usually responsible for differentiating instruction meaningfully for selected students. Kaplan (1974) described the three basic methods of differentiation for gifted in the regular classroom.

Exposure—Students are exposed for experiences, materials, and information which are outside the bounds of the regular curriculum, do not match age/grade expectancies and introduce smething new or unusual.

Extension—Students are afforded opportunities to elaborate on the regular curriculum through additional allocation of working time, materials, and experiences, and/or further self-initiated or related study.

Development—Students are provided with instruction which focuses on thorough or new explanation of a concept or a skill which is part of a general learning activity with the regular curriculum. (pp. 123–26)

In all cases it is important that the differentiation is designed as an integral part of the total program for the student.

Passow (1985) offers some generally accepted principles for differentiation of curriculum for the gifted: The content for curricula for gifted should:

1. Focus on and be organized to provide more elaborate, complex, and in-depth study of major ideas, problems, and themes that integrate knowledge with and across systems of thought.
2. Allow for the development and application of productive thinking skills to enable students to reconceptualize existing knowledge and genereate new knowledge.
3. Enable them to explore constantly changing knowledge and information and develop the attitude that knowledge is worth pursuing in an open world.
4. Encourage exposure to selection, and use of appropriate and specialized resources.
5. Promote self-initiated and self-directed learning and growth.
6. Provide for the development of self-understandings and the understandings of one's relationship to persons, societal institutions, nature and culture. (Adapted from Passow, 1985, p. 34)

Implementation of curricula for gifted may take a variety of formats, including ability grouping, acceleration, and enrichment. Research on ability grouping has been inconclusive and often confused because of philosophical stands for and against separating students by ability. In his review of literature on ability grouping, Gamoran (1986) cites expectations as a major influence on the effectiveness of grouping. "Students in higher groups may be 'chartered' to learn more, irrespective of what they are taught because they expect to enter high-status educational categories in subsequent years" (p. 185). The expectations of others also influence their achievement. "Parents, older siblings, peers, and teachers may communicate their beliefs about what the levels within the school system signify for one's future chances" (p. 187). Although providing positive reactions from students in the highest groups, these expectations provide negative reactions from students in the lowest ones.

Most educators who work with the gifted believe that some homogeneous grouping during part of the instruction is necessary so that gifted individuals can interact with others with similar characteristics. The amount and degree of separation, however, remains controversial. Goldberg and Passow addressed a major concern of some teachers that students not in the gifted program will be adversly affected when the gifted are absent. Their study, cited by Barbara Clark (1983), compared achievement between classes with both gifted and nongifted students and classed with nongifted students only. The trends that were evident were in science where the presence of the gifted seemed to have an upgrading effect, in social studies where the presence of the gifted helped only the brighter students, and mathematics where the presence of the gifted had a downgrading effect (p. 147).

Ability grouping for gifted may take any of several forms. At the elementary level the most common form is regular classroom with pull-out time provided for the gifted students. The advantage of this format is that the gifted students have opportunities to interact with each other at least part of the time, while maintaining contact with the rest of the class. A major disadvantage of this is that during general classroom instruction the educational strategies may be inappropriate to their abilities and characteristics. In addition, students in these gifted programs are sometimes penalized for their participation by having to make up work missed while attending the gifted program. To overcome this problem, effective communication and interaction between classroom teacher and the teacher of the gifted is absolutely vital.

Although separate classes for gifted are found in some elementary schools, this format is more common at the secondary level through tracking or leveling within subject areas in honors and advance placement classes. Because of its partial focus on interdisciplinary approaches, the International Baccalaureate may offer academic experiences that are more appropriate for gifted students than the traditional advance placement classes. A student in this 11th- and 12th-grade program takes six subjects including: native language, second language, Study of Man (e.g., philosophy, social anthropology, etc.), experimental science, mathematics, and arts (e.g., art, music, classical language). In addition, the student takes an interdisciplinary course (Theory of Knowledge), prepares a research paper, and participates in a "creative, aesthetic, or social activity" (Passow, 1986, p. 189). At the end of the program the student takes an international set of examinations. Except for the final tests, many high schools are requiring core curricula similar to this of all students. Needham High School (Needham, MA), for example, has recently implemented a core curriculum such as this with some differentiation for the more able students within classes or through levels (e.g., honors classes).

Acceleration is sometimes but not always a form of ability grouping. Often, individual students enter school early or skip grades, thereby accelerating their progression through school by participation in regular classes but at higher grade levels. Numerous studies on the effects of acceleration on gifted students have been conducted by a variety of researchers including Bish, 1960; Stanley, 1977; Jackson & Robinson, 1977; and Gold, 1965. All of these have concluded that acceleration has benefited the gifted learner. Indeed, Bish holds that emotional problems may result from "keeping gifted students in classes that do not challenge them, and that acceleration tends to contribute to increased social maturity in gifted students" (Tuttle, 1987, p. 17). This has been echoed by Stanley, who concluded that "non-acceleration often frustrates the learning pace of the gifted student and results in emotional and academic problems" (Tuttle, 1987, p. 17).

In some subjects the content and skill development are not necessarily sequential and linear. Rather, they may require ongoing refinement of processes and gradual addition and modification of content. Suhor (1988) found the goals of most English classes stress the development of processes more than the acquisition of knowledge. The learning requires time for exploration, experimentation, reflection, and reconsideration. Consequently, the acceleration model would be less appropriate for

English classes than for others in which the learning is more linear and knowledge based.

Enrichment programs involve supplementing the regular curriculum with opportunities for the gifted to explore topics of interest in-depth. The most effective enrichment programs "take into account the characteristics of the gifted such as their ability to draw abstract generalizations; to pursue topics of interest in great depth; to analyze, synthesize, and evaluate with little guidance; and to communicate ideas well in a variety of ways" (Tuttle, Becker & Sousa, 1988b, p. 32). Renzulli's "Enrichment Triad Model" exemplifies effective movement from group activities appropriate for many students to small group or individual enrichment activities designed for the motivated gift student. Renzulli (1977) describes the individual investigation:

Type III Enrichment differs from presented exercises in several important ways. First, the child takes an active part in formulation of both the problem and of the methods by which the problem will be attacked. Second, there is no routine method of solution or recognized correct answer although there may be appropriate investigative techniqies upon which to draw and criteria by which a product can be judged. Third, the area of investigation is a sincere interest to an individual rather than a teacher-determined topic or activity. And finally, the youngster engages in Type III activity with a producer's rather than a consumer's attitude, and in so doing, takes the necessary steps to communicate his or her results in a professionally appropriate manner. (p. 30)

Some schools have found that with special training, classroom teachers can often provide adequate differentiation within the class to accommodate the needs of most of the gifted, especially if this is supplemented with consultation for teachers and students and appropriate mentoring opportunities. A teacher may also use an integrated enrichment approach in a heterogeneously grouped class when enough gifted students are placed in that class so they may have opportunities to interact with each other at appropriate times. With this approach the gifted students may be exposed to the same concepts initially as other students but work with different materials and produce different products than the rest of the class. For example, during a unit on Greek mythology, a small group of gifted students substituted readings of Norse mythology for some of the Greek myths. Instead of writing essays describing Greek myths, their task was to compare and contrast the Greek and Norse myths on previously discussed elements of mythology, such as hero and societal values. Grouping for activities within a class allows for more flexibility and greater participation than pull-out programs or separate classes. Instead, groups may be defined by interest as well as by previous performance. This would encourage students who may not have performed well in the past to excel in particular areas of interest. The flexible grouping models is most appropriate for those who believe in the "incremental" theory of intelligence as it provides for change and risk-taking for a greater number of students than the more formal grouping strategies.

Of particular concern in program design is the need for appropriate programs at the middle school level where students experience "tumultuous changes in physical, cognitive, social, and emotional development" (Wright, 1983, p. 9). These changes often affect gifted students more than others because of their heightened perceptions and sensitivities to being different from other students. Consequently, they sometimes attempt to disguise these differences by acting counter to their abilities and characteristics. This is especially true of females with particular abilities in science and math that are often considered male domains. Jill Wright (1983) notes other difficulties encountered by gifted students in middle school, especially the underachieving student, advocating consideration of appropriate counseling as part of programs for gifted students.

First, throughout their elementary years they have been able to achieve adequately with a minimal amount of effort or planning. When suddenly confronted with work that requires more preparation and effort, some of these students are unable to do it since they have spent most of their school careers learning how not to prepare. In addition, if the classroom fails to challenge them, boredom and frustration may set in. This often leads to underachievement and/or unruliness.... Gifted children are caught in the middle of conflicting societal values. On one hand, society respects individual differences and feels that schools should recognize and provide for them. On the other hand, there is a tendency to view giftedness as elitist and therefore undesirable. Partially due to this conflict, gifted students suffer psychological abuse. They internalize society's schizophrenic attitude toward them. (p. 13)

TEACHING PRACTICES

In her review of 106 research studies on cognitive styles, development, and strategies of the gifted Rogers (1986) concludes that the characteristics assigned to gifted "are not exclusive to gifted students. Rather, they are dimensions of ability, development and attitudes on which gifted students tend to be favored. In the main, these differences are quantitative rather than qualitative" (p. 31). Similarly, differences in instruction should primarily be in degree rather than kind. As demonstrated in a variety of studies previously cited, a major characteristic of the intellectually gifted is their greater ability to draw relationships and perform several cognitive tasks simultaneously. Consequently, appropriate differentiation for the gifted should focus on synthesizing ideas and feelings, using a variety of media, and working on high level projects independently or in small groups.

According to Robinson (1986) differentiation for the gifted in language arts "involves shifting the emphasis of reading programs from basic skills to individualized selection of complete pieces of literature and content materials in order to support research and independent projects" (p. 180). Writing programs should not only include focus on the composing process of prewriting experiences and discussions, drafting, sharing, and rewriting, but should also encourage gifted students to explore a variety of modes of writing. Robinson, for example, advocates the use of technical writing for gifted students. "A key skill technical writers develop is the effective presentation of quantitative and visual information embedded in sections of written text" (p. 180). In her study of intellectually able students in grades 3–6, Masters (1987) also stressed the synthesis of tasks for gifted students, finding after instruction they were able to

incorporate plot structures and vocabulary effectively from literature studied into their own writing. Although many of these activities are certainly appropriate for all students, they are vital for the gifted as they allow them to participate in the class at their own levels and pace using their own styles with a minimal amount of repetitive review of skills and concepts they have already mastered.

Strategies appropriate for students gifted in English language arts are often similar to those associated with much older students. After examining the practices of finalists of the 1986 Scripps Howard National Spelling Bee, Olson, Logan, and Lindsay (1988) concluded that verbally gifted students use learning strategies of older students rather than those of students their own age. To address the instructional needs of the gifted in English and language-arts classes, teachers should focus on their synthesizing abilities, providing questions and experiences that encourage these students to make connections among content, prior knowledge, and other concepts. To be sure, this is important for all learners but at different stages and in different ways. The gifted require less structure and guidance from the teacher and can perform higher level tasks earlier than their age-mates, operating at levels usually associated with much older students.

If such instructional accommodation for gifted students is not made, the learning of gifted students may actually be inhibited. In many English classes, instruction in literature, for example, stresses recall questions and only toward the end of the lesson does it move into higher level questions. While this may be appropriate for many students, it is not sufficient for gifted students (Hafenstein, 1987; Scruggs & Mastropieri, 1985). Since the strategies employed by gifted students are beyond the literal and rote strategies used by others, gifted students may not respond effectively to the concrete questions comprising the majority of the discussion. By not participating in the class many of these students mentally withdraw from the class entirely. Scruggs and Mastropieri (1985) found that when instruction enhances the gifted students' ability to apply appropriate learning strategies, their performance increases in quality. Conversely, if their instruction does not focus on these strategies but rather primarily on strategies appropriate for other learners, the gifted students will tend to use the latter, less appropriate strategies used by their chronological peers instead of the more appropriate strategies used by older students. He concluded that "the performance of gifted learners may actually be inhibited by such rote, highly structured presentation" (p. 9).

Not only should the gifted students make connections among content, ideas, and feelings, but they should also be encouraged to communicate their insights to a variety of audiences. In their analysis of gifted students' (grade 6–11) reactions to psychological dilemmas expressed in five short stories, LeVine and Tucker (1986) concluded that the gifted exhibited more heightened sensitivity to the protagonists' dilemmas than other students. While they felt the precocious moral and ethical reasoning of the gifted has implications for differing counseling needs, this result also illustrates the abilities of the gifted to draw relationships between literature and value systems to a much greater degree than other students. Classroom instruction could take this into account by having these students discuss their insights among themselves using some initial evaluative questions as guides, followed by a sharing of their ideas with a specified audience or with other students after the class has had an opportunity to reach this point through a series of more structured discussions.

Although studies analyzing specific instructional techniques are valuable, those studies that explore cognitive processes of students may offer more general guidelines for teachers. Through these investigations teachers learn how their students may react to instructional practices and use skills and content most effectively. Even the methods used by the researchers to examine cognitive processes may also be adopted by teachers and students. For example, students could use the think aloud approach to explain their thoughts and strategies as they work through various stages of a cognitive activity (e.g., writing an essay or reading a short story). Because gifted students tend to use different strategies than other students, a discussion among a group of gifted students based on the findings of a think aloud activity would not only help the teacher design more appropriate lessons but would also demonstrate to the students that they are not alone in their approaches to problems. In addition, such discussions could also result in their own exploration of ways to improve these strategies.

PROGRAM EVALUATION AND RESEARCH DESIGN

Program evaluation is important not only for general program review but also for effective modification of instruction within the classroom. Although many schools have instituted programs for gifted students, few have been evaluated effectively. In her review of evaluation of gifted programs, Traxler (1987) found that of 192 programs throughout the nation, at least half were not evaluated at all and of those that were most did not use trained evaluators. Although many have provided guidelines for program evaluation (Renzulli, 197; Tuckman, 1979; Tuttle, Becker, & Sousa, 1988b), few of these guidelines have been followed by many of the programs, especially admonitions regarding early involvement of trained evaluators and design of the evaluation procedure prior to initiation of the program. Traxler (1987) found the most common methods of evaluation, usually established at the end of the program, were teacher observation and review of student products. In short, current program evaluations provide little consistent guidance for educators.

The classroom teacher may combine these approaches with less formal evaluation strategies to monitor the effectiveness of instruction. Tuttle, Becker, and Sousa (1988b) cite several factors that should be considered.

1. The evaluation should focus directly on the major goals of the specific program. . . .
2. Since in most programs for the gifted the learning revolves around classroom activity and interaction, the evaluation procedure should include observation and description of teacher and student behavior and the relationship between this behavior and the stated goals. . . .

3. Evaluators should be cautious about relying too heavily on standardized tests because these tests are usually designed for a different population. . . .
4. The evaluation should serve two functions:
   a. To continually modify the program to accomplish the goals more effectively
   b. To assess the overall relationship among program goals, student characteristics, identification procedures, and curriculum, ultimately evaluating the success of the program in attaining its goals. (pp. 78–79)

Because critical thinking, problem solving processes, and extensive student products are major aspects of most programs for verbally talented students, they should be major components of the evaluation. Although difficult to assess, these areas can be examined by the teacher using a combination of techniques including checklists of steps employed by students as they work through a problem, student interviews, an analysis of student products. Involvement of students in the evaluation procedure not only facilitates gathering of information, but it also provides a valuable learning experience for the students. Indeed, this activity is a realistic application of the critical thinking and communication skills often stressed in programs for the verbally talented.

Using a case study approach Kulieke (1986) examined appropriate research designs for gifted programs. Citing Cook and Campbell (1979), she stresses the importance of meeting the four conditions necessary for an experimental design: "(1) there must be a program for gifted learners that has an identifiable and distinguishable goal; (2) some type of product must be expected from the program; (3) there must be students that are assigned to the program in an identifiable way; and (4) there must be some comparison from which change can be inferred" (p. 194). To judge the suitablility of a particular instructional approach for gifted students, Carter (1986) established two criteria. "The first criterion measures the extent to which the instruction is unique from the regular classroom, while the second determines the degree to which the gifted require differentiated education from regular classroom students" (p. 51). All of these are important for both research as well as program evaluation design in gifted education.

As Kulieke states, program evaluation "needs to be viewed as a means to aid practitioners in providing gifted learners with the best programming possible given their unique needs" (p. 206). To accomplish this not only should the experimental conditions be met, but the program itself must be designed to meet the different learning characteristics of gifted individuals. Consequently, educators should take more care with program evauation, and conduct and review research in those cognitive and affective areas that differentiate gifted learners from their age-mates so that appropriate learning environments may be developed. As Rogers (1986) stated: "As educators, the primary goal of what is chosen to be done for gifted learners must not necessarily be to foster nor to encourage the differences. . . , but rather to meet the special needs and problems these differences may create. This is where the bulk of the future research efforts must lie" (p. 33). This is also where the focus of instruction should be for students gifted in English and language arts.

References

Bish, Charles E. "What Are the Advantages and Disadvantages of Acceleration?" *Administration Procedures and School Practices for the Academically Talented Student in the Secondary School.* Washington, D.C.: National Education Association, 1960.

Buchanan, N. K. (1987). Evaluating the identification process of a program for the gifted: A case study. *Roeper Review, 9.*

Carter, K. R. (1986). A coagnitive outcomes study to evaluate curriculum for the gifted. *Journal for the Education of the Gifted, 10* (1), 41–55.

Catron, R. M. & Wingenbach, N. (1986). Developing the potential of the gifted reader. *Theory into Practice, XXV* (2), 134–140.

Clark, B. (1983). *Growing up gifted.* (2nd ed.) Columbus, OH: Charles E. Merrill Publishing.

Cook, T., & Campbell, D. (1979). *Quasi-experimentation: Design and analysis issues for field settings.* Chicago: Rand McNally College Publishing.

Dweck, C. S., & Bempechat, J. (1983). Children's theories of intelligence: Consequences for learning. In S. G. Paris, G. M. Olson, & H. W. Stevenson (Eds.), *Learning and Motivation in the Classroom.* Hillsdale, NJ: Lawrence Erlbaum Associates.

Ericson, S. C. (1986, September). Education of gifted and talented in American public schools: A retrospective view. *Dissertation Abstracts International, 47A* (3), p. 800. DA 8610362.

Fehrenbach, C. R. (1987, October). Reader processing strategies of average and gifted field dependent and field independent eighth, tenth and twelfth grade students. *Dissertation Abstracts International, 48A* (4), p. 886. DA 8715208.

Fox, L., & Durden, W. G. (1982). *Educating verbally gifted youth.* Bloomington: Phi Delta Kappa.

Gagné, F. (1985). Giftedness and talent: Reexamining a reexamination of the definitions. *Gifted Child Quarterly, 29,* 103–112.

Gamoran, A. (1986). Instructional and institutional effects of ability grouping. *Sociology of Education, 59,* 185–198.

Gear, G. (1976). Accuracy of teacher judgement in identifying intellectually gifted children: A review of the literature. *Gifted Child Quarterly, 20,* 478–489.

Gear, G. (1978). Effects of training on teachers' accuracy in the identification of gifted children. *Gifted Child Quarterly, 22,* 90–97.

Gold, Milton. *Education of the Intellectually Gifted.* Columbus, OH: C. E. Merrill Books, 1965.

Hafenstein, N. (1987, April). The relationship of intellectual giftedness, information processing style, and reading ability in young gifted children. *Dissertation Abstracts International, 47A* (10), p. 3730. DA 8703296.

Jacobs, J. C. (1971). Effectiveness of teacher and parent identification of gifted children as a function of school levels. *Psychology in the Schools, 8.*

Kaplan, S. N. (1974). Providing programs for the gifted and talented: A handbook. Ventura, CA: N/S-LTI-GT.

Kempton, T. D. (1986, January). An analysis of the verbal behavior of gifted high school students engaged in creative problem solving. *Dissertation Abstracts International, vol. 46A* (7), p. 1877. DA8519195

Kulieke, M. (1986). Research design issues in the evaluation of programs for the gifted: A case study. *Journal for the Education of the Gifted, 1X* (3), pp. 193–207.

LeVine, E. S., & Tucker, S. (1986, Fall). Emotional needs of gifted children: A preliminary phenomenological view. *Creative child and Adult Quarterly, 11,* pp. 156–165.

Masters, D. Leff. (1987, May). A literature based writing curriculum for intellectually able elementary students. *Dissertation Abstracts International, 47A* (11), p. 3974. DA 8704304.

Olson, M. W., Logan, J. W., & Lindsay, T. P. (1988, March). Orthographic awareness and gifted spelling: Early experiences and practices. *Roeper Review, 3,* pp. 153–155.

Passow, A. H. (1985). Intellectual development of the gifted. In F. R. Link (Ed.), *Essays on the Intellect* (pp. 23–44). Alexandria, Va: ASCD.

Passow, A. H. (1986, Fall). Curriculum for the gifted and talented at the secondary level. *Gifted Child Quarterly, 30* (4).

Pegnato, C. W., & Birch, J. W. (1959, March). Locating gifted children in junior high schools: A comparison of methods. *Exceptional Children, 25.*

Renzulli, J. (1975). *A guide for evaluating programs for the gifted and talented.* Reston, Va: Council for Exceptional Children.

Renzulli, J. (1978). What makes giftedness? *Phi Delta Kappan* (November), 180–81, 261.

Richert, E. S. (1987). Rampant problems and promising practices in the identification of disadvantaged gifted students. *Gifted Child Quarterly, 31,* 149–154.

Roach, P., & Bell, D. (1986). Identifying the gifted. *The Clearing House, 59,* p. 59.

Robinson, A. (1986, Fall). Elementary language arts for the gifted: Assimilation and accommodation in the curriculum. *Gifted Child Quarterly, 30* (4).

Rogers, K. B. (1986). Do the gifted think and learn differently? A review of recent research and its implications for instruction. *Journal for the Education of the Gifted, x* (1).

Schofield, N. J., & Ashman, A. F. (1987, February). The cognitive processing of gifted, high average, and low average ability students. *British Journal of Educational Psychology, 57,* pp. 9–20.

Scruggs, T. E., & Mastropieri, M. A. (1985). Spontaneous verbal elaboration in gifted and non-gifted youths. *Journal for the Education of the Gifted, IX* (1), pp. 1–10.

Shore, B. M., & Dover, A. C. (1987, Winter). Metacognition intelligence and giftedness. *Gifted Child Quarterly, 31* (1), pp. 37–39.

Stanley, Julian C. "Educational Non-Accleration: An International Tragedy." Address at the Second World Conference on Gifted and Talented Children, University Center, University of San Francisco, August, 1977.

Sternberg, R. J. (1986, February). Identifying the gifted through IQ: Why a little bit of knowledge is a dangerous thing. *Roeper Review, VIII* (3), pp. 143–147.

Suhor, C. (1988). Content and process in the English curriculum. *Content of the Curriculum: ASCD Yearbook.* Reston, VA: ASCD.

Traxler, M. A. (1987). Gifted education programs evaluation: A national review. *Journal for the Education of the Gifted, X* (2), pp. 107–113.

Tuckman, B. W. (1979). *Evaluating instructional programs.* Rockleigh, NJ: Allyn and Bacon.

Tuttle, F. B. (1987). *Gifted and talented students.* Washington, DC: NEA.

Tuttle, F. B., Becker, L. A., & Sousa, J. (1988a). *Characteristics and identification of gifted and talented students* (3rd ed.). Washington, DC: NEA.

Tuttle, F. B., Becker, L. A., & Sousa, J. (1986b). *Program design and development for gifted and talented students* (3rd ed.). Washington, CD: NEA.

Van Tassell-Baska, J. (1986). The use of aptitude tests for identifying the gifted: The talent search concept. *Roeper Review, 8.*

Wallach, M. (1976). Tests tell us little about talent. *American Scientist, 64,* 57–63.

West, W. (1980). Teaching the gifted and talented in the English classroom. Washington, DC: NEA.

Whitmore, J. R. (1980). *Giftedness conflict, and underachievement.* Boston: Allyn & Bacon.

Wright, J. D. (1983). Teaching the gifted and talented in the middle school. Washington, DC: NEA.

·21·

TEACHERS AS LANGUAGE LEARNERS

21A. A HISTORY OF ENGLISH LANGUAGE ARTS TEACHER EDUCATION
Alfred H. Grommon

The purpose of this chapter is to offer some historical aspects of the ongoing process of preparing teachers of English language arts for the elementary and the secondary schools. This kind of research is not new, of course. An article, "A History of the Preparation of Teachers of English," was published in the *English Journal,* April, 1968. The entire issue of the *English Journal,* April, 1979, constitutes "An Historical Primer on the Teaching of English." The 12 interesting, informative articles report information about the teaching of segments of English throughout the nineteenth century and on up to the 1970s, but not about the preparation of teachers. The editors of the issue, David England and Stephen Judy, state, however, they hope "these articles will contribute in part to the development of teachers who can move more confidently into the future because of a better understanding of the past"(p.6). A study closer to this chapter is Kristine E. Marshall's article, "A Passion and an Aptitude: Turn-of-the -Centry Recommendations for English Teacher Preparation," which appeared in the *English Journal,* March, 1984, an issue featuring a "History of English Education."

But in some ways, this present review differs from others. It also includes materials on the preparation of elementry school teachers to fulfill their responsibilities of teaching aspects of English, on which they spend 40 to 60 percent of their teaching day. It presents evidence on the preparation of teachers as language learners and as teachers of students who are also language learners. And the search includes finding earlier statements of points of view and recommendations that may be precursors of more recent statements on the preparation of teachers of English.

The initial article in the first issue of *English Education,* Fall, 1969, this new professional journal in the field of English education, was James R. Squire's "The New Responsibilities of English Education." In identifying new responsibilities, he drew upon two national studies that he and Roger K. Applebee directed in the 1960s. *High School English Instruction Today: The National Study of High School English Programs* (1968) is based upon

visits to English classes in 158 high schools in 45 states. After the Dartmouth Seminar in 1966, they and their associates studied English teaching in 42 selected secondary schools, which they reported in *Teaching English in the United Kingdom* (1968).

He said these visits to a variety of English programs in the United States and the United Kingdom crystalized one central dilemma of American English education: "How to prepare today's teachers to face realistically, with enthusiasm and insight, the harsh realities of our classrooms"(p. 5).

He discerned five trends with "particular relevance to teacher education." The first two seem pertinent here:

- "The shift from an emphasis on teaching to an emphasis on learning ..."
- "From an emphasis on the acquisition of knowledge to an emphasis on the use of knowledge.... (p. 8,9).

This brief review of some of the historical information about the preparation and performance of teachers over the past 300 years might turn up earlier expression of these two trends and other points of view still relevant.

BEGINNINGS

Even in our earliest decades, communities were eager to have their children acquire facility in using the English Language. In 1642, Massachusetts' law ordered selectmen to see that their children, especially the able, could read and understand the principles of religion and the laws of the colony. Their specifying the relationship between reading and religion probably reflects the selectmen's and pupils' parents' experiences in English schools. The use of "primer" to identify such books seemed to have been based on school books published in Germany in 1415. They were called "Fibel," German for "Little Bible," according to R.R.Reeder's "Historical Development of School Readers and Methods of Teaching Reading" (1990, p.10).

Developments in the teaching of reading, writing, and even declamation continued in community schools and in colleges throughout the first 70 years of the nineteenth century. But the study of English as a school subject continued to languish. The study of Latin and Greek seemed to remain preeminent in secondary schools.

Interest in English as a secondary-school subject quickened considerably after 1869, however, when Charles W. Eliot was inaugurated as president of Harvard. He took that occasion to express his concern with the quality of English offered in schools and colleges. He stressed the "prevailing neglect of the systematic study of the English language." He complained that the "American college is obliged to supplement the American school. Whatever elementary instruction the schools fail to give, the colleges have to supply " (Eliot, 1898, p. 4).

A surprising coincidence occured 120 years later. On April 9, 1989, Vartan Gregorian was installed as president of Brown University. He, too, devoted part of his inaugural address to a harsh attack upon the inadequacy of American Public schools in preparing students for college, thereby forcing universities to "devote more time to introductory courses at the expense of more sophisticated subject matter"(*The New York Times,* April 10, 1989, p. A9).

Eliot, in his address, also announced that the Harvard faculty had decided to establish requirements for admission to Harvard, including writing of essays to demonstrate applicants' ability to write English and rhetoric acceptable to the Harvard faculty on a topic related to selections of literature.

This proliferation of entrance requirements baffled administrators and teachers in secondary schools. What kind or kinds of curricula should be offered to the very small percentage of their students preparing to enter college? The subsequent fomenting of teachers of English in opposition to these tests eventually led to the birth of the National Council of English in 1911.

The Committees

Eliot's deep concern over what he considered to be the sorry state of educational offerings in elementary and secondary schools, particularly in the teaching of English, led him, then in his 23rd year as president of Harvard, to accept in 1892 the chairmanship of what was to become the prestigious, influential Committee of Ten, established by the National Council of Education, a unit within the National Education Association. Almost simultaneously, other committees were also established to study particular aspects of schools and school systems, leading to other reports in the 1890s and the first decade of the twentieth century. But certainly the most important and best known of this cluster of committee reports is *The Report of the Committee of Ten,* 1894. Theodore R. Sizer states in the preface of his book *Secondary Schools at the Turn of the Century* that this report of the Committee of Ten "has had a profound influence on American education" (p. xi).

The committee had been instructed to bring some order out of the chaos of the nine subjects generally taught in secondary schools, to appoint conferences of ten each, and to summarize a final report. Of the 90 persons who worked on these conferences, 47 represented colleges and universities, 42 were from secondary schools, and one was the U.S. Commissioner of Education. As the base of the work ahead of them, they examined programs of study gathered from more than 40 high schools in many parts of the country. The Committee had requested courses of study from nearly 200 high schools (Committee of Ten, p. 4).

The Conference on English emphasized the importance of the study of English in primary and elementary grades, as well as in secondary schools. Its first recommendations relate to the place of English in the first years of school. It also strongly recommended that English be equal to that given to any other subject. The Committee of Ten approved that recommendation, particularly in the Modern Language and English Programs.

The conference also stated—still relevant today—that "in the case of high schools, as well as in the lower grades, every teacher of whatever department should feel responsible for the use of good English on the part of his pupils." All teachers and other departments should also help students develop their skills in writing. Moreover, the Conference on Geography recommended that English be a part of the teaching of geography. The Conference on History, one of whom was a Professor Woodrow Wilson of the College of New Jersey in Princeton, declared that "the teaching of history should be intimately connected with English." And even the Conference on Mathematics stated that "at the outset of concrete geometry the pupil should be required to express himself verbally." To see a much expanded, later treatment of these early calls for correlation among school subjects, consult *A Correlated Curriculum,* A Report of the Committee on Correlation of the NCTE, 1936.

Of even more direct relevance here, though, are the occasional references in this national document to the preparation of teachers. In his introductory comments on the reports of the nine Conferences, Eliot reminds the reader that throughout each report the Conference states that if schools were to adopt recommendations for improving the subjects studied in high schools, then teachers of higher academic caliber and with better preparation, especially in effective methods of teaching, would be needed in elementary and secondary schools, but also in modern schools, normal schools, and in colleges in which they are prepared.

The one specific recommendation made by the Committee of Ten, Conference on English is that the teacher of English should be prepared as both a learner and teacher of the language who

must of course be familiar with the more important facts of historical English grammar, and be able to use them in connection with the study of any branch of English, whenever they serve to explain difficulties or to fix grammatical principles. . . . And he must be able to teach dialects and literary language authority and usage, and the decay of inflections. (p. 92)

Here is evidence of early recognition of the English teacher's being both a learner and teacher of language, a point of view similar to Squire's expressed in 1969.

The makeup and procedures of this committee and its conferences are also extremely important. They set a pattern of close cooperation among universities, colleges, schools, and governmental agencies in working on educational problems that is followed to this day.

The work undertaken by the Committee of Ten led the National Council of Education, a unit of NEA, to appoint in 1893 also the Committee of Fifteen "to investigate the organizations of schools, the coordination of studies in primary and grammar schools, and the training of teachers." The Committee appointed three Sub-Committees to investigate each of these charges. At that time, the Department of Superintendence of NEA appointed the Committee of Twelve on Rural Schools.

The "Report of the Committee of Fifteen on Elementary Education, with the Reports of the Sub-Committees: on the Training of Teachers; on the Correlations of Studies in Elementary Education; on The Organization of City School Systems," was published in *Educational Review,* March, 1895. Later that year it was published by The American Book Company. The Committee of Fifteen was designated to be a companion of the Committee of Ten. The *Report of the Committee of Twelve on Rural Schools* was published by the University of Chicago Press in 1897.

The Sub-Committee on the Training of Teachers was composed of five superintendents of schools representing various sections of the country. On the basis of information and recommendations through a questionnaire and letters, the subcommittee made several recommendations for improving the preparation of teachers for elementary and secondary schools.

The sections of the subcommittee's report on the preparation of teachers does not specify teachers of English, of course, because at that time, though the aspects of what we now consider to be English—reading, writing, speaking, literature, rhetoric—were not then designated as a subject in elementary schools. It was so designed in secondary schools because, as we have seen, of Eliot, college entrance examinations, and the Committee of Ten report.

Of special note, however, is the level at which many prospective teachers were then being trained. One crucial issue much discussed at that time was whether academic studies "have any legitimate place in normal or training schools." In what kind or kinds of normal schools and training schools was the legitimacy of academic studies being debated? According to this 1895 report, "The great body of normal and training schools in the United States are secondary schools.... To put into those schools teachers whose scholarship is that of the secondary school is to narrow and depress rather than broaden and elevate" (Committee of Fifteen, 1895, p. 225).

One of the more practical, perhaps prophetic, suggestions is that prior to assuming full responsibility as a practice teacher, the student should begin by teaching for some time a small group of children to study the individual child learning new ideas. The student could then learn to modify lesson plans to adapt the subject matter and activities to the "child's taste and activities." Here then is an early version of what is more recently known as microteaching. It illustrates also what Squire recommends: focus upon the pupil as learner.

The subcommittee stressed also the importance of training teachers for secondary schools and for normal schools, claiming that secondary school teachers "give educational tone to communities as well as inspiration to the body of teachers," and

that those who teach in normal schools "need broad scholarship, thorough understanding of educational problems, and trained experiences...." (Committee of Fifteen, p. 34, 35).

In making its case for professional preparation of prospective teachers, the subcommittee states that:

If college students are put directly into teaching without special study and training, they will teach as they have been taught. The members of college teachers are not in all cases the best, and if they are, high school pupils are not to be taught nor disciplined as college students are (p. 35).

Some evidence emerging in current research on the relationship between teaching performance and professional preparation tends to support this generalization.

Pamela Lynn Grossman's unpublished Ph.D. dissertation in the Stanford School of Education (1988) is "A Study of the Pedagogical Content Knowledge for Secondary English." She made extensive, detailed case studies of six beginning secondary school English teachers and another case study of the curriculum and instruction course in which three of the candidates were enrolled. The other three entered teaching without formal preparation beyond their bachelor degrees in literature. Her information came from five extensive interviews and classroom observations for each of the six. She also attended regularly the C&I class in which three of the students were enrolled.

Throughout the year, marked contrasts emerged from the two groups in points of view toward the role of the English teacher, the understanding of adolescents, students' responses to the teachers, knowledge about planning, selecting materials, presentations in class, and class activities. One especially revealing contrast is in a chapter entitled "A Tale of Two Hamlets." Both students taught *Hamlet*. One student patterned his teaching after his professor's style in a Shakespeare seminar, which included *Hamlet*. When he encountered difficulties, he blamed them on dumb students. With the same kind of class, the second student, helped by a methods course, created an imaginative unit in which the students participated throughout. *The contrasts* showed up in all aspects of English the six were teaching.

Grossman summarizes that her study "suggests a need to investigate more closely the claim that beginning teachers learn nothing of value from their professional course work and poses implications for both research in professional education and policies that would waive professional education for prospective teachers." Though limited in scope, Grossman's study does support the statement by the subcommittee about the consequences of admitting college students into classrooms without having had any professional preparation for teaching.

One last example of this forward-looking subcommittee reporting in 1895 is a precursor of the fifth-year internship basic to many programs of teacher education of the past 20 to 30 years. In a section of the report on the postgraduate year (p. 38–39) the committee suggests that graduates who decide to prepare to teach may be offered further study in the department of pedagogy. Those in charge of relations with secondary schools may be able to place in the schools as many of these prospects the schools may need, on a 2- or 3-year basis. They would be paid one half of the usual salary for teachers without teaching experience. "Under the professor of pedagogy, the principal, and the head of the department, these student-teachers should do their work, receive advice, criticism, and illustrations as occasion requires. They should have two hours of teaching and one hour of general work or study. Their classroom work should be inspected as frequently as may be needed by the head of the department, the principal, and the professor of pedagogy." Such a training program for secondary school teachers in connection with Brown University and the Providence High School was then contemplated for the coming year, 1896.

This report on the preparation of teachers for elementary and secondary schools is richly supplemented by the Report of the Sub-Committee on the Correlation of Studies in Elementary Education.

The Sub-Committee on Correlation of Studies elected to change the word "coordination," which is used in the charge to the Committee of Fifteen, to "correlation." Consequently, the subcommittee felt obliged to explain what correlation means in its report. Apparently the mere coordination of the kind of intensive study the committee made of the five major subjects studied in elementary schools and also others.

In searching for elements of correlation within and among studies, they looked for such factors as logical and psychological features, the place of studies in the world of human learning, and the "correlation of a pupil's course of study with the world in which he lives—his spiritual and natural environment" (Committee of Fifteen, p. 40–41).

These features of correlation seem to relate closely with those specified later by the NCTE Committee on Correlation in its report, "A Correlated Curriculum" (1936, p. 4). An intergrated curriculum is "integrated in world pattern, in subject pattern, and in the psychological pattern of the individual being taught. . . . A curriculum so planned and executed will deal with life, with the subject-matter, with experience, and with the child as wholes." But the Committee also asks: "Is the program within the range of the training and ability of the teaching staff?" (p. 9).

A prime example of the subcommittee's application of its concept of correlation is its impressive, eight-page analysis of language studies, the pupil as a language learner, and of the center place these processes have in elementary education. The long section deserves much more attention than can be offered here. In an earlier section of the report on propositions unanimously approved by the full committee, it stated that "language of study has a distinct and definite relation to the introduction of the child into the civilization of his time, and has, therefore, a distinct pedagogical value, forming the true basis of correlating the elementary studies" (Committee of Fifteen, p. 14).

The longer statement on language studies also indicates what the subcommittee thought teachers in elementary schools should know about the English language, its roles in the school, and about teaching it. The writers state, in part, that because "language is the instrument that makes possible human social organization, it should have a prominent place in the program in elementary schools." They continue, "The written forms of speech preserve human knowledge and make progress in civilization possible. . . . Reading and writing are not so much means

in themselves as means for the acquirement of all other learning."

A second phase of the program is the reading of literature, including selections of prominent standard English and American authors. The third phase is formal grammar. But the subcommittee states that reading of works of literary art "will educate the child in the use of higher and better English style. Technical grammar can never do this."

The Committee of Ten and all its conferences (Committee of Ten, p. 16–17), and the Committee of Fifteen (Committee of Fifteen, p. 16) agreed that all pupils, no matter what their destinations, should take the same program of study. But a contrary point of view submitted to the Sub-Committee on the Correlation Study by a subcommittee led by Professor Paul Hanus of Harvard favored "the separation of the quick from the slow scholars, and the introduction of a double curriculum that will neither retard the process of the abler pupils nor unduly hurry the duller ones" (Committee of Fifteen (p. 174).

The final committee report of this productive decade to be mentioned here is the *Report of the Committee of Seventeen on the Professional Preparation of High-School Teachers, N.E.A., Proceedings and Addresses of the Forty-Fifth Annual Meeting,* 1907, p. 523–661. Two of the reports are on "Minimum Qualifications for Training and Certification of Secondary School Teachers" and the "Joint Recommendations of the Committee of Seventeen on the Professional Preparation of High-School Teachers." As these titles indicate, these segments are concerned with uniform standards of professional preparation and certification. One item of special interest in this list of joint recommendations is that "a year graduate work divided between academic and professional subjects is desirable," another recommendation that might lead to some kind of fifth-year internship (p. 537).

But the most relevant report here is the first of kind in all these reports: "Schedule of College Studies for a Teacher of English," by Paul H. Hanus, Professor of Education, Harvard. According to Hanus, Harvard would expect an incoming freshman to have completed three years of English, "four of Latin, two of Greek, two of German, and one year of French." This array of languages Hanus considered to be good linguistic preparation for the prospective teacher of English. But his "training in classics (in high school and college together) ought never be less than four years of Latin and two years of Greek. It is, of course, possible to enjoy English literature without some knowledge of the classics." If a would-be teacher of English.

has had no classics at all in his precollegiate training, he must at least know Greek and Roman literature thoroughly in translation. Even so, however, he will find himself handicapped at every turn because he lacks the elementary philosophical training, without which thorough understanding and appreciation of English are impossible. That a teacher of English ought to possess such understanding and appreciation goes without saying. Hence, the scheme recommended seems to me a safe basis for general guidance" (p. 567–568).

At the turn of the century, independent secondary schools might have been able to provide the substance of this kind of preparation in classics. But how many public high schools could have done so? Perhaps some in large cities. But where did a school find teachers qualified to offer such courses, to the small percentage of students preparing for college? As we have seen, some teachers had attended only high schools, some normal or training schools, and some a four-year college. Twelve years earlier, Hanus had been a member of that group favoring a double curriculum in elementary schools to accommodate the quick and slower pupils.

Harvard's program for prospective teachers of high-school English in 1907 is included in the *Report of the Committee of Seventeen.* Its heavy emphasis on classical languages, all in the freshman year, illustrates the commanding influence of Latin and Greek in schools and colleges beginning long before 1907, of course. We have already seen an earlier example of this influence in the four secondary school study programs recommended in 1894 by the Committee of Ten, chaired by Eliot, president of Harvard. The classical option required four years of Latin, two of Greek, and three years of German or French. The Latin-scientific elective required four years of Latin and three years of German or French. The Modern Languages courses required four years of two modern languages. The English option required four years of Latin, or French, or German. If a high-school student elected the English program, he might arrive at Harvard without having had any Latin. Imagine that freshman having to face those two daunting, year-long courses in Latin and Greek literature.

Yet with the exception of that burdensome first year, the courses in rhetoric and composition, English literature, debating and speech, natural and social sciences are still in keeping with what a university undergraduate would take to meet present-day requirements in general education and an English major. The courses in advanced composition and in debating and speech are still highly appropriate for a teacher of English. Added strength would come from courses in medieval, English, and American history, and the fine arts. Though American authors had been taught in public schools since the first decades of the nineteenth century (Joseph Mersand, 1960 p. 274–275), by 1907 Harvard apparently had not yet recognized teachers' need of courses in American literature. Neither did they have a course in the history and structure of the English language, even though the Committee of Ten Conference of English specified and described such a course in 1894, and even though the chairman of that conference was the distinguished Samuel Thurber, master of the Girls' High School in Boston, and even though the secretary was George Lyman Kittredge, Harvard's celebrated professor of English.

But no provisions were made here for the prospective teacher's professional preparation. Hanus was fully aware of this problem. He stated he considered courses in professional education to be as fundamental as the teacher's study of academic subjects. He thought the four full courses in professional education must be "assigned to a year of graduate study." But he also recognized the realities of a compromise in the undergraduate program between what ought to be and what can be reasonably demanded should, however, be recognized as temporary and to be outgrown at the earliest possible moment (Committee of Seventeen, p. 567). The compromise should make room for the essential minimum number of courses in professional education, presumably including practice teaching.

Though the report of the Committee of Ten made the greatest impact and continued to do so for many years, all of the four reports strongly recommended vast improvements in the preparation of teachers for elementary and secondary schools. All such improvements depended, of course, on great improvements in the quality of staff and facilities in secondary schools, normal schools, and the colleges who must accept their responsibilities for the preparation of teachers.

Eliot foresaw another contribution. After the *Report of the Committee of Ten* had been distributed throughout the country, had been reviewed—largely favorably—and had been much discussed, Eliot (1894, also 1898) addressed the American Institute of Instruction in New Hampshire, July 11, 1894, on "The Unity of Education Reform." Following his comments upon the pros and cons of reactions to the report, he closed with this observation:

On the whole, the greatest promise of usefulness that I see in The Report of the Committee of Ten lies in its obvious tendency to promote cooperation among school and college teachers, and all other persons intelligently interested in education, for the advancement of well-marked and comprehensive educational reforms.

Eliot's judgment is born out in that immediately the successive national committees of twelve, fifteen, and seventeen followed the pattern. So did the founders of the National Council of Teachers of English, the National Joint Committee responsible for the report on *Reorganization of English in Secondary Schools* (1917), the NCTE Commissions on the Curriculum, extensive committees representing the whole spectrum of English in the schools, colleges, and universities. Together, the first two commissions published eight books on aspects of English curricula and on the preparation of teachers for the whole range of schools, colleges, and universities. In addition to the lasting effects of the substance of these reports, the pattern of the make-up of committees, of their subcommittees, and their working procedures established by Eliot and his committee in 1892 have had lasting effect into the present, and probably into the future also.

TEXTBOOKS

For further developments in the growing concern with the preparation of teachers of English between the work of these committees, we need to turn to the writings of individual teachers, such as J. F. Genung and the prolific Samuel Thurber, who, as indicated earlier, was chairman of the Committee of Ten English Conference. Texts on the teaching of English, some with sections of chapters on qualifications and preparation of teachers, began to appear as early as 1887. Alexander Bain's *On Teaching English* (Longmans). B. A. Hinsdale, a professor of the art and science of teaching at the University of Michigan, published in 1896 *Teaching the Language-Arts: Speech, Reading, Composition* (Appleton), an early use of the term "language arts." In discussing qualifications of the teacher of language arts, he gives primary importance to "clear perception of the elements of the arts, their relations to real knowledge, and skill in bringing these elements into connection with young minds." This central principle continues to be stressed. Although Hinsdale doesn't seem to explain what he means by "real knowledge," he apparently means academic subject matter.

Percival Chubb's *The Teaching of English in the Elementary and the Secondary School,* an influential text, was published first by Macmillan in 1902, but went through revisions as late as 1929. Chubb was principal of the High School Department of the Ethical Culture Schools, New York. He bases his section of methods of teaching English on his teaching boys and girls in elementary and secondary schools and on his experiences of training teachers. He says in part:

We may take for granted the possession of those general attainments—disciplining power, sympathy, patience, etc.—which are essential in a teacher of anything; there being no need for special emphasis upon any of these qualities in connection with teaching English unless it be the possession of the imaginative sympathy with the child,—the power to take the child's point of view in the sphere of imagination, fancy, illusion, make-believe; to be the myth-maker, fetish-worshipper, idolator, play-actor, with him (p. 361).

Such wonderful qualities must abide also in teachers skilled in giving pupils rich experiences through, say, improvised dramatics, the kinds of teachers discussed throughout the Dartmouth Seminar and appreciatedly, warmly observed in some English schools.

Of far greater importance in this development is a textbook written by George R. Carpenter and Franklin T. Baker, professors of English at Columbia, and Fred N. Scott, professor of rhetoric at the University of Michigan: *The Teaching of English in the Elementary and the Secondary School,* published in 1903. It was revised and reissued up to 1927. Scott, James F. Hosic of Chicago Normal College, Edwin L. Miller, then assistant principal of Central High School in Detroit, and John M. Clapp of Lake Forest (Illinois) College led the way in founding NCTE in 1911. As the first president, Scott served for two years, 1912, 1913, the only president to do so. Baker followed as the second president, 1914.

Scott wrote the three chapters on "The Teacher and His Training." He discussed the purposes of training in the teaching of English, special and general qualifications, and some components of what the teacher should know and be able to teach. He believed that the main purpose of special training "is to give the teacher, not knowledge of his subject, but self-knowledge; not knowledge of methods of teaching, but resources to meet the exigencies of the classroom" (p. 307).

He presents much of value about preparing teachers, including this statement in his section of some of what the teacher should know about language learning: "From a study of the psychology of speech he will learn through what processes the child acquired his native tongue, and how the various elements of the language present themselves to the child-mind at different stages of its development" (p. 317).

The teacher should have extensive knowledge of both English and American literature and the history of these literatures. This is probably the earliest stipulation that an English teacher should also know American literature. The year was 1903.

During Scott's two years as the first president of the council,

he established much of what is still the pattern of the organization. Because of his prestige as a scholar, critic, author, teacher, and his stature in the Modern Language Association, his influence, according to James R. Squire, did much to win for the council the respect of members of college and university faculties.

The growing dissatisfaction with the influence of colleges upon high school programs of study, making them too restrictive and irrelevent for many, if not most, students led not only to the founding of NCTE but also to the appointment in 1912 or 1913 of one of the most important committees in the development of secondary education. As J. N. Hook points out in his indispensable history of NCTE, *A Long Way Together* (1979), the National Education Association

took the lead in an attempt at total reorganization of secondary school programs during the teens. One of its 16 committees was the National Joint Committee on the Reorganization of English in the High School, generally referred to as the Committee of Thirty or the Hosic Committee (p. 37). The word *Joint* meant NEA-NCTE" (p. 37). The members represented the newly-formed committee of NCTE on types of organization of high-school English programs and the NEA Committee on College Entrance Requirements in English. Of special importance to the council's role is that James Fleming Hosic, one of the founders of NCTE, the first secretary-treasurer, founder of the *English Journal,* president in 1920, was appointed chairman of this Joint Committee.

Although the Committee's report, *Reorganization of English in Seconday Schools* (1917), is best known for its recommendations for reorganizing English programs in public secondary schools, it also offers comments upon and recommendations for the preparation of teachers. It recognized, of course, the main facts and 450 widely distributed high-school English teachers replied to the NCTE committee's survey of teachers' preparation for teaching English. The report was published in the *English Journal,* May 1915. But the Joint Committee agreed also with that committee's conclusion "that as yet the question as to what constitutes the best preparation for the English teacher has not been widely and thoroughly considered."

In two statements expressing its point of view, the Joint Committee focused attention upon the quality of teachers:

- Finally, the success of English work is considered by certain material and personal factors, the most important of which are the number and size of classes, the library, and the preparation of the teacher. . . .
- The supreme essential to success in high-school English is the trained teacher—trained by the study of his subject, by the study of educational principles and methods, and trained by experience. . . . (Hosic, 1917, p. 28).

The Joint Committee did not make the needed comprehensive study of what constitutes the best preparation for high-school teachers of English. That attempt did not come until the 1960s. But it did comment generally upon the matter and offer a sample program of what it is talking about. It opened its special section on the preparation of teachers of English with the following statement about the act of teaching English and implications it saw for such teaching:

The difficulty is that mastery of English does not consist in the learning of facts and rules nor is it mere mechanical skill. Communication is an art. . . . . It is, indeed, not a task for a mere scholar accustomed to having bodies of facts presented in lecture form from the teacher's desk. It requires knowledge, but also skill—skill in using that knowledge in the important refrain of teachers' having the fundamental skill of recasting knowledge to reach the student's mind.

Although the committee had earlier acknowledged it did not know what "constitutes the best preparation of the teacher of English," it proceeded to do what others have since done: specify what *it* considered indispensables:

1. Studies in the nature and elements of the various literary types, in addition to a broad reading of English and American literature,
2. sufficient training in oral and written composition, including public speaking,
3. a course in the application of educational principles to the teaching of English in high schools,
4. active practice under direction. . . . . Preliminary steps have been taken in certain states to demand specific professional training of all high school teachers, and it is certain that it is only a question of time until this will be a common practice (p. 149).

Specialists in English education today might not quarrel much with what is included in these recommendations, but certainly will question serious omissions. Presently we might compare this modest program with the scope of later developments as the English Teacher Preparation Study (ETPS) (1968) and "A Statement on the Preparation of Teachers of English" prepared by the NCTE Standing Committee on Teaching Education and Certification (1976), or even with the Committee of Fifteen's strong section on language studies (1895) or Scott's calling in 1903 for an enlightened attitude toward language, for substantial training in the English language, and a foreign language, preparation in the psychology of speech, and in the processes through which children acquire their native language, and in the processes of writing and evaluating writing, the study of comparative literature, in addition to English and American literature.

But pointing out such contrast is a bit unfair. Hosic's Committee devoted only a small fraction of their landmark report on recommending a major reorganization of English programs in secondary schools and some emphasis on methods of teaching English. Their report had considerable influence on teachers and educators, and within 10 years upon NCTE's program.

Eliot and Hosic—a generation apart. Both made major contributions to the status and development of English as a school subject. Eliot's Committee of Ten Report (1894) succeeded in establishing English as a major study in elementary and secondary schools, giving it a status equal to that of any other study. In 1917, Hosic's Joint Committee, benefiting in working with a subject well established since Eliot's work but also struggling against the overbearing influence of college's influence upon English in high schools, an influence, ironically, probably initiated by Eliot's Harvard entrance tests in English in 1873–74, set

about unshackling English programs in secondary schools from the restrictive influence of colleges and universities. English teachers' protesting this influence became a major factor in the creation of the National Council in 1911.

How fortunate for all interested in the several facets of English as a school subject to have had among us two such wise, talented, foresighted, productive, prominent educational leaders as Charles W. Eliot and James F. Hosic. Eliot lived until 1926. He might have known about the founding of NCTE in 1911 and about Hosic's achievement in 1971, who thereby fulfilled a role somewhat similar to Eliot's in 1894.

PREPARING TEACHERS OF ENGLISH FOR ELEMENTARY SCHOOLS

Eliot, as were many others, was much concerned about qualifications of teachers in elementary schools. As mentioned earlier, he launched in his inaugural address his criticism of elementary and secondary school teachers and their programs of study. Then during the next few years, he gave several addresses on weaknesses he saw in elementary school teachers and their programs and also on his recommendations for both (Eliot, 1898). At the time he was probably the most prominent spokesman of these issues.

The NEA Committee of Fifteen through its Sub-Committee on the Training of Teachers and on The Correlation of Studies in Elementary Education contributed significantly to efforts to improve the quality of teachers and programs of study in elementary schools. The Sub-Committee on Training Teachers was composed of superintendents of schools in Providence, Rhode Island; Philadephia; Springfield, Massachusetts; Peoria, Illinois; and Galveston, Texas. The collected experiences and judgment represented their administrating city school systems, working with experienced teachers, and conducting teacher training programs in their high schools, normal schools, and hiring some teachers who had attended college. Their report offers helpful analyses and practical recommendations on such topics as training schools, academic studies, professional training, science of teaching, psychology, study of children, methodology, history of education, training in teaching, the practice school, tests of success, and a few items on the training of teachers for secondary schools. This program is surprisingly comprehensive for 1895 and serves well as companion volume to the Report of the Committee of Ten published the year before.

The Report of the Sub-Committee on the Correlation of Studies in Elementary Education is based on an innovative concept in 1895. The NCTE monograph, *A Correlated Curriculum,* was not published until 1936. The Sub-Committee report on correlation was written by William T. Harris, United States Commissioner of Education. He was also a member of the Committee of Ten. Through him, a much admired man, the committees decided that the Report of the Committee of Fifteen would be a companion volume of the Report of the Committee of Ten. This report is a rich response to the Committee of Ten's and Eliot's calls for improvement in the elementary school's program of study. Though the subcommittee does not encroach on the other Subcommittee by discussing the preparation of teachers, its substantial discussions of language studies, arithmetic, geography, history, and other branches present strong implications of the kind of teacher qualified to do justice to each part of the program rcommended here.

Of special interest is the subcommittee's designating language studies, especially reading, as the central study in elementary education. As reported in the preceding section, the committee held that the "whole elementary course may be described as an extension of the art of reading, not the mechanics." The long section on language studies includes several other aspects of the language arts the elementary school teacher is responsible for, including reading, of course, and grammar, writing, spelling, various kinds of vocabulary, writing style, and a list of selections of literature. In the 1940s and 1950s Dora V. Smith and other specialists in elementary education who were members of the NCTE Commission on the English Curriculum estimated that elementary school teachers devote about 40 percent of their teaching time to aspects of the language arts. The qualified teacher implementing the subcommittee's program guidelines would probably also be devoting almost half of his or her teaching to the pervasive aspects of language arts. And yet it will be a long time before even some elementary school teachers will begin to recognize themselves as being in large part teachers of the English language arts.

The NEA Committee of Twelve on Rural Schools reported in 1897 on the serious problems of preparing and supplying teachers for elementary schools in rural districts where, in those times "But few rural teachers know how to study or how to get the most out of books which fall into their hands" (p. 17). The subcommittee on Supply of Teachers stated that "Perhaps the most important subject entrusted to this subcommittee has reference to the training and preparation of teachers" (p. 15). Probably most of them went from high school graduation into their own classes as teachers. Although normal schools were established to prepare young people for teaching, many of them could not get to such schools. The subcommittee designed a one-year course of study extending for 40 weeks, offering elementary courses in the several subjects taught in elementary schools, including reading and literature, grammar and elements of rhetoric, and practice teaching each term. The committee hoped to attract experienced teachers for more extensive training and yet still keep them in their jobs. Because of teachers' miserable salaries ($25 to $30 a month in some districts), many teachers could not manage to attend. The subcommittee struggled with frustrating circumstances in striving to improve the quality of preservice and in-service programs for teachers in remote elementary schools.

A somewhat more detailed treatment of elementary school teachers' preparation to teach essential aspects of English was presented clearly and with some wit to a national meeting of the NEA Department of Superintendence by Ashley Van Storm, superintendent, City Schools, Iowa City, "Minimum Qualifications of the Elementary Teacher" (1907). He begins with the surprising statement that "Everyone from writers on pedagogy to the crossroads orator has for years expressed himself upon the qualifications that should distinguish the teacher from other and supposedly more common clay. I fear I cannot add anything to mountains of material heaped high long years ago and

thrashed annually or oftener ever since, regarding the qualifications of the ideal teacher" (p. 240).

This teacher should be able to distinguish between the knowledge gained from instructors and the ways to apply learning to young pupils. The teacher should have command, and yet pleasant use, of language in helping pupils acquire effective language, and realize she has "less use of grammatical rules and definitions than for the habit of correct and refined speech" (p. 248). The teacher should know how to spell the words used in the classroom, and the pupils should know how to spell the words in their writing vocabulary. She should help her pupils realize that to become a writer they must write. The teacher should place a minimum emphasis upon theory and mechanics of writing and a maximum upon substance and thought, and should know much about English literature and its history, including choice poems and stories appealing to pupils. She should be a good story teller. By "skillful questioning and wise suggestions she leads children to extract from the selections the nectar of knowledge and sentiment it possesses for them." She should be able to help her pupils acquire the mechanics of reading so that the pupil may become an independent reader. She should also know "how to correlate the other studies with reading that the child may come to each reading lesson with such aperception as will enable him to interpret readily the thought-content of what he reads" (p. 249).

Storm, a superintendent of schools, closed requesting attention be given rather to maximum qualifications. He gave this talk in 1907. How were teacher education programs then or even today going to produce the kind of teacher described by him?

The Elementary English Review

In 1924, W. Wilbur Hatfield, secretary-treasurer of the council, announced a new publication, *The Elementary English Review,* designed to appeal to teachers in elementary schools. As J. N. Hook points out in his history, *A Long Way Together,* the council from its beginning had difficulty attracting members from elementary school teachers, responsible for teaching a variety of subjects and skills, but consider themselves nonspecialists in any (p. 86). Yet, as indicated earlier, specialists in elementary education estimate these teachers devote about 40 percent of their teaching time to the English language arts.

C. C. Certain, an English teacher at Cass Technical High School in Detroit and a longtime active member of the Council and frequent speaker at meetings, designed and proposed this new magazine, was editor, publisher, and owner, just as Hatfield was for the *English Journal.* The first issue was published in 1924. Editor Certain selected largely articles telling his readers—teachers, supervisors, curriculum specialists, and college teachers—how to teach specific aspects of English to pupils in elementary schools. The initial article was "Teaching Literature for a Fuller Experience," written by Sterling Andrus Leonard, a prominent professor of English, Unversity of Wisconsin, president of NCTE in 1926. Other early articles were on "The Correlation of Language and Music in Intermediate Grades" and "Character Training Through History-English Projects." Not until 1927 did *The Review* begin to include articles related to the preparation of teachers of English in elementary schools.

The January 1927 issue included an article on the still current subject of "The Prevision Step in Composition." The May issue had a helpful, practical article, "Introducing Beginning Teachers to Classroom Practices in English Composition," and another one on the still debatable issue of "Professionalizing English Courses in Normal Schools." Mildred Dawson, then a graduate student at the University of Chicago, began a series of articles evaluating "Language Text Books."

But during most of the 1920s programs of the NCTE Annual Conventions apparently did not include any sessions on the preparation of teachers for elementary schools. The first meeting of the elementary school group was in Chicago, 1925; reports do not mention the preparation of teachers. When they met again in Chicago in 1927, they were then known as The Elementary-Normal School Section. The minutes of that section meeting again do not mention preparation of teachers. The same was true of the meeting in Baltimore in 1928. In the September 1928 issue of *The Review,* Certain's editorial (p. 29) identified seven categories of articles published in the first five years of *The Review.* He had no category on the preparation of teachers. Up to that time, the preparation of teachers apparently was not of sufficient importance to teachers themselves or to Certain to give the subject much attention in meetings and in *The Review.*

The 1929 convention held in Kansas City, Missouri, however, apparently was the first to pay any attention to the subject of preparing elementary school teachers to teach English. Carrie Belle Parks, State Teachers College, Indiana, Pennsylvania, reported for the Conference Related to Elementary English, which was published in *The Elementary English Review,* January, 1930 (p. 22–23). Her report is significant indication of the council's interest in preparing teachers for elementary schools.

In November 1929, Ruth Mary Weeks, newly-elected president of NCTE, presented to the Executive Committee a proposal that the committee establish a Curriculum Commission which "should build a course of study in English from kindergarten through graduate school." The Committee approved her proposal (*An Experience Curriculum in English,* p. ix). Hook reports that "she also established the machinery and led in the selection of most of the works on the extensive curriculum-building project" (1979, p. 111–112). The pattern of organization of the some 130 members of the commission representing many parts of the country, the whole range of our educational enterprise, and also six prominent national associations of teachers follows the pattern Eliot established in 1892 in forming the Committee of Ten and the nine subject-matter Conferences.

Earlier in this section Walter Barnes' article, "Opportunities in Elementary Education" (January, 1930) was cited. He stated that he thought the best hope of strengthening the growth of elementary schools' development "is to be found in strengthening the NCTE Elementary Section through contributions to the growing number of leaders and the available media of *The Elementary English Review* as a clearing house. His wishes were beginning to be fulfilled. Contributors to *The Review* included such leaders as Dora V. Smith, council president in 1936; Mildred Dawson, Paul McKee, Wilbur Hatfield, Lou LaBrant (1954),

Helene Hartley (1946), Walter Barnes (1933), James Hosic (1920), Helen K. Mackintosh (1957), Carrie Belle Parks, and others. Barnes played an important role as a member of the Steering Committee of the Curriculum Commission and as co-chair with Hatfield of the Subcommittee on Literature for the Secondary Level.

Further developments in strengthening the English background of teachers for elementary schools will be discussed in connection with later publications.

TEACHERS FOR SECONDARY SCHOOL

Earlier in this chapter, we saw initial efforts to formulate and comment upon preparing teachers for secondary schools: the Conference on English of the Committee of Ten (1894); the Committee of Fifteen's Sub-Committee on the Training of Teachers (1895); the *Report of the Committee of Seventeen on the Professional Preparation of High-School Teachers* (1907), especially the first-time introduction of a four-year program for prospective teachers of high-school English; and recommendations for the preparation of teachers of English included in the *Reorganization of English in Secondary Schools* (1917).

The publication of *An Experience Curriculum in English* in 1935 represents in a sense—almost two decades later—a fulfillment of the promise and directives in the Reorganization Report of 1917: "a pattern curriculum for English, Grades K through graduate school, based upon the principle that Experience is the best school of all" (p. 3).

Rich as the entire content of *An Experience Curriculum* is, of the 323 pages only Appendix C is relevant here: "Teacher Education in English," 11 1/2 pages. The Committee on Teacher Training introduces its program by properly stressing the importance of the careful selection of students preparing to become teachers of English. Timely, the program for the NCTE convention held in Indianapolis in November, 1935, included two sessions planned by members of the College Section who also had served on committees that produced *An Experience Curriculum:* one on "Selecting Candidates to be Trained to Teach English under the New Curriculum," and the other, "Training Teachers of Literature to Meet Changing Social Aims."

And it also emphasizes the importance of an experience curriculum within the program of teacher education, but only for the candidate. The rationale for the program and the criteria for selecting candidates are useful. The committee then presents sensible, detailed suggestions for a 4-year program for preparing teachers for elementary schools, 4- and 5-year programs for teachers of English in junior high schools, 5-year programs for teachers of English in high schools. The Committee's specifications in English, including advanced and creative writing, history of the English language, including usage problems and present day grammar, are comprehensive, especially for high-school teachers. The professional program is built around supervised teaching, methods, and methods of remedial teaching. These requirements in 1935 are quite in keeping, for example, with the English Teacher Preparation Guidelines (ETPS).

Nothing is said in this Appendix, however, about the importance of the candidate's knowing about *An Experience Curriculum in English* and about his being aware that the Commission considers "The ideal curriculum consists of well-selected experiences." That point of view necessitates the candidate's learning how to identify and capitalize upon the student's experiences during the candidate's experiences in working with case studies, and in observations in the schools, field work, supervised teaching, and, later, inservice education.

Apparently, the Committee on Teacher Training and, presumably, the Commission, had merely assumed the merits of the experience curriculum were sufficiently self-evident that college faculties, future teachers, and supervisors of directed teaching would, of course, automatically mine the gold therein.

During the decade *An Experience Curriculum* was published, several individuals published reports of various sorts on the teaching of English and preparing teachers. The most ambitious studies were those conducted by Dora V. Smith of the University of Minnesota, president of NCTE, 1936–37, and widely known as the premier leader in English education. Throughout much of the 1930s she was engaged in significant research on the teaching of English in public elementary and secondary schools. She reported her research in three volumes: *Instruction in English* (1932a), *Evaluating Instruction in English in Elementary Schools* (1941a), *Evaluating Instruction in Secondary School* (1941b). From these investigations, especially her inquiries into programs for the preparation of teachers of English, She extracted implications on the preparation of teachers of English. These are reported in two articles: "The Academic Training of High-School Teachers of English," in the *Harvard Education Review* (1932b) and "Implications of the New York Regents' Inquiry for the Teaching of English," in the *English Journal* (1939). For details of Professor Smith's findings and analysis see these publications. For some of the details and relationships see Grommon, "A History of the Preparation of Teachers of English" in the *English Journal* (1968).

Professor Smith's research and extensive writings during the 1920s, 1930s, and early 1940s constitute a benchmark in the development of programs for the education of teachers of English for elementary and for secondary schools. These notable achievements, her many other contributions to the profession, and her admirable personal qualities indicate clearly why the Executive Committee of NCTE unanimously chose her to be director of the second Commission of the English Curriculum established in 1945.

Thus began the most ambitious curriculum project yet undertaken by the council. The representations among the 31 members of the commission and the 175 members of the committees also follow the pattern established in 1892 by Eliot's Committee of Ten and nine Conferences, a pattern Eliot predicted would have lasting influence. It represented the full range of our educational system, including one college president and all parts of the country. According to the director, "more than 350 school systems tried out materials in the course of study, and contributed examples from their own systems" (NCTE 1952, p. viii).

The 1950's—1970's

The Executive Committee asked the Commission "to examine the place of the language arts in life today, to examine the

needs for learning for children and youth, and to prepare a series of volumes on the English Curriculum based on sound democratic principles and the most adequate research concerning how powers in the language arts can best be developed" (*Ibid.,* p. vi). To fulfill the Committee's charge, the Commission published five volumes known as the Curriculum Series: *The English Language Arts* (1952), *The Language Arts for Today's Children* (1954), *The English Language Arts in the Secondary School* (1956), *The Education of Teachers of English for American Schools and Colleges* (1963), and *The College Teaching of English* (1965).

In Smith's preface to Volume One, *The English Language Arts,* an overview of the curriculum in English language arts from preschool through the graduate school, she pointed out that in reexamining the English program one factor stands out: "the changing of learning brought about by the study of human development. . . . . . Language power is recognized today as a part of all growth" (p. v).

Of special concern in this chapter, of course, is Volume V, *The Education of Teachers of English for American Schools and Colleges* (1963). Also in 1963 appeared *The Education of American Teachers* by James Bryant Conant, a former president of Harvard. During his broad-gauged study, he and his staff also examined the preparation of elementary school teachers related to their functions as teachers of English and of teachers of English for secondary schools. Conant based his report substantially upon visits he and his staff made to 77 institutions in 22 states. He presents extensive information gathered throughout the project and many recommendations for changes in teacher preparation and certification.

Volume V, prepared for the NCTE Commission on the English Curriculum, represents by far the most comprehensive study yet of the recruitment and preservice and in-service education of teachers for elementary schools, secondary schools, and colleges. Thirty-eight specialists in English, in the teaching of English, and in English education contributed to this report.

The chapters on preparing teachers of English for secondary schools were written by prominent professors of English, linguistics, speech, and education, many of whom also had experience teaching in secondary schools. Their chapters present recommendations on background for planning programs, the academic and professional preparation for teachers of English and for continuing education. Others made a follow-up study of teachers of English on the job in elementary and secondary schools. The volume represents a synthesis of several points of view contributed by several Council members long dedicated to the preparation of teachers of English for the elementary and secondary schools. This report still remains the most comprehensive analysis of and recommendations for the education of teachers of English.

Guidelines

These programs and recommendations have been and can still be tested in accordance with at least three sets of guidelines over a 15-year period between 1961 and 1976. One of the significant developments during those years was the 1961 publication of the council's daring, revealing, influential document, *The Na-*

tional Interest and the Teaching of English, A report on the Status of the Profession.

The report was prepared to fulfill a resolution adopted at the 1960 convention that the Committee do all it could to gain support for the teaching of English, to inform the "nation's leaders in government, business, and education" of the neglect of English in trying "to persuade the Congress to extend the National Defense Act (NDEA) of 1958 to include English and the Humanities as a vital first step toward improving instruction in English and of stimulating program development in this important area." This report was distributed to each member of Congress, prior to Congress' every-three-year review of NDEA programs then in effect, to consider revisions.

The report's "A Standard of Preparation to Teach English" was developed initially by the NCTE Committee on Preparation and Certification of Teachers of English. In a sense, this outline is a skeletal precursor of the more detailed ETPS Guidelines developed in 1966–1967. The Committee introduces its outline with an overall statement about the teacher's personal qualities, the balanced nature of his or her general education, "including knowledge of a foreign language and a basic grounding in science, mathematics, the social sciences, and the arts," preparation in psychology and professional education, and being a person who "has dedicated himself to humanistic values" (p. 40).

The outline specifies the kinds of preparation in modern English language and its background, the scope of preparation in English, American, and world literature, ability to use modes of critical analysis, and the kinds of abilities he needs as a teacher to use effectively his knowledge of his subject (p. 40–42). From beginning with committee reports in the 1890s we have seen frequent references to the importance of teachers' being able to distinguish between the mere accumulation of knowledge and the ability to adapt knowledge to the mind, aptitude, and interest of students.

This flatout effort by the council's leaders to persuade the Congress in 1961 to include English and the humanities in the extension and revision of the NDEA failed, but not entirely. Before the Congress' next review and revision of the NDEA program in 1964, the resourceful Committee on National Interest produced a follow-up report, *The Continuing Education of Teachers of English.* Continous, relentless effort led to success. In 1964, Congress included English and the humanities in the NDEA program beginning in 1965 and appropriated $5.5 million for 105 institutes for teachers of English in elementary and secondary schools attended by 4,800 teachers in elementary and secondary schools. About 5,300 attended in 1966, and 3,400 in 1967 (Shugrue, 1967). By means of these institutes, thousands of English teachers were thereby brought up-to-date in recent developments and experimentation in the English curriculum and in methods of teaching English.

The Dartmouth Seminar

A highly influential event occured in the summer of 1966 related to the teaching of English in elementary and secondary schools and indirectly to the education of teachers of English: the Anglo-American Seminar on the Teaching of English held at Dartmouth College. Twenty-one representatives of schools and colleges in Great Britain, one from Canada, and 25 from U.S. schools and colleges met for almost a month. Twenty-one consultants from Great Britain, Canada, and the United States joined the seminar for brief periods.

All the publications on the Seminar were written by participants. One of the two reports is John Dixon's *Growth through English* (1967). The other was written by Herbert J. Muller of Indiana University, *The Uses of English* (1967). Of special interest here are the sections in the two reports on teacher education. In his brief discussion of teacher education, Dixon expresses his concern with the relationship between programs of teacher education and the kinds of points of view some British delegates expressed during the Seminar on the teacher and his pupils. He said in part:

> At present, college and university education in both countries, diverse as the systems are, is creating barriers to the teaching of English as envisaged in this report. Clearly students who intend to teach the subject need wide experience in drama, and particularly improvised drama; continuing experience and encouragement in imaginative writing; and a confident grouping in purposive talk that arises from group learning in an English workshop (p. 107).

The point of view of the British participants involving the teacher and pupils is refreshing. Their examples were impressive. Yet, we should not assume this basic point of view is entirely new in American education. As has been seen throughout this review, it began to appear as early as Eliot, it permeates much of what Walter Barnes said from 1918 on, and is basic to *An Experience Curriculum in English,* a report of the Curriculum Commission of the National Council of Teachers of English (1935), whose writers advocate that an English curriculum should be based upon selected experiences rather than upon specific titles. But somehow we seem to have lost this vision. Perhaps it succumbed to the back-to-basics combined with insistence upon accountability. The British at Dartmouth rendered us Americans a service not only in reminding us of the child in the classroom but also in showing us how to capitalize upon the individual's world and the collection of worlds represented in any class, especially now that any class contains many cultures.

ETPS Guidelines

The NCTE Committee that prepared "A Standard of Preparation to Teach English," included in *The National Interest and the Teaching of English,* had long urged that a national study build upon previous recommendations and the expertise of scholars and teachers to produce guidelines which could improve teacher preparation in English in the United States at all levels (Shugrue, 1968, p. 525).

Beginning in 1965, just such a national project began. With a grant from the Cooperative Research Program of the U.S. Office of Education to Western Michigan University, the National Association of State Directors of Teacher Education and Certification (NASDTEC), MLA, and NCTE began a 20-month national study, the English Teacher Preparation Study, under the direction of William P. Vail, executive secretary of NASDTEC (Shugrue, 1968). The project terminated with the publication of the guidelines in 1967. In the midst of this project, the Dartmouth Seminar met.

The ETPS was truly national in scope, involving regional and national conferences, thousands of teachers, professors of English and English education, and representatives of other education organizations. Each of the many drafts represented the suggestions and evaluations of all who participated and contributed. Through the full cooperation of Richard Alm, the editor of the *English Journal,* almost the entire issue of April, 1968, was devoted to publication of the Guidelines and several related articles.

As expressed in the preliminary statement, "the Guidelines are intended to suggest desirable competencies for teachers of English" at any level, that is, elementary or secondary school. One of the basic assumptions underlining these recommendations is that to "teach the content of his subject effectively the teacher not only must know the varied subject matter of English but also understand how to communicate this knowledge and appreciation to his students . . ."

The six Guidelines are based upon the tripod metaphor of language, literature, and composition advocated in the Commission on English report, *Freedom and Discipline in English* (1965). However, the detailed suggestions extend beyond the conservative tripod concept of English. They also reflect some suggestions emerging from the Dartmouth Seminar, such as preparation in speech, processes of communication, problems of bilingualism and multidialectalism, "understand and appreciate how writers order experience," stimulate students' "creative responses and reactions" to literature, "appropriate dramatic activities of all kinds," "help students find adequate means of expression in both imaginative and factual writing." The teacher should "have explored the creative and liberating functions of speaking and writing and other forms of expression, e.g., painting and pantomime," and much more. In these ETPS Guidelines, the tripod has acquired many additional legs.

To sense the magnitude of the growth of standards and guidelines for the preparation of teachers of English in elementary and secondary schools, just compare the ETPS Guidelines to those advocated in the Standards of Preparation to Teach English included in *The National Interest and the Teaching of English* (1961, p. 40–42). The ETPS Guidelines were published in the *English Journal* in April 1968, p. 529–536.

1976 Statement of Preparation

The last document to be included in this chapter is the 1976 "Statement of the Preparation of the Teacher of English" prepared by the NCTE Standing Committee on Teaching Preparation and Certification. Richard Larson, Herbert H. Lehman College of CUNY, Bronx, New York, was chairman of the Committee. Because the statement was published only nine years after publication of the ETSP Guidelines, Larson's Committee explains in its Preface why the committee thought its new statement was necessary. In its opening paragraph the committee pays its tribute to the 1967 Guidelines: These ETPS

guidelines disseminated throughout the country in the Council's publications and through its Committee on Teacher Preparation and Certification, have helped states and teacher-training institutions in the development of new programs in teacher education.

The Committee, however, objects to the pervasiveness of the "tripod" to symbolize the basic English curriculum and notes that the concept has virtually disappeared from the field of English curriculum. Instead, its point of view toward the basis of English reflects somewhat that emerging from the Dartmouth Seminar, particularly John Dixon's *Growth through English,* and Alan Purves' book and others' work on readers' responses to literature. On these matters the committee states that: "Today, many teachers agree that using English is also a means by which students grow emotionally; they respond to their experiences and learn about their worlds, their feelings, their attitudes, and themselves by using language about these subjects."

The Committee's final comment on the section presenting the questions is also a send-off to the future:

> Other important questions will no doubt occur to the planners of teacher education programs. The design they produce will show, by implication, how they have answered (a preceding list of questions). Accordingly, planners need to keep these questions before them as they work toward programs to assure that teachers have the knowledge, capabilities, and attitudes urged here (*English Education,* May 1976, p. 210).

This 1976 statement seems a suitable culmination for the time being of the long continuing efforts sketched in this chapter to prepare useful guidelines for preparing teachers of English for elementary and secondary schools. It offers sensible, stimulating guidelines presented in a clear, somewhat relaxed manner, not as rigid directions, but rather as practical suggestions and thought-provoking questions to be considered by planners and evaluators of programs of teacher education. The substance reflects directly fundamental experiences reminiscent of *An Experience Curriculum in English* and points of view discussed throughout the Dartmouth Seminar in 1966 and the follow-up publications. It is also in keeping with parts of the ETPS Guidelines.

What next may be in the expanding roles of computers, word processors, laser printers, and whatever else may already be in stages of developemt. But all this notwithstanding, how will all that is in the past and in the immediate future help the teacher of English in a public school system whose present students speak 72 different languages, as the California Superintendent of Public Instruction reported about the public schools in Los Angeles?

The September, 1987, issue of NCTE's "Council-Grams" had two articles relevant here. One was on the July Conference of the Coalition of the eight English Associations "currently responsible for setting policy for the teaching of English," a statement by Nancy S. McHugh, then president of the Council. In commenting on the meetings she said in part ". . . . We reached agreement in principle on a new phase for English education: a learner-centered curriculum in which students learn to become inquirers. . . . We want to empower all young people of all races, poor and rich, to do the kind of thinking this kind of participation requires" (p. 7). This point of view parallels Squire's 1969 statement on student as learner, which we have been following through the decades. Since at least 1894, we have seen the recurrence of injunctions that teachers should focus their attention and efforts upon their pupils as learners, especially the long section on language studies in the report of the Committee of Fifteen Sub-Committee on the Correlation of Elementary Education (1895). But this recent agreement should have much more force than did earlier urgings.

The other article is on the meeting of 40 college presidents who met in August, 1987, to see what they could do to improve teacher education on their campuses. Seven of these university presidents and deans of four leading schools of education met to plan the later, larger meeting. That group apparently considered themselves to be innovative in coming out as "partners and advocates" of public education. Then one history-minded participant called their attention to the contributions of Charles W. Eliot, president of Harvard, and several other college presidents who were members of the Committee of Ten and the impact their famous report of 1894 had upon the public schools the following years (Grommon, 1984, p. 26).

So, why should we look back? If we are not familiar with what our predecessors contributed to education, how then can we distinguish between what may be only a recent extension of what has been going on before and what is genuinely new?

References

Bain, A. (1887). *On teaching English.* New York: Longmans.

Barnes, Walter (1930). "Opportunities in Elementary Education." *The Elementary Review,* January.

Carpenter, G. R., Baker, F. T., & Scott, F. N. (1903). *The teaching of English in the elementary and the secondary schools.* New York: Longmans, Green, and Co.

Certain, C. C. (1924-passim.) *The Elementary English Review.*

Chubb, P. (1902). *The teaching of English in the elementary and the secondary school.* New York: The Macmillan Company.

Commission on English. (1965). *Freedom and discipline in English.* New York: College Entrance Examination Board.

Committee of Twelve of the National Education Association. (1897). Report on Rural Schools, University of Chicago Press.

Committee of Fifteen on Elementary Education of the National Education Association. (1895). *Report of the committee of fifteen, with the report of the sub-committees: On the training of teachers; on the correlation of elementary education; the organization of city schools.* New York: American Book Co.

Committee of Seventeen on the Professional Training of High-School Teachers. (1907). Report of the committee of seventeen on the professional preparation of high-school teachers. In *Proceedings and addresses of the forth-fifth annual NEA meetings.*

Committee of Ten of the National Education Association. (1894). *Report of the committee of ten on secondary schools, with the reports of the conferences arranged by the committee.* New York: American Book Co. for the National Education Association.

Conant, J. B. (1963). *The education of American teachers.* New York: McGraw-Hill Company, Inc.

Curriculum Commission of the National Council of Teachers of English. (1935). *An experience curriculum in English: A report of the curriculum commission of the National Council of Teachers of English.* English Monograph No. 4. New York: D. Appleton-Century Company.

Dixon, J. (1967). *Growth through English.* Reading, English: National Association for the Teaching of English.

Eliot, C. W. (1898). *Educational reform.* New York: The Century Co.

Eliot, C. W. (1894). The Unity of Education Reform. *Educational Review.*

Eliot, C. W. (November, 1905). The fundamental assumptions of the report of the committee of ten. *Educational Review.*

English teacher preparation study: Guidelines for the preparation of teachers of English—1968. *English Journal, 57,* 529–536. 528–536.

Gregorian, V. (April 10, 1989). *The New York Times,* p. A9.

Grommon, A. H. (Ed.). (1963). *The education of teachers of English for American schools and colleges.* New York: Appleton-Century-Crofts for NCTE.

Grommon, A. H. (April, 1968). A history of the preparation of teachers of English. *English Journal, 57.* 484–524

Grommon, A. H. (1984). Why look back? *English Journal, 73,* 24. 26–29.

Grossman, P. L. (1988). A study of pedagogical content knowledge for secondary English. An unpublished dissertation. School of Education, Stanford University.

Hinsdale, B. A. (1896). *Teaching language arts: Speech, reading, composition.* New York: D. Appleton.

Hook, J. N. (1979). *A long way together: A personal view of NCTE's first sixty-seven years.* Urbana, IL: National Council of Teachers of English.

Hosic, J. F. (Compiler). (1917). *Reorganization of English in secondary schools.* Bureau of Education, Bulletin No. 2. Washington, D.C.: Government Printing Office.

MacKenzie, J. G. (1894). The feasibility of modifying the programs of the elementary and secondary schools to meet the suggestions in the report of the committee of ten. *NEA Proceedings and General Sessions.*

Marshall, E. C. (March, 1984). A passion and an aptitude: Turn of the century recommendations for English teacher preparation. *English Journal, 73.* 63–70.

Mayo, A. D. (1884-1885). The common school in New England, from 1790 to 1840. Report of the Commissioner of Education, *U.S. Education Report, 1884-1885, II.*

Mersand, J. (1960). The teaching of literature in American high schools, 1865-1990. In R. C. Pooley (Ed.), *Perspectives on English: Essays to honor W. Wilbur Hatfield,* New York: Appleton-Century-Crofts. *273–302.*

Muller, H. (1967). *The uses of English.* New York: Holt, Rinehart, Winston.

NCTE Commission on the English Curriculum. (1952). *The English language arts.* New York: Appleton-Century-Crofts.

NCTE Commission on the English Curriculum. (1954). *Language arts for today's children.* New York: Appleton-Century-Crofts.

NCTE Commission on the English Curriculum. (1956). *The English language arts in the secondary school.* New York: Appleton-Century-Crofts.

NCTE Commission of the English Curriculum. (1963). *The education of teachers for American schools and colleges.*

NCTE Commission on the English Curriculum. (1965). *The college teaching of English.* New York: Appleton-Century-Crofts.

NCTE Committee on Correlation. (1936). *A correlated curriculum.* English Monograph No. 5. New York: D. Appleton-Century Company.

NCTE Hosic Committee (May, 1915). Survey of English Teachers Preparations.

NCTE Committee on National Interest. (1961). *The national interest and the teaching of English.* Champaign, IL: NCTE.

NCTE Committee on National Interest. (1964). *The continuing education of teachers of English.* Champaign, IL: NCTE.

NCTE Standing Committee on Teacher Preparation and Certification. (1976). A statement on the preparation of teachers of English. Urbana, IL: NCTE.

Parks, Carrie Belle (1930). Conference Related to Elementary English *The Elementary Review,* January.

Purves, A. C., & Beach, R. (1972). *Literature and the reader: Research in response to literature, reading interests, and the teaching of literature.* Urbana, IL: NCTE.

Reeder, R. R. (1900). *The historical development of school readers and methods of teaching reading.* Columbia University Contribution to Philosophy, Psychology, and Education (Vol. 8, No. 2). New York: The Macmillan Co.

Report of the Committee of Twelve on Rural Schools. (1897). Chicago: University of Chicago Press.

Shugrue, M. (April, 1968). The history of the ETPS. *English Journal, 57.* 525–527.

Sizer, T. R. (1964). *Secondary schools at the turn of the century.* New Haven: Yale University Press.

Smith, D. V. (1932a). Instruction in English. *Monograph No. 20, National Survey of Secondary Education,* (Bulletin No. 17). Washington, D. C.: Government Printing Office.

Smith, D. V. (1932b). The academic training of high school teachers of English. *Harvard Education Review.*

Smith, D. V. (March, 1939). Implications of the New York regents' inquiry for the teaching of English. *English Journal, 28,*

Smith, D. V. (1941a). *Evaluating instruction in English in elementary schools.* Research Bulletin No. 8. National Conference on Research in English.

Smith, D. V. (1941b). *Evaluating instruction in secondary school English.* English Monograph No. 11. NCTE.

Squire, J. R. (1969). The new responsibilities in English education. *English Education.*

Squire, J. R., & Applebee, R. K. (1968). *High school English instruction today: The national study of high school English programs.* New York: Appleton-Century-Crofts.

Squire, J. R., & Applebee, R. K. (1969). *Teaching English in the United Kingdom.* Urbana, IL: NCTE.

Van Storm, A. (1907). Minimum qualifications of the elementary school teachers. In *NEA Journal of Proceedings and Addresses, 45th Annual Meeting.*

21B. ISSUES IN THE RESTRUCTURING OF TEACHER PREPARATION

Miles Myers

Since *A Nation at Risk* (1983) and the subsequent nationwide debate about school reform (Boyer, 1983; Powell, Farrar, & Cohen, 1985; Sarason, 1983; and Sizer, 1984), two sets of reforms have been advanced for teacher education, one set focusing on the content of teacher education—what kinds of courses and topics should be included?—and another focusing on the structure of teacher education—where and when should teacher education take place and who should manage it? These two concerns go back nearly 150 years in this country (Mattingly, 1975) and have until recently involved a struggle between those emphasizing vocational competencies and those emphasizing academic knowledge in the undergraduate years (Borrowman, 1965).

This old struggle seems to have subsided largely because almost everyone now agrees that teacher candidates should complete a four year program of academic preparation prior to focusing on the vocational competencies of teaching. Not everyone, of course; some colleges still keep their budgets balanced by enrolling four-year education majors. But the major voices in teacher education, most of them in the Holmes Group, which is chaired by Judith Lanier of Michigan State University and which include education deans from 24 of the leading research universities, agree that prospective teachers should complete an undergraduate academic major before entering a teacher preparation program. A similar message appears in recent commission reports from Connecticut, Washington, and New York (Hammond & Berry, 1988).

An interesting debate is now developing over what should be the courses in those graduate years of teacher preparation. One group calls for intellectual rigor, another calls for remedial courses in the basic skills, and a third calls for technical training in pedagogy. On the side of intellectual rigor, are Ernest Boyer and John Goodlad, who call for courses in learning theory, the teaching of writing, the use of technology, the history of schooling in America, and inquiry methods (Boyer, 1983; Goodlad, 1984).

On the side of remediation are those who insist that courses in basic skills must be given at the graduate level to those who have failed or scored low on the basic skills tests now required by many states for entrance to teaching. In 1980, six states required that candidates for a teaching credential "pass" a basic skills test. Now 25 do (Hammond & Berry, 1988). Florida now gives its new teachers the SAT or ACT, Oklahoma gives a test in subject matter, and California gives a test in reading, writing, and mathematics (CBEST). To help teacher candidates overcome test deficits, many colleges now provide remediation courses during the graduate years of teacher preparation, and these remediation courses often undermine the intellectual rigor and status of teacher education within higher education. Yet many of those advocating remediation in the graduate years argue that without remediation, the country will face a shortage of teachers, especially a shortage of minority teachers who of-

ten, because of poverty, language difference, and racial discrimination, come to teacher preparation programs without adequate preparation for tests of basic skills.

Some candidates have not been required to write essays in their undergraduate education, and they come to an essay requirement without any preparation. Remediation of some kind seems essential as long as the quality of education continues to vary enormously from one secondary school to another, from one college to another. The issue I want to focus on is the debate between the Boyer-Goodlad advocates and those emphasizing lesson planning.

The Boyer-Goodlad emphasis on intellectual foundations has been severely criticized by those who believe competency in teaching, not intellectual foundations, is the purpose of teacher training, and teaching competency requires packages of what-to-do in the classroom, especially the "researched" what-to-dos like Madeline Hunter lessons, time-on-task programs, and direct instruction behaviors. Although these packages are now challenged by many as a deprofessionalization of teaching, they originally developed out of an effort to challenge Coleman's 1966 finding that variations among teachers were a minimal influence on student achievement (Coleman et al., 1966), a finding which threatened the very foundation of both teacher education and research on teaching.

To test Coleman's finding, the National Institute of Education funded several large scale correlational studies of basic skill instruction in elementary (Stallings & Kaskowitz, 1974; Brophy & Evertson, 1974; Good & Grouws, 1979; and others) and secondary classrooms (Evertson, Anderson, & Brophy, 1978; Good & Grouws, 1981; and others). In these process-product studies, the researchers used categorical scales to classify and to measure the frequency of various processes (teacher directions, teacher praise, peer group editing, reading time, and so forth) which were then correlated with results on tests of basic skills.

Barak Rosenshine (1979) concluded that the findings of these studies showed the effectiveness of what he called "direct instruction," a model which paralleled very closely Gagne's key "components of instruction" (Gagne, 1970) and Good and Grouws' "key instructional behaviors" (Good & Grouws, 1979):

... large groups, decision making by the teacher, limited choice of materials and activities by the students, orderliness, factual questions, limited exploration of ideas, drill, and high percentages of correct answers (Rosenshine, 1979, p. 47).

Some of the variables negatively associated with achievement were written assignments in class, many choices for the students, and conferencing with one student at a time (Stallings, 1980).

In an effort to determine why direct instruction worked, a second generation of process-product studies shifted the focus of classroom research from teacher behaviors to student-teacher interactions in the classroom. From 1972 to 1977, the Beginning Teacher Evaluation Study found that almost any kind of instruction worked if students had more Academic Learning Time (ALT), a formula combining the amount of time that the teacher assigned to such tasks (*allowed* time), and the amount of time students actually focused on the task (*engaged* time). *Engaged time* was dependent upon the student's success rate, which itself was a result of the teacher's diagnosis of the strengths and weaknesses of individual students, the quality of interactions between teachers and students, and the way the teacher designed the lesson (Beginning Teacher Evaluation Study, 1980).

These findings were almost immediately packaged as time-on-task measures *(engaged time),* models of Madeline Hunter's lesson designs *(allocated time),* and various forms of direct instruction and mastery learning *(success rate).* Time-on-task packages, probably the easiest component to package and implement in teacher preparation programs, were widely disseminated by the California Commission on Teacher Credentialing and the California State Department of Ecucation to K-12 school districts and teacher training institutions (California State Department of Education, 1980). The CTC gave grants to teacher preparation programs to train student teachers to improve their instruction by increasing *engaged time,* which meant literally to get their students to fix their eyes on a text or worksheet and appear to be "engaged" with it. One teacher trained in such a program told me, "I avoided discussions and student interactions because it was impossible for me to get a good time-on-task score in those activities."

Madeline Hunter's packaged lesson designs also became the training model for student teachers in many institutions throughout the country. Hunter's "Lesson Design" (Russell and Hunter, 1981) established a lesson format (anticipatory set, objectives, modelling, and guided practice) which allegedly ensured that more time was allocated for instruction and less time was "wasted." Hunter's lessons were often combined with some form of clinical coaching in which the student teacher's instructor or coach acted as a Rogerian analyst "leading" the student teacher to discover the anticipatory set or some other component.

An example of an *allocated-time* package is the "The Stallings Observation Strategy," a series of instruments developed by the Stallings' Teaching and Learning Institute of La Honda, California. These instruments provided a list of activities (written work, drill, and "practice"), a recommended percentage of time for activities in the observed class, and a recommendation for the teacher to continue present patterns, have more of particular activities, have fewer, or some combination thereof. This instrument was to be used to evaluate the classes of both beginning and experienced teachers and to define the teaching skills which teachers "studied" in teacher training and staff development programs. Few of the allocated time programs still continue.

The *success rate* packages were also adopted by various teacher preparation programs, usually as some form of either Benjamin Bloom's master learning theory (Bloom, 1968) or John B. Carroll's "A Model for School Learning" (Carroll, 1963). Many of these programs continue. Mastery learning programs

are organized around Bloom's claim that almost all students can achieve mastery if they are given the amount of instructional time they need and if they are introduced to instructional material at an appropriate level (Bloom, 1968). Bloom's taxonomy of six major classes of cognitive objectives provides a guide for diagnosing a lesson's level of difficulty and a student's level of reasoning (Bloom, 1968), from Knowledge and Comprehension at a lower level to Synthesis and Evaluation at a higher level. A major popularizer of Bloom's ideas is Thomas R. Guskey (1985), whose mastery learning program has been adopted by many teacher preparation and training programs in Pennsylvania and Fairfax County, Virginia.

All of these models for teacher preparation and in-service assume that there are generic teaching skills which are equally effective across all subjects and/or grades. Teacher preparation programs based on generic teaching skills have been challenged on two grounds, first for destroying the learning atmosphere in the classroom and second for imposing techniques in ways that go beyond the findings of research. First, changes that generic teaching models undermine classroom learning have come from a number of sources. Eleanor Duckworth, for example, has charged that mandated materials and behaviors undermine the learning atmosphere in the classroom by undermining the teacher's spirit of inquiry:

It is just as necessary for teachers as for children to feel confidence in their own ideas. It is important for them as people, and also important if they are really going to feel free to acknowledge the children's ideas. If teachers feel that their class must do things just as the book says, and that their excellence as a teacher depends upon that, they cannot possibly accept children's creations. A teacher's guide must give enough indications, enough suggestions, so the teacher has ideas to start with and to pursue in some depth. But it must also enable the teacher to feel free to move in directions of her own when other ideas arise (Duckworth, 1972).

Thomas Guskey, among others, acknowledges that many districtwide mastery learning programs are typically "mechanical" and provide "no personal ownership or pride for teachers" (Guskey, 1985, p. 93), a situation which constrains teachers and undermines their confidence in their own learning. At the same time, however, mastery learning appears to produce some short term gains on basic skills tests. (Guskey, 1985)

Arthur Wise has charged that these highly structured models of teaching effectiveness appear to be based on unproven techniques:

. . . the effort to rationalize beyond the bounds of knowledge . . . imposing means which do not result in the attainment of ends or the setting of ends which cannot be attained, given the available means—imposing unproven techniques, on the one hand, and setting unrealistic expectations on the other (Wise, 1979, p. 65).

The Beginning Teacher Evaluation study was hardly complete before the California State Department of Education called on teacher training programs to focus their instruction on generic teaching skills, even issuing grants to colleges and universities to establish direct instruction, time-on-task measures, and Madeline Hunter as essential components of teacher preparation.

Yet the BTES data, reports Brophy and Good (1986, p. 350), "did not support a basic assumption that led to BTES in the first place: The notion that there are 'generic' teaching skills that are appropriate and desirable in any teaching situation." Brophy and Good report that BTES and "most other data" support the conclusion that generic teaching behaviors for all situations have not been found by research studies of teaching.

Teacher preparation programs emphasizing generic teaching skills quickly encountered problems. For example, the Stallings instrument for measuring effective classrooms did not work in writing classes using the model of writing instruction recommended by Charles Cooper and others. Cooper emphasizes the importance of working individually with students on their writing, increasing the writing of pieces of at least paragraph length, decreasing short answer quizzes, and devoting much of class time to writing so that teachers can be available during the process to give help (Cooper, 1981). All of these traits were negatively associated with effective teaching in Stallings' allocated time model (Stallings, 1980).

In addition, Rosenshine's direct instruction behaviors did not work in English classes. Evertson, Anderson, and Brophy (1978) found little support for the direct instruction model in their study of 7th and 8th grade English classes, and they suggested that the reason might be that 7th and 8th grade English classes have instructional objectives more variable than those found in math or basic skill classes (reading, spelling, grammar), which were the usual data base for the direct instruction model. English classes, for example, depend upon collaborative efforts to learn composing skills in writing and interpretation skills in reading, both skills not easily measured by the tests usually used to measure the effectiveness in time-on-task and direct instruction studies.

Yet another study found that direct instruction did not work in problem solving classes. Peterson found that students who received direct instruction tended to do worse on problem solving tests than students who received what she calls more "open teaching" (Peterson, 1981, p. 63). Even Rosenshine and Stevens (1986) acknowledge in recent reviews that their general model of effective instruction is not well suited for all classes:

These findings are least applicable for teaching in areas which are "ill-structured," that is, where the skills to be taught do not follow explicit steps, or areas which lack a general skill which is applied repeatedly. Thus, the results of this research are less relevant for teaching composition and writing of term papers, analysis of literature, problem solving in specific content areas, discussion of social studies, or the development of unique or creative responses (p. 377).

The general failure to find an all-encompassing model of good teaching behaviors for all subjects led some researchers to attempt to find an all-encompassing model within single subject areas. George Hillocks picked composition classes as his target, and like Rosenshine, Hillocks used meta-analysis to identify his most effective model of instruction. After summing results across several studies of writing classes, Hillocks recommended that pre-service and in-service teacher education should recognize the environmental mode of instruction as the most effective (Hillocks, 1986). This mode is one in which writing assignments are embedded in actual or simulated "real life" situations—such things as preparing a tour package or preparing an investment report. Hillocks' recommendation is based on a meta-analysis of less than a dozen studies in which he sums statistics across different levels of student performance and across diverse situations in grades 6–13. His analysis does not include students above freshman composition classes or below the sixth grade, where, incidentally, over half the nation's K–12 children go to school.

The Hillocks study is one of many efforts to define good instruction in more global terms, going beyond a list of teacher behaviors. Another example is the Reading Recovery program developed in New Zealand and later offered as a year-long teacher training program at Ohio State University. This program defines good teaching as a theory-building process in which good teachers learn to make explicit their assumptions about reading by observing reading instruction and to test their notions in interchanges with other teachers and in lessons in which they design and teach (Clay, 1987). In the training for this program, teachers appear to shift from a skills orientation to a more integrated approach (Pinnell & Woolsey, 1985).

The general disenchantment with generic teaching skills has been reflected in a shift in some states to specialized credentials. For example, Nebraska has established 20, Montana 44, Massachusetts 52, Michigan 60 or more, and South Dakota 20 (Hammond & Berry, 1988, pp. 18–19). Some states which have specialized credentials have adopted misassignment laws. California, North Carolina and Washington have all passed laws aimed at preventing assignment outside the specialty of the credential. In California, teachers and principals involved in unapproved misassignment may lose their credentials.

FOUR KINDS OF KNOWLEDGE

The general disenchantment with teacher preparation models based on generic teaching skills has led a number of researchers to attempt to define the knowledge base of teaching in terms other than the rather global teaching approaches suggested by Hillocks' environmental mode or Clay's reading recovery. Lee Shulman, J. J. Schwab, and Donald Schon are examples of researchers who have attempted to specify the details of one or more of the four kinds of knowledge required to be teacher—*pedagogy, concepts, subject matter,* and *school structure. Pedagogical knowledge* has been defined by Schwab as an artistic combination of rules and cases:

Art arises as the knower of the rules learns to apply them appropriately to the particular case. Application, in turn, requires acute awareness of the particularities of the case and ways in which the rule can be modified to fit the case without complete abrogation of the rule. (Schwab, 1983, p. 265)

In Schwab's view, teaching rules do not have some kind of one-to-one correspondence with an all-purpose definition of good teaching, but instead are like maxims which must tested and illustrated by cases. As a result, it is the catalogue of cases, not the rules themselves, which define the central tendency or limits of a rule. Shulman describes the relationship as follows: "Both our scientific knowledge of rules and principles (properly construed as grounds, not prescriptions) and our knowledge of richly described and critically analyzed cases combine to define the knowledge base of teaching" (Shulman, 1986, p. 32). This makes teaching like other scientific communities in which exemplars "are far more effective determinants of community substructure than are symbolic generalizations" (Kuhn, 1977):

Acquiring an arsenal of exemplars, just as much as learning symbolic generalizations, is integral to the process by which a student gains access to the achievements of a disciplinary group. Without exemplars he would never learn much of what the group knows about such fundamental concepts as field and force, element and compound, or nucleus and cell. (p. 471).

The importance of cases and exemplars in the definition of knowledge has been substantiated by research findings in linguistics, anthropology, and psychology. In linguistics, for example, Kay and McDaniel (1978) have shown that there is no checklist of semantic features defining "redness," but rather "red" is a gradient quality whose category boundaries are defined by exemplars. As a result, George Lakoff (1972), Charles Fillmore (1976), Kay, and others have argued that checklist semantics should be replaced by prototype semantics in which word meaning is determined by a central prototype or typical use of the word, not the yes-no category boundaries of a list of features. One example of the problem is Fillmore's question "How old is a bachelor? Sixteen? Twenty-one? Thirty?"

In psychology, Eleanor Rosch has provided additional empirical evidence that people primarily use prototypes to define categories, not a list of features. Rosch (1977) had people compose sentences with category names like bird and fruit, then replaced the category name (for instance, bird) with a member of the category (for instance, robin, eagle, ostrich), and finally asked people to rate how sensible the resulting sentences were. It turns out that the prototypical bird is something like a robin, producing sensible results more often than chicken or ostrich or numerous other choices.

Prototypes or cases, by not defining issues with a yes/no list of features, allow for what Rosch and others have called fuzzy boundaries and areas of uncertainty. This is essential in teaching which has what Donald Schon has called indeterminate zone of practice—matters of "uncertainty, uniqueness, and value conflict" (Schon, 1987, p. 6). This uncertainty has primarily two sources—first, the nature of learning in the classroom. Paradigm shifts create contradictory ways of interpreting data (Kuhn, 1970)—for example, the tension between decoding and meaning theories in reading. Classroom learning also has an innate set of tensions creating uncertainty. Children come to school with different kinds of knowledge in which a given stimulus will not mean exactly the same thing to every child. Furthermore, the responses of the child tend to determine what stimulus the teacher might give next, and, as a result, the stimulus and the response are not always distinguishable, separate events. In such a situation, tightly structured procedures and

feature lists are relatively less helpful than they are in many technologically-dominant activities (McLaughlin & Marsh, 1978).

The point is that teaching is basically a case-study profession, a point that was brought home to me several years ago when Paul Diederich commented that the Bay Area Writing Project's major contribution to teaching preparation was that it introduced a way to do case studies of teaching. The BAWP Summer Institute presentations, he told me, are simply ways to begin organizing and reporting these cases. Thus, Rebecca Caplan's case begins as a summer institute presentation and evolves into a published report (Caplan, 1982). According to Diederich, BAWP's contribution was equivalent to Christopher Langdell's introduction of the case study method in law (Bay Area Writing Project Report, 1978). Other examples of the use of case studies are Judy Schulman's use of case studies as a way to train mentor teachers (Schulman & Colbert, 1987) and Lois Meyer's use of videotapes to train teachers (Meyer, 1989) at San Francisco State University.

The fact that case studies are the foundation of pedagogical knowledge does not meant that experimental, quantitative, and philosophical studies play no role in such knowledge. Controlled experiments, statistical surveys, and an examination of philosophical premises are all ways of describing and analyzing the problems suggested by a case. But it is the case which acts as the model, exemplar, or cultural motif anchoring the teaching community on a set of issues. An example of the way quantitative data helps explain cases is Mary Ellen Giacobbe's study of whether cases of good teaching of the writing process appear in 2nd and 5th grade textbooks (Giacobbe, 1988). Her basic "case" is James Moffett's model of what the writing process looks like. Her numbers show, for example, that parts of that case—for example—drawings are not considered in most texts. Her reports include both the bar graphs showing numerical trends and descriptions of the model case. What we discover is that the writing process as illustrated by Moffett's case is not presented in 2nd and 5th grade texts.

This process of using cases to explain and modify generalizations about teaching and learning requires that teachers be engaged in classroom research—in active inquiry into the how and why of student learning in their classrooms. Inquiry is essential because for teachers an examination of the learning task is more like problem solving than like mastering "proven" procedures.

Also, an inquiry approach releases teachers to learn, freeing them from a constraining fear of failure. For example, I asked one student teacher, who was always trying to begin class with the 7th graders yelling, to try waiting at the front for the students to quiet down before beginning. She could not wait beyond a few seconds. The next day I asked to try the same thing as an experiment and to focus on how many minutes it took the students to quiet down. Then she could do it. And the students did quiet down.

In summary, pedagogical knowledge must have inquiry methods and case studies as its foundation. This must include the basic statistics typically used to explain school results and an introduction to the critical cases or exemplars which define the foundations of pedagogical practice. Beginning attempts at introducing teacher research to student teachers has occurred at Stanford in Vickie LaBoskey's work (LaBoskey & Wilson, 1987) and at the University of California at Berkeley in the work of Kenneth Lane and others (Myers, 1985).

In addition to *pedagogical knowledge,* teacher preparation programs must examine the *conceptual knowledge* which underlies the following critical questions in teaching: What are the patterns of learning development, how do learners internalize culture, and what are the mismatches, if any, between culture and schooling? These questions have led many teacher preparation programs to introduce into their programs more collaborative learning (most teacher preparation programs still emphasize only individual learning), a variety of sign systems (most teacher preparation programs still give exclusive attention to words and numbers), a diversity of ways of talking in schools (most teacher preparation emphasize silent work and academic language), and more tool use (most teacher preparation programs emphasize the pencil and ignore computers, various graphic instruments, and video). Resnick has argued that these four areas—collaboration, contexts, tools, and sign use—are the critical disjunctions between schools and real world learning, disjunctions which schools must attend to (Resnick, 1987).

Why are these four areas critical? First, collaborative work. Students have two parallel levels of development, one being the things learners can do independently—for example, the things students get right on tests—and the other being the things learners can do only with help from tools or from adults and/or peers. This second level, the area of proximal development, comes first. Later one internalizes the help or scaffolding of others and of tools and begins to work independently (Vygotsky, 1981; Applebee & Langer, 1983). Lessons based on the concept of proximal development are quite different from those based on other theories of learning. In the concept of proximal development, the teacher is expected to recognize that the frontier of a student's learning is what the student can do with peers or with a new tool, not what the students can do alone when new knowledge has finally become fully internalized (Griffin & Cole, 1984).

The notion that new knowledge is assimilated through collaboration has spawned a great deal of valuable work on how people move from novice to expert on-the-job and in the classroom. In a learning model called cognitive apprenticeship, Collins, Brown, and Newman (in press) have brought together the new findings from math (Schoefeld, 1985), reading (Palincsar & Brown, 1984), writing (Scardamalia & Bereiter, 1983), and science (White, 1984). They have identified several learning concepts which run counter to the concepts in the direct instruction model, for example. First, in direct instruction, units of a lesson are narrowly focused and are carefully sequenced from simple to complex, from local to global. But Collins, Brown, and Newman emphasize the importance of global before local skills so that the "sequencing of activities provide learners with the opportunity to build a conceptual model of how all the pieces . . . fit together before attempting to produce the pieces" (Collins, Brown, & Newman, in press, p. 26).

Second, in direct instruction, lessons are tightly structured around one skill. But Collins, Brown, and Newman suggest that increasing the diversity of skills under consideration is as important as the issue of the increasing complexity of a single skill. This means in the development of reading skills one should intermix reading for pleasure, reading for memory or studying, and reading for a particular piece of information to complete a writing assignment (Collins, Brown, & Newman, in press). Finally, direct instruction assumes that the teacher knows everything in the lesson. In cognitive apprenticeship, the teacher is expected to solve new problems and read new texts in front of students so that students observe the teacher learn.

Some teacher preparation programs have begun to focus on the notion of cognitive apprenticeship and proximal development through frequent cooperative learning activities (Slavin, 1980), through the frequent use of a variety of tools, and through an examination of alternative ways of testing. Direct instruction, time-on-task, and mastery learning packages are focused on the independent development of students, as indicated by machine-scored tests, but cognitive apprenticeship focuses on different levels of proximal development. At the present time, the impact of the cognitive apprenticeship model has yet to be felt in most teacher preparation programs.

Second, sign shifting. In many teacher preparation programs, words and numbers are the only signs used to learn. The assumption of these programs is that the mind is a simple storage container for school information, and words and numbers can be used to store everything. However, the mind is not a simple storage container. Instead, it is an active information processor, constructing an internal reality by guessing and negotiating. This means that students must learn to guess, and teachers and students together must learn how to negotiate different forms of knowledge. Because sign systems are not transparent windows, but rather particular kinds of eye glasses through which one sees the world, the introduction of new sign systems (such as feminist images or pictures of the atom) changes one's views and constructs new realities. Mapping, picturing, different forms of talking, even such action routines as clapping and dancing, are all different ways of knowing and need to be part of the *conceptual* knowledge introduced into student teaching (Gardner, 1983).

Finally, teachers must become more self conscious about the cultural mismatch between community cultures and school cultures. The achievement gap between Black and White and between Hispanic and Anglo is the number one problem in public education, and this problem cannot be sensibly attacked without a much deeper understanding of how these cultures shape ways of learning and knowing (Heath, 1983) and how schools and communities are often a mismatch. The research on school culture mismatches has included an analysis of show-and-tell episodes in elementary classrooms (Michaels, 1981), of peekaboo and discourse at home and school (Cazden, 1983), of participant structures in classrooms (Erickson & Mohatt, 1982), and of school-as-culture (Lightfoot, 1983). In addition, a number of researchers have examined what teachers need to know when they teach limited-English students in one of the many approaches now used by school districts—Transitional Bilingual Education, Maintenance Bilingual Education, English-as-a-Second Language, Immersion, Sheltered English, and Submersion (Garcia, 1990). This knowledge, too, must find its way into new models of teacher preparation.

One of the key concerns in the area of cultural mismatch is professional ethics. What information told to a teacher by a student is confidential, if any? Is this confidentiality legally protected? Should the teacher grant a parent's request that a student not read a particular book? What are the differences between individual rights and professional rights? Do English teachers censor books when they select? When does parent choice of a student's educational needs begin to violate the professional norms of teacher? These issues raise the question of "Who owns the mind?" For doctors, the question of "Who owns the body?" has resulted in entirely new ways of dealing with patients. Now patients are consulted about what approaches to take in healing the body. Will we in the future consult with students and parents about the approaches we take to teaching? The potential contradictions between self interest and the public interest, between professional norms and individual rights, shape many of the critical professional decisions of teachers. Yet at present, teacher preparation programs and schools of education are the last places one would turn for some reflections about these kinds of questions.

In summary, changes in learning theory have modified the *conceptual* knowledge required of teachers—from telling to negotiating, from individual to collaborative work, from words and numbers only to many different sign systems, from one set of cultural assumptions to another, and finally from a relative indifference to issues of ethics to a keen interest.

SUBJECT MATTER KNOWLEDGE

In addition to *pedagogical knowledge* and *conceptual knowledge,* teaching practice needs a foundation in *subject matter knowledge* (Shulman, 1984). *Subject matter,* too, has undergone radical change in the last dozen years. For English teachers, the reading of the text is no longer just a matter of decoding words or patterns of text a la the New Criticism. Recent research has suggested that meaning is anchored in interpretative communities (Fish, 1980) and in relationships among different texts (Culler, 1975). For example, in one interpretive community, the relationship of Huck and Jim is racist, in another the relationship is redeeming, celebrating what is possible if one breaks away from the mainland, and in yet another Huck and Jim are read as a universal convention borrowed from texts going back to Homer in which rivers and oceans are read as metaphors for life itself.

What we bring to a reading shapes what we read, and part of what we bring is our experience with various texts and with the various interpretative communities in which we have lived. In the traditional approach to reading, meaning is delivered, not negotiated, and the selected materials are a restricted cannon, not a negotiated list. In our recent redefinitions of reading, interpretive communities within a given classroom must negotiate a text's meaning, and for this reason, a text may change its meaning from one class period to another, from one historical period to another (Scholes, 1985).

Writing, too, has changed (Myers & Gray, 1983). It is no longer simply a written product with a clear distinction between right and wrong conventions. It is now also a process,

from prewriting to writing and revising, and it is also a social context in which a set of social relationships are established between reader and writer. In both dimensions, conventions change. What is allowed in a memo or first draft may not be allowed in a published paper. What is allowed in conversational prose may not be allowed in academic papers.

An examination of writing as process requires that the teacher find the units in the process that the student can handle, for example, breaking the writing task into discussion, mapping, prewriting, and finally draft writing. An examination of writing as social context requires that the teacher develop a set of appropriate analogies between writing situations and oral speech events. For example, many teachers like to start with close audiences and move to more distant ones. In this new understanding of writing, all errors are no longer equal. Some represent a developmental advance, a mistake based on the effort to try something new and difficult, and others represent a miscue from old learning, using conventions from close audiences, for example, in writing to distant ones. In this new view of writing, the teacher's task is not a simple matter of circling the errors on the error list.

The precise strategies one uses in a task is governed by the subject matter of the task. For example, in writing, a good strategy is to begin by writing whatever introduction comes to mind, using it as a place holder and returning later for the rewrite. In reading it is a good strategy to mark with a paper clip sections not understood and to go on to the next section. Return to the marked sections after one has finished the first reading. Another strategy is to start reading a long text by reviewing the introduction and the conclusion.

Subject matter does not stay the same throughout the career of teachers. Beginning teachers must learn how to transfer the subject they knew as university students into experiences which are valuable for children and adolescents. Student teachers are attempting to make the transition while at the same time learning their pedagogical role as teachers—how to stop thinking first about what the teacher does and start thinking about how the students are responding. Thinking about student reactions is not easy for beginning teachers worried about filling up the time slots.

The recent research into the developmental history of teachers is telling a great deal about how to reform teacher preparation (Shulman, Sykes, & Phllips, 1983). One obvious inference from these insights is to think of teacher preparation as a multiyear, career project. In other words, universities must plan career programs for teachers, bringing them back to the campus in the summer for the second and third stages of teacher preparation. States have begun to restructure teaching as continuous preparation. For example, California's present credential law, which eliminated the life credential, requires that teachers, to keep their credentials, must complete 150 hours of professional studies every five years.

Shifts in *subject matter* cannot be understood and productively used without an understanding of the history of literacy in this country (Myers, 1984). Without this history, student teachers not only cannot understand many of the current critiques of public education but also cannot sustain a sense of their community with other teachers, both past and present.

Subject matter changes because our culture changes, and education researchers have done little to develop a history for teachers, although there are some promising beginnings (Cuban, 1984). In order to have a profession of teaching, one must have a history of teaching.

Second, in order to have a profession of teaching, one must have a science of teaching, and this science of teaching, like any system of rationality, has two functions. First, it provides a set of assumptions with which teachers can use to understand the teaching and learning problems in their room. Second, it distributes decision making authority on curriculum issues so that the school structure supports what must be done. *Pedagogical knowledge, concepts* about learning, and *subject matter* will not help a teacher who lacks some awareness about the relationship between these kinds of knowledge and knowledge about *school structure* (McNeil, 1986). One study of 14 classrooms (Myers & Thomas, 1982) found that urban classes were interrupted about six times each class period with a combination of messages (school bulletins and student messengers from various school offices, announcements over the loud-speaker in the classroom), attendance problems, discipline problems, and various other matters (Myers & Thomas, 1982).

Most of these interruptions were a direct result of explicit decisions about how to structure the school—discipline problems must be handled in the classroom and not sent to the office, attendance slips must be prepared by the teacher and be submitted everyday from every class, support personnel may interrupt classes at any time to complete their work (including administrative bulletins, state testing, and government surveys), and secondary teachers will teach at least five classes each day with an average of 33 students in each class (an average of 165 students per day). In addition, the system wants teachers to try to spend about 10 minutes each week on the writing and homework of each student (grading papers, recording progress), a total of 27 hours outside of class each week for secondary teachers (to be added to the minimum of 25 hours in classrooms, not counting prep periods and meetings).

Many beginning teachers, lacking awareness of these structural problems, think they are failures because they "can't find the time" or simply "can't do the job." This problem of overload is the major reason why over half of the beginning teachers leave teaching within five years. In order to handle the load, most experienced teachers design some slot-filling and copying exercises which are highly structured, keep students quiet in their seats, and require no assistance from the teacher. These exercises often make little or no contribution to the student's learning, but they do give the teacher some time to handle discipline and tardy problems, attendance, paper distribution, and so forth.

These slot-filling lessons are the kind that Cooper, Applebee, and others (Cooper, 1981; Applebee, 1981) think happen too often in K–12 writing classes. However, as long as school structures remain what they are, these lessons will remain. What is needed, of course, is to allow faculty and staff at the school site to change staffing, student assignments, and bell schedules to fit the needs at the site instead of trying to apply some standardized procedure at all sites and in all classrooms. Very few models of teacher preparation acknowledge the disabling contradictions between knowledge about *pedagogy, concepts about learning,* and *subject matter,* on the one hand, and knowledge about *school structure,* on the other.

An example of this contradiction is the set of assumptions in *Strategies for Teachers* by Paul D. Eggen, Donald P. Kauchak, and Robert J. Harder (1979), a book required for teachers in credential programs throughout the country. The book's learning conceptions are solid, based as they are interaction theorists like Jerome Bruner and Hilda Taba. But the book's assumptions about teacher roles and school structure are based on a division of labor appropriate for behaviorism and imprinting, not interaction learning. The authors see themselves telling teachers what to do, not providing the inquiry skills that teachers can use to shape teaching at the school site:

> Models are prescriptive teaching strategies.... The model chosen is specifically designed to achieve a particular set of objectives and will determine in large part the actions of the teacher. A teaching model, then, can be considered as a type of blue print for teaching.... The teacher is analogous to the builder.... (pp. 12–13).

Notice that in this book's professional hierarchy the architects of learning are the authors of the book, who feel that they can issue blue prints which "determine in large part the actions of the teachers" (p. 12). This is a form of mail-order architecture in which students are treated as standard, mass produced units and in which teachers are relegated to the nonprofessional roles of routine workers. In a sense, mail-order architecture is an adequate model for the teacher proof theories of behaviorist learning, for product theories of writing, and for the delivered information theories of reading. It is not adequate for an interaction concept of learning, for a process concept of writing and for a negotiation concept of reading.

The odd thing about K–12 teaching today is that many teacher preparation programs do exactly what Kauchak, et al. do—celebrate the best of what is known about *pedagogy, learning* and *subject matter* and at the same time distribute decision making authority in schools in ways which undermine the best of what is known about *pedagogy, learning,* and *subject matter.* Hargraves and Dawe have commented that as efforts to dictate the curriculum increase, "teachers are apparently being urged to collaborate *more,* just at the moment when there is less for them to collaborate about" (Hargraves & Dawe, 1989, p. 3).

Another example of the contradictions between school structure and claims about professionalism is the widespread use of Bruce Joyce's coaching model in teacher preparation and school staff development programs. The primary problem in Joyce's coaching model is his assumption that the way one coaches teachers is analogous to the way a physical education coach coaches tennis and football (Joyce & Showers, 1980). In other words, what should be communicated to teachers is a series of technical skills. Hargraves and Dawe, among others, have argued quite convincingly that the Joyce model undermines teaching effectiveness because "what is to be coached in teaching cannot be reduced solely to matters of technical skills and competence, but involves choices of a personal, moral, and sociopolitical nature" (Hargraves & Dawe, 1989, p. 20). Hargraves and Dawe also identify two other ways in which the Joyce coaching model undermines teaching effectiveness in schools.

First, the model does not adequately examine the problem of time in the school day: "... it seems to us that the time implications of implementing peer coaching are being treated a little too dismissively here" (Hargraves & Dawe, 1989, p. 13). The Joyce model looks at class time from the point of view of the distanced administrator, not from the point of view of the involved teacher.

Second, the Joyce model does not adequately understand what Bird and little have called the *norms of collegiality* (Bird & Little, 1986) Without cultures of collaboration in the school, without reciprocity in relationships, the Joyce model is "contrived collegiality," which works against the best that we know about teaching and learning:

We want to emphasize that such dangers and weaknesses attached to contrived collegiality within the technical coaching model are not temporary, local, or accidental. They are absolutely integral to a process of tightening administrative surveillance and bureaucratic control over curriculum design, instructional delivery and teacher 'development,' of which technical coaching is but one element (Hargraves & Dawe, 1989, p. 26).

IMPORTANCE OF SCHOOL STRUCTURES

Teacher preparation programs must examine carefully how school structures like Joyce's coaching model undermine professional assumptions. But what should the school structure be? The failure of researchers to find generic teaching skills for all grades, all developmental levels, and all subjects has lead some researchers to ask whether there are generic structures common to all effective schools. The answer to this question appears to be that effective schools do have some generic structures. They have, for example, a large degree of local, school site autonomy in their decision making and have substantive involvement of teachers (and sometimes parents) in school policy making (Edmonds, 1982). In general, teacher preparation programs do very little to prepare teachers to establish or to use school site decision making, either to help teachers acquire decision authority or to acquaint teachers with the influence of school structure on curriculum.

The effective schools research has also identified the critical importance of school structures which unite the community and the school. James Coleman's notion of social capital is critical here (Coleman, 1987), the notion being that youth and child services of all types are an essential foundation for schooling. What should teachers be doing? At present, very few teacher preparation programs examine the critical relations among teacher, parent, home, and school.

A good model of teacher education cannot ignore the way the university or college structures instruction. Are these institutions socializing teacher candidates into a profession of teaching in which these candidates will become school decision makers or are these institutions simply teaching graduate students to manage classes or to learn to write? The Bay Area Writing Project, for example, sees itself as first a professionalization project which identifies examples of best practice among practicing teachers. These teachers train other teachers, establishing the legitimacy of teacher knowledge and, at the same time, building a community of teacher leaders. Some writing proj-

ects, however, see themselves as courses to teach teachers how to teach and how to write, and these projects assign leadership to university professors or visiting lecturers with research and writing expertise (Newkirk, 1983). William Strong, who has studied both types of projects, concludes, "I came to see anew how NWP [National Writing Project] is as much about teacher empowerment as it is about the teaching and learning of writing" (Strong, 1988, p. 21).

Not one good idea of *content, pedagogy, subject matter* or *school structure* has a chance as long as the present politics of teacher education continue to decide questions about the structure of teacher preparation—who gives the courses and where? Many new models of teacher education are leaving the university and locating in the offices of school superintendents or private promoters. In fact, in some states, state policy is encouraging the separation of teacher preparation and the university. For example, the New Jersey Legislature voted to eliminate teacher education programs in higher education, and the California Legislature, responding to demands for more teachers, has given school districts the authority to train teachers for statewide credentials.

Why are these states and others abandoning the university? The reason is, as Herbert Simon notes, that "the natural sciences have almost driven the sciences of the artificial from professional school curricula" (Simon, 1981, p. 129–130). The natural sciences are the study of natural processes—memory, perception, digestion, reproduction, and so forth—all part of the *conceptual* knowledge teachers must learn. The artificial sciences study man's artificial creations—*school structures* and *pedagogy,* for instance.

The natural, therefore, involves only one area of teacher knowledge, *conceptual* knowledge. But the natural sciences dominate the course content of many teacher preparation programs. Many courses in credential programs are taught by professors who do not wish to examine their disciplines in terms of school structure, school subjects, or school pedagogy. Their commitments are to economics, history, sociology—the disciplines with status in university life. Thus, teachers are too often taught by professors and others who have little interest in schooling and teaching.

This general trend has led to many teacher preparation programs with little or no connection to teaching practice (Inman, 1984, p. 39) and has produced several legislative revolts in which states have mandated specific hours of field experience: Colorado has legislated 100 hours of field experience for student teachers, Kentucky 150 hours, Ohio 300 hours, North Carolina 10 weeks, North Dakota 10 weeks, New Mexico 14 weeks, Wisconsin 14 weeks, and 12 weeks in Oklahoma, Pennsylvania, South Carolina, and Mississippi (Hammond & Berry, 1988, p. 16). These state mandates ensure some field experience, but they also tend to stifle the creative development of diverse and intellectually respectable teacher preparation programs.

Many departments of education also use teacher preparation programs to fund jobs for graduate students who wish to take courses for higher degrees. It is one of the "dirty little secrets" surrounding teacher preparation in this country that teacher preparation has become a welfare program for graduate students (Sykes, 1983). These graduate students supervise student teachers, observe and advise student teachers at the school site, and teach methods courses. They are selected out of a pool of doctoral candidates who often have not taught K–12 or, if they did teach K–12, may have taught unsuccessfully. Graduate students do not constitute a pool of self-selected excellent teachers.

By assigning these graduate students to supervise and to teach student teachers, the university saves money, which it diverts to other university or school of education needs outside of teacher education. This, of course, deprofessionalizes teaching and increases Ph.D. enrollments. This employment pattern in teacher preparation programs has been institutionalized throughout the country, occurring even in prestigious places like Michigan, Harvard, Stanford, and Berkeley, and is part of an overall pattern of shifting tuitions and auxiliary support from teacher preparation to other university programs.

The problem of teacher preparation is not just a matter of having rigorous content—solid *pedagogical, conceptual, subject matter* and *structural* knowledge. Even when that is present, as is sometimes the case, the university often does not support such programs in its own structure and politics because the ruling faculty of schools of education lack an appropriate vision of what the teaching profession is or could be. As a result, universities are often involved in the training of "warm bodies" for classrooms without the slightest concern about the quality of preparation, accepting without comment the deterioration of credential standards when shortages develop. Witness the silence in Louisiana when Louisiana went to a two tier system in 1986 after the top level became too tough for many applicants. Witness the silence in Arizona when Arizona turned its emergency credential into an Associate Teacher Program in 1985 after shortages developed. Witness the silence of California universities when the credential commission gave school districts the authority to train and credential teachers.

New leadership in the universities is essential if the politics of schools of education are to change. In order to get support for promising models of teacher preparation maybe teacher preparation should be separated from other functions of the school of education. At least, then, teacher preparation could speak with a clear voice and could keep its own income to develop programs based on the best of *pedagogical, conceptual, subject matter* and *structural* knowledge. Teacher preparation needs what medicine got when medicine came to a crossroads in the preparation of doctors, an Alexander Flexner who used accreditation procedures to force changes in medical schools (Chapman, 1974).

Even if the university problem is solved, there still remains the problem of an adequate pool of candidates. No teacher preparation program can accomplish much if the candidates are not up to the task. Cremin argues, for example, that "progressive education demanded infinitely skilled teachers, and it failed because such teachers could not be recruited in sufficient numbers" (Cremin, 1965). Schools in the past staffed schools with talented people who were trapped and socially disadvantaged—women, ethnic minorities, and veterans discharged in mass from various wars (World War II, Korea, Vietnam). Many of these populations are now relatively free to pursue other, more high paying occupations, and for this reason and others, teachers' salaries must be raised to attract competent people to teaching (Hammond & Berry, 1988, p. 45). Many states have moved in that direction by providing incentives for higher beginning teacher salaries.

But salary alone may not create an adequate pool. School restructuring may require different levels of teacher licensing—for example, teacher assistant, teacher associate, and advanced teacher—so that those school tasks not requiring the judgment of a teacher may be assigned to paraprofessionals. This direction in many states has taken the form of programs to professionalize the paraprofessional and to establish career ladder programs. In such a structure, the fully professionalized teacher (the advanced teacher) may not always be in the room with students and may require different types of university credentialing at various stages in his/her career. Other types of teachers (teacher assistant) may require little more than permits from a two year college.

In this vision of the future, there would be fewer teacher preparation programs, but they would be of decidedly higher quality. Their essential characteristics would be a well developed knowledge base for teachers, a new kind of university structure which protects the resources of teacher preparation programs, and multilevel credentialing programs matched to different levels of teaching responsibilities. I think we have an adequate supply of good models which demonstrate the new knowledge base for teaching, but we lack, at the moment, the political will in state legislatures, in professional communities, and in universities and colleges to make the changes necessary on a large scale. Without some outside pressure, some outside threat, many insiders will not change very much. We need some ideas about how to make things go bump in the night! For example, maybe teacher's organizations should organize a boycott against schools of education now using antiprofessional practices in their teacher preparation programs. Such a proposed action might at least start an interesting exchange of views.

References

Applebee, Arthur. (1981). *Writing in the Secondary Schools.* Urbana, Illinois: National Council of Teachers of English.

Applebee, Arthur N., and Langer, Judith. (1983). "Instructional Scaffolding: Reading and Writing as Natural Language Activities," *Language Arts, 60,* (2), February 1983, 168–175.

Bay Area Writing Project (1978). *Evaluation Report.* University of California, Berkeley.

Beginning Teacher Evaluation Study: The Final Report (1980), Sacramento, California: California State Commission for Teacher Preparation and Licensing.

Bird, T. and Little, J. W. (1986). "How Schools Organize the Teaching Occupation," *The Elementary School Journal* 86 (4), 493–511.

Bloom, B. S. (1968). "Learning for Mastery." *Evaluation Comment.* UCLA-CSEIP, 1, n.p.

Borrowman, M. L. (1965). Liberal Education and Professional Education of Teachers." In M. L. Borrowman (Ed.), *Teacher Education in*

America: A Documentary History (pp. 1–53). New York, NY: Teachers of College Press, Columbia University.

Boyer, E. L. (1983). *High School: A Report on Secondary Education in America.* New York: Harper & Row.

Brophy, Jere & Good, Thomas L. (1986). "Teacher Behavior and Student Achievement." In Merlin C. Wittrock, (Ed.), *Handbook of Research on Teaching,* New York: MacMillan Publishing Company.

Brophy, J., & Evertson, C. (1974). *The Texas Teacher Effectiveness Project: Presentation of Non-Linear Relationships and Summary Discussion* (Research Report No. 74-6). Austin: University of Texas, R & D Center for Teacher Education, (ERIC Document Reproduction Service No. ED 099 345).

California State Department of Education. (1980). *Inservice Packet,* Sacramento, California.

Caplan, Rebecca. (1982). "Showing-Writing: A Training Program to Help Students Be Specific." In Gerald Camp (Ed.), *Teaching Writing,* Montclair, New Jersey: Boynton Cook.

Carroll, J. B. (1963). "A Model for School Learning." *Teachers College Record, 64* (8), 723–733.

Cazden, C. B. (1983). "Peekaboo as an Instructional Model: Discourse Development at School and at Home. In B. Bain (Ed.) *The Sociogenesis of Language and Human Conduct: A Multi-Disciplinary Book of Readings.* New York: Plenum.

Chapman, Carleton B. (1974). "The Flexner Report," *Daedalus, 103:* 1, 105–117.

Clay, M. (1987). "Implementing Reading Recovery: Systematic Adaptations to an Educational Innovation. *New Zealand Journal of Educational Studies, 22,* 35–58.

Coleman, James & Campbell, E. Q., Hobson, C. J., McPartland, J., Mood, A. M., Weinfeld, F. D., & York, R. L. (1966). *Equality of Education and Opportunity.* Washington, D.C.: U.S. Government Printing Office.

Coleman, James. (1987). "Families and Schools," *Educational Researcher.* AERA, August-September, 1987, 32–38.

Collins, Allan; Brown, John Sealy; & Newman, Susan E. (in press). "Cognitive Apprenticeship: Teaching the Craft of REading, Writing, and Mathematics." In L. B. Resnick (Ed.). *Cognition and Instruction: Issues and Agendas.* Hillsdale, NJ: Lawrence Erlbaum Associates.

Cooper, Charles, (1981). "Forward," in Arthur N. Applebee, *Writing in the Secondary Schools.* Urbana, Illinois: National Council of Teachers of English.

Cremin, Lawrence. (1965). *The Genius of American Education.* New York: Vintage Books.

Cuban, Larry. (1984). *How Teachers Taught: Constancy and Change in American Classrooms.* New York: Longman.

Culler, Jonathan. (1975). *Structural Poetics.* New York: Cornell University Press.

Duckworth, Eleanor. (1972). "The Having of Wonderful Ideas," *Harvard Educational Review, 42,* (2), 217–231.

Edmonds, Ron. (1982). "Programs of School Improvement: an Overview." *Educational Leadership: 403,* (3), 4–11.

Eggen, Paul D., Kauchak, Donald P., & Harder, Robert J. (1979). *Strategies for Teachers.* Englewood Cliffs, NJ: Prentice-Hall.

Erickson, F. & Mohatt, G. (1982). "Cultural Organization of Participant Structures in Two Classrooms of Indian Students." In G. D. Spindler (Ed.), *Doing the Ethnography of Schooling: Education Anthropology in Action.* New York: Holt, Rinehart and Winston.

Evertson, C., Anderson, L., & Brophy, J. (1978). *Texas Junior High School Study: Final Report of Process—Outcome Relationships* (Report No. 4061). Austin: University of Texas, R & D Center for Teacher Education.

Fillmore, Charles. (1976). "The Need for a Frame Semantics within Linguistics." In Karlgren (Ed.), *Statistical Methods in Linguistics.* Stockholm: Skriptor, p. 5–29.

Fish, Stanley. (1980). *Is There a Text in this Class?* Cambridge, Mass.: Harvard University Press.

Gagne, R. M. (1970). *The Conditions of Learning* (2nd ed.). New York: Holt, Rinehart, and Winston.

Garcia, Eugene E. (1990). "Educating Teachers for Language Minority Students." In W. Robert Houston (Ed.) *Handbook of Research on Teacher Education.* New York: MacMillan Publishing Company.

Gardner, Howard (1983). *Frames of Mind.* New York: Basic Books.

Giacobbe, Mary Ellen. (1988). "Choosing a Language Arts Textbook." In Thomas Newkirk and Nancie Atwell (Eds.). *Understanding Writing,* 2nd ed., pp. 253–273.

Good, T., & Grouws, D. (1975). *Process-Product Relationships in Fourth Grade Mathematics Classrooms.* Final Report of the National Institute of Education Grant (NEG-00-3-0123). Columbia: University of Missouri.

Good, T. L. & Grouws, D. A. (1979). "The Missouri Mathematics Effectiveness Project: An Experimental Study in Fourth-Grade Classrooms." *Journal of Educational Psychology, 71* (3), 355–362.

Good, T., & Grouws, D. (1981). *Experimental Research in Secondary Mathematics* (Final Report, National Institute of Education Grant No. NIE-G-79-0103). Columbia: University of Missouri, Center for the Study of Social Behavior.

Goodlad, J. (1984). *A Place Called School.* New York: McGraw-Hill.

Griffin, Peg, & Cole, Michael. (1984). "Current Activity for the Future: The Zo-Ped," In Barbara Rogoff & James V. Wertsch (Eds.), *Children's Learning in the "Zone of Proximal Development",* San Francisco: Jossey-Bass Inc., 45–64.

Guskey, T. R. (1985). *Implementing Mastery Learning.* Belmont, CA: Wadsworth Publishing Co.

Hammond, Linda Darling, & Berry, Barnett. (1988). *The Evolution of Teacher Policy.* Rand, Center for the Study of the Teaching Profession.

Hargraves, Andy & Dawe, Ruth. (1989). "Coaching as Unreflective Practice: Contrived Collegiality or Collaborative Culture." paper presented at ERA, March, 1989, San Francisco.

Heath, Shirley Brice. (1983). *Ways with Words.* Cambridge University Press.

Hillocks, George. (1986). *Research on Written Composition.* Urbana, Illinois: NCTE.

Hunter, M., & Russell, D. (1981). "Planning for Effective Instruction: Lesson Design." In *Increasing Your Teaching Effectiveness.* Palo Alto, CA: The Learning Institute.

Inman, V. "Certification of Teachers Lacking Courses in Education Stirs Battle in Several States." *Wall Street Journal,* January 6, 1984, p. 35.

Joyce, B. and Showers, B. (1980). "Improving Inservice Training: the Messages of Research. *Educational Leadership, 37* (5), 379–385.

Kay, P. and McDaniel, C. K. (1978). "The Linguistic Significance of the Meanings of Basic Color Terms." *Language, 54,* 610–646.

Kuhn, T. (1977). "Second Thoughts on Paradigms." In *The Structure of Scientific Theories,* Frederick Suppe, (Ed.). Chicago: University of Chicago Press.

Kuhn, T. S. (1970). *The Structure of Scientific Revolutions* (2nd ed.). Chicago: University of Chicago Press. (Original work published in 1964).

LaBoskey, Vickie Kubler & Wilson, Suzanne M. (1987). "The Gift of Case Study Pickle." Paper presented at AERA, April 1987.

Lakoff, G. (1972). "Linguistics and Natural Language." In D. Davidson & G. Harman (Eds.). *Semantics of Natural Language.* Dordrecht, Netherlands: D. Reidel Publishing, 545–665.

Lightfoot, Sarah. (1983). *The Good High School.* New York: Basic Books.

Mattingly, P. H. (1975). *The Classless Profession.* New York: New York University Press.

McLaughlin, Milbrey, & Marsh, David. (1978). "Staff Development and School Change," *Teachers College Record, 80* (1), 69–94.

McNeil, L. (1986). *Contradictions of Control: School Structures and School Knowledge.* New York, Methuen/Routledge and Kegan, Paul.

Michaels, Sarah. (1981). "Sharing Time: Children's Narrative Styles and Differential Access to Literacy." *Language in Society,* 10:423–42.

Meyer, Lois. (1989). Presentation to Student Teachers at San Francisco State University, February 1989.

Myers, Miles. (1984). "Shifting Standards of Literacy: The Teacher's Catch 22." *English Journal.* Urbana, Illinois: NCTE.

Myers, Miles (1985). *How To Do Teacher Research in the Classroom,* National Council of Teachers of English, Urbana, Illinois.

Myers, Miles A., & Gray, James. (1983). *Theory and Practice in the Teaching of Composition.* Urbana, Illinois: NCTE.

Myers, Miles A., & Thomas, Susan C. (1982). *The Interaction of Teacher Roles in the Teaching of Writing in Inner-City Secondary Schools.* NIE Contract Number 400-80-0024.

Newkirk, Tom. (1983). "Is the Bay Area Model the Answer?" *English Education,* 15, 161–166.

Palincsar, A. S., & Brown, A. L. (1984). "Reciprocal Teaching of Comprehension-Fostering and Monitoring Activities." *Cognition and Instruction, 1,* 117–175.

Peterson, Penelope. (1981). "Direct Instruction Reconsidered." In Penelope Peterson and Herbert Walbert (Eds.). *Research on Teaching.* pp. 57–69. Berkeley: McCutchan Publishing Company.

Pinnell, G. S. and Woolsey, D. (1985). Report of a study of teacher co-researchers in a project to prevent reading failure (Sponsored by a grant from the Research Foundation of the National Council of Teachers of English, Urbana, IL) Unpublished report submitted to NCTE and available from the first author at Ohio State University.

Powell, Arthur G., Farrar, Eleanor, & Cohen, David K. (1985). *The Shopping Mall High School.* Boston: Houghton Mifflin Company.

Resnick, Lauren B. (1987). "Learning in School and Out." *Educational Researchers. 16* (9), 13–20.

Rosch, E. (1977). "Human Categorization." In N. Warren, (Ed.). *Advances in Cross Cultural Psychology,* Vol. 1. London: Academic Press, 1977. Quoted in Herbert H. Clark and Eve Clark, *Psychology and Language.* Boston: Harcourt Brace, Inc.

Rosenshine, Barak, and Stevens, Robert. (1986). "Teaching Functions." In Merlin C. Wittrock (Ed.), *Handbook of Research on Teaching* (3rd ed., pp. 376–391). New York: Macmillan.

Rosenshine, Barak V. (1979). "Content, Time, and Direct Instruction." In Penelope Peterson & Herbert Walberg (Ed.) *Research on Teaching.* pp. 28–56. Berkeley: McCutchan Publishing Corporation.

Russell, Doug, & Hunter, Madeline, "Planning for Effective Instruction," unpublished paper, 1976.

Sarason, Seymour. (1983). *Schooling in America.* New York: Free Press.

Scardamalia, M. & Bereiter, C. (1983). "The Development of Evaluative, Diagnostic, and Remedial Capabilities in Children's Composing." pp. 67–95. In M. Martlew (Ed.) *The Psychology of Written Language: A Developmental Approach.* London: Wiley.

Schoenfeld, A. H. (1985). *Mathematical Problem Solving.* New York: Academic Press.

Scholes, Robert. (1985). *Textual Power.* New Haven: Yale University Press.

Schon, D. (1987). *Educating the Reflective Practitioner.* San Francisco: Jossey-Bass Publishers.

Schulman, Judith & Colbert, Joel. (1987). *The Mentor Teacher Case Book,* Far West Laboratory for Educational Research and Development.

Schwab, J. J. (1983). "The Practical 4: Something for Curriculum Professors To Do." *Curriculum Inquiry,* 13(3), 239–265.

Shulman, Lee. (1986). *Paradigms and Research Programs in the Study of Teaching.* In Merlin C. Wittrock (Ed.). *Handbook of Research on Teaching.*

Shulman, Lee. (1984). *The Missing Paradigm in Research on Teaching.* Paper presented at the Research and Development Center for Teacher Education. Austin, Texas.

Shulman, L. S., Sykes, G. & Phillips, D. (November 1983). *Knowledge Growth in a Profession: The Development of Knowledge in Teaching.* Proposal submitted to the Spencer Foundation, Stanford University, School of Education, Stanford, California.

Simon, Herbert. (1981). *The Sciences of the Artificial.* Cambridge, Mass.: The MIT Press, 1981.

Sizer, Theodore. (1984). *Horace's Compromise: The Dilemma of the American High School.* Boston: Houghton Mifflin.

Slavin, R. (1980). "Cooperative Learning." *Review of Educational Research,* 50, 315–342.

Stallings, J. (1980). "Allocated Academic Learning Time Revisited, or Beyond Time on Task," *Educational Researchers,* Washington, D.C.: AERA, December 1980, 11–16.

Stallings, J., & Kaskowitz, D. (1974). *Follow Through Classroom Observation Evaluation* 1972–1973 (SRI Project URU-7370). Stanford, CA: Stanford Research Institute.

Stallings, J. & Kaskowitz, S. (1978). "Effective Teaching and Learning in Urban Schools." Paper presented at the annual meeting of the AERA, 1978.

Strong, William. (1988). Report: Inside the New Hampshire Writing Project. *The Quarterly of the National Writing Project and the Center for the Study of Writing, 10* (4).

Sykes, G. (1983). Contradictions, Ironies, and Promises Unfulfilled: A Contemporary Account of the Status of Teaching. *Phi Delta Kappan,* Vol. 65 (2).

Vygotsky, L. S. (1981). *Mind and Society.* Cambridge, Mass.: Harvard University Press.

White, B. Y. (1984). "Designing Computer Games to Help Physics Students Understand Newton's Laws of Motion." *Cognition and Instruction, 1,* 69–108.

Wise, Arthur. (1979). *Legislated Learning.* Berkeley: University of California Press.

21C. TEACHER EVALUATION
Sheila Fitzgerald

The General Assembly of the state of North Carolina provides nearly 65 percent of the school budget for the 140 school districts in the state. It expects to have some say about the teachers working in North Carolina Schools—and it does. Along with 47 other states, North Carolina is evaluating the competencies of its teachers.

In 1979, the North Carolina General Assembly enacted a law requiring local boards of education to evaluate the performance of teachers annually following criteria established by the State Board of Education. It identified 28 generic teaching practices applicable across school subjects. Each school year since 1979, all first-year teachers in North Carolina and teachers whose certificates have expired are observed three times, at least once when the visit is unannounced. The observer, usually the principal, then prepares a narrative that becomes the basis for a conference with the teacher. Near the end of the school year when all three observations are completed, the principal rates the teacher numerically on eight subsets of the criteria, and the teacher and the principal formulate a Professional Development Plan to guide the teacher's efforts the following school year. (Holdzkom, 1987)

North Carolina is one of only seven states conducting performance tests of beginning teachers in their classrooms; most states test teachers earlier in their careers. These assessments are designed primarily to protect the public from incompetent and unethical educational practices, but they also attempt to improve teacher performance.

Why has there been a meteoric rise in legislature-mandated teacher evaluations in the last 10 years? What are the forms that preservice and in-service teacher tests take? How are teacher's language-arts skills tested, and how are their skills in teaching language arts measured? What impact will tests of teachers have on the goals for language-arts teachers? A few answers and many questions arise out of an examination of the current literature on state teacher-assessment efforts.

DEFINING TERMS

The terms testing, measuring, assessing, and evaluating are often used interchangeably, causing some of the confusion that abounds in the literature on teacher evaluation. Purves (1977) says that testing refers to formal means used to get people to perform so that their behavior can be measured, while measurement properly refers to any attempt to describe human behavior, usually in mathematical rather than verbal terms. He contrasts evaluation with measurement by noting that evaluation is the assignment of worth to human behavior (p. 245). The dictionary defines assessment as judging worth or importance, appearing to make it synonymous with evaluation, yet assessment is often used to refer to testing. In this chapter, testing will refer to the use made of standardized, largely computer-scored instruments. Measurement will refer to the accumulation of data, often from test results. Assessment and evaluation will both be used in describing judgments made about the worth of teachers.

Also, because the terms certification and licensure are often used interchangeably in publications, in this chapter the term certification will refer to both the licensing of teachers by the state and the endorsement of teachers proposed by independent agencies and professional associations. However, due to recent developments in teacher evaluation, some authorities are now making a clear distinction between licensure and certification:

Licensure is a legal process by which individual states set minimum standards for entry into a profession. These standards are designed to ensure that the individual is competent to practice, and, therefore, the standards protect the public ... Certification is a process which relies on high standards set by members of a profession through their own independent organizations for entry into the profession. Certification is a professional rather than a legal process, and it tends more toward knowledge-based assessments for processional entry. (Shive, 1988, p. 2)

In evaluating teachers, however, defining *good teaching* is a more central issue. Some authorities define teaching expertise in ways that seem to defy measurement. Rubin (1985) states:

There is a striking quality to fine classrooms. Students are caught up in the learning; excitement abounds; and playfulness and seriousness blend easily because the purposes are clear, the goals sensible, and an unmistakable feeling of well-being prevails.

Artist teachers achieve these qualities by knowing both their subject matter and their students; by guiding the learning with deft control—a control that itself is born out of perception, intuition, and creative impulse. (p. v)

In contrast, Berliner says:

We have identified a whole host of teacher behaviors and skills that are clearly related to achievement, pacing, structure, monitoring, feedback, certain kinds of questioning behavior. We have research on all sorts of academic climate variables. We know, in other words, what observable teacher characteristics are related to effective teaching. Now we want to go inside teachers' heads and ask them why they do the things they do. (Brandt, 1986, p. 9)

In 1974, a committee of the National Conference on Research in English (NCRE) produced a document defining teacher effectiveness in elementary school language arts. Its expressed purpose was "to guide the adaptation and/or creation of instruments for identifying and studying teachers' behaviors," (Robinson & Burrows, 1974, p. 89) and it said, "it could be argued that many behaviors of the mature-person-competent-professional are basic to all teaching, not limited to the language arts, and that particulars of teaching behaviors included in this concept come dangerously close to being personality factors." (p. 70) The committee identified five categories of criteria for excellence in teaching language arts in elementary schools:

Category I: Interactions with Pupils Applying Knowledge of Child Development and Individual Differences
Seeks to understand each learner's background—social, cultural, linguistic-in-relation to established sequences of child development.

Category II Interactions with Pupils Applying Knowledge of Teaching and Learning
Seeks to unify cognitive and affective learnings through action and reflection.

Category III Interactions with Pupils Showing Awareness of Societal Needs and Values
Acts upon knowledge that communication springs from, is supported by, and contributes to social interaction; utilizes children's language to capitalize on such interaction.

Category IV Interactions with Pupils Showing Maturity as a Person and as a Professional
Sees self as a guide, listener, questioner, reactor, and in general, as facilitator of language reading.

Category V Interaction with Pupils Demonstrating Knowledge of the Language Arts
Builds language on experience and experience on language; fosters genuine, purposeful, enjoyable communication among pupils and with others; shows appreciation for pupils' uniqueness and growth in the use of language. (p. 71–75)

The NCRE document demonstrates a commitment to process as central for learning. For the last 20 years, English language-arts teaching at both the elementary and secondary levels has focused on process approaches in instruction, on helping students use language for a variety of purposes, on helping them interact with peers and adults in written and oral forms, on helping them respond to their experiences in ways that enlighten themselves and others.

In a 1986 International Reading Association (IRA) publication, *Effective Teaching of Reading: Research and Practice* (Hoffman, Ed.) the history of research on elementary and secondary teaching is examined by Rupley, Wise, and Logan. They explain that teacher effectiveness research in the 1980's has taken on new dimensions due to concerns for process:

With the increased interest in cognitive psychology and cognitive information processing, many teacher effectiveness researchers are looking beyond direct instruction, management, and psychological conditions to determine goals, intentions, judgments, decisions, and information processing. Teacher effectiveness researchers have begun to examine the nature or teacher rationales. (p. 31–32)

The National Council of Teachers of English (NCTE) published *Guidelines for the Preparation of Teachers of English Language Arts* in 1986. In defining the roles of elementary and secondary teachers of English language arts, its authors recognized three categories: knowledge, pedagogy, and attitudes. They were careful to delineate *process* focused goals for each category but also recognized *mastery* modes in their use of per-

formance based concepts, and *heritage* models: the "traditions, history, the time-honored values of civilized thought and feeling (including the time-honored resistance to these values) and the skills that make it possible to share in one's culture and to pass it on." (Mandel, 1980, p. 8):

Knowledge: Teachers of English language arts need to know the following:

1. That growth in language maturity is a developmental process,
2. How students develop in understanding and using language,
3. How speaking, listening, writing, reading, and thinking are interrelated,
4. How social, cultural, and economic environments influence language learning,
5. The processes and elements involved in the acts of composing in oral and written forms (e.g., considerations of subject, purpose, audience, point-of-view, mode, tone, and style),
6. Major developments in language history,
7. Major grammatical theories of English,
8. How people use language and visual images to influence the thinking and actions of others,
9. How students respond to their reading and how they interpret it,
10. How readers create and discover meaning from print, as well as monitor their comprehension,
11. An extensive body of literature and literary types in English and its translation,
12. Literature as a source for exploring and interpreting human experience—its achievements, frustrations, foibles, values, and conflicts,
13. How nonprint and nonverbal media differ from print and verbal media,
14. How to evaluate, select, and use an array of instructional materials and equipment that can help students perform instructional tasks, as well as understand and respond to what they are studying,
15. Evaluate techniques for describing students' progrss in English,
16. The uses and abuses of testing instruments and procedures, and
17. Major historical and current research findings in the content of the English curriculum.

Pedagogy: Teachers of English language arts must be able to do the following:

1. Select, design, and organize objectives, strategies, and materials for teaching English language arts,
2. Organize students for effective whole-class, small-group, and individual work in English language arts,
3. Use a variety of effective instructional strategies appropriate to diverse cultural groups and individual learning styles,
4. Employ a variety of stimulating instructional strategies that aid students in their development of speaking, listening, reading, and writing abilities,

5. Ask questions at varying levels of abstraction that elicit personal responses, as well as facts and inferences,

6. Respond constructively and promptly to students' work,

7. Assess student progress and interpret it to students, parents, and administrators,

8. Help students develop the ability to recognize and use oral and written language appropriate in different social and cultural settings,

9. Guide students in experiencing and improving their processes of speaking, listening, and writing for satisfying their personal, social, and academic needs and intentions,

10. Guide students in developing an appreciation for the history, structure, and dynamic quality of the English language,

11. Guide students in experiencing and improving their processes of reading for personal growth, information, understanding, and enjoyment,

12. Guide students toward enjoyment, aesthetic appreciation, and critical understanding of literary types, styles, themes, and history,

13. Guide students toward enjoyment and critical understanding of nonprint forms,

14. Help students make appropriate use of computers and other emerging technologies to improve their learning and performance, and

15. Help students use oral and written language to improve their learning.

Attitudes: Teachers of English language arts need to develop the following attitudes:

1. A recognition that all students are worthy of a teachers' sympathetic attention in the English language arts classroom,

2. A desire to use the English language-arts curriculum for helping students become familiar with diverse peoples and cultures,

3. A respect for the individual language and dialect of each student,

4. A conviction that teachers help students grow by encouraging creative and responsible uses of language,

5. A willingness to seek a match between students' needs and teachers' objectives, methods, and materials for instruction in English language arts,

6. A willingness to respond critically to all the different media of communication and a willingness to encourage students to respond critically,

7. A commitment to continued professional growth in the teaching of English language arts,

8. A pride in the teaching of English language arts and a willingness to take informed stands on current issues of professional concern, and

9. A sensitivity to the impact that events and developments in the world outside the school may have on teachers, their colleagues, their students, and the English language arts curriculum.*

It is evident from NCTE's *Guidelines for the Preparation of Teachers of English Language Arts* and from IRA's *Guidelines for the Specialized Preparation of Reading Professionals* (Professional Standards and Ethics Committee, 1986) that the roles of teachers of English language arts are very complex, that knowledge of language and literature are hardly sufficient for meeting the needs of students, that teaching skills without knowledge are also inadequate. Personality, insight, knowledge, pedagogy, and attitudes of teachers intertwine with those same qualities in students in each language arts classroom.

HISTORICAL ROOTS OF TEACHER EVALUATION

In the United States, the control of teacher behavior has been the goal of supervision since the eighteenth century, and it has been accompanied "by a well-entrenced view that schools would be run according to the business management canons of efficiency, effectiveness, inspection, and quality control." (Gitlin & Smyth, 1988, p. 240) Furthermore, early twentieth century authorities claimed that using new, scientific perspectives on teaching would allow superintendents to remove teaching from the control of school boards who used teaching positions as patronage. Cubberley, author of the 1922 text *Public School Administration* "saw in testing the opportunity for the supervisor to change school supervision from guesswork to scientific accuracy, and (to) . . . establish . . . standards of work by which he may defend what he is doing" (Gitlin & Symth, 1988, p. 241).

As the number of schools in districts increased, supervision of teachers became the responsibility of the principal, a policy that continues in most school districts today. "Teachers anticipate that annual brief visit from the principal who, according to the stereotype, stands stone-faced at the back of the classroom filling out a form . . . judgments typically rest on assessment of generic teaching skills, which means that the evaluator need not have in-depth knowledge of the subject matter and grade-level pedagogical demands " (Wise & Darling-Hammond, 1985 p. 28, 30). Continuing dissatisfaction with administrators' evaluation of teachers, increasing calls for accountability in schooling, and the growing influence of federal and state governments in education prompted new approaches to controlling teacher behavior.

The profession of English language-arts teachers gained some measure of influence over the direction of teaching in 1961 with *The Basic Issues in the Teaching of English,* a publication resulting from four national conferences designed to reexamine the teaching of English from the elementary grades through graduate school. Influenced in strong measure by this document, the U.S. Office of Education (USOE) funded several Curriculum Study Centers at major research universities under the title Project English and funded conferences, research projects, and demonstration centers. As a result, Shugrue (1968) states, "The exhilaration of the profession late in 1963 can scarcely by overestimated." (p. 37)

---

*From Wolfe, D. (1986). *Guidelines for the preparation of teachers of English Language Arts*. Urbana, IL: National Council of Teachers of English. Copyright © 1986 by the National Council of Teachers of English. Reprinted with permission.

Among the influential reports coming out of Project English was *A Study of English Programs in Selected High Schools Which Consistently Educate Outstanding Students in English* (Squire & Appleby, 1966). This case study examination of 158 high schools in 45 states prompted Squire to comment, "if the quality of instruction which we have seen seems sometimes not quite good enough, one has only to imagine what may be characteristic of many practices in unselected high school English programs." (Squire, 1966, p. 614) Another striking example of the influence of Project English was the Illinois Statewide Curriculum Study Center in the Preparation of Secondary English Teachers (ISCPET) directed by J. N. Hook. Although designed as a statewide program involving 20 colleges and universities in Illinois, over 40,000 copies of its report were distributed nationally to assist teacher preparation institutions in measuring the quality of their programs for teacher education in English. The document listed minimal, good, and superior qualifications of teachers in five areas: knowledge of language, knowledge and skill in written composition, literature, oral communication, and the teaching of English. (Shugrue, 1968, p. 105–6)

Project English studies were addressing the needs of English teaching for model curricula and teaching units, yet nagging concerns about the quality of teacher preparation and measures of competency prevailed. State departments of eduction had emerged as powers in education in the 1940s and 1950s when the number of school districts expanded and inefficiency was suspected. In addition, an increasing need for more teachers in the early 1960s prompted state legislatures to authorize state departments of education to set guidelines for teacher preparation and certification. In the middle 1960s, USOE funded the *English Teacher Preparation Study: Guidelines for the Preparation of Teachers of English,* a joint effort of the National Association of State Directors of Teacher Education and Certification (NASDTEC), the Modern Language Association (MLA), and NCTE. The guidelines, "intended to suggest desirable competencies for teachers of English" (Viall, 1967, p. 885) emphasized not only the reading and appreciation of literature that characterized English studies in American colleges and universities but declared that

the preparation of the elementary school teacher and of the secondary school teacher of English must include work in the English language, in composition, and in listening, speaking, reading, and writing, both to extend the teacher's own background and to prepare him to meet the full range of his obligations as a teacher of English. (Viall, 1967, p. 886)

Brown vs. Board of Education of Topeka, however, escalated equity issues across the nation. Equity and the implications for American schooling of Russia's Sputnik launching shifted additional aspects of educational governance to the federal level. Yet, it was this federal involvement that was soon responsible for increasing influence of state departments of education. Title V of the Elementary and Secondary Act of 1965 strengthened state departments to insure that federal mandates would be implemented at the local level. Local control of education had eroded beginning in the 1950s, and when national reports critical of education appeared in the 1980s, catapulting states into renewed action, "cries of infringement on local control [of education] barely slowed the waves of reform and change." (Frazier, 1987, p. 107)

Over the years, principals and parents had quietly judged the abilities of school teachers, but in the late 1980s, the formal assessment of teacher competencies became a central educational issue in state reform packages. The previous decade, the 1970s, had demonstrated that the testing of students and the widespread publication of student test results fueled concerns over quality of schooling, and that the increasing sophistication of technology offered new possibilities for statistical analyses of large bodies of test data.

Standardized, computer-scored tests of students' learning, rising out of Skinnerian stimulus-response psychology and prompted by America's perceived loss of world stature following the Russians' successful launching of Sputnik, promoted science-based instruction as a cure-all for problems in American education, and legitimized numerical representations of education's results. Parents, students, administrators, legislators, and teachers themselves came to rely on test data to tell them about the quality of their school programs.

In the early 1970s, most standardized tests given to students were produced by commercial companies and selected by individual school districts to supplement teachers' evaluations of students' progress. Comparisons of test results among schools and school districts were not made in any formal way. Local school districts maintained control of the content of the curriculum for the most part, and the control of their test results.

The political potential of standardized tests, however, reached national attention with the creation of the National Assessment of Educational Progress (NAEP) in 1967. Designed by the National Commission of the States to obtain statistical evidence about school performance for use in federal policy formation, NAEP evaluated student learning on a yearly rotating cycle using a national matrix sampling of students, ages 9, 13, 17 and young adults ages 26 to 35. Although in later years NAEP expanded to include ten subject areas, test results in reading, writing and math continued to receive the most press.

The NAEP student test scores and other computer scored test results accumulated between the late 1960s and the middle 1980s did little to inspire public confidence in teachers, those perceived by the society to be primarily responsible for the learning of children from age 5 to 17. Inadequacies in teaching—not the limitations of the tests, the testing circumstances, or the backgrounds of the children—were blamed for low test scores. Increasing doubts about competitiveness of United States products in the world market, worries about the potential of workers educated in American schools, and fears about the growing power of teacher unions led Americans to seek reassurances about the education they were financing:

Evaluation is a form of reassurance. When living standards are rising, economic factors stable or expanding, and when there is optimism about national and world circumstances, the public mood is buoyant and confident and educational climate is secure and enterprising. But when forebodings arise about trading conditions, when money gets short and insularity prevails, activities like education which depend for their success on trust and optimism are particularly vulnerable to the climate of doubt and fear. (Holt, 1981, p. 26–7)

Individual teachers and school districts, however, could not be held accountable for NAEP scores which only projected national conditions based on a statistical sampling of students. The rise of student testing by individual state departments of education brought accountability closer to home. Starting in the 1960s and accelerated by the Back to the Basics movement of the 1970s, state departments of education began to develop basic skills tests, usually in reading and math, that were similar to the NAEP tests or adaptations of NAEP. By 1980, 37 of the 50 states had basic skills tests for students, and many were committed to every pupil testing, allowing the comparison of school districts, schools, and sometimes individual classrooms.

Up to the mid 1980s, the state tests, as well as most commercial tests, assessed student performance primarily in reading and math; for writing, only the ability to identify errors in usage, punctuation, or spelling were included. As a result, many elementary and secondary teachers neglected to teach composition in favor of the more readily testable subskills. The oral skills of listening and speaking, which were not amenable to paper and pencil measures, continued to be neglected in testing and in teaching, even after they were declared basic skills by Title II of the 1978 Elementary and Secondary Education Act.

If many students tested poorly, and if teachers were responsible for the learning of school children, then it seemed to follow that too many of those certified to teach in the nations' schools lacked needed skills. Therefore, authorization to teach granted with a degree from an approved teacher training college or university was no longer sufficient proof of competency. Tests of teachers, mandated by state legislatures and controlled by state departments of education, contributed to what some were calling the *evaluating eighties*. (Holt, 1981, p. 174)

TYPES OF STATE MANDATED TESTING OF TEACHERS

Admission Tests

The testing of applicants for admission to teacher education programs is a common form of teacher testing. Currently, 27 states are testing or planning to test applicants desiring majors in education. A few states have developed their own tests or required the colleges to design admission tests for in-coming education students. Some states require application to achieve a certain minimum percentile or a stated score on such tests as the Scholastic Aptitude Test, the American College Test, the California Test of Basic Skills, or the Pre-Professional Skills Test.

All state teacher tests include some measures of teacher's language competencies, particularly reading, but usually these measures take the form of multiple choice items. Some states, like Arizona, include essay testing or writing samples as well as multiple choice questions. Only Colorado requires applicants in teacher education to demonstrate oral English competency "by either completing a college level public speaking course with a B minus or better, or by passing an oral English competency assessment conducted by a panel of three judges." (Rudner, 1987, p. 55)

Currently, an average of 72 percent of applicants to teacher education programs in states requiring admissions tests reach or surpass the minimum passing grade.

Certification Tests

Certification tests given to the graduates of teacher education programs are the most common form of teacher assessment required by the states. Currently, 44 states have mandated or are in the process of initiating certification test requirements. The National Teacher Examination (NTE), developed originally in 1940 by the American Council on Education and now part of the Educational Testing Service (ETS), was the most used instrument for certification assessment until it was discontinued by ETS in October 1988. (Fiske, 1988) The complete battery of the NTE took 5½ hours to complete and contained 340 multiple choice items and one essay question. (Rudner, 1987, p. 33)

General and professional knowledge and communication skills, using a multiple choice format, are tested in most certification tests. For example, the communications skills measured by NTE included reading, writing, and listening—but not speaking, the language skill teachers seem to use the most. The communications content of the NTE included the following:

Reading: understanding the explicit content of a written message; clarifying a written message; judging the nature and merits of a written message.
Writing: grammar and syntax; sentence correction.
Listening: message comprehension; analysis of a message; evaluation of a message; feedback and response.

Under the General Knowledge category of the NTE, literature was tested along with fine arts:

Literature and Fine Arts: recognizing basic elements and works of literature and fine arts; analyzing and interpreting works of literature and art to one another.

States have set different minimum passing scores even on the same tests. For the NTE, scores ranged from 630 to 657; most states took into account the error of measurement by lowering the NTE minimum by an average of eight points. Even with passing scores set relatively low, passing rates for the states that required the NTE reached only 87 percent. (Rudner, 1987, p. 37.)

The NTE was strongly criticized over the years. The National Education Association (NEA) charged that it was racially biased. Teachers also argued that "the multiple choice format is gallingly simplistic because it implies that complex classroom management problems have predetermined answers." (Fiske, 1988, p. 6) In deciding to scrap NTE, the Educational Testing Service announced that it would be replaced by 1992 with a "multiple choice test of general knowledge to be taken after the sophomore year in college; a test of pedagogical knowledge using video and other new formats just before certification; and classroom observations once a new teacher is on the job." (Fiske, 1988, p. 6)

Performance Tests

Seven states currently have internship programs using observation instruments, and 17 additional states are considering using them in the future. Proponents of performance tests claim that classroom observation evaluations help beginning teachers in their first year, as well as determine if they will be eligible for regular certification (Rudner, 1987, p. 39)

Typically, the observation scales in use evaluate the following six phases of instruction:

Daily use of previous work;
Presentation of subject matter with an emphasis on the efficient use of time and materials;
Guided student practice, including a) frequent questioning to practice learned knowledge and skills and checking for comprehension, b) cuing to maintain academic focus, and c) instructing the whole group; feedback and correction, where the teacher either praises superior academic performance or corrects or clarifies incorrect student performance;
Independent practice, either seatwork or homework which is designed to reinforce the content being studied;
Regular review to maintain the currency of the material that has been studied over the year. (Rudner, 1987, p. 40)

The evaluation of the beginning teacher or intern is usually conducted during nine classroom visits by the principal, a teacher educator, and the supervisory teacher who is assigned to work with the beginning teacher throughout the school year. Instrument validity and the results of observation assessments are insufficient at this time for judging the effects of this form of teacher testing. (Rudner, 1987, p. 42)

Recertification Tests

Three states currently include a test in their recertification requirements for practicing teachers: Arkansas, Georgia, and Texas. Each uses a custom-made test.

Between 1985 and 1987, 35,000 Arkansas teachers took the Arkansas Educational Skills Assessment Test (AESAT) which measured reading, mathematics, writing and subject matter knowledge. To retain certification, all teachers were required to pass the AESAT by June 1987. Passing rates are not available. (Rudner, 1987, p. 52)

The Teacher Certification Test (TCT) was first required of Georgia teachers seeking initial certification after September 1, 1978. In 1986 it was expanded to require the test for all teachers seeking renewal of certificates after July 1, 1986. The 28 criterion-referenced tests which comprised the TCT measured subject matter content. Nearly 4,500 teachers were tested in Georgia in 1986, and no one was denied certification renewal that year. (Rudner, 1987, p. 65)

The State of Georgia declares two major purposes for its process of teacher certification: first, it claims to provide a formal method whereby an educator may be officially recognized as a professional person. Secondly, through certification, citizens may be assured that their state constitutional guarantee of an adequate educational opportunity for children and youth is being fulfilled in part through the employment of qualified teachers and other professional school personnel.

The Texas Examination for Current Administrators and Teachers (TECAT) was first administered in March 1986 to all persons certified to teach in Texas prior to May 1, 1986. Nearly 250,000 took the test of reading and writing skill that year. For reading, a minimum of 75 percent was expected on a multiple-choice test of 55 items; for writing, a "clearly acceptable essay." (Rudner, 1987, p. 118) The 150 word essay caused problems for the greatest number of Texas teachers, yet on the first try, 96.7 percent of the 202,000 teachers who first took the test passed, and 99 percent had passed after two tries. Shop teachers, special education teachers, and coaches were most likely to be among the failures.

Shepard and Kreitzer (1987) determined that $35.5 million in tax-supported funds were spent to develop, administer, and score TECAT, as well as to assign regular Texas Education Agency staff to the assessment task and provide inservice days so that teachers could take the test. These authors also state:

Politicians had expected the failure rates to be on order of 10,000 *after remediation,* not 1,200. Legislators had wanted to weed out social studies teachers who were deficient in American history and elementary teachers who didn't know the location of Alaska. The TECAT standard was too low to touch these teachers ...

At the same time that some incompetent social studies and English teachers surely passed, some teachers with badly needed skills were removed. More than half of those eliminated by TECAT were in vocational studies, special education, P.E. (physical education), kindergarten, health, and counseling. They were also disproportionately minority teachers in districts with high concentrations of minority children. (Shepard & Kreitzer, 1987, p. 30)

In summary, all states but Alaska and Iowa currently require some form of teacher assessment. Most are standardized, computer-scored instruments measuring reading, mechanical skills in writing, and math, but a few require written essays, and one has a measure of oral language competencies. Subject matter knowledge is tested by some states, but general and professional knowledge is more frequently measured. Preservice candidates and beginning teachers are the targets of most assessments, but veteran teachers have been tested in three states. Because the goals of the state mandated tests are not only to protect society from incompetent teachers but also to improve instruction, seven states currently assess beginning teachers' performance in their classrooms, and seventeen additional states have performance assessments under study.

EVALUATION OF TEACHERS FOR MERIT PAY AND CAREER LADDER PROMOTIONS

School reform procedures have sometimes taken the form of incentives for teachers to improve their performance so they can earn higher wages or qualify for somewhat different responsibilities. Merit pay plans reward teachers monetarily for doing their jobs in ways judged to be superior by systematic appraisal of their teaching in the classroom or by improvement in their students' test scores. Merit pay is in addition to base pay and increments for years of service and graduate degrees which have been established by collective bargaining. Career ladder promotions differ from merit pay schemes by qualifying teachers who are judged meritorious to participate in supervisory or research responsibilities as part of their assignments. Like merit pay, however, rising on the career ladder probably means an advance in pay as well. Career ladder plans assume that teachers desire advancement opportunities that give them job responsibilities outside of their classrooms in addition to teaching. Merit pay schemes assume that the primary concern of teachers is low pay, and that they would prefer to be paid on the quality of their teaching over and above their position on a specified pay scale. Both types of programs also assume that competition among teachers will motivate those teachers who are disinterested or unchallenged.

In 1983, 200 of 240 teachers in Niskayuna Central School district in Schenectady, New York, received from $1,000 to $2,000 in merit pay based on individual observations conducted by school principals. In this case and in the majority of merit pay programs, classroom performance is used as the basis of evaluation, assessing such matters as lesson preparation, knowledge of subject matter, and relationships with students (Johnson, 1984, p. 13–14).

Teachers in the Weber School District in Ogden, Utah qualify for $1,300 in merit pay on the basis of their student test scores. Dallas, Texas uses a group incentive plan: all teachers in schools achieving "exceptional progress" on student test scores receive bonus pay (Johnson, 1984, p. 13, 15). Yet, school districts using students' competency test scores as evaluations of teachers are being challenged in the courts. The American Federation of Teachers charged the St. Louis Public Schools with violations of constitutional equal protection and due process provisions for requiring at least half of teachers' students to perform at or above the national norm on the California Achievement Test ("Current Developments," 1987).

However, James Popham (1987) argues that measurement-driven instruction is the most cost-effective way of improving the quality of public education:

Whether they are concerned about their own self-esteem or their students' well-being, teachers clearly want students to perform well on such tests. Accordingly, teachers tend to focus a significant portion of their instructional activities on the knowledge and skills assessed by such tests. A high stakes test of educational achievement, then, services as a powerful "curricular magnet." Those who deny the instructional influence of high-stakes tests have not spent much time in public school classrooms recently. (p. 680)

Although she claims that "the money, time, and spirit spent trying to make merit pay work would be better spent elsewhere," Johnson (1984) assumes that merit pay will be adopted by many school districts. There is continuing public pressure for accountability and less opposition to merit pay from teachers and union leaders. Career ladders, on the other hand, require considerable funds to support substantially higher salaries, and they are administratively complex, Johnson says, so they are unlikely to replace merit pay proposals in school reform packages (p. 37).

RECENT INITIATIVES IN TEACHER EDUCATION

In 1988, *The Personnel Evaluation Standards* was published by the Joint Committee on Standards for Educational Evaluation, an incorporated organization of fourteen associations: American Association of School Administrators, American Association of School Personnel Administrators, American Educational Research Association, American Evaluation Association, American Federation of Teachers, American Psychological Association, Association for Measurement and Evaluation in Counseling and Development, Association for Supervision and Curriculum Development, Education Commission of the States, National Association of Secondary School Principals, National Council on Measurement in Education, National Education Association, and National School Boards Association. Beyond developing standards for teachers and other school personnel, the group also promotes the use of its standards through articles in the newsletters and journals of member associations and presentations at its conventions.

In addition to the assessment procedure, ETS plans as a replacement for the National Teacher exam, teacher performance is also the subject of another initiative for assessment of beginning teachers that is in the development state. The National Board of Professional Teaching Standards (NBPTS), funded by the Carnegie Foundation in 1987 as a result of its reprot, *A Nation Prepared: Teachers for the 21st Century* (1986), is a joint effort of business leaders, government officials, and teacher union representatives. It was created with a $5 million grant from the foundation's Forum on Education and the Economy "to project an image of the (teaching) profession," said board president James Kelly, "by setting up tough, voluntary certification standards" in any of twenty teaching specialties (1988, p. B:4).

Sykes (1987) notes that this effort is an attempt to change the control of teaching to an agency other than one directed by government, to an association similar to those that govern entrance to the medical and legal professions:

A profession agrees to devleop and enforce standards of good practice in exchange for the right to practice free of bureaucratic supervision and external regulation. At the policy level, this contract applies to standards for licensure, certification, and program accreditation. The state delegates substantial responsibility for such standards to the organizations that represent the occupation. At the practice level, this contract applies to the organization and management of work. Collegial norms and peer evaluation direct work that is amenable neither to administrative oversight nor to routinization. (p. 19)

Sykes goes on to establish NEA and the American Federation of Teachers (AFT) as the organizations that represent the occupation of teaching:

Now emerges in both teacher organizations a leadership vanguard at national, state, and local levels committed to change. In my opinion, their appearance is the most promising development in education in the last decade. The unadulterated industrial model is losing its hold on the imagination of teacher leaders, and this opens real possibilities for the future. Without a willingness on the part of organized teachers to take risks, to experiment with new forms of agreement and cooperation, there will be no genuine reform. Teacher organizations (NEA and AFT) are the key because they wield two forms of power. They can effectively veto top-down mandates at the implementation stage or, by genuinely supporting change, can help make it happen. (p. 20)

Marc Tucker, Carnegie Forum executive director, said that the NBPTS planning group is made up of members, half of whom "are themselves teachers or have been selected by teachers to represent teachers." ("Planning Group," 1987, p. 5). Most board members are NEA and AFT representatives; some also are associated with IRA and NCTE, but these organizations do not have official representation.

NBPTS is seeking federal government support and funding for its program. In February 1989, Senator Christopher Dodd of Connecticut introduced a bill in Congress to grant NBPTS up to $25 million over three years for targeting standards in mathematics, foreign languages, English literacy, and the sciences, particularly citing standards for teachers who work with special classifications of students: handicapped, gifted and talented, students with limited English language skills, and economically and educationally deprived. If the bill passes Congress, the Carnegie Board would be required to raise an equal amount in matching funds.

Certification of teachers on a national level by NBPTS is not intended to replace state licensure, but will certify nationally teachers who exceed certain evaluation standards set by the board, claiming to give those teachers recognition as among the best in their field. Lee Shulman and a team of researchers at Stanford University have set a target date of 1992 for the assessments they are developing for the NBPTS; they envision assessing provisionally certified teachers during a required one or two year internship to determine their capacities and performance. Several sources of data are apt to be accumulated, only one of which would be a conventional test, before a decision on permanent certification or tenure is made; this is now referred to as portfolio assessment. Shulman argues that generic checklists usually used to evaluate teachers in any discipline, such as those mandated in some state assessment programs, misinterpret current research on effective teaching. The assessments his team are working on will "call upon candidates to demonstrate both an understanding of the content of teaching, and [of the] pedagogy, but probably most important of all, the mutual adaptation of the content and the pedagogy to one another." ("Teacher Assessments," 1988, p. 1) Cost of certification by NBPTS for the individual application has yet to be determined.

THE RESPONSE OF PROFESSIONAL ENGLISH LANGUAGE-ARTS TEACHER ORGANIZATIONS TO TEACHER EVALUATION PROGRAMS

Both the IRA and NCTE have been studying the issues of teacher testing in the field of language arts. In 1986, the National Council of Teachers of English established a Taskforce on Teacher Competency Issues. (Mertz, 1987) The committee's report expressed concern over efforts to assess and regulate entry and continuance in the profession—and asserted NCTE's au-

thority as "the organization which is best qualified to define competency for English Language Arts teachers" (p. 188):

However well-intentioned many teacher evaluation efforts may be, we believe they could easily backfire. In particular and more strongly, we oppose any teacher assessment/testing/evaluation program that does not conform to guidelines established by NCTE committees for general test use, teacher certification and program accreditation. These guidelines have been spelled out in numerous council publications over the years. Of primary importance are the following considerations:

- The program must not focus on minimums; it must address comprehensively the skills and knowledge central to success in teaching reading, writing, literature, and other English-language related subjects.

- The program must be more than a "test," though a good examination might well be part of it. Candidate data should include observational materials, written work, interviews, and other indicators necessary for making reasonable and fair judgments.

- One dimension of the program must address instructional and individual improvement. Feedback from evaluation must be useful for those evaluated.

- The program must be developed by responsible faculty in each institution, working with teachers who are active in the classroom.

- The program should not be standardized across institutions. Complicated as that may make decisions, it is a necessary safeguard to protect diversity in higher education. (Mertz, 1987, p. 182)

Over the years, the Board of Directors of the National Council of Teachers of English has passed several resolutions related to testing of students and assessment of teachers (NCTE, 1987): In 1977:

RESOLVED that NCTE oppose legislatively mandated competency-based testing until such time as it is determined to be socially and educationally beneficial. RESOLVED that NCTE work with legislators and other policy makers to determine how language competence can be best assured; RESOLVED that appropriate NCTE standing committees and commissions examine alternative ways of assuring competence while determining through practice, theory, and research if competency-based education is in the best interest of all members of the educational community. (#77.6)

In 1978:

RESOLVED, that the NCTE Executive Committee or headquarters staff prepare a statement urging that state departments of education, when contemplating changes in requirements for certification, recertification, or licensor for English language arts teachers or for accreditation of English language arts teachers or for accreditation of English language arts teacher education programs, include on the comiittee as members or advisors a specialist in English Education, a classroom teacher of English language arts, and one or more representatives of National Council of Teachers of English affiliates. (#78.4)

In 1979:

RESOLVED that the National Council of Teachers of English (1) encourage the assignment to the teaching of English only those persons who have been prepared in accordance with the goals and emphases in the "Statement on the Preparation of Teachers of English"; (2) call upon its individual members and affiliate organizations to increase their support of the goals and emphases of the "Statement on the Preparation of Teachers of English"; and (3) urge the National Council of Teachers of English Executive Committee to intensify its efforts in cooperation with other Professional organizations to implement items (1) and (2) of this resolution. (#79.3)

In 1985: the essence of the 1979 resolution on teacher preparation was reaffirmed in a new resolution. (#85.2)

In July 1987, representatives of several professional organizations concerned with the teaching of English met for three weeks to address issues affecting language arts instruction, kindergarten through college, into the twenty-first century: the Modern Language Association (MLA), the Association of Departments of English (ADE), the Conference on English Education (CEE), the Conference of Secondary School Department Chairs (CSSEDC), the College English Association (CEA), the College Language Association (CLA), the Conference on College Composition and Communication (CCCC), and NCTE. In one of their resolutions, "Rights and Responsibilites for Students and Teachers," three statements refer to the rights of teachers in evaluation:

Evaluation [should be conducted] only by persons with current knowledge about the learning and teaching of English;
Evaluation [should be] aimed at improving instruction rather than at judging the person;
[There should be] reciprocal evaluation: teachers evaluate all those who evaluate them. (Lloyd-Jones & Lunsford, 1989, p. 48)

A 1988 resolution approved by IRA considered teacher qualifications in relation to emergency certificates sometimes granted to relieve teacher shortages, a practice the organization asserts "jeopardizes effective teaching and learning in the language arts":

Resolved, that all personnel responsible for teaching reading and language arts at both elementary and secondary levels be appropriately prepared, qualified and certificated (i.e., licensed); and that IRA urge local, state and national school board officials, accrediting agencies and teacher education institutions to adhere to the IRA guidelines for preparing appropriately qualified and certificated teachers. ("Resolutions Passed," p. 12)

ISSUES IN THE EVALUATION OF LANGUAGE ARTS TEACHERS

Who should evaluate teachers? Should those who evaluate teachers also be subject to evaluation? Who should make decisions about what constitutes quality language arts teaching? Will teachers and teacher educators limit curricula to what tests measure? Are there more profitable uses for the time, energy, and money that currently goes into evaluating teachers?

Remarkably little is written about the cost of producing the various forms of teacher evaluations now in use, costs that go beyond important monetary considerations to include the intangibles of time and effort that are very costly to school and college programs and to government. Rudner (1987) gives some figures on the money states spend to develop test instruments:

Costs to the state depend upon the tests selected, the complexity of the policy, the system on monitoring and reporting, and the charges to the examinee. The most expensive route is for the state to have a custom-made test developed and then to pay for its administration. Teacher tests cost approximately $50,000–$100,000 to develop and $5,000–$50,000 to validate. A test program consisting of a basic skills test and 25 subject matter tests can cost close to $1,000,000 to develop and over $100 per examinee to administer and score. These costs do not include the costs for a state department of education to manage and evaluate the program.

The least expensive route is to use a ready-made, nationally recognized instrument and have the candidates pay administration costs. A testing program using an off-the-shelf basic skills test and 25 subject matter tests would cost approximately $100,000 to validate. Scoring and administration costs would be the same, approximately $100 per examinee (p. 6).

Setting priorities for the use of education funds will always be in debate. Few will claim that passing a test makes any preservice or inservice teachers better at the art or craft of teaching, although many claim that there are long term benefits on teacher education programs and on the respect accorded teaching as a profession when teacher evaluation measures are expected. Yet there is ample evidence that current needs in instruction and money, time, and effort are sorely needed to improve teachers' competencies in many areas. In writing, for example, the latest NAEP assessment results indicate that fewer than one third of participating students report their teachers discusing the quality of their ideas with them and helping them rewrite unclear passages, yet these were precisely the skills on which many students failed in the NAEP writing test ("NAEP: Poor Writing," 1986).

In addition to concern over misplaced money and effort, many fear that tests disqualify teachers who are competent to teach but ill-prepared for the tests. Some individuals whose academic preparation is weak may be screened out of education by certification tests. Approximately 72 percent of current applicants pass the admissions tests to teacher education programs, and approximately 83 percent of college graduates pass certification tests in states requiring the exam (Rudner, 1987, p. 6). A high percentage of those who fail, however, are minorities. G. P. Smith estimates that 12.5 percent of the current national teaching force are minorities, but the percentage may be reduced to 5 percent or less by 1990 if current passing rates on tests, enrollment declines, and attrition rates for minorities in teaching continue (Rudner, 1987, p. 5).

Chaplin (1986) states that many minority students applying for teacher certification came to college as a result of equal access legislation, during a time of great upheaval in the English profession, yet:

English departments in many institutions are just beginning to adjust curricula to reflect new advancements; others continue to resist. Therefore, the incompetencies that the tests are revealing in minority applicants may more accurately slow the failure of the traditional English curriculum to meet the needs of a diverse student population than they indicate that minorities are inherently inferior prospects for teaching careers. Of course, it is also disturbing to realize that teacher competency testing, regardless of the underlying reason, is reducing the number of minority teachers at a time when minority student populations continue to increase. Since the reduction will lead to fewer role models for students, there may be a resurgence of the self-image problems experienced by minority students a decade ago (p. 119).

One could readily claim that the current practice of denying many minorities access to the teaching profession parallels the undemocratic ways used in the early intelligence and achievement tests to limit professional and managerial positions to those born into the middle classes or to those who could easily acquire the middle-class standards of language and speech. (Purves, 1977, p. 234)

English language-arts teachers are concerned not only about who will teach but also what will be taught in college preparatory classes and school classrooms as teacher evaluation programs have increasing impact on the content of teacher education curricula. Most tests of teachers currently in use, and most observation designs that measure competencies in classrooms, are poor reflections of the precise standards set by English teachers described in documents such as *Guidelines for the Preparation of Teachers of English Language Arts* (Wolfe, 1986). Knowledge of English must be an important consideration in evaluating all teachers, because it is through the English language that teaching and learning in all school subject areas will take place. In addition, the tests that measure teachers' knowledge of English and its pedagogy must be updated frequently as new understandings about language learning and literacy are gleaned from research and practice. Support for these views are not coming just from the organizations directly concerned for the English language arts but from other subject matter organizations. Fortunately, organizations of school administrators are also upholding the importance of teachers' current subject matter knowledge in their publication *Teacher Evaluation: Five Keys to Growth,* a joint effort of the American Association of School Administrators, National Association of Elementary School Principals, National Association of Secondary School Principals, and NEA. (Duke & Stiggens, 1986):

Technical knowledge of instruction is one thing; content knowledge is quite another. Content knowledge consists of two elements: knowledge of the subject matter to be taught and knowledge of the district's reflection of that content in the curriculum plan. How much a teacher knows about his or her subject can greatly influence the effect of the evaluation process. Teachers who are teaching a subject for the first time may be much more concerned about what they are teaching than how they are teaching it. The situation may be reversed for teachers with years of experience teaching the same content. Even so, these individuals may need to examine their content knowledge and be open to improving it. (p. 20)

This group also identifies six areas of credibility necessary for those who observe and evaluate teaching:

Knowledge of technical aspects of teaching;
Knowledge of subject area;
Years of classroom teaching experience;
Years of experience in the school and school district;
Recency of teaching experience;
Familiarity with the teacher's classroom and students. (p. 22)

Classroom observation evaluations are of particular concern for all teachers, including English teachers. Many aspects of classroom life affect instruction, but teachers have little or no control over them: the size and make-up of the classes, the students' home environments, students' attitudes, student absenteeism, and students' jobs outside of school. Teachers wonder if observers will take into account the time of day and year when the observation takes place, and if time will be given to preobservation and postobservation sessions with the teacher. Will they consider the effects on students of having an observer in the classroom? (Schlatter, 1985) English teachers are concerned, also, that observers, most often principals, have documented evidence that they are competent to judge the English teaching they observe at the grade level in which the observation occurs.

English teachers are concerned that all the documentation on teaching in tests and observations may direct evaluators and the teachers themselves from the heart of the matter, that it may make language-arts teaching a set of prescriptions. Is mechanical precision in English teaching a desirable goal anyway? Probably not, according to James Moffett (1968):

Untidy and amorphous as it is, "English" seems like a very unattractive candidate for a structural curriculum, which undoubtedly is a main reason for its being the caboose on the train of educational renovation . . . Although {the particle approach} pays lip service to the interrelations of elements, it cannot escape its own format. To cash in on current slogans like "sequential development," publishers often arrange these particles in an order of smaller to larger—from the word to the sentence to the paragraph to the whole composition. I do not know what development this corresponds to—certainly not to the functioning of either the language or the student . . . Atomizing a subject into analytical categories, inherent only in the subject, necessarily slights the internal processes of the student or language-user, who in any given instance of an authentic discourse is employing all the sub-structures, working in all the categories, at once. (p. 3, 5, 13)

Evaluators of English language-arts teachers, those who develop formal tests and those who observe in classrooms, need to be well-schooled in the broad field of English language arts and well experienced in classroom teaching. This is rarely the case, but there is evidence that state departments of education are increasing attention to the training of classroom observers, if not to improve their insight into subject matter teaching, at least to coach observers in general instructional methods. Florida, for example, gives principals and supervisors charged with observing teachers a three-day training session "followed by a criterion test of observation competence, an examination on teacher effectiveness research, a coding quiz, and periodic update sessions. Approximately 700 principals and supervisors and 3,000 teachers have qualified as observers." (Smith, Peterson, & Micceri, 1987, p. 19) Is this the most needed training for principals and supervisors in Florida school districts or might knowledge of subject matter and pedagogy be more productive? Will the additional time spent observing in classrooms and filling in the required forms improve the quality of teaching in their schools?

LEGAL IMPLICATIONS OF TEACHER TESTING

Of prime concern in a legalistic society is whether teacher competency tests of any kind will continue to stand up under challenge. In concluding his study of legal cases, Hammes (1985) determines that teacher testing is not apt to be challenged in the courts:

- The State has the power and the right to use any means it chooses to fulfill its compelling interest, which in this case is maintaining the quality of education in the state, as long as those means are consistent with the Federal and State Constitution and Federal Law . . .
- The use of a test constructed by teaching peers and validated appropriately has been upheld by the courts, but the case has limited generalization due to the fact that the plaintiffs were probationary teachers who had signed a contract with renewal conditional on their passing the test.
- The State cannot use means that are arbitrary, capricious, or discriminatory. Thus, when a State uses competency testing, it must be rationally related not only to a legal and acceptable state goal, but also to the job, or job-related (business necessity). This will rebut a Title VII challenge of adverse impact.
- If a use of a competency test can be proven to be intentionally discriminatory, its use will not be upheld by the courts.
- To prove a Constitutional violation, it is necessary for the plaintiff to prove that the purpose of a competency test by a board is to discriminate. Title VII disparate impact discrimination charges, however, do not require proof of a discriminatory motive; there does, however, appear to be a trend for the courts to place a heavier burden on the plaintiff to show that the state, in fact, did have discriminatory purpose. (p. 18–19)

Hammes ends by saying:

Thus, it appears that with all of the problems of competency testing for teachers—legal, measurement, and educational—the phenomenon is not only here to stay, but gives all indications of increased use throughout the United States. Under the correct conditions, it has and will pass legal muster. (p. 19)

Summary

A Nation at Risk (Gardner, 1983) the report of The National Commission on Excellence in Education, electrified the country when it appeared early in the 1980s. Among its recommendations for teaching were the following:

Persons preparing to teach should be required to meet high educational standards, to demonstrate an aptitude for teaching, and to demonstrate competence in an academic discipline. Colleges and universities offering teacher preparation programs should be judged by how well their graduates meet these criteria;

School boards, administrators, and teachers should cooperate to develop career ladders for teachers that distinguish among the beginning instructor, the experienced teacher, and the master teacher. (p. 30–31)

In the few years since the publication of *A Nation at Risk,* most states have rushed to put in place some type of teacher evaluation as one response to public pressure for better teaching in the nation's elementary and secondary schools. The 19th Annual Gallup Poll of the Public's Attitudes Toward the Public Schools (1987) seems to support the need for action to improve schooling: Only 26 percent of those surveyed rate the nation's school A or B and 56 percent grade them C or D, yet 69 percent give their own child's school an A or B and only 25 percent rate that school C or D. In addition, American teachers, at least those surveyed in The Metropolitan Life Survey of the American Teacher (1984), seem to give support to measures that evaluate their teaching performance:

90 percent were willing to have their overall performance evaluated by their administrator;

72 percent were willing to have their overall performance evaluated by a committee of teachers in their school, chosen by fellow teachers;

70 percent were willing to have the improvements their students make on standardized tests used to measure them as teachers;

60 percent were willing to use standardized tests to measure teachers' skills.

Yet, a May 1988 study of teachers by the Carnegie Foundation, "Report Card on School Reform: The Teachers Speak," indicates that 7 of 10 teachers given school reform efforts a "C" or less, and half of the 13,500 public school teachers surveyed feel that teacher morale is down in spite of gains on student test scores. A majority of teachers reported no improvement or a worsening of working conditions, study space for teachers, assigned teaching load, preparation time, class size, freedom from nonteaching duties, teacher awards, and money to support innovative ideas. (Mitgang, 1988)

There is little indication that the professional organizations of English language-arts teachers have had much impact on the designs for teacher evaluation so far, yet English teachers use language well, and as Dixon (1985) asserts "democratic power depends crucially on language." (p. 135) Elementary and secondary English language-arts teachers need to have a strong voice in the programs that determine quality instruction and quality teaching, and they are capable of exerting that influence.

Holt (1981) substantiates the need for an alliance between teachers and evaluation if instruction and learning are to improve:

Evaluation is an activity which cannot be meaningfully separated from curriculum action, and which is best left to those committing the action and therefore privileged to judge it. Formal evaluation is a needlessly elaborated search for inaccessible truths, and one which substitutes the drab routines of assessment and categorization for creative pleasures of planning, teaching, and learning. If instead we can promote the concept of the teacher as an autonomous professional, accountable to himself as a reasoning person, then curriculum will be a natural expression of the teacher's self understanding. (p. 175)

The National Governors' Association may be recognizing some of what Holt suggests. In *Time for Results: The Governors' 1991 Report on Education* ("Governors Propose," 1986) the state leaders call for fewer legislated requirements on school districts, allowing teachers and administrators a greater say in how money and time are spent and how staff and teaching materials are chosen. They state that greater employee involvement will raise morale and increase productivity. The report supports, however, the development of a national board on teaching standards and the governors' plan to reward schools for raising student achievement on mandated tests. "Educationally bankrupt schools," presumably those whose students do not reach stated minimums on tests, would be taken over by the state and reorganized. (p. 1)

In describing the growing power of state legislators, departments of education and governors' offices, Frazier (1987) states, "the educational train has returned from the nation's capitol, and for the foreseeable future the driving force for educational change is going to be the state." (p. 108) He warns:

If this country is to emerge from the present focus on education with a markedly stronger, self-correcting program in each of its elementary and secondary schools, then the first step in each state must be to reestablish the credibility of educators and thereby extend the focus of reform more strenuously to the school and school district level. Otherwise there will be no real and lasting change. (p. 109)

Do current teacher evaluation schemes add to the credibility of language arts educators? There is no evidence that they do. Is it reasonable to use evaluation instruments that make little use of the research and accumulated wisdom of the language arts field? Certainly not. Would language arts teachers support new initiatives in teacher evaluation that are based on what is known about good language arts instruction. Probably they would, although many would despair over massive expenditures for any type of teacher evaluation when there are critical instructional needs that go unattended year after year.

References

Basic Issues in the Teaching of English (1988). New York, N.Y.: Modern Language Association and National Council of Teachers of English.

Brandt, R. (1986). On the expert teacher: A conversation with David Berliner. *Educational Leadership, 44* (2), 4–9.

Carnegie Forum on Education and the Economy (1986). *A Nation Prepared: Teachers for the 21st Century.* Washington, D.C., Authors.

Certification project to lure top teachers. (1988, April 30). *Lansing (MI) State Journal,* (p. B:4).

Chaplin, M. (1986). The political issues since 1960. In M. Farmer (Ed.). *Consensus and Dissent* (pp. 113–125). Urbana, IL: National Council of Teachers of English.

Current developments in testing: Southern states compare SATs. (1987, January) NCTE *Council-Grams,* p. 6.

Dixon, J. (1985). Study group 1: Language, politics, and public affairs. In S. Tchudi (Ed.), *Language, schooling, and society* (pp. 135–144). Upper Montclair, NJ: Boynton/Cook.

Duke, D. & Stiggins, R. (1986). *Teacher evaluation: Five keys to growth.* Washington, D.C.: National Education Association.

Fiske, E. B. (1988, November 2). Lessons: A test for teachers dies as concern about professionalism rises. *New York Times,* p. 2:6.

Frazier, C. (1987). The 1980's: States assume educational leadership. *The ecology of school renewal.* Chicago, IL: National Society for the Study of Education.

Gallup, A. & Clark, D. (1987). The 19th annual Gallup poll of the public's attitudes toward the public school. *Phi Delta Kappan, 69* (1), 17–30.

Gardner, D. (1983). *A nation at risk.* Washington, D.C.: U.S. Department of Education.

Gitlin, A. & Smyth, J. (1988). 'Dominant' view of teacher evaluation and appraisal: an international perspective. *Journal of Education for Teaching, 14,* 237–257.

Governors propose new roles, responsibilities for teachers. (1986, November) NCTE *Council-Grams,* p. 1.

Hammes, R. R. (1985). Testing the teacher: A legal prospective. *Action in Teacher Education, 7* (3), 13–19.

Hoffman, J. V., Ed. (1986). *Effective teaching of reading: Research and practice.* Newark, DE: International Reading Association.

Holdzkom, D. (1987). Appraising teacher performance in North Carolina. *Educational Leadership, 44* (7), 40–44.

Holt, M. (1981). *Evaluating the evaluators.* London: Hodder and Stoughton.

Johnson, S. M. (1984). *Pros and cons of merit pay.* (Fastback No. 203). Bloomington, IN: Phi Delta Kappa Educational Foundation.

Joint Committee on Standards for Education Evaluation. (1988). *The Personnel Education Standards.* Beverly Hills, CA: Sage Publications.

Lloyd-Jones, R. & Lunsford, A. (Eds.). (1989). *The English coalition conference; Democracy through language.* Urbana, IL: National Council of Teachers of English.

Mandel, B. J. (Ed.). (1980). *Three Language Arts Curriculum Models: Pre-Kindergarten through College.* Urbana, IL: National Council of Teachers of English.

Mertz, M. P. (1987). *Report of the NCTE task force on teacher competency issues. English Education, 19,* 181–192.

Metropolitan Life survey of the American teacher. (1984). New York: Metropolitan Life Insurance Co.

Mitgang, L. (1988, May 22). Teachers work with spirits low, survey says. *Lansing (MI) State Journal,* p. A:3.

Moffett, James. (1968). Teaching the universe of discourse. Boston: Houghton Mifflin.

National Council of Teachers of English. (1987). *Handbook on Public Communication.* Urbana, IL: NCTE.

Planning group for certification board includes English teachers. (1987, January). NCTE *Council-Grams,* p. 5.

Popham, W. J. (1987). The merits of measurement-driven instruction. *Phi Delta Kappan, 68,* 679–682.

Professional Standards and Ethics Committee. (1986). *Guidelines for the Specialized Preparation of Reading Professionals.* Newark, DE: IRA.

Purves, A. (1977). Evaluating growth in English. In J. R. Squire (Ed.), *The teaching of English* (pp. 230–259). Chicago, IL: National Society for the Study of Education.

Resolutions passed at delegates assembly. (1988, June/July) IRA, *Reading Today, V* (6), 12–13.

Robinson, H. A. & Burrows, A. T. (1974). *Teacher effectiveness in elementary language arts: A progress report.* Urbana, IL: National Conference on Research in English.

Rubin, L. (1985). *Artistry in teaching.* New York: Random House. 1985.

Rudner, L. (1987). *What's happening in teacher testing.* Washington D.C.: U.S. Department of Education.

Rupley, W., Wise, B., Glogan, J. (1986). Research in effective teaching: an overview of its development. In Hoffman, J. Ed. (1986), *Effective Teaching of Reading.* Newark, Del: International Reading Association, 3–36.

Schlatter, F. (1985, March). Questions about merit pay and teacher evaluation that proponents must answer. NCTE *Slate* p. 1.

Shepard, L. A. & Kreitzer, A. E. (1987). The Texas Teacher Test. *Educational Researcher, 16* (6), 22–31.

Shive, J. J. (1988). Professional practices boards for teachers. *Journal of Teacher Education,* (39(6), 1–7.

Shugrue, M. F. (1968). *English in a decade of change.* New York: Western Publishing.

Smith, B. O., Peterson, D., & Micceri, T. (1987). Evaluation and professional improvement aspects of the Florida performance measurement system. *Educational Leadership, 44* (7), 16–19.

Squire, J. R. (1966). The national study of high school English programs. *College English, 27,* 613–619.

Squire, J. R. & Applebee, R. K. (1966). *A study of English programs in selected high schools which consistently educate outstanding students in English.* Urbana, IL: University of Illinois.

Sykes, G. (1987). Reckoning with the spectre. *Educational Researcher, 16* (6), 19–21.

Teacher assessments too simplistic. Shulman contends. (1988, May). ASCD *Update,* p. 1.

Viall, W. P. (1967). English teacher preparation study. *English Journal, 56,* 884–895.

Wise, A. E. & Darling-Hammond, L. (1985). Teacher evaluation and teacher professionalism. *Educational Leadership, 42* (4), 28–35.

Wolfe, D. (1986). *Guidelines for the preparation of teachers of English Language Arts.* Urbana, IL: National Council of Teachers of English.

·22·

CONTEMPORARY ISSUES AND FUTURE DIRECTIONS: ACTIVE LEARNERS AND ACTIVE TEACHERS

Courtney B. Cazden

The recent period of research on language learning has continued to be a period of research on the active learner. And it has been a period of continued unfortunate polarization, at least in the United States, between different views of the active teacher.

INSIGHTS AND LIMITATIONS IN RESEARCH ON THE ACTIVE LEARNER

The cognitive revolution of the last 25 years has dramatically changed our views of learning. Instead of inscription on an inert blank slate by means of the learner's practice and the culture's reinforcement, we now picture an active mind—from birth on—constructing knowledge through some internal integration of preconceptions and new information. In this psychological sea change, language acquisition has had pride of place as the most remarkable manifestation of human mental capacities (e.g. the work begun by Roger Brown [Kessel, 1988]). It has also been influential in arguments about language education.

Consider some examples of the complexity of the young language learner's task. Slobin (1982) illustrates this complexity by answers to the seemingly simple question, asked just after the action it refers to, "Who threw the ball?" Expressing the answer in English is such "first nature" to us that only a comparison of equivalent answers in other languages calls our attention to intrinsic complexities. In Table 22–1, showing answers in five languages, the three core semantic elements (agent, action and object) are indicated in capitals, and obligatory grammatical features are in square brackets.

The point of listing all these details is to show the complex learning that has to be done, and is done, by young children:

learning not only grammatical features of the language (including word order), but also those aspects of the event that must be attended to. The task is not simply to map verbal elements onto self-evident features of the nonverbal world, but also to learn which features of that world have to be encoded in language. In at least one of these non-English languages, children have to learn to attend to features that do not become "first nature" to us: the relation of the agent to the speaker (Turkish), whether the action was witnessed by the speaker (Turkish), the real-life gender of the agent (Hebrew) or the grammatical gender of the object (German), whether the past was recent or long ago (Kaluli), and whether the agent has made a transitive action and therefore must get a special "ergative" marking (Kaluli). Yet all these features are learned by children, without direct tuition, sometime during their preschool years.

Research on the acquisition of one language not included in the above set, a Bantu language of southern Africa (Demuth, 1989), provides an even more surprising contrast to our familiar experience. Sesotho is the language spoken by the people of Lesotho, a small African nation surrounded by South Africa although politically independent of it. In that language, there is a functional restriction in the grammar such that new information cannot be placed in the subject position in a sentence. Therefore, the question asking for information about who threw the ball would have to be asked in a passive construction, in English translation "The ball was thrown by whom?" And the corresponding answer would have to be, "The ball was thrown by Daddy."

Because of this functional restriction, passive constructions are much more common in everyday Sesotho conversation than in English, even in conversation with young children. And, pre-

TABLE 22–1. Answers to the Question, "Who Threw the Ball?"

English:	Daddy AGENT |focus|	threw ACTION |past|	the |definite|	ball. OBJECT	
German:	Vater AGENT |focus|	warf ACTION |past| |3rd per.| |sing.|	den |def.| |sing.| |masc.| |object|	Ball. OBJECT	
Hebrew:	Aba AGENT |focus|	zarak ACTION |past| |3rd per.| |sing.| |masc.|	et |obj. particle|	ha |def.|	kadur. OBJECT
Turkish:	Top- u OBJECT |def.| |obj.|	baba- AGENT	m |possessed by speaker|	at- ACTION	ti. |past| |3rd. per.| |sing.| |witnessed by speaker|
Kaluli: (Papua New Guinea)	Balow OBJECT	do- AGENT |possessed by speaker|	w |ergative agent|	sanditabe. ACTION |recent past|	

sumably because of this greater frequency, children growing up in that language community learn to use passives productively—that is, without an immediate model—at much younger ages. That is the surprising fact: Whereas children learning English, German and Hebrew do not control the comprehension and production of passive sentences until well into their elementary school years, children learning Sesotho do so before they are three. Whatever the intrinsic cognitive complexity of passive constructions, frequency of experience—in hearing and trying to say—seems to override the cognitive problems. There could be no better example of what Rommetveit calls, "the cultural development of attention" (1985, p. 194).

How is such success achieved? There is not yet agreement on the set of children's nonconscious mental "operating principles" that best fits this cross-linguistic evidence. (Compare Slobin, 1985 and Bowerman, 1985 for detailed discussion.) For example, while children may search for consistent patterns, they do learn irregular items, such as the irregular English past tense verb *threw*; they may search first for meaningful features, but they do learn the arbitrary markings of gender obligatory in many languages (as in the article preceding the object *ball* in German, above); and while they may search first for forms that are functionally necessary, they do learn complex constructions for which simpler alternatives are available, such as English tag questions (It's not hot, is it? or She can't go, can she?) for which "right?" would do just as well. No one language is harder or easier to learn overall; different languages, and the

cultural patterns with which they are used, are just hard and easy in different ways.

For us as teachers, this descriptive research on first language acquisition can be paralyzing or energizing. There is no question that young children's remarkable success contrasts dramatically with the considerably less universal success of much language learning—reading as well as writing—in school. As so, as one response to this disheartening contrast, we can let exaltation of the power inherent in all children's minds divert our attention from problems in the schools.

In a content analysis of 50 years of one journal, the *Harvard Educational Review* (HER), which in 1954 published Brown and Bellugi's first article on the language acquisition of Adam and Eve (pseudonyms for the first two children they studied) a sociologist of communication (Schudson, 1981) suggested why "language became a central concern of HER in the 1970s":

As educators have grown disheartened with the power of schools to affect students or change society, they have turned to a faith in the natural abilities of children to achieve for themselves. This emphasis is most evident in research on the child's capacity for learning language. . . .

That study of language touched on universal themes, revealed common human elements, and illuminated the biological nature of learners and, perhaps, their divine spark as well, was symbolized in Brown and Bellugi's decision to provide the two children they studied with the names Adam and Eve. . . .

An understanding of language, then, seemed to offer a way through social policy debacles and intellectual despair. A focus on language and the ability of the preschool child to show the most remarkable capacity for rule-governed behavior and the learning of exquisitely complex grammatical systems—regardless of genes, family background, or the quality of schooling—offered hope for the liberal position that the educational community had long tried to sustain. There was almost a new theology of education arising out of the study of language (pp. 20–21).

A second reason for paralysis, in addition to the disheartening contrast between learning at home and at school, is the stance of cultural relativity underlying much of the descriptive language acquisition research. For example, during discussion at the interdisciplinary symposium that resulted in the book, *Awakening to literacy* (Goelman, Oberg, & Smith, 1984), researchers could not even agree on a view of the child as an active learner. Editor Goelman reports:

Several speakers from the audience were eager to know if the participants could agree on a view of the child as an active learner. They referred to research findings presented at the symposium that supported this view and urged that if some sort of explicit, agreed-on-statement to this effect could be produced, it would be of great benefit for those working directly with children. The participants were not able to produce such an unequivocal statement. Schieffelin [the anthropologist who studied children learning Kaluli in Papua New Guinea] commented that this view of the child as an active learner is not universal across cultures or, in a historic sense, across time in our own culture. Such an unqualified statement, Schieffelin believed, might not be helpful when working with some children from a culture in which this view is not accepted within a larger cultural framework (Goelman in Goelman, Oberg, & Smith, p. 213).

If the researchers could not even agree on a view of the child as an active learner, they certainly could not agree on—and some were not even willing to discuss—implications for the role of the active teacher.

While such a cultural relativity stance is entirely appropriate for social science researchers, it is inherently impossible for teachers (Cazden, 1983). Teaching is value-laden, interventionist, work; and we have to answer the hard questions: What is wrong with school classrooms as environments for language learning? Why don't the language learning capacities that work so miraculously at home work the same magic in school? Why don't children who come to school speaking a nonstandard dialect of English acquire standard English? Why don't all children quickly pick up the ways of speaking expected in school (Cazden, 1988)—in Sharing Time, of large group lessons, or small group discussions? How can we help more children repeat their oral language learning successes in reading and writing in school? In short, how can the active child best be helped by the active teacher?

THE ACTIVE TEACHER

The most obvious implication from what we know about environments for successful language learning is epitomized by the report from Lesotho: children learn what they live, what they hear and try to speak, in a context of meaningful, functional use with people who care about them and have confidence that

they will learn. This, I assume, is the core message of what has come to be called "the whole language movement." As researcher, former primary school teacher, parent, and now grandparent, I'm convinced it is an essential part of the foundation for our work. But it seems to be only a part of that foundation, absolutely necessary but not sufficient for all children in school.

More than 20 years ago, psycholinguist John B. Carroll suggested answers to the same question I have asked here:

Might it not be possible for a child to learn to read [and, I would add, to write] in somewhat the same "natural" way that he learns his native language? Could reading perhaps be "acquired" through conditions and experiences analogous to those by which the child acquires his native language, rather than by the slow, careful teaching processes which we have thought necessary (1966, p. 577)?

After a careful comparison, Carroll concludes that school literacy programs could become more like the successful environments for oral language acquisition in specific ways:

1. The provision of a rich language environment that includes the full complexities, "irregularities and all;"
2. Writing and reading experienced as parallel and reciprocal processes, as speaking and comprehending speech are to the younger child; and
3. School reading and writing tasks "meaningful in the sense of having functional relations to [the child's] experiences, his desires, and his acts" (1966, p.579).

We get away without fully implementing Carroll's three requirements, yet without obvious failure, with those children whose out-of-school experiences provide them with "contexts-in-the mind" (Cazden, 1982) for more than decontextualized academic lessons. But for children without such experiences, Carroll's admonitions become more critical. And for all children, we still have a long way to go in providing the rich literacy environments he calls for. For example, we violate his second recommendation of reading and writing as parallel and reciprocal processes when we continue to provide fiction to read and yet assign expository texts to write. Children would not learn to speak a language they do not hear; how do we expect them to learn to write forms they do not read?

But no school provides a life-time for immersion in all the new literacy forms. And so Carroll also suggests that in school, "there is a certain efficiency to be gained" by teacher-initiated supplements:

In effect one appeals to the attention of the child on a periodic basis. The proper strategy, from this analysis, is to present a rich diet of reading [and again, I would add, writing] materials at every stage, but as a parallel tactic also to call the child's attention to particular items or patterns, in a systematic way, so as to facilitate his own developmental progress through spiraling levels of complexity (p. 581).

In the abstract, Carroll's recommendations may seem noncontroversial. But in specific cases, heated controversies continue more than 20 years later, seemingly unabated by needed research. The most obvious controversy is over the teaching of beginning reading—usually glossed as "phonics instruction" vs. "whole language" programs—for instance, between the recommendations of *Becoming a Nation of Readers* (Anderson Hiebert, Scott, & Wilkinson, 1985) and its critics in *Counterpoint and Beyond* (Davidson, 1988). Again and again, Davidson's authors argue against "contrived models of reading and writing experiences" (p. 18); they urge "focus on meaningful experiences and meaningful language rather than merely on isolated skill development" (p. 23); and they assert that "intensive formal instruction is totally inconsistent with the concept of emerging literacy" (p. 24). But there is still no research evidence that immersion in rich experience is sufficient for all children. And not all instruction is contrived, isolated, and inconsistent with development.

With respect to reading, Clay's research in New Zealand (1979, 1985) is a case in point. Her work is cited frequently in *Counterpoint and Beyond* (Davidson, 1988) to support whole language programs. But Clay and Cazden argue (in press) that Reading Recovery, the daily individual tutorial program for children who have not caught on to reading after one year in school (Clay, 1985), differs from whole language as well as phonics in significant ways:

It differs from most whole language programs in recognizing the need for temporary instructional detours in which the child's attention is called to particular cues available in speech or print. It differs from phonics in conceptualizing phonological awareness as an outcome of reading and writing rather than as their prerequisite, and in developing children's awareness of sounds in oral language rather than teaching letter/sound relationships. It differs from both in the frequent observation and recording of the reading and writing repertoire of the individual child as the basis for teacher initiative (as in choosing the next book) and response (in moment-to-moment decisions about when, and how, to help).

So, for example, during the writing segment of each daily tutorial, the teacher and child together transcribe a sentence that the child has composed. The teacher helps the child attend to the sounds in oral language by means of visual aids developed by Soviet psychologist Elkonin (1975). Then, once the sounds are figured out, and the letters written, the teacher asks the child to practice writing some of the words from visual memory. As the tutorial days and weeks go by, teacher help is reduced, and the child writes more and more alone.

In this program, children's sound awareness is developed in writing rather than reading, because getting to sounds from oral language rather than from letters builds on the resources children bring to literacy tasks. There are many assertions by Davidson's authors about the need to build on children's strengths. In the development of Reading Recovery, Clay and her colleagues have figured out how to do just that.

With respect to writing, three recent experiences may further explain my concern. First, language educators in both England and New Zealand have expressed ambivalence over the effect on classroom practice of descriptive U.S. research on children's invented spelling. Yes, they say, it is good to have this picture of children's intuitive knowledge. But unaccompanied by research on how to help children build on that knowledge,

the descriptive research seems to paralyze teachers and make them give up even reasonable and helpful aids.

Second, teachers who do in fact supplement rich immersion with mini-lessons may feel that the latter are old-fashioned and should not even be necessary in a perfect "whole language" world. For example, one 1st-grade teacher invited me to visit his classroom to see the writing program he was justifiably proud of. For more than an hour, the children wrote and then listened while many took turns reading aloud from "the author's chair." Only as I was leaving the room, with the teacher now engaged in shifting the class from writing to math, did I notice on the overhead projector a transparency with a child's story prepared for a class discussion of some editing conventions. Here was, in fact, a classroom with a rich main road to meaning *plus* what Cazden and Clay call an "instructional detour" to momentarily call the children's attention to matters of form. But that detour was not considered worthy of showing off, much as I would have valued it.

Finally, in two important articles, Black language arts educator Delpit (1986, 1988) argues for the important of deliberate teaching of the "culture of power" to Black children:

If you are not already a participant in the culture of power, being told explicitly the rules of that culture makes acquiring power easier.... Unless one has the leisure of a lifetime of immersion to learn them, explicit presentation makes learning immeasurably easier (1986, p. 283).

CONCLUDING COMMENTS

Delpit's phrase "explicit presentation" may be a critical point of controversy. In thinking about the implications of language acquisition research, philosopher Polanyi's (1964) distinction between focal and subsidiary awareness has been influential (e.g. Cazden, 1972). In one familiar example, when hammering in a nail, our focal attention is on the nail, with only subsidiary attention paid to the hammer. In early language acquisition, the child's focal attention is clearly on matters of intention and meaning; yet just as clearly, language structure—although attended to only subsidiarily—is acquired. So it is easy to conclude that focal attention to matters of language form should never be necessary; and that we can agree with the Dutchess who said to Alice in Wonderland, "and the moral of *that* is—'Take care of the sense, and the sounds will take care of themselves'."

But even Polanyi, much as he emphasized the importance of focal attention to meaning in all personal knowledge and skill, speaks also of the value of "maxims," or "rules of art:"

Maxims are rules, the correct application of which is part of the art which they govern. The true maxims of golfing or of poetry increase our insight into golfing or poetry and may even give valuable guidance to golfers or poets; but these maxims would instantly condemn themselves to absurdity if they tried to replace the golfer's skill or the poet's art. Maxims cannot be understood, still less applied by anyone not already possessing a good practical knowledge of the art.... Once we have accepted our commitment to personal knowledge, we can also face up to the fact that there exist rules which are useful only within the operation of our personal knowing, and can realize also how useful they can be as part of such acts (1964, p. 31).

Vygotsky's (1962) discussion of the relationship between spontaneous and scientific concepts fits here too. Scientific concepts (like Polanyi's maxims) can only be integrated into a foundation of spontaneous concepts that develop in the course of practical experience; but once that foundation is in place, scientific concepts can stimulate further development.

As a way of summing up his recommendations for an optimal mix of rich environment plus periodic instruction in the details of text forms, Carroll (1966) suggests the metaphor of "parallel tracks." Cazden and Clay (in press) suggest, instead, the metaphor of "instructional detours." The idea of a detour preserves what I believe to be essential: the prior establishment of a main road of meaningful language use, to which the detour is a momentary diversion when needed.

Or, in still another metaphorical contrast, we need to provide vitamins as well as food—vitamins that are concentrated forms of essential ingredients for those who need more specific nutrition than that provided by healthy diet alone.

To assert the need for such combined ingredients in an optimal environment for literacy learning in school does not tell us what to supply when, and how. But it does argue that this, rather than arguments between one extreme and the other, is where research and documentation—by teachers as well as university researchers—needs to be done. I have mentioned one program, Reading Recovery, because it exemplifies the kind of mix that I believe we need in other areas of English language arts, a mix that builds on children's strengths in comparable ways and continues the "cultural development of attention" (Rommetveit, 1985, p. 194) started at birth. Wolf (1988) documents analogous practices with older learners. We now know much about the active child; but we still have lots to learn about the active teacher.

References

Anderson, R. C., Hiebert, E. H., Scott, J. A., & Wilkinson, I. A. G. (1985). *Becoming a nation of readers.* Washington: National Institute of Education.

Bowerman, M. (1985) In D. I. Slobin (Ed.), *The crosslinguistic study of language acquisition, Vol. 2.* Hillsdale, NJ: Erlbaum.

Carroll, J. B. (1966). Some neglected relationships in reading and language. *Elementary English, 43,* 577–582.

Cazden, C. B. (1972). *Child language and education.* New York: Holt, Rinehart & Winston.

Cazden, C. B. (1982). Contexts for literacy: In the mind and in the classroom. *Journal of Reading Bheavior, 14,* 413–427.

Cazden, C. B. (1983). Can ethnographic research go beyond the status quo? *Anthropology and Education Quarterly, 14,* 33–41.

Cazden, C. B. (1988). *Classroom discourse: The Language of teaching and learning.* Portsmouth, N.H:Heinemann.

Clay, M. M. (1979). *Reading: The patterning of complex behavior.* Portsmouth, NH: Heinemann.

Clay, M. M. (1985). *The early detection of reading difficulties (3rd ed.).* Portsmouth, NH: Heinemann.

Clay, M. M. & Cazden, C. B. (in press) A Vygotskian interpretation of 'Reading Recovery.' In L. C. Moll (Ed.), *Vygotsky and education: Instructional implications and applications of socio-historical psychology.* Cambridge (UK) and New York: Cambridge University Press.

Davidson, J. L. (1988). *Counterpoint and beyond: A response to Becoming a Nation of Readers.* Urbana, Ill.: National Council of Teachers of English.

Delpit, L. (1986). Skills and other dilemmas of a progressive Black educator. *Harvard Educational Review, 56,* 379–385.

Delpit, L. (1988). The silenced dialogue: Power and pedagogy in educating other peoples' children. *Harvard Educational Review, 58,* 280–298.

Demuth, K. (1989). Maturation and the acquisition of the Sesotho passive. *Language, 65,* 56–80.

Elkonin, D. B. (1975). USSR. In J. Downing (Ed.), *Comparative reading: Cross-national studies of behavior and processes in reading and writing.* New York: Macmillan.

Goelman, H., Oberg, A., & Smith, F. (Eds.), (1984) *Awakening to literacy.* Portsmouth, NH: Heinemann.

Kessel, F. S. (Ed.) (1988). *The development of language and language researchers: Essays in honor of Roger Brown.* Hillsdale, NJ: Erlbaum, 1988.

Polanyi, M. (1964). *Personal knowledge: Towards a post-critical philosophy.* New York: Harper & Row (Torchbooks).

Rommetveit, R. (1985). Language acquisition as increasing linguistic structuring of experience and symbolic behavior control. In J. V. Wertsch (Ed.), *Culture, communication and cognition.* Cambridge (UK) and New York: Cambridge University Press.

Schudson, M. A. (1981). A history of the *Harvard Educational Review.* In J. R. Snarey, T. Epstein, C. Sienkiewicz & P. Zodhiates (Eds.), *Conflict and continuity: A history of ideas on social equality and human development.* Cambridge, MA: Harvard Educational Review Reprint Series No. 15.

Slobin, D. I. (1982). Universal and particular in the acquisition of language. In E. Wanner & L. R. Gleitman (Eds.), *Language acquisition: The state of the art.* Cambridge (UK)" Cambridge University Press.

Slobin, D. I. (1985). Crosslinguistic evidence for the Language-Making Capacity. In D. I. Slobin (Ed.), *The crosslinguistic study of language acquisition,* Vol. 2. Hillsdale, NJ: Erlbaum.

Vygotsky, L. S. (1962). *Thought and language.* Cambridge: MIT Press.

Wolf, D. (1988). *Reading reconsidered: Literature and literacy in high school.* New York: College Entrance Examinations Board.

Part

·IV·

ENVIRONMENTS FOR ENGLISH LANGUAGE ARTS TEACHING

·23·

THE ELEMENTARY SCHOOL CLASSROOM

Eileen Tway

Looking at the elementary school classroom as a learning environment can bring unexpected revelations. On the one hand, everyone seems to know that a classroom is for learning. It is the kind of knowledge that exists in the public domain and is taken for granted. On the other hand, few stop to consider whether the classroom by its very nature is really conducive to learning. A close look at what happens in the classroom reveals that classrooms are crowded places full of distracting events and that often individual students do not have much active learning time (Doyle, 1980, 1986; Jackson, 1968).

CHANGES IN CLASSROOM RESEARCH

Teachers have long been aware of the need to consider classroom environment as a factor in teaching, but often their consideration has been confined to cosmetic little gestures, making the room attractive or making adjustments to insure physical comfort, such as pulling down shades or turning up the thermostat. Yet these efforts are surface ones. There is a "deep" environment that a close look at classrooms can probe, and this deep environment consists of the social (and emotional) setting that influences the intellectual climate of the classroom. This climate has an effect on all the learning that goes on in the classroom, and, certainly, on language learning.

Philip W. Jackson (1968) took a close look at "life in classrooms" some 20 years ago to find what it was really like in the daily course of events, mostly humdrum, that make up the major part of school life. Jackson went into elementary school classrooms and spent considerable time observing what went on there, and his close-look research showed the unpredictable and sometimes chaotic nature of everyday classroom life. He pointed out that researchers who do not work in actual classroom environments (and most did not at that time, 20 or more years ago) are missing the social realities of classroom life. Researchers of two decades or more ago tended to stay in laboratory or clinical situations where they had more control over the variables involved, or they studied approaches to teaching "long distance" and never knew all of the variables involved.

Jackson's observational kind or research was one of the pioneer studies of its kind, and he predicted then that future researchers would do more observational research, working right inside classrooms.

Over the past two decades, Jackson's predictions have been fulfilled. Janet Emig (1971) made case-study observational research respectable as good research design and gave new direction to writing research in her shift from examining student's written products to studying the ongoing writing process in the secondary classroom. Donald Graves (1973, 1983) led the way to studying the writing process in the elementary classroom, and his followers are now almost legion.

As researchers have moved into the classroom to observe what actually goes on there, they have had to give up prior assumptions, or what Philip W. Jackson (1968) calls "comfortable beliefs" about what classroom life is really like. The classroom is different from a laboratory where outside distractions or variables can be largely controlled. The classroom situation is largely unpredictable, subject to all kinds of distractions and interruptions, such as nosebleeds, intercom messages, misunderstood directions, and so on. Effective teachers have to be opportunistic and make the most of the unexpected (Jackson, 1968, 166–167; Florio & Clark, 1982).

As researchers became more open to the social realities of the classroom, they began to look at social interaction between teacher and students and among students, since teaching seemed apparently to be a series of interactions all the day through. Research began to give a descriptive picture of what went on in classrooms. This new descriptive research brought together several disciplines, including sociology and anthropology, to aid in taking a close look at classroom interaction. Wilkinson (1982) refers to a "new wave" of multidisciplinary research on the functions of language in the classroom. She says,

Within the last decade (1972-1982), a new paradigm of research has developed for the study of social interaction in the classroom: the sociolinguistic approach. This approach focuses on descriptions of students' and teachers' use of language in the classroom. These descriptions provide us with a richer understanding of realities in classrooms . . . (p. xiii).

425

Fillion and Brause (1987) explain the new directions in research as follows: "In language education, the burgeoning research into cognitive and linguistic development has shifted attention from the teacher to the learner, and from learning as the retention of information or performance of discrete skills to learning as an active, dynamic process" (p. 203).

In short, classroom research has changed in the last 20 years from long-distance to close-up, and from a focus on knowledge gained (product) to a focus on how knowledge is gained (process). As the studies moved away from hypothesis testing to determine whether certain materials or approaches led to improved student performance and toward observation of how the materials or approaches influenced learning, it became clear that the classroom itself could influence the teaching-learning process. In fact, the classroom environment could be arranged in a way that made it an effective instructional tool (Loughlin & Suina, 1982). Interaction assessment has shown the classroom in its event context and has strong implications for providing for events that lead to language learning, sometimes called "literacy events" by the researchers (Cazden, 1986, p. 436; Lund & Duchan, 1988, p. 7).

In spite of research about language as social interaction, writing as a process, literacy events, and classroom environment as instructional tool, many elementary school classrooms still remain barren places where the teacher does most of the language producing and the class rarely gets beyond the supporting skills of spelling, handwriting, and grammar in language arts. Skills are developed out of context with nothing in the way of real language to support (Mehan, 1979; Wilkinson, 1982).

Research on language development in context is what this chapter is all about, and while much is still unknown about language learning and cannot be observed, new research is giving promising direction. In 1968, Philip W. Jackson suggested not only more direct, observational research, but also more research by teacher-practitioners in the classroom. This, too, has come to pass, and the 1980s have brought an era of collaborative classroom research between professional researchers and professional practitioners (See Goswami & Stillman, 1987; Mohr & MacLean, 1987.) With all of the promising classroom research in teaching-learning language arts today, limits must be set for the discussion in this chapter. The limits are presented below.

LIMITS ON A BROAD TOPIC

The elementary classroom as environment for teaching and learning language arts is a broad topic and can cover anything that happens in the classroom setting from teaching strategies to learning styles. Here, the focus will be on the classroom environment as instructional tool and on language learning as social interaction.

Studies of early (or first) language learning of preschool children have shown that an immersion-in-language environment is essential for language acquisition. (See Hoskisson & Tompkins, 1987, Chapter One for a discussion of studies of preschool language acquisition.) In school, the environment must be manipulated to provide immersion in language-rich experiences. Cazden calls this kind of manipulation, or influence, "environmental assistance" (Cazden, 1972). Loughlin and Martin (1987) speak of the "arranged environment." They say, "The arranged environment functions as an instructional tool, complementing and reinforcing other strategies the teacher uses to support children's learning" (p. 6). Loughlin and Suina (1982) report that the provision and arrangement of materials, such as trade books, influence their use and potential in encouraging student learning. This chapter will elaborate on these studies and others that show the potential of the classroom environment to influence the teaching and learning of language arts. As subtopics of "environment as instructional tool," class size and classroom climate will also be considered.

The interdisciplinary approach to classroom research has shown that language learning depends on social interaction (Johnson & Johnson, 1975). It follows that language learning in school is inextricably bound up with the classroom environment as scene for interaction. Hoskisson and Tompkins (1987) say that "instead of dispensing knowledge, the teacher must engage students with experiences . . . that require them to modify their cognitive structures and construct their own knowledge" as they interact with and adapt to their environment (p. 2; see also Piaget, 1969). Teaching becomes a linguistic process in which individuals in a classroom interact with language and each other as they move toward collaborative constructions of meaning (Cazden, 1986; Erickson, 1986; Genishi, McCarrier & Nussbaum, 1988).

A subtopic of the interactional environment as an aid to instruction will be "the school and classroom as a community of learners." Loughlin and Martin (1987) sum up the current emphasis on community by saying, "After a number of decades of research focusing on individual learners as if they were isolated from others, concern is once again turned to issues related to the classroom community as a social entity" (Foreword, p. xiii). Certainly language learning, while the creative activity of each learner, is not something that happens in individual isolation. It is a function of communication, and communication implies, even requires, two or more participants. These participants form a language community.

This chapter also will look at how language is learned in the classroom community. Barr and Dreeben (1983) stress that learning is a function of groups in a classroom. Wood (1984) says that in group work, "students are more intensely involved in learning because their chances of oral participation are increased" (p. 117). Interaction analysis of oral participation in the classroom enables researchers to determine who gets the talking time and what kinds of talk occur (Flanders, 1970). The results of interaction analysis are often surprising, especially in considering the ratio of teacher talk to student talk.

Cazden (1988) has used interaction analysis and other techniques to study classroom discourse. She points out, "Just as all speech has an accent, even though we are not made aware of our own until we travel somewhere where there is a different norm, so patterns of teacher-student interactions in typical classroom lessons are cultural phenomena . . ." (p. 67). Some children are culturally equipped to adapt better to the language life of the classroom than others are. Studies, such as those by

Heath (1983), show the need for adjustments on the part of teacher and students to make the classroom a rich language environment for all students. All of these considerations and more will be dealt with in this chapter under the topic, "Oral Communication in the Classroom Context."

Writing is "coming up on the outside," not overtaking reading yet as a prime concern in elementary education, but making a good show today in the race for attention. Research is showing the importance of writing as a way of learning and as an integral part of classroom life (Calkins, 1983; Graves, 1983; Murray, 1984a; Tway, 1984). Still, actual classroom practice is a long way from the realization of the ideal of the writing classroom, where real writing is a matter of course. According to a 1986 report on the 1984 National Assessment of the Writing Achievement of American School Children, very few school children are expected to write as much as a paragraph in continuous composition; they are evidently too busy circling words, underlining, and checking off on worksheets (Applebee, Langer, & Mullis, 1986).

Lucy Calkins (1983) said she started out her research in writing, purposely ignoring reading, because reading had had such a lion's share of attention for so long, but she found she could not ignore it; reading was there side by side with writing. Calkins was not alone in her discovery. Researchers in language learning have discovered, or rediscovered, writing and reading connections. Tway (1985) writes, "As glad as teachers of writing may be to see writing getting new respect they will want to guard against viewing writing in isolation" (p. 1). Goodman and Goodman (1983) advise that "people not only learn to read by reading and write by writing but they also learn to read by writing and write by reading" (p. 592). This chapter will look at research about the classroom as writing community and the interactions with and between writing and reading under the topic, "The Classroom as Context for Literacy Events."

THE CLASSROOM ENVIRONMENT AS INSTRUCTIONAL TOOL

As studies have moved from the laboratory to the real world of the classroom (see David Bloome, "Studying Literacy in the Real World," 1987), researchers have discovered the efficacy of the classroom environment as instructional tool. The classroom can be set up in such a way that it issues an invitation to learning. When books are attractively displayed, writing materials and tools are readily available, mobiles, bulletin boards, and posters offer challenges to curiosity, and interesting objects give children something to talk about and act upon, and when all of this is aesthetically arranged, not crowded or cluttered, then the classroom itself is part of the instructional method. Loughlin and Martin (1987) call this the arranged environment.

Other kinds of environments exist, of course, such as the built (architectural), the natural, and the social, psychological, institutional, and management aspects of settings for learning (Loughlin & Martin, p. 6). However, authors Loughlin and Martin say, "The arranged environment functions as an instructional tool, complementing and reinforcing other strategies the teacher uses to support children's learning" (p. 6). The use of the arranged environment is not always considered in elementary classrooms according to some observers. Yetta Goodman (1987) (see Foreword of *Supporting Literacy,* p. xiv) states that "instructional activities have been planned as if elementary school students are learning literacy in a vacuum . . ." Yet there is more and more support for filling the vacuum and creating a rich literacy environment in classrooms (see Barr & Dreeben, 1983; Loughlin & Martin, 1987). And still more needs to be done. Barr and Dreeben say, "While only the most exceptional of teacher effectiveness studies treat relations among the elements of instruction, virtually none identifies a connection between the activities of teachers and the characteristics of the setting in which teaching takes place—the classroom" (p. 34).

Studies that do consider the instructional setting include the classroom observation studies of Loughlin and Suina, 1982; Loughlin and Martin, 1987, mentioned above; Barr and Dreeben, 1983. also mentioned above; and McKenzie, 1985.

The arrangements of furniture, materials, centers, and art work of any classroom shape the behaviors of students and teachers by "giving very strong messages, encouraging them to act in particular ways," according to Loughlin and Martin (1987, p. 7). For example, a bright and colorful arrangement of a variety of books in easily accessible classroom space gives the message, "Come and read," and the provision of writing tools near subject area centers, such as science tables and social studies reference shelves, encourages students to make connections between the materials and to keep records, write letters, develop reports, and so on.

Students are less likely to make connections between materials or to combine them or to use them effectively when materials are widely scattered, according to Loughlin and Suina (1982). Much more direct teacher instruction is needed if scattered materials are to be combined in learning activities. When materials are arranged so that connections are easily inferred, teacher assignments are not required, and the teacher is freed to work with individual students or to "float" around the classroom as a guide, wherever needed. Loughlin and Martin (1987) advocate the placement of materials where possibilities for their use exist. This is not a "scattering" of materials, but carefully placed combinations that encourage effective use. Loughlin and Martin describe these careful placements as "decentralizing literacy materials" (p. 38).

Loughlin and Martin report on decentralizing literacy materials as follows:

The distribution of materials in small quantities in several locations stimulates literacy related to the activities involving other provisions in the area. In most literacy environments, holders containing a small number of common tools and materials for literacy are arranged with or near all other provisions. Two or three pencils, markers, and crayons, with recording materials such as pads or typing paper, some word lists and a dictionary for reference, and a few joining and display tools in each collection are often enough to remind children to report, display, or make notes about their activities. . . . Teachers in functioning literacy environments seem to place literacy stimuli in all areas, including some not commonly considered in connection with growth in literacy. Art materials, blocks, number rods, playground equipment, photo albums, window sill plants, sand tables, nature study collections, calculators, newspaper clippings, and any other imaginable information sources or materials collections seem to function as natural starting places for the uses of literacy (p. 39).

At any rate, Loughlin and Martin find that decentralizing literacy materials for better accessibility minimizes crowding or traffic congestion in classrooms and has a positive influence on use of the materials.

Jennie Ingham (1982) tells of a study in which sheer numbers of materials were used to "flood" a learning environment. She describes the Bradford Book Flood Experiment in which large numbers of additional books were made available to middle school children to see whether access to books in great numbers would improve reading development. The findings showed that a large number of additional books in a classroom is a necessary, but not sufficient, condition for reading improvement. The way in which the books were presented in the classroom seemed to be a key factor. Much depends on whether the books are stored in cupboards away from sight or whether they are displayed invitingly and attractively for a "book flood" to be effective.

Teachers' ability to place materials strategically in the environment is evidently crucial to the productivity of a language arts classroom. Smith (1978) argues that *immersion* in the language environment is essential for language acquisition. Teachers who provide book floods, writing centers near places that stimulate writing, experiences for discussion, etc., are giving the kind of help that Cazden (1972) calls "environmental assistance" and aiding students in continued language acquisition.

In planning the arranged environment, or environmental assistance, teachers must adapt their view of the classroom to the view of a child (Loughlin, 1977). Loughlin suggests that "because of differences in size, role, movement patterns, and experience background, adults and children have different visual and spatial experiences in the same environment; they occupy different spaces, see different surroundings, and perceive the content of the environment differently" (Loughlin & Martin, 1987, p. 6). Teachers who project their views of the classroom from a child's standpoint can better understand the effects of environmental arrangements. Even small adjustments such as moving posters and bulletin boards displays to child's eye level or moving alphabet writing models from the top of the chalkboard to child's eye level, perhaps even changing to individual desk models for easy reference, improve the learning environment.

Desks that can be moved together to form tables where from 2 to 4 students can work in community provide for far more language interaction than desks left in individual isolation all lined up in rows facing the teacher's desk. Loughlin and Suina (1982) report that "teachers can use spatial organization to design settings that stimulate language interaction, shelter a working child, or foster group inquiry" (p. 7). Flexible furniture arrangements can give whole group circle set-ups for face to face interaction, individual study carrels are needed, and small-group work spaces.

McCroskey (1980) reports that research with shy and apprehensive children suggests that a classroom that promotes communication helps children function more effectively in the learning environment (pp. 239–244). All children, not just the shy and apprehensive, actually benefit from arrangements that free them from isolation from their peers—that particular kind of loneliness in a crowd that is often found in schools—and enable them to interact with and learn from each other. Yetta Goodman (1987) says, "The classroom is greater than the sum of its parts. The classroom is more than one child plus one child plus one child. It is a community" (p. xiii). The classroom is also greater than the sum of its parts—teacher, students, space, furniture, materials, and so forth—in that beyond the surface interactions there is an atmosphere of perceived intent, feelings, rapport or lack of rapport, and degree of emotional security that could be called "classroom climate."

Classroom Climate

Seiler, Schuelke, and Lieb-Brilhart (1984) say, "Every school or classroom generates an atmosphere, which is often not articulated explicitly, but which leaves a distinct impression of the interrelationships of the educators and the students" (p. 19). The manner in which these interrelationships are conducted affects the classroom climate. Research on school climate shows that some climates promote learning while others do not, and may even hinder the learning process. According to Seiler, Schuelke, and Lieb-Brilhart, "evidence shows that effective and ineffective schools differ in the climates that they have established in a number of characteristics: openness vs. defensiveness, confidence vs. fear, acceptance vs. rejection, belonging vs. alienation, trust vs. suspicion, high expectations vs. low expectations, order vs. chaos, and control vs. frustration" (p. 19). These differences have strong implications for the quality of communication in a classroom. One that seems especially pertinent for success in language learning and which has a lot to do with influencing the other factors is the difference made by high expectations vs. low expectations.

Squires (1980) says, "If teachers believe that all of the students in their classroom will succeed in passing the grade, learning to read, or graduating from high school, then it appears that the teacher is more likely to structure the environment in accordance with that expectation" (p. 34). The high-expectation environment communicates an important message to children: *they can learn*. In the learning climate with positive expectations that children can succeed, the children behave accordingly, with more confidence, more inner motivation, more supportive cooperation with each other, and more self-respect.

Self-respect, or a positive self-concept, on the part of students is one of the most important outcomes of a positive classroom climate. Beane, Lipka, and Ludewig (1980) report that self-concept is related to productive social interaction among peers, active participation in class discussions, self-direction in learning, and strong school achievement in general (p. 85). It appears particularly important to foster the self-concept of children with learning disabilities who have repeatedly experienced frustration with their perceived lack of ability to succeed in the classroom. Dunn (1985) reports that learning disabled students differ significantly from high achievers on their perceptions of the classroom learning environment, especially in areas of perceived difficulty and class cohesiveness. He suggests that classroom intervention programs for learning disabled students should take into consideration the effects of the perceived environment. Positive expectations for these students and materials that insure step-by-step success should go far toward influencing favorable perceptions of the learning environment, or climate.

Many teachers believe that they will be justified in having higher expectations for students and that their classroom climate will be greatly improved with reduced class size. Research findings support the belief that climate is improved, but not that student achievement necessarily improves with smaller class size (Vincent & Olson, 1972; Cahen, Filby, McCutcheon, & Kyle, 1983).

Class Size

Researcher Leonard S. Cahen and his colleagues (1983) report on three years of collaborative research on class size and instruction. Their study was conducted in several sites and sponsored by the National Institute of Education through its Teaching and Learning Division. In this comprehensive study, changes did occur when class size was reduced. Cahen, et al., say, "Teachers and students were generally happier and more productive in the smaller classes ... On the other hand, the process of instruction looked very much the same, regardless of class size. The machinery functioned more smoothly, but the design of the machine remained the same" (p. 201). For example, in smaller classes, more individual attention was given to students in the form of more contact time, better record keeping of student progress, and closer physical proximity in group lessons. Teachers felt they could meet individual needs better, have time to talk personally to students, and be more supportive. Teachers were happier because they did not feel as pressured as they did when surrounded by crowds of students.

As one teacher put, "There is more of me left at the end of the day" (p. 204). As for the students, they were more attentive, more productive, and had more free time to explore different activities. However, these kinds of changes are not necessarily reflected on achievement tests; thus, sometimes it is difficult to show the true benefits of class size reduction. Cahen et al., say, "These factors may have long-term effects not in evidence on short-term achievement tests" (p. 206).

Another factor that may influence student achievement is whether or not the teacher takes advantage of reduced class size to change instructional strategies. In the study by Cahen, et al., teachers had more time for individual students, but they did not individualize the curriculum. Students in all classes were grouped for instruction in reading and mathematics as usual. Teachers did not attempt to individualize programs. "What teachers did do, however," according to the researchers, "was provide more individual contact time in support of the ongoing program" (p. 205). Changes in the curriculum were predominantly in the area of enrichment; the basic program remained the same. There were special afternoon programs, for example, but these were not additions that were integrated into the core curriculum.

Perhaps if teachers are given time to anticipate and plan for reduced class size, they would be more likely to enrich their classroom programs in ways that are integrative and more effectively individualized. Cahen, et al., speculate that their teacher-subjects did not have adequate time to prepare for smaller-class instruction and observe that change occurs slowly, especially when teachers have developed one kind of approach with which they have become comfortable over the years.

Current research is still unclear about whether or not student achievement in language arts or any other subject area improves directly due to smaller class size, but it does seem to be clear that the classroom climate improves with smaller class size and, thus, indirectly students may be encouraged to achieve more (see Glass, Cahen, Smith, & Filby, 1982, Chapter 3).

It is also evident that it is what teachers do within the framework of time and class size that counts, not the mere existence of small classes and big blocks of time (Fillion & Brause, 1987). Again, it becomes the responsibility of the teacher to make the most of the classroom environment as an aid to instruction.

Putting so much responsibility for creating a good classroom environment on teachers' shoulders could be interpreted as an unfair burden, but, it also can be seen as part of the teacher's role to create an environment conducive to learning. However, in reality, teachers cannot manipulate every aspect of the environment. Mayher and Brause (1986) say, "As individual teachers we can't control every aspect of the learning environment provided by the school we work in. But we can begin to change ourselves. And when we've changed ourselves, we can begin to change our classrooms" (p. 620). In effect, then, Mayher and Brause are saying that teachers can change their behaviors and expectations to make the most of the environment they are given. The teacher is key in developing the classroom environment as instructional tool—through manipulating materials, arranging physical space, and capitalizing on opportunities in the setting, such as reduced class size, to personalize instruction.

The Whole Environment: The Classroom and Beyond as Community

In examining the physical and educational characteristics of a classroom to see how conducive they are to learning, it is useful to have guidelines for observation. Moira G. McKenzie (1985) writes about "Classroom Contexts for Language and Literacy" and suggests that the following factors must be considered:

1. The whole environment of the classroom and school,
2. What is happening at a particular time,
3. The subject studied,
4. The books and materials used,
5. The ongoing activities,
6. The participants, that is the teacher (and any other adults) and the children, their roles and role relationships, i.e., the changing parts they play in interaction (p. 235).

More specifically, a literacy stimuli checksheet may be used by teachers and researchers to help them be more aware of what the classroom environment offers and to give them a tool

SURVEY RECORDING SHEET

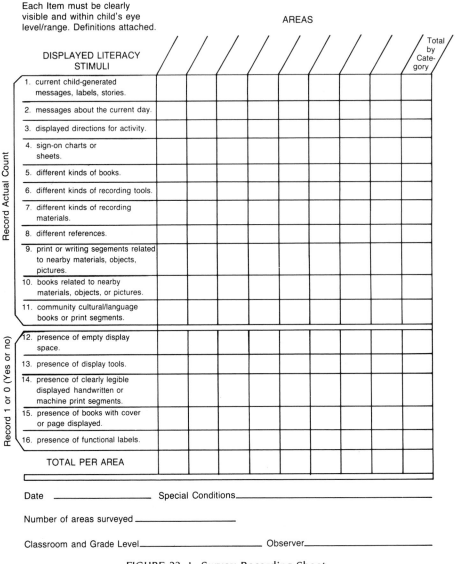

Each Item must be clearly visible and within child's eye level/range. Definitions attached.

AREAS

DISPLAYED LITERACY STIMULI

Record Actual Count

1. current child-generated messages, labels, stories.
2. messages about the current day.
3. displayed directions for activity.
4. sign-on charts or sheets.
5. different kinds of books.
6. different kinds of recording tools.
7. different kinds of recording materials.
8. different references.
9. print or writing segments related to nearby materials, objects, pictures.
10. books related to nearby materials, objects, or pictures.
11. community cultural/language books or print segments.

Record 1 or 0 (Yes or no)

12. presence of empty display space.
13. presence of display tools.
14. presence of clearly legible displayed handwritten or machine print segments.
15. presence of books with cover or page displayed.
16. presence of functional labels.

Total by Category

TOTAL PER AREA

Date _____ Special Conditions_____

Number of areas surveyed _____

Classroom and Grade Level_____ Observer_____

FIGURE 23–1. Survey Recording Sheet.

for evaluating the language-arts environment. Loughlin and Martin (1987) have developed a survey recording sheet that they find useful (see Figure 23–1).

This survey sheet will show where the stimuli for literacy are in the environment, the relative emphasis on different categories of literacy stimuli, such as books available or writing (recording) tools, the variety of stimuli, and the quantitative amount of support for literacy in the environment—plus the evidence that the outside-of-classroom community is represented (or not) in the classroom.

Researchers and teachers recognize that the classroom environment is affected by the larger setting around it. The school itself and the school administrators most certainly affect what happens in the classroom. King (1984) suggests that administra-

tors have an important role in developing a sense of community within a school. She says that academic achievement and social interactions are affected by issues of school climate and that administrators need to ensure a good working climate by encouraging greater discussion and participation on the part of all the members of the school population. Other studies support King's work and show the effects of various administrative behaviors on the total school environment including a study by Burford (1986) that shows even a principal's sense of humor can play an important part in the "robustness" of a school environment. The research indicates that as people become more involved in decision-making at the school and classroom level, they also become more involved in the life of the school (King, 1984).

As more and more studies look closely at "life in classrooms," it becomes clear that it is a community life that revolves around social interaction (Goswami & Stillman, 1987). Children who are involved in the decision-making process and encouraged to initiate interaction among themselves, as well as respond to teacher-initiated interaction, have more of a vested interest in classroom life. Graves (1983) speaks of the importance of students' "ownership" of their writing through being enabled to write about topics that are "real" and important to them and that they choose for themselves. This kind of ownership can extend to the classroom itself if children are part of the decision-making process. They will take pride in their classroom as "owners" instead of tenants. Interaction in this kind of classroom will be rich and purposeful.

LANGUAGE LEARNING AS SOCIAL INTERACTION: ORAL COMMUNICATION IN THE CLASSROOM CONTEXT

"In order to participate effectively in the life of classrooms, children must have more than academic knowledge alone" (Wilkinson, 1982, p. 4).

To do well in classrooms children must understand the communication context of the classroom and how to operate socially within the context. Language learning in particular comes about through social interaction. Recent enthnographical and discourse analysis studies "have produced a deeper appreciation of classrooms as dynamic environments in which participants and processes interact in complex ways to influence both instruction and learning," according to Fillion and Brause (1987), p. 203.

Courtney Cazden's studies of classroom discourse analysis show the complexities involved, even in everyday spoken language, or "talk." Cazden (1988) says that the study of classroom discourse is the study of situated language use in a social setting. She points out the special features of spoken language in the classroom setting. "First," Cazden says, "spoken language is the medium by which much teaching takes place, and in which students demonstrate to teachers much of what they have learned" (p. 2). Second, she observes that in classrooms, unlike other social situations, such as restaurants or buses, "one person, the teacher, is responsible for controlling all the talk that occurs . . .," and, third, she notes, "spoken language is an important part of the identities of all the participants" (p. 3).

Early research on analyzing classroom talk proved enlightening to researchers and teachers alike. Flanders' (1970) work on interaction analysis was a foundation on which many researchers (including Cazden) built as they studied oral communication in the classroom. Flanders' system of interaction analysis (see Figure 23–2) enabled researchers, and teachers, too, to determine the kinds of interaction going on in the classroom and the proportion of time devoted to the various kinds. It was often a revelation to teachers and observers to see the ratio of teacher talk to student talk and especially the ratio of teacher-initiated talk to student-initiated talk (initiation as opposed to response).

Flanders and those who worked with him did not put any

kind of judgment or priority on one kind of interaction over another; rather, they focused on the variety of kinds, the flexibility in the range of spoken language, the ratio of controlling kinds of teacher talk to freeing, encouraging kinds, and other ratios. It is a numerical, tally-taking kind of system that leaves interpretation to the teachers involved or to other observers.

Flanders does classify the categories of teacher talk according to initiation (direct influence) and response (indirect influence). Most interpreters, including Flanders, agree that when the teacher is direct, it minimizes children's freedom to respond and when the teacher is indirect, it maximizes the freedom of children in their oral expression. However, these interpretations or beliefs are not meant to be judgmental in the absolute sense, because there are times when the teacher's role calls for direct influence. What is gained from the analysis of direct versus indirect categories is an awareness of freeing and directing behaviors and whether or not there is some kind of balance in these behaviors; that is, approximately as much indirect as direct behavior. Both kinds of teacher-talk have their place, but teacher-response and indirect influence should not be neglected or relegated to second place, most interpreters stress (see Seiler, Schuelke, & Lieb-Brilhart, 1984, pp. 187–204).

Cultural differences among students have been found to affect the way they use language in the classroom, language growth, and freedom of expression. It appears to be more difficult for some students than others to be "free" to use their language in the classroom (Cazden, 1988). Interaction analysis, then, needs also to take into account whether the teacher directs and responds differently for different students. The tallies do not show this information on the Flanders scale, but observers and teachers (doing self-evaluation) could be especially alert for this phenomenon and keep field notes about which students receive more controlling teacher talk and which get more "freeing" teacher talk. Videotapes of classroom oral interaction are especially useful for this kind of analysis. Observers can replay the interaction to check the accuracy of their findings, and teachers can observe their own behaviors from a more detached point of view.

Cazden (1988) says that the patterns of teacher-student interactions in typical classroom lessons are cultural phenomena. She discusses possible culturally-related disadvantages for some children in their classroom language use as follows:

In some of its aspects, the demands of classroom discourse are new to all children. In the classroom, the group is larger than even the largest family gathered at meals, and so getting a turn to talk is much harder. When one does get a turn, acceptable topics for talk are more restricted and more predetermined by someone else. . . . But beyond these commonalities, some children may be at a special disadvantage. For some children there will be greater cultural discontinuity, greater sociolinguistic interference, between home and school (pp. 67–68).

A page from a student-teacher's log will serve to illustrate how an inexperienced or otherwise unaware teacher may react to cultural differences. The teacher in this case was observing in a small-town school in Ohio. She wrote about two boys who were both language-different in the small-rural-town community.

Flanders' Interaction Analysis Categories* (FIAC)

Teacher Talk	**Response**	1. *Accepts feeling.* Accepts and clarifies an attitude or the feeling tone of a pupil in a nonthreatening manner. Feelings may be positive or negative. Predicting and recalling feelings are included.
		2. *Praises or encourages.* Praises or encourages pupil action or behavior. Jokes that release tension, but not at the expense of another individual; nodding head, or saying "Um hm?" or "go on" are included.
		3. *Accepts or uses ideas of pupils.* Clarifying, building, or developing ideas suggested by a pupil. Teacher extensions of pupil ideas are included but as the teacher brings more of his own ideas into play, shift to category five.
	Initiation	4. *Asks questions.* Asking a question about content or procedure, based on teacher ideas, with the intent that a pupil will answer.
		5. *Lecturing.* Giving facts or opinions about content or procedures; expressing *his own* ideas, giving *his own* explanation, or citing an authority other than a pupil.
		6. *Giving directions.* Directions, commands, or orders to which a pupil is expected to comply.
		7. *Criticizing or justifying authority.* Statements intended to change pupil behavior from nonacceptable to acceptable pattern; bawling someone out; stating why the teacher is doing what he is doing; extreme self-reference.
Pupil Talk	**Response**	8 *Pupil-talk — response.* Talk by pupils in response to teacher. Teacher initiates the contact or solicits pupil statement or structures the situation. Freedom to express own ideas is limited.
	Initation	9. *Pupil-talk — initiation.* Talk by pupils which they initiate. Expressing own ideas; initiating a new topic; freedom to develop opinions and a line of thought, like asking thoughtful questions; going beyond the existing structure.
Silence		10. *Silence or confusion.* Pauses, short periods of silence and periods of confusion in which communication cannot be understood by the observer.

*There is *no* scale implied by these numbers. Each number is classificatory; it designates a particular kind of communication event. To write these numbers down during observation is to enumerate, not to judge a position on a scale.

FIGURE 23–2. Flanders' Interaction Analysis Categories* (FIAC).

One child in the class has a dialect which reflects his origin. He speaks with a severe country accent. His vocabulary is filled with words such as gonna, didn', and git. He frequently says, "don't got nutin'." He lives in the country and has told me about his 'coon dogs. His relatives live in Kentucky and they visit there frequently. His formal and informal language is more or less the same.

I am particularly intrigued by [another] child's language because it reflects his thorough and aware nature. His language is more formal than informal in most situations. He is very descriptive and likes to tell every detail. He is a well read child and watches educational television. He takes piano lessons and likes the movie, "Sound of Music." When asked to describe himself, he replied, "different."

(Anonymous, 1988)

The teacher-writer implied in her log that she valued the second boy's language over the first, perhaps because the second boy spoke a more standard English and spoke about things more familiar to her culture than 'coon dogs. In the classroom

situation, she would probably show her scale of values in subtle ways. She would no doubt respond more favorably and encouragingly to the second boy's detailed accounts of his activities and perhaps be direct or, controlling, in "correcting" the first boy's "severe country dialect." In short, the second boy would be encouraged in his oral expression, and the first boy would be limited. He would perhaps sense that his language was not appreciated as much in the classroom as that of the second boy.

Teachers are usually aware of individual differences among students and attempt to adapt the classroom situation accordingly, but the way in which the adaptation is done is a crucial consideration if all children are to benefit. In some cases, such as the one above where one boy exhibited a definitely nonstandard dialect, the teacher may adapt expectations and not expect as much in the way of language learning. This, in turn, may well keep children from meeting their growth potential.

Recent research points to the need for adaptive action that

would make classrooms more culturally-compatible places, where the transition between the home and school culture is positively supported and there is mutual adaptation; that is, the child is not required to do all of the adjusting to a new situation, but the situation is also adapted to cultural differences (Cazden, 1988; Heath, 1983; Jordan, 1981; Lucas & Borders, 1987).

A program founded in 1971 attempted to research and develop instructional procedures and curricula for improving the educational achievement of children of Hawaiian ancestry. The Kamehameha Early Education Program (KEEP) in Hawaii sought to find culturally-compatible classroom practices. The researchers looked for points where classroom contexts and relevant home-contexts touched, and developed a program accordingly. Cathie Jordan, research anthropologist with KEEP and the Kamehameha Educational Research Institute, says, "One of the distinguishing features of the KEEP program, and one of the probable reasons for its effectiveness, is that, at many key points, it is compatible with Hawaiian culture" (1981, p. 16).

An example of where home and school cultures touched is the social organization of the independent work centers in which KEEP children spend four fifths of their language arts period. Jordan says,

These learning centers' constitute a comfortable and effective learning context for Hawaiian children partly because the social organization of the centers is congruent in a number of ways with major non-school contexts in which Hawaiian children work and acquire new information and skills. The analogous home contexts are those of the sibling group, especially in its capacity as a work force, and to a lesser extent, the companion-peer group (p. 17).

Another study which focused on helping children adjust between the home culture and the school culture was a long-term ethnographical study of children and their language in two small communities, one African American, one white, in the Piedmont Area of the Carolinas (see Heath, 1983). The central question out of which the study grew was: "For each of these groups, what were the effects of the preschool home and community environment on the learning of those language structures and uses which were needed in classrooms and job settings?" (Heath, 1983, Prologue, p. 4).

Since Heath was also connected to a local institution of higher education and involved in teacher education at the time, she was able to work with teachers in the area in a research-partner relationship. She worked with teachers specifically to try new methods, materials and motivations to help the working-class African American and white children of the area learn more effectively than they had in the past. She reports that teachers "constructed curricula from the world of the home to enable students to move to the curricular content of the school" (p. 340). In constructing such curricula, teachers' goals were:

1. To provide a foundation of familiar knowledge to serve as context for classroom information.
2. To engage students in collecting and analyzing familiar ways of knowing and translating these into scientific or school-accepted labels, concepts, and generalizations.

3. To provide students with meaningful opportunities to learn ways of talking about using language to organize and express information. (p. 340)

The central focus was the promotion of ethnographic methods for students to look at their own language use at home and at school. With the new curricula, students improved their textbook unit test scores, standardized test results, attendance records, and attitudes toward school.

To build more bridges between the home community and the school community, teachers can bring in materials from the community to provision the classroom. Loughlin and Martin (1987) say, "When a teacher adds materials from the community's natural environment, from children's homes, and from other local sources, the environment [at school] begins to resemble the community, offering a message of welcome and acceptance, influencing children's feelings of comfort and their attitudes as they approach learning materials" (p. 33). Sea shells, indigenous stones, seed pods of the area, local crafts, community photographs old and new, etc., all give children something to talk about, something very real and related to their personal lives in the community. These materials have multiple uses and encourage children to share and celebrate community life along with helping children to connect the learning at school with the learning that occurs in the larger community setting.

Different cultures and different dialects do not have to interfere with language learning, but rather can enhance it, if teachers capitalize on the strengths attendant to the cultural or language differences and make positive adjustments, e.g., adjust the classroom environment to reflect some of the home culture. Lucas and Borders (1987) found that some children show a much wider range of functional language competence in situations in which their dialect features are considered acceptable. Teachers who capitalize on the already-existing functional language competence of their students will use this foundation to help the students develop sociolinguistic skills for a variety of settings, according to Lucas and Borders.

Halliday (1973) has developed useful categories for the various functions of language, which can help teachers become more aware of different competencies to encourage and develop. These categories range from instrumental language to get things done, to imaginative language to express creativity, to heuristic language to seek information.

In sum, classroom conducive to continued oral language development must be a place where children have a chance to use their language in *real,* purposeful ways and where they feel comfortable in doing so. If *all* children, no matter the diversity of their backgrounds, are to feel comfortable in their classroom talk, it appears that connections must be made between the classroom and the home-community. Bringing into the classroom artifacts, natural objects, and resources from the community can serve to give children something important-to-them to talk about. They can converse, report, discuss, debate, relate, interview, question, dramatize, and speculate about these materials. From there, they can bring their language to bear on more abstract community and school issues, related to what they have found in the community, such as, population and employment trends, environmental clean-up, noise control, etc. Foremost and finally, children need time to talk; the classroom should not be a place where the teacher does most of the talking.

THE CLASSROOM AS CONTEXT FOR LITERACY: READING AND WRITING AS LITERACY EVENTS

Cazden (1986), in describing the typical classroom day, says that it "divides easily into events with labels familiar to participants . . ." She gives reading as one example of an event, and says observers may ask a question such as, "When is reading?" and be readily understood (p. 436). However, reading events may happen both formally and informally, researchers find, and many researchers have been looking more closely at when (and how) reading and writing occur as literacy events in the classroom (Calkins, 1983; Florio & Clark, 1982; Graves, 1983; Hubbard, 1985).

Florio and Clark (1982) say that "in our society the classroom is one of the few places in which socialization into literacy occurs" (p. 269). Thus, reading and writing can be seen not just as academic events in a classroom day; they are also social events. In fact, enthnographers studying classrooms make a point of speaking of literacy as a social event (Bloome, 1981, 1984; Heath, 1983; see also Smith-Burke, 1987, p. 241). For researchers, the analytic task becomes one of identifying the literacy events and discovering "the attendant social roles and expectations of teacher and students on those occasions" (Florio & Clark, 1982, p. 269).

Griffin (1977) reports that reading events occur all day long in a classroom, not just in specified "reading periods." The reading events included the reading of trade books, daily schedules, labels, and each other's work, and listening to stories read aloud by the teacher. There were unofficial and official reading events, the official being the kind directed by the teacher in the reading period. In unofficial reading events, such as reading captions under each other's pictures or sharing a funny picture book with a friend, the interactive roles were cooperative, mutually supportive, and child-directed. In official reading events, roles were more formal and based on previous expectations, rather than spontaneous. It became important for children to know when to raise their hands, what the signals were for turn-taking, how the teacher indicated quality of performance, along with knowing how to understand the printed material. Most of the official events were teacher-directed. Yet the children were using reading all through the day and learning outside of as well as inside the official reading periods.

To accommodate the all-day nature of reading events, it appears, classrooms should provide a rich print environment, not just materials, such as basal readers, designed for teaching reading. Griffin suggests that classrooms should contain "materials that need to be read" (p. 382). Her study showed children in the 1st grade reading primers, trade books, resource books, menus, daily schedules, recipes, labels from a science experiment, and each other's work.

Florio and Clark (1982) report on a series of related expressive activities in a 2nd to 3rd grade class in an elementary school and a 6th grade class in a middle school. These observ-ers found that often writing, as a literacy event, began with a shared experience not originally planned by the teacher (as in the case of an unexpected assembly on safety, for example). Experiences that became successful writing activities had importance in both the school and nonschool lives of the students. In the example of the safety assembly, the children returned to the classroom and talked about safety rules during language-arts time. The children had difficulty remembering much of what went on at the assembly, and the teacher served as coach and memory guide in the discussion. When the teacher encouraged the children to make safety posters as a service and a reminder for other students in the school, the project changed from one that belonged to the teacher to one that belonged to the class. The children assumed the purpose and knew the audience for their posters, and completed them with zest. Later the 2nd and 3rd grade authors in this classroom read their posters to kindergarten students and talked about safety with the younger students. Florio and Clark say the safety poster event "took on a life of its own" and was typical of "literally hundreds of occasions for writing" that took place in the two classrooms in which they worked for a full school year (pp. 279, 281). These classroom researchers credited one of the teacher's planning for literacy events as typical of both: "She created writing curriculum with her students as the class jointly produced a situation that would both support the practice of writing and be supported by that writing" (p. 281).

Another study which examined literacy in its event context was that of Hickman (1981), in which she found seven responses that promoted reading, writing, discussion, and the enjoyment of literature:

1. Selecting quality books
2. Assuring and promoting access to these books
3. Reading aloud and introducing literature every day
4. Discussing books using appropriate terminology [language to talk about what happens in books]
5. Assuring time for extension activities
6. Allowing for sharing and displaying of [extension] work
7. Planning cumulative experiences to consider literature in a variety of ways over time (pp. 343–354).

In considering these responses, it seems evident that a classroom environment rich in a variety of good children's literature can become a literacy-teaching tool.

Whether the research studies focus on reading or whether they focus on writing, most soon reveal that one cannot be studied without the other. Researchers in the 1980s call attention to reading-writing connections (Hansen, Newkirk, and Graves, 1985; see also Jensen, 1984). Donald Murray (1984b) writes of the reintegration of reading and writing, realizing that researchers are only rediscovering the connections; the connections have always been there (p. 21).

In the set up and integration of the classroom, it appears that what the teacher does is the key factor in establishing an environment conducive to learning. A promising development in looking at the role of the teacher is the new emphasis on the teacher as researcher, as learner in the classroom (Goswami & Stillman, 1987; Mohr & MacLean, 1987). In the role of learner, the teacher sets the tone for what happens in the classroom, for whether or not it becomes a learning community. If teaching is not seen as pouring knowledge from the teacher as fountain into students as empty vessels, then teacher and students can work together on a variety of activities with a sense of inquiry.

Cullinan and Strickland (1986) say that "teacher researchers shape classroom conditions for systematic inquiry" (p. 805). Cullinan's and Strickland's experiences in working with teacher, as researchers show that these teachers see themselves as learners in the classroom, along with their students. They are continually seeking better opportunities for nurturing reading and writing, for creating important literacy events in the classroom. They are not afraid to question traditional assumptions and to encourage their students to be questioners. Teaching becomes, for them, a matter of designing situations and events for inquiry and learning.

"Teaching occurs as children use materials, work with each other, see demonstrations, and talk with the teacher . . .," according to Genishi, McCarrier, and Nussbaum (1988, p. 184). Discussing recent developments in looking at language in its event context would not be complete without considering computers as part of the materials that children will be using in modern classrooms. Genishi, McCollum, and Strand (1985) report that research suggests that computers *can* support learning in the language arts. They say, "Our observations lead us to conclude that computer activity can be highly sociable" (p. 531). For example, they tell how children helped each other solve problems as they worked at the computer. Reid (1985) conducted an enthnographic study of computer use in a 4th grade classroom, and found that the computer created a new writing environment, transforming writing from a private to a public activity. The presence of a computer or several computers in the classroom certainly adds to the event structure of the classroom setting.

An important literacy event in a classroom is the publishing of a class newspaper, newsletter, or story-bulletin. Newman (1988a) suggests that using the best features of several word processing programs and whatever computers are available and then doing a cut-and-paste job to get an acceptable layout works well. Children interact with each other, with various word processing programs, and with the computers themselves to solve problems connected with producing a class publication. They work together to compose, to read over, and to revise their articles and stories. Newman says, "Such inexpensive alternatives to 'professional' desktop publishing make it possible . . . to take writing beyond traditional classroom contexts with the teacher as the sole reader of students' efforts" (p. 732).

Newman, Vibert, Freeman, and Sharp (1988) point out that computers encourage collaborative learning, even in story games. Contrary to adult assumptions that these computer programs and games are solitary activities, they are almost always played in groups. The games seem to generate large-scale, collaborative, problem-solving activities. Chosen judiciously, these games can promote classroom interaction, encourage student planning and decision-making, and become an important part of the computer-literacy events in the classroom.

In order to capitalize on the potential of various computer word processors and story programs, teachers "have to be will-

ing to relinquish direct instruction" (Newman, 1988b, p. 605). The classroom learning context becomes interactive and collaborative when students are encouraged to experiment with programs and ideas and create their own literacy events.

CONCLUSION

George Hillocks, Jr. (1986), uses the term "environmental mode" to describe instruction that is "characterized by

1. Clear and specific objectives, e.g., to increase the use of specific detail and figurative language;
2. Materials and problems selected to engage students with each other in specifiable processes important to some particular aspect of writing [or other language art]; and
3. Activities, such as small-group problem-centered discussions, conducive to high levels of peer interaction concerning specific tasks" (p. 122).

These characteristics seem to apply to the instruction discussed in this chapter for making the most of the classroom environment as instructional tool and as a site of language learning through interaction. To borrow a term, then, from Hillocks, this chapter concludes with a recommendation that we teach language arts in the environmental mode.

Specific Recommendations

More specifically, the general recommendation can be divided into particular recommendations based on this chapter's review of the research and the characteristics of the environmental mode: objectives for better classroom situations; judicious use of materials; and provision for interactive learning. Specific recommendations are:

1. Recognize that classroom environment goes deeper than surface niceties like bulletin boards, that classroom environment includes human attitudes, emotions, motivations, and expectations.
2. Have lightweight, sturdy, flexible furniture that can be arranged to meet different objectives: whole class presentations, small group work, or individual pursuits.
3. See that classroom organization of furniture and supplies facilitate easy access to centers of learning and instructional materials.
4. Supply the classroom with books and writing materials and present them invitingly to extend the language context of the environment.
5. Adapt teaching to take advantage of opportunities to individualize language instruction more when class size is reduced.
6. Include in the classroom artifacts, visiting resource persons, and literature of the various cultures represented in the classroom so that bridges can be built between home and school cultures.
7. Provide for classroom interaction between and among pu-

pils; between pupils and teacher, initiated by pupils; and not just between teacher and pupils, initiated by teacher.

8. Permit students to explore the possibilities of whatever computers are available in the school and classroom by collaborating on programs, word processing, and problem-solving games.

9. Reach out to the larger community around the classroom—to the school and neighborhood to share in the community of learners.

10. Encourage students, through materials, classroom physical set-up, and indirect teaching, to create their own language and literacy events.

If teachers follow these recommendations, they can challenge Mayher and Brause (1986), who say, "One of the striking things about schools is how little they have changed for one hundred years or more. Our grandparents wouldn't recognize our clothes, or homes, or means of transportation, but they'd feel very comfortable in most classrooms" (p. 619). Classrooms of the late twentieth century could be unrecognizable to reincarnated grandparents—with learning centers actually in the center of the classroom, with flexible furniture, with banks of computers, with an abundance of colorful books, etc. It is the challenge of the classroom of the future.

References

Anonymous. (1988). *Student log*. Oxford, OH: Miami University. Unpublished student papers.

Applebee, A. N., Langer, J. A., & Mullis, I. V. S. (1986). *The writing report card: Writing achievement in American schools.* Princeton, NJ: Educational Testing Service.

Barr, R., & Dreeben, R. (1983). *How schools work*. Chicago: The University of Chicago Press.

Beane, J. A., Lipka, R. P., & Ludewig, J. W. (1980). Synthesis of research on self-concept. *Educational Leadership, 38,* 84–89.

Bloome, D. (1981). An ethnographic approach to the study of reading activities among black junior high students: A sociolinguistic enthnography. *Dissertation Abstracts International* 42:2992-A.

Bloome, D. (1984). Reading: A social process. In B. Hutson (Ed.), *Advances in Reading/Language Research,* Vol. 2. Greenwich, CT: JAI Press.

Bloome, D. (1987). *Literacy and schooling.* Norwood, NJ: Ablex Publishing Corporation.

Burford, C. T. (1986). The relationship of principals' sense of humor and job robustness to school environment. *Dissertation Abstracts International, 46,* 2856A.

Cahen, L. S., Filby, N., McCutcheon, G., & Kyle, D. W. (1983). *Class size and instruction.* Research on Teaching Monograph Series. New York: Longman.

Calkins, L. (1983). *Lessons from a child.* Exeter, NH: Heinemann.

Cazden, C. B. (1972). *Child language and education.* New York: Holt.

Cazden, C. B. (1986). Classroom discourse. In M. C. Wittrock (Ed.), *Handbook of research on teaching* (3rd ed.). New York: Macmillan, 432–463.

Cazden, C. B. (1988). *Classroom discourse.* Portsmouth, NH: Heinemann.

Cullinan, B. E., & Strickland, D. S. (1986). The early years: Language, literature, and literacy in classroom research. *The Reading Teacher, 39,* 788–806.

Doyle, W. (1980). *Classroom management.* West Lafayette, IN: Kappa Delta Pi.

Doyle, W. (1986). Classroom organization and management. In M. C. Wittrock (Ed.), *Handbook of research on teaching* (3rd ed.). New York: Macmillan, 392–431.

Dunn, M. L. (1985). A study of the differences in the perceptionsof the classroom learning environment by fourth-, fifth-, and sixth-grade learning disabled and achieving boys. *Dissertation Abstracts International, 47,* 146A.

Emig, J. (1971). *The composing process of twelfth graders.* Research report no. 13. Urbana, IL: National Council of Teachers of English (ED 058 205).

Erickson, F. (1986). Qualitative methods in research on teaching. In M. C. Wittrock (Ed.), *Handbook of research on teaching* (3rd ed.). New York: Macmillan, 119–161.

Fillion, B., & Brause, R. S. (1987). Research into classroom practices: What have we learned and where are we going? In J. R. Squire (Ed.), *The dynamics of language learning.* Urbana, IL: National Conference on Research in English and ERIC Clearinghouse on Reading and Communication Skills, 201–225.

Flanders, N. (1970). *Analyzing teacher behavior.* Reading, MA: Addison-Wesley.

Florio, S., & Clark, C. M. (1982). What is writing for? Writing in the first weeks of school in a second-third grade classroom. In L. C. Wilkinson (Ed.), *Communicating in the classroom.* New York: Academic Press, 265–282.

Genishi, C., McCarrier, A., & Nussbaum, N. R. (1988). Research currents: Dialogue as a context for teaching and learning. *Language Arts, 65,* 182–191.

Genishi, C., McCollum, P. & Strand, E. (1985). Research currents: The international richness of children's computer use. *Language Arts, 62,* 526–532.

Glass, G. V., Cahen, L. S., Smith, M. L., & Filby, N. N. (1982). *School class size: Research and policy.* Beverly Hills: Sage Publications.

Goodman, K., & Goodman, Y. (1983). Reading and Writing relationships: Pragmatic functions. *Language Arts, 60,* 590–599.

Goodman, Y. M. (1987). Foreword. In Loughlin, C. E., & Martin, M. D. *Supporting literacy.* New York: Teachers College Press, xiii–xiv.

Goswami, D., & Stillman, P. R. (Eds.). (1987). *Reclaiming the classroom: Teacher research as an agency for change.* Upper Montclair, NJ: Boynton/Cook.

Graves, D. (1973). Children's writing: Research directions and hypotheses based upon an examination of the writing process of seven-year-old children. *Dissertation Abstracts International, 34,* 6255A.

Graves, D. (1983). *Writing: Teachers and children at work.* Exeter, NH: Heinemann Educational Books.

Griffin, P. (1977). How and when does reading occur in the classroom? *Theory into Practice, 16,* 376–383.

Halliday, M. A. K. (1973). *Explorations in the functions of language.* London: Edward Arnold.

Hansen, J., Newkirk, T., & Graves, D. (1985). *Breaking Ground: Teachers Relate Reading and Writing in the Elementary School.* Portsmouth, NH: Heinemann.

Heath, S. B. (1983). *Ways with words.* New York: Cambridge University Press.

Hickman, J. (1981). A new perspective on response to literature: Research in an elementary school setting. *Research in the Teaching of English, 15,* 343–354.

Hillocks, G., Jr. (1986). *Research on Written Composition*. Urbana, IL: National Conference on Research in English and ERIC Clearinghouse on Reading and Communication Skills.

Hoskisson, K., & Tompkins, G. E. (1987). *Language arts: Content and teaching strategies*. Columbus, OH: Merrill.

Hubbard. (1985). In Hansen, et al., *Breaking ground*. Portsmouth, NH: Heinemann.

Ingham, J. (1982). *Books and reading development* (2nd ed.). Exeter, NH: Heinemann.

Jackson, P. W. (1968). *Life in classrooms*. New York: Holt, Rinehart, and Winston.

Jensen, J. (Ed.). (1984). *Composing and Comprehending*. Urbana, IL: NCTE.

Johnson, D. W., & Johnson, R. T. (1975). *Learning together and alone: Cooperation, competition, and individualization*. Englewood Cliffs, NJ: Prentice-Hall.

Jordan, C. (1981). "The selection of culturally-compatible classroom practices." In G. E. Speidel (Ed.), Journal of the College of Education, University of Hawaii at Manoa, *Educational Perspectives, 20*, 16–19.

King, S. P. (1984). The school as community: The importance of school environment. *Dissertation Abstracts International, 45*, 1593A.

Loughlin, C. E. (1977). Understanding the learning environment. *The Elementary School Journal, 78*, 126–131.

Loughlin, C. E., & Martin, M. D. (1987). *Supporting literacy: Developing effective learning environments*. New York: Teachers College Press.

Loughlin, C. E., & Suina, J. H. (1982). *The learning environment: An instructional strategy*. New York: Teachers College Press.

Lucas, C., & Borders, D. (1987). Language diversity and classroom discourse. *American Educational Research Journal, 24*, 119–141.

Lund, N. J., & Duchan, J. F. (1988). *Assessing children's language in naturalistic contexts* (2nd ed.). Englewood Cliffs, NJ: Prentice-Hall.

Mayher, J. S., & Brause, R. S. (1986). Learning through teaching: Is your classroom like your grandmother's? *Language Arts, 63*, 617–620.

McCroskey, J. C. (1980). Quiet children in the classroom: On helping not hurting. *Communication Education, 29*, 239–244.

McKenzie, M. G. (1985). Classroom contexts for language and literacy. In Jaggar, A., and Smith-Burke, M. T. (Eds.), *Observing the language learner*. Newark, DE: The International Reading Association with the National Council of Teachers of English, 232–249.

Mehan, H. (1979). *Learning lessons*. Cambridge: Harvard University Press.

Mohr, M. M., & MacLean, M. S. (1987). *Working together: A guide for teacher-researchers*. Urbana, IL: National Council of Teachers of English.

Murray, D. (1984a). Facets: The most important developments in the last five years for high school teachers of composition. *English Journal, 78*, 21.

Murray, D. (1984b). *Write to learn*. New York: Holt, Rinehart, and Winston.

Newman, J. M. (1988a). Online: Classroom publishing. *Language Arts, 65*, 727–732.

Newman, J. M. (1988b). Online: Logo and the language arts. *Language Arts, 65*, 598–605.

Newman, J. M., Vibert, A., Freeman, L. M., & Sharp, P. L. (1988). Online: Learning collaboratively. *Language Arts, 65*, 74–79.

Piaget, J. (1969). *The psychology of intelligence*. Patterson, NJ: Littlefield, Adams.

Reid, T. R. A. (1985). Writing with micro-computers in a fourth grade classroom: An ethnographic study. *Dissertation Abstracts International, 47*, 03A.

Seiler, W. J., Schuelke, L. D., & Lieb-Brilhart, B. (1984). *Communication for the contemporary classroom*. New York: Holt, Rinehart, and Winston.

Smith, F. (1978). *Reading without nonsense*. New York: Teachers College Press.

Smith-Burke, M. T. (1987). Classroom practices and classroom interaction during reading instruction: What's going on? In J. R. Squire (Ed.), *The Dynamics of Language Learning*. Urbana, IL: National Conference on Research in English & National Council on Teachers of English.

Squires, D. A. (1980). *Characteristics of effective schools: The importance of school processes*. Philadelphia: Research for Better Schools, Inc.

Tway, E. (1984). *Time for writing in the elementary school*. Urbana, IL: National Council of Teachers of English and ERIC Clearinghouse on Reading and Communication Skills.

Tway, E. (1985). *Writing is reading: 26 ways to connect*. Urbana, IL: National Council of Teachers of English and ERIC Clearinghouse on Reading and Communication Skills.

Vincent, W. S., and Olson, M. N. (1972). *Measurement of school quality and its determiners*. New York: Teachers College Institute of Administrative Research.

Wilkinson, L. C. (Ed.) (1982). *Communicating in the classroom*. New York: Academic Press.

Wood, B. S. (1984). Oral communication in the elementary school. In Thaiss, C., & Suhor, C. (Eds.), *Speaking and writing K–12*. Urbana, IL: National Council of Teachers of English, 104–125.

·24·

SECONDARY ENGLISH CLASSROOM ENVIRONMENTS

Allan A. Glatthorn

This chapter reviews and synthesizes the research on the learning environment of secondary English classrooms. It begins by presenting a conceptualization of that environment that is based upon four key components: the physical environment; the group environment; the work environment; and the psycho-social environment. That conceptualization provides an organizing system for the rest of the chapter.

The review of the literature was conducted by first locating sources that related to the topic addressed here; the author conducted a comprehensive examination of the ERIC data base, using these descriptors: *learning environment; classroom environment; English classroom environment; learning climate; school environment.* The same descriptors were used in reviewing *Dissertation Abstracts* and *Subject Guide to Books in Print.* Those publications that met generally accepted standards for research design were identified and examined.

The English Classroom Environment; an Alternative Conceptualization

In most of the related research, *classroom environment* has been conceptualized somewhat narrowly, focusing essentially on what is termed here the psycho-social environment. The best way to understand this narrowness is to examine the two most widely used scales for measuring secondary classroom learning environments—the Classroom Environment Scale (CES) (Moos & Trickett, 1974) and the Learning Environment Inventory (LEI) (Fraser, Anderson, & Walberg, 1982). The CES measures students' perceptions across three broad dimensions: relationship, the nature and intensity of personal realtionships within the environment; personal development, the basic directions along which personal growth happens; and system maintenance and system change, the extent to which the environment is orderly, clear in expectations, control-oriented, and responsive to change. These 3 broad dimensions subsume 9

subscales; the dimensions and subscales are identified and defined briefly in Figure 24–1. (The subscale definitions are paraphrased from Moos, 1980.)

The LEI (Secondary Level) includes 105 items descriptive of secondary school classes; these items are related to 15 scales. The scales and their definitions (paraphrased from Fraser, Anderson, & Walberg, 1982) are shown in Figure 24–2.

These two instruments seem to be both sound in their design and productive in their use. First, both have achieved a satisfactory degree of reliability and validity. As Fraser (1986) notes, the alpha reliability coefficents (a measure of internal consistency reliability) for the nine subscales of the CES range from 0.51 to 0.75; and those of the LEI, from 0.54 to 0.85. The mean correlations of one scale with other scales (a measure of discriminant validity) for the CES range from 0.09 to 0.40; those for the LEI, from 0.08 to 0.40. The two inventories have also produced a significant body of research. (For a review of that research, see the section below on "Psycho-social environments.")

However, both instruments seem somewhat narrow in their conceptualization of classroom environment. Except for the "Difficulty" and "Material Environment" scales of the LEI, both inventories address elements of only the psycho-social environment—the patterns of relationships and interactions between students and students and teacher and students. For the purposes of this review, a more inclusive conceptualization seems needed.

Such a conceptualization would begin by placing the classroom environment in a broader context. Here a synthesis of the research on educational productivity by Fraser and his colleagues (1987) seems useful. On the basis of their review of about 3,000 studies of educational research, they identified 9 factors (falling into 3 groups) that increase student learning. Three of the factors related to student aptitude: ability or prior achievement; development, as indexed by age or maturation; motivation, or self-concept. Two of the factors related to instruc-

438

Relationship Dimensions

1. **Involvement.** The extent to which students are attentive and interested.
2. **Affiliation.** Student friendship; the extent to which students cooperate and enjoy working together.
3. **Teacher support.** The help, trust, and friendship demonstrated by the teacher.

Personal Growth or Goal Orientation Dimensions

4. **Task orientation.** The importance of completing activities and sticking to the subject matter.
5. **Competition.** The emphasis placed on competition and grades and the difficulty of achieving good grades.

System Maintenance and Change Dimension

6. **Order and organization.** The emphasis on students behaving in an orderly manner and on the organization of assignments and class activities.
7. **Rule clarity.** The emphasis on establishing and following clear rules and on students knowing the consequences of not following them.
8. **Teacher control.** How strict the teacher is in enforcing rules and punishing rule infractions.
9. **Innovation.** How much students are involved in planning classroom activities and the number of innovative activities planned by the teacher.

FIGURE 24–1. Dimensions and Subscales of the Classroom Environment Scale.

tion: the amount of time students were engaged in learning; and the quality of the learning experience, including both psychological and curricular aspects. Four of the factors related to what they terms the "psychological environments": the home; the peer group outside school; the amount of leisure-time television viewing; and the classroom environment.

Thus, by a process of elimination, "classroom environment" seems to be used in the above work to mean all those classroom elements other than student aptitude and instruction (including the curriculum and time allocations). By excluding these elements and by reviewing the research on secondary English classrooms, one can analyze the construct *classroom environment* into four related elements, using a process that Hase and Goldberg (1967) have described as *intuitive-rational,* (See Figure 24–3 for a schematic representation of these elements.)

1. Physical environment. The physical environment of the classroom includes such elements as the presence or absence of walls, classroom design and furniture, and classroom density and crowding.
2. Group environment. The group environment (as the term is used here) involves the way students are grouped for learning—the size of the class and the tracking and grouping systems used to assign students to a class.

1. **Cohesiveness.** Extent to which students help and are friendly with each other.
2. **Diversity.** Extent to which students' differences are provided for.
3. **Formality.** Extent to which behavior is guided by formal rules.
4. **Speed.** Extent to which class work is covered rapidly.
5. **Material Environment.** Availability of adequate books, equipment, and space.
6. **Friction.** Amount of tension among students.
7. **Goal direction.** Degree of goal clarity.
8. **Favoritism.** Extent to which teacher treats some students more favorably than others.
9. **Difficulty.** Extent to which students find class work difficult.
10. **Apathy.** Extent to which the class feels no affinity with class activities.
11. **Democracy.** Extent to which students share equally in decision-making.
12. **Cliqueness.** Extent to which students refuse to mix with rest of class.
13. **Satisfaction.** Extent of enjoyment of class work.
14. **Disorganization.** Extent to which class activities are confusing and disorganized.
15. **Competitiveness.** Emphasis placed on students competing with each other.

FIGURE 24–2. Scales of the Learning Environment Inventory.

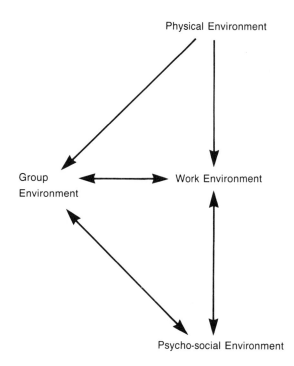

(Note: The lines and arrows are intended to suggest general relationships, not casual influences and directions.)

FIGURE 24–3. Elements of Classroom Learning Environment.

3. Work environment. The work environment is the nature of the academic work and its related activities, as construed by the teacher and the students.
4. Psycho-social environment. The psycho-social environment is the shared perceptions of the people in an environment about the nature of the psycho-social interactions of that environment.

These four elements are used as the organizing bases for the reviews that follow.

THE PHYSICAL ENVIRONMENT

The *physical environment of the classroom* is a comprehensive concept that includes the following elements: the presence or absence of walls ("open space" or "traditional" classrooms); classroom design and furniture; seating arrangements; the density and crowding of classrooms; and the amount of noise in the classroom. Surprisingly, perhaps, there have been only a handful of research studies that have specifically examined the relationship of the physical environment of the secondary English classroom to student achievement and student attitude.

The only major publication dealing with the issue of the physical nature of the English classroom was Whalen's (1972) report for the National Council of Teachers of English Committee on English Learning Environment. Since the committee functioned during the years when flexible grouping schemes

were popular with many educators, they predictably concluded that varied spatial arrangements were needed. They proposed a set of recommendations that from this vantage point seem somewhat unrealistic: a large auditorium for the presentation of plays and other artistic performances; several regular classrooms designed to accommodate up to 30 students; small-group seminar rooms; small conference spaces for 1 to 2 students; and numerous spaces for individual study. The committee provided little research support for their recommendations, relying solely on the recommendations of experts and their own experience. Somewhat similar recommendations were made by Krovetz (1977), although again without much research support.

Since there is thus a rather narrow research base on the specific issue of the physical environment of secondary English classrooms, the following review will examine the research on the general issue of the relationship of the physical environment of classrooms to student achievement and attitude. Those studies that used achievement as the dependent variable equated achievement with performance on either a subject-based test or a standardized test; those using attitude as the variable relied upon scores on some attitudinal measure. The review concludes by discussing the implications of that research for the secondary English classroom.

The Presence or Absence of Classroom Walls

During the school building boom of late 1960s and early 1970s, many school boards followed the recommendations of architects who advocated the construction of "open space" schools. In fact, a 1975 study by George reported that more than half of the schools built between 1967 and 1970 were open space schools. While there was much variation in how this concept was understood and implemented, most open space schools were characterized by the presence of several large general teaching and learning areas (often called "pods") that could accommodate up to 150 students and 5 teachers. In some open space schools, pods were assigned to grade levels; thus, an English teacher would share this open space with teachers of social studies and mathematics. In other open space schools, pods were assigned to departments; thus, five English teachers might share one pod.

Several studies examined the nature of student activity in open space schools. An early study by Burnham (1970) of open space and traditional schools determined that in the open environment, students were more often observed initiating activities, engaging in cooperative learning with teachers and each other, assuming personal responsibility, and in general demonstrating a "spirit of inquiry." Gump (1974) found that life in open space schools seemed more active: students entered more sites and spent much more time in transitions from space to space. However, as Durlak, Beardsley, and Murray (1972) note, it would be unwise to equate type of space and type of program: they discovered that some traditional schools supported rather open patterns of activity, while some open environments housed traditional programs.

One major study (Gump & Ross, 1977) examined the nature of teacher behavior in open space settings over a two-year period. As the school year progressed, teachers tended to close off and define space with the use of furniture. Tall furniture was used to create visual barriers, and low furniture to mark off territorial boundaries.

What are the effects of open space schools on teachers and students? In general open space seems to have a positive effect on teachers, although Weinstein (1979) notes that the problem of self-selection may be a confounding factor: teachers who prefer an open environment would be more likely to volunteer for assignment to open space schools. Given that limitation, teachers in open space schools, when compared with their counterparts in traditional buildings, tend to show the following characteristics: have increased interaction with peers (Meyer, 1971); have greater feelings of autonomy (Brunetti, 1971); express greater satisfaction (Meyer, 1971); spend less time on routine activities (Ellison, Gibert, & Ratsoy, 1969); and more often use variable group activities (Warner, 1971).

What is the effect of open space on student attitudes and learning? In general the evidence suggests that students in open space schools tend to have more positive attitudes than their counterparts in traditional schools: they have greater feelings of autonomy (Meyer, 1971); are more willing to take risks (Anifant, 1972); and show greater task persistence (Reiss & Dyhaldo, 1975). There also seem to be some important behavioral differences. Students in open space schools tend to interact with a larger number of teachers during the day (Gump, 1974) and engage in a greater variety of activities (Clem, Ahern, Dailey, Gary & Scantlebury, undated).

The evidence on the effects of open space schools on student achievement is somewhat conflicting. The only two studies that attempted to control curricular and other variables yielded different results. The study by Traub and others (1976) of 30 schools found no consistent relationship between space and achievement. However, the researchers did discover that students in open space schools displayed more positive attitudes towards school, their teachers, and themselves; they also scored higher on independence. Teachers in open space schools also seemed more positive towards their work and demonstrated more interactions with peers and administrators. However, Beck (1979) found in a study of 120 schools that students in traditional schools achieved at significantly higher rates in mathematics and reading than did students in open space schools; there were no significant differences insuch noncognitive outcomes as attitude toward school and locus of control. On the basis of his review of the evidence, George (1975) concluded that "neither the open space schools or the conventional schools have demonstrated a clear superiority" (p. 63).

Classroom Design and Furniture

If classrooms are separated by walls, then the next issue to examine is whether variations in classroom design and classroom furniture make any signficant difference.

First, how do teachers place themselves in classrooms? There is some evidence that teachers place themselves "front and center" regardless of whether the classroom is perceived as open or traditional. In Rivlin and Rothenberg's (1976) study of two schools using open classroom approaches, teachers tended to remain in the front center of the room, near the blackboard and the classroom door. The students in those classrooms tended to spend most of their time close to the teacher, even though more space was available in other portions of the room. When teachers varied from that standard pattern by placing their desks in the corner of the room, Zifferblatt (1972) determined that teachers moved around the room more and seemed more involved with students.

The general attractiveness of the classroom and the type and placement of classroom furniture seem to affect student attitudes and behavior, although there is no demonstrable relationship between these elements of the physical environment and student achievement. Early laboratory studies by Mintz (1956) concluded that there was a relationship between an "ugly" environment and feelings of discontent and fatigue. In the Zifferblatt study, the clustering of 2 or 3 student desks together seemed to be more satisfactory than clustering 10 or 12 desks together. An "alternative learning facility" for college students that made use of much color, movable panels, and comfortable sets seemed to result in better attendance, greater student participation, and increased group cohesiveness (Horowitz & Otto, 1973). And Santrock (1976) concluded that the affective quality of the environment seemed to influence student task persistence: students worked longer in a "happy" setting than in a "sad" or neutral one.

Although the conventional wisdom suggests that placing student desks in circles, squares or horseshoes should facilitate student participation, the available evidence does not support this belief. Johnson's (1973) study of the effect of furniture arrangement on student participation showed no significant differences in the patterns of verbal interaction. One study suggested that traditional rows are academically useful: Bennett and Blundell (1983) found that having students work independently in rows before they did gorup work resulted in an increased quantity of work with a similar level of quality. Despite this finding, the issue of furniture placement and student achievement seems unresolved. As Weinstein (1979) notes, it may be that the differences between rows, horseshoes, and circles are not powerful enough to affect achievement and verbal interaction.

Seating Arrangements

As noted above, the placement of furniture in general seems not be be an important environmental factor. However, where students sit in the classroom does seem to be important. When desks are arranged in traditional rows, students sitting in the front and center seem to get more than their share of teacher attention. Early studies by Adams (1969) and Adams and Biddle (1970) established that students who sat in the "action zone" (in the front and center of the room) interacted most frequently with the teacher. Later studies did not consistently support these early findings. The Koneya (1976) study substantiated the existence of the action zone; the Delefes and Jackson (1972) study did not.

Additional studies have analyzed seating arrangements with different constructs. Brooks, Silvern, and Wooten (1978) identified the front and center as the "social-consultive" zone, finding that students who sat in that zone received a more permissive and interactive type of communication from the teacher; students in the public zone (middle and back of the room) received more lecturing and one-way communication.

Several studies have tried to establish the causal direction of seating patterns and positions: do verbally active students choose front and center positions? or do front and center positions seem to increase student participation? The results are generally inconclusive. A study by Schwebel and Cherlin (1972) indicated that moving students to the action zone tended to increase students' on-task behavior and increased the number of favorable teacher ratings. Stires (1978) discovered that, whether or not students chose their own seats or were randomly assigned, those in the middle received higher grades and liked both the course and the instructor better than those on the side. However, Koneya (1976) discovered that highly verbal college students chose front-center seats when asked to indicate their preference on a seating chart. In the same study, the participation by highly and moderately verbal students was affected by seat placement; these students participated more frequently when they sat in the action zone, whereas the participation of low verbalizers was not affected by seat placement.

In her view of the research, Weinstein (1979) suggests that the better achievement, attitudes, and participation of students sitting in the action zone results from their greater proximity to the teacher, resulting in increased eye contact and greater opportunities for other kinds of nonverbal communication.

Density and Crowding

In analyzing the effects of the number of students in a given space, Stokols (1972) makes a useful distinction between density and crowding: density is a mathematical measure of the number of people in a given space; crowding is the perceived judgment of excessive density. Perceptions of crowding seem to depend upon several factors, including personal preferences and the kind of activity. According to Epstein and Karlin (1975), individuals have certain expectations about appropriate space for given kinds of interactions and feel that they are crowded when they are not provided with what they believe is appropriate distance.

Crowding would seem to be the more important measure in studying achievement. Yet when achievement of a complex task is the criterion, crowding does not seem to be a significant variable. Weinstein (1979) offers three explanations for this somewhat surprising conclusion: some studies examined only density, ignoring the more important phenomenon of crowding; in many of the studies, the tasks were not sufficiently complex, and even more complex tasks that do not require interaction are not impaired by high density.

However, density does seem to affect behavior. In general, high density classrooms have been found to be associated with increased aggression (Loo & Kennelly, 1979), decreased social interaction (Hutt & Hutt, 1970), and noninvolvement with lesson activities (Shapiro, 1975). And in a major study that systematically varied density and the resources available in a day-care classroom, Rohe and Patterson (1974) discovered that as density

was increased, aggressive, destructive, and uninvolved behavior increased. Finally, a study of college students by Schettino and Borden (1976) determined that increased density was associated with increased feelings of nervousness and crowdedness for women and increased feelings of aggressiveness for men.

Noise

Researchers investigating the effects of noise on learning usually make a distinction between short-term exposure to moderate within-school or within-classroom noise and long-term exposure to external noise, such as that from an airport or highway. In general within-classroom noise does not seem to have a deleterious effect on learning. An early (1968) study by Slater of 7th graders' performance on a reading test determined that noise levels within the classroom were not a factor in performance. A later (1979) study by Weinstein and Weinstein on the effect of noise in an open space school on reading comprehension also found no significant differences in performance under conditions of quiet and normal background noise.

However, studies of schools located near airports, busy highways, or elevated trains indicated that there may be effects from long-term exposure to increased noise levels. Children on the noisy side of a school near an elevated train had reading scores significantly lower than those on the less noisy side (Bronzaft & McCarthy, 1975). In classrooms facing a major traffic artery, almost 17 minutes were lost from teaching time on the noisy side of the building, whereas only 7.5 minutes were lost on the quiet side (Kyzar, 1977). Similar results were obtained in a study of schools close to the Heathrow Airport in London (Crook & Langdon, 1974).

Students' Individual Preferences

Some educators who advocate the importance of assessing student learning styles and adjusting instructional conditions accordingly view environmental factors as critical aspects of style preference. Thus, the Learning Style Profile published by the National Association of Secondary School Principals (Keefe, 1988) includes items on sound preference, lighting preference, and temperature preference; and the Learning Style Inventory (Dunn, Dunn, & Price, 1985) assesses learner preferences for sound, light, temperature, and need for either a formal or informal design.

Dunn and Dunn (1987) cite several studies supporting their belief that responding to such preferences will result in improved learning. Shea (1983) determined that when students who preferred sitting informally on cushions, couches, and carpeting were permitted to work that way they performed significantly better on an English comprehension test than when they were required to sit in conventional seats. Some adolescents, according to Price's (1980) study, seemed to think and remember best when studying with music. Some students performed better in low rather than bright light (Krimsky, 1982). Middle school students achieved better when they were tested in a thermal setting that matched their preferences (Murrain, 1983).

On the basis of this review, the Dunns recommend that teachers provide environmental options in classrooms and let students learn in the kind of environment they prefer.

Others are not persuaded either by this limited body of evidence or the assumptions that undergird it. David Kolb, who has done extensive research on the conceptual dimensions of learning styles, expresses this caution in his commentary on a 1981 article by Dunn and De Bello (1981):

I feel there are great dangers in the misuse of learning style concepts. Specifically, we must avoid turning these ideas into stereotypes used to pigeon hole individuals. Furthermore, we should not deny students the opportunity to develop themselves fully by only exposing them to educational environments that match their strengths. (p. 373)

Implications for the Secondary English Classroom

The assumption here is that school administrators and English teachers want learning environments that reflect these characteristics: students are engaged in a variety of learning tasks; much of the teaching-learning transactions involve group discussion; students seem to be achieving a broad range of outcomes; students are developing positive attitudes about themselves, the teacher, and the study of English.

What kind of physical environment would best reflect those characteristics? The first point to make is that the physical environment does not matter, if student achievement is the sole criterion. Weinstein's review of the research leads her to this conclusion:

Despite the objections voiced by many of these humanist educators to the hard "tight spaces" ... characteristic of our schools..., it would seem that the physical environment of the conventional classroom has little impact on achievement. (p. 598)

However, the physical environment does seem to make a difference in relation to student attitudes and behavior. In determining which of those characteristics would be important for the secondary English classroom, only tentative recommendations can be offered, since the research base is somewhat limited.

1. Open space schools would seem to provide a hospitable environment for teaching English.
2. English classrooms should be attractive and uncrowded places.
3. English teachers should vary the seating arrangements to accommodate the instructional activity. They should feel free to experiment with circles and horseshoes when discussion is important. They should have students sit in rows when independent work is desired.
4. English teachers should be sensitive to the effects of seating arrangements on student participation. If they wish to encourage particular students to become more actively involved in activities, they should seat those students in the action zone.
5. English teachers should learn to tolerate the moderate noise levels produced by active learning and discussion, without worrying that that noise is distracting.

GROUP ENVIRONMENT

As the term is used in this work, *group environment* refers to those aspects of the classroom learning environment that derive from administrative decisions about how many and which students are assigned to a class and teacher decisions about how that class is organized once those decisions have been implemented. Two aspects of the group environment seem important: class size; and tracking and ability grouping.

Class Size

Teachers have always wanted smaller classes. Over the years, they have been uniformly insistent in their claims that smaller classes create a more desirable learning environment, result in better student achievement, and make their own professional lives more rewarding. (See, for example, Millard, 1977; Haddad, 1978; and Cotton & Savard, 1980.) And, as Suhor (1986) notes, the National Council of Teachers of English has for several years undertaken numerous efforts to persuade the public and school administrators that smaller classes are especially important for English teachers. As he points out, as far back as the 1950s, the NCTE recommended maximum class loads of 100 students for each English teacher; during the 1960s it recognized schools that had made significant efforts in reducing class size and teacher workload by designating them "Honor Roll" schools. And during the past three decades, it has appointed several committees to study the issue, has published bibliographies, and has disseminated kits to its members to help them achieve the goal of smaller classes.

To what extent are these beliefs and their resulting actions supported by the research? As Smith (1986) indicates, there is little research on the effects of class size and the teaching of English. It therefore seems useful here to review the large body of research on class size in general and then draw some tentative inferences about its implications for English classes.

Class Size and Achievement. Although the issue continues to be debated by both researchers and practitioners, it now seems reasonably safe to conclude that greater achievement occurs in smaller classes than in larger ones. This finding was first firmly established by Glass and Smith (1978) in their meta-analysis of 76 studies of the issue. They summarized their findings in this manner:

As class size increased, achievement decreases. A pupil who would score at about the 63rd percentile on a national test when taught individually would score about the 37th percentile in a class of 40 pupils. The difference is being taught in a class of 20 versus a class of 40 is an advantage of ten percentile ranks.

They further noted that the greatest gains occurred in classes of 15 pupils or fewer; in classes of 20 to 40 students, gains were not as pronounced.

The Glass and Smith conclusions were strongly attacked by the authors of the Educational Research Service (1980) critique. They faulted the Glass and Smith meta-analysis on several grounds: a substantial number of the studies involved extremely small groups of 1 to 5 pupils; Glass and Smith relied on too few studies; they over-generalized from their results; and they ignored the political and fiscal realities that make the goal of very small classes almost impossible to achieve. However, a recent reanalysis of the Glass and Smith data by Hedges and Stock (1983) generally supports the Glass and Smith findings. They conclude that the "suboptimal statistical methods" used by Glass and Smith did not greatly affect the results of their meta-analysis.

Class Size and the Nature of Classroom Interactions. These generally positive effects of smaller classes can be understood by examining the research on the nature of classroom interactions in smaller and larger classes.

First, discipline is better in smaller classes. Several studies have concluded that in smaller classes, students are more likely to remain on task, the teacher is better able to manage disruptive behavior, and students seem to demonstrate greater self-control. (See, for example, Filby, 1980; Smith & Glass, 1979; and Noli, 1980.) Second, as determined in those same studies, student participation and involvement tends to increase when classes are small. This finding is perhaps predictable: students who are not so aggressive in their responding behaviors are more likely to gain the floor in smaller classes.

Third, teachers in smaller classes tend to give more and better feedback than those in larger classes (Noli, 1980; McDonald, 1980; Smith & Glass, 1979). Finally, students show general improvement in a range of attitudinal responses. Smith and Glass's 1979 meta-analysis indicated that students in smaller classes had stronger motivation, better self-concept, and less anxiety.

Surprisingly, perhaps, teachers do not seem to vary their teaching methods when they teach smaller classes. Although there are some conflicting findings here, two major studies found that giving teachers smaller classes did not result in different teaching practices. In a two-year study in Ontario, Shapson and his colleagues (1978) determined that smaller classes did not result in greater individualization of instruction, even though the teachers involved were sure that greater individualization would occur. Field studies conducted by the Far West Regional Laboratory of two urban schools and two rural schools reached the same conclusion. As Filby (1980) noted in reviewing the results of these studies, the teachers were not likely to try dramatically different methods of instruction even though they had smaller classes, perhaps because they were not trained in such approaches.

Class Size and the Teaching of English. As noted above, there have been relatively few studies that examined class size in teaching English. In a study of college instructional practices, Cheatham and Jordan (1976) determined that smaller classes of 20 were more desirable for what they termed "performance oriented" courses—and they included in this group English composition and speech communication. And McDonald (1980) concluded that classes of 15 or fewer were associated with improved student writing, because they made it possible for students to receive more feedback and do more revising

under supervision. This relative lack of research seemed to place the NCTE Task Force on Class Size and Workload in Secondary English Instruction in a somewhat awkward position. After reviewing the research, the task force seemed to be able to make only weak claims about the advantages of smaller classes. Here is one example of their tentativeness:

... if the goal is for students to analyze the theme and structure of any novel, common sense suggests that students will, at some point, have to engage in such analyses under the guidance of a teacher. In such cases, classes of thirty to forty may very well be too large. (Smith, 1986, p. 3)

After noting the value of such teaching/learning activities as mastery learning, peer group problem solving, and homework with feedback, they offer this observation.

All of these and other powerful instructional variables are quite time-consuming, however. *Class size, therefore, may determine whether or not they are ever put into practice, for class size influences the extent to which they can be successfully employed.* Yet there is no research on the relationship of these variables to class size. (Italics in original.) (p. 4).

Yet a later chapter in the same report concludes, as noted above, that teachers with smaller classes did not vary their instructional techniques.

The body of research on class size in general would seem to warrant stronger claims. Smaller classes are associated with better achievement. Smaller classes are also associated with other indicators of quality, such as better student discipline and increased student participation. And if English teachers are expected to respond to student writing and to involve students in discussion, then the argument about the need for smaller English classes would seem to be ended. Despite this evidence, school administrators seem relatively indifferent to the matter. The Applebee (1977) study of teaching conditions in English indicated that the typical secondary school English teacher taught five classes a day, with 26 to 30 students per class. There is no recent evidence to suggest that those conditions have changed substantially.

Curriculum Tracking and Ability Grouping

The second aspect of the group environment is the way in which students are grouped for instruction. In general three grouping practices are widely used in American secondary schools: curriculum tracking; ability grouping; and within-class grouping. Curriculum tracking is a practice of assigning secondary students to a particular curricular sequence (such as college preparatory, general, or vocational) and scheduling them as curricular groups for their instruction. Thus, a student would take college preparatory English, college preparatory mathematics, and so on. Ability grouping is a practice of assigning students to classes on the basis of their ability in that particular subject. Thus, a student might be in a high ability English class and a middle ability class in mathematics. Within-class grouping is a practice by which a teacher, once having been assigned a class, divides that class into instructional groups on the basis of their ability. In this instance, an English teacher might have in the same class one group of of excellent writers, one group of average writers, and one group of weaker writers.

Rather than organizing this discussion in relation to the type of grouping practice, it seems to make more sense to analyze the impact of ability grouping in general. After examining the evidence about the various processes by which students are assigned to instructional groups, Bolvin (1982) concluded that "... there is little difference between curriculum grouping and ability-achievement grouping" (p. 266). Although elementary teachers seem to make extensive use of within-class grouping (especially for reading), secondary English teachers are less likely to use within-class ability grouping. Therefore, the discussion that follows examines the evidence relative to ability grouping in general, noting distinctions between the types only when that seems important.

How Students Are Assigned to Groups. In examining how group assignments are determined, the distinction between curriculum tracking and ability grouping is important. In general, students (and their parents) choose the curriculum track; teachers and counselors usually determine ability group placement.

The research on how students choose curriculum tracts suggests a rather complex process. (The description that follows is a synthesis of three major sources: Alexander & Cook, 1982; Oakes, 1985; and Rosenbaum, 1980.) Early in the secondary years, the student begins to think about post-high school plans (influenced by school experience, parent expectations, and peer norms) and begins to make some early choices about curriculum. For example, early in the middle school years, one student may decide to take foreign language; another decides (or is told) to take a reading course. Those early choices begin he process of curriculum stratification. At the end of 8th or 9th grade, when the student is asked to make a definite commitment, the student talks with a guidance counselor, who gives the student advice, based on the counselor's perceptions of the student's interests and strengths. Rosenbaum points out several related problems here: counselors tend to spend more time with college preparatory students; counselors seem to give different advice depending upon students' social characteristics; and counselors tend to give information that is consonant with their advice. The result is that many students make choices on the basis of incomplete or inaccurate information and find themselves in a curriculum track not related to their career plans. Thus, as Rosenbaum notes, the supposedly "free" choice made by students and their parents is not really free at all, since it is made on the basis of incomplete and inaccurate information.

To what extent does class bias affect this process? While there is clear evidence that poor and minority students are over-represented in noncollege preparatory programs, the research is somewhat conflicting as to whether social class operates as a major and direct factor in curriculum tracking. While some earlier studies suggested that social class influenced track

assignments, a more recent study by Alexander and Cook (1982) found little evidence of SES background, race, or gender bias.

Ability group placement operates somewhat differently. In secondary schools the decision to place a student in a particular ability group for the coming school year is usually made by the student's teacher at the end of the school year when administrators begin to determine scheduling parameters. In making this critical decision, the teacher tends to place greatest reliance upon achievement and aptitude test scores, student motivation, and classroom performance (Schafer & Olexa, 1971; Heyns, 1974; Rehberg & Rosenthal, 1978; Metz, 1978; Finley, 1984). If the teacher is uncertain about placement, he or she usually consults with the department chair. The final decision is often influenced by the department head's assessment of several scheduling factors. How many teachers are available for low-ability classes? How many teachers want to teach honors sections? How many students should there be in low-ability classes?

The process by which these scheduling factors are analyzed and assessed is illuminated in Finley's (1984) study of how English teachers and the English department chair in a comprehensive high school made decisions about teacher assignments. As Finley described the process, it seemed to be a highly political one, fraught with sensitive issues of power and influence. All teachers wanted to avoid the "lemon" classes, the remedial sections designed for students in the lowest 25 percent in English achievement. At the end of each school year, English teachers filled out preference sheets listing courses they wanted to teach. The department chairperson and the vice-principal assigned classes based upon those requests, giving teachers some of the classes they preferred and filling out with the leftovers no one wanted. In this process, however, there were certain tacit assumptions operating about priorities in responding to preferences. Electives and advanced courses were seen as the property of those currently teaching them. Part-time English teachers (who taught part-time in some other department) were usually assigned remedial sections. Teachers new to the school were assigned only low-track classes at first, until they had proven themselves.

What effect do social class and ethnic identity play in the process of assigning students to certain ability groups? Here again there is some ambiguity about the effect of student's social class and race on the decision-making process. In one study of 49 elementary schools, Haller (1985) discovered that in making decisions about reading groups, teachers most frequently discussed students' reading skills, with general academic competence, behavior and personality traits, work habits, and home background also mentioned frequently. While he discovered that African American students were over-represented in lower ability groups, he concluded that "... these results do not suggest that teachers are illegitimately influenced by pupils' race in making group decisions ... the association of race with reading group assignments is primarily an artifact of its association with achievement" (p. 480). And Finley discovered that the English teachers in her study were primarily influenced by their assessments of student motivation. However, Oakes (1985) notes that most standardized tests are culturally biased. She also points out that the personal characteristics (such as speech patterns, dress, and ways of interacting with adults) that affect teachers' decisions about grouping are factors often influenced by race and class. Thus, she argues that race and class play an indirect but influential role in grouping decisions.

Major Differences between Low and High Ability Classes. Once students are placed in a particular section, they experience some important differences in curriculum, instruction, and classroom climate. And those differences would seem to argue for a more equitable heterogeneous grouping.

First, the curriculum for low-ability classes is significantly different. In her study of 25 of the secondary schools included in John Goodlad's major project (A Place Called School, 1984), Oakes discovered some key differences in the English curriculum of the 299 English classes examined. Students in high-ability English classes were exposed to what she calls "high status" knowledge: standard works of literature; historical development of literature; characteristics of literary genres; literary elements; the writing of expository essays; College Board vocabulary and reading skills. On the other hand, students in low-ability English classes were exposed to "low prestige" knowledge: they read young-adult fiction, used workbooks and reading kits, wrote short simple paragraphs, studied English usage, and learned how to complete application forms.

Instructional practices also vary widely between the two extremes, as Gamoran and Berends' (1987) review indicates. First, teachers of low-ability classes spend less time on instruction than those in high ability classes. The most comprehensive study of this aspect is Oakes' analysis. By examining teachers' perceptions of time spent on instruction, direct observation of time spent on instruction, teachers' expectations of homework time, and observations of on-task and off-task behavior, she determined ". . . that, without question, low-track classes have considerably less of both the necessary and the sufficient elements of classroom time for student learning" (p. 104). She also found significant differences in what she termed the "quality of instruction." In comparison with students in low-ability classes, students in high-ability classes reported that their teachers were more enthusiastic, were clearer about learning expectations, and were less punitive in their approach to discipline. The Finley study tends to supports Oakes' findings. While teachers of high-ability sections typically used large-group discussion and small-group projects, teachers of the low sections used lesson plans based upon individual worksheets dealing with grammar and mechanics.

Finally, there are some important differences in the classroom climate. The research suggests in general that the climate in high ability classes is a more desirable one than that in low ability classes. Students in high-ability classes seem to get to the learning task more quickly (Evertson & Hickman, 1981). Observers of high-ability classes report better work habits, higher levels of participation, and more dependable behavior (Veldman & Sanford, 1984). Also reported are more trust, cooperation, and good will among students in higher-track classes (Oakes, 1985). One problem in using heterogeneous grouping in junior high English classes was noted by Evertson, Sanford, and Emmer (1981). In their study of 27 junior high school English classes in a large metropolitan school district, they found that extreme heterogeneity limited teachers' ability to respond to individual students' needs, made it less possible for them to respond to students' affective concerns, and resulted in lower task engagement and cooperation.

Outcome Differences in Heterogeneous and Homogeneous Classes. The key question, of course, is whether heterogeneous or homogeneous classes achieve better outcomes. The discussion that follows reviews first the research on achievement outcomes and then that on noncognitive ones.

Recent reviews of the research on achievement outcomes suggest that there are no significant differences between heterogeneous classes and homogeneous classes in terms of school achievement, although the evidence is far from conclusive. A 1982 meta-analysis by Kulik and Kulik of 52 studies of grouping at the secondary level concluded that, in general, students in grouped classes outperformed nongrouped students only slightly; however, students in gifted and talented programs performed better than they would have in heterogeneous classes.

However, there are some important findings from individual studies that usefully supplement the conclusions from the meta-analyses. Veldman and Sanford's (1984) study of 135 junior high school mathematics and English classes indicated that both higher ability students and lower ability students achieved better in high ability classes and that the differences in classroom environment had a greater impact on lower ability students. The researchers infer that these students are more reactive to or dependent upon class norms than are their higher ability counterparts. Becker's (1987) analysis of state reading achievement test scores of 8,000 Pennsylvania 6th-graders suggested that the effects of tracking varied in relation to students' socioeconomic class. Among students of "low" background, test scores in reading were negatively associated with tracking. However, he also notes that tracking for English was associated with higher English test scores for both the low and high background groups.

A recent (1986) study of grouping conducted by Dar and Resh of Israeli middle schools yielded some differential effects in relation to student ability. They found that "high resource" students in homogeneous classes did not do significantly better than similar students in heterogeneous ones; however, "low resource" students found the heterogeneous classes more advantageous. They summarized their findings in this manner: "In separation (into homogeneous classes), the low-resource students' loss is greater than the high-resource students' profit, and in mixing (in heterogeneous classes), the high resource students' loss is smaller than the low-resource students' gain" (p. 357).

The same inconclusiveness characterizes the research on the noncognitive outcomes of grouping practices. The Kulik and Kulik meta-analysis concluded that students in grouped classes developed more positive attitudes toward the subject being studied; but grouping practices did not seem to influence students' attitudes toward themselves and their schools. However, in his (1980) review of the related studies, Rosenbaum reaches a different conclusion: ". . . the majority of studies find that ability grouping hurts the self-evaluations of average and low-ability students. . . ." (p. 372). The Newfield and McElyea (1983) study of ability grouping in English classes concluded that high achieving sophomores and seniors in homogeneous classes (in comparison with high achievers in heterogeneous classes) rated their school higher on academic instruction, expressed more interest in school, had more positive attitudes toward themselves, and perceived English as more useful. The researchers found no significant differences among low achievers in heterogeneous and homogeneous classes in attitudes towards self and school.

The inconclusiveness of all these findings is probably attributable to the difficulties noted by Good and Marshall (1984): many of the studies have been narrowly designed, focusing only on one variable when a complex set are operating; the concepts of *heterogeneous* and *homogenous* have been poorly defined and operationalized; and direct observations of classrooms have too often not been made.

Implications for Practitioners

The findings presented above yield no simple answer to English teachers, supervisors, and school administrators trying to find the best grouping arrangements for secondary English. Taken together, however, the research would suggest a compromise strategy of the following sort.

1. Separate gifted students into honors and advanced placement classes. There seems to be consistent evidence that such grouping results in better achievement for more able students.
2. Group the rest of the students heterogeneously. The dangers of tracking and the resulting stratification probably outweigh any slight advantage that might accrue with homogeneous grouping.
3. Provide teachers with the training needed to teach heterogeneous groups, giving special emphasis to the use of cooperative learning groups.

A special note might be made about this last suggestion. A substantial body of research suggests that cooperative learning approaches are very effective in achieving cognitive and noncognitive outcomes with heterogeneous classes. (See, for example, Slavin 1983). One form of cooperative learning, Cooperative Integrated Reading and Composition (CIRC), has been shown to be especially effective in English classes. As Slavin (1987) explains, students in the CIRC program work in mixed-ability teams on a series of reading activities (reading aloud to each other and completing several kinds of reading-related activities) and engage in peer response groups in a writing process model. He notes that in one 24-week study, students using the CIRC approach gained 64 percent of a grade equivalent more than control students in reading comprehension, language expression, and language mechanics.

THE WORK ENVIRONMENT

The work environment, as conceptualized here, is the nature of the academic work and its related activities, as construed by both the teacher and the students. The concept of *academic work* was initially developed by Doyle as a means of analyzing and understanding the nature of teaching-learning transactions as they occur in the classroom. (See his and Carter's 1984 publication for a detailed explication of the concept and its applications.) The discussion that follows represents this author's attempts to integrate Doyle's theory and research with that of other scholars who analyze the concept somewhat differently. (See, for example, Blumenfeld & Meece, 1988; and Anderson, Stevens, Prawat, & Nickerson, 1988.) It should be noted, of course, that other metaphors and constructs might be used in examining the teaching-learning transactions and would obviously yield different findings. However, the concept of *academic work* is so widely accepted by scholars in the field and seems potentially useful that it is accepted here as the operative construct.

Figure 24–4 presents a schematic representation of the major elements in academic work. Each is treated briefly here and explicated more fully in the discussion that follows. First, the teacher makes plans for what might be termed the intended work. Those plans are influenced by several sources—chiefly, the curriculum guides, the textbooks, the tests, and the teacher's knowledge and previous experience. As the teacher attempts to structure the intended work, those intentions are mediated by both external occurrences (such as a fire drill) and by internal events (such as students' questions or behaviors). Those internal events are themselves influenced by the students' goals for that classroom session and the pressures students exert to achieve those goals. Those external and internal events operating on the teacher's plans result in what might be termed the actual work—what finally occurs in the classroom.

Teachers' Plans for Academic Work

The processes by which teachers plan for academic work are complex, not yet fully understood either by researchers or teachers themselves. The general picture of those complex processes that is presented below must therefore be seen as a preliminary sketch, subject to further revision as additional research findings are generated. The difficulty of delineating a general process is complicated by the fact that, as both Favor-Lydecker (1981) and Sardo (1982) noted, teachers have different planning styles that cannot be completely captured in a general portrait.

Teachers consider unit planning as the most important type of planning; they view daily lesson planning as much less important. As Clark and Yinger (1979) discovered, unit planning is a cyclical and an incremental process that begins with a general idea and moves through phases of successive elaboration. In making those unit plans, teachers seem to respond differentially to several pressures. For most teachers, standardized and

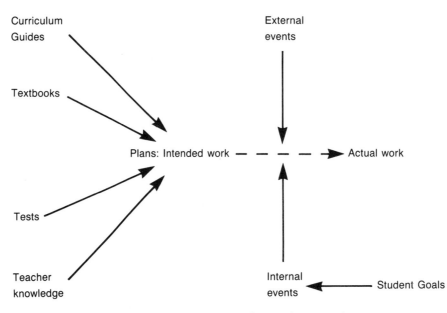

FIGURE 24–4. The Academic Work Environment.

curriculum-based tests exercise a powerful influence. For others the textbook is the primary determiner of what is taught. For most secondary teachers, their own knowledge and experience is dominant, with the district's curriculum guide exerting only a modest influence on their decisions. (For the research on factors influencing teachers' planning, see Clark & Elmore, 1981; Floden, Porter, Schmidt, Freeman & Schwille, 1980; Leithwood, Ross, & Montgomery, 1982.)

In making their plans, teachers seem to focus either on content ("It's time to start *Julius Caesar*"), activities ("I'll begin class with a quiz"), or tasks ("They should start writing their personal essay"). Although the research is not uniform on this issue of focus, most studies indicate that teachers do not use the rational planning approach of first identifying objectives and then selecting activities to achieve those objections. (See Zahorik, 1975; and Sardo, 1982.)

Although these plans for work are usually not implemented with a high degree of fidelity, the evidence suggests that long-term and short-term planning is important. First, the teacher's yearly, semester, and unit plans are the chief means by which the teacher makes decisions about content selection and time allocation. The research on teacher effectiveness suggests that student achievement is higher when teachers deal with the prescribed content of the curriculum and allocate time consistent with district priorities. (See the Brophy & Good 1986 review.) Second, well-organized instruction pays off, as Rosenshine and Stevens (1986) point out. While there is no direct relationship between the quality of the written lesson plans and the organization of the taught lesson, it seems safe to conclude, as Clark and Peterson (1986) do, that teacher planning does influence opportunity to learn, content coverage, grouping for instruction, and the general focus of classroom processes, all important elements of effective teaching.

External and Internal Events

As noted above, those plans are not always delivered as intended. First, there are external factors that require changes in the plans. As McCutcheon (1980) learned, many teachers view long-range planning as counterproductive because of unpredictable changes in the schedule and interruptions of class. An assembly scheduled at the last minute, an early dismissal because of threatening weather, an unannounced guest speaker who must be accommodated—such interruptions and intrusions require the teacher to make last-minute changes in the carefully planned unit.

Internal events also play an important role. Clark and Peterson (1986) observe that, once class begins, the plan moves to the background and interactive decision-making becomes more important. In this sense then the teacher's interactive decision-making is the process by which the intended work is transformed into the actual work. Teachers' reports of their interactive thoughts suggest that those thoughts are concerned primarily with the students and their responses ("they're starting to lose interest in the story"); instructional processes ("this would be a good time for a small-group discussion") are second in importance. (See the Clark & Peterson 1986 review.) Those thoughts about the students and the activities lead them to make numerous interaction decisions—one every two minutes, according to the Clark and Peterson review.

Student Pressures

As noted above, student behavior tends to play a major role in teachers' interactive decision-making. The research suggests that often this behavior is intended to reduce the complexity of classroom work, to make classroom life less demanding. Doyle and Carter's (1984) study of an English teacher teaching writing is instructive here. In this two-month observational study, the researchers noted significant changes from the time the task was introduced by the teacher to the time it was accomplished by the students: the writing task became less ambiguous and more explicit; the teacher did an increasing amount of work for the students by specifying the features of an acceptable product; and the accountability system was softened. These changes were brought about largely by the students: students influenced task demands by asking questions about content and procedures and by offering guesses to teacher questions in order to elicit clarifying instructions from the teachers. They also exerted indirect pressure on the task system by slowing down the pace of classroom events, frequently punctuating work periods with questions.

The Actual Work

All the above factors interact to produce the actual work of the classroom—work that, as Doyle (1986) notes, acts as the substance of classroom events, directs students' information processing, and affects their attitudes about participation and cooperation. This actual work can perhaps best be conceptualized as a series of academic tasks. Those tasks involve several components: content; resources; procedures; activities; goals or products; and an accountability system.

To understand the nature and interrelationships of these components of the academic task, consider the English teacher planning and teaching a unit on the persuasive essay. The content—the substantive focus—is the persuasive essay as a type of writing. The resources include models of persuasive essays, textbook explanations of how to write a persuasive essay, teacher presentations and questions, and the ideas and responses of other students. The procedures, the operations that the student brings to bear to transform the resources into the product, would include such processes as analyzing the audience, prioritizing arguments, selecting evidence, and organizing the essay. The activities, the specific teaching-learning transactions orchestrated by the teacher to help the student complete the product, might involve such things as reading a model essay, discussing the essay in small groups, and writing a brief response to the essay. The product, of course, is the essay the student submits; and the accountability system involves both the monitoring of the activities and the grading of the final product.

Activities in the English Class

In the foregoing analysis, the activity is seen as a component of the task, although some researchers focus on either activity or task, to the exclusion of the other. Several researchers have examined the nature and function of activities, which Doyle (1983) defines as "a bounded segment of classroom time characterized by an identifiable (a) focal content or concern and (b) pattern or program of action" (p. 2).

Doyle's (1983) study of seven junior high English teachers yielded useful insights about the importance of activities as a means of achieving order. First, he discovered that the school schedule acted as a major constraint for teachers; they often had problems fitting activities into the 55-minute period provided for English. In some cases, activities ran short and students had nothing to do for several minutes; in other cases the bell interrupted the last activity. He noted that more effective teachers were consistently able to fit activities to periods. Second, he discovered much mixing of activity types: teahcers often inserted questions into lectures or made announcements during seatwork. However, the more effective teachers in his study made sure that these activity mixes had a clear sense of purpose, working jointly towards a single theme.

Next, the successful managers had developed and used distinct patterns for opening the class session, for marking transitions, and for ending the period. They also demonstrated what Doyle called "situational awareness," frequently scanning the class for signs of confusion and inattention, making brief contacts with individual students, and making brief comments on events occurring in the room. They also protected activities by blocking any event or incident that might interrupt activity flow: "We can take care of that later." And they pushed students through the curriculum, focusing on content even when misbehavior seemed prevalent.

The Tasks of English Classes

The special nature of tasks in the English classroom has been the focus of several other studies. First, some studies have examined the intellectual or cognitive nature of tasks in the English class, in comparison with other subjects. Steele, Walberg, and House (1974) determined that there were some important differences in the cognitive press of secondary English language-arts classes when compared with secondary mathematics, science, and social studies classes: English language-arts classes were most divergent in their cognitive press (there is no right answer) and were most concerned with syntax over substance (focused more on having students synthesize, translate, and apply, rather than summarize and memorize). Their study was replicated by Kuert (1977) with essentially the same findings. However, Randhawa and Hunt (1982) in their study of the perceptions of 10th grade Canadian students found that English and mathematics were quite similar in their intellectual climate.

An analysis of tasks in middle school English, science, and social studies classes by Korth and Cornbleth (1982) concluded that the English curriculum was more diverse than the social studies and involved less seat work than social studies. However, in all three classes the dominant whole-class task involved what the researchers called "QATE," teacher question, student answer, and teacher elaboration.

One major study by Applebee (1984) examined the special nature of writing tasks in the English classroom, yielding some important findings. On the average the students in the study completed an average of approximately fourteen papers in the course of the school year. For two thirds of those papers, the audience was the "teacher-as-examiner." Informational writing accounted for close to 85 percent of the English papers written, with analysis and summary accounting for almost all of the informational tasks. The information for these writing tasks was drawn chiefly from the teacher or the text. For those advocating a diversified writing program emphasizing real problems and real audiences, the findings must seem rather discouraging.

Finally, a study by Doyle and Sanford (1982) of secondary English classes focused on managing student work in secondary classrooms, concluding with several "practical lessons" for English teachers for managing classroom work more effectively. First, they recommend that teachers should take special pains to communicate the task clearly to students, noting that students often misinterpret assigned tasks. In this explanation, they should clarify the assignment, identify the steps and strategies to be used, analyze a model response, call attention to the goal, and identify the criteria to be used for grading.

Second, they should carefully monitor students understanding of the work and the strategies for accomplishing it. In making long-term assignments, like reading a novel or writing an essay, the teacher should confer with individual students at the start of the task, to be sure that they understand both task and strategies. They should ask students "strategic questions" that probe for understanding and ask students to explain their answers. They should also monitor student group work and observe student-student interactions.

Third, they should encourage students to engage in novel tasks that involve more risk for the student. Since students will exert pressure for the teacher to do their work for them, teachers should determine which aspects of the task should be carried out completely by the students and insist that students carry out those aspects, regardless of student questions and requests. They should also provide "safety nets" for students doing novel work: let them revise and resubmit without penalty; provide for cooperative learning; and adjust the grading system.

Finally, and perhaps most importantly, teachers should help students find meaning in the tasks they are doing. The researchers noted that they seldom saw students doing tasks in which they were required to struggle with meaning. Grammar consisted of multiple-choice exercises that asked students to select the word that sounded right, instead of sentence combining and sentence writing. Literature consisted of memorizing the facts of a story or learning the standard interpretation of a passage, rather than struggling with what the work meant to the student. To help students find meaning in their classroom tasks, the authors recommend several strategies: when assignments are introduced, make explicit statements about the relationship between the current work and previous work; build a meaningful system of related tasks, instead of fragmented and disjointed ones; culminate units by assigning tasks that require students to review and integrate previous work.

Implications for Administrators and Supervisors

The research reviewed above suggests that administrators and supervisors concerned about making the English classroom a better work environment should provide English teachers

with systematic staff development focusing on the following skills.

1. Developing long-term plans that reflect curricular priorities and make appropriate time allocations.
2. Making effective interaction decisions in the classroom—knowing when to adhere to and when to deviate from the intended work, knowing when to respond and when to ignore student pressures to simplify the task.
3. Communicating the task clearly and monitoring student behavior to ensure that students understand both the task and the needed strategies.
4. Conducting activities effectively: marking activity boundaries; showing situational awareness; protecting the activity flow.
5. Presenting novel tasks when appropriate and providing students with the support needed to complete those tasks effectively.
6. Helping students find meaning in classroom tasks by showing them relationships and assisting them in making connections.

PSYCHO-SOCIAL ENVIRONMENT

The psycho-social environment is defined here as the shared perceptions of the people in an environment about the nature of the psycho-social interactions of that environment. The following discussion examines its nature more specifically, reviews the findings on the psycho-social environment in general, discusses the research on secondary English classroom environments, reviews the research on person-environment interactions, and concludes by discussing the implications of that complex body of research.

The Nature of the Psycho-social Environment

In analyzing the special nature of the psycho-social environment, the subscales of the Classroom Environment Scale (Moos & Trickett, 1974) seem to be especially useful. Although the Learning Environment Inventory (Fraser, Anderson, & Walberg, 1982) has been more widely used in research on the classroom environment, the LEI includes one subscale ("material environment") that in this chapter is considered as the "physical environment" and includes three subscales ("diversity," "speed," and "difficulty") that are here considered aspects of the work environment.

In the following discussion, therefore, the concept of the psycho-social environment will be considered as embodying the nine elements reflected in the CES: involvement; affiliation; teacher support; task orientation; competition; order and organization; role clarity; teacher control; and innovation. However, research findings from the LEI, as well as those from other measures, will be included in the review wherever appropriate.

The Importance of the Psycho-Social Environment

This section will review the research on the relationship between these environmental factors and student outcomes, first clarifying the general nature of that relationship, then examining broad environmental types, and finally considering specific environmental factors. Before reviewing that research, it would be useful to keep in mind Fraser's (1986) cautionary note: all the research up to this point has been correlational in nature; there are no experimental studies providing support for a causal relationship.

The research suggests rather clearly that the psycho-social environment is strongly associated with both achievement and attitudinal outcomes. Two major reviews of studies related to the psycho-social environment suggest that student perception of the classroom environment accounted for between 13 and 46 percent of the variance in cognitive, affective, and behavioral outcomes (Anderson & Walberg, 1974; Haertel, Walberg, & Haertel, 1981).

Supporting the general importance of the psycho-social environment is Moos's (1980) analysis of the major types of classroom environment. By using cluster analysis of data from 200 classes that had been assessed with the Classroom Environment Scale (CES), Moos was able to identify six basic types of classrooms. From his review of this large body of research, he was able to arrive at four conclusions concerning the relationship of these general types to student outcomes. First, those classes oriented towards relationships and innovation enhance social growth and personal growth, abut do less well in improving achievement scores. Second, classes that emphasize goal accomplishment and classroom maintenance can bring about high achievement but are associated with lower student interest, morale, and creativity. Third, control-oriented classrooms lead to dissatisfaction and alienation and at the same time are not related to personal, social, or academic growth. Finally—and most importantly—classrooms that combine warm and supportive relationships, an emphasis on academic tasks and accomplishments, and an orderly and well-structured milieu are associated with achievement gains, creativity, and personal growth.

Moos (1987) summarizes the general import of these findings in this manner:

Overall, these findings imply that basic skills programs will have more positive effects if they are supportive as well as task-oriented, whereas alternative school programs need more task focus, though not at the expense of engagement and support. (p. 4)

Several specific psycho-social factors seem to be important in relation to student outcomes. The meta-analysis by Haertel, Walberg, and Haertel (1981) concluded that the following psycho-social factors were positively associated with gains in learning in several subject areas: cohesiveness; satisfaction; formality; goal direction; and democracy. Adjusted gains in learning were negatively associated with these factors: friction; cliqueness; apathy; and disorganization.

The Psycho-Social Environment of the Secondary English Classroom

A comprehensive search of the ERIC data base and *Dissertation Abstracts International* failed to identify any study that fo-

cused on the psycho-social environment of the secondary English class alone; however, several studies have examined the differences between the environments of English classes and those of other secondary subjects. Anderson (1971) found several interesting differences and similarities between humanities classes (English literature and history) and science, mathematics, and French classes in Montreal: compared with mathematics classes, English classes were lower on friction, favoritism, disorganization, and cliqueness and higher on formality and goal direction; compared with science classes; humanities classes were seen as less formal and slower moving, with more friction, favoritism, cliqueness, and disorganization; compared with French classes, humanities classes were seen as lower on goal direction and higher on friction and disorganization.

Although Randhawa and Michayluk (1975) determined that subject content did not significantly affect the learning environment of the classroom, they concluded that mathematics and social studies classrooms seemed to the students to be more cohesive than English classrooms.

Hearn and Moos (1978) used a conceptualization of personalities and environments developed by Holland (1973) to classify school subjects as one of the following five types: realistic (vocational-technical shops); investigative (mathematics and science); artistic (English, music, foreign language and art); social (social studies); and conventional (business subjects). In a study of 209 classes, they found that students in the artistic classes had a high emphasis on task orientation and teacher control, with a lack of emphasis on involvement. affiliation, and innovation. Realistic classes were high on several factors (competition, rule clarity, teacher control, involvement, affiliation, and innovation) and low on task orientation. Conventional classes were high in involvement, affiliation, task orientation, competition, and rule clarity and low only on innovation. Social classes were low in several dimensions: task orientation, rule clarity, teacher control, involvement, and affiliation.

Although not specifically concerned with classroom environment as such, Evertson's (1979) study examined the affective behaviors of 39 junior high English teachers and 29 mathematics teachers over the course of one year. In both subjects, high-achieving classes were characterized as having good classroom management, effective teaching, a large proportion of time spent in teaching, and a positive student attitude. In focusing on English teachers, Evertson pointed out that the more effective teachers had an overall sense of purpose; less effective teachers seemed on the other hand to have a day-to-day attitude of survival, without a clear sense of instructional purpose. As she put it, less effective teachers were ". . . either marking time or filling it with activities whose functions appear to be 'making it through the period' " (p. 24).

Finally, Costello (1987) determined that students in high-track mathematics and English classes both assessed the learning environment more favorably than students in middle- and lower-ability tracks. He also concluded that the relationship between Classroom Environment Scale scores and student achievement on the Stanford Test of Academic Skills varied somewhat in relation to the ability level of the English classes. He found that English achievement on this standardized test was positively associated with these subscales of the CES: in low-track classes, with Task Orientation, Order and Organization, and Teacher Control; in middle-track classes, with Teacher Support and Order and Organization. Although there were no significant relationships between standardized test scores and CES subscales for the high track students, he discovered that semester grades for these students were positively associated with Affiliation, Teacher Support, Order and Organization, and Innovation.

These studies are so few in number, so different in their methodologies, and so varied in their findings that it would seem unwise to generalize about the special nature of English classroom environments.

The Person-Environment Fit

In general a relatively small body of research suggests that students will achieve more and have better attitudes when there is congruence between the actual learning environment and the preferred learning environment.

Several studies have provided general support for Hunt's (1975) Conceptual level are able to organize their environments, whereas those at a lower conceptual level learn better when the teacher provides a more structured environment. Harpin and Sandler (1979) found that junior high boys who were more comfortable with teacher-provided structure adjusted better in a classroom with high teacher control. In a later (1985) study they discovered that student perception of the relevance of the classroom environment was an important factor: internally-oriented students who viewed classroom control as relevant adapted better in low-control classrooms, whereas such congruence was not a factor with students who saw the environment as less relevant. Moos (1987) reaches this general conclusion about the importance of conceptual level: "In general, externally oriented students tend to adjust better in more flexibly organized settings. Similarly, students who want to explore and shape their environments and who exhibit a strong need for independence profit more from less structured learning environments" (p. 6).

Studies making use of other inventories have also provided tentative support for the importance of person-environment fit. Nielsen and Moos (1978) explored the relationship of students' preference for social exploration (the willingness to explore or change relationships) and the actual extent of classroom social exploration. Students high in exploration preference achieved better in classrooms high in actual exploration; there was no difference for students low in exploration preference. A study by Rich and Bush (1978) examined the effect of congruence between teacher style (direct or indirect verbal behavior) and student social-emotional development. Ten congruent groups were obtained by matching teachers with a natural direct style with students high in social-emotional development; 10 incongruent groups matched 5 direct teachers with students low in social-emotioinal development and 5 indirect teachers with students high in social-emotional development. The congruent groups performed better than the incongruent groups on reading achievement, time on task, and affective perception. Fraser (1986) observes, on the basis of this and other related studies,

that person-environment fit is at least as important as actual environment in predicting learning outcomes.

Since these studies have used the class as the level of analysis, Fraser's caution here seems appropriate. He points out that, although class achievement of certain outcomes might be enhanced by attempting to change the environment to make it more congruent with class preferences, it cannot be inferred that an individual's achievement will be improved by moving that student from an incongruent to a congruent environment. He reports three case studies he conducted in which a teacher was able to bring about such change through a problem-solving process: the teacher administered one of the learning environment surveys to students; the data were analyzed and presented to the teacher as profiles showing class means of actual and preferred environmental scores; after private reflection and informal discussion with the researchers, the teacher used several strategies to change the environment to achieve greater congruence.

Moos (1980) notes other cautions about trying to match the environment with individual student preferences. He points out first that students' preferences change over time, as they experience different settings. He also observes that students may prefer environments that are not sufficiently challenging. One final argument could be presented against matching individuals' preferences with the environment provided: one important outcome of schooling should be the ability to adjust to and learn in a variety of environments. Adults need to work in a variety of environments—many of which are not congruent with their preferences.

The Implications for Practice

What are the implications of the reserach on psycho-social environments for school administrators and English language arts supervisors? Since relatively little research has addressed the specific issue of secondary English environments, the following recommendations for practice are offered rather tentatively:

1. English teachers should be provided with the staff development that would enable them to examine and discuss the characteristics that seem to define an effective psycho-social environment. Those characteristics would seem to be the following:
   - There are supportive relationships between the teacher and the students and among the students.
   - There is an emphasis on accomplishing the academic tasks important in English language arts: writing effectively, reading intelligently, communicating clearly.
   - There is an orderly and well-structured classroom environment.
   - The English teacher has a clear sense of purpose and direction; there is a sense of intentionality about classroom events.
2. English teachers should receive constructive feedback about the type of environment they are providing. This feedback can come from two chief sources: observations by a trained

observer (an administrator, supervisor, or colleague); and feedback from students.

3. Administrators, supervisors, and teachers should collaborate in organizing and implementing staff development sessions that would enable teachers to make needed modifications in the environment.

A Concluding Note

Each of the sections of this chapter has concluded with an analysis of the implications of the research on the four chief components of the classroom learning environment: the physical environment; the group environment; the work environment; and the psycho-social environment. These analyses are not intended to offer a set of prescriptions for all secondary English classrooms; there is not yet sufficient knowledge about these crucial and sensitive issues to warrant prescriptive advice. Rather they are presented as tentative suggestions that need additional study and analysis.

An analysis of the literature suggests the need for three kinds of research here. First, there is clearly a need for carefully designed empirical studies that would focus on the learning environment of secondary English classroom, examining the relationship between certain environmental factors and student affective and cognitive outcomes. Second, there is a need for additional ethnographic studies of secondary English classrooms that would provide the rich detail that is so important in understanding learning environments. Finally, there is a need for action research of the collaborative sort recommended by Lieberman and Miller (1986) that would enable practitioners to diagnose and modify these environments for both teachers and students.

References

Adams, R. S. (1969). Location as a factor of instructional interaction. *Merrill Palmer Quarterly, 15,* 309–322.

Adams, R. S. & Biddle, B. J. (1970). *Realities of teaching: Explorations with video tape.* New York: Holt, Rinehart, & Winston.

Alexander, K. L. & Cook, M. A. (1982). Curricula and course work: A surprise ending to a familiar story. *American Sociological Review, 47,* 626–640.

Anderson, G. J. (1971). Effects of course content and teacher sex on the social climate of learning. *American Educational Research Journal, 8,* 649–663.

Anderson, G. J. & Walberg, H. J. (1974). Learning environments. In H. J. Walberg (Ed.), *Evaluating educational performance: A sourcebook of methods, instruments, and examples* (pp. 81–98). Berkeley, CA: McCutchan.

Anderson, L. M., Stevens, D. D., Prawat, R. S., & Nickerson, J. (1988). Classroom task environments and students' task-related beliefs. *Elementary School Journal, 88,* 281–295.

Anifant, D. C. (1972). Risk-taking behavior in children experiencing open space and traditional school environments. (Doctoral dissertation, University of Maryland, College Park, MD, 1971.) *Disseratation Abstracts International, 33,* 2491A.

Applebee, A. N. (1977). *A survey of teaching conditions in English, 1972.* Urbana, IL: ERIC Clearinghouse on Reading and Communication Skills, National Council of Teachers of English.

Applebee, A. N. (1984). *Contexts for learning to write: Studies of secondary school instruction.* Norwood, NJ: Ablex.

Beck, T. M. (1979, April). *An Australian study of school environments.* Paper presented at the annual meeting of the American Educational Research Association, San Francisco. (ERIC Document Reproduction Service No. ED 172 357.)

Becker, H. J. (1987). *Addressing the needs of different groups of early adolescents: Effects of varying school and classroom organization practices on students from different social backgrounds and abilities.* Baltimore, MD: Center for Research on Elementary and Middle Schools, Johns Hopkins University.

Bennett, N. & Blundell, D. (1983). Quantity and quality of work in rows and classroom groups. *Educational Psychology, 3,* 93–105.

Blumenfeld, P. C. & Meece, J. L. (1988). Task factors, teacher behavior, and students' involvement and use of learning strategies in science. *Elementary School Journal, 88,* 235–250.

Bolvin, J. O. (1982). Classroom organization. In H. E. Mitzell (Ed.), *Ency-* *clopedia of educational research* (5th ed.) (pp. 265–274). New York: Free Press.

Bronzaft, A. L. & McCarthy, D. P. (1975). The effect of elevated train noise on reading ability. *Environment and Behavior, 7,* 517–527.

Brooks, D. M., Silvern, S. B. & Wooten, M. (1978). The ecology of teacher-pupil verbal interaction. *Journal of Classroom Interaction, 14,* 39–45.

Brophy, J. E. & Good, T. L. (1986). Teacher behavior and student achievement. In M. C. Wittrock (Ed.), *Handbook of research on teaching* (3rd ed.) (pp. 328–375). New York: Macmillan.

Brunetti, F. A. (1971). The teacher in the authority structure of the elementary school: A study of open space and self-contained classroom schools. (Doctoral disseration, Stanford University, Stanford, CA, 1970.) *Dissertation Abstracts International, 31,* 4405A.

Burnham, B. (1970). *A day in the life: Case studies of pupils in open plan schools.* Toronto: York County Board of Education.

Cheatham, R. & Jordan, W. (1976). Cognitive and affective implications of class size in a lecture-practicum speech communicatio course. *Improving College and University Teaching, 24,* 251–254.

Clark, C. M. & Elmore, J. L. (1981). *Transforming curriculum in mathematics, science, and writing: A case study of teachers' yearly planning.* East Lansing, MI: Institute for Research in Teaching, Michigan State University.

Clark, C. M. & Peterson, P. L. (1986). Teachers' thought processes. In M. C. Wittrock (Ed.), *Handbook of research on teaching* (3rd ed.) (pp. 255–296). New York: Macmillan.

Clark, C. M. & Yinger, R. J. (1979). *Three studies of teacher planning.* East Lansing, MI: Institute for Research in Teaching, Michigan State University.

Clem, P., Ahern, K., Dailey, N., Gary, M., & Scantlebury, M. (n. d.) *A comparison of interaction patterns in an open space and a fixed paln school.* Blacksburg, VA: Virginia Polytechnical Institute and State University.

Costello, R. W. (1987). Relationships among ability grouping, classroom climate, and academic achievement in mathematics and English classes. In B. J. Fraser (Ed.), *The study of learning environments, Vol. 3* (pp. 60–67). Baton Rouge, LA: Louisiana State University College of Education.

Cotton, K. & Savard, W. G. (1980). *Class size research on school effectiveness project.* Portland, OR: Northwest Regional Laboratory.

Crook, M. A. & Langdon, F. J. (1974). The effects of aircraft noise in schools around London airport. *Journal of Sound and Vibration, 34,* 221–232.

Dar, Y. & Resh, N. (1986). Classroom intellectual composition and academic achievement. *American Educational Research Journal, 23,* 357–374.

Delefes, P. & Jackson, B. (1972). Teacher-pupil interaction as a function of location in the classroom. *Psychology in the Schools, 9,* 119–123.

Doyle, W. (1983). *Managing classroom activities in junior high English classes: An interim report.* Austin, TX: Research and Development Center for Teacher Education, University of Texas.

Doyle, W. (1986). Classroom management. In M. C. Wittrock (Ed.), *Handbook of research on teaching* (3rd ed.) (pp. 392–431).

Doyle, W. & Carter, K. (1984). Academic tasks in classrooms. *Curriculum Inquiry, 14,* 129–147.

Doyle, W. & Sanford, J. P. (1982). *Managing student work in secondary classrooms: Practical lessons from a study of classroom tasks.* Austin, TX: Research and Development Center for Teacher Education, University of Texas.

Dunn, K. & Dunn, R. (1987, March). Dispelling outmoded beliefs about student learning. *Educational Leadership, 44* (5) (pp. 55–62).

Dunn, R., Dunn, K., & Price, G. (1985). *Learning style inventory.* Lawrence, KS: Price Systems.

Durlak, J., Beardsley, B., & Murray, J. (1972). Observations of user activity patterns in open and traditional plan school environments. *Proceedings of the Environmental Design and Research Association Conference.* Los Angeles: University of California.

Educational Research Service. (1980). Class size research: A critique of recent meta-analyses. *Phi Delta Kappan, 62,* 239–241.

Ellison, M., Gilbert, L. L., & Ratsoy, E. W. (1969). Teacher behavior in open-area classrooms. *Canadian Administration Quarterly, 8,* 17–21.

Epstein, Y. M. & Karlin, R. A. (1975). Effects of acute experimental crowding. *Journal of Applied Psychology, 5,* 34–53.

Evertson, C. M. (1979). *Teacher behavior, student achievement, and student attitudes: Description of selected classrooms.* Austin, TX: Research and Development Center for Teacher Education.

Evertson, C. M. & Hickman, R. C. (1981). *The tasks of teaching classes of varied group composition.* Austin, TX: Research and Development Center for Teacher Education.

Evertson, C. M., Sanford, J. P., & Emmer, E. T. (1981). Effects of class heterogeneity in junior high school. *American Educational Research Journal, 18,* 219–232.

Favor-Lydecker, A. (1981, April). *Teacher planning of social studies units.* Paper presented at annual conference of the American Educational Research Association, Los Angeles.

Filby, N. A. (1980, February). *Evidence of class-size effects.* Paper presented at annual conference of the American Educational Research Association, Anaheim, CA.

Finley, M. K. (1984). Teachers and tracking in a comprehensive high school. *Sociology of Teaching, 57,* 233–243.

Floden, R. E., Porter, A. C., Schmidt, W. J., Freeman, D. J., & Schwille, J. R. (1980). *Responses to curriculum pressures: A policy capturing study of teacher decisions about content.* East Lansing, MI: Institute for Research on Teaching, Michigan State University.

Fraser, B. J. (1986). *Classroom environment.* Dover, NH: Croom Helm.

Fraser, B. J., Anderson, G. J., & Walberg, H. J. (1982). *Assessment of learning environments: Manual for Learning Environment Inventory (LEI) and My Class Inventory (MCI)* (3rd ed.). Perth: Western Australian Institute of Technology.

Fraser, B. J., Walberg, H. J., Welch, W. W., & Hattie, J. A. (1987). Syntheses of educational productivity research. *International Journal of Educational Research, 11,* 145–252.

Gamoran, A. & Berends, M. (1987). The effects of stratification in secondary schools: Synthesis of survey and ethnographic research. *Review of Educational Research, 57,* 415–435.

George, P. S. (1975). *Ten years of open space schools: A review of the research.* Gainesville, FL: Florida Educational Research and Development Council, University of Florida.

Glass, G. V. & Smith, M. L. (1978). *Meta-analysis of research on the relationship of class size and achievement.* San Francisco: Far West Laboratory for Educational Research and Development.

Good, T. L. & Marshall, S. (1984). Do students learn more in heterogeneous or homogeneous groups? In P. L. Peterson, L. C. Wilkinson, & M. Hallman (Eds.), *The social context of instruction: Group organization and group processes* (pp. 15–38). Orlando, FL: Academic Press.

Goodlad, J. (1984). *A place called school: Prospects for the future.* New York: McGraw-Hill.

Gump, P. V. (1974). Operating environments in schools of open and traditional design. *School Review, 82,* 575–593.

Gump, P. V. & Ross, R. (1977). The fit of milieu and programme in school environments. In H. McGurk (Ed.), *Ecological factors in human design.* New York: North-Holland.

Haddad, W. D. 91978). *Educational effects of class size.* World Bank Staff Working Paper #280. (Educational Document Reproduction Service No. ED 179 003.)

Haertel, G. D., Walberg, H. J., & Haertel, E. H. (1981). Socio-psychological environments and learning: A quantitative synthesis. *British Educational Research Journal, 7,* 27–36.

Haller, E. J. (1985). Pupil race and elementary school ability grouping: Are teachers biased against black children? *American Educational Research Journal, 22,* 465–483.

Harpin, P. & Sandler, I. (1979). Interaction of sex, locus of control, and teacher control: Toward a student-classroom match. *American Journal of Community Psychology, 7,* 621–632.

Harpin, P. & Sandler, I. (1985). Relevance of social climate: An improved approach to assessing persons by environment interactions in the classroom. *American Journal of Community Psychology, 13,* 381–392.

Hase, H. D. & Goldberg, L. R. (1967). Comparative validity of different strategies of constructing personality inventories. *Psychological Bulletin, 67,* 231–248.

Hearn, J. C. & Moos, R. H. (1978). Subject matter and classroom climate: A test of Holland's environmental propositions. *American Educational Research Journal, 15,* 111–124.

Hedges, L. V. & Stock, W. (1983). The effects of class size: An examination of rival hypotheses. *American Educational Research Journal, 20,* 63–85.

Heyns, B. (1974). Social selection and stratification within schools. *American Journal of Sociology, 79,* 1434–1451.

Holland, J. L. (1973). *Making vocational choices: A theory of careers.* Englewood Cliffs, NJ: Prentice Hall.

Horowitz, P. & Otto, P. (1973). *The teaching effectiveness of an alternative teaching facility.* (ERIC Document Reproduction Service No. ED 083 242). Alberta, Canada: University of Alberta.

Hunt, D. (1975). Person-environment interaction: A challenge found wanting before it was tried. *Review of Educational Research, 45,* 209–230.

Hutt, S. J. & Hutt, C. (1970). *Direct observation and measurement of behavior.* Springfield, IL: Thomas.

Johnson, R. H. (1973). The effects of four modified elements of a classroom's physical environment on the social-psychological environment of a class. (Doctoral dissertation, Oregon State University, Corvallis, OR, 1973.) *Dissertation Abstracts International,* 1973, *34,* 1002A.

Keefe, J. W. (Ed.) (1988). *Profiling and utilizing learning style.* Reston, VA: National Association of Secondary School Principals.

Kolb, D. (1981). Commentary on Dunn and De Bello article. *Educational Leadership, 38,* 372–375.

Koneya, M. (1976). Location and interaction in row and column seating arrangements. *Environment and Behavior, 8,* 265–270.

Korth, W. & Cornbleth, C. (1982, March). *Classroom activities as settings for cognitive learning opportunity and instruction.* Paper presented at annual meeting of the American Educational Research Association, New York.

Krimsky, J. S. (1982). *A comparative analysis of the effects of matching and mismatching fourth grade students with their learning style preferences for the environmental element of light and their subsequent reading speed and accuracy.* Doctoral dissertation, St. John's University, Jamaica, New York.

Krovetz, M. L. (1977). Who needs what when: Design of pluralistic learning environments. In D. Stokols (Ed.), *Perspectives on environment and behavior: Theory, research, and applications.* New York: Plenum Press.

Kuert, W. P. (1977). *Differences in course content at the high school level characterized by multivariate measures of cognitive and sociopsychological climate.* Doctoral dissertation, University of Tulsa, Tulsa, Oklahoma.

Kulik, C. L. & Kulik, J. A. (1982). Effects of ability grouping on secondar school students: A meta-analysis of evaluation findings. *American Educational Research Journal, 19,* 415–428.

Kyzar, B. L. (1977). Noise pollution and schools: How much is too much? *CEFP Journal, 4,* 10–11.

Leithwood, K. A., Ross, J. A. & Montgomery, D. J. (1982). An investigation of teachers' curriculum decision-making. In K. A. Leithwood (Ed.), *Studies in curriculum decision-making* (pp. 14–46). Toronto: Ontario Institute for Studies in Education.

Lieberman, A. & Miller, L. (1986). School improvement: Themes and variations. In A. Lieberman (Ed.), *Rethinking school improvement: Research, craft, and concept* (pp. 96–114). New York: Teachers College Press.

Loo, C. & Kennelly, D. (1979). Social density: Its effects on behaivor and perceptions of preschoolers. *Environmental Psychology and Nonverbal Behavior, 3,* 131–146.

McCutcheon, G. (1980). How do elementary school teachers plan? The nature of planning and influences on it. *Elementary School Journal, 81,* 4–23.

McDonald, S. P. (1980). Interpreting growth in writing. *College Composition and Communication, 31,* 301–310.

Metz, M. H. (1978). *Classrooms and corridors: The crisis of authority in desegregated schools.* Berkeley, CA: University of California Press.

Meyer, J. (1971). *The impact of the open space school upon teacher influence and autonomy: The effects of an organizational innovation.* Stanford, CA: Stanford University. (ERIC Document Reproduction Service No. 062 291.)

Millard, J. E. (1977). *Small classes? What research says about the effects of class size and possible alternatives to small classes.* Aukeny, IA: Heartland Educational Association. (ERIC Document Reproduction Service No. 133 897).

Mintz, N. L. (1956). Effects of esthetic surroundings, II: Prolonged and repeated experiences in a "beautiful" and "ugly" room. *Journal of Psychology, 41,* 459–466.

Moos, R. H. (1980). Evaluating classroom learning environments. *Studies in Educational Evaluation, 6,* 239–252.

Moos, R. H. (1987). Learning environments in contexts: Links between school, work, and family settings. In B. J. Fraser (Ed.), *The study of learning environments* (Vol. 2) (pp. 1–16). Baton Rouge, LA: Louisiana State University College of Education.

Moos, R. H. & Trickett, E. J. (1974). *Classroom environment scale manual.* Palo Alto, CA: Consulting Psychologists Press.

Murrain, P. G. (1983). *Administrative determinations concerning facilities utilization and instructional grouping: An analysis of the relationship(s) between selected thermal environments and preferences for temperature, an element of learning style, as they affect word recognition scores of secondary students.* Doctoral dissertation, St. John's University, Jamaica, New York.

Newfield, J. & McElyea, V. B. (1983). Achievement and attitudinal differences among students in regular, remedial, and advanced classes. *Journal of Experimental Education, 52,* 47–56.

Nielsen, H. D. & Moos, R. H. (1978). Exploration and adjustment in high school classrooms: A study of person-environment fit. *Journal of Educational Research, 72,* 52–57.

Noli, P. M. (1980, February). *Implications of class size research.* Paper presented at annual meeting of American Association of School Administrators, Anaheim, California. (ERIC Document Reproduction Service No. 184 237).

Oakes, J. (1985). *Keeping track: How schools structure inequality.* New Haven, CN: Yale University Press.

Price G. (1980). Which learning style elements are stable and which tend to change? *Learning Styles Network Newsletter, 4* (2), 38–40.

Randhawa, B. S. & Hunt, D. (1982, September). *Structure of learning environment variables in mathematics and English courses.* Paper presented at annual meeting of the British Educational Research Association, St. Andrews, Scotland. (ERIC Document Reproduction Service No. 223 667).

Randhawa, B. S. & Michayluk, J. O. (1975). Learning environments in rural and urban classrooms. *American Educational Research Journal, 12,* 265–285.

Rehberg, R. A. & Rosenthal, E. R. (1978). *Class and merit in the American high school,* New York: Longman.

Reiss, S. & Dyhaldo, N. (1975). Persistence, achievement, and open space environments. *Journal of Educational Psychology, 67,* 506–513.

Rich, H. L. & Bush, A. J. (1978). The effects of congruent teacher-student characteristics on instructional outcomes. *American Educational Research Journal, 15,* 451–457.

Rivlin, L. G. & Rothenberg, M. (1976). The use of space in open classrooms. In H. M. Proshansky, W. H. Ittelson, & L. G. Rivlin (Eds.), *Environmental psychology: People and their physical settings* (2nd ed.). New York: Holt, Rinehart, & Winston.

Rohe, W. & Patterson, A. J. (1974). The effects of varied levels of resources and density on behavior in a day care center. In D. H. Carson (Ed.), *Man-environment interaction: The evaluations and applications* (Part III). Stroudsburg, PA: Dowden, Hutchinson, & Ross.

Rosenbaum, J. E. (1980). Social implications of educational groupings. In D. C. Berliner (Ed.), *Review of research in education (Vol. 8)* (pp. 361–404.) Washington: American Educational Research Association.

Rosenshine, B. & Stevens, R. (1986). Teaching functions. In M. C. Wittrock (Ed.), *Handbook of Research on Teaching* (3rd ed.) (pp. 376–391.)

Santrock, J. W. (1976). Affect and facilitative self-control: Influence of ecological setting, cognition, and social agent. *Journal of Educational Psychology, 68,* 529–535.

Sardo, D. (1982, October). *Teacher planning styles in the middle school.* Paper presented to the Eastern Educational Research Association, Ellenville, New York.

Schettino, A. P. & Borden, R. J. (1976). Sex differences in response to naturalistic crowding: Affective reactions to group size and group density. *Personality and Social Psychology Bulletin, 2,* 67–70.

Schwebel, A. I. & Cherlin, D. L. (1972). Physical and social distancing in teacher-pupil relationships. *Journal of Educational Psychology, 63,* 543–550.

Schafer, W. E. & Olexa, C. (1971). *Tracking and opportunity.* Scranton, PA: Chandler.

Shapiro, S. (1975). Preschool ecology: A study of three environmental variables. *Reading Improvement, 12,* 236–241.

Shapson, S. M., Wright, E. N., Eason, G., & Fitzgeral, J. (1978, March).

Results of an experimental study of the effects of class size. Paper presented at the annual meeting of the American Educational Research Association, Toronto. (ERIC Document Reproduction Service No. 151 985.)

Shea, T. C. (1983). *An investigation of the relationship among preferences for the learning style element of design, selected instructional environments, and reading achievement of 9th grade students to improve administrative determinations concerning effective educational facilities.* Doctoral dissertation, St. John's University, Jamaica, New York.

Slater, B. (1968). Effects of noise on pupil performance. *Journal of Educational Psychology, 59,* 239–243.

Slavin, R. E. (1983). *Cooperative learning.* New York: Longman.

Slavin, R. E. (1987). *Grouping for instruction: Equity and effectiveness.* Baltimore, MD: Center for Research on Elementary and Middle Schools, Johns Hopkins University.

Smith, M. L. & Glass, G. V. (1979). *Relationship of class size to classroom processes, teacher satisfaction, and pupil affect: A meta-analysis.* San Francisco: Far West Laboratory for Educational Research and Development.

Smith, W. L. (Chair) and the NCTE Task Force on Class Size and Workload in Secondary English Instruction. (1986). *Class size and English in the secondary school.* Urbana, IL: National Council of Teachers of English.

Steele, J. M., Walberg, H. J. & House, E. R. (1974). Subject areas and cognitive press. *Journal of Educational Psychology, 66,* 363–366.

Stires, L. (1978, March). *The effect of classroom seating location on student grades and attitudes; Environment or self-selection?* Paper presented at the annual meeting of the Eastern Psychological Association, Washington, DC.

Stokols, D. (1972). On the distinction between density and crowding: Some implications for future research. *Psychological Review, 79,* 275–277.

Suhor, C. (1986). Introduction. In W. L. Smith (Chair). *Class size and English in the secondary school* (pp. ix–xii.) Urbana, IL: National Council of Teachers of English.

Traub, R., Weiss, J., Fisher, C., & Khan, Y. (1976). *Openness in schools: An evaluation study.* Toronto: Ontario Institute for Studies in Education.

Veldman, D. J. & Sanford, J. P. (1984). The influence of class ability level on student achievement and classroom behavior. *American Educational Research Journal, 21,* 629–644.

Warner, J. B. (1971). A comparison of students' and teachers' performance in an open space facility and in self-contained classrooms. (Doctoral dissertation, University of Houston, Houston, TX, 1970.) *Dissertation Abstracts International, 31,* 3851A.

Weinstein, C. S. (1979). The physical environment of the school: A review of the research. *Review of Educational Research, 49,* 577–610.

Weinstein, C. S. & Weinstein, N. D. (1979). Noise and reading performance in an open space school. *Journal of Educational Research, 72,* 210–213.

Whalen, H. L. (1972). *English Learning Environment.* Urbana, IL: National Council of Teachers of English.

Zahorik, J. A. (1975). Teachers' planning models. *Educational Leadership, 33,* 134–139.

Zifferblatt, S. M. (1972). Architecture and human behavior: Toward increased understanding of a functional relationship. *Educational Technology, 12,* 54–57.

·25·

BEYOND THE CLASSROOM

25A. FAMILY LITERACY: TEXT AS CONTEXT
Denny Taylor

My Mom is Best

I like my Mom
My Mom liks me

I love my mom
My mom loves
me

My mom is Busy
Sometimes. and
I can't Bother
her.

Sometimes I'm
Busy too.

My Mom is So
nice to me.

Sometimes I'm
not nice to her

Sometimes my
mom gets
angry.

Sometimes I get
angry too.

My mom
teaches me
all the right

things.

Sarah, who wrote this story, is one of the children in the family that helped me to construct a prose home movie of their reading of *Chester Cricket* (Taylor, 1986a). Several years ago,

Cullen, her mother, sent me a copy of Sarah's story, because she knew that I would enjoy reading it. Even the cover made me smile:

This Book is
called

My Mom
Is BEST!

For my
mom Cullen

Sarah, who must be in 5th grade by now, made the book at home sometime during her 1st grade year. It would be possible to use Sarah's story to construct a picture of what she knew about books and written language when she was in 1st grade, but I would prefer to use Sarah's story to create a picture, from a researcher's perspective, of what she knew about family. Sarah wrote the story *My Mom is Best!* for her mother, and the sharing of the book was used in the mediation of their experiences of one another. In essence, the text became the context. Sarah was able to express the nuances of her familial relationship with her mother through the construction of her story. She managed to balance family unity with individual diversity, while at the same time she demonstrated that, on some level, she had access to her mother's conceptual world.

Sarah could not talk about this "stuff," for these are adult interpretations of a child's intuitive understandings of the bond that exists between her and her mother. But by writing her story, Sarah reminds us of the complexity of her world. For her, to learn language is to live lanaguage. She uses it, incorporating print into her everyday activities, so that her personal understandings of literacy are both socially constructed and individually situated in the practical accomplishments of her family life.

Two of the studies, *Growing Up Literate: Learning From Inner-City Families,* and *Working Parents,* were funded, in part, by Elva Knight grants from the International Reading Association. I would like to thank David Bloome, Erwin Flaxman, Don Graves, Judith Green and Helen Schotanus for their much appreciated support. Most of all I would like to thank the families, teachers and administrators with whom I have worked over the past twelve years.

457

Thus we can state that her experiences with written language at home have been very different from her experiences of written language at school. At home, print is a means of communication and not an academic exercise. In both kindergarten and 1st grade, Sarah spent most of her time doing workbook pages, and there were very few opportunities for her to write stories.

In recent years, there has been increasing concern about both the artificiality of early reading and writing programs (Bloome & Nieto, in press; Goodman, Goodman, Freemamn & Murphy, 1988; Taylor, 1989) and the pacification of children through instruction that minimizes their opportunities to actively engage in the genuine constructions of the types and uses of reading and writing that are a part of their everyday lives (Heath, 1983; Juliebo, 1987; Taylor, 1988; Taylor & Dorsey-Gaines, 1988;). Hasan, 1987 states:

As the child crosses and recrosses the boundary between home and school, the separation of his linguistic experiences in one from that in the other can be no more than a questionable fiction (draft p. 3).

What Sarah teaches us is that it is not only her linguistic experiences that must be free to move between home and school, but also her complex understandings of the social world in which she lives. Sarah's short story gives us an intuitive sense of what is missing in many of our classrooms. By maintaining the status quo, we are not accommodating to the richness and complexity of literacy in the everyday lives of children. Fortunately, many teachers across the country have gained a voice in the educational community (see Bissex & Bullock, 1987; Hansen, Newkirk & Graves, 1985) and through their efforts classroom practices are changing to reflect their theoretically-grounded understandings of the social realities that are intricately connected with the emergence of literacy in young children. In our quest to understand reading and writing as social processes, many educators have realized that it becomes essential for us to study the "situated practical accomplishments" (McDermott & Roth, 1978) of young children as they live their daily lives.

My small part in this adventure has been to study literacy in family settings. In essence, I have learned to understand the families with whom I have worked through their uses of reading and writing in everyday life. I believe this is consistent with the experiences of the other authors in this book who have found that as they study the reading and writing behaviors of young children, they have learned about the young children themselves. It is from this perspective that we begin to see that for many young children linguistic experiences have been fractured and crushed beyond recognition, and their school learning has become totally disconnected from their everyday lives.

How can we help?
What have we learned that would help us as teachers?
How can we make it easier for children to learn to read and write in school?

I will address these questions directly in my conclusions to this chapter, but I will begin my response with a brief synthesis of some of the underlying patterns of family literacy that have emerged from my last 12 years of research in family settings. In this way, I hope to show how some of my interpretations of family literacy can be used to help teachers and students in school.

CONSERVATION AND CHANGE IN THE TRANSMISSION OF LITERACY STYLES AND VALUES

In Families:

1. Some rituals and routines of written language usage appear to conserve family traditions of literacy, while others appear to change the patterns of the past.
2. Patterns of family literacy are constantly evolving to accommodate the everyday experiences of both parents and children, and the introduction of a younger sibling can lead to the systematic restructuring of the routine.

These statements were first written in *Family Literacy* (Taylor, 1983), which describes a study of white middle-class families in which there were young children sucessfully learning to read and write. From the data collected in that research, it appears that the conservation of literacy styles and values occurs almost automatically, and only when the parent is intent on change is a conscious effort involved. Some parents spoke of wanting to provide alternate experiences for their children. One father explained, "Maybe I know that because I hated it so badly I'm going to guarantee her that she doesn't know that I disliked it so much." In *Growing Up Literate* (Taylor & Dorsey-Gaines, 1988), which was a study of Black families living below the poverty level, the underlying patterns of conservation and change were also evident. However, in this urban environment where both children and their parents were so desperately at risk, it was evident that conserving family rituals and routines as well as changing them took a conscious effort on the part of the parents. The families had to make a determined effort just to survive.

Each new study creates another opportunity to reflect upon the notion of multigenerational patterns of conservation and change. In my research on ethnographic assessment (Taylor, 1988; 1990; in press), I listened to parents as they talked about their children's difficulties in learning to read and write in school, and as they described what happened to them in their classrooms when they were young children. There is no doubt that literacy is both deeply embedded in and a part of the sociohistorical contexts of family life. Again, the notion of text as context emerges as we remember our own experiences and use them to parent our children, but what happens in families in which the children's early existence is very different from their later experiences of family life? In the *Working Parents* research (Taylor, 1986b, in progress), I have had the opportunity to explore this question with one family with whom I have lived as part of the research. The mother, Cindy, is a single parent who has adopted 7 childern and is the American guardian to the Chinese boy who is a refugee from Vietnam.

Emilie, one of Cindy's Korean-born daughters, helps us see the relationships between past and present in the essay that she

FIGURE 25–1.

wrote about her mother for "A Special Mother's Day Contest." (See Figure 25–1.) Emilie's essay won the grand prize. In it she writes:

Kind, Generous, Respectable, are only some words to describe my mom, I was adopted when I was three, and am now almost twelve. My mom has been the best mother any child could dream of. . . .

My mom is a single parent, and is the board vice president of . . ., an adoption agency that places Korean kids. She voluntarily makes a newsletter to help adoptive parents thinking about adopting, and children who were adopted to learn more about their Korean culture, and be proud of their birthplace. . . .

With all this work she still makes time to do things with her children. We go to the museums, fish hatcheries, fishing, parks, Disneyland, Great Adventure and many family trips to historical or just very pretty sites. I guess she proves the saying that goes "If you want anything done, ask a busy person."

Cindy has made a conscious effort to preserve the cultural heritage of her children while creating for them a place in American society. The photograph of Meredith, taken in 1986 when she had been in America for just eight days, is another vivid illustration of these processes of conservation and change. Meredith is wearing a hanbok, the traditional costume of her country of birth, and she is holding a cabbage patch doll which in many ways symbolizes her country of adoption. Cindy is managing to create sociohistorical contexts for her children that bring their past experiences into the present, and texts are a part of the context for this endeavor. Letters from family members in Korea and Vietnam and read, cherished and preserved. Letters and birthday cards that were sent back and forth between the children and their American grandparents (Cindy's parents), became an important way of remembering when their adopted grandmother (Omni) died (see Taylor & Strickland, 1988). Father's day cards and birthday cards continue to be sent

by the children to Cindy's father who is 79 years of age and is still an active member of the family.

In the ebb and flow of day-to-day living, both the indiviudal and combined life histories of the children and their mother become deeply embedded in the rituals and routines of family life. Understanding how such family patterns influence the learning opportunities of young children will help us as we strive to facilitate literacy learning in schools. When I visit, Cindy simetimes sits at the kitchen table and reminisces about her own childhood experiences, and she links some of the experiences that she had in school with the experiences of some of her children. At other times, we talk on the telephone, and again she makes the connection as she talks about some specific problem that she is trying to solve in the schooling of a particular child. Her family's experiences are important to her as she discusses the education of her children. Even this brief introduction to Cindy and her children underscores as well as confirms the complexity of family experiences, of which literacy is a part, that children bring to school.

THE MOMENT-TO-MOMENT LITERACY EXPERIENCES OF PARENTS AND CHILDREN

In Families:

1. Many of the literacy experiences that occur at home take place as parents and children go about their daily lives.
2. On many occasions, the act of reading is not the focus of attention, and the print has no intrinsic value. The message is embedded in some other event, useful within the context in which it was written or read, but otherwise appearing to be of little importance.

When children write at home, the event often goes by unnoticed. Strings of letters and emerging words signify meanings that sometimes pass by unnoticed, while at other times they are recognized and responded to in some special way. In *Family Literacy,* this is well-illustrated by Jill Langdon's comments when we looked at some of the papers she found in a cupboard drawer in her living room. She hesitated several times before designating ownership, and was often unsure if the papers were this year's writing or last year's endeavors. Jill found two typed pages. Reasoning aloud, she argued that she did not think Steven (4 years and 10 months) would have had the staying power to type so much, but that on the other hand, Ken (7 years, 9 months) would not have been content without writing something. Ken arrived and Jill asked him who had typed the two pages. Ken looked at them and replied, "Steven."

In *Growing Up Literate,* children wrote in a similar fashion. Jamaine often used odd pieces of paper to write and to draw, and again much of his activity went by unnoticed as his texts became a part of the situated practical accomplishments of his everyday life. On one occasion, when Taskmika was drawing a picture of her family, Jemma, her mother, told us that Jerry, the children's father, had died. Jemma and Jerry were separated but he had visited the children on a regular basis. The circumstances were such that he did not watch the children except to

FIGURE 25–2.

glance at them from time to time. Jamaine was close to Jemma as she talked, and it was then, without our knowing, that he drew the picture of his father before his death and becoming an angel when he died. When Jamine showed us his picture, he pointed to the figure he had drawn at the bottom of the piece of paper, and he told us it was a picture of his dad. Then he traced his finger along the line (arrow?) that he had drawn up to the figure at the top of his paper and told us it was his dad and that his dad was an angel. (See Figure 25–2.)

Doodles on paper, messages in print, unrecognized, scrumpled, dropped in the waste paper basket, forgotten, all of these descriptors can be used to characterize momentary writing activities. (See Figure 25–3.) This recurring pattern has appeared again in the *Working Parents* study. On one occasion when Alison was 5, she wrote her name on my note pad as I was taking photographs of her family. Alison has cerebral palsy, and it is difficult for her to control the movements that are necessary to write. Nevertheless she perseveres, and her messages are not affected by her motoric complications. She took the note pad on which I had been writing and wrote her name. She worked quietly with great concentration and when she had finished, her solitary, momentary activity became a shared event as she asked how to write the word camera.

Just as children's early writing goes by unnoticed, so does much of the written activity of the household. In every study in which I have been involved, evidence has been found of family members using print to fulfill many purposes in family life. Notes are written and quickly left. The following are examples from *Family Literacy:*

Laura—I ate pizza—rest on stove.
Margaret called again—wants to talk with
you. Dog gone when I got home. Put him on
chain if he arrives before you go out again
See you at—6:00. Will jog first. Barry.

Kathy and Debbie,
Please be very quiet—Nan is sleeping.
Thank you.
   Love, Mommy

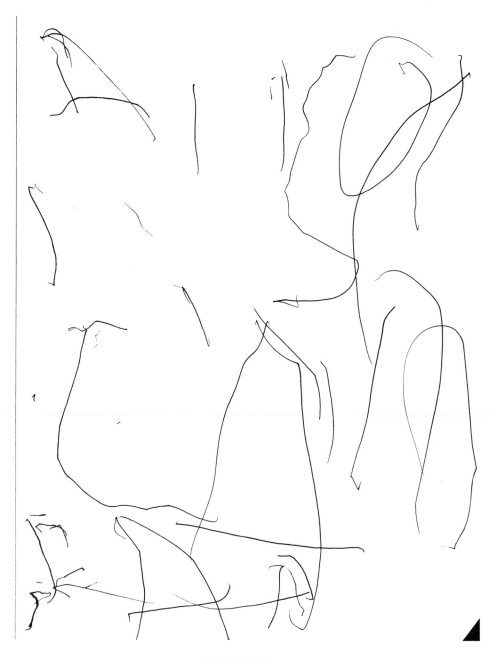

FIGURE 25–3.

Beth—Don't forget your violin Friday—
take a small hand towel for a chin rest.

In *Growing Up Literate,* similar notes were found. Until they separated, Jemma left notes for Jerry if she had to go out before he came home. She would tell him where she was, and sometimes she would ask him to go to the store or start preparing the evening meal. Jemma also wrote notes to Tasmika. One note was written to remind Tasmika that she had to bring her bicycle

into the apartment before 6 p.m. In the *Working Parents* study, such notes are a common occurrence in Cindy's family. My favorite note is one written by Meredith a year after she had arrived in America. Meridith wanted to take a cake to school for a special event, and so, knowing that her Mom was busy, she wrote a note both to ask Cindy for the cake and to help her remember. Again, we could say that Meredith's note was written to fulfill some purpose in everyday life, but the writing had no intrinsic value (except to an ethnographer whose irresistible

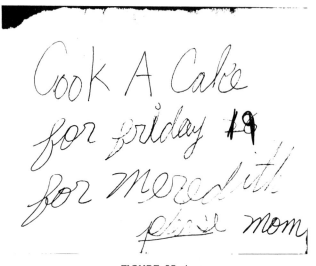

FIGURE 25–4.

tendency is to collect every piece of paper on which a person has made a mark). (See Figure 25–4.)

THE DELIBERATE USES OF LITERACY IN FAMILY SETTINGS

In Families:

1. Many of the deliberate uses of literacy found in family settings occur when "moment-to-moment" uses of literacy are specific events that become the focus of attention.
2. There are times when reading and writing become deliberate acts, when the text becomes as important as the message that it contains.

Clearly the designation of an event as one thing or another is an interpretive construction. In *Family Literacy,* I think the note that Bonnie King (7 years and 7 months) left for her mother's well-being. Thus, my interpretations suggest that even when literacy becomes the focus of specific attention the print is still contextually situated. Bonnie wrote:

Dear Mommie,

I really love you. Yes I do.
You care for me. And I know
why you tell me to have
gum olny every other day
I know it all. It is for my
own good. So I don't get
cavities you are the mother
I want for ever
and ever.
    Love Bonnie

    XXXX OOOOOO

    XXXX OOOOOO

    XXXX OOOOOO
    I love you

When Donna talked about the note she explained that she had been "feeling down" that morning and Bonnie had known that she was unhappy. Donna said that she thought Bonnie had written the note because she wanted her mother to know how much she loved her.

In *Growing Up Literate,* the letter Teko wrote to his mother, during the summer of 1976, when he was 11 years of age, can also be described as a specific literacy event. Teko was not happy to be away from home and he wrote:

Dear Mom,

I haven't had too much fun on this trip. First of all a boy named John Davidson he is on the stupidest kids here he thinks he can beat everybody. Second of all the lady who takes care of me is nice but she doesn't let us have too much fun. Thrid of all I have lost a dollar. I hope you are having as much luck as me. I have a surprise for you momma and Danny. I will be back soon.

    Sincerely yours,

    Teko

Again, we can describe the text as a part of the context of family life and parent-child relationships.

A final example comes from the study of *Working Parents.* It is the letter written by Emilie when she was 8 years old and her grandmother was dying. In talking about the letter, Emilie's mother Cindy commented that written communication is sometimes safer when emotions are too overwhelming for us to say how we feel. Thus Emilie's writing became a specific literacy event that helped her to cope with the imminent death of her grandmother. Emilie wrote:

My Grandmother is special to me because she doesn't yell she explains. She taught card games. She always has time for us. When each of us came she accepted us as a member of the family right away. She also met each one of us at the airport.

Omni is the name we gave to her when my brother came from Korea. It sound like Halmunee which means Grandmother in Korean. And I will never forget the day I went with her on my birthday. I was turning 8 years old. She went with me shopping. We bought stickers and construction paper and things like that. Omni went with me out to dinner. That was a great day. The thing that made it so special was that it was just Omni and me.

Right now Omni has cancer but she still tries to be the same old Omni. We pray for her every night. Each of us do the best we can to help her. We have been successful so far sort of.

Omni has been so kind to us that I wrote this poem to her last birthday. It is called "Love". people feel that way about Omni too. My godmothers who brought me to America made a song called "Omni" that we love to sing to her.
    Each Time I feel loved and safe
    I think of you Omni
    I feel your hand holding mine
    Stay near me my Omni
    Show me the way to live each day
    Making you proud of me
    I want you to see
    Your life in me
    I love you so
      Omni

Perhaps one of the most important insights that I have gained from *Growing Up Literate* and *Working Parents* is that at a fundamental level, parents and children *use* literacy to cope with the stress in their lives (see Taylor & Strickland, 1988). This is especially evident in the *Working Parents* research, which focuses upon family life when there is no primary caretaker at home on a full time basis. Tentative interpretations of the data collected in this study, which are supported by my other family literacy studies suggest, that communicating through print becomes one of the ways in which families learn to cope, and texts become a part of the context(s) of their everyday lives. School schedules and afterschool activities are juxtaposed and fitted in with parents' work schedules and late meetings. The memo on page 464 (Figure 25–5) was given by Cindy to her children at the beginning of the summer vacation:

All of the information that was written down was also shared verbally with the children. Cindy explained, "By the end of the first week of the summer vacation we were all going crazy. The summer presented a whole new routine that was not defined by school. No one knew the rules to make the family run smoothly and we had only two months. By putting them down on paper, when there was a question I could say, 'There are the rules. Take a look at them.' Our situation is the reverse of what exists when a mother is at home. When you're raised in a family where the mother is at home there is no need to put them up, but you need them when she goes back to work. Here, the rules were posted because the mother was at home for the summer and there was a new lack of structure."

THE IMPACT OF CHANGING FAMILY LIFE STYLES ON EARLY LITERACY LEARNING

In Families:

1. When both parents work or when there is a single working parent and time is at a premium, the moment-to-moment and specific uses of print that occur when one parent is at home full-time with a child will diminish.
2. However, literacy can become a key element in the ability of some families as they attempt to juggle all of the schedules, rituals and routines and time constraints that are a part of their daily lives.

When there is no primary caretaker at home family rituals and routines and the use of time and space radically change to accommodate the working life styles of family members. There is no doubt that in such families there is less time for parents and children just to be together, and moment-to-moment learning opportunities diminish (Taylor & Strickland, 1988). However, not all the effects of changing family lifestyles are negative. In *Working Parents* the research focuses upon **functioning** families in which there is no primary caretaker at home, and the initial data collected in this study suggests that literacy can become a key element in the ability of some families to juggle all of the schedules, rituals and routines, and time constraints that are a part of their daily lives. Print can change the procedural possibilities for problems solving as family members recast

problem-solution relationships by incorporating print into the environment to simplify tasks. Cindy's summer rules provide us with an opportunity to glimpse one of the ways in which she used literacy to provide a common structure for family life at a time when the rules were changing and the family was out of their working routine. Print provided her with the opportunity to find a "gap-closing" solution that she used to complement, clarify and reinforce the oral conversations that she had with her children.

In the summer of 1987 the "rules" were easy to write. There was a certain flexibility in who-goes-where-when, but throughout the school year there is very little leeway in the times, places and events that occupy the family. Cindy's work schedule is fixed. She can arrive early but not late, similarly for the children. Each of the schools that they attend start and end at designated times. The children are expected to be at their schools when the bells ring, with their homework done, and with a packed lunch or money to buy school food, their notices signed, carrying instruments to play and gym clothes in their bags. Each child's schedule must somehow be maintained, holidays coordinated, dental appointments arranged and sports events attended. Distances must be travelled and drop-offs and pick-ups negotiated. In Cindy's family there are nine individual schedules that must be adhered to, while at the same time they must be fitted into the daily routine. Negotiations begin in the evening for the following day's events and activities, continue at the breakfast table and are often completed in the car. What follows is an account of the beginning of a school day, which Cindy confirms is typical of the early morning routine at the time of the observation (Summer, 1987).

6:40 Chris is in the cooking area. Cindy is helping him with his shirt. He has on red shorts and a white shirt with red stripes. Cindy is putting tofu in soup. Chris is walking around with socks in his hand. Cindy tells Ben to check the report that she has typed for him to make sure there are no "typos." Cindy has oatmeal on the table for Alison and Chris. Emilie is here. Cindy asks Emilie to feed Alison. Vin and Ben are at the table eating soup with tofu.... Cindy is organizing the evening of baseball games. Chris says his game is cancelled. Ben talks about the playoffs. Emilie also has a game.... Meredith is emptying the dishwasher ready Cindy to fill it. Ben has taken Alison to the bus. Cindy is clearing up the kitchen. Meredith is now eating. Cindy is talking with Meredith about what she should do when she comes home from school. There is a load of washing that needs to be folded. They talk about getting Alison off the bus and about their schedules for tomorrow. Emilie shows her Mom her report card. Cindy gives her a kiss. She teases Emilie about the complimentary remarks about her musical ability. "Pure fake!" Cindy laughs. Emilie smiles.

Breakfast accomplished the family members begin their separate agendas for the day. Ben takes Alison to wait for her bus. The Vin and Meredith leave to get their bus. Caroline, Emilie, Ben and Chris travel with their mother. Cindy takes Caroline to the high school and then she drives to the elementary school that is attended by Emilie, Ben and Chris. Last minute arrangements are made about meeting after school, and there is more talk of coordinating baseball games.

To ensure that the family can cope, notices are kept and posted. On one occasion when I stayed with Cindy and her mm

SUMMER RULES FOR EASIER LIVING, 1987

mmmmmmmmmmmmmmmmmmmmmmmmmmmmmmmmmmmmmmmmmmmmmmmmmmmmmmmmmmmmmmmmmmmmmmmmmmmmmmmm

REMEMBER: Rules are not made to be broken, but they certainly <u>can</u> be discussed or negotiated! Don't wait until the last minute to do so, however!

1) Check in at home at noon either to a) find out when lunch will be ready or   b) make yourself a sandwich or whatever else you would like that is available

2) Be home by 6:00 for dinner!

3) Be ready to head upstairs by 9:00 <u>unless</u> there are special requests or circumstances arranged for in advance, such as a night-time outside game, a special TV program, a baseball game, etc.

4) Leave a note to tell me where you are if I am not at home to be told in person

5) If you want to watch daytime TV, earn the minutes to do so by reading

6) Plan to mow the lawn (boys) on alternate weekends. Sign your name on the calendar after the job is done.

These are the <u>BASIC RULES</u>. If you can't follow them, especially #1 and #2, be prepared to <u>pay the penalty</u>.   The penalty is what will be most effective for the specific person who can't follow the rules.

POINTS TO PONDER: (not really "rules," as such, but nice things to remember)

1) SMILE once in a while at the people around you. It will drive them crazy wondering what you're up to! (It will also make Mom feel appreciated)

2) Do something NICE for someone in the family who least expects it. It make <u>them</u> appreciate <u>you</u>!   You never know when it will pay off!

3) Say "thanks" to people in the family when it's appropriate. It shows that you <u>do</u> care.

4) If you **see** something that needs doing, do it. Why not?

FIGURE 25–5.

children, the following notices were among those displayed on the noticeboard in the family's kitchen:

1. Children's school schedules which list designated holidays and note the possibility of snow days. (On Alison's schedule Cindy had noted beside several of the dates "Same for all" and "Same for V. and M.")
2. Boy Scout's camp schedule for 1986-1987, with names and telephone numbers of the "adults responsible" for the various campouts and ski trips.
3. Baseball schedules with telephone numbers for players and coaches, dates of games and teams to be played.
4. Baseball practice schedules with lists for oranges and soda.

(The following directive was written about oranges and soda: "Below is the list for orange and soda—please remember your turn. Its very important that the boys have the orange and soda, so if you are not able to do your turn-*please* change with someone or call me.")
5. Soccer schedules, dates, times, telephone numbers, coaches, referees.
6. School menus. (Decisions regarding lunches were negotiated at the beginning of each week. It was in this way that the children decided for themselves on which days they would take a bag lunch and on which days they would take money.)
7. "Happenings" at one of the schools. Including spring concerts, class trips and class plays.

8. P.T.O. schedule of meetings and fund raising events.
9. Notices about the support group for parents of adopted Korean children, cultural events, fund raising activities, names and telephone numbers.

To be in the right place at the right time the children themselves take a great deal of responsibility. For example, during one of my visits Alison reminded Cindy that she had to phone her school principal to make sure that it was alright for me to accompany her to school the next day. Cindy was busy preparing supper, but Alison was persistent and eventually Cindy did find time to phone. However, she had lost the telephone number and several of the children helped her locate the appropriate paper while Alison offered advice on where to look for the number. Using print to get things done is a family affair in which all of the children can and do participate. What emerges from these observations is the beginning of an evidentiary base that enables us to recognize that when print is incorporated into family activities it becomes a part of the socially-constructed and individually-situated practical accomplishments of everyday life. Stated another way, literacy provides families with flexible (sometimes "short-cut") opportunities for dealing with problem solving in complex social situations. (This theoretical perspective is grounded in the studies of Carraher, 1986; Carraher, Carraher & Schliemann, 1985; LaRocha, 1985; Lave, 1985; Lave, Murtaugh & LaRocha, 1984; and Scribner, 1984).

TEXT AS CONTEXT: WHAT FAMILIES CAN TEACH US ABOUT LITERACY LEARNING IN SCHOOL

As these studies of family literacy continue, it is possible that they will provide us with new insights into the ways in which families use literacy to accommodate to the increasing complexity of everyday life. At the present time, these studies allow the following statements to be made about literacy in families:

1. At any one time, multiple interpretations of literacy as part of some family activity are possible, and the possibilities for different interpretations are created over time.
2. For each family member participating in an activity which involves literacy, the occasion is both socially constructed and personally interpreted through the interplay of the family members' individual biographies and educative styles.
3. Moment-to-moment and deliberate uses of literacy can be social events or solitary endeavors.
4. Solitary and shared, deliberate and momentary, literacy is a dynamic, complex, multi-dimensional phenomenon.

When we consider these descriptions of literacy, and we compare the richness and complexity of out-of-school print environments with the reading and writing environments that we often find in elementary school classrooms, the discontinuities are clearly visible. If we visit the 1st grade classroom in which Cindy's son Chris spends his day, we are provided with an opportunity to gain some understanding of what can happen to some children when the dialectical relationships that exist between the social and cognitive uses of print in classroom set-tings do not complement their experiences of the mutual dependence of purposes (socially constructed-complex mental activity) and uses (practical accomplishments) of print in their everyday lives (see Bloome & Nieto, in press; Coles, 1987). Cindy describes the school in which Chris spent his 1st grade years as "an upper-middle class community" in which there were "predominantly professional families." In Chris's classroom, his teacher works to fulfill the curriculum requirements expected of her through the use of the manual, basals, workbooks and dittos that have been provided. Most children accommodate to the system and thrive. Chris does not, and from this perspective some educators may consider him an atypical learner. It is important that we try to understand his experiences, for from his "uniqueness" we can learn lessons that will help us to look more closely at the ways in which we can incorporate literacy into school environments. The following is a narrative account of one morning during Chris' 1st grade year:

9.00 T: "Take out your calenders please."
Chris gets a folder out of his desk.
He takes out his calender and then goes back into his desk.
T. asks him what he is doing.
Chris goes on looking.
T: "pencil!"
Chris nods.
T. tells him it is on his desk.
Chris holds up the pencil and says, "It's green."
T. finds a pencil and gives it to him.

9:00 T. is at the board.
T: "I made some *serious* mistakes."
She asks the children to read out the sentences.
The children read.

T: "Now think about capital letters."
T: "How should the sentences begin?"
T: "How should *I* be written? The word *I*?"
T: "How about names?"
T: "A person's first name?"
T: "A person's last name?"
T: "Chris?"

"Capitals."

Back and forth. Questions are asked about the sentences. The children answer. Hands are up. Children are called upon.

Chris is sitting. Smiles. Watches. Appears to listen. . . .

9:12 T. tells the children to write the sentences correctly.
She tells them to get out their phonics workbooks and to tear out page 159.
Chris tears out the page. . . .
Chris puts the phonics book into his desk, puts the paper in the middle of his desk and his pencil across the top.

T. says "if you're ready your book is in your desk and your name is at the bottom of the paper."

Chris writes his name and puts his pencil down.

T. asks a boy to read the directions.

T. asks Chris to name the pictures. Chris points to each picture and names it.

T. tells the class to do the boardwork and phonics paper. She asks for the "Grizzly Bears." . . .

Chris quickly does one side of the phonics paper and turns the paper over. He looks at the first sentence. He gets up and goes over to the T. at the reading table.... Chris waits. T. does not speak to him and he returns to his desk. He reads the sentences quietly and adds the appropriate words, e.g.:

bay

It is safe to ------- bag

band

Chris chooses the word that fits into the sentence.

Chris is working down the page reading the sentences and choosing a word from the side.

9:25 Chris has finished the phonics page and has taken out a large piece of paper.

Chris copies the sentences from the board. He writes them exactly as they are written and then he circles the mistakes.

1. today is monday june 8.

9:30 Chris is writing the last sentence on the back of his paper. He turns it over and opens up his box of crayons.
He looks inside and his hand hovers above them as he chooses which crayon to use.
He gets up and goes to a basket of crayons behind the computer.
He turns them over and then takes the black.
He goes back to his table and begins to draw.

9:35 Chris draws:
Chris writes "Tarpets" above his drawing.
He gets up and shows me. He says "pits" and smiles.
I say "tarpits."
Chris smiles again and takes his paper to his T. She looks at it and says he did a fine job with his writing....
Chris folds the paper and puts it into his folder. He walks around by his desk.

T: "Chris. Do you have your extra work folder?"
Chris nods and sits.
T: "Then get on."

Chris looks inside the envelope. Inside are dittos. He pulls one out. He looks at it. Puts it back.

9:40 Chris takes out another ditto. Puts it on his desk. He turns and looks at a display of photos and laughs. Turns to his paper and works on a ditto....

9:43 T. calls Chris.
He goes up with his reading book on his own. He sits next to T. Children are coming up to get their work checked.
Chris opens his book.
On some paper on the easel beside table T. writes *woman*.
Chris looks at it and after a moment says, "woman?"

T: "right. One *woman*."
She shows him the plural *women*.
Then *to too two*
The she writes *flour* and *flower*

9:50 Chris reads from his reading book.
Two children wait with work while Chris reads.
Chris stops.
T. checks the work of the waiting children.
T. takes the workbook that Chris has brought with him. She tears out a page. She has the manual on her lap. T. reads "red." Chris has to name the vowel sound.
T. talks with him about short e.

Chris writes other words with short e that T. reads from her manual. She tells Chris to take the work back to his desk....

10:00 Chris sits down and works on the workbook page.
He points with his pencil to the words that he reads in the sentences and then he draws lines to the pictures....

Chris has put his work into the envelope.
One of the boys gives him a book with pop-up pictures.
Chris smiles and looks at the pop-ups as he turns the pages of the book.

T. tells him to put it away and work on a phonics paper. At the top of the workbook page is written, "Reviewing Initial and Final Consonants."

Chris begins working on the paper.
He stops.
He picks up the plum that he has brought to school.
He holds it up near his face and and appears to be daydreaming.

He puts it down and continues working on the ditto.

The morning continued with Chris working on dittos. At 11 a.m. the children went to see a play put on by another class. Later, I asked his teacher why she thought Chris had chosen to draw a picture of some tar pits. She said she didn't know, but she thought it might have something to do with dinosaurs. Later, I asked Cindy about the drawing. She talked about the visits to the Natural History Museum in New York. She said that Chris was fascinated by the dinosaurs and that it was there in the museum that Chris had learned about tar pits. The sentences that Chris had copied from the chalkboard and then corrected were as follows:

1. today is monday june 8.
2. where is mrs. brown.
3. kate is 5 years old.
4. tom moves to kansas.
5. we went to the museum.

It was after he had written the last sentence that Chris had drawn his picture of the tar pits. He had made his own sense out of a senseless activity. It was the only time that morning that Chris had brought his own understandings of written language into the classroom, and his efforts went unnoticed. Chris's personal understanding of literacy are what Bloome and Nieto (in press) refer to as "marginalized" by the basal reading instruction in his classroom which "disconnects" him "from conditions for learning, for intellectual and personal growth and development." Thus every aspect of Chris's life is affected by the way in which he is being taught to read and write in school.

Cindy moved at the end of Chris's 1st grade year and he attended another elementary school. At the beginning of his 2nd grade year, an individual educational plan (IEP) was written for Chris which graphically illustrates the separation that often takes place between the social lives of children and the ways in which they are often taught to read and write. His IEP states (among other directives) that to "develop prosocial skills Chris will:"

• Follow directions
• Ask appropriate questions

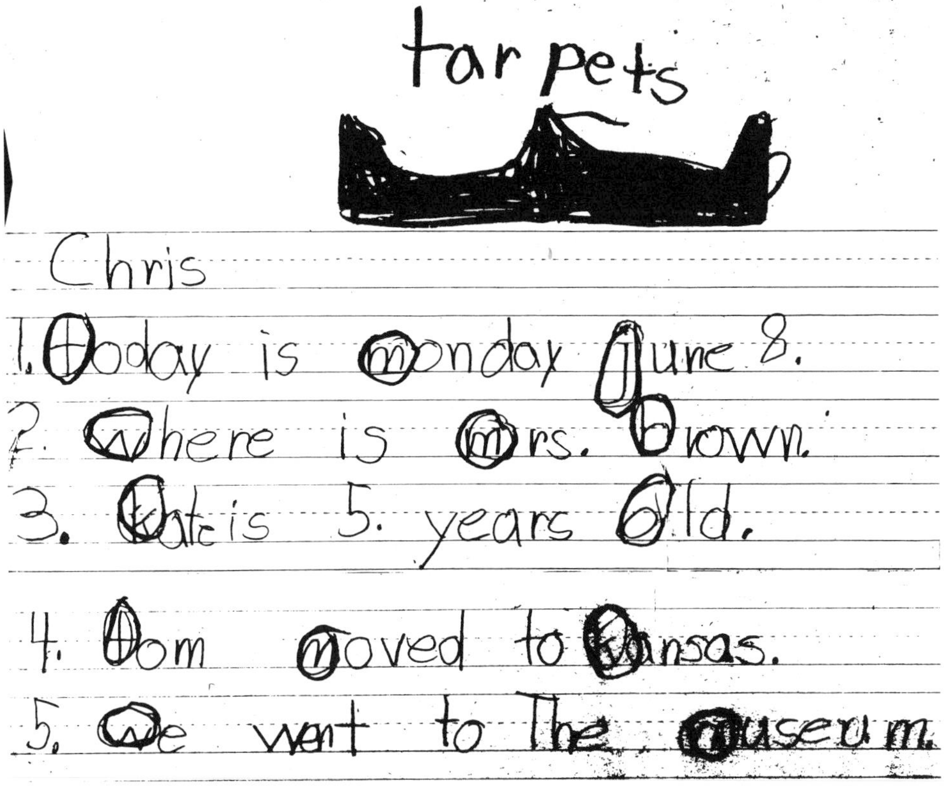

tar pets

Chris

1. Today is monday June 8.
2. Where is Mrs. Brown.
3. Ontc is 5. years Old.
4. Tom moved to Kansas.
5. We went to The museum.

FIGURE 25–6.

- Begin social conversation
- Identify potential problems before they occur
- Generate 2 alternative strategies when he is not included in an activity

In addition, "to improve reading skills (level 2) Chris will":

1. Recognize basic sight words in core program
2. Use vocabulary words from core program in sentences
3. Recall details from story read aloud
4. Find main idea of story read aloud
5. Sequence events
6. Learn context clues
7. Identify and decode consonant blends
8. Identify and decode silent consonants
9. Identify and decode long and short vowels
10. Learn rules governing vowel sounds
11. Learn prefixes, suffixes and root words
12. Follow printed directions
13. Read smoothly orally
14. Continue to develop good listening skills with correct posture
15. Follow 3-4 step oral direction

Among the instructional strategies in the reading section of the IEP is the following directive, "Encourage Chris to read silently without moving his lips."

Chris is now in 3rd grade and Cindy says he hates school. She speaks of his frustration with the demands that are being placed upon him. In the classroom his work includes reading (wordbox, sentences, tests), phonics, "ABC order" and spelling, on all of which he is graded; and upon behavioral objectives, which include "paying attention to the teacher," "following classroom directions," "neatness and accuracy," and "smiling/ happiness," for which he receives points. During the first week of December, 1988, Chris received one point for "smiling/hap-piness" and lost five points "for buying a pencil." In addition to these grades and points, Chris also receives a plus or a minus on his "behavior chart" which includes participation in the flag salute, getting into line and walking in line properly, entering and exiting the classroom properly, helping a person in need, playing and working with others without hurting them.

By his behavior in school, Chris continually demonstrates that his social and academic life cannot be artificially separated without disrupting his ability to learn in a school setting. At home Chris listens to stories, takes part in activities that are accomplished through the use of print, helps to care for his two younger sisters (both of whom have cerebral palsy), and plays with neighborhood children.

Several weeks ago, Cindy received a letter from the principal stating that if Chris's behavior in the playground did not im-prove he would be suspended. Cindy said, "He's 9 years of age. If they suspend him now, what are they going to do to him when he's 15?"

COMMENTARY

Bloome and Nieto state, "By equating education with schooling, we assume limited possibility in role relationships, organization, the structure of knowledge, and the assignment of meaning to behavior" (draft p. 6). Later these researchers speak of the need to "erase the boundaries between language as a topic of study and language as a means of social engagement, socialization and cultural transmission" (draft 12). In the Biographic Literacy Profiles Project (Taylor, 1990), teachers are attempting to blur these school-created boundaries through their observations of individual children as they read and write in early childhood (K–3) settings. In essence, they are learning about literacy from the children that they teach. The teachers participating in the project are attempting to get as close as possible to individual children's perspectives of "what's happening" in their classrooms. This involves close observation of children as they work at reading and writing, and it means giving children *real* opportunities to *use* language. Thus the teachers are attempting to engage in literacy activities that are both mutually supportive of and complementary to the literacy experiences of the children in out of school settings.

The teachers are recording their observations of the children in their classrooms, and they are using their notes, together with the writings that they have collected and placed in the children's literacy portfolios, to build literacy profiles of individual children. The profiles that the teachers are writing are intuitive as well as analytic, and their explanations reflect their awareness of current theories and practices as well as their own personal understandings of literacy. The following excerpts from some of their literacy profiles are offered in "answer" to the questions that I posed in the introduction to this chapter, for in the classrooms of these teachers texts are a part of the context of the everyday school lives of the children, and the profiles reflect the many ways in which the teachers are making it easier for the children to learn to read and write in school.

MAGGIE: KINDERGARTEN

In October Maggie is aware that print can be used for communication. When asked about one page in her journal which contained rows of curving connected lines, she said "It says this is a letter for my grandma and grandpa." She went back to work done earlier and added her new kind of writing to several pages announcing to me what each one said, sometimes with verbal labels (a house, the sun), sometimes in complete sentences (This is the door of a cave.) She does her writing with very quick, left to right, in rows usually top to bottom. Her writing resembles cursive writing with connected sections of various lengths and breaks in between.

TEACHER: SHARRON CADIEUX

EDDIE: FIRST GRADE

In October Eddie excitedly conveyed, "I can read a book!" He heard a friend read a book, then he read that book himself. Eddie then took that book home to read to his family. It appeared to be his first realization of his ability. In his writing you see the use of beginning sounds and ending sounds. He wrote his first complete sentence, IYWTITA = I went apple picking. He copied this sentence onto the next page, he knows that print carries meaning. Eddie numbers the pages in his writing book which shows he understands that books have a special order. Middle sounds appear in his spelling, PKN = pumpkin. Eddie again uses his invented spelling for pumpkin on following pages which may indicate an awareness that word spellings are stable and consistent. Eddie uses the print in the classroom and illustrates the meaning of each word he uses. The quantity of writing increases and some vowels and sight words (the) are emerging. Eddie seems to like to repeat and improve upon his writings. He now uses more complete sentences in his writing. When working with an adult, Eddie can focus and use more sounds in his spelling. The spelling of pumpkin, PKN, remains stable through the month. More sight words are apparent (my, I, is). Eddie likes to write notes to classmates and mail them into the boxes. He can use writing for social purposes.

TEACHER: MARGARET PELCZAR

ROBIN: FIRST GRADE

Robin's topics for his News have been things he likes to do, like soccer; places he has been, like Florida; home and friends, places he can find on his Globe when watching the Olympics. His pictures are brief pencil sketches, just enough to give an idea of the text. Robin is able to carry most of the information in his writing.

Robin writes in upper case letters, observing spaces between words. His texts may curl around to fit spaces around the pictures. He uses beginning, ending, middle consonants, and medial vowels. He has a number of sight words such as I, me, and, to, a. He records past tense word endings (ME AND BEN BALDD I DAM. "Me and Ben builded a dam"). . . .

Robin brought in from home *Windy Day* which he has enjoyed reading to friends and to the class. During independent reading time he has chosen stories with predictable texts and picture which point to the meanings ... (In October) Robin has branched out in his choices for independent reading. Among his choices are Rita Gelman's *More Spaghetti I Say,* Audrey Woods' *Quick as a Cricket,* and Mercer Mayer's *All By Myself,* Robin has read these books to himself, to friends, and to the class. He enjoys doing projects for his stories, and works hard to solve the problems he sets for himself with cardboard, paste, popsicle sticks, etc ...

TEACHER: LEE PROCTOR

As the boundaries between language as a topic of study and language as a means of social engagement fade, these teachers are blurring the boundaries between home and school. In their classrooms they are incorporating print into everyday activities so that the children's personal understandings of literacy are both socially constructed as well as individually situated. Children are not disenfranchised, nor are their experiences marginalized. When the text becomes the context, children 's lives change. Teachers lives change. Observing children enables teachers to rethink the ways in which they can provide realistic instruction in situations that make sense to the children as well as to themselves. In such classrooms:

1. Patterns of literacy are constantly evolving to accommodate the everyday experiences of both teachers and children, and new understanding of reading and writing can lead to the systematic restructuring of classroom routines.

2. Many of the literacy experiences that occur at school take place as teachers and children go about their daily lives.

3. On many occasions, the act of reading is not the focus of attention, and the print has no intrinsic value. The message is embedded in some other event, useful within the context in which it was written or read, but otherwise appearing to be of little importance.

4. Many of the deliberate uses of literacy occur when such moment-to-moment uses of literacy become specific events, and the focus of attention is placed upon the functions and uses of reading together with context-specific analysis of language structure and skills.

5. When reading and writing become deliberate acts (4), the text becomes as important as the message that it contains.

6. Literacy is a key element in the ability of teachers and children to juggle all of the schedules, rituals and routines and time constraints that are a part of their school lives.

In the classroom, literacy becomes a dynamic, complex, multidimensional phenomenon that is transformed through the mutual dependence of activity and setting, and a dialectical relationship is established between school and family life.

References

Bissex, Glenda, & Bullock Richard. (1987). *Seeing for Ourselves: Case-Study Research by Teachers of Writing*. Portsmouth, NH: Heinemann Educational Books.

Bloome, David. See Chapter 3D this Handbook.

Carraher, Terezinha Nunes. (1986). From Drawings to Buildings: Working With Mathematical Scales. *International Journal of Behavioral Development*. (9), 527–544.

Carraher, Terezinha Nunes, Carraher David William, & Schliemann Analucia Dias. (1985). Mathematics in the Streets and in Schools. *British Journal of Developmental Psychology*. 3, 21–29.

Coles, Gerald. (1987). *The Learning Mystique: A Critical Look at "Learning Disabilities"*. New York: Pantheon Books.

Hansen, Jane, Newkirk Thomas, & Donald Graves, (Eds.). (1985). *Breaking Ground: Teachers Relate Reading and Writing in the Elementary School*. Portsmouth, NH: Heinemann Educational Books.

Hasan, Ruqaiya. (1987). *Reading Picture Reading: Invisible Instruction at Home and in School*. Sydney: Australian Reading Association.

Heath, Shirley Brice. (1983). *Ways With Words Language, Life, and Work in Communities and Classrooms*. Cambidge: Cambridge University Press.

Juliebo, Moira Fraser & Elliott Jean. (1987). The Child Fits the Label . . . *Elements*. 19 (1), 19–21.

LaRocha, Olivia De La. (1985). The Reorganization of Arthmetic Practice in the Kitchen. *Anthropology and Education Quarterly*. 16, 193–198.

Lave, Jean, Murtaugh Michael, & Rocha Olivia de la. (1984). The Dialectic of Arthmetic in Grocery Shopping. In B. Rogoff, & J. Lave (Eds.), *Everyday Cognition: It's Development In Social Context*. pp. 67–94. Cambridge, MA: Harvard University.

Lave, Jean. (1985). The Social Organization of Knowledge and Practice: A Symposium. *Anthropology and Education Quarterly*. 16, 171–176.

McDermott, Ray, & Roth D.R. (1978). The Social Organization of Behavior: Interactional Approaches. *Annual Review of Anthropology*. 7, 321–345.

Scribner, Sylvia. (1984). Studying Working Intelligence. In B. Rogoff, & J. Lave (Eds.), *Everyday Cognition: Its Development in Social Context*. Cambridge, MA: Harvard University Press.

Taylor, Denny. (1983). *Family Literacy: Young Children Learning to Read and Write*. Portsmouth, NH: Heinemann Educational Books.

Taylor, Denny. (1986a). Creating Family Story, in W. Teale & E. Sulzby (Eds.) *Emergent Literacy: Writing and Reading*. Norwood, NJ: Ablex Publishing Corporation. pp. 139–155.

Taylor, Denny. (1986b). Working Parents adn their Children: A Study of Family Literacy and Learning. A proposal submitted to the Elva Knight Research Award Committee of the International Reading Association.

Taylor, Denny. (1988). Ethnographic Educational Evaluation for Children, Families, and School. *Theory Into Practice*. 27 (1), 67–76.

Taylor, Denny. (1989). Toward a Unified Theory of Literacy Learning and Instructional Practices. *Phi Delta Kappan*. 71 (3), 184–193.

Taylor, Denny. From the Child's Point of View: Alternate Approaches to Assessment, to be published in *Developing Context-Responsive Approaches to Assessment*, Jessie Roderick & Judith L. Green, National Council of Research in English. (In press).

Taylor, Denny. (1990). Teaching Without Testing: Assessing the Complexity of Children's Literacy Learning. *English Education*. 22(1), 4–74.

Taylor, Denny, & Dorsey-Gaines Catherine. (1988). *Growing Up Literate: Learning From Inner City Families*, Portsmouth, NH: Heinemann Educational Books.

Taylor, Denny, & Strickland, Dorothy S. (1988). Learning From Families: Implications For Educators and Policy Makers, in J. Allen & J. Mason (Eds.), *Reducing the Risks for Young Learners*, Portsmouth, NH: Heinemann Educational Books. pp. 251–277.

25B. THE COMMUNITY AND LANGUAGE ARTS
Walt Wolfram

The significant role of the community in shaping language should be indisputable. Whereas a child's primary caretakers are influential in molding early language norms, by the time children reach school age this influence has been largely supplanted by that of the surrounding community of peers. Those who doubt the significance of community norms in shaping children's language need only examine the bilingual status of children whose parents are monolingual speakers of another language. Children of monolingual Spanish or Vietnamese parents readily pick up English if it is used in the community, regardless of their parents' English proficiency. Similarly, the dialect patterns of families who move to a different locale indicate that children rapidly adopt dialect norms of the new area while the parents typically remain entrenched in the dialect of their original locale. Thus, a Northern family who moves to a Southern dialect area of the United States usually reflects two sets of norms—the "fossilized" Northern dialect pattern retained by the parents and the Southern, community-based local norm acquired by the children.

Language norms of the community may also compete with the language norms of the school, and when this happens, the community dialect often emerges as the dominant influence. The persistence of community-based nonstandard or vernacular dialects in the face of institutional pressure to purge them is ample testimony to the significance of the community language environment. When all the factors that determine the shape of language are considered, few have as much influence on students' linguistic behavior as the community outside of the school.

Why are community norms of language so strong, often resisting the pressures of school and family alike when these norms clash? The answer seems to lie in the underlying social basis of language. Language is more than a simple code for the transmission of information; it is also a type of behavior that plays an important sociopsychological role for its speakers. In its behavioral role, it carries symbolic social meaning that includes group and community identity. Language norms are invariably embedded in culture, whether it be the assumed "academic culture" of the school or the indigenous culture outside the school. From this perspective, language arts in school cannot be treated simply as another academic content to be mastered. Language-arts education must start with a fundamental recognition of the symbolic cultural significance of the language that students bring to school with them, and a realistic understanding that few student behaviors are more central to students' community role than their language.

DEFINING THE COMMUNITY

There are certainly many definitions of "community," and still further controversy over the sociolinguistic definition of a "language community," but the aspect of community relevant for our discussion here is a fairly simple one involving the local culture outside the school. This community culture that students bring with them is characterized by a number of social attributes such as locale, social class, and ethnicity, but more importantly, this community culture provides a basic set of values, beliefs, and shared interests about language, along with other kinds of behavior. Both interactional relationships with community members and more abstract cultural norms of language behavior are involved in this notion of community. This may seem like an inclusive, somewhat loose definition of community language, but it is in line with our more general focus on influences outside of the school that affect language within the school. Narrowly based details of language structure as well as broadly based beliefs and attitudes about language use and interaction may have a bearing on language arts within the school, so we prefer to operate with a deliberately inclusive referent for community language.

COMMUNITY AND SCHOOL LANGUAGE DISSONANCE

In the past several decades, much attention has been given to the potential dissonance between community language and "school language." Language norms assumed in the educational system are invariably embedded in middle-class culture that includes Standard American English, whereas the language norms of the community may or may not match this standard variety. Whenever the norms of the community and educational institution are dissimilar, there is the potential for conflict. The conflict may involve *language forms,* the particular linguistic structures characterizing the community language variety, or it may involve *language use,* the functional language strategies used to carry out communication. In the following sections, we briefly discuss some areas of the community-school differences before turning to the relationship of the community and school in language arts.

Community-Based Language Structure

Over the past several decades, social dialectologists have provided fairly extensive inventories of the structural features that distinguish community-based, vernacular dialects from their standard English counterparts, including descriptions of vernacular African American English (e.g., Baugh, 1983; Fasold & Wolfram, 1970; Labov, 1972), Southern white rural varieties (Feagin, 1979; Wolfram & Christian, 1976), Northern metropolitan dialects (Labov, 1966; Shuy, Wolfram, & Riley, 1967; Wolfram, 1974), and a number of vernacular varieties influenced by other languages as well, such as American Indian English (Leap, 1977; Wolfram, Christian, Leap, & Potter, 1979), Chicano English (Peñalosa, 1980), and Vietnamese English (Wolfram, Christian, & Hatfield, 1986).

The structures described in these studies typically carry

overt social stigma in a mainstream institutional setting such as the school. It is important to understand, however, that in an indigenous context outside of the school, these forms simply reflect community norms of linguistic behavior. In fact, sociolinguists (Trudgill, 1972; Labov, 1972) have shown that some of these overtly stigmatized forms may, at the same time, carry covert prestige from a community perspective. That is, forms may be valued for their symbolic significance in terms of local identity and solidarity despite the fact that the forms are widely recognized as nonstandard. For example, it is possible for a structure such as the multiple negative (e.g., *She ain't gonna do nothing*) or the invariant *be* form (e.g., *They always be messing around*) to carry overt social stigma in mainstream institutional settings at the same time they are valued on a covert level in the community as symbolic linguistic tokens of community language behavior.

The notion of covert prestige is of particular relevance in understanding some school-community language conflicts. For certain age-groups of students influenced by nonmainstream values and peer group influence, the covert prestige of nonstandard forms may be an important underlying reason why these speakers maintain vernacular dialects in the face of school pressures to adopt Standard English forms. It is well recognized that vernacular speakers do not rush to become standard dialect speakers, even when these speakers may evaluate the social value of linguistic forms on the surface in a way that matches that of the more widespread mainstream social evaluation of dialect forms. Students maintain vernacular dialect forms because of their essential sociopsychological community functions, not because they are unfamiliar with the standard variant. This is a fundamental sociolinguistic principle that must be understood in teaching language arts, particular in programs that aim to teach Standard English as an alternative to the vernacular community dialect.

There are a number of different ways that structural differences between the language norms of the community and school may impact language arts. One of the major areas of conflict involves *language assessment*. The notion of correctness in language structure is traditionally restricted to standard English forms, so that the use of community-based, nonstandard English forms would systematically lower the score of a student who resorts to community forms in a standardized test. As most standardized achievement tests have a section on language use focusing primarily on the identification of standard English grammar forms (e.g., California Achievement Test, Iowa Test of Basic Skills), it stands to reason that students who use community-based, nonstandard English forms will lag in their achievement scores for language. From a current sociolinguistic vantage point, the question of what language usage tests actually test, what they should test, and how the scores should be interpreted for vernacular dialect speakers are important to confront squarely by language-arts educators and testing and measurement specialists (Wolfram & Christian 1980).

The differential scores of vernacular dialect speakers on standardized tests that recognize only standard English as a correct response are often interpreted as an indication of a language deficit, but they may also be interpreted as a simple manifestation of a community language difference. The difference-deficit controversy has now been debated by educators and sociolinguists for several decades with considerable passion, but it is still quite alive in language arts. The deficit position maintains that speakers of community-based vernacular varieties have a linguistic handicap because of the language system they have acquired. Unfortunately, this interpretation is often based upon the assumption that the indigenous language variety is an imperfect version of the standard variety. The difference position maintains that speakers of vernacular, community-based dialects simply have a different linguistic system, but that no one system is inherently superior or inferior linguistically. Vernacular varieties have linguistic rules that are every bit as systematic and complex as their standard counterparts, albeit different (Labov, 1972). It is important to understand that the difference position does not deny the sociolinguistic reality of the institutional legitimacy of Standard English in settings such as the school, but it separates this socioeducational position from the fundamental question of linguistic and cognitive adequacy.

How community-based language forms are interpreted in the basic assessment of language capability remains a live debate in most contexts for language-arts education, even when educators agree about the utility of Standard English for mainstream institutional purposes. Furthermore, the interpretation of the community language apparently is not educationally irrelevant, as negative views and erroneous assumptions about vernacular varieties often lead to self-fulfilling prophecies about students' language abilities and development (Williams, 1976).

Particular educational skills may also be affected by the structural conflict between community and school language forms, such as aspects of reading and writing development. These language differences may influence a student's writing and reading, although "structural interference" is not always as direct and predictable as one might assume based upon a simple comparison of structural differences between the structure of vernacular dialect and the Standard English of the school (cf. Farr, 1981; Laffey & Shuy, 1973; Wolfram & Christian, 1989). Nonetheless, the following hypothesis seems reasonable: *The more distant a student's community language is from the standard English of the classroom, the greater the likelihood that the structures of this language variety will be evidenced in classroom language tasks such as reading and writing.*

Community-Based Language Use

Language differences may extend considerably beyond the structural details of pronunciation and grammar. Important differences may also exist in the communicative strategies used to convey a message. There are a variety of ways available to say the same thing, and speakers typically choose strategies based upon who they are talking to and the conditions that surround the speech event. For example, one may direct a person to take out the garbage through the use of a direct, literal command such as *Take out the garbage!* or select from a range of more indirect means, including a question such as *Would you mind taking out the garbage?* or a a declarative that implies the need to take out the garbage such as *Tomorrow is garbage collection.*

The choice of a strategy invariably takes into account a number of social and cultural factors that dictate the appropriate form for a given circumstance. The school, as a reflection of academic culture, may adopt one set of conventions for carrying out a communicative function whereas the community may have another set of conventions that governs its communicative interaction.

Language use differences cover a wide set of communicative functions, ranging from the structure of participation in verbal interaction to the specific details for carrying out particular speech acts. On one level, functional language differences in the community and classroom are quite like those found in linguistic structure, but the potential for social dissonance in a mainstream educational setting seems to be greater in language use differences. Without an appreciation of the sociolinguistic diversity in language use as well as language form, communication strategies that follow community rather than school norms may be interpreted as unsocialized, uncooperative, or even hostile behavior.

Some of the classic examples of classroom and community conflict over language use conventions come from studies of verbal participation styles in nonmainstream American Indian communities and in nonmainstream African American communities, although illustrations might have been taken just as readily from other minority communities in the United States. Philips (1972, 1982), for example, shows that the conventional classroom context creates sociolinguistic conditions that are unfamiliar and threatening for American Indian children from the Warm Springs Indian reservation in Oregon. The emphasis upon competitive verbal responses in the public forum of the classroom gives rise to the profile of the quiet Indian child. In reality, the children are simply subject to context-specific communication patterns that are at odds with the kind of verbal individualism promoted in the classroom. Philips finds that the classroom contexts in which children perform best are those similar in organization to the local community, where cooperation and sociality rather than competition and individuality are emphasized.

A number of researchers (e.g., Kochman, 1981; Smitherman, 1977) also have shown that verbal interactional styles found in the indigenous African American community may clash with the normative conventions of the classroom. For example, simultaneous verbal participation and responses from students whose turn to speak has not formally been recognized by the teacher may be viewed as inappropriate classroom behavior. These verbal participation strategies may, however, simply follow different community norms governing verbal interaction. Aspects of conversational turn-taking, conversational pacing, participatory listening, and even topic choice may reveal fundamental differences between the conventions of mainstream classroom culture and the indigenous community culture that provides a background for students' entry into the classroom.

Researchers have further shown that the structure and function of discourse styles may be different in the community and the school, and that this difference may systematically affect an instructor's evaluation and response to students' verbal contributions. For example, Michaels' (1981) study of the narrative styles of "sharing time" in the classroom indicates an important difference between the narrative styles of middle-class Anglo first graders and their working-class African American counterparts in describing an object or recounting a past time event for other students in the class. The middle-class Anglo children in her study tended to use a topic-centered style of narration, in which events were linked primarily on the basis of chronological sequencing, whereas many of the African American children used a topic-associated style of discourse, in which a series of events are linked on the basis of implicit association. Michaels found further that the topic-associated style of the African American children was systematically interrupted by the teacher's attempts to keep the children from straying from the topic, whereas the style of the middle-class children was encouraged and rewarded. Michaels concludes that when the child's narrative style matches that of the teacher's expectations "collaboration is rhythmically synchronized and allows for informal practice in the development of a literate discourse style" (1981, p. 423), but when it is at variance with the teacher's expectations "collaboration is often unsuccessful and, over time, may adversely affect performance and evaluation" (1981, p. 423). Such studies clearly show differential school performance in language arts, based upon traditions of discourse structure facilitated in the home community.

Heath (1983) supports and complements other research on school-community differences in language use with data from a rural setting in the Piedmont Carolinas. She compared the middle-class "teacher talk" to children in the classroom with the talk of caretakers in the indigenous community of rural, low-income children, finding different language socialization processes and modes of language use. For example, the use of known-information questions (e.g., *What time is it now?* when the teacher already knows the time), object labeling *(What is this?),* and the identification of features of objects (e.g., *What can a bird do?*) were common strategies used by teachers in the classroom; they were also used by the teachers in the socialization of their own children at home. However, these strategies were not paralleled in the language socialization of children from a local indigenous community. Similarly, the common use of classroom interrogatives as directives such as *"Would you like to give me your paper now?"* as a command to give the teacher the paper was a classroom strategy not typically found in local community language uses. Other studies comparing language use conventions in the classroom and community (e.g., Anderson & Teale, 1981; Cazden, 1979; Hu-Pei-Au, 1980) document a fairly broad inventory of school-community language use differences. It seems only reasonable to conclude that these kinds of differences may impact on a full range of educational tasks—tasks which include, but are certainly not limited to the teaching and learning of language arts. We thus conclude that there are important relationships between language use and language socialization in the community and school that have a direct bearing on differential school performance in the language arts (Mehan, 1984).

THE COMMUNITY ROLE IN TEACHING AND LEARNING

Up to this point, we have focused mostly on the kinds of differences that may arise in classroom and community language norms. We now turn to the question of the community role in teaching and learning. What role might the community have in language arts, and how might sociolinguistic conflicts between community and school be mediated? Although there is more discussion of the differences between community and classroom language than there is discussion of constructive educational programs aimed at resolving such dissonance, there are several models of community involvement that hold considerable educational promise. In this section, we briefly present several of these models, based upon actual programs that have been attempted in different educational settings. The models discussed here include one in which the community culture is used as a primary content resource in language arts, one in which community-based interactional models are adopted for classroom instructional purposes, and one in which community and classroom differences are mediated through mutual acculturation by teachers and students.

The Community as a Content Resource

One approach to the community in a language-arts program is typified by the Foxfire program initiated by Eliot Wigginton in Rabun Gap, Georgia, in the late 1960s (Wigginton, 1986). Of the various language-arts programs involving the community, this is certainly one of the most popular and well-known programs. The underlying theme of the secondary school language-arts program developed by Wigginton is a fairly simple one in which language arts skills, in this case journalism, are learned by focusing on the description of various facets of life in the nonmainstream culture of rural, southern Appalalachia. Students learn by going into the community and collecting oral histories, which they mold into written descriptions and narratives. The quarterly journal *Foxfire* published by Wigginton's students is entirely run by the students, who are responsible for the original collection of oral histories and subsequent writing, editing, layout, and publication of each journal issue. The book-length collections of *Foxfire* material now include over 20 volumes on indigenous themes ranging from the affairs of "plain living" to special customs and traditions. This model has served the students of Rabun Gap, Georgia, quite well, but there are features of the program that are generalizable far beyond this local community. Other communities may be very different from southern Appalachia but there is no reason why the cultural heritage of these communities might not be tapped in an analogous fashion.

One might also extend the community resource model more directly to the study of language. Language characteristics of a local language community can serve to illustrate fundamental notions about linguistic organization, including the nature of linguistic diversity, the dynamic nature of language change, and the sociolinguistic significance of language differences reflected in community dialects. A community-based program of dialect study might, for example, give students informed knowledge about the naturalness of dialects at the same time it provides students with direct experience in collecting and analyzing linguistic data. Firsthand experience with community dialects also can provide students with a realistic understanding of the sociolinguistic consequences of using mainstream, stan-

dard English varieties as· opposed to vernacular, community-based dialects. At this point, experimentation in a language-arts curriculum focused on dialect differences is only in its preliminary phase (Wolfram, forthcoming), but such a model for language study focused on the community dialect holds exciting potential in the language-arts curriculum.

Adopting Community-Based Interactional Models

A somewhat different approach to the role of the community incorporates local community models of interaction into the classroom as a basis for instruction. A prime example of this type of approach is the Kamehameha Early Education Project K–3 lab school for Hawaiian children (Hu-Pei-Au, 1980). In this project, a multidisciplinary team of teachers, anthropologists, educational psychologists, and linguists attempted to develop a set of teaching practices and classroom organization strategies that emulated the indigenous style of interaction and learning. The study of the community turned up a number of features that were at odds with conventional assumptions about classroom interaction, as reported in *The Harvard Educational Letter:*

Children were more accustomed to learning from one another and from older children than from adults. In addition, although taught to respect their parents, children did not automatically defer to other adults . . . In native Hawaiian communities, the model for the nonparental adult was the soft, supportive "aunty." (The Harvard Educational Letter Vol. IV, No. 2, p.2)

The instructional model adopted in the classroom capitalized upon children's peer orientation. With respect to language, a style of participation evolved that seized upon the indigenous "talk story," a style of conversational interaction in which participants assist one another in telling stories. Students told stories in ensembles, supporting and criticizing peer contributions, instead of following the traditional classroom practice of speaking as an individual when a student turn is recognized. Parenthetically, it should be noted that students were also permitted to use Hawaiian Creole, the community language, in relating their experiences although the texts were in standard English and the teachers spoke in the standard variety. Over time, the use of a community-based cultural model of interaction and communication was shown to enhance rather than inhibit the students' progress in conventional skills such as reading, and standardized test scores eventually showed significant gains.

The critical component of programs such as the Kamehameha project is the adoption of community-based models for classroom instructional purposes. This model brings community patterns into the classroom. In the previously described model, the emphasis was upon students reaching out to the community rather than the incorporation of community-based instructional models. In both cases, however, the community is considered an indispensable variable to be considered in the educational process. Naturally, the incorporation of community models of interaction and learning into the school setting requires a fairly comprehensive ethnographic understanding of the culture from which the students come, but in the case of Kamehameha, the investment seemed to be well worth the effort. The project apparently transformed an educational situation that was steeped in failure into a successful one by using the community to guide the restructuring of the instruction process. It is also important to understand that academic standards and teacher expectations were not lowered in the process, as the students made significant progress as measured by standardized achievement tests.

Bridging Community and School: Mutual Acculturation

We already noted that the academic context of the school and the local community from which students come may represent very different subcultures and different socialization processes in language may lead to quite different behavioral conventions in language form and use. From one perspective, instruction in literacy and language arts in the classroom is often a matter of acculturation to mainstream culture. Getting students and teachers to observe some of the cultural differences related to language may thus be an important part of bridging the school-community cultural gap. As Farr and Daniels (1986, p. 31–32) put it, "cultural differences in language practices that are part of very different ways of viewing and operating in the world must be taken very seriously indeed." Teachers need to take into instructional consideration sociolinguistic features of the community at the same time that students need to be socialized into the linguistic culture of the school. One cannot simply assume that this process will naturally and routinely take place, so that special attention may have to be paid to building a sociolinguistic bridge.

Heath's (1983) work with teachers in the Piedmont study mentioned earlier attempts to incorporate such knowledge into the instructional program. In this program, teachers, learning to function as ethnographic observers of language, were expected to understand some of the differences between school and community language socialization and to modify some of their classroom language behavior accordingly. Based on their observations of language behavior at school and outside the school, teachers began to understand why children had trouble answering some of the questions posed in class and why the children appeared inattentive to certain ways of framing directives. As a result, teachers adjusted some of their own uses of language with children from these communities, and began experimenting with alternative linguistic strategies with their students. At the same time, information about observed sociolinguistic differences was presented to students to enrich their understanding of language use in different contexts, as children were systematically introduced to school language uses. Mutual language accommodation by teachers and students thus took place. Although this model has not been carried out in an extended, formal instructional program, preliminary experimentation in this type of sociolinguistic bridging appears to hold considerable promise in terms of reconciling school-community language relations.

IMPLICATIONS FOR THE LANGUAGE-ARTS EDUCATOR

Given the array of community language influences that may impact students' lives, it seems essential that language-arts spe-

cialists become familiar with aspects of community language. As an underlying, attitudinal approach, it is critical that practitioners appreciate the complexity and naturalness of community language patterns. We have mentioned repeatedly that the conflict in the linguistic patterns of the community and school is not related to the inherent nature of the linguistic system, but to the social position of different communities in our society and diverse traditions in language socialization. This understanding should serve as the basis for developing a nonpatronizing respect of community language, and stimulate the natural curiosity about language that should be expected on the part of language-arts educators.

Knowledge of community language must, of course, extend beyond the attitudinal appreciation of the naturalness and complexity of community language systems. It should also involve knowlege of the structural details of the community language system. It seems reasonable to expect that a language-arts practitioner serving a rural Appalachian community or an urban African American community know what the major pronunciation and grammar rules of these varieties are, especially where these rules contrast with the norms of Standard English presumed in the classroom. Knowledge of the structural language details of the community language system serves as the basis for understanding how these language differences may influence basic education skills such as writing and reading. It may further serve as a basis for understanding some of the differences in the standardized testing of language-arts skills as well. As mentioned previously, there are now available linguistic descriptions of some of the major regional and social/ethnic language systems that comprise these community language systems such as vernacular African American English, Appalachian English, Puerto Rican English, and so forth. However, available summaries of these varieties tend to focus on shared characteristics across local communities, so that it is necessary to complement available descriptions with community-specific information. Insight into particular language forms found in various communities is not the exclusive domain of the linguist or dialectologist.

As observers of language behavior, language-arts specialists are in an excellent position to contribute to the understanding of structural differences between community and school language. This does not mean that language-arts specialists need to know the technical formulas for rules sometimes used by linguists, but it does obligate them to know what language forms are commonly used in the community and the kinds of linguistic structures in which they are found. A person who pays close attention to language and is willing to spend time where language is used naturally—on the playground, in shops, and in other natural community contexts—is in a good position to make observations about community language and to follow this up by examining how these language patterns may carry over to specific language-arts skills in the context of the school.

Knowledge of community language must also involve an understanding of community conventions for language use. These conventions may dictate how students from different communities will participate in classroom situations ranging from taking turns to specific details of directness and literalness in language use. On one level, such knowledge provides a perspective for understanding student language behavior. On another level, this information may provide an important contrastive basis for the eventual socialization of students into the norms of language behavior expected in a classroom context. Knowledge of language use conventions must also include information about community values and beliefs with respect to language use. What kinds of language styles are positively and negatively valued in the community, and how is school language valued in the community by comparison? How is learning standard English viewed in the community? Is it associated with "acting white," as found in some working-class African American communities; is it associated with acting "uppity," as it may be in some working-class white communities? Such community values cannot be ignored in programs that aim to teach Standard English. Underlying values about the relative social significance of community language and school language are not a frivolous adjunct for the language-arts practitioner; they may impact the language-arts curriculum in a fundamental way and determine how students respond to language-arts objectives set forth in the classroom.

Knowledge of language use must further consider community-specific language interactional styles as they may relate to the learning process. Is the community model for language interaction between a speaker and audience one which follows a "call-response" pattern (e.g., Smitherman, 1977) or is it one which calls for single, recognized-turn response as expected in many classroom situations? These considerations may define the notion of "interrruption" in a classroom context very differently for various communities, and must be understood by the language-arts practitioner if the classroom and community are to come together in the education process.

Finally, language-arts specialists should become aware of community resources in the language arts. Are there community language uses that dovetail with important language-arts skills to be taught in the classroom? Are there exceptional storytellers or recognized styles of creative language use that can unify the community and classroom? If so, students can build upon community language strengths. Furthermore, teachers and students together can turn to the community as a natural resource. A model that builds upon community strengths in language, even when different from those assumed by the institutional educational system, seems to hold a much greater potential for success than one which focuses exclusively upon conflicts between the community and school language uses. Language-arts specialists may choose to disregard the role of the community in the classroom, feeling that their task is to ensure that the acquisition of school-related traditions takes place, but such an approach may simply force students to make a language choice between school and community. A more reasonable alternative is to start with a fundamental understanding and recognition of the significance of the community language and build upon it wherever possible. The goals of language arts in mainstream education and indigenous language traditions do not invariably have to be set up as a forced choice for students; in fact, the community may just turn out to contain a camouflaged educational lodestone for language arts.

References

Anderson, A. B., & Teale, W. H. (1981). Literacy as cultural practice, *Simposio Internacional: Nuevas perspectivas en los procesos de lectura y escritura, Siglo, 21,* 817–846.

Baugh, J. (1983). *Black street speech: Its history, structure, and survival.* Austin, TX: The University of Texas Press.

Cazden, C. B. (1979). *Peekaboo as an instruction strategy: Discourse development at home and at school.* (Papers and reports on child development, No. 17). Department of Linguistics, Stanford University.

Christian, D. (1987, December). Vernacular dialects in U.S. schools. *ERIC Digest.* Washington, DC: ERIC Clearinghouse on Languages and Linguistics.

Erickson, F., & Mohatt G. (1982). Participation structures in two communities. In G. Spindler (Ed.), *Doing the ethnography of the classroom.* New York: Holt, Rinehart, Winston.

Farr Whiteman, M. (1981). Dialect influence in writing. In M. Whiteman Farr (Ed.), *Variation in writing: Functional and linguistic-cultural differences.* Hillsdale, NJ: Lawrence Erlbaum.

Farr, M., & Daniels, H. (1986). *Language diversity and writing instruction.* Urbana, IL: ERIC/Institute for Urban and Minority/National Council of Teachers of English.

Fasold, R. W., & Wolfram, W. (1970). Some linguistic features of Negro dialect. In R. W. Fasold & R. W. Shuy (Eds.), *Teaching Standard English in the inner city.* Washington, DC: Center for Applied Linguistics.

Feagin, C. (1979). *Variation and change in Alabama English: A sociolinguistic study of the white community.* Washington, DC: Georgetown University Press.

Heath, S. B. (1983). *Ways with words: Language, life and work in communities and classrooms.* Cambridge, England: Cambridge University Press.

Hu-Pei-Au, K. (1980). Participation structures in a reading lesson with Hawaian children: An analysis of a culturally appropriate instructional event. *Anthropology and Education Quarterly, 11*(2), 91–115.

Kochman, T. (1981). *Black and white: Styles in conflict.* Chicago: University of Chicago Press.

Labov, W. (1966). *The social stratification of English in New York City.* Washington, DC: Center for Applied Linguistics.

Leap, W. L. (Ed.). (1977). *Studies in Southwestern Indian English.* San Antonio, TX: Trinity University.

Labov, W. (1972). *Language in the inner city: Studies in the Black English vernacular.* Philadelphia: University of Pennsylvania Press.

Laffey, J., & Shuy, R. (Eds.). (1973). *Language differences: Do they interfere?* Newark, DE: Iternational Reading Association.

Mehan, H. (1984). Language and schooling. *Sociology of Education, 57,* 174–183.

Michaels, S. (1981). Sharing time: children narrative style and differential access to literacy. *Language in Society, 10,* 423–442.

Penalosa, F. (1980). *Chicano sociolinguistics: A brief introduction.* Rowley, MA: Newbury House.

Philips, S. U. (1972). Participant structures and communicative competence: Warm Springs children in community and classroom. In C. Cazden, V. P. John & D. Hymes (Eds.), *Functions of language in the classroom.* New York: Teachers College Press.

Philips, S. U. (1982). *The invisible culture: Communication in classroom and community on the Warm Springs Indian reservation.* New York: Longmans.

Shuy, R. W., Wolfram, W., & Riley, W. K. (1967). *Linguistic correlates of social stratification in Detroit speech.* (Report No. 6-1347). Washington, DC: U.S. Office of Education.

Smitherman, G. (1977). *Talkin and testifyin: The language of Black America*. Boston: Houghton Mifflin.

The Harvard Educational Letter, 4(2). (1988). Cultural differences in the classroom.

Trudgill, P. (1972). Sex, covert prestige and linguistic change in the urban British English of Norwich. *Language in Society, 1,* 179–195.

Wigginton, E. (1986). *Sometimes a shining moment: The Foxfire experience*. Garden City, NJ: Anchor/Doubleday.

Williams, F. (1976). *Explorations of the linguistic attitudes of teachers*. Rowley, MA: Newbury House.

Wolfram, W. (1974). *Aspects of assimilation: Puerto Rican English in New York City*. Washington, DC: Center for Applied Linguistics.

Wolfram, W. (forthcoming). A secondary school curriculum on dialects. Cincinnati Public Schools.

Wolfram, W., & Christian, D. (1976). *Appalachian speech*. Washington, DC: Center for Applied Linguistics.

Wolfram, W., & Christian, D. (1980). On the application of sociolinguistic information: Test evaluation and dialect differences in Appalachia. In T. Shopen & J. M. Williams (Eds.), *Standards and dialects in English*. Cambridge, MA: Winthrop.

Wolfram, W., & Christian, D. (1989). *Dialects and education: Issues and answers*. Englewood Cliffs, NJ: 1989.

Wolfram, W., Christian., D, & Hatfield, D. (1986). The English of young adult Vietnamese refugees in the United States. *World Englishes, 5,* 47–60.

Wolfram, W., Christian, D., Leap, W. L., & Potter, L. (1979). *Variability in the English of two Indian communities and its effect on reading and writing*. (Report No. 400-78-0057). Washington, DC: National Institute of Education.

·26·

CLASSROOM CONTEXTS FOR LITERACY LEARNING

Roselmina Indrisano
Jeanne R. Paratore

A systematic investigation of the research in organizing and managing instruction reveals that contrary to the assumptions of many educators, relevant studies are substantial in certain areas and sparse in others, and definitive conclusions reflect the same phenomenon. For these reasons, then, this chapter will include a review of the investigations that focus on the organization and management of instruction, conclusions drawn for the body of research, and questions yet to be answered.

Several limitations were imposed by the authors as this review was prepared: 1. the review is limited to studies reported within the last two decades; 2. the findings reported are generally limited to those that relate specifically to the theme of the chapter, although additional findings may have been reported by the researchers; and 3. related findings are reported only when these outcomes are essential to understanding and interpreting the outcomes that pertain specifically to organizing and managing instruction.

A REVIEW OF INVESTIGATIONS

The studies that follow have been clustered to suggest the major organizational emphasis on students, teaching behaviors, and curriculum/task. The classification of the investigation by the content of the hypothesis or questions is intended only to provide an orderly presentation and not to suggest that the complex phenomena of learning, teaching, and curriculum are inherently separable.

Students

In many contemporary elementary classrooms and secondary schools, grouping practices are used to organize students for instruction in the language arts. These practices include abil-

ity grouping, cooperative learning, and peer tutoring. In this section, the impact of these practices on both student achievement and attitudes toward learning and the self is examined.

Ability Grouping. Ability grouping, the practice of instructing students in groups according to academic performance and/or ability levels, is characterized in the literature by two basic organizational plans: within class or by class. When "within class" grouping is employed, students within heterogeneous classrooms are regrouped homogeneously for specific instruction during part of the school day. When "by class" grouping is used, students performing at similar achievement levels are assigned to a particular classroom for the entire school day. Often referred to as "tracking," by class groups typically move together from teacher to teacher and are more frequently observed within secondary school settings. Though ability grouping is sometimes discussed as a single phenomenon, research suggests that the type of grouping, i.e., in class or by class, results in different student outcomes (Slavin, 1986). Further, recent investigators have suggested that in addition to type of grouping, differential teaching behaviors within ability groups may also relate to varied learner outcomes (Heibert, 1983). Thus, this review includes an analysis of both studies that examine ability grouping as a variable in differential learning, as well as those that investigate the incidence of differential instruction within high and low ability groups.

Heterogeneous vs. Homogeneous Grouping. Ability grouping has long represented a practice for organizing and managing students within classrooms. Passow (1988) cites systematic efforts to group by ability as early as 1867 in St. Louis, and notes that "with the advent of group intelligence tests and standardized achievement tests around World War I, ability grouping became a commonplace practice by which schools attempted to cope with student diversity and provide for individual differences" (p. 205). According to Good and Stipek (1983), ability grouping continues to maintain its status in contemporary classrooms as the most common procedure to accommodate individual differences in rates of learning. Despite its long history and a substantial number of studies aimed at documenting outcomes related to grouping practices, several recent reviews of investigations have yielded few conclusive findings. Good and Marshall (1984) attribute the lack of consistent findings to several factors, including variation in the scope and purpose of studies, with differences occurring in number of students, number of groups and size of classrooms; variation in instructional content, including both curriculum and methods of teaching; and a failure to control for differential teaching qualities and behaviors. However, careful review of studies in which factors such as group composition, curriculum, and teaching behaviors were effectively controlled yield some insight into the efficacy of ability grouping. For example, examining observational studies in elementary and junior high schools, Good and Marshall found consistent evidence that assignment of students to lower tracks generally maintains or sustains student performance at a low level. Support for this finding is revealed in other studies. Sorensen and Hallinan (1986) report that in studies of fourth through seventh grade grouped and ungrouped classes, high ability groups provide more opportunities for learning than low ability groups. These findings are consistent with those of Rowan and Miracle (1983) who also found in a study of fourth-grade students that ability grouping had direct effects favoring high ability, but not low ability learners. Kulik and Kulik (1982) conducted a meta-analysis of findings from 52 studies of ability grouping carried out in secondary schools, including only investigations reporting on measured outcomes in grouped and ungrouped classes. They found that effects were largest in programs designed for talented and gifted students, who accomplished more in honors programs than they did in mixed ability classrooms. However, effects were near zero in programs designed especially for academically deficient students, with these students learning as much in heterogeneous as they did homogeneous classrooms. Similar findings are reported in earlier studies of first-grade students by Weinstein (1976) and of secondary students by Alexander and McDill (1976) in which initial inequalities in achievement between high and low ability groups actually increased over time.

In studies of the impact of ability grouping on factors other than achievement, Felmlee and Eder (1983) and Eder and Felmlee (1984) examined the development of different attention norms in low versus high ability first-grade reading groups. Controlling for individual characteristics and previous individual attention patterns, they report that students in low ability groups became inattentive at four times the rate of students in high ability groups. Of particular importance is the finding that the effect became greater over time, suggesting the impact of the learning environment on student behavior.

Reporting somewhat more positive findings in a review of five types of grouping plans for elementary school students, Slavin (1986) concludes that although by class grouping, or tracking, does not enhance student achievement, there are con-

ditions under which within class grouping can be highly effective. He reports that plans most apt to boost student achievement share at least three criteria: students are placed according to ability levels in the specific skill being taught; groups are flexible enough to allow teachers to reassign students to different ability groups if academic performance changes; and teachers vary the pace and level of instruction to respond to students' needs.

Differential Instruction. In addition to achievement studies, several researchers have investigated the differential instruction hypothesis in relation to ability grouping, exploring whether or not both quantity and quality of learning is distributed differently among different ability groups. Several factors have been examined, including pacing practices, instructional content, instructional techniques, and general learning environments. As with the achievement studies, findings are often inconsistent, varying by type of grouping and grade level.

Effective teaching research has consistently identified brisk pacing as a correlate of higher achievement. In exploring how teachers make pacing decisions, Barr (1975) interviewed first-grade teachers and found that in no case could teachers identify the cues they used to adjust pacing; further she found that pacing practices remained stable from year to year and that extreme similarity existed among pacing practices within particular schools. She concluded that first-grade pacing practices are more often a response to group placement than to individual need. In an observational study of the impact of in class versus by class grouping, Rowan and Miracle found by class grouping disadvantaged lower ability learners through slower pacing, but that in class grouping had opposite effects, with lower level reading groups involved in more direct interaction with teachers and paced faster than high ability groups. They suggested that in class grouping results in an attempt by teachers "to bring lower groups up to the level of higher groups through compensatory actions" (p. 141). Further evidence of pacing differences between high and low ability groups is provided by Allington (1984). In an analysis of teacher logs from 600 reading group sessions in grades 1, 3, and 5, he found better readers read more total words and read more words silently during instructional sessions at all grade levels. In a large scale study of junior high and high school practices, Oakes (1980) reports consistent data from teachers, students, and observers indicating that more time is spent on instruction in high than in low track classes, leading to faster pacing practices for high ability groups. At the high school level, pacing differences were observed not only in school-based assignments, but in homework assignments as well, with teachers having higher expectations for homework time of high ability versus low ability groups. The impact of differential pacing is highlighted in a study by Gamoran (1986). Examining first-grade classrooms that isolated instructional effects, he found that the number of words and phonics concepts taught to first graders, differentiated by reading groups, was the most important factor in student learning.

With regard to instructional content, Hiebert (1983) reviewed several studies and concluded that at the elementary level, low ability groups tend to spend more time on decoding tasks, while high ability groups are engaged in "critical thinking" activities. At the junior high and secondary level, Oakes (1980) reported significant differences in content taught in high track versus low track classes. Differences in instructional strategies are reported as well. For example, Hiebert cites evidence that low ability groups had fewer opportunities to answer analytic type questions. Eder and Felmlee (1984) report that teachers were less likely to rely on discussions in lower ability groups, placing emphasis on structured activities, resulting in fewer opportunities to develop important communication skills in lower ability groups. Good and Marshall (1984) conclude from their review that teachers in low groups make fewer demands on students and apply less exacting standards to both student performances and their own teaching. Oakes (1980) reports clear cut differences in cognitive levels required by instructional activities in classes at different track levels in both junior high and high school levels.

In addition, differences between high and low ability groups are reported in relation to the general instructional environment. Grant and Rothenberg (1986) examined first- and second-grade classrooms using ability groups and concluded that students in top groups are advantaged by having environments more conducive to learning, characterized by fewer interruptions, more opportunities to demonstrate competence, more practice with autonomous, self-directed modes of learning, and a generally warmer, socioemotional atmosphere. Similarly, Eder and Felmlee (1984) reported that first-grade teachers' use of management and underlying expectations varied across group levels, with teachers in high ability groups quick to manage any type of inattentiveness or disruption, while teachers in low ability groups ignored many inattentive or disruptive actions. These findings are consistent with those reported by Hiebert (1983) in a review of related studies that led her to conclude that engaged time in low ability groups is less than engaged time in high ability groups and that teachers allow fewer interruptions when working with high ability groups than low ability groups. At the junior high and high school levels, Oakes (1980) observed less variability in materials in high and low track classes, less clarity of instructional expectations, and less teacher enthusiasm for low track classes.

Finally, a few studies report peer effects in high versus low ability groups. In their study of first-grade students, Eder and Felmlee (1984) report high ability group students apply pressure to maintain attention during interruptions from outside the group, while low ability group members view interruptions as an opportunity to turn their attention from group work. In studies of elementary and junior high students, Schwartz (1981) reports consistent differences in student behavior in high and low track classes, with low track behavior characterized as challenging teachers, obstructing academic activity, and misusing educational resources. Though teachers tend to use more control statements and more positive reinforcement with low ability groups (Eder, 1983; Eder and Felmlee, 1984; Haskins, Walden, & Ramey, 1983), students are still more likely to exhibit off-task, often disruptive behavior. Findings such as these led Good and Marshall (1984) to conclude that "peer influences in low ability groups (i.e., inattentiveness; disruptive behavior)

tend to be unavoidable and strong enough to overwhelm the potential instructional advantages of grouping" (p. 22).

Collaborative Learning. Although ability grouping clearly represents the predominant grouping practice in elementary and secondary schools today, there is a growing interest in and implementation of organizational plans that facilitate and promote peer interaction. Largely in response to the Vygotskian principle that social interaction serves as a catalyst for intellectual growth (Vygotsky, 1962), plans such as cooperative learning and peer tutoring, each having a long but sparsely used history in American education, are experiencing increased interest from both researchers and classroom teachers. In this section, the impact of cooperative learning and peer tutoring on student achievement, attitudes toward learning and peers, and academic self-concepts will be explored.

Cooperative Learning. Cooperative learning is defined by Slavin (1980) as a technique "in which students work on learning activities in small groups and receive rewards or recognition based on their group's performance." Cooperative learning groups may differ from traditional classroom groups in three ways: authority structure, group tasks, and reward structures. Slavin (1980) defines the authority structure as the control that students exercise over their activities, and the extent of choice they have about what they will study, how they will learn, and what they will need to learn. Reward structures are defined as the means that teachers use to motivate students to perform school tasks. In traditional structures, each student strives for an individual grade. In cooperative learning structures, students work toward a group reward or grade.

Task structures represent the organization of the class activities that make up the school day, including seat work, lecture-discussion, individualized instruction, or peer tutoring. Recent studies have attempted to analyze the impact of cooperative learning structures on student outcomes. In a meta-analysis of 122 studies of the relative effectiveness of cooperation, cooperation with intergroup competition and interpersonal competition, and individualistic goal structures, Johnson, Maruyama, Johnson and Nelson (1981) report that for all subject areas and all age groups studied, cooperation is considerably more effective than interpersonal competition and individualistic efforts, and that cooperation with intergroup competition is superior to interpersonal competition and individualistic efforts. Slavin (1978) studied separate effects of the three components, a focused schedule of instructional activities (i.e., authority structure), tasks and rewards, on achievement and time on task of fourth- and fifth-grade students. Behavioral observations and academic achievement results support the importance of a group reward, which yielded significantly greater performance when compared to traditional reward structures, but did not support the group task, during which students in groups were observed to be off-task for significantly greater percentages of time when compared to students working independently. His most important finding, however, relates to the focused schedule of instruction that was found to be the most important variable in student outcomes. Slavin defines "schedule of instruction" as the extent of systematic instruction that occurs prior to cooperative learning activities.

Sharan (1980) conducted a review of investigations related to five cooperative learning methods and, in findings similar to Slavin's, concluded that the cooperative reward and the underlying instructional strategies, not the team task, represent the critical components of cooperative learning.

In addition to achievement outcomes, researchers report positive results from cooperative learning structures on attitudes toward learning and academic self-concepts (Slavin, 1978, 1980; Sharan, 1980). Further, Slavin (1980) and Sharan (1980) report strong and consistent positive effects on racial relationships, with evidence of increased cross-racial interaction both when students were and were not working on academic material.

Finally, in a study of the feasibility of teaching teachers cooperative learning strategies in a large school system, Talmage, Pascarella and Ford (1984) report that cooperative learning strategies can be learned by teachers through long-term, in-service programs, and that length of teacher experience with cooperative grouping is significantly associated with end of year reading achievement and student perception of the degree of cooperation in their own learning environment.

The literature related to cooperative learning is best summarized by a statement by Johnson (1981):

> The strength of the evidence concerning the importance of peer relationships, the constructive impact of cooperative learning experiences and the power of effectively managed controversy, highlight a number of discrepancies between current educational practice and knowledge. Competition, individualistic learning and the avoidance of conflict among ideas dominate most American classrooms. There is a need to bring current educational practice into closer correspondence with what we know about effective pedagogy. (p. 10)

Peer Tutoring. As outlined by Sharan (1980), peer tutoring differs from methods of cooperative learning in several ways. Organizationally, cooperative learning methods utilize groups or teams, while tutoring schemes are characterized by dyads. With regard to the nature of the learning task, tutoring is usually focused on transmitting very specific information, emphasizing information and skills acquisition, while cooperative learning groups stress problem-solving, interpretation, synthesis, and application of information. Further, peer tutoring usually maintains a traditional, individual reward system, although evaluation in cooperative groups is typically both individual and group-based. Finally, with regard to total classroom organization, under a peer-tutoring plan the class functions as an aggregate of teams that are uncoordinated or engaged in a uniform task, while under the cooperative learning plan the class functions as a "group of groups" with between group coordination and division of labor and tasks. Although no studies were located that compared the effectiveness of peer tutoring and cooperative learning, several researchers have investigated the effectiveness of peer tutoring in comparison to traditional organizational plans. As with other classroom organizational plans, studies of peer tutoring yield conflicting results, with success or failure highly dependent on the specific context for instruction.

Among the most comprehensive reviews is a meta-analysis of 65 studies of tutoring programs conducted by Cohen, Kulik and Kulik (1982). Studies included in the analysis were those that took place in actual elementary or secondary school settings, reported quantitatively measured outcomes in both tutored and untutored groups, and were identified as being free from methodological flaws such as differing aptitude levels and teaching to the test for one group but not the other. Reviewing 52 achievement studies, the investigators found superior achievement for students in tutored versus untutored programs in 45 of the studies. Statistically significant differences were found in 19 studies, with average effect sizes described as modest. Further analysis revealed that studies with the following features consistently reported strong effects: more structured programs; programs of shorter duration; lower level skills taught and tested on exams; locally developed tests rather than nationally standardized tests used for evaluation. With regard to attitude toward subject matter, eight studies were reviewed, all revealing more positive student attitudes in classrooms with tutoring programs. Data related to self concept revealed that neither tutors nor tutees changed in self-esteem as a result of tutoring programs. In a later review, Damon (1984) confirmed the achievement benefits of tutorial programs, stressing as well the importance of those features outlined by Cohen, Kulik and Kulik. Damon concluded that one-on-one tutoring seems most suitable to those situations where there is a need for supplementary bolstering of adult instruction, although collaborative groups are better suited to acquiring basic reasoning skills. Additional support for peer tutoring is found in a study by Brown and Palincsar (1985) on the reciprocal teaching procedure that enables peer tutors to raise the comprehension scores of their tutees by up to 70 percent. In a study of the effects of peer tutoring on analogy performance, Judy, Alexander, Kulikowich and Willson (1988) report that those who received peer tutoring not only did significantly better at solving analogy problems than those who did not, but in addition, those who were trained by peer tutors in only two sessions performed comparably on the analogy test to those who were trained by the investigators in three sessions. Although most tutorial studies focus on higher ability student tutoring lower ability learners, one study was located that assessed the effects of reverse-role tutoring, that is, handicapped students tutoring regular class students. Osguthorpe, Eiserman, Shiser, Top, and Scruggs (n.d.) examined the impact of fourth- to sixth-grade learning and behaviorally handicapped students tutoring regular education first graders who were identified as delayed in reading. Comparing tutors' and tutees' performance with appropriate comparison groups, results revealed higher reading performance for both tutors and tutees.

Other researchers have investigated the effectiveness of student dyads that function more as collaborators and less in the roles of teacher-learner. For example, in a study examining the cognitive benefits of peer collaboration, Forman (cited in Forman & Cazden, 1985) found that fourth-and fifth-grade collaborators solved many more problems than singletons in the same set of 11 sessions; further, she observed the pair that showed the most cooperative interactions and used the most combinational strategies solved the most problems. Such data led to the conclusion that "support from an observing partner seems to enable the two collaborators to solve problems together before they are capable of solving the same problems alone" (p. 341). Similarly, evidence from a study of first-grade sharing time led Michaels and Foster (1985) to conclude that peer teaching can enhance language learning even among very young children. With regard to the role of peer groups in the writing classroom, teachers and researchers cite many potential benefits. For example, DiPardo and Freedman (1987) suggest that peer groups provide a structure for development of a sense of audience, expand the actual audience to which children write, and provide increased opportunities to receive response to their writing during, rather than at the end of, the writing process. However, investigations of peer writing groups' effectiveness reveal conflicting results. For example, Freedman (1985) reported that in a survey of 560 teachers of writing, teachers and their students disagreed over the effectiveness of peer groups; students agreed that groups are relatively useless, although teachers disagreed among themselves about the usefulness of groups. In a case study of four children with low, average and high abilities in writing, Russell (1985) examined the relationship between peer conferencing and the revision process. Results suggested that poor writers can effectively conference with their peers but are dependent on the questions of others in order to revise their writing, while average and good writers seem to be able to distance themselves from their writing, serving as their own audience and revising on their own. Conflicting data such as these, and the general paucity of related research led DiPardo and Freedman (1987) to conclude that "we know little about precisely why groups work when they do, or perhaps more importantly, what accounts for their failures" (p. 2).

Teaching and Teachers

Emmer and Evertson (1982) defined effective classroom management as "teacher behaviors that produce high levels of student involvement in classroom activities, minimal amounts of student behaviors that interfere with the teacher's or other students' work, and efficient use of instructional time" (p. 342). In this section, classroom organization and management will be reviewed from the perspective of teachers and teaching behaviors.

Team Teaching

From research on effective staff utilization in the decade of the 1950s, the concept of team teaching emerged as a way to respond to the teacher shortage and to improve education. Armstrong (1977) provides an extensive review of the studies that investigated the impact of team teaching on academic achievement. Citing Cunningham, Armstrong notes four organizational patterns in team teaching.

1. Team leader type: In this arrangement one team member has a higher status than the other(s). He may well have a special title such as "team leader."

2. Associate type: In this arrangement there is no designated leader. Leadership may be expected to emerge as a result of interactions among individuals and given situations.

3. Master teacher—beginning teacher: In this arrangement team teaching is used to foster acculturation of new staff members to the school.

4. Coordinated team type: In this arrangement there is no joint responsibility for a common group of youngsters. What *is* involved is joint planning by two or more teachers who are teaching the same curriculum to different groups of youngsters. (pp. 2–3)

Comprehensive summaries of investigations comparing team-taught and solitary-teacher-taught students at the elementary level (Table 26–1) and the secondary level (Table 26–2) are provided by Armstrong.

In concluding his review, Armstrong cautions that methodological differences preclude valid generalizations across investigations and suggest that researchers provide specific information regarding the critical variables in team teaching. Further, he notes:

In summation, one is struck by the very basic nature of the questions for which research has failed, after fifteen or more years of team teaching, to supply at least tentative answers. Team teaching, it is evident, represents one of those educational practices that have not been subjected to truly intensive and systematic investigation. Support for team teaching has been more of a validation through affirmation than a validation based on empirical evidence. At this juncture, little in the research literature provides solace either for team teaching's critics or its most ardent supporters. (p. 83)

Characteristics of Effective Classroom Managers. Studies related to effective classroom practice have consistently yielded correlates of higher achievement. These include brisk pacing, increased allocated academic time, high rates of students engaged time, and high success rate (Rosenshine & Stevens, 1984). Beyond knowing exactly what factors correlate with higher achievement, researchers have attempted to determine what management behaviors enable teachers to achieve these correlates. In a study of effective classroom management at the beginning of the school year, Emmer, Evertson and Anderson (1980) observed the behaviors of 27 third-grade teachers. Included in the observations was a vast array of factors, including room arrangement, materials, assignments, introductions, classroom rules, consequences of misbehavior, initiation of activities, transitions, delays, student reactions, grouping patterns, the nature of individual work and organizational procedures, desired student activities, problems, response to inappropriate behavior, consistency of teacher responses, systems for contacting students, procedures for various teacher and pupil activities, the nature of group work, monitoring, feedback systems, reward and punishment systems, and teacher cues. Based on their observations and a measure of student engagement, the researchers reported that effective managers were distinguished from less effective managers by the degree to which the rules and procedures were integrated in a workable system, and how effectively the system was taught to the children. Effective managers explained rules and procedures clearly, providing stu-

TABLE 26–1. Investigations Comparing Team-Taught and Solitary-Teacher-Taught
Students—Elementary Level

Investigator	Significant Differences Favoring Team-Taught Pupils	Significant Differences Favoring Solitary-Teacher-Taught Pupils	No Significant Differences Between Team-Taught and Solitary-Teacher-Taught Pupils
Jackson (1964)	(5th graders) reading achievement (6th graders) work study skills		(5th graders) science, social studies, language, work study, arithmetic (6th graders) science, social studies, language, arithmetic, reading achievement
Lambert, Goodwin & Wiersma (1965)	(2nd year; 1st graders) reading, language, total achievement (2nd year; 2nd graders) language	(1st year; all pupils) reading, arithmetic, total achievement	(1st year; all pupils) language (2nd year; (1st graders) arithmetic (2nd year; 2nd graders) reading, arithmetic, total achievement (2nd year; grades 3–6) reading, arithmetic, language arts, total achievement
Burningham (1968)	(4th graders) mathematics, science		(4th graders) all remaining subject areas measured by Sequential Test of Educational Progress
Sterns (1969)			(4th graders and 6th graders) mental maturity, reading achievement
Rhodes (1971)		(K–6 pupils) average reading gain	(K–6) pupils) spelling, arithmetic, attitude toward school and learning
Cooper & Sterns (1973)			(4th graders and 6th graders) mental maturity, reading achievement

Source: David G. Armstrong, Team teaching and academic achievement. *Review of Educational Research*, 47, p. 70.

dents examples and reasons. They observed that effective managers spent considerable time during the first week of school explaining and reminding pupils of the rules and used a greater variety of rewards and signals for appropriate behavior. Further, during the initial phase of instruction, effective managers relied on whole-group instruction, allowing students to become familiar with classroom procedures before they were required to work independently. Investigators observed that although effective managers viewed the teaching of content as important, they stressed socialization into the classroom during the first few weeks of school. By the end of the first three weeks, these classes had acquired the management skills that would prepare them for the rest of the year. With regard to instructional management, Emmer, Evertson, and Anderson reported that better managers had smoother, shorter transitions between activities, that children had activities to do after completing "regular" work; directions were clear and usually written on the board; routines were established early and often taught step by step with the teacher monitoring to verify that each step was performed appropriately; seatwork and progress on assigned work was frequently monitored; activities had a sense of purpose and organization; climate was relaxed but work centered. A study of effective teaching in first-grade reading groups led Anderson, Evertson and Brophy (1979) to four major conclusions related to effective management behaviors: more effective teachers

spent more time with the group and covered more content, providing students more opportunities to learn; during group instruction, more effective teachers provided students opportunities to practice skills being taught, permitting immediate corrective feedback and lesson adjustments; effective teachers provided appropriate information about structure of skills involved, rather than focusing on memorizing rules or labels; good classroom management underlies all of the other principles and includes use of efficient routines; working without distraction; prevention of behavior problems, smooth transition times. Duffy, Roehler and Rackliffe (1986) report findings from a study of experienced fifth-grade teachers, however, that suggest although teaching behaviors such as time allocation and management routines that maximize time on task may be important, even when these conditions are present, differences in teachers' instructional talk may create differences in student understanding and achievement. Evertson, Anderson, Anderson and Brophy (1980) examined the relationships between classroom behaviors and student outcomes in junior high English and mathematics classes. Although results related to mathematics outcomes were in many ways similar to findings at the elementary level, results related to effective teaching behaviors in the English class were largely inconsistent, and not adequate to serve as the basis for an instructional framework. In a two-year study of secondary schools, Stallings (1979) identified several

TABLE 26–2. Investigations Comparing Team-Taught and Solitary-Teacher-Taught Students—Secondary Level

Investigator	Significant Differences Favoring Team-Taught Pupils	Significant Differences Favoring Solitary-Teacher-Taught Pupils	No Significant Differences Between Team-Taught and Solitary-Teacher-Taught Pupils
Johnson, Lobb & Patterson (1959, 1960)	None: 1959 Investigation English: 1960 Investigation	(1960) social studies, geometry, science, business education	(1959) language arts, English, plane geometry, American history
Taffel (1962)			physics
Georgiades & Bjelke (1964)			English
Oakland Public Schools (1964)			mathematics, reading, writing
Klausmeier & Wiersma (1965)	(low ability students, homogeneously-grouped classes) English, social studies		(low ability students, heterogeneously-grouped classes) English, social studies (average-ability students, homogeneously-grouped classes) English, social studies (average-ability students, heterogeneously-grouped classes) English, social studies
Georgiades & Bjelke (1966)	reading comprehension		reading vocabulary
Fraenkel (1967)	(using criterion instrument demanding higher level thinking skills) United States history		(using criterion instrument demanding recall and memory skills) United States history
Robinson (1968)			biology
Schlaadt (1969)			health
Lutenbacher (1970)			social studies, English
Gamsky (1970)	(after one semester) English		(after one semester) social studies (after two semesters) English, social studies

Source: David G. Armstrong, Team teaching and academic achievements. *Review of Educational Research*, 47, pp. 76–77.

factors positively related to reading gain, including discussing homework or reading content, instructing new work, appropriate drill and practice, oral reading, sustaining feedback, short quizzes, and praise and support. Factors that were negatively related to reading gain at the secondary level included outside intrusions, social interactions, misbehavior or negative interactions, offering student choices, too much written assignment time, too much silent reading time, and too much time spent working with students individually.

In a later report, Stallings (1986) suggested three major findings related to teaching processes and student achievement in secondary reading classes. First, teacher reinforcement of correct responses and guidance when incorrect responses are given are positively related to reading gains; two, frequency of reading related verbal interactions, including interactive instruction and oral reading, positively relates to achievement; and third, the number of social interactions and other off-task behaviors that occur during class have a negative relationship to achievement.

Instructional Models. Several researchers have used the findings from studies of effective teaching behaviors to support implementation of what has come to be known as the explicit teaching or direct instruction model. Rosenshine (1986), for example, summarized studies of effective teaching into six teaching functions, including daily review, presenting new material, conducting guided practice, providing feedback and correctives, conducting independent practice, and conducting weekly and monthly review. Instructional frameworks such as this have received substantial research support, particularly for promoting outcomes related to improved student achievement (Becker & Gersten, 1982; Gersten, Carnine, & Williams, 1981; Gersten & Keating, 1987; Meyer, Gersten, & Gutkin, 1983; Rosenshine, 1979; Rupley & Blair, 1981; Stallings, 1975, 1976). Other researchers, however, suggest that while the direct instruction model may favorably impact student achievement, other instructional models have greater impact on outcomes related to broader cognitive and affective outcomes. In a reanalysis of an extensive review conducted by Horwitz, plus a review of additional studies, Peterson (1979) compared traditional instructional models (which she equated with direct instruction) to open or nontraditional models. She reports that students instructed with open approaches tend to be more creative than students in traditional approaches, tend to have more positive attitudes toward teachers and school, demonstrate greater independence and curiosity. In all cases, effect sizes were relatively small and number of studies that met the criteria for the review were few. Peterson concluded that effectiveness of the instructional model depends on the type of outcome being sought.

Other researchers have attempted to investigate the impact of the direct instruction model on specific components of reading/writing instruction. For example, investigations by Baumann (1984), Gordon and Pearson (1983), Palinscar and Brown (1984), and Raphael and Pearson (1985) suggest that comprehension skills are effectively taught in a model that begins with teacher demonstration, provides opportunity for guided practice and gradually builds toward student independence.

With regard to writing instruction, Hillocks (1986) concludes that most effective approaches to teaching writing involve direct instruction in how to examine and analyze data and how to use formal knowledge. Applebee (1986) suggests that effective management in the teaching of writing includes student ownership of the learning event; a structured learning environment; shared responsibility; and transfer of control.

Bereiter and Scardamalia (1982) examined the impact of procedural facilitation or expert assistance as a method of writing assistance, and concluded that it holds potential as a way of facilitating cognitive processing.

More recently, researchers have begun to question exactly what elements of instruction warrant explicit teaching. Roehler, Duffy and Meloth (1984) argue that direct instruction aimed at content (e.g., answers to story line questions; linking specific experiences to story content) is misguided; rather, they suggest that students need direct instruction in mental processing involved in comprehension skills. Support for the "process into content" approach espoused by Roehler, Duffy and Meloth is found in a study reported by Duffy (1983) in which the researcher observed that effective teacher explanation included explicit information about what it taught and why it is important, clear explanations of how to do the task, monitoring students' cognitive processing during turn-taking, cohesive linkings across lessons and perceptions of what the outcomes of instruction will be. These findings are consistent with those of Paris (1984) who reports significant increases in comprehension test scores following instruction intended to increase students' explicit awareness about comprehension strategies.

Curriculum/Task

Researchers who are primarily concerned with curriculum and task have focused on the congruence (or lack thereof) be-

tween programs for students in regular education and those who are "at risk"; and on integrated language-arts programs. The largest body of recent investigations is concerned with program congruence.

Congruence between Regular and Special Education. Researchers in reading/language education have contributed, along with those in special education, to the literature on program congruence. A brief historical note will clarify the significant issues that have given rise to the shared interest in the topic. As a result of the social legislation that marked the "Great Society" of the 1960s, regular and special education were expanded to include a third type of program, compensatory education, intended to equalize educational opportunities for all children, particularly those who lived in poverty. The compensatory programs provided essentially separate curricula prior to (e.g., Head Start) or simultaneous with (e.g., Follow Through and Title/Chapter I) regular education.

In the decade of the 1970s, special education was itself expanded to include another group of learners who would require curriculum modification, the learning disabled. Largely as a result of parental efforts, the children who were classified as learning disabled were seen to be different from those learners who required special education because of intellectual, emotional, or physical differences.

Thus, in recent years, programs have been developed for special education, compensatory education, and special education for the learning disabled. Of critical concern are two issues: 1. the criteria that places students in such programs and 2. the congruence among the curricula provided to students in the various programs.

With regard to the ambiguities of classification, Hobbs concluded, as a result of his extensive research, that the means used to classify and place students constituted "a major barrier to the efficient and effective delivery of services to them and their families" (Hobbs, 1980, p. 274). More recently, Wang, Reynolds, and Walberg suggested that in special education the problem of confused criteria is particularly prevalent among the learning disabled population. "The widely varying percentages of students classified as learning disabled suggest disparities and anomalies that are difficult to resolve" (Wang, Reynolds, & Walberg, 1986, p. 27). Given the confusions that surround classification of students, researchers in both regular and special education have begun to call for the end of separate programs for most learners in favor of comprehensive approaches that combine the best features of regular and special education (Leinhardt, Bickel, & Pallay, 1982; Shepard, 1987; Stainback & Stainback, 1987, Wang, Reynolds, & Walberg, 1986). Until such a goal can be achieved, researchers continue to raise questions regarding the management of instruction for children at risk.

The Sustaining Effects Study of Compensatory Education Programs, funded by the U.S. Department of Education under the mandate of the Congress, is summarized by Carter (1984) who reports the following relevant findings. The typical mode of special instruction for compensatory education students was the "pullout setting" where teachers used different methods and practices for reading instruction than were used in the regular classroom. This finding is significant in light of another conclusion, "coordination of instruction. . . . is positively related to achievement and to achievement gain" (Carter, 1984, p. 9).

The congruence of classroom and remedial reading instruction was studied by Johnston, Allington, and Afflerbach (1985) through a series of interviews conducted with students, classroom and remedial reading teachers, and reading program supervisors at grades first through eighth. They report, "Encountering a full range of contrasts between classroom and remedial programs, we found a frequent lack of congruence between the regular class and remedial class settings" (p. 474). Among the possible reasons for the lack of congruence are the findings that teachers report a wide range in frequency of communication, restricted communication regarding goals between teachers and students, and supervisors' notions that lack of congruence is appropriate.

The Integrated Language Arts. In spite of the many philosophical and theoretical treatises on the integrated nature of the English language arts, only one study could be located that offers evidence regarding the use of this type of organizational plan. Schmidt, et al. (1983) studied six elementary teachers' classroom logs for evidence of the integration that teachers favored. Additionally, teachers were observed in the natural setting of the classroom. Logs and observations revealed that less than 10 percent of the time was spent in integrated language activities, generally in whole-class settings under direct teacher supervision.

CONCLUSIONS

The review of studies in organizing and managing instruction suggests the following conclusions. They are presented within the major emphases of the chapter: Students; Teachers and Teaching Behaviors; and Curriculum/Task.

Students

- When studies are comparable, the following results are noted. Students assigned to lower track classes maintain or sustain performance at a lower level and have higher rates of inattention. Exceptions to this pattern occur when students are grouped for particular learning objectives, when the grouping is flexible and when instruction is geared to rate and level of learning.
- Differences in instructional approaches employed to teach high and low ability groups may have a negative impact on the quality and quantity of learning of the low ability students. Instructional differences include content, pacing, and the nature of the learning environment.
- Cooperative efforts are considerably more effective than individualistic or competitive efforts when the schedule of instruction is focused.
- Cooperative learning impacts positively on attitudes toward learning and academic self-concept.
- Studies of peer tutoring yield conflicting results with success or failure highly dependent on the specific context for in-

struction. Comparable studies generally reveal superior achievement in tutored versus untutored programs when the programs were structured, short in duration, and employed specific abilities.
- Studies of peer collaborators reveal higher productivity in problem-solving. However, for writing, results are conflicting.

Teachers and Teaching Behaviors

- Correlates of higher achievement include brisk pacing, increased allocated academic time, high rates of student engaged time, and high success rate.
- Effective managers integrate a learning routine with instructional content so that the procedures are understood by the learners. Teacher guidance is provided within a model of effective instruction.
- The impact of factors that characterize effective management are virtually inseparable from those that characterize effective instruction.
- Due to the methodological inconsistencies in the studies, the impact of team teaching as compared to solitary teaching on achievement is inconclusive.
- Students instructed with open approaches differ from those instructed within more traditional approaches in more effective problem solving, increased creativity, more positive attitudes toward school and teachers, and greater independence and curiosity.
- When the measured outcome is achievement, studies of direct instruction yield consistently positive results.

Curriculum/Task

- Research in special and regular education reveals a serious lack of consistency in identifying categories of learners and a lack of congruence in planning and implementing instructional programs.
- Attempts to individualize instructions have been varied and results conflicting.
- Studies of integrated language arts instruction are too sparse to permit conclusions.

UNANSWERED QUESTIONS

Although there is a substantial body of research that has led to conclusive findings regarding classroom organization and management, there are also several unanswered questions. Given the evidence that organization and management of instruction in the classroom enhances or inhibits student learning, it is proposed that research efforts be directed toward the following areas of inquiry:

- Ability grouping has been found to favor high ability groups, but results in zero or negative impact on low ability groups. Questions remain, however, regarding whether negative findings are related to ability grouping itself, or to differential instruction. If lower ability groups received instruction quantitatively and qualitatively equal to that of high ability groups, would outcomes be more favorable for low ability groups?

- Although there is some evidence that reverse role tutoring is effective, studies are few. Replication and extension of research related to tutoring roles for children currently placed in special and remedial education is needed. In addition, results related to the impact of tutoring on the self-esteem of both tutor and tutee is promising, but not conclusive. What impact does peer tutoring have on self-esteem and attribution of learners at risk?

- The role of peer collaboration in writing has received some research support. Questions remain, however, regarding both developmental and curricular issues. Are there particular ages of learners and/or stages of the writing process when peer collaboration is more effective in facilitating learning?

- Although research related to effective teaching behaviors has yielded consistent findings at the elementary level, similar studies at the secondary level have been less definitive. Yet unanswered are questions regarding the impact of class discussion, question types, and independent learning on achievement of secondary school learners in reading and the language arts.

- With regard to issues related to organization of teachers, studies regarding team teaching were inconclusive. Studies designed to permit comparison of team teaching with solitary teaching models are needed to answer the following questions: Does team teaching have differential effects on elementary as compared with secondary level learners? Do team teaching models serve particular types of learners (e.g., learners at risk; gifted learners) better than solitary teaching models? Are team teaching models more effective for particular curricular designs, such as the integrated language arts?

- Evidence suggests that congruence does not currently exist between regular and special education program goals, instructional methodology and materials. What is unknown is how to effectively coordinate classroom and special programs when more than one teacher is involved in the instructional planning delivery.

- Despite positive intuitions and experiences, virtually no empirical evidence exists regarding the effects of integrating the language arts. Investigations are needed to answer the following questions: Are there particular stages of development when integrating the language arts is more effective? Are there particular learners for whom integrated language-arts approaches are more effective? What are characteristics of effective integrated language-arts approaches?

CONCLUDING STATEMENT

This chapter was intended to report the current state of knowledge regarding classroom organizaation and management, in order to gain insight into effective classroom contexts for literacy learning. Findings revealed multiple contexts for effective learning, but only one consistent variable within each context—the excellence of the teacher, whether that teacher was adult or peer. Perhaps these findings are best summarized by the following statement:

Classroom management is not simply a task that is accomplished once in a classroom, although it certainly needs to be accomplished first. Management is, rather, a pervasive and contributing feature of teaching in classrooms. In this sense, classroom management defines what it means to be a teacher. (Doyle, 1979, p. 74)

References

Alexander, K. L., & McDill, E. L. (1976). Selection and allocation within schools: Some causes and consequences of curriculum placement. *American Sociological Review, 41,* 963–980.

Allington, R. L. (1984). Content coverage and contextual reading in reading groups. *Journal of Reading Behavior, 16* 85–96.

Anderson, L. M., Evertson, C. M., & Brophy, J. E. (1979). An experimental study of effective teaching in first grade reading groups. *Elementary School Journal, 79,* 193–223.

Applebee, A. N. (1986). Problems in process approaches: Toward a reconceptualization of process instruction. In A. Petrosky & D. Bartholomae (Eds.), *The teaching of writing, eighty-fifth yearbook of the National Society for the Study of Education.* Chicago: University of Chicago Press.

Armstrong, D. G. (1977). Team teaching and academic achievement. *Review of Educational Research, 47,* 65–86.

Barr, R. (1975). How children are taught to read: Grouping and pacing. *School Review, 83,* 479–499.

Baumann, J. F. (1984). The effectiveness of the direct instruction paradigm for teaching main idea comprehension. *Reading Research Quarterly, 20,* 93–108.

Becker, W. C., & Gersten, R. (1982). A follow-up of follow through: The later effects of the direct instruction model on children in fifth and sixth grades. *American Educational Research Journal, 19,* 75–92.

Bereiter, C., & Scardamalia, M. (1982). From conversation to composition: The role of instruction in a developmental process. In R. Glazer (Ed.), *Advances in instructional psychology.* Hillsdale, NJ: Lawrence Erlbaum Associates.

Brown, A. L., & Palincsar, A. S. (1985). *Reciprocal teaching of comprehension strategies: A natural history of one program for enhancing learning* (Tech. Rep. No. 334). Urbana: University of Illinois, Center for Study of Reading.

Carter, L. F. (1984). The sustaining effects study of compensatory and elementary education. *Educational Researcher, 13,* 4–13.

Cazden, C. B. (1988). *Classroom discourse: The language of teaching and learning.* Portsmouth, NH: Heinemann Educational Books.

Cohen. P. A., Kulik, J. A., & Kulik, C. C. (1982). Educational outcomes of tutoring: A meta-analysis of findings. *American Educational Research Journal, 19,* 237–248.

Damon, W. (1984). Peer education: The untapped potential. *Journal of Applied Psychology, 5,* 331–343.

DiPardo, A., & Freedman, S. W. (1987). *Historical overview: Groups in the writing classroom* (Tech. Rep. No. 4). Berkeley, CA: Center for the Study of Writing.

Doyle, W. (1979). Making managerial decisions in classrooms. In D. L. Duke (Ed.), *Classroom management, seventy-eighth yearbook of the Society for the Study of Education*. Chicago: University of Chicago Press.

Duffy, G. G. (1983). From turn taking to sense making: Broadening the concept of teacher effectiveness. *Journal of Educational Research, 76,* 134–139

Duffy, G. G., Roehler, L. R., & Rackliffe, G. (1986). How teachers' instructional talk influences students' understanding of lesson content. *The Elementary School Journal, 87,* 3–16. Eder, D. (1983). Ability grouping and students' academic self-concepts: A case study. *The Elementary School Journal, 84,* 149–161.

Eder, D., & Felmlee, D. (1984). The development of attention norms in ability group. In P. L. Peterson, L. C. Wilkinson, & M. Hallinan (Eds.), *The social context of instruction*. New York: Academic Press.

Emmer, E. T., & Evertson, C. M. (1982). Synthesis of research in classroom management. *Educational Leadership, 39,* 342–347.

Emmer, E. T., Evertson, C. M., & Anderson, L. D. (1980). Effective management at the beginning of the school year. *The Elementary School Journal, 80,* 219–231.

Evertson, C. M., Anderson, C. W., Anderson, L. M., & Brophy, J. E. (1980). Relationships between classroom behaviors and student outcomes in junior high mathematics and English classes. *American Educational Research Journal, 17,* 43–60.

Felmlee, D., & Eder, D. (1983). Contextual effects in the classroom: The impact of ability groups on student attention. *Sociology of Education, 56,* 77–87.

Forman, E. A., & Cazden, C. B. (1985). Exploring Vygotskian perspectives on education: The cognitive value of peer interaction. In J. V. Wertsch (Ed.), *Culture, communication and cognition: Vygotskian perspectives*. New York: Cambridge University Press.

Freedman, S. W. (1985). Response to and evaluation of writing: A review. *Resources in Education* (ED 247 605).

Gamoran, A. (1986). Instructional and institutional effects of ability grouping. *Sociology of Education, 59,* 185–198.

Gersten R., Carnine, D., & Williams P. (1981). Measuring implementation of a structured educational model in an urban school district. *Educational Evaluation and Policy Analysis, 4,* 56–63.

Gersten, R., & Keating, T. (1987). Long term benefits from direct instruction. *Educational Leadership, 44,* 28–31.

Good, T., & Stipek, D. (1983). Individual differences in the classroom: A psychological perspective. In M. Fernstermacher & J. Goodlad (Eds.), *National Society for the Study of Education yearbook*. Chicago: University of Chicago Press.

Good, T., & Marshall, S. (1984). Do students learn more in heterogenous or homogeneous groups? In P. L. Peterson, L. C. Wilkinson, & M. Hallinan (Eds.), *The social context of instruction*. New York: Academic Press.

Gordon, C., & Pearson, P. D. (1983). *The effects of instruction in metacomprehension and inferencing on children's comprehension abilities* (Tech. Rep. No. 277). Urbana: University of Illinois, Center for the Study of Reading.

Grant, L., & Rothenberg, J. (1986). The social enhancement of ability differences: Teacher-student interactions in first and second grade reading groups. *The Elementary School Journal, 87,* 29–49.

Haskins, R., Walden, T., & Ramey, C. T. (1983). Teacher and student behaviors in high ability and low ability groups. *Journal of Educational Psychology, 75,* 865–876.

Heibert, E. H. (1983). An examination of ability grouping for reading instruction. *Reading Research Quarterly, 18,* 231–255.

Hillocks, G. (1986). The writer's knowledge: Theory, research and implications for practice. In A. Petrosky & D. Bartholomae (Eds.), *The teaching of writing, eighty-fifth yearbook of the National Society for the Study of Education*. Chicago: University of Chicago Press.

Hobbs, N. (1980). An ecologically oriented service-based system for the classification of handicapped children. In S. Salzinger, J. Antrobus, & J. Glick (Eds.), *The ecosystem of the "sick" child. Implications for classification and interventions for disturbed and mentally retarded children*. New York: Academic Press.

Johnson, D. W. (1981). Student-student interaction: The neglected variable in education. *Educational Researcher, 9,* 5–10.

Johnson, D. W., & Johnson, R. T. (1979). Conflict in the classroom: Controversy and learning. *Review of Educational Research, 49,* 51–70.

Johnson, D. W., Maruyama, G., Johnson, R., & Nelson, D. (1981). Effects of cooperative, competitive and individualistic goal structures on achievement: A meta-analysis. *Psychological Bulletin, 89,* 47–62.

Johnston, P., Allington, R., & Afflerbach, P. (1985). The congruence of classroom and remedial reading instruction. *Elementary School Journal, 85,* 465–477.

Judy, J. E., Alexander, P. A., Kulikowich, J. M., & Wilson, V. L. (1988). Effects of two instructional approaches and peer tutoring on gifted and ungifted sixth-grade students' analogy performance. *Reading Research Quarterly, 23,* 236–256.

Kulik, C. C., & Kulik, J. A. (1982). Effects of ability grouping on secondary school students: A meta-analysis of evaluation findings. *American Educational Research Journal, 19,* 415–428.

Leinhardt, G., Bickel, W., & Pallay, A. (1982). Unlabeled but still entitled: Toward more effective remediation. *Teachers College Record, 84,* 391–422.

Meyer, L., Gersten, R., & Gutkin, J. (1983). Direct instruction: A Project Follow Through success. Story in an inner-city school. *Elementary School Journal, 84,* 380–394.

Michaels, S., & Foster, M. (1985). Peer-peer learning: Evidence from a student run sharing time. In A. Jaggar & M. T. Smith-Burke (Eds.), *Observing the language learner*. Urbana, IL: National Council of Teachers of English/International Reading Association.

Oakes, J. (1980). *Tracking and inequality within schools: Findings from a study of schooling*. Paper presented at American Educational Research Association, Annual Meeting, Boston: (ED 187 814).

Osguthorpe, R. T., Eiserman, W., Shisler, L., Top, B. L., & Scruggs, T. E. (n.d.). *Reverse role tutoring: The effects of handicapped students tutoring regular class students*. (ED 255 027).

Palincsar, A., & Brown, A. (1984). Reciprocal teaching of comprehension fostering and comprehension monitoring activities. *Cognition and Instruction, 1,* 117–175.

Paris, S. G. (1984). Teaching children to guide their reading and learning. In T. Raphael (Ed.), *The contexts of school-based literacy*. New York: Random House.

Passow, A. H. (1988). Issues of access to knowledge: Grouping and tracking. In L. N. Tanner (Ed.), *Critical issues in curriculum, eighty-seventh yearbook of the National Society for the Study of Education*. Chicago: University of Chicago Press.

Peterson, P. L. (1979). Direct instruction reconsidered. In P. L. Peterson & H. J. Walberg (Eds.), *Research on teaching: Concepts, findings and implications*. National Society for the Study of Education Series on Contemporary and Educational Issues. Berkeley, CA: McCutchan Publishing Corporation.

Raphael, T. E., & Pearson, P. D. (1985). Increasing students' awareness of sources of information in answering questions. *American Educational Research Journal, 22,* 217–236.

Roehler, L. R., Duffy, G. G., & Meloth, M. S. (1984). What to be direct about the direction instruction in reading: Content-only versus process-into-content. In T. Raphael (Ed.), *The context of school-based literacy*. New York: Random House.

Rosenshine, B. V. (1979). Content, time and direct instruction. In P. L. Peterson, & H. J. Walberg (Eds.), *Research on teaching: Concepts, findings and implications*. National Society for the Study of Education Series on Contemporary and Educational Issues. Berkeley, CA: McCutchan Publishing Corporation.

Rosenshine, B. V. (1976). Recent research on teaching behaviors and student achievement. *Journal of Teacher Education, 27,* 61–64.

Rosenshine, B. V., & Stevens, R. (1984). Classroom instruction in reading. In P. D. Pearson (Ed.), *Handbook of reading research*. New York: Longman, Inc.

Rosenshine, B. V. (1986). Synthesis of research on explicit teaching. *Educational Leadership, 43,* 60–69.

Rowen, B., & Miracle, A. W. (1983). Systems of ability grouping and the stratification of achievement in elementary schools. *Sociology of Education, 56,* 133–144.

Rupley, W. H., & Blair, T. R. (1981). Specification of reading instructional practices associated with pupil achievement gains. *Educational and Psychological Research, 1,* 161–169.

Russell, C. (1985). *Peer conferencing and writing revision: A study of the relationship*. Unpublished manuscript. (ED 260 392).

Schmidt, W. H., Roehler, L. R., Caul, J. L., Diamond, B., Solomon, D., Cianciolo, P., & Buchmann, M. (1983). *Curriculum integration: Its use in language arts instruction* (Research Series No. 140). East Lansing, MI: The Institute for Research on Teaching.

Schwartz, F. (1981). Supporting or subverting learning: Peer group patterns in four tracked schools. *Anthropology and Education Quarterly, 12,* 99–121.

Sharan, S. (1980). Cooperative learning in small groups: Recent methods and effects on achievement, attitudes and ethnic relations. *Review of Educational Research, 50,* 241–271.

Shepard, L. A. (1987). The new push for excellence: Widening the schism between regular and special education. *Exceptional Children, 53,* 327–329.

Slavin, R. E. (1978). *Effects of student teams and peer tutoring on academic achievement and time on task* (Center Rep. No. 253). Baltimore, MD: Johns Hopkins University, Center for Social Organization of Schools.

Slavin, R. E. (1980). Cooperative learning. *Review of Educational Research, 50,* 315–342.

Slavin, R. E. (1986). *Ability grouping and student achievement in elementary school: A best evidence synthesis*. Baltimore, MD: Johns Hopkins University, Center for Research on Elementary and Middle Schools.

Sorenson, A. B., & Hallinan, M. T. (1986). Effects of ability grouping on growth in academic achievement. *American Educational Research Journal, 23,* 519–542.

Stainback, S., & Stainback, W. (1987). Integration versus cooperation: A commentary on "Educating children with learning problems: A shared responsibility". *Exceptional Children, 54,* 66–68.

Stallings, J. (1975). Implementation and child effects of teaching practices in follow through classrooms. *Monograph of the Society for Research in Child Development, 40*(163), 7–8.

Stallings, J. (1976). How instructional processes relate to child outcomes in a national study of follow through. *Journal of Teacher Education, 27,* 43–47.

Stallings, J. A. (1979). How to change the process of teaching reading in secondary schools. *Educational Horizons, 57,* 196–199.

Stallings, J. A. (1986). Effective use of time in secondary reading programs. In J. V. Hoffman (Ed.), *Effective teaching of reading: Research and practice*. Newark, DE: International Reading Association.

Talmage, H., & Pascarella, E. T., and Foed, S. (1984). The influence of cooperative learning strategies on teacher practices, student perceptions of the learning enviroment and academic achievement. *American Educational Research Journal, 21,* 163–179.

Vygotsky, L. S. (1962). *Thought and language*. Cambridge, MA: Massachusetts Institute of Technology Press.

Wang, M. C., Reynolds, M. C., & Walberg, H. J. (1986). Rethinking special education. *Educational Leadership, 43,* 26–31.

Weinstein, R. S. (1976). Reading group membership in the first grade: Teacher behaviors and pupil experience over time. *Journal of Educational Psychology, 68,* 103–116.

EVALUATING LANGUAGE DEVELOPMENT

27A. FORMAL METHODS OF EVALUATION

Roger Farr
Michael Beck

Formal methods of assessing language development usually have as their goal the determination of *how well* students are able to read, write, listen, or speak. Knowing *how well* students can use language skills is important to administrators, teachers, researchers, evaluators—and the public. However, the narrow focus on test scores and the predominant use of multiple-choice tests rather than broader forms of assessment seriously limits the usefulness of formal assessments. Despite these critical problems, the formal assessment of students' language development is both necessary and useful.

Assessment is of fundamental concern to language-arts teachers and curriculum leaders for providing information necessary to plan instruction. Some form of assessment is essential if educators are to understand what is working. Information concerning student growth and development in language performance is needed to evaluate the effectiveness of various teaching strategies, and the study of experimental programs must indicate whether intended results are being achieved. In addition, the focus on assessment forces language educators to define operationally what they mean by reading and writing, and what evidence they will accept as indicators of progress.

However, formal assessment is only one part of a total evaluation program, and as such, provides only a limited view of a program (c.f., Guba & Lincoln, 1981). In order to provide a complete understanding of a program, more comprehensive evaluations are needed (Guba, 1969; Scriven, 1973, McClellan, 1988). The issues in conducting a comprehensive evaluation are more extensive than can be treated in this chapter that focuses only on the formal assessment of students' language development. (See Guba, 1978; Popham, 1974; Stake, 1975; Tyler, 1969; Wolf, 1977.)

Although evaluation should be much more than a simple assessment of student achievement, there is no question that student achievement should generally be a significant component of a complete evaluation program. Even though new forms of assessment are regularly called for, formal assessment of some kind is always included in the pronouncements of the need for curriculum revision (*English-Language Arts Frame-work*, 1987; *A Nation at Risk*, 1983; *Becoming a Nation of Readers*, 1984). Indeed, many new (or perhaps rediscovered) types of tests and assessment techniques have been developed for reading, and to some extent writing, although very few formal methods are available for assessing listening and speaking (Anderson, 1982; Bock & Bock, 1981; Farr & Carey, 1986; Resnick, 1982; Rubin & Mead, 1984). Regardless of the type of assessment, the issues are the same. Assessment must produce information in a timely and efficient manner and the information that is rendered must be both valid and reliable.

Formal and Informal Assessment: Contrasts and Similarities

Comparing and contrasting formal and informal assessment may bring into clearer focus some of the relevant issues that concern both. Formal assessment is conducted to determine *how much* students have learned. Most often, formal assessment takes place at the end of some phase of instruction, such as the end of a school year or the completion of a unit of work or level of an instructional program. Formal assessment of this type is usually clearly identifiable. Students are told they are going to take a test, and the tests are presented in recognizable test format. There is no pretext that formal assessment is an integral part of instruction, and sometimes (though not often enough) students are told the use to which the test results will be put.

Informal assessment is an attempt to determine *why* students perform as they do rather than *how well* they perform. Informal assessment is exemplified by a teacher at a student's side looking over the student's shoulder and commenting that what the student has written might be organized more effectively. In these situations, students are often not even aware that they are being assessed. Indeed, they might view this assessment as the teacher simply commenting on their work, rather than as testing.

Formal assessment is an attempt to determine *whether a student can do something;* in informal assessment the aim is to determine *how a student does something*. Although this suggests that informal and formal assessments differ, the distinctions are often blurred or nonexistent. The timing of formal assessment, for example, need not be only at the end of an instructional period. Periodic assessments prior to and throughout an instructional period would provide better information about a student's language development than would a single test used at the end of instruction. For example, portfolio assessment (the collection of work samples gathered throughout an instructional period) is being espoused by many language educators as a useful formal assessment procedure.

The distinction that formal assessment is concerned with product *(how well)* and informal assessment is concerned with process *(how)* is often one of degree. All assessment must rely on student performance. That performance can be used to infer *how well* a student might perform on similar tasks. However, if the same exhibited behavior is used to infer *how* students performed as they did, it then becomes a process measure. For example, a student's writing can be compared to some standard of good writing (criterion referencing) or to other student essays (norm referencing). In either case, the writing sample is used to infer *how well* the student writes. The same writing sample can also be used to understand *how* the student writes by discussing the writing with the student and asking about the source of the ideas, how he/she wanted to make his points, as well as revisions that would make the ideas in the writing more compelling.

Even the typical distinction that formal tests are published and informal tests are unpublished is obscured when one considers the many tests published with the label of "Informal Assessment of . . ." as part of the title. A plethora of observation checklists, interview guides, and similar assessments are also readily available from publishers.

Perhaps the major element that distinguishes formal from informal assessments is the existence of performance indicators or scales. Formal assessment usually includes some predetermined scale against which a student's performance can be interpreted. Sometimes these are norm-referenced scales that relate test results to those students comparable in some way—sex, age, or grade most typically. Other times, these are criterion-referenced scales, which are comparisons of performance to acceptable levels as determined by some type of judgment or expectation. Informal evaluations, with the exception of some that are published, seldom include predetermined scales of interpretation. Teachers interpret the results according to their individual expectations of performance for a class or individual student, or in comparison to what has been taught.

Although formal and informal assessment may differ enough to be discussed in separate chapters, such a separation incorrectly suggests that formal and informal assessment involve different issues. It would be unfortunate if the division separates formal and informal assessments in the thinking of language-arts specialists. Assessment is best thought of as gathering a variety of information, at diverse times, and under differing conditions. Too many educators now see assessment as being of two types—that which teachers do to help students *(informal assessment)* and that which is forced on teachers and students by the administration *(formal assessment).*

Such differences should not exist. Formal assessment could be strengthened considerably through the addition of information gathered informally. On the other hand, the informal assessment conducted by teachers could be enhanced with greater attention to reliability and validity and with an eye toward using the information to communicate students' achievement to administrators and to the public.

While accepting the notion that formal and informal assessment have more similarities than differences, this chapter will focus on formal assessment used to evaluate students' language development. Formal assessment, for purposes of this chapter, will include published tests that generally provide product rather than process information, and that provide either norm-referenced or criterion-referenced scales for interpretation.

ISSUES IN LANGUAGE-ARTS ASSESSMENT

Purposes for Assessment: The Test User's Perspective

If language-arts educators are to foster the development of better tests, then they must clearly and explicitly define the purposes for which they need information. They also need to describe the language behaviors they want to test, which is a concern relating to the test's validity. It is not enough to know what performance one wants to know about. The first question to be answered is *why* the information is needed.

Improved test usage, as well as the development of better tests, is hampered by the expectations of some language-arts specialists that eventually *the best test will be developed.* That *best test* is viewed as one that would provide exactly what one needs to know and would be quick and easy to administer, interpret, and apply to instruction. Moreover, all students would experience success on this test. The problem is that the expectation for such a test is unrealistic. The answer lies not in the search for the elusive best test, but rather in setting clear and specific purposes for testing and then choosing/building an instrument to fit that purpose. Almost always the need will be for a variety of assessments collected concomitantly with instruction.

The ultimate goal in evaluating any language-arts program should be the improvement of instruction. Information is needed to plan instruction, but the purposes of evaluation must be more specific than merely the improvement of instruction. For example, the information a curriculum director needs to determine which students are making adequate progress differs from the information a teacher needs for planning tommorrow's lesson. There are a broad range of legitimate purposes for language assessments, and there are a broad range of formal and informal tests. Good assessment is possible only when information needs are matched with appropriate assessment types. Poor assessment results when a test is used for a purpose for which it was never intended. The purposes for which assessments are needed in language education are those that are responsive to program decision-making (Guba & Lincoln, 1981).

Tests in the area of language arts are sometimes administered when there is no clearly stated purpose for administering them. This leads to such questions as, "Now that we have given the tests, what do the results mean, and what do we do with them?" When there are clearly defined purposes for the test information, the use of the results will be obvious. Kaplan (1964) succinctly stated the importance of testing purposes:

Too often, we ask how to measure something without raising the question of what we would do with the measurement if we had it. We want to know *how* without thinking of *why*. I hope I may say without impiety, seek ye first what is right for your needs, and all these things shall be added to you as well. (p. 214)

In essence, the overriding purpose for assessment in language arts is to promote a broad understanding of the language arts that can lead to constructive change. To create this change, information must be collected about students' language behaviors. The assessment must be conducted in a timely and efficient manner, and the information produced by the assessment must be valid and reliable. But above all, the information must be focused on *the purpose to which the information will be put.*

Purposes for Assessment: The Test Taker's Perspective

Any assessment should pose a clear and realistic purpose to examinees. When students face a set of questions to answer with no purpose-setting question for their work, the test does not represent normal reading or writing activities, nor does it represent sound classroom instruction that emphasizes helping readers establish purposes for reading and helping writers focus on an audience and a purpose for their writing.

How an examinee interprets and internalizes a test task can significantly affect the response. For example, researchers in the area of writing assessment have suggested that the framing of the writing task may have an important influence on what students write (Odell, Cooper, & Courts, 1978). The issue goes beyond concern with the framing of the test task. Those who develop and interpret tests must realize that the task may be interpreted differently by different examinees (Greenberg, Weiner, & Donovan, 1986). Smith (1967) found that better readers established their own purposes for reading and these purposes facilitated comprehension. Betts (1954) made the same point years earlier when he wrote that, "The purpose of the reading controls comprehension" (p. 95).

In addition to the need to design test tasks that produce the behaviors being assessed, test tasks need to be realistic both to the examinees and to those who will interpret the test results. This issue may be at the heart of the concerns of those who question the validity of many language-arts tests. For example, English teachers often state that multiple-choice tests of language mechanics fail to assess actual writing; and reading teachers are concerned that fixed, one-choice answers fail to reflect the reading process as we have come to know it, or that short reading selections fail to reflect typical classroom reading activities. For many language specialists, the traditional tests don't match the tasks they have set as goals for their students. Kaplan (1964) made this very point when he wrote in his discussion of validity:

If you can measure it, that ain't it! For the student of human behavior

at any rate—so the view goes—measurement is pointless at best, and at worst, a hopeless distortion of what is really important. The exact sciences belong to the study of nature, not of man. (p. 207)

Kaplan explains that we can assess many aspects of human behavior, but we must emphasize the limitations of the measurement. For Kaplan, validity resides in an analysis of the use that will be made of the measurement and the purpose we establish for the test task. Tests must provide reasonable testing purposes and those purposes must appear to both examinees and test users to assess what is relevant. The test task should pose an activity and a purpose for engaging in that activity that corresponds with everyday language activities.

Much recent criticism of reading tests (e.g., Valencia & Pearson, 1987) concerns just this issue. There have been calls for reading tests to include "real literature" (generally defined as anything that was previously published), longer test passages, and questions that more clearly represent what one does when reading. These issues have been raised for reasons in addition to those of making the test task more closely resemble "real" language tasks. For example, the focus on passage length is based on the concern that certain important question types can't be asked unless there is more material to be read. However, the issue of short "test-type" passages has also been raised because short passages are purportedly not what students read in school or out. Nor, say the critics, do they read the contrived passages one finds on traditional reading tests.

Primary trait writing assessment clearly addresses the issue of providing a purpose for the test taker. In primary trait assessment, the writing task specifies the audience, the purpose to be served by the writing, and oftentimes the writing format. Writing a letter to school board members to persuade them to keep the school library open on Saturday mornings is an example of one such writing task. In primary trait scoring, the writing is evaluated in terms of whether the goal for the writing has been achieved. It is a more difficult task to evaluate an essay by determining whether it accomplished the writer's rhetorical goal than it is merely to judge whether the writing is of reasonable quality without regard to writing purpose (Brown, 1986). It is clear that primary trait writing assessment attempts to set task purposes that not only guide the examinee's response, but also make the task seem more realistic to the examinees.

In the area of reading assessment, Rowe and Rayford (1987) investigated whether setting a purpose for reading a test passage prior to reading helped students establish a schema for reading the passage. The types of purposes they examined were those that related reading purposes and passage content. For example, "Why did the neighbors plant trees?" "How good were Jules Verne's predictions?" and "How are these scientists trying to read your mind?" Rowe and Rayford found that readers were able to make valid predictions about the content and type of passages from reading these purpose-setting questions. In brief, the purposes did help the students develop a schema for reading. However, data as to whether such purposes actually produced better reading, and thus a better reading assessment were inconclusive. There is, however, no question that establishing a purpose for reading a selection makes the reading task more closely resemble typical reading.

Establishing purpose-setting questions in reading assessment also provides a focus for the questions that follow the reading. Questions that reflect the reading purpose will seem fair and reasonable to the test taker. Rather than asking an assortment of questions that merely relate to information presented in the reading selection, purpose-related questions direct the test developer to ask questions that respond to the established reader purpose. In this way, reading comprehension resembles primary trait writing assessment. Both are directed by clearly established purposes, and success is determined by how well those purposes are met.

Perhaps if tests with specific examinee purposes can be developed, there will be less concern with test wiseness (Carter, 1986). Rather than studying whether students can "psyche out" the test task and answer questions based on cues that are part of the test format, tests will more closely reflect realistic tasks.

Reliability and Validity

Reliability and validity are characteristic of all sound measurement procedures, whether formal or informal, commercial or teacher-developed. Opponents of standardized measures often object to such tests on the basis of (generally undocumented) claims that such assessments lack these qualities. The less ingenuous of these attacks may simply result from a lack of clear understanding of the meaning of the terms.

Reliability. Reliability is defined as the consistency of scores obtained when persons are reexamined with the same test on different occasions or with tests composed of parallel sets of items. Simply speaking, a test's reliability is an expression of the amount of error present in a set of scores. As such, it is important to note that reliability is a property *not* of the test per se, but of a particular set of scores resulting from the test. Thus, a test does not possess high or low reliability in general; a particular set of scores obtained from the test has this quality. It is possible, indeed, quite common, for a test with sound technical characteristics for most populations and uses to have poor reliability when applied to particular groups. This occurs most frequently when the group tested is small or atypical in performance, e.g., compensatory education samples or classroom-sized groups scoring very high or low on the test. For prospective users of a particular test, it is important to review reliability data collected on the group for which the test will be used or on groups comparable in ability and variability to those to whom the test will be given.

As a general rule of thumb, test specialists recommend reliability coefficients of .85 or higher for making decisions in isolation about individuals. When several sets of data are available for such decisions, tests with reliabilities significantly lower than this figure can be combined for reliable totals. This is because, as logic would indicate, the combined use of several somewhat reliable scores yield a more reliable total. This phenomenon is what allows the typical school language-arts grading process to have high reliability. The reliability of the various components of such a grade, scores on individual sets of homework, essays, quizzes, teacher-made tests, and textbook-imbedded tests, tends to be very modest, generally on the order of about .4 to .7. However, when several such assessments are combined into a single end-of-term grade, the total grade tends to have high reliability. Although this loose psychometric magic is certainly not the reason behind the typical school grading procedures, it does explain why such a process tends to yield fairly reliable indicators of performance. Interested readers are referred to an "instructional module" on the topic of reliability developed by Frisbie (1988). His article provides an excellent overview of reliability as a construct, the factors that influence it, common procedures for computing reliability estimates, and interpretive guidelines.

There are at least two common uses of language-arts test data today in which test reliability is a special concern. The first such case is in "criterion-referenced tests" (more accurately termed objectives-referenced tests in almost all educational situations). Most available objectives-referenced tests, whether commercially prepared or state assessments, tend to report performance based on "subtests" (objectives) of from 3 to 6 items. That is, small numbers of items are used to assess each objective. This is so due to the practical limitations of testing time. For various reasons (Berk, 1980; Popham, 1971), traditional reliability techniques are often inappropriate for such measures. Reliability estimates for criterion-referenced assessments are best determined by dividing the tested groups into "masters" and "nonmasters" or similar groups. Reliability can then be determined most accurately by testing examinees twice within a short period of time, although many procedures exist for estimating reliability of such tests based on a single testing. Subkoviak (1988), for example presents a useful summary of procedures for computing and interpreting reliability data for mastery-type tests, including shortcut tables for estimating reliability of these tests without laborious calculations.

Regardless of the procedures used, it should be obvious that scores based on 3, 4, or even 10 or 12 items are almost always less reliable than those based on 40 to 60 questions, the typical length of a complete test. Thus, while scores on objectives-referenced tests may be appealing and appear to offer instructional value, they must be interpreted with a great deal of caution and skepticism. Using traditional calculations, the reliability of such objectives-based test scores seldom exceed .40, a rather typical figure for a teacher-made quiz. Even when statistical procedures that are especially applicable to such tests are used, reliability results are seldom adequate for placing much confidence in the scores. They are probably of some worth as indicators, but can at best raise questions, not provide answers.

A second situation in which cautious interpretation is called for with regard to reliability is in essay exams. Reliability for essay scoring is typically defined as the correlation between two independently determined scores on the same set of papers, two scorers or one rater who rescores the papers after some period of time. The reliability of scores derived from a single essay scored by a pair of professionally trained readers using carefully selected orientation or scale-point selection papers and using a well-conceived scoring scheme is generally on a level of .75 ± .05. If a single reader is used, if training is less-than-comprehensive, if score points are not clearly defined and described, and if the essay topics have not been pretested, such figures drop dramatically. The upper practical limit of the reliability of such essay scores is the low .80s, the lower bound of the rule-of-thumb guideline for interpreting an individual's score. In most practical situations in which important test-based decisions are to be made (e.g., state-assessment graduation or promotion tests), essay scores must be combined in some way with the results of objectively scored items to increase the reliability of the total score.

Validity. The validity of a test relates to what the test assesses and how well it does so. As with reliability, validity is inherent not in the instrument, but in its application: a test has (or lacks) validity for a particular use or in a particular situation, not in general. The validity of a test is essentially determined by gauging the extent to which the test results yield information compatible with other independently determined information about the trait being assessed. (See Cronbach, 1971; Messick, 1975; and Yalow & Popham, 1983 for discussions of this, and related, validity issues.) Thus, a reading comprehension test has validity to the extent that its scores relate highly with other accepted indicators of comprehension.

Users of tests and, to an unfortunate extent, those who write about testing, often are confused by the inextricable relationships between reliability and validity. Reliability is a necessary, though not sufficient, precursor to validity. A test simply cannot be valid unless it is also reliable; said another way, a test's reliability sets an upper bound on its validity. Thus claims such as those referred to by Johnston (1983) that informal tests have low reliability but higher validity are simply nonsensical. In most typical test construction or test selection situations, the instrument first must be long enough (i.e., sample a sufficient portion of behavior) to yield stable (read reliable) scores. In order for such a test also to be valid, the sample of behaviors tested must be systematically representative of the underlying trait being assessed. Major aspects of the construct must be tested, and in proportion to their presence in the appropriate curriculum. Thus, almost by definition, a test of writing achievement that requires a single essay written on a particular assigned or student-selected topic, will lack high validity. Such a test simply samples too narrow a range of behavior. Those tempted by the face validity lure of essay exams as *the* way to assess writing would be well advised to consider the timeless warnings summarized by Anastasi (1982):

Objective items have largely replaced essay questions in standardized testing programs, not only because of time restriction in test scoring, but also—and more importantly—because they provide broader subject-matter coverage, yield more reliable and more valid scores, and are fairer to individuals. Essay writing should be encouraged and developed primarily as an instructional procedure to foster clear, correct, and effective communication in all content areas. (p. 399)

A related content validity issue arises in the new types of reading assessment instruments being developed in several states, led by Michigan and Illinois. The content validity issue involves the particular selections to be read by students on such tests. These newer tests typically require students to read two long passages, each roughly 1000 or more words in length. Tra-

ditional comprehension tests generally include 8 to 10 shorter passages. Although the total amount of reading required is usually higher on the traditional tests (Sonnenschein, 1988), the longer passages are more consistent with the types of materials that many reading researchers and theorists consider desirable (c.f., Michigan State Board of Education, 1987; Pearson & Valencia, 1987). The tradeoff here is obvious, use of only two passages restricts significantly the range of genre, topics, interest levels, and difficulty levels that can be examined. Clearly, this is another of the familiar "pay your money and take your choices" situations in the arena of practical test construction. Within the limits of time available, how should the developer best allocate content? Purely from the standpoint of range of content coverage, the traditional tests are on sounder ground. Clearly, it would be *most* desirable to use several long passages, the best of both worlds. As with most similar issues in testing, such an ideal is impractical.

A final point to this section of reliability and validity concerns an often expressed perception of formal testing. That perception generally translates into statements such as, "This test was a waste of time—it told me what I already knew." This confirmation that test results generally provide is one of their great strengths, NOT a weakness. Indeed, this confirmation is what reliability and validity means. That is, the tests, without observing and by using procedures and questions and approaches far different from those used by a sensitive, involved teacher, are validating that teacher's judgment. It is, of course, the exceptions to this confirmation that generally receive and deserve the bulk of the interpretive attention; however, the confirmations evidence their greatest strength.

Further, extensive research has clearly shown (Kellaghan, Madaus, & Airasian, 1981; Rudman et al., 1980; Salmon-Cox, 1981; Stetz & Beck, 1981) that when test scores and teacher judgments of pupil abilities differ, teachers are inclined to change their views to the benefits of children. That is, when a child's test scores are higher than the teacher would predict, the teacher tends to inflate his/her view of the child's ability; when scores are lower than teacher judgment would predict, the test scores are dismissed.

TRENDS IN LANGUAGE-ARTS ASSESSMENT

Curriculum-Driven Assessment

One of the important issues facing language educators is whether tests should lead or follow the curriculum. The debate over the influence of tests on what is taught in classrooms is a longstanding one. The issue is actually one of the influence of test results on curriculum, not whether tests lead or follow the curriculum. And, the issue has long been decided: tests *do* determine, at least to some extent, what is taught. Therefore, the issue is really a concern with whether what is tested is what ought to be taught, or whether the tests reflect important curriculum goals.

Recent commentators on the political use of high-stakes tests promote the merits of (Popham, 1987; Popham et al., 1985) or lament the narrowness or other evils of (Bracey, 1987; Madaus,

1985) "teaching to the test." Even in its most acceptable form of teaching the skills underlying the test, rather than the test content per se, the thought of tests leading, rather than following, the curriculum is embraced by few measurement specialists. Regardless of the persuasion of the present authors, however, there can be no doubt that such a trend is occurring. The natural extension of this phenomenon is that there can be no question that student scores on these high-stakes tests have improved (Stake, Bettridge, Metzer, & Switzer, 1987). The critical question that remains unanswered is whether the underlying, broader skills assessed on such tests have improved, or whether the change has been test, or even test-item specific. Although measurement philosophers disagree on the advisability of such a phenomenon (Airasian, 1988), pragmatists will argue that we should take pedagogical advantage of the situation, not lament it or turn ostrich. Because tests *do* drive instruction, and what is stressed in instruction is learned (Popham et al., 1985), the joint task of language-arts curriculum developers and language-arts test developers is to ensure that what is tested on such high stakes is what *should* be taught.

Curriculum-driven assessment would *not* be a major concern to language-arts educators if they believed the tests adequately assessed all important aspects of the language-arts curriculum. Witty (1949) recognized the problem that can result from a lack of curriculum/assessment congruence many years ago:

It is necessary to supplement the knowledge of a child's reading status derived from standard tests by an estimate of his success in comprehending whole episodes or stories. In addition, understanding of each child's reading can be enhanced by examining a record of the books he has read in and out of school. (p. 215)

Some 35 years later, Purves (1984), commenting on the influence of minimum competency tests on the language-arts curriculum, made the same point when he presented the criticisms of those who opposed minimum competency assessment in language arts: "Statements of competence produced a circumscribing of the curriculum to a point where it merely prepared students for the test rather than being concerned with broad educative functions."

The impact of testing on instruction is viewed as a positive influence by a growing number of language-arts curriculum leaders, or at least as a lever they can use to change curriculum. Airasian (1988) describes measurement-driven instruction (MDI) as a change from measurement that takes its direction from curriculum to one in which curriculum takes its direction from testing. MDI is not a new phenomenon; tests have always driven instruction to a lesser or greater extent, but earlier tests were usually written after the curriculum was developed. In MDI, the tests are written as, or even before, the curriculum is developed. In effect, MDI proponents are saying, *here is the goal for instruction (performance on this test); now you curriculum people do what needs to be done in instruction to produce good scores.*

There are those who applaud the MDI movement as one that will lead to a clarification of instructional goals and increased academic achievement (c.f., Popham, 1987). On the other hand, many educators, including a number of measurement special-

ists, are concerned that MDI narrows the curriculum and removes the last vestiges of decision-making from the teacher (Madaus, 1985). Airasian (1988) views MDI as more complex than it appears on the surface. He suggests three factors that determine the impact of assessment on instruction—the nature of the content being measured, the standards established for satisfactory test performance, and the test stakes (the decision to be made from the test results, e.g., promotion, graduation, and teacher salaries). He goes on to say that, "Depending on the interrelationship among these three factors, the instructional response may range from strong to weak."

The issues of MDI are those of curriculum control and decision-making in regard to what will be taught and how it will be taught. Language-arts curriculum leaders have always been concerned about these issues. Indeed, one of the strongest fears when the National Assessment of Educational Progress (NAEP) was first being established was its potential for dictating a national curriculum. Because of these concerns, NAEP was set up so that state comparisons and individual school districts comparisons were not possible. The goal of NAEP was to find out, in general and on a national basis, how students were achieving in various areas of the curriculum. Results were not to be used to determine curriculum or to foster specific course content. Recent reports, however, have called for a change in NAEP to provide more definite information about more precisely defined groups so the results of NAEP may be used to foster curriculum change (James, 1987).

Other educators and education reviewers have noted the impact of assessment on the control of education. Salganik (1985) believes that the reliance on test scores has weakened the authority of professional judgment and pushed schools toward more centralized governance. Moreover, she sees this trend as one that will accelerate.

Language education seems to be one area where the emphasis on test scores is growing concurrently with the development of new approaches to assessment and the use of a greater variety of assessments. Many language-arts curriculum leaders, who may in the past have paid little attention to assessment or merely been critics of assessment, now see assessment as a way to induce schools to incorporate into the curriculum what the leaders believe is important. Measurement-driven instruction is a fact of life, and the curriculum battles in language arts may revolve around the control of assessment.

This trend is almost sure to produce increased criticisms of tests regardless of their content because tests by themselves are too narrow and too insensitive to measure all those things schools are trying to achieve. The concern with the limits of test scores to assess the quality of education was emphasized by Sizer (1984), who declared that test scores cause educators and policymakers to focus on the wrong problems, and, more importantly, on the wrong solutions to those problems:

I have little confidence in the educational significance of the use of standardized achievement test scores. It's not that the scores have no meaning, it's simply that they tap much too slender a slice of what I believe is important in education. (p. 49)

In the language-arts field, recent years have witnessed a number of recommendations and test development projects that have had as their goal the influence of curriculum, or at the very least the influence of new knowledge about language growth on test development, with a subsequent influence on curriculum reform. This may seem like a chicken and egg issue, and indeed it is. The real issue is the effort to develop tests that more closely match instruction.

The English Language-Arts Framework (1987) calls for a much greater variety of assessments including student reading habits and writing activities. The report also endorses the California Department of Education's direct writing assessment that "will ask for student writing in a variety of types: reflective, autobiographical, critical and analytical." The assessment chapter of the California Framework concludes with the statement that, "Effective assessment must focus on identifying the extent to which the programs [California School District Language-Arts Programs] have accomplished these goals."

Michigan and Illinois have also attempted to bring their assessments into closer alignment with what many experts feel should be taught in reading instruction and with what is known about the reading process (Wixson, Peters, Weber, & Roeber, 1987; Valencia & Pearson, 1986). Both states have developed tests that include longer test passages because of the belief that shorter passages lack structural and topical integrity. They assert that shorter passages do not reflect the sustained reading that students do in typical classrooms. This move to longer passages has become prominent, and it is likely that the next editions of commercial reading achievement tests will include longer test passages.

What is not known at this time is whether longer passages provide a more valid measure of reading. It seems reasonable to hypothesize that such tests assess short-term memory, perhaps as much as they assess reading ability. Furthermore, it is reasonable to argue on the basis of classroom observations that when faced with long passages, many students will only skim the reading selection and will then move quickly to the questions, and skim back and forth from the questions to the passage searching for answers. Although skimming is a valuable skill and one that is frequently taught, it is doubtful that a skimming test adequately assesses reading. Finally, it is not known just how much sustained reading students do in school. It may be that most reading is of the short snippet variety. Even when one reads a complete chapter or book, there are constant pauses for reflection, summarization, and prediction before the reader picks up again with the reading. Short passages may actually be more reflective of the typical school reading process.

Longer passages that are not well organized and that do not have structural integrity are no better, or no worse, than shorter passages that suffer from the same problems. The issue is most accurately seen as the quality of the writing, not the length of what is to be read.

In addition to passage length, recent developments in reading assessment have focused on metacognition, defined as a reader's awareness of the cognitive demands of reading, how well the reader is comprehending, and what strategies the reader might use to improve comprehension. There is clear evidence that better readers use these strategies and poorer readers do not (Pritchard, 1987). There is also increasing evidence that metacognition can be tapped through various assessment approaches (Garner, 1988). Introspective and retrospec-

tive assessments have been used successfully be several researchers (Afflerbach & Johnston, 1984; Ericsson & Simon, 1980). However, these techniques have not been adopted very widely in schools.

It is not known in regard to metacognition whether a reader has to have these metacognitive skills developed to a conscious level. It may be that these skills function quite satisfactorily without any recognition by the reader that he or she is using them. If our assessment becomes intrusive (and is subsequently reflected in classroom instruction), we may produce readers who, at least during a developmental period, pay more attention to the process than to the content of what they are reading. One only needs to be reminded of the "grunt and groan" phonics readers to realize this possibility.

The recent move to writing assessment based on student writing samples is a clear attempt to more closely align curriculum and assessment in language arts, or at least what language arts curriculum leaders would like to see emphasized in schools. The desire to induce more schools to teach writing as a process and to prod teachers to provide students with more writing opportunities has had an impact on assessment. As well, the establishment of writing assessment programs has resulted in increased classroom writing activities. Writing samples are now used in well over half of the states as part of their statewide testing programs (Afflerbach, 1985), and numerous school districts include writing samples as part of their annual school assessments. In addition, most commercial standardized tests now include writing sample tests as part of their test batteries (Stiggins & Bridgeford, 1983).

The concern with higher-order thinking skills in the language arts is another curriculum movement that has found its way into the assessment area. Although some educators have argued that thinking skills cannot be taught through the typical state the objectives, teach the skills, and provide practice used for other skills (Sternberg, 1987), and others have argued that it is absurd to assume that thinking can be taught at all (Smith, 1989), the teaching and assessment of higher-order thinking skills has flourished (Norris, 1985; Paul, 1985).

This phenomenon may have originated with earlier reviews of the NAEP reading data, and the same conclusion has been reinforced in the most recent NAEP results. The general conclusion was that students were doing quite well with literal (lower-order) reading comprehension, but they were not doing well with inferential, critical, and evaluative (higher-order) reading comprehension. This gave rise to a school curriculum and testing emphasis on higher-order thinking skills (HOTS). Rather than attempting to look for ways to emphasize and teach these skills within the existing curriculum, and to assess the skills within already existing testing areas, a separate curriculum and assessment area developed. (See Nickerson (1988) for a well-developed review of research on the teaching of thinking skills).

Higher-order thinking skills are now commonly listed in the curriculum of many state and school district curriculum guides, and those who select tests insist that such skills be included on the tests. Regardless of the evidence for the validity of such assessment, because it is in the curriculum, it must be tested, and if it is on the tests, then teachers will attempt to teach the skills.

All of the examples of changes in language-arts assessment surveyed in this section have as their goal the closer tie of curriculum and assessment. It is not a matter of whether or not measurement-driven instruction is a reality in the language arts—it *is*.

Issues in Norm-Referenced and Criterion-Referenced Interpretation

Criterion-referenced tests (CRTs), first labeled and described by Glaser (1963), have now matured as a concept. Although these tests have brought with them some special concerns and even statistical techniques, they are now generally accepted, for better or for worse, as being not necessarily distinct from norm-referenced tests (NRTs). Most measurement specialists and commentators now acknowledge that any CRT could be normed, and that any NRT with carefully constructed content could offer CRT-type interpretations. The differences are more ones of primary purpose rather than of structure or substance. Attention to NRT and CRT interpretive issues varies with the purpose to be served by the assessment, i.e., whether performance should be referenced to relative standing within a normative group, whether a classroom or a national grade-level sample, or to standing relative to some judgmentally determined standard of performance.

As CRT theory has matured, recent action in the referencing arena has returned to NRTs. The most recent norm-referenced issue drawing broad professional and public attention has been the so-called "Lake Wobegon effect" (Cannell, 1987, 1988). This phenomenon, brought to the attention of the profession and the public by a physician, created much distress for both users and publishers. Cannell reports (1987) that all states, 90 percent of the school districts, and 70 percent of the students tested nationwide receive achievement scores above the national average. Such data, which on the surface at least sound not only incredible, but statistically impossible, have received wide comment. (Interested readers should consult the Summer 1988 issue of *Educational Measurement: Issues and Practice* for a summary of the Lake Wobegon effect, with commentaries by representatives of major test publishers and federal education officials.)

Suffice it is say that Cannell's data, although questionable from several perspectives, on the whole raises serious concerns about procedures used both in developing and reporting national normative data. The fidelity and comparability of national norms, selectively in testing particular groups of students in norming and in large-scale testing programs, issues of teaching to the test, and the stability of national norms over time are all important issues raised by this report. These issues range from political ones to fairly abstruse psychometric and statistical ones. The fallout from this report has not ended (Cannell, 1988), and both test publishers and state education departments are considering and/or implementing changes in procedures used to either develop or report normative data.

A somewhat related concern about the quality of normative data is represented by the work of Baglin (1981). His research, although methodologically flawed (Beck, 1981), highlighted

publicly a problem that test publishers have experienced to a growing degree over the past two decades. That problem is one of obtaining voluntary cooperation of school districts in national norming programs. The ever-increasing demands on a school's limited instructional time provide a partial explanation for the trend. A related cause is the similarly increasing intrusion of mandated testing programs, federal and state governments primarily, but also from the public's seemingly insatiable appetite for more data. Whether Baglin's claims that publisher norms are easy because of the nonrepresentative samples included in norming programs are true, or if so, whether this relates to Cannell's finding, are unanswered questions to date. Perhaps the next decade will provide answers to these serious concerns. If publishers are unable, for whatever reasons, to obtain accurate sets of normative data at a time when the demand for such data is ever increasing, new approaches for collecting these data will have to be implemented.

One proposed way of addressing the issue of datedness in national norms that has recently been discussed is that of annual norms—or "rolling norms." Such an approach is offered by some as a way of dealing with the concerns about the datedness of norms (c.f. Qualls-Payne, 1988). However, we see little appeal in such an approach. In many ways, the most valuable aspect of national norms for a test is the constant point of reference against which change can be assessed. Were test norms to change annually, this current positive feature would be lost, or at least obfuscated. Obviously, such essentially constant norming efforts would only exacerbate the concerns raised by Baglin. While "user norms," developed using only the results of current tests' users, may offer a way of dealing with the cooperation issue, this approach would introduce its own set of serious problems.

Evolving Assessments

Farr and Carey (1986) describe the limited change in the structure and content of standardized reading tests over the past 50 years. The same summary applies to the other areas of language-arts testing as well. The only possible exception to this is the area of writing assessment, where the use (though not the structure) of essay examinations has recently increased markedly. In the area of formal assessment, changes in language-arts testing have been evolutionary rather than revolutionary.

We identify under the evolving assessments heading three significant trends—new reading comprehension measures, performance assessments, and scores that carry interpretive meaning. The first two of these trends apply directly to assessments per se, the latter pertains more specifically to the portrayal of information resulting from the assessments.

Holistic Reading Comprehension Measures. Although it is likely that the soundness of traditional measures of reading comprehension has been questioned since the first day such tests were used, the current direction for comprehension assessment seems to have begun with Simons (1971). He attacked the several approaches to comprehension assessment used at that time and proposed that new measures be more attentive to reading processes than to the product of these processes.

The clearest illustration of such efforts is found in the reading tests resulting from several state assessment projects, notably those in Michigan and Illinois, though several other states (as is our wont in education) have joined the parade and are developing near clones of these two initial efforts. Minor and less minor differences exist among the several states now developing or using such measures, but all are characterized by their holistic nature. The theoretical underpinnings of these instruments are based on the current view of reading comprehension as a dynamic, interactive process.

With some differences in focus, wording, and item format, these new assessments generally have four interrelated parts:

1. Comprehension/constructing meaning,
2. Metacognition/reading strategies/knowledge about reading,
3. Topic familiarity/prior knowledge, and
4. Attitudes/self-perceptions/literary experiences.

Most traditional tests have focused almost exclusively on only the constructing meaning portion of the above group of factors, although commercial reading surveys and attitude scales have long been available, albeit seldom linked to comprehension measures.

Although proponents of these new measures may argue that the constructing meaning and attitude components differ in substance from those in traditional tests, clearly the most unique elements of the new measures are the portions assessing metacognition and prior knowledge. It remains to be seen empirically whether these new assessments work and, if so, what contribution they make to future large-scale reading assessments and, more importantly, to instruction. However, at the very least, such developments havé raised the consciousness of a broad range of developers and users of reading assessment instruments.

Perhaps the most significant potential for failure of these instruments is the mismatch between their structure and the tests' purpose. Recall that these tests are state assessment instruments, developed, interpreted, and used almost exclusively for ranking and sorting (accountability) purposes. Such instruments, regardless of how faithful they are to current reading theory, will be used or misused no less often or seriously than is predictable from their purpose. The Stanford-Binet is an excellent psychometric instrument, built to be consistent with a well-explicated theory of ability. However, it would not be the instrument of choice for planning tomorrow's instruction for a group of children. The instrumentation and the purpose for its use simply would not be well matched. So it is with the use of instructionally oriented reading tests built for state accountability purposes. We can only hope that the instruments will be used by insightful, caring educators in ways consistent with their development. Further, it is hoped that such extensive staff development, curriculum alignment, and instructional planning activities as have already taken place, most notably in Michigan, will become a model for others. In this instance, the test merely serves as a change agent to bring about a redirection of instruction.

Other nontraditional reading comprehension assessment procedures may offer as much, if not more, long-term promise, though they currently are receiving less attention in the measurement and instructional communities. We include here the work of Carver (1981) and of Royer and his colleagues (Royer, Hastings, & Hook, 1979). These two have conducted rather extensive research efforts relating to their proposed assessment procedures.

Performance Testing. Performance testing in language arts is most clearly and pervasively illustrated in the widespread use of student-generated writing as an assessment vehicle. Performance assessment, of course, takes place on a near-continual basis by all classroom teachers. We are addressing here, however, the development of formal procedures. The key characteristics of all sound assessment instrumentation, i.e., reliability and validity, apply to performance assessments in much the same way as they do to traditional multiple-choice tests. The two critical validity issues in performance tests are that they focus on the critical elements that define the attribute to be assessed, and that as representative a sample of behavior as possible be collected. In terms of reliability, the most significant challenge is making the judgment-based scoring as objective and replicable as possible. Three excellent sources of information on the development and use of sound performance assessment procedures are Priestly (1982), Berk (1986), and Stiggins (1987).

Powell (1988) studied the reading processes used by sixth-grade students as they engaged in four different reading activities, multiple-choice tests, cloze tests, written retellings, and a nonassessed reading task. Powell's study was designed to determine if students used different strategies in responding to each of these tasks. She found that written retellings and multiple-choice questions were the most alike and were the most similar to the nonassessed reading task. The cloze task produced quite different reading strategies on the part of these sixth-grade readers. The study concluded that the readers did not appear to be as involved cognitively with the text in the cloze test as they did in the other three tasks. Powell further concluded that "the multiple choice test, the written retelling and the nonassessed reading task are those that are considered to be associated with the task of reading, such as tieing prior knowledge in with the text, visualizing what is happening in the text, and paraphrasing the text." More studies comparing different assessment approaches in terms of the reading/thinking processes used by students will provide more clues as to the most valid ways of assessing language behaviors.

Assessment specialists and commentators alike have long urged for the use of fewer paper-and-pencil procedures and more performance measures. The combination of inertia, complexities of performance assessment development, and the several economies of paper-and-pencil instruments have made actual progress in performance assessment development in traditional education settings minimal to date. However, there are several signs that this long-slumbering area is coming alive. Several state assessment programs are conducting feasibility studies and even full-scale performance assessment programs. These procedures to date generally have not been in the language-arts area (c.f., *Learning by Doing,* 1987, a manual containing performance assessment procedures in science and mathematics developed for NAEP). However, it seems predictable the next few years will see increased attention to performance instrumentation in language arts (Burstall, 1986). The first signs of this are obvious in the snowballing informal assessment area. Such procedures as verbal and written retellings, and writing folders are examples of techniques that seem likely to be adapted from informal to formal assessments. As one example of this possibility, consider the translation of the long-used informal writing folders procedures into formal portfolio assessments now striking the fancy of test development specialists.

Instructionally Useful "Scores". Another trend in formal language assessment is the development of more meaningful scores. This trend is a natural outgrowth of the criterion-referenced testing movement and another reaction against the use of normative references for test interpretation. Early recognition of the potential value of such scores was made by Flanagan (1951) and Ebel (1962), two of the most creative and influential measurement specialists of our era. However, only recently have we witnessed any translation of these ideas into practice. Three primary examples of this trend, all in the area of reading, are in the scores of the NAEP, the *Degrees of Reading Power,* and the *Metropolitan Achievement Tests.* Each of these instruments attacks the meaning problem in different ways, using widely differing psychometric and test construction procedures, and with different aims. Yet all illustrate an attempt to portray a student's or group's test performance in a performance fashion *other than* in reference to others. In the case of the NAEP (Kirsch & Jungeblut, n.d.), the scores, described as comprising a "prose scale," range from 0 to 500, with increasing scores indicating increased proficiency. The unique element is the addition of performance descriptors for various score points. For example, a score of 210 is associated with the ability to locate information in a moderate length newspaper article, while the ability to synthesize the main argument of a lengthy newspaper article corresponds with a score of 340. Although not instructionally prescriptive, referencing of score points to concrete tasks is an attempt to give interpretive meaning to quantitative data.

In the *Degrees of Reading Power* (1980), scores on a set of passages presented in modified close format are related to performance on a broad range of reading materials by expressing both the test scores and the difficulty of materials on the same scale. The reading level of a wide assortment of texts and trade books is thus directly tied to a student's test performance, resulting in a predicted match of reader with reading materials at the appropriate instructional level.

The *Metropolitan Achievement Tests* (Prescott, Balow, Hogan, & Farr, 1984) use sets of graded, traditional looking reading passages and multiple-choice questions to arrive at an estimate of a student's instructional reading level. The key element of this link is the close matching of passage level with the difficulty of the questions assessing each passage. The tests, although also proving the usual assortment of norm-referenced scores, scale reading levels according to the grade levels of basal reading materials. Using a student's performance on the

questions based on the several graded reading passages, an estimate of the appropriate instructional reading level is provided.

The above three examples may not be a comprehensive demonstration of the trend to portraying test scores in interpretable metrics, but they are probably the best developed demonstrations thereof. We anticipate that as the demands continue to increase for tests to be instructionally relevant, evolution of such metrics will continue.

CONTINUING ISSUES

The theme most dominant in current discussions of language-arts assessment is process. The call has been for instruments more attentive to the processes of language development, rather than the products. This trend, first evidenced by the criterion-referenced testing movement of the 1960s and now seen in the new state-level reading tests initiated by the work in Michigan, is also obvious in the performance assessment developments outlined above.

The argument underlying this theme is that the processes of, say, reading, are more important than the product. Such an argument is specious in isolation. Clearly, both process and product are important, both for "formative" and "summative" assessment. The key element missing in such discussions is the *purpose* for which the information is being collected. Teachers, administrators, boards of education, and parents are all interested in both process and product, though in generally different ways. Teachers are obviously concerned primarily with process as they help a child move toward increased language proficiency; however, they are also by necessity concerned with the product of all the processes. Process assessment is critical in planning and guiding instruction, but product measurement is essential in gauging the success of a program or intervention. Similarly, administrators are primarily concerned with product, but cannot neglect the processes that lead to it.

To a significant extent, the process-product distinction is an illusion in that, by definition, all assessments must be of a product. Even with brilliantly conceived and developed assessment instruments, we could only observe a product, and infer the intervening or enabling processes that led to it.

It is certain from the trends of the past few years, that the next several years will witness increased use of writing, the development of portfolio assessment for both reading and writing, and a push for more approaches to the assessment of metacognitive skills in both reading and writing. If these approaches are to provide meaningful (valid) and useful (reliable) results for teachers and administrators, much work needs to be done. Moreover, the issue of teacher time to engage in these additional tasks needs to be addressed. Even if teachers find these new forms of assessment to be especially useful, time will need to be found in an already overloaded schedule for reviewing and using the information derived from these assessments. The efficiency of assessment will always be an issue in determining new directions.

Formal assessments were developed and have maintained their dominant position in the measurement armamentarium primarily because of their financial and temporal efficiency. Compared with "better" (read less-formal) techniques, the unchanging multiple-choice product measures are cheap and quick. In the efforts by instructional leaders and creative measurement specialists to evolve instrumentation that is more attentive to what we are coming to understand about the language development process (i.e., tests that are more valid), the efficiency is sacrificed. We must wonder whether the increase in fidelity/validity is proportionate with the increased cost in time and money. Our general conclusion is that it is easier, faster, and cheaper, and more valid, to approach the measurement of process indicators via informal procedures applied in a timely, as-needed way by the teacher in the privacy of his/her classroom. While there is a need to continue to progress in making formal product assessments more faithful to what we

know and are learning about reading or other language constructs, efforts to assess process through such tests are bound to lead to less than satisfying results.

This conclusion leads necessarily to a call to train, retrain, and otherwise assist classroom teachers in designing and conducting valid informal and semiformal assessments. Current indications (Carter, 1984; Gullickson & Ellwein, 1985; Rudman, et al., 1980; Stiggins & Bridgeford, 1985; Stiggins, Conklin & Bridgeford, 1986) are that most teachers do not have a high degree of knowledge about the development, analysis, and interpretation of assessment instruments, formal or informal. The challenges to teacher-training institutions and forward-looking school districts and state departments of education are obvious.

References

Afflerbach, P. (1985). *Statewide assessment of writing*. Princeton, NJ: ERIC Clearinghouse on Tests, Measurement, and Evaluation.

Afflerbach, P., & Johnston, P. (1984). On the use of verbal reports in reading research. *Journal of Reading Behavior, 16,* 307–322.

Airasian, P. W. (1988). Measurement driven instruction: A closer look. *Educational Measurement: Issues and Practice, 7*(4), 6–11.

Anastasi, A. (1982). *Psychological testing* (5th ed.). New York: Macmillan.

Anderson, B. (1982). Test use today in elementary and secondary schools. In A. K. Wigdor and W. R. Garner (Eds.), *Ability testing: Uses, consequences, and controversies,* Part 2. Washington, DC: National Academy Press.

Baglin, R. F. (1981). Does "nationally" normed really mean nationally? *Journal of Educational Measurement, 18,* 97–107.

Becoming a nation of readers: The report of the commission on reading. (1984). Prepared by the Richard C. Anderson and others. Washington, DC: The National Institute of Education, U.S. Department of Education.

Beck, M. D. (1981). Critique of *"Does 'nationally' normed really mean nationally?"* Unpublished manuscript. New York: The Psychological Corporation.

Bock, D. C., & Bock, E. H. (1981). *Evaluating classroom speaking.* Annandale, VA: Speech Communication Association.

Berk, R. A. (Ed.). (1980). *Criterion-referenced measurement: The state of the art.* Baltimore, MD: Johns Hopkins University Press.

Berk, R. A. (Ed.). (1986). *Performance assessment: Methods and applications* Baltimore, MD: Johns Hopkins University Press.

Betts, E. A. (1954). *Foundations of reading instruction.* New York: American Book Company.

Bracy, G. W. (1987). Measurement-driven instruction: Catchy phrase, dangerous practice. *Phi Delta Kappan, 68,* 683–686.

Brown, R. (1986). Evaluation and learning. In A. R. Petrosky & D. Bartholomae (Eds.), *The teaching of writing: Eighty fifth yearbook of the National Society for the Study of Education.* Chicago: University of Chicago Press.

Burstall, C. (1986). Innovative forms of assessment: A United Kingdom perspective. *Educational Measurement: Issues and Practice, 5*(1), 17–22.

Cannell, J. J. (1987). *Nationally normed elementary achievement testing in America's public schools: How fifty states are above the national average.* Daniels, WV: Friends of Education.

Cannell, J. J. (1988). The Lake Wobegon effect revisited. *Educational Measurement: Issues and Practice, 7*(4), 12–15.

Carter, K. (1984). Do teachers understand the principles for writing tests? *Journal of Teacher Education, 35*(6), 57–60.

Carter, K. (1986). Test wiseness for teachers and students. *Educational Measurement: Issues and Practice, 5*(4), 20–23.

Carver, R. P. (1981). *Reading comprehension and reading theory.* Springfield, IL: Charles C. Thomas. (Reprinted, 1987. Kansas City, MO: Revrac Publications).

Cronbach, L. J. (1971). Test validation. In R. L. Thorndike (Ed.), *Educational measurement* (2nd ed.). Washington, DC: American Council on Education.

Degrees of reading power. (1980). Brewster, NY: Touchstone Applied Science Associates.

Ebel, R. L. (1962). Content standard test scores. *Educational and Psychological Measurement, 22,* 15–25.

English-Language Arts Framework. (1987). Developed by the English-Language Arts Curriculum Framework and Criteria Committee. Sacramento, CA: California State Department of Education.

Ericsson, K. A., & Simon, H. A. (1980). Verbal reports as data. *Psychological Review, 87,* 215–251.

Farr, R., & Carey, R. F. (1986). *Reading: What can be measured?* Newark, DE: International Reading Association.

Flanagan, J. C. (1951). Units, scores, and norms. In E. F. Lindquist (Ed.), *Educational measurement.* Washington, DC: American Council on Education, 695–763.

Frisbie, D. A. (1988). NCME instructional module on reliability of scores from teacher-made tests. *Educational Measurement: Issues and Practice, 7*(1), 25–35.

Garner, R. (1988). *Metacognition and reading comprehension.* Norwood, NJ: Ablex Publishing Company.

Glaser, R. (1963). Instructional technology and the measurement of learning outcomes: Some questions. *American Psychologist, 18,* 519–521.

Greenberg, K., Weiner, H., & Donovan, R. (Eds.). (1986). *Writing assessment: Issues and strategies.* New York: Longman.

Guba, E. (1969). The failure of educational evaluation. *Educational Technology, 9,* 29–33.

Guba, E. G. *Toward a methodology of naturalistic inquiry in educational evaluation.* Monograph series No.8. Los Angeles: Center for the Study of Evaluation, University of California, 1978

Guba, E., & Lincoln, Y. (1981). *Effective evaluation.* San Francisco: Jossey-Bass.

Gullickson, A. R., & Ellwein, M. C. (1985). Post hoc analysis of teacher-made tests: The goodness-of-fit between prescription and practice.

Educational Measurement: Issues and Practice, 4(1) 15–18.

James, H. T. (1987). *The nation's report card: Improving the assessment of student achievement*. Cambridge, MA: The National Academy of Education.

Johnston, P. H. (1983). *Reading comprehension assessment: A cognitive basis*. Newark, DE: International Reading Association.

Kaplan, S. (1964). *The conduct of inquiry*. San Francisco: Chandler.

Kellaghan, T., Madaus, G. F., & Airasian, P. W. (1981). *The effects of standardized testing*. Boston, MA: Kluwer-Nijhoff.

Kirsch, I. S., Jungeblut, A. (n.d.). *Literacy: Profiles of America's young adults*. Princeton, NJ: Educational Testing Service, National Assessment of Educational Progress, Report No. 16-PL-OZ.

Learning by doing. (1987, May). Princeton, NJ: Educational Testing Service (Report No.: 17-Nos-80).

Madaus, G. F. (1985). Public policy and the testing profession: You've never had it so good? *Educational Measurement: Issues and Practice, 4,* 5–11.

McClellan, M. C. (1988). Testing and reform. *Phi Delta Kappan, 69,* 766–771.

Messick, S. (1975). The standard problem: Meaning and values in measurement and evaluation. *American Psychologist, 30,* 955–966.

Michigan State Board of Education. (1987). *Blueprint for the new MEAP reading test*. Lansing, MI: Michigan State Board of Education.

A Nation at Risk. (1983). The National Commission on Excellence in Education. Washington, DC: U.S. Department of Education.

Nickerson, R. S. (1988). On improving thinking through instruction. In E. Z. Rothkopf (Ed.), *Review of research in education,* (Vol. 15). Washington, DC: American Educational Research Association, 3–57.

Norris, S. P. (1985). Synthesis of research on critical thinking. *Educational Leadership, 42*(8), 40–45.

Odell, L., Cooper, C. R., & Courts, C. (1978). Discourse theory: Implications for research in composing. In C. R. Cooper & L. Odell (Eds.), *Research on composing: Points of departure*. Urbana, IL: National Council of Teachers of English.

Paul, R. W. (1985). Bloom's taxonomy and critical thinking instruction. *Educational Leadership, 42*(8), 36–39.

Pearson, P. D., & Valencia, S. (1987). *The Illinois State Board of Education census assessment in reading: An historical reflection*.

Popham, W. J. (1971). *Criterion-referenced measurement*. Englewood Cliffs, NJ: Educational Technology Publications.

Popham, J. W. *Evaluation in education*. Berkeley, CA: McCutchan Publishing Corp., 1974.

Popham, W. J. (1987). The merits of measurement-driven instruction. *Phi Delta Kappan, 68,* 679–682.

Popham, W. J., Cruse, K. L., Rankin, S. L., Sandifer, P. D., & Williams, P. L. (1985). Measurement driven instruction: It's on the road. *Phi Delta Kappan, 66,* 628–634.

Powell, J. (1988) *An examination of comprehension processes used by readers as they engage in different forms of assessment*. Unpublished doctoral dissertation, Indiana University, Bloomington.

Prescott, G. A., Balow, I. H., Hogan, T. P., & Farr, R. C. (1984). *Metropolitan achievement tests*. San Antonio, TX: The Psychological Corporation.

Priestly, M. (1982). *Performance assessment in education and training: Alternate techniques*. Englewood Cliffs, NJ: Educational Technology Publications.

Pritchard, R. (1987) *A cross-cultural study of the effects of cultural schemata on proficient reader's comprehension monitoring strategies and their comprehension of culturally familiar and unfamiliar passages*. Unpublished doctoral dissertation, Indiana University, Bloomington.

Purves, A. (1984). The challenge to education to produce literate citizens. In A. Purves & O. Niles (Eds.), *Becoming readers in a complex society: Eighty-third yearbook of the National Society for the Study of Education*. Chicago: University of Chicago Press.

Qualls-Payne, A. (1988). SRA response to Cannell's article. *Educational Measurement: Issues and Practice, 7*(2), 21–22.

Resnick, D. (1982). History of educational testing. In A. K. Wigdor and W. R. Garner (Eds.), *Ability testing: Uses, consequences, and controversies,* Part 2. Washington, DC: National Academy Press.

Rowe, D. W., & Rayford, L. (1987). Activating background knowledge in reading comprehension assessment. *Reading Research Quarterly, 2,* 160–176.

Royer, J. M., Hastings, C. N., & Hook, C. (1979). A sentence verification technique for measuring reading comprehension. *Journal of Reading Behavior, 11,* 355–363.

Rubin, D., & Mead, N. (1984). *Large-scale assessment of oral communication skills: Kindergarten through Grade 12*. Annandale, VA: Speech Communication Association.

Rudman, H. C., Kelly, J. L., Wanous, D. S.. Mehrens, W. A., Clark, C. M., & Porter, A. C. (1980). *Integrating assessment with instruction: A review*. East Lansing, MI: Institute for Research on Teaching, Michigan State University.

Salganik, L. H. (1985). Why testing reforms are so popular and how they are changing education. *Phi Delta Kappan, 66,* 628–634.

Salmon-Cox, L. (1981). Teachers and Tests: What's really happening? *Phi Delta Kappan, 62,* 631–634.

Scriven, M. (1973). Goal free evaluation. In E. R. House (Ed.), *School evaluation: The politics and process*. Berkeley, CA: McCutchan Publishing.

Simons, H. D. (1971). Reading comprehension: The need for a new perspective. *Reading Research Quarterly, 6,* 338–363.

Sizer, T. R. (1984). *Horace's compromise*. Boston: Houghton Mifflin.

Smith, F. (1989). Overselling literacy. *Phi Delta Kappan, 70,* 353–359.

Smith, H. K. (1967). The responses of good and poor readers when asked to read for different purposes. *Reading Research Quarterly, 3,* 56–83.

Sonnenschein, J. L. (1988). *Process vs. product: What test publishers can deliver*. Paper presented at the 12th World Congress in Reading. The Gold Coast, Australia.

Stake, R. E. Preordinate vs. responsive evaluation. (mimeographed) Urbana, IL: University of Illinois, 1975.

Stake, R. E., Bettridge, J., Metzer, D., & Switzer, D. (1987). *Review of literature on effects of achievement testing*. Champaign, IL: University of Illinois Center for Instructional Research.

Sternberg, R. (1987). Teaching critical thinking: Eight easy ways to fail before you begin. *Phi Delta Kappan, 68,* 456–459.

Stetz, F. P., & Beck, M. D. (1981). Attitudes toward standardized tests: Students, teachers, and measurement specialists. *Measurement in Education, 12*(1).

Stiggins, R. J. (1987). NCME instructional module on design and development of performance assessments. *Educational Measurement: Issues and Practice, 6*(3), 33–42.

Stiggins, R. J., & Bridgeford, N. J. (1983). An analysis of published tests of writing proficiency. *Educational Measurement: Issues and Practice, 2*(1), 6–10, 26.

Stiggins, R. J., & Bridgeford, N. J. (1985). The ecology of classroom assessment. *Journal of Educational Measurement, 22,* 271–286.

Stiggins, R. J., Conklin, N. F., & Bridgeford, N. J. (1986). Classroom assessment: A key to effective education. *Educational Measurement: Issues and Practice, 5*(2), 5–17.

Subkoviak, M. J. (1988). A practitioner's guide to computation and interpretation of reliability indices for mastery tests. *Journal of Educational Measurement, 25,* 47–55.

Tyler, R. W. (Ed.) *Educational evaluation: New roles, new means.* (68th Yearbook of the National Society for the Study of Education, Part 2) Chicago: University of Chicago Press, 1969.

Valencia, S., & Pearson, P. D. (1986). *New Models for reading assessment: Reading education report no. 71.* Urbana, IL: Center for the Study of Reading.

Valencia, S., & Pearson, D. (1987). Reading assessment: Time for a change. *The Reading Teacher, 40,* 726–732.

Witty, P. (1949). *Reading in modern education.* Boston, MA: D. C. Heath and Company.

Wixson, K. K., Peters, C. W., Weber, E. M., & Roeber, E. D. (1987). New directions in state wide assessment. *The Reading Teacher, 40,* 749–755.

Wolf, R. L. Toward more natural inquiry in education. *CEDR Quarterly,* 1977 *10* (Fall), 7–9.

Yalow, E. S., & Popham, W. J. (1983) Content validity at the crossroads. *Educational Researcher, 12*(8), 10–14, 21.

27B. INFORMAL METHODS OF EVALUATION
Yetta M. Goodman

Mary K. finishes talking to a small group of fifth graders about a story they are writing. She stands, moves over to the side of the room, looks around the class and notes to herself:

Chris and Isaac have their heads together over Isaac's radio play. Hopefully they are going to tape-record both of their plays with the help of a Halloween sound effects record. Chris has written Isaac in as a major character in his play and has shared it with Isaac and a few other classmates from beginning draft through two revisions. Isaac has read his draft to Chris but does not seem to be seeking more than approval. The class members worked on their radio plays on Tuesday and Wednesday. They revised Tuesday's "sloppy copy" into another "sloppy copy" on Wednesday. Some merely recopied the first draft, but a few incorporated a little more detail. I typed some of the more cohesive plays as best I could. Chris and Isaac are both working from typed versions, filling in what I couldn't make out from their invented spelling and making changes they now desire (Marek, Howard, et al., 1984).

Don H. is reading a story to his second graders and the text refers to somebody being horsewhipped. Kalman interrupts and reminds the class that being horsewhipped is like being hit with a whip made out of horses. "That's like the book we read a long time before about that king who reigned," he calls out excitedly. Don was struck by the fact that only four weeks earlier he had relegated a plan to have the children make books about homonyms to a good idea gone bad since the kids at that time hadn't responded to his suggestion. Now the children themselves had related this story to the previous one and from Kalman's suggestions the class made a set of books similar to Fred Gwynn's *The King Who Reigned* (unpublished paper).

Carol A. is having a writing conference with Marlene, one of her first graders. Carol describes her responses: I asked Marlene to read her writing to me. "I am outside, under a rainbow and beside a tree," she read as she moved her finger under the letters in a very precise, deliberate fashion."

"Tell me about these O's." I responded. Marlene looked at me and giggled that I didn't see what was so obvious.

"Those aren't O's," she said. "They're circles."

"Circles?" Now I was puzzled. "Well, why did you decide to put circles in the middle of your writing?"

"Because. See, I couldn't tell what letters make those sounds so I just put circles for what goes there because something goes there only I don't know what. I can't tell what letter makes that sound, so I just put circles."

Marlene read and pointed her way through the line again. "I am—oops, I forgot to write *I*." Her finger lands under the first circle as she says *am*. She continues on and I can see that Marlene has correctly written *S* for side, *RB* for rainbow, *BS* for beside, and *T* for tree. The sounds she was unable to identify are vowel sounds, but Marlene was able to develop a strategy to deal with this.

When I looked again at Marlene's writing and listened to her explanation, I understood that she could distinguish vowel sounds in words but could not identify them with a corresponding letter (Avery, unpublished paper).

Nancie Atwell transcribes an evaluation conference she had with one of her adolescent students in *In the Middle* (Atwell, 1987)

Atwell: Okay, Mike your goals for this past quarter were to try some new kinds of writing, going beyond personal experience narrative, and to work on proofreading finals so you don't end up making a lot of new mistakes on the published copy.

Mike: I really spent a lot of time on that:

A: So, that's a goal you've conquered . . . What about the other goal, trying something new?

M. I really didn't do much on that . . . But I'm going to try fiction this quarter.

Mary, Don, Carol, and Nancie are professionals. They know their students well. They use observations, questioning techniques, individual and small group interactions, conferences, and in-depth analysis of their students' oral and written productions to engage in daily evaluation of development. They understand what they are observing because they are knowledgeable about learning, language, and language learning. They are interested in both the process of their students' learning as well as the products that result in order: 1. to share their professional insights with their students and their parents; 2. to use their insights reflectively for purposes of continuous curriculum planning and professional growth; and 3. to provide permanent records as a history of their students' experiences in school. They are involved in ongoing interpretive evaluation. Over the years such evaluation has often been called informal, but I prefer to avoid that term since it reflects a view of evaluation that assumes that only controlled and quantifiable evaluation is worthy of being considered formal (Note the title for this article as compared with Roger Farr's in this volume).

Fred Erickson (1987) uses the term interpretive in a relevant and significant article on "Qualitative Methods in Research on Teaching" in relation to classroom research because of a "central research interest (among a range of qualitative researchers) in human meaning in social life and in its elucidation and exposition by the researcher" (p. 119). In a similar way, the term *interpretive evaluation* can be used to suggest evaluation that is integral to the ongoing daily experiences that teachers use to elucidate and explicate the nature of learning and teaching at the same time that they are building meanings about the social life of the classroom. The questions interpretive researchers and teachers who use interpretive evaluation ask and the uses they make of the information gathered in classroom settings are often different, but the methodology each uses to collect and analyze the information are similar. Teachers who are consciously aware of the significance of their role in interpretive

OOSOORB OB SOT

MARLENE

FIGURE 27B–1.

evaluation have similar views about the nature of human beings as do researchers who engage in interpretive research.

CALL FOR RESEARCH ON INTERPRETIVE EVALUATION

Ongoing interpretive evaluation has been little researched. In 1967 the Association for Supervision and Curriculum Devel-

opment published *Evaluation as Feedback and Guide* (Wilhelms, 1967) with the purpose of "understanding the role of evaluation in education." In a section of the book focusing on alternative views of evaluation, the authors explored the answers to questions such as:

How does a learner's ceaseless evaluation shape a lifetime of becoming? How does the teacher handle precise and clear evaluation in response to the learner so it leads to challenge rather than threat; to encouragement rather than defeat; to a richer more valid self-image rather than need-distortion; and to the involvement of the learner in a cooperative, ongoing inquiry rather than to imposition by the teacher (p. 47).

The ASCD Yearbook Committee called for research to understand the role of evaluation in education. In the past two decades, although there has been abundant research on the use of testing in response to the committee's recommendation, there has been little research that would address the issues related to alternative views of education including those of interpretive evaluation. In a special issue of *The Reading Teacher* (Squire, 1987) on the state of reading assessment, there are a number of articles that address issues of teacher evaluation in the classroom; however, there is no documentation of research on such evaluation.

What I hope to accomplish in this article is:

1. Explore why there is a paucity of research on interpretive evaluation;
2. Provide a theoretical rationale for the use of interpretive evaluation;
3. Explore why professionals must find ways to legitimatize research on the use of such evaluation techniques; and
4. Suggest some specific activities that might be included in doing such research.

THE PAUCITY OF RESEARCH ON INTERPRETIVE EVALUATION

Although classroom research has been gaining respectability in the field of educational research (Erickson, 1987), there are agencies that still won't fund research that does not have an experimental design, and there are institutions that still restrict graduate students from designing research to evaluate their own classroom practices and from applying ethnographic research techniques to classroom settings.

Classroom research has provided educationists with knowledge about classroom interactions and about the meanings being generated by students and teachers in classroom settings. At the present time there is still limited knowledge however, that documents:

1. Continuous interpretive evaluation teachers do;
2. Responses and understandings of students that result from ongoing interpretive evaluation;
3. Degree to which teachers are consciously aware of the evaluative processes they are engaged in;
4. Effectiveness of interpretive evaluation on teachers' professional development and the growth of students and;
5. Role such evaluation plays for parents, subsequent teachers, administrators, and other interested members of the school community.

The lack of research in this area is due, in part, to the belief that interpretive evaluation is informal and subjective and there

fore not to be valued or taken seriously. At the same time it is not uncommon to hear people say that such evaluation is too difficult and time consuming. Research on such evaluation calls for longitudinal studies for which there is little financial or institutional support. In addition, since such research is often not valued, researchers are reluctant to expend a great deal of energy on research that does not yield much recognition from the reward system within academic institutions.

Other issues that limit research on interpretive evaluation are related to the knowledge and time needed to analyze, interpret, and discuss the information collected. Research, especially when the focus is the English/language-arts classroom, involves careful analysis of language experiences and products, often after school hours, as well as the continuous observation and interaction with students within the classroom setting. It takes a good deal of knowledge and understanding about language processes—reading, composition, oral discourse, and text analysis—and about curriculum and evaluation in order to do research on interpretive evaluation. Such research is not easy nor can it be done quickly or neatly.

Yet, from the point of view of scholars who support a constructionist point of view of learning, knoweledgable evaluative interpretation of what students are doing is precisely the kind of evaluation that ultimately has the most impact on students' growth in all language areas, on the professional development of teachers, and on the potential for significant changes for teaching and curriculum development. Research is necessary to document this impact.

RATIONALE FOR RESEARCH ON ONGOING INTERPRETIVE EVALUATION

All teachers are constantly involved in evaluation whether they are consciously aware of doing so or not. This ongoing evaluation reflects their beliefs about schooling, their theories and knowledge about language, about humans, about development and learning. Teachers are involved in evaluating individual students, groups of students, and whole classrooms. They make decisions about instruction based on these evaluations and in so doing are reflecting on themselves as professionals. In other words, as they evaluate their students, they are not only involved in curriculum development but in the process of self-evaluation as well.

Teachers' comments and behaviors in classrooms and teachers' lunchrooms, at conferences and social gatherings indicate the wide range of evaluative judgements they make about their students. Researchers have documented that teachers respond differently to different kinds of students in classrooms. They may correct the oral reading miscues of their slower students, yet when their better readers make the same miscues, they seem to overlook or not be aware of their productions. Students with different language backgrounds get more or less wait time from teachers when they are asked questions. Teachers ask certain students more difficult questions than others based on their often unexamined views of the students' abilities (Allington, 1980; Hoffman, 1987; McDermott, 1974). Teachers frequently comment that one class is more difficult than another; that one group of children is working more independently than another. These responses indicate the degree to which teachers are continuously involved in evaluation and suggest that their evaluative judgements are the basis for instructional decisions that teachers make daily about the lives of their students. It is interesting to note that in reviews on teachers' decision-making, although there is discussion about teacher judgement, there is no obvious link expected between teachers' ongoing decision-making and the evaluation of students (Shavelson & Stern, 1981). I believe this is related to viewing evaluation as an end product of teaching and not as an ongoing and continuous process. Unfortunately, if the field of education does not consider continuous evaluation significant to the teaching/learning process and does not develop ways to study such evaluation, then we allow the subtle unstated actions in classrooms to impact students' lives without any consideration whatsoever.

If we accept the assumption that teachers are indeed evaluating at all times, then it is necessary to call for serious research into such activities. Such research will help teachers who are not yet consciously aware of their tacit evaluation to become more reflective about their responses to students. For informed teachers such as Mary, Don, Carole, and Nancie, who talk and write about the power of such evaluation on their own teaching and the growth of their students, research will legitimatize their professional inquiry into their teaching and their evaluation of students (Goodman, Goodman, & Hood, 1989).

Research that is to have any important impact on interpretive evaluation must include the teachers being studied, either as principal investigators or as collaborators. Interpretive research (Erickson, 1987) is one of the best methodologies to use to study interpretive evaluation in classroom settings. In this way the meanings that teachers have about the impact of ongoing interpretive evaluation in classroom settings will be well understood. Through such understandings, professional educators will become more consciously tuned into the power of interpretive evaluation on teacher change, learning, and the development of students.

Teachers who observe students with a perspective based on the latest knowledge and theories about language and learning, who question students in ways that support their development, who know the significance of the nature of error, who organize the kinds of environments in which students are willing to take risks in their language use promote language development in their classrooms and are reflective about their teaching. Dewey argued for the importance of reflective thinking on the part of teachers:

It (reflective thinking) emancipates us from merely impulsive and merely routine activity . . . (It) enables us to direct our activities with foresight and to plan according to . . . purposes of which we are aware. It enables us to act in deliberate and intentional fashion to . . . come into command of what is now distant and lacking. By putting the consequences of different ways and lines of action before the mind, it enables us to know what we are about when we act. It converts action that is merely appetitive, blind, and impulsive into intelligent action. (Archambault, 1964, p. 212).

Professionals who understand their power and their ability to observe development in students make use of inquiry for their own purposes. They begin to realize that they are developing professional responses to their students' language activities. They know how to ask questions that reflect their own theoretical view of teaching, learning, and language. They find ways to answer their own questions and to solve their own problems through reading, involvement with other professionals, careful evaluation of the oral and written language of their students, and continuous evaluation of their English/language-arts curriculum. They confidently question educational theory, the results of the research, and new innovations in curriculum and material development (Moll, 1988). They are learners and inquirers of their own professional activities.

There are growing numbers of teachers seriously taking on the role of learner and inquirer. Many have begun writing about their experiences. Some call themselves writing process teachers, others whole language teachers, teachers who believe in language across the curriculum, integrated curriculum, or curriculum devoted to serious problem solving on the part of their students. Nancie Atwell has described such teachers, reflecting on herself as a teacher/researcher (NCTE Conference Presentation, Boston, 1988).

LEGITIMIZING ONGOING INTERPRETIVE EVALUATIVE RESEARCH IN THE CLASSROOM

Erickson (1987) states that fieldwork for purposes of interpretive research involves:

(a) intensive, long-term participation in a field setting;
(b) careful recording of what happens in the setting by writing field notes and collecting other kinds of documentary evidence;
(c) analytic reflection on the . . . record obtained and reporting by means of detailed description. (p. 118)

In ongoing interpretive evaluation, the teacher has an intensive and long-term relationship with those being evaluated (the teacher and the students); the teacher keeps careful notes and collects other kinds of documentary evidence, reflecting continuously on the nature of what the records and other related evidence mean in terms of student growth and professional self-evaluation.

Teachers may not be able to be as thorough as the researcher in analyzing all the data, but they may be even more reflective. Teachers are not studying the activities of outsiders but trying to understand the meanings of what they are doing, what the students are doing, and how these activities relate to each other and influence development and growth in students.

Evaluation like research is also based on asking questions, although many of the questions teachers ask about evaluation will be different than the questions researchers ask.

Teachers questions might include: How does what I do influence what students are doing? What do the students' productions reveal about their linguistic and conceptual knowledge and their intellectual functioning? In what ways do classroom experiences with reading, writing, speaking, and listening influence the students' products? To what degree are students consciously aware of their own processes? How does this conscious awareness or lack of it influence students' compositions and comprehension?

At the same time that teachers use the answers to their questions to continuously plan instructional experiences for students, researchers will ask a different set of questions in order to explore the nature of interpretive evaluation. Their questions might include: What are the interaction patterns that influence evaluation by the teacher and self-evaluation on the part of students? What kinds of questions do teachers ask of themselves and of students in order to evaluate? How do teachers learn to ask different types of questions? What devices do teachers use to answer their own questions about students' development, about curriculum, and about their own professional development? In what ways do outside-of-school language experiences influences students' compositions and comprehension? Answers to these kinds of questions among many others will inform the profession in general about the nature of ongoing interpretive evaluation. If researchers are working collaboratively with teachers, answers to these questions will provide teachers with information about the growth of individual students, about how various groups of students work together in classroom settings, and about how the community outside of the classroom influences teaching and learning.

Erickson (1987) lists reasons for interpretive research on teaching. One is the "need for specific understanding through documentation of concrete details of practice." As has been stated, teachers are involved in ongoing evaluation in all phases of teaching. They make judgments constantly about students that may support or hinder student growth. Although classroom research has focused on many aspects of classroom practice, it needs to more specifically focus on the kinds of influences that ongoing interpretive evaluation has on teaching and learning English/language arts.

SUGGESTIONS FOR RESEARCH ON INTERPRETIVE EVALUATION

We need to examine various aspects of ongoing interpretive evaluation through the use of interpretive research methodology using participant-observation fieldwork for researchers and for classroom teachers as well. Erickson argues that "The results of interpretive research are of special interest to teachers, who share similar concerns with the interpretive researcher. Teachers too are concerned with specifics of local meaning and local action; that is the stuff of life in daily classroom practice" (p. 156).

Collaboration between teachers and researchers is important because teachers working alone in the classroom may not always have the time or the opportunity to observe carefully enough. Together with a researcher, however, the teacher has another informed person's perspective on the meanings being expressed in the classroom setting. The researcher on the other hand gains a view of the classroom from someone who is extremely knowledgeable about daily life in that contextual setting and who can explain meanings that might take a researcher as a participant observer months and years to understand. When teacher and researcher collaborate by reading each other's field notes and deliberate carefully about their respective meanings, they build a stronger case for their understandings and conclusions (Matlin & Wortman, 1989).

Whether researchers or teachers are working collaboratively or alone, there are a number of techniques especially relevant to the English/language arts to help gather the kinds of information that would result in answering questions and developing important insights.

Many instruments that can be used to collect such information are documented in *Measures for Research and Evaluation in the English Language Arts, Vol. 2* (Fagan, Jensen, & Cooper, 1985). Others can be found in recent publications that feature writing process and whole language teachers' descriptions of their own classrooms (Goodman, Goodman, & Hood, 1989; Hanson, Newkirk, & Graves, 1985; Meek, Armstrong, Austerfield, Graham, & Pakcett, 1983).

Checklists, Inventories, and Interviews

Checklists, inventories, and interviews allow teachers to see change in their students and in their teaching. Answers to questions that focus on students' attitudes about language, the kinds of materials they read, and the range of topics they write about provide insight into students' beliefs about the power of language and its influence on their lives. Changes in such beliefs and attitudes can be traced across time and to specific curricular activities. Students can also be involved in recording their own work with a focus on self-evaluation. Research can document the use of such record keeping, its impact on students and reveal what understanding students and teachers have regarding the meanings of record keeping, its uses, and its purposes.

Portfolios and Samples of Work

In programs where students write regularly and participate in literature-based reading programs, teachers keep portfolios of students' written work, which may include tapes of oral reading, lists of readings, reading responses, results of reading conferences between the teacher and the student, and selections of oral and written compositions. It would be important to document:

1. Ways that teachers collect, store, and analyze students' speech acts and literacy events;
2. Students' behaviors as they participate in reading, writing, and oral language activities;
3. ways teachers respond to students during such activities;
4. How students respond to teacher's comments, interactions, and questions;
5. Kinds of information teachers want to know in order to make the best use of the student's work portfolio;

6. Ways that the analysis of such work influences teachers' views about language processes and instruction

Other questions that research can detail include: Do teachers make use of special trait scoring, holistic scoring, miscue analysis, or other ways of analyzing students' work? How do such ways of evaluating become internalized? Do teachers use them in informal and incidental situations or only in carefully planned and formal ways? In what ways do teachers believe such knowledge helps them in working with students? In what ways do teachers use such knowledge to help students develop techniques of self-evaluation?

Teacher educators and researchers who have examined the use of miscue analysis by teachers (Long, 1985) report that teachers discuss the reading process in more sophisticated ways and often indicate that they will never be able to listen to students read in the same way that they did prior to learning miscue analysis procedures (Goodman, Watson, & Burke, 1987). Teachers who involve their students in writing on a regular basis often question the use of holistic scoring when they realize that it masks specific growth over time. They begin to ask insightful questions about linguistic systems, cohesive analysis, voice, sense of story, and genre variations in order to be able to analyze and understand more about their students' development. I am more aware of this growth from working with teachers in in-service courses and professional development workshops. It would be important to know how these changes that teachers are able to talk about is manifest in their actual daily interactions with their students.

Dialogue Journals and Learning Logs

For those teachers who use dialogue journals (Staton, 1984) or learning logs with their students on a regular basis, it would be helpful to document teachers' responses to journals or logs to discover what this reveals about teacher evaluation, how teachers help students reflect on their own learning, and how teachers reflect in their curriculum planning what they've learned from such experiences. Analysis of teachers' responses to classroom experiences kept regularly in logs or as field notes would also yield important information about interpretive evaluation. Questions that researchers and teachers could explore include: In what ways do teachers respond to students' journals to allow students to become more reflective about their own processes? In what ways are different kinds of responses from the teacher reflected in what the students write or think about? In what ways do journals and logs reveal the meanings students and teachers have about classroom contexts, especially as it relates to evaluation? In what ways do journals and logs reveal self-evaluation on the part of teachers and students?

In Japan there are teachers who analyze carefully the impact their written responses to students' writing have on the writing development of students (Kitagawa & Kitagawa, 1987). Similar insights gained from the analysis of teachers' responses to dialogue journals and learning logs would provide important information about the impact journals and logs have on student growth, teacher evaluation of students, self-evaluation on the part of both teachers and students, and teacher change.

Anecdotal Records

Discussions about anecdotal records are usually found in sections labeled informal assessment techniques in professional language-arts textbooks. However, a carefully documented record of the setting of a particular significant event accompanied by information about time, persons involved, and other important aspects of the social context is one of the most useful pieces of evaluative information a teacher can have. It provides a record that a number of interested parties can review independently or discuss together to interpret its possible meanings. It provides opportunities for students to verify the teacher's perceptions. In many ways, anecdotal records are akin to the anthropologist's field notes or to a psychologist's case study.

Discussions about anecdotal records often assume that the records are kept in the same way, at exact specified intervals, and in the same form throughout a school year. However, my experiences verified by others who also use anecdotal records suggest that such records change over time depending on the time of the year, the knowledge the teacher has accumulated about the student, and the particular kinds of information the teacher is trying to gather. Early in the year teachers may make very regular and detailed entries about many aspects of reading, writing, speaking, and listening, but as teachers get to know their students, the type of entries change focusing more specifically and are recorded only when a relevant activity occurs. The dynamic nature of whole language classrooms suggest that teachers who take responsibility for their own evaluation change the kinds of use they make of their evaluative instruments as well as the form of the instrument and the kinds of information they decide to document (Goodman, Goodman, & Hood, 1989). The ways that teachers change their documentation of student growth, why and when they change the instruments they use are all kinds of understandings that need to be carefully researched to understand how anecdotal records help teachers in the evaluation of their students and at the same time help both teachers and students in self-evaluation.

Observation Techniques: Kidwatching

As teachers are working directly with the students, they often step back to observe students and, in such moments of professional observation, make evaluative judgements about the students that inform instructional planning. Research questions that can provide needed documentation about professional observations include: How do teachers build a professional sense across time that helps them understand what they are looking at, what they are looking for, and what their observations mean in terms of student evaluation and curriculum planning? Why are some teachers more confident about their abilities in professional decision making about student evaluation than others? How do teachers' interpretive evaluations match the perceptions of students?

I call this kind of observation "kidwatching" (Goodman, 1978, 1985) to highlight its ongoing and interpretive nature within the classroom setting in the hands of a professional. Kidwatching may be one of the major forces that influences teachers' reflective thinking about evaluation of students and the planning of instructional activities in the classroom. Kidwatching is not as conscious as it probably needs to be for teachers to gain the greatest insights from it. The ways teachers react to these observational moments in the classroom deserve serious study in order to understand the nature and the influences of kidwatching on curriculum development and instruction. Indeed, such study will provide understandings about the nature of teaching itself. It will reveal the development of a professional sense: the ability of teachers to understand how to respond to students in order to enhance their growth. This relates significantly to the concept of the zone of proximal development (Vygotsky, 1986).

Questioning and Interactions

There is a wide range of issues concerning the nature of questions and interactions between teachers and students relating to ongoing interpretive evaluation in the classroom that can be addressed through research. How do the kinds of questions teachers ask of students reflect what teachers understand about language and language learning? When do teacher questions and interactions and what types of questions and interactions move students toward greater intuitive leaps in thinking and conceptual development? What kinds of teachers' questions focus students' attention on aspects of language learning that help them learn about language in appropriate ways? What is the nature of teachers questions and interactions that enhance learning or interfere with learning? How do interactions and questions by teachers and students differ in large-group settings, small-group settings and in one-on-one relationships? How do students' questions reflect the use of questions by teachers?

Conferences

A major aspect of the writing process curriculum that has become popular in recent years includes the use of different kinds of conferences between the teacher and the students in response to their writing. Teacher-student conferences have also focused on students' reading and other language activities and provide important avenues to both student and teacher evaluation. Although a good deal has been written about such conferences, there has been a lack of in-depth research detailing different kinds of conferences, their various procedures and purposes, the language structures that occur during such conferences, the meanings students and teachers have about such conferences, and its impact on student growth.

Collaborative Learning

There is growing insight into the nature of collaborative learning in classrooms (Pontecorvo, 1987; Pontecorvo & Zuc-

chermaglio, 1990; Teberosky, 1982). This includes not only peer interactions but the collaborations between students and the teacher. Ongoing interpretive research would be helpful to gain in-depth understandings of how these learnings influence interpretive evaluation.

Student Self-Evaluation

Self-evaluation and record keeping by students and how parents are involved in the evaluation are also an important aspect of the kind of evaluation that has been under discussion. The analysis of how students develop self-evaluation techniques, how teachers support such a process, and how parents are involved in a student's evaluation would be most informative.

IN ANTICIPATION

The purpose here is not to be exhaustive concerning the potential research within the classroom that will result in significant and necessary information to help educational professionals understand constant and ongoing interpretive evaluation. Rather, I have suggested possibilities for research that will result in greater legitimacy for the kind of evaluation that I have been advocating. Once interpretive evaluation is taken seriously, valued in an appropriate manner, and understood better, the ways that such techniques can be used and studied in classroom settings will grow dynamically.

It is fitting therefore to conclude by quoting from a parent's evaluative response to a teacher's evaluation system that results in the kind of interpretive evaluation that has been explored in this article. It reflects the issue that the total school community is an integral part of ongoing interpretive evaluation and would benefit from the research on such evaluation.

Dear Ms. D.

I just finished reading R.'s self evaluation form and I had to sit down and tell you about how I feel. With teachers of three children to see, a parent often has to stop and see teachers in trouble areas first and catch the others later or miss them totally. Unfortunately, I put your class in that trouble free category. After talking with you at open house and talking with R., I felt quite comfortable with skipping you at conference time.

R.'s dad and I know that R. is quite capable in doing her schoolwork and if problems arise they are probably in social areas as she is approaching her teen age years.

Back to the evaluation. Your developing this tool was an excellent idea in my estimation. Of course I know it's a pleasure to read that your child is doing well and is able to express it and why in writing. But I also think that if my child were having problems, reading this form would help to point them out.

As a parent involved for the past twelve years in this school, I have never received a form that dealt so clearly with communicating to parents the child's progress and ability and reason for the grade. I appreciate your effort in developing and using this form of communication. Keep talking to kids and parents and you will have reached us all.

Thanks so much for all your efforts.

F. D.

References

Allington, R. (1980). Teacher interruption behaviors during primary-grade oral reading. *Journal of Educational Psychology, 72,* 371–377.

Archambault, R. (Ed.). (1964). *John Dewey on education.* Chicago: University of Chicago Press.

Atwell, N. (1987). *In the middle.* Portsmouth, NH: Boynton Cook.

Atwell, N. " 'Wonderings to Pursue': The Writing Teacher as Researcher," NCTE Conf. Presentation, Boston, 1988.

Erickson, F. (1987). Qualitative methods in research in teaching. *Handbook on research in teaching.* In V. K. Richardson (Ed.), American Education Research Association. pp. 119–160.

Fagan, J., Jensen, J., & Cooper, C. (1985). *Measures for research and evaluation in the English language arts, Vol 2.* Urbana, Il: ERIC/ NCTE.

Goodman, K., Goodman Y., & Hood, W. (Eds.). (1989) *The whole language evaluation book.* Portsmouth, NH: Heinemann Educational Books.

Goodman, Y. (1978, June) Kidwatching: An alternative to testing. *The National Elementary Principal.* pp. 41–45.

Goodman, Y. (1985) Kidwatching: Observing children in the classroom. In A. Jaggar & M. T. Smith-Burke (Eds.). *Observing the language learner.* Urbana, IL and Newark, DE: NCTE and IRA. pp. 9–18.

Goodman, Y., Watson, D., & Burke, C. (1987). *Reading miscue inventory: Alternative procedures.* New York: R. C. Owen.

Hanson, J., Newkirk, T., & Graves, D. (Eds.). (1985) *Breaking ground* Portsmouth, NH: Heinemann.

Hoffman, J. (1987). Rethinking the role of oral reading in basal instruction. *The Elementary School Journal, 87* (3), 367–374.

Kitagawa, M. M., & Kitagawa, C. (1987). *Making connections with writing.* Portsmouth, NH: Heinemann.

Long, P. (1985). *The effectiveness of reading miscue instruments.* (Occasional Paper #13). Program in Language and Literacy. Tucson, AZ: University of Arizona.

Marek, A., Howard, D., Disinger, J., Jacobson, D., Earle, N., Goodman, Y., Hood, W., Woodley, C., Wortman, J., Wortman, R. (1984). *The kidwatchers's guide: A whole language guide to assessment.* (Occasional Paper #9). Program in Language and Literacy. Tucson, AZ: University of Arizona.

Matlin, M. and Wortman, R. "Observing readers and writers: A teacher and a researcher learn together" In Pinell, G. S. and Matlin, M. L. (Eds.) *Teachers and Research: Language Learning in the Classroom* Newark, DE: International Reading Association, 1989.

McDermott, R. (1974). Achieving school failure: An antropological approach to illiteracy and social stratification. In G. D. Spindler, (Ed.), *Education and Cultural Processes* (pp. 82–118). N.Y: Holt, Rinehart and Winston.

Meek, M., Armstrong, S., Austerfield, V., Graham, J., & Pakcett, E. (1983). *Achieving literacy: Longitudinal studies of adolescents learning to read.* London: Routledge & Kegan Paul.

Moll, L. (1988). Some key issues in teaching Latino students. *Language Arts.* 65 (5), pp. 465–473.

Pontecorvo, C. (1987). Discussing for reasoning: The role of argument in knowledge construction. In E. De Corte, J. G. L. C. Lodewjks, R. Parmentier, & P. Span (Eds.), *Learning and instruction.* European Association for Research for Learning and Instruction Oxford/Leuven: Pergamon Press/Leuven University Press.

Pontecorvo C., & Zuccermaglio, C. 1990. A passage to literacy: Learning in a social context. In Y. Goodman (Ed.), *How children construct literacy: Piagetian perspectives.* Newark DE: International Reading Association.

Shavelson, R. J., & Stern, P. (1981). Research on teachers' pedagogical thoughts, judgements, decisions, and behavior. *Review of Educational Research 51* (4), pp. 455–499.

Staton, J. (1984, November). Research ideas: Using school records. *Dialogue 2,* 3. p. 6. Washington, DC: Center For Applied Linguistics.

Squire, J. (Ed.). (1987, April). A special Themed Issue: The state of assessment in reading. *The Reading Teacher, 40* (8).

Teberosky, A. (1982). Construccion de escritura atraves de la interaccion grupal. In E. Ferriero & M. Gomez Palacio (Eds.), *Nuevas perspectivas sobres los procesos de lectura y escritura.* Mexico City: Siglo Veintiuno Editores.

Vygotsky, L. (1986). In Kozulin, (Ed.), *Thought and language.* Cambridge, MA: The MIT Press.

Wilhelms, F. (Ed.). (1967). *Evaluation as feedback and guide.* Washington DC: Association for Supervision and Curriculum Development.

27C. TEACHER-BASED ASSESSMENT OF LITERACY LEARNING

Elfrieda H. Hiebert

Teachers have an abundance of information about their students' literacy accomplishments and about their classrooms as literate environments. As teachers examine students' writing, they can see the influence of particular authors whose books the class has read. As teachers listen to students in a social studies lesson, they can detect whether a critical perspective toward authors' points of view taught in reading extends to discussions with expository content.

Teachers' knowledge of their students' accomplishments and learning opportunities is quite different than the view that comes from standardized tests. Tests give an index of an individual's standing relative to other students on a specific task and at a particular point in time; they cannot provide the insight of a teacher into students' abilities to extend strategies to new types of text or to oral language contexts.

Over the years, and even more so in the last decade as school reform efforts have interpreted evidence of learning as higher test scores, tests have come to drive instruction. Although the concern of the school reform movement for better learning is well-intentioned, the outcome of this emphasis on multiple-choice tests has been less than desirable. An overemphasis on test scores appears to have trivialized the curriculum (McNeil, 1988).

Standardized tests provide one type of information and undoubtedly will remain as one means of describing children's school learning. Recent changes in tests such as longer passages and better questions (Valencia & Pearson, 1987; Wixson, Peters, Weber, & Roeber, 1987) promise to better capture higher-level reading processes. Despite these encouraging efforts, the thesis of this chapter is that attention must also be paid to information gathered by teachers and students as part of classroom life.

Two arguments can be made for increased attention to teacher-based assessment. First, critical literacy goals like students' ability to self-select high-quality literature or to detect bias in their writing cannot be assessed adequately through multiple-choice tests. If students' progress toward such goals is to be captured, data from children's participation in classroom literacy events must be added to that from tests. Second, teacher-based assessment underlies effective instruction. If even a small fraction of the resources devoted to standardized testing was devoted to improving teachers' assessment skills, many teachers would be better equipped to create more effective learning environments for students.

This chapter reviews existing literature with the aims of synthesizing work on teacher-based assessment into a unified perspective and suggesting next steps to align current practice with available knowledge on teacher-based assessment. Assessment of literacy will be the focus in this review. Although outside the classroom, comprehension and composition processes are more likely to occur through oral than written language, little attention has been given to assessment of students' abilities to compose and comprehend orally. Illustrations will be given of ways that comprehension and composition can be assessed through speaking and listening, but space does not permit a thorough discussion of issues involved in assessment of oral language capabilities. Nor, for that matter, can all issues related to assessment of composition and comprehension of written language be presented here. The aim is to raise fundamental issues related to teacher-based assessment of literacy, with the acknowledgement that everything could not be included or dealt with as comprehensively as might be needed.

While studies of teacher-based assessment practices are few, a growing body of scholarship is available. The literature on portfolios illustrates this work. Suggestions for practice are many; studies that consider implementation and effects on students, classrooms, and teachers are infrequent. Many of these ideas, however, derive from theoretically sound rationales and proven practice. This chapter presents current work in the field, some emanating from research but much more deriving from scholarship that summarizes or outlines effective practice.

A MODEL OF TEACHER-BASED ASSESSMENT

Some elements of teacher-based assessment have a long history. For example, informal reading inventories date back at least to the 1920s (Gray, 1920). This tradition, as Johnston (1984) notes, was not the path chosen by policymakers. However, many suggestions regarding informal or alternative assessment techniques are aimed at teachers. Most teachers appear to follow this advice in only a limited way. A variety of explanations for this failure can be given, not the least of which is the lack of value given to these data beyond classrooms. For such data to have credibility beyond classrooms and to be useful to teachers, integrated views of teacher-based assessment are required.

Expanding on Cronbach's (1960) identification of careful observations, a variety of methods and measures, and integration of information as the three principal features of assessment, Calfee and Hiebert (1988) have proposed that teachers participate in several processes. These processes are setting goals and purposes, gathering information, and interpreting and acting on information. These activities are synonymous with the processes of effective instruction. In other words, assessment in this view is embedded in instruction, rather than seen to run parallel to or compete with instruction.

The underlying assumption is that assessment occurs in the service of some instructional purpose. Information about students' strategies and knowledge assists teachers in their instructional planning. When goals and purposes are clear, the nature of the required information becomes apparent. For example, the number of samples and level of documentation may be quite different when teachers are gathering information to guide students in new genres in writing than when they are communicating information to parents about children's progress.

Typically, teachers are interpreting and acting on information as they gather it. As teachers listen to students respond in a discussion, they are assessing students' knowledge and processes. These on-the-spot interpretations may lead to changes in the questions that a teacher asks or in the activities themselves. For example, when a teacher realizes that students are unfamiliar with a topic, semantic mapping may be added to a lesson. Although occasions for teachers to reflect on student work occur rarely as part of formal school structures, such opportunities are caught in bits and pieces throughout the school day or after school. Times for interpretation and decision-making, even informal ones, are necessary. The processes of purpose-setting, information-gathering, and interpreting and acting on information are recursive, rather than linear, but at times, each phase becomes the center of attention. How this occurs is described next.

Setting Goals and Purposes

The basis of assessment is the teacher's vision of literacy. A technique like observation can be used to capture trivialities just as easily as it can be used to sample profound aspects of literacy. The questions that guide teachers' assessment and their interpretations of children's products and processes will be determined by a view of literacy. Teachers who believe that children must be able to verbalize phonics generalizations will focus on that ability, while teachers who view literacy as the construction of meaning will focus on children's interpretations of different texts.

Even in the immediate past, very different visions of literacy can be found. Within the mastery-learning model that dominated the 1960s and 1970s, reading was viewed as the acquisition of a hierarchical set of skills (Otto, 1977). Consensus has formed for an alternative view that emphasizes the construction of meaning. Descriptions of this view can be found in a variety of sources (Anderson, Hiebert, Scott, & Wilkinson, 1985; Calfee, 1988; Goodman, Shannon, Freeman, & Murphy, 1988). Although educators may disagree about some elements of this model (e.g., the amount of attention to specific features of print that novices require), they agree on its general framework. Literacy, in this view, is the process of constructing meaning, either from text written by others or in generation of text for others. Successful readers and writers employ strategies for monitoring their progress in constructing meaning. Manifestations of these strategies may appear quite differently with first graders than sixth graders. Consequently, visions of literacy require some clarification as to how a literate individual appears at different points of development. The same fundamental processes such as acting strategically, however, underlie comprehension and composition at all stages.

As well as drawing teachers' attention to particular dimensions of literacy, the focus of the constructive model on intentional, strategic activity impacts teacher-based assessment in another way. This emphasis means that teachers attend to the processes in which students are engaged, not just the products. Products are not disregarded; however, how readers and writers plan, monitor, and revise their interpretations as they read and write becomes of interest as well. As teachers delve into students' thinking processes rather than simply examine products, they will uncover surprises. For example, when students' reasoning behind incorrect responses on multiple-choice tests is elicited, their explanations often indicate inferences much more sophisticated than the simple responses expected by the testmaker (Langer, 1987).

Discussions of teacher-based assessment are pertinent only in so far as teachers' purposes for using information are clear. Teachers use information for a variety of purposes, the primary of which is to plan instructional experiences for children. Information on students' existing strategies and knowledge is necessary for choosing materials and activities, forming groups, and determining the appropriate amount of teacher direction. Information-gathering can also assist teachers as they guide children in setting goals and as they talk with parents or children about progress toward these goals.

Information-Gathering

A survey of reading methodology textbooks produces a variety of assessment techniques that are usually termed informal: performance samples, conferences, questioning, observations, checklists, portfolios, inventories, surveys, and interviews. A list of techniques is not helpful to teachers without some understanding of their functions. Techniques can be collapsed into three basic activities on the part of the teacher: 1. observing, 2. talking with students through questioning or interviewing, and 3. sampling student work. A description of the methods involved in observing, questioning or interviewing, and sampling student work follows. A final component examines methods of furthering students' self-assessment. Within a view of literacy users as active participants, the ability of students to monitor and assess their progress toward critical goals is viewed as an important outcome of a literacy program.

Observing. As students work in the many contexts of classrooms, teachers are observing them and gaining information about their knowledge and strategies. Sometimes, these observations occur in unlikely settings, such as casual comments that students make on the playground or on the way to lunch. The wealth of information gained from observations makes it understandable that teachers identify these as their most important source of information and downplay standardized test results in comparison (Dorr-Bremme & Herman, 1986; Salmon-Cox, 1981).

Although most scholars would agree with Goodman (1985, this volume) on the critical role of teacher as "kid-watcher," the systematicity of teachers' observations is another matter. Because human beings observing the same event can see very different things, it is not surprising that teachers see different things when observing the same instructional episode (Berliner, 1986). A lack of consistency in teachers' conclusions about classroom events or students' actions is understandable, considering the nature of guidance that teachers receive in preparation programs. Attention to assessment is limited in most teacher education programs (Schafer & Lissitz, 1988), and

TABLE 27C–1. Examples of Information Gained From Observing

Observations of Children's Library Selection Strategies
1. Looked for particular topic, author, illustrator, or title
2. Thumbed through book(s)
3. Sampled print or examined pictures
4. Discussed book(s) with peer or adult
5. Chose book(s) without looking inside

Discussions of Children's Library Selection Strategies
1. Topic or story
2. Author or series
3. Illustrations
4. Information from a book talk or a friend
5. Easiness or difficulty of book
6. Familiarity or unfamiliarity of book

Source: K. B. Mervar, 1989, pp. 93–94. Unpublished doctoral dissertation, University of Colorado, Boulder.

even that tends to be devoted to standardized tests. Rarely do preservice teachers discuss commonalities or disagreements in observations of instruction, either videotaped or on-the-spot. More typically, preservice teachers observe in separate classrooms, for short periods of time, and with little more than their own attitudes to orient observations or guide interpretations. A preservice teacher, viewing children engaged in writing groups, may be more concerned with the teacher's maintenance of order than with students' comments about writing. Once teachers have their own classrooms, opportunities are even fewer to observe other teachers or to share interpretations of commonly observed instructional events with other teachers. When teachers are guided in evaluation, outcomes are positive. A training session as short as a month can increase considerably the consistency of teachers' evaluation of information (Gil, Polin, Vinsonhaler, & Van Roekel, 1980).

Although teachers cannot possibly begin to document all their observations, documentation on some occasions can assist reflection and sharing information with students, parents, administrators, and the next year's teacher. Telling a parent that his or her child has a difficult time contributing to writing groups becomes more meaningful when the teacher's notes show that the child failed to participate in the group on four of the five observed occasions.

Checklists can be helpful in teachers' documentation in that they specify particular dimensions for observation and provide a means for summarizing observations. Table 27C–1 illustrates information that was gained through observations of students while they selected books. These categories, and those that evolved out of discussions with students about their reasons for selecting books, can be used to guide future observations. Teachers may also wish to substitute or supplement such category schemes with notes. For example, a note written down during independent reading time that some children are repeatedly soliciting assistance from others in figuring out unknown words may remind the teacher of the need for guidance in alternative strategies.

Observations have a benefit in that information can be gained on students' behaviors in everyday settings. Evaluative contexts like tests can produce less than optimal performances for many students (Hill, 1984; Mosenthal & Na, 1980). Observations permit teachers to gain information about students in everyday settings that do not have the constraints of tests. When this information is combined with analyses of student work samples, a comprehensive view of students' processes and products within particular domains is gained.

Observations should not be limited to children's accomplishments but should also consider the nature of literacy experiences. It may well be that children's failure to progress reflects lack of opportunities to participate in activities or to receive guidance rather than any deficiency in capability. For instance, problems in children's reports may be explained by a lack of opportunities to learn how to integrate information from different sources. Without such guidance, children may merely be copying facts from one information source, followed by the facts from another. Assessing the instructional experiences that are available to children provides another critical source of information for teachers.

Questioning and Interviewing. Included under the rubric of questioning and interviewing are several activities that involve teacher-student interaction. Questioning will be used here to refer to the interaction between students and teachers that occurs in typical classroom contexts. Interviewing implies more structured interactions than those that occur daily in classrooms. These interactions typically involve individual students and are organized around a specific task or set of questions. When faced with large classes, teachers may find it impossible to interview children as often as they would like. On some dimensions like establishing interest in topics for writing or reading, teachers may choose to administer questionnaires or surveys that involve written responses. Such surveys pose a different context than do questioning in daily classroom contexts or individual interviews. Thus, the three types of interaction are treated separately.

The most frequent type of classroom interaction is for teachers to question students (Cazden, 1986). Often, teachers' question fail to engage children in high-level thinking and do little more than test students' recognition of facts (Durkin, 1978, 1979). Recent work, however, provides guidance for teachers in both the content and process of questioning.

A number of frameworks are available to guide teachers in interactions about the comprehension and composition of narrative. One such framework delineates the elements of stories like problem and resolution (Beck & McKeown, 1981). Whether students are talking about stories they are reading or ones that they are writing, story structure elements provide a useful guide for capturing students' thinking about narrative text.

Pearson and Johnson's (1978) scheme directs teachers' attention to considering the relationship of their questions to the text and background knowledge of students. Raphael (1986) has taken this framework one step further in that students are taught about question-answer relationships. In the case of "Right There" questions, for example, students look in the text for the material, while students need to draw on their background knowledge with "On My Own" questions. Similarly, an understanding of the structures of expository text can assist teachers in their questioning of students and students in asking questions of themselves and one another. When students are made aware of different structures in expository text, such as compare-contrast and cause-effect, their writing and comprehension can improve (Raphael, Englert, & Kirschner, 1986).

Dynamic assessment guides teachers in how to interact with students. This concept comes from the work of Vygotsky (1962) and has been extended by Brown & Reeve (1985). Vygotsky's notion of the zone of proximal development suggests that students may perform at one level when working independently but, with guidance, may be capable of higher levels of performance. This band between students' independent functioning and their performances with guidance is termed the zone of proximal development. Assessment is dynamic in the sense that teachers provide a framework or scaffold that requires students to increasingly rely on their own devices. The dynamic assessment perspective has much to offer teachers in their questioning and, also, in an overall stance toward assessment of students. This perspective makes it clear that teachers need to consider various factors that impact students' performances such as texts (e.g., narrative, expository) and tasks (an evaluative setting versus a cooperative one) (Brown, Campione, & Day, 1981).

As teachers interact with students, an awareness that different linguistic and cultural backgrounds typically mean unique communicative patterns can go a long way in creating classroom contexts where children express themselves adequately. The discontinuity between interaction patterns of children's culture and that of the school has been illustrated with a variety of cultures (e.g., Au & Mason, 1981; Heath, 1982; Phillips, 1983). Studies have also shown that classroom environments can be created that allow the communicative patterns of children from nonmainstream cultures to be recognized (Au & Jordan, 1981; Heath, 1982). Some general shifts in participation structures in classrooms can create interaction that is more amenable for all children. For example, moving from rigid test question formats that originate only with the teacher to formats where children are encouraged to contribute questions and comments creates more student participation and learning (Palincsar & Brown, 1984).

Guidance for classroom interaction also comes from recent work in writing as a process (Calkins, 1986; Graves, 1983). In writing workshops, several contexts create different opportunities for students to interact with one another and the teacher. The "author's chair" provides opportunities for students to question one another in a large group, while small peer groups allow children to interact more intensively about their compositions. Teachers' questioning occurs primarily in individual settings as they conference with children about their compositions.

Although teacher-student interactions during writing conferences are not structured interviews, they illustrate the translation of interviewing into classroom routines. In addition to quick, frequent interactions that occur as part of teacher-student conferencing, teachers need opportunities to talk in-depth with individual students about specific topics or tasks. Among the interviews used by teachers are those developed by Johns

TABLE 27C–2. Planning Questions of the Index of Reading Awareness

1. If you could only read some of the sentences in the story because you were in a hurry, which ones would you read?	
0^1	a. Read the sentences in the middle of the story.
2	b. Read the sentences that tell you the most about the story.
1	c. Read the interesting, exciting sentences.
2. When you tell other people about what you read, what do you tell them?	
2	a. What happened in the story.
0	b. The number of pages in the book.
1	c. Who the characters are.
3. If the teacher told you to read a story to remember the general meaning, what would you do?	
2	a. Skim through the story to find the main parts.
1	b. Read all of the story and try to remember everything.
0	c. Read the story and remember all of the words.
4. Before you start to read, what kind of plans do you make to help you read better?	
0	a. You don't make any plans. You just start reading.
1	b. You choose a comfortable place.
2	c. You think about why you are reading.
5. If you had to read very fast and could only read some words, which ones would you try to read?	
1	a. Read the new vocabulary words because they are important.
0	b. Read the words that you could pronounce.
2	c. Read the words that tell the most about the story.

Source: J.E. Jacobs & S.G. Paris, "Children's metacognition about reading: Issues in definition, measurement and instruction," *Educational Psychologist*, 22, p. 269. Copyright © 1987 by Educational Psychologist.

[1]Indicates score given to the response; 2 = strategic responses that were planful and exhibited awareness of reading goals and strategies, 1 = responses that describe a general cognitive act indicating an understanding that some extra effort and special thinking will be required to remember the material; 0 = inappropriate responses.

(1986) and Burke (1980) on the nature and processes of reading. One question, for example, in Burke's interview queries students as to what they would do to help someone who has difficulty reading. These questions can easily be adapted to writing. Information in these interviews can be even more insightful when questions are asked with respect to particular compositions or books. Because time is teachers' most precious commodity, they will not be able to interview students frequently. Even so, setting time aside periodically to talk with individuals can provide teachers with information they might not gain otherwise.

Surveys are one response to the time constraints of interviewing. Jacobs and Paris's (1987) Index of Reading Awareness can give teachers insight into large groups of students' strategies in evaluating, planning, and regulating their reading. The questions on planning one's reading that appear in Table 27C–2 could be used in an interview, but Jacobs and Paris' categorization of typical responses assists teachers who wish to get information quickly on many students. Numerous measures can also be found that survey children about their interests in different topics and their feelings toward reading and writing (see, e.g., Estes, 1971; Heathington, 1979). Since children's interests in topics can change frequently (Asher, 1977), surveys of topics and interests can assist children in developing an awareness of how these factors enter into their reading and writing, as well as aid teachers in making choices about topics of demonstration lessons in writing and in selecting books for instruction, reading aloud, and the classroom library.

Sampling Student Work. Performance samples refer to some form of student work that remains as an artifact that teachers, students, and others can reflect upon. Sampling student work is not a new idea, although the notion has been rejuvenated recently through portfolio assessments. Even tests can be regarded as samples of performances, although the samples are gained in an atypical situation and with limited response modes. Recent efforts by teachers, districts, and state departments of education illustrate a broader interpretation of sampling student work through portfolios (see, e.g., Flood & Lapp, 1989). The original use of the term portfolio came from the collections that artists and architects have of their best work. In education, portfolios more typically consist of samples that represent particular genres or tasks over a period of time rather than students' best work. Even so, the idea of examining samples of work that come from everyday settings, rather than from test settings, is restructuring assessment in many classrooms, school districts, and even state departments of education (see, e.g., Brewer, 1989). Of course, teachers can sample student work without a portfolio system. Students' written comments about point-of-view in narrative passages might be compared to their analyses of point-of-view in expository passages.

Sampling students' writing presents unique issues and has a different history than sampling students' reading. Because compositions are concrete and can be gained easily, written samples have been very much in the limelight as part of the current portfolio movement. In summarizing students' written work, teachers are guided by a long tradition of evaluation in the field of writing. The first is a differentiation between quantitative and qualitative aspects of writing. Simple counts of elements like adjectives, T-units, words, or sentences can be used as gross indicators of progress. For example, if children write stories of only several lines, lessons on story structure have little application.

The insight gained from counting features gives only part of the picture of students' knowledge and strategies. Holistic scoring techniques allow teachers to consider students' writing in-depth. Two basic types of scoring are included among the various holistic techniques (see Cooper, 1977). In the first, pieces are given one rating for overall quality (often in reference to prototypical pieces). For example, on the last National Assessment of Educational Progress for reading, students' summaries of the author's purpose in a passage that they had read were scored on a four-point scale—inadequate, minimal, satisfactory, and elaborated (Applebee, Langer, & Mullis, 1988).

In the second type of holistic scoring, ratings are given to a number of different dimensions of a set of compositions, frequently referred to as features or primary traits. An example of a scoring scheme used to assist teachers in their assessment and instruction of writing, as well as a district's evaluation, is presented in Table 27C–3. This scheme illustrates the manner in which criteria for scores related to a feature such as message quality can be defined.

Single global ratings of students' compositions (such as inadequate or satisfactory) may be helpful for accountability purposes but usually will not provide sufficient information for the classroom teacher in planning instructional experiences. For classroom purposes, schemes that focus on specific dimensions are more helpful. The compositions of children who have been working on mysteries, for example, might be rated for creation of setting and maintenance of suspense. Reports might be rated for coherence of the organization and elaboration of ideas within paragraphs. Aspects of students' oral communication and reading can also be scored holistically. Students' oral reports, for example, might be rated for organization and use of examples. Oral reading could be scored holistically for fluency and retellings could be scored for critical elements of stories.

Historically, the evaluation of reading has been somewhat different than the holistic scoring schemes of writing. Analyses in the form of the informal reading inventory have been used for decades (see, e.g., Gray, 1920). In informal reading inventories, children's errors when reading graded passages orally have been analyzed for quantity, and their responses to questions have been analyzed as right or wrong. Informal reading inventories go beyond simple counting of errors, in that errors are classified by type (e.g., omissions, insertions) and error patterns are used to ascertain areas of needed work such as context clues or main idea. Despite this emphasis on patterns of errors, the use of informal reading inventories has remained largely quantitative in that numbers of oral reading errors or incorrect comprehension responses are used to establish students' frustration, instruction, and independent reading levels.

Goodman (1968), while still sampling children's oral reading and retelling, used students' miscues or deviations from texts to establish their underlying understandings of semantic, syntactic, and graphophonic systems of written language. Children's miscues were viewed as windows into their knowledge of those systems. Thus, the concern was not with establishing the right grade level for oral reading but in sampling students' reading appropriately so that their strategies would become apparent.

Administration and analysis of either the miscue analysis or informal reading inventory techniques take a considerable amount of time. A recent survey shows that even those teachers who have been trained in using informal reading inventories do not use them frequently (Harris & Lalik, 1987). Miscue analyses and informal reading inventories are frequently presented in their entirety to teachers, leaving the expectation that it is all or nothing. Because the process is costly in terms of time, teachers fail to use these measures. Such a rejection is unfortunate because teachers can find a variety of suggestions for applying miscue analysis techniques in everyday settings, without administering the complete miscue procedure (see, e.g., Marzano, Hagerty, Valencia, & DiStefano, 1987). In small groups or teacher-student conferences, teachers can take notes on students' oral reading. Or teachers might periodically have students read a short passage or two (e.g., self-chosen versus teacher-chosen

TABLE 27C–3. Criteria for Evaluating Writing[1]

Trait	Level	Criteria
Message Quality	1–2	Unclear focus; no elaboration of ideas; no evidence of awareness of intended reader
	3–4	Message is communicated, although focus may change; elaboration occurs through additional evidence or details; ideas, information, genre, register not consistent.
	5–6	Tightly focused message; ideas and details create a mood, tone; ideas, information, genre, register are chosen to communicate message.
Coherence	1–2	No relationships among ideas; lacks clear organizational design; no transitions.
	3–4	Organizational design, differentiation of important from less important ideas, and some transitions linking ideas beginning to appear.
	5–6	Relationships among ideas are established through order or subordination; organizational design is compatible with purpose; transitions used effectively to move ideas in a smooth, clear sequence.
Language	1–2	Flat, unimaginative language is used; sentences are incomplete, run-on, or simple.
	3–4	Simple sentences are used effectively and attempts are made in variety of imaginative language, word order, and type and length of sentences.
	5–6	Fresh, imaginative language is used to create an image and capture reader's interest such as leads, strong verbs, vivid descriptions, figures of speech; word order and type and length of sentences are varied for emphasis or effect.
Language Conventions	1–2	Many spelling, grammatical, punctuation, capitalization, and format errors make message difficult to understand.
	3–4	Some errors are made in spelling, grammar, capitalization, punctuation, and format.
	5–6	Conventions of spelling, grammar, capitalization, punctuation, and format are observed at developmental level.

[1]This is a modified version of the Criteria for Evaluating Writing developed by School District #12, Adams County (CO).

or narrative versus expository) and get a grasp of their strategies.

Furthermore, a critical contribution of miscue analysis should not be lost sight of by teachers. Miscue analysis provides a stance toward children's errors, whether these are in oral reading, speaking, or writing. When teachers view children's attempts as evidence of their underlying strategies and knowledge, they can obtain valuable information. Although children's early spelling efforts may miss the mark when judged by conventional spelling, thoughtful examination of these efforts can indicate the nature of children's underlying knowledge about relationships between letters and sounds (Read, 1986). In listening to children's retellings of stories for underlying strategies and knowledge rather than for the right answer, teachers may find that children are making conclusions that fit in perfectly with their background knowledge. Rather than viewing what children do as mistakes to be corrected, the stance of miscue analysis calls for teachers to view children's deviations from the expected as clues to what they do know.

Frequently, performance-based assessment of reading uses written samples, such as summaries of what has been read, literature logs, or journals. This use of writing to assess reading reflects the recognition of reading and writing connections (Pearson & Tierney, 1984). The emphasis on language use as a constructive, strategic process has also contributed to moving attention away from decoding in oral reading to comprehen-

sion. Furthermore, it is much easier to obtain written samples for a class of children than samples of their oral reading and retellings. Although the ability to express one's self in writing is obviously a critical dimension of sharing interpretations from reading, too heavy an emphasis on writing can skew the evaluation process for some students. However, ways can be found that use writing to capture children's comprehension but do not place excessive demands on writing skill. In one assessment (Massachusetts Assessment of Educational Progress, 1987), fourth-grade students write phrases that predict the contents of a passage, based on the beginning sentences of an article. This task assesses the fundamental reading strategy of activating prior knowledge relative to a topic, without overly taxing writing ability.

Teachers' understanding of cultural and linguistic uniquenesses can influence their evaluation of performance samples, just as they do their observations and discussions. Sometimes, children's use of African American English dialect is interpreted as evidence of decoding problems (Burke, Pflaum, & Krafle, 1982). Misjudgments can also be made with children for whom English is a second language on the basis of their fluency or lack thereof. Bilingual children can be quite proficient at retelling, despite numerous miscues in their oral renditions of passages (Miramontes & Commins, 1989).

The manner in which misjudgments related to children's cultures and languages enter into teachers' assessments of writing is less clear, although some studies suggest that surface indicators such as grammar and handwriting influence teachers' judgments about written products more than message quality or coherence of ideas (Chase, 1979; Stewart & Grode, 1979). Much of the research from which that conclusion derives occurred before extensive staff development efforts in writing as a process. It would be assumed that teachers trained in writing as a process would respond more to the quality of the message and the organization of the composition than to usage. There can be no doubt that a view toward alternative interpretations of students' efforts can go a long way in creating an understanding of students' capabilities and needs.

Self-Assessment by Students. In the majority of classrooms and for the majority of time, assessment emanates from the teacher. On those infrequent occasions when students participate in the assessment process, their involvement is nominal such as checking a fellow student's spelling list against the answers that the teacher has placed on the board. Much more rare is the classroom where children are asked to identify goals and monitor their progress toward those goals. The consequences of externally driven assessment systems in classrooms are evident (Ames & Ames, 1984; Johnston & Winograd, 1985). When students are driven by external rewards such as grades, the consequences on their learning can be negative.

Several promising developments in literacy instruction suggest greater student involvement in planning and monitoring learning. The emphasis of the last decade on metacognition is one such development. Although instructional interventions in classrooms illustrate the manner in which teachers can guide children in becoming more metacognitive about a variety of dimensions of reading and writing (see, e.g., Duffy et al., 1987), no evidence exists on how a metacognitive stance has impacted the assessment practices of most teachers. It would be expected that guidance in metacognition would support students' participation in the assessment process along with that of the teacher.

Another promising development for enhancing the self-assessment of children lies in the peer interaction that is part of writing experiences (Calkins, 1986; Graves, 1983). There are at least two points in writing activities where peer response is elicited. One is through peer conferences, when children meet in groups of two or three to discuss one another's pieces. The other is through large group sessions where children sit in the "author's chair" and share their efforts. The reports of many teachers suggest that children become more knowledgeable about what they are doing as a result of such experiences.

Peer interactions as part of reading instruction have not received the same amount of attention as they have in writing, although suggestions for such involvement have been made (Hiebert, 1980). One component of the successful cooperative learning program in reading of Slavin and his colleagues (Stevens, Madden, Slavin, & Farnish, 1987) involves peers working with one another but, at least in the existing reports of this program, the efficacy of this practice is difficult to extract from the program's many components. The success of peer involvement in writing, however, suggests that such interactions hold promise for students' involvement in monitoring, planning, and assessing their comprehension.

TABLE 27C–4. Example of a Self-Evaluation Form
While I was reading how did I do? (Put an X in the appropriate column.)

	Not very much	A little bit	Much of the time	All of the time
Made predictions				
Formed pictures				
Used "like-a"				
Found problems				
Used fix-ups				

Source: B. Davey, "Think Aloud—Modeling the cognitive processes of reading comprehension." *Journal of Reading, 27,* p. 46. Copyright © 1983 by Journal of Reading. Reprinted with permission of Beth Davey and the International Reading Association.

Guides to assist students in self-assessment or in peer assessment are also springing up in books and journals for teachers and in commercial programs. Although such guides are popular in writing programs, especially for editing and revising, some instruments are also oriented to aiding students in assessing their planning and monitoring in reading. The self-evaluation guide in Table 27C–4 stems from research on the strategies of good readers. Students monitor their application of strategies during reading, with the goal of increasing the use of these strategies.

Another example of guiding students in self-assessment comes from Project Zero (Wolf, 1989), which uses portfolios for assessment of writing and fine arts. While teachers interact with students in deciding what to put into portfolios, students are responsible for their selections. Furthermore, portfolios include a diary or journal in which students reflect on the progress that they can detect in their portfolio entries.

Assessing one's abilities and gauging the next step is an important part of learning of any type. This element has not been a major concern in literacy programs, although there are indications that emphases on metacognition and writing as a process are beginning to create more opportunities for students to assess their progress.

Interpreting and Acting on Information

Teaching is not a process where activities fall into neat categories. Consequently, assessment does not begin with goal-setting, move next to gathering information, and end with interpreting and acting on information. Teachers often alter their course in the midst of an activity, whether its aim be instruction or assessment. A teacher's line of questioning may change quickly, as an insight is gained into students' strategies or knowledge. Even though the school environment may not be structured for times of collegial or even individual reflection, teachers constantly reflect on their students and activities but often at unexpected times and places. In the case of the teacher whom Kidder (1989) studied, a commute to and from school was used to reflect on students and activities. Even during the hiatus between one school year and the next, teachers' minds are busy, reviewing what happened with their students during the previous year and using this information to plan the curriculum and activities of the next year.

Although times for reflection and collegial interaction in decision-making are a goal of school restructuring efforts (see, e.g., Hiebert & Calfee, 1989; Schaefer, 1967), the concern here will not be on the nature of decision-making when such restructuring has occurred but with decision-making within the circumstances that many teachers find themselves. Several ideas should underlie teachers' thinking as they reflect on the information they have gathered. These ideas can easily be integrated into preservice and inservice courses and may even contribute to making teacher-based assessment more credible and usable beyond the classroom.

The first idea has to do with the reliability of information. Reliability directs teachers to reflect on consistency of performances in the same situations from day to day. Teachers' thoughts turn to variables that might have impinged upon students' performances. For example, a disruptive recess preceding a writing period may contribute to dramatic shifts in a student's writing from one day to the next. Before they make conclusions, teachers should consider alternative explanations about students' products and processes.

A second idea is related to the validity of teacher-based assessments. The question here is whether the particular information that has been gathered reflects the crucial representations of the domain. Typical standardized tests of reading comprehension evaluate students' responses to questions about short paragraphs. Many argue, however, that other procedures such as assessments of students' ability to capture the author's purpose in an extended text are more accurate representations of comprehension. Similarly, before they make conclusions about students' accomplishments in a particular domain, teachers should question whether or not their information captures the critical aspects of the domain of interest. For example, in the criteria for evaluating writing in one school district, mechanical aspects of compositions dominated, with less emphasis on the meaning conveyed (Hagerty, Owens, Hiebert, & Fisher, 1989). Even though samples of student work were being used as the basis for assessment, the evaluation criteria were not capturing the goals of teachers' writing programs that emphasized mechanics in the service of the message. A new scheme was devised that placed heavier emphasis on the quality of the message, language, and coherence (see Table 27C–3).

Especially critical to teachers' interpretations of the information they have gathered is understanding the impact of cultural and linguistic uniquenesses on classroom performances. It may well be that some children's performances are easily explained, if viewed from another vantage point. Even children's willingness to express themselves in classroom contexts may be a function of different cultural norms or facility with English. Because children from nonmainstream cultures are often placed in programs that emphasize skill and drill (Moll, Estrada, Diaz, & Lopez, 1980), teachers should think about previous learning experiences before they make generalizations about children's capabilities. For example, children's lack of fluency in writing may reflect few previous opportunities to write in literature logs or journals.

Even though information may be shared with parents or administrators, the primary reason for teachers to gather information in their classrooms is to assist student learning. At one point or another, teachers use information to adapt, initiate, or eliminate learning experiences in their classrooms.

DIRECTIONS

For practice to align with the existing knowledge base on teacher-based assessment requires effort on at least two fronts. The first is preservice and inservice experiences; the second is a solid research base that verifies the nature and effects of teacher-based assessment practices.

Preservice and Inservice Experiences in Teacher-Based Assessment

Analyses of textbooks, course content, and inservice programs lead to the same conclusion. Guidance for teachers in teacher-based assessment has been minimal (Calfee & Hiebert, 1988; Dorr-Bremme & Herman, 1986; Schafer & Lissitz, 1988). Even those who advocate teachers as evaluation experts (e.g., Goodman, 1985; Johnston, 1987) provide little indication of the manner in which teachers gain this expertise. Teaching has been a profession very different than a field like clinical psychology, which also relies on expertise in assessment. Clinical psychologists have internships in the hundreds of hours. At best, teachers have a course on evaluation and assessment that most likely emphasizes test development.

To date, no research has been concerned with verifying the features of staff development or teacher education programs that are successful in creating teacher expertise in assessing students. Some informed predictions can be made about the form that such expertise would take, based on experiences with a variety of school districts in several states. A composite has been developed from these school districts.

In this school district, teams of teachers identified goals of their literacy programs. These goals were large enough in scope to be significant but not so large that it would be unclear if a student had accomplished the goal. For example, one goal was for students to understand the themes of different kinds of texts. The manner in which these goals would be manifest at different developmental levels was identified. Even though first-grade students might be expected to understand that there are problems in stories that characters need to resolve, their abilities to extract themes from stories and to develop these themes in their own writing would be expected to be less well developed than the efforts of third- or fifth-grade students.

Once goals had been identified, ways of assessing student' acquisition of goals within and beyond instructional activities were established. The school district is now in the process of offering inservice sessions in which teachers at school sites work on implementing instructional and assessment activities for particular goals. Part of this inservice consists of teachers observing one another in implementing instructional and assessment strategies in their classrooms.

Several characteristics of this program should be noted. The first is that the changes emanated from teachers' concerns. As state mandates have focused more on test scores, teachers have protested that standardized tests do not capture the goals of their classroom programs. The district responded by supporting ways to supplement standardized test data.

A second characteristic is the school site as the unit of change. A very different sense of collegiality exists among teachers when, performance samples in hand, they interact about their students' progress than when teachers meet with ill-defined goals.

The concentration to this point on directions for inservice programs is not meant to diminish the need for changes in preservice teacher education programs. Expertise in observing children, analyzing samples of their work, and conducting interviews would result from the laboratory experiences that Berliner (1985) has described as critical to teacher education programs. In this proposal, Berliner describes university-based laboratories in addition to field-based ones. Field-based situations give prospective teachers the opportunity to apply knowledge as they interview youngsters and observe them in the busyness of day-to-day classroom life. In laboratory contexts, prospective teachers can reflect on students' processes and products as they mull over videotapes of classroom events, analyze transcripts of class discussions, and study samples of student work.

Research

On the basis of scholarship and good practice, a rather coherent argument can be made that classroom environments are more conducive to learning when students and teachers are involved in planning, monitoring, and assessing as part of daily classroom tasks. Sooner or later, however, some data confirming the nature and effects of teacher-based assessments will be needed. The proof of teacher-based assessment cannot be expected through the simplistic evaluations of classroom practice that measure effectiveness solely by student test performances. A broader view of what constitutes evidence for practices is required. Two lines of research illustrate the form that this evidence could take.

The first line of research has to do with descriptive research of existing practices in the classrooms of expert teachers. Information on the ways that assessment weaves through the instruction and planning of expert teachers will provide models for other teachers and also substantiate the notion that assessment is very much tied to good instruction.

A second line of research would describe changes in classroom environments when assessment is a more integral part of teachers' instructional practices. This research would document changes in teacher-student interaction, student tasks, and student outcomes as teachers become more facile at observing, questioning, and sampling student work. A critical part of this work would be the documentation of changes in students' perceptions and performances, as their self-assessments are integrated into classroom decision-making.

Conclusion

The conversation about assessment is beginning to shift to include teacher-based assessment, as evidenced by reports from policy centers (e.g., Archbald & Newman, 1988), journals (e.g., Brandt, 1989; Squire, 1987), and state policies (e.g., Brewer, 1989). If critical goals of literacy are to be captured and if teachers are to become more adept in creating optimal instructional environments, teacher-based assessment must be a critical dimension of this conversation. Teachers' expertise in assessment depends on support from a number of different sources. For one, school and district administrators need to value teachers' expertise as a legitimate source of information about students' attainment of the goals of literacy. Another group whose practices must change dramatically are schools of education because a solid foundation in teacher-based assessment should be part of teachers' training, not something to be acquired on the job. Hopefully, educators at all levels will unite to facilitate greater expertise in teacher-based assessment among the nation's teachers.

References

Ames, R., & Ames, C. (Eds.). (1984). *Motivation in Education: Student Motivation* (Vol. 1). New York: Academic Press.

Anderson, R. C., Hiebert, E. H., Scott, J. A., & Wilkinson, I. A. (1985). *Becoming a nation of readers*. Champaign, IL: Center for the Study of Reading.

Applebee, A. N., Langer, J. A., & Mullis, I. V. S. (1988). *Who reads best? Factors related to reading achievement in Grades 3, 7, and 11*. Princeton, NJ: National Assessment of Educational Progress & Educational Testing Service.

Archbald, D. A., & Newman, F. M. (1988). *Beyond standardized testing*. Reston, VA: NASSP.

Asher, S. R. (1977). *Sex differences in reading achievement* (Reading Education Rep. #2). Champaign, IL: Center for the Study of Reading.

Au, K. H., & Jordan, C. (1981). Teaching reading to Hawaiian children: Finding a culturally appropriate solution. In H. T. Treuba, G. P. Guthrie, & K. H. Au (Eds.), *Culture and the bilingual classroom: Studies in classroom ethnography*. Rowley, MA: Newbury House.

Au, K. H., & Mason, J. M. (1981). Social organizational factors in learning to read: The balance of rights hypothesis. *Reading Research Quarterly, 17*, 115–152.

Beck, I. L., & McKeown, M. G. (1981). Developing questions that promote comprehension: The story map. *Language Arts, 58*, 913–918.

Berliner, D. C. (1986). In pursuit of the expert pedagogue. *Educational Researcher, 15*, 5–13.

Berliner, D. C. (1985). Laboratory settings and the study of teacher education. *Journal of Teacher Education, 36*, 2–8.

Brandt, R. (Ed.). (1989). Special issue on "Redirecting Assessment." *Educational Leadership, 46*.

Brewer, R. (1989, June). *State assessments of student performance.* Presentation at the 19th Annual Assessment Conference sponsored by Education Commission of the States, Colorado Department of Education. Boulder, CO.

Brown, A. L., Campione, J. C., & Day, J. D. (1981). Learning to learn: On training students to learn from text. *Educational Researcher, 10,* 14–21.

Brown, A. L., & Reeve, R. A. (1985). *Bandwidths of competence: The role of supportive contexts in learning and development* (Tech. Rep. No. 336). Urbana IL: University of Illinois, Center for the Study of Reading.

Burke, C. L. (1980). Reading interview. In B. R. Farr & D. J. Strickler (Eds.). *Reading comprehension: An instructional videotape series* p. 71. (Resource Guide). Bloomington, IN: Indiana University Press.

Burke, S. M., Pflaum, S. W., & Krafle, J. D. (1982). The influence of Black English on diagnosis of reading in learning-disabled and normal readers. *Journal of Learning Disabilities, 15,* 19–22.

Calkins, L. M. (1986). *The art of teaching writing.* Portsmouth, NH: Heinemann.

Calfee, R. C. (1988). *Indicators of literacy: A monograph for the Center for Policy Research in Education.* Santa Monica, CA: The Rand Corporation.

Calfee, R. C., & Hiebert, E. H. (1988). The teacher's role in using assessment to improve literacy. In C. U. Bunderson (Ed.), *Assessment in the service of learning* (pp. 45–61). Princeton, NJ: Educational Testing Service.

Cazden, C. B. (1986). Classroom discourse. In M. C. Wittrock (Ed.), *Handbook of Research on Teaching* (3rd Ed.) (pp. 432–463). New York: Macmillan Publishing.

Chase, C. I. (1979). The impact of achievement expectations and handwriting quality on scoring essay tests. *Journal of Educational Measurement, 16,* 39–42.

Cooper, C. R. (1977). Holistic evaluation of writing. In C. R. Cooper & L. Odell (Eds.), *Evaluating writing: Describing, measuring, judging* (pp. 3–31). Champaign, IL: NCTE.

Cronbach, L. J. (1960). *Essentials of psychological testing* (3rd Ed.). New York: Harper Row.

Davey, B. (1983). Think aloud—Modeling the cognitive processes of reading comprehension. *Journal of Reading, 27,* 44–47.

Dorr-Bremme, D. W., & Herman, J. L. (1986). *Assessing student achievement: A profile of classroom practices* (CSE Monograph #11). UCLA: Center for the Study of Evaluation.

Duffy, G., Roehler, L., Sivan, E., Rackliffe, G., Book, C., Meloth, M. S., Vavrus, L. G., Wesselman, R., Putnam, J., & Bassiri, D. (1987). Effects of explaining the reasoning associated with using reading strategies. *Reading Research Quarterly, 22,* 347–366.

Durkin, D. (1978, 1979). What classroom observations reveal about reading comprehension instruction. *Reading Research Quarterly, 14,* 481–533.

Estes, T. H. (1971). A scale to measure attitudes toward reading. *Journal of Reading, 15,* 135–138.

Flood, J., & Lapp, D. (1989). Reporting reading progress: A comparsion portfolio for parents. *The Reading Teacher,* 508–514.

Gil, D., Polin, R. M., Vinsonhaler, J. F., & Van Roekel, J. (1980). *The impact of training on diagnostic consistency* (Technical Report No. 67). East Lansing, MI: The Institute for Research on Teaching.

Goodman, K. S. (1968). The psycholinguistic nature of the reading process. In K. S. Goodman (Ed.), *The psycholinguistic nature of the reading process* (pp. 13–26). Detroit: Wayne State University Press.

Goodman, K. S., Shannon, P., Freeman, Y., & Murphy, S. (1988). *Report card on basal readers.* New York: Richard C. Owen Publishers.

Goodman, Y. (1985). Kidwatching: Observing children in the classroom. In A. Jaggar & M. T. Smith-Burke (Eds.), *Observing the language learner.* Newark, DE: International Reading Association.

Graves, D. (1983). *Writing: Teachers and children at work.* Exeter, NH: Heinemann.

Gray, W. S. (1920). The value of informal tests of reading achievement. *Journal of Educational Research,* 103–11.

Hagerty, P., Owens, M. K., Hiebert, E. H., & Fisher, C. W. (1989, December). *Growth in comprehension, metacognition, and writing in literature-based classrooms: A follow-up study.* Paper presented at the annual meeting of the National Reading Conference, Austin, TX.

Harris, L. A., & Lalik, R. M. (1987). Teachers' use of informal reading inventories: An example of school constraints. *The Reading Teacher, 40,* 624–630

Heath, S. B. (1982). Questioning at home and at school: A comparative study. In G. Spindler (Ed.), *Doing the ethnography of schooling: Educational anthropology in action* (pp. 102–131). New York: Holt, Rinehart & Winston.

Heathington, B. S. (1979). What to do about reading motivation in the middle school. *Journal of Reading, 22,* 709–713.

Hiebert, E. H. (1980). Peers as reading teachers. *Language Arts, 57,* 877–881.

Hiebert, E. H., & Calfee, R. C. (1989). Advancing academic literacy through teachers' assessments. *Educational Leadership, 46,* 50–54.

Hill, K. T. (1984). Debilitating motivation and testing: A major educational problem—Possible solutions and policy. In R. Ames & C. Ames (Eds.), *Research on motivation in education: Student Motivation (Vol. 1).* New York: Academic Press.

Jacobs, J. E., & Paris, S. G. (1987). Children's metacognition about reading: Issues in definition, measurement, and instruction. *Educational Psychologist, 22,* 255–278.

Johns, J. L. (1986). Students' perceptions of reading: Thirty years of inquiry. In D. B. Yaden, Jr., & S. Templeton (Eds.), *Metalinguistic awareness and beginning literacy: Conceptualizing what it means to read and write* (pp. 31–40). Portsmouth, NH: Heinemann.

Johnston, P. H. (1984). Assessment in reading. In P. D. Pearson (Ed.), *Handbook of reading research.* New York: Longman.

Johnston, P. H. (1987). Teachers as evaluation experts. *The Reading Teacher, 40,* 744–748.

Johnston, P. H., & Winograd, P. N. (1985). Passive failure in reading. *Journal of Reading Behavior, 17,* 279–301.

Kidder, T. (1989). *Among schoolchildren.* Boston: Houghton Mifflin.

Langer, J. A. (1987). The construction of meaning and the assessment of comprehension: An analysis of reader performance on standardized test items. In R. O. Freedle & R. P. Duran (Eds.), *Cognitive and linguistic analyses of test performance.* Norwood, NJ: Ablex.

Marzano, R. J., Hagerty, P. J., Valencia, S. W., & DiStefano, P. P. (1987). *Reading diagnosis and instruction: Theory into practice.* Englewood Cliffs, NJ: Prentice-Hall.

Massachusetts Department of Education (1987). *Reading and thinking: A new framework for comprehension.* Massachusetts Educational Assessment Program.

McNeil, L. M. (1988). Contradictions of control, Part 2: Teachers, students, and curriculum. *Phi Delta Kappan,* 433–438.

Mervar, K. B. (1989). *Amount of reading in and out of school and book-selection skills of second-grade students in textbook-based and literature-based programs.* Unpublished doctoral dissertation, University of Colorado-Boulder.

Miramontes, O., & Commins, N. L. (1989, April). *A study of oral and reading proficiency of mixed dominant Hispanic students.* Paper presented at the annual meeting of the American Educational Research Association, San Francisco, CA.

Moll, L. C., Estrada, E., Diaz, E., & Lopes, L. M. (1980). The organization of bilingual lessons: Implications for schooling. *The Quarterly Newsletter of the Laboratory of Comparative Human Cognition, 2,* 53–58.

Mosenthal, P., & Na, T. J. (1980). Quality of children's recall under two classroom testing tasks: Towards a socio-psycholinguistic model of reading comprehension. *Reading Research Quarterly, 15,* 504–528.

Otto, W. (1977). *Wisconsin design for reading skill development.* Minneapolis, MI: National Computer Systems.

Palincsar, A. S., & Brown, A. L. (1984). Reciprocal teaching of comprehension-fostering and comprehension-monitoring activities. *Cognition and Instruction, 1,* 117–175.

Pearson, P. D., & Johnson, D. (1978). *Teaching reading comprehension.* New York: Holt, Rinehart & Winston.

Pearson, P. D., & Tierney, R. J. (1984). *On becoming a thoughtful reader: Learning to read like a writer* (Reading Ed. Rep. No. 50). Champaign, IL: Center for the Study of Reading.

Philips, S. U. (1983). *The invisible culture: Communication in the classroom and community on the Warm Springs Indian Reservation.* New York: Longman.

Raphael, T. E. (1986). Teaching question answer relationships, revisited. *The Reading Teacher, 39,* 516–523.

Raphael, T. E., Englert, C. S., & Kirschner, B. W. (1986). *The impact of text structure instruction and social context on students' comprehension and production of expository text.* (Research Series No. 177). East Lansing, MI: Michigan State University Institute for Research on Teaching.

Read, C. (1986). *Children's creative spelling.* Boston: Routledge & Kegan Paul.

Salmon-Cox, L. (1981). Teachers and standardized achievement tests: What's really happening? *Phi Delta Kappan, 62,* 631–634.

Schaefer, R. J. (1967). *The school as a center of inquiry.* New York: Harper & Row.

Schafer, W. D., & Lissitz, R. W. (1988, April). *The current status of teacher training in measurement.* Paper presented at the annual meeting the National Counil on Measurement in Education, New Orleans, LA.

School District #12 (1989). *Criteria for evaluating writing (Grades 2-6).* Thornton, CO: School District #12, Adams County.

Squire, J. (Ed.). (1987). The state of reading assessment. *The Reading Teacher, 40* (8).

Stevens, R., Madden, N., Slavin, R., & Farnish, A. (1987). Cooperative integrated reading and composition: Two field experiments. *Reading Research Quarterly, 22,* 433–454.

Stewart, M. F., & Grode, C. H. (1979). Syntactic maturity, mechanics of writing, and teachers' quality ratings. *Research in the Teaching of English, 9,* 37–46.

Valencia, S., & Pearson, P. D. (1987). Reading assessment: Time for a change. *The Reading Teacher, 40,* 726–732.

Vygotsky, L. (1962). *Thought and language.* Cambridge, MA: MIT Press.

Wiggins, G. (1989). Teaching to the (Authentic) test. *Educational Leadership, 46,* 41–47.

Wixson, K. K., Peters, C. W., Weber, E. M., & Roeber, E. D. (1987). New directions in statewide reading assessment. *The Reading Teacher, 40,* 749–754.

Wolf, D. P. (1989). Portfolio assessment: Sampling student work. *Educational Leadership, 46,* 35–39.

·28·

MATERIALS

28A. THE SELECTION AND USE OF LANGUAGE ARTS TEXTBOOKS

Janice A. Dole
Jean Osborn

> As long as the text dominates curricula, to ignore it as simply not worthy of serious attention is to live in a world divorced from reality.
> (Apple, 1985, p. 159)

Many observers of American education today have commented on the ubiquitous presence of textbooks in American classrooms. In a survey conducted in the early 1980s, teachers reported using instructional materials during 90 to 95 percent of classroom time, and textbooks about 70 percent of that time (Komoski, 1985). While Komoski argued that textbooks have been used by teachers and students quite extensively in the past, it appears that textbooks have become even more relied upon in recent years. Komoski believes that "many states and local districts essentially delegate-by-default their curriculum design work and instructional decision making to the developers and publishers of instructional materials" (1985, p. 32).

Various scholars concur with Komoski's assertions. For example, Apple (1985) asserted that textbooks have come to legitimize the knowledge made available in schools, and that standardized grade level textbooks have come to define not only a national curriculum but instructional programs in all subject areas. A number of classroom observers have noted how much of the decision-making about curriculum and instructional issues is left up to textbooks (Brophy, 1982; Duffy & McIntyre, 1982; Hodges, 1980; Jackson, 1981; Resnick and Resnick 1985; Talmage & Eash, 1979; Woodward, 1986).

Despite the long-standing and widespread use of reading and language arts textbooks in particular, the contents and instructional effectiveness of these textbooks have only recently been examined. Additionally, although some recent research has focused on the evaluation and selection of reading textbooks, relatively little is known about the textbook selection process in general or about the selection of other language-arts texts such as English composition texts, literature anthologies or spelling and handwriting textbooks. Research is even more scant regarding how these language-arts textbooks are used by teachers—how much of the textbooks are used, how often, to what extent textbooks are adapted and modified and how textbooks affect student interest and learning of the language arts.

This chapter reviews and summarizes the research that exists on the selection and use of reading and language-arts textbooks. We begin with a definition of textbooks and a delineation of the types of materials we have in mind for this review. Next we review the research on the textbook selection process, with an emphasis on the growing body of research on the evaluation and selection of basal reading textbooks. We follow with a review of the emerging research on the uses of language-arts textbooks by teachers and students. The chapter closes with a discussion of issues related to the future of these textbooks.

LANGUAGE ARTS TEXTBOOKS: A DEFINITION

For the purposes of this chapter we use the definition of a textbook presented by Warren (1981). Warren defined textbooks as "printed instructional material in bound form, the contents of which are properly organized and intended for use in elementary or high school curricula" (p. 43). According to this definition, student textbooks and teachers' manuals of commercial programs are considered textbooks, since both are used to organize and guide elementary and secondary curricula. Language-arts texts therefore include the student textbooks and teachers' manuals of the comprehensive programs—basal reading programs and English programs—as well as the more specific programs developed for the teaching of handwriting, spelling, composition and grammar.

THE SELECTION OF LANGUAGE-ARTS TEXTBOOKS

A cursory look at research on textbooks reveals that we have, at best, only a beginning understanding of how some language-arts textbooks are evaluated and selected. A number of articles have addressed the complex set of issues involved in selecting textbooks, often noting the lack or rigor in the textbook selection process and the enormous social and political obstacles that can exert undue influence over that process. Critics have come from within the textbook industry (Follett, 1985; Maxwell, 1984; Squire, 1982, 1985) and from without (Apple, 1985; Crane, 1975; English, 1980; Goodman, Freeman, Murphy & Shannon, 1987; Koops, 1978; McCutcheon, 1982). What critics and researchers alike have agreed upon is that the textbook selection process is a complex and multidimensional one and is influenced by numerous pressures on those who evaluate and select textbooks (Apple, 1985; Courtland, Farr, Harris, Tarr, & Treece, 1983; Far & Tulley, 1985; Marshall, 1985; Powell, 1985).

Outside Influences on the Textbook Evaluation and Selection Process

The process of evaluating and selecting textbooks for use in school districts is most often conducted by textbook adoption committees. These committees consist of a group of teachers, administrators, and sometimes lay citizens who examine the available textbooks on the market and select one or more for use in their schools. The ostensible, if not explicit, goal of textbook adoption committees is to select the best textbook(s) on the market. However, it is not that simple. Textbook adoption committees are pressured by a number of different constituents, some outside the control of the committee members. These include state-level adoption policies, specific protesters concerned with the content of the textbooks, and the publishing companies themselves. These factors sometimes influence the decisions of adoption committees and the content of the textbooks themselves.

State level adoption policies are one highly influential factor on textbook evaluation and selection. In order to understand the influence of state level adoption policies, it is necessary to understand how textbooks are adopted in different states (see Marshall, 1985; Farr, Tulley & Powell, 1987; and Tulley, 1985 for more extensive discussions of this topic.) The 50 states are roughly divided into what publishers call "closed" and "open" territories. In "closed" territories, commercially developed reading materials are first examined by a statewide adoption committee. The committee evaluates and selects three to five acceptable textbooks which are placed on an "approved" list

(Marshall, 1985). Adoption committees of local school districts then can examine and select their textbooks from the approved state list. Publishers refer to these states, 22 of them currently, as "closed," because they cannot sell their textbooks in those states unless they make the approved adoption list. In "open" territory states local school districts can examine and select from all commercially produced textbooks. Because there is no state list, local adoption committees can select from any program on the market. Publishers refer to these states as "open" because they are free to sell their textbooks to all school districts in those states.

State level adoption policies in closed territory states have important consequences for the textbook selection process at both the state and local levels. For example, the evaluation procedures used by large states can determine the content of textbooks examined by school districts throughout the country. Marshall (1987) noted the strong influence of the state proclamations in guiding Texas state level committees in their evaluation of textbooks. He found that these proclamations, written by state board members and lay persons, were more important to adoption decisions than were the opinions of the committee members themselves. And, since these proclamations are in the public domain, they are used by textbook publishers to develop their textbooks (Marshall, 1985, 1987). In this way, Texas's proclamation procedures influence the content of all textbooks on the market.

A second and related consequence of state level adoption is that the social, political and sometimes moral agendas of protesters in large states like California, Florida or Texas become agendas and often mandates for textbook publishers (Crane, 1975; English, 1980; Squire, 1982). Jenkinson (1985) documented the powerful influence of protesters like the Gablers who forced changes in a number of textbooks in the 1980s. McCutcheon (1982) and Jenkinson (1985) reported that publishers may consult with state adoption boards when deciding which stories to include in their literature anthologies or what "objectionable content" should be removed from these and other texts. These researchers argued that the values of these large states influence what is included and excluded from textbooks. And, once these changes have been made, it is not profitable for publishers to change other editions sold in other states (Jenkinson, 1985). In this way, protesters and would-be censors influence the content and curriculum of textbooks throughout the country.

While state level adoption exerts pressure on adoption committees at both the state and local levels, other pressures exist as well. Powell (1985) described the receptions, dinner meetings and other kinds of marketing strategies used by publishers to influence the decisions of adoption committee members. Committee members in her study reported that these marketing strategies were sometimes effective and sometimes not. Courtland et al. (1983) found that members of the adoption committee they studied said that the publishers and their representatives did not influence their decisions in any way. Yet they also said that poor sales presentations by publishers' representatives could cause them to look no further into a given textbook. Marshall (1987) argued that "the data leave little doubt that [textbook] decisions were, in many cases, influenced by members of the textbook publishing industry who pitch their books to committee members in various public and private settings" (p. 11).

Undoubtedly, the information from these studies does not identity all of the outside pressures on textbook adoption committees, nor does it provide a complete picture of the scope and complexity of the adoption process. We have an insufficient data base to determine exactly what and how specific state level adoption policies affect the instructional content of textbooks and the decision-making process. We also have insufficient data to identify adequately the influence of publishers and their representatives on that process. What we do know, however, is that many factors unrelated to the instructional quality of textbooks can, and in fact do, influence the textbook evaluation process and the final selection of a textbook.

Inside Influences on the Textbook Evaluation and Selection Process

While it is true that outside factors influence textbook selection decisions, it is also true that many factors within textbook adoption committees themselves exert an influence on selection decisions. Studies of textbook adoption committees have uniformly identified several key influences: 1) the evaluation criteria used to examine and select textbooks; 2) the amount of time allotted to examining and evaluating textbooks; 3) the past experiences of the members of textbook adoption committees; and 4) the amount of training committee members have had evaluating textbooks.

Researchers examining the textbook selection process have found that one of the critical factors influencing the decisions made by committee members at all levels is the criteria they use to evaluate textbooks (Comas, 1983; Courtland et al., 1983; Farr, Powell & Tulley, 1987; Marshall, 1985, 1987). For example, in Texas, proclamations have been developed that serve as evaluation criteria. In a study of these proclamations, Marshall (1985, 1987) found that they most frequently regulated the social and moral content of textbooks. He found that special provisions were included to cover topics such as the use of offensive language, the illustration of varying life styles, and the presentation of traditional as well as changing roles of men and women. The proclamation criteria did not, however, provide guidance for evaluators to examine and evaluate the instructional content and quality of the textbooks. This evaluation was left to individual committee members.

On the other hand, in studies by Courtland et al. (1983) and Winograd and Osborn (1985), researchers found that state guidelines in Indiana and Kentucky did contain pedagogical criteria designed to assist in the evaluation of reading textbooks. Examination of these criteria, however, revealed numerous problems. For example, Courtland et al. (1983) reported that two sources of evaluation criteria were used in the Indiana adoption process they examined. First, a state-written set of criteria were developed and served as a more sensible evaluation checklist. But Indiana textbook reviewers also used other checklists developed independently by each of the seven commissioners who led the adoption process. Thus, in addition to

the state written *Criteria* seven different checklists were developed, and further, were interpreted differently by the many textbook reviewers assisting the commissioners. This proliferation of checklists resulted in reviewers being vague about what it was they were evaluating when they evaluated textbooks. Courtland et al.'s conclusions about the vagueness of evaluation criteria on checklists have been corroborated by other researchers (Comas, 1983; Dole, Rogers & Osborn, 1987a,b, Farr & Tulley, 1985; Marshall, 1987; Powell, 1985).

Researchers have found other problems with checklists. Farr and Tulley (1985) concluded that checklists encouraged committee members to check off the listing of skills or topics in scope and sequence charts, rather than encouraging them to examine the instructional quality of those skills or topics in the teacher and student materials. Dole and Osborn (1989) observed that committee members could easily look up skills in the scope and sequence charts, find these skills covered on many pages in the program, and conclude that the program really teaches and develops those skills. These researchers, along with others (Farr and Tulley, 1985; Keith, 1985) suggested that what was being evaluated was the appearance of the skills or topics but not how well they were translated into instruction or other learning experiences.

A second factor that appears to play a major role in the textbook selection process is the amount of time allotted for examining and evaluating textbooks. Committee members from studies by Courtland et al. (1983), Dole et al., (1987b), and Powell (1985) all commented on the enormity of the evaluation task itself and the relatively little amount of time allocated to that task. Researchers reported that committee members complained about the lack of adequate time, despite wide variability in time frames for evaluating textbooks. Complaints were voiced from adoption committees who had a few months to conduct the evaluation process (Dole et al., 1987b), but also from those who were involved in a two year selection process (Powell, 1985). Committee members in both these studies felt overwhelmed with what they perceived to be too little time to evaluate too much material. How the factor of time affects the quality of the evaluations and whether more time would result in the selection of better textbooks, though, remain unknown but important issues in textbook selection.

A third critical factor that appears to influence adoption committee decisions is the past experiences of committee members. Most committee members are experienced teachers, but have had little experience or training in evaluating the instructional quality and effectiveness of textbooks. It should not be surprising, therefore, that Courtland et al., (1983), Dole et al., (1987a,b), Farr, Tulley, & Powell, (1985), Marshall (1985, 1987) and Powell (1985) all found that adoption committee members tended to rely on their own personal pedagogical knowledge to make decisions about selecting textbooks. Powell (1985) found that committee members evaluated most positively those materials that were similar to the ones they were already using. Marshall (1987) reported that although committee members said they "knew what they were looking for" (Marshall, 1987, p. 14), they were actually quite vague when they tried to verbalize what that was. Marshall (1987), Courtland et al., (1983) and Powell (1985) all documented the wide-spread use of the "flip test" that committee members used to evaluate the quality of textbooks. Considering that adoption committee members have had little or no training in how to evaluate textbooks, it makes sense that they resort to that with which they are most familiar.

Thus, many forces both within textbook adoption committees and outside of them appear to exert strong influences on which reading textbooks and literature anthologies are selected for use in American schools. We do not know the extent to which these same pressures influence the choice of other language-arts texts. We imagine there is variability; for example, protesters may be a strong factor in influencing the selection of literature anthologies, but they may not care so much about the selection of spelling or grammar books.

What is particularly problematic about the research to date is this: While the unstated goal of textbook adoption is to choose the textbook of the highest instructional quality, research indicates that many factors unrelated to this goal often predominate. Why this is so remains a critical research question. Research in a number of areas outside of language arts—group process and decision-making, communication and persuasion, policy analysis—may help language arts educators better understand the complex set of issues involved in textbook evaluation and selection.

THE USE OF LANGUAGE ARTS TEXTBOOKS

Regardless of how language-arts textbooks are selected, the fact remains that they are widely used in schools at all grade levels. In this section we review the research to date regarding the nature and degree of use of different textbooks for language instruction. We also discuss some of the reasons for teachers' continued reliance on these materials. Once again, research is not extensive. The handful of studies that do exist do not address the range of textbooks used for literacy instruction. They do, however, provide a beginning look at how and why teachers use at least some language-arts textbooks.

How Language Textbooks are used by Teachers

Remarkably, we know of no systematic and detailed study that documents how teachers use textbooks in any subject area. Reading has received the most attention, although the research is fragmented and incomplete. Writing has received some research attention, yet none of the research on writing textbooks has addressed how teachers actually use those textbooks. What we are left with are a few studies whose purpose is often not related to describing how teachers use their textbooks, and whose data are sketchy at best. Because the data are so few, the textbook focus—student textbooks or teachers' manuals—addressed in each study guides the discussion.

How do teachers use their language textbooks? Do they use them *carte blanche* or do they modify, adapt, omit and add to what is in them? Several studies of teacher planning indicate that teachers adapt the materials contained in their teachers' manuals. For example, Clark and Elmore (1981) studied one elementary teacher's preliminary long-term planning of several

subjects, including writing. They found that as this teacher thought-through and organized her writing instruction for the year, she relied on her English textbook for both the content and sequence of instruction for her students. In addition, though, she used her own teaching experiences and her knowledge of students' successes in the past to modify and adjust the content, sequencing and pacing of her instruction.

In another study of teacher planning, Kyle (1980) found that teachers also relied upon, but modified, the information found in the teachers' manuals of their reading and spelling textbooks. Kyle observed that one teacher in the study "modified textbook materials by varying the methods of presentation and by making connections between topics" (p. 85). On the other hand, McCutcheon (1980) concluded that most teachers in her study relied almost exclusively on reading textbooks for their planning and implementation of reading instruction. These teachers' lessons were fragmented, mirroring the fragmentation of corresponding lessons in their textbooks. McCutcheon found, however, that many teachers recognized serious instructional shortcomings in their reading textbooks. Some teachers foresaw difficulties and revised their lessons; other teachers "were caught by difficulties during the course of the lesson and had to revise the plan on the spur of the moment" (p. 15).

Studies in reading corroborate data from the more general research on teacher planning. In a questionnaire sent out by Rosecky (1978), for example, 90 percent of the teachers she sampled said they used basal reader teachers' manuals. Seventy five percent of the teachers said they omitted certain parts of the suggested directed reading activity components of the teachers' manuals, most often the follow-up or enrichment activities. But how these materials were used by teachers was not clear from this study.

Durkin's (1983) well-known study of teachers' manuals provides important information not in the Rosecky study, because Durkin interviewed teachers and observed them as well. Overall, Durkin's results were similar to those of Rosecky. Teachers were indeed selective in using the directed reading activity component of basal teachers' manuals, and did not appear to spend much time on new vocabulary, background information or prereading questions. On the other hand, she found that considerable time was spent on comprehension assessment questions and written practice assignments—usually workbooks.

Mason (1983) obtained comparable results in her observational study. She found that little actual instructional time was spent on activities that were related to the story in the student reader and the directed reading activity suggestions provided in the teachers' manuals. Rather, Mason found that the majority of time was spent on disjointed lessons—drill and chalk exercises—and extensive written practice assignments. It was not clear from Mason's study whether these activities and assignments also came from the teachers' manuals and if so were used in the sequence suggested by the manuals. Since these teachers extensively modified and adapted suggestions for the directed reading activity, we could reasonably conclude that they also modified and adapted additional practice assignments found in the manuals.

A study by Shake & Allington (1985) presents a somewhat

different picture of teachers' use of manuals in basal reading programs. The six teachers in their study more often than not (79 percent to 21 percent of the time) made up their own questions about the selections they asked students to read, rather than relying on questions in teachers' manuals. Shake & Allington concluded, however, that the teachers' manual questions were superior to the ones asked by the teachers.

Shake and Allington's results contradict most of the research to date on teachers' use of basal reading program manuals. Their findings certainly contradicted those of Durkin (1978–79; 1983), especially in indicating that teachers do not use the questions contained in the teachers' manuals of basal textbooks. These disparate results could be explained, however, by the variability in teachers' use of different suggestions in the teachers' manuals. Intrapersonal variability is likely to occur not only within a given textbook in one subject area, but across subject areas. It is also reasonable to assume that there is variability across teachers in their use of the same language textbooks—sometimes to the dismay of administrators! We may speculate on reasons for this variability—experience of the teacher, needs of students, teachers' pedagogical knowledge and confidence, administrative demands, and so forth. But further research is needed to understand the relationship between the content of textbooks and the instructional decisions of teachers.

When we turn to studies of writing and/or English composition textbooks, we find a different research framework and tradition, and different questions asked and answered about these textbooks. Numerous studies have focused extensively on the types of tasks in writing books and the discrepancy between these tasks and current theory about the writing process (Applebee, 1974, 1981, 1984; Bridge & Hiebert, 1985; Graves, 1977). We have found no research, however, that examines directly how teachers use these textbooks—either the teachers' manuals or the student textbooks—in classes with their students. We know that they do, or at least that they used to. In a survey conducted as part of the National Study of Writing in the Secondary School, Applebee (1981) found that 91 percent of the teachers who responded said they regularly used textbooks as part of their instruction. But researchers have not examined how teachers use these textbooks and the extent and degree to which teachers modify, adapt, omit or add to the writing tasks assigned to students in their texts. Similarly, researchers have not examined the degree to which teachers rely on the teachers' manuals of the writing textbooks their students use.

Throughout this discussion, we have not mentioned the nature and extent of students' use of their reading and writing textbooks. For example, how much of the basal stories are actually read by students? And, how much of the writing tasks in traditional English language-arts textbooks are actually completed by students? How do teachers plan and make decisions about the textbook tasks that are completed by students? Data provided by Duffy, Roehler and Putnam (1987) and Shannon (1983) in particular suggest that many school districts have strong administrative mandates about adherence to reading textbooks. Perhaps students in these districts use their reading and writing textbooks to a greater extent than students in districts that are decentralized. Does it make a difference in the quality of instruction that students receive? These remain important questions that need to be addressed for a full understanding of the role of textbooks in language instruction.

Why Teachers Rely on Textbooks for Language Teaching and Learning

If you ask teachers why they rely so heavily on textbooks, they say one of two things: first, it is easier to use a textbook than to develop a new curriculum; and/or second, the people who wrote the textbooks must know what they are talking about. Research provides us with data that support these two assertions.

Research on teacher decision-making and teacher planning indicate why it is easier for teachers to rely on a textbook than to develop their own curriculum. Research indicates that teaching is a highly complex activity placing heavy cognitive demands on teachers. Apple and Tietelbaum (1986), Duffy and Ball (1986) and Stern and Shavelson (1983) delineated some of the daily demands placed on teachers—facing the complexities of managing an entire class, meeting difficult scheduling demands, meeting the needs of a diverse and heterogeneous group of students, and covering the curriculum in a number of subject areas. Brophy (1982) argued that such demands on teachers' time limit the extent to which teachers can develop their own curricula and materials. As a result, Brophy asserted, teachers tend to concentrate on the what and how of instruction rather than on the objectives of instruction. Perhaps this is why teachers do not appear to "rely upon rational models to make decisions about developing student understanding but, instead, focus on procedural concerns regarding classroom organization and management" (Duffy & Ball, 1986, p. 173).

Doyle (1983) argued that teachers and students engage in a complex negotiation process to simplify academic tasks. Thus, the behaviors of teachers, including their concern for smooth organization and management and their focus on simpler instructional procedures, result in part from students' reactions to their academic work, and their implicit, if not explicit, attempt to negotiate the level of task difficulty down. Given these pressures, teachers, like students, often become preoccupied with "getting work accomplished" (Doyle, 1986, p. 418). And, getting work accomplished is often translated into completing tasks in the textbook. Interviews with teachers appear to support these observations (Duffy, Roehler & Putnam, 1987; Shannon, 1983; 1989a).

A second reason for teachers' heavy reliance on textbooks comes from Shannon (1983, 1989a) In his 1983 study, Shannon provided data that highlighted teachers' and administrators' beliefs about the programs they used. These educators believed that these programs were "scientifically valid and the direct technology developed during research on reading and instruction" (p. 61). He found that many teachers believed that basal reading textbooks were written by experts who developed materials superior to what teachers could provide. This thinking reflected Shannon's (1983) notion of the "reification of the basal." Teachers do not think they are in a position to question what is in the textbook. Because of this attitude, teachers in essence give up their teaching to the textbooks.

More recently, Shannon (1989a) traced the development and use of basal reading programs throughout the early twentieth century and attempted to explain teachers' heavy reliance on basal textbooks in terms of critical theory. According to critical theorists (also see Apple, 1985; Giroux & Freire, 1989; Shannon, 1989b), the relationship between teachers and textbooks must be analyzed and will ultimately be understood and changed only through an examination of the larger ideological, social, political and economic forces that affect them. Shannon argued that management issues related to power and domination over the teaching profession exert a strong influence over what materials are used, how often and to what extent.

Our discussion has been concerned with possible reasons for teachers' continued reliance on language textbooks. The focus of discussion has been on reading textbooks, although the reasons behind teachers' reliance on reading textbooks are probably similar to their reliance on other language-arts texts as well. It is clear that research is needed in many areas. First, teachers' reliance on textbooks should be examined within the larger context of instructional decision-making. Within this framework, an issue that has not been addressed but that appears to be critical, is teachers' perceptions of their own pedagogical knowledge and how that knowledge relates to their use of language textbooks. Do teachers rely more heavily on textbooks when they perceive themselves to be less knowledgeable about the content of what they teach?

Second, we need to know more about the relationship between administrators and teachers in their reliance on textbooks. Shannon's research (1983) provides a beginning step in understanding this complex relationship, but important questions remain. To what extent do district and state mandates tell teachers in some districts that they *must* use textbooks for language instruction? Who makes these kinds of policy decisions and how are they made? Further, why do some teachers ignore mandates that are there? On the other hand, why do other teachers perceive mandates when they are not there? Research on policy analysis is scant (Mitchell, 1984), but may offer some help in addressing these issues.

SOME FINAL THOUGHTS: THE FUTURE OF LANGUAGE-ARTS TEXTBOOKS

We believe that textbooks have never been under such a siege of attack from both outside and inside the educational community as they are today, and this is especially true of language-arts textbooks. Some inside critics of language-arts textbooks question the value of all existing textbooks in literacy instruction. They ask such questions as: Can writing ever be taught out of a textbook? Can children ever learn the function and form of our phonetic language through a spelling textbook? Can literature anthologies or basal textbooks ever capture the richness and texture of high quality literature for children? Can teachers ever create a literate environment so long as they rely on teachers' manuals?

Research conducted on the content and instructional quality of reading and writing textbooks would lend support for skepticism about the use of textbooks to improve literacy instruction.

Whether examining reading instruction (Beck, McKeown, McCaslin, & Burkes, 1979; Bruce, 1984; Durkin, 1978-79; Osborn, 1984) or writing instruction (Applebee, 1974; Bridge & Hiebert, 1985; Graves, 1977), studies uniformly indicate that current theory and research about reading and writing are not reflected in the reading and writing practices of current textbooks.

But, we do not know the extent to which the quality of different language-arts textbooks currently on the market affect literacy learning. Are there textbooks that are significantly better than others and that do, in fact, make a difference in the quality of language instruction offered to American children? While almost everyone has a strong opinion on this critical question, the field does not have a data base to provide a reasonable answer. The question remains empirical.

Now, we are left with an additional question: What should we do? One possible answer is reflected in two new movements in literacy instruction today. In particular, whole language and process writing advocates regard textbooks with suspicion at best. These advocates recommend the use of children's trade books instead of basal textbooks, and the use of extensive writing instead of English composition books (see, for example, Calkins, 1986; Hansen, 1987; and Newman, 1985). Additionally, instead of teachers' manuals, these advocates recommend that teachers rely on their own pedagogical knowledge and expertise in planning and developing the curricula, and in organizing, managing, and implementing the instructional program in literacy.

Much of what whole-language and process writing advocates say appears to be educationally sound and reasonable. The problem arises from research data which reveals the extent to which teachers rely on textbook programs and their reasons for doing so. Research on teacher planning and decision-making point to the extreme cognitive complexity of developing curricula and organizing and managing instruction. Critical theorists point to the social, political and ideological forces shaping a strong tradition of teachers' use of textbooks. If information from these lines of research present an accurate picture of teachers' reliance on commercially developed textbooks, then teachers in all probability will continue to use them.

There is an alternative to the elimination of language textbooks for literacy learning. This alternative is to change the textbooks. One very positive result of the current controversy over literacy textbooks is the pressure on textbook publishers to improve the quality of the language textbooks they produce. Squire (1985) and Follet (1985) have argued that textbook publishers produce the kinds of textbooks that educators want (see, also, Dole et al., 1987a). They believe that as teachers become better acquainted with current theory and research on literacy, they will make demands for textbooks that incorporate this theory and research into meaningful practice.

What should new literacy textbooks look like? Guthrie (1981) suggested that educators first examine the role of the textbook in the curriculum. Will the text be the sole basis of the information presented? Will it be a minor resource for students or a laboratory guide? Guthrie argued that these purposes imply very different textbooks. We can ask ourselves: What should ideal language arts textbooks look like? What should be their purpose? How should they help students progress in language learning? And, how should they assist teachers in developing a curriculum that fosters language learning?

We think that Guthrie had an idea whose time has come. It is time to rethink the functions, purposes, and forms of literacy textbooks. It also may be a time when creative and innovative thinking based on sound theoretical notions about literacy instruction can result in vastly improved textbooks and improved instruction as well.

References

Apple, M. W. (1985). The culture and commerce of the textbook. *Journal of Curriculum Studies, 17,* 147–162.

Apple, M. W., & Tietelbaum, K. (1986). Are teachers losing control of their curriculum? *Journal of Curriculum Studies, 18,* 177–184.

Applebee, A. N. (1974). *Tradition and reform in the teaching of English: A history.* Urbana, IL: National Council of Teachers of English.

Applebee, A. N. (1981). *Contexts for learning to write: Studies of secondary school instruction.* New Jersey: Ablex.

Applebee, A. N. (1984). *Writing in the secondary school.* Urbana, IL: National Council of Teachers of English.

Beck, I. L., McKeown, M. G., McCaslin, E. S., & Burkes, A. M. (1979). *Instructional dimensions that may affect reading comprehension: Examples from two commercial reading programs.* Pittsburgh: University of Pittsburgh, Learning and Research Development Center.

Bridge, C. A., & Hiebert, E. H. (1985). A comparison of classroom writing practices, teachers' perceptions of their writing instruction, and textbook recommendations on writing practices. *The Elementary School Journal, 86,* 155–172.

Brophy, J. E. (1982). How teachers influence what is taught and learned in classrooms. *The Elementary School Journal, 83,* 1–13.

Bruce, B. (1984). A new point of view of children's stories. In R. C. Anderson, J. Osborn, & R. J. Tierney, (Eds.), *Learning to read in American schools: Basal readers and content texts* (pp. 153–174). Hillsdale, NJ: Lawrence Erlbaum Associates.

Calkins, L. M. (1986). *The art of teaching writing.* Portsmouth, NH: Heinemann.

Clark, C. M., & Elmore, J. L. (1981). *Transforming curriculum in mathematics, science, and writing: A case study of teacher yearly planning.* (Research Series No. 99). East Lansing: Michigan State University, Institute of Research on Teaching.

Comas, J. (1983). *Item analysis: Basal reading evaluation forms.* Unpublished manuscript, Indiana University.

Courtland, M. C., Farr, R., Harris, P., Tarr, J. R., & Treece, L. J. (1983). *A case study of the Indiana state reading textbook adoption process.* Bloomington, IN: Center for Reading and Language Studies.

Crane, B. (1975). The "California effect" on textbook adoptions. *Educational Leadership, 32,* 283–285.

Dole, J. A., & Osborn, J. (1989). Evaluation, selection and use of reading materials. In S. B. Wepner, J. T. Feeley, & D. S. Strickland (Eds.), *The administration and supervision of reading programs* (pp. 109–130). NY: Teachers College Press.

Dole, J. A., Rogers, T., & Osborn, J. (1987a). Improving the selection of basal reading programs: A report of the Textbook Adoption Guidelines Project. *The Elementary School Journal, 87,* 283–298.

Dole, J. A., Rogers, T., & Osborn, J. (1987b). Improving the textbook selection process: Case studies of the Textbook Adoption Guidelines Project. *Book Research Quarterly, 3*(3), 18–36.

Doyle, W. (1983). Academic work. *Review of Educational Research, 53,* 159–199.

Doyle, W. (1986). Classroom organization and management. In M. C. Wittrock (Ed.), *Handbook of research on teaching* (pp. 392–431). NY: Macmillan Publishing.

Duffy, G. G., & Ball, D. L. (1986). Instructional decision making and reading teacher effectiveness. In J. V. Hoffman (Ed.), *Effective teaching of reading: Research and practice* (pp. 163–180). Newark, DE: International Reading Association.

Duffy, G. G., & McIntyre, L. (1982). A naturalistic study of instructional assistance in primary-grade reading. *The Elementary School Journal, 83,* 15–23.

Duffy, G. G., Roehler, L. R., & Putnam, J. (1987). Putting the teacher in control: Basal reading textbooks and instructional decision-making. *The Elementary School Journal, 87,* 357–366. And *What basal reader manuals recommend?* (Reading Education Report No. 44). Urbana: University of Illinois, Center for the Study of Reading.

Durkin, D. (1978/1979). What classroom observations reveal about reading comprehension instruction. *Reading Research Quarterly, 14,* 481–533.

Durkin, D. (1983). *Is there a match between what elementary teachers do and what basal reader manuals recommend?* (Technical Report No. 44). Champaign, ILL: Center for the Study of Reading, University of Illinois.

English, R. (1980). The politics of textbook adoption. *Phi Delta Kappan, 62,* 275–278.

Farr, R., & Tulley, M. A. (1985). Do adoption committees perpetuate mediocre textbooks? *Phi Delta Kappan, 66,* 467–471.

Farr, R. Powell, D., Tulley, M. A. (1987). The evaluation and selection of basal readers. *The Elementary School Journal, 87,* 267–282.

Follett, R. (1985). The school textbook adoption process. *Book Research Quarterly, 1*(2), 19–23.

Giroux, H. A., & Freire, P. (1989). Reading instruction and critical pedagogy. In P. Shannon, *Broken promises: reading instruction in twentieth-century America* (p. ix-xii). Granby MA: Bergin & Garvey Publishers.

Goodman, K. S., Freeman, Y., Murphy, S., & Shannon, P. (1987). *Report card on basal readers.* Urbana, IL: National Council of Teachers of English.

Graves, D. H. (1977). Language arts textbooks: A writing process evaluation. *Language Arts, 54,* 817–823.

Guthrie, J. T. (1981). Forms and functions of textbooks. *Journal of Reading, 24,* 554–556.

Hansen, J. (1987). *When writers read.* Portsmouth, NH: Heinemann.

Hodges, C. A. (1980). Commentary: Toward a broader definition of comprehension instruction. *Reading Research Quarterly, 15,* 229–306.

Jackson, S. A. (1981). About publishers, teachers and reading achievement. In J. H. Cole & T. C. Sticht (Eds.), *The textbook in American society.* Washington, DC: The Library of Congress.

Jenkinson, E. B. (1985). Protecting Holden Caulfield and his friends from the censors. *English Journal, 74,* 26–33.

Keith, S. (1985). Choosing textbooks: A study of instructional materials selction processes for public education. *Book Research Quarterly, 1,* 24–37.

Komoski, P. K. (1985). Instructional Materials will not improve until we change the system. *Educational Leadership, 42,* 31–37.

Koops, J. B. (1978). Warmed up leftovers and hot apple pie: A report on widely used secondary schools writing textbooks. *English Education, 10,* 17–24.

Kyle, D. W. (1980). Curriculum decisions: Who decides what? *The Elementary School Journal, 81,* 77–85.

Marshall, J. D. (1985). *The politics of curriculum decisions manifested through the selection and adoption of textbooks for Texas.* Unpublished doctoral dissertation, The University of Texas at Austin.

Marshall, J. D. (1985, April). *Better textbooks, better criteria: The role of research in directing efforts for reform.* Paper presented at the meeting of the American Educational Research Association, Washington, DC.

Mason, J. M. (1983). An examination of reading instruction in third and fourth grades. *The Reading Teacher, 36,* 906–913.

Maxwell, J. (1984). *The future of textbooks.* NASSP Bulletin. Urbana, IL: National Council of Teachers of English.

McCutcheon, G. (1980). How do elementary school teachers plan? The nature of planning and influences on it. *The Elementary School Journal, 81,* 4–23.

McCutcheon, G. (1982). Bait/Rebait: Publishers' influence on curricula. *English Journal, 17,*(7), 16–18.

Mitchell, D. E. (1984). Educational policy analysis: The state of the art. *Educational Administration Quarterly, 20,* 129–160.

Newman, J. M. (1985). *Whole language: Theory in use.* Portsmouth, NH: Heinemann Press.

Osborn, J. (1984). The purposes, uses and content of workbooks and some guidelines for publishers. In R. C. Anderson, J. Osborn, & R. J. Tierney (Eds.), *Learning to read in American schools* (pp. 45–112). Hillsdale, NJ: Lawrence Erlbaum.

Powell, D. A. (1985). *Retrospective case studies of individual and group decision making in district-level elementary reading textbook selection.* Unpublished doctoral dissertation, Indiana University.

Resnick, D. P., & Resnick, L. B. (1985). Standards, curriculum and performance: A historical and comparative perspective. *Educational Researcher, 14*(4), 5–20.

Rosecky, M. (1978). Are teachers selective when using basal textbooks? *The Reading Teacher, 32,* 381–385.

Shake, M. C. & Allington, R. L. (1985). Where do teachers' questions come from? *The Reading Teacher, 38,* 432–438.

Shannon, P. (1983). The use of commercial reading materials in American elementary schools. *Reading Research Quarterly, 19,* 68–85.

Shannon, P. (1989a). *Broken promises: Reading instruction in twentieth-century America.* Granby, MA: Bergin & Garvey Publishers.

Shannon, P. (1989b). Paradigmatic diversity within the reading research community. *Journal of Reading Behavior, 21,* 97–108.

Stern, P., & Shavelson, R. J. (1983). Reading teachers' judgments, plans and decision-making. *The Reading Teacher, 37,* 280–286.

Squire, J. R. (1982). Bait/Rebait: Publishers' influence on curriculum. *English Journal, 17*(7), 16–18.

Squire, J. R. (1985). Textbooks to the forefront. *Book Research Quarterly, 1*(2), 12–18.

Talmage, H., & Eash, M. J. (1979). Curriculum, instruction, and materials. In P. L. Peterson, & H. J. Walberg (Eds.), *Research on teaching: Concepts, findings, and implications* (pp. 161–179). Berkeley, CA: McCutchan Publishing.

Tully, M. A. (1985). A descriptive study of the intents of selected state level textbook adoption processes. *Educational Evaluation and Policy Analysis, 7:* 289–308.

Warren, C. C. (1981). Adopting textbooks. In J. Y. Cole & T. G. Sticht (Ed.), *The textbook in American society* (pp. 43–45). Washington, DC: Library of Congress.

Winograd, P., & Osborn, J. (1985). How adoption of reading textbooks works in Kentucky: Some problems and some solutions. *Book Research Quarterly, 1*(3), 3–22.

Woodward, A. (1986). Over-programmed materials: Taking the teacher out of the teaching. *American Educator, 10,* 26–31.

28B. LITERATURE FOR LITERACY:
WHAT RESEARCH SAYS ABOUT THE BENEFITS OF
USING TRADE BOOKS IN THE CLASSROOM

Lee Galda
Bernice E. Cullinan

Children's and young adult literature—trade books—are good for children. Parents spend millions of dollars each year, publishers produce thousands of books each year, librarians purchase hundreds of books each year, and teachers make countless instructional decisions based on this premise. What is the research evidence for this claim and how powerful is it? Why are some teachers, schools, school districts, and states committed to using literature in their classrooms? This chapter explores reasons for using trade books as an integral part of an instructional program, presenting what current research tells us about the effectiveness of such a practice.

Theorists have long argued that reading to children will help prepare them for literacy and develop their literacy skills (Cullinan, 1989; Huey, 1908; Snow, 1983). Noted authorities in the field of children's and young adult literature stress the importance of reading to and with students of all ages and of providing them with ample opportunity to read and respond to a variety of excellent trade books in the classroom as well as the library media center (Cullinan, 1989; Donelson & Nilsen, 1989; Huck, Hepler, & Hickman, 1987). These authorities note that being surrounded by trade books and supportive adults helps children in their active acquisition of literacy much as being surrounded by oral language is a necessary factor in learning to talk. Further, they reason, frequent and positive contact with trade books engenders interest in reading; increased interest results in reading more; reading more results in reading better. It also is widely held that vocabulary and syntax are developed by extensive use of trade books. Others argue that listening to trade books helps children build a schema for stories that is crucial for comprehending text presented in story form. Writing is also said to be affected by reading trade books, as the lexical choices, style, and content of what children read becomes a part of their reading and writing repertoire. Despite these widely held claims for the efficacy of using trade books for literacy development, however, many teachers are frustrated in their attempts to incorporate literature into their daily schedule, because there is not time. Too often, literature is not given its place as a central part of the curriculum. A look at research in the use of trade books demonstrates the importance of literature in building literacy, and argues for the planned inclusion of trade books in all classrooms.

THE PRESCHOOL YEARS

Children's educational achievement is related to early experiences listening to stories both at home and school.

The Home

Researchers who examine the beginnings of literacy in the preschool years find that interactions between adults and children around books at home promote literacy (Baghban, 1984; Clark, 1984; Durkin, 1974; Teale, 1978, 1981; Holdaway, 1979; Moon & Wells, 1979). Relationships between learning to read at an early age and being read to have been documented time and again. An early study by Durkin (1966) showed that children who learned to read before entering first grade were ones who were read to by siblings, parents, or another caring adult. Neither race, ethnicity, socioeconomic level, nor I.Q. distinguished between readers and nonreaders; access to print, being read to, parents valuing education, and early writing did. Durkin called these early readers "paper and pencil kids," kids who liked to make marks on paper. Wells (1986) spent 15 years in a longitudinal study of 32 children from shortly after their first birthdays until the last year of their elementary schooling. In *The Meaning Makers,* Wells presents case studies of six of those children to identify the major linguistic influences on their later educational achievement. Wells found that stories are the way that children make sense of their lives; they give meaning to observable events by making connections between them and the real world; and the number of stories children heard before schooling had a lasting effect. Experience with books at age 5 was directly related to reading comprehension at age 7 and again at 11. Primarily case and correlational, these studies of early literacy show that children who are read to at home come to school reading or ready to learn to read.

Many researchers have looked closely at what children who are read to come to know about books. They point out several positive outcomes of involvement with storybooks in the home. Children who are read to develop highly positive associations for books (Holdaway, 1979). Reading books is a pleasurable activity, one that children seek and value. This pleasure is true not only for the child listener but also for the reader, thus providing a positive social model (Hiebert, 1981). How children percieve their parents' attitudes toward reading is an important influence on their own attitudes (Ransbury, 1973). Research also indicates a positive relationship between the number of books in the home and children's reading ability (Durkin, 1966; Lamme, 1985; Sheldon & Carrillo, 1952). A greater number of books was associated with high reading achievement and fewer books with low reading achievement.

Being read to helps children develop familiarity with the conventions of print (Clay, 1979; Doake, 1981; Taylor, 1983) as well as metalinguistic awareness about print (Schickedanz,

529

1986). Hearing books read aloud helps develop children's vocabulary (Ninio, 1980; Ninio & Bruner, 1978) and other language skills. Early exposure to books in the home helps children come to know two essential things. They learn how print works and that reading is worth the effort it takes.

Listening to storybooks also acquaints a child with the special use of language found in storybooks: not language to get something done, but language to represent experience, language which encourages the contemplation and evaluation of experience (Britton, 1970). Being read to also helps children understand the differences between oral and written language (Clark, 1976; Smith, 1978). And because storybook language is often the language of narrative, knowledge about narrative structure is yet another benefit for those children who are read to (Meyer & Rice, 1984). Finally, being read to increases young children's knowledge of the world, helping to provide a broad base of experience from which to comprehend and interpret other texts (Steffensen, Joag-Dev & Anderson, 1979). Anderson, Hiebert, Scott, and Wilkinson, in *Becoming a Nation of Readers* (1985), say that independent reading is a major source of building background knowledge. Research on emergent literacy clearly demonstrates that trade books play a significant role in helping preschool children become literate. Simply put, children who spend time interacting with adults around books develop understandings about the functions and the processes of reading that help them develop literacy skills when they enter traditional classrooms. There is a strong body of research that documents the importance of reading trade books in the home. What of books in the classroom?

The Classroom

Reading to children in preschool classrooms positively affects their literacy development. Research that examines the use of literature in preschool classrooms provides an excellent base from which we can extrapolate to elementary school classrooms. Morrow (1988) attempted to replicate one-to-one storybook reading at home in a low socioeconomic strata daycare center. The 4-year-olds in her study who were read to for ten weeks became better and more frequent question askers, gave more interpretive responses to the stories they read, and responded more often to the print and the story structure. Cochran-Smith, in *The Making of A Reader* (1984), describes how story reading happened in one middle class preschool class and what the consequences were of the literacy events that occurred in that classroom. Although the children she studied were not being taught to read, their interactions with adults around books did result in the growth of important knowledge about books and print. The children learned, among other things, that reading and writing were important parts of their world and could help them accomplish many purposes. They learned how to interpret and use contextualized and decontextualized print, and how they could use their real-world experiences to understand texts and their experiences with texts to understand the real world. This ethnographic study of one preschool classroom has increased our knowledge of the effect of reading trade books with preschoolers.

THE SCHOOL YEARS

Experiences with literature during the school years promote interest in reading, language development, reading achievement, and growth in writing ability. A number of recent studies have described both classroom contexts and teacher behaviors which surround the use of trade books.

Interest

Reading and listening to a variety of good books increases interest in reading. Both elementary (Mendoza, 1985) and high school (Bruckerhoff, 1977) students affirm that they like to be read to and that being read to is an important factor in their positive attitude towards books. Positive associations with trade books encourage school-age children to practice the skill of reading until they become good at it. Being read to increases reading interest (Porter, 1969).

The level of reading comprehension, the amount of reading done, and the attitude toward reading are all affected by the student's interest in the materials. We understand materials best when we are interested, we read more when we find materials that interest us, and we have a more positive attitude toward reading when we can choose materials of interest. For example, Asher (1980), Asher and Markell (1974), and Matthewson (1985) found that the interest level of the material was a determining factor in reading comprehension. Asher assessed fifth grade students' interests and later gave them three reading passages corresponding to their highest rated topics and three passages corresponding to their lowest rated topics. All children comprehended the high interest materials better than they did the low interest materials.

Language Development

Being read to from trade books also positively affects children's general language development. Chomsky (1972) found a strong positive relationship between the stages of children's development and their exposure to literature; the greater the exposure to literature the more advanced the stage of linguistic development. Harste, Woodward and Burke (1984) described children feeding their "linguistic data pool" from encounters with stories, and using those experiences with stories to help make sense of subsequent language encounters. Language skills such as vocabulary and syntax are positively influenced by listening to trade books read aloud (Cohen, 1968; Feitelson, 1988). Anderson et al. (1985) report that independent reading is probably a major source of vocabulary growth. Nagy, Herman and Anderson (1985) found that children in grades 3 through 12 learn the meanings of about 3,000 new words a year. Although some of these words are taught in school, direct instruction could only account for a modest proportion of the total since learning 3,000 words a year would require learning about 15 words every school day. Nagy, et al., believe that beyond the third grade, children incidentally acquire the majority of the new words they learn while reading books and other material.

In a study which investigated the effects of reading several stories from a series, Feitelson, Kita and Goldstein (1986) found that "disadvantaged" first graders who were read to outscored their non-read-to peers on measures of decoding, reading comprehension, and vocabulary. The results of these studies and others strongly suggest that reading trade books to children benefits their general language development.

Reading Achievement

Reading literature develops readers' schemata for narrative form and life experiences. Many trade books read aloud or on classroom bookshelves are narratives. Listening to these books helps children develop a narrative schema which aids in their ability to comprehend the stories they encounter in their reading (Rumelhart & Ortony, 1977; Spiro, 1977). Schema theory, as set forth by Anderson (1977), and Rumelhart and Ortony (1977) among others, stresses that readers bring their own knowledge to the texts they encounter. It is this knowledge, in conjunction with the signals or clues that the text provides, which guides comprehension. Thus more knowledge leads to better comprehension. Exposure to trade books is one way to provide this knowledge.

Exposure to narrative patterns through extensive use of trade books increases knowledge about story structure, which in turn improves comprehension of narrative texts (Adams & Collins, 1979; Stein & Glenn, 1979). Further, as one would expect, these schema begin to develop in young children as the result of exposure to stories (usually gained through interaction with adults around trade books) and continue to develop in complexity throughout the school years and into adulthood (Stein & Glenn, 1979).

In like manner, trade books provide windows (Cullinan, 1989) on other worlds and other experiences, windows that become virtual experience as we read. These virtual experiences are then added to children's knowledge of the world. This increase in knowledge, in turn, increases the possibilities for responding to the world. Reading extensively in trade books not only increases children's sense of narrative patterns but also their storehouse of experiences. This aids in the comprehension of texts, especially narratives, and in the composition of texts.

Reading widely from real books that bring enjoyment and information is what makes fluent readers. The research evidence on how much time children spend reading independently in school or out of school, however, is discouraging. Anderson, et al., (1985) report that the amount of independent, silent reading children do is significantly related to gains in reading achievement. They also report that the amount of time children spend reading in the average classroom is small. Children in primary grade classrooms average 7 or 8 minutes a day reading silently—less than 10 percent of the total time devoted to reading. Students in the middle grades average 15 minutes per school day reading silently. Obviously, children do not get much reading practice in school.

What is the picture outside of school? Anderson and his colleagues also report that the amount of reading students do out of school is consistently related to gains in reading achievement. In a study by Fielding, Wilson, and Anderson (1986), 5th graders completed a daily log of after-school activities for periods ranging from 2 to 6 months. They found that 50 percent of the children read books for an average of 4 minutes or less a day, 30 percent read 2 minutes or less per day, and fully 10 percent never reported reading any book on any day. For the majority of children, reading from books occupied less than 1 percent of their free time. In contrast, the children averaged 130 minutes of television viewing per day.

The avid readers in this study did as much as 20 times more independent reading than did the children who chose to read less often. As a result, these avid readers got a great deal more practice in reading, a factor that helps to explain why children who read a lot make more progress in reading. Independent reading is undoubtedly a major source of reading fluency. In a study of the leisure reading habits of Irish fifth-grade students Greaney (1980) found that even reading the comics was positively related to reading achievement and that those students who spent little time reading for pleasure tended to score low on the achievement measure.

Studies conducted by the National Assessment of Educational Progress have also shown that students who read most read best. In the recent report, *Who Reads Best? Factors Related to Reading Achievement in Grades 3, 7, and 11,* Applebee, Langer, and Mullis (1988) report similar findings. There were dramatic differences between the amount of independent reading reported by the better and poorer students, particularly in school. In the third grade 75 percent of the readers in the highest quartile reported reading daily in school, compared to 57 percent of the readers in the lowest quartile. The same discrepancy appeared in the results for reading independently outside of school: 56 percent of the better readers read at home every day while only 48 percent of the poorer readers did. For grades 7 and 11, student reports were combined into a composite variable reflecting both frequency and variety of materials read. At both grade levels, the greater the breadth of materials the students reported reading, the better the student's reading performance was likely to be. There were also differences between how better and poorer 7th graders reported using the library. Students in the highest quartile reported using the library to read on their own, to look up facts for school, and to take out books. Students in the lowest quartile reported using the library as a quiet place to study and to find books about their hobbies. Similarly, the 11th grade better readers used the library more frequently for academic purposes and the poorer readers used it more frequently to find out about their hobbies (pp. 37–43).

Composing

Reading literature is linked to success in becoming a proficient writer. Many similarities have been noted between the acts of comprehending and composing (Goodman & Goodman, 1983; Tierney & Pearson, 1983; Squire, 1983; Wittrock, Marks & Doctorow, 1975) and it seems that doing one affects one's ability to do the other, and vice versa (Smith, 1983). Contact with literature exposes writers to a variety of lexical and syntactic choices as well as to a variety of narrative patterns that they then may call on in their own production of written text (Chomsky, 1972).

There is evidence that success in writing is predicted by reading scores (Loban, 1963). But what kind of reading is important? Eckhoff (1983) studied second grade children's writing and their basal reading texts. She found that those children who worked in a reading text that "more closely matched the style and complexity of literary prose" (p. 608) used more elaborate linguistic structures in their own writing than did those children who used a more traditional basal containing simplified sentence structures. DeFord's (1981) work documents the same phenomenon with first-grade children. Thus is seems that the language of the trade books that children read significantly affects the language they use in composition.

The narrative structures found in trade books also help children become better writers. King, Rentel, Pappas, Pettigrew, and Zutell (1981) argued that children have a basic understanding of folktale structure by the time they enter school, as evidenced by their oral stories (Applebee, 1978; Leondar, 1977). The findings in their longitudinal study of first and second grade children indicate that the folktales that children encounter in their contacts with trade books serve as "rhetorical models" for beginning writers. Comprehending and remembering familiar folktales seemed to result in a rudimentary rhetorical scheme from which young children could draw during their written production of folktale-like narratives. One child borrowed freely from "The Ugly Duckling," *Frog and Toad,* "The Gingerbread Boy," and "Little Red Riding Hood" as he created his own original story. The literature children hear is reflected in the content and form of their language and their stories. Blackburn (1985) described children's use of the stories they heard in the stories they wrote as "borrowings" in a cycle of never-ending story. Reading and discussing both trade books and their own compositions can also help children become aware of the choices authors make, make them more critical consumers of texts, and increase their sense of authorship (Graves, 1983; Hansen, 1987).

Social Context

Theorists agree that language learning is social and collaborative (Jaggar & Smith-Burke, 1985; Vygotsky, 1962, 1978). Children acquire language in meaningful interactions with others who provide models and support their learning by responding to what they are trying to say and do, rather than to the form. Interactive social experiences are also at the heart of literacy learning. Such experiences involve children as active learners in cooperative social environments where an adult serves as a model, structures the environment, or offers direct instruction that helps learners complete tasks they could not have completed alone (Langer, 1987). Children learn to think about and approach literacy tasks by seeing adults, classmates, and teachers engage in those activities. Eventually, they internalize the rules needed to complete the tasks alone.

LITERATURE-RICH CLASSROOMS

Books, time to spend with books, and a supportive, enthusiastic teacher are essential elements in the creation of readers. Kiefer (1988) spent many hours observing children responding to picture books in literature-rich settings from grades K–4. She recorded their reactions during read-aloud sessions with their teachers, in small-group peer interaction, and in interviews. She demonstrated that children can and do respond in profound ways to the meaning making choices of artists, but their insights do not develop by chance. Such insights grow best in very special classrooms which develop the potential for communication of meaning between the child and the picture book. The context for communication and for learning was found in classrooms in which teachers and students pursued thematic units involving numerous experiences. One of the prime features of the classroom context was time—time to look at books, to think about the experience, to listen to books read aloud, to respond to books, and to read independently. Another feature was availability. There were numerous books in the classrooms and children had easy access to them. Most importantly, teachers played the key role in creating rich classroom contexts, providing children with the opportunities to develop literacy and to deepen aesthetic and literary response. In one of the classrooms Kiefer describes, the teacher's knowledge and enthusiasm about literature, her invitations to find "secrets" in books, and her encouragement to notice and appreciate details were all factors in creating an effective context for literacy.

Hickman (1981) studied the responses of 90 children in three classrooms spanning kindergarten through grade 5 by serving as a participant observer for four months. She found that the responses to the literature children read were closely tied to the settings in which they occurred and were influenced by the teachers who created those settings. Her work underscores the importance of a rich literacy environment and the teacher's enthusiasm for literature.

Hepler (1982) spent a year in a combined fifth and sixth grade classroom to determine the patterns of response to literature. Among other things, she learned that response is social—that children use the classroom community to "pick their way to literacy." Hepler and Hickman (1982) use the phrase "a community of readers" to describe what they observed happening in middle grade classrooms. Comments such as "Everyone in the class read it, so I figured I ought to, too" . . . "I usually read what Tammy reads," showed the effect of belonging to a community of readers. Hepler (1982) also found that students read more books when they were in a literature-rich environment. Students read from 24 to 122 books over the year. In this class, book discussions occurred daily during the last 15 minutes of an hour-long period for sustained silent reading. The children supported each other in their selections of books and in their evaluations as a community of readers.

Hepler and Hickman (1982) point out that talk helps children negotiate meanings. Talk in the literature-rich classrooms was made easier by having others who shared the same context. Clusters, pairs, and small groups shared comments about books that were based on mutual understanding from having read the same books. Hepler and Hickman state, "Perhaps the single most important function of the community of readers is to provide a model set of reader behaviors which tell children how readers act. Readers enjoy books, thinks the child, and I do, too." Further, once children discern that the teacher values reading, they are most anxious to let the teacher know that they *are* reading (p. 282).

Teachers of young children spend a great deal of time behind the scenes, playing the role of community planner. At any grade level, the teacher is also the person who functions to hold the group history in memory and to ask questions that allow children to range back over what they have read. By asking students to relate their current reading to other things they have read, they help them see reading as a part of a wider literary framework. Behind one child lost in a good work stands a community of other children and interested adults who help the reader choose, respond, and enjoy (Hepler & Hickman, 1982, p. 283). Books, time, and interactions with interested others create avid readers.

TEACHER BEHAVIORS

How teachers read books affects their students' understanding of how to listen and respond to books. A number of researchers interested in the use of trade books in the classroom have noted that in many studies of the use of trade books in the classroom one important variable has often been ignored. Quite often, trade books are read aloud by a teacher to a class. Thus teacher behaviors become an important factor in examining the effective use of trade books. Green and Harker (1982) argue that how teachers present trade books to their students makes the difference between effective and ineffective story reading situations. The manner in which teachers present stories is influenced by "factors such as developmental differences, teacher's goals, the nature of the text, as well as skills and abilities of students, all [of which] influence the instructional process and potentially influence the effectiveness of a given set of strategies" (Green & Harker, 1982, p. 197). Reading to children involves at least three components—children, teachers, and texts—and these factors must be considered when planning lessons involving trade books. However, Green and Harker point out that it is the implementation of these plans in the highly interactive context of a classroom that holds the key to effective teaching. Their research shows how two teachers with similar goals had very different ways of "orchestrating" the interactions of children around the same trade book. It was suggested that these differences in orchestration influenced student performance on a story retelling measure of comprehension.

Using a similar analytic strategy, Cochran-Smith (1984) looked closely at the use of trade books in a preschool classroom. She closely examined the literacy events she observed and described in detail three ways in which the storybook reader mediated the text for her audience. The reader initiated or guided three main interactions during storybook reading. Type I interactions (readiness for reading) involved appropriate behaviors when listening and responding to a story. Type II interactions (life-to-text) involved making sense of the books read aloud by bringing life-knowledge to bear on the text. This included but was not limited to "knowledge of lexical labels, literary and cultural heritage, narrative structures, human nature, and literary conventions" (p. 173). Type III interactions (text-to-life) involved "helping children discover the meaning that a book's message, theme or information might have in their own lives" (p. 173). These interactions were crucial to the development of literacy in this preschool classroom. One of the important contributions Cochran-Smith makes is that she, also, shows how important it is for researchers to examine what actually occurs during a storybook reading session rather than simply assuming that all such sessions share the same characteristics.

The importance of knowing how books are presented to children as well as knowing how often they are presented is amply documented in these studies as well as other studies of book-reading with preschoolers at home (e.g., Ninio & Bruner, 1978) and at school (e.g., Morrow, 1988). Mason and her colleagues have shown how kindergarten children's story recall was best when teachers read a story and then followed with a thorough discussion of story events. Further, what teachers stressed during book-reading episodes influenced children's comprehension (Mason, Peterman, Powell & Kerr, 1989). Another group of researchers have looked closely at story-reading interaction patterns in elementary classrooms.

Studies such as Green and Harker's (1982) and Cochran-Smith's (1984) as well as studies of home storybook reading events (Heath, 1982; Teale, 1978, 1981) describe the great variability in interactional patterns during book reading. Building on the idea that literacy learning is a social process, Teale, Martinez, and Glass (in press) have developed a method for describing what occurs when a teacher reads aloud to a class. Teale, et al. focus on the story, categorizing its content in a story grammar format, and the teachers' behaviors during reading and discussion. They, like Green and Harker, found great differences in interactional style among teachers. Their method for describing classroom storybook reading holds promise for future research in reading trade books in the classroom.

FUTURE RESEARCH

By considering closely both the texts being read and teacher behavior, researchers now can measure more accurately the effects of reading aloud on children's interest, language development, reading achievement, and writing ability. Further, researchers should be able to describe the most effective ways to read and discuss trade books by attending closely to teacher behaviors.

At the present time, in addition to the research discussed above, there are literally hundreds of articles by K–12 teachers that describe effective uses of trade books in their classrooms. These articles testify to increased interest in reading, increased enjoyment of reading, and increased ability in reading and writing. While these articles represent a different type of research, the sheer number of teachers saying the same thing, regardless of differences in demographics, student ability, grade level, and teacher styles, should at least be considered a strong indicator of the central place of literature in the development of literacy.

It may also be that the essential nature of the importance of literature in literacy learning cannot be measured fully. Litera-

The authors wish to thank Lesley Mandel Morrow and Susan Cox for their critical reading of this manuscript.

ture in most of its guises appears in a narrative form and, as Hardy (1978) has so aptly put it, narrative is a "primary act of mind." Beyond its use as a pedagogical tool, literature seems to speak to our elemental need for story. Bruner (1984) calls for using literature as a way into literacy because it is most constitutive of human experience. Literature, he says, is an "instrument for entering possible worlds of human experience" that is the driving force in language learning (p. 200).

Young children learn to talk by engaging in talk with supportive others. Smith has said that we "learn to read by actually reading," both independently and within a supportive social context in the classroom. Child language researchers have demonstrated that children learn to talk in part because it is a meaningful, indeed essential, part of life. Meaningfulness in reading, rarely captured in textbooks or basal readers, is surely present in literature that readers can make their own, creating as they read stories that speak to their own needs, desires, and expectations. This is the literature found in the thousands of trade books readily available in school and public libraries. Why read trade books to children and encourage them to read for themselves? Because reading literature is a most effective way into literacy. Being able to read literature is one basic reason for becoming literate and for making reading a lifelong habit.

References

Adams, M. J. & Collins, A. (1979). A schema-theoretic view of reading. In R. Freedle (Ed.) *New directions in discourse processing.* Norwood, NJ: Ablex.

Anderson, R. C. (1977). *Schema-directed processes in language comprehension* (Technical Report No. 50). Cambridge, MA: Bolt, Beranek and Newman, Inc.; Urbana, IL: Center for the Study of Reading.

Anderson, R. C., Hiebert, E. H., Scott, J. A., and Wilkinson, I. A. G. (1985). *Becoming a nation of readers: The report of the commission on reading.* Washington, DC: National Institute of Education.

Applebee, A. N. (1978). *The child's concept of story: Ages two to seventeen.* Chicago: University of Chicago Press.

Applebee, A. N., Langer, J. A., & Mullis, V. S. (1988). *Who reads best? Factors related to reading achievement in grades 3, 7, and 11* (Report No. 17-R-01). National Assessment of Educational Progress. Princeton, NJ: Educational Testing Service.

Asher, S. R. (1980). Topic interest and children's reading comprehension. In R. J. Spiro, B. Bruce, W. Brewer (Eds.) *Theoretical issues in reading comprehension.* Hillsdale, NJ: Erlbaum.

Asher, S. R. and Markell, R. A. (1974). Sex differences in comprehension of high- and low-interest reading material. *Journal of Educational Psychology, 66,* 680–687.

Baghban, M. J. M. (1984). *Our daughter learns to read and write: A case study from birth to three.* Newark, DE: International Reading Association.

Blackburn, E. (1985). Stories never end. In J. Hansen, T. Newkirk, & D. Graves (Eds.), *Breaking ground: Teachers relate reading and writing in the elementary school* (pp. 3–13) Portsmouth, NH: Heinemann.

Britton, J. (1970). *Language and learning.* London: Penguin.

Bruckerhoff, C. (1977). What do students say about reading instruction? *The Clearing House, 51,* 104–107.

Bruner, J. (1984). Language, mind, and reading, In H. Goelman, A. Oberg, & F. Smith (Eds.), *Awakening to literacy.* (pp. 193–200) Portsmouth, NH: Heinemann.

Chomsky, C. (1972). Stages in language development and reading exposure. *Harvard Educational Review, 42,* 1–33.

Clark, M. M. (1976). *Young fluent readers.* London: Heinemann.

Clark, M. M. (1984). Literacy at home and at school: Insights from a study of young fluent readers. In J. Goelman, A. Oberg, & F. Smith (Eds.), *Awakening to literacy.* (pp. 122–130) Portsmouth, NH: Heinemann.

Clay, M. M. (1979). *Reading: The patterning of complex behavior* (2nd ed.). Auckland: Heinemann.

Cochran-Smith, M. (1984). *The making of a reader.* Norwood, NJ: Ablex.

Cohen, D. (1968). The effect of literature on vocabulary and reading. *Elementary English, 45,* 209–213.

Cullinan, B. E. (1989). *Literature and the child* (2nd ed.). San Diego: Harcourt Brace Jovanovich.

DeFord, D. E. (1981). Literacy: Reading, writing and other essentials. *Language Arts, 58,* 652–658.

Doake, D. (1981). *Book experience and emergent reading in preschool children.* Unpublished doctoral dissertation, University of Alberta, Canada.

Donelson, K. L., & Nilsen, A. P. (1989). *Literature for today's young adults* (3rd Edition). Glenview, IL: Foresman & Co.

Durkin, D. (1966). *Children who read early.* Teachers College Press.

Durkin, D. (1974). A six-year study of children who learned to read in school at the age of four. *Reading Research Quarterly, 10,* 9–61.

Eckhoff, B. (1983). How reading affects children's writing. *Language Arts, 60,* 607–616.

Feitelson, D. (1988). *Facts and fads in beginning reading: A cross-language perspective.* Norwood, N.J.: Ablex

Feitelson, D., Kita, B., & Goldstein, Z. (1986). Effects of listening to series stories on first graders' comprehension and use of language. *Research in the Teaching of English, 20,* 339–356.

Fielding, L, Wilson, P. T., & Anderson, R. (1986). A new focus on free reading: The role of trade books in reading instruction. In T. E. Raphael (Ed.), *The contexts of school-based literacy* (pp. 149–160). Random House.

Goodman, K. & Goodman Y. (1983). Reading and writing relationships: Pragmatic functions. *Language Arts, 69,* 590–599.

Graves, D. H. (1983). *Writing: Teachers and children at work.* Portsmouth, NH: Heinemann.

Greaney, V. (1980). Factors related to amount and type of leisure time reading. *Reading Research Quarterly, 15,* 337–357.

Green, J. L., & Harker, J. O. (1982). Reading to children: A communicative process. In J. A. Langer & M. T. Smith-Burke (Eds.), *Reader meets author: Bridging the gap.* (pp. 196–122) Newark, DE: International Reading Association.

Hansen, J. (1987). *When writers read.* Portsmouth, NH:Heinemann.

Hardy, B. (1978). Towards a poetics of fiction: An approach through narrative. In M. Meek, A. Warlow, & G. Barton (Eds.), *The Cool Web.* (pp. 12–23) New York: Atheneum.

Harste, J., Woodward, V., & Burke, C. (1984). *Language stories and literacy lessons* Portsmouth, NH: Heinemann.

Heath, S. B. (1982). What no bedtime story means: Narrative skills at home and school. *Language in Society, 11,* 49–76.

Hepler, S. (1982). *Patterns of response to literature: A one-year study of fifth- and sixth-grade classrooms.* Unpublished doctoral dissertation, The Ohio State University, Columbus.

Hepler, S. I., Hickman, J. (1982). The book was okay, I love you—Social aspects of response to literature. *Theory into Practice, 21,* 278–283.

Hickman, J. (1981). A new perspective on response to literature: Research in an elementary school setting. *Research in the Teaching of English, 15*(4), 353–354.

Hiebert, E. H. (1981). Developmental patterns and interrelationships of preschool children's print awareness. *Reading Research Quarterly, 16,* 236–260.

Holdaway, D. (1979). *The foundations of literacy,* Sydney: Ashton Scholastic.

Huck, C., Hepler, S., & Hickman, J. (1987). *Children's literature in the elementary school* (4th ed.) New York: Holt Rinehart & Winston.

Huey, E. B. (1908). *The psychology and pedagogy of reading.* New York: Macmillan.

Jaggar, A. and Smith-Burke, M. T. (1985). *Observing the language learner.* Newark, DE: International Reading Association/NCTE.

Kiefer, B. (1988). Picture books as contexts for literary, aesthetic, and real world understandings. *Language Arts, 65*(3), 260–271.

King, M., Rentel, V., Pappas, C., Pettigrew, B., & Zutell, J. (1981) *How children learn to write: A longitudinal study* (ERIC Document No. 213 050). Columbus, OH: National Institute of Education Grant G-79-0137.

Lamme, L. (1985). *Growing up reading.* Washington, D.C.: Acropolis Books.

Langer, J. (1987). Book review: The contexts of school-based literacy. *Journal of Reading Behavior, 19*(4), 437–440.

Leondar, B. (1977). Hatching plots: Genesis of storymaking. In D. Perkins and B. Leondar (Eds.), *The arts and cognition.* (pp. 172–191) Baltimore: Johns Hopkins University Press.

Loban, W. (1963). *The language of elementary school children* (Research Report No. 1). Urbana, IL: National Council of Teachers of English.

Mason, J. M., Peterman, C. L., Powell, B. M. and Kerr, B. M. (1989). Reading and writing attempts by kindergartners after book reading by teachers, in J. M. Mason (Ed.) *Reading and writing connections.* Boston: Allyn and Bacon.

Mathewson, G. C. (1985) Toward a comprehensive model of affect in the reading process. In Harry Singer and Robert B. Ruddell (Eds.) *Theoretical models and processes of reading* (3rd ed.) Newark, DE: International Reading Association. 841–856.

Mendoza, A. (1985). Reading to children: Their preferences. *The Reading Teacher, 38,* 522–527.

Meyer, B. J., & Rice, G. E. (1984). The structure of text. In P. D. Pearson (Ed.), *Handbook of reading research* (pp. 319–351) New York: Longman.

Moon, C., & Wells, G. (1979). The influence of the home on learning to read. *Journal of Research in Reading, 2,* 53–62.

Morrow, L. M. (1988). Young children's responses to one-to-one story readings in school settings. *Reading Research Quarterly, 23,* 89–107.

Nagy, W. E., Herman, P. A., & Anderson, R. C. (1985). Learning words in context. *Reading Research Quarterly, 20,* 233–253.

Ninio, A. (1980). Picture-book reading in mother-infant dyads belonging to two sub-groups in Israel. *Child Development, 51,* 587–590.

Ninio, A., & Bruner, J. (1978). The achievement and antecedents of labelling. *Journal of Child Language, 5,* 5–15.

Porter, J. (1969). *The effect of a program of reading aloud to middle grade children in the inner city.* Unpublished doctoral dissertation, The Ohio State University, Columbus.

Ransbury, M. K. (1973). An assessment of reading attitudes. *Journal of Reading, 17,* 25–28.

Rumelhart, D. E. & Ortony, A. (1977). Representation of knowledge. In R. C. Anderson, R. J. Spiro, & W. E. Montague (Eds.), *Schooling and the acquisition of knowledge.* (pp. 99–135) Hillsdale, NJ: Erlbaum.

Schickedanz, Judith A. (1986). *More than ABCs: The early stages of reading and writing.* Washington, DC: National Association for the Education of Young Children.

Sheldon, W., & Carrillo, R. (1952). Relation of parent, home and certain development characteristics to children's reading ability. *Elementary School Journal, 52,* 262–270.

Smith, F. (1978). *Understanding reading* (2nd ed.). New York: Holt, Rinehart & Winston.

Smith, F. (1983). Reading like a writer. *Language Arts, 60,* 558–567.

Snow, C. E. (1983). Literacy and language: Relationships during the preschool years. *Harvard Educational Review, 55,* 165–189.

Spiro, R. J. (1977). Remembering information from text: The 'state of schema' approach. In R. C. Anderson, R. J. Spiro, and W. E. Montague (Eds.), *Schooling and the acquisition of knowledge.* (pp. 137–165) Hillsdale, NJ: Erlbaum.

Squire, J. R. (1983). Composing and comprehending: Two sides of the same basic process. *Language Arts, 60,* 581–589.

Stein, N. L., & Glenn, C. G. (1979). An analysis of story comprehension in elementary school children. In R. O. Freedle, *Advances in discourse processes (Vol. 2): New directions in discourse processing.* (pp. 53–120). Norwood, N.J.: Ablex.

Steffensen, M. W., Joag-Dev, C., & Anderson, R. C. (1979). A cross-cultural perspective on reading comprehension. *Reading Research Quarterly, 15,* 10–29.

Taylor, D. (1983). *Family literacy: Young children learning to read and write.* Exeter, NH: Heinemann.

Teale, W. H. (1978). Positive environments for learning to read: What studies of early readers tell us. *Language Arts, 55,* 922–932.

Teale, W. H. (1981). Parents reading to their children: What we know and need to know. *Language Arts, 58,* 902–911.

Teale, W. H., Martinez, M. G., & Glass, W. L. (in press). Describing classroom storybook reading. In D. Bloome (Ed.), *Learning to use literacy in educational settings.* Norwood, NJ: Ablex.

Tierney, R. J., & Pearson, P. D. (1983). Toward a composing model of reading. *Language Arts, 60,* 568–580.

Vygotsky, L. S. (1962) *Thought and language.* Cambridge, MA: MIT Press.

Vygotsky, L. S. (1978). *Mind in society.* Cambridge, MA: Harvard University Press.

Wells, G. (1986). *The meaning makers.* Portsmouth, NH: Heinemann.

Wittrock, M. C., Marks, C. B., & Doctorow, M. J. (1975). Reading as a generative process. *Journal of Educational Psychology, 67,* 484–489.

28C. ROLES FOR COMPUTERS IN TEACHING THE ENGLISH LANGUAGE ARTS

Bertram Bruce

New information technologies such as computers and electronic networks are now being used in all facets of teaching the English language arts. These wide-ranging applications raise the question, "What role should these technologies play in teaching and learning?" This chapter discusses examples of applications grouped into five roles: (1) tutor, (2) tool, (3) language exploration, (4) medium, and (5) communication environment.

The time is near when computers, and other new information technologies, such as video, telecommunications, and speech synthesis, will play such important roles in English and language-arts classrooms that it will not be possible to write a chapter like this one. Pervasive and multifaceted, information technology is beginning to mirror all the traditional topics, methods, and goals of teaching. Thus, research on the use of computers must be examined in the context of noncomputer methods. It makes more sense to talk about a computer program designed to enhance literacy appreciation in comparison to other methods for teaching literature, computer-based or not, than in comparison to computer language arts programs in general.

A narrow conception of the computer's use within English language-arts teaching today would see the computer as a device with some well-defined function, such as drill on basic skills. Under this conception, it would make sense to examine critically the research that has been done specifically on computer use, with the aim of identifying the programs that are most effective and the populations of students who could be most helped. One would look for evidence of the effectiveness of this technique in comparison to other technologies, such as the use of film strips, to learn about famous authors, or playing word games as a way to build vocabulary.

A broader conception sees computers as flexible tools, which can be employed in such diverse ways that the basic question shifts from "Are computers good for English language arts?" to "How can computers be used to accomplish pedagogical goals?" or "How are computers being used?" Thus, rather than looking at technology as a new method to be assessed in toto, we must focus on the underlying educational issues first, and then ask how technology can best be used in each specific area. A computer program for teaching beginning reading using a phonics method would then be examined in relation to other approaches to teaching beginning reading, and only incidentally to other computer programs. This chapter presents five such roles for the computer.

Roles for the Computer

Computers are now being used in classrooms for instruction in composition, literature, decoding, reading comprehension, spelling, vocabulary, grammar, usage, punctuation, capitalization, brainstorming, planning, reasoning, outlining, reference use, study skills, rhetoric, handwriting, drama, and virtually every other area of language arts. There are also programs specifically designed for learners in preschool, primary, upper elementary, middle school, high school, and college grades, as well as those in adult, English as a second language, foreign language, bilingual, and special needs classes.

These wide-ranging applications of technology raise the question, "What role should the computer play in teaching and learning?" Some of the most important research on the use of computers in teaching English language arts has paralleled that of other research on computers in education, in trying to answer this question. This work has been a process of discovery, and at times, of contention between rival camps. There are divergent conceptions regarding whether, why, and how the computer should be used for instruction.

Turkle (1984) has suggested that the computer acts like a Rorschach ink blot in the way it evokes diverse responses from people. She argues that these responses tell more about people than about the computer. Similarly, the ways the computer is used in schools reveals more about conceptions of learning than it does about what computers can or cannot do.

Below are some possible responses one might make to the question of how a computer should be used. Each is indexed, not simply to features of the technology, but to assumptions about the enterprise of schooling. Thus, depending upon one's assumptions about education, the computer can be:

1. A *tutor*. It can individualize instruction, provide learning material at a controlled pace, and record student progress.
2. A *tool*. It aids in reading; it allows students to produce and format texts easily; it facilitates revision of texts; it checks for spelling errors. It stores in a compact and easily accessible form all sorts of information that learners need, from style sheets to encyclopedic data.
3. A *way to explore language*. It makes the regularities, the beauties, and the difficulties of language something that students can examine and interact with in new ways.
4. A *medium*. It makes possible new modes of communication, and "hypertexts," or "hypermedia," which allow the intermixing of tables, charts, graphs, pictures, sounds, video, and text.
5. An *environment for communication*. It is a new social realm that permits new forms of meaningful communication and reconfigures the relationships among students and teachers.

It is not possible to present a survey of computer use within each of these roles that is both comprehensive and brief. Instead, this chapter presents some representative uses as a way of suggesting possible directions. Because computer use is still rapidly evolving, the examples represent categories of applications, not necessarily formal research studies on classroom effectiveness. There should be more such studies, for the few that exist highlight the diversity of the impact, positive and negative, that computers may have.

Computers as Tutors

Artificial intelligence research has led to the specification of criteria for so-called "intelligent tutoring systems." An intelligent tutor should have the ability to perform the task being taught, and to discuss it articulately. Thus, a spelling tutor should be able to correct misspellings and to identify them as instances of general spelling rules. A second important requirement is a representation of the student's evolving knowledge, so that misconceptions can be diagnosed and addressed appropriately. Third, the system should have strategies for teaching. It should know how to present material, how to pose problems, and how to achieve the appropriate balance between tutor-direction and support for student-directed inquiry.

Not surprisingly, designing an intelligent tutoring system for language use is difficult. Little of such software exists today, and the most successful computer tutors have been designed for well-constrained topics within mathematics and science. One such program for language is *Iliad* (Bates & Wilson, 1982), which was designed to tutor deaf children who have difficulties mastering language forms such as negation and question formation (see Knapp, 1986, for a discussion of computer use for other special needs). *Iliad* can generate syntactic variations of a core sentence. For example, from the sentence "John ate the apple" *Iliad* might generate:

Did John eat the apple?
What did John eat?
Who ate the apple? etc.

The tutoring component asks the child to carry out similar transformations and comments on the result. *Iliad* could, in principle, be extended to allow children to design their own transformation rules, either using a simple grammar notation, or by using examples. Thus, a child might propose: "Which apple did John eat?" as a new transformation of "John ate the apple" and then test it on other sentences. The child would type 'Mary sees the cat' and the system would use the rule to produce "Which cat did Mary see?"

A related program is VP^2 (Schuster, 1986), which tutors non-native speakers in English. It incorporates an explicit model of the student's developing grammar. Hundreds of simpler tutoring programs also exist—programs for teaching letters of the alphabet, spelling, vocabulary, synonyms and antonyms, grammar, punctuation, capitalization, and word usage. These skill development programs are useful for specific purposes, but extensive reliance on them may interfere with addressing a greater need: helping students to learn purposeful use of language in its complete forms (Warren & Rosebery, 1988).

Computers as Tools

Word processing (see Olds, 1985) has become such a commonplace fixture within English and language-arts classrooms that some people now take it for granted, saying, "We only do word processing; when will we start real computer use?" Of course, word processing is real computer use, and serves an important function, even if it only helps with the practical details of creating and sharing texts within a classroom. Moreover, there is some, albeit mixed, evidence that in making it easier to compose and revise, to see problems with a text, and to share texts, students learn to be better writers and readers (Bruce, Rubin, & Barnhardt, in press; Bruce & Michaels, 1989; Daiute, 1985; Levin, Boruta, & Vasconcellos, 1982; Rubin & Bruce, 1985, 1986; Wresch, 1984).

There are now hundreds of word processing programs, which allow writers to enter and revise text. Some, like *Bank Street Writer* (Scholastic), present menus of functions from which the author chooses, thus making it easy to learn and to use the system, but with some sacrifice of flexibility. More complex programs, such as *Wordbench* (Addison-Wesley) allow writers to control details of text format, permit access to indexed notes, and have capabilities for tables of contents, lists, footnotes and endnotes, biliographies, and indexes.

Assistance in Reading. But word processing is only one of the ways computers serve as tools for writing and reading (see Wresch, 1988). Programs with speech synthesizers, or stored speech, now assist readers who encounter unfamiliar words (McConkie & Zola, 1985; Rosegrant & Cooper, 1983). On-line dictionaries help with word meanings. Hypertext systems, which allow the storage of multiple, linked texts, can provide further explanations, additional examples, or commentaries on the text at hand (see section on "Computers as Media").

Generating Ideas and Planning. It is in the area of writing that we find the widest range of tool-like uses of computers. Several software programs have been designed to help with the tasks of planning and generating ideas (see Pea & Kurland, 1986). One program, called *CAC,* offers children advice on composing persuasive text. For instance, the student might ask for advice about choosing the next sentence. The computer suggests actions based on keywords it finds in the preceding text written by the student. Several word processing programs have an option to turn off the screen, when text is being entered, so that the student is not distracted by the visual image of what is written. This technique is called "invisible writing" (see Marcus & Blau, 1983). It is one way of facilitating "free writing" (Elbow, 1973) and encourages students not to focus on editing prematurely. Idea generation activities are included in many other programs such as: *SEEN* (H. Schwartz), a literature-oriented program; *Writer's Helper* (Conduit), which displays the tree of ideas developed by the writer; *Writing Workshop* (Milliken), which includes three prewriting programs; and *Writing a Narrative* (MECC), a tutorial on narrative structure and point of view.

The computer also offers the capability of moving text around in various ways and of viewing it from different vantage points. For instance, some outline generating programs, such as *Framework* (Ashton-Tate), create empty, numbered outline structures within a word processing program. Related programs include *ThinkTank* (Living Videotex), *MaxThink* (MaxThink), and *Freestyle* (Summa Technologies). These programs have become known as "idea processors."

Finding Information. Data bases of information make it possible for students to browse text as a method of stimulating their reading and writing. There are now large data bases available on compact disk. These include dictionaries (for instance, the *Oxford English Dictionary*), encyclopedias (for instance, *Grolier's*), and complete statistics from recent Olympics games. The NeXT computer comes with its own built-in library, including a thesaurus, a dictionary, and the *Oxford Complete Works of Shakespeare*. There are also many microcomputer-based data bases, such as Australia's *Bushrangers* (KnowWare), which allow students to explore new worlds of information.

Viewing a Text. One program included in the *Writer's Workbench* (AT&T Bell Laboratories) strips away all text except headings and the beginning and end of paragraphs, giving the author an uncluttered view of text transitions. Similar features in *Writer's Assistant* (Interlearn) allow the user to see only the first sentence of each paragraph, or to flip between a sentence-by-sentence format and the conventional paragraph organization.

Seeing a text in which each sentence starts at the left margin makes it easier for writers to discover for themselves problems with capitalization, punctuation, run-on sentences, sentence fragments, repetitions, beginnings of sentences, and other technical points. The *Electronic English Handbook* (Technology Training Associates) provides a related sort of help: It is an on-screen reference tool that allows the writer to access usage rules and examples during the composition process.

Other programs exist to support composition within a genre, or discourse mode, such as poetry. These include poetry generators such as *Compupoem* (Marcus, 1982) and *Poetry Prompter* (Interlearn). Other programs help in analyzing or revising a poem. The *Poetry Processor* (Newman, 1986) aids the developing poet by displaying a line of a poem in a specified meter. For example, the first line of Shakespeare's Sonnet 18 (in iambic pentameter) would appear as:

Shall I comPARE thee TO a SUMmer's DAY?

If a student wanted to try the same line in trochaic pentameter, the program would show:

SHALL i COMpare THEE to A sumMER'S day?

Reading the line to himself, he might decide to rewrite the line or change the meter.

Writer's Workbench includes over 40 programs that provide feedback on spelling, diction, style, and other text characteristics. An interactive version of the program works within a text editor; it suggests correct spellings for words, and will automatically replace them if the author desires. The *Writer's Assistant* (Levin, Boruta, & Vasconcellos, 1982), checks spelling and other features, and allows students to try out various sentence combinations. *Epistle* (IBM) has a parser that detects complex linguistic problems, such as subject-verb agreement. The *Random*

House Electronic Thesaurus provides word alternatives to facilitate revision. These programs are advisory, rather than tutorial.

Viewing the Writing Process. Despite extensive research on writing in recent years (Graves, 1982; Hillocks, 1986), we still know too little about how writers generate ideas, how they revise, how they use what they have read in writing, or how their writing changes over time. One reason is that such processes occur in the writer's head, and external manifestations, such as pauses, backtracking, use of resources, oral interactions with others, and so on, are difficult to record and interpret.

With text being produced and stored on the computer, there arise new possiblities for examining the writing process. Some text editors offer a 'replay' facility, which re-enacts an entire editing session, allowing student and teacher to see the process of text creation. Sirc (1988) describes how he uses this approach to model revision. He records every keystroke he makes during his revision of a student paper. Then he replays the revision session discussing the reasons for each step in the process. This approach allows students to peer inside the expert writer's process of revision.

Computers as Ways to Explore Language Structure

Computer-based microworlds have been developed in various areas of science and mathematics to allow students to explore new domains, test hypotheses, construct models, and discover new phenomena (Papert, 1980). The same technology can be used to create microworlds for language. Investigations within these microworlds can be highly motivating for students; moreover, they lead students to think deeply about language patterns, conceptual relationships, and the structure of ideas. We are only at the beginning of this potentially powerful role for computers in language instruction.

An example of this approach is the use of the programming language, *Logo,* to construct models of language structure and use (Goldenberg & Feurzeig, 1987). Students work within any genre, or mode of discourse, to build up their theories about meaning and form. For instance, they can write programs that gossip.

In this case, gossip is viewed as comprising descriptions of actions that someone else has allegedly taken, actions which are newsworthy because they involve surprising revelations about the other's character. Thus, there is a predication about a subject. In *Logo,* this might be expressed by the following procedure:

```
TO GOSSIP
    OUTPUT (SENTENCE PERSON DOESWHAT)
END
```

This procedure is a small computer program, which, when executed, produces a sentence composed of a first part, which is the name of a person, and a second part, which is a description of some action that person did. Now, this only works if the procedures, PERSON and DOESWHAT, are appropriately defined. For example:

```
TO PERSON
        OUTPUT PICK |SANDY DALE DANA CHRIS|
END

TO DOESWHAT
        OUTPUT PICK |CHEATS. |LOVES TO WALK.|→
                    |TALKS A MILE A MINUTE.| YELLS.|
END
```

The first procedure, PERSON, selects one person from a list. The second procedure, DOESWHAT, selects a predicate to apply to that person. In this case, the predicate is expressed by an unanalyzed verb phrase. With these procedures, a student can then ask the computer to print out any number of gossip statements. At first, the interest for students comes from the fact that they can be playful, making the computer print out funny, and sometimes, surprising statements, even though they provided it with all its data. As they continue to explore the gossip domain, though, the interest comes from something deeper, a developing appreciation of the complexities, beauties, and regularities of language.

For example, students can revise the original procedures to produce more versatile GOSSIP programs. They can break apart the predication into transitive verbs with objects, or expand the range of possible subjects. They can add conditional actions to the procedures, for instance, that only certain people can do particular actions. As they construct their GOSSIP programs, they are forced to confront fundamental questions about language, such as, "What is the relationship between syntax and semantics?," "What is a word?," or "What makes a sentence interesting?" While the program has no means for answering such questions, it provides an environment in which students can seek answers themselves; it allows them to see the consequences of their own hypotheses about language.

This approach is but one example drawn from a family of programs and activities designed to encourage students to explore language. *Phrasebooks and Boxes* (Sharples, 1985) are two extensions of *Logo* that allow children to classify words, create their own dictionaries and phrasebooks, devise a quiz, write a program that will converse in natural language, or build their own 'Adventure Games,' in which other students explore a student-created fantasy world. *Crossword Magic* (Mindscape) allows students to create crossword puzzles. The activity encourages exploration of word meanings and relationships, as well as spelling. *Missing Links* (Sunburst) supports activities in which students try to decipher a text in which various letters or words have been left out. In doing so, they develop reading and problem-solving skills. *Storymaker* (Rubin, 1980) allows students to create and manipulate text units larger than the sentence. Story structures are represented as a tree consisting of nodes connected by branches. The nodes contain sentences or paragraphs. The student creates a story by choosing branches to follow. The program adds each selected text segment to the story as the child moves through the story tree. The student can also write new text segments, which then become available for other students to choose. There is still little research regarding classroom use of these constructive approaches to language understanding.

Computers as Media

Increasingly, computer-based writing is never published as words on a printed page. Electronic mail, on-line documentation, and electronic encyclopedias are read directly from a video screen. The computer has thus become a new communications medium, one which facilitates traditional paper-based writing, but allows other forms of writing as well. There are now multi-media messaging and conferencing systems that allow users to send not just text, but images, graphics, spread sheets, voice and video, e.g., *Diamond* (Thomas, Forsdick, Crowley, Robertson, Schaaf, Tomlinson, & Travers, 1985). These systems are being equipped with a variety of fonts, to permit writing in languages such as Arabic, Russian, and Japanese; they can also display text in appropriate orientations, such as right-to-left, or down a column. Current research (Levy, 1988) is exploring how our current concepts of texts, documents, and media must change as these systems are used, and to understand the possibilities for enhancing communication and exploring language.

Moreover, the computer can be used to create webs of related information. Explicit connections between texts allow readers to travel from one document to another, or from one place within a document to another. The computer can help a reader to follow trails of cross-reference without losing the original context. Electronic document systems also facilitate co-authoring of text. A group of children can create a common electronic notebook, by making their own contributions, viewing and editing one another's items, then linking the items together.

Authors and readers can now be given the same set of integrated tools to create, browse, and develop text. They can move through material created by other people, add their own links and annotations, and merge the material with their own writings. In consequence, the boundaries between author and reader may begin to disappear. Research is needed to understand these changes and the consequences they have for reading and writing instruction.

Several programs help writers organize thoughts using a tool described as linked note cards. *Notecards* (Xerox) includes a multiwindowed display that allows a writer to create individual notes that can be linked to other notes. Notes can contain graphic images or text. With the hypertext editing system IRIS (Brown University), a person reading an article about cars has a choice of how much detail to see about the history of cars, their manufacture, their relation to the rubber industry, and so on. Hypertext has now become available on microcomputers (e.g., Apple's *Hypercard*). These systems open up new possibilities for communication. The challenge is to use this powerful medium in more open and enriching ways.

Computers as Learning Environments

Computers can be used to foster social interaction and thereby contribute to language development and learning. It is through feedback from others, peer tutoring, and sharing ideas, that reading and writing skills develop. Several writing programs, such as the *Quill Mailbag* and *Library* facilities, make it easier for writers to share their products (Rubin & Bruce, 1985, 1986). *Mailbag* is a simple electronic mail system in which writers can send messages to individuals (other students or the teacher) to groups, or to the whole class. *Library* allows texts to be stored with complete titles and author's names, and keywords to facilitate finding the text by selecting a topic. It allows students to store two author's names with a text as a way of supporting collaborative writing.

Electronic networks are being used increasingly for communication among students and teachers. For example, the Computer Chronicles News Network allows children to share news items from around the world. Research in now underway (see Riel, 1988) to explore different ways of organizing such networks. Some networks are focused on a task; others have a looser conference structure. Some have centralized direction and others do not. It is too soon to say what the full implications of different network participant structures might be.

Teachers are also beginning to use electronic networks for communicating. In a project in Alaska (Bruce, Rubin, & Barnhardt, in press), teachers developed a community through the use of electronic mail. Their shared need to learn better ways of teaching for nonmainstream students was partially met through the exchange of classroom ideas and mutual encouragement over an electronic network. The network made exchange of messages much faster than ordinary mail and greatly eased the task of sending the same message to many people at once. Moreover, other writing already in electronic form, such as students' texts or a teacher's text written for a university course, could also be easily transmitted and shared with other teachers. There is now a *Computers and Composition Digest* used primarily in its electronic form. Teachers, researchers, and software developers interact through issues of the digest, which are constructed out of electronic mail messages and went via networks to over 600 sites.

Research on using real-time communication networks to teach English language skills or composition is also underway, as in the ENFI consortium (Batson, 1988; Sirc, 1988; Thompson, 1987). In these systems, students engage in a written form of conversation. Their typed messages are transmitted immediately to others in the group. Such an environment requires students to formulate their ideas as written text but allows faster response than traditional writing or even electronic mail. Many students find these environments more conducive to writing than traditional writing classes.

Conclusion

Technology can be used to change writing instruction in a variety of ways. Computers can aid at places where teacher time and attention are insufficient. They can facilitate the processes of generating ideas and organizing text. Unlike teachers, they can give feedback at any convenient moment. They can comment upon features of written texts. With the aid of a text editor, revision of text is more efficient and rewarding. Computers can increase the time-on-task and can help lessen the teaching load. They can thus create time and opportunity for teacher involvement with essential aspects of writing processes that are beyond the reach of the computer.

New technologies can also help to realize a more functional way of teaching writing. Ideals of writing across the curriculum may become more feasible with the support of computers. By means of computer networking, communities of student-writers can be established. Real audiences and meaningful goals can stimulate the development of competency in written communication as well as enhance motivation.

But the potential value of computers is far from full realization. Many of the uses described here require a rethinking of student and teacher roles, of curricula, and of school activities. Moreover, current programs and models for computer-based activities are often clumsy to use or difficult to integrate with other learning. Costs are still high, especially when viewed as only a portion of the meager resources available for instructional materials. And too often, the best computer resources are inequitably distributed. Despite these problems, the use of computers for English language-arts instruction is in fact growing and promises to be an increasingly important aspect of learning in the future.

References

Bates, M. & Wilson, K. (1982). *ILIAD: Interactive language instruction assistance for the deaf* (BBN Report No. 4771). Cambridge, MA: Bolt Beranek and Newman, Inc.

Batson, T. (1988, February). The ENFI Project: A networked classroom approach to writing instruction. *Academic Computing, 2*(5), 32–33, 55–56.

Beeman, W. O. (1988). *Intermedia: A case study of innovation in higher education*. Final Report to the Annenberg/CPB Project. Providence, RI: IRIS, Brown University.

Bruce, B., & Michaels, S. (1989). *Classroom contexts and literacy development: How writing systems shape the teaching and learning of composition (Technical Report)*. Urbana, IL: Center for the Study of Reading, University of Illinois at Urbana-Champaign.

Bruce, B., Rubin, A. & Barnhardt (in press). *Electronic Quills*. Hillsdale, NJ: Erlbaum.

Daiute, C. (1985). *Writing and computers*. Reading, MA: Addison-Wesley.

Elbow, P. (1973). *Writing without teachers*. London: Oxford University Press.

Goldenberg, E. P., & Feurzeig, W. (1987). *Exploring language with Logo*. Cambridge, MA: The MIT Press.

Graves, D. H. (1982). *Writing: Teachers and children at work*. Exeter, NH: Heinemann Educational Books.

Hillocks, G. (1986). *Research on written composition: New directions for teaching*. Urbana, IL: National Conference on Research in English.

Knapp, L. R. (1986). *The word processor and the writing teacher*. Englewood Cliffs, NJ: Prentice-Hall.

Levin, J. A. (1982). Microcomputers as interactive communication media: An interactive text interpreter. *The Quarterly Newsletter of the Laboratory of Comparative Human Cognition, 4*, 34–36.

Levin, J. A., Boruta, M. J., & Vasconcellos, M. T. (1982). Microcomputer-based environments for writing: A writer's assistant. In A. C. Wilkinson (Ed.), *Classroom computers and cognitive science* (pp. 219–232). New York: Academic Press.

Levy, D. M. (1988). *Topics in Document Research*. Paper presented at ACM Conference on Document Processing Systems, Santa Fe, New Mexico, December 5–9, 1988.

Marcus, S. (1982). Compupoem: CAI for writing and studying poetry. *The Computing Teacher*, 28–31.

Marcus, S. & Blau, S. (1983). Not seeing is relieving: Invisible writing with computers. *Educational Technology*, 11: 12–15.

McConkie, G. W., & Zola, D. (1985). *Computer aided reading: An environment for developmental research*. Paper presented at the Society for Research on Child Development, Toronto, Canada.

Michaels, S. & Bruce, B. (1989). *Classroom Contexts and literacy development: How writing systems shape the teaching and learning of composition*. (Technical Report No. 476). Urbana-Champaign: University of Illinois, Center for the Study of Reading.

Olds, H. F. (1985). A new generation of word processors. *Classroom Computer Learning*, 22–25.

Papert, R. D. & Kurland, D. M. (1987) *Mindstorms: Children*, computers, and powerful ideas. New York: Basic Books.

Pea, R. D., & Kurland, D. M. (1987). Cognitive technologies for writing. In Frase, H. (Ed.) *Review of Research in Education, 14*: 277–326.

Riel, M. (1988). *Telecommunication: Connections to the future*. California State Educational Technology Committee.

Rosegrant, T., & Cooper, R. (1983). *Talking screen texturiting program manual: A word processing program for children using a micro-computer and a speech synthesizer*. Glendale, Arizona: Computer Adventures, Ltd.

Rubin, A. D., & Bruce, B. C. (1985). QUILL: Reading and writing with a microcomputer. In B. A. Hutson (Ed.), *Advances in reading and language research*, 97–117. Greenwich, CT: JAI Press.

Rubin, A. D., & Bruce, B. C. (1986). Learning with QUILL: Lessons for students, teachers and software designers. In T. E. Raphael (Ed.), *Contexts of school based literacy* (pp. 217–230). New York: Random House.

Schuster, E (1986) VP2: The role of user modeling in correcting errors in second language learning. *Journal of Structural Learning, 9*: 175–190.

Sharples, M. (1985). Phrasebooks and Boxes: Microworlds for Language. Paper presented at the World Conference of Computers and Education, Norfolk, Virginia.

Sirc, G. (1988, April). Learning to write on a LAN. *T.H.E. Journal, 15*(8), 99–104.

Thomas, R. H., Forsdick, H. C., Crowley, T. R., Robertson, G. G., Schaaf, R. W., Tomlinson, R. S., & Travers, V. M. (1985). Diamond: A multimedia message system built upon a distributed architecture. *IEEE Computer, 18*: 1–31.

Thompson, D. (1987). Teaching writing on a local area network. *T.H.E. Journal, 15*(2), 92–97.

Turkle, S. (1984). *The second self: Computers and the human spirit*. New York: Simon and Schuster.

Warren, B., & Rosebery, A. S. (1988). Theory and practice: Uses of the computer in reading. *Remedial and Special Education, 9*(2), 29–38.

Wresch, W. (Ed.) (1984). *The computer in composition instruction*. Urbana, IL: National Council of Teachers of English.

28D. THE MEDIA ARTS AND ENGLISH LANGUAGE ARTS TEACHING AND LEARNING

Carole Cox

Research on film and other media arts has looked at many things, depending on how the role of media in education is viewed. Several lenses have been used to focus investigations of media over time, such as the uses and influence of mass media, effectiveness of media in instruction, and the relationship of nonprint media and reading (Allen, 1960; Dillingofski, 1979; Hoban & van Ormer, 1972; Wartella & Reeves, 1985).

Within the field of teaching the English language arts there have been many film and media arts advocates, but little research focused on their role in the curriculum (Hennis, 1981). Knowledge about the media arts in the lives of children and adolescents has emerged primarily in answer to questions about the use and gratification, or direct effects of the mass media (Luke, 1985) in social contexts outside the classroom, where media is most used (Chu & Schramm, 1967; Himmelweit, Oppenheim, & Vince, 1958; Jamison, Suppes, & Wells, 1974; Lyle & Hoffman, 1972; Schramm, 1973; Schramm, Lyle, & Parker, 1961; Wartella, Alexander, & Lemish, 1979). Furthermore, much of what has been accomplished in the area of media research has used a behaviorally grounded cause-and-effect model for hypothesis generating, for often simplistic empirical studies of the medias' effects on children and adolescents (Meadowcroft & McDonald, 1986), and has been typically atheoretical in nature (Salomon, 1979).

There has been a lack, then, not only of research on the media arts in the teaching of the English language arts, but also possible theoretical explanations of the role of film and other visual and aural medial in relation to English, of the sort that grounds other disciplines in the field (Polito, 1965; Suhor, 1986). Attempts to develop theories and models of use of media have emerged primarily from the work of educational psychologists, mass media researchers, and visual arts and communication theorists who have questioned and examined this issue primarily in explorations of the complex relationship of the symbol system of television to children's learning (Olson, 1974).

RELEVANT RESEARCH ON THE MEDIA ARTS IN RELATION TO ENGLISH

This chapter will focus on research that seems most relevant to understanding film and other media arts in learning environments for teaching the English language arts. These studies include those that examined comparative effects of media arts, preference and response studies, and those that have analyzed film and media arts education in schools.

Comparative Effects of the Media Arts on Learning from Narrative

Certain studies have compared the effects of film and other nonprint media and print, on learning, cognitive skills, attitudes, and behaviors relevant to teaching the English language arts, particularly learning from narrative. Modes of narrative presentation such as storytelling, picture books read aloud, sound and silent film and video, filmstrip, audio-cassettes, and recording of a storyteller have been analyzed and compared for either a generalized or isolatable effect on specific learning from narrative such as story vocabulary, comprehension, identification with characters, enjoyment, or listening skills (Cowgill, 1975; Levinson, 1964; Ruch & Levin, 1977; Stevenson & Siegel, 1969; Sullivan, 1985; Taylor, 1976). These studies have consistently failed to show that one medium is consistently more effective than another for any general effects on learning from narrative.

Other studies, however, have shown that the media arts differ in their effectiveness for conveying different types of information from narrative (Alwitt, Anderson, Lorch, & Levin, 1980; Barrow & Westley, 1959; Greenfield, 1984; Hayes, Kelly, & Mandel, 1986; Huston & Wright, 1983; Meringoff, Vibbert, Kelly, & Charr, 1981; Pezdek, Lehrer, & Simon, 1984; Salomon, 1983). There is some evidence that aural renditions enhance verbal comprehension (Beagles-Roos & Gat, 1983), and others have shown that young children remember more visual than auditory information, especially the most important, or central characteristics of the story (Calvert, Huston, Watkins, & Wright, 1982; Gibbons, Anderson, Smith, Field, & Fischer, 1986; Hayes & Birnbaum, 1980; Hayes, Chemelski, & Birnbaum, 1981; Pezdek & Hartman, 1983; Stoneman & Brody, 1983). In a study that compared children's apprehension of an unfamiliar story either read to them from an illustrated book or presented as a televised film, for example, Meringoff (1980) measured recall of story content and inferences about characters and events. She found that children who saw the film remembered more story actions, and relied more on visual content as a basis for inferences, and those who were read the story in picture-book form remembered more vocabulary, and relied more on textual content as a basis for inferences, providing support for Salomon's (1979) notion that differences in the symbol systems used by media to represent content, rather than media per se, influence learning: ". . . if their unique symbolic capabilities are capitalized upon, each medium adresses itself to different . . . mental skills, thus benefits learners of different aptitudes and serves different educational ends" (p. 144).

Others offer theoretical perspectives sensitive to these media differences with regard to the nature of symbolization. Gardner, Howard, and Perkins (1974) point out that the same medium (television) may be a vehicle for different symbol systems (language, visual imagery), and the same symbol system (language) may occur in different media (book, television). The extent to which, then, students are exposed to certain media may result in the cultivation of the unique cognitive skills necessary to gain meaning from the particular symbol system used by each different media.

Preference and Response Studies in the Media Arts

Many studies have looked at film and media preferences since the turn of the century (Wartella & Reeves, 1985), and most recent studies have analyzed use and interest in commercial television programs (Comstock, Chaffee, Katzman, McCombs, & Roberts, 1978; Lyle & Hoffman, 1972; Schramm, Lyle, and Parker, 1961; Streicher & Bonney, 1974).

The National Assessment of Educational Progress (1981) reports, however, that given a choice of watching television, going to a movie, reading a book, or reading a magazine, one half of the 9-year-olds and nearly two thirds of the 17-year-olds sampled chose film first. Despite this high interest in film among students, only a few studies have looked exclusively at preference patterns of children for short entertainment films of the type most often used in the classroom (Cox, 1978, 1982). These have shown that 9- to 11-year-old students preferred narrative films with stories of familiar experience, similar to their interests in literature at this age. They also preferred live-action over animation as a film technique, and they least liked non-narrative films with highly abstract visual content.

The role of interest in the evaluation, comprehension, and attitudes of viewer orientation towards film was investigated earlier by Robinson (1974) who found that more analytical film viewers had been interested in and had experiences with the medium since childhood; were around adults with an interest in film as a child; attended more artistic and cultural events as children than less analytical viewers; and continued to view films and enjoy their study, value the film medium for self-enhancement rather than just entertainment, are selective about films to view, and are more critical during viewing.

Secondary students' responses to film have been examined by Lewis (1972), who found that 10th-grade students interpreted both lyric and narrative film more than literature, and narrated literature more than film. Freden (1974) found few clear cut differences in 9th-grade students' responses analyzed according to categories developed for literary response (Purves & Rippere, 1968), but showed that interest was related to enjoyment and their willingness to extend responses.

Elementary students' response to film has recently been explored by Cox, Beach, & Many (1988) in a descriptive study of types of responses and response strategies of elementary-age children to short films, and the relationship of these responses to film type and preference. Response to film centered on content rather than form, and the types of responses varied according to the film type, and student preference for films. Children were much more likely to explain and expand their responses to the realistic narrative films they liked most, and only describe their responses to the more abstract, non-narrative films they liked less. It appears that children's responses to film are most influenced by content and interest, much as they are in other print and nonprint media such as literature and television. Also similar to their responses to other print and nonprint media is their preference for narrative, or more story-like, linear, and literary, to non-narrative presentations.

In contrast to the numerous studies on students' literature and print preferences (Purves & Beach, 1972), little research on preferences for the media arts exists other than for television, although the role of interest in understanding response has long been suggested as important (Cooper, 1985). Further research may more clearly define this relationship in terms of the schemata, or knowledge structures, representing what a learner feels as well as knows about something (Bandura, 1978; Salomon, 1979; Watzlawick, Beavin, & Jackson, 1967), and Wartella, Alexander, and Lemish (1979) have suggested several hypotheses that may ground future research in this area.

Creating and Communicating Through the Media Arts

A few studies have selected to focus exclusively on film as a constructed object, looking for links between the film form and possibly other mass media forms, such as television, with the interpretive, creative or cognitive skills of audiences. This type of research has analyzed films made by children, hoping to gain insights about both the development of learning processes in general, and, more specifically, the communication of meaning in the context of the development of literacy, particularly as a cultural phenomenon (Chalfen, 1981; Durkin, 1970; Larson & Meade, 1969, Sutton-Smith, Eadie, & Griffin, 1983; Sutton-Smith, Eadie, Griffin, & Zarem, 1979; Worth & Adair, 1972).

Griffin (1985) had observed students becoming more intelligent and skillful filmmakers and became interested in both the topics and events that were most important to them in the creation of their own films. He identified patterns of editing and narrative structure, and the variance among these patterns supported Gross's (1974) hypothesis that symbolic modes "are partially but not totally susceptible to translation into other modes . . . and are basically learned only through actions appropriate to the particular mode" (p. 57). Although age was a factor in the development of filmmaking abilities, even more important was familarity with television content and a desire to incorporate it into films, and technical competence was more related to experience in filmmaking than age. The most consistent finding underlying developmental differences as students became more proficient filmmakers was their increased use of television as a model for narrative form, theme, camera work, and editing style. These findings suggest the great extent to which television as a cultural model may be shaping the unique symbolic patterns children draw on to organize and represent the world to others.

Other studies of students' composing processes through audio-visual symbol systems have found that the experience of transforming ideas and images from one medium to another, such as words to pictures, stimulated a challenge to children's intellectual powers and a desire to be analytical and thorough and provide specific concrete examples of abstract ideas as they communicated through media creation (Weiss, 1982), and that the experience of active communication in cinematic codes through filmmaking significantly affected mental skills, especially the effect of editing activity on children's ability to form logical inferences (Tidhar, 1984).

Findings such as these on the relationship of skills requisite to creating and communicating through media, and cognitive development, lend support to Salomon's notion that the mastery of such skills represents a high level of literacy involving involving "top down" elaboration processes that are not specific to any symbol system, but can be transferred across mediums.

Film and Media Arts Education

Several surveys have focused on media use in English language-arts education. Barry (1979) replicated the Squire and Applebee survey of secondary schools for 1968, finding an increase in the use of media over the earlier study, but also finding that media was still not used with any consistency in English education.

In a review of surveys of film use in education (Lynch, 1983; McKeever, 1972; Pryluck & Hemenway, 1982), Lynch (1986) described the types and sources of films used, purposes for film use, film teaching methods, and film related background of those who teach film. At both the secondary and elementary level, film is taught primarily by English and language-arts teachers and is strongly tied to the teaching of literature with little attention paid to the teaching of film as a constructed object. In general, however, film education is not well defined.

In high schools, for example, there is no real consensus of what even constitutes an introductory course on film. The less teachers use films, the more likely they are to use an instructional film or a filmed version of a book to support the teaching of literary terms. More frequent film users are more likely to use film to encourage students to think, as a common topic for discussion, for less able students, or in lieu of literature. Overall, decisions about how much to use film, which films to use, and how to approach film in the classroom, i.e. film study, mass media study, filmmaking and TV production, interdisciplinary courses using film, or film as literature, is highly idiosyncratic.

At the elementary level, film is taught even less than at the secondary level. Elementary teachers tend to use film to support curriculum, and primarily use instructional films for this purpose, or films of children's fiction. The percentage of film use is about equally divided among high, medium, low, and nonusers, the latter citing lack of time, problems with access to equipment and films, and lack of familiarity with films as reasons they do not tend to use film.

A model to test the efficacy of a classroom-taught course on television, including televised films, was recently piloted and put into effect in Great Britain in response not only to the broad goal of learning about the media, but more specifically because the study of television and film has become part of English literature. The television film *Flying into the Wind* has become the first film to be studied as a 'set text' in an English literature 'O' level examination in Britain (Kelley, Gunter, & Buckle, 1987; Kelley, Gunter, & Kelley, 1985). The six-week course for 14- and 15-year-olds included a study and production of video programs, and critical evaluation of television drama, documentary, and news programming. Results on tests indicated that students were better able to understand the medium and programs and make sophisticated evaluations. This model will be part of plans to implement the study of media in schools in Britain as part of the Media Studies and English literature GSCE examinations. While no such mandate for the inclusion of media studies in American schools exists, as Lynch has indicated, Kelley, Gunter and Buckle refer to several successful television literacy projects that have been carried out in the United States (Idaho State Department of Education, 1978; Media Action Research Centre, 1979; Singer, Zuckerman, & Singer, 1980; WNET, 1980).

Beyond specific media studies programs, others have articulated the role of the media arts in English education, and in the curriculum at large. In *Double Exposure,* Costanzo (1984) describes an approach to composing through writing and film that is well-grounded in current theory and research and offers a way of thinking about seeing, writing, and thinking in the classroom based on what he calls "the collaborative powers of the visual image and the written word" (preface). Suhor (1984, 1986) has articulated a semiotics-based curriculum as a basis for making clear the meaning of the media in educational settings, as well as all other sign systems.

RESEARCH, PRACTICE, AND THE MEDIA ARTS: A VIEW TO THE FUTURE

Much of what we already know about the media arts in learning and instruction can be traced to a research tradition that has focused on questions of media effectiveness, but many have questioned this tradition as meaningful (Jamison, Suppes, & Wells, 1974; Winn, 1986). Clark (1983) maintains that this work has not produced meaningful results because such studies have simply not asked the right questions. Neither have they used useful methods, for by controlling for everything other than medium, including method, it is not reasonable to expect that differences would be found. He argues that simple medium-differences do not make a difference, and that the learning context and methods that are used should center further work in the field.

A promising direction for future research and practice has been suggested by the work of Salomon (1981, 1983, & 1984) who suggests that media's role in education is determined by students' perceptions that affect the amount of mental effort they are willing to invest in learning from media (Shannon 1985). Framed against the background of a theoretical approach to considering all verbal and visual media in education from an educational-psychological perspective, which is that essential differences among these media are the unique ways in which their symbol systems structure and convey contents, Salomon (1979) describes an interactive model of the visual media experience that draws from recent work in schema theory as explanation for the processing of text discourse (Ausubel, 1968; Nelson, 1977) and Bandura's scheme of reciprocal determinism (1978). Within this model, the meaning of a communication is what is attributed to it by the viewer, and not an intrinsic and immutable property of the message itself. This model acknowledges the viewer's prior knowledge, considers viewing as active communication, and emphasizes the need for critical and literate viewing instuction in schools (Luke, 1985).

A basis for such a model is much of the recent research on media which has rejected the traditional cause and effect model and replaced it with one that considers students as active, schema-guided viewers (Collins, 1981; Dorr 1981; Lorch, Bellack, & Augsback, 1987; Rice & Wartella, 1981). Rather than simply comparing the effects of one presentation mode with another, the comparative effects of unmediated and mediated, with adult interaction or instructional intervention, viewing are under investigation (Buerkel-Rothfuss, Greenberg, Atkin, & Neuendorff, 1982; Desmond & Jeffries-Fox, 1983).

This model seriously calls into question the notion of a linear and mindless affect of a medium such as television viewers (Postman 1979, 1982; Trelease, 1982; Winn, 1977; Zuckerman, Singer, & Singer, 1980), and is supported by studies that have shown that viewers actively mediate the effects of a medium (Anderson, Lorch, Field, & Sanders, 1981; Collins, 1981; Levin & Anderson, 1976). Calvert, Huston, Watkins, and Wright (1982), for example, showed that although children all understood the same animated film, they used widely different reasons for their answers.

One of Salomon's (1979) suggested research hypotheses in his efforts to further theoretically around research in visual media, is that early exposure to a medium's symbol system in the context of interactions with adults who support the learner's efforts to address themselves to symbolic modes they might not explore otherwise, will make a difference in their learning from these systems. His own research (Salomon, 1977) showed that when "Sesame Street" was first introduced in Israel, coobserving mothers caused children to invest more effort in the viewing experience, and as a result gain more knowledge.

Recent research supports to this theory. Alexander, Ryan, Munoz (1984) investigated the nature of siblings' verbal interaction during television viewing and found that children plan an active role in interpreting the television world for each other. Others (Anderson, 1980; Cohen & Salomon, 1979; Collins, Sobol, & Westby, 1981; Corder-Bolz, 1980; Corder-Bolz & O'Bryant, 1978; Crowell & Au, 1981; Dorr, Graves, & Phelps, 1980; Lee, 1980; Rapaczynski, Singer & Singer, 1982; Singer, Zuckerman, & Singer, 1980) have also shown the positive influence of adults and significant others on children's critical viewing during media use, similar to research on the importance of adult child interaction during reading (Flood, 1977).

A promising approach for future research and practice is one that would view film primarily as art or narrative, able to offer the same set of possibilities for understanding and meaning as other forms of narrative and art, and all the media arts as part of a literacy of many codes, looking at the unique ways each visual and aural media symbol system shapes meaning in order to better understand how individuals make meaning across all such systems. Such a view increases the complexity of the task, since film theorists and critics as yet do not agree on how meaning is made and understood in the film medium (Nichols, 1976). But neither do all literary theorists agree on how meaning is made through experiences with literature (Cooper, 1985; Probst, 1988), and comparisons of the New Critical theories (Richards, 1929), transactional theory (Iser, 1978; Rosenblatt; 1978), and subjective criticism (Bleich, 1978; Holland, 1985) keep the discussion open. Unlike attempts to understand the role of media arts in learning and teaching, however, few would question the central role of literature in English education.

There has also been danger in decontextualizing media arts in past research. It appears more useful now to acknowledge, explore, and even celebrate the understanding and use of symbol systems across all print and nonprint media across both home and school contexts. Also of interest are a more complete understanding of the links between narrative form and content and preferences and response, students efforts at composing, comprehending, and communicating through the media arts, and the nature of the cultural context in approaches to mediating interactive viewing experiences in school settings. In a year-long study of upper elementary students' responses to literature, film, television, and other media experiences both at home and in the classroom. Cox and Many (in press) have collected data via personal journals, free written responses, small group and teacher-led whole-class discussions, and case-studies, to describe both types and patterns of responses, the role of intertextual and autobiographical knowledge, and mediated viewing, reading, and responding across all contexts as students make meaning from their experiences with all these media.

Current theory, research, and practice indicate a shift from the traditional view of film and other media arts in teaching as received knowledge toward one of self-knowledge among students, based on a view of the viewer as an active participant in the process of making meaning from the whole range of possible experiences with verbal and visual media.

References

Alexander, A., Ryan, M. S., & Munoz, P. (1984). Creating a learning context: Investigations on the interaction of siblings during television viewing. *Critical Studies in Mass Communication, 1,* 345–364.

Allen, W. H. (1960). Audio-visual communication. In C. W. Harris (Ed.), *Encyclopedia of educational research* (3rd ed.). (pp. 115–137). New York: Macmillan.

Alwitt, L. F., Anderson, D. R., Lorch, E. P., & Levin, S. R. (1980). Preschool children's visual attention to attributes of television. *Human Communication Research, 7,* 52–67.

Anderson, J. (1980). The theoretical lineage of critical viewing curricula. *Journal of Communication, 30,* 64–70.

Anderson, D., Lorch, E., Field, D., & Sanders, J. (1981). The effects of television program comprehensibility on preschool children's visual attention to television. *Child Development, 52,* 151–157.

Ausubel, D. P. (1968). *Educational psychology: A cognitive view.* New York: Holt Rinehart & Winston.

Bandura, A. (1978). The self system in reciprocal determinism. *American Psychologist, 33,* 344–358.

Barrow, L. C., & Westley, B. H. (1959). Comparative teaching effectiveness of radio and television. *Audio-Visual Communication Review, 7,* 14–23.

Barry, R. V. (1979). Using media in the classroom: A selected replication of the Squire-Applebee survey. *English Education, 11,* 48–52.

Beagles-Roos, J., & Gat, I. (1983). The specific impact of radio and television on children's story comprehension. *Journal of Educational Psychology, 75,* 128–137.

Bleich, D. (1978). *Subjective criticism.* Baltimore, MD: John Hopkins University Press.

Buerkel-Rothful, N. L., Greenberg, B. S., Atkin, C. K., & Neuendorff, K. (1982). Learning about the family from television. *Journal of Communication, 32,* 191–201.

Calvert, S. L., Huston, A. C., Watkins, B. A., & Wright, J. C. (1982). The relation between selective attention to television forms and children's comprehension of content. *Child Development, 53,* 601–610.

Chalfen, R. (1981). A sociovidistic approach to children's filmmaking: The Philadelphia Project. *Studies in Visual Communication, 7,* 2–32.

Chu, G. C., & Schramm, W. (1967). *Learning from television: What the research says.* Stanford, CA: Institute for Communication Research.

Clark, R. E. (1983). Reconsidering research on learning from media. *Review of Educational Research, 53,* 445–460.

Cohen, A., & Salomon, G. (1979). Children's literate TV viewing: Surprises and possible exceptions. *Journal of Communication, 29,* 156–163.

Collins, W. A. (1981). Recent advances in research on cognitive processing during television viewing. *Journal of Broadcasting, 25,* 327–334.

Collins, W. A., Sobol, B. L., & Westby, S. (1981). Effects of adult commentary on children's comprehension and inferences about a televised aggressive portrayal. *Child Development, 52,* 158–163.

Comstock, G., Chaffee, S., Katzman, N., McCombs, M., & Roberts, D. (1978). *Television and human behavior.* New York: Columbia University Press.

Cooper, C. (Ed.). (1985). *Researching response to literature and the teaching of literature: Points of departure.* Norwood, NJ: Ablex.

Corder-Bolz, C. R. (1980). Mediation: The role of significant others. *Journal of Communication, 30,* 106–108.

Corder-Bolz, C. R., & O'Bryant, S. L. (1978). Teacher vs. program. *Journal of Communication, 28,* 97–103.

Costanzo, W. V. (1984). *Double exposure, composing through writing and film.* Upper Montclair, NJ: Boynton/Cook.

Cowgill, G. A. (1975). A study of the differential effects of short films, audio-tapes, and class discussions on the unstructured written responses of senior students to poetry (Doctoral dissertation. University of Pittsburgh, 1975). *Dissertation Abstracts International, 36,* 7976A.

Cox, C. (1978). Films children like—and dislike. *Language Arts, 55,* 334–338, 345.

Cox, C. (1982). Children's preferences for film form and technique. *Language Arts, 59,* 231–238.

Cox, C., Beach, R., & Many, J. E. (1988, April). *Response to film art: Commonalities within a community of young viewers.* Paper presented at the meeting of the American Educational Research Association, New Orleans, LA.

Cox, C. & Many, J. E. (in press). Stance towards a literary work: Applying the transactional theory to children's responses. In J. E. Many & C. Cox (Eds.), *Readers stance and literary understanding.* Norwood, NJ: Ablex.

Cox, C. & Many, J. E. (in process). Children's response to literature and film narrative: Patterns of response and levels of interpretation.

Crowell, D., & Au, K. (1981). Developing children's comprehension in listening, reading, and television viewing. *Elementary School Journal, 82,* 129–135.

Desmond, J. D., & Jeffries-Fox (1983). Elevating children's awareness of television advertising: The effects of a critical viewing program. *Communication Education, 32,* 107–115.

Dillingofski, M. S. (1979). *Nonprint media and reading.* Newark, DE: International Reading Association.

Dorr, A. (1981). Television and affective development and functioning: Maybe this decade. *Journal of Broadcasting, 25,* 335–345.

Dorr, A., Graves, S., & Phelps, E. (1980). Television literacy for young children. *Journal of Communication, 30,* 71–83.

Durkin, R. (1970). *Involvement and making movies: A study of the introduction of movie making to poverty boys.* (Final Report). New York: Columbia University. (ERIC Document Reproduction Service No. ED 045 648)

Flood, J. (1977). Parental styles in reading episodes with young children. *The Reading Teacher, 30,* 864–867.

Freden, S. E. (1974). The effects of planned introductions on the written responses of selected ninth grade students to selected short experiential films (Doctoral dissertation, University of Colorado at Boulder, 1973). *Dissertation Abstracts International, 34,* 7464 A.

Gardner, H., Howard, V., & Perkins, D. (1974). Symbol systems: A philosophical, psychological, and educational investigation. In D. R. Olson (Ed.) *Media and symbols: The forms of expression, communication, and education.* (pp. 27–55). Chicago, IL: University of Chicago Press.

Gibbons, J., Anderson, D. R., Smith, R., Field, D. E., & Fischer, C. (1986). Young children's recall and reconstruction of audio and audio-visual narratives. Child Development, 57, 1014–1023.

Greenfield, P. M. (1984). *Mind and media: The effects of television, video games, and computers.* Cambridge, MA: Harvard University Press.

Griffin, M. (1985). What young filmmakers learn from television: A study of structure in films made by children. *Journal of Broadcasting & Electronic Media, 29,* 79–92.

Gross, L. (1974). Modes of communication and the acquisition of symbolic competence. In D. R. Olson (Ed.). *Media and symbols: The forms of expression, communication and education* (pp. 56–80). Chicago, IL: University of Chicago Press.

Hayes, D. S., & Birnbaum, D. W. (1980– Preschoolers' retention of televised events: Is a picture worth a thousand words? *Developmental Psychology, 16,* 410–416.

Hayes, D. S., Chemelski, B. E., & Birnbaum, D. W. (1981). Young children's incidental and intentional retention of televised events. *Developmental Psychology, 17,* 230–232.

Hayes, D. S., Kelly, S. B., & Mandel, M. (1986). *Journal of Educational Psychology, 78,* 341–346.

Hennis, R. S. (1981). Needed: Research in the visual language. *English Journal, 70,* 79–82.

Himmelweit, H. T., Oppenheim, A. N., & Vince, P. (1958). *Television and the child.* London: Oxford University Press.

Hoban, C. F., & van Ormer, E. B. (1972). Instructional film research 1918–1950. New York: Arno Press.

Holland, N. N. (1975). 5 readers reading. New Haven and London: Yale University Press.

Huston, A. C., & Wright, J. C. (1983). Children's processing of television: The informative functions of formal features. In J. Bryant & D. R. Anderson (Eds.). *Children's understanding of television: Research on attention and comprehension* (pp. 35–58). New York: Academic Press.

Idaho State Department of Education. (1978). *The way we see it: A program to improve critical viewing skills.* Idaho State Department of Education.

Iser, W. (1978). *The act of reading: A theory of aesthetic response.* Baltimore, MD: John Hopkins University Press.

Jamison, D., Suppes, P., & Wells, S. (1974). The effectiveness of alternative instructional media: A survey. *Review of Educational Research, 44,* 1–67.

Kelley, P., Gunter, B., & Buckle, L. (1987). 'Reading' television in the classroom: More results from the Television Literacy Project. *Journal of Educational Television, 13,* 7–19.

Kelley, P., Gunter, B., & Kelley, C. (1985). Teaching television in the classroom: Results of a preliminary study. *Journal of Educational Television, 11,* 57–63.

Larson, R., & Meade, E. (1969). *Young filmmakers.* New York: Dutton.

Lee, B. (1980). Prime-time in the classroom. *Journal of Communication, 30,* 175–180.

Levin, S., & Anderson, D. (1976). The development of attention. *Journal of Communication, 26,* 126–135.

Levinson, E. (1964). Effects of motion pictures on the response to narrative: A study of the effects of film versions of certain short stories on the responses of junior high school students (Doctoral dissertation, New York University, 1963). *Dissertation Abstracts International, 25,* 2297.

Lewis, W. J. (1972). A comparison of responses of adolescents to narrative and lyric literature and film (Doctoral dissertation, The Florida

State University, 1972). *Dissertation Abstracts International, 25,* 2297.

Lorch, E. P., Bellack, D. R., & Augsback, L. H. (1987). Young children's memory for televised stories: Effects of importance. *Child Development, 58,* 453–463.

Luke, C. (1985). Television discourse processing: A schema theoretic approach. *Communication Education, 34,* 91–105.

Lyle, J. & Hoffman, H. (1972). Children's use of television and other media. In E. Rubenstein, D. Comstock, and J. Murray (Eds.), *Television and social behavior 4* (pp. 129–256). Washington, DC: Government Printing Office.

Lynch, J. D. (1983). Film education in secondary schools. New York: Garland.

Lynch, J. D. (1986). Film education research: An overview. *Teaching English in the Two-Year College, 13,* 245–253.

McKeever, J. (1972). *The cooperative film program for the Philadelphia secondary schools teacher's guide.* Philadelphia, PA: School District of Philadelphia.

Meadowcroft, J. M., & McDonald, D. G. (1986). Meta-analysis of research on children and the media: Atypical development? *Journalism Quarterly, 63,* 474–480.

Media Action Research Center. (1979). *Television awareness training.* New York: Media Action Research Center.

Meringoff, L. K. (1980). Influence of the medium on children's story apprehension. *Journal of Educational Psychology, 72,* 240–249.

Meringoff, L. K., Vibbert, M., Kelly, H., & Charr, C. (1981, April). *How shall you take your story: With or without pictures?* Paper presented at the meeting of the Society for Research in Child Development, Boston.

National Assessment of Educational Progress (1981). Reading, thinking, and writing: Results from the 1979–1980 National Assessment of reading and literature. Denver, CO: Education Commission of the States.

Nelson, K. (1977). Cognitive development and the acquisition of concepts. In R. C. Anderson, R. J. Spiro, & N. S. Hontague (Eds.) *Schooling and the acquisition of knowledge.* Hillsdale, NJ: Lawrence Erlbaum.

Nichols, B. (1976). *Movies and methods.* Berkeley and Los Angeles, CA: University of California Press.

Olson, D. R. (Ed.). (1974). *Media and symbols: The forms of expression, communication, and education.* Chicago, IL: University of Chicago Press.

Pezdek, K., & Hartman, E. F. (1983). Children's television viewing: Attention and comprehension of auditory versus visual information. *Child Development, 54,* 1015–1023.

Pezdek, K., Lehrer, A., & Simon, S. (1984). The relationship between reading and cognitive processing of television and radio. *Child Development, 55,* 2072–2082.

Pezdek, K., & Stevens, E. (1984). Children's memory for auditory and visual information on television. *Developmental Psychology, 20,* 212–218.

Polito, R. (1965). The history of film teaching in the American school system. *Screen Education, September/October,* 10–18.

Postman, N. (1979). *Teaching as a conserving activity.* New York: Delta.

Postman, N. (1982). *The disappearance of childhood.* New York: Delacorte.

Probst, R. E. (1988). *Response and analysis, teaching literature in junior and senior high school.* Portsmouth, NH: Boynton Cook/Heinemann.

Purves, A., & Beach, R. (1972). *Literature and the reader: Research in response to literature, reading interests, and the teaching of literature.* Urbana, IL: National Council of Teachers of English.

Purves, A., & Rippere, V. (1968). *Elements of writing about a literary work: A study of response to literature.* Urbana, IL: National Council of Teachers of English.

Pryluck, C., & Hemenway, P. T. M.'(1982). *The American Film Institute second survey of higher education.* Los Angeles, CA: American Film Institute.

Rapaczynski, W., Singer, D., & Singer, J. (1982). Teaching television: A curriculum for young children. *Journal of Communication, 32,* 46–55.

Rice, M., & Wartella, E. (1981). Television as a medium of communication: Implications for how to regard the child viewer. *Journal of Broadcasting, 25,* 365–372.

Richards, I. A. (1929). *Practical criticism.* New York: Harcourt Brace.

Robinson, D. C. (1974). Film analycity: Variations in viewer orientation (Doctoral dissertation, University of Oregon, 1974). (ERIC Document Reproduction Service No. ED 096 725)

Rosenblatt, L. (1978). *The reader, the text, the poem: The transactional theory of the literary work.* Carbondle, IL: Southern Illinois University Press.

Ruch, M., & Levin, J. (1977). Pictorial organization versus verbal repetition of children's prose: Evidence for processing differences. *Audio Visual Communication Review, 25,* 269–280.

Salomon, G. (1977). Effects of encouraging Israeli mothers to co-observe 'Sesame Street' with their five-year olds. *Child Development, 45,* 1146–1151.

Salomon, G. (1979). *Interaction of media, cognition, and learning.* San Francisco, CA: Jossey-Bass Publishers.

Salomon, G. (1981). *Communication and education: social and psychological interaction.* Beverly Hills, CA: Sage.

Salomon, G. (1983). Television watching and mental effort: A social psychological view. In J. Bryant & D. R. Anderson (Eds.), *Children's understanding of television: Research on attention and comprehension* (pp. 265–296). New York: Academic Press.

Salomon, G. (1984). Television is 'easy' and print is 'hard': the differential investment of mental effort in learning as a function of perceptions and attributes. *Journal of Educational Psychology, 76,* 647–648.

Schramm, W. (1973). Big media, little media. Palo Alto, CA: Stanford University, Institute for Communication Research.

Schramm, W., Lyle, J., & Parker, E. B. (1961). *Television and the lives of children.* Palo Alto, CA: Stanford University Press.

Shannon, P. (1985). Print and television: Children's use of the medium is the message. *The Elementary School Journal, 85,* 663–672.

Singer, D. G., Zuckerman, D. M., & Singer, J. L. (1980). Helping elementary children learn about TV. *Journal of Communication, 30,* 84–93.

Squire, J. R., & Applebee, R. K. (1968). *High school English instruction today.* New York: Appleton-Century-Crofts.

Stevenson, H. W., & Siegel, A. (1969). Effects of instructions and age on retention of filmed content. *Journal of Educational Psychology, 60,* 71–74.

Stoneman, Z., & Brody, G. H. (1983). Immediate and long-term recognition and generalization of advertised products as a function of age and presentation mode. *Developmental Psychology, 19,* 56–61.

Streicher, L. H., & Bonney, N. L. (1974). Children talk about television. *Journal of Communication, 24,* 54–61.

Suhor, C. (1984). Towards a semiotics-based curriculum. *Journal of Curriculum Studies, 16,* 247–257.

Suhor, C. (1986). Media and English: What happened? *Teaching English in the Two-Year College, 13,* 254–260.

Sullivan, J. E., & Rogers, B. G. (1985). Listening retention of third-grade pupils as a function of mode of presentation. *Journal of Experimental Education, 53,* 227–229.

Sutton-Smith, B., Eadie, F., Griffin, M. (1983). Filmmaking by young filmmakers. *Studies in Visual Communication, 9,* 65–75.

Sutton-Smith, B., Eadie, F., Griffin, M., & Zarem, S. (1979). *A develop-*

mental psychology of childrens' filmmaking. New York, NY: Ford Foundation. (ERIC Document Reproduction Service No. ED 148 330).

Taylor, M. (1976). A study of the effects of presenting literature to first-grade students by means of five visual-verbal presentation modes (Doctoral Dissertation, University of Southern California, 1976). *Dissertation Abstracts International, 37,* 1393A.

Tidhar, C. (1984). Children communicate in cinematic codes: Effects on cognitive skills. *Journal of Educational Psychology, 76,* 957–965.

Trelease, J. (1982). *The read aloud handbook.* New York: Penguin.

Wartella, E., Alexander, A., & Lemish, D. (1979). The mass media environment of children. *American Behavioral Scientist, 23,* 33–52.

Wartella, E., & Reeves, B. (1985). Historical trends in research on children and the media: 1900–1960. *Journal of Communication, 35,* 118–133.

Watzlawick, P., Beavin, J. H., & Jackson, D. D. (1967). *Pragmatics of human communication: A study of interactional patterns, pathologies, and paradoxes.* New York: Norton.

Weiss, M. (1982). Children using audiovisual media for communication: A new language? *Journal of Educational Television, 8,* 109–112.

Winn, M. (1977). The plug-in drug. New York: Viking.

Winn, W. (1986). Trends and future directions in educational technology research from a North American perspective. *Programmed Learning and Educational Technology, 23,* 346–355.

WNET Project. (1980). Critical television viewing. New York: Cambridge Publishers.

Worth, S., & Adair, J. (1972). *Through Navajo eyes: An exploration in film communication and anthropology.* Bloomington, IN: Indiana University Press.

Zuckerman, D., Singer, D., & Singer, J. (1980). Television viewing, children's reading, and related classroom behavior. *Journal of Communication, 30,* 166–174.

·29·

ENVIRONMENTS FOR LANGUAGE TEACHING AND LEARNING: CONTEMPORARY ISSUES AND FUTURE DIRECTIONS

Arthur N. Applebee

The 1970s and 1980s have been a period of sharp debate about the nature of effective environments for learning, for the curriculum as a whole as well as for the teaching of the English language arts. Calls for a return to the "basics," to a traditional liberal arts curriculum, to the classical works of Western civilization, and to direct instruction have echoed against calls for contemporary relevance, content reflecting the contributions of minorities and of women, process-oriented approaches, and student-centered classrooms. These debates are far from over, but the profession may now be moving toward a consensus about many of the most important components of effective environments for learning. This chapter will review some of the dimensions of that consensus, as well as the issues that remain to be resolved. The discussion will be organized around changing perceptions of three components of effective environments for language learning—the teacher, the student, and the curriculum—and of the metaphors that govern how these components interact in teaching and learning.

THE TEACHER

The teacher plays an obvious and central role in creating effective environments for language teaching and learning, and some of the most important developments in the language arts during the past decades have focused directly on the teacher. The recurring theme has been the need for the teacher to be regarded, and to act, as a professional within the larger environment of the school. The image of teacher as professional carries with it a clear set of responsibilities for planning and decision-making, as well as a clear set of obligations in terms of knowledge and competence in structuring the environment for learning in the language arts classroom.

The emphasis on professionalism has come from a variety of directions, some essentially "top down" and others "bottom up." The growing strength of teacher unions, with their insistence that their collective voice be included in dialogues about school reform, has certainly played an important role. So too has the influence of the National Writing Project, with its stress on articulating and sharing the classroom knowledge that successful, experienced teachers possess. At a more academic level, the movement has gained momentum from a reexamination of the nature of pedagogical knowledge in general, and that of subject-specific pedagogical knowledge in particular. This reexamination has challenged the notion that effective teaching can be described in terms of a limited set of generic teaching skills, and has led to an exploration of the knowledge of the subject area teacher, including the teacher of English (Grossman, 1988; Shulman, 1987). The most practical, and potentially the most far-reaching, of the outcomes of this movement have been the prototype examination questions developed for the teacher certification project of the Carnegie Foundation by Shulman and his colleagues.

One aspect of the emphasis on teacher-as-professional has been a movement to legitimate the teacher-as-researcher. The most important influence of this movement has been to open up a dialogue about the nature of educational reform in general, and about the various kinds of new knowledge that interact to create changes in environments for learning the English language arts. In its most naive form, teacher-as-researcher has encouraged a blurring between the expertise of teachers and that of other professionals interested in educational issues. Rather than recognizing various kinds of expertise, this version of teacher-as-researcher has fostered a leveling of expertise, and led inevitably to frustration and discontent as teachers have found that reports of their research rarely make it into traditional research journals.

A more productive version of teacher-as-researcher has linked the metaphor to the role of the professional as a reflective practitioner, engaged in a constant cycle of experimentation and commentary upon the content and process of teaching and learning. The teacher operates with different concerns than the psychologist, anthropologist, or sociologist who also studies classrooms; the teacher brings different expertise to bear upon suggestions for educational reform. The strength of this conception is that it reconstrues the role of everyone involved in the process of educational change. Because the teacher has unique expertise, proposals for change must take account of that expertise. The results of research in one or another of the academic disciplines may provide useful information to be considered in the reform of classrooms, but for that information to be effectively utilized it must be evaluated and reformulated by teachers themselves. Conversely, teachers' reactions may play an important part in forcing a reexamination of emerging theories in one or another of the scholarly disciplines, but the reshaping of those theories will usually be undertaken by scholars in those disciplines.

On one point there is considerable consensus: improvement of the environment for teaching and learning in the language arts can come only through the direct involvement of teachers. This involvement has two major purposes. One is simply a question of ownership for the changes that occur: if teachers do not have a vested interest in a proposal for change, they will adapt it to suit their own interests. That process of adaptation may change the proposal in ways so fundamental that it no longer functions to carry out its original purposes. The second is that most proposals for change reflect one or two major concerns or conclusions of research; classroom environments, on the other hand, reflect a creative balance among a wide variety of differing agenda. To be effective, any change must be incorporated into that complex web of interactive forces—and that requires the commitment and expertise of the professional teacher.

Efforts at reform that ignore the expertise of the practicing teacher are doomed to fail, as they have in the past (Cuban, 1984). Teacher-proof curricula, mandated management systems, state-level guidelines that specify detailed content—all misconstrue the central role of the professional teacher in the process of education and the process of reform. In the coming decades, reforms that begin with the recognition of the central role of the professional teacher are much more likely to succeed.

The role of the teacher, however, is only one part of the configuration of factors that shapes the nature of effective teaching and learning. The decisions the teacher makes are shaped in part by perceptions of the students—who they are and what they need to know.

CONCEPTIONS OF THE STUDENT

The second component shaping environments for language teaching and learning is the underlying conception of the student. Such conceptions begin with perceptions of who the students are and what they know, and proceed from there to assumptions about the learning objectives that are most appropriate for them. Our understandings about both of these dimensions have altered considerably during the 1980s.

One of the long-standing findings in research on student language skills is that achievement is influenced by the resources that students have available in the home. Students are likely to do better in all aspects of literacy if they come from supportive home environments, with abundant literacy material in the home, and with caregivers who are themselves well-educated and who value academic achievement (Applebee, Langer, & Mullis, 1988; Heath, 1984). Such students often do well whatever the characteristics of the educational program at their schools. Conversely, students who come from less-supportive home environments pose a particular challenge to schools.

During much of the 1980s, the education of such "at-risk" students received relatively little attention. The situation began to change late in the decade, in the face of a continuing pattern of unacceptably low performance for at-risk groups (Applebee, Langer, & Mullis, 1987) and of the recognition that minority students may soon be the majority in our schools—as they already are in California. Although there has been some narrowing of the gap in performance between historically at-risk and historically successful groups of students, the gap remains unacceptably large. In 1986, for example, African American and hispanic school children averaged nearly 4 grade levels below their white peers in reading and writing achievement (Applebee, Langer, & Mullis, 1987; Chall and Curtis, this handbook). On equity grounds alone, such imbalances require special attention.

At the same time that educators have begun to turn their attention to at-risk students, the demands for literacy skills have been increasing. The same assessment studies that have suggested some narrowing of the performance gap have also indicated that this narrowing has occurred almost entirely through improvements in lower-level or basic skills. These skills for the most part reflect rote or routine performance, rather than the ability to use literacy skills in broader contexts. Indeed, National Assessment results suggest that very few students in any group—historically at-risk or historically high-achieving—do well on tasks that require them to justify conclusions or elaborate upon particular points of view.

In our conceptions of students, then, we seem to be reaching a consensus on two points: the need to renew our efforts to develop effective programs for students who have been historically at-risk for school failure, and the need to provide programs that will help all students develop the interwined reading, writing, and reasoning skills that are the cornerstones of reasoned and disciplined thinking.

THE CURRICULUM

The curriculum is the third component of effective environments for language learning; it represents a translation of teachers' goals and perceptions of students' needs into specific content and activities. Some of the major changes in environments for language learning during the past decade have involved the curriculum, particularly in the teaching of writing. Here the conventional wisdom has shifted from a focus on the characteristics of the final written text, to a focus on the process skills that a writer utilizes in producing that text.

Traditional approaches to the teaching of writing have treated the subject as a body of knowledge concerned with the characteristics of effective text. In order to write well, the argument went, students would have to learn the "rules" or formulae governing sentences, paragraphs, and larger units. The curriculum that resulted usually ended up specifying a variety of rules, and providing various exercises in which the rules could be applied and practiced. The amount of practice varied inversely with the level at which the rule applied: the greater part of the curriculum usually focused on sentence-level rules; the next largest segment on paragraph-level structures; and the least on how to put these components together into larger texts.

During the 1970s and 1980s, this traditional approach to the writing curriculum faced a number of challenges, some internal and some external. Internal challenges questioned the validity of the rules themselves: Braddock (1974), for example, found that textbook prescriptions for the use of topic sentences in paragraphs bore little relationship to topic-sentence usage in published articles; Mead and Ellis (1970) posed similar questions about textbook prescriptions for paragraph organization. The adequacy of grammar rules received an even greater challenge, as the field of linguistics passed successively through structural, transformational, and posttransformational approaches to syntactic description. The effect of such internal challenges was to weaken traditional approaches to writing instruction, leaving the profession open, even eager, for an alternative approach.

The alternative that has been widely advocated shifts the focus of the curriculum away from the final written text toward the various cognitive and linguistic skills that effective writers draw upon in the process of shaping that text. Such process-oriented approaches to the curriculum have a number of appeals: they parallel attention in cognitive psychology to processes of problem solving; they support a student-centered rather than a content-centered pedagogy; and they lead to a variety of specific teaching suggestions. The characteristics of process-oriented instruction vary from classroom to classroom, but as a group they share an emphasis on prewriting and revision activities, multiple drafts, small group instruction, peer response, the provision of audiences for student work, and the postponement of evaluation until late in the process.

The emergence of process-oriented writing instruction has been part of a more general shift in emphasis toward the cognitive and linguistic processes underlying school learning. Similar changes in emphasis have occurred in reading instruction, for example, as scholars have untangled the complicated and interacting processes that govern comprehension. These changes have reinforced calls for whole-language programs and movements away from basal readers, but changes in reading programs have not been as widespread or universally accepted as have those in writing instruction.

The emergence of process-oriented approaches to the teaching of writing has led to a somewhat schizophrenic approach to the teaching of English. The idealized process-oriented writing class is organized around student activities, with the teacher in the role of fostering the newly-emerging process skills. The literature lesson, however, has remained very traditional in orientation, utilizing a lecture-and-discussion format designed to lead students toward a canonical interpretation of standard texts (Applebee, Langer, & Mullis, 1987; Ravitch & Finn, 1987).

Such discrepancies have led to a reconsideration of the goals of literature instruction, and the search for a conception of literary knowledge that may be more compatible with the emerging image of successful writing instruction. Prescriptions for process-oriented writing instruction in fact offer some useful guidelines for what such a conception of literature might look like. Rather than focusing on lecture and whole-class discussion, process-oriented approaches to the teaching of writing emphasize drafting and redrafting of the evolving text, which is shaped in interaction with teacher and peers, allowing understanding to grow over time, through the process of writing and discussion. A model for the teaching of literature might similarly focus on the process of literary understanding: extending over time, with interpretation drafted and redrafted in interaction with teacher and peers, and with evaluation of students' understanding of a text postponed until late in the process, instead of assuming that comprehension is complete upon reading the final words of a text. Although the dimensions of process-oriented approaches to the teaching of composition have been fairly well developed, those of the teaching of literature are just beginning to be outlined by scholars and teachers alike (cf. Langer, 1989).

There is a consensus in the profession, then, about the usefulness of process-oriented approaches to the teaching of the English language arts. As process-oriented approaches have become more widespread, however, a variety of new problems have begun to emerge. These include issues of structure and sequence in the curriculum, and issues of assessment of student learning.

Structure and Sequence

When the language-arts curriculum was defined in terms of particular content knowledge, the task of imposing structure and sequence on the curriculum was straightforward (if somewhat imposing, given the large number of items of content that remained to be put into coherent order). The usual approach was to develop a detailed curriculum guide or a scope-and-sequence chart. When the curriculum is defined in terms of process-related cognitive and linguistic skills, however, the task of laying out an orderly, sequential curriculum becomes quite different. Rather than an external order based on the subject matter, the curriculum has to be structured to foster the growth of problem-solving skills that may develop quite differently from student to student, depending upon background and previous experiences. The issue for curriculum theory becomes one of providing an orderly, coherent set of experiences, each of which is flexible enough to provide the appropriate degrees of challenge and support to students whose knowledge and skills may differ widely from each other.

In practice, this is likely to mean that the external curriculum is highly indeterminate, with few constraints on school-level decisions about materials and activities assigned to various grades and classes. These decisions will be guided by local considerations, such as the ethnic background of the community, concerns of parents, and preferences of the teachers involved. Though arbitrary, these decisions are still important, because the curriculum framework that results provides stability to the program and guidance to teachers and students—a necessary sense of order and coherence.

The critical curriculum decisions, those that shape the teaching and learning that will take place within these broad frameworks, will have to be made by the individual teacher for the individual class. These are decisions about the individual assignments that will be constructed and the structure of the environment for teaching and learning that will surround the assignments. The principles governing this structure are just beginning to be explored, but clearly they will look very different from the scope-and-sequence chart that they will replace. Indeed, they are likely to be principles that rely for their implementation on the day-to-day judgment of the professional teacher, rather than on the prescriptions of an external curriculum. There is as yet, however, little consensus about what such ordering principles should look like.

Assessment

The movement toward process-oriented approaches to writing instruction was contemporaneous with a movement toward direct assessment of writing skills—that is, of testing writing abilities by asking students to write, rather than by asking them to complete more easily scored multiple-choice tasks (usually, focused on grammar and usage). Direct assessment of writing skills posed a variety of technical problems for measurement specialists—complications introduced because of the variability of rater judgments as well as by variations in response to such factors as test length and item topic. Many of these problems have been overcome, to the point where reliabilities above .9 are routinely reported by National Assessment (cf. Applebee, Langer, & Mullis, 1986), which has been one of the leading agencies in the development of direct assessments of writing abilities.

As assessments have become more technically accurate, however, other problems have begun to become apparent. Just as multiple-choice tests were attacked because of their lack of correspondence to the kinds of activities desired in the English language-arts curriculum, direct assessments of writing skills are vulnerable to complaints that they do not allow students to utilize or display the process-related writing skills emphasized in their classrooms. The tension between the constraints of the assessment situation and the more natural conditions of classroom writing are real, and have not been successfully addressed in any of the major state or national assessments of writing abilities.

Assessment issues are also emerging in other areas of the language arts curriculum. In reading, the typical test does a reasonable job of rank-ordering students, but again does little to assess (or reflect) the process-related reading skills that lead to good comprehension (Langer, 1985; 1987). This makes the results of questionable diagnostic value, and (as with writing assessment) leads to a situation in which the testing program conflicts at a relatively fundamental level with the principles of effective instruction. Literature assessment is the least well-developed, with most tests of specifically literary knowledge taking the form either of multiple-choice tests of content (authors, titles) or of reading comprehension, with little distinction between the skills needed for comprehending literary as opposed to expository texts (Brody, DeMilo, & Purves, 1989). Oral language skills, though a traditional part of the language arts curriculum, are rarely assessed at all, at least in the United States. (See also the chapters on assessment in this Handbook by Farr and Beck, Goodman, and Hiebert.)

Implementation of Process-Oriented Approaches

By the middle-1980s, process-oriented approaches to writing instruction had replaced product-oriented approaches as the conventional wisdom—at least in the professional literature. Various studies of classroom instruction, however, suggested that more traditional, text-oriented approaches continued to dominate in many (perhaps the majority of) classrooms. This discrepancy may be attributable in part to the traditional lag between theory and practice, but in the case of process-oriented approaches to instruction there may be a more troubling problem: put simply, the emphasis on process-oriented instruction may conflict in fundamental ways with traditional models of teaching and learning.

Curriculum theory in the United States has many ancestors, but two of the most powerful traditions trace their roots to behavioral psychology and industrial design (Callahan, 1962). It is these traditions that gave rise to the detailed scope-and-sequence charts, mentioned earlier, and to the conception of teaching and learning that they represent. In this conception, education is guided by a building-block or assembly-line metaphor: the final product is a body of knowledge made up of discrete component parts, and these parts must be assembled in a coherent, specified order if they are to function properly. In developing a reading curriculum, for example, such an analysis often begins with hand-eye coordination activities that allow proper letter identification, followed by sound discrimination and phonics skills that lead to the identification of individual words, and these in turn to reading of simple, and eventually to more complex, passages. Vocabulary, syntax, and discourse structure all need to be controlled, to encourage the development of a coherent foundation of skills upon which to build. In writing, a comparable sequence begins with handwriting exercises, moving from there to single words (sometimes embedded in drawing or labelling activities), simple sentences, paragraphs, and finally whole texts.

The teacher's role in such a teaching and learning process is carefully constrained, and in theory at least replaceable by an automated delivery system such as computer-assisted instruction. The most common pattern consists of diagnosis of what students already know and can do (i.e., determining which of the building blocks are already in place), teaching the next set of missing information or requisite skills, testing to see what has now been learned, and reteaching the knowledge that is still missing or the skills that are insufficiently routinized.

Whether explicit or implicit, this model of diagnose, teach, test, and reteach is deeply engrained in the American educational system (Langer, 1984). It is embedded in our curricula and our textbooks; it is part of our teacher training programs; and it has been internalized by many, if not most, teachers, as a guiding framework in their day to day teaching. It is a comfortable model, because it implies clear standards for success and failure, providing teachers and students alike with clear evidence of how well they are doing. It lends itself well to a complex organizational structure such as the American education system, with its demands for monitoring of performance at the individual student, classroom, and building level. And with its accompanying curriculum guides and scope-and-sequence charts, it insures at least the semblance of clearly specified goals and efficient organization of resources.

Process-oriented approaches to instruction, on the other hand, are based on the assumption that learning is not linear and sequential, but instead will involve a variety of false starts and tentative explorations. Understanding will change and grow as learning progresses. Premature evaluation will short-circuit this process, curtailing risk-taking and placing a premium on correctness rather than growth and exploration. The teacher and student in a process-oriented classroom must accept error as a matter of course, rather than using it as a measure of failure and misunderstanding.

Initial proposals for process-oriented approaches to instruction ignored the tensions between these approaches and the traditional model of instruction. Instead, process-oriented instruction was treated largely as a question of new and more effective activities that could replace traditional product oriented materials. Changes in the role of the teacher, in the patterns of interaction among students, and in the focus of evaluation were expected to follow more or less inevitably with the new activities. Results in practice, however, have not conformed to the initial theory. However effective and well-motivated new activities may be in the hands of their initial developers, as they have become more widespread they have been assimilated into traditional models of instruction. And in turn, it is not clear that they are any more effective than the product-oriented approaches that they are replacing.

These issues have become particularly apparent in writing instruction. Writing fits quite comfortably into the traditional pattern of diagnose-teach-test-reteach, filling the "diagnose" and "testing" slots, and the variety of prewriting, revision, and editing activities are transformed quite easily into practice in important skills. But when these activities are assimilated in this way, their role as part of a process-oriented approach quickly disintegrates. The focus shifts back toward recitation of previous learning, toward an emphasis on right and wrong, and away from the tentative exploration of new ideas, of developing and changing understandings. The failure, like that of many previous generations of curriculum reform, is not in the initial conceptualization, but in the transformation of that conceptualization into favored activities rather than into broad principles of effective teaching—principles that must be put into practice by the professional teacher.

METAPHORS FOR TEACHING AND LEARNING

Problems in implementation do not necessarily mean that process-oriented approaches should be abandoned, but they do highlight one of the major tasks of this decade: the development of a new metaphor governing the structure of effective teaching and learning, a metaphor that will support rather than subvert process-oriented approaches to instruction. Such metaphors are important, because they provide teachers with an overarching framework for thinking about issues of teaching and learning. These frameworks, in turn, shape the curriculum that students experience, and the learning that results.

Although no single metaphor has yet emerged to replace the traditional model of teaching and learning, there is considerable consensus on the conceptual underpinnings that will give that metaphor its depth and power. Educators and scholars have turned increasingly during the past decade toward constructivist theories of language and learning, initially as a way to explain processes of child language development, and more recently as a framework for understanding school learning as well.

Constructivist approaches have a variety of roots, with related frameworks emerging in fields as seemingly diverse as linguistics (Halliday, 1977), psychology (Bruner, 1974; Donaldson, 1978; Vygotsky, 1962), history of science (Kuhn, 1962), sociology (Berger & Luckmann, 1966), and philosophy (Cassirer, 1944; Langer, 1942; Polanyi, 1958). What these various scholars share is a view of knowledge, and of mind, as an active construction built up by the individual acting within a social context that shapes and constrains that knowledge, but does not determine it in an absolute sense.

Constructivist orientations have become popular in education in part because they provide a powerful framework for thinking about teaching and learning (Britton, 1970). Rather than focusing either on specific content to be learned or on the nature of the learner, they lead to a consideration of learning-in-context—to how knowledge develops within a particular environment for teaching and learning. Such a framework seems particularly compatible with educational approaches that emphasize process-oriented instruction, and provides a way to approach the problem of defining broad underlying principles that govern effective contexts for effective teaching and learning. In the language arts, a number of scholars have built on this framework to move research on teaching away from previous process/product or treatment-group studies, looking in more detail at the ways the structure of interaction with a particular learning environment shapes the knowledge and skills that students develop (e.g., Griffin & Cole, 1984; Heath, 1984; Langer & Applebee, 1987; Palincsar & Brown, 1984; Raphael, 1985).

Langer & Applebee (1986), building on work by Bruner (e.g., Wood, Bruner, & Ross, 1976), Cazden (1979), and others, have used the metaphor of "instructional scaffolding" as one alternative to traditional models of teaching and learning. In this metaphor, the task of the teacher is seen to be much like that of the parent in previous studies of early language development: a process of providing scaffolds (Wood, Bruner, & Ross, 1976) or support for the child's efforts to do new things with language. As the student attempts new tasks, the instructional scaffolding provided by the teacher provides the necessary support—and at the same time models or leads the student through effective strategies for completing that task. Over time and with repetition, these strategies become internalized, and the student becomes capable of carrying them out without additional support. The notion of instructional scaffolding can be extended to encompass a variety of dimensions of the environment for teaching and learning language—from classroom dialogue to the material in the textbook to the activities and study materials that the teacher initiates or provides.

Basing their work on studies of process-oriented approaches to instruction, Langer and Applebee (1986) have suggested 5 criteria for effective instructional scaffolding. These criteria are not meant as a complete model of teaching and learning, but focus instead on problems that occur in traditionally-oriented classrooms. They represent one attempt to describe the dimensions of effective environments for teaching and learning of the English language arts.

1. Ownership. Effective instructional environments must allow room for students to make their own contribution to ongoing tasks. They must establish their own purposes for what they are doing with language, for it is these purposes that integrate and give point to the specific skills and strategies they may draw upon as a task is carried out.

The need for ownership militates against traditional demands for recitation of previous learning and demonstration of skills, where the purposes are simply to display information that is already better-known by the teacher. Instead, it requires tasks where specific answers are less certain, depending not only on what the teacher or textbook has presented but also on how the student makes use of that new information. In writing, opportunities for ownership occur when topics call for students to explore their own experiences and opinions, or to elaborate upon a point of view. In reading and literature, similar opportunities for ownership occur when students are encouraged to develop—and defend—their own interpretations, rather than being led to accept the teacher's predetermined point of view.

When instructional environments are structured to encourage students to take ownership, questions of right and wrong become of lesser importance, but students must take responsibility for the conclusions they reach, and be able to justify and defend them in the light of what others may say or do. Thus classrooms that provide opportunities for students to take ownership for their work are not abandoning standards of excellence; on the contrary, they lead to the development of rigorous standards of argument and evidence in defense of the positions that students adopt. As an important byproduct, classroom environments that stress ownership are also likely to be environments that lead to the develop of more effective reasoning and thinking skills.

The notion of ownership is related to a variety of other recent suggestions for educational reform. Graves (1983) has used the term to argue for the importance of writing about self-selected rather than teacher-provided topics. Britton et al.

(1975) have pointed out the emptiness of "dry runs" in school writing, and pointed to the motivating effect of "real" writing tasks. Moffett (1981) has argued for the importance of writers finding their own voice in the assignments they undertake, and the deadliness of the "English" that results when students write without vesting themselves and their own opinions and experiences in the task. In literature, Rosenblatt (1978) and others have argued the importance of the individual transaction between reader and work—a transaction without which the work does not in any real sense exist for the reader.

2. Appropriateness. Effective instructional tasks will build on literacy and thinking skills that students already have, helping them to accomplish tasks that they could not otherwise complete on their own. In Vygotsky's (1962) terms, teaching and learning will be aimed "not so much at the ripe, but at the ripening functions."

This is a commonsense principle, often phrased in terms of "starting where the students are," but it is a principle that is easily violated in practice. An environment for teaching and learning that is built around scope-and-sequence charts targeted at particular grade levels almost inevitably means that many of the activities that take place will be inappropriate for many of the children present. The activities either will involve repetition of things that many students already know how to do, or will lead to unsuccessful struggles with tasks that are too difficult for many students to complete.

The ways around this problem are related to the earlier discussion of scope and sequence in the curriculum. When tasks become more open-ended, rather than focused on achieving a particular correct solution, students have more chance of working at the appropriate level. Their interpretations of literature will be more or less abstract, more or less complex, for example; their writing will move further along a continuum from narrative commentary to tight argument. And in turn, the responses that the student receives, whether from the teacher or from other students working on related problems within the same classroom environment, will adjust to the appropriate level.

The specification of task-appropriateness is closely intertwined with issues of scope and sequence in the curriculum as a whole, and like those issues, remains as one of the major agenda that the profession needs to address.

3. Support. To be an effective vehicle for learning, instructional tasks must make the structure of the activity clear and must guide the student through in a way that will provide effective strategies for use in other contexts. Put another way, the task must support a natural sequence of thought and language, providing effective routines for the student to internalize.

This criteria lies at the heart of the notion of instructional scaffolding; it focuses on the interaction between the student and the supporting context that provides the structure and knowledge that makes it possible for learning to occur. The implications of this criteria for the shape of instruction are dramatic, for it implies that the teaching of skills out of their context for use will not be effective.

At the same time, this criteria places the teacher, in the role of mentor or guide who structures the instructional environment, at the heart of the teaching and learning process—for students need help and support if they are to continue to grow as language learners and language users. The teacher must understand the kinds of knowledge and skill that need to be drawn upon in particular tasks, and must structure the tasks so that students will be introduced to appropriate knowledge and skills at the point at which this information is needed. In writing, for example, this may take the form of suggesting appropriate prewriting activities to help students gather and organize pertinent information, ways to segment the task to make it easier to accomplish, or the provision of constructive critical response (either from teacher the or from other students) to help shape initial ideas into a more effective draft. In reading and literature, it may include prereading activities to provide a context for the work to be read, carefully constructed guide questions to lead the student through difficult sections of the text itself, or mutual exploration of first interpretations as students first work their way into and then back out of a text (Langer, 1989).

Traditional critical apparatus and technical terminology may play an important role in these processes, they will do so by being introduced in contexts where they help students elaborate upon and make sense of what they are reading or writing.

Hillocks' (1979; Hillocks, Kahn, & Johannessen, 1983) examples of "environmental learning" offer some of the most carefully worked out illustrations of such structure in the teaching of writing. In his approach, writing activities involve real problems to be solved, with appropriate problem-solving strategies introduced as they are needed in the course of the task. The problems and the tasks are both highlighted, so that the students understand the instrumental nature of the activities they are asked to do. In a meta-analysis of experimental studies since 1962, Hillocks (1986) concludes that such environmental teaching was some 3 times as effective in developing writing skills as were more traditional approaches.

These examples also highlight another important feature of the notion of instructional scaffolding as a way to think about teaching and learning: it works by providing a way to think about and organize familiar activities and approaches, rather than by asking teachers to abandon what they already know. Instructional scaffolding is a beginning at the complex problem of codifying principles of effective teaching and learning.

4. Collaboration. In effective environments for teaching and learning, the teacher's role needs to be one of collaboration rather than evaluation. Evaluation has an important role in most classrooms, but it is a role that needs to be separated from the teaching-learning process (instead of embedded in it, as it is in traditional models of instruction). Only in this way can the teacher offer support that allows tentative explorations of new learning, with the inevitable false starts and initial misapprehensions that such explorations entail. If evaluation intrudes too soon, students will retreat to safer, and in many ways simpler, routines of recitation and display of previous learning.

5. Internalization. As students, peers, and teachers tackle new problems and carry their language activities through to comple-

tion, the young learners internalize the strategies and skills that were involved in solving those problems. These skills and strategies become resources to be drawn upon in new contexts; the socially embedded and transmitted knowledge that they represent becomes part of the individual student's repertoire. It is this process that leads to the astonishingly rapid emergence of language skills in the infant, and it is this same process that lies at the heart of language learning during childhood, adolescence, and adulthood.

Effective environments for teaching and learning will be structured to welcome this process, providing opportunities for young learners to take greater control of their language activities as they develop new skills. They must have room to initiate as well as respond, to explore the strengths as well as the limitations of their new knowledge and strategies. For this to happen, the teacher must be ready to step back as well as forward, providing room for students to use the skills they have as well as providing support for new skills that students are still in the process of developing. It is this process that provides the real structure and sequence in the curriculum, a structure and sequence that will emerge from the developing oral and written language skills of the individual learner.

Palincsar and Brown's (1984) notion of "reciprocal teaching" emphasizes this process of internalization, as well as the stepping back that is essential to success. In their approach, developed in the context of reading instruction, students' understanding is supported initially through a series of questions that the teachers ask about difficult passages. Gradually, students learn to take over these questions, using them overtly as they enter reciprocally into the teaching practice within small groups of their peers, and covertly as they read new passages on their own.

Griffin and Cole (1984) have similarly stressed the importance of interaction in the process of completing new tasks as a mechanism for the internalization of new knowledge and skills.

CONCLUSION

Many of the changes discussed so far could be cast another way, as changes in the nature of the interaction that will take place within effective environments for teaching and learning of the language arts. In the classrooms of the past, interaction has been one-sided; the teacher has delivered new information (through lecture or textbook), and has tested students to see what they have learned (either formally in writing or informally through questions and responses in class discussion). In such classrooms, students have few opportunities to initiate interactions with the teacher or with their peers. Such classrooms have worked relatively well in promoting basic skills among relatively well-motivated and high-achieving students; they have done less well in engaging traditionally at-risk students, or in promoting reasoned and disciplined thinking among any groups.

In the successful classroom of the future, the interaction will look rather different. The teacher will still play a central role, choosing the material that will be introduced, providing the structure that insures learning can take place, helping students complete the tasks they undertake. But in doing so the teacher will be encouraging the students to take a more central role in the classroom dialogue: advancing their own interpretations and opinions, defending them against alternatives rasied by their teachers and peers, checking them against their own experience and the logic and rigor of the texts with which they deal.

Such classrooms will be more complicated and less predictable than classrooms based on an orderly transmission of basic knowledge and skills. To run smoothly and effectively, they will require the guidance of the professional teacher, empowered to shape and support the interactions that emerge in ways that will help each student continue to progress and grow. Until we vest teachers with the authority to implement such approaches in the classrooms for which they are responsible, no amount of rhetoric, research, or curriculum planning is likely to make a significant difference in the nature of teaching and learning of the English language arts.

References

Applebee, A. N., Langer, J. A., & Mullis, I. (1986). *Writing: Trends across the Decade, 1974-1984.* Princeton, NJ: National Assessment of Educational Progress.

Applebee, A. N., Langer, J. A., & Mullis, I. (1987). *Learning to be literate in America.* Princeton, NJ: National Assessment of Educational Progress.

Applebee, A. N., Langer, J. A., & Mullis, I. (1988). *Who Reads Best? Factors Related to Reading Achievement.* Princeton, NJ: National Assessment of Educational Progress.

Applebee, A. N., Langer, J. A., & Mullis, I. (1987). *Literature and U.S. History: The Instructional Experiences and Factual Knowledge of High School Juniors.* Princeton, NJ: National Assessment of Educational Progress.

Berger, P. L., & Luckmann, T. (1966). *The social construction of reality.* NY: Anchor Books.

Braddock, R. (1974). The frequency and placement of topic sentences in expository prose, *Research in the Teaching of English 8,* 287–302.

Britton, J. N. (1970). *Language and learning.* London: Allen Lane The Penguin Press.

Britton, J. N., Burgess, T., Martin, N., McLeod, A., & Rosen, H. (1975). *The development of writing abilities (11–18).* London: Macmillan Educational for the Schools Council.

Brody, P., DeMilo, C., & Purves, A. (1989). *The current state of assessment in literature.* Report Number 3.2. Albany, NY: Center for the Learning and Teaching of Literature, The University at Albany, SUNY.

Bruner, J. (1974). *Beyond the information given: Studies in the psychology of knowing.* London: George Allen and Unwin.

Callahan, R. E. (1962). *Education and the cult of efficiency.* Chicago: Chicago University Press.

Cassirer, E. (1944). *An essay on man: An introduction to a philosophy of human culture.* New Haven: Yale University Press.

Cazden, C. (1979). Peekaboo as an instructional model: Discourse development at home and at school. *Papers and Reports on Child Language Development, 17,* 1–19.

Cuban, L. (1984). *How teachers taught.* New York: Longman.

Donaldson, M. (1978). *Children's minds.* Glasgow: Collins.

Graves, D. (1983). *Writing: Teachers and children at work.* Exeter, NH: Heinemann.

Griffin, P., & Cole, M. (1984). Current activity for the future: The zo-ped. In B. Rogoff & J. Wertsch (Eds.), *Children's learning in the zone of proximal development* (New Directions for Child Development, No. 23). San Francisco, Jossey-Bass.

Grossman, P. (1988). *A study in Contrast: Sources of Pedagogical Content Knowledge for Secondary English.* Doctoral dissertation, Stanford University.

Halliday, M. (1977). *Learning how to mean.* New York: Elsevier.

Heath, S. B. (1984). *Ways with words.* NY: Cambridge University Press.

Hillocks, G., Jr. (1979). The effects of observational activities on student writing, *Research in the Teaching of English, 13,* 23–35.

Hillocks, G., Jr. (1986). *Research on Written Composition.* Urbana, IL: National Conference on Research in English.

Hillocks, G., Jr., Kahn, E., & Johannessen, L. (1983). Teaching defining strategies as a mode of inquiry, *Research in the Teaching of English 17* (3), 275–84.

Kuhn, T. S. (1962). *The structure of scientific revolutions.* International encyclopedia of unified sciences, vol. 2, no. 2. Chicago: University of Chicago Press.

Langer, J. A. (1984). Literacy instruction in American schools: Problems and perspectives, *American Journal of Education, 93* (1), 23–35.

Langer, J. A. (1985). Levels of questioning: An alternative view, *Reading Research Quarterly 20* (5), 586–602.

Langer, J. A. (1987). The construction of meaning and the assessment of comprehension: An analysis of reader performance on standardized test items. In R. Freedle (Ed.), *Cognitive and linguistic analyses of strandardized test performance.* Norwood, NJ: Ablex, 1987, 225–244.

Langer, J. A. (1989). *The process of understanding literature.* Report No. 2.1. Albany, NY: Center for the Learning and Teaching of Literature, The University at Albany, SUNY.

Langer, J. A., & Applebee, A. N. (1986). Reading and writing instruction: Toward a theory of teaching and learning. In E. Z. Rothkopf (Ed.), *Review of Research in Education, 13,* 171–194.

Langer, J. A., & Applebee, A. N. (1987). *How Writing Shapes Thinking: A Study of Teaching and Learning.* Research Report No. 22. Urbana, IL: National Council of Teachers of English.

Langer, S. (1942). *Philosophy in a new key.* Cambridge: Harvard University Press.

Meade, R. A., & Ellis, W. G. (1970). Paragraph development in the modern age of rhetoric, *English Journal 59,* 219–226.

Moffett, J. (1981). *Active voice.* Montclair, NJ: Boynton Cook.

Palincsar, A. S., & Brown, A. L. (1984). Reciprocal teaching of comprehension-fostering and monitoring activities. *Cognition and Instruction, 1* (2), 117–175.

Polanyi, M. (1958). *Personal knowledge.* London: Routledge and Kegan Paul.

Raphael, T. E. (1985). *The contexts of school-based literacy.* NY: Random House.

Ravitch, D., & Finn, C. E. (1987). *What Do Our 17-Year-Olds Know?* New York: Harper & Row.

Rosenblatt, L. (1978). *The reader, the text, the poem.* Carbondale, IL: Southern Illinois University Press.

Shulman, L. (1987). Knowledge and teaching: Foundations of the new reform. *Harvard Educational Review, 57,* 1–22.

Vygotsky, L. S. (1962). *Thought and language.* Cambridge: MIT Press.

Wood, D., Bruner, J. S., & Ross, G. (1976). The role of tutoring in problem solving, *Journal of Child Psychology and Psychiatry, 17,* 89–100.

Part

·V·

RESEARCH ON TEACHING SPECIFIC ASPECTS OF THE ENGLISH LANGUAGE ARTS CURRICULUM

·30·

LANGUAGE, THE LANGUAGE ARTS, AND THINKING

Robert J. Marzano

The last decade has seen a growing educational interest in thinking and the ways it can be enhanced in the classroom. Calls for improved instructional techniques to enhance thinking arise in Congressional hearings as demands for graduates better able to take in work that requires responsibility and judgment (Resnick, 1987). Reports from the National Assessment of Educational Progress have noted that students appear to be performing less well on items which require higher-order thinking (Burns, 1986).

The current emphasis on thinking is not new. One can trace the call for an emphasis on enhanced thought back to Dewey (1933). In their analysis of the history of the literacy movement in this country, Resnick and Resnick (1977) noted that since there have been books and writing there have also been schools (mostly private and religious) established to train students in reasoning, rhetoric, mathematics and scientific thought. What is new about the current emphasis on thinking is that it is recommended for all students: "Although it is not new to include thinking, problem solving and reasoning in *someone's* school curriculum, it is new to include it in *everyone's* curriculum" (Resnick, 1987, p. 7).

In response to the perceived need to increase student thinking, a plethora of programs have been developed. Although many of the practices within these programs are drawn from fields traditionally not considered cognate to the language arts, much of what is currently being proposed to enhance thinking has its roots in language and many practices are direct applications of language-arts strategies. To highlight these relationships, this chapter is organized around three principles:

1) Language and thinking are inextricably linked,
2) Many of the current practices designed to enhance thinking have strong roots or corollaries within the language arts, and
3) Some of the theory and practice which has been developed to enhance thinking can be used to augment current conceptions of language arts.

To expand on these principles, the chapter is organized into three sections. The first section describes the interrelationship of thought and language. The second describes current approaches to the teaching of thinking and discusses the relationship of these approaches to the language arts. Finally, the third section describes ways in which current theory and practice in the teaching of thinking can expand on traditional views of the language arts.

THE PRIMACY OF LANGUAGE IN COGNITION

Language and thought are related in a number of ways. In this section three relationships are discussed:

1) Language as a form of thought,
2) Language as a mediator of thought and
3) Language as a tool for enhancing thought.

Language as a Form of Thought

Language is fundamentally linked to thought by the manner in which information is stored. There are many theories and models of information storage and representation in long-term memory (LTM). Researchers in hemisphericity (e.g., Gazzaniga,

This publication is funded, in part, by the Office of Educational Research and Improvement, Department of Education, under Contract Number 400-86-0002. The content of this publication does not necessarily reflect the views of OERI, the Department or any other agency of the U.S. Government.

1985; Gazzaniga & LeDoux, 1978; Gazzaniga & Sperry, 1967; Sperry, 1965) and those involved in the study of the neural aspects of cognition (Luria, 1961, 1969; Sokolov, 1972) assert that language is a unique form of coding which augments and, over time, synthesizes the other nonlinguistic codes. For example, Gazzaniga and LeDoux stated that "the behaviors that these separate (nonlinguistic) systems emit are monitored by the one system we come to use more and more, namely, the verbal natural language system" (1978, p. 150). Tulving (1972) in his landmark paper described the integrative nature of language in his discussion of semantic memory as opposed to episodic. Episodic memory is comprised of records of experienced events stored as perceptual (e.g., auditory, olfactory, tactile, kinesthetic, etc.) characteristics. Semantic memory contains decontextualized information that is fundamentally linguistic in form. Input to semantic memory comes directly from episodic memory and from the cognitive products of semantic memory itself. In other words, the semantic code for information in LTM is derived from translating and synthesizing the other codes. It also is derived from cognitive operations performed on itself.

Language philosophers go a step further in their assertions about the relationship of language to human thought. Some argue that language is at the root of intentional behavior, which ultimately is the characteristic separating human behavior from that of other animal forms. Whether language causes intentional behavior or enables it is subject to debate. Some language philosophers (e.g., Fodor, 1975) postulate the existence of a deep level, linguistically-based abstract code that is at the root of all thinking and intention. Similarly, Schlesinger (1971) posited the existence of abstract linguistic "intention markers" that form the basis of thought while Schank and Reiger (1974) identified twelve primitive actions that form the basis for human perception of all actions. However, Bishop (1983) asserted that a valid argument for language as the source of human intentions has yet to be developed. He concluded that a more defensible position is that language is a necessary, but not sufficient, condition for intentionality.

Although it cannot be shown that language is the basis for human intentions, strong arguments have been put forth for the influence of language in shaping human thought and, consequently, human intentions. For example, drawing from the work of case grammarians (Chafe, 1970; Fillmore, 1968), McNeil (1975) noted that language is organized around such conceptual entities as objects, agents, states and events. Even abstract content where there may or may not be real objects, actions, states or events must be organized into these structures. Thus, the semantic structure of language is a frame or matrix around which the somewhat random array of information initially received in sensory information storage is organized (Lindsay & Norman, 1977). Whorf's concept of linguistic relativity epitomizes the principle that language shapes perception. Building on the teaching of Sapir (1921), Whorf (1956) proposed that we dissect nature along the lines laid down by our native languages. The thoughts we isolate from the world of sensory stimuli are not there because they stare every observer in the face: "On the contrary, the world is presented in a kaleidoscopic flux of impressions which has to be organized by

our minds—and this means largely by the linguistic system in our minds (p. 213). (For a discussion of current interpretations of linguistic relativity, see Clarke, Losoff & Rood, 1982.)

In recent years, the role of language as a form of thought has been further described by the discipline of semiotics or the study of signs. Modern semiotic theorists (Deely, 1982, Eco, 1976, 1984) explain human cognition as an interactive triad composed of objects, signs and an interpretant. Objects are those physical entities and events external to the individual. Signs are abstract mental representations commonly expressed in linguistic form. The interpretant is a parallel representation that helps one place meaning on, or interpret, the abstract code. From this perspective, language is the mediator between objective reality and personal interpretation of that reality. Individuals within a society have subjective interpretations of reality but through language can share commonalities within these experiences. There is a growing interest in analyzing domain-specific knowledge from the semiotic perspective as language-based sign systems (Cunningham & Luk, 1985; Dickson, 1985; Suhor, 1984).

Even if language does not organize thought, the study of language has greatly enhanced our understanding of thought. Specifically, much of the research in cognitive science is linguistically based (Graesser, Millis & Long, 1986). For example, Schank and Abelson (1977) identified scripts, plans, and goals as fundamental cognitive structures in LTM that account for much of human behavior. Similarly, de Beaugrande (1980) identified frames, scripts and schemata. All of these structures are presumably comprised of nonlinguistic information organized and marked by a linguistic code.

The work in cognitive science on different types of cognitive structure has been greatly enabled by the research on discourse structures. In fact, some discourse structures directly parallel cognitive structures in LTM (van Dijk, 1980). Harris (1952) is commonly credited as being among the first to propose a serious model for linguistic analysis that extended beyond the sentence. Since then, there have been a number of models developed to describe inter- and intra-sentential semantic links (e.g., Marzano, 1983; Nold & Davis, 1980), the most influential of which were Young, Becker and Pike's (Pike, 1964; Young & Becker, 1965; Young, Becker & Pike, 1970) work on tagmemics and Halliday and Hasan's *Cohesion in English* (1976). (For a review of semantically based surface structure models see Cooper, 1983.) These models of surface-level discourse characteristics formed the basis for models that could be used not only to describe surface-level, textual characteristics but also the mental representation of those textual characteristics. A number of such systems have been proposed (Frederiksen, 1977; Meyer, 1975; Stein & Glenn, 1979; Turner & Greene, 1977). From these systems came theories of the process by which surface-level, textual characteristics are translated into LTM cognitive structures. To illustrate, one theory asserts that the process is one of translating or transforming a microstructure to a macrostructure (van Dijk, 1977, 1980; Kintsch & van Dijk, 1978). The microstructure of discourse is the "local structure," the literal meaning of the words, phrases, sentences and the relationships among them within discourse. The macrostructure is the global meaning extracted and inferred from the microstructure via such macrorules as deletion, construction and generalization. It is the macrostructure rather than the microstructure of text that is stored in LTM. This explains why an individual will tend to recall the "gist" or general theme rather than the detail of information read or heard (Frederiksen, 1977; Meyer, 1975; van Dijk & Kintsch, 1983). Analogous structures to micro- and macrostructures along with accompanying transformational processes have also been proposed (Crothers, 1979).

Language as a Mediator of Thought

A second relationship language has to thought is that of mediator of cognition. As mediator, language allows one cognitive system to interact with, and sometimes control, another system. For example, the different cognitive systems used within complex skills are often mediated by language until they have been developed to the level of automaticity (Sokolov, 1972). That is, a learner will commonly rehearse the various components of a complex skill at the early stages of skill development (Fitts, 1964). Consequently, many programs and practices that attempt to enhance the development of complex skills use inner or covert speech as a basic learning device. Inner speech signifies soundless mental speech at the instant one thinks about something. In short, we think and learn with the aid of words that we articulate to ourselves (Meichenbaum, 1977; Sokolov, 1972).

The use and development of inner speech as a mediational tool for learning complex cognitive skills can be traced to the late 1960s and the early 1970s (Meichenbaum, 1985). Many of the current programs and practices that use inner speech evolved partially from laboratory-based investigations of children's self-mediated cognitive strategies in social situations (Kanfer & Goldfoot, 1966; Kanfer & Phillips, 1970). This research demonstrated that young children quite naturally use inner or covert speech to enhance their understanding and use of the rules and principles of social behavior within peer groups. A second area of influence on the role of inner speech in enhancing learning was the verbal mediation literature that reinforced the role of inner speech in the development and use of specific strategies to enhance performance in specific learning tasks such as reading and problem solving (Bem, 1971; Flavell, Beach & Chinsky, 1966; Reese, 1962). A third area of influence was the work of Russian psychologists. For example, Luria (1961, 1969) proposed three stages by which the initiation and inhibition of voluntary behaviors come under verbal control. In the first stage, the speech of others controls and directs a child's behavior. In the second stage, the child's own overt speech becomes an effective regulator. Finally, in the third stage, a child's covert or inner speech is used to regulate behavior and cognition. (See Meichenbaum, 1975; and Wozniak, 1972, for reviews of the Soviet position on inner speech.)

One model for teaching the use of inner speech as a mediational tool for enhancing learning includes:

1) Cognitive modeling—an adult model performs the task while talking to himself out loud;
2) Overt, external guidance—the child performs the same task under the direction of model;

3) Overt self-guidance—the child performs the task while instructing himself out loud;
4) Faded, overt, self-guidance—the child whispers the instructions to himself as he progresses through the task; and
5) Covert self-instruction—the child performs the task while guiding his performance via inaudible or private speech (Meichenbaum, 1985).

The process of going from external to internal speech is key to the instructional sequence and should not be considered, warned Meichenbaum, a simple matter of faded overt speech. Rather, covert speech is a unique form of language with properties distinct from overt speech. Similarly, Vygotsky (1962) noted that the transfer from overt to covert speech is a change to a distinctly different form of cognition both in purpose and content.

Using the instructional model described above or variations of it, programs and practices have been constructed that purport to successfully develop varying levels of control over the disruptive behavior of hyperactive children (Douglas, Parry, Marton & Garson, 1976), the overt negative behaviors of aggressive children (Camp, Blom, Hebert & van Dournick, 1977) and the impulsivity of children (Bender, 1976; Meichenbaum & Goodman, 1971).

Language as a Tool for Enhancing Thought

A third type of relationship language has to thought is as a tool to enhance one's own thinking and that of others. Used in this way, language does not mediate the interactions of cognitive systems; rather, it is used as a somewhat artificial tool for eliciting certain types of thinking and as a tool for making more salient the type of thinking occurring at any given time so that it can be analyzed and subsequently improved. Language used to enhance thinking is always overt. In this section is discussed:

1) Overt speech as a tool for enhancing thinking and
2) Writing as a tool for enhancing thinking.

Overt Speech as a Tool for Enhancing Thinking. The importance of overt speech as a tool for enhancing thinking was evidenced in 1974 when the National Institute of Education identified overt speech in the classroom as one aspect of its research agenda. Green (1983) provided a summary of the research funded at that time. Cazden (1986) explained that much of that research focused on identifying the linguistic rules which govern speech in specific classroom situations. A broader perspective for studying overt speech in classrooms, asserted Cazden, is to view it as the vehicle that creates classroom context. Building on the work of Bateson (1972) and Erickson (1975), Cazden (1979) has shown that the use of oral language by both teachers and students serves to establish a classroom atmosphere that either elicits or discourages certain types of thinking. Cuing and questioning are two primary ways that teachers use overt speech to elicit specific types of thought.

Cuing involves teachers' use of overt speech to signal specific learning episodes. That is, teachers verbally signal the type of learning expected within a given period of time. Ideally students then retrieve appropriate mental scripts to match the learning episode. Elaborate coding schemes have been developed to describe the different forms of teacher language used as cues for various episodes (Mehan, 1979; Sinclair & Coulthard, 1975). Cues such as verbal advanced organizers that signal the structure of content are among the most powerful. That is, when students learn new content, the structure that information takes in the LTM is greatly influenced by how the teacher talks about the content (Moore, 1977). A number of studies have shown that structure of content as stored in students' LTM corresponds more closely to the a priori structure of the content after verbal instruction (Johnson, 1967, 1969; Johnson, Cox & Curran, 1970; Shavelson & Geeslin, 1973).

One of the primary ways that teachers signal the cognitive structure of content is through staging (Clements, 1979). Staging refers to a set of decisions that a teacher (or any speaker or writer) makes to communicate information in the most efficient manner. Based on the work of Clark & Haviland (1977), Frederiksen (1977) and Grimes (1975), Clements identified such staging rules as:

1. Identification of topic;
2. Determination of what is known and unknown; and
3. Coordination with other topics.

Where the research on staging has shown the effects of cuing on students' understanding of textual information, the research on scaffolding has provided evidence for the importance of teachers' use of language to signal the structure of nontextual information. The distinguishing feature of scaffolded instruction is the prominent role of dialogue between teacher and students to provide the learner with enough support and guidance to comprehend information and perform tasks in a manner that would be beyond unassisted efforts (Wood, Bruner & Ross, 1976). Scaffolded instruction involves reducing a task to a somewhat hierarchic, well-structured format. The teacher then keeps the learner in pursuit of the task, demonstrates an idealized version of the task and marks the critical features of the task for the learner. Scaffolding derives its theoretical base from theorists such as Vygotsky (1978) and Wertsch (1984) who asserted that an individual's learning of higher-order cognitive processes is enhanced by shaping those processes via verbal interaction with expert models. This assertion is also supported by many of the current pedagogical models (Davies, 1980; Pask, 1975; Reigeluth & Stein, 1983).

Questioning is a second way that teachers use overt speech to elicit specific types of thought. Christenbury and Kelly (1983) have described and critiqued many of the taxonomic and classification systems used to study teacher questioning. In general, teachers ask far more questions than they are aware of. For example, elementary teachers who thought they were asking 12 to 20 questions every half hour were actually asking 45 to 150 (Nash & Shiman, 1974). There is some evidence that asking questions improves students' comprehension and retention of content (Yost, Avila & Vexler, 1977). When questions are given after content has been presented and students are required to construct answers rather than select from among alternatives,

the benefits tend to be strongest (Christenbury & Kelly, 1983). Higher-level questions also appear to be instrumental in enhancing student thinking (Redfield & Rousseau, 1981) although there is considerable disagreement as to what constitutes higher-level questions (Fairbrother, 1975; Wood, 1977). One powerful distinction is that between recitation questions (those requiring students to simply retrieve information previously learned) and construction questions (those requiring students to construct new ideas or conclusions relative to information in LTM). Christenbury and Kelly (1983) described a system of questioning that is neither sequential nor hierarchic, yet allows a teacher to systematically ask construction questions that stimulate various types and levels of thought.

A subset of the research on teacher questioning is the research on teacher use of "wait time." Expanding on Rowe's (1974) original definition of wait time as pausing for several seconds after asking a question to give students time to think before being called on to answer, Tobin (1987) identified a number of different types of wait time (e.g., the pause following any teacher utterance and any student utterance, the pause following any student utterance and preceding any teacher utterance). He concluded that extended teacher wait time after asking questions should be viewed as a necessary but insufficient condition for higher, cognitive-level achievement. Results obtained by Granato (1983) and Knickerbocker (1984) suggest that a longer wait time after questions provides students with opportunities to get involved in verbal interactions. Similarly, extended wait time has been associated with more student discourse (Swift & Gooding, 1983), more student-to-student interactions (Fowler, 1975; Honea, 1982), decrease in student confusion (DeTure & Miller, 1985), higher achievement (Riley, 1986; Tobin, 1986) and increase in complexity and cognitive level of student responses (DeTure & Miller, 1985; Fagan, Hassler & Szabo, 1981).

Just as teachers use overt speech to enhance learning, so, too, do students. This assertion is supported by much of the research on small-group interactions within the cooperative learning literature. It is a basic assumption of many cooperative learning strategies that student-to-student verbal interactions about content improve learning and increase the level of thinking: "It is through the medium of this interaction and communication within small groups cooperating on academic tasks that these team-learning methods strive to influence pupils' cognitive learning" (Sharan, 1980, p. 242).

A number of studies on the relationship between small-group interaction and achievement have highlighted the importance of helping behavior in improving student learning (Hanelin, 1978; Johnson, 1979; Slavin 1978a, 1978b). (For a review of the research on the effects of small-group interaction on student learning, see Webb, 1982.) Further studies differentiated the effects for the individual providing the help from those obtained by the individual receiving the help. A majority of studies that analyzed the effects of providing help to peers in the form of verbal explanations (Peterson & Janicki, 1979; Peterson, Janicki & Swing, 1981; Webb, 1980a, 1980c, 1980d) found that it increased achievement. However, the effects of receiving help are much less robust. Specifically, receiving help positively affects achievement when it is elicited by the individual receiving help rather than volunteered by the help giver (Webb, 1980b, 1980c). In fact, it has been found that terminal feedback—providing a correct answer in the absence of an explanation of why the error is incorrect—is negatively related to achievement (Anderson, Evertson & Brophy, 1979). The explanation for the powerful effect of verbalization when helping a peer is that it forces the help-giver to critically analyze and sometimes restructure known information (Bargh & Schul, 1980).

Writing as a Tool for Enhancing Thinking. In terms of the relationship of writing to thinking, Nickerson has stated that: "Writing is viewed not only as a medium of thought but also as a vehicle for developing it" (Nickerson, 1984, p. 33). It is the robust nature of the difficulty of the writing task that renders it a powerful tool for enhancing thinking. By definition, the composing process is a highly-complex cognitive task. For example, in a study of writing performance within a number of disciplines, Perkins (1981) found that the ability to produce final copy easily and on the first draft is rare even among professionals.

In a series of studies Flower and Hayes (1980a, 1980b, 1981) developed a model for the writing process. Although it has been criticized (Cooper & Holzman, 1983), it is still the most widely cited. As Applebee (1984) noted, it is "the most thoroughly formalized model of the writing process" (p. 582). Flower and Hayes characterized writing as a set of iterative, recursive phases, which include planning, translating and reviewing, all of which are under the control of an executive monitor. Within each phase the writer is continually weighing the effects of current decisions on those previously made. The longer the process continues and the more the quantity of written discourse increases, the more interdependency is effected. Over time the process becomes one of making decisions based on increasingly more numerous and complex conditions.

From this perspective, writing is one of the most taxing of cognitive acts because it maximizes the load of information that must be maintained in working memory during its execution. Specifically, Johnson-Laird (1983) characterized thinking within any task as the execution of "mental models" somewhat like mental programs with variables. The more variables a program contains the more difficult its execution. Similarly, Anderson's (1983) production model of cognition postulates that the more branch decisions involved in a cognitive act the more difficult its execution. The numbers of decisions, then, that must be made during writing, and the interdependence of these decisions makes it one of the most difficult cognitive processes. As writers becomes more skilled, their ability to monitor and control the many variables involved increases. It is this control that is hypothesized to generalize to other tasks (de Beaugrande, 1984).

Presumably, practice in writing should enhance performance in any cognitive process in which executive control over a number of variables is a factor (e.g., some forms of problem solving); however, not all forms of writing instruction will enhance such executive control. Specifically, in his meta-analysis of writing research, Hillocks (1986) concluded that it is only when teachers plan instructional activities that result in a high level of student autonomy and interaction about the problems faced in composing that writing instruction has a powerful effect on student thinking. Hillocks referred to this as the environmental mode of instruction.

In summary, language and thought are inextricably linked. Language can be viewed as a separate form of thinking that is at the root of human cognition. It can also be viewed as a mediator to thought, using covert speech to control and orchestrate one's own thinking. Finally, it can be viewed as a tool used by both teacher and student for enhancing thought, using spoken and written language to elicit and improve specific types of cognition.

APPROACHES TO THE TEACHING OF THINKING AND THEIR BASES IN THE LANGUAGE ARTS

The recent interest in thinking has spawned the development of a myriad of programs and practices designed to enhance thinking. (For reviews of these programs and practices, see Chance, 1986; Costa, 1985a; Nickerson, Perkins & Smith, 1985). Although there are many ways to categorize the different approaches to teaching thinking (e.g., Resnick, 1987; Segal, Chipman & Glaser, 1985), the following four categories are useful in highlighting the role of the language arts in the teaching of thinking:

1) Metacognitive approaches,
2) Componential approaches,
3) Heuristic approaches,
4) Critical and creative thinking approaches.

In this section programs and practices within those four categories are discussed along with the related language-arts research within each category.

Metacognitive Approaches

Metacognition as defined by Flavell (1976, 1977, 1978) refers to one's knowledge concerning one's own cognitive processes and products or anything related to them. Brown (1978) breaks metacognition into two components: awareness and control of the factual or declarative knowledge necessary to complete a specific task and awareness and control over the necessary processes or procedural knowledge to complete a task. "Awareness and control" refer to the executive monitoring of knowledge. Others (Paris & Lindauer, 1982; Paris, Lipson & Wixson, 1983) have broadened the notion of metacognition beyond the awareness and control of declarative and procedural knowledge to include the executive monitoring of one's self system and how that self system interacts with the task. In this section programs and practices that emphasize executive control of the self system are first described. Next are described programs and practices that emphasize executive control over task-related declarative and procedural knowledge.

Control of the Self System. A number of studies have emphasized the interaction of the self system with the task. In a series of studies McCombs (1984, 1986, 1987), building on the work of others (Baird & White, 1984; Bandura, 1977; Connell & Ryan, 1984; Harter, 1982; Shavelson & Bolus, 1982), established that an individual's motivation for and efficiency at a given task are, at least, partially a function of the attitudes and beliefs the individual has relative to such factors as: control over the task, the perceived value of the task, and the perceived competence for the task. Programs and practices that attempt to improve students' knowledge and control of self usually employ some form of verbal mediation (use of covert speech) to generate positive affect and enhance efficacy. (For reviews of programs see McCombs, 1984; Reynolds & Stark, 1983.) For example, drawing on the work of Ellis (1962), Luria (1961) and Vygotsky (1962), Meichenbaum (1977) has developed verbal mediation strategies that provide the learner with an awareness of the effect (both negative and positive) of specific self statements on task performance. Meichenbaum's strategies are based on the assumption that negative self statements reflect the structure of the self system through which a given task is processed. He asserted that by rehearsing positive self statements in specific task situations one gradually changes the structure of the self system relative to the task. To illustrate the relationship between self statements and performance on creativity, Henshaw (1978) studied the verbalizations of high-creative versus low-creative college students and found that the high-creative students differed significantly from low-creative in the frequency with which they emitted self statements that were supportive and in the amount of positive affect they experienced for the task. Low-creative students produced significantly more negative self statements and experienced more negative affect for the task. Working with army recruits, McCombs (1984, 1986) found that training in techniques to monitor and control the self system improved subjects' perceptions of control and their ability to perform specific tasks. Allen (1972), however, has warned that strategies aimed at mediating the self system have long-term effects only when coupled with counseling.

Control of Task. Programs and practices emphasizing metacognitive control over task-related declarative and procedural knowledge are growing in number. In fact, over the last decade scores of "learning strategies" for increasing students' control over the processing of a task have been developed and tested. (For a review see Derry & Murphy, 1986.) Snowman and McCown (1984) have made a distinction between *learning strategies* and *learning tactics*. A learning strategy is an overall plan one makes for performing a task, whereas a tactic is a more specific skill one uses in the service of a strategy. Strategies are metacognitive. In fact, they are sometimes referred to as *metastrategies* or *metacognitive strategies* (Dansereau, 1978; Pressley, Borkowski & O'Sullivan, 1984). Pressley, Levin and Ghatala (1984) have coined the acronym MAPS, Metamemory Acquisition Procedures, to stand for instruction that enhances students' abilities to evaluate the tactics they are using to complete a specific task. For example, a strategy that teaches students a particular method for taking notes and then asks the student to evaluate the effectiveness of that strategy would be considered a MAPS technique. In general, MAPS techniques have been found to improve students' use of the specific tactics used in the task and their general metacognitive control over the task (Brown,

1978; Flavell, 1981). Metacognitive programs that are considered part of the mainstream emphasis to enhance thinking include the Productive Thinking Program and paired problem solving.

The Productive Thinking Program (Covington, 1985) is designed for upper elementary school children and reinforces a variety of metacognitive strategies such as setting goals, planning and monitoring progress toward goals. The program also emphasizes monitoring such self-system variables as resisting immobilization caused by failure anxiety. As compared to other programs, Productive Thinking has been evaluated rather extensively (Covington, 1983, 1985). Subjects who have gone through the program exhibit more efficient use of the metacognitive strategies presented and, more importantly, states Resnick (1987), they tend to use the strategies in tasks not covered in the program such as writing a report, studying for a test, or approaching a problem.

Whimbey and Lochhead (1982, 1984) stress a paired problem-solving process in which students alternate the roles of problem solver and listener-critic. Its intent is to improve student abilities in such metacognitive strategies as analyzing tasks, formulating plans, and evaluating outcomes. According to Lochhead (1985) few formal evaluations have been conducted to assess the effectiveness of paired problem solving. The most carefully designed studies have involved courses that used paired problem solving in conjunction with other approaches with advanced secondary or post-secondary students. For example, Lochhead cites a 1979 summer program for 34 prefreshmen students who had scored below twelfth grade on a standardized reading achievement test. These students were subjected to a multi-approach course that included use of the text, *Problem Solving and Comprehension* (Whimbey & Lochhead, 1982). Pre-post results indicated that subjects increased their use of metacognitive strategies and exhibited significant grade-level gains in reading comprehension.

Metacognition and the Language Arts. Although metacognition as it relates to a knowledge and control of the self system has received little attention from the English language arts, metacognition as it relates to a knowledge and control of task has received a great deal of attention particularly within the research and theory on writing. For example, a key component of the Hayes and Flower (1980) model of writing is the monitor that exerts executive or metacognitive control over the component processes. Key to this metacognitive control of the task is goal setting. Specifically, writers translate high-level goals into subgoals. The result is that subgoals tend to pile up creating a potential overload on working memory (Flower & Hayes, 1981). The writer, in turn, develops strategies for handling this "memory overload" condition taking advantage of situations where the creation of one subgoal generates an opportunity for the completion of another (Hayes-Roth & Hayes-Roth, 1979). Thus, the generation of subgoals in the writing process is dynamic rather than a priori (Matsuhashi, 1982). The result is that high-level goals are sometimes replaced by subgoals generated relatively late in the writing process. Thus, the end product of the composing process is often a surprise to the writer (Murray, 1978).

It is the metacognitive ability to monitor this highly complex process of juggling goals and subgoals that separates the writing of skilled versus novice writers and the writing of adults from that of children (Scardamalia, Bereiter & Steinbach, 1984). However, it has been shown that children's metacognitive control over goals can be improved by giving them verbal prompts about possible next steps in the writing process as they "think aloud" while engaged in the task (Bereiter & Scardamalia, 1982; Scardamalia & Bereiter, 1983, 1985).

The influence of the research and theory on metacognition in the language arts is also evidenced in the literature on reading (Paris, Lipson & Wixson, 1983). Parallels have been drawn between metacognition in reading and metacognitive behavior in other disciplines such as mathematics, memory and problem solving (Brown, 1975; Kail & Hagen, 1982; Resnick & Ford, 1981; Siegler, 1983). The strategic reader, like the strategic mathematician or problem solver, juggles goals and subgoals relative to the purpose of reading, the changing nature of the text, and the extent to which information is new or old (Clark & Haviland, 1977). In fact, one of the more powerful reading interventions is Palincsar and Brown's (1984) reciprocal teaching, which is fundamentally metacognitive in nature. Reciprocal teaching employs a process of cooperative question-asking between teacher and students to highlight many of the metacognitive demands of reading. The teacher models the overt summarizing, questioning, clarifying, and predicting processes, which are assumed to be internal processes executed during reading, while students comment on the quality of questions, and summaries, and try to construct better ones. After an intervention period of several weeks in which reciprocal teaching was practiced daily, middle-school students who had received instruction had higher reading performance than control groups and maintained this higher performance even after an eight-week period without instruction (Palincsar & Brown, 1984). More strikingly, noted Resnick (1987), scores on science and social studies comprehension tests given in the classroom rather than in the reciprocal teaching laboratory also rose significantly for the experimental subjects.

Componential Approaches

Componential approaches to teaching thinking are those that attempt to develop specific cognitive operations. Although many componential approaches also enhance metacognition, it is not a necessary by-product of such approaches. That is, specific cognitive operations can be enhanced without enhancing a general knowledge and control of self and task. Using the terminology of Snowman and McCown (1984), componential approaches stress learning tactics rather than learning strategies. Componential approaches can be organized into three categories:

1) Model-based approaches,
2) Eclectic approaches, and
3) Single-tactic approaches.

Model-Based Approaches. Some componential approaches attempt to operationalize a complete model of intelligence or learning. For example, the Structure of Intelligence or SOI pro-

gram (Meeker, 1969) is based on Guilford's model of intelligence (Guilford, 1967; Guilford & Hoepfner, 1971), which proposes 120 intellectual abilities that are combinations of *operations* (e.g., comprehending, remembering and analyzing); *content* (e.g., words, forms and symbols); and *products* (e.g., single words, groups and relationships). SOI reportedly reinforces 90 of Guilford's 120 components using materials that range from primary through high-school grades. Evaluations of SOI are based on tasks specifically designed to measure Guilford's components and generally show an increase in subjects' abilities to perform these tasks as a result of using the materials. However, its transfer to non-SOI tasks has not been established (Nickerson, Perkins & Smith, 1985). Yet, this same criticism can be leveled at many of the programs which purport to enhance thinking (Resnick, 1987).

Instrumental Enrichment (Feuerstein, Rand, Hoffman & Miller, 1980) is a program composed of a series of problem-solving tasks and exercises that are grouped in 14 areas. Exercises are called *instruments* rather than lessons because their intent is to be content free (Link, 1985). The goal of each instrument is to reinforce the cognitive operations relative to the *input* phase (e.g., gathering relevant information relative to a problem), the *elaboration* phase (e.g., operating on input information) and the *output* phase (e.g., reporting the desired result) of problem solving.

Feuerstein's model assumes that cognitive deficits occur when processing breaks down relative to the operations within any of the three phases (Messerer, Hunt, Meyers & Lerner, 1984). The initial two-year evaluation of Instrumental Enrichment in Israeli schools with students ages 12 to 15 (Feuerstein et al., 1980) indicated that IE produced substantial gains in performance in a variety of intellectual tasks including general cognitive tasks as measured by Thurstone's Primary Mental Abilities test and content-specific cognitive abilities as measured by standardized achievement tests. In a replication of the original Feuerstein study, Ruiz and Castaneda (in Savell, Twohig & Rachford, 1986) administered IE to experimental and control Venezuelan children ages 10 to 14 over a two-year period. The results indicated that subjects in the experimental group scored significantly higher than control subjects in all measures, which included intelligence tests, math, and language-achievement tests. Similar studies have been conducted in Nashville, Toronto and other cities. (For a review see Savell et al., 1986). Relative to the effectiveness of IE, Campione, Brown and Ferrara (1982) have suggested that the materials themselves have less to do with the program's success than the reinforcement of the specific cognitive components (input, elaboration, output) that are emphasized.

Eclectic Approaches. There are many componential approaches to teaching thinking that can be classified as eclectic— they employ multiple tactics but draw their components from various models of learning and intelligence as opposed to a single model. Included in such programs are Project Intelligence and BASICS.

Begun in 1979, Project Intelligence was a joint effort by researchers at Harvard University, Bolt, Beranek and Newman, Inc., and the Venezuelan Ministry of Education to develop methods and materials that enhance the ability of students to perform a wide variety of cognitive operations including inferential use of information in long-term memory, hypothesis generation, predicting, classifying, problem solving, and decision making (Nickerson et al., 1985). The backbone of the program is approximately 100 lessons aimed at teaching and reinforcing these tactics.

The materials were initially tested using 12 experimental and 12 control classes. All participating classes were designated by Venezuelan authorities as being part of "Barrio" schools, indicating that students came from families of low-socioeconomic status and minimal parental education. A variety of tests were administered to both groups including a number of general-abilities tests and some special-abilities tests developed by the researchers to measure specific skills within the program. A detailed discussion of the results appears in the project's final report (Harvard University, 1983). As summarized by Nickerson et al., (1985), in the large majority of cases the gains shown by students in the experimental group were greater than those shown by the control. The differences were both statistically significant and substantial in size especially for the special abilities tests.

BASICS is an acronym for Building and Applying Strategies for Intellectual Competencies in Students (Ehrenberg, Ehrenberg & Durfee, 1979). It is designed to enhance thinking in eighteen thinking/learning tactics, which include such cognitive operations as noting differences and similarities, grouping, classifying, generalizing, and inferring causes and effects. Detailed, almost algorithmic processes are presented for each of the thinking tactics.

Although no formal evaluation of the BASICS program has been published, Nickerson et al. (1985) critiqued the program relative to its construct validity. They noted that the program appears conceptually sound in that the tactics are sequenced so that later ones build on earlier ones. "Also, all of the strategies (tactics) repeat certain characteristics that seem designed to foster a sound cognitive style. There is emphasis throughout on systematizing, thoroughness, checking judgments, storing or communicating results, justifying conclusions, and producing overt 'thought products' " (p. 180). However, they also noted that the program has some conceptual flaws in that some of the tactics are based on conceptions of thinking that do not reflect the latest research and theory in psychology. They stated that the effectiveness of the BASICS program "must remain an open question until the necessary evaluation studies are undertaken (p. 181).

Single-Tactic Approaches. A number of componential approaches emphasize a single cognitive operation which is directly or indirectly related to some model of intelligence or learning. Within such approaches subjects are usually presented with tactics rather than strategies for enhancing the underlying cognitive operation. Below are described five general categories of such tactics:

1) Encoding,
2) Matching,
3) Analyzing,
4) Representing, and
5) Extending.

1. Encoding Tactics. Encoding involves representing selected information in such a way as to make it more easily retrieved from LTM. Encoding tactics include rehearsal and mnemonics. In their review of a wide variety of tactics of which rehearsal is one type, Weinstein and Mayer (1986) reported that rehearsal includes verbatim rehearsal and generative rehearsal. Verbatim rehearsal involves the repetition of information to be remembered, either overtly or covertly, using words or mental pictures. Generative rehearsal involves the selection of information from a text via copying, underlining or highlighting and then subsequently repeating this selected information either covertly or overtly. Flavell, Friedrichs, and Hoyt (1970) found that students' spontaneous use of rehearsal tactics increases in frequency and effectiveness with age. In addition, it has been shown that students can be overtly taught to effectively use both verbatim rehearsal tactics (Kenney, Cannizzo, & Flavell, 1967) and generative rehearsal tactics (Rickards & August, 1975), yet younger students (e.g., below the age of seven) are not adept at selecting appropriate rehearsal tactics across different tasks (Appel, Cooper, McCarrell, Sims-Knight, Yussen, & Flavel, 1972) nor are students below a certain age (e.g., sixth grade) adept at identifying important information on which to use rehearsal tactics (Brown & Smiley, 1977).

Mnemonic devices are learning tactics that enhance the recall of information (Belleza, 1981). A number of studies have shown rather dramatic effects on recall performance when using such mnemonic devices as the method of loci (Ross & Lawrence, 1968), the peg-word mnemonic (Bugelski, 1968), the link mnemonic (Delin, 1969), and the story mnemonic (Bower, 1972; Bower & Clark, 1969). Belleza explained that mnemonic devices have often been considered "artificial memory devices," because they use cognitive structures that, "somewhat disturbingly, have little or no relationship to the conceptual content of the material being learned" (1981, p. 247). Belleza noted that much of the past research has, unfortunately, focused on the visual imagery aspects of mnemonics creating the inaccurate perception that mnemonics and visual imagery mediation are synonymous. In fact, mnemonics operate by the creation and use of a variety of types of *cognitive cuing structures* which include selection of important information, organization of that information, and creation of salient cues which are nonlinguistic and linguistic in nature.

2. Matching Tactics. A number of componentially based approaches fall under the general rubric of what Anderson (1983) refers to as matching, determining how one or more entities are alike and/or different on one or more characteristics and then using those distinctions to reorganize the information. Matching tactics include comparing, categorizing and ordering.

Comparing is identifying and articulating the similarities and differences between elements. It is basic to many other cognitive operations and one of the first steps in higher forms of analysis (Feuerstein et al., 1980). Although the difficulty of a comparison task is partially a function of the individual's knowledge of the content being compared (Mandler, 1983), skill at comparing can be improved. For example, Raphael and Kirschner (1985) found that students' comprehension, and their production of comparative written summaries, improved when they were taught specific types of comparison structures (e.g., whole/whole, part/part and mixed).

Classifying also is a central component of many theories of cognition and learning. For example, Nickerson et al., (1985) along with others (Mervis, 1980; Smith & Medin, 1981) have asserted that the ability to form conceptual categories is so basic to human cognition that it can be considered a necessary condition of thinking. To classify, individuals must be able to identify the common features or attributes of various entities which form a group or groups. There is evidence that young children can categorize information with which they are very familiar but have difficulty using categorization as a tool for processing unfamiliar content unless they receive explicit instruction to do so (Moely, 1977). Jones, Amiran and Katims (1985) found that students' ability at categorizing can be improved with explicit instruction, yet extended practice and feedback is needed for transfer to occur.

Closely related to classifying is ordering, which is sequencing or ordering entities on selected characteristics or attributes. Although Piaget concluded that children do not usually master ordering until the concrete operational stage, usually about age 7 or 8 (Piaget & Szeminska, 1941), Feuerstein et al., (1980) found that low-achieving and very young children can develop competence in ordering tasks when specific tactics are reinforced. Similarly, matrix outlining strategies (discussed in conjunction with representing components) have proven to be effective tools for enhancing the ability to order.

3. Analyzing Tactics.

Analyzing tactics are those which help the learner identify component parts of information and articulate the subordinate and superordinate relationships among those parts. From this perspective analyzing tactics are fairly direct applications of Kintsch and van Dijk's (1978) theory of macro- and micro-structures, Anderson's (1982, 1983) principle of generalization, and Bransford and Frank's (1976) concept of decontextualizing. Tactics in this category include summarizing, note taking, and finding main idea.

Brown, Campione and Day (1981) used a rule-based approach to summarizing which includes deleting trivial and redundant material, substituting superordinate terms for lists and selecting or inventing a topic. Their research suggests that younger and low-achieving students have difficulty using these rules especially the last one, which requires them to select or invent a topic. Often, they will select what interests them rather than what is a good organizer for the information that is to be summarized.

Note taking is another tactic that can be classified as analyzing. DiVesta and Gray (1972) found that note taking provides both encoding and storage functions. It aids the learner in creating a macro-structure for information and provides a form of external storage for later review. In general, results of note taking have shown better recall of information at a time proximal to the presentation of the information, but there have been mixed results at distal points (Peper & Mayer, 1978; Barnett, DiVesta & Rogozinski, 1981).

Finding the main idea is another cognitive process that includes the properties of analysis. However, main idea as a construct is not well defined. For example, Cunningham and Moore (1986) listed ten different ways of conceptualizing main idea and the task of finding it. From an instructional perspective, main idea is commonly approached as the topic sentence within textual information (Braddock, 1974). Ashton, O'Hear, and Pherson (1985) found that many of the linguistic cues for identifying topic sentences taught in study skill texts apply quite well to sociology textbooks. However, studies of other types of textbooks indicate that topic sentence is not an effective method for teaching main idea (Alexander, 1976; Axelrod, 1975). Another perspective of main idea is that it is the most salient discourse structure within the text (Anderson & Armbruster, 1985). From this perspective much of the work on superordinate discourse structures (Meyer, 1975, 1985; van Dijk & Kintsch, 1983) supports the viability of instruction in main idea. For example, it has been found that informal oral summarizing can be effectively elicited from students before, during, and after reading text segments via teacher- and student-directed questions that focus attention on the subordinate and supeordinate structure of discourse (Jones, Palincsar, Ogle, & Carr, 1987).

4. Representing Tactics.

Representing tactics are those used to change the form of information to improve understanding and ease of recall. A key characteristic of representation is that the learner encodes the information in a new form or new modality. That is, the learner transforms linguistic information into some form that uses symbols and diagrams to represent semantic relationships among concepts. Within this category fall graphic organizing tactics (e.g., webs and maps). Graphic organizers have been shown to enhance both comprehension and recall of information (Holley & Dansereau, 1984; Jones, Tinzmann, Friedman & Walker, 1987; Van Patten, Chao & Reigeluth, 1986). Also included in this category are the matrix outlining tactics that have been used to help students classify, identify, and articulate main ideas (Jones et al., 1985). Presumably, these tactics aid recall because they increase the number of association points with which information can be retrieved. Similarly, they aid understanding because they increase the variety of information representation allowing for information linkages not possible in a strictly linguistic mode.

5. Extending Tactics.

Extending tactics are those that enable the learner to go beyond what is explicitly stated in textual information. Bartlett (1932) is usually credited as being the first psychologist to document the fact that individuals' recall of information read or heard is inaccurate; elements are distorted to conform to prior knowledge. He interpreted these results as an indication that information in LTM shapes and extends incoming information. In recent years, a number of types of information-shaping and extending tactics have been identified, most of them fall within the general rubric of inference. (For a review of extending tactics see Reder, 1980.) For example, many typologies and thinking skills programs have defined various types of inductive and deductive tactics (Nickerson et al., 1985; Costa, 1985b). Many of these are based on inductive and deductive rules from syllogistic models. Some theorists have criticized the traditional definitions of induction and deduction (Deely, 1982; Eco, 1976, 1979, 1984) asserting that the normal process of inference is nonlinear and far more "messy" than that described within the inductive/deductive models.

Instructionally, extending is commonly reinforced by presenting students with tactics for creating analogies and metaphors. They have been shown to be powerful cognitive tools in developing ideas in oral discourse, in composing, and in creative thinking (Bransford, Sherwood, Rieser & Vye, 1986: Mayer, 1984; Weinstein & Mayer, 1986). In addition, Koch (1970, 1974) has developed tactics for eliciting strikingly original metaphoric language from children of all ages.

Componential Approaches and Language Arts. Many of the single-tactic componential approaches described above have roots or corollaries in the language arts. For example, a significant proportion of the previously-described matching tactics for comparison and contrast were initially field tested and evaluated in language arts settings (Jones et al., 1987; Raphael & Kirschner, 1985). Similarly, summarizing tactics have been used extensively within reading. For example, Day (in Raphael, 1987) developed a series of six summarization rules designed for use with poor readers and writers. Working with average and above-average eleventh-grade students, Bean, Singer, Sorter and Frazee (1983) found that instruction in summarization rules increased students' ability to retrieve information from memory and express it in a succinct way although it did not increase their ability to select key ideas. Similarly, McNeil and Donant (1982) found that sixth graders could be taught to use summarization rules that significantly affected their comprehension scores. (See Hidi & Anderson, 1986, for a review of research on summarization.)

Note taking is an analyzing tactic that also has been studied within the context of the language arts. For example, note taking traditionally has been taught within language-arts based study skills courses or as a part of composition courses (Weinstein & Mayer, 1986). A number of studies have demonstrated its effect on recall for information in notes although instruction in note taking does not insure that students will identify important information on which to take notes (Einstein, Morris & Smith, 1985).

Main idea also is traditionally based in the language arts. For example, the International Reading Association published an edited work (Bauman, 1986) in teaching main idea as an aid to comprehension. Strategies covered include generating hypotheses before reading and then testing the accuracy of these hypotheses during and after reading, looking for superordinate structures, looking for linguistic cues, and looking for topic sentences. (See Cunningham & Moore, 1986, and Winograd & Bridge, 1986, for reviews of the different conceptions of main idea and the different tactics for teaching it.)

Representing tactics are relatively new in the language arts, although incidents of their use are rapidly increasing. Such tactics have been effectively used as tools for enhancing reading comprehension (Miccinati, 1988). For example, Singer and Bean (1984) found that students who created a graphic organizer for information read recalled more information than those who outlined. Similarly, Slater, Graves and Piche (1985) found that representing in visual form produced better recall of information than taking notes. Representational techniques have also been used with the language arts as tools for improving vocabulary development (Marzano, Hagerty, Valencia & DiStefano, 1987), for taking notes (Dansereau, 1985) and developing content-area schemata (Freedman & Reynolds, 1980).

Extending tactics have received language-arts attention primarily in the area of inferences made while reading. For example, Warren, Nicholas and Trabasso (1979) developed a hierarchy of the types of reading inferences commonly made. The taxonomy includes logical inferences (e.g., motivation, psychological causation, physical causation), informational inferences (e.g., spatiotemporal, world frame) and value inferences (e.g., evaluative). Similarly, Crothers (1979) identified two major categories of text inferences (implicational and referential). Instructionally, within the language arts, a number of tactics have been developed that aid students in making and checking elaborative inferences. For example, Pearson and Johnson (1978) proposed a three-way relationship among questions, the text, and prior knowledge of the content being read. Using this basic framework, Raphael (1982, 1984) developed a QARS tactic (Question-Answer Relationships) in which students differentiate between questions for which the answers is "right there" in the text and is cued directly by the question stem, versus questions that are in the text but must be found via a "think and search" process, versus questions for which the student will have to generate the answers "on their own."

Heuristic Approaches

A number of approaches to teaching thinking are heuristically based. Heuristics are general rules that, when followed, increase the likelihood of success at a given task. At their core, heuristic approaches provide the learner with actions that, when followed, increase the likelihood of successful completing specific cognitive operations. Heuristic approaches differ from componential approaches in that they are more "macro" in nature; they deal with more global cognitive operations. Arguably, the techniques presented within heuristic approach are quite similar to the tactics presented within componential programs.

Although heuristics have been developed for a number of cognitive operations (e.g., Beyer, 1988), problem solving and decision making are commonly the focus of heuristically-based approaches. Both problem solving and decision making have been identified as central to cognition of all types (Anderson, 1982, 1983; Rowe, 1985). Studies on expert versus novice approaches to problem solving indicate that experts differ from novice problem solvers in their knowledge and use of general problem-solving heuristics such as devising a plan, representing the problem, carrying out a plan, and checking results (Gick & Holyoak, 1980; Schoenfeld, 1980; Simon, 1980). Schoenfeld (1983a, 1983b) stressed that expert problem solvers are better than novice problem solvers even when dealing with problems outside of their domain of expertise, because they use their general problem-solving heuristics better.

Most programs that attempt to foster thinking use a problem-solving orientation. For example, the Productive Thinking Program (previously discussed) by Covington, Crutchfield, Davies, & Olton, (1974) and Instrumental Enrichment (previously discussed) by Feuerstein et al., (1980) use problem-solving as the primary instructional vehicle. Wales and Stager (1977, see also Nardi & Wales, 1985) have developed a heuristically-based approach to enhancing problem solving and decision making that they refer to as Guided Design. Guided Design has been offered in high schools and colleges as a course to accompany a wide variety of disciplines (e.g., the humanities, the social sciences, the physical sciences and engineering). Using freshmen in engineering at West Virginia University, Wales (1979) found increases in grade point averages after four years even after controlling for grade inflation. As described by Resnick: "Before the introduction of Guided Design, engineering students' average freshman GPA's were well below the university average; after Guided Design, their GPA's were well above the average. Students who had participated in the Guided Design program as freshmen also had higher four-year GPA's than (transfer) students who had not participated" (1987, p. 21).

Many of the processes within the CoRT Thinking Program (de Bono, 1976, 1983, 1985) also can be classified as decision-making and problem-solving heuristics. The materials are as content free as possible, reflecting de Bono's desire to develop heuristics for "real life" thinking versus artificial, academic situations. This position is echoed by Frederiksen (1984), who noted that most of the problems presented to students in academic situations are well structured with straightforward paths to a solution, whereas problems faced in life are not.

Although it is probably the most widely used program for teaching thinking, CoRT has not been extensively evaluated (Resnick, 1987). De Bono (1976) reported several experiments involving idea counts contrasting students who had received CoRT instruction with control groups. Results indicated that CoRT instruction leads to the production of more ideas and a more balanced and less egocentric view of problems. Edwards and Baldauf (1983) reported a study in which tenth-grade students in a science course were exposed to the CoRT materials. The researchers found a statistically significant relationship between gain scores on items testing CoRT heuristics and science exam scores after controlling for IQ. "This says that those who learned CoRT better also learned science better, discounting IQ, suggesting that CoRT addresses some aspect of ability in science other than IQ" (Nickerson et al., 1985, p. 218).

Heuristic Approaches and the Language Arts. Again, given their close connections, many of the language-arts tactics discussed previously also might be described as heuristics (e.g., Brown et al., 1981; Raphael, 1982, 1984). Within the language arts, many of the approaches to processing textual information are heuristically based. For example, Ogle's (1986) K-W-L is a heuristically-based approach for improving student comprehension of textual material. It involves having students identify what they know (K), what they would like to know (W), and what they have learned (L) within the process of reading. Similarly, PReP, which is an acronym for Pre-Reading Plan, is a three-step procedure intended to help students access and use prior

knowledge while reading (Langer, 1982). Closely related is ARC developed by Estes (in Marzano et al., 1987). ARC, which is an acronym for Anticipation, Realization and Contemplation, helps students articulate what they think they know in a text, note what they would like to know, and then summarize their findings after reading.

One of the most popular text processing heuristics is Dansereau's MURDER (1985), which also is an acronym for:

1) Setting the *mood* to study;
2) Reading for *understanding;*
3) *Recalling* the material without referring to the text;
4) *Digesting* the material by recalling and amplifying it;
5) *Expanding* knowledge by self-inquiry; and, finally,
6) *Reviewing* mistakes.

The research on MURDER indicates that it is a highly-generalizable technique that can be learned with relative ease and produces positive effects on student understanding and recall of information (Chance 1986; Dansereau, 1985).

Critical and Creative Thinking Approaches

The approaches to teaching thinking described thus far spring from a psychological tradition. However, it was not until the mid-nineteenth century that scholars viewed the human mind as a working mechanism with underlying operations that could be studied from a psychological perspective (Rowe, 1985). In contrast, the roots to the philosophical interest in thinking reach back to the classical past. Greene (1984) noted that in the Western World, philosophy preceded by at least 2,000 years the growth of what we now call psychology. At the heart of the philosophic perspective of thinking is the use of reason to guide behavior. For example, Aristotle described the process of discerning truth through rational thought as grasping the design or *telos* of reality.

Most critical-thinking approaches to enhancing thinking are rooted in philosophy. Although once defined in a narrow sense as assessing the accuracy of statements, critical thinking is now defined in a more robust manner as "reasonable reflective thinking that is focused on deciding what to do or believe" (Ennis, 1985, p. 54). This broader conception of critical thinking is consistent with the adopted educational goals of most states and school systems (Goodlad, 1984) primarily because critical thinking is considered essential for democratic citizenship (Remy, 1980).

As opposed to componential and heuristic approaches which focus on fairly specific cognitive operations, critical-thinking approaches attempt to enhance use of informal logic and dispositions of thought neither of which are easily reduced to a series of steps. Teaching informal logic as a means of enhancing thinking presupposes the existence of a mental logic. Johnson-Laird (1983) explained that, in an attempt to describe how humans can draw conclusions that must be true given that the premises are true, some have postulated the existence of a mental logic (e.g., Gentzen, 1964; Lakoff, 1970). An extreme form of this idea is that "reasoning is nothing more than the propositional calculus itself" (Inhelder & Piaget, 1958, p. 305). It is well known that many nineteenth-century logicians (e.g., Boole, 1854; Mill, 1874) regarded logic as providing the basis of everyday reasoning. That is, they assumed that one is always using logic to make decisions, solve problems, and complete tasks. However, in recent years a number of studies have shown that, in everyday thinking, highly intelligent individuals often fall prey to a variety of errors in logic (Perkins, Allen & Hafner, 1983; Staudenmayer, 1975). It is now more commonly assumed that people have the power to use mental logic within their daily endeavors but frequently misunderstand or forget premises and infuse additional and unwarranted assumptions into their reasoning (Henle, 1978).

Until recently, many theorists (e.g., Chapman & Chapman, 1959; Henle, 1962) assumed that mental logic was akin to Aristotelian logic. However, a number of researchers (e.g., Braine, 1978; Johnson-Laird, 1983) have demonstrated that pure Aristotelian logic does not account for many common inferences. Consequently, modern theories conceptualize mental logic in a way that incorporates many of the principles of schema-driven models of inference (e.g., Warren, Nicholas & Trabasso, 1979).

Some critical thinking programs have attempted to develop mental logic through the teaching of syllogistic rules of reasoning. For example, Instrumentation Enrichment (Feuerstein et al., 1980) contains instruments that deal with syllogisms. Similarly, Philosophy for Children (Lipman, Sharp & Oscanyan, 1980) includes exercises in syllogistic reasoning. More commonly, though, critical-thinking programs include practice in recognizing informal fallacies (e.g., the gambler's fallacy, equivocation) that purportedly introduce error into one's normally error-free system of mental logic (e.g., Beyth-Marom & Dekel, 1985; Negin, 1987; Toulmin, Rieke & Janik, 1981).

Although there has been research on the ability of both children and adults to reason in ways consistent with principles of logic (e.g., Johnson-Laird, 1975; Johnson-Laird & Steedman, 1978), studies linking the teaching of formal or informal logic with achievement are inconclusive. Bransford (1979) noted that it is generally assumed that practice in performing logic problems and recognizing informal fallacies will increase the accessibility of these skills in everyday reasoning situations. However, there is evidence that students who receive only formal reasoning exercises such as these may have a very limited idea of the purpose of the exercises; they might, therefore, be able to activate appropriate logic-related skills when presented with familiar problems yet not be able to transfer these skills to other situations (Bransford, Arbitman-Smith, Stein, & Vye, 1985; Brown, Bransford, Ferrera, & Campione, 1986; Maratsos, 1977). Outside of the classroom there is, however, a growing interest in using informal logic as a clinical tool for increasing patients' ability to control dysfunctional emotions through increased emphasis on rational thought. For example, based on the work of Ellis (1977), Cohen (1987) has described how therapy patients can be taught to use an adaptation of Aristotle's practical syllogisms to gain insight into and control over their irrational behaviors.

A second approach to teaching critical thinking is dispositional in nature. Dispositions, as described here, are habits of thought, cognitive "mental sets" for specific situations (Resnick,

1987). There have been a number of attempts to identify the dispositions of effective reasoning. For example, building on the work of Dewey (1933), Baron (1985) identified a number of dispositions for "good thinking." These include such mental habits as recognizing a sense of disequilibrium or doubt, identifying goals, searching for evidence, and revising one's plans when appropriate. Similarly, Ennis (1985) identified a set of critical thinking dispositions that include many of Baron's along with seeking precision, looking for alternatives, and seeing others' points of view.

Reinforcing critical thinking dispositions is a far less straightforward process than reinforcing the skills of informal logic. Here the tools are discussion (commonly Socratic) and modeling of dispositions around issues gleaned from literature or current events. One model for enhancing critical thinking dispositions is Philosophy for Children (Lipman et al., 1980). Although (as mentioned previously) the program does contain activities designed to enhance informal logic, its main function is to enhance critical thinking dispositions by developing a community of inquiry in the classroom (Chance, 1986). This is accomplished by teacher and students' interactions around a set of booklets (Lippman 1974, 1978, 1980) specially designed to highlight issues that elicit specific critical-thinking dispositions.

Relative to other programs, Philosophy for Children is one of the most thoroughly evaluated. (For reviews see Lipman, 1985; Chance, 1986.) For example, Haas (in Chance, 1986) studied the effects of Philosophy for Children on 200 fifth and sixth graders over a six-month period while 200 students from other schools acted as controls. A comparison of reading scores on the Metropolitan Achievement Test revealed that those who had studied Philosophy for Children gained an average of 8 months in reading ability, while the comparison subjects advanced 5 months in the same time. In the initial evaluation of the program, 40 fifth-grade students were randomly assigned to experimental and control groups. The experimental group received 18 40-minute sessions on Philosophy for Children over a period of 9 weeks. Both groups were initially tested in the California Test of Mental Maturity. The groups were not significantly different in pretesting, but in posttesting the experimental group's mental age scores were 27 months higher than those of the control group. Two years after the study, the experimental group had significantly-higher reading scores in the Iowa Achievement Test even though the two groups were not significantly different at pretesting. The program also has produced positive effects on student participation in class, social behavior and motivation (Chance, 1986).

Closely related to critical thinking is creative thinking. Both require a certain precision and rigor of thought, yet creative thinking is geared more toward the production of information whereas critical thinking is geared more toward the analysis of information. Halpern (1984) stated that "creativity can be thought of as the ability to form new combinations of ideas to fulfill a need" (p. 344). Perkins (1984) also stressed the notion of new and unique combinations of ideas but emphasized the importance of generating a product (mental or physical) that fulfills a specific function in an appropriate yet unique way. A number of approaches to creative thinking are highly dispositional in nature (e.g., Amabile, 1983; Marzano et al., 1988) stressing the fact that creative products spring from a set of high-level operating principles (dispositions) engaged in by an individual.

In spite of its highly dispositional nature, the teaching of creativity is commonly approached from a heuristics or tactics perspective and is usually practiced on gifted populations (Mitchell, 1980, 1984). Many approaches to enhancing creativity focus on solving novel and sometimes unstructured problems in new and unusual ways. For example, two international, interscholastic competitions, the Future Problem Solving Program (Crabbe, 1982; Torrance, 1980) and Olympics of the Mind (Gourley, 1981) use a problem-solving format to enhance creative thinking. It is estimated that over 150,000 gifted students participate each year in each of these programs (Torrance, 1986). Both programs use a game format in which teams compete with one another in solving specially-selected problems. Team responses are scored on a number of criteria including originality and divergence of thinking.

In a review of 166 experimental studies of teaching creativity skills at elementary and secondary levels since 1972, Torrance (1986) found that 17 percent used some type of creative problem-solving process similar to those used in Olympics of the Mind and Future Problem Solving. Torrance reported that other approaches included the use of media and reading, the creative arts, training in affective components, tactics to effect altered awareness, and packaged materials. Of these, the creative problem-solving approaches had a 77 percent success rate.

Critical and Creative Thinking and the Language Arts. Critical and creative thinking is grounded in the English language arts in a variety of ways. For example, language-arts teachers have traditionally used oral and written language as tools for enhancing critical and creative thought. Similarly Socratic questions that induce thoughtful student response, large and small group discussions, in-depth analysis of texts, the study of language in relation to nonprint media, propaganda, and persuasion, among others, have been means to this end. Indeed, critical and creative thought are at the very core of literacy.

Defined in the "low" sense, literacy is the ability to read and write in a manner consistent with the adult norms in a society (Resnick, 1987). However, defined in the "high" sense, literacy includes many of the critical and creative-thinking skills and dispositions (Resnick, 1987). For example, Tuman (1987) described the low model of literacy as the ability to read with understanding anything that one could understand if it had been spoken and the ability to write so that it could be read, anything that one can say. The high model of literacy, asserted Tuman, includes all characteristics of the low model but also involves the cultivation of the habits of critical and creative thinking.

Although the high-literacy tradition is less popular (with many of the national reports being concerned with functional and normal literacy for adults), there are a growing number of examples of attempts to frame literacy in the high fashion. For example, The College Board (1983) in its description of the necessary skills for success in postsecondary education explicitly, listed reasoning and a number of critical and creative thinking dispositions as fundamental literacy requirements. Similarly, in 1986 the Massachusetts Department of Education made

critical and creative thinking an integral part of their assessment of the reading ability of third- seventh- and eighth-grade students (Swartz, 1987).

The high literacy tradition has emphasized critical and creative thinking under the general rubric of rhetorical invention (Clanchy, 1983; Clifford, 1984). Kinneavy's (1980) work on the invention process is of particular importance here. Also, included in the high literacy tradition are new theories of the nature and process of reading. Specifically, Rosenblatt's (1978) work on the transactional nature of reading has helped elevate reading to a process that, by definition, includes critical and creative thought. Perhaps the most comprehensive attempt to incorporate the high-literacy tradition within the framework of the language arts is Moffett's "interaction" approach (1968; Moffett & Wagner, 1983). He conceptualized the "universe of discourse" to encompass: the linguistic modes of listening, speaking, reading and writing; the different forms of audience; and the egocentricity versus the exo-centricity (decentration) of the thought being experienced. The ultimate goal of a language-arts program in Moffett's scheme is to create flexible language users and thinkers, those capable of using different modes of discourse for different audiences at differing levels of decentration. Instructionally, Moffett's model calls for a classroom laid out for simultaneous group and individual activities (e.g., games, the arts, drama) with no set curriculum. Rather, students progress through self-selected, and teacher-directed activities. Interaction among peers and teachers and students is the key to the curriculum. The high-literacy nature of Moffett's approach is evident in its emphasis on student's creation of new products (e.g., essays, plays, poems), which implicitly demand attention to invention, arrangement, style, delivery, synthesis, extension, and other activities associated with critical and creative thought.

Although Moffett's approach has received some criticism for its lack of empirical testing (Nickerson et al., 1985), it has for years served as a model for those curricular and instructional changes that can, and perhaps should, occur when one tries to operationalize high literacy.

In summary, the various approaches to teaching can be described as metacognitive, componential, heuristic and critical/creative. Metacognitive approaches emphasize strategies that help the learner control the general processing of a task and components of the self system as they relate to the task. Componential approaches attempt to reinforce single, or sets of, cognitive operations by presenting the learner with tactics designed to enhance performance in the target cognitive operations. Heuristically based approaches focus on slightly more global cognitive operations and provide the learner with rules which facilitate the execution of these operations. Finally, critical and creative approaches are geared toward enhancing use of informal logic as well as various dispositions toward critical and creative thought.

Many of the current practices designed to enhance thinking have their roots or strong corollaries in the language arts. Metacognition, especially as it relates to control of task, is emphasized in the research and practice on both writing and reading. Some of the componential approaches (e.g., comparing, summarizing, note taking, finding main idea, representing, and tactics) have explicit tactics developed and used within the language arts. Similarly, many techniques designed to improve comprehension are heuristically based. Finally, critical and creative thinking are reinforced in the language arts through various approaches to reinforcing high literacy.

THE TEACHING OF THINKING AND THE LANGUAGE ARTS

Just as the teaching of thinking owes much to the language arts, the language arts can benefit from the advances in the teaching of thinking. Specifically, the scope of the language arts can be considerably broadened by incorporating some of the current work on thinking. Shuell (1986) has asserted that the stage is set for the development of a comprehensive theory of learning, one that would illustrate the interrelationship of the various types of thinking within a successful learning experience.

There have been a number of attempts to describe fairly robust frameworks of intelligence and learning (e.g. Baron, 1982, Sternberg, 1985). In spite of the breadth of these efforts, no single model exists that is readily translatable into classroom pedagogy. However, from the models and frameworks which do exist, a number of principles can be identified that have significant implications for language-arts instruction. Below, five such principles are described.

Principle #1: Learning Occurs in a Mental Context.

Learning of any type takes place in a mental environment that either enables or inhibits learning. Simply stated, one is or is not "mentally set" for learning at any given time. Technically stated, one's thinking at any time can be mathemagenic (i.e., conducive to learning) or mathemathanic (i.e., detrimental to learning) (Loman, 1986, Rothkopf, 1970). Marzano and Marzano (1987) have identified three aspects of thought that affect the mathemagenic versus mathemathanic nature of one's mental environment:

1) Affect,
2) Attitude, and
3) Focus.

Affect. Many theories of cognition emphasize the connection between affect and intellect (e.g., Piaget, 1962, Meichenbaum, 1977). The terms affect and emotion are frequently used interchangeably when discussing responses of relatively short duration, whereas the term mood is used to describe a disposition persisting over time (Owens & Maxmen, 1979). It is generally accepted that affect is generated by a set of related systems of the midbrain, which regulate the "backdrop of emotion" for a situation. This emotional backdrop determines the intensity with which one responds to situations—how strong or weak reactions will be (Mandler, 1983). Effective learning occurs in an emotional backdrop which is neutral to positive. That is, the learner does not necessarily have to have high positive affect, but cannot be experiencing high negative affect (Combs, 1982; Ellis, 1977, Meichenbaum, 1977).

Attitudes. Closely related to one's emotional tone at any time are one's attitudes. Specifically, Weiner (1972, 1983) asserted that behavior is a product of two factors: affect and attitudes. Affect occasionally shapes attitudes, attitudes occasionally shape affect. Three general categories of attitudes that contribute to one's mental set for learning are:

1) Attitudes about self as related to the environment,
2) Attitudes about self as related to the learning task, and
3) Attitudes about self as related to others.

1. Attitudes About Self and Environment. Within any learning situation, the learner is concerned with such environmental factors as safety, order, and general level of comfort. Maslow (1968) emphasized the importance of these concerns in his hierarchy of needs. Similarly, much of the effective schools' literature of the late 1970s and early 1980s identified environmental concerns that have an effect on learning (e.g., Brophy & Good, 1986; Emmer, Evertson & Anderson, 1980). Metaphorically, one might say that learners ask themselves such questions as whether they are safe, and relatively comfortable, and whether the setting is orderly. Negative answers to these questions influence students' propensity to learn.

2. Attitudes About Self and Task. When engaged in any task, individuals usually assess the task in terms of:

1) The extent to which it is considered valuable,
2) The extent to which the necessary knowledge and abilities to complete the task are possessed, and
3) The extent to which there is perceived control over the task.

Continuing the metaphor, learners ask: Is this important to me? Can I do it? Do I have some control over the situation? Again, negative answers to these questions render one's mental set mathemathanic.

3. Attitudes About Self and Others. Attitudes about self and others also impinge on learning, although sometimes not as directly as attitudes about self as it relates to task. For example, Combs (1982) has noted that individuals must have a sense of acceptance by the teacher to function efficiently in any learning situation. Similarly, Johnson, Johnson, Roy and Holubec (1984) described the importance of peer acceptance to learning. Attitudes about self and others, then, include:

1) Attitudes about self and teacher, and
2) Attitudes about self and peers.

In short, the learner metaphorically asks, Am I respected by the teacher? Will this situation affect my status with my peers?

Focus. Focus refers to the ability to attend to specific information at any time when "attend" refers to the selective transfer of information from sensory information storage to working memory (Norman, 1969). Broadbent (1958) was one of the first to demonstrate that human beings selectively attend to the multitude of stimuli bombarding them at any time. At a very basic level, one attends to the stimuli that is most salient within the environment. This form of attention is commonly exhibited by infants (Luria, 1973). However, a much more efficient form of attention is that focused because of a previously-established goal. So important is goal-directed attention, that a number of psychologists have postulated that it represents a unique cognitive state. For example, Neisser (1967) referred to goal-directed attention as a "controlled state," Lindsay and Norman (1977) called it a "conscious state."

Focus, as described here, is attention that is goal driven. The research on goal-directed learning is relatively clear. Over 40 years ago, Sears (1940) found that successful students tended to set explicit goals. More recently, Brophy (1982) found that successful students set increasingly more difficult goals in academic situations.

In summary, the extent to which learning occurs is at least partially a function of the learner's

1) Affective tone;
2) Attitudes about self and environment, self and task, and self and others; and
3) Awareness of and attention to explicit goals.

Values on these parameters represent the mental context in which the learner functions from moment to moment. Certain values enable learning (are mathemagenic), others do not (are mathemathanic).

Implications for the Language Arts. The principle that learning occurs within a mental context has fairly clear implications for the language arts. Specifically, language-arts instruction should attend to the mental context or environment of the learner, and, perhaps, provide students with specific strategies for establishing an awareness and control of their mental set. Relative to the learner's emotional backdrop, research indicates that when it is of high intensity it is relatively difficult to change (Heliman & Satz, 1983); however, an awareness of a high-intensity backdrop can allow one to mediate its possible negative affects (Meichenbaum, 1977; Santostefano, 1986). In addition, a low intensity backdrop can be changed by rehearsing the behaviors of higher intensity affect (Bettencourt, Gillett, Gall & Hull, 1983). Similarly, attitudes regarding self, whether they relate to the environment, task, or others, can be effectively controlled by an awareness of their existence and a combined use of positive verbal mediation and strategies for shifting the focus of control to the learner (Ellis, 1962, Meichenbaum, 1977). Finally, the research on goal setting indicates students should be presented with clear-cut goals and required to set and articulate their own learning goals (Brophy, 1982). Developmentally speaking, Bandura and Schunk (1981) found that it is better to introduce students to proximal goals before presenting them with techniques for accomplishing distal goals.

Principle #2: Learning Involves Making Distinctions Between Different Types of Information.

A number of theorists have either directly or indirectly asserted that learning content of any type is fundamentally a con-

structive process (e.g., Vosniadou & Brewer, 1987; Wittrock, 1974). Learners do not passively receive new information as presented by a teacher or a textbook; rather, they make distinctions about different types of incoming information. Different types of information are structured in different ways. There have been a number of theories about the different types of information (e.g., semantic versus episodic, linguistic versus non-linguistic). Relative to domain-specific content, one of the more useful distinctions is that between declarative and procedural information.

Declarative Information. Declarative information is factual in nature and can be subdivided into at least four basic types:

1) Concepts,
2) Facts,
3) Principles and
4) Schemata.

Concepts are abstract structures usually represented by a word within a society (Klausmeier, 1985). Relative to classroom learning, Marzano (1987) has identified four broad categories of concepts:

1) Animate entities (e.g., animals, plants),
2) Inanimate objects (e.g., weapons, tools),
3) Locations (e.g., North America, Denver), and
4) Events (e.g., festivals, carnivals).

Facts are statements of relationships between or among concepts. Linguistically, facts are commonly communicated as propositions—"conceptual structures that are the minimal bearers of truth" (van Dijk, 1980, p. 107). For example, *Columbus, discovery,* and *America* are concepts but are not information that can be examined for truth or falsity. However, "Columbus discovered America" is a proposition, because one can ask and answer whether it is true or false. Facts, then, are propositions important to a given content area.

Like facts, principles are propositional in form. However, principles assert information that can be exemplified whereas facts do not. Also principles tend to be used as major organizers of domain specific content whereas facts do not (Klausmeier, 1985). Katz (1976) has identified four types of principles important to various content areas:

1) cause/effect (e.g., "Tuberculosis is caused by the organism microbacterium tuberculosis."),
2) correlational (e.g., "The increase in lung cancer among women is directly proportional to the increase in the number of women who smoke."),
3) probability (e.g., "The chances of giving birth to a boy during any one pregnancy is .52.") and
4) axiomatic (e.g., "All people ar created equal.").

Schemata represent the broadest and, perhaps, loosest category of declarative information. Rumelhart (1980) described schemata as "packages" of information stored in long-term memory. A commonly used example of a schema is that knowledge associated with going to a restaurant. That is, people in our culture have an internalized restaurant schema that includes knowledge about reading a menu, ordering food, waiting for it to come, eating with an array of utensils, and paying the bill. Theorists and researchers in artificial intelligence (e.g., Schank & Abelson, 1977) subdivide the broad notion of schemata into a number of distinct types, whereas psycholinguists commonly do not make fine distinctions as to different categories or types of schemata. For educational purposes, schemata can be divided into four different types (Marzano, 1987):

1) Time lines (e.g., the events that occurred between two specific dates in history),
2) Problems and solutions (e.g., the different, possible ways of fixing a faulty distributor in an automobile engine),
3) Causal networks (e.g., the events leading up to the bombing of Pearl Harbor), and
4) Episodes (e.g., the circumstances surrounding "Watergate").

Declarative information, then, involves concepts, facts, principles and schemata. As the learner interacts with the learning situation, she organizes the information contained therein into salient concepts, facts, principles, and schemata either with the guidance of teacher or textbook or on her own.

Procedural Information. Procedural information is sometimes characterized as knowledge of *how* (Paris & Lindauer, 1982; Paris, et. al., 1983). For example, knowing how to read a bar graph or how to perform long division is procedural. Procedural knowledge includes process knowledge and conditional knowledge. Processes involve steps that are either ordered or unordered. For example, the process for reading a bar graph involves a relatively unordered set of steps. The process for performing long division, on the other hand, has a rather rigid order to the steps involved. Along with knowledge of process, procedural knowledge includes knowing when the process should be used or "conditional knowledge." For example, along with knowledge of the process in performing long division, one has (or should have) an understanding of the situations in which it is useful (e.g., in certain types of problems and not in others.)

Procedural knowledge, then, is comprised of both process knowledge and conditional knowledge or knowledge about when to use specific processes. The extent to which a learner organizes information presented by the teacher, the textbook, or a learning experience into appropriate procedural structures determines the effectiveness of the learning.

The Interaction of Declarative and Procedural Information. Although declarative and procedural knowledge have been discussed separately above, they of course, are not separate in long-term memory. In fact, procedural knowledge is highly dependent on declarative knowledge. Theorists in artificial intelligence (Anderson, 1983; Newell & Simon, 1972) represent the interaction of declarative and procedural knowledge as "productions"—*if/then* structures in long-term memory. For example, consider the following:

IF: 1. two short sentences are adjacent in an essay, and
2. both have a S-LV-Adj structures, and
3. both have the same subject,
THEN: embed the adjective in one sentence in the other.

The process knowledge in this production is about combining sentences. The conditional knowledge is represented in statements 1, 2, and 3. Together the process and conditional knowledge make up the procedure. Yet, contained within the procedure are such declarative components as the concepts, *sentence, subject* and the fact that S-LV-Adj represents a particular syntactic structure. Hence, this production contains both declarative and procedural information integrated in a unified whole.

In summary, learning content within any discipline involves the learner recognizing and organizing the content into appropriate declarative and procedural structures unified into integrated blocks of working knowledge.

Implications for the Language Arts. The distinction and interrelationship between declarative and procedural information implies that the language arts can be partitioned into specific types of inter-related information. To illustrate, consider the reading process. Using a production model one can conclude that effective reading involves the interaction of both declarative and procedural information. This is the basic premise underlying Rumelhart's (1977) interactive model of reading. On the declarative side, reading involves knowledge of concepts, facts, principles, and schemata covering topics which range from letter/sound relationships to the conventions of paragraphing, to the format of different text types, to the characteristics of different discourse types and genre. To a great extent much of this declarative information can be organized hierarchically from information that is fairly atomic and discrete (e.g., letter/sound relationships) to information that is more global (e.g., discourse types).

Although reading instruction has traditionally included (and most probably over-emphasized) a coverage of declarative information relative to letter/sound relationships and some reading conventions, it has only recently expanded to include explicit instruction on types of discourse and genre. For example, McNeil (1984) described strategies for instruction in specific discourse types and ways that students can use such knowledge to understand and structure information they read. Similarly Sadow (1982) has developed questioning techniques that highlight the basic discourse structure of text. Finally, Fowler (1982) described a "macro-close" technique that focuses on the structure of discourse and genre type.

On the procedural side reading involves processes ranging from letter recognition, to word recognition, to comprehension of whole texts, to the application of information. Again reading has traditionally emphasized instruction in such microprocesses as letter recognition and word recognition commonly under the rubric of "decoding strategies" (e.g., Eckwall, 1977; Finn, 1985). However, recent years have seen a shift to more macrolevel processing. For example, Jones and her colleagues (Jones, et al. 1987; Jones et al. 1987) have described what they refer to as strategic teaching, which is the overt presentation of strategies to students for learning in specific situations. Indeed, virtually all of the learning strategies research (Derry & Murphy, 1986) underscores the importance of strategies instruction when teaching complex skills such as reading or writing.

Underlying the production model is the assertion that declarative and procedural information are used in an integrated fashion. A direct implication is that these types of information should be taught in an integrated fashion relative to any complex skill. This speaks against "skills" approaches to reading or writing that teach the components as isolated and discrete parts and speaks for those approaches that present the declarative and procedural components of reading in a specific yet integrated manner. To this end, much of what has been roughly referred to as a "whole language" approach to reading and writing instruction would appear to have a sound theoretical base. For example, Goodman (1986) noted that academic tasks in the language arts should be organized around topics or themes of natural interest to students (p.31). In general those tasks should be holistic in nature covering a variety of important declarative and procedural components. Such a holistic approach to language and instruction is also the foundation of the systems advocated by Calkins (1986) and Graves (1983). However, the production model also validates the importance of teaching discrete pieces of information important to complex process under study. This was basically the conclusion reached by the Commission on Reading (Anderson, Hiebert, Scott & Wilkinsen, 1985). Unfortunately, some descriptions of holistic approaches seem to explicitly forbid the teaching of declarative information especially that at lower levels. A production model would seem to legitimize both declarative and procedural aspects of reading, not emphasizing one to the exclusion of the other.

Principle #3: Knowledge in LTM is Stored in Different Forms.

There are a number of theories relative to information storage in LTM. Most differentiate between declarative and procedural information. That is, the way declarative information is stored in long-term memory is qualitatively different from the way procedural information is stored.

Storage of Declarative Information. Paivio (1969, 1971) and Bower (1972) assert that declarative knowledge is stored in long-term memory in two primary forms: linguistic and nonlinguistic. This has been referred to as the "dual coding" theory. The linguistic encoding of declarative knowledge is commonly manifested as inner speech (Sokolov, 1972; Vygotsky, 1962). It is a misconception, however, to think that linguistic thought is represented only as words. Linguistic thought is probably represented in its most basic form as highly abstract semantic units (Kintsch, 1974; van Dijk, 1980). Consequently, storage of declarative information can also occur as symbolic representations.

When information is represented nonlinguistically, it can contain visual, auditory, kinesthetic, tactile, olfactory, and emotional components (Gazzaninga, 1985; Gazzaniga & LeDoux, 1978; Underwood, 1969). Perhaps the most powerful form of nonlinguistic coding for learning purposes is visual—some mental, visual representation of information. Mental, visual representations fall in a continuum that runs from episodic to symbolic. Episodic visual representations are those mental pictures that come from "true-to-life" episodes or fabricated episodes. Symbolic, visual, mental representations are not true to life. That is, they are not comprised of pictures of real people, places, and things organized as events. Instead, they are comprised of abstract shapes and forms that convey meaning to the learner about the information being represented. Symbolic mental representations are quite common within the domains of mathematics and science (Tweney, Doherty & Mynatt, 1981).

Storage of Procedural Information. Information that is organized as procedural structures has a different form of representation from that which is declarative. Specifically, procedural information is first stored (in a fashion similar to declarative information) in linguistic and nonlinguistic codes. However, in its final form, procedural information is stored in highly abstract production units (see discussion of Principle #2) that take very little room in working memory when accessed. This gradual progression of procedural knowledge to abstract production unit form is a developmental process that includes cognitive, associated, and autonomous stages (Anderson, 1983; Fitts, 1964). During the cognitive stage, learners deal with procedural information just as they would declarative information, attempting to understand its component parts. During the associate stage, learners begin to smooth out the process, adding to and deleting from the information understood at the associated stage. Finally, during the autonomous stage, learners store the information as abstract production units that can be accessed and executed with little conscious thought.

In summary, content-area information, both declarative and procedural, is initially represented in the mind in linguistic and nonlinguistic forms. Procedural information is then rehearsed to the point at which it is stored as highly abstract structures that can be accessed and executed with little conscious effort. The extent to which the learner represents and stores declarative information in a linguistic and nonlinguistic manner and the extent to which the learner represents procedural information as abstract production units easily accessed dictates the usefulness of the learner's knowledge. Information not stored efficiently is not usable to the learner at a later date.

Implications for the Language Arts. One of the main implications of the fact that information is encoded in both linguistic and nonlinguistic modes is that language-arts instruction should involve more and varied nonlinguistic modes of processing information. Although there are many strategies for enhancing nonlinguistic modes of processing information, few appear in the language-arts literature. For example, McCarthy's (1980) 4MAT System provides for ways of enhancing the visual, auditory, olfactory, tactile, and kinetic aspects of processing information within reading, writing, and oral language. Similarly, Carbo, Dunn & Dunn (1986) describe ways of utilizing multisensory approaches to language-arts instruction. The common criticism of such approaches is their lack of a supporting research base, yet Fernald (1988) established the utility of the "multi-sensory" aspects of the language arts as far back as 1921. Similarly the legitimacy and importance of different cognitive styles in processing information has a rich research base. (See Shipman & Shipman, 1985 for a review of the related research and theory.)

A second implication is that the processes in the language arts should be thought of developmentally—processing through a series of stages in which learners gradually shape the process to conform to their own styles while still meeting certain accepted standards. Here great strides are being made. Specifically, Scardamalia & Bereiter (1985) documented differences between the writing of children and unskilled writers that emphasized the developing complexity of the writing tasks. (For a review of writing development see Stein, 1986.) Children and unskilled writers view the process as simply recording what they know. This is referred to as "associative writing" (Bereiter, 1980). The writer records on paper whatever comes to mind, searches for another thought, and then transcribes that. Bereiter and Scardamalia (1982) refer to this strategy as "knowledge telling"—telling what one knows in the simplest possible way. Additional stages of writing include "performative writing"—similar to the associative stage but adding control of grammar, spelling and other mechanics; "communicative writing"—writing which includes control of mechanics and is shaped by the needs of different audiences; "unified writing"—writing in which the writer uses herself as a critical reader and editor; and, finally, "epistemic writing"—writing which functions as a tool for developing knowledge within a discipline (Bereiter, 1980).

Similarly, Gentry (1982, 1987) building on the work of others (Hanna, Hanna, Hodges & Rudorf, 1966) characterized the various phases within the acquisition of spelling strategies. Finally, at a very general level the entire emergent literacy field has begun to identify developmental components of all language-arts-related cognitive processes (Clifford, 1984; Sulzby, 1985, 1986; Teale, 1987). For example, Mason and Allen (1986) characterize the development of reading and writing ability as an integrated complex process of the learner gradually identifying and then developing their own strategies and rules for particular situations.

Principle #4: Learning involves the Shaping and Sharpening of Known Information.

Declarative and procedural knowledge, once represented in long-term memory is not static; it is developed in a number of ways, some of which are quite surprising and unpredictable (Vosniadou & Brewer, 1987). There are a number of different descriptions of the structural changes that occur to information in long-term memory. For example, Piaget (1959) characterized changes in one's knowledge structures as accommodation. He characterized learning as a continual reorganization of existing knowledge as a result of a mismatch or disequilibrium between what is known and as external experiences. Experiences that do not match existing knowledge force the learner to reorganize existing structures to accommodate the new experiences.

Rumelhart and Norman (1981) identified three ways in which existing knowledge (schemata) can be modified: accretion, tuning, and restructuring. Accretion refers to the changes in knowledge in LTM over time due to the gradual accumulation of information. It involves additive components. Tuning refers to the creation of generalizations about existing schema and the identification of default values. Finally, restructuring refers to the creation of new structures either to reinterpret old information or create new information. Changes in knowledge structures, then, can be placed on a continuum that ranges from gradual additive changes (accretion) to drastic reorganization (restructuring).

Vosniadou and Brewer (1987) distinguished between global restructuring and domain-specific restructuring. Global restructuring refers to changes in cognitive operations that work on knowledge in LTM. For example, it is global restructuring that distinguishes among Piaget's stages. The child's capacity for representational thought marks the difference between the sensorimotor and the preoperational stages; whereas, the cognitive processes of transition, association, and reversibility mark the difference between preoperational and operational stages.

In contrast to global restructuring is domain-specific restructuring, which is not a change in logical operations but a change in the knowledge within a domain. This is not to say that global restructuring does not occur, only that global and domain-specific restructuring interact to create different levels and types of knowledge change within a specific area. Vosniadou and Brewer identified three categories of domain-specific restructuring:

1) Weak restructuring,
2) Strong restructuring, and
3) Paradigm shift.

Much of the basis for the descriptions of weak and strong restructuring is derived from the research on experts and novices within various domains (e.g., di Sessa, 1982; Larkin, 1979, 1981). Weak restructuring involves the creation of new and more numerous links among conceptual nodes for information in LTM. It also involves the use of more abstract schemata to link conceptual nodes. Radical restructuring involves the development of totally new theories to explain and organize information. That is, where weak restructuring makes a knowledge base more complex and abstract, radical restructuring changes the theory base or exploratory system that guides the organization of information. For example, di Sessa (1982) and White (1983) found that novices in physics use explanatory theories that resemble those of Aristotle more than those of Newton. Finally, paradigm shifts are major reorganizations of assumptions underlying a domain. Kuhn (1962) described paradigm shift as a radical reorganization of the beliefs within a domain such that new insights are possible. Sawada and Caley (1985) explained that new paradigms do not emerge in a linear fashion as a natural outgrowth of existing paradigms. Rather, new paradigms emerge via a radical restructuring of old paradigms which occurs when a system maintains a state "far from equilibrium" for a prolonged period of time. To illustrate, any system can exist in three states:

1) At equilibrium with respect to its environment,

2) Near-equilibrium with respect to its environment, or

3) Far-from-equilibrium with respect to its environment.

When systems approach a far-from-equilibrium state, which Sawada and Caley referred to as the "threshold of becoming," they are subject to spontaneous reorganization or "bifurcation."

Implications for the Language Arts. One of the major implications of the principle that knowledge is shaped and sharpened by the learner is that the scope of activities within the language-arts curriculum should be expanded to enhance the restructuring of information. Here the programs and practices designed to enhance thinking have much to offer the language arts. For example, Gubbins (in Sternberg, 1985) lists over 30 types of tasks which engage the learner in shaping and sharpening forms of cognition. Similarly, Marzano et al. (1988) identified a number of cognitive tasks that require the learner to rethink and reorganize information. Unfortunately, such tasks are not a common occurrence within a language arts (or any other type of) classroom. Specifically, such knowledge restructuring activities as problem finding, formulating questions, establishing criteria, and verifying are seldom part of classroom practices (Frederiksen, 1984). However, there have been efforts to reshape the language-arts classroom so as to emphasize more cognitively complex tasks. Specifically, Jones et al. (1987) have shown that language-arts instruction can incorporate such cognitively complex tasks as problem solving and decision making into the standard curriculum.

A second implication is that many components of the language arts are themselves shaping and sharpening vehicles. Specifically, Vosniadou and Brewer (1987) identify classroom dialogue as one of the primary vehicles for knowledge restructuring. Similarly, Marzano et al. (in press) assert that oral discourse and composing are two major knowledge restructuring tools. From this perspective, the writing across the curriculum movement can be considered an effort to establish writing as a tool for restructuring domain-specific knowledge (Applebee, 1977). Similarly, efforts have been put forth to frame reading as a process of both comprehending the information contained in text as well as shaping and sharpening that information (Palincsar, Ogle, Jones & Carr, 1986).

Principle #5: Higher Order Thinking is Dispositional in Nature.

There have been many attempts to distinguish higher-order versus lower-order types of thought. Most attempts have focused on hierarchies of information processing skills. In education Bloom, Englehart, Furst, Hill & Krathwohl's (1956) taxonomy of cognitive objectives is perhaps the most well known. Unfortunately, Bloom's taxonomy suffers from an indeterminacy at the higher levels (as do most taxonomies). Specifically, tasks that are at higher levels cannot be differentiated from tasks supposedly at lower levels (Fairbrother, 1975; Wood, 1977), although some evidence for hierarchic structures similar to Bloom et al.'s has been found for questions pertaining to different discourse types

(Hillocks & Ludlow, 1984). Similarly, hierarchies of cognitive operations have been articulated and validated from developmental perspectives (Case, 1985; Gagne, 1975). For example, Fischer (1980) has noted that complex tasks are built on substructures of less complex cognitive operations performed at an automatic level. Higher-order processes are those which cannot be performed automatically although they rely on the execution of subprocesses that are executed automatically. The implication of such theories is that higher-order processes invariably become lower-order as the learner progresses through stages of development within a domain. As Anderson (1982, 1983) and Fitts (1964) have noted, the learner inevitably progresses to a stage where a cognitive process can be executed automatically without much conscious thought. From this perspective higher-order thinking varies from individual to individual depending on one's skill development within a domain.

Resnick (1987) has taken another perspective. She asserts that higher-order thinking is not so much the use of one set of cognitive processes versus another, but the dispositions within which cognitive processes are executed. In effect Resnick's dispositions toward higher-level thinking are combinations of:

1) Metacognitive dispositions relative to knowledge and control of both task and self,

2) The dispositions that render thinking critical and,

3) The dispositions that render thinking creative.

That is, higher-order thinking occurs when an individual regulates learning as well as renders it critical and creative.

Implications for the Language Arts. The major implication of the fact that higher-order thinking is dispositional is that ultimately the language arts (or any other discipline) cannot be reduced to a set of processes and algorithms. Although such content is important (see discussion of principle #2), language-arts instruction must include a balance between a thorough and somewhat automatic knowledge of important declarative and procedural knowledge and a certain "mindfulness" about the tasks being performed. Although mindfulness is not a common topic with the psychological literature, it is at the center of philosophic discussions of thought. For example, Heidegger (1968) asserted that what is commonly called thinking is fundamentally a reactive process—the automatic execution of what modern psychologists would call productions. True thought is observing and controlling one's own cognition. Similar assertions have been made by Searle (1984) and Dewey (1957), who objected to what he called "bloodless reason" or cognition without deliberation.

Operationally mindfulness is difficult to describe because by definition it does not lend itself to a set of heuristics or algorithms that can be taught. Rather, Csikszentmihalyi (1975) notes that mindfulness is most common within "flow experiences"—those actions selected by an individual as expressions of their individuality and self-actualization. Key to flow experiences are the freedom of selection of task and establishment of criteria for success. This would imply that language-arts instruction should involve many more tasks that are selected, planned, developed, and evaluated by students. Unfortunately, more often than not, language-arts instruction is characterized by tasks that are teacher directed, controlled, and evaluated (Fisher & Hiebert, 1988).

In summary, five principles can be drawn from the current research and theory in the teaching of thinking. These principles imply that:

1) Language-arts instruction should address the mental context of the learner,
2) Language-arts instruction should include integrated attention to both declarative and procedural information,
3) The language arts should include more multimodal forms of processing information,
4) Language arts-instruction should include more varied and cognitively complex tasks, and

5) Language-arts instruction should include an emphasis on the dispositions toward higher-order thinking.

SUMMARY

Language, the language arts, and thinking are inextricably linked. First, language itself represents a type of thinking. It also is a vehicle by which thought is mediated and enhanced. Recently, a number of programs and practices have been developed that are designed to teach thinking. Many of the strategies and tactics employed within these programs are based in the language arts. Finally, the current research and theory on the teaching of thinking suggests a number of principles that can significantly affect language-arts instruction.

References

Alexander, C. F. (1976). Strategies for finding the main idea. *Journal of Reading, 19,* 299–301.

Allen, G. J. (1972). The behavioral treatment of test anxiety. *Behavior Therapy, 3,* 253–262.

Amabile, T. M. (1983). *The social psychology of creativity.* New York: Springer-Verlag.

Anderson, J. (1982). Acquisition of cognitive skills. *Psychological Review, 89,* 369–406.

Anderson, J. (1983). *The architecture of cognition.* Cambridge, MA: Harvard University Press.

Anderson, L. M., Evertson, C. M., & Brophy, J. E. (1979). An experimental study of effective teaching in first-grade reading groups. *The Elementary School Journal, 79,* 193–273.

Anderson, R. C., Hiebert, E. H., Scott, J. A., & Wilkinsen, I. A. (1985). *Becoming a nation of readers.* Washington, DC: National Institute of Education.

Anderson, T. H., & Armbruster, B. B. (1985). Studying. In P. D. Pearson (Ed.), *Handbook of reading research.* New York: Longman.

Appel, L. F., Cooper, R. G., McCarrell, N., Sims-Knight, J., Yussen, S. R., & Flavell, J. H. (1972). The development of the distinction between perceiving and memorizing. *Child Development, 43,* 1365–1381.

Applebee, A. N. (1977). Eric/RCS Report: Writing across the curriculum: The London projects. *English Journal, 66*(9), 81–85.

Applebee, A. N. (1984). Writing and reasoning. *Review of Educational Research, 54,* 577–596.

Ashton, P. J., O'Hear, M. F., & Pherson, V. E. (1985). The presence of main idea clues in college textbooks. *Journal of College Reading and Learning, 18,* 59–67.

Axelrod, J. (1975). Getting the main idea is still the main idea. *Journal of Reading, 18,* 383–387.

Baird, J. R., & White, R. T. (1984). *Improving learning through enhanced metacognition: A classroom study.* Paper presented at the annual meeting of the American Educational Research Association, New Orleans.

Bandura, A. (1977). Self-efficacy: Toward a unifying theory of behavioral change. *Psychological Review, 84*(2), 191–215.

Bandura, A., & Schunk, D. H. (1981). Developing competence, self-efficacy and intrinsic interest through proximal self-motivation. *Journal of Personality and Social Psychology, 41*(3) 586–598.

Bargh, J. A., & Schul, Y. (1980). On the cognitive benefits of teaching. *Journal of Educational Psychology, 72,* 593–604.

Barnett, J. E., DiVesta, F. J., & Rogozinski, J. T. (1981). What is learned in note-taking? *Journal of Educational Psychology, 73,* 181–191.

Baron, J. (1982). Personality and intelligence. In R. J. Sternberg (Ed.). *Handbook of human intelligence* (pp. 308–351). London: Cambridge University Press.

Baron, J. (1985). *Rationality and intelligence.* New York: Cambridge University Press.

Bartlett, F. C. (1932). *Remembering: A study in experimental and social psychology.* Cambridge, England: Cambridge University Press.

Bateson, G. (1972). *Steps to an ecology of mind.* New York: Ballantine Books.

Bauman, J. F. (Ed.) (1986). *Teaching main idea comprehension.* Newark, DE: International Reading Association.

Bean, T. W., Singer, H., Sorter, J., & Frazee, C. (1983). Acquisition of summarization rules as a basis for question generation in learning from expository text at the high school level. In J. A. Niles & L. A. Harris (Eds.), *Searching for meaning in reading/language processing and instruction* (pp. 43–49). Thirty-second yearbook of the National Reading Conference. Rochester, NY: The National Reading Conference.

Belleza, F. (1981). Mnemonic devices: Classification characteristics and criteria. *Review of Educational Research, 51,* 247–275.

Bem, S. (1971). The role of comprehension in children's problem solving. *Developmental Psychology, 2,* 351–354.

Bender, N. (1976). Self-verbalization versus tutor verbalization in modifying impulsivity. *Journal of Educational Psychology, 68,* 347–354.

Bereiter, C. (1980). Development in writing. In L. W. Gregg & E. R. Steinberg (Eds.), *Cognitive processes in writing.* Hillsdale, NJ: Lawrence Erlbaum Associates.

Bereiter, C., & Scardamalia, M. (1982). From conversation to composition: The role of instruction in a developmental process. In R. Glaser (Ed.), *Advances in instructional psychology* Vol. 2, pp. 1–64). Hillsdale, NJ: Lawrence Erlbaum.

Bereiter, C., & Scardamalia, M. (1985). Cognitive coping strategies and the problem of "inert knowledge." In S. F. Chipman, J. W. Segal, & R. Glaser (Eds.), *Thinking and learning skills: Vol. 2. Research and open questions* (pp. 65–80). Hillsdale, NJ: Lawrence Erlbaum Associates.

Bettencourt, E. M., Gillet, M. H., Gall, M. D., & Hull, R. E. (1983). Effects of teacher enthusiasm training on student on task behavior and achievement. *American Education Research Journal, 20,* 435–450.

Beyer, B. E. (1988). *Developing a thinking skills program.* Boston, MA: Allyn & Bacon.

Beyth-Marom, R., & Dekel, S. (1985). *An elementary approach to thinking under uncertainty.* Hillsdale, NJ: Lawrence Erlbaum.

Bishop, J. C. (1983). Can there be thought without language? In W. Maxwell (Ed.), *Thinking, the expanding frontier* (pp. 13–24). Philadelphia, PA: The Franklin Institute Press.

Bloom, B. S., Englehart, M. D., Furst, E. J., Hill, W. H. & Krathwohl, D. R. (Eds.). (1956). *Taxonomy of educational objectives: The classification of educational goals. Handbook I: Cognitive domain.* New York: David McKay.

Boole, G. (1854). *An investigation of the laws of thought.* London: Walton & Manerly.

Bower, G. (1972). Analysis of a mnemonic device. In M. Coltheart (Ed.), *Readings in cognitive psychology.* (pp. 399–426) Toronto: Holt, Rinehart & Winston.

Bower, G. H., & Clark, M. C. (1969). Narrative stories as mediators for serial learning. *Psychonomic Science, 14,* 181–182.

Braddock, R. (1974). Frequency and placement of topic sentences in expository prose. *Research in Teaching English, 8,* 287–302.

Braine, M. D. S. (1978). On the relation between the natural logic of reasoning and standard logic. *Psychological Review, 85,* 1–21.

Bransford, J. D. (1979). *Human cognition: Learning, understanding and remembering.* Belmont, CA: Wadsworth Publishing Co.

Bransford, J. D., Arbitman-Smith, R., Stein, B. S., & Vye, N. J. (1985). Improving thinking and learning skills: An analysis of three approaches. In J. W. Segal, S. F. Chipman, & R. Glaser (Eds.), *Thinking and learning skills: Vol. 1. Relating instruction to research* (pp. 133–206). Hillsdale, NJ: Lawrence Erlbaum.

Bransford, J. D., & Franks, J. J. (1976). Toward a framework for understanding learning. In G. H. Bower (Ed.), *Psychology of learning and motivation* (Vol. 10, pp. 93–127). New York: Academic Press.

Bransford, J. D., Sherwood, R., Rieser, J., & Vye, N. (1986). Teaching thinking and problem solving: Research foundations. *American Psychologist, 41,* 1078–1089.

Broadbent, D. (1958). *Perception and communication.* London: Pergamon Press.

Brophy, J. (1982). *Classroom organization and management.* Washington, DC: National Institute of Education.

Brophy, J. & Good, T. L. (1986). Teacher behavior and student achievement. In M. C. Wittrock (Ed.), *Handbook of research on teaching* (3rd ed.) (pp. 328–375). New York: Macmillan Publishing Co.

Brown, A. L. (1975). The development of memory: Knowing knowing about knowing, and knowing how to know. In H. W. Reese (Ed.), *Advances in child development and behavior.* (Vol. 10.) New York: Academic Press.

Brown, A. L. (1978). Knowing when, where and how to remember: A problem of metacognition. In R. Glaser (Ed.), *Advances in instructional psychology* (Vol. 1, pp. 77–165). Hillsdale, NJ: Lawrence Erlbaum and Associates.

Brown, A. L., Bransford, J. D., Ferrara, R., & Campione, J. (1986). Learning, understanding and remembering. In J. H. Flavell & E. Markman (Eds.), *Mussen handbook of child psychology: Vol. 1. Cognitive development.* (4th ed.). New York: John Wiley & Sons.

Brown, A. L., Campione, J. C., & Day, J. (1981). Learning to learn: On training students to learn from texts. *Educational Researcher, 10,* 14–24.

Brown, A. L., & Smiley, S. S. (1977). Rating the importance of structural units of prose passages: A problem of metacognitive development. *Child Development, 48,* 1–8.

Bugelski, B. R. (1968). Images as mediators in one-trial paired-associate learning. II: Self-timing in successive lists. *Journal of Experimental Psychology, 77,* 328–334.

Burns, M. (1986). Teaching "what to do" in arithmetic vs. teaching "what to do and why." *Educational Leadership, 43,* 34–38.

Calkins, L. M. (1986). *The art of teaching writing.* Portsmouth, NH: Heinemann.

Camp, E., Blom, G., Herbert, P., & Van Dournick, W. (1977). Think Aloud: A program for developing self-control in young aggressive boys. *Journal of Abnormal Child Psychology, 8,* 157–169.

Campione, J. C., Brown, A. L., & Ferrara, R. A. (1982). Mental retardation and intelligence. In R. J. Sternberg (Ed.), *Handbook of human intelligence* (pp. 392–490). New York: Cambridge University Press.

Carbo, M., Dunn, R., & Dunn, K. (1986). *Teaching students to read through their individual styles.* Englewood Cliffs, NJ: Prentice Hall.

Case, R. (1985). *Intellectual development, birth to adulthood.* New York: Academic Press.

Cazden, C. B. (1979). Language in education: Variation in the teacher-talk register. In J. Alatis & R. Rucker (Eds.), *Language in public life.* (pp. 120–147) Washington, DC: Georgetown University Round Table in Language and Linguistics.

Cazden, C. B. (1986). Classroom discourse. In M. C. Wittrock (Ed.), *Handbook of research on teaching* (3rd ed.) (pp. 432–463). New York, NY: Macmillan Publishing Co.

Chafe, W. L. (1970). *Meaning and structure of language.* Chicago, IL: University of Chicago Press.

Chance, P. (1986). *Thinking in the classroom,* New York: Teacher's College Press.

Chapman, L. J., & Chapman, J. P. (1959). Atmosphere effects reexamined. *Journal of Experimental Psychology, 58,* 220–226.

Christenbury, L., & Kelly, P. P. (1983). *Questioning: A Path to critical thinking.* Urbana, IL: Clearinghouse on Reading and Communication Skills, the National Council of Teachers of English.

Clanchy, M. T. (1983). Looking back from the invention of printing. In D. P. Resnick (Ed.), *Literacy in historical perspective,* (pp. 7–22). Washington, DC: Library of Congress.

Clark, H. H. & Haviland, S. E. (1977). Comprehension and the given-new contract. In R. O. Freedle (Ed.), *Discourse production and comprehension.* (Vol. 1) (pp. 1–40) Norwood, NJ: Ablex Publishing Co.

Clarke, M., Losoff, A., & Rood, D. S. (1982). Untangling referent and reference in linguistic relativity studies: A response from Clark et al. *Language learning, 32,* 209–217.

Clements, P. (1979). The effects of staging on recall from prose. In R. O. Freedle (Ed.), *New directions in discourse processing.* (Vol. 2.) (pp. 287–330) Norwood, NJ: Ablex Publishing Co.

Clifford, G. J., (1984). Buch and lesen: Historical perspectives on literacy and schooling. *Review of Educational Research, 54,* 472–500.

Cohen, E. D., (1987). The use of syllogism in rational-emotive therapy. *Journal of Counseling and Development, 66,* 37–39.

Combs, A. W. (1982). *A personal approach to teaching.* Boston: Allyn & Beacon.

Connell, J. P., & Ryan, R. M. (1984). A developmental theory of motivation in the classroom. *Teacher Education Quality, 11*(4), 64–77.

Cooper, C. R., (1983). Procedures for describing written texts. In P. Mosenthal, L. Tamor & S. A. Walmsley (Eds.), *Research on writing* (pp. 287–313). New York: Longman.

Cooper, C., & Holzman, M. (1983). Talking about protocols. *College Composition and Communication, 34,* 284–293.

Costa, A. L. (Ed.). (1985a). *Developing minds: A resource book for teaching thinking.* Alexandria, VA: Association for Supervision and Curriculum Development.

Costa, A. L. (1985b). Toward a model of human intellectual functioning. In A. L. Costa (Ed.), *Developing minds: A resource book for teaching thinking* (pp. 62–65). Alexandria, VA: Association for Supervision and Curriculum Development.

Covington, M. V. (1983). Motivated cognitions. In S. G. Paris, G. M. Olson & H. W. Stevenson (Eds.), *Learning and motivation in the classroom* (pp. 139–164). Hillsdale, NJ: Erlbaum.

Covington, M. V. (1985). Strategic thinking and the fear of failure. In J. W. Segal, S. F. Chipman, & R. Glaser (Eds.), *Thinking and learning skills: Vol. 1. Relating instruction to research* (pp. 389–416). Hillsdale, NJ: Erlbaum.

Covington, M. V., Crutchfield, R. S., Davies, L., & Olton, R. M. (1974). *The productive thinking program: A course in learning to think.* Columbus, OH: Merrill.

Crabbe, A. B. (1982). Creating a brighter future: An update on the Future Problem Solving Program. *Journal for the Education of the Gifted, 5,* 2–11.

Crothers, E. J. (1979). *Paragraph structure inferences.* Norwood, NJ: Ablex.

Csikszentmihalyi, M. (1975). *Beyond boredom and anxiety.* San Francisco: Jossey-Bass.

Cunningham, D. & Luk, H. (March, 1985). *Student as semiotician.* Paper presented at the annual meeting of American Educational Research Association. Chicago.

Cunningham, J. W., & Moore, D. W. (1986). The confused world of main idea. In J. F. Bauman (Ed.), *Teaching main idea comprehension.* (pp. 1–17). Newark, DE: International Reading Association.

Dansereau, D. F. (1978). The development of a learning strategy curriculum. In H. F. O'Neill, Jr. (Ed.), *Learning strategies* (pp. 1–29). New York: Academic Press.

Dansereau, D. F. (1985). Learning strategy research. In J. W. Segal, S. F. Chipman & R. Glaser (Eds.), *Thinking and learning skills, Vol. 1, Relating instruction to research* (pp. 209–240). Hillsdale, NJ: Lawrence Erlbaum.

Davies, I. K. (1980). *Instructional technique.* New York, NJ: McGraw-Hill.

de Beaugrande, R. (1980). *Text, discourse and process: Toward a multidisciplinary science of text.* Norwood, NJ: Ablex.

de Beaugrande, R. (1984). *Text production: Toward a science of composition.* Norwood, NJ: Ablex.

de Bono, E. (1976). *Teaching thinking.* London: Temple Smith.

de Bono, E. (1983). The cognitive research trust (CoRT) thinking program. In Maxwell, W. (Ed.), *Thinking: The expanding frontier.* Philadelphia: The Franklin Institute Press.

de Bono, E. (1985). The CoRT thinking program. In J. W. Segal, S. F., Chipman, & Glaser, R. (Eds.), *Thinking and learning skills: Vol. 1. Relating instruction to research* (pp. 363–388). Hillsdale, NJ: Erlbaum.

Deely, J. (1982). *Semiotics: Its history and doctrine.* Bloomington, IN: Indiana University Press.

Delin, P. S. (1969). The learning to criterion of a serial list with and without mnemonic instructions. *Psychonomic Science, 16,* 169–170.

Derry, S., & Murphy, D. (1986). Designing systems that train learning ability. *Review of Educational Research, 56,* 1–39.

DeTure, L. R., & Miller, A. P. (1985). *The effects of a written protocol model on teacher acquisition of extended wait-time.* Paper presented at the annual meeting of the National Science Teachers Association, Cincinnati, OH.

Dewey, J. (1983). *How we think: A restatement of the relation of subjective thinking to the educative process.* Boston, MA: D. C. Heath.

Dewey, J. (1957). *Human nature and conduct.* New York: Modern Library.

Dickson, W. P. (1985). Thought-provoking software: Juxtaposing symbol systems. *Educational Research, 14,* 30–38.

di Sessa, A. (1982). Unlearning Aristotelian physics: A study of knowledge-based learning. *Cognitive Science, 6,* 37–75.

DiVesta, F. J., & Gray, G. S. (1972). Listening and note-taking. *Journal of Educational Psychology, 63,* 8–14.

Douglas, V., Parry, P., Martin, P., Garson, C. (1976). Assessment of a cognitive training program for hyperactive children. *Journal of Abnormal Child Psychology, 4,* 389–410.

Eckwall, E. E. (1977). *Locating and correcting reading difficulties.* Columbus, OH: Charles E. Merrill.

Eco, U. (1976). *A theory of semiotics.* Bloomington, IN: Indiana University Press.

Eco, U. (1979). *The role of the reader.* Bloomington, IN: Indiana University Press.

Eco, U. (1984). *Semiotics and the philosophy of language.* Bloomington, IN: Indiana University Press.

Edwards, J., & Baldauf, R. B. (1983). Teaching thinking in secondary science. In W. Maxwell (Ed.), *Thinking: The expanding frontier.* Philadelphia, PA: The Franklin Institute Press.

Ehrenberg, S. D., Ehrenberg, L. M., & Durfee, D. (1979). *BASICS: Teaching/learning strategies.* Miami Beach, FL: Institute for Curriculum and Instruction.

Einstein, G. C., Morris, J., & Smith, S. (1985). Note-taking, individual differences, and memory for lecture information. *Journal of Educational Psychology, 77,* 522–532.

Ellis, A. (1962). *Reason and emotion in psychotherapy.* New York: Lyle Stuart.

Ellis, A. (1977). The basic clinical theory of rational-emotive therapy. In A. Ellis & R. Grieger (Eds.), *Handbook of rationale-emotive therapy.* New York: Springer.

Emmer, E. T., Evertson, C. M., & Anderson, L. (1980). Effective management at the beginning of the school year. *Elementary School Journal, 80,* 219–231.

Ennis, R. H. (1985). Goals for a critical thinking curriculum. In A. Costa (Ed.), *Developing minds: A resource book for teaching thinking* (pp. 54–57). Alexandria, VA: Association for Supervision and Curriculum Development.

Erickson, F. (1975). Gate-keeping and the melting pot: Interaction in counseling interviews. *Harvard Educational Review, 45,* 44–70.

Fagan, E. R., Hassler, D. M., & Szabo, M. (1981). Evaluation of questioning strategies in language arts instruction. *Research in the Teaching of English, 15,* 267–273.

Fairbrother, R. (1975). The reliability of teachers' judgments of the abilities being tested by multiple choice items. *Educational Researcher, 17,* 202–210.

Fernald, G. M. (1988). Remedial techniques in basic school subjects. (L. Idol, Ed.). Austin, TX: Pro-ed.

Feuerstein, R., Rand, Y., Hoffman, M. B., & Miller, R. (1980). *Instrumental enrichment: An intervention program for cognitive modifiability.* Baltimore, MD: University Park Press.

Fillmore, C. J. (1968). The case for case. In E. Beck & R. T. Harms (Eds.), *Universals in linguistic theory* (pp. 1–210). New York: Holt, Rinehart & Winston.

Finn, P. J. (1985). *Helping children to learn to read.* New York Random House.

Fischer, K. W. (1980). A theory of cognitive development: The control and construction of hierarchies of skills. *Psychological Review, 87*(6), 477–531.

Fisher, C. W., & Hiebert, E. F. (1988). Characteristics of literacy learning activities in elementary schools. Paper presented at the annual meeting of the *National Reading Conference,* Tucson.

Fitts, P. M. (1964). Perceptual-motor skill learning. In A. W. Melton (Ed.). *Categories of human learning.* New York: Wiley.

Flavell, J. H. (1976). Metacognitive aspects of problem solving. In L. B. Resnick (Ed.), *The nature of intelligence.* Hillsdale, NJ: Lawrence Erlbaum.

Flavell, J. H. (1977). *Cognitive development.* Englewood Cliffs, NJ: Prentice-Hall.

Flavell, J. H. (1978). Metacognitive development. In J. M. Scandura & C. J. Brainerd (Eds.), *Structural/process theories of complex human behavior.* (pp. 213–245) The Netherlands: Sijthoff and Noordoff.

Flavell, J. H. (1981). Cognitive monitoring. In W. P. Dickson (Ed.), *Children's oral communication skill,* (pp. 35–60). New York: Academic Press.

Flavell, J. H., Beach, D., & Chinsky, J. (1966). Spontaneous verbal rehearsal in a memory task as a function of age. *Child Development, 37,* 283–299.

Flavell, J. H., Friedrichs, A. H., & Hoyt, J. D. (1970). Developmental changes in memorization processes. *Cognitive psychology, 1,* 324–340.

Flower, L. A. & Hayes J. R. (1980a). The cognition of discovery, defining a rhetorical problem. *College Composition and Communication, 13,* 21–32.

Flower, L. A. & Hayes, J. R. (1980b). The dynamics of composing: Making plans and juggling constraints. In L. W. Gregg & E. R. Steinberg (Eds.), *Cognitive processing in writing.* Hillsdale, NJ: Lawrence Erlbaum.

Flower, L. A. & Hayes, J. R. (1981). A cognitive process theory of writing. *College Composition and Communication, 32,* 365–387.

Fodor, J. (1975). *The language of thought.* New York: Crowell.

Fowler, G. L. (1982). Developing comprehension skills in primary students through the use of story frames. *Reading Teacher, 36,* 176–179.

Fowler, T. W. (1975, March). *An investigation of the teacher behavior of wait-time during an inquiry science lesson.* Paper presented at the Annual Meeting of the National Association for Research in Science Teaching, Los Angeles. (ERIC Document Reproduction Service No. ED 108 872).

Frederiksen, C. H. (1977). Semantic processing units in understanding text. In R. O. Freedle (Ed.), *Discourse production and comprehension.* (Vol. 1, pp. 57–88). Norwood, N.J.: Ablex.

Frederiksen, N. (1984). Implications of cognitive theory for instruction in problem solving. *Review of Educational Research, 54,* 363–407.

Freedman, G. & Reynolds, E. G. (1980). Enriched basic reader lessons with semantic webbing. *Reading Teacher, 33,* 677–683.

Gagne, R. M. (1975). *The conditions of learning.* (3rd. ed.). New York: Holt, Rinehart & Winston.

Gazzaniga, M. S. (1985). *The social brain.* New York: Basic Books.

Gazzaniga, M. S., & LeDoux, J. E. (1978). *The integrated mind.* New York: Plenum Press.

Gazzaniga, M. S., & Sperry, R. W. (1967). Language after section of the cerebral commissures. *Brain, 90,* 131–148.

Gentry, J. R. (1982). An analysis of developmental spelling in GYNS AT WRK. *Reading Teacher, 36,* 192–200.

Gentry, J. R. (1987). *Spel . . . is a four-letter word.* Portsmouth, NH: Heinemann.

Gentzen, G. (1964). Investigations into logical deduction. *American Psychological Quarterly, 1,* 288–306.

Gick, M. L., & Holyoak, K. J. (1980). Analogical problem solving. *Cognitive Psychology, 12,* 306–355.

Goodlad, J. I. (1984). *A place called school.* New York: McGraw-Hill.

Goodman, K. (1986). *What's whole in whole language.* Portsmouth, NH: Heinemann.

Gourley, T. J. (1981). Adapting the varsity sports model of non-psychomotor gifted students. *Gifted Child Quarterly, 25,* 164–166.

Graesser, A. C., Millis, K. K., & Long, D. L. (1986). The construction of knowledge structures and inferences during text comprehension. In N. E. Sharkey (Ed.), *Advances in cognitive science* (pp. 125–157). New York, NJ: Ellis Horwood.

Granato, J. M. (1983, April). *The effects of wait time on the verbal behavior of kindergarten children.* Paper presented at the Annual Conference of the New England Educational Research Organization, Rockport, ME.

Graves, D. (1983). *Writing: Teachers and children at work.* Portsmouth, NH: Heinemann.

Green, J. L. (1983). Research on teaching as a linguistic process. A state of the art. In E. W. Gordon (Ed.). *Review of research in education.* (Vol 10, pp. 151–252.) Washington, DC: American Educational Research Association.

Greene, M. (1984). Philosophy, reason and literacy. *Review of Educational Research, 54,*(4), 547–559.

Grimes, J. E. (1975). *The thread of discourse.* The Hague: Mouton.

Guilford, J. P. (1967). *The nature of human intelligence.* New York: McGraw-Hill.

Guilford, J. P., & Hoepfner, R. (1971). *The analysis of intelligence.* New York: McGraw-Hill.

Halliday, M. & Hasan, R. (1976). *Cohesion in English.* London: Longman.

Halpern, D. F. (1984). *Thought and knowledge: An introduction to critical thinking.* Hillsdale, NJ: Lawrence Erlbaum.

Hanelin, S. J. (1978). *Learning, behavior and attitudes under individual and group contingencies.* Unpublished doctoral dissertation, University of California, Los Angeles.

Hanna, P., Hanna, J., Hodges, R., & Rudorf, E. (1966). *Phoneme grapheme correspondence as cues to spelling improvement.* Washington, DC: U.S. Government Printing Office.

Harris, Z. S. (1952). Discourse analysis. *Language, 28,* 1–30.

Harter, S. (1982). A developmental perspective on some parameters of self-regulation in children. In P. Karoly & F. H. Kanfer (Eds.), *Self-management and behavior change: From theory to practice* (pp. 165–204). New York: Pergamon Press.

Harvard University (1983). *Project intelligence: The development of procedures to enhance thinking skills:* Final report, submitted to the Minister of the Development of Human Intelligence, Republic of Venezuela.

Hayes, J. R., & Flower, L. S. (1980). Writing as problem solving. *Visible Language, 14,* 383–399.

Hayes-Roth, B., & Hayes-Roth, F. (1979). A cognitive model of planning. *Cognitive Science, 3,* 275–310.

Heidegger, M. (1968). *What is called thinking?* (J. G. Gray, Trans.) New York: Harper & Row. (Original work published 1954.)

Heliman, K. M., & Satz, P., (Eds.). (1983). *Neuropsychology of human emotions.*

Henle, M. O. (1962). On the relation between logic and thinking. *Psychological Review, 69,* 366–378.

Henle, M. O. (1978). Forward to R. Revlin and R. E. Mayer (Eds.), *Human reasoning.* Washington, DC: Winston.

Henshaw, D. (1978). *A cognitive analysis of creative problem-solving.* Unpublished doctoral dissertation, University of Waterloo.

Hidi, S., & Anderson, V. (1986). Producing written summaries: Task demands, cognitive operations, and implications for instruction. *Review of Educational Research, 56,* 473–494.

Hillocks, G., Jr. (1986). *Research on written composition.* Urbana, IL: ERIC Clearinghouse on Reading and Communication Skills.

Hillocks, G., Jr., & Ludlow, L. H. (1984). A taxonomy of skills in reading and interpreting fiction. *American Educational Research Journal, 21*(1), 7–24.

Holley, C. D., & Dansereau, D. F. (1984). *Spatial learning strategies: Techniques, applications, and related issues.* New York: Academic Press.

Honea, M. J. (1982). Wait time as an instructional variable: An influence on teacher and student. *Clearinghouse, 56*(4), 167–170.

Inhelder, B., & Piaget, J. (1958). *The growth of logical thinking from childhood to adolescence.* London: Routledge & Kegan Paul.

Johnson, D. W., Johnson, R. T., Roy, P. & Holubec, E. J. (1984). *Circles of learning: Cooperation in the classroom.* Alexandria, VA: Association for Supervision and Curriculum Development.

Johnson, J. A. (1979). Learning in peer tutoring interactions: The influence of status, role change, time-on-task, feedback and verbalization. (Doctoral dissertation, University of California, Los Angeles, 1978). *Dissertation Abstracts International, 39,* 5469A-5470A. (University Microfilms No. 79-06, 175).

Johnson, P. E. (1967). Some psychological aspects of subject-matter structure. *Journal of Educational Psychology, 58,* 75–83.

Johnson, P. E. (1969). On the communication of concepts in science. *Journal of Educational Psychology, 60,* 32–40.

Johnson, P. E., Cox, D. L., & Curran, T. E. (1970). Psychological reality of physical concepts. *Psychonomic Science, 19,* 245–247.

Johnson-Laird, P. N. (1975). Models of deduction. In R. J. Falmagne

(Ed.), *Reasoning: Representation and process in children and adults.* Hillsdale, NJ: Lawrence Erlbaum.

Johnson-Laird, P. N. (1983). *Mental models,* Cambridge, MA: Harvard University Press.

Johnson-Laird, P. N., & Steedman, M. J. (1978). The psychology of syllogisms. *Cognitive Psychology, 10,* 64–99.

Jones, B. F., Amiran, M., & Katims, M. (1985). Teaching cognitive strategies and text structures within language arts programs. In J. W. Segal, S. F. Chipman, & R. Glaser (Eds.), *Thinking and learning skills, Vol. 1: Relating instruction to research* (pp. 259–295). Hillsdale, NJ: Lawrence Erlbaum.

Jones, B. F., Palincsar, A. S., Ogle, D. S., & Carr, E. G. (1987). *Strategic teaching: Cognitive instruction in the content areas.* Alexandria, VA: Association of Supervision and Curriculum Development.

Jones, B. F., Tinzmann, M., Friedman, L. B., & Walker, B. J. (1987). *Teaching thinking skills in English/Language Arts.* Washington, DC: National Education Association.

Kail, R. V., & Hagen, J. W. (1982). Memory in childhood. In B. Wolman (Ed.), *Handbook of developmental psychology.* Englewood Cliffs, NJ: Prentice-Hall.

Kanfer, F., & Goldfoot, D. (1966). Self-control and tolerance of noxious stimulation. *Psychological Reports, 18,* 79–85.

Kanfer, F., & Phillips, J. (1970). *Learning foundations of behavior therapy.* New York: John Wiley.

Katz, S. E. (1976). *The effect of each of four instructional treatments on the learning of principles by children.* Madison, WI: Wisconsin Research and Development Center for Cognitive Learning, The University of Wisconsin.

Kenney, T. J., Cannizzo, S. R., & Flavell, J. H. (1967). Spontaneous and induced verbal rehearsal in a recall task. *Child Development, 38,* 953–966.

Kinneavy, J. (1980). *A theory of discourse.* New York: Norton.

Kintsch, W. (1974). *The representation of meaning in memory.* Hillsdale, NJ: Erlbaum.

Kintsch, W. & van Dijk, T. A. (1978). Toward a model of text comprehension and production. *Psychological Review, 85,* 363–394.

Klausmeier, H. J. (1985). *Educational psychology* (5th ed.). New York: Harper & Row.

Knickerbocker, M. E. (1984). *The effects of wait time on verbal behavior of kindergarten children: A replication.* (Unpublished master's thesis, University of New York at Oswego).

Koch, K. (1970). *Wishes, lies, and dreams.* New York: Chelsea.

Koch, K. (1974). *Rose, where did you get that red?* New York: Random House.

Kuhn, T. (1962). *The structure of scientific revolutions.* Chicago: University of Chicago Press.

Lakoff, G. (1970). Linguistics and natural logic. *Syntheses, 22,* 151–271.

Langer, J. A. (1982). Facilitating text processing: The elaboration of prior knowledge. In M. Trika Burke-Smith (Eds.), *Reader meets author: Bridging the gap.* Newark, DE: International Reading Association.

Larkin, J. H. (1979). Information processing models and science instruction. In J. Lochhead & J. Clement (Eds.), *Cognitive process instruction* (pp. 109–118). Philadelphia, PA: The Franklin Institute Press.

Larkin, J. H. (1981). Enriching formal knowledge: A model of learning to solve textbook physics problems. In J. Anderson (Ed.), *Cognitive skills and their acquisition* (pp. 311–334). Hillsdale, NJ: Laurence Erlbaum.

Lindsay, P. H., & Norman, D. A. (1977). *Human information processing.* New York: Academic Press.

Link, F. (1985). Instrumental enrichment. In A. Costa (Ed.), *Developing minds: A resource book for teaching thinking* (pp. 193–195). Alexandria, VA: Associates for Supervision and Curriculum Development.

Lipman M. (1974). *Harry.* Upper Montclair, NJ: Institute for the Advancement of Philosophy for Children.

Lipman, M. (1976). *Lisa.* Upper Montclair, NJ: Institute for the Advancement of Philosophy for Children.

Lipman, M. (1978). *Suki.* Upper Monclair, NJ: Institute for the Advancement of Philosophy for Children.

Lipman, M. (1980). *Mark.* Upper Montclair, NJ: Institute for the Advancement of Philosophy for Children.

Lipman, M. (1985). Thinking skills fostered by philosophy for children. In J. W. Segal, S. F. Chipman, & R. Glaser (Eds.), *Thinking and learning skills: Vol. 1. Relating instruction to research* (pp. 83–108). Hillsdale, NJ: Lawrence Earlbaum.

Lipman, M., Sharp, A. M., & Oscanyan, F. S. (1980). *Philosophy in the classroom* (2nd ed.). Philadelphia, PA: Temple University Press.

Lochhead, J. (1985). Teaching analytic reasoning skills through pair problem solving. In J. W. Segal, S. F. Chipman & R. Glaser (Eds.), *Thinking and learning skills: Vol. 1. Relating instruction to research* (pp. 109–131). Hillsdale, NJ: Lawrence Erlbaum.

Loman, D. F. (1986). *Predicting mathemathanic effects in the teaching of higher order thinking skills.* Unpublished manuscript. The University of Iowa, School of Education, Iowa City, IA.

Luria, A. (1961). *The role of speech in the regulation of normal and abnormal behaviors.* New York: Liveright.

Luria, A. (1969). Speech and formation of mental processes. In M. Cole & I. Maltzman (Eds.), *A handbook of contemporary Soviet psychology.* (pp. 519–541) New York: Basic Books.

Luria, A. (1973). *The working brain.* New York: Basic Books.

Mandler, G. (1983). The nature of emotions. In J. Miller (Ed.), *States of mind* (pp. 136–153). New York, NY: Pantheon Books.

Maratsos, M. P. (1977). Disorganization in thought and word. In R. Shaw & J. Bransford (Eds), *Perceiving, acting and knowing.* (pp. 171–189) Hillsdale, NJ: Lawrence Erlbaum.

Marzano, R. J. (1983). *A quantitative grammar of meaning and structure: A methodology for language analysis and measurement.* Technical Report. Denver, CO: Mid-continent Regional Educational Laboratory (ERIC Document Reproduction Service No. ED 239 491).

Marzano, R. J. (1987). *Decomposing curricular objectives for specivity of instruction.* (Technical Report) Aurora, CO: Mid-continent Regional Educational Laboratory. (ERIC Document Reproduction Service No ED 290 220).

Marzano, R. J., Arredondo, D., Blackburn, G., Brooks, D., Ewy, R., & Pickering, D. (in press). Creating a learner-centered paradigm of instruction. *Educational Leadership.*

Marzano, R. J., Brandt, R. S., Hughes, C. S., Jones, B. F., Presseisen, B. Z., Rankin, S. C., & Suhor, C. (1988). *Dimensions of thinking: A framework for curriculum and instruction.* Alexandria, VA: Association for Supervision and Curriculum Development.

Marzano, R. J., Hagerty, P. J., Valencia, S. W., & DiStefano, P. P. (1987). *Reading diagnosis and instruction: Theory into practice.* Englewood Cliffs, NJ: Prentice-Hall.

Marzano, R. J., & Marzano, J. S. (1987). *Contextual thinking: The most basic of the cognitive skills.* (Technical Report) Aurora, CO: Mid-continent Regional Educational Laboratory. (ERIC Document Reproduction Service No. ED 286 634).

Maslow, A. H. (1968). *Toward a psychology of being.* New York: Van Nostrand Reinhold.

Mason, J. M., & Allen, J. (1986). A review of emergent literacy with implications for research and practice in reading. In E. Z. Rothkopf (Ed.). *Review of research in education, Vol. 13* (pp. 3–47). Washington, DC: American Educational Research Association.

Matsuhashi, A. (1982). Explorations in the real-time production of written discourse. In M. Nystrand (Ed.), *What writers know: The language, process, and structure of written discourse* (pp. 269–290). New York: Academic Press.

Mayer, R. E. (1984). Aids to text comprehension. *Educational Psychologist, 19,* 30–42.

McCarthy, B. (1980). *The 4MAT system.* Oak Harbor, IL: Excel Inc.

McCombs, B. (1984). Processes and skills underlying continuing intrinsic motivation to learn: Toward a definition of motivational skills training intervention. *Educational Psychologist, 19,* 197–218.

McCombs, B., (1986). The role of the self system in self-regulated learning. *Contemporary Educational Psychology, 11,* 314–332.

McCombs, B. (1987, April). *Issues in the measurement by standardized tests of primary motivation variables related to self-regulated learning.* Paper presented at the annual meeting of the American Educational Research Association, Washington, DC.

McNeil, D. (1975). Semiotic extension. In R. L. Solso (Ed.), *Information processing and cognition: The Loyola symposium.* Hillsdale, NJ: Lawrence Erlbaum.

McNeil, J., & Donant, L. (1982). Summarization strategy for improving reading comprehension. In J. A. Niles & L. A. Harris (Eds.), *New inquiries in reading research and instruction.* (pp. 215–219) Thirty-first yearbook of the National Reading Conference. Rochester, NY: National Reading Conference.

McNeil, J. D. (1984). *Reading comprehension. New directions for classroom practice.* Glenview, IL: Scott, Foresman.

Meeker, M. N. (1969). *The structure of intelligence: Its interpretation and uses.* Columbus, OH: Charles E. Merrill.

Mehan, H. (1979). *Learning lessons.* Cambridge, MA: Harvard University Press.

Meichenbaum, D. (1975). Theoretical and treatment implications of developmental research on verbal control of behavior. *Canadian Psychological Review, 16,* 22–27.

Meichenbaum, D. (1977). *Cognitive behavior modification.* New York, NY: Plenum Press.

Meichenbaum, D. (1985). Teaching thinking: A cognitive-behavioral perspective. In S. F. Chipman, J. W. Segal, & R. Glaser (Eds.), *Thinking and learning skills: Vol. 2. Research and open questions* (pp. 407–426). Hillsdale, NJ: Lawrence Erlbaum.

Meichenbaum, D. & Goodman, S. (1971). Training impulsive children to talk to themselves: A means of developing self-control. *Journal of Abnormal Psychology, 77,* 115–126.

Mervis, C. B. (1980). Category structure and the development of categorization. In R. J. Spiro, B. C. Bruce & W. F. Brewer (Eds.), *Theoretical issues in reading comprehension* (pp. 279–307). Hillsdale, NJ: Lawrence Erlbaum.

Messerer, J., Hunt, E., Meyers, G. & Lerner, J. (1984). Feuerstein's instrumental enrichment: A new approach for activating intellectual potential in learning disabled youth. *Journal of Learning Disabilities, 17,* 322–325.

Meyer, B. J. F. (1975). *The organization of prose and its effects on memory.* New York, NY: American Elsevier.

Meyer, B. J. F. (1985). The structure of text. In P. D. Pearson (Ed.), *Handbook of reading research.* New York: Longman.

Miccinati, J. L. (1988). Mapping the terrain: Connecting reading with academic writing. *Journal of Reading, 31,* 542–552.

Mill, J. S. (1874). *A system of logic* (8th ed.). New York: Harper.

Mitchell, B. M. (1980). What's happening to gifted education in the U.S. today? *Roeper Review, 2,* 7—10.

Mitchell, B. M. (1984). An update on gifted/talented education in the U.S. *Roeper Review,6,* 161–163.

Moely, B. E. (1977). Organization factors in the development of memory. In R. V. Kail & J. W. Hagen (Eds.), *Perspectives on the development of memory and cognition. Hillsdale,* (pp. 314–352) NJ: Lawrence Erlbaum.

Moffett, J. (1968). *Teaching the universe of discourse.* Boston: Houghton-Mifflin.

Moffett, J., & Wagner, B. J. (1983). *Student-centered language arts and reading, K–13: A handbook for teachers.* (3rd ed.). Boston, MA: Houghton Mifflin Company.

Moore, C. A. (1977). Verbal teaching patterns under simulated teaching conditions. In R. O. Freedle (Ed.). *Discourse production in comprehension.* (Vol. 1) (pp. 271–305) Norwood, NJ: Ablex Publishing Co.

Murray, D. M. (1978). International revision: A process of discovery. In C. R. Cooper & L. Odell (Eds.), *Research on composing* (pp. 85–103). Urbana, IL: National Council of Teachers of English.

Nardi, A. H., & Wales, C. E. (1985). Teaching decision-making with guided design. In A. L. Costa (Ed.), *Developing minds: A resource book for teaching thinking* (pp. 220–225). Alexandria, VA: Association for Supervision and Curriculum Development.

Nash, R. J., & Shiman, D. A. (1974). The English teacher as questioner. *English Journal, 63,* 42–45.

Negin, G. (1987). *Inferential reasoning for teachers.* Dubuque, IA: Kendall/Hunt.

Newell, A., & Simon, H. A. (1972). *Human problem solving.* Englewood Cliffs, NJ: Prentice-Hall.

Neisser, V. (1967). *Cognitive psychology.* New York: Appleton.

Nickerson, R. S. (1984). Kinds of thinking taught in current programs, *Educational Leadership, 42,* 26–37.

Nickerson, R. S., Perkins, D. N. & Smith, E. E. (1985) *The teaching of thinking.* Hillsdale, NJ: Erlbaum.

Nold, E. W., & Davis, B. E. (1980). The discourse matrix. *College Composition and Communication, 31,* 141–147.

Norman, D. (1969). *Memory and attention.* New York: Wiley.

Ogle, D. (1986). The K-W-L: A teaching model that develops active reading of expository text, *The Reading Teacher, 39,* 564–576.

Owens, H., & Maxmen, J. S. (1979). Moods and affect: A semantic confusion. *American Journal of Psychiatry, 136,* 97–99.

Palincsar, A. S. & Brown, A. L. (1984). Reciprocal teaching of comprehension-fostering and comprehension-monitoring activities. *Cognition and Instruction, 1,* 117–175.

Palincsar, A. S., Ogle, D. S., Jones, B. F., & Carr, E. G. (Eds.). *Teaching reading as thinking.* Alexandria, VA: Association for Supervision and Curriculum Development.

Paivio, A. (1969). Mental imagery in associative learning and memory. *Psychological Review, 76,* 241–263.

Paivio, A. (1971). *Imagery and verbal processing.* New York: Holt, Rhinehart and Winston.

Paris, S. G. & Lindauer, B. K. (1982). The development of cognitive skills during childhood. In B. W. Wolman (Ed.), *Handbook of developmental psychology.* Englewood Cliffs, NJ: Prentice-Hall.

Paris, S. G., Lipson, M. Y., & Wixson, K. K. (1983). Becoming a strategic reader. *Contemporary Educational Psychology, 8,* 293–316.

Pask, G. (1975). *Conversations, cognition and learning.* Amsterdam: Elsevier.

Pearson, P. D. & Johnson, D. D. (1978). *Teaching reading comprehension.* New York: Holt, Rhinehart & Winston.

Peper, R. J., & Mayer, R. E. (1978). Note-taking as generative activity. *Journal of Educational Psychology, 70,* 514–522.

Perkins, D. N. (1981). *The mind's best work.* Cambridge, MA: Harvard University Press.

Perkins, D. N. (1984). Creativity by design. *Educational Leadership, 42,* 18–25.

Perkins, D. N., Allen, R., & Hafner, J. (1983). Difficulties in everyday reasoning. In W. Maxwell (Ed.), *Thinking: The expanding frontier.* Philadelphia, PA: The Franklin Institute Press.

Peterson, P. L., & Janicki, T. C. (1979). Individual characteristics and children's learning in large-group and small-group approaches. *Journal of Educational Psychology, 71,* 677–687.

Peterson, P. L., Janicki, T. C., & Swing, S. R. (1981). Ability x treatment interaction effects on children's learning in large-group and small-group approaches. *American Educational Research Journal, 18,* 453–473.

Piaget, J. (1959). *Language and though of the child.* Cleveland, OH: World.

Piaget, J. (1962). The relationship of affectivity to intelligence in the mental development of the child. *Bulletin of the Menninger Clinic, 26,* 129–137.

Piaget, J. & Szeminska, A. (1941). *The child's conception of number.* Atlantic Highlands, NJ: Humanities Press.

Pike, K. L. (1964). A linguistic contribution to composition: A hypothesis. *College Composition and Communication, 15,* 82–88.

Pressley, M., Borkowski, J. G., & O'Sullivan, J. T. (1984). Memory strategy instruction is made of this: Meta-memory and durable strategy use. *Educational Psychologist, 19,* 94–107.

Pressley, M., Levin, J. R. & Ghatala, E. S. (1984). Memory strategy monitoring in adults and children. *Journal of Verbal Learning and Verbal Behavior, 23,* 270–288.

Raphael, T. E. (1982). Question-answering strategies for children. *Reading Teacher, 36,* 186–190.

Raphael, T. E. (1984). Teaching learners about sources of information for answering comprehension questions. *Journal of Reading, 27,* 303–311.

Raphael, T. E. (1987). Research on reading: But what can I teach on Monday? In V. Richardson-Koehler (Ed.), *Educator's handbook: A research perspective* (pp. 26–49). New York: Longman.

Raphael, T. E., & Kirschner, B. M. (1985). *The effects of instruction in compare/contrast text structure on sixth-grade students' reading comprehension and writing products* (Research Series 161). East Lansing, MI: Michigan State University, Institute for Research on Teaching.

Reder, L. M. (1980). The role of elaboration in the comprehension of prose: A critical review. *Review of Educational Research, 50,* 5–53.

Redfield, D. L., & Rousseau, E. W. (1981). A meta-analysis of experimental research on teacher questioning behavior. *Review of Educational Research, 51,* 237–245.

Reese, H. (1962). Verbal mediation as a function of age. *Psychological Bulletin, 59,* 502–509.

Reigeluth, C. M., & Stein, F. S. (1983). The elaboration theory of instruction. In. C. M. Reigeluth (Ed.), *Instructional design theories and models: An overview of their current status* (pp. 335–381). Hillsdale, NJ: Lawrence Erlbaum Associates.

Remy, R. C. (1980). *Handbook of basic citizenship competencies: Guidelines for comparing materials, assessing instruction, and setting goals.* Alexandria, VA: Association for Supervision and Curriculum Development.

Resnick, D. P., & Resnick, L. B. (1977). The nature of literacy: An historical exploration. *Harvard Educational Review, 47,* 370–385.

Resnick, L. B., (1987). *Educational and learning to think.* Washington, DC; National Academy Press.

Resnick, L. B., & Ford, W. W. (1981). *The psychology of mathematics for instruction.* Hillsdale, NJ: Lawrence Erlbaum.

Reynolds, W., & Stark, F. (1983). Cognitive behavior modifications: The clinical application of cognitive strategies. In M. Pressley & J. Levin (Eds.), *Cognitive strategy research: Psychological foundations* (pp. 221–266). New York, NJ: Springer-Verlag.

Rickards, J., & August, G. J. (1975). Generative underlining strategies in prose recall. *Journal of Educational Psychology, 67,* 860–865.

Riley, J. P., II. (1986). The effects of teachers' wait-time and knowledge comprehension questioning on pupil science achievement. *Journal of Research in Science Teaching, 23*(4), 335–342.

Rosenblatt, L. (1978). *The reader, the text, the poem.* Carbondale, IL: Southern Illinois University Press.

Ross, J., & Lawrence, K. A. (1968). Some observations on memory artifice. *Psychonomic Science, 13,* 107–108.

Rothkopf, E. Z. (1970). The concept of mathemagenic activities. *Review of Educational Research, 40,* 325–336.

Rowe, H. (1985). *Problem solving and intelligence.* Hillsdale, NJ: Erlbaum.

Rowe, M. (1974). Wait-time and rewards as instructional variables, their influence on language, logic and fate control. Part 1 wait-time. *Journal of Research in Science Teaching, 11,* 81–94.

Rumelhart, D. E. (1977). Toward an interactive model of reading. In S. Dornic (Ed.). *Attention and performance. VI.* Hillsdale, NJ: Laurence Erlbaum.

Rumelhart, D. E. (1980). Schemata: The building blocks of cognition. In R. J. Spiro, B. C. Bruce, & W. F. Brewer (Eds.), *Theoretical issues in reading comprehension* (pp. 33–58) Hillsdale, NJ: Lawrence Erlbaum.

Rumelhart, D. E., & Norman, D. A. (1981). Accretion, tuning and restructuring: Three modes of learning. In J. W. Colton & R. Klatzky (Eds.), *Semantic factors in cognition.* Hillsdale, NJ: Lawrence Erlbaum.

Sadow, M. W. (1982). The use of story grammar in the design of questions. *Reading Teacher, 35,* 263–265.

Santostefano, S. (1986). Cognitive controls, metaphors and contexts. An approach to cognition and emotion. In D. J. Bearson & H. Zimiles (Eds.), *Thought and emotions: Developmental perspectives.* Hillsdale, NJ: Lawrence Erlbaum.

Sapir, E. (1921). *Language: An introduction to the study of speech.* New York: Harcourt Brace Jovanovich.

Savell, J. M., Twohig, P. T., & Rachford, D. L. (1986). Empirical status of "Feuerstein's instrumental enrichment" technique as a method of teaching thinking skills. *Review of Educational Research, 56,* 38–410.

Sawada, D., & Caley, M. T. (1985). Dissipative structures: New metaphors for becoming in education. *Educational Researcher, 14,* 3–19.

Scardamalia, M., & Bereiter, C. (1983). Child as co-investigator: Helping children gain insight into their own mental processes. In S. Paris, G. Olson, & H. Stevenson (Eds.), *Learning and motivation in the classroom* (pp. 61–82). Hillsdale, NJ: Lawrence Erlbaum.

Scardamalia, M., & Bereiter, C. (1985). Fostering the development of self-regulation in children's knowledge processing. In S. F. Chipman, J. W. Segal & R. Glaser (Eds.), *Thinking and learning skills: Vol. 2. Research and open questions* (pp. 563–578). Hillsdale, NJ: Erlbaum.

Scardamalia, M., & Bereiter, C. (1986). Research on written composition. In M. C. Wittrock (Ed.), *Handbook of research on teaching* (3rd ed.) (pp. 778–803). New York: MacMillan Publishing Company

Scardamalia, M., Bereiter, C., & Steinbach, R. (1984). Teachability of reflective processes in written composition. *Cognitive Science, 8*(2), 173–190.

Schank, R. C. & Abelson, R. (1977). *Scripts, plans, goals and understanding.* Hillsdale, NJ: Erlbaum.

Schank, R. C., & Rieger, C. J. (1974). Inference and the computer understanding of natural language. *Artificial Intelligence, 5,* 373–412.

Schlesinger, M. (1971). Production of utterances in language acquisition. In D. I. Slobin (Ed.), *The ontogenesis of grammar* (pp. 63–101). New York: Academic Press.

Schoenfeld, A. H. (1980). Teaching problem-solving skills. *American Mathematical Monthly, 87*(10), 794–805.

Schoenfeld, A. H. (1983a). Episodes and executive decisions in mathematical problem solving. In R. Lesh & M. Landau (Eds.), *Acquisition of mathematical concepts and processes.* New York: Academic Press.

Schoenfeld, A. H. (1983b, April). *Theoretical and pragmatic issues in the design of mathematical "problem solving" instruction.* Paper presented at the annual meeting of the American Educational Research association. Montreal.

Searle, J. (1984). *Minds, brains, and science.* Cambridge, MA: Harvard University Press.

Sears, P. S. (1940). Levels of aspiration in academically successful and unsuccessful children. *Journal of Abnormal and Social Psychology, 35,* 498–536.

Segal, J. W., Chipman, S. F., & Glaser, R. (Eds.). (1985). *Thinking & learning skills. Vol. 1. Relating instruction to research.* Hillsdale, NJ: Lawrence Erlbaum.

Sharan, S. (1980). Cooperative learning in small groups: Recent methods and effects on achievement, attitudes and ethnic relations. *Review of Educational Research, 50,* 241–272.

Shavelson, R. J., & Bolus, R. (1982). Self-concept: The interplay of theory and methods. *Journal of Educational Psychology, 74,* 3–17.

Shavelson, R. J., & Geeslin, W. E. (1973). A method for examining subject matter structure in written material. *Journal of Structural Learning, 4,* 101–111.

Shipman, S., & Shipman, V. C. (1985). Cognitive styles: Some conceptual, methodological, and applied issues. In E. W. Gordon (Ed.) *Review of research in education. Vol. 12* (pp. 229–291). Washington, DC: American Educational Research Association.

Shuell, T. J. (1986). Cognitive conceptions of learning. *Review of Educational Research, 56,* 411–436.

Siegler, R. S. (1983). Information processing approaches to development. In W. Kessen (Ed.), *Manual of child psychology: History, theories, and methods.* (pp. 420–442) New York: Wiley.

Simon, H. A. (1980). Problem solving and education. In D. T. Tuma & F. Reif (Eds.), *Problem solving and education: Issues in teaching and research* (pp. 81–96). Hillsdale, NJ: Lawrence Erlbaum.

Sinclair, J. McH., & Coulthard, R. M. (1975). *Towards an analysis of discourse: The English used by teachers and pupils.* London: Oxford University Press.

Singer, H., & Bean, T. (Eds.). (1984). *Learning from texts: Selection of friendly texts.* Proceedings of the Lake Arrowhead Conference on Learning from Text. Arlington: VA. (ERIC Document Reproduction Service No. ED 251 512).

Slater, W., Graves, M., & Piche, G. (1985). Effects of structural organizers on ninth-grade students' comprehension and recall of four patterns of expository text. *Reading Research Quarterly, 20,* 189–202.

Slavin, R. E. (1978a). Effects of student teams and peer tutoring on academic achievement and time-on-task. *Journal of Experimental Education, 48,* 252–257.

Slavin, R. E. (1978b). Student teams and comparison among equals: Effects on academic performance and student attitudes. *Journal of Educational Psychology, 70,* 532–538.

Slobin, D. I. (1979). *Psycholinguistics.* Glenview, IL: Scott, Foresman.

Smith, E. E., & Medin, D. L. (1981). *Categories and concepts.* Cambridge, MA: Harvard University Press.

Snowman, J., & McCown, R. (1984, April). *Cognitive processes in learning: A model for investigating strategies and tactics.* Paper presented at the annual meeting of the American Educational Research Association, New Orleans, LA.

Sokolov, A. N. (1972). *Inner speech and thought* (G. T. Onischenko, Trans). New York: Plenum Press.

Sperry, R. W. (1985). Brain bisection and mechanisms of consciousness. In J. C. Eccles (Ed.), *Brain mechanisms and conscious experience.* New York: Springor-Verlag.

Staudenmayer, H. (1975). Understanding conditional reasoning with meaningful propositions. In R. Falmagne (Ed.), *Reasoning: Representation a process in children and adults.* Hillsdale, NJ: Lawrence Erlbaum.

Stein, N. L. (1986). Knowledge and process in the acquisition of writing skills. In E. Z. Rothkopf (Ed.), *Review of research in education* (Vol. 10, pp. 255–258). Washington, DC: American Educational Research Association.

Stein, N. L., & Glenn, C. G. (1979). An analysis of story comprehension in elementary school children. In R. O. Freedle (Ed.), *New directions in discourse processing* (Vol. 1) (pp. 53–120). Norwood, NJ: Ablex.

Sternberg, R. J. (1985). *Beyond IQ.* Cambridge University Press.

Suhor, C. (1984). Toward a semiotics-based curriculum. *Journal of Curriculum Studies, 16,* 247–257.

Sulzby, E. (1985). Kindergartners as writers and readers. In M. Farr

(Ed.), *Advances in writing research: Vol. 1. Children's early writing development* (pp. 127–199). Norwood, NJ: Ablex.

Sulzby, E. (1986). Writing and reading: Signs of oral and written language organization in the young child. In W. H. Teale & E. Sulzby (Eds.), *Emergent literacy: Writing and reading* (pp. 50–89). Norwood, NJ: Ablex.

Swartz, R. J. (1987). *Reading and thinking: A new framework for comprehension.* Boston, MA: Massachusetts Department of Education.

Swift, J. N., & Gooding, C. T. (1983). Interaction of wait time feedback and questioning instruction on middle school science teaching. *Journal of Research in Science teaching, 20*(8), 721–730.

Teale, W. H. (1987). Emergent literacy: Reading and writing development in early childhood. In J. E. Readence & R. S. Baldwin (Eds.), *Research in literacy: Merging perspectives* (pp. 45–74). Thirty-sixth yearbook of the National Reading Conference. Rochester, NJ: The National Reading Conference.

The College Board (1983). *Academic preparation for college: What students need to know and be able to do.* New York: The College Board.

Tobin, K. (1986). Effects of teacher wait time on discourse characteristics in mathematics and language arts classes. *American Educational Research Journal, 23,* 191–200.

Tobin, K. (1987). The role of wait time in higher cognitive level learning. *Review of Educational Research, 57,* 69–95.

Torrance, E. P. (1980). More than the ten rational processes. *Creative Child and Adult Quarterly, 5,* 9–19.

Torrance, E. P. (1986). Teaching creative and gifted learners. In M. C. Wittrock (Ed.), *Handbook of research on teaching* (3rd ed.) (pp. 630–647) New York: Macmillan Publishing Company.

Toulmin, S., Rieke, R., & Janik, A. (1981). *An introduction to reasoning.* New York: Macmillan.

Tulving, E. (1972). Episodic and semantic memory. In E. Tulving & W. Donaldson (Eds.), *Organization of memory* (pp. 185–191). New York: Academic Press.

Tuman, M. C. (1987). *A preface to literacy: An inquiry into pedagogy, practice, and progress.* Tuscaloosa, AL: The University of Alabama Press.

Turner, A., & Greene, E. (1977). *The construction of a propositional text base.* Boulder, CO: Institute for the Study of Intellectual Behavior, The University of Colorado at Boulder.

Tweney, R. D., Doherty, M. E., & Mynatt, C. R. (1981). *On scientific thinking.* New York: Columbia University Press.

Underwood, B. J. (1969). Attributes of memory. *Psychological Review, 76,* 559–573.

van Dijk, T. A. (1977). *Text and context.* London: Longman.

van Dijk, T. A. (1980). *Macrostructures.* Hillsdale, NJ: Erlbaum.

van Dijk, T. A. & Kintsch, W. (1983). *Strategies of discourse comprehension.* Hillsdale, NJ: Erlbaum.

Van Patten, J. R., Chao, C. I., & Reigeluth, C. M. (1986). A review of strategies for sequencing and synthesizing information. *Review of Educational Research, 56,* 437–472.

Vosniadou, S., & Brewer, W. F. (1987). Theories of knowledge restructuring in development. *Review of Educational Research, 51*(1), 51–67.

Vygotsky, L. (1962). *Thought and language.* New York: Wiley.

Vygotsky L. (1978). *Mind in society.* Cambridge, MA: Harvard University Press.

Wales, C. E. (1979). Does how you teach make a difference? *Engineering Education, 69,* 394–398.

Wales, C. E., & Stager, R. A. (1977). *Guided design.* Morgantown, WV: West Virginia University Center for Guided Design.

Warren, W. H., Nicholas, D. W., & Trabasso, T. (1979). Event chains and inferences in understanding narratives. In R. O. Freedle (Ed.), *New directions in discourse processing, Vol. 2.* (pp. 23–52). Norwood, NJ: Ablex Publishing Corp.

Webb, N. M. (1980a). A process-outcome analysis of learning in group and individual settings. *Educational Psychologist, 15,* 69–83.

Webb, N. M. (1980b). An analysis of group interaction and mathematical errors in heterogeneous ability groups. *British Journal of Educational Psychology, 50,* 1–11.

Webb, N. M. (1980c). Group process and learning in an interacting group. *The Quarterly Newsletter of the Laboratory of Comparative Human Cognition, 2,* 10–15.

Webb, N. M. (1980d). Group process: The key to learning in groups. *New Directions for Methodology of Social and Behavioral Science: Issues in Aggregation, 6,* 77–87.

Webb, N. M. (1982). Student interaction and learning in small groups. *Review of Educational Research, 52,* 421–445.

Weiner, B. (1972). Attribution theory, achievement motivation and the educational process. *Review of Educational Research, 42,* 203–215.

Weiner, B. (1983). Speculations regarding the role of affect in achievement-change programs guided by attributional principles. In J. M. Levine & M. C. Wang (Eds.), *Teaching and student perceptions: Implications for learning* (pp. 57–73). Hillsdale, NJ: Lawrence Erlbaum.

Weinstein, C. E., & Mayer, R. E. (1986). The teaching of learning strategies. In M. C. Wittrock (Ed.), *Handbook of research on teaching* (3rd ed.) (pp. 315–327). New York: Macmillan Publishing Co.

Wertsch, J. V. (1984). The zone of proximal development: Some conceptual issues. In B. Rogoff & J. Wertsch (Eds.), *Children's learning in the zone of proximal development* (pp. 7–18). San Francisco: Josey-Bass.

Whimbey, A., & Lochhead, J. (1982). *Problem solving and comprehension.* Philadelphia: The Franklin Institute Press.

Whimbey, A. & Lochhead, J. (1984). *Beyond problem solving and comprehension.* Philadelphia,: The Franklin Institute Press.

White, B. Y. (1983). Sources of difficulty in understanding Newtonian dynamics. *Cognitive Science, 7,* 41–65.

Whorf, B. L. (1956). *Language, thought and reality.* Cambridge, MA: MIT Press.

Winograd, P. N., & Bridge, C. A. (1986). The comprehension of important information in written prose. In J. F. Bauman (Ed.), *Teaching main idea comprehension* (pp. 18–48). Newark, DE: International Reading Association.

Wittrock, M. C. (1974). Learning as a generative process. *Educational Psychologist, 11,* 87–95.

Wood, P., Bruner, J., & Ross, G. (1976). The role of tutoring in problem-solving. *Journal of Child Psychology and Psychiatry, 17,* 89–100.

Wood, R. (1977). Multiple choice: A state of the art report. *Evaluation in Education, 1,* 191–280.

Wozniak, R. (1972). Verbal regulation of motor behavior: Soviet research and non-Soviet replications. *Human Development, 15,* 13–57.

Yost, M., Avila, L., & Vexler, E. B. (1977). Effects of learning of post-instructional responses to questions of differing degrees of complexity. *Journal of Educational Psychology, 69,* 398–401.

Young, R. E., & Becker, A. L. (1965). Toward a modern theory of rhetoric: A tagmemic contribution. *Harvard Educational Review, 35,* 450–468.

Young, R. W., Becker, A. L., & Pike, K. L. (1970). *Rhetoric: Discovery and change.* New York: Harcourt Brace.

·31·

TEACHING THE ROOTS OF MODERN ENGLISH

31A. THE HISTORY OF THE LANGUAGE IN THE LANGUAGE ARTS CLASS

James W. Ney

Any chapter on the teaching of the history of the English language in elementary or high school for a *Handbook of Research on Teaching the English Language Arts* must start with a caveat. For, as Marckwardt (1963) pointed out at the Allerton Park Conference there is a vacuum on research on how to teach ANY linguistics in the schools, including the teaching of the history of the language.

At this point, it is interesting to note that language-arts texts seem to follow the emphasis set by Savage (1977), for treating aspects of the history of the English language by concentrating largely on etymology. As a result, very little of the history of the English language is taught in the schools unless it is related to brief etymological excerpts. Quandt rationalizes the current situation by stating:

One implication of linguistic discoveries is that children learn to communicate by experimenting with language and practicing it in meaningful ways. It would seem to be a contradiction to the work of linguists if we made linguistics a major part of the language arts content. (Quandt 1983, p. 30)

He neglects the intermediate position, the teaching of *some* linguistics, and appears to advocate the teaching *none*. In fairness to Quandt, he does recommend the study of synonyms, dialects, and "a few historical aspects of English" (1983, p. 30). He also states that: "individuals who become interested in language study should be encouraged and supported by the teacher . . ." After this he indicates that when children are regularly forced to memorize the facts of language, they do not develop an interest in language, but, if some young students do develop an interest in language then, ". . . the teacher can also provide resources on language histories . . ." (1983, p. 31) He closes his discussion, reiterating his previous sentiments and stating that "linguistic content . . . should not become a major component in the language arts curriculum . . ." thereby consigning a generation of students to ignorance of the history and the structure of the language that they speak. All of this is reminiscent of one participant at the Dartmouth conference who is reported to have said: "English has no content; there are virtually no facts to transmit" (Muller 1967, p. 12).

During the 1960s members of the Commission on the English Curriculum of the National Council of Teachers of English (1963) took the position that the history of the English language had no real place in the English curriculum except on the graduate level where they recommended two courses for Ph.D. students. Members of the commission have no trouble in recommending "social studies and science and all learning experiences of the school" as "occasions and materials for developing power in . . . outlining for a purpose, and various other types of speech and writing" (1963, p. 390). But they seem to have overlooked the fact that such activities could be planned around studies in the history of the English language in the schools.

The Commission's and Quandt's position is not necessarily typical, however. In the 1960s, several ambitious projects were designed to include work on the history of the English language in school curricula. Some of these probably owed their impetus to the Woods Curriculum Workshop (1961) and, later, the 1966 Dartmouth conference. In the latter, participants such as Kitzhaber, Gleason and Britton helped to form a consensus, producing statements about language becoming the "integrating centre, about which a new curriculum" was to be built (Kitzhaber as quoted by Allen, 1980, p. 30). As a result, ambitious curriculum guides were produced that dealt with all aspects of language including the history of the English language. For the elementary through high schools these include: the Nebraska Curriculum (1966), the Atlanta Regional Curriculum Project (1968), Muinzer's "History: The Life in Language" (1960), the Minnesota Center for Curriculum Development in English (1968a,b,c), Kitzhaber, "History of English" (1968), the Oregon Elementary English Project (1971), and the North Carolina State Board of Education (1968). One of these, those of the Minnesota Center for Curriculum Development in English (1968c), follows the procedure of Savage (above) by approaching the teaching of the history of the English language through etymology. (Milosh (1972) makes drudgery of the study of the history of the English language.)

Some of these curricula were quite ambitious. For instance, the Atlanta Regional Curriculum Project is summarized in the following statement:

This curriculum guide, developed for prekindergarteners through grade 12 as part of the total English curriculum, is concerned with the English language as it is now known and as it evolved from its Indo-European roots. Materials include:

1. an overview of the origin and development of the English language from Old English through Middle English to Modern English.
2. a design for teaching sequentially the underlying principle that the English language has changed drastically from its beginnings and is being changed now.
3. 23 items of selected knowledge to be grasped during the course of study, from the simplest concept of English as a member of a language family to the more complex concept, the historical and cultural influences contributing to language changes.
4. recommended learning experiences, which at an elementary level provide such activities as hearing and discussing a recording and improvising a meeting between a Viking and an Englishman; on the junior high level, charting family trees and researching the Teutonic Conquest; on the high school level, examining an example of modern English for its syntax and tracing word origins in *The Oxford English Dictionary.*

Some suggestions for introducing the history of the English language into the schools are novel. For instance, Harder (1967) uses study of place names, Ali (1969) attempts the same through the use of slang, jargon, colloquialisms, and regional dialects, such as Appalachian English (Peterson 1987), and also the study of etymology as in previously cited instances (Lesiak 1978, Tompkins & Yaden, 1986).

It is difficult to assess the impact of suggested curricula on the schools. One study (Cleaver 1976) would seem to indicate that teaching the history of the English language is spotty and mixed. According to Cleaver, most of the teaching of this subject is done in conjunction with discussions about usage. Similarly, a survey of language-arts texts would seem to indicate the same haphazard treatment on the history of the English language. For instance, in the recent Laidlaw Language Experience for grades three through eight (Hand, Harsh, Ney & Shane, 1972e), only the sixth grade book, *Progress in English,* includes material that overtly discusses the history of the English language. Of the 375 pages in the text, it devotes only 16 of 60 pages to linguistic matters. References to the history of the English language also occur in treatments of spelling, naming and dictionary skill in this and other books in the series. Even in the trend-setting Robert's Linguistics Program little space is devoted to matters pertaining to the history of the English language and most of it deals with dictionaries and etymologies. Perhaps the most that can be expected of the commercial texts under review is illustrated in the American Book Company series (Conlin, Herman and Martin, 1966), in which the sixth-, seventh- and eighth-grade books have a single page at the beginning of each chapter on "The English Language and How It Grew." Of the texts under review, only the work by Horn (1967) devotes a reasonable amount of space to the topic, fully one third of the work.

The views of Quandt and the silence of other methodologists on the issue of teaching the history of the English language may be a result of the focus of contemporary linguistics. For the last two decades, linguistics has focused on transformational generative grammar. As a result, educator/statesmen/linguists such as A. H. Marckwardt and H. B. Allen have not been on the scene or center stage to focus attention on other types of linguistics and the history of the English language. This is evident from a perusal of the proceedings of the Fourth International Conference of English teachers (Tchudi, Boomer, Maguire, Creber, D'Arcy & Johnson 1986) under the auspices of the International Federation for the Teaching of English. Hardly a word is printed there in favor of teaching language as a content area, even though linguists such as Fries and Ney were present during the proceedings. Another sign of the same syndrome can be found works such as Crystal's book on applied linguistics (1981) that have nothing to say on the history of the English language; evidently, linguists working in this area have nothing worthy of application to classroom settings. It is no wonder that methods books published in the 1980s show little concern for teaching the history of the English language (Anderson, 1988, Chenfield, 1987, Cushenbery, 1986, Glatthorn, 1980, Hadley, 1985, Mangieri, Moffett & Wagner, 1983, Myers, 1984, Staley & Wilhide, 1984, and Staub, 1986).

If the teaching of one part of cultural heritage, the history of the English language, is in such a state of neglect, a question arises as to what can be done to strengthen the teaching of this subject matter in the schools? It is strange that educators do not raise the spectre of boredom when the history of colonial America is the topic to be presented in the social studies class. But, that spectre is raised when linguistic studies, in particular, studies on the history of the English language, are mentioned (Quandt 1983, p. 30). Several suggestions have been made, however, for making the study of the history of the English language more interesting.

Peterson (1987) has suggested that study of the history of the English language can be made more interesting by relating that history to the current scene through the study of an English dialect. The Minnesota Center for Curriculum Development (1968b) suggests the use of Old English to Modern English versions of the Prodigal Son and the Lord's Prayer to lighten the study of the history of the language. Kitzhaber (1968) suggests teaching the history of the English language through the literature of Old English, Middle English and Early Modern English. The Oregon curriculum (1971) would have fifth and sixth graders study the history of the various periods correlated with the study of the history of the English language. Muinzer (1960) tries to lighten his approach to the teaching the history of the English language for high school students by presenting "... two major ingredients of linguistic history (which) are illustrated with plans for short classroom discussions on four aspects of linguistic change: error, intentional innovations, semantic change, and the linguistic impact of history...." A

National Council of Teachers of English (1967) publication suggests that interest can be added to the study of the history of the language by reading actual texts. Milosh (1972, p. 20) suggests that the subject matter itself can set students aglow with interest.

Certainly, with state, local and federally mandated requirements focusing on skills such as reading and writing, little time can be spent on subject matter that is perceived as being a frill in spite of arguments to the contrary (Moss 1987). One method, frequently exploited, for avoiding the appearance of frivolity in the study linguistic history is to link that study to the development of dictionary skills, considered a necessity. This technique is apparent in the materials of the Center for Curriculum Development in English (1968) and suggested by Corcoran (1970, pp. 160–2), The Minnesota Center for Curriculum Development (1968a), Chenfield (1987) and is used by Hand, Harsh, Ney and Shane (1972e). Thus, it would appear that there is no shortage of ideas for the implementation of study of the history of the English language in the schools. What is lacking is the will to implement the studies and the research showing that such implementation is not only feasible but also beneficial for the students.

References

Ali, F. (1969). "Do You Know Where I Come From?" *Use of English* 21(1), 35–37. See also ERIC EJ 038 183.

Allen, D. (1980). *English Teaching Since 1965: How much Growth?* London: Heinemann Educational Books.

Anderson, P. S. (1988). *Language Skills in Elementary Education.* New York: Macmillan.

Atlanta Regional Curriculum Project. (1968). "History of the English Language." Atlanta, Ga. Regional Curriculum Project. Atlanta, Ga. (ERIC Document Reproduction Service No. ED 042 743)

Chenfield, M. B. (1987). *Teaching Language Arts Creatively.* San Diego, CA: Harcourt Brace Jovanovich.

Cleaver, B. P. (1976). Teaching the History of the English Language: A Study of English Programs in North Carolina Schools, 1974–1975. *Dissertation Abstracts International, 77,* 3573A. (University Microfilms No. 76-27,960).

Commission on the English Curriculum of the National Council of Teachers of English. (1952). *The English Language Arts.* New York: Appleton-Century-Crofts, Inc.

Commission on the English Curriculum of the National Council of Teachers of English. (1963). *The Education of Teachers of English.* New York: Appleton-Century-Crofts, Inc.

Commission on the English Curriculum of the National Council of Teachers of English. (1954). *Language Arts for Today's Children.* New York: Appleton-Century-Crofts, Inc.

Conlin, D. A., G. R. Herman & J. Martin (1966). *Our Language Today.* New York: American Book Co.

Corcoran, G. B. (1970). *Language Arts in the Elementary School: A Modern Linguistic Approach.* New York: The Ronald Press.

Crystal, David. (1981). *Directions in Applied Linguistics.* New York: Academic Press.

Donahue, M. R. (1985). *The Child and the English Language Arts.* Dubuque, IA: Wm. C. Brown Publishers.

Cushenbery, D. C. (1986). *Directing an Effective Language Arts Program for Your Students.* Springfield, IL: Charles C. Thomas.

Glatthorn, A. A. (1980). *A Guide for Developing an English Curriculum for the Eighties.* Urbana, IL.: National Council of Teachers of English.

Hadley, E. (1985). *English in the Middle Years.* London: Edward Arnold.

Hand, J. S., W. Harsh, J. W. Ney & H. G. Shane (1972a). *Adventures in English: Experiences in Language.* River Forest, IL: Laidlaw Brothers.

Hand, J. S., W. Harsh, J. W. Ney & H. G. Shane (1972b). *Discovering in English: Experiences in Language.* River Forest, IL: Laidlaw Brothers.

Hand, J. S., W. Harsh, J. W. Ney & H. G. Shane. (1972c). *Exploring in English: Experiences in Language.* River Forest, IL: Laidlaw Brothers.

Hand, J. S., W. Harsh, J. W. Ney & B. Folta. (1972d). *Growth in English: Experiences in Language.* River Forest, IL: Laidlaw Brothers.

Hand, J. S., W. Harsh, J. W. Ney & H. G. Shane. (1972e). *Progress in English: Experiences in Language.* River Forest, IL: Laidlaw Brothers.

Harder, Kelsie B. (1967). "Place Names in the Classroom." (ERIC Document Reproduction Service No. ED 017 500.)

Horn, R. E. (1967). *A Programmed Course in Language Change and Communication.* Chicago: Science Research Associates.

King, M. (1986). What is Language for?: A Functional View of the Language Arts. In P. Demers *The Creating Word* (pp. 158–177). London: Macmillan.

Kitzhaber, Albert R. (1968). *History of English, Parts 3 and 4—Old English to Early Modern—Language Curriculum V and VI, Teacher and Student Versions.* Eugene, OR: The University of Oregon. (ERIC Document Reproduction Service No. ED 015 920)

Lesiak, J. (1978). "The Origin of Words: A Unit of Study: Briefs." *Language Arts* 55(3), 317–9.

Mangieri, J. N., N. K. Staley & J. A. Wilhide. (1984). *Teaching Language Arts: Classroom Applications.* New York: McGraw Hill.

Marckwardt, A. H., (1963). "Research in the teaching of English language and Linguistics (A Summary)," *Proceedings of the Allerton Park Conference on Research in the teaching of English.* Robert W. Rogers, (ed.) Urbana: Unpublished Report of a USOE Project, #G-1006.

Milosh, J. E. Jr. (1972). *Teaching the History of the English Language in the Secondary Classroom.* Urbana, IL.: ERIC Clearinghouse on the Teaching of English and the National Council of Teachers of English, 1972.

Minnesota Center for Curriculum Development in English. (1968a). *A Historical Study of the English Lexicon.* Minneapolis, MN: The University of Minnesota, Center for Curriculum Development in English. (ERIC Document Reproduction Service No. ED 027 326.)

Minnesota Center for Curriculum Development in English. (1968b). *A Historical Study of English Phonology, Morphology, and Syntax.* Minneapolis, MN: The University of Minnesota, Center for Curriculum Development in English. (ERIC Document Reproduction Service No. ED 028 182)

Minnesota Center for Curriculum Development in English. (1968c). *The Dictionary: Describer or Prescriber?* Minneapolis, MN: The University of Minnesota, Center for Curriculum Development in English. (ERIC Document Reproduction Service No. ED 041 881)

Moffett, J. & B. J. Wagner. (1983). *Student-centered Language Arts and Reading K–13: A Handbook for Teachers.* Boston: Houghton Mifflin.

Moss, R. F. (1987). "Plumbing the Surfaces: The Value of Frivolous Subjects in Developmental English," *The English Record, 38,* 18–21.

Muinzer, L. A. (1960). "History: The Life in Language; and Historical Linguistics in the Classroom." (ERIC Document Reproduction Service No. ED 041 894, 1960. Reprinted from *The Illinois English Bulletin,*" 47(8), (May 1960) and 48(1), (October 1960).

Muller, Herbert J. (1967). *The Uses of English: Guidelines for the Teaching of English from the Anglo-American Conference at Dartmouth College.* New York: Holt, Rinehart and Winston.

Myers, D. T. (1984). *Understanding Language.* Upper Montclair, NJ: Boynton/Cook Publisher, Inc.

National Council of Teachers of English. (1967). *Comments and Exercises on Historical Linguistics.* Urbana, IL: National Council of Teachers of English. Also (ERIC Document Reproduction Service No. ED 144 086)

Northern Illinois Project English Curriculum Center. (1966). *History of the Language, Material for Incorporation in Curricula of Grades 11 and 12.* De Kalb, IL: Northern Illinois University, Project English Curriculum Center (ERIC Document Reproduction Service No. ED 019 259)

Nebraska Curriculum Development Center. (1966). *A Curriculum for English: Language Explorations for the Elementary Grades.* Lincoln, NE: University of Nebraska Press.

Ney, J. W., W. Harsh, D. Lapp, M. L. Myerson, & M. Armstead. (1979). *Good English: Blue Book.* River Forest, IL: Laidlaw Brothers.

North Carolina State Board of Education. (1968). *We speak with the tongue of men and of angels: Essays in the history of the english language.* Raleigh, NC: North Carolina State Board of Education, Dept. of Public Instruction. (ERIC Document Reproduction Service No. ED 029 886)

Oregon Elementary English Project. (1971). "History of the English Language: Language V-VI (Grades Five and Six); Teacher's Guide." Eugene, OR: University of Oregon, Oregon Elementary English Project. (ERIC Document Reproduction Service No. ED 075 838)

Peterson, B. (1987). "Why They Talk That Talk: Language in Appalachian Studies." *English Journal, 76*(6), 53–56.

Quandt, Ivan J. (1983). *Language Arts for the Child.* Englewood Cliffs, NJ: Prentice Hall.

Roberts, P. (1966). *The Roberts English Series: A Linguistics Program.* New York: Harcourt, Brace and World, Inc.

Savage, J. F. (1977). *Effective Communication: Language Arts Instruction in the Elementary School.* Chicago: Science Research Associates.

Staub, M. (1986). *Educational Linguistics.* Oxford: Basil Blackwell.

Tchudi, S., G. Boomer, M. Maguire, J. W. P. Creber, P. D'Arcy & F. Johnson (Eds.) (1986). *English Teachers at Work.* Upper Montclair, NJ: Boynton/Cook, Inc.

Tompkins, G. E. & D. B. Yaden Jr. (1986). *Answering Students' Questions about Words.* Urbana, IL: ERIC Clearinghouse on Reading and Communication Skills, National Council of Teachers of English. (ERIC Document Reproduction Service No. ED 268 548)

31B. GRAMMAR AND USAGE

George Hillocks, Jr.
Michael W. Smith

For two millennia, grammar has been central to school curricula. It was the subject of one of the earliest textbooks, antedated only by Euclid's text about geometry (Casson, 1985). Though grammar is ancient, conflicting views of what it is and what it is worth continue to haunt teachers. Research over a period of nearly 90 years has consistently shown that the teaching of school grammar has little or no effect on students. Still it seems to usurp a major portion of time available for the English curricula of today's schools. This chapter may not be able to explain that paradox but it will examine the questions surrounding it:

1. What meanings do we attach to the word grammar?
2. How did grammar develop as a school subject?
3. What is the evidence for the effects of teaching grammar on learning it, on thinking, on correctness, and on writing?

SOME DEFINITIONS OF GRAMMAR

In classical Greek and Latin, the *Oxford English Dictionary* (OED) explains, the word for *grammar* "denoted the methodical study of literature ... including textual and aesthetic criticism, investigation of literary history and antiquities, explanation of allusions," and so forth. Postclassically, *grammatica* came to apply largely to the linguistic rather than literary portion of this ancient discipline. The OED explains that in the Middle Ages grammar meant Latin grammar and was "often used as synonymous with learning in general, the knowledge peculiar to the learned class." Because the knowledge of the learned class was popularly supposed to include magic and astrology, grammar came to include these meanings that survive in what the OED calls corrupt forms: French, *grimoire* (book of spells or black book) and English, glamour (OED: magic, enchantment; a magical or fictitious beauty attaching to any person or object). Interestingly, the latter has appeared in English as a verb: to cast a spell on. We might say, then, that grammar has glamoured English teachers.

Hartwell (1985), building on an important article by Francis (1954), enumerates five "meanings" of grammar:

1. The set of formal patterns which speakers of a language use automatically to construct and construe larger meanings. These patterns are shared by all speakers though few may be able to explain what they are and how they work. Hartwell provides several examples of such internalized rules: e.g., the rule for the distribution of plural phonemes /s, iz, z/ in speech.
2. The scientific study (description, analysis, and articulation) of the formal patterns of a language. In some senses, traditional school grammar is of this type, but Francis really had structural linguistics in mind. We would have to include other kinds of grammar as well, generative, tagmemic, and case grammar, for example. This is the primary meaning provided by the OED.
3. A set of rules governing how one ought to speak or write. In this

sense, grammar is prescriptive rather than simply descriptive as is the case above. This is the third meaning offered by the OED.
4. The grammar taught in schools. This is somewhat misleading, suggesting, as it does, that school grammar is a distinct variety. It is not, however, for it combines all three of Francis' types. It assumes the existence of type one grammar in students. It provides what many teachers see as a "description" of language, although that "description" has little to do with the reality of language. And it certainly provides type three grammar, prescriptions for usage.
5. Grammatical terms and concepts used to help teach prose style. This has had little effect on the schools, yet such grammars and adaptations of them are being widely used by those who teach professionals and business people about clear style (e.g., Williams, 1981b).

THE DEVELOPMENT OF GRAMMAR AS A SCHOOL SUBJECT

In the ancient world grammar developed largely as a result of two needs. One was the philosophical desire "to understand nature in order to live a harmonious and therefore virtuous life" (Huntsman, 1983, p. 61). This tradition emanated from Aristotle and the Stoics, who saw language as imposing order on reality and grammar as a means of understanding language. However, they believed that grammar could not provide a complete understanding of language because as a product of man's nature, language is "subject to anomalies inexplicable within any strict system of grammar" (Huntsman, 1983, p. 61). The Alexandrian grammarians, on the other hand, worked in the world's first great library with texts several hundred years old. These they found to be filled with language they could no longer understand. They assumed, unlike the stoics, that language had once reflected reality. They attempted to find as many regularities as possible in order "to explain unusual or archaic forms by analogy" (Huntsman, 1983, p. 61). This practical need gave rise to dictionaries and to the first grammar text, published by Dionysios of Thrace late in the second century BC.

This grammar became the standard grammar for Greek school boys up until the twelfth century AD and the model upon which Latin grammars were based (Casson, 1985). And it has had a continuing impact on school grammars. Its assumptions that language forms can be explicated by analogy and that "right" forms are discoverable determined from the outset both the paradigmatic character of school grammars and their emphasis on correctness. Over two thousand years later these are still with us.

That first grammar by Dionysios of Thrace was short, treating only the phonological values of the alphabet and eight parts of speech: nouns, verbs, participles, articles, pronouns, prepositions, adverbs, and conjunctions. The parts of speech were defined primarily by their formal attributes although semantic definitions crept in. Later grammars, especially that by Appolonios Dyskolos, provided a description of Greek syntax and a model for describing syntax. The ideas of these Greek grammarians passed directly into their Roman successors' texts and from there into the works of two premedieval grammarians, Donatus and Priscian, whose works dominated school grammar study throughout the Middle Ages to the Renaissance. Donatus (fourth century) preserved the eight parts of speech of Dionysios' work, even though Latin had no article. He simply substituted the interjection. His parts of speech were defined by a mixture of formal and semantic features. Priscian (sixth century) defined the parts of speech primarily through semantic as opposed to formal characteristics. Thus, a verb is defined as signifying action or being, and an adverb as qualifying a verb. Even when the works of these two men were no longer in actual circulation, their ideas and procedures continued to influence school grammars.

School grammars for English first developed late in the eighteenth century. English was not a highly inflected language, although it once had been, and was, therefore, not suitable to the same paradigmatic treatment afforded Latin and Greek. Nonetheless, these grammars present nouns in paradigms that include nominative and objective cases. They treat other parts of speech and aspects of syntax much as had the medieval Latin grammars preceding them.

Although in the library of Alexandria, grammar had to be invented as a tool to help in the decoding of archaic forms in ancient texts, by the Middle Ages it had gone far beyond the status of mere tool. It had become the foundation of all knowledge. The beginning point of education in the seven liberal arts was the word. Grammar became, for most of the Middle Ages, the chief subject of the trivium (grammar, rhetoric, and logic), which was key to the quadrivium. Grammar was the "gateway" to all of knowledge, particularly sacred knowledge. "Grammar was thought to discipline the mind and the soul at the same time, honing the intellectual and spiritual abilities that the future cleric would need to read and speak with discernment" (Huntsman, 1983, p. 59). The major task of the cleric, according to Morrison (1983), was to use the arts, chief of which was grammar, first "to disclose the hidden mysteries of Scripture; and, second, to express esoteric doctrine for the wise, while disguising it from the simple without falsifying it" (p. 38). When Christians turned from Scripture to the arts themselves, they once again trusted to the power of grammar: "Their object was to examine . . . valid processes of reasoning, the operations of the mind itself. God had established these in the order of nature, but they too were hidden . . . by the fallacious content and methods of instruction in the arts" (Morrison, 1983, p. 39). The object of education then involved the near paradox of revealing the hidden truth of Scripture by means of arts that are themselves cloaked in error. In the Middle Ages grammar was the key to the entire enterprise.

Early English school grammar evolved from a direct application of Latin grammars to the English language. As Applebee (1974) explains, "Grammatical studies in the classical languages had traditionally emphasized two elements: the learning of rules, and their 'use' or practical application. An extensive methodology had grown up around both aspects, and this was transferred more or less intact to studies of English grammar" (p. 6). Indeed, school grammars commonly treated English as though it were a highly inflected language. One text, for example, by T. S. Pinneo (1850) presents nouns as having four cases:

nominative, possessive, objective, and independent. "Case," the author claims, "is that property of a noun which denotes its *relation to other words*" (p. 35). The case endings of Latin nouns did indeed denote the relationships among words. Indeed, they did in Old English. But they do not for modern English. These Latinate grammars taught that nouns are the names of things, that verbs denote actions or being, that sentences are complete thoughts. These grammars require that students parse sentences by attending to each word in turn and naming its part of speech, its properties (for nouns these include person, gender, number, and case), and its relationships to other words in the sentence.

For the most part, current grammar texts are direct descendants of these late eighteenth-century Latinate grammars and present what we will call traditional school grammar (TSG), Hartwell's type three. Except for less emphasis on the case and gender of nouns and mode of verbs, the declarations about the grammar of English found in most contemporary texts are essentially the same as those in their counterparts of nearly 200 years ago. However, since the 1950s, two more modern kinds of grammar, structural and generative, have had some impact on curricular thinking and instructional practice.

ATTACKS ON TRADITIONAL SCHOOL GRAMMAR (TSG)

Textbooks on grammar have remained largely impervious to direct criticisms of what they offer as knowledge worth having and to developments in the field of grammar.

The strongest and most typical criticism appears in C. C. Fries' *The Structure of English* (1952). First, Fries argues that TSG ignores many crucial features of English (e.g., phonology, morphology, pitch, stress, juncture), features that make differences in meaning. Second, he demonstrates that the categories of language that traditional school grammar attempts to establish are hopelessly ambiguous. TSG presents definitions that cannot function with desired results unless the person using them has more information about language than the definition provides. For example, traditional grammars tell us that a noun is the name of a person, place, or thing—and some add idea to the list. *Blue, red,* and *yellow* are the names of colors but would not be considered nouns in the phrase, the *blue* shirt. *Up, down,* and *across* are the names of directions but would not pass as nouns to most traditional grammarians. Fries points out that a large part of this difficulty arises because the definitions are not parallel. That is, a word like *blue* is the name of a color but, at the same time, can be used to modify a noun. It fits two definitions. The definition for nouns attempts to classify words according the lexical meanings, while that for adjectives classifies words by function (cf. Fries, 1952, pp. 65–86). In chapter after chapter Fries enumerates the ambiguities and unexplained paradoxes of TSG.

STRUCTURAL GRAMMAR

Structural grammarians believed that to avoid the difficulties of earlier grammars, they would have to examine a body of real language and describe it by means of its structural features rather than by semantic content. Gleason (1965) assigns the origins of such grammar to the work of nineteenth-century cultural anthropologists and philologists who wished to describe languages previously unknown to European and American scholarship and for which there was often no written version. Indeed, the purpose in describing the spoken language was often to devise a system of writing for the language.

The basic technique involves finding native speakers of the language and recording what they say. When a sufficient sample of the spoken language has been collected in its phonetic form, linguists analyze it into three levels: the phonological (significant sounds or alphabet), the morphological (words and parts of words that carry distinctive meaning), and the syntactic (sentence structures and substructures such as clauses and phrases). The grammar of a language is a description of all the elements in each of these levels.

Linguists identify the elements of these levels through structural features. At the phonological level, for example, they show that voicing was a structural contrastive feature of consonants, such that certain pairs of consonants differ only in that vocal cords vibrate for one but not the other. That is, the lips, teeth, and tongue are in the same positions for each member of a given pair. But the members of the pair contrast because one is voiced while the other is not: /b/ and /p/; /d/ and /t/; and /g/ and /k/, for instance.

In a similar way structural grammarians analyze parts of speech through structural features. Nouns, for example, take plural and possessive inflections; use certain derivational affixes as *-er, -ism,* and *-tion;* and fit in frames of the following kind: One _____ is here. A complete analysis of any form class in English is quite complex. (See, for example, Francis, 1958, pp. 237–288.)

Structural grammar examines syntax most commonly through immediate constituent analysis, a technique based on the assumption that linguistic structures may be analyzed by dichotomous cuts to the level of individual words and sometimes meaningful segments of words (morphemes). Although this analysis helps to show certain relationships among the words and phrases that constitute sentences, the rules for making the cuts were never clearly laid out. Structural grammar does not provide much insight into syntax.

The purpose of structural linguistics is to describe the structures in the language as it is used by native speakers. In doing that, the discipline had profound effects on the study of language. It provided a scientific basis for the study of language, allowed for far greater accuracy and detail in description, and avoided the prescriptivism of TSG that was often based on uninformed personal bias (Williams, 1981a).

However, certain basic assumptions of structural linguistics were to come under sharp criticism. One was its rejection of meaning as a criterion for the analysis of language. Some critics argued that the structuralists' own techniques contradicted this belief. That is, although a linguist may not know the meaning of a language, the native informant's identification of contrastive features depends upon the informant's knowledge of meaning.

A second important assumption inherent in descriptive procedures also came under attack: the philosophical view that language is what comes out of the mouth of a speaker. Assuming

that to be true, then no matter how large a sample of language is collected, it will remain a tiny proportion of what may be spoken. The experience of any speaker with a particular language is likely to be limited to a very small proportion of that language. His or her experience is likely to be accidental rather than systematic. Yet the speaker will be able to produce an infinite number of utterances he/she has not heard before but which will be recognized by other native speakers as "grammatical," that is, recognizable as an English utterance. ("Grammatical" here has nothing to do with correctness in the usual TSG sense.) Structural grammar provides no explanation of how that is possible.

GENERATIVE GRAMMAR

In a sense, generative grammar developed as a response to these problems in structural linguistics. One of the first questions Chomsky raises in *Syntactic Structures* (1957) is that of how a speaker whose experience with language is finite and essentially accidental "can produce or understand an indefinite number of new sentences" (p. 15). No matter how accurate a description of language structural linguistics might provide, the description cannot explain how sentences are formed or predict what might be formed. Beyond that, descriptive techniques, because they are limited to observations, can never explain structures that *can not* occur in a language. For example, no English speaker would produce the following utterance even though each word is an English word: Blinking drinks of into boxes fleas.

Descriptive techniques commonly used by structuralists for generalizing about rules for clusters within sentences are limited as well. For example, the test frame for adjective presented by Francis (1958) is "The _____ *noun* is very _____."

True adjectives are said to fit in both slots. If we fill the noun slot with the word *woman,* the adjectives *old, young, decrepit,* and *happy* fit both slots. If we change, the noun to *plate,* however, we find that although old, and possibly *decrepit,* fit both slots, *happy* and *young* fit only as metaphor. (*Young* cannot fit literally because the semantically appropriate contrast for *old* with inanimate nouns is *new.*) The structuralist attempt to reject meaning as a basis for analysis of relationships results in the failure to produce rules that account for such relationships.

Generative grammars reject the view that the whole of language is contained in actually observed utterances. On the contrary, they argue that language is an abstract entity and that utterances actually spoken represent epiphenomenal evidence of the existence of the abstract language. Many believe that Saussure's (1959) dichotomy of *langue* and *parole* is the source of this idea.

Chomsky (1957, 1965) and many others view grammar as theory of the language. Native speakers intuit the grammar of their languages. The task of grammarians is to make explicit the rules of the grammar operating the language. (It is important to note that the use of the term *rule* here has nothing to do with rules for correctness found in TSG.) In generative grammar, rules account for the production of sentences. Early generative grammars comparable to those used in a variety of studies (e.g., Elley, Barham, Lamb, & Wyllie, 1976; Mellon, 1969) regard a sentence as a "deep structure" containing

elements of semantic content such as boy play. The rules of the grammar act upon this deep structure and result in the "surface structure" that actually occurs: "The boy is playing." This sentence is only one of many possible surface structures that the grammar might generate: "A boy plays; a boy does play; a boy was playing; was a boy playing; where is the boy playing; etc."

The purpose of studying grammar, then, is to develop the rules that will explain how surface structures are generated from deep structures and to state these rules so that they have the widest possible generality in their application. (Hillocks, McCabe, & McCampbell, 1971, p. 427)

Chomsky was very careful to warn enthusiasts that his theoretic model did not represent the psychological processes of readers. In 1965 he wrote,

To avoid what has been a continuing misunderstanding, it is perhaps worthwhile to reiterate that a generative grammar is not a model for a speaker or a hearer. It attempts to characterize in the most neutral possible terms the knowledge of the language that provides the basis for actual use of language by a speaker-hearer. When we speak of a grammar as generating a sentence with a certain structural description, we mean simply that the grammar assigns this structural description to the sentence. (p. 9)

Since the advent of generative grammar, research in linguistics has continued, actively generating new insights and theories. Grammatical studies have displayed a constantly changing knowledge base. However, school curricula in grammar have ignored these developments. Schools contemplating the serious study of grammar should at least consider grammars more consistent with current linguistic theory.

DIALECT

The focus of descriptive linguists on the variation of actual utterances led quite naturally to the study of dialect. Dialecticians, working within the traditions of structural linguistics, have shown that most differences in usage among speakers cannot be considered aberrations from some standard preferred speech with its origins in a distant Edenic past when all things were perfect. Rather, most variations in usage derive from different language communities that develop their own varying norms. Labov (1972) has argued forcefully, for example, that what he calls Black Vernacular English (BVE) is not simply a mass of error as was thought by earlier researchers. On the contrary, Labov shows clearly that BVE is "a distinct subsystem within the larger grammar of English" (pp. 63–64) with its own regular conventions and a few clearly different rules for the production of utterances.

One such rule, for example, allows for what Labov (1972) calls a remote present perfect in the use of *been* in an expression usch as, "I been know your name" (pp. 53–55), in which *been know* means *have known for a long time* and *still know*. Heath (1983) explains that such forms cause difficulty in classrooms when teachers do not know BVE usage, for they often interpret them as Standard English past perfect as in the following revealing incident related by Heath:

A teacher asked one day: "Where is Susan? Isn't she here today?" Lem answered "She ain't ride de bus." The teacher responded: "She doesn't ride the bus, Lem." Lem answered: "She do be ridin' de bus." The teacher frowned at Lem and turned away. Within the system of Black English Lem used, ain't was used as equivalent to didn't, the negative of the past tense of auxiliary do; thus his answer had to be interpreted as "She didn't ride the bus." The teacher heard the ain't as equivalent to doesn't and corrected Lem accordingly; he rejected this shift of meaning and asserted through his use of do be ridin' that Susan did indeed regularly ride the bus. (pp. 277–278)

In addition to demonstrating the internal regularities of BVE and how failures to comprehend it lead to serious misunderstandings by educators, linguists have also demonstrated that speakers of BVE develop a finely honed sense of logic and argument within their own language conventions (Labov, 1972, pp. 201–240). Further, Heath (1983) has shown in rich detail how conflicting language conventions of people living and working in the same community lead to misunderstandings on the part of teachers and students, to inappropriate judgments of the students, and hence to failure to learn on both sides of the desk. Heath has also provided accounts of how teachers in one community found ways to overcome such problems.

GRAMMAR: KNOWLEDGE AND LEARNING

Knowledge about language has been systematized in various ways and taught for over 2000 years. Reasons for such study have varied: in the ancient world to recover the meaning of old texts and in the Middle Ages to provide the foundation for art and knowledge. In general, modern proponents of grammar instruction cite three reasons for teaching it:

1. The insight it offers into the way the language works,
2. Its usefulness in mastering standard forms of English, and
3. Its usefulness in improving composition skill.

A great deal of research in the past nine decades has been devoted to investigating the validity of these and other reasons for studying grammar. At the same time, it has become clear that native speakers intuit a grammar of greater complexity than has so far been described by linguists. Further, it is doubtful that this complexity can be taught. What follows briefly reviews studies of tacit knowledge and then turns to studies that investigate effectiveness of teaching grammar 1) to understand language as a supreme human achievement, 2) to improve compositions, and 3) to improve usage. Finally, the chapter will examine the use of tacit grammatical concepts to enhance students' syntactic versatility—sentence combining and sentence construction.

STUDENTS' TACIT KNOWLEDGE OF GRAMMAR

If knowledge of grammar is defined as the ability to produce and understand a wide range of grammatical structures, then students have a substantial knowledge of grammar before they receive any formal instruction. In her extensive study of the language of elementary school children in grades 1 through 6, Strickland (1962) concludes "that children learn fairly thoroughly at an early age the basic structures of their language" (p. 106). Strickland's finding has been corroborated by a variety of researchers. Hunt (1965) notes that "the average child in the fourth grade produces virtually all the grammatical structures ever described in a course in school grammar ..." (p. 156). O'Donnell, Griffin, and Norris (1967) in their study of kindergarten and elementary school children found that kindergarteners produced essentially the same sentence patterns as seventh graders. Labov (1970) argues on the basis of his study of speakers of nonstandard dialects that "the child who comes to school is already in possession of an extremely complex set of linguistic rules—more complex than any linguist is now able to describe" (p. 48). He explains that "most linguistic roles ... are not consciously recognized and are never violated" (p. 29).

One example of such an "automatic rule" is the rule of contracting *is* to *'s*. Labov explains that even though no one is taught the complex conditions under which one can make the contraction, native speakers would say He's here, but would never say *Here he's*. Hartwell (1985) offers another example. He reports asking a variety of people, from sixth graders to high school teachers, to cite the rule for combining adjectives of age, nationality, and number in English. No one is able to do so. However, when he asked these same people to arrange the words *French the young girls four* in a natural order, all native speakers immediately produce "the four young French girls." Interestingly, when he provided the rule for using the definite article, the indefinite article, or no article and asked native speakers to apply it in a passage in which the articles were deleted, he found that most native speakers reported "a great deal of frustration." He concludes that "the rule ... is, for the most part, simply unusable for native speakers of the language" (p. 116). Shaughnessy (1977) in her study of basic writers in college composition explains that "despite their difficulties with common errors, their intuitions about English are the intuitions of native speakers. Most of what they need to know has already been learned—without teachers" (p. 129). Quite clearly, students have an immense amount of grammatical knowledge without any formal instruction.

The fact that students enter school with this knowledge already in place does not imply that they do not develop during their years of formal schooling. Hunt (1965) notes that the younger student

does not produce as many [grammatical structures] at the same time—as many inside each other, or on top of each other—as older students do. He does subordinate some clauses to others, but not as many. He does reduce some coordinate clauses to coordinations inside a single clause, but not enough.... He does write some complicated nominals, but his are never most highly complicated. It is what the older students does *in extremis* that especially distinguishes him. (p. 156)

Hunt's findings that more mature writers produce longer T-units with more embeddings were supported by O'Donnell, Griffin, and Norris (1967) who especially note an increase in

making structures more compact through deletion transformations. Loban (1976) noted that these two characteristics together with increased elaboration and a reduction in mazes (confused patterns) most clearly distinguished the language of proficient subjects as compared with those who use language ineffectively. Each of the groups (high, random, and low) in his longitudinal study of childrens' language from kindergarten through twelfth grade was characterized by "steady nondramatic chronological development" (p. 84) in most of the language behavior he studied.

GRAMMAR FOR APPRECIATION OF HUMAN LANGUAGE

Since the 1960s, one of the most frequently cited reasons for studying grammar is its humanistic value. Weaver (1979) lists it first among various reasons offered for teaching grammar. "The study of grammar is important simply because language is a supreme (and perhaps unique) human achievement which deserves to be studied as such" (p. 3). This, of course, is not an empirically arguable claim, but it has an empirical dimension. That is, researchers can ask whether students are successful in learning the system of grammar taught in order to understand the working of language.

Generally speaking, as indicated above, linguists regard TSG as an inadequate description and explanation of how the English language works. If we wish to teach grammar for humanistic reasons, it seems to follow that the curriculum should make use of relatively current knowledge about grammar. Structural grammar had some currency during the 1960s. Alva (1960), for example, reports that structural grammar was generally taught in California schools in 1960 and seemed to be increasing in popularity. Also in the 1960s, structural and generative grammars were incorporated into the curricula developed by the Project English Curriculum Centers at Nebraska and Oregon and by the Euclid (Ohio) Western Reserve Project English Demonstration Center.

Some researchers have considered the newer effects of grammars. For example, Bateman and Zidonis (1966) contrast the effects on ninth graders of two years of instruction in a generative grammar as compared with a control group that studied no grammar. They report a statistically significant difference in the number of well-formed sentences written by the experimental group. Working with classes from 21 schools, Smith and Sustakowski (1968) compared the effects of a structural grammar to the effects of traditional grammar. As one might expect, they report large gains on the *Modern Language Aptitude Test* by the group that studied structural grammar. The MLAT measures sensitivity to phonological, morphological, and syntactic structures, something the structural group studied but the traditional group did not. (However, the researchers did not find significant differences on a variety of measures of correctness.)

In 1966, the Dartmouth Conference of British and American scholars and teachers concerned with the teaching of English agreed in principle that language study "may be justified simply as a humanistic study, valuable in itself" (Muller, 1967, p. 72). However, when they considered a curricular document purporting to teach a newer grammar, in Muller's words, "Disaster struck.... It looked just as dreary as the old exercises in grammar. The British were appalled by it; they wanted to know how these ghastly exercises could be considered 'humanistic' " (p. 72). Muller himself states that "the clearest contribution of linguistics to the teaching of English remains its studies of usage, not the new modes in grammatical exercises" (p. 73). The Dartmouth Conference may have sounded the death knell of newer grammars in the schools.

The value of studying grammar for humanistic reasons is dependent on the extent to which students learn it and on how they feel about learning it. Some studies examine the extent to which students learn the grammar they are taught. Briggs (1913) reports that groups with considerable training in TSG did less well on a test of formal grammar than students with no such instruction. The test included items examining the ability to parse and to identify types of clauses and complete sentences. One item included parsing a predicate attribute of the object that "represents the effect of the act expressed in the predicate on that which the object represents" (p. 294).

Macauley (1947) examines knowledge of grammar using a seemingly simpler test. He presented Scottish students at various levels sets of sentences and asked that they identify the nouns, verbs, adjectives, and adverbs. He administered the test to 131 students who had completed primary school with 30 minutes of grammar instruction daily for four years. With passing set at 50 percent, only one student passed. Thirty-seven percent passed on nouns, 21 percent on verbs, and only 5 and 4 percent passed on adjectives and adverbs respectively. He administered the same tests to students completing the elite senior secondary school that, in Scotland, admitted only the top 20 percent of junior secondary school graduates. These students had studied grammar for nine years. Of these top students only 42 percent were able to identify 50 percent of the items correctly. In other words, in Macauley's study, a majority of even the most capable students failed to learn what teachers think of as fundamental concepts of TSG.

It may be that the inherent ambiguities of TSG identified by Fries (1952) make learning parts of speech extremely difficult even for the best students. Or it may be that the subject of grammar is so abstract that it is difficult to learn. Whatever the reason, if students cannot or do not learn the fundamental concepts, the class time spent on the study of grammar in order to appreciate language as a human achievement is wasted.

A few studies inquire into student attitudes toward the study of language. Hillocks (1971) surveyed attitudes toward English of over 3000 high school students in three predominantly blue-collar suburban communities. He reports that students rated the study of TSG and mechanics as the least interesting part of their English programs. Elley, et al. (1976), whose study included two different grammar treatments (TSG and generative), reports that both groups found English less "interesting" than the no-grammar group. In regard to feelings about sentence study and language textbooks, the generative grammar group "showed predominantly negative attitudes, especially on such dimensions as 'useless,' 'unimaginative,' 'repetitive,' 'passive,' 'complicated,' and 'unpleasant.' Clearly, the [generative gram-

mar] strand of the Oregon Curriculum was not popular" (p. 16).

In short, there is little to suggest that students either learn grammar or enjoy it. Such findings seem to weaken the case for promoting formal grammar study in the schools in the hope that students will appreciate language as "a supreme (and perhaps unique) human achievement" (Weaver, 1979, p. 3).

GRAMMAR AND COMPOSITION

In their 1963 review of research in written composition, Braddock, Lloyd-Jones, and Schoer make this now-famous pronouncement: "The teaching of formal grammar has a negligible or, because it usually displaces some instruction and practice in actual composition, even a harmful effect on the improvement of writing" (pp. 37–38). Hillocks (1986) in his review of research in written composition done from 1963 to 1982 makes an equally strong statement:

School boards, administrators, and teachers who impose the systematic study of traditional school grammar on their students over lengthy periods of time in the name of teaching writing do them a gross disservice which should not be tolerated by anyone concerned with the effective teaching of good writing. (p. 248)

Hillocks bases his conclusion both on his narrative review (with Smith) of studies and his meta-analysis of composition studies (1986), 14 of which involved grammar as either the experimental or control treatment.

Of all of the studies Hillocks and Smith reviewed, by far the most impressive is by Elley, et al. (1976). Meckel (1963) comments that the training periods in many studies "have been comparatively short, and the amount of grammar instruction has frequently been small" (p. 981). In contrast, Elley and associates consider the achievement of New Zealand high school students as they moved through the third, fourth, and fifth forms and in a follow-up one year after the completion of instruction. The time period is notable. The sample is large (248 students at the outset and 166 after three years) and carefully controlled. Students were divided into eight classes matched on the basis of four test scores, sex, ethnicity, contributing school, and subject option. Three of these classes studied the Oregon curriculum, which included generative (transformational) grammar. Three other classes studied the same curriculum, replacing the study of transformational grammar with extra literature and creative writing. The final two classes studied TSG. The instruction in literature for these classes was centered on the study of six to eight sets of popular fiction. During each year of the study, teachers taught a different treatment so that no one method was taught by the same teacher for more than one year. The researchers used a variety of measures after each year of the study: tests of reading, listening, English usage, spelling, English literature, and sentence combining; criterion reference scales on essays the students had written; and attitude surveys.

The findings are notable, not for the differences that

emerged, but rather for the lack of differences. At the end of the first year, no significant differences among groups existed on any of the measures. At the end of the second year the traditional grammar group's essay content was significantly better than the no grammar group, and the generative grammar group's attitude toward writing and literature was significantly worse than the other two groups. At the end of the third year the generative grammar group and the no grammar group performed significantly better on the sentence combining test. Both grammar groups performed significantly better on the English usage test. However, there were no significant differences in the quality or correctness of students' actual writing. The fact that the differences among groups was small is clear. Indeed, even the superiority of the grammar groups on the test of English usage is questionable because it "was dispersed over a wide range of mechanical conventions, and was not clearly associated with sentence structure" (Elley et al., 1976, p. 15). This advantage must be weighed against the negative effect of studying grammar on students' attitudes toward English.

A variety of studies corroborate the most important finding of Elley and associates: Teaching grammar does not have a beneficial effect on students' writing. White (1965), Whitehead (1966), J. L. Sullivan (1969), and Bowden (1979) all compared the effects of teaching traditional school grammar with the effects of teaching no grammar and found no significant differences.

Perhaps the strongest support for the conclusion of Elley et al. is Hillocks' (1986) meta-analysis of composition studies. To be included in the meta-analysis a study had to meet several criteria, among them consideration of students' actual writing and not standardized measures of writing quality, appropriate scoring procedures, at least minimal teacher controls, and reporting of data that allowed the computation of effect size.

Meta-analysis has several important advantages as an analytic tool. In the first place, it focuses on the size of gains (effect size), and not simply on statistical significance, which depends in part on the number of subjects in a study. Secondly, because it pools data from several sources and tests the similarity of findings through a homogeneity statistic, it can determine whether or not a study's findings are merely idiosyncratic.

For the purposes of the meta-analysis, Hillocks groups treatments that focus on grammar with those that focus on mechanics and those that combine instruction in grammar and mechanics. Of all of the studies on grammar and mechanics, only three, Elley et al. (1976), A. E. Thibodeau (1964), and A. L. Thibodeau (1964), meet the criteria for inclusion and, in addition, compare the study of grammar and/or mechanics to some other instruction. These three studies include a total of five treatments. Hillocks reports that students in the grammar and/or mechanics treatments score .29 standard deviations lower than students in the control no grammar and/or mechanics treatments. Further, this is a highly homogeneous effect.

Hillocks also examines the pre- to posteffect sizes of all treatments focusing on grammar in studies qualifying for the meta-analysis. This allows inclusion of nine control treatments that appear in other categories when experimental/control effects are examined. The resulting 14 treatments of grammar and/or

mechanics produce a mean pre- to postgain of .06 standard deviations. In contrast, the mean pre- to postgain for the 75 treatments that include no instruction in grammar and/or mechanics is .44 of a standard deviation. This difference is quite large and highly significant (p < .0001). Apparently any focus of instruction is more effective in improving the quality of writing than grammar and mechanics.

Nonetheless, many classroom teachers reject this finding and are suspicious of those who offer it. Taylor (1986) explains that "teachers working with student writing know that their students need some knowledge of language and its conventions" (p. 95). She notes further: "When 'experts' tell teachers that the research says that grammar should not be taught at all, teachers are suspicious of the research and inclined to reject it" (p. 95). This is especially true when teachers equate the recommendation not to teach grammar with a lack of concern with "correctness."

GRAMMAR AND USAGE

Supporters of grammar instruction argue that the study of grammar is essential in improving writing quality because grammar instruction will reduce error rates in mechanics and usage. As we have seen, many items that teachers regard as errors (e.g., he don't) are not. They simply follow the rules of the dialect spoken by the person using them. It is unreasonable to expect a few minutes of studying TSG each day to result in changing patterns learned and reinforced over many years. Deviations from the conventions of formal written Standard English (e.g., punctuation and capitalization) are of a different sort and are treated elsewhere in this volume. (See the chapter by Hodges.) Briefly, however, research suggests that the study of formal grammar has little effect on learning these conventions. As noted earlier, Elley et al. (1976) found no significant difference between the grammar and no grammar groups on the mechanics rating of students' actual writing.

Supporters of grammar instruction also argue that students must learn grammar so that teachers and students have a common vocabulary to discuss writing. The question of the importance of grammatical terminology is one the research has not fully answered. Research does make it clear that students have difficulty applying their knowledge of grammatical terms. As we have seen, students tend not to learn even the fundamental concepts of grammar (Macauley 1947). Teaching grammatical terms to provide teachers a quick way to grade papers does not seem justified. Hartwell (1985) explains that the rules of traditional grammar are "COIK," clear only if known. Hillocks, McCabe, and McCampbell (1971) come to a similar conclusion: "If the student understands the error he has made, the problem is not grammar but proofreading and should consequently be treated differently. If he does not understand the error, the teacher's reference to it will be futile" (p. 411).

Shaughnessy (1977) explains that to be useful a student's knowledge of grammatical terms must go well beyond the ability to state definitions. She advocates teaching four key concepts: the sentence, inflection, tense, and agreement. She makes it clear that learning something as complex as the third person singular inflections requires far more detailed knowledge than provided by most traditional instruction in grammar. At present, however, research does not suggest how much or what kinds of instruction in grammar writers must have to reduce errors significantly.

The analysis of errors students make may suggest directions for instruction. For example, Kagan (1980) presents two tests to 202 remedial college freshmen. One test consists of 15 different syntactic structures together with five complete sentences randomly ordered. She asks students to identify which are sentences or parts of sentences. She finds that students most often mistake a verb plus a subordinate clause, a verb plus a direct object and a prepositional phrase, and two prepositional phrases for sentences. Her analysis of a similar test on run-on sentences reveals that the most common errors relate to combinations of long and short sentences. This study suggests that learning to identify basic sentence patterns and expand them in a variety of ways might help students identify sentence boundaries more consistently.

Taylor (1986) argues that teachers cling to traditional grammar because they have not developed alternative approaches. Unfortunately, ways to improve students' "correctness," an issue important to teachers, have been largely neglected by researchers.

SENTENCE COMBINING

In his preface to Hunt's 1965 study, G. Robert Carlsen states that "the school's program should facilitate the student's moving in the direction of mature writing patterns" (p. vi). Mellon's 1969 study was the first consideration of instruction designed to do just that. Mellon theorized that applying a knowledge of transformational grammar to concrete sentence combining (SC) problems would result in greater "syntactic fluency." (Other researchers use the term syntactic maturity.) That is, he believed that the experimental treatment would result in students' writing longer T-units that would display enhanced growth in the use of the types of transformations that Hunt found characterized mature syntax. He was right, and this "pioneering experiment . . . laid the foundations for subsequent experimental research in sentence combining" (Kerek, Daiker, & Morenberg, 1980, p. 1061).

However, SC did not become an important focus of instruction until O'Hare's 1973 study. O'Hare hypothesized that the gains in Mellon's experimental group were the result of sentence-combining practice rather than knowledge of transformational grammar. To test his hypothesis, O'Hare's experimental group worked with combining sets of sentences into increasingly complex structures. The combinations were cued by connecting words rather than by grammatical terminology. O'Hare reports significant increases in syntactic fluency on a variety of measures as well as an overall growth in quality.

Since O'Hare's study, SC has been enormously popular. Cooper (1975) argues that "no other single teaching approach has ever consistently been shown to have a beneficial effect on syntactic maturity and writing quality" (p. 72). Mellon (1979)

concurs: "The best evidence I can give teachers today, relative to sentence combining, is—Do it!" (p. 35).

Sentence Combining and Syntactic Fluency. Kerek, Daiker, and Moreberg (1980) report that SC "has been proven again and again to be an effective means of fostering growth in syntactic maturity" (p. 1067). In a later review Hillocks and Mavrogenes (1986) consider the "host" of SC studies done from 1973 to 1982. They report that "the overwhelming majority of these studies have been positive, with about 60 percent of them reporting that work in sentence combining, from as low as grade 2 through the adult level, results in significant advances (at least $p < .05$) on measures of syntactic maturity" (pp. 142–143). Further, they report that an additional 30 percent of the studies found some improvement at a nonsignificant level. Only 10 percent of the studies that Hillocks and Mavrogenes review are negative, showing no differences or mixed results.

In addition to working with all ages of subjects, SC appears to increase syntactic fluency in all types of students. Hunt and O'Donnell (1970), Ross (1971), Perron (1975), Schuster (1976, 1977), and Waterfall (1978) report that remedial or disadvantaged students especially benefit from sentence-combining instruction. Stoddard and Renzulli (1983) indicate that SC is effective for above-average students.

Research, however, does not provide unqualified support for using SC. Perhaps the most important question is whether longer T-units, the most common measure of syntactic fluency, are desirable. Hake and Williams (1979) argue that when students who were initially judged to be incompetent writers become competent writers, their T-unit length decreases.

A variety of correlational studies also question whether syntactic fluency as it is commonly measured is an important curricular goal. Faigley (1979) examines the correlations between measures for a set of pretest and posttest narratives by college freshmen. He finds that measures related to elaboration (words in final free modifiers, percent of T-units with final free modifiers, and overall length) were significantly related to the quality of writing. Syntactic measures unrelated to elaboration, however, are not significant.

Other studies have also shown a very low correlation between mean T-unit length and quality ratings: Belanger (1978), Nold and Freedman (1977), Stewart and Grobe (1979), and Wille (1982). The only significant correlation between T-unit length and writing quality was for Stewart and Grobe's fifth graders, and their other results strongly suggest that the significance of this relationship decreases as students continue in school. These findings question whether the overwhelming evidence that SC increases syntactic fluency is sufficient justification for recommending its use.

Other studies question the reliability of T-unit length as a measure of syntactic fluency. Martinez San Jose (1973), Perron (1977), and Crowhurst and Piche (1979) all strongly suggest that different modes of discourse produce different syntactic structures as well as different mean T-unit lengths. It may be that mean T-unit length is a function of the writer's purpose in a specific piece of writing. If so, mean T-unit length cannot be an effective measure of syntactic fluency.

Even if one accepts the importance of syntactic fluency measures, however, questions about SC remain. A variety of studies have considered whether gains in syntactic fluency are maintained. Several studies (Combs, 1977; Maimon & Nodine, 1979; Morenberg, Daiker, & Kerek, 1978; Pederson, 1978) suggest that gains are maintained for a period of several months. Other studies, however, offer clearly negative (Callaghan, 1978; Green, 1973) or somewhat negative (Combs, 1976; Ofsa, 1975; M. A. Sullivan, 1978, 1979) answers to this question.

Strong (1986) labels the Morenberg, Daiker, and Kerek study "probably the best designed, best funded, and most carefully executed SC study to date" (p. 7). In their 1978 study of 290 college freshmen, Morenberg, Daiker, and Kerek report that the experimental group, whose instruction focused on whole-discourse, open SC problems scored significantly higher on holistic and analytic measures than the control group, whose instruction focused on modes of discourse. They also report that these gains were maintained for several months. However, 28 months after the instruction Kerek, Daiker, and Morenberg (1980) gave their subjects a delayed posttest and found that although the experimental group's scores did not decline, the control group gained significantly without specific instruction. These results suggest that syntactic fluency may be, in part, the result of maturity. They raise a question of the ultimate benefits of accelerating what may be natural development.

A related question is whether SC acutally increases students' skill in manipulating syntax or rather simply cues them to make use of resources they already have. Smith and Combs (1980) study this question. They presented three assignment conditions to college freshmen:

1. The assignment with no cue about structure,
2. The assignment plus a cue indicating that the audience would be impressed with long, complex sentences, and
3. A covert cue of two days of SC.

Their results indicate that a combination of the overt and covert cues over one week produced mean gains in words per clause comparable to those gains produced by a semester of SC practice in other studies. Smith and Hull (1985) also consider the power of SC as a cue. Their study targets three syntactic structures: relative clauses, appositives, and infinitive nominals. They selected students who used these three structures significantly more or less than average on the basis of a pretest writing sample. They explained to these high-use and low-use students that because the students had an idiosyncratic problem, they were to do SC exercises. The results indicate that the high-use groups reduced their use of each of the targeted structures while the low-use group increased their use of the structures on a posttest. The authors theorize that the SC exericises act as a cue to increase or decrease the structures. Further, they report that the cue retained its strength for the low-use group when they revised both the pretest and the posttest. However, they report that the strength of the cue diminished for the high-use group who increased their use of the targeted structures on their revisions of the pretest and the posttest.

On balance, the evidence strongly suggests that SC increases syntactic maturity, but by itself this evidence does not stand as an unqualified endorsement of SC. A Far more important question is, What are the effects of SC on writing quality?

Sentence Combining and Writing Quality. A variety of studies (Combs, 1976, 1977; Howie 1979; Morenberg, Daiker & Kerek, 1978; Obenchain 1979; Ofsa 1975; O'Hare, 1973; Pederson, 1978; Schuster, 1976, 1977; Stewart, 1978; Stoddard & Renzulli, 1983; Waterfall, 1978) examine the effect of SC on writing quality.

Hillocks (1986) examines each of these studies in his meta-analysis of composition studies, with the exception of Stoddard and Renzulli (1983), which was published after Hillocks had collected his data. He includes four in his meta-analysis (Howie, 1979; Morenberg, Daiker, & Kerek, 1978; Pederson, 1978; Waterfall, 1978), grouping them with Faigley's 1979 study of sentence construction, one of the few studies that considers an experimental treatment derived from Christensen's (1967) generative rhetoric.

Hillocks' meta-analysis reports a highly homogeneous effect size of .35 standard deviations. This effect is significantly greater than the average effect of grammar ($-.29$), free writing (.16), and the study of models (.22). The mean effect size of SC is approximately the same as the effect size of treatments using rating scales (.36). Only the inquiry focus (.56) has a significantly greater effect size than SC. A subsequent meta-analysis by William Asher (1988) includes the studies Hillocks uses as well as several that failed to meet Hillocks' criteria, and found the same effect size without the homogeneity.

In light of the question about the importance of syntactic fluency to writing quality, what could explain these results. Hillocks (1986) cites research by Bereiter and Scardamalia (1982) as one possible explanation. He notes that Bereiter and Scardamalia found that when children revise, they avoid changing basic sentence plans. Shaughnessy's (1977) analysis of sentence consolidation errors suggests that basic writers are plagued by the same tendency. Perhaps sentence combining provides students with a more systematic repertoire of syntactic choices and helps them avoid this difficulty.

Crowhurst (1983) offers three possible explanations. She notes that the increase in writing quality may be the result of

1. Increased practice in writing sentences,
2. Greater facility in constructing sentences, and
3. An increased attention to other aspects of composing as a consequence of students' facility in constructing sentences.

Strong (1986) supports Crowhurst's third alternative. He believes that "SC may help with automaticity in syntax, freeing up mental energy so that learners can concentrate on planning and composing" (p. 3). He also argues that revising and editing are the main skills affected by SC practice.

Freedman (1985) believes that SC promotes skill in perceiving relationships on the T-unit level and that this skill transfers to the whole-text level. She contends that because SC causes students to search for these relationships, they develop a habit of mind that, in turn, extends conceptual knowledge.

Why does SC improve students' writing? Experimental research has raised an important question that can best be answered by descriptive studies, for example, case studies of why writers make certain syntactic choices or how concern for syntax assists or interferes with planning and composing. A consideration of questions like these would be a fruitful direction for future research.

Sentence Combining and Error. Another area of concern for researchers is the effect of SC on error. Ross (1971) finds that her experimental group had fewer inaccurate sentences in their posttest essays than did her control group, but the results were not statistically significant. Schuster's (1976, 1977) experimental groups also exhibit fewer errors on their posttest essays, both in usage and mechanics. Obenchain (1979) finds substantial decreases in errors of emphasis, punctuation, and spelling. Argall (1982) reports her success in reducing a variety of errors in her developmental students' writing through the use of sentence combining. Strong (1986) cites Powell's (1984) conclusion that "SC appeared to reduce errors over a sixteen-week period" (p. 9). On the other hand, Maimon and Nodine (1978, 1979) find that SC practice results in more errors on a rewriting passage, though this is not true for free writing. Hake and Williams (1979) report a higher "flaw count" with increased T-unit length. In their study, flaws include problems of content and organization as well as uage and punctuation. Strong cites Guttry (1982) who finds that SC is no more effective in reducing errors of community college freshmen, Jackson (1982) who finds that SC practice does not reduce the errors of basic writers, and Hayes (1984) who finds that SC instruction is no more effective than regular instruction in reducing error.

Clearly, these findings produce mixed results. Perhaps that is to be expected. If instruction results in students' experimenting with more complex structures, errors are bound to result. On the other hand, if SC practice focuses on producing specific structures and learning how to punctuage those structures, it is likely to prove effective.

This raises another set of questions that researchers could profitably pursue, for example, How do teachers use SC? What instructional techniques promote what sort of changes? Researchers might sharpen their focus in their consideration of SC. Strong notes that only Henderson (1980) considers the relative effects of different SC treatments. (She finds that signaled exercises promote a greater gain in clauses per T-unit, but that open exercises produce more nonclausal embeddings and a greater improvement in quality.)

Sentence Combining and Reading. Kerek, Daiker, and Morenberg (1980) state that "after 10 years of prolific research and in spite of some promising results, Mellon's early remark that sentence combining practice 'may contribute to the development of reading ability' (1969, p. 75) still remains more a reasonable possibility than an unassailable fact" (p. 1072). Not only the inconsistent results of this body of research, but also the variety of measures and control groups employed make generalization extremely difficult. For example, Straw and Schreiner (1982) compare the results of 25 lessons of SC to the results of labelling and identifying sentence parts for fourth graders. They found a significant difference favoring SC on a cloze test, but no significant difference on a standardized test of reading comprehension. On the other hand, Levine (1977) compares the results of 96 lessons combining SC exercises with instruction from a basal

text to without SC for third graders. She reports a significant difference on a standardized test favoring the SC group, but no significant difference between the groups on a cloze test. Several studies report significant results on one set of measures, but no significant results on others. Until researchers can agree on effective measures of reading comprehension that would be sensitive to changes that might come as a result of lessons in SC, it is unlikely that any clear conclusions in this area will emerge.

IMPLICATIONS FOR TEACHING AND RESEARCH

From all accounts, despite the huge body of research over the past 90 years, grammar remains a potent force in the curriculum of today's schools. Curriculum outlines and guides in many schools demand that great blocks of time be spent on grammar. Publishers say privately that composition texts lacking the usual thorough (and lengthy) grammar section will lose sales to texts that have it. State guidelines (e.g., Texas) insist on extensive treatments of grammar in textbooks.

Why does grammar retain such glamour when research over the past 90 years reveals not only that students do not learn it and are hostile toward it, but that the study of grammar has no impact on writing quality? Many explanations have been adduced, some not so flattering: it is easy to teach by simply assigning page and exercise numbers; it is easy to grade; it provides security in having "right" answers, a luxury not so readily available in teaching writing or literature; it helps to demarcate social distinctions, at the same time raising the teacher to a higher class by virtue of at least seeming to possess a prestige dialect; and it is an instrument of power by which one may hold those unable to learn in thrall. The more generous explanations for the persistence of grammar have to do with the lingering legacy of the Middle Ages—the belief that grammar is the key to something else. At the very least, teachers say, grammar provides the basis for "correctness" in writing, for putting commas and periods in the conventional places.

Unfortunately, the research provides no evidence to suggest that the study of grammar helps students become more proficient at placing punctuation in the spots designated by the style sheets. We assume that to proofread with any care, some knowledge of grammar must be necessary. What knowledge that is and how it is acquired are questions that have not been explored. It may be that a less ambiguous grammar that proceeded from basic sentence patterns (cf. Roberts, 1962) to increasingly complex expansions would help students learn to identify clause, phrase, and sentence boundaries. Perhaps more research of the kind conducted by Kagan (1980) will provide insight into student conceptions of sentences. Research in these areas may provide some solutions to the nagging problems of correctness.

Until we have such knowledge, the grammar sections of a textbook should be treated as a reference tool that might provide some insight into conventions of mechanics and usage. It should *not* be treated as a course of study to improve the quality of writing. Several far more successful paths to improving writing are available (Hillocks, 1986). If grammar is to be treated as a humanistic study, TSG alone is inadequate. It must be supplemented with more accurate, less ambiguous grammars with greater explanatory power.

References

Alva, C. A. (1960). Structural grammar in California high schools. *English Journal, 49,* 606–611.

Applebee, A. N. (1974). *Tradition and reform in the teaching of English: A history.* Urbana, IL: National Council of Teachers of English.

Argall, R. (1982). *Sentence combining: An incisive tool for proofreading.* Paper presented at the Annual Meeting of the Conference on College Composition and Communication, San Francisco. (ERIC Document Reproduction Service No. ED 214 186)

Asher, W. (1988). *The effects of sentence-combining interventions on children's and adolescents' written language development and some data on methodological concerns in writing research.* Paper presented at the Annual Meeting of the American Educational Research Association, New Orleans.

Bateman, D. R., & Zidonis, F. J. (1966). *The effect of a study of transformational grammar on the writing of ninth and tenth graders.* Champaign, IL: NCTE.

Belanger, J. F. (1978). *Reading skill as an influence on writing skill.* Unpublished doctoral dissertation, University of Alberta. (ERIC Document Reproduction Service No. ED 163 409)

Bowden, S. P. (1979). The effects of formal, traditional grammar study on the writing ability of secondary school students. *Dissertation Abstracts International, 40,* 1389A. (University of Microfilms No. 790025)

Braddock, R., Lloyd-Jones, R., & Schoer, L. (1963). *Research in written composition.* Champaign, IL: NCTE.

Briggs, T. H. (1913). Formal English grammar as a discipline. *Teachers College Record, 14,* 251–343.

Callaghan, T. F. (1978). The effects of sentence-combining exercises on the syntactic maturity, quality of writing, reading ability, and attitudes of ninth grade students. *Dissertation Abstracts International, 39,* 637A. (University Microfilms No 7813980)

Casson, L. (1985). Breakthrough at the first think tank. *Smithsonian, 16* (3), 158–168.

Chomsky, N. (1957). *Syntactic structures.* The Hague: Mouton & Co.

Chomsky, N. (1965). *Aspects of the theory of syntax.* Cambridge: The M.I.T. Press.

Christensen, F. (1967). *Notes toward a new rhetoric: Six essays for teachers.* New York: Harper & Row.

Combs, W. E. (1976). Further effects of sentence-combining practice on writing ability. *Research in the Teaching of English, 10,* 137–149.

Combs, W. E. (1977). Sentence-combining practice: Do gains in judgments of writing "quality" persist? *Journal of Educational Research, 70,* 318–321.

Cooper, C. (1975). Research roundup: Oral and written composition. *English Journal, 64* (9), 72–74.

Crowhurst, M. (1983). Sentence combining: Maintaining realistic expectations. *College Composition and Communication, 34,* 62–72.

Crowhurst, M., & Piche, G. L. (1979). Audience and mode of discourse effects on syntactic complexity in writing at two grade levels. *Research in the Teaching of English, 13,* 101–109.

Elley, W. B., Barham, I. H., Lamb, H., & Wyllie, M. (1976). The role of grammar in a secondary school English curriculum. *Research in the Teaching of English, 10,* 5–21.

Faigley, L. (1979). The influence of generative rhetoric on the syntactic maturity and writing effectiveness of college freshmen. *Research in the Teaching of English, 13,* 197–206.

Francis, W. N. (1954). Revolution in grammar. *Quarterly Journal of Speech, 40,* 299–312.

Francis, W. N. (1958). *The structure of American English.* New York: The Ronald Press Co.

Freedman, A. (1985). Sentence combining: Some questions. In A. Freedman (Ed.), *Carleton Papers in Applied Language Studies, Volume II* (pp. 17–32). (ERIC Document Reproduction Service No. ED 267 602)

Fries, C. C. (1952). *The structure of English.* New York: Harcourt, Brace, and World.

Gleason, H. A., Jr. (1965). *Linguistics and English grammar.* New York: Holt, Rinehart, and Winston.

Green, E. A. (1973). An experimental study of sentence-combining to improve written syntactic fluency in fifth-grade children. *Dissertation Abstracts International, 33,* 4057A. (University Microfilms No. 73-4169)

Hake, R. L., & Williams, J. M. (1979). Sentence expanding: Not can, or how, but when. In D. A. Daiker, A. Kerek, & M. Morenberg (Eds.), *Sentence combining and the teaching of writing* (pp. 134–146). Conway, AR: University of Akron and University of Central Arkansas.

Hake, R. L., & Williams, J. M. (1985). Some cognitive issues in sentence combining: On the theory that smaller is better. In D. A. Daiker, A. Kerek, & M. Morenberg (Eds.), *Sentence combining: A rhetorical perspective* (pp. 86–106). Carbondale, IL: Southern Illinois University Press.

Hartwell, P. (1985). Grammar, grammars, and the teaching of grammar. *College English, 47,* 105–127.

Heath, S. B. (1983). *Ways with words: Language, life, and work in communities and classrooms.* New York: Cambridge University Press.

Hillocks, G., Jr. (1971). *An evaluation of Project Apex, a nongraded phase-elective English program.* Trenton, MI: Trenton Public Schools.

Hillocks, G., Jr. (1986). *Research on written composition: New directions for teaching.* Urbana, IL: ERIC and NCTE.

Hillocks, G., Jr., & Mavrogenes, N. (1986). Sentence combining. In *Research on written composition: New directions for teaching* (pp. 142–146). Urbana, IL: ERIC and NCRE.

Hillocks, G., Jr., McCabe, B. J., & McCampbell, J. F. (1971). *The dynamics of English instruction:* Grades 7–12. New York: Random House.

Hillocks, G., Jr., & Smith, M. J. (1986). Grammar. In *Research on written composition: New directions for teaching* (pp. 134–141). Urbana, IL: ERIC and NCRE.

Howie, S. M. H. (1979). A study: The effects of sentence combining practice on the writing ability and reading level of ninth grade students. *Dissertation Abstracts International, 40,* 1980A. (University Microfilms No. 7923248)

Hunt, K. (1965). *Grammatical structures written at three grade levels.* Champaign, IL: NCTE.

Hunt, K. W., & O'Donnell, R. C. (1970). *An elementary school curriculum to develop better writing skills.* Tallahassee, FL: Florida State University. (ERIC Document Reproduction Service No. ED 050 108)

Huntsman, J. F. (1983). Grammar. In D. L. Wagner (Ed.), *The seven liberal arts in the Middle Ages* (pp. 58–95). Bloomington, IN: Indiana University Press.

Kagan, D. M. (1980). Run-on and fragment sentences: An error analysis. *Research in the Teaching of English, 14,* 127–138.

Kerek, A., Daiker, D., & Morenberg, M. (1980). Sentence combining and college composition. *Perceptual and Motor Skills, 51,* 1059–1157.

Labov, W. (1970). *The study of nonstandard English.* Champaign, IL: NCTE.

Labov, W. (1972). *Language in the inner city: Studies in the Black English vernacular.* Philadelphia: University of Pennsylvania Press.

Levine, S. S. (1977). The effect of transformational sentence-combining exercises on the reading comprehension and written composition of third-grade children. *Dissertation Abstracts International, 37* 6431A. (University Microfilms No. 77-7653)

Loban, W. (1976). *Language development: Kindergarten through grade twelve.* Urbana, IL: NCTE.

Macauley, W. J. (1947). The difficulty of grammar. *British Journal of Educational Psychology, 17,* 153–162.

Maimon, E. P., & Nodine, B. F. (1978). Measuring syntactic growth: Errors and expectations in sentence-combining practice with college freshmen. *Research in the Teaching of English, 12,* 233–244.

Maimon, E. P., & Nodine, B. F. (1979). Words enough and time: Syntax and error one year after. In D. A. Daiker, A. Kerek, & M. Morenberg (Eds.), *Sentence combining and the teaching of writing* (pp. 101–108). Conway, AR: University of Akron and University of Central Arkansas.

Martinez San Jose, C. P. (1973). Grammatical structures in four modes of writing at fourth grade level. *Dissertation Abstracts International, 33,* 5411A. (University Microfilms No. 73-9563)

Meckel, H. C. (1963). Research on teaching composition and literature. In N. L. Gage (Ed.), *Handbook of research on teaching* (pp. 966–1006). Chicago: Rand McNally.

Mellon, J. C. (1969). *Transformational sentence-combining: A method for enhancing the development of syntactic fluency in English composition.* Champaign, IL: NCTE.

Mellon, J. C. (1979). Issues in the theory and practice of sentence combining: A twenty year perspective. In D. A. Daiker, A. Kerek, & M. Morenberg (Eds.), *Sentence combining and the teaching of writing* (pp. 1–38). Conway, AR: University of Akron and University of Central Arkansas.

Morenberg, M., Daiker, D., & Kerek, A. (1978). Sentence combining at the college level: An experimental study. *Research in the Teaching of English, 12,* 245–256.

Morrison, K. F. (1983). Incentives for studying the liberal arts. In D. L. Wagner (Ed.), *The seven liberal arts in the Middle Ages* (pp. 32–57). Bloomington, IN: Indiana University Press.

Muller, H. J. (1967). *The uses of English: Guidelines for the teaching of English from the Anglo-American conference at Dartmouth College.* New York: Holt, Rinehart, and Winston.

Nold, E. W., & Freedman, S. W. (1977). An analysis of readers' responses to essays. *Research in the Teaching of English, 11,* 164–174.

Obenchain, A. (1979). Developing paragraph power through sentence combining. In D. A. Daiker, A. Kerek, & M. Morenberg (Eds.), *Sentence combining and the teaching of writing* (pp. 123–133). Conway, AR: University of Akron and University of Central Arkansas.

O'Donnell, R. C., Griffin, W. J., & Norris, R. C. (1967). *Syntax of kindergarten and elementary school children: A transformational analysis.* Champaign, IL: NCTE.

Ofsa, W. J. (1975). An experiment in using research in composition in the training of teachers of English. *Dissertation Abstracts International, 35,* 7174A. (University Microfilms No. 75-11,711)

O'Hare, F. (1973). *Sentence combining: Improving student writing without formal grammar instruction.* Urbana, IL: NCTE.

Pederson, E. L. (1978). Improving syntactic and semantic fluency in the writing of language arts students through extended practice in sentence-combining. *Dissertation Abstracts International, 38,* 5892A. (University Microfilms No. 7802703)

Perron, J. D. (1975). An exploratory approach to extending the syntactic development of fourth-grade students through the use of sentence-combining methods. *Dissertation Abstracts International, 35,* 4316A. (University Microfilms No. 75-1744)

Perron, J. D. (1977). *Written syntactic complexity and the modes of discourse.* Paper presented at the Annual Meeting of AERA, New York. (ERIC Document Reproduction Service No. ED 139 009)

Pinneo, T. S. (1850). *Analytical grammar of the English language.* Cincinnati, OH: W. B. Smith & Co.

Roberts, P. (1962). *English sentences.* New York: Harcourt, Brace & World.

Ross, J. (1971). A transformational approach to teaching composition. *College Composition and Communication, 22,* 179–184.

Saussure, F. de. (1959). *Course in general linguistics* (W. Baskin, Trans.). New York: Philosophical Library.

Schuster, E. H. (1976). *Forward to basics through sentence combining.* Paper presented at the Annual Meeting of the Pennsylvania Council of Teachers of English, Harrisburg. (ERIC Document Reproduction Service No. ED 133 774)

Schuster, E. H. (1977). *Using sentence combining to teach writing to inner-city students.* Paper presented at the Annual Meeting of NCTE, New York. (ERIC Document Reproduction Service No. ED 150 614)

Shaughnessy, M. P. (1977). *Errors and expectations: A guide for the teacher of basic writing.* New York: Oxford University Press.

Smith, H. L., Jr., & Sustakowski, H. J. (1968). *The application of descriptive linguistics to the teaching of English and a statistically-measured comparison of the relative effectiveness of the linguistically-oriented and traditional methods of instruction.* Buffalo: State University of New York. (ERIC Document Reproduction Service No. ED 021 216)

Smith, W. L., & Combs, W. E. (1980). The effects of overt and covert cues on written syntax. *Research in the Teaching of English, 14,* 19–38.

Smith, W. L., & Hull, G. A. (1985). Differential effects of sentence combining on college students who use particular structures with high and low frequencies. In D. A. Daiker, A. Kerek, & M. Morenberg (Eds.), *Sentence combining: A rhetorical perspective* (pp. 17–32). Carbondale, IL: Southern Illinois University Press.

Stewart, M. F. (1978). *Sentence-combining and syntactic maturity in first year university.* Report prepared at the University of New Brunswick, Canada. (ERIC Document Reproduction Service No. ED 153 240)

Stewart, M. F., & Grobe, C. H. (1979). Syntactic maturity, mechanics of writing, and teachers' quality ratings. *Research in the Teaching of English, 13,* 207–215.

Stoddard, E. P., & Renzulli, J. S. (1983). Improving the writing skills of talent pool students. *Gifted Child Quarterly, 27,* 21–27.

Straw, S. B. & Schreiner, R. (1982). The effect of sentence manipulation on subsequent measures of reading and listening comprehension. *Reading Research Quarterly, 17,* 339–352.

Strickland, R. G. (1962). The language of elementary school children: Its relationship to the language of reading textbooks and the quality of reading of selected children [entire issue]. *Bulletin of the School of Education, Indiana University, 38* (4).

Strong, W. (1986). *Creative approaches to sentence combining.* Urbana, IL: ERIC and NCTE.

Sullivan, J. L. (1969). A study of the relative merits of traditional grammar, generative-transformational grammar, or no grammar in an approach to writing in Communication One at Colorado State College. *Dissertation Abstracts International, 29,* 2686A.

Sullivan, M. A. (1978). The effects of sentence-combining exercises on syntactic maturity, quality of writing, reading ability, and attitudes of students in grade eleven. *Dissertation Abstracts International, 39,* 1197A. (University Microfilms No. 7814240)

Sullivan, M. A. (1979). Parallel sentence-combining activities in grades nine and eleven. In D. A. Daiker, A. Kerek, & M. Morenberg (Eds.), *Sentence combining and the teaching of writing* (pp. 79–93). Conway, AR: University of Akron and University of Central Arkansas.

Taylor, S. J. (1986). Grammar curriculum—back to square one. *English Journal, 75* (1), 94–98.

Thibodeau, A. E. (1964). Improving composition with grammar and organization exercises utilizing differentiated group patterns. *Dissertation Abstracts International, 25,* 2389. (University Microfilms No. 64-4048)

Thibodeau, A. L. (1964). A study of the effects of elaborative thinking and vocabulary enrichment exercises on written composition. *Dissertation Abstracts International, 25,* 2388. (University Microfilms No. 64-4041)

Waterfall, C. M. (1978). An experimental study of sentence-combining as a means of increasing syntactic maturity and writing quality in the compositions of college-age students enrolled in remedial English classes. *Dissertation Abstracts International, 38,* 7131-A. (University Microfilms No. 7808144)

Weaver, C. (1979). *Grammar for teachers: Perspectives and definitions.* Urbana, IL: National Council of Teachers of English.

White, R. H. (1965). The effect of structural linguistics on improving English composition compared to that of prescriptive grammar or the absence of grammar instruction. *Dissertation Abstracts, 25,* 5032.

Whitehead, C. E., Jr., (1966). The effect of grammar-diagraming on student writing skills. *Dissertation Abstracts, 26,* 3710. (University Microfilms No. 66-508)

Wille, S. C. (1982). *The effects of pre-writing observational activities on syntactic structures.* Unpublished master's thesis, University of Chicago.

Williams, J. M. (1981a). The phenomenology of error. *College Composition and Communication, 32,* 152–168.

Williams, J. M. (1981b). *Style: Ten lessons in clarity and grace.* Glenview, IL: Scott, Foresman and Company.

31C. RESEARCH ON VOCABULARY INSTRUCTION: ODE TO VOLTAIRE

James F. Baumann
Edward J. Kameenui

Language is very difficult to put into words.

Voltaire (1694–1778)

It seems only fitting in the midst of a virtual explosion in the research on vocabulary learning and instruction that we recall the wistful admonition by a poet-writer-philosopher who knew intimately the beguiling charm and character of words. As we began writing this chapter, we quickly came to appreciate the veracity of Voltaire's seemingly glib statement—it was indeed challenging to find the proper words to describe what we know (and don't know) about word meanings and how to teach them.

Words. According to one recent estimate, printed school English, as represented by the materials in grades 3 to 9, contains 88,533 distinct word families (Nagy & Anderson, 1984). This results in a total volume of nearly one-half million graphically distinct word types when one includes all proper names. Interestingly, roughly one-half of these 500,000 or so words occurs once or less in a billion words of text. Some of these words are encountered fairly often, and others appear quite infrequently. The challenge facing language users, learners, and teachers is literally and figuratively immense.

When preparing this chapter, we were tempted to follow the literary precedent set by Francois Marie Arouet (alias Voltaire) and adopt pen names to conceal our real identities. We were convinced we did not have much that was new to say about vocabulary instruction that had not already been said and repeated (e.g., see extensive reviews by Beck & McKeown, in press; Calfee & Drum, 1986; Graves, 1986; Herman & Dole, 1988; Mezynski, 1983; McKeown & Curtis, 1987; Miller & Gildea, 1987; Stahl & Fairbanks, 1986). Our dilemma, we came to recognize, was in sharp contrast to the conclusion reached by Petty, Herold, and Stoll (1967) more than a two decades ago after reviewing vocabulary instruction research: "The teaching profession seems to know little of substance about the teaching of vocabulary" (p. 85). Thus, we cannot take cover behind Petty et al.'s conclusion. Instead, we find ourselves facing just the opposite dilemma: We know too much to say we know too little, and we know too little to say that we know enough. Indeed, language is difficult to put into words.

Within the last two decades, there has been a great deal of ambitious, rigorous, and focused research on all aspects of vocabulary learning and instruction; hence, we are in a position to be clearer about what we know and do not know about this topic. We are hopeful that this chapter will provide educators substance and guidance in the quest to provide students with a sensible, pedagogically sound, and empirically based program of vocabulary instruction.

Because this is a language arts handbook, our charge is to present research on both expressive vocabulary (speaking, writing) and receptive vocabulary (listening, reading). However, given the limited space we have to address this broad topic, and in light of the limited research on teaching speaking and writing vocabularies (Duin & Graves, 1987), we have devoted our greatest efforts to presenting and evaluating the research on reading vocabulary instruction and its relationship to text comprehension.

We have organized this chapter into three major sections. First, we address several theoretical and pedagogical issues that continue to haunt the research on vocabulary instruction. Second, we examine the research on vocabulary instruction. Here we review and highlight selected studies from the voluminous body of research that attempts to answer the question, "How can we best teach students vocabulary?" Finally, we sum up our review by discussing what we know and do not know about teaching vocabulary and extend it by considering what this knowledge might mean for practice.

ISSUES RELATED TO VOCABULARY KNOWLEDGE AND INSTRUCTION

It is difficult to have a sensible discussion about vocabulary knowledge, learning, and instruction without first examining several important theoretical and pedagogical issues. These issues are not new to the research on vocabulary knowledge (cf., Anderson & Freebody, 1981; Russell & Fea, 1963), but they must be addressed in order to appreciate the nature of the task facing teachers and researchers concerned with vocabulary instruction. In this section we examine two general sets of issues related to the development of an empirically based program of vocabulary learning. First, we examine the quality and quantity of children's vocabulary knowledge. Second, we attempt to determine what this information says about the importance of vo-

The authors thank Isabel Beck, Michael Graves, Joseph Jenkins, Dale Johnson, Mark McDaniel, Susan Pittelman, Deborah Simmons, and Steven Stahl for their most helpful comments on earlier versions of this chapter.

cabulary instruction and its influence on reading comprehension.

The Quality and Quantity of Student's Vocabulary Knowledge

We attempt to answer two questions about vocabulary knowledge: What does it mean to know a word? and How many words do students know?

What Does it Mean to Know a Word? The study of vocabulary knowledge is as much a study about *knowing* and how we as researchers and practitioners decide when a student really knows something as it is a study about words and students. Determining what a student knows, how much is known, when it is known, and how the depth and breadth of that knowing changes developmentally have been issues at the heart of vocabulary inquiry for at least a century. For example, in the first *Handbook of Research on Teaching* (Gage, 1963), Russell and Fea point out that attempts to measure "children's vocabularies have been numerous during the past 75 years" and that "investigators cannot agree as to what evidence indicates that the word is 'known' by the child" (p. 889).

Our historical and logical sensibilities tell us that it simply does not make sense to discuss the number of words a child knows or must know without first defining what it means to know a word. In his extensive review of vocabulary learning and instruction, Graves (1986) states twice "there has been little research on depth of word knowledge in school-age children" (pp. 54–55). If we ponder Graves' iterative assessment of this issue today and Russell and Fea's (1963) similar observation a number of years ago, it is fairly clear that we have advanced very little, if at all, in addressing the question, "What does it mean to know a word?"

If our assessment of this situation is correct, we must ascertain why it is that we know so little about what it means to know a word. This task obviously hides more than it reveals. Were it an easy, straightforward task, it would have been settled more than 75 years ago. However, in our judgment, this issue remains unsettled for two primary reasons: (a) The difficulty of delimiting the boundaries of a word, especially when a word can be defined in numerous ways; and (b) the inherent difficulty in deciding when something is known (or not known). In the next two sections, we examine each of these issues.

What is a Word? The concept word can be defined along various dimensions: semantic, graphic, psychological, sociological, historical, or philosophical. Each dimension is likely to reflect a particular theory or ideology that gives primacy to one feature or another (Mezynski, 1983; Mosenthal, 1984). For example, according to Vygotsky (1962) a word is a unit of "verbal thought" that is "already a generalization" (p. 5). Vygotsky views word meanings as "dynamic rather than static formations. They change as the child develops; they change with the various ways in which thought functions" (p. 124). Vygotsky notes in the final sentence of *Thought and Language,* "A word is a microcosm of human consciousness" (p. 153). Vygotsky's definition appears to reify the concept of word as a psychological state that ultimately shapes human behavior and action.

On the other hand, Serra (1953; cited in Russell & Fea, 1963) speaks of words as "verbalized concepts." These concepts represent "through general agreement certain sounds, symbolized in writing by certain combinations of letters ... and certain meanings attached to certain words" (p. 888). Knowing a word, according to Serra, is simply a matter of determining "whether a child is aware of, and in accord with, the common agreement concerning each word" (p. 888).

If we were to appreciate fully Vygotsky's (1962) insights about words, we would be saddled with the Sisyphean task of having to continuously uncover or disentangle an intricate and complex psychological network of meanings, intentions, affective tendencies, emotions, and so on. The Vygotskian standard of using words as a psychological tool for measuring students' consciousness reveals the potential drama of words. However, Serra's (1953) definition of word knowledge leaves little of the complexity and charm of words. To appreciate this definition, we need only to assess if a student's awareness of a word as a graphically distinct sequence of letters matches the agreed upon meaning of the word.

In contrast to the definitions offered by Vygotsky (1962) and Serra (1953), Nagy and Anderson (1984) define the concept word in terms of the semantic relatedness of words to each other.

We analyzed relatedness among words, not in terms of their historical derivations, but in terms of similarity of their current meanings. For example, the relationship of a derivative word to its base (e.g., *business* to *busy* or *darkness* to *dark*) was viewed in terms of the relative ease or difficulty with which an individual who knew the meaning of only one of the words could guess or infer the meaning of the other when encountering it in context while reading. (p. 307)

Using this definition, Nagy and Anderson (1984) identified 15 different types of relationships (e.g., regular inflections: *walks* and *walk;* suffixation: *frustration* and *frustrate*) between a target word and an "immediate ancestor" (p. 309), that is, a word that was most closely related to the target word. In addition, they identified six different levels of semantic relatedness between a target word and its immediate ancestor. These relationships ranged from "semantically transparent" (e.g., *cleverness* and *clever*), words that could be comprehended without assistance from the context, to "semantically opaque" (e.g., *dash* and *dashboard*), words that were not connected semantically.

So, what is a word? Well, it depends. It depends upon your purpose for asking the question and your view of thought and language. *Word* may be defined in a very pragmatic way (Serra, 1953); it may be defined in order to answer a specific question (e.g., "How many words are there?", Nagy & Anderson, 1984); or it may be defined in a psychological or philosophical manner (Vygotsky, 1962). For us, like Nagy and Anderson, word will be defined operationally according to the questions we ask about their various dimensions, that is, questions that help us evaluate students' abilities to know and be taught word meanings.

When is a Word Known? When we speak of vocabulary knowledge, we implicitly recognize four different vocabularies that can be thought of as either expressive (i.e., speaking and writing) or receptive (i.e., reading and listening). *Expressive vocabulary* requires the speaker or writer *to produce* a specific label (e.g., *dope*) for a particular meaning (e.g., a thick, pasty liquid used as a lubricant or absorbent). In contrast, *receptive vocabulary* requires the reader or listener *to associate* a specific meaning with a given label as in reading or listening (Kameenui, Dixon, & Carnine, 1987).

In order for a word to be used in expressive vocabulary, the word must be adequately learned or acquired, retained in memory, and retrieved either "out of the blue" (Crowder, 1976, p. 4) or as part of a common expression. In short, the word and its attendant meanings must be fairly well-known and established in memory. Hence, if a student is unable to produce a specific vocabulary word in attempting to express a particular meaning during the acts of writing or speaking, we could say with confidence that the child simply does not know the word. However, as Crowder insightfully notes, unpacking the "fundamental ambiguity" (p. 4) as to exactly why something is not known is a most intricate undertaking.

In receptive vocabulary, however, a student need not know a word in the same way a word is known in expressive vocabulary in order to appreciate its meaning. In fact, in some instances, a word does not need to be known at all, and the reader or listener can still derive a meaning for the unknown label or word. For example, in the following sentence, it is not imperative for the reader or listener to know the meaning of *altercation: The altercation left Rocky smiling at his powerful fists and Herbert holding his broken jaw with one hand and his broken ribs with the other.* The reader or listener can rely on the unknown word's immediate environment (i.e., the verbal context surrounding the word) for assistance. The unknown word does not just appear from "out of the blue" but in the context of other words that will determine how much prior knowledge the child must possess to understand it.

However, as Freebody and Anderson (1983) suggest, an unknown word's immediate environment may need to be fairly obvious and helpful (as in the *altercation* example), or "readers, upon encountering a word they do not know, [may] simply skip it, avoiding a drain on resources" (p. 286). This is not to suggest that difficult words will be skipped automatically or that readers and listeners are instantly paralyzed by such words. Comprehension performance usually suffers when the text contains difficult vocabulary (Kameenui, Carnine, & Freschi, 1982), but the suffering is not akin to comprehension death, as Freebody and Anderson have argued.

If a word does appear from "out of the blue," either in isolation or in a hostile context surrounded by unknown words, the learner might infer the word's meaning from individual parts of the unknown word itself. As Wysocki and Jenkins (1987) note, this process is called morphological generalization. For example, knowledge of the base word *altercate* may allow a learner to decipher the meanings of *altercation* or *altercative*. It appears that children's ability to utilize morphological clues is influenced significantly by learning and reading experience (Nagy & Anderson, 1984; Wysocki & Jenkins, 1987). Specifically, adults and adolescents tend to use the internal clues more suc-

cessfully than younger children. These findings suggest that word meanings must be fairly well-known in order for morphological generalization to occur. The reliance on morphology as a strategy may also depend upon motivated and word-wise readers or listeners. Therefore, an unknown word can be known in degrees, depending upon the internal clues of the word itself or the accompanying verbal context that influences the degree of prior knowledge the learner must have about the word.

In summary, expressive vocabulary requires a learner to know a word rather well before using it; not knowing a word is likely to result in the learner not using the word at all. On the other hand, the standards for knowing a word in receptive vocabulary are not as stringent. In fact, a word need not be known prior to its use in a receptive task, and the learner may still be able to discern its meaning. As Freebody and Anderson (1983) state, "it takes a surprisingly high proportion of difficult vocabulary to produce reliable decrements in comprehension measures" (p. 293).

If a word in a receptive task is known in degrees, then it is important that we examine the research on degrees of vocabulary knowledge, a topic we now address.

Degrees of Word Knowledge. It has been argued that vocabulary knowledge is often more than merely the sum of its parts. As Kameenui et al. (1987) point out, "it is conceivable that two students might know the same number of words, and possibly, even roughly the same words, but . . . have 'different vocabularies,' due to differences in the quality or extensiveness of their knowledge of particular words" (p. 133). McKeown and Beck (1988) succinctly capture the issue by noting that "word knowledge is not an all-or-nothing proposition. Words may be known at different levels" (p. 42).

Reviews and analyses on the degrees of word knowledge (Anderson & Freebody, 1981; Dixon & Jenkins, 1984; Graves, 1986; Kameenui et al., 1987) have, for all practical purposes, relied upon the concept learning and development research. For example, Graves (1986) analyzed the developmental concept learning models of Clark (1973), Carey (1978), and Anglin (1977), all of whom relied upon a features analysis of word meanings. For young children, acquiring word meanings is a gradual process based upon the experiences a child has with words. Initial learning of word meanings tends to be useful but incomplete. A child's awareness of critical features of words (i.e., those common to *all* instances of a concept) and variable features of words (i.e., those common to *some* concepts) appears to be highly stipulated by the use of words in limited contexts. Naturally, the more experiences a child has, the more mature and complete the word knowledge becomes (Miller and Gildea, 1987). However, as Graves (1986) notes, "Such findings . . . do no say much about the development of the meanings of individual words or suggest specific ways of characterizing the richness of the word knowledge children of various ages have developed" (p. 54).

Dixon and Jenkins (1984) and Kameenui et al. (1987) also rely on a concept analysis of word learning. However, their analyses are not derived from the results of descriptive studies documenting children's developmental acquisition of word meanings. Instead, these researchers argue that determining the qualities of receptive vocabulary knowledge requires not only a logical analysis of the features of word meanings but also an analysis of the attributes of the vocabulary tasks and contexts in which those words are found. Knowing the meaning of a word, they reason, also requires knowing the conditions of the task in which the word is nested because words rarely occur in isolation. Vocabulary knowledge involves determining more than what is known about a word per se; it also involves assessing the dimensions of the immediate task environment in which the word is embedded.

The notion that a word can be known at different levels is well accepted (Graves, 1984; McKeown & Beck, 1988; Nagy & Anderson, 1984). However, less accepted are the various approaches that have been offered to characterize these levels and to capture the salient features that differentiate one level from another. For example, Beck, McCaslin, and McKeown (1980) suggest scaling the qualities of word knowledge according to three different levels of lexical access: unknown, acquainted, and established word knowledge. A word, according to this scale, would be judged broadly as either well-known (i.e., easily and rapidly accessed in memory), known but not well-known, or known.

Stahl (1985, 1986) suggests an intuitive scale consisting of three successively deeper levels of processing word meanings during reading: association, comprehension, and generation. Generative processing requires the child to produce the target word in a novel context, which is considered to reflect a deeper level of cognitive processing than the association and comprehension of the word. According to Beck et al. (1980) and Stahl, a word is really known when a child is able to retrieve that word from memory rapidly and use it correctly in an uninstructed context. This standard of knowing word meanings is akin to the standard we discussed earlier for expressive vocabulary.

Like Beck et al. (1980) and Stahl (1985, 1986), Kameenui et al. (1987) propose three continuous levels of word knowledge: full concept knowledge, partial concept knowledge, and verbal association knowledge. In addition, they propose a framework for thinking about the influence contexts have on words. For example, when a word is embedded in a rich context of supportive and redundant information, the learner might be more likely to acquire its meaning than when the same word is found in a lean context (i.e., it is surrounded by other equally difficult words). In the former context, knowledge of a word is said to be derived, prompted, or assisted by the verbal context (reading or listening). In the latter situation, word knowledge is considered to be unprompted and therefore unassisted by the immediate context. According to this analysis, knowing the meaning of a word also requires scrutinizing the word's immediate environment and understanding the task conditions under which the word is being assessed.

Assessing Vocabulary Knowledge. Determining when a word is known also depends to a great extent on how knowledge of that word is assessed. Graves (1986), like Russell (1954) before

him, points out that word knowledge typically is assessed through the use of a multiple-choice format that measures vocabulary knowledge by the recognition of a synonym or definitional phrase. Although this form of assessing vocabulary knowledge is widely used, convenient, and differentiates between "those who have no knowledge of a word and those who have some knowledge" (Graves, 1986, p. 56), some argue that multiple-choice vocabulary tasks "are useless at best and dangerous at worst" (Kameenui et al., 1987, p. 138) because they are not sensitive to the various dimensions of vocabulary knowledge (see Anderson & Freebody, 1981; Curtis, 1987).

Attempts have been made recently to modify the traditional multiple-choice test format. Noting the insensitivity of vocabulary measures to the incremental and partial learning of word meanings from context, Nagy, Herman, and Anderson (1985) designed a set of multiple-choice questions to explicitly measure degrees of word knowledge. Instead of relying on one multiple-choice test item per word, they developed test items that assessed three different levels of difficulty for each word. Test items in which the distractors were the most semantically and syntactically similar to the target word were considered the most difficult. The least difficult test items included distractors that were very dissimilar in meaning and speech part to the target word. Nagy et al. also utilized an interview test that called for students to produce the meanings of target words. Although this modification of the multiple-choice test represents a significant improvement of the traditional format, it also implicitly acknowledges the importance of matching assessment task conditions to the dimensions of vocabulary knowledge one is interested in assessing, especially if the objective involves acquisition of partial word knowledge.

Kameenui et al. (1987) argue that the focus on assessing knowledge of specific word meanings has resulted in researchers and practitioners neglecting other equally important dimensions of vocabulary learning. Specifically, they call attention to the relationship between vocabulary instruction and assessment. Such a focus, they argue, "holds that the relationship between vocabulary learning and reading comprehension is dependent on consistencies of objectives, instructional tasks, and assessment tasks within an intricate set of requirements that vary" (p. 139).

In summary, what does it mean to know a word? Well, again it depends. It depends upon how you define *word* (cf., Nagy & Herman, 1984; Serra, cited in Russell & Fea, 1963; Vygotsky, 1962), and it depends upon how you measure them. For us, how you measure words depends upon the kinds of questions one asks about a student's word knowledge. These might include questions such as: Can a student identify a synonym for a word? Can a student generate an oral definition? Can a student place a word within a semantic category? Can a student discriminate a word's denotative and connotative meanings? Can a student express the obvious and subtle differences in meanings among a set of synonyms? Can a student use a word sensibly in an oral or written context?

Our lack of clarity and closure on the question "What does it mean to know a word?" may not be very satisfying—it isn't for us—but for now our best response to what it means to know a word is captured by the exchange between Humpty Dumpty and Alice in Lewis Carroll's *Through the Looking Glass:*

"When I use a word," Humpty Dumpty said in a rather scornful tone, "it means just what I choose it to mean—neither more nor less."

"The question is," said Alice, "whether you *can* make words mean so many different things."

"The question is," said Humpty Dumpty, "which is to be master—that's all."

How Many Words Do Students Know? According to Graves' (1986) review, estimating vocabulary size is not a new endeavor. In citing Dale, Razik, and Petty's *Bibliography of Vocabulary Studies* (1973), he notes that 35 studies investigating vocabulary size were published between 1891 and 1960. Graves, and Nagy and Anderson (1984) point out that research on vocabulary size prior to the 1980s suffered from numerous methodological problems (e.g., poor sampling procedures, imprecise definition of *word*). As a result, estimates of vocabulary size for first graders ranged from 2,562 to 26,000 words, and for university graduate students from 19,000 to 200,000 (Graves, 1986, p. 50).

For a long time, estimates of vocabulary size were viewed primarily as numerical and theoretical artifacts with little real pedagogical significance. However, Becker (1977) added a sharp edge to this issue by linking estimated vocabulary size to the academic achievement of disadvantaged children. Becker asserted that deficiencies in vocabulary knowledge were primary in accounting for the academic failure of disadvantaged students in grades 3 through 12. His call for teaching these students a core vocabulary of basic 8,000 words (Becker, Dixon, & Anderson-Inman, 1980) served in part to prompt a closer scrutiny of vocabulary size (Graves, 1980, 1986).

However, as Nagy and Anderson (1984) suggest, if only a handful of words is required to be known, then a "ruthlessly systematically direct instruction" (p. 304) program could perhaps muscle its way into making a significant difference. On the other hand, if the number of words was much, much greater, then a different kind of instructional program would be required.

If students must learn 8,000 words by their senior year in high school, an ambitious program of direct instruction might hope to cover every word. If, on the other hand, the number of words to be learned were closer to 80,000, this goal would be beyond the reach of even the most intensive direct instruction that could be accomplished in the time available. (Nagy & Anderson, 1984, p. 305)

The real number appears to be 10 times greater than what Becker (1977) proposed. Nagy and Anderson (1984) estimate that printed school English contains 88,533 word families. There appears to be wide agreement with this estimate and its accuracy (e.g., Graves, 1986; Kameenui et al., 1987). However, as Graves (1986) cautions, this figure does not represent the "number of different word families that any one 3rd through 9th grader will ever deal with," nor is it the "number of words known by any one student" (p. 52). Instead, this figure is based on a sample of words taken from school materials (e.g., textbooks, workbooks, novels, magazines, encyclopedias) used in

grades 3 through 9. Furthermore, this figure does not represent the total number of word families that Nagy and Anderson identified. Instead, approximately 180,000 semantically related words were identified. The 88,533 distinct word families represent only the morphological basic words they identified that they defined as "a group of morphologically related words such that if a person knows one member of the family, he or she will probably be able to figure out the meaning of any other member upon encountering it in text" (p. 315).

Nagy and Anderson's (1984) analysis also offered some interesting insights into the number of words students would actually encounter in grades 3 through 9, as well as the distribution of words by frequency. For example, they note that approximately half of the words in printed school English occur "roughly once in a billion words of text or less" (p. 320). However, these frequencies betray the real utility of some of these words. Specifically, words such as *seagull, deform, billfold,* and *inflate* were counted as occurring less than three times in a billion words of text (p. 321).

Nagy and Anderson (1984) also estimate that a student in grades 6 through 9 is likely to encounter approximately 3,000 or 4,000 new vocabulary words each year, assuming he or she reads between 500,000 and a million running words of text in a school year, which is not an unrealistic range (see Anderson, Wilson, & Fielding, 1986). Nagy and Herman's (1987) recalibration of this extrapolation suggests a similar finding in which an average student in grades 3 through 12 is likely to learn approximately 3,000 new vocabulary words each year.

White, Graves, and Slater (1990) evaluated reading vocabulary knowledge for middle-class and disadvantaged children in grades 1 through 4. Although minority students' vocabularies were generally one half to two thirds that of middle-class students, White et al. reported estimated yearly increases of vocabulary in excess of Nagy and Herman's (1987) recalibrations. For example, White et al. estimated that between grades 1 and 3, minority students' vocabularies increased by about 3,500 words a year and middle-class students' vocabularies increased by about 5,000 words a year.

The task facing school-age children and teachers is an enormous one, if we accept Nagy and Anderson's (1984) appraisal of the number of word families in printed school English, and there is no reason to doubt their estimates. However, as Beck, McKeown, and Omanson (1984) note in the face of Nagy and Anderson's appraisal (1984; see also Nagy & Herman, 1984), there is much debate over the role of instruction in vocabulary learning. In the following section, we examine the implications of the research on the quality and quantity of vocabulary knowledge for designing a program of vocabulary instruction.

Dimensions of Vocabulary Instruction and Their Effects on Reading Comprehension

Factor analytic studies document that vocabulary knowledge is an important predictor of reading comprehension (Davis, 1944, 1968; Singer, 1965; Spearritt, 1972; Thurstone, 1946). However, the evidence of a causal link between vocabulary and comprehension is historically long but empirically soft (Kameenui et al., 1982; McKeown, Beck, Omanson, & Pople, 1985), although its intuitive appeal is as solid as granite (Kameenui et al., 1987). It is probably because of this sleight-of-hand intuition that practitioners have insisted on teaching vocabulary words as a way to influence comprehension (Cole, 1946).

We now know that the relationship between vocabulary instruction and comprehension is more complex than simply teaching students more words (Nagy & Anderson, 1984; Stahl & Fairbanks, 1986) and that the causal association between vocabulary and comprehension is tricky and elusive, as Beck, McKeown, and Omanson (1987) note:

The causal links between vocabulary knowledge and reading comprehension are not well understood. For instance, are people good comprehenders because they know a lot of words, or do people know a lot of words because they are good comprehenders and in the course of comprehending text, learn a lot of words, or is there some combination of directionality? (p. 147)

In this section, we explore some of the issues related to the vocabulary/comprehension connection. Specifically, we present what has been referred to as the fertility/futility debate; then we review what we know about learning words incidentally from context.

To Teach or Not to Teach Words: That Is Not the Question.
The sheer volume of printed school English appears to defy direct systematic instruction. It is also obvious from the nature of receptive tasks that children learn new words, albeit incompletely and gradually, through reading and hearing unknown words in context (Nagy et al., 1985; Nagy, Anderson, & Herman, 1987). What has not been obvious until recently is the nature and degree of vocabulary learning from context and its effects on reading comprehension (Jenkins, Stein, & Wysocki, 1984).

We know that children's vocabulary increases at a rate of approximately 3,000 new words per year (Nagy & Anderson, 1984; Nagy & Herman, 1987). We also know that children's vocabulary size, regardless of the method used to count specific vocabulary words, approximately doubles between grades 3 and 7 (Jenkins & Dixon, 1983). It is also evident, as Nagy et al. (1985) point out, that this "massive vocabulary growth seems to occur without much help from teachers" (p. 235), as systematic, intensive vocabulary instruction may not be a prominent feature of basal reading programs (Jenkins & Dixon, 1983), and we have little evidence that teachers demonstrate significant amounts of direct instruction in vocabulary (Durkin, 1978–1979). To reconcile the massive growth in children's vocabulary with the lack of vocabulary instruction in schools, Nagy et al. argue that "The only plausible explanation seems to be some type of incidental learning from context" (p. 234).

The plausibility of this explanation is greeted skeptically by Beck, McKeown, and McCaslin (1983) in an article titled cleverly, "All contexts are not created equal." Beck et al. distinguish between natural contexts, those in which words reside in honestly written materials, and pedagogical contexts, those that are contrived for teaching or testing contextual analysis ability. Beck et al. point out that natural contexts do not necessarily provide strong clues to word meanings. In fact, they argue that

some natural contexts might be *nondirective*, those "which seem to be of no assistance in directing the reader toward any particular meaning for a word," or even *misdirective*, "those that seem to direct the student to an incorrect meaning for a target word" (p. 178). Baldwin and Schatz (1985; Schatz & Baldwin, 1986) also argue that many contexts are misdirective, and they have provided additional empirical support for this assertion. In short, it has been argued that natural contexts at best may be insufficient to help readers infer word meanings and at worst may be misleading to readers.

The contrasting positions represented by Nagy and his colleagues and Beck and her colleagues characterize what has been called the "fertility versus futility" debate (cf., Beck et al., 1984; Nagy & Herman, 1984). The debate captures the dilemma facing practitioners and researchers in determining the role of instruction in learning and using vocabulary (Glaser, 1984). Those who argue for *fertile* vocabulary instruction point to the unreliability of natural contexts to assist readers in understanding an unknown word (Beck et al., 1983; Kameenui et al., 1982). They also argue that learning word meanings from natural contexts is less efficient than direct instruction (Miller & Gildea, 1987; Stahl & Fairbanks, 1986).

In contrast, those who see direct instruction as *futile* note that there are just too many words to be taught directly and too little instructional time to do it for direct instruction to be an effective means of sustained vocabulary development (Nagy & Herman, 1987; Sternberg, 1987). They also point out that vocabulary development is a gradual process that takes place within a broader learning context of acquiring other knowledge structures or schemata (Nagy & Herman, 1987). Finally, it is argued that experimental evidence supporting the relationship between vocabulary instruction and reading comprehension is less than robust (Freebody & Anderson, 1981).

As in the case of most debates, the fertility versus futility debate tends to accentuate contrasting views, while it masks subtle, more complex issues that need to be addressed. For example, those who argue of the futility of vocabulary instruction do not call for direct instruction to cease altogether: "We would not care to maintain that no direct instruction in vocabulary should ever be undertaken (Nagy et al., 1985, p. 252). Similarly, those who argue for fertility of direct vocabulary instruction do not call for direct instruction alone but for "carefully crafted, multifaceted instruction" (Beck et al., 1984, p. 8). As Stahl (1988) suggests, the real issue is that of striking a *balance* between direct instruction and learning from context. We address the specifics of a balanced vocabulary program at the conclusion of this chapter.

We now turn to the topic of incidental word learning, information germane to our later discussion of instruction in contextual analysis.

Incidental Learning of Word Meanings from Context. We noted earlier that receptive language processes—reading and listening—provide learners with a context for discerning the meanings of unknown words. These contexts can be generous or parsimonious, helpful or hostile in the amount of assistance they provide the reader or listener (Beck et al., 1983). Studies that have investigated the effects of these contexts on students' ability to learn uninstructed words have relied on either experimenter-contrived texts or natural, ecologically valid texts selected from basal reading programs or content textbooks.

In general, these studies suggest that children of varying ages (8-year-olds to college students) and abilities (low-ability versus high-ability) are able to derive the meanings of unknown words from context (Carnine, Kameenui, & Coyle, 1984; Daalen-Kapteijns & Elshout-Mohr, 1981; McKeown, 1985; Sternberg, Powell, & Kaye, 1983; Werner & Kaplan, 1952). As Herman, Anderson, Pearson, and Nagy (1987) point out, in most of these studies, readers were directed to figure out the meanings of specific words that were highlighted in some fashion. They also note that "few studies have investigated the *incidental* learning of word meanings from written context. That is, few studies have examined how much word learning occurs when students are reading selections for a purpose, such as to understand and remember information in a text or to enjoy a story" (p. 265). To date, four studies have examined incidental learning from context.

Jenkins et al. (1984) required average and above-average fifth-grade students to read experimenter-contrived texts in which difficult vocabulary words were embedded 0, 2, 6, or 10 times. The unknown words were contained in passages that were fairly generous with redundant information about the targeted words. Results showed that 6 or 10 encounters with a word resulted in greater word learning than 2 encounters; 2 encounters did not promote word learning; and the above-average students learned more word meanings than the average ability students.

Herman et al. (1987) noted, however, that in the Jenkins et al. (1984) study, "students may have been alerted to the nature of the study because they read aloud the target words beforehand. Thus, learning may not have been entirely incidental" (p. 265). Also, Nagy et al. (1985) noted that the contexts Jenkins et al. constructed were most likely richer than natural ones. To address these concerns, Nagy and his colleagues conducted several experiments.

In their first study, Nagy et al. (1985) required eighth-grade average and above-average students to read 1,000-word narrative and expository basal reader excerpts containing 15 difficult words. On several dependent measures sensitive to complete and partial word knowledge (see earlier discussion), students demonstrated a context effect that was "small in absolute terms" but "statistically robust and very consistent across types of text, methods of measurement, and level of scoring." (p. 245). Nagy et al. concluded that "There can be no doubt that the effect was real" (p. 245).

In an extended replication of this experiment, Nagy et al. (1987) found a similar effect with a larger sample of students in grades 3, 5, and 7. Again, "small but reliable gains in knowledge of words from the passages read were found at all grade and ability levels" (p. 237) for both narrative and expository passages.

In a third study, Herman et al. (1987) investigated the extent to which variations in text features influenced incidental word learning. Eighth-grade students read either an original, unedited science textbook excerpt or one of three revised versions each designed to enhance text comprehension. Results indicated that both able and less able students who read a revised version that thoroughly explains key concepts and the relations between them acquired more word meanings incidentally than those who read either the original version or the other two revised versions.

The results of the research on incidental word learning from context are perhaps best summarized by Jenkins et al. (1984) who note that learning word meanings incidentally during reading "apparently does not come easily or in large quantities" (p. 782). However, the evidence that incidental word learning does occur is unequivocal as Nagy et al. concluded from their 1987 experiment: "Our results demonstrate beyond a reasonable doubt that incidental learning of word meanings does take place during normal reading" (p. 261). Nagy et al. state further that "The results of this study support our earlier contention (Nagy, Herman, & Anderson, 1985) that regualr, wide reading must be seen as the major avenue of large-scale, long-term vocabulary growth" (p. 266). We certainly agree with Nagy et al. that word learning does occur during normal reading; we also concur that wide reading is a necessary factor in vocabulary growth. However, we believe that instruction has a distinct role in vocabulary development, as will be demonstrated in the remaining sections of this chapter.

RESEARCH ON TEACHING VOCABULARY

In this section, we examine the research on vocabulary instruction. We begin with a description of the state of vocabulary instruction in schools. We then examine those intervention studies that have compared and contrasted the effectiveness of various kinds of curriculum and instruction in vocabulary. This includes a brief discussion of classic research on teaching vocabulary, followed by a detailed review of more contemporary studies that are representative of the resurgent interest in researching vocabulary that began in the 1970s.

The State of Vocabulary Curriculum and Instruction in Schools

Vocabulary Curriculum. Because basal readers are the pervasive curricular vehicle of reading instruction in schools (a 94 percent usage estimate in elementary grades, Educational Products Information Exchange, 1977), we have restricted our discussion here to basal materials. Criticisms of basal readers have included many dimensions (cf., Goodman, Shannon, Freeman, & Murphy, 1988; Squire, 1987), but the quantity and quality of vocabulary instruction has come under especially careful scrutiny (Beck, 1984; Beck & McKeown, 1987; Beck, McKeown, McCaslin, & Burkes, 1979; Jenkins & Dixon, 1983; Sorenson, 1985).

For example, Jenkins and Dixon (1983) reported that at best no more than 300 words per year were taught in three basal programs they examined, and at worst virtually no words were taught. Further, they stated that "program developers seem not to rely much on direct teaching to produce growth in vocabulary knowledge" (p. 247). In short, they noted that few words were taught and even fewer were taught well.

Beck et al. (1979) examined two basal series and found vocabulary instruction in each lacking in both intensity and scope. To illustrate the range of quality in basal reader vocabulary instruction, Beck (1984) described the best and worst instances of vocabulary instruction:

Let us now for a moment consider the best case of vocabulary instruction that we found in the programs we studied. A new vocabulary word is presented in a sentence that elucidates the meaning of the new word; the word is encountered in the text selection, and the student looks it up in the glossary if she/he does not remember its meaning; the word appears a third time in an independently completed, after-reading activity. The word does not appear again in subsequent selections or in vocabulary work. Remember, this is the *best* instance of new word experience that we encountered. It does not necessarily occur with any regularity.

At worst, a new word appers solely in a selection and the student skips over it because she/he either does not recognize it as an unknown word or does not want to be bothered with the disruptive glossary step. (pp. 11–12)

Durkin (1981a) evaluated the suggestions for comprehension instruction found in the teachers' manuals (kindergarten through grade six) for five basal reading series. One of her categories of analysis involved prereading activities that she called "preparation" and included "attention to new vocabulary, word meanings, background knowledge, and prereading questions" (p. 520). Durkin reported finding 1,929 total instances of preparation suggestions across the five series, an average of 386 per series (i.e., across the K–6 manuals) and interpreted these values as indicative of "limited attention given new vocabulary, especially in the middle- and upper-grade manuals" (p. 525). She concluded her analysis of the preparation suggestions as follows: "That manuals and teachers may need to do much more with new words before children attempt to read a selection is something that merits serious consideration" (p. 526).

Jitendra and Kameenui (1988) reviewed and analyzed the concept teaching procedures in five recently published (1980–1986) basal language programs for the early grades. They based their analysis on five design-of-instruction criteria that were drawn from three empirically based models of concept teaching. They found that in *every* lesson of all five basal language programs, the majority of the design-of-instruction principles for conept teaching were violated.

In conclusion, the quantity and quality of vocabulary instruction in basal reader programs has been criticized for lack of depth and substance. It should be noted, however, that the materials Beck et al. (1979), Jenkins and Dixon (1983), and Durkin (1981a) examined were basal programs with copyrights of the mid to late 1970s, so their findings may not be generalizable to contemporary programs. Whether authors and publishers of current basal reading programs have included more comprehensive vocabulary instructional components that are compatible with the growing research literature is a question that must yet be answered.

Vocabulary Instruction. What do we know about the quantity and quality of vocabulary instruction that teachers actually administer in schools? Several teacher observation studies and one interview study have addressed this question.

Durkin (1978–1979) reported that not much attention was given to vocabulary instruction in fourth-grade classrooms. Of the 4,469 minutes of reading instruction she and her assistants observed in 24 different classrooms, 19 minutes were devoted to what she labeled "word meanings: instruction," 4 minutes were devoted to "word meanings: review," and 94 minutes were devoted to "word meanings: application." These three categories accounted for 2.6 percent of the *total* observed time. Even if one includes whatever attention was given to vocabulary during prereading activities (what she called "comprehension: preparation for reading"), this encompassed only an additional 247 minutes, and it is undetermined what proportion of the prereading activities actually involved vocabulary. At one extreme, all four of these categories account for about 8 percent of the total observed time; however, if one includes only the "word meaning: instruction" and "word meaning: review,"— what we consider to be explicit vocabulary instructional activities—then only about *one-half of 1 percent* of the observed time involved vocabulary instruction.

Durkin's (1978–1979) data were corroborated by findings of a similar observational study briefly noted by Roser and Juel (1982). They observed reading lessons in 12 grade 1–5 classrooms. Of approximately 1,200 minutes of observation, only 65 minutes, about 5 percent, were devoted to vocabulary instruction, a mean of 1.67 minutes per lesson. Word meaning instruction per lesson ranged from 0 to 12 minutes, but the modal value was 0.

However, as Durkin's (1981a) evaluation of basal reader manuals indicated, teachers may not be provided much guidance in how to teach vocabulary, so the lack of attention to vocabulary should come as no surprise. To pursue this issue further, Durkin (1984) returned to elementary classrooms to find out if there was a match between what basal manuals recommended and what teachers actually did. She found little match.

Durkin (1984) observed 16 first-, third-, and fifth-grade teachers for 1,920 minutes as they taught reading usual basal readers. She compared what they did to the recommendations present in the basal manuals they were using. Regarding vocabulary, there were suggestions in the basal manuals to present new vocabulary in context for 13 of the 16 teachers. However, only three teachers presented the words in context as the manual directed; the other 10 simply wrote the words in lists on the board or on charts, and the explanation they gave for doing this according to Durkin was "writing the context sentences took too much time" (p. 737). One might interpret these data to suggest that even if publishers do provide good, strong prereading vocabulary activities in basal materials, some teachers will still choose not to use them.

What about vocabulary instruction in secondary school classrooms? Graves (1987) stated that he was aware of no extant research, but he did provide the following comment:

However, 14 years of teaching secondary reading courses to inservice teachers, talking to secondary content teachers in a variety of subject areas, and observing secondary classrooms has convinced me that even less vocabulary instruction occurs at that level [i.e., secondary versus elementary levels]. More specifically, I believe that anything other than a very brief introduction to some words from an upcoming selection is extremely rare, and that even such brief instruction is quite rare. (p. 166)

Clearly, the observational research by Durkin (1978–1979; 1984) and Roser and Juel (1982), as well as Graves' (1987) testimony, suggest that vocabulary instruction may not be a high priority for elementary and secondary teachers. In contrast to this rather pessimistic picture of vocabulary instruction in schools, two more recent investigations suggest that the situation may not be quite so dismal after all.

Johnson, Levin, and Pittelman (1984) surveyed 228 teachers in grades 1 to 5 in seven different geographic regions in the U.S. about their beliefs and practices regarding vocabulary instruction. When asked if they teach vocabulary to prepare students to read a basal selection, the majority of teachers responded affirmatively. Approximately 75 percent of the primary grade teachers and 85 percent of the intermediate grade teachers reported that they "almost always" introduced new vocabulary before students read a basal selection. However, less than one third of those surveyed indicated that they related new vocabulary to past experiences. Ninety-six percent responded that they teach vocabulary as part of content instruction, and about three fourths of the teachers said they spend more than 15 minutes each week on vocabulary in content subjects. Whether the teachers' perceptions of their behaviors were accurate representations of what they actually did cannot be determined, of course, but it is clear that the respondents indicated that much more vocabulary instruction was occurring than prior observational studies had indicated (Durkin 1978–1979; Roser & Juel, 1982).

Blachowicz (1987) reported the results of a study in which she observed six fourth-grade reading groups as they each completed three basal reader selections (10–15 observation days per teacher, 20–40 minutes per observation). Results revealed that time spent on vocabulary ranged from 14 percent of the reading instructional time (according to a strict definition of vocabulary instruction) to 19 percent of instructional time (according to a lenient definition). When asked how much time they thought they spent on vocabulary instruction, the teachers estimated about 15 percent of the time was spent on vocabulary. Almost all of the time devoted to vocabulary (1,075 total minutes) involved prereading activities. Forty-five percent of this time involved determining the meanings of words in context, and 28 percent was spent on defining or pronouncing specific words. Activities such as categorizing words, reminders to use context clues, and teaching word structure clues consumed the balance of vocabulary instructional time.

The teachers Blachowicz (1987) observed spent more time on vocabulary than those observed by other researchers (cf., Durkin 1978–1979; Roser & Juel, 1982). One possible explanation for this difference is that because the basal materials used by the teachers Blachowicz observed were more recent (1982 editions of the Ginn and Houghton Mifflin reading programs), they provided more guidance in how to each vocabulary. In fact, Blachowicz noted that one basal series had a "high vocabulary load (the Ginn Reading Program, 1982), one that emphasized preparation of vocabulary and routinely introduced 10–15 words per lesson" (p. 136). Durkin's (1984) findings would seem to refute the hypothesis that more emphasis on vocabulary in the basal materials would result in greater attention to vocabulary, because she reported that teachers often did not adhere to basal manual suggestions. However, Blachowicz noted that teachers followed the manuals very closely and "teachers of the high load series [Ginn Reading Program] spent more time on vocabulary instruction and introduced more words" (p. 136).

In spite of the more positive results of Blachowicz' (1987) observations, she noted the following qualification:

All of these observations suggest that the major vocabulary goal in the observed 4th grade classrooms was to develop discrete word meanings rather than to develop vocabulary related to the conceptual framework of the selection or independent word learning strategies. (p. 135)

In other words, the quantity of vocabulary instruction apparently had improved compared to prior observations of teachers, but the quality of the time spent on vocabulary still left much to be desired.

In conclusion, most of the data on the state of vocabulary instruction in schools indicate that (a) teachers may not get much guidance for teaching vocabulary from the commercial materials on which they so regularly rely, and (b) teachers do not spend much time actually teaching vocabulary. However, it will be interesting to see if more recent editions of basal reading series demonstrate improved treatment of vocabulary instruction, as suggested by Blachowicz' (1987) report, and if the apparent trend toward more vocabulary instruction in classrooms, as noted by Blachowicz and Johnson, Levin, and Pittelman (1984), can be verified.

Instructional Research on Vocabulary: Pre-1970

Research on vocabulary instruction is hardly a recent phenomenon. In 1963 Dale and Razik published a bibliography of vocabulary research that included 3,125 entries. However, the interest in vocabulary instruction and the volume of research it produced failed to advance the state of knowledge significantly; much of the research was inconclusive, at least with respect to the persistently asked question about the comparative effectiveness of one approach to vocabulary teaching versus another. McKeown and Curtis (1987) commented on the equivocal results of much of the extant vocabulary research when they noted that "Clearly, missing answers have not resulted from a reluctance to search for them" (p. 1).

What, if anything, was learned about vocabulary instruction prior to about 1970? The conclusions drawn by Petty et al. from their 1967 literature review of 80 instructional studies typify the state of the art of vocabulary instruction research in the late 1960s:

The studies investigated show that vocabulary can be taught; they do not show that a "direct" method is better than an "indirect" one, that teaching words in isolation is better than teaching them in context, that an inductive appraoch is better than a deductive one. That is, it is not clear that these or any other dichotomies—other than that of teaching vocabulary versus not teaching it—have been resolved as a consequence of the designing, executing, and reporting of these many studies. (p. 25)

In other words, they acknowledged that some kind of instruction was better than no instruction in vocabulary, but the superiority of one strategy over another could not be established. The authors admitted that they initially conducted their review on the assumption that "there is some best way to teach vocabulary," but concluded that "This simply is not the case" (p. 25).

Chall (1987) found it interesting that the results of the Petty et al. (1967) review have often been interpreted pessimistically by researchers and practitioners. Rather than recognizing that direct teaching of vocabulary works (i.e., some kind of instruction was better than no instruction), the results of the review were often interpreted as a lack of support for direct teaching because there was no clearly superior method. We agree with Chall that as unsatisfying as the early research on vocabulary may have been, it was valuable in that it answered affirmatively at least one important research question: Can vocabulary be taught? It would be left to the next generation of vocabulary researchers, however, to tease out the discriminating features of the various instructional methods and to evaluate their relative effectiveness.

Instructional Research on Vocabulary: Post-1970

There are several ways that a discussion of research and practice in vocabulary instruction can be structured (cf. Beck & McKeown, in press; Herman & Dole, 1988; Mezynski, 1983; Stahl & Fairbanks, 1986). We have organized our review of recent instructional research according to a scheme similar to one used by Graves (1986) that places studies within one of two categories: (a) research on strategies designed to teach the meanings of specific words, or (b) research on generalizable and transferable strategies designed to promote the acquisition of new word meanings. We acknowledge that this dichotomy is not perfect (e.g., some research includes or compares both specific word and generalizable/transferable instructional methods), but it does enable us to organize our review in a manner that brings some structure to an otherwise diverse and expansive body of literature.

Teaching Specific Words. Many strategies have been recommended for teaching students the meanings of specific words (see collections of techniques in Carnine, Silbert, & Kameenui, 1990; Dale, O'Rourke, & Bamman, 1971; Johnson, 1986; Johnson & Pearson, 1984; Klein, 1988; McNeil, 1987; Nagy, 1988; Tierney, Readence, & Dishner, 1985; Wilson & Gambrell, 1988). Until recently, strategy selection could be based only on intuition, face validity, or testimony regarding the efficacy of a particular instructional approach. However, there now exists some empirical evidence on which strategy selection can be based.

In this section, we review recent research on various strategies for teaching specific words. Again, we draw upon Graves' (1986) organizational scheme. He identifies two specific-word-learning instructional tasks: "learning new labels" and "learning new concepts." The former involves teaching alternate names

(synonyms) or definitions for known concepts (e.g., a learner is taught that *irate* means about the same as *very angry*); the latter involves teaching words that represent difficult or entirely new concepts (e.g., a learner is taught words and corresponding concepts such as *spectroscope, democracy,* or *photosynthesis*). First, we present research on teaching students new labels for known concepts, which is achieved primarily through instruction in definitions or synonyms. Second, we present research on teaching students new concepts, which is achieved primarily through the use of semantic relatedness and prior knowledge strategies.

Learning New Labels: Research on Strategies Designed to Teach Word Definitions or Synonyms. Learning labels for words involves associative learning, which is pairing or associating two ideas—a concept and a label (learning definitions for words) or a known label with a new label (learning synonyms). Two different types of associative vocabulary learning approaches will be discussed: rote learning and mnemonic learning. Rote associative vocabulary learning involves drill and practice so that students learn or memorize definitions or synonyms. Mnemonic associative vocabulary learning involves use of specific strategies to help students remember concepts and their accompanying labels.

Rote Vocabulary Learning: Research on Teaching Definitions or Synonyms. Historically, the most common approach to teaching vocabulary was through a rote method; students learned definitions or synonyms through the use of a dictionary, glossary, or selected list of words and their definitions (Manzo & Sherk, 1972; Petty et al., 1967). Typically, vocabulary learning was self-directed. Students looked up words, wrote their definitions, used them in sentences, found synonyms or antonyms, and/or engaged in oral or written drill by way of worksheets or workbooks.

Indeed, students can be taught definitions or synonyms for specific words as Petty et al. (1967) noted in their review of early studies on vocabulary. This finding has been replicated in more recent experiments (e.g., Kameenui et al., 1982; McKeown et al., 1985; Pany & Jenkins, 1978; Pany, Jenkins, & Schreck, 1982; Parker, 1984; Stahl, 1983). For example, Stahl (1983) reported that fifth-grade students who looked up words in a dictionary, wrote their definitions, and discussed their meanings (definitional treatment) learned more word meanings than controls who worked in a comprehension skills book. Similarly, McKeown et al. (1985) found that students who were given "traditional" vocabulary instruction (drill, practice, and games designed to teach definitions or synonyms for target words) learned the meanings of more words, as measured by a multiple-choice test, than students in an uninstructed control group.

Further, the more intense or direct definitional vocabulary instruction is, the greater the gains in word knowledge. For example, like Stahl (1983) and McKeown et al. (1985), Pany et al. (1982) found that students who were provided simple definitional information (Meanings Given condition) learned more word meanings than control subjects. However, students who were provided intensive, teacher-led drill and practice on target words (Meanings Practiced condition) outperformed students in the Meanings Given group. Therefore, there is evidence that intensive, teacher-led definitional instruction (McKeown et al.'s Traditional group being a prime example) is superior to independent, student-directed vocabulary study.

The effectiveness of instructing students in word definitions is supported by Stahl and Fairbanks' (1986) meta-analysis. For the 29 vocabulary training studies that compared a "definitional only" or a "definitional emphasis" treatment to a no-exposure control group, the average effect size for dependent measures that assessed word knowledge was significantly different from zero (effect size of 1.37 for definitional only and 1.62 for definitional emphasis). In other words, students who were taught definitions consistently outperformed control group subjects on tests of word knowledge. However, simple definitional instruction did not enhance passage comprehension.

Although teaching definitions or synonyms does work, it may not be the most effective vocabulary teaching method. In studies that compared a definition or synonym approach (usually involving dictionary look-up), other strategies typically surpassed definition instruction. Specifically, students who were trained according to a semantic feature analysis approach (Anders, Bos, & Filip, 1984), a context method (Gipe, 1978–1979), a semantic relatedness approach (McKeown et al., 1985), a vocabulary with writing approach (Duin & Graves, 1987), and a definition-plus-context approach (Stahl, 1983) all exceeded students who received rote definitional/synonym instruction only. In summary, definition instruction works; however, as Beck et al. (1987) note, definitional training is effective only when the instructional objective is limited knowledge of new vocabulary items.

When one examines the impact learning definitions or synonyms has on comprehension of text that contains taught words, the limitation of rote vocabulary instruction becomes apparent. With the exception of only a few experiments (e.g., Kameenui et al., 1982), training in definitions or synonyms *only* has not improved students' understanding of texts that contain those words (e.g., Ahlfors, 1979; Jackson & Dizney, 1963; McKeown, et al., 1985; Pany & Jenkins, 1978; Pany et al., 1982; Tuinman & Brady, 1974).

For example, in the McKeown et al. (1985) experiment, students in the Traditional treatment learned word meanings (as measured by a multiple-choice test) as well as students in a Rich or an Extended Rich treatment (intensive instruction on sets of semantically related words), and all groups outperformed uninstructed controls. However, only subjects in the Rich and Extended Rich groups demonstrated improved passage comprehension. Similarly, Stahl (1983) reported that his Definitional treatment did not promote comprehension, whereas a Mixed treatment (students provided both definitional and contextual information) did enhance passage comprehension. On the basis of their meta-analysis, Stahl and Fairbanks (1986) reached the following conclusion regarding this issue:

Methods that provided only definitional information about each to-be-learned word did not produce a reliable effect on comprehension. . . . Also, drill-and-practice methods, which involve multiple repetitions of the same type of information about a target word using only associative processing, did not appear to have reliable effects on comprehension. (p. 101)

Therefore, definitional instruction alone is not likely to promote comprehension of passages that contain taught words. Additional instructional dimensions—contextual information or semantic relatedness, for example—must support or extend definition instruction.

In conclusion, students can learn word meanings according to rote vocabulary learning methods. However, other approaches may be more effective, especially if the objective is a richer, deeper understanding of words. Further, if passage comprehension is the objective of vocabulary instruction, then it is unlikely that rote definition/synonym strategies will achieve this goal.

Mnemonic Vocabulary Learning: Research on the Keyword Method. The word *mnemonic* refers to memory and strategies intended to improve memory or memorizing (Harris & Hodges, 1981). Nonacademic mnemonics include the use of phrases such as "Thirty days has September . . ." to remember the number of days in each month or "*Every good boy does fine*" to remember the notes represented by the lines on the treble clef.

One specific form of academic mnemonic strategy designed to teach definitions for words is the keyword method (Pressley, Levin, & McDaniel, 1987). Like rote learning of definitions or synonyms, the keyword method involves associative learning, but associative learning that includes a mental crutch. In its most common version, the keyword method requires the learner to construct an interactive visual image between the definition of the to-be-learned word and a familiar, concrete word that shares some common features. For example, to teach the English word *carlin,* which means *old woman,* the keyword *car* could be used to have the learner generate the image of an old woman driving a car (example from Pressley et al., 1987). When later asked to recall the definition of *carlin,* the learner would retrieve *car,* because of its acoustic similarity, and then recall the visual image and hence the meaning of *carlin.* An alternate version of the keyword method is a verbal-only one (Atkinson, 1975; Rohwer, 1973) that uses a sentence containing the keyword and definition to retrieve the target word, for example, "The *car* was driven by an *old woman*" (also from Pressley et al., 1987).

The keyword method has been heavily researched, and results favoring its efficacy as a definition-remembering technique have been consistent and robust (see reviews by Pressley, Levin, & Delaney, 1982; Pressley et al., 1987). Further, the keyword method has been shown to be effective for learning a variety of vocabulary item types (Levin, 1985) and across many diverse populations of learners that include normally achieving students (Levin et al., 1984; Levin, McCormick, Miller, Berry, & Pressley, 1982; Pressley, Ross, Levin, & Ghatala, 1984), learning-disabled children (Mastropieri, Scruggs, & Levin, 1985), university students (McDaniel & Pressley, 1984), and mentally handicapped students (Scruggs, Mastropieri, & Levin, 1985).

However, as Stahl and Fairbanks (1986) have noted, because the purpose of such keyword research has been to establish its validity as a viable strategy for vocabulary learning, it often has been compared only to no-strategy control groups, in which subjects typically were directed to read and study words and their definitions but without the aid of any specific strategy or training (Levin & Pressley, 1985; Pressley et al., 1982). Hence, those studies are not helpful in evaluating the comparative effectiveness of keyword learning with other vocabulary learning approaches. However, in several recent experiments with children, the keyword method has been compared to other ecologically valid approaches for learning word meanings. For example, Levin et al. (1984) reported that the keyboard method was superior to semantic mapping and a contextual analysis strategy for teaching high-achieving fourth- and low-achieving fifth-grade students the definitions of 12 low-frequency target words, although the keyword group's advantage was not evident one week later on a definition-matching test.

The keyword method has also been compared to a contextual analysis method. Working with 10- to 13-year-old students, Pressley et al. (1984) compared the keyword method to a context approach in which students constructed sentence contexts for 22 low-frequency English nouns. Results revealed that students recalled definitions for 51 percent of the words presented according to the keyword method versus only 8.5 percent presented through the use of the context items. In two experiments with fourth graders, Levin et al. (1982) compared the keyword method to a study method that presented subjects with the same low-frequency words in a meaningful sentence or paragraph context. Again, the keyword method resulted in significantly greater recall of definitions for target words. Similar experiments with adult subjects (e.g., McDaniel, Pressley, & Dunay, 1987; McDaniel & Tillman, 1987) support the conclusion that the keyword method is more effective than passage context alone for learning the meanings of specific words.

To summarize, the results of these and other studies with children and adult learners (Pressley et al., 1987) indicate that the keyword method is more effective in promoting recall of definitions of words when compared to a contextual presentation of the same target words (e.g., Levin et al., 1982, 1984; Pressley et al., 1984). Also, there is some indication that it is superior to a semantic mapping procedure (Levin et al., 1984) when training individual students and the criterion measure is definition recall. However, there is little evidence that keyword training has a positive effect on the comprehension of texts containing taught words.

Learning New Concepts: Research on Semantic Relatedness and Prior Knowledge Strategies. Semantic relatedness and prior knowledge strategies involve presenting new words in relation to words of similar meaning and/or relating new words or concepts to those that lie within the learner's realm of experience. Unlike rote and mnemonic associative approaches for learning new labels, semantic relatedness and prior knowledge approaches involve organizational processing and learning (Just & Carpenter, 1987, p. 402). In organizational learning, the emphasis is on acquiring new concepts rather than learning labels for known concepts.

Theoretical support for semantic relatedness and prior knowledge strategies comes from the *knowledge hypothesis,* which Anderson and Freebody (1981, 1983) have posed to explain the relationship between vocabulary and comprehension. The knowledge hypothesis is founded on a schema-theoretic view of comprehension (Adams & Collins, 1979; Anderson & Pearson, 1984), which asserts that understanding involves an integration of textual information and a comprehender's prior knowledge, or schemata. Thus, understanding is relational and occurs within the context of what the learner already knows or believes. As a result, semantic relatedness strategies, which present new words and concepts in relation to known words and concepts, are viewed as the pedagogical extension of the knowledge hypothesis.

Many strategies for teaching vocabulary fall under the rubric of semantic relatedness or prior knowledge. These include (a) semantic mapping (Hagen-Heimlich & Pittelman, 1984; Hanf, 1971; Heimlich & Pittelman, 1986; Johnson, 1984; Johnson & Pearson, 1984; Johnson, Pittelman, & Heimlich, 1986) and semantic feature analysis (Anders & Bos, 1986; Johnson, 1984; Johnson & Pearson, 1984); (b) other clustering and labeling strategies such as the List-Group-Label procedure (Taba, 1967), word or concept maps (Schwartz, 1988; Schwartz & Raphael, 1985a), webbing (Calfee & Drum, 1986; Cooper, 1986), and hierarchical classification (Calfee & Drum, 1986); (c) a comprehensive semantic relatedness program involving cognitive, physical, and affective dimensions (Beck & McKeown, 1983; Beck et al., 1980); and (d) other semantic relatedness, prior knowledge, experiential, or personalized approaches that purport to capitalize on learners' schemata (Bean, Singer, and Cowan, 1985; Carr, 1985; Cunningham, 1987; Duffelmeyer, 1985; Duin & Graves, 1988; Haggard, 1982, 1985, 1986; Ignoffo, 1980; Johnson & Johnson, 1986; Manzo, 1983; Marzano, 1984; Marzano & Marzano, 1988; Powell, 1986; Thelen, 1986). Because of the great volume of research on semantic relatedness and prior knowledge strategies, we have organized this research into four categories, each of which is discussed in a separate section.

Research on Semantic Mapping and Semantic Feature Analysis. Semantic mapping (see Figure 31C–1) is a categorization procedure that organizes words related to a core concept into meaningful clusters. The steps of semantic mapping (see Heimlich & Pittelman, 1986, pp. 5–6; Johnson & Pearson, 1984, pp. 37–38) typically include:

a. selecting a key or central word from a reading selection about which the teacher can assume that the students have some familiarity,

b. having the students free associate on the core word and generate a list of related words,

c. organizing the words into categories (and perhaps labeling them), and

d. discussing alternate ways of categorizing the words, adding new words, and forming new categories.

Semantic feature analysis (see Figure 31C–2) also draws on a learner's prior knowledge, but unlike semantic mapping in which a group of words is organized according to common features (i.e., placed into categories), students examine how a

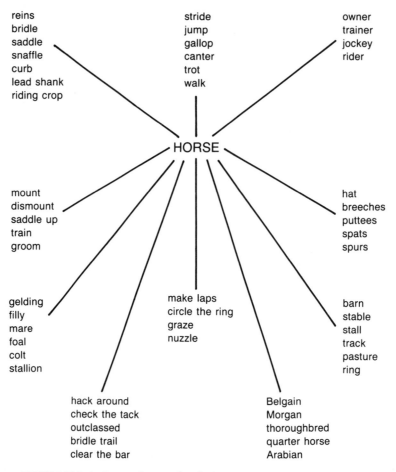

FIGURE 31C–1. Semantic map for *horse*.

Source: Dale D. Johnson & P. David Pearson, *Teaching Reading Vocabulary* (2nd ed.), New York: Holt, Rinehart and Winston, p. 162. Copyright © 1984 by Holt, Rinehart and Winston, Inc., reprinted by permission of the publisher.

group of related words differs—that is, how they can be discriminated from one another according to their features. Typical procedures for semantic feature analysis (see Johnson, 1984, pp. 32–33; Johnson & Pearson, 1984, p. 42) include:

a. selecting a key or central word from a reading selection about which the teacher can assume that the students have some familiarity,

b. listing, in a column on a matrix, several words that fall within the category,

c. listing, in a row on the matrix, characteristics or attributes (i.e., semantic features) of some but not all of the words,

d. determining which words do or do not possess those features, for example, using plus (+) and minus (−),

e. adding additional words and features and completing the matrix, and

f. discussing how words that are semantically related are alike and different.

Several investigations have examined the effectiveness of semantic mapping and semantic feature analysis for teaching the meanings of specific sets of related words. Johnson, Toms-Bronowski, and Pittelman (1982) and Toms-Bronowski (1983) reported that intermediate grade students who were taught target words according to semantic mapping and semantic feature analysis procedures outperformed students (on immediate and delayed measures) who learned the words through contextual analysis. Pittelman, Levin, and Johnson (1985) reported that semantic mapping was also an effective vocabulary building strategy when used with poor readers, and that it was equally effective when the poor readers were organized in small groups or in a whole class setting.

Johnson, Pittelman, Toms-Bronowski, and Levin (1984) used either semantic mapping, semantic feature analysis, or a modification of a traditional basal approach for prereading instruction with fourth-grade students. The two semantic-based strategies proved to be equally effective and, in some cases, more effective than the modified basal technique for general vocabulary development. All three treatments resulted in improved passage comprehension with a tendency for the comprehension scores for students in both semantic groups to be higher than scores for students who received the modified basal instruction.

	large	small	exquisite	lovely	rustic
villa	+	–	+	+	–
cabin	–	+	–	–	+
shed	–	+	–	–	+
barn	+	–	–	–	+
tent	–	+	–	–	–

FIGURE 31C–2. Semantic feature analysis for *shelters*.
Source: Dale D. Johnson & P. David Pearson, *Teaching Reading Vocabulary* (2nd ed.), New York: Holt, Rinehart and Winston, p. 42. Copyright © 1984 by Holt, Rinehart and Winston, Inc., reprinted by permission of the publisher.

Hagen (1980) also experimented with semantic mapping as a prereading strategy with fourth- and fifth-grade students. She found that in addition to enhancing vocabulary knowledge and comprehension, semantic mapping was a valuable diagnostic tool for assessing prior knowledge. The strategy also encouraged divergent thinking, and it was an effective motivator.

As noted in the prior section on mnemonic strategies, Levin et al. (1984) compared the effectiveness of semantic mapping, a contextual analysis method, and the keyword method for teaching high-achieving fourth- and low-achieving fifth-grade students the definitions of words. Keyword subjects outperformed semantic mapping students on an immediate definition recall test, but not on a delayed definition matching test. Also, the keyword and semantic mapping groups did not differ on two measures of sentence comprehension. Levin et al. interpreted their results as support for the use of the keyword method as the preferred method to teach immediate definition recall.

Stahl and Vancil (1986) sought to isolate the effect of the visual map itself from the effect of an accompanying class discussion of the semantic map. Sixth-grade students received one of three approaches to semantic mapping instruction: (a) Full Treatment, in which students generated and discussed semantic maps; (b) Discussion Only treatment, in which students only discussed the relationships among a cluster of words but saw no visual semantic map; or (c) Map Only treatment, in which a semantic map was provided for the students, but no discussion occurred. Results revealed that both the Full Treatment and Discussion Only treatments were superior to the Map Only treatment as documented by students' ability to identify synonyms for taught words and to insert them in those sentences, although neither discussion group differed on these measures. Stahl and Vancil concluded that discussion is a critical element in semantic mapping. Their finding perhaps explains the somewhat poor performance of the semantic mapping group in the Levin et al. (1984) study, since all instruction in their experiment was conducted individually, thus precluding the opportunity for discussion.

There also is evidence that semantic mapping and semantic feature analysis are effective strategies when used with disabled readers, learning-disabled students, and culturally diverse populations. Margosein, Pascarella, and Pflaum (1982) compared semantic mapping to contextual analysis and found that semantic mapping was superior for teaching vocabulary to reading disabled seventh and eighth graders of Hispanic background.

Karbon (1984) investigated the use of semantic mapping with rural Native American, inner city African Americans, and suburban sixth-grade students. She found that semantic mapping enabled students to rely on their prior knowledge and experiences as a means to expand their vocabulary. Jones (1984) replicated the Johnson, Pittelman, Toms-Bronowski, and Levin (1984) study with African American inner city fifth graders. In addition, there is evidence that semantic mapping and semantic feature analysis are effective when used with an ideographic language such as Chinese (Johnson, Pittelman, Toms-Bronowski, Chu-Chang, Tsui, Yin, Chien, & Chin, 1982).

Anders et al. (1984) used semantic feature analysis as a prereading and postreading strategy to teach high school learning-disabled students information covered in a social studies chapter. Students who received this instruction outperformed comparable control group subjects (who looked up difficult words from the chapter in a dictionary and wrote out their definitions) on both a vocabulary test of the words that were covered as well as a general comprehension test over the material. Bos, Anders, Filip, and Jaffe (1985) readministered the identical posttests to the same subjects six months later and found the same pattern of results: experimental subjects outperformed controls on both vocabulary and comprehension.

In conclusion, in the majority of studies (Levin et al., 1984, being somewhat the exception), semantic mapping and semantic feature analysis appear to be effective strategies for teaching students the meanings of new words that lie within a semantically related category of which students are familiar. In addition, there is evidence that these techniques also promote passage comprehension and are effective with learners of diverse ages, ethnic backgrounds, and reading abilities.

Research on Other Clustering and Labeling Strategies. The effectiveness of several other procedures that involve clustering semantically related words and labeling them have also been researched. One such procedure is Taba's (1967) List-Group-Label. LGL involves selecting a topic, brainstorming terms that relate to the topic, and grouping and labeling clusters of related terms. LGL is similar to semantic mapping except that a visual representation of the relationships among the words is typically not included. Bean, Inabinette, and Ryan (1983) evaluated the effectiveness of LGL for teaching 10–12th-grade students a series of literary terms (e.g., *allusion*). The LGL treatment group read an essay that discussed a particular literary element, were presented with an explanation of the element by the teacher, read a story that exemplified the element, and then completed a LGL lesson on the literary element. Results revealed that students in the LGL were more successful in learning literary terms than students who received the same sequence of instruction but without the LGL component.

Thames and Readence (1988) examined the effects of three forms of prereading vocabulary instructino used in conjunction with basal reader stories on second-grade students' vocabulary learning and comprehension. Students engaged in one of three approaches for dealing with preselected vocabulary: (a) use of the List-Group-Label (Taba, 1967) procedure; (b) use of the Reconciled Reading Lesson (Reutzel, 1985), in which enrichment or extension activities commonly found at the end of the basal reader lesson are used before the story is read; or (c) use of a traditional directed reading activity as prescribed in the basal manual (i.e., words are presented in context and discussed). Students read three basal stories using one of these procedures and after each responded to objective-item posttests that evaluated pretaught vocabulary and story comprehension. Results across all stories revealed that the RRL group outperformed both other groups, but the LGL and basal DRA groups did not differ. The authors suggested that the active, energetic responses promoted by the RRL approach might account for its superior performance and that the LGL might be a more appropriate postreading, rather than prereading, activity (i.e., how LGL was used by Bean et al., 1983).

Schwartz and Raphael (1985a; see also Schwartz, 1988) proposed a "concept of definition" approach to vocabulary learning that teaches students what types of information make up a definition and how they can use context and their own knowledge to learn word meanings. The strategy includes the use of a modified semantic map, which they call a word or concept map and context clues. Using the word map, students are taught to answer three questions that specify a word's definition: What it is? What is it like? and What are some examples? The concept of definition procedure involves high levels of teacher direction at the onset of the instructional sequence, but students are taught to use the procedure independently by gradually assuming more responsibility for applying it in later lessons.

The efficacy of the concept of definition approach has been tested in two experiments involving fourth- and fifth-grade students (Schwartz & Raphael, 1985b). In both experiments, students taught the concept of definition strategy outperformed students in a practice-control group (subjects worked independently to define the same words) or a no-treatment-control group (subjects only participated in pre- and posttesting) on posttests that required them to write definitions for words presented with and without supporting context. Schwartz and Raphael concluded from their work that the concept of definition procedure has promise, especially in content area instruction, for teaching students an independent strategy to help them understand new concepts and associated texts.

To summarize, there is some indication that the use of other clustering and labeling strategies, such as List-Group-Label and the concept of definition, may be effective in teaching vocabulary that is central to the understanding of basal reader and content area selections. However, the equivocal findings of research on LGL (cf., Bean et al., 1983; Thames & Readence, 1988)

and the limited research on concept of definition suggest that additional studies are needed before strong claims regarding their efficacy as vocabulary instruction or comprehension-enhancing techniques can be justified.

Research on the Beck and McKeown Program of Rich Vocabulary Instruction. A comprehensive program of vocabulary research and development using a semantic relatedness perspective has been initiated by Beck, McKeown, and colleagues. Their instructional program (see Beck & McKeown, 1983; Beck et al., 1980) presents words to students in semantic categories, not unlike a semantic mapping exercise, but instruction also includes multimodal tasks such as definition, sentence generation, and oral production. Game-like activities to promote response speed, interest in vocabulary and word play, and the use of learned words in new contexts beyond the classroom are additional components of their program. Also, instruction is intensive (30-minute lessons) and long term (up to 6 months in duration).

In their first two experiments involving fourth graders, Beck and her colleagues (Beck, Perfetti, & McKeown, 1982; McKeown, Beck, Omanson, and Perfetti, 1983) evaluated the effectiveness of their instructional program compared to control subjects who participated in regular reading and language arts activities. Results demonstrated that the rich vocabulary instruction received by experimental subjects was superior in three ways: (a) instructed students learned the meanings of more of the words that were taught; (b) they demonstrated greater speed of lexical access (as measured by reaction time on a word categorization task); and (c) comprehension of stories that contained taught words was superior for instructed students.

In a third study, McKeown et al. (1985) systematically examined the effects of the nature of vocabulary instruction and the frequency of instructional encounters of taught words. Fourth-grade students received one of three kinds of instruction: Traditional instruction (learning definitions for words), Rich instruction, or Extended/Rich instruction. The latter two treatments involved variations of their intensive program of vocabulary instruction (i.e., Beck et al., 1982; McKeown et al., 1983); what discriminated them was that Extended/Rich instruction encouraged students to be aware of and use the taught words outside of class, whereas the Rich instruction did not include this component. An uninstructed control group was also included in the experiment. Frequency was manipulated by providing either 4 or 12 encounters with each word. Dependent variables were measures of definition knowledge, fluency of access to word meanings, context interpretation, and story comprehension. Results indicated that the three instructional groups did not differ on simple definitional word knowledge, although any instruction was superior to no instruction (control group). Extended/Rich instruction was superior to Rich in fluency of access and story comprehension, and Rich was superior to Traditional in context interpretation and story comprehension. High frequency resulted in better performance on all measures. In a review of their work, Beck et al. (1987) drew the following conclusions from this experiment:

First of all, even a few, in this case four, encounters with a word within rather narrow instructional activities [Traditional treatment] will produce some, albeit limited, results. Second, a greater number of encounters with words is generally more helpful toward a variety of vocabulary learning goals. One exception to this was that even a higher number of encounters with traditional instruction did not enhance reading comprehension. Only rich instruction, and only in the high encounter condition, was powerful enough to affect comprehension. Finally, extending instruction beyond the classroom held advantage in making knowledge about the words more readily available for processing. (p. 154)

In conclusion, the work of Beck, McKeown, and their colleagues has demonstrated that an intensive, long-term program of semantic relatedness instruction can have positive effects not only on students' word learning but also on their comprehension of texts that contain taught words. They also have clarified somewhat the conditions of vocabulary instruction that influence passage comprehension. It appears that only frequent, rich instruction on words critical to story understanding, particularly when instruction extends beyond the confines of the classroom, affects comprehension. In contrast, traditional, definitional training in word meanings, even when such instruction is frequent, does not enhance passage comprehension. However, definitional training is effective and efficient when the instructional goal is only limited facility with new vocabulary.

Research on Other Semantic Relatedness or Prior Knowledge Approaches. Additional experiments have investigated the effectiveness of various other semantic relatedness or prior knowledge strategies for teaching word meanings. For example, Bean, Singer, and Cowan (1985) developed a procedure for using analogical study guides for use in content area subjects as a means to relate familiar words and concepts to unfamiliar ones. In an experiment with high school biology students (Bean, Singer, & Cowan, 1984), an analogical study guide that compared cell anatomy to a factory (e.g., cell wall = factory wall; cytoplasm = work area; lysosomes = clean-up crew) was used to teach cell structure/function associations. Results revealed that the analogical study guide was more effective in teaching structure/function associations than a traditional study method (cell parts related to their function but no analogy used) for students who were weak in comprehension abilities; however, neither method was superior for students who were above average in comprehension ability.

Duin and Graves (1987) explored the impact instruction in a set of semantically related words has on essay writing. Seventh-grade students were taught 13 target words over 6 days according to one of three methods: (a) Intensive Vocabulary and Writing Instruction (similar to the McKeown et al., 1985, Extended/Rich instruction, but it included many writing activities), (b) Intensive Vocabulary Alone (same as Intensive Vocabulary and Writing, but no writing activities were included), or (c) Traditional Vocabulary Instruction (worksheet/definition activities). As measured by a multiple-choice vocabulary knowledge test, an analysis of the students' use of target words in essays, and holistic analyses of the essays, the Vocabulary and Writing group consistently outperformed the other two groups, and the Vocabulary Alone group outperformed the Traditional Vocabulary group. The authors concluded that teaching a set of related words to students before they write not only results in students

learning the meanings of those words but also improves the quality of their essays.

Wixson (1986) contrasted the effectiveness of two approaches to preteaching vocabulary for basal reader selections: (a) a traditional dictionary word look-up method, and (b) a concept method using the Frayer model (Frayer, Frederick, & Klausmeir, 1969), in which students list attributes for target words and generate examples and nonexamples for each. Results indicated that preteaching unfamiliar central story words enhanced understanding of the selection, but both methods were equally effective in achieving this effect. Wixson stated that the comparison of methods was equivocal due to an interaction with instructional texts and that future research was needed to explore the relative effectiveness of a dictionary method versus the Frayer model.

Carr (1985) developed the Vocabulary Overview Guide (VOG), a procedure that requires students to draw from their prior knowledge in order to learn the meanings of semantically related groups of words contained in a selection they must read. The words along with synonyms and personal clues to their meanings are displayed in a graphic organizer. The VOG also has a metacognitive component that enables students to quiz themselves on words they are learning and employ review or corrective strategies as needed. To test this procedure, Carr and Mazur-Stewart (1988) taught developmental college readers to use the VOG and compared its effectiveness to a List Treatment, in which comparable students read the same passages but simply underlined and listed unknown vocabulary and ascertained their meanings from context. Results indicated that the VOG students demonstrated superior performance on a vocabulary test that evaluated their knowledge of the 100 words dealt with during intervention; this was true at the conclusion of training and 4 weeks later when the same test was readministered. VOG students also demonstrated greater awareness and control of vocabulary learning strategies as measured by a metacognitive awareness posttest.

Duffelmeyer (1980) tested the effectiveness of an "experiential" approach to vocabulary learning. Students in a college reading/study skills course were taught low frequency words according to one of two methods: (a) an experiential method, in which students enacted brief skits that involved the use of a target word and then related personal experiences that also exemplified the target word; or (b) a traditional approach, in which the same words were taught through contextual analysis, structural analysis, and dictionary usage. As measured by "paragraph-to-word" posttests that required students to match target words to paragraphs that described them, subjects in the experiential group consistently outperformed students in the traditional group.

Eeds and Cockrum (1985) experimented with a teacher prior knowledge/teacher interaction approach for teaching fifth-grade students the meanings of unknown words that appeared in a novel students were reading. Four target words contained in each day's segment of the novel were presented by having the students respond to questions that tapped their prior knowledge and experiences related to each target word. Students also generated examples and nonexamples of each target word and composed a definition for each. Compared to a dictionary look-up group and a control gorup that only read the novel, prior knowledge/interaction group students' performance on immediate and delayed multiple-choice posttests of target words exceeded the performance of both other groups.

Finally, in an experiment with third-grade students, Reutzel and Hollingsworth (1988) compared two strategies for teaching inferential comprehension: (a) a strategy that taught students to highlight vocabulary critical for the understanding of specific inference types (Johnson & Johnson, 1986), and (b) regular basal reader inferential comprehension instruction. Students receiving strategy instruction outperformed the basal group and controls on a series of near and far measures of inferential comprehension. Although the Reutzel and Hollingsworth strategy did not directly include a semantic relatedness dimension (rather, it involved a combination of text generation activities and aspects of reciprocal teaching), their experiment is noteworthy because it demonstrates further that a rich, elaborated form of vocabulary instruction does promote comprehension abilities.

In conclusion, research on a potpourri of other instructional strategies suggests that iterations of semantic relatedness and/or prior knowledge procedures are effective in teaching students word meanings. Specifically, an analogical study guide, intensive vocabulary and writing instruction, the Frayer concept model, the vocabulary overview guide, and experiential or interaction procedures have all been shown to enhance students' understanding of word meanings. Future research is required to evaluate the effectiveness and efficiency of these procedures relative to one another and to other semantic relatedness instructional techniques.

Summary of Research on Strategies for Teaching Specific Words.

The following statements summarize what we have learned from our review of research on teaching specific words.

1. Students can learn word meanings by rote vocabulary learning methods, such as definition or synonym instruction, and these procedures are sensible if the instructional objective is limited or partial knowledge of fairly large numbers of words. However, other approaches may be more effective if a deeper and fuller understanding of word meanings is desired. If passage comprehension is the objective of vocabulary instruction, then it is unlikely that rote definition/synonym strategies will achieve this goal.

2. The mnemonic keyword method is effective in teaching diverse groups of students definitions or synonyms. It is unknown if students can learn and retain word meanings for large numbers of words according to the keyword method, and the keyword's impact on text comprehension, if any, is yet to be established empirically.

3. Various semantic relatedness and prior knowledge approaches, such as semantic mapping and semantic feature analysis, are effective techniques for teaching new concepts to students of varied abilities and different racial and ethnic backgrounds. Further, there is some evidence that these methods also enhance passage comprehension.

4. The Beck and McKeown comprehensive program of rich vocabulary instruction has been shown to be effective in teach-

ing fourth-grade students word meanings, and there is strong evidence that such instruction positively affects the comprehension of texts that contain taught words.

Teaching Transferable and Generalizable Vocabulary Learning Strategies.

In this section we present research on teaching students transferable and generalizable vocabulary learning strategies. Unlike procedures designed to teach *specific* words (e.g., definition or mnemonic keyword instruction) or concepts (e.g., semantic relatedness techniques), the objective of strategies discussed here is to teach students skills and abilities that will enable them to acquire the meanings of *many* words. Research on two sets of strategies will be reviewed: research on teaching contextual analysis and research on teaching morphemic analysis.

Research on Teaching Contextual Analysis.

Contextual analysis is a strategy readers or listeners use to infer or predict the meaning of a word by scrutinizing the semantic and syntactic cues present in the preceding and following words, phrases, and sentences. As we noted earlier in this review, descriptive research provides evidence that extensive reading promotes word learning. This is true of students in grade 3, 5, 7, and 8 who read narrative and expository texts (Nagy et al., 1985, 1987) as well as kindergarten children who listened to picture books (Eller, Pappas, & Brown, 1988). There are a number of factors that affect learning from context such as frequency of occurrence (Jenkins et al., 1984), proximity of a clue to an unknown word (Carroll & Drum, 1982; Kameenui, Simmons, & Darch, 1987; Madison, Carroll, & Drum, 1982), the explicitness of a clue (Carnine, Kameenui, & Woolfson, 1982; Carroll & Drum, 1983), the proportion of difficult words (Nagy et al., 1985, 1987), the ability level of the student (Jenkins et al., 1984; McKeown, 1985), and the considerateness or clarity of the text (Herman et al., 1987; Konopak, 1988). Further, not all contexts are equally rich (Beck et al., 1983) and some may be ineffective or unreliable in providing meaning clues (Baldwin & Schatz, 1985; Schatz & Baldwin, 1986). Nevertheless, the accumulated evidence indicates that words are learned incidentally by reading or listening (Drum & Konopak, 1987; Nagy & Herman, 1987; Sternberg, 1987).

Although it is clear that words are learned incidentally through context, what does the research say about the effectiveness and efficiency of *teaching* students contextual analysis as a vocabulary acquisition strategy? To answer this question, results of two different sets of experiments on instruction in contextual analysis are reviewed.

Research Comparing the Effectiveness of Contextual Analysis and Specific Word Learning Strategies.

Several studies have compared contextual analysis to strategies designed to teach the meanings of specific words. In most instances, contextual analysis has not fared very well in these experiments. As indicated by studies reviewed in preceding sections of this chapter, contextual analysis was found to be less effective than semantic mapping (Johnson et al., 1982; Margosein, et al., 1982; Toms-Bronowski, 1983) and the keyword method (Levin et al., 1982, 1984; Pressley et al., 1984) for teaching students definitions or synonyms. These findings are supported by Stahl and Fairbank's (1986) meta-analysis which demonstrated that strategies representing a balanced mixture of definitional and contextual information were superior to strategies emphasizing only definitional or only contextual information.

In contrast, results of a few studies suggest that contextual analysis may be an effective method for teaching specific word meanings. Most notably, Gipe (1978–1979) reported that what she called a context method was superior to an association method (an associative labeling task), a category method (a semantic relatedness approach), and a dictionary look-up method for teaching word meanings. Somewhat similarly, Kameenui et al. (1982) found that when vocabulary definition training was integrated with passage reading (i.e., students were required to recall the meanings of previously taught words as they read them in context), it resulted in greater word learning and passage comprehension than when definition instruction was not integrated with passage reading.

However, as Kameenui et al. (1982) pointed out, neither Gipe's (1978–1979) experiment nor their own exclusively involved context clues. Rather, contextual and definitional information were combined to produce the positive effects. In fact, Stahl and Fairbanks (1986) labeled both Gipe's context method and Kameenui et al.'s passage integration method as being "balanced" approaches, which they defined as providing "a balance or near balance between definitional and contextual information" (p. 75). Therefore, it is safe to say that *purely* contextual approaches are not as effective in teaching new labels or concepts for specific words as are other direct, associative approaches, most notably the mnemonic keyword method (Pressley et al., 1987).

Does this mean that instruction in contextual analysis is never justified? Not at all. The experiments noted above (e.g., Johnson et al., 1982; Levin et al., 1984) suffer from an apples and oranges limitation: Specific-word methods (e.g., semantic mapping, keyword) were contrasted to a generalizable strategy (contextual analysis) that is not bound to specific words. It is true that strategies such as the keyword method are more effective than context for teaching synonyms or definitions for specific words, but they are not easily generalizable and transferable. In contrast, instruction in the *process* of contextual analysis has the potential to help students acquire the meanings of many words they encounter, not just those they are taught directly. Sternberg (1987) made this point very well as he elaborated on his claim that most vocabulary is learned from context:

What the claim does imply is that teaching people to learn better from context can be a highly effective way of enhancing vocabulary development. What the claim does not imply is that teaching specific vocabulary using context is the most effective, or even a relatively effective, way of teaching that vocabulary. Unfortunately, many believers in learning from context, as well as their detractors, have drawn the second inference rather than the first. As a result, they are on the verge of throwing out a perfectly clean and healthy baby with its, admittedly, less than sparkling bath water. (p. 89)

An analogue to this situation is instruction in word pronunciation. We can teach students to pronounce specific words through a look-say or sight word method, or we can teach them transferable and generalizable word pronunciation rules through instruction in phonic analysis. The former teaches the pronunciations of specific words; the latter teaches a process to pronounce many words. No doubt, a sight word method is more effective for teaching students to pronounce *specific* words, but one is limited in the number of specific words that can be taught. Each approach is justifiable and useful, but the objectives and outcomes differ significantly. So, too, teaching contextual analysis and the meanings of specific words, though both justifiable and useful, have very different objectives and outcomes. In the following section, we examine research on teaching contextual analysis as an independent word learning strategy.

Research on Teaching Contextual Analysis as an Independent Word Learning Strategy. What research has been conducted on teaching the process of contextual analysis as a transferable and generalizable strategy to acquire vocabulary? Unfortunately, the volume of research is fairly limited. As noted in an earlier section, Jenkins et al. (1984) reported that high ability fifth-grade students were able to supply definitions for words presented in contrived passages after 6 or 10 exposures, but not with only 2 exposures. However, when students were provided informal instruction for target words, preexposure to synonyms prior to reading the selection, they were much more efficient in using the context. Thus, even minimal instruction may enhance the effect context has on acquiring word meanings.

Sampson, Valmont, and Allen (1982) provided indirect instruction in contextual analysis to third-grade children by training them in the use of instructional cloze. They reported that cloze-trained students outperformed controls on an experimenter-conducted cloze test as well as on a standardized reading comprehension test; however, experimentals and controls did not differ on a standardized vocabulary measure. This latter finding requires some qualification, however, for the standardized vocabulary test used (*Gates-MacGinite Reading Tests,* MacGinite, 1978) employed a synonym matching format that presented the target word in isolation. Therefore, students were unable to rely on context clues when completing this test.

Instruction in contextual analysis is also a part of the Vocabulary Overview Guide proposed by Carr (1985) as well as the "concept of definition" strategy proposed by Schwartz and Raphael (1985a), and each procedure was designed to enable students to achieve independence in acquiring word meanings from context as they read content area selections. However, the strategies involve a combination of semantic relatedness procedures and instruction in contextual analysis, and research on the efficacy of these approaches is limited (Carr & Mazur-Stewart, 1988; Schwartz & Raphael, 1985b). Therefore, more research on these procedures is required, particularly experiments that contrast these approaches to others intended to teach independent word learning, before conclusions can be drawn regarding the relative effectiveness of these promising instructional strategies.

Several other experiments have been conducted in which more systematic and intensive instruction in contextual analysis has occurred. Hafner (1965) conducted a month-long experiment in which fifth-grade students were taught to use context clues; however, experimentals did not outperform controls. Askov and Kamm (1976) trained third-, fourth-, and fifth-grade students to use cause/effect and description context clues. After 4 hours of training, experimentals outperformed controls on a criterion-referenced test specifically designed to measures use of context.

Sternberg and several colleagues have described a set of context clue types and an accompanying theory for their use by readers (Sternberg & Powell, 1983; Sternberg et al., 1983). They have provided evidence in support of their theory (Sternberg & Powell, 1983) and have conducted two experiments to see if students could be taught to improve their use of context clues (see descriptions of both experiments in Sternberg, 1987). In their first training study, 10th- and 11th-grade students were taught to use six types of context clues. Instruction spanned six class periods. Experimentals outperformed controls on a test that included neologisms (invented, newly-coined words) and cloze blanks, although the pretest/posttest gains were modest. In a second experiment, adult subjects who received 45 minutes of training according to one of three different procedures based upon the Sternberg theory outperformed controls who either memorized words or who practiced using context clues. Although the results of these studies are promising, few conclusions can be drawn since Sternberg (1987) has only presented summaries of these studies, not complete research reports.

Building upon the work of Carnine et al. (1984), Patberg, Graves, and Stibbe (1984) taught fifth-grade students synonym and contrast context clues according to an "active teaching" procedure based upon teacher effectiveness principles. Comparison groups consisted of students who practiced contextual analysis on worksheets and an uninstructed control group. Results indicated that the active teaching group outperformed both the practice and control groups in ability to determine the meanings of low-frequency, novel words that were presented in short texts that contained synonym and contrast context clues.

In a somewhat similar study, Jenkins, Matlock, and Slocum (1989) taught fifth-grade students a general strategy for deriving the meanings of words from context. The strategy required students to scrutinize the context, supply a plausible synonym, evaluate the sensibility of the substitution, and generate another synonym if necessary. Results indicates that when the context strategy was provided in medium or high intensities (i.e., over 11 or 20 sessions, respectively), as opposed to low intensity (9 sessions), experimentals demonstrated small but reliable gains in ability to use context to infer the meanings of untaught words when compared to students who received word definition instruction.

In summary, research on teaching the process of contextual analysis as a transferable and generalizable skill is somewhat limited and at times equivocal (cf., Askov & Kamn, 1976; Hafner, 1965). However, experiments by Jenkins et al. (1989), Patberg et al. (1984), and Sternberg (1987) provide some evidence that training in context analysis may enable students to infer the meanings of words that have not been taught directly. In conclusion, we see promise in this line of inquiry but limited data to support the efficacy of extensive instruction in contextual analysis. Unfortunately, the situation today remains about the same it was in 1984 when Johnson and Baumann reviewed the instructional research on contextual analysis and reached the following conclusion:

So, while there is little doubt that contextual clues are potentially powerful aids in identifying unknown words, much additional educational research is warranted in order to determine what specific pedagogical procedures will be most effective in teaching children to learn and apply this skill. (p. 602)

Research on Teaching Morphemic Analysis. Morphemic analysis is a word identification strategy in which the meanings of words can be determined or inferred by examining their meaningful parts. A *morpheme,* the smallest unit of meaning in language, can occur in two forms: free and bound. Free morphemes function independently and are often referred to as base words or roots words (e.g., *walk, girl, happy*). Bound morphemes *(ing, s, un, ness)* also convey meaning, but they cannot stand alone; they must be attached to free morphemes. By combining free and bound morphemes, many different words can be formed (e.g., *walking, girls, unhappiness*). Morphemic analysis, which is also called structural analysis, typically includes four components:

(a) affixes—how the addition of various prefixes and suffixes affects word meaning, (b) inflections—how plurals, comparatives, verb tenses, and possessives alter word meanings, (c) compound words—how the conjoining of two free morphemes can result in a new word that is different in meaning but still retains some kernel of meaning of each of the base words, and (d) contractions—the merging and condensing of two free morphemes through usage. (Baumann, 1988, p. 202)

The rationale that underlies instruction in morphemic analysis is that if students can be taught basic and recurring free and bound morphemes, knowledge of many semantically related words can be acquired. For example, knowing the base word *add* and the meanings of various bound morphemes could enable students to understand *adds, added, adding, addend, addition, additional, additive,* and *additives* (example from Nagy & Anderson, 1984, p. 309).

Nagy and Anderson (1984) have estimated that about 230,000 words, 170,000 inflections, and another 100,000 proper names are to be found in printed school English (reading materials for students in grades 3 through 9). However, they estimate that this volume reduces to 88,533 word families, which are defined as follows:

A word family consists of the set of words for which there is a transparent, predictable relationship in both form and meaning. For example, *persecute, persecution,* and *persecutor* would all be considered as constituting a single word family, along with regular inflections such as *persecuted* and *persecutions.* (Nagy & Herman, 1987, p. 20)

Nagy and Anderson state that "for every word a child learns, we estimate that there are an average of one to three additional words that should also be understandable to the child, the exact number depending on how well the child is able to utilize context and morphology to induce meanings" (p. 304). Therefore, instruction in morphemic analysis is potentially a powerful and fruitful means for students to acquire new vocabulary.

Many strategies for teaching morphemic analysis have been proposed (e.g., Becker, 1977; Durkin, 1981b; Johnson & Pearson, 1984), and reading experts suggest that structural or morphemic analysis be a part of developmental (Duffy & Roehler, 1986; Mason & Au, 1986) and corrective/remedial (e.g., Carnine, Silbert, & Kameenui, 1990; Taylor, Harris, & Pearson, 1988) reading instruction. Further, all basal reading programs contain instruction in structural elements such as base words, inflections, contractions, and compound words. In spite of the conventional wisdom that instruction in morphemic analysis is an appropriate transferable and generalizable vocabulary strategy, research on the efficacy of such instruction is fairly limited.

Otterman (1955) taught seventh-grade students various morphological elements. Results revealed that although experimentals outperformed controls on tests of spelling and the instructed morphemic elements, they did not demonstrate superior performance on tests of new words, general vocabulary, or comprehension. Similarly, Freyd and Baron (1982) taught fifth-grade students specific suffixes but found that they were no more adept than controls at using this knowledge to understand untaught derived words. Freyd and Baron attributed this finding to the limited amount of time the experimental subjects were provided for instruction and practice. Hanson (1966) reported success in teaching first-grade students inflected endings but that this knowledge was not manifest on measures of general reading ability. In contrast, Thompson (1958) reported success in teaching college students 20 prefixes and 14 roots. Students not only learned the prefixes and roots and were able to identify them in words, but they also improved their ability to recognize words that possessed the prefixes.

One of the more technically sound morphemic analysis training studies was conducted by Graves and Hammond (1980). They taught seventh-grade students the meanings of nine commonly occurring prefixes (prefix group) and how to use them to discover the meanings of unfamiliar words that contained the prefixes. A second group of students (whole word group) was taught definitions for the same set of words as the prefix group (each of which contained one of the nine prefixes), but no mention was made of the prefixes. Results indicated that the prefix group learned the prefixes that they were taught when compared to the whole word group and an uninstructed control group; both treatments outperformed the controls on the set of taught words; but the prefix group outperformed both the whole word and control group on a set of transfer words, difficult vocabulary words that contained taught prefixes. Graves and Hammond concluded that "students can use their knowledge of the prefixes they are taught as a generative tool that will help them unlock the meaning of novel words" (p. 187).

In several more recent, small-scale studies, elementary children have been taught the meanings of prefixes as a generative tool. White, Sowell, and Yanagihara (1989) taught high ability third-grade children selected prefixes and reported that those students outperformed uninstructed controsl on two transfers tests involving unfamiliar prefixed words. Nicol and Graves (1990) reported similar findings for high-, middle-, and low-ability fourth-, fifth-, and sixth-grade students; further, the instructed students maintained their advantage over uninstructed controls on a delayed measure administered three weeks after instruction.

Wysocki and Jenkins (1987) examined the effect of instructing 135 fourth-, sixth-, and eight-grade students in derivational morphemes. Students were taught definitions or synonyms of six words for which there was a paired morphological derivative. Each set consisted of a stimulus word in which the students were instructed (e.g., *melancholic*) and a transfer word that was not taught (e.g., *melancholia*). Posttesting required the students to provide a definition for (a) transfer words in weak context, (b) transfer words in strong context, and (c) stimulus words in weak context. Results indicated that all students demonstrated morphological generalization ability (i.e., ability to define *melancholia* after have been taught *melancholic*), although this finding was much more robust under a lenient, as opposed to strict, scoring criteria. Stronger context also enhanced students' ability to make morphological generalizations, although unexpectedly, the effects of morphological generalization and context did not appear to be additive. In other words, unlike Nagy and Anderson's (1984) suggestion that morphology and rich context should enhance vocabulary acquisition, Wysocki and Jenkins found no evidence that their subjects combined these two sources of information.

In conclusion, similar to the research on teaching contextual analysis, research on teaching morphological analysis to both limited and oftentimes equivocal. Although several studies suggest that instruction in morphological elements may not be fruitful (e.g., Freyd & Baron, 1982; Otterman, 1955), other, perhaps more methodologically and pedagogically sound, experiments suggest that such training may be effective. Specifically, it appears as though elementary and middle grade students can be taught specific morphemic elements (e.g., Graves & Hammond, 1980) and that they are able to spontaneously generalize (infer) the meaning of one word from a morphologically similar derivative (Wysocki & Jenkins, 1987).

Summary of Research on Teaching Transferable and Generalizable Vocabulary Learning Strategies. The following statements summarize what we have learned from our review of research on contextual analysis and morphological analysis.

1. Use of context clues is a relatively ineffective means for inferring the meanings of specific words; rather, semantic relatedness procedures and mnemonic methods are preferred approaches for teaching the meanings of specific words.
2. When definitional information is combined with contextual cues, students are more apt to learn specific new vocabulary than when contextual analysis is used in isolation.
3. Research on teaching contextual analysis as a transferable and generalizable strategy for word learning is promising but limited. However, further research is required before

statements about the effectiveness of contextual analysis instruction can be made with much conviction.

4. Research on teaching morphological analysis as a transferable and generalizable strategy for word learning is limited. There is some indication that students can be taught specific morphemes (e.g., prefixes) that may enable them to unlock the meanings of unknown words containing these elements; also, there is some evidence that teaching students the meanings of unfamiliar words enables them to infer the meanings of morphologically related words. However, additional research is required in this area.

WHAT WE KNOW AND DON'T KNOW ABOUT VOCABULARY INSTRUCTION

In the final section of this chapter, we sum up what we have learned from our review of the literature on vocabulary acquisition and instruction and what we believe we have yet to learn. We have organized this section into three parts: (a) what we know and don't know about the breadth and depth of students' vocabulary knowledge, (b) what we know and don't know about teaching vocabulary, and (c) several conclusions about vocabulary teaching and learning.

The Breadth and Depth of Students' Vocabulary Knowledge: What We Know and Don't Know

What We Know. We know that students are faced with many words in the oral language they hear and the written language they read. Nagy and Anderson (1984) estimate that there are over 88,500 distinct word families in printed school English for students in grades 3 to 9. With an average family size of about 4.5 words, this means that there are nearly 400,000 graphically distinct word types in books used in schools, and this does not even include an estimated 100,000 proper names. Of course not all students will encounter all these word types, but clearly, the printed vocabulary presented to students is immense.

We know that students do learn the meanings of many words. Nagy and Herman (1987) estimate that students learn approximately 3,000 new words per year during the school years, and that a high school senior's vocabulary measures approximately 40,000 words. Data by White et al. (1990) suggest that these estimates may even be conservative. There are individual differences, of course (e.g., disadvantaged students know about 50 to 70 percent of the words known by middle class students; White et al.), but vocabulary learning does proceed at a fairly high rate throughout the school years.

We know that students encounter many unknown words as they read. Based upon work by Nagy and Anderson (1984) and Anderson and Freebody (1983), Nagy and Herman (1987) estimate that an average fifth-grade student who does only a modest amount of reading (3,000 words per school day) is likely to encounter almost 10,000 different unknown words a year. So, in spite of the vocabulary growth that occurs by way of instruction, incidental learning, or natural development, students are faced with many unknown words.

We know that students learn word meanings incidentally through oral and written context. Estimates of word learning from oral context (e.g., conversation, television, films) are unavailable; however, it is clear that students learn vocabulary from context while reading (Nagy et al., 1985, 1987). Such gains are modest but nonetheless real. Although the probability of learning the meaning of a word from a single encounter of it in text is low (about 1 in 20), if students read regularly for even modest amounts of time (e.g., 25 minutes per day for 200 days a year), they will learn from 750 to 1,500 words a year (all estimates from Nagy & Herman, 1987). Thus, from 25 to 50 percent of the estimated annual growth of vocabulary can be attributed to incidental learning from context while reading.

We know that vocabulary knowledge is related to and affects comprehension. The relationship between word knowledge and comprehension is unequivocal (e.g., David, 1944, 1968). Further, instruction in vocabulary, if done in systematic, intense, and rich ways, does positively affect comprehension (Beck et al., 1987; Mezynski, 1983; Stahl & Fairbanks, 1986).

What We Don't Know. What don't we know about the breadth and depth of student's vocabulary knowledge? Researchers are still not in agreement on several basic issues and questions such as, What is a word? and When is a word known? Such issues may never be resolved completely, but more attention must be given to specifying the basic concept of word and when one is known (see Anderson, in press).

More needs to be learned about incidental vocabulary learning. We have just begun to explore the effects of school and recreational reading on word learning. We know it occurs, but the interactions of factors such as type of material read, the volume of reading students do, the number of incidental encounters with a given unknown word, a reader's skill level and motivation, and the like are essentially unknown.

We know little about the impact oral context plays on vocabulary learning. How does the volume and quality of language that students are exposed to affect vocabulary learning? What are the individual and combined effects of oral and written context? What can be done to enhance the environment to optimize learning words from oral contexts? Longitudinal and developmental research is needed to address these questions.

Much remains to be learned about the relationship between vocabulary and comprehension. We know there is one and that it probably is causal. However, our power to predict what words will influence comprehension is weak, and the subtleties of the relationship between depth of word knowledge and the type and level of understanding remain elusive.

Teaching Vocabulary: What We Know and Don't Know

What We Know. What do we know about teaching vocabulary? First, we know that vocabulary instructional materials, basal reading series with 1970s' copyrights in particular, have been criticized for a lack of breadth and depth of vocabulary instruction (Beck et al., 1979; Durkin, 1981a; Jenkins & Dixon, 1983). Second, apparently elementary and secondary teachers don't teach vocabulary very often or very intensively (Durkin, 1978–1979, 1984; Graves, 1987; Roser & Juel, 1982), although there is some indication that this situation is improving (Blachowicz, 1987; Johnson, Levin, & Pittelman, 1984).

We know that early vocabulary research (before 1970) was not particularly illuminating. We learned that some form of vocabulary instruction was better than no instruction, an important but oftentimes ignored fact (Chall, 1987), but little could be stated about the relative effectiveness of one approach versus another (Petty et al., 1967).

We know that since 1970 there has been increased interest in vocabulary research, with many experiments comparing the effectiveness of different approaches to teaching vocabulary. A brief summary of the results of those comparative studies follows:

- Students can be taught labels (definitions, synonyms) for specific words through associative teacher-led definitional methods (e.g., Kameenui et al., 1982; Pany et al., 1982; Stahl, 1983). However, definitional instruction alone is not likely to result in enhanced comprehension of text that contains taught words (e.g., McKeown et al., 1983; Pany & Jenkins, 1978; Stahl & Fairbanks, 1986).

- Students also can be taught labels for specific words very effectively through the associative mnemonic approach known as the keyword method (e.g., Levin et al., 1982). Further, the keyword method has been shown to be more effective than semantic relatedness methods (Levin et al., 1984) and simple use of context (Pressley et al., 1987) for learning specific word labels.

- Various semantic relatedness approaches such as semantic mapping (e.g., Johnson, Pittelman, Toms-Bronowski, & Levin, 1984), semantic feature analysis (e.g., Anders et al., 1984), and other similar approaches (e.g., Bean, Inabinette, & Ryan, 1983; Schwartz & Raphael, 1985b) have been shown to be effective for teaching students new concepts and labels for them. In addition, there is evidence that such approaches postively affect the comprehension of texts that contain taught words (e.g., Anders et al., 1984; Johnson, Pittelman, Toms-Bronowski, & Levin, 1984).

- The intensive program of rich vocabulary instruction devised and tested by Beck and McKeown (e.g., Beck et al., 1982; McKeown, et al., 1983, 1985) has been shown to be effective in teaching concepts and improving the comprehension of texts that contain such concepts.

- Compared to associative tasks (e.g., keyword) or semantic relatedness approaches (e.g., semantic mapping), context clues are relatively inefficient for inferring the meanings of specific words (e.g., Johnson et al., 1982; Levin et al., 1984).

- When definitional information is combined with contextual cues, students are more likely to learn new vocabulary than when contextual analysis is used in isolation (e.g., Stahl, 1983).

- There is some evidence that teaching contextual analysis (e.g., Jenkins et al., 1989; Sternberg, 1987) and morphemic analysis (e.g., Graves & Hammond, 1980) as transferable and generalizable strategies are effective means for students to learn word meanings independently.

What We Don't Know. What is still unknown about vocabulary instruction? What are areas in need of further inquiry? We don't know if current commercial materials, basal reading series in particular, provide teachers stronger, richer, more comprehensive programs of instruction than the 1970s programs that have been extensively analyzed and found lacking. Further, we know virtually nothing about the quantity and quality of (a) vocabulary instructional methods, suggestions, and procedures found in supplemental vocabulary programs, and (b) vocabulary instruction that might be incorporated into content textbooks. In sum, much descriptive materials evaluation and analysis needs to be done to determine if current instructional materials provide sufficient attention to vocabulary instruction and if such instruction reflects our current knowledge base.

We don't know if classroom instructional practices in vocabulary have improved or are improving. Evidence reported by Blachowicz (1987) and Johnson, Pittelman, and Levin (1984) suggests that this may be happening, but more data are needed to document this apparent trend. Large scale, long-term classroom observational studies of elementary and secondary teachers and students are required to establish what attention is given to vocabulary within reading/language arts and content instruction.

There are things we don't know about specific vocabulary instructional approaches, strategies, and programs. For example, regarding rote vocabulary learning, we don't know what the most effective and efficient means are to provide students initial, limited definitional knowledge of vocabulary such that it will serve as the foundation for subsequent deeper, richer instruction or the acquisition of meanings from context.

We know that it takes more than definitional knowledge of words to affect comprehension, but we don't know what the optimal ratio of definitional knowledge to contextual/semantic relatedness information might be. How much emphasis on definitions relative to the use of new words in context or in semantically related ways is required to positively affect comprehension of texts containing taught words?

We don't know if the keyword method, which is very effective for teaching new labels for words and concepts, can positively affect the comprehension of text containing taught words. Also, as with any specific-word instructional strategy, one must question the efficiency of keyword instruction (cf., Beck et al., 1984; Nagy & Herman, 1984): Will students be able to retain mnemonic keys for large numbers of words taught across time according to the keyword method? Will long-term instruction in keyword become tiring as Graves (1986) suggests? What about polysemous words? Can the keyword method be used to teach multiple meanings?

What are the critical features of semantic relatedness instruction? We know that many different strategies work, but what are the underlying general principles? What is the relative power of focusing on word *similarities* (e.g., semantic mapping) versus focusing on *differences* in meaning (e.g., semantic feature analysis)? What are the individual and interactive effects of discussion and visual displays that appear to be central to semantic relatedness procedures?

We don't know if students can be taught to use contextual and morphemic analysis independently to learn the meanings of unknow words. If so, for which ages and grades of learners is this instruction effective? What role do students' individual differences play in contextual and morphemic analysis instruction? What types of context clues and morphemic elements are the most efficient to teach students? Might it be possible to define a scope and sequence of instruction in generalizable word learning skills? How efficient is instruction in generalizable vocabulary strategies? Do students who are taught to use contextual or morphemic clues learn significantly more words than what they might acquire incidentally through reading or listening? The promise of providing students transferable and generalizable tools for independent word learning through contextual and morphemic analysis is great, but the promise currently outstrips the evidence we possess on the efficacy of such instruction.

What Does It All Mean?

Can our knowledge of vocabulary instruction be reduced or synthesized? Are there any general, global principles that teachers, teacher trainers, supervisors, curriculum developers, or educational publishers might adhere to as they develop or administer vocabulary curriculum and instruction? Several writers have proposed guidelines for teaching vocabulary (e.g., Blachowicz, 1985, pp. 879–880; Blachowicz, 1986, p. 644; Carr & Wixson, 1986, pp. 589–592; Marzano & Marzano, 1988, pp. 11–12; Mezynski, 1983, p. 273; Stahl, 1985, pp. 19–20; Stahl & Fairbanks, 1986, p. 101). Stahl's (1986) three principles for effective vocabulary instruction are representative of many of these guidelines: (a) "Principle 1: Give both context and definitions," (b) "Principle 2: Encourage 'deep' processing" and (c) "Principle 3: Give multiple exposures" (663–665).

For the most part, we find existing sets of principles or guidelines like Stahl's (1986) sensible, empirically based, and practical. However, we typically find them to be linked to a specific vocabulary instructional objective, usually one involving teaching specific words. For example, Stahl's suggestions are appropriate if one's objective is to promote students' comprehension of texts. In order to achieve this goal, research suggests that it makes sense to provide deep instruction with multiple exposures with words for which both context and definitional information is provided. However, if one's objective were different, for example, to make students skillful in independent word learning strategies (e.g., ability to use contextual analysis), then Stahl's three principles would not be applicable.

It is not our intent to criticize Stahl (1986) or others who have made recommendations for vocabulary instruction (e.g., Graves, 1987; Kameenui et al., 1987; Nagy, 1988). In fact, we applaud them for their efforts in translating research into practice. However, we believe that there needs to be an alignment between instructional objectives and the instructional means to achieve them. Actually, we see the need for two related sets of decision-making guidelines: a global set and a specific set. At the global level, we see the need for a set of decision-making principles that must be superordinate to, but complementary with, specific instructional principles like Stahl's. These principles would guide the design of a comprehensive program of vocabulary instruction. What would we recommend? We admit we are on thin ice at this point; nevertheless, here are our suggestions for making *global* instructional decisions regarding vocabulary instruction.

1. Establish vocabulary learning goals for your students.
2. Include goals that provide for teacher-initiated vocabulary learning as well as ones that strive for student independence in vocabulary learning.
3. Include instruction in both specific-word and transferable and generalizable strategies.
4. Select instructional strategies and procedures that are carefully aligned with each of your goals.
5. Provide poor readers and at-risk learners a systematic and sustained program of vocabulary instruction that teaches them more words and strategies in less time (Kameenui & Simmons, 1990; Stanovich, 1986).
6. Select assessment tasks and formats that are consistent with your instructinal strategies and desired outcomes.
7. Consider the costs and benefits of instruction (Graves & Prenn, 1986) in terms of student and teacher time and effort when matching instructional methods to goals.
8. Select the most effective and efficient strategy(ies) for each instructional objective.
9. Do not limit yourself to a narrow set of vocabulary instructional techniques. Select suitable strategies from a range of empirically validated instructional procedures that are compatible with your instructional objectives.
10. Continually evaluate your vocabulary learning objectives and the procedures and techniques you have chosen to address each.

At the *specific* level would come guidelines like those Stahl (1986) has recommended. For example, given a decision to provide vocabulary instruction that will enhance text comprehension, then a procedure that employs Stahl's three principles could be selected (e.g., the Beck and McKeown, 1983, program of rich instruction).

What help can be provided when deciding which specific strategy to select? We agree with McKeown and Beck (1988) that "the choice of the kind of instruction to use in specific instances depends on the goal of the instruction, the kinds of words being presented, and the characteristics of the learners" (p. 44). In other words, the method you select for teaching vocabulary depends upon the instructional objective you have.

Graves and Prenn (1986) have elaborated on the relational nature of vocabulary instruction. They argue, quite convincingly, we believe, that methods must be selected by weighing their costs and benefits.

Different methods of teaching words are appropriate in difference circumstances. . . . Our purpose is to make the point that there is no one best method of teaching words—that various methods have both their costs and their benefits and will be very appropriate and effective in some circumstances and less appropriate and effective in others. (pp. 596–597)

For example, if one's objective were to teach the meanings of a relatively few specific words in a content subject like science, the least costly approach might be to use a definitional method. However, if one wished to teach meanings for many words, or if the goal were to enhance passage comprehension, another method, perhaps a semantic relatedness procedure, would be preferred. If one's goal were long-term, expansive, independent vocabulary learning, regular independent reading combined with instruction in use of contextual and morphemic analysis would be the logical approach. In short, the simplicity of Graves and Prenn's statement, "there is no one best method of teaching words," should not mask its importance.

What about a comprehensive program of vocabulary instruction? We have outlined 10 principles above that might be used to guide decision making in vocabulary instruction, but what about the substance or content of such a comprehensive program? What would be the objectives of it, and what would be the means to reach those objectives? Relatively few writers have addressed this issue directly (Beck et al., 1987; Kameenui et al., 1987; and McKeown & Beck, 1988; being the exceptions), perhaps because the ice gets even thinner here. Nevertheless, we conclude our review with three instructional objectives and corresponding means to achieve each. In doing this, we draw from the empirical evidence on vocabulary teaching and learning; a similar plan outlined by Graves (1987); and our own intuition, common sense, biases, and beliefs. We have organized the components according to an objective/means format.

Objective 1: Teach students to learn words independently.

Means to Achieve Objective 1:

- Have students listen to live and recorded oral discourse. Read to them and have them listen to stories, books, plays, songs, poems, fiction and nonfiction prose, and simple conversation. It would be unwise to underestimate the power of simple oral exposure to vocabulary.
- Promote wide independent reading at home and school. Make independent reading a regular, significant part of the language-arts curriculum. We believe in the power of incidental learning of vocabulary, but incidental word learning cannot rely on accidental reading.
- Engage students in oral and written composition on a regular basis. Have students express themselves in writing and speech daily. Generative processes must be used and exercised if receptive vocabulary is to become expressive.
- Teach students formally and directly the transferable and generalizable vocabulary learning strategies of morphemic and contextual analysis. It is likely that this instruction will enhance students' ability to acquire word meanings incidentally from written and oral texts.
- Teach students to use regular and specialized dictionaries and the thesaurus. This instruction may be mundane, but skilled use of these tools is essential for later sustained and independent vocabulary growth.

Objective 2: Teach students the meanings of specific words.

Means to Achieve Objective 2:

- Teach synonyms or definitions for specific words through rote or mnemonic strategies. There will be times when students must learn labels for limited numbers of words; in those situations, select the most efficient and cost effective approaches.
- Provide students partial knowledge of many unknown words. Simple definitional strategies or preexposure prior to reading or listening will provide students a foot-in-the-door level of knowledge for words that they may learn more deeply and fully over time with additional subsequent exposures.
- Preteach critical vocabulary necessary to comprehend selections students read in basal readers and in content area textbooks. Deep, rich levels of word knowledge are needed in order to affect text comprehension, and costly strategies such as semantic relatedness or definitional/context methods must be employed in order to achieve this objective.

Objective 3: Help students to develop an appreciation for words and to experience enjoyment and satisfaction in their use.

Means to Achieve Objective 3:

- Set a positive model. Demonstrate how word play can be interesting and enjoyable by expressing the value in possessing a versatile vocabulary and by demonstrating how word learning can be interesting and fun.
- Have fun with words. Play word games linked to content topics and ones that may be done purely for entertainment and enjoyment.
- Promote student use of vocabulary learned at school in nonschool contexts (e.g., Beck & McKeown's 1983, "Word Wizard").

We acknowledge that several of the preceding objectives and means are based as much upon our intuition and beliefs as on hard data. We do not apologize for this, for we offer them more to challenge researchers and developers than to present them as truth. We await eagerly the generation of data that will affirm or refute what we now conceive to be an appropriately balanced vocabulary instructional program. Stated alternately, time will tell whether we should have selected pseudonyms when we wrote this chapter.

In closing, having completed this review, we now recognize that it was relatively easy to express what we know and don't know about vocabulary acquisition and what works and does not work in vocabulary instruction. It was quite another matter to translate this knowledge into sound pedagogy. In short, the bridge from theory to practice is shrouded in mist and haunted by all sorts of insalubrious creatures. Therefore, we agree with Voltaire that "Language is very difficult to put into words." However, as educators, we find the reciprocal of Voltaire's statement even more challenging: Words are indeed very difficult to put into language (instruction).

====================== *References* ======================

Adams, M., & Collins, A. (1979). A schema-theoretic view of reading. In R. Freedle (Ed.), *New directions in discourse processing.* Norwood, NJ: Ablex.

Ahlfors, G. (1979). *Learning word meanings: A comparison of three instructional procedures.* Unpublished doctoral dissertation, University of Minnesota, Minneapolis.

Anders, P. L., & Bos, C. S. (1986). Semantic feature analysis: An interactive strategy for vocabulary development and text comprehension. *Journal of Reading, 29,* 610–616.

Anders, P. L., Bos, C. S., & Filip, D. (1984). The effect of semantic feature analysis on the reading comprehension of learning-disabled students. In J. A. Niles & L. A. Harris (Eds.), *Changing perspectives on research in reading/language processing and instruction,* Thirty-third yearbook of the National Reading Conference (pp. 162–166). Rochester, NY: National Reading Conferece.

Anderson, R. C. (in press). Inferences about word meanings. In A. Graesser & G. Bower (Eds.), *The psychology of learning and motivation.*

Anderson, J. C., & Freebody, P. (1981). Vocabulary knowledge. In J. T. Guthrie (Ed.), *Comprehension and teaching* (pp. 77–117). Newark, DE: International Reading Association.

Anderson, R. C., & Freebody, P. (1983). Reading comprehension and the assessment and acquisition of word knowledge. In B. Hutson (Ed.), *Advanced in reading/language research: A research annual* (pp. 231–256). Greenwich, CT: JAI Press.

Anderson, R. C., & Pearson, P. D. (1984). A schema-theoretic view of basic processes in reading comprehension. In P. D. Pearson (Ed.), *Handbook of reading research* (pp. 255–291). New York: Longman.

Anderson, R. C., Wilson, P. T., & Fielding, L. G. (1986). *Growth in reading and how children spend their time outside of school.* (Tech. Rep. No. 389). Urbana: University of Illinois, Center for the Study of Reading.

Anglin, J. M. (1977). *Word, object, and conceptual development.* New York: Norton.

Askov, E. N., & Kamm, K. (1976). Context clues: Should we teach children to use a classification system in reading? *Journal of Educational Research, 69,* 341–344.

Atkinson, R. C. (1975). Mnemotechnics in second-language learning. *American Psychologist, 30,* 821–828.

Baldwin, R. S., & Schatz, E. L. (1985). Context clues are ineffective with low frequency words in naturally occurring prose. In J. A. Niles & R. V. Lalik (Eds.), *Issues in literacy: A research perspective,* Thirty-fourth yearbook of the National Reading Conference (pp. 132–135). Rochester, NY: National Reading Conference.

Baumann, J. F. (1988). *Reading assessment: An instructional decision-making perspective.* Columbus, OH: Merrill.

Bean, T. W., Inabinette, N. B., & Ryan, R. (1983). The effect of a categorization strategy on secondary students' retention of literary vocabulary. *Reading Psychology, 4,* 247–252.

Bean, T. W., Singer, H., & Cowan, S. (1984, December). *Acquisition of a topic schema in high school biology through an analogical study guide.* Paper presented at the meeting of the National Reading Conference, St. Petersburg, FL.

Bean, T. W., Singer, H., & Cowan, S. (1985). Analogical study guides: Improving comprehension in science. *Journal of Reading, 29,* 246–250.

Beck, I. L. (1984). Developing comprehension: The impact of the directed reading lesson. In R. C. Anderson, J. Osborn, & R. J. Tierney (Eds.), *Learning to read in American schools* (pp. 3–20). Hillsdale, NJ: Erlbaum.

Beck, I. L., McCaslin, E. S., & McKeown, M. G. (1980). *The rational and design of a program to teach vocabulary to fourth-grade students* (LRDC Publication 1980/25). Pittsburgh: University of Pittsburgh, Learning Research and Development Center.

Beck, I. L., & McKeown, M. G. (1983). Learning words well—A program to enhance vocabulary and comprehension. *The Reading Teacher, 36,* 622–625.

Beck, I. L., & McKeown, M. G. (1987). Getting the most from basal reading selections. *Elementary School Journal, 87,* 343–356.

Beck, I. L., & McKeown, M. G. (in press). Conditions of vocabulary acquisition. In P. D. Pearson (Ed.), *Handbook of reading research* (2nd ed.). New York: Longman.

Beck, I. L., McKeown, M. G., & McCaslin, E. S. (1983). Vocabulary development: All contexts are not created equal. *Elementary School Journal, 83,* 177–181.

Beck, I. L., McKeown, M. G., McCaslin, E. S., & Burkes, A. M. (1979). *Instructional dimensions that may affect reading comprehension: Examples from two commercial reading programs* (LRDC Publication 1979/20). Pittsburgh: University of Pittsburgh, Learning Research and Development Center.

Beck, I. L., McKeown, M. G., & Omanson, R. C. (1984, April). *The fertility of some types of vocabulary instruction.* Paper presented at the meeting of the American Educational Research Association, New Orleans.

Beck, I. L., McKeown, M. G., & Omanson, R. C. (1987). The effects and uses of diverse vocabulary instructional techniques. In M. G. McKeown & M. E. Curtis (Eds.), *The nature of vocabulary acquisition* (pp. 147–163). Hillsdale, NJ: Erlbaum.

Beck, I. L., Perfetti, C. A., & McKeown, M. G. (1982). Effects of long-term vocabulary instruction on lexical access and reading comprehension. *Journal of Educational Psychology, 74,* 506–521.

Becker, W. C. (1977). Teaching reading and language to the disadvantaged—what we have learned from field research. *Harvard Educational Review, 47,* 518–543.

Becker, W. C., Dixon, R., & Anderson-Inman, L. (1980). *Morphographic and root word analysis of 26,000 high frequency words* (Tech. Rep. 1980–1). Eugene: University of Oregon Follow Through Project, College of Education.

Blachowicz, C. L. Z. (1985). Vocabulary development and reading: From research to instruction. *The Reading Teacher, 38,* 876–881.

Blachowicz, C. L. Z. (1986). Making connections: Alternatives to the vocabulary notebook. *Journal of Reading, 29,* 643–649.

Blachowicz, C. L. Z. (1987). Vocabulary instruction: What goes on in the classroom? *The Reading Teacher, 41,* 132–137.

Boorstin, D. J. (1983). *The discoverers: A history of man's search to know his world and himself.* New York: Random House.

Bos, C. S., Anders, P. L., Filip, D., & Jaffe, L. E. (1985). Semantic feature analysis and long-term learning. In J. A. Niles & R. V. Lalik (Eds.), *Issues in literacy: A research perspective,* Thirty-fourth yearbook of the National Reading Conference (pp. 42–47). Rochester, NY: National Reading Conference.

Calfee, R., & Drum, P. (1986). Research on teaching reading. In M. C. Wittrock (Ed.), *Handbook of research on teaching* (3rd ed.) (pp. 804–849). New York: Macmillan.

Carey, S. (1978). Child as word learner. In M. Halle, J. Bresnam, & G. Miller (Eds.), *Linguistic theory and psychological reality,* (pp. 264–293). Cambridge, MA: MIT Press.

Carnine, D. W., Kameenui, E. J., & Coyle, G. (1984). Utilization of contextual information in determining the meaning of unfamiliar words. *Reading Research Quarterly, 19,* 188–204.

Carnine, D. W., Kameenui, E. J., & Woolfson, N. (1982). Training textual dimensions related to text-based inferences. *Journal of Reading Behavior, 14,* 331–340.

Carnine, D. W., Silbert, J., & Kameenui, E. J. (1990). *Direct instruction reading* (2nd ed.). Columbus, OH: Merrill.

Carr, E. M. (1985). The vocabulary overview guide: A metacognitive strategy to improve vocabulary comprehension and retention. *Journal of Reading, 28,* 648–689.

Carr, E. M., & Mazur-Stewart, M. (1988). The effects of the vocabulary overview guide on vocabulary comprehension and retention. *Journal of Reading Behavior, 20*(1), 43–62.

Carr, E. M., & Wixson, K. K. (1986). Guidelines for evaluating vocabulary instruction. *Journal of Reading, 29,* 588–595.

Carroll, B. A., & Drum, P. A. (1982). The effects of context clue type and variations in content on the comprehension of unknown words. In J. A. Niles & L. A. Harris (Eds.), *New inquiries in reading research and instruction,* Thirty-first yearbook of the National Reading Conference (pp. 89–93). Rochester, NY: National Reading Conference.

Carroll, B. A., & Drum, P. A. (1983). Definitional gains for explicit and implicit context clues. In J. A. Niles & L. A. Harris (Eds.), *Searches for meaning in reading/language processing & instruction.* Thirty-second yearbook of the National Reading Conference (pp. 158–162). Rochester, NY: National Reading Conference.

Chall, J. S. (1987). Two vocabularies for reading: Recognition and meaning. In M. G. McKeown & M. E. Curtis (Eds.), *The nature of vocabulary acquisition* (pp. 7–17). Hillsdale, NJ: Erlbaum.

Clark, E. V. (1973). What's in a word? On the child's acquisition of semantics in his first language. In T. E. Moore (Ed.), *Cognitive development and the acquisition of language* (pp. 65–110). New York: Academic Press.

Cole, L. (1946). *The elementary school subjects.* New York: Rinehart.

Cooper, J. D. (1986). *Improving reading comprehension.* Boston: Houghton Mifflin.

Crowder, R. G. (1976). *Principles of learning and memory.* Hillsdale, NJ: Erlbaum.

Cunningham, P. M. (1987). Are your vocabulary words lunules or lupulins? *Journal of Reading, 30,* 344–348.

Curtis, M. E. (1987). Vocabulary testing and instruction. In M. G. McKeown & M. E. Curtis (Eds.), *The nature of vocabulary acquisition* (pp. 37–51). Hillsdale, NJ: Erlbaum.

Daalen-Kapteijns, M. M. van, & Elshout-Mohr, M. (1981). The acquisition of word meanings as a cognitive verbal process. *Journal of Verbal Learning and Verbal Behavior, 20,* 386–399.

Dale, E., O'Rourke, J., & Bamman, H. A. (1971). *Techniques of teaching vocabulary.* Palo Alto, CA: Field Educational Publications.

Dale, E., & Razik, T. (1963). *Bibliography of vocabulary studies.* Columbus, OH: Ohio State University Bureau of Educational Research and Service.

Dale, E., Razik, T., & Petty, W. (1973). *Bibliography of vocabulary studies.* Columbus, OH: Ohio State University.

Davis, F. B. (1944). Fundamental factors in reading comrehension. *Psychometrika, 9,* 185–197.

Davis, F. B. (1968). Research in comprehension in reading. *Reading Research Quarterly, 3,* 499–545.

Dixon, R. C., & Jenkins, J. R. (1984). *An outcome analysis of receptive vocabulary knowledge.* Unpublished manuscript, University of Illinois, Champaign-Urbana.

Drum, P. A., & Konopak, B. C. (1987). Learning word meanings from written context. In M. G. McKeown & M. E. Curtis (Eds.), *The nature of vocabulary acquisition* (pp. 73–87). Hillsdale, NJ: Erlbaum.

Duffelmeyer, F. A. (1980). The influence of experience-based vocabulary instruction on learning word meanings. *Journal of Reading, 24,* 35–40.

Duffelmeyer, F. A. (1985). Teaching word meaning from an experience base. *The Reading Teacher, 39,* 6–9.

Duffy, G. G., & Roehler, L. R. (1986). *Improving classroom reading instruction: A decision-making approach.* New York: Random House.

Duin, A. H., Graves, M., F. (1987). Intensive vocabulary instruction as a prewriting technique. *Reading Research Quarterly, 22,* 311–330.

Duin, A. H., Graves, M., F. (1988). Teaching vocabulary as a writing prompt. *Journal of Reading, 32,* 204–212.

Durkin, D. D. (1978–1979). What classroom observations reveal about reading comprehension instruction. *Reading Research Quarterly, 14,* 481–533.

Durkin, D. D. (1981a). Reading comprehension instruction in five basal reader series. *Reading Research Quarterly, 16,* 515–544.

Durkin, D. D. (1981b). *Strategies for identifying words* (2nd ed.). Boston: Allyn and Bacon.

Durkin, D. D. (1984). Is there a match between what elementary teachers do and what basal reader manuals recommend? *The Reading Teacher, 37,* 734–744.

Education Products Information Exchange. (1977). *Report on a national survey of the nature and the quality of instructional materials most used by teachers and learners* (Tech. Rep. No. 76). New York: EPIE Institute.

Eeds, M., & Cockrum, W. A. (1985). Teaching word meanings by expanding schemata vs. dictionary work vs. reading in context. *Journal of Reading, 28,* 492–497.

Eller, R. G., Pappas, C. C., & Brown, E. (1988). The lexical development of kindergarteners: Learning from written context. *Journal of Reading Behavior, 20*(1), 5–24.

Frayer, D. A., Frederick, W. C., & Klausmeir, H. J. (1969). *A schema for testing the level of concept mastery* (Working Paper No. 16). Madison, WI: University of Wisconsin, Wisconsin Research and Development Center for Cognitive Learning.

Freebody, P., & Anderson, R. C. (1981). *Effects of differing proportions and locations of difficult vocabulary on text comprehension* (Tech. Rep. No. 202). Champaign: University of Illinois, Center for the Study of Reading.

Freebody, P., & Anderson, R. C. (1983). Effects of vocabulary difficulty, text cohesion, and schema availability on reading comprehension. *Reading Research Quarterly, 18,* 277–294.

Freyd, P., & Baron, J. (1982). Individual differences in acquisition of derivational morphology. *Journal of Verbal Learning and Verbal Behavior, 21,* 282–295.

Gage, N. L. (Ed.). (1963). *Handbook of research on teaching.* Chicago: Rand McNally.

Gage, N. L. (1978). *The scientific basis for the art of teaching.* New York: Teachers College Press.

Gipe, J. P. (1978–1979). Investigating techniques for teaching word meanings. *Reading Research Quarterly, 14,* 624–645.

Glaser, R. (1984, April). (Chair). *What is the role of instruction in learning and using vocabulary?* Symposium conducted at the meeting of the American Educational Research Association, New Orleans.

Goodman, K. S., Shannon, P., Freeman, Y. S., & Murphy, S. (1988). *Report card on basal readers.* Katonah, NY: Richard C. Owen.

Graves, M. F. (1980, April). *A quantitative and qualitative study of students' reading vocabularies.* Paper presented at the meeting of the American Educational Research Association, Boston.

Graves, M. F. (1984). Selecting vocabulary to teach in the intermediate and secondary grades. In J. Flood (Ed.), *Promoting reading comprehension* (pp. 245–260). Newark, DE: International Reading Association.

Graves, M. F. (1986). Vocabulary learning and instruction. In E. Z. Rothkopf (Ed.), *Review of research in education,* vol. 13 (pp. 49–89). Washington: American Educational Research Association.

Graves, M. F. (1987). The roles of instruction in fostering vocabulary development. In M. G. McKeown & M. E. Curtis (Eds.), *The nature of vocabulary acquisition* (pp. 165–184). Hillsdale, NJ: Erlbaum.

Graves, M. F., & Hammond, H. K. (1980). A validated procedure for teaching prefixes and its effect on students' ability to assign meaning to novel words. In M. L. Kamil & A. J. Moe (Eds), *Perspectives on reading research and instruction,* Twenty-ninth yearbook of the National Reading Conference (pp. 184–188). Washington, D.C.: National Reading Conference.

Graves, M. F., & Prenn, M. C. (1986). Costs and benefits at various methods of teaching vocabulary. *Journal of Reading, 29,* 596–602.

Hafner, L. E. (1965). A one-month experiment in teaching context aids in fifth grade. *Journal of Educational Research, 58,* 471–474.

Hagen, J. E. (1980). The effects of selected prereading vocabulary building activities on literal comprehension, vocabulary understanding, and attitudes of fourth and fifth grade students with reading problems (Doctoral dissertation, University of Wisconsin-Madison, 1980). *Dissertation Abstracts Internatinal, 40,* 6216A. (University Microfilms No. 80-07, 553)

Hagen-Heimlich, J. E., & Pittelman, S. D. (1984). *Classroom application of the semantic mapping procedure in reading and writing* (Program Report No. 84-4). Madison, WI: Wisconsin Center for Education Research, University of Wisconsin.

Haggard, M. R. (1982). The vocabulary self-collection strategy: An active approach to word learning. *Journal of Reading, 26,* 203–207.

Haggard, M. R. (1985). An interactive strategies approach to content reading. *Journal of Reading, 29,* 204–210.

Haggard, M. R. (1986). The vocabulary self-collection strategy: Using student interest and word knowledge to enhance vocabulary growth. *Journal of Reading, 29,* 634–642.

Hanf, M. B. (1971). Mapping: A technique for translating reading into thinking. *Journal of Reading, 14,* 225–230.

Hanson, I. W. (1966). First grade children work with variant word endings. *The Reading Teacher, 19,* 505–507, 511.

Harris, T. L., & Hodges, R. C. (Eds.) (1981). *A dictionary of reading and related terms.* Newark, DE: International Reading Association.

Herman, P. A., Anderson, R. C., Pearson, P. D., & Nagy, W. E. (1987). Incidental acquisition of word meaning from expositions with varied text features. *Reading Research Quarterly, 22,* 263–284.

Herman, P. A., & Dole, J. (1988). Theory and practice in vocabulary learning and instruction. *Elementary School Journal, 89,* 43–54.

Ignoffo, M. F. (1980). The thread of thought: Analogies as a vocabulary building method. *Journal of Reading, 23,* 519–521.

Jackson, J. R., & Dizney, H. (1963). Intensive vocabulary training. *Journal of Developmental Reading, 6,* 221–229.

Jenkins, J. R., & Dixon, R. (1983). Learning vocabulary. *Contemporary Educational Psychology, 8,* 237–260.

Jenkins, J. R., Matlock, B., & Slocum, T. A. (1989). Approaches to vocabulary instruction: The teaching of individual word meanings and practice in deriving word meaning from context. *Reading Research Quarterly, 24,* 215–235.

Jenkins, J. R., Stein, M. L., & Wysocki, K. (1984). Learning vocabulary through reading. *American Educational Research Journal, 21,* 767–787.

Jitendra, A., & Kameenui, E. J. (1988). A design-of-instruction analysis of concept teaching in five basal language programs: Voltaire from the bottom up. *Journal of Special Education, 22,* 199–219.

Johnson, D. D. (1984). Expanding vocabulary through classification. In J. F. Baumann & D. D. Johnson (Eds.), *Reading instruction and the beginning teacher: A practical guide* (pp. 28–38). Minneapolis, Burgess.

Johnson, D. D. (Ed.). (1986). Vocabulary [Special issue]. *Journal of Reading, 29*(7).

Johnson, D. D., & Baumann, J. F. (1984). Word identification. In P. D. Pearson (Ed.), *Handbook of reading research* (pp. 583–608. New York: Longman.

Johnson, D. D., & Johnson, B. V. (1986). Highlighting vocabulary in inferential comprehension instruction. *Journal of Reading, 29,* 622–625.

Johnson, D. D., & Levin, K. M., & Pittelman, S. D. (1984). *A field assessment of vocabulary instruction in the elementary school classroom* (Program Rep. No. 84-3). Madison, WI: Wisconsin Center for Education Research, University of Wisconsin.

Johnson, D. D., & Pearson, P. D. (1984). *Teaching reading vocabulary* (2nd ed.). New York: Holt, Rinehart, and Winston.

Johnson, D. D., Pittelman, S. D., & Heimlich, J. E. (1986). Semantic mapping. *The Reading Teacher, 39,* 778–783.

Johnson, D. D., Pittelman, S. D., Toms-Bronowski, S., Chu-Chang, M., Tsui, G., Yin, M. C., Chien, C. Y., & Chin, P. (1982). *Studies of vocabulary development techniques in the United States of America and the Republic of China* (Program Rep. No. 83-4). Madison, WI: Wisconsin Center for Education Research, University of Wisconsin.

Johnson, D. D., Pittelman, S. D., Toms-Bronowski, S., & Levin, K. M. (1984). *An investigation of the effects of prior knowledge and vocabulary acquistion on passage comprehension* (Program Rep. No. 84-5). Madison, WI: Wisconsin Center for Education Research, University of Wisconsin.

Johnson, D. D., Toms-Bronowski, S., & Pittelman, S. D. (1982). *An investigation of the effectiveness of semantic mapping and semantic feature analysis with intermediate grade level students* (Program Rep. No. 83-3). Madison, WI: Wisconsin Center for Education Research, University of Wisconsin.

Jones, S. T. (1984). *The effects of semantic mapping on vocabulary acquisition and reading comprehension of innercity black students.* Unpublished doctoral dissertation, University of Wisconsin, Madison.

Just, M. A., & Carpenter, P. A. (1987). *The psychology of reading and language comprehension.* Newton, MA: Allyn and Bacon.

Kameenui, E. J., Carnine, D. W., & Freschi, R. (1982). Effects of text construction and instructional procedures for teaching word meanings on comprehension and recall. *Reading Research Quarterly, 17,* 367–388.

Kameenui, E. J., Dixon, D. W., & Carnine, R. C. (1987). Issues in the design of vocabulary instruction. In M. G. McKeown & M. E. Curtis (Eds.), *The nature of vocabulary acquisition* (pp. 129–145). Hillsdale, NJ: Erlbaum.

Kameenui, E. J., & Simmons, D. (1990). *Designing instructional strategies for the prevention of academic learning problems.* Columbus, OH: Merrill.

Kameenui, E. J., Simmons, D., & Darch, C. (1987). Learning disabled children's comprehension of selected textual characteristics: Proximity of critical information. *Learning Disabilities Quarterly, 10,* 237–248.

Karbon, J. C. (1984). *An investigation of the relationships between prior knowledge and vocabulary development using semantic mapping with culturally diverse students.* Unpublished doctoral dissertation, University of Wisconsin-Madison.

Klein, M. L. (1988). *Teaching reading comprehension and vocabulary: A guide for teachers.* Englewood Cliffs, NJ: Prentice Hall.

Konopak, B. C. (1988). Effects of inconsiderate vs. considerate text on secondary students' vocabulary learning. *Journal of Reading Behavior, 20*(1), 25–41.

Konopak, B. C. (1988). Eighth graders' vocabulary learning from inconsiderate and considerate text. *Reading Research and Instruction, 27,* 1–14.

Levin, J. R. (1985). Educational applications of mnemonic pictures: Possibilities beyond your wildest imagination. In A. A. Sheikh (Ed.), *Imagery in the educational process* (pp. 63–87). Farmingdale, NY: Baywood.

Levin, J. R., Johnson, D. D., Pittelman, S. D., Levin, K. M., Shriberg, L. K., Toms-Bronowski, S., & Hayes, B. L. (1984). A comparison of semantic- and mnemonic-based vocabulary learning strategies. *Reading Psychology, 5,* 1–15.

Levin, J. R., McCormick, C. B., Miller, G. E., Berry, J. K., & Pressley, M. (1982). Mnemonic versus nonmnemonic vocabulary-learning strategies for children. *American Educational Research Journal, 19,* 121–136.

Levin, J. R., & Pressley, M. (1985). Mnemonic vocabulary instruction: What's fact, what's fiction. In R. F. Dillon (Ed.), *Individual differences in cognition* (Vol. 2) (pp. 145–172). Orlando, FL: Academic Press.

MacGinite, W. H. (1978). *Gates-MacGinite reading tests.* Boston: Houghton Mifflin.

Madison, J. Y., Carroll, B. A., & Drum, P. A. (1982). The effects of directionality and proximity of context clues on the comprehension of unknown words. In J. A. Niles & L. A. Harris (Eds.), *New Inquiries in reading research and instruction,* Thirty-first yearbook of the National Reading Conference (pp. 105–109). Rochester, NY: National Reading Conference.

Manzo, A. V. (1983). "Subjective approach to vocabulary" acquisition ("or . . . I think my brother is arboreal!"). *Reading Psychology, 3,* 155–160.

Manzo, A., & Sherk, J. (1972). Some generalizations and strategies to guide vocabulary acquistion. *Journal of Reading Behavior, 4,* 78–89.

Margosein, C. M., Pascarella, E. T., & Pflaum, S. W. (1982, April). *The effects of instruction using semantic mapping on vocabulary and comprehension.* Paper presented at the annual meeting of the American Educational Research Association, New York.

Marzano, R. J. (1984). A cluster approach to vocabulary instruction. *The Reading Teacher, 38,* 168–173.

Marzano, R. J., & Marzano, J. S. (1988). *A cluster approach to elementary vocabulary instruction.* Newark, DE: International Reading Association.

Mason, J. M., & Au, K. H. (1986). *Reading instruction for today.* Glenview, IL: Scott Foresman.

Mastropieri, M. A., Scruggs, T. E., & Levin, J. R. (1985). Maximizing what exceptional children can learn: A review of research on the keyword method and related mnemonic techniques. *Remedial and Special Education, 6,* 39–45.

McDaniel, M. A., & Pressley, M. (1984). Putting the keyword method in context. *Journal of Educational Psychology, 76,* 598–609.

McDaniel, M. A., & Pressley, M., & Dunay, P. K. (1987). Long-term retention of vocabulary learning after keyword and context learning. *Journal of Educational Psychology, 79,* 87–89.

McDaniel, M. A., & Tillman, V. P. (1987). Discovering a meaning versus applying the keyword method: Effects on recall. *Contemporary Educational Psychology, 12,* 156–175.

McKeown, M. G. (1985). The acquisition of word meaning from context by children of high and low ability. *Reading Research Quarterly, 20,* 482–496.

McKeown, M. G., & Beck, I. L. (1988). Learning vocabulary: Different ways for different goals. *Remedial and Special Education, 9,* 42–46.

McKeown, M. G., Beck, I. L., Omanson, R., & Perfetti, C. A. (1983). The effects of long-term vocabulary instruction on reading comprehension: A replication. *Journal of Reading Behavior, 15,* 3–18.

McKeown, M. G., Beck, I. L., Omanson, R., & Pople, M. T. (1985). Some effects of the nature and frequency of vocabulary instruction on the knowledge and use of words. *Reading Research Quarterly, 20,* 522–535.

McKeown, M. G., & Curtis, M. E. (Eds.). (1987). *The nature of vocabulary acquisition.* Hillsdale, NJ: Erlbaum.

McNeil, J. D. (1987). *Reading comprehension: New directions for classroom practice* (2nd ed.). Glenview, IL: Scott Foresman.

Mezynski, K. (1983). Issues concerning the acquisition of knowledge: Effects of vocabulary training on reading comprehension. *Review of Research in Education, 53,* 253–279.

Miller, G. A., & Gildea, P. M. (1987). How children learn words. *Scientific American, 257,* 94–99.

Mosenthal, P. (1984). The problem of partial specification in translating reading research into practice. *Elementary School Journal, 85,* 1–28.

Nagy, W. E. (1988). *Teaching vocabulary to improve reading comprehension.* Newark, DE: International Reading Association.

Nagy, W. E., & Anderson, R. C. (1984). How many words are there in printed school English? *Reading Research Quarterly, 19,* 303–330.

Nagy, W. E., Anderson, R. C., & Herman, P. A. (1987). Learning word meanings from context during normal reading. *American Educational Research Journal, 24,* 237–270.

Nagy, W. E., & Herman, P. A. (1984). *Limitations of vocabulary instruction.* (Tech. Rep. No. 326). Urbana: University of Illinois, Center for the Study of Reading. (ERIC Document Reproduction Service No. ED 248 498).

Nagy, W. E., & Herman, P. A. (1987). Breadth and depth of vocabulary knowledge: Implications for acquisition and instruction. In M. G. McKeown & M. E. Curtis (Eds.), *The nature of vocabulary acquisition* (pp. 19–35). Hillsdale, NJ: Erlbaum.

Nagy, W. E., Herman, P. A., & Anderson, R. C. (1985). Learning words from context. *Reading Research Quarterly, 20,* 233–253.

Nicol, J. E., & Graves, M. F. (1990). *Building vocabulary through prefix instruction.* Unpublished manuscript, University of Minnesota.

Otterman, L. M. (1955). The value of teaching prefixes and word-roots. *Journal of Educational Research, 48,* 611–616.

Pany, D., & Jenkins, J. R. (1978). Learning word meanings: A comparison of instructional procedures and effects on measures of reading comprehension with learning disabled students. *Learning Disability Quarterly, 1,* 21–32.

Pany, D., Jenkins, J. R., & Schreck, J. (1982). Vocabulary instruction: Effects on word knowledge and reading comprehension. *Learning Disability Quarterly, 5,* 202–215.

Parker, S. L. (1984). *A comparison of four types of initial vocabulary instruction.* Unpublished master's thesis, University of Minnesota, Minneapolis.

Patberg, J. P., Graves, M. F., & Stibbe, M. A. (1984). Effects of active teaching and practice in facilitating students' use of context clues. *Changing perspectives on research in reading/language processing and instruction,* Thirty-third yearbook of the National Reading Conference (pp. 146–151). Rochester, NY: National Reading Conference.

Petty, W., Herold, C., & Stohl, E. (1967). *The state of the knowledge about the teaching of vocabulary* (Cooperative Research Project No. 3128). Champaign, IL: National Council of Teachers of English. (ERIC Document Reproduction Service No. ED 012 395)

Pittelman, S. D., Levin, K. M., & Johnson, D. D. (1985). *An investigation of two instructional settings in the use of semantic mapping with poor readers* (Program Rep. No. 85-4). Madison, WI: Wisconsin Center for Education Research, University of Wisconsin.

Powell, W. R. (1986). Teaching vocabulary through opposition. *Journal of Reading, 29,* 617–621.

Pressley, M., Levin, J. R., & DeLaney, H. D. (1982). The mnemonic keyword method. *Review of Educational Research, 52,* 61–92.

Pressley, M., Levin, J. R., & McDaniel, M. A. (1987). Remembering versus inferring what a word means: Mnemonic and contextual approaches. In M. G. McKeown & M. E. Curtis (Eds.), *The nature of vocabulary acquisition* (pp. 107–127). Hillsdale, NJ: Erlbaum.

Pressley, M., Ross, K. A., Levin, J. R., & Ghatala, E. S. (1984). The role of strategy utility knowledge in children's strategy decision making. *Journal of Experimental Child Psychology, 38,* 491–504.

Reutzel, D. R., (1985). Reconciling schema theory and the basal reading lesson. *The Reading Teacher, 39,* 194–197.

Reutzel, D. R., & Hollingsworth, P. M. (1988). Highlighting key vocabulary: A generative-reciprocal procedure for teaching selected inference types. *Reading Research Quarterly, 23,* 358–378.

Richek, M. A. (1988). Relating vocabulary learning to world knowledge. *Journal of Reading, 32,* 262–267.

Rohwer, W. D. (1973). Elaboration and learning in childhood and adolescence. In H. W. Reese (Ed.), *Advances in child development and behavior* (Vol. 8, pp. 1–57). New York: Academic Press.

Roser, N., & Juel, C. (1982). Effect of vocabulary instruction on reading comprehension. In J. A. Niles & L. A. Harris (Eds.), *New Inquiries in reading: Research and instruction,* Thirty-first yearbook of the National Reading Converence (pp. 110–118). Rochester, NY: National Reading Conference.

Russell, D. H. (1954). The dimensions of children's meaning vocabulary in grades four through twelve. *University of California Publications in Education, 11,* 315–414.

Russell, D. H., & Fea, H. R. (1963). Research on teaching reading. In N. L. Gage (Ed.), *Handbook of research on teaching* (pp. 865–928). Chicago: Rand McNally.

Sampson, M. R., Valmont, W. J., & Allen, R. V. (1982). The effects of instructional cloze on the comprehension, vocabulary, and divergent production of third-grade students. *Reading Research Quarterly, 17,* 389–399.

Schatz, E. K., & Baldwin, R. S. (1986). Context clues are unreliable predictors of word meanings. *Reading Research Quarterly, 21,* 439–453.

Schwartz, R. M., (1988). Learning to learn vocabulary in content area textbooks. *Journal of Reading, 32,* 108–118.

Schwartz, R. M., & Raphael, T. E. (1985a). Concept of definition: A key to improving students' vocabulary. *The Reading Teacher, 39,* 198–205.

Schwartz, R. M., & Raphael, T. E. (1985b). Instruction in the concept of definition as a basis for vocabulary acquisition. In J. A. Niles & R. V. Lalik (Eds.), *Issues in literacy: A research perspective,* Thirty-fourth yearbook of the National Reading Conference (pp. 116–123). Rochester, NY: National Reading Conference.

Scruggs, T. E., Mastropieri, M. A., & Levin, J. R. (1985). Vocabulary acquisition of retarded students under direct mnemonic instruction. *American Journal of Mental Deficiency, 89,* 546–551.

Serra, M. C. (1953). How to develop concepts and their verbal representations. *Elementary School Journal, 53,* 275–285.

Singer, H. A. (1965). A developmental model of speed of reading in grades 3 through 6. *Reading Research Quarterly, 1,* 29–49.

Sorenson, N. L. (1985). Basal reading vocabulary instructions: A critique and suggestions. *The Reading Teacher, 39,* 80–85.

Spearitt, D. (1972). Identification of subskills of reading comprehension by maximum likelihood factor analysis. *Reading Research Quarterly, 8,* 92–111.

Squire, J. R. (1987, November). *A publisher responds to that basal reader report card.* Paper presented at the meeting of the National Council of Teachers of English, Los Angeles.

Stahl, S. (1983). Differential word knowledge and reading comprehension. *Journal of Reading Behavior, 15*(4), 33–50.

Stahl, S. A. (1985). To teach a word well: A framework for vocabulary instruction. *Reading World, 24*(3), 16–27.

Stahl, S. A. (1986). Three principles of effective vocabulary instruction. *Journal of Reading, 29,* 662–668.

Stahl, S. A. (1988). [Review of *The nature of vocabulary acquisition*]. *Journal of Reading Behavior, 20*(1), 89–95.

Stahl, S. A., & Fairbanks, M. M. (1986). The effects of vocabulary instruction: A model-based meta-analysis. *Review of Educational Research, 56,* 72–110.

Stahl, S. A., & Vancil, S. J. (1986). Discussion is what makes semantic maps work in vocabulary instruction. *The Reading Teacher, 40,* 62–67.

Stanovich, K. E. (1986). Matthew effects in reading: Some consequences of individual differences in the acquisition of literacy. *Reading Research Quarterly, 21,* 360–407.

Sternberg, R. B. (1987). Most vocabulary is learned from context. In M. G. McKeown & M. E. Curtis (Eds.), *The nature of vocabulary acquisition* (pp. 89–105). Hillsdale, NJ: Erlbaum.

Sternberg, R., & Powell, J. S. (1983). Comprehending verbal comprehension. *American Psychologist, 38,* 878–893.

Sternberg, R., Powell, J. S., & Kaye, D. B. (1983). The nature of verbal comprehension. In A. C. Wilkinson (Ed.), *Communicating with computers in classrooms: Prospects for applied cognitive science* (pp. 121–143). New York: Academic Press.

Taba, H. (1967). *Teacher's handbook for elementary social studies.* Reading, MA: Addison-Wesley.

Taylor, B., Harris, L. A., & Pearson, P. D. (1988). *Reading difficulties: Instruction and assessment.* New York: Random House.

Thames, D. G., & Readence, J. E. (1988). Effects of differential vocabulary instruction and lesson frameworks on the reading comprehension of primary grade children. *Reading Research and Instruction, 27,* 1–12.

Thelen, J. N. (1986). Vocabulary instruction and meaningful learning. *Journal of Reading, 29,* 603–609.

Thompson, E. (1958). The "master word" approach to vocabulary training. *Journal of Developmental Reading, 2,* 62–66.

Thurstone, L. L. (1946). A note on a reanalysis of Davis' reading tests. *Psychometrika, 11,* 185–188.

Tierney, R. J., Readence, J. E., & Dishner, E. K. (1985). *Reading strategies and practices: A compendium* (2nd ed.). Newton, MA: Allyn and Bacon.

Toms-Bronowski, S. (1983). An investigation of the effectiveness of selected vocabulary teaching strategies with intermediate grade level students (Doctoral dissertation, University of Wisconsin-Madison, 1983). *Dissertation Abstracts International, 44,* 1405A. (University Microfilms, No. 83-16, 238)

Tuinman, J. J., & Brady, M. E. (1974). How does vocabulary account for variance on reading comprehension tests: A preliminary instructinal analysis. In P. Nacke (Ed.), *Twenty-third national reading conference yearbook* (pp. 176–184). Clemson, SC: National Reading Conference.

Vygotsky, F. (1962). *Thought and language.* Cambridge, MA: MIT Press.

Werner, H., & Kaplan, B. (1952). The acquisition of word meanings: A developmental study. *Monographs of the Society for Research in Child Development, 15* (Serial No. 51, No. 1).

White, T. G., Graves, M. F., & Slater, W. H. (1989). Growth of reading vocabulary in diverse elementary schools. *Journal of Educational Psychology.*

White, T. G., Sowell, J., & Yanagihara, A. (1989). Teaching elementary students to use word-part clues. *The Reading Teacher, 42,* 302–308.

Wilson, R. M., & Gambrell, L. B. (1988). *Reading comprehension in the elementary school: A teacher's practical guide.* Newton, MA: Allyn & Bacon.

Wixson, K. K. (1986). Vocabulary instruction and children's comprehension of basal stories. *Reading Research Quarterly, 21,* 317–329.

Wysocki, K., & Jenkins, J. R. (1987). Deriving word meanings through morphological generalization. *Reading Research Quarterly, 22,* 66–81.

31D. RHETORIC

James L. Kinneavey

Both throughout history and at the present time, the term *rhetoric* has been used to refer to seveal quite distinct, though related, things. It might be useful to group these different meanings in a descending and order of generality. Possibly the most general meaning can be seen in phrases such as: the rhetoric of architecture, the rhetoric of fashion, the rhetoric of confrontation, and so on. In these cases, rhetoric almost comes to mean the effect of impact of something. This most general meaning is a modern meaning, almost limited to the second half of this century. A somewhat narrower meaning is the use of rhetoric to refer to the study of discourse generally, usually with the aim of ensuring more effective writing or speaking or narrating, or science, or propaganda. This usage of the term occurs frequently in Antiquity, both in Greece and in Rome; it persists throughout history and is still a major meaning of the term today, particularly in America. The most dominant meaning of the term throughout history, however, is at a lower level of generality: rhetoric is the study of persuasive discourse, particularly as used in law courts and in politics, and later in sermons. In classical studies, this is frequently the most dominant meaning. Finally, the most constricted meaning of the term limits its reference to stylistic concerns; we often speak of a rhetorical analysis of figures of speech in a poem or speech. This use also runs the course of history; it is possibly the most common use of the term in Europe at the present time.

In the context of teaching language arts, rhetoric usually takes on the second meaning above: the study of discourse generally. Consequently, it will be given that meaning in this chapter. As such, it includes the more specific meaning of persuasion, but it also includes the study of literature, expository writing and reading, exploratory uses of language, and self-expression on the part of the student. These areas are called by some the functions of language (Britton, 1975; passim) and by others the aims of discourse (Kinneavy, 1971; Morris, 1955, pp. 95 ff.). Historically these functions were called the trivium of the liberal arts tradition: logic was the study of proof in language and dialectic was the study of exploration in language; grammar was the study of the literacy texts of the tradition and the study of the language itself; and rhetoric was the study of persuasive discourse. Possibly the most thorough treatment of this tradition from a modern perspective has been that of Kenneth Burke, who follows the tradition in writing a major book on science and dialectic (1952), another on rhetorical persuasion (1969, 1950), and a third on literature (1973).

In addition to the aims of discourse, rhetoric throughout history has included a study of the modes of discourse. These have included narration, description, classification and definition, exposition, and evaluation. Traditionally, these were called the issues or matters—the writer took a stand on one of these aspects of the subject matter.

At the current time, rhetoric is often a synonym for the study of the language arts of reading, writing, speaking, and listening.

And, of course, these arts have been a consistent concern of the study of discourse throughout history.

Finally, since the eighteenth century considerably more attention in the teaching about language has been devoted to the study of the grammar, mechanics, and vocabulary aspects of language. These aspects have not usually been called rhetorical, however.

All of these issues will be given some attention in the remainder of this chapter. Although a cursory presentation may make them seem rather discrete and fragmented, they are all carefully related in a systematic view of language study (see Beale, 1977, 1987; Kinneavy, Chapter I, 1980).

RHETORIC AS PERSUASION

Rhetoric arose in the transition in the city-states of Greece and Sicily from monarchies to oligarchies to democracies from the sixth to the fifth century B. C. The division of the land of the oligarchs and tyrants among commoners occasioned many legal disputes, and techniques to persuade in court were codified. At the same time, the new commoners had a say in the political decisions of the city-state and needed to learn how to persuade their fellow citizens. Thus the legal and political rhetoric of persuasion arose at the same time, and these remained for centuries the two main subjects of rhetoric. In addition, teachers of rhetoric often composed fictional speeches to display their virtuosity in order to attract students—these were called epideictic (display) speeches. Often these display speeches embodied the fundamental aspirations and values of a writer, so that some epideictic speeches took on a second important psychological and cultural function.

Authorities

There are many rhetorical treatises from both Greece and Rome teaching students how to write these legal, political, and display speeches. But the dominating works in the rhetorical tradition of persuasion are Aristotle, Cicero, and Quintilian and they dominated not only Antiquity, but also the Middle Ages and the Renaissance. Both Cicero and Quintilian adopted the systematic framework of Aristotle; as a result, Aristotle's system has been widely adopted as a beginning system for teaching rhetoric as persuasion, even at the present time (see Corbett, 1971, and Horner, 1988; for basic texts and translations, see Aristotle, 1926; Cicero, 1942, 1948; Quintilian, 1920–1922).

Subject Matters

Persuasion, in this narrow sense, meant initially the kind of legal and political conviction characteristic of democratic insti-

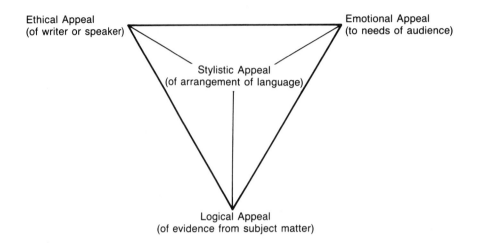

FIGURE 31D–1. The persuasive appeals.

tutions in Antiquity. Later, the notion of religious persuasion by sermons was grafted onto the notion of rhetoric, especially by St. Augustine (*De Doctrina Christiana,* Bk. IV, 1958; see Murphy, 1978, 1981). Still later commercial persuasion by advertising was added, with the rise of modern journalism (see, for a typical treatment, Sandage, 1960). At the present time, it is recognized that almost any subject matter can be the topic of a persuasion.

The Four Appeals

The classical view of persuasion taught students to use four main types of appeal: writers or speakers can persuade by the credibility engendered by their personalities as projected in the text; or writers can engender belief in the readers by appealing to the emotions, interests, and biases of the readers; or authors can bring about conviction by the more intellectual means of logical arguments; and, finally, persuaders can get an audience to adopt a given position by the effectiveness of their style. Most of the time, of course, a speaker uses all or at least several of these appeals in a given text, and a given slogan, for instance, often will embody a rational argument, an appeal to the audience's emotions, and a clever wording. The four appeals are often represented graphically by grouping them around the communication triangle, as it is called (see Figure 31D–1).
These four appeals have been the core of the persuasion teaching throughout history. For a thorough commentary on Aristotle on these issues, see Cope, 1867. For full modern treatments of them, see Corbett, 1971; Horner, 1988; Kinneavy, 1980.

The first appeal, the author's personal credibility, was called in classical rhetoric the "ethical argument," although both terms in the phrase are used in rather unorthodox manners in this case to mean the conviction carried about by the image presented of the author's seeming ethical (in the usual meaning of the term) sincerity, his sympathy for the audience, and his knowledgeability and decisiveness. A major modern study of these character or charisma appeals parallels Aristotle's three factors: the author's trustworthiness, intentions, and expertness are the main dimensions of "ethical appeal" (Hovland, 1953).

Usually beginning writers are urged to incorporate the ethical appeal early in the paper, often when giving the background and importance of the topic. This establishes credibility at the outset of the paper. Of course, it is directly reenforced by references throughout the paper, underscoring any of the three dimensions. Usually these are done somewhat subtly. Of course the image of the speaker is also indirectly reenforced by the three other appeals, that is, by the manner that the writer appeals to the audience's interests and emotions, by the writer's subject matter arguments, and by the writer's style. Directly or indirectly, the establishment of credibility is paramount; if the writer is not believed, the rest of the speech is wasted on the audience. As Aristotle himself says, the speaker's "character may almost be called the most efficient means of persuasion he possesses" (1960, p. 1356a (13).

The second rhetorical appeal is based on incentives grounded in the interests and emotions of the audience. These emotions and interests may even change with different cultures or subcultures, but this "pathetic" appeal, as it was traditionally called, has been a staple of rhetoric in all cultures. The history of political propaganda, religious sermons, commercial advertising, and legal rhetoric attests to the importance of appealing to the audience's emotions and self-interest.

Aristotle in the fourth century B. C. and Madison Avenue in this century devote more attention to this appeal than to any other—and this is true of many rhetoricians in between. It is the basis for most of the marketing research carried on by advertising agencies, by political pollsters, and public relation firms. These groups carefully discriminate among various ages, genders, geographic regions, economic, educational, and ethnic backgrounds, in their attempts to differentiate the various interests of different audiences, even within the same culture. This is even more true when attempts are made to persuade other cultures; psychologists and anthropologists and propagandists and market managers have all come to recognize that what may sell in Peoria may be spurned in Vladivostok (see Brown, 1963, pp. 40–41).

The third appeal consists of rational appeals grounded in the subject matter under consideration. Aristotle called this the logical argument. It can be based on principles or axioms that the writer and readers share, and from which inferences may be drawn that apply to the issue at hand. This is the application of deductive reasoning to rhetoric. Secondly, it can be based on reasoning from particulars to a generalization, which can be applied to the relevant topic. This is the use of induction in rhetoric. Particular deductive or inductive patterns in favor with a particular subculture Aristotle called topics. Thus in his society, Aristotle found that an argument with an a fortiori base like the following would be convincing to a Greek audience: If even the gods are not omniscient, certainly human beings are not (1397b 12). He gave examples of topics used in special areas like politics and law. Today, with the emphasis on specialized audiences the study of topics has received considerable recent attention, especially in legal, political, literary, and ethical discourse (see Bornscheuer, 1976; Curtius, 1973; Perelman, 1969).

The fourth appeal of classical rhetoric is based on style. In most of the major rhetoricians, style was treated under the headings of the four virtues of style: dignity, propriety, clarity, and correctness. These four correspond in emphasis to the four elements of the communication triangle referred to above: dignity enhances the credibility of the speaker, propriety realizes the adaptability of the style to the audience, clarity ensures an accurate transmission of the subject matter, and correctness takes care of the conventions of the language. Dignity of style was usually looked upon as being secured by figures of speech, such as metaphor, synecdoche, hyperbole, and irony, intended to clarify the meaning of concepts and to embellish the speech. Historically the number of these figures increased to more than 150 in some rhetoric manuals in the Renaissance. Just as important as the figures of speech were the figures of sound, based on rhythm, rhyme, alliteration, and assonance. Almost one third of the rhetorical manuals from Greek Antiquity were limited to these and other stylistic considerations. Cicero, for instance, painting the picture of the perfect speaker in the *Orator,* "devotes three-quarters of the treatise to *elocutio* [style]," as his translator and editor, H. M. Hubbell, says in the introduction to the Loeb edition (1952, p. 297).

These figures of rhetoric were so important throughout history that, as was pointed out above, one of the main meanings of the term related to figurative language and analysis. Just as important historically was the doctrine of the three styles that established the propriety or decorum of the style in relation to the audience primarily, and secondarily to the other elements of the rhetorical situation. The three styles were usually referred to as the high (grand, Asian) style, the middle (Rhodian), and the low (plain, Attic) style. Cicero relates the three styles to the three duties of the orator: to move in the grand style, to delight in the middle style, and to teach in the plain style (*Orator,* Sec. xxii). The grand style was highly ornamental in its use of figures of speech, often bombastic in diction, and characterized by striking and obvious sound structures (Cicero, *Orator,* Sec. xxviii, XCVII–XCIX). The plain style is described by Cicero as not emphasizing rhythm at all, as not adorned (except with a few metaphors), as elegant and neat, as humorous and witty, as purist in grammar, and especially as clear (*Orator,* Sec. 23, pp. 76–90). The middle style is characterized by a "minimum of vigor and a maximum of charm;" it uses all types of figurative

language, but in a restrained way; it is the language of the philosophers (Cicero, *Orator,* Sec. xxvi–xxvii). Cicero describes the best orator in a famous passage that dominated rhetorical history for 1700 years, "He is in fact eloquent who can discuss commonplace matters simply, lofty matters impressively, and topics ranging in between in a tempered style" (*Orator,* Sec. xxix).

The third virtue of style is the virtue of clarity. To achieve clarity Aristotle insisted again on the use of figurative language, the uses of both ordinary and extraordinary language, and especially on the use of lively and dynamic imagery (*Rhetoric,* Bk. III, Chaps. 2, 4, 11). At some times in the rhetorical tradition, clarity almost preempted all other considerations. This is true of the period of Ramus and his influence from the sixteenth till the nineteenth century. For some writers, Tolstoy, for example, clarity becomes a matter of ethics.

The final virtue of the rhetorical tradition was correctness. This has often been given a chauvinistic interpretation, dignifying a prestige dialect and demeaning other (usually more provincial) dialects. This began with the Greeks and the Romans and has been true of nearly all modern European dialectics. It has only recently been challenged in this country by modern linguistics. In teaching composition, this challenge is reflected in a position taken by the Conference on College Composition and Communication, called the "Students' Rights to Their Own Language," a position intended to honor African American, Hispanic, and other minority American dialects (see "Students' Rights," 1974).

These four appeals of rhetoric can all be abused and used to manipulate audiences, rather than to attempt to lead them to a free and rational decision. And rhetoric has been under attack for these abuses since its foundation. Plato lead the attack against these abuses in the *Gorgias* (1925), and many others have followed him through the centuries. At the present time, political propaganda, much commercial advertising, some religious proselytism, some types of education, and various other forms of persuasion have been called immoral (for propaganda, see Doob, 1961; Lasswell, 1965; for advertising see Packard, 1980, and Kaldor and Holdren in Harris, 1962, pp. 69–72).

The manipulative use of rhetoric tends to change the nature of all the proofs. Persuasion by personal credibility can degenerate into projection of a false image; appeals can be made to base instincts and biases; logic can be only apparent logic or even deceptive fallacy; and style can sometimes take over as the main appeal, in the absence of any substantial argument.

Despite the abuses to which it has been put, rhetoric has had its champions from an ethical point of view. Tacitus in Antiquity maintained that rhetoric only prospered in free societies and declined and languished under tyrants and emperors (*Dialogue,* 1958). Harris echoes this defense in our time (1962, p. 161), and he also defends commercial advertising from an economic point of view (see Robertson in Harris, 1962, p. 102). Brown also contends that commercial advertising "played a major part in making newspapers honest and moderately respectable" (1963, p. 13). Possibly the most significant defense of rhetoric from a moral point of view has been that of Kierkegaard, who condemns both science (1959) and literature (1962) as being too neutral and noncommitted to issues. Only rhetoric is "engaged," he says, to use a word much employed in existential philosophy.

RHETORIC AND THE OTHER AIMS OF LANGUAGE

Rhetoric in the large sense includes, besides persuasion, expository discourse, literary discourse, and expressive discourse. The current general framework of these distinctions comes from the classical liberal arts tradition (see above) and, more recently, from the literary critic Roman Jakobson (1967) as adopted both by Britton, 1975, and Kinneavy, 1980.

Expository Writing

Expository writing is called transactional by Britton. It usually includes today the traditional thesis type of writing that proves a point by logical argument, the hypothesis type of writing that explores a topic without necessarily taking a stand or considering the issue settled, and the informative type of writing.

The thesis paper, covered traditionally by logic in the liberal arts tradition, is today usually considered divided into theses proved by deductive inference or by inductive inference or by a combination of both. At the present time, in composition theory two groups challenge this traditional approach. Stephen Toulmin's (1964) challenge has been largely adopted by many authorities in speech communication departments. He discards these customary methods of proof and analyzes arguments by their various claims and the levels of warrants that can be made for them. A second group of writers prefers to distinguish between the careful claims made by professional logicians and the more informal logic used in such fields as law, ethics, esthetics, politics, and the like (see Maimon, 1981, 1984, for the humanities generally; Nisbet, 1980, for psychology; Baier, 1958, for ethics and law; Perelman and Tyteca, 1969). Ehninger (1974) and McCleary (1979) have applied Toulmin, and Maimon et al. have applied informal logic to composition and rhetoric, but only at the college level.

The hypothesis or exploratory theme is the modern counterpart of dialectic in the liberal arts tradition. At the elementary and secondary level, this is most frequently presented as the problem-solving technique, following Dewey's (1938) methodology. At the college level it is frequently presented as an honest exploration, following the scientific method. The most influential paradigm of this method in rhetorical studies has been that of Thomas Kuhn (1967), which has been adopted by Kinneavy and Zeiger, among others (Kinneavy, 1980, pp. 141–151; Zeiger, 1985). A different theoretical basis, that of the linguist Kenneth Pike, has been used as the basis for *Rhetoric: Discovery and Change* (Pike, Young, and Becker, 1970). Writing of this type recommended by these five authors issues at best in a question, not a definitive answer. Many students find this a healthy alternative to the thesis theme. Acutally we often live in an exploratory world rather than a world of definitive answers, and students reflect this reality.

In the use of writing in different subject matter fields, as opposed to writing in English departments, there has been considerable uses of writing as a way of learning the material. This was one of the major concerns of the work of James Britton and his colleagues in England (1975). One of the more influential essays in this country has been that by Janet Emig, "Writing as a Mode of Learning," 1977. Both the Michigan and the Michigan Tech programs in writing across the curriculum emphasized this kind of writing (see Fulwiler, 1980; Stock, 1983). One of the best collections of essays on this is edited by Ann Ruggles Gere, *Roots in the Sawdust: Writing to Learn Across the Disciplines* (1985), and the emphasis in the essays can be seen in the subtitle. Another influential essay has been Anne J. Herrington's "Writing to Learn: Writing Across the Disciplines," 1981.

Creative Writing

This term is today usually reserved for poetry, dramas, novels, and short stories. The unfortunate implication is that there is not much creativity involved in other types of writing. Sometimes in high school textbooks the term *imaginative* writing is used, but this suffers from the same objection. Throughout history, creative writing was taught in texts usually called *poetics*, which handled drama, epic, and lyric poetry. Historically, teaching students how to write belle-tristically took place within the liberal art of grammar, understood as the study and writing of literature. The two dominant texts in this history have been the *Poetics* of Aristotle (1960) and the *Ars Poetica* of Horace (1940). Aristotle argues for a structionalist view: literature is intended to satisfy a craving for the perception of structures, of suspense in plot, of character juxtaposition, of thematic unity, of scenic relevance, and of sound patterns. Horace generally agrees, although he emphasizes the local conventions of plot, character, and dialect more than does Aristotle.

Today creative writing at the college level is almost universally determined by the individual theories of the teacher, often a poet or a novelist or a dramatist who also happens to teach. There is hardly any textbook used; most of the texts are anthologies of creative writing, and the teacher moves from these collections in any direction he or she wishes. At the secondary and elementary level, there are some more obvious influences.

The liberal arts tradition, emphasizing the influences of Aristotle and Horace, had some good and some harmful effects. One of the best effects was to keep the importance of creative writing in the forefront of academic education. Our forefathers in western culture who went to school, in general, wrote more poetry than most of us ever attempt. And this emphasis continued throughout the nineteenth century. Even when the poetics and rhetorics of the liberal arts tradition no longer dominated the educational scene, for instance, in the approach of Alexander Bain (1887), heavily influential in this country, in Great Britain, and in South America for over a century, most of the assignments continued to be literary giants of British and American literature, and the models for exposition were the essayists of the same tradition: Irving, Newman, Ruskin, Carlyle.

Beginning in the latter part of the nineteenth century and especially in this century, this emphasis has shifted, particularly in the secondary schools and in the colleges. Frequently, creative writing is neglected in favor of expository writing, both in this country and in Great Britain. Britton's study of writing in England found that only 17.6 percent of the writing in his 1,992 samples from ages 11 to 18 were poetic, whereas 63.4 percent were transactional, 5.5 percent were expressive and 13.5 percent mixed and miscellaneous, including persuasive (1975, Table 164, p. 52). The emphasis has clearly shifted from the creative to the transactional. The shift in this country has been exacerbated by the scientific threat from Russia in 1957, with the launching of Sputnik, Russia's first rocket, and today by the economic threat posed by Japan and West Germany.

For the better part of a century, one pervasive counterpart to this expository emphasis has come from the progressive school movement of the thirties and forties, largely based on Dewey's educational philosophy, which culminated in individual self-expression. For Dewey (1934), self-expression ideally eventuated in the esthetic experience. Consequently, it is not surprising that the pedagogical application of self-expression in the progressive schools heavily emphasized the esthetic. Dewey's massive influence on education both in America and in many other parts of the world as well have probably done more in this century to stem the tide towards the emphasis on the expository than almost any other figure.

Recently in this country, another healthy opposition to this movement was made by the popularity of Kenneth Koch's *Wishes, Lies, and Dreams: Teaching Children to Write* (1971), in which he described his success in teaching poetry in Harlem, using repeated general sentence types calling for concrete images as structures on which to hang the poem. Thus the imagery structure of "I wish I were with Charlie Brown in a blue shirt in France" is repeated 25 times, with each student supplying a similar line, like "I wish I was Blondie in the color sea green and the state of California." Koch (1977) repeated his success with elderly people in The American Nursing Home in New York City.

Expressive Writing

There was no explicit provision for self-expression, as such, in the liberal arts tradition, although there has always been an informal practice of such writing in western culture. But, beginning explicitly in the Renaissance and reaching a full tide in the nineteenth century, the notion that students might write simply to express their own ideas, ideals, frustrations, gripes, and reactions to situations, without any prior persuasive, expository, or literary aim, began to emerge more and more frequently. The notion was linked to the Romantic idea of individualism, the Freudian idea of expression of the unconscious, and the Hegelian idea of full development of the individual (*The Phenomenology of Mind,* 1967), which came into American thought through Croce and Dewey.

This notion was further developed philosophically by Heidegger, Sartre, Cassirer, and Gusdorf (see Kinneavy (1980, pp. 398–409) for the application of this to teaching self-expression. During the 1960s, when these theories hit the American scene, there were a number of composition practicioners whose ideas embodied in a practical way the theories of the existentialists and phenomenologists. Lou Kelley, in *From Dialogue to Discourse,* 1972, Ken Macrorie, in *Uptaught,* 1970, and other books, and Peter Elbow, in *Writing Without Teachers,* 1973, all emphasized the psychological primary of expressive discourse, though with no conscious affiliation to existential thought. The ideas of Dewey, Macrorie, Kelley, Elbow, and Kinneavy emphasizing expressive discourse have had a strong influence on the American educational scene—some have felt too strong. And there has been a pendulum swing away from too strong an emphasis on this kind of writing, especially when it is done to the exclusion of other kinds of writing. Most of these authorities would agree with this corrective.

Some of these writers see expressive discourse as a psychological beginning for all types of writing, and consequently that tend to place it at the beginning of syllabuses or textbooks and even to emphasize it more at the elementary and secondary levels and to ignore it at the college level. Thus it is not surprising that Lynn Phillips (1978), examining writings from 52 university departments, found that there was less than 1 percent of the writings that were dominantly expressive. This American figure thus parallels Britton's low figure of 5.5 percent for the high school scene in England. In America, with the exception of textbooks for freshman writing, there is scarcely any explicit provision structurally for self-expression in the curriculum at the college level.

The practice of expressive writing is quite varied at both the secondary school and college levels. Possibly the most frequent format is the use of the journal. For some, the journal is used almost as a private sanctuary of reactions to parents, teachers, fellow students, boyfriends, girlfriends, events, movies—almost anything. As such, it is frequently not graded, occasionally not even read except by the teacher. Sometimes the journal is later rewritten into a more polished paper. Occasionally, the reactive journal has been used in an exploratory way in writing across the curriculum programs. Toby Fulwiler's article "Journals Across the Disciplines," 1980, summarizes this.

Other formats are also used for expressive discourse. The personal movie or book reaction (rather than a formal review) has proven very popular at the secondary and college level. Expressive descriptions of places or of persons are also used. Some teachers have used music, to which the students then react in personal and imaginative ways. The personal letter is still also used for expressive writing.

A somewhat more systematic heuristic for self-expression has been written by Cynthia Selfe and Sue Rodi in "An Invention Heuristic for Expressive Writing," 1980, based on the existential notion of self-expression found in Jean-Paul Sartre. It can be applied at any level.

WRITING AND THE MODES OF DISCOURSE

Paralleling the traditional liberal arts throughout history, there has been a concern for the perspective from which the subject matter is approached. Thus if a student is doing a paper about George Washington, the concern may be a historical and biographical approach, or it can be a description of his character, or it may be an attempt to use Washington to define the nature of the presidency at the beginning of the country, or it may be an evaluation of Washington as a politician or as a general. The first paper would be a narrative, the second a description, the third a definition, and the fourth an evaluation. These types of writing are currently called the modes of discourse, although there is some disagreement on the various categories. In the nineteenth century and the early twentieth century, they were called the forms of discourse. Throughout most of history they were called the *status,* from the Latin term used by Cicero and others.

Historically, the modes paralleled the liberal arts in teaching writing, usually, though not always, in a subordinate position. At least one third of the extant Greek rhetorics, as well as many of the Latin rhetorics, focus on the modes. In the Middle Ages, the primary rhetorical text was Cicero's *On Invention,* the primary concern of which is the modes (see Cicero, *De Inventione,* 1949). The modes were also important throughout the Renaissance, mainly through the work of Hermogenes, the most read Greek rhetorician in the Renaissance (see Nadeau, 1964, for an English translation and commentary of "On Stases"). Finally, the modes again dominated composition practice in America and in Latin America from the middle of the nineteenth century till the 1970s, owing to the influence of Alexander Bain (1887), a Scotch rhetorician of the nineteenth century.

Cicero considered the status mainly from a lawyer's point of view. What aspect of the case should the lawyer emphasize in his speech? Should he stay with the facts of the case: Did Brutus actually stab Caesar, did the event happen as the prosecution alleged? Or should the lawyer concede the fact that Brutus did stab Caesar and attempt to prove that it was not really a murder, but rather a case of self-defense? In this second instance, the issue becomes a matter of definition. Or, finally, should the lawyer concede the fact of the stabbing, concede also the classification of the case as a murder, but argue that this factual murder was justified by the circumstances because Caesar was threatening the Roman republic? This third defense turns the case into an evaluation of an event in the light of a possibly unjust law. These three perspectives of fact, definition, and value were summarized by Cicero in a classic rule: *Sitne? quid sit? quale sit?* (Is it? What is it? What value does it have?), which occurs in his most famous treatise *De Oratore* (II, 1948, 30, 132). These were also adopted by Quintilian and Hermogenes and many others, although there were sometimes other status added. Each is given a lengthy treatment, and they were taught throughout history from Antiquity through the Renaissance.

Beginning in the seventeenth century and becoming stronger in the eighteenth and nineteenth century, there was a movement to link the modes with the faculties of the mind: to enlighten the understanding, to please the imagination, to move the passions, and to influence the will. Boswell, 1987, has an article chronicling this development. Bain, for example (1887, p. 19), said that description, narration, and exposition enlightened the understanding; that persuasion moved the will; and that poetry gave pleasure to the feelings. Later, poetry was dropped as a major kind of discourse for pedagogical purposes, and persuasion was changed to argumentation. These four structured composition books for over a century, at all levels of schooling.

They were eventually challenged by Kinneavy (1971, 1980) and Britton (1975), who maintained that the modes were really only means to achieve the aims or functions of language. Robert J. Connors has an influential essay on "The Rise and Fall of the Modes of Discourse" (1981). Connors, unfortunately almost dismisses the baby with the bath, assigning no importance to the modes at all. On the other hand, James Moffett's use of the modes (he calls them "kinds of discourse") in *Teaching the Universe of Discourse,* 1968, has been quite influential and relates them to semantics and to the psychologist Jean Piaget. So also has the use of them as an exploratory heuristic by the tagmemicists Kenneth Z. Pike et al. (1970). Frank J. D'Angelo approaches the modes more historically through the classical topics and parallel figurative language in a theoretical work, *A Conceptual Theory of Rhetoric,* 1975, and in a textbook that has gone through several editions, *Process and Thought in Composition,* 1980. A program at Maryland unabashedly uses the status as the framework for an entire upper division writing course, required of all university undergraduates. The text used is written by Jeanne Fahnstock and Marie Secor and is called *The Rhetoric of Argument,* 1982. Kinneavy, whom Connors invokes to dethrone the modes, still uses them in his theory and in his texbooks (see *Writing in the Liberal Arts Tradition,* Part II, 1985). These texts and programs are not atypical: The modes continue to be an integral part of nearly all writing texts from elementary school through college, as well as technical writing manuals.

THE SUBJECT MATTER OF WRITING

The subject matter of writing is often not given explicit attention by contemporary rhetoricians, although their theories and textbooks may take it for granted that some subjects are important and others are not. The recent concern with writing in the content areas (the school terminology) and writing across the curriculum (the college terminology) has radically challenged this placid oversight.

It might be worthwhile to give a brief historical sketch of this issue and then to outline some of the contemporary thinking about it. In Antiquity, the early composition exercises, called the *progymnasmata* because they were written prior to the college experience in the *gymnasion,* seemed to draw heavily from mythology and fables and to be embodied in imitation of models of description, narration, and other types of discourse drawn from canonical writers (see Nadeau, 1952, for a translation of Aphthonius' *Progymnasmata*). In the *gymnasion,* the two main subjects were already oriented to training for legal oratory by writing a persuasive piece (called a *suasoria*), to give advice, for instance to Alexander about whether he should cross the ocean after he had conquered everything on land. The subjects were often drawn from history (or fictional history) and were supposed to train the student for the courtroom. The more difficult of the subjects, however, was the dispute topic (called *controversia*), which was intended to prepare the student for political speeches. The topics usually revolved around issues of morality or laws, and, like the legal topic, were often given an imaginary situational context (see Kennedy, 1972, pp. 316–318, for a quick overview of these two topics).

The third main topic in Antiquity was handled in speeches intended to display the orator's cleverness and technique; these were called epideictic speeches. Often they too were based on history or fictional history. Frequently, the writer presents himself as the spokesman for a whole culture and embodies the aspirations and ideals of the culture. Pericles' speech to the Athenians on the occasion of the funeral for the first dead in the Peloponnesian war is often cited as the exemplar for such a topic (see Thucydides, 1954, for the reconstructed version of the speech, pp. 395–399). Later, the topics often became more trivial, mythological, and imaginary.

With the advent of Christianity, rhetoric was turned to the service of religion, which became the dominant topic of rhetoric for centuries, displacing both law and politics in importance. The major text in this displacement was Book IV of Augustine's *De Doctrina Christiana*, 1958, in which he channels classical rhetoric into the study of the Bible. This religious dominance was not challenged until the seventeenth and eighteenth centuries, at which time the rise of science and the rise of journalism both questioned the techniques and style of classical rhetoric to handle the presentation of the new sciences and the beginning reportorial writing of journalistic media.

Thus new topics, the many new sciences and current events of all types, invaded the hitherto sequestered domain of legal, political, and religious rhetoric. A classic presentation of this movement can be seen in Williamson's *The Senecan Amble*, 1951. Eventually commerce and trade and the beginning of modern advertising added new subjects to the range of writing topics, so that finally composition topics could be about anything. However, the textbooks of the eighteenth and nineteenth centuries did not reflect this universality.

Rather, religious topics and para-literary topics came to dominate the textbooks. Religion remained as an important topic because many of the most important rhetoricians of the period were ministers, for example, George Campbell, 1963, in Scotland, and Richard Whately, 1946, in England. But Campbell and others exerted another influence in subject matter. He continually overlapped the concerns of rhetoric with those of the belletristic writers of poetry, essays, and novels and chose his examples from these sources. Thus the models whom the students were to imitate were largely drawn from the literary canon, not from science or advertising or politics. This trend continues in Bain, whose influence in this country and South America has been discussed above.

As a result of these nineteenth century rhetoricians, the topics for writing in textbooks for almost a hundred years continued to be para-literary and religious.

The major break with these topics came with the advent of the progressive school, based on Dewey, also discussed above. With the emphasis on the individual, students were encouraged to write about anything that they desired, especially anything that they considered important to them. This, of course, was the subject matter corollary of the expressive movement spearheaded by Dewey and his disciples. This has made its way into elementary, secondary, and college texts on writing for the past 40 years. This universal tolerance is sometimes decried by teachers who get tired of perennial topics, such as "How I Spent My Summer Vacation."

This universalism has only recently been challenged by the recent attempt to have students write about all of their content areas, the movement usually called "writing across the curriculum." Mike Rose, in an important article, "Remedial Writing Courses: A Critique and a Proposal" (1983), questions the rather meaningless topics of the typical freshman English texts and proposes instead that the students write about the subject matter of their major (physics, economics, English, history, and so on). Rose here attempts to infuse into the college freshman composition program the strong writing across the curriculum movement that had begun with Britton and his associates in England and continued in this country by such efforts as the Michigan program (see Stock, 1983), the Michigan Tech program (see Fulwiler and Young, 1982), and the Beaver College program (see Maimon et al., 1981 (2), 1984). All three of these programs have been highly influential in spreading the movement in this country (see Kinneavy, 1983).

From almost nothing in the early 1980s to the present, the writing across the curriculum movement has become probably the most important movement in this country in writing in the past 10 years. A survey by the Modern Language Association in 1984 showed that more than 50 percent of its members claimed to have some kind of writing across the curriculum program (1985).

The programs generally were divided into two types, the program that insisted on a writing component in the traditional content courses in chemistry, art education, sociology, civil engineering, philosophy, and soon, and the program that had the students write about their specific subject matter in a centralized writing department (usually English). The prototype of the first program has been the program in the College of Letters, Arts and Sciences at the University of Michigan (see Stock, 1983). The prototype of the second was the program at Brigham Young University pioneered by John Harris. There has been more written about the Maryland program, which is very similar to the Brigham Young University program, however. Especially significant is the text used for the program, unabashedly based on the status of Cicero, *A Rhetoric of Argument*, by Jeanne Fahnstock and Marie Secor, 1982. For a discussion of the advantages and disadvantages of both types of programs, see Kinneavy, 1983, who contends that both types of program are needed in a full composition program: We must teach students to address their peers in the language of the specific discipline with its disciplinary sophistication in methodology and language, and we must also teach students to address the general public in language that it can understand in order to make intelligent political and moral decisions.

RHETORIC AND THE LANGUAGE ARTS

At the present time, the curricular pattern for the teaching of rhetoric at the elementary and high school level is the language-arts structure, that based on reading, writing, speaking, and listening. The listing is significant: Reading is accorded a primary importance, with writing as secondary, and speaking and listening in distant third and fourth rankings. Yet several studies, first in the 1920s and then in the 1940s have repeatedly shown that listening is quantitatively the most dominant of the language arts, with listening as a language art, occupying over

50 percent of our communication hours. Then comes speaking, taking about one third of our communicative life. Reading then takes about one eighth of our language time (depending on our career). And finally, writing may occupy as much as one twelfth of our time spent communicating. These early studies have to be modified by the heavy influence of television and radio on our lives. Any society in which the average person spends 6 hours a day watching television has obviously increased the listening time in communicating and decreased the time spent in speaking, reading, and writing.

Considerations like these have prompted authorities in curricula at all levels to reconsider the time devoted to the various language arts. At the school level, the movement resulted in the restructuring of entire programs into the language-arts segments (although the literature-grammar structure continued to dominate the texts adopted). At the college level, the communication arts (as they were called) initiated the organization of the Conference on College Composition and Communication—notice the last word of the organization. It emphasized the neglected arts of speaking and listening in the freshman composition progams. In 1949 the first meeting of the organization was held, and the organization has come to be the most important influence in writing in America for the past 49 years. Initially, the movement encouraged the incorporation of speaking and listening into college writing programs at the freshman level in such places as the universities of Minnesota, Iowa, and Denver. At the present time, however, this emphasis has almost totally disappeared, although the organization continues to be the torchbearer for composition studies in this country, and, indeed, in the world at large.

There are some studies that have compared the time spent on various arts in American schools as contrasted to those in Great Britain. Mina Shaughnessy reports that there is a dramatic difference in the amount of classroom time spend on writing in the two school systems. As she says,

Compared with the 1000 words a week that a British student is likely to have written in the equivalent of an American high school or even the 350 words a week that an American student in a middle-class high school is likely to have written, the basic writing [remedial] student is more likely to have written 350 words a semester. (1977, 14)

RHETORIC AND GRAMMAR

Today the word *grammar* usually means the study of a language's structures. Earlier, however, grammar, in the context of the liberal arts tradition, meant the study of the literature and language of a culture. Consequently, grammar, in the liberal arts tradition of the western world, meant the study of literature and was distinguished from rhetoric, which meant the study of how to produce persuasive discourse (legal, political, or religious). Both rhetoric and grammar were distinguished from logic and dialectic, which were the study of how to prove a point or how to explore an issue.

Of secondary importance in the liberal arts tradition was the second meaning of grammar, that is, the study of the structures of a language. This meaning of the term was applied to English only in the seventeenth century. And this meaning was even more clearly distinguished from rhetoric. Rhetorical treatises usually presumed a knowledge of the grammar of the language.

At some times, however, since rhetoric presupposes grammar as a prerequisite, the assumption has been made that a mere knowledge of grammar will produce literature prose. The corollary of this is that much of the time in teaching writing should be spent in teaching the rules of grammar. This formal teaching of grammar has been a characteristic of a good deal of teaching writing in the 1940s, 1950s, 1960s, and even 1970s. The English syllabus was often broken down into the teaching of grammar and the teaching of literature, and a good deal of speaking, listening, and writing, as well as thinking and viewing were somehow accommodated in the grammar/literature framework.

As a result, even from the beginning of the century, there has been research inquiring into the usefulness of formal teaching of grammatical rules and analysis as a tool to teaching effective writing. There have been three major summaries of this research, one in 1960 by Ingrid Strom, one in 1963 by Richard Braddock, Richard Lloyd-Jones, and Lowell Schoer, and one in 1987 by George Hillocks. There is a fairly strong consensus on the conclusions to be drawn from nearly 90 years of research on this topic, and possibly Braddock, Lloyd-Jones, and Schoer's statement summarizes it best:

In view of the widespread agreement of research studies based upon many types of students and teachers, the conclusion can be stated in strong and unqualified terms: the teaching of formal grammar has a negligible or, because it usually displaces some instruction and practice in actual composition, even a harmful effect on the improvement of writing. (1963, p. 38)

Hillock's book, it might be poined out, is a superb review of much of the major research in many areas of writing instruction at the present time.

References

Aristotle. (1926). *The "art" of rhetoric.* (J. H. Freese, Trans.). The Loeb Classical Library. Cambridge, MA: Harvard University Press.

Aristotle. (1960). *The poetics.* (W. R. Fyfe, Trans.). Longinus. *On the sublime.* (W. R. Roberts, Trans.). Demetrius. *On style.* (W. R. Roberts, Trans.) The Loeb Classical Library. Cambridge, MA: Harvard University Press.

Augustine. (1958). *On Christian doctrine.* (D. W. Robertson, Trans.). Library of Liberal Arts, 80. New York: Bobbs-Merrill.

Baier, K. (1958). *The moral point of view: A rational basis for ethics.* Ithaca, NY: Cornell University Press.

Bain, A. (1887). *English composition and rhetoric: A manual.* New York: D. Appleton and Co.

Beale, W. H. (1977, Spring). "On the classification of discourse performance. *Rhetoric Society Quarterly, VII,* 31–40.

Beale, W. H. (1987). *A pragmatic theory of rhetoric.* Carbondale, IL: Southern Illinois University Press.

Bornscheuer, L. (1976). *Topik. Zur struktur der gesellschaftlichen einbildungskraft.* Frankfurt am Main: Suhrkamp.

Boswell, G. (1988). The disfunction of rhetoric: Invention, imaginative excess, and the origin of the modes of discourse. *Rhetoric Society Quarterly, 18*(3, 4), 237–248.

Braddock, R., Lloyd-Jones, R. & Schoer, L. (1963). *Research in written composition.* Urbana, IL: National Council of Teachers of English.

Britton, J. N., Burgess, T., Martin, N., McCleod, A., Rosen, H. (1975). *The development of writing abilities* (pp. 11–18). London: Macmillan Education.

Brown, J. A. C. (1963). *Techniques of persuasion, from propaganda to brainwashing.* Baltimore, MD: Penguin Books.

Burke, K. (1969). *A Grammar of Motives.* Berkeley, CA: University of California Press. (Original work published 1945.)

Burke, K. (1973). *The philosophy of literary form.* Berkeley, CA: University of California Press. (Original work published 1941).

Burke, K. (1969). *A rhetoric of motives.* Berkeley, CA: University of California Press. (Original work published 1950).

Campbell, G. (1963). *The philosophy of rhetoric.* L. F. Bitzer (Ed.). Carbondale, IL: Southern Illinois University Press.

Cicero. (1952). *Brutus.* (G. L. Hendrickson, Trans.). *Orator.* (H. M. Hubbell, Trans.). The Loeb Classical Library. Cambridge, MA: Harvard University Press.

Cicero. (1949). *De inventione. De optimo genere oratorum. Topica.* (H. M. Hubbell (Trans). The Loeb Classical Library. Cambridge, MA: Harvard University Press.

Cicero. (1948). *De oratore, Books I–II.* (E. W. Sutton and H. Rackham, Trans.). The Loeb Classical Library. Cambridge, MA: Harvard University Press.

Cicero. (1942). *De oratore, Book III. De fato. Paradoxoa stoicorum. De partitione oratoria.* (H. Rackham Trans.). The Loeb Classical Library. Cambridge, MA: Harvard University Press.

College Composition and Communication, Committee on CCCC Language Statement. (1974, October). Students' right to their own language. *College Composition and Communication, 25,* 1–18.

Connors, R. J. (1981). The rise and fall of the modes of discourse. *College Composition and Communication, 32,* 444–455.

Cope, E. M. (ca. 1967). *An introduction to Aristotle's rhetoric: with analysis, notes.* Dubuque, IA: Wm. C. Brown Reprint Library. (Original work published 1867, London: Macmillan)

Corbett, E. P. J. (1971). *Classical rhetoric for the modern student.* New York: Oxford University Press. (Original work published 1965)

Curtius, E. R. (1973). *European literature and the Latin Middle Ages.* (W. R. Trask, Trans.). Princeton, NJ: Princeton University Press. (Original work published 1953)

D'Angelo, F. J. (1975). *A conceptual theory of rhetoric.* Cambridge, MA: Winthrop Publishers.

D'Angelo, F. J. (1980). *Process and thought in composition* (2nd ed.). Cambridge, MA: Winthrop Publishers.

Dewey, J. (1958). *Art as experience.* New York: Capricorn. (Original work published 1934)

Dewey, J. (1955). *Logic: The theory of inquiry.* New York: Henry Holt and Co. (Original work published 1938)

Doob, L. W. (1961). *Communication in Africa: A search for boundaries.* New Haven, CT: Yale University Press.

Ehninger, D. (1974). *Influence, belief, and argument: An introduction to responsible persuasion.* Glenview, IL: Scott, Foresman and Co.

Elbow, P. (1973). *Writing without teachers.* New York: Oxford University Press.

Emig, J. (1977). Writing as a model of learning. *College Composition and Communication, 28,* 122–128.

Fahnstock, J., & Secor, M. (1982). *A rhetoric of argument.* New York: Random House.

Fulwiler, T. (1986). Journal-writing across the curriculum. In *Classroom practices in teaching English 1979-80: How to handle the paper load.* Urbana, IL: National Council of Teachers of English.

Fulwiler, T. & Young, A. (1982). *Language connections: Writing and reading across the curriculum.* Urbana, IL: National Council of Teachers of English.

Gere, A. R. (Ed.). (1985). *Roots in the sawdust: Writing to learn across the disciplines.* Urbana, IL: National Council of Teachers of English.

Harris, R., & Seldon, A. (1962). *Advertising and the public.* London: A. Deutsch.

Hegel, G. W. F. (1967). *The phenomenology of mind.* (J. B. Baillie, Trans.). Introduction, G. Lichtheim. New York: Harper & Row.

Herrington, A. J. (1981). Writing to learn: Writing across the disciplines. *College English, 43,* 379–387.

Hillocks, G. (1986). *Research on written composition: New directions for teaching.* Urbana, IL: National Council of Teachers of English.

Horace. (1940). Ars poetica. In *literary criticism from Plato to Dryden* (Pp. 128–143). (E. Blakeney, Trans.). A. H. Gilbert, (Ed.). New York: American Book Company.

Horner, W. B. (1988). *Rhetoric in the classical tradition.* York: St. Martin's Press.

Hovland, C. I., Janis, I. R., and Kelly, H. H. (1953). *Communication and persuasion.* New Haven: Yale University Press.

Jakobson, R. (1967). Linguistics and poetics. In S. Chatman & S. R. Levin (Eds.), *Essays on the Language of Literature* (pp. 296–322). Boston: Houghton Mifflin.

Kelley, L. (1972). *From dialogue to discourse: An open approach to competence and creativity.* Glenview, IL: Scott, Foresman and Co.

Kennedy, G. (1972). *The art of rhetoric in the Roman world.* Princeton, NJ: Princeton University Press.

Kierkegaard, S. (1959). Concluding unscientific postscript. In *a Kierkegaard anthology* Tr. (W. Lowrie, Trans.). R. Bretall (Ed.). New York: Modern Library.

Kierkegaard, S. (1962). *The point of my work as an author: A report to history and related writings.* Lowrie (Trans.). B. Nelson (Ed.). New York: Harper & Row.

Kinneavy, J. L. (1980). *A theory of discourse.* New York: Norton. (Original work published 1971)

Kinneavy, J. L., McCleary, W., & Nakadate, N. (1983). Writing across the curriculum. *Profession, 83,* 13–20.

Kinneavy, J. L., McCleary, W., & Nakadate, N. (1985). *Writing in the liberal arts tradition.* New York: Harper & Row.

Kinneavy, J. L., McCleary, W., & Nakadate, N. (1987). Writing across the curriculum. In G. Tale (Ed.), *Teaching composition: Twelve bibliographical essays* (pp. 353–377). Fort Worth, TX: Texas Christian University Press.

Koch, K. (1977, January 20). I never told anybody: Teaching poetry writing in a nursery home. Supplement to *The New York Review of Books,* pp. 36–47.

Koch, K. and the Students of P. S. 61 in New York City. (1971). *Wishes, lies, and dreams: Teaching children to write poetry.* New York: Vantage Books, Chelsea Publishing.

Kuhn, T. (1967). *The structure of scientific revolutions.* Chicago: University of Chicago Press. (Original work published 1962)

Lasswell, H. D., Leites, N., Janis, I. L., Kaplan, A., Goldsen, J. M., Grey, A., Kaplan, D., Mintz, A., Yakobson, S., de Sola Pool, I. (1965). *Language of politics.* Cambridge, MA: M. I. T. Press. (Original work published 1949)

Macrorie, K. (1970). *Uptaught.* Rochelle Park, NJ: Hayden Book.

Maimon, E., Belcher, G. L., Hearn, G. W., Nodine, B. F., O'Connor, F. W. (1981). *Writing in the arts and sciences.* Cambridge, MA: Winthrop Publishers.

Maimon, E. (1984). *Readings in arts and sciences.* Boston, MA: Little, Brown and Co.

McCleary, W. J. (1979). *Teaching deductive logic: A test of the Toulmin and Aristotelian models for critical thinking and college composition.* Unpublished doctoral dissertation, Austin, TX.

Modern Language Association Commission on Writing and Literature. (1985, May 2). *Survey of the Profession.* Unpublished manuscript.

Moffett, J. (1968). *Teaching the universe of discourse.* Boston: Houghton Mifflin.

Morris, CH. W. (1955). *Signs, language and behavior.* Englewood Cliffs, NJ: Prentice-Hall. (Original work published 1946)

Murphy, J. J. (Ed.). (1978). *Medieval eloquence: Studies in the theory and practice of medieval rhetoric.* Berkeley, CA, and London: University of California Press.

Murphy, J. J. (Ed.). (1981). *Rhetoric in the Middle Ages: A history of rhetorical theory from Saint Augustine to the Renaissance.* Berkeley, CA, and London: University of California Press. (Original work published 1974).

Nadeau, R. (1964). Hermogenes' on *Stases:* A translation with an introduction and notes. *Speech Monographs, 31,* 361–424.

Nadeau, R. (1952, November). The progymnasmata of Aphthonius in translation. *Speech Monographs, XIX,* 264–285.

Nisbet, R., & Ross, L. (1980). *Human inference: Strategies and shortcomings of social judgement.* Century Psychology Series. Englewood Cliffs, NJ: Prentice-Hall.

Packard, V. (1980). *The hidden presuaders.* New York: Pocket Books. (Original work published 1957)

Perelman, C., & Olbrechts-Tyetca, L. (1969). *The new rhetoric: A treatise on argumentation.* (J. Wilkinson and Purcell Weaver, Trans.). Notre Dame, IN: University of Notre Dame Press.

Phillips, L. A. (1978). *An assessment of the preparatory value of a college course in freshman composition.* Unpublished doctoral dissertation, Austin, TX.

Pike, K. Z., Young, R., & Becker, A. (1970). *Rhetoric: Discovery and change.* New York: Harcourt, Brace and World.

Plato, (1925). *Lysis. Symposium. Gorgias* (W. R. M. Lamb, Trans.). The Loeb Classical Library. Cambridge, MA: Harvard University Press.

Quintilian. (1920–1922). *The Institutio Oratoria of Quintilian* (Vols. 1–4). (H. E. Butler, Trans.). The Loeb Classical Library. Cambridge, MA: Harvard University Press.

Rose, M. (1983). Remedial writing courses: A critique and a proposal. *College English, XLV,* 109–126.

Sandage, C. H. & Fryburger, V. (1960). *Advertising theory and practice.* Homewood, IL: Richard D. Irwin Inc., 1960 and 1979.

Selfe, C. L., & Rodi, S. (1980, May). An invention heuristic for expressive writing. *CCC, XXXI,* 169–174.

Shaughnessy, M. P. (1977). *Errors and expectations: A guide for the teacher of basic writing.* New York: Oxford University Press.

Stock, P. (Ed.). (1983). *Fforum: Essays on Theory and Practice in the Teaching of Writing.* Montclair, NJ: Boynton/Cook.

Strom, I. (1960). Research in grammar and usage and some implications for teaching writing. *Bulletin of the School of Education, Indiana University.*

Tacitus, C. (1958). *Dialogues, Agricola, Germania.* (W. Peterson, Trans.). The Loeb Classical Library. Cambridge, MA: Harvard University Press.

Thucydides. (1952). The history of the Peloponnesian War. In *The history of Herodotus* (G. Rawlinson, Trans.). *The history of the Peloponnesian War, Thucydides* (R. Crawley, Trans.). Rev. by R. Feetham. Great Books of the Western World, 6. Ed. R. M. Hutchins (Ed.). Chicago: Encyclopedia Britannica.

Toulmin, S. E. (1964). *The uses of argument.* Cambridge, MA: Cambridge University Press. (Original work published 1958)

Whately, R. (1963). *Elements of logic, comprising an analysis of the laws of moral evidence and of persuasion, with rules for argumentative composition and elocution.* D. Ehninger (Ed.). (D. Potter, Foreword). Carbondale, IL: Southern Illinois University. (Original work published 1828)

Williamson, G. (1951). *The senecan amble: A study in prose form from Bacon to Collier.* Chicago, IL: University of Chicago Press.

Zeiger, W. (1985, September). The exploratory essay: Enfranchising the spirit of inquiry in college composition. *College English, XLVII* (5), 454–464.

32

LITERATURE

32A. CHILDREN'S RESPONSES TO LITERATURE

Miriam G. Martinez
Nancy L. Roser

A 2-year-old pats a page of his picture book with a cut-away illustration of a two-story house: "This won't work," he says emphatically. "There's no way to get upstairs." (Sure enough, no staircase is pictured.)

A 5-year-old carries his poetry book to his kindergarten teacher: "I listen," he smiles, "but I don't do motions on the outside."

A 7-year-old listens to *The Twits* (Dahl, 1981) gasping with laughter: "I love funny books like this! Wait! Read that again about those guys stuck on the ceiling."

A 13-year-old closes *Isaac Asimov's Robot City 4: Prodigy* (Cover, 1988): "This is the first book I've ever read I haven't liked," he sighs. "Isaac Asimov is encouraging other writers to go on writing like him. The first three books were so close to Asimov's style I couldn't tell them apart. But *this* author didn't think the same way. His characterization was all wrong, and he used vocabulary he didn't have to to be clear."

In each of the above cases, the respondent was the same child, registering varying degrees of personal satisfaction with the logic, language, forms, and consistency of different texts over the course of time. Britton (1968) posits that growth in response to literature lies in

perceiving gradually more complex patterns of events, in picking up clues more widely separated and more diverse in character, and in finding satisfaction in patterns of events less directly related to [readers'] expectations (pp. 4–5)

By carefully attending to spontaneous as well as elicited responses to literature, researchers have begun to gain access to the premises of children's responses. Further, research has begun to describe varying influences on response, features of mature response, and how responses reveal children's efforts to construct meaning.

Harding (1968) has asserted that response is active rather than passive, that it includes both immediate and delayed effects, and that overt responses (i.e., verbal) may not be the total indicator of the inner responses that occur. In Harding's view, the emergence of response to literature is sequential, stemming from children's earliest experiences listening to rhymes, songs,

and stories. Although it is not yet feasible to propose a definitive model of this development, it does seem reasonable to suggest that children's responses to literature develop as their experiences with literature broaden. Therefore, as Britton (1968) suggests, our teaching goals should be "to refine and develop responses the children are already making" (p. 4) rather than to instruct those responses. And indeed, attention to "response to literature" has not been so much the search for an instructional tool as it has been an attempt to understand the nature of the reader (or listener's) literary experience.

Until recently, research in responses to literature has focused largely on what can be learned from the written responses of university or secondary students to particular literary works (cf. Purves & Rippere, 1968). These studies served to sensitize teachers of literature at all levels to the complexity of students' responses:

Response to literature is mental, emotional, intellectual, sensory, physical. It encompasses the cognitive, affective, perceptual, and psychomotor activities that the reader of a poem, a story, or a novel performs as he reads or after he has read. (p, xi)

Researchers are now turning more attention to using alternative methods to study the variety of responses produced by young children in order to understand the ways that young readers and listeners come to consider, reflect, manipulate, and verbalize their feelings and opinions about text. Contributing to this broadened perspective are changes that have occurred in the view of the reader/learner (cf. Donaldson, 1978; Lindfors, 1987; Teale, 1987), in the view of the reading process itself (cf. Pearson, 1986; Rosenblatt, 1978), and in the ways that responses have been productively investigated (Galda, 1983; Hickman, 1981). (Also see chapter by Rosenblatt in this Handbook)

Increasingly, the young child is viewed as an active constructor of language, and as an active processor/learner in general, capable of inference and abstract thought, who in literate environments is "continuously learning to read and write" (Teale, 1987, p. 47). With more credence given the young child as learner, more attention has been given to describing what young children know about story and about print, to investigating their efforts to construct meaning, and to observing ways they respond to literature.

Changes in perspective on the reading act result from the contributions of cognitive psychologists who have demonstrated that reading is the active construction of meaning guided by printed symbols. Reading is viewed as a transaction between reader and text. The term *transaction* as used by Rosenblatt (1976) describes the relationship between reader and text, with the reader as constructor of the literary experience guided by the text, rather than one seeking a precise interpretation of text. Text, to Rosenblatt (1985), consists only of contrasting marks on a page. The literary work, "the poem", is evoked in this transaction of reader and text. Readers must attend *both* to the text and to the "qualitative overtones of the ideas, images, situations, and characters" being evoked (p. 38). Because the reader/learner is critical to the transaction, it becomes important to discern how readers of all ages engage in transactions with literary texts.

Finally, there have been changes in the ways that researchers study responses to literature. For decades, descriptions, comparisons, and analyses were drawn from students' written responses to prescribed text. Squire (1964) and others attended to students' oral responses. More recently, these methodologies have been supplemented with ethnographic techniques, including participant-observer and case study, describing a wide variety of types of response, including the nonverbal modes associated with young children. Recent research conducted both in home and classroom settings has attended to spontaneous 'literacy events" and the responses they evoke, as well as to the talk that occurs during storytime, finding both settings to offer rich opportunities for attending to children's responses.

Rosenblatt (1985) urges researchers to "reflect on the 'fit' of a problem into a broader perspective related to human development." By considering the research question in view of its broadest implications, investigations into responses to literature are likely to produce teaching effects "that foster the capacity for more and more rewarding transactions between readers and text" (p. 51).

When Purves and Beach (1972) produced their comprehensive review of research on responses to literature nearly 20 years ago, they noted in the Foreword (p. vii) that they faced two major problems in their effort: The first was finding some way of classifying the studies being examined; the second was weighing the merits of those studies. Based on the advice of an advisory board of eminent scholars, Purves and Beach decided that a classification system must grow from consideration of the studies themselves rather than from a preordained formulation; second, they decided the contribution of any study would be gauged from the importance of the question being considered, the conception of a worthwhile problem, rather than solely from the sophistication of its statistical properties. Following the lead provided by Purves and Beach, this chapter attempts to take stock of the increasing number of investigations of children's responses to literature both in home and classroom settings. Its organization grew from the studies themselves; its authors have tried to be vigilant for the thoughtful question, the

use of logical procedures, and for appropriately aged participants.

FACTORS THAT AFFECT CHILDREN'S RESPONSES TO LITERATURE

The nature of the reading event suggests several vantage points from which to view responses to literature. Responses (as described earlier) are the result of a transaction between a reader and a text, and this transaction occurs within a particular context. Each of these elements—text, reader, and context—serves as a perspective from which to examine and better understand readers' responses (Purves, 1985). Because all three elements are essential to any literary transaction, it is impossible to discuss one independently of the others. Nevertheless, the studies of children's responses to literature have focused primarily on reader and context factors that influence response. This chapter is organized to attend to each factor, but offers a fuller discussion of the reader and context variables.

Reader Factors

The reader as well as the text shapes the transaction that occurs in a reading event. Researchers have identified numerous reader characteristics that influence response, including reader beliefs and expectations, reading ability, socioeconomic status, cultural background, personality, cognitive development, sex, and personal style (Applebee, 1973, 1978; Cooper, 1969; Cullinan, Harwood, & Galda, 1983; Galda, 1982; Hickman, 1983; Petrosky, 1976; Purves, 1973; Squire, 1964). Despite the increased attention to the reader-responder, research in this area is in its infancy. The major thrust of investigations of children's responses has been on a single reader characteristic, that of age and how responses to literature change across age levels.

Britton (1968) noted that although a child's responses to literary text may appear to be naive and unsophisticated, those responses are better viewed as the "tender shoots" from which more mature responses emerge. Increasingly, researchers have investigated how children respond to literature across age levels, and from these efforts a clearer picture is emerging of how children's responses evolve into those of mature readers.

Applebee (1978) conducted the first major work on developmental differences in children's responses to literature. Drawing on a number of lines of evidence to describe the responses of 6-, 9-, 13-, and 17-year-olds, Applebee found differences across age levels in the children's objective responses (i.e., those responses concerned with the story's publicly verifiable characteristics such as details of character, structure, point of view, theme) and their subjective or personal responses.

The objective responses of Applebee's younger subjects (the 6- and 9-year-olds) focused on story action rather than other characteristics of stories such as point of view or theme. Young children organized their discussions of story action in one of three ways, through a retelling, a synopsis, or a summary. Although both 6- and 9-year-olds used each of these three organizational forms, 6-year-olds typically favored retellings and synopses, while 9-year-olds primarily produced synopses and very short summaries. The children's subjective responses or evaluations of stories also assumed characteristic forms across the different age levels in the study. Most of the 6-year-olds evaluated stories globally (e.g., "It's good."). When pressed to explain why they liked or disliked a story, the children singled out a single memorable incident or detail in the story (e.g., "I liked it because the troll fell in the water."). The 9-year-olds evaluated stories by placing them into categories with clearly marked attributes. For example, stories were evaluated as "dreary" or "interesting."

Applebee found that 6- and 9-year-olds responded literally whether they discussed action or evaluated stories. To determine if children at these age levels could also recognize a more generalized meaning, he asked his subjects to explain the meaning of two common sayings ("When the cat is away, the mice will play" and "You must have gotten out of the wrong side of the bed this morning"). Most of the 6-year-olds offered literal interpretations of the sayings; by age 9, however, some of the children began to offer more sophisticated interpretations.

Although the 6- and 9-year-olds produced retellings, synopses, and summaries, Applebee found that the 13- and 17-year olds' objective responses to stories changed dramatically. The adolescents were concerned with analyzing the structures of stories and forming generalizations about their meanings. Further, their objective and subjective responses were closely linked, as their evaluations emerged from their analyses of the structure of literary works. These avenues of response did not yet appear to be open to the 6- and 9-year-olds for whom the story remained "primarily a patterning of events" (p. 115).

Cullinan, Harwood, and Galda (1983) also studied developmental differences in children's responses to literature. Eighteen children in grades 4, 6, and 8 were asked to read *Bridge to Terabithia* (Paterson, 1977) and *A Wizard of Earthsea* (LeGuin, 1968). Following the reading of each book, the children were interviewed individually and later in same-sex groups of three to elicit their responses. The students were asked to tell about the story, to tell what made it good or not so good, whether the title or symbol had any special meanings, and whether the book reminded them of any others they had read. Cullinan and her colleagues found strong developmental trends in the form and content of the children's story recall and in their metaphoric and thematic comprehension. To analyze the form of the students' individual recall protocols, the researchers used Applebee's categories. They found that the fourth graders, like Applebee's 9-year-old subjects, tended to use synopsis and retelling. Of the sixth graders, half used synopsis and half used summary in recalling the story. The eighth graders in this study, like the 13-year-olds in Applebee's study, responded to the task of recalling the story by giving summaries ending in analysis. Findings of both studies indicate that children use different processes in recalling stories at different ages.

Cullinan et al. also examined the ways that children responded to story content, whether literally, by interpreting, and/or by evaluating. The fourth graders responded at a literal level; although, in recalling one story, they all omitted a crucial event, the death of a major character. When this event was brought up in group discussion, the children insisted the char-

acter had come back to life. The expectation that stories have happy endings, an expectation that Squire (1964) calls "happiness binding," clearly interfered with the literal comprehension of the fourth graders. Sixth graders comprehended both of the stories at a literal level and occasionally at an interpretive level. Although they recounted the death scene omitted by the fourth graders, the sixth graders expressed shock over it. Eighth graders comprehended at the literal and interpretive levels and were also able to make judgments about the meaning of the stories in their own lives. However, the boys' evaluations were influenced by peers. In discussing *Bridge to Terabithia* in the interview situation, the boys indicated that they viewed the friendship of the male and female characters as idyllic, but in the group discussions they made light of this relationship.

The fourth, sixth, and eighth graders also responded differently to probes designed to elicit symbolic and thematic comprehension. The fourth graders did not see any special meaning in the symbols used by the authors, and the sixth graders gave only tentative explanations. However, the eighth graders saw numerous possible meanings in these same symbols. To tap thematic comprehension, the researcher asked the children to describe the most important part or idea of each book; children's responses revealed increasingly more in-depth and insightful thematic analyses across age levels. The fourth graders seemed to know that books are thematic, and they tried to articulate themes. However, they saw only a very simple message in each text. Even though the sixth graders perceived more subtle messages than the fourth graders, their responses were markedly less sophisticated than those of the eighth graders, who saw multiple messages in the novels and drew implications for their own lives from those messages.

Lehr (1988) also found developmental trends in children's ability to identify and articulate story themes. In her study of kindergarten-, second-, and fourth-grade children, Lehr found that students who had had more exposure to literature were better able to generate thematic statements. Kindergarten children's statements were generally most different from those generated by adults. Nevertheless, even the youngest children were able to generate thematic statements that were consistent with story content. Unlike Applebee and Cullinan et al., Lehr found that the second and fourth graders from the high exposure group were able to analyze and make generalizations about stories.

In exploring children's responses to literature, most researchers have focused on developmental patterns, an aspect of response that Hickman also (1981) examined. Yet Hickman's work in this field is particularly noteworthy in that she pioneered the study of children's responses to literature in naturally occurring contexts. In doing so, she was able to tap dimensions of response that had remained untouched by more conventional approaches. Further, in addition to examining developmental differences in response, she identified significant social and temporal factors influencing children's responses. Using primarily an ethnographic research method, she became a participant-observer in three multiage classrooms (K–1, 2–3, and 4–5). Data were field notes, taped interviews, and photographs gathered in the three classrooms that Hickman described as sites "where literature was much in evidence" (p. 525). Hickman viewed a response event as any behavior occurring in the classroom that revealed some connection between children and literature. This definition was broader in scope than those underlying preceding studies of children's responses, in which oral or written responses about particular stories were elicited using researcher-posed questions. Although others (e.g., Harding, 1968) had recognized that children's responses may be qualitatively different than those of adolescents and adults, Hickman was the first researcher to employ a research design capable of taking into account a variety of modes of naturally occurring response. Harding, in his report on the proceedings of the Dartmouth Seminar, had included in his description of young children's responses those made by children as they physically respond to the sounds of literature, or correct the storyteller who fails to render a word perfect reading, or assume the role of a storybook character in dramatic play, or talk about the world created by the storyteller. Hickman's study attended to these forms of response as well as others.

In the three classrooms in which she gathered data, Hickman identified seven different types of responses. These categories of response were:

a. Listening behaviors such as applause or joining in refrains,
b. Contact with books such as browsing or keeping books at hand,
c. Acting on the impulse to share by reading together or sharing discoveries,
d. Oral responses such as retelling or freely commenting on stories,
e. Actions and drama,
f. Making things such as pictures or games, and
g. Writing about literature or using literary models in one's writing.

Although all categories of response events occurred in each of the three classes, some modes were characteristic of different age groups. For example, the kindergarten/first-grade children were more likely to use their bodies to respond. These children often echoed the action in stories during reading and in teacher-led discussions; parts of stories appeared frequently in their dramatic play. Hickman described the second/third-grade level as a transitional one in which children seemed at different times more like the younger or older groups. However, the children in this class were distinguished by their dedication to the task of becoming readers, as evidenced by the amount of time they devoted to reading together and sharing. Many of the spontaneous comments of the second/third graders revealed a concern with the conventions of print and a preference for books that could be read independently. Hickman characterized the children in the fourth/fifth-grade level as intensely attentive to books. Only at this level did children become so engrossed in text as to be described as "lost in a book."

Hickman was primarily interested in children's naturally occurring responses. However, she recognized that verbal responses in a question/answer format are, nonetheless, the most frequently occurring type of response event in most classrooms. Therefore, as part of the larger study, she elicited children's responses to the book *The Magical Drawings of Moony*

B. Finch (McPhail, 1978). Twenty-eight children were asked to listen to or read the book and then use a tape recorder to "tell what you think about it; say anything you wish" (p. 10). Following this, the children were individually interviewed about the book. In their taped responses, children of all ages used similar approaches. Most made global evaluative statements, referring to the story as "neat" or "funny" or "good." Generally they chose to make references to the illustrations in the book. The younger children tended to produce partial retellings and summaries, strategies used by Applebee's subjects when they were asked to tell about a favorite story. The older children in Hickman's study appeared to have a greater repertoire of things to say about stories, and hence relied less on retellings and summaries.

The results of the focused interview also revealed distinct patterns across age levels. When asked to classify the book, all the children made global evaluative statements. However, only the older children used conventional literary terminology to classify the book. As part of the interview, the children were asked to provide explanations about the fantasy element of the story. The younger children tended to offer literal explanations based on their own experiences. By contrast, questions related to realism/fantasy elements posed no problem for the older children who, according to Hickman, "had developed a confident sense of the distance between the real world and the world of the story" (p. 11). When asked if the main character had learned anything in the story, some of the younger children were able to offer a thematic statement of sorts, but one that was clearly embedded in the situation of the story. The older children, by contrast, handled the question in a far more sophisticated manner, offering a disembedded thematic statement that was clearly appropriate for the story.

Examining a somewhat related aspect of response, Pillar (1983) found that the responses of children also reflected their levels of moral development. She elicited second-, fourth-, and sixth-graders' responses to moral dilemmas presented in fables without four dimensions—intentionality, relativism, punishment, and independence of sanctions (Kohlberg, 1964; Piaget, 1965). Developmental differences emerged within each dimension. Responding to questions related to intentionality, the younger children judged the actions of characters to be bad when those actions resulted in negative physical consequences. Older children took intentionality or characters' motives into account in making their decisions. Within the dimension of relativism, younger children viewed acts as totally good or totally bad, and they allowed no room for diversity of opinion. Older students recognized that shades of gray may exist and that people can legitimately disagree in their beliefs about what is right and wrong. Responding to questions about punishment, younger children favored severe punishment to show offenders their guilt, while older ones expressed a belief that explanation and reproach might be a more appropriate way to deal with an offender. The final dimension of moral development that Pillar examined was independence of sanctions. She found that young children identified rules with duties; that is, they viewed any act obedient to a rule as good. In contrast, the older, more mature responders viewed story acts in terms of their effects on others; that is, they took into account how actions affected the rights and feelings of others. Within each of the four dimensions examined by Pillar, there were strong developmental patterns in the responses of second, fourth, and sixth graders to the moral situations in fables.

Researchers who have examined children's responses to literature from a developmental perspective have generally argued that the changes across age levels can be accounted for in terms of children's level of cognitive development. Applebee, in particular, espouses such a view. However, a too rigid cognitive developmental interpretation must be questioned on a number of bases. First, Galda's research, examining children's responses from a personal style perspective, calls into question the role of cognitive development in constraining responses.

Studying the responses of three fifth-grade girls matched on reading ability, Galda found that the readers had distinctive, individual styles of response to two novels, *Bridge to Terabithia* (Paterson, 1977) and *Beat the Turtle Drum* (Greene, 1976). For example, Emily, the first of the three fifth graders, read stories primarily for the plot. She wanted to find out what happened in a story and was especially responsive to unusual twists in the plot. Evaluation was Emily's most frequent mode of response, and her evaluations employed general labels (e.g., "good," "nice style") that were rarely supported with references to the stories. Galda found that Emily was unable to assume the spectator role and thereby accept the world created by the author on its own terms. Rather, her responses were governed by her personal view of reality, and she criticized characters and events that did not conform to her reality.

In contrast to Emily, Charlotte focused on the central conflict and the main characters' reactions to that conflict. However, she took deliberate steps to maintain a distance from the conflict to prevent personal involvement in the story. One way in which she did this was by assuming the role of the observer-critic. In this role Charlotte, like Emily, criticized the story in terms of her own perceived reality, but she couched her criticism in objective terms by comparing characters' behavior with what she called "typical" behavior. Unlike Emily, Charlotte supported her evaluations with examples from the texts.

Galda characterized the third respondent, Ann, as a mature responder, one who analyzed both the text and her responses to it. Unlike Emily and Charlotte, Ann focused on characters' feelings, personalities, and motives rather than solely on story events. She was able to assume what Britton (1970) has termed a spectator stance as she "entered into the experience the text offered" (Galda, 1982, p. 16), accepting realities present in the story that were not her own. Finally, rather than evaluating a text on a piecemeal basis, she focused on the text as a whole.

The diversity in the responses of Emily, Charlotte, and Ann suggests that factors other than cognitive development may also influence response. For example, the degree of exposure to literature may be one such factor, as Lehr's findings suggest. Although Lehr found developmental trends in children's responses across age groups (as did Applebee, Cullinan et al., and Hickman), these differences were most evident among children with low or limited contact with children's literature. Children with greater experience with literature were able to use more sophisticated forms in retelling stories than their age-mates in other studies, and were also able to engage in more analysis

and generalization than reported by other investigators studying same-age children.

Not only does degree of exposure to literature appear to influence children's responses, but the contextual situation in which responses are invited appears to be important as well. In fact, these efforts to understand the settings in which responses occur, and in particular the interactions that occur there, contribute the second major strand of research in children's responses to literature, the study of the context for responses.

Context Factors

In recent years, a number of researchers have focused directly on how context factors influence children's responses within school and home settings. Hickman, whose work was reviewed in the previous section, first studied children's naturally occurring responses in a school setting, finding that the responses were very obviously tied to the context in which they occurred. Throughout the school that Hickman observed, children's literature was a central part of the students' experience, and this was clearly apparent in the three focal classrooms. Although the classroom literature programs organized by the teachers were not identical, Hickman (1981) was able to identify some common strategies used by the teachers:

1. The teachers selected titles for classroom use with an emphasis on quality and relatedness. Titles might be related by genre, topic, theme, author, or illustrator. Hickman found that the presentation of related selections influenced the children's responses in at least two ways. First, these units of study appeared to encourage the children to make explicit connections among literature selections. In addition, Hickman found that where related selections were less available, the children had less to say about the formal properties of a selection.
2. The teachers assured children of access to books by displaying the books attractively and by providing ample time for children to read. Hickman found that children more readily expressed their responses when they had the book in hand. Although they made brief comments about books not physically available, more reflective thinking (expressed through artwork, writing, or discussion) emerged when children had direct access to a book.
3. The teachers presented literature to the children daily, both by reading aloud and by introducing books to the children. Books read aloud or introduced by the teacher were the ones most often sought by the children. These were also the titles that generated the most talk and the greatest variety of response events (e.g., artwork, writing).
4. The teachers discussed books with the children, using critical terminology to support children who had an idea, but needed words to express that idea.
5. The teachers provided the space, time, materials, and suggestions for book related activities.
6. The teachers provided for the formal sharing and display of completed book extensions.
7. The teachers planned for cumulative experiences with literature. They allowed the children to consider some selections and genre in depth, and in a variety of ways over time. This temporal dimension of response, which is in part under the influence of teachers, is of special note because Hickman found that the children's responses to particular books frequently changed over time. Hickman noted that "both the length involved (allowing reflection and repetition)

and the cumulative effect of employing a variety of modes seems to be important in determining qualitative shifts in the content of responses." (p. 349)

Kiefer (1983) extended one aspect of Hickman's dissertation study by focusing on children's naturally occurring responses to picture books in a classroom setting. The classroom was a multilevel first/second grade, in which picture books played a central role; in fact, picture books served as the basis for reading instruction. Like Hickman, Kiefer found that the teacher played a key role in influencing response. In this classroom, the teacher chose to read and reread books, and Kiefer found a marked deepening and broadening of response as the children had repeated opportunities to interact with a book. The language the teacher chose to use in discussing books also influenced the children, who in turn frequently used specialized terminology such as "media," "collage," and "acrylics" in talking about illustrations in books. In addition, the teacher used open-ended discussion strategies to elicit a variety of responses, and Kiefer found the children talked among themselves, expressing feelings, making predictions and inferences, asking questions, exchanging information, and connecting new books with others they had read.

Using a participant-observer stance, McClure (1985) studied a class of fifth/sixth grade children's responses to poetry over the course of one school year, focusing especially on the relationship of their responses to the context in which they occurred. She chose to look within a classroom in which poetry already held a significant place in order to describe the classroom factors that seemed to support the students' responses. She observed episodes related to sharing published poetry, writing poetry, and extending poetry through art. Students both shared and critiqued poetry with peers or teachers in large or small group settings. McClure noted that it was eivdent that the two teachers in whose classroom she observed had "created a physical and emotional climate which supported children's emerging responses to poetry" (p. 274) by interweaving the context factors of time, space, materials, and the teachers' own convictions. Their nondirective teaching role appeared to nurture an active, exploratory learner role. McClure described the aspects of the classroom environment that seemed to be supportive of children's tentative, exploratory poetic responses. These included sanctioning peer interaction, teacher support for experimentation and divergent thinking, communication of adult fallibility, offering praise and feedback, teachers' acknowledgement of the struggle required to create poetry, as well as their establishment of clear-cut expectations, from which children could operate comfortably and with much self-determination.

Children's responses across time to the same story have received attention from a number of researchers (cf. Crago & Crago, 1976; Hickman, 1979; Kiefer, 1986; White, 1956, Yaden, 1988). The opportunity to have repeated exposures to the same story is often a naturally occurring context variable of storytime that also seems to be related to children's responses. In two case studies, Martinez and Roser (1985) examined changes in children's naturally occurring responses as they listened to stories read aloud more than one time. Focusing on the story-time interactions of a 4-year-old and her father and a group of 4-year-olds and their preschool teacher, Martinez and Roser described at least four changes that signaled the differences in children's responses as they listened to stories repeatedly. First, the children in both settings talked more about familiar than unfamiliar stories. Second, the form of the children's responses changed when listening to unfamiliar and familiar stories. The child reading with her father asked more questions when a story was read for the first time and made more comments when listening to familiar stories. In the preschool, the children also made more comments when stories were familiar. The focus of responses (i.e., talk centering on characters, events, details, titles, setting, story language, or theme) changed over repeated readings of stories. Although the pattern of change varied from story to story, the shifts in focus suggest that, as children gain control over particular aspects of stories, they are able to attend to other dimensions. Finally, when children chose to discuss a particular aspect of a story across multiple readings, the discussion indicated that the children were probing the story more deeply than they had initially. For these preschoolers then, increased opportunities to listen to a story resulted in more complex responses.

As part of an experimental study designed to increase the number and complexity of 4-year-olds' responses to literature, Morrow (1988) also investigated children's responses to stories read to them repeatedly. The children, all of low socioeconomic status attending urban day-care centers, were assigned to two experimental groups and one control group. In the first experimental group, the children were read a different book each week for 10 weeks on a one-to-one basis. Children in the second experimental group heard repeated readings of only three different books, while those in the control group were involved in traditional reading readiness activities. Morrow found that participation in one-to-one read-aloud events increased the quantity and complexity of the children's responses. On the post-treatment measure, children in both experimental groups asked more questions and made more comments than those in the control group. Children in the different-book experimental group asked more questions, while those in the repeated-book experimental group asked more questions, while those in the repeated-book experimental group made more comments about the stories they heard. In addition, repeated experiences with stories fostered a wider variety of responses and more complex, interpretive comments than did single readings of stories.

The work reviewed in this section has thus far revealed the extent to which adults can support and encourage growth in children's responses through the organization and management of the setting in which responses occur. There is need to understand more fully the ways that children's responses to literature are shaped by cultural characteristics (Purves, 1981) as well as by the physical and social characteristics of the classroom. Because each classroom is a community, the members of that community may assume positions that enable them to promote rich and diverse responses to literature. The teacher seems a key member of the classroom response community, and in talking about books with children, the teacher may have the opportunity to promote children's growth as responders.

Certainly Eeds and Wells (1989), in their study of fifth-grade literature discussion groups, found that children and teachers "built meaning by working together" (p. 26).

As another indicator of the teacher's effects on students' responses, Kiefer (1986) observed that the language the teacher used in talking about stories was adopted by the children. Further, the open-ended discussion strategies she employed appeared to elicit a variety of responses from the children. However, a systematic description of the teacher's discussion strategies was beyond the scope of Kiefer's study. Yet, Rosenblatt (1985) suggests that this would be a promising avenue of research. She notes that "much remains to be done through study of classroom dynamics to discover how the teacher's guidance (without domination) of group discussion can contribute to growth in students' ability to handle and reflect on their transactions with texts" (p. 49). Few investigators have addressed the question of how the teacher in the role of story discussant can promote children's growth as responders. There is, however, a rapidly growing body of research on story-time interactions at home and in school which, although not generally assuming a literary response perspective, nonetheless suggests that such a perspective would be of value. This research has demonstrated that storybook reading involves far more than reading aloud the words of an author. Integral to the story-time experience is the discussion among readers and listeners that occurs in response to the shared text (e.g., Cochran-Smith, 1984; Heath, 1982; Snow, 1983; Sulzby & Teale, 1987; Teale & Sulzby, 1987). Further, this body of research suggests that the role of the adult reader is highly significant (Ninio & Bruner, 1978; Snow & Goldfield, 1982; Teale & Sulzby, 1987). For example, by analyzing the storybook interactions of a mother and child across repeated readings of a book, Teale and Sulzby found that in early readings of the book the mother provided the scaffolding needed to support the social interaction centering around the book. In latter readings it became apparent that the child had internalized the language and social interaction of earlier readings.

Roser and Martinez (1985) explored how the adult's storybook reading style may influence children's responses to literature. They observed preschoolers involved in a series of storytime interactions with adults in two preschools and in two homes. The children expressed a broad range of similar responses whether at home or at school. However, the more striking finding was that in both settings children tended to respond to literature more like the adult in the situation than they did like children in another setting. The cooperative nature of the read-aloud in these four cases made it difficult to discern who was assuming the lead in discussing the story, the adult or children. To gain insight into the role of adults in storytime, Roser and Martinez analyzed story language according to the functions it served. They found clues to the richness of the children's responses in two of the roles that the parents and teachers assumed: (a) coresponder and (b) informer/monitor. As coresponders, the adults initiated topics of discussion for the purposes of describing information in illustrations, recounting parts of stories, sharing personal reactions to stories, and inviting the children to share responses. In this role, the parents and teachers appeared to model for the children the process of

the mature reader in interaction with the text. In the second role, that of informer/monitor, the adult explained different aspects of stories, provided information to broaden the child's story-related world knowledge, and assessed and monitored the children's understanding of stories. By using language for these purposes, the adults signaled the importance of making sense from print and modeled strategies for attempting this.

Cochran-Smith also examined the adult's role in promoting children's growth as responders. Studying the storybook interactions of a nursery school teacher and her 3- to 5-year-old students, Cochran-Smith found that the teacher acted as a mediator during storybook readings, assisting the children in two major ways: (a) by helping them learn to take the knowledge they had gained outside of book reading experiences and use this knowledge to make sense within texts; and (b) by helping them learn to apply the meanings and messages gained from books to their own lives. One of the types of knowledge that the teacher assisted the children to gain was knowledge of how to respond as a member of a reading audience. The teacher used a variety of strategies to accomplish this:

a. She modeled for the students her own responses to the story;
b. She used questions to signal feelings the children ought to have;
c. She used questions to explore feelings they might have; and
d. She used prosodic features while reading aloud to signal appropriate ways to respond to stories.

Hepler and Hickman (1982) noted that "the literary transaction, the one-to-one conversation between author and audience, is frequently surrounded by other voices" (p. 279); the work of Roser and Martinez and Cochran-Smith suggests that what those "other voices" say influences the child's development as a responder. There is a need to attend even more closely to those other voices—what they say and how they say it. Strategies used by adults in storybook reading have been described by a number of researchers, and although this work has not been conceptualized from a response-to-literature perspective, it can nonetheless inform those interested in the social dimension of response. A number of investigators have found that there are marked differences in the storybook reading discussion strategies of adults (e.g., Heath, 1982; Martinez & Teale, 1989). Martinez and Teale (1989), for example, examined the storybook reading styles of three kindergarten teachers. Although they found that all three controlled the content of discussions, there were, nonetheless, notable differences in their storybook reading discussion styles. First, the three diverged dramatically on the issue of the importance of the story information they chose to discuss, with two of the teachers focusing on key story information that advanced the story line and one focusing almost exclusively on story details that fleshed out the story. In addition, the three teachers chose to emphasize different types of information (e.g., textually explicit, inferential, personal association) in discussing stories. Finally, the three teachers differed in the extent to which they elicited and invited responses from students, reviewed and recapitulated textual information, and shared their own reactions to texts. Not only have investigators found variations in teachers' storybook reading styles, but in some instances these variations have been tied to differences in children's comprehension of stories (e.g., Green & Harker, 1982; Green, Harker, & Golden, 1986). What remains to be investigated is how, if at all, these different styles affect children's growth as responders.

Students are also integral to the social community of the classroom; therefore, peer response merits study, especially in light of Dyson's (1987) and others' (Cooper, Marquis, & Ayers-Lopez, 1982) discussions of children's spontaneous talk in the classroom. These researchers argue that when children share experiences, ideas, and opinions, they are engaging in their most intellectually demanding work. The observations of a number of investigators support this assertion and suggest a need for more systematic study of how peers affect one another's responses to literature. Hickman (1979) underscored this need by noting the social nature of response events in the classrooms that she observed. Although she did not systematically explore this influence of peers, most of the response events she observed involved children together in pairs, in small groups, or as a class, and many of these events involved what she termed "honest exchanges of information." Hepler and Hickman (1982) found that the informal talk about books that occurs among peers serves a number of functions. First, children, especially those in the middle grades, exchange information about what to read. Further, the opportunity to talk about a book enables the reader to rehearse or organize the content of the book. Hepler and Hickman also contend that children's talk helps them negotiate meanings; for example, the struggles to express what one means offer opportunities to explore that meaning more fully.

This supportive context was also described by McClure in her investigation of intermediate students' responses to poetry. She documented a strong social network within the classroom in which children "supported and refined each other's tentative responses to poetry" (p. 278) in significant ways. She noted that children formed both flexible and stable peer reading/writing communities, and by so doing supplied support to their peers in various ways. For example, the students worked with the less able; they provided ideas to one another for topics, titles and extensions of themes; they helped one another refine and clarify meanings; they supported one another in positive and increasingly focused ways; they served as audiences for one another, and they shared their collective memory. McClure concluded that the complexity of response in this group of students depended more on contextual than developmental factors (also a contention of those who subscribe to the tenets of cooperative learning).

Eeds and Wells (1989) present further compelling evidence that children support one another in their efforts to understand and reflect on stories. In describing the discussion of fifth graders in literature groups, the researchers found that the children helped one another respond more fully to the stories under discussion by collaborating in the construction of simple meaning, by sharing personal stories inspired by the books, by actively questioning what they read in order to uncover meaning, and by addressing issues of what they liked about the author's writing and why. Working together and with their teachers, the children participated in what these researchers describe as "grand conversations."

Yet, Eeds and Wells, like others, noted that the text being discussed also seemed to influence the quality of those classroom conversations. This focus on text factors that affect responses forms the third group of studies that are reviewed.

Text Factors

A number of strands of research indicate that text factors also affect children's responses. Certainly studies of children's book interests suggest such an influence (Purves & Beach, 1972; Tucker, 1976, 1981). This strand of research has focused on both the content and genre of literature in which children are interested. Findings focusing on how the content of stories influences students' reading interests have been relatively consistent over the decades (Purves & Beach, 1972). Although distinctions can be made both across grade levels and exceptions within individuals, researchers have found that, in general, elementary-aged children are interested in adventure, fairy tales, making things, humor, biography, true-event stories, and animal stories. In addition, in reviewing studies as early as 1899, Purves and Beach found that elementary students preferred literary presentations (e.g., fiction, drama, or poetry) to nonliterary ones. Narrative material is of special interest to children, particularly that with a suspenseful plot, much action, humor, and nonsense. Although interest can not be equated with response, these findings do suggest some broad areas that might guide initial research on the influence of text on children's responses to literature.

The work of investigators like Rubin and Gardner (1985) and Green (1982), although not specifically focusing on responses to literature, nonetheless indicate that children are sensitive to text features. Rubin and Gardner asked first, third, and sixth graders to devise a conclusion to one of two versions of a researcher-developed fairy tale and then to retell the story. There were differences across grade levels; nonetheless, the children's responses to these tasks revealed their sensitivity to a variety of narrative features of fairy tales. Although the children made no explicit references to these features, their inclusion of the features in the endings they devised and in their retellings reflected an implicit awareness of form. Similarly, Green found that approximately half of her 5-year-old subjects were able to discriminate among diverse literary styles in children's books (the styles of Bill Peet, Virginia Kahl, Beatrix Potter, Dr. Seuss, and Margaret Wise Brown) as evidenced by their success in identifying the authors of books presented by audiotape. Further, when asked how they were able to identify the correct authors, some of the children were able to verbalize responses that indicated they were at least somewhat aware of certain stylistic features. Green's work indicates that children even at very young ages may respond to this particular aspect of form.

Within broader studies of response, a limited number of researchers have noted text features that appear to affect children's responses. Lehr, in her study of kindergarten, second-, and fourth-grade students' responses to theme, found that the children were generally far more likely to identify and generate themes for realistic stories than for folktales. She accounted for this difference by noting that "common folktale themes such as greed, sacrifice, gaining independence, and overcoming evil or danger, are abstract concepts, especially when related in settings removed from everyday experience" (p. 352–53).

In their study of four groups of fifth graders responding to four different novels, Eeds and Wells found that the group discussing *Tuck Everlasting* (Babbitt, 1975) responded more reflectively than did the other groups as they "discussed the central truth that the work held for them" (p. 27). The researchers discerned no substantive differences among the teachers' abilities to lead discussions that could account for the differences in the quality of the groups' discussions. Nor were there any evident differences in the student make-up of the groups. Rather, Eeds and Wells maintained that the exceptional quality of *Tuck Everlasting*, relative to the books read by the other groups, accounted for the difference in the depth of discussions among the groups. *Tuck Everlasting* is, in effect, a book that offers the reader a great deal with which to grapple and hence can evoke in-depth responses from the reader.

Galda (1982) addressed the issue of how text factors influence response in her study of three fifth-grade girls' responses to *Beat the Turtle Drum* and *Bridge to Terabithia*. The two texts were matched for genre (each is a work of contemporary realistic fiction) and topic (each deals with friendship and the death of a child). However, the books differ in terms of style and structure, and one of these structural differences affected the children's responses to the texts: Unlike the end of *Beat the Turtle Drum*, the ending of *Bridge to Terabithia* offers closure, and each of the children clearly preferred this ending to that of *Beat the Turtle Drum*. In addition, the authors' use in both texts of minor characters and events appeared to influence the children's responses. The only student who preferred these texturizing effects was the one Galda termed a more mature literary responder, capable of assuming a spectator stance. The other girls questioned why these elements, which they deemed superfluous, were included in the stories.

Summary

Only in the last 10 to 15 years have children's responses to literature emerged as a focus of investigation, and in that time a number of dimensions of response have been explored. Research has confirmed what Harding noted some 20 years ago—that children express their responses to literature in a variety of ways. Further, children more frequently express response to the content of stories than to their form. In describing verbal and nonverbal responses to literature, investigators have most often used researcher-constructed probes to elicit response. Researchers employing ethnographic techniques to study naturally occurring responses in classrooms have extended this work and offered new insights. Whether examining children's verbal or nonverbal responses, a number of investigators have found that children respond to literature in diverse ways at different age levels. For example, the form of older children's story recalls and evaluations differs from that of younger children. In addition, children's metaphoric and thematic comprehension becomes increasingly sophisticated across grade levels. In discussing their findings, a number of investigators have concluded that diversity across age levels is a function of differ-

ences in cognitive development. Perhaps these conclusions should be viewed tentatively in view of Galda's research on personal styles of response, and of Hickman's, Kiefer's, McClure's and others' research on the effects of context and text on response, suggesting that responses are far more sensitive to contextual and text variables than to developmental factors alone.

CONSIDERATIONS FOR A RESEARCHER COMMUNITY

The research on response has begun to sketch a picture of the child as a responder, yet the picture that is emerging is by no means complete. First, even though efforts have been directed toward describing children's naturally occurring responses, these efforts represent only a beginning. There is still need for systematic, detailed descriptions of these responses. Anecdotal accounts, diaries, and case studies of storybook reading in home and school settings support the argument that such in-depth investigations promise valuable insights into the richness and diversity of children's responses to literature (Baghban, 1984; Butler, 1979; Crago & Crago, 1976; Paley, 1981; White, 1956).

Also necessary to complete the emerging picture are studies that *systematically* examine the influence of text factors on children's responses. Indeed, in the research on adolescents' and adults' responses to literature, text has been found to play a critical role in shaping reader response (Booth, 1961; Galda, 1983; Squire, 1968; Zaharias, 1986). Therefore, through increased attention to text, both researchers and practitioners may better understand how young children respond to literature. However, to successfully explore the effect of text factors requires careful attention to methodology. If researcher-elicited probes are used, they must be carefully structured to elicit children's responses to text features rather than just to story content. In addition, researchers should be sensitive to the notion that children's responses that occur naturally in their talk about stories, as well as in their writing and dramatic play, may provide evidence of text features' influence on response.

Peer interactions can serve as another valuable avenue for studying children's growth as respondents. In light of Dyson's (1983) research on children's writing development, it seems sensible to attend to the peer dynamics surrounding literary response in the classroom. She has argued that "given tasks worth talking about and the right to talk, children's interactions can contribute substantially to intellectual development in general and literary growth in particular" (Dyson, 1987, p. 397). Certainly, the search for avenues for increased intellectual development and literary growth are worthy aims for future research.

Just as there is much remaining to be learned about the contribution of peer interactions to children's growth as responders, so too is there a need to explore the ways in which teachers function as leaders in literary response groups. Too often, perhaps, as Eeds and Wells note, teachers lead "gentle inquisitions" rather than "grand conversations." Although there is intuitive support for movement away from "gentle inquisitions," there is little hard evidence that questioning itself interferes with insights or impedes children's personal constructions of text. One promising effort that helps to reveal how teachers can promote "grander conversations" is the work of Saul (1989) who argues that teachers must learn to view story as literary text, and to use authentic language in discussion of that text in order to elicit children's authentic responses.

A number of questions clearly remain to be explored in order to understand the influences of cognitive development and social factors on children's responses to literature: How widespread are the differences in response styles within given age groups? How do differences in response styles emerge? How can context factors be manipulated to foster increasingly mature responses to both the content and form of literature? What is the role of the teacher in guiding response? How can peer interactions be structured to promote growth in responses? How does valuing story in classrooms affect the nature of children's responses? To understand fully how the child-respondent at the beginning of this review grew in his responses to literature requires answers to these and related questions.

IMPLICATIONS FOR A PRACTITIONER COMMUNITY

If experts are correct, "Teachers are tackling with new zest questions which ask about the relationship of literature to life" (Meek, Warlow, & Barton, 1977, p. 4). Classrooms where responses to literature thrive seem to be characterized by teachers' valuing of responses as the crux of literacy growth. Valuing of response in the classroom is evident when teachers (a) provide opportunities for response, (b) provide response models, and (c) receive children's responses (in all their diversity).

Providing Opportunities for Response. The provision of opportunities to respond to literature requires teachers who are committed to the place of literature within their classrooms. This commitment is demonstrated through the flexible use of time, space, and materials. For example, well selected classroom libraries offer opportunities to read, but teachers are discovering that providing of literature in itself is not sufficient for ensuring that children do read and respond. Morrow and Weinstein (1986), for example, found that books that were provided in appealing and comfortable *library centers* were chosen for reading and response. In addition, it seems that books that are highlighted by teachers in some way—either through read-alouds or through specific introductions—are more likely to be selected for reading. Classrooms in which children read and respond are also distinguished by the provision of time for

reading, clearly designated time for meeting books. Teachers in these responsive classrooms not only sanction peer interactions about books, but structure the classroom environment so that it occurs. Seemingly, the classroom organization that fosters response has clearcut expectations, so there can be comfort with its consistent features, and therefore the freedom to create. Teachers with children who respond to books offer them both time and opportunity for talking about books, as well as for responding in a variety of other ways. Their children may also draw, write, dramatize, or represent their responses in still other forms. These divergent responses require that the teacher offer choices of materials and, initially, guidance for using those materials to represent the range and depth of the reader's thoughts and feelings.

Providing Response Models. Research suggests the powerful effect of the teachers' modeling of response to literature on the subsequent responses of young children. There is evidence that responders (expert and naive) in the same setting tend to react in the same ways toward text. The teacher who conjectures, connects, appreciates, muses, challenges, and questions aloud shows the child how the mature responder interacts with text. By modeling these responses both during and after the reading of stories, the teacher encourages children's active participation. Just as adults serve as models, children also appear to affect one another's responses, as evidenced by their book conversations, the similarities of the selected modes of response that occur within classrooms, and through the social interactions that signal permission has been granted for constructing both individual and group meanings. As mentioned above, to take advantage of these peer relationships, the teacher must value interactions and provide time and opportunities for these negotiations, joining the community of responders as an equal partner who also proposes, retracts, and amends thinking in collaborative situations.

Receiving Responses. The classroom climate that nurtures unique and personal interpretations is the one in which the teacher values children's responses and is open to receiving those responses in all their diversity. Such a classroom values experimentation and divergence. Teachers are discovering that children respond in many of the same ways that adults respond. They infer, predict, evaluate, connect, and link text with their own lives. Although children respond in accordance with their own experiences and hence differently from adults, their responses nonetheless represent a rich diversity to be welcomed and encouraged in the classroom.

References

Applebee, A. (1973). *The spectator role: Theoretical and developmental studies of ideas about and responses to literature with special reference to four age levels*. Unpublished doctoral dissertation, University of London.

Applebee, A. (1978). *The child's concept of story*. Chicago: University of Chicago Press.

Babbitt, N. (1975). *Tuck everlasting*. New York: Farrar, Straus & Giroux.

Baghban, M. (1984). *Our daughter learns to read and write: A case study from birth to three*. Newark, DE: International Reading Association.

Booth, W. C. (1961). *The rhetoric of fiction*. Chicago: University of Chicago Press.

Britton, J. (1968). Response to literature. In J. R. Squire (Ed.), *Response to literature* (pp. 3–9). Champaign, IL: National Council of Teachers of English.

Britton, J. (1970). *Language and learning*. London: Allen Lane, The Penguin Press.

Butler, D. (1979). *Cushla and her books*. London: Hodder & Stoughton.

Cochran-Smith, M. (1984). *The making of a reader*. Norwood, NJ: Ablex.

Cooper, C. R. (1969). Preferred modes of literary response: The characteristics of high school juniors in relation to the consistency of their reactions to three dissimilar short stories. *Dissertation Abstracts International, 31,* 1680A-1681A. (University Microfilms No. 70-17, 535).

Cooper, C. R., Marquis, A., & Ayers-Lopez, S. (1982). Peer-learning in the classroom: Tracing developmental patterns and consequences of children's spontaneous interactions. In L. C. Wilkinson (Ed.), *Communicating in the classroom* (pp. 69–84). New York: Academic Press.

Cover, A. B. (1988). *Isaac Asimov's robot city 4: Prodigy*. New York: Ace Books.

Crago, H., & Crago, M. (1976). The untrained eye? A preschool child explores Felix Hoffman's "Rapunzel." *Children's Literature in Education, 22,* 135–151.

Cullinan, B., Harwood, K., & Galda, L. (1983). The reader and the story: Comprehension and response. *Journal of Research and Development in Education, 16,* 29–37.

Dahl, R. (1981). *The Twits*. New York: Alfred A. Knopf.

Donaldson, M. (1978). *Children's minds*. London: Croom Helm Ltd.

Dyson, A. H. (1983). The role of oral language in early writing. *Research in the Teaching of English, 17,* 1–30.

Dyson, A. H. (1987). The value of "time off task": Young children's spontaneous talk and deliberate text. *Harvard Educational Review, 57,* 396–420.

Eeds, M., & Wells, D. (1989). Grand conversations: An exploration of meaning construction in literature study groups. *Research in the Teaching of English, 23,* 4–29.

Galda, L. (1982). Assuming the spectator stance: An examination of the responses to three young readers. *Research in the Teaching of English, 16,* 1–20.

Galda, L. (1983). Research in response to literature. *Journal of Research and Development in Education, 16,* 1–7.

Green, G. M. (1982). Competence for implicit text analysis: Literary style discrimination in five-year olds. In D. Tanner (Ed.), *Analyzing discourse: Text and talk*. Washington, D.C: Georgetown University Press.

Green, J. L., & Harker, J. O. (1982). Reading to children: A communicative process. In J. A. Langer & M. T. Smith-Burke (Eds.), *Reader meets author/bridging the gap: A psycholinguistic and sociolinguistic perspective*. Newark, DE: International Reading Association.

Green, J., Harker, J., & Golden, J. (1986). Lesson Construction: Differing views. In G. Noblit & W. T. Pink (Eds.), *Schooling in social context: Qualitative studies*. Norwood, NJ: Ablex.

Greene, C. (1976). *Beat the turtle drum*. New York: Viking.

Harding, D. W. (1968). Response to literature: The report of the study group. In J. R. Squire (Ed.), *Response to literature* (pp. 11–27). Champaign, IL: National Council of Teachers of English.

Heath, S. B. (1982). What no bedtime story means: Narrative skills at home and school. *Language in Society, 11,* 49–76.

Hepler, S., & Hickman, J. (1982). "The book was okay. I love you"—social aspects of response to literature. *Theory into Practice, 21,* 278–283.

Hickman, J. (1979). *Response to literature in a school environment, grades K through 5*. Unpublished doctoral dissertation, The Ohio State University.

Hickman, J. (1981). A new perspective on response to literature: Research in an elementary school setting. *Research in the Teaching of English, 15,* 343–354.

Hickman, J. (1983). Everything considered: Response to literature in an elementary school setting. *Journal of Research and Development in Education, 16,* 8–13.

Keifer, B. (1983). The responses of children in a combination first/second grade classroom to picture books in a variety of artistic styles. *Journal of Research and Development in Education, 16,* 14–20.

Keifer, B. (1986). The child and the picture book: Creating live circuits. *Children's Literature Association Quarterly, 11,* 63–68.

Kohlberg, L. (1964). Development of moral character and moral ideology. In M. L. Hoffman (Ed.), *Review of Child Development Research*. New York: Russell Sage Foundation.

Le Guin, U. K. (1968). *A wizard of earthsea*. Boston: Parnassus.

Lehr, S. (1988). The child's developing sense of theme as a response to literature. *Reading Research Quarterly, 23,* 337–357.

Lindfors, J. (1987). *Children's language and learning* (2nd ed.). Englewood Cliffs, NJ: Prentice Hall.

Martinez, M., & Roser, N. (1985). Read it again: The value of repeated readings during storytime. *The Reading Teacher, 38,* 782–786.

Martinez, M., & Teale, W. H. (1989). Classroom storybook reading: The creation of texts and learning opportunities. *Theory into Practice, 28,* 126–135.

McClure, A. A. (1985). *Children's responses to poetry in a supportive context*. Unpublished doctoral dissertation, The Ohio State University.

McPhail, D. (1978). *The magical drawings of Moony B. Finch*. New York: Doubleday.

Meek, M., Warlow, A., & Barton, G. (Eds.) (1977). *The cool web: The pattern of children's reading*. London: The Bodley Head.

Morrow, L. M. (1988). Young children's responses to one-to-one story readings in school settings. *Reading Research Quarterly, 23,* 89–107.

Morrow, L. M., & Weinstein, C. S. (1986). Encouraging voluntary reading: The impact of a literature program on children's use of library centers. *Reading Research Quarterly, 21,* 330–46.

Ninio, A., & Bruner, J. (1978). The achievement and antecedents of labelling. *Journal of Child Language, 5,* 5–15.

Patey, V. G. (1981). *Wally's stories*. Cambridge, MA: Harvard University Press.

Paterson, K. (1977). *Bridge to Terabithia*. New York: Avon Books.

Pearson, P. D. (1986). Twenty years of research in reading comprehension. In T. Raphael (Ed.), *The contexts of school-based literacy* (pp. 43–62). New York: Random House.

Petrosky, A. R. (1976). The effects of reality perception and fantasy on response to literature: Two case studies. *Research in the Teaching of English,* 239–258.

Piaget, J. (1965). *The moral judgment of the child*. New York: Free Press.

Pillar, A. C. (1983). Aspects of moral judgment in response to fables. *Journal of Research and Development in Education, 16,* 39–46.

Purves, A. C. (1973). *Literature education in ten countries: An empirical study*. New York: John Wiley & Sons.

Purves, A. C. (1981). *Reading and literature: American achievement in internatinal perspective*. Urbana, IL: National Council of Teachers of English.

Purves, A. C. (1985). That sunny dome. Those caves of ice. In C. Cooper (Ed.), *Researching response to literature and the teaching of literature: Points of departure* (pp. 54–69). Norwood, NJ: Ablex.

Purves, A. C., & Beach, R. (1972). *Literature and the reader: Research in response to literature, reading interests, and the teaching of literature*. Urbana, IL: National Council of Teachers of English.

Purves, A. C., & Rippere, V. (1968). *Elements of writing about a literary work: A study of response to literature*. Urbana, IL: National Council of Teachers of English.

Rosenblatt, L. M. (1976). *Literature as exploration*. New York: Noble and Noble. (Original work published in 1938).

Rosenblatt, L. M. (1978). *The reader, the text, the poem: The transactional theory of the literary work*. Carbondale, IL: Southern Illinois University Press.

Rosenblatt, L. (1985). The transactional theory of literary work: Implications for research. In C. Cooper (Ed.), *Researching response to literature and the teaching of literature. Points of departure.* Norwood, NJ: Ablex.

Roser, N., & Martinez, M. (1985). Roles adults play in preschoolers' response to literature. *Language Arts, 62,* 485–490.

Rubin, S., & Gardner, H. (1985). Once upon a time: The development of sensitivity to story structure. In C. R. Cooper (Ed.), *Researching response to literature and the teaching of literature.* Norwood, NJ: Ablex.

Saul, E. W. (1989). 'What did Leo feed the turtle?' and other nonliterary questions. *Language Arts, 66,* 295–303.

Snow, C. E. (1983). Literacy and language: Relationships during the preschool years. *Harvard Educational Review, 53,* 165–189.

Snow, C. E., & Goldfield, B. A. (1982). Building stories: The emergence of information structures from conversation. In D. Tanner (Ed.), *Analyzing discourse text and talk.* Washington, D.C: Georgetown University Press.

Squire, J. R. (1964). *The responses of adolescents while reading four short stories* (NCTE Research Report No. 2). Urbana, IL: National Council of Teachers of English.

Squire, J. (1968). *Response to literature.* Champaign, IL: National Council of Teachers of English.

Sulzby, E., & Teale, W. H. (1987). *Young children's storybook reading: A longitudinal study of parent-child interaction and children's independent functioning.* Final Report to the Spencer Foundation, Ann Arbor, MI: University of Michigan.

Teale, W. (1987). Emergent literacy: Reading and writing development in early childhood. In J. E. Readence & R. S. Baldwin (Eds.), *Research in literacy: Merging perspectives.* Rochester, NY: National Reading Conference.

Teale, W. H., & Sulzby, E. (1987). Literacy acquisition in early childhood: The roles of access and mediation in storybook reading. In D. A. Wagner (Ed.), *The Future of Literacy in a Changing World.* New York: Pergamon Press.

Tucker, N. (1976). How children respond to fiction. In G. Fox, G. Hammond, T. Jones, F. Smith, & K. Sterck (Eds.), *Writers, critics, and children.* New York: Agathon Press.

Tucker, N. (1981). *The child and the book: A psychological and literary exploration.* Cambridge: Cambridge University Press.

White, D. N. (1956). *Books before five.* Wellington, New Zealand: New Zealand Council for Educational Research.

Yaden, D. (1988). Understanding stories through repeated read-alouds: How many does it take? *The Reading Teacher, 41,* 556–560.

Zaharias, J. A. (1986). The effects of genre and tone on undergraduate students' preferred patterns of response to two short stories and two poems. *Research in the Teaching of English, 20,* 56–68.

32B. RESPONSE TO LITERATURE
Robert E. Probst

Within the past 20 years or so, more and more teachers and researchers have begun to take serious interest in the concept of response to literature. That is not to say that the questions about the reader's role in making sense of literary texts are all new. They had been asked at least as early as the late 1920s.

In England, Richards had raised many of them in *Practical Criticism* (1956), one of the first experimental looks at response to literature. In the United States, Rosenblatt had raised the issue as long ago as 1938 with *Literature as Exploration,* another of the progenitory works in this area. In that text she argued persuasively that the uniqueness of individual readers must shape their understandings of a text. Because readers differed, because they bring to texts different histories, different beliefs, different values, different contexts, and different purposes, their readings must inevitably differ. Meaning, she proposed, does not reside purely and simply within a text, to be extracted whole and complete, rather, it lies in the transaction between reader and text. It is the result of a meeting between reader and text. Thus, she argued, we must not just look at the characteristics of texts if we wish to understand literary experience, but also at people reading texts.

Harding was raising similar questions at about the same time. In one of many essays in *Scrutiny* (1937), he examined in great detail the behavior of onlookers, suggesting the importance of understanding their attitudes and practices if we are to understand the nature of literary art. "The playwright, the novelist, the song-writer and the film-producing team," he says, "are all doing the same thing as the gossip" (p. 257). That is to say, they are each inviting "the audience to agree that the experience he portrays is possible and interesting, and that his attitude to it, implicit in his portrayal, is fitting" (pp. 257–258). Harding suggests that literary experience involves an important social dimension and urges us to examine it: "Is our taste in gossip the same kind of thing, or not, as our taste in films and trivial fiction? And is this latter continuous, or not, with our taste in literature (p. 258)?" Such questions clearly point us toward investigation of the reader's role in literary experience.

Richards' *Practical Criticism* had begun that investigation. He asked students to respond to poems offered them with no clues about authorship to source. "The attempt to read without this guidance puts a strain upon us that we are little accustomed to," he reported (p. 316). Lacking the provenance of that supporting information, students were, he found, virtually unable to function. They felt confused, desperate, unsure. Richards suggested that they had come to rely heavily upon the established, accepted critical opinions, simply applying them as labels in accordance with the judgments they had learned, but had not learned to make. And when deprived of those approved opinions, they often succumbed to other temptations, and their statements about the poems were characterized by reliance upon stock responses, expressions of sentimentality, overindulgence in irrelevant memories, and the like. Richards found his students little able to make sense themselves of the texts, and

his final recommendation is to teach them self-reliance: "The lesson of all criticism is that we have nothing to rely upon in making our choices but ourselves. The lesson of good poetry seems to be that, when we have understood it, in the degree in which we can order ourselves, we need nothing more" (p. 351).

That lesson, and all that it has led to, has proved to be an exciting but problematic notion. Some teachers—respecting the uniqueness of their students, believing in the value of their students' idiosyncratic and personal readings of texts, sensing perhaps that even the digressions, the departures from the text, the excursions into memories or personal narrative, may be legitimate responses to literary works—have tried to attend to response in their classrooms. The classroom, and the curricula in general, occasionally seem inhospitable. Students trained to produce answers to multiple-choice questions, taught to find out precisely what they need to know, expected to accumulate information and develop skills, conditioned to regard the teacher as the source of knowledge and the voice of judgment, may look askance at the teacher who invites them to respond. It does not look like school work, and they may not trust it. It does not lend itself to grades, for one, and if it doesn't clearly earn points, then its value is likely to be suspect for any student who sees grades as either the achievement to be pursued or the penalty to be avoided.

Further, planning instruction to elicit and respect students' responses to texts seems difficult. Response may be unpredictable, diverse, digressive; it is hard to plan the carftsman-like lesson, moving logically from objective to evaluation, its purpose always clearly evident, and still allow for the uncertainties of response. On a broader scale, the curriculum, too, looks more difficult to design. If we organize the literature program based on historical principles, then we arrange things chronologically, and if we choose to study formal elements, then we may arrange texts by genre, but what pattern do we have if we decide to focus on the unique readings of our students? No such pattern presents itself.

If the concept of response to literature has posed problems for teachers, it may have been even more unwieldy for researchers who've taken an interest in it. It is an elusive concept, hard to define and difficult to assess. Response takes place in the black box of the mind, and it has been difficult to look inside and see what's going on. All that researchers have had to work with is expressed response (though some have tried to gain access to unexpressed response by measuring brain waves, galvanic skin response, and other physiological indications of mental or emotional activity), and it is likely that expressed response reveals only part of the transaction. Hansson (1973) observed in his studies that "the PASSIVE ability of the less educated readers to notice and judge linguistic, literary and experiential qualities is much more developed than their ACTIVE ability to verbalize their interpretations and experiences in a written statement" (p. 268). The connections between what is expressed and what has actually happened can only be hypothesized.

THE ANALYSIS OF RESPONSES

Nonetheless, most of the early studies concentrated attention upon expressed, recorded, resposes. Purves and Rippere had provided, in *The Elements of Writing about a Literary Work* (1968), a scheme for analyzing the content of responses, and researchers immediately put it to use. The Purves-Rippere system identified, in the writings of both critics and students, the kinds of statements that might be made about a literary work. The unwieldy list numbers over 100, but the statements cluster more conveniently into four major categories:

1. Engagement-involvement: These are statements indicating the writer's involvement in the work, the strength of its emotional impact upon him or her or the degree of interest it has aroused within him/her.
2. Perception: Statements describing the work itself. They may be retellings of the story, summaries of the content, comments about formal elements or historical context, and the like.
3. Interpretation: Interpretive statements are attempts to ascribe meaning to the text, to explain or generalize about it, perhaps to move beyond it to issues broader or more inclusive than those dealt with in the text itself.
4. Evaluation: Judgments about the quality of the work. They may be, at one extreme, simplistic or unelaborated, or at the other, complex analyses based upon carefully articulated criteria.

The categories, derived as they were from written statements of response, gave researchers a tool for analyzing other written statements of response. Analyses using these categories (or adaptations of them such as the expansion of the four original categories into nine subcategories proposed by Purves and Beach [1972] and then modified slightly by Odell and Cooper [1976]) proliferated during the 10 or 15 years following the publication of *Elements*. Summarizing the results of many of those studies, Applebee's ERIC/RCS Report (1977) noted several generalizations toward which the research was leading. The finding that he saw as most important was that "the approach to literature adopted by the individual teacher does affect the content of the response from the teacher's pupils" (p. 256). The patterns of response, in other words, are learned. Students figure out the expectations of their teachers, or perhaps, more broadly, of their culture, and conform to them.

Data from the International Association for the Evaluation of Educational Achievement confirmed that observation dramatically, revealing some striking differences among the response patterns of students in the 10 countries participating. Purves (1973), in his report of the IEA, suggests that

Because the patterns differ not simply in degree but also in kind as one moves from population to population within a country, and because there exist national differences in patterns, one's best inference in that the differences result from education rather than from a general progress through adolescence. . . .

Response to literature is a learned behavior. (pp. 314–315)

In light of that observation, some of the other findings are less than surprising. Studies that examined differences across grades or ages, such as the massive National Assessment of Educational Progress, found a clear tendency to shift with age toward more interpretive responses and fewer engagement-involvement responses. Considering the emphasis in secondary literature programs upon interpretation, and the New Critical disparaging of personal, especially emotional, responses, that seems an entirely predictable trend. Students learn that interpretive statements are valued, and that expressions of involvement in the text are of less significance.

There are, of course, other influences upon the choice of mode. Sex is one such variable, though Applebee's survey found that differences in response preferences (not in reading interests or in achievement) were minor, with girls slightly more willing than boys to express engagement with literary works. Beach and Brunetti (1976) looked at both age and sex as variables influencing readers' perceptions of characters in short stories, and observed that although there was marked difference in the way males and females judged themselves, there was little difference in the characteristics they attributed to male and female characters in the fiction they read.

The text itself is another variable shaping responses. Angelotti (1972), for example, compared responses to an adolescent novel and to an adult novel, and observed that students were more willing to attempt interpretive statements with the easier book, relying on description, statements of perception, with the more difficult text. He suggested the importance of identifying material within the students' grasp if we intend to give them practice in literary analysis. Student ability also played a role, though again a small one, with those students who scored higher on achievement tests, indicating a stronger preference for the interpretive responses.

Cornaby (1975) concluded that differences between patterns of response to traditional and nontraditional novels, to poems and short stories, and to traditional novels and poems, could be attributed to textual differences in the genre. Corcoran (1979) also found different response patterns resulting from differences in the genre, with poetry generally more problematic than stories, and yielding fewer retellings. Zaharias (1986) looked at the effects of both tone and genre on response preferences, using adapted IEA Response Preference Measures, and discovered that lighter readings tended to evoke a descriptive response, while a more serious tone resulted in personal, interpretive, and evaluative statements. Poetry tended to yield descriptive statements, and short stories led to expressions of personal response.

The research clearly indicates that selection of texts cannot be based solely on a conception of literary merit without taking into account the interests and abilities of the readers, and the range of response the curriculum hopes to encourage, or allow.

RESPONSE CATEGORIES AND READER CHARACTERISTICS

Efforts to sharpen the analysis of response led some researchers to look for relationships between the response categories and other aspects of psychology or of intellectual functioning. Odell and Cooper (1976), for instance, in their adaptation of the Purves-Beach categories, suggested that the concept of "intellectual strategies" borrowed from Young, Becker, and Pike (1970) might contribute some insight into the processes readers engaged in as they read. They argued that although the four categories—engagement, perception, interpretation, and evaluation—even in their expanded nine-subcategory version, may tell us something about *what* the responses were, but not enough about *how* they came to be. They sought to sharpen their insight into the processes by combining those categories with the intellectual processes Young et al. had deduced. Those processes, as Odell and Cooper adopted them, included: focus (the segmenting of experience so that particular aspects might be investigated), contrast (the making of distinctions between items or events), classification (the recognition of similarities or groupings among items), change (the awareness of movement, evolution, or development), and reference to chronology, logical order, and context. The resulting categories were these:

Personal Statement
1. about the reader, an "auto biographical digression"
2. about the work, expressing personal engagement with it

Descriptive Statement
3. narrational, retelling part of the work
4. descriptive of aspects of the work: language, characters, setting, etc.

Interpretive Statement
5. of parts of the work
6. of the whole work

Evaluative Statement
7. about the evocativeness of the work
8. about the construction of the work
9. about the meaningfulness of the work (Odell & Cooper, 1976 pp. 205–206)

Odell and Cooper suggested that the refined analysis made possible by this slightly more complex scheme could tell us something about the strategies students actually employed to make meaning out of literary experience. They pointed out that Somers's (1972) earlier study using the four Purves categories had failed to reveal differences among seventh-, ninth-, and eleventh-graders' responses, and speculated about the questions that raised:

In view of this rather surprising finding, we wonder if use of the nine categories of the Purves and Beach scheme would show that students in these different grades make different responses. Also: when seventh, ninth, and eleventh graders' make the same sort of response, are there differences in the sort of intellectual strategies they use? If so, can we (should we) help seventh graders use intellectual strategies in the same ways that eleventh graders do? (p. 224)

Their parenthetical question implies, of course, the problem that this sort of research cannot fully answer. And that is the question of what we value in our teaching. The Purves categories are descriptive, but not necessarily hierarchical. That is, no one of the categories is assumed to be better, or higher, or more desirable, than the others. The schools have, of course, seemd to value the interpretive most highly, though this research doesn't speak to that issue at all. Whether they should place such emphasis upon interpretation or not is another question, and it demands that we not only acquire information about what happens as students read in school, but also pass some judgment on what happens and how we wish to affect it. It is, in other words, a philosophical question as much, or more, than it is a research problem.

Other psychological research has also provided us with concepts or strategies useful in examining response. Piaget's work on cognitive development, for example, and Kohlberg's on the development of moral reasoning were employed by Parnell (1984), who looked into the matter of development by interviewing students at four grade levels. He concluded that response matured in ways predicted both by Kohlberg's levels of moral reasoning and by Piaget's levels of cognitive development.

Construct theory (Kelly, 1955, 1970) has also offered a tool for these studies. Kelly suggests that people develop intellectual constructs, bipolar scales ("good-bad," "kind-cruel") with which they organize their social experience. Hynds (1985), arguing that "readers must often invoke social perceptual skills in interpreting the actions and motivations of literary characters" (p. 387), examined the relationship between the complexity of readers' constructs and their response preferences, their impressions of characters, their comprehension of texts, and their attitudes toward literature. She concluded that students with more complex constructs for interpersonal relationships tended also to have more complex understandings of characters in the stories they read. She found further that "interpersonal cognitive complexity is related to inferential comprehension, but not to literal comprehension of a literary work" (p. 398), thus calling into question the appropriateness of literal questions in judging students' understanding of texts.

Hynds study is especially interesting because it ties together our dealings with texts and our dealings with the world. "If," she says, "there is a relationship between cognitive complexity in the social environment and complexity in the realm of literature, the teaching of literature takes on yet another dimension and offers another challenge" (p. 399), suggesting that literary experiences may have implications for the way readers deal with social experiences. "Literature provides a vehicle for enlarging students' understanding of the people they are likely to encounter in the social world" (p. 399).

A more recent study by Hynds (1989) looks further into the connection between social and literary understanding. In this project Hynds was especially interested in how adolescent readers used their understandings of people as they read literary texts, and in the influence of other social and home experiences on attitudes toward reading. For a case study design, Hynds chose four student representing each of four prototypes. One tended to have high complexity ratings on interpersonal constructs for peers, less complex for literary characters. One showed the opposite pattern: less complex interpersonal constructs for peers, and more complex for literary characters. The third had high complexity ratings on constructs for both peers and literary characters, and the fourth, lower ratings for both peers and literary characters (p. 33).

Hynds observed that students do use their social understandings "to predict what will happen next in the story or to speculate beyond it; to understand people around them; to reflect on their own personal lives; and to compare the world of the text with the everyday world in which they live" (p. 49). She pointed out, however, that how much they do so depends a great deal on such factors as the encouragement they find at home for reading, the strength of their motivation to perform in the classroom, and, of course, their competence.

The comments of the students themselves offered Hynds some insight into their conception of the literature classroom. They reported to her the "constraining influence" (p. 57) of ceaseless evaluation and of having their interpretations rejected by teachers too strongly devoted to their own. They noted, too, the pleasure, rare though it was, of working with teachers "who were willing to act as 'co-learner' in the process of literary analysis" (p. 57). Their observations indicated to Hynds that they would see clearer connections between literature and their lives "when teachers model literature as a way of learning about and reflecting upon life, when they are willing to act as co-learner rather than expert in that process, and when they offer choices of response modes and assessment measures" (p. 58).

Beach and Wendler (1987) also examined cognitive complexity, looking particularly at the developmental differences in student ability to draw inferences about characters' acts, perceptions, and goals. They hypothesized that as readers matured from adolescence to adulthood they would begin to judge characters' acts less as "autonomous physical behaviors" (p. 288) and instead speak of their social or psychological significance. Similarly, they would see characters' perceptions less in terms of apparent emotions or feelings and more as evidence of the characters' beliefs or values. And they would come to understand not just the immediacy of characters' goals, but also their longer range implications. Examining 8th and 11th graders, and college freshmen and juniors, Beach and Wendler did observe the predicted development of their inferential abilities.

Such research may help us clarify our expectations of readers at different levels of schooling, and suggest directions for our teaching. Beach and Wendler noted, for example, that younger readers tended to discuss characters' acts in simpler terms of their feelings; older readers were more likely to consider "conflicting perceptions between characters" (p. 295). Understanding something of the pattern of development in ability to infer about literary works may help us decide what issues are suitable for particular grades, what depth of thought we may expect of or encourage in students. Younger students' tendency to think about characters' acts as physical behaviors and to ignore their broader social or psychological implications may make it difficult for them to move from event to theme in literary works, requiring us to provide some sort of assistance with that process.

Most of these studies obtained their data through the analysis of written responses to texts, or, in some cases, such as Zaharias's study, simply through response preference inventories that ask students to rate the relative importance of 20 or so questions representing the categories of personal, descriptive, interpretive, and evaluative response. Such methods enabled researchers to segment responses, to discriminate among them, to correlate them with other variables, but it did not allow them

to see the responses as living, changing processes. As Odell and Cooper (1976) remark:

Purves (1968) suggests a number of ways of describing the kinds of responses students make. He is, however, much less helpful in providing ways to describe the *processes* by which students formulate their responses. (p. 204)

Just as composition research had at one time focused almost exclusively on the written product rather than on the act of writing, so much of this research had concentrated upon the written report of response rather than on the vital act of responding. It gave us, consequently, a still picture of response—response frozen, divided, counted. It told us something about what we had after the reading, but little about what happened as the reading progressed.

The fundamental question of course, is what does happen as a reader reads. Several studies had begun to explore this problem.

THE ANALYSIS OF TRANSACTIONS

Squire's (1964) examination of responses to short stories, predating the Purves-Rippere *Elements* by 4 years, may be one of the first that attempted to do this. He thought that asking students to respond orally, rather than in writing, would elicit from them a clearer and more accurate picture of their responses to the works. Dividing the stories into several parts, he interviewed students after they had read each section, and thus was able to view the reading as a sequence of events, a process, rather than as a static entity.

His analysis suggested seven categories of response, similar to those that Purves would later identify:

1. Literary judgments,
2. Interpretational responses,
3. Narrational reactions,
4. Associational responses,
5. Self-involvement,
6. Prescriptive judgments,
7. Miscellaneous.

Tracking the responses through six divisions of each story revealed some interesting relationships among the categories of response, relationships that would have been obscured in a written record produced at the conclusion of the reading. He noted, for instance, that narrational and associational responses, that is, retellings of the story and departures from the text to talk about the reader's own experience, tended to remain constant throughout the reading, suggesting that readers might find their own history insinuating itself into the reading at almost any point. Students do not necessarily "comprehend" the work first, and then extend into their own experiences: rather, it may well be that they call upon their history throughout the reading of a literary text. Literary judgments, however, were concentrated in the first divisions of the story and in the last. Readers may, perhaps, pass a hasty judgment upon the story as they begin it, quickly assessing its potential for pain or pleasure, then gradually become absorbed in the story, withholding further evaluation until they've completed it.

Self-involvement responses, statements indicating that the readers associate themselves with the actions or the feelings of the character, increase quickly after the first division and then hold fairly constant throughout the reading. Squire noted a curious relationship betwen the involvement and the judgmental responses, observing that during the time readers were deeply involved they made fewer judgments. Nonetheless, those students who were more emotionally involved tended also to offer more literary judgments about the texts. Speculating about that observation, Squire suggested that this "calls into question the tendency to assume an unnecessary opposition between intellectual and emotional responses to literature" (p. 22).

Squire's study followed the students through the process of reading and responding and thus was able to give us some picture of the movement. He shows us a reader passing early judgment upon the merits of a text, becoming absorbed in the narration, attending occasionally throughout the reading to memories and associations called to mind by the text, and at the end, evaluating the text once again. If he had become deeply involved in the story, he was also likely to evaluate it more extensively. With Squire's study we began to develop a picture, not just of the categories of response, but also of the active, responding reader.

Later studies would fill out the picture. Mauro (1983), for instance, conducted case studies of five high school students in a effort to see how their construct system might shape the process of response. Drawing upon suggestions in Applebee's (1978) study of the development of a sense of story, Mauro investigated three construct systems that she thought might shape response: constructs of experience or content, constructs of literary conventions and form, and constructs of process. Her strategy for investigating the readings was similar to Squire's. She asked the individual students to read the items—stories and poems—and to interrupt their readings, whenever they thought appropriate, to respond. (She did not divide the stories or poems for the students, as Squire had done, relying instead upon their felt need, with occasional prompting, to speak.) Mauro taped all of the sessions and was present for all but one, which she intentionally skipped so that she might assess the effect of reading and responding in solitude.

Her analysis of the students' transactions with the texts suggested that the individual's construct systems would be likely to shape his/her responses (making unlikely a unanimity in interpretation). One of the students, for example, revealed such strong disapproval of suicide that it seemed difficult for her to address any other topic when discussing a text that dealt with that issue. Another student, for whom suicide was not an important construct, scarcely mentioned it.

Mauro noticed also that students had certain expectations of texts, constructs of form, that in some cases seemed to shape responses more powerfully than did constructs of content. Stories, for some, were expected to provide vivid, living characters. Stories that did not ("The Sniper" was one such story) were likely to be viewed by those students as defective and unsatisfactory.

Perhaps most interesting of all, however, were Mauro's observations about the construct of process. Students, she found, had developed a notion of what was appropriate and what was not in the reading of a literary work. Analyzing and generalizing were, as might be predicted, assumed by all of the students to be suitable behaviors. There was more variation on other matters. One student demonstrated a strong interest in sharing his thoughts with others; another showed no inclination whatsoever to do so. One indicated clearly that the sharing of personal response was not an academically responsible behavior, and regardless of how interesting it might be, was not relevant or important in the literature classroom. One seemed to think that the appropriate behavior was to sit patiently and wait for the researcher to ask questions rather to initiate any discussion on his own.

Mauro noticed also that the "permeability," that is, the openness to change, of the constructs was a significant factor. Students whose constructs were relatively impermeable—rigid and inflexible—tended to reject texts that did not confirm them. The student, for example, who was deeply offended by the concept of suicide found it extremely difficult to deal with such texts as "Richard Corey." More flexible readers, tolerating if not approving, could at least consider the texts and reflect upon them without serious discomfort.

Langer's (1989) recent study focusses not so much on what students bring to the text but on what they do with it. She attempts to describe the nature of literary experience in terms of changing "stances" toward the text as readings progress. Thirty-six students in grades 7 through 11 were asked to think aloud while reading six texts—two short stories, two poems, one science text, and one social studies text. Her analysis of transcripts of the readings suggested that "readers were always actively engaged in creating meanings when they read. However, as they developed their meanings across time, their stance (the way they related to the text) changed, with each stance adding a somewhat different dimension to the reader's understanding of the entire piece" (p. 7). The stances she identified were these:

"Being Out and Stepping Into an Envisionment"—this is the reader's attempt, drawing upon prior knowledge and upon characteristics of the text, to begin to comprehend what is happening in the text.

"Being In and Moving Through an Envisionment"—the reader is involved in the text, has some understanding of what is transpiring, and is building more complex understandings.

"Stepping Back and Rethinking What One Knows"—here the reader reflects, using the envisionment offered by the text to reconsider knowledge, assumptions, attitudes brought to the reading.

"Stepping Out and Objectifying the Experience"—the reader moves away from the text, reflecting on it and the experience of reading it. (1989, p. 7)

Studies such as this one may offer us some interesting implications for the classroom. It clearly suggests, for instance, a pattern for questioning and discussing in the literature classroom. Teachers might experiment with plans devised to assist the students to move through these four stances and see if such designs yield more satisfying experiences.

Studies such as these remind us that response to literature is a complex phenomenon. It is not simply a matter of liking or disliking, feeling or not feeling. Nor can it simply be viewed as a transaction between a solitary reader and a single text. Rather, it is that transaction as it has been shaped by all the social and pedagogic experiences that precede it. The student comes to any text with ideas about its content, with expectations about what the text should offer, and with notions about his own responsibilities as a reader. The response is, in part at least, the consequence of all of those factors. And it may be the teacher's responsibility to consider all of those factors. We have occasionally been encouraged, by tests in teacher's handbooks, by the ominous specter of Scholastic Aptitude and Achievement Tests, and by other forces, to view student accomplishment in simple terms. We may look to see if they understand the text, judging them by their ability to produce, reproduce, or at least identify acceptable interpretations. The research into the nature of response suggests that we should perhaps consider more. Mauro's study in particular suggests that we consider the complex set of expectations and intellectual habits students bring with them or develop in our classes, and Langer's urges us to look carefully at the actual process of making sense of literary texts.

THE ANALYSIS OF DEVELOPMENT

Much of the research drawing upon the Purves-Beach system of analyzing responses, in an effort to objectively describe readers and reading, intentionally avoids making value judgments about the categories of response. Yet the efforts to describe the processes of response and to depict its "natural" development have revealed that there is no such thing as natural development. Response patterns mature within a cultural context that reinforces some patterns and discourages others. When New Criticism dominated, and it may dominate still, students learned to analyze and interpret literature, suppressing personal response and resisting, if they were good students, the desire to digress to their own stories or to other matters outside the text. As attention to response grows more and more respectable, it is likely that students will learn to respond and to express those responses in academically approved ways.

Thus it is hard to speak of development without considering how we channel it, encourage it, interfere with it—the value judgments lurk close to the surface. Developmental models have consequently grown more sophisticated. The model Protherough (1983) proposes would analyze students responses on four dimensions: awareness of theme, ability to empathize with characters, understanding of motivation, and ability to predict beyond the story. He argues that levels of response identified within each of these dimensions provide a model of development indicating "a shift away from reacting to isolated, particular details towards more perceptive responses to the total meaning of a text" (p. 45). We may note, in this model, that the text still dictates. Maturity in reading is a matter of more perceptive responses *to the text*.

Thomson, however, in 1987, proposes a somewhat more comprehensive model. He suggests six stages:

1. Unreflective interest in action.
2. Empathising.

3. Analogising.
4. Reflecting on the significance of events (theme) and behaviour (distanced evaluation of characters).
5. Reviewing the whole work as the author's creation.
6. Consciously considered relationship with the author, recognition of textual ideology, and understanding of self (identity theme) and of one's own reading process. (360–61)

The fifth and sixth stages are most interesting because it is here that he most clearly indicates his attention to the investigations into response. We may note here some parallels with Mauro's study. She had observed the influence of construct systems related to the three points at issue in these stages. The construct of content is echoed in Thomson's idea of recognizing textual ideology; both have to do with understanding the values or ideas carried by both text and reader. Mauro's construct of process is Thomson's notion of understanding one's own reading process. And Mauro's construct of form is recalled by the fifth stage, seeing the work as an author's creation. Thomson has broadened the picture to include not just attention to text, but also to writer, to culture, to self, and to self-as-reader.

The extent of the change may be even more apparent in the "process strategies" that amplify each stage. At stage three, "Analogising," he suggests that the process is one of "drawing on the repertoire of personal experiences, making connections between characters and one's own life." Clearly he would have the student go beyond the text, and he would consider reading to be more than simply comprehending what transpires within the text itself. At the fifth stage he sees students "drawing on literary and cultural repertoires," comparing the "author's representations with one's own," and recognizing the "implied author" behind the text. Here again response and comprehension consist of a great deal more than simple submission to text. Finally, in the sixth stage, he calls for awareness of the expectations of the reader implicit within the text. Drawing upon Iser (1978) and Booth (1961), he suggests that the process involves the recognition of the "implied reader in the text, and the relationship between implied author and implied reader." The last strategy in his list of 13 is reflexiveness—"understanding of textual ideology, personal identity and one's own reading processes."

With Thomson's developmental model, response to literature takes into consideration text, author, reader, and culture. If any element is missing in this conception it may be the teacher.

THE ANALYSIS OF INTERACTIONS

One critically important question for research on response has to do with the shaping effects of teaching. As the IEA study had pointed out, response to literature is learned. To ask what a natural, uncontaminated response would be is to ask an impossible question because literary response is not a biological phenomenon but a cultural one—it occurs, that is to say, within a social context, the context of the school. Efforts to examine developmental stages in response may give us some indications about how the reader's mind, ability, and attitudes change over time, but whether those changes are attributagle to natural processes, or to the consequences of schooling, or, more likely, to some infinitely complex combination of those and other factors is difficult to assess.

A number of studies had noted the narrowing of our range of responses, with the focus gradually, over the years of schooling, coming to bear upon interpreting texts. We had assumed that interpretation was what we wanted, but the Purves-Beach categories reminded us that there was more that we might do with literature. Rosenblatt's vision of the reader, first articulated at length in *Literature as Exploration* (1983; published originally in 1938), compelled us to look more closely at the reader reading. She suggested that a formal, distanced interpretation, one that failed to take into account the uniqueness of the reader, neglected essential elements in the literary experience. It failed, in particular, to consider the aesthetic and emotional. On the one hand, our instruction was having its effects; on the other hand, we were beginning to doubt that these were the effects we wanted.

Lucking (1976) attempted to assess the effects of different questioning strategies on the responses to short stories. Comparing no instruction, traditional instruction, and instruction arranged according to the hierarchy dictated by Bloom's taxonomy, Lucking noted several sharp differences in response patterns. Compared to no instruction, the traditional instruction yielded fewer engagement and evaluation responses, and more perception and miscellaneous. The major difference observable between traditional and experimental was a dramatic increase in interpretational responses after the hierarchically arranged questioning session. Though there is some uncertainty about what the traditional instruction consisted of, because Lucking seemed to be relying on the training and instincts of the teachers to mold them to some traditional patterns, and though patterns of questioning suggested by Bloom's taxonomy could hardly be said to respect individual response, it was fairly clear that differences in questioning did yield differences in response patterns, suggesting the importance of considering the shaping influence of classroom discourse on the students' thinking.

A recent study by Marshall looked not at oral questioning, but at the writing students were expected to undertake. He examined the effects of several conditions, no writing, restricted writing, personal analytical writing, and formal analytical writing, on the responses of 11th-grade students to each of four short stories. The restricted writing assignments consisted of eight short answer questions, all of which seemed, from the examples provided, to focus on the text itself. Similarly, the formal writing assignments directed the students' attention to the text, asking them to interpret in somewhat more extensive form than was expected in the restricted assignments. The personal writing asked the students to "elaborate upon their responses to the story, drawing on their own values and personal experience to make sense of their reactions to the text" (p. 43).

Marshall observed that the three different writing tasks did in fact shape the responses of the students in fairly predictable ways. The short answers evoked predominantly interpretive statements, with some description offered, presumably as support for the interpretation. The formal analytical assignment, predictably, did the same, interpretive statements supported by description of the text. The personal analytical, however, also elicited interpretive statements, though not as high a percentage as the other two forms. Here, though, the interpretations

were supported or developed with personal statements, connecting the reading with the students' other experiences as well as with descriptions of the text. Invitation to address personal reactions did not, as some have feared it might, lead the students into orgies of self-revelation or otherwise distract them entirely from the text. Instead, it allowed them to consider the text in the light of their own lives. As Marshall (1987) puts it,

Because the form was more flexible, the students could employ in their personal writing a language more clearly consonant with their initial experience of the stories. Because the tasks asked them to address that experience directly, their personal essays were less a report on shared knowledge than an opportunity to begin the process of independent analysis. (p. 59)

Hansson (1973), reporting on studies he had done in Sweden, suggested four possible effects of teaching: "The intellectual understanding of a poem could often be enriched and diversified, while the emotional qualities of the experience remained more or less unchanged; shallow and impersonal experiences could be influenced if the reader was not wholly indifferent to the poem; strongly personal experiences were not open to outside influences except for details; well-founded and well-defined critical opinions were hard to change" (p. 263). It may be more important, however, to note the reservations he expressed. Students who were engaged in analysis and discussion of a short story "acquired a more uniform understanding of the text and reached more uniform interpretations" (p. 274) than did individuals who were allowed to study it on their own. Unfortunately, he notes, "at the same time the attitude of these students had grown more negative, and they felt less keen on reading more texts by the same author than did the students who had not been taught in class" (p. 274). He suggested that it might be appropriate, especially in the United States where New Critical analyses of texts seemed to be the dominant approach, to examine the various effects, both academic and psychological, of the methods of the literature classroom.

Purves also had observations to make on this very point, first in the report of the IEA (1973), and later in his assessment of the IEA data most directly relevant to American schools (1981). In the first, *Literature Education in Ten Countries,* he concludes,

The IEA study implies that there are alternatives as to what might be learned. One could learn a single pattern of response which is the cultural norm and which could seek to override any tendency to be influenced by the specific text. One could learn a pattern that is determined by the text—again on a norm of how most people respond to that text. One could learn—or be encouraged—to follow one's whim regardless of cultural norm or textual norm. One could learn a variety of patterns and be left free to apply one or another pattern as one sees fit. There are other possibilities as well. To choose among them, one must consider the implications of each possibility for the student, for literature as an art form, and for the society of which that student will be a part. (p. 315)

FINAL COMMENTS

The impossibility of defining natural response processes in the reading of literature forces us to move at some point from empirical research to philosophy. The efforts to categorize response, to correlate it with features of texts, with personality traits, with instructional methods, may tell us something about what happens in the literature classroom, but ultimately we are left with the question, "What should happen in literature teaching?" and that question leads not to multivariate statistics, nor even to ethnography, but to philosophy. Our answers will depend on our vision of the good life, on our hopes for our children, as much as upon the information, valuable as that is, that research gives us.

Much of the current research in response to literature lends strength, however, to a democratic vision of the classroom. It suggests that significant and enjoyable learning can occur when the classroom respects the unique responses of readers, encouraging them to make meaning of texts in personally significant ways. The possibilities remain both exciting and problematic for teachers. On the one hand, they have the prospects for classroom exchanges in which the learning may take on a much more significant role in the lives of their students. Literary experience, in classes shaped by this body of research, may bring texts and lives to bear upon one another in ways that enliven and enrich the discourse. On the other hand, teachers will face the problems of working within a tradition that discourages their efforts. The emphasis schools have always placed on correctness, on the gathering of information whether assimilated or not, and on measuring learning, will likely prove discouraging to teachers hoping to work with the notions of literature instruction sustained by this research.

The research, however, promises ultimately to provide arguments against this tradition. It has begun to defend the notion that alternative readings of texts are both natural and desirable, and thus to reject the idea that literary experiences can be simply and easily judged as correct or incorrect. It has begun to demonstrate the great importance of connecting the text with the other experiences, the prior knowledge of the reader, and thus to reject the notion that simply acquiring information—facts, dates, memorized judgments, and the like—amounts to significant learning. And it has surely begun to indicate the complexity of literary experience, suggesting that efforts to reduce it to discrete, isolable, measurable units will likely be either futile or immensely difficult.

Teachers, and schools, will have to respond to the notion, fundamental in the work on response, that literary experience is much more than the acquiring of information. The sense that literature touches the individual and shapes his/her vision of human possibilities explains its enduring in the curriculum, despite this culture's seduction by the quantifying methods of empirical science. The vision of literature and literature instruction that informs much of the research on response accepts and sustains that notion of literature's place.

References

Angelotti, M. (1972) A comparison of elements in the written free response of eighth graders to a junior novel and an adult novel. *Dissertation Abstracts International, 33*:06A.

Applebee, A. N. (1977, Winter). ERIC/RCS Report: The elements of response to a literary work: What we have learned. *Research in the Teaching of English, II*, 255–271.

Applebee, A. N. (1978). *The child's concept of story.* Chicago: University of Chicago Press.

Beach, R. & Brunetti, G. (1976). Differences between high school and university students in their conceptions of literary characters. *Research in the Teaching of English, 10*, 259–268.

Beach, R., & Wendler, L. (1987, October). Developmental differences in response to a story. *Research in the Teaching of English, 21*, 286–297.

Booth, W. (1961). *The rhetoric of fiction.* Chicago: University of Chicago Press.

Corcoran, W. T. (1979). *A study of the responses of superior and average students in grades eight, ten, and twelve to a short story and a poem.* Alberta: University of Alberta.

Cornaby, B. J. (1975). A study of the influence of form on responses of twelfth-grade students in college-preparatory classes to dissimilar novels, a short story, and a poem. *Dissertation Abstracts International, 35*, 4856-7A.

Hansson, G. (1973). Some types of research on response to literature. *Research in the Teaching of English, 7*, 260–284.

Harding, D. W. (December, 1937). The role of the on-looker. *Scrutiny, 6*, 247–258.

Hynds, S. D. (1985, December). Interpersonal cognitive complexity and the literary response processes of adolescent readers. *Research in the Teaching of English, 19*, 386–402.

Hynds, S. D. (1989, February). Bring life to literature and literature to life: Social constucts and contexts of four adolescent readers. *Research in the Teaching of English, 23*, 30–61.

Iser, W. (1978). *The act of reading: A theory of aesthetic response.* Baltimore, Johns Hopkins University Press.

Kelly, G. A. (1955). *A theory of personality.* New York: Norton.

Kelly, G. A. (1970). A brief introduction to personal construct psychology. In D. Bannister (Ed.), *Perspectives in Personal Construct Theory.* London: Academic Press.

Langer, J. (1989, April). *The process of understanding literature* (Report Series 2.1). Albany, NY: Center for the Learning and Teaching of Literature, State University of New York.

Lucking, R. A. (1976, Winter)I A study of the effects of a hierarchically-ordered questioning technique on adolescents' responses to short stories. *Research in the Teaching of English, 1*, 269–76.

Marshall, J. D. (1987, February). The effects of writing on students' understanding of literary texts. *Research in the Teaching of English, 21*, 30–63.

Mauro, L. H. (1983). Personal constructs and response to literature: Case studies of adolescents reading about death (Doctoral dissertation, Rutgers University). *Dissertation Abstracts International,* 4407A.

Odell, L., & Cooper, C. (1976). Describing responses to works of fiction. *Research in the Teaching of English, 10*, 203–225.

Parnell, G. (1984). Levels of Aesthetic Experience with Literature. *Dissertation Abstracts International,* 45,06A.

Protherough, R. (1983). *Developing response to fiction.* Milton Keynes: Open University Press.

Purves, A. C. and Rippere, A. (1968). *Elements of writing about a literary work: A study of response to literature.* Urbana, IL: National Council of Teachers of English.

Purves, A. C. (1973). *Literature education in ten countries.* New York: John Wiley and Sons.

Purves, A. C. (1981). *Reading and literature: American achievement in international perspective*. Urbana, IL: National Council of Teachers of English.

Purves, A. C., & Beach, R. (1972). *Literature and the reader*. Urbana, IL: National Council of Teachers of English.

Richards, I. A. (1956). *Practical criticism*. New York: Harcourt, Brace and Co. (Original work published 1929)

Rosenblatt, L. M. (1983). *Literature as exploration* (4th ed.). New York: Modern Language Association. (Original work published 1938)

Somers, A. B. (1972). Responses of advanced and average readers in grades seven, nine, and eleven to two dissimilar short stories. *Dissertation Abstracts International, 3308A.*

Squire, J. (1964). *The responses of adolescents while reading four short stories,* NCTE Research Monograph #2. Urbana, IL: National Council of Teachers of English.

Thomson, J. (1987). *Understanding teenagers' reading: Reading processes and the teaching of literature*. New York: Nichols Publishing Co.

Young, R. E., Becker, A. L., & Pike, K. L. (1970). *Rhetoric: Discovery and change*. New York: Harcourt, Brace, and World.

Zaharias, J. A. (February, 1986). The effects of genre and tone on undergraduate students' preferred patterns of response to two short stories and two poems. *Research in the Teaching of English, 2,* 56–68.

32C. READING PREFERENCES

Dianne L. Monson
Sam Sebesta

The reading interests of children and adolescents have been the subject of widespread study. Jordan, in 1921, reviewed 10 substantial published interest studies, the earliest done in 1897. Meckel (1963) grouped reading-interest studies according to their variables (e.g. maturity, sex, intelligence; literary characteristics, satisfactions derived by readers), speculating on the influence of such studies on the teaching of literature. In 1967, King noted that over 300 reading-interest studies had been reported since the beginning of the century. About this time, Spache (1963) wrote that "Research in determining children's reading interests has diminished greatly from the peak period in the 1920s and 1930s. The basic trends have been confirmed in so many repetitive studies that there appear to be few fresh facts to be discovered" (p. 166).

Perhaps. But researchers and practitioners continue their interest in *interests*. What are the factors that underlie the interests of readers and would-be readers? As children have changed over the past 20 years, have interest patterns also changed? What differences appear in findings, attributable to differences in research design and research strategy? Certainly, interests are based on past experience; are they substantially broadened or altered, then, by present experience, by planned treatment? Or are interests independent of immediate influence, derived instead from "a variety of internal drives and needs" (Spache, 1963, p. 171)?

These and other interest-related questions persist despite what seems to be an abundance of studies. More broadly, knowledge about reading interests has proved elusive. Expressed interests may not represent real interests. An interest of the moment or based on single exposure or on an out-of-context aspect of literature may not be reliable or valid. As Weintraub (1969) points out, there are problems of interpretation:

A pupil may select a book for a reason quite different from that identified by an adult. The category "animals" or the topic "horses" may not mean that the child is interested in just any story about horses or in all animal tales. He may be equating horse stories with adventure tales or some other facet of his interest. Researchers have often failed to identify the particular features, stylistic or otherwise, of a piece of material that makes it appealing to children. (p. 651)

Researchers doubt the stability of interest study data. When intermediate-grade subjects responded to Ashley's (1972) list of interest categories and open questions about reading interests, the researcher concluded, "It became clear that many youngsters do not indicate specific kinds of reading so much as a choice of books which they have recently read, which were then 'translated' into the type of reading they appeared to 'fit'" (p. 27).

One difficulty in designing and interpreting reading-interest research is to devise a theory-based, agreed-upon operational definition of the term. Dewey's (1913) definition of interest—"a form of self-expressive activity, that is, of growth that comes through acting upon nascent tendencies" (p. 101)—suggests criteria. For instance, a "self-expressive activity" might not be indicated by response to a structured questionnaire. "Nascent tendencies" (coming into existence) might need to be distinguished from less dynamic, more entrenched beliefs. Dewey's definition may be especially suited to the study of apparently often-changing reading interests of young people. Getzels (1966) prefaces a classic definition of interest with this distinction: "The difference between a preference and an interest is that the preference is relatively passive, while the interest inevitably dynamic" (p. 7). According to Getzels (1966), an interest is "a characteristic disposition, organized through experience, which impels an individual to seek out particular objects, activities, understandings, skills, or goals for attention or acquisition" (p. 7).

The reading-interest studies that we summarize, discuss, or suggest in this chapter may or may not align with such definitions as those of Dewey and Getzels. When children respond to a questionnaire ("What books do you like best?"), there is no measure of "seeking out" behavior. When they indicate that they "like" one poem better than another, the choice may be a preference, not an interest. Reading-interest studies seem particularly vulnerable to criticism derived from the rigors of research. But, we shall see, many problems in reading-interest research arise not from ignorance or negligence but from complexity.

A HISTORY OF READING-INTEREST RESEARCH

The Early Studies—A Mission to Change

Jordan's (1921) summary of reading-interest studies done up to the time of his own investigation notes "substantial agreement" among findings, including preference for fiction over nonfiction, with girls choosing "sentiment and emotion" and boys favoring adventure and history. Neither sex appeared to prefer books about travel or science. One of the studies (Wissler, 1898) found a rapid increase in liking for poetry as children grew older, attributing the increase to the study of *Evangeline*, "Thanatopsis", and *Snowbound*. Mainly, the studies used three types of data collection:

1. *open questionnaires* (Subjects in one study were asked to comment on "quantity, quality, harmfulness, and interest" in their reading.);
2. *lists of topics* (e.g. Great Men, Great Women, Ghosts, Love, War) on which students were asked to underline preferences;
3. *lists of literary titles* (For example, Abbott, in 1902, provided a list of 178 recommended books, asking students to indicate by 0, +, or + + their opinion of those they had read.).

Jordan's own study, employing an open questionnaire, is notable for one innovation: after listing adolescents' favorite-listed titles, he studied the content and designated "Satisfiers" and "Annoyers"—attributes that might account for preferences and nonpreferences.

An extensive study comparing the reading interests and reading habits of approximately 1000 gifted (IQ 135+) and "unselected" elementary-age pupils is that of Terman and Lima (1925). For two months, subjects kept a day-by-day record of books read and opinions about books read (e.g. "Do you think you will want to read it again?" p. 54). Vast differences were found between gifted and average in regard to quantity; gifted pupils read three or four times as many books. Large sex differences were found in book choices: only 4 of the top 20 "most liked books" (grades 1–8) appear on both boys' and girls' lists. As in past studies, fiction predominates; boys preferred "adventure and mystery," girls "stories of home and school life" (p. 75).

Underlying these early studies is a sense of mission. Jordan (1921) notes, "If we could determine what the child's major interests are, be those interests good or bad, it would be possible to direct those forces along lines which are desirable" (p. 1). Terman and Lima (1925) devote a chapter to "The Undesirable Book," leading to "wasted hours, a perverted reading taste, a false sense of reality, and a direct loss of education" (p. 81); two thirds of their report presents an annotated list of "desirable" books. Reading interests are to be studied and, when necessary, changed.

Preference Studies

No such mission appears in Gates' (1930) study to determine primary-level children's preferences regarding "literary characteristics." The study seems aimed at gathering information to help the author select and prepare high-interest material for basal readers and comprehension test items. As such, it differs from the broader intent of earlier studies. It also represents a departure in methodology, although Gates acknowledges that it is derived from an earlier study by Dunn (1921).

Gates devised a list of 14 literary characteristics drawn partly from the Dunn study. He hired "several persons highly familiar with children's materials and highly capable of judging such qualities" (p. 74) to estimate the weighting of each characteristic in each of 30 selections considered to be "representative of the range of children's literature" (p. 73). Selections were randomly paired and read to classes whose pupils indicated which of the paired selections was preferred. Gates estimated that about 15,000 individual votes were collected. Then, through partial correlations, the independent weighting of each literary characteristic across preferences was determined. The ranking, from highest preferred to lowest, is as follows: *surprise, liveliness, animalness, conversation, humor, plot, narrativeness, poeticalness, familiarity, repetition, fancifulness, realism, verse form, moralness.* Gates concluded that the first six characteristics are "the six main elements among those here studied to weave into a selection" (p. 89). *Moralness* appeared to decrease interest, as did what some adults appraise as *humor:* "We must

conclude that we have much yet to learn about what is, fundamentally, funny to young children" (p. 90).

This study foreshadows attempts to pinpoint characteristics, other than merely topic, that might describe appeal, based on preference or self-chosen selections. It is probably among the earliest attempts at market research in juvenile literature, attempting to discern preferences in order that new materials may conform to readers' approval.

A long tradition of studies is concerned with the influence of age, intelligence, and sex upon children's preferences in literature. Huber, Bruner, and Curry (1927) determined grade level rankings of poems preselected by experts and from courses of study and textbooks. They concluded that "present placement is only 39 percent right" (p. 71). Huber (1928) compared the preferences of what she termed dull, average, and bright groups (mean IQs 74.4, 98.5, and 114.6, respectively) in special classes and in grades 1 through 5. Overall, a "striking similarity" was found among the preferences of the three groups. Pupils of lower intelligence, however, evidenced greater liking for "familiar experience" stories and poems and less liking for humor than did the other two groups.

A decade later, Lazar (1937) used the results of an extensive inventory of 4,000 New York children, ages 10 to 12, to conclude:

Girls read more and with greater enjoyment than boys, with substantial differences between the two in regard to interests. [Citing cultural comparisons from Margaret Mead, Lazar stated her belief that such differences exist "because social opinion has prescribed them" (p. 92).];

Pupils categorized as "dull" in intelligence did less reading and displayed less interest in reading in general than did their counterparts.

They found greater appeal in "fanciful, unrealistic" books, literature that Lazar considered of questionable value. Dull groups also appeared to like poetry better than the bright and average groups. Lazar's rather puzzling conclusion, citing "marked differences in the reading interests, activities, and opportunities of children of different levels of intelligence" (p. 104), is that: "The aim of the schools should be to reduce these differences between the various groups of pupils as far as possible" (p. 104).

Researchers have inferred interests from subjects' citation of real titles. They have attempted to discern preferences on the basis of subjects' choices from selections read to them. A potential threat to validity in both instances is that specifics (a single title, a single selection) may not warrant such generalization. On the other hand, preference studies cited in this section of our review involve large numbers of subjects. The percentages of agreement reported in early studies and the more sophisticated statistics of later studies indicate verification across large samples.

"Interest Score" Studies

R. L. Thorndike (1941) tried to avoid the generalization fallacy by preparing a fictitious annotated title questionnaire, "to escape in some measure from the influence of a single specific reading experience" (p. 5). The questionnaire was answered by 2,891 subjects, grades 4–12, who responded by circling "Yes," "No," "?" as to whether they would like to read a selection based on the fictitious title and annotation. The 88 items on the questionnaire were designed so that reactions to two or more items could be combined to indicate an interest. (For example, positive responses to "Buster Bear's Birthday" and "Bob the Beaver Builds a Dam" were considered to indicate an interest in Talking Animal Stories.) Using such categories, Thorndike derived an "interest score" for subgroups based on age, sex, and intelligence. This "interest score," subsequently used by other investigators, was compiled by counting "Yes" votes plus one-half "?" and dividing by the total number of subjects responding to an item. Correlations among interest scores could then lead to comparisons among subgroups, and Thorndike from these decided that:

Sex accounts for much greater differences in interests than does age or intelligence: "The differences associated with sex obscure any effect of level of maturity" (p. 36);

Within the same sex, interests across levels of IQ show a "substantial positive correlation," with "bright" subjects revealing interests comparable to "mentally slower" subjects who are 2 to 3 years older.

In all, Thorndike was able to indicate by age, sex, and intelligence factors the "Maximum Interest Level" of 14 fiction and 10 nonfiction categories. For example, "Realistic Animal Stories" were designated "moderate to high" interest for boys and for girls, ages 9–11 for "bright groups" and ages 10–14 for "slow groups."

Norvell (195) used Thorndike's interest score concept to explore opinions of 50,000 secondary-level students regarding 1,700 selections identified by teachers as "studied or read by the class this school year" (p. 10). A typical class balloted 40 to 50 selections, rating each as very interesting, fairly interesting, or uninteresting—a total of 1.59 million ratings gathered from 200 New York schools. From these data, Norvell published indices for each selection by sex, grade, and genre (novels, plays, poems, short stories, biographies, and essays). In this study, neither age nor intelligence appeared to bring major differences in choices at the secondary level, but "sex is a dominating factor which attains its maximum during the junior high school period" (p. 48). Norvell notes, however, that stories and poems dealing with adventure, obvious humor, animals, and patriotism appealed to both sexes, while neither group liked many selections about the supernatural or with didactic themes.

In a second study, Norvell (1958) used an identical procedure to obtain 960,000 opinions from 24,000 children in grades 3–6, yielding interest scores on 1,576 selections studied in class, read independently, or read by teachers with discussion. Compared with the earlier study, age played a greater part in accounting for differences: fewer selections rated consistently high or low across intermediate-grade groups. Sex differences appeared to vary by genre and, at least in regard to poetry, by individual selections. Such differences were not, however, the major concern of the author, who began his report with an at-

tack on "the ineptness of expert judgment on children's reading interests" (p. 4). Norvell cited, as evidence, an assortment of authors and works praised or negatively reviewed by critics. In each instance, interest scores of children indicate an opposite opinion. Norvell's conclusion: "That adult standards for literature are not children's standards has been emphasized through this report" (p. 149). He argued for "relinquishment" of adult selection "in favor of the acceptance of children's own choices" (p. 174).

The issue raised by Norvell is important because it pertains to the implications of all interest and preference studies. Should findings be used literally in selecting literature for young people and helping them select their own? Or, presuming that judgment of authorities differs from judgment of young readers, is the dual system of selection to be desired? Norvell was adamant in his rejection of the latter. It should be noted, however, that his studies are an inadequate basis for an opinion on the issue. First, the selections which Norvell identified as the choices of secondary and intermediate-grade pupils are drawn mainly from those provided in school, many of them presented by teachers or included in literary anthologies. The choices do not represent "seeking out" behavior so much as preferences among literary examples in the curriculum. Second, Norvell's citation of critical selections and rejections in literature was haphazard. He made no systematic attempt to survey critics' choices in order to contrast these with what he identified as the choices of children and adolescents.

Intermediate-graders' preferences in poetry were explored by Terry (1974), who presented 113 poems, audiotaped by an expert reader, to be rated by 422 pupils in 42 classrooms in four regions of the United States. Overall, interest in poetry was highest in grade 4, steadily declining in grades 5 and 6. Inner-city subjects expressed highest interest, with metropolitan, rural, and suburban subjects displaying, respectively, less favorable reactions. The 25 most popular poems in this study were characterized by narrative form, rhyme, rhythm, sound, humor, and pleasant familiar experience. The 25 most disliked poems included free verse, imagery that tended to obscure meaning, and "traditional" rather than modern authorship. On the basis of teacher questionnaires, Terry concluded that "poetry is sadly neglected in upper elementary school classrooms" (p. 47).

The largest continuing study, described by Leibowicz (1983) as providing "the most visible and perhaps most directly useful information on children's reading interests" (p. 184), is the Children's Choices survey sponsored by a joint committee of the International Reading Association and the Children's Book Council (Roser & Frith, 1983). Beginning in 1974, the committee annually submits multiple copies of 500+ newly-published trade books to five regions throughout the United States, where team leaders make the books available to and solicit the votes and opinions from more than 10,000 children. The results, presented annually in *The Reading Teacher*, comprise a list of approximately 100 annotated titles considered, on the basis of the survey, to be "Children's Choices." Numerous studies have resulted from researchers' attempts to deduce factors defining interests based on Children's Choices lists. Some of these are discussed in the following section of this chapter. In 1986 a similar annual project was begun under the auspices of the International Reading Association: Young Adults' Choices. (See October issues of *Journal of Reading.*)

Conclusions

What can be learned from these past attempts to explore reading interests and preferences? One use would be to subject them to a meta-analysis (Jackson, 1980), to determine whether a profile of childhood reading-interest factors can be drawn. Certainly there is much general agreement in the findings if we include the researchers' divisions by sex and age. Shortcomings in design and sampling limitations might be compensated in such an over-all attempt to find consistency.

The opposite conclusion might be drawn: that these studies have *imposed* generalization and that, ultimately, children's interests are individual and idiosyncratic. This is a view experssed by Summers and Lukevich (1983): "The best approach for the teacher is to treat 'norms' lightly and analyze preferences for a particular class, within a specific school and community " (p. 358). If this is true, then these and further studies are misleading. Researchers might then examine the ample field of interest studies as the exploration of a construct whose reality was not supported.

Surprisingly, none of these past studies appears to have attempted a pragmatic test of findings. For example, if subjects are besieged with selections to match their interests as measured, are there indeed discernible results: an increase, say, in amount of voluntary reading, in response factors, in attitude? One recent study (Anderson, Shirey, Wilson, & Fielding, 1987) compared children's comprehension of sentences representing a wide range in interest, concluding that "interestingness" as a factor accounts for 30 times as much variance as does readability. It might be conjectured, then, that interest study findings, if they are valid, might be powerfully verified through a study of their application to subjects' subsequent reading.

The history of preference and interest studies appears to reveal a trend in researchers' motives for conducting them. Early studies seem to have been done, at least in part, for the purpose of discovering preferences in order that these might be altered or compensated by "good" literature—that is, literature selected and approved by adults. A reversal in this position comes with studies to discern children's preferences so that reading materials can be matched to them. Whether to change or to match interests, or to attempt to do both, remains an issue.

CONTEMPORARY STUDIES OF READING INTERESTS

Content Factors

A number of studies have examined reading interests in terms of subject matter and genres that appear to have the greatest appeal. The results of a good number of studies reveal agreement on types of subject matter that appeal to students of a particular age level and support the notion that interests change with age. Underlying those generalizations, however, is the plain fact that the commonly used subject matter categories (such as adventure, animal stories, realistic stories, make-believe, nature, science, biography, etc.) borrow from topic choice as well as from genre choice. Furthermore, the so-called "subject matter" categories are not mutually exclusive; that is, a child who chooses to read animal stories may choose those that are realistic or those that are make believe, or a mixture of both. The common ground is simply a focus on animals as characters. There is also a problem with a category such as make-believe, because it does not give information about specific elements of the genre that appeal to the child. More specific descriptors such as fables, myths, or folk tales might be more revealing.

It is somewhat useful to look at reading interests of students according to level of schooling. Studies that cut across the elementary grades highlight the general interest in animals, mystery, science, history, make-believe, and people (Beta Upsilon, 1974; Chiu, 1984). In their discussion of interest patterns, Purves and Beach (1972) identify changes that occur by stages of growth. Animals, nature, fantasy and child characters appear to be preferred by children in grades 1 and 2 (Consuelo, 1967; Nelson, 1966; Witty, Coomer, & McBean, 1946). Primary grade children have also indicated interest in reading general informational material, history, and science informational materials (Carter, 1976; Huus, 1979; Itzkowitz, 1982; Kirsch, 1975). Children in grades 3 and 4 continue to be interested in reading about nature and animals and begin to develop interest in adventure and familiar experiences, but show decreased interest in fables (Curley, 1929; Graham, 1986). By fifth and sixth grades, interests begin to differ by sex with boys more interested in reading about war, travel and mystery (Row, 1968) and girls interested in animal stories, westerns, and fairy tales (Shores, 1954). More recent studies indicate increasing interest in history and science in intermediate grade students, as well as a continuing interest in reading mystery and adventure (Bundy, 1983; Graham, 1986; Hawkins, 1983).

There is evidence that at least by fourth grade the reading interests of boys and girls are beginning to diverge. Boys show stronger preference for nonfiction and girls for realistic fiction (Landy, 1977; Lynch-Brown, 1977; Wolfson, Manning, & Manning, 1984). Furthermore, it appears that when interests are examined over a 24-year period, boys show increased interest in books about personal problems and decreased interest in physical science, whereas girls show greater preference for stories about family life and children and decreased interest in animal stories.

In junior high, reading interests continue to differ according to sex. Seventh and eighth grade girls prefer mystery, romance, animals, religion, career stories, comedy, and biography. Boys prefer science fiction, mystery, adventure, biography, history, animals and sports. Both boys and girls show increased interest in nonfiction, historical fiction, romantic fiction, and books dealing with adolescence (Carlsen, 1967; Carter & Harris, 1982; Gallo, 1983; Leafe, 1951; McBroom, 1981; Smith & Eno, 1961; Strang, 1946). Contemporary realism is an important genre for this age group, too (Coomer & Tessmer, 1986). Smith and Eno (1961) used a strategy of asking students what type of story they would want an author to write. They found students preferred characters between the ages of 15 and 19 who were attractive, intelligent, and physically strong. Other studies have also revealed students' liking for characters who are clever, bright, and successful (Malchow, 1937). Two studies, one looking at books in the IRA Children's Choices list (Greenlaw & Wielan, 1979) and the other a survey of library users ages 11 to 20 (Goodhope, 1982) reinforce the cross-age appeal of books that contain humor and adventure. In a 1969 review of reading interests, Squire noted that "scientific themes and such elements as humor, surprise, and a stirring plot appeal to most young readers" (p. 467). He also indicated that the research in reading interests published over a period of time tended to show that patterns of interest remain fairly constant over several generations of children.

Poetry

The contemporary study of poetry interests provides information about the poetry preferences of children in the primary school years (Fisher & Natarella, 1982). This study derives from the earlier study by Terry (1974). Responses to the poems included in this study indicated preference for rhythm and rhyme and a liking for alliteration and onomatopoeia. The children disliked poems that rely on metaphor, simile or personification. These and other studies indicate that humor is a popular element in poems and that narrative poetry is well-liked (Ingham, 1980). The popularity of humorous poems and poems about animals is evident from responses by English as well as U.S. children (Cullingford, 1979).

An interesting finding from the studies suggests that students in the middle grades prefer to read poems rather than to listen to them (Cullingford, 1979; Kutiper, 1985). These studies add something to what we know from earlier work. They also indicate that the reasons for poetry preference may not have changed greatly over the years since Mackintosh published her study in 1924. Favorite poems may change for each generation according to what is available to them, but it is clear that today students use many of the criteria Mackintosh identified: funny, tells a good story, has adventure and excitement, has romantic and dramatic qualities, deals with material understandable and interesting, and has rhythm and rhyme.

Literary Forms and Devices

Historically, many studies have indicated that students preferred narrative material to informational material. Even as far back as 1899, Wissler pointed out that preferences went to plots with suspense and action and stories with humor. Studies by Dunn (1921) and Gates (1930) agree. More recent studies have tended to support the liking for action and humor. Within the broad category of narrative, it is not really clear whether children prefer realistic stories or fantasy. Studies tend to suggest that fantasy is preferred more by primary age children and realism more by those in the intermediate grades (Peltola, 1965). However, Smith (1926) found that first-graders liked realistic stories more than nursery rhymes.

The matter of preference for informational books shows some change over time. A number of studies reported during the last two decades single out informational books as highly interesting to children in upper grades and high school and particularly to boys. Recent studies also show strong interest in biography for this group of students. It is difficult to view this finding, or any other related to reading choices, as unrelated to publishing trends. It is surely true that, in the last decade, students have had access to far more well-written informational books than at any time in the past. There has also been an increase in publication of biographies of popular figures in sports and entertainment so that access must be considered as a possible factor in a shift in reading preferences.

Literary devices, too, can influence reading interests. Humor is one factor that has emerged in a number of studies. Some forms of humor seem to have greatest appeal and perhaps are better understood by children in elementary and junior high school than others. The totally ridiculous situation and humorous characters are well liked, as is the humor associated with exaggeration, a surprising event, and play on words (Monson, 1968; McNamara, 1984; Wells, 1934). There is some evidence that readers in the middle grades also enjoy satirical literature, though they may not associate it with their own lives (McNamara, 1984).

Attention to literary characteristics as an influence on reading interests is evident in responses of elementary school children. Unfortunately, relatively few studies have attempted to examine this dimension of reading preference or interest. It appears that elementary school students prefer books with happy endings (Mendoza, 1983) and episodic plots (Abrahamson, 1979; Abrahamson & Shannon, 1983). The development of characterization also appears to influence reader interest. Students prefer books in which characters are shown to have contrasting points of view (Abrahamson & Shannon, 1983). Adolescents also prefer characters they view as being like themselves and pay attention to the age and sex of the protagonist (Carter & Harris, 1982; Ingham, 1982; Johnson, Peer, & Baldwin, 1984; Yoder, 1978). Increased identification with characters appears to produce more suspense (Jose & Brewer, 1984).

Abrahamson's analysis of responses to *Children's Choices* picture books suggests a liking for books with qualities of good literature (characters confronting a problem and seeking a solution, plots that focus on characters with different points of view or who experience the same thing in contrasting ways). Ingham, however, found that her English subjects' responses to Enid Blyton's books indicated a liking for books written to a formula that provided for predictability and security.

Cross-National Comparisons

Cross-national study of reading interests is useful from the standpoint of identifying similarities as well as differences among young people from a variety of countries. Kirsch, Pehrsson and Robinson (1976) examined interests of a large number of children from 10 countries and reported more similarities than differences among them. Other studies, though not all of them cross-national, tend to support the notion that reading interests do not vary greatly from country to country, yet they also enlarge our understanding of qualities that draw children to books. A study of Japanese 5-year-olds revealed an interest in books that contained unexpected developments and books in which main characters attempted to solve problems in order to attain a goal (Tokogi, 1980). A comparison of reading preferences of British and American children ages 7 to 10 showed similarities in favorite categories for boys and girls in both countries, with adventure, animals, fantasy, hobbies, and travel the most preferred categories. The group diverged in response to poetry, with British children preferring to read about poetry rather than people, but American children preferred to read about people (Schofer, 1981). A study of the reading interests of intermediate grade Canadian children indicated that both boys and girls preferred themes of mystery, adventure, and fantasy (Summers & Lukevich, 1983). The pattern is not unlike what is known of U.S. children's interests, although the preference for fantasy is not a favorite with this age group in most U.S. studies. Intermediate grade children in Australia were surveyed to determine factors that influence book choices (Hill, 1984). Content and cover or title were strong influences and most books read came from a school or classroom library. It appears that secondary students in Greece prefer books with similar themes to those preferred by U.S. adolescents, choosing adventure, crime, social problems, novels, politics, and sports as favorite topics (Sikiotis, 1981). A study of responses by Canadian High School students to Canadian and New Zealand poems suggested a tendency for those students to prefer Canadian poems (Ross, 1978). Overall, while there amy be some national differences in interests, perhaps related to availability of materials, interests across cultures appear quite consistent.

External Factors

As students progress through the middle grades and into adolescence, they rely less on teachers and parents for reading guidance and more on peers (Shore, 1986; Wendelin & Zinck, 1983). Response to questionnaires as well as observational studies suggest that children in this age group select books according to favorite authors and are influenced by the appearance of a book, including the cover and the content of the first page, the length, and the illustrations as well as the title (Burgess, 1985; Higgins & Elliott, 1982; Wendelin & Zinck, 1983).

Format of a book, title, cover, and size may also act as an influence on expressed interests and preferences. Several recent studies have examined factors related to format of books. For some lower achieving students, physical elements of a book such as print, illustration, and length join with the title to assist in determining book selection (Higgins & Elliott, 1982; White, 1973; Wilson, 1985). Although numerous instruments have been used in reading interest studies, rarely have the instruments been subjected to tests of reliability (Weintraub, 1969). Joels and Anderson (1983) used a Reading Interest Survey, Forms A and B, consisting of fictitious titles. Form A was administered initially and Form B was administered after one week and again after a six-month interval. Correlation coefficients were computed for each of the six interest categories: fantasy, love and romance, mystery/adventure, religion, science, and

sports. Coefficients ranged from .65 to .82 after one week and from .58 to .76 after six months. Although the interests did change, the change does not appear to be great.

MEANS OF ELICITING AND MEASURING READING INTERESTS

Examination of a large number of interest studies reveals a great variety of strategies used to gain access to information about interests. These include questionnaires, interviews, checklists of book titles assumed to be popular, checklists of fictitious titles, paired comparisons of fictitious story synopses, paired comparisons questionnaire with content categories, reading records kept by students or teachers, library withdrawal records, student ratings of samples from a text, free response measures, semantic differential formats. Reading interests or preferences also have been examined by means of interest inventories, analysis of library selections (Smith, 1926), open-ended questionnaires (Shore, 1968), relating freely discussed topics to interests (Byers, 1964), and nonverbal evaluations (Ford & Koplyay, 1968).

It is immediately clear that some strategies are constructed from preconceived ideas of what students will be interested in reading. Others leave the matter open, relying on reader response to an open-ended interview or questionnaire. Clearly, the information resulting from a forced choice situation may be considerably different from information gained through open-ended response.

On another dimension, there is a disctinction between strategies that rely on fictitious titles and synopses (Thorndike, 1941; Zais, 1969) and those that draw from samples of actual texts. The use of fictitious titles and synopses can remove the interference of previous experience with a text. That strategy assumes that the titles and synopses actually represent those characteristics of literary genres or devices that are intended. Purves and Beach (1972) point out that samples from a text may fail to reflect key qualities of that book. In that way, the results can be misleading. On the other hand, this method can reveal interest in specific literary qualities or devices, response to writing style or to genre. Furthermore, a mechanism like the semantic differential allows for response to fairly specific qualities of a text, but it does not necessarily give an indication of a reader's preference for or interest in that genre as opposed to other genres. The semantic differential has been employed in a number of studies (Hansson, 1973; Klein, 1968). A Likert-type scale has also been used successfully to document response to excerpts from reading texts (Coleman & Jungeblut, 1961). Reading records kept by students or teachers and library withdrawal records may be quite easily obtained and classified by genre, but such records do not necessarily mean that the student was interested enough in the book to complete it. Free response measures are more likely to reveal factors related to interests but are complicated by the need to maintain reliability of judges in content analysis of those responses. As an example, Peltola (1965) asked children to name their favorite character from all the books they had read and to give the name of the book. Responses were then categorized as to reviewers' rating of the books as recommended or not recommended books, real or make believe, and sex of the character named.

The effectiveness of a strategy for eliciting information about reading interests comes down to the question of which strategy or strategies provide the most accurate assessment. Purves and Beach (1972) report one study conducted in Finland by Lehtovaaro and Saarinen (1964) comparing results from four strategies for data gathering: questionnaire, fictitious title booklist; text sample, and paired comparisons. The subjects were 2,000 Finnish students, ages 10 to 16. Results indicated that the booklist and the text samples showed the closest correspondence and that the booklist and questionnaire were the next most similar in outcomes. Paired comparisons produced results different from the other three strategies. However, Lehtovaaro and Saarinen reported paired comparison measures to be highly accurate.

The difference in assumptions underlying these strategies adds to difficulties in making any kinds of comparisons of findings across studies. It would appear that there is a need for research that focuses on accuracy and reliability of the strategies used.

FUTURE RESEARCH ON INTERESTS

Future reading-interest research undoubtedly will continue to examine likenesses and differences in preferred reading fare according to age, sex, and intelligence. Current social trends and increased availability of reading materials, sometimes significantly augmented by cassettes (Roberts, 1987), may lead to greater commonality of interests, if some recent studies are indicators. For instance, G. Anderson, Higgins, and Wurster (1985) found that level of achievement accounted for little difference among topic interests in a large (N = 476) intermediate-grade sample. McKenna (1986) concluded a study of reading-interest topics submitted to secondary students with a "universal" list of subjects "not differentially preferred by age or sex" (p. 349).

Such findings should not be generalized to the point of overlooking uniqueness of interests. At a time when voluntary reading ranks low among activities, the greatest hope of raising attitudes toward reading still lies in appraising individuals' interests, meeting them, and expanding them. In such light, studies may be of little help if their research questions are too narrow ("At what grade level should this poem be taught?") or, conversely, too broad ("What award-winning selections should appeal to all readers?").

A hopeful sign is that inquiry has expanded beyond lists of topics, titles, and forced-choice preferences. The possibility of international studies comparing genre choices of young readers in various countries is suggested by Apseloff (1985), who collected data regarding distribution from publishers' representatives at a world-wide exhibit; her evidence suggests considerable divergence in genre choice by country. The Children's Choices project, described earlier in this chapter, provides an annual list of 100 + preferred books, based upon reports from about 10,000 children in naturalistic settings. Munn (1986) used a sample of Children's Choices to explore criteria used by inter-

mediate-age pupils when selecting a book, finding that title, author, book cover, and summary ranked, respectively, highest as determiners. Abrahamson (1980) analyzed plot structures of Children's Choices picture books: he found a balance of confrontation, episodic, and contrast plots, with infrequent use of travel, quest, and plotless stories. Sebesta (1980) compared Children's Choices selections with a sampling of books *not* chosen in the project, compiling a list of preferred qualities (fast pace, detailed description of settings, didactics, warmth). While none of the Children's Choices-based studies to date can be called rigorous or exhaustive, the accumulating list of preferred works comprises a vast sample inviting investigation. Content analysis of the books themselves and inquiry into children's reasons for choosing them may yield useful in-depth information regarding reading interests. Parallel studies of Young Adults' Choices (see October issues of *Journal of Reading*) also offer promising possibilities.

Inevitably, studies of reading interests overlap with research in a wider, more recent area of investigation: children's response to literature. Hickman (1979) notes the relationship: "To many teachers . . . response and choice are synonymous; children's expressions of interest may be the most obvious of their classroom responses" (p. 3). How these expressions of interest are best elicited may depend upon situation and access, but the promising trend is toward ethnographic study. The researcher acting as participant-observer accumulates "a broad range of evidence" to be subjected to "careful reflection," resulting in an organized, verifiable description of the phenomenon (Hickman, 1985). Far from the compilation of topics or titles, ethnographic research is described as a "semiliterary genre of anthropological discourse" (Marcus & Fischer, 1986, p. 5), leading to "a cultural critique of ourselves [offering] today a renewed potential for development" (p. 20).

The prospect of ethnographic study of interests, using data collection procedures such as interviews, journals, and observation, suggests the feasibility of teachers and librarians in the role of researcher. The resulting synthesis of practice and research into the field of reading interests may be a trend toward the future, following participant-observer training studies along the lines of those laid down by Heath (1983) in her report of oracy/literacy traditions by social strata. Ethnographic study of interests may help alleviate apparent incongruence between school literacy and the quality of literacy deemed desirable in modern culture (Erickson, 1984).

As research encompasses the dynamics of the classroom and other contexts, the feasibility of studying the effects of treatments upon reading interests increases. What happens, for instance, when a teacher presents intensive schema-building and imagery building activities in an attempt to increase interest in a hitherto unpopular genre, such as historical fiction? The outcome, as Quiocho (1984) has shown, may run counter to prediction. On the other hand, the apparent interest-raising effects of read-aloud tutoring (O. Anderson, 1984), interactive book club sessions to encourage the reading of Newbery Medal selections (Pileri, 1981), and systematically introducing sex-fair reading materials (Scott, 1986) are at least partially supported. The effects of a computer program to match interests with "just the right book" (Cunningham, 1981) can be studied. Burgess

(1985) speculated that if children were provided book reviews written specifically for them, their ability to select materials to match their interests would be vastly increased; such a possibility needs trying and evaluating. But in all cases, effects upon interests and assignment of causality to treatment conditions will require closer scrutiny and insight into complex events than seems apparent in much reading-interest research of the past.

The importance of the reading-interest construct seems fully established. Its centrality in promoting voluntary or free reading (Morrow, 1987, Fielding, Wilson, & Anderson, 1984), reading instruction (Anderson, Scott, Hiebert, & Wilkinson, 1985), and assessment (Asher, 1980) is recognized. For a time there was speculation that prior knowledge rather than interest in and of itself accounts for increased performance on high interest materials, compared with performance on materials of less interest to the reader. Asher (1980), Anderson et al. (1985), and Baldwin, Peleg-Bruckner, & McClintoch (1985) each examined the question in a different way. For example, Asher extrinsically raised interest in hitherto uninteresting selections but did not provide "prior knowledge" in order to discover whether heightened interest alone increased comprehension; Baldwin weighted students' prior knowledge and level of interest, then did analysis of variance on comprehension to determine the weighting of each factor. The conclusion is that interest is an "autonomous" factor, with generally low correlation with prior knowledge.

So far, so good; the construct has been established. But it is not easily understood. A notable outside view provided by a developmental psychologist is this: "Research on children's interests has been empirically driven, not theoretically driven. It has been more like market research than scientific research. A worthwhile challenge would be to propose a theoretically based program of work into children's interests. This need not reduce its practical impact, but should focus research efforts more sharply, perhaps even more usefully" (Butterfield, 1989).

Given such a theory, we may find that we have underestimated the valence of the interest construct, perhaps through neglect, narrowness of definition, or inadequate assessment of its causes and effects. It is a crucial construct for further study.

References

Abrahamson, R. F. (1979). Children's favorite picture storybooks: An analysis of structure and reading preferences. (ERIC Documents Reproduction Service No. ED 174 977)

Abrahamson, R. F. (1980, November). An analysis of children's favorite picture storybooks. *The Reading Teacher, 34,* 167–170.

Abrahamson, R. F., & Shannon, P. (1983, October). A plot structure analysis of favorite picture books. *Reading Teacher, 37,* 44–48.

Anderson, G., Higgins, D., & Wurster, S. R. (1985). Differences in the free-reading books selected by high, average, and low achievers. *The Reading Teacher, 39,* 326–330.

Anderson, O. S. (1984, Fall). Read aloud tutoring: A program to enhance reading interests. *Reading Horizons, 24,* 14–17.

Anderson, R. C., Scott, J. A., Hiebert, E. H., & Wilkinson, I. A. G. (Eds.). (1985). *Becoming a nation of readers: The report of the Commission on Reading.* Washington, D.C.: The National Institute of Education.

Anderson, R. C., Shirey, L. L., Wilson, P. T., & Fielding, L. G. (1987). Interestingness of children's reading materials. In R. E. Snow & M. J. Farr, (Eds.). *Aptitude, learning, and instruction, 3,* Cognative and Affective Process Analyses, pp. 287–299.

Apseloff, M. F. (1985). New trends in children's books from Europe and Japan. *School Library Journal, 32,* 30–32.

Asher, S. R. (1980). Topic interest and children's reading comprehension. *Theoretical issues in reading comprehension.* In R. J. Spiro, B. C. Bruce, & W. F. Brewer (Eds.). Hillsdale, NJ: Lawrence Erlbaum, 525–532.

Ashley, L. F. (1972). *Children's reading in the 1970's.* Toronto: McClelland and Stewart.

Baldwin, R. S., Peleg-Bruckner, Z., & McClintock, A. H. (1985). Effects of topic interest and prior knowledge on reading comprehension. *Reading Research Quarterly, 20,* 497–504.

Beta Upsilon Chapter, Pi Lambda Theta. (1974). Children's reading interests classified by age level. *Reading Teacher, 27,* 694–700.

Bundy, B. A. (1983). The development of a survey to ascertain the reading preferences of fourth, fifth and sixth graders. Dissertation Abstracts International *44,* 68A, University Microfilms No. DA 8312392.

Burgess, S. A. (1985, January). Reading but not literate: The ChildRead Survey. *School Library Journal, 31,* 27–30.

Butterfield, E. C. (1989). Personal communication.

Byers, L. (1964). Pupils Interests in the Content of Primary Reading Texts. *The Reading Teacher, 17,* 227–233.

Carlsen, G. R. (1967). *Books and the teen-age reader.* New York: Harper & Row.

Carter, B. & Harris, K. (1982, October). What junior high students like in books. *Journal of Reading, 26,* 42–46.

Carter, S. M. (1976). Interpreting interests and reading interests of pupils in grades one through three. Unpublished Doctoral Dissertation, University of Georgia.

Chiu, Lian-Hwang. (1984, June). Children's attitudes toward reading and reading interests. *Perceptual and Motor Skills, 58,* 960–962.

Coleman, J. H. & Jungeblut, A. (1961, February). Children's likes and dislikes about what they read. *Journal of Educational Research, 54,* 221–228.

Consuelo, Sr. M. (1967). What do first graders like to read? *Catholic School Journal, 67,* 42–43.

Coomer, J. W. & Tessmer, K. M. (1986). 1986 books for young adults poll. *English Journal, 75,* 58–61.

Cullingford, C. (1979). Children and poetry. *English in Education, 13,* 58–61.

Cunningham, P. (1981). Finding "just the right book." *The Reading Teacher, 34,* 720–722.

Curley, A. M. (1929). An analysis of the textbooks used in investigating children's interests and a summary of the findings. In W. S. Gray and R. Munroe (Eds.), *The Reading Interests and Habits of Adults,* pp. 108–110. New York: Macmillan Company.

Dewey, J. (1913). *Interest and effort in education.* New York: Houghton Mifflin.

Dunn, F. W. (1921). Interest factors in primary reading material. *Teachers College Contributions to Education,* No. 113. New York: Bureau of Publications, Teachers College, Columbia University.

Erickson, F. (1984). School literacy, reasoning, and civility: An anthropologist's perspective. *Review of Educational Research, 54,* 525–546.

Fielding, L. G., Wilson, P. T., & Anderson, R. C. (1984). A new focus on free reading: Role of trade books in reading instruction. *In T. E. Raphael and R. E. Reynolds (Eds.). The contexts of school-based literacy.* New York: Random House.

Fisher, C. J. & Natarella, M. A. (1982). Young children's preferences in poetry: A national survey of first, second, and third graders. *Research in the Teaching of English, 16,* 339–354.

Ford, R. C. & Koplyay, J. (1968). Children's story preferences. *The Reading Teacher, 22,* 232–237.

Gallo, D. R. (1983). Students' reading interests—A report of a Connecticut Survey. ERIC Documents Reproduction Service No. ED 232 143.

Gates, A. I. (1930). *Interest and ability in reading.* New York: Macmillan.

Getzels, J. W. (1966). The problem of interests: A reconsideration. In H. A. Robinson (Ed.), *Reading: Seventy-five years of progress.* Supplementary Educational Monographs, *96,* pp. 97–106. Chicago: University of Chicago Press.

Goodhope, Jeanie. (1982). Into the eighties: BAYA's fourth interest survey." *School Library Journal, 29,* 33.

Graham, S. A. (1986). Assessing reading preferences: A new approach. *New England Reading Association Journal, 21,* 8–11.

Greenlaw, M. J. & Wielan, O. P. (1979). Reading interests revisited. *Language Arts, 56,* 432–433.

Hansson, G. (1973). Some types of research on response to literature. *Research in the Teaching of English, 7,* 260–284.

Hawkins, S. (1983). Reading interests of gifted children. *Reading Horizons, 24,* 18–22.

Heath, S. B. (1983). *Ways with words: Language, life, and work in communities and classrooms.* Cambridge: Cambridge University Press.

Hickman, J. (1985). Looking at response to literature. *Observing the language learner,* pp. 111–119. In A. J. and M. T. Smith-Burke (Eds.). International Reading Association/National Council for the Teachers of English.

Hickman, J. (1979). *Response to literature in a school environment, Grades K–5.* Unpublished Doctoral Dissertation, The Ohio State University.

Higgins, D. & Elliott, D. (1982). Shadowing kids in the library: Observational study of the free reading behavior and book selection process of lower achieving fourth grade students. *Arizona Reading Journal, 21,* 5–7.

Hill, S. (1984). What are children reading? *Australia Journal of Reading, 7,* 196–199.

Huber, Miriam. (1928). *The influence of intelligence upon children's reading interests.* New York: Bureau of Publications, Teachers College, Columbia University.

Huber, M., Bruner, H. B., & Curry, C. M. (1927). *Children's interests in poetry.* Chicago: Rand McNally.

Huus, H. (1979). A new look at children's interests. In J. E. Shapiro (Ed.). *Using literature and poetry affectively.* International Reading Association, 37–45.

Ingham, Jennie. (1982). Middle school children's responses to E. Blyton in "The Bradford Book Flood Experience." *Journal of Research in Reading, 5,* 43–56.

Ingham, R. O. (1980). The poetry preferences of fourth and fifth grade students in a suburban setting in 1980. University of Houston, Dissertation Abstracts International, 1981, *42,* 984A, No. 8112331.

Itzkowitz, S. G. (1982). Reading interests of first grade students and basal story content. *The Reading Instruction Journal, 26,* 18–19.

Jackson, G. B. (1980). Methods for integrative reviews. *Review of Educational Research, 50,* 438–460.

Joels, R. W. & Anderson, B. (1983). Reliability of reading interest assessment: An applied study. *Reading Horizons, 23,* 230–234.

Johnson, D. M., Peer, G. R., & Baldwin, R. S. (1984). Protagonists preference among juvenile and adolescent readers. *Journal of Educational Research, 77,* 147–50.

Jordon, A. M. (1921). *Children's interests in reading.* New York: Bureau of Publications, Teachers College, Columbia University.

Jose, P. E. & Brewer, S. F. (1984). Development of story liking: Character identification, suspense, and outcome resolution. *Developmental Psychology, 20,* 911–924.

King, E. (1967). Critical appraisal of research on children's reading interests. *Canadian Education and Research Digest, 7–8,* 312–326.

Kirsch, D. (1975). From athletes to zebras–Young children want to read about them. *Elementary English, 52,* 73–78.

Kirsch, D., Pehrsson, R., & Robinson, H. A. (1976). Expressed reading interests of young children: An international study, In J. E. Merritt (Ed.) *New Horizons in Reading.* Newark, Delaware: International Reading Association, pp. 45–56.

Klein, H. A. (1968). Interest and comprehension in sex-typed materials. Doctoral Dissertation at Syracuse University.

Kutiper, K. S. (1985). A survey of the adolescent poetry preferences of seventh, eighth, and ninth graders. Dissertation Abstracts International 47, 02A, No. 86-07, 020.

Landy, S. (1977). Why Johnny can read ... but doesn't. *Canadian Library Journal, 34,* 379–387.

Lazar, M. (1937). *Reading Interests, Activities, and Opportunities of Bright, Average, and Dull Children.* New York: Bureau of Publications, Teachers College, Columbia University.

Leafe, B. (1961). A survey of reading interests and habits of high school students in the Sacramento area, pp. 258–260. In H. A. Bammen, U. Hogan, and C. E. Greene (Eds.). *Reading Instruction in the Secondary School.* New York: David McKay Company.

Lehtovaaro, A. & Saarinen, P. (1964). *School-age reading interests: A methodological approach.* Helsinki, Finland: Suomalainen Tiedeakatemia.

Leibowicz, J. (1983). Children's reading interests. *The Reading Teacher, 37,* 184–187.

Lynch-Brown, C. (1977). Procedures for determining children's book choices: Comparison and criticism. *Reading Horizons, 17,* 243–50.

Mackintosh, H. K. (1924). A study of children's choices in poetry. *The Elementary English Review, 1,* 85–89.

Malchow, E. C. (1937). Reading interests of junior high school pupils. *School Review, 45,* 175–185.

Marcus, G. & Fischer, M. (1986). *Anthropology as Cultural Critique.* Chicago, IL: University of Chicago Press.

McBroom, G. (1981). Research: Our defense begins here. *English Journal, 70,* 75–77.

McKenna, M. (1986). Reading interests of remedial secondary school students. *Journal of Reading, 29,* 346–351.

McNamara, S. G. (1984). Children respond to satire in picture books. *Reading Improvement, 21,* 303–323.

Meckel, H. C. (1963). Research on teaching composition and literature. In N. Gage, (Ed.), *Handbook of Research on Teaching,* pp. 966–1006. Chicago, IL: Rand, McNally.

Mendoza, A. (1983). Elementary school children's preference in literature. *Childhood Education, 59,* 193–197.

Monson, D. L. (1968). Children's test responses to seven humorous stories. *Elementary School Journal, 68,* 334–339.

Morrow, L. M. (1987). Field-based research on voluntary reading: A process for teachers' learning and change. *The Reading Teacher, 39,* 331–337.

Munn, N. (1986). Choosing books that appeal to children. *Louisiana Library Association, 49,* 79–81.

Nelson, R. C. (1966). Children's poetry preferences. *Elementary English, 43,* 247–251.

Norvell, G. W. (1950). *The reading interests of young people.* Boston: Heath.

Norvell, G. W. (1958). *What boys and girls like to read.* Morristown, New Jersey: Silver Burdett.

Peltola, B. J. (1965). A study of the indicated literary choices and measured literary knowledge of fourth and sixth grade boys and girls. Doctoral Dissertation at the University of Minnesota.

Pileri, I. M. (1981). Newbery medal books are alive and well at Court Street School. *School Library Journal, 27,* 93–95.

Purves, A. C. & Beach, R. (1972). Literature and the reader: Research in response to literature, reading interests, and the teaching of literature. National Council of Teachers of English.

Quiocho, A. M. L. L. (1984). *The effects of schema development strategies on fifth-sixth graders' comprehension of responses to, and interest in historical fiction: A classroom study.* Unpublished doctoral dissertation at the University of Washington.

Roberts, G. Z. (1987). Listen, learn, enjoy: Cassettes for all uses. *School Library Journal, 33,* 34–37.

Roser, N. & Frith, M. (Eds.) (1983). *Children's choices: Teaching with books children like.* Newark, Delaware: International Reading Association.

Ross, C. A. (1978). A comparative study of the responses made by grade 11 Vancouver students to Canadian and New Zealand poems. *Research in the Teaching of English, 12,* 297–306.

Row, B. H. (1968). Reading interests of elementary school pupils in selected schools in Muscogee County, Georgia. Doctoral Dissertation at Auburn University.

Schofer, G. (1981). Reading preferences of British and American elementary children. *Reading Improvement, 18,* 127–131.

Scott, K. P. (1986). Effects of sex-fair reading materials on pupils' attitudes, comprehension, and interest. *American Educational Research Journal, 23,* 105–116.

Sebesta, S. (1980). What do young people think about the literature they read? *Reading Newsletter, 8,* 1–2.

Shore, R. B. (1968). Perceived influence of peers, parents, and teachers on fifth and ninth graders' preferences of reading material. Dissertation Abstracts International 47, 05A, No. 86-16, 829.

Shores, J. H. (1954, December). Reading interests and informational needs of children in grades four to eight. *Elementary English, 31,* 493–500.

Sikiotis, N. (1981, April). Reading habits and preferences of secondary-school pupils in Greece. *English Language Teaching Journal, 35,* 300–306.

Smith, M. L. & Eno, I. V. (1961, May). What do they really want to read? *English Journal, 50,* 343–345.

Smith, N. B. (1926, February). An investigation in children's interests in different types of stories. *Detroit Educational Bulletin, 9,* 3–4.

Spache, G. D. (1963). *Toward better reading.* Champaign, Illinois: Garrard.

Squire, J. R. (1969). English literature. In R. Ebel, (Ed.) *Encyclopedia of Educational Research,* (4th ed.).

Strang, R. E. (1946). Reading interests. *English Journal, 35,* 477–482.

Summers, E. G. & Lukevich, A. (1983). Reading preferences of intermediate-grade children in relation to sex, community, and maturation (grade-level): A Canadian perspective. *Reading Research Quarterly, 18,* 347–360.

Terman, L. M. & Lima, M. (1925/1926). *Children's reading: A guide for parents and teachers.* New York: Appleton.

Terry, A. (1974). Children's poetry preferences: A national survey of upper elementary grades. Urbana, Illinois: NCTE Research Report, No. 16.

Thorndike, R. L. (1941). *A comparative study of children's reading interests.* New York: Bureau of Publications, Teachers College, Columbia University.

Tokogi, K. (1980). Interests in picture books of Japanese five-year-olds. *Reading Teacher, 33,* 442–444.

Weintraub, S. (1969). Children's reading interests. *The Reading Teacher, 22,* 655–659.

Wells, R. E. (1934). A study of tastes in humorous literature among pupils of junior and senior high schools. *Journal of Educational Research, 28,* 81–91.

Wendelin, K. H. & Zinck, R. A. (1983). How students make book choices. *Reading Horizon, 23,* 84–88.

White, S. F. (1973). A study of the relationship between racial illustrations accompanying stories in basal readers and children's preferences for these stories. Dissertation Abstracts International, 34, 77A.

Wilson, R. J. (1985). Children's classics: A reading preference study of fifth and sixth graders. Dissertation Abstracts International 47, 02A, No. 86-09,031.

Wissler, C. (1898). Interests of children in reading in the elementary school. *Pedagogical Seminary, 5,* 523–540.

Witty, P., Coomer, A., & McBean, D. (1946). Children's choices of favorite books: A study conducted in ten elementary schools. *Journal of Educational Psychology, 37,* 266–278.

Wolfson, B. J., Manning, G., & Manning, M. (1984). Revisiting what children say their reading interests are. *Reading World, 24,* 4–10.

Yoder, J. M. (1978). The relative importance of four narrative factors in the reading interests of male and female adolescents in grades ten through twelve. Dissertation Abstracts International, 39, 219A.

Zais, R. S. (1969). A scale to measure sophistication of reading interests. *Journal of Reading, 12,* 273–276.

32D. THE SCHOOL SUBJECT LITERATURE
Alan C. Purves

The school subject literature has been variously defined over the past hundred years or more, but through those definitions there have remained certain constants (Applebee, 1974; Burton, 1964; Purves, 1971, 1975; Squire & Applebee, 1968). Those writers have suggested that the emphasis of the subject may stray within certain bounds, but that the bounds themselves are impervious to change. The arguments about the curriculum are arguments of emphasis, and although they may have strong effects on student learning, they generally exist within a framework of content and behavior. That is to say, the literature curriculum consists of literary texts and information surrounding those texts, on the one hand, and various acts related to reading the texts, talking about the reading, and writing about the reading. What texts, what information, what focus in the reading, what sort of talk, and what sort of writing, form the nub of the various arguments. The focus of this discussion will be on the secondary school curriculum; I realize only too well the importance of literature in the elementary school and have long been an advocate. The issues surrounding literature and the language arts and initial reading instruction would lead to a totally different approach to the topic. In this chapter, I want to focus on literature as a school subject.

The content of literature instruction is usually limited to four basic groups of items: literary works, background information, literary terminology and theory, and cultural information. Some curricula have made a point of introducing a fifth group, the responses of the students themselves (Cooper & Purves, 1973; see also Tompkins, 1980); but others have argued that this introduction is tantamount to a reinterpretation of the work as content, since all that can be known is the work as it is perceived and responded to (Fish, 1980; Rosenblatt, 1978). In terms of behavior, the foci of the curriculum range from recognition and recall through interpretation and evaluation to the categories of preference and value.

The shifts of emphasis within these boundaries depend upon the purposes of the curriculum-makers and their particular philosophic penchants. In his review of European curricula, Van de Ven (1987) has shown how the various influences of nationalism, scientism, pragmatism, and moralism have exerted themselves on the literature curriculum, and these influences have been approximately simultaneous across national boundaries. His review suggests striking parallels to that of Applebee's (1974) depiction of the United States curriculum, and to the analysis of international curricula by Purves (1973, 1975).

All of these reviews suggest that the subject literature is seen through one of three main sets of lenses. One sees it primarily as a body of knowledge to be acquired; the second sees it as the vehicle for training in the skills of analysis and interpretation, and the third sees it as the vehicle for social and moral development. Many curriculum makers have sought to combine these three approaches in various ways, and many actual curricula represent pragmatic choices to reconcile the different objectives. The three basic approaches, however, clearly have implications for the choice of content and for the relative emphasis on specific behavior (Purves, 1971). The first and third approaches suggest that a curriculum planner must attend to the selection from the canon, either focusing on the author or on the ostensible moral and social content of the text. Both approaches suggest that the major behaviors are those of knowledge and preference, rather than analysis and interpretation. Both also can be used by political conservatives or liberals, as witness the debate on "cultural literacy," which shall be the primary focus of the rest of this article, because it raises sharply the various positions concerning texts and activities surrounding texts, and because, more than any other phenomenon, it has served to turn the attention of the profession away from language and composition towards the neglected field of literature.

The ideas of the second approach, which can be seen in some aspects of a "new critical," "deconstructive," "Marxist," or "reader response" approach to literature, to name but a few, or in the curricula that have literature subserve something called "generic critical thinking skills," persist in some of the curricula and testing programs, but they do not serve to focus the debate on the subject literature. The argument that it matters little what the text is as long as one focuses on skills has generally been dismissed; increasingly people have come to see that the choice of text is the crux of the curricular issue in literature education.

CULTURAL LITERACY

Although cultural literacy came into the news, thanks to the article and book by E. D. Hirsch, Jr. (1983, 1987) and the measure of cultural knowledge in The National Assessment initiated by Diane Ravitch and Chester Finn, Jr. (1987), the idea is far from new. The call for a limited curriculum goes back to the work of Eliot and Erskine in the early twentieth century, the Lynch and Evans (1963) report on secondary literature in the late 1950s, and, more recently to Mortimer Adler's (1982) Paideia proposal. The concept of "culture" goes back at least as far as Vico and Herder, and may best be defined by Edward Said (1983) as all that an individual possesses and that possesses an individual. As he writes:

culture is used to designate not merely something to which one belongs but something that one possesses, and along with that proprietary process, culture also designates a boundary by which the concepts of what is extrinsic or intrinsic to the culture comes into forceful play (pp. 8–9).

Anthropologists tend to see culture somewhat differently from literary people, but this root definition of possession and being possessed seems to apply both to those societies that operate through what might be called natural filiation (a system of intergenerational and familial relationships), and those that operate through affiliation to some arbitrarily instituted set of relationships. Current "American" culture is a culture of affiliation, whether it be the culture of Hawthorne and Harriet Beecher Stowe, the culture of African American Studies, the culture of feminism, or the culture of punk.

Any culture serves to isolate its members from other cultures and any culture is elitist in some senses, as Said points out:

What is more important in culture is that it is a system of values saturating downward almost everything within its purview; yet paradoxically culture dominates from above without at the same time being available to everything and everyone that it dominates (1983, p. 9).

Cultures are exclusionary by definition; people who have a culture see others as outside or beneath them; and certainly very few people transcend cultures or are full members of more than one culture, although they may be members of several subcultures, such as the subculture of reader-response researchers in the United States, which has its body of shared knowledge, its sets of allegiances to I. A. Richards, Louise Rosenblatt, and James Squire, and its tendency to exclude those who, even though very well educated in other respects, fail to share certain knowledge and beliefs. The members of this subculture may also be members of such other subcultures as that of mycologists, joggers, or film aficionados as well as of the broader culture of literate Americans.

To be a member of a culture, one must possess a fair amount of knowledge, some of it tacit, concerning the culture: its rules, rituals, mores, heroes, gods, and demigods. This knowledge lies at the heart of cultural literacy, and the knowledge is brought into play when people read and respond to a piece of literature that comes from the same culture. It is such knowledge that, in fact, enables them to read that literature. By knowledge one must include semantic knowledge, knowledge of text structures and models, and pragmatic knowledge or knowledge as to how to act before, during, and after reading a particular text in a given situation (Purves, 1987). It is these kinds of knowledge that are brought into play when we read and write as social beings. The lack of such knowledge keeps us outside, as witness the problems of visitors to our culture who often suffer trifling embarrassments or serious misunderstandings.

CULTURE AND CURRICULAR GOALS

Kádár-Fülop (1988) has written that there are three major functions of the language curriculum in school. Basing her argument on a survey of curriculum goals in fifteen countries, she finds that these three functions accord with the earlier definitions of language functions proposed by Weinreich (1963). The first of these functions is the promotion of cultural communication so as to enable the individual to communicate with a wider circle than the home, the peers, or the village. Such a function clearly calls for the individual to learn the cultural norms of semantics, morphology, syntax, text structures, and pragmatics and some of the common metaphors and allusions particularly to folklore and legend as well as procedural routines so as to operate within those norms and be understood.

The second function is the promotion of cultural loyalty or the acceptance and valuing of those norms and the inculcation of a desire to have them remain. A culturally loyal literate would have certain expectations about how texts are to be written or to be read as well as what they should look like, and would expect others in the culture to follow those same norms. A culturally literate American would expect to hear nothing but praise for Mark Twain and is offended when some call for the banning of *Huckleberry Finn*.

The third function of literacy education may be the development of individuality. Once one has learned to communicate within the culture and developed a loyalty to it, then one is able to become independent of it. Before then, independence of those norms and values is seen as naive, illiterate, or childish. For example, teachers of English in the United States will accept this statement in a student's composition on *The Red Pony*. "When I think of Jody's father I want to hit him for being so shitty," on two conditions. The first is that that the student has assured them of full awareness of the rules of critical detachment. The second is that the student acknowledges that such a statement is aberrant in a composition. As Lev Vygotsky wrote (1956): "In reality a child's thought progresses from the social to the individual not from the individual to the socialized." This view is specifically exemplfied with respect to language learning by A. K. Markova (1979), who explicitly sets forward a curriculum in which social norms predominate, particularly in the upper elementary and lower secondary schools.

When writers such as Hirsch speak of cultural literacy they are clearly echoing Eliot, Adler and others and advocating the first two goals set forth by Kádár Fülop; they restrict the sense of the term to literacy in a particular culture, such as F. R. Leavis's "Great Tradition" or that aspect of general education which is defined as "the humanities" or "American classics." Hirsch and other advocates of cultural literacy refer to a definite body of knowledge and suggest that specific titles are necessary. It is this common knowledge that enables readers to read certain kinds of texts—notably texts that are shared by a group that one might define as "highly literate Americans." These would be people, for example, who can read *The New York Times* with understanding and can also read journals and books such as *The Atlantic Monthly* or Katherine Paterson's *Jacob Have I Loved*.

There are two versions of the argument for this sort of cultural literacy. The first is the argument that supported the Chicago Great Books Program, Harvard's General Education proposal, and Columbia's Humanities program that such literacy brings together a disparate immigrant population and helps the melting pot do its job (Bell, 1966). Such proposals bore with them the arguments of people like Matthew Arnold, F. R. Leavis, and T. S. Eliot that a common culture or the Judeo-Christian heritage forged society into unity through affiliation. It does so not without cost; again to cite the comments of Edward Said:

When our students are taught such things as 'the humanities' they are almost always taught that these classic texts embody, express, represent what is best in our, that is, the only, tradition. Moreover, they are taught that such fields as the humanities and such subfields as "literature" exist in a relatively neutral political element, that they are to be appreciated and venerated, that they define the limits of what is acceptable, appropriate, and legitimate as far as culture is concerned (1983, p. 21).

Other critics such as Eagleton and Tompkins suggest that thanks to Matthew Arnold, literature came to form a secular religion and the study of literature came to parallel seminary training. To a great extent, this is the argument made by such writers as Randall Jarrell in the 1950s and by William Bennett in the controversial report, *To Reclaim A Legacy* (1983) as well as in his attacks on any attempt to broaden the canon.

A second strand of the argument is partly that of Hirsch (1987) and more clearly that of Ravitch and Finn (1987). This argument is a pragmatic political argument that a mobile school population needs stability for common communication and the schools can best provide this stability through the texts chosen. The literature curriculum has this stability only in the eleventh grade where American literature is taught. The argument has raised a number of political responses (Simonson & Walker, 1988). The political issue, as Hirsch points out, is who is to select the unifying texts, an issue to which this paper will return.

At this point, there exists another political question: how in the history of our educational system did the idea of a cultural heritage come to disappear and why should such writers as Jarrell, Bennett, Finn and Ravitch, and Hirsch have come to decry the lack of a cultural center? There were a number of groups that began to coalesce over the middle third of the century to drive literature and the notion of cultural literacy out of the curriculum. These groups existed not just in the United States, but in most of the European nations as well (Ball, 1984). The first is the group that advocated comprehensive secondary schools, the second is the linguists, the third is the functionalists, and the fourth is the literature teachers themselves. The sources for these arguments are many and diverse, but they constitute much of the theme of such documents as those of the Dartmouth Seminar, the writing surrounding the student-centered curriculum of James Moffett, the various articles and editorial stands in *The English Journal* for the past twenty years, and such books as the 1973 edition of *How Porcupines Make Love* (Purves, 1973a). These forces had the curious additional side-effect of drawing the attention of researchers, curriculum makers, and teacher trainers away from literature towards language and composition.

The arguments of these groups against teaching a cultural heritage with a single canon can be enumerated as follows:

1. Given a comprehensive secondary school system (or initial tertiary system), more diverse groups are now passing through the system and we must attend to the cultural needs of these groups. The current canon does not address these minority groups and it certainly does not address the concerns of women. Coupled with this claim that the world is multi-cultural and students need to learn a smattering about all cultures. Perhaps it is simpler to drop the heritage strand from the curriculum.

2. A mother-tongue education should be dominated by language study and the appropriate teaching of the uses of language, whether one adopts a skills approach or whether one adopts an approach that looks at the personal growth of the individual student; thus there is no time for literature as such.

3. A mother-tongue education should meet the functional needs of the students and the work-place; there is little room in life for the cultural heritage.

4. Many of the works in the canon are simply too difficult for the new students and beyond their range of experience; they are appropriate for people of greater and broader experience of life. Rather than bowdlerize them or present them in film, we should turn to the kinds of works that students can read, particularly adolescent and popular fiction. The curriculum in literature should echo Henry Ford's "History is bunk," and turn to relevance as the only criterion for text selection (Purves, 1973a).

It seems that those who argue for cultural literacy using the argument of the unification of a diverse nation through cultural literacy have not addressed these counterarguments, some of which are palpably specious. Hirsch does argue for the basic democratic nature of his version of cultural literacy, but he does not counter the attack. The argument is not *whether* cultural literacy, for all literature curricula imply a body of works that constitute a de facto canon and thus serve to acculturate youth as does television and other nonschool phenomena; the argument is *what* should serve to define the culture or cultures of our society.

CULTURAL LITERACY AND READING

One should notice, however, that Hirsch also sets forth a subtler argument, one devolving from the study of literature as a subject, particularly that of such structuralists as Northrop Frye. Hirsch bolsters this view with current research in reading, which has demonstrated that prior knowledge is a key factor in reading comprehension. Most of that research has looked at substantive knowledge of the material in the text, such as knowledge about automobiles with reference to a text concerning automobiles. It has not dealt with the more literary or metaphorical schemata. This argument begins with the assertion that texts within a culture, particularly literary texts, build upon each other, so that contemporary texts employ a complex web of allusion or metaphor building upon previous texts. Such metaphors control how writers think about their material, and writers trade on the cumulative nature of literary texts as well as commentaries upon texts. Katherine Paterson's novel, *Jacob Have I Loved,* alludes to the Biblical story of Jacob and Esau, as she points out directly by quotation. But she also relies on the reader's knowing something of the whole story of Jacob and Esau and the foundation of the tribes of Israel. The use of allusion was one of the bases of the "Nebraska Curriculum" of the 1960s (Olson, 1977). Many other contemporary novels, poems, and play, not to mention cartoons and comic strips build upon other works in even more subtle ways—works such as Joyce's *Ulysses* serve as primary examples.

But there are other examples as well. A typical piece in *The New York Times* reads:

Pandora Shamed

Thirteen hundred years ago in Japan, three slender documents—letters? shopping lists? birth certificates?—were placed in a thin box which was then wrapped in brocade.

Over the centuries the box was put in three larger boxes each one of which was wrapped in cloth.

In 1606 the letter box was placed in yet another box and adorned with a covering note. Don't open this, it read, unless you don't mind being tossed out of the Horyuji, a temple in Nara containing the country's oldest Buddhist compound. Eighty-five years later the fourth box was put into a fifth, and the warning was repeated.

This week art scholars who had found the package on the temple grounds opened the fifth, fourth, third, second and first boxes. But did they open the final box? Not on your life. Hadn't the letters said that was a no-no? Instead they X-rayed it, which is how the world knows that it holds three documents.

That, then, is all the world will ever know about that box—and all it needs to know. In putting Pandora to shame, the Japanese have turned what may be three ordinary missives into three extraordinary mysteries.

The New York Times 7 November 1985, p. 25.

Aside from the fact that the article deals with a somewhat exotic topic, it is unexceptional to many readers. Yet it uses an allusion to Pandora, and fails to provide any context to help the reader determine who Pandora is and why this action of Japanese scholars might put her (or possibly him or it) to shame. In articles on various topics, the pages of *The New York Times* frequently contain this sort of allusion to Greek and Old Testament mythology. Clearly the writers have a set of expectations about their readers, and certainly the set differs from that held by the editors of *People* or *Car and Driver*.

A study that was conducted by Broudy (1982) set out to examine what he refers to as the uses of learning. Using several passages from *The New York Times,* as well as a poem, he asked students in the first year of graduate school to read them and comment upon them as they read. Broudy selected students on the basis of their background, including an artist, a dancer, and a student each in the humanities, in engineering, in law, in commerce, in social sciences, and in the hard sciences. The results clearly showed that some of the respondents had trouble with passages like "Pandora Shamed"; they did not know how to respond to it, and shut themselves off from it, primarily because they did not have the specific piece of information that allowed them to understand the passage. In some cases the allusion was to mythology; in other cases it was to "general knowledge" from science, the arts, or economics or history.

One might draw two conclusions from this study; the first is that writers of all sorts do indeed presume a certain fund of knowledge on the part of their prospective readers, and that writers for a "general circulation" and perhaps "middlebrow" publication like *The New York Times* presume a level of general knowledge similar to that possessed by someone who has had a course in something not unlike an undergraduate program in General Education—say, two semesters each in the humanities, the social sciences, and the natural sciences. That is to say, the editors assume, as does a writer like Hirsch, that their readers are culturally literate to the level of Mortimer Adler's Great Books. Such an assumption may be elitist; it may be the bane of an educational liberal of the Arizona school; it may be seen as opposed to the liberation literacy of a Jonathan Kozol or a Richard Ohmann (both of whom possess exactly that sort of cultural literacy they decry—which makes it easy for them to decry it); but it is simply a fact of the world of media in the 1980s. *The New York Times* assumes a lesser body of knowledge

than did Matthew Arnold or Henry David Thoreau or Joseph Addison or William Shakespeare, but it assumes more than is covered in the curriculum of many elementary and secondary schools in this country.

The second conclusion one might draw from this study goes directly to the heart of this chapter. Texts contain various sorts of allusion, and readers are expected to have sufficient knowledge of the allusion to fill in gaps, just as readers are expected to know the referents of metaphoric language as in a phrase such as "the ship plowed the seas." When readers find they haven't that knowledge, they "stop" reading or responding to the text. This situation leads to a necessary reconsideration of the literature curriculum and particularly its content.

THE USES OF LEARNING

At this point, one might refer again to Broudy's idea of the "uses of learning." He sets forth four uses: replicative, applicative, interpretive, and associative. The replicative and applicative uses are those he finds to be most frequently addressed in schools and colleges: that is, people are to give back what they learn or apply it directly to a new situation. The interpretive use, where the individual at some later point takes what has been learned in order to come to an understanding of a phenomenon that may or may not be directly related to the item learned, can be seen in the ways by which a reader is expected to use knowledge about the legend of Pandora in construing the brief article or the knowledge about Jacob and Esau in construing Paterson's novel. The associative use of learning is seen when something in the new phenomenon elicits an indirect connection with an item previously learned. This sort of learning is displayed in reading and response to literature, when the reader makes a connection between the story of *Hamlet* and that of *Oedipus Rex.* No explicit connection exists, but for the reader steeped in Greek drama, the implicit connections appear present. So too such connections as that between Conrad's *The Heart of Darkness* and Dante's *Inferno,* or many other sets of works as discussed by critical readers.

The dividing line between explicit and implicit connections among texts is not a clear one. Some poets, like Keats, Shelley, or T. S. Eliot use a great deal of overt allusion to various earlier literatures, and in the case of the first two appear to have expected their readers to share the world of allusion, while the last often provided appropriate glosses, something that Ezra Pound did not. A writer like Faulkner tends to be somewhat less explicit in his use of allusion in a story such as "The Bear," and one like Carl Sandburg appears to have virtually no explicit literary allusions, and each reader will infer whatever connections are adduced. Thus, there seems to be a continuum of texts based on their apparent dependency on prior texts and therefore the amount of shared cultural knowledge assumed by the writer. This dimension differs from the dimension of topicality, which distinguishes a writer like Swift, who continually refers to events of his day, from a writer like Emily Bronte, who, if not otherworldly, creates a self-contained world outside of history. Critics such as Hirsch are less concerned with topicality than they are with allusiveness, although he does make extensive reference to Grant and Lee. The reason may be that for a large number of allusive writers in the "Western Culture" the circle of allusion is relatively circumscribed and relatively common, just as it is for writers in other cultures such as that of Japan or Iran.

Another of the findings from the study that Broudy conducted was that the sort of learning that was used interpretively was not *what* but *how*. In most instances, he found that the subjects had learned certain "mannerisms" of reading (for want of a better word), such as one student's immediate distrust of anything that contained metaphor, or another student's manner of reading all literature that derived from the critical theory of Maritain. On subsequent interviews, the readers recalled precisely where they had learned to read certain texts in the ways that they did. Given this particular interpretive use of learning, one might well suspect that analogizing is a mannerism learned in reading certain kinds of texts, particularly literary ones.

To turn to the curricular implications of the Broudy study: the idea of cultural literacy like the idea of bilingualism has both educational and political overtones. Although only the brain-damaged are culturally illiterate in one sense; in the Arnoldian sense, a large proportion of our society is culturally illiterate. It is hard to be against cultural literacy; the problem is how one establishes the boundaries of the culture (Simonson & Walker, 1988). Hirsch would like to have a National Board of Education like the New York State Regents or the examining boards in countries like England and New Zealand. At the same time he realizes that such a board will not come about, and worries lest the National Board be *de facto* The College Entrance Examination Board (Hirsch, 1983, pp. 167–168). Former Secretary of Education William Bennett, at this writing, as well as Lynne Cheney of the National Endowment for the Humanities have sought to influence the canon, either by attacking the addition of minorities, non-western culture or female writers as Bennett has done or by producing summer reading lists as Cheney has done. Whether these efforts have an effect remains to be seen.

THE DETERMINERS OF THE LITERATURE CURRICULUM

From prior observations of the forces that affect the literature curriculum, it would appear that The College Entrance Examination Board and the Federal government are less formidible than are the publishers, not only the text publishers, but those trade or reprint houses that cater to the schools and school libraries. In different ways they seek to create a conon or canons so as to sell their merchandize. One group works at "watering down" the classics with bowdlerized versions. There is a question as to whether these watered-down versions considered appropriate for high-school students or nonreaders can provide the same experience as the original no matter how difficult. There have been some attempts by publishers to make the classics available without watering them down; the most notable example is the series of "comic book" versions of Shakespeare done by distinguished British illustrators and using the uncut Quarto texts without footnotes.

Another group within publishing, abetted by such authors' lobbies as the Children's Book Council and the Adolescent Lit-

erature Assembly, touts the latest trade book and the latest writer and has virtually no interest in any culture but the culture of the present. This group has helped expand the market for the adolescent novel in school classes as well as out of them and has worked to have what was essentially spare-time reading incorporated into the new canon. Even *A Catcher in the Rye* is old hat to the adolescent literature lobby and who would want to read *Tom Sawyer?* Stocking the bookstores and school libraries does not provide sufficient sales, particularly when library budgets have to include computer software. The classroom book budget is a useful source of income.

This group vies with the anthology publishers, often from the text division of the same house. The latter are more than willing to have the older writers in their texts because, being dead, they do not request reprint fees. They are also less controversial than the living writers, and the publishers need to appeal to the large adoption states which attract the most censors. Anthologies are good money-makers particularly if they seldom have authors who receive royalties. Even a cursory glance at the current anthologies leads one to see that there is less contemporary literature and certainly less literature by minorities and women than one or even two decades ago.

THE IDEAL AND REAL CANON

One question that needs to be studied is the nature of the canon or canons that actually exist in our primary and secondary schools. What works are taught to how many students where? What are the most frequently taught texts? We do not know whether there is an adolescent literature canon, an anthology canon, or a Harlequin romance canon in the schools of The United States. The most recent study is a replication by The Center for the Teaching and Learning of Literature (Applebee, 1989) of the study done over 20 years ago by Anderson (1964). Based on a questionnaire sent to several hundred secondary schools, it shows that the most frequently-taught long works have changed little in the past generation. Shakespeare leads the list, and the only woman to make the top ten is Harper Lee. There are no African Americans or other minorities among the most-read authors. This study only includes "full-length works" and does not mention short stories, short plays, or poems. The schools say they are teaching the classics and have not admitted a multicultural and double-gendered culture, but one is unsure whether they have omitted the more popular works such as adolescent or young-adult fiction, because they do not "teach" it, or because this appears more frequently in reading programs. The survey will be followed by a study of anthologies, which should say more about the actual canon. Clearly it is important to match an ideal canon with the actual canon. Any assessment of knowledge of "what should be read" can then be matched to the opportunity of students to have read those texts.

LITERATURE AND KNOWLEDGE

The assessment question raised in conjunction with the idea of cultural literacy forms the final curricular issue. The question is both an epistemological and an empirical one, and may be

TABLE 32D–1. School Literature

Knowledge		Practice		Preference	
Textual	Extra-Textual	Reading	Writing	Aesthetic	Habits
Specific Text	History	Decoding	Retelling	Evaluating	Reading
Cultural allusion	Author	Envisioning	Criticizing single works	Selecting	Criticizing
	Genres	Analyzing		Valuing	
	Styles	Personalizing	Generalizing across works		
	Critical terms	Interpreting			

phrased as "what do you mean by know?" At the same time that Hirsch's essay appeared, the game *Trivial Pursuit* swept the nation. Is the level of cultural literacy to be assessed at the level of trivia? Certainly that sort of knowledge, naming authors and titles, perhaps citing such a character as Scrooge is a popular form of testing of literature, and one that has long been attacked by New Critics as well as reader-response critics. That replicative learning is a starting point cannot be denied, and such learning can be had without the experience of reading the text. A large number of people in this country can tell something about Romeo or Thor without having read the play or the Norse myths. Some items of cultural knowledge have become common nouns like kleenex. It would appear that the interpretative and associative uses of learning require more than recall and recognition. We have already seen that literature uses allusion and builds upon itself at a "deeper" level than simply that of names. *West Side Story* is a complex retelling of *Romeo and Juliet* and requires a knowledge not simply of names, which are irrelevant, but of character relationships, scenes, and images. If one could construct a hierarchy of knowledge, such might be useful, ranging from recognition of name, for example, to identification in a parody, to recognition in a transformation, to thematic recognition. One might then develop a series of measures that would text exactly how culturally literate a group of students might be.

Knowledge of texts, of course, is not the only kind of knowledge that operates in the school subject literature, although it is the most controversial aspect of knowledge. There is clearly knowledge of genres, of styles, or authors and history, and of literary terminology and critical approaches. All of these forms of knowledge constitute the main distinction of the literature as against a reading or writing curriculum.

The domain of school literature is usually seen as one of the language arts, which have often been defined in terms of reading, writing, speaking and listening. Since literature involves texts that people read or write, and since when students read literature they often write about what they have read, literature is often seen as simply a subset of reading and writing, with an occasional nod to speaking and listening. But those who take a serious interest in literature as a school subject are uneasy with this definition. They become more uneasy when they look at the world of tests and see that literature is simply a vehicle for reading comprehension tests or for measures of writing skill or proficiency. There seems to many to be the need for something more. To define the literature curriculum as simply a subset of

reading and writing neglects a number of the acts that go on within the activity of literature education.

Some would define literature as a school subject that has its own body of knowledge. Narrowly defined, the body refers to the names associated with a particular set of texts: authors, characters, plots, and themes. But the body might well be broadened to include such matters as critical terms like metaphor and simile as well as genres, schools or styles of writing, and whole critical approaches.

There is another group that would see literature as something that is not simply read as other kinds of texts are read but is to be read differently. Louise Rosenblatt calls this kind of reading aesthetic and opposes it to the reading that one does with informational texts such as those of social studies and science. From this approach, one sees that a part of literature education is the development of what one might call preferences, which is to say habits of mind in reading and writing. In addition, literature education is supposed to develop something called "taste" or the love of "good literature," so that literature education goes beyond reading and writing in the inculcation of specific sets of preferences and habits of reading and writing about that particular body of texts that is called literature.

We may then conclude that the domain of school literature can be divided into three interrelated aspects: knowledge, practice, and preference. The interrelationships are complex in that one uses knowledge in the various acts that constitute the practice and the preferences, and that the practices and preferences can have their influence on knowledge. At the same time one can separate them for the purposes of testing and curriculum planning. We may schematize the three subdomains as shown in Table 32D–1.

The Center for the Learning and Teaching of Literature study of the current tests of literature available through the anthology series, the proprietary testing companies, and the university entrance groups suggests that, except for the last group (and there only for the Advanced Placement Examination of the College Entrance Examination Board), the tests treat literature as little more than fodder for reading scores. They neglect the aesthetic dimension entirely, and they see cultural literacy as knowledge of particulars and vocabulary in the style of a reading test. Knowledge of the canon is measured as superficial knowledge if at all (Brody, DeMilo, & Purves, 1989). There is relatively little application or interpretation. Only where there are writing measures attached to the objective tests does there seem to be any tapping of generalizing or interpreting and occasionally evaluating.

It appears that the "Cultural Literacy" phenomenon has forced a whole generation of critics and educational researchers and planners to reconsider literature. These people have neglected literature in part because of the dominance of the linguistic and cognitive perspective. The concept of cultural literacy is important and necessary to the reading of and responding to literature, as well as to the political and psychological need for affiliation to both the dominant culture and to the various subcultures. The concept needs to be incorporated as an aspect of the schools' concern with response to literature and the teaching of literature. One form of that concern would be for teachers to look at the ways by which individuals use their knowledge interpretively and associatively. A second form of that concern would be a careful deliberation about the operating literacy canons in America's schools. A third form of that concern would deal with the question of knowledge and its assessment. If teachers and curriculum-makers were to take these three forms of concern with cultural literacy seriously, their efforts might lead to a resurrection of interest in the school subject literature, and the profession of English teaching might at last have something of importance to offer educational policy makers in the classroom and at the state and national levels.

References

Adler, M. (1982). *The paideia proposal*. New York: Macmillan.

Anderson, S. (1964). *From the Grimms to the group*. Princeton, NJ: Educational Testing Service.

Applebee, A. (1974). *Tradition and reform in the teaching of English: A history*. Urbana, IL: National Council of Teachers of English.

Applebee, A. (1989). A study of book-length works taught in high school English courses. Report 1.2. Albany, NY: Center for the Learning and Teaching of Literature.

Ball, S. (1984). Conflict, panic and inertia. Mother tongue teaching in England 1970–1983. In Herrlitz, W., A. Kamer, S. Kroon, H. Peters and J. Sturm eds. *Mother tongue education in Europe: A survey of standard langauge teaching in nine European Countries*. Enschede Netherlands: International Mother Tongue Education Network.

Bell, D. (1966). *The reforming of general education*. New York: Columbia University Press.

Bennett, W. (1983). *To Reclaim a Legacy*. Washington: US Government Printing Office.

Brody, P., DeMilo, C., and Purves, A. C. (1989). The current state of assessment in literature. Albany, NY: Center for the Learning and Teaching of Literature. Report 3.1.

Broudy, H. (1982). Report: On case studies on uses of knowledge. Chicago: Spencer Foundation (ERIC Documents Reproduction Service No. ED 224016).

Burton, D. (1964). *Literature study in the high schools*. New York: Holt, Rinehart and Winston.

Cooper, C. & Purves, A. (1973). *Responding: Guide to evaluation*. Lexington, MA: Ginn and Co.

Fish, S. (1980). *Is there a text in this class? The authority of interpretation communities*. Cambridge, MA: Harvard University Press.

Hirsch, E. D. Jr. (1983). Cultural literacy. *The American Scholar* (Spring 1983), 159–169.

Hirsch, E. D. Jr. (1987). *Cultural literacy*. Boston: Houghton Mifflin.

Kádár-Fülop, J. (1988). Culture, writing, curriculum. In Purves, A. C., (Ed.). *Writing across languages and cultures: Issues in contrastive rhetoric*. pp. 25–50. Newbury Park, CA: Sage.

Lynch, J. J. and Evans, B. (1983). *High-school English Textbooks: A critical examination*. Boston: Little Brown.

Markova, A. K. (1979). *The teaching and mastery of language*. White Plains, NY: M. E. Sharpe.

Olson, D. (1977). From utterance to text: The bias of language in speech and writing. *Harvard Educational Review, 47*, 257–281.

Purves, A. C. (1971). Evaluation of learning in literature. In B. S. Bloom, J. T. Hastings, & G. Madaus (Eds.), *Handbook of formative and summative evaluation of student learning*. New York: McGraw-Hill.

Purves, A. C. (1973a). *How porcupines make love*. Lexington, MA: Xerox College Publishing.

Purves, A. C. (1973b). *Literature education in ten countries: An empirical study. International studies in evaluation*. Stockholm: Almqvist and Wiksell.

Purves, A. C. (1975). Culture and deep structure in the literature curriculum. *Curriculum Theory Network, 2*, 139–150.

Purves, A. C. (1987). Literacy, culture and community. In Wagner, D. A. (Ed.). *The future of literacy in a changing world*. Oxford: Pergamon Press. 216–232.

Ravitch, D. and Finn, C. E. Jr. (1987). *What seventeen-year olds know*. Boston: Houghton Mifflin.

Rosenblatt, L. (1978). *The reader, the text and the poem*. Carbondale, IL: Southern Illinois University Press.

Said, E. (1983). *The world, the text and the critic*. Cambridge, MA: Harvard University Press.

Simonson, R. and Walker, S. (1988). *The Graywolf annual five: Multicultural literacy*. St. Paul, MN: Graywolf Press.

Squire, J. R. and Applebee, R. (1968). *High-school English instruction today*. New York: Appleton-Century Crafts.

Tompkins, J. ed. (1980). *Reader response criticism: From formalism to post-structuralism*. Baltimore, MD: Johns Hopkins University Press.

Van de Ven, P. H. (1987). Some histories of mother tongue teaching in western Europe. *Mother Tongue Education Bulletin, 2*, 40–49.

Vygotsky, L. S. (1956). *Izbrannye psikhologicheskie isseldovaniia*. Moscow: RSFR Academy of Pedagogical Sciences.

Weinreich, U. (1963). *Languages in contact: Findings and problems*. The Hague: Mouton.

32E. PROMOTING VOLUNTARY READING

Lesley Mandel Morrow

"We must reignite our romance with the written word."

(Spielberg, 1987)

Because a thoroughly democratic society depends on the cultivation and practice of literacy, the promotion of voluntary reading among children should rank high as a goal of both parents and teachers. Both at home and in school, voluntary reading should be cultivated as a habit of personal choice beginning in a child's very earliest years. Through voluntary reading children learn to associate reading with pleasure, especially while they are very young. If youngsters enjoy looking at books, then eventually reading them, they will tend to read more, which in turn can lead to improved reading ability. Voluntary or recreational reading must be an integral part of the total developmental reading program.

In this chapter the terms *voluntary reading* and *recreational reading* are used to connote children's own decisions to spend portions of their time reading or participating in reading-related activities, including listening to stories and looking at books. The practice includes voluntary reading of newspapers, magazines, pamphlets, and brochures, of listening to taped stories, and of reading directions and other informational literature.

The problem of illiteracy in the United States is well-documented. According to *A Nation at Risk* (1983), 23 million American adults are functionally illiterate, a number that is reported to be increasing by approximately 2.3 million annually; 40 percent of all 17-year-olds cannot draw inferences from written material: 25 percent of our military recruits cannot read at the ninth grade level.

While these statistics are staggering, they reflect only part of the problem. In a 1984 report to Congress entitled *Books in our Future,* Daniel Boorstin, Librarian of Congress, warned that *aliterates*—individuals who can read but choose not to do so—constitute a threat at least equal to that of *illiterates* in a democratic tradition built on books and reading. The practice or absence of voluntary reading, he wrote, "will determine the extent of self-improvement and enlightenment, the ability to share wisdom and the delights of our civilization, and our capacity for intelligent self-government" (p. iv).

Teaching people to read is certainly the most prevalent goal of American schooling. It is all but impossible to identify a goal more basic or more traditional. It is remarkable, therefore, that so little attention is paid in instructional programs, especially in the early years of schooling, to developing voluntary readers, youngsters who will choose to read widely and often on their own.

History attests to the tremendous impact that common literacy has had on the development of societies and civilization. As early as 1647, American dedication to literacy was established in a belief that ability to read was necessary not only to a well-ordered society, but to the moral welfare of the individual as well. That was the year the General Court of Massachusetts enacted legislation mandating universal reading instruction so . . .

That learning might not be buried in the grave of our fathers in church and commonwealth. . . . It is therefore ordered that every township in this jurisdiction, after the Lord hath increased them to the number of fifty householders, shall then forthwith appoint one within their town to teach all such children as shall resort to him to write and read (Clews, 1899, in Smith, 1970).

Little more than a century later, Thomas Jefferson spelled out three beliefs about literacy and education that remain fundamental in our national ethos. First, democratic functioning depends on every citizen's ability to read. Second, because of that fact, it is the general public's responsibility to support the teaching of reading to all youngsters. Third, reading should be taught during the earliest years of schooling. Among the reasons he cited, "none is more important, none more legitimate, than that of rendering the people safe, as they are the ultimate guardians of their own liberty" (Koch & Peden, 1944).

Nineteenth century America not only accepted those fundamental beliefs, but extended them into everyday practicality. Anyone who was to tame the wilderness, work the soil, and later fuel the factories of industrial society needed certain reading and writing skills to do so. Even in our present age of electronic audio and video communication, the most literate person is generally considered to be also the most civilized and knowledgeable. The implication is pervasive and clear that a democratic, moral, productive society depends on citizens who can and do read.

The purpose of this chapter is to review the professional literature concerning the promotion of voluntary reading and to provide a statement of its significance and a rationale for its greater role in the reading instructional program, including research that describes successful programs in promoting voluntary reading. In the review, the following areas will be addressed:

1. The extent of voluntary reading,
2. benefits associated with voluntary reading,
3. Characteristics of voluntary readers and their homes,
4. A theoretical framework for promoting voluntary reading at school, and
5. Strategies for promoting voluntary reading in school.

THE EXTENT OF VOLUNTARY READING

Unforunately, it is clear that substantial numbers of children and adults read neither for pleasure nor for information. Studies by Morrow and Weinstein (1982), for example, observed that few primary-grade children choose to look at books during free-choice time in school. Greaney (1980) found that fifth-grade students spent only 5.4 percent of their leisure time engaged in reading, and 22 percent did not read at all. Similar studies by Walberg and Tsai (1984), Greaney and Hegarty (1987), Anderson, Wilson and Fielding (1985), found that children did not choose to read very much in their spare time. Whitehead, Capey, Maddren, and Wellings (1977) studied the voluntary reading of 8,000 English children. The investigation revealed a decline in reading as children became older. They found that at age 10, nine percent of the children studied did not read voluntarily; by age 14, that figure rose to 40 percent. A survey of 233,000 sixth graders by the California Department of Education (1980) found that 70 percent almost never read for pleasure. A 1972 Gallup survey revealed that 80 percent of the books read in the United States were read by only 10 percent of the population (Spiegel, 1981); half the adults sampled admitted never having completed a book. An extensive investigation by the Book Industry Study Group (BISG) (1984) indicated that the number of young people under the age of 21 identified as readers dropped from 75 percent in 1976 to 63 percent in 1984.

The BISG hypothesized that the new forms of electronic equipment introduced during those eight years may have diverted the attention of youth from books. The attraction of electronic entertainment could be one reason for the low level of voluntary reading among the young. However, studies that have compared television viewing and leisure reading have not substantiated the hypothesis. Researchers have found inconclusive data. There are apparently both heavy and light readers who watch a substantial amount of televison and heavy and light readers who do not watch much television. These studies also confirm that television does not interfere with the reading of books (Childers & Ross, 1973; La Blonde, 1967; Neuman, 1980; Quissenberry & Klasek, 1976). In a longitudinal survey from 1949 to 1965, Witty (1967) found that even though children increased in the amount of television they viewed, the number of books they read remained the same.

Another factor in the low frequency of voluntary reading may be that most instructional programs in reading are skills-oriented and provide little opportunity for students to read for enjoyment (Lamme, 1976; Spiegel, 1981). The possibility is bolstered somewhat by reports from schools in which recreational reading, or reading for enjoyment, is incorporated as a regular element in instructional programs. Such systematic promotion of pleasurable literary activities seems to enhance enthusiasm and foster positive attitudes among students toward reading (Irving, 1980; Manley & Simon, 1980; Rosler, 1979; Yatvin, 1977).

Despite obvious needs, common assumptions, and documented benefits, it appears that use of literature and systematic development of voluntary reading remain quite limited in early childhood and elementary classrooms. Unfortunately, schools tend to define initial reading instruction almost universally as an array of psychological and linguistic skills and subskills, and teachers schedule and use few literary activities (Hall, 1971; Morrow, 1982). The skill-drill, teach-and-test approach dominates instructional programs throughout the United States to the infrequent use of literary activities and personal immersion in stories and other pupil-selected reading materials.

Schools generally gauge the success of their reading programs not by the personal reading habits of their students, but by "successful" scores on standardized reading tests (Irving, 1980; Spiegel, 1981). General comprehension skills, not application of such skills to personal use and benefit, are commonly considered the ultimate goal of a reading program. Children are taught to read but not to develop the habit of reading. On the occasions when literacy activities are introduced into the classroom, they are considered motivational techniques, supplementary rewards, or classroom extras, rather than keys to the development of voluntary reading. Ironically, schools spend a great deal of time teaching literary skills, then leave little room for children to practice those skills (Holdaway, 1979). It is therefore not surprising that substantial numbers of children choose not to read.

Children's reading habits develop early in life, no later than sixth grade (Bloom, 1964). If schools do not deliberately and thoughtfully attract children to reading during these early years, voluntary reading may never become a life-long habit.

BENEFITS ASSOCIATED WITH VOLUNTARY READING

Some of the studies that found that children do not spend a lot of time involved in voluntary reading conversely revealed strong relationships between the amount of leisure reading and success in reading. The amount of leisure reading and reading achievement are correlated (Connor, 1954; Greaney, 1980). In a recent study by Anderson, Fielding & Wilson (1988), children recorded the number of minutes of their out-of-school reading. The number of minutes correlated positively with reading achievement. For example, children who score at the 90th percentile on a reading test spend five times as many minutes per day reading books as children at the 50th percentile, and more than two hundred times as many minutes per day reading books as the child at the 10th percentile. Children who do a substantial amount of vocabulary reading also demonstrate positive attitudes towards reading (Greaney, 1980; Long & Henderson, 1973; Maxwell, 1977; Whitehead, Capey & Maddren, 1975). Apparently, an element of personal motivation in voluntary reading leads to greater interest and skill development (Irving, 1980). In a study of kindergarten children Morrow (1983) found that those who demonstrated a voluntary interest in books were rated by their teachers as displaying high performance in fine motor control, social and emotional maturity, work habits and general school achievement. They also performed well on a standardized reading-readiness test.

The cultural benefits of reading are taken for granted in every academic institution and in many of America's corporate headquarters. It is commonly recognized that reading enables, develops, or informs technological know-how, intellectual stimulation and growth, leisure, cultural identification, and transfer of information. Since before Jefferson's day, universal literacy has supported and informed our democratic political processes. Our faith in literacy is established firmly in American law through the doctrines of free speech and free press, both in development since before the War for Independence. We recognize that citizens need to read widely and deeply if they are to make informed decisions about self-government. That fact was recognized in Colonial America no less than it is now, in the depth and breadth of analysis, reflection, and perspective on political issues available only through the printed page.

Literacy also supports and informs morality, a fact evident in the central positions of liturgy, discourse, law, and commentary in all major Western religions. It is conversely evident in the attacks on specific books and instructional materials by various doctrinaire or sectarian groups in attempts at censorship within the schools.

One obvious assumption underlies all these benefits—cultural, political, moral, and educational: the well-educated person will choose to read because it is socially, individually, and educationally beneficial to do so. We teach youngsters to read so they can participate fully in a civilized society. For such participation, they must become readers by choice, not by coercion. How else will they or our society realize all the benefits that ability to read brings with it.

The promotion of voluntary reading, then, is appropriate among children from their very earliest years. As educators, we need to study and promote the techniques of developing voluntary readers at least to the same extent as we explore the process of training children to decipher the printed page (Morrow, 1986a).

CHARACTERISTICS OF VOLUNTARY READERS AND THEIR HOMES

Researchers have investigated the characteristics of home environments in which children have demonstrated eary voluntary interest in books and established voluntary reading habits.

According to Himmelweit and Swift (1976) in a study with elementary grade children, and Morrow (1983) in a study of kindergarteners, families of children who show a voluntary interest in books are more likely to be small and parents are likely to hold a college or graduate degree. Greaney and Hegarty (1985) agree that the more formal education parents have, the more positive home support they seem to offer for reading. Hansen (1969) found that a rich literary environment was the most significant contributor to children's voluntary reading behavior. Other researchers have found that socioeconomic status is a factor in voluntary reading (Neuman, 1986), but certainly not the most important. Voluntary readers have been found to come from homes where they were given a certain amount of independence and responsibility. They participated in diverse leisure activities, and, most of all, their parents encouraged reading, which proved to be the most significantly related factor to children's leisure reading behavior.

Many studies also have found that a rich literacy environment at home contributes to children's voluntary interest in literature. Results of many investigations (Clay, 1976; Moon & Wells, 1979; Morrow, 1983; Sakamoto & Kiyoski, 1973) have demonstrated that parents with children who showed an early voluntary interest in books served as reading models for their children, since they read often in their leisure time. They read novels, magazine, newspapers, and work-related materials. Parents with children who were not interested in books tended to read only newspapers and work-related materials. A distinction emerges: newspapers and work-related materials were read by all, but novels and magazines, which are linked more closely with recreation and voluntary choice, were read more often by parents of children who showed an early voluntary interest in books. Other characteristics of homes where children were voluntary readers became evident. There were more books found in these homes and the books were placed in many different rooms, including playrooms, kitchens, and children's bedrooms. Parents of voluntary readers took their children to the library often and read to them daily. They enforced television rules that included amount of TV viewing allowed and selective viewing habits (Whitehead, Capey, & Maddren, 1975).

Some of the same home literacy characteristics appeared in studies of children who demonstrated an early voluntary interest in books and from homes where children learned to read early without direct instruction before coming to school (Briggs & Elkind, 1973; Clark, 1976; Durkin, 1966; Taylor, 1983; Teale, 1984). Such an environment has a large supply of accessible books, plus parents who read to children regularly, who are responsive to their children's questions about books and print, and who read a great deal themselves, thus serving as reading models. These children are in a natural setting that provides the interaction between adult and child that is socially, emotionally, and intellectually conducive to literacy growth (Holdaway, 1979).

Children who are voluntary readers demonstrate distinct characteristics. They tend to be girls who are high achievers in school and particularly successful in reading performance (Greaney, 1980; Long & Henderson, 1973; Whitehead, Capey, & Maddren, 1975). Young children who demonstrate a voluntary interest in books tend to spend their playtime at home writing and drawing with paper and crayons as well as looking at books, whereas children who show a low interest prefer playing outdoors and with toys and trucks. Children who demonstrate an interest in books watch less television daily than those who do not demonstrate an interest in books (Durkin, 1966; Hansen, 1969; Lomax 1976; Morrow, 1983). Most of the research reviewed also indicates that voluntary readers and children with strong interest in books score well on reading tests at school.

In one investigation (Morrow, 1983), however, some children were identified who had low interest in books, but who received mean percentile scores on a reading-readiness test higher than the average of the total high-interest group. Conversely, there were children in the high-interest group who received mean percentile scores on the test similar to the average for the total low-interest group. These findings present an interesting consideration. It has been generally accepted that school achievement and recreational reading are related, but according to the study, skilled readers are not necessarily voluntary readers. Even though a child demonstrates academic ability when tested, if a supportive literary environment is not present at home or in school, voluntary reading habits may not develop. On the other hand, a child exposed to literature at home and in school may develop a strong interest in books in spite of lower academic ability as indicated on scores from standardized tests. Anderson, Fielding & Wilson (1988) found that children who were in classrooms that promoted voluntary reading did more reading at home than children from classrooms where there was little emphasis in this direction.

A THEORETICAL FRAMEWORK FOR PROMOTING VOLUNTARY READING AT SCHOOL

The importance of promoting voluntary reading as an integral part of the reading program is based on the premise that "skills-only" reading instruction does not produce or encourage a literate society whose members read fluently, frequently, and voluntarily. If success in reading is influenced by children's attitudes toward reading, by their association of reading with pleasure, by the opportunity to practice skills through actual reading, and by exposure to a rich literacy environment, then the development of voluntary reading must be a key component of efforts to foster literacy. Such a program integrates a voluntary reading program and regular reading instruction. The program complements direct instruction of skills with equal time for the following components:

1. Regularly scheduled adult-guided literature activities to promote enjoyment;
2. The creation of library centers in the classroom for housing books and related literature materials to be used and read in school and taken home; and
3. Time set aside on a regular basis for recreational reading in school.

This proposed framework for reading instruction is guided by Holdaway's (1979) developmental literacy theory and Teale's (1982) discussion of natural literacy development. Teale argues that "the typical literacy curriculum with its progression from part to whole and its hierarchy of skills" does not reflect the way children learn to read:

The belief is that literacy development is a case of building competencies in certain cognitive operations with letters, words, sentences and texts, competencies which can be applied in a variety of situations. A critical mistake here is that the motives, goals, and conditions have been abstracted away from the activity in the belief that this enables the student to "get down to" working on the essential process of reading and writing. But ... these features are critical aspects of the reading and writing themselves. By organizing instruction which omits them, the teacher ignores how literacy is practiced (and therefore learned) and thereby creates a situation in which the teaching is an inappropriate model for the learning (p. 567).

Teale views literacy learning as the result of children's involvement in reading and writing activities that are mediated by literate others. It is the interaction accompanying these activities that makes them so significant to the child's development. Not only do interactive literacy events teach children the societal functions and conventions of literature, they also link reading and writing with enjoyment and satisfaction, and thus increase children's desire to engage in literacy activities.

Teale's emphasis on the social aspects of literacy development reflects the influence of Vygotsky's (1981) more general theory of intellectual development. Vygotsky has defined "all higher mental functions (as) internalized social relationships." This movement from interpsychological learning to intrapsychological learning is apparent as children become increasingly able to engage independently in literacy activities that previously required interaction with more literate others.

Holdaway's (1979) theory of literacy development is consistent with Teale's positions. According to Holdaway,

The way in which supportive adults are induced by affection and common sense to intervene in the development of their children proves upon close examination to embody the most sound principles of teaching. Rather than provide verbal instructions about how a skill should be carried out, the parent sets up an emulative model of the skill in operation and induces activity in the child which approximates towards use of the skill. The first attempts of the child are to do something that is like the skill he wishes to emulate. This activity is then "shaped" or refined by immediate rewards.... From this point of view, so-called "natural" learning is in fact supported by higher quality teaching intervention than is normally the case in the school setting. (p. 22)

Holdaway contends that this form of "developmental" teaching is appropriate for school-based literacy instruction. Characterized by self-regulated, individualized activities, frequent peer interaction, and an environment rich with materials, Holdaway's model is derived from observations of home environments where children have learned to read without direct instruction. Such supportive home literacy environments have a large supply of accessible reading and writing materials; moreover, parents read to children regularly, are responsive to their children's questions about books and print, view reading as a key to achievement, and read a great deal themselves (Teale, 1978).

Four processes are defined that enable children to acquire literacy abilities. The first is *observation* of literacy behaviors—being read to, for example, or seeing adults read and write. The second is *collaboration*, interaction of another individual with the child, providing encouragement, motivation, and help. The third is *practice*, during which the learner tries out alone what has been learned, reading for pleasure or to others, for instance, without direction or adult observation. Practice gives children opportunities to evaluate their own performances, make corrections, and increase skills. In the fourth process, *performance*, the child shares what has been learned and seeks approval from adults who are supportive and interested (Calkins, 1983; Clark, 1976; Holdaway, 1986; Snow, 1983).

The theoretical perspectives of Teale, Holdaway, and Vygotsky are reflected in recreational reading programs proposed from research investigations. These programs provide children with the opportunity to

1. *Observe* and emulate the behavior of literate adults who read to them and read themselves;

2. enjoy the support of adults who *collaborate* or interact with them during literature activities and reward literacy behaviors;

3. have the opportunity to *practice* skills learned by engaging in free reading during recreational reading periods, using materials from classroom library centers; and

4. *perform* or share literature experiences with others, demonstrating what has been learned, through pleasurable experiences such as telling stories and discussing books that have been read.

STRATEGIES FOR PROMOTING VOLUNTARY READING IN SCHOOL

There is widespread agreement among educators that encouraging student to develop lifelong, voluntary reading habits is important. Although a great deal has been written about the important role of literature in the early childhood/elementary classroom (Cullinan, 1987; Galda & Cullinan, in press; Huck, 1976; Stewig & Sebesta, 1978), the use of literature appears to be quite limited (Hall, 1971). An investigation of literature use in early childhood rooms (Morrow, 1982), for example, found that most teachers had no regular literature program and that no time was set aside for children to use books. An explanation for these findings is provided by a subsequent study (Morrow, 1986b) of the attitudes of parents, principals, and teachers toward the development of voluntary reading as a responsibility of the school. While programmatic development of voluntary reading was ranked and rated fourth in importance by all three groups when compared with comprehension, word recognition skills, and study skills, its ratings were fairly high—an indication that teachers, principals, and parents considered it an important area, though simply not one to which they would assign top priority. The three groups also indicated that they believe there would be only a moderate amount of space for classroom materials necessary for library centers, limited money for materials, and insufficient time for classroom activities.

The findings may reflect the influence of many basal-reading programs that are used in school districts throughout the United States. Typical of such commercial materials is a strong emphasis on word recognition and skill development, with converse lack of attention to the promotion of recreational reading. This was verified in a study of six sets of basal readers, in which 14 elements found to have a positive relationship toward promoting voluntary reading (Morrow, 1982; 1983; 1987b; Morrow & Weinstein, 1982; 1986) were counted for frequency of occurrence in the lesson plans in teacher's manuals. The 14 elements were;

1. Discussing story meaning,
2. Reading to children,
3. Using children's literature in basal stories,
4. Scheduling recreational reading,
5. Doing art activities related to stories,
6. Maintaining a classroom library,
7. Asking children to record books read,
8. Asking children to write stories for the classroom library,
9. Encouraging children to read to each other,
10. Encouraging children to tell stories,
11. Using the school and public library,
12. Sharing books read at home and school,
13. Discussing authors and illustrators,
14. Asking children to keep records of books they've read.

Of the 14 activities sought, the first five appeared in the teachers manuals in 5 percent or more of the stories and mostly in supplementary sections of the teacher's manual. Elements 6 through 14 appeared in fewer than 1 percent of the 2,733 selections analyzed (Morrow, 1987a). Findings like these suggest that school personnel have been assigned or have assigned themselves the role of teaching literacy skills with no one in particular taking the responsibility for conveying the enjoyment of reading. Although some basal readers have included literature selections in their programs, they are often used for skill development and the promotion of voluntary reading is not emphasized. No matter how many literature selections may be included, a basal cannot substitute for actual books in their original size, shape and form.

The teacher plays a critical role in influencing children's attitudes toward reading. Children live what they learn. If children associate reading only with repetition of skill, drill, teach and test, they will never reach for a book on their own initiative. As Niles wrote in the foreword to *Reading for Pleasure: Guidelines* (Spiegel, 1981), "If we teach children to read, but do not instill the desire to read, what will we have accomplished?" (p. v). If, on the other hand, children live in an environment that associates reading with pleasure and enjoyment as well as with skill development, they are likely to become voluntary readers. How children live and learn in the classroom ultimately determines whether they will live their lives as literate or alliterate individuals. Irving (1980) contended:

One of the clear points to emerge from research into reading failure is that there was no association between reading and pleasure. . . . The role of teachers in stimulating voluntary reading among children and young people is . . . potentially the most powerful of all adult influences upon the young. (p. 7)

Research that incorporates correlational data, experimental paradigms and anecdotal observations had been carried out to describe programs designed to promote voluntary reading. These investigations, which are discussed in the next section made use of children's literature as a strong component in the program.

THE ROLE OF LITERATURE IN THE VOLUNTARY READING PROGRAM AT SCHOOL

There isn't a great deal of research concerning the value of promoting voluntary reading in the school program. Early investigations on promoting interest in books and the use of literature in the classroom were mainly anecdotal in nature. Schools have emphasized the importance of literature by supplementing their regular reading programs with "Spring Reading Campaigns," "Reading Awareness Weeks," and "Reading Celebrations" (Irving, 1980; Manley & Simon, 1980; Manning & Manning, 1984; Rosler, 1979; Yatvin, 1977). These anecdotal reports suggest that such programs invariably enhance students' enthusiasm and foster positive attitudes toward books.

In three similar "Book Flood" studies, classrooms were filled with large numbers of trade books, and teachers were asked to encourage free reading. The results of these investigatios reported improvement in children's reading achievement, gains in vocabulary and comprehension, increased reading, and better attitudes toward reading than exhibited by children in comparison schools who did not participate in such programs (Elley & Mangubhai, 1983; Fielding, Wilson & Anderson, in press; Ingham, 1981). Research by Morrow & Weinstein (1982, 1986) found that literature use increased dramatically when teachers incorporated enjoyable literature activities into the daily program, when library centers were created in the classrooms, and when recreational reading periods were regularly scheduled. Interestingly, there was no difference in the frequency with which high-achievers and low-achievers chose to use literature; the recreational reading program succeeded in attracting even poor readers to literature. In a similar study of inner-city minority children in after-school and summer daycare centers for youngsters from 6 to 11 years of age, a significant increase in book reading occurred from the beginning to the end of the program (Morrow, 1987b).

Empirical research by Morrow (1982; 1987b) and Morrow and Weinstein (1982; 1986) suggests specific activities in preschool through sixth grade classroom recreational reading programs that increased the use of literature by children. The results of their studies indicate that one practice of utmost importance is to read to children daily. Storytelling by teachers and use of storytelling props, such as feltboard stories, puppets, filmstrips and taped stories, were all found to be valuable in creating interest in books. When props were used to tell stories, the teachers involved made sure that the actual storybooks were available for children to use later on. All story-related materials, such as feltboards and roll movies, were left for children to use. Discussions that focused on interpretive and critical issues within the stories also served to heighten interest in books. Authors and illustrators were discussed and compared. Children's books brought from home and those written by the children themselves were extremely popular. Using literature related to content area topics correlated positively with children's increased use of literature, as did time set aside specifically for voluntary reading. All these activities promoted voluntary reading when carried out regularly.

The research reviewed to this point has focused on the use of literature in the promotion of voluntary reading. But, such exposure to literature is beneficial to children in so many other ways that it seems important to mention some of them at this point. As voluntary reading is being promoted through the use of literature, other skills are also being acquired. Reading to children and actively involving them before, during, and after a story helps with general literacy development.

Clay (1979) and Smith (1978) suggest that reading to young children helps them differentiate written language from oral, learn that printed words have sounds, and recognize that print carries meaning. A number of correlations have been reported between frequent experiences with storybook reading in early childhood and development of certain literacy skills. Parents of early readers, of more successful readers, and of children who entered school already knowing how to read report having read to their youngsters often during their early years (Clark, 1984; Durkin, 1966; Holdaway, 1979; Teale, 1978; Walker & Kuerbitz, 1979). Similar home and school experiences with reading have correlated with children's language development in syntactic complexity and vocabulary (Burroughs, 1972; Chomsky, 1972; Fodor, 1966). Experimentally, Cohen (1968) and Feitelson, Kita & Goldstein (1986) found that frequent storybook reading in the classroom significantly improved children's vocabulary, comprehension, and decoding ability.

Research has focused on trying to identify specific beneficial behaviors during story book readings. It has been found that kind and amount of verbal interaction between adult and child during such events can influence literacy development (Flood, 1977; Heath, 1982; Ninio, 1980; Teale, 1981; Teale & Sulzby, 1987). Teachers' reading styles were found to affect children's comprehension (Dunning & Mason, 1984; Green & Harker, 1982). The social interaction between readers and listeners during read-aloud events seems to help participants actively construct meaning based on text (Bloome, 1985; Ninio & Bruner, 1978). Story reading also leads children to practice reading on their own by reenacting the story reading and modeling the adult-child interaction. The nature of the interaction may even affect how much information the child learns as well as the child's skills and attitudes towards reading (Teale & Sulzby, 1987). The read-aloud event itself does not necessarily enhance literacy, but certain methods, environmental influences, attitudes, and interactive behaviors do contribute.

Experimental treatments in school settings have been studied in other attempts to define specific story reading elements that enhance literacy skills (Brown, 1975; Morrow, 1985a; Pellegrini & Galda, 1982). Children were read stories, then asked to respond by role playing, retelling, or reconstructing the stories with pictures. Children in the experimental groups improved more than those in control groups. Eliciting children's responses to literature seemed to enable them to integrate information and see relationships among various parts of a story. Besides enticing them to books, storybook-reading has been found to help children construct meaning about the text through the interaction of adult and child. During story reading, the adult helps the child understand and interpret text according to experiences, background, and beliefs (Altwerger, Diehl-Faxon & Dockstader-Anderson, 1985).

THE ROLE OF THE CLASSROOM ENVIRONMENT AND THE PROMOTION OF VOLUNTARY READING AT SCHOOL

Researchers have studied the effects of manipulating the physical environments of the classroom. Studies by Bumsted (1981), Phyfe-Perkins (1979), Sutfin (1980), and Weinstein (1977) have shown that changes in classroom environment can bring about desirable changes in students' choices of activities. Classroom environment is often overlooked in instructional planning. Energies are directed almost exclusively toward varying teaching strategies. When program and environment are not coordinated, "setting deprivation" often results, a situation in which physical environment fails to support the activities and needs of the students (Spivak, 1973).

The research on voluntary reading has demonstrated the important role that physical setting plays. It is an active and pervasive influence on children's attitudes and selection of classroom activities during the school day. Appropriate physical arrangement of furniture, material selection, and the aesthetic quality of different parts of a classroom, in this case the library center, can provide a setting that contributes to teaching, learning, and the promotion of voluntary reading (Morrow, 1982; 1983; Prescott, Jones & Kritchevksy, 1967).

Studies by Morrow (1982), Rosenthal (1973), and Shure (1963) found that library corners as they typically existed were among the least popular areas in early childhood classrooms during free play periods. In most rooms, library centers consisted simply of a bookshelf with books shelved in a disorderly fashion. Frequently, the area was difficult to find, little care was taken to make it attractive and physically accessible, nor did it contain interesting literature-related materials. According to Coody (1973) and Huck (1976), the effort of creating an inviting atmosphere for a classroom library corner is rewarded by children's increased interest in reading and reading achievement. Stauffer (1970) suggested that the classroom library be the focal area in the room, since it is a principal source of knowledge. According to Beckman (1972), although it is important to maintain a central library in a school, classroom libraries are essential for providing immediate access to reading materials. Bissett (1969) found that children in classrooms containing literature collections read 50 percent more books than children in classrooms wthout such collections. The findings of a similar study by Powell (1966) demonstrated that the more immediate the access to library materials, the greater the amount of recreational reading by pupils.

Correlational and experimental studies have identified many positive relationships between the frequency with which young children use literature in the classroom and physical design characteristics of library centers. Studies also report increased use of literature during free-choice periods in classrooms where library corners featured specific design characteristics (Anderson, Fielding & Wilson, 1985; Ingham, 1981; Morrow, 1982; 1983; 1987b; Morrow & Weinstein, 1982; 1986). Library centers that promoted children's voluntary use of books:

• were physically accessible and visually attractive;
• were partitioned off from the rest of the room on at least two sides to give a feeling of privacy;
• were large enough to hold about five children at a time;
• offered comfortable seating, such as a rocking chair, pillows to lean on, and a rug;
• provided five to eight books per child, books of varied reading levels;
• held a wide variety of children's literature, including picture

story books, novels, magazines, informational books, newspapers, poetry, fairy tales, fables, realistic literature and biographies;
• categorized books for selection;
• circulated new books regularly;
• offered a simple procedure for checking books in and out;
• had open-faced bookshelves to feature particular books;
• had attractive posters and literature-related bulletin boards
• provided story props such as a feltboard and cutout characters as well as puppets for storytelling;
• offered taped stories with headsets.

Studies have illustrated that characteristics of the physical environment play an important role in promoting voluntary reading in the classroom. However, the very same studies indicate that without the support of teachers who introduce the materials and feature books in daily routines, the physical factors alone will not succeed.

DISCUSSION

Becoming a Nation of Readers (Anderson, Heibert, Scott, & Wilkinson, 1985) refers to independent reading as a major source of reading fluency. Opportunities for recreational reading in school allow children to practice skills they are taught in typical reading instruction. Practice must be easy enough to give them a sense of success and enjoyable enough that they will continue to read by choice. The literature review reveals the benefits of voluntary reading and the characteristics of voluntary readers and provides documentation of the fact that children's voluntary reading habits can be increased when teachers carry out literature activities designed to create an interest in books, along with a supportive physical environment. Home studies identify characteristics that foster the development of voluntary readers. Teachers can share this information with parents about home environments and activities to help increase their children's voluntary reading.

Research needs to be continued concerning the promotion of voluntary reading to demonstrate its importance. It has too often become the "forgotten goal" in reading instruction. If the promotion of voluntary reading is to take its place as an integral part of reading programs, we must present data to confirm its importance. Although anecdotal and correlational data are available to support its importance, there have been few experimental studies. We need to carry out longitudinal, experimental research on the promotion of voluntary reading with children from different socioeconomic levels, from both urban and suburban environments, and with different cultural backgrounds to identify the benefits of such programs on literacy development. The research should include parent involvement, which the literature review demonstrates is an important element in creating voluntary readers (Morrow, 1985b). Assuming that the results of these experimental data reinforce the positive findings already documented for voluntary reading, they will help to change current practices in reading instruction.

Shavelson & Borko (1979) have studied factors that affect

teachers' decision-making about classroom instruction. In addition to a teacher's personal attitudes, they found that institutional constraints, external pressure, and instructional materials shape beliefs and consequently affect classroom practice. Teachers perceive money, space, and time as institutional constraints that hinder the promotion of voluntary reading. The external pressures to improve standardized test scores are felt rather generally by teachers, pressures from local and state officials as well as from parents. Teachers feel pressured to use classroom time for the skill development that they believe will help children achieve high scores on such tests. Skills-oriented programs are more easily measured on standardized tests, the results of which are in turn appreciated by the school boards, parents and taxpayers. Voluntary reading, by contrast, is a matter that requires qualitative evaluation as well as quantitative. The benefits of voluntary reading as intellectual stimulation and growth, acculturation, and general transfer of information are a matter of long-range development rather than of immediate payoff.

Finally, there is the pressure to use and the influence of basal reading programs. Typical of such commercial materials is strong emphasis on word recognition and skill development, with converse lack of attention to the promotion of recreational reading. As mentioned earlier, although more recent basal materials have incorporated literature in their selections, they still do not focus on promoting voluntary reading. Teachers who use basal reading material without personal input tend to become technicians who are proficient in the application of materials, but who have relinquished to the textbook their role as decision-maker (Hoover, 1983). Yet, there is no reason why recreational reading and basal instruction cannot work together. Basal readers can be used for skill development at the same time activities that promote voluntary reading are given equal importance. Teachers also need to use real selections of children's literature to read, just for pleasure. Editors of basals can help with this plan by including specific suggestions for promoting voluntary reading, and doing so in prominent sections of the teacher's manual, rather than among optional or supplementary suggestions.

Recent instructional practices tend to define reading as process somewhat at the expense of essence. Our schools seem to be teaching children how to read, rather than paying attention to what they read or why they should want to read at all. There are more things to be read and more reasons to read them that at any other time in history. But the classroom priority evident for at least a decade or more apparently short-circuits fundamental motivation to read. Are we teaching youngsters to read

in order to raise reading test scores, or to nurture individuals who will choose to read throughout their lives?

It is time for schools to look beyond achievement test performance and to implement reading programs that include as a major purpose the development of voluntary reading. If we believe fundamentally that we teach children to read because their own voluntary reading throughout life is necessary if they are to participate to their fullest in a democratic, civilized society, with all the benefits a literate society affords, then we need to remedy our approaches to reading instruction in the elementary school. Foremost in that remedy is a general commitment to systematic, programmatic development of voluntary reading. That development should be the primary objective of education, especially of early childhood and elementary education.

Such a developmental approach to literacy requires classroom environments rich in literary activities, classroom library corners bountifully stocked, frequent use of such areas by children of all ability levels and interests, children reading for their own purposes and practicing skills learned from direct instruction. As various research reports have found, incorporating recreational reading and pleasurable literary activities into instructional programs both enhances enthusiasm and fosters positive attitudes toward reading at the same time it improves vocabulary, comprehension, and language development.

To remedy the current situation, we must develop and regularly use appropriate instructional activities. We must adjust or reallocate resources, redirect the preservice and inservice preparation of teachers and encourage mutual support among all concerned, especially teachers, administrators, and parents. As primary decision-makers in curriculum and instruction, teachers must recognize that they not only influence instruction but also determine what children learn. They must be encouraged by administrators and colleagues to act on their beliefs in the value and importance of developing voluntary readers. It requires no great expenditure of time, effort, or money to regain out ultimate goal in teaching children to read. Techniques and materials are readily available. We need only the will to put them to use in general practice.

No one suggests that skill development is unimportant or unnecessary. It is simply by itself incomplete. Systematically integrating direct instruction with the promotion of voluntary, recreational reading endows skill development with a reason for being and points the reader toward lifetime fulfillment and continued growth. Every classroom can and should become a literary-rich environment in which children read not because they have to but because they want to.

References

Altwerger, A., Diehl-Faxon, J., & Dockstader-Anderson, K. (1985). Read aloud events as meaning construction. *Language Arts, 62,* 476–484.

Anderson, R. C., Fielding, L. G., & Wilson, P. T. (1988). Growth in reading and how children spend their time outside of school. *Reading Research Quarterly, 23,* 285–304.

Anderson, R. C., Hiebert, E. H., Scott, J. A., & Wilkinson, I. A. G. (1985).

Becoming a nation of readers. Washington, D.C.: The National Institute of Education.

Anderson, R. C., Wilson, P. T., & Fielding, L. G. (1985). *A new focus on free-reading.* Symposium presentation at the National Reading Conference, San Diego, California.

Beckman, D. (1972). Interior space: The things of education. *National Elementary Principal, 52,* 45–49.

Bissett, D. (1969). *The amount and effect of recreational reading in selected fifth grade classes*. Unpublished doctoral dissertation, Syracuse University.

Bloom, B. (1964). *Stability and change in human characteristics*. New York: John Wiley & Sons.

Bloom, D. (1985). Bedtime reading as a social process. In J. A. Niles & R. V. Lalik (Eds.), *Issues in literacy: A research perspective*. Rochester, NY: The National Reading Conference.

Book Industry Study Group. (1984). *The 1983 consumer research study on reading and book publishing*. New York.

Boorstin, D. (1984). Letter of transmittal. *In books in our future: A report from the librarian of congress to the congress* (p. iv). Washington, D.C.: U. S. Congress, Joint Committee on the Library.

Briggs, C., & Elkind, D. (1973). Cognitive development in early readers. *Developmental Psychology, 9,* 279–280.

Brown, A. (1975). Recognition, reconstruction and recall of narrative sequences of preoperational children. *Child Development, 46,* 155–166.

Bumstead, L. A. (1981). Influencing the frequency of children's cooperative and learning task-related behavior through change in the design and management of the classroom. Unpublished master's thesis, Cornell University.

Burroughs, M. (1972). The stimulation of verbal behavior in culturally disadvantaged three-year-olds. Unpublished doctoral dissertation, Michigan State University.

California Department of Education. (1980). *Student acievement in California schools: 1979–1980 annual report*. Sacramento, CA: California Department of Education.

Calkins, L. M. (1983). *Lessons from a child*. Porstmouth, NH: Heinemann Educational Books.

Childers, P. R., & Ross, J. (1973). The relationship between viewing television and school achievement. *The Journal of Educational Research, 66,* 317–319.

Chomsky, C. (1972). Stages in language development and reading. *Harvard Educational Review, 42,* 1–33.

Clark, M. M. (1976). *Young fluent readers*. London: Heinemann Educational Books.

Clark, M. M. (1984). Literacy at home and at school: Insights from a study of young fluent readers. In J. Goelman, A. A. Oberg, & F. Smith (Eds.), *Awakening to literacy*. London: Heinemann Educational Books.

Clay, M. (1976). Early childhood and cultural diversity in New Zealand. *Reading Teacher, 29,* 333–342.

Clay, M. M. (1979). *Reading: The patterning of complex behavior*. Auckland: Heinemann Educational Books.

Clews, E. W. (1899). Quoted by Nila B. Smith, *American Reading Instruction*. p. 13. New York: Silver, Burdett, 1934.

Cohen, D. (1968). The effect of literature on vocabulary and reading achievement. *Elementary English, 45,* 209–213, 217.

Connor, D. V. (1954). The relationship between reading achievement and voluntary reading of children. *Educational Review, 6,* 221–2217.

Coody, B. (1973). *Using literature with young children*. Dubuque, Iowa: Wm. C. Brown.

Cullinan, B. (Ed.). (1987). *Children's literature in the reading program*. Newark, DE: International Reading Association.

Dunning, D., & Mason, J. (1984). An investigation of kindergarten children's expressions of story character intentions. Paper presented at the 34th Annual Meeting of the National Reading Conference, St. Petersburg, Florida.

Durkin, D. (1966). *Children who read early: Two longitudinal studies*. New York: Teachers College Press.

Elley, W. B., & Mungubhai, F. (1983). The impact of reading on second language reading. *Reading Research Quarterly, 19,* 53–67.

Feitleson, D., Kita, B., & Goldstein, Z. (1986). Effects of listening to series stories on first graders' comprehension and use of language. *Research in the Teaching of English, 20,* 339–256.

Fielding, L. G., Wilson, P. T., & Anderson, R. C. (In press). A new focus on free reading: The role of trade books in reading instruction. In Ralphael, T. E., & Reynolds, R. (Eds.), *Contexts of literary*. New York: Longmans.

Flood, J. (1977). Parenting styles in reading episodes with young children. *The Reading Teacher, 30,* 846–867.

Fodor, M. (1966). The effect of systematic reading of stories on the language development of culturally deprived children. Unpublished doctoral dissertation.

Galda & Cullinan (In press). Literature for literacy. In Jensen, J., Lapp, D., Flood, J., & Squire, J. (Eds.), *Handbook of Research on Teaching the English Language Arts*. NY: Macmillan.

Greaney, V. (1980). Factors related to amount and type of leisure reading. *Reading Research Quarterly, 15,* 337–357.

Greaney, V., & Hegarty, M. (1985). Correlated of leisure-time reading. Unpublished paper. Educational Research Centre. St. Patricks College, Dublin, Ireland.

Greaney, V., & Hegarty, M. (1987). Correlates of leisure-time reading. *Journal of Research in Reading, 10,* 3–20.

Green, J. L., & Harker, J. O. (1982). Reading to children: A communicative process. In J. A. Langer & M. T. Smith-Burke (Eds.). *Reader meets author/bridging the gap: A psycholinguistic and sociolinguistic perspective,* pp. 196–221. Newark, DE: International Reading Association.

Hall, M. (1971). Literature experiences provided by cooperating teachers. *Reading Teacher, 24,* 425–431.

Hansen, J. S. (1969). The impact of the home literacy environment on reading attitude. *Elementary English, 46,* 17–24.

Heath, S. B. (1982). What no bedtime story means: Narrative skills at home and school. *Language in Society, 11,* 49–76.

Himmelweit, H. T., & Swift, B. (1976). Continuities and discontinuities in media usage and taste: A longitudinal study. *Journal of Social Issues, 32,* 133–156.

Holdaway, D. (1979). *The foundations of literacy*. New York: Ashton Scholastic.

Holdaway, D. (1986). The structure of natural learning as a basis for literacy instruction. In M. Samson, (Ed.), *The pursuit of literacy: Early reading and writing*. Dubuque, Iowa: Kendall/Hunt.

Hoover, N. (1983). Teacher's self-reports of critical decisions in teaching reading. Paper presented at the National Reading Conference, Austin, Texas.

Huck, S. (1976). *Children's literature in the elementary school* (3rd ed). New York: Holt, Rinehart & Winston.

Ingham, J. L. (1981). *Books and reading development: The Bradford books flood experiment*. Exeter, NH: Heinemann Educational Books.

Irving, A. (1980). *Promoting voluntary reading for children and young people*. Paris: UNESCO.

Koch, A., & Peden, W. (Eds.). (1944). *The life and selected writings of Thomas Jefferson* (p. 265). New York: Random House.

LaBlonde, J. A. (1967). A study of the relationship between television viewing habits and scholastic achievement of fifth grade children. *Dissertation Abstracts, 27,* 2284A.

Lamme, L. (1976). Are reading habits and abilities related? *Reading Teacher, 30,* 21–27.

Lomax, L. M. (1976). Interest in books and stories at nursery school. *Educational Research, 19,* 100–112.

Long, H., & Henderson, E. H. (1973). Children's uses of time: Some personal and social correlates. *Elementary School Journal, 73,* 193–199.

Manley, M. A., & Simon, E. A. (1980). A reading celebration from k to 8. *Reading Teacher, 33,* 552–554.

Manning, G. L., & Manning, M. (1980). What models of recreational reading make a difference? *Reading World, 23,* 375–380.

Maxwell, J. (1977). *Reading progress from 8 to 15.* Slough, Bucks: National Foundation for Educational Research.

Moon, C., & Wells, G. (1979). The influence of home on learning to read. *Journal of Research in Reading, 2,* 53–62.

Morrow, L. M. (1982). Relationships between literature programs, library corner designs and children's use of literature. *Journal of Educational Research, 75,* 339–344.

Morrow, L. M. (1983). Home and school correlates of early interest in literature. *Journal of Educational Research, 76,* 221–230.

Morrow, L. M. (1985a). Retelling stories: A strategy for improving young children's comprehension concept of story structure, and oral language complexity. *The Elementary School Journal, 85,* 647–661.

Morrow, L. M. (1985b). *Promoting vocabulary reading at school and at home.* Bloomington, IN: Phi Delta Kappa Educational Foundation.

Morrow, L. M. (1986a). Voluntary reading: Forgotten goal. *Educational Forum, 50,* 159–168.

Morrow, L. M. (1986b). Relationships between principals, teachers', and parents' attitudes towards the development of voluntary reading. *Reading Research and Instruction, 25,* 116–130.

Morrow, L. M. (1987a). Promoting voluntary reading activities represented in basal reader manuals. *Reading Research and Instruction, 26,* 189–202.

Morrow, L. M. (1987b). Promoting inner city children's recreational reading. *Reading Teacher, 41,* 266–274.

Morrow, L. M., & Weinstein, C. S. (1982). Increasing children's use of literature through program and physical design changes. *Elementary School Journal, 83,* 131–137.

Morrow, L. M., & Weinstein, C. S. (1986). Encouraging voluntary reading. The impact of a literature program on children's use of library centers. *Reading Research Quarterly, 21,* 330–346.

National Commission on Excellence in Education. (1983). *Nation at risk: The imperative for educational reform.* Washington, DC: U.S. Department of Education.

Neuman, S. B. (1980). Television: Its effects on reading and school achievement. *The Reading Teacher,* 801–805.

Neuman, S. B. (1986). The home environment and fifth-grade students' leisure reading. *Elementary School Journal, 86,* 335–342.

Ninio, A. (1980). Picture-book reading in mother-infant dyads belonging to two subgroups in Israel. *Child Development, 51,* 587–590.

Ninio, A., & Bruner, J. S. (1978). The achievement and antecedents of labelling. *Journal of Child Language, 5,* 5–15.

Pellegrini, A., & Galda, L. (1982). The effects of thematic-fantasy play training on the development of children's story comprehension. *American Educational Research Journal, 19,* 443–452.

Phyfe-Perkins, E. (1979). *Application of the behavior-person-environment paradigm to the analysis and evaluation of early childhood programs.* Doctoral dissertation, State University of New York at Buffalo.

Powell, W. R. (1966). Classroom libraries: Their frequency of use. *Elementary English, 43,* 395–397.

Prescott, E., Jones, E., & Kritchevsky, S. (1967). Group daycare as a child rearing environment: An observational study of daycare programs. Pasadena, CA: Pacific Oaks College. (ERIC Document Reproduction Service No. ED 024-453)

Quissenberry, N., & Klasek, C. (1976). The relationship of children's television viewing to achievement at the intermediare level.

Rosenthal, B. A. (1973). An ecological study of free play in the nursery school. Unpublished doctoral dissertation, Wayne State University, Detroit.

Rosler, F. (1979). Spring reading campaign. *Reading Teacher, 32,* 397–398.

Sakamoto, T., & Kiyoski, M. (1973). Japan. In J. Downing (Ed.), *Comparative reading.* New York: Macmillan.

Shavelson, R. J., & Borko, H. (1979). Research on teacher's pedagogical thoughts, judgments, decisions, and behaviors. *Review of Educational Research, 51,* 455–498.

Shure, M. B. (1963). Psychological ecology of a nursery school. *Child Development, 34,* 979–992.

Smith, F. (1978). *Understanding reading* (2nd ed.). New York: Holt, Rinehart and Winston.

Smith, N. B. (1970). *American Reading Instruction.* (Rev. ed.) Newark, DE: International Reading Association. (originally published 1934)

Snow, C. E. (1983). Literacy and language: Relationship during the preschool years. *Harvard Educational Review, 53,* 165–189.

Speigel, D. L. (1981). *Reading for pleasure: Guidelines.* Newark, Delaware: International Reading Association.

Spielberg, S. (1987). Acceptance speech at the Academy Awards. Los Angeles, California.

Spivak, M. (1973). Archetypal place. *Architectural Forum, 40,* 44–40.

Stauffer, R. G. (1970). A reading teacher's dream come true. *Wilson Library Bulletin, 45,* 292–292.

Stewig, J. W., & Sebesta, S. (Eds.). (1978). *Using literature in the elementary classroom.* Urbana, IL: National Council of Teachers of English.

Sutfin, H. (1980). The effect of children's behavior of a change in the physical design of kindergarten classroom. Unpublished doctoral dissertation, Boston University.

Taylor, D. (1983). *Family literacy: Young children to read and write.* Exeter, NH: Heinemann Educational Books.

Teale, W. (1978). Positive environments for learning to read: What studies of early readers tell us. *Language Arts, 55,* 922–932.

Teale, W. H. (1981). Parents reading to their children: What we know and need to know. *Language Arts, 59,* 555–570.

Teale, W. (1984). Reading to young children: Its significance for literacy development. In H. Goelman, A. Oberg, & F. Smith (Eds.)., *Awakening to literacy.* London: Heinemann Educational Books.

Teale, W. H., & Sulzby, E. (1987). Literacy acquisition in early childhood: The roles of access and mediation in storybook readings. In D. A. Wagner (Ed.), *The future of literacy in a changing world.* New York: Pergamon Press.

Vygotsky, L. S. (1981). The genesis of higher mental functions. In J. V. Wetsch (Ed.), *The concept of activity in society psychology.* White Plains, NY: M. E. Sharpe.

Walberg, H. J., & Tsai, S. (1984). Reading achievement and diminishing returns to time. *Journal of Educational Psychology, 76*(3), 442–451.

Walker, G. M., & Kuerbitz, I. E. (1979). Reading to preschoolers as an aid to successful beginning reading. *Reading Improvement, 16,* 149–154.

Weinstein, C. S. (1977). Modifying student behavior in an open classroom through changes in the physical design. *American Educational Research Journal, 14,* 249–262.

Whitehead, F. Capey, A. C., & Maddren, W. (1975). *Children's reading interests.* London, UK: Evans and Matheun.

Whitehead, F., Capey, A. C., Maddren, W., & Wellings, A. (1977). *Children and their books.* London: Macmillan.

Witty, P. (1967). Children of the television era. *Elementary English, 44,* 528–535, 554.

Yatvin, J. (1977). Recreational reading for the whole school. *Reading Teacher, 31,* 185–188.

33

ORAL LANGUAGE: SPEAKING AND LISTENING IN THE CLASSROOM

Gay Su Pinnell
Angela M. Jaggar

Daily life is conducted in spoken language. Human beings constantly converse, negotiate, discuss, and debate the issues and decisions of their lives; the ability to speak and listen effectively often makes the critical difference between success or failure. Speaking and listening, traditionally treated as separate areas of the curriculum, together comprise the oral language arts. Should speaking and listening be taught in school? The answer must be "yes"; a better question is how? Research on the teaching of oral language in elementary and secondary schools must ultimately address that question.

The intent of this chapter is to review the pertinent research on how children learn to be effective speakers and listeners (that is, users of oral language), and to discuss the implications for teaching. Theory and research from a number of disciplines are examined, particularly child language research, speech communication research, psycholinguistics, sociolinguistics, pragmatics, and discourse analysis. In addition, relevant pedagogical literature in language arts and speech communication education is discussed.

This review was undertaken within a framework suggesting that language is learned through use, first in the home, family, and social community, and then in the social context of the classroom and school. Moreover, in both formal and informal social contexts, speaking and listening are not separate processes. Instead, they are interrelated as participants engage in the give and take of oral communication. The processes of speaking (producing messages) and listening (comprehending messages) require the same underlying knowledge of language, including knowledge of the linguistic structures and the social rules that determine how language is used in context. Furthermore, oral language development is inextricably related to literacy development and to learning in the content areas. For language-arts instruction, this means teachers at all levels must create classroom environments, and interact with students in ways that will help them to develop and effectively use oral language as a tool for communication and learning.

First, to provide historical perspective, the chapter begins with an overview of the status of instruction in speaking and listening, and then a review of traditional lines of research that treats each as a separate area of study. This review is not exhaustive, but rather highlights the major trends and their impact on curriculum. Although traditional lines of inquiry have provided some insight into the nature of listening and speaking processes, it has been a compartmentalized approach that has not yielded an adequate knowledge base to formulate conceptually sound instructional programs.

Current research on oral language development and use at home and in the classroom treats speaking and listening as aspects of an integrated system, and it focuses on the nature and development of communicative competence and on the role of talk in learning. Findings from this research have greater potential for developing a coherent theoretical framework to guide oral language teaching. Thus, the remainder of the chapter contains an overview of new directions in language research and, in following sections, reviews current research in three areas:

1. Communicative competence, surveying findings on children's language functions, interactional skills, and discourse development;
2. Comparisons of home and school language, and
3. The nature of classroom talk and its impact on student's communication development and learning.

Finally, the implications of the research will be discussed in terms of principles for teaching oral language in classrooms.

THE STATUS OF INSTRUCTION IN SPEAKING AND LISTENING

Educators and researchers have talked about speaking and listening as interrelated processes, but in research and pedagogy the two have remained separate until recently. Twenty-five years ago, a joint statement (Mackintosh, 1964) by the National Council of Teachers of English and other professional organizations confirmed the importance of oral language for social development and for learning, and presented suggestions for instruction and evaluation. The authors of this document summed up their position by saying:

We share with all educators the concern about written communication and the recognition that reading skills are basic to all learning. But we have voiced the need for equal concern about educating all children to be effective speakers and listeners ... the ability to speak and listen effectively is probably the most important asset that he can acquire and maintain throughout a lifetime. (p. 36)

A supplementary document (Petty, 1967) presented research-based articles by noted educators. Those scholars examined what was known about the relationship of oral language to areas such as personal and social development, reading, writing, home environment, sex differences, classroom context, and teacher behavior. The articles suggested the interrelatedness of speaking and listening; but the two areas were discussed in separate chapters, and different conceptual models were used to describe them. In one of the statements on needed research, Strickland, Blake and Amato, and Petty (1967) reported they had found an almost complete void of studies on oral language. They called for greater attention to research related to defining and teaching oral communication skills and for more investigations into the relations between speaking and listening, and among all the language arts.

Research on oral language development increased during the 1960s, and is reviewed in more detail in subsequent actions. Findings from this research challenged the highly structured traditional approach to language teaching that dominated instruction in both the United States and the Britain. This approach emphasized learning of "correct" form and rules of grammar through exercises and drills that would, it was assumed, improve reading, writing, and speaking (Czerniewska, 1981). New research suggested, however, that by the time children entered school, they already know the basic patterns and "have mastered the fundamental rules of their native language, rather than being empty vessels into which teachers somehow pour language" (Hendricks, 1980, p. 366). According to Czerniewska (1981), exercises were rejected in favor of creative and individual activities that could tap the child's language resources. "Teachers began to use real-life contexts, instead of lists of abstract rules, as starting points for langauge work.... The teacher merely supplies the stimulus—from seashells to poetry—and the child is left the freedom to respond in the form of language of his choosing" (p. 168–169).

This shift in language teaching was part of a shift in the approach to education as a whole during the 1960s, with the former subject-centered approach being replaced by a child-centered approach (Czerniewska, 1981). In the field of English education, there was a surge of activity that led to the Anglo-American Seminar held in Dartmouth, New Hampshire, in 1966 and to the book *Growth through English* by John Dixon (1967) that described the personal growth model of English teaching supported by many seminar participants. "Basically the assumption of this model is that the individual learner should be the focus. He develops in no small measure through language: by language he is able to understand his world" (Wilkinson, Barnsley, Hanna, & Swan, 1980, p. 7). For an interesting discussion of the impact of the Dartmouth Seminar see Allen, 1980.

The child-centered approach enjoyed favor for a while but in the 1970s and early 1980s, several events led to demands for change in oral language teaching. Most significant was the mounting concern about the quality of education in the United States generally and the teaching of basic skills, which eventually resulted in the back-to-the-basics movement and emphasis on competency based instruction.

In 1978 the Federal government amended Title II of the Elementary and Secondary Act of 1965 to include, for the first time, speaking and listening as "basic skills" along with reading and writing. This legislation, Public Law 95-561, called upon Federal, State, and local authorities to reevaluate their curricula so that all children are able to master the basic skills of effective communication, written and *spoken,* and to either restructure or create new programs that placed greater emphasis on oral language skills.

Further support for improvement in oral language instruction came from:

1. Twenty-five professional education associations that in 1979 endorsed the *Essentials of Education Statement* (1981), which listed the ability to use langauge to communicate and think effectively as essential,
2. National Council of Teachers of English that affirmed the importance of oral communication skills in its *Essentials of English Statement* (1983),
3. National Commission on Excellence in Education (1983), and
4. The College Board (1983) that listed speaking and listening as one of six basic competencies needed for college.

In addition, a number of state and local education agencies began to accept speaking and listening as basic skills. Van Rheenan, McClure, and Backlund (1984) reported that by 1983, 23 states had enacted policies and were developing goals for oral language curriculum and assessment, and 9 others were planning to do so. This was a substantial increase over the number found 2 years earlier in a survey conducted by Backlund, Booth, Moore, Parks, and Van Rheenan (1982).

Two years prior to the passage of the new basic skills legislation, Allen and Brown (1976) published the final report of the Speech Communication Association's National Project on Speech Communication Competencies. Initiated in 1973, this large scale project was motivated by:

two convictions held widely by communication scholars and educators: (1) that functional communication behaviors are of such crucial significance that they must be emphasized progressively and continuously throughout the school experience and (2) that our nation's schools have largely ignored the the functional communication needs of children and youth. (p. 3)

The purpose of the study was to identify the most fruitful directions for the development of speech communication programs in the schools. The report contains a review of over 1000 studies considered pertinent to communication development, a list of the communication competencies derived from the literature review, and a report on a final synthesis conference where the participants attempted to define communication competence and to specify some implications for research and instruction.

Based on the findings of this project, the Speech Communication Association (SCA) and the American Speech-Language-Hearing Association (ASHA) issued *Standards for Effective Oral Communication Instruction* (see Lieb-Brilhart, 1982). This document defined oral communication as the process of interacting through heard and spoken messages in a variety of situations. The definition stressed the interrelatedness of the two processes, depicting communication as a transactional process wherein speakers and listeners exchange roles in the course of interacting.

With passage of the new basic skills legislation, speech communication and English language-arts educators undertook a number of projects to disseminate research on the processes involved in oral communication development and to translate theory and research into useful suggestions for classroom practice. Examples of this work include Brown et al. (1981), Brown (1984), Book (1978); Freidrich (1981), Holdzkom, Reed, Porter, and Rubin (1982); Hopper and Wrather, 1978; Parkay, O'Bryan and Hennessy (1984); Thaiss and Suhor (1984); and Wood (1977a, 1977b, 1981). Because evaluation is an essential part of the education process, several other projects were undertaken to review and critique procedures for assessing oral communication skills and to suggest research and development priorities for the 1980s. For examples, see Larson (1978), Larson, Backlund, Redmond and Barbour (1978), Rubin and Mead (1984), Stiggins (1981), and Powers (1984).

The focus on speaking and listening as basic competencies stimulated interest in oral language instruction; however, these projects seem to have had little impact on practice. According to studies conducted in the 1980s, the status of instruction in speaking and listening has not changed much despite their designation as basic skills and the initial availability of federal funds to support curriculum improvement in oral communication.

In both elementary and secondary education, listening (Devine, 1982; Strother, 1987) as well as speaking (Backlund et al., 1982; Hendricks, 1980; Rubin, 1985) are still not priorities. As observed more than 20 years ago (Petty, 1967), instruction in oral language continues to take a back seat to reading and writing. Even where oral language skills are emphasized, there is generally not a strong conceptual base for the curriculum.

As we move into the 1990s, English educators at all levels are again focusing on ways to further the development of students' spoken language abilities as evidenced in the recent report *The Coalition Conference: Democracy through Language* (Lloyd-

Jones & Lundsford, 1989). Educators now recognize the centrality of talk in both communication and learning and are searching for more effective approaches to developing students' "oracy" skills. Andrew Wilkinson (1965) coined the term "oracy" in the 1960s in England on the analogy of literacy to stress the importance of speaking and listening language skills.

Although there has been a great deal of work on the nature and teaching of oracy in Britain, it is only in relatively recent years that the concept of oracy has received much attention in the United States. Both countries, have two current views of oracy, each with different implications for practice (MacLure, 1988; Rubin, 1985). One view defines oracy as communicative competence and calls for programs directed at teaching and assessing oral skills and competencies in their own right (MacLure, 1988). This view of oracy finds support among members of the Speech Communication Association and others who advocate a deliberate approach to the teaching of specific oral communication competencies. The second views oracy as a tool for learning and calls for programs that give students many opportunities to talk for learning across the curriculum (Bullock, 1975; MacLure, 1988; Marland, 1977; Corson, 1988). This view of oracy is finding support in both the "whole language" and "language across the curriculum" movements now gaining popularity in the United States.

LISTENING AND SPEAKING AS SEPARATE AREAS OF INQUIRY: A HISTORICAL SKETCH

Traditionally research and pedagogy have treated listening and speaking as separate areas of study. To provide historical perspective, this section sketches some directions research has taken in these two areas and discusses the implications for practice that have been drawn from that work.

Listening

The words *ignored* and *neglected* frequently appear in the literature on listening (Landry, 1969; Pearson & Fielding, 1982; Schaudt, 1983; Strother, 1987). Although reading research began in the 1880s, research on listening was not published until the 1920s. By 1948 only three research reports had been published on listening; although over 3,000 studies had been published on reading (Anderson, 1952). The *Encyclopedia of Educational Research* (Harris, 1960) did not include "Listening: Teaching of" and "Tests of" until 1960; and in 1969, Landry described listening as being "crowded out" by reading.

One wonders why listening has been so neglected considering how much time students spend listening in school. In an often cited study, Wilt (1950) discovered that elementary school children were expected to listen 2 and one-half hours per day, more than 60 percent of the time they were in the classroom, and more time than on any other activity. Moreover, for most of that time, students listened to the teacher talk; yet, teachers appeared to be unaware of the amount of time children were expected to listen, estimating only 74.3 minutes per day. Wilt suggested that teachers need to become more aware of listening as a factor in learning. Her findings on time spent listening in classrooms were comparable to Rankin's (1928) much earlier study. He brought attention to the importance of listening in everyday life when he discovered people devote forty-five percent of their time to listening, thirty percent to speaking, sixteen percent to reading, and only nine percent to writing.

With the recognition that students were engaged in listening for much of their school day, researchers began to investigate the relations between listening ability and other areas of school achievement. For example, Ross (1964) found high correlations between poor listening and poor school achievement. Early studies (Larsen & Feder, 1940; Young, 1936) reported relationships between listening and reading; later studies (reviewed in more detail in Devine, 1978; Duker, 1961, 1966, 1969; Lundsteen, 1979; Sticht, Beck, Hauke, Kleiman, & James, 1974) found substantial correlations between listening comprehension, reading comprehension, and reading achievement. In addition, studies of the relationship between listening comprehension and reading comprehension (Hampleman, 1958) suggested that listening is an important vehicle for learning, particularly in elementary school and particularly for students who are slower.

Another line of research during the 1950s and 1960s focused on the effects of instruction in listening. This research addressed the question: Does listening skill develop "naturally," or can it be taught directly? Studies showed that direct instruction in listening (Canfield, 1961; Hollow, 1955; Lundsteen, 1964, 1965; Pratt, 1956; Trivette, 1961) led to measurable gains in listening comprehension. Lundsteen's (1964, 1971) influential studies of critical listening suggested the direct teaching of critical thinking skills is related to an improvement in listening comprehension. Lundsteen (1971) recommended that students be given experience in critical listening and that researchers work to identify hierarchies of skills in this area. Lundsteen (1979) provided a suggested hierarchy that could be used for instructional purposes.

In their review of listening research, Pearson and Fielding (1982) concluded that by the 1960s there was "considerable proof that elementary children can improve in listening comprehension through training" (p. 619). Though the training methods used in the studies "generally focused on skills commonly taught in reading, such as getting the main idea, sequencing, summarizing and remembering facts," the important thing is that "the instruction occurred in listening, *not* in reading, and that the children were aware that they were receiving listening instruction (p. 619). Pearson and Fielding review some more recent studies and suggest that "one promising approach to listening comprehension may lie in combining listening with oral responses from the listeners" (p. 620). Active involvement following listening activities may help more than do passive activities.

Following the work on the relations between listening and other areas, particularly reading comprehension, investigations into the nature and attributes of listening took a new direction. According to Horrworth (1966), the research suggested that listening is not a discrete skill or a generalized ability, but a cluster of specific abilities closely related to those needed in the reading task (Russell, 1964). Caffrey (1955) and later Spearritt (1962), reported in Duker (1968), sought to define this cluster

of abilities and suggested that there may be factors in listening ability, or "auding" that are different from those involved in reading. Based on this work, Horrworth (1966) defined auding as "the gross process of listening to, recognizing, and interpreting spoken symbols. This definition is holistic in nature and embraces the hearing act, the listening act, and the comprehending act" (p. 857). She expressed this definition as a paradigm: Auding = Hearing + Listening + Cognizing.

Though Horrworth considered listening as a part of a cluster of abilities, new research followed that attempted to further integrate listening and overall comprehension. Sticht's work (Sticht, Beck, Hauke, Kleiman & James, 1974) challenged the idea of a special "listening comprehension" different from other language abilities. His (Sticht, 1972) model of the reading/writing, auding/speaking process assumed that reading and auding access the same language and conceptual bases. In other words, people use the same basic kinds of adaptive processes to build cognitive competence and acquire language skill, first in auding and speaking and then later in reading and writing, with additional competencies added to enable the decoding of print.

Using recordings that artificially compressed speech into a shorter time period, Stitch (Foulke & Sticht, 1969; Sticht et al., 1974) and several other researchers (Orr, Friedman & Williams, 1965; Zemlin, Daniloff & Shriner, 1968) investigated the rate at which individuals could track and process information presented orally. Spoken discourse usually ranges from 125 to 200 words per minute (WPM), the rate that news broadcasters and readers for the blind read (Foulke & Sticht, 1969). The maximum listening rate appeared to be about 300 WPM (Goldstein, 1940; Sticht et al., 1974). When speech was presented at a faster rate, comprehension was severely diminished, although intelligibility was less affected. In other words, intelligibility scores fell off less rapidly than comprehension scores when the rate of listening was increased (Foulke & Stitch, 1969).

Experiments with compressed speech also indicated that short phrases were more intelligible than isolated words; common words were more intelligible than less common words; and, as in reading, words presented in context were more intelligible than the same words presented in isolation. Sticht interpreted the results of these experiments as evidence of a reciprocal relationship between intelligibility and understanding. The listener makes predictions about what the input of the messages should be and then checks out the elements only as thoroughly as needed to confirm the predictions. Not only does the intelligibility of the message affect comprehension; the listener's knowledge and comprehension also affect intelligibility.

Sticht's model raises questions about assuming that reading problems are the only obstacles to learning. In a study of adults, Sticht (1972) found that men who are marginally literate learned equally poorly by listening as by reading. This research suggested that much of the reading difficulty may actually be a general difficulty in comprehending language. Thus, converting tasks to listening rather than reading does not necessarily mean greater learning of content. In both listening and reading, greater learning may be achieved with the use of advanced organizers (Ausubel, 1960; Ausubel & Robinson, 1969). The idea is that learning new material is facilitated when the learner already has the concepts within which to integrate the new information. This "frame of reference," if effective in reading, should also be helpful in listening. Sticht argued that both listening and reading are part of a larger and more general langauge ability. Teaching listening, then, really means teaching "learning (comprehending) by listening" and should include the same kinds of practices suggested for helping students "read to learn." He proposed attention to the acoustic, linguistic, and semantic features of listening.

Pearson and Fielding (1982) find Sticht's line of research important because it suggests that "once lower level reading skills are mastered, both reading and listening are controlled by the same set of cognitive processes" (p. 623). They conclude that after students have become mature readers, then what benefits reading (e.g., instruction in reading strategies) will benefit listening comprehension. However, at earlier stages of reading, cross modal transfer may be possible but less likely. They also call for more investigations into the implications of schema theory and models of text comprehension for listening comprehension curricula. Pearson and Fielding suggest that they may be even more applicable to listening comprehension than to reading comprehension.

In the early 1970s, Wilt (1973) expressed concern that the field of listening research had progressed little since the 1950s, claiming that studies had been based on narrow definitions of listening and had come out with limited results applicalbe only to small populations. Wilt suggested that listening research may have been based on faulty notions of the nature of listening and warned that listening must be considered as part of a much larger whole. She argued that speaking, listening, reading, and writing cannot be taught as discrete lessons. The task of improving listening is one of expanding the child's thinking and learning. According to Wilt (1973), the "efficacy of listening will need to be found in observation of a person's ability to interact in a communication situation with all of its ramifications rather than in whether an individual can remember facts he hears" (p. 69).

Much listening research is open to criticism for using artificial rather than naturalistic situations, and employing inadequate measurement techniques (Kelly, 1971; Rubin & Mead, 1984; Wilt, 1973). Back in 1955, Wilt observed that techniques such as observational checklists (Farrell & Flint, 1967) and standardized tests like the *Durrell Listening-Reading Series* (1969) measured only a minute aspect of listening. Fifteen years later, Wilt (1973) proposed that real assessment of listening must take into account the complex combination of understandings and behaviors that make up effective listening in various social situations. More recent reviews of assessment procedures (for example, see Rubin & Mead, 1984) suggest little progress in the development and use of naturalistic techniques for assessing listening. Most listening assessment takes the form of pencil and paper tests that typically resemble reading comprehension tests.

The importance of listening in school success is widely accepted, but listening is largely ignored in instruction. Research over the years has spanned from considering listening as an isolated activity to the more recent view that listening is intertwined with the child's overall communication development. Certainly much more theory and research, especially naturalis-

tic studies, are needed on the linguistic, cognitive, and social processes involved in listening; the course of listening development; the factors that affect that development; and on ways teaching can further the development of listening as a tool for communication and learning.

Speaking

Prior to the 1900s, elocution, skill in oral expression, was considered an essential part of competence, but the emphasis on oral expression declined in the 1920s and 1930s when research and practice shifted its focus to silent reading. Since the 1940s, emphasis on oral skills in the language-arts curriculum has increased, although assessment practices have contributed to maintaining the primary focus on literacy. In summarizing trends in oral communication instruction at the secondary level, Lieb-Brilhart (1984) claims that "the rise of silent reading . . . and the emphasis on literature and composition helped foster the view of oral communication as 'speech arts,' reducing it to an elective or extra curricula activity in the English curriculum" (p. 69).

Speaking occupies more school time than any other activity (reading, writing, and so on) except listening (Wilt, 1955). Although speaking does not receive large amounts of instructional time (DeLawter & Eash, 1966; Rubin, 1985), educators believe that the ability to speak effectively is an important fundamental skill that is necessary for success in school. At the surface level, teachers are still concerned with distinct articulation, enunciation, and pronunciation. Beyond that, they recognize that children need to be able to organize and present ideas, give clear directions, and display their knowledge.

During the 1960s studies of oral expression focused on the use of structures and on developmental changes in speech patterns. For example, O'Donnell, Griffin and Norris (1967) studied the oral language of kindergarten, first-, second-, third-, fifth-, and seventh-grade students and found increasing complexity in use of syntax between kindergarten and first-year students and between fifth- and seventh-grade students. It was not until fifth grade that the syntax of written language compositions began to overtake oral language in complexity. Thus, for younger children, using oral language means expressing ideas in complex language, and as indicated by C. Chomsky's (1969) research, school-age children are still developing the use of new structures in their oral language throughout the elementary school years.

As with listening, the view that development of oral expression is valuable mainly in its relation to literacy learning has been at least partially justified by important investigations in the 1960s that either directly or tangentially linked oral language development with literacy. For example, studies by Loban (1963, 1976), Strickland (1962), and Ruddell (1965, 1966), demonstrated the close relationship between sentence patterns, vocabulary, and speech rhythms of oral language and the speaker's proficiency in reading and writing. Loban's (1963, 1976) longitudinal work indicated that children who were advanced in language ability at the kindergarten level used language in flexible ways. They could take "moveables," that is, parts of a sentence that may occur several different places, and distribute them in various ways. According to Loban, such skill represented control over language, and children who could demonstrate such oral skill eventually scored higher in reading achievement. Differences in this skill between high and low reading groups increased from year to year.

The research described above focused on children's use of language structure, and on developmental changes in speech patterns and their relations to reading achievement. At the same time, other studies focused on how to help students become better at oral expression. For example, in an analysis of children's tape recorded interviews after hearing unfinished stories, DeLawter and Eash (1966) noted errors that signaled a lack of the skill they claimed was critical for mature listening and should be used to plan oral language curricula. These areas of need included failure to focus and to clarify questions, poor organization of ideas, lack of supporting ideas and appropriate subordination of ideas, stereotyped vocabulary, and inadequate descriptions. To help students overcome such errors, DeLawter and Eash recommended greater use of small group discussion to give children practice, the use of devices such as tape recorders to help students evaluate their own oral speech, and integration of speaking with the other language arts.

Just as in listening studies, much early research on the effects of spoken language instruction involved use of contrived situations that do not tap students' true language abilities; however, during the 1960s researchers and English teachers at all levels began to recognize the power of learning language while using it in more realistic social situations. They advocated that the traditional approach to language teaching, while emphasized learning of skills through exercises and drills, be replaced by more creative oral language activities, such as storytelling, discussion, and creative dramatics. They found support for this approach in the linguistic studies that seemed to show children learn linguistic rules and structures before they enter kindergarten, and that speaking and listening are learned "naturally" and require no further direct instruction from the teacher (Czerniewska, 1981; Hendricks, 1980; Lieb-Brilhart, 1984).

With the designation of speaking and listening as basic skills in the 1970s, many speech communication and English language-arts educators called for more deliberate teaching of oral communication skills. Based on an extensive survey of the research on the development of children's oral communication available at the time (see Allen & Brown, 1976), they advocated that the popular activities approach be replaced by a more deliberate approach to teaching listening and speaking.

These researchers (for example, Book, 1981; Brown, 1984; Brown et al., 1981; Hopper and Wrather, 1978; Lieb-Brilhart, 1984; Rubin & Kantor, 1984; and Wood, 1977a, 1977b, 1981, 1984) attempted to define oral communication competence, specified the goals of instruction, identified the skills to be taught, and outlined programs for elementary and secondary education that were based on a functional approach to oral communication. According to Brown (1984), instruction in this approach focuses on using language for five major functions identified by Wells (1973). Experience with each of the five functions is gained through games, simulations, and problem situations that are "designed to help students: (a) develop a wide repetoire of communication strategies and skills, (b) select skills which seem appropriate to the situation, (c) implement the skills through practice, and (d) evaluate the effectiveness and the appropriateness of the skills employed" (Brown et al. 1981, pp. 79–80).

The functional approach received a great deal of attention in language-arts and speech communication publications in the late 1970s and early 1980s; however, little recognized research establishes the effects of the approach on students' speaking and listening abilities. In addition, several researchers (Hendricks, 1980; McCrosky, 1982; Weimann & Backlund, 1980; and others) have questioned the approach for equating competence and performance, and for being too behavioristic in tone. They suggest that definitional problems and theoretical issues about what knowledge, abilities, and factors are involved in communicative competence must be resolved before conceptually sound pedagogy can be designed.

Given the continuing priority placed on literacy and the problems in defining oral communication competence as a pedagogical objective, it is not surprising that surveys show oral language curricula in the United States have changed little since the 1960s. Oral language curricula at the elementary and at the secondary level tend to emphasize performance rather than the natural uses of language needed to use language effectively in a variety of different social/academic settings.

In the elementary schools, listening and speaking are taught primarily by engaging children in activities such as telling stories, discussion, conversation, creative dramatics, singing, games, and exercises used to strengthen skills in one or the other area (Brown, 1984; Brown et al., 1981), or as "incidental means to an end" (Rubin, 1985, p. 32). Because evaluation and testing practices tend to emphasize written language skills, much of the value attached to listening and speaking lessons at the elementary level has been associated with developing the foundation for literacy. In the 1980s some researchers were even beginning to express doubt about the assumed relationship between oral language competence and school performance in reading and writing. Reviews (Gray, Saski, McEntire, & Larsen, 1980; Hammill & Groff, 1978; McNutt, 1980) of a large number of studies conducted in the 1960s and 1970s revealed that the correlations between specific oral language skills (e.g., grammatical usage) and measures of reading and writing were generally low, suggesting that achievement in written language may not be related to oral language proficiency. However, as in all such studies, low correlations may reflect problems associated with the validity of the measures used to investigate the constructs assumed to be under study.

Surveys of secondary schools (Book, 1981; Book & Pappas, 1981; Lieb-Brilhart, 1984; Rubin, 1985) suggest that little curriculum change has been implemented and that speech and listening, along with the other language arts, are still viewed as separate curriculum areas. Although secondary students appear to spend most of their time listening to the teacher (Devine, 1978), attention to listening is minimal; however, students may be engaged in discussion, making reports, panel presentations, brainstorming, and role playing in their various courses of study.

Formal speech instruction generally takes place in separate elective courses (e.g., public speaking) or as part of extracurricular activities such as debate or drama.

Defining and assessing competence in speaking presents problems for both educators and researchers. If the organized instructional program "neglects" speaking, it may be because competence in this area cannot be measured through group standardized pencil and paper measures. Teachers can use tape recorded samples and checklists to evaluate student progress (Kopp, 1967), and assess group discussions and other oral activities using observation guides and checklists or participation charts (Rubin & Mead, 1984). However, valid assessment of students speaking abilities must include facility in using spoken language in a variety of social/academic contexts and for a range of different purposes (see Barnes, 1980; Gorman, 1985; Wilkinson, 1965).

CURRENT RESEARCH FOCUS: ORAL LANGUAGE USE AND COMMUNICATIVE DEVELOPMENT

Current language research confirms the importance of oral communication in the child's social and cognitive development, and provides the impetus not only to integrate speaking and listening, but to define competence in new ways, this time with emphasis on the interactive nature of communication and on contextual factors that influence such communication. This research provides the evidence necessary for new directions in practice. First, language research (King, 1984) confirms the human potential to construct meaning through language and to use language to learn. Second, language research (Cazden, John, & Hymes, 1972) brings attention to the functions of language and to communicative competence within the social context of the classroom. Third, it leads to new definitions of competence that account for the complexities of human learning and provides the basis for an integrated language-arts curriculum that acknowledges the interrelatedness of the social and intellectual functions of language.

Shifting Views of Oral Language Development

Linguists in the 1940s and 1950s studied the structure of language. They were concerned with describing the phonology, morphology, and syntax of the language, and they studied the elements and rules of the language. These studies of language form and structure provided accurate information about the nature of language and generated a concept of what must be learned. At the same time studies of language development concentrated on establishing norms for language learning. Educators and language development scholars focused on when, and in what sequence, children learned the forms of language. They established milestones that allowed for comparisons between groups and for evaluation of individuals, but they did not take into account the social, cultural, and contextual factors that may have influenced language development or the role of the child in that development (Bloom, 1975).

By the 1960s, researchers realized that children were not just acquiring collections of words; instead, they were abstracting systems of rules that they could use to generate their own language structures. This research revealed that all children appear to have this ability to learn and use a system for language. This linguistic competence (N. Chomsky, 1957, 1965) is made up of their acquired knowledge of the forms of language and of the rules for generating those forms. (For reviews of this early work on children's language development, see Bloom, 1975; DiVesta & Palermo, 1974.) In the 1960s scholars also recognized that all dialects and varieties of a language are systematic and rule-governed, complex, and useful as a tool for cognitive and social development (for example, Labov, 1969), and that language learning could be studied across languages and cultural groups. (See Wells & Nicholls, 1985, for interesting discussions of the major issues in language research in both Britain and the United States during this period.)

By the 1970s, research on language, particularly children's language learning, had shifted from concern with form and structure to the study of language in use. Linguists, sociolinguists, and ethnographers began to focus on larger units of language and to give attention to the context in which language is used and developed. "This gradual development of language knowledge, from phonology, to morphology, to syntax, to discourse, paralleled by a gradual development from form to function, now places language knowledge in a position to be most helpful to educators and students alike" (Shuy, 1984, p. 168).

Communicative Competence

The new views of language signaled a new definition of competence. To use language effectively, one must know more than the complex or "mature" linguistic structures identified in previous research. As researchers examined language use in naturalistic contexts, it became clear that one must know how to use language as a social instrument. This shift in focus is illustrated by the difference between N. Chomsky's (1957, 1965) notion of linguistic competence (knowledge of the system) and Hymes' (1972) notion of communicative competence (a repertoire of language strategies that are appropriate for different contexts).

Hymes (1971) introduced the concept, saying that communicative competence meant "the most general term for speaking and hearing capabilities of a person.... Competence is understood to be dependent on two things: (tacit) passive knowledge and (ability for) use" (p. 16). It is the totality of knowledge that enables a speaker to produce speech that is socially appropriate as well as grammatical in culturally determined contexts, and to understand the speech of others in those contexts (Gumperz & Hymes, 1964; Hymes, 1971). This "knowledge" is used in both the production and comprehension of language.

The purpose of instruction, then, should be to help students develop a repertoire of strategies (forms) for different functions of language that would enable them to select a particular strategy in a given context, to communicate using that strategy, to evaluate the effectiveness of that strategy and modify it, if necessary, and to do so while simultaneously engaged in social dialogue. Current research on children's language development provides important information that can be used to design classroom situations that will foster rather than hinder this development. This research is reviewed in the next section.

Language Functions and Interactional Competence

Piaget (1959) did not consider the speech of young children to be truly social. However, research on young children younger than 7 or 8 years old were "egocentric" (Piaget, 1959), unable to consider the listener's viewpoint. Children may be better described as "sociocentric." Apparently, even infants are interested in their peers (Vandell & Mueller, 1980), and even very young children seek social interaction (Genishi & Dyson, 1984). Evidence from studies of caregivers (Bates, 1976; Nelson, 1973; Snow, 1977; Snow & Ferguson, 1977) show that for young children, and older children (Ross & Goldman, 1976), interaction with adults appears to promote language development, especially when the child's utterances are treated as meaningful (Wells, 1981).

Studies of young children's language learning (Bloom, 1970; Dore, 1974; 1979; Ervin-Tripp, 1973; Halliday, 1973, 1975; Weeks, 1979) suggest that function precedes form. Children use language for a wide range of social functions before they enter school. Through this intentional use of language, children increase their repertoire of forms and language strategies. In a study of preschool children's everyday motives for talking, Schachter, Kirshner, Klips, Friedricks, and Sanders (1974) used an observational checklist to score children's functional use of language. The analysis of data revealed that children from 2 to 5 years old gradually moved toward using more sophisticated speech in addressing adults and in adapting their forms of speech to the needs of the listener depending on their intention.

Studies of children's language use (variously called development pragmatics or discourse analysis) provide insights about how listening and speaking abilities develop. The following is a review of selected research on a range of social functions and interactional skills needed to use language effectively in context. (For comprehensive reviews see Lindfors, 1987; Menyuk, 1988; McTear, 1985; Romaine, 1984. See Franklin & Barten, 1988, for a collection of studies that represent significant areas in which there is on-going theoretical controversy and productive research. Also see chapters in this handbook by Menyuk, Clay, Farr, Bloome, and Taylor.)

Conversational Discourse. Conversation has been one of the most studied forms of discourse. Researchers have been interested to learn how children develop their sense of the structure and design of a conversation, and how those structures and designs vary accordingly to culture (Tannen, 1982, 1985).

Studies of infants and caregivers (Snow, 1977; Stern, 1977; Stern, Jaffe, Beebe, & Bennett, 1975; Whiten, 1977) reveal the beginnings of children's knowledge about the social processes involved in oral language interaction. In these "protoconversations" (McTear, 1984, 1985) adults and infants apparently en-gage in patterns of behavior such as turn taking (Snow, 1977; Whiten, 1977), and sometimes the infant takes the lead (Foster, 1979; Trevarthen, 1979). Gestures are related to intentions, such as requests and imperatives, and form the basis for later verbalizations (Bates, Camaioni, & Volterra, 1975). Mothers tend to treat infants as if they are conversing, and they build a structure around the child's responses as if they were engaged in turn taking, with the mother gradually decreasing her role, while the child develops more extensive contributions (Snow, 1977).

In a study of the development of dialogue strategies among preschool children, McTear (1984) videorecorded and analyzed free-play conversations. He found that in the early stages interactions are usually closed and do not develop into sustained dialogue. In later stages, however, children learn to link exchanges topically and to sustain talk, an important feature of mature conversation. The interest in conversation and the importance attached to learning the rules of conversation conflicts with the lack of attention to conversation in school settings.

Sensitivity to Audience. Part of what must be learned in the communication situation is how to adjust language according to the characteristics of one's audience. People talk differently to others based on factors such as age and previous knowledge. Even young children appear to practice conversational rules, including the adjustment of speech to their audience. For example, they may vary length of utterances and number or pattern of pausing. This evidence suggests that even young children are aware of the cooperative principles (Grice, 1975) required for social interaction and improve as they get older (Garvey & Ben-Debba, 1974; Shatz & Gelman, 1973; Welkowitz, Cariffe, & Feldstein, 1976). Studies of children's use of specific functions of language confirm this.

Arguing, Persuading, and Controlling Others. Eisenberg & Garvey (1981) studied argument and the resolution of conflict in conversations among 3- to 5-year-olds playing in pairs in laboratory settings. The results indicated that preschool children were able to use complex strategies such as giving reasons and requesting explanations or justifications for behavior. When preschool children's arguing strategies were recorded in more naturalistic settings, however, results demonstrated the powerful influence of the social context on the kinds of strategies children employed (Genishi & DiPaolo, 1982). These findings indicated that children in a preschool setting could be distracted by the activity around them and generally argued to establish their own authority rather than to resolve conflicts by reasoning or compromising. They did not necessarily need to resolve conflict to continue in their interaction with others.

Studies of children's arguments in preschool settings (Genishi & Di Paolo, 1982) provided evidence that although children's frequently occurring arguments were simple in structure, the children had internalized knowledge of a particular form and the social rules for engaging in that form of discourse. Children were learning to establish their relative status and defend themselves. In a study of interaction within first-grade reading classrooms, Wilkinson and Dollaghan (1979) found that children were consistently engaged in a kind of trial and error process for communication strategies. Another first-grade study by Ervin-Tripp (1982) focused on children's ability to control others and get what they wanted. Children demonstrated a repertoire of strategies and selected from that repertoire based on an awareness of factors such as closeness and familiarity of partners and status differences. Wood's (1981) study of directives indicated that children appeared to move from simple, direct requests to subtle directives that included more complex, adult-like forms such as hints. The ability to use a range of control strategies, including hints, indicated a sensitivity to contextual factors that influenced the structure of their conversation.

Studies of persuasive strategies (see Delia & Clark, 1977) demonstrate children's ability to analyze and have impact on listeners. Specific stages were identified (Delia & Clark, 1977; Delia, Kline, & Burleson, 1979). Delia and Clark's studies of 6-, 8-, 10-, and 12-year-olds and Alvy's (1973) studies of children from varying social backgrounds showed that children could use persuasive strategies and that those strategies became more effective as children got older. Perspective taking appears to be the underlying cognitive skill that is developed in this trial and error process. These findings suggest that children need the opportunity to use persuasive talk in a variety of different situations; for example, dramatic play was found to be a particularly rich situation by both Pinnell (1975) and Black (1979a, 1979b).

Making Requests and Asking for Information. As children explore alternative ways of expressing their intentions, they are obliged to respond to elements of the social system. This process is illustrated by Ervin-Tripp's (1974) study of the comprehension and production of requests by children. She found that by the middle of the third year, children had a variety of alternative ways to produce requests. For example, they could make requests through questions, statements of need, direct requests, or persuasive rhetoric. She also found that children showed a systematic social distribution in the forms of requests they used. Even among 2-year-olds there were systematic differences between requests made to children and those made to adults. Moreover, their requests of adults differed depending on a variety of factors. Children in nursery schools appeared to give negative requests and imperatives more often to children than to adults. They addressed their need statements and general condition statements more often to adults. At age 4, children addressed imbedded imperatives and permission-request forms more often to adults than peers. Even very young children seem to be aware of questions (Halliday, 1975), although they might not be able to provide an appropriate response (Dore, 1977). Studies of response to questions indicate that there is change between ages 1 and 6 (Ervin-Tripp, 1970), and that children grow in ability to more directly answer their questioners (McTear, 1984).

Informing. Much research on functions of children's language has concentrated on referential communication or the informing function (see Dickson, 1981; Flavell, Speer, Green, & August, 1981; Glucksberg & Krauss, 1967) and has focused on school-age children. For example, in a sociolinguistic study, Cook-Gumperz (1977) recorded fifth-grade children who were engaged in instruction and direction-giving situations that were subject to constraints similar to testing. Children were required

to lexicalize the details of the activities and their own interpretations. Pairs of children were asked to make a tinkertoy model, with one child as the blindfolded builder and the other as instructor. Differences in success were related to differing strategies of "doing instruction-giving." The researchers identified two main patterns in the interaction between instructor and builder: 1) cooperative and based on dialogue, and 2) controlling and taking the form of a monologue. Children tended to use direct imperatives and relied on prosodic features to convey information, strategies that were efficient in this situation but resulted in a reduced amount of lexicalized information.

Dickson (1981) wrote that research done from two separate perspectives, experimental research on referential communication skills and sociolinguistic approaches to the study of communicative competence in natural settings, "portrays an optimistic view of children's ability to communicate, both in the sense of specific communication skills such as speaking and listening and in the broader aspects of communicative competence" (pp. xiii). Careful study of children in natural settings has revealed many instances in which children are highly competent communicators. The experimental studies show, however, that "children can [also] be taught to encode more informative measures and to ask for more information when given inadequate messages. In addition, children can be taught that communication is a two-person activity, and that successful communication depends on the efforts of both" (p. xiv). In a subsequent publication, Dickson (1982) discusses how experimental referential training tasks might be translated into communication games to improve speaking and listening in the classroom.

Imagining. Irwin's (1975) study of dramatic play of children age 2 to 7 indicated that children used words to symbolize their feelings and thoughts, suggesting that language use in such situations can play an important role in children's social and intellectual development. Imagining has been shown to arise from play (Garvey, 1977). In their play, even very young children vary their speech patterns as they take on various roles. Role-taking is an important skill in mature communication, indicating that social/dramatic play for young children, improvisation, and more structured forms of drama for older children are effective means of facilitating growth in communicative competence. According to Garvey (1974), Genishi and Dyson (1984), and others, participation in social play and drama requires, among other things, that children abstract the conversational rules (e.g., turn-taking) for structuring the play and that they be able to select and use linguistic features that are appropriate to the roles played.

Galda (1984) has proposed that children's play in the narrative mode (narrative play) is also related to narrative development. She reviewed several studies and concluded that, although the studies had methodological flaws, dramatic play does seem to be an effective facilitator of narrative competence. In a subsequent study, Pellegrini and Galda (1988) documented ways children use personal narratives under two conditions and found that use of narrative language was related to age and the context of the situation; children more often generated personal narratives in ambiguous and more natural peer-play situations than in explicit storytelling situations. They conclude that the "formality of the storytelling interview may have may have suppressed children's narrative competence. It may be that other more natural contexts, such as dramatic play, may be more appropriate for eliciting children's narratives" (p. 188). (See the chapter in this handbook for a more detailed treatment of the research on teaching and the imaginative uses of language, including drama.)

Telling Stories: Development of Narrative Discourse. Children's stories, both oral and written, have been the subject of important research on the development of children's ability to construct coherent texts (for example, Haslett, 1983; King & McKenzie, 1988; Rentel & King, 1983; Stenning & Michell, 1985). Story-telling is probably the first situation in which the child must sustain a monologue without the support of a conversational partner (Stenning & Michell, 1985). Stories also have a defined structure and require complex cognitive processes such as the use of explanation (Stenning & Michell, 1985), however, even very young children have been shown to display story sense through paralinguistic features before syntactic and lexical systems are in place (Wade, 1983).

To tell a story, children must learn, among other things, how narratives are structured. A number of researchers (Hasan, 1984a, 1984b, 1984c; Johnson & Mandler, 1980; Labov, 1972; Stein & Glenn, 1979) have identified the overall structure of narrative discourse. Learning a sense of story means learning this "story grammar" and being able to produce it (Applebee, 1978; Botvin & Sutton-Smith, 1977; Westby, 1984). Bower (1976) and Thorndyke (1977) indicate that structure is also important in listening comprehension; a coherent story is remembered better than a series of unrelated events. The issue is that each type of discourse has its own structure or "script" (Nelson, 1986; Mandler, 1984). It is this structure (mental schema) that must be learned and used in producing (speaking and writing) and understanding (listening and reading) a particular form of discourse.

Research on children's narrative competence has focused mainly on primary grade children. For example, using a Piagetian framework, Applebee (1978) found that children's concept of story and ability to maintain a different point of view developed with maturity. He found that children's use of conventions, attitudes toward story, and organizational patterns reflected general cognitive developmental trends.

King and Rentel (1981) studied structural features of children's told (dictated) and retold stories. They analyzed story structure and cohesion using procedures developed by Propp (1968) and Halliday and Hasan (1976) respectively. Their findings show that children's narratives became increasingly complex as they progressed from the end of first through the second grade. As the children matured, their narratives contained more elements of story structure, such as conflict, character development, and definite endings. In addition, students were also better able to use language that was not context bound. Very young storytellers believed that their audiences knew all the things that they knew, but as the children matured and developed a better sense of audience, they provided information a listener needed to understand. Further, the type of cohesive devices in their narratives changed as they grew older. They

increased their use of lexical cohesion and conjunctions and decreased their use of exophoric reference, thereby showing increasing sensitivity to audience.

Many recent studies have shown that as young children hear stories told and read, children learn the structure as well as the linguistic features of narrative discourse (King & Rentel, 1981; Pappas, 1985; Cox & Sulzby, 1984). They often display their knowledge by "talking like a book" when they reenact or pretend to read their favorite stories (Butler, 1980; Clay, 1977, 1979; Cochran-Smith, 1984; Doake, 1985; Fox, 1985, 1988; Heath, 1983; King & McKenzie, 1988; McKenzie, 1977; Pappas & Brown, 1987; Schickedanz & Sullivan, 1984; Sultzby, 1985; Taylor, 1983). These studies suggest that reading aloud to children facilitates the development of narrative competence, particularly literate narrative.

Descriptions of narrative discourse have arisen in several different fields and have shown to be highly related to cultural factors (Labov, 1972). Tannen (1982) claims that oral discourse can be sorted into oral and literate categories. For example, in storytelling, some adults dramatize rather than state the point of the story, or they utilize exaggerated paralinguistic features to convey meaning, a style Tannen labeled as more "oral." In oral style there is a scarcity of explicit verbal information. Tannen (1985) further suggested that the differences between oral and literate traditions lie in the focus, whether it is on interpersonal involvement or on information and explicit messages.

"Sharing time" is a common discourse activity in primary school classrooms. Analyses of "sharing time" (Michaels 1981, 1984, 1985, 1986; Michaels & Cook-Gumperz, 1979; Michaels & Foster, 1985) provide evidence that divided African American and white children according to their performance, the reinforcement they received from the teacher, and the practice in literate-style discourse they received during the event. Teachers appeared to have difficulty recognizing the special intonation patterns that some African American children used to emphasize points or create cohesion in messages. These students tended to come from cultural backgrounds different from that of the teacher. Conversely, "sharing stories" that had a main point and used explicitly stated connections were more highly rated by teachers. Those strategies were characteristic of white children who came from backgrounds similar to the teachers'.

In another study, Michaels and Collins (1984) were able to identify oral-based and literate-based strategies in spoken narratives. Children's narratives, produced in response to a short film, were used to characterize children as literate-style or oral-style speakers. These two groups both attempted to establish cohesion, but they used different strategies to do so. Oral-style children relied on context, paralinguistic cues, and audience involvement more than on lexicalization, the strategy used more by the literate-style children.

Story structure varies by cultural group (Tannen, 1985). Michaels' work indicates that children learn the narrative structures used in their families and communities; but when they attempt to use the structure they know in social settings, they may encounter another concept of the structure of narrative. Stories are related to culture, context, and purpose, and assessment of children's narrative knowledge should be based on performance in several different contexts (Pappas, 1981, 1985).

Pedagogical Significance of Child Language Research. This research shows that by the time children go off to school they know a great deal about their native language and how to use that language to communicate with others. Although not specifically related to teaching oral language in the classroom, the studies provide important insights about the basic processes involved in language learning.

The studies illustrate that:

1. Children learn how language is used while they are learning language;
2. Children learn language by using it for real purposes within social situations; and
3. Factors in the social context heavily influence language use and learning.

They show that children do become increasingly sophisticated at using spoken language for a variety of functions (making requests, asking for information, controlling others, informing, imagining, and telling stories) and different forms of discourse (conversation, argument, narrative), and in monitoring and adjusting their language to the context of the situation (setting, audience, task). Whether or how these competencies can be further developed in the classroom, remains an open question.

Development of communicative competence is a complex process. Children need to learn the functions of language, the rules that govern social interaction, and the structure of various forms of discourse in order to use language effectively in both speaking and listening. The three aspects of communicative competence are interrelated in language use and learning, and are also related to literacy development (for discussions of the potential relationships see Dickinson, 1987; Fitzgerald, 1989, Kretschmer, 1989; Myers, 1987; Torrence & Olson, 1984). Although we need more research to describe and explain the process and to determine the conditions that will promote learning, the research does suggest that "communicative competence in the classroom cannot be broken down into fragments out of context, without destroying the essence of the process" (Wilkinson & Spinelli, 1982, p. 327).

FROM HOME TO SCHOOL

When children enter school, they encounter a new language environment; and for many, it is an environment greatly different from their homes. An aspect of learning to be a pupil is the mastery of a code of oral language interactions, including rules that are rarely made explicit by teachers (Willes, 1983).

Willes (1983) found that teachers who taught children entering school for the first time took a great deal for granted about children's knowledge of this system of rules. Teachers frequently asssumed that instructions would be understood by pupils who did not understand the context to which those instructions referred and who had not been provided with relevant explanations of procedures. Because this was the children's first school experience, it might have been reasonable to expect teachers to ease the transition from home to school, including explanations, demonstrations, and time to practice the ways of

talking and behaving that are important in school settings. Instead, the whole process of acquiring competence as a student is somewhat haphazard and left to chance. According to Willes, many children receive far less support than they need. Children do not start at a common level of experience in school-like settings; the required knowledge is not easily communicated through direct instruction. Some children remain "baffled and silent."

Through detailed studies of children in both home and school settings, Wells (1985, 1986a, 1986b; Wells & Wells, 1984) discovered that young children's home environments provide interactions characterized by collaboration in the negotiation of meaning and intention. Wells' data were collected through recording language in naturalistic settings and then systematically analyzing the transcribed data. A total of 128 children were recorded at intervals over 2 and one-half years, with a subgroup followed through primary school. Wells was able to observe children in both home and school settings and to note differences among children and between the settings. School language was basically teacher dominated. Compared to the home setting, children initiated fewer interactions, played a much more passive role in conversations, took fewer turns, and asked fewer questions. Children in school produced syntactically less complex utterances with a narrower range of meaning content than in home settings. Teachers were twice as likely to develop their own meanings as they were to respond to children's meanings, while parents were twice as likely to respond to children's contributions. Wells explained the "impoverished" talk between teachers and pupils by proposing that teachers probably do not believe that pupils' own talk has value in their learning.

Wells suggested that homes tended to provide richer oral language environments than did classrooms. Educators have assumed that children's lack of language skills, resulting from deficient home environments, contributes to a lack of success in school. Wells' research raises doubts about this assumption and suggests that schools do not provide a context that demands children use language in new ways. Classrooms may not provide opportunities for children to learn through talk and, at the same time, to expand their repertoire for talking in different ways.

Tizard and Hughes (1984) drew similar conclusions from their comparisons of 4-year-olds in conversations with their mothers and in conversations with their teachers at nursery school. The conversations at home revealed the children to be persistent and logical thinkers, puzzling to grasp new ideas. The children's talk with teachers lacked such richness, depth, and variety. There was not the same sense of intellectual struggle and mutual attempt to communicate found at home. DeStefano and Kantor (1988) had similar findings in their study of the differences between the language used at home and that used in school with Appalachian children.

Heath (1983) studied aspects of learning behavior in southern U.S. African American and white communities. She found that each community had its own values and conventions for instructional encounters. Strategies that outside observers might label as dysfunctional behaviors were actually firmly grounded in the interactive practices and learning styles of the home. These differences in discourse patterns had consequences for children's ability to profit from instruction in the school classroom. Heath (1983) concluded that educators must account for variations in interactive norms and continuously seek to be sure that information is conveyed to students. Accomplishing this goal would mean viewing teaching and learning as interactive processes.

These and other studies (Phillips, 1972) of the differences between conversations at home and in school and among different cultural groups throw doubt on the theory that some children underachieve at school because of a language deficit at home, and raise serious issues about how schools affect students of different sociocultural and economic backgrounds. Tizard and Hughes (1984) conclude: "The schools' problem, as we see it, is how to foster the interest and curiosity which children show at home. An environment is required that will allow the 'puzzling' to flourish, and which will help the young child . . . develop her intellectual and communication skills" (p. 261).

The studies reviewed above focus on differences in patterns of language *use* that are the result of differences in the social system, the rules that govern a speaker's interactions with others. Differences in language *structure* (e.g., phonology and syntax) are also potential sources of interference in communication and learning. Many teachers, though aware of the differences, still hold the view that children who speak a language that is different from the accepted standard are poor language users (Goodman, Smith, Meredith, & Goodman, 1987). In fact, every version of a language is appropriate and useful for the culture within which it is constructed (DeStefano, 1973; Labov, 1969).

Goodman et al. (1987) caution that educators must not ignore dialect differences because they might make unconscious assumptions about language and text that will cause problems in instruction, such as presenting rhyming words that do not rhyme for the divergent speaker. All children, as they encounter new situations, must learn to expand their ability to use language in different ways. The teacher, however, must not subvert this expansion process by rejection or negative attitude towards children's own speech (Kiefer & DeStefano, 1985). Children who experience such rejection may be reluctant to risk speaking in new ways; and, they may not make full use of their language resources in the learning situation.

Children may speak different idiolects, different regional or social dialects of the same language, or different languages. They may even be hard of hearing and use the sign language of the deaf as a primary communication system. Research in these areas is reviewed in other sections of this volume; however, it is particularly important to acknowledge the existence of language differences in this chapter. It is through oral language that teachers notice characteristics of divergent speech.

RESEARCH ON ORAL LANGUAGE IN THE CLASSROOM: THREE PERSPECTIVES

Research on classroom language has provided important information about the uses of oral language in schools, the characteristic features of classroom discourse, and the potential consequences of students' oral language development and learning. This section describes three perspectives from which classroom discourse has been studied: one developed in the United States and dominated classroom research for years, another that developed in Britain and focuses on the role of talk in learning, and a third that focuses on classrooms as contexts for social interaction and has had a significant impact on classroom research in both countries. The subsequent section will review the results of classroom language research for insights about the state of practice.

U.S. Tradition: Using Coding Systems to Describe Classroom Interaction

During the 1960s and 1970s almost all the classroom research in the United States, and some in Britain, involved the creation and use of coding approaches for analyzing classroom social systems. As reviewed in Dunkin and Biddle (1974), the systematic tradition, stemming from psychology, resulted in a large number of studies designed to provide clues to the kinds of social interactions and social systems that were related to higher achievement or positive outcomes in education. Studies of social interaction rose from three sources: 1) educators who were concerned with conditions for learning; 2) psychologists concerned with mental health in schools; and 3) social scientists studying the behavior of groups in social settings such as the classroom (Withall & Lewis, 1971).

In order to quickly and efficiently code classroom talk into quantifiable data, a large number of techniques were designed (Amidon & Hough, 1967; Amidon & Hunter, 1967; Flanders, 1966; Simon & Boyer, 1974). As indicated in one review (Dunkin & Biddle, 1974), these methods were "systematic." They used instruments for noting or measuring events and used them consistently for a number of observations. These investigators systematically observed what happened in classrooms and quantified those observations for descriptive and correlational studies.

The results of these observational studies suggested that "the majority of classrooms are dominated by a style of teaching that has remained virtually unchanged since the beginning of modern schooling in the nineteenth century, and probably since the beginning of the age-graded school class" (Young & Watson, 1981, p. 82). Teachers do most of the talking, estimates go as high as 72 to 75 percent. Moreover, teachers ask almost all the questions in classrooms (90 to 95 percent), and the recitation pattern (with teachers' instructions, questions, and reactions to student responses making up 70 to 75 percent of the talk, and student responses constituting 25 to 30 percent) dominates classroom discourse in studies done across different levels and areas of the curriculum, including English and language-arts instruction (Young & Watson, 1981).

Although these systematic studies offer educators information about classroom language, they have been criticized by English educators (Barnes, 1972) and by language researchers working in other disciplines (Edwards, 1976; Edwards & Furlong, 1978; Edwards & Westgate, 1987; Delamont, 1976, 1981; Delamont & Hamilton, 1984; Gumperz, 1986; Hammersley,

1986b; Mehan, 1981; Sevigny, 1981). They claim, among other things, that the coders/observers were subject to cultural blinders, ignored the perspectives and intentions of the participants involved in the interactions, did not record actual data for more systematic and reliable analysis, and, as a result, failed to see the complexity and patterns of interaction in classroom discourse. Evertson and Green (1986) have identified many common sources of error in this research and note that these problems need attention if one is to observe accurately in classrooms.

Delamont and Hamilton (1984) criticized prespecified coding schemes because

1. Such schemes seek to produce only numerical and normative data;
2. The procedures tend to ignore the context in which data are gathered;
3. The coding schemes are usually concerned only with overt, observable behavior, and not with the intentions behind the behavior;
4. They focus on things that can be categorized and measured, and distort or ignore the qualitative features;
5. The systems focus on small bits of behavior rather than global concepts;
6. Categories are prespecified and thus may assume rather than explain social processes; and
7. Arbitrary boundaries are pre-established, thus creating an initial bias that "freezes" reality (p. 8–10).

Despite these problems, research using interactional analysis systems provided important information about language use in classrooms. These studies created the notion of objective feedback to assist teachers in becoming aware of their own language as a means of improving their teaching (Good & Brophy, 1987). Furthermore, the results raised issues for English educators and researchers in Britain and the United States who were already concerned about the impact of classroom language on students' learning and communication development (for example, see Allen & Brown, 1976; Barnes, 1972; Barnes, Britton & Rosen, 1971; Dixon, 1967; Moffett, 1968).

British Approach: Recognizing the Role of Oral Language

In the 1960s and 1970s, research emerging in the United Kingdom brought increased attention to the development of oral language in school settings. Exemplified by the new term "oracy," coined to parallel "literacy" that at the time dominated the curriculum (Wilkinson, 1965; Wilkinson, 1970), a new scholarly direction emphasized the integrated nature of listening and speaking and the importance of talking in learning.

Seminal studies of talk in primary and secondary classrooms were produced by Barnes, Britton and Rosen (1971), Barnes (1976), and Rosen and Rosen (1973). These studies were important because they provided pictures of what classrooms were and could be like and had implications that seemed sensible and real to teachers on both sides of the Atlantic. These researchers tended not to focus on language itself, but to view language as providing a window on students' learning and social development.

A major policy document, the Bullock (1975) report, *A Language for Life* presented a forward-looking language policy that would create what Marland (1977) called "a 'virtuous circle': if a school devotes thought and time to assisting language development, learning in all areas will be helped; if attention is given to language in the content and skill subjects, language development will be assisted powerfully by the context and purpose of those subjects" (p. 3). Though the report focused on secondary schools, the ideas were equally applicable to education in primary schools.

The climate was right for this report, being already influenced by the "language across the curriculum movement" advocated by the National Association for the Teaching of English (1976). The origin of the movement could be traced to an interest in theories of language and learning derived from the work of Piaget (1959), Vygotsky (1962, 1978), Kelly (1955), and Bruner (1975). The work by Barnes (1971, 1972, 1973); Barnes et al. (1971); Britton (1970, 1971); Doughty, Pearce, & Thornton (1972); Halliday (1969, 1971, 1973, 1975, 1978); Wilkinson (1971, 1972, 1975); and Wilkinson, Stratta and Dudley (1974) provided theoretical foundations for the movement. In their work, they addressed such issues as the functions of language, language as part of the social system, the relations between language and situation, classroom environments for language use, and the relations between talking and learning. Others attempted to translate theory into teachers' guides for language work in the school. For example, in *Language in Use,* Doughty, Pearce, and Thornton (1971), developed Halliday's ideas into a set of classroom activities that would allow secondary students to explore, discover, and experiment with the variety of uses of language.

Moreover, following Barnes' (1972) criticism of the systematic approach to investigating classrooms and his call for more naturalistic studies, English educators (Barnes, 1976; Jones & Mulford, 1971; Martin, Williams, Wilding, Hemmings, & Medway, 1976; Martin, D'Arcy, Newton, & Parker, 1976; Mallet & Newsome, 1977; Rosen & Rosen, 1973; Torbe & Protherough, 1976) published case studies and anecdotal reports that provided powerful descriptive portraits of how language use shares learning when primary and secondary students are given opportunities to use language—talk and write, read and listen—to learn across the curriculum.

These British scholars had a significant impact on views of oral language competence and moved language teaching into the future by envisioning a curriculum for listening and speaking based on broad communicative competence. Their view suggested that when engaged in the process of "languaging," a speaker looks outward, towards the audience, as well as inward, at his/her own linguistic resources. Competence is an individual's ability to select and use language in a way that communicates what he/she wants to "mean" in that context (Halliday, 1973, 1975). Competence, then, is a mediating factor between the speaker's potential for making meanings and the demands of the situation.

This view of competence suggests that students who perform poorly may have considerable "meaning potential" and resources, but may lack experience using language in the contexts concerned. The task for the curriculum, then, is to provide experiences in the classroom that require the growth of this competence. Variety in learning situations is necessary; these must constantly change and should demand a range of oral language use (Britton, 1970, 1971; Halliday, 1969, 1973, 1978).

Both kinds of classroom research—systematic observation and naturalistic case studies—have provided important information on the uses of oral language in the classroom, however, still another line of research sprang from theories of classroom discourse emerging in the fields of educational sociology, linguistics, sociolinguistics, and anthropology (Cicourel et al., 1974; Coulthard, 1977; Delamont, 1983; Erickson & Shultz, 1977; Gumperz & Humes, 1972; Hymes, 1962, 1967, 1972, 1974; Mehan, 1979, 1981; Sinclair & Coulthard, 1975; Stubbs, 1983; Stubbs & Delamont, 1976; Young, 1971). These new theories influenced the direction of classroom research in the United States and the United Kingdom.

Classrooms as Contexts for Social Interaction: An Ethnographic Perspective

Sociologists who studied schools in the 1960s found that children previously thought unresponsive and lacking in verbal ability were actually skilled communicators in peer group situations (Labov, 1969). Their speech showed reflection of underlying grammatical rules and indicated the use of complex cognitive abilities. It was still unclear, however, how language entered into the social environment of the school.

In 1962, Hymes called for an ethnography of communication that signalled the blending of different perspectives to study language use in social contexts. Techniques from anthropology, sociology, linguistics, and sociolinguistics were used to create detailed observations of the ways language is used in different speech communities (Hymes, 1962, 1967), including the classroom (Gumperz, 1981, 1986).

Hymes' work was given greater attention with the publication of *Functions of Language in the Classroom* (Cazden, John, & Hymes, 1972). In the introduction to that volume, Hymes (1972) restated his previous position concerning the way language should be studied. He maintained that it must be studied in the social context and in terms of the way it is organized to meet social needs. Accepting each child's culture, language, and ways of using language was a primary theme of the volume. The educative process is based on what the child brings to the situation and on the relationship between ways of using language and ways of learning in the classroom.

The early work, in particular, focused on the discrepancy between language use at home among various cultural and socioeconomic groups and use at school (see Bernstein, 1971, 1973, 1974; Boggs, 1972; Philips, 1972). For more recent work see Au, 1980; Erickson & Mohatt, 1982; and Heath, 1983). Recognition of the relations between language and culture contributed significantly to knowledge of oral language use in classrooms. In the search for ways to understand cultural differences, researchers in a number of disciplines began to study the classroom as a social system and developed new ways

to analyze communication in this speech community (Hymes, 1967). (See also chapters in this handbook by Bloome and by Zaharlick and Green.)

Communication is a critical component of classroom teaching and learning; it is important because of its role in social interaction and in gaining and displaying knowledge. As Mehan (1979) states:

Students not only must know the content of academic subjects, they must learn the appropriate form in which to cast their knowledge. That is, competent membership in the classroom community involves employing interactional skills and abilities in the display of academic knowledge. They must know with whom, when, and where they can speak and act, and they must provide the speech and behavior that are appropriate for a given classroom situation. (p. 133)

Examples of research done from an ethnographic perspective are included in the discussion in the next section. For more comprehensive reviews of this work see Cazden, 1986, 1988; Edwards and Furlong, 1978; Edwards and Westgate, 1987; Edwards and Mercer, 1987; Green, 1983; Green and Smith, 1983. (For collections of representative studies see Gilmore and Glatthorn, 1982; Green, 1979; Green and Wallat, 1981a; Hammersley, 1986a; Trueba, Guthrie, and Au, 1981; and Wilkinson, 1982). Findings from research on the nature of classroom discourse and on the role of talk in learning provide significant information about the state of practice and the nature of classrooms as contexts for communication development and learning.

CLASSROOMS AS CONTEXTS FOR COMMUNICATION AND LEARNING: THE STATE OF PRACTICE

Many researchers have explored the communication demands of the classroom. They have studied the functions of language and various features of the discourse used in urban and suburban schools, across grade levels (K–12), in whole-class and small-group instruction, in various activities (free play, role play, lessons, discussions), and in different curriculum areas (reading, math, science, social studies, English, and the humanities). The results provide important insights about the kinds talking and learning that take place in elementary and secondary classrooms.

Functions of Language in the Classroom

Language is functional; it serves important purposes in people's lives. It is used to establish and maintain relationships, influence others, tell stories, ask questions and give information, and analyze and speculate about the world. Its primary function is for communication, but it is also a tool for learning. The study of the functions of language, then, focuses on what people do with language.

Various approaches have been used to study the functions of oral language in classrooms. The particular approach depends on the researcher's purpose and the way that language is conceptualized. For example, Halliday (1973, 1978) conceptualized language as "meaning potential," which is actualized in various social situations through communication. He argued that language development is a process of "learning how to mean," that is, learning what one can do with language in interaction with others. For Halliday, then, meaning is defined in terms of function.

Halliday (1969, 1973) identified seven models or social functions of language. Halliday (1975) found that these functions evolve over time, but that children use language for all of these functions before they enter school. He found that children's language initially expresses:

1. An *instrumental* function to satisfy basic needs;
2. A *regulatory* function to influence the behavior of others;
3. An *interactional* function to mediate relationships with others; and
4. A *personal* function to express self. These are followed by
5. A *heuristic* function to explore and find out about the environment;
6. An *imaginative* function to pretend and explore an imagination world and, finally,
7. An *informative* or representational function to inform or communicate information to others.

Halliday (1975, 1978) also argued that these seven functions, which are discrete and independent language uses in young children, merge into three more general functions that characterize adult language. These include: the *pragmatic or interpersonal* function that has to do with maintaining social relationships; the *mathetic or ideational function* that has to do with reflecting on personal experience and exploring the environment, and the *textual function* that involves the use of language resources to construct oral texts (e.g., stories, conversation) that are coherent within themselves and within the context of the situation. In adult language, all three of these functions are used simultaneously.

Halliday (1969, 1978) stressed the importance of children experiencing the full range of language functions in the classroom. Pinnell (1975) used Halliday's seven categories to study children's uses for language in informal first-grade classrooms in the United States and to determine what elements of the classroom context seemed to foster a range of language functions. She found that although these classrooms provided opportunities for children to use language for all the functions, some functions were not used as frequently as might be expected. She concluded that "even in the best of educational situations, encouragement for talking and an array of materials are not enough. Teachers' . . . subtle communication through which they invite children to use language for a variety of purposes makes the critical difference" (p. 325). Although it is important for teachers to accept and appreciate the language children have when they come to school, it is also important for them to provide the conditions whereby children can increase their range of competence.

The way young children use language in educational settings has been the subject of Tough's (1973, 1977a) work in England. Her studies of the language of 3-, 4-, and 5-year-old children

provide evidence that when children come to the school situation they have already established certain orientations to language and expectations about ways of using it. Tough agreed with Halliday (1973) and Bernstein (1971, 1973, 1975) that differences in children's language use may reflect differences in the set of meanings they hold. As they attempt to deal with the new experiences of the school situation, they must refer to the set of meanings developed through prior experience. For some, this task is relatively simple because the school requires using language in many of the same ways they have used it at home. For others, school may mean adjustment to many unaccustomed ways of using language.

Tough (1973, 1977a) analyzed her language data to compare advantaged and disadvantaged groups of children. She concluded that the socially disadvantaged group talked as much and had the same general knowledge and language resources as the advantaged group; however, they were inexperienced in the ways schools expect students to verbalize thought. Tough (1976, 1977b) then proposed procedures teachers could use to provide more supportive and demanding contexts for language development. Tough's work has been criticized (Shuy, 1984) for being "reductionist," that is, she reduced her analysis to sets of categories rather than probing responses within each interaction; but her close look at children's development of language functions in classroom settings revealed powerful "under the surface" factors in children's oral language learning.

Tough, 1973, described one classroom situation in which children were "immersed in teachers' language." The adult teachers in the classroom created a warm and accepting environment but offered little invitation for children to talk. Teachers found it quicker and easier to anticipate students' needs and thus failed to seize opportunities that would make the children want and need to talk. They were providing a situation in which children could have time to talk and interact with each other; but not a situation that would foster the development of new language abilities. Pinnell's (1975) study provides evidence that supports Tough's research. After analyzing written transcripts of talk recorded in naturalistic classroom settings, she found a range of language functions to exist among child-to-child interactions, but described teachers' roles as managerial and facilitative of activity rather than critical in extending children's use of language.

Tough (1973, 1977a) drew implications from her research for classroom practice. She recommended that the teacher carefully observe children and listen to their language. Then, the teacher must seek ways to provide opportunities for expanding talk. Tough claimed that the listening, alert, and knowledgeable teacher can consciously influence children's talk and help them pursue ideas and develop new meanings. Teachers may need to raise their own awareness of their oral language interactions with children. Tough (1976, 1977b, 1979) went on to create materials to assist teachers in observing children's uses of language. Her function categories included among others, self-maintaining language to reveal personality and reflect social adjustment, reporting present or past experiences, projecting into possibilities or feelings of others, and moving into logical reasoning.

Britton (1970, 1971) developed a theory of language functions based on a continuum of language roles. He emphasized the importance of "starting where the child is" and gradually developing the differences in language use by refining the various language roles into which children enter. He created a continuum from the participant role in which the speaker uses language for practical matters such as informing, persuading, and explaining, to the spectator role in which the speaker uses language to daydream, chat about experiences, contemplate events, tell stories, and preserve delight in utterance. These roles are seen to cover all uses of language: the transactional or informative uses at the participant end of the continuum, the expressive uses in the middle, and the poetic uses at the spectator end.

Britton (1970, 1971) proposed that the young child's language is primarily expressive, but with experience it gradually moves outward toward the kinds of language used in both the participant (transactional) or spectator (poetic) roles in response to different contexts. However, expressive language, out of which the other two functions grow, continues to be important for learners of all ages. Britton (1971) argues that expressive speech is not only the means by which we get to know one another; it is the means by which we "rehearse the growing points of our formulation and analysis of experience. . . . It is our principal means of exchanging opinions, attitudes, and beliefs in face-to-face situations" (p. 207–208). Thus, expressive language is used to speculate and to explore new ideas and, as such, plays a central role in learning.

Britton's framework of expressive, transactional, and poetic functions was initially developed to analyze written language (Britton, Burgess, Martin, Mcleod & Rosen (1975), nevertheless, it is equally applicable to spoken and written discourse. Britton (1971) saw the scheme as providing a framework for planning language activities across the curriculum that engage students in roles where they have opportunities to use language—spoken and written—for the full range of functions. "We hope, for instance, the expressive language may be increasingly seen to play a role in all learning (even the most subject oriented) as well as in learning to use language; and that the educational value of spectator activities may come to be better understood and more convincingly argued" (p. 218).

In his now classic survey of secondary classrooms, Barnes (Barnes et al., 1971) found little or no exploratory talk during formal lessons in the general area of the humanities and in science subjects, areas where one would expect to find students engaged in inquiry. Instead, teachers did most of the talking; students were cast in a passive role. However, in another study, Barnes (1976) analyzed relatively unstructured peer conversations and found students more frequently used exploratory talk in their discussions of science, history, and poetry. Based on close analysis of language use in small-group student discussions, Barnes and Todd (1977) and other investigators (Chilver & Gould, 1982; Phillips, 1985) advocate use of small-group discussions without a teacher as a way to avoid the constraints placed on talk and learning in teacher-led lessons. Recent reviews of research indicate, however, that true discussion is rare in classrooms (Dillon, 1984). Based on her study of secondary English classrooms, Alverman (1986) called discussion the "forgotten language art."

Whole-class, teacher-led "discussions" predominate, particu-

larly at the secondary level, in the United States as well as other countries. Watson (1987) suggests that we need alternatives to the teacher-dominated patterns of whole-class lessons, patterns that will give students more activity and opportunities to explore through language. Watson (1980) found such patterns in a study of 90 English lessons in New South Wales. He observed three distinct types of whole-class discussion, each characterized by a different kind of conversational control (Stubbs, 1976). The first type (60 percent of lessons) was a classroom in which closed questions predominated and teachers were content with one-word or very brief answers. The discourse in these lessons was similar to what Barnes (1973) described as a transmission model of teaching. The second (30 percent of lessons) was a class in which the teacher still retained conversational control over choice of topic, and who and when students could speak, but there were more open questions and the teacher responded to students' replies instead of simply evaluating them. In this type of classroom, students were encouraged to engage in some exploratory talk (Barnes, 1976).

In the third type (observed in four to five lessons), Watson found less conversational control. Pupil initiated responses were more common and teachers generally used open questions and did not demand that all comments be funneled through the teacher. Watson described the second and third types as more conducive to critical thinking. The discourse in these classrooms was more reflective of Barnes' (1973) interpretation style of teaching. Follow-up interviews revealed that teachers in the first category believed that they were encouraging pupils to develop their answers and were responding rather than simply evaluating. They tended to exaggerate the involvement of pupils in the discussion. Since whole-class discussion appears to be the predominate mode of instruction in most of the upper grades, teachers need to be more aware of the effects of conversational control and of their own tendency to deceive themselves about the nature of students' experiences.

Many researchers have used Britton's framework to study classroom talk. Several (Barr, D'Arcy, Healey, 1982; Berrill, 1988; Hickman & Kimberley, 1988; Mallet & Newsome, 1977; Martin, 1983; Martin, D'Arcy, Newton, & Parker, 1976; Martin, Williams, Wilding, Hemmings, & Medway, 1976; Robertson, 1980; Torbe & Protherough, 1976; Torbe & Medway, 1981) have shown how students, given the opportunities to talk and listen, can and do use spoken language in productive ways to learn in all areas of the curriculum. These studies highlight the kinds of curriculum activities, learning tasks, and conditions that are likely to encourage students to use language to learn and, in the process, learn how to use language.

Research on language use in the classroom points to the fact that language, even for young children, is functionally complex and that any segment of talk can serve many purposes (Halliday, 1973, 1975). It has also demonstrated that language use is related to the type of activities students engaged in (Genishi & Dyson, 1984; Pinnell, 1975, Shure, 1963). For example, language used in dramatic play has been found to be unusually rich and productive, as evidenced in Black's (1979b) comparisons of young children's language during play and test situations. Other studies have shown that language use is related to physical arrangements and materials (Doke & Risley, 1972) and to group size and/relationship (Berk, 1973; Schacter et al., 1974).

The research reviewed here also points to the need for teachers to be aware of how oral language is used in their classrooms. Cahir and Kovac (1981) have developed sets of materials to help teachers become more aware of student's uses for language as well as their own. Others (for example, Allen, Brown & Yatvin, 1986; Doughty & Doughty, 1974; Doughty, Pearce & Thornton, 1971; Gorman, 1985; Klein, 1977, 1979; Lund & Duchan, 1988; Moffett, 1968; Moffett & Wagner, 1973; Pinnell, 1985; Shafer, Staab, & Smith, 1983; Wilkinson, 1975; Wilkinson, *et al.*, 1980; Wood, 1977a, 1977b) have explored theory and research on functions of language and have suggested ways teachers can use various category systems to observe and assess students' use of spoken language and to design curriculum activities that give them practice in talking and listening for a full range of social and intellectual functions.

Classroom Communication and Learning: A Sociolinguistic Perspective

Much current research focusses on classroom communication processes and is framed from a sociolinguistic perspective. This research draws on methodologies and interpretive frameworks from a variety of disciplines (Cazden, 1986; Green, 1983; Green & Harker, 1988; Wilkinson, 1982). Sociologists, linguists, and sociolinguists are interested in the classroom as a social context for language use because it has recognizable and well defined roles and traditions (Hymes, 1972; Gumperz, 1986; Gumperz & Herasimchuk, 1975; Edwards, 1976, 1979; Sinclair & Coulthard, 1975). Language is seen as a window to provide information on learning and social development; but researchers also find it valuable to focus on the window itself, to learn about how people learn to communicate and use language in classroom contexts.

This research has revealed the special characteristics of speech routines that occur in classroom situations. These routines are similar across classroom contexts and serve as "speech events" for study (Gumperz, 1986). In general, this research shows that teachers and children in classrooms interact in very patterned, rule-governed ways. These rules or norms for behavior are continually monitored, signaled, and interpreted by the people involved, and part of learning is finding out how to read cues and make inferences necessary to be successful in classrooms (Gilmore & Glatthorn, 1982; Green & Wallat, 1981b). This process is complex because expectations vary by situational factors (Gumperz, 1981), such as the background of people involved. Also, the context constantly changes as signals interact with the background experiences and assumptions of participants, and they are often interpreted differently.

Many of the sociolinguistic studies of classroom communication have focused on the nature of the social relationships underlying the distinctive discourse produced in the spoken language of the classroom. Primarily two kinds of relationships exist within any K–12 classroom: relationships between teachers and students, and between students and students.

Teacher and Student Talk: Studying Classroom Lessons. According to Edwards (1976, 1979), classroom talk typically consists of working out the power relationships between teacher and students. Classrooms seem to be environments in which teachers place severe functional constraints upon what students say. Knowledge is framed by the teacher and communicated by the authority to the pupils (Edwards, 1979). In some classroom environments, "elaborated codes" (Bernstein, 1964, 1975) predominate. Students who are not accustomed to reconstructing their knowledge and expressing it explicitly may find themselves at a disadvantage and teachers may view them as inferior in learning ability. Studies of teacher and student talk reveal that not only must students learn the content of school lessons, they must learn the behaviors and language teachers connect with successful students (Cazden, 1988; Edwards, 1981; Mehan, 1979).

A fruitful area of investigation in sociolinguistic studies of classroom language has been the teacher-led lesson that, as documented in many studies (Bellack, Kleibard, Hyman, & Smith, 1966; Mehan, 1979; Sinclair & Coulthard, 1975; Griffin & Shuy, 1978), takes place in an orderly and patterned way. The basic lesson structure includes a three-part sequence of turns in which the teachers asks a question that requires a response, a student responds, and the teacher comments on the response, evaluating or reformulating the student's response (Mehan, 1979). This has become known as the recitation pattern. Shavelson and Stern (1981) found that when teachers prepare lessons they follow implicit "scripts" that guide the lesson and determine the overall structure and flow of the action.

Lessons provide a predictable environment, within which, once established, the teacher can use simple utterances that would be ambiguous without knowledge of the context (Mehan, 1979). In a year-long study of a first-grade classroom, Gumperz (1986) found that the manner of articulation is more important than the actual content of lessons. The teacher used phrases and intonation to set up a predictable structure within which children could understand what was expected. Erickon and Shultz (1977) suggest that the teacher "sets them up" for prediction through the words and phrases used in the lesson (Erickson & Schultz, 1977).

Lessons are different from ordinary conversation. In everyday conversation, speakers share responsibility and they negotiate turns. In situations where it is very difficult to get a turn, speakers often reform into smaller groups. In classrooms, however, the number of speakers are contained in one space for a long period of time. The teacher is pressed to keep order so that information can be transmitted; so, teachers control turns (Edwards, 1979). There is one speaker at a time, to which everyone is supposed to listen, few gaps in conversation, and little overlap of speakers. Teachers usually speak between each turn. The teacher allocates turns, monitors what is said, repairs breakdowns, and sums up, thereby having complete control of who speaks, and what and how much is said (Edwards, 1979). Based on what he observed in secondary English classrooms, Stubbs (1976) describes classroom talk as "asymmetrical . . . almost never used by pupils and, when it is, it is a sign that an atypical teaching situation has arisen" (p. 162).

In the classroom situation, questions are asked by a person who already knows the answer (Cazden, 1988; Edwards, 1979). This particular circumstance means that the person asking the question retains the power to evaluate the response (Sinclair & Coulthard, 1975). When teachers ask questions, students are obligated to respond, to wait for an assessment of what they say, and to look for cues as to how they should modify their responses (Hammersley, 1977; Mehan, 1978, 1979). As Edwards (1979) explains, the teacher in the classroom "owns" instructional talk, with the prerogative to direct speakership and to make at least most of the decisions concerning duration, and content of the talk. The critical element in the pattern is the teacher's prior knowledge that is to be transmitted to the students. The teacher retains the preallocated rights of the "expert" and the students are assumed to be unknowing; thus, the teacher's questions function as "tests"; the pupil's meanings are defined in relationship to the body of knowledge that defines what is relevant and irrelevant. This pattern of interaction is not unique to the classroom. It is typical of any hierarchical relationship in which one person holds the knowledge and power and attempts to instruct another.

Given this constrained view of classroom discourse, it appears that the gap between middle- and lower-class children's ability to cope with school is not so much being able to be explicit or talk in elaborated ways as it is knowing how and when to talk and how to display knowledge in talk. Edwards (1979) suggests that middle-class children, who seem to have more experience with adults in tutorial roles, may be more successful in school situations where information exchange and knowledge testing are primary. "They seem to be more accustomed to having their knowledge tested, more concerned with getting their answers right, more constrained by what they perceive as being relevant to the adult listener, and more experienced in ... drills which prepare them to ignore verbally the fact that the questioner already knows" (Edwards, 1979, p. 251).

Dillon and Searle (1981) conducted an ethnographic study of a first-grade class that supported Edwards' description of classroom language as constrained. They observed one teacher judged as "good," and six children considered "successful" at home and at school. Out of school, children were more likely to be partners with adults in conversations, resembling Bernstein's (1964) "elaborated" code. In school, however, a "restricted" code was more likely to be the norm. Their findings are similar to those of Wells (1981) and Tizard and Hughes (1984) who also found the home a richer context for communication and learning.

In a review of 10 studies funded by National Institute of Education in the late 1970s, Green and Smith (1983) provided a list of constructs that define teaching and learning as linguistic processes. These same constructs represent basic assumptions pertinent to the study of speaking and listening as integrated oral language actions. Their list included the following:

1. Classrooms are communicative environments;
2. Communication is a rule-governed activity;
3. Inferencing is required for conversational comprehension;
4. Meaning is context-specific; and
5. Contexts are constructed during interaction.

Teachers appear to provide contextualization cues to help students understand the classroom language. These contextualization cues and students' ability to understand and use them are critical to the transmission and construction of meaning in the classroom (Green & Smith, 1983).

In a comprehensive study of classroom processes, one that combined examination of recorded language, interviews to gain perspective, and achievement data, Morine-Dershimer (1985) found that achievement seemed to be related to a close "fit" between pupil perspectives and interpretations and the teacher's use of classroom language. Morine-Dershimer concluded that teachers were confirming and acknowledging pupils' understandings about the rules for discourse in the classroom. Thus, learning was a complex interaction of teachers' use of contextualization cues and pupils' belief systems about the nature of how to learn in classrooms. This study provides an example of the complexity of contextual variables in classroom communication processes. The context is affected by all past experiences participants bring into the setting and is constantly built in a dynamic way on everything that went before (Green, 1983).

Studies such as Morine-Dershimer's (1985) illustrate that tasks and activities do not necessarily structure the learning that goes on. Acting together on tasks and on each others' messages and behaviors, teachers and children construct the learning that takes place (Erickson & Shultz, 1977; Green & Wallat, 1981b; Gumperz, 1981). Students must not only acquire academic knowledge; they must learn how and when to display it (Bloome & Theodorou, 1988; Mehan, 1979; Mehan, 1981). This requires that educators reexamine language use in the classroom. They must be alert to the hidden curriculum that implicitly "teaches" students to present themselves through speech as "good students."

Student Talk: Child-to-Child Interactions. In recent years, a number of researchers have studied how students talk with peers in situations where the teacher is not present. Some researcher focus on the potential benefits of peer interaction for communication or social development, while others are interested in the benefits for students' learning and cognitive growth. As the earlier section on children's communicative competence indicated, children acquire considerable communication skills in the years before they enter school.

Most research on peer-peer interaction among school-age children has focused on students in the lower grades and points to the value of these situations for students' social development. For example, Lazarus (1984) recorded kindergarten pupils in peer interactions in informal settings and more formal settings with the teacher. She found children are aware of regularities in language use in classrooms, including address forms, greetings, and norms of interaction. She also found that young children are able to announce their learning confusions, solicit help from peers or teacher, and adjust their strategies depending on the audience.

Black (1979a) and Ross (1983) found that kindergarten children use a wide range of language strategies to deal with problems in situations away from adult supervision. Their studies indicate the value of such situations for learning the social skills necessary for working together. Children develop understandings of cooperation, independence, and competition that are learned not so much through formal instruction as through opportunities to engage in peer interaction. Through oral language activities, children learn to maintain their own relative status with peers and to engage in learning situations in cooperation with others. Black emphasizes the importance of teachers focusing on communicative, rather than linguistic, competence and proposes that the opportunity for children to practice and use language with peers as they work and play in the natural classroom environment could be the most effective language program.

Cooper, Marquis and Ayers-Lopez (1982) studied the roles children assume, the developmental trends, and the discourse patterns in spontaneous peer-peer learning situations in kindergarten, first- and second-grade classrooms. They found wide variation in children's competence to take on roles related to forming working relationships and accomplishing tasks in peer learning situations. They also found evidence of developmental differences. Second graders formed more long-lasting relationships with others in their class, while kindergarten children had more transitory contacts with peers. Older children were more successful at asking for help, getting and giving information, managing others' behavior, engaging the listener's attention, and participating in collaborative learning groups, though there continued to be varying degrees of social competence within grades and across peer learning situations.

In a series of studies (Wilkinson, 1984; Wilkinson & Calculator, 1982; Wilkinson & Dollaghan, 1979), Wilkinson focused on first- through third-grade children's use of requests for action and requests for information in small peer reading and math groups. The results show that children in first, second and third grade, on the whole, use language effectively to obtain responses in peer learning situations, and that their skills improve as they get older. The research also shows that the effective communicators are those students who produce requests that are direct, sincere, on task, and directed to a specific peer, and who can revise their requests if not initially successful. She also found that the way children talk in peer groups is related to achievement in reading and math. Wilkinson's research points to the value of small group, peer-peer interaction for promoting academic and social learning.

In addition to the opportunity for social development, so necessary in a pluralistic society, Cazden (1988, pp. 123–135) identifies four potential cognitive benefits of discourse among peers that apply to all ages and cites studies that support each. The benefits include discourse: 1) as *relationship with an audience* in which an orientation to Other is achieved in speech when immediate feedback is available (Heap, 1986); (2) as *enactment of complementary rules* through which peers scaffold one another to perform tasks together when they would not be able to do so alone (Forman, 1981); (3) as *catalyst for development of logical reasoning skills* in which students hear different points of view and collaborate to solve problems (Paley, 1981); and (4) as *exploratory talk* in which the learner can "rehearse" knowledge before formalizing it into a "final draft," such as an oral presentation or report (Barnes, 1976). Barnes (1976) suggested that exploratory small-group talk supports forms of learning that rarely take place in full group, teacher-led discussions.

Several maxims (Grice, 1975) or social rules guide human interaction and make effective communication possible. One is the "cooperative principle" that consists of a willingness to believe that the statements of those with whom we interact mean something and that our job as listeners is to discern that meaning. Grice (1975) also listed Quantity, provide what is required but no more than needed; Relevance, make contributions that are related to ongoing conversation; and Manner, be clear rather than ambiguous and wordy. As listeners, we scan talk and context in search of meaning and test our interpretations in various ways as we negotiate our way through a conversation. As we attempt to persuade others or to explain to others, we hear ourselves say what we think and in the process organize our thinking. This process of "talking things through" provides the basis for developing the internalizations (Vygotsky, 1962) that support cognitive processes.

All teachers, elementary or secondary, English language arts or subject matter specialists, can take advantage of the social and cognitive benefits derived from peer-peer learning by creating classroom situations that foster interaction around tasks, issues, and problems that are meaningful to their students. In such contexts, students are more likely to assume greater responsibility for their own learning.

IMPLICATIONS OF RESEARCH FOR TEACHING ORAL LANGUAGE

The conclusion to this chapter is organized around five principles for oral language teaching that are worth pondering. Researchers are still developing good descriptions of classroom processes and gaining insights into how spoken language is used to form social relationships, to communicate, and to learn. The implications of current research are so powerful, however, that educators must begin to interpret the findings and to define new directions for practice. This goal is particularly important when we consider the current state of oral language teaching.

With regard to elementary classrooms, research points to the neglect of oracy in favor of teaching reading and writing, the expectation that students will spend most of their time listening to teacher-talk, and the potential gap between home language and school language some young children face when they enter school. Many children have difficulty because of differences between their home and school environments and these difficulties are sometimes so severe that children are restricted in using their language skills and competencies to help them in school learning.

As students advance through the grades, opportunities for them to use oral language in the classroom appear to decrease. Olson (1977) contends that beyond the third grade, little verbal output is expected or even tolerated by teachers. Students are programmed for input, not output. Whole-class teaching still predominates in secondary schools in the United States and other countries. Research shows that the patterns of discourse in this style of teaching severely restrict students' use of talking, thus ignoring the learning potential of students' own spoken language.

The research reviewed in this chapter indicates that the situation must change for both elementary and secondary school students. From simple descriptions of classroom interaction to complex mappings of the sociolinguistic context, research supports the integration of speaking and listening, and the development of language curricula that provide students with opportunities to use language (i.e., talk) for a wide variety of purposes, in different situations, and with different audiences.

1. English Language-Arts Curricula Should Offer Students Many Opportunities To Engage in Talking.

Systematic classroom research (Dunkin & Biddle, 1974) points to the need, at all levels of schooling, for less teacher-talk and more pupil-talk to help students increase their competence in oral communication. Child language research (McTear, 1985; Wells, 1981) shows that children learn language and how to use it through social interaction in situations where spoken language serves genuine purposes for them and those around them. Through interaction with others, children learn the functions of language, the structure of different forms of spoken discourse, and the social rules that govern how language is used in different contexts.

Naturalistic studies of the use and functions of language in classrooms illustrate the value of talking for exploration and learning (Barnes, 1976; Britton, 1970, 1971). Studies also demonstrate that students of all ages use language creatively, effectively, and productively in classrooms where they are encouraged to interact with their peers as well as the teacher (Cazden, 1988; Chilver & Gould, 1982; Mallet & Newsome, 1977; Pinnell, 1975; Rosen & Rosen, 1973; Tough, 1973). Furthermore, research on classroom communication processes (Cazden, 1988; Edwards & Mercer, 1987; Green & Smith, 1983) offers compelling evidence that students need opportunities to talk not only to learn, but to learn how to use language to meet the academic and social demands of the classroom.

2. English Language-Arts Curricula Should Provide Students with Opportunities To Engage in Many Kinds of Talking.

Research done in the 1950s and 1960s suggested that listening and speaking skills could be taught separately, and that those skills are related to school success. But current theory and research indicates that the knowledge and skills needed for speaking and listening are inextricably intertwined and, therefore, the two should not be treated as separate from one another, or separate from reading and writing. All four processes are language processes; experiences that enhance development in one area should benefit development in the others areas. Nor can the skills and knowledge needed to use language effectively be taught through narrow lessons, or isolated drills and exercises; instead, the school experience should help students learn how to *use* language (i.e., talk and listen) effectively in real life circumstances.

The entire body of research, whatever the perspective, affirms the importance of language programs that foster speaking and listening skills through situations that engage students, from nursery through high school, in many different kinds of talking. Based on current theory and research, English language-arts educators in the United States, Britain, and other countries (Barnes, 1976; Barnes & Todd, 1977; Corson, 1988; Dougill & Knott, 1988; Jones, 1988; Knowles, 1983; Moffett &

Wagner, 1983; Watson, 1987) generally agree that the most effective techniques for promoting oral language development are small-group student discussions and project work, informal conversations between students and their peers and teachers, language games, story-telling, creative dramatics, role playing, improvisation, and, for older students, more formal drama.

One issue that remains, however, is how to organize and sequence oral language activities to form a coherent and developmentally sound curriculum, K–12. The student-centered, "activities approach" of the late 1960s and 1970s, which remains popular at the elementary level and in some junior high and high schools, is considered by many to be haphazard, fragmented, and inadequate. Czerniewski (1981), Watson (1987), and others discuss the limitations of the activities approach and suggest alternative ideas.

For example, Watson (1987) examines the strengths of a thematic approach to teaching secondary English that engages students in a wide variety of language activities around a given topic or theme, for example, The Sea, Fear. The approach provides for sustained, serious "explorations of the given theme or topic, as well as purposeful speaking, listening, reading and writing" (p. 99). Thus, the approach is a means of integrating the language arts. Strickland (1989) and Gamberg, Kwak, Hutchings and Altheim (1988), and other whole-language specialists see the same advantages for younger children and, therefore, advocate an integrated thematic approach to teaching language arts in the early childhood and elementary years. Moffetts' (1968) familiar theory of teaching the universe of discourse offers another approach to organizing and sequencing language activities. Others, however, propose functional approaches to language teaching. These are discussed below.

3. The English Language-Arts Curriculum Should Not Leave Oral Language Teaching To Chance but Should Guarantee Opportunities for Students To Develop the Skills Necessary To Use Language for the Full Range of Social and Intellectual Functions.

Based on current research and theories of language use and learning, many language-arts and speech communication educators advocate a functional approach to language learning. The particular approach depends, however, on how the theorist interprets the pedagogical implications of the research and perceives the goals and purposes of oracy instruction.

For example, several speech communication educators advocate a deliberate approach to the teaching of oral communication. As exemplified by Allen and Brown (1976), Allen, Brown, and Yatvin (1986), Klein (1977, 1979), Wood (1977a, 1977b, 1984), Rubin (1985), and Rubin and Kantor (1984) the curriculum should be comprised of activities that give students opportunities to practice different language functions and communication skills in specifically planned situations. According to these theorists, the purpose of instruction is to help students learn a repertoire of strategies for using language appropriately and effectively in different social situations.

Advocates of this functional approach to oral communication suggest that students should be aware that they are studying speech communication, just as they might know they are studying biology (Rubin, 1985). This view of language teaching holds that, while communication skills and functions of language can be developed within any subject matter area, it is also necessary to have an explicitly defined curriculum for teaching speaking and listening skills and to focus on that specifically at certain times each day (Rubin, 1985).

British educators MacLure (1988), Barnes (1988), and others argue that this functional approach, also evident in the United Kingdom, is based on a narrow concept of oracy, which MacLure calls "oracy as communication." The assumption is that oracy is an aspect of communicative competence and teachers have the obligation to teach children to speak and listen, just as they have the responsibility to teach them to read and write. "In this view, oracy tends to be seen as primarily the concern of English teachers and language specialists; and oral *assessment* means the assessment of oral skill and competencies in their own right, rather than as a vehicle or expression of learning in other curriculum subjects" (p. 5).

MacLure (1988) and others call for a different view of oracy, "oracy as a tool for learning." Those who hold this view (Barnes, 1988; Britton, 1970, 1971; Corson, 1988; Jones, 1988; Marland, 1977; Tarleton, 1988; Thaiss, 1986; and Wilkinson, 1965) advocate an indirect approach to fostering development of students' oral language abilities. In this view oracy is the medium for learning in every subject area of the curriculum, not just English language arts. All teachers are seen as language teachers. These theorists argue that students in elementary and in secondary schools should be involved in settings and circumstances across the curriculum that regularly require them to actively learn by talking. The assumption is that through talking students construct their knowledge of the content and, at the same time, develop skill in different modes of discourse (exploratory, transactional, and poetic), become aware of the contextual constraints on language, and learn how to modify their language depending on the setting, audience, topic, and purpose. As appropriate, the teacher may hold up language for explicit examination or instruction; most of the time, however, the teaching is indirect.

Recently, based on the body of research showing the critical relations between language knowledge and school success, some scholars (Christie, 1985a, 1985b, 1987) have called for greater attention to the forms of discourse students will need in order to participate successfully in discourse required by the subject areas. For example, Christie (1985a) argues that successful participation in any context or situation requires the ability to recognize and use the relevant discourse patterns or generic structures. This knowledge is important in two ways: (1) in production and (2) in comprehension. Thus the same knowledge is needed by speaker/listener in order to successfully engage in discourse in a particular situation.

Christie (1985a) goes on to say that learning in any "content area"—math, science, history—is "primarily a matter of learning language: a matter, that is, of learning," not only the vocabulary or lexical items, "but the discourse patterns or genre . . . which are characteristic of the different subjects" (p. 37). Both the content and the ways of working together, the methods of inquiry, find expression in the discourse patterns that are characteristic of the field. Christie emphasizes the importance of exploratory talk in learning, but proposes that more attention

be paid to the forms of discourse students need to learn in order to talk, write, and read successfully in the different content areas. She also suggests that when planning, "whatever the age group and whatever the subject matter, teachers need to consider two questions: 1. What do my students need to be able to do in language in order to be successful in mastering this content? and 2. What kind of context of situation for working and learning should be generated in order that the students will be assisted to master the required language patterns?" (1985, p. 31).

4. English Language-Arts Curricula Must Account for the Fact That Context Plays a Central Role in Language Use and Learning. Oral language is the primary medium through whcih the business of learning is carried out (Cazden, 1986) in the classroom. As this review of research indicates, the classroom context can have a significant impact on language use and learning. Teachers must be aware of the language environment in their classrooms and understand the conditions that may foster or hinder oracy development. Several theorists provide models or frameworks that teachers and curriculum developers can use to identify and observe situational factors (e.g., audience, setting, task) that affect language use in the classroom.

For example, Halliday's (1978) concepts of field, tenor, and mode of discourse provide a useful framework for understanding the complex ways that classrooms vary as language learning environments. He proposed three components of any situation that influence language use:

1. The *field of discourse* that refers to the activity participants are engaged in and the topic or subject matter of their talk that affects language use, not just the vocabulary but the ways of expressing concepts and relationships between phenomenon in the field;
2. The *tenor of the discourse* that refers to the role relationships among the participants and affects the style of discourse; and
3. The *mode of discourse* that refers to the medium (spoken/written) and to the distance among the participants, e.g., close as in conversation or distant as in writing. (Mode interacts with the speaker's purpose to determine, in large measure, the genre or form of discourse used, e.g., story, conversation, discussion.)

In a study of rich classroom environments, Platt (1984) found that children's oral and written language varied according to the nature of the interpersonal situation (tenor) and the content (field). Learning oral and written language was scaffolded through both peer and teacher interaction that helped children to make connections between the familiar and the new. She described the teacher's goal as establishing a familial sense of community within which children could practice sharing time and space, working out conflicts, coping with and reconciling difficulties, and generally learn to function in a more complex social environment than had thus far been presented by the home. Children learned self direction through working in small groups, and they also interacted with a range of others, including the principal, other teachers, and community members. Content was integrated across subject matter lines and first experiences were both exploratory and concrete. Gradually children moved toward more formal categories of knowledge and representations of knowledge in oral and written language.

Classroom descriptions such as that provided by Platt (1984), illustrate Barnes' (1973) earlier assertion that children need a rich classroom experience and high quality interactions with a knowledgeable adult. Barnes described the classroom alternatives by contrasting teachers who see language as transmission of information and those who view it as a means of interpretation. Teachers who view their role as transmitting knowledge to pupils who are ignorant, will be likely to establish the traditional patterns of discourse in their classrooms. Those who believe students should bring their own knowledge to the new learning will base instruction on the assumption that students do have knowledge, and quite different forms of discourse may be the result (Edwards, 1979).

5. Teachers Must Understand That Oral Language Is One Means By Which Students Gain Access To Learning and Display Their Competence. Studies of classroom processes (Delamont, 1983; Green & Wallat, 1981a) have made it clear that oral language functions in subtle, yet immensely important ways to give students access to learning. Oral language is subtly evaluated by teachers and other students as students attempt to display what they know in classroom lessons. Teachers' awareness of these processes is the first step toward finding ways to provide greater access for and participation from all students.

Coda

The research on speaking and listening justifies the present interest in developing school curricula to help all students become more competent oral language users. In light of current assessment practices and the continued emphasis on reading and writing, it is difficult to keep oral language in the forefront of curriculum development. yet, the accumulating body of evidence, from diverse perspectives and different fields, indicates the centrality of talking and listening in students' learning.

More research is needed, but we already know enough to make substantial revisions in practice. The indicated revisions may be difficult for some because they do not lend themselves to packaged programs or written materials. Oral language skills and concepts are best developed in situations that imitate life. Constructing such learning experiences will not be easy and will require extensive study and development on the part of teachers. With that in mind, it appears that an immediate start is warranted. Children entering schools today will need high level "oracy" skills when they become the ones to debate the issues and negotiate the decisions of the twenty-first century.

References

Allen, D. (1980). *English teaching since 1965: How much growth?* London: Heinemann Educational Books.

Allen, R. R., & Brown, K. L. (Eds.). (1976). *Developing communication competence in children.* Skokie, IL: National Textbook Co.

Allen, R. R., Brown, K. L., & Yatvin, J. (1986). *Learning language through communication.* Belmont, CA: Wadsworth.

Alverman, D. E. (1986). Discussion: The forgotten art: Becoming literate in the secondary school. Paper presented at the Annual Meeting of the American Educational Association, San Francisco. (ERIC Document Reproduction Service No. 269 717)

Alvy, K. T. (1973). The development of listener adapted communications in grade-school children from different social-class backgrounds. *Genetic Psychology Monograph, 87,* 33–104.

Amidon, E. J., & Hunter, E. (1967). *Improving teaching: The analysis of verbal interaction.* New York: Holt, Rhinehart & Winston.

Anderson, H. A. (1952). Needed research in listening. *Elementary English, 29,* 215–224.

Applebee, A. (1978). *The child's concept of story.* Chicago: University of Chicago Press.

Au, K. H. (1980). On participation structure in reading lessons. *Anthropology & Education Quarterly, 11* 91–115.

Ausubel, D. P. (1960). The use of advance organizers in the learning and retention of meaningful verbal material. *Journal of Educational Psychology, 51,* 267–272.

Ausubel, D. P., & Robinson, F. G. (1969). *School learning: An introduction to educational psychology.* New York: Holt, Rhinehart & Winston.

Backlund, P., Booth, J., Moore, M., Parks, A. M., & Van Rheenan, D. (1982). A national survey of state practices in speaking and listening skill assessment. *Communication Education, 31,* 125–130.

Barnes, D. (1971). Classroom contexts for language and learning. *Educational Review, 23,* 235–248.

Barnes, D. (1972). Language and learning in the classroom. In *Language in education: A source book* (pp. 112–118). London: Routledge & Kegan Paul in association with Open University Press.

Barnes, D. (1973). Styles of communication and thinking in the classroom. In *Language in the classroom* (pp. 14–17). Ed. 262, Block 4, Milton Keynes, England: Open University Press.

Barnes, D. (1976). *From communication to curriculum.* Hardmonsworth: Penguin.

Barnes, D. (1980). Situated speech strategies: Aspects of the monitoring of oracy. *Educational Review, 32* 123–131.

Barnes, D., & Todd, F. (1977). *Communication and learning in small groups.* London: Routledge & Kegan Paul.

Barnes, D., Britton, J., & Rosen, H. (1971). *Language, the learner and the school.* Harmondsworth: Penguin.

Barr, M., D'Arcy, P., & Healy, M. K. (1982). *What's going on: Language episodes in British and American classrooms, grades 4–13.* Montclair, NJ: Boynton/Cook.

Bates, E. (1976). *Language and context: The acquisition of pragmatics.* New York: Academic Press.

Bates, E., Camaioni, L., & Volterra, V. (1975). (rev. ed.). The acquisition of performatives prior to speech. *Merrill–Palmer Quarterly, 21,* 205–224.

Bellack, A. A., Kliebard, H. M., Hyman, R. T., & Smith, F. L. (1966). *The language of the classroom.* New York: Teachers College Press.

Berk, L. E. (1973). *An analysis of activities in preschool settings (Final report).* Washington, DC: National Center for Educational Research and Development. (ERIC Document Reproduction Service No. ED 099 131)

Bernstein, B. (1964). Elaborated and restricted codes: Their social origins and some consequences. In J. J. Gumperz & D. Hymes (Eds.), The ethnography of communication. *American Anthropology, 66,* 55–69.

Bernstein, B. (1971). *Class, codes, and control. Vol. I: Theoretical studies toward a sociology of language.* London: Routledge & Kegan Paul.

Bernstein, B. (1973). *Class, codes, and control. Vol. II: Applied studies towards a sosiology of language.* London: Routledge & Kegan Paul.

Bernstein, B. (1974). *Class, codes and control.* (2nd rev. ed.). New York: Schocken Books.

Bernstein, B. (1975). *Class, codes, and control. Vol. III: Towards a theory of educational transmissions.* London: Routledge & Kegan Paul.

Berrill, D. P. (1988). Anecdote and the development of oral argument in sixteen-year-olds. In M. MacLure, T. Phillips, & A. Wilkinson (Eds.), *Oracy Matters* (pp. 57–68). Milton Keynes: Open University Press.

Black, J. (1979a). Assessing kindergarten children's communication competence. In O. K. Garnica & M. L. King (Eds.), *Language, children and Society* (pp. 37–52). Oxford, England: Pergamon Press.

Black, J. (1979b). Formal and informal means of assessing the communicative competence of kindergarten children. *Research in the Teaching of English, 13,* 49–68.

Bloom, L. (1970). *Language development: Form and function in emerging grammars.* Cambridge, MA: The M.I.T. Press.

Bloom, L. (1975). Language development. In F. D. Horowitz (Ed.), *Review of child development research, 4,* (pp. 245–303). Chicago: University of Chicago Press.

Bloome, D., & Theodorou, E. (1988). Analyzing teacher-student and student-student discourse. In J. L. Green & J. O. Harker (Eds.), *Multiple perspective analyses of classroom discourse* (pp. 217–248). Norwood, NJ: Ablex.

Boggs, S. T. (1972). The meaning of questions and narratives to Hawaiian children. In C. B. Cazden, V. P. John, & D. Hymes (Eds.), *Functions of language in the classroom* (pp. 299–327). New York: Teachers College Press.

Book, C. L. (1978). Teaching functional communication skills in the secondary classroom. *Communication Education, 27* 322–327.

Book, C. L. (1981). Speech communication in the secondary school. In G. W. Friedrich (Ed.), *Education in the 80's: Speech communicatation* (pp. 22–29). Washington, DC: National Education Association.

Book, C. L., & Pappas, E. J. (1981). The status of speech communication in secondary schools in the United States: An update. *Communication Education, 30,* 199–208.

Botvin, G., & Sutton-Smith, B. (1977). The development of structural complexity in children's fantasy narratives. *Developmental Psychology, 13,* 377–88.

Bower, G. H. (1976). Experiments on story understanding and recall. *Quarterly Journal of Experimental Psychology, 28,* 511–534.

Bremme, D. W., & Erickson, F. (1977). Relationships among verbal and nonverbal behaviors. *Theory into Practice, 16,* 153–161.

Britton, J. (1970). *Language and learning.* England: Penguin Books.

Britton, J. (1971). What's the use? A schematic account of language functions. *Educational Review, 23,* 205–19.

Britton, J., Burgess, T., Martin, N., McLeod, A., & Rosen, H. (1975). *The development of writing abilities (11–18).* London: Schools Council Publications & MacMillan Education.

Brown, K. L. (1984). Teaching and assessing oral language. In F. W. Parkay, S. O'Bryan, & M. Hennessy (Eds.), *Quest for quality: Improving basic skills instruction in the 1980's* (pp. 78–87). Lanham, MD: University Press of America.

Brown, K. L., Burnett, N., Jones, G. Matsumoto, S., Langford, N. J.,& Pacheco, M. (1981). *Teaching speaking and listening skills in the elementary and secondary schools.* Boston: Massachusetts Department of Education.

Bruner, J. S. (1975). Language as an instrument of thought. In A. Davies (Ed.), *Problems of language and learning* (pp. 61–81). London: Heinemann.

Bullock, A. (1975). *A language for life.* London, England: Department of Education and Science, HMOS.

Butler, D. (1980). *Cushla and her books.* Boston: The Horn Book.

Caffrey, J. (1955). Auding. *Review of Educational Research, 25,* 121–132.

Cahir, S. R. & Kovac, C. (1981). *Exploring functional language.* Washington, DC: Center for Applied Linguistics.

Canfield, R. G. (1961). How useful are lessons for listening? *Elementary School Journal, 62,* 147–151.

Cazden, C. (1979). Peekaboo as an instructional model: Discourse development at home and at school. *Papers and Reports on Child Development, 17,* 1–29.

Cazden, C. (1986). Classroom discourse. In M. C. Wittrock (Ed.), *Handbook of research on teaching* (3rd ed.) (pp. 432–463). New York: Macmillan.

Cazden, C. (1988). *Classroom discourse: The language of teaching and learning.* Portsmouth, NH: Heinemann.

Cazden, C., John, V. P., & Hymes, D. (1972). *The functions of language in the classroom.* New York: Teachers College Press.

Chilver, P., & Gould, G. (1982). *Learning and language in the classroom.* Oxford: Pergamon.

Chomsky, C. (1969). *The acquisition of syntax in children from 5 to 10.* Cambridge, MA: M.I.T. Press.

Chomsky, N. A. (1957). *Syntactic structures.* The Hague: Mouton.

Chomsky, N. A. (1965). *Aspects of the theory of syntax.* Cambridge, MA: M.I.T. Press.

Christie, F. (1985a). *Language education.* Victoria, Australia: Deakin University.

Christie, F. (1985b). Language and schooling. In S. N. Tchudi (Ed.), *Language, schooling and society* (pp. 21–40). Upper Montclair, NJ: Boynton/Cook.

Christie, F. (1987). Young children's writing: From spoken to written genre. *Language and Education, 1,* 3–13.

Cicourel, A. V., Jennings, K. H., Jennings, S. H. M., Leiter, K. C. W., MacKay, R., Mehan, H., & Roth, D. R. (1974). *Language use and school performance.* New York: Academic Press.

Clay, M. M. (1977). *Reading: The patterning of complex behavior.* Portsmouth: NH: Heinemann.

Clay, M. M. (1979). *The early detection of reading difficulties* (3rd ed.). Portsmouth, NH: Heinemann.

Cochran-Smith, M. (1984). *The making of a reader.* Norwood, NJ: Ablex.

College Board (1983). *Academic preparation for college: What students need to know and be able to do.* New York: College Entrance Examination Board.

Cook-Gumperz, J. C. (1977). Situated instructions: Language socialization of school age children. In S. Ervin-Tripp & C. Mitchell-Kernan (Eds.), *Child discourse* (pp. 103–124). New York: Academic.

Cooper, C. R., Marquis, A., & Ayers-Lopez, S. (1982). Peer learning in the classroom. Tracing developmental patterns and consequences of children's spontaneous interactions. In L. C. Wilkinson (Ed.), *Communicating in the classroom* (pp. 69–84). New York: Academic Press.

Corson, D. (1988). *Oral language across the curriculum.* Clevedon and Philadelphia: Miltilingual Matters.

Coulthard, M. (1977). *An introduction to discourse analysis.* London: Longman.

Cox, B., & Sulzby, E. (1984). Children's use of reference in told, dictated, and handwritten stories. *Research in the Teaching of English, 18,* 345–365.

Czerniewski, P. (1981). Teaching children language. In N. Mercer (Ed.), *Language in school and community* (pp. 161–178). London: Edward Arnold.

Delamont, S. (1976). Beyond Flanders fields: The relationship of subject matter and individuality to classroom style. In M. Stubbs & S. Delamont (Eds.), *Explorations in classroom observation* (pp. 101–131). London: John Wiley.

Delamont, S. (1981). All too familiar: A decade of classroom research, *Educational Analysis, 3,* 69–83.

Delamont, S. (1983). *Interaction in the classroom: Contemporary sociology of the school* (2nd ed.). London: Methuen.

Delamont, S., & Hamilton, D. (1984). Revisiting classroom research: A cautionary tale. In S. Delamont (Ed.), *Readings on interaction in the classroom* (pp. 3–38). London: Methuen.

DeLawter, J. A., & Eash, M. J. (1966). Focus on oral communication. *Elementary English, 43,* 880–883.

Delia, J. D., & Clark, R. A. (1977). Cognitive complexity, social perception, and the development of listener-adapted communication in six-, eight-, ten-, and twelve-year-old boys. *Communication Monographs, 44,* 236–245.

Delia, J. D., Kline, S. L., & Burleson, B. R. (1979). The development of persuasive communication strategies in kindergarteners through twelfth graders. *Communication Monographs, 46,* 241–256.

DeStefano, J. S. (Ed.). (1973). *Language, society and education: A Profile of Black English.* Worthington, OH: Jones.

DeStefano, J. S., and Kantor, R. (1988). Cohesion in spoken and written dialogue: An investigation of cultural and textual constraints. *Linguistics and Education, 1,* 105–124.

Devine, T. G. (1978). Listening: What do we know after fifty years of research and theorizing? *Journal of Reading, 21,* 269–304.

Devine, T. G. (1982). *Listening skills schoolwide.* Urbana, IL: ERIC Clearinghouse on Reading and Communication Skills and the National Council of Teachers of English.

Dickson, W. P. (Ed.). (1981). *Children's oral communication skills.* New York: Academic Press.

Dickson, W. P. (1982). Creating communication-rich classrooms: Insights from sociolinguistic and referential traditions. In L. C. Wilkinson (Ed.), *Communicating in the classroom* (pp. 131–152). New York: Academic Press.

Dickinson, D. K. (1987). Oral language, literacy skills, and response to literature. In J. R. Squire (Ed.), *The dynamics of literacy learning: Research in reading and English* (pp. 147–183). Urbana, IL: ERIC Clearinghouse on Reading and Communication Skills & National Conference on Research in English.

Dillon, J. T. (1984). Research on questioning and discussion. *Educational Leadership, 42,* 50–56.

Dillon, D., & Searle, D. (1981). The role of language in one first grade classroom. *Research in the Teaching of English, 15,* 311–28.

DiVesta, F. J., & Palermo, D. S. (1974). Language development. In F. N. Kerlinger & J. B. Carroll (Eds.), *Review of research in education* (pp. 55–107). Itasca, IL: Peacock.

Dixon, J. (1967). *Growth through English.* London: Oxford University.

Doake, D. B. (1985). Reading-like behavior: Its role in learning to read. In A. Jaggar & M. T. Smith-Burke (Eds.), *Observing the language learner* (pp. 82–98). Newark, DE & Urbana, IL: International Reading Association & National Council of Teachers of English.

Doke, L. A., & Risley, T. R. (1972). The organization of day-care environments: Required versus optional activities. *Journal of Applied Behavior Analysis, 5,* 205–420.

Dore, J. (1974). A description of early language development. *Journal of Psycholinguistic Research, 4,* 423–430.

Dore, J. (1977). "Oh them sheriff": A pragmatic analysis of children's responses to questions. In S. Ervin-Tripp & C. Mitchell-Kernan (Eds.), *Child Discourse* (pp. 139–64). New York: Academic Press.

Dore, J. (1979). Conversation and preschool language development. In P. Fletcher & M. Garman (Eds.), *Language acquisition: Studies in first language development* (pp. 337–362). Cambridge, England: Cambridge University Press.

Doughty, A., & Doughty, P. (1974). *Using language in use: A teacher's guide to language work in the classroom.* London: Edward Arnold.

Doughty, P., Pearce, J., & Thornton, G. (1971). *Language in use.* London: Edward Arnold.

Doughty, P., Pearce, J., & Thornton, G. (1972). *Exploring language.* London: Edward Arnold.

Dougill, P., & Knott, R. (1988). *The primary language book.* Milton Keynes: Open University Press.

Duker, S. (1961). Listening. *Review of Educational Research, 31,* 145–151.

Duker, S. (1966). *Listening: Readings.* Metuchen, NJ: Scarecrow Press.

Duker, S. (1968). *Listening bibliography.* Metuchen, NJ: Scarecrow Press.

Duker, S. (1969). Listening. In R. L. Ebel (Ed.), *Encyclopedia of Educational Research* (4th ed.). London: Collier-Macmillan.

Dunkin, M. J., & Biddle, B. J. (1974). *The study of teaching.* New York: Holt, Rhinehart & Winston.

Durrell listening-reading series. (1969). New York: Harcourt, Brace & World.

Edwards, A. D. (1976). *Language in culture and class.* London: Heinemann.

Edwards, A. D. (1979). Patterns of power and authority in classroom talk. In P. Woods (Ed.), *Teacher strategies: Explorations in the sociology of the school* (pp. 237–253). London: Croom Helm.

Edwards, A. D. (1976). *Language in culture and class.* London: Heinemann.

Edwards, A. D. (1979). Patterns of power and authority in classroom talk. In P. Woods (Ed.), *Teacher strategies: Explorations in the sociology of the school* (pp. 237–253). London: Croom Helm.

Edwards, A. D. (1981). Analysing classroom talk. In P. French & M. MacLure (Eds.), *Adult-child conversation* (pp. 291–308). London: Croom Helm.

Edwards, A. D., & Furlong, V. J. (1978). *The language of teaching: Meaning in classroom interaction.* London: Heinemann.

Edwards, A. D., & Westgate, D. P. G. (1987). *Investigating classroom talk.* London: Falmer Press.

Edwards, D., & Mercer, N. (1987). *Common knowledge: The development of understanding in the classroom.* London: Methuen.

Eisenberg, A., & Garvey, C. (1981). Children's use of verbal strategies in resolving conflict. *Discourse processes, 4,* 149–170.

Erickson, F., & Mohatt, G. (1982). Cultural organization of participant structures in two classrooms of Indian students. In G. Spindler (Ed.), *Doing the ethnography of schooling: Educational anthropology in action* (pp. 132–174). New York: Holt, Rhinehart & Winston.

Erickson, F., & Schultz, J. (1977). When is a context? Some issues and methods in the analysis of social competence. *Quarterly Newsletter for Comparative Human Development, 1,* 5–10. Also in J. Green & C. Wallat (Eds.), *Ethnography and language in educational settings.* 1981, Norwood, NJ: Ablex.

Ervin-Tripp, S. (1970). Discourse agreement: How children answer questions. In J. R. Hayes (Ed.), *Cognition and the development of language* (pp. 79–108). New York: John Wiley.

Ervin-Tripp, S. (1973). *Language acquisition and communicative chance.* Palo Alto: Stanford University Press.

Ervin-Tripp, S. (1974). The comprehension and production of requests by children. In *Papers and reports on child language development* (special issue, pp. 188–95). Stanford: Sixth Child Language Research Forum.

Ervin-Tripp, S. (1982). Structures of control. In L. C. Wilkinson (Ed.), *Communicating in the classroom* (pp. 27–48). New York: Academic Press.

Ervin-Tripp, S., & Mitchell, Kernan, C. (Eds.). (1977). *Child discourse.* New York: Academic Press.

Essentials of Education Statement. (1981). In A. C. Purves, "The essentials of education: An overview". In L. Y. Mercier (Ed.), *The essentials approach: Rethinking the curriculum for the 80's* (pp. 3–5). Washington, DC: U.S. Department of Education, Basic Skills Improvement Program.

Essentials of English: A document for reflection and dialogue. (1983). *English Journal, 72,* 51–53.

Evertson, C. M., & Green, J. L. (1986). Observation as inquiry and method. In M. C. Wittrock (Ed.), *Handbook of research on teaching* (3rd ed.) (pp. 162–213). New York: Macmillian.

Farrell, M., & Flint, S. H. (1967). Are they listening? *Childhood Education, 43,* 528–529.

Fitzgerald, J. (1989). Research on stories: Implications for teachers. In K. D. Muth (Ed.), *Children's comprehension of text: Research into practice* (pp. 2–36). Newark, DE: International Reading Association.

Flanders, N. A. (1966). *Interaction analysis in the classroom: A manual for observers* (rev. ed.). Ann Arbor, MI: School of Education, University of Michigan.

Flavell, J. H., Speer, J. R., Green, F. L., & August, D. L. (1981). The development of comprehension monitoring and knowledge about communication. *Monographs of the Society for Research in Child Development, 46*(5, Serial No. 192).

Forman, E. A. (1981). *The role of collaboration in problem solving in children.* Unpublished doctoral dissertation, Harvard University.

Foster, S. (1979). *From non-verbal to verbal communication: A study of the development of topic initiation strategies during the first two-and-a-half years.* Unpublished doctoral dissertation, University of Lancaster.

Foulke, E., & Sticht, T. (1969). Review of research on the intelligibility and comprehension of accelerated speech. *Psychological Bulletin, 72,* 50–62.

Fox, C. (1985). Talking like a book: Young children's oral monologues. In M. Meek (Ed.), *Opening moves: Work in progress in the study of children's language development* (pp. 12–25). Institute of Education, University of London.

Fox, C. (1988). 'Poppies will make them grant'. In M. Meek & C. Mills (Eds.), *Language and literacy in the primary school* (pp. 53–68). East Sussex, England: Falmer Press.

Franklin, M. B., & Barten, S. S. (1988). *Child language: A reader.* Oxford: Oxford University Press.

Friedrich, G. W. (Ed.) (1981). *Education in the 80's: Speech communication.* Washington, DC: National Education Association.

Galda, L. (1984). Narrative competence: Play, storytelling, and story comprehension. In A. D. Pellegrini & T. Yawkey (Eds.), *The development of oral and written language in social contexts* (pp. 105–117). Norwood, NJ: Ablex.

Gamberg, R., Kwak, W., Hutchings, M., & Altheim, A. (1988). *Learning and loving it: Theme studies in the classroom.* Portsmouth, NH: Heinemann.

Garnica, O. K., & King, M. L. (Eds.). (1979). *Language, children and society: The effect of social factors on children learning to communicate.* Oxford, England: Pergamon.

Garvey, C. (1974). Some properties of social play. *Merrill-Palmer Quarterly, 20,* 163–180.

Garvey, C. (1977). Play with language and speech. In S. Ervin-Tripp & C. Mitchell-Kernan (Eds.), *Child Discourse* (pp. 27–47). New York: Academic Press.

Garvey, C. & BenDebba, M. (1974). Effects of age, sex, and partner on children's dyadic speech. *Journal of Child Development, 45,* 1159–1161.

Garvey, C., & Hogan, R. (1973). Social speech and social interaction: Egocentrism revisited. *Child Development, 44,* 562–568.

Genishi, C., & DiPaolo, M. (1982). Learning through argument in a preschool. In L. C. Wilkinson (Ed.), *Communicating in the classroom* (pp. 49–68). New York: Academic Press.

Genishi, C., & Dyson, A. H. (1984). *Language assessment in the early years.* Norwood, NJ: Ablex.

Gilmore, P., & Glatthorn, E. (1982). *Children in and out of school.* Washington, DC: Center for Applied Linguistics.

Glucksberg, S., & Krauss, R. (1967). What do people say after they have learned how to talk? Studies of the developmental of referential communication. *Merrill Palmer Quarterly, 13,* 309–316.

Goldstein, H. (1940). *Reading and listening comprehension at various controlled rates.* New York: Teachers College Press.

Good, T. L., & Brophy, J. E. (1987). *Looking in classrooms* (4th ed.). New York: Harper & Row.

Goodman, K. S., Smith, E. B., Meredith, R., & Goodman, Y. M. (1987). *Language and thinking in school* (3rd ed.). New York: Richard C. Owen.

Gorman, T. (1985). Language assessment and language teaching: Innovation and interaction. In G. Wells & J. Nicholls (Eds.), *Language & learning: An interactional perspective* (pp. 125–134). England: Falmer.

Gray, R. A., Saski, J., McEntire, M. E., & Larsen, S. C. (1980). Is proficiency in oral language a predictor of academic success? *The Elementary School Journal, 80,* 260–268.

Green, J. L. (Ed.). (1979). *Communicating with young children. Theory into practice, 18.*

Green, J. L. (1983). Research on teaching as a linguistic process: A state of the art. *Review of Research in Education, 10,* 151–252.

Green, J. L., & Harker, J. O. (Eds.). (1988). *Multiple perspective analyses of classroom discourse* (pp. 11–47). Norwood, NJ: Ablex.

Green, J. L., & Smith, D. (1983). Teaching and learning: A linguistic perspective. *The Elementary School Journal, 83,* 353–391.

Green, J. L., & Wallat, C. (Eds.). (1981a). *Ethnography and language in educational settings.* Norwood, NJ: Ablex.

Green, J. L., & Wallat, C. (1981b). Mapping instructional conversations: A sociolinguistic ethnography. In J. L. Green & C. Wallat (Eds.), *Ethnography and language in educational settings* (pp. 161–205). Norwood, NJ: Ablex.

Grice, H. P. (1975). Logic and conversation. In P. Cole & J. Morgan (Eds.), *Syntax and semantics, Vol. 3: Speech acts* (pp. 41–58). New York: Academic Press.

Griffin, P., & Shuy, R. W. (1978). *Children's functional language and education in the early years.* Final report to Carnegie Corporation of New York: Arlington, VA: Center for Applied Linguistics.

Groff, P. (1978). Children's oral language and their written composition. *The Elementary School Journal, 78,* 180–191.

Gumperz, J. J. (1981). Conversational inference and classroom learning. In J. L. Green & C. Wallat (Eds.), *Ethnography and language in educational settings* (pp. 3–24). Norwood, NJ: Ablex.

Gumperz, J. J. (1986). Interactional sociolinguistics in the study of schooling. In J. Cook-Gumperz (Ed.), *The social construction of literacy* (pp. 45–68). London: Cambridge University Press.

Gumperz, J. J., & Herasimchuk, E. (1975). The conversational analysis of social meaning: A study of classroom interaction. In M. Sanches & B. Blount (Eds.), *Sociocultural dimensions of language use* (pp. 81–116). New York: Academic Press.

Gumperz, J. J., & Hymes, D. (1964). The ethnography of communication. *American Anthropology, 66,* Pt. 2.

Gumperz, J. J., & Hymes, D. (Eds.). (1972). *Directions in sociolinguistics: The ethnography of communication.* New York: Holt, Rhinehart & Winston.

Halliday, M. A. K. (1969). Relevant models of language. *Educational Review, 22,* 26–37.

Halliday, M. A. K. (1971). Language in a social perspective. *Educational Review, 23,* 165–188.

Halliday, M. A. K. (1973). *Explorations in the functions of language.* London: Edward Arnold.

Halliday, M. A. K. (1975). *Learning how to mean: Explorations in the development of language.* London: Edward Arnold.

Halliday, M. A. K.,(1978). *Language as social semiotic: The social interpretation of language and meaning.* London: Edward Arnold.

Halliday, M. A. K., & Hasan, R. (1976). *Cohension in English.* London: Longman.

Hammersley, M. (Ed.). (1986a). *Case studies in classroom research.*

Philadelphia, PA & Milton Keynes, England: Open University Press.

Hammersley, M. (Ed.). (1986b). *Controversies in classroom research*. Philadelphia, PA & Milton Keynes, England: Open University Press.

Hammersley, M. (1977). School learning: The cultural responses required by pupils to answer a teacher's question. In P. Woods & M. Hammersley (Eds.), *School experience: Explorations in the sociology of education* (pp. 57–86). New York: St. Martin's Press.

Hammill, D. D., & McNutt, G. (1980). Language abilities and reading: A review of the literature on their relationship. *The Elementary School Journal, 80,* 269–277.

Hampleman, R. S. (1958). Comparison of listening and reading comprehension ability of fourth and sixth grade pupils. *Elementary English, 35,* 49–53.

Harris, C. W. (Ed.). (1960). *Encyclopedia of educational research*. New York: Macmillan.

Hasan, R. (1984a). The structure of the nursery tale: An essay in text typology. *Proceedings of the XVth Congress of S.L.I.*

Hasan, R. (1984b). Coherence and cohesive harmony. In J. Flood (Ed.), *Understanding reading comprehension: Cognition, language, and the structure of prose* (pp. 181–219). Newark, DE: International Reading Association.

Hasan, R. (1984c). The nursery tale as a genre. *Nottingham Linguistic Circular, 13,* 71–102.

Haslett, B. (1983). Children's strategies for maintaining cohesion in their written and oral stories. *Communication Education, 32,* 91–106.

Heap, J. L. (1986). Sociality and cognition in collaborative computer writing. Paper presented at the University of Michigan School of Education Conference on Literacy and Culture in Educational Settings. Reprinted in D. Bloome (Ed.), *Classrooms and literacy* (pp. 135–158). Norwood, NJ: Ablex.

Heath, S. B. (1983). *Ways with words: Language, life, and work in communities and classrooms*. Cambridge: Cambridge University Press.

Hendricks, B. L. (1980). The status of elementary speech communication education. *Communication Education, 29,* 364–369.

Hickman, J., & Kimberley, K. (1988). *Teachers, language and learning*. London: Routledge.

Holdzkom, D., Reed, L. J., Porter, E. J., & Rubin, D. L. (1982). *Research within reach: Oral and written communication: A research-guided response to the concerns of educators*. St. Louis, MO: CEMREL.

Hollow, Sr. M. K. (1955). Listening comprehension at the intermediate grade level. *The Elementary School Journal, 56,* 158–161.

Hopper, R., & Wrather, N. (1978). Teaching functional communication skills in the elementary classroom. *Communication Education, 27.*

Horrworth, G. L. (1966). Listening: A facet of oral language. *Elementary English, 43,* 856–864, 868.

Hymes, D. (1962). The ethnography of speaking. In T. Gladwin & W. C. Sturtevant (Eds.), *Anthropology and human behavior* (pp. 15–33). Washington: Anthropological Society of Washington.

Hymes, D. (1967). Models of the interaction of language and social setting. *Journal of Social Issues, 23,* 8–29.

Hymes, D. (1971). Competence & performance in linguistic theory. In R. Huxley & E. Ingram (Eds.), *Language Acquistion: Models and methods* (pp. 3–24). New York: Academic Press.

Hymes, D. (1972). Introduction. In C. Cazden, V. P. John, & D. Hymes (Eds.), *Functions of language in the classroom* (pp. xi–liv). New York: Teachers College Press.

Hymes, D. (1974). *Foundations in sociolinguistics: An ethnographic approach*. Philadelphia: University of Pennsylvania Press.

Irwin, E. C. (1975). Play and language development. *Speech Teacher, 24,* 15–23.

Johnson, N. S., & Mandler, J. M. (1980). A tale of two structures: Underlying and surface forms in stories. *Poetics, 9,* 51–86.

Jones, P. (1988). *Lipservice: The story of talk in schools*. Milton Keynes: Open University Press.

Jones, A., & Mulford, J. (Eds.). (1971). *Children using language: An approach to English in the primary school*. London: Oxford University Press.

Kelly, C. M. (1971). Listening: Compex of activities—and a unitary skill? In S. Duker (Ed.), *Listening: Readings* (Vol. 2) (pp. 213–229). Metuchen, NJ: Scarecrow Press.

Kelly, G. A. (1955). *The psychology of personal constructs*. New York: Norton.

Kiefer, B. Z., & DeStefano, J. S. (1985). Cultures together in the classroom: "What you saying?". In A. Jaggar & M. T. Smith-Burke (Eds.), *Observing the language learner* (pp. 159–172). Newark, DE & Urbana, IL: International Reading Association & National Council of Teachers of English.

King, M. L. (1984). Language and school success: Access to meaning. *Theory Into Practice, 23,* 175–182.

King, M. L., & McKenzie, M. G. (1988). Research currents: Literary discourse from the child's perspective. *Language Arts, 65,* 304–314.

King, M. L., & Rentel, V. (1981). Research Update: Conveying meaning in written texts. *Language Arts, 58,* 721–728.

Klein, M. L. (1977). *Talk in the language arts classroom*. Urbana, IL: ERIC Clearinghouse on Reading and Communication and National Council of Teachers of English.

Klein, M. L. (1979). Designing a talk environment for the classroom. *Language Arts, 56,* 647–656.

Knowles, L. (1983). *Encouraging talk*. New York: Methuen.

Kopp, O. W. (1967). The evaluation of oral language activities: Teaching and learning. *Elementary English, 44,* 121–122.

Kretschmer, R. E. (1989). Pragmatics, reading, and writing: Implications for hearing impaired individuals. *Topics in Language Disorders, 9,* 17–32.

Labov, W. (1969). The logic of non-standard English. In J. Alatis (Ed.), *Linguistics and the teaching of standard English to speakers of other languages* (pp. 1–44). Georgetown: Georgetown University Press.

Labov, W. (1972). *Language in the inner city*. Philadelphia: University of Pennsylvania Press.

Landry, D. L. (1969). The neglect of listening. *Elementary English, 46,* 599–605.

Larson, C. (1978). Problems in assessing functional communication. *Communication Education, 27,* 304–309.

Larson, C., Backlund, P., Redmond, M., & Barbour, A. (1978). *Assessing functional communication*. Urbana, IL & Falls Church, VA: ERIC Clearinghouse on Reading and Communication Skills & Speech Communication Association.

Larson, R. P., & Feder, D. D. (1940). Common and differential factors in reading and hearing comprehension. *Journal of Educational Psychology, 31,* 241–252.

Lazarus, P. G. (1984). What children know and teach about language competence. *Theory into Practice, 23,* 225–31.

Lieb-Brilhart, B. (1982). Standards for effective oral communication programs. In L. Reed & S. Ward (Eds.), *Basic skills, issues and choices* (Vol. 2). St. Louis: CEMREL.

Lieb-Brilhart, B. (1984). Oral communication instruction: Goals and teacher needs. In F. W. Parkay, S. O'Bryan, & M. Hennessy (Eds.), *Quest for quality: Improving basic instruction in the 1980's* (pp. 69–77). Lanham, MD: University Press of America.

Lindfors, J. W. (1987). *Children's language and learning* (2nd. ed.). Englewood Cliffs, NJ: Prentice-Hall.

Lloyd-Jones, R., & Lunsford, A. A. (Eds.). (1989). *The English coalition conference: Democracy through language*. Urbana, IL: National Council of Teachers of English

Loban, W. D. (1963). *The language of elementary school children* (National Council of Teachers of English Research Report No. 1). Urbana, IL: National Council of Teachers of English.

Loban, W. D. (1976). *Language development: Kindergarten through grade twelve* (National Council of Teachers of English Research Report No. 18). Urbana, Il: National Council of Teachers of English.

Lund, N. J. & Duchan, J. F. (1988). *Assessing children's language in naturalistic contexts* (2nd. ed.). Englewood Cliffs, NJ: Prentice-Hall.

Lundsteen, S. W. (1964). Teaching and testing critical listening in the fifth and sixth grades. *Elementary English, 41,* 743–747, 752.

Lundsteen, S. W. (1965). Critical listening—permanency and transfer of gains made during and experiment in fifth and sixth grades. *California Journal of Educational Research, 16,* 210–216.

Lundsteen, S. W. (1971). Critical listening and thinking: A recommended goal for future research. In S. Duker (Ed.), *Listening: Readings* (Vol. 2) (pp. 233–248). Metuchen, NJ: Scarecrow Press.

Lundsteen, S. W. (1979). *Listening: Its impact on reading and the other language arts* (rev. ed.). Urbana, IL: National Council of Teachers of English and ERIC Clearinghouse on Reading and Communication.

Mackintosh, H. K. (1964). *Children and oral language.* A joint statement of the Association for Childhood Education International, Association for Supervision and Curriculum Development, International Reading Association, National Council of Teachers of English.

MacLure, M. (1988). Introduction oracy: Current trends in context. In M. MacLure, T. Phillips, & A. Wilkinson (Eds.), *Oracy matters.* Philadelphia, PA & Milton Keynes, England: Open University Press.

Mallett, M., & Newsome, B. (1977). *Talking, writing and learning 8-13.* London: Evans/Methuen.

Mandler, J. M. (1984). *Stories, scripts, and scenes: Aspects of schema theory.* Hillsdale, NJ: Lawrence Erlbaum.

Marland, M. (1977). *Language across the curriculum.* London: Heinemann Educational Books.

Martin, N. (1983). *Mostly about writing: Selected essays.* Upper Montclair, NJ: Boynton/Cook.

Martin, N., D'Arcy, P., Newton, B., & Parker, R. (1976). *Writing and learning across the curriculum 11-16.* London: Schools Council Publications.

Martin, N., Williams, P., Wilding, J., Hemmings, S., & Medway, P. (1976). *Understanding children talking.* Harmondsworth: Penguin.

McCrosky, J. M. (1982). Communication competence and performance: A research and pedagogical perspective. *Communication Education, 31,* 1–7.

McKenzie, M. (1977). The beginnings of literacy. *Theory into Practice, 16,* 315–324.

McTear, M. G. (1984). Structure and process in children's conversational development. In S. A. Kuczaj (Ed.), *Discourse development: Progress in cognitive development research* (pp. 37–76). New York: Springer-Verlag.

McTear, M. G. (1985). *Children's conversations.* Oxford: Blackwell.

Mehan, H. (1974). Accomplishing classroom lessons. In A. V. Cicourel, K. H. Jennings, H. M. Sybillyn, K. C. Leiter, R. MacKay, H. Mehan, & D. R. Roth (Eds.), *Language use and school performance* (pp. 76–142). New York: Academic Press.

Mehan, H. (1978). Structuring school structure. *Harvard Educational Review, 48,* 32–64.

Mehan, H. (1979). *Learning lessons: Social organization in the classroom.* Cambridge, MA: Harvard University Press.

Mehan, H. (1981). Ethnography of bilingual education. In H. T. Trueba, G. P. Guthrie, & K. H. Au (Eds.), *Culture and the bilingual classroom: Studies in classroom ethnography* (pp. 36–55). Rowley, MA: Newbury House.

Menyuk, P. (1988). *Language development: Knowledge and use.* Glenview, IL: Scott Foresman.

Michaels, S. (1984). Listening and responding: Hearing the logic in children's classroom narratives. *Theory into Practice, 23,* 218–224.

Michaels, S. (1985). Hearing the connections in children's oral and written discourse. *Journal of Education, 167,* 36–56.

Michaels, S. (1986). Narrative presentations: An oral preparation for literacy with first graders. In J. Cook-Gumperz (Ed.), *The social construction of literacy* (pp. 94–116). London: Cambridge University Press.

Michaels, S., & Collins, J. (1984). Oral discourse style: Classroom interaction and the acquisition of literacy. In D. Tannen (Ed.), *Coherence in spoken and written discourse* (pp. 219–244). Norwood, NJ: Ablex.

Michaels, S., & Cook-Gumperz, J. (1979). A study of sharing time with first grade students: Discourse narratives in the classroom. *Proceedings of the Fifth Annual Meeting of the Berkeley Linguistics Society* (pp. 51–80).

Michaels, S., & Foster, M. (1985). Peer-peer learning: Evidence from a student run sharing time. In A. Jaggar & M. T. Smith-Burke (Eds.), *Observing the language learner* (pp. 143–158). Newark, DE & Urbana, IL: International Reading Association & National Council of Teachers of English.

Moffett, J. M. (1968). *Teaching the universe of discourse.* New York: Houghton Mifflin.

Moffett, J. M., & Wagner, B. J. (1973). *Student-centered language arts and reading, k-13.* Boston: Houghton Mifflin.

Moffett, J. M., & Wagner, B. J. (1983). *Student-centered language arts and reading, k-13* (3rd ed.). Boston: Houghton Mifflin.

Morine-Dershimer, G. (1985). *Talking, listening, and learning in elementary classrooms.* New York: Longman.

Myers, M. (1987). The shared structure of oral and written language and the implications for teaching writing, reading, and literature. In J. R. Squire (Ed.), *The dynamics of language learning: Research in reading and English* (pp. 121–146). Urbana, IL: ERIC Clearinghouse on Reading and Communication Skills & National Conference on Research in English.

National Association for the Teaching of English (1976). *Language across the Curriculum: Guidelines for schools.* London: Ward Lock.

National Commission on Excellence in Education (1983). *A nation at risk: The imperative for educational reform.* Washington, DC: U.S. Government Printing Office.

Nelson, K. (1973). Structure and strategy in learning to talk. *Monographs of the Society for Research in Child Development, 149,* (38 Pt. 1,2).

Nelson, K. (1986). *Event knowledge: Structure and function in development.* Hillsdale, NJ: Lawrence Erlbaum.

O'Donnell, R. C., Griffin, W. J., & Norris, R. C. (1967). *Syntax of kindergarten and elementary school children: A transformational analysis* (National Council of Teachers of English Research Report No. 8). Urbana, IL: National Council of Teachers of English.

Olson, D. (1977). From utterance to text: The bias of language in speech and writing. *Harvard Educational Review, 47,* 257–81.

Orr, D. B., Friedman, H. L., & Williams, J. C. (1965). Trainability of listening comprehension of speeded discourse. *Journal of Educational Psychology, 56,* 148–156.

Padak, N. (1986). Teachers' verbal behaviors: A window to the teaching process. In J. A. Niles & R. V. Lalik (Eds.), *Solving problems in literacy: Learners, teachers, and researchers* (pp. 185–91). Thirty-fifth Yearbook of the National Reading Conference.

Paley, V. G. (1981). *Wally's stories.* Cambridge, MA: Harvard University Press.

Pappas, C. C. (1981). *The development of narrative capabilities within a synergistic, variable pespective of language development: An examination of cohesive harmony of stories produced in three con-*

texts—Retelling, dictating, and writing. Unpublished doctoral dissertation, The Ohio State University, Ohio.

Pappas, C. C. (1985). The cohesive harmony and cohesive density of children's oral and written stories. In J. D. Benson & W. S. Greaves (Eds.), *Advances in discourse processes* (Vol. 16). *Systematic perspectives on discourse: Selected applied papers from the ninth international systemic workshop* (Vol. 2) (pp. 169–86). Norwood, NJ: Ablex.

Pappas, C. C., & Brown, E. (1987). Learning to read by reading: Learning how to extend the functional potential of language. *Research in the Teaching of English, 21,* 160–184.

Parkay, F. W., O'Bryan, S., & Hennessy, M. (Eds.). (1984). *Quest for quality: Improving basic skills instruction in the 1980's.* Lanham, MD: University Press of America.

Pearson, P. D., & Fielding, L. (1982). Research update: Listening comprehension. *Language Arts, 59,* 617–629.

Pellegrini, A. D., & Galda, L. (1988). The effects of age and context on children's use of narrative language. *Research in the Teaching of English, 22,* 183–195.

Petty, W. T. (1967). *Research in oral language* (A Research Bulletin). Urbana, IL: National Council of Teachers of English.

Philips, S. (1972). Participant structures and communicative competence: Warm Springs children in community and classroom. In C. Cazden, V. P. John, & D. Hymes (Eds.), *Functions of language in the classroom* (pp. 370–94). New York: Teachers College Press.

Philips, S. (1976). Some sources of cultural variables in the regulation of talk. *Language in Society, 5,* 81–96.

Phillips, T. (1985). Beyond lip-service: Discourse development after the age of nine. In G. Wells & J. Nicholls (Eds.), *Language & learning: An interactional perspective* (pp. 59–82). England: Falmer Press.

Phillips, T. (1988). On a related matter: Why "successful" small-group talk depends upon not keeping to the point. In M. MacLure, T. Phillips, & A. Wilkinson (Eds.), *Oracy matters* (pp. 69–81). Milton Keynes: Open University Press.

Piaget, J. (1959). *The language and thought of the child.* London: Routledge and Kegan Paul.

Pinnell, G. S. (1975). Language in primary classrooms. *Theory into Practice, 24,* 318–327.

Pinnell, G. S. (1985). Ways to look at the functions of children's language. In A. Jaggar & M. Trika Smith-Burke (Eds.), *Observing the language learner* (pp. 57–72). Newark, DE & Urbana, IL: International Reading Association & National Council of Teachers of English.

Platt, N. G. (1984). How one classroom gives access to meaning. *Theory into Practice, 23,* 239–245.

Powers, D. E. (1984). *Considerations for developing measures of speaking and listening.* New York: College Entrance Examination Board.

Pratt, E. (1956). Experimental evaluation of a program for the improvement of listening. *Elementary School Journal, 56,* 315–320.

Propp, V. (1968). *Morphology of the folktale* (Lawrence Scott, trans). Austin: University of Texas Press.

Rankin, P. T. (1928). The importance of listening ability. *English Journal* (College Ed.), *17,* 623–630.

Rentel, V., & King, M. L. (1983). Present at the beginning. In P. Mosenthal, L. Tamor, & S. Walmsley (Eds.), *Research on Writing: Principles and methods* (pp. 139–176). New York: Longman.

Robertson, I. (1980). *Language across the curriculum: Four cast studies.* London: Metheun.

Romaine, S. (1984). *The language of children and adolescents: The acquisition of communicative competence.* Oxford: Basil Blackwell.

Rosen, C., & Rosen, H. (1973). *The language of primary school children.* London: Schools Council Publications, Penguin Books.

Ross, D. D. (1983). Competence, relational status, and identity work: A study of the social interactions of young children. Paper presented at Annual Conference of National Association for the Education of Young Children, Washington, D.C.

Ross, H. S., & Goldman, B. M. (1976). Establishing new social relationships in infancy. In T. Alloway, L. Krames, & P. Pliner (Eds.), *Advances in communication and affect* (Vol. 4). New York: Plenum Press.

Ross, R. (1964). A look at listeners. *The Elementary School Journal, 64,* 369–372.

Rubin, D. L. (1985). Instruction in speaking and listening: Battles and options. *Educational Leadership, 42,* 31–36.

Rubin, D. L., & Kantor, K. (1984). Talking and writing: Building communication competence. In C. Thaiss & C. Suhor (Eds.), *Speaking and writing K-12* (pp. 29–73). Urbana, IL: National Council of Teachers of English.

Rubin, D. L., & Mead, N. A. (1984). *Large scale assessment of oral communication skills: Kindergarten through grade 12.* Urbana, IL & Annandale, VA: ERIC Clearinghouse on Reading and Communication Skills & Speech Communication Association.

Ruddell, R. B. (1965). Effect of the similarity of oral and written patterns of language structure on reading comprehension. *Elementary English, 42,* 403–410.

Ruddell, R. B. (1966). Oral language and the development of other language skills. *Elementary English, 43,* 489–498.

Russell, D. H. (1964). A conspectus of recent research on listening abilities. *Elementary English, 41,* 262–267.

Schachter, F. F., Kirschner, K., Klips, B., Friedricks, M., & Sanders, K. (1974). Everyday preschool interpersonal speech usage: Methodological, developmental, and sociolinguistics studies. *Monograph of the Society for Research in Child Development, 39*(3, Serial No. 156).

Schaudt, B. A. (1983). Relationships between listening and reading: A historical survey. Paper presented at the annual meeting of the Great Lakes Regional conference of the International Reading Association, Springfield, IL. (ERIC Document Reproduction Service No. ED 240 544)

Schickedanz, J. A., & Sullivan, M. (1984). Mom, what does U-F-F spell? *Language Arts, 61,* 7–17.

Sevigny, M. J. (1981). Triangulated inquiry: A methodology for the analysis of classroom interaction. In J. Green & C. Wallat (Eds.), *Ethnography and language in educational settings* (pp. 65–86). Norwood, NJ: Ablex.

Shafer, R. E., Staab, C., & Smith, K. (1983). *Language functions and school success.* Glenview, IL: Scott Foresman.

Shatz, M., & Gelman, R. (1973). The development of communication skills: Modifications in the speech of young children as a function of listeners. *Monograph of the Society for Research in Children's Development, 38,* 55.

Shavelson, R. J., & Stern P. (1981). Research on teachers' pedagogical thoughts, judgments, decisions, and behavior. *Review of Educational Research, 51,* 455–498.

Shure, M. B. (1963). Psychological ecology of a nursery school. *Child Development, 34,* 979–992.

Shuy, R. (1984). Language as a foundation for education: The school context. *Theory into Practice, 23,* 167–174.

Simon, A., & Boyer, B. G. (Eds.). (1974). *Mirrors for behavior III: An anthology of observation instruments.* Wyncote, PA: Communications Materials Center.

Sinclair, J. McH., & Coulthard, M. (1975). *Towards an analysis of discourse: The English used by teachers and pupils.* London: Oxford University Press.

Snow, C. (1977). The development of conversation between mothers and babies. *Journal of Child Language, 4,* 1–22.

Snow, C., & Ferguson, C. (Eds.). (1977). *Talking to children: Language input and acquisition.* New York: Cambridge University Press.

Spearritt, D. (1962). *Listening comprehension: A factoral analysis* (Australian Council for Educational Research, Research Series No. 76). Melbourne: G. W. Green & Sons.

Stein, N., & Glenn, C. (1979). An analysis of story comprehension in elementary school children. In R. Freedle (Ed.), *New directions in discourse processing* (Vol. 2) (pp. 53–120). Norwood, NJ: Ablex.

Stenning, K., & Michell, L. (1985). Learning how to tell a good story: The development of content and language in children's telling of one tale. *Discourse Processes, 8,* 261–279.

Stern, D. (1977). *The first relationship: Infant and mother.* London: Open Books.

Stern, D., Jaffe, J., Beebe, B., & Bennett, S. (1975). The infant's stimulus world during social interactions. In H. R. Schaffer (Ed.), *Studies of mother-infant interactions.* New York: Academic Press.

Sticht, T. (1972). Learning by listening. In R. O. Freedle & J. B. Carroll (Eds.), *Language comprehension and the acquisition of knowledge* (pp. 285–314). Washington, DC: V. H. Winston & Sons.

Sticht, T., Beck, L., Hauke, R., Kleiman, G., & James, J. (1974). *Auding and reading: A developmental model.* Alexandria, VA: Human Resources Research Organization.

Stiggins, R. J. (Ed.). (1981). *Perspectives on oral communication assessment in the 80's.* Portland, Oregon: Northwest Regional Educational Laboratory.

Strickland, D. S. (1989). A model for change: Framework for an emergent literacy program. In D. S. Strickland and L. M. Morrow (Eds.), *Emerging literacy: Young children learn to read and write* (pp. 135–146). Newark, DE: International Reading Association.

Strickland, R. G. (1962). The language of elementary school children: Its relationship to the language of reading textbooks and the quality of reading of selected children. *Bulletin of the School of Education, 38*(4). Bloomington, IN: Bureau of Educational Studies and Testing, School of Education, Indiana University.

Strickland, R. G., Blake, H. E., & Amato, A. J., & Petty, W. T. (1967). Three statements regarding needed research in oral language. In W. T. Petty (Ed.), *Research in oral language* (pp. 60–67). Urbana, IL: National Conference on Research in English.

Strother, D. B. (1987). Practical applications of research: On listening. *Phi Delta Kappan, 68,* 625–628.

Stubbs, M. (1976). *Language, schools and classrooms.* London: Methuen.

Stubbs, M. (1983). *Discourse analysis: The sociolinguistic analysis of natural language.* Oxford: Blackwell.

Stubbs, M., & Delamont, S. (Eds.). (1976). *Explorations in classroom observation.* London & New York: John Wiley.

Sulzby, E. (1985). Children's emergent reading of favorite storybooks: A developmental study. *Reading Research Quarterly, 20,* 458–481.

Tannen, D. (1982). Oral and literate strategies in spoken and written narrative. *Language Arts, 58,* 1–21.

Tannen, D. (1985). Relative focus on involvement in oral and written discourse. In D. R. Olson, N. Torrance, & A. Hildyard (Eds.), *Literacy, language and learning: The nature and consequences of reading and writing* (pp. 124–47). New York: Cambridge University Press.

Tarleton, R. (1988). *Learning and talking: A practical guide to oracy across the curriculum.* New York: Routledge.

Taylor, D. (1983). *Family literacy.* Portsmouth, NH: Heinemann.

Thaiss, C. (1986). *Language across the curriculum in elementary grades.* Urbana, IL: National Council of Teachers of English.

Thaiss, C., & Suhor, C. (Eds.). (1984). *Speaking and writing K-12.* Urbana, IL: National Council of Teachers of English.

Thorndyke, P. W. (1977). Cognitive structures in comprehension and memory in of narrative discourse. *Cognitive Psychology, 9,* 77–110.

Tizard, B., & Hughes, M. (1984). *Young children learning: Talking and thinking at home and at school.* London: Fontana Press.

Torbe, M., & Medway, P. (1981). *The climate for learning.* Montclair, NJ: Boynton/Cook.

Torbe, M., & Protherough, R. (Eds.). (1976). *Classroom encounters: Language and English teaching.* London: Ward Lock in association with The National Association for the Teaching of English.

Torrence, N., & Olson, D. R. (1984). Oral language comptence and the acquisition of literacy. In A. D. Pellegrini & T. Yawkey (Eds.), *The development of oral and written language in social contexts* (pp. 167–181). Norwood, NJ: Ablex.

Tough, J. (1973). *Focus on meaning: Talking to some purpose with young children.* London: George Allen & Unwin.

Tough, J. (1976). *Listening to children talking: A guide to the appraisal of children's use of language.* London: Ward Lock.

Tough, J. (1977a). *The development of meaning: A study of children's use of language.* London: George Allen & Unwin.

Tough, J. (1977b). *Talking and learning: A guide to fostering communication skills in nursery and infant schools.* London: Ward Lock.

Tough, J. (1979). *Talk for teaching and learning.* London: Ward Lock.

Trevarthen, C. (1979). Communication and cooperation in early infancy: A description of primary intersubjectivity. In M. Bullowa (Ed.), *Before speech: The beginning of interpersonal communication* (pp. 321–347). Cambridge: Cambridge University Press.

Trivette, S. E. (1961). The effect of training in listening for specific purposes. *Journal of Educational Research, 54,* 276–277.

Trueba, H. T., Guthrie, G. P., & Au, K. H. (1981). *Culture and the classroom: Studies in classroom ethnography.* Rowley, MA: Newbury House.

Vandell, D. L., & Mueller, E. (1980). Peer play and friendships during the first two years. In H. C. Foot, A. J. Chapman, & J. R. Smith (Eds.), *Friendship and social relations in children.* New York: John Wiley.

Van Rheenan, D., McClure, E., & Backlund, P. (1984). *State policies in speaking and listening skill assessment through 1983.* Orono: Department of Speech Communication, University of Maine.

Vygotsky, L. (1962). *Thought and language.* Cambridge, MA: M.I.T. Press.

Vygotsky, L. (1978). *Mind in society: The development of higher psychological processes* (M. Cole, V. John-Steiner, S. Scribner, & E. Souberman, trans.). Cambridge, MA: Harvard University Press.

Wade, B. (1983). Story and intonation features in young children: A case study. *Educational Review, 35,* 175–186.

Watson, K. (1980). A close look at whole class-discussion. *English in Education, 14,* 39–44.

Watson, K. (1987). *English teaching in perspective* (2nd ed.). Milton Keynes: Open University Press.

Webb, N. M. (1982). Student interaction and learning in small groups. *Review of Educational Research, 52,* 521–545.

Weeks, T. E. (1979). *Born to talk.* Rowley, MA: Newbury House.

Weimann, J. M., & Backlund, P. (1980). Current theory and research in communicative competence. *Review of Educational Research, 50,* 185–199.

Welkowitz, J., Cariffe, G., & Feldstein, S. (1976). Conversational congruence as a criterion of socialization in children. *Child Development, 47,* 269–72.

Wells, G. (1973). *Coding manual for the description of child speech.* Bristol, England: University of Bristol School of Education.

Wells, G. (1981). *Learning through interaction: The study of language development.* Cambridge: Cambridge University Press.

Wells, G. (1985). *Language, learning and education.* England: NFER-NELSON.

Wells, G. (1986a). *The meaning makers: Children learning language and using language to learn.* Portsmouth, NH: Heinemann.

Wells, G. (1986b). The language experience of five-year-old children at home and at school. In J. Cook-Gumperz (Ed.), *The social construction of literacy* (pp. 69–93). London: Cambridge University Press.

Wells, G., & Nicholls, J. (Eds.). (1985). *Language & learning: an interactional perspective* (pp. 18). England: Falmer Press.

Wells, G., & Wells, J. (1984). Learning to talk and talking to learn. *Theory into Practice, 23,* 190–197.

Westby, C. (1984). Development of narrative language abilities. In G. Wallach & K. Butler (Eds.), *Language learning disabilities in school-age children* (pp. 347–74). Baltimore, MD: Williams and Wilkins.

Whiten, A. (1977). Assessing the effects of perinatal events on the success of the mother-infant relationship. In H. R. Schaffer (Ed.), *Studies in mother-infant interaction.* New York: Academic Press.

Wilkinson, A. M. (1965). *Spoken English,* with contributions by A. Davies and D. Atkinson. Birmingham, England: University of Birmingham.

Wilkinson, A. M. (1970). The concept of oracy. *English Journal, 59,* 70–77.

Wilkinson, A. M. (1971). *The foundations of language: Talking and reading in young children.* Oxford: Oxford University Press.

Wilkinson, A. M. (1972). Total communication. *English in Education, 6,* 55–62.

Wilkinson, A. M. (1975). *Language and education.* Oxford: Oxford University Press.

Wilkinson, A. M., Barnsley, G., Hanna, P., & Swan, M. (1980). Assessing language development. Oxford: Oxford University Press.

Wilkinson, A. M., Stratta, L., & Dudley, P. (1974). *The quality of listening.* England: Schools Council Research Study, Macmillan Education.

Wilkinson, L. C. (Ed.). (1982). *Communicating in the classroom.* New York: Academic Press.

Wilkinson, L. C. (1984). Research currents: Peer group talk in elementary school. *Language arts, 61,* 164–169.

Wilkinson, L. C., & Calculator, S. (1982). Effective speakers: Students' use of language to request and obtain information and action in the classroom. In L. C. Wilkinson (Ed.), *Communicating in the classroom* (85–99). New York: Academic Press.

Wilkinson, L. C., & Dollaghan, C. (1979). Peer communication in first-grade reading groups. *Theory into Practice, 18,* 267–274.

Wilkinson, L. C., & Spinelli, F. (1982). Conclusion: Application for education. In L. C. Wilkinson (Ed.), *Communicating in the classroom* (pp. 323–327). New York: Academic Press.

Willes, M. (1983). *Children into pupils.* London: Routledge & Kegan Paul.

Wilt, M. E. (1950). A study of teacher awareness of listening as a factor in elementary education. *Journal of Educational, Research, 43,* 626–636.

Wilt, M. E. (1955). Children's experiences in listening. In V. E. Herrick & L. B. Jacobs (Eds.), *Children and the language arts.* Englewood Cliffs, NJ: Prentice-Hall.

Wilt, M. E. (1973). Listening! What's new? In M. L. King, R. Emans, & P. J. Cianciolo (Eds.), *A forum for focus* (pp. 63–72). Urbana, IL: National Council of Teachers of English.

Withall, J., & Lewis, W. W. (1971). Social interaction in the classroom. In A. H. Yee (Ed.), *Social interaction in educational settings* (pp. 25–57). Englewood Cliffs, NJ: Prentice-Hall.

Wood, B. S. (Ed.). (1977a). *The development of functional communication competencies: Pre-K through grade 6.* Urbana, IL: ERIC Clearinghouse on Reading and Communication Skills.

Wood, B. S. (Ed.). (1977b). *The development of functional communication competencies: Grades 7–12.* Urbana, IL: ERIC Clearinghouse on Reading and Communication Skills. (ERIC Document Reproduction Service No. ED 137 859)

Wood, B. S. (1981). *Children and communication: Verbal and nonverbal language development* (2nd ed.). Englewood Cliffs, NJ: Prentice-Hall.

Wood, B. S. (1984). Oral communication in the elementary classroom. In C. Thaiss & C. Suhor (Eds.), *Speaking and writing, K–12* (pp. 104–125). Urbana, IL: National Council of Teachers of English.

Young, M. F. D. (1971). An approach to the study of curricula as socially organized knowledge. In M. F. D. Young (Ed.), *Knowledge and control.* London: Collier-Macmillan.

Young, R., & Watson, K. (1981). Verbal communication: The nature of classroom discourse. In Deakin University, *Classroom communication: Classroom processes* (pp. 81–100). Victoria, Australia: Deakin University Press.

Young, W. E. (1936). The relation of reading comprehension and retention to hearing comprehension and retention. *Journal of Experimental Education, 5,* 30–39.

Zemlin, W. R., Daniloff, R. G., & Shriner, T. H. (1968). The difficulty of listening to time-compressed speech. *Journal of Speech and Hearing Research, 11,* 869–874.

34

READING

34A. CHILDREN'S DEVELOPING KNOWLEDGE OF WORDS

Jana M. Mason
Patricia A. Herman
Kathryn H. Au

Over time, research on the acquisition of knowledge about words and an understanding of the larger process of reading for meaning has led to changes in views of reading and its development. In this chapter we review research on two aspects of beginning reading: word identification and vocabulary knowledge. Word identification and vocabulary knowledge are critical in the sense that reading for meaning cannot take place in their absence. We do not intend this to mean that other aspects of reading such as knowledge of the functions of literacy (Heath, 1983) or concepts about print (Clay, 1979, 1985), or story forms (Applebee, 1980) are unimportant. It would be inaccurate to speak of word identification and vocabulary knowledge as the only skills basic to reading.

In fact, one of the major themes in this chapter is that children's understanding of words is best understood from the perspective of developing sensitivities to the English language. In the case of word identification, for example, experiences in writing, spelling, and reading words make a significant contribution. Vocabulary knowledge takes place through word play and talk about language as well as through wide-ranging opportunities to express, hear, and read new words in meaningful contexts.

A second major theme is that acquisition of word identification skills and vocabulary knowledge centers around discovery of the regularity of the language. Of course, the English language is quite complex, so the process of discovery is not simple. In some cases words may be identified or their meanings interpreted through the application of rather simple understandings. In other cases, though, more complicated understandings must be invoked.

The first section of this chapter deals with word identification and the second with vocabulary knowledge. We decided not to address the two topics in a strictly parallel manner. Research conducted with adults receives much less attention in the section on word identification than in the section on vocabulary.

The reason for this difference is that children's learning of word identification involves striking developmental changes. Children typically shift from identifying words one by one, in piecemeal fashion, to identifying words using a variety of approaches based on extensive knowledge of context, letter sounds, and syllable patterns. A similar shift in approaches does not seem to occur with acquisition of vocabulary knowledge. Thus, research conducted with adults may be less informative in the case of word identification than in the case of vocabulary knowledge, especially when it comes to instructional implications.

The research reviewed in this chapter presents a synthesis of information from both qualitative and quantitative studies. The literature on word identification and vocabulary development is vast, go the studies cited here should be considered illustrative. These studies stem from different theoretical, as well as methodological, orientations. Nevertheless, it appears that the patterns of findings in both bodies of research are gradually converging and tend to provide support for many of the same conclusions. It is these patterns that we have tried to convey.

WORD IDENTIFICATION

The typical 4-year-old relies on idiosyncratic cues to identify words. For example, a child might recognize the word *monkey* because there is a tail on the *y* (Gates & Bocker, 1923), or *look* because it seems to have two eyes in the middle. In a word learning study, Gough and Juel (in press) even found that young children were more likely to notice and rely on a thumb print on a word card than on the letter information. These examples make the point that children do not intuitively make use of letter-sound information to recognize words. By the end of the elementary school years, however, children can usually read and understand words using a vast array of information about letter-sound patterns, clusters of letters, and syllables.

Children can then identify words quickly and with little effort. They are better able to place word identification in the background and focus on comprehension. Children with inadequate word identification skills, however, continue to rely principally on context cues and are almost invariably poor readers (Simon & Leu, 1987; Stanovich, in press).

Clearly, proficiency in word identification is central to the reading act. How might proficient word identification be characterized? What course do children generally follow in developing the ability to identify words? What types of classroom experiences appear most valuable for strengthening chidlren's ability to identify words? These questions are addressed below.

Proficient Word Identification

Skilled readers have the ability to identify words fluently and effortlessly. According to McConkie and Zola (1987) reading is carried out "by making a series of eye fixations, each of which exposes the processing system to a large and complex stimulus array. . . . During reading these displaced views of the text occur four times per second, on the average. Thus, about every quarter of a second the reader selects from the stimulus array the information that is needed to further an understanding of the text" (pg. 385). The processes of identifying words becomes subservient to text meaning and overall understanding.

There appear to be two mechanisms for the word identification process (Rayner & Pollatsek, 1989). One mechanism, a direct route, involves rapid or automatic recognition of words and their pronunciation and meaning. Most common words, words that appear frequently in texts such as pronouns, articles, and frequently read nouns and verbs, are recognized rapidly by skilled readers. Less common words and words never before seen cannot be recognized by this process. The other mechanism seems to operate through an ongoing construction process of plausible pronunciations. Words are recognized through a process of similarity or analogy to known words and by knowing spelling pattern rules. You might pronounce, "barbet," for example, through analogy to other known words, such as *barber* or *sherbet*. You would not think that it is pronounced like "ba-rbet" because you know that *rbet* is not a legal syllable in English. You usually can make appropriate generalizations to new words based on this sort of extensive knowledge of words and word patterns.

In summary, we can say that there are two systems for identifying words. One is a direct, lexical mechanism in which the pronunciation is "looked up" after the eye fixates on the word. The other is a slower, pattern-based mechanism whereby the pronunciation of a word is generated by a complex analysis of analogous words. This works in coordination with spelling or pronunciation rules. The direct route results in rapid recognition of very frequently occurring words, regardless of their letter-sound regularity. The analytic system results in recognition of most other words based on knowledge of similarly formed words and rules for analyzing words into letter-sounds, syllables, roots, and affixes.

This picture of skilled reading indicates that children need to be able to identify common words effortlessly and to figure out less common words through knowledge of word structures. How do most children arrive at this point? The beginnings of word identification can be traced back to children's early experiences with literacy. If we follow the development from that period through the primary grades, we can see how word identification develops systematically and can be related to instruction.

Development of Word Identification Skills

Becoming literate builds upon the production and understanding of speech, but also goes far beyond. Literacy requires an awareness that the words in books, on signs, and in other places are intended to convey a message that may be interesting, amusing, or important (Mason & Au, 1990). Literacy also involves an ability to separate oneself from meaning, that is, to take a distant or analytic position, to judge as well as to understand text information and to think of language as a tool (Egan, 1987; Olson, 1984).

Children first become aware that language can be observed and analyzed into words and letters by seeing its written form in familiar contexts. For example, while looking at an alphabet book with a parent, the young child may see the word *apple* accompanied by the letter *A* and a picture of an apple. At breakfast there may be Special K cereal with an oversized *K* on the box. On outings, the child visits a McDonald's restaurant and sees the sign with the golden arches. These early experiences with environmental print may play a role in children's early understanding of words by helping children view printed words as meaningful representations of objects, unchanging in their context (Mason, 1980).

A further contribution of these experiences to later word identification, however, has not been clearly established. Masonheimer, Drum and Ehri (1984), for example, found that children noticed nothing different about the *PEPSI* logo when the letters were changed to read *XEPSI*. Nonetheless, although children are not processing all letter information, their responses suggest that they are gaining an understanding of the function of familiar environmental print. Mason and Stewart (1988) found in testing preschool children's understanding of print that they were likely to give the response "stop sign" when asked to read *STOP* when it was printed on the familiar octagon-shaped sign. This erroneous response was only a temporary stage in their reading development.

It may be, then, that environmental print serves in a preliminary way to make children aware of some words and helps to illustrate some of the purpose served by print. Having a sense of these purposes would also make the print more meaningful, and thus more memorable (Doake, 1985), and it could help motivate children to begin attending more closely to print.

Another indication that word identification has its roots in children's general understandings of print is provided by the work of Peterman and Mason (1984). They showed kindergarten children labeled pictures. They found that some children could point to the print when asked where there is something to read, but then would ignore the print when asked to read what it says. That is, children knew that reading involved print, but had the idea that they could read without using the letter information. Children further along realized that they should attend both to pictures and print when trying to identify the labeled pictures or when trying to recall a page of text that had been read to them. Even then, however, where a word ends or where to begin and stop reading was still uncertain for some children. For example, when shown the phrase "wood blocks" and asked how many words there were, some children did not distinguish letters from words and counted the letters instead.

As children have more opportunities to watch others read and try to read by themselves, they come to the realization that printed words can be differentiated on a page. They might try to remember words by the initial letter, especially if a word begins with the same letter as their name. They might overuse letter names when they write, spelling *are* as R, and *you* as U, indicating that they cannot yet break words into letter sounds.

As part of becoming literate in English, though, children must come to realize that words can be further analyzed and that there are predictable patterns of letters and sounds. That is, they must understand the regularity of spelling-to-sound correspondence (Ehri, 1991). As with learning about the visual properties of print, initial learning about the relationships between letters and sounds often begins through home literacy activities. A variety of experiences appear to support the development of these concepts: hearing nursery rhymes, stories, and interesting words; discussing words with parents; invented spelling and writing; and having words pointed out in context (Bissex, 1980; Taylor, 1983). Maclean, Bryant and Bradley (1987) determined that knowledge of nursery rhymes at age 3 was strongly related to early reading performance.

Before making much use of spelling-to-sound regularities in English words, children tend to use other types of information. Context cues provided by pictures and sentences make it easier for beginning readers to identify words. When these cues are unavailable, beginners generally experience much more difficulty. Less advanced first graders, for example, find words easier to identify if they are presented in the sentences in which they were learned than in other sentences or lists (Francis, 1977). Beginning readers are likely to make oral reading errors that are consistent with sentence context but not with spelling-to-sound information (Stanovich, Cunningham, & Feeman, 1984; Underwood, 1985). According to a compensatory model of reading performance, it is said that beginners are compensating for their limitations in using spelling-to-sound correspondence by relying heavily on context cues.

Considerable research has verified that an ability to break the sounds of words into phonemes, which is referred to as *phonemic awareness*, is the initial step in lessening the importance of context. Phonemes are the sounds of letters and letter groups in words (e.g., *m-ea-t, g-r-i-pe, sh-e-ll-s*). Early on, children are not aware of phonemes. Rather, they seem first to recognize the syllable as a unit, and then notice that a syllable has two major subunits, called the onset and the rime (Treiman, in press). The onset is the initial portion of the syllable (e.g., *m* in *meat, gr* in *gripe*, or *sh* in *shells*). The rime includes the vowel and ending consonants (e.g., *eat* in *meat, ipe* in *gripe, ells* in *shells*). Treiman found that young children could analyze spoken syllables into onsets and rimes before they could identify

phonemes. This suggests that children can be helped to hear syllables in words, then onset/rimes, and then individual phonemes. Instructionally, it suggests that breaking spoken words into syllables by clapping could be a useful beginning step. Initial sounds of words could be introduced through ABC books, where the first letter in a word is highlighted, and ending sounds of words could be presented through rhymes.

After children can distinguish onset/rime units in words, they will be able to separate other phonemes in words and to manipulate phonemes. Bissex (1980), for example, reported her son's discovery that he could remove the *l* from *please* and have the word *peas(e)*). With these and related discoveries, children begin to realize the regularities of spelling-to-sound patterns. They begin to figure out words they have never seen in print before based on their knowledge of letter patterns and knowing the words orally. This knowledge can be tested with various word and letter-sound analysis tasks, which Stanovich, Cunningham, and Cramer (1984), and Yopp (1988) showed are all highly intercorrelated.

More generally, word and letter-sound analysis ability is significantly correlated with later reading achievement (e.g., Calfee, Lindamood, & Lindamood, 1973; Lundberg, 1986; Share, Jorm, Maclean, & Matthews, 1984). An ability to analyze words into letter sounds appears to allow children to discover and exploit the alphabetic principle of spelling-to-sound regularities. Understanding this aspect of written language structure provides "a basis for constructing a large and expandable set of words—all the words that ever were, are, and will be—out of two or three dozen signal elements (phonemes)" (Liberman & Shankweiler, 1985, p, 9).

Can children be taught an awareness of phonemes in words? Apparently, yes. Two studies have shown that phonemic awareness training in kindergarten benefits children's later reading. Bradley and Bryant (1983) worked with children who had obtained low scores on a test of phonemic awareness. One treatment group was given 40 individual tutoring sessions on identifying beginning, middle, and final sounds in words and connecting sounds to letters. Those in comparison and control groups did not fare as well as this group in later school years in reading. Lundberg, Frost, and Petersen (1988) found that children's reading and spelling benefited from metalinguistic training given in daily, whole-class lessons during the kindergarten year. Teachers provided the following types of activities in approximately this sequence: listening to nonverbal and verbal sounds; nursery rhymes and stories and games for rhyming production; segmentation of sentences into words; segmentation of words into syllables (clapping, marching, dancing, walking followed by use of plastic markers and games using puppets); segmentation of initial letters of words from remainder; and segmentation of two-letter words into phonemes.

Word Reading and Spelling Development in the Primary Grades

Ehri (1986) and Ehri and Wilce (1987) proposed that knowledge of how to match letters to sounds progresses in a developmental fashion. At first children use knowledge of letter names to spell parts of words, usually the initial or initial and final parts. Thus, they might spell *cat* as *K* or *KT*. After this semiphonetic stage, children master vowel spellings and phonemic segmentation, enabling them to place all the letter sounds in the words, though not necessarily correctly. During this time *cat* might be spelled correctly or phonetically (*kat*). Finally, sometime during the first grade of reading instruction, children move into the morphemic stage, "when the principle of one-letter-for-every-sound loses its grip and spellers begin to utilize word-based spelling regularities to generate spellings" (p. 62). At this point children are learning about conventional spellings through the texts they are reading.

When children first turn to the use of spelling-to-sound information, the presence of the more consistent or regular spelling-to-sound patterns (as in words such as *pat, paid, pave*) becomes important. For a short time, children might even have more difficulty identifying words that form inconsistent patterns or are exceptions to regular patterns (e.g., *put, said, have*). Gradually though, they recognize exceptions as unique words. Most of these words would be recognize directly. Recognition of less common words builds on an understanding of regular word patterns and leads to recognition through the other word identification mechanism (Tunmer, Herriman, & Nesdale, 1988).

This means that knowledge of spelling-to-sound correspondence not only enables readers to recognize words they know, but also to identify words never encountered previously. Glushko (1981) showed that adults use their knowledge of common, regular words to identify unknown words by using familiar, analogous words. Goswami (1988) found that even beginning readers figure out new words by analogy, that is, by thinking of similar (rhyming or alliterative) words. For example, a child may recognize a new word, *peak*, by recalling the pronunciation of the analogous word, *beak*. Goswami found that children who had acquired letter-sound knowledge used decoding by analogy both when reading words in lists and when the new words were in connected texts. In a second study, she found that children who were taught words with regular patterns (e.g., *beak*) made more analogies than children who were taught words inconsistent in pattern (e.g., *break*). Goswami pointed out that these results are congruent with Treiman's (in press) view that "phonemic awareness progresses from an analysis of syllable into onsets and rimes, and only subsequently to the ability to analyze onsets and rimes into phonemes" (p. 41). Similarly, in an unpublished study, Mason found that a number of second-grade children figured out how to pronounce pseudowords by analogy, for example, explaining that they could pronounce *moke* by taking the *s* off from *smoke*.

Knowledge that letters form predictable sequences is also important, beginning at about second grade (Adams, 1990). Children find it easier to identify words containing commonly occurring letter sequences. For example, words such as *ten* and *the* will be easier to identify then *tsar* or *two* because *t* as the first letter of a word is more likely to be followed by *e* or *h* than *s* or *w*. Children gradually become knowledgeable about the predictability of letter sequences and at about fourth grade they can use this knowledge to recognize syllable patterns and boundaries in multisyllable words. They can determine where breaks between syllables are likely to occur and how the syllables might be pronounced (e.g., *mon-key* rather than *mo-nkey* because *nkey* is not a legitimate syllable; *fa-ther* rather than *fat-her* because *th* is a letter sequence that usually appears in the same syllable).

In brief, by the end of first grade, many children are reading easy texts fluently, and some have even gained the ability to identify common syllable patterns. At this point, most children are well on their way to becoming effective word readers, able to make good use of common and less common patterns in written English. By the end of third or fourth grade, only uncommon multisyllable words are difficult for most children to recognize.

Connecting Word Recognition Development to Other Aspects of Literacy

Recent developmental models of reading connect early with more skilled reading and introduce an interplay between word identification and text comprehension. Lundberg (in press), for example, proposes that reading emerges from two related but separate roots. One, word recognition, is related to phonology, and the other is related to comprehension. When learning to read, children use internal representations of words from their own language to begin the analysis of written words. Children begin reading using highly contextualized skills and then move on to relatively decontextualized skills. Book reading, listening to stories at an early age, and learning to read easy stories appear to contribute to effective reading development.

Brugelmann (1986) suggests that both writing and spelling are coordinated with reading because all three aspects of literacy require similar knowledge about the written language. Children's writing moves from aimless traces, beginning with toddlers who might experiment by touching pencil to paper, and then to directed scribbling, such as zig-zags across the page. Next, children imitate letter shapes, constructing letter-like scribbles, then single letters, and then multiple letters. Finally, recognizing that the letters can form words and phrases they construct letters that are connected. Just as writing develops from scribbles, so spelling develops from drawings that are intended to represent words, and then letters are added arbitrarily to the drawings. Next, letters that represent particular words are used, such as *R* for the word *are*. A sound-oriented shorthand, an invented spelling, is then developed to represent the sounds the child hears in words. A child might spell *kite* as *kt*. Children eventually replace these with specific learned spellings, filling in the vowels and applying learned orthographic patterns. Earliest aspects of reading are listening to stories and telling stories. Then, mock or pretend-reading, imitations of being read to, occur. Lartz and Mason (1988), for example, showed how a 4-year-old child could say a substantial part of a story from remembering what was read to her and with the aid of the illustrations on successive pages. For all three aspects of literacy, context is used, and then gradually superseded by attention to letter-sound information and more complex patterns of English.

Brugelmann's proposal reminds us that word identification is only one part of literacy activity: knowledge about how to recognize words is initiated with rough attempts to carry out the whole act, whether reading, writing, or spelling, and continues to become more accurate and realistic.

Instructional Implications

Children face a major cognitive challenge to understand the regularity of written English for identifying, writing, and spelling words effortlessly. Word recognition research points to the complexity of the learning children must do to become proficient word identifiers. They must develop phonemic awareness, come to an understanding of spelling-to-sound correspondence, and then progress to applying knowledge of letter patterns and syllables.

It is not surprising, then, that research supports the importance of systematic instruction in spelling-to-sound correspondences, commonly called phonics instruction, during the early grades (Anderson, Hiebert, Scott, & Wilkinson, 1985). Early studies tended to pit approaches incorporating systematic phonics instruction against approaches that emphasized text reading and relied on children's learning of words as wholes. We believe this tendency had the inadvertent effect of creating a false dichotomy. It seemed to lead some educators to infer that reading programs including systematic instruction in spelling-to-sound regularities should minimize comprehension, book reading, and writing. At times, this led to the implementation of beginning reading programs in which book reading played little or no role, and children received lesson after lesson on letter-sound-relationship (Durkin, 1983; Mason, 1984). Other educators, in turn, rejected what they viewed as an overemphasis on phonics instruction and tried to promote programs that emphasized book reading, writing, and the development of positive attitudes toward literacy (Allen, 1989).

In our view, an integrated reading and writing program and systematic instruction in spelling-to-sound regularities need not be diametrically opposed because word recognition and comprehension have common roots in story book reading, vocabulary, and listening activities (Mason, in press). Moreover, because reading and spelling can support the development of the other skills (Clarke, 1988; Dobson; 1989), they will foster word recognition if taught together. Let us be more specific about how systematic instruction in spelling-to-sound regularities and holistic approaches could work in concert.

Research on children's reading development suggests that essential concepts about word identification usually are acquired informally at home in the context of meaningful reading and writing activities. School programs for introducing written words would be more supportive if children could experience reading and writing informally. A number of new kindergarten programs are moving in this direction. There are successful ways to provide instruction as well as child-directed activity (Allen and Mason, 1989; Crowell, Kawakami, & Wong, 1986). In these programs, literacy goals are accomplished through activities that are staged by teachers. Teacher-directed activities might include activities in which children talk about and learn

to recite or read books that are read to them, hearing and playing letter-and word-sound games, writing and analyzing words in a message that the teacher has written, shared reading and writing, and reading to children. Child-directed activities might include reading and writing, story listening centers that are changed weekly to include inviting new materials, and dramatic and block play centers in which reading and writing material are available and become part of the situations that children create.

If children can begin reading by using a variety of context-supported materials, they will be less likely to lose the sense of text meaning and will know to rely on pictures as well as letter and sentence information to begin reading (Clay, 1985). As letter and sound cues in words become more apparent, children will use their knowledge of context in conjunction with spelling patterns to become more proficient readers.

An integrated reading and writing instructional program should extend into the primary grades as well, and there still ought to be both systematic and informal opportunities for children to learn about word identification. Phonics instruction alone is not sufficient for building proficient word identification skills, a conclusion that is also supported by phonics advocates. Phonics instruction supports only one strategy for word identification, namely, analysis of words into their constituent phonemes. To avoid giving the impression that phonetic analysis is the only way to identify words, teachers should encourage children to decode words by analogy. Moreover, since early growth in word reading is linked with opportunities to read connected text (Anderson et al, 1985), teachers should provide opportunities for children to listen to stories and read and write on their own.

Creative writing is an example of an informal activity that will support the development of other word identification strategies. In a study comparing first graders who used conventional spelling with those who invented their own spellings of words, Clarke (1988) found that allowing children to invent word spellings in their creative writing assignments led to longer pieces, knowledge of more written words, and superior spelling and phonetic analysis skills.

Lesgold, Resnick, and Hammond (1985) point to another advantage of context-supported instruction. Children's learning is supported when easy reading materials are presented in a meaningful context. Drawing an analogy to skiing, the authors note that when skiing was taught using a skills approach, each aspect "was separately learned and practiced. Learning was slow. Then, skis started to be made in a graded series of lengths. Short skis allowed novices to engage in the integrated activity of skiing from the start, without significant risk. Learning became much more rapid" (p. 110). The idea is that reading development may proceed more rapidly if children have the opportunity to engage in all aspects of the process at once. This is in contrast to always having their attention narrowly focused on just one aspect of reading, without regard for the whole process.

It is hard to learn to identify words in our language. As a result, developmental change in word identification involves an understanding of many subtle concepts. What must be learned cannot be completely taught or satisfactorily supervised by teachers. Thus, we recommend that teachers keep children's meaningful text reading as the primary goal and encourage them to apply more inductive word identification approaches. If teachers coach children to use word identification strategies in meaningful contexts and encourage them to use more than one strategy, children will learn how to navigate independently and find their own way through the thicket of letters and sounds, word patterns and irregularities, phrases and text context. As Clay (1985) directs, children need to learn how to monitor their own reading, use strategies involving letter information, word patterns, and text interpretation, and cross-check for meaningful renditions of the text. Practicing with complete texts—stories, and expository text, and children's own writings—is probably the best approach.

These conclusions point to the need for significant changes in typical kindergarten and primary grade reading lessons. Among the changes are the following:

1. A shift from assuming that learning to read and write is initiated in first grade to the notion that literacy can and often does begin to develop earlier and can be fostered with context-supported reading and writing activities in kindergarten.
2. A shift from teaching word recognition as isolated words and skills to teaching them in the context of a wide range of meaningful reading and writing activities.
3. A realization that word identification skills are acquired over several years, and so new literacy concepts should be built upon those already learned and understood.
4. An understanding that children need a range of word-reading experiences in order to acquire word identification processing mechanisms that lead to accurate, rapid access of common words and analyses of letters and word patterns in other words.

Word Identification Summary

The instructional changes we advocate are in keeping with the two major themes of this chapter, one being that children learn to identify words more effectively if they are presented within a larger, more meaningful context, whether it be a story, sentence, picture book, phrase, or advertisement. Extensive opportunity to read and listen to texts of all sorts is recommended. If words are learned in context, children will be able to keep the goal of understanding in mind as they see, learn about, and figure out new words. Teachers will then find it easier to model the act of reading for children, which in turn will aid children to better understand both the processing steps of word identification and the purposes for reading and learning words.

The second theme in this chapter is that the very complexity of written English requires children to develop a number of different strategies for learning to identify words. Children need to supplement the instruction they receive in school with their own discoveries about language patterns. To that end, we recommend systematic instruction that encourages phonemic awareness and then leads children to knowledge of spelling-to-sound correspondences. We also recommend that the teacher establish opportunities in the classroom for children to read and write informally. Children can learn to read and write accurately and fluently if they are allowed to experience invented spelling, approximations to conventional text reading, and story rereadings.

VOCABULARY KNOWLEDGE

Word knowledge is, of course, not limited to word identification. As word forms are identified, they are immediately connected to their meanings, whether by direct, lexical access, or by the slower word analysis mechanism. Thus, recognition and knowledge of word meanings leads to text comprehension. Moreover, skilled readers possess an extensive vocabulary. For example, an average high school senior understands an amazing number of words, about 27,000 (Nagy & Herman, 1984). Top students and many adults know literally thousands more.

How might extensive, well-developed vocabulary knowledge be characterized? What systems and processes might be involved? How might teachers best utilize what is currently known about vocabulary knowledge to expand and sharpen their students' developing vocabulary knowledge? The next section addresses these questions. Instructional implications follow.

Extensive, Well-developed Vocabulary Knowledge

Adults and older students who have extensive vocabularies possess not only systematic knowledge of English pronunciations but also a vast array of concepts about meaning-related connections among words. (Anderson & Nagy, 1991) They understand how the English language works, and they use vocabulary skills appropriately in any number of situations. They use these systems interactively as they construct and convey meaning while reading, speaking, writing, and listening.

Systems of Words. Words are labels for concepts, and recognizing words in ordinary use brings to mind a contextually appropriate meaning rather than a well-articulated definition (Anderson & Freebody, 1981; Clark, 1983; Johnson-Laird, 1987; Miller, 1985). When words are well understood, in fact, the richness of understanding far exceeds any definition you might read or write down.

For example, the word *restaurant* immediately brings to mind "a place where you go to buy food and eat." A bit more thought brings to mind types of restaurants (e.g., elegant, fast-food, the one your aunt took you to), available services (e.g., head waiters, busboys), kinds of furnishings (e.g., counters, chopsticks, the decor of your favorite one), ways of paying, appropriate manners for a given establishment, acceptable clothing to wear while there, actions likely to occur (e.g., ordering, spilling, sizzling), feelings (hunger, impatience, satisfaction), and so on.

Thus, a whole network of concepts is activated; in the above case, a network of knowledge about restaurants. Cognitive psychologists term such networks *schemata* (e.g., Anderson, 1984a); psycholinguists describe such organization as *semantic fields* (e.g., Kuczaj, 1982). People with comprehensive vocabulary knowledge know many of these topically related systems and draw upon their understanding of them to construct meaning while reading or listening (Anderson & Pearson, 1984; Bransford & Nitsch, 1978).

In addition to understanding words as topical networks, people have extensive knowledge of how whole families of English words are related *morphologically* (that is, by their root meanings and affixes). For example, you understand the concept of the root word, *act,* and how its meaning is the basic ingredient woven through *react, activation, actor, inactivity,* and so on. You also understand that groups of words are related by function. For instance, you can grasp how the basic function of seeing is a bit different when one is *glancing, staring, looking, leering, or glimpsing.*

Although an exact understanding of what it means to know a word is currently being debated (cf. Carey, 1982), knowing a word clearly involves possessing a fleshed out understanding of the concept itself, and understanding how that concept fits in with related groups of words—words related by topic, by morphology, or by function. "A vocabulary is a coherent, integrated *system* of concepts" (Miller, 1986, p. 175).

Patterns of Word Meaning. In addition to and in conjunction with well-developed systems of words, people with good vocabulary knowledge have a rich understanding of how systematically the English language operates (Nagy & Gentner, 1987; Nagy, Scott, Schommer, & Anderson, 1987). Such knowledge encompasses what people know "about words as words, about how words and their meanings are put together, and how they are used in text" (Nagy et al., 1987, p. 3).

Much of what people know about words as words, or patterns of word meaning, is at the unconscious level. "For example, [people] know, at least implicitly, that English verbs of motion typically tell something about the *way* an object moves (e.g., *slide, wobble, plunge, spin*), but not, for example, what shape it is. . . . people have to have rich word schemas—expectations about what words are like and constraints on what types of information can be encoded in words" (Nagy et al., 1987, pp. 2–3). Nonetheless, such tacit knowledge is an integral part of a person's vocabulary knowledge and plays an important role in constraining word meanings (Nagy et al., 1987).

The English language depends heavily upon word order to communicate meaning. Words are positioned as English grammar (syntax) dictates. Such syntactic structure enables people to know that the three missing words in the sentences below must be a noun, verb, and an adjective (Johnson & Pearson, 1978, p. 116):

The _____ went to the game.
We tried to _____ the table.
She blew up the big _____ balloon.

Again, proficient word users apply their understanding of English grammar so automatically that they are little aware of its role in their construction of meaning (Nagy & Gentner, 1987).

An integral part of vocabulary knowledge is an extensive understanding of appropriate usage of words. A key expectation is that words appear in contexts that make sense. People with vast vocabulary knowledge are likely to have read many books (Anderson, Wilson, & Fielding, 1988) and, over the course of time, to have developed expectations about what kind of words authors are prone to use. So, one might expect to find *putative* in a scholarly article, but not in a romance novel or in most conversations. Much of this systematic knowledge apparently operates so automatically that people are not aware of its role

in constructing meaning unless an anomaly arises (e.g., if we were to insert, "What's up Doc?" in this chapter).

In summary, people with well-developed vocabulary knowledge possess rich, interconnecting networks of concepts with words to label much of that knowledge, rather than long lists of dictionary-like definitions in their heads (Miller, 1986). Woven into such understanding is a keen sense of how the English language operates and a set of expectations about appropriate uses. Much of this knowledge is processed so interactively and automatically that people are rarely, if ever, aware of the role of any one part in constructing meaning. Like word identification, then, application of vocabulary knowledge during reading involves sophisticated, instantaneous use of regular patterns and meaningful connections among words.

Understanding New Words. Persons who have depth of vocabulary knowledge have efficient procedural knowledge for gaining an understanding of new words. Such people are competent comprehenders (e.g., Anderson & Freebody, 1981; Davis, 1944, 1968) and monitor information-bearing contexts for sense (Brown, 1985). When they detect an unfamiliar word that is important to their continued construction of meaning, they bring to bear their knowledge of integrated word-meaning systems, how words fit in text contexts, problem-solving skills, and a compelling motivation to figure it out.

For example, while reading a text on the development of river systems, suppose a new term *rills* is encountered in the following text excerpt: "A river system has several parts. Small rills form first. They join to form creeks, which join to form streams."

Sensing its importance because it initiates a description of the topic, the reader draws upon the meaning envisioned from the text so far, automatically notices from context that *rills* is a plural noun with some tangible properties, and assumes that it is connected to river systems. After this fairly rapid initial mapping, the reader makes a hypothesis about the meaning of *rills* and forms a mental model of the word/concept (Elshout-Mohr & van Daalen-Kapteijns, 1987). The reader continues through the text, gains more information about the word, consciously adjusting the model within the framework of river systems concepts or schema and unconsciously within the constraints of the English language. The reader may end up with a fairly well fleshed out understanding of rills or, as is often the case, may end up with some level of partial knowledge, such as: Rills are small waterways. Fuller understanding, such as how rills fits into the entire river system schema, may be mapped out more slowly as further encounters with rills occur over time (cf. Nelson, in press).

Instructional Implications for Developing Vocabulary Knowledge

With the foregoing picture of extensive, well-developed vocabulary knowledge, what can be said about how children might acquire vocabulary knowledge? First, it is not possible to teach children as many words a year as they typically learn, that is, 3000 words a year. Moreover, because teachers usually introduce far fewer words a year, most words students learn over the course of a year cannot be acquired from direct instruction (Nagy & Herman, 1987). Instead, words must be acquired informally and outside of school, principally through voluntary reading. Incidental word learning is possible because we know that children are able to learn something about the meaning of a new word from a single exposure *if* the word is embedded in a context that is meaningful to students (Carey, 1982; Markman, 1984; Nagy, Herman, & Anderson, 1985). For example, some concepts about new words could be acquired through conversations about dinosaurs at an exhibit, from listening to a dramatic reading of *Julius Caesar,* or by reading an article about baseball. In fact, students who engage in a wide range of reading and other experiences encounter thousands of words in meaningful context and acquire partial knowledge for hundreds of them—one of the most profitable avenues for acquiring vocabulary knowledge (Nagy, Herman, & Anderson, 1985; Nagy, Anderson, & Herman, 1987). Therefore, it makes pedagogical sense to encourage voluntary reading and to provide instruction that enhances the likelihood that students will acquire more vocabulary knowledge on their own.

By contrast, consider the common types of school activities that are meant to teach vocabulary: words and meanings to match on workbook pages, packaged programs that drill on lists of unrelated words, guessing a word meaning by reading a sentence or two, looking up lists of words in the dictionary, and brief introductions of words before students read. If the words are already known, these activities are of no help; they are busywork. If the words are not known, much more support for learning is needed. None of the activities listed above produces the kind of vocabulary knowledge that affects overall comprehension (e.g., Ahlfors, 1979; Tuinman & Brady, 1974), although some level of partial knowledge may be gained when these activities are repeated with a small number of words (Beck & McKeown, 1985).

What does the research suggest as a starting point for vocabulary instruction? Because students' understanding of concepts, networks of concepts, and the words used to label them is critical to vocabulary learning and yet varies greatly, determining what partial knowledge or analogous knowledge students already have about the words they are to learn is recommended. This step will help anchor vocabulary instruction not only to the reading task before students, but also to their level of understanding.

One technique for assessing background knowledge is brainstorming and visually displaying what students know about key words/concepts (Carr, 1985; Heimlich & Pittelman, 1986). Often students know bits and pieces related to a schema (Anderson, 1984b) and have limited understanding of its scope (Bransford & Nitsch, 1978). Once students' background knowledge has been assessed, the teacher can initiate a discussion to show students how these pieces fit together and to broaden their understanding of how words/concepts belong to larger schemata (Stahl & Vancil, 1986; see Marzano & Marzano, 1988, for examples of word clusters). For example, students can be led to see how *frenzy* relates to *hysterical, excitement, calmness,* and to the more general concept of emotions in a novel; how *veins* not only relates to *arteries, carbon dioxide,* and so on, but also to the circulatory system schema in a science unit.

Quality instruction establishes ties between new words, background knowledge, larger schemata, and the naturally occurring contexts of instruction. Instruction in such depth takes time and, therefore, needs to be centered on words that are critical to maintaining comprehension and words that are encountered quite often. Thus, for a novel, words integral to the setting, main characters, developing plot, and resolution would be prime candidates. In an exposition or on a field trip, words related to the main network of concepts would also be central. Instruction must build on concepts and systems of concepts and not rely on giving students superficial contact with individual, seemingly unrelated, words. Such knowledge-based development (Anderson & Freebody, 1981) enhances comprehension (Bos, Anders, Filip, & Jaffe, 1985; McKeown, Beck, Omanson, & Perfetti, 1983; Swaby, 1977) and provides students with a base for actively reasoning about the meaning of new words encountered in a variety of contexts.

In addition, students need to understand *how* their knowledge can be used to infer meanings of new words. This is not an easy task because of the complexity of using schemata, along with an understanding of the English language and expectations about appropriate usage. Research supports instruction that explicitly models such integrated thinking for students, then gradually releases responsibility to them (Pearson & Gallagher, 1983). Instruction that allows students gradually to take over the tasks of figuring out word meanings in context may provide students with strategies for acquiring word knowledge independently (Carr, 1985; Herman & Dole, 1988; Schwartz & Raphael, 1985).

An important component in such reasoning about word meanings is an understanding of English morphology. Instruction that reveals how affixes systematically change word meanings has the potential for unlocking understanding of large groups of words. For instance, "for each root word, children who employ this strategy can probably work out the meanings of seven new words. This includes about four words formed with regular or irregular inflections, and about three formed with affixes or as compounds" (Mason & Au, 1986, p. 119). Given the number of words in printed school materials, around 88,000 (Nagy & Anderson, 1984), such generative power is extremely important for students to grasp.

English syntax (grammar) is another systematic aspect of the English language that students can use to constrain their reasoning about new words embedded in context. For instance, when young children were "shown a picture of a strange action on a strange container filled with strange stuff," they demonstrated an action when they were asked to show *sebbing,* they pointed to the container when asked to show a *seb,* and they indicated the "stuff" when asked to show *some seb* (Brown, 1957, cited in Carey, 1982, p. 375). Their responses indicated that new words can be easily connected to *common* syntactical patterns.

However, complicated or implicit, syntactical patterns, especially in some forms of written English, may not be easily understood (e.g., Irwin, 1980). For example, children have more difficulty understanding (1) "The car wouldn't start. It was raining." than (2) "The car wouldn't start because it was raining." The reason is that explicit meaning ties are not given in the first sentence. Unfortunately, some school texts that children are asked to read and learn from often omit these ties. Thus, teachers need to be wary of expecting children to learn from short, choppy texts that lack meaning cues.

Another important instructional component is to bolster children's comprehension strategies for inferring word meanings, as well as providing opportunities for them to become more familiar with patterns in written English. One way is to make many stories available for them to read at home, to read many stories to them, and to include opportunities for them to discuss words and meanings in context. These experiences, furthermore, promote an awareness of appropriate usage of words, such as expecting a fairy tale to contain a certain flavor and style of language. Such a language-rich environment may do a great deal to develop children's grasp of English language structures, especially when children come from language environments where they have had few opportunities to learn about the syntactic properties of written English (Heath, 1983).

The final instructional principle is that not all words in a text can or should be taught. Students must have the opportunity to apply what they understand about the topic at hand and aspects of the English language just outlined to figure out meanings of unfamiliar words in meaningful contexts. One such context is after reading a story. Students look back, identify a new word and, under the guidance of the teacher, reason about its meaning (for an example see Herman & Dole, 1988, or Duffy, Roehler, & Rackliffe, 1986).

Above all, students who have become infected with a love for and fascination with words possess a key ingredient in continuing to develop vocabulary knowledge (Deighton, 1960; McKeown et al., 1983). In fact, "establishing motivation and desire to acquire new vocabulary is at the very heart of vocabulary acquisition" (Ruddell, 1986, p. 587)—and within the inspirational power of teachers.

CONCLUSION

Implications of current research on the topics of word identification and vocabulary knowledge have two characteristics in common. The first is that children's learning should be viewed in the context of their overall development in literacy. Learning is cumulative, not disjointed. Young children's understanding affects later acquisition, and acquisition generally takes place in informal as well as formal instructional settings, proceeding best when reading and writing activities are meaningful. In our view, the research supports instructional activities with a broad, rather than a narrow focus, so that children can read or attempt to read and understand many words in a number of text contexts and learn to apply varying strategies for recognition and understanding.

The second characteristic is that word identification ability and vocabulary knowledge involve and appreciation of the regularity of the English language. We hope we have succeeded in communicating that understanding this systematicness is not a trivial task. Many strategies are needed for identifying words and for building vocabulary knowledge. Simple processes of memorization, letter-sound associations, or of word meanings are not sufficient and cannot form the basis for skilled performance. It follows, then, as the research shows and as we have portrayed in this chapter, that instruction must also be better tuned to children's existing knowledge than was previously assumed. Quite varied formal as well as informal instruction is required so that children have opportunities to rely on lower and higher order thinking skills, including rapid recognition of printed words and inference of their meanings, analysis and synthesis of words into sounds and morphemes, rule-constructing and generalization of those rules to new and related words. Word identification and vocabulary knowledge may be "basic" skills, but they are far from being simple or simply taught.

References

Ahlfors, G. (1979). *Learning word meanings: A comparison of three instructional procedures.* Unpublished doctoral dissertation, University of Minnesota, Minneapolis.

Adams, M. J. (1990). *Beginning to read: Thinking and learning about print.* Cambridge, MA: MIT Press.

Allen, J. B. (1989). Reading and writing development in whole language kindergartens. In J. Mason (Ed.), *Reading and writing connections.* (pp. 121–146) Needham Heights, MA: Allyn & Bacon.

Allen, J. & Mason, J. (1989). *Risk makers, risk takers, risk breakers: Reducing the risks for young literacy learners.* Portsmouth, NH: Heinemann.

Anderson, R. C. (1984a). Role of the reader's schema in comprehension, learning, and memory. In R. Anderson, J. Osborn, & R. Tierney (Eds.), *Learning to read in American schools* (pp. 243–258). Hillsdale, NJ: Erlbaum.

Anderson, R. C. (1984b). Some reflections on the acquisition of knowledge. *Educational Researcher, 13,* 5–10.

Anderson, R., & Freebody, P. (1981). Vocabulary knowledge. In J. Guthrie (Ed.), *Comprehension and teaching: Research reviews* (pp. 77–117). Newark, DE: International Reading Association.

Anderson, R., & Pearson, P. D. (1984). A schema-theoretic view of basic processes in reading comprehension. In P. D. Pearson (Ed.), *Handbook of reading research* (pp. 255–292). New York: Longman.

Anderson, R., Hiebert, E., Scott, J., & Wilkinson, E. (1985). *Becoming a nation of readers: The report of the Commission on Reading.* Urbana-Champaign: University of Illinois, Center for the Study of Reading.

Anderson, R., Wilson, P., & Fielding, L. (1988). Growth in reading and how children spend their time outside of school. *Reading Research Quarterly, 23,* 285–303.

Anderson, R., & Nagy, W. (1991). Word Meanings. In R. Barr, M. Kamil, P. Mosenthal, & P. D. Pearson (Eds.) *Handbook of Reading Research,* Vol II (pp. 690–724). New York: Longman.

Applebee, A. N. (1980). Children's narratives: New directions. *The Reading Teacher, 34,* 137–42.

Beck, I., & McKeown, M. (1985). Teaching vocabulary: Making the instruction fit the goal. *Educational Perspectives, 23,* 11–15.

Bissex, G. (1980). GYNS AT WRK: *A child learns to write and read.* Cambridge, MA: Harvard University Press.

Bos, C., Anders, P., Filip, D., & Jaffe, L. (1985). Semantic feature analysis and long-term learning. In J. Niles & R. Lalik (Eds.), Issues in literacy: *A research perspective* (pp. 42–47). Rochester, NY: National Reading Conference.

Bradley, L., & Bryant, P. (1983). Categorizing sounds and learning to read—a causal connection. *Nature, 301,* 419–421.

Bransford, J., & Nitsch, K. (1978). Coming to understand things we could not previously understand. In J. Kavanagh & W. Strange (Eds.), *Speech and language in the laboratory, school, and clinic* (pp. 267–327). Cambridge, MA: The MIT Press.

Brown, A. (1985). *Teaching students to think as they read: Implications for curriculum reform* (Reading Education Report. No. 58). Champaign, IL: University of Illinois, Center for the Study of Reading.

Brown, R. (1957). Linguistic determinism and the part of speech. *Journal of Abnormal and Social Psychology, 55,* 1–5.

Brugelmann, H. (1986). *No future for graded reading schemes.* 11th IRA World Congress on Reading, London.

Calfee, R., Lindamood, P., & Lindamood, C. (1973). Acoustic-phonetic skills and reading—kindergarten through 12th grade. *Journal of Educational Psychology, 64,* 293–298.

Carey, S. (1982). Semantic development: the state of the art. In W. Wanner & L. Gleitman (Eds.), *Language acquisition: The state of the art* (pp. 345–489). New York: Cambridge University Press.

Carr, E. (1985). The vocabulary overview guide: A metacognitive strategy to improve vocabulary comprehension and retention. *Journal of Reading, 28,* 588–595.

Clark, E. (1983). Meanings and concepts. In P. Mussen (Ed.), *Handbook of child psychology* (pp. 787–840). New York: John Wiley & Sons.

Clarke, L. (1988). Invented versus traditional spelling in first graders' writings: Effects on learning to spell and read. Research in the Teaching of English, 22, 281–309.

Clay, M. (1979). *Reading: The patterning of complex behavior.* Portsmouth, NH: Heinemann.

Clay, M. (1985). *Early detection of reading difficulties* (3rd ed.). Portsmouth, NH: Heinemann.

Crowell, D., Kawakami, A., & Wong, J. (1986). Emerging literacy: Experiences in a kindergarten classroom. *The Reading Teacher, 40,* 144–149.

Davis, F. (1944). Fundamental factors of comprehension in reading. *Psychometrika, 9,* 185–197.

Davis, F. (1968). Research in comprehension in reading. *Reading Research Quarterly, 3,* 499–545.

Deighton, L. (1960). Developing vocabulary: Another look at the problem. *English Journal, 49,* 82–87.

Doake, D. (1985). Reading-like behavior: Its role in learning to read. In A. Jaggar & M. T. Smith-Burke (Eds.), *Observing the language learner.* (pp. 82–98). Newark DE: IRA.

Dobson, L. (1989). Connections in learning to write and read: A study of children's development through kindergarten and grade one. In J. Mason (Ed.), *Reading and writing connections.* (pp. 83–104). Needham Heights, MA: Allyn & Bacon

Duffy, G., Roehler, L., & Rackliffe, G. (1986). How teachers' instructional talk influences students' understanding of lesson content. *Elementary School Journal, 87,* 3–16.

Durkin, D. (1983). What classroom observations reveal about reading comprehension instruction. *Reading Research Quarterly, 14,* 481–533.

Egan, K. (1987). Literacy and oral foundations of education. *Harvard Educational Review, 57,* 445–472.

Ehri, L. (1991). Development of the ability to read words. In R. Barr, M. Kamil, P. Mosenthal, and P. D. Pearson (Eds.), *Handbook of Reading research* (Vol II) pp. 383–417). New York: Longman.

Ehri, L. (1986). Sources of difficulty in learning to spell and read words. In M. Wolraich & D. Routh (Eds.), *Advances in developmental and behavioral pediatrics.* (pp. 121–195). Greenwich, CT: JAI Press.

Ehri, L., & Wilce, L. (1987). Does learning to spell help beginners learn to read words? *Reading Research Quarterly, 22,* 47–65.

Elshout-Mohr, M., & van Daalen-Kapteijns, M. (1987). Cognitive processes in learning word meanings. In M. McKeown & M. Curtis (Eds.), *The nature of vocabulary acquisition* (pp. 53–71). Hillsdale, NJ: Lawrence Erlbaum.

Francis, H. (1977). Reading abilities and disabilities: Children's strategies in learning to read. *British Journal of Educational Psychology, 47,* 117–125.

Gates, A., & Bocker, E. (1923). A study of initial stages in reading by preschool children. *Teachers College Record, 24,* 469–688.

Glushko, R. J. (1981). Principles for pronouncing print: The psychology of phonography. In A. Lesgold and C. Perfetti (Eds.), *Interactive processes in reading.* (pp. 61–84). Hillsdale, NJ: Erlbaum.

Gough, P., & Juel, C. (in press). In P. Gough, L. Ehri, & R. Treiman (Eds.), *Reading acquisition.* Hillsdale, NJ: Erlbaum.

Goswami, U. (1988). Orthographic analogies and reading development. *Quarterly Journal of Experimental Psychology, 40,* 239–268.

Heath, S. B. (1983). *Ways with words: Language, life, and work in communities and classrooms.* Cambridge, MA: Cambridge University Press.

Heimlich, J., & Pittelman, S. (1986). *Semantic mapping: Classroom Applications.* Newark, DE: International Reading Association.

Herman, P., & Dole, J. (1988). Theory and practice in vocabulary learning and instruction. *The Elementary School Journal, 89,* 41–52.

Irwin, J. (1980). The effecrs of explicitness and clause order on the comprehension of reversible causal relationships. *Reading Research Quarterly, 15,* 477–488.

Johnson, D., & Pearson, P. D. (1978). *Teaching reading vocabulary.* New York: Holt, Rinehart and Winston.

Johnson-Laird, P. (1987). The mental representation of the meaning of words. *Cognition, 25,* 189–211.

Kuczaj, S. (1982). Acquisition of word meaning in the context of the development of the semantic system. In C. Brainerd & M. Pressley (Eds.), *Verbal processes in children: Progress in cognitive developmental research* (pp. 95–121). New York: Springer-Verlag.

Lartz, M., & Mason, J. (1988). Jamie: One child's journey from oral to written language. *Early Childhood Research Quarterly, 3,* 193–208.

Lesgold, A., Resnick, L., & Hammond, K. (1985). Learning to read: A longitudinal study of word skill development in two curricula. In G. E. Mackinnon and T. G. Waller (Eds.), *Reading research, advances in theory and practice,* Volume 4. (pp. 107–138). New York: Academic Press.

Liberman, I. & Shankweiler, D. (1985). Phonology and the problems of learning to read and write. *RASE, 6*(6), 8–17.

Lundberg, I. (in press). Two dimensions of decontextualization in reading acquisition. In P. Gough, L. Ehri, & R. Treiman (Eds.), *Reading acquisition.* Hillsdale, NJ: Erlbaum.

Lundberg, I., Frost, J., & Petersen, O. (1988). Effects of an extensive program for stimulating phonological awareness in preschool children. *Reading Research Quarterly, 23,* 263–284.

Maclean, M., Bryant, P., & Bradley, L. (1987) Rhymes, nursery rhymes, and reading in early childhood. *Merrill-Palmer Quarterly, 33,* 255–281.

Markman, E. (1984). *How children constrain the possible meanings of words.* Unpublished manuscript, Stanford University.

Marzano, R., & Marzano, J. (1988). *A cluster approach to elementary vocabulary instruction.* Newark, DE: International Reading Association.

Mason, J. (1980). When do children begin to read? *Reading Research Quarterly, 15,* 203–227.

Mason, J. (1984). A question about reading comprehension instruction. In G. Duffy, L. Roehler, & J. Mason (Eds.), *Comprehension instruction: Perspectives and suggestions.* (pp. 39–56). New York: Longman.

Mason, J. (in press). Reading stories to preliterate children: A proposed connection to reading. In P. Gough, L. Ehri, & R. Treiman (Eds.), *Reading acquisition.* Hillsdale, NJ: Erlbaum.

Mason, J., & Au, K. (1986, 1990). *Reading instruction for today,* First and second editions. Glenview, IL: Scott, Foresman & Company.

Mason, J., & Stewart, J. (1989). Testing emergent literacy in kindergarten. L. Morrow and J. Smith (Eds.), In *Assessment for instruction in early literacy,* (pp 155–175). Englewood Cliffs, NJ: Prentice Hall.

Masonheimer, P., Drum, P., & Ehri, L. (1984). Does environmental print identification lead children into word reading? *Journal of Reading Behavior, 16,* 257–271.

McConkie, G., & Zola, D. (1987). Visual attention during eye fixations while reading. In M. Coltheart (Ed.), *Attentions and performance XII: The psychology of reading.* Hillsdale NJ: Earlbaum.

McKeown, M., Beck, I., Omanson, R., & Perfetti, C. (1983). The effects of long-term vocabulary instruction on reading comprehension: A replication. *Journal of Reading Behavior, 15,* 3–18.

Miller, G. (1986). Dictionaries in the mind. *Language and Cognitive Processes, 1,* 171–185.

Nagy, W., & Anderson, R. (1984). The number of words in printed school English. *Reading Research Quarterly, 19,* 304–330.

Nagy, W., Anderson, R., & Herman, P. (1987). Learning words meanings from context during normal reading. *American Educational Research Journal, 24,* 237–270.

Nagy, W., & Gentner, D. (1987). *Semantic constraints on lexical categories.* (Tech. Report. No. 413). Champaign, IL: University of Illinois, Center for the Study of Reading.

Nagy, W., & Herman, P. (1987). Breadth and depth of vocabulary knowledge: Implications for acquisition and instruction. In M. McKeown & M. Curtis (Eds.), *The nature of vocabulary acquisition* (pp. 19–36). Hillsdale, NJ: Erlbaum.

Nagy, W., Herman, P., & Anderson, R. (1985). Learning words from context. *Reading Research Quarterly, 20,* 233–253.

Nagy, W., Scott, J., Schommer, M., & Anderson, R. (December, 1987). *Word schemas: What do people know about words they don't know?* Paper presented at the National Reading Conference, St. Petersburg Beach, FL.

Nelson, K. (in press). Constraints on Word Meaning. Cognitive Development.

Olson, D. (1984). "See! Jumping!" Some oral language antecedents of literacy. In H. Goelman, A. Oberg, & F. Smith (Eds.), *Awakening to literacy.* (pp 185–192). Portsmouth, NH: Heinemann.

Pearson, P. D., & Gallagher, M. (1983). The instruction of reading comprehension. *Contemporary Educational Psychology, 8,* 317–345.

Peterman, C., & Mason, J. (1984). *Kindergarten children's perceptions of the forms of print in labelled pictures and stories.* Paper presented at National Reading Conference, St. Petersburg, Florida.

Rayner, K., & Pollatsek, A. (1989). *The Psychology of Reading.* Englewood Cliffs, NJ: Prentice Hall.

Ruddell, R. (1986). Vocabulary learning: A process model and criteria for evaluating instructional strategies. *Journal of Reading, 29,* 581–587.

Schwatz, R., & Raphael, T. (1985). Concept of definition: A key to improving students' vocabulary. *The Reading Teacher, 39,* 198–205.

Share, D., Jorm, A., Maclean, R., & Matthews, R. (1984). Sources of individual difference in reading acquisition. *Journal of Educational Psychology, 76,* 1309–1324.

Simon, H., & Leu, D. (1987). The use of contextual and graphic information in word recognition by second-, fourth-, and sixth-grade readers. *Journal of Reading Behavior, 19,* 33–47.

Stahl, S., & Vancil, S. (1986). Discussion is what makes semantic maps work in vocabulary instruction. *The Reading Teacher, 40,* 62–69.

Stanovich, K. (in press). Speculations on the causes and consequences of individual differences in early reading acquisition. In P. Gough, L. Ehri, & R. Treiman (Eds.), *Reading acquisition.* Hillsdale, NJ: Erlbaum.

Stanovich, K., Cunningham, A., & Feeman, D. (1984). Relation between early reading acquisition and word decoding with and without context: A longitudinal study of first-grade children. *Journal of Educational Psychology, 76,* 668–677.

Stanovich, K., Cunningham, A., & Cramer, B. (1984). Assessing phonological awareness in kindergarten children: Issues of task comparability. *Journal of Experimental Child Psychology, 38,* 175–190.

Swaby, B. (1977). The effects of advance organizers and vocabulary introduction on the reading comprehension of sixth grade students. *Dissertation Abstracts International, 39,* A115 (University Microfilms 78–09, 754).

Taylor, D. (1983). *Family literacy.* Portsmouth, NH: Heinemann.

Treiman, R. (in press). The role of intrasyllabic units in learning to read and spell. In P. Gough, L. Ehri, & R. Treiman (Eds.), *Reading acquisition.* Hillsdale, NJ: Erlbaum.

Tuinman, J., & Brady, M. (1974). How does vocabulary account for variance on reading comprehension tests: A preliminary instructional analysis. *Twenty-third yearbook of the National Reading Conference.* Clemson, SC: National Reading Conference.

Tunmer, W., Herriman, M., & Nesdale, A. (1988). Metalinguistic abilities and beginning reading. *Reading Research Quarterly, 23,* 134–158.

Underwood, G. (1985). Information processing in skilled readers. In G. E. Mackinnon and T. G. Waller (Eds.), *Reading research, advances in theory and practice,* Volume 4. (pp. 139–181) New York: Academic Press.

Yopp, H. K. (1988). The validity and reliability of phonemic awareness tests. *Reading Research Quarterly, 23,* 159–177.

34B. READING COMPREHENSION INSTRUCTION

James Flood
Diane Lapp

In the past few years, a great deal has been written about "state-of-the-art" reading comprehension instructional practices (Duffy, Roehler, & Mason, 1983; Duffy et al., 1984; Durkin, 1978–1979; Flood, 1984a, 1984b; Guthrie, 1981; Pearson, 1984; Robinson, Farsone, Hittleman, & Unruh, in press; Tierney and Cunningham, 1984; Tierney and Pearson, 1984). Each of these authors has maintained that comprehension instruction is dependent upon the interaction of four sets of critical variables: reader variables (age, ability, affect, motivation), text variables (genres, type, features, considerateness); educational-context variables (environment, task, social grouping, purpose); and teacher variables (knowledge, experience, attitude and pedagogical approach). Each author maintains that an adequate explanation of effective comprehension instruction is impossible without taking each of these key variables into consideration.

In this paper, each of these sets of variables will be discussed as they relate to our most current understanding of effective comprehension instruction. The paper is divided into two major sections: 1) What we know about the competent comprehender, and 2) What we know about instructing for competent comprehension.

WHAT WE KNOW ABOUT THE COMPETENT COMPREHENDER

Although research in reading comprehension instruction is incomplete and still developing, most educators agree that competent comprehenders exhibit a set of discernible characteristics. Researchers have found that competent readers actively construct meaning through an integrative process in which they "interact" and "transact" with the words on the page, integrating new information with preexisting knowledge structures (Anderson, Hiebert, Scott, & Wilkinson, 1985; Anderson & Pearson, 1984; Brown, Campione & Day, 1981; Jensen, 1984; Lapp & Flood, 1986; Paris, 1986; Rosenblatt, 1938, 1982, this volume). Further, it has been found that a reader's prior knowledge, experience, attitude, and perspective determine the ways that information is perceived, understood, valued, and stored (Anderson et al., 1985; Flood, 1984a,b; Holbrook, 1987; Pearson, 1984; Rumelhart, 1981; Squire, 1983).

The Competent Comprehender: A Strategic Reader

Good readers are strategic readers who actively construct meaning as they read; they are self-motivated and self-directed (Paris, Lipson, & Wixson, 1983); they monitor their own comprehension by questioning, reviewing, revising, and rereading to enhance their overall comprehension (Baker & Brown, 1984). Good readers have learned that it is the reader in the *reading* process who creates meaning, not the text or even the author of the text. Iser (1978) explained this view of the reading process when he stated:

The significance of the work, then, does not lie in the meaning sealed within the text, but in the fact that meaning brings out what had previously been sealed within us.

Bleich (1978) also maintained that "the work itself would have no existence at all if it were not read" (p. 3).

There is also some agreement among contemporary researchers about the mental processes that readers engage in while reading. Most agree that reading is essentially a thinking activity (Anderson & Pearson, 1984; Baker & Brown, 1984; Duffy & Roehler, 1987; Rumelhart, 1981) in which the reader engages in a series of complex processes. First the reader previews the text by noting its general features (print size, pictures, headings); then, as reading begins, four different kinds of knowledge are used by the reader to process the information of the text:

1. Knowledge of letters and sound correspondences;
2. Knowledge of words and word forms;
3. Knowledge of syntax, i.e. the grammatical structures of sentences and their functions; and
4. Knowledge of meanings and semantic relations.

Throughout, the reader uses metacognitive processes to monitor, control, and advance the search for meaning. Flavell (1981) suggests that there are four components of metacognitive monitoring that readers use as they process texts:

1. They establish learning goals;
2. They generate cognitive associations to achieve these goals;
3. They evaluate their own metacognitive experiences through questioning and reflection; and
4. They use their own metacognitive knowledge to monitor their own understanding.

In his description of the ways that readers use these strategies, Paris (1986) suggests that competent readers exhibit three kinds of knowledge about the reading process as they read: 1) declarative knowledge (the what of comprehension); 2) procedural knowledge (the how of comprehension); and 3) conditional knowledge (the when of comprehension).

There is also consensus among researchers that good readers, competent comprehenders, have a plan for comprehending; they use their metacognitive knowledges in an orderly way to implement their plan. Although each reader's plan varies for each text and task, the following steps seem to be part of the competent reader's generalizable plan for many different kinds of texts:

Before reading, the strategic reader:

- **PREVIEWS** the text by looking at the title, the pictures, and the print in order to evoke relevant thoughts and memories
- **BUILDS BACKGROUND** by activating appropriate prior knowledge through self-questioning about what he/she already knows about the topic (or story), the vocabulary, and the form in which the topic (or story) is presented
- **SETS PURPOSES** for reading by asking questions about what he/she wants to learn (know) during the reading episode

During reading, the strategic reader:

- **CHECKS UNDERSTANDING** of the text by paraphrasing the author's words
- **MONITORS COMPREHENSION** by using context clues to figure out unknown words and by imaging, imagining, inferencing, and predicting
- **INTEGRATES** new concepts with existing knowledge; continually revising purposes for reading

After reading, the strategic reader:

- **SUMMARIZES** what has been read by retelling the plot of the story or the main idea of the text
- **EVALUATES** the ideas contained in the text
- **MAKES APPLICATIONS** of the ideas in the text to unique situations, extending the ideas to broader perspectives

Many researchers have discussed the similarity of the writing process to the reading process. It has been argued that in reading, the student constructs meaning, while in writing the student reconstructs meaning (Flood & Lapp, 1987; Squire, 1983; Tierney & Pearson, 1984). Jensen (1984) explains that "both reading and writing processes require similar abilities, similar analysis and synthesis—comparing and contrasting, connecting and reevaluating—the same weighting and judging of ideas" (p. 4).

WHAT WE KNOW ABOUT READING COMPREHENSION INSTRUCTION

If the preceding section accurately reflects the processes that the competent comprehender engages in, one might wonder: Is there a role for the teacher *or* does comprehension ability merely occur as a result of practice, of extensive and frequent reading?

Can Comprehension Be Taught?

Although some educators have suggested that the controversial question, "Can Comprehension Be Taught?" is no longer a burning, lingering issue (Pearson, 1984; Tierney & Cunningham, 1984) it seems to have been reignited recently in both its old form and in a newer form. Carver (1987), in his article entitled "Should Reading Comprehension Skills Be Taught?" argues that the evidence for teaching comprehension is "weak, nonex-istent, or directly counter (to the data)." He argues that the evidence for teaching reading comprehension is based on a series of studies that violate three basic principles of reading research:

1. The Easiness Principle (comprehension levels can be increased by reading easier materials);
2. The Reading Time Principle (students can improve their comprehension by spending more time reading and rereading a text); and
3. the Practice Principle (comprehension is improved through practice).

After reviewing several of the seminal studies that serve as the basis for maintaining that reading comprehension can be taught and has been taught and learned effectively, he states:

The evidence presented to support the case for teachers spending more time teaching reading comprehension skills is frail at best. Too often the Easiness Principle and the Reading Time Principle are not accounted for in research, and there is no solid evidence that gains due to the Reading Practice Principle will transfer to reading ability in general. It makes more sense to regard comprehension skills as study skills in disguise, and teaching them to unskilled readers is a questionable practice. (Page 125).

Carver argues that the question "Can Comprehension Skills Be Taught?" can be answered with a resounding "No." He proceeds to argue that the more pertinent question is "Should those skills that have been (falsely) labeled as comprehension skills be taught?" From his review of the available literature, he suggests that the most cogent and compelling evidence for teaching comprehension comes from Palincsar and Brown's (1985) study on the effects of reciprocal teaching, but even these data are suspect for him: "Certain study skills can be taught that are likely to help students comprehend more of the materials at the frustration level, but these skills are not likely to help students comprehend any more of the materials at the instructional level unless they spend more time reading them. (Page 125).

The debate has also been reignited by Haller, Child, and Walberg (1988) in their article entitled "Can Comprehension Be Taught? A Quantitative Synthesis of Metacognitive Studies." They examined the results of 20 seminal studies involving 1,553 students on the effects of "metacognitive instruction" on reading comprehension performance. Although the exact nature of metacognition is still being debated, it was defined in their study as three mental activities that constitute metacognition: being aware, monitoring, and regulating in order to aid faltering understanding.

Their results argued strongly that comprehension can be taught; their data suggested that sufficient evidence exists for encouraging teachers to instruct their students in reading comprehension based on a series of research studies that were rigorously conducted. Three specific findings were highlighted in their analysis:

1. There were age effects especially for seventh/ eighth graders and second graders;

2. Reinforcement was the single most effective part of reading comprehension instruction; and

3. The more instructional features involved in the learning episode, the more significant the results.

It seems that the real answer to this question is not a simple yes or no, but a qualified one that clearly explains definition and purpose. All of the studies cited in both Carver's study and the series of studies examined by Haller, Child, and Walberg are dependent upon their own kind of comprehension measurement for legitimacy. In almost all of these cases, comprehension was assessed and determined by measures of understanding elements included in or derivable from a specific text, either through a formal norm-referenced test or an informal reading/writing measure. All of the studies used measures that tested how well the student performed on one text. None used longitudinal data, collected over the course of many years, to examine other aspects of comprehension, like reading freely and reading widely. Although the purpose of these studies was to directly and immediately assess the instruction students received for specific texts, clearly, these broader purposes need to be taken into consideration when attempting to ultimately answer the question of whether comprehension can be taught and whether such teaching is effective. In asking the question "Can comprehension be taught?" one has to be careful to add "Comprehension of what, by whom, under what conditions, and for what purposes?"

Although one has to attend to the possibility that the question is still open, there is ample and ever increasing evidence that comprehension instruction has been effective in many different studies. The purpose of this chapter is to review representative samples of these studies to determine elements of comprehension instruction that seem generalizable and useful for teachers at various grade levels in various settings. Naturally not all relevant studies can be included in this chapter, rather only a modest number will be included as illustrations of what we currently know about comprehension instruction.

Such a listing and review of the studies that point to the effectiveness of comprehension instruction would not be particularly useful without placing the studies within a framework that evolves into a specific approach that capitalizes on students' current levels of functioning as well as their experiences, knowledges, and values. In order to provide this framework, a brief historical review of comprehension instruction in the United States will be presented.

Historical Perspectives on Teaching Reading Comprehension in the United States

The history of reading comprehension instruction in the United States is actually very brief. The term comprehension seems first to have been used by J. Russell Webb in the third reader of his series, *Normal Readers* in 1856 (Smith, 1965). Prior to that time, comprehension *per se* was not discussed—one presumes it was thought about but not researched or reported. Although it is dangerous to try to guess what our predecessors thought, there does seem to be evidence that com-

prehension was not included as a major thrust in reading instruction in the early years because it was thought to be a logical by-product of learning to read (Smith, 1965).

In the nineteenth century, the term *meaning* came into use and it evolved into *understanding what one reads* in the early twentieth century. The definition of comprehension in the late nineteenth century was one in which comprehension was thought to be the product of reading; the aggregated total of comprehending many small units. Perhaps the most significant shift in emphasis in reading comprehension instruction that is observable from published research reports occurred in the early part of the twentieth century when educators shifted their emphasis from the improvement of oral reading as a means for "getting meaning" to an emphasis on improving comprehension during silent reading (Mathews, 1966, Roser, 1984; Smith, 1965).

This movement seems to have signaled (and foreshadowed) a growing interest in contemporary efforts that encourage students to be in control of their own comprehension processes. This early twentieth-century movement seems to have resulted in a contemporary concern to move the focus of learning from external control of comprehension (prescribed materials and predetermined activities) to internal control in which students generate their own perspectives, interpretations, and understandings.

Another gradual shift in comprehension instruction was the movement away from "subskills" approaches, in which students were taught isolated skills in the belief that the accumulation of these skills would result in comprehension, to holistic strategic approaches in which students are taught about the what, how, and when of comprehension.

Farr (1971) referred to the period between 1940 and 1980 as the period of subskill proliferation. In one of the earliest attempts to isolate specific subskills that affect comprehension, Davis (1944), using factor analysis techniques, found five skills that contributed to reading comprehension performance:

1. Knowledge of word meaning
2. Reasoning in reading
3. Concentration on literal sense meaning
4. Following the structure of a passage
5. Recognizing the mood and literary techniques of a writer

The first two, word knowledge and reasoning, accounted for 89 percent of the variance in his study. Although there were criticisms of the factor analysis techniques he used, Davis' later work (1968) continued to demonstrate that reading comprehension can be affected by specific skills.

Many attempts to isolate the "skills" of comprehension based upon Davis' findings followed to the point where long lists of comprehension skills were developed. Simons (1971) found that some checklists contained more than 200 separate comprehension skills. Roser (1984) explained that attempts to systematically organize these skills (sometimes discussed as taxonomies) were not successful for three basic reasons:

1. The skills identified in the list were ambiguous and confusing; there was no logic for their grouping. Some of these

skills described "uses" of comprehension, some described instructional practices, and some described cognitive processes.

2. Each skill could be listed under a variety of labels.
3. The lists/taxonomies suggested greater scientific precision than they actually had.

Although some studies have examined the beneficial effects of training in individual skills on overall comprehension, some current theorists are suggesting that comprehension is a unitary phenomenon. Although the debate of whether comprehension is best understood as a unitary process or a set of discernible skills will rage on for the foreseeable future, Roser (1984) suggests a practical explanation—it may be both. She maintains that an endorsement of this explanation gives credence "to the efforts of the cognitive psychologists as they search for ways to explain the unity, as well as the efforts of the practitioners who must interpret the whole into transferable good." (Page 58).

A final major movement in comprehension instruction is the movement toward the explicit teaching of comprehension strategies with guided and independent practice (Robinson et al., in press).

Evidence appears to be mounting that explicit instruction in comprehension increases reading comprehension ability for specific texts. In several frequently cited studies that examined the effectiveness of explicit instruction at various grade levels, it has been demonstrated that explicit instruction results in enhanced understanding of texts (Baumann, 1983, 1986; Rosenshine & Stevens, 1984). Successful explicit reading comprehension instruction usually includes four stages in which responsibility gradually shifts from the teacher to the students:

1. Setting purposes for reading. The teacher uses a structured overview to introduce the students to the task, including the purpose for the lesson. The teacher assumes the major responsibility for this part of the instruction.
2. Modeling. The teacher tells, shows, and/or demonstrates *how* comprehension occurs. The teacher again assumes the greatest responsibility for this part of the lesson.
3. Guided Practice. The students attempt to follow the model provided by the teacher; feedback and conferencing are an integral part of this step. Students and teachers share the responsibility during this stage.
4. Independent Practice. The student practices independently with "novel" materials. The student accepts the major share of the responsibility for this part of the instruction.

These shifts in practice over the years seem to reflect a growing understanding of the mental processes that are involved in comprehension and an understanding that these processes can be acquired and developed through instruction and practice. These radical changes over the years acknowledge the changing perspective of the teacher's role in fostering comprehension and the learner's role in controlling his/her own comprehension.

Appropriately, from a historical perspective, there does not seem to be a single model for comprehension instruction that can be immediately implemented in every classroom. Rather, many models, approaches, methods, heuristics, and practices seem to hold promise for helping students develop their own comprehension.

The framework that seems most appropriate after reviewing the evidence from many studies attempting to find the "best practices in reading comprehension instruction research" seems to favor a process approach that builds upon what we know about the ways that students read and learn.

An Instructional Process Approach Built Upon Constructivist Principles

In recent years we have learned that students develop comprehension skills and strategies most successfully through a process approach that emphasizes the underlying cognitive and linguistic skills that are prerequisites for understanding and appreciating texts. Just as has been the case for some time in writing instruction, reading instruction is undergoing a profound change in its theoretical orientation and ensuing pedagogy. Educators are moving away from fragmented component skills approaches in which reading is taught as a series of subskills to a holistic approach in which comprehension is viewed as a unitary process (Robinson et al., in press). As a result, contemporary comprehension instruction should be based on constructivist principles that acknowledge the student's role as the meaning-maker in the reading act.

What are the instructional implications of such an approach? Can constructivism be the basis for effective instruction in which students learn to internalize rules and strategies for comprehending? Applebee (in this volume) argues that it can be—if there is a shift from the metaphor of "diagnosis and prescription" that has been traditionally used to discuss teaching and learning to a new metaphor that adequately advances constructivist notions of teaching and learning. He argues for the use of instructional scaffolding as the most fitting metaphor for teaching and learning, suggesting that it more fully describes teaching and learning because it focuses on the notion of dynamic learning within a specific context. The metaphor of instructional scaffolding supports a process-oriented approach that perceives the teacher's role as one that provides necessary and meaningful support where and when necessary and the student's role as one in which the learner is the maker of meaning. His notion of "instructional scaffolding" requires the student to take ownership for learning and the teacher to provide appropriate direction and support. It requires a form of collaboration between teachers and students in which teachers and students work together to ensure that students internalize rules and strategies for meaning-making.

Instructional Methods for Implementing A Process Approach to Reading Comprehension Instruction

There are several methods for implementing a process approach that fosters constructivist notions. Two methods that have been particularly successful in helping to develop competent comprehension strategies will be reviewed. The first method, Reader Response to Literature, is generally thought to be a method used for instruction with literary texts (narratives, poetry, drama), but it can also be used in some instances with certain forms of information texts. The second method, reciprocal teaching, has sometimes been classified as an instructional activity rather than as a method of teaching. For our purposes in this review, we will classify it as a method because it is a comprehensive way to instruct students through an entire text. Reciprocal teaching has also sometimes been thought to be a method of instruction to be used with information texts exclusively. However, evidence suggests that it can be used effectively with many different forms of texts, including narrative pieces.

Reader Response Method For Teaching Literature

As early as 1938, Rosenblatt proposed a "new" method for teaching literature; an essentially reader-based method that attended directly to what "real" readers thought of the literature they were reading. In more recent years, this method has become known as "Reader Response." She argued that reader response instruction, in which readers' personal interpretations of texts were of primary importance, would provide for more meaningful and effective teaching than the critical interpretative methods that were traditionally used.

A reader-response based method of teaching literature is a fundamental shift from the viewpoint that literary interpretation is a right/wrong entity to a view that perceives literary interpretation as a transaction between the reader and the text. Four basic assumptions underlie a response-based approach:

1. Literary meaning is a "transaction" between the reader and the text.
2. The meaning of literature is not contained in a static text.
3. Readers comprehend differently because every reader is unique.
4. Readers' personal responses to text are a critical element in meaning-making.

Loban (1987) further explained the need for this shift arguing that "only by learning to respond fully to the [literary] journey itself will pupils gain genuine appreciation of literature" (p. 17).

Although Mailloux (1982) referred to the literature on reader response as "meta-critical chaos," he argued that there was a shared view among reader response theorists that reading is not the discovery of meaning but the creation of it.

In arguing for a shift to a reader response approach to the teaching of literature, which is essentially a constructivist process approach, Holbrook (1987) argued that such a change will take tremendous support because of the powerful and lasting effects of *New Criticism* on teaching and learning theory. In New Criticism theory, it is argued that meaning resides principally in the text, and students must be taught a great deal *about* literature before they can appropriately interpret a text. In advocating a reader response methodology, researchers are essentially arguing for a fundamental change in thinking and in teaching. Educators are being asked to alter their belief that each text has one, true accurate meaning to accepting what Rosenblatt (1982) calls "transaction," or interrogation between text and reader.

Reader response methodology is not a new phenomenon; it has its roots in the work of I. A. Richards (1929) who believed that reader response was the only powerful route to literature teaching because readers are unique and their responses will always be individualistic, unique, and idiosyncratic. He believed in a process that allowed readers to interpret any way they want (provided that their responses adhere to principles of logical thought).

Reader response has been investigated in many areas and it has been found to be affected by age (Applebee, 1978; Cullinan, Harwood, & Galda, 1983; Farnan, 1988; Hickman, 1983; Martinez & Roser, in this volume), ability level (Farnan, 1988; Petrosky, 1976; Squire, 1964), sex (Squire, 1964), and type of text that is read (Purves, 1973; Wagner, 1985).

In the area of cognitive development, Cullinan, Harwood and Galda (1983) investigated selected developmental aspects of response and found that fourth graders' responses were concrete, literal and context-bound; sixth graders' responses were primarily literal with some interpretive responses, and eighth graders exhibited literal patterns with some responses containing interpretive and evaluative statements.

In Applebee's (1978) seminal study, he found that children at Piaget's preoperational stage (2 to 6 years of age) displayed step-by-step retellings: at the concrete stage (6 to 11 years of age) children used summarizations; at the formal stage (Level I) (12 to 15 years of age) children displayed empathy in their responses and at Level II (16 years of age to adulthood) students were able to make generalizations.

The results of these studies taken collectively argue for the effectiveness of a response-based approach, but the researchers associated with these studies caution that there are factors that will impinge upon the effectiveness of the approach at various age levels, with various students and with various types of texts.

Reciprocal Teaching Methods

Palincsar and Brown (1985) and Palincsar (1982, 1984a, 1984b, 1986) have developed a paradigm that has been effective for developing constructivist, process-oriented reading comprehension abilities. In their methodology, students and teachers take turns assuming the role of the teacher through a structured dialogue. The teacher models four distinct comprehension strategies and the students have opportunities to practice these strategies. Students are asked to 1. Summarize the paragraph that was read in a simple sentence, 2. Generate a question about the paragraph that was read to ask a fellow student, 3. Ask for clarity (or resolution) of anything in the text that was unclear, and 4. Make a prediction about what will happen next in the text. In their studies, students were shown how to do this by teacher modeling; adult support was withdrawn gradually as students exhibited their ability to perform the task independently. Palincsar (1984a) reported gains of 35 percent and more on comprehension assessments after 20 days of instruction.

Palincsar and Brown's (1985) original formulation was based on Vygotsky's (1978) notions about the zone of proximal development which he described as:

The distance between the actual developmental level as determined by independent problem solving and the level of potential development as determined through problem solving under adult guidance or in collaboration with more capable peers. (p 117).

The foundation of Palincsar and Brown's notions rests upon the premise that children can be taught to internalize rules for comprehending over a period of time through the gradual removal of supportive scaffolds (Palincsar, 1984, 1986; Wood, Bruner, & Ross, 1976). This notion rests on the assumption that scaffolds are adjustable as well as temporary and that learning is a natural interactive process because it occurs in social contexts. It is highly dependent upon discussions between students and teachers. Duffy and Roehler (1987) explain that discussion is a critical part of this type of teaching and learning; they argue that it is:

the process whereby the teacher structures an interaction, learns from student response what is in the students' minds, and restructures the situation to clarify or correct student responses. (pp. 70–71)

Instructional Activities That Foster Constructivist Principles

Several teaching and learning activities foster constructivist notions that lead to the development of comprehension abilities. These activities are based on the premise that comprehension is a gradual, emerging process in which readers grow in comprehension abilities by processing texts in a generative manner, building on their own experiences, knowledges, and values. Eight categories of activities that have proven to be successful in helping students develop their comprehension abilities will be discussed. These include:

1. Preparing for reading activities,
2. Developing vocabulary activities,
3. Understanding and using text structure knowledge activities,
4. Questioning activities,
5. Information processing activities,
6. Summarizing activities,
7. Notetaking activities, and
8. Voluntary/recreational reading activities.

Preparing for Reading

Three activities that help students ready themselves for reading will be discussed. These include: PReP, Previewing, and Anticipation Guides.

Many of these activities have been used by teachers for generations. Although most of these have been practiced in classrooms around the world for some time, the successful research base for some of them has only been recently established, although others have a long historical research base. The research study references that are included with these activities are selective, tending to be recent studies because space limits a historical review of the research base of all of these activities. It is in no way our intent to suggest that these are new ideas. Rather, we hope to show that effective instructional activities

sustain themselves and remain in practice over time with modifications, revisions, and additions precisely because they help students to construct meaningful understandings of texts.

Prereading Plan (PReP). Langer (1982, 1984) has proposed an activity that prepares students for reading by activating their prior knowledge that is relevant to the text through a series of prompt questions. She proposes three stages to PReP—initial associations' reflections about initial associations and reformulation of knowledge. In the initial association stage, the teacher selects a word, phrase, or picture about the key concept in the text and initiates a discussion to induce concept-related associations. For example, in teaching a lesson about the American Revolution, the teacher might ask "What comes to mind when you hear the words 'Revolutionary War'?" During the reflection stage students are asked to explain their associations, for example, "Why do those ideas come to mind?" Langer (1984) found that the social context of this activity advanced students understanding—they expanded and/or revised their knowledge through listening to and interacting with their peers. In the final stage, reformulation of knowledge, students might be asked "Have you gained any new ideas of the Revolutionary War?" She found that students' knowledge was expanded through the generative processes in which they were engaged. She found that students responses changed from remotely related personal experiences to an understanding of relations between pieces of knowledge. In this stage, responses consisted of superordinate concepts with characteristics, traits, and examples as well as analogies.

Previewing. Graves, Penn, and Cooke (1985) tested a procedure in which students listened to a lengthy preview of the assigned text. The preview was prepared by the teacher and had as its purpose to motivate students by: 1) activating prior personal experiences that are relevant to the text; 2) building necessary background knowledge for the text; and 3) establishing an organizational framework for the text that is consistent with the framework the author used to present information. Students who listened to the previews before reading the text significantly outperformed students who did not have previews on several measures of comprehension.

Anticipation Guides. Herber (1978) designed a previewing guide in which students were encouraged to predict the information they expected to encounter in the text. As they read the text, their predictions were compared with the information that was actually contained in the text. This active form of processing text helped children develop effective comprehension strategies.

Developing Vocabulary

Nagy (1988) documented the relationship between word knowledge and reading comprehension, cogently arguing that one cannot understand oral and written language without knowing what most words mean. The extent of one's vocabulary (receptive and/or expressive) has been considered to be a measure of one's world knowledge (Freebody & Anderson, 1983) and one's active ability to comprehend (Nagy, 1988; Nagy & Herman, 1987). In several studies of effective vocabulary instruction, Beck, McKeown, and Omanson (1984, 1987) and Beck, Perfetti, and McKeown (1982) found that vocabulary needed to be taught in semantically and topically related networks in order to improve overall comprehension. Beck, Perfetti, and McKeown (1982) found that a semantic network approach improved both knowledge of word meanings and background knowledge that was necessary to comprehend the text.

Several researchers have found that vocabulary instruction that is not tied to building broad background knowledge relevant to the text will not result in vocabulary or comprehension growth (Beck, McKeown, & Omanson, 1987).

Two activities seem especially pertinent for helping to develop vocabulary within a network that encourages students to relate their knowledges (old information, experience, and new information) in an effort to create broader formulations of meaning. These activities have been found to enhance reading comprehension performance (Johnson & Pearson, 1978).

Semantic Mapping. Johnson and Pearson (1978) and Anders and Bos (1986) found that vocabulary words that were taught and learned in networks were better learned than words that were taught through contextual approaches.

Semantic Feature Analysis. Anders and Bos (1986) and Beck, McKeown, and Omanson (1987) found that students who were taught vocabulary words through a semantic feature analysis paradigm learned the words more thoroughly than students who learned the target words in other ways.

Understanding and Using Text Structure Knowledge

In recent years, there has been a great deal of attention given to the role that understanding of text structure plays in students' comprehension.

Narrative Texts. Some researchers argue that explicit instruction of story structure is unnecessary because students will automatically acquire this knowledge indirectly as a by-product of story listening/viewing (Moffett, 1983). Schmitt and O'Brien (1986) argued against instruction in narrative structure, suggesting that this form of instruction was both unnecessary and counterproductive; it emphasized only one piece of a story and deemphasized story content. However, there are other researchers who have found that instruction in narrative structure positively affects students reading about writing studies (Lapp & Flood, 1986). Further, Buss, Ratliff, and Irion (1985) found that students who had little knowledge of story structure benefited considerably from direct instruction in story grammars.

Information Texts. Many researchers have reported that students at all grade levels can be taught the structures that underlie expository texts (Berkowitz, 1986; Flood, 1986; Flood, Lapp, & Farnan, 1986; Slater, Graves, & Piche, 1985; Taylor & Beach,

1984). It has also been discovered that students who consistently use their knowledge of text structure while they are processing texts recall and comprehend more than students who do not know or use text structure knowledge (Armbruster, Anderson, & Ostertag, 1987; Baumann, 1984). Further, students who had the knowledge but did not use it were more negatively affected when reading texts with unfamiliar material than texts with familiar material (Meyer, Brandt, & Bluth, 1980; Taylor & Beach, 1984).

Questioning

QARs and Inference Training activities have been found to improve reading comprehension for students at several different grade levels.

Question/Answer Relationships (QARs). In several studies, Raphael (1982, 1986) demonstrated that students were capable of generating and answering questions that enhanced their comprehension and led to independent processing. Four types of QARs were designed, tested, and found to be successful in helping students to comprehend:

1. Text-based QARs in which the answers are "right there" explicitly stated in the text;
2. Text-based QARs in which the student has to "think and search" for relevant information throughout the text;
3. Knowledge-based QARs in which the reader has to read the text to understand the question, but the answer is not in the text; and
4. Knowledge-based QARs in which the student can answer the question without reading the text.

In the beginning stage of this process, the teacher accepts total responsibility for the five key elements of the activity: 1) assigning the text, 2) generating the questions, 3) providing answers, 4) identifying the QAR, and 5) providing a justification for the QAR identified. Eventually, control is released to the student after guided practice is offered to the student. Students who were trained in the QAR activity demonstrated significant gains in comprehension.

Inference Training. Hansen (1981), Hansen and Hubbard (1984), and Hansen and Pearson (1983) tested a paradigm for inference training in which the teacher generates two questions—one to activate prior experience and one to generate predictions. Answers were shared in a group to expose students to many possible ideas. Students were able to answer the questions and to generate their own questions to novel texts.

Information Processing

KWL: What We Know, What We Want To Find Out, What We Learn and Still Need to Learn. The KWL procedure, developed by Ogle (1986), rests upon constructivist principles: it is the reader who ultimately must create meaning. The emphasis of responsibility in this activity is on the students' deciding what is known and what needs to be learned. Initially, the student is shown how to use the guide. This is followed by the teacher's question "How do you know that?" which reminds the student to seek evidence from the text or from previous knowledge. This procedure is intended to activate, review, and develop background knowledge, and to set useful purposes that will enable the student to be an active, independent learner.

Concept-Task-Application (C-T-A). Wong and Au (1984) found that asking focused prereading discussion questions about critical concepts contained in the text enhanced students' background knowledge before reading. During this first phase, students set purposes for reading, and the goal of the questions is twofold: 1) to find out what students already know about a topic and 2) to determine what they will need to know. During the second stage, the task stage, the teacher asks cueing questions that focus the students' attention to important sections of the text, directing them to formulate satisfactory answers to the questions. When the students' answers indicate that comprehension is inaccurate or incomplete, the teacher asks questions that enable the student to realize they have a need for more information, which is frequently only available from an outside source, in order to "fix" their comprehension. The third stage, application, occurs through a summarization process in which the teacher repeats the initial question and the student summarizes all the information that has been discussed throughout the teaching/learning episode.

Analogies. Several researchers have demonstrated the effectiveness of using analogies to enhance comprehension (Hayes & Tierney, 1982; Peabody, 1984). Bean, Singer, and Cowen (1985) developed an Analogical Study Guide to help students in biology understand the concepts they were learning. In their study, they used the analogy of a factory functioning to understand the working of cells in the human body. Students who were given the analogical guide outperformed students who were taught the information in more traditional ways.

Summarizing

A renewed interest in summarization as a means for improving reading comprehension has occurred during the past few years. Much of this contemporary interest has been a result of Kintsch and Van Dijk's (1978) work that tied summarization ability to reading comprehension, and this renewed interest is documented and detailed in Hidi and Anderson's 1986 report in *Review of Educational Research*. The antecedents to this contemporary work can be found in a series of research studies conducted in the 1920s and 1930s. In 1934, Salisbury reported on the efficacious results of using outlines as the basis for summaries that positively affected reading comprehension.

In its more recent development, summary writing has been difficult to describe because the summary itself has no universally accepted definition. Therefore, appropriate instruction that results in informal summaries is often difficult to describe. However, even with that caveat, summary writing in its various forms still seems to be one of the best vehicles available for

implementing a constructivist, process-oriented approach to teaching reading comprehension (Bean & Steenwyk, 1984; Hare & Borchardt, 1984). As Annis (1985) has explained there are three cognitive/linguistic requirements for comprehending prose: 1) orientation of attention toward task; 2) recording the information in the text into one's own words; and 3) making connections between the new material and one's prior knowledge. As readers work through these three requirements, they are building summaries of the text.

Notetaking

Although the studies on the effectiveness of notetaking as an aid to comprehension and learning have yielded mixed results, Lapp and Flood (1986) argue that notetaking is essentially a complex task of rehearsal that requires time for the reader to learn how to select and practice strategies that lead to information acquisition. In the studies in which notetaking has been found to be an aid to comprehension and learning, it has been argued that performance increases because the reader is directed to specific text ideas and permitted to reflect on these ideas that have been presented in a meaningful context.

The recording of a group discussion about texts is another form of notetaking. The "think alouds" have been found to be effective during reading as a means for facilitating recall, and during writing as a means for organizing written work (Hare & Smith, 1982; Hayes & Flower, 1980; Olshavsky, 1976–1977). However, in several studies (Fuerstein, 1979), it has been found that rehearsal strategies alone did not aid readers in making connections between ideas contained in the text and their prior knowledge.

Many researchers have argued that some form of mediation in addition to rehearsal strategies is needed to enhance learning (Fuerstein, 1979; Vygotsky, 1978; Wood, Bruner, & Ross, 1976). Novak and Gowin (1984) have found that this mediation can occur through activities such as conceptual mapping in which students make decisions about the importance of ideas in texts and the relations between these ideas. Further, some researchers believe that mediated learning activities that provide opportunities for the student to elaborate on the content of the text enhance comprehension significantly (Anderson & Reder, 1979; Risko & Alvarez, 1986).

Voluntary/Recreational Reading

Several studies have indicated that few children or adults choose reading as a source of information or as a recreational activity (Anderson, Wilson, & Fielding, 1988; Greaney & Hegarty, 1987; Morrow & Weinstein, 1982). Greaney and Hegarty's 1987 statistics on how many fifth graders read at all were alarming—almost one quarter of the students in his study said that they did no leisure reading. Conversely, several studies have revealed convincing data that suggests students who engage in voluntary reading significantly outperform students who do not (Long & Hendersey, 1973; Irving, 1980; Morrow, 1983).

One contemporary approach to addressing the problems associated with literacy (those who can read but don't) has been the use of voluntary reading programs within and outside school. These programs forward the tenets of a constructivist approach to developing reading comprehension because they foster self-selection by the student that, in turn, encourages personal meaning-making by the student. When students select their own literature, they are taking a first step toward being responsible for their own comprehension development.

Several studies that examined the effectiveness of voluntary literature programs, in which classrooms were filled with high quality trade books, reported success in overall reading comprehension as well as improved attitudes toward reading (Fielding, Wilson, & Anderson, in press; Ingham, 1981).

Summary

The story of reading comprehension instruction has moved from a period of no awareness of the importance of instruction to a period of emphasis on the subskills that were thought to be the underpinnings of comprehension to the present that views comprehension as a gradual, emerging process in which the reader constructs meaning through a transaction with the text.

Contemporary trends suggest that instructional activities need to be based on basic constructivist principles that acknowledge the reader as the meaning-maker. The activities need to be conducted in such a way that readers are encouraged to build meaning based upon their experiences and knowledge. Assessment techniques, which have always driven the ways in which comprehension has been perceived as a construct and the ways in which it has been taught (or not taught), are gradually changing. More change is needed to help teachers and students understand that comprehension is a complex phenomenon that cannot be easily measured, and it almost certainly cannot be measured with a single instrument.

Finally, there are still many unanswered questions and many questions unframed and unasked. In the future, teachers will need to know more about the delicate instructional balances between preparing for reading and reading; guided reading and independent reading; reading and writing; reading and discussing; reading primary and secondary text sources; vocabulary knowledge and reading; and language variation and reading.

The current climate in education argues well for continued research in comprehension because most educators now agree that the fundamental purpose for reading instruction is to help develop lifelong, independent readers.

References

Anders, P. L., & Bos, C. S. (1986). Semantic feature analysis: An interactive strategy for vocabulary development and text comprehension. *Journal of Reading, 29*, 610–616.

Anderson, R. C., & Pearson, P. D. (1984). A schema-theoretic view of basic processes in reading comprehension. In P. David Pearson (ed.), *Handbook of reading research.* New York: Longman.

Anderson, R. C., Hiebert, E. H., Scott, J. A., & Wilkinson, I. A. (1985). Becoming a nation of readers: The report of the commission on reading (Contract No. 400-83-0057). Washington, DC: National Institute of Education.

Anderson, J. R., & Reder, L. M. (1979). An elaborative processing explanation of depth of processing. In L. S. Cermak & F. I. M. Craik (Eds.), *Levels of processing and human memory.* Hillsdale, NJ: Laurence Erlbaum Assoc.

Anderson, R. C., Wilson, P., & Fielding, L. (1988). Growth in reading and how children spend their time outside of school. *Reading Research Quarterly, 23*, 285–303.

Annis, L. F. (1985). Student-generated paragraph summaries and the information-processing theory of prose learning. *Journal of Experimental Education, 54*, 4–10.

Applebee, A. N. (1978). *The child's concept of story: Ages 2 to 17.* Chicago: The University of Chicago Press.

Armbruster, B. B., Anderson, T. H., and Ostertag, J. (1987). Does text structure/summarization instruction facilitate learning from expository text? *Reading Research Quarterly, 21*, 331–346.

Baker, L., & Brown, A. L. (1984). Metacognition skills and reading. In P. D. Pearson (Ed.), *Handbook of reading research.* New York: Longman.

Baumann, J. F. (1983). A generic comprehension instruction strategy. *Reading World, 22*, 284–294.

Baumann, J. F. (1984). The effectiveness of a direct instruction paradigm for teaching main idea comprehension. *Reading Research Quarterly, 20*, 93–115.

Baumann, J. F. (1986). Teaching third grade students to comprehend anaphoric relationships. The application of a direct instruction model. *Reading Research Quarterly, 21*, 70–90.

Bean, T. W., Singer, H., and Cowen, S. (1985). Acquisition of a topic schema in high school biology through an analogical study guide. In J. A. Niles and R. V. Lalik (Eds.), *Issues in literacy: A research perspective,* Thirty-fourth Yearbook of the National Reading Conference. Rochester, NY: National Reading Conference.

Bean, T. W., & Steenwyk, F. L. (1984). The effect of three forms of summarization instruction on sixth graders' summary writing and comprehension. *Journal of Reading Behavior, 16*, 297–306.

Beck, I. L., McKeown, M. G., & Omanson, R. C. (April 1984). *The fertility of some types of vocabulary instruction.* Paper presented at the meeting of the American Educational Research Association, New Orleans.

Beck, I. L., McKeown, M. G., & Omanson, R. C. (1987). The effects and uses of diverse vocabulary instructional techniques. In M. G. McKeown & M. E. Curtin (Eds.), *The nature of vocabulary acquisition.* Hillsdale, NJ: Erlbaum.

Beck, I. L., Perfetti, C. A., & McKeown, M. G. (1982). Effects of long-term vocabulary instruction on lexical access and reading comprehension. *Journal of Educational Psychology, 74*, 506–521.

Berkowitz, S. J. (1986). Effects of instruction in text organization on sixth grade students' memory for expository reading. *Reading Research Quarterly, 21*, 161–178.

Bleich, D. (1978). *Subjective criticism.* Baltimore: Johns Hopkins University Press.

Brown, A. L., Campione, J. C., & Day, J. D. (1981). Learning to learn: On training students to learn from texts. *Educational Researcher, 10*, 14–21.

Buss, R. R., Ratliff, J. L., and Irion, J. C. (1985). Effects of instruction on the use of story starters in composition of narrative discourse. In J. A. Niles and R. V. Lalik (Eds.), *Issues in literacy: A research perspective.* Rochester, NY: National Reading Conference.

Carver, R. (1987). Should reading comprehension skills be taught? In J. E. Readence & R. S. Baldwin (Eds.), *Research in literacy: Merging perspectives,* Thirty-sixth Yearbook of the National Reading Conference. Rochester, NY: National Reading Conference.

Cullinan, B. E., Harwood, K. T., and Galda, L. (1983). The reader and the story: Comprehension and response. *Journal of Research and Development in Education, 16,* 29–38.

Davis, F. B. (1944). Fundamental factors of comprehension. *Reading Psychometrika, 9,* 185–197.

Davis, F. B. (1968). Research in comprehension in reading. *Reading Research Quarterly, 3,* 499–545.

Duffy, G. G., & Roehler, L. R. (1987). Characteristics of responsive elaboration which promote the mental processing associated with strategy use. Paper presented at annual meeting, National Reading Conference, St. Petersburg Beach, FL.

Duffy, G., Roehler, L., & Mason, J. (Eds.). (1984). *Comprehension instruction.* New York: Longman.

Duffy, G. G., Roehler, L. R., Sivan, E., Rackliffe, G., Book, C., Meloth, M. S., Vavrus, L. G., Wesselman, R., Putnam, J., & Bassiri, D. (1987). Effects of explaining the reasoning associated with using reading strategies. *Reading Research Quarterly, 22,* 347–368.

Durkin, D. (1978–1979). What classroom observations reveal about reading comprehension instruction. *Reading Research Quarterly, 14,* 481–533.

Farnan, N. C. (1988). *Reading and responding: Effects of a prompted approach to literature.* Unpublished doctoral dissertation, Claremont Graduate School, San Diego State University, CA.

Farr, R. (1971). Measuring reading comprehension: A historical perspective. In F. Greene (Ed.), *Reading: The right to participate.* Twentieth Yearbook of the National Reading Conference.

Fielding, L. G., Wilson, P. T., & Anderson, R. C. (in press). A new focus on free reading: The role of trade books in reading instruction. In T. E. Raphael, & R. Reynolds, (Eds.), *Contexts of literacy.* New York: Longman.

Flavell, J. H. (1981). Cognitive monitoring. In W. P. Dickson (Ed.), *Children's oral communication skills.* New York: Academic Press.

Flood, J. (Ed.). (1984a). *Promoting reading comprehension.* Newark, DE: International Reading Association.

Flood, J. (Ed.). (1984b). *Understanding reading comprehension.* Newark, DE: International Reading Association.

Flood, J. (1986). The text, the student, and the teacher: Learning from exposition in middle schools. *The Reading Teacher, 39,* 784–791.

Flood, J., & Lapp, D. (1987). Reading and writing relations: Assumptions and directions. In J. Squire (Ed.), *The dynamics of language learning.* Urbana, IL: National Conference on Research in English.

Flood, J., Lapp, D. & Farnan, N. (1986). A reading writing procedure that teaches expository text structure. *The Reading Teacher, 39,* 556–561.

Freebody, P., & Anderson, R. (1983). Effect of vocabulary difficulty, text cohesion and schema availability on reading comprehension. *Reading Research Quarterly, 18,* 277–294.

Fuerstein, R. (1979). *Instrumental enrichment.* Baltimore, MD: University Park.

Graves, M. F., Penn, M. C., & Cooke, C. L. (1985). The coming attraction: Previewing short stories. *Journal of Reading, 28,* 594–598.

Greaney, V., & Hegarty, M. (1987). Correlates of leisure-time reading. *Journal of Research in Reading, 10,* 3–20.

Guthrie, J. (Ed.). (1981). *Comprehension and teaching: Research views.* Newark, DE: International Reading Association.

Haller, E. P., Child, D. A., & Walberg, H. J. (1988). Can comprehension be taught? A quantitative synthesis of "metacognitive" studies. *Educational Researcher, 17,* 5–8.

Hansen, J. (1981). The effect of inference training and practice on young children's reading comprehension. *Reading Research Quarterly, 16,* 391–417.

Hansen, J., & Hubbard, R. (1984). Poor readers can draw inferences. *The Reading Teacher, 37,* 586–589.

Hansen, J., & Pearson, P. D. (1983). An instructional study: Improving the inferential comprehension of good and poor fourth-grade readers. *Journal of Educational Psychology, 75,* 821–829.

Hare, V. C., & Borchardt, K. M. (1984). Direct instruction of summarization skills. *Reading Research Quarterly, 20,* 62–78.

Hare, V. C., & Smith, D. C. (1982). Reading to remember: Studies of metacognitive reading skills in elementary school-aged children. *Journal of Educational Research, 75,* 157–164.

Hayes, J. R., & Flower, L. S. (1980). Identifying the organization of writing processes. In L. W. Gregg & E. R. Steinberg (Eds.), *Cognitive processes in writing.* Hillsdale: Lawrence Erlbaum Association.

Hayes, D. A., & Tierney, R. J. (1982). Developing readers' knowledge through analogy. *Reading Research Quarterly, 17,* 256–280.

Herber, H. (1978). *Teaching reading in content areas* (2nd ed.). Englewood Cliffs, NJ: Prentice-Hall.

Hickman, J. (1983). Everything considered: Response to literature in an elementary school setting. *Journal of Research and Development in Education, 16,* 8–13.

Hidi, S., & Anderson, V. (1986). Producing written summaries: Task demands, cognitive operations, and implications for instruction. *Review of Educational Research, 56,* 473–493.

Holbrook, H. T. (1987). Reader response in the classroom. *Journal of Reading, 30,* 556–559.

Ingham, J. L. (1981). *Books and reading development: The Bradford books flood experiment.* Exeter, NH: Heinemann Educational Books.

Irving, A. (1980). *Promoting voluntary reading for children and young people.* Paris: UNESCO.

Iser, W. (1978). *The act of reading: A theory of aesthetic response.* Baltimore, MD: Johns Hopkins University Press.

Jensen, J. (1984). Introduction. In J. Jensen (Ed.), *Composing and comprehending.* Urbana, IL: ERIC Clearinghouse, ED 243 139.

Johnson, D., & Pearson, P. D. (1978). *Teaching reading vocabulary.* New York: Holt, Rhinehart & Winston.

Kintsch, W., & Van Dijk, T. A. (1978). Toward a model of text comprehension and production. *Psychological Review, 85,* 363–394.

Langer, J. A. (1982). Facilitating text processing: The elaboration of prior knowledge. In J. A. Langer & M. T. Smith-Burke (Eds.), *Reader meets author/bridging the gap: A psycholinguistic and sociolinguistic perspective.* Newark, DE: International Reading Association.

Langer, J. A. (1984). Examining background knowledge and text comprehension. *Reading Research Quarterly, 19,* 468–481.

Lapp, D., & Flood, J. (1986). *Teaching students to read.* New York: Macmillan.

Loban, W. (1987). Literature and the basic reading skills. *The California Reader, 20,* 15–17.

Long, H., & Henderson, E. H. (1973). Children's uses of time: Some personal and social correlates. *Elementary School Journal, 73,* 193–199.

Mailloux, (1982). *Interpretive conventions: The reader in the study of American fiction.* Ithaca, NY: Cornell University Press.

Mathews, M. (1966). *Teaching to read: Historically considered.* Chicago: University of Chicago Press.

Meyer, B. J. F., Brandt, D. H., & Bluth, G. J. (1980). Use of author's textual schema: Key for ninth graders' comprehension. *Reading Research Quarterly, 16,* 72–103.

Moffett, J. (1983). *Teaching the universe of discourse.* Boston: Houghton Mifflin.

Morrow, L. M. (1983). Home and school correlates of early interest in literature. *Journal of Educational Research, 76,* 221–230.

Morrow, L. M., & Weinstein, C. S. (1982). Increasing children's use of literature through program and physical design changes. *Elementary School Journal, 83,* 131–137.

Nagy, W. E., & Herman, P. A. (1987). Breadth and depth of vocabulary knowledge: Implications for acquisition and instruction. In M. G. McKeown & M. E. Curtis (Eds.), *The nature of vocabulary acquisition*. Hillsdale, NJ: Lawrence Erlbaum.

Nagy, W. E. (1988). *Vocabulary instruction and reading comprehension* (Tech. Rep. No. 431). Champaign, IL: University of Illinois, Center for the Study of Reading.

Novak, J. D., & Gowin, B. D. (1984). *Learning how to learn*. Cambridge, MA: Cambridge University Press.

Ogle, D. (1986). K-W-L: A teaching model that develops active reading of expository text. *The Reading Teacher, 39,* 564–570.

Olshavsky, J. E. (1976–1977). Reading as problem solving: An investigation of strategies. *Reading Research Quarterly, 12,* 654–674.

Palincsar, A. S. (1982). Improving the reading comprehension of junior high students through the reciprocal teaching of comprehension-monitoring strategies. *Dissertation Abstracts International, 43,* 3744A.

Palincsar, A. S. (April, 1984a). *Working with the zone of proximal development*. Paper presented at the 68th meeting of the American Educational Research Association, New Orleans.

Palincsar, A. S. (1984b). Reciprocal teaching of comprehension fostering and comprehension monitoring activities. *Cognition and Instruction, 2,* 117–175.

Palincsar, A. S. (1986). The role of dialogue in providing scaffolded instruction. *Educational Psychologist, 21,* 73–98.

Palincsar, A. S., & Brown, A. L. (1985). Reciprocal teaching activities to promote reading with your mind. In E. J. Cooper (Ed.), *Reading, thinking, and concept development: Interactive strategies for the class*. New York: The College Board.

Paris, S. G. (1986). Teaching children to guide their reading and learning. In T. E. Raphael (Ed.), *The contexts of school-based literacy*. NY: Random House.

Paris, S. G., Lipson, M. Y., & Wixson, K. K. (1983). Becoming a strategic reader. *Contemporary Educational Psychology, 8,* 293–316.

Peabody, M. B. (1984). *The effect of concrete examples on transitional and formal students in the instruction of chemical bonding*. Unpublished doctoral dissertation, Northern Arizona University.

Pearson, P. D. (Ed.). (1984). *Handbook of Reading Research*. New York: Longman.

Petrosky, A. R. (1976). Genetic epistemology and psychoanalytic ego psychology: Clinical support for the study of response, to literature. *Research in the Teaching of English, 10,* 28–38.

Purves, A. C. (1973). *Literature education in ten countries: An empirical study*. New York: John Wiley & Sons.

Raphael, T. (1982). Question-answering strategies for children. *The Reading Teacher, 36,* 186–190.

Raphael, T. (1986). Teaching question answer relationships, revisited. *The Reading Teacher, 39,* 516–522.

Richards, I. A. (1929). *Practical criticism: A study of literary judgment*. New York: Harcourt, Brace and World.

Risko, V. J., & Alvarez, M. C. (1986). An investigation of poor readers' use of a thematic strategy to comprehend text. *Reading Research Quarterly, 21,* 298–316.

Robinson, H. A., Farsone, V., Hittleman, D., & Unruh, E. (in press). *Reading comprehension instruction, 1783-1987: A review of trends and research*. Newark, DE: International Reading Association.

Rosenblatt, L. M. (1938). *Literature as exploration*. New York: Noble & Noble.

Rosenblatt, L. M. (1982). The literary transaction: Evocation and response. *Theory Into Practice, 21,* 268–277.

Rosenshine, B., & Stevens, R. (1984). Classroom instruction in reading. In P. D. Pearson, R. Barr, M. Kamil, & P. Mosenthal (Eds.), *Handbook of reading research*. New York: Longman.

Roser, N. (1984). Teaching and testing reading comprehension: A historical perspective on instructional research and practices. In J. Flood (Ed.), *Promoting reading comprehension*. Newark, DE: International Reading Association, 48–60.

Rumelhart, D. E. (1981). Schemata: The building blocks of cognition. In J. T. Guthrie (Ed.), *Comprehension and teaching: Research reviews*. Newark, DE: International Reading Association.

Salisbury, R. (1934). A study of the transfer effects of training in logical organization. *Journal of Educational Research, 38,* 241–254.

Schmitt, M. C., & O'Brien, D. (1986). Story grammars: Some cautions about the translation of research into practice. *Reading Research and Instruction, 26,* 1–8.

Simons, H. (1971). Reading comprehension: The need for a new perspective. *Reading Research Quarterly, 6,* 338–363.

Slater, W. H., Graves, M. F., & Piche, G. L. (1985). Effects of structural organizers on ninth grade students' comprehension and recall of four patterns of expository text. *Reading Research Quarterly, 20,* 189–202.

Smith, N. B. (1965). *American reading instruction*. Newark, DE: International Reading Association.

Squire, J. R. (1964). *The responses of adolescents while reading four short stories*. (NCTE Research Report No. 2). Urbana, IL: National Council of Teachers of English.

Squire, J. R. (1983). Composing and comprehending: Two sides of the same basic process. *Language Arts, 60,* 581–89.

Taylor, B. M., & Beach, R. W. (1984). The effects of text structure instruction on middle grade students' comprehension and production of expository text. *Reading Research Quarterly, 19,* 134–146.

Tierney, R. J., & Cunningham, J. (1984). Research on teaching reading comprehension. In P. D. Pearson (Ed.), *Handbook of reading research*. New York: Longman.

Tierney, R., & Pearson, P. D. (1984). Toward a composing model of reading. In J. Jensen (Ed.), *Composing and comprehending*. Urbana, IL: ERIC Clearinghouse, ED 243 139.

Vygotsky, L. S. (1978). *Mind in society: The development of higher psychological processes*. In M. Cole, V. John-Steiner, S. Scribner, & E. Soubermann (Eds. and Trans.), Cambridge, MA: Harvard University Press.

Wagner, C. (1985). *Factors affecting young children's response to literature*. Unpublished master's project, San Diego State University, CA.

Wong, J. A., & Au, K. H. (1984). The concept-text application approach: Helping elementary students comprehend expository text. *The Reading Teacher, 38,* 612–618.

Wood, P., Bruner, J., & Ross, G. (1976). The role of tutoring in problem solving. *Journal of Child Psychology and Psychiatry, 17,* 89–100.

34C. STUDYING: SKILLS, STRATEGIES, AND SYSTEMS

Thomas G. Devine

The term *studying* implies a deliberate effort by the student to understand, remember, and use specified knowledge or procedures. Although often associated with reading, it is not the same. Studying frequently occurs in a variety of nonverbal contexts (as when one deliberately tries to play a musical passage on an instrument, develop computational skills, or master intricate physical maneuvers in basketball or a similar activity). Studying is also unlike reading in its emphasis on memory and the later use of studied material; that is, students study to remember and demonstrate at another time some competence or understanding (through performance, testtaking, or writing). Students may read but not study and study but not read.

The term *study skills* has come to embrace a wide variety of competencies associated with academic learning, from alphabetizing to using a table of contents and index, from taking lecture notes to writing a library research paper. Many study-skills textbooks and programs, from elementary school to college levels, aim to introduce students to a vast array of discrete and often unrelated skills. However, some of the skills described in popular student guides and textbooks appear to be distinctly peripheral to the central purposes of study (to understand, remember, and use knowledge or procedures), and overemphasis on their acquisition may be uneconomical in terms of teacher and student time and energy. A smaller number of these skills may be better viewed as *study strategies* that directly promote comprehension, retention in memory, and the ability to demonstrate learning. Teachers and researchers have sometimes combined two or more of these specific strategies as *study systems* on the grounds that related strategies when used together somehow become more effective. All three—study skills, study strategies, and study systems—are bound by a common goal: each is intended to assist students to learn on their own. They are suggested as aids for independent learning, for student rather than teacher use.

Reasons for providing instruction in study skills, strategies, and systems are evident. Students clearly benefit from the competencies included in traditional study skills programs (that is, using a table of contents, library reference systems, a glossary, and so on). They obtain even greater benefits, however, from the use of specific study strategies, such as defining and previewing an assignment, taking effective notes, outlining, self-recitation, or summarizing, as well as the ability to use specific study systems such as SQ3R, PORPE, or SPIN. Instruction in how to study can help learners recognize their own cognitive capabilities, realize how to define and analyze study tasks, and be aware of the array of learning methods available to them. While teachers need to better understand and use available tools for improving teaching (such as, lesson frameworks, effective study guides, and various instructional strategies), it is important that they also understand and promote those tools that will allow students to strike out on their own.

Many useful books and guides are available to promote independent learning (see, for example, Bragstad & Stumpf, 1987; Devine, 1987; Graham & Robinson, 1984; Kahn, 1984; Palmer & Pope, 1984). Although several present information about research and theory, most focus on study skills and strategies and suggest ways that teachers may develop them in students. This chapter examines research findings underlying several widely-used study strategies and often-recommended study systems, and concludes with discussion of instructional issues.

SPECIFIC STUDY STRATEGIES

Research findings on specific study strategies, though sometimes anfractuous and equivocal, tend to support the belief that students may be given tools to help them better understand, remember, and apply knowledge and procedures that are new to them. Several widely-used strategies are examined here. The first two, Defining Study Tasks and Previewing, are often viewed as instructional rather than learning strategies but are often used by students as ways to improve their own learning; the last, Writing, although presently recommended and studied as a teaching strategy, is seen here as a tool for improving independent learning.

Defining Study Tasks

Students who know exactly what they are supposed to learn tend to outperform those who simply "study." While some teachers continue to tell students to "Study Chapter 8" or "Learn the causes of the American Revolution," research findings suggest that such assignments handicap students. Anderson and Biddle (1975) for example, noted in a review of 14 studies that students given information, while studying, about the questions to be asked at the conclusion of a reading assignment, tended to do significantly better on tests than students who were not given such information. Further studies by Anderson (1980) and Glynn (1978) suggest that the more specific the knowledge provided, the better the performance. After examining studies done since the 1930s, Anderson and Armbruster (1984) noted that several lines of research suggest that "the more specific the knowledge about the criterion event, the greater the effectiveness of studying" (p. 660), especially when students realize that modifying their study habits to conform to the task will result in better performance. Time spent with students, whether in elementary school or college, in defining the study task so that they understand what is expected of them is evidently time well spent. After repeated experiences under teacher guidance, task definition may become a study strategy for students to use independently so that they can, on their own, try to spell-out the goals and parameters of an assignment and see the ways it relates to course or curriculum objectives.

Previewing

Related to task definition is previewing (sometimes also called *overviewing* or *surveying*). Previewing an assignment helps students see its purpose, the lines of demarcation separating it from other study tasks, and how its components fit into a larger task. In addition, previewing before study can activate relevant background knowledge and may enrich and refine new schemata.

Research on various forms of previewing tends to be positive, although most has focused on previewing as an instructional rather a study strategy. Many studies have examined the value of previewing as a means of activating or providing prior knowledge: Graves (1980; 1981; 1983), for example, used previews in story reading and found that building background knowledge increased learning by significant amounts; Stevens (1982) also found previewing and providing relevant background knowledge helped 10th-grade students better understand passages in a history textbook; Hayes and Tierney (1982) discovered that giving students information about the topic treated in the text prior to reading helped readers learn more from the text.

Informal types of previewing have long been used by many teachers as instructional strategies: class discussions, informal lectures, examination of illustrations, viewing appropriate films, reading outlines, and so on. Some teachers have also used more structured previews. *Advance organizers,* for example, were first suggested by Ausubel (1960) as "introductory material at a higher level of abstraction, generality and inclusiveness than the learning passage itself" (Ausubel, 1978, p. 252). They are intended to serve as ideational scaffolding for the incorporation of new material. Some research indicates that they are effective (Corkill, Bruning, & Glover, 1988; Tudor, 1986); other research is less conclusive (Tierney & Cunningham, 1984). *Structured overviews* are designed to serve the same purpose but present visual overviews of the concepts and relationships in the text (for examples, see Devine, 1986). *Structural organizers* (Slater, Graves, & Piche, 1985) focus student attention on the ways a text is organized: before they read, they are given its basic rhetorical framework, such as cause-effect, claim-support-conclusion, problem solution, and so on, with paragraph plans, main idea sentences, and signal words and phrases highlighted.

Previewing as a study strategy rather than a teaching approach has not been carefully examined by researchers. Clearly, previewing can be—and is—used independently by many students. They have learned to examine illustrations prior to reading to get a notion of the assignment; many read chapter summaries first; others study an available outline before they read, while still others have learned to check typographical aids or even the first sentences of paragraphs before beginning to read and study an assignment. Previewing to create questions to be answered during reading is a strategy developed by many teachers as a result of frequent experience with the study system SQ3R (see Study Systems below): they have internalized an approach recommended and used by their teachers. Many of the highly-structured previewing strategies used by teachers may also, in time, become internalized by students to become parts of their personal study strategy repertoires. Teachers should probably encourage students to make classroom previewing strategies their own by regularly reminding them to: check titles, subtitles, and headings; look at typographical aids; study illustrations, maps, charts, and graphs prior to reading; examine ends of previous chapters and beginnings of subsequent ones; note any study material provided; read summaries first; create their own guide questions, and so on.

Questioning

Questioning, as a study strategy, may take at least three forms:

1. Students may use teacher or textbook questions to guide them through a reading assignment or lecture;
2. they may generate their own questions for the same purpose; or
3. they may use other-or self-generated questions for self-recitation and/or review.

The values of teacher and textbook prequestions have been fairly well established. They can, for example, focus student attention on key points, thus better defining the study task. In one recent study, Wade and Trathen (1989) found that prereading questions seemed to reduce the amount of unimportant information subjects noted, and that, particularly, they also improved the recall of important information for lower ability groups. In another study, Rickards and McCormick (1988) found that conceptual prequestions in a lecture situation seemed to encourage more elaborate processing. Prequestions by teachers and others, however, fall in the category of instructional, not learner, strategies. What evidence supports the belief that student-generated prequestions are effective? Unfortunately, most studies on student-generated questioning have focused upon questioning during, not before, study. In his examination of the SQ3R study system Martin (1985) attributed the effectiveness of the system to its structure of which self-generated prequestioning is an intrinsic component. (He also discovered that self-questioning *during* reading was not significantly superior to SQ3R.) Studies of self-generated questioning during reading have sometimes been negative (King, Biggs, & Lipsky, 1984; Morse, 1975), sometimes positive. Duell (1978) found that college students who developed their own questions from instructional objectives outperformed those who simply studied the material with knowledge of the objectives. Frase and Schwartz (1975) found that students who wrote out questions while studying did better than those in control group who read only. As Anderson and Armbruster (1984) have noted, "It seems plausible that when student questioning *is* effective, it is so because students are forced to encode the information more than they might if they simply read it" (p. 672). They also noted that the actual writing of questions required students to paraphrase or perform some other transformation of the text, thus entailing processing.

The research on self-recitation, or self-testing, goes back more than 70 years (Gates, 1917). It seems to be one of the most-used as well as oldest of study strategies. Recall during practice (that is, reciting to oneself as material is studied) clearly increases the chances of retention of material being studied. When based on teacher-prepared questions and lists, it is especially effective, because usually the teacher develops the questions or lists with the test in mind. Thus, the problem of task definition is minimized if not resolved in advance of study. When material to be studied is generated by students, they may select inappropriate material unless they are competent in task definition. However, enough research support of student-generated questions exists (see above) to encourage students to continue self-recitation. They need to be shown such activities as

1. The use of 3x5 inch "flip" cards (with questions on one side and answers on the back),
2. The Self Test in which they write out answers to their own questions,
3. Matching puzzles to connect names and dates with events, and so on,
4. The use of charts, graphs, and maps to be filled in to verify their learnings, and similar self-recitation devices.

Self-recitation remains a viable study strategy. When coupled with guidance in task definition, it seems an especially powerful study tool.

Underlining

Underlining (also called *underscoring,* or *highlighting*) seems to be the most popular study strategy. It probably owes its effectiveness to the Von Restorff effect, a laboratory finding that the isolation, or highlighting, of one item from a homogeneous background leads to increased recall of that item (McAndrew, 1983). For example, when a word or phrase is printed in a different color or type from others on a list, viewers tend to remember it better than other items. It is used more in college than in elementary or secondary school and, indeed, is the most-used study technique for many college students (Policastro, 1975).

While some studies show positive results from underlining texts (for example, Rickards & August, 1975, and Schell & Rocchio, 1975), others indicate that it is no more effective than other study strategies (for a summary, see Anderson & Armbruster, 1984, p. 665). In a study of its use at the college level, Policastro (1975) noted,

1. Students usually underline too much. The average textbook runs to 400 pages. If just 20 percent of each page were underlined, it would result in 80 pages of rereading (while turning all 400) for a review in preparation for an exam.
2. The underlined section will often lose some, if not all, of its significance when reread at some future time. The student then has to reread surrounding material in order to reconstruct the original meaning, requiring extra time and effort.
3. Underlining is a comparatively passive activity and has the effect of psychologically deferring the active (learning) process to some future point. Often a student will underline something that is assumed (rightly or not) to be important, though not fully understood, with the intention of rereading the item at a more "opportune" time in order to discover the complete meaning. (pp. 372–375)

In another study at the college level, Nist and Hogrebe (1987) investigated opposing theoretical viewpoints as explanations of the effect of underlining. Four groups of provisionally-admitted college freshmen were given preunderlined material (a passage from a "typical" college textbook on American government). Group 1 received the passage with information marked that was considered important by a panel of experts; Group 2 received the same markings but with accompanying annotation; Group 3 received the passage with underlining under information that was not selected unaminously by the panel of experts; Group 4 received the same underlining as Group 3 but with accompanying annotation. Group 5 were instructed to generate their own underlining. All students took a test of prior knowledge, read the assigned passage, and took a 24-item multiple-choice test consisting of 12 high-relevant and 12 low-relevant questions. Data analysis indicated that when text material was underlined or underlined and annotated, students directed their attention to the information highlighted, thus supporting the operation of the Von Rostoff effect. Students in Groups 1 and 2 correctly answered more questions about information deemed important by the experts. Students in Groups 3 and 4 answered correctly more of the questions about information not considered important by the experts. The researchers note, "These results suggest that text material which had been marked by the researchers, regardless of the quality of that marking, had a rather strong influence on directing the reader's attention to certain parts of the text" (p. 22). Students who generated their own underlining did not perform significantly better than those who were given experimenter-generated underlining.

Probably better than underlining are *marginal comments* and personal *coding systems.* Writing their own questions, rephrasing difficult sentences, and defining unfamiliar words indicate that the student is more engaged in the process of learning than when tracing lines across the page. Coding systems involving colored symbols for key ideas, lines drawn from main ideas to supporting examples, arrows to show relationships, boxes containing related ideas, marginal numbers indicating chronological patterns, question marks noting unsupported references, hearts and flowers to signal emotional language, and so on also tend to encourage active processing of new information. Simple underlining may be more effective than passive reading, but marginal comments and/or personal coding systems involve students more directly with the text.

Notetaking

The values of notetaking seem clear. It assists students in focusing attention and processing new material. It aids in memory retention and provides students with a record for later review and study. More specifically, as Anderson and Armbruster (1984) note, it allows students "to record a reworked (perhaps more deeply processed) version of the text in a form appropriate for the criterion task" (p. 666). Studies on notetaking, however, have generally produced mixed results.

Some studies (for example, Arnold, 1942; Poppleton Austwick, 1964; Todd & Kessler, 1971; Schultz & DiVesta, 1972) showed notetaking to be only as effective, or distinctly less effective, than rereading, the use of programmed text, underlining, or making marginal comments. Other studies indicated positive effects. Kulhavy, Dyer, and Silver (1975) compared notetaking with reading-only and underlining, and found students in their notetaking group outperformed students in the other two groups. In an older study, Mathews (1938) compared groups who reread, took marginal notes, and outlined, and found that although there were no significant differences on test scores for the three groups, the outlining group scored better when required to give back information in outline form. Bizinkauskas (1970) compared outlining with underlining, reading-only, and tape-recording key ideas and words; he found notetaking in outlines superior.

Recent studies have examined other aspects of notetaking. Kiewra, DuBois, Christian, and McShane (1988), for example, showed college students a videotaped lecture but did not allow them to take any kinds of notes. They then provided the students with one of three forms of notes for review: a complete text, a linear outline including all 121 key ideas of the lecture, and a matrix with the 121 ideas arranged in organized cells. Another group of students in a control group were given no notes and asked to review mentally. Post-testing indicated that students using any of the three forms of preprepared notes outperformed those who reviewed mentally and that outline and matrix notes were more effective than no-notes. In another study, Rickards and McCormick (1988) found that notetaking alone resulted in "more shallow, literal, or paraphrased listing of passage material" (p. 592) than notetaking guided by questions inserted at intervals to guide notetaking. Kiewra and Frank (1988) compared personal notes, complete forms of detailed instructor's notes, and skeletal forms of instructor's notes, and found that detailed instructor's notes provided for better review. Shrager and Mayer (1989) instructed college students to take notes or not take notes during a videotaped lecture. They found that notetakers outperformed non-notetakers for students with low prior knowledge of the topic but not for students with high prior knowledge of the topic.

Sometimes study results vary because student notetaking varies. Some students jot down single words, phrases, sentences, dates, or computations; other try to copy verbatim, from both books and lectures. Some students paraphrase, draw illustrations, make up questions, summarize as they go along, add personal examples, and so on. Clearly, copiousness, quality, and character of notes affect their value. Some recent research suggests a relationship between copiousness and achievement on examinations. Kiewra (1984) found that students who were not permitted to review their study notes nevertheless recalled up to 78 percent of the material they had recorded but only from 5 to 34 percent of that they did not record. Some of the benefits of notetaking result evidently from greater attention to the material noted, as well as deeper processing of it (Kiewra & Fletcher, 1983). Indeed, any notetaking that maximizes processing (such as, paraphrasing, summarizing, elaborating, or personalizing) seems to help. (See, for example, Barnett, DiVesta, & Rogozinski, 1981, and Einstein, Morris, & Smith, 1985.) Bretzing and Kulhavy (1979) compared high school groups who took verbatim notes with groups who wrote summaries, paraphrased

main ideas, and simply wrote down words that began with upper-case letters. On tests requiring integration of information, students who wrote summaries or paraphrased main ideas outperformed those who took verbatim notes or simply copied certain words. In another study, Bretzing and Kulhavy (1981) compared groups of college students who read only, took notes to deliver a lecture to other students, and took notes to lecture professionals. On tests, both groups of notetakers did significantly better than students who read only.

Outlining, Traditional and Free-form

Both traditional outlining and forms of diagrammatic outlining need further research. Traditional outlining encourages students to read texts carefully enough to note main ideas, distinguish between main and subordinate points, locate and list supporting examples and details, be aware of sequence and use of transitional elements, note patterns of organization, and, usually, rewrite material in their own words. Traditional outlining, therefore, appears to be a powerful study strategy, and, indeed, studies lend support to this view. Barton (1930), Salisbury (1935), Mathews (1938), Bisinkauskas (1970) and others found that students who outlined texts outperformed others. On the other hand, other studies (for example, Arnold, 1942; Todd & Kessler, 1971; Willmore, 1966) found outlining to be less, or no more, effective than other study strategies. An important point to note, however, is that traditional outlining, with its highly structured and codified format, demands instruction. As Courtney (1965) pointed out, the ability to recognize organization in spoken or printed texts is rarely a natural accomplishment nor a quality of native intelligence (p. 78). To realize the full potential of traditional outlining as a study tool, it must be taught, probably in early grades with regular review and further application through secondary school and college. Questions that need to be asked about outlining are: When should instruction begin? How much is required? What approaches to instruction are most effective?

Recently, variations of traditional outlining have been studied and found effective. *Mapping* (sometimes called *graphing* or *networking*) allows students to note text relationships visually, in a nonlinear rather than linear way. Rather than list main and subordinate ideas and supporting examples or details consecutively as found in the printed text, students may indicate relationships in circles, constellations, or other ways. *Array-outlining* (Hansell, 1978) has students identify key points in an assignment, copy these onto small pieces of paper, and arrange the pieces on their desktops in some order. After discussion with other students and teacher, students then copy their arrangements, or outlines, onto a larger sheet for study and review. *Pyramid outlines* (Walker, 1979) are drawings students prepare with key ideas at the top of a pyramid and with subordinate ideas arranged below.

Recent research on graphic organizers (Hawks, McLeod, and Jonassen, 1985) has led to the use of *structured notetaking* (Smith & Tompkins, 1988). Structured overviews and structural organizers (discussed above) are explained to students who are then given extensive practice in their use. Once students understand that such organizers represent text structures pictorially, they are encouraged to work collaboratively to prepare their own graphic organizers and then to use these as notetaking strategies. They learn to outline textual material diagrammatically and, with further practice, apply the strategy to both lecture notetaking and the development of their own written compositions.

Diagrammatic outlining offers many of the advantages of traditional outlining and, unlike traditional outlining, may be used to take lecture notes when lecturers fail to follow standard outline form. Again, more studies need to be done on both linear and nonlinear outlining, especially on variations of nonlinear.

Summarizing

Many studies have examined the value of summarizing as a study strategy. Some have found that it seems to improve both retention and recall (Doctorow, Wittrock, & Marks, 1978; King, Biggs, & Lipsky, 1984; Brown, Campione & Day, 1980; Winograd, 1984); reading comprehension (Palincsar & Brown, 1983; McNeil & Donant, 1982; Rinehart, Stahl & Erickson, 1986); and written summaries (Hare & Borchardt, 1984; McNeil & Donant, 1982).

Summarizing actually is a series of separate operations. Students must decide what to include or eliminate (evaluation), what to combine (condensation), and what language to use (transformation) (Hidi & Anderson, 1986). At least two sets of cognitive operations seem to be necessary: a selection process in which conscious judgments are continuously made of what is important and what is not, and a reduction process in which ideas are deliberately condensed through a variety of highorder transformations. In the classroom, summarizing encourages students to:

1. Identify the writer's main ideas,
2. Recognize the purpose or intent of the selection,
3. Distinguish between relevant and irrelevant material,
4. Note the key evidence offered in support of a thesis or main idea,
5. See the underlying structure of organization,
6. Note the transitional, or signal, expressions used in the text, and
7. Follow the sequence of the material (Devine, 1986).

Specific rules for summarizing have been described by McNeil and Donant (1982):

1. Delete unnecessary or trivial material,
2. Delete material that is important but redundant,
3. Substitute a superordinate term for a list of terms,
4. Substitute a superordinate term for components of an action,
5. Select a topic sentence, and
6. Invent one when there is no topic sentence.

In addition to such rule-governed approaches to instruction, Cunningham (1982) has suggested a more intuitive strategy called GIST (for Generating Interactions between Schema and

Text). GIST restricts students' summaries to 15 blanks: as they read, they must delete all trivial propositions and select macrolevel ideas.

Is summarizing an effective study strategy? Its values seem apparent: it forces students to more carefully examine texts and record their reworked versions in their own language; it assists retention and is readily adoptable in a variety of classroom situations. Clearly, summarization training makes students more aware of the structure of ideas within the reading assignment and how the individual ideas relate to each other. In addition, such training causes students to spend more time with reading assignments, and, as has been frequently noted (see, for example, Rinehart et al., 1986), time spent on reading correlates highly to reading achievement. Study findings in general suggest that summarizing can be powerful study tool. However, to be effective, it requires some instruction: children do not summarize naturally.

Skillful mature readers discriminate among portions of a text as they summarize, basing their choices of summary material on their knowledge of the content and their understanding of the author's intentions and the textual structure. Children, on the other hand, tend to overlook textual cues and make decisions about what to include or eliminate on a sentence-bysentence basis (Hare & Borchardt, 1984). They also tend to include material they consider interesting outstanding, sometimes disregarding topic sentences and implicit main ideas (Brown & Day, 1983). In one study, Winograd (1984) found poorer readers unable to select the same material as adult and better readers. Without guidance, eighth-graders in the study seemed to have difficulty using textual cues. In another study (Pichert, 1979), third-graders were able to rate the relative importance of a passage's idea units but only after they had received instruction.

Instruction does seem to pay dividends. Summarization training has been found to improve written summaries (Brown, Campione, & Day, 1981; Hare & Borchardt, 1984; Palincsar & Brown, 1983). Baumann (1984) found the reading comprehension of sixth-graders improved through summarization training. Bean and Steenwyk (1984) used two different methods of teaching summarization to sixth-grade students: a rule-governed approach (see McNeil & Donant, 1982, noted above) and the intuitive GIST approach (Cunningham, 1982, also described above). They found that both treatment groups significantly outperformed the control group on both paragraph summarization measures and a standardized reading comprehension test. A study at the college level (King et al., 1984) also found that students trained in summary writing not only wrote better summaries but achieved higher scores on a reading comprehension test than students in a control group that received no training.

Writing

Related to summarizing, particularly the writing of summaries, is writing as a study approach or strategy. Although observation and experience seem to indicate that writing about what one is learning is an effective way to improve learning, few studies have been undertaken to study writing as a study tool.

Clearly, writing can make students aware of what they know and do not know, thus serving to monitor learning. In addition, the active researching that takes place before and during writing may add to students' knowledge, while the writing itself helps them discover meanings for themselves. Little research evidence is available, however, to explain the effects of writing upon learning and study (Applebee, 1984).

Evidence exists that students may use written summaries as a means of retaining new content area knowledge in memory (Dansereau, D. F., McDonald, B. A., Long, G. L., Atkinson, T. R., Ellis, A. M., Collins, K. W., Williams, S., & Evans, S. H. 1974; Doctorow et al, 1978, Linden & Wittrock, 1981; Pio & Andre, 1977), especially after they have received training in how to write a summary. Further evidence seems to indicate that personal (learner-oriented) summaries, used by students to facilitate and monitor their own learning, are more effective than those prepared for teachers and others (audience-oriented summaries) (Jenkins, 1979; Hidi & Anderson, 1986). Evidence exists, too, that the writing of analytic essays aids students learning. In studies by Langer (1986) and Newell (1984), high school students were asked to read a selection and respond in one of three ways: answer questions, take notes, or write an analytic essay that applied the new ideas to a new situation. Newell found the writing group produced a more abstract set of associations for key ideas in the selection; Langer found that content area knowledge increased most from essay writing (with notetaking next, and question-answering last). They both concluded that writing analytic essays seems to require students to be less bound by the text in front of them and more involved in organizing, integrating, and assimilating new ideas and information. Simpson, Hayes, Stahl, Connor & Weaver (1988) attempted to structure essay writing in a study system called PORPE (see Study Systems below) and reported that students trained in this writing approach tended to write significantly more organized and coherent essays. They concluded that this writing approach led to an efficient independent study strategy.

Feathers (1987) found that journal writing also seemed to facilitate learning and study. College students were encouraged to predict, underline, make notes, prepare maps, charts, and written summaries, as well as generate their own questions. While studying chapters from college-level textbooks, they kept journals, writing four times a week. Analysis of the journals revealed that students not only learned the study strategies they were being taught but also grew in their metacognitive awareness of learning. Students demonstrated an understanding of the textbook material and alternative ways of studying it.

STUDY SYSTEMS

Study systems are combinations of specific strategies, joined to increase their effectiveness. Among the oldest and most-often-recommended is SQ3R (Robinson, 1970). Using this approach, students first *survey* the assignment to get a general idea of what the passages are about; then they make up their own *questions* (often from headings and subtitles in the text). They next *read* to discover answers to their own questions, *recite* (in writing or aloud) these answers, and finally *review* by rereading parts of the assignment to verify their answers.

Clearly, SQ3R provides students with both an overview and opportunity to better define the study task, as well as opportunities for notetaking and self-recitation. Since Francis Robinson first described this system in the early 1940s, SQ3R has been widely used by teachers and students at all grade levels and has stimulated the development of many similar systems: PQRST: Preview, Question, Read, State, Test (Staton, 1954); the Triple S Technique: Scan, Search, Summarize (Farquhar, Krumboltz, & Wrenn, 1960); OARWET: Overview, Achieve, Write, Evaluate, Test (Norman & Norman, 1968); OK5R: Overview, Key Idea, Read, Record, Recite, Review, Reflect (Pauk, 1974); PQ4R: Preview, Question, Read, Reflect, Recite, Review (Thomas & Robinson, 1972; S4R: Survey, Read, Recite, Record Review (Stetson, 1981); and PQ5R: Preview, Question, Read, Record, Recite, Review, reflect (in Graham & Robinson, 1984).

Study systems continue to be devised. ERICA (for Effective Reading in Content Areas) was developed in Brisbane, Australia (Stewart-Dore, 1982). It consists of four stages: preparing for reading, thinking through information, extracting and organizing information, and translating information. ERICA differs from other study systems in its focus on writing; students use graphic organizers, visual arrays, frames, flow charts, and Venn diagrams, as well as essays and narrative forms. Bailey (1988) describes a variation of SQ3R devised for college students; in SRUN, students Survey, Read, Underline, and take Notes. In HEART, Santeusanio (1988) has students ask "How much do I know about this topic?," establish a purpose for study, ask questions as they study, record their answers, and, finally, test themselves. PORPE (for Predict, Organize, Rehearse, Practice, and Evaluate) was also developed for college students (Simpson, et al., 1988). Students are asked to predict possible essay questions, organize key ideas pertinent to the questions, rehearse through self-recitation, practice by actually writing an essay, and evaluate their work for completeness and accuracy. PSRT (Simons, 1989) has students Prepare, Structure, Read, and Think, with preparation focusing on activating prior knowledge, structure on noting how the text is organized, and thinking as summarizing and developing thought-provoking questions. SPIN (Aylward, 1990) has students Summarize, Predict, Infer, and take Notes.

Do study systems work? The individual components of most study systems rest on some research base. Defining study tasks, overviewing, notetaking, summarizing, and others (see previous section) are supported by study findings (although findings are in some instances equivocal or open to various interpretations). Study systems themselves usually are recommended by teachers who have devised and used them successfully but not tested them in controlled studies. Many are known primarily because of a single article in a professional journal or advocacy in a textbook or program.

SQ3R is a notable exception. Since its first promotion as an effective tool for studying expository text, many studies have been conducted on its usefulness (Gustafson & Pederson, 1985). Johnson (1973) reviewed the research on SQ3R and concluded that research evidence did not support its widespread use but that the value of its component parts is generally substantiated. Spencer (1978) reviewed the research and concurred with Harris (1971) that SQ3R "seems to be well grounded in the experimental psychology of learning, but has not been subjected to much experimentation" (p. 440). Johns and McNamara (1980) noted that its wide use stems less from controlled studies than endorsements by reading educators. Maxwell (1980) noted, too, that while studies support the separate components, SQ3R needs further research as a total method. She also pointed out that "For the fearful student, faced with a long, difficult text to read, the SQ3R method provides a technique for getting started." Moreover, she noted, "it makes explicit the steps that a skilled learner automatically follows" (p. 306). Santeusanio (1983) found a lack of specific research evidence to support SQ3R but recommended its continued use as a study tool.

Martin (1985) focused on the self-questioning aspect of SQ3R. College freshmen in three groups were trained in SQ3R, self-questioning, and the REAP study system (Eanet & Manzo, 1976). REAP was selected because it does not include a self-questioning component. It requires students to read the passage, encode the meaning in the reader's language, annotate the meaning by writing personal notes, and then ponder the passage's meaning, now in annotated form, either through internal "dialectic thinking" or through discussion with others. (In the annotation stage, the reader is expected to "discriminate and synthesize the ideas presented by the writer, translate these into his own language, and crystalize the result in writing", Eanet & Manzo, 1976). After six weeks of practice students were given an infamiliar passage and told to apply the specific approach they had learned. Two weeks later students were again tested to determine the effects of the treatment on longer-term retention. Students who used SQ3R significantly outperformed those who used REAP. However, the SQ3R group did not significantly outperform the self-questioning group, although self-questioning was not significantly superior to SQ3R. Martin concluded that SQ3R owes its effectiveness to its step-by-step structured procedure. Evidently, it does help students concentrate upon those areas of a passage that could be of most importance: "By surveying headings and subheadings, and converting them into questions, subjects are better able to focus in on the important information" (p. 78).

Two other studies of study systems are described here. PORPE (for Predict, Organize, Rehearse, Practice, and Evaluate) was developed as an integrated study systems that focuses on writing, particularly on writing as a postreading strategy to assist students in the assimilation and synthesis of concepts (Simpson et al. 1988). In their study, the researchers wanted to determine the extent which writing as an integrated component of a study system improved the learning of content area material. Predicting possible essay questions, they believed, would promote self-generated questions to encourage active and elaborative processing and act as a catalyst for the subsequent steps in the system; organizing key ideas would help students plan and arrange information for later writing much as they would do in the drafting stage of writing. Rehearsing would engage them in active self-recitation and self-testing, thus helping them to monitor and question themselves and take corrective actions when needed; practicing would help students create from memory their own text which would answer their self-predicted essay questions, while evaluating would help them check whether they had created meaningful text that demonstrated their understanding of the content. Sixty-five college freshmen

were trained over a 3-week period to use either a question-answer recitation format or PORPE. All students took both pre- and post-study essay and multiple-choice tests. The results indicated that the students trained in the Porpe Study System scored significantly higher than students using a recitation format with questions similar to those found in textbooks or usually used by teachers. They scored higher on both recall and recognition items on the multiple-choice tests and on an essay scored for content, organization, and cohesion. It was concluded that "PORPE can be a potent, durable, and efficient study strategy for college students in their efforts to learn content area concepts" (p. 149).

In SPIN, Aylward (1990) focused on summarizing, predicting, inferencing, and notetaking. Using summary rules suggested by Brown and Day (1983), 50 eighth-grade students were trained to summarize and take notes. Through teacher modeling and worksheets they were given practice in predicting and making inferences about stories and content area materials. These students were given 10 weeks of continued practice in the use of SPIN in content area classes, while an equated control group studied the same material without instruction in SPIN. A comparison of pre- and post-test scores on measures of content indicated that students in the SPIN group scored significantly higher in knowledge of content as well as in ability to summarize, predict, infer, and take notes. SPIN differs from other study systems in that students are not advised to use the separate study strategies in sequence; that is, there are no "stages": they are not told to, first, predict, then read, and then, infer and take notes, and, finally, summarize. Instruction stresses all four strategies and encourages students to use them together.

Study systems, such as SQ3R, PORPE, or SPIN, should not be confused with teacher-directed lesson frameworks. Lesson frameworks help teachers structure and control learning in the classroom. In the Directed Reading Activity, or DRA, for example, Betts (1955) suggested stages in a reading lesson: exploring and building background knowledge, reading, discussion, and extension. By moving sequentially through the stages, teachers are better able to control student learning. The Directed Reading-Thinking Activity, or DR-TA (Stauffer, 1969), moves students through prediction and verification to considered judgments in 5 steps. The Guided Reading Procedure, or GRP (Manzo, 1975), has 8 steps to guide students, under the teacher's direction, from prereading to evaluation. K-W-L Plus (Carr & Ogle, 1987) has students recall what they know about the topic of a passage, decide what they want to learn from reading, and then identify what they have learned, using both mapping and summarizing. Such approaches may in time be internalized by students and become personal study systems for them, but their primary intent is to aid teachers.

IMPROVEMENT OF STUDY: FURTHER CONSIDERATIONS

At the present time, the convergence of a number of research areas seems to promise fresh insights into how students learn. Studies in learning theory, cognitive psychology, cognitive styles, reading, the writing process, and other areas are revealing interconnections between areas that point to new understandings about ways to improve study. Different theories and data lead to different data and theories; all lead to different ways of looking at learning. However, several concerns, questions, and issues, although certainly affected by research findings, need to be addressed less in terms of statistical analysis and measures and more in terms of professional considerations. Three such concerns are examined here.

First, students need a repertoire of study tools. Although enthusiastic advocates regularly promote one specific type of, say, notetaking, the latest version of SQ3R, or some particular strategy as a panacea, no single study skill, strategy, or system is demonstrably superior to others. The quick-and-easy ones often work only at certain times, for certain students, in certain situations. Those that do seem to focus attention effectively and promote deeper processing often demand great expenditures of time and effort on the part of students. In addition, the tools that show great promise—such as summarizing and both linear and diagrammatic outlining—usually require considerable training. Some study tools have demonstrated power but only in specific contexts, with students of a certain age, in one content area but not in another, with one kind of materials but not with others, and so on. To complicate matters further, not enough is yet known about cognitive styles (see, for example, Goodenough, 1976, or Kardash, Lukowski, & Bentmann, 1988) to generalize about the best strategies for independent learning. Due to these reasons and the fact that some research questions remain unaddressed while others are equivocal, it seems appropriate to introduce students to a wide array of study tools and encourage them to experiment to discover those that work most effectively for them in various situations.

Second, students need help in test-taking. Study skills, strategies, and systems are developed in school settings where achievement is measured by tests. Many teachers have suggested, therefore, that test-taking skills need to be developed along with study tools. They cite the positive relationship between test performance and the skills required to take tests (Crehan, Koehler, & Slakter, 1974; Kubistant, 1981; Lee & Alley, 1981; Taylor & White, 1982) and note the value to students of knowledge of test characteristics and formats to improve performance (Millman, Bishop, & Ebel, 1965). Many teachers show students how to prepare for tests by defining the content area to be studied, noting specialized vocabulary, as well as ideas and information stressed in class, and examining previous exams, study guides, outlines, notes, and assignments. They have encouraged students to generate their own questions for study, summarize difficult points, check other sources, and given tips about controlling test anxiety. In addition, many teachers at all levels have shared with students specific information about test formats, pacing during exams, writing essay tests, dealing with multiple-choice items, and so on. A variety of articles and handbooks are available to assist teachers in showing students how to take tests (see, for example, Pauk, 1984, or Devine & Meagher, 1989). Many teachers use specific strategies such as SCORER (S—Schedule your time; C—Check clue words; O—Omit difficult questions; R—Read Carefully; E—Estimate your answer; R—Review your work). Devised by Carman and Adams (1972), the strategy has been further developed and used in several studies (see Lee & Alley, 1981; Alley & Deshler, 1979; Ritter & Idol-Maestas, 1983). In a recent study, Ritter and Idol-Maestas (1986) found that the SCORER strategy worked successfully with both poor and above-average comprehenders and recommended such a test-taking strategy to help students earn optimal scores on tests. Although there may be ethical concerns about test coaching, which is specific to the content being examined (Rawl, 1984), test-wiseness (or test-sophistication) seems a reasonable objective of any program designed to improve independent study.

Third, students need study help in *all* classes. In many schools, guidance in independent learning is often relegated to special classes or courses taught by special teachers. Instructional programs in elementary and secondary schools (especially middle schools) meet one, two, or three times a week to introduce students to basic strategies, a study system, usually SQ3R, and a variety of so-called study skills, ranging from alphabetizing to using the card catalog. Such arrangements may make students more aware of the need to study, help foster positive study habits and attitudes, and introduce important study skills, strategies, and systems. However, no evidence exists that these arrangements lead to transfer or further growth. Most college-level programs have been similarly arranged: students, usually freshmen, meet one, two, or three times a week with a specialist who introduces basic skills, explains time-management, encourages the use of assignment books, and so on (Sherman, 1985; Reed, 1986). Again, no evidence exists that students transfer such learning to other college courses. Another point of view about the improvement of independent study has gained prominence in recent years (Devine, 1989). It suggests that instruction in how to study begin in the primary grades and continue through to the final college years and that it take place in content area classes under the guidance of content area teachers. A similar position is now taken by many college teachers and administrators who suggest that study techniques be taught not in separate freshman-year courses by specialists but by all college teachers (Donohoe, 1989). Learning how to learn on one's own may be too important to be the exclusive concern of specialists. It is the core of education.

References

Alley, G. R., & Deshler, D. D. (1979). *Teaching the learning disabled adolescent: Strategies and models.* Denver, CO: Love.

Anderson, R. C., & Biddle, W. B. (1975). On asking people questions about what they are reading. In G. H. Bower (Ed.), *The psychology of learning and motivation* (Vol. 9, pp. 89–132). New York: Academic Press.

Anderson, T. H. (1980). Study strategies and adjunct aids. In R. J. Spiro, B. C. Bruce, & W. F. Brewer (Eds.), *Theoretical issues in reading comprehension* (pp. 483–502). Hillsdale, NJ: Erlbaum.

Anderson, T. H., & Armbruster, B. B. (1984). Studying. In P. D. Pearson (Ed.), *Handbook of reading research* (pp. 657–679). New York: Longman.

Applebee, A. N. (1984). Writing and reasoning. *Review of Educational Research, 54,* 577–596.

Arnold, H. F. (1942). The comparative effectiveness of certain study techniques in the field of history. *Journal of Educational Psychology, 33,* 449–457.

Ausubel, D. P. (1960). The use of advance organizers in the learning and retention of meaningful verbal material. *Journal of Educational Psychology, 51,* 267–272.

Ausubel, D. P. (1978). In defense of advance organizers: A reply to critics. *Review of Educational Research, 48,* 251–257.

Aylward, M. (1990). *The SPIN reading/study skills system.* Unpublished doctoral dissertation. Lowell, MA: University of Lowell.

Bailey, N. S. (1988). S-RUN: Beyond SQ3R. *Journal of Reading, 32,* 170–171.

Barnett, J. E., Divester, F. J., & Rogozinski, J. T. (1981). What is learned in notetaking? *Journal of Educational Psychology, 73,* 181–192.

Barton, W. A. (1930). *Outlining as a study procedure.* New York: Teachers College, Columbia University.

Baumann, R. (1984). The effectiveness of a direct instruction paradigm for teaching main idea comprehension. *Reading Research Quarterly, 20,* 93–115.

Bean, T. W., & Steenyk, F. L. (1984). The effect of three forms of summarization instruction on sixth graders' summary writing and comprehension. *Journal of Reading Behavior, 16,* 297–307.

Betts, E. (1955). Reading as a thinking process. *The National Elementary Principal, 35,* 90–99.

Bizinkauskas, P. A. (1970). *An evaluation of the effectiveness of tape-recorded note-taking versus written note-taking versus rereading as a study technique.* Unpublished doctoral dissertation. Boston, MA: Boston University.

Bragstad, B. J., & Stumpf, S. M. (1987). *A guidebook for teaching study skills and motivation.* Needham, MA: Allyn and Bacon.

Bretzing, B. B., & Kulhavy, R. W. (1979). Note taking and depth of processing. *Contemporary Educational Psychology, 4,* 145–153.

Bretzing, B. B., & Kulhavy, R. W. (1981). Note taking and passage style. *Journal of Educational Psychology, 73,* 242–250.

Brown, A. L., Campione, J. C., & Day, J. D. (1980). *Learning to learn: On training students to learn from texts.* (Report No. CS 006 135). Cambridge, MA: Bolt, Beranek and Newman, Inc. (ERIC Document Reproduction Service No. ED 203 297).

Brown, A. L., Campione, J. C., & Day, J. D. (1981). Learning to learn: On training students to learn from texts. *Educational Researcher, 10,* 14–21.

Brown, A. L., & Day, J. D. (1983). Macrorules for summarizing texts: The development of expertise. *Journal of Verbal Learning and Verbal Behavior, 22,* 1–14.

Carman, R. A., & Adams, W. R. (1972). *Study skills: A student's guide for survival.* New York: John Wiley.

Carr, E., & Ogle, D. (1987). K-W-L Plus: A Strategy for comprehension and summarization. *Journal of Reading, 30,* 626–631.

Corkill, A. J., Bruning, R. H., & Glover, J. A. (1988). Advance organizers: Concrete versus abstract. *Journal of Educational Research, 82,* 76–81.

Courtney, L. (1965). Organization produced. In H. L. Herber (Ed.), *Developing study skills in secondary schools* (pp. 77–96). Newark, DE: International Reading Association.

Crehan, K. D., Koehler, R. A., & Slakter, M. J. (1974). Longitudinal studies on test-wiseness. *Journal of Educational Measurement, 11,* 209–212.

Cunningham, J. R. (1982). Generating interaction between schemata and text. In J. A. Niles & L. A. Harris (Eds.), *New inquiries in reading research and instruction* (pp. 42–47). Rochester, NY: National Reading Conference.

Dansereau, D. F. McDonald, B. A., Long, G. L., Atkinson, T. R., Ellis, A. M., Collins, K. W., Williams, S., & Evans, S. H. (1974). *The development and assessment of an effective learning strategy program.* (Rep. No. 3). Fort Worth, TX: Texas Christian University.

Devine, T. G. (1986). *Teaching reading comprehension: From theory to practice.* Needham, MA: Allyn and Bacon, Inc.

Devine, T. G. (1987). *Teaching study skills: A guide for teachers, Rev. Ed.* Needham, MA: Allyn and Bacon, Inc.

Devine, T. G. (1989). Not just reading—Study skills, too. *New England Reading Association Journal, 25,* 7–14.

Devine, T. G., and Meagher, L. D. (1989). *Mastering study skills: A student guide.* Englewood Cliffs, NJ: Prentice Hall.

Doctorow, M, Wittrock, M. C., & Marks, C. (1978). Generative processes in reading comprehension. *Journal of Educational Psychology, 70,* 109–118.

Donohoe, J. S. (1989). *The impact of faculty participation in a college study skills program.* Unpublished doctoral dissertation. Boston, MA: Northeastern University.

Duell, O. K. (1978). Overt and covert use of objectives of different cognitive levels. *Contemporary Journal of Educational Psychology, 3,* 239–245.

Eanet, M. G., & Manzo, A. V. (1976). REAP—A strategy for improving reading/writing/study skills. *Journal of Reading, 19,* 647–652.

Einstein, G. O., Morris, J., Smith, S. (1985). Notetaking, individual differences, and memory for lecture information. *Journal of Educational Psychology, 77,* 522–532.

Farquhar, W. W., Krumboltz, J. D., & Wrenn, C. G. (1960). *Learning to study.* New York: Ronald Press.

Feathers, K. M. (1987). Learning to learn: Case studies of the process. *Reading Research and Instruction, 26,* 264–274.

Frase, L. T., & Schwartz, B. J. (1975). Effect of question production and answering on prose recall. *Journal of Educational Psychology, 67,* 628–635.

Gates, A. I. (1917). Recitation as a factor in memorizing. *Archives of Psychology, 40* (1917).

Glynn, S. M. (1978). Capturing reader's attention by means of typographic cueing strategies. *Educational Technology, 18,* 7–12.

Goodenough, D. R. (1976). The role of individual differences in field dependence as a factor in learning and memory. *Psychological Bulletin, 83,* 675–694.

Graham, K. G., & Robinson, H. A. (1984). *Study skills handbook: A guide for all teachers.* Newark, DE: International Reading Association.

Graves, M. F., & Cooke, C. L. (1980). Effects of previewing difficult short stories for high school students. *Research on Reading in Secondary Schools, 6,* 38–54.

Graves, M. F., Cooke, C. L., & La Berge, M. J. (1983). Effects of previewing difficult short stories in low ability junior high school students' comprehension, recall, and attitude. *Reading Research Quarterly, 18,* 262–276.

Graves, M. F., & Palmer, R. J. (1981). Validating previewing as a method of improving fifth and sixth grade students' comprehension of short stories. *Michigan Reading Journal, 15,* 1–3.

Gustafson, D. J., & Pederson, J. E. (1985). SQ3R: Surveying and questioning the relevant, recent (and not so recent) research. (Report No. CS 008 436). Milwaukee, WI: Great Lakes regional Conference of the International Reading Association. (ERIC Document Reproduction Service No. ED 269 736).

Hansell, T. S. (1978). Stepping up to outlining. *Journal of Reading, 22,* 248–252.

Hare, V. C., & Borchardt, K. M. (1984). Direct instruction of summarization skills. *Reading Research Quarterly, 20,* 62–78.

Harris, A. J. (1971). *How to increase reading abilities.* 5th ed. New York: McKay.

Hawks, P., McLeod, N. P., & Jonassen, D. H. (1985). Graphic organizers in texts, courseware, and supplementary materials. In D. H. Jonassen

(Ed.), *Technology of text,* Vol. 2. (pp. 250–262). Englewood Cliffs, NJ: Educational Technology Publications.

Hayes, D. A., & Tierney, R. J. (1982). Developing readers' knowledge through analogy. *Reading Research Quarterly, 17,* 256–280.

Hidi, S., & Anderson, V. (1986). Producing written summaries: Task demands, cognitive operations, and implications for instruction. *Review of Educational Research, 56,* 473–493.

Jenkins, J. J. (1979). Four points to remember: A tetrahedral model and memory experiments. In L. S. Cermak, & F. I. M. Craik (Eds.), *Levels of processing in human memory* (pp. 429–446). Hillsdale, NJ: Erlbaum.

Johns, J. L., & McNamara, L. P. (1980). The SQ3R study technique: A forgotten research target. *Journal of Reading, 23,* 705–708.

Johnson, S. (1973). A system for the diagnosis and treatment of test study problems. In G. Kerstiens (Ed.), *Proceedings of the sixth annual conference of the Western College Reading Association.* Santa Fe Springs, CA: Western College Reading Association.

Kahn, N. (1984) *More learning in less time: A guide for effective study.* Upper Montclair, NJ: Boynton/Cook Publishers.

Kardash, C. M., Lukowski, L., & Bentmann, L. (1988). Effects of cognitive style and immediate testing on learning from a lecture. *Journal of Educational Research, 81,* 360–364.

Kiewra, K. A. (1984). Acquiring effective notetaking skills: An alternative to professional notetaking. *Journal of Reading, 27,* 299–302.

Kiewra, K. A., DuBois, N. F., Christian, D., & McShane, A. (1988). Providing study notes: Comparison of three types of notes for review. *Journal of Educational Psychology, 80,* 595–597.

Kiewra, K. A., & Fletcher, H. J. (1983). A levels of processing approach for determining the relationship between note encoding and achievement. Paper presented at the southwest Psychological Association, San Antonio, Texas.

Kiewra, K. A., & Frank, B. M. (1988). Encoding and external-storage effects of personal lecture notes, skeletal notes, and detailed notes for field-independent and field-dependent learners. *Journal of Educational Research, 81,* 143–148.

King, J. R., Biggs, S., & Lipsky, S. (1984). Students' self-questioning and summarizing as reading-study strategies. *Journal of Reading Behavior, 16,* 205–218.

Kubistant, T. (1981). Test performance: The neglected skill. *Education, 102,* 53–55.

Kulhavy, R. W., Dyer, J. W., & Silver, L. (1975). The effects of note-taking and test expectancy on the learning of text material. *Journal of Educational Research, 68,* 363–365.

Langer, J. A. (1986). Learning through writing: Study skills in the content areas. *Journal of Reading, 29,* 400–406.

Lee, P., & Alley, G. G. (1981). *Training junior high LD students to use a test-taking strategy.* (Research Report No. 38) Lawrence, KS: University of Kansas, Institute for Research in Learning Disabilities.

Linden, M., & Wittrock, M. C. (1981). The teaching of reading comprehension according to the model of generative learning. *Reading Research Quarterly, 17,* 44–57.

Manzo, A. (1975). Guided reading procedures. *Journal of Reading, 18,* 287–291.

Martin, M. A. (1985). Students' applications of self-questioning study techniques: An investigation of their efficiency. *Reading Psychology, 6,* 69–83.

Mathews, C. O. (1938). Comparison of methods of study for immediate and delayed recall. *Journal of Educational Psychology, 29,* 101–106.

Maxwell, M. (1980). *Improving student learning skills.* San Francisco, CA: Jossey-Bass.

McAndrew, D. A. (1983). Underlining and notetaking: Some suggestions from research. *Journal of Reading, 27,* 103–108.

McNeil, J., & Donant, L. (1982). Summarization strategy for improving reading comprehension. In J. A. Niles & L. A. Harris (Eds.), *New inquiries in reading research and instruction.* Rochester, NY: The National Reading Conference.

Millman, J., Bishop, C. H., & Ebel, R. (1965). An analysis of test-wiseness. *Educational and Psychological Measurement, 25,* 707–726.

Morse, J. M. (1975). *The effects of question generation, question answering, and reading on prose learning.* Unpublished doctoral dissertation. Eugene, OR: University of Oregeon. *Dissertation Abstracts International,* 1977, *37,* 5709A-5710A. (University microfilms No. 77–4750).

Newell, G. E. (1984). Learning from writing in two content areas: A case study/protocol analysis. *Research in the Teaching of English, 18,* 265–285.

Nist, S. L., & Hogrebe, M. C. (1987). The role of underlining and annotating in remembering textual information. *Reading Research and Instruction, 27,* 12–25.

Norman, M. H., & Norman, E. S. (1968). *Successful reading.* New York: Holt, Rinehart and Winston.

Palincsar, A. S., & Brown, A. L. (1983). *Reciprocal teaching of comprehension-monitoring activities.* (Technical Report No. 269). Champaign, IL: University of Illinois, Center for the Study of Reading. (ERIC Document Reproduction Service No. ED 225 135).

Palmer, R., & Pope, C. (1984). *Braintrain: Studying for success.* London: E. & F. N. Spoon.

Pauk, W. (1974). *How to study in college,* 2nd ed. Boston: Houghton Mifflin.

Pauk, W. (1984). Preparing for exams. *Reading World, 23,* 386–387.

Pichert, J. W. (1979). *Sensitivity to what is important in prose.* (Report No. CS 005 172). Cambridge, MA: Bolt, Beranek and Newman. (ERIC Document Reproduction Service No. ED 179 946).

Pio, E., & Andre, M. L. D. A. (1977). Paraphrasing highlighted statements and learning from prose. Paper presented at the annual meeting of the American Educational Research Association, New York, NY, April, 1977.

Policastro, M. (1975). Notetaking: The key to college success. *Journal of Reading, 18,* 372–375.

Poppleton, P. K., & Austwick, K. (1964). A comparison of programmed learning and note-taking at two age levels. *British Journal of Educational Psychology, 34,* 43–50.

Rawl, E. H. (1984). Test-taking strategies can be the key to improving test scores. *National Association of Secondary School Principals Bulletin, 68,* 108–112.

Reed, M. E. B. (1986). Management strategies to assist students in improving learning skills. *Journal of Developmental Education, 9,* 2–4.

Rickards, J. P., & August, G. J. (1975). Generative underlining strategies in prose recall. *Journal of Educational Psychology, 67,* 860–865.

Rickards, J. P., & McCormick, C. B. (1988). Effect of interspersed conceptual prequestions on note-taking in listening comprehension. *Journal of Educational Psychology, 80,* 592–594.

Rinehart, S. D., Stahl, S. A., & Erickson, L. G. (1986). Some effects of summarization training on reading. *Reading Research Quarterly, 21,* 422–436.

Ritter, S. A., & Idol-Maestas, L. (1983). Training EMH senior high school students to use a test-taking strategy. Unpublished manuscript. Urbana-Champaign, IL: Department of Special Education, University of Illinois.

Ritter, S. A., & Idol-Maestas, L. (1986). Teaching middle school students to use a test-taking strategy. *Journal of Educational Research, 79,* 350–357.

Robinson, F. (1970). *Effective Study,* 4th ed. New York: Harper and Row.

Salisbury, R. (1935). Some effects of training in outlining. *English Journal, 24,* 111–116.

Santeusanio, R. P. (1983). *A practical approach to content area reading*. Reading, MA: Addison-Wesley.

Santeusanio, R. P. (1988). *Study skills and strategies*. Baltimore: College Skills Center.

Schell, T. R., & Rocchio, D (1975). A comparison of underlining strategies for improving reading comprehension and retention. In G. H. McNinch & W. D. Miller (Eds.), *Reading: Convention and Inquiry* (pp. 391–399). Clemson, SC: National Reading Conference.

Schultz, C. B., & DiVesta, F. J. (1972) Effects of passage organization and note-taking on the selection of clustering strategies and on recall of textual material. *Journal of Educational Psychology, 63,* 244–252.

Sherman, T. M. (1985). Learning improvement programs: A review of controllable influences. *Journal of Higher Education, 56,* 85–100.

Shrager, L., & Mayer, R. E. (1989). Note-taking fosters generative learning strategies in novices. *Journal of Educational Psychology, 81,* 263–264.

Simons, S. M. (1989). PSRT—A reading comprehension strategy. *Journal of Reading, 32,* 419–427.

Simpson, M. L., Hayes, C. G., Stahl, N., Connor, R. T., & Weaver, D. (1988). An initial validation of a study strategy system. *Journal of Reading Behavior, 20,* 149–180.

Slater, W. H., Graves, M., & Piché, G. L. (1985). Effects of structural organizers on ninth-grade students' comprehension and recall of four patterns of expository prose. *Reading Research Quarterly, 20,* 189–202.

Smith, P. L., & Tompkins, G. E. (1988). Structured notetaking: A new strategy for content area readers. *Journal of Reading, 32,* 46–53.

Spencer, F. (1978). SQ3R: Several queries regarding relevant research. In J. L. Vaughan & P. J. Gaus (Eds.), *Research on reading in secondary schools* (pp. 285–293). Tucson, AZ: University of Arizona.

Staton, T. H. (1954). *How to study*. Nashville, TN: McQuiddley Printing Co.

Stauffer, R. G. (1969). *Directing reading maturity as a cognitive process*. New York: Harper and Row.

Stetson, E. G. (1981). Improving textbook learning with S4R: A strategy for teachers, not students. *Reading Horizons, 22,* 129–135.

Stevens, K. C. (1982). Can we improve reading by teaching background information? *Journal of Reading, 25,* 326–329.

Stewart-Dore, N. (1982). Where is the learning we have lost in information?: Strategies for effective reading in content areas. Paper presented at the 9th World Congress in Reading, International Reading association, Dublin, Ireland, July, 1982. (ED 322 138)

Taylor, C., & White, K. R. (1982). The effect of reinforcement and training on group standardized test behavior. *Journal of Educational Measurement, 19,* 199–209.

Thomas, E., & Robinson, H. A. (1972). *Improving reading in every classroom*. Boston, MA: Allyn and Bacon.

Tierney, R. J., & Cunningham, J. W. (1984). Research in teaching reading comprehension. In P. D. Pearson (Ed.), *Handbook of reading research* (pp. 609–655). New York: Longman.

Todd, W., & Kessler, C. C. (1971). Influence of response mode, sex, reading ability and level of difficulty as four measures of recall of meaningful written material. *Journal of Educational Psychology, 62,* 229–234.

Tudor, I. (1986). Advance organisers as adjuncts to L2 reading comprehension. *Journal of Research in Reading, 9,* 103–115.

Wade, S. E., & Trathen, W. (1989). Effect of self-selected study methods on learning. *Journal of Educational Psychology, 81,* 40–47.

Walker, J. (1979). Sequeezing study skills (into, out of) content areas. In R. T. Vacca & J. A. Meagher (Eds.), *Reading through Content* (pp. 137–148). Storrs, CT: University of Connecticut.

Willmore, D. J. (1966). *A comparison of four methods of studying a textbook*. Unpublished doctoral dissertation. Minneapolis, MN: University of Minnestota.

Winograd, P. N. (1984). Strategic difficulties in summarizing texts. *Reading Research Quarterly, 19,* 404–425.

·35·

WRITING

Anne Haas Dyson
Sarah Warshauer Freedman

Five-year-old Sharon had been standing a few feet from the classroom writing center, observing her friends at work. Anxious to involve Sharon in the writing, the adult observer inquired, "You gonna' write today too, Sharon?"

"Well," said Sharon, "how do you do it?" (Dyson, 1981, 776).

While few children are as straightforward as Sharon, most student writers, including adults, expect their teachers to help them answer the "How-do-you-do-it?" question. And, despite the deceptively simple nature of the question, providing supportive answers is a complex challenge.

Some of the complexity of teaching writing comes from the nature of writing itself. As we illustrate in this chapter, writing can be an avenue for individual expression and, at the same time, it can serve to reflect or proclaim the individual author's membership in a social group. Further, writing is conceived of as a skill and yet, at the same time, that skill is itself a process dependent upon a range of other skills and, moreover, a process that is kaleidoscopic, shaped by the author's changing purposes of writing.

Some of the complexity of teaching writing comes from the nature of classrooms as educational settings. Teachers negotiate between the class as a social group and individual students in that group, a challenging task when individuals number in the twenties and thirties or more and when social/cultural member-

ship is diverse. Moreover, teachers often negotiate between their desires to teach writing as a purposeful process and to teach the varied "skills" conceived of as integral to that process, skills differentially controlled by their students.

To manage this complex teaching act, teachers of all levels must become comfortable with and careful observers of writers and of writing, seeking the sort of information about students that helps them as teachers respond to the questions—the challenges—inherent in their students' efforts. In the following three sections of this chapter, we review the kinds of interrelated research knowleege about writing that may inform teachers' observations of their students and their decisions about how to best support their students' efforts.

First, since ways of using written language vary with different social situations, we review research on how literacy functions in varied communities, including both the classroom and the larger community the student inhabits outside the classroom. This research may support teachers' efforts to build on the foundation of each student's literacy experiences.

Second, since writing is a complex process, one involving the orchestration of many kinds of skills, we review research on the composing process. Such knowledge may support teachers' efforts to observe individual writer's ways of composing, including their successes and challenges. On the basis of such obser-

The project presented, or reported herein, was performed pursuant to a grant from the Office of Educational Research and Improvement/Department of Education (OERI/ED) for the Center for the Study of Writing. However, the opinions expressed herein do not necessarily reflect the position or policy of the OERI/ED and no official endorsement by the OERI/ED should be inferred.

This chapter is a major revision of Freedman, S. Warshauer, Dyson, A. Haas, Flower, L., and Chafe, W. *Research in Writing: Past, Present, and Future,* Technical Report No. 1 of the Center for the Study of Writing, University of California, Berkeley, California. That report was itself based on the Mission Statement from "A Proposal to Establish a Center for Study of Writing" submitted to the National Institute of Education by The University of California at Berkeley in collaboration with Carnegie Mellon University, March, 1985. In parts of the process of writing that missions statement, we worked closely with Arthur Applebee, Shirley Brice Heath, and Judith Langer at Stanford University. They deserve credit for their contributions to many of the ideas behind the mission statement. In addition, we would like to thank Peg Griffin, Luis Moll, and Michael Cole of the University of California at San Diego for their assistance at many points in its development. Special thanks go to Dean Bernard Gifford at Berkeley, who not only made substantive contributions throughout the development of the proposal, but who also gave his full support, constant encouragement, and substantial help in putting the proposal together. Finally, we would like to thank Carol Heller and Alíce Guerrero for their assistance in producing this manuscipt.

754

vations, teachers may help writers overcome difficulties that cannot be seen on the page, ward off problems before they occur in print, and thus, ease students' ways into writing.

Finally, since writing is a developmental process, one in which today's ways of composing change in complex ways into tomorrow's, we review research on the development of writing. Such knowledge may help teachers appreciate the signs of progress that may be hidden amidst students' sighs and scratch-outs. Too, such knowledge may support teachers' efforts to understand the questions students cannot articulate and to appreciate the answers they figure out for themselves. Further, knowledge about developmental processes may guide teachers to see the kinds of support individual students might find most helpful.

The research we review can provide information for teachers, but it can not provide prescriptions to follow, techniques proven to work for all learners. Rather, it can provide information that might help focus teacher observations, deepen insights, and, in the end, inform the crucial decision-making that is the daily work of all teachers—when to push a student for more, when to praise what may seem to be "errors," when to encourage students to write collaboratively, when to call a parent in.

As suggested by our review, this decision-making is informed by observations of both the classroom community and individual class members. Each student has a unique rhythm, a particular pitch, but that individual quality is a part of, and is shaped by, the rhythm and pitch—the communal quality—of the classroom as a whole. Just as musical notes play differently in varied compositions, so do our students reveal themselves differently in different combinations of others. We, then, aim through this review to contribute to educators' understanding of writing's compositional possibilities, of the promise and challenges of each student, and of their own potentials, in collaboration with their students, to further literacy growth in their classrooms.

THE USES OF WRITING

Five-year-old Sharon's "how-do-you-do-it" question is difficult to answer, in part, because the hows are shaped by the whys, whos, and whats: Who wants to write, to or for whom, about what, and why? Indeed, in the lives of children, as in the lives of whole communities, literacy prospers if and when compelling reasons exist for writing and when the information conveyed through that writing is a valued part of the social network—when it helps people mediate relationships with other people and reflect on their own lives (Heath, 1986; Schieffelin & Cochran-Smith, 1984).

In fact, children like Sharon are first introduced to literacy within their homes and communities and within the social and emotional context of relationships. For example, in their families, list-making may be at the center of family planning for a shopping trip, an illegible phone message or returned check may be surrounded by a family argument, a note from a teacher may elicit parental confusion, pride, or anger, while an "I love you" note from a child might evoke an oral response and a

hug. Children first learn of print's social significance within the context of familial occasions, where things happen around and through particular kinds of print (Gundlach, McLane, Scott, & McNamee, 1985; Heath, 1983; Taylor, 1983; Tizard & Hughes, 1984). Writing, then, like speech, is a cultural tool, one that members of a society use to carry on their lives together and that they pass on to their children (Scribner & Cole, 1981).

Variation in Writing's Function and Forms

The tool of writing is viewed by many scholars as contributing to human cultures in unique ways (Goody, 1968; Goody & Watt, 1963; Olson, 1977; Ong, 1982). For example, Goody argues:

The importance of writing lies in its creating a new medium of communication between [people]. Its essential service is to objectify speech, to provide language with a material correlative, a set of visible signs. In this material form, speech can be transmitted over space and preserved over time; what people say and think can be rescued from the transitoriness of oral communication. (1968, pp. 1–2)

In the last decade anthropologists, linguists, and psychologists have tried to specify writing's varied functions and forms—its usefulness—in a range of situations. Some scholars have worked to characterize the features of written language that make it such a potentially powerful medium of communication in particular situations. In this work, written language is contrasted with oral language. Written language, researchers and theorists argue, can be constructed so that it is ultimately less dependent upon a specific context. Authors can pack much meaning onto the printed page, weaving words together tightly through such linguistic features as subordinate clauses, prepositional phrases, and adjective phrases (Chafe, 1982, 1985; Johnston, 1979; Tannen, 1982, 1984a, 1984b).

By tightly structuring words, meanings are made explicit—that is, the connections between ideas and the qualifications of those ideas are deliberately put into words. "On the other hand," "however," "despite this" are the sorts of phrases we expect in written essays. Other scholars argue that the development of writing had intellectual consequences in the history of humankind, leading to the development of abstract, logical reasoning (Goody & Watt, 1963; Olson, 1977).

Yet, this vision of writing as explicit—as able to exist on its own, meaningful for anyone in any situation—contrasts sharply with the sorts of cozy home literacy scenes just discussed. Clearly there are varied styles of written language, just as there are varied styles of oral language (Chafe & Danielewicz, 1987). For this reason, the theory that the development of writing skill leads inevitably to the production of expository prose has been challenged. Ways of using both oral and written language are interrelated not only with contexts for using language but also with ways of living—historical and geographical conditions; social and economic resources and opportunities; religious beliefs, values, and motivations (Cole & Nicolopoulous, in press; Gee, 1988; Heath, 1983; Philips, 1975; Scribner & Cole, 1981). In this sense, written language is always "embedded"—it always figures into particular kinds of communicative events. Its form varies depending upon its uses.

Many scholars have investigated how writing varies from situation to situation. For example, the study of literature and rhetoric has produced taxonomies of textual types (e.g., Kinneavy, 1971; Lundsford & Ede, 1984; Winterowd, 1975). And authors concerned with the teaching of writing have produced other categories (Britton, Burgess, Martin, McLeod, & Rosen, 1975; Emig, 1971). They distinguish kinds of writing according to the purpose for writing (e.g., to persuade or to inform) and the features associated with those purposes.

Others have investigated how writing varies across situations, considering how the activity of writing is socially organized within the ongoing life of particular groups (Basso, 1974; Philips, 1975; Szwed, 1981). Researchers working within this tradition are called "ethnographers of communication" (Gumperz & Hymes, 1972; Hymes, 1962). They study social activities that are centered around reading or writing, activities often termed "literacy events" (Heath, 1982; Teale, Estrada, & Anderson, 1981). Like "speech events" (Hymes, 1972), literacy events are characterized by varied components, including setting, participants (senders, recipients), purposes and goals, message form, content, channel, key or tone, and rules governing the sort of writing and talking that should occur (Basso, 1974). For example, informal letter-writing events differ from joint committee-report-writing events, which differ from list-making events.

Both the social and the cognitive consequences of written language, then, depend upon the specific nature of the written language events, including the goals and the cognitive processes those events entail. In other words, it is not writing per se but the sorts of social situations in which writing is embedded that determine its ultimate human effects. For example, writing to memorize texts may influence individuals' rote memory, but such literacy practice would not affect performance on a logical reasoning task (Scribner & Cole, 1981). From a social point of view, a person who finds writing a letter to a relative a comfortable use of literacy may not be comfortable writing an academic essay—such impersonal writing for an unknown audience may be contrary to that individual's sense of self in relationship to other people (Scollon & Scollon, 1981).

The most extensive study of how literacy is used in a contemporary American community has been done by Heath (1983). She studied language use in two working-class communities and in the homes of middle-class teachers in the Piedmont Carolinas. Individuals in all three settings were literate, in that all made some use of written language, but only the middle-class community used written language—and talked about written language—in ways compatible with the literacy models used in school. For example, people in all communities made lists and wrote notes, but only those in the middle-class neighborhood would bring home expository sorts of writing tasks, such as writing summaries or reports.

Heath worked with teachers to develop strategies for making school ways of using and talking about written language sensible to students from working-class as well as middle-class communities. For example, a primary grade teacher incorporated environmental print (e.g., labels on cans and boxes, street signs, store advertisements and price tags) into her classroom. Heath (1980) describes the philosophy of this teacher:

Reading and writing are things you do all the time—at home, on the bus, riding your bike, at the barber shop. You can read, and you do everyday before you ever come to school. You can also play baseball and football at home, at the park, wherever you want to, but when you come to school or go to a summer program at the Neighborhood Center, you get help on techniques, the gloves to buy, the way to throw, and the way to slide. School does that for reading and writing. We all read and write a lot of the time, lots of places. School isn't much different except that here we work on techniques, and we practice a lot—under a coach. I'm the coach (pp. 130–131).

An intermediate grade teacher helped her students become ethnographers, who talked, read, and wrote of the folk concepts about agriculture in their local community and the relationship of those concepts to "scientific" concepts. A high school teacher encouraged students to create documents and videos explaining to senior citizen groups the meanings of complex written forms, like housing regulations and warranties. At all levels, students discussed differences in how people used oral and written language, thereby developing their comfort with the talk about oral and written language so prevalent in schools as well as developing their capacity to deliberately manipulate language to suit different social occasions.

Although studies of literacy in varied cultural groups are helpful, sensitizing us to the rich diversity of literacy use in our society, clearly teachers cannot all do extensive studies in the homes of students. But teachers can provide curricular time and space for students to talk about their out-of-school lives, providing teachers with insight into possible ways of building bridges, making connections (Hymes & Cazden, 1980).

Too, the variability of writing's forms and functions suggests that the formal school curriculum recognize variable functions and forms (Florio & Clark, 1982). Defining writing more broadly might allow more students to see themselves officially as writers and would allow teachers more footholds from which to build—more ways of tapping students' interest in print. (For an illustration of such as rich literacy curriculum, see Edelsky & Smith's [1984] description of a sixth-grade curriculum that recognized a variety of writing purposes and forms, including signs, lists, and more extended discourse forms, in a variety of content areas.)

Literacy in the Classroom Community

A "literacy community" is not synonymous with a "cultural community" (Teale, Estrada, & Anderson, 1981). Just as speech communities (Gumperz, 1971) may be occupational or interest specific, so may literacy communities. The classroom itself can be considered a literacy community, one with special ways of using and talking about written language. Thus, the classroom can create or restrict the sorts of opportunities students have to become literate. In this section, we look closely at the nature of the classroom as a context for writing.

In trying to understand how literacy functions in the classroom community, a basic question is, what is the nature of the kinds of literacy activities that occur there? This kind of question can allow teachers insight into the sorts of bridges they are building for children, both from the literacy uses in the home to the classroom and from the classroom to the workplace (Gundlach, Farr, & Cook-Gumperz, in press). In addition, it can allow teachers to evaluate the ways in which literacy becomes meaningful inside classrooms.

For example, Applebee (1981), at the secondary school level, and Florio and Clark (1982; Clark & Florio, 1981; Clark, et al., 1981), at the elementary school level, have documented how many school writing opportunities restrict children from intellectually and socially engaging in the writing process. For example, writing's format and much of its content might be provided by a commercial publisher on a worksheet or by the teacher, as in boardwork; in such cases, students do not have to formulate their own thoughts. As Hudson (1988) illustrates, the more students control the form and content of their writing, the more likely they may be to perceive even assigned writing as they own.

Other researchers have focused on unofficial (child-controlled) writing, the kind that may exist in the "underground writing curriculum" (Dyson, 1985c). These researchers are primarily interested in how students create their own opportunities to learn. For example, Fiering (1981) and Gilmore (1983) studied the unofficial writing activities of intermediate-grade students in inner-city schools, noting that students who may be viewed as poor writers by their teachers may in fact make extensive use of writing for their own purposes. Asher (1988) provides similar findings for inner city high school students.

In order to look in more fine-grained ways at classroom writing events—to begin to understand exactly how teachers and students interactively create them—we must step back and consider how teachers and students interactively create schooling itself. The concept of the classroom as a social system jointly constructed by teachers and students has been dramatized by studies that began in the 1950s (Henry, 1955, 1963; Jackson, 1968; Leacock, 1969; Rist, 1970, 1973; see reviews by Bogdan & Biklen, 1982, and Hamilton, 1983).

In the 1970s, researchers began to focus specifically on the language of the classroom, arguing that it was, after all, through language that teaching and learning occurred and, thus, through language that insight could be gained into the social context of learning (see review, Cazden, 1986; also Cazden, 1988). This research, much of which has been conducted in elementary classrooms, has revealed the varied demands made by classroom activities. It is not enough for students to know in an academic sense—they must know how to display what they know through appropriate talk (e.g., Bremme & Erickson, 1977; Green & Wallat, 1979; Mehan, 1979; Merritt, 1982; Shultz & Florio, 1979; Wilkinson, 1982). That is, they must be familiar and comfortable with the kinds of questions that teachers ask, with the ways people take turns speaking, or with the sorts of relationships expected among the children themselves (relationships that are often competitive rather than cooperative).

In the schools, writing is taught as teachers and students talk about writing. Thus, the literature on classroom language can inform teachers' efforts to take advantage of the rich interac-

tional potential of the classroom. For example, some kinds of relationships between teachers and students may be particularly productive for written language growth. Britton (1989) argues for the importance of collaborative relationships between teachers and students, in which teachers do not relinquish their authority but do allow children choices in their daily activities. Wells (1986) discusses the instructional implications of his study of parent/child interaction during first language acquisition; he stresses the importance of teachers, like parents, responding to students' written initiatives, helping them develop *their* ideas, an emphasis compatible with the recent pedagogical emphasis on dialogue journals (Staton, Shuy, Peyton, & Reed, 1988) and on teacher-student writing conferences (e.g., Applebee, 1984; Calkins, 1983, 1986; Graves, 1983; Freedman, 1987a) to be discussed in a later section.

Despite teachers' best intentions for planning productive writing activities, students may not interpret those writing opportunities as teachers have planned them. The writing opportunities seemingly available to students from a teacher's or an observer's point of view may not, in fact, be realized in students' interpretations of those events. Students may differ in their social interpretations of the events (e.g., who, in fact, the audience is, what the actual purpose of the event is, what the evaluative standards are) (Clark & Florio, 1981; Dyson, 1985b; Freedman, 1987a; Sperling & Freedman, 1987). They may also have differing conceptions about writing and written language than those underlying an activity planned by the teacher. For example, they may not assume the analytic approach to language that underlies and is taken for granted by many beginning literacy programs (Dyson, 1984a, 1984b). They may have differing notions of how narratives are structured or even what stories are (Heath, 1983; Michaels & Cook-Gumperz, 1979; Cazden, 1988).

One particularly potent source of tension between teachers and students is the relationship among students themselves that is expected in the classroom. The peer social network interacts in complex ways with teaching and learning, at times supporting and, at other times, interfering. For example, peers have been found to be effective teachers and collaborative learners (Cooper, Marquis, & Ayers-Lopez, 1982; Gere, 1987; Newman, Griffin, & Cole, 1984; Steinberg & Cazden, 1979; Wilkinson, 1982). On the other hand, if peer group values conflict with classroom values, children may reject academic demands; among those aspects of school life most often cited as divisive are those that touch on children's relationships with each other—children having to work silently, to value adult more than self and peer approval, to compete with friends for that adult approval (Gilbert & Gay, 1985; Gilmore, 1983; Labov, 1982; Philips, 1972; Tharp et al., 1984). In writing classrooms in particular, students having to evaluate each other's work can generate tension (Freedman, 1987b).

Nonetheless, students' desires for each others' companionship and approval can be exploited. Through informal talk during writing, children may learn how it is that writing figures into human relationships, as peers respond both critically and playfully to their efforts (Daiute, 1989; Dyson, 1987b, 1988a). Through more structured peer conferences, modeled after teacher/student conferences, students may be guided to attend to each other's writing in particular ways (Bruce, 1987; Gere, 1987; Graves, 1983; Nystrand, 1986; Sowers, 1985). Students can also use written language to establish relationships with students in other grade levels, other schools, cities, or states, or even other countries (e.g., Freedman & McLeod, 1988; Green, 1985; Heath & Branscombe, 1985), relationships that can provide them with engaging but potentially demanding audiences.

No doubt we have much to learn about how particular kinds of relationships between teachers and students and among students themselves—and the sorts of talk that enact those relationships—influence students' learning in our very diverse society. For example, many pedagogical strategies for writing stress teacher questioning of students; that questioning is meant to help students expand and develop their ideas. And yet, much research has documented how uncomfortable some students may be in situations where adults repeatedly question them about their work; this discomfort has been particularly noted in children who are not of the same ethnic or social class as their teacher (Labov, 1970; Tizard & Hughes, 1984). As we explore the characteristics of varied classrooms serving students from varied backgrounds we may be able to articulate better the sorts of experiences that are critical for writing growth (e.g., opportunity to talk about, reflect upon writing in particular ways) from the particular shapes that critical experience can take (the variety of ways such opportunities can be provided).

The Evaluation of Written Language

In the classroom community, Sharon's "How-do-you-do-it?" question may soon be overshadowed by her teacher's inquiry, "How well can *you* do it?". For a major educational issue is determining how well the writing of individual students, whole classes, whole school districts, indeed whole countries is progressing. How can student progress be measured? How can successful instruction be identified? And, an even more basic question, what is "good" writing? As will be discussed in the section on writing development, there is no one description of what writing progress looks like throughout the school years. Still, there are ways to document progress, ways which we will discuss here.

Inside Classrooms. The most common classroom practices for evaluating student writing have proven problematic: writing comments on student papers and, particularly for intermediate and secondary school students, grading (Searle & Dillon, 1980). Comments on mechanics (spelling, handwriting, grammar) may overshadow any comment on students' ideas (Petty & Finn, 1981). Too, when papers are graded, comments may serve primarily to justify the grade, rather than to help students learn; further, written comments tend to be phrased so generally that they carry little meaning (Butler, 1980; Hahn, 1981; Sommers, 1982; Sperling & Freedman, 1987). And, when every piece of writing is commented upon by the teacher, students have little opportunity to practice evaluating their own progress, an activity critical to student growth (Graves, 1983; Hilgers, 1986; Hillocks, 1986; Wolf, 1988). To become reflective writers, students must take communication, not grades, as their end goal (Applebee, 1984; Britton et al., 1975; Freedman, 1987a).

An alternative to comments and grades, one applicable across all levels of schooling, is informal assessment based on teacher observation and careful record keeping (e.g., anecdotal records, folders of children's work samples). Through such techniques, student progress is revealed by patterns in behaviors over time (British National Writing Project, 1987; Dixon & Stratta, 1986; Genishi & Dyson, 1984; Graves, 1983; Jaggar & Smith-Burke, 1985; Newkirk & Atwell, 1988). These patterns are not likely to display smooth forward motion, but, rather, will be characterized by ups and downs; some kinds of writing activities pose more difficulties than others, and, too, students themselves sometimes take on more challenges when they write than they do at other times (Flower, 1988; Lucas, 1988a, 1988b; Ruth & Murphy, 1988).

As teachers move toward keeping folders of their students' writing, perhaps giving a grade to the entire folder or to selected pieces, they may involve students in the evaluation process. Teachers can ask students to discuss their ways of writing and their products, articulating changes in processes and products over time and across kinds of writing activities; students are thus helped to formulate concepts about "good" writing, including the variability of "good" writing across situations and audiences (Gere & Stevens, 1985; Knoblauch & Brannon, 1984). As part of their folder evaluation, students can select for evaluation pieces they feel most proud of and explain specifically why they like those pieces better than others (Burnham, 1986; Graves, 1983).

In Schools, Districts, and States. Outside the classroom, writing evaluation plays a major role in the educational decision-making of the school, the school district, and the state. For example, writing programs within a school or a district must be evaluated, and students must be assessed for placement in courses or schools or even for promotion and certification. Too, through an evaluation procedure, teachers may be brought together to develop community standards for "good" writing.

In the last decade, the most popular large-scale assessments of writing have been modeled after the evaluations developed and commonly used by the Educational Testing Service (Davis, Scriven & Thomas, 1987; Diederich, 1974; Myers, 1980; White, 1985). In these evaluation procedures, students write on an assigned topic, in a relatively short time, and in a testing situation. Teachers are then brought together to rate the papers, giving a single score to each paper. The teachers discuss their rating standards, and more than one teacher rates each paper, to be certain that raters agree. When the goal is to make judgments about individuals, evaluators advise that more than one writing sample be gathered from each writer.

These "holistic" evaluation procedures are a major advance over older methods of judging writing that were based on multiple-choice grammar tests, and they are also very useful for helping communities of teachers develop standards together. Yet, there are serious problems with holistic assessments (Brown, 1986; Lucas, 1988a, 1988b; Witte, Cherry, Meyer & Trachsel, in press). Writing for a test has little function for the student writers other than for them to be evaluated. Too, students must write on topics they have not selected and may not be interested in. Further, they are not given sufficient time to engage in the elaborated processes that, as will soon be discussed, are fundamental to how good writers write.

The current alternative is similar to the kind of in-classroom folder evaluation just discussed. Termed "portfolio assessment," this procedure, which is common in England, is now in experimental stages at several sites in the United States. For this kind of assessment, students submit a folder of their work, created as part of their normal instructional activity, to be evaluated in a formal evaluation setting (Camp, 1985; Camp & Belanoff, 1987; Elbow, 1986; Elbow & Belanoff, 1986). This alternative, although less controlled and standardized than holistic assessment, may provide an accurate picture of individual writers and writing programs. And, as teachers work together to analyze portfolios, they may develop analytic tools that may prove useful in their teaching. Official evaluations in schools, districts, and states often influences the nature of instruction in writing (Cooper, 1981; Cooper & Odell, 1977; Diederich, 1974; Mellon, 1975; Myers, 1980), and so the more harmonious the assessment is with what successful practitioners do, the more valuable the assessment for the classroom.

In the Nation. In the United States, there are two ongoing national assessments: the writing portion of the National Assessment of Educational Progress (NAEP), for 9-, 13-, and 17-year-olds (Applebee, Langer, & Mullis, 1986a, 1986b; Lloyd-Jones, 1977) and the College Entrance Examination Board's Achievement Test in English Composition given to a select population of high school seniors. In addition, in the early 1980s, the International Writing Assessment, collected writing samples in 14 countries from students in elementary school, at the end of compulsory secondary education, and at the end of academic secondary education (Gorman, Purves, & Degenhart, 1988; Gubb, Gorman & Price, 1987; Purves, 1988).

These national writing assessments all evaluate relatively short samples of writing collected under formal testing conditions. Thus, the samples present the same validity problems as the impromptu writing scored for school, district, and state assessments. Only NAEP has published claims about the state of writing in our nation, and these claims must be interpreted with great caution, given that their conclusions are based on students' performance on impromptu writing completed in 15 minutes (Mellon, 1975; Nold, 1981; Silberman, in press).

There is reason, then, for educators to seriously consider a potentially more valid alternative, national portfolio assessments; such assessments have not been used for national evaluation purposes in the United States, but they are in England (Dixon & Stratta, 1986; O'Hear, 1987).

The concerns discussed in this opening section of our review, on the uses of literacy, will be echoed in our succeeding two sections, on writing processes and writing development respectively. Even as we focus in to look at how individual students engage with writing—and how their engagement changes over time—we must bear in mind the purposes and situations that are couching their efforts, including the people among whom and for whom they are writing. As we have argued, the meaning of writing for individual students, like that of individual notes, is best revealed in composition with others.

THE PROCESSES OF WRITING

Sharon's "how do you do it" question is central to research on writing processes, not just for 5-year-olds but also for older writers, their teachers, and researchers. All involved want to know how writers write—what problems writers face, how they solve their problems, and what support they need along their journey from first idea to final version.

In the past two decades researchers shifted their attention from studies of pieces of writing, the written products, to studies of "how you do it," of writers' composing processes. They investigate what writers think about and the decisions they make—in essence how they manage the complex task of putting thoughts on paper. This shift from studying writing itself to studying how writers write has been accompanied by a similar shift in the orientation of many classroom teachers (Applebee, Langer, Mullis, 1986a,b; Freedman, 1987a; Hairston, 1982). And yet, process approaches in actual classroom practice have not been universally successful (Applebee, 1981, 1984; Freedman, 1987; Hillocks, 1986; Langer & Applebee, 1987; Swanson-Owens, 1986). One difficulty is that there is no "writing process," but a flexible process, one influenced by the kind of writing being attempted, the writer's purpose and the situational conditions—by, in other words, the complex dimensions of literacy events discussed in our first section. Thus, process research—like all research—does not offer any simple prescriptions for practice. But it can offer a vocabulary for talking about the nature of writing—planning, revising, editing—and insight into how these processes work for particular writers in particular situations.

Describing Writers at Work

Research on how writers write began with Emig's (1971) case studies of 12th-graders. She pioneered the think-aloud protocol as a way of studying how writers compose. These protocols consist of what writers say they are thinking about while they are actually in the process of writing. Protocols, then, give researchers some access to the thinking processes of teenage and adult writers who do not naturally talk as they write. Emig, though, not only used protocols; she used many sources of data, of information, to understand her students' writing, including, in addition to the think-aloud protocols, extensive interviews with the students about their experiences with school writing and analysis of their written products.

Emig learned that the highly successful, middle-class, 12th-grade students she studied found school-assigned writing generally unengaging; they spent little time planning what they would say and less time revising it. In essence, school writing was a well-learned, fairly routinized, mechanical activity; its purpose for the students was not to communicate to someone about something or to help them grapple with difficult new material. By contrast, the story and poetry writing these students did for themselves, outside of school, engaged their interest; on such writing, they spent substantial amounts of time writing, planning, and revising.

Since Emig, many researchers have studied students' writing

processes. Some have used Emig's case study methods (Perl, 1979; Pianko, 1979; Stallard, 1979). Others have used protocols but from a somewhat different research tradition, most notably, Flower & Hayes (1981a, 1981b, 1981c, 1983) from rhetoric and cognitive psychology. Others have observed writers' behaviors while they write, most notably examining when writers pause and when they write fluently (Matsuhashi, 1981; Chafe, 1982, 1985).

A Model of Adult Composing

While trying to understand how writers compose, some researchers have begun to generate a model or parts of a model of a prototypical expert adult's composing process (de Beaugrande, 1984; Bracewell, Fredericksen, & Fredericksen, 1982; Cooper & Matsuhashi, 1983; Hayes & Flower, 1980; Kintsch & van Dijk, 1978; Nold, 1981; Witte, 1985, 1987). This model construction has involved much research on the composing processes of adults, usually mainstream college students and sometimes high school students, and has suggested widely-accepted characteristics of the adult model.

First, writing is viewed as consisting of several main processes—planning, transcribing text, reviewing—that do not occur in any fixed order. Thought in writing is not linear but jumps from process to process in an organized way that is largely determined by the individual writer's goals. Britton et al. (1975) and Emig (1971) fully describe these processes, although their descriptions are more linear than more recent researchers. Flower & Hayes (1980b, 1981a), along with many other researchers (de Beaugrande, 1984; Bridwell, 1980; Daiute, 1981; Faigley & Witte, 1981; Matsuhashi, 1981; Perl, 1979; Sommers, 1980; Witte, 1983, 1985, 1987), define these processes recursively, showing how the subprocesses interrupt each other.

If the subprocesses of writing are recursive, any classroom structures that demand that all students plan, write, and revise on cue or in that order are likely to run into difficulty. Writers need flexibility, and they need time to allow the subprocesses to cycle back on each other.

A second characteristic of the adult model describes writing as a hierarchically organized, goal-directed, problem-solving process. Whatever one writes poses an intellectual problem to be solved on multiple levels, with some goals overarching others (Bereiter & Scardamalia, 1980, in press; Collins & Gentner, 1980; Hayes & Flower, 1980; Flower & Hayes, 1981b). For many kinds of school writing, writers try to achieve the more global goal of communicating an intended message to a reader by setting up that goal as the overriding problem to be solved. In order to solve that problem, the writer sets up subgoals and solves subproblems. For example, when writing an essay in school, the writer must solve the subproblems of how to form letters, how to punctuate and spell, how to construct felicitous written sentences, how to get ideas, how to order those ideas, and so on. Some of these processes become quite automatic and unconscious as the writer matures, while others take time, attention, and skill, even for experienced adults.

Thinking about writing as problem-solving can be helpful for teachers, guiding them to attend to the particular problems their student writers are grappling with. As will be further discussed in a later section, teachers' help is more likely to be effective if it is directed toward specific difficulties students are facing.

Novice/Expert Differences

Another key strand of research on composing shows that "experts" and "novices" solve the problems posed by the task of writing differently. The concept of the novice has been used to include

1. Students at all levels whose skills are developing;
2. Basic writers who are behind their peers or age group; and
3. Young writers or children.

Each group, however, is distinctive, having differing characteristics and needs. And too, all writers, even the "experts," may continually develop, as they pose new problems and thus meet new challenges.

When college-age experts write essays, they write what Flower (1979) calls reader-based prose. Their less-skilled peers, on the other hand, often create what Flower calls writer-based prose. They are described as not consciously attending to, and Flower and Hayes (1977) conclude they do not think about, their reader while they are writing; instead, they are most concerned with the text. Thinking about the reader seems to help the experts plan their essays and generate ideas.

Findings from other expert-novice studies show that secondary, college-age, and adult experts who are given the same task as novices make global revisions while novices revise mostly on the word level (Bridwell, 1980; Sommers, 1980). Sommers compared the changes adult student and expert writers made as they revised their written work. In analyzing interviews with the writers about their revision process, she found that expert writers revised on the discourse level and made changes in meaning, while student writers revised mostly on the word level and made changes in form. Bridwell came to similar conclusions on the basis of her comparisons of the revision process of more and less competent 12th-graders.

Differences in what writers revise are related to how they detect and diagnose problems. Hayes, Flower, Schriver, Stratman & Carey (1987), in describing the cognitive processes of revision, found that professionals detected more problems than did instructors, who detected more than students. Similarly, professionals displayed a larger repertoire of revision strategies than instructors, who displayed more strategies than students for solving local and global problems. Students attempted to solve problems simply by rewriting, without analyzing them.

Witte's (1987) studies, however, suggest caution in drawing conclusions about the extensiveness and meaning of writers' revisions by only looking at the marks made on the page. His work has allowed insight into the words in adult writers' heads before the words appear on the page, what he calls "pre-text," and thus demonstrates that much revision may occur mentally, before anything is written on the page.

The ability to revise demands flexibility as a writer, a willingness to reconsider, to try again. Rose (1980) discovered that writers who suffer from writer's block may follow rigid rules and have inflexible plans. Students who have this type of writing difficulty are stymied because they apply rules rigidly to situations where the rules do not apply. Unblocked writers work with flexible plans rather than rigid rules.

Basic college-age writers may have difficulty following through on their plans; they may lose their train of thought because they spend so much of their energy during composing attending to mechanical concerns (Perl, 1979). Too, basic writers may have a different grammar of written language, an intermediate grammar between speech and writing (Bartholomae, 1980; de Beaugrande 1982; Shaughnessy, 1977); thus, they may be less able than more expert writers to attune to the flow of their text, that is, to detect errors by relying on their sense of the sounds of written text (Hull, 1987).

Relating What One Writes to How One Writes

Another line of research on composing examines how the nature of the writing task affects the writer's strategies. Researchers have demonstrated the effects of different modes of discourse or types of writing on parts of the composing process, be it the amount of attention to audience or engagement with the task itself (Applebee, Langer, Durst, Butler-Nalin, Marshall, & Newell 1984; Britton et al., 1975; Chafe, 1982; Durst, 1987; Emig, 1971; Hidi & Hildyard, 1984; Kroll, 1978; Langer, 1986; Marshall, 1987; Perron, 1974; Tannen, 1982). For example, as writers see their topics as more abstract, they spend more time planning. Writers tend to pause more when writing pieces that require generalizations than when writing reports; further, writers tend to pause more before abstract than concrete sentences (Matsuhashi, 1981).

Evidence is growing that given the same writing assignment, different college students will interpret it differently and thus will pose qualitatively different writing problems to themselves (Flower, 1987; Nelson & Hayes, 1988). Flower finds that students show only minimal awareness that they and others in their class may be solving very different writing problems. Nelson and Hayes show that college students expend significantly more effort and tackle more difficult tasks when their teachers monitor and support them throughout their writing processes, giving them guidance on references and asking them questions along the way. Too, college students stretch themselves more when they must present their work orally to the class as well as in written form to the teacher.

The Writing Process in the Classroom

We began this review of process research by pointing out that many teachers have begun using "the process approach," an approach to teaching writing that recognizes the many kinds of activities writers may engage in, including planning, drafting, revising, editing, and publishing. We noted too, though, that, in the country as a whole, the approach has seemed to have only minimal success in improving students' writing. Indeed, there seems to be confusion over exactly what a process approach is.

In his meta-analysis of the effects of different classroom approaches, Hillocks (1984, 1986) equates the process approach with "the natural process approach." As he describes it, teachers following this tack are concerned with having their students "go through a process" or essentially follow a set of procedures that include planning and revising, something more than just transcribing words onto paper. This approach, outlined in some detail in the *California Handbook for Planning an Effective Writing Program* (1986), may yield a set of unconnected "process" activities that fit well into the usual organizational structure of the school—and that do not require teacher decision-making to put into place.

Thus, many instructional leaders have expressed concern that the writing process may become a rigid set of activities in the school week: "Monday we plan; Tuesday we draft; Wednesday we respond to drafts; Thursday we revise," and so on (for an example of such concern, see introduction to Newkirk & Atwell, 1988). Viewing writing as a problem-solving process demands flexibility and room for a recycling through its various subprocesses. Students may not always need to revise, for example, or they may not benefit from response on the day response is scheduled (DiPardo & Freedman, 1988; Freedman, 1987a).

Moreover, there has yet been little attention to the varied language situations of writers in our classrooms. For example, non-native speakers of English and bilinguals may use more than one language as they compose, with their oral and written language development intertwined in patterned ways, depending on their levels of proficiency in the language in which they are writing (see Valdés, 1988, for a review of research on the writing of non-native speakers and for specific suggestions for future research).

In summary, taken alone, knowledge about how adult writers compose provides an inadequate theoretical base for reforming instruction. Since the research on writing processes reveals something about how individuals write, its best use seems to be to help individual teachers better understand the writing processes of their individual students. This teacher knowledge, coupled with an understanding of how writing functions for and is used by writers, can lead to suggestions for reforming the teaching and learning of writing.

Needed as well, though, is an understanding of how writing develops, for the writing process varies, not only across contexts, but also over time. Children do not develop as writers by simply imitating "experts." Many educators have offered insight into the potential of child writers when not stymied by overemphasis on handwriting and spelling (e.g., Ashton-Warner, 1963; Britton, 1970; Burrows, 1959; Evertts, 1970; Rosen & Rosen, 1973). Beginning most notably during the mid-1970s, though, formal studies of young writers began to yield visions of writing that looked very different from those of adults. In her research, Clay introduced 5-year-olds who clearly did not plan in any adult-like way, hence the title of her book: *What Did I Write?* (1975). Graves (1973) described second-graders whose processes involved much talk to themselves and much drawing as well—neither critical variables in the adult writing literature. Development, then, takes its own course and must be examined as it unfolds, from the child's point of view, not from the adult's.

For this reason, we now turn to a discussion of children's writing development.

THE DEVELOPMENT OF WRITING

When kindergartener Sharon finally decided to have a go at writing, she filled her paper with letters and letter-like shapes, hoping that indeed she had succeeded in "doing" writing, but not at all sure of what exactly she had done. Particularly in the past 15 years, language-arts educators have gained new appreciation of both young children's ability to "explore with a pencil," to use Marie Clay's words (1977), and of the complex changes that occur in students' writing over time.

As discussed earlier, children are initiated into the use of writing as a tool for communication—as a holistic process—during the preschool years. As a basic means of communication, one that is interwoven throughout their environment, writing is available for them to investigate, to play with, and to use in personally satisfying ways. And, as they do in learning other symbol systems (Werner, 1948), children experiment and approximate, gradually becoming aware of the specific features of written language and the relationships between meanings and symbols and between symbol makers and symbol receivers.

Written language learning, like oral language learning, is complex, for written language too is a "complex of interconnecting systems," including phonological (more accurately for writing, orthographic), syntactic, semantic, and discourse rule systems (Nelson & Nelson, 1978, p. 225). The complexity of the written language system is reflected in the diverse perspectives of the literature on writing development. Some researchers have focused on children's exploration of the visual features of print, for example, its directionality and arrangement on a page (e.g., Clay, 1975). Others have studied how children come to understand the orthographic encoding system (e.g., Ferreiro & Teberosky, 1982; Read, 1975) and the intricacies of graphic segmentation and punctuation (e.g., Cazden, Cordeiro, & Giacobbe, 1985; Edelsky, 1983), tracing the evolution from early forms, like a 5-year-old's *ILVBS*, to the more conventional, like *I love (ILV) spaghetti* (pronounced " 'basghetti", hence *BS*). Still others have examined such text level features as the changing structural organization of children's stories or reports (e.g., Applebee, 1978; King & Rentel, 1981; Langer, 1986; Newkirk, 1987) or changes in children's control of the varied processes involved in forming such texts (e.g., Graves, 1975, 1983; Perl, 1979).

Within each area or strand of written language, general patterns in how children perform particular sorts of writing tasks can be identified. Often researchers and educators talk about what developmental stage of writing particular children are in, and, by "stage" they have in mind one aspect of written language use. For example, in the literature on young children's writing, "stage" is most often used in reference to spelling. But when we look at a child, like Sharon, with consideration for the whole of her development as a symbol-maker, commenting on what stage she is in is quite a different matter.

Although writing can be logically analyzed into its varied aspects, a learner comes as a whole, not displaying knowledge of these aspects in neat sequential order, but in clumps which the researcher and the teacher (not the learner) must separate into neatly organized categories. Further, written language, like oral, is an independent entity but is subject to the demands of the situation. Like a kaleidoscope, its parts are ever newly arranged, newly revealed. And, finally, the person controlling the kaleidoscope has his or her own intentions and style, his or her own sense of what's interesting; thus individuals who share similar knowledge about written language may have different stylistic preferences for organizing and using that knowledge for acting, thinking, and expressing meaning (Bussis, Chittenden, Amarel, & Klausner, 1985). In brief, the nature of the individual learner, the nature of the situational context, and the complex nature of the writing system itself all interact in written language growth, just as they do in oral language growth (Dyson, 1985a, 1987a).

The interplay of these factors suggests that we cannot offer a one-dimensional description of writing development that can serve as a template for all learners (Dyson, in press). However, as educators, we can ask varied kinds of broad questions that will inform our decisions about the challenges facing and the potential sources of support for students. For example, we can ask, how does the young child as a symbolizer—one virtually blooming with symbolic capacity in the preschool and early school years—approach this relatively more difficult form of symbolization (Donaldson, 1984; Dyson, 1988a, 1989; Ferreiro & Teberosky, 1982; Gundlach, 1982)? How do other symbol systems, like those of drawing or of talk, support written language growth? How do they pose tensions, challenges to be resolved?

We can also ask, within a developing strand of the system, what sorts of patterns of change have been observed? How do those developmental patterns relate to broader patterns of cognitive, linguistic, and social development (e.g., Bartlett, 1981; Bereiter & Scardamalia, 1982; Edelsky, 1986; Graves, 1975)? And we can offer insight into the varied ways these developmental strands may be interwoven as individual learners grow and change: What dimensions of behavior (stylistic, situational, linguistic, cultural) influence the ways in which students orchestrate these varied dimensions of writing (Bussis et al., 1985; Dyson, 1987a; Edelsky, 1986)?

Finally, we can ask about the sorts of environments that give rise to these challenges. That is, in a Vygotskian sense, what sorts of collaborations with others initiate children into written language? In a Piagetian sense, how do productive tensions, between self and others, between meaning intended and meaning formed, get set into motion? And we can consider the work of the many teachers who have shared their insight into the workings and unfoldings of writing in their particular environments, which particulars may yield insight into the kinds of environments that are helpful to developing composers and their teachers (Newkirk & Atwell, 1988).

In the following sections we consider these questions. Our review is selective, intended to capture a sense of development and of the kinds of environmental resources supporting development. Since other chapters in this volume discuss students' developing control of conventions, we emphasize here changes in their ways of composing text worlds.

FIGURE 35–1. Sance's writing and drawing.

The Nature of Writing Development

Children's Early Ways of Writing. Although children are initiated into the use of written symbols during infancy, they control first-order symbols systems, like speech and drawing, before they control second-order systems like written language (systems in which one symbol stands for another, as the written graphics stand for the spoken word). Researchers have pointed out that children use drawing and talk to support their early exploration of and use of print (Dyson, 1982, 1988a; Graves, 1981; Gundlach, 1981).

Children themselves make clear this linking, as they declare their interest in "writing houses and stuff." They understand that writing, like drawing, is a way of representing experiences. Children may, in fact, initially view writing as similar to drawing in the way that meaning is encoded in both. That is, they may view writing as direct symbolism: children may not form letters to represent speech, but to directly represent known people or objects or the names of those figures (Ferreiro & Teberosky, 1982). In their view, readers may then elaborate upon, talk about, the written names (Dyson, 1983).

For example, 5-year-old Sance's piece (Figure 35–1) is similar to many products written spontaneously by young children.

Following are Sance's comments on her graphics:

That's my Mama's name [Patty]. That's my phone number [1626]. That's my house. That's a whale. That's grass.
This is my name. HBO. That's my neighbor. That's my brother's name [Troy]. That's love. And that's my dog.

Sance graphically depicted figures with letters or with drawings, and then she talked about these important people and things. As her piece suggests, children's first conventionally written words are usually their own names, and, from those names, they reach out to learn more about written language: For example, 5-year-old Mark comments, "That's me," pointing to the letter *M;* his peer Rachel remarks, "That goes in Brian's name," when she spots a *B.*

Children's early behavior reflects the complex and hierarchical nature of the symbol system, for they seem to initially explore all aspects of written language (Clay, 1975; Hiebert, 1981). In addition to finding personally meaningful connections with these new symbol systems, they often explore the medium itself, with no concern for a specific message; in their exploring, they play with print's basic graphic features, for example, its linearity and the arrangement of print lines upon the page (Clay, 1975). Children also repeat for pragmatic or exploratory purposes familiar sentence or phrase routines ("I love you"), and they may even write whole texts (stories); these extended texts may be written with children's least sophisticated encoding procedures (e.g., cursive [~] writing) (Dyson, 1981; Sulzby, 1985). Their efforts to write for immediate audiences, as in letters and cards, may result in more conventional words than their writing for less specific audiences (as in book writing) (Lamme & Childers, 1983).

Once children gain some initial understanding of the unique nature of the symbol system, including its alphabetic nature—that precisely what is read depends on precisely what letters are written and that particular oral/written relationships define the precise letters—writing may become more difficult. Children may be less willing to randomly put down well-known letters, or to simply trust that a reader will find a message in their printed graphics (Clay, 1975). They must work hard to orchestrate the complex message creating and encoding process of writing. And in so doing, they lean on other people, other symbol systems, and their understanding of the sort of activity they are participating in (i.e., their knowledge of the kind of writing expected in any particular situation).

Patterns in Discourse Development. Children's early writing often consists of well-known words, simple statements, or repetitive sentence structures (Clay, 1975; Edelsky, 1986; McCaig, 1981; Sowers, 1981). The text is often just a reference point for an experience, which may well have been recorded more fully elsewhere, in talk or, less ephemerally, in drawing. Depending on the child's intentions, a label could be the written tip of an imaginary world (Dyson, 1983, 1988b) or the seedling of an essay on a topic of interest (Newkirk, 1987). Thus, to gain insight into children's efforts—and to help them reflect on what exactly they have done—teachers may have to listen to children's talk during the drawing and writing as well as "read" both their pictures and their text.

Children's early written texts, like their spelling (Henderson, 1981; Read, 1975) and syntax (Loban, 1976; O'Donnell, Griffin, & Norris, 1967), undergo transformations during the school years (Gundlach, 1981). They not only become longer, they also become more coherent and internally cohesive. For example, children become less likely to make references outside the texts themselves (e.g., to begin texts with "This is") or to use pronouns without references (e.g., to use "He is" when who "he" actually "is" is not clear). Still, even middle-school children have difficulties making clear these internal connections in particular situations, for example in disambiguating two "he's" when a text involves two same-sex characters (Bartlett, 1981).

In addition to changes in length and internal connectedness, the global structure of children's texts becomes more complex over time. Even preschoolers are aware of differences in text structures or genres. Through their experiences with the print world surrounding them, they come to realize that surface forms of letters, maps, and stories, for example, may all vary (Harste, Woodward, and Burke, 1984). Yet, as just discussed, children's initial authoring, their stories and reports in school, may consist of statements and labels.

A number of researchers have traced the increasing complexity and structural integrity of children's texts, particularly their written stories. By the time they begin formal schooling, young children generally display an understanding of many underlying features of narratives, that is, of their culture's way of storytelling (Applebee, 1978; Leondar, 1977; Stein & Glenn, 1979; Wolf, 1985). Children can often tell stories with recognizable characters engaged in simple plots, with beginnings, middles, and ends. They know the conventional "once upon a time" beginning and, less often, the "happily ever after" ending, and they place intervening events in the past tense.

King and Rentel (1981, 1982) illustrate how, over the course of the first two years of schooling, children's written stories ac-

quired the structural complexity evident from the very beginning of school in their orally told stories. This progress in writing was less evident for non-middle-class than middle-class children in their study; the former children began with less knowledge of written language-like story structures, but, in addition, they had fewer opportunities in their school to hear, produce, and talk about stories.

Although basic narrative knowledge is evident quite early, it does continue to develop throughout the school years. For example, it is not until the middle school years that detailed information about characters' motivations and reactions is regularly included in students' stories. Similarly, elaborate accounts of how events unfolded are not consistently given until the middle and junior high years (Bartlett, 1981). Indeed, even fluent adolescent writers may be far from skilled in embedding the quality of an experience in textual description and narration of actors and their actions (Dixon & Stratta, 1986); secondary students, like elementary ones, may discover that, in visualizing and dramatizing their stories (in making use of other media), characters' unarticulated emotions emerge in facial expressions, gestures, movement and dialogue—all aspects of the living "text" that must somehow be translated into words.

There is less information available on the development of expository prose, but what is available suggests a more gradual development. Young children do use exposition (Bissex, 1980; Langer, 1986; Newkirk, 1984; Taylor, 1983), but much research has emphasized how middle and junior high students grapple with nonfictional forms (e.g., Bereiter, 1980; Scardamalia, 1981). Bereiter and Scardamalia suggest that students' difficulty with these forms has to do with their general cognitive development—that is, students have difficulty integrating the multiple ideas contained in exposition into an orderly whole. But students may simply have less exposure to models of expositions and, in the primary grades, fewer opportunities for practice (Langer, 1986; for a discussion of the development of expository materials for, and with the help of, young school children, see Comber & Badger, 1987).

From the work of Newkirk (1987) with primary-grade children and Langer (1986) with intermediate- and middle-school children comes a sense of how children's expository writing may be gradually transformed. Without claiming that there is a rigid developmental sequence, Newkirk presents a general progression of structural complexity in children's texts. Simple written labels for pictures may evolve into a series of labels or linked information statements, attributes, or reasons. For example, an early label like *bird* or a simple listing of figure names (*bird, dog, house, flower*) may appear before two-unit clauses—"couplets"—which can link the "litany-like repetition," for example:

> This is my kneaf My knife is sharp [one couplet]
> This is a bowy knife Bowie knifs are sharp [another couplet]
> (Newkirk, 1987, p. 131, p. 133)

Still more complex are texts containing paragraphs in which the statements are in some kind of logical order, even though paragraphs themselves may not yet be ordered.

Like Newkirk's, Langer's (1986) findings also suggest that students gradually transform structures they already control. For example, as late as ninth grade, students did not regularly use such complex expository forms as problem/solution, causality, or comparison of alternatives to globally organize their texts. But, when she examined lower-level, more circumscribed structures, Langer found that indeed more complex expository structures did gradually appear across the school years.

As just illustrated, forms of discourse, like children's drawing schemata (Goodnow, 1977) and grammatical structures (Slobin, 1979), undergo gradual transformations. Rather than adopting wholly new structures, students seem to solve new text-forming problems by gradually adapting forms already controlled. This transformation process is conservative; text features are added on before internal restructuring occurs (Bartlett, 1981).

Similarly, the very process of rethinking—revising—texts develops conservatively. With Sowers (1985) and Calkins (1980), Graves (1983) studied 16 elementary school children (grades 1–4) in a middle-class community school over a 2-year period. One of the researchers' major means for studying the children, which became a major means for teaching them as well, was the workshop conference in which researchers and teachers talked to individual children about their writing processes and products. The children's responses to these conferences illustrated the gradual development of an awareness of text malleability and of the means to deliberately act on that awareness.

For example, children seem willing to change spelling and handwriting earlier than they do structure and content. Indeed, they might find abandoning drafts easier than reworking them (Calkins, 1980). Too, as Graves (1983) notes, children may find little use for revision unless they are grappling with ordering ideas—a list of names or statements makes sense in any arrangement.

The research reviewed on discourse forms, and the insight it offers into students' ways of structuring texts, may help teachers respond in helpful ways to possibilities present in individuals' work. That is, by looking analytically at students' efforts, teachers may find new structures in their products, structures that can be talked about and built upon (e.g., "You know how you arranged the sentences in that paragraph? I wonder if the paragraphs themselves should be rearranged?")

As argued throughout this section, developmental changes in students' writing processes and products are linked, not only to changes in writing itself, but to changes in how students use writing vis a vis other symbol systems, particularly drawing and speech. To gain insight into the changing role of writing in children's symbol-making, Dyson (1988b, 1989) conducted a longitudinal study of eight primary (K–third grade) grade children in an urban magnet school, examining their drawing, talking and writing (and, in the kindergarten, dictating) during a daily composing period.

As in others' studies, the observed children initially relied on drawing and talking to carry much of their story meaning. Moreover, the social functions of composing time were accomplished primarily through drawing and talking. Through those media, children not only represented imaginative worlds, they also connected with their friends, as peers talked about and at times playfully dramatized each others' texts. And they also commented on their experiences, as they evaluated the "realness" of each others' pictures. In time, children began to comment on each other's texts, as well as pictures; gradually they tried to accomplish, through writing, the social and evaluative functions previously accomplished primarily through other media. That is, over time, writing allowed the children connections with, and writing became more embedded in, their social and experienced worlds.

Yet, the children faced challenges in accomplishing through writing what they had earlier done through drawing and talking. The overlapping symbolic worlds of text, talk, and pictures, the ongoing social world, and the wider world of experiences all exist in different space/time structures; tensions among these structures were evident in the children's talk during writing and also in their texts (e.g., in shifts of tense and of person). That is, children's often awkward texts, with their unstable time frames and points of view, result not only from children's grappling with discourse forms—with textual worlds—but from their grappling with multiple worlds. For example, consider second-grader Jake's piece, written as he played inside—and outside—his text with his friend Manuel:

Once there was a boy that is named Manuel. Manuel is going to fly the fastest jet and I am going to fly the the jet too. But Manuel's headquarters is going to blow up But I am OK. But I don't know about Manuel but I am going to find Manuel [and on the story goes as Jake finds Manuel, assures himself of his safety (Manuel are you OK? Yes I am OK.) and then saves him by shooting the bad guys "out of the universe."]

"Simple" narrations, then, are not so simple (cf. Perera, 1984), considering the different media and different "worlds" writers move among. Nonetheless, in time, straightforward chronologies may be manipulated into time expansions and condensations, foreshadowing and remembering (Graves, 1983; Dixon & Stratta, 1986), as students develop new ways of structuring experiences—and connecting with readers.

The Developmental Role of Form. As the research just reviewed illustrates, a major developmental difficulty is that any discourse form serves multiple functions. To internalize the forms modeled for them in school, students must understand what those forms, in both their substantive and social functions, are meant to do—how functions and forms may place authors in particular stances toward the experienced world and toward anticipated readers (Bruner, 1986; Dyson, 1988b; for a recent review of the "social dimensions" of writing, see Rubin, 1988).

The concern that discourse forms be meaningful for children is related to Britton's (1970; Britton, Burgess, Martin, McLeod, & Rosen, 1975) caution against overemphasizing the forms of students' writing. In a study of the written products produced in school by secondary students, Britton and his colleagues (1975) found a predominance of "transactional" writing, writing to accomplish some practical aim in the world (e.g., giving information). They argued that students may become more comfortable and fluent as writers—and be better able to reflect on their experiences—when initially allowed to write "expressively," that is, in a relaxed, conversational way. To illustrate, Britton et al. (1975) present a number of student texts, including the following text by a young girl:

It is quite easy to make oxygen if you have the right equipment necessary. You will need a test tube (a large one), a stand with some acid in it. You will need also a Bunston burner. Of course you must not forget a glass tank too. A thin test tube should fix neatly in its place. When you have done that fill the glass tank and put the curved end upwards. Put the glass tank on the table and fill with water. Very soon you will find that you have made oxygen and glad of it. (p. 196)

Moffett (1968; Moffett & Wagner, 1983) has also written persuasively about the importance of writing that is infused, like the above science report, with the writer him or herself. And indeed, many successful writing programs have followed this dictate; students begin by writing about familiar subjects for known others (for example, see earlier discussion on Heath's work with teachers).

The emphasis on conversational writing predated the more recent emphasis on young children's early writing, which is decidedly unlike speech. Students' interest in varied kinds of writing may well have been underestimated. Further, students' familiarity with particular written discourse forms, and thus with their "comfort" with those forms, no doubt varies.

Nonetheless, it is developmentally sensible that control of formal discourse forms will happen gradually and that many students will build from more comfortable conversational forms. Indeed, it is this concept that underlies "dialogue journal" programs, which have been used to help students from varied backgrounds learn to write (Staton, et al., 1988; see also Fulwiler, 1987).

The Challenge of Orchestration. This section on the nature of writing growth illustrates just how very complex writing is, particularly for the inexperienced. For they must worry not only about how their ideas are taking shape but also about how to spell out those ideas, where their periods and commas go, and, even, how certain letters are formed. (A classroom teacher, Martha Rutherford, reported her second-grade daughter's worry that she had, once again, spelled "raddit" rather than "rabbit").

Thus, this section closes with a return to the earlier introduced concept of orchestration (Bussis et al., 1985). Students cannot control all aspects of the written system at once (Graves, 1982; Jacobs, 1985; Weaver, 1982). There are individual differences—stylistic differences—in how students get a handle on the process, that is, in which aspects of the process they do or do not attend to at any given writing moment. Moreover, to this orchestration, students bring varied resources—different understandings of the encoding system, of text structure, and of literacy's purposes—and they bring diverse ways of interacting with other people and with other symbolic media (Dyson, 1987a).

The task of supporting students—the task of teaching—is therefore also very complex. Teachers are supported in their own efforts by their understandings of the nature of writing and of the developmental challenges inherent in writing. And they are supported as well by their ability to observe in students' processes and products signs of what students are grappling with and by their understanding and ability to make use of the resources available to them in the classroom environment. The most important of those resources are the human ones—themselves and their students. It is to these resources that we now turn.

The Support System for Writing Development

Our understanding of the role of others in learning has been influenced by the theoretical ideas of Vygotsky and, more specifically, by research on children's acquisition of language. Vygotsky (1978) argued that learning is a social process; children are initiated into the use of their culture's signs and tools, such as written language, by their interactions with other people:

From the very first days of the child's development, his activities acquire a meaning of their own in a system of social behavior and, being directed towards a definite purpose, are refracted through the prism of the child's environment. (p. 30)

Children, then, grow and learn as they join in ongoing social activities, engaging in problem-solving with others. Gradually, they begin to internalize the processes they intially performed collaboratively. Just as a symphony gives meaning to the individual notes it contains, the social system in which children participate shapes the cognitive development of individuals (Rogoff & Lave, 1984). Schools, therefore, can promote development best if they are very social places, places where students have ample opportunities to interact with one another and with their teacher. Schools can maintain order and organization, but they cannot remain halls of silence.

The Role of Interaction in Development. Vygotsky suggests that social interaction leads the child's development forward. Learning does not wait upon but in fact leads development, as the instructor aims for the learner's "zone of proximal development . . . the distance between the actual developmental level as determined by independent problem solving and the level of potential development as determined through problem solving under adult guidance or in collaboration with peers" (1978, p. 86).

Researchers have focused on understanding more precisely how thinking is influenced by social interaction in a variety of home, work, and school settings (see literature review by Rogoff, Ellis, & Gardner, 1984). In daily life, teachers do not simply direct the learner's performance but, rather, collaborate with the learner; teachers model both the problem-solving process and involve the learner in that process.

The following classroom example illustrates a collaborative social interaction about a piece of writing between Art Peterson (AP) and his student, ninth-grade Gina. The two are discussing a draft of a paper she has written about her friend Dianne. After reading Gina's draft, Peterson models how Gina might go back and forth between generalization and support for her generalizations:

AP: All right. . . . What . . . is Dianne's main quality as you see it?
Gina: Uhm, well, she is pretty phony.
AP: Phony.

Gina: ... That's the main word. Phony. Uhm ... she has a lot of money and she uses it to get people to like her. She thinks that ... her money is the only thing that's ... in her that's worth anything. So in a lot of ways she's very uhm—

AP: Insecure.

Gina: Insecure. Well she's also secure in that ... she tries to act as if she is secure. You can really see through that after you get to know her. ... She uses her friends as a sort of shield. If she wants to do something, and because of her insecurity she feels bad about it, she tells her friend, "Go do this for me." For example, if she wants to uh ask somebody to do something for her ... Her friend said she wanted me to go to the movies with her. She was insecure about me saying "yes" or "no," whether or not I liked her. So she asked her friend to ask me.

AP: Okay. Okay. So you've got this insecure person, but she has certain uh uhm ...

Gina: But she tells people in a lot of ways. A lot of people think that she is the most secure person that they've ever seen.

AP: Yeah. Because she has these little uh tricks or devices, one of which is money.

Gina: Yeah. Uh hum.

AP: Another, another, another ...

Gina: She has lots of clothes, her tennis ability, her skiing ability. That stuff.

AP: Okay, and then she has all these other little manipulative techniques.

Gina: Yeah. She uses her friends.

AP: Yeah right.

Gina: Yeah.

AP: Okay. So that's good. You've got a person who is basically insecure, but is able to cover it up. Of course you've got to establish her insecurity. You can't just say she's insecure.

Gina: Uh hum.

AP: I mean you've got to (unclear) give me some examples of how this shows through sometimes. /Uh hum/ But then, you get in to the way you, these little techniques that she uses. That could be good.

Peterson's questions allow Gina to articulate her essential understanding of Dianne. Through this collaborative problem-solving with her teacher, Gina comes to new understandings of Dianne's insecurity, as she sorts out the appearance from the reality. Gina moves from describing Dianne as phony, to insecure, to apparently secure. Peterson does not impose his ideas; after all, he has never met Dianne. Instead, playing the roles of an interested listener and reader, as well as teacher, he draws an inference from what Gina has said about Dianne, gives Gina opportunity to elaborate on the reasons others perceive Dianne as secure, coaches Gina in synthesizing her thoughts by taking one of her judgments (Dianne appears secure although she is really insecure), models the process of supporting a generalization by adding a piece of support from what Gina has already said (Dianne's use of money), and then asks Gina to independently add further elaboration and thereby show that she understands the process he has just modelled. Finally, he summa-

rizes what he and Gina have constructed, what will become the essence of Gina's paper: "You've got a person who is basically insecure, but is able to cover it up." Peterson has led Gina to verbalize more than the surface phoniness, to understand its source and its effects. Gina has used oral language in the form of a student-teacher conversation to bring her thoughts together (example and discussion excerpted from Freedman, 1987a).

As Peterson illustrates, teachers need to be sensitive to their students' current skills and understandings and provide collaborative support to help them move along (Cole & Griffin, 1980; Wertsch McNamee, McLane, & Budwig, 1980).

"In instruction using the zone of proximal development, the adult oversees the construction of an instructional context by establishing references to what the child already knows. This context allows the child to build new information or skills into the existing knowledge structure" (Rogoff & Gardner, 1984, p. 100).

Clearly, successful instruction is dependent on the adults' "headfitting," Brown's (1979) term: the closer the distance between what the learner already knows and the information to be acquired, the more likely it is that instruction will be successful.

In this conception of teaching and learning, there is a sense of Stern's (1977) description of adult-infant communication as a dance, in which mother and child accommodate to each other. In fact, it is the child-language literature that provides perhaps the clearest illustrations of the learning of information and skills through interaction (e.g., Cross, 1975; Snow & Ferguson, 1977; Wells, 1981). Researchers have examined the nature of caregiver/child interaction, as well as the nature of the learning that results. Particularly relevant here are the mother/infant studies by Bruner and his colleagues (Bruner, 1978; Ninio & Bruner, 1978; Ratner & Bruner, 1978). They have characterized the adult role as one of providing "scaffolding" that supports early language learning. Adult/child interaction is built around familiar and routinized situations, such as peekaboo games and storytime rituals, that serve both as immediate ends in themselves and as the contexts within which the child gradually learns more sophisticated language functions: mothers "would introduce a new procedure and gradually 'hand it over' to the child as his skills for executing it developed" (Bruner, 1983, p. 60). Studies of early language learning in nonmainstream homes and communities indicate that scaffolding dialogues may take different forms in different cultures (Heath, 1983; Schieffelin, 1979).

Bereiter and Scardamalia (1982) also describe the support teachers give writers, referring to it as "procedural facilitation." This teaching practice, which aims at developing students' composing strategies, focuses on learners' cognitive activities, not on the actual content of their texts. The teacher, or mechanical support system (word processor, cuing cards), enables students to carry out more complex strategies during such tasks as content generation and revising than the student could carry out alone.

Instructional Procedures. This conception of the interactive nature of instruction is beginning to be used as a framework for examining instruction. In 1979, Cazden summarized recent research on discourse learning and proposed Bruner's studies of "peekaboo" as a starting point for a new instructional model, and many such efforts have begun (e.g., Applebee & Langer, 1983; Langer & Applebee, 1984; Brown, Palincsar, & Purcell, 1986; Palincsar & Brown, 1984).

These efforts to apply the concept of scaffolding to teaching and learning in schools are appealing. However, as Cazden (1988) cautions, the scaffolding metaphor is static while the process of teaching and learning is dynamic, the participation of the learner affects the teacher just as the teacher affects the learner, as both move to build a support structure that meets the learners' needs. Freedman (1987a) uses the term collaborative problem-solving in an attempt to capture the dynamic role of interaction in the process of teaching and learning.

In assisting developing writers, teachers can provide a variety of kinds of social interaction around writing—both between themselves and their students as in the Peterson example (see also Graves, 1983; Murray, 1984; Sperling, 1988; Witte, Meyer, Miller, & Faigley, 1981) and among the students themselves. Student interaction can take many forms. In classrooms, writers may talk to one another about their writing informally as they work side-by-side on their individual papers (Dyson, 1987b, 1988a) or as they collaborate on a joint piece (Daiute, 1989; Daiute & Dalton, 1988). As Daiute & Dalton (1988) argue, the informal and playful talk of elementary school children sounds quite different from more formal teacher-student conferences. But its playfulness—its childlikeness—is in fact its value, for language play involves modeling, exploring, and negotiating the sounds and meanings of language.

Students, particularly secondary-school students, may also interact in highly structured peer response groups (Beaven, 1977; Berkenkotter, 1984; Freedman, 1984, 1987a; Gere & Abbott, 1985; Gere & Stevens, 1985; Healy, 1980; Macrorie, 1970, 1984; Moffett, 1968; Newkirk, 1984); in special peer tutor-

ing programs (Bruffee, 1973, 1978, 1984, 1985; Hawkins, 1976); in classrooms organized specifically to allow for peer writing groups (Elbow, 1973; Murray, 1984; Nystrand, 1986); and even in writing groups that are based in communities rather than schools (Gere, 1987; Heller, in press). (For reviews of peer talk about writing, see DiPardo & Freedman, 1988, and Gere, 1987 and for questions about the efficacy of peer groups see Newkirk, 1984, and Berkenkotter, 1984).

In the end, for teachers or peers to provide meaningful support to developing writers, they must work in environments that are flexible, where they can be attentive to the highly varied needs of individual writers. Indeed, writers and teachers of writing will need to become "members of a diversified community of learners—dynamically interacting and, like the business of becoming a writers, forever in process" (DiPardo & Freedman, p. 145).

CONCLUSION

Sharon's task is complex, but she has many years, indeed a lifetime, in which to build a repertoire of skills that will enable her to create the music of her written language portfolio. She will need the help and encouragement of many people along her way—members of her community and of her family, teachers, friends, and classmates.

As she grows up, Sharon's developmental path may take different directions from the paths of some of her other 5-year-old friends. The challenge for the schools is to understand Sharon's needs and the needs of Sharon's friends and to provide the support they all will need throughout their years in the classroom. Through supportive and responsive classroom environments, schools may best help each generation grow into literacy in ways that enable them to use written language productively and fulfillingly throughout their lives.

References

Applebee, A. N. (1978). *The child's concept of story: Ages two to seventeen*. Chicago, IL: University of Chicago Press.

Applebee, A. N. (1981). *Writing in the secondary school: English and the content areas* (NCTE Research Report No. 21). Urbana, IL: National Council of Teachers of English.

Applebee, A. N. (1984). Writing and reasoning. *Review of Educational Research, 54*(4), 577–596.

Applebee, A. N., & Langer, J. A. (1983). Instructional scaffolding: Reading and writing as natural language activities. *Language Arts, 60,* 168–175.

Applebee, A. N., Langer, J., Durst, R. K., Butler-Nalin, K., Marshall, J. D., & Newell, G. E. (1984). *Contexts for learning to write: Studies of secondary school instruction*. Norwood, NJ: Ablex.

Applebee, A. N., Langer, J. & Mullis, I. (1968a). *The writing report card: Writing achievement in American schools*. Princeton NJ: National Assessment of Educational Progress, National Testing Service.

Applebee, A. N., Langer, J., & Mullis, I. (1986b). *Writing: Trends across the decade, 1974–1984*. Princeton, NJ: National Assessment of Educational Progress, National Testing Service.

Asher, C. (1988). *Writing on our own: The function of self-sponsored writing in the lives of six low economic status high school students*. Unpublished doctoral dissertation, New York University.

Ashton-Warner, S. (1963). *Teacher*. New York: Simon & Schuster.

Bartholomae, D. (1980). The study of error. *College Composition and Communication, 31*(3), 253–69.

Bartlett, E. J. (1981). *Learning to write: Some cognitive and linguistic components*. Washington, DC: Center for Applied Linguistics.

Basso, K. (1974). The ethnography of writing. In R. Bauman & J. Sherzer (Eds.), *Explorations in the ethnography of speaking*. Cambridge: Cambridge University Press.

de Beaugrande, R. (1982). Psychology and composition: Past, present, and future. In M. Nystrand (Ed.), *What writers know: The language, process and structure of written discourse* (pp. 211–268). New York: Academic Press.

de Beaugrande, R. (1984). *Advances in discourse processes: Vol. 11. Text production: Toward a science of composition*. Norwood, NJ: Ablex.

Beaven, M. (1977). Individualized goal setting, self-evaluation, and peer evaluation. In C. Cooper and L. O'Dell (Eds.), *Evaluating writing: Describing, measuring, judging* (pp. 135–156). Urbana, IL: National Council of Teachers of English.

Bereiter, C. (1980). Development in writing. In L. W. Gregg & E. R. Steinberg (Eds.), *Cognitive processes in writing* pp. 73–93. Hillsdale, NJ: Erlbaum.

Bereiter, C. & Scardamalia, M. (1980). *Fostering the development of self-regulation in children's knowledge processing*. Paper presented at the NIE-LRDC Conference on Thinking and Learning Skills, Pittsburgh, PA.

Bereiter, C. & Scardamalia, M. (1982). From conversation to composition. In R. Glaser (Ed.), *Advances in instructional psychology* (Vol. 2). Hillsdale, NJ: Erlbaum.

Bereiter, C. & Scardamalia, M. (in press). Cognitive coping strategies and the problem of "inert knowledge." In S. Chipman et al., (Eds.), *Thinking and learning skills*. Hillsdale, NJ: Erlbaum.

Berkenkotter, C. (1984). Student writers and their sense of authority over text. *College Composition and Communication, 34,* 312–319.

Bissex, G. L. (1980). *Gnys at wrk*. Cambridge, MA: Harvard University Press.

Bogdan, R. C., & Biklen, S. K. (1982). *Qualitative research for education: An introduction to theory and methods*. Boston: Allyn & Bacon.

Bracewell, R. J., Frederiksen, C. H., & Frederiksen, J. D. (1982). Cognitive processes in composing and comprehending discourse. *Educational Psychologist, 17,* 146–164.

Bremme, D. W., & Erickson, F. (1977). Relationships among verbal and nonverbal classroom behaviors. *Theory into Practice, 16,* 153–161.

Bridwell, L. (1980). Revising strategies in twelfth grade students' transactional writing. *Research in the Teaching of English, 3,* 197–222.

British National Writing Project. (1987). *Ways of looking at children's writing: The National Writing Project response to the task group on assessment and testing* (Occasional Paper No. 8). London: School Curriculum Development Committee Publications.

Britton, J. (1970). *Language and learning*. Harmondsworth, Middlesex, England: Penguin.

Britton, J., Burgess, T., Martin, N., McLeod, A., and Rosen, H. (1975). *The development of writing abilities: 11–18*. London: Macmillan Education Ltd.

Britton, J. (1989). Writing and reading in the classroom. In A. Haas Dyson (Ed.), *Collaborating through writing and reading: Exploring possibilities* (pp. 217–246). Urbana, IL: National Council of Teachers of English.

Brown, A. L. (1979). Theories of memory and the problems of development: Activity, growth, & knowledge. In L. S. Cermak & F. I. M. Craik (Eds.), *Levels of processing in human memory* (pp. 225–258). Hillsdale, NJ: Erlbaum.

Brown, A. L., Palincsar, A. S., & Purcell, L. (1986). Poor readers: Teach, don't label. In U. Neisser (Ed.), *The academic performance of minority children: A new perspective* (105–144). Hillsdale, NJ: Erlbaum.

Brown, R. (1986). A personal statement on writing assessment and education policy. In K. Greenberg, H. Weiner, & R. Donovan (Eds.), *Writing assessment: Issues and strategies* (pp. 44–52). New York: Longman.

Bruce, B. C. (1987). An examination of the role of computers in teaching language and literature. In J. R. Squire (Ed.), *The dynamics of language learning: Research in reading and English* (pp. 277–293). Urbana, IL: NCTE.

Bruffee, K. (1973). Collaborative learning: Some practical models. *College English, 34*(5), 579–86.

Bruffee, K. (1978). The Brooklyn plan: Attaining intellectual growth through peer-group tutoring. *Liberal Education, 64,* 447–468.

Bruffee, K. (1984). Peer tutoring and the "conversation of mankind." *College English, 56*(7), 635–652.

Bruffee, K. (1985). *A short course in writing* (3rd Ed.). Boston: Little, Brown and Company.

Bruffee, K. (1986). Beginning a tasting program: Making lemonade. In K. Greenberg, H. Wiener, & R. Donovan, *Writing assessment: Issues and strategies* (pp. 93–97). New York: Longman.

Bruner, J. (1978). The role of dialogue in language acquisition. In A. Sinclair (Ed.), *The child's conception of language* (pp. 241–256). New York: Springer-Verlag.

Bruner, J. (1983). *Child's talk: Learning to use language*. London: Oxford University Press.

Bruner, J. (1986). *Actual minds, possible worlds*. Cambridge, MA: Harvard University Press.

Burnham, C. (1986). Portfolio evaluation: Room to breathe and grow. In C. Bridges (Ed.), *Training the teacher of college composition* (pp. 125–138). Urbana, IL: National Council of Teachers of English.

Burrows, A. T. (1959). *Teaching composition: What research says to the classroom teacher*. Washington, DC: National Education Association.

Bussis, A. M., Chittenden, E. A., Amarel, M., & Klausner, E. (1985). *Inquiry into meaning: An investigation of learning to read*. Hillsdale: Erlbaum.

Butler, J. (1980). Remedial writers: The teacher's job as corrector of papers. *College Composition and Communication, 31,* 270–277.

California Handbook for Planning an Effective Writing Program. (1986). Sacramento, CA: California State Department of Education.

Calkins, L. M. (1980). Childrens rewriting strategies. *Research in the Teaching of English, 14,* 331–341.

Calkins, L. M. (1983). *Lessons from a child on the teaching of writing*. Exeter, NH: Heinemann.

Calkins, L. M. (1986). *The art of teaching writing*. Portsmouth, NH: Heinemann.

Camp R. (1985). The writing folder in post-secondary assessment. In P. J. A. Evans (Ed.), *Directions and misdirections in English evaluation* (pp. 91–99). Ottowa, Canada: The Canadian Council of Teachers of English.

Camp, R., & Belanoff, P. (1987). Portfolios as proficiency tests. *Notes from the National Testing Network in Writing, 7*(8).

Cazden, C. (1979). Peekaboo as an instructional model: Discourse development at home and at school. *Papers and Reports on Child Language Development, 17,* 1–19.

Cazden, C. (1986). Classroom discourse. In M. C. Wittrock (Ed.), *Handbook of research on teaching* (3rd ed.) (pp. 432–463). New York: Macmillan.

Cazden, C. (1988). *Classroom discourse: The language of teaching and learning*. Portsmouth, NH: Heinemann.

Cazden, C., Cordeiro, P., & Giacoabbe, M. E. (1985). Spontaneous and scientific concepts: Young children's learning of punctuation. In G. Wells & J. Nicholls (Eds.), *Language and learning: An interactional perspective* (pp. 107–124). Phildaelphia, PA: The Falmer Press.

Chafe, W. (1982). Integration and involvement in speaking, writing, and oral literature. In D. Tannen (Ed.), *Spoken and written language: Exploring orality and literacy*. Norwood, NJ: Ablex.

Chafe, W. (1985). Linguistic differences produced by differences between speaking and writing. In D. Olson, A. Hildyard, & Torrance (Eds.), *Language, literacy, and education*. Cambridge: Cambridge University Press.

Chafe, W., & Danielewicz, J. (1987). Properties of spoken and written language. In R. Horowitz & J. Samuels (Eds.), *Comprehending written language* (pp. 83–113). New York: Academic Press.

Clark, C. M., & Florio, S. (1981). *Diary time: The life history of an occasion for writing*. East Lansing, MI: The Institute for Research on Teaching.

Clark, C. M., & Florio, S., with J. Elmore, J. Martin, R. Maxwell & W. Metheny. (1982). *Understanding writing in school: A descriptive study of writing and its instruction in two classrooms*. East Lansing, MI: The Institute for Research on Teaching.

Clay, M. (1975). *What did I write?* Auckland: Heinemann.

Clay, M. (1977). Exploring with a pencil. *Theory into Pratice, 16,* 334–341.

Cole, M., & Griffin, P. (1980). Cultural amplifiers reconsidered. In D. R.

Olson (Ed.), *The social foundations of language and thought* (pp. 343–364). New York: Norton.

Cole, M., & Nicolopoulous, A. (in press). The intellectual consequences of literacy. *The Oxford international encyclopedia of linguistics.* London: Oxford University Press.

Collins, A., & Gentner, D. (1980). A framework for a cognitive theory of writing. In L. Gregg and E. Steinberg (Eds.), *Cognitive processes in writing* (pp. 51–72). Hillsdale, NJ: Lawrence Erlbaum.

Comber, B., & Badger L. (1987). *Enjoying non-fiction with young children.* Paper presented at the South Pacific Reading Conference.

Cooper, C. R. (Ed.). (1981). *The nature and measurement of competency in English.* Urbana, IL: National Council of Teachers of English.

Cooper, C. R., Marquis, A., & Ayer-Lopez, S. (1982). Peer learning in the classroom: Tracing developmental patterns and consequences of children's spontaneous interactions. In L. C. Wilkinson (Ed.), *Communicating in the classroom* (pp. 69–84). New York: Academic Press.

Cooper, C. R., & Matsuhashi, A. (1983). A theory of the writing process. In M. Martlew (Ed.), *The psychology of written language* (pp. 3–39). London: John Wiley and Sons.

Cooper, C. R., & Odell, L. (Eds.). (1977). *Evaluating writing: Describing, measuring, judging.* Urbana, IL: National Council of Teachers of English.

Cross, T. (1975). Some relationships between mothers and linguistic levels in accelerated children. *Papers and reports on child language development* (Vol. 10). Stanford, CA: Stanford University.

Daiute, C. (1981). Psycholinguistic foundations of the writing process. *Research in the Teaching of English, 15,* 5–22.

Daiute, C. (1989). Play as thought: Thinking strategies of young writers. *Harvard Educational Review, 59,* 1–23.

Daiute, C., & Dalton. (1988). "Let's brighten it up a bit": Collaboration and cognition in writing. In B. Ratoth & D. Rubin (Eds.), *The social construction of written communication* (pp. 249–272). Norwood, NJ: Ablex.

Davis, B., Scriven, M., & Thomas, S. (1987). *The evaluation of composition instruction* (2nd ed.). New York: Teachers College Press.

Diederich, P. (1974). *Measuring growth in English.* Urbana, IL: National Council of Teachers of English.

DiPardo, A., & Freedman, S. (1988). Peer response groups in the writing classroom: Theoretic foundations and new directions. *Review of Educational Research, 58*(2), 119–149.

Dixon, J., & Stratta, L. (1986). *Writing narrative—and beyond.* Upper Montclair, NJ: Boynton/Cook.

Donaldson, M. (1984). Speech and writing as modes of learning. In H. Goelman, A. A. Oberg, & F. Smith (Eds.), *Awakening to literacy* (pp. 174–184). Exeter, NH: Heinemann

Durst, R. (1987). Cognitive and linguistic demands of analytic writing. *Research in the Teaching of English, 21*(4), 347–376.

Dyson, A. H. (1981). Oral language: The rooting system for learning to write. *Language Arts, 58,* 776–784.

Dyson, A. H. (1982). The emergence of visible language: Interrelationships between drawing and early writing. *Visible Language, 6,* 360–381.

Dyson, A. H. (1983). The role of oral language in early writing processes. *Research in the Teaching of English, 17,* 1–30.

Dyson, A. H. (1984a). Emerging alphabetic literacy in school contexts: Toward defining the gap between school curriculum and child mind. *Written Communication, 1,* 5–55.

Dyson, A. H. (1984b). Learning to write/learning to do school: Emergent writers' interpretations of school literacy tasks. *Research in the Teaching of English, 18,* 233–264.

Dyson, A. H. (1985a). Individual differences in emerging writing. In M. Farr (Ed.), *Advances in writing research: Vol. 1. Children's early writing development* (pp. 59–126). Norwood, NJ: Ablex.

Dyson, A. H. (1985b). Second graders sharing writing: The multiple social realities of a literacy event. *Written Communication, 2*(2), 189–215.

Dyson, A. H. (1985c). Research currents: Writing and the social lives of children. *Language Arts, 62,* 632–639.

Dyson, A. H. (1987a). Individual differences in beginning composing: An orchestral vision of learning to compose. *Written Communication, 4,* 411–442.

Dyson, A. H. (1987b). The value of "time off task": Young children's spontaneous talk and deliberate text. *Harvard Educational Review, 57*(4), 396–420.

Dyson, A. H. (1988a). Unintentional helping in the primary grades: Writing in the children's world. In B. A. Rafoth & D. L. Rubin (Eds.), *The social construction of written communication* (pp. 218–248). Norwood, NJ: Ablex.

Dyson, A. H. (1988b). Negotiating among multiple words: The space/time dimensions of young children's composing. *Research in the Teaching of English, 22*(4), 355–391.

Dyson, A. H. (1989). *Multiple worlds of child writers: Friends learning to write.* New York: Teachers College Press.

Dyson, A. H. (in press). The word and the world: Reconceptualizing written language development. *Research in the Teaching of English.*

Edelsky, C. (1983). Segmentation and punctuation: Developmental data from young writers in a bilingual program. *Research in the Teaching of English, 17,* 135–156.

Edelsky, C. (1986). *Writing in a bilingual program: Habia una vez.* Norwood, NJ: Ablex.

Edelsky, C., & Smith, K. (1984). Is that writing—or are those marks just a figment of your curriculum? *Language Arts, 61*(1), 24–32.

Elbow, P. (1973). *Writing without teachers.* London: Oxford University Press.

Elbow, P. (1986). Portfolio assessment as an alternative in proficiency testing. *Notes from the National Testing Network in Writing, 6, 3,* and *12.*

Elbow, P., & Belanoff, P. (1986). State University of New York, Stony Brook Portfolio-based evaluation program (pp. 95–105). In P. Connolly & T. Vilardi (Eds.), *New methods in college writing programs: Theories into practice.* New York: Modern Language Association.

Emig, J. (1971). *The composing processes of twelfth graders* (Research Report No. 13). Urbana, IL: National Council of Teachers of English.

Evertts, E. (1970). *Explorations in children's writing.* Urbana, IL: National Council of Teachers of English.

Faigley, L., & Witte, S. (1981). Analyzing revisions. *College Composition and Communication, 32,* 400–414.

Ferreiro, E., & Teberosky, A. (1982). *Literacy before schooling.* Exeter, NH: Heinemann.

Fiering, S. (1981). Commodore School: Unofficial writing. In D. H. Hymes (Ed.), *Ethnographic monitoring of children's acquisition of reading/language arts skills in and out of the classroom* (Final Report to the National Institute of Education).

Florio, S., & Clark, C. (1982). The functions of writing in an elementary classroom. *Research in the Teaching of English, 16,* 115–129.

Flower, L. (1979). Writer-based prose: A cognitive basis for problems in writing. *College English, 41,* 19–37.

Flower, L. (1987). Interpretive acts: Congnition and the construction of discourse. *Poetics, 16,* 109–130.

Flower, L. (1988). Taking thought: The role of conscious processing in the making of meaning. In E. Maimon, B. Nodine, & F. O'Connor (Eds.), *Thinking, reasoning, and writing.* New York: Longman.

Flower, L., & Hayes, J. R. (1977). Problem-solving strategies and the writing process. *College English, 39*(4), 449–61.

Flower, L., & Hayes, J. R. (1980b). Identifying the organization of writing processes. In L. W. Gregg & E. R. Steinberg (Eds.), *Cognitive processes in writing* (pp. 31–50). Hillsdale, NJ: Erlbaum.

Flower, L., & Hayes, J. R. (1981a). A cognitive process theory of writing. *College Composition and Communication, 32,* 365–387.

Flower, L., & Hayes, J. R. (1981b). Plans that guide the composing process. In C. H. Frederiksen, & J. F. Dominic (Eds.), *Writing: The nature, development and teaching of written communication: Vol. 2. Writing: Process, development and communication* (pp. 39–58). Hillsdale, NJ: Erlbaum.

Flower, L., & Hayes, J. R. (1981c). The pregnant pause: An inquiry into the nature of planning. *Research in the Teaching of English, 15,* 229–243.

Flower, L., & Hayes, J. R. (1983). Uncovering cognitive processes in writing: An introduction to protocol analysis. In P. Mosenthal, L. Tamor, & S. Walmsley (Eds.), *Research on written language: Principals and methods* (pp. 206–219). New York: Guilford Press.

Freedman, S. (1984). *Response to, and evaluation of writing: A review.* Paper presented at the annual meeting of the American Educational Research Association, New Orleans. (ERIC Document Reproduction Service No. ED 247 605).

Freedman, S. with C. Greenleaf and M. Sperling. (1987a). *Response to student writing* (Research Report No.23). Urbana, IL: National Council for the Teachers of English.

Freedman, S. (1987b). *Peer Response Groups in Two Ninth-Grade Classrooms* (Technical Report No. 12). Berkeley: University of California, Center for the Study of Writing.

Freedman, S., & McLeod, A. (1988). *National surveys of successful teachers of writing and their students: The United Kingdom and the United States* (Technical Report No. 14). Berkeley: University of California, Center for the Study of Writing.

Fulwiler, T. (Ed.). (1987). *The journal book.* Portsmouth, NH: Heinemann. 1987.

Gee, J. (1988). The legacies of literacy: From Plato to Freire through Harvey Graff. *Harvard Educational Review, 58*(2), 195–213.

Genishi, C. & Dyson, A. H. (1984). *Language assessment in the early years.* Norwood, NJ: Ablex.

Gere, A. (1987). *Writing groups: History, theory, and implications.* Carbondale, IL: Southern Illinois University Press.

Gere, A., & Abbott. (1985). Talking about writing: The language of writing groups. *Research in the Teaching of English, 19*(4), 362–379.

Gere, A., & Stevens, R. (1985). The language of writing groups: How oral response shapes revision. In S. W. Freedman (Ed.), *The acquisition of written language: Response and Revision* (pp. 85–105). Norwood, NJ: Ablex.

Gilbert, S. H., & Gay, G. (1985). Improving the success in school of poor black children. *Phi Delta Kappan, 67*(2), 133–137.

Gilmore, P. (1983). Spelling "Mississippi": Recontextualizing a literacy-related speech event. *Anthropology & Education Quarterly, 14*(4), 235–256.

Goodnow, J. (1977). *Children drawing.* Cambridge, MA: Harvard University Press.

Goody, J. (1968). *Literacy in traditional societies.* Cambridge: Cambridge University Press.

Goody, J., & Watt, I. (1963). The consequences of literacy. *Comparative Studies in Society and History, 5,* 304–26, 332–45.

Gorman, T., Purves, A., & Degenhart, R. E. (Eds.). (1988). *The international writing tasks and scoring scales: International study of achievement in writtten composition* (Vol. 1.). Oxford: Pergamon Press.

Graves, D. (1973). *Children's writing: Research directions on hypotheses based upon an examination of the writing process of seven-year-old children.* Unpublished doctoral dissertation, State University of New York at Buffalo.

Graves, D. (1975). An examination of the writing processes of seven-year-old children. *Research in the Teaching of English, 9,* 227–41.

Graves, D. (1981). *A case study observing the development of primary children's composing, spelling and motor behaviors during the writing process* (Final Report to the National Institue of Education). Durham: University of New Hampshire.

Graves, D. (1982). Patterns of child control of the writing process. In R. D. Walsh (Ed.), *Donald Graves in Australia* (pp. 17–28). Exeter, NH: Heinemann.

Graves, D. (1983). *Writing: Teachers and children at work.* Exeter, NH: Heinemann.

Greene, J. (1985). Children's writing in an elementary postal system. In M. Farr (Ed.), *Advances in writing: Vol. 1. Children's early writing development* (pp. 201–296). Norwood, NJ: Ablex.

Green, J., & Wallat, C. (1979). What is an instructional context? An exploratory analysis of conversational shifts over time. In O. Garnica & M. King (Eds.), *Language, children, and society* (pp. 159–188). New York: Pergamon.

Gubb, J., Gorman, T., & Price, E. (1987). *The study of written composition in England and Wales.* Windsor, England: NFER-NELSON Publishing Co. Ltd.

Gumperz, J. (Ed.). (1971). *Language in social groups.* Stanford: Stanford University Press.

Gumperz, J., & Hymes, D. H. (Eds.). (1972). *Directions in sociolinguistics: The ethnography of communication.* Oxford: Basil Blackwell.

Gundlach, R. (1981). On the nature and development of children's writing. In C. Fredericksen & J. Dominic (Eds.), *Writing: The nature, development and teaching of written communication: Vol. 2. Writing: Process, development and communication* (pp. 133–152). Hillsdale, NJ: Erlbaum.

Gundlach, R. (1982). Children as writers: The beginnings of learning to write. In M. Nystrand (Ed.), *What writers know* (pp. 129–148). New York: Academic Press.

Gundlach, R., Farr, M. & Cook-Gumperz, J. (1989). Writing and reading in the community. In A. Haas Dyson (Ed.), *Collaborating through writing and reading: Exploring possibilities* (pp. 91–130). Urbana, IL: National Council of Teachers of English.

Gundlach, R., McLane, J. B., Scott, F. M., & McNamee, G. D. (1985). The social foundations of children's early writing development. In M. Farr (Ed.), *Advances in writing: Vol. 1. Children's early writing development* (pp. 1–58). Norwood, NJ: Ablex.

Hahn, J. (1981). Students' reactions to teachers' written comments. *National Writing Project Network Newsletter, 4,* 7–10.

Hairston, M. (1982). The winds of change: Thomas Kuhn and the revolution in the teaching of writing. *College Composition and Communication, 33*(1), 76–88.

Hamilton, S. F. (1983). The social side of schooling: Ecological studies of classrooms and schools. *The Elementary School Journal, 83*(4), 313–334.

Harste, J. C., Woodward, V. A., & Burke, C. L. (1984). *Language stories & literacy lessons.* Portsmouth, NH: Heinemann.

Hawkins, T. (1976). *Group inquiry techniques for teaching writing.* Urbana, IL: NCTE/ERIC.

Hayes, J. R., & Flower, L. S. (1980). Identifying the organization of writing processes. In L. W. Gregg & E. R. Steinberg (Eds.), *Cognitive processes in writing* (pp. 3–30). Hillsdale, NJ: Erlbaum.

Hayes, J. R., Flower, L., Schriver, K., Stratman, J., & Carey, L. (1987). Cognitive processes in revision. In Rosenberg, S. (Ed.), *Advances in applied psycholinguistics: Reading, writing, and language processing* (pp. 176–240). Cambridge, England: Cambridge University Press.

Healy, M. K. (1980). *Using student writing response groups in the classroom.* Berkeley: University of California, Bay Area Writing Project.

Heath, S. B. (1980). The functions and uses of literacy. *Journal of Communication, 30,* 123–133.

Heath, S. B. (1982). Protean shapes in literacy events: Evershifting oral and literate traditions. In D. Tannen (Ed.), *Spoken and written lan-*

guage: Exploring orality and literacy (pp. 91–118). Norwood, NJ: Ablex.

Heath, S. B. (1983). *Ways with words: Language, life, and work in communities and classrooms.* Cambridge: Cambridge University Press.

Heath, S. B. (1986). Critical factors in literacy development. In S. deCastell, A. Luke, & K. Egan (Eds.), *Literacy, society, & schooling: A reader* (pp. 209–229). Cambridge: Cambridge University Press.

Heath, S., & Branscombe, A. (1985). "Intelligent writing" in an audience community: Teacher, students and researchers. In S. W. Freedman (Ed.), *The acquisition of written language: Response and revision* (pp. 3–32). Norwood, NJ: Ablex.

Heath, S. B. & Branscombe, A. with C. Thomas. (1986). The book as narrative props in language acquisition. In B. Schieffelin & P. Gilmore, *The acquisition of literacy: Ethnographic perspectives* (pp. 16–34). Norwood, NJ: Ablex.

Heller, C. (in press). *Women writers of the Tenderloin* (Technical Report). Berkeley, CA: University of California, Center for the Study of Writing.

Henderson, E. H. (1981). *Learning to read and spell: The child's knowledge of words.* DeKlab, IL: Northern Illinois University Press.

Henry, J. (1955). Docility or giving teacher what she wants. *The Journal of Social Issues, 11*(2), 33–41.

Henry, J. (1963). *Culture against man.* New York: Random House.

Hidi, S., & Hildyard, A. (1984). The comparison of oral and written productions in two discourse modes. *Discourse Processes, 6*(2), 91–105.

Hiebert, E. H. (1981). Developmental patterns and interrelationships of preschool children's print awareness. *Reading Research Quarterly, 49,* 1231–1234.

Hilgers, T. L. (1986). How children change as critical evaluators of writing: Four three-year case studies. *Research in the Teaching of English, 20,* 36–55.

Hillocks, G., Jr. (1984). What works in teaching composition: A meta-analysis of experimental treatment studies. *American Journal of Education, 93*(1), 107–132.

Hillocks, G. (1986). *Research on written composition: New directions for teaching.* Urbana, IL: ERIC Clearinghouse on Reading and Communication Skills.

Hudson, S. A. (1988). Children's perceptions of classroom writing: Ownership in a continuum of control. In B. Rafoth & D. Rubin (Eds.), *The social construction of written language* (pp. 37–69). Norwood, NJ: Ablex.

Hull, G. (1987). The editing process in writing: A performance study of more skilled and less skilled college writers. *Research in the Teaching of English, 21*(1), 8–29.

Hymes, D. H. (1962). The ethnography of speaking. In T. Gladwin & W. C. Sturtevant (Eds.), *Anthropology and human behavior* (pp. 13–53). Washington DC: Anthropology Society of Washington.

Hymes, D. H. (1972). Models of the interaction of language and social life. In J. J. Gumperz & D. Hymes (Eds.), *Directions in sociolinguistics* (pp. 35–71). New York: Holt, Rinehart & Winston.

Hymes, D. H., with Cazden, C. (1980). Narrative thinking and storytelling rights: A folklorist's clue to a critique of education. In D. Hymes, *Language in education* (pp. 126–138). Washington, DC: Center for Applied Linguistics.

Jackson, P. (1968). *Life in classrooms.* New York: Holt, Rinehart, & Winston.

Jacobs, S. E. (1985). The development of children's writing: Language acquisition and divided attention. *Written Communication, 2,* 414–433.

Jaggar, A. & Smith-Burke, T. (1985). *Observing the language learner.* Urbana, IL: National Council of Teachers of English.

Johnston, R. (1979). Development of a literary mode in the language of nonliterary communities. In S. A. Wurm (Ed.), *New Guinea and neighboring areas: A sociolinguistic laboratory* (pp. 129–155). The Hague: Mouton.

King, M., & Rentel, V. (1981). *How children learn to write: A longitudinal study.* Columbus, OH: Ohio State University.

King, M., & Rentel, V. (1982). *Transition to writing.* Columbus, OH: Ohio State University.

Kinneavy, J. (1971). *A theory of discourse.* New York: Norton.

Kinstch, W., & van Dijk, T. (1978). Toward a model of text comprehension and production. *Psychological Review, 85,* 363–394.

Knoblauch, C., & Brannon, L. (1984). *Rhetorical traditions and the teaching of writing.* Upper Montclair, NJ: Boynton-Cook.

Kroll, B. (1978). Cognitive egocentrism and the problem of audience awareness in written discourse. *Research in the Teaching of English, 12,* 269–281.

Labov, W. (1982). Competing value systems in inner-city schools. In P. Gilmore & A. A. Glatthorn (Eds.), *Children in and out of school* (pp. 148–171). Washington, DC: Center for Applied Linguistics.

Labov, W. (1970). The logic of nonstandard English. In F. Williams (Ed.), *Language and poverty.* Chicago: Markham Publishing.

Lamme, L. & Childers, N. (1983). The composing processes of three young children. *Research in the Teaching of English, 17,* 31–50.

Langer, J. (1986). *Children reading and writing: Structures and strategies.* Norwood, NJ: Ablex.

Langer, J. A., & Applebee, A. N. (1984). Language, learning, and interaction: A framework for improving the teaching of writing. In A. Applebee (Ed.), *Contexts for learning to write: Studies of secondary school instruction* (pp. 169–182). Norwood, NJ: Ablex.

Langer, J. A., & Applebee, A. N. (1987). *How writing shapes thinking: A study of teaching and learning* (Research Report No. 22). Urbana, IL: National Council of Teachers of English.

Leacock, E. (1969). *Teaching and learning in city schools.* New York: Basic Books.

Leondar, B. (1977). Hatching plots: Genesis of storymaking. In D. Perkins and B. Leondar (Eds.), *Arts and cognition* (pp. 172–191). Baltimore, MD: Johns Hopkins University Press.

Lloyd-Jones, R. (1977). The politics of research into the teaching of composition. *College Composition and Communication, 28,* 218–222.

Loban, W. (1976). *Language development: Kindergarten through grade twelve.* Urbana, IL: National Council of Teachers of English.

Lucas, C. Keech. (1988a). Recontextualizing literacy assessment. *The Quarterly, 10*(2), 4–10.

Lucas, C. Keech. (1988b). Toward ecological evaluation. *The Quarterly, 10*(1), 1–3, 12–17.

Lundsford, A., & Ede, L. (1984). Classical rhetoric, modern rhetoric, and contemporary discourse studies. *Written Communication, 1,* 78–100.

Macrorie, K. (1970). *Uptaught.* New York: Hayden Book Co.

Macrorie, K. (1984). *Twenty teachers.* New York: Oxford University Press.

Marshall, T. (1987). The effects of writing on students' understanding of literary texts. *Research in the Teaching of English, 21*(1), 30–63.

Matsuhashi, A. (1981). Pausing and planning: The tempo of written discourse. *Research in the Teaching of English, 15,* 113–134.

McCaig, R. (1981). A district-wide plan for the evaluation of student writing. In S. Haley-James (Ed.), *Perspectives on writing in grades 1–8* (pp. 73–92). Urbana, IL: National Council of Teachers of English.

Mehan, H. (1979). "What time is it, Denise?": Asking known information questions in classroom discourse. *Theory into Practice, 28,* 285–294.

Mellon, J. C. (1975). *National assessment and the teaching of writing.* Urbana, IL: National Council of Teachers of English.

Merritt, M. (1982). Distributing and directing attention in primary classrooms. In L. C. Wilkinson (Ed.), *Communicating in the classroom* (pp. 223–244). New York: Academic Press.

Michaels, S., & Cook-Gumperz, J. (1979). A study of sharing time with first grade students: Discourse narratives in the classroom. *Proceedings of the Fifth Annual Meeting of the Berkeley Linguistics Society.* Berkeley, CA.

Moffett, J. (1968). *Teaching the universe of discourse.* Boston: Houghton Mifflin.

Moffett, J., & Wagner, B. J. (1983). *Student-centered language arts and reading, K–13: A handbook for teachers* (3rd ed.). Boston: Houghton-Mifflin.

Murray, D. (1984). *A writer teaches writing* (2nd ed.). Boston: Houghton-Mifflin.

Myers, M. (1980). *A procedure for writing assessment and holistic scoring.* Urbana, IL: National Council of Teachers of English.

Nelson, J., & Hayes, J. (1988). *How the writing context shapes college students' strategies for writing from sources* (Technical Report No. 16). Berkeley: University of California, Center for the Study of Writing.

Nelson, K. E., & Nelson, K. (1978). Cognitive pendulums and their linguistic realization. In K. E. Nelson (Ed.), *Children's language* (Vol. 1) (pp. 233–285). New York: Gardner.

Newkirk, T. (1984). How students read student papers: An exploratory study. *Written Communication, 3,* 283–305.

Newkirk, T. (1987). The non-narrative writing of young children. *Research in the Teaching of English, 21,* 121–145.

Newkirk, T., & Atwell, N. (Eds.). (1988). *Understanding writing.* (2nd ed.). Portsmouth, NH: Heinemann.

Newman, D., Griffin, P., & Cole, M. (1984). Social constraints in laboratory and classroom. In B. Rogoff & J. Lave (Eds.), *Everyday cognition: Its development in social context* (pp. 172–193). Cambridge, MA: Harvard University Press.

Ninio, A., & Bruner, J. (1978). The achievement and antecedents of labeling. *Journal of Child Language, 5,* 1–15.

Nold, E. (1981). Revising. In C. H. Fredericksen & J. F. Dominic (Eds.), *Writing: The nature, development, and teaching of written communication: Vol. 2. Process, development, and communication* (pp. 67–80). Hillsdale, NJ: Lawrence Erlbaum.

Nystrand, M. (1986). Learning to write by talking about writing: A summary of research on intensive peer review in expository writing instruction at the University of Wisconsin-Madison. In M. Nystrand (Ed.), *The structure of written communication* (pp. 179–211). Orlando, Fl: Academic Press.

O'Donnell, R. C., Griffin, W. J., & Norris, R. C. (1967). *Syntax of kindergarten and elementary school children: A transformational analysis.* Urbana, IL: National Council of Teachers of English.

O'Hear, P. (1987). Which syllabus at 16+: An English Magazine Guide to GCSE. *English Magazine, 14,* 4–13.

Olson, D. (1977). From utterance to text. *Harvard Educational Review, 47,* 257–279.

Ong, W. (1982). *Orality and literacy: The technologizing of the word.* London: Methuen.

Palinscar, A. S., & Brown, A. L. (1984). Reciprocal teaching of comprehension-fostering and monitoring activities. *Cognition and Instruction, 1*(2), 117–175.

Perera, K. (1984). *Children's writing and reading.* Oxford: Basil Blackwell.

Perl, S. (1979). The composing processes of unskilled college writers. *Research in the Teaching of English, 13,* 317–336.

Perron, J. (1974). *An exploratory approach to extending the syntactic development of fourth-grade students through the use of sentence-combining methods.* Bloomington: Indiana University Press.

Petty & Finn. (1981). Classroom teachers' reports on teaching composi-

tion. In S. Haley-James (Ed.), *Perspectives on writing in grades 1-8* (pp. 19–34). Urbana, IL: National Council of Teachers of English.

Philips, S. U. (1972). Participant structure and communicative competence: Warm Springs children in community and classroom. In C. B. Cazden, V. P. John, & D. Hymes (Eds.), *The functions of language in the classroom* (pp. 370–393). New York: Teachers College Press.

Philips, S. U. (1975). Literacy as a mode of communication on the Warm Springs Indian Reservation. In E. H. Lenneberg & E. Lenneberg (Eds.), *Foundations of language development* (pp. 367–381). New York· Academic Press and Paris: UNESCO.

Pianko, S. (1979). A description of the composing process of college freshman writers. *Research in the Teaching of English, 13,* 5–22.

Purves, A. (Ed.). (1988). *Written Communication Annual: Vol. 2. Writing across languages and cultures: Issues in contrastive rhetoric.* Newbury Park: Sage Publications.

Ratner, N., & Bruner, J. (1978). Games, social exchange and the acquisition of language. *Journal of Child Language, 5,* 391–401.

Read, C. (1975). *Children's categorizations of speech sounds in English.* Urbana, IL: National Council of Teachers of English.

Rist, R. C. (1970). Student social class and teach expectations: The self-fulfilling prophesy in ghetto education. *Harvard Educational Review, 40*(3), 411–451.

Rist, R. (1973). *The urban school: A factory for failure.* Cambridge, MA: Massachusetts Institute of Technology Press.

Rogoff, B., Ellis, S., & Gardner, W. (1984). The adjustment of maternal-child instruction according to child's age and task. *Developmental Psychology, 20,* 193–199.

Rogoff, B., & Gardner, W. (1984). Adult guidance of cognitive development. In Rogoff, B. & Lave, J. (Eds.), *Everyday cognition: Its development in social context* (pp. 95–116). Cambridge, MA: Harvard University Press.

Rogoff, B., & Lave, J. (Eds.). (1984). *Everyday cognition: Its development in social context.* Cambridge, MA: Harvard University Press.

Rose, M. (1980). Rigid rules, inflexible plans, and the stifling of language: A cognitive analysis of writer's block. *College Composition and Communication, 31,* 389–401.

Rosen, C. & Rosen, H. (1973). *The language of primary school children.* Hardmonsworth, Middlesex, England: Penguin Education.

Rubin, D. (1988). Introduction: Four dimensions of social construction in written communication. In B. Rafoth & D. Rubin (Eds.), *The social construction of written language* (pp. 1–33). Norwood, NJ: Ablex.

Ruth, L. & Murphy, S. (1988). *Designing writing tasks for the assessment of writing.* Norwood, NJ: Ablex.

Scardamalia, M. (1981) How children cope with the cognitive demands of writing. In C. H. Frederiksen & J. F. Dominic (Eds.), *Writing: The nature, development, and teaching of written communication: Vol. 2. Process, development, and communication* (pp. 81–104). Hillsdale, NJ: Lawrence Erlbaum.

Schieffelin, B. B. (1979). Getting it together: An ethnographic approach to the study of the development of communicative competence. In E. Ochs & B. B. Schieffelin (Eds.), *Developmental pragmatics* (pp. 73–108). New York: Academic Press.

Schieffelin, B. B., & Cochran-Smith, M. (1984). Learning to read culturally: Literacy before schooling. In H. Goelman, A. A. Oberg, & F. Smith (Eds.), *Awakening to literacy* (pp. 3–23). Exeter, NH: Heinemann.

Scollon, R. & Scollon, S. B. K. (1981). *Narrative, literacy, and face in interethnic communication.* Norwood, NJ: Ablex.

Scribner, S., & Cole, M. (1981). *The psychology of literacy.* Cambridge, MA: Harvard University Press.

Searle, D. & Dillon, D. (1980). The message of marking: Teacher written responses to student writing at intermediate grade levels. *Research in the Teaching of English, 14*(3), 233–242.

Shaughnessy, M. P. (1977). *Errors and expectations: A guide for the teacher of basic writing.* New York: Oxford University Press.

Shultz, J., & Florio, S. (1979). Stop and freeze: The negotiation of social and physical space in a kindergarten-first grade classroom. *Anthropology and Education Quarterly, 10*(3), 166–181.

Silberman, A. (in press). *Growing up writing.* New York: Time Books.

Slobin, D. (1979). *Psycholinguistics.* Glenview, IL: Scott Foresman.

Snow, C., & Ferguson, C., (Eds.). (1977). *Talking to children.* Cambridge: Cambridge University Press.

Sommers, N. (1980). Revision strategies of student writers and experienced adult writers. *College Composition and Communication, 31,* 378–88.

Sommers, N. (1982). Responding to student writing. *College Composition and Communication, 33,* 148–156.

Sowers, S. (1981). Young writers' preference for non-narratiave modes of composition. In D. H. Graves (Ed.), *A case study observing the development of primary children's composing, spelling, and motor behavior during the writing process, final report* (NIE Grant No. 6780174) (pp. 189–206). Durham, NH: University of New Hampshire.

Sowers, S. (1985). Learning to write in a workshop: A study in grades one through four. In M. F. Whiteman (Ed.), *Advances in writing research: Vol. 1. Children's early writing development* (pp. 297–342). Norwood, NJ: Ablex.

Sperling, M. (1988). *The writing conference as a collaborative literacy event: Discourse analysis and descriptive case studies of conversation between ninth grade writers and their teachers.* Unpublished doctoral dissertation, University of California, Berkeley.

Sperling, M. & Freedman, S. (1987). A good girl writes like a good girl: Written response and clues to the teaching/learning process. *Written Communication, 4,* 343–369.

Stallard, C. (1979). An analysis of the writing behavior of good writers. *Research in the Teaching of English, 8,* 206–18.

Staton, J., Shuy, R., Peyton, J., & Reed, L. (1988). *Dialogue journal communication.* Norwood, NJ: Ablex.

Stein, N. L., & Glenn, C. G. (1979). An analysis of story comprehension in elementary school children. In R. O. Freedle (Ed.), *New directions in discourse processing II* (pp. 53–120). Norwood, NJ: Ablex.

Steinberg, Z., & Cazden, C. (1979). Children as teachers—of peers and ourselves. *Theory into Practice, 18*(4), 258–266.

Stern, D. (1977). *The first relationship: Infant and mother.* Cambridge, MA: Harvard University Press.

Sulzby, E. (1985). Kindergartners as writers and readers. In M. Farr (Ed.), *Advances in writing research: Vol. 1. Children's early writing development* (pp. 127–200). Norwood, NJ: Ablex.

Swanson-Owens, D. (1986). Identifying natural sources of resistance: A case study of implementing writing across the curriculum. *Research in the Teaching of English, 20*(1), 68–97.

Szwed, John F. (1981). The ethnography of literacy. In M. F. Whiteman (Ed.), *Writing: The nature, development, and teaching of written communication: Vol. 2. Variation in writing: Functional and linguistic-cultural differences* (pp. 13–24). Hillsdale, NJ: Erlbaum.

Tannen, D. (1982). Oral and literate strategies in imaginative fiction: A comparison of spoken and written narratives. *Language, 58,* 1–22.

Tannen, D. (1984a). *Coherence in spoken and written discourse.* Norwood, NJ: Ablex.

Tannen, D. (1984b). *Conversational style: Analyzing talk among friends.* Norwood, NJ: Ablex.

Taylor, D. (1983). *Family literacy: Young children learning to read and write.* Exeter, NH: Heinemann.

Teale, W. H., Estrada, E., & Anderson, A. B. (1981). How preschoolers interact with written communication. In M. L. Kamil (Ed.), *Directions in reading: Research and instruction* (Thirtieth Yearbook of the National Reading Conference) (pp. 257–265). Washington, DC: National Reading Conference.

Tharp, R., Jordan, C., Speidel, G. E., Au, K., Klein, T., Calkins, R., Sloat, K., & Gallimore, R. (1984). Product and process in applied developmental research: Education and the children of a minority. In M. E. Lamb, A. L. Brown, & B. Rogoff (Eds.), *Advances in developmental psychology* (pp. 91–144). Hillsdale, NJ: Erlbaum.

Tizard, B. & Hughes, M. (1984). *Young children learning.* Cambridge, MA: Harvard University Press.

Valdes, G. (1988). *Identifying priorities in the study of writing of Hispanic background students.* Final Report to the Office of Educational Research and Inprovement. Berkeley: University of California, Center for the Study of Writing.

Vygotsky, L. S. (1978). *Mind in society.* Cambridge, MA: Harvard University Press.

Weaver, C. (1982). Welcoming errors as signs of growth. *Language Arts, 59,* 438–444.

Wells, G. (1981). *Learning through interaction: The study of language development* (Vol. 1). Cambridge, England: Cambridge University Press.

Wells, G. (1986). Variation in child language. In P. FLetcher & M. Garman (Eds.), *Language acquisition,* (2nd ed.) (pp. 109–140). Cambridge: Cambridge University Press.

Werner, H. (1948). *Comparative psychology of mental development.* New York: International Universities Press.

Wertsch, J. V., McNamee, G. W., McLane, J. B., & Budwig, N. A. (1980). The adult-child dyad as a problem-solving system. *Child Development, 51,* 1215–1221.

White, E. (1985). *Teaching and assessing writing.* San Francisco: Fossey-Bass.

Wilkinson, L. C. (1982). Introduction: A sociolinguistic approach to communicating in the classroom. In L. C. Wilkinson (Ed.), *Communicating in the classroom* (pp. 3–12). New York: Academic Press.

Winterowd, R. (1975). *Contemporary rhetoric: A conceptual background with readings.* New York: Harcourt Brace Jovanovich.

Witte, S. (1983). Topical structure and revision: An exploratory study. *College Composition and Communication, 34,* 313–341.

Witte, S. (1985). Revising, composing theory and research design. In S. W. Freedman (Ed.), *The acquisition of written language: Response and revision* (pp. 250–284). Norwood, NJ: Ablex.

Witte, S. (1987). Composing and pre-text. *College Composition and Communication, 38,* 297–425.

Witte, S. P., Meyer, P. R., Miller, T. P., & Faigley, L. (1981). *A national survey of college and university writing program directors* (Final report to the Fund for the Improvement of Postsecondary Education).

Witte, S. P., R. Cherry, P. Meyer, & M. Trachsel. (in press). *Holistic assessment of writing: Issues in theory and practice.* New York: Guildford Press.

Wolf, D. P. (1985). Ways of telling: Text repertoires in elementary school children. *Journal of Education, 167,* 71–87.

Wolf, D. P. (1988). Opening up assessment. *Educational Leadership,* 24–29.

·36·

THE CONVENTIONS OF WRITING

Richard E. Hodges

This chapter examines research concerning teaching *conventions of writing,* a component of general written language instruction that includes spelling, handwriting, and typographical elements including capitalization, segmentation, and punctuation. Spelling and handwriting once held prominent positions in the school curriculum, while the teaching of other writing conventions has traditionally been subsumed within spelling and composition instruction. As a result, punctuation and capitalization are, for the most part, auxiliary footnotes in an extensive English language-arts literature.

A review of the literature covering the conventions of writing reveals a decline in the past 25 years in the number of investigations into the nature and teaching of handwriting. Such has not been the situation for spelling, however. Spelling continues to be a source of considerable interest for researchers, especially for those looking into the general acquisition of written language because orthographic skills are involved in both writing and reading. It is also the case that, in the more recent work on spelling development, punctuation, segmentation, and capitalization are becoming objects of study in view of their relevance in understanding the development of general print literacy.

Over 80 years have elapsed since B. C. Gregory, superintendent of schools in Chelsea, Massachusetts, observed that

Of all the blind teaching we teachers do, the teaching of spelling is the blindest. It is empirical in most cases; reason (much less psychology) enters very little into our methods. We differ as to oral and written spelling, we differ as regards the use of spelling-books and the degree of difficulty of words used; but why we differ, or what is the psychological basis of this or that method, few of us can say. (Gregory, 1907–1908)

Much has been accomplished in the intervening years to allay Superintendent Gregory's concern. In many respects, spelling has been one of the most studied areas of the school curriculum. This is not to say that consensus has been achieved about the nature of spelling ability; nor, for that matter, about the instructional practices that are believed to foster this ability. On the contrary, spelling remains a subject about which widely divergent views are held regarding both theory and practice.

Although a primary purpose of this chapter is a consideration of teaching practices in spelling, contemporary research has largely centered on the nature and development of spelling ability rather than on instructional issues (cf. Read & Hodges, 1982). This emphasis is not typical of the traditional spelling research literature that prior to 1970 was largely concerned with curriculum and method. (cf. Horn, 1941, 1950, 1960; T. Horn, 1969; Sherwin, 1969).

In addition, spelling research has seldom been extended beyond the elementary school years, in large part because direct instruction in spelling is uncommon past eighth grade. Interestingly, studies of spelling sometimes reappear at the college level, usually to identify and remediate spelling difficulties (Shaughnessy, 1977; Fischer, Shankweiler, & Liberman, 1985). Given the dearth of research on spelling during the high school years, the picture of spelling development from its onset to maturity remains incomplete.

HISTORICAL FRAMEWORKS

Spelling has maintained a secure position as a subject in the school curriculum (Hanna & Hanna, 1959; Hodges, 1977; Hodges, 1987; Towery, 1979; Venezky, 1980.), mainly because of the importance attributed to correct spelling by the larger society. The first large-scale American scientific study of classroom learning, for instance, included an appraisal of the outcomes of spelling instruction as a measurement of school effectiveness (Rice, 1987; Venezky, 1980).

Contemporary spelling instruction still reflects the brunt of two forces—one societal, the other psychological—that altered the traditional school curriculum in the early twentieth century. An intensified sense of the social purposes that schooling plays led to a new guide for the selection of content—*the principle of social utility,* a principle that proposed that what is learned in school should have utility in life outside of school (McKee, 1939). At the same time, views of learning also changed as mental discipline gave way to the formation of bonds between stimulus and behavior (Thorndike, 1929).

The principle of social utility and behaviorist psychology affected the spelling curriculum in the form of a number of influential publications devoted to explicating new views of spelling theory and practice, especially those set forth by Ernest Horn (Horn, 1919, 1926) whose influence is still felt (cf. Fitzsimmons & Loomer, 1974; Graham, 1983; Johnson, Langford, & Quorn, 1981; Sherwin, 1969).

Traditional Research and Its Implications

A basic question early spelling researchers asked was "What words should be learned?" In response, two lines of attack were taken, investigations of the frequencies of words that writers use (Ayres, 1913; Bauer, 1916; Buckingham & Dolch; 1936; Chancellor, 1910; Dolch, 1927; Fitzgerald, 1951; Hillerich, 1978; Horn, 1926; Jones, 1913; Rinsland, 1945; Tidyman, 1926) and investigations of the words that writers have the most difficulty spelling (Bauer, 1916; Brittain & Fitzgerald, 1942; Fitzgerald, 1932, 1938; Furness & Boyd, 1958; Gates, 1937; Johnson, 1950; Pollack, 1953).

Hanna and Hanna (1959) have reported that well over 600 hundred such studies were undertaken up to 1940. The number may be excessive; but these inquiries had lasting effects on spelling instruction and established an ongoing examination of the frequency distributions of words (cf. Carroll, Davis, & Richman, 1971; Kucera & Francis, 1967). What have studies such as these revealed? The answer is perhaps most succinctly stated by J. A. H. Murray, founding editor of the *Oxford English Dictionary,* who observed that the "English language has a well-defined center but no discernible circumference" (Horn, 1938).

Studies to determine optimal instructional methods in spelling paralleled those that were intended to determine utilitarian word lists. Spelling became one of the most thoroughly researched school subjects, leading Horn (1919) to conclude that ample experimental data were available to develop a definitive course of study and to prepare a list of 41 instructional principles that set the course of spelling instruction for nearly the next half century.

CURRENT UNDERSTANDINGS

Orthography

English orthography has a widely held reputation as an inadequate writing system with unstable correspondences between letters and sounds. Were it a true alphabetic writing system, its critics assert, English orthography would include only as many letters as are needed to represent the number of speech sounds of spoken language. Such a one-to-one correspondence would make learning to spell and read a relatively simple matter (Hodges, 1972).

Proposals to reform the alphabetic vagaries of English orthography date at least as far back as the thirteenth century (Hodges, 1964; Venezky, 1980). Like the language that it represents, an orthography is an instrument that is influenced and shaped by cultural forces and events. Invasions by Danes and

Normal French, a rebirth of classical studies during the Renaissance, Gutenberg's printing press, interactions with other cultures and languages, changes in English phonology over time, and Samuel Johnson's dictionary are among the significant forces and events that have shaped present-day English orthography (Scragg, 1974).

Despite the orthography's apparently erratic nature and calls for its reform (cf. Dewey, 1971; Pitman, & St. John, 1969; Yule 1986), it is worth noting that in-depth investigations and analyses of the nature of English orthography have primarily taken place within the past 30 years (Adams, 1981; Albrow, 1972; Hodges, 1972; Becker, Dixon, & Anderson-Inman, 1980; Chomsky & Halle, 1968; Gleitman & Rozin, 1977; Hall, 1961; Hanna, Hanna, Hodges, & Rudorf, 1966; Henderson, 1982; Reed, 1969; Russell, 1975; Smith, Jr., 1968; Stubbs, 1980; Venezky, 1967, 1970). These investigations have revealed that English orthography is more complex than its surface appearance suggests. The English writing system is more than an apparently flawed graphic transcription of phonology; it also represents lexical, grammatical, and semantic features of language (cf. Chomsky & Halle, 1968; Venezky, 1970).

The findings of these orthographic studies have significance for the spelling curriculum. For, if the orthography is a closer representation of language than a surface inspection suggests, then a spelling course of study can emphasize an examination of structural relationships among written words rather than treating the spelling of each word as a specific act of learning.

Models of Spelling

Several attempts have been made to devise models of spelling behavior that explain what transpires in the minds of persons as they spell. Such models reflect theorists' conceptions of the nature of language and the nature of learning. Simon and Simon (1973) and Simon (1976) have proposed an information processing model of spelling behavior that is comprised of word recognition memory and phonetic knowledge. Nicholson and Schacter (1979) have developed a three-tiered model in which spelling ability grows out of general language knowledge, visual associations, and internalized orthographic rules. Nelson (1980) has described two routes to spelling achievement, one that translates the phonemic elements of words into graphemes and one that moves directly from word meaning to spelling.

Ehri (1987b) has recently proposed that spellings of specific words systematically accumulate in memory through a process that assimilates the spellings of known words into memories of their meanings and pronunciations, especially when those spellings conform to known orthographic regularities. In Ehri's "amalgamation" model, spelling and reading development are closely related. Her model contains three knowledge sources: 1) alphabetic letters; 2) the orthographic system; and 3) memory of spellings of specific words, including their visual configurations and such features as letter symbolizations of phonemes and morphemes.

Yellin (1986) has placed learning to spell within a context of general written language literacy and has attempted to classify spelling processes and practices in terms of "bottom-up," "top-down," and "interactive-compensatory" models. Bottom-up models, according to Yellin, describe texts and teachers as controllers of student learning; such models emphasize rules, word lists, and rote memory in spelling instruction, with little connection with actual writing (cf. Fitzsimmons & Loomer, 1974). Top-down models, on the other hand, describe students as controllers of their own learning; these models emphasize the development of generalizations about the nature of the writing system that emerge during the course of active involvement in writing and reading (cf. Gentry, 1984; Henderson & Beers, 1980; Read; 1986). Interactive compensatory models describe spelling behavior in terms of phonological information and higher level processing skills (cf. Jorm, 1983).

A recent, provocative, spelling model is that proposed by Bouffler (1984) who views language as functional, social, and contextual. In her socio-psycholinguistic (semiotic) model, children learn to spell as needs arise for writing. Bouffler maintains that developmental stage theory is incorrect because it posits an endpoint—adult language—toward which learners strive. She counters this view with one in which children draw upon many of the same strategies that adults employ in writing (including spelling), although lacking knowledge of the full range of the language system to draw upon because of less experience with language.

Recent models of spelling share a common foundation, that learning to spell is a complex cognitive undertaking to which formal instruction and reading and writing in daily life contribute. As Frith (1980a) has noted, learning to spell is richer in intellectual texture than commonly pictured.

Spelling-Reading Relationships

That spelling ability grows in context with the development of other written language abilities is not a new idea (Cornman, 1902; Thorndike, 1929). Spelling and reading instruction, for example, were at one time directly linked, becoming separate subjects during the nineteenth century (Hodges, 1987).

At the same time, it should be recognized that the processes of reading and spelling differ in some significant ways. Spelling in English orthography is a more complex process than reading because spelling requires an accurate reproduction of all the letters of words, many of which have complex links to phonology. Spelling requires that the writer pay close attention to the fine details of printed words, a process that hinders efficient reading. Such differences suggest that good readers who are poor spellers appear to have developed very functional sampling strategies for reading, but ill-defined strategies for looking at words in detail for spelling (Frith, 1978, 1980b).

Both reading and spelling behavior rely on the concept of *orthographic word,* that spoken words can be represented graphically. Orthographic words provide a visual and spatial form that facilitates word memory (Ehri, 1987a, 1987b; Templeton, 1979b), both in recognizing words when reading and in recalling words when writing (Invernizzi, 1984). A knowledge of orthographic words develops from numerous, varied, interactions with written language—being read to, observing

print in the environment, exploring books, and writing (cf. Ehri, 1980; Fearing, 1983).

The Development of Word Knowledge and Spelling Strategies

R. S. Thompson (1930) observed that "Theorists who have been fortunate in a special aptitude (for spelling), or have forgotten their early struggles with the subject, have sometimes been disposed to consider the matter a simple one" (p. 1). Thompson's admonition has not been lost on contemporary spelling researchers. Their descriptions of the development of spelling ability and how it emerges in concert with maturing intellectual processes, work knowledge, and functional experiences with written language in various social contexts reveal the complex nature of spelling behavior (Henderson, 1981; Templeton, 1986).

That young learners view the world differently than adults do has special consequence for understanding spelling development. Read's (1971, 1975) groundbreaking observations of young children's early spelling strategies, their invented spellings, set the stage for a wealth of studies that, in aggregate, describe the active roles learners play in developing knowledge about the nature and uses of written language.

Young learners' acquaintance with written language begins with a kind of global understanding, a *gestalt,* of its nature and purposes (Wood, 1982); that writing is, for example, a graphic representation of meaning and that orthography contains some basic attributes, such as directionality and linearity (Clay, 1975; Ferreiro & Teberosky, 1982). A child's scribbling, for instance, globally represents an intended meaning (Harste, Woodward, & Burke, 1984; Heald-Taylor, 1984). Random letters and other graphic markers used in early writing attempts represent various semantic units such as paragraphs, sentences, and phrases (Hall & Hall, 1984). Children's early writing, in short, reveals the emergent beginnings of literacy.

The initial phase of spelling development has been variously termed as *precommunicative* (Gentry, 1982) and *preliterate* (Henderson & Templeton, 1986), the latter term more appropriate because early writing has a communicative function, however primitive. Although preliterate spelling demonstrates a young child's awareness of the purposes of writing, it also demonstrates that a concept of *word* is lacking, and that words can be segmented into phonemes (Read, 1986). Later use of letter-name spellings more nearly approximates true spelling, as children associate letters to sounds on the basis of shared phonetic features (Read, 1971, 1975.).

Several investigators have described the transition from a phonetic letter-name spelling strategy to a phonemic spelling strategy in which conventional spellings begin to appear (Beers, 1980; Beers & Henderson, 1977; Bissex, 1980; Gentry, 1978). These *transitional* spellings (Gentry, 1984) are illustrative of a young child's recognition of important orthographic features, such as vowel spellings, *e*-markers and vowel digraph patterns, orthographic inflectional patterns, and frequently used letter sequences. The use of these features is indicative of a child's growing visual memory of spelling patterns within *words* (Fearing, 1983; Ehri, 1980; Sloboda, 1980) where more abstract (and more powerful) orthographic relationships are to be found.

Morton Hunt (1982) has pointed out that "The human mind . . . makes order out of its experiences not only by grouping them into categories but by noticing patterns or regularities in the way things happen" (p. 177). For the development of spelling ability, an awareness of orthographic patterns within words marks an important advance (Schlagal, 1982). Yet, many riddles abound for young spellers to solve as their understandings of the working of English spelling move beyond the limitations of sound-letter relationships and toward the orthographic nature of words, riddles about letter constraints, and about ways that syllables, bases, prefixes, and suffixes are joined in polysyllabic words (Beers & Henderson, 1977 Beers, Beers, & Grant (1977); J. Gentry, 1981; Marino, 1979; Schwartz & Doehring, 1977; Schlagal, 1982; Thomas, 1982; Wilde, 1986; Zutell, 1979).

A significant strategy emerges in the elementary school years for most developing spellers, as early as second grade for some (Beers & Beers, 1980), an *analogical* spelling strategy in which orthographic knowledge of known words is used to spell other words whose spellings have not been secured in memory (Baron, 1978; Marsh, Friedman, Welsh, & Desberg, 1980; Nolen and McCartin, 1984; Phillips, 1980; Radebaugh, 1985). Analogical spelling is a high-order strategy that draws on a writer's knowledge of orthographic relationships among related words, requires a well-stocked memory store of words, and emphasizes visual strategies over phonological ones (Marsh, Friedman, Welsh, & Desberg, 1980).

Another important orthographic principle involves the spellings of words with shared roots and bases (Chomsky & Halle, 1968; Venezky, 1970) in which the root spellings remain essentially the same even when the words are differently pronounced. Awareness of this principle makes it possible for spellers to break words with unfamiliar spellings into morphemic segments and to seek analogies to morphemically related words they do know that will help in spelling the unfamiliar ones (Hodges, 1982; Radebaugh, 1985).

The use of knowledge of morphemic representations in orthography is one of the later spelling strategies to develop (Thomas 1982; Zutell, 1979). Children before fourth grade exhibit little control over derivational spelling patterns (Marino, 1979; Zutell, 1979). Although derivational spelling strategies are displayed by some fifth and sixth graders (Invernizzi, 1984; Templeton 1979a, 1979b, 1986), the development of this strategy usually continues into maturity (Baker, 1980; Fischer, Shankweiler, & Liberman, 1985; Read, 1986).

Few studies have examined the spelling behaviors of high school students. Templeton (1979b) compared sixth, eighth, and tenth graders in their abilities to pronounce and spell derived words. Templeton and Scarborough-Franks (1985) looked at the ability of sixth and tenth graders to produce orthographic and phonetic derivatives of three vowel alternation patterns found in derived words. The results of both studies indicate that many students are more knowledgeable of the orthography than of the phonology of derived words.

A few investigations of the spelling behaviors of adults suggest inferences about spelling development in later school years. Fischer, Shankweiler, and Liberman (1985) found in comparing college-level good and poor spellers that, although poor spellers were deficient at all levels (phonetic, orthographic rules, morphophonemic/derived), they mostly lacked a knowledge of morphophonemic structure. Bookman (1984) compared college-level poor spellers' performance on the spelling section of the WRAT with those of fifth graders on the same test and found that the adult poor spellers who read poorly performed much like the fifth graders, when analyzed in a developmental framework. Marcel (1980) compared the spelling behaviors of adults in a literacy class, a dyphasic/dysgraphic adult patient, and 8- and 9-year-old children and found developmental similarities among the three groups.

Studies such as these demonstrate that older students with spelling difficulties have a limited knowledge of the multilevel nature of English orthography and a limited apprehension of word structure (Anderson, 1985). It seems in learning to spell that, as Shipley has remarked about the lexicon in general, "words repay the attention they are accorded" (1977, p. 52).

Analyses of Spelling Errors

Investigations of spelling behavior from a developmental perspective provide a significant observation: that spelling errors are graphic expressions of a writer's knowledge of linguistic/orthographic reality. Individuals make few random spelling errors in their writing (Hodges, 1981).

The first extensive study of spelling errors took place in 1918 (Hollingsworth, 1918). Numerous studies followed, usually in hope of determining causes of spelling difficulties that would suggest ways to groups words to facilitate their learning (cf. Book & Harter, 1929; Carroll, 1930; Foran, 1934; Gates, 1937; Masters, 1927; Mendenhall, 1930; Robinson, 1940; Spache, 1940a, 1940b, 1940c).

Spelling errors have been variously classified, but usually on the basis of *word difficulty* (Johnson, 1950; Fitzgerald, 1932, 1938; Jones, 1913); *word frequency* (Brittain & Fitzgerald, 1942; Goyen & Martin, 1977; Johnson, 1970; Pollack, 1953); *word meaningfulness* (Bloomer, 1961; Mangieri & Baldwin, 1979); *serial-position effects* (Jensen, 1962; Kooi, Schutz, & Baker, 1965; Mendenhall, 1930); and *phonetic factors* (Petty, 1957). (cf. Cahen, Craun, & Johnson, 1971, for a comprehensive discussion of spelling difficulties.)

Spelling error classifications have mainly focused on surface characteristics such as letter omissions, additions, substitutions, and transpositions. Following Read's exploration of underlying causes of invented spellings (1971, 1975), however, attention has been turned to identifying perceptual, linguistic, and cognitive factors involved in spelling that errors reveal (Bouffler, 1984; Frith, 1980b; Ganschow, 1984; Henderson, 1981; cf. Henderson & Beers, 1980; Invernizzi; 1984; Marino, 1981; Nelson, 1980; Schlagal, 1982; Weiner, 1980; Wilde, 1986, 1987) and that focus more on the writer's own contributions to spelling performance than on the effects of various instructional methods and materials (Francis, 1984).

Spelling errors provide clues to a writer's personal system

of orthographic rules that are drawn upon when spelling (Zutell, 1979) and reveal a developmental progression of the logical processes involved (Francis, 1984; Marino, 1981). It seems, as John Dryden observed, that "Errors like straws upon the surface flow; He who would search for pearls must dive below" (1972, p. 27).

Differences Between Good and Poor Spellers

Spelling remains, of course, a difficulty for many writers. A developmental perspective helps to clarify some of the reasons. Unlike reading, as noted earlier, a thorough knowledge of orthographic word structures is inherent in correct spelling (Ehri, 1987c). However, although poor spellers' misspellings are more diverse and deviant than those of typical spellers (Manolakes, 1975; Schlagal, 1982), the misspellings approximate those made by typical spellers at earlier developmental phases. Similar findings have been reported for mentally retarded spellers (Holmes & Peper, 1977), and also for learning disabled spellers whose error patterns are analogous to those of writers three to four years younger (Gerber, 1984). The profiles of dyslexic spellers have also been found to be similar to those of normal spellers in early stages of writing (Moats, 1983). What emerges from an accumulation of research into spelling difficulty is a picture of spellers who, for whatever reason, have incomplete information about the orthographic structures of words (Drake & Ehri, 1984).

Poor spellers who are poor readers, for example, appear to have little knowledge of phoneme-grapheme relationships, as well as a diminished word memory (Drake & Ehri, 1984; Fox & Routh, 1983; Frith, 1980b; Perin, 1982). Better readers who are yet poor spellers, however, make misspellings that more closely correspond to plausible phoneme-grapheme patterns (Frith, 1980b). Nevertheless, they tend to stay with a phonological strategy, even when there is insufficient knowledge about the sound structure of a word (Frith & Frith, 1980). They also tend to spell phoneme by phoneme, as though naive about word structure (Radebaugh, 1985).

Poor spellers who are further along the developmental path appear to have a limited, poorly organized, knowledge about word structure and orthography that is not easily accessed when needed (Gerber, 1984). They are less able than typical spellers to determine whether nonsense words approximate standard English spelling (Wallace, Klein, & Schneider, 1968) They lack knowledge of morphographic root patterns (Drake & Ehri, 1984), and they have difficulty identifying misspelled segments of text (Ormrod, 1985).

Proofreading

Being able to detect and correct misspelled words, however, is not readily achieved by average spellers. Part of the difficulty is that strategies used for reading mitigate against proofreading. Proficient readers do not usually read word by word; nor, for that matter, do they delve into the structures of words unless it become necessary to do so. Yet proofreading requires both of these operations. In addition, having once written some text, that text is highly predictable to the writer (Bouffler, 1984). It is for this reason that errors are more likely to be detected when a text is set aside for a period of time after it is written.

Being able to detect and correct one's spelling errors is a necessary aspect of spelling behavior. Yet, few inquiries have been made into the manner in which proofreading skills develop (Lydiatt, 1984) or into the kinds of proofreading strategies that appear to be most effective (Personke & Knight, 1967). The scant available research evidence indicates that text familiarity enhances proofreading, since attention can be focused on the proofreading task (Levy & Begin, 1984); that it is easier to detect spelling errors that both look wrong and sound wrong (Cohen, 1980); and that poor spellers have difficulty identifying and reading their own misspellings (Frith, 1978).

Common wisdom has often advocated reading text backwards (to obscure meaning and highlight word analysis), subvocalizing or reading text out loud (to relate orthographic words with spoken ones), allowing a "cooling off" period before proofreading new written material, exchanging papers with others, and reading text aloud while another students proofreads as effective proofreading techniques. Riefer (1987), however, reports that reading through a text more than once is a more effective proofreading procedure than reading text backwards. Lydiatt (1984) describes several proofreading strategies based on assumptions that effective proofreading is a function of a reader's sensitivity to the existence of errors and the extent of certainty in making a judgment that a word is incorrectly spelled. Drake & Ehri (1984) suggest converting spelled words to their spoken forms to see if the spelling conforms to correct pronunciation. Whatever techniques are taught, direct instruction of proofreading techniques appears to have positive outcomes (Frasch, 1965; Personke & Knight, 1967).

Punctuation, Segmentation, and Capitalization

Although the emphasis of this chapter has been on spelling, writers also need to be conversant with other graphic features that make up written language; namely, punctuation, segmentation, and capitalization. Wilde (1986) has described the important functions of these writing conventions. Punctuation sets apart syntactic units, and provides intonational cues and semantic information. Segmentation (the spaces between words in print) identifies word boundaries. In conjunction with periods, capital letters have both semantic and syntactic uses in indicating proper names and sentence boundaries.

Instruction in the uses of these graphic conventions has long been a part of teaching spelling and composition (Cronnell, 1980; L. Gentry, 1980, 1981). Yet, how young writers conceptualize those uses has only recently become a subject of empirical investigation. (cf. Wilde, 1986 1987, for a comprehensive review.)

Knowledge of the functions of various punctuation markers progresses slowly, even with instruction (Cordeiro, 1986; Cordeiro, Giacobbe, & Cazden, 1983). Milz (as cited in Wilde, 1986) reports that some first graders are likely to omit punctuation altogether, except a period, which might be placed at the end of every line, or at the end of a written discourse (Edelsky, 1983). Some young writers even invent their own punctuation marks (Calkins, 1980; Cordeiro, Giacobbe, & Cazden, 1983). The idiosyncratic use of periods and other punctuation marks is most likely a consequence of an absence of simple rules that would explain their functions to young writers (Edelsky, 1983).

Gradually, however, knowledge about the uses of graphic conventions stabilizes, probably as much from using them in functional writing as from formal instruction and practice, especially if functional writing is frequent (Calkins, 1980; Edelsky, 1983; Harste, Woodward, & Burke, 1984). At the present state of understanding, it appears clear that growth of knowledge about functional uses of punctuation, capitalization, and segmentation can be accounted for within the context of the development of general written language ability.

Handwriting

The importance that is attributed to correct spelling in school and in the larger society was pointed out previously, and legible handwriting has also had a share of that importance. The quality of a student's handwriting, for example, can influence raters' judgments of the quality of content of compositions (Marschall & Powers, 1969).

Handwriting enjoyed a featured place in the common school curriculum as a separate subject until the early 1930s when it began to be taught in connection with spelling and composition. Other subjects moved into the curriculum to take its place and less attention was given to methods of teaching handwriting in teacher preparation (Currie, 1981). Systematic handwriting instruction became largely relegated to the early school years (Sassoon, 1983).

Numerous surveys of existing handwriting research and practices have been published (cf. Askov & Peck, 1982; Graham & Miller, 1980; Masters, 1987; Peck, Askov & Fairchild; 1980). Yet, perhaps more than any other subject, handwriting instruction has been largely guided by tradition and pragmatic factors, with considerable reliance on commercial materials as vehicles of instruction (Froese, 1981).

Summaries of current practices indicate that handwriting instruction is fairly uniform throughout the United States, typically beginning with manuscript writing in the first grade, with a transition to cursive writing sometime before the third grade. Direct handwriting instruction is commonly a whole class activity; nearly a third of the classes use commercial workbooks, most often for copying practice. Teacher observation rather than some uniform scale remains the predominant form of handwriting assessment (Masters, 1987). Legibility (well proportioned, uniformly arranged, letters and words) and fluency (rate of writing) are critical criteria in determining handwriting quality. Freeman's (1959) legibility classification scheme is the most commonly used; namely, letter form, uniformity of slant, letter alignment, quality of line, and spacing between letters and words. Writing speed is sometimes considered in assessing handwriting skill, especially in activities where speed may be a factor, such as notetaking and timed practice exercises (Graham & Miller, 1980). Phelps, Stempel, and Speck (1985) have reported that writing speed is perceived as a bigger problem than legibility for many children.

The preferred form of writing, cursive or manuscript, has generated considerable debate among handwriting specialists since 1920 when manuscipt writing was transplanted to the United States from Great Britain. Yet, by 1962, nearly 86 percent of American schools taught manuscript as an initial writing device, followed by a transition to cursive (Froese, 1981), even though evidence is sparse to show that cursive is faster to write or more legible to read (Koenke, 1986; Peck, Askov, & Fairchild, 1980). Research evidence is similarly equivocal concerning the superiority of particular approaches or commercial systems to ease the transition from manuscript to cursive (Masters, 1987). Perhaps, as Froese (1981) has concluded, the transition from manuscript to cursive, if even necessary, should be an individual decision; and, if so, that both writing forms should be maintained (Peck, Askov, & Fairchild, 1980).

Evidence is also inconclusive with respect to superiority of styles of writing (e.g., italic, cursive, D'Nealian). In general, proponents of respective writing styles have found their own system to be the most beneficial. One is reminded of Bruner's comment that "common sense (and scientific puritanism) warns against: Better not know too early at the start what you are looking for lest you find it" (1983 p. 3).

Finally, literature on handwriting provides only limited insights into successful teaching practices (Askov & Peck, 1982; Masters, 1987). What appears to be important in the development of handwriting is the amount of emphasis teachers place on legible, neat writing (Koenke, 1986; Milone & Wasylyk, 1981; Peck, Askov, & Fairchild, 1980), and also the presence in the classroom of good handwriting models (Milone & Wasylyk, 1981).

CURRICULAR AND INSTRUCTIONAL IMPLICATIONS

This chapter began with an observation made by a Massachusetts school superintendent who early in the present century deplored the absence of a sensible rationale for teaching spelling (Gregory, 1907–1908). The remainder of the chapter has centered on an examination of current understandings of the nature and functions of spelling development and other conventions of writing from which such a rationale might be established.

Perhaps the most significant insight stemming from this examination is a recognition of the active involvement of developing writers in their own learning as they extract fundamental characteristics about the conventions of writing from an orthography whose surface appearance belies the existence of an underlying rationale. Bissex' (1980) illuminating description of her son's emergence as a mature writer concludes with the comment that "The logic by which we teach is not always the logic by which children learn" (1981 p. 199). What, then, might be concluded from the areas of research that have been reviewed here that places the logic of instruction in closer proximity with the logic of the learner?

It is evident that learning about the conventions of writing is a part of a process in which general written literacy develops from experiences both in and out of school. Ferreiro and Teberosky (1982), among others reported elsewhere in this *Handbook,* have vividly described how many young learners access the print environment in which they live in formulating early conceptions of the nature and purposes of written language. For such children, school becomes a place in which these conceptions are expanded and refined.

A recently reported study (Clarke, 1988), for example, in which first-grade children who were encouraged to use invented spelling in creative writing were compared with other first graders who were prompted to use correct spellings reveals that more of the inventive spellers were able to write independently early in the school year. Significant differences favoring the inventive spellers were also found with respect to text length and variety of words used. Moreover, the children using invented spelling scored higher on subsequent posttests of spelling and word recognition, even though their written productions showed no increase in the percentage of correct spelling over the term of the study. Clearly, these young writers were expanding their understandings of the nature and functions of spelling, even in the absence of direct instruction.

Herein lies a basic issue concerning the treatment of spelling and other writing conventions in the English language-arts curriculum in the years ahead; namely, whether students' control over the conventions of writing is most effectively achieved by teacher-directed instruction using texts and other prepared materials or whether such control grows incidentally out of students' uses of these conventions in natural writing. The issue is not a trivial one. For at its heart lie basically different views about the nature and purposes of the English language arts-curriculum (and curriculum in general), views that provide fuel to a general ongoing debate concerning the merits of "student-centered" versus "teacher-centered" approaches to curriculum development.

In support of student-centered approaches, numerous reports have appeared in recent years that call attention to how teachers' utilization of children's invented spellings in daily writing can provide opportunities to help young students extend their emerging knowledge of English orthography (cf. Anderson, 1985; DiStefano & Hagerty, 1985; Lehr, 1986; Lutz, 1986; Wilde, 1989). These, and other, reports cited in this chapter point out students' active roles in determining the nature and uses of writing conventions through reading and writing and how they develop strategies for coping with a complex orthography. In this regard, Wilde (1990) set forth a rationale for a student-centered spelling curriculum that is predicated on these findings, one in which the pace and direction of learning about English spelling are determined primarily by students themselves.

Conversely, others (cf. Henderson, 1985; Henderson & Templeton, 1986; Morris, Nelson, & Perney, 1986) have drawn upon developmental spelling research data to describe spelling programs in which formal, direct instruction using textual materials provides the basis for student learning. In either case, the research base concerning the nature and development of spelling ability is now sufficiently rich to focus once again on investigations of instructional methods and on the development of materials that draw upon this research base to promote spelling literacy throughout the school years.

Regardless of which instructional approaches are advocated, the research reviewed in this chapter points to an important conclusion—that learning about and using the conventions of writing is an *intellectual* process. Providing for spelling instruction as though the ability to spell is only a product of memorizing specific words fails to acknowledge that, like the acquisition of other language behavior, much of what is learned about spelling is gained by noticing recurring patterns encountered in functional settings and trying out and revising hypotheses about these patterns in other writing situations.

That the orthography operates at more abstract levels than sound-letter correspondence has been cogently pointed out elsewhere (Bookman, 1984; Read, 1975). These levels are revealed when groups of words are associated by their phonological, lexical, and syntactic, and semantic relationships, relationships that many students make intuitively (Radebaugh, 1985; Schlagal, 1982; Thomas, 1982), and that creative instruction can foster for others (Chomsky, 1979). The more information about the logic of word structure to which students become sensitive, the more sophisticated and responsive become their uses of this knowledge in spelling words (Hodges, 1982; Templeton, 1979a, 1979b). The discovery of relationships among words of similar structure, then, is an important step in advancing the development of useful spelling strategies (Elliott, 1982; Zutell, 1979).

Learning to spell is, after all, learning about the structures and uses of words in written language. Wide reading in a variety of contexts contributes to the development of a word reservoir that can be used as a data base for exploring orthographic relationships (Zutell, 1979) and that makes possible an analogical spelling strategy. Instructional strategies such as word sorts (Gillet & Kita, 1979) and semantic mapping (Johnson & Pearson, 1984) further help in the formation of analogies among related words.

Students' spelling and their use of other writing conventions in functional writing provides the discerning teacher with important information about their orthographic knowledge. A qualitative analysis of spelling errors reveals the different levels of word knowledge and learning rates that exist in classrooms and provides information that makes it more likely that instruction can be matched to learners' levels of understanding (Marcel, 1980; Schlagal, 1982), both for individual students (Ganschow, 1981; 1984; Marino, 1981; Wilde, 1989) and for students who are grouped at similar instructional levels (Morris, Nelson, & Perney, 1986).

In a 1930 review of spelling instruction, R. S. Thompson made the following observation:

"Neither more nor better methods of drill, nor the most ingenious methods of individual and specific attack on words will make up for the ignorance of exactly how the learning of spelling goes on, incidentally and within the spelling period." (p.1)

The aim of this chapter has been to consider the extent to which such ignorance has been supplanted by recent understandings that have been gained about the nature and functions of spelling behavior and other writing conventions, understandings that might shed light on how the uses of these fundamental tools of writing can effectively be presented in English language arts. At the least, curriculum makers and teachers should be constantly mindful of the contributions that students make to their own learning and, in doing so, create instructional settings and materials that promote students' active explorations of the conventions of writing, just as they do naturally.

References

Adams, M. J. (1981). What good is orthographic redundancy? In O. J. L Tzeng and H. Singer (Eds.), *Perception in print: Reading research in experimental psychology* (pp. 197–221). Hillsdale, NJ: Lawrence Erlbaum Assoc.

Albrow, K. H. (1972). *The English writing system: Notes towards a description.* London: Longman.

Anderson, K. F. (1985). The development of spelling ability and linguistic strategies. *The reading teacher, 39,* 140–147.

Askov, E. N., & Peck, M. (1982). Handwriting. In H. E. Mitzel (Ed.), *Encyclopedia of educational research* (5th ed.) (pp. 764–769). New York: Macmillan.

Ayres, L. P. (1913). *The spelling vocabularies of personal and business letters.* New York: Russell Sage Foundation.

Baker, R. G. (1980). Orthographic awareness. In U. Frith (Ed.), *Cognitive processes in spelling* (pp. 51–68). London: Academic Press.

Baron, J. (1978). Using spelling-sound correspondences without trying to learn them. *Visible Language, 12,* 55–70.

Bauer, N. (1916). *The New Orleans public school spelling list.* New Orleans, LA: F. F. Hansell & Bros.

Becker, W. C., Dixon, R., & Anderson-Inman, L. (1980). *Morphographic and root word analysis of 26,000 high frequency words* (Technical report 1980-1). Eugene: University of Oregon Follow Through Project.

Beers, J. W. (1980). Developmental strategies of spelling competence in primary school children. In E. H. Henderson & J. W. Beers (Eds.), *Developmental and cognitive aspects of learning to spell* (pp. 36–45). Newark, DE: International Reading Association.

Beers, J. W., & Beers, C. S. (1980). Vowel spelling strategies among first and second graders: A growing awareness of written words. *Language Arts, 57,* 166–172.

Beers, J. W., Beers, C. S., & Grant, K. (1977). The logic behind children's spelling. *The Elementary School Journal, 77,* 238–242.

Beers, J. W., & Henderson, E. H. (1977). A study of developing orthographic concepts among first graders. *Research in the Teaching of English, 11,* 133–148.

Bissex, G. L. (1980). *Gyns at wrk: A child learns to read and write* Cambridge, MA: Harvard University Press.

Bloomer, R. H. (1961). Concepts of meaning and the reading and spelling difficulty of words. *Journal of Educational Research, 54,* 178–182.

Book, W. F., & Harter, R. S. (1929). Mistakes which pupils make in spelling. *Journal of Educational Research, 19,* 106–118.

Bookman, M. O. (1984). Spelling as a cognitive-developmental linguistic process. *Academic Therapy, 20,* 21–32.

Bouffler, C. M. (1984). *Case study explorations of functional strategies in spelling.* Unpublished doctoral dissertation, Indiana University.

Brittain, F. J., & Fitzgerald, J. A. (1942). The vocabulary and spelling errors of second-grade children's themes. *Elementary English Review, 19,* 43–50.

Bruner, J. (1983). *In search of mind: Essays in autobiography.* NY: Harper & Row.

Buckingham, B. R., & Dolch, E. W. (1936). *A combined word list.* Boston: Ginn.

Cahen, L. S., Craun, M. J., & Johnson, S. K. (1971). Spelling difficulty: A survey of the research. *Review of Educational Research, 41,* 281–301.

Calkins, L. M. (1980). Research update—When children want to punctuate: Basic skills belong in context. *Language Arts, 57,* 567–573.

Carroll, H. E. (1930). *Generalization of bright and dull children: A comparative study with special reference to spelling.* NY: Teachers College, Columbia University, Contributions to Education, No. 439.

Carroll, J. A., Davies, P., & Richman, B. (1971). *The American heritage word frequency book.* NY: Houghton Mifflin Company and American Heritage Publishing Co.

Chancellor, W. E. (1910). Spelling: 1000 words. *Journal of Education, 71,* 488–489, 517, 522, 545–546, 573, 578, 607–608.

Chomsky, C. (1979). Approaching reading through invented spelling. In. L. B. Resnick & P. Weaver (Eds.), *Theory and practice in early reading* (Vol II, pp. 43–65). Hillsdale, NJ: Lawrence Erlbaum Assoc.

Chomsky, N., & Halle, M. (1968). *The sound pattern of English.* NY: Harper & Row.

Clarke, L. K. (1988). Invented versus traditional spelling in first grades' writings: Effects on learning to spell and read. *Research in the Teaching of English, 22,* 281–309.

Clay, M. M. (1975). *What did I write?* London: Heinemann.

Cohen, G. (1980). Reading and searching for spelling errors. In U. Frith (Ed.), *Cognitive processes in spelling* (pp. 135–155). London: Academic Press.

Cordeiro, P. A. (1986). Punctuation in a third grade class: An analysis of errors in period placement. *Dissertation Abstracts International, 47,* 05A. (University Microfilms No. 86-16, 763).

Cordeiro, P., Giacobbe, M. E., & Cazden, C. (1983). Apostrophes, quotation marks, and periods: Learning punctuation in the first grade. *Language Arts, 60,* 323–332.

Cornman, O. P. (1902). *Spelling in the elementary school.* NY: Ginn.

Cronnell, B. (1980). *Punctuation and capitalization: A review of the literature.* Los Alamitos, CA: Southwest Regional Laboratory for Educational Research and Development. (ERIC Document Reproduction Service No. ED 208 404)

Currie, A. B. (1981). *Instruction in handwriting in Ontario schools.* Toronto, Canada: Ontario Department of Education. (ERIC Document Reproduction Service No. ED 205 983)

Dewey, G. (1971). *English spelling: Roadblock to reading.* NY: Teachers College Press.

DiStefano, P., & Hagerty, P. (1985). Teaching spelling at the elementary level: A realistic perspective. *The Reading Teacher, 38,* 372–377.

Dolch, E. (1927). Grade vocabularies. *Journal of Educational Research, 16,* 16–26.

Drake, D. A., & Ehri, L. C. (1984). Spelling acquisition: Effects of pronouncing words on memory for their spellings. *Cognition and Instruction, 1,* 297–320.

Dryden, J. (1972). *All for love.* D. M. Veith (Ed.). Lincoln, NE: University of Nebraska Press. (Original work published in 1678)

Edelsky, C. (1983). Segmentation and punctuation: Developmental data from young writers in a bilingual program. *Research in the Teaching of English, 17,* 135–136.

Ehri, L. C. (1980). The development of orthographic images. In U. Frith (Ed.), *Cognitive processes in spelling* (pp. 311–338). London: Academic Press.

Ehri, L. C. (1987a). Does learning to spell help beginners learn to read words? *Reading Research Quarterly, 22,* 47–65.

Ehri, L. C. (1987b). Learning to read and spell. *Journal of Reading Behavior, 19,* 5–31.

Ehri, L. C. (1987c). Sources of difficulty in learning to spell and read. In M. L. Wolraich & D. K. Routh (Eds.), *Advances in developmental and behavioral pediatrics* (Vol. 8, pp. 5591–5666). Greenwich, CT: JAI Press.

Elliott, I. (1982). *Learning to spell: Children's development of phoneme-grapheme relationships* (Research report 4/82). Carlton, Victoria: Curriculum Services Unit, Education Department of Victoria.

Fearing, H. (1983). *Learning to spell: The role of visual memory* (Research report 1/83). Carlton, Victoria: Curriculum Services Units, Education Department of Victoria.

Ferreiro, E., & Teberosky, A. (1982). *Literacy before schooling.* Exeter, NH: Heinemann.

Fischer, F. W., Shankweiler, D., & Liberman, I. (1985). Spelling proficiency and sensitivity to word structure. *Journal of Memory and Language, 24,* 423–441.

Fitzgerald, J. A. (1932). Words misspelled most frequently by children of the fourth, fifth, and sixth grade levels in life outside the school. *Journal of Educational Research, 26,* 213–218.

Fitzgerald, J. A. (1938). The vocabulary and spelling errors of third-grade children's life-letters. *The Elementary School Journal, 38,* 518–527.

Fitzgerald, J. A. (1951). *A basic life spelling vocabulary.* Milwaukee, WI: The Bruce Publishing Co.

Fitzsimmons, R. J., & Loomer, B. M. (1974). *Improved spelling through scientific investigation.* Des Moines and Iowa City, IA: Iowa State Department of Public Instruction and Iowa Center for Research in School Administration, University of Iowa.

Foran, G. T. (1934). *The psychology and teaching of spelling.* Washington, DC: The Catholic Education Press.

Fox, B., & Routh, D. K. (1983). Reading disability, phonemic analysis and sysphonetic spelling: A follow-up study. *Journal of Clinical Child Psychology, 12,* 28–32.

Francis, H. (1984). Children's knowledge of orthography in learning to read. *British Journal of Educational Psychology, 54,* 8–23.

Frasch, D. K. (1965). How well do sixth-graders proofread for spelling errors? *The Elementary School Journal, 65,* 381–385.

Freeman, F. (1959). New handwriting scale. *The Elementary School Journal, 35,* 366–372.

Frith, U. (1978). Annotation: Spelling difficulties. *Journal of Child Psychology and Psychiatry, 19,* 279–285.

Frith, U. (Ed.). (1980a). *Cognitive processes in spelling.* London: Academic Press.

Frith, U. (1980b). Unexpected spelling problems. In U. Frith (Ed.), *Cognitive processes in spelling* (pp. 495–515). London: Academic Press.

Frith, U., & Frith, C. (1980). Relationships between reading and spelling. In J. F. Kavanaugh & R. L. Venezky (Eds.), *Orthography, reading and dyslexia* (pp. 287–295). Baltimore, MD: University Park Press.

Froese, V. (1981). Handwriting: Practice, pragmatism, and progress. In V. Froese & S. B. Straw (Eds.), *Research in the language arts: Language and schooling* (pp. 227–243). Baltimore, MD: University Park Press.

Furness, E. L., & Boyd, G. A. (1958). Real spelling demons for high school students. *The English Journal, 47,* 267–270.

Ganschow, L. (1981). Discovering children's learning strategies for spelling through error analysis. *The Reading Teacher, 34,* 676–680.

Ganschow, L. (1984). Analyze error patterns to remediate severe spelling difficulties. *The Reading Teacher, 38,* 288–293.

Gates, A. I. (1937). *Spelling difficulties of 3876 words.* New York: Bureau of Publications, Teachers College, Columbia University.

Gentry, J. R. (1978). Early spelling strategies. *The Elementary School Journal, 79,* 88–92.

Gentry, J. R. (1981). Learning to spell developmentally. *The Reading Teacher, 34,* 378–381.

Gentry, J. R. (1982). Developmental spelling: Assessment. *Diagnostique, 8,* 52–61.

Gentry, J. R. (1984). Developmental aspects of learning to spell. *Academic Therapy, 20,* 11–19.

Gentry, L. A. (1980). *Capitalization instruction in elementary school textbooks* (Techinical Note TN 2-81-01). Los Alamitos, CA: Southwest Regional Laboratory for Educational Research and Development. (ERIC Document Reproduction Service No. ED 199 756)

Gentry, L. A. (1981). *Punctuation instruction in elementary school textbooks.* Los Alamitos, CA: Southwest Regional Laboratory for Educational Research and Development. (ERIC Document Reproduction Service No. ED 199 757)

Gerber, M. M. (1984). Orthographic problem-solving ability of learning disabled and normally achieving students. *Learning Disability Quarterly, 7,* 157–164.

Gillet, J. W., & Kita, M. J. (1979). Words, kids and categories. *The Reading Teacher, 32,* 538–542.

Gleitman, L. L., & Rozin, P. (1977). The structure and acquisition of reading. 1: Relations between orthographies and the structure of language. In A. S. Reber & D. L. Scarborough (Eds.), *Toward a psychology of reading: The proceeding of the CUNY Conference* (pp. 1–53). Hillsdale, NJ: Erlbaum.

Goyen, J. D., & Martin, M. (1977). The relation of spelling errors to cognitive variables and word type. *British Journal of Educational Psychology, 47,* 268–273.

Graham, S. (1983). Effective spelling instruction. *The Elementary School Journal, 83,* 560–567.

Graham, S., & Miller, L. (1980). Handwriting research and practice: A unified approach. *Focus on Exceptional Children, 13,* 1–15.

Gregory, B. C. (1907–1908). The rationale of spelling. *The Elementary School Teacher, 8,* 40–55.

Hall, R. A., Jr. (1961). *Sound and spelling in English.* Philadelphia and New York: Chilton.

Hall, S., & Hall, C. (1984). It takes a lot of letters to spell 'Erz'. *Language Arts, 61,* 822–827.

Hanna, P. R., & Hanna, J. S. (1959). Spelling as a school subject: A brief history. *National Elementary Principal, 38,* 8–23.

Hanna, P. R., Hanna, J. S., Hodges, R. E., & Rudorf, E. H. (1966). *Phoneme-grapheme correspondences as cues to spelling improvement.* Washington, DC: U.S. Government Printing Office, U.S. Office of Education.

Harste, J. C., Woodward, V. A., & Burke, C. L. (1984). *Language stories and literacy lessons.* Portsmouth, NH: Heinemann.

Heald-Taylor, B. G. (1984). Scribble in first grade writing. *The Reading Teacher, 38,* 4–8.

Henderson, E. H. (1981). *Learning to read and spell: The child's knowledge of words.* Dekalb, IL: Northern Illinois University Press.

Henderson, E. (1985). *Teaching spelling.* Boston: Houghton Mifflen.

Henderson, E. H., & Beers, J. W. (Eds.) (1980). *Developmental and cognitive aspects of learning to spell: A reflection of word knowledge.* Newark, DE: International Reading Association.

Henderson, E. H., & Templeton, S. (1986). A developmental perspective of formal spelling instruction through alphabet, pattern, and meaning. *The Elementary School Journal, 86,* 304–316.

Henderson, L. (1982). *Orthography and word recognition in reading.* London: Academic Press.

Hillerich, R. L. (1978). A writing vocabulary of elementary Children. Springfield, IL: Charles C. Thomas.

Hodges, R. E. (1964). A short history of spelling reform in the United States. *Phi Delta Kappan, 45,* 330–332.

Hodges, R. E. (1972). Theoretical frameworks of English orthography. *Elementary English, 49,* 1089–1097, 1105.

Hodges, R. E. (1977). In Adam's fall: A brief history of spelling instruction in the United States. In H. A. Robinson (Ed.), *Reading and writing instruction in the United States: Historical trends* (pp. 1–16). Urbana, IL and Newark, DE: ERIC Clearinghouse on Reading and Communication Skills and the International Reading Association.

Hodges, R. E. (1981). *Learning to spell.* Urbana, IL: ERIC Clearinghouse on Reading and Communication Skills and the National Council of Teachers of English.

Hodges, R. E. (1982). *Improving spelling and vocabulary in the secondary school.* Urbana, IL: ERIC Clearinghouse on Reading and Communication Skills and the National Council of Teachers of English.

Hodges, R. E. (1987). American spelling instruction: Retrospect and prospect. *Visible Language, 21,* 215–235.

Hollingsworth, L. S. (1918). *The psychology of special disability in spelling.* NY: Teachers College, Columbia University. Contributions to Education, No. 88.

Holmes, D. L., & Peper, R. J. (1977). Evaluation of the use of spelling error analysis in the diagnosis of reading disabilities. *Child Development, 48,* 1708–1711.

Horn, E. (1919). Principles of teaching spelling, as derived from scientific investigation. In G. M. Whipple (Ed.), *Fourth Report of Committee on Economy of Time in Education* (pp. 52–77). (Eighteenth Yearbook of the National Society for the Study of Education, Part 2). Bloomington, IL: Public School Publishing Co.

Horn, E. (1926). *A basic writing vocabulary: 10,000 words most commonly used in writing.* (University of Iowa Monographs in Education No. 4). Iowa City, IA: College of Education, University of Iowa.

Horn, E. (1938). Contributions of research to special methods: Spelling. In F. N. Freeman (Ed.), *The Scientific Movement in Education* (pp. 107–114). (Thirty-seventh Yearbook of the National Society for the Study of Education, Part 2). Chicago: University of Chicago Press.

Horn, E. (1941). Spelling. In W. S. Monroe (Ed.), *Encyclopedia of Educational Research* (pp. 1166–1183). New York: Macmillan.

Horn, E. (1950). Spelling. In W. S. Monroe (Ed.), *Encyclopedia of Educational Research* (rev. ed.) (pp. 1247–1264). New York : Macmillan.

Horn. E. (1960). Spelling. In C. W. Harris (Ed.), *Encyclopedia of Educational Research* (3rd ed.) (pp. 1337–1354). New York: Macmillan.

Horn, T. D. (1969). Spelling, In R. L. Ebel (Ed.), *Encyclopedia of Educational Research* (4th ed.) (pp. 1282–1299). New York: Macmillan.

Hunt, M. (1982). *The universe within: A new science explores the human mind.* New York: Simon & Schuster.

Invernizzi, M. (1984). *Memory for word elements in relation to stages of spelling power.* Paper presented at annual meeting of the International Reading Association, Atlanta.

Jensen, A. (1962). Spelling errors and the serial-position effect. *Journal of Educational Psychology, 53,* 105–109.

Johnson, D. D., & Pearson, P. D. (1984). *Teaching reading vocabulary* (2nd ed.). NY: Holt, Rinehart & Winston.

Johnson, J. B. (1970). *An analysis of spelling difficulties of common words used with high frequency.* Unpublished doctoral dissertation, University of Wyoming, Laramie.

Johnson, L. W. (1950). One hundred words most often misspelled by children in the elementary grades. *Journal of Educational Research, 44,* 54–55.

Johnson, T. D., Langford, K. G., & Quorn, K. C. (1981). *Characteristics of an effective spelling program.* Language Arts, 58, 581–588.

Jones, W. F. (1913). *Concrete investigation of the material of spelling.* Vermillion, SD: University of South Dakota.

Jorm, A. F. (1983). *The psychology of reading and spelling disabilities.* London: Routledge & Kegan Paul.

Koenke, K. (1986). Handwriting instruction: What do we know? *The Reading Teacher, 40,* 214–216.

Kooi. B. Y., Schutz, R. E., & Baker, R. L. (1965). Spelling errors and the serial position effect. *Journal of Educational Psychology, 56,* 334–336.

Kucera, H. and Francis, W. N. (1967). *Computational analysis of present-day American English.* Providence, RI: Brown University Press.

Lehr, F. (1986). Invented spelling and language development. *The Reading Teacher, 39,* 452–454.

Levy, B. A., & Begin, J. (1984). Proofreading familiar text: Allocating resources to perceptual and conceptual processes. *Memory and Cognition, 12,* 621–632.

Lutz, E. (1986). Invented spelling and spelling development. *Language Arts, 63,* 742–744.

Lydiatt, S. (1984). Error detection and correction in spelling. *Academic Therapy, 20,* 33–40.

Mangieri, J. N., & Baldwin, R. S. (1979). Meaning as a factor in predicting spelling difficulty. *Journal of Educational Research 72,* 285–287.

Manolakes, G. (1975). The teaching of spelling: A pilot study. *Elementary English, 52,* 243–247.

Marcel, T. (1980). Phonological awareness and phonological representation: investigation of a specific spelling problem. In U. Frith (Ed.), *Cognitive processes in spelling* (pp. 373–403). London: Academic Press.

Marino, J. L. (1979). *Children's use of phonetic, graphemic, and morphophonemic cues in a spelling task.* Unpublished paper. (ERIC Document Reproduction Service No. ED 188-235)

Marino, J. L. (1981). Spelling errors: From analysis to instruction. *Language Arts, 58,* 567–572.

Marschall, J. C., & Powers, J. M. (1969). Writing neatness, composition errors, and essay grades. *Journal of Educational Measurement, 6,* 72–101.

Marsh, G., Friedman, M., Welch, V., & Desberg, P. (1980). The development of strategies in spelling. In U. Frith (Ed.), *Cognitive processes in spelling* (pp. 339–353). London: Academic Press

Masters, D. G. (1987). *Handwriting* (English Language Arts Concept Paper, No. 2). Salem, OR: Oregon State Department of Education. (ERIC Document Reproduction Service No. ED 284 265)

Masters, H. V. (1927). *A study of spelling errors* (Studies in Education, No. 4). Iowa City, IA: University of Iowa.

McKee, P. (1939). *Language in the elementary school: Composition, spelling, writing.* Boston: Houghton Mifflin.

Mendenhall. J. E. (1930). *An analysis of spelling errors: A study of factors associated with word difficulty.* New York: Bureau of Publications, Teachers College, Columbia University.

Milone, M. N. Jr., & Wasylyk, T. M. (1981). Handwriting in special education. *Teaching Exceptional Children, 14,* 58–61.

Moats, L. C. (1983). A comparison of spelling errors of older dyslexic and second-grade normal children. *Annals of Dyslexia, 33,* 121–140.

Morris, D., Nelson, L., & Perney, J. (1986). Exploring the concept of 'spelling instructional level' through analysis of error types. *The Elementary School Journal, 87,* 181–200.

Nelson, H. E. (1980). Analysis of spelling errors in normal and dyslexic children. In U. Frith (Ed.), *Cognitive processes in spelling* (pp. 475–493). London: Academic Press.

Nicholson, T., & Schacter, S. (1979). Spelling skill and teaching practice: Putting them back together again. *Language Arts, 56,* 804–809.

Nolen, P., & McCartin, R. (1984). Spelling strategies on the Wide Range Achievement Test. *The Reading Teacher, 38,* 148–158.

Ormrod, J. (1985). Proofreading the cat in the hat: Evidence for different reading styles of good and poor spellers. *Psychological Reports, 57,* 863–867.

Peck, M., Askov, E. N., & Fairchild, S. H. (1980). *Another decade of research in handwriting: Progress and prospect in the 1970s. The Journal of Educational Research, 73,* 293–298.

Perin, D. (1982). Spelling strategies in good and poor readers. *Applied Psycholinguistics, 3,* 1–14.

Personke, C., & Knight. L. (1967). Proofreading and spelling: A report and a program. *Elementary English,* 44, 768–774.

Petty, W. (1957). Phonetic elements as factors in spelling difficulty. *Journal of Educational Research, 51,* 209–214.

Phelps, J., Stempel, L, & Speck, G. (1985). The children's handwriting scale: A new diagnostic tool. *Journal of Educational Research, 79,* 46–50.

Phillips, L. P. (1980). *Strategies children use in spelling.* Unpublished doctoral dissertation, University of Denver, Denver.

Pitman, J., & St. John, J. (1969). *Alphabets and reading: The initial teaching alphabet.* New York: Pitman.

Pollack, T. C. (1953). *Words most frequently misspelled in the seventh and eighth grades* (In Teachers Service Bulletin in English). New York: Macmillan.

Radebaugh, M. R. (1985). Children's perceptions of their spelling strategies. *The Reading Teacher, 38,* 532–536.

Read, C. (1971). Pre-school children's knowledge of English phonology. *Harvard Educational Review, 42,* 1–34.

Read, C. (1975). *Children's categorizations of speech sounds in English* (Research Report No. 17). Urbana, IL: National Council of Teachers of English.

Read, C. (1986). *Children's creative spelling.* London: Routledge & Kegan Paul.

Read, C., & Hodges, R. E. (1982). Spelling. In H. Mitzel (Ed.), *Encyclopedia of Educational Research* (5th ed.) (pp. 1758–1767). New York: Macmillan.

Reed, D. W. (1969). A theory of language, speech, and writing. In H. Singer and R. B. Ruddell (Eds.), *Theoretical models and processes of reading* (pp. 219–228). Newark, DE: International Reading Association.

Rice, J. M. (1897). The futility of the spelling grind. *The Forum, 23,* 163–172, 409–419.

Riefer, D. M. (1987). *Is 'backwards reading' an effective proofreading strategy?* (ERIC Document Reproduction Service No. ED 281 175)

Rinsland, H. D. (1945). *A basic vocabulary of elementary-school children.* New York: Macmillan.

Robinson, F. P. (1940). Misspellings are intelligent. *Educational Research Bulletin, 19,* 436–442.

Russell, P. (1975). *An outline of English spelling* (Technical Report No. 55). Los Alamitos, CA: Southwest Regional Laboratory for Educational Research and Development.

Sassoon, R. (1983). *The practical guide to children's writing.* London: Thames and Hudson.

Schafer, J. C. (1988). Invented spelling and teacher preparation. *English Education, 20,* 97–108.

Schlagal, R. (1982). A qualitative inventory of word knowledge: A developmental study of spelling, grades one through six. Unpublished doctoral dissertation, University of Virginia, Charlottesville. *Dissertation Abstracts International 47,* 915A.

Schwartz, S., & Doehring, D. G. (1977). A developmental study of children's ability to acquire knowledge of spelling pattern. *Developmental Psychology, 13,* 419–420.

Scragg, D. G. (1974). *A history of English spelling.* Manchester: Manchester University Press.

Shaughnessy, M. (1977). *Errors and expectations.* New York: Oxford University Press.

Sherwin, S. J. (1969). *Four problems in teaching English: A critique of research.* Scranton, PA: International Textbook Co.

Shipley, J. T. (1977). *In praise of English.* New York: New York Times Books.

Simon, D. P. (1976). Spelling: A task analysis. *Instructional Sciences, 5,* 277–302.

Simon, D. P., & Simon, H. A. (1973). Alternative uses of phonemic information in spelling. *Review of Educational Research, 43,* 115–137.

Sloboda, J. A. (1980). Visual imagery and individual differences in spelling. In U. Frith (Ed.), *Cognitive processes in spelling* (pp. 231–248). London: Academic Press.

Smith, H. L., Jr. (1968). *English morphophonics: Implications for the teaching of reading Monograph No. 10.* New York State English Council.

Spache, G. (1940a). A critical analysis of various methods of classifying spelling errors, I. *Journal of Educational Psychology, 31,* 111–134.

Spache, G. (1940b). Validity and reliability of the proposed classification of spelling errors, II. *Journal of Educational Psychology, 31,* 204–214.

Spache, G. (1940c). Spelling disability correlates I-Factors probably causal in spelling disability. *Journal of Educational Research, 34,* 561–586.

Stubbs, M. (1980). *Language and literacy: The sociolinguistics of reading and writing.* London: Routledge & Kegan Paul.

Templeton, S. (1979a). The circle game of spelling: A reappraisal for teachers. *Language Arts, 56,* 789–797.

Templeton, S. (1979b). Spelling first, sound later: The relationship between orthography and higher order phonological knowledge in older students. *Research in the Teaching of English, 13,* 255–264.

Templeton, S. (1986). Synthesis of research on the learning and teaching of spelling. *Educational Leadership, 43,* 73–78.

Templeton, S., & Scarborough-Franks, L. (1985). The spelling's the thing: Knowledge of derivational morphology in orthography and phonology among older students. *Applied Psycholinguistics, 6,* 371–390.

Thomas, V. (1982). *Learning to spell: The way children make use of morphemic information* (Research Project 1/82). Carlton, Victoria: Curriculum Services Unit, Education Department of Victoria.

Thompson, R. S. (1930). *The effectiveness of modern spelling instruction.* New York: Bureau of Publications, Teachers College, Columbia University. Contributions to Education No. 436.

Thorndike, E. L. (1929). The need of fundamental analysis of methods of teaching. *The Elementary School Journal, 30,* 189–191.

Tidyman, W. F. (1926). *The teaching of spelling.* Yonkers, NY: World Book.

Towery, G. (1979). Spelling instruction through the nineteenth century. *English Journal, 68,* 22–27.

Vachek, J. (1973). *Written language.* The Hague: Mouton.

Venezky, R. L. (1967). English orthography: Its graphical structure and its relation to sound. *Reading Research Quarterly, 2,* 75–105.

Venezky, R. L. (1970). *The structure of English orthography.* The Hague: Mouton.

Venezky, R. L. (1980). From Webster to Rice to Roosevelt: The formative years for spelling instruction and spelling reform in the U.S.A. In U. Frith (Ed.), *Cognitive processes in spelling* (pp. 9–30). London: Academic Press.

Wallace, J., Klein, R., & Schneider, P. (1968). Spelling ability and probability structure of English. *Journal of Educational Research, 61,* 315–319.

Weiner, E. S. (1980). Diagnostic evaluation of writing skills. *Journal of Learning Disabilities, 13,* 48–53.

Wilde, S. (1986). An analysis of the development of spelling and punctuation in selected third and fourth grade children. Unpublished doctoral dissertation, University of Arizona, Tucson. *Dissertation Abstracts International, 47,* 2452A.

Wilde, S. (1987). *Spelling and punctuation development in selected third and fourth grade children* (Occasional Paper No. 17). Arizona Center for Research and Development, University of Arizona, Tucson.

Wilde, S. (1989). Looking at invented spelling: A kidwatcher's guide to spell, Part 1. In K. S. Goodman, Y. M. Goodman, and W. J. Hood (Eds.), *The whole language evaluation book* (pp. 213–226). Portsmouth, NH: Heinemann.

Wilde, S. (1990). A proposal for a new spelling curriculum. *The Elementary School Journal,* 90, 275–289.

Wood, M. (1982). Invented spelling. *Language Arts, 59,* 707–717.

Yellin, D. (1986). *Connecting spelling instruction to reading and writing.* Paper presented at the annual meeting of Southwest Regional Conference of the International Reading Association, San Antonio. (ERIC Document Reproduction Service No. ED 268 486)

Zutell, J. (1978). Some psycholinguistic perspectives on children's spelling. *Language Arts, 55,* 844–850.

Yule, V. (1986). The design of spelling to match needs and abilities, *Harvard Educational Review, 56,* 278–297.

Zutell, J. (1979). Spelling strategies of primary school children and their relationships to Piaget's concept of decentration. *Research in the Teaching of English, 13,* 69–80.

·37·

IMAGINATIVE EXPRESSION

Betty Jane Wagner

The focus of this chapter is research on teaching discourse that is primarily imaginative. One could argue, of course, that all expressive discourse, or even all discourse for that matter, is at least in part imaginative. However, for this chapter, imaginative expression encompasses only the writing of poems, fictional narratives, and plays; improvisational classroom drama; and the performing of texts of literary works. Omitted are writing solely to express personal feeling, opinion, or acutal experience; and expressive discourse used as brainstorming, free-writing, or journal entries to prepare for writing informative or conative discourse, which Britton, Burgess, Martin, McLeod, & Rosen (1975) term *transactional*.

Therefore, this chapter encompasses only written or oral expressive discourse with an imaginative aim, which Britton terms *poetic* discourse—poems, stories, play scripts—orally improvised or crafted in writing. This includes the discourse aim Kinneavy (1971) identifies as literary, but more than that; it also considers the whole "let's pretend" function as Halliday (1977) distinguishes it from the other six functions of language: "The imaginative function of language ... is the ... [one] whereby the child creates an environment of his own ... a world initially of pure sound, but which gradually turns into one of story and make-believe and let's pretend, and ultimately into the realm of poetry and imaginative writing" (p. 20). This imaginative function often co-occurs with others, of course, so the scope of this chapter unavoidably overlaps that of most of the chapters in Part V of this *Handbook*. This chapter ends with a discussion of oral interpretation, storytelling, or choral reading, but it omits reading and responding to imaginative discourse, which is reviewed in the chapters on response to literature.

First, a caveat: by separating a discussion of imaginative expression from chapters on language, literature, speaking, listening, reading, and written composition, the editors of this text unwittingly tend to perpetuate a view of the field of language arts as separate skills strands rather than as an integrated interweaving of all of these. Their goal is a worthy one: by including this chapter they mean to highlight the importance of imaginative expression and to provide a place to consider dramatic inventing, which is not subsumed in other chapters. The organiza-

tion of this book, however, does not represent the view presented in some current discussions of literacy acquisition or in efforts, at the elementary level, to integrate the language arts with each other and with other curricular areas, or to apply what is sometimes termed "whole language." The need to focus separately on segments of the English teacher's task is practical in a handbook of this kind, but one should never forget that the fountain of imaginative expression splashes over all of the English language-arts curriculum.

In this discussion of imaginative expression, claims for the centrality of this type of discourse come first. Then follows a presentation of the need for researching stages of development of imaginative expression, noting the value of H. Gardner's multiple intelligences for such study. The rest of the chapter considers the following in turn: written imaginative expression, improvisational classroom drama, and performing texts.

CLAIMS AND PERSPECTIVES

Several major theorists have asserted that imaginative discourse is central to language-arts development: Barnes (1968), Britton (1970), Moffett (Moffett & Wagner, 1983), not to overlook the guiding philosopher of the early decades of this century, Dewey (1959). Moreover, Piaget (1962) and Vygotsky (1967) showed how pretend play, especially the use of objects in a non-literal fashion, parallels cognitive development.

Most English teachers were lured into their profession in the first place by imaginative discourse, what Dryden termed that "fairy kind of writing which depends only upon the force of imagination" (*King Arthur,* Dedication). Berthoff's (1984) call to "reclaim the imagination" echoes the concerns of the 1960s, with its outpouring of works on creativity and the rethinking of the goals of English teaching that followed the historic Anglo-American Dartmouth Conference in 1966. This profession seems to need continual reminding of Susanne K. Langer's insight: "Imagination is the primary talent of the human mind, the activity in whose service language was evolved."

Despite this call to imaginative expression and English for

personal growth, as bodied forth in the widely acclaimed but short-lived *Interaction* curriculum of the early 1970s, edited by Moffett, the apex of commitment to imaginative expression was in the 1920s and 1930s. The progressive movement in education reflected a larger society's values. Today the nurturing of imaginative expression is too often considered simply a way to develop fluency in preparation for the sterner stuff that is the real business of school. In many schools, this means that imaginative discourse is relegated to early elementary grades, elective options, or to programs for the gifted and talented. Howell (1982) notes, "the place given to 'creative expression' in the curriculum is a barometer of the society's attitudes towards spontaneity, freedom, and individuality" (p. 16).

The current cries of despair about the sorry state of cultural literacy and the closing of the American mind have led to new public affirmations for more literature and dramatic art in the schools, as typified by the National Endowment for the Arts publication (1988), *Toward Civilization.* Of course, each educational reformer has his or her own idea as to what constitutes the cultural heritage the schools should transmit. Such calls reflect the conservative side of the conservative vs. progressive conflict that has marked the history of American education (Kantor 1975). Advocacy of imaginative expression tends to characterize those on the progressive side of the conflict, who point out that cultural transmission is never enough. They argue that what makes the difference in students' lives is not just cultural literacy but cultural *renewal.* Through imaginative expression students make a cultural heritage their own, first by choosing among what should be available to them—a rich array of attractive alternatives—and by creatively transforming what they select into something that is personally meaningful. Hughes Mearns was a catalyst in the 1920s and the 1930s for the flowering of imaginative expression. Like, among others, Koch and Kohl in the 1970s and Dyson and Moffett in the 1980s, Mearns showed, by publishing children's literary pieces, that they were capable of powerful imaginative writing. He advocated releasing children's potential by accepting their efforts, selectively approving of them, presenting appropriate criticism, and teaching indirectly.

Few Studies of Teacher Effectiveness

Very few studies of effective teaching strategies focus solely on imaginative expression. This is not surprising in light of the fact that the goal of such discourse is divergent not convergent thinking, and thus does not lend itself to easy measurement either of student achievement or of teacher effectiveness. Perhaps the reason Piaget's stages of development have been so widely embraced is that the cognitive end-state he posits not only is comparatively easy to measure, but also is the intelligence of a scientist, which happens to coincide with a researcher's personal goal. Cognitive development, according to Piaget, is toward a mode of problem solving familiar to scientists. Moffett (1979) sees the whole society as out of balance with its overemphasis on linear, analytic thinking that skews schooling (p. 115). Brownowski (1978) has called this "an age when nonsci-

entists are feeling a kind of loss of nerve" (p. 112). H. Gardner (1983) is helping clear the land for research in imaginative expression by positing the idea of multiple intelligences, only one of which is scientific intelligence. More on his theory appears in the next section.

When a teacher aims for imaginative expression, he or she is inevitably drawn into a consideration of the development of artistic sensibility. The teacher's work at least in part must be to help students become artists. Such a teacher must enable students to learn how to grapple with material, reorder it, *reconstruct* it, as Dewey or Kelly would say; or, to make of it an object of *personal knowledge,* in Polyani's (1962) terms. Archambault (1968) saw the teacher as primarily a catalyst for students' artistic development. Students are improvisational players, making something of their own by mixing their labor with the inspiration the teacher gives and discipline he or she imposes. What is artistic growth in imaginative expression, and what are its stages of development?

Development of Imaginative Expression

Imaginative expression begins even before a child can use language. Examples are popular infant games like "peek-a-boo" and deliberate child-initiated fantasy such as Britton (1983) describes as the "play face" mode of interaction his granddaughter adopted even before she could say only a few words. When she hunched up one shoulder and looked slightly askance with a gleam of mischief in her eye, she felt free to pretend to misbehave. This "play face" behavior disappeared when she was a little older and could understand and tell stories. Before they are 3 years old, many children can tell surprisingly complete imaginative stories (A. Applebee, 1978; Pitcher & Prelinger, 1963; Scollon & Scollon, 1981). Preschoolers characteristically engage in highly imaginative play and enjoy hearing, telling, and enacting fantasies (Paley, 1987). Emergent literacy studies document the vitality of imaginative discourse in kindergarten and first grade (Dyson 1986; Harste, Woodward, & Burke, 1984). Many teachers report their primary children much prefer the imaginative to the transactional or nonfictive aims of discourse.

In order to assess the effectiveness of teaching imaginative expression, inasmuch as it differs from teaching other areas of the curriculum, one needs a comprehensive understanding of its development. Such research has only recently begun to emerge. Comprehensive studies are needed to determine and to chronicle stages in the growth of divergent thinking and artistic creation that is the goal of imaginative expression. Such comprehensive developmental research will depend on the collaboration both of developmental psychologists and of artists—poets, fiction writers, actors, and playwrights. The end-state for the artist is imaginative expression; the ideal toward which he or she strives is not the same as the end-state for the scientist.

H. Gardner (1980, 1983, 1985), in his work with Project Zero at Harvard, has hypothesized the existence of multiple intelligences. His theoretical position has grown out of a deep dissatisfaction with the notion of a single intelligence, one that can be measured in a brief time with a paper and pencil test. His theory has a rich heuristic value for researchers in teaching the arts. By positing appropriate end-states and stages of development that are different for each of his different intelligences, Gardner has provided those who study English teaching a new way to envision their purview. If students are progressing toward an end-state of linguistic or dramatic artistry, then their teacher is effective. For example, Gardner has posited the poet as the epitome of what he terms *linguistic intelligence*. Development of imaginative expression in language is toward an ever greater sensitivity to style, composition, balance, and cadence of sound.

He has also done English teachers a great service by considering linguistic expression as a type of intelligence rather than as a creative talent. As he notes, if he had called his multiple intelligences *talents,* no one would have paid much attention to his theory. By calling them intelligences, he gives them equal status with logical-mathematical intelligence.

An actor needs to have several highly developed intelligences: linguistic, interpersonal, and bodily-kinesthetic. Dramatic competence encompasses the ability to represent with gesture, to have a facial expression or movement stand for something else. Thus, pantomime development can be seen as moving from a preschool child's spreading his arms wide and swooping with abandon about the room as an eagle in spontaneous fantasy play to the precise gesturing of Marcel Marceau's pensive plucking of a petal from an imaginary daisy. Colby's (1988) work on describing dramatic intelligence and its U-shaped trajectory in development it manifests is a provocative extension of Gardner's work, one that could guide future studies of growth in dramatic intelligence and teaching strategies appropriate to each stage. Colby posits successive reorganizations of understanding that account for, for example, growth from the preschool stage of *being* a character to the middle childhood stage of *playing* a character, and from that to the adolescent stage of return to the "notion of *being* a character, but on a higher level and with the discoveries of the previous stages available" (p. 183).

Interestingly, Colby's U-shaped trajectory in development for school-age students is the opposite from the inverted U-shaped trajectory cognitive psychologists have noted in the growth of spontaneous pretend play of early childhood. These researchers have found that of all the types of play young children engage in (functional, constructive, pretend, and games with rules), the proportion of time spent in spontaneous pretend play increases steadily from the second year of life until around 7 years, and then it declines, largely because games with rules replace it. Spontaneous pretend play moves from solitary to social or interactive pretense. Children who have drama instruction in school often begin their study at about seven, so for them the spontaneous play of the preschool years is replaced by teacher-led drama. Colby characterizes this middle childhood stage as that of *playing* a character. It's as if children see acting as a game with rules, which is their predominant mode of play. Only later do they return to a greater identification with a character. Thus, when the cognitive developmental

view is combined with Colby's trajectory, an S-shaped pattern of development emerges.

Implications for Teaching

If the end-state of linguistic or dramatic intelligence is different from the end-state of other intelligences, then perhaps teachers of imaginative expression must themselves be aware of and capable of engaging in strategies central to growth in language or dramatic arts. In other words, they need to show students what linguistic and dramatic craft looks like. They need to be more like masters modeling imaginative expression for apprentices; the more transparent they can make their own creative processes, the more their apprentices will be able to experiment with the master's strategies for the apprentices' ends. But the masters are not building a scaffold, to use a currently popular metaphor, for students to stand on as they learn to solve the same problems the teacher has long since mastered. Rather, the teachers are publicly struggling anew with their material with the goal of creating a product unique in the world. Teachers need to model the way an artist works. When students write imaginatively, subject and object distinctions blur. Through the imagination they create a new thing out of the many different elements of experience. For example, when a teacher and students together improvise a drama, in Courtney's (1985) words "they engage in problem-solving in a deep personal way through the fictional present" (p. 49). In both writing and drama the individual is intuitively aware of the relatedness of the self and the object of creation. The process of imagining generates feeling and enables the student to align feeling with ideas, images, and action. Teachers need to model this imaginative process.

Thus, teaching for growth along an artistic spectrum is somewhat different from teaching for other goals of the English curriculum. A model such as the six-step presentational mode developed by Madelyn Hunter may actually inhibit rather than foster the growth of imaginative expression. As Peters (1987) puts it, "Direct instruction and similar strategies that have successfully improved basic skills may not be as effective as other strategies for creativity, complex problem solving, or independent thinking" (p. 36). In a RAND report, Wise, Darling-Hammond, McLaughlin, & Bernstein (1984) note no one unidimensional construct called *effective teaching* exists. "The more complex and variable one considers the educational environment, the more one relies on teacher judgment to guide the activities of classroom life and the less one relies on generalized rules for teacher behavior" (pp. 10–11). It follows that the more varied human intelligences and their ideal end-states are, the more varied effective teaching strategies are. What kind of teacher judgment can most aptly guide student growth in imaginative expression, and how can it be described?

Naturalistic studies of imaginative discourse show much about the climate that fosters such language; rich descriptions typically include long verbatim quotations of student's oral and written output. The best accounts of oral imaginative expression come from studies of preschoolers, probably because at that age many children spontaneously engage in social symbolic play; after the preschool years they have very few opportunities for this kind of "as if" language in schools.

Ryans' study in 1960 for the American Council on Education may well apply most aptly to teachers of imaginative expression. He found that teachers of all subjects who had

more successful patterns of classroom behavior tended to have strong interests in many areas, to prefer student-centered learning situations, to be independent, to have superior verbal intelligence, and to be willing to allow nondirective classroom procedures. Teachers with less successful behavior patterns tended to prefer teacher-directed learning situations, to value exactness, orderliness, and "practical" things, and to be less tolerant toward the expressed opinions of pupils. They were also more restrictive and critical in appraising the behavior and motives of other persons. (Peters, 1987, p. 29)

Harris reported in 1973 that students increase their own creative behavior if their teacher is flexible, divergent, or creative in contrast to students whose teachers do not have these characteristics. Witkin (1974) is convinced that teachers need to understand the praxis of creative expression and must "enter the creative process at the outset" (p. 69). He contends that teacher involvement is essential to the setting, making, holding, and resolving of expressive acts. Without it, teachers, whether habitually or intentionally, remain on the periphery of their students' expressive acts.

In summary, although claims for the centrality of imaginative expression in the school curriculum are solid, few studies exist of effective teaching strategies to foster its growth. H. Gardner's model of multiple intelligences, with its potential for guiding studies of the development of linguistic and dramatic intelligence, shows promise for identifying stages of growth upon which an understanding of effective teaching depends. The rest of this chapter is a summary of recent research on imaginative expression with a focus of teaching.

WRITTEN IMAGINATIVE EXPRESSION

In recent years, techniques of teaching writing have received increasing attention, but little of this focuses specifically on the production of literary forms—poems, stories, and plays. Writing Projects based on the Bay Area Writing Project model, over 160 of which sprang up across the country in the late 1970s and 1980s, have provided forums for teachers to hone their strategies for teaching all types of writing. These Writing Projects bring teachers and administrators of all grade levels together for two levels of training: an intensive Summer Institute and a 30-hour Professional Development Program. At both levels, participants re-engage in the writing process themselves; testimonies from Writing Project participants show that many have found to their surprise they can write in genres they may not have ever tried before, poetry, fiction, or drama, and can help their students do the same.

One study shows that imaginative writing itself is an effective way to improve growth in language arts. Shumaker (1982) found sixth graders taught expressive writing three times a week improve significantly more than students who follow a textbook language-arts program. The differences are significant in word knowledge, reading, language, and creative writing, but not spelling and mechanics.

Ideology of Teachers

Several quasi-experimental studies have identified general characteristics of effective teachers. Writing teachers who teach reading in a more open-ended manner have students who produce better imaginative writing. Mosenthal (1984) found what he termed "cognitive-developmental" ideology to be significantly more effective than "academic" ideology in developing fourth graders' ability to draw on a variety of meaning sources in writing stories about a baseball game from a picture stimulus. Those teachers with a cognitive-developmental ideology tend to generate stories with more developed motive structures and goals appropriate to the game of baseball. Such teachers are those most likely to improvise rather than follow the basal reader guide exactly, to ask reconstructive questions and give reconstructive directives, and to accept or prompt plausibly correct responses rather than to insist that responses be based only on the book the children are currently reading (p. 683). Teachers reflecting an academic ideology are those most likely to reproduce the basal reader guide, to ask reproductive questions and give reproductive directives, and to reject plausibly correct responses drawn from sources other than the current text (p. 683).

In a subsequent study, Mosenthal, Conley, Colella, and Davidson-Mosenthal (1985) found the following contrasts in the cognitive-developmental teachers' classes: Fourth graders with high prior knowledge produce significantly more auxiliary-action propositions than those with low prior knowledge do. Low-knowledge children produce significantly more irrelevant propositions than the high-knowledge children do. High-knowledge children produce significantly more significance-statement propositions than do low-knowledge students. "No such differences were found in the academic teachers' classes" (p. 629). If the goal of writing is to encourage full elaboration of what children know, then clearly to encourage is better than to inhibit the inclusion of prior knowledge in writing a story from a set of pictures.

Calkins (1986), Florio and Clark (1982), and Graves (1973) have found that for all types of writing, not just imaginative, the most effect teaching strategies are those that:

a. Create an informal environment and climate of risk-taking,
b. Encourage students to generate their own topics,
c. Provide stimulating prewriting experiences,
d. Recognize and allow for individual and sometimes unique processes of writing,
e. Set up real purposes and real audiences, and
f. Confer during the writing process in a nondirective way to facilitate the writer's achieving his or her own intentions.

In contrast to the findings of Calkins, Florio and Clark, Graves, and Mosenthal, Bennett (1976) found no significant differences between imaginative essays written by British primary children whose teachers were "formal" and those who were "informal."

Teachers Accomplished at Linguistic Craft

In this section are descriptions of five teachers, each of whom is an able writer himself. Three of these were successful in stimulating student writing, but the other two met with less than complete success because their stimuli and modeling did not carry over into student efforts. Thus, although a teacher's ability to demonstrate the craft he or she teaches is a highly desirable attribute, it is by no means the only essential element in successful teaching.

The first three reports show the variety of ways teacher nurturing and response to student writing can foster development. The first two are ethnographic studies of high school creative writing teachers noted for their effectiveness in motivating student writing and the third is a self report. In all three cases, the teacher is an exemplar of the craft he is teaching. In the first study by Dunn, Florio-Ruane, and Clark (1985), the teacher is himself a poet, and in the second by Kantor (1984), a story writer. The success of these two teachers suggests that the teaching of imaginative writing by a teacher who is a linguistic craftsman may be qualitatively different from other teaching. Teachers who represent the end-state toward which students are striving may be, as suggested earlier, assuming a role more like a master with apprentices than like an explicit lesson giver.

Dunn et al. (1985) closely observed a teacher in a multigrade elective creative writing class in a suburban high school. The teacher was concerned that the students' commitment to academic writing might make them reluctant to take the risk of engaging in more personally meaningful writing. To get his students to write evocative haiku poetry, he carefully modulated the roles he assumed. At some times he was a stimulator of ideas; at others, a model; at still others, a coach; and, most importantly, perhaps, the provider of a real-world audience, not only in the classroom but outside in the writing contests he urged his students to enter. He sufficiently distanced himself "from the putative role of 'teacher as evaluator' to enable his students to take greater power and responsibility for their roles as authors" (p. 39). The role the teacher chose at any particular time depended on his instructional purpose and also on a sensitive response to context, which meant frequently negotiating his role with the students. His classroom walls were laden with his own photographs and paintings as well as charcoal sketches, airbrush designs, and oil paintings done by his students. When introducing a new poetry topic, he read aloud the poetry of other authors, played recordings of poems set to music, presented slides and photographs, and provided a rich array of stimulating books. To help students see how visual images could make statements about the world, he had them do photo montages. He shared his own photos, and montages done by former students. He also advised them to write frequently by suggesting that his own photography and poetry efforts often failed, but that successive trials paid off. As he wrote in his teacher journal, his goal was "to get people into spaces where

they are really thinking about what they have to say and are being honest" (Dunn et al., p. 44). One of his students wrote in his journal: "The spaces my teacher talks of can only be entered when I feel like writing true feelings and not what people want to read" (p. 44).

Kantor (1984) documents the effectiveness of providing students with an opportunity to write for their peer communities as a way to allow writing to intersect personal and social spheres. He also shows how much can be learned from an examination of instruction in imaginative writing that includes not only teaching strategies but also a thick description of the conditions under which students write and of the personalities, attitudes, and interpersonal styles of both the students and the teacher. His description of one teacher's work with a group of bright and academically successful 12th graders in a creative writing class highlights the effectiveness of nondirective teaching with such a group. Kantor describes how the teacher helped students become more comfortable and willing to take risks in a situation unfamiliar to them. The teacher encouraged them to choose their own topics and modes of discourse; he gave no grades until the end of the quarter.

A short story writer himself, the teacher assumed the role of responder and fellow writer, and he carried on the class discussion in a low-keyed and informal manner. He, the students, and the participant observer, Kantor, sat in a circle. All of them wrote and shared their writing with the group. The teacher tried to read each student's piece on the author's terms, not his own. He was unfailingly encouraging, patient, and accepting, effectively helping the students move from a perception of him as authority to one of trusted adult. He admitted his difficulties with writing and showed his own processes—how he dealt with blocks and how he revised. He read them statements by various professional writers and shared how he had come to see writing as a discovery process and to trust his own writing intuitions. He modeled the way he wanted students to receive one another's work by responding spontaneously after a student read a finished or unfinished piece, making suggestions but avoiding formulas. Occasionally he gave them what he called a "sermonette," providing advice such as the value of using concrete and sensory detail. The teacher created a social interaction, encouraging talk about associations and experiences, thus engendering camaraderie and solidifying community as well as contributing to the richness and vividness of the writing. Kantor documents individual student growth toward stronger sensory details, toward revealing feeling and personal voice, toward experimentation with new genres, toward an awareness of the appropriateness of a particular genre for an individual writer, toward greater imagination and humor, and toward use of a wider range of revising strategies.

A third example of successful teaching is Carl Hirsch's (1984) description of his own experience, as Artist in the Schools, with a ninth-grade creative writing class. He described his reluctance to "show off" his own writing efforts for fear that would inhibit his students. He started the class by having them remember a traumatic experience in their past, and then day by day he went through a series of suggestions for fictionalizing and expanding that incident into a story. Because he deliberately went for the most personal of experiences, he sensed that students would be reluctant to share with each other, just as the students were in the classroom described below in Perl and Wilson's (1986) study. However, instead of forcing the issue as the unsuccessful teacher they described did, he invited them to turn in their papers to him, clipping each successive draft to the preceding ones. His first responses were invariably encouraging. By the end of the 8-week session, some of the students were willing to own and share their by now fairly fictionalized stories, not only with the teacher and each other, but with an outside observer as well.

Being a linguistic craftsman, however, is not all that is needed. Even when teachers themselves have refined their own skill and can provide good models of an end-state of a writer, they do not always find it easy to effect student development of the craft of imaginative writing. Perl and Wilson (1986) have documented a painful failure by a usually effective eighth-grade teacher who one year simply could not connect with his students. However,

by outside standards he was quite successful: his students wrote, worked in writing groups, revised, and edited; they produced writing in many different forms and published both whole-group and individual magazines; they sent articles, many of which were published, to the district's newsletter; they read and wrote and grew and changed. (p. 119)

This teacher used many of the strategies one or more of the three high school teachers described above did. He provided a model by reading his own poems to the class, and his walls were covered with stimulating posters on popular culture or environmental issues. He had handy an impressive array of media equipment. He began the year by asking the students to engage in 10 minutes of uninterrupted writing, and he wrote with them. Perhaps what he lacked was the patience Kantor's (1984) teacher showed. This was first seen when instead of inviting students to read their 10-minute free writes, he volunteered to go first, and then, when no one volunteered to read next, he called on the students. He was fairly directive in what would be expected of them—to memorize and recite a poem, to keep all drafts of their writing, to keep a process journal and a social studies journal, and to bring to class a notebook for in-class writing and "a writing implement" (p. 122).

This teacher's room had a dramatic appeal, but he usually took center stage. Frequently the action revolved around him and his writing. He composed out loud in front of the students and asked them to notice how he wrote. When one of the students noticed, "You use the biggest vocabulary I ever heard" (Perl & Wilson, p. 123) and others agreed they couldn't write like that, the teacher got up from his chair in the center of the group and moved to the chalkboard, saying, "What you are talking about now is ownership. This is the vocabulary I've become comfortable with." The teacher continued to be, in his terms, "the educational leader in the classroom . . . the driving force behind what happens" (p. 124), but at the same time, outside of class, he began to wonder if he were too strong a writer

and too forceful in a discussion. Indeed, such fears were well founded; he set a less-than-accepting tone in the class with his lack of patience with students who didn't listen. Although he continued to write verses and parodies to commemorate school events, his own joy of performance did just the opposite of what he had hoped. Unlike the first two teachers described above, this teacher's willingness to share his own writing made the students feel less able rather than empowered. This teacher felt confused, tense, and uneasy when the small writing groups met. He was afraid they might not be doing what they were supposed to be doing. He didn't feel comfortable with the feeling of not being "in charge." Whenever he found students who seemed to be wasting time, he scolded them and got mad at himself for not having structured the task more clearly. He felt the students were doing rushed, sloppy work because he was not giving them grades.

By midyear the students were resisting; except for a few dutiful ones, they didn't volunteer to read their writing aloud or share their observations and ideas about their writing processes. Class camaraderie was missing. Stalemates continued, followed by outright hostility on both sides. Perhaps this teacher was confusing his artistic role as a poet who carefully controls and crafts language with his less satisfying (for him) role of enabler of student growth. In any case, his efforts to control the class and force their output became increasingly difficult, and he became more and more tense and depressed. The students also sensed something was wrong. When a multimedia show his social studies class was rehearsing became hopelessly bogged down, the teacher asked the students to write letters about what had happened, their feelings, and what he should do to improve (p. 136). One girl captured not only how the students felt about this show but what might have been at the source of their resistence in the creative writing class as well: "We (some of us) don't feel that the show is ours anymore. You do everything (well almost everything). It's sort of like you are taking over" (p.137).

In this example, the master was perceived as one who did not relish apprentices; their limitations irritated him. His modeling was not firing student energy; it was dampening it.

One final report is that of Lopate (1978), a widely published author of poetry and fiction. He observed that an interesting discussion or a collaborative composition with an elementary school class does not necessarily serve as a model to improve the quality of children's individual poems, as he had hoped it would. He found that although some children pick up on the visual model of modern verse they and the teacher have created as a class poem, most of them return to their usual style when they write individually. "Certainly the reckless tempo, linguistic freedom, and subject leaps which characterize the collaborative class poem rarely carry over to the individual student's work" (p. 138). Lopate advises teachers to let the writer choose his or her own moment to compose. "The best single incentive to creative writing is a classroom atmosphere in which everyone knows he or she has permission to go off and write at any given time in the day" (p. 148). He sees that the process of serious creative writing requires withdrawal and learning to be alone.

Studies of Specific Teaching Strategies

A few studies have assessed the effectiveness of particular heuristics for developing imaginative expression. Several descriptive studies confirm Lopate's observation that success in evoking poetry and stories is largely a by-product of allowing students to choose their own topics and their own time to write on them (Calkins, 1986; Emig, 1971; Graves, 1973; McLure, 1985; Perl & Wilson, 1986). These studies describe some of the same qualities of successful teaching Dunn et al. (1985) and Kantor (1984) identified and described.

McClure (1985) described a supportive context that was critical to developing mature responses to poetry and experimentation in writing poems by a group of intermediate children. The teacher sanctioned peer interaction, gave focused praised and feedback, acknowledged frustration, had clear behavioral expectations, allowed flexibility in time and space, and helped the children create a strong social network. The children generally enjoyed reading and writing poetry, developing preferences for more complex and challenging poems as they continued to enjoy light humorous pieces.

Perl and Wilson (1986) described the teaching of a fourth/ fifth- and of an eighth-grade teacher, both of whom were successful in evoking poetry and stories, largely as a by-product of allowing students to choose their own topics. Although neither of these teachers was an accomplished writer, their students often burst into imaginative expression and produced some carefully crafted pieces. What characterized the classrooms of these two successful teachers was that the teachers were no longer the sole sources of knowledge. Students wrote for and learned from each other. When freed from "the need to write merely to please their teachers, some students, some of the time, discovered a freedom and depth of expression they had rarely known before" (p. 251).

Effect of Basal Readers. Scardamalia and Bereiter (1986) in their review of the literature on writing instruction note the common view that much of what students learn about writing has to come from exposure to examples. The next three studies focus on the texts primary children read and their influence on their writing styles.

Phillips (1986) found first graders whose teachers read and discuss poems and stories rather than use basal readers write significantly more and better than control groups. Their stories and poems are more original and show such elements as simile, metaphor, personification, exaggeration, and repetition. The vocabulary is more richly figurative and sensory. Burton (1985) found that third and fourth graders in an open classroom borrow and improvise on the language of the classroom literature. Children's literature provides a necessary source of authentic experience for the writers. Eckhoff (1983) found second graders who read basal reading texts that have unelaborated stories with simple sentences and one sentence per line write that way, whereas those reading a basal text that has more elaborate structures write more elaborated and mature sentences. All too often when children start handwriting and encoding practice in workbooks in school, they halt the progress they have made as

preschoolers in creative and innovative epxlorations into producing printed language (Dyson, 1982).

Story Elements. Although the quality of the imaginative literature children read seems to influence their writing, direct teaching of models is not the most effective way to improve writing (Hillocks, 1986). Instead of teaching through models and examples, teaching specific knowledge about the structure or schema, based on Stein's (1983, 1984, & 1986) work on story comprehension, seems to improve story-writing skills.

Fitzgerald, Spiegel, and Teasley (1987) show that story structure instruction to poor-reading fourth graders improves the overall quality and organization of written stories, but not coherence and creativity. Reynolds (1982) found a similar effect with low-achieving high school students (mostly sophomores); they write significantly better stories after 12 weeks of "traditional" writing instruction than they do after 12 weeks of expressive writing instruction. However, high-achieving students do not. Traditional instruction as Reynolds defines it includes an overview of story elements and then presentations of the different characteristics of four types of fiction: gothic, romance, hero, and mystery. The teacher spells out the different audiences for and structures of each of these types of literature. Students engage in many activities including describing pictures to blindfolded students, writing dialogues, and naming a character based on a description. Students choose a story type and answer a set of questions such as "How was the evil unleashed?" before they write their story. Then they do an outline of scenes. The other instructional condition, expressive writing, is essentially experience in freewriting as brainstorming. Students are asked to list 100 possible audiences for writing. Then they do the same for purposes and forms for writing. They choose their own topics, putting one item from each list at the top of their papers. They also write expressive responses to filmstrips or books. In both modes of instruction, students meet in small groups to share and respond to drafts and work in progress.

Direct teaching of story elements is not always effective, however. Scardamalia and Bereiter (1986) report that when third and seventh graders are exposed to instruction and/or a model suspense story, they do not, when asked to do so, revise a suspenseful story they have written earlier to make it more suspenseful. "Only 26 percent of their original stories were rated as at least moderately suspenseful, and there was no increase in this percentage on revision" (p. 790).

Stimuli for Elaborative Thinking. Hillocks (1986), in his meta-analysis of 60 studies of writing instruction, includes a few that are of imaginative expression (as defined in this chapter). However, Hillocks does not report these separately from other modes of writing. He found the instruction he categorizes as "environmental" has the greatest power for effecting student improvement in a variety of types of writing, largely because it stimulates elaboration. Although Hillocks distinguishes the environmental mode of instruction from what he terms "natural process," it is actually "structured process," a version of a process-oriented approach, one that, as A. Applebee (1986) notes, "draws on the panoply of techniques [Hillocks] . . . seems to be attacking" (p. 105).

One of the effective environmental instructional modes for imaginative writing Hillocks describes is Sager's (1973) approach. Teachers gave inner-city sixth graders a set of scales for evaluating compositions. For example, experimental subjects were asked to read an unelaborated story on "The Green Martian Monster" and then asked to do a series of tasks such as quickly listing "all the reasons why a mouthless, green Martian monster might land in the USA" (Hillocks, 1986, p. 123). They worked with scales that focused on elaboration, vocabulary, organization, and structure. After 8 weeks, the experimental control effect size was 0.93, nearly a full standard deviation, but Hillocks does not include this in his meta-analysis because of inadequate teacher controls. Coleman (1982) confirmed Sager's results with second- and third-grade gifted students. Thibodeau (1964) presented sixth graders with problems involving elaborative thinking. They worked in pairs or small groups to list, for example, all the reasons a diver might suddenly realize he must fight his way back to the surface. The effect size of this instruction is 0.35.

Bereiter and Scardamalia (1982) found that when sixth graders are given the task of composing a story to fit with an ending sentence, they discuss the problem of how to develop the story in a manner that reflects the flavor of adult planning (p. 24). Hilyard and Hidi found when they gave third and fifth graders two inconsistent sentences—one for the story beginning sentence and the second for the ending—children were about twice as likely to resolve the inconsistency as if they are given the same two sentences as the beginning of the story (Bereiter & Scardamalia, 1982, p. 27).

In contrast to these findings, Kelley (1984) found that a flexible six-step (aiming, extending, organizing, expressing, refining, and communicating) creative approach for teaching story writing is not significantly more effective than a sentence/paragraph structure approach in improving the story-writing ability of sixth graders, but is significantly more effective than an equivalent amount of time in sustained silent reading.

Roubicek (1983) and Ridel (1975) found creative drama improves creative writing as noted below in the discussion of the effects of improvisational drama.

Visual Stimuli. Two researchers examined the effect of visual stimuli on writing. Golub (1983) found that third- through sixth-grade children tend to see the narrative-descriptive possibilities in concrete black and white pictures and write more, in contrast to three other types of pictures: abstract black and white, concrete color, or abstract color. Children responding to concrete black and white pictures use more subordinate adverbial clauses, more adverbs other than time, place, and manner modifiers, and more medial adverbs. They also tend to tell a story rather than simply descibe what they see (p. 111). Golub concludes that black and white concrete pictures provide enough stimulus to energize and direct the student's creative and linguistic imagination. Kafka (1971) found that intermediate-grade children write significantly worse narratives after auditory and tactile stimuli than with no stimuli. Visual stimuli produce better compositions than auditory or tactile, but not significantly better.

Mental Imagery. Gambrell (1982) found induced mental imagery to be more effective with third graders than instructions to "think about" what was read. The children in the imagery group write more words than the other group. Gambrell suggests that "mental imagery encourages reflection and contemplation" (p. 8), which have been shown to play a significant role in the composing process (Graves, 1978; King, 1978; Stallard, 1974).

A final important method of teaching imaginative expression, one that has shown astonishing improvement in the writing of open-admissions college students, is the Story Workshop technique (Schultz, 1982). High school teachers who use it report similar results. The highly prescribed technique incorporates oral word association, oral telling, oral reading, writing, and recall exercises, with the emphasis on seeing an image in the mind, using precise gesture, and addressing a present audience.

Surveys and Assessments

Just how much imaginative writing actually goes on, and how much do teachers value it? Even the National Assessment of Educational Progress (NAEP) did not include imaginative writing until its second round. Some NAEP evidence suggests that, at least outside of school, students are engaging in imaginative writing. According to the 1984 NAEP survey of writing achievement, students report they write stories or poems that are not schoolwork; the percentage declines after fourth grade: 27 percent at 4th, 11.2 percent at 8th, and 12.8 percent at 11th grade (A. Applebee, Langer, & Mullis, 1986). In school, there seems to be a shift toward process-oriented teaching activities, a shift that should facilitate the generation of poetic as well as other aims of discourse. The NAEP assessment reports that a growing proportion of students engage in at least one process-oriented activity. For example, nearly half report that they talk with a teacher about a paper while they are working on it (Applebee et al., 1990).

Despite the effect Writing Projects may be having on some teachers, a large number of high school teachers still neither embrace the so-called "process approach" to writing nor foster imaginative expression in their classrooms. A. Applebee (1984) in his analysis of what he saw as the failure of the "process approach" to writing instruction in high schools pinpointed the major factor that works against widespread acceptance of more open-ended strategies for teaching writing: the real threat such teaching poses "to the teachers' conception of their instructional role. To implement such activities effectively, the teacher must shift from a position of knowing what the students' response should be to a less secure position in which there are no clear right or wrong answers (p. 187)." Such a shift is essential if the goal is student production of a unique piece of discourse, one the teacher cannot sketch ahead of time. S. Gardner's (1985) findings confirm those of Applebee. She found that secondary teachers who feel less threatened will risk letting students assume more control of their learning. Those who are uncertain about what students are capable of doing are those who exert more control and are more cynical about student abilities. A second reason some teachers do not teach writing as a process is rooted in the fact that teachers who are uncomfortable with writing themselves and have never enjoyed the satisfaction of producing their own compositions are unlikely to create classroom climates conducive to it.

For whatever reasons, one thing is certain: in school, high school students do not write much fiction, poetry, or drama. In A. Applebee's (1981) nationwide survey of 754 high school teachers, he found that students in English classes spend only 10 percent of their class time generating "extended writing," a paragraph or more, in contrast to nonwriting activities and to filling in workbook or mimeographed exercises. One can guess that this 10 percent does not include much imaginative writing. Applebee's finding is all the more disheartening because the survey includes only "good teachers," those nominated by their building principals as representing "good practice." Applebee asked them to check, from the following list, the two most important reasons for asking students to write:

a. To remember important information,
b. To correlate experience with topic,
c. To test learning of content,
d. To share imaginative experiences (e.g., through stories and poems),
e. To summarize class material,
f. To express feelings,
g. To explore out-of-class material,
h. To practice writing mechanics,
i. To force thinking,
j. To apply concepts to new situations,
k. To teach proper essay form, and
l. To test clear expression.

Only 30 percent of the English teachers include imaginative experiences as one of the two most important reasons (p. 64).

Freedman and McLeod (1988) used the same survey for 560 teachers selected as the most successful in their communities by National Writing Project directors throughout the country. They found more high school teachers (42.2 percent) than Applebee found (30 percent) who choose "to share imaginative experiences" as one of their two most important reasons for asking students to write. They also found significantly more elementary (68.8 percent) than high school teachers who choose imaginative experiences. Freedman and McLeod also surveyed a comparable sample of teachers in the United Kingdom. They were designated as especially capable by members of the executive board of the National Association of English Advisors, who are curriculum consultants to schools. In contrast to their U.S. counterparts, 67.8 percent of the secondary and 84.4 percent of the elementary teachers in the United Kingdom select "to share imaginative experiences" as one of the two most important reasons to ask students to write. The percentage of secondary teachers in the United Kingdom choosing imaginative experiences is statistically significantly higher than that of the U.S. high school teachers (Freedman & McLeod, 1988, p. 20).

Thus, despite the enthusiasm with which U.S. educators since the Dartmouth Conference have embraced the goals of British education, even the best secondary teachers of writing tend not to include stories and poems as most important. A. Applebee (1984) found in secondary school textbooks significantly more imaginative writing assignments in literature anthologies than in any of the other textbooks he examined. The assignments, however, "are either very abrupt, with little development, or very analytic, asking students to examine the workings of a selection very closely, and then to imitate its content or form" (p. 26).

Even in Great Britain, where imaginative writing has assumed, at least until the recent development of the National Curriculum, a larger part of the English curriculum than in the U.S., some reports reflect the view of a group of teachers cited in the Bullock report, who believe that overemphasis on creative, personal, or freewriting has meant, in actuality, artificially stimulated colorful or fanciful language at the expense of ordinary language with vivid imagery.

Perhaps not surprisingly, on the 1984 and 1988 NAEP assessments of writing achievement of American school children, "students found it moderately difficult to write well-developed stories" (A. Applebee et al., 1986, p. 9). An adequate story is one with clear evidence of a plot and descriptions of events, characters, and settings. In the 1988 NAEP assessment only 9.1 percent of the fourth graders, 32.5 percent of the eighth graders, and 40.1 percent of the twelfth graders wrote an adequate or better ghost story in 10 minutes for the fourth graders or in 15 minutes for the eighth and twelfth graders. However, when given twice as much time to respond (20 or 30 minutes), the proportion went up to 17.1 percent for fourth graders, 50.6 percent for eighth graders, and 55.7 percent for the twelfth graders (Applebee et al., 1990). One conclusion is clear: 10 or 15 minutes is too short a time for most students at all grade levels to produce adequate imaginative writing.

Summary

What works best in imaginative writing is not simply finding a teacher who is a master of the craft he or she is presenting but also finding one who can create an appropriately safe and supportive climate for risk taking, can introduce a wide array of stimuli and models without overwhelming the students or teaching the models directly, and can set up a real-world audience without inhibiting the privacy needed for what Lopate refers to as that dive into the deepest part of oneself. A good teacher of imaginative writing needs a well-tuned sensitivity to each student's own inner ripeness for writing, a flexibility that enables the teacher to negotiate his or her role with the students, and an ability to enable students to get started in the process and at the same time encourage their own selection of material to write about. The successful teacher must be a patient respondent who acknowledges writing difficulties but continues to enable movement out of a morass, and an advisor and information-giver when the time is right. Indirect but engaged teaching, an ability to let the students have center stage, a capacity for stimulating mental imagery and elaborative thinking—all are effective. Somehow a good imaginative writing teacher must provide literature that fosters at least an unconscious awareness of schema and form, and at the same time allow students to ignore or transcend such models. A good teacher improvises and confers with students during their writing in a nondirective way to enable them to realize their own intentions. The order is a tall one; it is a wonder any teachers ever realize it. A number of studies and reports of classroom observers show that many of them do. However, after fourth grade, imaginative writing that is not part of schoolwork declines; and very little writing of fiction, poetry, or drama goes on in U.S. high schools.

IMPROVISATIONAL CLASSROOM DRAMA

Improvisational drama in the classroom is a type of oral imaginative expression through which students work together in a fictive enterprise. By its nature, drama is a more social medium than writing. It is not exclusively imaginative, however. Some social dramatic play, especially in infants and toddlers, is merely a ritualistic reenactment of real-world scripts. In the elementary, as opposed to the preschool, classroom, informal improvisational drama is usually led by a teacher either in or out of role. Such drama builds on the experience of informal pretend play that usually arises spontaneously in early childhood. Improvisational classroom drama is the term used in this chapter to encompass not only teacher-sponsored drama but also spontaneous social pretend play if it takes place in a classroom.

This section presents the claims made for informal classroom drama and an overview of major studies of its effectiveness on an array of attitudes and skills. The focus is on its effect on language-arts development: oral language, reading, and writing. Despite the claims for and some research supporting it, very little informal classroom drama is actually taking place in schools. This section concludes with suggestions for further study.

Claims and Overview

Oral language is commonly held to be the seedbed for later growth in literacy. Drama particularly has been advocated as a way to develop not only oral language facility but reading and writing as well (Barnes, 1968; Britton, 1970; Britton, Burgess, Martin, McLeod, & Rosen, 1975; Creber, 1965; Dixon, 1975; Heathcote, 1981; Hoetker, 1969; Moffett & Wagner, 1983). However, convincing empirical research to support these general claims is sparse, and many of the existing studies are not comparable or are faulty in method (Galda, 1984). In preparation for a longitudinal study of children and drama, Collins (1985) surveyed 55 empirical studies, 46 of which assessed drama's effect on other attitudes and skills. He too concludes that one cannot generalize confidently from these studies. Moreover, no replication studies clearly confirm earlier findings.

Much of the work on drama has been done by psychologists concerned with cognition. Basing their work on Piaget and Vygotsky, seminal theorists in the field hypothesized a relationship between symbolic play and sociocognitive development. Some classroom studies assessing the effects of classroom drama have been done, in part, in response to the accountabil-

ity pressures of the 1970s. To justify the arts in the schools, some proponents have shown their effect on skills of recognized value, such as the development of literacy. Such a bias for justifying drama is not new, however; in sixteenth-century Europe, schoolboys' performance of plays was defended as an aid to the study of the art of rhetoric and classical drama.

Recent empirical studies show drama has an effect on a wide variety of attitudes and perspective taking, mental imagery and creative thinking, oral language, reading, and writing. Studies of drama have been conducted by cognitive psychologists to chronicle growth in role taking (Flavell, Botkin, Fry, Wright, & Jarvis, 1968), by speech communication researchers to chronicle growth in persuasion (Clark & Delia, 1976; Delia, Kline, & Burleson, 1979; Lein & Brenneis, 1978; Mitchell-Kernan & Kernan, 1977; Piche, Rubin, & Michlin, 1978), by educators interested in environments and activities that foster language growth (Galda, 1984; Pellegrini, 1985), or by creative dramatics experts interested in assessing the effect of drama on other skills (Isenberg & Jacob, 1983; Wagner, 1986, 1988). Only one study compares two creative dramatic approaches, the Rutgers imagination method and traditional creative dramatics: Chrein (1982) found traditional instruction consisting of warmups and acting out a story leads to a higher level of dramatic behavior, but does not lead to greater mental imagery.

Kardash and Wright (1987) did a meta-analysis of 36 effect sizes drawn from 16 studies of drama between 1965 and 1984 with children (kindergarten to grade seven). The results show that drama has a moderate, positive effect (mean size of 0.67) on children's achievement in four skill areas: reading, communication, person perception, and drama (p. 15). An effect size of 0.67 means that the average child in a drama program is better than almost 75 percent of those in a control group. The three studies that examined effects on diverse populations show that "creative drama appears to have extremely beneficial effects for gifted children, a very small effect for remedial readers, and a moderate, positive effect on learning disabled students" (p. 16). Drama also appears to be most beneficial for younger students, verbal rather than written instructions are more effective, and the largest effect size (+1.53) is found in the only study in which a creative drama specialist led the drama.

Several studies have shown that drama has a positive effect on personal attitudes often associated with language growth: self-confidence, self-concept, self-actualization, empathy, helping behavior, and cooperation (Clore & Jeffery, 1972; DeCourcy-Wernette, 1977; Garner, 1972; Johnson, 1975). Role taking, which shows an awareness of audience, is also usually associated with growth in effective communication. Drama "appears to have an extremely beneficial effect on role taking ability" (Kardash and Wright, 1987, p. 17).

Studies show that training in drama produces positive effects on oral language, reading, and writing; a summary of each follows.

Effect on Oral Language

Six studies show drama correlates with oral language development (McIntyre, 1975; Norton, 1973; Smilansky, 1968;

Snyder-Greco, 1983; Stewig & Young, 1978; Vitz, 1984), but four show no significant effect (Dunn, 1977; Kassab, 1984; Stewig & Vail, 1985; Youngers, 1977). Smilansky's (1968) pioneering research on the effects of drama on oral language and on other areas of the cognitive and social development of disadvantaged Israeli 3- to 6-year-olds shows significant improvement in both oral language and social behavior.

Norton (1973) found a program of pantomime and improvisation improves second graders' oral communication, which is significantly more flexible, original, coherent, fluent (in total number of words but not total number of sentences), but not more elaborated than a control group. Vitz (1984) found that drama, with a group of recent, predominantly Southeast Asian immigrants in a grades-one-to-three classroom, results in a significant increase in the number of words and a greater mean length of communication utterance, indicating greater sentence or utterance complexity. She found no significant difference in the number of communication utterances. The control group participated in an audio-lingual English as a Second Language program (listen-repeat-transform procedure). To measure language proficiency, she evaluated pre- and postsamples of oral language students used in telling the story of a wordless picture book. Stewig and Young (1978) found that after 20 creative drama lessons fourth and seventh graders improve significantly in total verbal output, total T-units, words per T-unit, and ratio of clauses to T-unit. McIntyre (1975) found drama and other creative activities significantly reduce the number of consonant articulation errors in preadolescent and adolescent students with speech disorders.

Snyder-Greco (1983) showed that students who engage in drama make a significant gain in the number of words spoken and in projective language. Projective language forecasts events, anticipates consequences of actions or events, surveys possible alternatives, forecasts related possibilities of something that might happen, and recognizes problems and predicts solutions (pp. 10–11).

In contrast to the research cited above, four studies show drama has no significant effect on oral language (Dunn, 1977; Kassab, 1984; Stewig & Vail, 1985; Youngers, 1977).

Pellegrini (1980, 1982) and his colleagues have done a series of studies with lower socioeconomic children in kindergarten through second grade to examine the effect of dramatic play on a wide range of language and cognitive skills. They show that children engaging in symbolic play use literate language and thus are doing orally what they will later need to transfer to writing. They tend to delineate roles and props precisely at the beginning of play episodes, typically defining pronouns linguistically, introducing topics explicitly, and clarifying roles when they are ambiguous. Because drama involves explicitly separating symbols and the concepts they stand for, Pellegrini (1984a) suggests it may facilitate the use of explicit language.

From the mixed results of these studies one cannot conclude that improvisational classroom drama has a measurable effect on oral language development, although evidence shows that the language used in drama is more explicit and unambiguous than other oral language. New studies need to describe more fully the structure of drama teaching to determine which teacher behaviors and interactions with the students are critical to the effect of drama on oral language and thus might account for the differences in the results of the studies reported here.

Effect on Reading

Piaget (1962) and Vygotsky (1967) laid the theoretical foundations for the relationship of pretend play to the development of literacy. Piaget shows the child moving from egocentric symbolic play to social symbolic play. Through play and imitation, the child learns to separate signifiers from the signified, to attach meanings to symbols, using experiences from the real world to engage in object substitutions and decontextualized behavior. Vygotsky (1967) saw play, which for him was synonymous with pretense, as part of the process of learning to engage in symbol manipulation.

Children in dramatic play often use symbols or signs to represent objects that are absent, and almost always use language, the signifier par excellence (Galda, 1984, p. 106). In drama, language transforms roles, objects, and situations from their real to a pretense function (p. 107). As children get older, they are increasingly apt to use explicit language to define what the object stands for (Pellegrini, 1985). This use of decontextualized language and enactment of role-appropriate behavior in a make-believe situation represents a major step toward literacy, or what Vygotsky terms *second-* rather than *first-order symbolism*. In reading and writing, children engage in a form of conscious symbolization; they assign meaning to arbitrary forms (letters) just as they do to objects in drama (Clay, 1975; Moffett & Wagner, 1983).

Researchers have attempted to study the relationship between symbolic play and the development of literacy. Observational studies show similar mental processes: decontextualized language and narrative sequencing are involved in both; but the experimental studies, with kindergarteners and first graders, that attempt to show a *causal relationship* are not particularly supportive (Pellegrini, 1985). Research shows convincingly, however, that drama *correlates* with literacy skills, especially in kindergarten and first grade (Pellegrini, 1980; Wolfgang, 1973).

Observational studies have shown that nursery-school and kindergarten children often incorporate into their drama social behaviors associated with specific uses of print (Hall, 1988). Durkin's (1966) observations of children who read early show that such children often play "school" with older siblings, who help them by incorporating literacy content into drama. Isenberg and Jacob (1983) reported Wolfgang's 1973 finding that the opposite is also characteristic: first-grade boys who have not reached high levels of dramatic play have "difficulty in reading as well as in other academic areas involving the use and manipulation of symbols and signs" (p. 273).

Pellegrini (1980) found among kindergarteners a significant relationship between symbolic play and reading achievement, this in contrast to sex and socioeconomic background, which do not significantly correlate. Children who engage primarily in social symbolic play have significantly higher scores in word comprehension and in understanding a variety of syntactic structures than other children. They score higher on the Prereading Composite score of the Metropolitan Reading Readiness Test, which consists of audiovisual skills and productive and receptive language skills. Tucker (1971) also found that creative dramatics improves the reading readiness of kindergarten children.

Galda and Pellegrini (1982) found that adult-directed drama is more significantly correlated with the recall of literal details than either discussion or drawing for kindergarten to second-grade children, and more for younger than for older ones. However, a later study (Pellegrini, 1985) shows a significant effect only when the children are measured right after the dramatic enactment, but not when measured a week later. Galda (1984) found that, for second graders, dramatizing a story "seems to result in a greater understanding of cause and effect and the motivations and emotional responses of the characters" (p. 114). It probably helps children shift from a focus on physical to a focus on character or on psychological events. Other studies found a significant positive relationship between dramatic activities and general cognition, response to literature, language, empathy for characters, and comprehension (Conner, 1974; Demmond, 1977; Galda, 1984; Green, 1974).

In addition to the observational correlational studies reported above, three empirical studies show a *causal* effect for drama on reading achievement. Saltz, Dixon, and Johnson (1977) found that lower socioeconomic preschoolers trained in enacting stories construct stories, from a sequence of pictures, that contain significantly more words, connectives, and inferences. Two studies of primary children, one by Henderson and Shanker (1978) and one by Strickland (1973), show that comprehension of literature can be significantly improved through story dramatization compared to basal reader workbook skill activity.

On the other hand, two studies show no significant effect for improvisational classroom drama for older students. Harris and Rosenberg (1983) found creative dramatics does not significantly change high school sophomores' affective engagement with literature when compared with teacher-directed lecture-discussion and with a self-directed small-group strategy. The categories of affective response are empathy, identification, association, and moral reaction (p. 23). Burke (1980) found no significant differences between the reading abilities or self-concepts of two groups of seventh graders who had creative dramatics and who had had reading instruction through a laboratory program.

Isenberg and Jacob (1983), in their literature review of dramatic play and literacy, conclude that dramatic play fosters literacy development in two ways: (a) children's use of representational skills serves as a basis for representation in literacy, and (b) dramatic play provides a safe environment for practicing "the skills and social behaviors associated with literacy activities" (p. 272). On the other hand, Pellegrini (1985) concludes that research does not particularly support a theory that dramatic play facilitates literate behavior. Certainly more research is needed to determine if there really is a causal effect of drama on reading and just what kind of instruction effects the greatest gains.

Effect on Writing

If Bereiter and Scardamalia's (1982) conclusion from evidence is valid, namely, that children's main problem in writing

is accessing and giving order to what they know (p. 17), then drama should help them discover and shape their ideas. The kinesthetic element of assuming an appropriate posture and using apt gestures should enable students to access not only oral but also written persuasive competence. Moffett and Wagner (1983) posit that experience is first coded by the muscles, then by the senses, then by memory, and, finally, by reason (p. 530). Vygotsky (1978) provides the theoretical foundation for the assumption that gesture is akin to writing. Both, like drawing, are accomplished with the hand, and their significance lies in what the gesture symbolizes. As Emig (1978) implies, writing may be even closer to gesture than to speech, and, if so, giving students an opportunity to use gesture in drama may help them kinesthetically to identify with a particular posture and stance, and to produce the natural language that goes with it. Emergent literacy studies (Calkins, 1980; Cioffi, 1984; Dyson, 1981, 1986; Graves, 1982, 1983; Harste, Woodward, & Burke, 1984; Sowers, 1979) show that children give their early writing a multimodality associated with gesture and graphics.

Monson (1986) describes several ways that drama serves as an effective prewriting strategy, clarifying for children concepts they might want to explore through writing. Many observations, such as that of the much discussed Plowden Report (1967) on British schools, attest to the effect of drama on writing. British examiners wrote, "What is most remarkable now in many infant schools is the variety of writing: writing rising out of dramatic play" (p. 218).

However, empirical studies are few. Only five studies test the claim that drama improves writing: Pellegrini (1984b), Ridel (1975), Roubicek (1983), Troyka (1973), and Wagner (1986). Pellegrini (1984b) showed that drama is significantly correlated with word-writing fluency in kindergarten, as measured by performance on Robinson's test of "writing one's own name, writing others' names, writing names of colors, and a miscellaneous category" (p. 277). By contrast, sex and age are not significantly correlated, and socioeconomic status, though significant, accounts for only 12 percent of the variation in total fluency. A correlation, of course, does not mean a cause, but this finding suggests to Pellegrini that pretend play is a powerful predictor of writing achievement in kindergarten. Although word writing is only the beginning of sustaining a monologue using graphic symbols, both it and drama demand moving from the here-and-now perceptions of the moment to displaying internal mental constructions. With growth, a child shows an increasing independence from the limitations of current stimuli and an increasing control of self through internal direction. When children engage in social symbolic or fantasy play, they need to define their symbolic representations socially just as they do when they write words. Both pretend play and word writing "may be related to the child's general representational competence" (p. 276).

Roubicek (1983) found that acting out a story is significantly more effective than a structured discussion for improving subsequent writing among fifth graders. The childrens' compositions show significant differences from the control group in elaboration, and in the "ideas" and "flavor" features on the Diederich Writing Assessment Scale.

Wagner (1986) found role playing to be significantly effective in improving the persuasive letter writing of fourth and eighth graders when compared to either a presentation of models and rules for persuasive letters, or to no instruction. The writing samples were scored for their level of target orientation, or tailoring of the persuasion to its audience. Ridel (1975) showed that ninth graders write more original creative stories after a creative drama program based on theater games. Troyka (1973) showed an effect of drama on writing of 0.75 for the persuasive essays of remedial college freshmen. Cohen (1977) defines 0.10 as a small effect size derived from an F ratio, 0.25 as medium, and 0.40 as large (p. 348).

These five studies show dramatic play in kindergarten correlates with writing achievement, and improvisational classroom drama under a teacher's guidance is effective in improving subsequent writing in studies at fourth-, fifth-, eighth-, and ninth-grade levels and at the remedial college freshmen level.

Surveys

Despite strong claims and a few studies that show classroom drama helps students achieve some very important language-arts goals, two surveys suggest very little drama instruction is part of even the best of language-arts programs. Stewig (1986b) examined the programs of schools named by the National Council of Teachers of English as Centers of Excellence, 150 schools chosen from among 700 applications. Of the 150 programs, only four mention *drama* by name in their title in contrast to 38 that include the word *writing*. On the grounds that drama programs may exist in high schools in departments other than English, and thus might not be mentioned in descriptions of English programs, Stewig looked more closely at the 46 of the 150 Centers that include elementary schools. Only 11 of these have some instance of drama mentioned either in their application form or their evaluation (p. 26). In another survey, Stewig (1986a) found only five elementary school principals out of 20 who report that over half of their teachers use drama once a week or more.

No evidence has surfaced that American language-arts and English teachers have embraced improvisational drama any more than they had when R. Applebee and Squire (1969) did their report on English teaching in the United Kingdom. They noted then the much greater emphasis in classrooms in the United Kingdom on creative uses of language, particularly in the teaching of writing, oral English, and drama (p. 240). "Improvisation, mime, role playing, basic movement, re-creation of basic stories—these are essential" (p. 197). Two movements in the last two decades—emphasis on the process rather than exclusively on the product of writing, and writing across the curriculum—have reflected United Kingdom practice, but there is no evidence that this trend has led also to more improvisational drama in American language-arts or English classrooms. In A. Applebee's (1984) survey of secondary instruction, he makes no mention of drama programs as appropriate contexts for learning to write. (See the discussion of Performing Texts below for more on high school theater programs.)

Need for Naturalistic Observation

Those who have led groups of children or have heard them interact in role in a classroom drama have often marveled at their maturity of expression. Surely this is the quality of language that should be fostered. What both the research community and teachers need are more richly detailed observations of teacher-led classroom drama, descriptions that capture the immediacy and power of the student's struggle to make meaning. They also need the analytical insight that Dyson (1981), Florio and Clark (1982), Giffen (1984), Hall (1988), and Paley (1987) have provided for preschool spontaneous pretend play, emergent literacy events, and classroom interaction. Their rich descriptions have powerful implications for classroom instruction.

The chief weakness of all of the studies of drama reviewed above is their lack of descriptive detail of the teaching act. In contrast to the varied research methods reflected in Part II of this *Handbook,* studies of improvisational classroom drama have not been characterized by naturalistic observation. Drama research has not reflected the tilt in both oral language and literacy research toward hypothesis-generating studies, studies that Eisner (1988) describes as recognizing the primary of experience. He sees the emerging climate for research leading to a rediscovery of "the qualities, complexities, and the richness of life in classrooms" (p. 19). For example, oral language study has encompassed ethnographic observations, pragmatic considerations, sociolinguistic examination, and analyses of function. Reading research is increasingly focused on case and longitudinal studies and analyses of process. Current studies of writing tend to center either on the process in the contexts in which it takes place or on the cognitive mental processing that goes on in the act of writing, and have increasingly encompassed case studies, ethnographic explorations, protocols of the process, sociolinguistic analyses, and close observations of writing behaviors and teacher responses to student efforts. In addition, a lively interest is evident in the similarities and differences between spoken and written texts. The common element in all of these studies is their focus primarily on characteristics of the process, text, instruction, or the culture of the classroom, rather than on the effects of alternative teaching strategies. Because of the limited methods used in drama research, the teaching profession knows too little about what actually goes on in an effective lesson. What are the teacher's goals and how does he or she achieve them? What types of student response indicate growth? What kind of cognitive processing takes place?

To answer such questions, teachers need rich descriptions, focusing on drama teaching in its classroom context like those done on Dorothy Heathcote (Herbert, 1985; Wagner, 1976, 1983, 1985, 1990). Researchers also need to examine the oral texts students produce in role as Beach and Anson (1988) have done with texts written in role and analyze them systematically to document qualitative differences. Empirical studies of classroom drama at this point provide little to go on if one is to pinpoint instruction that leads to specific student changes in oral language, reading, or writing. Teachers would benefit both from longitudinal studies identifying stages in dramatic growth such as Colby's (1988) work and from participant-observer and ethnographic field studies, in which trained observers code standardized categories of teacher-student interaction and participant behaviors. A combination of cognitive and ethnomethodological perspectives could enlighten the field. More comprehensive surveys of the actual time devoted to improvisational drama in classrooms at all levels and of teaching practices are needed to guide the profession in moving toward more optimum emphasis on this medium for learning.

PERFORMING TEXTS

Frequent calls for more oral reading of poems and telling and reading of stories by both teachers and students has characterized the profession for decades. If narrative and poetry are to be nurtured, the sound of language as well as its sense must be valued (Moffett & Wagner, 1983). Educators are rediscovering the value of modeling expressive oral reading, choral reading, and individual performing of longer texts (Hoffman, 1987) in contrast to procedures of sounding out words and round-robin turn-taking in the primary grades. However, very few studies have been done of the effect of classroom performances of texts; what evidence there is, however, seems to point to the value of hearing literature interpreted orally.

Children respond enthusiastically to the entertainment of a well-told story. Even college students who rank their teachers as effective perceive them to tell more stories in the classroom than teachers ranked as less effective (Holladay, 1987). Speech communication researchers who have analyzed storytelling view it as a dense achievement sustained through the interactional cooperation of both tellers and recipients, one that has the effect of bonding group participants.

Orally presented stories show significant effects on the learning of young children. Milner (1982) found that preschool teachers who base their curriculum on orally presented fairy tales have children who are significantly higher than a control group in level of empathy, reading readiness, oral language, and concept of story. Pelias (1979) showed that a course in oral interpretation improves the perspective-taking abilities of college undergraduates.

The value for children of telling stories as well as hearing them is widely claimed. Rosen (1986) makes a strong case for retelling familiar stories in one's own words. In the retelling they become transformed. As the context changes, new meaning potential asserts itself.

We elaborate, compress, innovate, and discard, take shocking liberties, delicately shift nuances. In some cultures there are [authoritative] privileged tales ... which must be retold; but every authentic teller must turn them into internally persuasive discourse or be reduced to a mere reciter, an inflexible mimic. (p. 235)

Thus, storytelling is like all other types of imaginative expression: a creative art. It depends on the same two abilities on which creativity depends: divergent production and transformation.

Teachers who ask children to tell stories need to be sensitive to diverse ethnic and cultural patterns of oral storytelling. For example, instead of a sustained monologue, a cooperative, conversational "talk story" is the conventional pattern in the Athabaskan (Scollon & Scollon, 1981) and in the Hawaiian cultures (Hu-pei Au & Kawakami, 1985).

Story dramatization is another form of presenting a text that has a long history of claims for its value. Page (1983) compared the effects of story dramatization with storytelling on primary children. First graders, particularly low readers, comprehend more after drama, but interesting differences emerge in the effect of the two approaches. Drama is more effective for building understanding of enacted words and details, whereas storytelling is more effective for understanding descriptive details and words. Drama is better for facilitating comprehension of main idea, character motivation, and identification; storytelling is better for inference. To help children empathize with a character and bring to a story their own experience, dramatizing is better, taking a particular moment in time and living it at life rate, tearing the story apart and exploding it into its twisted moments. On the other hand, to make literary forms familiar, to help children internalize story schema, and to stimulate reflection and evaluation of the universal theme inherent in a tale, storytelling is the better medium.

The Arizona State University Seven-Year Longitudinal Study, though not yet completed, has shown that regularly scheduled classroom creative drama sessions *and* frequent theater viewing have a measurable effect on the way children perceive and respond to theater as compared to a control group (Saldaña, 1987).

Readers theater, a group form of oral interpretation, is another oral mode of performance that has strong support among reading and English educators (Bacon, 1972; Coger & White, 1973; Moffett & Wagner, 1983; Post, 1974; Winegarden, 1980). Mayberry (1975) compared the effect of readers theater and solo performance with silent reading. He found that, for both comprehension and appreciation, readers theater and solo performance are more effective than silent reading, with readers theater the most powerful in effect: means are 7.40, 7.09, and 6.43.

Almost no research exists on the effects on students of high school theater programs and on successful teaching or coaching strategies for such programs. However, Waack's (1982) comparison of the number of curricular and co-curricular programs during 1981–1982 in high schools affiliated with the International Thespian Society with programs reported in Joseph Peluso's 1971 survey show that such programs either grew or remained stable in the 1970s. Nearly all of the schools (97.8 percent) produce plays for the general public, and 86 percent offer theater courses for credit.

CONCLUSION

Effective teaching of imaginative expression calls for a special commitment to artistry in addition to a set of informal instructional strategies and styles that are effective for the rest of the English curriculum. If teachers are to enable students to call into existence something new in the world, to draw out of their kinesthetic knowing, their sensory experience, and these memories authentic expressions wrought into symbols, these teachers need to know how to inspire and challenge them for this bracing task. If the flexible and holistic teaching strategies described in this chapter are central to success, then what is currently known about the development of imaginative expression and effective ways to foster it in the classroom points to a holistic, integrated curriculum, one that is the subject of the next chapter.

References

Applebee, A. N. (1978). *The child's concept of story.* Chicago: University of Chicago Press.

Applebee, A. N. (1981). *Writing in the secondary school: English and the content area.* Urbana, IL: NCTE.

Applebee, A. N. (Ed.). (1984). *Contexts for learning to write: Studies of secondary school instruction.* Norwood, NJ: Ablex.

Applebee, A. N. (1986). Problems in process approaches: Toward a reconceptualization of process instruction. In A. Petrosky & D. Bartholomae (Eds.), *The teaching of writing.* Urbana, IL: NCTE.

Applebee, A. N., Langer, J. A., Jenkins, L. B., Mullis, I. S., & Foertsch, M. A. (1990). *Learning to write in our nation's schools.* U. S. Department of Education: Office of Educational Research and Improvement.

Applebee, A. N., Langer, J. A., & Mullis, I. V. S. (1986). *The writing report card: Writing achievement in American schools.* Princeton, NJ: Educational Testing Service.

Applebee, R. K., & Squire, J. R. (1969). *Teaching English in the United Kingdom: A comparative study.* Champaign, IL: NCTE.

Archambault, R. D. (1968). Education and creativity. In Kosinski, L. V. (Ed.), *Readings on creativity and imagination in literature and language.* Champaign, IL: NCTE.

Bacon, W. (1972). *The art of interpretation* (3rd ed.). New York: Holt, Rinehart, & Winston.

Barnes, D. (1968). *Drama in the English classroom.* Champaign, IL: NCTE.

Beach, R., & Anson, C. M. (1988). The pragmatics of memo writing: Developmental differences in the use of rhetorical strategies. *Written Communication.*

Bennett, N. (1976). *Teaching styles and pupil progress.* Cambridge: Harvard University Press.

Bereiter, C., & Scardamalia, M. (1982). From conversation to composition: The role of instruction in a developmental process. In R. Glaser (Ed.), *Advances in instructional psychology* (Vol. 2, pp. 1–64). Hillsdale, NJ: Lawrence Erlbaum Associates.

Berthoff, A. E. (1984). *Reclaiming the imagination.* Upper Montclair, NJ: Boynton/Cook.

Britton, J. N. (1970). *Language and learning.* Baltimore, MD: Penguin.

Britton, J. N. (1983). Writing and the story world. In B. M. Kroll & G. Wells (Eds.), *Explorations in the development of writing* (pp. 3–30). New York: John Wiley & Sons.

Britton, J. N., Burgess, T., Martin, N., McLeod, A., & Rosen, H. (1975). *The development of writing abilities (11–18).* Urbana, IL: NCTE.

Bronowski, J. (1978). *The origins of knowledge and imagination.* New Haven: Yale University Press.

Bullock, A. L. C. (1975). *A language for life: Report of the Committee of Inquiry appointed by the Secretary of State for Education and Science under the chairmanship of Sir Alan Bullock.* London: Her Majesty's Stationery Office.

Burke, J. J., Jr. (1980). *The effect of creative dramatics on the attitudes and reading abilities of seventh grade students.* Unpublished doctoral dissertation, Michigan State University. *Dissertation Abstracts International, 41/12-A,* 4887. (UMI No. D81-12054)

Burton, F. R. (1985). *The reading-writing connection: A one year teacher-as-researcher study of third-fourth grade writers and their literary experiences.* Unpublished doctoral dissertation, Ohio State University. *Dissertation Abstracts International, 46/12-A,* 3595. (UMI No. DA86-02976)

Calkins, L. M. (1980). Children's rewriting strategies. *Research in the Teaching of English, 14,* 331–341.

Calkins, L. M. (1986). *The art of teaching writing.* Portsmouth, NH: Heinemann.

Chrein, G. H. (1982). *The relative effects of two creative drama approaches on the dramatic behavior and mental imagery ability of elementary school students.* Unpublished doctoral dissertation, Rutgers University. *Dissertation Abstracts International, 44/02A,* 433. (UMI No. DA83-13431)

Cioffi, G. (1984). Observing composing behaviors of primary-age children: The interaction of oral and written language. In R. Beach & L. Bridwell (Eds.), *New directions in composition research* (pp. 171–190). New York: Guilford.

Clark, R. A., & Delia, J. G. (1976). The development of functional persuasive skills in childhood and early adolescence. *Child Development, 47,* 1008–1014.

Clay, M. M. (1975). *What did I write?* Exeter, NH: Heinemann Educational Books.

Clore, G. L., & Jeffery, K. M. (1972). Emotional role playing, attitude change, and attraction toward a disabled person. *Journal of Personality and Social Psychology, 23,* 105–111.

Coger, L. I., & White, M. R. (1973). *Readers theatre handbook: A dramatic approach to literature* (rev. ed.). Glenview, IL: Scott, Foresman & Co.

Cohen, J. (1977). *Statistical power analysis in the behavioral sciences* (rev. ed.). New York: Academic Press.

Colby, R. W. (1988). *On the nature of dramatic intelligence: A study of developmental differences in the process of characterization by adolescents.* Unpublished doctoral dissertation, Harvard University. *Dissertation Abstracts International, 49/06B,* 239.

Coleman, D. R. (1982). *The effects of pupil use of a creative writing scale as an evaluative and instructional tool by primary gifted students.* Unpublished doctoral dissertation, Kansas State University. *Dissertation Abstracts International, 42,* 3409-A. (UMI No. 81278860)

Collins, R. (1985). Appendix H: Results of published, empirical drama studies, *Arizona State University Longitudinal Study of Children and Drama.* Tempe, AZ: Arizona State University Child Drama Department.

Conner, M. C. (1974). *An investigation of the effects of selected educational dramatics techniques on general cognitive abilities.* Unpublished doctoral dissertation, Southern Illinois University. *Dissertation Abstracts International, 34* (1975), 6162A. (UMI No. 74-6189, 119)

Courtney, R. (1985). The dramatic metaphor and learning. In J. Kase-Polisini (Ed.), *Creative drama in a developmental context.* New York: University Press of America.

Creber, J. W. P. (1965). *Sense and sensitivity.* London: University of London Press.

DeCourcy-Wernette, E. E. (1977). *Defining, implementing, and assessing the effects of human focus drama on children in two settings—drama workshops and a social studies class.* Unpublished doctoral dissertation, University of Wisconsin, Madison. *Dissertation Abstracts International, 38/08-A,* 4451. (UMI No. D77-19755)

Delia, J. G., Kline, S. L., & Burleson, B. R. (1979). The development of persuasive communication strategies in kindergarteners through twelfth graders. *Communication Monographs, 46,* 241–256.

Demmond, J. (1977). *The use of role-playing, improvisation and performance in the teaching of literature.* Unpublished doctoral dissertation, Georgia State University. *Dissertation Abstracts International, 38/07A,* 3906.

Dewey, J. (1959). *Art as experience.* New York: G. P. Putnam's Sons.

Dixon, J. (1975). *Growth in English.* Urbana, IL: NCTE.

Dunn, J. (1977). *The effect of creative dramatics on the oral language abilities and self-esteem of Blacks, Chicanos, and Anglos in the sec-*

ond and fifth grades. Unpublished doctoral dissertation, University of Colorado. *Dissertation Abstracts International 38/07-A,* 3907. (UMI No. 77-29908)

Dunn, S., Florio-Ruane, S. Clark, C. M. (1985). The teacher as respondent to the high school writer. In S. W. Freedman (Ed.), *The acquisition of written language* (pp. 33–50). Norwood, NJ: Ablex.

Durkin, D. (1966). *Children who read early.* New York: Teachers College Press.

Dyson, A. H. (1981). Oral language: The rooting system for learning to write. *Language Arts, 58,* 776–784.

Dyson, A. H. (1982). Teachers and young children: Missed connections in teaching learning to write. *Language Arts, 59,* 674–680.

Dyson, A. H. (1986). The imaginary worlds of childhood: A multimedia presentation. *Language Arts, 63,* 799–808.

Eckhoff, B. (1983). How reading affects children's writing. *Language Arts, 60,* 607–616.

Eisner, E. W. (1988). The primacy of experience and the politics of method. *Educational Researcher,* 15–20.

Emig, J. (1971). *The composing process of twelfth graders.* (Research Report No. 13). Urbana, IL: NCTE.

Emig, (1978). Hand, eye, brain: Some "basics" in the writing process. In C. R. Cooper & L. Odell (Eds.), *Research on composing: Points of departure* (pp. 59–71). Urbana, IL: NCTE.

Fitzgerald, J., Speigel, D. L., & Teasley, A. B. (1987). Story structure and writing. *Academic Therapy, 22,* 255–263.

Flavell, J., Botkin, P. J., Fry, C. L., Wright, J. W., & Jarvis, P. E. (1968). *The development of role-taking and communication skills in children.* New York: John Wiley.

Florio, S., & Clark, C. M. (1982). What is writing for? Writing in the first weeks of school in a second-third-grade classroom. In L. C. Wilkinson (Ed.), *Communicating in the classroom* (pp. 265–282). New York: Academic Press.

Freedman, S. W., & McLeod, A. (1988). *National surveys of successful teachers of writing and their students: The United Kingdom and the United States* (Technical Report No. 14). Berkeley, CA: Center for the Study of Writing.

Galda, L. (1984). Narrative competence: Play, storytelling, and story comprehension. In A. Pellegrini & T. Yawkey (Eds.), *The development of oral and written language in social contexts* (pp. 105–117). Norwood, NJ: Ablex.

Galda, L., & Pellegrini, A. D. (1982) The effects of thematic-fantasy play training on the development of children's story comprehension. *American Educational Research Journal, 19,* 443–452.

Gambrell, L. B. (1982). *Induced mental imagery and the written language expression of young children.* Paper presented at the Annual Meeting of the National Reading Conference, Clearwater, FL.

Gardner, H. (1980). Children's literary development: The realms of metaphors and stories. In P. E. McGhee & A. J. Chapman (Eds.), *Children's humor.* New York: John Wiley.

Gardner, H. (1983). *Frames of mind: The theory of multiple intelligences.* New York: Basic.

Gardner, H. (1985). Towards a theory of dramatic intelligence. In J. Kase-Polisini (Ed.), *Creative drama in a developmental context.* New York: University Press of America.

Gardner, S. (1985). *The teaching of writing from the perspective of secondary English teachers.* Unpublished doctoral dissertation, University of Michigan. *Dissertation Abstracts International, 46/04-A,* 915. (UMI No. DA85-12409)

Garner, R. C. (1972). *Effects of a simulation learning game on student attitudes and on the learning of factual information.* Unpublished doctoral dissertation, New Mexico State University. *Dissertation Abstracts International, 33/02-A,* 662. (UMI No. D72-22775)

Giffen, H. (1984). Coordination of meaning in shared make believe. In I. Bretherton (Ed.), *Symbolic play: The development of social understanding.* New York: Academic Press.

Golub, L. S. (1983). Stimulating and receiving children's writing: Implications for an elementary writing curriculum. In M. Myers, & J. Gray (Eds.), *Theory and practice in the teaching of composition: Processing, distancing, and modeling* (pp. 103–115). Urbana, IL: NCTE.

Graves, D. H. (1973). *Children's writing: Research directions and hypotheses based upon an examination of the writing processes of seven-year-old children.* Unpublished doctoral dissertation, State University of New York at Buffalo. *Dissertation Abstracts International, 34/10-A,* 6255. (UMI No. 74-8375)

Graves, D. H. (1978). Balance the basics: Let them write. *Learning, 6,* 30–33.

Graves, D. H. (1982). *A case study observing the development of primary children's composing, spelling, and motor behaviors during the writing process* (Final report, September 1, 1978-August 31, 1981). Department of Education, Durham, NH. (ERIC Document Reproduction Service No. ED 218 653)

Graves, D. H. (1983). *Writing: Teachers and children at work.* Exeter, NH: Heinemann.

Green, B. T. (1974). *The effects of dramatic techniques on selected learning outcomes.* Unpublished doctoral dissertation, Clark University. *Dissertation Abstracts International, 35/05-A,* p. 2767. (UMI No. D74-24186)

Hall, N. (1988). Playing at literacy. *London Drama,* 7(5), 11–15.

Halliday, M. A. K. (1977). *Learning how to mean: Explorations in the development of language.* New York: Elsevier.

Harris, M. B. (1973). Modeling and flexible problem-solving. *Psychological Reports, 33*(1), 19–23.

Harris, L. F., & Rosenberg, H. S. (1983). Creative drama and affective response to literature. *Children's Theatre Review, 31,* 27–43.

Harste, J., Woodward, V. A., Burke, C. (1984). *Language stories & literacy lessons.* Portsmouth, NH: Heinemann.

Heathcote, D. (1981). Drama as education. In Nellie McCaslin (Ed.), *Children and drama* (2nd ed., pp. 78–90). New York: Longman.

Heathcote, D., & Herbert, P. A. (1985). A drama of learning: Mantle of the expert. *Theory into Practice, 24,* 173–180.

Henderson, L. C., & Shanker, J. L. (1978). The use of interpretative dramatics versus basal reader workbooks for developing comprehension skill. *Reading World, 17,* 239–243.

Hillocks, G. (1986). *Research on written composition: New directions for teaching.* Urbana, IL: National Conference on Research in English.

Hirsch, S. C. (1984). Understanding fiction through writing it. *English Journal, 73*(5), 77–81.

Hoetker, J. (1969). *Dramatics and the teaching of literature.* Champaign, IL: NCTE.

Hoffman, J. V. (1987). Rethinking the role of oral reading in basal instruction. *The Elementary School Journal, 87,* 367–373.

Holladay, S. J. (1987). *Narrative activity and teacher effectiveness: An investigation of the nature of storytelling in the classroom.* Paper presented at the annual meeting of the Speech Communication Association, Boston.

Howell, S. (1982). *The role of expressive writing in the writing program.* Unpublished doctoral dissertation, Southern Illinois University. *Dissertation Abstracts International, 43/05-A,* 1454. (UMI No. DA82-21940)

Hu-Pei, Au, K., & Kawakami, A. J. (1985). Research currents: Talkstory and learning to read. *Language Arts, 62,* 406–411.

Isenberg, J., & Jacob, E. (1983). Literacy and symbolic play: A review of the literature. *Childhood Education, 59,* 272–276.

Johnson, D. W. (1975). Cooperativeness and social perspective taking. *Journal of Personality and Social Psychology, 31,* 241–244.

Kafka, T. T. (1974). *A study of the effectiveness of four motivational stimuli on the quality of composition of intermediate students in one school district.* Unpublished doctoral dissertation, St. John's University. *Dissertation Abstracts International, 32,* 2549A. (UMI No. D71-30213)

Kantor, K. J. (1975). Creative expression in the English curriculum: An historical perspective. *Research in the Teaching of English, 9,* 5–29.

Kantor, K. J. (1984). Classroom contexts and the development of writing intuitions: An ethnographic case study. In R. Beach & L. S. Bridwell (Eds.), *New directions in composition research.* New York: Guilford.

Kardash, C. A. M., & Wright, L. (1987). Does creative drama benefit elementary school students: A meta-analysis. *Youth Theater Journal, 2* (1), 11–18.

Kassab, L. J. (1984). *A poetic/dramatic approach to facilitate oral communication (oral interpretation, reticence).* Unpublished doctoral dissertation, Pennsylvania State University. *Dissertation Abstracts International, 45/10-A,* 3026. (UMI No. D84-29098)

Kelley, K. R. (1984). *The effect of writing instruction on reading comprehension and story writing ability.* Unpublished doctoral dissertation, University of Pittsburgh. *Dissertation Abstracts International, 45/06-A,* 1703. (UMI No. D84-21346)

King, M. (1978). Research in composition: A need for theory. *Research in the Teaching of English, 12,* 193–202.

Kinneavy, J. L. (1971). *A theory of discourse.* New York: Norton.

Lein, L., & Brenneis, D. (1978). Children's disputes in three speech communities. *Language in Society, 7,* 299–324.

Lopate, P. (1978). Helping young children start to write. In C. R. Cooper & L. Odell (Eds.), *Research on composing: Points of departure* (pp. 135–149). Urbana, IL: NCTE.

Mayberry, D. R. (1975). *A comparison of three techniques of teaching literature: Silent reading, solo performance, and readers theatre.* Unpublished doctoral dissertation, North Texas State University. Abstract in *I.D. Newsletter, 16,* 10.

McIntyre, B. M. (1957). *The effect of a program of creative activities upon the consonant articulation skills of adolescent and pre-adolescent children with speech disorders.* Unpublished doctoral dissertation, University of Pittsburgh. *Dissertation Abstracts International, 17/05,* 1152. (UMI No. DOO-21006)

McLure, A. A. (1985). *Children's responses to poetry in a supportive literary context.* Unpublished doctoral dissertation, Ohio State University. *Dissertation Abstracts International, 46/09-A,* 2603. (UMI No. DA85-26218)

Milner, S. C. (1982). *Effects of a curriculum intervention program using fairy tales on preschool children's empathy level, reading readiness, oral language development and concept of a story.* Unpublished doctoral dissertation, University of Florida. *Dissertation Abstracts International, 44/2,* 430-A. (UMI No. DA83-13664)

Mitchell-Kernan, C., & Kernan, K. (1977). Pragmatics of directive choice among children. In C. Mitchell-Kernan & S. Ervin-Tripp (Eds.), *Child discourse.* New York: Academic Press.

Moffett, J. (1979). Commentary: The word and the world, *Language Arts, 56,* 115–116.

Moffett, J., & Wagner, B. J. (1983). *Student-centered language arts and reading, K–13: A handbook for teachers.* Boston: Houghton Mifflin.

Monson, D. (1986). Drama and narrative: The link to literature and composition in the elementary school. In J. Kase-Polisini (Ed.), *Children's theater: Creative drama and learning.* New York: University Press of America.

Mosenthal, P. B. (1984). The effect of classroom ideology on children's production of narrative text, *American Educational Research Journal, 21,* 679–689.

Mosenthal, P. B., Conley, M. W., Colella, A., & Davidson-Mosenthal, R. (1985). The influence of prior knowledge and teacher lesson structure on children's production of narratives, *The Elementary School Journal, 85,* 621–634.

National Endowment for the Arts. (1988). *Toward civilization.* Washington DC: Public Information Office.

Norton, N. J. (1973). *Symbolic arts: The effect of movement and drama upon the oral communication of children in grade two.* Unpublished doctoral dissertation, Boston University. *Dissertation Abstracts International, 34/04-A,* 1491. (UMI No. 73-23589)

Page, A. (1983). *Children's story comprehension as a result of storytelling and story dramatization: A study of the child as spectator and as participant.* Unpublished doctoral dissertation, University of Massachusetts. *Dissertation Abstracts International, 44/04-A,* 985. (UMI No. DA83-17447)

Paley, V. (1987). *Wally's stories: Conversations in the kindergarten.* Cambridge: Harvard University Press.

Pelias, R. J. (1979). *Oral interpretation as a method for increasing perspective-taking abilities.* Unpublished doctoral dissertation, University of Illinois at Urbana-Champaign. *Dissertation Abstracts International, 40/10-A,* 5248. (UMI No. 80-09127)

Pellegrini, A. D. (1980). The relationship between kindergarteners' play and achievement in prereading, language, and writing. *Psychology in the Schools, 17,* 530–535.

Pellegrini, A. D. (1982). The construction of cohesive text by preschoolers in two play contexts. *Discourse Processes, 5*(1), 101–108.

Pellegrini, A. D. (1984a). The effect of dramatic play on children's generation of cohesive text. *Discourse Processes, 7*(1), 57–67.

Pellegrini, A. D. (1984b). Symbolic functioning and children's early writing: The relations between kindergarteners' play and isolated word-writing fluency. In R. Beach & L. S. Bridwell (Eds.), *New directions in composition research* (pp. 274–284). New York: Guilford.

Pellegrini, A. D. (1985). The relations between symbolic play and literate behavior: A review and critique of the empirical literature. *Review of Educational Research, 55*(1), 107–121.

Perl, S., & Wilson, N. (1986). *Through teachers' eyes.* Portsmouth, NH: Heinemann.

Peters, W. H. (1987). Research on teaching: Presage variables. In W. H. Peters & Conference on English Education Commission on Research in Teacher Effectiveness (Eds.), *Effective English teaching.* Urbana, IL: NCTE.

Phillips, L. M. (1986). *Using children's literature to foster written language development* (Research/Technical Report No. 143). (ERIC Document Reproduction Service No. ED 276 027)

Piaget, J. (1962). *Play, dreams, and imitation in childhood.* New York: Norton. (Original work published 1945)

Piche, G. L., Rubin, D. L., & Michlin, M. L. (1978). Age and social class in children's use of persuasive communicative appeals. *Child Development, 49,* 773–780.

Pitcher, E., & Prelinger, E. (1963). *Children tell stories.* New York: International Universities Press.

Plowden, Lady B. (1967). *Children and their primary schools,* Plowden Report. London: Her Majesty's Stationery Office.

Polyani, M. (1962). *Personal knowledge: Towards a post-critical philosophy.* Chicago: University of Chicago Press.

Post, R. M. (1974). Readers theatre as a method of teaching literature, *English Journal, 63*(6), 69–72.

Reynolds, A. L., Jr. (1982). *The effects of teaching expressive writing (integrated within the writing process) on the improvement of student writing skills at the high school level.* Unpublished doctoral dissertation, Northern Illinois University. *Dissertation Abstracts International, 44/04-A,* 1011. (UMI No. D83-18312)

Ridel, S. J. H. (1975). *An investigation of the effects of creative dramatics on ninth grade students.* Unpublished doctoral dissertation, Florida

State University. *Dissertation Abstracts International, 36/06A*, 3551-A. (UMI No. 75-26, 811, 238)

Rosen, H. (1986). The importance of story. *Language Arts, 63*, 226–237.

Roubicek, H. L. (1983). *An investigation of story dramatization as a pre-writing activity.* Unpublished doctoral dissertation, University of Maryland. *Dissertation Abstracts International, 45/02-A*, 403. (UMI No. 84-12051)

Sager, C. (1973). *Improving the quality of written composition through pupil use of rating scale.* Unpublished doctoral dissertation, Boston University. *Dissertation Abstracts International, 34*, 1496-A. See also, Sager writing scale (ERIC Document Reproduction Service No. ED 091 723).

Saldaña, J. (1987). Statistical results in progress for the theatre for children component of the ASU longitudinal study. *Youth Theatre Journal 2*(2), 14–27.

Saltz, E., Dixon, D., & Johnson, J. (1977). Training disadvantaged preschoolers on various fantasy activities: Effects on cognitive functioning and impulse control. *Child Development, 48*, 367–380.

Scardamalia, M., & Bereiter, C. (1986). Research on written composition. In M. C. Wittrock (Ed.), *Handbook of research on teaching* (3rd ed., pp. 778–803). New York: Macmillan.

Schultz, J. (1982). *Writing: From start to finish.* Portsmouth, NH: Heinemann Boynton/Cook.

Scollon, R., & Scollon, B. K. S. (1981). *Narrative, literacy, and face in interethnic communication.* Norwood, NJ: Ablex.

Shumaker, C. L. (1982). *A study to determine if planned weekly instruction in expressive writing in grade six improves pupils' language arts achievement scores.* Unpublished doctoral dissertation, Temple University. *Dissertation Abstracts International, 43/03-A*, 709. (UMI No. DA82-17798)

Smilansky, S. (1968). *The effects of sociodramatic play on disadvantaged preschool children.* New York: John Wiley.

Snyder-Greco, T. (1983). The effects of creative dramatic techniques on selected language functions of language disorders children. *Children's Theatre Review, 32*, 9–13.

Sowers, S. A. (1979). A six year old's writing process: The first half of first grade. *Language Arts, 56*, 829–835.

Stallard, C. K. (1974). An analysis of the writing behavior of good student writers. *Research in the Teaching of English, 8*, 207–218.

Stein, N. (1983). On the goals, functions, and knowledge of reading and writing. *Contemporary Educational Psychology, 8*, 261–292.

Stein, N. (1984). Critical issues in the development of literacy education: Toward a theory of issues and instruction. *American Journal of Education, 93*(1), 171–197.

Stein, N. (1986). Knowledge and process in the acquisition of writing skills. In E. Z. Rothkopf (Ed.), *Review of research in education, 13* (pp. 225–258). Washington, DC: American Educational Research Association.

Stewig, J. W. (1986a). The classroom connection: Elementary school principals and creative drama. *Youth Theater Journal, 1*(2), 15–18.

Stewig, J. W. (1986b). NCTE Centers of Excellence: A place for drama. *Youth Theater Journal, 1*(2), 25–27.

Stewig, J. W., & Vail, J. (1985). The relation between creative drama and oral language growth. *Clearing House, 58*, 261–264.

Stewig, J. W., & Young, L. (1978). An exploration of the relations between creative drama and language growth. *Children's Theatre Review, 27*(2), 10–12.

Strickland, D. S. (1973). A program for linguistically different Black children. *Research in the Teaching of English, 7*, 79–86.

Thibodeau, A. L. (1974). *A study of the effects of elaborative thinking and vocabulary enrichment exercises on written composition.* Unpublished doctoral dissertation, Boston University. *Dissertation Abstracts International, 25/04-A*, 2388. (UMI No. D64-04041)

Troyka, L. Q. (1973). *A study of the effect of simulation-gaming on expository prose competence of college remedial English composition students.* Unpublished doctoral dissertation, New York University. *Dissertation Abstracts International, 34* (1974), 4092-A. (UMI No. 73-30, 136) (ERIC Document Reproduction Service No. ED 090 541)

Tucker, J. K. (1971). *The use of creative dramatics as an aid in developing reading readiness with kindergarten children.* Unpublished doctoral dissertation, University of Wisconsin. *Dissertation Abstracts International, 32/06-A*, 3471. (UMI No. 71-25508)

Vitz, K. (1984). The effects of creative drama in English as a second language. *Children's Theatre Review, 33*, 23–26, 33.

Vygotsky, L. S. (1967). Play and its role in the mental development of the child. *Soviet Psychology, 12*, 62–76.

Vygotsky, L. S. (1978). *Mind in society: The development of higher psychological processes.* M. Cole, V. John-Steiner, S. Scribner, & E. Souberman (Eds.). Cambridge: Harvard University Press.

Waack, W. L. (1982). *A survey of the status of curricular and co-curricular theatre programs in International Thespian Society affiliated high schools in the United States.* Unpublished doctoral dissertation, University of Iowa. *Dissertation Abstracts International, 43/08-A.* (UMI No. D82-29981)

Wagner, B. J. (1976). *Dorothy Heathcote: Drama as a learning medium.* Washington, DC: National Education Association.

Wagner, B. J. (1983). The expanding circle of informal classroom drama. In B. A. Busching & J. I. Schwartz (Eds.), *Integrating the language arts in the elementary school.* Urbana, IL: NCTE.

Wagner, B. J. (1985). Elevating the written word through the spoken: Dorothy Heathcote and a group of 9- to 13-year-olds as monks. *Theory into Practice, 24*, 166–172.

Wagner, B. J. (1986). *The effects of role playing on written persuasion: An age and channel comparison of fourth and eighth graders.* Unpublished doctoral dissertation, University of Illinois at Chicago. *Dissertation Abstracts International, 47/11-A*, 4008. (UMI No. 87-05196)

Wagner, B. J. (1988). Research currents: Does classroom drama affect the arts of language? *Language Arts, 65*, 46–51.

Wagner, B. J. (1990). Dramatic improvisation in the classroom. In D. L. Rubin & S. Hynds (Eds.), *Perspectives on talk and learning.* Urbana, IL: NCTE.

Winegarden, A. D. (1980). The value of readers theatre: Claims, programs, and research. *Research in Education.* (ERIC Document Reproduction Service No. ED 182 793)

Wise, A. E., Darling-Hammond, L., McLaughlin, M. W., & Bernstein, H. T. (1984). *Teacher evaluation: A study of effective practices.* Santa Monica, CA: Rand Corporation. (ERIC Document Reproduction Service No. ED 246 559)

Witkin, R. W. (1974). *The intelligence of feeling.* London: Heinemann Educational Books.

Wolfgang, C. H. (1973). *An exploration of the relationship between reading achievement and selected developmental aspects of children's play.* Unpublished doctoral dissertation, University of Pittsburgh. *Dissertation Abstracts International, 34/08-A.*

Youngers, J. S. (1977). *An investigation of the effects of experiences in creative dramatics on creative and semantic development in children* (Volumes I and II). Unpublished doctoral dissertation, University of Iowa. *Dissertation Abstracts International, 39/117-A.* (UMI No. 7810 405, 922)

38

UNIFYING THE ENGLISH LANGUAGE ARTS CURRICULUM

38A. THE LANGUAGE ARTS INTERACT

Jane Hansen
Donald H. Graves

Whether teachers have kindergarten children or PhD candidates as their students, a dilemma about the teaching of reading, writing, talking, and listening faces them. They must choose between two definitions of literacy. One school of thought defines it as simply the ability to read and write, while others define literate persons as those whose actions reveal an understanding of ways to put print to use. Plus, countless gray areas dwell between the two poles. Researchers, whether they research their own teaching or that of others, face the same dilemma when they study the language arts.

All researchers focus on what they feel are the qualities of a literate person. The emphasis they choose reflects their values. Those who rest research results on test scores, or, similarly, choose teaching methods that originate in such research, may possess the first assumption: Someone who can read and write is literate. Such persons may perform the acts of reading and writing, but not connect literacy to their own lives. They read and write because they're told to, rather than initiate reading and writing on their own. Regardless, they can receive high test scores and be judged successful students.

On the other hand, researchers who look to social behaviors in the work place, home, school, or classroom, as necessary components of literacy, may make the second assumption: Literate persons seek and use knowledge for purposes they think are useful. They not only read and write to satisfy their own quests, but they consider talk an important learning mode. They also listen. They listen to their equals, rather than only to authorities. Many versions of the two definitions span the distance between the extremes and provide theories for educators. Thus, as authors of this chapter, we have our belief system.

To us, literacy has been simplified by both researchers and practitioners. It is now time to focus on its complexity in order to create better opportunities for powerful learning.

If literacy is complicated, and if literate persons seek and use information for purposes they think are useful, they must be persons who can find purposes. Thus, research on literacy cannot be simply researcher-driven. It must emanate from the persons being studied. Similarly, teachers in literate classrooms do not develop the habit of always setting the purposes of the lesson. The students also participate. It's the teacher's responsibility to teach children how to choose purposes for reading, writing, talking, and listening. The leader helps the learners create situations in which their thinking will have meaning for them. Language use is not mechanistic.

In this chapter, we use the following format to show where and how the various language arts (reading, writing, talking, and listening) take on significance in the lives of literate researchers, teachers, and students. First, we examine the influences of community, home, and school on classroom language use. Second, since the use of language requires people to interact, we examine how children and adults learn from each other, as well as how children learn from each other. Third, we explore ways to change these settings where people interact: the language classroom, school and beyond.

THE INFLUENCES OF COMMUNITY, HOME AND SCHOOL ON CLASSROOM LANGUAGE USE

The participants in any language event may have different purposes. When two people read, one may be hiding behind the book to shield a preoccupation with a personal problem and the other may be reading a book recommended by a best friend in order to gain insights into the friend. Similarly, when one person calls another to ask about the hospitalization of a mutual friend, the caller may have made the call because of worries about whether her own shaky health will go downhill as fast as her friend, but the other's mind is somewhere else, quickly thinking of ways to help the friend in the hospital.

Thus, any interaction must be framed by this question, "What is language for?" When someone reads, teachers need to know the answer to "Why are you reading that?" before they ask "What does it mean to you?" The first question only works, however, if students are reading self-selected material.

Because the forces affecting a child may be very different than those the teacher has on her mind, the teacher seeks to learn from the student, to understand the other viewpoint. To value the influence of everything that might affect a particular situation—home, community, school and language class—is an issue that has surfaced repeatedly over the years but educators have often pushed it aside because it complicates the ability to predict success. However, the consideration of many elements in the students' overall life underlies the simpler question of how to teach the language arts as interdependent ways of learning. In order to understand language in the classroom, teachers must understand the school. Similarly, the school must be studied in terms of the community it serves and leads.

The Role the Home and Community Play in the Shaping of Language Use

Families are minisocieties where children learn basic social values and ways to interact. They use more kinds of language patterns in their homes and communities than in school. School restricts their language use. Language patterns used in many families are often not permitted in schools, even though learning in families works. Children do learn a great deal in their homes and communities, and they bring this knowledge with them when they enter school. Many schools, however, do not build upon the skills children bring with them (Heath, 1983). Conflict can arise very soon if the interaction patterns children have learned are not understood and valued by schools. Thus, knowledge of the influence of home and community is crucial to a study of the language arts.

In programs for the children of the Northern Cheyenne Indian tribe and of Spanish-speaking migrant families in a border area in Texas along the Rio Grande, very low success rates in school changed when interaction between the community and classroom became a reality (McConnell, 1989). When local leaders managed programs and parents became part of the teaching staff, rather than all the teachers being outsiders, the children's test scores rose significantly. The hiring of teachers from ethnic and language-minority groups "minimized the cultural shock for the child. . . . If the teacher in the school is more like the adults at home there is less shock than if the child encounters someone . . . using . . . a different manner of relating to other people, insofar as these patterns are culturally determined."

Home patterns, regardless of the community, shed light on children's learning patterns. Gundlach, McLane, Stott & McNamee (1985) found that children's interactions with their families contributed greatly to their writing. One 5-year-old girl learned from, with, and despite her 7-year-old sister. One day when they had fun making a magic potion, they spontaneously wrote a list of their ingredients and this activity stretched the younger sister's writing ability.

On another occasion, however, the older sister didn't want to include the younger, but the neighborhood children overrode the older sister and, thus, the younger one became involved in a group writing game that helped her writing skills. In both situations, the younger sister did not get better on her own. Interactions with others contribute to children's learning. This aspect of an effective learning environment is important for educators to think about when learning environments are planned. In order to be comfortable with scenes of interaction among students, teachers must trust the students' knowledge. Unfortunately, teachers often do not honor the lives their students bring into their classrooms.

In *The Education of Little Tree* (Carter, 1986), written about Little Tree's childhood during the 1930s, a Cherokee with cause to be bitter shows Little Tree, his grandson, to see worth in others. Even though the federal government uprooted the Cherokee nation, Grandpa teaches Little Tree to value the needs of others, such as the sharecroppers and trees. When Little Tree goes to school, however, because his knowledge base is different from that of his teachers, his interpretations of texts are foreign to them, and they thrash him.

Many readers hear themselves in the voices of these teachers. This callousness goes farther back, to the end of the Civil War. In *Beloved* (Morrison, 1987), a young mother cannot cope with freedom from slavery. Readers shudder and wonder what was taught in schools at that time, when home and community was valued so little that the pressures and prides prevalent in the homes of African Americans were typically omitted from the mainstream of education.

The notion of understanding the whole person has only recently come to the forefront, even to a limited degree. Cazden (1986) shows different talk patterns set up by teachers in their classrooms, and says these patterns often reflect the "extra-classroom influences" of the country's stratified society. In other words, the classroom society is often divided into groups who have less than equal status and the teacher uses different language with the various groups; the teacher's expansive language with "top" groups serves to expand their learning while the language used in "low" groups pinpoints the children's thinking toward specific bits of information. Differentiation among social groups is one of the basic characteristics of language.

Halliday (1979) reveals the interactive nature of social class and language. Dialect reveals class, but register (the variation in talk depending upon whether a person talks to the retired gentleman next door or the lively toddler across the street) shows the variations used to fit into a situation. If people cannot adjust to a situation, then those to whom they talk, get confused. A situation determines the language people use, and language affects their ability to make meaning in, and of, an event. The more diverse someone's language experiences are, the greater is the person's chance to use and understand language effectively.

Because "speech unites the cognitive and the social" (Cazden, 1986) educators must consider many contexts when bringing the notion of interaction into classrooms. Who speaks to whom, about what, when, and for what purpose sets the groundwork upon which language instruction rests. If teachers value the learning that occurs when children talk to each other, and value what they, as adults, learn when they listen to children, then the phrase "interaction among the language arts" has a different meaning than in a classroom where children must be quiet because the teacher thinks her students will learn best by listening to her language rather than, also, by listening to each other and constructing meaning themselves by talking with both adults and children.

The Role the School Plays in Shaping Language Use

In Goodlad's (1984) study of *A Place Called School,* he describes the emotions, atmosphere, and environments of schools as "flat." Many students do not commit energy to their work; they do not care. Educators must decide whether to let students pursue their own interests, and, in those contexts, to teach them how to pursue new ideas. Because learning processes vary so much from person to person, task to task, and situation to situation, frequent interaction among learners (the teacher is one of the learners) can help the learners reflect on their own strategies and those of others.

Presently, such interaction is seldom valued in schools and universities. Rather, teachers make the decisions about what and how students will learn and students have one overriding decision to make, "Should I bother to learn or not?" The school, because of its unengaging climate, does not teach children to think about, talk about, explore, or become excited about content, information, or meaning. The main thing students learn in school is not subject matter, but what their relationship is to authority (Wilcox, 1982). The children constantly decide when, and when not, to comply.

This role of schools as socializing institutions provides a less-than-ideal climate for both students and adults. Discontent reigns among students, educators, and the community at large. Solutions bound. Different camps vow they have the way to improve schools.

In-services and brochures tempt teachers with information about a wholistic approach to teaching, and, at the same time, other pamphlets and workshops entice teachers to learn about Effective Schools, which emphasize a much different form of instruction, based on the hierarchical arrangement of bits and pieces. Effective Schools (Hunter, 1982, 1984) do not rest on one dimension; they are complex. However, a salient feature is a belief in the "psychological" principle that simple concepts must be learned before more complex ideas can be understood. This general model for teaching has direct relevance for teachers of the language arts.

The educator, in this model, breaks learning experiences into small bits and presents those pieces to children in stepwise fashion. In other words, for reading, teachers would have children learn to identify letters first, then sounds, next would come phrases and sentences, then short stories, and, much later, books. Similarly, in writing, teachers would have children print letters, copy sentences, compose sentences and paragraphs, and compose essays that followed a prescribed format.

This picture of language instruction changes, however, in the presence of other research.

Jensen's (1988) book of chapters written by teacher-researchers shows schools that challenge children to grapple with complex environments. Young children start to write by composing entire thoughts and children learn to read from entire books. Children in these classrooms turn the Effective-Teacher literature upside down, because they do not move from simple to complex. Children learn written language as they learn oral language, by first getting a sense of the entire sound and use of it (Lindfors, 1980). As toddlers, they lived a life immersed in the oral language of a variety of people. Similarly, in order to get a sense of how printed language works, children benefit from the heterogeneous use of the written word by diverse children.

Rather than plan situations where children work in homogeneous groups in traced classrooms, all students can share the responsibility for finding something worthwhile in books and/or for extending their thoughts beyond books. However, the Effective-Teacher literature tells teachers to direct easier questions to the "less able students and difficult questions to more able students." The problem with this reasoning is that the less able students remain so from first grade through high school (Weinstein, 1986). They seldom receive challenges; they get farther and farther behind. Schools shape language use in a negative way when they do not focus on higher-level thinking and segregate children into high and low groups.

Grouping helps to ensure the failure of low students (Oakes, 1985), but educators establish groups to give additional help under the false assumption that success gained in a low group will increase student motivation to learn. Our profession overlooks the overriding effect of the socialization we enforce when we make it our practice to put someone down. Being in a bottom group every day for 12 years does not increase motivation. Instead, it robs students of the learning skills they brought to school at the age of five.

Children talk to create meaning and understand their world. There are so many things children do not understand about what goes on around them. Unfortunately, when they start school, teachers place some of them in top, middle, and bottom groups, depending on their previous experiences. The very children who have not put their world together, according to school terms, as meaningfully as others, are placed in the bottom group. Less exposure to comprehension, less constructive use of oral language in connection with reading, occurs in low reading groups, with the children who need it most. Stratification hinders their learning. In both of Collins' (1982) schools, the high groups "improved dramatically during the year and the low groups improved little."

Some children do not match the system of groups and tracks. They have learning problems and spend time in special classrooms. The help provided for these children is often narrow compared to the help we give to children without difficulties. Teachers often keep students in resource rooms and other low groups from performing thinking tasks they can do. For example, children evaluated themselves at age two when their block towers fell down and continued, at age three, four and five, to perform at the top level of Bloom's taxonomy, evaluation, a level meant to be reserved until later by effective teachers. Children, however, do not learn to think in a hierarchical fashion. They perform all the thinking skills of adults (Donaldson, 1977).

For years, however, educators have thought that children's thinking skills develop from simple to more complex. To give children credit for what they can do is difficult. As changes in our knowledge about children occur, we find discrepancies in our thinking. We try to incorporate the new, but the old roots are deep. To see learning as an interaction of many levels of understanding at any one point in time rather than as a hierarchical progression confuses teachers, administrators, and, also, researchers (Neilsen, 1989).

Gartner & Lipsky (1987) advocate a shift away from segregated education for learning disabled students and, at the same time, as if the two approaches do not conflict, they advocate the need to maintain teacher-directed instruction, reinforcement, and individual instruction. These latter conditions inherently segregate the children from each other and the teacher from the children, as the teacher serves the role of evaluator. The children work for the teacher. In special education, "learned helplessness" sets in, as the children learn from the ever-present teacher to not rely on themselves. Children with academic and social problems can, however, learn in classrooms where the teacher has taught the children to take responsibility for many of their decisions rather than following the dominant model where the teacher is the prime decision-maker.

Wansart (1989) describes the benefits to children who have learning disabilities labels and normal children when they interact for reading and writing. His findings show benefits that learning disabilities research failed to document when resource rooms focused on the isolation of skills from a context of real writing and reading, separated those skills into discrete units arranged into a hierarchy, and isolated coded children from normal children. In Wansart's study of one learning disabled child in a fourth grade classroom, the

community mileau (of the classroom supported) the idea that writing is hard work for everyone. This sense of community allows students with writing disabilities to become integrated into the classroom learning process and to feel a connection with other students, rather than feeling isolated and incapable. . . .

Because this learning disabled child started to stay in her regular classroom during reading and writing, and because the children in her classroom did not work in isolation, but helped each other daily, Jessica (the child with problems) could not only admit to having a question but could ask for and receive help.

As Jessica worked on her reading journal one morning, she was having difficulty reading some of the comments the teacher had written about her book. Finally she asked another student for help. Brandy and then Kristin came over to Jessica's desk. . . .

Kristen read the teacher's question out loud. As Jessica wrote the answer, the two helpers read over her shoulder. Brandy suggested an incorrect spelling for a word and Kristin corrected her. Brandy pointed to the writing and said, "OK, Put a period in there." . . . .

Jessica then continued on her own. As Brandy walked away she said, "OK, if you need me you know what to do!"

Children, literate people, need to be able to relate well, or at least realize the importance of good relations, and strive for them. Their desire and ability to initiate positive interactions with others often helps them with their learning. However, at a special education placement meeting, this comment was considered irrelevant, "Johnny has been a problem on the playground ever since first grade" (Poplin, 1987). Contrary to the special education team's belief, Johnny's ability to get along with his peers is relevant. The ability to use language to solve problems and celebrate is at the heart of any language situation, whether it be on the playground or in the classroom.

The Role the Classroom Plays in the Shaping of Language

Expansive Language. During reading groups in Lynn Parson's grade 5 class in Stratham, New Hampshire (Hansen, submitted), children not only encourage their teacher, but interact with each other more than with her. The groups in this classroom are heterogeneous, not ability-leveled groups. On a day in April of 1988 6 children and 2 adults met to share the various books they were reading. Their discussion shows how the children talked to each other, as well as how they interacted with the teacher.

Kate was the second child to share and she shared *Anastasia Again* by Lois Lowry. She introduced the book, read a part, and the children responded to the section.
Then Ms. Parsons spoke, "You've read a lot of Anastasia books. Why?"
    Kate: "I kind of identify with them."
Another child: "I like them too, because. . . ."
Another child: "So do I. . . ."
    Kate: "I've really only read two. . . . I think Anastasia's funny, the way she talks to her parents, like they're children."

      . . . .

Ms. Parsons told about the book she had just finished, *Up the Road Slowly* by Irene Hunt, ". . one morning she woke up and felt life again."
    A child: "Do you have a part to read?"
  Ms. Parsons: "Well, I wasn't going to, but I could."
      Child: "Read the part where she woke up and felt life again."
Ms. Parsons read and the children responded.
Then one child said, "I've got that book but I haven't started it yet."
  Ms. Parsons: "It has lots of incidences . . . like you. I think you could identify with it. Abey, I think you'd like it, too."
      Child: "Has she written others?"
They found four.

Abey shared *Nothing's Fair in Fifth Grade* by Barth DeClements, ". . . . It's wicked funny." She read a portion of the book. The children enjoyed what she shared, so she read another part! The children responded and a comment reminded someone of

The TV Kid by Betsy Byars. That book reminded children of five others.

When someone mentioned *After the Goatman,* Ms. Parsons said, I read that last fall."

A child bridged from that book to *The Midnight Fox* and the children discussed it.

Ms. Parson's, in response to one child's comments about it, said: ".... That reminds me of *Otherwise Known as Sheila the Great.*"

A child responded to her: "Yes, 'cause they're afraid to go swimming."

Ms. Parson's: "Afraid of lots of things!"

... ...

The last child shared *Dear Mr. Henshaw* by Beverly Cleary.

As the discussion of it drew to a close, Ms. Parsons said, "That's one Beverly Cleary I haven't read. Do you think I would enjoy it?"

Child: "Probably, 'cause you like books!"

A literate teacher establishes an environment that supports children's attempt to understand and revise their place in their world. As one child said when Ms. Parsons asked the children to reflect on their reading group discussions now, compared to previous years when reading groups sounded quite different, "I can talk to adults better now.... We talk normally in the groups and I'm learning how to talk to you and that helps me talk to other adults."

In classrooms where children and teachers talk and listen to each other, use oral language to explore their reading and writing, and think about how their reading and writing connect with their lives, their dialogue reveals the rich learning that can take place in classrooms, as different from the fragmented dialogue in the following reading group (Moll & Diaz, 1987):

> **T:** I am going to let Sylvia read first, she has her hand up.
> **Sylvia:** " 'You can't guess where we are going,' said David."
> **T:** OK, just a minute, please, Carla, we need you to follow with us. (Carla was not looking at her book.)
> **Carla:** OK.
> **T:** Delfina, we need you to follow right along. (Addressing Sylvia) Would you start all over again?
> **S:** OK, I'll start over again. " 'You can't guess ...' "
> **T:** (Interrupting) OK, what is this? (Points at a word in the text)
> **S:** Can't?
> **T:** Can't. What does that mean? (Pause)
> **C:** Uhmmm ...
> **T:** OK, Carla, if I say you can guess or you can't guess.
> **D:** (Raising her hand) Oh! Can't is like no ...
> **C:** Don't do that.
> **T:** Uh, yeah, uh huh. Read the sentence, the whole sentence again and let's see what it says ...
> **S:** " 'You can't guess where we are going,' said David Lee."
> **T:** Good.
> **S:** "It's going to be a ..." (Looks at teacher)
> **C:** Surprise.
> **T:** Surprise.

> **S:** Surprise. " 'I like surprises,' said Isabel. 'You bet, I'll bet you can't guess where we are all going,' said David."

This excerpt illustrates the deliberate, slow pace of lessons with students in the low reading groups, including the frequent interruptions to help with pronunciation or define words. The children display similar difficulties when they are required to report verbally what they have understood from the reading; they were tentative in their speech and their answers were fragmentary, as in the next transcript when the teacher asked them why the children in the story thought that one of the girls, Isabel, was lost in the fire station.

> **D:** Because, the boys and girls, um, looked ... (Sylvia raises her hand)
> **T:** Sylvia
> **S:** Uh, because the boys and girls, uh (pauses, laughs) the ... um ...
> **D:** Had to go home
> **S:** Because the boys and girls go ...
> **T:** Mhm ...
> **S:** ... out in the first place and the girls not say "I am here."

Teachers interrupt children in low reading groups (Moll & Diaz, 1987), because the teachers want to break the subject matter down into simple components within the grasp of the poor students. Such practices, however, underestimate and constrain what children can do. This "discriminatory treatment" perpetuates differences between high- and low-group students because the low students are "denied" access to practice in comprehension of print (Collins, 1982). The poor students do not interact with what they read in meaningful ways.

Language Focused on the Reader's Meaning. School tasks often require students to focus on what the writer meant rather than on what a passage means to a student. However, "both reading and writing must be meaningful activities ..." (Shanklin, 1981). In both processes, readers and writers construct a message by gradually moving from a global notion of what to write or what to expect of a reading, toward a more specific idea of what a text might become.

"Generally, (however), reading has not been viewed as a constructive process. Instead it has been viewed as a process by which readers' jobs are to recode and then to reconstruct a writer's message. Recent theories of reading would suggest, instead, that the real meaning of a text does not reside in the material itself, but in the transactions that take place between readers and text" (Shanklin, 1981).

When this interaction between print and the thoughts that spiral from it are not the center of a discussion, then reading is no longer reading.

Lehr (1988) studied the benefits to children's reading when complexity was the hallmark of the class. She analyzed children's sense of theme in literature and her students surpassed those in previous studies. She hypothesized that this was because she used real books in her study. In other words, in previous research on children's sense of theme, researchers used artificially-created text, sometimes simplified. "None of the former studies used book-length texts with extended plot, setting, and characterization and with multiple themes (and) none had been conducted in naturalistic settings where children were allowed to see and touch the actual books as they were read aloud." Lehr's results, found in this naturalistic setting, showed that children can do more than they could in the previous, restricted contexts.

When these kindergarten, second- and fourth-grade children responded to books such as *The Carrot Seed* by Pat Hutchins, *The Hating Book* by Charlotte Zolotow, and *When I Was Young in the Mountains* by Cynthia Rylant, they often generated themes that compared books. The setting in which the books were shared and the multifaceted plots and characterizations helped the children's understanding of them. Thus, when researchers simplify texts, they remove the interactions typically found in realistic fiction, and these simplifications interfere with children's ability to understand a story.

The complexities of books, classrooms, and language help learners create meaning when they write, also. The core of writing is meaning. Writing that is hard to understand is not good writing, even if it looks perfect (Graves, 1983). Graves writes about the children's and teachers' initial focus on information as indication of a shift away from a focus on mechanics. Such teachers know it is unwise for them to frequently assign topics or give story starters. Those devices rest on the assumption that th child's life does not contain something meaningful, but we know that children come to school with strong opinions, desires, and various kinds of knowledge. It is our task to believe children know something, find out what that something is for each child, help the children become aware of what they know, and help them believe in the significance of it.

We make time to listen to them tell us about their delights and concerns. Then we make time for them to write about what they know, whether it is hurricane Gilbert or Uncle Herbert. When we respond to the child's writing, we begin by listening. The children read their writing to us or tell us about it. Mr. Metson, a third-grade teacher, heard some facts and feelings about the hurricane when Amy told him about her writing. Metson wondered about supportive details, so he said, "Amy, if Gilbert was the swiftest hurricane ever, how fast was it?"

Responsive questions are specific, meaning-based, honest queries to which teachers do not know the answer. In time, Amy not only answers questions, but must decide whether this draft needs more information, whether she wants to read old newspapers and magazines for more data, whether the draft contains irrelevant or incorrect information, needs sequencing and/or characters, should be shared with children, should be hidden in a portfolio, can be considered a final draft in its initial state, or needs editing. The child has many decisions to make, and these various decisions affect each other in diverse ways.

The Complexity of Language Skills. Dyson (1982) refers to this complexity as the Written Language Puzzle. "Coming to understand written language . . . involve(s) learning at several levels all at once." We must simultaneously "grapple with (and) interact with" reading, writing, and talking. "As with most puzzles, children cannot solve (the Written Language Puzzle) by being given only one piece at a time."

To value the interaction among several components of language presents a tough challenge in teaching skills, the specific tasks children must learn in order to say /ch/ when they see the letters 'ch' and to find a book on the library shelves, once they have gotten its call number from the card catalogue. Traditionally, we have taught these skills apart from real situations where children need them, which defies what we know about the basic way children learn langauge.

Children learn in social situations where "please" is not an isolated word to repeat again and again, but, instead, is a plea young toddlers quickly learn to use effectively, at times where it counts. Similarly, two fifth-grade girls who have taken part in numerous library skills lessons on how to find books with certain call numbers, finally learned that skill one day in September of 1988 when they "had" to find scary books to read. This was their own goal. No one had told them to read scary books, but several of their friends were and they wanted to be a part of the action.

They found five call numbers of books to locate and beseeched Jane Hansen (who works as a researcher in the Stratham, NH, elementary school library), "Can you help us find these, please?" She steered them in the general direction of one, but they came back, "Can you help us? We can't find it." It was not on the shelf. Jane continued to give some direction for the next two books, less direction for book four, and, when they found book five by themselves, they literally squealed with delight at their new found skill (and book).

These two girls can now teach others. I.e., Jane Hansen can refer the next similar request to those two girls, who will be truly honored to help someone else. The adult only has to teach a skill once, and ideally, she should not even have done that. She could have found another child to help the two girls with the skill they needed to learn.

Children want to learn skills and feel good when they do not have to depend on someone else, but lessons to teach skills are often taught out of context and tend to fall on unfertilized ground. This learning often sprouts, but soon dies when unused.

As teachers, it scares us to think of teaching skills by need rather than via a list. We worry, "But, what if I don't ever hear anyone need /ch/, then I'll never teach it!" The answer to this worry is not simple, but for teachers who spend their teaching time among writers and readers, not apart from them, at the teacher's desk or running a reading group, the children's needs, or lack thereof, often become quite clear. If no one in the class ever errs on a /ch/ word, it does not need to be taught. They know it.

When we do not let students sit quietly in isolated desks, but insist that they get help from each other when they have a concern or question, lots of learning and teaching happens continuously. The possibilities for learning multiply, not only because of the increased availability of help, but because the help is pertinent, applicable, ad usable.

THE USE OF LANGUAGE REQUIRES PEOPLE TO INTERACT

When children have something to say, they want someone to listen. Schools in which teachers expect children to say what they think, and in which teachers resolve to listen to children, give educators pause to reexamine the roles of both children and adults. In this section, we will show the importance of children and adults learning from each other, and children learning from each other.

Children and Adults Learn from Each Other

Historically, children were not considered sources of information. Teachers were. The teacher's task was to give students information, and the children's task was to learn. Wells (1986), however, says we must reconsider what it means to be a teacher. "The conception of teaching as 'transmission' must be a mistaken one. First, it is not possible, simply by telling, to cause students to come to have the knowledge that is in the mind of the teacher. Knowledge cannot be transmitted." It is, instead, constructed, and it must be constructed by each individual.

Whether child or adult, any person who comes across new information will make sense of it based on the

. . . learner's existing internal model of the world. The process (of learning) is therefore essentially *interactional* in nature, both within the learner and between the learner and the teacher, and calls for the *negotiation* of meaning, not its unidirectional transmission. . . . For those of us who are . . . teachers—the responsibility is clear: to interact with those in our care in such a way as to foster and enrich *their* meaning making." (Wells, 1986)

We must build upon what children say. Wells gives this example to show how a teacher's questions can create in children a sense that they know something, and, therefore, can learn more:

Amanda: Mrs. M, if he put this bit in the belt and this bit in the back with the oxygen, it might look like a real diver.

Matthew: That's what I'm going to do.

Teacher: Do you think it looks like a real diver at the moment?

Matthew: No.

Amanda: No.

Maxine: Not much. It hasn't got the equipment on it.

Amanda: Yes, but if you put the feet too small, it could easily fall down.

Teacher: How do you know about a real diver, Matthew?

Matthew: I read a lot about it.

Maxine: Why? Have you got a book about divers?

Matthew: Two. Two great big annuals of divers at home and I read 'em . . . every night 'fore I go to bed. But I'm in—I'm in the middle book one and in book two it tells you about deep-sea divers. In book one it tells you about frogmen.

Maxine: How to make it?

Matthew: Not how to make 'em.

Teacher: What's the difference between frogmen and deep-sea divers?

Matthew: 'Cos deep-sea divers aren't like frogmen—deep-sea divers haven't got flippers and—and they have different kinds of—Frogmen don't have helmets, but

deep-sea divers do. So frogmen are quite different, 'cos they haven't got helmets.

The teacher asks questions to learn, not to check the child's knowledge. This kind of questioning sets a tone of support for the student, but, because it is not the usual mode of questioning used by teachers, it may be difficult to learn. Most teachers who want to understand the concept of interaction find they talk too much and ask too many questions that require children to provide short answers requiring only the lowest level of intellectual activity. To want to learn from the child, to listen, rests on a belief that the child's knowledge has value.

Cochran-Smith (1984) documented nursery school teachers' story reading sessions and heard them build on what the children noticed in the text and pictures. "Storyreading was not a recitation of set reader-questions and listener-responses." The discussions were negotiated, nonfocused interactions. The teachers were aware of the sense-making of the children and two readings of the same book did not bring forth the same thoughts. The cooperative negotiation of the story depended on what the children said about their confusions, interpretations, and what they understood. The teacher responded to the meaning the group seemed to make of the story. The teacher wanted to know what the children heard in books.

Hubbard (1989) studied young children's art and found that children's explanations of their drawings differed from adult explanations. Adult insights into children's work were deprived compared to the children's own knowledge. Adults shortchanged the children.

Goodman (1988), also, listens to children to learn what they know. Some children, upon etnry into school do poorly on placement tests but know much when Goodman listens to them in social contexts away from and in school. The child who says, "Brake car," when he sees a stop sign knows what reading is all about. However, if he does not know his letters, he may be placed in a low group where his central experiences with reading will not be meaning-based and, over time, his notion of reading may suffer. Goodman says, "(An) instructional system that focuses on mastery of one skill before another loses sight of the complexity of learning written language."

However, it is this complexity that scares us as teachers. We want some way of finding out, from among the many activities of the child, what it is the child might learn next so we can effectively teach. We need to find out, from the child, where the child is coming from. For example, when Mark sticks this note on his teacher's desk:

ZRHC DEN EY   (We need chairs.)
YE RELE NED CHRZ!!!! (We really need chairs!)

and Ms. Salisa asks him to read it to her, she not only responds to his message, "We DO need chairs," and they proceed to get some, she learns that Mark is on the verge of understanding that writing goes from left to right. A session on it is a wiser choice than a prescribed lesson on /CH/, a skill he shows he may understand. Teachers' objectives appear on the spot when they see and think, "Mark has been writing backwards all year, but this last sentence goes from left to right!"

Later, when his message has been attended to, the teacher

shows Mark his left to right sentence. He shrugs. She asks him to bring the book he is reading. As he reads, he moves his finger under the words. She points out his behavior to him and says, "Your own writing moves in the same direction as the writing in *Very Hungry Caterpillar!*" Mark smiles. He later writes:

I RED S YA   (I read this way.)

Ms. Salisa asks Mark to share this latest piece of writing with his class. He struggles to juggle the book and his writing as he explains what he has learned. A child instantly responds, "Now you're a real writer!"

Ms. Salisa thinks about her objectives, the hallmarks of her teacher preparation days. Every lesson must begin with the Teacher's Objectives. However, when teachers and children learn from each other, they share the responsibility for setting objectives (Barnes, 1975). Rather than look to the curriculum to see what to teach next, the children share what they have learned, get ideas for goals from each other, and the teacher and children teach what is timely. The items on the teacher's "Lists of What to Teach" are still the topics they teach, but the guide no longer determines when.

To know when to teach also influences how. If a lesson has spun off from a child's newly found knowledge, the child becomes the teacher, or coteacher. No longer is the teacher the authority who determines the lesson she will teach each day. The children starts to feel their influence, and this determines the "what" of the curriculum.

The what is not simply a skill or strategy someone needs to know, nor is the curriculum confined to the academic content of a discipline. Instead, the curriculum is both the content and the way the teachers and children pursue the study of the material. The What I Learned in School Today, is not only a lesson in directionality, but a lesson in values. The child learned that his knowledge counts. So does he.

He plays a role in his own learning. He influences the lesson of the day. He and his teacher accommodate each other in a way that determines the direction of the class. This basic interaction between teacher and child enables interaction among the various facets of the language arts. The language of instruction in a classroom opens, or closes, the doors to possibilities. As children realize the privileged status given to their knowledge, they gain in confidence, and their language use takes on even greater dimensions.

Wertsch (1984) writes about the importance of the teacher's ability to sense what the child is on the verge of knowing. He elaborates on Vygotsky's (1978) notion of the zone of proximal development (ZPD). Children learn best when they interact with adults at the point where the child is. Thus, it is up to the adult to find out what the child needs and/or wants. This information or strategy is what is most learnable; it lies within the ZPD.

Sometimes a child's actions do not lead to as clear a resolution as March achieved with his note. At times, both child and teacher may have specific goals in mind, but they differ. When the teacher knows the child's goal, the teacher may share her goal with the children, and they may appreciate each others' goal.

This can happen, for example, when children and teachers talk about books. The teacher who considers children's viewpoints, hears their voices when they tell her what a book means to them. The children, in turn, hear the teacher's insights. Both honor each others' thoughts, because the ability to use reading to mediate between oneself and one's world determines our success as readers. Print helps people interpret themselves and aids interactions with nature and society. Reading has a social element in it, a committment that goes beyond the text and the reader. The denial of this responsibility toward others has caused many of the problems we have in much reading pedagogy.

"Up until—roughly speaking—1968, the majority of American critics seemed preoccupied by one crucial question, 'What does this text mean?' . . . they held at least one conviction in common, namely that the most important thing to do was to determine as accurately as possible what the text was trying to say" (Todorov, 1985).

However, in the last two decades we have learned more of the true meaning of the term "language arts." If literature is an art, then it "opens us to dilemmas, to the hypothetical, to the range of possible worlds that a text can refer to . . ." (Bruner, 1986).

This notion scares many parents and educators, because where does the "range of possible worlds" end? Certainly there must be some limit to what is acceptable and what is not. At this point, "values" enter the picture. Values are things people passionately believe in, things they stand up for, argue for, defend to the hilt. When we open our classrooms to discussions in which teachers and children express their values, boredom may no longer reign. "Literature, in this spirit, is an instrument of freedom, lightness, imagination, and yes, reason. It is our only hope against the long gray night" (Bruner, 1986).

Thus, literature helps us mediate our place in society. A sociohistorical look at written language helps us understand the concept of reading as a process of meditation, and thus, to look at what should be the heart of remediation. As a process of mediation, reading is a means by which we mediate our world. Thus, when students do not use reading to help them understand their world, they need help, or remediation. At the core of this assistance are strategies to help readers see relationships between themselves and others (Five, 1986).

The sharing and caring of children who support each other promotes a group belief where there "affective identity" is an "effective identity" (Turnbull, 1983). The anthropological view of Turnbull highlights the benefits of learning in society rather than in isolation, as prevails in schools. The reciprocity and mutual responsibility that can thrive between teacher/student may be the core of thinking (John-Steiner, 1985). In John-Steiner's book, she interviews reknowned thinkers and pulls together a triangle of new notions about learning.

In general, thinking results from various interactions, all of which a mentor supports in a young learner. One interaction is a back and forth movement between known concepts and new, which is different from a prevailing notion in education where we more frequently hear about the necessity of building new information on old. However, exceptional learners zigzag from new to known when they regularly test and reaffirm their knowledge.

Another feature of thinking as its combination of bursts of exploration and continuity. Both are characteristics of thinkers. They dash after new "I wonders" and they stay for endless periods of time on one idea. These inner drives to move ahead or to rehash familiar data, need the support of a mentor who can reflect and stretch the learner's thoughts. The mentor is sensitive to whether the learner is on a plateau or shooting ahead.

Finally, intensity is the overriding feature of creative thinkers. John-Steiner found no well-known thinkers who spent isolated periods of time on many barely-related, short-term tasks in which they were only minimally involved. Her research encourages us to serve as mentors for our students as they become more intense people who may pursue, under our guidance, concentrated areas of study that are important to them. In so doing, we also consider her findings on the important role of a support group.

Children Learn from Each Other

Groups have personalities and local knowledge (Geertz, 1983). They have a code of behavior, ways to interact that are appropriate and inappropriate. In some classrooms the code is: "Sit quietly. Do your work alone. If you don't understand, try your best. When you finish put it in my basket and I'll correct it later. Then read a book." In other classrooms the norm is: "Experiment so you can decide when you'd rather work alone or with others. If you don't understand, get help. When you finish, share with someone if you'd like. Decide if you want to continue or start something new. Reading books and writing are part of your work."

The notion of working together can increase learning opportunities in a classroom, but it is difficult for us, as teachers, to trust our students to learn from each other. Brady and Jacobs (1988) write about the transition Brady made, as a fourth- and fifth-grade teacher who learned to stay away from her children when they met in response groups for writing. She is available for help, but her students meet on their own. She decided not to be a regular part of groups when she saw a video of her children and noticed how much they needed each other. "The direction of learning is not one-way: social learning is both cause and effect of academic learning."

These children learned, at a young age, about the value of the communities Booth (1974) writes about. He gives two major bases for all teaching, one being the only clear value he believes everyone shares:

It is always good to maintain and improve the quality of our symbolic exchange with our fellow "selves"—to sharpen our symbolic powers so that we can understand and be understood, "taking in" other selves and thus expanding our own. What we say matters, and it matters how we say it.

We want to understand and be understood, because we live in a world threatened by alienation and the loss of community. Thus, his second premise comes into being. He wants to belong to a "community of those who want to discover good reasons together."

Children who work together in classrooms where their goal is to find worth in each other's contributions, tend to put forth a great deal of effort. Hansen (1987) writes about a third-grade classroom where a new student entered in April. The class knew how to discover good qualities in each other's writing and, even though Meredith had not written or shared her writing for supportive response in her previous school, the ability of the children, in a teacherless writing group, to find worth in each other's contributions gave Meredith the boost she needed to join a classroom of believers on her fourth day of immersion in that setting. The other children extended an invitation to her that she could not refuse.

She wrote and shared about her pets. The children started to get to know her. She became real. The complexity of people forbodes the danger educators flirt with when children are asked to divide themselves into two halves and leave the personal half, for example, outside the door. Similarly, as teachers, we often feel we must divide ourselves so we are less than whole. To be someone, it helps to be decisive. To be decisive, it is beneficial for a person to be a unified self.

Rousseau (1762) stresses this necessity and cautions educators against simplifying and impoverishing the human experience. It is the task of building a oneness for self that preoccupies people throughout their lives, and it is the task of teachers to help children with this goal. This places great demands on teachers to help children create harmony among beauty, anger, and goodness. Every side of the child strives to develop, trying to outstrip every other side. Development is inherently uneven. Unfortunately, we educators often view this unevenness as indication of something wrong and forget to aid the harmony of development. This is the eternal mistake of pedagogical theories.

Our focus on one part of a child is especially detrimental if we let a child come to believe that the activity of learning is not a pursuit we value (Papert, 1980). We forget that when people are learning, they are trying something new. They do not know how to do it. They will make mistakes. Errors are a sign of trying new things, taking risks, the hallmarks or learners. Our response to people's mistakes influences their willingness to try again and their enthusiasm for even the things they can not do well.

Children develop irregularly; they do some things well and others clumsily, but no matter how irregular the development of a child, the primitive features of harmony always exist. To children's detriment, we adults often focus teaching a false vision of perfection and, enroute, not only become impatient with irregularities but believe we can correct them. We have a hard time comprehending and *valuing* the primitive beauty of a child or ourselves.

However, our ability to appreciate children has increased during the last several years as we have learned to appreciate what children do and, consequently, that they have much to offer each other.

WAYS TO CHANGE SETTINGS WHERE PEOPLE INTERACT

Insights into *Children's Minds* (Donaldson, 1977) challenge us, as teachers, to assess our traditions in education. We contemplate change. Some of us seek a revolution (Harste, Woodward, & Burke, 1984). In this section, we explore possible ways to improve our larger society, school, and language instruction.

Toward Improvements in Language Instruction

New knowledge causes us, as educators, to challenge many of our prevailing assumptions. For example, in a classic book in the world of reading instruction, *Learning to read: The great debate,* Chall (1967) argued that a molecular emphasis in the teaching of beginning reading was superior to a more holistic approach. Berlak (1981), however, writes about the "continued skepticism of Chall's conclusions" and attributes the controversy to the nature of the evidence Chall used to support her conclusions.

Initially, Chall's research question was, "What is the best way to teach a young child to read?" Chall, however, did not study the processes used by teachers because the complicated process of teaching could not be segmented to fit into the prevailing research methods—methods which required Chall to compare discrete pieces of behavior to each other.

Therefore, what Chall did was "transform her initial question into a form that was acceptable" for the research method she would use. Thus, rather than compare the

consequences of methods in use, she compared the effects on children of teachers who reported that they used materials that emphasized either a code or a meaning approach. The relative effects of ... materials type A v. B upon children were determined by comparing scores on standardized reading tests" (Berlak, 1981).

Contributions of "social, cultural and intellectual differences" were eliminated by statistical means.

Thus, a question which began as a puzzle over the consequences upon children of different ways to teaching reading, in order to meet the

"methodological rigors of empirical science, was transformed into a comparison of the effects upon standardized reading test scores of types of teaching materials classified by researchers in terms of their relative emphasis on drill of sounds.

In bypassing the process of teaching, Chall reduced differences in methods to a single dimension: ... (whether) learning is molecular or holistic. To conceive of teaching in terms of a resolution of a single dilemma is distorting because a whole range of dilemmas that deal with social and knowledge control are simultaneously being resolved. The practical implication of this transformation is of no small consequence. It can easily mislead us into accepting standardized tests as a reasonable, if not fully adequate, index of whether teachers and school heads are doing a good job, and whether children are learning.

An alternative way to pose the question of the effects of differing approaches to teaching reading is to ask what are the meanings about control, knowledge and society children take from different (processes) used by teachers in the teaching of reading and language." (Berlak, 1981)

If new ways of assessment could be derived, more defensible teaching methods could emerge. It is hard for teachers to change what they do when they teach it, if outdated assessments are used. In reality, tests dictate the what and how of teaching.

However, if teachers could assume leadership in assessment, then they could design evaluations that would encourage more recent teaching ideas. Then they could have the nerve, for example, to take time away from paper and pencil tasks and let other uses of language enrich the children's learning.

Because of what language development experts have learned within the last two decades, teachers should encourage talk in the classroom more than in the past. Oral language may underlie success in both writing and reading (Tannen, 1985) because children know that their talk gets them something, or, at times, fails. Thus, they learn from oral language that words have a purpose and that the better one puts those words together, the better off one is. They also know that talk does not exist in a vacuum. When someone talks, someone else is present, and, hopefully, listens.

The involvement of the two (or more) people determines the success of the interaction; the degree to which they both care is more influential than anything else in whether or not communication will occur. To permit and encourage child involvement asks for a break with tradition. In the world of reading instruction, for example, the pattern of interaction in reading groups has not been direct interaction between children nor between children and books. The teacher has monitored interactions among children and between children and their interpretations of what they read. However, as teachers, we now realize the children's stances regarding a story they read will most likely be different from ours.

Their years of experience and types of experiences vary from the adult world. Children and teacher learn each others' points of view when they interact and enlarge their world view from literature. Even authors enlarge their perspective on their own work when they learn the variety of meanings children create from their books. Letters Jane Yolen (1985) received from her young readers showed her the impossibility of stating *the* one meaning that resides in any of the books she authors.

Similarly, teacher and children learn each others' viewpoints when they share compositions. This has come to our attention within the surge of research on writing that started in 1971 when Janet Emig wrote,

In this inquiry we have seen that the most significant others in the ... writing of twelfth graders are peers.... American high schools and colleges must seriously and immediately consider that the teacher-centered presentation of composition, like the teacher-centered presentation of almost every other segment of a curriculum, is pedagogically, developmentally, and politically an anachronism.

So ends Emig's book. She certainly wants change.

Emig slams the five-paragraph essay and, when she hypothesizes about its existence in instruction, she wonders if teachers read and assumes not. Because teachers are not well-read in current and classic literature, they do not realize that the five-paragraph essay is not a form used by real writers. It is something created only for students and has no purpose. However, if teachers possessed substantial knowledge about reading and writing, they would realize the emptiness of the five-paragraph form.

When writing, as Emig hypothesizes, is divorced from reading, it becomes nonsense. Reading and writing cannot interact for students if they do not interact for teachers. Teachers cannot teach something they do not do. Besides not reading, teachers do not write.

They have no recent, direct experience with a process they purport to present to others.... (B)ecause they have no direct experience with composing, teachers of English err in important ways. They underconceptualize and oversimplify the process of composing. Planning degenerates into outlining; reformulating becomes the correction of minor infelicities.

Teaching goes awry when someone simplifies it.

Graves (1983) extended Emig's work into elementary classrooms and learned not only that young children can write but that they want to write and will. Because children do think important thoughts, it is valuable for them to share those thoughts with each other, not only with the teacher. Not only is it important for children to learn to interact socially in our pluralistic society, but they learn from each other when they talk about their school work.

Children who go to each other for help and offer assistance to each other, learn more than children who work alone (Cazden, 1988). This, however, scares teachers, and rightfully so. It is one thing to know that children should share their perceptions with each other and something else to know how to structure a classroom so children will successfully interact.

The ability to permit talk, rather than keep children apart, underlies whether the language arts will ever come together. One high school English teacher and her class (Eidman-Aadahl, 1988) researched reading and started to question the beliefs about reading that they had inherited from their former teachers. They had been taught that reading was a solitary activity, as opposed to an activity that may bring people together. These grade 11 students quoted former teachers who had said, "Stop talking boys," even when the teacher knew the boys were talking about a book. Another teacher had said, "Don't talk, this is reading time." Still another, "I don't want you sharing a book because you'll talk," or "You should be reading. I shouldn't hear any talking going on."

In general, their former teachers convinced these students that reading is a solitary, not a social act. However, via the insights of their secondary teacher, they started to realize otherwise. They started to think about the possibility of book-talk as a social bond. The probability that reading could serve as an interpersonal glue was the only hope for the survival of reading, because their peer network was more influential than anything else in most of their lives. These students' emerging belief in the social nature of reading can now bring reading into the center of their lives. This type of change in our understanding of what reading can do for us may drastically influence the types of interaction we encourage in our language classrooms and schools.

Toward Improvements in Schools

Are students' points of view valuable? School personnel who answer yes, learn from their students. Such teachers move out from behind their lecterns, the hiding places of many teachers, especially those of us in higher education. Traditionally, we have not considered our students' point of view, even though the ability to take another point of view plays a large role in one's literacy. Literate people look for the welfare of others and themselves in each context. Thus, for teachers to look for children's point of view is crucial.

The old roles in classroom language did not consider children's points of view. The old roles followed this form: Initiate—respond—evaluate (Goodwin, 1981). The teacher began, the children responded, and the teacher evaluated. Ms. Jones said, "What was the main idea of the story?" Fred said, "That successful people aren't always happy." Ms. Jones said, "Right! Good thinking!"

Teachers and children learned their lines for these parts very well, but in order for change to occur in schools, the roles everyone plays must be reconsidered. It is what is conveyed by this exchange pattern that has a significant effect on what is learned in classrooms. Even though teachers may have created this pattern because we think it is the best way to teach children to comprehend what they read, it is not consistent with what we now know about reading. Readers must learn to set their own purposes and decide for themselves whether they've understood a text to their satisfaction.

With the prevalent model, children do not learn the primary skills of independent learners. Instead of learning to comprehend, which is the intention of the format, students learn to submit. They learn that when they read, they must figure out what the teacher thinks is important in the passage. The three parts of the routine—initiate, respond, evaluate—could remain, but the students could assume the roles, and, thus, the implications for learning would shift.

Initiate: Children, as well as teachers, can initiate. Because language use in the real world bounces back and forth between at least two participants, children must learn to play both roles. The social nature of learning implies that, because each context is different, participants must always evaluate what to say, consider options, and make choices. One choice is when and how to initiate an interaction with someone. Learning rests on these risks into the unknown (Cook-Gumperz, 1986).

Respond: The response to an attempt determines the ongoing nature of the learning. If the response is not supportive, the learner may quit. However, if the response brings, in turn, a supportive response from the learner, learning may continue. The interaction builds vertically on the previous response. The success of the interaction depends on each person's ability to take the other point of view. Response is everyone's domain: teachers and children.

Evaluate: Children and teachers have opinions of what they read, write, and hear. They can talk about the overall program, about themselves, and about what they want to learn and how it's going. Evaluation, in those situations, is an ongoing, continuous process. All participants evaluate whether their attempts at learning are fruitful or could be changed.

Such efforts at learning involve teachers learning new ideas, as well as students, and, in their case, the teachers will interact with each other and with administrators. The patterns of discourse used by the adults in a school influence the environment for the classrooms. Who initiates, responds, and evaluates among the adults, and whether these roles are reciprocal or stratified, sets the overall stage that makes any kind of interplay among people and subject matter more or less feasible.

In *Taking Charge of Change* (Hord, Rutherford, Huling-Austin & Hall, 1987), the primary fault for the death of changes in schools is given to evaluators who do not follow the daily practices of teachers. Changes involve individuals, and their personal concerns, if supported, need not be roadblocks against different ways of teaching. Administrators should attend sessions in which teachers are informed of a new instructional procedure, visit classrooms and listen to teachers' feelings about their attempts. The key to the success of a new orientation to teaching is the personal attention administrators give to individual teachers in acceptance of the teacher's concerns.

The ongoing nature of interactions is crucial to the notion that various people and disciplines in a school affect each other and should not be studied in isolation. Differences expand the opportunities for learning if those differences can be capitalized on. Scollon and Scollon (1981) studied the unusual nature of Athabaskan's responses—unusual by European standards—and learned how their unique communication system can help us with insights into our own.

He learned the value of reserving judgment. He coined the term "deferred politeness," as more effective than "solidarity politeness" to bring about a cohesive community rather than a community fraught with stress. People who practice deferred politeness listen carefully to others in order to understand their point of view, but not necessarily to accept it. This contrasts with the notion that it is necessary to agree in order to maintain a close-knit community of learners. With a deferred politeness model, people listen in order to give the other person room.

Evaluation, of course, often becomes more formal and the formal measures typically value something other than the child's interpretation of a situation or ability to use language to mediate social situations. Because learning interactions cannot yet be structured as simulations on a computer or with mathematical models, high scores on a single dimension can determine a child's future. Brown (1987) worries about this and pushes for change in schools. He says,

"... there are too few incentives for thoughtfulness and too many incentives for just getting by.

... many of us are captivated by theories of teaching and learning that tell us to break knowledge into discrete pieces and to teach and test these pieces one by one, starting with the simplest elements. We then find that knowledge can be broken into so many pieces that we wind up spending all our time covering the simple elements and never get to the more complicated stuff....

Finally, many of us undoubtedly fear thoughtfulness because it cannot be easily controlled....

No doubt another reason we attend so faithfully to minimums and basics is that state and local policy makers hold us strictly accountable for them. It is the policy makers' job to establish minimum standards in housing, health matters, prison conditions, building codes, and so forth. We all benefit from the enforcement of such standards, and it is perfectly reasonable for policy makers to establish and monitor minimum standards for education, as well.

The problem with a policy that is minimum-oriented, however, is that it requires a free market or some other such device to push it

toward excellence. Take health codes in the restaurant business, for example.... (They) greatly boost my confidence in dining out. But ... the marketplace serves to promote excellence and run mediocrity out of business.

Education policy has been strong on enforcing minimums, but it has had not system of comparable strength to push for maximums....

If we want an accountability system that will gather data for maintaining minimum standards without thwarting constructive growth and change, we will have to redesign the existing system.

Such wholesale restructuring has happened before. Testing as we know it today became a part of schooling at a time when great demands were being placed on the educational system to absorb large numbers of people who had not previously sought schooling. A national need to sort people and a desire to do so 'objectively' ran head-on into the long-established practice of 'subjective' evaluation. Slowly but surely, subjectivity was driven to the margins....

The best way to restore balance ... would be to create a strong counterculture within the system that values inquiry and thoughtfulness above all else.... Since we have not yet made a strong commitment to the proposition that *all* students can learn—and can learn a great deal more than they do today—we do not really know what our educational system can do. To the extent that we show it to be capable of doing much more than it now does, we will be held accountable for much more.

Besides quantity, we want to take responsibility for the quality of learning. We are not only interested in how much our students learn, but we want them to learn beyond the concrete, easily-measurable data of machine-scorable tests. As teachers of language, we want to know how students use oral and written language to clarify their thoughts. The ideal accountability system will give students a chance to show what they think are their unique thoughts derived from a book.

Toward Improvements Beyond School

Literacy is not merely a number on a test. It is also knowing oneself, others, and the collective knowledge of groups. It includes knowledge of society's expectations, and the realization that changes came about because people sensed the necessity to go beyond existing social rules (de Castell, Luke & Egan, 1986). In language class, this means that teachers and students must go beyond print to explore the ideas it gives them about how to make their own world, this entire world, a better place.

Someone, maybe the students in today's reading classes, will affect the direction of the rapid change our world is in the midst of. The world is a place of diversity. To learn from various disciplines may be the route to pursue. The disciplines of law, art history, moral philosophy, and the history of science offer more help in a search for a way through perplexities than supposedly more scientific avenues (Geertz, 1983). The principle of *interaction* dominates.

As educators, we let the interaction of knowledge from various disciplines inform us. We let our interaction with various people gives us insights. "In our world, nobody leaves anybody else alone and isn't ever again going to (Geertz, 1983)." It is with this world in mind that we interact with children, help them interact with each other, and, as adults, interact among themselves.

Those of us who research must talk to practitioners, if we

are not practicing teachers, and vice versa. As teachers, other educators, and children learn to trust their evaluations of what is happening in schools, classrooms, among themselves, and within themselves, research will be not only the systematic collection of data but the daily scrutiny of interactions. Fenstermacher (1986) argues that research will only make a difference if it rests on the practical arguments in the minds of teachers.

Natural scientists have begun to reveal the limitations of the paradigm of inquiry they invented and social scientists adopted (Poplin, 1987). Their quantitative methods strip problems from their context by narrowing the range of variables to be studied. When many aspects of a classroom are not included in a research project, results may be unrealistic. Learning is part of a social system and to isolate it from its context distorts its character.

Qualitative insights can be as credible as quantitative. In *Chaos* James Gleick (1987) explains such a movement in the hard sciences. Scientists have recently begun to sense the futility of their traditional approach to research. For decades, they sought answers to problems by breaking the problems down into smaller and smaller pieces, but, finally they realized that they were still far from solutions. The notion of *chaos* is to accept the fact that one little change in a system does not necessarily reveal insights that make the system easier to understand. Instead, one change may bring about changes in the overall environment. It is this larger environment, with its many component parts that chaos scientists study. The sum of all the systems' little pieces do not add up to the whole because one small change may trigger many other changes.

Similarly, the world of education now senses that learning is not an accumulation of facts, nor, more specifically, is reading an accumulation of sounds, then words, then sentences, then, then, then. Nor is writing the accumulation of neat letters, then proper punctuation, and finally an original text. Nor do toddlers first utter isolated sounds, then words, then sentences, and, finally, express complete thoughts. They begin to talk by grappling with the complete communication patterns of those around them, then they decide on something they want to say, then they try to say the whole thing. The one word we hear is not one, isolated word. It represents an entire, purposeful message. These patterns give us guidelines for classrooms.

Children can continue their struggle to unravel a complete communication system if educators immerse the students in the banter of language. They hear back-and-forth talk, become involved in talk where they take turns with peers and teachers, talk which they often initiate, and they pursue reading and writing that emanates from their talk. To teach listening apart from reading is unnecessary. Writers listen to their texts when they write and readers listen to those texts when they read them and when they share them. To isolate one part makes it artificial.

To isolate reading from life, makes reading artificial. Tchudi (1985) learned this from her daughter and son, at home. When her daughter received an assignment to read a story and answer questions, the daughter could not answer the questions because she became emotionally involved in the story and raised concerns that went way beyond the teacher's prepared list of questions. Tchudi, her daughter, and preschool son talked

about books in ways that led "to the richest of experiences" for her and for them. These rich interchanges can happen in classrooms, as well.

The challenge for educators and scientists is to embrace complexity. Part of this responsibility is not only to ensure that disciplines cross lines, but that specialists cross lines. The scientific community, as the education community, has become tightly compartmentalized. "Biologists had enough to read without keeping up with the mathematics literature—molecular biologists had enough to read without keeping up with population biology. Physicists had better ways to spend their time than sifting through the meteorology journals (Gleick, 1987)." However, the power of the new research is in the interaction among the fields, just as the power of the English language lies in its power to help all of us interact with each other.

We began this chapter with a presentation of both the teacher and researcher's dilemma. The dilemma is a tug between those who examine the language arts separately and those who view language as primarily interactive. That is, for the language processes to develop, they require effective audiences within the family, classroom, school and community. Furthermore, in order to understand them, we must examine their complexity in the very settings in which our students find them important. Too many students fail to become lifelong readers and writers, or have the confidence to speak before groups, or understand the function of heightened listening as a learning medium.

We attribute much of this problem to a failure of function—i.e., the lack of a connection between teachers' and students' self interests in school and outside of that edifice.

In spite of these positions, however, it is too easy to dismiss the importance of heightened focus on particular skills. In the context and timeliness of learning in the classroom, occasions arise when students must focus on sound/symbol correspondence, use of possessives, the organization of a speech, or redirected questioning to become better listeners. Problems enter, however, when the student's diet is essentially skills divorced from function, divorced from the student's need to understand the place of the skill in his own self interest.

If change is to be made in society's literacy, we, as educators, cannot restrict our focus to a single context, such as school. When L. Neilsen (1989) studied literate adults in their homes, communities, and workplaces, she revealed the complexities of literacy in contrast to the stark models of literacy represented in curricular packages. No evolution or real growth can occur until "reassessment of underlying assumptions occurs."

These assumptions can be challenged even further when we move into inner-city homes. The complex social and thinking abilities used by inner-city children in their daily lives go way beyond the definitions of learning practiced in schools, which are limited to test-like worksheets and workbooks. Taylor and Dorsey-Gaines (1988) found an unnecessary discrepancy between what the schools and families expected of the children they studied.

Taylor and Dorsey-Gaines show the poignant interactions valued for the children in their families and neighborhoods, plus the complex problems the children solve daily. Then, when the children go to school, their real life is not mentioned, social interaction is limited and the problems given to them on worksheets are trivial pursuits.

Educators apparently do not value these children's families' determination to become competent and independent. "The vividness of children's experiences should not be dulled by the pedantry of programs that lack respect for their everyday lives (Taylor & Dorsey-Gaines, 1988)."

Our overall goal is extremely complex and difficult to put into practice, but our own literacy helps us understand our role in schools and classrooms. Unless the language arts interact in our own lives, the full implementation of a sound interactive program for children is unlikely. The professionals' own understandings of literacy provide the insights we need to use the various arts of language.

References

Barnes, D. (1975). *From communication to curriculum.* NY: Penguin Books.

Berlak, A. & Berlak, H. (1981). *Dilemmas of schooling: Teaching and social change.* London: Methuen.

Booth, W. C. (1974). *Modern dogma and the rhetoric of assent.* Notre Dame, Indiana: University of Notre Dame Press.

Brady, S. & Jacobs, S. (1988). Children responding to children: Writing groups and classroom community. In T. Newkirk & N. Atwell (Ed.), *Understanding writing: Ways of observing, learning, and teaching* (pp. 142–150). Portsmouth, NH: Heinemann.

Brown, R. (1987). Who is accountable for 'thoughfulness'? *Phi Delta Kappan,* September, 49–52.

Bruner, J. (1986). *Actual minds, possible worlds.* Cambridge, MA: Harvard University Press.

Carter, F. (1986). *The education of little tree.* Albuquerque: University of New Mexico Press.

Cazden, C. B. (1986). Classroom discourse. In M. C. Wittrock (Ed.), *Handbook of research on teaching,* (3d ed.) NY: Macmillan.

Cazden, C. B. (1988). *Classroom discourse: The language of teaching and learning.* Portsmouth, NH: Heinemann.

Chall, J. S. (1970). *Learning to read: The great debate.* NY: McGraw.

Cochran-Smith, M. (1984). *The making of a reader.* Norwood, NJ: Ablex.

Collins, J. (1982). Discourse style, classroom interaction and differential treatment. *Journal of Reading Behavior, 14,* 429–438.

Cook-Gumperz, J. (1986). *The social construction of literacy.* Cambridge: Cambridge University Press.

de Castell, S., Luke, A. & Egan, K. (Eds.) (1986). *Literacy, society, and schooling: A reader.* Cambridge: Cambridge University Press.

Donaldson, M. (1977). *Children's minds.* NY: Norton.

Dyson, A. H. (1982). Reading, writing, and language: Young children solving the written language puzzle. *Language Arts, 59,* (8), 829–839.

Eidman-Aadahl, E. (1988). The solitary reader: Exploring how lonely reading has to be. *The New Advocate. 1,* (3), 165–176.

Emig, J. (1971). *The composing processes of twelfth graders.* NCTE Research Report No. 13. Urbana, IL: National Council of Teachers of English.

Fenstermacher, G. D. (1986). Philosophy of research on teaching: Three aspects. In M. C. Whittwock (Ed.). *Handbook of Research on Teaching.* NY: MacMillan.

Five, C. (1986). Teresa: A reciprocal learning experience for teacher and child. In J. Harste & D. Stephens (Eds.), *Toward practical theory.* Bloomington, IN: Indiana University.

Gartner, A. & Lipsky, D. K. (1987). Beyond special education: Toward a quality system for all students. *Harvard Educational Review, 57,* (4), 367–395.

Geertz, C. (1983). *Local knowledge: Further essays in interpretive anthropology.* NY: Basic Books.

Gleick, J. (1987). *Chaos: Making a new science.* NY: Viking.

Goodlad, J. (1984). *A place called school.* NY: McGraw.

Goodman, Y. (1988). The development of initial literacy. In E. R. Kintgen, M. Kroll & M. Rose (Eds.), *Perspectives on literacy.* Carbondale: Southern Illinois University Press.

Goodwin, C. (1981). *Conversational organization: Interaction between speakers and hearers.* San Diego: Academic Press.

Graves, D. (1983). *Writing: Teachers and children at work.* Portsmouth, NH: Heinemann.

Gundlach, R., McLane, J. B., Stott, F. M. & McNamee, G. D. (1985). The social foundations of children's early writing development. In M. Farr (Ed.), *Advances in writing research, Volume One: Studies in children's writing development.* Norwood, NJ: Ablex.

Halliday, M. A. K. (1979). *Language as social semiotic: The social interpretation of language and meaning.* London: Edward Arnold.

Hansen, J. (submitted for publication). Writers and readers evaluate themselves.

Hansen, J. (1987). *When writers read.* Portsmouth, NH: Heinemann.

Hord, S. M., Rutherford, W. L., Huling-Austin, L. & Hall, E. (1987). *Taking charge of change.* Alexandria, VA: Association for Supervision and Curriculum Development.

Hubbard, R. (1989). *Authors of pictures: Draftsmen of words.* Portsmouth, NH: Heinemann.

Hunter, M. (1982). *Mastery teaching: Increasing instructional effectiveness in secondary schools, colleges, and universities.* El Segundo, CA: TIP Publications.

Hunter, M. (1984). Knowing, teaching, and supervising. In Hosford, P. L. (Ed.), *Using what we know about teaching.* Alexandria, VA: Association for Supervision and Curriculum Development.

Jensen, J. M., Editor (1988). *Stories to grow on: Demonstrations of language learning in K–8 classrooms.* Portsmouth, NH: Heinemann.

John-Steiner, V. (1985). *Notebooks of the mind.* Albuquerque, NM: University of New Mexico Press.

Lehr, S. (1988). The child's developing sense of theme as a response to literature. *Reading Research Quarterly, 23,* (3), 337–357.

Lindfors, J. W. (1980). *Children's language and learning.* Englewood Cliffs, NJ: Prentice-Hall.

McConnell, B. (1989). Education as a cultural process: The interaction between community and classroom in fostering learning. In J. Allen & J. Mason (Eds.), *Rick makers, risk takers, risk breakers: Reducing the risks for young literacy learners* (pp. 201–221). Portsmouth, NH: Heinemann.

Moll, L. C. & Diaz, S. (1987). Change as the goal of educational research. *Anthropology and Education Quarterly, 18,* (4), 300–311.

Morrison, T. (1987). *Beloved.* NY: Knopf.

Neilsen, A. (1989). *Critical thinking and reading: Impowering learners to think and act.* Monographs on Teaching Critical Thinking, Vol. 2, Bloomington, IN: ERIC Clearinghouse on Reading and Communication Skills. Urbana, IL: National Council of Teachers of English.

Neilsen, L. (1989). *Literacy and living.* Portsmouth, NH: Heinemann.

Oakes, J. (1985). *Keeping track: How schools structure inequality.* New Haven, CT: Yale University Press.

Papert, S. (1980). *Mindstorms.* New York: Basic Books.

Poplin, M. S. (1987). Self-imposed blindness: The scientific method in education. *Remedial and Special Education, 8,* (6), 31–37.

Rousseau, J. J. (1762). Translation by A. Bloom, 1979– *Emile or on education.* NY: Basic Books.

Scollon, R. & Scollon, S. B. K. (1981). *Narrative, literacy and face in interethnic communication.* Norwood, NJ: Ablex.

Shanklin, N. K. L. (1981). *Relating reading and writing: Developing a transactional theory of the writing process.* Monograph in Language and Reading Studies. Bloomington, IN: Monographs in Teaching and Learning/School of Education/Indiana University.

Tannen, D. (1985). Relative focus on involvement in oral and written discourse. In D. R. Olson, N. Torrance & A. Hildyard (Eds.), *Literacy, language, and learning: The nature and consequences of reading and writing.* Cambridge: Cambridge University Press, 124–147.

Taylor, D. & Dorsey-Gaines, C. (1988). *Growing up literate: Learning from inner-city families.* Portsmouth, NH: Heinemann Educational Books.

Tchudi, S. (1985). The roots of response to literature. *Language Arts, 62,* (5), 463–468.

Todorov, T. (1985). All against humanity. *Times Literary Supplement,* October 4, 1093–1094.

Turnbull, C. (1983). *The human cycle.* NY: Simon and Schuster.

Vygotsky, L. S. (1978). *Mind in society. The development of higher psychological processes.* Cambridge, MA: Harvard University Press.

Wansart, W. (1988). The student with learning disabilities in a writing process classroom: A case study. *Journal of Reading, Writing, and Learning Disabilities International.* 4:311–319

Weinstein, R. (1986). Teaching reading: Children's awareness of teacher expectancy. In T. Raphael (Ed.), *Contexts of school-based literacy.* New York: Longman, 233–252.

Wells, G. (1986). *The meaning makers: Children learning language and using language to learn.* Portsmouth, NH: Heinemann.

Wertsch, J. V. (1984). The zone of proximal development: Some conceptual issues. In B. Rogoff and J. V. Wertsch (Eds.), *Children's learning in the "Zone of Proximal Development,"* New Directions for Child Development, No. 24. San Francisco, Jossey Bass, March, 7–18.

Wilcox, B. (1982). School self-evaluation. The benefits of a more focused approach. *Educational Research,* Vol. 34, November, 185–193.

Yolen, J. (1985). The story between. *Language Arts, 62,* (6), 590–592.

Yolen, J. (1987). *Owl moon.* NY: Philomel Books.

38B. LANGUAGE ACROSS THE CURRICULUM

Mary K. Healy
Mary Barr

The phrase "language across the curriculum" has become synonymous, since the 1960s, with a particular curricular and methodological focus on the role pupils' oral and written language plays in the learning of a range of subjects in school. Although, as Parker (1985) has described, the focus of interest in language across the curriculum differs in the Unites States, England, Canada, and Australia, the recognition that language use is instrumental to both language development and concept learning is common in all these countries. This notion runs counter to the one prevailing in schools where reading and writing, and to a lesser extent, speaking and listening, are viewed as separate skills to be practiced and learned in English and language arts classes.

The principles underlying language across the curriculum in schools emphasize the necessary link between language and thought, build on the prior experiences all pupils bring to school, and acknowledge the learners' intentions to make sense of new information, including subject matter concepts. Although these principles appear simple and straightforward, they are profound, because they could have a radical effect on pupils' learning in school. When acknowledged in practice, they shift pupils' and teachers' attention from the use of language as a means of displaying what has been learned (testing and reporting) to the use of language as an integral part of the learning process itself. Peter Medway (1984) likens this shift in attention to the change caused by the translation of the Bible from Latin and Greek to English, a change that made the Bible accessible, without intermediaries, to commoners for the first time. The pedagogical shift from language as a product to be examined to language as an accompaniment to learning of all kinds is, as yet, occurring slowly. But, as the theory, research, and practice reviewed in the chapter indicate, the argument for such a shift is compelling.

Using language to aid learning requires that teachers provide regular occasions for pupils to discuss and write about the new ideas they are encountering in all subjects. Instead of depending solely on teacher or text to point out the significance of new ideas, pupils need to engage in informal uses of writing and talking to discover what meanings these ideas have for them. In order for pupils to develop lines of argument or to reflect on the causes of historical events, they must have an interested partner, usually the teacher, who encourages both their process of discovery and their application of this new knowledge to different situations. The language used during these formulating stages of learning is characterized by its informality, the questions it raises, and the tentativeness of the conclusions reached. Unfortunately, in the more typical school situation when the teacher serves only as an examiner of student knowledge, language is viewed as a product to be assessed, and attention is focused solely on what has been learned.

Although edited language use for public audiences is impor-
tant to learn, it is the informal use of writing and talk *during* learning activities that causes the deeper understanding of subject area content found to be lacking currently in pupils' preparation. As a recent National Assessment of Educational Progress report (Applebee, Langer, Mullis, March, 1987) points out, pupils across the nation are failing to develop full literacy ability, that is "the ability to reason effectively about what one reads and writes in order to extend one's understanding of the ideas expressed" (p. 9).

THEORETICAL BACKGROUND

Over the past 30 years, psychologists and language theorists have explored the importance of language for extending and developing human learning. Lev Vygotsky's pioneering work in *Thought and Language* (1962) focused on language as promoting and accompanying the growth of thought. He provided the image of two overlapping circles—one labeled thought, the other language—to explain the way thought and language, though separate human endowments, combine to produce the verbal thought necessary to school success. Each circle maintains a portion of itself exclusively, to account for preverbal and nonverbal thought on the one hand, and nonthoughtful, sometimes ritualistic, language on the other. The overlapped portion represents verbal thought: the language that both discovers and clarifies thought in concert with the thought which permeates and constructs language (pp. 47–48). Vygotsky thus accounts for the way that verbalization of ideas and feelings often leads to understanding of them, that is, language serves in the "deliberate structuring of meaning" (p. 100).

Another property of language is its provision of distance from experience, a property that allows us to speculate about events, reflect on them, and shape them. In other words, language allows us to think about events and, therefore, to select from them, even though they are past, significant lessons for use in the present. Bruner (1964) speaks of this property in this way:

Once language becomes a medium for the translation of experience, there is a progressive release from immediacy. For language . . . has the new and powerful features of remoteness and arbitrariness: it permits productive combinatorial operations in the absence of what is presented. (p. 14)

Janet Emig (1977), working with Burner's categories for how humans represent and deal with experience, credits writing with special powers to aid learning. She notes that all three of Bruner's categories—the enactive, the iconic, and the symbolic—are simultaneously deployed in writing: ". . . the symbolic transformation of experience through the specific symbol system of verbal language is shaped into an icon (the graphic product) by the enactive hand" (p. 124).

The editors express their appreciation to Gordon M. Pradl (New York University), who served as a reviewer for this chapter.

Vygotsky, Bruner, and Emig share a conception of an active language user, spurred by intention, deliberately translating experience into words and structuring meaning. Through this process of generation and combination, the writer produces a text that is available for immediate response and revision and that serves as a starting point for future speculation and reorganization of experience.

Putting the learner in charge of his or her own translations of experience is a radical departure from practices which encourage teacher-and-text centered classrooms. James Britton supports such a power shift, arguing that it is not only possible but desirable in terms of improving pupil achievement. In *Language and Learning* (1970), Britton synthesized Vygotsky's and Bruner's theories for education and urged that schools build on the inclination human learners have to use their talk, their reading, and their writing for real, life-serving purposes. He advocated an interrelated use of the language arts, the "marriage of the process of composing in written language to that of reading, and the relating of both to the learner's spoken language resources" (1970, p. 159). Britton emphasized that schools must move away from focusing on the products of learning in order that pupils can have sufficient time to delve into the processes by which those products are constructed; that is, the reconstructing of what is observed or read or remembered by exploring its meaning and relevance in the course of explaining or interpreting it for others. The teacher may intervene to offer assistance or, in Bruner's terms, provide the scaffold to support the journey from what is known to what is to be learned, but the journey belongs, ultimately, to the learner.

Teachers, in Britton's view, encourage the learners' own intentions when they provide the time and the occasions for pupils to talk and write spontaneously about the ideas, values, and issues in the subject matter they are studying. In the process of such examining and questioning, pupils create their own interpretations of experience. Besides encouraging this human propensity to use language to shape and therefore control life's events, Britton would have teachers build on what comes naturally, "the intention to share, inherent in spontaneous utterance, [that] sets up a demand for further shaping (1982, p. 141).

If teachers are to enable learners to learn in any subject, they must provide opportunities for the generation and sharing of language and ideas in classrooms where the pupils' values and beliefs about issues raised in readings and lectures can be honored as fundamental to intellectual development. Pupils, encouraged in this kind of classroom to make sense of experience, would frequently use the informal, spontaneous, expressive language that is of central importance in implementing a language across the curriculum program. The term "expressive" was used by Britton, Burgess, Martin, McLeod and Rosen (1975) to describe the language we use when we are first working through our understanding of new ideas.

THE CENTRALITY OF PUPILS' EXPRESSIVE LANGUAGE

To accomplish the goal of deepening pupils' understandings of subject area concepts, British and American theorists and practitioners suggest that teachers encourage expressive lan-

guage—both spoken and written—as a regular part of instruction. Mike Torbe and Peter Medway in *The Climate for Learning* (1981), for example, argue that the complexities of the learning situation require that students use their "own familiar language" to make sense of new information, because it focuses their attention on the task at hand.

After all, we are asking it to perform the function of thinking, and it will need to come easily and naturally as thought; that is why it needs to be the language the students wear as close to them as their skin. (p. 42)

Expressive language used throughout the process of learning becomes the ally of understanding because it helps to make explicit the lessons of experience. As Torbe and Medway put it, "It is language that externalizes our first stages in tackling a problem or coming to grips with an experience" (p. 197). Pat D'Arcy (1977), too, discussed the appropriateness of using expressive writing to think aloud on paper. As she put it, such language will "allow for the initial sorting out processes which are necessary steps toward assimilating new knowledge ..." (p. 34).

Teachers need to encourage expressive language both for the benefits it affords pupils and for the insights it provides teachers into the pupils' learning processes. Because learning means connecting new ideas to what is already known, pupils must have opportunities to verbalize their unique understandings in order to create the context that encourages further learning. Others—whether teachers or peers—cannot do that for them, because only the pupil themselves have lived the lives out of which they make sense of new experiences.

From these descriptions of the benefits of expressive language, it follows that writing and talking in school can be more than modes of communication with others. Of equal importance is the use of language to connect new information with what is already known. This expressive use of writing is essential to complete what Freisinger (1980) calls the "binary character of language," its use for both thinking/discovering and reporting/informing. As he puts it, "The former gets us in touch with ourselves; the latter connects us to others" (p. 155).

Peter Medway, in his introduction to *Language in Science* (1980a) discussed the specific qualities characteristic of expressive language:

The pupil's language, spoken and written, will have to express uncertainty, tentativeness, speculation, argument, sudden insight, patient worrying, 'seeing the funny side'—all the states and attitudes to be found in our own heads when we're preoccupied with something unfamiliar: The point is to get it out of the head and into overt language so that those embryonic thoughts and perceptions and questions can be fanned into life and amplified by the stimulus of communicating with someone who is listening seriously and sympathetically to what one has to say. (p. 6)

Collaborative and extended oral discussions provide natural settings for pupils to discover and sort out their responses to what they read and observe. Douglas Barnes and Frankie Todd, who have done extensive work with pupils' talk in small groups across the curriculum, analyzed the benefits of such activity (1977):

When children are talking in a group without an adult present, responsibility for the management of the talk falls on themselves. They must negotiate who talks, when, and how. They must cope with occasional episodes of conflict, and with silences. They must encourage group members with useful contributions to make, and at the same time, control any attempts to dominate the talk for irrelevant purposes. They must judge the relevance of contributions, and monitor whether they are germane to the problem set; they must also maintain some overall judgment of the quality of the discussion, so as to assess when they have reached a point where it is reasonable to stop. (pp. ix, x)

In addition, pupils' small group discussion of subject matter concepts can be enriched when they first reflect on their ideas in writing and later extend them by reading further in texts and trade books. Such activities, Tierney, R. V., Caplan, R., Ehri, L., Healy, M. K., & Hurdlow, M. (1988) remind us, mirror those in the world outside the classroom where "writing and reading are naturally intertwined" (p. 2).

In a national report on the growth and development of all aspects of language in British schools (Bullock, 1975), writing was cited as having specific and basic cognitive benefits for pupils. The report suggested that when pupils write often to "generate knowledge for themselves" (p. 50), they are rehearsing mental strategies useful to all language and learning processes.

Although from the 1960s onward there has been considerable interest in the uses of expressive language for learning across the curriculum at the teacher organization/education journal level, this interest has not, as yet, turned into widespread curricular and methodological change in schools. In fact, quite the opposite has been shown to be true. Researchers in the United States, England, Canada, and Australia have investigated the nature and amount of student writing done in secondary school classes across the curriculum (Applebee, 1980; Bennett, 1979; Britton, Burgess, Martin, McLeod, and Rosen, 1975; Fillion, 1979). The Britton et al. study involved the nation-wide solicitation and subsequent analysis of 2,122 pieces of connected discourse from various subject area classes in 65 secondary schools in Great Britain. The research team developed two major categories—audience and function—to describe the writing they collected. Their audience categories covered a range beginning with the self and moving outward to trusted adult, teacher as partner in dialogue, teacher as examiner, peers of the writer, and the most distant—an unknown audience. The findings revealed that 95 percent of the students were writing for the teacher as an audience. The researchers subdivided the function category into

1. Transactional—writing to inform, instruct or persuade
2. Expressive—the informal writing that was closest to speech; and
3. Poetic—writing in which language is used as an art medium. Sixty-three percent of the writing they collected was transactional, 18% was poetic, and 5.5% was expressive.

Subsequent surveys, employing different methodologies but using or revising the categories of audience and function that the work of Britton et al. established, had similar findings. To discover the amount and kind of writing done by students across the curriculum, Bryant Fillion (1979) conducted 2-week surveys in three Toronto, Canada area secondary schools and reported few cases of students writing about or reflecting on their own experiences or commenting informally on the subject matter. In addition, he found that most "directed writing" involved answers to factual, recall questions, or longer "reports" that were largely paraphrased versions of encyclopedia or textbook information. In Australia, as part of a 3-year study of the development of writing abilities of students in the senior years (ages 15–17) of four secondary schools, Bruce Bennett (1979) of the University of Western Australia and his colleagues surveyed the writing done in all subjects by 551 students over a 2-week period in 1977. These scripts were also classified according to the function categories developed by Britton et al. Here transactional writing accounted for 86.9 percent of all writing sampled. Poetic accounted for 9.2 percent, and expressive writing accounted for only 2.9 percent of the sample. In the United States, Arthur Applebee (1980) carried out a yearlong study of writing across the curriculum in secondary school that drew from two major sources of data: a national questionnaire survey of teachers in six major subject areas—English, foreign language, mathematics, science, social science, business education, and recorded observations of single classes in two high schools over the course of a year in the same subject areas. As in the British, Canadian, and Australian surveys, Applebee's study also revealed that pupils had few opportunities for doing expressive writing to aid their learning in content area classrooms. Instead, two major types of writing prevailed: mechanical writing tasks (for example, short answer and fill-in-the-blank exercises) and writing to demonstrate whether required content or skills had been learned. This study, as well as further studies conducted by Applebee in collaboration with Judith Langer (1987), indicate that students had few genuine opportunities to use writing to aid their learning in content area classrooms. Instead, as in the British, Canadian, and Australian surveys, writing to demonstrate what one had learned prevailed. As Applebee (1983, p. 3) pointed out, such an emphasis had the instructional consequences of limiting both prewriting activities and teacher or peer assistance during the writing process and focusing attention solely on "accuracy" or "correctness."

RECONCEPTUALIZING THE TEACHER'S ROLE IN THE CLASSROOM

The movement to increase attention paid to the uses of language for learning in classrooms will make little difference unless there is a corresponding shift in how teachers at all levels and of subjects across the curriculum conceive of their role (Barnes, 1976; Medway, 1980b; Cummins, 1986, Swanson-Owens, 1986). Traditionally, the role of the teacher has been to impart a body of information and teach specific skills, and then monitor and assess pupils' progress in learning. This view of the teacher's role is clearly at odds with the findings of investigations into language use across the curriculum. Douglas Barnes, in an observation study of a variety of classes across the curriculum in eleven British secondary schools (Barnes, 1976), looked at teachers' view of learning as exemplified in their classroom practices. He developed two major categories—

Transmission and Interpretation—to describe the teachers he observed. The Transmission teacher fulfills the traditional role described above. For this teacher, writing and talk have little to do with the students' acquisition of knowledge. Knowledge in these classrooms is to be found intact in the language of the teacher and the text. The role of the student in such classrooms is that of passive recipient. Interpretation teachers, on the other hand, understand that to learn pupils must reinterpret information for themselves. These teachers carry on productive dialogues with their pupils in order to support the learners' attempts to interpret text and actual experience. An Interpretation teacher insists on the active engagement of pupils in what they are learning.

In a discussion of his findings, Barnes argued against transmission methods and the debilitating expectation that the pupils' role is to reproduce thought rather than to generate it. To improve this situation, Barnes described how teachers of subjects like science, literature and history can help pupils develop confidence in their abilities to reason when they verbalize their thinking. In dialogue transcripts, he showed a science teacher, for instance, who, in his careful attention to what his pupils said during discussions of a science experiment and this thoughtful follow-up questions, helped his pupils see the consequences of their responses. In so doing, he fostered more respect for learning than a teacher who simply asked for answers and then labeled them right or wrong. By treating pupils' responses as clues to their thinking, Barnes suggests, teachers encourage further thought. When teachers provide the occasions for the verbalizing and thinking-through of abstract concepts in their disciplines, pupils can, by making these concepts explicit through language, gain control over their own learning.

In reconceptualizing their role, teachers also must realize the dangers of prematurely directing the learners' attention to the correctness of their language use rather than their meaning (Kelly, 1988; Krashen, 1981; Smith, 1984). By attending initially to the meanings being expressed, rather than to the errors in the pupils' developing text, teachers are actually creating rhetorical occasions for the fluency that both helps writing serve learning and carries pupils to the next stage of language growth. Furthermore, this attention by the teacher to the pupils's meaning will accommodate to the diversity of learning styles of students in today's classrooms.

Another focus for reconceptualizing the teacher's role to promote the use of language for learning is to help teachers recognize the markers of literacy's developing stages so they can set up classroom situations in which pupils can grow. In these classrooms, subject teachers will help their students use talking, writing, reading, and listening to make sense of a range of content area experience—lectures, readings, experiments, discussions. They will encourage pupils in collaborative settings to explore ideas, concepts, and relevant personal experiences. In summary, this reconceptualized teacher's role will provide the occasions, resources, and enabling climate for the pursuit of individual meaning.

With the understanding that language is actually an instrument of thought comes the realization that teaching and learning are comprised of the use of language for a variety of purposes and audiences. A teacher's own language can provide a

model of what it means to be a learner: one who examines experience, questions it, and treats meaning from it. Pupils' classroom experiences will vary from discipline to discipline, with the sciences exploring the logic of the natural world using both linguistic and mathematical symbol systems and the humanities exploring the varieties of truths revealed in human dilemmas. The questions asked by the scientist, and therefore the learner of science, pursue what happened or happens. And the meanings created are those that can be verified publically. In the humanities, questions are posed as speculations about the effects of experience, and answers are interpretations based on the world view held by the learner. With support for the validity of their own experiences, pupils can learn to describe with increasing clarity their initial understandings, compare them with the responses of others, and return to the teacher or text for verification—and deeper comprehension. Thus, in subjects across the curriculum, an ongoing and crucial aspect of the teacher's role is to demonstrate confidence in the pupils' abilities to make sense out of what they read and discuss.

LANGUAGE ACROSS THE CURRICULUM IN PRACTICE

Peter Medway, commenting on what happened when teachers in a range of school subjects began tape-recording and listening to pupils' small groups discussions said: "In the tapes we could observe, in ways Piaget and Vygotsky had alerted us to, the thought developing as the language flowed" (Torbe and Medway, 1981, p. 154). Medway's image of thought developing through the increasing flow of language turns up again and again as teachers involved in pursuing the role of language in learning describe what happens when they encourage a wide range of exploratory language activities in subjects across the curriculum.

In Britain the report of the Bullock Committee, *A Language for Life* (1975), focused attention on language use across the curriculum through one of its major recommendations: "Each school should have an organized policy for language across the curriculum, establishing every teacher's involvement in language and reading development throughout the years of schooling" (p. 514). This national call for school-wide, agreed-upon language policies resulted in a critical appraisal of some of the report's short-comings (Rosen, 1975), an analysis of the research and teacher training implications of the report (Davis & Parker, 1978; Bailey, 1983), and a range of publications designed to aid teachers and schools in completing the task (Marland, 1977; Sutton, 1981).

One of the earliest systematic inservice efforts to work with teachers in subjects across the curriculum was the Writing Across the Curriculum Development Project funded by the British Department of Education and Science to work with teachers of all subjects to explore ways for pupils' writing to aid personal development and learning. As Nancy Martin, the Project's director, described, "the problem of the writing development project was to get the teachers of subjects across the curriculum to recognize language . . . as a major intellectual tool and go on to examine the part language—and in particular—writing played in the teaching of their subjects. In effect, this meant a shift of focus from how they viewed language to how they viewed learning." (1983, p. 103)

This project conducted numerous workshops for teachers in all disciplines during which the teachers both looked at their own writing and discussion and examined the writing and talk of students to discover how language use can enable—or impede—learning. At the conclusion of the Project's term, a text (Martin, D'Arcy, Newton & Parker, 1976) was published, which contained extensive descriptions of the classroom contexts in which significant use of language to aid learning took place. Subsequently, Pat D'Arcy, one of the original members of the Development Project, organized—from 1983 to 1989—an ambitious publishing effort producing 25 monographs written by classroom teachers of various subjects from both primary and secondary schools, who were involved in the Wiltshire and Somerset (England) Language for Learning Projects. These booklets were the result of year-long classroom investigations of how pupils' language functioned to aid their learning. Subsequently, in an Anglo-American volume (Barr, D'Arcy & Healy, 1982), British primary and secondary teachers in a range of subject areas joined their American colleagues in describing how they organized their classrooms and their curricular offerings to encourage pupils' use of oral and written language.

In the United States, the interest in language across the curriculum focused more narrowly, in many cases, on writing across the curriculum, perhaps because the initial interest in focusing specifically on cross-disciplinary writing came from college and university instructors. The work of Toby Fulwiler and his colleagues at the Michigan Technological Universtiy (Fulwiler & Young, 1982; Young & Fulwiler, 1986) and Elaine Maimon and her colleagues at Beaver College (Maimon, E. P., Belcher, G. L., Hearn, G., Nodine, B. F., O'Connor, F. W., 1981) revealed cross-disciplinary faculty collaboratively looking at their students' writing and, while postponing evaluation, debating the efficacy of the writing for their students' learning. An appraisal of other implications of the writing across the curriculum movement at the college/university level (McLeod, 1989) emphasized the diversity of these programs.

Unlike the focus at the university level, teachers in grades K–12 moved beyond this focus on writing to look at how all language modes contributed to pupils' learning. Many of the summer institutes and school year inservice programs of the sites of the National Writing Project include teachers from a range of subject areas in grades K–12 who demonstrate the methods they have developed to aid their students' learning (Gere, 1985; Wotring & Tierney, 1981). In an ambitious project sponsored by the Virginia State Department of Education, Judy Self (1987) collected accounts of classroom and district uses of language to learn by K–12 teachers across the state. These teachers described specifically how they had used a range of language activities to improve learning in their classrooms. In Hawaii, Ann Bayer, working with elementary and secondary teachers, developed a teaching model that places student language and thinking at center stage with the teacher as guide and learner. Calling this model a collaborative apprenticeship learning process based on Vygotsky's notions of the social ori-

gin of learning (Bayer, in press), Bayer and her K–12 colleagues describe how they experimented in their classrooms with collaborative teaching-learning strategies that made extensive use of language as a tool for learning.

Common to many of these accounts of language use for learning by subject area teachers across the levels of schooling has been the use of learning logs or journals (Fulwiler, 1987; Healy, 1981, 1983). In these logs, pupils reformulate new information learned from teachers or textbooks by writing informally, trying to make sense of this information by putting it into their own words, raising questions about what they do not understand and making connections between the new information and their prior knowledge of the subject. For example, Lynda Chittenden worked extensively with learning logs in her class of fourth and fifth graders at Old Mill School in Mill Valley, California as they wrote and illustrated *Our Friends in the Waters* (1979), an 80-page professionally-published source book about marine mammals. Writing this book provided an authentic and functional goal for a year's work in science, reading, literature and language arts. In an article describing the processes which culminated in the production of the book, Chittenden (1982) discussed her rationale:

Puzzling, questioning, imagining, dreaming, pondering: these are all accepted mental activities of learning. They are, however, an even more profound part of learning logs and reflect on the questions, confusions and fantasies that are included in active, involved learning. Also, the learning process is enhanced when kids are surrounded by the language of the unit they're studying: they need to read good works of fiction and non-fiction that deal with the content; they need to be involved in animated discussions in which they ponder and exclaim over the wonder of the content. (p. 37)

As the classroom practice of the teachers mentioned above and others (Giroux, 1979; Jacobs, 1970; Mayher, Lester, Pradl, 1983; Salem, 1982) illustrate using oral and written language as a means of inquiry and discovery can be encouraged whether pupils are studying the rules of sports or games in physical education, are creating or solving word problems in math classes, are writing directions, instructions, or reports in industrial arts or home economics classes, or are collaborating and writing up their lab data in science classes. For example, what if the expectation for pupils in a science class were that they talk or write like scientists: conjecturing, speculating, posing questions, probing reactions, seeking to unlock the secrets of natural phenomena? What if they were encouraged to think about the idea of, say, entropy, in terms of their own experiences with personal relationships? What if these pupils kept observation journals and class time permitted oral sharing of individual perceptioins about the effects of heat, plant growth, mood swings, or cat behavior? This litany of "what ifs" could, of course, also include expectations about what it means to study literature, history, math and other outer subject matter. In schools where pupils are expected to think about the ideas in the respective disciplines, they will construct interpretations of those ideas; that is, they will write and talk about them: speculating, creating analogies, comparing perceptions. They will actively and regularly *use* language across the curriculum.

CONCLUSION

Language used in the pursuit of meaning integrates reason, emotion and action. Attention to language use in learning contexts, where the discovery, clarification, and conveyance of personal knowledge serves cross-curricular purposes, is an emphasis naturally suited to the challenge facing schools: the need for all students to become literate. It is ironic, however, that with a body of evidence accumulating to support a holistic view of language use as the way to promote scholastic achievement in any discipline, that language for learning activities remain unavailable to most pupils.

Research in reading and writing, too, remain, for the most part, unintegrated. However, increased interest in language use across the curriculum may provide the impetus and the pedagogy to go beyond the separation between reading and writing and reintegrate the language arts in the minds of researchers and teachers. The necessary collaboration among teachers of different subjects, as they put language across the curriculum practices to work, opens classroom doors, relieving the isolation of teaching. The respect for informal dialogue among learners—both written and oral—about ideas in different kinds of texts makes emerging thoughts acceptable, despite ellipses and untidiness. And, too, teachers of all subjects, who are aware of the ways language promotes or restricts learning, can themselves remain tentative and curious as they collaboratively study how language is used in each discipline.

The use of one's own words as one is learning subject matter relieves the abstract nature of school knowledge, causing reverberations and establishing resonances between what is to be learned and what is already known. When students of any background must foreshorten this natural process which they have used since birth to make sense of their experiences, their achievement suffers. It is that simple.

References

Applebee, A. (1980). *A study of writing in the secondary school.* Final Report NIE-G-79-0174. Urbana, IL: National Council of Teachers of English.

Applebee, A. (1983). *Learning to write in the secondary school.* Final Report, Grant No. NIE-G-80-0156. Stanford, CA: Stanford University, School of Education.

Applebee, A., Langer, J. A., & Mullis, I. V. S. (1987). *The nation's report card: Learning to be literate in America.* Princeton, NJ: National Assessment of Educational Progress.

Bailey, R. W. (1983). Writing across the curriculum: The British approach. In P. Stock (Ed.) *Fforum: Essays on theory and practice in the teaching of writing* (pp. 24–32). Portsmouth, NH: Boynton/Cook.

Barnes, D. (1976). *From communication to curriculum.* Harmondsworth, England: Penguin Books.

Barnes, D. and Todd, F. (1977). *Communication and learning in small groups.* London: Routledge & Kegan Paul.

Barr, M., D'Arcy, P., & Healy, M. K. (1982). *What's going on?: Language/learning episodes in British and American classrooms, grades 4–13.* Portsmouth, NH: Boynton/Cook.

Bayer, Ann. (in press). *Collaborative apprenticeship learning: A teaching model using collaborative strategies to promote language and thinking across the curriculum.* Mountain View, CA.: Mayfield Publishing Co.

Bennett, B. (1979). *The process of writing and the development of writing abilities, 15–18.* Paper presented at the Annual Meeting of the Canadian Council of Teachers of English, Ottawa. (ERIC Document Reproduction Service No. ED 174 984).

Britton, J. (1970). *Language and learning.* Harmondsworth, England: Penguin Books.

Britton, J. (1982). Shaping at the point of utterance. In G. Pradl (Ed.) *Prospect and retrospect: Selected essays of James Britton* (pp. 139–145). Portsmouth, NH: Boynton/Cook.

Britton, J., Burgess, T., Martin, N., McLeod, A., & Rosen, H. (1975). *The development of writing abilities (11–18).* London: Mac Millian Education.

Bruner, J. S. (1964). Course of cognitive growth. *American Psychologist, 19* (1), 14.

Bullock, A. (1975). *A language for life.* (Report of the Committee of Inquiry appointed by the Secretary of State for Education and Science). London: Her Majesty's Stationery Office.

Chittenden, L. (1982). "What if all the whales are gone before we become friends?" In M. Barr, P. D'Arcy & M. K. Healy (Eds.), *What's going on? Language/learning episodes in British and American classrooms, grades 4–13* (pp. 36–51). Portsmouth, NH: Boynton/Cook.

Cummins, J. (1986). Empowering minority students: A framework for intervention. *Harvard Educational Review, 56*(1), 18–36.

D'Arcy, P. (1977). *Writing across the curriculum: Language for learning.* Exeter, England: Exeter University School of Education.

Davis, F. & Parker, R. (1978). *Teaching for literacy: Reflections on the Bullock report.* New York: Agathon Press, Inc.

Emig, J. (1977). Writing as a mode of learning. *College Composition and Communication, 28* (May), 122–128.

Fillion, B. (1979). Language across the curriculum. *McGill Journal of Education, XIV*(1), 47–60.

Freisinger, R. (1980). Cross-disciplinary writing workshops: Theory and practice. *College English, 42,* 154–166.

Fulwiler, T. (Ed.) (1987). *The journal book.* Portsmouth, NH: Boynton/Cook.

Fulwiler, T. & Young, A. (1982). *Language connections: Writing and reading across the curriculum.* Urbana, IL: National Council of Teachers of English.

Gere, A. (Ed.) (1985). *Roots in the sawdust: Writing to learn across the disciplines.* Urbana, IL: National Council of Teachers of English.

Giroux, H. (1979). Teaching content and thinking through writing, *Social Education, 43*(3), 190–193.

Healy, M. K. (1981). Purpose in learning to write: An approach to writing in three curriculum areas. In C. H. Frederiksen & J. F. Dominic (Eds.), *Writing: the nature, development, and teaching of written communication,* Vol. 2 (pp. 223–232). Hilldale, NJ: Lawrence Erlbaum.

Healy, M. K. (1983). Writing across the curriculum at all grade levels: A state-mandated revolution in writing instruction. *Teacher Education Quarterly, 10* (3), 9–21.

Jacobs, G. (1970). *When children think*. New York: Teachers College Press.

Kelly, L. P. (1988). Relative automaticity without mastery: The grammatical decision making of deaf students. *Written Communication, 5*(3), 325–351.

Kids in Room 14 (1979). *Our friends in the waters*. (Available from 40 Millside Lane, Mill Valley, CA 94941).

Krashen, S. D. (1981). *Second language acquisition and second language learning*. Hayward, CA: The Alemany Press.

Maimon, E. P., Belcher, G. L., Hearn, G. W., Nodine, B. F., & O'Connor, F. W. (1981). *Writing in the arts and sciences*. Cambridge, MA: Winthrop Publishers, Inc.

Marland, M. (1977). *Language across the curriculum*. London: Heinemann.

Martin, N. (1983). Language across the curriculum: A paradox and its potential for change. In *Mostly about writing: Selected essays by Nancy Martin*. (pp. 100–111). Portsmouth, NH: Boynton/Cook.

Martin, N., D'Arcy, P., Newton, B., and Parker, R. (1976). *Writing and learning across the curriculum 11–16*. London: Ward Lock Educational.

Mayher, J. S., Lester, N., & Pradl, G. M. (1983). *Learning to write/writing to learn*. Portsmouth, NH: Boynton/Cook.

McLeod, S. H. (Ed.), (Winter 1989). *Strengthening programs for writing across the curriculum*. New directions for teaching and learning, No. 36. San Francisco: Jossey-Bass.

Medway, P. (1980a). *Language in science*. Hatfield, England: Language in Science Working Party, The Association for Science Education.

Medway, P. (1980b). *Finding a language: Autonomy and learning in school*. London: Writers and Readers Publishing Cooperative.

Medway, P. (1984). The bible and the vernacular: The significance of language across the curriculum. In J. Britton (Ed.), *English teaching: An international exchange*. (pp. 153–157). Portsmouth, NH: Boynton/Cook.

Parker, R. (1985). The "language across the curriculum" movement: A brief overview and bibliography. *College Composition and Communication, 36* (2), 173–177.

Rosen, H. (Ed.), (1975). *Language and literacy in our schools: Some appraisals of the Bullock report*. London: University of London Institute of Education.

Salem, J. (1982). Using writing in teaching mathematics. In M. Barr, P. D'Arcy, M. K. Healy (Eds.), *What's going on? Language/learning episodes in British and American classrooms, grades 4–13*. Portsmouth, NH: Boynton/Cook.

Self, J. (Ed.). (1987). *Plain talk about learning and writing across the curriculum*. Richmond, VA: Virginia Department of Education.

Smith, F. (1984). Reading like a writer. In Jensen, J. M. (Ed.), *Composing and comprehending*, (pp. 47–56). Urbana, IL: ERIC Clearinghouse on Reading and Communication Skills and National Conference on Research in English.

Sutton, C. (Ed.) (1981). *Communicating in the classroom: A guide for subject teachers on the more effective use of reading, writing and talk*. London: Hodder and Stoughton.

Swanson-Owens, D. (1986). Identifying natural sources of resistance: A case study of implementing writing across the curriculum, *Research in the Teaching of English, 20*(1), 69–97.

Tierney, R. J., Caplan, R., Ehri, L., Healy, M. K., & Hurdlow, M. (1988). Writing and reading working together. Occasional paper no. 5, Center for the Study of Writing. University of California, Berkeley, and Carnegie Mellon University.

Torbe, M. and Medway, P. (1981). *The climate for learning*. London: Ward Lock Educational.

Vygotsky, L. S. (1962). *Thought and language*. Cambridge, MA: MIT Press.

Wotring, A. & Tierney, R. (1981). *Two studies in high school science*. Classroom research study #5. Berkeley, CA: Bay Areas Writing Project.

Young, A. & Fulwiler, T. (Eds.). (1986). *Writing across the disciplines: Research into practice*. Portsmouth, NH: Boynton/Cook.

39

CURRENT ISSUES AND FUTURE DIRECTIONS

James Moffett

Research is a kind of rhetoric, one among many ways of persuading. Our society seems to revere scientific research but actually ignores its findings when some other rhetoric better matches motives. In education, for example, research results are used to justify traditional teaching practices far more than to innovate, for which less motivation exists. For financial and political reasons, most research is short and slight and tends to confirm teaching methods that are short and slight. This means, in language arts, that the direct teaching of subskills in isolation—the particle approach—is automatically favored over the holistic approach, by which phonics, spelling, punctuation, vocabulary, syntax, usage, and other components and subskills of comprehending and composing are taught only by massive practice of the language arts themselves through whole discourses. Segmental research can validate only segmented teaching methods.

The only experimental research that could fairly test the whole-discourse approach would require totally committing to the approach a sizeable student population for their first 8 or so years of schooling—a risk no school typical enough to inspire credibility has ever run. This forfeiture leaves the impression that the particle approach is tried and true, whereas it never had to win a berth because it was already on board, and leaves also the impression that the holistic approach has failed to prove itself, whereas it is simply unprovable except under special long-range, full-scale conditions that are financially and politically unwelcome. Most managers, moreover, of educational institutions, curriculum industries, and funding sources tend to prefer the particle approach because it lends itself, respectively, to authoritarian systematization, commercial production, and reigning notions of cost benefits. Because quick-pay-off research is consonant with this current short-term mode of management—if indeed it does not derive from it—such segmental research forms a closed loop with our public psyche that makes it difficult to change and that obscures its inherent futility.

Experimental research in education exemplifies well how dangerous become the pieces out of the whole. No research that reports learning success in one component or subskill, such as vocabulary or sentence complexity or identifying main

points in a text, should be enacted into curriculum without knowing other effects of the procedure tested. Much serious damage is done by forcing results—usually short-lived—for one highly targeted skill at the expense of other, often more important, factors in thought and language or overall personal development. But controlling for unintended effects is rarely built into experimental design and indeed would in most cases be impossible, because too many effects are unforeseeable and widely scattered across the mental life. And since every segregated-skill experiment does similar damage, together they add up to an intolerable price—the betrayal of the real goals of speaking, thinking, reading, and writing for the sake of ensuring periodic "progress" in the subskills alleged to comprise them.

The only way to avoid this trap is to refer research to a more comprehensive framework. Without it, moreover, we do not know what to make of, or what to do with, even good research with whole-language activities, because we don't understand well enough the relationships among the various thinking and verbalizing faculties to know what we are doing in working with any one of them. Besides practical literacy, what, finally, are we really trying to accomplish through language in the bigger picture of individual and social life? Ultimate values must enter into any thoughtful overview of present and future. For all these reasons, literacy and literature are best discussed in constant relation to culture and consciousness.

Researchers are in the position of trying to investigate those same physical, psychological, social, and cultural environments that determine the nature and conditions of their research itself. To be of any great use to education in the future, research must rise to a new sophistication in the kind of self-examination that we are familiar with, for example, in literary criticism. Like textual interpretation, research needs to undergo a kind of deconstruction. Just as the contexts of the author, text, and reader must be taken into account in dealing with the meaning of a text, so must the circumstances of the investigator, the project, and the applier of the findings in making sense of research. What are the personal and cultural *subtexts* of the research report? Just as current hermeneutics penetrates well beyond the truism that people read into a text some of their own inner life, and that authors say more than they realize, this new self-examination should far exceed the mere reminder that any research is vulnerable to bias.

In their efforts to make their disciplines as "hard" as those in the natural sciences, behavioral scientists have often taken on a scientific swagger that, interestingly, the phycicist has been forced to drop. The harder the science, the harder does the scientist run up against the limits of the scientific method. After Einstein's relativity and Heisenberg's uncertainty have come other principles, like that of probability, to attenuate and qualify the realities of matter. The more one views holistically, from multiple vantage points and expanded perspectives, the more relativistically one thinks. As the interplay of "particles" in a nucleus dissipates the very idea of a particle, the meaning of a single text extends out across the whole network of reciprocally defining words and cross-referring intertextuality that makes up signification for writer and reader. If both literature and physics operate today on a principle of relativity, behavioral scientists should be able to drop the defensive effort to pretend their disciplines are "hard."

Within this framework of new self-awareness, the subject matter of research should be drastically and daringly enlarged. It remains far too physical, partly in allegiance to a lingering behaviorism and partly in adherence to an old-fashioned doctrine of nineteenth-century positivism, according to which nothing is real that cannot be hefted, counted, or perceived by the senses. In an era when theoretical physics sounds stranger than scholastic theology, and the most important "things" in science are mathematical constructs, this materialism seems inappropriate indeed. Researchers have got to quit intimidating each other by disparaging attempts to explore the intangible—especially when investigating the mental life! The old positivistic scientism has created a climate we still live in that I call the "scientific inquisition," whereby the research establishment punishes its members for dealing with taboo subjects, as the church did before it.

In *The Body Electric: Electromagnetism and the Foundation of Life* (1985), orthopedic surgeon Robert Becker not only gives an account of his pioneering experimentation on the healing power of electricity but also makes of this research a case history of how scientists may reject for a long time well-substantiated findings if these contradict established beliefs. Since the eighteenth century, when Volta challenged Galvani's assertion that frogs' legs operated electrically, most biologists have squelched or ignored evidence of animal electricity. Becker chronicles in detail how clear findings presented by many others as well as himself were repeatedly brushed off right up into the 1960s, when the scientific community finally began to accept that bodies generate electricity and are influenced by electromagnetic fields—a finding of far-reaching significance and practical value. In a postscript titled "Political Science" Becker exposes how the politics of funding determines the kind of research and therefore the kind of knowledge that is permitted. Even today, prejudices against electrical healing, a heavy medical committment to treating by drugs, and commercial protection of microwaves ovens and other electronically hazardous appliances still starve funding for research on electrical physiology.

But besides these worldly factors, ever since Galvani's and Volta's day the mysterious and invisible power of electricity had been associated with the philosophy of vitalism, according to which the universe, as Plato and most other philosophers taught, is animated from beyond itself by an immaterial force. Vitalists backed electricity as the candidate for this force while mechanists fought strenuously to disprove the presence of electricity in living beings, which it would appear to animate from another dimension. So a metaphysical dispute, potentially threatening the material basis of science itself, has underlain into our own time any research in bodily electricity. If researchers like Becker, well grounded in both medical practice and orthodox experimentation, have encountered such resistance in investigating purely physical phenomena, imagine the difficulty one may meet investigating less material phenomena.

Even Freud and Jung were intimidated by this conformist pressure, as Arthur Koestler points out in *The Roots of Consciousness: An Excursion into Parapsychology* (1972). Though not personally inclined toward the paranormal, Freud came to believe in telepathy from direct experience of it with his patients and joined both the British and American Society for Psychical Research. Ernest Jones dissuaded him from speaking or publishing about it, though Freud's papers on the relations between telepathy and psychoanalysis appeared posthumously. For most of his career, Jung felt obliged to explain his own numerous psychic experiences and his theory of the collective unconscious as somehow existing or happening in the individual mind, but near the end of his life he acknowledged that these had reality beyond the physical brain.

Though this sort of censorship has lifted somewhat today, physicist Fritjof Capra suffered career difficulties because he compared nuclear theory to oriental metaphysics in *The Tao of Physics* (1977). Biologist Rupter Sheldrake was castigated in an editorial in science's most prestigious and traditional journal, *Nature,* for the theory he set forth in *A New Science of Life: The Hypothesis of Formative Causation* (1981), which *Nature* said was "the best candidate for burning there has been for a long time" (p. 245). Sheldrake hypothesizes that, along with heredity and environment, a nonmaterial field for each species may govern the formation of its members. It may be intellectually chic to speak of a "shift of paradigm" in the sciences, but it is not professionally very safe yet to propose one.

These examples are not idle. Not only is telepathy related to the idea of a collective unconscious or group mind like Sheldrake's formative field but both, if real, bear a tremendous amount on language learning. So let us use them further as examples of the bolder and broader research that educators might do well to foster and follow. Actually, the notion of intelligence as a force field exerting action across time and space has a tradition in modern biology including many others than Freud and Jung, who certainly took seriously the likelihood of such fields, since telepathy presupposes some such means of communication and since a collective unconscious would also depend on a nonphysical transmission in the present. ("Racial memory" begs the question of how individuals can remember experiences others had before them.)

One idea that recurs among scientists goes well beyond the now-demonstrable fact that organisms give off an electromagnetic field. It is that members of a set of living beings, including humans, participate in some kind of force field, escaping the detection of physical instruments, which individuals at once collectively generate and are in some measure directed by. Sheldrake calls these fields "morphogenetic" (from the traditional study of morphogenesis or developmental forces) to indicate that some characteristics of species are beamed to members in the present, beyond what genetic transmission can account for. Generally, according to this hypothesis, repeated action builds up a "morphic resonance" to which members are tuned and that perpetuates such action in the field until new actions should be repeated enough to change the field (as in evolution). The idea curiously resembles the Hindu *samskaras,* which are habits based on the self-perpetuating repetition of thoughts, words, and deeds that likewise generate a formative field by which the past determines the present. Experiments with people and animals before and after Sheldrake proposed his theory tend to indicate individuals may learn new behavior more easily after others have mastered it, a phenomenon that could explain the constant setting of new records in sports and of achievements in other fields that seem to extend human capacity. But certain proof for this controversial "new science for life" awaits, precisely, further research, which the *Brain Mind Bulletin* faithfully covers, as it did the original controversy.

In the fall of 1982 issue of *Revision,* Sheldrake placed his hypothesis within a lineage deriving from vitalists like Hans Driesch, an embryologist who defected from mechanism at the turn of the century because it could not explain how bits of an embryo could regenerate themselves, and from Alfred North Whitehead's organismic framework of the 1920s. Sheldrake's geneology of biologists proposing some sort of morphogenetic fields includes Alexander Gurwitsch of Russia, Paul Weiss of Vienna, C. H. Waddington, René Thom, and Brian Goodwin (p. 41). Writing before Sheldrake, in *The Roots of Consciousness,* Koestler mentions that biologist Sir Alistair Hardy thought that the highly skilled and coordinated activities of some lower animals "could only be explained by a kind of group-mind where each individual shared a 'psychic blueprint'" (1972, p. 101–102).

In *Lifetide: The Biology of the Unconscious* (1979) another biologist, Lyall Watson, uses lifetide as a metaphor to evoke a field of interconnectedness among living things that may explain "paranormal" events such as the now famous "hundredth monkey" phenomenon. A young female monkey on a Japanese island began washing potatoes in the sea before eating them, a significant innovative behavior soon imitated by her peers and from them by her elders. Then on other Japanese islands other monkeys started washing their potatoes who could not have been learning from observation. Watson conjectures that after a certain critical mass has been reached—the hundredth monkey, say—the behavior becomes directly available to the whole collective unconscious of that group. This would, of course, exemplify exactly Sheldrake's idea, but, pertinently enough, Watson had to tell anecdotally the island-leaping part of the story, because some researchers involved did not believe what was happening and those who did fear for their reputation if they reported it officially. Having to fill in this crucial gap in the journals with unofficial oral accounts brought Watson in for

heavy criticism, especially from organizations that specialize in debunking quacks.

The common motive behind these various concepts of invisible formative fields has been to explain certain material observations that materialist frameworks cannot account for. Scientists who oppose an hypothesis like Sheldrake's tend to be biochemists, he points out, who work with a microview that obviates the inexplicable facts that zoologists and botanists encounter in the larger time-space scope of whole organisms and their evolution. Physicist David Bohm has proposed in *Wholeness and the Implicate Order* (1980) a theory comparable to Sheldrake's and for the similar reason that Bohm believes present-day quantum mechanics "does not have any concept of movement or process or continuity in time" because it too takes a microview, the observations of one moment, "but out of this truncated view physicists are trying to explain everything" (from a discussion between him and Sheldrake in the fall 1982 issue of *Revision,* p. 45). This from a highly respected former coworker with Einstein and an author of a widely used textbook on quantum mechanics. Like the morphogenetic field, the implicate order is a formative ground unmanifest itself but determining the particulars of what we do see. It is the enfolded, potential order behind the unfolded, manifested order and so corresponds, as Bohm does not hesitate to say, to metaphysical concepts of a nonphysical reality emanating the familiar material world. Sheldrake and Bohm agree on the similarity of their theories and of the theories' function, to make sense of the more comprehensive findings in their respective fields.

The limitations of physicalist assumptions have been forcefully impressed upon all the great brain researchers of the last 100 years. Michael Aron points out in the December 1975 issue of *Harper's* that I. V. Pavlov, Sir Charles Sherrington, Sir John Eccles, A. R. Luria, Wilder Penfield, and Karl Pribram all had to resort to positing some nonphysical plane or order of reality that, as in Sheldrake's and Bohm's theories, acts as a field governing what one observes. In *The Mystery of the Mind* (1975), after reporting his famous experiments with electrical stimulation of the brain, Wilder Penfield wrote:

Because it seems to me certain that it will always be quite impossible to explain the mind on the basis of neuronal action within the brain, and because it seems to me that the mind develops and matures independently throughout an individual's life as though it were a continuing element, and because a computer (which the brain is) must be programmed and operated by an agency capable of independent understanding, I am forced to choose the proposition that our being is to be explained on the basis of two fundamental elements.

Here Penfield is quite deliberately picking up a problem in the philosophy of science that was old in Newton's day—the one referred to earlier, about whether the universe is utterly mechanical or is animated by a force from another dimension. One of the "fundamental elements" would be physical and the other not. But like most other scientists today, Penfiled hesitates to employ a term like 'nonphysical' or 'immaterial' because the definition of physical matter could simply be changed to fit the findings, as indeed may soon happen in a reconstrual of the nature of 'nature' that can comfortably include the 'supernatural.' Contrast Penfield's conclusion here, the same as his mentor Sherrington's and his other predecessors, with a statement in *The Dragons of Eden* by astronomist Carl Sagan, who was trying (in 1977) to head off just such a line of thinking in the public: "My fundamental premise about the brain is that its workings—what we sometimes call 'mind'—are a consequence of its anatomy and physiology, and nothing more" (p. 7 of the Introduction).

The current successor to the brain researcher's dilemma, Karl Pribram, has brought theoretical physics and mathematics to bear on the brain/mind duality in such a way as to transcend the division into physical and nonphysical, natural and supernatural. He has adopted a holographic model based on the realization from Karl Lashley's and his own research that a memory has no particular brain site but is distributed over such a large portion of the brain that most removal or damage cannot destroy the memory. Just as each part of a hologram contains an image of the whole photographed object, different parts of the brain contain a record of a given experience.

Furthermore, as converging lasar beams create a pattern of wave interference photographed as a hologram, although the pattern looks nothing like the photographed image, sensory wave frequencies intersecting at junctions between neurons register a pattern as a memory that also does not resemble the perceived object. "Images are mental constructions," Pribram writes in *The Holographic Paradigm*. "But the process of image construction involves . . . a transformation into the frequency (holographic) domain. This domain is characteristic not only of brain processing . . . but of physical reality as well. Bohm refers to it as the implicate order . . ." (p. 33). Continues Pribram, ". . . Time and space are collapsed in the frequency domain. . . . In the absence of space-time coordinates, the usual causality upon which scientific explanation depends must also be suspended" (1982, p. 34). However much we might share Sagan's concern that knowledge not be polluted by popular superstition, educators must recognize that the scientific paradigm is rapidly shifting among leading researchers to accommodate formally what Sir Arthur Eddington said for some scientists even several decades ago, that the stuff of the universe is mind-stuff.

An hypothesis should not be ruled out of serious consideration because it is physically untestable. After all, the more comprehensive and important an idea, the harder we should expect it to be to confirm empirically. If we insist on material evidence, we doom our understanding of nature to the less consequential. Rather, we may avail ourselves of other ways of testing an hypothesis. First, how well does it explain otherwise inexplicable phenomena? Second, how well generally does it fit knowledge already accepted? Third, though no experiment may be devised to test it directly, does a synthesis of empirical evidence culled over time from across different disciplines tend to bear it out? Finally, are there logical ways to reason a case for it? Research that truly contributes to English education in the future will have to help us understand better the relations among thought, language, and consciousness. This will not happen without considering seriously some ideas not so honored so far in education, though given considerable thought on the growing edge of the scientific community.

Entertaining the idea, for example, of mental force fields acting in exemption from time and space would make enormous difference in how we might think about language learning. If collective consciousness and telepathy are real, what new truths might these imply, and what light would these shed on old facts? Koestler says that Freud "theorised that ESP was an archaic method of communication between individuals, which was later supplanted by the more efficient method of sensory communication" (*The Roots of Consciousness*, 1972, p. 101). Reflect a moment on the many implications of such an idea for language acquisition. And if morphogenetic fields exist, a human individual must be participating in several at once—familial, ethnic, linguistic, cultural. How do these interplay? Of the several fields to which an individual is tuned, which field dominates in influence? Dominates by virtue of which factors? What is the relation between knowledge beamed directly and constantly to the individual from these group minds and knowledge learned by personal experience or by oral and written transmission? Are people in fact gaining access to knowledge telepathically that is attributed to deliberate teaching? What opens or blocks attunement to these fields (and some perhaps beyond the human families)? Can people learn to control attunement so as to choose which field to resonate with at a certain moment?

What role does language play in all of this? Does it, for example, supplant telepathy for the child, as Freud theorized it once did for humanity as a whole? If so, in what sense does the child gain? Are there losses? Let us begin to move this inquiry closer to language learning by using as transition a couple of lines of valuable research already in progress.

One was begun some 30 years ago by H. A. Witkin, who proposed a psychological dimension running from field-dependent to field-independent where "field" refers to a physical or social environment. Originated in investigations of how much people orient themselves spatially by internal versus external references, this initially perceptual dimension has since become a common dimension of cognitive style and of personality and has even been usefully applied to cultural comparison as in the finding that individuals in hunter-gatherer societies tend toward independence from the social field whereas members of herder-farmer societies tend to depend more on the group, differences reflected in their respective ways of rearing children. Because language is social in origin and in function, the degree of individual dependence on the group must affect considerable how one learns and practices language, especially as this degree itself is in part culturally determined. But this whole promising line of investigation of one's relation to the social field might take a quantum leap if researchers saw fit to consider research subjects within several sorts of fields, perhaps simultaneously sometimes, one possibility being physically detectable fields such as those of gravity and electromagnetism, another being the more inferential fields of society and culture, and another being the "immaterial" fields of collective, telepathic knowledge.

With a more enabling concept of 'field', research might yield greater understanding about familiar practical learning issues. Does truly mastering a foreign language, for example, entail participation in a new group mind, a new attunement? Do small children learn both a native language so rapidly and foreign languages so much more readily than elders because they are more telephathically receptive? Does our current concept of literacy, that the learner joins a community of readers and writers, mean more than we know, in the sense that joining is not just learning by interacting with people physically present but tapping into the whole pool of the literate field from an oral field? Putting the question anew like this might help us make better use of what a Walter Ong or Erick Havelock tells us about the relations of orality to literacy.

The most neglected problem in education may be why children go into a slump by the end of primary school, around the age of 8. As psychologist Joseph Chilton Pearce described probably most forecefully, in *The Magical Child* (1977), a prodigious creative learning capacity enjoyed during the preschool and primary years seems to wither then. Do language acquisition and external acculturation cause this as a side-effect by over-molding experience? This paramount question might become more answerable if researchers were willing to recast it into terms of group-mind resonance. Does orality first, and then literacy again later, alter the receptivity of the individual to such resonance—reduce telepathy and hence make it harder to gain direct access to the pool of collective knowledge? Does shifting cultural transmission from telepathy to oral and written language free individuals from the tyranny of an unconscious group mind, but also cut them off from the genius of the genus, with all its accumulated knowledge and capacity, and set them plodding to piece this all together bit by bit? Researchers are going around and around, as in the debate between the followers of Chomsky and Piaget, about how much environment and heredity, nurture and nature, contribute respectively to human formation. This forum may need another dimension—the ways in which morphogenetic fields are forming the mind directly, interplaying with these physical and social fields.

The work of psychologist Julian Jaynes exemplifies both some directions for new research and some limitations of the old. In *The Origin of Consciousness in the Breakdown of the Bicameral Mind* (1976) he sets forth a daring thesis based on an admirable synthesis of knowledge from art and archaeology, physiology and psychiatry, myth and history. Before about 3,000 years ago, he argues, individuals did not experience personal consciousness and could not think for themselves. They depended almost totally on the culture and had a 'bicameral mind,' by which he means a two-chambered mind of which half carried out orders received from the other half, which was really a program of cultural imperatives perceived by the individual as voices of gods or ancestors. Jaynes hypothesizes as the mechanism for this bicamerality that these standing orders were transmitted from an area in the right hemisphere of the brain to a corresponding area in the left hemisphere (Wernicke's area, a major site of speech), where they were translated into hallucinated voices. So people felt directly commanded to act by the gods, as in the *Iliad,* and were indeed run from the outside.

Two developments broke down the bicameral mind, says Jaynes, and made today's personal consciousness develop as a necessity. Mobility confused the cultures, and literacy silenced the voices. When cultures began to mix, individual action was confounded beyond the capacity of programmed commands. At the same time, laws inscribed to be posted or circulated replaced the hallucinated vocal directives. (Moses' bringing down

of the tablets would presumably represent a transition.) Individual mentation became necessary for action, and literacy made it possible by teaching people to metaphorize and hence to build an inner model of the world. So consciousness evolves from group to individual but with many throw-backs to remote authority as in the auditory hallucinations of modern schizophrenics.

In its ingenious weaving of disparate information and its application in turn to different domains, the theory is brilliant if only one-quarter true, because even what may not be true catalyzes very productive thinking in the reader. Here are some thoughts from this reader. First, some notion of evolution in consciousness does seem prerequisite for discussing in depth the other matters of language acquisition, cognitive development, and cultural heritage. Second, such a comprehensive framework does entail a rare sort of scanning across areas of knowledge and across periods of history. It was heroic to attempt this alone. Third, the direction of the evolution of consciousness that Jaynes indicates, from collective to individual, seems well confirmed by many other things he does not refer to, as does also his splendid evocation of the waning of the gods and the fading of the voices, so well attested in a vast mythology and literature of lost paradises and in the long subsequent history of efforts to reestablish contact through divination, auguries, prophecies, and other seership by those still gifted to hear divine or ancestral voices. ("The falcon can no longer hear the falconer.") Finally, and this does not exhaust the riches of the theory, Jaynes illuminates past and present by bringing them to bear on each other in a living continuity pertinent to the purposes of education.

Even where it may not hold up, the theory inspires valuable thought. Jaynes' date for the origin of our sort of consciousness is too late. His timetable of causation obliged him to place it after the advent of writing, but in writings as early as the Vedas meditation practices are referred to as antedating writing and presuppose a personal consciousness already so developed that it needed to be quieted and reattuned to fields beyond. The metaphorization that Jaynes sees as inaugurating individual consciousness more likely *prepared* for writing than *resulted* from it. That is, it seems easier to imagine metaphorization deriving from visual homologs such as tree-limbs/body-limbs, from which in turn could develop the categorical concepts needed for common nouns and further verbalization.

Here I feel Jaynes is following our common cultural assumption that thought is beholden to language. Our culture bears nearly as strong a bias against the nonverbal as it does against the nonphysical. Language is revered out of all measure, at least by those who make their living by it, to the point that we can hardly imagine the mind developing without it, whereas as Hans Furth, for one, has pointed out in *Thinking Without Language: Psychological Implications of Deafness* (1966), thought can grow independently of language. But the very perceptiveness of the rest of Jaynes' theory calls our attention to this telling assumption that, precisely, needs much more thought and research.

More important, the materialist framework of the scientific establishment within which Jaynes is still trying to work obliges him to contain the voices within the physical brain, as hallucination, whereas I think the bicameral or externally directed mind can be better explained by telepathy and better developed by the concept of a collective mental force field operating from the past and within the present. This adjustment would not seriously disrupt Jaynes' thesis, but it would alter the relations among thought, speech, writing, and consciousness—which are all the more important for educators as children may pass through whatever sequence humanity may have undergone. According to my own theorizing, thought evolved before speech—conceptualization independently of verbalization—but was indeed group-thought, shared by telepathy, which can be wordless.

The mixing of bloods and cultures did indeed muddy each group mind, however, and did force individuals to think for themselves. The emergence of individual consciousness, speech, and literacy are indeed related to each other and to the disappearance of the gods and voices, but it could as easily have happened as follows. If speech evolved out of the necessity to replace telepathy, it was because the development of personal consciousness was already weakening the attunement with the collective consciousness, the direction of evolution being, precisely, from group to individual. Effect rather than cause of this evolution, literacy would nevertheless have made personal consciousness at once more necessary and more possible as it replaced telepathy. Hallucination probably did occur as a frantic effort to renew contact with the authoritarian imperatives. Being in touch with the culture externally but out of touch with the group mind internally could have left us with the nostalgia for ethnocentricity that today plagues not only world peace but haunts cultural research itself. Understanding the direction of the evolution of consciousness deserves top priority, because educators need to think about how schooling should fit this development.

Another cultural bias may play a part in Jaynes' theory that is critical to thinking about the evolution of consciousness, namely, the notion that our age is superior to the past. Thus a pathological behavior like hallucination is posited to explain how our former mind was externally directed, not a positive faculty like telepathy, which modern people usually do not have access to or do not believe in but would envy in earlier people were they indeed endowed with it (as all the esoteric literature consistently states).

A notion of progress that condescends to the past destroys the very concept of evolution in consciousness, which must acknowledge that trade-offs occur over history among human faculties. Memory and reason, let us say for example, became respectively necessary to create and retain knowledge as human beings became more individuated and lost telepathic touch with the group field. Misleading value judgments can enter here. Moderns are more willing to concede that preliterate peoples had a better memory, because we regard memory as an inferior faculty, whereas telepathy, if accepted, would appear to be "higher." But if consciousness is evolving from collective to individual, then of course telepathy would be most appropriate to the earlier, collective stage. And also, the evolution of consciousness may well spiral so that, for example, telepathy might return as a willed capacity individuals might switch on and off rather than, as previously, an unconscious, involuntary bond to

which no alternative for knowledge existed before memory and reason. Thus, just as personal memory of acquired experience would have taken the place of the waning telepathic group mind, so memory would have had to decline before logic could emerge. If literacy triggers intellectual growth, it may be because it undercuts memory and makes reason needed as a supplanting means to knowledge. If you cannot tune in or recall, figure it out. Maybe we should regard reason as both a third-best and a cumulative achievement. So it is in this evolutionary way that we must consider the interplay of faculties, and not mourn this loss or vaunt that gain. It may come about that as the technology of printing made memory less necessary but brought reason to the fore, the technology of computers may cause logic to atrophy and force a yet more sophisticated knowledge-making faculty to emerge.

Still, isn't all this too speculative, unprovable? How can research be research and depart so far from the evidence of the senses? Part of the point is that research has always been more speculative than it appears. And the more "proof" accumulates the more it topples of its own weight. Hence the "deconstruction" occurring now in philosophy: greater knowledge has led to greater uncertainty about the larger, more important matters. Research needs to become more frankly speculative, philosophical, and even metaphysical, because frameworks cannot truly be omitted, they can only be secreted or disregarded. As biases emerge from our increasing knowledge of the world, the more we realize that this knowledge is self-knowledge. Partialities are not just personal and partisan but cultural. In fact, it is from the cultural that we discover how much we still function as a group mind. Ethnocentricity, more than anything else, limits understanding. Personal and partisan biases can detect and counter each other, and a synthesis of disciplines can offset the limitations of each field of formal investigation, but what is to correct cultural partialities? Yes, other cultures, at least to a great degree, but research rarely crosses cultures. The corrective is to draw not only on other current cultures but on those of the past, for impartiality—the whole truth—requires tension over time as well as space.

To focus these considerations and relate them more to the classroom, let us cast them into the terms of the "cultural literacy" debate, which concerns whether schools should identify and teach certain key ideas, values, and works deemed to characterize the culture in which the education is to occur. Immediately one wonders how a culture is defined for this purpose. Most states have required their students to take courses in the history and culture of their state or region, and most U.S. schools have required courses in American history and American literature, often leaving ancient or European history, or British or European literature, as options, though sometimes the course in the larger culture may be required as well.

Advocates of "great books" have in mind a coverage or sampling of "Western" culture, alleged to have begun with the Greeks but allowing that Christianity had roots in Judaism. To designate those classics that culturally literate students ought to have read, educators often refer to them, by analogy with holy writ, as the "canon" (other books being presumably apocryphal). Of course actually "covering" a culture so defined necessitates sutdents' reading a great deal in translation and instructors' surveying for students a vast amount that their charges could not be expected to read for themselves. So besides the partialities built into the culture itself, we must take into account the endless possibilities for misrepresentation that inhere in all this purveying of three millenia of culture, at each stage of which the inheritors are selecting, translating, and summarizing according to their bents and lights. Characterizing a culture poses a profoundly compounded problem in research, inasmuch as each generation of researchers is somewhat at the mercy of all its predecessors as well as of its own predilections.

The question of what is a culture arises not only about books but about the environments of the students who are to read them. So both scholarly research and school populations are at issue together. America comprises a plurality of living cultures and derives from a multitude of contemporary as well as ancient sources. In fact, new efforts in the 1980s to make "cultural literacy" a central curriculum goal may well owe to the threat posed to national and cultural identity by trends of the last 20 years. Not only have established minorities like African Americans and chicanos asserted their identities and insisted on representation of their cultures, but new immigrations of southeast Asians, Central and South Americans, West Indians, and Middle-easterners have aroused consternation in some quarters about whose country and culture America really is. But the threat to identity comes from without as well as from within. Commerce, finance, politics, and ecological safety are rapidly becoming internationalized. The interdependence among countries is creating so sensitive and intricate a fabric that the very viability and validity of nations is coming into question, and the need for planetary regulation and cooperation is coming to the fore. At the same time, the United States has been losing the supreme position it enjoyed following World War II and is becoming just another nation striving to hold its own in international competition. Backlashes of nationalism and ethnocentricity have resulted from all this.

During this period we have seen in education the movement to cancel bilingualism and the resurgence of the old "great books" curriculum under the rubric of "cultural literacy." Renewal of the curriculum mandate to transmit "our Western heritage" is being challenged today, however, and research can play a perhaps salvational role in dealing with the conflicts inherent in such an educational goal. When in 1988 Stanford changed its required course in Western civilization to include nonEuropean cultures and works by women and member of minorities, U.S. Education Secretary William Bennett charged that this was "primarily a political, not an educational decision" and that ethnicity had nothing to do with it (*San Francisco Chronicle*, April 19, 1988). But the very definition of a culture is political, and nothing has so much to do with a culture as ethnicity. This inability or unwillingness to acknowledge these substrata of books and ideas is something the future will not abide. If we can own up to the hidden politics of literature surely we can in the more obvious case of whole civilizations.

Not only must the "our" be scrutinized, in "our Western heritage," but also the "Western." As Europeans and Americans have had increasingly to share scholarly authority with researchers of other cultures, a less parochial perspective of civilization has emerged. In his trilogy *Black Athena: The Afroasiatic Roots of Classical Civilization* (1987) historian Martin Bernal argues on considerable evidence that the Greek language and culture derived from Egypt and Phoenicia, as stated by the Greeks themselves, but that European scholars of the eighteenth and nineteenth centuries, mostly British and German, discredited these derivations from Africa and the Orient for ethnocentric and racist reasons, establishing instead an "Aryan Model" that kept the founts of "Western" civilization in Europe and hence its great works in the family. He traces in great detail how European vogues for Rome, Egypt, China, India, and Greece succeeded themselves during the last two centuries until preference settled on Greece, around which many great scholars of the period constructed a god-like mystique befitting caucasian and Christian superiority. This Hellenophilia influences powerfully today even an eminent classicist like Eric Havelock. When he claims in *The Muse Learns to Write* (1986) that the Greeks invented the first real alphabet and thereby became the first philosophers, he combines this cultural assumption of Greek primacy with the cultural assumption that intellectual achievement awaits literacy.

It is true, as one can see for oneself, that many if not most of the great scholars of the last century, on whose work we often rely, were startlingly chauvinistic. In the introduction to his 1882 translation of the Chinese classic, *The I Ching: Book of Changes,* James Legge's irritation with his subject erupts more than once. He makes invidious comparisons with Western texts, calls the hexagrams themselves a "farrago" (p. 25), and disparages the philosophy when it does not resemble Christian doctrine. This was the standard translation until Richard Wilhelm's in 1950, published by Princeton's Bollingen Foundation and introduced by Jung. But consider a far more recent work, also much relied on, Montague Rhodes James' *The Apocryphal New Testament,* put out in 1924 by Oxford University. In his preface, James cheerfully explains that a main reason for making the texts available is to show how they deserved to be excluded from the Bible. He then gives as reasons for his excluding Gnostic texts from his Apocrypha that Gnostics were not "normal or Catholic Christians" (p. xvii); that the texts, which he named, were unavailable (though he deemed it his job to translate and make scores of other texts available); and that they were not readable or made little sense. Thus this twentieth century scholar carried on the censorship of the Gnostic literature that Irenaeus and other church fathers had initiated so successfully in the second century that Gnostics rarely spoke for themselves until the accidental discovery in 1945 of the Gnostic Gospels in Upper Egypt, buried there in the fourth century to escape Roman Christian scourging.

In *The Sufis* (1964) and others of his works scholar Idries Shah has pointed out how much more the sources of Western literature and other culture lie in Arabic civilization than most Americans and Europeans realize. He refers not just to known works such as *A Thousand and One Nights,* which provided the concept of a frame story for a collection of stories, borrowed by Ovid for *The Decameron* and from Ovid by Chaucer for *The Canterbury Tales,* nor merely to the Sufi allegory, "The Rubaiyat of Omar Khayam," which Edward Fitzgerald fashioned into a classic of wine, women, and song, but to the troubadour and Grail literature of the twelfth to thirteenth centuries, medieval scholasticism, and the work of such figures as Dante, Roger Bacon, and St. John of the Cross. Europeans have never fully acknowledged how much "Western" culture has drawn from, interacted with, or at least been preserved and transmitted by this "other" culture.

Ever since studying Chaucer in college, I have wondered where he got the strange idea of this *Parliament of Fowls,* until my wife came across a copy of *The Conference of the Birds,* a twelfth century Sufi allegory by Farid Ud-din Attar. In the full-year course in Chaucer that I took at Harvard in 1952 no such source was mentioned. Could American scholars not have known of a work four times translated into English and so well regarded in Islam that a new edition of it has appeared every few years since the twelfth century in one or another country of the Near East? If not known, why not? And if known, why not mentioned?

It is difficult to distinguish cultural chauvinism from religious competition. Christian censorship over the centuries deliberately removed knowledge of other religious and cultural influences such as Manicheism, which was Persian, and Gnosticism, which was Egyptian and Oriental. The show-down during the first centuries after Christ between Rome and Alexandria, which Rome of course won, typify the West's periodic efforts to purge itself of the East. The chief reason for the Christian burning of libraries at Alexandria (the Sarcens also burned some later) and for the murder by monks of the brilliant, renowned female mathematician/philosopher, Hypatia, was to destroy that great Afrosiatic pagan culture, which succeeded that of Athens and surpassed that of Rome. Bernal's point that European civilization was never limited to the northern shores of the Mediterranean—to Europe—involves controversies about which cultures were antecedent and which derivative. Many Christian scholars have tried to prove, for example, that both Egyptian and Greek religions derived from the teachings of Moses.

But an equally important point, typified by Alexandria, concerns the constant synthesis of cultures occurring not only in the ancient world but all through history. Ideas have been so syncretized, inventions and discoveries so cycled around cultures and built on from one to another, that it becomes ludicrous to start assigning credit, especially to one's "own." When Aristotle's pupil Alexander founded his Greek city in Egypt he was bringing back to the "East" in a new form ideas that came from there, and his Hellenism then became utterly fused with cultures stretching from Iran to India that were, like Egypt, now receiving back through his conquests a transformation of what they had earlier contributed to.

What Alexandria was to the ancient world, the Languedoc area of southern France was to the medieval world—a rich cross-fusion of cultures that the Christian empire destroyed because it was offering a whole alternative civilization. Up over the Pyrenees in the eleventh to thirteenth centuries there spilled an astonishing hybrid culture that was part Christian, part Jewish, and part Islamic but harmonious. From it was generated not only part of the troubadour Grail literature but the Albigensian or Cathar heresy and the Knights Templar, both of which the church and the government of France ruthlessly exterminated. Jewish Cabalism, Moslem Sufism, and Christian mysticism not only coexisted for a while in Spain and southern

France but enriched each other and produced an illuministic strain of culture which, had it been allowed to survive, could have vastly improved "Western civilization" and that in any case was to prolong subterraneanly into modern times the multicultural esoteric doctrine of antiquity.

Here we come upon some little discussed matters that future research should certainly bring into the open and deal with if cultural literacy is to be more than a kind of academically glamorized jingoism. Beneath cultures we think of as different, there seems to run a universal substrate, but this does not come through in traditional history partly because history is usually written ethnocentrically from within one culture (or even a faction of a culture) and partly because what is common to different cultures is a universalist metaphysic transmitted more or less secretly and quite often in oral forms that escape most historians. See Rudolf Steiner's *Occult History* (1957) as an antidote. Because it is about the cosmic, this underground culture is cosmopolitan—international, cross-cultural, and remarkably consistent over time despite its many transformations. Moot and buried as it is, this sort of metaphysical common denominator may deserve highest priority in future research, for several reasons. Substantiating it could show that

1. All cultures are at bottom kin and can identify with each other;
2. Minorities belong to whatever culture they are in because whatever other culture they originated from has contributed to the one they are now in, as African, Asiatic, and Semitic have to "Western"; and
3. To become culturally literate about one culture has to mean about all cultures, simultaneously—about culture and acculturation.

Furthermore, searching for that universal metaphysic may provide just the sort of comprehensive framework for future research that can most benefit literacy and literature.

My own studies for many years have focused on what is variously called the "perennial philosophy" (the title of Aldous Huxley's work on the subject, taken from Leibnitz), the "wisdom literature," the "esoteric doctrine," etc. This is the universal metaphysic, just mentioned, which has been transmitted across cultures from preliterate times to the present, taught in the ancient world through various "mysteries" and in the Middle Ages through Christian heresies and such channels as the Knights Templar and the Cabalists. It surfaced during the Renaissance as Rosicrucianism (Spencer's Red Cross Knight reflects it) and in the eighteenth century as Freemasonry, the form of it that so profoundly influenced the Enlightenment and the men who founded the United States. Today it is best represented by the Theosophists, Rudolf Steiner's Anthroposophy, some Rosicrucians and various New Age groups. Steiner's many books build up a stunning presentation of its thought, history, and applications to the twentieth century. Max Heindel's *The Rosicrucian Cosmo-Conception* (1909) treats it most fully in a single book.

At times the teaching took on the transformative language of alchemy or the force-field language of astrology, both of which, like official church teachings themselves, were frequently debased by people unready to understand their symbols. Indeed, the danger of misunderstanding and consequent abuse was the chief reason this doctrine was kept esoteric, secret—a later reason being to escape persecution. People today, perhaps more even than then, are almost bound to misunderstand the language and imagery of these traditions, because we read the symbols too materially and read into them the "prescientific" ignorance and superstition we expect to find and that indeed abounded all about this subtle metaphysic, often as popular degenerations of it. Jung, however, spent the last 17 years of his life studying alchemy, because he knew better, and because he knew the esoteric tradition perhaps better than any other investigator at our time not actually transmitting the teaching like Steiner and Heindel.

Most of the West's great philosophers were participating, more or less awarely, in this tradition, as Liebnitz acknowledged in his term *philosophia perennia*. The esoteric literature takes for granted part of what Martin Bernal is so painstakingly documenting in *Black Athena* (1987), that Pythagoras, Plato, and the other Greek philosophers and Neo-Platonists were all working off of Egyptian Hermeticism. But the latter itself is regarded by esotericists as incorporating elements from Mesopotamia and India and having antecedents as well in whatever the civilization of Atlantis was. We may find it hard to believe that preliterate cultures could have had thoughts deep and subtle enough to have been worthy of transmission and transformation by the finest minds of "our" civilization. Indeed, we tend to date a culture from its first texts—Homer and the Bible—as if there were not vestiges of oral and nonverbal traditions predating writing by many centuries.

Most scholars still argue, for example, that the Hermetic texts cannot represent an expression of Egyptian thought because they were written in Latin and Greek circa the first couple of centuries after Christ and clearly contain Platonic and Stoic ideas! In the only version most English-language readers are likely to find of these texts, another publication by Oxford in 1924, *Hermetica,* editor-translator Walter Scott first rules half of the corpus out of his collection on grounds that they are "pseudoscience" and "rubbish" not connected to the religious philosophy of the other half (p. 4 of the Introduction). He then proceeds to speculate that these anonymous authors ascribed their texts to Hermes (Egyptian Thoth, scribe of the gods and inventor of writing) only because "It had long been accepted as a known historical fact that both Pythagoras and Plato had studied in Egypt" and so their writings would gain prestige from associating them with this illustrious geneology. Of the original Egyptian writings themselves, such as *The Book of the Dead,* this authority writes on the same page that "it may seem strange to us that anyone should have imagined them to contain a profound philosophy." Though Scott believes that these writers were merely recasting Greek thought for themselves, he acknowledges that they themselves "were teaching what they held to be the supreme and essential truth towards which Greek philosophy pointed; and it was taken as known that Greek philosophy was derived from the Egytian books of Hermes, in which that essential truth was taught" (p. 5 of the Introduction).

The very founders of modern science—Newton, Bacon, and

Descartes—were so steeped in the esoteric doctrine that half of what they said has been passed over in embarrassment by those moderns who do not realize that physics cannot be disembedded from metaphysics. When Descartes said that the seat of the soul is in the pineal gland he was merely passing on an idea transmitted to him from the esoteric doctrine and found in the Vedanta as well as in the Hermetica (and made less embarrassing perhaps by recent research on the pineal). For the same reason, however, that some Christians do not want to admit influences from pagan and heretical sources, some members of the scientific community do not want to acknowledge how much the fathers of modern science were inspired by their background in the esoteric doctrine, which includes of course the now-anathematized alchemy and astrology.

In one of periodic efforts to stave off such an unholy relationship, a conference was held at University of California at Los Angeles in 1974 to counter the credence that some of the scientific community was showing in such theses as historian Francis Yates', that Giordano Bruno and other esotericists of his time adopted the Copernican theory because it corresponded to their Hermetic metaphysic. One of the papers delivered there, published in *Hermeticism and the Scientific Revolution* (Westman and McGuire, 1977), was by a Newton specialist, J. E. McGuire, who says, "Although Newton's alchemical manuscripts lend support to the position that the general character of his pre-1680 views on the aether and the powers of light may derive from alchemical texts, this claim should be treated with caution" inasmuch as, he continues weakly, we do not know from his reading notes on them or from his commentary on them what he thought of them (p. 119). Despite this ignorance, McGuire goes on to say that "no matter how it is interpreted, alchemy cannot explain the genesis and nature of Newton's claim that light and bodies are 'convertible into one another'" because McGuire sees nothing compatible to this idea in alchemy, although in the same breath he says that "Newton probably saw alchemy as a deep and esoteric expression of true knowledge that had to be properly interpreted . . ." (p. 120). Indeed, the idea is more than compatible. Here, surely, by the way, is a precursor of the idea that energy and matter are convertible into one another, formulated as $E = mc$ by Einstein, who was not at all embarrassed by metaphysics, of whoever's culture.

In *The New View Over Atlantis* (1985) archaeologist John Michell wrote, in regard to the world-wide megalithic culture of monuments, mounds, and alignments, that we live amid the fragments of a vast human creation we do not see the whole of or the purpose of. This is exactly how I have come to feel about the esoteric doctrine. We know bits of it from literature, religion, history, and philosophy, but scholars have never put it together so as either to interpret the pieces properly or to discern its coherence and continuity through ours and other cultures. For research, it poses the inherent problems of having been transmitted secretly, often orally, or nonverbally through glyphs, so that it does not always manifest in texts, and when it does, the texts may be regarded as about something else, or as unintelligible, like Plato's *Timaeus,* his most esoteric and probably least-read work today. Indeed, I suspect that many important texts have been ill translated by scholars not conversant enough with esoteric tradition to understand fully the content of the texts, like even the great translator of the Egyptian *Book of the Dead,* Wallace Budge, who could have better rendered the intricate Egyptian spectrum of realities had he known better its counterpart in esoteric Christian, Jewish, and Islamic teachings. This might in turn have helped Walter Scott to translate and edit the *Hermetica.* But, paradoxically, the very ubiquity of the esoteric doctrine makes it accessible if researchers know to look for it and enjoy a spacious enough purview to be able to connect its scattered and various manifestations.

The more serious problem is that modern academics and intellectuals have been little inclined to pursue it for fear of being associated with superstition or "occultism," which has sensationalist connotations in America, where also the scientific inquisition has reigned most punitively. Ironically, the scientific establishment inherited this taboo from the religious establishment, which profoundly resented a teaching more spiritual than its own exoteric popularizations of it and that was, furthermore, transmitted outside the church. Thus both establishments have kept from public awareness and from standard American history books, for example, the fact that a majority of the founding fathers including George Washington, Thomas Jefferson, and Benjamin Franklin were Freemasons and/or Rosicrucians, like Voltaire and virtually every other Enlightenment figure, and that international Freemasonry played a decisive role in establishing modern democracy (the subject of Bernard Fay's *Revolution and Freemasonry: 1680–1800,* 1935). This role was proclaimed negatively by Jesuits in the form of a conspiracy theory still much alive today in extreme right circles that correctly traces Freemasonry back through the esoteric chain to Egyptian Hermeticism but that makes of it a satanic force bent on destroying Christian civilization. For example, *Secret Societies and Subversive Movements* (Webster, 1924), a scholarly book by a British lady of the 1920s, published by the Christian Book Club of America and distributed by the John Birch Society, opens with this sentence: "The East is the cradle of secret societies." The lineage she reconstructs matches remarkably the one that esotericists trace for themselves, only she is unearthing it in order to warn the world of its conspiracy. But she shares with many academic people of the twentieth century a revulsion to the esoteric doctrine and a repudiation of the "East" that engendered it.

Modern scholars can best avoid rebukes from both scientific and religious quarters if they just leave alone the whole matter of the role in overt events of this underground strand of the culture, even though this strand most likely constitutes the single most important continuity in it if not the very subtrate of it. This buried but all-pervasive cosmology must be declassified, nevertheless, history deconstructed, and culture reconstructed on pain of much interim research merely compounding the problems and their attendant distortions.

To circle closer now to English education in particular, my own modest studies in the esoteric traditions have greatly impressed on me how profoundly they have influenced literature even in the common cases, like those cited earlier of *The Parliament of Fowls* and "The Rubaiyat," where the authors may not be aware of all that is in the stories or symbols they are taking over. Of course, literary scholars already know a lot about neo-

Platonism or the terms and tropes of a tradition like alchemy if only to be able to gloss the allusions to them in Medieval or Renaissance texts. But the full relation between literature and the esoteric teachings has hardly begun to emerge. Most American literature professors who know of *The Occult Philosophy in the Elizabethan Age* (1979) by the much-honored contemporary British historian Dame Francis Yates, do not take her work seriously, though George Steiner and other scholars abroad praised it, probably because she was pioneering in precisely the threat-laden direction just indicated. She relates key works like *The Faerie Queen, The Alchemist,* Marlowe's *Faust,* and *The Tempest* to Christian Cabalists such as Raymond Lull, Pico della Mirandola, Cornelius Agrippa, and the much-caricatured John Dee, resident magus of Elizabeth's court. If we are to acclaim great writers, we should not be ashamed to take seriously what they took seriously. (Shakespeare and Spenser honored the esoteric tradition while Jonson and Marlowe repudiated it.) We have only to look at the work of the Romantics, the French Symbolists, Yeats, Eliot, Joyce, and Pound to realize how intimately this tradition has remained a part of literature.

But the most far-reaching aspect of the relationship concerns less the conscious participation of authors in the tradition as the subtle workings of it on the most profane writers. In fact, I would like to see researchers take on the hypothesis that all literature in any culture is a secularization of some holy writ. The earliest literature is sacred and cosmological, and the following literature does a kind of exegesis on the first, and so on. Thus holy writ also sets in motion forms and processes that evolve and revolve throughout later literature, themes that are orchestrated and tropes that are transformed. The first literature is always poetry because scripture is poetry, and scripture is poetry because only language at once multilevelled and incantatory can do justice to the reality it evokes and invokes. However secular it becomes, literature never severs itself from holy writ, because the impact and meaning of any text any time depends on a colossal intertextuality that evolves from one epoch into another and one culture into another.

More gingerly than I hope will be necessary in the future, two great critics of our day have in some way already taken on this hypothesis—Kenneth Burke in *The Rhetoric of Religion: Studies in Logology* (1961) and Northrop Frye in *The Secular Scripture: A Study of the Structure of Romance* (1976), *Creation and Recreation* (1980), and *The Great Code: The Bible and Literature* (1981). The best way to understand verbalization, Burke says, is to look to theology, the supreme model, because through words referring to the natural world it manages to refer to a supernatural world. From among Frye's complicated analogies between literature and scripture arises also the notion of holy writ as a master code by which to understand language and literature. Esoteric doctrine, I believe, is the code to the code, precisely because it is a universal metaphysic underlying the holy writs of various cultures and therefore permeating their gradually secularizing literatures.

The American Transcendentalist and innovative educator Bronson Alcott (father of Louisa May) set up a very interesting experiment at his Temple School in Boston. A man who took seriously his cultural inheritance, he taught his pupils by a kind of Socratic dialogue, and the experiment was to test a belief dear to Plato and the whole esoteric transmission—that knowledge is recollection. This is one of those "great Western ideas" that advocates of cultural literacy are not apt to list as such, perhaps because they do not believe it squares with science. It accords perfectly, however, with a metaphysic that includes a master force field or cosmic mind having a cosmic memory—like the "reverberating circuits" some neurophysiologists have posited for personal memory—which individuals may access by attunement. In one of the classics of English literature, "Ode: Intimations of Immortality from Recollections of Early Childhood," Wordsworth characterizes the newborn child as "trailing clouds of glory" from the spirit state and "haunted forever by the Eternal Mind."

Alcott asked his students to explain passages from the Gospels on the grounds that, for the very reasons Wordsworth alludes to, they are best qualified to do Biblical exegesis. In 1837, he published his transcriptions as *Conversations with Children on the Gospels*. Even allowing for how his own beliefs about the Gospels must have polluted his research, the children's commentary is remarkable. Community disapproval of the book and of his teaching methods forced Alcott to close the Temple School. But the transcendental tradition and its allied idea of knowing as recollecting is a major cultural heritage that some researchers are again taking seriously, as Thomas Armstrong makes clear in *The Radiant Child* (1985). Ideas worth transmitting are worth investigating.

There is another reason for cultural reexamination and the pursuit of the universalist metaphysic. Except for members of certain organizations like the Association for Moral Education and the Philosophy of Education Society, most educators have avoided issues of moral or spiritual education, though the laity often raises them, as in fundamentalist objections to school curriculum and textbooks. Understandably, researchers especially do not want to appear to violate either the separation of church and state or the separation of science from religion. But issues of value underlie research as much as any other activity, as we have seen, and so it would be only honest to include them as part of the subject. What might help this situation would be to distinguish spirituality, which is a universal perception of wholeness, from religion, which is the embodiment of this perception in a particular culture and set of human institutions. In wisely separating church from state, the founding fathers did by no means intend to separate state from spirituality. Nor would they have seen the slightest need to separate spirituality from science, since the essence of both is the holistic connectedness of the universe. A main tenet of the esoteric doctrine in which they believed is that all things are in correspondence with one another, expressed in "As above, so below" and "I am that." Nor should researchers feel legally or professionally barred from dealing with the practical effects of spirituality, that is, morality, which is a natural result of identifying with others across material differences. Such expansive identification must surely be a large part of the English teachers' claim that literature educates the moral sensibility.

Researching the hypothesis that literature is a secularization of sacred scripture—and especially of a universal metaphysic—might ease several problems at once. Exploring this relationship could clarify the claim that literature is an essential part of moral education and could open the way for schools to deal with scripture as scripture, not just as literature, without "teaching religion." By framing literature cosmologically, metaphysically, English classrooms can deal with spiritual and religious connections while improving the professional offering of literature, which badly needs this dimension. (This of course contrasts with a merely moralistic application of literature to life.) Literature is a cornucopia of diverse riches, but this very profusion affects us more when read against its ultimate ground, which the total intertextuality of scripture and literature itself provides.

What is today called literary criticism has in fact turned sharply in the direction of philosophy and metaphysics and has done so by using cross-disciplinary, cross-cultural knowledge to conduct political, personal, and cultural self-examination. Derrida has most recently focused on Spinoza's theology in relation to the contention about whether literacy destroys the sacred aspect of language (an issue, incidentally, for Navajos today). A book that caps such trends in typifying fashion is Mark C. Taylor's *Erring: A Post-Modern A/Theology* (1984), the title itself expressing how the far-reaching explorations of contemporary literature criticism have brought it back, with perhaps exactly the phycisist's ironic ambiguity, to those cosmological considerations that literature secularizes. But then literary interpretation has always been an extension of Biblical exegesis. At any rate, the hypothesis I am proposing would automatically generate the metaphysical framework that, it seems to me, researchers should frame themselves within for the future.

References

Alcott, B. (Ed.). (1837). *Conversations with children on the Gospels* (Vols. 1–2). New York: Arno Press.

Armstrong, T. (1985). *The radiant child*. Wheaton, IL. and London: Theosophical Publishing House.

Aron, M. (1975, December). The world of the brain. *Harper's* Magazine, 251, 3–4.

Attar, Farid Ud-Din. (1954). *The conference of the birds* (C. S. Nott, Trans.). New York: Samuel Weiser.

Becker, Robert O. & Selden, G. (1985). The body electric: electromagnetism and the foundation of life. New York: William Morrow.

"Bennett Says Stanford 'Capitulated,' " *San Francisco Chronicle,* April 19, 1988.

Bernal, M. (1987). *Black Athena: The Afroasiatic roots of classical civilization* (Vols. 1–3). London: Free Association Books.

Bohm, D. (1980). *Wholeness and the implicate order*. London and Boston: Ark.

Budge, E. A. W. (1895). *The Egyptian book of the dead*. New York: Dover.

Burke, K. (1961). *The rhetoric of religion: studies in logology*. Berkeley: University of California Press.

Capra, F. (1977). *The tao of physics*. New York: Bantam.

Faÿe, B. (1935). *Revolution and Freemasonry, 1680–1800*. Boston: Little, Brown.

Frye, N. (1976). *The Secular Scripture: A study of the structure of romance*. Cambridge: Harvard University Press.

Frye, N. (1980). *Creation and recreation*. Toronto: University of Toronto Press.

Frye, N. (1981). *The great code: The Bible and literature*. New York: Harcourt, Brace, Jovanovich.

Furth, H. (1966). *Thinking without language: Psychological implications of deafness*. New York: Free Press.

Havelock, E. A. (1986). *The muse learns to write: Reflections on orality and literacy from antiquity to the present*. New Haven: Yale University Press.

Heindel, M. (1909). *The Rosicrucian cosmo-conception*. Oceanside, CA: The Rosicrucian Fellowship.

Huxley, A. (1944). *The perennial philosophy*. New York: World.

James, M. R. (1924). *The apocryphal New Testament*. Oxford: Clarendon Press.

Jaynes, J. (1976). *The origins of consciousness in the breakdown of the bicameral mind*. Boston: Houghton-Mifflin.

Koestler, A. (1972). *The roots of consciousness: An excursion into parapsychology*. New York: Vintage.

Legge, J. (Trans.). (1882). *I Ching: Book of changes*. New York: Causeway.

Michell, J. (1985). *The new view over Atlantis*. New York: Harcourt, Brace, Jovanovich.

Penfield, W. (1975). *The mystery of the mind*. Princeton: Princeton University Press.

Pearce, J. C. (1977). *The magical child*. New York: E.P. Dutton.

Plato. (1929). *Timaeus* (Vol. 7 of Plato in the Loeb Classical Library). Cambridge: Harvard University Press.

Pribram, K. H. (1982). What the fuss is all about. In K. Wilber (Ed.), *The holographic paradigm and other paradoxes* Cambridge, MA: Shambhala, pp. 27–34.

Sagan, C. (1977). *The dragons of Eden*. New York: Random House.

Scott, W. (1924). *Hermetica: The ancient Greek and Latin writings which contain religious or philosophic teachings ascribed to Hermes Trismegistus* (Vols. 1–4). London: Dawsons of Pall Mall.

Shah, I. (1964). *The sufis*. Garden City: Doubleday Anchor.

Sheldrake, R. (1981). *A new science of life: the hypothesis of formative causation*. Los Angeles: J.P. Tarcher.

Sheldrake, R. & Bohm, D. (1982). Sheldrake, Bohm, and morphogenetic fields and the implicate order. *Revision: A journal of consciousness and change, 5,* 41–48.

Steiner, R. (1957). *Occult history*. London: Rudolf Steiner Press.

Taylor, M. C. (1984). *Erring: A postmodern a/theology*. Chicago and London: University of Chicago Press.

Watson, L. (1982). Lifetide: The biology of the unconscious. New York: Simon and Schuster.

Webster, N. (1924). *Secret societies and subversive movements*. Christian Book Club of America.

Westman, R. S. & McGuire, J. E. (1977), Hermeticism and the scientific revolution. Los Angeles: William Andrews Clark Memorial Library, University of California.

Wilhelm, R., Trans. (1950). *I ching or book of changes*. Princeton: Princeton University Press.

Yates, F. (1979). *The occult philosophy in the Elizabethan age*. London: Ark.

EPILOGUE: THE SHAPING OF THE ENGLISH LANGUAGE ARTS

James Flood

Julie M. Jensen

Diane Lapp

James R. Squire

For the cover-to-cover reader of this *Handbook,* the contributors have answered central questions about research in the teaching of the English language arts during the waning years of the twentieth century: Who is doing the research? What questions are they asking about whom? Where are they finding answers to their questions? What methods are they using and for what purposes? Why are they doing research at all? And what lies ahead? The research included in the *Handbook* points to several dramatic changes during the past two decades alone. Not only is the *what* and *how* of research changing but so is the *who* and *where.* For the more typical, selective reader, the editors close with a few, brief reflections on these and related questions.

The What and How of Contemporary Research

Two notable changes in research emphasis are the developments of interest in the early years of language acquisition and the emergence of studies on multiple aspects of the language arts and their relations to one another. In both cases, the approach to studying the English language arts involves a paradigm shift in which language development is viewed in a broader context than it had been previously. For example, the recent work in emergent literacy by Clay, Sulzby and Teale, and Roser and Martinez, all described in chapters within this *Hand-*

book, emphasizes the ways in which children learn to use the language arts in relation to one another. These researchers' emphasis on the developmental aspects of learning the language arts suggests that their view of language learning is at once continuing *and* interactive and can best be studied and understood in natural contexts.

A third and related area of research that has changed in recent years is the emphasis on studying extended oral and written discourse, rather than smaller, discrete units. This research is born of the same paradigm shift noted earlier, a belief that language is studied most meaningfully when it is whole. Halliday and Hasan's seminal work, *Cohesion in English,* influenced this trend considerably; their argument that cohesion in discourse extends not only beyond word boundaries but also beyond sentence boundaries enlightened language-arts researchers and encouraged them to examine the language user's discourse in a fuller, more holistic way.

Discourse analysts have also looked at whole texts, both literary and informational, to study issues of readability and comprehensibility. Previously, the emphasis in readability research had been placed on individual syllables, words, and sentences. In analyzing text readability, contemporary researchers also look at many of the issues involved in discourse analysis, e.g., cohesion within and among sentences, cohesion within and among paragraphs, synonymy, examples, transitions, and metadiscourse. In some ways, the changes in text analysis have been more dramatic than any other area of language-arts research. Current emphasis on pure texts in students' anthologies, (i.e., unabridged, unrevised, unadapted), is one product of increased attention to the findings from discourse-analysis studies.

A fourth area of change in research in the English language arts is in the area of computer technology and its applications to language learning. Speech synthesizers, interactive computers and video, and word processing advances have enabled educators to use technology in more meaningful ways than ever before in their language teaching. Bruce, in his chapter in this *Handbook,* argues that the current interest in the uses of computers for writing development is the most significant educational application of computers. The findings from several studies have, in fact, confirmed the beneficial effects of computers on students' writing development.

Significant changes in studying the language arts have also been occurring in the area of methodology. Traditionally, almost all research in the language arts was conducted from an empirical, quantitative perspective. More recently, attempts have been made to study the language arts from a variety of perspectives including anthropology (Green, this volume), developmental aspects of psychology (Schallert, this volume), and linguistics (Menyuk, this volume). Multiple perspectives have also been used in many of the contemporary ethnographic studies of language-learning environments (Cazden, this volume). A further change in the way research gets done is the renewed interest in large-scale studies like those conducted by the National Assessment of Educational Progress, and longitudinal studies like those previously conducted by Loban and Strickland (for a review see Tierney, this volume). Both types of research are being conducted regularly and both are receiving renewed attention from the field.

Much attention during the past few years has also focused on the issue of creating tests/assessment instruments that reflect contemporary holistic notions of the ways in which people learn language. For example, if it is the case that language users process longer, more natural units of discourse more fully than abbreviated, shorter units of discourse, then longer units should be included in assessments of reading ability. Further, if it is the case that prior knowledge, world view, and personal orientation affect comprehension, then these issues should be addressed in any meaningful assessment effort. Several states (e.g., Illinois and Michigan) have designed statewide tests that profess to be consistent with these findings about language learning. Others, like California, seek to provide a more broadly based assessment of student writing that will evaluate pupil progress in various dimensions of language use. Although interest in new forms of assessment is widespread, substantial research is yet to be reported. Assessment efforts to date are better characterized as development projects than research studies. Indeed, this phenomenon seems to be somewhat of a trend. A number of development projects undertaken in recent years have been producing promising results although they are not yet reported as research studies. Examples of these projects include the Reading Recovery Project from Ohio State University and the Bay Area Writing Project from the University of California at Berkeley.

The *Who* and *Where* of Contemporary Research

During the past two decades a great deal of research has emerged from settings like the home, the community, the job, and the school. These studies are reflected in most of the chapters in this collection. This shift from laboratory or laboratory-like settings to natural settings was based on the belief that language learning is situational and must be studied as such, examining various roles and functions of language, e.g., listener-speaker relations; superordinate-subordinate social roles; and turn-taking conventions. At the heart of the school-based research is a new emphasis on the role played by the teacher as researcher.

This line of research frequently shifts the focus from university-based research to a team approach involving a collaboration between teachers and university educators. Often, these collaborations develop over a long period of time. They are most effective when they recognize the complementary types of expertise of each member of the team. This kind of research is essentially ethnographic and is often presented in a case study format.

Lee Shulman's notions of the "wisdom of practice" and his case study, autobiographical approach to examining the nature of good teaching is related methodologically to the collaborative efforts described above (see Shulman, 1986). In his studies, teachers reflect upon their decisions, revisions, and deletions before, during, and after teaching. The critical emphasis in this line of research is metacognitive. Teachers are asked to think about how they think and how they know what they know, i.e., to provide evidence about their own "knowings." In this research the teacher as reporter is of primary importance.

The range of research in the teaching of the English language arts thus far seems broader than a decade ago, with ethnographic studies, case study methods and qualitative and philosophical analyses yielding important insights. Even so, the overwhelming body of studies in the English language arts still reflects experimental approaches. The research traditions of many disciplines are affecting inquiry in English language-arts education—but not always wisely and certainly not in any integrated fashion. For instance, studies of schema theory and of the impact of prior knowledge on comprehension seem often to be providing an empirical justification for teaching strategies long since espoused by reading response theorists, but no one yet has brought together the cognitive psychologists and the literary scholars to forge a comprehensive strategy for teaching literature based on insights from the different disciplines. Indeed, better communication is needed across disciplines (and across countries) as scholars from diverse contexts begin to address similar questions.

Further, too little research today stems from questions about what to teach and how to teach, perhaps because too few teachers are involved in setting a research agenda. The recent rise of interest in teacher-researchers seek to alleviate the discrepancy between a knowledge base for teaching emanating only from the work of university scholars, often without reference to the accumulated practical insights and lore of classroom teachers. See, for example, the discussion by Burton earlier in this *Handbook.* Theorists such as Lytle and Cochran-Smith (1989), and Mohr (1989) argue eloquently that teacher research is essential to enhance professionalism of teachers, and an increasing number of professional leaders call for teacher involvement in research (Squire 1987). Yet perusal of current journals reporting research reveals few reports of teacher-researcher studies. An occasional article (see, for example, Hiebert & Calfee, 1989) points up the significance of sharing insights accumulated by teachers, but the first reports on teacher research seem to be appearing in journals for general practitioners and may not always reach researchers. Thus, the profession as a whole has yet to find effective ways of communicating much of the teacher work already under way.

Other kinds of research also seem to be needed. We have, for example, too much single-skill research; e.g., studies that emphasize the teaching or learning of a discrete competency, often in isolation. But a priority need of today's profession is research on the teaching and learning of skills in context. Indeed, the strong fragmentation of research in the English language arts may have long since contributed to fragmentation in instruction.

Recent research has been enriched by many ethnographic and qualitative studies. No longer does experimental, quantifiable study dominate work in the field. But often the different kinds of studies are built on different assumptions and ask different questions. Still, on the really crucial questions of language learning and language teaching, we need to bring insights from different kinds of research—qualitative and quantitative, experimental, and ethnographic.

Longitudinal studies would seem particularly important in a field in which language development is a major concern. Yet our reviews of research make clear how neglected such studies have been. Until we have a clearer understanding of how children develop, we cannot be certain that what we know about reading or writing or literary response at one developmental level can be applied to another. Cross-sectional studies offer a quick way of generating hypotheses about long-range growth, but seem at best a short term substitute for the real thing.

We have already commented at length on the imperative need to involve more teachers in defining research questions and in interpreting findings. But in no area of research is teacher participation more essential than in research in measurement and assessment.

Current professional criticism of today's assessment procedures has been widespread; so is the widespread assumption that assessment drives curriculum and instruction. Yet little data can be found to indicate exactly how and when testing instruments have the greatest impact. Certainly research into the impact of the processes of assessment could be as potent as research seeking to improve the instruments. But through it all the classroom teacher must be central. It is his or her teaching strategies most likely to be affected by new measurement instruments, and it is the teacher who best understands the dimensions of learning and teaching for which we currently lack adequate assessment approaches.

How Research is Reviewed and Assessed

The past two decades has also seen a noticeable increase in interest in educational research. The growth in circulation of research journals such as *Reading Research Quarterly* and *Research in the Teaching of English,* the steady acceleration of interest in research activities within I.R.A. and N.C.T.E. (such as I.R.A.'s recognition of outstanding dissertations and N.C.T.E.'s organization of the Research Assembly), the expansion of activities by the National Conference on Research in English, the steady stream of research-based monographs emanating from ERIC and the R&D centers, and particularly the growing number of research reports from commercial publishers—all testify to an increased interest in research in the teaching of the English language arts.

But this interest in the findings of educational research is too seldom matched by critical analyses of the design of the research, the reliability of its instruments, the validity of its conclusions. In our eagerness to identify research that either seems to confirm or deny particular teaching or learning strategies, we too seldom evaluate critically the point of view, the design, the instrumentation, and the analyses of even our most important studies. The very organization of many of the teaching-effectiveness studies conducted during the 1970s foreshadowed inevitable findings: the importance of academic emphasis, time on task, and direct instruction. What otherwise could we have expected to find in schools selected because students achieve high scores in tests of specific skills in mathematics or reading? The assumptions that underlie particular studies need to be assessed as those studies are evaluated. Indeed, more critical analyses and fewer summaries of research could elevate the profession's dialogue about research.

Those who interpret research need to consider carefully whether research findings that apply to students at one particular level of development can validly be applied to another level. We know that learning to speak or write or read differs significantly from level to level. Prepubescent boys and girls bring different perceptions to literature than do preschool children. The writing problems of young adults are radically different from those of the young child. Why, then, do we so often assume that teaching and learning strategies that emerge from the study of college freshman will help to solve the writing problems of the middle-school child?

The reverse of this situation also creates problems, the more so when researchers at college and secondary school levels seem willfully uninformed about or unwilling to consider implications about what researchers in elementary school have found about student-centered learning in the language arts.

Issues of this kind are too seldom addressed by our major research journals, even by those which have achieved admirable success in reporting results of recent studies. More attention, then, to assessing the quality of the designs and the appropriateness of the implications of research findings is a critical need. Mandatory is greater attention to the universality of research.

Encouraging more teacher reviews of research might help to bring balance. In the last analysis, the ultimate criterion for evaluating the quality of a study may be the extent to which it affects (or illuminates) classroom practice. Why not, then, involve more practitioners in reviewing and synthesizing recent research? In addition to engaging individually or cooperatively in defining issues to be studied and methods to be employed, teachers can be critically importnat reviewers of the current literature. Indeed, a summative teaching assessment of accumulated research in each of the critical dimensions of the English language (literature, reading, oral language, writing, etc.) every half-decade could provide critical guidelines for future studies as well as important guidelines for school practice.

The World of the Classroom

A look inside the classrooms of most urban schools reveals increasing numbers of economically disadvantaged, limited English-speaking and ethnic minority children. Although many of these students have successful school experiences, others lack motivation, proficiency in English, financial support, parental involvement, and awareness of the customs, needs, and characteristics of the dominant culture of which the school is a part. These are often the students who are not succeeding in current school programs or structures, yet they are a major segment of the work force of tomorrow. "Our collective future depends on them" (Hodginson, 1988).

With the changes in the demographics of public schools (see Farr, Allen, Chall, and Curtis for elaboration), instructional practices are needed that demonstrate awareness of and appreciation for such diversity. We must provide experiences that encourage learning for *all* students including both genders, exceptional students, and students from various socioeconomic, religious, ethnic, and cultural groups. In order to do so, researchers on teaching will need to ask questions and select subjects with a diverse student population in mind.

As Marcia Farr suggests in this *Handbook,* instructional practices sensitive to the needs of all language learners are coming none too soon. Clearly, future language-arts research needs to more systematically address the needs of a diverse school population and the teachers and administrators with whom it interacts. In order to more fully explore and define effective language-arts methods, we need to focus on issues related to:

1. The effects of bilingualism, socioeconomic status, and academic performance in determining school success,
2. The impact of learning one language on learning a second language,
3. The development of instructional strategies that encourage participation by *all* students,
4. The preparation of *all* teachers to teach *all* students.

A study of these and other related language-arts issues is necessary if instructional strategies are to be designed by well-prepared teachers who know the research that gives credence and direction to the belief that linguistic and cultural-minority students can succeed in school.

The Role of Research

Finally, we ask, why did we compile research on English language-arts teaching into this *Handbook?* Why did the researchers conduct it in the first place? And, why are you reading it? Because, though we all know that its effects are neither immediate nor widespread, nor its influence singular, the influence of research is unique. George Henry, reflecting on our profession's respect for and reliance on research for the improvement of English teaching, concluded that "Education, like politics or religion or economics, must have recourse to some form of authority to lend stability to it as an institution. Education at present has no Supreme Court, no Vatican Council" (1966, p. 230). Given that teaching makes a difference in students' lives, we are obligated to learn ever-more about it. Research may be complicated and imperfect; it does not lead to quick and simple payoffs in education; but what are alternative ways to find the knowledge that it can provide? Indeed, research should, and does play a critical role in the improvement of English language-arts instruction.

We devote our energies to research in teaching knowing it is but one of many forces that affect classroom practice. Teaching is influenced by theories from a range of disciplines. Fields such as anthropology, linguistics, literary theory, and psychology are affecting the questions that are asked, the way they are asked, the methods that are used, and the conclusions that are drawn. Thus, teaching is touched by theories that are not grounded in questions about what and how to teach. Neither are some of the forces that influence practice theoretical. The media, pressures from parents, tradition, and the economic, social, and political conditions of our society all vie with research and theory to affect instruction in English language-arts classrooms. Among other influences on practice are development efforts discussed earlier in this chapter and the traditional wisdom of teaching, the general maxims that teachers believe though they have no necessary derivation from a theoretical base, research data, or development efforts. Sometimes good practice predates research, with studies of practice than serving to test, refine, confirm, or elaborate earlier conceptual work.

All of these factors—theoretical or not, education-based or not—affect the substance of research on teaching. All of them help to shape perennial questions (e.g., What is English?), cyclical questions (e.g., Why can't students read and write?), and new questions (e.g., How do we best use high technology?). They account for our longstanding issues (e.g., teaching load, class size, testing, evaluation, teacher preparation, censorship) and our emerging fields (e.g., computer applications). They determine how research gets done (e.g., through federally funded research centers and institutes). They account for certain aspects of the language-arts curriculum reflecting an explosion of interest (e.g., comprehension, writing) while others are virtually ignored (e.g., policy studies, listening, handwriting), as is evident in preceding chapters in which some authors had difficulty finding significant research to report, while others could only skim a vast surface. In sum, for complex and multiple reasons, one can observe great variation in the quantity and character of scholarly attention paid to the various language arts. Diverse communities of researchers, practitioners, and policymakers comprise and define the universe of research in teaching the English language arts.

Diminishing the potential impact of research on teaching is the fact that researchers represent only a small segment of language-arts educators, as do readers of research. The professional literature amply demonstrates that professors and graduate students both produce the most research and comprise its major reading audience. Indeed, enthusiasm for and belief in the promise of research on teaching is not universal.

With only exceptional teachers as consumers or producers, the influence of research findings on classroom practice is, at best, indirect and delayed, and, at worst, nil. That research has had a limited effect on practice may be because too many researchers have forgotten, or never knew, that classrooms are practical places where teachers make countless instructional decisions every day. Studies undertaken by researchers removed from the reality of life in the classroom, and too often written in a form that is accessible to few, are unlikely to have an immediate impact on practice, no matter how much we hope that instructional decisions are influenced by research findings.

But it is heartening to note that this *Handbook* reflects signs of change. More than ever before it demonstrates a bridging of research and practice, of researcher and practitioner. The studies reported here show growing evidence of classroom teachers having a hand in planning and executing research, with the potential result being both better research and better practice.

We close with an observation that research seems as much an *attitude* as an *act*. More than one who sees a problem, makes relevant observations, determines the meaning of those observations, and sets an objectively informed course, a researcher is one who is curious and sensitive, aware and purposeful, objective and honest.

Likewise, this *Handbook* is intended to be more than assembled facts and observations on English language-arts instruction for kindergarten through grade 12 teachers. It is an opportunity for those teachers to see how ways of studying students' language learning are growing and developing. It invites them, as it did the contributors, to go beyond data—to find relationships, to reconcile conflicts, to assess significance for life in the classroom.

As its editors, we have noted in this *Handbook* signs of admirable vigor and promising progress within the ranks of a diverse community of researchers. We hope, most of all, that our product is a lesson in attitude—that we have helped our readers to view themselves not only as interpreters of the research of others, but as active participants in an ongoing search. Such professionals, armed with new ways of thinking about what they do, are better poised to see, examine, and act on the countless questions of English language-arts teaching which surround us—waiting to be answered.

References

Halliday, M. & Hasan, R. (1976). *Cohesion in English*. London: Longmans.

Henry, G. H. (1966). English teaching encounters science. *College English, 28,* 220–235.

Hiebert, E. H. & Calfee, R. C. (1989). Advancing academic literacy through teacher assessments. *Educational Leadership, 46*(7), 50–54.

Hodginson, H. (1988). The right schools for the right kids. *Educational Leadership, 45,* 10–14.

Lytle, S. L. & Cochran-Smith, M. (1989). Teacher research: Toward clarifying the concept. *The Quarterly of the National Writing Project, 11*(2), 1–3, 22–27.

Mohr, M. et al. (1989). Teacher-researchers: Their voices, their continued stories. *The Quarterly of the National Writing Project, 11*(2), 4–7, 19.

Shulman, L. S. (1986). Paradigms and research programs in the study of teaching: A contemporary perspective. In M. C. Wittrock (Ed.), *Handbook of Research in Teaching* (3rd. ed.). New York: Macmillan Co.

Squire, J. R. (Ed.). (1987). *The dynamics of language learning.* Urbana, IL: National Council of Teachers of English and National Council on Research in English.

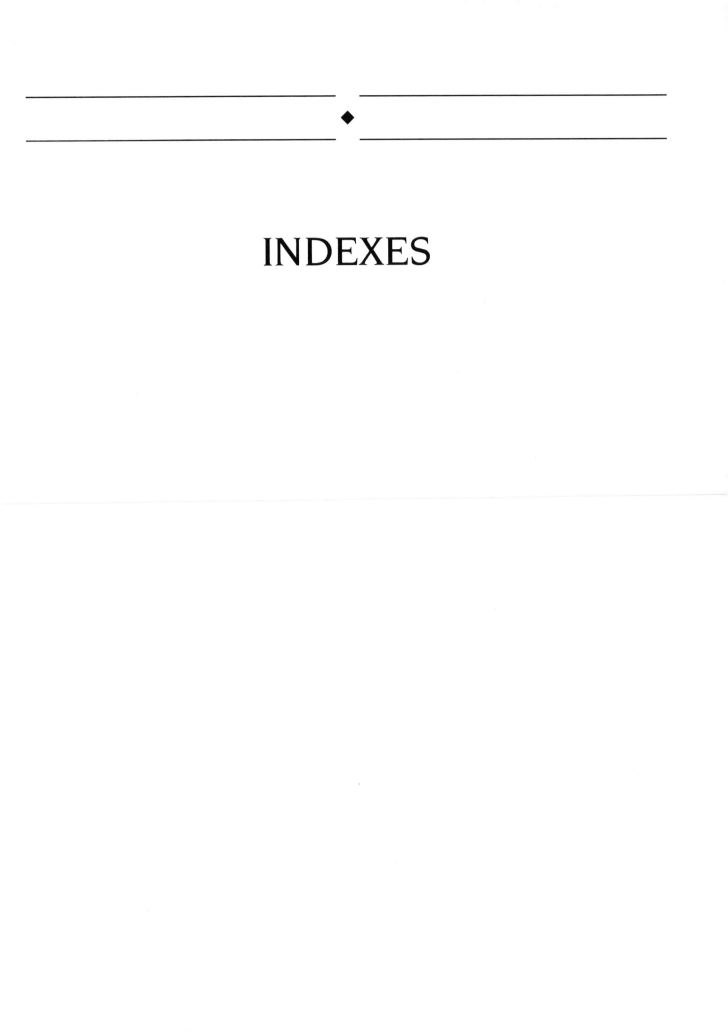

INDEXES

SUBJECT INDEX